Part VI: Mentally Disordered Offenders

Part VII: Legal Aid and Costs

ARCHBOLD

2012

Published in 2011 by
Sweet & Maxwell
100 Avenue Road, London NW3 3PF
part of Thomson Reuters (Professional) UK Limited
(Registered in England and Wales, Company No. 1679046. Registered Office and address for service: Aldgate House, 33 Aldgate High Street, London EC3N 1DL)
(http://www.sweetandmaxwell.co.uk)

For further information on our products and services, visit:
www.sweetandmaxwell.co.uk

Typeset by Sweet & Maxwell Ltd, 100 Avenue Road, London NW3 3PF
Printed and bound by CPI Group (UK) Ltd Croydon, CR0 4YY

ISBN 9780414048478

No natural forests were destroyed to make this product; only farmed timber was used and replanted

A CIP catalogue record for this book is available from the British Library

ARCHBOLD

MAGISTRATES' COURTS CRIMINAL PRACTICE

2012

SWEET & MAXWELL

THOMSON REUTERS

EDITOR

BARBARA BARNES
District Judge (Magistrates' Courts)

CONTRIBUTING EDITORS

WILLIAM CARTER, B.A. (OXON.)
of Gray's Inn, Barrister

PAUL CLARK, M.A. (OXON.)
District Judge (Magistrates' Courts)

JEREMY COLEMAN
District Judge (Magistrates' Court)

STEPHEN LEAKE, LL.M.
of the Middle Temple, Barrister

KEVIN MCCORMAC, O.B.E., M.A. (OXON.)
of Gray's Inn, Barrister

QUENTIN PURDY, B.A. (Hons), LL.M. (LOND.)
of Gray's Inn, Barrister
a District Judge (Magistrates' Courts)

THOMAS RING, LL.B. Hons
Clerk to the Justices for North & East London
of Inner Temple, Barrister

STEPHEN SHAY, B.A. (OXON.)
of the Middle Temple, Barrister

DR MICHAEL STOCKDALE Ph.D., LL.B.,
Director of the Centre for Criminal and Civil Procedure and Evidence, School of Law, Northumbria University

ASSISTANT EDITOR

LOUISE COWEN, M.Phil (CANTAB.), Ph.D. (CANTAB.)
of Gray's Inn, Barrister

PREFACE TO THE 2012 EDITION

We are pleased to publish this 8th edition of *Archbold Magistrates' Courts Criminal Practice*. Originally designed as a companion volume to the *Archbold* in use in the Crown Courts, we hope that this book will continue to prove useful to District Judges, legal advisers and advocates working in the magistrates' courts as well as to students of magistrates' courts practice.

Although the stream of criminal justice legislation has abated somewhat, this edition still includes several new legislative measures brought in under the *Coroners and Justice Act* 2009, the *Crime and Security Act* 2010 and the *Police (Detention and Bail) Act* 2011, all of which affect procedure. In addition the *Bribery Act* 2010 is covered in full which completely changed the law on bribery and corruption.

There is new case law included in every chapter and also the new *Sentencing Council Guidelines* on assault are covered in the relevant chapter.

The appendices include the revised and updated *Codes of Practice* under the *Police and Criminal Evidence Act* 1984 together with the new *Criminal Procedure Rules* 2011 which were published by way of Statutory Instrument in July 2011 and will come into force in October. The new rules, amongst other things, make provision for electronic service of certain documents and also extend the time limits in relation to notification of bad character and hearsay applications and make changes to reporting restrictions.

There have been extensive changes to the editorial team consequent on retirements. I am pleased to welcome District Judges (Magistrates' Court) Quentin Purdey and Paul Clark; Justices' Clerk Tom Ring and the academic Michael Stockdale as contributing editors. I am very grateful to them all for their impressive work on their areas of expertise. I must also thank Stephen Shay, Stephen Leake, Louise Cowen, Will Carter, Kevin McCormac and Jeremy Coleman who have continued to work tirelessly in refining and updating their contributions.

I am exceedingly grateful to Lindsay Emerson and her team at Sweet and Maxwell for support and reassurance during the long, hard process of bringing this publication to fruition.

Finally, I would like to say special thanks to Gaynor Houghton-Jones for her seven years of tireless commitment and assistance as a contributing editor. She will be greatly missed.

This edition is published including the law as it stood in July 2011.

Barbara Barnes
District Judge (Magistrates' Court) July 2011

CONTENTS

ABBREVIATIONS

The following abbreviations have been adopted throughout.

ASBO .... Anti-Social Behaviour Order

CCSU .... Council of Civil Service Unions
CDRO .... Criminal Defence Representation Order
CJA .... Criminal Justice Act
CJCSA .... Criminal Justice and Court Services Act
CJPOA .... Criminal Justice and Public Order Act
CLA .... Criminal Law Act
CPIA .... Criminal Procedure and Investigations Act
CPS .... Crown Prosecution Service
CRO .... Community Rehabilitation Order
CYPA .... Children and Young Persons Act

DCW .... Designated Case Worker
DTTO .... Drug Treatment and Testing Order

FACT .... Federation Against Copyright Theft

ISSP .... Intensive Supervision and Surveillance Program

JOPI .... Joint Operational Instructions

MDO .... Mentally Disordered Offenders

PACE .... Police and Criminal Evidence Act
PCC(S)A .... Powers of Criminal Courts (Sentencing) Act
POCA .... Protection of Children Act
PSR .... Pre-Sentence Report

RIPA .... Regulation of Investigatory Powers Act
RTA .... Road Traffic Act

SOA .... Sexual Offences Act
SSR .... Specific Sentence Report

YJCEA .... Youth Justice and Criminal Evidence Act
YOT .... Youth Offending Team

SERVICE INFORMATION

The Archbold Magistrates' service

Archbold Magistrates' Criminal Practice consists of one main text volume (including the tables and index). This volume is re-issued annually, and is updated by an annual supplement.

The supplement, containing updated material for the main volume, is published once a year as part of the service.

After consulting the main work on any given subject, reference should always be made to the same paragraph number in the current supplement to check that there have been no new developments since the main text volume was published. The supplement will also track material which has been removed or relocated as part of the re-issue process.

All references in the text to cases, statutes and statutory instruments are contained in the tables printed at the beginning of this supplement.

TABLE OF STATUTES

[Paragraph numbers in bold type denote where the text of the statute is printed]

TABLE OF STATUTORY INSTRUMENTS

[Paragraph numbers in bold type denote where the text of the statutory instrument is printed]

Practice Directions

TABLE OF CASES

Part I

Pre-Trial Issues

Chapter 1

CRIMINAL INVESTIGATIONS

I. INVESTIGATORY POWERS

A. Introduction

The law governing the police's powers in conducting criminal investigations is primarily contained in the *Police and Criminal Evidence Act* 1984 as amended, and as supplemented by a series of Codes of Practice (see *post*, Annex A). The 1984 Act is not, however, a complete code of a police officer's powers or duties. Common law powers (such as the power to arrest for breach of the peace) remain. Further powers subsequently have been enacted, such as the *Police Act* 1997, ss.91–108 (authorisation of covert entry upon and interference with property or with wireless telegraphy by the police, Revenue and Customs officers, and others); the *Regulation of Investigatory Powers Act* 2000 (dealing with all forms of covert surveillance which do not involve covert entry upon or interference with property or wireless telegraphy); the *Criminal Justice and Police Act* 2001 (see *post*, §§ 1–67 *et seq.*); and the *Serious Organised Crime and Police Act* 2005, ss.60–70 (prosecution powers to compel individuals to answer questions or produce relevant documents pursuant to disclosure notices). **1–1**

B. Police and Criminal Evidence Act 1984 (PACE) and Codes of Practice

(1) Legislative background

Police and Criminal Evidence Act 1984, s.66

Codes of practice

66.—(1) The Secretary of State shall issue codes of practice in connection with— **1–2**

(a) the exercise by police officers of statutory powers—

(i) to search a person without first arresting him;

(ii) to search a vehicle without making an arrest;

or

(iii) to arrest a person;

(b) the detention, treatment, questioning and identification of persons by police officers;

(c) searches of premises by police officers; and

(d) the seizure of property found by police officers on persons or premises.

(2) Codes shall (in particular) include provision in connection with the exercise by police officers of powers under section 63B above.

(3) Nothing in this section requires the Secretary of State to issue a code of practice in relation to any matter falling within the code of practice issued under section 47B(1) of the *Terrorism Act* 2000 (as that code is revised from time to time) (code of practice in relation to terrorism powers to stop and search in specified locations).

[This section is printed as amended by the *Criminal Justice and Court Services Act* 2000, s.57(4); the *Serious Organised Crime and Police Act* 2005, ss.110(3) and 174(2), and Sched. 17; and the *Terrorism Act 2000 (Remedial) Order* 2011 (S.I. 2011 No. 631).]

As from a day to be appointed, codes of practice under s.66 of the *PACE Act* 1984 must make provision about the questioning of a person by a constable in accordance with s.22 of the *Counter-Terrorism Act* 2008 (post-charge questioning in relation to terrorist offences): 2008 Act, s.22(7).

1–3 Section 63B (*post*, § 18–76) allows the police to test a person in police detention for the presence of Class A drugs.

1–4 There are eight Codes of Practice. The full text is in Appendix A and also on the Police Home Office website at *http://www.homeoffice.gov.uk*. The Codes are:

A. Code of Practice for the Exercise by; Police Officers of Statutory Powers to Stop and Search; Police Officers and Police Staff of Requirements to Record Public Encounters.

B. Code of Practice for Searches of Premises by Police Officers and the Seizure of Property found by Police Officers on Persons or Premises.

C. Code of Practice for Detention, Treatment and Questioning of Persons by Police Officers.

D. Code of Practice for the Identification of Persons by Police Officers.

E. Code of Practice on Tape Recording of Interviews with Suspects.

F. Code of Practice on Visual Recording of Interviews with Suspects.

G. Code of Practice for the Statutory Power of Arrest by Police Officers.

H. Code of Practice for Detention, Treatment and Questioning of Persons under section 41 of and Sched. 8 to the *Terrorism Act* 2000.

1–5 The original Codes first came into force as follows: Codes A to D on January 1, 1986; Code E on July 29, 1988; Code F on May 7, 2002.; Code G on January 1, 2006; and Code H on July 20, 2006. The latest revision of Codes A, B and D came into force on March 7, 2011: *Police and Criminal Evidence Act 1984 (Codes of Practice) (Revision of Codes A, B and D) Order* 2011 (S.I. 2011 No. 412). The revisions implement a reduced level of recording of stop and search encounters, provide guidance on the use of mobile fingerprinting technology and on the enhanced powers to take samples and fingerprints, and reflect other minor changes in legislation and practice. The latest revision of Code C came into force on February 1, 2008:*Police and Criminal Evidence Act 1984 (Codes of Practice) Order* 2008 (S.I. 2008 No. 167). However, the legal advice changes in Code C took effect on that day only in Greater Manchester, the West Midlands and West Yorkshire; they took effect elsewhere on April 21, 2008. As from May 1, 2010, revised Codes E and F came into force: *Police and Criminal Evidence Act 1984 (Codes of Practice) (Revisions to Codes E and F) Order* 2010 (S.I. 2010 No. 1108). The revisions permit the recording of interviews with suspects by a secure digital network as an alternative to the use of audio tapes (Code E), and enable visual recordings of interviews to be digitally recorded (Code F). For the full text of the current codes, see Appendix A, *post*.

(2) Status of the Codes

1–6 The Codes are admissible in evidence and the court may take account of any relevant provision: *PACE Act* 1984, s.67(11), *post*, § 1–8. However, s.67(11)does not render admissible something which would otherwise be hearsay, merely because the statement is made during processes properly conducted in accordance with the relevant code: *R. v. Lynch* [2008] 1 *Archbold News* 2, CA (not following *R. v. McCay*, 91 Cr.App.R. 84, CA).

Annexes elaborate upon aspects of the Codes and must be observed. Notes for guidance advise upon the application of the Codes and Annexes but do not have the binding effect of the codes themselves although they are there to be followed. **1–7**

Copies of the Codes should be available at Police Stations for public consultation and for reference for police officers and detained persons.

(3) Application of the Codes

Police and Criminal Evidence Act 1984, s.67

Codes of Practice—supplementary

67.—(1–7D) [*Provisions for the issue and revision of codes of practice.*] **1–8**

(8) [*Repealed.*]

(9) Persons other than police officers who are charged with the duty of investigating offences or charging offenders shall in the discharge of that duty have regard to any relevant provision of a code.

(9A) Persons on whom powers are conferred by—

(a) any designation under section 38 or 39 of the *Police Reform Act* 2002 (police powers for police authority employees); or

(b) any accreditation under section 41 of that Act (accreditation under community safety accreditation schemes),

shall have regard to any relevant provision of a code of practice to which this section applies in the exercise or performance of the powers and duties conferred or imposed on them by that designation or accreditation.

(10) A failure on the part—

(a) of a police officer to comply with any provision of a code; or

(b) of any person other than a police officer who is charged with the duty of investigating offences or charging offenders to have regard to any relevant provision of a code in the discharge of that duty, or

(c) of a person designated under section 38 or 39 or accredited under section 41 of the *Police Reform Act* 2002 to have regard to any relevant provision of a code in the exercise or performance of the powers and duties conferred or imposed on him by that designation or accreditation,

shall not of itself render him liable to any criminal or civil proceedings.

(11) In all criminal and civil proceedings any code shall be admissible in evidence; and if any provision of a code appears to the court or tribunal conducting the proceedings to be relevant to any question arising in the proceedings it shall be taken into account in determining that question.

(12), (13) [*Armed forces etc.*]

[This section is printed as amended, and repealed in part, by the *Armed Forces Act* 1996, s.5 and Sched. 1, Pt IV, para. 105; the *Police Act* 1996, s.103(3) and Sched. 9; the *Criminal Justice and Police Act* 2001, ss.76(2) and 77; the *Police Reform Act* 2002, s.107(1) and (2), Sched. 7, para. 9(6)–(8), and Sched. 8; the *Criminal Justice Act* 2003, ss.11(1) and 332, and Sched. 37, Pt 1; and as amended, October 31, 2009 (*Armed Forces Act 2006 (Commencement No. 5) Order* 2009 (S.I. 2009 No. 1167)) by the *Armed Forces Act* 2006, s.378(1), and Sched. 16, para. 101 (substitution of subss (12) and (13) for subs. (12)).]

The Codes of Practice apply to: **1–9**

(a) police officers (sections 60(1), 60A(1), 66(1) and 67(10) of the *PACE Act* 1984)—this includes police forces such as the British Transport Police; and

(b) persons "other than police officers who are charged with the duty of investigating offences or charging offenders" (s.67(9)).

As to category (b), the court will consider whether a duty exists either in common law, statute or contract. A store detective has been held to have a duty to investigate incidents (*Bayliss* (1993) 98 Cr.App.R. 235) but a headteacher has not (*DPP v. G, The Times*, November 24, 1997). An inspector of the RSPCA may be bound (*RSPCA v. Eager* [1995] Crim.L.R. 59) as was an officer of the Federation Against Copyright Theft (*Joy v. FACT* [1993] Crim.L.R. 588)

The codes also apply to Revenue and Customs officers (*R. v. Okafor* (1994) 99 Cr.App.R. 97, CA); officers of the Serious Fraud Office (*R. v. Director of SFO, ex p. Saunders* [1988] Crim.L.R. 837, DC); and Inland Revenue special compliance officers investigating tax fraud (*R. v. Gill* [2004] 1 Cr.App.R. 20, CA), but not local tax inspectors (*R. v. Doncaster* (2008) 172 J.P. 202, CA).

In *R. v. Devani (Maya)* [2008] 1 Cr.App.R. 4, CA, it was held that the codes applied to a prison officer with powers of arrest equivalent to a constable (apparently a reference to the *Prison Act*, s.8), but not to operational support grade officers within the same prison who had no such powers. However, even though the codes do not apply to the latter, the judge should consider whether there is a breach of the spirit or substance of the codes: ibid., and *R. v. Ristic* (2004) 148 S.J. 942, CA.

In *R. v. Welcher* [2007] Crim.L.R. 804, CA (see also § 10–124, *post*), it was held that a line manager conducting interviews in accordance with his employers' disciplinary policy, with a view to reporting to the employers' disciplinary panel as to whether the defendant should be dismissed, was not "charged with the duty of investigating offences".

Where the Code refers to duties to be carried out by police officers at a police station it may be impractical for investigators who are not police officers to comply with those requirements. A Social Security investigator was held not to be in breach of the Code in failing to advise of the right to free legal advice on interview. This provision of the Code was held only to apply to investigators at the police station where the free Legal Aid representation scheme applied and a duty solicitor could be called: *R. (Social Security Secretary) v. South Central Division Magistrates, Daily Telegraph*, November 28, 2000, DC.

As to the exclusion of evidence obtained in breach of the Codes, see *post*, §§ 10–130 *et seq.*

C. STOP AND SEARCH

(1) Introduction

1–10 Section 1 of the *Police and Criminal Evidence Act* 1984 gives the police power to stop and search in England and Wales. Other statutory powers of stop and search also exist, *e.g. Firearms Act* 1968, s.47(3); *Misuse of Drugs Act* 1971, s.23(2), and *Terrorism Act* 2000, s.44. Under s.60 of the *Criminal Justice and Public Order Act* 1994, extended powers of search were introduced. Even where consent to a search is given, a statutory power of search must exist and the Code will still apply.

General

1–11 Code A sets out the principles governing the power of the police to stop and search persons and vehicles. Under s.117 of the *Police and Criminal Evidence Act* 1984, officers are permitted to use "reasonable force" if necessary in the exercise of this and other powers conferred under the Act.

(2) Reasonable grounds for suspecting

1–12 When exercising the power to stop and search persons or vehicles a constable must have reasonable grounds for suspecting that stolen or prohibited articles will be found. The existence of a reasonable suspicion is crucial to the existence of the power to stop and search.

"Reasonable suspicion" is not defined in the Act. Code A, paras 2.2 to 2.9, provide guidance on what amounts to a reasonable suspicion. There must be an objective basis for the suspicion based on facts, information or intelligence which are relevant to the likelihood of finding prohibited articles or stolen property: para. A:2.2. A reasonable suspicion cannot be based only on personal factors relevant to the suspect, (*e.g.* age, appearance or known record). There must also be reliable supporting intelligence or information or some specific behaviour by the person concerned giving rise to the suspicion. A reasonable suspicion cannot be based on generalisations or stereotypical images of certain groups or categories of people as more likely to be involved in criminal activity. See *post*, Appendix A.

The test as to whether reasonable grounds for the suspicion to justify an arrest existed is partly subjective, in that the arresting officer must have formed a genuine suspicion that the person being arrested was guilty of an offence, and partly objective, in that there had to be reasonable grounds for forming such a suspicion; such grounds could arise from information received from another (even if it subsequently proves to be false), provided that a reasonable man, having regard to all the circumstances, would regard them as reasonable grounds for suspicion; but a mere order from a superior officer to arrest a particular individual could not constitute reasonable grounds for such suspicion: *O'Hara v. Chief Constable of the Royal Ulster Constabulary* [1997] A.C. 286, HL. *O'Hara* was followed in *Commr of Police of the Metropolis v. Raissi* [2008] L.S. Gazette, November 27, 19, CA (Civ. Div.), where it was held that the arresting officer could not establish reasonable grounds for suspicion merely by inferring that his superiors must have had such grounds before instructing him to arrest a suspect.

See also *Siddiqui v. Swain* [1979] R.T.R. 454, 457, DC, in which "reasonable grounds to suspect" in the *Road Traffic Act* 1972, s.8(5) (now the *Road Traffic Act* 1988, s.7) were said to "import the further requirement that the constable in fact suspects"; *Parker v. Chief Constable of the Hampshire Constabulary*, unreported, June 25, 1999, CA (Civ. Div.), where it was held that an officer who had reasonable grounds to think it "possible" that one of two people in a car was someone he was entitled to arrest had been justified in arresting that person; and *Cumming v. Chief Constable of Northumbria Police, The Times*, January 2, 2004, CA (Civ. Div.) (there is nothing in principle to prevent (a) opportunity from amounting to reasonable grounds for suspicion, or (b) the police arresting more than one person even if the crime can only have been committed by one person).

As to having reasonable grounds for suspecting that an offence has been committed (see s.24(2), *post*, § 1–106), it is not necessary that an officer should have in mind specific statutory provisions, or that he should mentally identify specific offences with technicality or precision. He must, however, reasonably suspect the existence of facts amounting to an offence of a kind that he has in mind; unless he can do that, he cannot comply with his obligation under s.28(3) (*post*, § 1–114) to inform the suspect of the grounds of arrest: *Chapman v. DPP* (1988) 89 Cr.App.R. 190, DC; *Mossop v. DPP* [2003] 6 *Archbold News* 1, DC.

In *Kynaston v. DPP* (1987) 87 Cr.App.R. 200, DC, it was held that where the validity of an arrest is in issue, if the defence do not raise the question whether there were reasonable grounds for suspicion, it is open to the court, in appropriate circumstances, to infer that such grounds existed.

If the arresting officer knows at the time of arrest that there is no possibility of a charge being made, the arrest would be unlawful as he must have acted on an irrelevant consideration or for some improper motive: *Plange v. Chief Constable of South Humberside Police, The Times*, March 23, 1992, CA (Civ. Div.). *Plange* was referred to, without disapproval, in *Chalkley and Jeffries* [1998] 2 Cr.App.R. 79, CA, but the court seems to have thought that an arrest would be lawful if there were reasonable grounds to suspect the person arrested to be guilty of the offence for which he was told he was being arrested, even though the arresting officer knew that there was no intention to prosecute him for that offence, provided that the true reason for the arrest was to facilitate the investigation and prevention of more serious crime. This was *obiter*, as the officers who made the arrest knew nothing of their superiors' motives, and because, in any event, the validity of the arrest was irrelevant to the determination of the appeal.

(3) Power of constable to stop and search persons and vehicles

Police and Criminal Evidence Act 1984, s.1

Power of constable to stop and search persons, vehicles etc

1–13 **1.**—(1) A constable may exercise any power conferred by this section—

(a) in any place to which at the time when he proposes to exercise the power the public or any section of the public has access, on payment or otherwise, as of right or by virtue of express or implied permission; or

(b) in any other place to which people have ready access at the time when he proposes to exercise the power but which is not a dwelling.

(2) Subject to subsection (3) to (5) below, a constable—

(a) may search—

(i) any person or vehicle;

(ii) anything which is in or on a vehicle,

for stolen or prohibited articles, any article to which subsection (8A) below applies or any firework to which subsection (8B) below applies; and

(b) may detain a person or vehicle for the purpose of such a search.

(3) This section does not give a constable power to search a person or vehicle or anything in or on a vehicle unless he has reasonable grounds for suspecting that he will find stolen or prohibited articles, any article to which subsection (8A) below applies or any firework to which subsection (8B) below applies.

(4) If a person is in a garden or yard occupied with and used for the purposes of a dwelling or on other land so occupied and used, a constable may not search him in the exercise of the power conferred by this section unless the constable has reasonable grounds for believing—

(a) that he does not reside in the dwelling; and

(b) that he is not in the place in question with the express or implied permission of a person who resides in the dwelling.

(5) If a vehicle is in a garden or yard occupied with and used for the purposes of a dwelling or on other land so occupied and used, a constable may not search the vehicle or anything in or on it in the exercise of the power conferred by this section unless he has reasonable grounds for believing—

(a) that the person in charge of the vehicle does not reside in the dwelling; and

(b) that the vehicle is not in the place in question with the express or implied permission of a person who resides in the dwelling.

1–14 (6) If in the course of such a search a constable discovers an article which he has reasonable grounds for suspecting to be a stolen or prohibited article, an article to which subsection (8A) below applies or a firework to which subsection 8B below applies he may seize it.

(7) An article is prohibited for the purposes of this Part of this Act if it is—

(a) an offensive weapon; or

(b) an article—

(i) made or adapted for use in the course of or in connection with an offence to which this sub-paragraph applies; or

(ii) intended by the person having it with him for such use by him or by some other person.

(8) The offences to which subsection (7)(b)(i) above applies are—

(a) burglary;

(b) theft;

(c) offences under section 12 of the *Theft Act* 1968 (taking motor vehicle or other conveyance without authority);

(d) fraud (contrary to section 1 of the *Fraud Act* 2006); and

(e) offences under section 1 of the *Criminal Damage Act* 1971 (destroying or damaging property).

(8A) This subsection applies to any article in relation to which a person has committed, or is committing or is going to commit an offence under section 139 of the *Criminal Justice Act* 1988.

(8B) This subsection applies to any firework which a person possesses in contravention of a prohibition imposed by fireworks regulations.

(8C) In this section—

(a) "firework" shall be constructed in accordance with the definition of "fireworks" in section 1(1) of the *Fireworks Act* 2003, and

(b) "fireworks regulations" has the same meaning as in that Act.

(9) In this Part of this Act "offensive weapon" means any article—

(a) made or adapted for use for causing injury to persons; or

(b) intended by the person having it with him for such use by him or by some other person.

[This section is printed as amended by the *Criminal Justice Act* 1988, s.140, Pt 1; the *Criminal Justice Act* 2003, ss.1 and 332 and Sched. 37; the *Serious Organised Crime and Police Act* 2005, s.115; and the *Fraud Act* 2006, s.14(1) and Sched. 1, para. 21.]

The term "constable" covers every police officer of whatever rank: *Lewis v. Cattle* [1938] 2 K.B. 454. **1–15**

As to "reasonable grounds for suspecting", see *ante*, § 1–12.

Section 139 of the *Criminal Justice Act* 1988 refers to unlawful possession of a bladed article.

(4) Provisions relating to search under section 1

Police and Criminal Evidence Act 1984, s.2

Provisions relating to search under s.1 and other powers

2.—(1) A constable who detains a person or vehicle in the exercise— **1–16**

(a) of the power conferred by section 1 above; or

(b) of any other power—

(i) to search a person without first arresting him; or

(ii) to search a vehicle without making an arrest,

need not conduct a search if it appears to him subsequently—

(i) that no search is required; or

(ii) that a search is impracticable.

(2) If a constable contemplates a search, other than a search of an unattended vehicle, in the exercise—

(a) of the power conferred by section 1 above; or

(b) of any other power, except the power conferred by section 6 below and the power conferred by section 27(2) of the *Aviation Security Act* 1982—

(i) to search a person without first arresting him; or

(ii) to search a vehicle without making an arrest,

it shall be his duty, subject to subsection (4) below, to take reasonable steps before he commences the search to bring to the attention of the appropriate person—

(i) if the constable is not in uniform, documentary evidence that he is a constable; and

(ii) whether he is in uniform or not, the matters specified in subsection (3) below;

and the constable shall not commence the search until he has performed that duty.

(3) The matters referred to in subsection (2)(ii) above are— **1–17**

(a) the constable's name and the name of the police station to which he is attached;

(b) the object of the proposed search;

(c) the constable's grounds for proposing to make it; and

(d) the effect of section 3(7) or (8) below, as may be appropriate.

(4) A constable need not bring the effect of section 3(7) or (8) below to the attention of

the appropriate person if it appears to the constable that it will not be practicable to make the record in section 3(1) below.

(5) In this section "the appropriate person" means—

(a) if the constable proposes to search a person, that person; and

(b) if he proposes to search a vehicle, or anything in or on a vehicle, the person in charge of the vehicle.

(6) On completing a search of an unattended vehicle or anything in or on such a vehicle in the exercise of any such power as is mentioned in subsection (2) above a constable shall leave a notice—

(a) stating that he has searched it;

(b) giving the name of the police station to which he is attached;

(c) stating that an application for compensation for any damage caused by the search may be made to that police station; and

(d) stating the effect of section 3(8) below.

(7) The constable shall leave the notice inside the vehicle unless it is not reasonably practicable to do so without damaging the vehicle.

(8) The time for which a person or vehicle may be detained for the purposes of such a search is such time as is reasonably required to permit a search to be carried out either at the place where the person or vehicle was first detained or nearby.

(9) Neither the power conferred by section 1 above nor any other power to detain and search a person without first arresting him or to detain and search a vehicle without making an arrest is to be construed—

(a) as authorising a constable to require a person to remove any of his clothing in public other than an outer coat, jacket or gloves; or

(b) as authorising a constable not in uniform to stop a vehicle.

(10) This section and section 1 above apply to vessels, aircraft and hovercraft as they apply to vehicles.

1–18 Section 6 of the Act confers defined powers of stop and search on constables employed in undertakings related to railways, road and water transport and docks and harbours, etc. Searches may be carried out on vehicles before they leave the goods areas of the relevant premises. The *Aviation Security Act* 1982 confers powers to stop and search persons and vehicles leaving a cargo area of an aerodrome.

Under the Code, a constable may stop and question a suspect and then has a discretion not to proceed with a search if it is unnecessary or impracticable. If the search is to proceed the officer has a duty to comply with the requirements of this section, providing the information specified. All these details must be recorded in writing and the person involved has a right to be given a copy of this record either in person or if the search was of an unattended vehicle, then the record must be left with the vehicle. Any failure to comply with the section means a constable is not acting in the execution of his duty and a search will not be lawful: *Osman v. DPP* (1999) 163 J.P. 725, DC. See also *R. (Bonner) v. DPP* [2005] A.C.D. 227 (56), QBD, where it was held that the requirements of section 2 and the Codes had to be strictly observed prior to an intended search even where the person apprehended knew that the search was being conducted by a police officer and there were fears for the safety of an officer; *R. v. Bristol* (2007) 172 J.P. 161, CA, where a police officer's failure to state his name and the police station to which he was attached rendered his subsequent search of the suspect unlawful, notwithstanding the officer's belief that the suspect was in possession of drugs and was about to swallow the drugs and *Michaels v. Highbury Corner Magistrates' Court* [2010] Crim.L.R. 506, DC (officer's failure to inform suspect of officer's name and the police station to which he was attached fatal to search, even though the suspect knew the officer).

(5) Duty to make records concerning searches

Police and Criminal Evidence Act 1984, s.3

Duty to make records concerning searches

1–19 **3.**—(1) Where a constable has carried out a search in the exercise of any such power as is mentioned in section 2(1) above, other than a search—

(a) under section 6 below; or
(b) under section 27(2) of the *Aviation Security Act* 1982,

a record of the search shall be made in writing unless it is not practicable to do so.

(2) If a record of a search is required to be made by subsection (1) above—

(a) in a case where the search results in a person being arrested and taken to a police station, the constable shall secure that the record is made as part of the person's custody record;
(b) in any other case, the constable shall make the record on the spot, or, if that is not practicable, as soon as practicable after the completion of the search.

(3)–(5) [*Repealed by the Crime and Security Act 2010, s.1*]

(6) The record of a search of a person or a vehicle— **1–20**

(a) shall state—
  (i) the object of the search;
  (ii) the grounds for making it;
  (iii) the date and time when it was made;
  (iv) the place where it was made;

  [except in the case of a search of an unattended vehicle, the ethnic origins of the person searched or the person in charge of the vehicle searched (as the case may be); and;

  (vi) [Repealed by the *Crime and Security Act* 2010, s.1]
(b) shall identify the constable who carried out the search.

(6A) The requirement in subsection (6)(a)(v) above for a record to state a person's ethnic origins is a requirement to state—

(a) the ethnic origins of the person as described by the person, and
(b) if different, the ethnic origins of the person as perceived by the constable.]

(7) If a record of a search of a person has been made under this section the person who was searched shall be entitled to a copy of the record if he asks for one before the end of the period specified in subsection (9) below.

(8) If—

(a) the owner of a vehicle which has been searched or the person who was in charge of the vehicle at the time when it was searched asks for a copy of the record of the search before the end of the period specified in subsection (9) below; and
(b) a record of the search of the vehicle has been made under this section.

the person who made the request shall be entitled to a copy.

(9) The period mentioned in subsections (7) and (8) above is the period of 3 months beginning with the date on which the search was made.

(10) The requirements imposed by this section with regard to records of searches of vehicles shall apply also to records of searches of vessels, aircraft and hovercraft.

[This section is printed as amended by the *Crime and Security Act* 2010, s.1 (omission of italicised words, insertion of words in square brackets).]

(6) Road checks

Police and Criminal Evidence Act 1984, s.4

Road checks

4.—(1) This section shall have effect in relation to the conduct of road checks by police officers for the purpose of ascertaining whether a vehicle is carrying— **1–21**

(a) a person who has committed an offence other than a road traffic offence or a vehicle excise offence;
(b) a person who is a witness to such an offence;
(c) a person intending to commit such an offence; or
(d) a person who is unlawfully at large.

(2) For the purposes of this section a road check consists of the exercise in a locality of the power conferred by section 163 of the *Road Traffic Act* 1988 in such a way as to stop during the period for which its exercise in that way in that locality continues all vehicles or vehicles selected by any criterion.

(3) Subject to subsection (5) below, there may only be such a road check if a police officer of the rank of superintendent or above authorises it in writing.

(4) An officer may only authorise a road check under subsection (3) above—

(a) for the purpose specified in subsection (1)(a) above, if he has reasonable grounds—

(i) for believing that the offence is an indictable offence; and

(ii) for suspecting that the person is, or is about to be, in the locality in which vehicles would be stopped if the road check were authorised;

(b) for the purpose specified in subsection (1)(b) above, if he has reasonable grounds for believing that the offence is an indictable offence;

(c) for the purpose specified in subsection (1)(c) above, if he has reasonable grounds—

(i) for believing that the offence would be an indictable offence; and

(ii) for suspecting that the person is, or is about to be, in the locality in which vehicles would be stopped if the road check were authorised;

(d) for the purpose specified in subsection (1)(d) above, if he has reasonable grounds for suspecting that the person is, or is about to be, in that locality.

1–22 (5) An officer below the rank of superintendent may authorise such a road check if it appears to him that it is required as a matter of urgency for one of the purposes specified in subsection (1) above.

(6) If an authorisation is given under subsection (5) above, it shall be the duty of the officer who gives it—

(a) to make a written record of the time at which he gives it; and

(b) to cause an officer of the rank of superintendent or above to be informed that it has been given.

(7) The duties imposed by subsection (6) above shall be performed as soon as it is practicable to do so.

(8) An officer to whom a report is made under subsection (6) above may, in writing, authorise the road check to continue.

(9) If such an officer considers that the road check should not continue, he shall record in writing—

(a) the fact that it took place; and

(b) the purpose for which it took place.

(10) An officer giving an authorisation under this section shall specify the locality in which vehicles are to be stopped.

(11) An officer giving an authorisation under this section, other than an authorisation under subsection (5) above—

(a) shall specify a period, not exceeding seven days, during which the road check may continue; and

(b) may direct that the road check—

(i) shall be continuous; or

(ii) shall be conducted at specified times, during that period.

1–23 (12) If it appears to an officer of the rank of superintendent or above that a road check ought to continue beyond the period for which it has been authorised he may, from time to time, in writing specify a further period, not exceeding seven days, during which it may continue.

(13) Every written authorisation shall specify—

(a) the name of the officer giving it;

(b) the purpose of the road check; and

(c) the locality in which vehicles are to be stopped.

(14) The duties to specify the purposes of a road check imposed by subsections (9) and (13) above include duties to specify any relevant indictable offence.

(15) Where a vehicle is stopped in a road check, the person in charge of the vehicle at the time when it is stopped shall be entitled to obtain a written statement of the purpose of the road check if he applies for such a statement not later than the end of the period of twelve months from the day on which the vehicle was stopped.

(16) Nothing in this section affects the exercise by police officers of any power to stop vehicles for purposes other than those specified in subsection (1) above.

[This section is printed as amended by the *Road Traffic (Consequential Provisions) Act* 1988, s.4, and Sched. 3, para. 27; and the *Serious Organised Crime and Police Act* 2005, s.111, and Sched. 7, para. 43.]

Road Traffic Act 1988, s.163

Power of police to stop vehicles

163.—(1) A person driving a mechanically propelled vehicle on a road must stop the vehicle on being required to do so by a constable in uniform or a traffic officer. **1–24**

(2) A person riding a cycle on a road must stop the cycle on being required to do so by a constable in uniform or a traffic officer.

(3) If a person fails to comply with this section he is guilty of an offence.

(4) [*Repealed.*]

[This section is printed as amended by the *Road Traffic Act* 1991, s.48, and Sched. 4, para. 67; the *Police Reform Act* 2002, s.49(1); the *Traffic Management Act* 2004, s.6(4); and, as repealed in part, by the *Serious Organised Crime and Police Act* 2005, ss.111 and 174(2), Sched. 7, para. 27(3), and Sched. 17, Pt 2.]

Section 4 extends the power to stop vehicles on the road to enable searches to be made. A constable in uniform has power under the *Road Traffic Act* 1988, s.163 to stop vehicles. Section 4 allows for the power under s.163 to be used for a specified time, not exceeding seven days, in a specified locality for the purposes of carrying out searches of vehicles under s.1. There is no requirement for a reasonable suspicion to attach to the individual vehicles that are stopped but *PACE* 1984, ss.1 and 2 must still be complied with as any search is carried out. The checks must be authorised by a senior officer unless it is a matter of urgency. The authorisation may only be given if the authorising officer has reasonable grounds for believing the matters listed in s.4(4).

(7) Power to stop and search in anticipation of violence

Criminal Justice and Public Order Act 1994, s.60

Powers to stop and search in anticipation of, or after, violence

60.—(1) If a police officer of or above the rank of inspector reasonably believes— **1–25**

(a) that incidents involving serious violence may take place in any locality in his police area, and that it is expedient to give an authorisation under this section to prevent their occurrence, or:

(aa) that —

(i) an incident involving serious violence has taken place in England and Wales in his police area;

(ii) a dangerous instrument or offensive weapon used in the incident is being carried in any locality in his police area by a person; and

(iii) it is expedient to give an authorisation under this section to find the instrument or weapon;

(b) that persons are carrying dangerous instruments or offensive weapons in any locality in his police area without good reason,

he may give an authorisation that the powers conferred by this section are to be exercisable at any place within that locality for a specified period not exceeding 24 hours.

(2) [*Repealed.*]

(3) If it appears to an officer of or above the rank of superintendent that it is expedient to do so, having regard to offences which have, or are reasonably suspected to have, been committed in connection with any activity falling within the authorisation, he may direct that the authorisation shall continue in being for a further 24 hours.

(3A) If an inspector gives an authorisation under subsection (1) he must, as soon as it is practicable to do so, cause an officer of or above the rank of superintendent to be informed.

(4) This section confers on any constable in uniform power—

(a) to stop any pedestrian and search him or anything carried by him for offensive weapons or dangerous instruments;

(b) to stop any vehicle and search the vehicle, its driver and any passenger for offensive weapons or dangerous instruments.

(4A) [*Repealed.*]

(5) A constable may, in the exercise of the powers conferred by subsection (4) above, stop any person or vehicle and make any search he thinks fit whether or not he has any grounds for suspecting that the person or vehicle is carrying weapons or articles of that kind.

(6) If in the course of a search under this section a constable discovers a dangerous instrument or an article which he has reasonable grounds for suspecting to be an offensive weapon, he may seize it.

(7) This section applies (with the necessary modifications) to ships, aircraft and hovercraft as it applies to vehicles.

(8) A person who fails

(a) to stop, or to stop a vehicle

(b) [*Repealed.*]

when required to do so by a constable in the exercise of his powers under this section shall be liable on summary conviction to imprisonment for a term not exceeding *one month* [51 weeks] or to a fine not exceeding level 3 on the standard scale or both.

(9) Subject to subsection (9ZA), authorisation under this section shall be in writing signed by the officer giving it and shall specify the grounds on which it is given and the locality in which and the period during which the powers conferred by this section are exercisable and a direction under subsection (3) above shall also be given in writing or, where that is not practicable, recorded in writing as soon as it is practicable to do so.

(9ZA) An authorisation under subsection (1)(aa) need not be given in writing where it is not practicable to do so but any oral authorisation must state the matters which would otherwise have to be specified under subsection (9) and must be recorded in writing as soon as it is practicable to do so.

1–26 (9A) The preceding provisions of this section, so far as they relate to an authorisation by a member of the British Transport Police Force (including one who for the time being has the same powers and privileges as a member of a police force for a police area), shall have effect as if the references to a locality in his police area were references to a place in England and Wales specified in section 31(1)(a) to (f) of the *Railways and Transport Safety Act* 2003 and as if the reference in subsection (1)(aa)(i) above to his police area were a reference to any place falling within section 31(1)(a) to (f) of the Act of 2003.

(10) Where a vehicle is stopped by a constable under this section, the driver shall be entitled to obtain a written statement that the vehicle was stopped under the powers conferred by this section if he applies for such a statement not later than the end of the period of twelve months from the day on which the vehicle was stopped as respects a pedestrian who is stopped and searched under this section.

(10A) A person who is searched by a constable under this section shall be entitled to obtain a written statement that he was searched under the powers conferred by this section if he applies for such a statement not later than the end of the period of twelve months from the day on which he was searched.

(11) In this section—

"dangerous instruments" means instruments which have a blade or are sharply pointed;

"offensive weapon" has the meaning given by section 1(9) of the *Police and Criminal Evidence Act* 1984 or, in relation to Scotland, section 47(4) of the *Criminal Law (Consolidation) (Scotland) Act* 1995; but in subsections (1)(aa), (4), (5) and (6) above and subsection (11A) below includes, in the case of an incident of the kind mentioned in subsection (1)(aa)(i) above, any article used in the incident to cause or threaten injury to any person or otherwise to intimidate; and

"vehicle" includes a caravan as defined in section 29(1) of the *Caravan Sites and Control of Development Act* 1960.

(11A) For the purposes of this section, a person carries a dangerous instrument or an offensive weapon if he has it in his possession.

(12) The powers conferred by this section are in addition to and not in derogation of, any power otherwise conferred.

[This section is printed as amended and repealed in part by the *Knives Act* 1997, s.8; the *Crime and Disorder Act* 1998, s.25; the *Anti-Terrorism, Crime and Security Act* 2001, ss.101 and 125, and Scheds 7 and 8; the *Railways and Transport Safety Act* 2003, s.73(1) and Sched. 5, para. 4(1) and (2)(f); the *British Transport Police (Transitional and Consequential Provisions) Order* 2004 (S.I. 2004 No. 1573), Art. 12(3)(a); and the *Serious Crime Act* 2007, s.87; and, as from a day to be appointed, by the *Criminal Justice Act* 2003, s.280(2), and Sched. 26, para. 45(1) and (2) (substitution of words in square brackets for italicised words).]

This section allows for random stop and search powers to be exercised by any police constable in uniform in any locality where an authorisation has been given. This is a temporary extension of police powers available in the specific situations outlined. The Notes for Guidance state that the authorisation given under the section must have an objective basis such as intelligence or information about a history of violence at a particular location or an increase in crime involving weapons in the area. The authorising officer must determine the geographical area that constitutes a "locality". The power can be authorised for 24 hours and extended for a further 24 hours if the conditions of the section are met. **1–27**

Part I

The power of search is limited to offensive weapons or dangerous instruments that have a blade or are sharply pointed. Unlike the power to stop and search in s.1 of *PACE Act* 1984, a constable in uniform may exercise the powers conferred under s.60(4) if he or she thinks fit, regardless of whether there are any grounds for suspecting that the person or vehicle is carrying offensive weapons or dangerous articles. If during the course of a search under this section a constable discovers a dangerous instrument or an article which he or she has reasonable grounds for suspecting to be an offensive weapon, it may be seized. Items seized may be retained in accordance with s.60A of the *Criminal Justice and Public Order Act* 1994 and regulations made by the Secretary of State. Section 2 of the 1984 Act applies with the requirements to explain and record the searches.

(8) Power to require removal of disguises

Criminal Justice and Public Order Act 1994, s.60AA

Powers to require removal of disguises

60AA.—(1) Where— **1–28**

(a) an authorisation under section 60 is for the time being in force in relation to any locality for any period, or

(b) an authorisation under subsection (3) that the powers conferred by subsection (2) shall be exercisable at any place in a locality is in force for any period,

those powers shall be exercisable at any place in that locality at any time in that period.

(2) This subsection confers power on any constable in uniform—

(a) to require any person to remove any item which the constable reasonably believes that person is wearing wholly or mainly for the purpose of concealing his identity;

(b) to seize any item which the constable reasonably believes any person intends to wear wholly or mainly for that purpose.

(3) If a police officer of or above the rank of inspector reasonably believes—

(a) that activities may take place in any locality in his police area that are likely (if they take place) to involve the commission of offences, and

(b) that it is expedient, in order to prevent or control the activities, to give an authorisation under this subsection,

he may give an authorisation that the powers conferred by this section shall be exercisable at any place within that locality for a specified period not exceeding twenty-four hours.

(4) If it appears to an officer of or above the rank of superintendent that it is expedient to do so, having regard to offences which—

(a) have been committed in connection with the activities in respect of which the authorisation was given, or

(b) are reasonably suspected to have been so committed,

he may direct that the authorisation shall continue in force for a further twenty-four hours.

(5) If an inspector gives an authorisation under subsection (3), he must, as soon as it is practicable to do so, cause an officer of or above the rank of superintendent to be informed.

(6) Any authorisation under this section—

(a) shall be in writing and signed by the officer giving it; and

(b) shall specify—

(i) the grounds on which it is given;

(ii) the locality in which the powers conferred by this section are exercisable;

(iii) the period during which those powers are exercisable;

and a direction under subsection (4) shall also be given in writing or, where that is not practicable, recorded in writing as soon as it is practicable to do so.

1–29 (7) A person who fails to remove an item worn by him when required to do so by a constable in the exercise of his power under this section shall be liable, on summary conviction, to imprisonment for a term not exceeding *one month* [51 weeks] or to a fine not exceeding level 3 on the standard scale or both.

(8) The preceding provisions of this section, so far as they relate to an authorisation by a member of the British Transport Police Force (including one who for the time being has the same powers and privileges as a member of a police force for a police area), shall have effect as if references to a locality or to a locality in his police area were references to any locality in or in the vicinity of any policed premises, or to the whole or any part of any such premises.

(9) [...]

(10) The powers conferred by this section are in addition to, and not in derogation of, any power otherwise conferred.

(11) This section does not extend to Scotland.

[This section was inserted by the *Anti-terrorism, Crime and Security Act* 2001, s.94(1). It is printed as repealed in part by the *Railways and Transport Safety Act* 2003, s.73 and Sched. 5, para. 4(1) and (2)(f); and as amended, as from a day to be appointed, by the *Criminal Justice Act* 2003, s.280(2), and Sched. 26, para. 45(1) and (3) (substitution of words in square brackets for italicised words).]

1–30 The authorisation itself must be properly documented but the exercise of this power has not been held to be a search so the requirements of s.2 of *PACE* 1984 do not apply: *DPP v. Avery* [2002] 1 Cr.App.R. 31, DC.

D. ENTRY, SEARCH AND SEIZURE

(1) Introduction

1–31 Part II of the *PACE Act* 1984 (*i.e.* ss.8 to 23) consolidates many, but not all, police powers of entry, search and seizure. It contains provisions relating to search warrants, privileged material (ss.8–16), and seizure (ss.19–22). Section 8 creates a general power to obtain a search warrant from a justice of the peace in the case of an indictable offence. Sections 15 (search warrants—safeguards), 16 (execution of warrants) and 19 (general power of seizure), relate to all powers of entry, including those not repealed by the 1984 Act. There are many statutes enabling a justice of the peace to issue a warrant authorising a constable to search for and seize certain items and to enter premises for the purpose of doing so: see the statutes listed *post*, § 1–84 (powers to which the *Criminal Justice and Police Act* 2001, s.50, applies). There are also statutory powers relating to search and seizure, not printed in this work, exercisable in the Crown Court: see the *PACE Act* 1984, s.9 and Sched. 1; the *Drug Trafficking Act* 1994, ss.55–59A; and the *Proceeds of Crime Act* 2002, ss.343–379.

1–32 Where an officer wishes to gain entry to premises for the purposes of a search and he believes consent is either unforthcoming or impracticable, application will be made to a magistrate or district judge for a search warrant. The warrant from the court will authorise the officer to enter and search named premises for specific items. Such applications will be made in writing generally in standard format and will be signed and substantiated on oath or affirmation. The application can be made to the magistrate or district judge in court, in the retiring room or, in urgent situations, out of hours to the magistrate or district judge at home. The requirements of s.8 of *PACE* 1984 must be fully complied with and the principles of the European Convention on Human Rights must be considered, particularly Art. 8 which provides the right to respect for privacy and family life. The granting authority must be satisfied that the issue of a warrant is a proportional step and that the infringement of Art. 8 rights is in accordance with the law and necessary in a democratic society in the interests of national security, public safety or the economic well-being of the country, for the prevention of disorder or crime, for the protection of health and morals or for the protection of the rights and freedom of others.

A search of premises has been held to be an interference with Art. 8 rights (see *Funke v. France* (1993) 16 E.H.R.R. 297; *Chappell v. UK* (1990) 12 E.H.R.R. 1) and justification for the infringement is necessary. The prevention of crime or the protection of others would form the required qualification on the enjoyment of the right to privacy. Questions of proportionality must also be considered not only in the issue of the warrant but also the way in which it is to be executed. Magistrates may inquire into the nature of the premises and whether families and neighbours will be treated with respect and sensitivity within the remit of the warrant.

The powers of seizure under the *PACE Act* 1984 and many other statutes were considerably extended by the provisions of *Criminal Justice and Police Act* 2001, Pt 2. The intention was first to remedy the problem highlighted by the decision in *R. v. Chesterfield JJ., ex p. Bramley* [2000] Q.B. 576, DC (no entitlement to seize items for purpose of sifting through them later to see whether they fall within scope of warrant), and secondly, to give the police and others power to seize and retain material which could not itself be seized but which is inextricably linked with material which is liable to be seized. The second of these purposes is related to the difficulties encountered with modern technology and the increasing use of computers. For the text of Pt 2, see *post*, §§ 1–67 *et seq.* Guidance in relation to the new powers is included in the Code of Practice for the Searching of Premises by Police Officers and the Seizure of Property found by Police Officers on Persons or Premises (Code B): see paras B:7.7 *et seq.* (Appendix A).

As to entry on or interference with property for the purpose of preventing or detecting serious crime under the *Police Act* 1997, see *post*, § 1–87. As to entry under a warrant to search for and seize documents required under a disclosure notice issued pursuant to the *Serious Organised Crime and Police Act* 2005, see *post*, §§ 1–89 *et seq.*

(2) Warrant to enter and search premises

Police and Criminal Evidence Act 1984, s.8

Power of justice of the peace to authorise entry and search of premises

8.—(1) If on an application made by a constable a justice of the peace is satisfied that there are reasonable grounds for believing— **1–33**

(a) that an indictable offence has been committed; and
(b) that there is material on premises mentioned in subsection (1A) below which is likely to be of substantial value (whether by itself or together with other material) to the investigation of the offence; and
(c) that the material is likely to be relevant evidence; and
(d) that it does not consist of or include items subject to legal privilege, excluded material or special procedure material; and
(e) that any of the conditions specified in subsection (3) below applies in relation to each set of premises specified in the application,

he may issue a warrant authorising a constable to enter and search the premises.

(1A) The premises referred to in subsection (1)(b) above are—

(a) one or more sets of premises specified in the application (in which case the application is for a "specific premises warrant"); or
(b) any premises occupied or controlled by a person specified in the application,

including such sets of premises as are so specified (in which case the application is for an "all premises warrant").

(1B) If the application is for an all premises warrant, the justice of the peace must also be satisfied—

(a) that because of the particulars of the offence referred to in paragraph (a) of subsection (1) above, there are reasonable grounds for believing that it is necessary to search premises occupied or controlled by the person in question which are not specified in the application in order to find the material referred to in paragraph (b) of that subsection; and

(b) that it is not reasonably practicable to specify in the application all the premises which he occupies or controls and which might need to be searched.

(1C) The warrant may authorise entry to and search of premises on more than one occasion if, on the application, the justice of the peace is satisfied that it is necessary to authorise multiple entries in order to achieve the purpose for which he issues the warrant.

(1D) If it authorises multiple entries, the number of entries authorised may be unlimited, or limited to a maximum.

(2) A constable may seize and retain anything for which a search has been authorised under subsection (1) above.

(3) The conditions mentioned in subsection (1)(e) above are—

(a) that it is not practicable to communicate with any person entitled to grant entry to the premises;

(b) that it is practicable to communicate with a person entitled to grant entry to the premises but it is not practicable to communicate with any person entitled to grant access to the evidence;

(c) that entry to the premises will not be granted unless a warrant is produced;

(d) that the purpose of a search may be frustrated or seriously prejudiced unless a constable arriving at the premises can secure immediate entry to them.

(4) In this Act "relevant evidence", in relation to an offence, means anything that would be admissible in evidence at a trial for the offence.

(5) The power to issue a warrant conferred by this section is in addition to any such power otherwise conferred.

(6) This section applies in relation to a relevant offence (as defined in section 28D(4) of the *Immigration Act* 1971) as it applies in relation to an indictable offence.

(7) Section 4 of the *Summary Jurisdiction (Process) Act* 1881 (execution of process of English courts in Scotland) shall apply to a warrant issued on the application of an officer of Revenue and Customs under this section by virtue of section 114 below.

[This section is printed as amended by the *Immigration and Asylum Act* 1999, s.169(1), and Sched. 14, para. 80(1) and (2); the *Serious Organised Crime and Police Act* 2005, ss.111, 113(1)-(4), and 114(1) and (2), and Sched. 7, para. 43(1) and (3); and the *Finance Act* 2007, s.86]

For "items subject to legal privilege", see s.10, *post*, § 1–37; for "excluded material", see ss.11 to 13, *post*, §§ 1–40 *et seq.*; and for "special procedure material", see s.14, *post*, § 1–43. As to the extension of Pt II so as to have effect as if the references to indictable offences in s.8 included any conduct which is an offence under the law of a country or territory outside the United Kingdom and would constitute an indictable offence if it had occurred in any part of the United Kingdom, see s.16 of the *Crime (International Co-operation) Act* 2003 (as amended by the *Serious Organised Crime and Police Act* 2005, s.111, and Sched. 7, para. 51(1) and (2)). "Material" in s.8(1) is wide enough to embrace a computer and its hard disk: *R. (Faisaltex Ltd) v. Preston Crown Court*, , [2009] 1 Cr.App.R. 37.

1–34 This section confers on district judges and magistrates the power to authorise constables to enter and search premises. The exercise of the power is also subject to the safeguards contained in s.15—see *post*, § 1–45.

The power under s.8 is draconian. In *Redknapp v. Commr of the City of London Police Department* [2009] 1 W.L.R. 2091, DC (see also *post* § 1–50) it was said that obtaining a search warrant is never a formality, as it authorises invading a person's home; all the material necessary to justify the warrant's grant should be contained in the information provided on the application form; if the magistrate requires any further information to satisfy himself that the warrant is justified, a note should be made of the additional information so that there is a proper record of the full basis upon which the warrant has been granted; where the required information is not contained in the application form or in such a note the warrant is unlawfully issued.

In *R. (Wood) v. North Avon Magistrates' Court* (2009) 174 J.P. 157, DC (see also *post*, § 1–57), the observations in *Redknapp*, *ante*, were approved. It was said also that, as a matter of good practice, a police officer applying for a search warrant under s.8 should, save in exceptional circumstances, be an officer directly involved in the investigation; and, in making the application, the police should make full and frank disclosure of any earlier search of the premises, because that would be material as to whether evidence of substantial value or relevance would still be on the premises (s.8(1)(b), (c)), and also as to whether the purposes of a search would be frustrated or seriously prejudiced if advance warning were to be given (s.8(3)(d)), which would depend on whether or not the defendant had co-operated with the earlier search.

Furthermore, before issuing a warrant, a magistrate must be satisfied, amongst other requirements set out in the section, that the material in question is not *prima facie* subject to legal privilege within s.10(1) or special procedure material as defined by s.14; and, if there is any doubt, the application should be refused, leaving the applicant to apply to a Crown Court judge under s.9 and Sched. 1 (Crown Court judge's power to make production order or issue warrant in relation to excluded material or special procedure material): *R. v. Guildhall Magistrates' Court, ex p. Primlaks Holdings Co (Panama) Inc* [1990] 1 Q.B. 261, CA.

Before a warrant to enter and search premises may be issued the district judge or magistrate before whom the information is laid must be satisfied that there are reasonable grounds for believing that the conditions set out in the section exist. This means they must:

a.) Identify the indictable offence.

b.) Check whether the warrant is for specific premises or for all premises. Check the details of all addresses or locations to be searched, which can include premises or vehicles. In the case of multi-occupancy premises such as hostels or offices care must be taken to clarify the parameters of the search. For an all premises warrant, check the details of the person named as being in occupation or control of the premises specified and also check that there is good reason why all the premises in his control or occupation cannot be specified in view of the nature of the offence alleged and the material sought.

c.) Check the number of entries required under the warrant and the reasons for requesting multiple entries either limited or not.

d.) Check the list and specification of the items being sought and confirm that they are likely to be of substantial value to the investigation.

e.) Check why these items would be relevant and admissible at the trial and confirm that the items being sought are not subject to legal privilege or in any other way confidential. (A search of business or office premises—especially a lawyer's office may give rise to immediate concerns under this provision).

f.) Inquiries should also be made about the nature of the premises and whether any vulnerable people such as children or the elderly may be affected by the execution of a warrant.

g.) Check whether a search warrant has been issued previously for the same premises and confirm the history of any earlier application.

The officer may be questioned on oath to ascertain this information and a record of **1–35**
any answers should be appended to the information. See *Redknapp* case, *ante*.

It is not a condition precedent to granting a search warrant under section 8 that other methods of obtaining the material have been tried without success or have not been tried because they are bound to fail: *R. v. Billericay Justices, ex p. Frank Harris (Coaches)* [1991] Crim.L.R. 472.

For a case in which the police were criticised for applying to a justice of the peace under s.8 of the 1984 Act, instead of to the Crown Court under s.9, see *Power-Hynes v. Norwich Magistrates' Court* (2009) 173 J.P. 573, DC, where it was held that there was no jurisdiction under section 8(1)(d) in relation to an accountant acting as company secretary to various companies, some of which were unconnected to the police investigation, given the likelihood that the documents in his possession included special procedure material. It was not sufficient that the application for the warrant purported to exclude special procedure material. There should have been a specific exclusion of such material in the warrant itself. See also *post*, § 1–46.

1–36 If an item is seized as apparently falling within the scope of the warrant, but subsequently transpires to be subject to legal professional privilege, its seizure does not thereby become unlawful unless the officer had reasonable grounds to believe it to be subject to legal privilege at the time of seizure (see section 19(6) of the 1984 Act (*post*, § 1–56)): *ex p. Bramley*, *ante*, § 1–32. The court said that if an officer comes across material which may be privileged, he should try to reach agreement at the time of the search as to whether it is privileged but, if agreement is impossible, it would be wise to package any such items separately for later analysis: he is not bound to accept at face value a claim to privilege. As to packaging separately items falling within the search criteria, but which may be privileged, see also *R. v. Customs and Excise Commrs, ex p. Popely* [1999] S.T.C. 1016, DC. In both *ex p. Bramley* and *ex p. Popely*, the court dissented from the view expressed in *R. v. Southwark Crown Court, ex p. Gross* [1998] C.O.D. 445, DC, that the innocent seizure of privileged material is unlawful. As to the duty to return legally privileged material that has been seized, see s.54 of the *Criminal Justice and Police Act* 2001 (*post*, § 1–74). Note also that s.19(6) of the 1984 Act (*ante*) is disapplied in relation to the extended powers of seizure provided for in ss.50 and 51 of the 2001 Act (*post*, §§ 1–67 *et seq.*).

(3) Items subject to legal privilege, excluded material, special procedure material

Police and Criminal Evidence Act 1984, s.10

Meaning of "items subject to legal privilege"

1–37 **10.**—(1) Subject to subsection (2) below, in this Act "items subject to legal privilege" means—

(a) communications between a professional legal adviser and his client or any person representing his client made in connection with the giving of legal advice to the client;

(b) communications between a professional legal adviser and his client or any person representing his client or between such an adviser or his client or any such representative and any other person made in connection with or in contemplation of legal proceedings and for the purposes of such proceedings; and

(c) items enclosed with or referred to in such communications and made—

(i) in connection with the giving of legal advice; or

(ii) in connection with or in contemplation of legal proceedings and for the purposes of such proceedings, when they are in the possession of a person who is entitled to possession of them.

(2) Items held with the intention of furthering a criminal purpose are not items subject to legal privilege.

1–38 Records of a conveyancing transaction, including details of the financing, are not privileged, but correspondence between the solicitor and his client about the conveyance could be privileged if the letters contained advice: *R. v. Inner London Crown Court, ex p. Baines and Baines* [1988] Q.B. 579. Attendance notes of a solicitor on his client were held not to be privileged, as they simply provided a record of time and did not amount to the giving of legal advice: *R. v. Crown Court at Manchester, ex p. Rogers* [1999] 2 Cr.App.R. 267. A completed application form for legal aid was held to be privileged as being made in contemplation of legal proceedings: *R. v. Crown Court at Snaresbrook, ex p. DPP* [1988] Q.B. 532.

Where a scientist carried out tests on a blood sample provided by the defence, it was held that the sample was an item made for the purposes of legal proceedings and so was covered by s.10: *R.* [1995] 1 Cr.App.R. 183.

In *R. v. Central Criminal Court, ex p. Francis and Francis* [1989] A.C. 346, it was held that communications made between a lawyer and his client in the furtherance of a criminal purpose could not be protected by legal privilege (following the leading case at common law, *Cox and Railton* (1884) 14 Q.B.D. 153). Legal privilege could not extend to cover such advice irrespective of the innocence of the lawyer and s.10 was interpreted widely to remove that privilege no matter which party had the intention of furthering a criminal purpose. In this case the documents in dispute were to be used in the furtherance of money laundering by drug traffickers.

A court is entitled to look at an item to determine whether it is held with the intention of furthering a criminal purpose: *R. v. Governor of Pentonville Prison, ex p. Osman* (1988) 90 Cr.App.R. 281, DC. In relation to documents held by a solicitor acting for a defendant in pending criminal proceedings, a claim to legal professional privilege can be defeated where there is evidence of a specific agreement to pervert the course of justice, which is freestanding and independent, in the sense that it does not require any judgment to be reached in relation to the issues to be tried in the pending proceedings: *R. (Hallinan Blackburn Gittings & Nott (a firm)) v. Crown Court at Middlesex Guildhall* [2005] 1 W.L.R. 766, DC (applied in *Kuwait Airways Corp v. Iraqi Airways Co (No. 6)* [2005] 1 W.L.R. 2734, CA (Civ. Div.)).

Where legal privilege does not attach to documents, there could still be special procedure material under section 14 if there exists an express or implied undertaking to hold them in confidence: *R. v. Guildhall Magistrates' Court, ex p. Primlaks Holdings Co (Panama) Inc* [1990] 1 Q.B. 261, CA. **1–39**

In *R. (Malik) v. Manchester Crown Court* [2008] 4 All E.R. 403, DC, judicial review proceedings were brought in relation to a production order issued pursuant to provisions in the *Terrorism Act* 2000 analogous to those in the *PACE Act* 1984. The court reviewed the authorities on whether the privilege against self-incrimination can be invoked in relation to pre-existing documents. The majority decision in *C. Plc v. P.* [2008] Ch.1, CA (Civ. Div.), was to the effect that no such privilege exists, but the House of Lords have granted leave to appeal against this decision. Pending the House of Lords' ruling, the court in *Malik* recommended that circuit judges adopt the majority's approach in *R. (Bright) v. Central Criminal Court*; *R. (Alton) v. Same*; *R. (Rusbridger) v. Same* [2001] 1 W.L.R. 662, DC, that is to treat the privilege against self-incrimination as an important relevant factor to be taken into account when deciding how to exercise discretion in respect of the disclosure of pre-existing documents. The following non-exhaustive factors should be considered: (1) the true benefit to the investigation of the material in question, including the extent to which the material can be (a) obtained by other means, (b) disclosed in stages, the non-privileged material being disclosed first, and (c) redacted; (2) the importance of the privilege itself, convincing justification being needed to compel a person to forego its protection; (3) the gravity of the offence with which the person required to surrender the privilege might be charged, disclosure requiring greater justification for more serious offences; (4) the risk of prosecution, although in the absence of an offer of immunity the court should be slow to treat a prosecution as unlikely; and (5) the trial judge's power to exclude evidence under s.78 of the 1984 Act.

Police and Criminal Evidence Act 1984, ss.11, 12

Meaning of "excluded material"

11.—(1) Subject to the following provisions of this section, in this Act "excluded material" means— **1–40**

(a) personal records which a person has acquired or created in the course of any trade, business, profession or other occupation or for the purposes of any paid or unpaid office and which he holds in confidence;

(b) human tissue or tissue fluid which has been taken for the purposes of diagnosis or medical treatment and which a person holds in confidence;

(c) journalistic material which a person holds in confidence and which consists—

(i) of documents; or

(ii) of records other than documents.

(2) A person holds material other than journalistic material in confidence for the purposes of this section if he holds it subject—

(a) to an express or implied undertaking to hold it in confidence; or

(b) to a restriction on disclosure or an obligation of secrecy contained in any enactment, including an enactment contained in an Act passed after this Act.

(3) A person holds journalistic material in confidence for the purposes of this section if—

(a) he holds it subject to such an undertaking, restriction or obligation; and

(b) it has been continuously held (by one or more persons) subject to such an undertaking, restriction or obligation since it was first acquired or created for the purposes of journalism.

Meaning of "personal records"

1–41 **12.** In this Part of this Act "personal records" means documentary and other records concerning an individual (whether living or dead) who can be identified from them and relating—

(a) to his physical or mental health;

(b) to spiritual counselling or assistance given or to be given to him; or

(c) to counselling or assistance given or to be given to him, for the purposes of his personal welfare, by any voluntary organisation or by any individual who—

(i) by reason of his office or occupation has responsibilities for his personal welfare; or

(ii) by reason of an order of a court has responsibilities for his supervision.

Hospital records of admission to or discharge from hospital can fall under the definition of "personal records" because they relate to a person's physical or mental health: see *R. v. Cardiff Crown Court, ex p. Kellam*, *The Times*, May 3, 1993, DC.

Police and Criminal Evidence Act 1984, ss.13, 14

Meaning of "journalistic material"

1–42 **13.**—(1) Subject to subsection (2) below, in this Act "journalistic material" means material acquired or created for the purposes of journalism.

(2) Material is only journalistic material for the purposes of this Act if it is in the possession of a person who acquired or created it for the purposes of journalism.

(3) A person who receives material from someone who intends that the recipient shall use it for the purposes of journalism is to be taken to have acquired it for those purposes.

Meaning of "special procedure material"

1–43 **14.**—(1) In this Act "special procedure material" means—

(a) material to which subsection (2) below applies; and

(b) journalistic material, other than excluded material.

(2) Subject to the following provisions of this section, this subsection applies to material, other than items subject to legal privilege and excluded material, in the possession of a person who—

(a) acquired or created it in the course of any trade, business, profession or other occupation or for the purpose of any paid or unpaid office; and

(b) holds it subject—

(i) to an express or implied undertaking to hold it in confidence; or

(ii) to a restriction or obligation such as is mentioned in section 11(2)(b) above.

(3) Where material is acquired—

(a) by an employee from his employer and in the course of his employment; or

(b) by a company from an associated company,

it is only special procedure material if it was special procedure material immediately before the acquisition.

(4) Where material is created by an employee in the course of his employment, it is only special procedure material if it would have been special procedure material had his employer created it.

(5) Where material is created by a company on behalf of an associated company, it is only special procedure material if it would have been special procedure material had the associated company created it.

(6) A company is to be treated as another's associated company for the purposes of this section if it would be so treated under section 449 of the *Corporation Tax Act* 2010.

[This section is printed as amended by the *Corporation Tax Act* 2010, s.1177, and Sched. 1, para. 193.]

Frequent applications are made to search for and seize "special procedure material". **1–44** This includes records held by solicitors and accountants or banks and building societies and also films or photographs held by the media.

In *R. v. Leeds Magistrates' Court, ex p. Dumbleton* [1993] Crim.L.R. 866, DC, it was held that the protection of special procedure material could not attach to forged documents, as they could not have been acquired or created in the course of the profession of a solicitor. Furthermore, a dishonest solicitor could not be said to hold a forged document subject to an express or implied undertaking to hold it in confidence, there being no confidence in iniquity.

(4) Safeguards

Police and Criminal Evidence Act 1984, s.15

Search warrants—safeguards

15.—(1) This section and section 16 below have effect in relation to the issue to constables **1–45** under any enactment, including an enactment contained in an Act passed after this Act, of warrants to enter and search premises; and an entry on or search of premises under a warrant is unlawful unless it complies with this section and section 16 below.

(2) Where a constable applies for any such warrant, it shall be his duty—

(a) to state—

(i) the ground on which he makes the application;

(ii) the enactment under which the warrant would be issued; and

(iii) if the application is for a warrant authorising entry and search on more than one occasion, the ground on which he applies for such a warrant, and whether he seeks a warrant authorising an unlimited number of entries, or (if not) the maximum number of entries desired;

(b) to specify the matters set out in subsection (2A) below; and

(c) to identify, so far as is practicable, the articles or persons to be sought.

(2A) The matters which must be specified pursuant to subsection (2)(b) above are—

(a) if the application relates to one or more sets of premises specified in the application, each set of premises which it is desired to enter and search;

(b) if the application relates to any premises occupied or controlled by a person specified in the application-

(i) as many sets of premises which it is desired to enter and search as it is reasonably practicable to specify;

(ii) the person who is in occupation or control of those premises and any others which it is desired to enter and search;

(iii) why it is necessary to search more premises than those specified under sub-paragraph (i); and

(iv) why it is not reasonably practicable to specify all the premises which it is desired to enter and search.

(3) An application for such a warrant shall be made ex parte and supported by an information in writing.

(4) The constable shall answer on oath any question that the justice of the peace or judge hearing the application asks him.

(5) A warrant shall authorise an entry on one occasion only unless it specifies that it authorises multiple entries.

(5A) If it specifies that it authorises multiple entries, it must also specify whether the number of entries authorised is unlimited, or limited to a specified maximum.

(6) A warrant—

(a) shall specify—

(i) the name of the person who applies for it;

(ii) the date on which it is issued;

(iii) the enactment under which it is issued; and

(iv) each set of premises to be searched, or (in the case of an all premises warrant) the person who is in occupation or control of premises to be searched, together with any premises under his occupation or control which can be specified and which are to be searched; and

(b) shall identify, so far as is practicable, the articles or persons to be sought.

(7) Two copies shall be made of a warrant which specifies only one set of premises and does not authorise multiple entries; and as many copies as are reasonably required may be made of any other kind of warrant.

(8) The copies shall be clearly certified as copies.

[This section is printed as amended and repealed in part by the *Serious Organised Crime and Police Act* 2005, ss.113(1) and (5)-(8), 114(1) and (3)-(7), and 174(2), and Sched. 17; and the *Serious Organised Crime and Police Act 2005 (Amendment) Order* 2005 (S.I. 2005 No. 3496).]

Subject to modifications, s.15 of the 1984 Act has effect in relation to the issue of a warrant under ss.19(4) or 23(1) of the *Animal Welfare Act* 2006: *Animal Welfare Act* 2006, s.53 and Sched. 2.

1–46 There is now a line of Divisional Court authority establishing that the effect of s.15(1) is that non-compliance with either s.15 (as to the content of the warrant) or s.16 (as to its execution) will render any entry, search and seizure unlawful: see *R. v. Chief Constable of Lancashire, ex p. Parker* [1993] Q.B. 577; *R. v. Chief Constable of the Warwickshire Constabulary, ex p. Fitzpatrick* [1999] 1 W.L.R. 564; *R. v. Chesterfield JJ., ex p. Bramley, ante*, § 1–32; and *R. (Bhatti) v. Croydon Magistrates' Court* (2011) 1 W.L.R. 948, DC. The suggestion canvassed in *R. v. Longman* (1988) 88 Cr.App.R. 148, CA, that "it" in subs. (1) merely refers to the warrant, may now safely be ignored.

In *Power-Hynes v. Norwich Magistrates' Court* (2009) 173 J.P. 573, DC (see also *ante*, § 1–35), it was held that a warrant seeking "documents and records (electronic or otherwise) relating to high value financial transactions", in relation to an accountant acting as company secretary to various companies, some of which were unconnected to the police investigation, was too vague to comply with s.15(6)(b); nor could it be rescued by its reference to searching "for the material in respect of which the application is made", as both the statute and principle require a search warrant to be a self-contained statement of the articles for which the search is authorised, since both those who execute a warrant and those whose property is affected should be able to ascertain, from the warrant, whether any individual document or class of documents falls within it (applying *R. (Energy Financing Team Ltd) v. Bow Street Magistrates' Court* [2006] 1 W.L.R. 1316, DC). The decision in *Paul da Costa & Co (a firm) v. Thames Magistrates' Court* [2002] S.T.C. 267, DC (not referred to in *Power-Hynes*) is difficult to reconcile with this approach. It was there held that a warrant that referred to items in general terms (e.g. "bank accounts") did not contravene s.15(6)(b) where it was clear, reading the warrant as a whole, that the references related to the suspected offences identified in the supporting information.

In *R. v. Chief Constable of Lancashire, ex p. Parker, ante*, the court observed that it is highly desirable for the copying and certification of copies under s.15(7) and (8) to be carried out by the issuing court, compliance with those provisions being the responsibility of the judge or magistrate who issues the warrant (although he can delegate the issuing process to court staff). The court held that copies of the warrant have to be clearly certified as such, and that it would be contrary to the legislature's purpose if a judge could authorise the police to replace the whole or part of the original warrant, for the purpose of its execution, by an uncertified photocopy which he has not seen. It was suggested *obiter* that, where a warrant consists of more than one page, something more than the judge's signature and the court stamp on one page would be desirable as a means of authenticating the whole: the judge might, for example, initial the other pages, and in the case of a three-page warrant the pages might be numbered 1/3, etc.

Both the information and the warrants must be signed and dated by the person granting the application. The time of the application will also be noted on the documents so that time limits can be observed. The information is lodged with the Court and the original warrant and copies are taken by the officer.

Sometimes requests are made for copies of informations as well as warrants. Such copies can be provided to other Courts or to legal representatives if the Court is satisfied of the reason why the information is required. There are issues about the protection of informants so disclosure of the information may not be automatic to the individual whose premises were searched.

Part I

(5) Execution of the warrant

Police and Criminal Evidence Act 1984, s.16

Execution of warrants.

16.—(1) A warrant to enter and search premises may be executed by any constable. **1–47**

(2) Such a warrant may authorise persons to accompany any constable who is executing it.

(2A) A person so authorised has the same powers as the constable whom he accompanies in respect of—

(a) the execution of the warrant, and

(b) the seizure of anything to which the warrant relates.

(2B) But he may exercise those powers only in the company, and under the supervision, of a constable.

(3) Entry and search under a warrant must be within three months from the date of its issue.

(3A) If the warrant is an all premises warrant, no premises which are not specified in it may be entered or searched unless a police officer of at least the rank of inspector has in writing authorised them to be entered.

(3B) No premises may be entered or searched for the second or any subsequent time under a warrant which authorises multiple entries unless a police officer of at least the rank of inspector has in writing authorised that entry to those premises.

(4) Entry and search under a warrant must be at a reasonable hour unless it appears to the constable executing it that the purpose of a search may be frustrated on an entry at a reasonable hour.

(5) Where the occupier of premises which are to be entered and searched is present at the time when a constable seeks to execute a warrant to enter and search them, the constable—

(a) shall identify himself to the occupier and, if not in uniform, shall produce to him documentary evidence that he is a constable;

(b) shall produce the warrant to him; and

(c) shall supply him with a copy of it.

(6) Where—

(a) the occupier of such premises is not present at the time when a constable seeks to execute such a warrant; but

(b) some other person who appears to the constable to be in charge of the premises is present,

subsection (5) above shall have effect as if any reference to the occupier were a reference to that other person.

(7) If there is no person present who appears to the constable to be in charge of the premises, he shall leave a copy of the warrant in a prominent place on the premises.

(8) A search under a warrant may only be a search to the extent required for the purpose for which the warrant was issued. **1–48**

(9) A constable executing a warrant shall make an endorsement on it stating—

(a) whether the articles or persons sought were found; and

(b) whether any articles were seized, other than articles which were sought,

and, unless the warrant is a warrant specifying one set of premises only, he shall do so separately in respect of each set of premises entered and searched, which he shall in each case state in the endorsement.

(10) A warrant shall be returned to the appropriate person mentioned in subsection (10A) below—

(a) when it has been executed; or

(b) in the case of a specific premises warrant which has not been executed, or an all premises warrant, or any warrant authorising multiple entries, upon the expiry of the period of three months referred to in subsection (3) above or sooner.

(10A) The appropriate person is—

(a) if the warrant was issued by a justice of the peace, the designated officer for the local justice area in which the justice was acting when he issued the warrant;

(b) if it was issued by a judge, the appropriate officer of the court from which he issued it.

(11) A warrant which is returned under subsection (10) above shall be retained for 12 months from its return—

(a) by the designated officer for the local justice area, if it was returned under paragraph (i) of that subsection; and

(b) by the appropriate officer, if it was returned under paragraph (ii).

(12) If during the period for which a warrant is to be retained the occupier of premises to which it relates asks to inspect it, he shall be allowed to do so.

[This section is printed as amended by the *Access to Justice Act* 1999, s.90(1), and Sched. 13, para. 126; the *Criminal Justice Act* 2003, s.2; the *Courts Act* 2003, s.109(1), and Sched. 8, para. 281; the *Serious Organised Crime and Police Act* 2005, ss.113(1) and (9), and 114(1) and (8); and the *Serious Organised Crime and Police Act 2005 (Amendment) Order* 2005 (S.I. 2005 No. 3496).]

Subject to modifications, s.16 of the 1984 Act has effect in relation to the issue of a warrant under ss.19(4) or 23(1) of the *Animal Welfare Act* 2006: *Animal Welfare Act* 2006, s.53 and Sched. 2.

1–49 Section 16 provides safeguards for the execution of warrants under s.8 as amended. A search warrant is valid for three months. If it has not been executed during that time it must be returned to the court issuing it. With respect to multiple entries and entry to unspecified premises allowed on a warrant the written authorisation of a senior officer is required before such a power may be exercised. This ensures that the execution of such warrants is subject to proper scrutiny and is properly recorded. The outcome of all searches must be endorsed on the warrant separately in respect of each of the sets of premises searched. The police may execute the warrant and there is power for members of other agencies involved in the investigations leading to the issue of the warrant to execute it and seize items under the supervision of the constable. Such authorised persons must observe the Codes of Practice. Officers of other agencies may be authorised to accompany the police but the number should be restricted and those persons must not exceed their authority: *R. v. Reading Justices, Chief Constable of Avon and Somerset and Intervention Board for Agricultural Produce, ex p. South West Meat Ltd* [1992] Crim.L.R. 672.

1–50 As soon as possible after entry and before search the officer should identify himself and if not in uniform a warrant card should be produced for inspection. The original search warrant itself should also be produced and be made available for inspection. The procedure relating to the warrant must comply with both ss.15 and 16 or the entry and search will be unlawful: *Longman* [1988] 1 W.L.R. 619, CA. The Administrative Court has considered the extent of officers' powers on the execution of search warrants. In *DPP v. Meaden* [2004] Crim.L.R. 587, it was held that officers executing a search warrant were not exceeding their duty when they restricted individuals to certain rooms on the premises during the currency of the search.

The endorsed warrant will be returned to the Court and kept with the information for at least 12 months.

Where police officers failed to show the occupier of premises which were being searched the whole of the warrant, and failed to supply her with a copy of it, there was a breach of s.16(5) of the 1984 Act, making the execution of the search unlawful; and this was so even where the police did not wish the occupier to see the addresses of other premises listed in the warrant, because the police could avoid that problem by obtaining separate warrants or by redacting those addresses: *Redknapp v. Commr of the City of London Police Department* [2009] 1 W.L.R. 2091, DC (see also *ante*, § 1–34). The requirement to provide the occupier with a copy is fulfilled only by the provision of a copy of the warrant in its entirety, not a copy of part only supplemented by further information given (in writing) by the executing officer: *R. (Bhatti) v. Croydon Magistrates' Court, Commr of Police of the Metropolis and Secretary of State for the Home Department*, *ante*, § 1–46.

Part I

(6) Entry to arrest

Police and Criminal Evidence Act 1984, s.17

Entry for purpose of arrest etc.

17.—(1) Subject to the following provisions of this section, and without, prejudice to any other enactment, a constable may enter and search any premises for the purpose— **1–51**

(a) of executing—

(i) a warrant of arrest issued in connection with or arising out of criminal proceedings; or

(ii) a warrant of commitment issued under section 76 of the *Magistrates' Courts Act* 1980;

(b) of arresting a person for an indictable offence;

(c) of arresting a person for an offence under—

(i) section 1 (prohibition of uniforms in connection with political objects) of the *Public Order Act* 1936;

(ii) any enactment contained in section 6 to 8 or 10 of the *Criminal Law Act* 1977 (offences relating to entering and remaining on property);

(iii) section 4 of the *Public Order Act* 1986 (fear or provocation of violence);

(iiia) section 4 (driving etc. when under influence of drink or drugs) or section 163 (failure to stop when required to do so by a constable in uniform) of the *Road Traffic Act* 1988;

(iiib) section 27 of the *Transport and Works Act* 1992 (which relates to offences involving drink or drugs,

(iv) section 76 of the *Criminal Justice and Public Order Act* 1994 (failure to comply with interim possession order);

(v) any of sections 4, 5, 6(1) and (2), 7 and 8(1) and (2) of the *Animal Welfare Act* 2006 (offences relating to the prevention of harm to animals);

(ca) of arresting, in pursuance of section 32(1A) of the *Children and Young Persons Act* 1969, any child or young person who has been remanded or committed to local authority accommodation under section 23(1) of that Act;

(caa) of arresting a person for an offence to which section 61 of the *Animal Health Act* 1981 applies;

(cb) of recapturing any person who is, or is deemed for any purpose to be, unlawfully at large while liable to be detained—

(i) in a prison, remand centre, young offender institution or secure training centre, or

(ii) in pursuance of section 92 of the *Powers of Criminal Courts (Sentencing) Act* 2000 (dealing with children and young persons guilty of grave crimes), in any other place;

(d) of recapturing any person whatever who is unlawfully at large and whom he is pursuing; or

(e) of saving life or limb or preventing serious damage to property.

(2) Except for the purpose specified in paragraph (e) of subsection (1) above, the powers of entry and search conferred by this section— **1–52**

(a) are only exercisable if the constable has reasonable grounds for believing that the person whom he is seeking is on the premises; and

(b) are limited, in relation to premises consisting of two or more separate dwellings, to powers to enter and search—

(i) any parts of the premises which the occupiers of any dwelling comprised in the premises use in common with the occupiers of any other such dwelling; and

(ii) any such dwelling in which the constable has reasonable grounds for believing that the person whom he is seeking may be.

(3) The powers of entry and search conferred by this section are only exercisable for the purposes specified in subsection (1)(c)(ii) or (iv) above by a constable in uniform.

(4) The power of search conferred by this section is only a power to search to the extent that is reasonably required for the purpose for which the power of entry is exercised.

(5) Subject to subsection (6) below, all the rules of common law under which a constable has power to enter premises without a warrant are hereby abolished.

(6) Nothing in subsection (5) above affects any power of entry to deal with or prevent a breach of the peace.

[This section is printed as amended by and repealed in part by the *Public Order Act* 1986, s.40(2), and Sched. 2, para. 7; the *Criminal Justice and Public Order Act* 1994, s.168(2), and Sched. 1, para. 53; the *Prisoners (Return to Custody) Act* 1995, s.2(1); the *Powers of Criminal Courts (Sentencing) Act* 2000, s.165(1), and Sched. 9, para. 95; the *Police Reform Act* 2002, s.49(2); the *Serious Organised Crime and Police Act* 2005, s.111, and Sched. 7, paras 43(1) and (4), and 58; and the *Animal Welfare Act* 2006, s.24.]

1–53 The power of entry pursuant to s.17(1)(b) is only available to an officer who has reasonable grounds for suspicion, but such grounds can be inferred: *Kynaston v. DPP* (1987) 87 Cr.App.R. 200, DC, *ante*, § 1–12.

A police officer exercising his power pursuant to s.17 to enter premises may use reasonable force, if necessary: the *PACE Act* 1984, s.117, *post*, § 1–119. He should, unless the circumstances make it impossible, impracticable or undesirable, give any occupant present the reason for his exercising that power of entry: *O'Loughlin v. Chief Constable of Essex* [1998] 1 W.L.R. 374, CA (Civ. Div.). If the real reason is to arrest a person inside (s.17(1)(b)), it is insufficient to tell the occupants that he wishes to "speak to" that person about the offence: *ibid*.

Where police officers are invited onto premises by an occupier or other person authorised to do so, who had been told by them the reason for their entry, they are lawfully on the premises, and they do not have to comply with s.17, which applies to entry and search in the absence of consent: *Riley v. DPP* (1989) 91 Cr.App.R. 14, DC; *Hobson v. Chief Constable of the Cheshire Constabulary* (2003) 168 J.P. 111, DC.

Section 17(1)(d) contemplates an act of pursuit, a chase, however short in time and distance, and does not cover a situation where the police form an intention to arrest and decide to put it into practice by resorting to the premises where they believe that the person sought might be found: *D'Souza v. DPP* (1992) 96 Cr.App.R. 278, HL.

In *Baker v. CPS*, 173 J.P. 215, DC, the court considered the power of search conferred by s.17(1)(e) of the 1984 Act. The following propositions, all *obiter*, are derived from the judgments: (i) the power is wide enough to cover saving a person from seriously harming himself, as well as seriously harming third parties; (ii) entry will be lawful provided that the officer reasonably believes that this is necessary to save life or limb or to prevent serious damage to property; (iii) there is no need for an officer to explain the reason for his entry to the occupier where this is impossible, impractical or undesirable, as in cases of emergency; (iv) the power of search extends to a search of the person, provided that it is limited to the object of saving life and limb where the risk thereto is properly regarded as imminent; and (v) an officer who has entered lawfully under this power is entitled to remain on the premises until he is reasonably satisfied that life, limb or property are no longer in danger and, while he is thus lawfully on the premises, he may search for anything he reasonably believes may be used to endanger life, limb or property. See also *Blench v. DPP* (2004) 69 J.C.L. 98, DC (police responding to emergency call to effect that man was trying to take baby from house).

The words "saving life or limb" in section 17(1)(e) relate to serious bodily injuries, not mere concern for the welfare of someone inside the premises: *Syed v. DPP* [2010] 1 Cr.App.R. 34, DC.

The question whether premises consist of two or more separate dwellings (s.17(2)(b))is one of fact; where the terms of occupation of a three-bedroom flat, which police officers visited pursuant to s.17 to effect an arrest of one of the occupants, were that each occupant had a licence to occupy, for a day, his bedroom, with its own lock and number, and the communal area, the occupiers of the rooms each had a sufficient degree of occupation and control to make each bedroom a separate dwelling, and thus the right to exclude police officers from entering their room without the proper authorisation: *Thomas v. DPP*, *The Times*, November 25, 2009, DC.

Part I

Police and Criminal Evidence Act 1984, s.18

Entry and search after arrest

18.—(1) Subject to the following provisions of this section, a constable may enter and search any premises occupied or controlled by a person who is under arrest for an indictable offence, if he has reasonable grounds for suspecting that there is on the premises evidence, other than items subject to legal privilege, that relates— **1–54**

(a) to that offence; or

(b) to some other indictable offence which is connected with or similar to that offence.

(2) A constable may seize and retain anything for which he may search under subsection (1) above.

(3) The power to search conferred by subsection (1) above is only a power to search to the extent that is reasonably required for the purpose of discovering such evidence.

(4) Subject to subsection (5) below, the powers conferred by this section may not be exercised unless an officer of the rank of inspector or above has authorised them in writing.

(5) A constable may conduct a search under subsection (1) above—

(a) before the person is taken to a police station or released on bail under section 30A; and

(b) without obtaining an authorisation under subsection (4) above,

if the condition in subsection (5A) is satisfied

(5A) The condition is that the presence of the person at a place (other than a police station) is necessary for the effective investigation of the offence.

(6) If a constable conducts a search by virtue of subsection (5) above, he shall inform an officer of the rank of inspector or above that he has made the search as soon as practicable after he has made it.

(7) An officer who—

(a) authorises a search; or

(b) is informed of a search under subsection (6) above, shall make a record in writing—

(i) of the grounds for the search; and

(ii) of the nature of the evidence that was sought.

(8) If the person who was in occupation or control of the premises at the time of the search is in police detention at the time the record is top be made, the officer shall make the record as part of his custody record.

[This section is printed as amended by the *Police Reform Act* 2002, s.107(1), and Sched. 7, para. 9(1); the *Criminal Justice Act* 2003, s.12, and Sched. 1, paras 1 and 2; and the *Serious Organised Crime and Police Act* 2005, s.111, and Sched. 7, para. 43(1) and (5).]

Section 18(1) is modified in relation to Revenue and Customs officers by the *Police and Criminal Evidence Act 1984 (Application to Customs and Excise) Order* 1985 (S.I. 1985 No. 1800) as amended. The effect of the modification is to replace "an indictable offence" with "any indictable offence which relates to an assigned matter, as defined in s.1 of the *Customs and Excise Management Act* 1979". **1–55**

For the power to search premises where an arrest takes place, see s.32 of the Act, *post*, § 1–130.

In *Khan v. Commr of Police of the Metropolis, The Times*, June 16, 2008, CA (Civ. Div.), it was held that the power of entry and search under section 18 of the 1984 Act applies only where the premises searched are in fact occupied or controlled by the person under arrest; if they are not, the search is unlawful, even if the officer conducting the search has a reasonable belief that they are.

The reasoning in *O'Loughlin v. Chief Constable of Essex, ante*, § 1–53, applies equally to s.18: *Linehan v. DPP* [2000] Crim.L.R. 861, DC (officers proposing to enter premises by force should have told the occupier their purpose, *i.e.* to search for the proceeds of a burglary for which the occupier's son had been arrested).

The word "anything" in s.18(2) entitles a constable to seize a vehicle and not just its parts or contents, even though the vehicle itself is "premises" for the purposes of the Act (s.23, *post*, 1–65): *Cowan v. Condon* [2000] 1 W.L.R. 254, CA (Civ. Div.).

Section 18(7) is directory only; non-compliance does not automatically invalidate the search: *Krohn v. DPP* [1997] C.O.D. 345, DC.

For a case where evidence obtained through a search was held to be properly admitted notwithstanding a breach of s.18(8), see *Wright* [1994] Crim.L.R. 55, CA.

Section 18 does not have the effect of abolishing common law rules as to entry and search after arrest, it being a well established principle that a rule of law is not extinguished by a statute unless the statute makes that clear by express provision or clear implication: *R. (Rottman) v. Commr of Police of the Metropolis* [2002] 2 A.C. 692, HL. At common law, a police officer who entered a house and arrested a suspect pursuant to a warrant of arrest had power to search the entire house and seize any articles which provided evidence against the suspect; that power applied to extradition crimes as well as domestic crimes; and it survived the 1984 Act: *ibid*.

In *R. (Hewitson) v. Chief Constable of the Dorset Police, The Times*, January 6, 2004, DC, the court refused to extend the police's common law power of search, as explained in *Rottman, ante*, to searching a flat in circumstances where (a) the suspect was arrested away from the flat and its curtilage, (b) the search was more than two hours after the arrest, and (c) the link between the suspect and the flat was tenuous, the flat belonging to a friend and the suspect being only an occasional visitor.

(7) General power of seizure

Police and Criminal Evidence Act 1984, s.19

General power of seizure etc.

1–56 **19.**—(1) The powers conferred by subsections (2), (3) and (4) below are exercisable by a constable who is lawfully on any premises.

(2) The constable may seize anything which is on the premises if he has reasonable grounds for believing—

(a) that it has been obtained in consequence of the commission of an offence; and

(b) that it is necessary to seize it in order to prevent it being concealed, lost, damaged, altered or destroyed.

(3) The constable may seize anything which is on the premises if he has reasonable grounds for believing—

(a) that it is evidence in relation to an offence which he is investigating or any other offence; and

(b) that it is necessary to seize it in order to prevent the evidence being concealed, lost, altered or destroyed.

(4) The constable may require any information which is stored in any electronic form and is accessible from the premises to be produced in a form in which it can be taken away and in which it is visible and legible or [from which it can readily be produced in a visible and legible form] if he has reasonable grounds for believing—

(a) that—

(i) it is evidence in relation to an offence which he is investigating or any other offence; or

(ii) it has been obtained in consequence of the commission of an offence; and

(b) that it is necessary to do so in order to prevent it being concealed, lost, tampered with or destroyed.

(5) The powers conferred by this section are in addition to any power otherwise conferred.

(6) No power of seizure conferred on a constable under any enactment (including an enactment contained in an Act passed after this Act) is to be taken to authorise the seizure of an item which the constable exercising the power has reasonable grounds for believing to be subject to legal privilege.

[This section is printed as amended by the *Criminal Justice and Police Act* 2001, s.70, and Sched. 2, para. 13.]

For the disapplication of subs. (6) in relation to the powers of seizure under ss.50 and 51 of the *Criminal Justice and Police Act* 2001, see subs. (4) of those sections, *post*, §§ 1–68, 1–70. **1–57**

Unlike s.17, *ante*, § 1–51, which by subs. (5) expressly abolished with one exception all the rules of common law under which a constable had power to enter premises, s.19(5) provides that the powers conferred by the section are in addition to any power otherwise conferred.

For the meaning of "anything" (s.19(2)), see *Cowan v. Condon, ante*, § 1–55.

Where the scope of a warrant was limited to a flat within a block of flats, the "premises" (s.19(2)) to which the warrant related could not be assumed to include the surrounding car park, and thus the seizure of a car from the car park was unlawful; the position might have been otherwise if the warrant had specified that the premises included any other part of the premises within the property demised by the lease, or surrounding the flat or the common parts: *R. (Wood) v. North Avon Magistrates' Court* (2009) 174 J.P. 157, DC. See also *ante*, § 1–34.

Section 19 refers to "evidence" (s.19(3),(4)), as opposed to "relevant evidence", which is defined in s.8(4) (*ante*, § 1–33), in relation to an offence, as "anything that would be admissible in evidence at a trial for the offence".

The references to an "offence" in s.19(3) do not include foreign offences; in the absence of an express provision to the contrary, "offence" in a statute means a domestic offence: *R. (Rottman) v. Commr of Police of the Metropolis, ante*, § 1–55.

In *R. (Cook) v. Serious Organised Crime Agency* [2011] 1 W.L.R. 144, DC, it was held that s.19 of the 1984 Act does not permit the re-seizure at the police station of material unlawfully obtained pursuant to an unlawful seizure and unlawfully brought to the police station; the mere obtaining of a signature on a receipt for the material is insufficient to engage the section; to hold otherwise, the court said, would deny the structure of the legislation and fail entirely to have regard to the way in which the serious interference, which is the power to enter premises and seize property, is controlled. Once the property has been properly restored, however, a further warrant may then be sought and obtained; and, whilst the history would have to be disclosed, the application for the further warrant would not be adversely affected by the failed warrant, provided sufficient grounds were established; and if this warrant failed to produce the documents sought, one (if not the only) appropriate inference might be that the material is adverse to those who have kept it away from the prosecuting authorities: *ibid*. In the particular circumstances, the court ordered the return of the unlawfully seized property, but refused orders for the destruction of any copies or prohibiting the use of any knowledge gained as a result of the unlawful search and seizure.

(8) Power to seize computerised information

Police and Criminal Evidence Act 1984, s.20

Extension of powers of seizure to computerised information

20.—(1) Every power of seizure which is conferred by an enactment to which this section applies on a constable who has entered premises in the exercise of a power conferred by an enact- **1–58**

ment shall be construed as including a power to require any information stored in any electronic form and accessible from the premises to be produced in a form in which it can be taken away and in which it is visible and legible or from which it can readily be produced in a visible and legible form.

(2) This section applies—

(a) to any enactment contained in an Act passed before this Act;

(b) to sections 8 and 18 above;

(c) to paragraph 13 of Schedule 1 to this Act; and

(d) to any enactment contained in an Act passed after this Act.

[This section is printed as amended by the *Criminal Justice and Police Act* 2001, s.70, and Sched. 2, para. 13.]

(9) Access and copying

Police and Criminal Evidence Act 1984, s.21

Access and copying

1–59 **21.**—(1) A constable who seizes anything in the exercise of a power conferred by any enactment, including an enactment contained in an Act passed after this Act, shall, if so requested by a person showing himself—

(a) to be the occupier of premises on which it was seized; or

(b) to have had custody or control of it immediately before the seizure,

provide that person with a record of what he seized.

(2) The officer shall provide the record within a reasonable time from the making of the request for it.

(3) Subject to subsection (8) below, if a request for permission to be granted access to anything which—

(a) has been seized by a constable; and

(b) is retained by the police for the purpose of investigating an offence,

is made to the officer in charge of the investigation by a person who had custody or control of the thing immediately before it was so seized or by someone acting on behalf of such a person, the officer shall allow the person who made the request access to it under the supervision of a constable.

(4) Subject to subsection (8) below, if a request for a photograph or copy of any such thing is made to the officer in charge of the investigation by a person who had custody or control of the thing immediately before it was so seized, or by someone acting on behalf of such a person, the officer shall—

(a) allow the person who made the request access to it under the supervision of a constable for the purpose of photographing or copying it; or

(b) photograph or copy it, or cause it to be photographed or copied.

(5) A constable may also photograph or copy, or have photographed or copied, anything which he has power to seize, without a request being made under subsection (4) above.

(6) Where anything is photographed or copied under subsection (4)(b) above, the photograph or copy shall be supplied to the person who made the request.

(7) The photograph or copy shall be so supplied within a reasonable time from the making of the request.

(8) There is no duty under this section to grant access to, or to supply a photograph or copy of, anything if the officer in charge of the investigation for the purposes of which it was seized has reasonable grounds for believing that to do so would prejudice—

(a) that investigation;

(b) the investigation of an offence other than the offence for the purposes of investigating which the thing was seized; or

(c) any criminal proceedings which may be brought as a result of—

(i) the investigation of which he is in charge; or

(ii) any such investigation as is mentioned in paragraph (b) above.

(9) The references to a constable in subsections (1), (2), (3)(a) and (5) include a person authorised under section 16(2) to accompany a constable executing a warrant.

[This section is printed as amended by the *Criminal Justice Act* 2003, s.12, and Sched. 1, paras 1 and 3.]

A refusal to grant access under s.21(8) should be challenged by way of judicial review: *Allen v. Chief Constable of Cheshire Constabulary*, *The Times*, July 16, 1988. **1–60**

Where company documents have been seized the person who had control immediately before the seizure has right of access. This right is vested in the company and not the directors or former directors: *Re DPR Futures Ltd* [1989] 1 W.L.R. 778.

(10) Retention

Police and Criminal Evidence Act 1984, s.22

Retention

22.—(1) Subject to subsection (4) below, anything which has been seized by a constable or taken away by a constable following a requirement made by virtue of section 19 or 20 above may be retained so long as is necessary in all the circumstances. **1–61**

(2) Without prejudice to the generality of subsection (1) above—

(a) anything seized for the purposes of a criminal investigation may be retained, except as provided by subsection (4) below—

(i) for use as evidence at a trial for an offence; or

(ii) for forensic examination or for investigation in connection with an offence; and

(b) anything may be retained in order to establish its lawful owner, where there are reasonable grounds for believing that it has been obtained in consequence of the commission of an offence.

(3) Nothing seized on the ground that it may be used—

(a) to cause physical injury to any person;

(b) to damage property;

(c) to interfere with evidence; or

(d) to assist in escape from police detention or lawful custody,

may be retained when the person from whom it was seized is no longer in police detention or the custody of a court or is in the custody of a court but has been released on bail.

(4) Nothing may be retained for either of the purposes mentioned in subsection (2)(a) above if a photograph or copy would be sufficient for that purpose.

(5) Nothing in this section affects any power of a court to make an order under section 1 of the *Police (Property) Act* 1897.

(6) This section also applies to anything retained by the police under section 28H(5) of the *Immigration Act* 1971.

(7) The reference in subsection (1) to anything seized by a constable includes anything seized by a person authorised under section 16(2) to accompany a constable executing a warrant.

[This section is printed as amended by the *Immigration and Asylum Act* 1999, s.169(1), and Sched. 14, para. 80(1) and (3); and the *Criminal Justice Act* 2003, s.12, and Sched. 1, paras 1 and 4.]

The police are not entitled to retain property where the seizure was not in compliance with ss.15 and 16 of the *Police and Criminal Evidence Act* 1984 and so was unlawful. This section only applies to property which is lawfully in the possession of the police: *R. v. Chief Constable of Lancashire, ex p. Parker* (1993) 97 Cr.App.R. 90. **1–62**

The police are permtted to continue to retain any property for a short period, after detention is no longer necessary under section 22, while they are considering the position: *Gough and another v. Chief Constable of West Midlands Police*, *The Times*, March 4, 2004, CA (Civ. Div.); *R. (Iqbal)* v. Luton & South Bedfordshire Magistrates' Court [2011] A.C.D. 57, DC.

In *Settelen v. Metropolitan Police Commissioner*, *Daily Telegraph*, October 7, 2004, Ch.D., the court held that, where material was lawfully seized in a search during one investigation, the police could only retain the material pursuant to s.22 in relation to a subsequent unrelated investigation if it was "necessary" to do so.

In *Scopelight Ltd v. Chief Constable of Northumbria* [2010] 1 Cr.App.R. 19, CA (Civ. Div.), it was held that the police can retain property after the CPS decide not to prosecute, if a private prosecution is being contemplated or is taking place. Section 22(1) ("anything which has been seized by a constable may be retained so long as is necessary in all the circumstances") requires the police to consider each case on its own individual facts, at each stage in the process of investigation and prosecution. Where a body other than the CPS wishes to pursue a private prosecution, the relevant circumstances include, but are not limited to: the potential prosecutor's identity and motive; the gravity of the allegations together with the reasons why the CPS declined to prosecute, and thus the extent to which the public have a legitimate interest in prosecution; the police view of the significance of what has been retained; and any material fact concerning the proposed defendant.

1–63 The system for recovery of property retained by Customs officers was considered in *R. v. Southampton Justices, ex p. Newman* (1988) 88 Cr.App.R. 202. Documents had been seized from the defendant's home on his arrest by Customs officers. He applied to the court for an order under s.48 of the *Magistrates' Courts Act* 1980 for the return of this property. It was held that s.48 did not apply, because it referred to the return of property taken from the defendant's person and not from his home at the time of arrest. The Court conceded that this left the defendant with no direct remedy as, although the *Police and Criminal Evidence Act* 1984, ss.17 and 19, applied to Customs officers by virtue of the *PACE (Application to Customs and Excise) Order* 1985 (S.I. 1985 No. 1800), s.22(5) did not and neither did the *Police Property Act* 1897. It was suggested that the court has an inherent power to control the proceedings, so it might in these circumstances adjourn or refuse to proceed if it thought it in the interests of justice that the documents should be returned to the defendant to enable him to prepare his defence.

1–64 The provisions of s.48 of the *MCA* 1980, and the *Police Property Act* 1897, whereby application may be made to the magistrates court for the return of property in police possession to the owner or any person as the court thinks meet are preserved. See *post*, §§ 20–130 *et seq.*

(11) Meaning of "premises" etc.

Meaning of "premises" etc.

1–65 **23.** In this Act—

"premises" includes any place and, in particular, includes—

(a) any vehicle, vessel, aircraft or hovercraft;

(b) any offshore installation;

(ba) any renewable energy installation;

(c) any tent or movable structure; and

"offshore installation" has the meaning given to it by section 1 of the *Mineral Workings (Offshore Installations) Act* 1971;

"renewable energy installation" has the same meaning as in Chapter 2 of Part 2 of the *Energy Act* 2004.

[This section is printed as amended by the *Energy Act* 2004, s.103(2).]

(12) Additional powers of seizure from premises

1–66 The powers of seizure under the *PACE* 1984 were considerably extended under the provisions of the *Criminal Justice and Police Act* 2001. See *ante*, § 1–32.

Criminal Justice and Police Act 2001, s.50

Additional powers of seizure from premises

1–67 **50.**—(1) Where—

(a) a person who is lawfully on any premises finds anything on those premises that he has reasonable grounds for believing may be or may contain something for which he is authorised to search on those premises,

(b) a power of seizure to which this section applies or the power conferred by subsection (2) would entitle him, if he found it, to seize whatever it is that he has grounds for believing that thing to be or to contain, and

(c) in all the circumstances, it is not reasonably practicable for it to be determined, on those premises—

(i) whether what he has found is something that he is entitled to seize, or

(ii) the extent to which what he has found contains something that he is entitled to seize,

that person's powers of seizure shall include power under this section to seize so much of what he has found as it is necessary to remove from the premises to enable that to be determined.

(2) Where—

(a) a person who is lawfully on any premises finds anything on those premises ("the seizable property") which he would be entitled to seize but for its being comprised in something else that he has (apart from this subsection) no power to seize,

(b) the power under which that person would have power to seize the seizable property is a power to which this section applies, and

(c) in all the circumstances it is not reasonably practicable for the seizable property to be separated, on those premises, from that in which it is comprised,

that person's powers of seizure shall include power under this section to seize both the seizable property and that from which it is not reasonably practicable to separate it.

(3) The factors to be taken into account in considering, for the purposes of this section, whether or not it is reasonably practicable on particular premises for something to be determined, or for something to be separated from something else, shall be confined to the following— **1–68**

(a) how long it would take to carry out the determination or separation on those premises;

(b) the number of persons that would be required to carry out that determination or separation on those premises within a reasonable period;

(c) whether the determination or separation would (or would if carried out on those premises) involve damage to property;

(d) the apparatus or equipment that it would be necessary or appropriate to use for the carrying out of the determination or separation; and

(e) in the case of separation, whether the separation—

(i) would be likely, or

(ii) if carried out by the only means that are reasonably practicable on those premises, would be likely,

to prejudice the use of some or all of the separated seizable property for a purpose for which something seized under the power in question is capable of being used.

(4) Section 19(6) of the 1984 Act and Article 21(6) of the *Police and Criminal Evidence (Northern Ireland) Order* 1989 (S.I. 1989 No. 1341 (N.I. 12)) (powers of seizure not to include power to seize anything that a person has reasonable grounds for believing is legally privileged) shall not apply to the power of seizure conferred by subsection (2).

(5) This section applies to each of the powers of seizure specified in Part 1 of Schedule 1.

(6) Without prejudice to any power conferred by this section to take a copy of any document, nothing in this section, so far as it has effect by reference to the power to take copies of documents under section 28(2)(b) of the *Competition Act* 1998, shall be taken to confer any power to seize any document.

(13) Additional powers of seizure from the person

Criminal Justice and Police Act 2001, s.51

Additional powers of seizure from the person

51.—(1) Where— **1–69**

(a) a person carrying out a lawful search of any person finds something that he has reasonable grounds for believing may be or may contain something for which he is authorised to search,

Part I

(b) a power of seizure to which this section applies or the power conferred by subsection (2) would entitle him, if he found it, to seize whatever it is that he has grounds for believing that thing to be or to contain, and

(c) in all the circumstances it is not reasonably practicable for it to be determined, at the time and place of the search—

(i) whether what he has found is something that he is entitled to seize, or

(ii) the extent to which what he has found contains something that he is entitled to seize,

that person's powers of seizure shall include power under this section to seize so much of what he has found as it is necessary to remove from that place to enable that to be determined.

(2) Where—

(a) a person carrying out a lawful search of any person finds something ("the seizable property") which he would be entitled to seize but for its being comprised in something else that he has (apart from this subsection) no power to seize,

(b) the power under which that person would have power to seize the seizable property is a power to which this section applies, and

(c) in all the circumstances it is not reasonably practicable for the seizable property to be separated, at the time and place of the search, from that in which it is comprised,

that person's powers of seizure shall include power under this section to seize both the seizable property and that from which it is not reasonably practicable to separate it.

1–70 (3) The factors to be taken into account in considering, for the purposes of this section, whether or not it is reasonably practicable, at the time and place of a search, for something to be determined, or for something to be separated from something else, shall be confined to the following—

(a) how long it would take to carry out the determination or separation at that time and place;

(b) the number of persons that would be required to carry out that determination or separation at that time and place within a reasonable period;

(c) whether the determination or separation would (or would if carried out at that time and place) involve damage to property;

(d) the apparatus or equipment that it would be necessary or appropriate to use for the carrying out of the determination or separation; and

(e) in the case of separation, whether the separation—

(i) would be likely, or

(ii) if carried out by the only means that are reasonably practicable at that time and place, would be likely,

to prejudice the use of some or all of the separated seizable property for a purpose for which something seized under the power in question is capable of being used.

(4) Section 19(6) of the 1984 Act and Article 21(6) of the *Police and Criminal Evidence (Northern Ireland) Order* 1989 (S.I. 1989 No. 1341 (N.I. 12)) (powers of seizure not to include power to seize anything a person has reasonable grounds for believing is legally privileged) shall not apply to the power of seizure conferred by subsection (2).

(5) This section applies to each of the powers of seizure specified in Part 2 of Schedule 1.

(14) Procedure for exercise of additional powers

Criminal Justice and Police Act 2001, s.52

Notice of exercise of power under s.50 or 51

1–71 **52.**—(1) Where a person exercises a power of seizure conferred by section 50, it shall (subject to subsections (2) and (3)) be his duty, on doing so, to give to the occupier of the premises a written notice—

(a) specifying what has been seized in reliance on the powers conferred by that section;

(b) specifying the grounds on which those powers have been exercised;

(c) setting out the effect of subsections 59 to 61;
(d) specifying the name and address of the person to whom notice of an application under section 59(2) to the appropriate judicial authority in respect of any of the seized property must be given; and
(e) specifying the name and address of the person to whom an application may be made to be allowed to attend the initial examination required by any arrangements made for the purposes of section 53(2).

(2) Where it appears to the person exercising on any premises a power of seizure conferred by section 50—
(a) that the occupier of the premises is not present on the premises at the time of the exercise of the power, but
(b) that there is some other person present on the premises who is in charge of the premises,

subsection (1) of this section shall have effect as if it required the notice under that subsection to be given to that other person.

(3) Where it appears to the person exercising a power of seizure conferred by section 50 that there is no one present on the premises to whom he may give a notice for the purposes of complying with subsection (1) of this section, he shall, before leaving the premises, instead of complying with that subsection, attach a notice such as is mentioned in that subsection in a prominent place to the premises.

(4) Where a person exercises a power of seizure conferred by section 51 it shall be his duty, on doing so, to give a written notice to the person from whom the seizure is made— **1–72**
(a) specifying what has been seized in reliance on the powers conferred by that section;
(b) specifying the grounds on which those powers have been exercised;
(c) setting out the effect of subsections 59 to 61;
(d) specifying the name and address of the person to whom notice of any application under section 59(2) to the appropriate judicial authority in respect of any of the seized property must be given; and
(e) specifying the name and address of the person to whom an application may be made to be allowed to attend the initial examination required by any arrangements made for the purposes of section 53(2).

(5) The Secretary of State may by regulations made by statutory instrument, after consultation with the Scottish Ministers, provide that a person who exercises a power of seizure conferred by section 50 shall be required to give a notice such as is mentioned in subsection (1) of this section to any person, or send it to any place, described in the regulations.

(6) Regulations under subsection (5) may make different provision for different cases.

(7) A statutory instrument containing regulations under subsection (5) shall be subject to annulment in pursuance of a resolution of either House of Parliament.

(15) Return or retention of seized property

Criminal Justice and Police Act 2001, ss.53–58

Examination and return of property seized under s.50 or 51

53.—(1) This section applies where anything has been seized under a power conferred by section 50 or 51. **1–73**

(2) It shall be the duty of the person for the time being in possession of the seized property in consequence of the exercise of that power to secure that there are arrangements in force which (subject to section 61) ensure—
(a) that an initial examination of the property is carried out as soon as reasonably practicable after the seizure;
(b) that that examination is confined to whatever is necessary for determining how much of the property falls within subsection (3);
(c) that anything which is found, on that examination, not to fall within subsection (3) is separated from the rest of the seized property and is returned as soon as reasonably practicable after the examination of all the seized property has been completed; and

Part I

(d) that, until the initial examination of all the seized property has been completed and anything which does not fall within subsection (3) has been returned, the seized property is kept separate from anything seized under any other power.

(3) The seized property falls within this subsection to the extent only—

(a) that it is property for which the person seizing it had power to search when he made the seizure but is not property the return of which is required by section 54;

(b) that it is property the retention of which is authorised by section 56; or

(c) that it is something which, in all the circumstances, it will not be reasonably practicable, following the examination, to separate from property falling within paragraph (a) or (b).

(4) In determining for the purposes of this section the earliest practicable time for the carrying out of an initial examination of the seized property, due regard shall be had to the desirability of allowing the person from whom it was seized, or a person with an interest in that property, an opportunity of being present or (if he chooses) of being represented at the examination.

(5) In this section, references to whether or not it is reasonably practicable to separate part of the seized property from the rest of it are references to whether or not it is reasonably practicable to do so without prejudicing the use of the rest of that property, or a part of it, for purposes for which (disregarding the part to be separated) the use of the whole or of a part of the rest of the property, if retained, would be lawful.

Obligation to return items subject to legal privilege

1–74 **54.**—(1) If, at any time after a seizure of anything has been made in exercise of a power of seizure to which this section applies—

(a) it appears to the person for the time being having possession of the seized property in consequence of the seizure that the property—

(i) is an item subject to legal privilege, or

(ii) has such an item comprised in it,

and

(b) in a case where the item is comprised in something else which has been lawfully seized, it is not comprised in property falling within subsection (2),

it shall be the duty of that person to secure that the item is returned as soon as reasonably practicable after the seizure.

(2) Property in which an item subject to legal privilege is comprised falls within this subsection if—

(a) the whole or a part of the rest of the property is property falling within subsection (3) or property the retention of which is authorised by section 56; and

(b) in all the circumstances, it is not reasonably practicable for that item to be separated from the rest of that property (or, as the case may be, from that part of it) without prejudicing the use of the rest of that property, or that part of it, for purposes for which (disregarding that item) its use, if retained, would be lawful.

(3) Property falls within this subsection to the extent that it is property for which the person seizing it had power to search when he made the seizure, but is not property which is required to be returned under this section or section 55.

(4) This section applies—

(a) to the powers of seizure conferred by sections 50 and 51;

(b) to each of the powers of seizure specified in Parts 1 and 2 of Schedule 1; and

(c) to any power of seizure (not falling within paragraph (a) or (b)) conferred on a constable by or under any enactment, including an enactment passed after this Act.

Obligation to return excluded and special procedure material

1–75 **55.**—(1) If, at any time after a seizure of anything has been made in exercise of a power to which this section applies—

(a) it appears to the person for the time being having possession of the seized property in consequence of the seizure that the property—

(i) is excluded material or special procedure material, or

(ii) has any excluded material or any special procedure material comprised in it,

(b) its retention is not authorised by section 56, and

(c) in a case where the material is comprised in something else which has been lawfully seized, it is not comprised in property falling within subsection (2) or (3),

it shall be the duty of that person to secure that the item is returned as soon as reasonably practicable after the seizure.

(2) Property in which any excluded material or special procedure material is comprised falls within this subsection if—

(a) the whole or a part of the rest of the property is property for which the person seizing it had power to search when he made the seizure but is not property the return of which is required by this section or section 54; and

(b) in all the circumstances, it is not reasonably practicable for that material to be separated from the rest of that property (or, as the case may be, from that part of it) without prejudicing the use of the rest of that property, or that part of it, for purposes for which (disregarding that material) its use, if retained, would be lawful.

(3) Property in which any excluded material or special procedure material is comprised falls within this subsection if—

(a) the whole or a part of the rest of the property is property the retention of which is authorised by section 56; and

(b) in all the circumstances, it is not reasonably practicable for that material to be separated from the rest of that property (or, as the case may be, from that part of it) without prejudicing the use of the rest of that property, or that part of it, for purposes for which (disregarding that material) its use, if retained, would be lawful.

(4) This section applies (subject to subsection (5)) to each of the powers of seizure specified in Part 3 of Schedule 1. **1–76**

(5) In its application to the powers of seizure conferred by—...

(b) section 56(5) of the *Drug Trafficking Act* 1994,

(c) [*Northern Ireland*], and

(d) section 352(4) of the *Proceeds of Crime Act* 2002,

this section shall have effect with the omission of every reference to special procedure material.

(6) In this section, except in its application to—

(a) the power of seizure conferred by section 8(2) of the 1984 Act,

(b) [*Northern Ireland*],

(c) each of the powers of seizure conferred by the provisions of paragraphs 1and 3 of Schedule 5 to the *Terrorism Act* 2000, and

(d) the power of seizure conferred by paragraphs 15 and 19 of Schedule 5 to that Act of 2000, so far only as the power in question is conferred by reference to paragraph 1 of that Schedule,

"special procedure material" means special procedure material consisting of documents or records other than documents.

[This section is printed as amended and repealed in part by the *Proceeds of Crime Act* 2002, ss.456 and 457, Sched. 11, para. 40(2), and Sched. 12.]

Property seized by constables etc.

56.—(1) The retention of— **1–77**

(a) property seized on any premises by a constable who was lawfully on the premises,

(b) property seized on any premises by a relevant person who was on the premises accompanied by a constable, and

(c) property seized by a constable carrying out a lawful search of any person,

is authorised by this section if the property falls within subsection (2) or (3).

(2) Property falls within this subsection to the extent that there are reasonable grounds for believing—

(a) that it is property obtained in consequence of the commission of an offence; and

(b) that it is necessary for it to be retained in order to prevent its being concealed, lost, damaged, altered or destroyed.

(3) Property falls within this subsection to the extent that there are reasonable grounds for believing—

(a) that it is evidence in relation to any offence; and

(b) that it is necessary for it to be retained in order to prevent its being concealed, lost, altered or destroyed.

(4) Nothing in this section authorises the retention (except in pursuance of section 54(2)) of anything at any time when its return is required by section 54.

(4A) Subsection (1)(a) includes property seized on any premises—

(a) by a person authorised under section 16(2) of the 1984 Act to accompany a constable executing a warrant, or

(b) by a person accompanying a constable under section 2(6) of the *Criminal Justice Act* 1987 in the execution of a warrant under section 2(4) of that Act.

(5) In subsection (1)(b) the reference to a relevant person's being on any premises accompanied by a constable is a reference only to a person who was so on the premises under the authority of—

(a) a warrant under section 448 of the *Companies Act* 1985 authorising him to exercise together with a constable the powers conferred by subsection (3) of that section;

(b) [*repealed by Companies Act 2006 (Consequential Amendments, Transitional Provisions and Savings Order* 2009 (S.I. 2009 No. 1941), *Sched. 1, para. 189(1) and (2)*].

(c)-(e) [*repealed by* Financial Services and Markets Act 2000 (Consequential Amendments and Repeals) *Order 2001 (S.I. 2001 No. 3649), art. 364*].

[This section is printed as amended by the *Criminal Justice Act* 2003, s.12, and Sched. 1, para. 14.]

Retention of seized items

1–78 **57.**—(1) This section has effect in relation to the following provisions (which are about the retention of items which have been seized and are referred to in this section as "the relevant provisions")—

(a)-(r) [*see* post].

(2) The relevant provisions shall apply in relation to any property seized in exercise of a power conferred by section 50 or 51 as if the property had been seized under the power of seizure by reference to which the power under that section was exercised in relation to that property.

(3) Nothing in any of sections 53 to 56 authorises the retention of any property at any time when its retention would not (apart from the provisions of this Part) be authorised by the relevant provisions.

(4) Nothing in any of the relevant provisions authorises the retention of anything after an obligation to return it has arisen under this Part.

The provisions listed in subs. (1) (as amended) are: (a) the *PACE Act* 1984, s.22; (f) the *Companies Act* 1985, s.448(6); (g) the *Weights and Measures (Packaged Goods) Regulations* 2006 (S.I. 2006 No. 659), Sched. 7; (k) the *Human Fertilisation and Embryology Act* 1990, s.40(4) (to be substituted, as from a day to be appointed, by a reference to para. 7(4) of Sched. 3B to the 1990 Act: *Human Fertilisation and Embryology Act* 2008, s.65, and Sched. 7, para. 19); (l) the *Knives Act* 1997, s.5(4); (m) the *Data Protection Act* 1998, Sched. 9, para. 7(2); (n) the *Competition Act* 1998, s.28(7); (o) the *Financial Services and Markets Act* 2000, s.176(8); (p) the *Freedom of Information Act* 2000, Sched. 3, para. 7(2); (pa) the *Enterprise Act* 2002, s.227F; (q) the *Human Tissue Act* 2004, Sched. 5, para. 5(4); and (r) the *Animal Welfare Act* 2006, Sched. 7, para. 12(3). Paragraphs (b) and (d) relate to Northern Ireland. Paragraphs (e), (h) and (j) were repealed by S.I. 2001 No. 3649 (*ante*, § 1–77), Art. 364. Paragraph (c) was repealed by the *Finance Act* 2007, ss.84(4) and 114, Sched. 22, paras 3 and 13(1)(a), and Sched. 27, Pt 5. Paragraph (i) was repealed by S.I. 2009 No. 1941 (*ante*, § 1–77), Sched. 1, para. 189(1) and (3).

Person to whom seized property is to be returned

1–79 **58.**—(1) Where—

(a) anything has been seized in exercise of any power of seizure, and

(b) there is an obligation under this Part for the whole or any part of the seized property to be returned, the obligation to return it shall (subject to the following provisions of this section) be an obligation to return it to the person from whom it was seized.

(2) Where—

(a) any person is obliged under this Part to return anything that has been seized to the person from whom it was seized, and

(b) the person under that obligation is satisfied that some other person has a better right to that thing than the person from whom it was seized,

his duty to return it shall, instead, be a duty to return it to that other person or, as the case may be, to the person appearing to him to have the best right to the thing in question.

(3) Where different persons claim to be entitled to the return of anything that is required to be returned under this Part, that thing may be retained for as long as is reasonably necessary for the determination in accordance with subsection (2) of the person to whom it must be returned.

(4) References in this Part to the person from whom something has been seized, in relation to a case in which the power of seizure was exercisable by reason of that thing's having been found on any premises, are references to the occupier of the premises at the time of the seizure.

(5) References in this section to the occupier of any premises at the time of a seizure, in relation to a case in which—

(a) a notice in connection with the entry or search of the premises in question, or with the seizure, was given to a person appearing in the occupier's absence to be in charge of the premises, and

(b) it is practicable, for the purpose of returning something that has been seized, to identify that person but not to identify the occupier of the premises,

are references to that person.

(16) Remedies and safeguards

Section 59 of the 2001 Act allows any person with a relevant interest in seized property to make an application to the "appropriate judicial authority". By s.64, this means a Crown Court judge in England and Wales (or, in relation to specified statutes, the High Court). Where such an application is made, ss.60 and 61 provide for a duty to secure the seized property, and s.62 provides for inextricably linked property. **1–80**

(17) Construction of Pt 2 of the Criminal Justice and Police Act 2001

Criminal Justice and Police Act 2001, s.63

Copies

63.—(1) Subject to subsection (3)— **1–81**

(a) in this Part, "seize" includes "take a copy of", and cognate expressions shall be construed accordingly;

(b) this Part shall apply as if any copy taken under any power to which any provision of this Part applies were the original of that of which it is a copy; and

(c) for the purposes of this Part, except sections 50 and 51, the powers mentioned in subsection (2) (which are powers to obtain hard copies etc. of information which is stored in electronic form) shall be treated as powers of seizure, and references to seizure and to seized property shall be construed accordingly.

(2) The powers mentioned in subsection (1)(c) are any powers which are conferred by—

(a)–(i) [*see* post].

(3) Subsection (1) does not apply to section 50(6) or 57.

The provisions listed in subs. (1) are: (a) the *PACE Act* 1984, ss.19(4) and 20; (c) the *Firearms Act* 1968, s.46(3); (d) the *Gaming Act* 1968, s.43(5)(aa); (f) the *Food Safety Act* 1990, s.32(6)(b); (h) the *Competition Act* 1998, s.28(2)(f); and (i) the *Nuclear Safeguards Act* 2000, s.8(2)(c). Paragraphs (b) and (g) relate to Northern Ireland. Paragraph (e) was repealed by the *Finance Act* 2007, ss.84(4) and 114, Sched. 22, paras 3 and 13(1)(b), and Sched. 27, Pt 5.

For s.64 of the 2001 Act, see *ante*, § 1–80.

Criminal Justice and Police Act 2001, s.65

Meaning of "legal privilege"

1–82 **65.**—(1) Subject to the following provisions of this section, references in this Part to an item subject to legal privilege shall be construed—

(a) for the purposes of the application of this Part to England and Wales, in accordance with section 10 of the 1984 Act (meaning of "legal privilege");

(b) [*Scotland*];

(c) [*Northern Ireland*.]

(2) In relation to property which has been seized in exercise, or purported exercise, of—

(a) the power of seizure conferred by section 28(2) of the *Competition Act* 1998, or

(b) so much of any power of seizure conferred by section 50 as is exercisable by reference to that power,

references in this Part to an item subject to legal privilege shall be read as references to a privileged communication within the meaning of section 30 of that Act.

(3) [...]

(3A) In relation to property which has been seized in exercise, or purported exercise, of—

(a) the power of seizure conferred by section 352(4) of the *Proceeds of Crime Act* 2002, or

(b) so much of any power of seizure conferred by section 50 as is exercisable by reference to that power,

references in this Part to an item subject to legal privilege shall be read as references to privileged material within the meaning of section 354(2) of that Act.

(4) An item which is, or is comprised in, property which has been seized in exercise, or purported exercise, of the power of seizure conferred by section 448(3) of the *Companies Act* 1985 shall be taken for the purposes of this Part to be an item subject to legal privilege if, and only if, the seizure of that item was in contravention of section 452(2) of that Act (privileged information).

(5) [...]

(6) [*Corresponds to subs. (4) with substitution of references to* Timeshare, Holiday Products, Resale and Exchange Contracts Regulations *2010 (S.I. 2010 No. 2960), reg. 33(3) and (8).*]

(7) [*Corresponds to subs. (4) with substitution of references to* Data Protection Act *1998, Sched. 9, para. 1 and para. 9.*]

(8) [*Corresponds to subs. (4) with substitution of references to* Freedom of Information Act *2000, Sched. 3, para. 1 and para. 9.*]

(8A) [*Corresponds to subs. (4) with substitution of references to* Enterprise Act *2002, s.227C and s.227B(4).*]

(9) An item which is, or is comprised in, property which has been seized in exercise, or purported exercise, of so much of any power of seizure conferred by section 50 as is exercisable by reference to a power of seizure conferred by—

(a)-(f) [*the powers of seizure mentioned in subss. (4) to (8A) respectively*],

shall be taken for the purposes of this Part to be an item subject to legal privilege if, and only if, the item would have been taken for the purposes of this Part to be an item subject to legal privilege had it been seized under the power of seizure by reference to which the power conferred by section 50 was exercised.

[This section is printed as amended by the *Proceeds of Crime Act* 2002, s.456, and Sched. 11, para. 40(5); the *Enterprise Act 2002 (Amendment) Regulations* 2006 (S.I. 2006 No. 3663); the *Timeshare, Holiday Products, Resale and Exchange Contracts Regulations* 2010 (S.I. 2010 No. 2960), reg. 36(3), and Sched. 6, para. 2(1) and (2); and the *Timeshare (Amendment) Regulations* 2011 (S.I. 2011 No. 1065), reg. 2(4); and as repealed in part by the *Finance Act* 2007, s.84(4), and Sched. 22, paras 3 and 13(1); and S.I. 2009 No. 1941, *ante*, § 1–77.]

Criminal Justice and Police Act 2001, s.66

General interpretation of Part 2

1–83 **66.**—(1) In this Part—

"appropriate judicial authority" has the meaning given by section 64;

"documents" includes information recorded in any form;

"item subject to legal privilege" shall be construed in accordance with section 65;

"marine installation" has the meaning given by section 262 of the *Marine and Coastal Access Act* 2009;

"premises" includes any vehicle, stall or moveable structure (including an offshore installation or other marine installation) and any other place whatever, whether or not occupied as land;

"offshore installation" has the same meaning as in the *Mineral Workings (Offshore Installations) Act* 1971;

"return", in relation to seized property, shall be construed in accordance with section 58, and cognate expressions shall be construed accordingly;;

"seize", and cognate expressions, shall be construed in accordance with section 63(1) and subsection (5) below;;

"seized property", in relation to any exercise of a power of seizure, means (subject to subsection (5)) anything seized in exercise of that power; and

"vehicle" includes any vessel, aircraft or hovercraft.

(2) In this Part references, in relation to a time when seized property is in any person's possession in consequence of a seizure ("the relevant time"), to something for which the person making the seizure had power to search shall be construed—

(a) where the seizure was made on the occasion of a search carried out on the authority of a warrant, as including anything of the description of things the presence or suspected presence of which provided grounds for the issue of the warrant;

(b) where the property was seized in the course of a search on the occasion of which it would have been lawful for the person carrying out the search to seize anything which on that occasion was believed by him to be, or appeared to him to be, of a particular description, as including—

(i) anything which at the relevant time is believed by the person in possession of the seized property, or (as the case may be) appears to him, to be of that description; and

(ii) anything which is in fact of that description;

(c) where the property was seized in the course of a search on the occasion of which it would have been lawful for the person carrying out the search to seize anything which there were on that occasion reasonable grounds for believing was of a particular description, as including—

(i) anything which there are at the relevant time reasonable grounds for believing is of that description; and

(ii) anything which is in fact of that description;

(d) where the property was seized in the course of a search to which neither paragraph (b) nor paragraph (c) applies, as including anything which is of a description of things which, on the occasion of the search, it would have been lawful for the person carrying it out to seize otherwise than under section 50and 51; and

(e) where the property was seized on the occasion of a search authorised under section 82 of the *Terrorism Act* 2000 (seizure of items suspected to have been, or to be intended to be, used in commission of certain offences), as including anything—

(i) which is or has been, or is or was intended to be, used in the commission of an offence such as is mentioned in subsection (3)(a) or (b) of that section; or

(ii) which at the relevant time the person who is in possession of the seized property reasonably suspects is something falling within sub-paragraph (i).

(3) For the purpose of determining in accordance with subsection (2), in relation to any time, whether or to what extent property seized on the occasion of a search authorised under section 9 of the *Official Secrets Act* 1911 (seizure of evidence of offences under that Act having been or being about to be committed) is something for which the person making the seizure had power to search, subsection (1) of that section shall be construed—

(a) as if the reference in that subsection to evidence of an offence under that Act being about to be committed were a reference to evidence of such an offence having been, at the time of the seizure, about to be committed; and

(b) as if the reference in that subsection to reasonable ground for suspecting that such an offence is about to be committed were a reference to reasonable ground for suspecting that at the time of the seizure such an offence was about to be committed.

(4) References in subsection (2) to a search include references to any activities authorised by virtue of any of the following—

(a) [see *post*].

(5) References in this Part to a power of seizure include references to each of the powers to take possession of items under—

(b)-(i) [*see* post],

and references in this Part to seizure and to seized property shall be construed accordingly.

(6) In this Part, so far as it applies to England and Wales —

(a) references to excluded material shall be construed in accordance with section 11 of the 1984 Act (meaning of "excluded material"); and

(b) references to special procedure material shall be construed in accordance with section 14 of that Act (meaning of "special procedure material").

(7) [*Northern Ireland.*]

(8) References in this Part to any item or material being comprised in other property include references to its being mixed with that other property.

(9) [*Northern Ireland.*]

[This section is printed as amended by the *Marine and Coastal Access Act* 2009, s.253(6).]

The provisions listed in subsection (4) (as amended) are: (a) the *Trade Descriptions Act* 1968, s.28(1); (b) the *Fair Trading Act* 1973, s.29(1); (c) the *Prices Act* 1974, Sched., para. 9; (d) the *Consumer Credit Act* 1974, s.162(1); (e) the *Estate Agents Act* 1979, s.11(1) to (1c); (g) the *Weights and Measures Act* 1985, s.79, and the *Weights and Measures (Packaged Goods) Regulations* 2006 (S.I. 2006 No. 659), Sched. 7; (h) the *Consumer Protection Act* 1987, s.29; (j) the *Food Safety Act* 1990, s.35(2); (ja) the *Human Fertilisation and Embryology Act* 1990, Sched. 3B, para. 5 (inserted, as from a day to be appointed, by the *Human Fertilisation and Embryology Act* 2008, s.65, and Sched. 7, para. 20); (k) the *Property Misdescriptions Act* 1991, Sched., para. 3; (m) the *Timeshare Act* 1992, Sched. 2, para. 3; (ma) the *Enterprise Act* 2002, s.227C; (n) the *Human Tissue Act* 2004, Sched. 5, para. 2; (o) the *General Product Safety Regulations* 2005 (S.I. 2005 No. 1803), reg. 22; (repealed) (p) the *Animal Welfare Act* 2006, ss.26(1), 27(1), 28(1) and 29(1); (q) the *Business Protection from Misleading Marketing Regulations* 2008 (S.I. 2008 No. 1276), reg. 23; (r) the *Consumer Protection from Unfair Trading Regulations* 2008 (S.I. 2008 No. 1277), reg. 21; and (s) the *Timeshare, Holiday Products, Resale and Exchange Contracts Regulations* 2010 (S.I. 2010 No. 2960), reg. 33(3). Paragraphs (f), (i) (repealed) and (l) relate to Northern Ireland.

The provisions listed in subs. (5) are: (b) the *Companies Act* 1985, s.448(3); (f) the *Criminal Justice Act* 1987, s.2(5); (h) the *Competition Act* 1998, s.28(2)(c); and (i) the *Financial Services and Markets Act* 2000, s.176(5). Paragraphs (a), (c) and (e) were repealed by S.I. 2001 No. 3649, Art. 364 (*ante*, § 1–77). Paragraph (d) was repealed by S.I. 2009 No. 1941 (*ante*, § 1–77), Sched. 1, para. 189(1) and (6). Paragraph (g) was repealed by the *Human Fertilisation and Embryology Act* 2008, s.65, and Sched. 7, para. 20.

(18) Powers of seizure under 2001 Act (Schedule 1)

Powers to which section 50 applies (list 1)

1–84 Schedule 1, Pt 1, lists the powers of seizure conferred by the following enactments: (1) the *PACE Act* 1984, Pts II and III; (3) the *Official Secrets Act* 1911, s.9(1); (4) the *Children and Young Persons (Harmful Publications) Act* 1955, s.3(1); (5) the *Obscene Publications Act* 1959, s.3(1) and (2); (8) the *Firearms Act* 1968, s.46; (9) the *Trade Descriptions Act* 1968, s.28(1)(c) and (d); (10) the *Theft Act* 1968, s.26(3); (14) the *Misuse of Drugs Act* 1971, s.23(2) and (3); (15) the *Immigration Act* 1971, ss.28D(3), 28E(5) and 28F(6); (16) the *Fair Trading Act* 1973, s.29(1)(c) and (d); (17) the *Biologi-*

cal Weapons Act 1974, s.4(1)(b), (c) and (d); (18) the *Prices Act* 1974, Sched., para. 9(2); (19) the *Consumer Credit Act* 1974, s.162(1)(c) and (d); (21) the *Protection of Children Act* 1978, s.4(2); (23) the *Customs and Excise Management Act* 1979, s.118C(4); (24) the *Estate Agents Act* 1979, s.11(1)(c); (25) the *Indecent Displays (Control) Act* 1981, s.2(3); (26) the *Forgery and Counterfeiting Act* 1981, ss.7(1) and 24(1); (27) the *Betting and Gaming Duties Act* 1981, Sched. 1, para. 16(2); (34) the *Video Recordings Act* 1984, s.17(2); (35) the *Companies Act* 1985, s.448(3); (36) the *Weights and Measures Act* 1985, s.79(2)(b); (39) the *Protection of Military Remains Act* 1986, s.6(3); (41) the *Greater London Council (General Powers) Act* 1986, s.12; (44) the *Criminal Justice Act* 1987, s.2(5); (45) the *Consumer Protection Act* 1987, s.29(4), (5) and (6); (48) the *Copyright, Designs and Patents Act* 1988, ss.109(4), 200(3A) and 297B(4); (50) the *Food Safety Act* 1990, s.32(6); (51) the *Computer Misuse Act* 1990, s.14(4); (52) the *Human Fertilisation and Embryology Act* 1990, s.40(2) (to be substituted, as from a day to be appointed, by a reference to para.7(1) and (2) of Sched. 3B to the 1990 Act: *Human Fertilisation and Embryology Act* 2008, s.65, and Sched. 7, para. 21); (53) the *Property Misdescriptions Act* 1991, Sched., para. 3(3); (54) the *Dangerous Dogs Act* 1991, s.5(2); (56A) the *Charities Act* 1993, s.31A(3); (58A) the *Trade Marks Act* 1994, s.92A(4); (59) the *Drug Trafficking Act* 1994, s.56(5); (60) the *Chemical Weapons Act* 1996, s.29(2)(c), (d) and (e); (63) the *Knives Act* 1997, s.5(2); (64) the *Nuclear Explosions (Prohibitions and Inspections) Act* 1998, s.10(2)(c), (d) and (e); (65) the *Data Protection Act* 1998, Sched. 9, para. 1; (66) the *Landmines Act* 1998, s.18(3)(c), (d) and (e); (67) the *Competition Act* 1998, s.28(2); (68) the *Nuclear Safeguards Act* 2000, s.8(2); (69) the *Financial Services and Markets Act* 2000, s.176(5); (70) the *Terrorism Act* 2000, s.82(3); (71) *ibid.*, Sched. 5, paras 1, 3, 11, 15 and 19; (73) the *Freedom of Information Act* 2000, Sched. 3, para. 1; (73A) the *Proceeds of Crime Act* 2002, s.352; (73A [*sic*]) the *International Criminal Court Act* 2001, Sched. 5, para. 9; (73B) the *Enterprise Act* 2002, s.194(2); (73BA) the *Enterprise Act* 2002, s.227C; (73C) the *Crime (International Co-operation) Act* 2003, ss.17 and 22; (73D) the *Extradition Act* 2003, ss.156(5), 160(5), 161(4), 162(6) and (7), and 164 (6) and (7); (73E) the *Human Tissue Act* 2004, s.56, and Sched. 6, para. 5(1) and(2); (73E [*sic*]) the *Licensing Act* 2003, s.90; (73F) the *Serious Organised Crime and Police Act* 2005, s.66; (73F [*sic*]) the *Gambling Act* 2005, s.317; (73G) the *General Product Safety Regulations* 2005 (S.I. 2005 No. 1803), reg. 22(4)-(6); (73G [*sic*]) the *Weights and Measures (Packaged Goods) Regulations* 2006 (S.I. 2006 No. 659), Sched. 5, para. 4; (73H) the *Terrorism Act* 2006, s.28; (73I) the *Animal Welfare Act* 2006, Sched. 2 and para. 10(2)(j); (73J) the *Money Laundering Regulations* 2007 (S.I. 2007 No. 2157), reg. 39(6);(73K) the *Transfer of Funds (Information on the Payer) Regulations* 2007 (S.I. 2007 No. 3298), reg. 9(6) (73J [*sic*]) the *Business Protection from Misleading Marketing Regulations* 2008 (S.I. 2008 No. 1276), reg. 23(1)(c) and (d); (73K [*sic*]) the *Consumer Protection from Unfair Trading Regulations* 2008 (S.I. 2008 No. 1277), reg. 21(1)(c) and (d); (73L) the *Marine and Coastal Access Act* 2009, s.252(1) and (3); (73M) the *Cluster Munitions (Prohibitions) Act* 2010, s.22(2)(c), (e), (f) and (g); and (73N) the *Timeshare, Holiday Products, Resale and Exchange Contracts Regulations* 2010 (S.I. 2010 No. 2960), reg. 33(3).

Paragraph 7 was repealed by the *Licensing Act* 2003, s.199, and Sched. 7. Paragraphs 6, 11 and 20 were repealed by the *Gambling Act* 2005, s.356, and Sched. 16, para. 18. Paragraphs 13, 28, 29, 57, 58, 61 and 72 were repealed by the*Finance Act* 2007, ss.84(4) and 114, Sched. 22, paras 3 and 13(2), andSched. 27, Pt 5. Paragraphs 32, 40 and 43 were repealed by S.I. 2001 No. 3649, art. 364 (*ante*, § 1–77). Paragraph 37 was repealed by the *Weights and Measures (Packaged Goods) Regulations* 2006 (S.I. 2006 No. 659), reg. 1(2), and Sched. 1, Pt 2, paras (24) and (27)(b). Paragraph 47 was repealed by the *Proceeds of Crime Act* 2002, s.457 and Sched. 12. Paragraph 49 was repealed by the *Crime (International Co-operation) Act* 2003, s.91, and Sched. 6. Paragraph 56 was repealed by the *Timeshare, Holiday Products, Resale and Exchange Contracts Regulations* 2010 (S.I. 2010 No. 2960), reg. 36(3) and (5), Sched. 6, para. 2(1) and (4), and Sched. 8, Pt 1. Paragraph 56A was inserted by the *Charities Act* 2006, s.26(2). The first para. 73A was inserted by the *Proceeds of Crime Act* 2002, s.456, and Sched. 11, para. 40(6). Paragraph 73(B) (renumbered by a correction slip) was inserted by the *Enterprise Act* 2002, s.194(5). Paragraph 73(BA) was inserted by the *Enterprise Act 2002 (Amendment) Regulations* 2006 (S.I. 2006 No. 3363), regs. 24 and 28. Paragraph 48 was amended, and para. 58A and the second para. 73A were inserted, by the *Criminal Justice and Police Act 2001 (Powers of Seizure) Order* 2003 (S.I. 2003 No. 934). Paragraphs 73C and 73D were inserted by the *Crime (International Co-operation) Act* 2003, s.26(3), and the *Extradition Act* 2003, s.165(2), respectively. Paragraph 73E was inserted by the *Human Tissue Act* 2004, s.56, and Sched. 6, para. 5(1) and (4). A second para.73E (renumbered erroneously by the *Gambling Act* 2005, s.356, and Sched. 16, para. 18) was inserted by the *Licensing Act* 2003, s.198, and Sched. 6, paras 119 and 128(a). Paragraph 73F was inserted by the *Serious Organised Crime and Police Act 2005*, s.68. A second para.73F was inserted by the *Gambling Act* 2005, s.356, and Sched. 16, para. 18. The first para. 73G was inserted by the *General Product Safety Regulations* 2005 (S.I. 2005 No. 1803), reg. 47(3). A second para. 73G was inserted by S.I. 2006 No. 659 (*ante*), reg. 1(2), and Sched. 1, Pt 2, paras (24) and (27)(c). Paragraph 73H was inserted by the *Terrorism Act* 2006, s.28(6)(a). Paragraph 73I was inserted by the *Animal Welfare Act* 2006, s.64, and Sched. 3, para. 14. The first para. 73J was inserted by the *Money Laundering Regulations* 2007 (S.I. 2007 No. 2157), reg. 51, and Sched. 6, para. 3. The first paragraph 73K was inserted by the *Transfer of Funds (Information on the Payer) Regulations* 2007 (S.I. 2007 No. 3298), reg. 19, and Sched. 3, para. 3. The second paragraphs 73J and 73K were inserted by the *Consumer Protection from Unfair Trading Regulations* 2008 (S.I. 2008 No. 1277), reg. 30, and Sched. 2, para. 64. Paragraph 73L was inserted by the *Marine and Coastal Access Act* 2009, s.253(7). Paragraph 73M was inserted by the *Cluster Munitions (Prohibitions) Act* 2010, s.31, and Sched. 3, para. 1. Paragraph 73N was inserted by the *Timeshare, Holiday Products, Resale and Exchange Contracts Regulations* 2010 (S.I. 2010 No. 2960), reg. 36(3) and (5), and Sched. 6, para. 2(1) and (4), and was amended by the *Timeshare (Amendment) Regulations* 2011 (S.I. 2011 No. 1065), reg. 2(4).

Paragraphs 2, 12, 22, 30, 31, 33, 38, 42, 46 (repealed), 55 and 62 relate to Northern Ireland.

Powers to which section 51 applies (list 2)

1–85 Schedule 1, Pt 2, lists the powers of seizure conferred by the following enactments: (74) the *PACE Act* 1984, Pt III; (76) as (8) in list 1; (77) as (14) in list 1; (78) the *Immigration Act* 1971, s.28G(7); (79) as (17) in list 1; (81) the *Criminal Justice and Public Order Act* 1994, s.139(10); (82) the *Terrorism Act* 2000, s.43(4); (83) as (71) in list 1; and (83A) the *Extradition Act* 2003, s.163(6) and (7) (inserted by s.165(3) of that Act). Paragraphs 75 and 80 relate to Northern Ireland.

Powers to which section 55 applies (list 3)

1–86 Schedule 1, Pt 3, lists the powers of seizure conferred by the following enactments: (84) the *PACE Act* 1984, s.8(2); (86) as (3) in list 1; (87) as (4) in list 1; (88) as (5) in list (1); (91) as (8) in list 1; (92) as (10) in list 1; (95) the *Immigration Act* 1971, s.28D(3); (96) as (17) in list 1; (98) as (21) in list 1; (100) as (25) in list 1; (101) as (26) in list 1; (103) as (34) in list 1; (106) as (48) in list 1; (107) as (51) in list 1; (107A) as (58A) in list 1; (108) as (59) in list 1; (109) (i) the *Terrorism Act* 2000, Sched. 5, paras 1 and 3, and (ii) *ibid.*, paras 15 and 19, but so far only as the power in question is conferred by reference to para. 1 of that Sched.; (110) the *Proceeds of Crime Act* 2002, s.352(4); (111) the *Licensing Act* 2003, s.90; (112) the *Gambling Act* 2005, s.317; (113) the *Terrorism Act* 2006, s.28. Paragraphs 85, 94, 99, 102 and 104 relate to Northern Ireland.

Paragraphs 89, 93 and 97 were repealed by the *Gambling Act* 2005, s.356, and Sched. 16, para. 18. Paragraph 90 was repealed, and para. 111 (as renumbered by the *Gambling Act*, *ibid.*) inserted, by the *Licensing Act* 2003, ss.198 and 199, and Scheds 6, paras 119 and 128(b), and 7. Paragraph 105 was repealed, and para. 110 was added, by the *Proceeds of Crime Act* 2002, ss.456 and 457, and Scheds 11, para. 40(7), and 12. Paragraph 106 was amended, and para.107A was inserted, by S.I. 2003 No. 934 (*ante*). Paragraph 112 was inserted by the *Gambling Act*, *ibid*. Paragraph 113 was inserted by the *Terrorism Act* 2006, s.28(6)(b).

Part I

(19) Interception of communications and surveillance

Police Act 1997, ss.91–108 and Regulation of Investigatory Powers Act 2000, ss.5–11

Part III of the *Police Act* 1997, ss.91–108, allows for authorisation of covert entry **1–87** upon and interference with property or with wireless telegraphy by the police, Revenue and Customs and others. These powers are supplementary to existing police powers: s.93(7). A similar system has existed in this field in relation to the intelligence services since the *Security Services Act* 1989 and the *Intelligence Services Act* 1994.

All forms of covert surveillance which do not involve covert entry upon or interfer- **1–88** ence with property or wireless telegraphy came under the *Regulation of Investigatory Powers Act* 2000. The Act is an attempt to put covert policing on a statutory footing and an implicit acceptance that a non-statutory basis for such activity would breach the *Human Rights Act* 1998: see *Hansard*, H.C., Vol. 345, col. 677, and the remarks of the Home Office Minister in the press notice accompanying the draft codes (Notice 291/2000). The Act distinguishes between directed (section 26(2)) and intrusive surveillance (s.26(3)–(5)). "Directed surveillance" is defined as covert surveillance that is undertaken in relation to a specific investigation or a specific operation which is likely to result in the obtaining of private information about a person. "Intrusive surveillance" is defined as covert surveillance carried out in relation to anything taking place on residential premises. The Act also provides for the use of "covert human intelligence sources". This is defined as a person who establishes or maintains a personal relationship with a person for the covert purpose of using the relationship to obtain information or provide access to information to another person or covertly disclosing information obtained by the use of such a relationship or as a consequence of the existence of such a relationship (s.26(8)); and it has been held to included an undercover police officer: *Hardy* [2003] 1 Cr.App.R. 30, CA. The protections for any suspect are greater in respect of intrusive surveillance than in respect of directed surveillance or the use of covert human intelligence sources.

As from February 26, 2010, directed surveillance which is carried out in relation to anything taking place on so much of any specified premises as is, at any time during the surveillance, used for the purpose of legal consultations is to be treated for the purposes of Part II of the 2000 Act as intrusive surveillance: *Regulation of Investigatory Powers (Extension of Authorisation Provisions: Legal Consultations) Order* 2010 (S.I. 2010 No. 461) (where the specified premises are set out). These provisions would appear to address the concerns expressed in *McE. v. Prison Service of Northern Ireland (Northern Ireland Human Rights Commission intervening); C. v. Chief Constable of the Police Service of Northern Ireland (Same intervening); M. v. Same (Same intervening)* [2009] 1 A.C. 908, HL.

All conduct defined in s.26 will be lawful provided it is carried out in relation to the authorisation to which it relates (s.27). The Act does not make a failure to obtain an authorisation a criminal offence, but the explanatory notes accompanying the Act (para. 180) recognise that such a failure may mean that the law enforcement agency had acted unlawfully under the *Human Rights Act* 1998, s.6. Such covert activity must be both necessary and proportionate (ss.28, 29 and 32) and the Act sets out specific criteria. The Act sets up a system of authorisations and supervision by a number of commissioners and tribunals. Revised codes of practice, entitled "Covert Human Intelligence Sources" and "Covert Surveillance and Property Interference", relating to the conduct and use of covert human intelligence sources under Pt II of the 2000 Act, the carrying out of covert surveillance under that part of that Act and to interference with property or wireless telegraphy under the 1994 Act, s.5, or Pt III of the 1997 Act, came into force on

April 6, 2010: *Regulation of Investigatory Powers (Covert Human Intelligence Sources: Code of Practice) Order* 2010 (S.I. 2010 No. 462); and *Regulation of Investigatory Powers (Covert Surveillance and Property Interference: Code of Practice) Order* 2010 (S.I. 2010 No. 463). As to the importance of compliance with the Act and the Codes, see *Harmes and Crane* [2006] 7 *Archbold News* 1, CA.

As from February 18, 2010, the *Regulation of Investigatory Powers (Covert Human Intelligence Sources: Matters Subject to Legal Privilege) Order* 2010 (S.I. 2010 No. 123) makes provision in relation to authorisation under the 2000 Act of activities involving conduct or use of covert human intelligence sources to obtain, provide access to, or disclose matters subject to legal privilege. See also S.I. 2010 No. 461, *ante*, § 1–88.

Neither the 1997 Act nor the 2000 Act purports to deal with the question of the admissibility of evidence obtained under their provisions. Their relevance is confined to the fact that they provide a framework of law by which the legality of the actions of the police may be judged; where evidence has been unlawfully obtained, this is a matter to be taken into account by a court in deciding whether it is fair to admit it (*PACE Act* 1984, s.78, *post*, § 10–130). It is the effect on the fairness of the proceedings that is important, rather than the illegality of the police's conduct: Lord Nolan in *Khan (Sultan)* [1997] A.C. 558 at 582, HL, at p. 582. Fairness, however, is not to be confined to procedural fairness, and evidence may be excluded because it has been obtained by unfair means: per Lord Nicholls (paras 11 and 12) and Lord Scott (para. 122) in *Looseley* [2002] 1 Cr.App.R. 29, HL.

(20) Serious Organised Crime and Police Act 2005, ss.60–70 (Chapter 1)

Disclosure notices—summary

1–89 Sections 60 to 70 of the 2005 Act are headed "Investigatory Powers of DPP, etc.". Section 60 provides for the DPP, the Director of Revenue and Customs Prosecutions, and the Lord Advocate to give "disclosure notices" in connection with the investigation of offences to which Ch. 1 of Pt 2 applies. Each may delegate such powers. Section 61 lists the offences to which the powers apply. They are "lifestyle offences" under the *Proceeds of Crime Act* 2002, offences under the *Terrorism Act* 2000, ss.15 to 18, any offence which is a qualifying offence (as to which see subs. (2)) under the *Customs and Excise Management Act* 1979, s.170, the *Value Added Tax Act* 1994, s.72, the *Theft Act* 1968, s.17, or any qualifying common law offence of cheating in relation to the public revenue, or an attempt or conspiracy to commit any such offence.

Section 62 provides for a disclosure notice (as to which, see s.62(3)) to be given to a person where it appears to the investigating authority that there are reasonable grounds for suspecting that an offence to which Ch. 1 applies has been committed, that any person has information which relates to a matter relevant to the investigation of that offence, and that there are reasonable grounds for believing that information which may be provided by that person in compliance with a disclosure notice is likely to be of substantial value (whether or not by itself) to that investigation. Section 63 contains provision as to the production of documents where a disclosure notice has been given. Section 64 contains restrictions on the requirement to produce information (privileged information, "excluded material" within the *PACE Act* 1984, information subject to obligation of confidence, etc.). Section 65 restricts the use of statements made in response to a requirement imposed under s.2 or 63. The statement may not be used against the maker in criminal proceedings, except in the specified circumstances. Sections 66 and 67 provide for enforcement. Section 66 sets out the procedure for the issue and execution of a warrant in order to seize documents subject to a disclosure notice. Section 67(1) makes it a summary offence for a person, without reasonable excuse, to fail to comply with a requirement imposed on him under s.62 or 63. Section 67(2) provides for an either way offence where a person, in purported compliance with any such requirement, knowingly or recklessly makes a statement that is false or misleading in a material particular. Section 67(3) creates a summary offence of wilfully obstructing any person in the exercise of any rights conferred by a warrant under s.66. Section 68 inserts a reference to the power of seizure under s.66 into Pt 1 of Sched. 1 to the *Criminal Justice and Police Act* 2001 (*ante*, § 1–84). Section 69 prescribes the manner in which a disclosure notice may be given. Section 70 provides for the interpretation of Ch. 1.

Commencement

1–90 Sections 60 to 70 came into force on April 1, 2006: *Serious Organised Crime and Police Act 2005 (Commencement No. 1, Transitional and Transitory Provisions) Order* 2005 (S.I. 2005 No. 1521).

Legislation

Investigatory powers of DPP etc.

1–91 **60.**—(1) This Chapter confers powers on—

(a) the Director of Public Prosecutions,

(b) the Director of Revenue and Customs Prosecutions, *and*

(c) [*Scotland*]

(d) [*Northern Ireland*],

in relation to the giving of disclosure notices in connection with the investigation of offences to which this Chapter applies or in connection with a terrorist investigation.

(2) The Director of Public Prosecutions may, to such extent as he may determine, delegate the exercise of his powers under this Chapter to a Crown prosecutor.

(3) The Director of Revenue and Customs Prosecutions may, to such extent as he may determine, delegate the exercise of his powers under this Chapter to a Revenue and Customs Prosecutor.

(4) [*Scotland*.]

(4A) [*Northern Ireland*.]

(5) In this Chapter "the Investigating Authority" means—

(a) the Director of Public Prosecutions,

(b) the Director of Revenue and Customs Prosecutions, *or*

(c) [*Scotland*]

(d) [*Northern Ireland*.]

(6) But, in circumstances where the powers of any of those persons are exercisable by any other person by virtue of subsection (2), (3) (4) or (4A), references to "the Investigating Authority" accordingly include any such other person.

(7) In this Chapter "terrorist investigation" means an investigation of—

(a) the commission, preparation or instigation of acts of terrorism,

(b) any act or omission which appears to have been for the purposes of terrorism and which consists in or involves the commission, preparation or instigation of an offence, or

(c) the commission, preparation or instigation of an offence under the *Terrorism Act* 2000 or under Part 1 of the *Terrorism Act* 2006 other than an offence under section 1 or 2 of that Act.

[This section is printed as amended by the *Terrorism Act* 2006, s.33(1) and (2); and the *Northern Ireland (Miscellaneous Provisions) Act* 2006, s.26(2), and Sched. 3, paras 1 and 2. The italicised words are repealed as from a day to be appointed: *ibid*., s.30(2), and Sched. 5.]

Offences to which this Chapter applies

1–92 **61.**—(1) This Chapter applies to the following offences—

(a) any offence listed in Schedule 2 to the *Proceeds of Crime Act* 2002 (lifestyle offences: England and Wales);

(b) [*Scotland*];

(ba) [*Northern Ireland*];

(c) any offence under sections 15 to 18 of the *Terrorism Act* 2000 (offences relating to fund-raising, money laundering etc.);

(d) any offence under section 170 of the *Customs and Excise Management Act* 1979 (fraudulent evasion of duty) or section 72 of the *Value Added Tax Act* 1994 (offences relating to VAT) which is a qualifying offence;

(e) any offence under section 17 of the *Theft Act* 1968 or [*Northern Ireland*] (false accounting), or any offence at common law of cheating in relation to the public revenue, which is a qualifying offence;

(f) any offence under section 1 of the *Criminal Attempts Act* 1981 or [*Northern Ireland, Scotland*] of attempting to commit any offence in paragraph (c) or any offence in paragraph (d) or (e) which is a qualifying offence;

(g) any offence under section 1 of the *Criminal Law Act* 1977 or [*Northern Ireland, Scotland*] of conspiracy to commit any offence in paragraph (c) or any offence in paragraph (d) or (e) which is a qualifying offence;

(h) *in England and Wales—*

(i) *any common law offence of bribery;*

(ii) *any offence under section 1 of the Public Bodies Corrupt Practices Act 1889 (corruption in office);*

(iii) *the first two offences under section 1 of the Prevention of Corruption Act 1906 (bribes obtained by or given to agents). [any offence under the Bribery Act 2010]*

(2) For the purposes of subsection (1) an offence in paragraph (d) or (e) of that subsection is a qualifying offence if the Investigating Authority certifies that in his opinion—

(a) in the case of an offence in paragraph (d) or an offence of cheating the public revenue, the offence involved or would have involved a loss, or potential loss, to the public revenue of an amount not less than £5,000;

(b) in the case of an offence under section 17 of the *Theft Act* 1968 or [*Northern Ireland*], the offence involved or would have involved a loss or gain, or potential loss or gain, of an amount not less than £5,000.

(3) A document purporting to be a certificate under subsection (2) is to be received in evidence and treated as such a certificate unless the contrary is proved.

(4), (5) [*Provision for amendment of subss. (1) and (2) by order.*]

[This section is printed as amended by the *Serious Organised Crime and Police Act 2005 (Amendment of s.61(1)) Order* 2006 (S.I. 2006 No. 1629); by the *Northern Ireland (Miscellaneous Provisions) Act* 2006, s.26(2), and Sched. 3, paras 1 and 3; and as amended, as from a day to be appointed, by the *Bribery Act* 2010, s.17(2), and Sched. 1, para. 8 (substitution of words in square brackets, omission of italicised words in subs. (1)(h)).]

Disclosure notices

1–93 **62.**—(1) If it appears to the Investigating Authority—

(a) that there are reasonable grounds for suspecting that an offence to which this Chapter applies has been committed,

(b) that any person has information (whether or not contained in a document) which relates to a matter relevant to the investigation of that offence, and

(c) that there are reasonable grounds for believing that information which may be provided by that person in compliance with a disclosure notice is likely to be of substantial value (whether or not by itself) to that investigation,

he may give, or authorise an appropriate person to give, a disclosure notice to that person.

(1A) If it appears to the Investigating Authority—

(a) that any person has information (whether or not contained in a document) which relates to a matter relevant to a terrorist investigation, and

(b) that there are reasonable grounds for believing that information which may be provided by that person in compliance with a disclosure notice is likely to be of substantial value (whether or not by itself) to that investigation

he may give, or authorise an appropriate person to give, a disclosure notice to that person.

(2) In this Chapter "appropriate person" means—

(a) a constable,

(b) a member of the staff of SOCA who is for the time being designated under section 43, or

(c) an officer of Revenue and Customs.

[*Saving in relation to Northern Ireland.*]

(3) In this Chapter "disclosure notice" means a notice in writing requiring the person to whom it is given to do all or any of the following things in accordance with the specified requirements, namely—

(a) answer questions with respect to any matter relevant to the investigation;

(b) provide information with respect to any such matter as is specified in the notice;

(c) produce such documents, or documents of such descriptions, relevant to the investigation as are specified in the notice.

(4) In subsection (3) "the specified requirements" means such requirements specified in the disclosure notice as relate to—

(a) the time at or by which,

(b) the place at which, or

(c) the manner in which,

the person to whom the notice is given is to do any of the things mentioned in paragraphs (a) to (c) of that subsection; and those requirements may include a requirement to do any of those things at once.

(5) A disclosure notice must be signed or counter-signed by the Investigating Authority.

(6) This section has effect subject to section 64 (restrictions on requiring information etc.).

[This section is printed as amended by the *Terrorism Act* 2006, s.33(3); and the *Northern Ireland (Miscellaneous Provisions) Act* 2006, s.26(2), and Sched. 3, paras 1 and 4.]

Production of documents

63.—(1) This section applies where a disclosure notice has been given under section 62. **1–94**

(2) An authorised person may—

(a) take copies of or extracts from any documents produced in compliance with the notice, and

(b) require the person producing them to provide an explanation of any of them.

(3) Documents so produced may be retained for so long as the Investigating Authority considers that it is necessary to retain them (rather than copies of them) in connection with the investigation for the purposes of which the disclosure notice was given.

(4) If the Investigating Authority has reasonable grounds for believing—

(a) that any such documents may have to be produced for the purposes of any legal proceedings, and

(b) that they might otherwise be unavailable for those purposes,

they may be retained until the proceedings are concluded.

(5) If a person who is required by a disclosure notice to produce any documents does not produce the documents in compliance with the notice, an authorised person may require that person to state, to the best of his knowledge and belief, where they are.

(6) In this section "authorised person" means any appropriate person who either—

(a) is the person by whom the notice was given, or

(b) is authorised by the Investigating Authority for the purposes of this section.

(7) This section has effect subject to section 64 (restrictions on requiring information etc.).

Restrictions on requiring information etc.

64.—(1) A person may not be required under section 62 or 63— **1–95**

(a) to answer any privileged question,

(b) to provide any privileged information, or

(c) to produce any privileged document,

except that a lawyer may be required to provide the name and address of a client of his.

(2) A "privileged question" is a question which the person would be entitled to refuse to answer on grounds of legal professional privilege in proceedings in the High Court.

(3) "Privileged information" is information which the person would be entitled to refuse to provide on grounds of legal professional privilege in such proceedings.

(4) A "privileged document" is a document which the person would be entitled to refuse to produce on grounds of legal professional privilege in such proceedings.

(5) A person may not be required under section 62 to produce any excluded material (as defined by section 11 of the *Police and Criminal Evidence Act* 1984 or [*Northern Ireland*]).

(6), (7) [*Scotland.*]

(8) A person may not be required under section 62 or 63 to disclose any information or produce any document in respect of which he owes an obligation of confidence by virtue of carrying on any banking business, unless—

(a) the person to whom the obligation of confidence is owed consents to the disclosure or production, or

(b) the requirement is made by, or in accordance with a specific authorisation given by, the Investigating Authority.

(9) Subject to the preceding provisions, any requirement under section 62 or 63 has effect despite any restriction on disclosure (however imposed).

[This section is printed as amended by the *Northern Ireland (Miscellaneous Provisions) Act* 2006, s.26(2), and Sched. 3, paras 1 and 5.]

Restrictions on use of statements

1–96 **65.**—(1) A statement made by a person in response to a requirement imposed under section 62 or 63 ("the relevant statement") may not be used in evidence against him in any criminal proceedings unless subsection (2) or (3) applies.

(2) This subsection applies where the person is being prosecuted—

(a) for an offence under section 67 of this Act, or

(b) for an offence under section 5 of the *Perjury Act* 1911 (false statements made on oath otherwise than in judicial proceedings or made otherwise than on oath), or

(c) for an offence under [*Scotland*] or at common law for an offence of attempting to pervert the course, or defeat the ends, of justice.

(3) This subsection applies where the person is being prosecuted for some other offence and—

(a) the person, when giving evidence in the proceedings, makes a statement inconsistent with the relevant statement, and

(b) in the proceedings evidence relating to the relevant statement is adduced, or a question about it is asked, by or on behalf of the person.

Power to enter and seize documents

1–97 **66.**—(1) A justice of the peace may issue a warrant under this section if, on an information on oath laid by the Investigating Authority, he is satisfied—

(a) that any of the conditions mentioned in subsection (2) is met in relation to any documents of a description specified in the information, and

(b) that the documents are on premises so specified.

(2) The conditions are—

(a) that a person has been required by a disclosure notice to produce the documents but has not done so;

(b) that it is not practicable to give a disclosure notice requiring their production;

(c) that giving such a notice might seriously prejudice the investigation of an offence to which this Chapter applies.

(3) A warrant under this section is a warrant authorising an appropriate person named in it—

(a) to enter and search the premises, using such force as is reasonably necessary;

(b) to take possession of any documents appearing to be documents of a description specified in the information, or to take any other steps which appear to be necessary for preserving, or preventing interference with, any such documents;

(c) in the case of any such documents consisting of information recorded otherwise than in legible form, to take possession of any computer disk or other electronic storage device which appears to contain the information in question, or to take any other steps which appear to be necessary for preserving, or preventing interference with, that information;

(d) to take copies of or extracts from any documents or information falling within paragraph (b) or (c);

(e) to require any person on the premises to provide an explanation of any such documents or information or to state where any such documents or information may be found;

(f) to require any such person to give the appropriate person such assistance as he may reasonably require for the taking of copies or extracts as mentioned in paragraph (d).

(4) A person executing a warrant under this section may take other persons with him, if it appears to him to be necessary to do so.

(5) A warrant under this section must, if so required, be produced for inspection by the owner or occupier of the premises or anyone acting on his behalf.

(6) If the premises are unoccupied or the occupier is temporarily absent, a person entering the premises under the authority of a warrant under this section must leave the premises as effectively secured against trespassers as he found them.

(7) Where possession of any document or device is taken under this section—

(a) the document may be retained for so long as the Investigating Authority considers that it is necessary to retain it (rather than a copy of it) in connection with the investigation for the purposes of which the warrant was sought, or

(b) the device may be retained for so long as he considers that it is necessary to retain it in connection with that investigation,

as the case may be.

(8) If the Investigating Authority has reasonable grounds for believing—

(a) that any such document or device may have to be produced for the purposes of any legal proceedings, and

(b) that it might otherwise be unavailable for those purposes,

it may be retained until the proceedings are concluded.

(9) Nothing in this section authorises a person to take possession of, or make copies of or take extracts from, any document or information which, by virtue of section 64, could not be required to be produced or disclosed under section 62 or 63.

(10), (11) [*Scotland, Northern Ireland.*]

[This section is printed as amended by the *Northern Ireland (Miscellaneous Provisions) Act* 2006, s.26(2), and Sched. 3, paras 1 and 7.]

Offences in connection with disclosure notices or search warrants

67.—(1) A person commits an offence if, without reasonable excuse, he fails to comply with any requirement imposed on him under section 62 or 63. **1–98**

(2) A person commits an offence if, in purported compliance with any requirement imposed on him under section 62 or 63—

(a) he makes a statement which is false or misleading, and

(b) he either knows that it is false or misleading or is reckless as to whether it is false or misleading.

"False or misleading" means false or misleading in a material particular.

(3) A person commits an offence if he wilfully obstructs any person in the exercise of any rights conferred by a warrant under section 66.

(4) A person guilty of an offence under subsection (1) or (3) is liable on summary conviction—

(a) to imprisonment for a term not exceeding 51 weeks, or

(b) to a fine not exceeding level 5 on the standard scale,

or to both.

(5) A person guilty of an offence under subsection (2) is liable—

(a) on conviction on indictment, to imprisonment for a term not exceeding two years or to a fine, or to both;

(b) on summary conviction, to imprisonment for a term not exceeding 12 months or to a fine not exceeding the statutory maximum, or to both.

(6), (7) [*Scotland, Northern Ireland.*]

[This section is printed as amended by the *Northern Ireland (Miscellaneous Provisions) Act* 2006, s.26(2), and Sched. 3, paras 1 and 8.]

Procedure applicable to search warrants

68. [*Amends* Criminal Justice and Police Act *2001, Sched. 1, ante,* § 1–84.] **1–99**

Manner in which disclosure notice may be given

1–100 **69.**—(1) This section provides for the manner in which a disclosure notice may be given under section 62.

(2) The notice may be given to a person by—

(a) delivering it to him,

(b) leaving it at his proper address,

(c) sending it by post to him at that address.

(3) The notice may be given—

(a) in the case of a body corporate, to the secretary or clerk of that body;

(b) in the case of a partnership, to a partner or a person having the control or management of the partnership business;

(c) in the case of an unincorporated association (other than a partnership), to an officer of the association.

(4) For the purposes of this section and section 7 of the *Interpretation Act* 1978 (service of documents by post) in its application to this section, the proper address of a person is his usual or last-known address (whether residential or otherwise), except that—

(a) in the case of a body corporate or its secretary or clerk, it is the address of the registered office of that body or its principal office in the United Kingdom,

(b) in the case of a partnership, a partner or a person having the control or management of the partnership business, it is that of the principal office of the partnership in the United Kingdom, and

(c) in the case of an unincorporated association (other than a partnership) or an officer of the association, it is that of the principal office of the association in the United Kingdom

(5) This section does not apply to Scotland.

Interpretation of Chapter 1

1–101 **70.**—(1) In this Chapter

"act of terrorism" includes anything constituting an action taken for the purposes of terrorism, within the meaning of the *Terrorism Act* 2000 (see section 1(5) of that Act);

"appropriate person" has the meaning given by section 62(2);

"the Investigating Authority" is to be construed in accordance with section 60(5) and (6);

"disclosure notice" has the meaning given by section 62(3);

"document" includes information recorded otherwise than in legible form;

"terrorism" has the same meaning as in the *Terrorism Act* 2000 (see section 1(1) to (4) of that Act);

"terrorist investigation" has the meaning given by section 60(7).

(2) In relation to information recorded otherwise than in legible form, any reference in this Chapter to the production of documents is a reference to the production of a copy of the information in legible form.

[This section is printed as amended by the *Terrorism Act* 2006, s.33(4).]

E. ARREST AND DETENTION

(1) Introduction

1–102 In general, an arrest is constituted by a physical seizure or touching of the arrested person's body, with a view to his detention: (see, *e.g.*, *Brosch* [1988] Crim.L.R. 743, CA), but touching by a police officer cannot constitute an arrest unless the officer intends an arrest: *Wood v. DPP* [2008] 6 *Archbold News* 2, DC, following *Kenlin v. Gardner* [1967] 2 Q.B. 510, DC. But there may also be an arrest by mere words: see, *e.g.*, *Alderson v. Booth* [1969] 2 Q.B. 216; 53 Cr.App.R.301, DC (arrest is constituted when any form of words is used which is calculated to bring to the suspect's notice, and does so, that he is under compulsion, and he thereafter submits to that compulsion); and *Inwood* (1973) 57 Cr.App.R. 529, CA (no magic formula, only the obligation to make it plain to the suspect by what is said and done that he is no longer a free man; different procedures might be needed according to the person's age, ethnic origin, knowledge of English, intellectual qualities, physical or mental disabilities).

A constable may use reasonable force, if necessary, to effect an arrest: the *PACE Act* 1984, s.117, *post*, § 1–119.

An arrest is unlawful unless at the time of the arrest or as soon as practicable after the arrest the arrested person is informed that he is under arrest and of the ground of the arrest, regardless of whether the fact of arrest is obvious (*PACE Act* 1984, s.28 (*post*, § 1–114)). This is subject to an exception in the case of a person who escapes (s.28(5)).

Powers of arrest, whether by police or any other persons are governed by statute and common law. Any arrest has to have a legal basis or it may amount to a criminal offence or give rise to civil liability. **1–103**

The main police powers of arrest are—

1. Arrest without a warrant under the *PACE Act* 1984, Pt III (ss.24-33), *post*, §§ 1–106 *et seq.*
2. Arrest without a warrant under other statutes, either specifically preserved by the 1984 Act (s.26(2) and Sched. 2, *post*, § 1–111), or enacted subsequently (*e.g.* the *Public Order Act* 1986, s.5(4)).
3. Arrest for failure to comply with a requirement to provide fingerprints or samples under Sched. 2A to the 1984 Act (*post*, §§ 1–175 *et seq.*).
4. Arrest with a warrant issued by a magistrate or district judge—*Magistrates' Courts Act* 1980, s.1 (*post* § 4–76).
5. Arrest with or without a warrant under the *Criminal Justice and Public Order Act* 1994, Pt X (Cross-border enforcement).
6. Common law power of arrest for breach of the peace.

Code G (*post*, Appendix A) applies to the police's powers of arrest under the 1984 Act, s.24, as substituted by the *Serious Organised Crime and Police Act* 2005.

Consequences of arrest

Where a private citizen makes a lawful arrest either at common law or under statute, he should take the arrested person before a justice of the peace or a police officer, not necessarily forthwith, but as soon as reasonably possible: *John Lewis & Co Ltd v. Tims* [1952] A.C. 676, HL. **1–104**

As to the obligations of a constable when he arrests someone for an offence, or takes someone into custody after he has been arrested for an offence by a person other than a constable, at any place other than at a police station, see s.30 of the *PACE Act* 1984 (*post*, § 1–122).

A person who is at a police station under arrest must be further arrested where it appears that if he were released he would be liable to arrest for some other offence (*PACE Act* 1984, s.31, *post*, § 1–129).

Section 32 provides for the search of a person upon arrest and for entry and search of any premises in which he was when arrested or immediately before he was arrested (*post*, § 1–130).

For the conditions and duration of the detention of an arrested person, see the *PACE Act* 1984, Pt IV, ss.34-52. Sections 34 to 46 are found *post*, §§ 1–133 *et seq.* For bail after arrest, see s.47, *post*, § 5–100. For the questioning and treatment of persons in custody, see ss.53-65, *post*, §§ 1–150 *et seq.*

(2) Reasonable grounds for suspecting

See *ante*, § 1–12. **1–105**

(3) Arrest without warrant

Police and Criminal Evidence Act 1984, s.24

Arrest without warrant: constables

24.—(1) A constable may arrest without a warrant— **1–106**

(a) anyone who is about to commit an offence;

(b) anyone who is in the act of committing an offence;
(c) anyone whom he has reasonable grounds for suspecting to be about to commit an offence;
(d) anyone whom he has reasonable grounds for suspecting to be committing an offence.

(2) If a constable has reasonable grounds for suspecting that an offence has been committed, he may arrest without a warrant anyone whom he has reasonable grounds to suspect of being guilty of it.

(3) If an offence has been committed, a constable may arrest without a warrant—
(a) anyone who is guilty of the offence;
(b) anyone whom he has reasonable grounds for suspecting to be guilty of it.

(4) But the power of summary arrest conferred by subsection (1), (2) or (3) is exercisable only if the constable has reasonable grounds for believing that for any of the reasons mentioned in subsection (5) it is necessary to arrest the person in question.

(5) The reasons are—
(a) to enable the name of the person in question to be ascertained (in the case where the constable does not know, and cannot readily ascertain, the person's name, or has reasonable grounds for doubting whether a name given by the person as his name is his real name);
(b) correspondingly as regards the person's address;
(c) to prevent the person in question—
(i) causing physical injury to himself or any other person;
(ii) suffering physical injury;
(iii) causing loss of or damage to property;
(iv) committing an offence against public decency (subject to subsection (6)); or
(v) causing an unlawful obstruction of the highway;
(d) to protect a child or other vulnerable person from the person in question;
(e) to allow the prompt and effective investigation of the offence or of the conduct of the person in question;
(f) to prevent any prosecution for the offence from being hindered by the disappearance of the person in question.

(6) Subsection (5)(c)(iv) applies only where members of the public going about their normal business cannot reasonably be expected to avoid the person in question.

[This section was substituted by the *Serious Organised Crime and Police Act* 2005, s.110(1) and (4).]

1–107 In *Shields v. Chief Constable of Merseyside Police*, *The Times*, March 3, 2011, CA (Civ. Div.), the effect of s.24 was summarised as follows (at [14]):

> In short, under the scheme a summary arrest by a police officer will be lawful if (a) the person arrested is about to commit, is committing or has committed an offence or (b) the police officer has reasonable grounds for suspecting this to be so, provided in every case that the arresting officer has reasonable grounds for believing that the arrest is necessary for any of the reasons identified in s.24(5). There are thus three pairs of alternatives, depending on whether the arrest relates to future, present or past behaviour or suspected behaviour of the person arrested. As to future behaviour, a police officer may arrest a person who is about to commit an offence (s.24(1)(a)) or whom he has reasonable grounds for suspecting to be about to commit an offence (s.24(1)(c)). As to present behaviour, he may arrest someone who is in the act of committing an offence (s.24(1)(b)) or whom he has reasonable grounds for suspecting to be committing an offence (s.24(1)(d)). As to past behaviour, he may arrest someone who has committed an offence (s.24(3)(a)) or whom he has reasonable grounds for suspecting to be guilty of an offence (ss.24(2)/24(3)(b)).

The statutory code contemplated by s.24 does not require a police officer who has reasonable grounds for believing that an offence has been committed (see subs. (2)), and who reasonably believes that it is necessary to arrest the person in question (see subs. (4)), to go through any further mental process before carrying out the arrest: *Shields v. Chief Constable of Merseyside Police, ante*. Where the arresting officer wrongly believed that a fellow officer had already decided to arrest the appellant, that belief did not prevent the arrest being lawful, and the arresting officer was not obliged to exercise an independent discretion: *ibid*.

The power of arrest under s.24(3)(a) is legitimately exercised where the offence for which the detainee is arrested is sufficiently correlated to the offence which in fact has been committed:*Shields v. Chief Constable of Merseyside Police, ante*. So an arrest for assaulting a police officer in the execution of his duty is lawful even though the offence actually committed was common assault, but an offence for theft would be unlawful if the only offence actually committed was a motoring offence: *ibid*.

"Necessary" (s.24(4)) is an ordinary English word which can be applied without paraphrase: *Richardson v. Chief Constable of West Midlands Police* [2011] 2 Cr.App.R. 1, QBD (Slade J.), where an arrest of a voluntary attendee at a police station was held unlawful on the basis that the arresting officer failed to consider whether arrest was necessary or whether voluntary attendance would achieve the desired investigative objective under s.25(5)(e).

As to "reasonable grounds for suspecting", see *ante*, § 1–12. **1–108**

(4) Arrest without a warrant by other persons

Police and Criminal Evidence Act 1984, s.24A

Arrest without warrant: other persons

24A.—(1) A person other than a constable may arrest without a warrant— **1–109**

(a) anyone who is in the act of committing an indictable offence;

(b) anyone whom he has reasonable grounds for suspecting to be committing an indictable offence.

(2) Where an indictable offence has been committed, a person other than a constable may arrest without a warrant—

(a) anyone who is guilty of the offence;

(b) anyone whom he has reasonable grounds for suspecting to be guilty of it.

(3) But the power of summary arrest conferred by subsection (1) or (2) is exercisable only if—

(a) the person making the arrest has reasonable grounds for believing that for any of the reasons mentioned in subsection (4) it is necessary to arrest the person in question; and

(b) it appears to the person making the arrest that it is not reasonably practicable for a constable to make it instead.

(4) The reasons are to prevent the person in question—

(a) causing physical injury to himself or any other person;

(b) suffering physical injury;

(c) causing loss of or damage to property; or

(d) making off before a constable can assume responsibility for him.

(5) This section does not apply in relation to an offence under Part 3 or 3A of the *Public Order Act* 1986.

[This section was inserted by the *Serious Organised Crime and Police Act* 2005, s.110(1) and (4). Subsection (5) was inserted by the *Racial and Religious Hatred Act* 2006, s.2.]

As to "reasonable grounds for suspecting", see *ante*, § 1–12.

As from January 1, 2007 (*Electoral Administration Act 2006 (Commencement No. 2, Transitional and Savings Provisions) Order* 2006 (S.I. 2006 No. 3412)), s.71 of the *Electoral Administration Act* 2006 disapplies section 24A in relation to the arrest of a person inside a polling station who has committed or is suspected of committing an offence contrary to s.60 (personation) of the *Representation of the People Act* 1983.

Where the defendant was acquitted at trial of the substantive offence it was held to **1–110** invalidate the arrest by a citizen under the predecessor of s.24A(2) because no arrestable (now indictable) offence had been committed: *Self* (1992) 95 Cr.App.R. 42; *Walters v. W.H. Smith & Son Ltd* [1914] 1. K.B. 595.

Part I

(5) Other statutory powers of arrest without warrant

Police and Criminal Evidence Act 1984, s.26, Sched. 2

Repeal of statutory powers of arrest without warrant or order

1–111 **26.**—(1) Subject to subsection (2) below, so much of any Act (including a local Act) passed before this Act as enables a constable—

(a) to arrest a person for an offence without a warrant; or

(b) to arrest a person otherwise than for an offence without a warrant or an order of a court,

shall cease to have effect.

(2) Nothing in subsection (1) above affects the enactments specified in Schedule 2 to this Act.

SCHEDULE 2

PRESERVED POWERS OF ARREST

1–112 Section 2 of the *Emergency Powers Act* 1920.

Section 49 of the *Prison Act* 1952.

Section 13 of the *Visiting Forces Act* 1952.

Section 32 of the *Children and Young Persons Act* 1969.

Section 24(2) of the *Immigration Act* 1971 and paragraphs 17, 24 and 33 of Schedule 2 and paragraph 7 of Schedule 3 to that Act.

Section 7 of the *Bail Act* 1976.

Schedule 5 to the *Reserve Forces Act* 1980.

Sections 18, 35(10), 36(8), 38(7), 136(1) and 138 of the *Mental Health Act* 1983.

Section 5(5) of the *Repatriation of Prisoners Act* 1984.

[This Schedule is printed as amended, and repealed in part, by the *Representation of the People Act* 1985, s.25(1); the *Prevention of Terrorism (Temporary Provisions) Act* 1989, s.25(2) and Sched. 9, Pt I; the *Road Traffic (Consequential Provisions) Act* 1988, s.4 and Sched. 1; the *Children Act* 1989, s.108(5) and (7), Sched. 13 and Sched. 15; the *Serious Organised Crime and Police Act* 2005, ss.111 and 174(2), Sched. 7, para. 24(1) and (4), and Sched. 17; the *Electoral Administration Act* 2006, s.74(2), and Sched. 2; and the *Armed Forces Act* 2006, s.378(2), and Sched. 17.]

(6) Arrest for failing to comply with fingerprinting requirement

1–113 See now Sched. 2A to the 1984 Act (*post*, §§ 1–175 *et seq.*).

The actual taking of fingerprints is provided for by s.61, *post* § 1–156.

(7) Information to be given on arrest

Police and Criminal Evidence Act 1984, s.28

Information to be given on arrest

1–114 **28.**—(1) Subject to subsection (5) below, where a person is arrested, otherwise than by being informed that he is under arrest, the arrest is not lawful unless the person arrested is informed that he is under arrest as soon as is practicable after his arrest.

(2) Where a person is arrested by a constable, subsection (1) above applies regardless of whether the fact of the arrest is obvious.

(3) Subject to subsection (5) below, no arrest is lawful unless the person arrested is informed of the ground for the arrest at the time of, or as soon as is practicable after, the arrest.

(4) Where a person is arrested by a constable, subsection (3) above applies regardless of whether the ground for the arrest is obvious.

(5) Nothing in this section is to be taken to require a person to be informed—

(a) that he is under arrest; or

(b) of the ground for the arrest,

if it was not reasonably practicable for him to be so informed by reason of his having escaped from arrest before the information could be given.

In *Taylor v. Chief Constable of Thames Valley Police* [2004] 1 W.L.R. 3155, CA (Civ. Div.), the court said that s.28(3) reflects the common law as laid down in *Christie v. Leachinsky* [1947] A.C. 573, HL, and explained that the underlying rationale is that a person is entitled to know why he is being arrested; one reason for that is that he should have the opportunity of explaining any misunderstanding, or of calling attention to others for whom he might have been mistaken. The court said that the modern approach to s.28(3) is to ask whether, having regard to all the circumstances, the person arrested was told in simple, non-technical language that he could understand, the essential legal and factual grounds for his arrest (*Fox, Campbell and Hartley v. UK* (1990) 13 E.H.R.R. 157, ECtHR, para. 40, considering art. 5(2) of the European Convention); in future wrongful arrest cases, it will be unnecessary and undesirable to consider authority besides *Fox, ante*; thus, upon making an arrest for violent disorder, it had been sufficient to refer to "violent disorder" with a reference to the time and place; there had been no need to specify the precise way in which the arrestee was said to be taking part in the disorder. **1–115**

As to there being no intent to prosecute the suspect for the offence for which he is arrested, see *ante*, § 1–12. As to the unfairness of arresting and questioning for a lesser offence, when in fact the investigation relates to a more serious offence arising out of the same incident, see *Kirk* [2000] 1 Cr.App.R. 400, CA. **1–116**

In *Wheatley v. Lodge* [1971] 1 W.L.R. 29, DC, it was held that a police officer arresting a deaf person or somebody who could not speak English had to do what a reasonable person would do in the circumstances.

Where an arrest is unlawful, on the ground that the accused has not been told what acts are alleged to have constituted the offence for which he was arrested, this unlawfulness ceases when he is informed of the details at the police station: *Kulynycz* [1971] 1 Q.B. 367; 55 Cr.App.R. 34, CA. Where the initial arrest is valid and at the time of the arrest it is impracticable, because of the accused's physical resistance to the arrest, to inform him of the reason for the arrest, the initial arrest does not become invalid retrospectively when the officer fails to state the ground of arrest at the police station: *DPP v. Hawkins* (1988) 88 Cr.App.R. 166, DC (applied in *Blench v. DPP* (2004) 69 J.C.L. 98, DC). **1–117**

In *Dawes v. DPP* [1995] 1 Cr.App.R. 65, DC, the defendant was detained by the automatic activation of the door locks inside a car specially adapted by the police as a trap. It was held on appeal that he was arrested the moment that he was trapped inside the car, and that at that point the police were obliged to inform him of his arrest and his grounds of arrest as soon as practicable. Once the police discharged this duty, the arrest was made lawful. On the facts, the police had fulfilled the duty, but the court recommended that in future the police fix such cars with a device which automatically tells the offender that he has been arrested and why. **1–118**

On arrest there is also a duty to caution in accordance with Code C, para. 10 either immediately prior to arrest or on arrest. Paragraph 10.1 explains when the caution must be given if there are grounds to suspect an offence may have been committed. Questions may be put to establish identity or ownership of items or in furtherance of the conduct of a search but once there are grounds to suspect an offence the person must be cautioned before any further questions about his involvement in the offence are put.

The requirement of cautioning before questioning does not extend to the asking of routine questions designed to establish ownership of an item. In *Senior* (2004) 148 S.J. 300 it was held that it was not necessary to caution a suspect before asking questions about the ownership of a suitcase known to contain drugs. Such a question had no element of surprise or unfairness but once a person identified himself as the owner the caution should be given. Also a person who came to the airport to meet a passenger who was suspected of carrying drugs in their luggage did not need to be cautioned before being asked questions. Such preliminary questions were designed to determine whether there were any reasonable objective grounds to suspect any involvement in the drug smuggling. Once suspicions arise the caution is necessary: *Perpont (Hutil Percena)* [2004] EWCA Crim 2562. See also *Kemsley v. DPP* [2004] WL 229280 where it was held that questions put about who was driving a car at the scene of an accident were an attempt to elicit information and a caution was not necessary. Similarly in *Ridehalgh v. DPP* [2005] EWHC 1100, Admin, it was held that the existence of grounds to suspect an offence is a pre-condition to the necessity to give a caution before questioning. Where an officer had asked questions about whether a defendant had been drinking alcohol and whether he had driven it was open to the magistrates to find that such questions were posed before the officer had grounds to suspect an offence of drinking and driving and so the provisions of Code C requiring a caution did not apply at that stage.

The words of the caution are—

> "You do not have to say anything. But it may harm your defence if you do not mention when questioned something which you later rely on in court. Anything you do say may be given in evidence."

Minor deviations are not a breach of the code as long as the sense of it is preserved.

(8) Use of force in making arrest

Police and Criminal Evidence Act 1984, s.117

Power of constable to use reasonable force

1–119 **117.** Where any provision of this Act—

(a) confers a power on a constable; and
(b) does not provide that the power may only be exercised with the consent of some person, other than a police officer,

the officer may use reasonable force, if necessary, in the exercise of the power.

(9) Voluntary attendance at police station

Police and Criminal Evidence Act 1984, s.29

Voluntary attendance at police station, etc.

1–120 **29.** Where for the purpose of assisting with an investigation a person attends voluntarily at a police station or at any other place where a constable is present or accompanies a constable to a police station or any such other place without having been arrested—

(a) he shall be entitled to leave at will unless he is placed under arrest;
(b) he shall be informed at once that he is under arrest if a decision is taken by a constable to prevent him from leaving at will.

(10) Arrest elsewhere than at police station

1–121 Section 4 of the *Criminal Justice Act* 2003 introduces a scheme of "street bail" which allows for police officers to arrest a person on the street or elsewhere and then to grant bail without the need to escort them to a police station. No conditions may be imposed on the bail and the person involved is under a duty to attend later at a police station. Written notice must be given before the person is released which records the offence for which he has been arrested and the grounds of arrest. Failure to answer to street bail may lead to arrest without warrant. Section 4 amends s.30 of the *Police and Criminal Evidence Act* 1984 and adds ss.30A–30D to cover the arrangements for "street bail".

As from April 1, 2007 (*Police and Justice Act 2006 (Commencement No. 2, Transitional and Savings Provisions) Order* 2007 (S.I. 2007 No. 709)), the *Police and Justice Act* 2006, s.10 and Sched. 6, inserts ss.30CA and 30CB (dealing respectively with variation of s.30A bail by police and the court) after s.30C.

As from June 29, 2007 (*Police and Justice Act 2006 (Commencement No. 3) Order*

2007 (S.I. 2007 No. 1614)), ss.24A (arrest for failure to comply with conditions attached to conditional caution) and 24B (application of *PACE* provisions) are inserted into the *Criminal Justice Act* 2003 by the *Police and Justice Act* 2006, s.18(1). Where a person is arrested under s.24A, s.24B(1) and (2) applies various provisions of the 1984 Act, with such modifications as are necessary, to the arrest. Sections 30 to 30D (including new ss.30CA and 30CB) of the 1984 Act are all such provisions.

Police and Criminal Evidence Act 1984, ss.30–30D

Arrest elsewhere than at police station

30.—(1) Subsection (1A) applies where a person is, at any place other than a police station— **1–122**

(a) arrested by a constable for an offence,or

(b) taken into custody by a constable after being arrested for an offence by a person other than a constable.

(1A) The person must be taken by a constable to a police station as soon as practicable after the arrest.

(1B) Subsection (1A) has effect subject to section 30A (release on bail) and subsection (7) (release without bail).

(2) Subject to subsections (3) and (5) below, the police station to which an arrested person is taken under subsection (1A) above shall be a designated police station.

(3) A constable to whom this subsection applies may take an arrested person to any police station unless it appears to the constable that it may be necessary to keep the arrested person in police detention for more than six hours.

(4) Subsection (3) above applies—

(a) to a constable who is working in a locality covered by a police station which is not a designated police station; and

(b) to a constable belonging to a body of constables maintained by an authority other than a police authority.

(5) Any constable may take an arrested person to any police station if—

(a) either of the following conditions is satisfied—

(i) the constable has arrested him without the assistance of any other constable and no other constable is available to assist him;

(ii) the constable has taken him into custody from a person other than a constable without the assistance of any other constable and no other constable is available to assist him; and

(b) it appears to the constable that he will be unable to take the arrested person to a designated police station without the arrested person injuring himself, the constable or some other person.

(6) If the first police station to which an arrested person is taken after his arrest is not a designated police station, he shall be taken to a designated police station not more than six hours after his arrival at the first police station unless he is released previously.

(7) A person arrested by a constable at any place other than a police station must be released without bail if the condition in subsection (7A) is satisfied.

(7A) The condition is that, at any time before the person arrested reaches a police station, a constable is satisfied that there are no grounds for keeping him under arrest or releasing him on bail under section 30A.

(8) A constable who releases a person under subsection (7) above shall record the fact that he has done so.

(9) The constable shall make the record as soon as is practicable after the release.

(10) Nothing in subsection (1A) or in section 30A prevents a constable delaying taking a person to a police station or releasing him on bail if the condition in subsection (10A) is satisfied.

(10A) The condition is that the presence of the person at a place (other than a police station) is necessary in order to carry out such investigations as it is reasonable to carry out immediately.

(11) Where there is any such delay the reasons for the delay must be recorded when the person first arrives at the police station or (as the case may be) is released on bail.

(12) Nothing in subsection (1A) above shall be taken to affect—

(a) paragraphs 16(3) or 18(1) of Schedule 2 to the *Immigration Act* 1971;

(b) section 34(1) of the *Criminal Justice Act* 1972; or

(c) any provision of the *Terrorism Act* 2000.

(13) Nothing in subsection (10) above shall be taken to affect paragraph 18(3) of Schedule 2 to the *Immigration Act* 1971.

[This section is printed as amended by the *Prevention of Terrorism (Temporary Provisions) Act* 1989, s.25(1), and Sched. 8; the *Terrorism Act* 2000, s.125, and Sched. 15, para. 5(2); and the *Criminal Justice Act* 2003, s.4(1)-(6).]

In *Khan* [1993] Crim.L.R. 54, the Court of Appeal warned police and customs officers that, even if they were justified (by virtue of s.30(10)) in delaying taking a subject to a police station in order to carry out a search, they should not abuse the opportunity by asking a lengthy series of questions to circumvent the codes of practice and that, if they did, they risked having the answers excluded under s.78. The warning was not heeded in *Raphaie* [1996] Crim.L.R. 812, CA, where the police asked a series of questions during a search lasting one-and-three-quarter hours. It was held that in so behaving the officers abused the power given to them by s.30(10), particularly as most of the admissions attributed to the appellant during the search were not relevant to it.

Bail elsewhere than at police station

1–123 **30A.**—(1) A constable may release on bail a person who is arrested or taken into custody in the circumstances mentioned in section 30(1).

(2) A person may be released on bail under subsection (1) at any time before he arrives at a police station.

(3) A person released on bail under subsection (1) must be required to attend a police station.

(3A) Where a constable releases a person on bail under subsection (1)—

(a) no recognizance for the person's surrender to custody shall be taken from the person,

(b) no security for the person's surrender to custody shall be taken from the person or from anyone else on the person's behalf,

(c) the person shall not be required to provide a surety or sureties for his surrender to custody, and

(d) no requirement to reside in a bail hostel may be imposed as a condition of bail.

(3B) Subject to subsection (3A), where a constable releases a person on bail under subsection (1) the constable may impose, as conditions of the bail, such requirements as appear to the constable to be necessary—

(a) to secure that the person surrenders to custody,

(b) to secure that the person does not commit an offence while on bail,

(c) to secure that the person does not interfere with witnesses or otherwise obstruct the course of justice, whether in relation to himself or any other person, or

(d) for the person's own protection or, if the person is under the age of 17, for the person's own welfare or in the person's own interests.

(4) Where a person is released on bail under subsection (1), a requirement may be imposed on the person as a condition of bail only under the preceding provisions of this section.

(5) The police station which the person is required to attend may be any police station.

[Section 30A was inserted by the *Criminal Justice Act* 2003, s.4. It is printed as amended by the *Police and Justice Act* 2006, s.10(1), and Sched. 6, paras 1 and 2.]

Bail under section 30A: notices

1–124 **30B.**—(1) Where a constable grants bail to a person under section 30A, he must give that person a notice in writing before he is released.

(2) The notice must state—

(a) the offence for which he was arrested, and

(b) the ground on which he was arrested.

(3) The notice must inform him that he is required to attend a police station.

(4) It may also specify the police station which he is required to attend and the time when he is required to attend.

(4A) If the person is granted bail subject to conditions under section 30A(3B), the notice also—

(a) must specify the requirements imposed by those conditions,

(b) must explain the opportunities under sections 30CA(1) and 30CB(1) for variation of those conditions, and

(c) if it does not specify the police station at which the person is required to attend, must specify a police station at which the person may make a request under section 30CA(1)(b).

(5) If the notice does not include the information mentioned in subsection (4), the person must subsequently be given a further notice in writing which contains that information.

(6) The person may be required to attend a different police station from that specified in the notice under subsection (1) or (5) or to attend at a different time.

(7) He must be given notice in writing of any such change as is mentioned in subsection (6) but more than one such notice may be given to him.

[Section 30B was inserted by the *Criminal Justice Act* 2003, s.4. It is printed as amended by the *Police and Justice Act* 2006, s.10(1), and Sched. 6, paras 1 and 3.]

Bail under section 30A: supplemental

30C.—(1) A person who has been required to attend a police station is not required to do so if he is given notice in writing that his attendance is no longer required. **1–125**

(2) If a person is required to attend a police station which is not a designated police station he must be—

(a) released, or

(b) taken to a designated police station,

not more than six hours after his arrival.

(3) Nothing in the *Bail Act* 1976 applies in relation to bail under section 30A.

(4) Nothing in section 30A or 30B or in this section prevents the re-arrest without a warrant of a person released on bail under section 30A if new evidence justifying a further arrest has come to light since his release.

[Section 30C was inserted by the *Criminal Justice Act* 2003, s.4.]

Bail under section 30A: variation of conditions by police

30CA.—(1) Where a person released on bail under section 30A(1) is on bail subject to conditions— **1–126**

(a) a relevant officer at the police station at which the person is required to attend, or

(b) where no notice under section 30B specifying that police station has been given to the person, a relevant officer at the police station specified under section 30B(4A)(c), may, at the request of the person but subject to subsection (2), vary the conditions.

(2) On any subsequent request made in respect of the same grant of bail, subsection (1) confers power to vary the conditions of the bail only if the request is based on information that, in the case of the previous request or each previous request, was not available to the relevant officer considering that previous request when he was considering it.

(3) Where conditions of bail granted to a person under section 30A(1) are varied under subsection (1)—

(a) paragraphs (a) to (d) of section 30A(3A) apply,

(b) requirements imposed by the conditions as so varied must be requirements that appear to the relevant officer varying the conditions to be necessary for any of the purposes mentioned in paragraphs (a) to (d) of section 30A(3B), and

(c) the relevant officer who varies the conditions must give the person notice in writing of the variation.

(4) Power under subsection (1) to vary conditions is, subject to subsection (3)(a) and (b), power—

(a) to vary or rescind any of the conditions, and

(b) to impose further conditions.

(5) In this section "relevant officer", in relation to a designated police station, means a custody officer but, in relation to any other police station—

(a) means a constable who is not involved in the investigation of the offence for which the person making the request under subsection (1) was under arrest when granted bail under section 30A(1), if such a constable is readily available, and

(b) if no such constable is readily available—

(i) means a constable other than the one who granted bail to the person, if such a constable is readily available, and

(ii) if no such constable is readily available, means the constable who granted bail.

[This section is inserted into the 1984 Act, as from April 1, 2007, by the *Police and Justice Act* 2006, s.10 and Sched. 6, paras 1 and 4. It is printed as amended by the *Policing and Crime Act* 2009, s.112(1) and (2), Sched. 7, para. 123(1) and (2), and Sched. 8, Pt 13.]

Section 30CA is subject to s.24B(3)(a) of the 2003 Act, which modifies s.30CA(5)(a) to substitute, for the reference to being involved in the investigation of the offence, the following:
"a reference to being involved—

(i) in the investigation of the offence in respect of which the person was given the conditional caution, or

(ii) in investigating whether the person has failed, without reasonable excuse, to comply with any of the conditions attached to the conditional caution;".]

Bail under section 30A: variation of conditions by court

1–127 **30CB.**—(1) Where a person released on bail under section 30A(1) is on bail subject to conditions, a magistrates' court may, on an application by or on behalf of the person, vary the conditions if—

(a) the conditions have been varied under section 30CA(1) since being imposed under section 30A(3B),

(b) a request for variation under section 30CA(1) of the conditions has been made and refused, or

(c) a request for variation under section 30CA(1) of the conditions has been made and the period of 48 hours beginning with the day when the request was made has expired without the request having been withdrawn or the conditions having been varied in response to the request.

(2) In proceedings on an application for a variation under subsection (1), a ground may not be relied upon unless—

(a) in a case falling within subsection (1)(a), the ground was relied upon in the request in response to which the conditions were varied under section 30CA(1), or

(b) in a case falling within paragraph (b) or (c) of subsection (1), the ground was relied upon in the request mentioned in that paragraph,

but this does not prevent the court, when deciding the application, from considering different grounds arising out of a change in circumstances that has occurred since the making of the application.

(3) Where conditions of bail granted to a person under section 30A(1) are varied under subsection (1)—

(a) paragraphs (a) to (d) of section 30A(3A) apply,

(b) requirements imposed by the conditions as so varied must be requirements that appear to the court varying the conditions to be necessary for any of the purposes mentioned in paragraphs (a) to (d) of section 30A(3B), and

(c) that bail shall not lapse but shall continue subject to the conditions as so varied.

(4) [*Identical to s.30CA(4), ante,* § 1–126.]]

[This section is inserted into the 1984 Act, as from April 1, 2007, by the *Police and Justice Act* 2006, s.10 and Sched. 6, paras 1 and 4.]

Failure to answer to bail under section 30A

1–128 **30D.**—(1) A constable may arrest without a warrant a person who—

(a) has been released on bail under section 30A subject to a requirement to attend a specified police station, but

(b) fails to attend the police station at the specified time.

(2) A person arrested under subsection (1) must be taken to a police station (which may be the specified police station or any other police station) as soon as practicable after the arrest.

[(2A) A person who has been released on bail under section 30A may be arrested without a warrant by a constable if the constable has reasonable grounds for suspecting that the person has broken any of the conditions of bail.

(2B) A person arrested under subsection (2A) must be taken to a police station (which may be the specified police station mentioned in subsection (1) or any other police station) as soon as practicable after the arrest.]

(3) In subsection (1), "specified" means specified in a notice under subsection (1) or (5) of section 30B or, if notice of change has been given under subsection (7) of that section, in that notice.

(4) For the purposes of—

(a) section 30 (subject to the obligations in subsections (2) and (2B)), and

(b) section 31,

an arrest under this section is to be treated as an arrest for an offence.

[Section 30D was inserted by the *Criminal Justice Act* 2003, s.4. It is printed as amended by the *Police and Justice Act* 2006, s.10(1), and Sched. 6, paras 1 and 5.]

(11) Arrest for further offence

Police and Criminal Evidence Act 1984, s.31

Arrest for further offence

31. Where— **1–129**

(a) a person—

(i) has been arrested for an offence; and

(ii) is at a police station in consequence of that arrest; and

(b) it appears to a constable that, if he were released from that arrest, he would be liable to arrest for some other offence,

he shall be arrested for that other offence.

As from June 29, 2007, s.31 is another provision applied to arrest for failure to comply with conditions attached to a conditional caution: see *ante*, § 1–121.

The purpose of this section is to prevent the release and re-arrest of a suspect that would result in an artificial extension of the detention periods regulated by s.41 of the 1984 Act, *et seq*. There is no requirement that the further arrest should occur as soon as practicable, only that it must be done before expiry of the relevant detention period: *Samuel* [1988] Q.B. 615.

(12) Search following arrest

Police and Criminal Evidence Act 1984, s.32

Search upon arrest

32.—(1) A constable may search an arrested person, in any case where the person to be searched has been arrested at a place other than a police station, if the constable has reasonable grounds for believing that the arrested person may present a danger to himself or others. **1–130**

(2) Subject to subsections (3) to (5) below, a constable shall also have power in any such case—

(a) to search the arrested person for anything—

(i) which he might use to assist him to escape from lawful custody; or

(ii) which might be evidence relating to an offence; and

(b) if the offence for which he has been arrested is an indictable offence, to enter and search any premises in which he was when arrested or immediately before he was arrested for evidence relating to the offence.

(3) The power to search conferred by subsection (2) above is only a power to search to the extent that is reasonably required for the purpose of discovering any such thing or any such evidence.

(4) The powers conferred by this section to search a person are not to be construed as authorising a constable to require a person to remove any of his clothing in public other than an outer coat, jacket or gloves but they do authorise a search of a person's mouth.

(5) A constable may not search a person in the exercise of the power conferred by subsection (2)(a) above unless he has reasonable grounds for believing that the person to be searched may have concealed on him anything for which a search is permitted under that paragraph.

(6) A constable may not search premises in the exercise of the power conferred by subsection (2)(b) above unless he has reasonable grounds for believing that there is evidence for which a search is permitted under that paragraph on the premises.

(7) In so far as the power of search conferred by subsection (2)(b) above relates to premises consisting of two or more separate dwellings, it is limited to a power to search—

(a) any dwelling in which the arrest took place or in which the person arrested was immediately before his arrest; and

(b) any parts of the premises which the occupier of any such dwelling uses in common with the occupiers of any other dwellings comprised in the premises.

(8) A constable searching a person in the exercise of the power conferred by subsection (1) above may seize and retain anything he finds, if he has reasonable grounds for believing that the person searched might use it to cause physical injury to himself or to any other person.

(9) A constable searching a person in the exercise of the power conferred by subsection (2)(a) above may seize and retain anything he finds, other than an item subject to legal privilege, if he has reasonable grounds for believing—

(a) that he might use it to assist him to escape from lawful custody; or

(b) that it is evidence of an offence or has been obtained in consequence of the commission of an offence.

(10) Nothing in this section shall be taken to affect the power conferred by section 43 of the *Terrorism Act* 2000.

[This section is printed as amended by the *Prevention of Terrorism (Temporary Provisions) Act* 1989, s.25(1), and Sched. 8; the *Criminal Justice and Public Order Act* 1994, s.59(2); the *Terrorism Act* 2000, s.125, and Sched. 15, para. 5(3); and the *Serious Organised Crime and Police Act* 2005, s.111, and Sched. 7, para. 43(1) and (6).]

1–131 In its application to an offence under s.31(1) of the *London Olympic Games and Paralympic Games Act* 2006 (selling an Olympic ticket in a public place or in the course of a business otherwise than in accordance with a written authorisation issued by the London Organising Committee), this section permits the searching of a vehicle which a constable reasonably thinks was used in connection with the offence: 2006 Act, s.31(7).

A search under s.32 must be made at the time of the arrest and not several hours later: *Badham* [1987] Crim.L.R. 202, Crown Court (H.H. Judge Compston). *Cf.* s.18, *ante*, § 1–54.

A suspected burglar's car keys were not "evidence relating to an offence" under s.32(2)(a)(ii): *Churchill* [1989] Crim.L.R. 226, CA.

It is a question of fact where officers rely on s.32 to justify a search whether that was the genuine reason for the officers in making the entry: *R. v. Beckford (Junior)* (1991) 94 Cr.App.R. 43, CA. The issue as to the officers' motive may go to the weight to be attached to their evidence: *ibid.*

"Premises" includes "any vehicle": s.23, *ante*, § 1–65. As to the use of force, see s.117, *ante*, § 1–119.

As to the extent of the power of seizure where a constable is making a search of premises in exercise of the power conferred by subs. (2)(b), see s.19 of the Act, *ante*, § 1–56.

(13) Detention after arrest

The Act and Codes provide a framework regulating the detention of suspects in police custody. Reasons for detention must be given and the length of time that a person may be detained is limited and subject to review. Rights of the suspect are protected covering the conduct of searches and the taking of forensic samples. A custody officer is appointed at designated police stations with specific duties and responsibilities for detained persons. A person is in detention when he or she is arrested for an offence and taken to a police station or when he attends voluntarily at a police station and is then arrested: the *PACE Act*, s.118. The time for recording detention starts to run from arrival at the police station or from 24 hours after arrest, whichever is earlier: s.41. The timetable for review is as follows— **1–132**

6 hours	First review by police
+ 9 hours	Second review by police
+ 9 hours	Further review by police
24 hours	Charge required UNLESS
+ 12 hours	Authorised by senior officer. Then charge required UNLESS
36 hours	Application to court for warrant of further detention
+ 36 hours	Further detention order by court
+ 36 hours	Extension of further detention ordered by court BUT
96 hours	Maximum length of detention allowed before charge.

Longer periods of detention may be authorised under counter–terrorism provisions: see the *Terrorism Act* 2000.

Police and Criminal Evidence Act 1984, s.34

Limitations on police detention

34.—(1) A person arrested for an offence shall not be kept in police detention except in accordance with the provisions of this Part of this Act. **1–133**

(2) Subject to subsection (3) below, if at any time a custody officer—

(a) becomes aware, in relation to any person in police detention, that the grounds for the detention of that person have ceased to apply; and

(b) is not aware of any other grounds on which the continued detention of that person could be justified under the provisions of this Part of this Act,

it shall be the duty of the custody officer, subject to subsection (4) below, to order his immediate release from custody.

(3) No person in police detention shall be released except on the authority of a custody officer at the police station where his detention was authorised or, if it was authorised at more than one station, a custody officer at the station where it was last authorised.

(4) A person who appears to the custody officer to have been unlawfully at large when he was arrested is not to be released under subsection (2) above.

(5) A person whose release is ordered under subsection (2) above shall be released without bail unless it appears to the custody officer—

(a) that there is need for further investigation of any matter in connection with which he was detained at any time during the period of his detention; or

(b) that, in respect of any such matter, proceedings may be taken against him or he may be reprimanded or warned under section 65 of the *Crime and Disorder Act* 1998

and, if it so appears, he shall be released on bail.

(6) For the purposes of this Part of this Act a person arrested under section 6D of the *Road Traffic Act* 1988 or section 30(2) of the *Transport and Works Act* 1992 is arrested for an offence.

(7) For the purposes of this Part a person who—

(a) attends a police station to answer to bail granted under section 30A,

(b) returns to a police station to answer to bail granted under this part, or

(c) is arrested under section 30D or section 46A,

is to be treated as arrested for an offence and that offence is the offence in connection with which he was granted bail.

But this subsection is subject to section 47(6) (which provides for the calculation of certain periods, where a person has been granted bail under this Part, by reference to time when the person is in police detention only).

[(8) Subsection (7) does not apply in relation to a person who is granted bail subject to the duty mentioned in section 47(3)(b) and who either—

(a) attends a police station to answer to such bail, or

(b) is arrested under section 46A for failing to do so,

(provision as to the treatment of such persons for the purposes of this Part being made by section 46ZA).]

[This section is printed as amended by the *Road Traffic (Consequential Provisions) Act* 1988, s.4 and Sched. 3, para. 27(2); the *Criminal Justice and Public Order Act* 1994, s.29(3); the *Criminal Justice and Court Services Act* 2000, s.56(2); the *Police Reform Act* 2002, s.53(1); the *Railways and Transport Safety Act* 2003, s.107, and Sched. 7, para. 12; the *Criminal Justice Act* 2003, s.12, and Sched. 1, paras 1 and 5. Subsection (8) was inserted by the *Police and Justice Act* 2006, s.46(1) and (2), but is only in force in the following local justice areas: as from April 1, 2007, in Lambeth and Southwark (*Police and Justice Act 2006 (Commencement No. 2, Transitional and Savings Provisions) Order* 2007 (S.I. 2007 No. 709)); and, as from November 14, 2008 (*Police and Justice Act 2006 (Commencement No. 10) Order* 2008 (S.I. 2008 No. 2785)), (i) in London, Barking and Dagenham, Barnet, Bexley, Brent, Bromley, Camden and Islington, City of London, City of Westminster, Croydon, Ealing, Enfield, Greenwich and Lewisham, Hackney and Tower Hamlets, Hammersmith and Fulham and Kensington and Chelsea, Haringey, Harrow Gore, Havering, Hillingdon, Hounslow, Kingston-upon-Thames, Merton, Newham, Redbridge, Richmond-upon-Thames, Sutton, Waltham Forest, and Wandsworth; and (ii) in Kent, Central Kent, East Kent and North Kent and by the *Police (Detention and Bail) Act* 2011, with effect from July 12, 2011 and as regards those amendments to subsection (7) they are retrospective in effect.]

As from June 29, 2007, s.34 is another provision applied to arrest for failure to comply with conditions attached to a conditional caution: see *ante*, § 1–121.

1–134 The reference to s.65 of the *Crime and Disorder Act* 1998 in subs. (5)(b) relates to the system of court diversion for children and young persons.

The *Road Traffic Act* 1988 gives an officer power to arrest without warrant anyone who has provided a positive breath test at the roadside or who has failed to provide a specimen but the officer has reasonable cause to suspect that the person has alcohol his body. Section 46A gives power for a constable to arrest without warrant any person who has failed to answer their police bail back to the police station. In these situations an offence may not have been committed but this section means the defendant may be treated as if it had.

For the meaning of "police detention", see *ante*, § 1–132 (summarising s.118(2) of the 1984 Act).

Police and Criminal Evidence Act 1984, ss.35–36

Designated police stations

1–135 **35.**—(1) The chief officer of police for each police area shall designate the police stations in his area which, subject to sections 30(3) and (5), 30A(5) and 30D(2) above, are to be the stations in that area to be used for the purpose of detaining arrested persons.

(2) A chief officer's duty under subsection (1) above is to designate police stations appearing to him to provide enough accommodation for that purpose.

(2A) The Chief Constable of the British Transport Police Force may designate police stations which (in addition to those designated under subsection (1) above) may be used for the purpose of detaining arrested persons.

(3) Without prejudice to section 12 of the *Interpretation Act* 1978 (continuity of duties) a chief officer—

(a) may designate a station which was not previously designated; and

(b) may direct that a designation of a station previously made shall cease to operate.

(4) In this Act "designated police station" means a police station for the time being designated under this section.

[This section is printed as amended by the *Anti-terrorism, Crime and Security Act* 2001, s.101, and Sched. 7; and the *Criminal Justice Act* 2003, s.12, and Sched. 1, paras 1 and 6.]

Custody officers at police stations

36.—(1) One or more custody officers shall be appointed for each designated police station. **1–136**

(2) A custody officer for a police station designated under section 35(1) above shall be appointed—

(a) by the chief officer of police for the area in which the designated police station is situated; or

(b) by such other police officer as the chief officer of police for that area may direct.

(2A) A custody officer for a police station designated under section 35(2A) above shall be appointed—

(a) by the Chief Constable of the British Transport Police Force; or

(b) by such other member of that Force as that Chief Constable may direct.

(3) No officer may be appointed a custody officer unless he is of at least the rank of sergeant.

(4) An officer of any rank may perform the functions of a custody officer at a designated police station if a custody officer is not readily available to perform them.

(5) Subject to the following provisions of this section and to section 39(2) below, none of the functions of a custody officer in relation to a person shall be performed by an officer who at the time when the function falls to be performed is involved in the investigation of an offence for which that person is in police detention at that time.

(6) Nothing in subsection (5) above is to be taken to prevent a custody officer—

(a) performing any function assigned to custody officers—

(i) by this Act; or

(ii) by a code of practice issued under this Act;

(b) carrying out the duty imposed on custody officers by section 39 below;

(c) doing anything in connection with the identification of a suspect; or

(d) doing anything under sections 7 and 8 of the *Road Traffic Act* 1988.

(7) Where an arrested person is taken to a police station which is not a designated police station, the functions in relation to him which at a designated police station would be the functions of a custody officer shall be performed—

(a) by an officer who is not involved in the investigation of an offence for which he is in police detention, if such an officer is readily available; and

(b) if no such officer is readily available, by the officer who took him to the station or any other officer.

(7A) Subject to subsection (7B), subsection (7) applies where a person attends a police station which is not a designated station to answer to bail granted under section 30A as it applies where a person is taken to such a station.

(7B) Where subsection (7) applies because of subsection (7A), the reference in subsection (7)(b) to the officer who took him to the station is to be read as a reference to the officer who granted him bail.

(8) References to a custody officer in section 34 above or in the following provisions of this Act include references to an officer other than a custody officer who is performing the functions of a custody officer by virtue of subsection (4) or (7) above.

(9) Where by virtue of subsection (7) above an officer of a force maintained by a police authority who took an arrested person to a police station is to perform the functions of a custody officer in relation to him, the officer shall inform an officer who—

(a) is attached to a designated police station; and

(b) is of at least the rank of inspector,

that he is to do so.

(10) The duty imposed by subsection (9) above shall be performed as soon as it is practicable to perform it.

[This section is printed as amended by the *Road Traffic (Consequential Provisions) Act* 1988, s.4 and Sched. 3, para. 27(3); the *Criminal Justice Act* 2003, s.12, and Sched. 1, paras 1 and 7; the *Policing and Crime Act* 2009, s.112(1) and (2), Sched. 7, para. 123(1) and (3), and Sched. 8, Pt 13; and the *Serious Organised Crime and Police Act* 2005, s.121(1), (5).]

As from June 29, 2007, s.36 is another provision applied to arrest for failure to comply with conditions attached to a conditional caution: see *ante*, § 1–105. This is subject to modifications specified in the *Criminal Justice Act* 2003, s.24B(3). The references in the 1984 Act, s.34(5) and (7), to being involved in the investigation of an offence for which the person is in police detention, are substituted by references to being involved in the investigation of the offence in respect of which the person was given the conditional caution, or in investigating whether the person has failed, without reasonable excuse, to comply with any of the conditions attached to the conditional caution.

1–137 Sections 7 and 8 of the *Road Traffic Act* 1988 give the power to a constable to require specimens of breath or blood for analysis in road traffic investigations. The custody officer may perform these functions.

The Chief Constable has a duty to appoint at least one custody officer (of at least the rank of sergeant) for each designated station, but there is no requirement to ensure that a custody officer will always be available at a designated station to perform the duties of the custody officer: *Vince v. Chief Constable of Dorset Police* [1993] 1 W.L.R. 415, CA (Civ. Div.).

The functions of the investigating officer and the custody officer are to be kept separate under subs. (5). This provision was not breached where the custody officer, who was acting in co-operation with the investigating officers, placed the defendants in a bugged cell. The bugging of the cell was held not to be an oppressive or unfair method of obtaining the relevant evidence: *Bailey and Smith* (1993) 97 Cr.App.R. 365.

For the duties of a custody officer in general, see the 1984 Act, ss.37, 37A–D, and 38, *post*, §§ 4–41 *et seq*.

Police and Criminal Evidence Act 1984, s.39

Responsibilities in relation to persons detained

1–138 **39.**—(1) Subject to subsections (2) and (4) below, it shall be the duty of the custody officer at a police station to ensure—

(a) that all persons in police detention at that station are treated in accordance with this Act and any code of practice issued under it and relating to the treatment of persons in police detention; and

(b) that all matters relating to such persons which are required by this Act or by such codes of practice to be recorded are recorded in the custody records relating to such persons.

(2) If the custody officer, in accordance with any code of practice issued under this Act, transfers or permits the transfer of a person in police detention—

(a) to the custody of a police officer investigating an offence for which that person is in police detention; or

(b) to the custody of an officer who has charge of that person outside the police station,

the custody officer shall cease in relation to that person to be subject to the duty imposed on him by subsection (1)(a) above; and it shall be the duty of the officer to whom the transfer is made to ensure that he is treated in accordance with the provisions of this Act and of any such codes of practice as are mentioned in subsection (1) above.

(3) If the person detained is subsequently returned to the custody of the custody officer, it shall be the duty of the officer investigating the offence to report to the custody officer as to the manner in which this section and the codes of practice have been complied with while that person was in his custody.

(4) If an arrested juvenile is transferred to the care of a local authority in pursuance of

arrangements made under section 38(6) above, the custody officer shall cease in relation to that person to be subject to the duty imposed on him by subsection (1) above.

(5) [*Repealed by* Children Act *1989, s.108(7) and Sched. 15.*]

(6) Where—

(a) an officer of higher rank than the custody officer gives directions relating to a person in police detention; and

(b) the directions are at variance—

(i) with any decision made or action taken by the custody officer in the performance of a duty imposed on him under this Part of this Act; or

(ii) with any decision or action which would but for the directions have been made or taken by him in the performance of such a duty,

the custody officer shall refer the matter at once to an officer of the rank of superintendent or above who is responsible for the police station for which the custody officer is acting as custody officer.

[This section is printed as amended by the *Children Act* 1989, s.108(5), and Sched. 13, para. 54; and the *Policing and Crime Act* 2009, s.112(1) and (2), Sched. 7, para. 123(1) and (4), and Sched. 8, Pt 13.]

As from June 29, 2007, s.39 is another provision applied to arrest for failure to comply with conditions attached to a conditional caution: see *ante*, § 1–105. This is subject to modifications specified in the *Criminal Justice Act* 2003, s.24B(3). The references in the 1984 Act, s.39(2) and (3), to an offence, are substituted by references to failure to comply with conditions attached to a conditional caution.

(14) Review of detention

Police and Criminal Evidence Act 1984, s.40

Review of police detention

40.—(1) Reviews of the detention of each person in police detention in connection with the investigation of an offence shall be carried out periodically in accordance with the following provisions of this section— **1–139**

(a) in the case of a person who has been arrested and charged, by the custody officer; and

(b) in the case of a person who has been arrested but not charged, by an officer of at least the rank of inspector who has not been directly involved in the investigation.

(2) The officer to whom it falls to carry out a review is referred to in this section as a "review officer".

(3) Subject to subsection (4) below—

(a) the first review shall be not later than six hours after the detention was first authorised;

(b) the second review shall be not later than nine hours after the first;

(c) subsequent reviews shall be at intervals of not more than nine hours.

(4) A review may be postponed—

(a) if, having regard to all the circumstances prevailing at the latest time for it specified in subsection (3) above, it is not practicable to carry out the review at that time;

(b) without prejudice to the generality of paragraph (a) above—

(i) if at that time the person in detention is being questioned by a police officer and the review officer is satisfied that an interruption of the questioning for the purpose of carrying out the review would prejudice the investigation in connection with which he is being questioned; or

(ii) if at that time no review officer is readily available.

(5) If a review is postponed under subsection (4) above it shall be carried out as soon as practicable after the latest time specified for it in subsection (3) above.

(6) If a review is carried out after postponement under subsection (4) above, the fact that it was so carried out shall not affect any requirement of this section as to the time at which any subsequent review is to be carried out.

(7) The review officer shall record the reasons for any postponement of a review in the custody record.

(8) Subject to subsection (9) below, where the person whose detention is under review has not been charged before the time of the review, section 37(1) to (6) above shall have effect in relation to him, but with the modifications specified in subsection (8A).

1–140 (8A) The modifications are—

(a) the substitution of references to the person whose detention is under review for references to the person arrested;

(b) the substitution of references to the review officer for references to the custody officer; and

(c) in subsection (6), the insertion of the following paragraph after paragraph (a)—

'(aa) asleep;'.

(9) Where a person has been kept in police detention by virtue of section 37(9) or 37D(5) above, section 37(1) to (6) shall not have effect in relation to him but it shall be the duty of the review officer to determine whether he is yet in a fit state.

(10) Where the person whose detention is under review has been charged before the time of the review, section 38(1) to (6B) above shall have effect in relation to him, but with the modifications specified in subsection (10A).

(10A) The modifications are—

(a) the substitution of a reference to the person whose detention is under review for any reference to the person arrested or to the person charged; and

(b) in subsection (5), the insertion of the following paragraph after paragraph (a)—

'(aa) asleep;'.

(11) Where—

(a) an officer of higher rank than the review officer gives directions relating to a person in police detention; and

(b) the directions are at variance—

(i) with any decision made or action taken by the review officer in the performance of a duty imposed on him under this Part of this Act; or

(ii) with any decision or action which would but for the directions have been made or taken by him in the performance of such a duty.

the review officer shall refer the matter at once to an officer of the rank of superintendent or above who is responsible for the police station for which the review officer is acting as review officer in connection with the detention.

(12) Before determining whether to authorise a person's continued detention the review officer shall give—

(a) that person (unless he is asleep); or

(b) any solicitor representing him who is available at the time of the review,

an opportunity to make representations to him about the detention.

(13) Subject to subsection (14) below, the person whose detention is under review or his solicitor may make representations under subsection (12) above either orally or in writing.

(14) The review officer may refuse to hear oral representations from the person whose detention is under review if he considers that he is unfit to make such representations by reason of his condition or behaviour.

[This section is printed as amended by the *Police Reform Act* 2002, s.52; and the *Criminal Justice Act* 2003, s.28, and Sched. 2, para. 4.]

As from June 29, 2007, s.40 is another provision applied to arrest for failure to comply with conditions attached to a conditional caution: see *ante*, § 1–105. This is subject to modifications specified in the *Criminal Justice Act* 2003, s.24B(4), so as to omit subs (8) and (8A), and to substitute in subs. (9), for the reference to "section 37(9) or 37D(5)", a reference to the second sentence of s.24A(5).

1–141 Amendments inserted in the 1984 Act by the *Criminal Justice and Police Act* 2001 provide for reviews to be carried out by telephone (s. 40A) and video-conferencing (s.45).

Section 6 of the *Criminal Justice Act* 2003 substitutes s.40A to allow for a review to be carried out by means of a discussion, conducted by telephone, with one or more persons at the police station where the arrested person is held. This does not apply though if the review could be carried out using video-conferencing facilities. The section came into force on January 29, 2004, and is dependent on equipment being available and regulations authorising its use.

(15) Time limit

Police and Criminal Evidence Act 1984, ss.41–42

Limits on period of detention without charge

41.—(1) Subject to the following provisions of this section and to sections 42 and 43 below, a person shall not be kept in police detention for more than 24 hours without being charged. **1–142**

(2) The time from which the period of detention of a person is to be calculated (in this Act referred to as "the relevant time")—

(a) in the case of a person to whom this paragraph applies, shall be—
 (i) the time at which that person arrives at the relevant police station; or
 (ii) the time 24 hours after the time of that person's arrest,
 whichever is the earlier;

(b) in the case of a person arrested outside England and Wales, shall be—
 (i) the time at which that person arrives at the first police station to which he is taken in the police area in England or Wales in which the offence for which he was arrested is being investigated; or
 (ii) the time 24 hours after the time of that person's entry into England and Wales,
 whichever is the earlier;

(c) in the case of a person who—
 (i) attends voluntarily at a police station; or
 (ii) accompanies a constable to a police station without having been arrested,
 and is arrested at the police station, the time of his arrest;

(ca) in the case of a person who attends a police station to answer to bail granted under section 30A, the time when he arrives at the police station.

(d) in any other case, except where subsection (5) below applies, shall be the time at which the person arrested arrives at the first police station to which he is taken after his arrest.

(3) Subsection (2)(a) above applies to a person if—

(a) his arrest is sought in one police area in England and Wales;
(b) he is arrested in another police area; and
(c) he is not questioned in the area in which he is arrested in order to obtain evidence in relation to an offence for which he is arrested;

and in sub-paragraph (i) of that paragraph "the relevant police station" means the first police station to which he is taken in the police area in which his arrest was sought.

(4) Subsection (2) above shall have effect in relation to a person arrested under section 31 above as if every reference in it to his arrest or his being arrested were a reference to his arrest or his being arrested for the offence for which he was originally arrested.

(5) If— **1–143**

(a) a person is in police detention in a police area in England and Wales ("the first area"); and
(b) his arrest for an offence is sought in some other police area in England and Wales ("the second area"); and
(c) he is taken to the second area for the purposes of investigating that offence, without being questioned in the first area in order to obtain evidence in relation to it,

the relevant time shall be—
 (i) the time 24 hours after he leaves the place where he is detained in the first area; or
 (ii) the time at which he arrives at the first police station to which he is taken in the second area,
whichever is the earlier.

(6) When a person who is in police detention is removed to hospital because he is in

need of medical treatment, any time during which he is being questioned in hospital or on the way there or back by a police officer for the purpose of obtaining evidence relating to an offence shall be included in any period which falls to be calculated for the purposes of this Part of this Act, but any other time while he is in hospital or on his way there or back shall not be so included.

(7) Subject to subsection (8) below, a person who at the expiry of 24 hours after the relevant time is in police detention and has not been charged shall be released at that time either on bail or without bail.

(8) Subsection (7) above does not apply to a person whose detention for more than 24 hours after the relevant time has been authorised or is otherwise permitted in accordance with sections 42 or 43 below.

(9) A person released under subsection (7) above shall not be re-arrested without a warrant for the offence for which he was previously arrested unless new evidence justifying a further arrest has come to light since his release but this subsection does not prevent an arrest under section 46A below.

[This section is printed as amended by the *Criminal Justice and Public Order Act* 1994, s.29; and the *Criminal Justice Act* 2003, s.12, and Sched. 1.]

Authorisation of continued detention

1–144 **42.**—(1) Where a police officer of the rank of superintendent or above who is responsible for the police station at which a person is detained has reasonable grounds for believing that—

(a) the detention of that person without charge is necessary to secure or preserve evidence relating to an offence for which he is under arrest or to obtain such evidence by questioning him;

(b) an offence for which he is under arrest is an indictable offence; and

(c) the investigation is being conducted diligently and expeditiously.

he may authorise the keeping of that person in police detention for a period expiring at or before 36 hours after the relevant time.

(2) Where an officer such as is mentioned in subsection (1) above has authorised the keeping of a person in police detention for a period expiring less than 36 hours after the relevant time, such an officer may authorise the keeping of that person in police detention for a further period expiring not more than 36 hours after that time if the conditions specified in subsection (1) above are still satisfied when he gives the authorisation.

(3) If it is proposed to transfer a person in police detention to another police area, the officer determining whether or not to authorise keeping him in detention under subsection (1) above shall have regard to the distance and the time the journey would take.

(4) No authorisation under subsection (1) above shall be given in respect of any person—

(a) more than 24 hours after the relevant time; or

(b) before the second review of his detention under section 40 above has been carried out.

(5) Where an officer authorises the keeping of a person in police detention under subsection (1) above, it shall be his duty—

(a) to inform that person of the grounds for his continued detention; and

(b) to record the grounds in that person's custody record.

(6) Before determining whether to authorise the keeping of a person in detention under subsection (1) or (2) above, an officer shall give—

(a) that person; or

(b) any solicitor representing him who is available at the time when it falls to the officer to determine whether to give the authorisation,

an opportunity to make representations to him about the detention.

(7) Subject to subsection (8) below, the person in detention or his solicitor may make representations under subsection (6) above either orally or in writing.

(8) The officer to whom it falls to determine whether to give the authorisation may refuse to hear oral representations from the person in detention if he considers that he is unfit to make such representations by reason of his condition or behaviour.

(9) Where—

(a) an officer authorises the keeping of a person in detention under subsection (1) above; and

(b) at the time of the authorisation he has not yet exercised a right conferred on him by section 56 or 58 below, the officer—

(i) shall inform him of that right;
(ii) shall decide whether he should be permitted to exercise it;
(iii) shall record the decision in his custody record; and
(iv) if the decision is to refuse to permit the exercise of the right, shall also record the grounds for the decision in that record.

(10) Where an officer has authorised the keeping of a person who has not been charged in detention under subsection (1) or (2) above, he shall be released from detention, either on bail or without bail, not later than 36 hours after the relevant time, unless—

(a) he has been charged with an offence; or
(b) his continued detention is authorised or otherwise permitted in accordance with section 43 below.

(11) A person released under subsection (10) above shall not be re-arrested without a warrant for the offence for which he was previously arrested unless new evidence justifying a further arrest has come to light since his release but this subsection does not prevent an arrest under section 46A below.

[This section is printed as amended by the *Criminal Justice Act* 2003, s.7; and the *Serious Organised Crime and Police Act* 2005, s.111, and Sched. 7, para. 43(1) and (7).]

These provisions permit detention without charge for 24 hours from arrest or arrival at the police station, whichever is earlier. Section 41 gives details as to how the time should be computed. Section 42 permits a senior officer to authorise continued detention on the grounds given for a further 12 hours making a total of 36 hours detention without charge. The authorisation to extend the detention must be given within the first 24-hour period but after the second review which must occur at the latest 15 hours after the detention was first authorised. If authorisation is given then for a period of less than the 12 hours allowed it may be further extended up to the maximum of 12 hours as long as any authorisation is made during the currency of the extended period of detention: *Taylor (Leroy)* [1991] Crim.L.R. 541. After 36 hours the person must be released from detention and at that stage he can either be bailed to return to the police station or simply released. If he is not bailed or released he must be charged or application for further detention in custody can be made to a Court under the 1984 Act, s.43. **1–145**

Police and Criminal Evidence Act 1984, s.43

Warrants of further detention

43.—(1) Where, on an application on oath made by a constable and supported by an information, a magistrates' court is satisfied that there are reasonable grounds for believing that the further detention of the person to whom the application relates is justified, it may issue a warrant of further detention authorising the keeping of that person in police detention. **1–146**

(2) A court may not hear an application for a warrant of further detention unless the person to whom the application relates—

(a) has been furnished with a copy of the information; and
(b) has been brought before the court for the hearing.

(3) The person to whom the application relates shall be entitled to be legally represented at the hearing and, if he is not so represented but wishes to be so represented—

(a) the court shall adjourn the hearing to enable him to obtain representation; and
(b) he may be kept in police detention during the adjournment.

(4) A person's further detention is only justified for the purposes of this section or section 44 below if—

(a) his detention without charge is necessary to secure or preserve evidence relating to an offence for which he is under arrest or to obtain such evidence by questioning him;
(b) an offence for which he is under arrest is an indictable offence; and
(c) the investigation is being conducted diligently and expeditiously.

(5) Subject to subsection (7) below, an application for a warrant of further detention may be made—

(a) at any time before the expiry of 36 hours after the relevant time; or
(b) in a case where—
(i) it is not practicable for the magistrates' court to which the application will be made to sit at the expiry of 36 hours after the relevant time; but
(ii) the court will sit during the 6 hours following the end of that period,

at any time before the expiry of the said 6 hours.

(6) In a case to which subsection (5)(b) above applies—
(a) the person to whom the application relates may be kept in police detention until the application is heard; and
(b) the custody officer shall make a note in that person's custody record—
(i) of the fact that he was kept in police detention for more than 36 hours after the relevant time; and
(ii) of the reason why he was so kept.

(7) If—
(a) an application for a warrant of further detention is made after the expiry of 36 hours after the relevant time; and
(b) it appears to the magistrates' court that it would have been reasonable for the police to make it before the expiry of that period,

the court shall dismiss the application.

(8) Where on an application such as is mentioned in subsection (1) above a magistrates' court is not satisfied that there are reasonable grounds for believing that the further detention of the person to whom the application relates is justified, it shall be its duty—
(a) to refuse the application; or
(b) to adjourn the hearing of it until a time not later than 36 hours after the relevant time.

(9) The person to whom the application relates may be kept in police detention during the adjournment.

(10) A warrant of further detention shall—
(a) state the time at which it is issued;
(b) authorise the keeping in police detention of the person to whom it relates for the period stated in it.

(11) Subject to subsection (12) below, the period stated in a warrant of further detention shall be such period as the magistrates' court thinks fit, having regard to the evidence before it.

(12) The period shall not be longer than 36 hours.

(13) If it is proposed to transfer a person in police detention to a police area other than that in which he is detained when the application for a warrant of further detention is made, the court hearing the application shall have regard to the distance and the time the journey would take.

(14) Any information submitted in support of an application under this section shall state—
(a) the nature of the offence for which the person to whom the application relates has been arrested;
(b) the general nature of the evidence on which that person was arrested;
(c) what inquiries relating to the offence have been made by the police and what further inquiries are proposed by them;
(d) the reasons for believing the continued detention of that person to be necessary for the purposes of such further inquiries.

(15) Where an application under this section is refused, the person to whom the application relates shall forthwith be charged or, subject to subsection (16) below, released, either on bail or without bail.

(16) A person need not be released under subsection (15) above—
(a) before the expiry of 24 hours after the relevant time; or
(b) before the expiry of any longer period for which his continued detention is or has been authorised under section 42 above.

(17) Where an application under this section is refused, no further application shall be made under this section in respect of the person to whom the refusal relates, unless supported by evidence which has come to light since the refusal.

(18) Where a warrant of further detention is issued, the person to whom it relates shall

be released from police detention, either on bail or without bail, upon or before the expiry of the warrant unless he is charged.

(19) A person released under subsection (18) above shall not be re-arrested without a warrant for the offence for which he was previously arrested unless new evidence justifying a further arrest has come to light since his release; but this subsection does not prevent an arrest under section 46A below.

[This section is printed as amended by the *Criminal Justice and Public Order Act* 1994, s.29; and the *Serious Organised Crime and Police Act* 2005, s.111, and Sched. 7, para. 43(1) and (8).]

The maximum length of time for detention authorised by the police is 36 hours. If more time is required before a person can be charged application on a sworn information may be made to a court for a warrant of further detention. The application should be made within court sitting hours if at all possible but the period of detention of 36 hours may sometimes expire at a weekend or other time when a court is not sitting. The time limits should be closely monitored and if the application will need to be made out of court sitting hours the justices' clerk should be notified in advance as a bench must be convened and legal representation for the person detained must be provided. There is also a period of six hours grace if it is impracticable to convene a court within the 36 hours. The court must be satisfied that the grounds of s.43(4) are made out and further detention may be ordered for as long as the court thinks fit up to a maximum of 36 hours. Application may be made on a sworn information to the court to extend a warrant of further detention for up to another 36 hours. The longest period of detention in total must not exceed 96 hours from when it first started to run. **1–147**

In *R. v. Slough JJ., ex p. Stirling* [1987] Crim.L.R. 576, DC, it was held that s.43(5)(b) was not limited to a situation in which the 36-hour period expired at a time when the magistrates were not sitting at all. Where a magistrates' court was already sitting, the justices had a discretion upon being notified of the intention of a constable to make an application either to hear the application straightaway or to wait, provided they did not do so for longer than six hours after the end of the 36-hour period. However, the requirements of s.43(7) were mandatory. Here, the information to support the application was drafted eight minutes before the expiry of the 36-hour period. The clerk advised the court that it was not practicable to hear the application at that time and the application was adjourned to a time beyond the 36-hour period although within the extra six hours. The Divisional Court held that the application should have been refused as it could not be said that it would have been unreasonable for the police to draft the information earlier so as to ensure that the application was heard by the court before the expiry of the 36-hour period.

Police and Criminal Evidence Act 1984, s.44

Extension of warrants of further detention

44.—(1) On an application on oath made by a constable and supported by an information a magistrates' court may extend a warrant of further detention issued under section 43 above if it is satisfied that there are reasonable grounds for believing that the further detention of the person to whom the application relates is justified. **1–148**

(2) Subject to subsection (3) below, the period for which a warrant of further detention may be extended shall be such period as the court thinks fit, having regard to the evidence before it.

(3) The period shall not—

(a) be longer than 36 hours; or

(b) end later than 96 hours after the relevant time.

(4) Where a warrant of further detention has been extended under subsection (1) above, or further extended under this subsection, for a period ending before 96 hours after the relevant time, on an application such as is mentioned in that subsection a magistrates' court may further extend the warrant if it is satisfied as there mentioned; and subsections (2) and (3) above apply to such further extensions as they apply to extensions under subsection (1) above.

(5) A warrant of further detention shall, if extended or further extended under this section, be endorsed with a note of the period of the extension.

(6) Subsections (2), (3) and (14) of section 43 above shall apply to an application made under this section as they apply to an application made under that section.

(7) Where an application under this section is refused, the person to whom the application relates shall forthwith be charged or, subject to subsection (8) below, released, either on bail or without bail.

(8) A person need not be released under subsection (7) above before the expiry of any period for which a warrant of further detention issued in relation to him has been extended or further extended on an earlier application made under this section.

In *R. (Chief Constable of Greater Manchester Police) v. City of Salford Magistrates' Court and Hookway*, unreported, May 19, 2011, QBD (McCombe J.) ([2011] EWHC 1578 (Admin.)) it was held that where a warrant of further detention for 36 hours had been granted in respect of a suspect under section 43 of the 1984 Act (*ante*, § 1–146), where the suspect was released on bail six hours before the expiry of the period of detention authorised by the warrant, and where he was re-detained upon his surrender to bail several weeks later, police had no power to detain him and it was not then open to police to make an application for an extension of the warrant of further detention under section 44; section 44(3) was conclusive in that it provided that any period of extension granted under that section should not "end later than 96 hours after the relevant time", and that the relevant time was dictated by section 41 (*ante*, § 1–142) as the time of the suspect's arrival at the police station following his initial arrest. For a criticism of this decision, and in particular for a submission that for these purposes the key provision of the 1984 Act is section 34(7) ("a person who ... returns to a police station to answer bail granted under this Part ... is to be treated as arrested for an offence and that offence is the offence in connection with which he was granted bail") (*ante*, § 1–133), the point being that the relevant provisions of Part IV of the Act start over again when the suspect answers to his bail, albeit the suspect gets credit for time already spent in detention. (s.47(6), *post*, § 5–106). For the avoidance of doubt, the *Police (Detention and Bail) Act* 2011 was passed on July 12, 2011 with immediate and retrospective effect. This Act amends section 34 (see § 1–133) and s.47 (see § 5–104) so that this time limit does not include any time spent on bail.

Police and Criminal Evidence Act 1984, s.45

Detention before charge—supplementary

1–149 **45.**—(1) In sections 43 and 44 of this Act "magistrates' court" means a court consisting of two or more justices of the peace sitting otherwise than in open court.

(2) Any reference in this Part of this Act to a period of time or a time of day is to be treated as approximate only.

F. QUESTIONING AND TREATMENT OF DETAINED PERSONS

(1) Search of detained persons

1–150 The police have powers to search persons in detention and to seize and retain anything found on them. Such personal searches are not only undertaken to discover, identify and look for evidence but also to remove anything that may be used to cause harm to people or property or assist escape. During detention the police may take fingerprint evidence and also intimate and non-intimate samples for forensic purposes and to obtain a DNA profile. The conduct of searches is regulated by the *PACE Act* 1984 as amended and Code C.

Police and Criminal Evidence Act 1984, s.54

Searches of detained persons

1–151 **54.**—(1) The custody officer at a police station shall ascertain everything which a person has with him when he is—

(a) brought to the station after being arrested elsewhere or after being committed to custody by an order or sentence of a court; or

(b) arrested at the station or detained there, as a person falling within section 34(7), under section 37 above [or as a person to whom section 46ZA(4) or (5) applies].

(2) The custody officer may record or cause to be recorded all or any of the things which he ascertains under subsection (1).

(2A) In the case of an arrested person, any such record may be made as part of his custody record.

(3) Subject to subsection (4) below, a custody officer may seize and retain any such thing or cause any such thing to be seized and retained.

(4) Clothes and personal effects may only be seized if the custody officer—

(a) believes that the person from whom they are seized may use them—

(i) to cause physical injury to himself or any other person;

(ii) to damage property;

(iii) to interfere with evidence; or

(iv) to assist him to escape; or

(b) has reasonable grounds for believing that they may be evidence relating to an offence.

(5) Where anything is seized, the person from whom it is seized shall be told the reason for the seizure unless he is—

(a) violent or likely to become violent; or

(b) incapable of understanding what is said to him.

(6) Subject to subsection (7) below, a person may be searched if the custody officer considers it necessary to enable him to carry out his duty under subsection (1) above and to the extent that the custody officer considers necessary for that purpose.

(6A) A person who is in custody at a police station or is in police detention otherwise than at a police station may at any time be searched in order to ascertain whether he has with him anything which he could use for any of the purposes specified in subsection (4)(a) above.

(6B) Subject to subsection (6C) below, a constable may seize and retain, or cause to be seized and retained, anything found on such a search.

(6C) A constable may only seize clothes and personal effects in the circumstances specified in subsection (4) above.

(7) An intimate search may not be conducted under this section.

(8) A search under this section shall be carried out by a constable.

(9) The constable carrying out a search shall be of the same sex as the person searched.

[This section is printed as amended, and repealed in part, by the *Criminal Justice Act* 1988, s.147; the *Criminal Justice and Public Order Act* 1994, s.168(2) and Sched. 10, para. 55; the *Criminal Justice Act* 2003, s.8; and, as from April 1, 2007, in the local justice area of Lambeth and Southwark (*Police and Justice Act 2006 (Commencement No. 2, Transitional and Savings Provisions) Order* 2007 (S.I. 2007 No. 709)), and as from a day to be appointed elsewhere, the *Police and Justice Act* 2006, s.46(1) and (2) (addition of words in square brackets in subs (1)(b)).]

As from June 29, 2007, s.54 of the 1984 Act applies to a person falling within the *Criminal Justice Act* 2003, s.24A(3) (persons bailed after having been arrested for failure to comply with conditions of caution and then attending police station to answer to bail or having been arrested for failure to answer to bail), and who is detained under that section, as it applies to a person falling within s.34(7) of the 1984 Act, and who is detained under s.37 of that Act: *Criminal Justice Act* 2003, s.24B(6), as inserted by the *Police and Justice Act* 2006, s.18(1).

An intimate search is defined in s.65 as a physical examination of body orifices other **1–152**
than the mouth. See also s.62, *post*, § 1–165.

(2) Searches and examination to ascertain identity

Police and Criminal Evidence Act 1984, s.54A

Searches and examination to ascertain identity

1-153 **54A.**—(1) If an officer of at least the rank of inspector authorises it, a person who is detained in a police station may be searched or examined, or both—

(a) for the purpose of ascertaining whether he has any mark that would tend to identify him as a person involved in the commission of an offence; or

(b) for the purpose of facilitating the ascertainment of his identity.

(2) An officer may only give an authorisation under subsection (1) for the purpose mentioned in paragraph (a) of that subsection if—

(a) the appropriate consent to a search or examination that would reveal whether the mark in question exists has been withheld; or

(b) it is not practicable to obtain such consent.

(3) An officer may only give an authorisation under subsection (1) in a case in which subsection (2) does not apply if—

(a) the person in question has refused to identify himself; or

(b) the officer has reasonable grounds for suspecting that that person is not who he claims to be.

(4) An officer may give an authorisation under subsection (1) orally or in writing but, if he gives it orally, he shall confirm it in writing as soon as is practicable.

(5) Any identifying mark found on a search or examination under this section may be photographed—

(a) with the appropriate consent; or

(b) if the appropriate consent is withheld or it is not practicable to obtain it, without it.

(6) Where a search or examination may be carried out under this section, or a photograph may be taken under this section, the only persons entitled to carry out the search or examination, or to take the photograph, are constables.

(7) A person may not under this section carry out a search or examination of a person of the opposite sex or take a photograph of any part of the body of a person of the opposite sex.

(8) An intimate search may not be carried out under this section.

(9) A photograph taken under this section—

(a) may be used by, or disclosed to, any person for any purpose related to the prevention or detection of crime, the investigation of an offence or the conduct of a prosecution; and

(b) after being so used or disclosed, may be retained but may not be used or disclosed except for a purpose so related.

1-154 (10) In subsection (9)—

(a) the reference to crime includes a reference to any conduct which—

(i) constitutes one or more criminal offences (whether under the law of a part of the United Kingdom or of a country or territory outside the United Kingdom); or

(ii) is, or corresponds to, any conduct which, if it all took place in any one part of the United Kingdom, would constitute one or more criminal offences;

and

(b) the references to an investigation and to a prosecution include references, respectively, to any investigation outside the United Kingdom of any crime or suspected crime and to a prosecution brought in respect of any crime in a country or territory outside the United Kingdom.

(11) In this section—

(a) references to ascertaining a person's identity include references to showing that he is not a particular person; and

(b) references to taking a photograph include references to using any process by means of which a visual image may be produced, and references to photographing a person shall be construed accordingly.

(12) In this section "mark" includes features and injuries; and a mark is an identifying mark for the purposes of this section if its existence in any person's case facilitates the ascertainment of his identity or his identification as a person involved in the commission of an offence.

(13) Nothing in this section applies to a person arrested under an extradition arrest power.

[This section was inserted by the *Anti-terrorism, Crime and Security Act* 2001, s.90(1). It is printed as amended by the *Police Reform Act* 2002, s.107(1), and Sched. 7, para. 9(2); and the *Extradition Act* 2003, s.169(2).]

Part I

The *Criminal Justice Act* 2003, s.24B(7) (inserted as from June 29, 2007 by the *Police and Justice Act* 2006, s.18(1)), applies s.54A of the 1984 Act to a person detained at a police station under s.24A of the 2003 Act (arrest for failure to comply with conditions of caution), with the following modifications: **1–155**

(a) in subsections (1)(a) and (12), after "as a person involved in the commission of an offence" there are inserted the words "or as having failed to comply with any of the conditions attached to his conditional caution"; and
(b) in subsection (9)(a), after "the investigation of an offence" there are inserted the words ", the investigation of whether the person in question has failed to comply with any of the conditions attached to his conditional caution".

Appropriate consent is defined in s.65 as being the consent of the person to be searched if they are over 17 years of age; the consent of the person himself and that of his parent or guardian where the person to be searched is aged 14 to 16; and the consent of the parent or guardian of the person to be searched where the person is 13 years of age or less.

As from December 14, 2009 (*Coroners and Justice Act 2009 (Commencement No. 1 and Transitional Provisions) Order* 2009 (S.I. 2009 No. 3253)), the *Coroners and Justice Act* 2009, s.108(1), inserts new sections 54B and 54C in the 1984 Act, but only in certain local justice areas.

Police and Criminal Evidence Act 1984, ss.54B

Searches of persons answering to live link bail

54B.—(1) A constable may search at any time—

(a) any person who is at a police station to answer to live link bail; and
(b) any article in the possession of such a person

(2) If the constable reasonably believes a thing in the possession of the person ought to be seized on any of the grounds mentioned in subsection (3), the constable may seize and retain it or cause it to be seized and retained.

(3) The grounds are that the thing—

(a) may jeopardise the maintenance of order in the police station;
(b) may put the safety of any person in the police station at risk; or
(c) may be evidence of, or in relation to, an offence.

(4) The constable may record or cause to be recorded all or any of the things seized and retained pursuant to subsection (2).

(5) An intimate search may not be carried out under this section

(6) The constable carrying out a search under subsection (1) must be of the same sex as the person being searched.

(7) In this section "live link bail" means bail granted under Part 4 of this Act subject to the duty mentioned in section 47(3)(b).

Police and Criminal Evidence Act 1984, s.54C

Power to retain articles seized

54B.—(1) Except as provided by subsections (2) and (3), a constable may retain a thing seized under section 54B until the time when the person from whom it was seized leaves the police station.

(2) A constable may retain a thing seized under section 54B in order to establish its law-

ful owner, where there are reasonable grounds for believing that it has been obtained in consequence of the commission of an offence.

(3) If a thing seized under section 54B may be evidence of, or in relation to, an offence, a constable may retain it—

(a) for use as evidence at a trial for an offence; or

(b) for forensic examination or for investigation in connection with an offence.

(4) Nothing may be retained for either of the purposes mentioned in subsection (3) if a photograph or copy would be sufficient for that purpose.

(5) Nothing in this section affects any power of a court to make an order under section 1 of the *Police (Property) Act* 1897.

(6) The references in this section to anything seized under section 54B include anything seized by a person to whom paragraph 27A of Schedule 4 to the *Police Reform Act* 2002 applies.

(3) Fingerprinting, DNA profiling and samples

Police and Criminal Evidence Act 1984, s.61

Finger-printing

1–156 **61.**—(1) Except as provided by this section no person's fingerprints may be taken without the appropriate consent.

(2) Consent to the taking of a person's fingerprints must be in writing if it is given at a time when he is at a police station.

(3) The fingerprints of a person detained at a police station may be taken without the appropriate consent if—

(a) he is detained in consequence of his arrest for a recordable offence; and

(b) he has not had his fingerprints taken in the course of the investigation of the offence by the police.

(3A) Where a person mentioned in paragraph (a) of subsection (3) or (4) has already had his fingerprints taken in the course of the investigation of the offence by the police that fact shall be disregarded for the purposes of that subsection if—

(a) the fingerprints taken on the previous occasion do not constitute a complete set of his fingerprints; or

(b) some or all of the fingerprints taken on the previous occasion are not of sufficient quality to allow satisfactory analysis, comparison or matching (whether in the case in question or generally).

1–157 (4) The fingerprints of a person detained at a police station may be taken without the appropriate consent if—

(a) he has been charged with a recordable offence or informed that he will be reported for such an offence; and

(b) he has not had his fingerprints taken in the course of the investigation of the offence by the police.

(4A) The fingerprints of a person who has answered to bail at a court or police station may be taken without the appropriate consent at the court or station if—

(a) the court, or

(b) an officer of at least the rank of inspector,

authorises them to be taken.

(4B) A court or officer may only give an authorisation under subsection (4A) if—

(a) the person who has answered to bail has answered to it for a person whose fingerprints were taken on a previous occasion and there are reasonable grounds for believing that he is not the same person; or

(b) the person who has answered to bail claims to be a different person from a person whose fingerprints were taken on a previous occasion.

1–158 (5) An officer may give an authorisation under subsection (4A) above orally or in writing but, if he gives it orally, he shall confirm it in writing as soon as is practicable.

(5A) The fingerprints of a person may be taken without the appropriate consent if (before or after the coming into force of this subsection) he has been arrested for a recordable offence and released and—

(a) in the case of a person who is on bail, he has not had his fingerprints taken in the course of the investigation of the offence by the police; or

(b) in any case, he has had his fingerprints taken in the course of that investigation but subsection (3A)(a) or (b) above applies.

(5B) The fingerprints of a person not detained at a police station may be taken without the appropriate consent if (before or after the coming into force of this subsection) he has been charged with a recordable offence or informed that he will be reported for such an offence and—

(a) he has not had his fingerprints taken in the course of the investigation of the offence by the police; or

(b) he has had his fingerprints taken in the course of that investigation but subsection (3A)(a) or (b) above applies.

(6) Subject to this section, the fingerprints of a person may be taken without the appropriate consent if (before or after the coming into force of this subsection)—

(a) he has been convicted of a recordable offence,

(b) he has been given a caution in respect of a recordable offence which, at the time of the caution, he has admitted, or

(c) he has been warned or reprimanded under section 65 of the *Crime and Disorder Act* 1998 for a recordable offence, and

either of the conditions mentioned in subsection (6ZA) below is met.

(6ZA) The conditions referred to in subsection (6) above are—

(a) the person has not had his fingerprints taken since he was convicted, cautioned or warned or reprimanded;

(b) he has had his fingerprints taken since then but subsection (3A)(a) or (b) above applies.

(6ZB) Fingerprints may only be taken as specified in subsection (6) above with the authorisation of an officer of at least the rank of inspector.

(6ZC) An officer may only give an authorisation under subsection (6ZB) above if the officer is satisfied that taking the fingerprints is necessary to assist in the prevention or detection of crime.

(6A) A constable may take a person's fingerprints without the appropriate consent if—

(a) the constable reasonably suspects that the person is committing or attempting to commit an offence, or has committed or attempted to commit an offence; and

(b) either of the two conditions mentioned in subsection (6B) is met.

(6B) The conditions are that—

(a) the name of the person is unknown to, and cannot be readily ascertained by, the constable;

(b) the constable has reasonable grounds for doubting whether a name furnished by the person as his name is his real name.

[(6BA) A constable may take a person's fingerprints without the appropriate consent if the person is subject to a control order.]

(6C) The taking of fingerprints by virtue of subsection (6A) [or 6(BA)] does not count for any of the purposes of this Act as taking them in the course of the investigation of an offence by the police.

(6D) Subject to this section, the fingerprints of a person may be taken without the appropriate consent if—

(a) under the law in force in a country or territory outside England and Wales the person has been convicted of an offence under that law (whether before or after the coming into force of this subsection and whether or not he has been punished for it);

(b) the act constituting the offence would constitute a qualifying offence if done in England and Wales (whether or not it constituted such an offence when the person was convicted); and

(c) either of the conditions mentioned in subsection (6E) below is met.

(6E) The conditions referred to in subsection (6D)(c) above are—

(a) the person has not had his fingerprints taken on a previous occasion under subsection (6D) above;

(b) he has had his fingerprints taken on a previous occasion under that subsection but subsection (3A)(a) or (b) above applies.

(6F) Fingerprints may only be taken as specified in subsection (6D) above with the authorisation of an officer of at least the rank of inspector.

(6G) An officer may only give an authorisation under subsection (6F) above if the officer is satisfied that taking the fingerprints is necessary to assist in the prevention or detection of crime.

(7) Where a person's fingerprints are taken without the appropriate consent by virtue of any power conferred by this section—

(a) before the fingerprints are taken, the person shall be informed of—
   (i) the reason for taking the fingerprints;
   (ii) the power by virtue of which they are taken; and
   (iii) in a case where the authorisation of the court or an officer is required for the exercise of the power, the fact that the authorisation has been given; and

(b) those matters shall be recorded as soon as practicable after the fingerprints are taken.

(7A) If a person's fingerprints are taken at a police station, or by virtue of subsection (4A), (6A) [or 6(BA)] at a place other than a police station, whether with or without the appropriate consent—

(a) before the fingerprints are taken, an officer (or, where by virtue of subsection (4A), (6A) or (6BA) the fingerprints are taken at a place other than a police station, the constable taking the fingerprints) shall inform him that they may be the subject of a speculative search; and

(b) the fact that the person has been informed of this possibility shall be recorded as soon as is practicable after the fingerprints have been taken.

(8) If he is detained at a police station when the fingerprints are taken, the matters referred to in subsection (7)(a)(i) to (iii) above and, in the case falling within subsection (7A) above, the fact referred to in paragraph (b) of that subsection shall be recorded on his custody record.

(8A) [*repealed by* Policing and Crime Act 2009, *s.112(1) and (2), Sched. 7, para. 127(1) and (2), and Schedule 8, Pt 13.*]

(8B) Any power under this section to take the fingerprints of a person without the appropriate consent, if not otherwise specified to be exercisable by a constable, shall be exercisable by a constable.

(9) Nothing in this section—

(a) affects any power conferred by paragraph 18(2) of Schedule 2 to the *Immigration Act* 1971 [, section 141 of the *Immigration and Asylum Act* 1999 or regulations made under section 144 of that Act]; or

(b) applies to a person arrested or detained under the terrorism provisions.

(10) Nothing in this section applies to a person arrested under an extradition arrest power.

[This section is printed as amended by the *Criminal Justice and Public Order Act* 1994, s.168(2) and Sched. 10, para. 56; the *Terrorism Act* 2000, s.125 and Sched. 15, para. 5(7); the *Anti-Terrorism, Crime and Security Act* 2001, s.90(2); the *Criminal Justice and Police Act* 2001, s.78(2)-(7); the *Police Reform Act* 2002, s.107(1), and Sched. 7, para. 9(3); the *Extradition Act* 2003, s.169(3); the *Criminal Justice Act* 2003, s.9; the *Serious Organised Crime and Police Act* 2005, s.117(1), (2) and (4)(a); and the *Crime and Security Act* 2010, ss.2(1)–(4), 3(1) and 4(1)–(3); and, as from a day to be appointed, by the *Immigration and Asylum Act* 1999, s.169(1), and Sched. 14, para. 80(1) and(4) (insertion of words in square brackets in subs. (9)); and the *Counter-Terrorism Act* 2008, s.10(1) and (6) (insertion of subs. (6BA) and consequential amendments in square brackets). The amendments made by the 2008 Act, s.10, have effect from the commencement of that section regardless of when the control order was made: 2008 Act, s.13.

1–159 Fingerprints are defined in s.65 as a record in any form and produced by any method, of the skin pattern and other physical characteristics or features of a person's fingers or either of his palms.

Appropriate consent is that of the person to be fingerprinted himself, or in the case of a youth aged 14–16 his consent and that of his parent or guardian, and in the case of a youth under the age of 14 the consent of his parent or guardian.

Fingerprints after conviction can be taken under the *PACE Act* 1984, Sched. 2A (*post*, §§ 1–175 *et seq.*).

A person is detained at a police station, and so prints can be taken, when he is held there temporarily having been remanded in custody by the magistrates' court: *Seymour* [1995] 9 *Archbold News* 1, CA.

Part I

Police and Criminal Evidence Act 1984, s.61A

Impressions of footwear

61A.—(1) Except as provided by this section, no impression of a person's footwear may be taken without the appropriate consent. **1–160**

(2) Consent to the taking of an impression of a person's footwear must be in writing if it is given at a time when he is at a police station.

(3) Where a person is detained at a police station, an impression of his footwear may be taken without the appropriate consent if—

(a) he is detained in consequence of his arrest for a recordable offence, or has been charged with a recordable offence, or informed that he will be reported for a recordable offence; and

(b) he has not had an impression taken of his footwear in the course of the investigation of the offence by the police.

(4) Where a person mentioned in paragraph (a) of subsection (3) above has already had an impression taken of his footwear in the course of the investigation of the offence by the police, that fact shall be disregarded for the purposes of that subsection if the impression of his footwear taken previously is—

(a) incomplete; or

(b) is not of sufficient quality to allow satisfactory analysis, comparison or matching (whether in the case in question or generally).

(5) If an impression of a person's footwear is taken at a police station, whether with or without the appropriate consent—

(a) before it is taken, an officer shall inform him that it may be the subject of a speculative search; and

(b) the fact that the person has been informed of this possibility shall be recorded as soon as is practicable after the impression has been taken, and if he is detained at a police station, the record shall be made on his custody record.

(6) In a case where, by virtue of subsection (3) above, an impression of a person's footwear is taken without the appropriate consent—

(a) he shall be told the reason before it is taken; and

(b) the reason shall be recorded on his custody record as soon as is practicable after the impression is taken.

(7) The power to take an impression of the footwear of a person detained at a police station without the appropriate consent shall be exercisable by any constable.

(8) Nothing in this section applies to any person—

(a) arrested or detained under the terrorism provisions;

(b) arrested under an extradition arrest power.

[This section was inserted by the *Serious Organised Crime and Police Act* 2005, s.118.]

Intimate searches and samples

Police and Criminal Evidence Act 1984, s.55

Intimate searches

55.—(1) Subject to the following provisions of this section, if an officer of at least the rank of inspector has reasonable grounds for believing— **1–161**

(a) that a person who has been arrested and is in police detention may have concealed on him anything which—
 (i) he could use to cause physical injury to himself or others; and
 (ii) he might so use while he is in police detention or in the custody of a court; or
(b) that such a person—
 (i) may have a Class A drug concealed on him; and
 (ii) was in possession of it with the appropriate criminal intent before his arrest,

he may authorise an intimate search of that person.

(2) An officer may not authorise an intimate search of a person for anything unless he has reasonable grounds for believing that it cannot be found without his being intimately searched.

(3) An officer may give an authorisation under subsection (1) above orally or in writing but, if he gives it orally, he shall confirm it in writing as soon as is practicable.

(3A) A drug offence search shall not be carried out unless the appropriate consent has been given in writing.

(3B) Where it is proposed that a drug offence search be carried out, an appropriate officer shall inform the person who is to be subject to it—

(a) of the giving of the authorisation for it; and
(b) of the grounds for giving the authorisation.

(4) An intimate search which is only a drug offence search shall be by way of examination by a suitably qualified person.

(5) Except as provided by subsection (4) above, an intimate search shall be by way of examination by a suitably qualified person unless an officer of at least the rank of inspector considers that this is not practicable.

(6) An intimate search which is not carried out as mentioned in subsection (5) above shall be carried out by a constable.

(7) A constable may not carry out an intimate search of a person of the opposite sex.

(8) No intimate search may be carried out except—

(a) at a police station;
(b) at a hospital;
(c) at a registered medical practitioner's surgery; or
(d) at some other place used for medical purposes.

(9) An intimate search which is only a drug offence search may not be carried out at a police station.

(10) If an intimate search of a person is carried out, the custody record relating to him shall state—

(a) which parts of his body were searched; and
(b) why they were searched.

(10A) If the intimate search is a drug offence search, the custody record relating to that person shall also state—

(a) the authorisation by virtue of which the search was carried out;
(b) the grounds for giving the authorisation; and
(c) the fact that the appropriate consent was given.

1–162 (11) The information required to be recorded by subsections (10) and (10A) above shall be recorded as soon as practicable after the completion of the search.

(12) The custody officer at a police station may seize and retain anything which is found on an intimate search of a person, or cause any such thing to be seized and retained—

(a) if he believes that the person from whom it is seized may use it—
 (i) to cause physical injury to himself or any other person;
 (ii) to damage property;
 (iii) to interfere with evidence; or
 (iv) to assist him to escape; or
(b) if he has reasonable grounds for believing that it may be evidence relating to an offence.

(13) Where anything is seized under this section, the person from whom it is seized shall be told the reason for the seizure unless he is—

Part I

(a) violent or likely to become violent; or
(b) incapable of understanding what is said to him.

(13A) Where the appropriate consent to a drug offence search of any person was refused without good cause, in any proceedings against that person for an offence—
(a) the court, in determining whether there is a case to answer;
(b) a judge, in deciding whether to grant an application made by the accused under paragraph 2 of Schedule 3 to the *Crime and Disorder Act* 1998 (applications for dismissal); and
(c) the court or jury, in determining whether that person is guilty of the offence charged,

may draw such inferences from the refusal as appear proper.

(14) Every annual report—
(a) under section 22 of the *Police Act* 1996; or
(b) made by the Commissioner of Police of the Metropolis,

shall contain information about searches under this section which have been carried out in the area to which the report relates during the period to which it relates.

(14A) Every annual report under section 57 of the *Police Act* 1997 (reports by Director General of the National Crime Squad) shall contain information about searches authorised under this section by members of the National Crime Squad during the period to which the report relates.

(15) The information about such searches shall include—
(a) the total number of searches;
(b) the number of searches conducted by way of examination by a suitably qualified person;
(c) the number of searches not so conducted but conducted in the presence of such a person; and
(d) the result of the searches carried out.

(16) The information shall also include, as separate items—
(a) the total number of drug offence searches; and
(b) the result of those searches.

(17) In this section—

"the appropriate criminal intent" means an intent to commit an offence under—
(a) section 5(3) of the *Misuse of Drugs Act* 1971 (possession of controlled drug with intent to supply to another); or
(b) section 68(2) of the *Customs and Excise Management Act* 1979 (exportation etc. with intent to evade a prohibition or restriction);

"appropriate officer" means—
(a) a constable,
(b) a person who is designated as a detention officer in pursuance of section 38 of the *Police Reform Act* 2002 if his designation applies paragraph 33D of Schedule 4 to that Act.

"Class A drug" has the meaning assigned to it by section 2(1)(b) of the *Misuse of Drugs Act* 1971;

"drug offence search" means an intimate search for a Class A drug which an officer has authorised by virtue of subsection (1)(b) above; and

"suitably qualified person" means —
(a) a registered medical practitioner; or
(b) a registered nurse.

[This section is printed as amended by the *Criminal Justice Act* 1988, Sched. 15, para. 99; the *Criminal Justice and Police Act* 2001, s.79; the *Drugs Act* 2005, s.3 and the *Policing and Crime Act* 2009, s.112(1) and (2), Sched. 7, para. 123(1) and (5), and Sched. 8, Pt 13.]

An intimate search is physical examination of body orifices other than the mouth: the **1–163**
PACE Act 1984, s.65. The Code of Practice for the Detention, Treatment and Questioning of Persons, Code C; Annex A gives specific guidance on the conduct of intimate searches. Customs officers have power to conduct intimate searches under s.55(1)(a) only: S.I. 1985 No. 1800.

Police and Criminal Evidence Act 1984, s.55A

X-rays and ultrasound scans

1–164 **55A.**—(1) If an officer of at least the rank of inspector has reasonable grounds for believing that a person who has been arrested for an offence and is in police detention—

(a) may have swallowed a Class A drug, and

(b) was in possession of it with the appropriate criminal intent before his arrest,

the officer may authorise that an x-ray is taken of the person or an ultrasound scan is carried out on the person (or both).

(2) An x-ray must not be taken of a person and an ultrasound scan must not be carried out on him unless the appropriate consent has been given in writing.

(3) If it is proposed that an x-ray is taken or an ultrasound scan is carried out, an appropriate officer must inform the person who is to be subject to it—

(a) of the giving of the authorisation for it, and

(b) of the grounds for giving the authorisation.

(4) An x-ray may be taken or an ultrasound scan carried out only by a suitably qualified person and only at—

(a) a hospital,

(b) a registered medical practitioner's surgery, or

(c) some other place used for medical purposes.

(5) The custody record of the person must also state—

(a) the authorisation by virtue of which the x-ray was taken or the ultrasound scan was carried out,

(b) the grounds for giving the authorisation, and

(c) the fact that the appropriate consent was given.

(6) The information required to be recorded by subsection (5) must be recorded as soon as practicable after the x-ray has been taken or ultrasound scan carried out (as the case may be).

(7) Every annual report-

(a) under section 22 of the *Police Act* 1996, or

(b) made by the Commissioner of Police of the Metropolis,

must contain information about x-rays which have been taken and ultrasound scans which have been carried out under this section in the area to which the report relates during the period to which it relates.

(8) The information about such x-rays and ultrasound scans must be presented separately and must include—

(a) the total number of x-rays;

(b) the total number of ultrasound scans;

(c) the results of the x-rays;

(d) the results of the ultrasound scans.

(9) If the appropriate consent to an x-ray or ultrasound scan of any person is refused without good cause, in any proceedings against that person for an offence—

(a) the court, in determining whether there is a case to answer,

(b) a judge, in deciding whether to grant an application made by the accused under paragraph 2 of Schedule 3 to the *Crime and Disorder Act* 1998 (applications for dismissal), and

(c) the court or jury, in determining whether that person is guilty of the offence charged,

may draw such inferences from the refusal as appear proper.

(10) In this section "the appropriate criminal intent", "appropriate officer", "Class A drug" and "suitably qualified person" have the same meanings as in section 55 above.

[This section was inserted by s.5 of the *Drugs Act* 2005.]

A person who has been arrested may be X-rayed or scanned to see if there are drugs in his body. It relates only to Class A drugs and the power is only available if there are reasonable grounds to believe that the person arrested was in possession of the drugs with the appropriate criminal intent. That intent is defined as being an intention to commit an offence of possessing controlled drugs with intent to supply or drug smuggling under the *Customs and Excise Management Act* 1979. Consent must be given in writing and the search must be conducted under the proper medical conditions and fully recorded. If consent is refused without good cause the court may draw an adverse inference from that refusal at trial.

Police and Criminal Evidence Act, s.62

Intimate samples

62.—(1) Subject to section 63B below an intimate sample may be taken from a person in police detention only— **1–165**

(a) if a police officer of at least the rank of inspector authorises it to be taken; and
(b) if the appropriate consent is given.

(1A) An intimate sample may be taken from a person who is not in police detention but from whom, in the course of the investigation of an offence, two or more non-intimate samples suitable for the same means of analysis have been taken which have proved insufficient—

(a) if a police officer of at least the rank of inspector authorises it to be taken; and
(b) if the appropriate consent is given.

(2) An officer may only give an authorisation under subsection (1) or (1A) above if he has reasonable grounds—

(a) for suspecting the involvement of the person from whom the sample is to be taken in a recordable offence; and
(b) for believing that the sample will tend to confirm or disprove his involvement.

(2A) An intimate sample may be taken from a person where—

(a) two or more non-intimate samples suitable for the same means of analysis have been taken from the person under section 63(3E) below (persons convicted of offences outside England and Wales etc) but have proved insufficient;
(b) a police officer of at least the rank of inspector authorises it to be taken; and
(c) the appropriate consent is given.

(2B) An officer may only give an authorisation under subsection (2A) above if the officer is satisfied that taking the sample is necessary to assist in the prevention or detection of crime.

(3) An officer may give an authorisation under subsection (1) or (1A) or 2A above orally or in writing but, if he gives it orally, he shall confirm it in writing as soon as is practicable.

(4) The appropriate consent must be given in writing.

(5) Before an intimate sample is taken from a person, an officer shall inform him of the following—

(a) the reason for taking the sample;
(b) the fact that authorisation has been given and the provision of this section under which it has been given; and
(c) if the sample was taken at a police station, the fact that the sample may be the subject of a speculative search.

(6) The reason referred to in subsection (5)(a) above must include, except in a case where the sample is taken under subsection (2A) above, a statement of the nature of the offence in which it is suspected that the person has been involved.

(7) After an intimate sample has been taken from a person, the following shall be recorded as soon as practicable—

(a) the matters referred to in subsection (5)(a) and (b) above;
(b) if the sample was taken at a police station, the fact that the person has been informed as specified in subsection (5)(c) above; and
(c) the fact that the appropriate consent was given.

(8) If an intimate sample is taken from a person detained at a police station, the matters required to be recorded by subsection (7) *or (7A)* above shall be recorded in his custody record.

(9) In the case of an intimate sample which is a dental impression, the sample may be taken from a person only by a registered dentist.

(9A) In the case of any other form of intimate sample, except in the case of a sample of urine, the sample may be taken from a person only by—

(a) a registered medical practitioner; or

(b) a registered health care professional.

1–166 (10) Where the appropriate consent to the taking of an intimate sample from a person was refused without good cause, in any proceedings against that person for an offence—

(a) the court, in determining—

(i) *whether to commit that person for trial; or*

(ii) whether there is a case to answer; and

(aa) a judge, in deciding whether to grant an application made by the accused under—

(i) *section 6 of the* Criminal Justice Act *1987 (application for dismissal of charge of serious fraud in respect of which notice of transfer has been given under section 4 of that Act); or*

(ii) *paragraph 5 of Schedule 6 to the* Criminal Justice Act *1991 (application for dismissal of charge of violent or sexual offence involving child in respect of which notice of transfer has been given under section 53 of that Act; and* [paragraph 2 of Schedule 3 to the *Crime and Disorder Act* 1998 (applications for dismissal); and]

(b) the court or jury, in determining whether that person is guilty of the offence charged, may draw such inferences from the refusal as appear proper.

(11) Nothing in this section applies to the taking of a specimen for the purposes of any of the provisions of sections 4 to 11 of the *Road Traffic Act* 1988 or of sections 26 to 38 of the *Transport and Works Act* 1992.

(12) Nothing in this section applies to a person arrested or detained under the terrorism procedures; and subsection (1A) shall not apply where the non-intimate samples mentioned in that subsection were taken under paragraph 10 of Schedule 8 to the *Terrorism Act* 2000.

[This section is printed as amended and repealed in part by the *Road Traffic (Consequential Provisions) Act* 1988, s.4 and Sched. 3, para. 27(4); the *Criminal Justice and Public Order Act* 1994, ss.54(1)-(5) and 168(1)-(3), and Scheds 9, para. 24, 10, paras 57 and 62(4)(a) and 11; the *Terrorism Act* 2000, s.125 and Sched. 15, para. 5(8); the *Criminal Justice and Court Services Act* 2000, s.74 and Sched. 7, para. 78; the *Criminal Justice and Police Act* 2001, s.80(1); the *Police Reform Act* 2002, ss.53(2) and 54(1); and the*Crime and Security Act* 2010, ss.3(2) and (3) and 4(4) and (5). Subparas (i) and (ii) of subs. (10)(aa) are replaced by the words in square brackets that follow them by the *Criminal Justice Act* 2003, s.41, and Sched. 3, para. 56(1) and (2)(b). This amendment came into force on May 9, 2005 (*Criminal Justice Act 2003 (Commencement No. 9) Order* 2005 (S.I. 2005 No. 1267)) in relation to cases sent for trial under ss.51 or 51A(3)(d) of the *Crime and Disorder Act* 1998. Otherwise, it comes into force on a day to be appointed. Subsection (10)(a)(i) is repealed as from a day to be appointed by the *Criminal Justice Act* 2003, ss.41 and 332, Sched. 3, para. 56(2)(a), and Sched. 37, Pt 4.]

Intimate samples

1–167 Intimate samples are defined in s.65 as a sample of blood, semen or any other tissue fluid, urine or pubic hair; a dental impression; a swab taken from a person's body orifice other than the mouth. For appropriate consent, see *ante*, § 1–165.

Authorisation does not have to be sought before consent, but if authorisation were granted first any subsequent consent given may be on a dubious basis: *Butt*, unreported, February 20, 1998, CA. An analysis of the result of intimate samples taken under the provisions of this section in the course of an investigation can be used in proceedings for a separate investigation into a different offence: *Kelt* (1993) 99 Cr.App.R. 372.

Other samples

Police and Criminal Evidence Act 1984, s.63

Other samples

1–168 **63.**—(1) Except as provided by this section, a non-intimate sample may not be taken from a person without the appropriate consent.

(2) Consent to the taking of a non-intimate sample must be given in writing.

(2A) A non-intimate sample may be taken from a person without the appropriate consent if two conditions are satisfied.

(2B) The first is that the person is in police detention in consequence of his arrest for a recordable offence.

(2C) The second is that—

(a) he has not had a non-intimate sample of the same type and from the same part of the body taken in the course of the investigation of the offence by the police, or

(b) he has had such a sample taken but it proved insufficient.

(3) A non-intimate sample may be taken from a person without the appropriate consent if—

(a) he is being held in custody by the police on the authority of a court; and

(b) an officer of at least the rank of inspector authorises it to be taken without the appropriate consent.

(3ZA) A non-intimate sample may be taken from a person without the appropriate consent if (before or after the coming into force of this subsection) he has been arrested for a recordable offence and released and—

(a) in the case of a person who is on bail, he has not had a non-intimate sample of the same type and from the same part of the body taken from him in the course of the investigation of the offence by the police; or

(b) in any case, he has had a non-intimate sample taken from him in the course of that investigation but—

(i) it was not suitable for the same means of analysis, or

(ii) it proved insufficient.

(3A) A non-intimate sample may be taken from a person (whether or not he is in police detention or held in custody by the police on the authority of a court) without the appropriate consent if he has been charged with a recordable offence or informed that he will be reported for such an offence and—

(a) he has not had a non-intimate sample taken from him in the course of the investigation of the offence by the police; or

(b) he has had a non-intimate sample taken from him in the course of that investigation but—

(i) it was not suitable for the same means of analysis, or

(ii) it proved insufficient; or

(c) he has had a non-intimate sample taken from him in the course of that investigation and—

(i) the sample has been destroyed pursuant to section 64ZA below or any other enactment, and

(ii) it is disputed, in relation to any proceedings relating to the offence, whether a DNA profile relevant to the proceedings is derived from the sample.

(3B) Subject to this section, a non-intimate sample may be taken from a person without the appropriate consent if (before or after the coming into force of this subsection)—

(a) he has been convicted of a recordable offence,

(b) he has been given a caution in respect of a recordable offence which, at the time of the caution, he has admitted, or

(c) he has been warned or reprimanded under section 65 of the *Crime and Disorder Act* 1998 for a recordable offence, and

either of the conditions mentioned in subsection (3BA) below is met.

(3BA) The conditions referred to in subsection (3B) above are—

(a) a non-intimate sample has not been taken from the person since he was convicted, cautioned or warned or reprimanded;

(b) such a sample has been taken from him since then but—

(i) it was not suitable for the same means of analysis, or

(ii) it proved insufficient.

(3BB) A non-intimate sample may only be taken as specified in subsection (3B) above with the authorisation of an officer of at least the rank of inspector.

(3BC) An officer may only give an authorisation under subsection (3BB) above if the officer is satisfied that taking the sample is necessary to assist in the prevention or detection of crime.

(3C) A non-intimate sample may also be taken from a person without the appropriate consent if he is a person to whom section 2 of the *Criminal Evidence (Amendment) Act* 1997 applies (persons detained following acquittal on grounds of insanity or finding of unfitness to plead).

[(3D) A non-intimate sample may also be taken from a person without the appropriate consent if the person is subject to a control order.]

(3E) Subject to this section, a non-intimate sample may be taken without the appropriate consent from a person if—

(a) under the law in force in a country or territory outside England and Wales the person has been convicted of an offence under that law (whether before or after the coming into force of this subsection and whether or not he has been punished for it);

(b) the act constituting the offence would constitute a qualifying offence if done in England and Wales (whether or not it constituted such an offence when the person was convicted); and

(c) either of the conditions mentioned in subsection (3F) below is met.

(3F) The conditions referred to in subsection (3E)(c) above are—

(a) the person has not had a non-intimate sample taken from him on a previous occasion under subsection (3E) above;

(b) he has had such a sample taken from him on a previous occasion under that subsection but—

(i) the sample was not suitable for the same means of analysis, or

(ii) it proved insufficient.

(3G) A non-intimate sample may only be taken as specified in subsection (3E) above with the authorisation of an officer of at least the rank of inspector.

(3H) An officer may only give an authorisation under subsection (3G) above if the officer is satisfied that taking the sample is necessary to assist in the prevention or detection of crime.

(4) An officer may only give an authorisation under subsection (3) above if he has reasonable grounds—

(a) for suspecting the involvement of the person from whom the sample is to be taken in a recordable offence; and

(b) for believing that the sample will tend to confirm or disprove his involvement.

1–169 (5) An officer may give an authorisation under subsection (3) above orally or in writing but, if he gives it orally, he shall confirm it in writing as soon as is practicable.

(5A) An officer shall not give an authorisation under subsection (3) above for the taking from any person of a non-intimate sample consisting of a skin impression if—

(a) a skin impression of the same part of the body has already been taken from that person in the course of the investigation of the offence; and

(b) the impression previously taken is not one that has proved insufficient.

(6) Where a non-intimate sample is taken from a person without the appropriate consent by virtue of any power conferred by this section—

(a) before the sample is taken, an officer shall inform him of—

(i) the reason for taking the sample;

(ii) the power by virtue of which it is taken; and

(iii) in a case where the authorisation of an officer is required for the exercise of the power, the fact that the authorisation has been given; and

(b) those matters shall be recorded as soon as practicable after the sample is taken.

(7) The reason referred to in subsection (6)(a)(i) above must include, except in a case where the non-intimate sample is taken under subsection (3B) or (3E) above, a statement of the nature of the offence in which it is suspected that the person has been involved.

(8B) If a non-intimate sample is taken from a person at a police station, [or by virtue of subsection (3D) at a place other than a police station] whether with or without the appropriate consent—

(a) before the sample is taken, an officer [, or, in a subsection (3D) case, a constable,] shall inform him that it may be the subject of a speculative search; and

(b) the fact that the person has been informed of this possibility shall be recorded as soon as practicable after the sample has been taken.

(9) If a non-intimate sample is taken from a person detained at a police station, the matters required to be recorded by *subsection (8) or (8A) or (8B)* [subsection (6) or (8B)] above shall be recorded in his custody record. **1–170**

(9ZA) The power to take a non-intimate sample from a person without the appropriate consent shall be exercisable by any constable.

(9A) Subsection (3B) above shall not apply to [—

(a)] any person convicted before 10th April 1995 unless he is a person to whom section 1 of the *Criminal Evidence (Amendment) Act* 1997 applies (persons imprisoned or detained by virtue of pre-existing conviction for sexual offence, etc.)[; or

(b) a person given a caution before 10th April 1995.]

(10) Nothing in this section applies to a person arrested or detained under the terrorism provisions word substituted by *Criminal Justice and Police Act* 2001, Part 3 section 80(1).

(11) Nothing in this section applies to a person arrested under an extradition arrest power.

[This section is printed as amended by the *Criminal Justice and Public Order Act* 1994, ss.55(1)-(5) and 168(2), and Sched. 10, paras 58 and 62(4)(b); the *Criminal Evidence (Amendment) Act* 1997, ss.1(2) and 2(2); the *Terrorism Act* 2000, s.125 and Sched. 15, para. 5(9); the *Criminal Justice and Police Act* 2001, s.80(1),(3); the *Police Reform Act* 2002, s.107(1), and Sched. 7, para. 9(4); the *Extradition Act* 2003, s.169(4); the *Criminal Justice Act* 2003, s.10; the *Policing and Crime Act* 2009, s.112(1) and (2), Sched. 7, para. 127(1) and (3), and Sched. 8, Pt 13; and the *Crime and Security Act* 2010, ss.2(5)-(8) and 4(7)-(8); and as amended, as from a day to be appointed by the *Counter-Terrorism Act* 2008, s.10(6)(b) (insertion of words in square brackets, omission of italicised words). As to the taking effect of the 2008 Act amendments, see the note to s.61, *ante*, § 1–158.]

Non-intimate samples include saliva, skin impressions, mouth swabs, hair (other than pubic hair) and samples from under the nails: *PACE* 1984, s.65.

For "appropriate consent", see *ante*, § 1–165.

Supplementary provisions

Police and Criminal Evidence Act 1984, s.63A

Fingerprints and samples: supplementary provisions

63A.—(1) Where a person has been arrested on suspicion of being involved in a recordable offence or has been charged with such an offence or has been informed that he will be reported for such an offence, [or he is or has been subject to a control order] fingerprints, or impressions of footwear or samples or the information derived from samples taken under any power conferred by this Part of this Act from the person may be checked against— **1–171**

(a) *other fingerprints, or impressions of footwear or samples to which the person seeking to check has access and which are held by or on behalf of any one or more relevant law-enforcement authorities or which are held in connection with or as a result of an investigation of an offence;*

(b) *information derived from other samples if the information is contained in records to which the person seeking to check has access and which are held as mentioned in paragraph (a) above.*

[(a) other fingerprints, impressions of footwear or samples-

(i) to which the person seeking to check has access and which are held by or on behalf of any one or more relevant law-enforcement authorities or are held in connection with or as a result of an investigation of an offence, or

(ii) which are held by or on behalf of the Security Service or the Secret Intelligence Service;

(b) information derived from other samples-

(i) which is contained in records to which the person seeking to check has access and which are held as mentioned in paragraph (a)(i) above, or

(ii) which is held by or on behalf of the Security Service or the Secret Intelligence Service.]

(1ZA) Fingerprints taken by virtue of section 61(6A) above may be checked against *other fingerprints to which the person seeking to check has access and which are held by or on behalf of any one or more relevant law-enforcement authorities or which are held in connection with or as a result of an investigation of an offence.*
[other fingerprints-
(a) to which the person seeking to check has access and which are held by or on behalf of any one or more relevant law-enforcement authorities or which are held in connection with or as a result of an investigation of an offence, or
(b) which are held by or on behalf of the Security Service or the Secret Intelligence Service.]

(1A) In subsection (1) [and (1ZA)] above "relevant law-enforcement authority" means—
(a) a police force;
(b) the Serious Organised Crime Agency;
(c) [....];
(d) a public authority (not falling within paragraphs (a) to (c)) with functions in any part of the British Islands which consist of or include the investigation of crimes or the charging of offenders;
(e) any person with functions in any country or territory outside the United Kingdom which—
(i) correspond to those of a police force; or
(ii) otherwise consist of or include the investigation of conduct contrary to the law of that country or territory, or the apprehension of persons guilty of such conduct;
(f) any person with functions under any international agreement which consist of or include the investigation of conduct which is—
(i) unlawful under the law of one or more places,
(ii) prohibited by such an agreement, or
(iii) contrary to international law, or the apprehension of persons guilty of such conduct.

(1B) The reference in subsection (1A) above to a police force is a reference to any of the following—
(a) any police force maintained under section 2 of the *Police Act* 1996 (police forces in England and Wales outside London);
(b) the metropolitan police force;
(c) the City of London police force;
(d) any police force maintained under or by virtue of section 1 of the *Police (Scotland) Act* 1967;
(e) the Police Service of Northern Ireland;
(f) the Police Service of Northern Ireland Reserve;
(g) the Ministry of Defence Police;
(h) the Royal Navy Police;
(i) the Royal Military Police;
(j) the Royal Air Force Police;
(k) [...];
(l) the British Transport Police;
(m) the States of Jersey Police Force;
(n) the salaried police force of the Island of Guernsey;
(o) the Isle of Man Constabulary.

1–172 (1C) Where—
(a) fingerprints, impressions of footwear or samples have been taken from any person in connection with the investigation of an offence but otherwise than in circumstances to which subsection (1) above applies, and
(b) that person has given his consent in writing to the use in a speculative search of the fingerprints or of the samples and of information derived from them,

the fingerprints or impressions of footwear or, as the case may be, those samples and that information may be checked against any of the fingerprints, impressions of footwear, samples or information mentioned in paragraph (a) or (b) of that subsection.

(1D) A consent given for the purposes of subsection (1C) above shall not be capable of being withdrawn.

(1E) Where fingerprints or samples have been taken from any person under section 61(6) or 63(3B) above (persons convicted etc), the fingerprints or samples, or information derived from the samples, may be checked against any of the fingerprints, samples or information mentioned in subsection (1)(a) or (b) above.

(1F) Where fingerprints or samples have been taken from any person under section 61(6D), 62(2A) or 63(3E) above (offences outside England and Wales etc), the fingerprints or samples, or information derived from the samples, may be checked against any of the fingerprints, samples or information mentioned in subsection (1)(a) or (b) above.

(2) Where a sample of hair other than pubic hair is to be taken the sample may be taken either by cutting hairs or by plucking hairs with their roots so long as no more are plucked than the person taking the sample reasonably considers to be necessary for a sufficient sample.

(3) Where any power to take a sample is exercisable in relation to a person the sample may be taken in a prison or other institution to which the *Prison Act* 1952 applies.

(3A) Where—

(a) the power to take a non-intimate sample under section 63(3B) above is exercisable in relation to any person who is detained under Part III of the *Mental Health Act* 1983 in pursuance of—
   (i) a hospital order or interim hospital order made following his conviction for the recordable offence in question, or
   (ii) a transfer direction given at a time when he was detained in pursuance of any sentence or order imposed following that conviction, or
(b) the power to take a non-intimate sample under section 63(3C) above is exercisable in relation to any person,

the sample may be taken in the hospital in which he is detained under that Part of that Act.

Expressions used in this subsection and in the *Mental Health Act* 1983 have the same meaning as in that Act.

(3B) Where the power to take a non-intimate sample under section 63(3B) above is exercisable in relation to a person detained in pursuance of directions of the Secretary of State under section 92 of the *Powers of Criminal Courts (Sentencing) Act* 2000 the sample may be taken at the place where he is so detained.

(4) Schedule 2A (fingerprinting and samples: power to require attendance at police station) shall have effect. **1–173**

[This section was inserted by the *Criminal Justice and Public Order Act* 1994, s.56. It is printed as amended by the *Criminal Procedure and Investigations Act* 1996, s.64(1); the *Criminal Evidence (Amendment) Act* 1997, ss.3 and 4; the *Powers of Criminal Courts (Sentencing) Act* 2000, s.165(1) and Sched. 9, para. 97; the *Criminal Justice and Police Act* 2001, s.81; the *Serious Organised Crime and Police Act* 2005, ss.59, 117(5) and 118(1) and (3), and Sched. 4, paras 43 and 46; the *Armed Forces Act* 2006, s.378(1) and (2), and Sched. 16, para. 100; and the *Crime and Security Act* 2010, ss.5(1) and 6(1); and as amended, as from a day to be appointed, by the *Counter-Terrorism Act* 2008, ss.10(3) and (6) (insertion of subs. (6A) and consequential amendments in square brackets), and 14(1)-(3) (substitution of new words in subss. (1) and (1ZA) in square brackets, omissions in italics); As to the taking effect of the 2008 Act amendments, see the note to s.61, *ante*, § 1–158.]

Detention under s.92 of the *Powers of Criminal Courts (Sentencing) Act* 2000 relates to offenders under the age of 18 convicted of murder or other serious offences who are ordered to be detained at her Majesty's pleasure or other specified period. **1–174**

By s.118(1) of the 1984 Act, "recordable offence" means any offence under which regulations to s.27(4) apply. The *National Police Records (Recordable Offences) Regulations* 2000 (S.I. 2000 No. 1139) (as amended by the *National Police Records (Recordable Offences) (Amendment) Regulations* 2003 (S.I. 2003 No. 2823)) were made under subs. (4). They provide that there may be recorded in national police records convictions for, or cautions, reprimands and warnings given in respect of, offences punishable with imprisonment or for an offence included in a list of over 40 non-imprisonable offences. The reference to offences punishable with imprisonment is to be construed without regard to any prohibition or restriction imposed by or under any enactment on the punishment of young offenders. The regulations also provide that where a person's convictions are recordable, there may also be recorded his convictions for any other offences in the same proceedings.

This section allows for the checking of fingerprints and samples through several databases as an aid to detection.

Police and Criminal Evidence Act 1984, Sched. 2A

SCHEDULE 2A

FINGERPRINTING AND SAMPLES: POWER TO REQUIRE ATTENDANCE AT POLICE STATION

PART 1

Fingerprinting

Persons arrested and released

1–175 1.—(1) A constable may require a person to attend a police station for the purpose of taking his fingerprints under section 61(5A).

(2) The power under sub-paragraph (1) above may not be exercised in a case falling within section 61(5A)(b) (fingerprints taken on previous occasion insufficient etc) after the end of the period of six months beginning with the day on which the appropriate officer was informed that section 61(3A)(a) or (b) applied.

(3) In sub-paragraph (2) above "appropriate officer" means the officer investigating the offence for which the person was arrested.

Persons charged etc.

2.—(1) A constable may require a person to attend a police station for the purpose of taking his fingerprints under section 61(5B).

(2) The power under sub-paragraph (1) above may not be exercised after the end of the period of six months beginning with—

(a) in a case falling within section 61(5B)(a) (fingerprints not taken previously), the day on which the person was charged or informed that he would be reported, or

(b) in a case falling within section 61(5B)(b) (fingerprints taken on previous occasion insufficient etc), the day on which the appropriate officer was informed that section 61(3A)(a) or (b) applied.

(3) In sub-paragraph (2)(b) above "appropriate officer" means the officer investigating the offence for which the person was charged or informed that he would be reported.

Persons convicted etc. of an offence in England and Wales

3.—(1) A constable may require a person to attend a police station for the purpose of taking his fingerprints under section 61(6).

(2) Where the condition in section 61(6ZA)(a) is satisfied (fingerprints not taken previously), the power under sub-paragraph (1) above may not be exercised after the end of the period of two years beginning with—

(a) the day on which the person was convicted, cautioned or warned or reprimanded, or

(b) if later, the day on which this Schedule comes into force.

(3) Where the condition in section 61(6ZA)(b) is satisfied (fingerprints taken on previous occasion insufficient etc), the power under sub-paragraph (1) above may not be exercised after the end of the period of two years beginning with—

(a) the day on which an appropriate officer was informed that section 61(3A)(a) or (b) applied, or

(b) if later, the day on which this Schedule comes into force.

(4) In sub-paragraph (3)(a) above "appropriate officer" means an officer of the police force which investigated the offence in question.

(5) Sub-paragraphs (2) and (3) above do not apply where the offence is a qualifying offence (whether or not it was such an offence at the time of the conviction, caution or warning or reprimand).

Persons subject to a control order

[4. A constable may require a person to attend a police station for the purpose of taking his fingerprints under section 61(6BA).]

Persons convicted etc of an offence outside England and Wales

5. A constable may require a person to attend a police station for the purpose of taking his fingerprints under section 61(6D).

Multiple attendance

6.—(1) Where a person's fingerprints have been taken under section 61 on two occasions in relation to any offence, he may not under this Schedule be required to attend a police station to have his fingerprints taken under that section in relation to that offence on a subsequent occasion without the authorisation of an officer of at least the rank of inspector.

(2) Where an authorisation is given under sub-paragraph (1) above—

(a) the fact of the authorisation, and

(b) the reasons for giving it,

shall be recorded as soon as practicable after it has been given.

PART 2

Intimate Samples

Persons suspected to be involved in an offence

7. A constable may require a person to attend a police station for the purpose of taking an intimate sample from him under section 62(1A) if, in the course of the investigation of an offence, two or more non-intimate samples suitable for the same means of analysis have been taken from him but have proved insufficient. **1–176**

Persons convicted etc. of an offence outside England and Wales

8. A constable may require a person to attend a police station for the purpose of taking a sample from him under section 62(2A) if two or more non-intimate samples suitable for the same means of analysis have been taken from him under section 63(3E) but have proved insufficient.

PART 3

Non-Intimate Samples

Persons arrested and released

9.—(1) A constable may require a person to attend a police station for the purpose of taking a non-intimate sample from him under section 63(3ZA). **1–177**

(2) The power under sub-paragraph (1) above may not be exercised in a case falling within section 63(3ZA)(b) (sample taken on a previous occasion not suitable etc) after the end of the period of six months beginning with the day on which the appropriate officer was informed of the matters specified in section 63(3ZA)(b)(i) or (ii).

(3) In sub-paragraph (2) above, "appropriate officer" means the officer investigating the offence for which the person was arrested.

Persons charged etc

10.—(1) A constable may require a person to attend a police station for the purpose of taking a non-intimate sample from him under section 63(3A).

(2) The power under sub-paragraph (1) above may not be exercised in a case falling within section 63(3A)(a) (sample not taken previously) after the end of the period of six months beginning with the day on which he was charged or informed that he would be reported.

(3) The power under sub-paragraph (1) above may not be exercised in a case falling within section 63(3A)(b) (sample taken on a previous occasion not suitable etc) after the end of the period of six months beginning with the day on which the appropriate officer was informed of the matters specified in section 63(3A)(b)(i) or (ii).

(4) In sub-paragraph (3) above "appropriate officer" means the officer investigating the offence for which the person was charged or informed that he would be reported.

Persons convicted etc of an offence in England and Wales

11.—(1) A constable may require a person to attend a police station for the purpose of taking a non-intimate sample from him under section 63(3B).

(2) Where the condition in section 63(3BA)(a) is satisfied (sample not taken previously), the power under sub-paragraph (1) above may not be exercised after the end of the period of two years beginning with—

(a) the day on which the person was convicted, cautioned or warned or reprimanded, or

(b) if later, the day on which this Schedule comes into force.

(3) Where the condition in section 63(3BA)(b) is satisfied (sample taken on a previous occasion not suitable etc), the power under sub-paragraph (1) above may not be exercised after the end of the period of two years beginning with—

(a) the day on which an appropriate officer was informed of the matters specified in section 63(3BA)(b)(i) or (ii), or

(b) if later, the day on which this Schedule comes into force.

(4) In sub-paragraph (3)(a) above "appropriate officer" means an officer of the police force which investigated the offence in question.

(5) Sub-paragraphs (2) and (3) above do not apply where—

(a) the offence is a qualifying offence (whether or not it was such an offence at the time of the conviction, caution or warning or reprimand), or

(b) he was convicted before 10th April 1995 and is a person to whom section 1 of the *Criminal Evidence (Amendment) Act* 1997 applies.

Persons subject to a control order

[12. A constable may require a person to attend a police station for the purpose of taking a non-intimate sample from him under section 63(3D).]

Persons convicted etc of an offence outside England and Wales

13. A constable may require a person to attend a police station for the purpose of taking a non-intimate sample from him under section 63(3E).

Multiple exercise of power

14.—(1) Where a non-intimate sample has been taken from a person under section 63 on two occasions in relation to any offence, he may not under this Schedule be required to attend a police station to have another such sample taken from him under that section in relation to that offence on a subsequent occasion without the authorisation of an officer of at least the rank of inspector.

(2) Where an authorisation is given under sub-paragraph (1) above—

(a) the fact of the authorisation, and

(b) the reasons for giving it,

shall be recorded as soon as practicable after it has been given.

PART 4

General and Supplementary

Requirement to have power to take fingerprints or sample

1–178 15. A power conferred by this Schedule to require a person to attend a police station for the purposes of taking fingerprints or a sample under any provision of this Act may be exercised only in a case where the fingerprints or sample may be taken from the person under that provision (and, in particular, if any necessary authorisation for taking the fingerprints or sample under that provision has been obtained).

Date and time of attendance

16.—(1) A requirement under this Schedule—

(a) shall give the person a period of at least seven days within which he must attend the police station; and

(b) may direct him so to attend at a specified time of day or between specified times of day.

(2) In specifying a period or time or times of day for the purposes of sub-paragraph (1) above, the constable shall consider whether the fingerprints or sample could reasonably be

taken at a time when the person is for any other reason required to attend the police station.

(3) A requirement under this Schedule may specify a period shorter than seven days if—

(a) there is an urgent need for the fingerprints or sample for the purposes of the investigation of an offence; and

(b) the shorter period is authorised by an officer of at least the rank of inspector.

(4) Where an authorisation is given under sub-paragraph (3)(b) above—

(a) the fact of the authorisation, and

(b) the reasons for giving it,

shall be recorded as soon as practicable after it has been given.

(5) If the constable giving a requirement under this Schedule and the person to whom it is given so agree, it may be varied so as to specify any period within which, or date or time at which, the person must attend; but a variation shall not have effect unless confirmed by the constable in writing.

Enforcement

17. A constable may arrest without warrant a person who has failed to comply with a requirement under this Schedule.

[This schedule is inserted into the 1984 Act by the *Crime and Security Act* 2010, s.6(2), save that paras 4 and 12 come into force on a day to be appointed: see the *Crime and Security Act 2010 (Commencement No. 3) Order* 2011 (S.I. 2011 No. 414).]

Testing for the presence of Class A drugs

Under ss.63B and 63C of the 1984 Act the police have power to take a sample from a detained person to test for Class A drugs. The Act has been amended by the *Criminal Justice Act* 2003 and the *Drugs Act* 2005, s.7, so that such tests can now be done when a person is either arrested or charged. The power is exercisable in respect of trigger offences (listed in Sched. 6 to the *Criminal Justice and Court Services Act* 2000) or when a senior police officer has reasonable grounds to suspect that the misuse of Class A drugs was a causal or contributory factor to the offence. Once a sample has been taken and proves positive the result can be used in court to inform bail and sentencing decisions. It may also give rise to the police requiring the defendant to attend for drug assessment and treatment. For full details of the statutory provisions refer to Ch.18, Offences Involving Drugs. **1–179**

Destruction of fingerprints and samples

Police and Criminal Evidence Act 1984, s.64

Destruction of fingerprints and samples

64.—(1A) *Where—* **1–180**

(a) *fingerprints, impressions of footwear or samples are taken from a person in connection with the investigation of an offence, and*

(b) *subsection (3) below does not require them to be destroyed,*

the fingerprints, impressions of footwear or samples may be retained after they have fulfilled the purposes for which they were taken but shall not be used by any person except for purposes related to the prevention or detection of crime, the investigation of an offence, the conduct of a prosecution or the identification of a deceased person or of the person from whom a body part came] *[except as described in subsection (1AB)].*

[(1AA) *Where fingerprints or samples are taken from a person who is subject to a control order the fingerprints or samples may be retained after they have fulfilled the purposes for which they were taken but shall not be used by any person except as described in subsection (1AB).]*

[(1AB) *The fingerprints, impressions of footwear or samples may be used—*

(a) *in the interests of national security,*

(b) *for purposes related to the prevention or detection of crime, the investigation of an offence or the conduct of a prosecution, or*

(c) *for purposes related to the identification of a deceased person or of the person from whom the material came.]*

(1B) *In subsection (1A) [, (1AA)] [or (1AB)] above—*

(a) *the reference to using a fingerprint or an impression of footwear includes a reference to allowing any check to be made against it under section 63A(1) or (1C)[above and to disclosing it to any person;*

(b) *the reference to using a sample includes a reference to allowing any check to be made under section 63A(1) or (1C) above against it or against information derived from it and to disclosing it or any such information to any person;*

(c) *the reference to crime includes a reference to any conduct which—*

(i) *constitutes one or more criminal offences (whether under the law of a part of the United Kingdom or of a country or territory outside the United Kingdom); or*

(ii) *is, or corresponds to, any conduct which, if it all took place in any one part of the United Kingdom, would constitute one or more criminal offences;*

and

(d) *the references to an investigation and to a prosecution include references, respectively, to any investigation outside the United Kingdom of any crime or suspected crime and to a prosecution brought in respect of any crime in a country or territory outside the United Kingdom.*

(1BA) *Fingerprints taken from a person by virtue of section 61(6A) above must be destroyed as soon as they have fulfilled the purpose for which they were taken.*

(3) *If—*

(a) *fingerprints, impressions of footwear or samples are taken from a person in connection with the investigation of an offence; and*

(b) *that person is not suspected of having committed the offence,*

they must, except as provided in the following provisions of this section, be destroyed as soon as they have fulfilled the purpose for which they were taken.

1–181 (3AA) *Samples, fingerprints and impressions of footwear are not required to be destroyed under subsection (3) above if—*

(a) *they were taken for the purposes of the investigation of an offence of which a person has been convicted; and*

(b) *a sample, fingerprint, (or as the case may be) an impression of footwear was also taken from the convicted person for the purposes of that investigation.*

(3AB) *Subject to subsection (3AC) below, where a person is entitled under subsection (1BA) or (3) above to the destruction of any fingerprint or sample taken from him (or would be but for subsection (3AA) above), neither the fingerprint, nor the impression of footwear, nor the sample, nor any information derived from the sample, shall be used—*

(a) *in evidence against the person who is or would be entitled to the destruction of that fingerprint, impression of footwear or sample; or*

(b) *for the purposes of the investigation of any offence;*

and subsection (1B) above applies for the purposes of this subsection as it applies for the purposes of subsection (1A) above.

(3AC) *Where a person from whom a fingerprint, impression of footwear or sample has been taken consents in writing to its retention—*

(a) *that fingerprint, impression of footwear or sample need not be destroyed under subsection (3) above;*

(b) *subsection (3AB) above shall not restrict the use that may be made of the fingerprint, impression of footwear or sample or, in the case of a sample, of any information derived from it; and*

(c) *that consent shall be treated as comprising a consent for the purposes of section 63A(1C) above;*

and a consent given for the purpose of this subsection shall not be capable of being withdrawn.

This subsection does not apply to fingerprints taken from a person by virtue of section 61(6A) above.

(3AD) *For the purposes of subsection (3AC) above it shall be immaterial whether the consent is given at, before or after the time when the entitlement to the destruction of the fingerprint, impression of footwear or sample arises.*

(4) [Repealed by Criminal Justice and Police Act 2001, s.137, and Sched. 7, Pt II.]

(5) *If fingerprints or impressions of footwear are destroyed—*

(a) *any copies of the fingerprints or impressions of footwear shall also be destroyed; and*

(b) *any chief officer of police controlling access to computer data relating to the fingerprints or impressions of footwear shall make access to the data impossible, as soon as it is practicable to do so.*

(6) *A person who asks to be allowed to witness the destruction of his fingerprints or impressions of footwear or copies of them shall have a right to witness it.*

(6A) *If—*

(a) *subsection (5)(b) above falls to be complied with; and*

(b) *the person to whose fingerprints or impressions of footwear the data relate asks for a certificate that it has been complied with,*

such a certificate shall be issued to him, not later than the end of the period of three months beginning with the day on which he asks for it, by the responsible chief officer of police or a person authorised by him or on his behalf for the purposes of this section.

(6B) *In this section—*

"the responsible chief officer of police" means the chief officer of police in whose police area the computer data were put on to the computer.

(7) *Nothing in this section—* **1–182**

(a) *affects any power conferred by paragraph 18(2) of Schedule 2 to the Immigration Act 1971 or section 20 of the Immigration and Asylum Act 1999 (disclosure of police information to the Secretary of State for use for immigration purposes); or*

(b) *applies to a person arrested or detained under the terrorism provisions.*

[This section is printed as amended by the *Criminal Justice Act* 1988, s.148; the *Criminal Justice and Public Order Act* 1994, s.57; the *Police Act* 1996, s.103, and Sched. 7, para. 37; the *Criminal Justice and Police Act* 2001, s.82; and the *Serious Organised Crime and Police Act* 2005, ss.117(6)–(10) and 118(1) and (4); and as amended, as from a day to be appointed by the *Counter-Terrorism Act* 2008, ss.10(4) and (6) (insertion of subs. (1AA) and consequential amendments in square brackets), and 14(1), (4)-(6) (insertion of subs. (1AB) and consequential amendments in square brackets, omissions not italicised). As from a day to be appointed, this version of s.64 is substituted by a new s.64, *post*, § 1–179a: *Crime and Security Act* 2010, s.14(1).]

For "fingerprints", see *ante*, § 1–159; for "intimate sample", see *ante*, § 1–167; and **1–183** for "non-intimate sample", see *ante*, § 1–170. Section 18 of the *Counter-Terrorism Act* 2008 (not in force as at July 20, 2010) provides a statutory framework for the use and retention of DNA samples or profiles and fingerprints that are not held subject to other statutory provisions, and there are limitations on their use (in subs. (2)) that match those in s.64(1AB) of the 1984 Act, as amended (*ante*). However, s.18(3) contains a condition that the samples and fingerprints cannot be used for such purposes unless either they have been (i) obtained by the law enforcement authority that holds them pursuant to an authorisation under Part of the *Police Act* 1997 or Pt 2 of the *Regulation of Investigatory Powers Act* 2000, (ii) supplied to the authority by another law enforcement authority, or (iii) otherwise lawfully obtained or acquired by the authority for any of the purposes set out in subsection (2).

In *Att.-Gen.'s Reference (No. 3 of 1999)* [2001] 1 Cr.App.R. 34, CA, it was held that the combined effect of the previous version of s.64(1) and (3B) was to enact an absolute prohibition on the use of samples which should have been destroyed, or information derived therefrom, in any subsequent proceedings. In the House of Lords ([2001] 2 A.C. 1), it was held that such evidence was not inadmissible merely because of a breach of these provisions, but such a breach was a relevant factor for the judge to take into account in exercising his discretion to exclude such evidence. Section 64 has now been amended by the *Criminal Justice and Police Act* 2001, s.82, so that the only "prohibition" relates to a person who provides a sample but who is not suspected of an offence. Following the reasoning in *Att.-Gen.'s Reference (No. 3 of 1999)*, if the sample in respect of such a person is improperly retained, this will not lead to the automatic exclusion of evidence derived therefrom.

In *S. v. UK* (2009) 48 E.H.R.R. 50, ECtHR, it was held, contrary to the domestic courts' view (see [2004] 1 W.L.R. 2196, HL), that the retention of fingerprints and samples under section 64(1A), pursuant to guidelines issued by the Association of Chief Police Officers, was incompatible with art. 8(1) of the ECHR, in that the blanket and indiscriminate nature of the power failed to strike a fair balance between the competing public and private interests and overstepped any acceptable margin of appreciation in that regard; of particular concern was that unconvicted persons, entitled to the presumption of innocence, were to be treated in the same way as convicted persons; and the retention of an unconvicted person's data was especially harmful in the case of minors, given their special situation and the importance of their development and integration into society.

However, in *R. (G.C.) v. Commr of Police of the Metropolis and Secretary of State for the Home Department (interested party)*; *R. (C.) v. Same and Same (interested party)*, *The Times*, May 19, 2011, SC, it was held by a majority that section 64(1A) does not require the police to hold the relevant data indefinitely; the discretion afforded by the existing ACPO guidelines (despite modification, after the European Court of Human Rights' decision in *S. v. U.K.*, to remove all samples relating to children under the age of 10) are unlawful, because they are in breach of the ECHR. The court noted that the government proposes to amend the legislative regime so that data in relation to unconvicted persons may only be retained for a limited time and only in relation to particular crimes. It seems doubtful whether the new s.64 and ss.64ZA to 64ZN (*post*, §§ 1–184 *et seq.*), inserted into the 1984 Act as from a day to be appointed by the *Crime and Security Act* 2010 in response to *S. v. U.K.*, will be brought into force.

The restriction in subs. (1A) applies to fingerprints and samples taken from volunteers and victims, as well as from suspects: *Lambeth London Borough v. S., C., V. and J. (by his guardian)* [2007] 1 F.L.R. 152, Fam. D. (Ryder J.).

[Police and Criminal Evidence Act 1984, s.64

Retention of samples and fingerprints, etc generally

1–184 **64.**—(1) This section applies to the following material—

(a) fingerprints, samples or impressions of footwear—

(i) taken from a person under any power conferred by this Part of this Act, or

(ii) taken in connection with the investigation of an offence with the consent of the person from whom they were taken, and

(b) a DNA profile derived from a DNA sample falling within paragraph (a).

(2) Material to which this section applies may be retained after it has fulfilled the purpose for which it was taken or derived.

(3) This section is subject to sections 64ZA to 64ZJ.

(4) This section and sections 64ZA to 64ZH do not apply to material to which paragraph 14 of Schedule 8 to the *Terrorism Act* 2000 applies.

(5) Any reference in those sections to a person being arrested for or charged with an offence does not include a reference to a person—

(a) being arrested under section 41 of the *Terrorism Act* 2000, or

(b) being charged with an offence following an arrest under that section.

(6) Nothing in this section, or sections 64ZA to 64ZN, affects any power conferred by—

(a) paragraph 18(2) of Schedule 2 to the*Immigration Act* 1971 (power to take reasonable steps to identify a person detained), or

(b) section 20 of the*Immigration and Asylum Act* 1999 (disclosure of police information to the Secretary of State for use for immigration purposes).]

[This section is substituted for the previous version of s.64, as from a day to be appointed, by the *Crime and Security Act* 2010, s.14(1).]

For the previous version of s.64, and the relevant case-law, see *ante*, §§ 1–176 *et seq.*

Destruction, etc., of samples

Section 14(2) of the *Crime and Security Act* 2010 inserts (as from a day to be appointed) new ss.64ZA to 64ZN into the 1984 Act. These sections, together with new s.64 (*ante*), establish a framework for the retention and destruction of fingerprints, impressions of footwear and samples taken under the powers conferred by Pt V, or with consent in connection with the investigation of an offence. **1-185**

Whereas the default position is that material to which s.64 applies may be retained after it has fulfilled the purpose for which it was taken or derived (s.64(2)), ss.64ZA to 64ZJ provide for circumstances in which this indefinite retention of samples and data is limited. By virtue of s.64ZA, a DNA sample must be destroyed as soon as a DNA profile has been derived from it; and all samples, including DNA samples, must be destroyed within six months of their being taken. Fingerprints, impressions of footwear and DNA profiles derived from DNA samples that have been given by an individual with his consent must also be destroyed as soon as they have fulfilled the purpose for which they were taken, unless the individual is subsequently convicted, has previous convictions or consents to its retention, or it is material to which any of ss.64ZC to 64ZH applies (s.64ZB). Where material has been taken from a person who is subject to a control order (but who has no convictions other than an "exempt conviction" (as to which, see s.64ZC(5)(b))), it must be destroyed within two years of the order ceasing to have effect (s.64ZC), unless the person is convicted of a recordable offence within that period. The retention period for material relating to an adult with no convictions other than an "exempt conviction", who has been arrested but not convicted of a recordable offence, or a 16- or 17-year-old with no convictions other than an "exempt conviction" arrested but not convicted of a "qualifying offence" (as defined in s.65A), is six years (ss.64ZD and 64ZG). The retention period for material relating to a person under 18 with no previous convictions convicted of a recordable offence other than a qualifying offence is five years (s.64ZH); and the retention period for all other persons under 18 with no convictions other than an "exempt conviction" who are arrested but not convicted of a recordable or (persons under 16 only) a qualifying offence is three years (ss.64ZE and 64ZF). Destruction is not, however, required under ss.64ZD to 64ZH where the relevant person has subsequently been arrested for, charged with or convicted of a further recordable offence. Section 64ZJ provides that fingerprints taken from a person by virtue of s.61(6A) must be destroyed as soon as they have fulfilled the purpose for which they were taken. Section 64ZI contains supplementary provision, including as to when a conviction is "exempt".

Section 64ZK enables DNA profiles and certain fingerprints that would otherwise be required to be destroyed to be retained for a further two years for the purposes of national security, and such period may be further extended for further periods of two years. Section 64ZL provides for the retention of material where the person to whom the material relates consents; but consent may be withdrawn at any time. When fingerprints, impressions of footwear or DNA profiles are to be destroyed by virtue of any of these sections, all copies must also be destroyed except copies of DNA profiles kept in a manner which does not identify the persons to whom they relate (s.64ZM(1) and (2)). By virtue of s.64ZM(3), a person may request the police to notify him within three months of anything relating to him being destroyed under these sections. The purposes for which retained material (including material which is required to be destroyed) may be used are set out in s.64ZN. These are confined to national security, a terrorist investigation, the prevention or detection of crime, the investigation of an offence, the conduct of a prosecution and the identification of a deceased person or of the person to whom the material relates.

Section 18 of the *Counter-Terrorism Act* 2008 (not in force as of July 20, 2010) provides a statutory framework for the use and retention of DNA samples or profiles and fingerprints that are not held subject to other statutory provisions. As amended (as from a day to be appointed) by s.21(1) to (7) of the *Crime and Security Act* 2010, it now also contains provisions relating to the destruction of such material, which broadly **1-186** correspond to those in the 1984 Act (*ante*). Section 18A (inserted, as from a day to be appointed, by the 2010 Act, s.21(8)) contains interpretation provisions in respect of s.18.

Photographing of suspects

Police and Criminal Evidence Act 1984, s.64A

Photographing of suspects etc

1–187 **64A.**—(1) A person who is detained at a police station may be photographed—

(a) with the appropriate consent; or

(b) if the appropriate consent is withheld or it is not practicable to obtain it, without it.

(1A) A person falling within subsection (1B) below may, on the occasion of the relevant event referred to in subsection (1B), be photographed elsewhere than at a police station—

(a) with the appropriate consent; or

(b) if the appropriate consent is withheld or it is not practicable to obtain it, without it.

(1B) A person falls within this subsection if he has been—

(a) arrested by a constable for an offence;

(b) taken into custody by a constable after being arrested for an offence by a person other than a constable;

(c) made subject to a requirement to wait with a community support officer under paragraph 2(3) or (3B) of Schedule 4 to the *Police Reform Act* 2002 ("the 2002 Act");

(d) given a penalty notice by a constable in uniform under Chapter 1 of Part 1 of the *Criminal Justice and Police Act* 2001, a penalty notice by a constable under section 444A of the *Education Act* 1996, or a fixed penalty notice by a constable in uniform under section 54 of the *Road Traffic Offenders Act* 1988;

(e) given a notice in relation to a relevant fixed penalty offence (within the meaning of paragraph 1 of Schedule 4 to the 2002 Act) by a community support officer by virtue of a designation applying that paragraph to him; or

(f) given a notice in relation to a relevant fixed penalty offence (within the meaning of paragraph 1 of Schedule 5 to the 2002 Act) by an accredited person by virtue of accreditation specifying that that paragraph applies to him.

(2) A person proposing to take a photograph of any person under this section—

(a) may, for the purpose of doing so, require the removal of any item or substance worn on or over the whole or any part of the head or face of the person to be photographed; and

(b) if the requirement is not complied with, may remove the item or substance himself.

(3) Where a photograph may be taken under this section, the only persons entitled to take the photograph are constables.

(4) A photograph taken under this section—

(a) may be used by, or disclosed to, any person for any purpose related to the prevention or detection of crime, the investigation of an offence or the conduct of a prosecution or to the enforcement of a sentence; and

(b) after being so used or disclosed, may be retained but may not be used or disclosed except for a purpose so related.

(5) In subsection (4)—

(a) the reference to crime includes a reference to any conduct which—

(i) constitutes one or more criminal offences (whether under the law of a part of the United Kingdom or of a country or territory outside the United Kingdom); or

(ii) is, or corresponds to, any conduct which, if it all took place in any one part of the United Kingdom, would constitute one or more criminal offences; and

(b) the references to an investigation and to a prosecution include references, respectively, to any investigation outside the United Kingdom of any crime or suspected crime and to a prosecution brought in respect of any crime in a country or territory outside the United Kingdom; and

(c) "sentence" includes any order made by a court in England and Wales when dealing with an offender in respect of his offence.

(6) References in this section to taking a photograph include references to using any process by means of which a visual image may be produced; and references to photographing a person shall be construed accordingly.

(6A) In this section, a "photograph" includes a moving image, and corresponding expressions shall be construed accordingly.

(7) Nothing in this section applies to a person arrested under an extradition arrest power.

[This section was inserted by the *Anti-Terrorism, Crime and Security Act* 2001, s.92. It is printed as amended by the *Police Reform Act* 2002, s.107(1), and Sched. 7, para. 9(5); the *Extradition Act* 2003, s.169(5); and the *Serious Organised Crime and Police Act* 2005, s.116.]

For "appropriate consent", see *ante*, § 1–165.

(4) Tape recording of interviews

Police and Criminal Evidence Act 1984, s.60

Tape-recording of interviews

60.—(1) It shall be the duty of the Secretary of State— **1–188**

(a) to issue a code of practice in connection with the tape-recording of interviews of persons suspected of the commission of criminal offences which are held by police officers at police stations; and

(b) to make an order requiring the tape-recording of interviews of persons suspected of the commission of criminal offences, or of such descriptions of criminal offences as may be specified in the order, which are so held, in accordance with the code as it has effect for the time being.

(2) An order under subsection (1) above shall be made by statutory instrument and shall be subject to annulment in pursuance of a resolution of either House of Parliament.

Code E is the relevant code for the Tape Recording of Interviews with Suspects. The relevant order by the Secretary of State has been made for all police areas and now all interviews of those suspected of the commission of indictable offences must be tape recorded at police stations. The only exemption is for terrorism offences. **1–189**

The latest revision of Code E came into force on May 1, 2010, and applies to interviews carried out after that date, notwithstanding that the interview may have commenced before that time: see the preamble to the code itself. The revised code permits audio recording of interviews to secure digital network as an alternative to removable media format.

In addition there is a Practice Direction ([2002] 1 W.L.R. 2870) about the tape recording of police interviews in relation to the preparation for proceedings in the Crown Court which may also assist for magistrates' court proceedings.

Equipment is available for tapes to be played in the magistrates' courts and either full or edited transcripts may be adduced as evidence by the interviewing officer.

(5) Visual recording of interviews

Police and Criminal Evidence Act 1984, s.60A

Visual recording of interviews

60A.—(1) The Secretary of State shall have power— **1–190**

(a) to issue a code of practice for the visual recording of interviews held by police officers at police stations; and

(b) to make an order requiring the visual recording of interviews so held, and requiring the visual recording to be in accordance with the code for the time being in force under this section.

(2) A requirement imposed by an order under this section may be imposed in relation to such cases or police stations in such areas, or both, as may be specified or described in the order.

(3) An order under subsection (1) above shall be made by statutory instrument and shall be subject to annulment in pursuance of a resolution of either House of Parliament.

(4) In this section—

(a) references to any interview are references to an interview of a person suspected of a criminal offence; and

(b) references to a visual recording include references to a visual recording in which an audio recording is comprised.

[This section was inserted by the *Criminal Justice and Police Act* 2001, s.76(1).]

Orders making visual recordings of interview mandatory in certain police areas were revoked in November 2003. Police officers retain a discretion to record interviews visually.

Code F is the Code of Practice covering the Visual Recording of Interviews with Suspects.

The latest revision of Code F came into force on May 1, 2010, and applies to interviews carried out after that date, notwithstanding that the interview may have commenced before then: see the preamble to the code itself. The revised code permits visual recording of interviews by secure digital network as an alternative to the use of removable media format.

(6) Right to have someone informed when arrested

Police and Criminal Evidence Act 1984, s.56

Right to have someone informed when arrested

1–191 **56.**—(1) Where a person has been arrested and is being held in custody in a police station or other premises, he shall be entitled, if he so requests, to have one friend or relative or other person who is known to him or who is likely to take an interest in his welfare told, as soon as is practicable except to the extent that delay is permitted by this section, that he has been arrested and is being detained there.

(2) Delay is only permitted—

(a) in the case of a person who is in police detention for an indictable offence; and

(b) if an officer of at least the rank of inspector authorises it.

(3) In any case the person in custody must be permitted to exercise the right conferred by subsection (1) above within 36 hours from the relevant time, as defined in section 41(2) above.

(4) An officer may give an authorisation under subsection (2) above orally or in writing but, if he gives it orally, he shall confirm it in writing as soon as is practicable.

(5) Subject to subsection (5A) below an officer may only authorise delay where he has reasonable grounds for believing that telling the named person of the arrest—

(a) will lead to interference with or harm to evidence connected with an indictable offence or interference with or physical injury to other persons; or

(b) will lead to the alerting of other persons suspected of having committed such an offence but not yet arrested for it; or

(c) will hinder the recovery of any property obtained as a result of such an offence.

(5A) An officer may also authorise delay where he has reasonable grounds for believing that—

(a) the person detained for an indictable offence has benefited from his criminal conduct, and

(b) the recovery of the value of the property constituting the benefit will be hindered by telling the named person of the arrest.

(5B) For the purposes of subsection (5A) above the question whether a person has benefited from his criminal conduct is to be decided in accordance with Part 2 of the *Proceeds of Crime Act* 2002.

(6) If a delay is authorised—

(a) the detained person shall be told the reason for it; and

(b) the reason shall be noted on his custody record.

(7) The duties imposed by subsection (6) above shall be performed as soon as is practicable.

(8) The rights conferred by this section on a person detained at a police station or other premises are exercisable whenever he is transferred from one place to another; and this section applies to each subsequent occasion on which they are exercisable as it applies to the first such occasion.

(9) There may be no further delay in permitting the exercise of the right conferred by subsection (1) above once the reason for authorising delay ceases to subsist.

(10) Nothing in this section applies to a person arrested or detained under the terrorism provisions.

[This section is printed as amended and repealed in part by the *Drug Trafficking Offences Act* 1986, s.32; the *Criminal Justice Act* 1988, s.99(2); the *Terrorism Act* 2000, s.125, and Sched. 15, para. 5(5); the *Criminal Justice and Police Act* 2001, s.74; the *Proceeds of Crime Act* 2002, s.456, and Sched. 11, para. 14(2); and the *Serious Organised Crime and Police Act* 2005, s.111, and Sched. 7, para. 43(1) and (9).]

Code C deals with the right of a person detained at the police station not to be held incommunicado (para. C5) and Annex B deals with the delay in notifying arrest or allowing access to legal advice. **1–192**

(7) Additional rights of children and young persons

Children and Young Persons Act 1933, s.34

34.—(1) [*Repealed by* Criminal Justice Act *1991, s.56.*] **1–193**

(2) Where a child or young person is in police detention, such steps as are practicable shall be taken to ascertain the identity of a person responsible for his welfare.

(3) If it is practicable to ascertain the identity of a person responsible for the welfare of the child or young person, that person shall be informed, unless it is not practicable to do so—

(a) that the child or young person has been arrested;

(b) why he has been arrested; and

(c) where he is being detained.

(4) Where information falls to be given under subsection (3) above, it shall be given as soon as it is practicable to do so.

(5) For the purposes of this section the persons who may be responsible for the welfare of a child or young person are—

(a) his parent or guardian; or

(b) any other person who has for the time being assumed responsibility for his welfare.

(6) If it is practicable to give a person responsible for the welfare of the child or young person the information required by subsection (3) above, that person shall be given it as soon as it is practicable to do so.

(7) If it appears that at the time of his arrest a supervision order, as defined inPart IV of the *Children Act* 1989, is in force in respect of him, the person responsible for his supervision shall also be informed as described in subsection (3) above as soon as it is reasonably practicable to do so.

(7A) If it appears that at the time of his arrest the child or young person is being provided with accommodation by or on behalf of a local authority under section 20 of the *Children Act* 1989, the local authority shall also be informed as described in subsection (3) above as soon as it is reasonably practicable to do so.

(8) The reference to a parent or guardian in subsection (5) above is in the case of a child or young person in the care of a local authority, a reference to that authority.

(9) The rights conferred on a child or young person by subsections (2) to (8) above are in addition to his rights under section 56 of the *Police and Criminal Evidence Act* 1984.

(10) The reference in subsection (2) above to a child or young person who is in police

detention includes a reference to a child or young person who has been detained under the terrorism provisions; and in subsection (3) above "arrest" includes such detention.

(11) In subsection (10) above "the terrorism provisions" has the meaning assigned to it by section 65 of the *Police and Criminal Evidence Act* 1984.

[Subsection (2) to (11) were substituted by the *PACE Act* 1984, s.57. They are printed as subsequently amended and repealed in part by the *Children Act* 1989, s.108(5) and (7), and Scheds 13, para. 6(2) and (3), and 15; the *Powers of Criminal Courts (Sentencing) Act* 2000, s.165(1), and Sched. 9, para. 1; and the *Criminal Justice and Immigration Act* 2008, s.149, and Sched.28, Pt 1.]

(8) Right of access to a solicitor

Police and Criminal Evidence Act 1984, s.58

Access to legal advice

1–194 **58.**—(1) A person arrested and held in custody in a police station or other premises shall be entitled, if he so requests, to consult a solicitor privately at any time.

(2) Subject to subsection (3) below, a request under subsection (1) above and the time at which it was made shall be recorded in the custody record.

(3) Such a request need not be recorded in the custody record of a person who makes it at a time while he is at a court after being charged with an offence.

(4) If a person makes such a request, he must be permitted to consult a solicitor as soon as is practicable except to the extent that delay is permitted by this section.

(5) In any case he must be permitted to consult a solicitor within 36 hours from the relevant time, as defined in section 41(2) above.

(6) Delay in compliance with a request is only permitted—

(a) in the case of a person who is in police detention for an indictable offence; and

(b) if an officer of at least the rank of superintendent authorises it.

(7) An officer may give an authorisation under subsection (6) above orally or in writing but, if he gives it orally, he shall confirm it in writing as soon as is practicable.

(8) Subject to subsection (8A) below an officer may only authorise delay where he has reasonable grounds for believing that the exercise of the right conferred by subsection (1) above at the time when the person detained desires to exercise it—

(a) will lead to interference with or harm to evidence connected with an indictable offence or interference with or physical injury to other persons; or

(b) will lead to the alerting of other persons suspected of having committed such an offence but not yet arrested for it; or

(c) will hinder the recovery of any property obtained as a result of such an offence.

(8A) An officer may also authorise delay where he has reasonable grounds for believing that—

(a) the person detained for the indictable offence has benefited from his criminal conduct, and

(b) the recovery of the value of the property constituting the benefit will be hindered by the exercise of the right conferred by subsection (1) above.

(8B) For the purposes of subsection (8A) above the question whether a person has benefited from his criminal conduct is to be decided in accordance with Part 2 of the *Proceeds of Crime Act* 2002.

(9) If delay is authorised—

(a) the detained person shall be told the reason for it; and

(b) the reason shall be noted on his custody record.

(10) The duties imposed by subsection (9) above shall be performed as soon as is practicable.

(11) There may be no further delay in permitting the exercise of the right conferred by subsection (1) above once the reason for authorising delay ceases to subsist.

(12) Nothing in this section applies to a person arrested or detained under the terrorism provisions.

[This section is printed as amended by the *Drug Trafficking Offences Act* 1986, s.32;

the *Criminal Justice Act* 1988, s.99(3); the *Terrorism Act* 2000, s.125, and Sched. 15, para. 5(6); the *Proceeds of Crime Act* 2002, s.456, and Sched. 11, para. 14(3); and the *Serious Organised Crime and Police Act* 2005, s.111, and Sched. 7, para. 43(1) and (9).]

Right of access to a solicitor

Section 58 grants a person arrested and "held in custody in a police station or other premises" the right to consult a solicitor "if he so requests". Section 23 (*ante*, § 1–65) defines "premises" as including "any place" and specifies a number of examples such as vehicles. In *Kerawalla* [1991] Crim.L.R. 451, CA, it was held that "held in custody" is narrower than "in custody", so that a person arrested and detained may be in custody but not yet "held in custody" for the purposes of s.58 until his custody has been authorised, as by a custody officer who satisfies himself that continued detention is authorised. *Cf. Sanusi* [1992] Crim.L.R. 43, CA (Customs officers' area at airport tantamount to a police station). **1–195**

As to the duty to inform a person under arrest at a police station of his right to consult privately with a solicitor and that free independent legal advice is available, see Code C:3.1 and 6.1; and as to the duty to remind a person being interviewed at a police station or other authorised place of detention of these rights, see Code C:11.2. As to the duty to take an arrestee to a police station as soon as practicable after arrest, see s.30 (*ante*, § 1–122).

The right of access to a solicitor under s.58(1) does not extend to a person on remand in custody at a magistrates' court, but there is a right of access at common law to be permitted to consult a solicitor as soon as reasonably practicable: *R. v. Chief Constable of South Wales, ex p. Merrick* [1994] 1 W.L.R. 663, DC.

A person, not under arrest, who is interviewed under caution by a trading standards officer other than at a police station, has no entitlement to non-means tested free legal advice: *R. (Beale) v. South East Wiltshire Magistrates' Court*, 167 J.P. 41, DC.

Denial of access

In *Samuel* [1988] Q.B. 615, 87 Cr.App.R. 232, CA, the right of access to legal advice was described as "one of the most important and fundamental rights of a citizen" (at pp. 630, 245). Where it was sought to justify denial of the right of access to a solicitor on "reasonable grounds", that could not be done except by reference to specific circumstances including evidence about the person detained or the actual solicitor involved. The word "will" in s.58(8) is deliberately restrictive implying, in conjunction with "belief", a belief that it would very probably happen. Such a belief would have to relate to an individual solicitor rather than solicitors generally or, in most instances, a duty solicitor (see also, on this point, *Silcott, Braithwaite and Raghip*, *The Times*, December 9, 1991, CA). Cases where solicitors were inadvertently used to pass on coded messages would be rare (although the court in *Alladice* (1988) 87 Cr.App.R. 380, CA, seemed to think otherwise). **1–196**

A chief constable is not entitled to make a blanket order banning a probationary solicitor's representative from attending the police station to advise persons in custody. He could, however, under Code C:6.12A and 6.13, advise his officers that a particular representative was likely to hinder an investigation and the appropriate officer in a particular case could then decide whether he should be excluded: *R. (Thompson) v. Chief Constable of Northumbria Police* [2001] 1 W.L.R. 1342, CA.

Consequences of breach of section 58

Where there is a breach of s.58, a decision about admissibility will be governed by ss.76 and 78 of the 1984 *Act*: *Alladice, ante*. For cases where it was held on appeal that interviews in breach of s.58 should have been excluded under s.76, see *McGovern* (1990) 92 Cr.App.R. 228, CA (defendant aged 19, six months' pregnant, of limited intelligence), and *Chung* (1990) 92 Cr.App.R. 314, CA; and, under s.78, see *Samuel, ante*, *Absolam* (1988) 88 Cr.App.R. 332, CA; *Parris* (1988) 89 Cr.App.R. 68, CA; *Walsh* **1–197**

(1990) 91 Cr.App.R. 161, CA; and *Beycan* [1990] Crim.L.R. 185, CA. For cases where breaches of s.58 did not prevent the interviews' admissibility, see *Alladice*, *ante*, and *Dunford* (1991) 91 Cr.App.R. 150, CA.

Section 58 and drink driving cases

1–198 In *DPP v. Billington* (1988) 87 Cr.App.R. 68, DC, it was held:

(a) that there was nothing in s.58 or Code C which required the police to delay the taking of a specimen of breath, blood or urine for analysis under the *Road Traffic Act* 1988, s.7; and

(b) that failure to accord the defendant the right of consulting a solicitor as soon as practicable under s.58 did not thereby furnish the defendant with a reasonable excuse for failing to provide a specimen for analysis.

Billington was applied in *DPP v. Skinner*; *DPP v. Cornell* [1990] R.T.R. 254, DC, which was itself followed in *DPP v. Whalley* [1991] R.T.R. 161, DC: the effect of these decisions is that an arrested person cannot justify failure to supply a specimen on the ground that he is reading the codes of practice. This also applies to specimens taken under s.8 of the 1988 Act: *DPP v. Ward* [1999] R.T.R. 11, DC. See also *DPP v. Varley*, 163 J.P. 443, DC.

Whilst the public interest requires that the breath test procedure cannot be delayed to any significant extent, if there happens to be a solicitor in the charge room whom the detainee wishes to consult "for a couple of minutes" before deciding whether or not to provide specimens of breath he must be allowed to do so; similarly, if the detainee asks at that stage to speak to his solicitor or to the duty solicitor on the telephone for a couple of minutes and the solicitor is immediately available, he should be allowed to do so. If the detainee does no more than indicate a general desire to have legal advice, this is not a reason to delay the procedure: *Kennedy v. DPP* [2004] R.T.R. 6, DC; followed in *Kirkup v. DPP* [2004] Crim.L.R. 230, DC (where it was observed that a duty solicitor will not necessarily be immediately available or respond promptly), *Whitley v. DPP* [2004] Crim.L.R. 585, DC (what is practicable should be considered from the point of view of those at the police station at the time, rather than in hindsight), *Myles v. DPP* [2005] R.T.R. 1, DC (Commonwealth cases of limited assistance) *Causey v. DPP*, 169 J.P. 331, DC, *Gearing v. DPP* [2008] R.T.R. 7, DC (police in breach of s.58 in making no attempt to give effect to defendant's request for legal advice until immediately after she had refused to provide breath specimens, and *Chalupa v. CPS* (2009) 174 J.P. 111, DC (where the authorities are summarised)).

Compatibility with the European Convention on Human Rights

1–199 Article 6(3) of the ECHR normally requires that an accused be allowed the benefit of legal advice in the initial stages of interrogation. The right of private consultation may be limited for good cause: *Murray v. UK*, 22 E.H.R.R. 29, ECtHR. If an accused's right to an effective exercise of his defence rights has been infringed, it is not necessary to prove that the restriction had a prejudicial effect on the course of the trial: *Brennan v. UK* (2002) 34 E.H.R.R. 18, ECtHR.

In the context of legislation which permits adverse inferences to be drawn from silence, the right of access to legal advice is of "paramount importance": *Murray v. UK*, *ante*, at 67. Delaying access to legal advice in such cases, whatever the justification, is incompatible with the right to a fair trial guaranteed by art. 6(1) of the Convention and the right of access to legal advice under art. 6(3)(c): *ibid.*; and reiterated in a number of subsequent European Court of Human Rights cases: see *Condron v. UK* (2001) 31 E.H.R.R. 1; *Magee v. UK* (2001) 31 E.H.R.R. 35; *Averill v. UK* (2001) 31 E.H.R.R. 36. See also *Aspinall* [1999] 2 Cr.App.R. 115 at 121–122, CA; and Code C:10, and Annex C.

Chapter 2

CONSTITUTION AND JURISDICTION

I. INTRODUCTION

The magistrates' court is a creature of statute and although the office of justice of the peace dates back to the 14th century, the powers of the present day magistrate are based on more recent Acts of Parliament. The relevant statutes are the *Magistrates' Courts Act* 1980, which essentially outlines the jurisdiction and powers of the court and the *Courts Act* 2003, which provides for the appointment of magistrates, justices' clerks and district judges and the administration of the court. Parts 1–3 of the Act cover the court system, justices of the peace and the magistrates' courts specifically. **2–1**

Magistrates' Courts Act 1980, s.148

"Magistrates' court"

148.—(1) In this Act the expression "magistrates' court" means any justice or justices of the peace acting under any enactment or by virtue of his or their commission or under the common law. **2–2**

(2) Except where the contrary is expressed, anything authorised or required by this Act to be done by, to or before the magistrates' court by, to or before which any other thing was done, or is to be done, may be done by, to or before any magistrates' court acting in the same local justice area as that court.

A magistrates' court has no jurisdiction unless it is specifically conferred by statute. It is an inferior court and has no inherent jurisdiction. It is not a court of record so transcripts are not taken. The legal adviser may take a manual note of proceedings but this is not a verbatim record. The final record of all decisions and adjudications is the court register, which is generally computer generated and stored. Decisions of the magistrates' courts are subject to appeal to the Crown Court on fact and by way of case stated or judicial review to the High Court on cases of law or mixed fact and law. See Ch.11. **2–3**

A magistrates' court normally comprises of a district judge or magistrates. A district judge sits alone and magistrates sit in benches of not less than two or more than three magistrates: *Magistrates' Courts Act* 1980, s.121; *Justices of the Peace (Size and Chairmanship of Bench) Rules* 2005 (S.I. 2005 No.553). Normally there are three magistrates and objection may be taken to less than that number particularly when trials are to be heard. The problem with a bench of only two is the potential for disagreement. Some exceptions apply where magistrates may sit alone to conduct committals or to adjourn cases and also to give directions in early administrative hearings: *Magistrates' Courts Act* 1980, ss.4, 10; *Crime and Disorder Act* 1998, ss.49 and 50.

II. JUDGES OF THE MAGISTRATES' COURTS

(1) General

2–4 The jurisdiction of the magistrates' courts may be exercised by magistrates or District Judges (Magistrates' Courts) sitting in court with the justices' clerk or a qualified legal adviser.

Magistrates, otherwise known as justices of the peace or lay justices, are part-time unpaid volunteers and district judges are lawyers appointed to a full-time salaried post.

(2) Justices of the Peace

Courts Act 2003, ss.9–11

Meaning of "lay justice"

2–5 **9.** In this Act "lay justice" means a justice of the peace who is not a District Judge (Magistrates' Courts).

Appointment of lay justices etc.

2–6 **10.**—(1) Lay justices are to be appointed for England and Wales by the Lord Chancellor by instrument on behalf and in the name of Her Majesty.

(2) The Lord Chief Justice—

(a) must assign each lay justice to one or more local justice areas, and

(b) may change an assignment so as to assign the lay justice to a different local justice area or to different local justice areas.

(2A) The Lord Chancellor must ensure that arrangements for the exercise, so far as affecting any local justice area, of functions under subsections (1) and (2) include arrangements for consulting persons appearing to him to have special knowledge of matters relevant to the exercise of those functions in relation to that area.

(3) Every lay justice is, by virtue of his office, capable of acting as such in any local justice area (whether or not he is assigned to it); but he may do so only in accordance with arrangements made by Lord Chief Justice.

(4) Rules may make provision about the training courses to be completed before a person may exercise functions as a lay justice in any proceedings or class of proceedings specified in the rules.

(5) Subsection (3) is subject to section 12 (the supplemental list).

(6) The functions conferred on the Lord Chief Justice by subsections (2) and (3) may be exercised only after consulting the Lord Chancellor.

(7) The Lord Chief Justice may nominate a judicial office holder (as defined in section 109(4) of the *Constitutional Reform Act* 2005) to exercise his functions under subsection (2) or (3).

Resignation and removal of lay justices

2–7 **11.**—(1) A lay justice may resign his office at any time.

(2) The Lord Chancellor may remove, with the concurrence of the Lord Chief Justice, a lay justice from his office by an instrument on behalf and in the name of Her Majesty—

(a) on the ground of incapacity or misbehaviour,

(b) on the ground of a persistent failure to meet such standards of competence as are prescribed by a direction given by the Lord Chancellor with the concurrence of the Lord Chief Justice, or

(c) if he is satisfied that the lay justice is declining or neglecting to take a proper part in the exercise of his functions as a justice of the peace.

Justices of the peace, also referred to as magistrates, do not receive a salary for their work but they may claim expenses for travel, subsistence and financial loss: *Courts Act* 2003, s.15. No legal qualification is needed but conversely, there is no bar to barristers or solicitors holding office as a magistrate. Rules may make provision for the training, appraisal and development of lay justices, both at induction stage and for taking the chair in court: *Courts Act* 2003, s.19. **2–8**

Magistrates are addressed in court through the Chairman as "Sir" or "Madam" and collectively as "Your Worships".

(3) District Judges (Magistrates' Courts)

Courts Act 2003, ss.22, 23, 25 and 26

Appointment etc.

22.—(1) Her Majesty may, on the recommendation of the Lord Chancellor, appoint a person who has a 7 year general qualification to be a District Judge (Magistrates' Courts). **2–9**

(2) A District Judge (Magistrates' Courts) must, before acting as such, take the oath of allegiance and judicial oath in accordance with the *Promissory Oaths Act* 1868 and the *Promissory Oaths Act* 1871.

(3) The Lord Chancellor may pay to a District Judge (Magistrates' Courts) such allowances as he may determine.

(4) Any such allowances are in addition to the salary charged on and paid out of the Consolidated Fund under section 9 of the *Administration of Justice Act* 1973.

(5) The Lord Chancellor may, with the concurrence of the Lord Chief Justice, remove a District Judge (Magistrates' Courts) from office on the ground of incapacity or misbehaviour.

Senior District Judge (Chief Magistrate)

23. Her Majesty— **2–10**

(a) may designate one of the District Judges (Magistrates' Courts) to be Senior District Judge (Chief Magistrate), and

(b) if he does so, may designate another of them to be the deputy of the Senior District Judge (Chief Magistrate).

District Judges (Magistrates' Courts) as justices of the peace

25.—(1) A District Judge (Magistrates' Courts) is by virtue of his office a justice of the peace for England and Wales. **2–11**

(2) It is the duty of a District Judge (Magistrates' Courts) to act as a justice of the peace in any local justice area in accordance with arrangements made the Lord Chief Justice, after consulting the Lord Chancellor.

(3) The Lord Chief Justice may nominate a judicial office holder (as defined in section 109(4) of the *Constitutional Reform Act* 2005) to exercise his functions under subsection (2).

District Judges (Magistrates' Courts) able to act alone

26.—(1) Nothing in the 1980 Act— **2–12**

(a) requiring a magistrates' court to be composed of two or more justices, or

(b) limiting the powers of a magistrates' court when composed of a single justice,

applies to a District Judge (Magistrates' Courts).

(2) A District Judge (Magistrates' Courts) may—

(a) do any act, and

(b) exercise alone any jurisdiction,

which can be done or exercised by two justices, apart from granting or transferring a licence.

(3) Any enactment making provision ancillary to the jurisdiction exercisable by two justices of the peace also applies to the jurisdiction of a District Judge (Magistrates' Courts), unless the provision relates to granting or transferring a licence.

(4) This section does not apply to the hearing or determination of family proceedings (as defined by section 65 of the 1980 Act).

(5) "The 1980 Act" means the *Magistrates*' Courts Act 1980.

2–13 District Judges (Magistrates' Courts) are professional, salaried members of the judiciary. Until 1997 they were called stipendiary magistrates and were appointed to particular commission areas generally within large metropolitan areas such as London, Manchester and Leeds. The *Justices of the Peace Act* 1997, s.10A changed the description of the judicial office to District Judge (Magistrates' Courts) and established a national bench led by the Senior District Judge (Chief Magistrate). The district judge will be assigned to a local justice area but may be directed to sit at any court in England and Wales as required: *Courts Act* 2003, s.25.

2–14 Deputy District Judges may also be appointed under s.24 of the *Courts Act* 2003. They are appointed for a rolling fixed term of five years and they sit for up to 50 days a year on a part-time basis. They must have the same qualifications as a full-time District Judge and they have the powers of a full time District Judge.

Unlike magistrates, a district judge will always sit alone in all criminal proceedings: *Courts Act* 2003, s.26. This provision allowing for District Judges (Magistrates' Court) to sit alone extends to their not needing to be accompanied by a legal adviser when sitting in court although the present practice remains for them generally to be so assisted. A recent pilot has been introduced whereby 'court associates' are in court with District Judges. The associates are not legally qualified and they have only an administrative responsibility in court for recording proceedings and organising documentation. They do not provide legal advice to the court. This role is considered to be sufficient as the District Judge is a legally qualified full-time judicial office holder as opposed to the lay justices who are neither required nor expected to have any legal qualification and so rely on the legal advisers for legal advice and assistance. In order to develop the flexibility of judicial resources, s.65 of the *Courts Act* 2003 amends s.8 of the *Supreme Court Act* 1981 to allow District Judges (Magistrates' Courts) to exercise the jurisdiction of the Crown Court. Other functions are also conferred by Sched. 4 to the *Courts Act*. Exercise of this jurisdiction will depend on any future allocation of work that may be made by the Lord Chancellor.

The Judicial College is responsible for training district judges and delivers induction and continuing training. Certain district judges are designated by the Lord Chancellor or the senior district judge to deal with particular types of specialist work such as youth court cases, extradition and applications for warrants of further detention under the *Terrorism Act* 2000.

A district judge is addressed as "Sir" or "Madam".

(4) Justices' clerks

2–15 The justices' clerk and legal advisers give advice on law, practice and procedure to the justices of the peace.

Courts Act 2003, ss.27, 28, 29

Justices' clerks and assistant clerks

2–16 **27.**—(1) A justices' clerk is a person who is—

(a) appointed by the Lord Chancellor, after consulting the Lord Chief Justice, under section 2(1), and

(b) designated by the Lord Chancellor as a justices' clerk.

(2) A person may be designated as a justices' clerk only if he—

(a) has a 5 year magistrates' court qualification,

(b) is a barrister or solicitor who has served for not less than 5 years as an assistant to a justices' clerk, or

(c) has previously been a justices' clerk.

(3) The Lord Chancellor—

(a) must, after consulting the Lord Chief Justice, assign each justices' clerk to one or more local justice areas, and

(b) subject to subsections (4A) to (4C), may change an assignment so as to assign the justices' clerk to a different local justice area or to different local justice areas.

(4A) The Lord Chancellor may change an assignment of a justices' clerk so that he is no longer assigned to a local justice area ("the relevant area") only if the conditions in subsections (4B) and (4C) are met.

(4B) Before changing the assignment, the Lord Chancellor must consult—

(a) the chairman of the lay justices assigned to the relevant area, or

(b) if that is not possible or not practicable, the deputy chairman or such of the lay justices assigned to or acting in the relevant area as it appears to the Lord Chancellor appropriate to consult.

(4C) The Lord Chief Justice must agree to the change.

(5) An assistant to a justices' clerk is a person who is—

(a) appointed by the Lord Chancellor under section 2(1) or provided under a contract made by virtue of section 2(4), and

(b) designated by the Lord Chancellor as an assistant to a justices' clerk.

(6) The Lord Chancellor may by regulations provide that, subject to such exceptions as may be prescribed by the regulations, a person may be designated as an assistant to a justices' clerk only if he—

(a) has a 5 year magistrates' court qualification, or

(b) has such qualifications as may be prescribed by, or approved by the Lord Chancellor in accordance with, the regulations.

(6A) The Lord Chief Justice may nominate a judicial office holder (as defined in section 109(4) of the *Constitutional Reform Act* 2005) to exercise his functions under this section.

(7) In this Part "assistant clerk" is short for "assistant to a justices' clerk".

Functions

28.—(1) Rules may make provision enabling things authorised to be done by, to or before a single justice of the peace to be done instead by, to or before a justices' clerk. **2–17**

(2) Rules may also make provision enabling things authorised to be done by, to or before a justices' clerk (whether by virtue of subsection (1) or otherwise) to be done instead by, to or before an assistant clerk.

(3) An enactment or rule of law which—

(a) regulates the exercise of any jurisdiction or powers of justices of the peace, or

(b) relates to things done in the exercise or purported exercise of any such jurisdiction or powers,

applies in relation to the exercise or purported exercise of any such jurisdiction or powers by a justices' clerk by virtue of subsection (1) as if he were a justice of the peace.

(4) The functions of a justices' clerk include giving advice to any or all of the justices of the peace to whom he is clerk about matters of law (including procedure and practice) on questions arising in connection with the discharge of their functions, including questions arising when the clerk is not personally attending on them.

(5) The powers of a justices' clerk include, at any time when he thinks he should do so, bringing to the attention of any or all of the justices of the peace to whom he is clerk any point of law (including procedure and practice) that is or may be involved in any question so arising.

(6) For the purposes of subsections (4) and (5) the functions of justices of the peace do not include functions as a judge of the Crown Court.

(7) Subsections (4) and (5) do not limit—

(a) the powers and duties of a justices' clerk, or

(b) the matters on which justices of the peace may obtain assistance from their clerk.

(8) In this section "rules" means rules made by the Lord Chancellor with the concurrence of the Lord Chief Justice.

(9) Before making any rules for the purposes of this section the Lord Chancellor must consult—

(a) the Criminal Procedure Rule Committee,

(b) the Family Procedure Rule Committee, and

(c) the Magistrates' Courts Rule Committee.

(10) The Lord Chief Justice may nominate a judicial office holder (as defined in section 109(4) of the *Constitutional Reform Act* 2005) to exercise his functions under this section.

Independence

2–18 **29.**—(1) A justices' clerk exercising—

(a) a function exercisable by one or more justices of the peace,

(b) a function specified in section 28(4) or (5) (advice on matters of law, including procedure and practice), or

(c) a function as a member of the Criminal Procedure Rule Committee or the Family Procedure Rule Committee,

is not subject to the direction of the Lord Chancellor or any other person.

(2) An assistant clerk who is exercising any such function is not subject to the direction of any person other than a justices' clerk.

2–19 The role of the justices' clerk is to advise the magistrates on law, practice and procedure. These areas often overlap so advice is required on issues of mixed fact and law. The justices' clerk manages a team of legal advisers to whom powers are delegated to give legal advice to magistrates both in and out of court. Most legal advisers are solicitors or barristers and others hold recognised Court Clerk qualifications. The magistrate is not obliged to accept the advice and it is the bench, not the legal adviser, who is the ultimate decision-maker on questions of law and fact. However, it is accepted practice that they should do so, see *Jones v. Nicks* [1977] R.T.R. 72 when the bench acted against the advice of the legal adviser and accepted that the adverse effect on employment was a special reason not to endorse a driving licence. On appeal, it was held that the legal adviser had correctly explained the law to them and their decision against this advice was a nullity. Any magistrate will ignore legal advice at their peril for if a decision is made unsupported by the advice of the legal adviser, they could be held liable for errors affecting the liberty of the subject, *etc*. The *Consolidated Criminal Practice Direction* at V.55 gives detailed explanation of the role of the legal adviser including the method in which advice should be tendered (see Appendix F).

Legal advisers are required under the *Consolidated Criminal Practice Direction* to advise on questions of law (including Human Rights), questions of mixed law and fact, matters of practice and procedure, other issues relevant to the matter before the court and structured decision making. The legal adviser will also assist the court in drawing up and recording the reasons for decisions. At all times the legal adviser must exercise care not to trespass on the judicial responsibility of the bench by usurping its functions.

2–20 The legal adviser's role is to advise on these matters only and they must not appear to be trying to influence the magistrate's factual decisions: *Stafford Justices, ex p. Ross* [1962] 1 W.L.R. 456. In this case the clerk to the justices was seen to pass a note to the magistrates which contained an argument on the facts pointing to the guilt of the accused. The conviction was quashed on appeal as it was held that the clerk was attempting to influence the decision of the magistrates on matters of fact.

The legal adviser has a duty to ensure that every case is conducted fairly and that responsibility may incorporate assisting unrepresented defendants, taking notes of the evidence as a reminder and also asking questions of witnesses and parties to clarify evidence or issues in the case.

The legal adviser should not retire with the magistrates as a matter of course when they consider their verdict. If once the magistrates leave court, the legal adviser becomes aware that there is a point of law upon which they might require assistance then an approach may be made to the magistrates in the retiring room, see *Uxbridge Justices, ex p. Smith* (1985) 149 J.P. 620, where counsel for the defence referred to a passage in a legal text book as support for his submission. The bench retired and the legal adviser took the opportunity of reading the passage in full and then informed counsel that she was going to see the magistrates in the retiring room to advise them of her view on the law. On appeal the court held that in the absence of any indication or suspicion that the legal adviser had taken part in deciding questions of fact or the verdict, she was just carrying out her responsibility to advise the bench on the law. In *Consett Justices, ex p. Postal Bingo Ltd* [1967] 2 Q.B. 9, the interventions of the justices' clerk were even more marked but nevertheless on appeal the court held that he was acting in accordance with his duties to advise the bench. The case involved a complex matter of mixed law and fact. The justices' clerk went out with the magistrates to the retiring room together with his assistant and stayed there for over two hours of deliberations. The High Court held that the bench were entitled to his advice on "entangled questions of law and fact" and that his presence on their retirement did not invalidate the decision. In *Eccles Justices, ex p. Fitzpatrick* (1989) 89 Cr.App.R. 324, the clerk initially refused to allow the defendant to apply to the magistrates to change his plea and then went out to join the bench in the retiring room for about 25 minutes without being requested to do so. After a guilty plea was entered the clerk left court again with the bench and stayed in the retiring room with them for 30 minutes. The magistrates' decision to commit the defendant to the Crown Court for sentence was quashed on appeal. It was held that the clerk should not retire with the magistrates unless clearly requested to do so. In the absence of any dispute on the law, the magistrates did not need the advice of their clerk and his querying the motives behind a request to have the plea put again was improper. There was a reasonable suspicion of interference by the clerk which made the process unsafe.

The law has moved on since these cases and it is doubtful that such a wide interpretation would now be given to the advisory role of the justices' clerk. The *Human Rights Act* 1998 has had an impact on the transparency of communications between magistrates and legal advisers as expressed in the *Consolidated Criminal Practice Directions* (see Appendix F). The courts will be expected to limit and explain all consultations that take place out of court so that justice is seen to be done and art. 6 of the ECHR is observed. **2–21**

Legal advice should be given in open court. Where advice is given in the retiring room without having been previously canvassed in open court it will be given on a provisional basis only to the magistrates. The substance of the advice should be repeated in open court allowing the parties to make representations and then the advice will be stated in open court with amendments as required.

In *R. (Murchison) v. Southend Magistrates' Court* (2006) 170 J.P. 230, it was held that legal advisers should only attend on magistrates in the retiring room when called upon to do so. Previous convictions of the defendant should only be referred to after the verdict has been delivered in open court. Where the record had been made available by the legal adviser to the justices prior to the announcement of verdict this was inappropriate practice but in the circumstances of the case it was decided that the conviction was not unsafe.

Where the defendant is unrepresented the legal adviser is under a duty to assist both the defendant and the court. This will consist of explaining procedures to the defendant and where evidence is given in a trial, identifying the points in issue and ensuring appropriate questions are put to witnesses and assisting the defendant to give evidence if they so wish so that opportunity is provided to put the defence case fully: *Chichester Justices, ex p. DPP* (1993) 157 J.P. 1049.

Under the *Justices' Clerks Rules* 2005, r.2, justices' clerks may perform tasks which are authorised to be done by, to or before a single magistrate. The powers are specified in the Schedule to the Rules and include the issue of summonses, allowing agreed adjournments, granting criminal defence representation orders and the giving of directions in trials. The justices' clerk may delegate these powers to the legal advisers. In practice this means that the legal adviser will often deal with cases whilst the Bench retire to consider other matters. The justices' clerk may also sit alone to conduct early administrative hearings where the powers allow for pleas to be taken; remands on agreed bail and directions relating to trials to be given: *Crime and Disorder Act* 1998, s.50.

III. CONSTITUTION OF THE MAGISTRATES' COURTS

Magistrates' Courts Act 1980, s.121

Constitution and place of sitting of court

121.—(1) A magistrates' court shall not try an information summarily or hear a complaint **2–22**

except when composed of at least 2 justices unless the trial or hearing is one that by virtue of any enactment may take place before a single justice.

(2) A magistrates' court shall not hold an inquiry into the means of an offender for the purposes of section 82 above or determine under that section at a hearing at which the offender is not present whether to issue a warrant of commitment except when composed of at least 2 justices.

(3) [Repealed]

(4) Subject to the provisions of any enactment to the contrary, a magistrates' court must sit in open court if it is

(a) trying summarily an information for an indictable offence,

(b) trying an information for a summary offence,

(c) imposing imprisonment,

(d) hearing a complaint,

(e) holding an inquiry into the means of an offender for the purposes of section 82.

(5) A magistrates' court composed of a single justice, shall not impose imprisonment for a period exceeding 14 days or order a person to pay more than £1.

(6) Subject to the provisions of subsection (7) below, the justices composing the court before which any proceedings take place shall be present during the whole of the proceedings; but if during the course of the proceedings any justice absents himself, he shall cease to act further therein and, if the remaining justices are enough to satisfy the requirements of the preceding provisions of this section, the proceedings may continue before a court composed of those justices.

(7) Where the trial of an information is adjourned after the accused has been convicted and before he is sentenced or otherwise dealt with, the court which sentences or deals with him need not be composed of the same justices as that which convicted him; but, where among the justices composing the court which sentences or deals with an offender there are any who were not sitting when he was convicted, the court which sentences or deals with the offender shall before doing so make such inquiry into the facts and circumstances of the case as will enable the justices who were not sitting when the offender was convicted to be fully acquainted with those facts and circumstances.

(8) This section shall have effect subject to the provisions of this Act relating to family proceedings.

[This section is reprinted as amended by the *Children Act* 1989, Sched. 11, para. 8(c) and the *Courts Act* 2003, Sched. 8, para. 237.]

2–23 The minimum number of magistrates to hear a trial is two and it cannot be more than three: *Justices of the Peace (Size and Chairmanship of Bench) Rules* 2005.

IV. IMPARTIALITY OF MAGISTRATES

A. GENERAL

2–24 A magistrate is disqualified from sitting or adjudicating on a case if:

(a) a statutory disqualification applies;

(b) he would be a judge in his own cause;

(c) there is evidence of actual bias; or

(d) there is evidence of apparent bias.

Where a defendant demonstrates partiality or prejudice on the part of a judge there are irresistible grounds for objecting to the trial of the case by that judge.

Article 6 of ECHR guarantees a right to a fair and public hearing by "an independent and impartial tribunal". This includes the concept of subjective and objective impartiality. The subjective test is on the basis of the personal conviction of the particular judge and the objective test is ascertaining whether the judge offers guarantees sufficient to rule out any legitimate doubt as to the judge's impartiality: *Hauschildt v. Denmark* (1990) 12 E.H.R.R. 266.

If a magistrate is disqualified, he should declare an interest and withdraw from court.

It is possible for the interest to be declared and the parties to waive any objection on the basis of bias.

B. STATUTORY DISQUALIFICATION

Courts Act 2003, s.41

Disqualification of lay justices who are members of local authorities

41.—(1) A lay justice who is a member of a local authority may not act as a member of the Crown Court or a magistrates' court in proceedings brought by or against, or by way of an appeal from a decision of— **2–25**

(a) that local authority,

(b) a committee or officer of that local authority, or

(c) if that local authority is operating executive arrangements (within the meaning of Part 2 of the *Local Government Act* 2000)—

(i) the executive of that local authority (within the meaning of that Part), or

(ii) any person acting on behalf of that executive.

(2) A lay justice who is a member of the Common Council of the City of London may not act as a member of the Crown Court or a magistrates' court in proceedings brought by or against, or by way of an appeal from a decision of—

(a) the Corporation of the City,

(b) the Common Council, or

(c) a committee or officer of the Corporation or the Common Council.

(3) A joint committee, joint board, joint authority or other combined body—

(a) of which a local authority, the Corporation or the Common Council is a member, or

(b) on which the local authority, the Corporation or the Council is represented,

is to be regarded for the purposes of this section as a committee of the local authority, Corporation or Common Council.

(4) Any reference in this section to an officer of—

(a) a local authority,

(b) the Corporation, or

(c) the Common Council,

is to a person employed or appointed by, or by a committee of, the local authority, Corporation or Common Council in the capacity in which he is employed or appointed to act.

(5) No act is invalidated merely because of the disqualification under this section of the person by whom it is done.

(6) "Local authority" means–

(a) a local authority within the meaning of the *Local Government Act* 1972,

(b) a local authority constituted under section 2 of the *Local Government etc. (Scotland) Act* 1994,

(c) a police authority established under section 3 of the *Police Act* 1996, the Metropolitan Police Authority or the Serious Organised Crime Agency,

(d) the London Fire and Emergency Planning Authority,

(e) a joint authority established under Part 4 of the *Local Government Act* 1985,

(ea) an economic prosperity board established under s.88 of the *Local Democracy, Economic Development and Construction Act* 2009,

(eb) a combined authority established under s.103 of that Act,

(f) a National Park Authority,

(g) the Broads Authority, or

(h) a housing action trust established under Part 3 of the *Housing Act* 1988.

A "local authority" means a London borough council, a district council, a county council, a parish council or a community council: *Local Government Act* 1972, s.270. **2–26**

A magistrate who is a local councillor should not sit in court when the local authority is bringing a prosecution. He should declare an interest and withdraw from court. The case can continue with two magistrates sitting.

C. PARTY TO A CASE

It is one of the most fundamental principles of justice that a person cannot be a judge **2–27** in his own cause: *Dimes v. Proprietors of Grand Junction Canal* (1852) 3 H.L. Cas. 759.

Once it is shown that a magistrate is a party to a case or has an interest in the subject matter of the case he is disqualified without the need for any investigation into any actual bias. A direct pecuniary interest or proprietary interest in the outcome of a case acts as an automatic disqualification and an assumption of bias: *Bow Street Magistrates, ex p. Pinochet Ugarte (No.2)* [1999] 1 All E.R. 577.

D. ACTUAL BIAS

2–28 It is rare that actual bias is shown, but where it is the magistrate must disqualify himself: *Gough* [1993] 1 A.C. 646.

E. APPARENT BIAS

2–29 A judge is not disqualified from trying a case because he expresses a personal view before the start of a case which touches upon issues of law and practice which then arise in the case: *Browne*, *The Times*, August 23, 1997.

In *Incal v. Turkey* (2000) 29 E.H.R.R. 449, the European Court of Human Rights summarised the convention jurisprudence. It held that in order to establish whether a tribunal is independent, regard must be had to the manner of appointment of its members and their terms of office, the existence of safeguards against outside pressure and the question whether it presents an appearance of impartiality. There are two tests as to the condition of impartiality: the first consists of trying to determine the personal conviction of a particular judge in a given case (the subjective approach) and the second in ascertaining whether the judge offered guarantees sufficient to exclude any legitimate doubt in this respect (the objective approach). Appearances may be important but what is at stake is the confidence which the courts in a democratic society must inspire in the public and with regard to the criminal courts, in the defendant. In deciding whether there is a legitimate reason to fear that a particular court lacks independence or impartiality, the perspective of the defendant is important, what is decisive however is whether his doubts as to the impartiality of the tribunal are objectively justified.

The law was reviewed in detail in *Gough* [1993] 1 A.C. 646 which concerned a claim of apparent bias by a juror who was the neighbour of the defendant's brother. The court went on to consider the authorities on apparent bias and sought to identify the test to be applied. In the case of magistrates it was said that the court should consider if there was a real danger of bias on the part of the magistrate in the sense that he might unfairly regard with favour or disfavour the case of a party before him. The test of bias is whether there is a real risk that the defendant might have been denied a fair trial.

2–30 In *Bow Street Magistrate, ex p. Pinochet Ugarte (No. 2)* [1999] 1 All E.R. 577; [1999] 2 W.L.R. 272, HL, a member of the tribunal dealing with the applicant's case was connected to a charity called Amnesty International, which had intervened in the case. It was held on appeal that it is an automatic disqualification if a judge acts in his own cause. The court was reluctant to extend the ambit of automatic disqualification to cover the present case but it was a fundamental principle that justice should not only be done, but be seen to be done. The judge's connection with a party to the case disqualified him from hearing the case.

In *Harris (Joseph)* [2007] 2 Cr.App.R (S) 37 the defendant, an animal rights protestor, pleaded guilty to several offences including causing criminal damage to the property of a company associated with Huntingdon Life Sciences. An appeal against sentence was lodged because it was discovered that the judge some years previously had been a member of a pro-hunting group and had spoken in that cause at a meeting of the RSPCA to try and persuade the members to relax their view on criminalising hunting. It was held that although judges are entitled to hold views about matters that affect society there could be an appearance of bias if those views are not disclosed and fully considered before trial or sentence. In this case the judge had been actively involved

Part I

in an issue central to the case and the risk of apparent bias was so high that the appeal against sentence was allowed

There are many ways in which apparent bias might be claimed and it will depend on the circumstances of each case whether there is a risk that requires disqualification.

A remark by a magistrate that it was not the practice of the court to describe police officers as liars was held to amount to apparent bias as it demonstrated a strong reaction in favour of the police witnesses: *Highgate Justices, ex p. Riley* [1996] R.T.R. 150. The fact that solicitors representing a party in proceedings also advised the judge about personal matters did not mean that he would necessarily be biased in their favour and did not require him to disqualify himself after the connection had been disclosed: *Taylor v. Lawrence* [2002] 2 All E.R. 353. Where a magistrate had been a teacher at a defendant's school but had neither taught him nor had any other personal dealings with him but did recognise his name it was held that a "fair-minded and informed observer"would not conclude in these circumstances that there was a real possibility of apparent bias so the conviction was upheld—*R. (on the application of B) v. Wolverhampton Youth Court* [2009] EWHC 2706 (Admin).

In *Michel v. R.* [2010] 1 Cr.App.R. 24 the court restated the test to be applied in cases of apparent bias. This was an appeal to the Privy Council from Jersey. It was said that the right to a fair trial could be infringed by an unacceptable level of hostile and sarcastic remarks or questions from the Judge. In this case the excessive number and character of interventions from the Judge were held to render the conviction unsafe even though the case against the defendant was formidable. It was said that what needed to be considered was not only that the defendant should feel he had had a fair trial but that the "reasonable observer" would also regard it as such.

But in *Piggott* [2010] 2 Cr.App.R.(S.) 16, sceptical comments made by a judge in the context of a lengthy trial suggesting that a defendant's account was "manipulative and dishonest" were held to be justified and not to amount to real or apparent bias.

Where the judge described an agreed basis of plea as "fatuous" and then reserved the *Newton* hearing to himself it was held that despite the robust language it was clear that the hearing was conducted with scrupulous fairness and a complaint of bias was not upheld (*George* [2006] Crim.L.R. 164, CA). But *Steadman-Byrne v. Amjad* [2007] 1 W.L.R. 2484 (a civil case), illustrates the principle that a judge's remarks may give rise to the appearance of bias. The judge had invited the lawyers in a case into chambers at the end of the claimant's evidence and had given a clear indication of his thinking and expressed views adverse to the party yet to give evidence. It was held that the same test applies in chambers as in open court and that the judge's comments indicated a prematurely closed mind which gave the appearance of bias. Excessive discourtesy from a judge to a defendant can so affect due process and the fairness of a trial that it may amount to apparent bias which will lead to a conviction being quashed irrespective of the strength of the evidence in the case. In *Cordingley* (2008) Crim.L.R. 299 the judge was held to have acted oppressively to the defendant by his cross manner and also in withdrawing bail peremptorily. This was held to have inevitably inhibited the defendant in the course of his defence as he clearly felt that the judge's behaviour showed he was prejudiced against him. The appeal against conviction was allowed as the trial had not been fair because of the discourtesy demonstrated by the judge and the disregard for the presumption of innocence. In *Copsey and Copsey* [2008] EWCA Crim 2043 interruptions by the judge during the witnesses' evidence were held to lead to an unsafe conviction. The judge asked several questions of the defendants and appeared to side with the prosecution. The nature and frequency of his interventions together with a remark that part of the defence case was "bizarre" were held to affect the fairness of the trial. In *Harirbafan* [2008] EWCA Crim 1967 excessive interruptions by the judge were held to affect the appearance of impartiality and to disrupt the process of the defence case to such an extent that the conviction was held to be unsafe despite the strength of the evidence. See also *Cole, The Times*, March 16, 2009 where hostility shown by the judge towards the defence coupled with his handing an offensively critical note to defence counsel was held to make the trial unfair and the conviction unsafe. Where the judge in his questioning of the defendant acted as if he were an advocate for the prosecution, his interventions were held to be deeply prejudicial so that a fair and balanced approach had not been maintained. The conviction was quashed on appeal: *Andrew* [2010] EWCA Crim 798. See also *Zarezadeh* [2011] EWCA Crim 271. Also in *Tedjame-Mortty* [2011] EWCA Crim 950 where the judge was described as "haranguing"the defendant just before the defence case started over an allegation that he had intimidated a young visitor to the court, the conviction was quashed on the grounds that the quality of the defendant's evidence could have been adversely affected by the judge's wholly inappropriate behaviour. There must be very clear evidence of unfairness or an extreme lack of courtesy before apparent bias is shown and the appeal court will scrutinize the remarks and conduct of a bench to identify whether there is a genuine appearance of bias or whether a defendant may simply be aggrieved by a decision which has been quite properly arrived at. In *R. (on the application of Lawson) v. Stafford Magistrates' Court* (2007) 104 (40) LSG 26, the defence in a road traffic case raised issues of evidence in the closing speech that had not been dealt with during trial. It was held that the justices' decision to adjourn the case to allow the prosecution to bring evidence about those points could not be impugned for bias or the appearance of it. They were held to have acted properly in the case where the defendant had attempted to ambush the prosecution and their decision was not perverse. Present or past professional connections between the judge and any lawyer appearing before him was held not of itself to give rise to bias or an appearance of bias. In such circumstances a party may waive his right to object but only if fully aware of all the circumstances and the consequences of the choices open to him (*Smith v. Kvaerner Cementation Foundations Ltd & the Bar Council* [2006] 150 S.J. 401). Where judicial bias is apparent then disqualification of the judge is automatic. Inconvenience, cost and delay are not matters to be taken into account; *AWG Group Ltd (formerly Anglian Water Plc) v. Morrison* [2006] 1 W.L.R. 1163. In the case of *Russell* [2006] Crim.L.R. 862 the defendant escaped from the dock and attacked the judge during the summing up. The judge retired and discussed security arrangements with the officer in the case who had given evidence and then returned to continue the trial. An application to discharge the jury was refused. An appeal was lodged on the basis that the trial was unfair as the judge would have been biased having been attacked and having spoken in private to a prosecution witness and that the decision of the jury might have been affected as a result. On appeal it was held that any criticism of the judge was unfounded. The summing up was fair and balanced and no observer could conclude that for the judge to continue with the trial was unfair, particularly as the defendant had disrupted the trial by his own actions and could not thus demand a re-trial. The conviction was upheld. It is no doubt reassuring for those holding judicial office to know that being subjected to an unprovoked physical attack cannot entitle a defendant to choose the tribunal.

It has also been held that a judge need not recuse themselves from sentencing when an allegation of jury tampering and a threat to kill the judge had been made. The Appeal Court said that it was important that the sentence should be passed by the judge who dealt with the lengthy trial. No bias was perceived as the judge would be able to put from her mind the unsubstantiated allegations regarding the threats made towards her when considering sentence for the defendant, *Mehta* [2008] EWCA Crim 1491.

2–31 The magistrates must also be seen to be giving their clear and undivided attention to the proceedings. Apparently falling asleep, dealing with other paperwork or reading other documents during a trial have all resulted in convictions being quashed as unsafe; *Weston-Super-Mare Justices, ex p. Taylor* [1981] Crim.L.R. 179; *Marylebone Stipendiary Magistrate, ex p. Perry* [1992] Crim.L.R. 514; and *South Worcestershire Justices, ex p. Daniels* [1997] 161 J.P. 121.

The test for apparent bias for a magistrate also applies to justices' clerks because they are part of the judicial process in the magistrates' courts: *Gough* (*ante*).

V. RIGHTS OF AUDIENCE AND COURT DRESS

2–32 Defendants in person, barristers and solicitors with rights conferred by the *Courts and Legal Services Act* 1990 may address the court.

Magistrates' Courts Act 1980, s.122

Appearance by counsel or solicitor

122.—(1) A party to any proceedings before a magistrates' court may be represented by a legal representative. **2–33**

(2) Subject to subsection (3) below, an absent party so represented shall be deemed not to be absent.

(3) Appearance of a party by a legal representative shall not satisfy any provision of any enactment or any condition of a recognizance expressly requiring his presence.

Barristers and solicitors regularly appear in the magistrates' courts to represent defendants. A defendant may not be in court, either because he is ill or has been removed for misconduct or he may simply choose not to attend. It is possible for the proceedings to continue with the lawyer acting in the interests of the absent defendant. Lawyers will also represent bodies corporate and enter pleas on their behalf without the need for company officers to be present. **2–34**

In certain instances, statute requires that the defendant be present in court. Where a defendant has been released on bail to appear before the court, it is not sufficient for his legal representative to attend at court; bail must be answered in person as there is a duty to surrender to the custody of the court: *Bail Act* 1976, s.3. Bail may only be enlarged in absence if there is a reasonable cause for the failure to surrender. There are further specific provisions which require the defendant's presence even when represented, *e.g.* plea before venue should be dealt with in the presence of the accused unless he is removed from court because of his disorderly conduct: *Magistrates' Courts Act* 1980, s.17B; committal for trial to the Crown Court: *Magistrates' Courts Act* 1980, s.6(2) which requires the court to commit the accused for trial and the *Criminal Procedure Rules* 2011, r.10.2 which require the charge on which the defendant is to be committed to be read to him as part of the process. Under s.51 of the *Crime and Disorder Act* 1998, a person may only be sent for trial when he "appears" or is "brought before the court". Community penalties may be imposed only in the defendant's presence because of the legal requirement on the court to explain to the offender in ordinary language the effect of the order and the consequences of breach (see *Powers of Criminal Courts (Sentencing) Act* 2000). Similarly there is a legal requirement to explain to an offender the reasons why the court is imposing a custodial sentence: *Powers of Criminal Courts (Sentencing) Act* 2000, s.79.

Rights of audience are conferred by ss.27 and 28 of the *Courts and Legal Services Act* 1990. Duly qualified barristers and solicitors have a right of audience under these provisions. The court may also grant an individual right of audience to specified persons for specific proceedings under s.27(2)(c) of the Act. This discretion extends to any person in any proceedings: *Southwark Crown Court, ex p. Tawfick*, *The Times*, December 1, 1994.

Professional Codes of Conduct dictate the dress code for courts. Although wigs and gowns are not worn in the magistrates' court, a smart standard of dress is expected of all professionals appearing before the court.

VI. ADMINISTRATION OF THE MAGISTRATES' COURTS

The *Courts Act* 2003 makes provision about the courts and their procedure and practice. It unifies the Supreme Court, county courts and magistrates' courts into one court system, called Her Majesty's Court Service (HMCS) and the Lord Chancellor has a duty to maintain the new court system. The Home Office has responsibility for the police, crime reduction, immigration and asylum, security and counter-terrorism. The Ministry of Justice has responsibility for criminal law, sentencing, prisons and probation. **2–35**

VII. GENERAL JURISDICTION

(1) Legislation

Courts Act 2003 s.1

The general duty

2–36 **1.**—(1) The Lord Chancellor is under a duty to ensure that there is an efficient and effective system to support the carrying on of the business of—

(a) the Senior Courts,

(aa) the Court of Protection,

(b) county courts, and

(c) magistrates' courts,

and that appropriate services are provided for those courts.

(2) In this Part—

(a) "the Senior Courts" includes the district probate registries, and

(b) "magistrates' court" includes a committee of justices.

(3) In this Part references to the Lord Chancellor's general duty in relation to the courts are to his duty under this section.

(4) The Lord Chancellor must, within 18 months of the coming into force of this section, and afterwards annually, prepare and lay before both Houses of Parliament a report as to the way in which he has discharged his general duty in relation to the courts.

2–37 The Lord Chancellor in order to discharge his duty has power to appoint officers and staff under s.2 of the *Courts Act* 2003 and he also has power to provide accommodation for court houses and offices: *Courts Act* 2003, s.3. Courts Boards are established under s.5 of the Act and their function is to scrutinise the arrangements made by the Lord Chancellor and to make recommendations on how his duty should be discharged.

2–38 The *Courts Act* 2003 creates a national commission area for the whole of England and Wales. This is divided into local justice areas.

(2) The commission of the peace and local justice areas

Courts Act 2003, ss.7, 8

The commission of the peace for England and Wales

2–39 **7.** There shall be a commission of the peace for England and Wales—

(a) issued under the Great Seal, and

(b) addressed generally, and not by name, to all such persons as may from time to time hold office as justices of the peace for England and Wales.

Local justice areas

2–40 **8.**—(1) England and Wales is to be divided into areas to be known as local justice areas.

(2) The areas are to be those specified by an order made by the Lord Chancellor.

(3) Each local justice area established by order under subsection (2) is to be known by such name as is specified in the order (but subject to subsection (4)).

(4) The Lord Chancellor may make orders altering local justice areas.

(5) "Altering", in relation to a local justice area, includes (as well as changing its boundaries)–

(a) combining it with one or more other local justice areas,

(b) dividing it between two or more other local justice areas, and

(c) changing its name.

(5A) Before making any order under subsection (2) or (4), the Lord Chancellor must consult the Lord Chief Justice.

(6) Before making an order under subsection (4) in relation to a local justice area the Lord Chancellor must consult—

(a) the justices of the peace assigned to the local justice area,

(b) any courts board whose area includes the local justice area or a part of the local justice area, and

(c) unless the alteration consists only of a change of name, any local authorities whose area includes the local justice area or a part of the local justice area.

(7) "Local authority" means–

(a) any council of a county, a county borough, a London borough or a council of a district,

(b) the Common Council of the City of London, or

(c) a police authority established under section 3 of the *Police Act* 1996 or the Metropolitan Police Authority.

(8) The Lord Chief Justice may nominate a judicial office holder (as defined in section 109(4) of the *Constitutional Reform Act* 2005) to exercise his functions under this section.

Lay justices on appointment are assigned to a local justice area where they will sit to dispense justice. District Judges (Magistrates' Courts) have a national jurisdiction and may be directed to sit anywhere in England and Wales but they will also be assigned to sit usually in one or more local justice areas. **2–41**

(3) Jurisdiction for offences

Magistrates' Courts Act 1980, s.2

Trial of summary offences

2.—(1) A magistrates' court has jurisdiction to try any summary offence. **2–42**

(2) A magistrates' court has jurisdiction under sections 51 and 51A of the *Crime and Disorder Act* 1998 in respect of any offence committed by a person who appears or is brought before the court.

(3) Subject to—

(a) sections 18 to 22, and

(b) any other enactment (wherever contained) relating to the mode of trial of offences triable either way, a magistrates' court has jurisdiction to try summarily any offence which is triable either way.

(4) A magistrates' court has jurisdiction, in the exercise of its powers under section 24, to try summarily an indictable offence.

(5) This section does not affect any jurisdiction over offences conferred on a magistrates' court by any enactment not contained in this Act.

Once a defendant has been brought before a court in a local justice area under the relevant legal process the magistrates have power to deal with the case. **2–43**

(4) Places, date and time of sittings of courts

Courts Act 2003, s.30

Places, dates and times of sittings

30.—(1) The Lord Chancellor may, after consulting the Lord Chief Justice, give directions as to the places in England and Wales at which magistrates' courts may sit. **2–44**

(2) In exercising his powers under subsection (1), the Lord Chancellor shall have regard to the need to ensure that court-houses are accessible to persons resident in each local justice area.

(3) The Lord Chancellor may, with the concurrence of the Lord Chief Justice, give directions as to the distribution and transfer of the general business of magistrates' courts between the places specified in directions under subsection (1).

(4) Directions under subsection (3) may, in particular, contain provision that, where a person is charged with an offence and is being required to appear before a magistrates' court, the place where he is required to appear is one of the places described in subsection (5).

(5) The places are—

(a) a place in the local justice area in which the offence is alleged to have been committed;

(b) a place in the local justice area in which the person charged with the offence resides;

(c) a place in the local justice area in which the witnesses, or the majority of the witnesses, reside;

(d) a place where other cases raising similar issues are being dealt with.

(6) "The general business of magistrates' courts" does not include family proceedings (as defined in section 65 of the 1980 Act).

(7) The Lord Chancellor may, after consulting the Lord Chief Justice, give directions as to the days on which and times at which magistrates' courts may sit.

(8) Subject to any directions under subsection (7), the business of magistrates' courts may be conducted on any day and at any time.

(9) The Lord Chief Justice may nominate a judicial office holder (as defined in section 109(4) of the *Constitutional Reform Act* 2005) to exercise his functions under subsection (1) or (7).

2–45 In the national commission area all summary offences can be heard at any magistrates' court in England and Wales as can either way or indictable offences. The Lord Chancellor may make directions to ensure that the business of the courts is run efficiently. He may direct where magistrates' courts may sit and also how cases should be distributed amongst the courts in different areas. The directions recognise that the convenience of the defendant and the witnesses may dictate where a case should be heard which need not necessarily be in the court local to where the offence is alleged to have been committed.

VIII. TERRITORIAL JURISDICTION

A. INTRODUCTION

2–46 Generally, the courts are not concerned with conduct which occurs overseas: *Cox v. Army Council* [1963] A.C. 48.

Criminal offences may have a foreign element and in such cases the court will investigate the parliamentary intention in defining offences when deciding on any geographical limitation. In the absence of clear words to the contrary parliament is presumed not to have intended to make conduct occurring outside the territorial jurisdiction of the Crown a criminal offence triable in an English court: *Air India v. Wiggins* (1980) 71 Cr.App.R. 213. In the case of blackmail where the letter making the demand was posted in England the offence was held to be triable in England although the letter was directed to the intended victim abroad: *Treacy v. DPP* [1971] A.C. 537, HL.

Certain offences may be prosecuted in this country even where the offence was committed abroad, *e.g.* murder abroad by a British subject: *Offences against the Person Act* 1861, s.9; and terrorist acts committed in certain foreign countries: *Suppression of Terrorism Act* 1978, s.4.

2–47 There is provision for offenders to be extradited to England and Wales from foreign countries for offences committed here and similarly offenders may be extradited out of this jurisdiction if they are found in England and Wales and are subject to trial abroad. See Ch.3. The complexities of international crime were recognised by the *Criminal Justice Act* 1993, which extends and clarifies the jurisdiction of the criminal courts in the UK in relation to crimes with a foreign element.

B. EMBASSIES AND CONSULATES

2–48 The building occupied by a foreign embassy or consulate and the land upon which it stands remain the territory of the United Kingdom but diplomatic and consular premises are inviolable. The consent of the head of the mission is required before the local investigating authorities may gain entry. This can present problems in the magistrates' court when diplomatic representatives or their staff commit criminal offences.

Vehicles bearing diplomatic plates can incur parking tickets or other road traffic violations. Before these offences can be successfully prosecuted there must be effective service of a summons or enforcement notice at the diplomatic premises. In such cases the prosecution may choose not to proceed. For more serious offences warrants of entry or arrest can only be executed with official consent from the Embassy authorities.

C. SHIPS

English courts have jurisdiction in respect of offences committed on board United Kingdom ships if the defendant is a British citizen and is charged with having committed the offence on board any United Kingdom ship on the high seas, or in any foreign port or harbour, or on board any foreign ship to which he does not belong: *Merchant Shipping Act* 1995, s.281(a). If the defendant is not a British citizen English courts have jurisdiction if he is charged with having committed an offence on board any United Kingdom ship on the high seas: *Merchant Shipping Act* 1995, s.281(b). Section 3(A) of the *Magistrates' Courts Act* 1980 makes it clear that ss.280, 281 and 282 of the *Merchant Shipping Act* 1995 apply generally to offences under the law of England and Wales and not simply to specific offences under the Act. **2–49**

D. AIRCRAFT

Offences committed on aeroplanes are covered by specific statutes (see Ch.20— Aeroplanes and Airports) and the court has jurisdiction over any offences committed in the aircraft whilst it is in flight over the United Kingdom. Under s.92 of the *Civil Aviation Act* 1982, any act or omission taking place on board an aeroplane while on flight elsewhere than in or over the United Kingdom, if it constitutes an offence if committed on land, will be an offence in the air. Foreign aircraft are not affected by this Act unless the next landing of the aircraft is in the UK and where the vessel is registered elsewhere than the UK that the offence would constitute a criminal offence in the country of registration. The consent of the DPP is needed to prosecute offences committed on aircraft when not over UK airspace: s.92(2). **2–50**

IX. SOVEREIGN AND DIPLOMATIC IMMUNITY

Diplomatic agents enjoy immunity from the criminal jurisdiction of the state of residence: *Diplomatic Privileges Act* 1964, Sched. 1, art. 31. **2–51**

Members of diplomatic, administrative and technical staff of a mission and members of their families forming part of their household and domestic service staff are exempt from criminal proceedings: *Diplomatic Privileges Act* 1964, Sched. 1, art. 37. Private servants of members of the mission rather than servants of the mission itself enjoy no such immunity. Members of the families of diplomatic staff and members of the technical and administrative staff and their families who are British nationals or permanent residents do not enjoy immunity from criminal jurisdiction.

Where the question as to whether a defendant is entitled to diplomatic immunity under the *Diplomatic Privileges Act* 1964 arises, a certificate issued by or under the authority of the Secretary of State is conclusive evidence: *Diplomatic Privileges Act* 1964, s.4. In *Secretary of State for Foreign and Commonwealth Affairs, ex p. Trawnik, The Times*, April 18, 1985, the court held in a case of state immunity that a minister's certificate could not be challenged by way of judicial review except on the ground that it was a nullity or was issued beyond the scope of the minister's statutory power.

Diplomatic privilege cannot be pleaded successfully unless the Foreign and Commonwealth Office has been notified of the entry of the individual into the United Kingdom in accordance with the Vienna Convention on Diplomatic Relations, art.10 even though art.10 is not reproduced in the Schedule to the *Diplomatic Privileges Act* 1964: *Lambeth J.J., ex p. Yusufu* [1985] Crim.L.R. 510. **2–52**

It is possible for the immunity to be waived. Waiver must be made by or on behalf of the representative of the country concerned and cannot be made by the defendant. Until such a waiver is made the proceedings are without jurisdiction and are void: *Madan* [1961] Crim.L.R. 253.

X. CHILDREN AND YOUNG PERSONS

2–53 Under s.68 of the *Criminal Justice Act* 1991 the magistrates' courts have jurisdiction in respect of summary and indictable offences only where the offender is aged 18 years and over. Offenders under the age of 18 years are dealt with by the youth court.

The magistrates' court has power to deal with young people under the age of 18 in restricted circumstances.

a) If a person aged 17 or under appears alone before a magistrates' court, unless there is an adult co-defendant, the case must be adjourned to a youth court (*Children and Young Persons Act* 1933, s.46). The defendant may be remanded either on bail, in custody if aged 17 or to local authority accommodation if younger. A young person aged 15 or 16 can also be remanded to secure accommodation. Youth courts rarely sit on Saturdays or Bank Holidays so the youth will be produced at the adult court and will be remanded under this section to the next convenient youth court.

b) If a young person aged under 18 is jointly charged with an adult the magistrates' court (as opposed to the youth court) may deal with him: *Children and Young Persons Act* 1933, s.46. If the adult elects or is committed for jury trial at the Crown Court, the magistrates may commit the young person for trial at the Crown Court if it is in the interests of justice to do so: *Magistrates' Courts Act* 1980, s.24. If the adult consents to summary trial and pleads not guilty then the magistrates can direct that the young person be tried jointly with the adult. The court also has discretion to sever the co-defendants if it is in the interests of justice and may remit the young person to a youth court for trial: *Magistrates' Courts Act* 1980, s.29. Factors to consider are the age and plea of the young person and the advisability of duplication of trials.

c) The magistrates' court must remit a young person who is convicted of a joint charge with an adult to the youth court for sentence unless satisfied it would be undesirable to do so. The appropriate youth court will be the court acting for the same area as the adult court or the youth court that has jurisdiction for the area where the young person resides: *Powers of Criminal Courts (Sentencing) Act* 2000, s.8(1) and (2). The circumstances in which a magistrates' court may find it undesirable to remit the young person are set out in s.8 of the Act. Instead of remittal the court may make a referral order if the case falls within the relevant conditions. The magistrates' court has power to sentence a young person on conviction in a joint matter with an adult if the court is of the opinion that the case is one which can properly be dealt with by means of an absolute or conditional discharge, a fine not exceeding £250 in the case of a young person aged 10–13 inclusive or £1,000 for a young person aged 14–17, or an order for the offender's parent or guardian to enter into a recognisance to take proper care of him and exercise proper control over him: *Powers of Criminal Courts (Sentencing) Act* 2000, s.8(6)–(8).

2–54 A co-defendant who is a young person may become an adult during the process of the case. If he was 17 at the time of commission of the offence but reaches 18 before the first court appearance the adult court has jurisdiction and may hear the case. His young age should be taken into account on sentencing. If he appears as a youth co-defendant and reaches the age of 18 by the date of conviction, then he should be treated by the adult court as if he were still a young person with the restrictions on sentencing powers applying.

In *Ghafoor* [2002] Crim.L.R. 739, the defendant was 17 at the time of commission of an offence of rioting but was 18 by the time he was convicted. On appeal his sentence of four and a half years detention in a Young Offenders Institution was reduced to 18 months on the basis that taking his age into account at the time of the offence, this period of detention was equal to the length of any detention and training order that could properly have been imposed in the youth court. The relevant age for determining sentencing powers was the age at the time of the offence.

The case of *Ghafoor* was considered further in *Bowker* [2008] 1 Cr.App.R.(S) 72, where it was said that the decision in *Ghafoor* remained the starting point in that the level of sentence is that which was appropriate to the age of the defendant at the time the offence was committed but it was said that this still envisages flexibility. In *Bowker* the defendant was convicted of violent disorder which was committed two days before his eighteenth birthday. Although it was confirmed that his culpability should be judged by reference to his age at the time of the offence, because he was sentenced when aged 18, more general public policy matters, such as deterrence, could be taken into account under s.142 *Criminal Justice Act* 2003. The maximum sentence that could have been imposed at the time of the offence was held to be a "powerful" factor but not the sole or determinative one.

CHAPTER 3

EXTRADITION

I. INTRODUCTION

Extradition is the handing over by one country of a person who is alleged to have committed a crime or who has been convicted of a criminal offence to another country, which has jurisdiction to deal with the crime. **3–1**

Throughout the centuries it has been traditional for states to grant asylum to fugitives from other countries. It also became established that countries would not give asylum to those who had committed crimes unless it was considered that those crimes were political in nature. A state may extend the cloak of its own immunity over state officials but it cannot be a blanket immunity as some activities cannot in international law be legal: *Bow Street Metropolitan Stipendiary Magistrate, ex p. Pinochet Ugarte (No.3)* [2000] 1 A.C. 147. When determining whether a claim should succeed against a state official, the court should consider and balance at one and the same time all relevant factors: *Jones v. Ministry of the Interior of the Kingdom of Saudi Arabia (Secretary of State for Constitutional Affairs as intervenors)*: *Mitchell v. Al-Dali*, *The Times*, November 1, 2004. **3–2**

Treaties between countries exist to facilitate the return of those who have committed or are alleged to have committed serious offences. The United Kingdom seeks extradition from elsewhere while other countries seek extradition from this country.

The City of Westminster Magistrates' Court, being the office of the Senior District Judge (Chief Magistrate) and those other district judges designated to hear extradition proceedings, is the centre for outward extradition in England and Wales.

This chapter is concerned with magistrates' courts proceedings for outward extradition only. The proceedings are now covered by the *Extradition Act* 2003 which came into force on January 1st, 2004 (any proceedings either before the courts or the Home Office prior to that date must be considered under the *Extradition Act* 1989—very few such cases are believed to exist—save for Isle of Man and Guernsey which remain subject to the 1989 Act, Jersey has its own 2004 legislation). All statutory references are to that Act, the interpretation of which must be approached on the twin assumptions that Parliament did not intend the provisions of Pt 1 to be inconsistent with any Framework Decisions adopted by the European Council: *Office of the King's Prosecutor (Brussels) v. Armas* [2005] UKHL 67; [2006] 1 All E.R. 647. There is now a system of free movement of judicial decisions in criminal matters and practical solutions to legislative problems true to the spirit and the requirements of Framework Decisions, while properly safeguarding the liberty of the individual. **3–3**

Part I

Case law from previous legislation remains authoritative when considering provisions that have been replicated in this Act. Prior to the Act cases ran at about 50-60 per year. *Hansard* (9/11/10 Column 190W) records the Home Secretary's written reply to the 2009/10 business year for the UK in Pt 1 European Arrest Warrant (EAW) cases only as 699 (excluding Scotland) (516 pervious year) surrenders from the UK and 71 (including Scotland) (88 previous year) to the UK. Of these 425 went to Poland the next biggest number being 55 to Lithuania, which gives a clear flavour of the current operation of EAW requests to the UK. Other data has Scottish requests being 152 in total for 2010 of which those from Poland comprised 67.5 per cent next 5.5 per cent to Lithuania and just 6 of the total being non Pt 1 (EAW).

3–4 The Act categorises the United Kingdom's extradition partners into two. The Secretary of State for the Home Office designates countries into each category and those categories may change, for example, a country may migrate from category two to category one. No country may be designated under Pt 1 where the death penalty would be available if the person were found guilty: s.1(3). Section 94 (Pt 2 cases) allows extradition where the death penalty has been or could be imposed only if the Secretary of State receives an assurance it will not be imposed or carried out if imposed—s.94(2). There may also be special arrangements with modifications of the Act where a treaty is not in existence but there are memoranda of understanding: s.194, *e.g. Brown v. Gov. of Rwanda* [2007] EWHC 498 — genocide in Rwanda..

3–5 The difference in procedure between the two categories is that the Secretary of State for the Home Office still has a role to play so far as category 2 countries are concerned. Part 1 EAW cases should be **clearly understood** as being judicial authority to judicial authority not state to state and involving no political oversight or review. Citation of case law by reference to country in EAW cases in this chapter is for brevity only; strictly the actual requesting court or judge, not country, should be used. A check will need to be made to ascertain which countries have been designated to which category at any particular time. In addition the designation of category 2 countries may give special terms, *e.g.* the USA, in common with many other states, does not have to provide *prima facie* evidence. This was decided not to be unlawful or irrational: *R. (Ian Norris) v. Secretary of State for the Home Department* [2006] 3 All E.R. 1011. The Attorneys General of the UK and USA have issued guidance for handling cases where there is concurrent jurisdiction. It is concerned with cases that are the subject of separate investigations in the UK and USA in relation to which early contact between the authorities of the two countries would be beneficial. An extradition request is insufficient of itself to engage the guidance and it does not require consideration to be given to the prosecution in the UK of a person who is the subject of an extradition request by the USA, where there has been no investigation of his case in the UK and the DPP has not been seized of the case as prosecutor: *R. (on the application of Syed Talha Ahsan) v. DPP & USA etc.* [2008] EWHC 666 (Admin).

A request may be withdrawn and the person discharged.

See overview flowcharts for Pt 1 E.A.W. and Pt 2 cases at §§ 3–101 and 3–102 *ante*.

II. JURISDICTION

3–6 Extradition proceedings are dealt with by district judges who have been designated by the Lord Chief Justice after consulting with the Lord Chancellor and are known as the "appropriate Judge" see: ss.67 and 139. There are currently nine such Judges. Jurisdiction lies with the designated judge as opposed to the area or courthouse. The judge will normally sit at the City of Westminster Magistrates' Court but can sit elsewhere. A magistrate may deal with an application for a provisional warrant and arrangements are in place for such applications to be made both in and out of normal court hours. There is an established out of hours rota for the designated Judges to deal with provisional warrants in Pt 2 cases, Pt 1 E.A.W.'s are certified by S.O.C.A. having been issued by the Requesting Judicial Authority with no UK judicial involvement.

III. ARREST

The subject of an extradition request will be arrested on a warrant. The type of warrant will differ according to which part of the Act applies to the requesting state. The warrant may be a Pt 1 warrant (European Arrest Warrant), or a Pt 2 Provisional or certified warrant. Part 3 warrants refer to incoming extradition and are not dealt with here. **3–7**

Part I

(1) Part 1 warrant

This has commonly been called the European Arrest Warrant (EAW). The provisions are contained in s.2 of the Act. **3–8**

Extradition Act 2003, s.2

Part 1 warrant and certificate

2.—(1) This section applies if the designated authority receives a Part 1 warrant in respect of a person. **3–9**

(2) A Part 1 warrant is an arrest warrant which is issued by a judicial authority of a category 1 territory and which contains—

(a) the statement referred to in subsection (3) and the information referred to in subsection (4), or

(b) the statement referred to in subsection (5) and the information referred to in subsection (6).

(3) The statement is one that—

(a) the person in respect of whom the Part 1 warrant is issued is accused in the category 1 territory of the commission of an offence specified in the warrant, and

(b) the Part 1 warrant is issued with a view to his arrest and extradition to the category 1 territory for the purpose of being prosecuted for the offence.

(4) The information is—

(a) particulars of the person's identity;

(b) particulars of any other warrant issued in the category 1 territory for the person's arrest in respect of the offence;

(c) particulars of the circumstances in which the person is alleged to have committed the offence, including the conduct alleged to constitute the offence, the time and place at which he is alleged to have committed the offence and any provision of the law of the category 1 territory under which the conduct is alleged to constitute an offence;

(d) particulars of the sentence which may be imposed under the law of the category 1 territory in respect of the offence if the person is convicted of it.

(5) The statement is one that—

(a) the person in respect of whom the Part 1 warrant is issued has been convicted of an offence specified in the warrant by a court in the category 1 territory, and

(b) the Part 1 warrant is issued with a view to his arrest and extradition to the category 1 territory for the purpose of being sentenced for the offence or of serving a sentence of imprisonment or another form of detention imposed in respect of the offence.

(6) The information is—

(a) particulars of the person's identity;

(b) particulars of the conviction;

(c) particulars of any other warrant issued in the category 1 territory for the person's arrest in respect of the offence;

(d) particulars of the sentence which may be imposed under the law of the category 1 territory in respect of the offence, if the person has not been sentenced for the offence;

(e) particulars of the sentence which has been imposed under the law of the category 1 territory in respect of the offence, if the person has been sentenced for the offence.

(7) The designated authority may issue a certificate under this section if it believes that the authority which issued the Part 1 warrant has the function of issuing arrest warrants in the category 1 territory.

(8) A certificate under this section must certify that the authority which issued the Part 1 warrant has the function of issuing arrest warrants in the category 1 territory.

(9) The designated authority is the authority designated for the purposes of this Part by order made by the Secretary of State.

(10) An order made under subsection (9) may—

(a) designate more than one authority;

(b) designate different authorities for different parts of the United Kingdom.

[This section is printed as amended by the *Police and Justice Act* 2006, s.42 and Sched. 13.]

3–10 An EAW will be issued by a judicial authority and sent via that State's Central Authority to the UK for execution. Each jurisdiction within the EAW scheme has a central authority which provides administrative support and acts as the route of communicating incoming and outgoing EAWs or additional information that may have been requested or volunteered in response to some query or challenge. The central authority in England and Wales is the Serious Organised Crime Agency (SOCA) in Scotland, The Crown Office.

The EAW must have been issued by a judicial authority and will state whether the person to be arrested is to be prosecuted or has been convicted. Or both; see *Extradition Act 2003 (Multiple Offences) Order* 2003. It is insufficient to state that an arrest is sought "for legal proceedings" since the wording leaves the court unclear as to the stage the proceedings have reached in the requesting state; the precise wording on the head of the *pro forma* warrant annexed to the framework decision should be used and great care should be taken to ensure that there is nothing in the body of the warrant which detracts from that unequivocal statement: *Thompson v. France* [2009] A.C.D. 15, DC. It will give details of identity, particulars of the offence, how it was committed or the fact of a conviction, the possible or actual sentence together with details of any other outstanding warrants. Particulars of sentence must be contained within the warrant itself and it is not permissible to have regard to information supplied outside the warrant except in the case of ambiguity: *Tristan Haynes v. Malta* [2007] EWHC 2651. In that case the warrant referred to a number of offences but only one maximum sentence was specified. It was not clear whether that maximum was for a single offence or for all the offences. In a case involving multiple offences in which an aggregate sentence was imposed, s.2(6)(e) does not require Pt 1 requesting states to segregate the separate components of the aggregate sentence in respect of each individual offence: *Trepac v. Slovakia* [2006] EWHC 3346 (Admin); the only question that needs to be asked is whether the sentence for the conduct taken as a whole meets the requirement that it is a term of at least four months *Pilecki v. Poland* [2008] UKHL 7. It is common practice for member states to impose a single sentence of imprisonment to reflect the overall criminality of a defendant who has been convicted of multiple offences. Where this happens it is the only information which can be entered in the warrant and is compliant: *Jan Kucera v. Czech Republic* [2008] 4 All E.R. 80, DC. The warrant does not have to state the remaining period of sentence that a person has to serve: *Banasinski v. Poland* [2008] All E.R. (d) 253. A misstatement in the arrest warrant as to the remaining sentence to be served by an extraditee who had escaped from custody in the requesting state does not render the warrant invalid as it is information over and above that expressly required by the Framework Desicion 2002/584 art. 8: *Pietrzak v. Poland* [2008] EWHC 2138 (Admin).

The additional material set out in the pro forma warrant annexed to the Framework Decision goes way beyond what is required by art. 8(1) of that decision and its inclusion is not essential to the validity of the warrant; s.2(6) does not require it either. So where a warrant contains accurate details of the sentence which has been imposed but misstates the length of sentence left, the misstatement does not render the warrant invalid: *Pietzak v. Regional Court in Wloclawek, Poland* [2009] 1 W.L.R. 866. Neither the Framework Decision nor s.2(4)(c) explicitly require the victim to be named, nor did it have to include the precise date and time of an alleged offence: *Hewitt v. Spain* [2009] EWHC 2158 (Admin).

Where a warrant fails to identify the provision of law under which the person's conduct is alleged to constitute an offence, it does not conform to the requirements of s.2 and is invalid: *Hunt v. Belgium* [2006] EWHC 165; [2006] 2 All E.R. 735; *Hall v. Germany* [2006] EWHC 462; [2006] Extradition L.R. 94

The warrant must include particulars of the conduct which will be capable of constituting an extradition offence. Following *Dabas v. Spain* (2007) 2 All E.R. 641 a judge is entitled to limit the conduct alleging the offence to that which took place outside the UK: *Osunta v. Germany* [2008] 3 W.L.R 26. Charges must not be vague, *e.g.* in English terms "obtaining by deception" would not suffice: *Von der Pahlen v. Austria* [2006] EWHC 1672, where on a second application the warrant complied as it identified the victims, the number and size of advance payments and the nature of the fraudulent misrepresentations, the knowledge of misuse of other people's money by making unwarranted withdrawals from a business account and the period during which the withdrawals had been made. There is no need to become tied up in particular words. A description "misappropriation" is sufficient to satisfy particulars of conduct alleged as it is clearly theft and therefore there is no lack of specificity: *Sidlauskaite v. Prosecutor General's Office of the Republic of Lithuania* [2006] All E.R. (D) 276. The warrant must be read as a whole and due allowance must be made for the effects of translation; the warrant does not have to set out all the evidence against the fugitive: *Gabriel v. Spain* [2009] EWHC 1282 (Admin.). It is not necessary for a warrant to state that the individual is "unlawfully at large" if it can be inferred from the warrant as a whole: *Kuprevicius v. Lithuania* [2006] EWHC 1518.

There is no need to specify or identify the relevant *mens rea* of the English offence: so long as the information is capable of sustaining an inference as to the existence of the necessary *mens rea*; *Zak v. Poland* [2008] EWHC 470 (Admin).

Although there can be no formula for appropriate particularisation, in a post-conviction warrant, the requested person would need sufficient details of the circumstances of the underlying offences to enable him to understand what he has been convicted of and to consider whether any bars to extradition apply. It will almost always be necessary for a warrant to contain the number of offences of which the person has been convicted, and some information about when and where the offences were committed, and the person's participation in them, although not necessarily in the same level of detail as required in an accusation warrant. More particulars are appropriate in more complex crimes: *Sandi v. Romania* [2009] EWHC 3079 (Admin).

In considering the meaning of the words "any other warrant" in s.2(4)(b), art. 8 (1)(c) does not require an European arrest warrant to contain evidence of an earlier European arrest warrant on which it is not based but it does require it to contain evidence of the relevant domestic warrant on which it is based: *Louca v. Germany* [2010] 1 All E.R. 402. The Framework Decision is not intended to go so far as to require details of all previous warrants which may have been rejected. In *Jaso, Lopez, Hernandez v. Spain* [2008] 1 W.L.R. 2798 it was also made clear that the correct meaning of s.2(4)(b) is that a warrant is only required to contain particulars of an enforceable judgment on which the warrant is actually based, rather than any enforceable judgment that may have been issued in the past in relation to the relevant offences.

The effect of an inaccuracy in translation depends on its significance: where it has no material effect it does not invalidate the arrest warrant: *Glica v. Poland* [2008] EWHC 1111 (Admin). A typographical error as to the date of issue of a warrant does not affect its validity: *Aryantash v. France*, [2008] EWHC 2115 (Admin).

A warrant must be considered as a whole to decide whether a person is required for the purposes of prosecution or simply for investigation: *Harvey v. Portugal* [2007] EWHC 3282 (Admin). Here the judge had correctly decided that as the preamble to the warrant stated that the person be returned for "purposes of legal procedure" and further for "judicial interrogation" the reason for return was for the purposes of prosecution. Consideration has to be had for the conceptual and cultural differences between European countries in the way that they processed investigations and prosecutions. Where a fugitive has been convicted and sentenced in his absence in the requesting state, but the conviction and sentence are neither final nor enforceable, his case can be treated as an accusation case under s.2(3) even though he would not enjoy an unqualified right to a re-trial on the merits: *Caldarelli v. Italy* [2008] UKHL 51. A European arrest warrant for an accused person is still valid after conviction under Czech law as the conviction is not final and enforceable: *Usti Nad Labem Regional Court v. MJ* [2010] EWHC 463 (Admin). Providing as they do for international co-operation between states with different procedural regimes, the Framework Decision and the 2003 Act cannot be interpreted on the assumption that procedures which obtain in the UK obtain elsewhere. In *Sonea v. Mehedinti District Court* [2009] 2 All E.R. 821, DC (Admin) it was held that *Calderelli* was fact specific. In this case *Sonea* had submitted that, as he had a right to a retrial, having been convicted in his absence, the warrant should have been drafted as an accusation rather than a conviction warrant. The court stated that the Act envisaged a step by step approach. Where the warrant contains the statement required by s.2(2)(b), the judge has to decide whether the offence specified in the warrant is an extradition offence. If it isn't the person has to be discharged; if it is then the judge has to decide whether there are any bars to extradition. If there are not then the tests in s.11(4) and s.11(5) have to be considered and the outcome will depend on whether a person is unlawfully at large. If he is then the judge proceeds under s.20 and it is only then that a judge has to consider whether a person has been convicted in his presence or whether he had deliberately absented himself. Questions dealt with by s.20 cannot be dealt with as issues that determine the nature of the warrant. The plurality of functions of investigating magistrate, the police and the public prosecutor in other jurisdictions means that it is not always easy to see whether a particular case has crossed the boundary from suspicion or investigation into accusation. It is a question of fact and it is essential to keep in mind the "cosmopolitan approach" referred to in *Re Ismail* (1999) 1 A.C. 320 HL: *Arturo Paschayan v. Switzerland* [2008] EWHC 388 (Admin). This approach was endorsed in *Asztaslos v. Hungary* [2010] EWHC 237 (Admin). The phrases "is accused ... of the commission of an offence" and "for the purpose of being prosecuted" are not to be treated as terms of art. It is a question of fact whether the surrender is sought of an accused person and whether for the purposes of being prosecuted. It is wrong to approach the construction of the phrases solely from the perspective of English and Welsh criminal procedure. It is necessary to adopt a purposive construction to accommodate the differences between legal systems. Consideration of extrinsic factual or expert evidence to ascertain the warrant's purpose should be a last resort and in exceptional cases only. In *Belgium v. Bartlett* [2010] EWHC 1390 (Admin) it was said that extrinsic evidence should not be considered. A reference to pre-trial investigation rather than prosecution is irrelevant; although a distinct procedure in English law, it cannot be assumed that it is the case in civil law: *Rytmetis v. Lithuania* [2010] EWHC 1048 (Admin).

If the warrant is not valid there is no jurisdiction to order extradition: *Boudhiba v. Spain* [2006] 3 All E.R. 574. It is not necessary or appropriate to subject a warrant to the requirements of specificity accorded to particulars of, or sometimes required of, a count in an indictment or an allegation in a civil pleading in this country: *Fofana v. Thubin* [2006] EWHC 744. The warrant itself can amount to a certificate required under s.64(2)(b) and (c): *Dabas v. Spain*. Lord Bingham said that Pt 1 of the Act had to be read in the context of the Framework Decision which intends to simplify and expedite procedures and which is binding on the UK. That Framework makes no mention of a certificate but sets out the requirements for a warrant. The warrant in this case complied with these requirements and a decision that a separate certificate is required would re-introduce an element of technicality which the Framework Decision intended to banish and would frustrate the intention that a warrant in common form should be uniformly acceptable in all member states.

It is not for the court to consider the merits of any proposed prosecution but there must be clarity in relation to the stage which proceedings have reached in the foreign jurisdiction: *Vey v. Public Prosecutor of Montlucon* [2006] EWHC 760. In this case the issue was whether the person was merely wanted for questioning or whether an accusation had been made.

The designated authority for England and Wales is the Serious Organised Crime Agency (SOCA). That authority will certify whether the judicial authority has the function of issuing arrest warrants in the requesting country. The designation by European Member States of a body as a judicial authority is determinative of that body being a judicial authority for the purposes of s.2: *Enander v. Governor of HM Prison Brixton* [2005] Extradition L.R. 135.

Once refugee status has been granted a refugee cannot be extradited to his country of nationality while his refugee status remains: ss.39, 121. A judge cannot determine that status in an extradition hearing and it would only be in rare cases, where there was some factual basis for regarding the refugee status as questionable that it would be appropriate to adjourn the hearing pending a determination by the secretary of state of the continuation of refugee status: *Poland v. Dytlow* [2009] EWHC 1009 (Admin.).

If an asylum claim is made in the course of extradition proceedings the judge **must** adjourn until the claim is "finally determined"—s.39 (3)/121(3).

Chickvarkin v. S. of S. [2011] EWCA Civ. 91 provides powerful *obita* that if an asylum claim is being "actively considered" and involves (as is likely) human rights issues extradition proceedings should be adjourned until that claim is determined.

Where a person is unlawfully at large from serving a sentence in a country other than the convicting country under special arrangements for the transfer of prisoners a warrant may be issued by either the convicting country or the country where he is serving the sentence: s.63. **3–11**

Once the certificate has been issued by the designated authority a police or customs officer may execute the foreign warrant against a member of the public and, may do so, even if the warrant is not in his possession. There are also provisions for service personnel to be arrested by service policemen: s.3.

In cases of urgency a person may be arrested without warrant. This is called a provisional arrest and may take place where an officer has reasonable grounds for believing that a Pt 1 warrant has been or will be issued: s.5.

Extradition Act 2003, s.5(1)–(2)

Provisional arrest

5.—(1) A constable, a customs officer or a service policeman may arrest a person without a warrant if he has reasonable grounds for believing— **3–12**

(a) that a Part 1 warrant has been or will be issued in respect of the person by an authority of a category 1 territory, and

(b) that the authority has the function of issuing arrest warrants in the category 1 territory.

(2) A constable or a customs officer may arrest a person under subsection (1) in any part of the United Kingdom.

(2) Part 2 warrant

A warrant may be a provisional or certified warrant. **3–13**

A certified warrant will be considered where a certificate has been sent from the Secretary of State to a designated district judge. The certificate will be issued where a category two country requests the extradition of someone either alleged to have committed an offence or who has been convicted of an offence and provides valid supporting documentation through the diplomatic channels to the Secretary of State. It is a matter for the Secretary of State whether the documents sent to him as the formal requisition comply with requirements: *Governor of Brixton Prison, ex p. Cuoghi, The Times*, May 12, 1998.

Extradition Act 2003, s.70

Extradition request and certificate

70.—(1) The Secretary of State must issue a certificate under this section if he receives a valid request for the extradition to a category 2 territory of a person who is in the United Kingdom. **3–14**

(2) But subsection (1) does not apply if the Secretary of State decides under section 126 that the request is not to be proceeded with.

(3) A request for a person's extradition is valid if—

(a) it contains the statement referred to in subsection (4), and

(b) it is made in the approved way.

(4) The statement is one that the person—

(a) is accused in the category 2 territory of the commission of an offence specified in the request, or

(b) is alleged to be unlawfully at large after conviction by a court in the category 2 territory of an offence specified in the request.

(5) A request for extradition to a category 2 territory which is a British overseas territory is made in the approved way if it is made by or on behalf of the person administering the territory.

(6) A request for extradition to a category 2 territory which is the Hong Kong Special Administrative Region of the People's Republic of China is made in the approved way if it is made by or on behalf of the government of the Region.

(7) A request for extradition to any other category 2 territory is made in the approved way if it is made—

(a) by an authority of the territory which the Secretary of State believes has the function of making requests for extradition in that territory, or

(b) by a person recognised by the Secretary of State as a diplomatic or consular representative of the territory.

(8) A certificate under this section must certify that the request is made in the approved way.

(9) If a certificate is issued under this section the Secretary of State must send these documents to the appropriate judge—

(a) the request;

(b) the certificate;

(c) a copy of any relevant Order in Council.

3–15 The Secretary of State may choose not to issue a certificate if there are competing claims. He may defer the claim: s.126.

Upon receipt of the relevant documentation a designated judge may issue a warrant of arrest with or without bail: s.71.

It is important that a state requesting extradition fairly and properly describes the conduct alleged: *R. (Castillo) v. Spain* [2005] 1 W.L.R. 1043. The Secretary of State can infer from the whole of the documentation sent by the requesting state whether the person is an accused or convicted person: *Akaroglu v. Romania* (2008) 1 All E.R. 27. The facts must be clear and courts should be reluctant to fill a gap: *R. (Bleta) v. Secretary of State for the Home Department* [2005] 1 All E.R. 810. It has been held, under the old law, that the Secretary of State could issue a further authority to proceed to clarify the first: *Fernandes, Fernandes, Trevasso v. Governor of Brixton Prison, The Commonwealth of the Bahamas* [2004] EWHC 2207.

Extradition Act 2003, s.71(1)–(7)

Arrest warrant following extradition request

3–16 **71.**—(1) This section applies if the Secretary of State sends documents to the appropriate judge under section 70.

(2) The judge may issue a warrant for the arrest of the person whose extradition is requested if the judge has reasonable grounds for believing that—

(a) the offence in respect of which extradition is requested is an extradition offence, and

(b) there is evidence falling within subsection (3).

(3) The evidence is—

(a) evidence that would justify the issue of a warrant for the arrest of a person accused of the offence within the judge's jurisdiction, if the person whose extradition is requested is accused of the commission of the offence;

(b) evidence that would justify the issue of a warrant for the arrest of a person unlawfully at large after conviction of the offence within the judge's jurisdiction, if the person whose extradition is requested is alleged to be unlawfully at large after conviction of the offence.

(4) But if the category 2 territory to which extradition is requested is designated for the purposes of this section by order made by the Secretary of State, subsections (2) and (3) have effect as if "evidence" read "information".

(5) A warrant issued under this section may—

(a) be executed by any person to whom it is directed or by any constable or customs officer;

(b) be executed even if neither the warrant nor a copy of it is in the possession of the person executing it at the time of the arrest.

(6) If a warrant issued under this section in respect of a person is directed to a service policeman, it may be executed in any place where the service policeman would have power to arrest the person under the appropriate service law if the person had committed an offence under that law.

(7) In any other case, a warrant issued under this section may be executed in any part of the United Kingdom.

The designated district judge must be satisfied that the offence is an extradition offence and that a warrant for similar circumstances in the UK would be justified. The warrant may be executed even if it is not in the possession of the arresting officer. **3–17**

It is not necessary for a warrant to slavishly follow the language of the statute but it has to make clear in some way that the person concerned is unlawfully at large. It is not the issue of a warrant which sets the process of extradition in train but the issue of a warrant which complies with the prescribed conditions: *Pinto v. Governor of Brixton Prison* [2004] EWHC 2986. In that case the person was described as not having, on the term of a precarious prolonged exit presented himself at the State Prison. This was held not to state clearly that the person was unlawfully at large.

A provisional warrant may be issued under s.73 as a preliminary step at a time when no formal request for extradition has been made.

Extradition Act 2003, s.73(1)–(7)

Provisional warrant

73.—(1) This section applies if a justice of the peace is satisfied on information in writing and on oath that a person within subsection (2)— **3–18**

(a) is or is believed to be in the United Kingdom, or

(b) is or is believed to be on his way to the United Kingdom.

(2) A person is within this subsection if—

(a) he is accused in a category 2 territory of the commission of an offence, or

(b) he is alleged to be unlawfully at large after conviction of an offence by a court in a category 2 territory.

(3) The justice may issue a warrant for the arrest of the person (a provisional warrant) if he has reasonable grounds for believing that—

(a) the offence of which the person is accused or has been convicted is an extradition offence, and

(b) there is written evidence falling within subsection (4).

(4) The evidence is—

(a) evidence that would justify the issue of a warrant for the arrest of a person accused of the offence within the justice's jurisdiction, if the person in respect of whom the warrant is sought is accused of the commission of the offence;

(b) evidence that would justify the issue of a warrant for the arrest of a person unlawfully at large after conviction of the offence within the justice's jurisdiction, if the person in respect of whom the warrant is sought is alleged to be unlawfully at large after conviction of the offence.

(5) But if the category 2 territory is designated for the purposes of this section by order made by the Secretary of State, subsections (3) and (4) have effect as if "evidence" read "information".

(6) A provisional warrant may—

(a) be executed by any person to whom it is directed or by any constable or customs officer;

(b) be executed even if neither the warrant nor a copy of it is in the possession of the person executing it at the time of the arrest.

(7) If a warrant issued under this section in respect of a person is directed to a service policeman, it may be executed in any place where the service policeman would have power to arrest the person under the appropriate service law if the person had committed an offence under that law.

3–19 It is quite common for this type of warrant to be sought where it is deemed urgent. Many people wanted for extradition crimes are found to be in transit or about to leave the country or are on their way to this country and there is no time for a formal request under s.70. Information is often received from Interpol through police channels pending receipt of a formal extradition request and supporting documentation. The information should state that extradition will be sought and give sufficient facts about the person, the offence and the possible penalty.

Although an application may be made to any magistrate, applications are generally dealt with at the City of Westminster Magistrates' Court by a designated judge. The police will make contact with the justices' clerk or one of the legal advisers who will check the information for any defects and either draft a warrant for the judge's consideration or check a warrant which has already been prepared by the police. The practice of the legal adviser checking the process was approved in *Governor of Pentonville Prison, ex p. Osman (No.3)* [1990] 1 All E.R. 999.

The judge must be satisfied on the written information that the allegation would amount to an extradition offence and that a warrant is justified. In *Evans, ex p. Pinochet Ugarte, The Times*, November 3, 1998, a second provisional warrant was issued on the same information when the first warrant, having been issued in a very tight timescale, was found to be defective. That practice was upheld although Lord Bingham C.J. stated that it was unusual and generally undesirable.

In *Deuss v. Attorney General of Bermuda* [2009] UKPC 38, the statutory definition of an "extradition crime" in relation to British territories was discussed. It was said that a magistrate is entitled to issue a provisional warrant provided he receives evidence that satisfies him that the defendant is accused of conduct within the jurisdiction of another country which would, if committed in a British territory, justify the issue of a warrant for his arrest; there is no requirement that a magistrate must satisfy himself that the conduct constitutes an extradition crime.

3–20 The case of *Bow Street Magistrates' Court, ex p. Allison, The Times*, June 5, 1997 under the previous legislation defined an urgent case as one that is urgent at the time of the issue of the warrant, regardless of the cause of the urgency. In that case the person, who had been in custody awaiting extradition to the USA for other offences, was likely to be released very soon and was liable to abscond.

If a person is "on his way" s.73(1)(b) the judge should be satisfied that he has actually boarded a flight to this country and that there are no stops en route where he might get off. Information that a flight is booked to or via the UK will ordinarily be deemed sufficient. So long as the person has boarded the flight/ship.

The warrant may be executed even if it is not in the possession of the arresting officer. Premises may be entered and searched to facilitate an arrest. Upon arrest the person and the premises where the person was found or had recently been at, may be searched for evidence relating to the offence or the identity of the person: ss.161, 162 and 163.

3–21 After arrest the police also have powers in relation to entry and search of premises, seizure of material, the taking of photographs, fingerprints and other samples: ss.164–168. Codes of Practice are in existence.

The warrant may be issued with or without bail. A decision to bail is very rare and not generally good practice. Occasionally arrests take place by arrangement with the police within the City of Westminster Magistrates' Court building with the purpose of bringing a person before a designated judge without delay. Where the police bail the person, a police officer will liaise with the court to take account of the court lists and statutory time limits. The Secretary of State will be informed because where the person is arrested on a provisional warrant the court will need the Secretary of State's order before it can proceed. It should be noted that the judge must receive the certificate and supporting documentation within 45 days from the date of arrest (or any longer period agreed with a particular state) otherwise the person may be discharged.

Part 1

IV. REPRESENTATION

The requesting state will in most cases be represented by the Crown Prosecution Service, which acts as an agent. Many of its powers, being peculiar to the law of England and Wales, *e.g.* discontinuance, do not apply in extradition matters. The requesting state may alternatively instruct a firm of solicitors. See *DPP ex.p Thom* [1996] C.L.R. 116 and *Germany v. Kleinschmidt* [2005] EWHC 1373 (Admin). The CPS allocates all extradition cases to the Extradition Unit of its Specialist Crime Division using in-house lawyers or counsel. A Chinese walls policy is applied with these lawyers declining to prosecute domestic UK offences, which often bring Requested Persons before an extradition court following arrest by police for domestic offences following which the extradition request comes to light. This is to preserve the agent or quasi solicitor client relationship in both Pt 1 and Pt 2 cases: see *R. (on the application of Syed Talha Ahsan) v. DPP and the USA* [2008] EWHC 666 (Admin). Crown Prosecution Service lawyers drafting an EAW for a Judicial Authority without the latter's knowledge and consent risks being deemed an abuse of process: *Central Examining Court of the National Court of Madrid v. City of Westminster Magistrates' Court* [2007] EWHC 2059(Admin). The C.P.S. should ordinarily be expected to follow instructions in Pt 1 and Pt 2 cases but remains a public authority (s.6 *Human Rights Act* 1998) and must not act contrary to that role – see *R. (on the application of Lotfi Rassi) v. Secretary of State for the Home Department* [2007] EWCA Civ 243. **3–22**

The person arrested may instruct solicitors and may apply for a legal representation order. Representation orders in extradition cases follow the same requirements as for domestic proceedings. Access to a Duty Solicitor at the first (Initial Hearing) is not only permissible but actively encouraged by the designated judges at the City of Westminster Magistrates' Court. Almost all duty solicitors accepting these cases have some experience of this area of law and in many cases extensive expertise. Counsel may be instructed, including, unusually for the Magistrates' Court, Queen's Counsel subject to meeting the requirements of the Legal Aid Regulations. In practice such applications are considered upon written application by a designated judge. In *Bow Street Magistrates' Court, ex p. Shayler* [1999] 1 All E.R. 98 (albeit a potential inward extradition) the refusal of legal aid at the stage that a warrant had been issued but not executed was upheld.

V. PROCEDURE

A. First Appearance Before the Court

Once a person is arrested he must be brought before a designated judge as soon as practicable except in the case where a person has been provisionally arrested under s.5 when he must be brought before the judge within 48 hours: ss.4, 6 and 72. **3–23**

Weekends and certain specified holidays are excluded from the calculation of the 48 hour period and. the time limit for the provision of documents may be extended under s.6 (3B).

Habeas corpus is available to challenge a decision not to bring the arrested person before the court as soon as practicable: *Nikonovs v. Governor of Brixton Prison* [2005] EWHC 2405; [2006] 1 All E.R. 927. Here the person arrested had erroneously been taken before the court on a Monday instead of the previous Saturday due to a mistake of fact in believing a court was not sitting on that day.

In each case a copy of the warrant must be given to the person arrested as soon as practicable after arrest. Failure to do so may result in the person's discharge.

The need for a court to have sight of the warrant under s.8(2)(d) is in order to ensure that there are proceedings abroad but there is no requirement that every offence alleged is included in the warrant: *Hashmi v. United States of America* [2007] EWHC 564, Admin. On the other hand information is not limited to that which is in the originating request; a letter in response to proposed admissions and which comes to light later is admissible: *Mauro v. United States of America* [2009] EWHC 150 (Admin).

The prosecutor may prepare "charges" in the form of offences known to the law of England and Wales but they have no formal status; they are there to assist the judge: *Bow Street Magistrates' Court, ex p. Kline*, unreported, June 30, 1999. With the increase in the volume of cases most prosecutors, save in complex cases, identify orally the charges or offences that mirrors the conduct in the EAW or Pt 2 request.

3–24 The judge will want to establish identity and whether the person will consent to extradition. If consent is not forthcoming the judge must fix the date of the extradition hearing and timetable the rest of the proceedings. He may adjourn the proceedings and remand the person in custody or bail: ss.8, 71. The presumption of bail applies unless the person is alleged to be unlawfully at large after conviction: s.198. Both defence and prosecution may appeal an adverse decision which will be determined upon by the High Court, s.22(1A) *Criminal Justice Act* 1967—defence appeal and s.200 of the Act prosecution appeal. Where a person is remanded in custody the judge may give a direction that any attendance at a hearing other than the extradition hearing itself may be via a live link so long as it is not contrary to the interests of justice: s.206A. This order may be rescinded under s.206B.

Where the judge is informed that the person is charged with an offence in the United Kingdom he must grant an adjournment; he may also adjourn where the person is in custody in the United Kingdom serving a sentence of imprisonment or other form of detention: ss.8A, 8B, 22,23, 76A, 76B, 88 and 89. Where an adjournment is granted and the hearing of the offence has been concluded or the sentence has been served, extradition proceedings should recommence: s.216.

An extradition hearing does not begin simply because the case is called on in court—*Gronostajski v. Poland* [2007] EWHC 3314; something has to be said or done to show that extradition has started; merely adjourning proceedings is not enough. It is sufficient for the judge to make a statement in open court that proceedings have started, even if that is followed immediately by a decision to adjourn. Although the act of ordering an adjournment is a step in the extradition process, it does not, in itself, amount to taking a step in the process: *Kozluk v. Poland* [2010] 4 C.D. 83. A common practice is for the designated judge to say words to the effect "deemed opened no rulings".

Identity

3–25 The question of identity must be established on a balance of probabilities: ss.7, 78. It is to be determined at the initial hearing. If resolved in the affirmative, the extradition follows. The 2003 Act does not contemplate that there could be a second chance to raise identity at a later hearing: *Nur v. Van Der Valk* [2005] EWHC 1874. It is doubtful whether a judge has the jurisdiction to review the finding of identity previously made at an earlier hearing; the appropriate route is judicial review: *Hilali v Central Court of Criminal Proceedings, Madrid* [2006] 4 All E.R. 435.

The defendant may admit that he is the person concerned. If identification is in dispute, however, evidence must be brought before the court. Photographic or video evidence may be submitted: *Bradshar, Re*, unreported, February 28, 1984; *Governor of Pentonville Prison, ex p. Rodriguez, The Times*, November 29, 1984, DC; *Governor of Pentonville Prison, ex p. Voets* [1986] 2 All E.R. 630.

3–26 A passport linking the fugitive to the papers was approved in *Khan, Re*, unreported,

June 30, 1995. Evidence of what was said at the time of arrest has also been approved: *Governor of Pentonville Prison, ex p. Boettlicher*, unreported, April 28, 1993. In that case the fugitive had given his name, address and date of birth as contained in the papers and had remarked that the alleged assault was against his girlfriend.

In *Osawe v. Government of HM Prison Brixton* [2003] EWHC 2140, fingerprints and photographs overruled the fact that the person's name was different from that on the papers. In *Artan Brahja v. 1) the Governor of HM Prison Brixton 2) the Government of Italy* [2003] EWHC 509 Admin, it was held, where details on the person's driving licence were different, that minor discrepancies were not sufficient to raise doubts over identity.

If there is insufficient evidence to show that the person is the one to whom the warrant refers he must be discharged.

An unusual name, date of birth, abode and passport number even if the latter is found in papers relating to a co-defendant is sufficient evidence for identification: *Savvas v. Govt. of Italy* [2004] EWHC 1233. It is helpful to give reasons for a decision on identity: *Stefan v. Albania* [2007] EWHC 267 (Admin).

The proceedings may be adjourned to allow for evidence to be called.

Consent to extradition

The court must inform the person of his right to consent to extradition and the fact that consent will be irrevocable: ss.7 and 45 for Pt 1 cases and ss.127 and 128 for Pt 2 cases. They are in similar terms. **3–27**

If the person wishes to consent there is no reason why the judge cannot proceed to order extradition or in Pt 2 cases forward the case to the Secretary of State for his decision. The person must either be legally represented or has been offered legal aid but has refused or failed to apply or it has been refused or withdrawn. The consent must be recorded in writing. This is intended to provide a speedy process and protection is afforded through legal advice. A common practice is to ensure, where necessary, a court appointed interpreter countersigns the Requested Person's signature acknowledging that the standard form setting out the consequences of consenting has been translated. This document is then signed by the designated Judge.

Where consent is given before any date is fixed for an extradition hearing there is no obligation to fix a hearing and that consent reverses s.22 so that the extradition proceedings do not have to be adjourned until domestic proceedings have been concluded: *R. (on the application of Governor of Wandsworth Prison) v. Kinderis* [2007] EWHC 998 (Admin), *The Times*, June 26, 2007. The decision in *Kinderis* is now avoided in almost all cases by the operation of ss.8A, 76A which says the designated judge "**must** order further proceedings in respect of the extradition to be adjourned" until the conclusion of domestic proceedings or in ss.8B/76B "may order" an adjournment until "released from detention pursuant to the sentence (whether on licence or otherwise)". The practice is to adjourn proceedings, without dealing with consent, until conclusion of any outstanding domestic trial or to a date shortly before release would otherwise take place.

Where consent is not forthcoming, the judge will set the hearing date. In Pt 1 proceedings the time limit set in s.8 is 21 days from the date of arrest but there is provision for a later date to be fixed if it is in the interests of justice. Subsequently the hearing may be adjourned further. The judge is expected to manage the progress of the case to ensure there is no undue delay. The person will either be remanded in custody or on bail.

So far as Pt 2 proceedings are concerned the judge will proceed to timetable the case in accordance with the statutory time limits. Where the arrest is under a certified warrant the hearing date must not be later than two months from the date that the person first appears before the court although this period may be extended if the interests of justice so require: s.75. Where the arrest is under a provisional warrant, a hearing must **3–28** be fixed within two months from the date that the certificate from the Secretary of State is due to be received by the court.

B. THE EXTRADITION HEARING

(1) Extradition proceedings

3–29 Extradition proceedings are classified as a type of summary proceeding. They are criminal proceedings for the purposes of legal representation under the *Access to Justice Act* 1999. The general right to bail under the *Bail Act* 1976 applies unless the person is alleged to be unlawfully at large after conviction. Statutory time limits must be complied with and extensions granted only in exceptional circumstances. Abuse of process can be considered in extradition proceedings but the rules of disclosure do not apply as they form part of an adversarial process which differs from extradition proceedings in which the court must satisfy itself that the requirements for making an order are satisfied. There is a presumption that requesting states act in good faith when making an extradition request and a court will be slow to find that a requesting state has acted in bad faith. An argument can only be sustained if a person can (a) identify with specificity what conduct is said to be an abuse; (b); satisfy the court that such conduct is capable of constituting abuse and (c) that such conduct has occurred. If all three conditions are met then the court will require an explanation from the requesting state: *United States v. Tollman* [2008] 3 All E.R. 150. It is not an abuse where a third count had erroneously slipped into a warrant by mistake: *Haynes v. Malta* [2007] EWHC 2651 Admin and [2007] Extradition L.R. 295 . Where the requesting authority or state will not supply further information or evidence then the judge should hold that fair process is impossible and discharge the person. If a judge fears an abuse of process he should call for the necessary information or evidence for determining that issue and where fairness requires that material to be disclosed and the requesting authority or state will not agree, a judge should hold that fair process is impossible and discharge the person. An abuse of process argument may be a delaying tactic and a judge should be alert to that: *R. (United States of America) v. Bow Street Magistrates' Court and R. (Central Examining Court, Madrid) v. Bow Street Magistrates' Court* (2007) 1 W.L.R. 1157. The simple provision of drafting assistance by the Crown Prosecution Service to the claimant court in the preparation of a European arrest warrant is not, in law, capable of constituting an abuse of process: *Spain v City of Westminster Magistrates Court* [2007] EWHC 2059 (Admin). In *McKinnon v. USA* [2008] 1 W.L.R. 1739, on appeal, abuse of process was alleged on the grounds of being placed under the pressure of plea bargaining. The appeal was dismissed; UK law provides for credit for guilty pleas and the difference between the two countries is not as stark as had been suggested; a discount would have to be very substantially more generous than anything promised in this case before it could constitute unlawful pressure such as to vitiate the process; similarly, the predicted consequences of non-cooperation would need to go significantly beyond what could properly be regarded as a defendant's just deserts on conviction to constitute unlawful pressure: [2008] 1 W.L.R. 1739 .

A diplomatic note is, in international law, regarded as binding on the issuing state. Diplomatic notes issued by the United States government guaranteeing that on extradition to the United States alleged terrorists will not be put on trial before a military commission nor designated as enemy combatants can be relied upon, in the absence of strong contrary evidence, as providing a sufficient guarantee that, if extradited, their human rights will be protected: *Ahmad v. Government of the United States of America* [2006] EWHC 2927; [2007] H.R.L.R. 8. Similarly in *Gomes & Goodyer v. Govern of Trinidad & Tobago* [2009] UKHL 21 a diplomatic note as to which prison the men would be placed in was deemed acceptable, all other prisons, save the one in the Note, being deemed, on agreed expert evidence, accommodation contrary to art. 3 ECHR.

Extradition Act 2003, ss.9(1), (4), (5); 77(1), (4), (5)

Judge's powers at extradition hearing

3–30 **9. & 77.**—(1) In England and Wales, at the extradition hearing the appropriate judge has the same powers (as nearly as may be) as a magistrates' court would have if the proceedings were the summary trial of an information against the person in respect of whom the Part I warrant was issued.

(4) If the judge adjourns the extradition hearing he must remand the person in custody or on bail.

(5) If the judge remands the person in custody he may later grant bail.

The extradition hearing will be conducted as if it were a summary trial but no plea is taken as the person is not being tried in this country. The advocate for the requesting country will open the case and deal with preliminary matters. For EAW requests the warrant will be relied upon as the detailed basis for extradition. **No evidence** of any kind is required. Many Pt 2 countries, as designated by the Secretary of State, are not required to establish a prima facie case—see Extradition Arrangements at the end of this chapter for those countries currently so designated. See 3–100. Documentation supplied to the Secretary of State, often including affidavits from investigating police officers and prosecutors outlining the case, will be considered. Those jurisdictions required to produce a prima facie case generally provide much the same material but it must be "receivable" s.202 and comply with s.205. Live evidence need not be called and, in practice, rarely is by a prosecuting authority.The judge may call for further information from the country seeking extradition pursuant to art. 15 of the European Council Framework Decision of June 13, 2002 on the European arrest warrant and the surrender procedures between Member States (2002/584/JHA; OJ/2002/L190). In practice requests usually are from the CPS to the requesting Judicial Authority. However, a designated judge may, of their own motion, seek further information to clarify a point raised directly with another Judicial Authority in Pt 1 EAW cases. For Pt 2 cases all communications go via the Home Office. In Pt 1 cases, especially where translation of documents may be required, via SOCA as the central authority. **3–31**

There is power to adjourn: *Raffile v. United States of America* [2004] EWHC 2913; [2005] 1 All E.R. 889. In *Handa v. High Instance Court of Paris* [2004] EWHC 3116, it was stated that it is irrational to refuse to adjourn proceedings in circumstances where there is no statutory power enabling a serving prisoner to be released earlier than he should be in order that he could be extradited and where there is no reasonable cause for delay and no reasons not to adjourn.

The court may adjourn for the purposes of obtaining psychiatric reports: *Olah v. Regional Court in Plzen, Czech Republic* [2008] EWHC 2701 (Admin).

In Pt 2 cases the judge must ensure he has: **3–32**

— the certificate from the Secretary of State;

— particulars of the person whose extradition is requested;

— particulars of the offence specified in the offence; and

— an arrest warrant issued in the requesting state or a certificate of conviction from the requesting state and details of the sentence, if any.

He must satisfy himself that the documents have been served upon the person: s.78. Where the Secretary of State certifies that special extradition arrangements have been made he may extend the time in which the judge ought to receive the papers: *Brown v. Governor of Belmarsh Prison* [2007] 2 W.L.R. 1184. This was a particularly involved and lengthy case involving four defendants and allegations of genocide in Rwanda.

Extradition Act 2003, s.78

Initial stages of extradition hearing

78.—(1) This section applies if a person alleged to be the person whose extradition is requested appears or is brought before the appropriate judge for the extradition hearing. **3–33**

(2) The judge must decide whether the documents sent to him by the Secretary of State consist of (or include)—

(a) the documents referred to in section 70(9);

(b) particulars of the person whose extradition is requested;

(c) particulars of the offence specified in the request;

(d) in the case of a person accused of an offence, a warrant for his arrest issued in the category 2 territory;

(e) in the case of a person alleged to be unlawfully at large after conviction of an offence, a certificate issued in the category 2 territory of the conviction and (if he has been sentenced) of the sentence.

(3) If the judge decides the question in subsection (2) in the negative he must order the person's discharge.

(4) If the judge decides that question in the affirmative he must decide whether—

(a) the person appearing or brought before him is the person whose extradition is requested;

(b) the offence specified in the request is an extradition offence;

(c) copies of the documents sent to the judge by the Secretary of State have been served on the person.

(5) The judge must decide the question in subsection (4)(a) on a balance of probabilities.

(6) If the judge decides any of the questions in subsection (4) in the negative he must order the person's discharge.

(7) If the judge decides those questions in the affirmative he must proceed under section 79.

(8) The reference in subsection (2)(d) to a warrant for a person's arrest includes a reference to a judicial document authorising his arrest.

3–34 The judge must decide whether the offence is an extradition offence and whether extradition is barred within the terms of the Act but he is not concerned with proof of the facts or possibilities of other relevant factors as those are matters for trial. It is sufficient that the conduct described in the request amounts to an offence in English law: *Kadre v. France* [2006] A.C.D. 26.

Service of documents under s.78(4) is mandatory but there is nothing in the statute to say that the documents must be served before the commencement of the extradition hearing. Neither does the Act expressly state by whom or by when service is to be effected. Normally service should be effected before the commencement of the hearing but in appropriate circumstances the court may adjourn the hearing under s.77(4) to enable service to be effected and in practice, it will be the CPS which will have to undertake service:*Germany v. Kleinschmidt* [2005] 3 All E.R. 759. A poor translation of a prosecution document detailing allegations cannot be treated as particularising conduct alleged to constitute an offence and therefore fails to meet the requirements of s.78(2)(c): *Dudko v. Russia* [2010] EWHC 1125 (Admin).

The *Criminal Procedure Rules* apply to extradition proceedings but they govern procedure only; they are not to be used to modify or change Parliament's intention so as to create an additional exception to the Act: *Hubner v. Czech Republic* [2009] EWHC 2929 (Admin).

Normal rules of criminal evidence and procedure apply so long as they are construed in the context of extradition proceedings and subject to the express provisions of the Act: *The Governor of Brixton Prison ex. p Levin* [1997] A.C. 741 and *USA, R. (on the application of) v. Senior District Judge, Bow Street Magistrates' Court* [2007] 1 W.L.R. 1157 (DC). The hearsay rules in the CJA 2003 do not apply to extradition proceedings: *Friesel v. USA* [2009] EWHC 1659 (Admin) (DC).

(2) Extradition offence

3–35 The Act differentiates between those convicted of offences and sentenced and those who are merely accused of committing offences.

Offenders who have been sentenced

3–36 Part 1 cases are dealt with under s.65.

Extradition Act 2003, s.65

Extradition offences: person sentenced for offence

3–37 **65.**—(1) This section applies in relation to conduct of a person if—

(a) he is alleged to be unlawfully at large after conviction by a court in a category 1 territory of an offence constituted by the conduct, and

(b) he has been sentenced for the offence.

(2) The conduct constitutes an extradition offence in relation to the category 1 territory if these conditions are satisfied—

(a) the conduct occurs in the category 1 territory and no part of it occurs in the United Kingdom;

(b) a certificate issued by an appropriate authority of the category 1 territory shows that the conduct falls within the European framework list;

(c) the certificate shows that a sentence of imprisonment or another form of detention for a term of 12 months or a greater punishment has been imposed in the category 1 territory in respect of the conduct.

(3) The conduct also constitutes an extradition offence in relation to the category 1 territory if these conditions are satisfied—

(a) the conduct occurs in the category 1 territory;

(b) the conduct would constitute an offence under the law of the relevant part of the United Kingdom if it occurred in that part of the United Kingdom;

(c) a sentence of imprisonment or another form of detention for a term of 4 months or a greater punishment has been imposed in the category 1 territory in respect of the conduct.

(4) The conduct also constitutes an extradition offence in relation to the category 1 territory if these conditions are satisfied—

(a) the conduct occurs outside the category 1 territory;

(b) a sentence of imprisonment or another form of detention for a term of 4 months or a greater punishment has been imposed in the category 1 territory in respect of the conduct;

(c) in corresponding circumstances equivalent conduct would constitute an extra-territorial offence under the law of the relevant part of the United Kingdom punishable with imprisonment or another form of detention for a term of 12 months or a greater punishment.

(5) The conduct also constitutes an extradition offence in relation to the category 1 territory if these conditions are satisfied—

(a) the conduct occurs outside the category 1 territory and no part of it occurs in the United Kingdom;

(b) the conduct would constitute an offence under the law of the relevant part of the United Kingdom punishable with imprisonment or another form of detention for a term of 12 months or a greater punishment if it occurred in that part of the United Kingdom;

(c) a sentence of imprisonment or another form of detention for a term of 4 months or a greater punishment has been imposed in the category 1 territory in respect of the conduct.

(6) The conduct also constitutes an extradition offence in relation to the category 1 territory if these conditions are satisfied—

(a) the conduct occurs outside the category 1 territory and no part of it occurs in the United Kingdom;

(b) a sentence of imprisonment or another form of detention for a term of 4 months or a greater punishment has been imposed in the category 1 territory in respect of the conduct;

(c) the conduct constitutes or if committed in the United Kingdom would constitute an offence mentioned in subsection (7).

(7) The offences are—

(a) an offence under section 51 or 58 of the *International Criminal Court Act* 2001 (genocide, crimes against humanity and war crimes);

(b) an offence under section 52 or 59 of that Act (conduct ancillary to genocide etc committed outside the jurisdiction);

(c) an ancillary offence, as defined in section 55 or 62 of that Act, in relation to an offence falling within paragraph (a) or (b);

(d) an offence under section 1 of the *International Criminal Court (Scotland) Act* 2001 (genocide, crimes against humanity and war crimes);

Part I

(e) an offence under section 2 of that Act (conduct ancillary to genocide etc committed outside the jurisdiction);

(f) an ancillary offence, as defined in section 7 of that Act, in relation to an offence falling within paragraph (d) or (e).

(8) For the purposes of subsections (3)(b), (4)(c) and (5)(b)—

(a) if the conduct relates to a tax or duty, it is immaterial that the law of the relevant part of the United Kingdom does not impose the same kind of tax or duty or does not contain rules of the same kind as those of the law of the category 1 territory;

(b) if the conduct relates to customs or exchange, it is immaterial that the law of the relevant part of the United Kingdom does not contain rules of the same kind as those of the law of the category 1 territory.

(9) This section applies for the purposes of this Part.

3–38 The definition of an extradition offence where a person has been sentenced depends upon whether the conduct has occurred within or outside the territory of the requesting state.

Where the conduct has occurred in the territory of the requesting state, it is an extradition offence if it is certified as conduct within the European Framework list and he has been sentenced to a minimum of 12 months' imprisonment or detention or it is an offence also within the UK and a sentence of four months' or more imprisonment or detention has been imposed.

Where the conduct has occurred outside the territory of the requesting state, it is an extradition offence if a minimum four-month sentence of imprisonment or detention has been imposed and the conduct amounts to an extra-territorial offence in the UK punishable with a minimum of 12 months or the conduct amounts to an offence punishable with a minimum of 12 months in UK and a minimum of four months has been imposed in the requesting state or a minimum sentence of four months has been imposed in the requesting state and the offence is one of genocide, crimes against humanity or war crimes or an ancillary offence. A European arrest warrant can be validly executed for the surrender of a fugitive whose criminal conduct took place partly in the state issuing the warrant and partly in the UK. Conduct in s.65 means the conduct complained of or relied on in the warrant, s.65(3) does not require that all conduct takes place in the category 1 territory. It is enough that some of the conduct takes place in that territory: *R. (Okandeji) v. Bow Street Magistrates' Court* [2006] 1 W.L.R. 674.

A court may also order extradition in repatriation cases under s.63 where a person is at large when he should be serving a sentence under the repatriation arrangements and outside the territory where he was originally convicted. The phrase "unlawfully at large" in s.63(2)(a) is not limited to what, in vernacular terms, is "over the wall", *i.e.* an escape from prison. If the draftsman had intended to mean "escape" he would have used that word. The words "in which he was serving a sentence" seem to qualify territory rather than prison: *Chalitovas v. Lithuania* [2006] EWHC 1978. Therefore, as is common in civil law jurisdictions, a person sentenced to imprisonment with a duty to surrender to prison at a later date is covered by this provision.

3–39 Part 2 cases are dealt with under s.138.

Extradition Act 2003, s.138

Extradition offences: person sentenced for offence

3–40 **138.**—(1) This section applies in relation to conduct of a person if—

(a) he is alleged to be unlawfully at large after conviction by a court in a category 2 territory of an offence constituted by the conduct, and

(b) he has been sentenced for the offence.

(2) The conduct constitutes an extradition offence in relation to the category 2 territory if these conditions are satisfied—

(a) the conduct occurs in the category 2 territory;

(b) the conduct would constitute an offence under the law of the relevant part of the

United Kingdom punishable with imprisonment or another form of detention for a term of 12 months or a greater punishment if it occurred in that part of the United Kingdom;

(c) a sentence of imprisonment or another form of detention for a term of 4 months or a greater punishment has been imposed in the category 2 territory in respect of the conduct.

(3) The conduct also constitutes an extradition offence in relation to the category 2 territory if these conditions are satisfied—

(a) the conduct occurs outside the category 2 territory;

(b) a sentence of imprisonment or another form of detention for a term of 4 months or a greater punishment has been imposed in the category 2 territory in respect of the conduct;

(c) in corresponding circumstances equivalent conduct would constitute an extra-territorial offence under the law of the relevant part of the United Kingdom punishable with imprisonment or another form of detention for a term of 12 months or a greater punishment.

(4) The conduct also constitutes an extradition offence in relation to the category 2 territory if these conditions are satisfied—

(a) the conduct occurs outside the category 2 territory and no part of it occurs in the United Kingdom;

(b) the conduct would constitute an offence under the law of the relevant part of the United Kingdom punishable with imprisonment or another form of detention for a term of 12 months or a greater punishment if it occurred in that part of the United Kingdom;

(c) a sentence of imprisonment or another form of detention for a term of 4 months or a greater punishment has been imposed in the category 2 territory in respect of the conduct.

(5) The conduct also constitutes an extradition offence in relation to the category 2 territory if these conditions are satisfied—

(a) the conduct occurs outside the category 2 territory and no part of it occurs in the United Kingdom;

(b) a sentence of imprisonment or another form of detention for a term of 4 months or a greater punishment has been imposed in the category 2 territory in respect of the conduct;

(c) the conduct constitutes or if committed in the United Kingdom would constitute an offence mentioned in subsection (6).

(6) The offences are—

(a) an offence under section 51 or 58 of the *International Criminal Court Act* 2001 (genocide, crimes against humanity and war crimes);

(b) an offence under section 52 or 59 of that Act (conduct ancillary to genocide etc committed outside the jurisdiction);

(c) an ancillary offence, as defined in section 55 or 62 of that Act, in relation to an offence falling within paragraph (a) or (b);

(d) an offence under section 1 of the *International Criminal Court (Scotland) Act* 2001(genocide, crimes against humanity and war crimes);

(e) an offence under section 2 of that Act (conduct ancillary to genocide etc committed outside the jurisdiction);

(f) an ancillary offence, as defined in section 7 of that Act, in relation to an offence falling within paragraph (d) or (e).

(7) If the conduct constitutes an offence under the military law of the category 2 territory but does not constitute an offence under the general criminal law of the relevant part of the United Kingdom it does not constitute an extradition offence; and subsections (1) to (6) have effect subject to this.

(8) The relevant part of the United Kingdom is the part of the United Kingdom in which—

(a) the extradition hearing took place, if the question of whether conduct constitutes an extradition offence is to be decided by the Secretary of State;

(b) proceedings in which it is necessary to decide that question are taking place, in any other case.

(9) Subsections (1) to (7) apply for the purposes of this Part.

3-41 Here conduct will amount to an extradition offence if it:

1) occurs in the requesting state, the conduct would constitute an offence in England and Wales punishable with a minimum of 12 months' imprisonment or detention and a minimum of four months' imprisonment or detention has been imposed;
2) occurs outside the requesting state and a minimum of four months' imprisonment or detention has been imposed in the requesting state and the conduct would constitute an extra territorial offence under the law of England and Wales punishable with a minimum of 12 months' imprisonment or detention;
3) occurs outside the requesting state and no part of it has occurred within the UK and it would constitute an offence in England and Wales punishable with a minimum of 12 months' imprisonment or detention and a minimum sentence of four months' imprisonment or detention has been imposed in the requesting state;
4) occurs outside the requesting state and no part occurs within the UK, a minimum of four months' imprisonment or detention has been imposed in the requesting state and the conduct if committed in the UK would constitute an offence of genocide, crimes against humanity and war crimes or ancillary offences.

A certificate of conviction, the indictment and a transcript of the proceedings can establish the conviction: *Re Parkyn-Jackson (Bruce)* [1989] C.O.D. 188. More commonly affidavit or other evidence from a prosecutor or investigating police officer is adduced although copies of court judgements are often tendered.

Those accused of crimes or unlawfully at large after conviction but before sentence

3-42 Part 1 cases are dealt with under s.64.

Extradition Act 2003, s.64

Extradition offences: person not sentenced for offence

3-43 **64.**—(1) This section applies in relation to conduct of a person if—

(a) he is accused in a category 1 territory of the commission of an offence constituted by the conduct, or
(b) he is alleged to be unlawfully at large after conviction by a court in a category 1 territory of an offence constituted by the conduct and he has not been sentenced for the offence.

(2) The conduct constitutes an extradition offence in relation to the category 1 territory if these conditions are satisfied—

(a) the conduct occurs in the category 1 territory and no part of it occurs in the United Kingdom;
(b) a certificate issued by an appropriate authority of the category 1 territory shows that the conduct falls within the European framework list;
(c) the certificate shows that the conduct is punishable under the law of the category 1 territory with imprisonment or another form of detention for a term of 3 years or a greater punishment.

(3) The conduct also constitutes an extradition offence in relation to the category 1 territory if these conditions are satisfied—

(a) the conduct occurs in the category 1 territory;
(b) the conduct would constitute an offence under the law of the relevant part of the United Kingdom if it occurred in that part of the United Kingdom;
(c) the conduct is punishable under the law of the category 1 territory with imprisonment or another form of detention for a term of 12 months or a greater punishment (however it is described in that law).

(4) The conduct also constitutes an extradition offence in relation to the category 1 territory if these conditions are satisfied—

(a) the conduct occurs outside the category 1 territory;
(b) the conduct is punishable under the law of the category 1 territory with imprisonment or another form of detention for a term of 12 months or a greater punishment (however it is described in that law);
(c) in corresponding circumstances equivalent conduct would constitute an extra-territorial offence under the law of the relevant part of the United Kingdom punishable with imprisonment or another form of detention for a term of 12 months or a greater punishment.

(5) The conduct also constitutes an extradition offence in relation to the category 1 territory if these conditions are satisfied—
(a) the conduct occurs outside the category 1 territory and no part of it occurs in the United Kingdom;
(b) the conduct would constitute an offence under the law of the relevant part of the United Kingdom punishable with imprisonment or another form of detention for a term of 12 months or a greater punishment if it occurred in that part of the United Kingdom;
(c) the conduct is so punishable under the law of the category 1 territory (however it is described in that law).

(6) The conduct also constitutes an extradition offence in relation to the category 1 territory if these conditions are satisfied—
(a) the conduct occurs outside the category 1 territory and no part of it occurs in the United Kingdom;
(b) the conduct is punishable under the law of the category 1 territory with imprisonment or another form of detention for a term of 12 months or a greater punishment (however it is described in that law);
(c) the conduct constitutes or if committed in the United Kingdom would constitute an offence mentioned in subsection (7).

(7) The offences are—
(a) an offence under section 51 or 58 of the *International Criminal Court Act* 2001 (genocide, crimes against humanity and war crimes);
(b) an offence under section 52 or 59 of that Act (conduct ancillary to genocide etc committed outside the jurisdiction);
(c) an ancillary offence, as defined in section 55 or 62 of that Act, in relation to an offence falling within paragraph (a) or (b);
(d) an offence under section 1 of the *International Criminal Court (Scotland) Act* 2001 (genocide, crimes against humanity and war crimes);
(e) an offence under section 2 of that Act (conduct ancillary to genocide etc committed outside the jurisdiction);
(f) an ancillary offence, as defined in section 7 of that Act, in relation to an offence falling within paragraph (d) or (e).

(8) For the purposes of subsections (3)(b), (4)(c) and (5)(b)—
(a) if the conduct relates to a tax or duty, it is immaterial that the law of the relevant part of the United Kingdom does not impose the same kind of tax or duty or does not contain rules of the same kind as those of the law of the category 1 territory;
(b) if the conduct relates to customs or exchange, it is immaterial that the law of the relevant part of the United Kingdom does not contain rules of the same kind as those of the law of the category 1 territory.

(9) This section applies for the purposes of this Part.

For conduct to amount to an extradition offence it must either: **3–44**

1) occur in the requesting state with no part occurring within the UK and is punishable with a minimum of three years' imprisonment or detention; or
2) occur in the requesting state and is punishable by a minimum of 12 months' imprisonment or detention and would constitute an offence in the UK if committed there; or
3) occur outside the requesting state and is punishable with a minimum of 12 months' imprisonment or detention and would be an extra territorial offence under UK law punishable with a minimum of 12 months' imprisonment or detention; or

4) occur outside the requesting state with no part of it occurring within the UK and would be an offence in the UK punishable with a minimum of 12 months' imprisonment or detention and is similarly punishable in the requesting state; or

5) occur outside the requesting state with no part of it occurring within the UK and is punishable with a minimum of 12 months' imprisonment or detention and would also be an offence of genocide, war crimes or crimes against humanity or ancillary crimes if committed in the UK.

3–45 Section 64(3) does not preclude the extradition of a person who is alleged to have committed a crime in a category 1 territory simply because some of his criminal conduct might have allegedly occurred within the United Kingdom: *Convery v. High Court of Rotterdam* [2005] EWHC 566.

Extradition offences are often transnational offences. In order to constitute an extradition offence not all the conduct constituting the offence has to occur in one territory. The word "also" in ss.(3) to (6) does not of itself indicate that each subsection is exclusive of every other subsection. Subsections (2) to (6) form a list and conduct constitutes an extradition offence if any of them apply: *King's Prosecutor; Brussels v. Armas* [2005] 2 All E.R. 181.

It is not for the court to decide whether a person should be prosecuted in England and Wales or extradited with a view to prosecution abroad; that is a decision for the Director of Public Prosecutions; and, in making his decision, it is not for him to take account of any possible violation of the person's ECHR rights were he to be extradited; the fact that a person is suffering from Asperger Syndrome, and that suicide and self harm can be associated with that disorder, falls short of establishing a risk of infringement of art. 3: *R. (on the application of McKinnon) v. Secretary of State for Home Affairs; R. (McKinnon) v. DPP* [2009] EWHC 2021 (Admin).

3–46 Section 64(3)(c) is satisfied when actions which had taken place in UK have been intentionally felt in another country so could be said to have occurred in that other country as well as the UK: *Hosseini v. France* [2006] EWHC 1333. The case of *Derevianko v. Lithuania* [2005] EWHC 1212 heard under the previous legislation, has held that an offence punishable by imprisonment for a term of "up to one year" incorporates a term of imprisonment for one year.

Part 2 cases are dealt with under s.137.

Extradition Act 2003, s.137

Extradition offences: person not sentenced for offence

3–47 **137.**—(1) This section applies in relation to conduct of a person if—

(a) he is accused in a category 2 territory of the commission of an offence constituted by the conduct, or

(b) he is alleged to be unlawfully at large after conviction by a court in a category 2 territory of an offence constituted by the conduct and he has not been sentenced for the offence.

(2) The conduct constitutes an extradition offence in relation to the category 2 territory if these conditions are satisfied—

(a) the conduct occurs in the category 2 territory;

(b) the conduct would constitute an offence under the law of the relevant part of the United Kingdom punishable with imprisonment or another form of detention for a term of 12 months or a greater punishment if it occurred in that part of the United Kingdom;

(c) the conduct is so punishable under the law of the category 2 territory (however it is described in that law).

(3) The conduct also constitutes an extradition offence in relation to the category 2 territory if these conditions are satisfied—

(a) the conduct occurs outside the category 2 territory;

(b) the conduct is punishable under the law of the category 2 territory with imprisonment or another form of detention for a term of 12 months or a greater punishment (however it is described in that law);

(c) in corresponding circumstances equivalent conduct would constitute an extra-territorial offence under the law of the relevant part of the United Kingdom punishable with imprisonment or another form of detention for a term of 12 months or a greater punishment.

(4) The conduct also constitutes an extradition offence in relation to the category 2 territory if these conditions are satisfied—

(a) the conduct occurs outside the category 2 territory and no part of it occurs in the United Kingdom;

(b) the conduct would constitute an offence under the law of the relevant part of the United Kingdom punishable with imprisonment or another form of detention for a term of 12 months or a greater punishment if it occurred in that part of the United Kingdom;

(c) the conduct is so punishable under the law of the category 2 territory (however it is described in that law).

(5) The conduct also constitutes an extradition offence in relation to the category 2 territory if these conditions are satisfied—

(a) the conduct occurs outside the category 2 territory and no part of it occurs in the United Kingdom;

(b) the conduct is punishable under the law of the category 2 territory with imprisonment for a term of 12 months or another form of detention or a greater punishment (however it is described in that law);

(c) the conduct constitutes or if committed in the United Kingdom would constitute an offence mentioned in subsection (6).

(6) The offences are—

(a) an offence under section 51 or 58 of the *International Criminal Court Act* 2001 (genocide, crimes against humanity and war crimes);

(b) an offence under section 52 or 59 of that Act (conduct ancillary to genocide etc committed outside the jurisdiction);

(c) an ancillary offence, as defined in section 55 or 62 of that Act, in relation to an offence falling within paragraph (a) or (b);

(d) an offence under section 1 of the *International Criminal Court (Scotland) Act* 2001 (genocide, crimes against humanity and war crimes);

(e) an offence under section 2 of that Act (conduct ancillary to genocide etc committed outside the jurisdiction);

(f) an ancillary offence, as defined in section 7 of that Act, in relation to an offence falling within paragraph (d) or (e).

(7) If the conduct constitutes an offence under the military law of the category 2 territory but does not constitute an offence under the general criminal law of the relevant part of the United Kingdom it does not constitute an extradition offence; and subsections (1) to (6) have effect subject to this.

(8) The relevant part of the United Kingdom is the part of the United Kingdom in which—

(a) the extradition hearing took place, if the question of whether conduct constitutes an extradition offence is to be decided by the Secretary of State;

(b) proceedings in which it is necessary to decide that question are taking place, in any other case.

(9) Subsections (1) to (7) apply for the purposes of this Part.

Conduct constitutes an extradition offence if it: **3–48**

1) occurs in the category 2 state and is punishable there with a minimum of 12 months' imprisonment or detention and it also constitutes an offence in the UK similarly punishable;
2) occurs outside the category 2 state, is punishable with a minimum of 12 months' imprisonment or detention and would also be an extra-territorial offence in the UK similarly punishable;
3) occurs outside the category 2 state and no part of it occurred in the UK, is punishable with a minimum of 12 months' imprisonment or detention and is an offence in the UK similarly punishable;

Part I

4) occurs outside the category 2 state and no part occurred in the UK, is punishable with a minimum of 12 months' imprisonment or detention and the offence if committed in the UK would be one of genocide, crimes against humanity or war crimes or ancillary crimes.

3–49 The correct approach is to look at the essentials of the conduct relied on and consider whether if it had occurred in England, at the time it was alleged to have occurred, it would have constituted an English offence. The words "constitute an offence" in s.137 (2) (b) do not mean that a requesting state has to prove the guilt of the person in English law. They simply mean that, if proved, it would constitute the comparable English offence: *Mauro v. United States of America* [2009] EWCA Civ 150. That test should be applied consistently throughout the 2003 Act. A district judge is not tied to considering the peculiarities of a requesting country's institutions, officials and procedures: *Norris v. United States of America* [2008] 2 W.L.R. 673, 2 All E.R. 1103.

Although a judge has an implied jurisdiction to hold that the prosecutor is abusing the process of the court, no finding of abuse can be justified in a case where the category 2 territory, in this case the USA, does not have to prove that there is a case to answer, on the grounds that the prosecutor has refused or failed to disclose evidential material beyond what is contained in the extradition request: *R. (Bermingham) v. Director of the Serious Fraud Office*; *Bermingham v. United States of America* [2006] 3 All E.R. 239.

It is not an extradition offence if it is an offence under the military law of the category 2 state but is not an offence under UK law. Extraterritoriality under s.137(2)(a) was discussed in *The Government of the United States of America v. Bentley* [2005] EWCH 1078. It was said that it is the court's duty, at least if the point is taken, to determine whether the conduct is punishable under the law of the category 2 territory. This may be done by means of a duly authenticated document under s.202(4)(a).

In deciding whether the conduct alleged discloses dual criminality a court is limited to the facts alleged in "the offence specified in the request" together with any document which it incorporates by express reference, and cannot take into account any narrative or explanation tendered by the requesting state: *J D Edwards v. USA* [2007] EWHC 1877 (Admin).

Where a warrant alleges that a person has alienated movable property on which an Inland Revenue official has "levied an attachment", the conduct does not satisfy the dual criminality test: *Luczak v. Poland* [2009] EWHC 2753(Admin).

(3) Restrictions or bars to extradition ss.11–25, 79, 95, 96

3–50 Extradition will not be ordered where any of the following bars are found to apply:

— Double jeopardy;
— Extraneous considerations;
— Passage of time;
— Age (Part 1 only);
— Hostage-taking considerations;
— Speciality (Part 1 only);
— The person's earlier extradition to the UK from another country (Part 1 only).

For each bar the Act is predicated with the phrase "if (and only if)". Thus it is necessary to ensure any bar that is raised, there may be more than one, is clearly identified for the purposes of the full extradition hearing. A very substantial body of case law now exists, given the automatic right of appeal given to both parties, especially in Pt 1, EAW cases, although given the mirror provisions of the bars for Pt 2 cases (in almost all instances) the decided cases are equally applicable save, sometimes, with greater emphasis for those jurisdictions which apply the ECHR—these include as a precondition **all** Pt 1 (EAW jurisdictions) but others *e.g.* Albania and Russia. Only some cases are cited under each bar to illustrate the current approach. Passage of time s.14, 82— despite active discouragement from the House of Lords in *Gomes v. Goodyer v. Govern of Trinidad*

& Tobago [2009] UKHL 21—continues to generate a significant volume of litigation. In many instances, given the replication of some of the bars found in the Act from earlier extradition statutes, the old case law remains sound.

If the judge concludes that a bar or bars is/are established "he **must** order the person's discharge": s.11(3).

Double jeopardy: ss.12, 80

No-one should be extradited if he would be entitled to claim double jeopardy. The rule of double jeopardy covers both an acquittal or conviction of a criminal offence and the situation where following a trial for any offence founded on the same or substantially the same facts where the court would stay the prosecution as an abuse of process unless it could show that there are special circumstances why another trial should take place: *Connelly* [1964] A.C. 1254; *Humphries* [1977] A.C.T. 1; *Beedie* [1998] Q.B. 356; *Z* [2000] 2 A.C. 483. The fact that a person has stolen the cars in the UK is irrelevant to the extradition on aiding and abetting charges relating to those cars elsewhere: *Mitchell v. High Court of Boulogne Sur Mer* [2007] EWHC 2006 (Admin). *Fofana v. France* [2006] EWHC 744 (Admin) DC held that there are two ways in which double jeopardy is engaged. Firstly, per *Connelly, ante*, if classic autrefois acquit or convict principles apply. Secondly if "the same or substantially the same facts" are relied upon such that a domestic trial would be stayed as an abuse of process unless the prosecution can show "special circumstances" why another trial should be permitted. In considering any abuse of process the judge must also determine if the current allegations should have been pursued at the first trial: *Maxwell-King v. USA* [2006] EWHC 3033 (Admin) (DC). An acquittal of a co-accused is not a matter which the court should take into account: *Rottman v. Governor of HM Prison Brixton* [2003] EWHC 496. Extradition is not barred on the ground of double jeopardy by reason of the fact that a person has faced proceedings in relation to three, being convicted on one occasion, out of very many overt acts contained in an indictment for conspiracy. The conspiracy alleged in the case of *John v. Government of the United States of America* [2006] All E.R. (D) 357 was, in its duration, scale and reach of a wholly different order to the conduct which led to the person's conviction. **3–51**

A prosecution appeal failed in *Hamburg Public Prosecutor's Office, Germany v. Altun* [2011] All E.R. (D) 25, [2011] EWHC 397 (Admin) when A had been tried, convicted and served a period in custody (prior to release by virtue of an amnesty) in Turkey and could not face the same offences in Germany (armed robberies). The fact the amnesty made for a very lenient sentence was irrelevant. The court made clear it was not for UK courts to ignore the legal effect of legislation of friendly foreign states when asking if, by those laws, conviction and sentence had occurred unless those laws could be held offensive to international legal norms.

It must be noted that the *Criminal Justice Act* 2003 provides for the possibility of a retrial on indictment in certain circumstances where there is new and compelling evidence and it is in the interests of justice that the crime is reinvestigated. **3–52**

As in *Altun ante* careful examination of the reasons for that which may appear prima facie to offend s.12, 80 is necessary if this bar is argued. Expert evidence on foreign substantive law and procedure may well be appropriate.

Extraneous considerations: ss.13, 81

If it appears that a person will be prosecuted, prejudiced in his trial, punished or detained on the grounds of race, religion, nationality, gender, sexual orientation or political opinion the judge must refuse extradition. **3–53**

The legal test by which a fair trial has to be judged is whether a defendant would suffer a real risk of a flagrant denial of justice if extradited. In *Fernandez v. Government of Singapore* [1971] 1 W.L.R. 987 H.L. Lord Diplock held "a reasonable chance", "substantial grounds for thinking", "a serious possibility" reflected the test to be met.

This is for the Requested Person to establish on evidence, not merely assert. However, while a forward looking exercise, that which has happened previously may be highly relevant: *Tamarevichute v. Russia* [2008] EWHC 534 (Admin) (DC). *Fernandez ante* was applied in a Pt 1 (EAW) case: *Hilali v. Spain* [2006] EWHC 1239 (Admin), DC. A "real risk" does not mean proof on balance of probabilities, but is merely a risk which is substantial and not merely fanciful which might be established by something less than proof of a 51 per cent probability: *Brown v. Rwanda* [2009] EWHC 770 (Admin.)—a successful defence appeal involving a proposed trial for genocide in Rwanda.

Passage of time: ss.14, 82

3–54 This bar applies if it would be "unjust" and/or "oppressive" to extradite by reason of the passage of time. That time runs from the date of the offence in an accusation case or when they became unlawfully at large in a conviction case. The period includes the hearing date of any appeal: *Gomes & Goodyer v. Govern of Trinidad & Tobago* [2009] UKHL 21. Lord Diplock in *Kakis v. Govern of the Republic of Cyprus* [1978] 1 WLR 779 H.L. set out an approach that has stood the test of much litigation p.782–783:

> "unjust" I regard as directed primarily to the risk of prejudice to the accused in the conduct of the trial itself, "oppressive" as directed to hardship to the accused resulting from changes in his circumstances that have occurred during the period to be taken into consideration, but there is room for overlapping, and between them they cover all cases where to return him would not be fair. Delay in the commencement or conduct of extradition proceedings which is brought about by the accused himself by fleeing the country, concealing his whereabouts or evading arrest cannot, in my view, be relied upon as a ground for holding it to be either unjust or oppressive to return him. . . delay which is brought about by the acts of the accused himself. . . is not generally relevant. What matters is not so much the cause of such delay as its effect".

Kakis ante was again considered by the House of Lords in *Gomes* ante and strongly approved. In *Gomes* a "classic fugitive" *i.e.* one who had evaded due process is very unlikely indeed to successfully establish the bar. A delay caused without any fault by the Requested Person is the only circumstance in which the state may be required to explain the delay or face a discharge of the extradition proceedings. In *Barone v. Italy* [2010] EWHC 3004 (Admin) although upholding, on other grounds, a first instance decision to discharge the request (for murder) the High Court held a passage of time bar finding of oppression was wrongly found given an escape from a Turin prison in 1976, a successful challenge to earlier extradition proceedings (*H.M. Prison Brixton ex. p Barone* [1997] EWHC Admin 988) and time running from then and an unsuccessful petition by the Italian Government to the House of Lords until Pt 1 EAW proceedings following rearrest in 2010. *Barone* had had no indication of indifference form the Italian authorities, any solace he had came from the UK courts only (*i.e.* in dismissing the earlier request) which could not support this bar. *Gomes* expressly approved five principles relating to the injustice limb derived from *Knowles v. USA* [2007] 1 W.L.R. 47 (PC): (i) would it be unjust/oppressive to extradite (not try)? (ii) if the UK court is bound to concluded a fair trial is impossible (iii) regard should be had to fair trial safeguards, with a strong presumption those apply to all ECHR jurisdictions and that such is the case in all jurisdictions with whom the UK has agreed extradition treaties (iv) each case will depend on its own facts in assessing when a fair trial by virtue of the passage of time can no longer take place (v) there is no cut off point when it will be presumed to be unjust/oppressive to extradite. Oppression will require establishing far greater hardship to oneself and/or one's immediate family or dependents than is inevitable in the extradition process. The presumption, which is clear form the jurisprudence, of honouring the enforcement of cross border criminal justice *inter alia* via the extradition process is deemed very much in the public interest. This repeats similar sentiments in *Croatia v. Spanovic EWHC* [2007] 1770 (Admin) see also *Norris v. USA* [2007] 1 W.L.R. 1730.

Age: s.15

3–55 A person under the age of criminal responsibility (10 years of age—see s.50 *Children* *and Young Person's Act 1933*) had the offence occurred within England and Wales will not be extradited. Youths will be brought before designated judges on extradition matters and will not be taken to a youth court.

Hostage-taking considerations: ss.16, 83

Where communication between the person and the appropriate consular authorities would not be possible and the conduct constitutes an offence or an attempt to commit an offence under s.1 of the *Taking of Hostages Act* 1982 extradition is barred. **3–56**

Speciality: ss.17, 95

The rule of speciality limits the offences for which the person may be tried in the country requesting extradition. In Pt 1 extradition is barred unless arrangements have been made with the country concerned. Extradition is limited to those offences upon which a person has been extradited, those which are disclosed from the same facts, those to which consent has been given by a judge and those which are not punishable by imprisonment or detention. If the offence does not fall within the exceptions he must be given an opportunity to leave the country within 45 days from the date of his arrival. It does not apply if the person has consented to extradition or has waived his rights. A certificate issued by the Secretary of State is conclusive proof that there are arrangements between the UK and the other country. **3–57**

In *Sutej v. Governor of Holloway Prison* [2005] EWHC 465, it was said that where a person had previously been discharged from extradition to Switzerland on particular criminal charges, the fact that the authorities indicated that a ruling would be made on those criminal charges, upon her return to Switzerland in respect of other related criminal charges, did not mean that the extradition on related charges breached the principle of speciality protection. Where there are a large number of offences it is a matter for the local court to decide which charges to pursue. Courts or the Secretary of State can only consider whether there is a law in place to respect the speciality rule or whether there is cogent evidence that the speciality rule would not be followed: *Arain v. Germany*, *The Times*, March 24, 2006; [2006] EWHC 1702.

It is only in exceptional circumstances that, considering art. 8 ECHR, it will be disproportionate to extradite an individual. The individual would have to show in respect of each offence why it was disproportionate. In *Arain* it was held that it was impossible to see how extradition for conduct disclosing a large number of offences could be proportionate but then became disproportionate because a district judge had held that part of the conduct alleged did not amount to an offence in the UK. The application of speciality in US courts is affected by the view of the sending state. If a superseding indictment alleges offences not covered by the terms of the Act, the US authorities will not prosecute. Where the consent of the Secretary of State is required under s.95(4)(c) for prosecutions falling outside the scope of ss.95(4)(a), (b) and (d), that consent is not to be inferred but must be expressly given otherwise any subsequent trial will breach the speciality rule: *Welsh v. Secretary of State for the Home Department* [2006] 3 All E.R. 204.

In *Hilali v. Spain* [2006] EWHC 1239 (Admin) (DC) the court held Pt 1 and Pt 2 cases required the same consideration namely did effective procedural arrangements exist in the requesting jurisdiction to ensure trial only in respect of the offence for which extradition is sought? Any challenge will require compelling evidence.

Following extradition a request for "consent" to prosecute for additional charges may be made — see ss.54–58 and *post* 3–99 *ante*.

Earlier extradition to United Kingdom from another country: s.18

A person cannot be extradited where the consent of the first country is necessary before he is extradited to another country and that consent has not been given: s.96. **3–58**

Part I

In Pt 2 cases, it is for the Secretary of State to decide the issue of speciality as well as other matters which might render extradition inappropriate. Section 19 deals with non Pt 1 jurisdictions and s.19A earlier transfer to the UK by the International Criminal Court. In practice instances of cases under s.18-19A are very rare with no case law on point. Should such a case arise the provisions of the Act should be followed with care.

(4) Other considerations

Convictions in absence: ss.20, 86

3–59 A person who has been convicted in his absence is protected by the terms of the Act. In Pt 1 cases the judge must decide whether the person absented himself from the trial deliberately. This is essentially a question of fact. If he decides in the affirmative then he must decide whether the extradition would be compatible with the *Human Rights Act* 1998, s.21. If the extradition is not compatible then the person must be discharged. In the case of *Falanga v. Italy* [2007] EWHC 268, DC it was said *obiter* that the court had difficulty with the proposition that s.21 only applied to prospective breaches of human rights and it did not enable a court to refuse extradition on the basis of reference to a past trial that was not in compliance with art. 6 ECHR.

If the judge decides that the person had not deliberately absented himself he must go on to decide whether the person would be entitled to a retrial or an appeal which would be heard as a retrial and that the person would be entitled to defend himself and to examine witnesses in person or through legal assistance of his own choosing and for that legal assistance to be free if he could not pay. If the person is not so entitled he must be discharged. "Entitlement" in s.20(5) means a right under the law of the requesting state and it is not necessary to consider what a requesting state might do in practice. It is for the requesting state to establish compliance with s.20. Where a requesting state is a member of the Council of Europe it can be assumed that, as a signatory to ECHR, it is capable of protecting against an unjust trial pursuant to art. 6; letters from the Hungarian judge were sufficient *prima facie* evidence to satisfy compliance with s.20: *Benko v. Hungary* [2009] EWHC 3530 (Admin). In *France v. Wade* [2006] EWHC 1909, DC the person was held not to have absented himself from an appeal as he had been advised by the authorities that there would be no consequences of his failure to attend.

This case was disapproved in *Atkinson v. Supreme Court of Cyprus*, [2010] 1 W.L.R. 570, where the Divisional Court said that too much reliance had been placed on a domestic approach. Whether proceedings before the appellate court can be seen as part of the trial process has to be considered from a cosmopolitan perspective. Where, as in Cyprus, the appellate court is a jurisdiction in which the prosecution can discharge the burden of proof and rebut the presumption of innocence, proceedings before such a court are axiomatically part of the trial process. Misinformation given by a legal adviser will not make a decision by an individual to absent himself from a trial not deliberate.

An order of a foreign court cancelling the deferral of a sentence of imprisonment does not constitute a fresh conviction or imposition of sentence and does not therefore amount to a conviction at which an offender is not present for the purposes of s.20(1): *Baksys v. Lithuania* [2007] EWHC 2838.

Section 19A, 83A remain provisions that have not been brought into force. This may change following the publication of the Scott Baker Review into Extradition Law due to be submitted to the Government in the summer of 2011. For the present a potential bar arising out of a contention a significant part of the alleged conduct occurred in the UK and should be tried in the UK cannot be pursued as a bar save in so far as an order for extradition is incompatible with a person's human rights: *Onwuzulike v. USA* [2009] EWHC 1395 (Admin) (DC).

The ongoing nature of proceedings with no finalisation despite a trial at first instance (in absence), remained an accusation case denying retrial protections but still afforded s.21 safeguards: *Caldarelli v. Italy* [2008] UKHL 51.

In Pt 1 EAW cases the steps for the Judge are therefore (i) was conviction in presence?—if yes go to s.21 (human rights), (ii) If not convicted in presence, did the person "deliberately" absent themselves—if yes go to s.21, (iii) if not deliberately absent does a retrial or review amounting to a retrial with all art. 6 ECHR safeguards exist? If yes proceed to s.21, if no discharge the extradition request. Unlike common law jurisdictions, where an absent Defendant is comparatively rare (although by no means unknown) in many Civil Law jurisdictions trials in absence are very common. Therefore anyone who appears to have formal notice of trial process is at grave risk of being held "deliberately" absent for s.20, 86 purposes.

In Pt 2 cases it is for the judge to decide whether the person was convicted in his absence and if so, whether he deliberately absented himself from his trial: s.85. The applicable standard of proof for a determination under s.85(3) is the criminal standard: *Mitoi v. Romania* [2006] EWHC 1977, DC. "His trial" contemplates a specific event and not the entire legal process: *Albania v. Bleta* [2005] 3 All E.R. 351. If the judge decides the person has deliberately absented himself he must then proceed under s.87—see *post*. If not, then he decides whether the person has a right to a retrial or a review amounting to a retrial where the person has the right to defend himself and with free legal representation where he has not the means to pay as well as the right to examine and call witnesses. If he is so entitled then the judge goes on to decide whether, on the evidence supplied to him, a case to answer has been made out as if it were a summary trial against the person in this country: s.86. In *Lodhi v. 1) Governor of HM Prison Brixton 2) Government of the United Arab Emirates* [2001] EWCA Admin 178, it was stated that a person whose extradition was sought should be treated as a person accused rather than *autrefois convict* where he had been convicted in his absence but where the conviction would be set aside on his return.

In construing material from other countries it is important for the court to have the best guidance available. A court may adjourn proceedings so that extra material may be admitted by the requesting state. It is unnecessary for the court to examine what the requesting state has done in practice as it is the law of the requesting state which either does or does not confer the right to retrial: *Bogdani v. Albania* [2008] EWHC 2065 (Admin).

It is not for a court to examine the sufficiency of evidence leading to a conviction in the requesting State and come to a conclusion about the safety of the conviction: *Mariotti v. Italy* [2005] EWHC 2745. Where there is evidence that a trial in absence breached Article 6 ECHR because a person had not been afforded an adequate opportunity to challenge evidence adduced at the trial, a court is entitled to examine that evidence and reach a decision that the trial was not ECHR compliant and refuse jurisdiction: *Migliorelli v. Italy (No.3)* [2006] EWHC 243, Admin. In *Slovakia v. Badi* [2008] EWHC 2913 (Admin) it was held that the District Judge's decision to refuse to extradite was correct where the extraditee could not satisfy the sixth month limit for requesting a retrial and where, in those circumstances, a retrial would be permitted only if certain conditions were met, namely if facts or evidence unknown at the time of the conviction were to emerge. Where an individual who is sought for extradition has been absent from a sentencing appeal conducted in the sentencing state, which appeal results in an extension of his term of imprisonment, that absence does not render the sentencing appeal a conviction in the individual's absence as it was neither a trial nor a conviction but an appeal by way of review of the trial at which the individual had been convicted in his presence: *Virciglio v. Graz High Court of Austria* [2006] EWHC 3197, DC.

An accusation must be made in good faith: *Ingrid Sutej v. (1) Governor of HM Prison Holloway (2) Government of Switzerland* [2003] EWHC 1940, Admin; *Gulay Asliturk v. Government of Turkey* [2002] EWHC 2326. In *Popa v. Czech Republic* [2011] EWHC 329 (Admin) bad faith required proof to a high threshold albeit the Court found CPS incompetent and confused in its conduct of proceedings that was not bad faith. **3–60**

Domestic charges: ss.22, 88

Domestic charges take precedence and the extradition proceedings must be **3–61** adjourned until their conclusion. See also s.8A, 76A. The Court must review such cases every 28 days usually via video link if the person is in custody.

Persons serving sentences: ss.23, 89

3–62 Where a person for whom an extradition warrant has been issued is found to be serving a sentence in the UK, the extradition hearing may be adjourned until the sentence has been served. See also s.8B, 76B. On an application for an adjournment a judge was said to have been irrational not to have considered that it was appropriate to determine the matters under ss.11 and 21 where the person would not be released from prison for at least three years and when any act of extradition would not occur until then: *R. (Slator) v. Bow Street Magistrates' Court* (2007) A.C.D. 28. A review not less than every six months is required, usually via video link to the relevant prison.

Competing claims: ss.24, 90

3–63 Other claims may be deferred. Such instances are in practice rare. See also s.126.

Physical or mental condition: ss.25, 91

3–64 Medical evidence may be introduced to show that it would be unjust or oppressive to extradite the person on the grounds of his physical or mental condition whereupon the judge may order his discharge. In *R. (Warren) v. Secretary of State for the Home Department* [2003] EWHC 1177, it was stated that the question of mental fitness to stand trial as opposed to be extradited was a matter for the requesting state. The presence of a risk to a person's physical condition by the physical act of extradition does not mean that extradition cannot be effected provided that proper assessment of the risk posed is undertaken prior to extradition: *McCaughey v. (1) USA (2) Secretary of State for the Home Department* LTL 20/01/06; *Niziol v. Poland*, unreported, April 18, 2007.

In *Boudhiba v. Spain* [2007] 1 W.L.R. 124(DC) it was held the test to be considered was whether to extradite would be unjust/oppressive due to physical and/or mental condition not the fact of such condition(s). As a general proposition most jurisdictions are deemed to provide adequate (ECHR compliant) medical facilities even for those in custody. The gravity of the offence may be a relevant factor: *Hutton v. Australia* [2009] EWHC 564 (Admin) in that case murder albeit over 20 years before. In *Tollman v. USA* [2008] EWHC 184 (Admin) how the requesting state considers fitness to plead issues is relevant but not determinative. The key always being the wording of s.25, 91. In practice this is a growth area often pursued in conjunction with s.21/87 human rights concerns. An example is *Laskowski v. Poland* [2011] All E.R. (D) 10, Collins, J. reiterating the jurisprudence namely an assumption that medical treatment will be available in Poland, if not necessarily as good as in the UK, but then permitted an extension of time prior to removal to finish current (heart) treatment. See also *Wrobel v. Poland* [2011] EWHC 374 (Admin) re threat of suicide and adequacy of (mental health) treatment. See also *Griffin v. France* [2011] EWHC 943 (Admin) regarding threat of suicide.

Human rights: s.21, 87

3–65 This is now a growth area of litigation with an increasing volume of case law. There is a positive duty to consider whether the person's extradition would be compatible with ECHR but it is neither necessary nor right to examine what a requesting state does in practice provided that the Convention is unequivocally incorporated into the state's body of laws and that the terms of the Convention would prevail if any conflict arose between it and the state's laws: *Da An Chen v. Romania* (2008) 1 All E.R. 851. It is to be assumed that a country designated a Category 1 territory would respect a person's human rights and in the absence of any cogent evidence to the contrary it is appropriate to order extradition: *Kotwa v. Poland* [2010] EWHC 1000 (Admin). As French law fully incorporates ECHR, there is no risk that a person will not receive a fair trial if extradited to France for alleged offences in relation to terrorism: *R. (Mustapha Labsi) v. Secretary of State for the Home Department* [2005] EWHC 2931, Admin.

Human rights issues must be raised at the extradition hearing; it is too late to raise them at the judicial review stage: *R (on the application of Navadunskis) v Serious Organised Crime Agency* [2009] EWHC 1292

Following *Dabas v. Spain ante* the Framework Decision provides a safeguard and a disincentive to signatory states to act in breach of art. 3 as sanctions are available. Courts have to act on the basis that the confidence required extends to the executive arm of the government party to the Framework Decision. The risk on return has to be assessed on the evidence before the court on the date of the hearing: *Khemiri v. Italy* [2008] EWHC 1988 (Admin).

Where allegations are made that art. 3 might be engaged there must be an assessment of the conditions in the requesting country and its compliance with art. 3 and this would necessitate an examination of the foreseeable consequences of sending the person to that country, having regard to both the general situation there and his personal circumstances; the provision of diplomatic assurances does not remove the need to examine whether in practice there are sufficient guarantees that the rights of the individual would be properly protected: *Kaboulov v. Ukraine,* 50 E.H.R.R. 970.

In *Agius v. Malta* [2011] EWHC 759 (Admin) Sullivan, L.J. and Maddison, expressly disapproved of three decisions of Mitting, J. sitting alone (*Dabowski v. Poland* [2010] EWHC 1712 (Admin), *Rot v. Poland* [2010] EWHC 1820 (Admin) and *Klimas v. Poland* [2010] EWHC (2076) (Admin) making clear any view a judge was not required to consider ECHR safeguards or only in wholly exceptional circumstances was wrong. Section 21 was in mandatory terms. The correct approach was a presumption ECHR states would honour their obligations, any contrary assertion needed clear and cogent evidence but it was not for a person to show exceptional circumstances: see also *Janiga v. Czech Republic* [2011] All E.R. (D) 236—consensual agreement to chemical castration (for a serious child sex offender) as part of treatment, refusal of which could well result in continued detention, did not breach arts 3, 5 or 8.

The risk of suicide, on sufficiently well established and clear evidence, can form the basis of a proper plea that an individual's rights under art. 3 might be infringed by any action which could trigger suicide: *Kwietniewski v. Poland* [2008] EWHC 3121 (Admin). Where it is argued that suicide is a risk, it might be desirable for the requesting state to commission its own psychiatric report; in cases where diagnosis is difficult, the views of two psychiatrists might be better than one: *Sbar v. Italy* [2010] EWHC 1184 (Admin).

In *Jansons v. Latvia* [2009] EWHC 1845 (Admin), Sir Anthony May P held ". . . an assessment, so far as the evidence enables one to do so, that the risk that he will succeed in committing suicide, whatever steps are taken, is on the evidence, sufficiently great to result in a finding of oppression". Considering *Jansons* ante in *Wrobel v. Poland* [2011] EWHC 374 (Admin), Bean J. set out a four stage approach: (i) regard to be had to the public interest in honouring treaty obligations (ii) a presumption states had adequate facilities (even if not those of the UK) to treat mental illness (iii) a high threshold has to be surmounted for a finding of oppression and (iv) "independent and convincing evidence of a very high risk of suicide if the fugitive is returned".

In the UK, the imposition of a whole life sentence is not of itself an infringement of Article 3. An irreducible life sentence might raise an issue under art. 3 but would not necessarily infringe it; a prisoner would have to contend that his continued detention would be inhuman or degrading. In the extradition context a very strong case has to be made out. In *R. (on the application of Wellington) v. Secretary of State for the Home Department* [2009] 2 W.L.R. 48 this case was not made out where the state of Missouri gave its governor the power to pardon a prisoner or commute his sentence to one of life imprisonment with the possibility of parole. "Special administrative measures" which might be imposed (*i.e.* special confinement of prisoners where there is a risk of death or serious bodily injury) do not of themselves cross the art. 3 threshold for inhuman or degrading treatment so as to militate against extradition to the USA; whether the conditions of detention cross art. 3 depends on the facts of the individual case: *R. (on the application of Bary) v. Secretary of State for the Home Department* [2009] EWHC 2068 (Admin). The fact that a person is likely to share prison in a vulnerable prisoner unit in order to protect him from reprisals with those he considers to be undesirable does not give rise to a claim under arts 2 and 3: *Radzizewski v. Poland* [2010] EWHC 601 (Admin).

The publication of a prison report, expressing concerns about the provision of health care to individuals suffering from HIV in Latvia is insufficient to prevent extradition: *Valts v. Latvia* [2010] EWHC 999 (Admin) as is a wife's mental health difficulties in relation to the upbringing of a child necessitating help from the extraditee:*A v. Croatia* [2010] EWHC 918 (Admin).

Article 6, in principle, is not applicable to extradition proceedings but European case law provides that exceptionally an issue might be raised in circumstances where the fugitive risks a flagrant denial of a fair trial in the country of destination; in assessing that risk, the contracting state must refer as a priority to circumstances of which it has or should have had knowledge at the time of the extradition: *Olaechea Cahuas v. Spain* 48 E.H.R.R. 572, E.C.H.R.

See also *Olszewska v. Poland* [2011] All E.R. (D) 166, [2011] EWHC 514 (Admin) inter alia a contention of innocence based on alibi (in UK at material time) was a matter properly left to a trial court and was not for an extradition court to purport to determine. Also *Jaso and others v. Spain* [2007] EWHC 2983(Admin) —art. 3, 5, 6 and 8 considered.

A trial of a British national is not unfair if the entire proceedings are not translated into English: *Daniels v. Governor of Holloway Prison* [2005] EWHC 148, DC. From the moment of conviction when considering art. 5, the relevant part is art. 5(1)(a) rather than 5(1)(c) and art. 5(3). It is, therefore, just and appropriate to extradite in those circumstances even where a defendant is not allowed to apply for bail on his return: *Ceausescu v. (1) Secretary of State for the Home Office (2) Romania* [2007] EWHC 1423, Admin. The use of evidence from an anonymous witness does not deprive a person of a fair trial: *R. (Al-Fawwaz) v. Governor of Brixton Prison* [2001] 1 W.LR. 1234. Evidence obtained through torture is inadmissible: *A v. Secretary of State for the Home Department* [2006] 1 All E.R. 575.

It is not sufficient to show that widespread discrimination exists. An extraditee must demonstrate that there exists a reasonable chance or a serious possibility of prejudice at trial or that he would be punished, detained or restricted in personal liberty because of his race: *Tamarevichute v. Russia* [2008] EWHC 2838.

A default judgment entered in civil proceedings in the USA is not prejudicial to a criminal trial and does not breach *ECHR* art. 6; it is open to a defendant to say that the only reason there is a judgement against him is that he did not put forward a defence and steps can be taken to ensure that a jury would not be prejudiced: *Taylor v. USA* [2007] EWHC 2527 (Admin). The fact that German courts are not under a duty to take into account offences of fraud committed in the UK that were similar to offences of fraud in respect of which extradition is sought is not a bar based on art. 6: *Ezeanaka v. Germany* [2010] EWHC 741 (Admin).

Extradition of itself invades art. 8 ECHR, the right to family life, and it, therefore has to be shown that the extradition is in accordance with law and is proportionate: *Launder v. UK* [1997] App 27279/95. Appellants who seek to rely upon art. 8 have to be able to demonstrate a real risk of a flagrant breach of their Convention rights upon extradition: *Colda v. Romania* [2006] EWHC 1150. It is only in exceptional circumstances that the extradition of a person to face trial on serious charges would be held to be an unjustified or disproportionate interference with the right to family life: *Government of the United States of America v. Bentley, ante*. In *Norris v. Government of USA* [2010] 2 W.L.R. 572 it was agreed that there could be no absolute rule that any interference with art. 8 rights as a consequence of extradition would be proportionate; an assumption of the importance of extradition is an essential element in the task of weighing the public interest in extradition against its effects on individual human rights. The reality is that only if some quite exceptionally compelling feature, or combination of features, is present that interference with family life consequent upon extradition would be other than proportionate to the objective that extradition serves. There is no reason why the relative seriousness of the extradition offence should not be a factor to be taken into account when assessing whether extradition would breach art. 8 (or be barred for passage of time): *Zak v. Regional Court in Bydoszcz* [2009] Crim.L.R. 31; the judiciary questioned whether the issue of an European Arrest warrant for an offence of receiving a stolen mobile telephone was to use a sledgehammer to crack a nut.

The fact that an extraditee is a nursing mother and might be separated from her child for a long period of time at a critical stage in the child's development is not an exceptional circumstance so as to amount to a violation of her right to family life under art. 8 ECHR: *Spain v. Reid* 2009 G.W.D.6-101 (Scottish case). The triviality of an extradition offence or the imposition of a seemingly disproportionately lengthy sentence cannot amount to "striking and unusual facts" so as to render extradition a disproportionate interference with an individual's art. 8 rights: *Sandru v. Romania* [2009] EWHC 2879 (Admin).

H.H. & P.H. v. *Italy* [2011] EWHC 1145 (Admin) raised the welfare of young children if parent(s) is/are extradited – the matter is due to be heard by the Supreme Court (late 2011) who will have the opportunity to review its own decision in *Norris, ante*. Two decisions of Collins J. (yet to be reported) both decided on June 21, 2011 further illustrate the approach to art.8 see; *Radvilavicious v. Lithuania* – pregnant partner in UK not sufficient to prevent extradition to serve 12 months for theft and *Rzeczkowski v. Poland* – although 17 years old at the time of offence (attempted robbery in 1996) and having served 2 years of 5 imposed then absconding overseas, despite 10 years in the UK with a family and employment, although "borderline" it was not disproportionate to extradite.

Substantial grounds must exist for finding that there would be a violation of human rights: *Mamatkulov v. Turkey* (2005) 41 E.H.R.R. 25. The test for substantial grounds is not on a balance of probabilities but whether there is a real risk of the violation occurring: *Miklis v. Lithuania* [2006] 4 All E.R. 808. The test for an art. 2 breach is one of "almost certainty": *Osman v. UK* (1998) 29 E.H.R.R. 245; *Soering v. UK* (1989) 11 E.H.R.R. 439. The "real risk" test can be applied to art. 3: *James McLean v. Ireland* [2008] EWHC 547 (Admin). In that case it was said that the extraditee had not only to show that there was a real risk to his life but that as it was from non-state agents that there was also a lack of reasonable protection in the receiving country. Following *Dabas v. Spain, ante* the Framework Decision provides a safeguard and a disincentive to signatory states to act in breach of art. 3. Courts have to act on the basis that the confidence required extends to the executive arm of the government party to the Framework Decision. The risk on return has to be assessed on the evidence before the court on the date of the hearing: *Khemiri v. Italy* [2008] EWHC 1988 (Admin). Extradition was upheld where the appellants were afraid that they would be deported from Italy to Tunisia following extradition as they had been convicted or been subject of criminal proceedings there and would thus suffer a breach of their rights. The standard of proof is "beyond reasonable doubt", which may follow from the coexistence of sufficiently strong, clear and concordant inferences or of similar un-rebutted presumptions of fact. Where the events in issue lie wholly, or in large part, within the exclusive knowledge of the authorities, as in the case of persons in custody under their control, strong presumptions of fact will arise in respect of any injuries occurring during such detention and, in such cases, it will be up to the authorities to provide a satisfactory and convincing explanation, in the absence of which the court is able to draw unfavourable inferences. Ill treatment must attain a minimum level of severity if it is to fall within art. 3; the assessment is relative and depends on the circumstances of the case, such as the duration of the treatment, its physical and mental effects and, in some case, the sex, age and state of health of the victim. Although the purpose of the treatment is a factor to be taken into account, in particular whether it was intended to humiliate or debase the victim, the absence of any such purpose will not inevitably lead to a finding that there has been no violation: *Khudobin v. Russia,* 48 E.H.R.R. 523, E.C.H.R. The risk of suicide, on sufficiently well established and clear evidence, can form the basis of a proper plea that an individual's rights under art. 3 might be infringed by any action which could trigger suicide: *Kwietniewski v. Poland* [2008] EWHC 3121 (Admin). The case of *McKinnon ante* held that the fact that a person was suffering from Asperger Syndrome, and that suicide and self harm could be associated with that disorder, fell short of establishing a risk of infringement of art. 3.

Asylum claim: ss.39, 40, 121

3–66 Where the person makes an application for asylum during the course of the proceedings there is no need for the proceedings to be adjourned but the person cannot be extradited until the asylum claim is finally determined. The bar does not extend to claims made before the extradition request and the person may be extradited: *Dos Santos v. Portugal,* June 15, 2010, unreported. In *Poland v. Dytlow* [2009] EWHC 1009 (Admin) it is "implicit" per Keene L.J. that if a claim is upheld a person cannot then be extradited.

Chickvarkin v. S. of S. [2011] EWCA Civ. 91 provides powerful *obita* that if an asylum claim is being "actively considered" and involves human rights issues (as is likely) extradition proceedings should be adjourned until that claim is determined.

VI. EVIDENCE

3–67 EAW Pt 1 cases have no evidence requirements whatsoever. If a requested person calls evidence including expert evidence (*e.g.* medical, prison conditions, racial hostility) a Judicial Authority should be given the opportunity to reply. This is usually in the form of additional information from the issuing judge not a formal statement.

The evidence necessary for an extradition order under Pt 2 for many but by no means all (see *post* 3–100) of the category 2 countries will be that which is sufficient for a case to be answered See: s.84 *ante* evidence akin to that in a summary trial: *Re Nielsen* [1984] 2 All E.R. 81, HL; *The Government of the United States of America v. McCaffery* [1984] 1 W.L.R. 867, HL; *Parekh* [1988] Crim.L.R. 832. There is no obligation on the requesting state to provide evidence from complainants or police officers involved: *Stepp v. USA* [2006] EWHC 1033. In considering an application a judge must distinguish between what might be material that was relevant and admissible at a trial in the requesting state and what was material that was relevant and admissible in extradition proceedings in the UK: *R. (Kaupitis) v. Prosecutor General's Office (Lithuania)* [2006] EWHC 2185. The essentials of extradition are to be decided on the criminal standard of proof: *The Government of the United States of America v. Bentley, ante,* although identity is to be determined under s.78(5) on a balance of possibilities. It is not for the court to weigh the evidence of the witnesses: *Hashmi v. United States of America, ante.*

It is necessary to determine firstly whether the conduct alleged to constitute the criminal offence charged occurs in the category 2 territory and then secondly whether any of the conduct was within that territory. The offender's evidence may be heard: *Re Gross* [1998] 3 All E.R. 624.

In these circumstances the test in *Galbraith*—see Pt 3, *post*—will be used. That was commended by the House of Lords in *Alves v. DPP* [1992] 4 All E.R. 787. The UK government has agreed to dispense with the *prima facie* rule for certain countries, *e.g.* USA. Designation orders will need to be checked. See *Extradition Act* 2003 (Designation of Part 2 Territories) Orders S.I. 3334/2003. Such states only need to provide "information" not "evidence".

3–68 The court may receive properly authenticated evidence in the form of statements or affidavits received from the requesting state. It can also receive statements made in this country as well as hear evidence on oath or affirmation. Formal admissions may also be made. Live link evidence, in some instances, can be used s.206A.

Extradition Act 2003, ss.202, 205(1)–(2)

Receivable documents

202.—(1) A Part 1 warrant may be received in evidence in proceedings under this Act. **3–69**

(2) Any other document issued in a category 1 territory may be received in evidence in proceedings under this Act if it is duly authenticated.

(3) A document issued in a category 2 territory may be received in evidence in proceedings under this Act if it is duly authenticated.

(4) A document issued in a category 1 or category 2 territory is duly authenticated if (and only if) one of these applies—

(a) it purports to be signed by a judge, magistrate or officer of the territory;

(aa) it purports to be certified, whether by seal or otherwise by the Ministry or Department of the territory responsible for justice or for foreign affairs.

(b) it purports to be authenticated by the oath or affirmation of a witness.

(5) Subsections (2) and (3) do not prevent a document that is not duly authenticated from being received in evidence in proceedings under this Act.

Written statements and admissions

205.—(1) The provisions mentioned in subsection (2) apply in relation to proceedings under this Act as they apply in relation to proceedings for an offence. **3–70**

(2) The provisions are—

(a) section 9 of the *Criminal Justice Act* 1967 (proof by written statement in criminal proceedings);

(b) section 10 of the *Criminal Justice Act* 1967 (proof by formal admission in criminal proceedings);

Extradition proceedings are not, in any way, a trial on the merits, however most of the rules governing admissibility of evidence in England and Wales will apply. **3–71**

Those termed rules of law, *e.g.* hearsay, will apply whereas those termed rules of practice, *e.g.* refreshing memory, will not: *Governor of Gloucester Prison, ex p. Miller* [1979] 2 All E.R. 1103. A summary of a witness'evidence can be given as hearsay evidence by another person: s.84(4): *India v. Rajarathinam* [2007] 1 W.L.R. 1593 (DC). Where oral evidence has been introduced a district judge may refuse cross-examination where it would not be procedurally correct or not allowed in English law: *Fernandes, Fernandes, Travasso v. Governor of Brixton prison, The Commonwealth of the Bahamas, ante*. Where an extraditee alleges that extradition would be unjust or oppressive the burden is on him to prove it. See *Brown & others v. Rwanda* [2009] EWHC 770 (Admin) (DC) for the approach a judge should take in considering evidence.

The meaning of "accused person" was considered in *Re Ismail* [1999] A.C. 320. The House of Lords stated that it is more than mere suspicion that an individual has committed an offence and courts ought to adopt a purposive interpretation.

> "It is necessary for our courts to adopt a cosmopolitan approach to the question whether as a matter of substance rather than form the requirement of there being an 'accused' person is satisfied. . .the Divisional court in this case posed the right test by addressing the broad question whether the competent authorities in the foreign jurisdiction had taken a step which can fairly be described as the commencement of a prosecution. But in the light of the diversity of cases which may come before the courts it is right to emphasise that ultimately the question whether a person is 'accused'…will require an intense focus on the particular facts of each case".

Where a person has not been convicted the provisions covering documentary evidence are found in s.84. **3–72**

Extradition Act 2003, s.84(1)–(7)

Case where person has not been convicted

84.—(1) If the judge is required to proceed under this section he must decide whether there **3–73**

is evidence which would be sufficient to make a case requiring an answer by the person if the proceedings were the summary trial of an information against him.

(2) In deciding the question in subsection (1) the judge may treat a statement made by a person in a document as admissible evidence of a fact if—

(a) the statement is made by the person to a police officer or another person charged with the duty of investigating offences or charging offenders, and

(b) direct oral evidence by the person of the fact would be admissible.

(3) In deciding whether to treat a statement made by a person in a document as admissible evidence of a fact, the judge must in particular have regard—

(a) to the nature and source of the document;

(b) to whether or not, having regard to the nature and source of the document and to any other circumstances that appear to the judge to be relevant, it is likely that the document is authentic;

(c) to the extent to which the statement appears to supply evidence which would not be readily available if the statement were not treated as being admissible evidence of the fact;

(d) to the relevance of the evidence that the statement appears to supply to any issue likely to have to be determined by the judge in deciding the question in subsection (1);

(e) to any risk that the admission or exclusion of the statement will result in unfairness to the person whose extradition is sought, having regard in particular to whether it is likely to be possible to controvert the statement if the person making it does not attend to give oral evidence in the proceedings.

(4) A summary in a document of a statement made by a person must be treated as a statement made by the person in the document for the purposes of subsection (2).

(5) If the judge decides the question in subsection (1) in the negative he must order the person's discharge.

(6) If the judge decides that question in the affirmative he must proceed under section 87.

(7) If the judge is required to proceed under this section and the category 2 territory to which extradition is requested is designated for the purposes of this section by order made by the Secretary of State—

(a) the judge must not decide under subsection (1), and

(b) he must proceed under section 87.

3–74 Where the person has been convicted in his absence the evidential requirements are found in s.86.

Extradition Act 2003, s.86(1)–(7)

Conviction in person's absence

3–75 **86.**—(1) If the judge is required to proceed under this section he must decide whether there is evidence which would be sufficient to make a case requiring an answer by the person if the proceedings were the summary trial of an information against him.

(2) In deciding the question in subsection (1) the judge may treat a statement made by a person in a document as admissible evidence of a fact if—

(a) the statement is made by the person to a police officer or another person charged with the duty of investigating offences or charging offenders, and

(b) direct oral evidence by the person of the fact would be admissible.

(3) In deciding whether to treat a statement made by a person in a document as admissible evidence of a fact, the judge must in particular have regard—

(a) to the nature and source of the document;

(b) to whether or not, having regard to the nature and source of the document and to any other circumstances that appear to the judge to be relevant, it is likely that the document is authentic;

(c) to the extent to which the statement appears to supply evidence which would not be readily available if the statement were not treated as being admissible evidence of the fact;

(d) to the relevance of the evidence that the statement appears to supply to any issue likely to have to be determined by the judge in deciding the question in subsection (1);

(e) to any risk that the admission or exclusion of the statement will result in unfairness to the person whose extradition is sought, having regard in particular to whether it is likely to be possible to controvert the statement if the person making it does not attend to give oral evidence in the proceedings.

(4) A summary in a document of a statement made by a person must be treated as a statement made by the person in the document for the purposes of subsection (2).

(5) If the judge decides the question in subsection (1) in the negative he must order the person's discharge.

(6) If the judge decides that question in the affirmative he must proceed under section 87.

(7) If the judge is required to proceed under this section and the category 2 territory to which extradition is requested is designated for the purposes of this section by order made by the Secretary of State—

(a) the judge must not decide under subsection (1), and

(b) he must proceed under section 87.

In *Ginova v. Government of the Czech Republic* [2003] EWHC 2187, it was said that the burden of proof on the requesting state to show that a person was unlawfully at large was proof beyond reasonable doubt. It is for a person to displace the presumption that the court document from the requesting state recording the hearing accurately reflects what happened: *Prenga v. Albania* [2006] EWHC 1616. See also *Patel v. Germany* [2011] EWHC 155(Admin) regarding the presumption of good faith in documentary replies from the Judicial Authority notwithstanding defence expert evidence purporting to contradict it. **3–76**

Where authentication of documents is required it is not necessary for each and every statement on oath to be certificated: *Oskar v. Government of Australia* [1988] A.C. 366. It is sufficient to have a certificate which adequately identifies all the statements which it certifies. In that case the statements were all tied together.

In *Lodhi, ante*, it was said that statements in English made by a non-English speaker had to be accompanied by a signature to a document written in his own language coupled with an attested translation of his signed affidavit into English.

It has been held that an affidavit is a document containing evidence whereas a deposition is a document recording evidence and both are admissible: *Fernandez v. Government of Singapore* [1971] 2 All E.R. 691.

In *Orechovsky v. Government of Slovakia* [2003] EWHC 2758, it was held that the court could consider articles drawn from the internet concerning human rights abuse in the requesting state. The court was not restricted to hearing evidence in the strict sense. In practice an increasing amount of material derived from the internet is adduced, usually by the defence. The weight to be given to such material is the issue not its general receipt at the hearing per se. **3–77**

There is no right of access to unused material: *Governor of Pentonville Prison, ex p. Lee* [1993] 3 All E.R. 504. This was approved in *Lodhi v. Governor of HM Prison Brixton* [2001] EHWC Admin 178. In *Kashamu* [2002] Q.B. 887, the extradition order was quashed on the grounds that the extradition proceedings were unfair as aresult of the non-disclosure of crucial evidence. The foregoing are all cases decided before the Act. In *Jenkins v. USA* [2005] EWHC 1051 (Admin) there was express approval of *Serbeh v. Governor of HMP Brixton* [2002] EWHC 2356 (Admin) DC—holding that it is for a requesting Judicial Authority/state to decide what material to disclose, all of which is to be considered on a presumption of good faith. While a judge may request additional information there is no power, unsurprisingly, to compel a response and a failure to respond, given the underlying presumptions of the Act, is not per se to be held in any way against the requesting body: see inter alia *Central Examining Court of the National Court of Madrid v. City of Westminster Magistrates' Court* [2007] 2089(Admin) (DC).

The *Police and Criminal Evidence Act* 1984 does not strictly apply to extradition proceedings as a person has not been arrested for an offence. Case law has, however, confirmed that s.78 of that Act does apply: *Governor of Pentonville Prison, ex p. Walters* [1987] Crim.L.R. 577; *Governor of Pentonville Prison, ex p. Chinoy* [1992] 1 All E.R. 317; *Governor of Brixton Prison, ex p. Levin* [1997] 3 W.L.R. 117. In the latter case Lord Hoffman stated that extradition proceedings were criminal proceedings but of a very special kind. He confirmed that s.78 applied. He said:

> "The question is, therefore, whether the admission of the evidence would have such an adverse effect on the fairness of the decision to... extradite the accused for trial, even if the trial is a fair one... It would undermine the effectiveness of international treaty obligations if the courts were to superimpose discretions based on local notions of fairness upon the ordinary rules of admissibility. I do not wish to exclude the possibility that the discretion may be used in extradition proceedings founded upon evidence which, although technically admissible, has been obtained in a way which outrages civilised values. But such cases are also likely to be very rare."

3–78 In *R. (Saifi) v. Governor of Brixton Prison* [2001] 1 W.L.R. 1134, Rose L.J., in rejecting a burden of proof test for s.78, stated that:

> "Under section 78 any circumstance which can reasonably have a bearing on fairness should be considered. The weight to be attached to an individual circumstance may increase or decrease because of the presence of other related or unrelated circumstances. The preponderance of all the circumstances may show that the admission of the evidence would have such an adverse effect on fairness as to require its exclusion."

In practice such challenges are now rare given the significant number of jurisdictions (all Pt 1 and many Pt 2) that do not require a prima facie case, *e.g. Hutton v. Australia* [2009] EWHC 564 (Admin) (DC) confession evidence to police being agreed as the crucial material (a murder) could not be challenged under s.76/78 *PACE* in extradition proceedings that being a matter for trial.

Evidence of identity is admissible—see *ante*, § 3–25, ss.7, 78 being expressed as upon the balance of probabilities. In the case of *Anthony*, June 27, 1995, it was stated that when there is an issue as to whether the person brought before the magistrate is the person requested by the foreign state, that is a question which is fundamental to the jurisdiction of the magistrate.

The burden of proof is in accordance with the person being accused of a summary offence. The judge will weigh up the evidence but will not weigh the evidence: *Governor of Pentonville Prison, ex p. Osman* [1989] 3 All E.R. 701,

> "... it was the magistrate's duty to consider the evidence as a whole, and to reject any evidence which he considered worthless. In that sense was his duty to weigh up the evidence. But it was not his duty to weigh the evidence. He was neither entitled nor obliged to determine the amount of weight to be attached to any evidence, or to compare one witness with another. That would be for the jury at the trial. It follows that the magistrate was not concerned with the inconsistencies or contradictions in...evidence, unless they were such as to justify rejecting or eliminating his evidence altogether ... As a working guide, we could not do better than adopt the language of the magistrate ... substituting 'consider' for 'weigh'."

VII. THE DECISION

3–79 In Pt 1 cases, the judge will make an extradition order (s.21 (3)) or will discharge the person. If there is no appeal the extradition will then take place within ten days unless a later date is agreed: ss.35, 46. As the opportunity to consider any appeal is 7 days for the defence or the Judicial Authority (s.26, 28) which cannot be waived the timescale is 7 days to lodge an appeal. If this is not done (and in correct form) then a further 10 days is allowed for SOCA to arrange surrender, a total of 17 days. In Pt 2 cases the judge will either commit the person in custody or on bail to await the Secretary of State's decision on extradition or will discharge him.

See s.87 (3). The judge **must** inform the defendant of the right to lodge an appeal (ss.103 and 104) albeit that no appeal can be heard until the Secretary of State has made a decision s.103(5). A discharge order by the judge is subject to a State's appeal (ss.105

and 106). For appeals against the Secretary of State's decision to order extradition see ss.108 and 109 and against his decision to order extradition see ss.110 and 111. Section 93 requires the Secretary of State to consider four matters—usually within 2 months of the Judge's decision under s.87 (3)—as follows:

(i) has or will the person face the death penalty (if yes he cannot be extradited unless a "written assurance" is received it will not be carried out: s.94).
(ii) Whether speciality arrangements exist.
(iii) Whether he has previously been extradited from elsewhere and consent for onward extradition has not been obtained; and
(iv) Whether he has previously been transferred to the UK by the International Criminal Court which has not consented to onward extradition.

If all matters are determined in favour of the Requesting State extradition will be ordered, subject to appeal to the High Court, if not discharge must follow subject to the Requesting State's right of appeal (see above).

The power to grant an extension of time under s.35(4)(b) is not restricted to circumstances in which extradition within the normal time limit has been prevented by circumstances beyond the control of the member States: *Szklanny v. City of Westminster Magistrates Court* (2008) 1 W.L.R. 789. Where there are other European Arrest Warrants outstanding and an appeal is unsuccessful the extradition may not actually take place within the 10 days: *Calderelli v. Italy* [2009] EWHC 107 (Admin). Here *Calderelli* applied for a discharge of the original order for extradition under s.36(8) as he had not been extradited within the ten day period. The District Judge had held that there had been reasonable cause to delay the extradition because *Calderelli* was entitled to contest the proceedings under the new warrants. On appeal the District Judge was upheld and it was said that it is an entirely reasonable view to take that the overall objective of the Framework Decision, which is to ensure the swift and orderly extradition between Member States, would be met by the judicial authority of the requested state dealing as swiftly as practicable with all outstanding warrants

For the purposes of s.36(2) and (3) the "required period" does not begin to run until the period permitted for applying for leave to appeal to the Supreme Court ends; it makes no difference that certification of a point of law of general public importance has been requested and refused: *Owens v. City of Westminster Magistrates' Court* [2009] A.C.D. 56 .

While *Bow Street Magistrates' Court, ex p Allison, The Times* June 2 1998 held that there is no legal duty to give reasons this must now, with respect, be doubted since the*Human Rights Act* 1998 and the unchallenged ECHR jurisprudence based on the need for reasoned rulings, however brief, in all contested matters. In practice if no issues are raised a short ex tempore judgement is given. Any other matter is dealt with by written reasons, delivered orally in open court, provided to the parties and, if requested, the press.

If a person has been ordered to be extradited under Pt 1 and he is serving a sentence in this country, the judge may make the order subject to a condition that extradition is not to take place unless he has received an undertaking on behalf of the requesting state that the person will be returned to the UK to serve the remainder of his sentence on the conclusion either of the proceedings or the sentence to be served there: ss.37, 52 and 186. There is no provision in the Act for the removal of persons serving domestic sentences and this undermines ss.37 and 186: *Handa v. High Instance Court of Paris*; *R. (Handa) v Bow Street Magistrates' Court, ante*.

In Part 2 cases the Secretary of State will not make a decision until the charge is disposed of, withdrawn or discontinued and where a sentence of imprisonment is imposed for that offence or the person is already serving a prison sentence the decision may be deferred until the person is released: ss.97, 98. A judge can reconsider an order if a basic error, including a procedural error, emerges from the terms of the judgement and is brought to his attention immediately after delivery of the judgement and the pronouncement of the order: *R. (on the application of Berners) v. Westminster Magistrates' Court* [2010] EWHC 1010 (Admin).

3–80 Where a person has been discharged and an appeal is pending then he will be remanded in custody or on bail pending the conclusion of the appeal: s.30.

Once a fugitive has been extradited under Pt 1, an appropriate judge has no power: (i) to make inquiries of the requesting state about the conduct of the criminal process or any other aspect of the way in which the extradited person is being dealt with; or (ii) to request the return of the extradited person, and the High Court has no jurisdiction to grant a declaration that the authorities of the requesting state are acting in breach of the speciality rule or to order the return of an extradited person where he is being dealt with in breach of that rule; there is no statutory provision which requires or enables the appropriate judge or the High Court to supervise the treatment of an extradited person following surrender to another category 1 territory: *R. (Hilali) v. City of Westminster Magistrates' Court* [2009] 1 All E.R. 834, DC.

In *Pilecki v. Poland* [2008] 1 W.L.R. 325 (H.L.), the UK authorities had failed to appreciate a petition was awaiting determination by the House of Lords and surrendered P. to the Polish authorities. The House of Lords made clear this should never be repeated but that P. had agreed to remain in a Polish prison while his appeal was considered (ultimately dismissed). Had he been successful, securing his release or return to the UK, absent Polish cooperation, would have been legally impossible.

VIII. CHALLENGING THE DECISION

3–81 An appeal may be made by the requesting state against discharge and by the person concerned against the order for extradition.

In Pt 1 cases the appeal is to the High Court on a question of law and fact: s.26. The High Court may allow or dismiss the appeal: s.27. In Pt 2 cases no appeal from a decision to "send" the case per s.87 (3) shall lie until the Secretary of State has made his decision: s.103. An appeal will lie from the High Court to the Supreme Court ss.32, 114, and in certain instances the House of Lords (now Supreme Court) may remit the case back to the district judge.

Habeas corpus is not available where there is a statutory appeals system: *Re Hilali* [2008] 1 A.C. 805. This was confirmed in *Ignauoua v. Italy* [2008] EWHC 2619 (Admin) which went on to say that where fresh evidence is available the proper course is to apply to re-open the Divisional Court's decision under the *Civil Procedure Rules* r.52.17. See also *Hungary v. Fenyvesi post* 3–84.

Extradition Act 2003, ss.26, 27

Appeal against extradition order

3–82 **26.**—(1) If the appropriate judge orders a person's extradition under this Part, the person may appeal to the High Court against the order.

(2) But subsection (1) does not apply if the order is made under section 46 or 48.

(3) An appeal under this section may be brought on a question of law or fact.

(4) Notice of an appeal under this section must be given in accordance with rules of court before the end of the permitted period, which is 7 days starting with the day on which the order is made.

The permitted period for submitting a notice under s.26(4) starts on the day on which the judge makes the order. The fact that a hearing has been concluded after hours does not mean that the period starts on the following business day: *R. (on the application of Kofi Amoako) v. DPP* [2004] 4 All E.R. 230. This means 7 days including weekends and public holidays. Therefore, to comply, a party needs to be aware of when, especially at periods of longer closure around Christmas and New Year, the High Court is open for business.

The Act envisages a strict timetable and provisions under the *Civil Procedure Rules* whereby the court can extend the time for the taking of any step or make an order dispensing with service cannot be invoked to extend a statutory time limit or to avoid service required by statute.; an appeal can only be brought validly if there is strict compliance with the time limits: *Mucelli v. Albania*; *Moulai v. France* [2009] 1 W.L.R. 276 (joined appeals to the House of Lords of a Pt 1 and Pt 2 case). All that s.26 (4) and s.103 (9) require is that the notice of appeal is filed within the specified period. Where a document is transmitted by fax after 4pm it is deemed to be served on the business day after it is transmitted: CPR r.6.7. There is an express provision in r.5.3(9) advising that a "fax" should not be used as a means to file a notice of appeal "except in an unavoidable emergency". Where the office of the recipient is closed during the whole of the last day for service then the notice will be filed validly if it is given at any time during the next business day. An email cannot amount to the filing of notice: *Gercans v. Latvia* [2008] EWHC 884 (Admin). The previous case of *R. (on the application of Mendy) v. Crown Prosecution Service* [2007] A.C.D. 90 had suggested that this could possibly happen in extreme circumstances where it is asserted that the decision of the judge was wrong in law or in fact and there is a real danger of a breach of human rights should the remedy be denied. In *Bergman v. Czech Republic* [2011] EWHC 267 (Admin), Irwin J. reviewed the case law, even for "unrepresented litigants in custody", holding "in almost every other circumstance, the court would be able to look behind the formalities . . . in this regime [*viz. Extradition Act*] one is not able to do so. There is no appeal; there can be no appeal; I am not able to extend any time limit to permit an appeal".

On an appeal in the case of *Moulai*, *ante* to the House of Lords which was dismissed the court stated that there is power to extend the timetable under s.31(5) and this can be exercised even after the time has expired if the court believes that it is in the interests of justice, in this case because he was serving a custodial sentence. See also *Pomiechowski v. Poland* [2011] All E.R. (D) 96. While generally the court could cure defects in formal notice procedures—*Civil Procedure Rules* r.3.10—in extradition appeals all three requirements *per* s.26(4) had to be met or an appeal notice could not be cured.

Where a supervening event has occurred after the exhaustion of statutory appeal rights, e.g. a coup in the requesting state leading to a change of government or the outbreak of genocide, that would render it wholly inappropriate to surrender an individual then: (a) if the case is one where there has been a properly constituted appeal that has run its course, then an application can be made under CPR r.52.17 to reopen the case; (b) if it is a Pt 2 case and there was no appeal representations should be made to the Secretary of State for the Home Department; (c) if it is a Pt 1 case and there was no appeal then representations should be made to the agency which could advise that permission might be sought from the Divisional Court to seek judicial review: *R. (on the application of Navadunskis) v. Serious Organised Crime Agency, ante*.

Once the time limit for appeal under Pt 1 has expired the order is final; there is no jurisdiction to judicially review the order unless an intervening circumstance of the type outlined in *Navadunskis* occurs after the time limit has expired, even if the failure has occurred through the incompetence of legal representatives: *R. (on the application of Mann) v. Westminster Magistrates' Court* [2010] EWHC 48 (Admin). The court doubted s.142 *Magistrates Courts Act* 1980 could be used to reopen an extradition decision.

Court's powers on appeal under s.26

27.—(1) On an appeal under section 26 the High Court may— **3–83**

(a) allow the appeal;

(b) dismiss the appeal.

(2) The court may allow the appeal only if the conditions in subsection (3) or the conditions in subsection (4) are satisfied.

(3) The conditions are that—

(a) the appropriate judge ought to have decided a question before him at the extradition hearing differently;

(b) if he had decided the question in the way he ought to have done, he would have been required to order the person's discharge.

(4) The conditions are that—

(a) an issue is raised that was not raised at the extradition hearing or evidence is available that was not available at the extradition hearing;

(b) the issue or evidence would have resulted in the appropriate judge deciding a question before him at the extradition hearing differently;

(c) if he had decided the question in that way, he would have been required to order the person's discharge.

(5) If the court allows the appeal it must—

(a) order the person's discharge;

(b) quash the order for his extradition.

3–84 The High Court may allow the appeal only if it believes that the judge should have decided a question before him differently and that difference would have led to the person's discharge. Its powers are to dismiss the application or to quash the extradition order and discharge the person.

It is inappropriate to adduce fresh evidence when it could have been introduced at the extradition hearing through the exercise of due diligence; it is trite law that those who are involved in litigation should advance all the case at first instance: *Kalniets v. Latvia* [2009] EWHC 534 (Admin). Evidence which is not available at the extradition hearing means evidence which, either does not exist at the time, or which is not at the disposal of the party wishing to adduce it and which cannot with reasonable diligence be obtained: *Hungary v. Fenyvesi* [2009] 4 All E.R. 324.

In *Sziraki v. Romania* [2011] All ER (D) 128, Silber, J. refused to consider medical evidence on appeal when "no reason" for it not being before the District Judge had been given.

In *Hoholm v. Government of Norway* [2009] EWHC 1513 (Admin) however, it was said that where an issue is available to be raised at an extradition hearing, that issue may be raised on appeal to the Divisional court, even though it has not been raised before. The law seems to be that the High Court expects all evidence and legal argument to be considered at first instance. However, if good cause can be shown why that has not been done the High Court has the discretion to hear and consider fresh evidence and legal argument.

Extradition Act 2003, s.28

Appeal against discharge at extradition hearing

3–85 **28.**—(1) If the judge orders a person's discharge at the extradition hearing the authority which issued the Part 1 warrant may appeal to the High Court against the relevant decision.

(2) But subsection (1) does not apply if the order for the person's discharge was under section 41.

(3) The relevant decision is the decision which resulted in the order for the person's discharge.

(4) An appeal under this section may be brought on a question of law or fact.

(5) Notice of an appeal under this section must be given in accordance with rules of court before the end of the permitted period, which is 7 days starting with the day on which the order for the person's discharge is made.

3–86 The requesting Judicial Authority may appeal against discharge within seven days on a question of law or fact. On appeal the High Court may allow the appeal if the judge ought to have decided a question differently and that would not have led to the person's discharge or a new issue has been raised or new evidence is available and that if heard by the judge would not have led to the person's discharge. There is no power to extend the time limit for serving the notice of appeal and a court's general powers of management found in CPR r.3 apply only to compliance with rules, practice directions and court orders and not statutory provisions. Even where a notice cannot be filed because of a court's electrical blackout or closure compliance will fail: *Lithuania v. Barcys* (2008) 1 All E.R. 733

Extradition Act 2003, s.29

Court's powers on appeal under s.28

29.—(1) On an appeal under section 28 the High Court may— **3–87**

(a) allow the appeal;

(b) dismiss the appeal.

(2) The court may allow the appeal only if the conditions in subsection (3) or the conditions in subsection (4) are satisfied.

(3) The conditions are that—

(a) the judge ought to have decided the relevant question differently;

(b) if he had decided the question in the way he ought to have done, he would not have been required to order the person's discharge.

(4) The conditions are that—

(a) an issue is raised that was not raised at the extradition hearing or evidence is available that was not available at the extradition hearing;

(b) the issue or evidence would have resulted in the judge deciding the relevant question differently;

(c) if he had decided the question in that way, he would not have been required to order the person's discharge.

(5) If the court allows the appeal it must—

(a) quash the order discharging the person;

(b) remit the case to the judge;

(c) direct him to proceed as he would have been required to do if he had decided the relevant question differently at the extradition hearing.

(6) A question is the relevant question if the judge's decision on it resulted in the order for the person's discharge.

Section 29(4) is expressed in terms which appear to give the court no discretion and the court, in order to decide whether the result would have been different if evidence had been adduced, should consider evidence which was not available at the hearing with some care; admitting evidence which would require a full rehearing in the High Court must be regarded as exceptional: *Szombathely City Court and others v. Fenyvesi and another* [2009] 4 All E.R. 324, DC. See commentary 3-84.

The specific procedure for Pt 2 cases is contained in the following provisions. **3–88**

Extradition Act 2003, ss.103–106

Appeal where case sent to Secretary of State

103.—(1) If the judge sends a case to the Secretary of State under this Part for his decision whether a person is to be extradited, the person may appeal to the High Court against the relevant decision. **3–89**

(2) But subsection (1) does not apply if the person consented to his extradition under section 127 before his case was sent to the Secretary of State.

(3) The relevant decision is the decision that resulted in the case being sent to the Secretary of State.

(4) An appeal under this section may be brought on a question of law or fact.

(5) If an appeal is brought under this section before the Secretary of State has decided whether the person is to be extradited the appeal must not be heard until after the Secretary of State has made his decision.

(6) If the Secretary of State orders the person's discharge the appeal must not be proceeded with.

(7) No appeal may be brought under this section if the Secretary of State has ordered the person's discharge.

(8) If notice of an appeal under section 110 against the decision which resulted in the order for the person's discharge is given in accordance with subsection (5) of that section—

(a) subsections (6) and (7) do not apply;

(b) no appeal may be brought under this section if the High Court has made its decision on the appeal.

(9) Notice of an appeal under this section must be given in accordance with rules of

court before the end of the permitted period, which is 14 days starting with the day on which the Secretary of State informs the person under section 100(1) or (4) of the order he has made in respect of the person.

It is not appropriate for a court to exercise its power under the *Civil Procedure Rules* r.6.9 to dispense retrospectively with the need for service under s.103(9) where an appellant makes no attempt to serve a notice of appeal in time and where it is tantamount to dispensing with statutory time limits: *Vullnet Mucelli v. Albania* (2008) 2 All E.R. 340.

It would ordinarily be wrong for the Secretary of State to be made a respondent to an appeal under s.103 as he would not normally be required to consider afresh whether the extradition is incompatible with ECHR: *Nisbet v. Secretary of State for the Home Dept & Ors* [2007] EWHC 1768(Admin).

Court's powers on appeal under s.103

3–90 **104.**—(1) On an appeal under section 103 the High Court may—

(a) allow the appeal;

(b) direct the judge to decide again a question (or questions) which he decided at the extradition hearing;

(c) dismiss the appeal.

(2) The court may allow the appeal only if the conditions in subsection (3) or the conditions in subsection (4) are satisfied.

(3) The conditions are that—

(a) the judge ought to have decided a question before him at the extradition hearing differently;

(b) if he had decided the question in the way he ought to have done, he would have been required to order the person's discharge.

(4) The conditions are that—

(a) an issue is raised that was not raised at the extradition hearing or evidence is available that was not available at the extradition hearing;

(b) the issue or evidence would have resulted in the judge deciding a question before him at the extradition hearing differently;

(c) if he had decided the question in that way, he would have been required to order the person's discharge.

(5) If the court allows the appeal it must—

(a) order the person's discharge;

(b) quash the order for his extradition.

(6) If the judge comes to a different decision on any question that is the subject of a direction under subsection (1)(b) he must order the person's discharge.

(7) If the judge comes to the same decision as he did at the extradition hearing on the question that is (or all the questions that are) the subject of a direction under subsection (1)(b) the appeal must be taken to have been dismissed by a decision of the High Court.

Where a remitted question has been decided adversely to an appellant, the effect of s.104(7) is that the original appeal is taken to have been dismissed by the High Court. This is to avoid successive and repeated applications. That decision is not subject to judicial review and the only route of appeal is to the Supreme Court. Remission can only be of a question which was originally decided at the extradition hearing. If a district judge goes beyond that question he acts beyond his powers under the section and judicial review is available: *Chen v. Romania* [2009] 1 W.L.R. 257. In *Gomes v. Goodyer v. Goverment Trinidad and Tobago* [2009] 1 W.L.R. 1038 (H.L.), the House of Lords accepted that the District Judge, to whom the case had been remitted, had to consider a divergence of High Court cases that had arisen since the original first instance decision.

Appeal against discharge at extradition hearing

3–91 **105.**—(1) If at the extradition hearing the judge orders a person's discharge, an appeal to the High Court may be brought on behalf of the category 2 territory against the relevant decision.

(2) But subsection (1) does not apply if the order for the person's discharge was under section 122.

(3) The relevant decision is the decision which resulted in the order for the person's discharge.

(4) An appeal under this section may be brought on a question of law or fact.

(5) Notice of an appeal under this section must be given in accordance with rules of court before the end of the permitted period, which is 14 days starting with the day on which the order for the person's discharge is made.

Court's powers on appeal under section 105

106.—(1) On an appeal under section 105 the High Court may— **3–92**

(a) allow the appeal;

(b) direct the judge to decide the relevant question again;

(c) dismiss the appeal.

(2) A question is the relevant question if the judge's decision on it resulted in the order for the person's discharge.

(3) The court may allow the appeal only if the conditions in subsection (4) or the conditions in subsection (5) are satisfied.

(4) The conditions are that—

(a) the judge ought to have decided the relevant question differently;

(b) if he had decided the question in the way he ought to have done, he would not have been required to order the person's discharge.

(5) The conditions are that—

(a) an issue is raised that was not raised at the extradition hearing or evidence is available that was not available at the extradition hearing;

(b) the issue or evidence would have resulted in the judge deciding the relevant question differently;

(c) if he had decided the question in that way, he would not have been required to order the person's discharge.

(6) If the court allows the appeal it must—

(a) quash the order discharging the person;

(b) remit the case to the judge;

(c) direct him to proceed as he would have been required to do if he had decided the relevant question differently at the extradition hearing.

(7) If the court makes a direction under subsection (1)(b) and the judge decides the relevant question differently he must proceed as he would have been required to do if he had decided that question differently at the extradition hearing.

(8) If the court makes a direction under subsection (1)(b) and the judge does not decide the relevant question differently the appeal must be taken to have been dismissed by a decision of the High Court.

Where the High Court remits a question to the district judge for reconsideration on further evidence but the district judge comes to the same conclusion as at the original extradition hearing, the second decision of the district judge is deemed by statute to be a decision of the High Court as there is no purpose in the district judge's sending the case to the Secretary of State again under s.87(3): *R. (Okandeji) v. Bow Street Magistrates' Court, ante*.

Where no point of law has ever been certified, there is no permitted period for applying to the Supreme Court for leave to appeal to it: *Wood v. City of Westminster Magistrates Court & ors* [2007] EWHC 2080.

IX. COSTS

Where extradition has been ordered costs may be awarded under s.60 for category 1 cases and s.133 for category 2. **3–93**

Extradition Act 2003, ss.60(2), (4); 133(2), (4)

Costs where extradition ordered

60. & 133.—(2) ... the appropriate judge may make such order as he considers just and reasonable with regard to the costs to be paid by the person. **3–94**

(4) An order for costs under this section—

(a) must specify their amount;

(b) may name the person to whom they are to be paid.

3–95 Where extradition is ordered, the person may be ordered to pay a specific sum of costs which is considered just and reasonable. Where the person has been discharged or taken to be discharged, costs may be ordered under s.61 for category 1 cases and s.134 for category 2.

Extradition Act 2003, ss.61(2), (5)–(8);134(2), (5)–(8)

3–96 **61. & 134.**—(2) ... an order under subsection (5) in favour of the person may be made by—

(a) the appropriate judge, if the order for the person's discharge is made by him;

(5) An order under this subsection in favour of a person is an order for a payment of the appropriate amount to be made to the person out of money provided by Parliament.

(6) The appropriate amount is such amount as the judge or court making the order under subsection (5) considers reasonably sufficient to compensate the person in whose favour the order is made for any expenses properly incurred by him in the proceedings under this Part.

(7) But if the judge or court making an order under subsection (5) is of the opinion that there are circumstances which make it inappropriate that the person in whose favour the order is made should recover the full amount mentioned in subsection (6), the judge or court must—

(a) assess what amount would in his or its opinion be just and reasonable;

(b) specify that amount in the order as the appropriate amount.

(8) Unless subsection (7) applies, the appropriate amount—

(a) must be specified in the order, if the court considers it appropriate for it to be so specified and the person in whose favour the order is made agrees the amount;

(b) must be determined in accordance with regulations made by the Lord Chancellor for the purposes of this section, in any other case.

3–97 Here there are three options:

1) where the judge considers that a person should not receive all his costs he should specify the amount of costs ordered;
2) where the judge considers that the person should receive all his costs he may specify the sum where the sum is agreed by the person; or
3) where the judge considers that the person should receive all his costs he may order that they may be taxed by the determining officer: s.62.

3–98 The Secretary of State for the Home Department operates an *ex gratia* scheme for the payment of compensation to those persons unlawfully detained from a wrongful conviction or charge. This also applies in the context of extradition proceedings: *R. (on the application of Lotfi Raissi) v. Secretary of State for the Home Department* (2008) 2 All E.R. 340.

X. POST EXTRADITION

3–99 Under Pt 1 where the extradition order has been made with consent, then, if a request is made by the requesting state for extradition on another offence, the judge will hold a hearing to determine whether the offence is an extradition offence and whether he would order extradition if he had proceeded in the normal way: s.55. In Pt 2 cases that is a matter for the Secretary of State. In practice these consent applications are most common from Polish Judicial Authorities. An issue can arise in ensuring notice is given to the Requested Person who has, almost always, been long since surrendered. The form of the consent documents mirrors that of an EAW. Representations are rarely received challenging the Request.

XI. *EXTRADITION ARRANGEMENTS*

(i) All EU countries are EAW (Pt 1) no evidence requirement jurisdictions and follow the EU Framework Decision 2002 and ECHR. **3–100**

(ii) The following have been "designated" by the Secretary of State (under Pt 2) as category 2 territories not required to establish prima facie evidence at an extradition hearing: [see *Extradition Act 2003 (Designation of Part 2 Territories) Order* 2003 (S.I. 2003 No.3334) as amended—there are several]

Albania, Andorra, Armenia, Australia, Azerbaijan, Canada, Croatia, Georgia, Hong Kong, Iceland, Israel, Liechtenstein, Macedonia, Moldova, Montenegro, New Zealand, Norway, Russian Federation, Serbia, South Africa, Switzerland, Turkey, Ukraine, USA.

(iii) All other countries, with whom the UK has a treaty, seeking extradition will be subject to Pt 2 and required to establish a prima facie case.

EXTRADITION PROCEEDINGS EAW (PT 1 EX. ACT 2003)

3–101 **ISSUE EAW & certify by SOCA** — Judicial Authority from requesting jurisdiction

ARREST — Provide copy EAW-s.4(2)—or provisional arrest s.5—and transfer to City of Westminster MC.

INITIAL HEARING

BAIL—presumption in favour unless conviction case, as per *Bail Act* 1976. Any appeal to High Court (both parties have automatic right of appeal).

(1) Must produce before "appropriate judge" s.4(3) "as soon as practicable" or s.5—provisional arrest—within 48 hours—or "discharge" EAW.

(2) Establish I.D—s.7—"on balance of probabilities"—may adjourn for evidence.

(3) Consent—s.8(3)—must be legally represented and if agreed confirmed in writing —extradited within 10 days (no appeal possible)

(4) If no consent—proceed to full hearing—ss.8/9—either immediately or within 21 days of arrest—may adjourn beyond this date.

(5) If judge "informed" domestic proceedings are outstanding must adjourn —s.8A—review every 28 days; if serving a sentence may (should) adjourn until near release date—s.8B—review at least every 6 months.

EXTRADITION HEARING	Consider—s,2—particulars alleged—s.10 (also ss.64/65)—extradition offence/dual criminality —s.11 (1)(a-i) bars and, s.20 retrial rights (if not "deliberately" absent at trial), s.25 physical/mental health: s.21 (2) ECHR compatibility—Discharge or order extradition/ surrender s.21 (3): 7 days to lodge appeal, if none, extradite 10 days thereafter *i.e.* 17 days.
APPEAL: High Court	Automatic right of appeal: Def S26 or Pros s.28—strict 7 days **and** in correct form (including day of order and weekends etc). High Court will not usually hear new evidence/submissions of law.
FURTHER APPEAL: SUPREME COURT	Point of law of "general public importance" certified by High Court and by leave only of High Court or Supreme Court: s.32 (3).

Part I

EXTRADITION PROCEEDINGS CATEGORY 2 TERRITORIES (PT 2 EX. ACT 2003)

3–102 **START OF PROCESS**	Requesting State: s.70. S. of S "must";
i) Full Certified extradition request:	certify if receives "valid" request.
ii) Provisional arrest:	S.71. An "appropriate judge" may issue a warrant if "reasonable grounds for believing" the allegation/conviction is an extradition offence and there is "evidence" (or if a "designated" State "information") justifying arrest. S.73 Any J.P. "satisfied on oath in writing" a person is "believed to be in. . .. . .or on his way" to UK and accused/convicted of an extradition offence and there is "evidence" (or if a "designated" State "information") "justifying arrest" may issue a warrant.
ARREST	Provide copy of warrant "as soon as practicable"—s.72 full request; s.74 provisional request—and brought "as soon as practicable" before an "appropriate judge" (ss.72/74).

FIRST APPEARANCE
(Certified Request) :-
(Provisional arrest) :-

"Appropriate Judge" "must" "inform" the person of the contents of the request and explain "consent" option. If "consents" must be legally represented and sign in writing-case sent (without more) to S. of S. (no appeal possible)—ss.127/128. Otherwise fix a date for the full hearing which must be no more than 2 months from first appearance-s.72.

"Appropriate Judge" "must" "inform" the person he is accused/convicted and explain "consent" (as above). If no consent must adjourn for receipt of the full certified request within 45 days-once received fix a date for the full hearing within 2 months of receipt of papers by the court (extendable if "in the interests of justice")—s.74. If judge "informed" of domestic proceedings "must" adjourn until concluded—s.76A-must review every 28 days. If "informed" of a domestic prison sentence "may" (should) adjourn until near end of term—s.76B-must review every 6 months.

BAIL —consider at first appearance—presumption in favour unless conviction case, as per *Bail Act* 1976. Any appeal to High Court (both parties have automatic right of appeal)

EX. HEARING

(1) The judge must be "satisfied" the documentation provided "consist of" the S of S's certificate, the formal request & particulars of: (a) the requested person, (b) the offence(s), (c) the arrest warrant (accusation) or memorandum of conviction (conviction) and that the offences are extradition offences (ss.137/138)-s.78.

(2) Consider "bars"—s.79(1) (a-d), any competing extradition claims—s.90 and any physical/mental health issue—s.91...

(3) Consider if evidence establishes a prima facie case-only applicable in non designated territories—s.84.

(4) Consider retrial rights (if person not "deliberately" absent at trial)—s.85.

(5) Consider if "extradition would be compatible" with ECHR—s.87 (2).

If **not** satisfied of any of the above "must" discharge, if satisfied "must" send to S of S—s.87 (3) & "inform" the person of the right of appeal to High Court—s.92.

SECRETARY OF STATE'S CONSIDERATION	Considers—s.93—within 2 months (extendable if "in the interests of justice"): (a) Is the death sentence faced (s.94),(b) Speciality (s.95),(c) earlier extradition to the UK (s.96),(d) earlier transfer to UK from International Criminal Court (s.96A). If any apply "must" discharge if not "must" order extradition.
APPEAL: HIGH COURT	Automatic right by unsuccessful State or requested person against decision of "appropriate judge" &/or S of S (ss.103-116). Strict time limits apply for lodging-no power to extend. No appeal will be heard until after decision of S of S. High Court will not usually hear new evidence/submissions of law. High Court may remit to an "appropriate Judge" to "decide again" any question determined at first instance—s.104 (1) (b).
FURTHER APPEAL: SUPREME COURT	Point of law of "general public importance" certified by High Court & by leave only ofHigh Court or Supreme Court—s.114.

Part I

CHAPTER 4

COMMENCEMENT OF PROCEEDINGS

I. INTRODUCTION

A prosecution consists of the institution and pursuance of legal proceedings against named persons or bodies. When a decision is made to prosecute a criminal case it will generally be started in the magistrates' court. Cases may be commenced in a variety of ways and by a number of different people, including private individuals, corporations and representatives of statutory organisations such as the police. **4–1**

The Crown Prosecution Service on behalf of the police prosecutes the majority of cases in the magistrates' courts. Prosecutions may also be brought by other prosecuting authorities such the Serious Fraud Office and the Revenue and Customs Prosecution Office. Government departments and local authorities are also empowered by specific statutes to institute and carry on prosecutions of certain offences. **4–2**

The named individual who commences the prosecuting process may be described as the prosecutor, even if little or no role is taken by him or her personally in the subsequent court proceedings. Where the prosecution begins with the accused being charged at the police station, a police officer will commence the prosecution by signing the charge sheet. Where the prosecution begins with the laying of an information before a magistrate, the person who laid the information commences the prosecution. The prosecution may then be taken over from the individual prosecutor by the relevant prosecuting body which in the case of police officers will be the Crown Prosecution Service. A private individual either acting alone or on behalf of a body corporate may also prosecute a case through the criminal courts by applying to the court for a summons to commence the proceedings.

4–3 Anyone who appears in the magistrates' court to commence or carry on a prosecution will either be a private individual or a corporation both of whom may instruct a legal representative at their own expense or they will be an individual employed by a public authority which is publicly funded with statutory powers to conduct prosecutions. Public authorities may also instruct lawyers as agents to conduct prosecutions.

II. THE PROSECUTOR

A. THE LAW OFFICERS OF THE CROWN

Law Officers Act 1997, s.1

The Attorney General and the Solicitor General

4–4 **1.**—(1) Any function of the Attorney General may be exercised by the Solicitor General.

(2) Anything done by or in relation to the Solicitor General in the exercise of or in connection with a function of the Attorney General has effect as if done by or in relation to the Attorney General.

(3) The validity of anything done in relation to the Attorney General, or done by or in relation to the Solicitor General, is not affected by a vacancy in the office of Attorney General.

(4) Nothing in this section—

(a) prevents anything being done by or in relation to the Attorney General in the exercise of or in connection with any function of his; or

(b) requires anything done by the Solicitor General to be done in the name of the Solicitor General instead of the name of the Attorney General.

(5) It is immaterial for the purposes of this section whether a function of the Attorney General arises under an enactment or otherwise.

4–5 The Law Officers of the Crown (the Attorney-General and the Solicitor-General, together with the Advocate General of Scotland) are the chief legal advisers to the government and are responsible for all Crown litigation. The Attorney-General is the Chief Law Officer and the Solicitor-General is his or her deputy. Neither office has any statutory basis; and both officers are politicians and members of the government and Parliament.

4–6 The three main functions of the Attorney-General are to act as guardian of the public interest, to act as the chief legal advisor to the government, and to act as a criminal justice minister. These functions include powers to bring or intervene in legal proceedings in the public interest and to act as advocate for the Crown in important cases; to terminate criminal proceedings on indictment by issuing a *nolle prosequi*; to bring proceedings for contempt of court; and to bring proceedings to restrain vexatious litigants, including private prosecutors. Further, certain criminal prosecutions can only be brought with the Attorney-General's consent (see *post*). The Attorney-General has a statutory responsibility for superintendence of the main prosecuting authorities (the Crown Prosecution Service, the Serious Fraud Office, and the Revenue and Customs Prosecutions Office) and is generally considered responsible for other prosecuting authorities. Superintendence encompasses answering for the prosecuting authorities in Parliament; responsibility for the overall policies of those authorities; responsibility for the overall effective and efficient administration of those authorities, including matters of resources; a right for the Attorney-General to be consulted and informed about difficult, sensitive and high-profile cases; but not responsibility for every individual prosecution decision, or for the day-to-day running of the organisation. There is no statutory power according to which the Attorney-General may direct the prosecuting authorities to prosecute (or not to prosecute) a particular case, or to take (or not to take) any other form of action. Additionally, the Attorney-General is responsible for the appointment of counsel to represent the Crown in criminal proceedings; and is the leader of the Bar *ex officio*.

4–7 The Solicitor-General is entitled to exercise any function of the Attorney-General, including the power to give consent for certain prosecutions to be brought.

B. THE CROWN PROSECUTION SERVICE (INCORPORATING THE REVENUE AND CUSTOMS PROSECUTION OFFICE)

(1) General

Prosecution of Offences Act 1985, s.1

The Crown Prosecution Service

1.—(1) There shall be a prosecuting service for England and Wales (to be known as the "Crown Prosecution Service") consisting of— **4–8**

(a) the Director of Public Prosecutions, who shall be head of the Service;

(b) the Chief Crown Prosecutors, designated under subsection (4) below, each of whom shall be the member of the Service responsible to the Director for supervising the operation of the Service in his area; and

(c) the other staff appointed by the Director under this section.

(2) The Director shall appoint such staff for the Service as, with the approval of the Treasury as to numbers, remuneration and other terms and conditions of service, he considers necessary for the discharge of his functions.

(3) The Director may designate any member of the Service who has a general qualification (within the meaning of section 71 of the *Courts and Legal Services Act* 1990) for the purposes of this subsection, and any person so designated shall be known as a Crown Prosecutor.

(4) The Director shall divide England and Wales into areas and, for each of those areas, designate a Crown Prosecutor for the purposes of this subsection and any person so designated shall be known as a Chief Crown Prosecutor.

(5) The Director may, from time to time, vary the division of England and Wales made for the purposes of subsection (4) above.

(6) Without prejudice to any functions which may have been assigned to him in his capacity as a member of the Service, every Crown Prosecutor shall have all the powers of the Director as to the institution and conduct of proceedings but shall exercise those powers under the direction of the Director.

(7) Where any enactment (whenever passed)—

(a) prevents any step from being taken without the consent of the Director or without his consent or the consent of another; or

(b) requires any step to be taken by or in relation to the Director;

any consent given by or, as the case may be, step taken by or in relation to, a Crown Prosecutor shall be treated, for the purposes of that enactment, as given by or, as the case may be, taken by or in relation to the Director.

[This section is printed as amended by the *Courts and Legal Services Act* 1990, Sched. 10.]

The Crown Prosecution Service was established by s.1(1) of the *Prosecution of Offences Act* 1985. It consists of the Director of Public Prosecutions (who is head of the service), qualified lawyers designated by the DPP as Chief Crown Prosecutors and Crown Prosecutors, and other employees. Each Chief Crown Prosecutor is responsible for a particular area of England and Wales assigned to him or her by the DPP. The functions of the CPS are set out in s.3 of the Act (see *post*) as being matters which it is the duty of the DPP to discharge. Each Crown Prosecutor is entitled to exercise the powers of the DPP as to the institution and conduct of proceedings, provided that he or she does so under the direction of the DPP. The DPP is also permitted to appoint qualified lawyers in private practice to act as agents on behalf of the CPS with powers to institute or take over the conduct of criminal proceedings or extradition proceedings (see s.5, *post*); and to designate non-legally qualified members of staff of the CPS as Associate Prosecutors (formerly known as Designated Case Workers, DCWs) to exercise limited rights of audience in the magistrates' courts (see s.7A, *post*) **4–9**

At the present time, the CPS also incorporates the Revenue and Customs Prosecution Office. This has no statutory basis, the RCPO being established as a separate entity under s.34 *et seq.* of the *Commissioners for Revenue and Customs Act* 2005. However, with effect from January 2010, the DPP concurrently holds the office of Director of Rev- **4–10** enue and Customs Prosecutions and thus, as a matter of administrative convenience, the CPS incorporates the RCPO. As to the RCPO generally, see *post*, § 4–38.

(2) The Director of Public Prosecutions and the functions of the CPS

(a) *Introduction*

4–11 The DPP is appointed by, and required to discharge his functions under the superintendence of, the Attorney-General: see ss.2(1) and 3(1) of the *Prosecution of Offences Act* 1985. The various duties which the DPP is required to discharge (and which, by implication, are the responsibility of the CPS as a whole) are set out in s.3(2) and (3).

(b) *Legislation*

Prosecution of Offences Act 1985, ss.3 and 15(2)–(5)

Functions of the Director

4–12 **3.**—(1) The Director shall discharge his functions under this or any other enactment under the superintendence of the Attorney General.

(2) It shall be the duty of the Director, subject to any provisions contained in the *Criminal Justice Act* 1987—

(a) to take over the conduct of all criminal proceedings, other than specified proceedings, instituted on behalf of a police force (whether by a member of that force or by any other person);

(aa) to take over the conduct of any criminal proceedings instituted by an immigration officer (as defined for the purposes of the *Immigration Act* 1971) acting in his capacity as such an officer;

(b) to institute and have the conduct of criminal proceedings in any case where it appears to him that—

(i) the importance or difficulty of the case makes it appropriate that proceedings should be instituted by him; or

(ii) it is otherwise appropriate for proceedings to be instituted by him;

(ba) to institute and have the conduct of any criminal proceedings in any case where the proceedings relate to the subject-matter of a report a copy of which has been sent to him under paragraph 23 or 24 of Schedule 3 to the *Police Reform Act* 2002 (reports on investigations into conduct of persons serving with the police);

(c) to take over the conduct of all binding over proceedings instituted on behalf of a police force (whether by a member of that force or by any other person);

(d) to take over the conduct of all proceedings begun by summons issued under section 3 of the *Obscene Publications Act* 1959 (forfeiture of obscene articles);

(e) to give, to such extent as he considers appropriate, advice to police forces on all matters relating to criminal offences;

(ea) to have the conduct of any extradition proceedings;

(eb) to give, to such extent as he considers appropriate, and to such persons as he considers appropriate, advice on any matters relating to extradition proceedings or proposed extradition proceedings;

(ec) to give, to such extent as he considers appropriate, advice to immigration officers on matters relating to criminal offences;

(f) to appear for the prosecution, when directed by the court to do so, on any appeal under—

(i) section 1 of the *Administration of Justice Act* 1960 (appeal from the High Court in criminal cases);

(ii) Part I or Part II of the *Criminal Appeal Act* 1968 (appeals from the Crown Court to the criminal division of the Court of Appeal and thence to the Supreme Court); or

(iii) section 108 of the *Magistrates' Courts Act* 1980 (right of appeal to Crown Court) as it applies, by virtue of subsection (5) of section 12 of the *Contempt of Court Act* 1981, to orders made under section 12 (contempt of magistrates' courts);

(fa) to have the conduct of applications for orders under section 1C of the *Crime and Disorder Act* 1998 (orders made on conviction of certain offences) [, section 6 of the *Violent Crime Reduction Act* 2006 (orders on conviction in criminal proceedings)] and section 14A of the *Football Spectators Act* 1989 (banning orders made on conviction of certain offences);

(faa) where it appears to him appropriate to do so, to have the conduct of applications made by him for orders under section 14B of the *Football Spectators Act* 1989 (banning orders made on complaint);

(fb) where it appears to him appropriate to do so, to have the conduct of applications under section 1CA(3) of the *Crime and Disorder Act* 1998 for the variation or discharge of orders made under section 1C of that Act;

(fc) where it appears to him appropriate to do so, to appear on any application under section 1CA of that Act made by a person subject to an order under section 1C of that Act for the variation or discharge of the order.

[(fd) where it appears to him appropriate to do so, to have the conduct of applications under section 8(1)(b) of the *Violent Crime Reduction Act* 2006 for the variation or discharge of orders made under section 6 of that Act;

(fe) where it appears to him appropriate to do so, to appear on any application under section 8(1)(a) of that Act by a person subject to an order under section 6 of that Act for the variation or discharge of the order.]

(ff) to discharge such duties as are conferred on him by, or in relation to, Part 5 or 8 of the *Proceeds of Crime Act* 2002 (civil recovery of the proceeds etc. of unlawful conduct, civil recovery investigations and disclosure orders in relation to confiscation investigations);

(g) to discharge such other functions as may from time to time be assigned to him by the Attorney-General in pursuance of this paragraph.

(2A) Subsection (2)(ea) above does not require the Director to have the conduct of any extradition proceedings in respect of a person if he has received a request not to do so and—

(a) in a case where the proceedings are under Part 1 of the *Extradition Act* 2003, the request is made by the authority which issued the Part 1 warrant in respect of the person;

(b) in a case where the proceedings are under Part 2 of that Act, the request is made on behalf of the territory to which the person's extradition has been requested.

(3) In this section—

"the court" means—

(a) in the case of an appeal to or from the criminal division of the Court of Appeal, that division;

(b) in the case of an appeal from a Divisional Court of the Queen's Bench Division, the Divisional Court; and

(c) in the case of an appeal against an order of a magistrates' court, the Crown Court;

"police force" means any police force maintained by a police authority under the *Police Act* 1996 and any other body of constables for the time being specified by order made by the Secretary of State for the purposes of this section; and

"specified proceedings" means proceedings which fall within any category for the time being specified by order made by the Attorney-General for the purposes of this section.

(4) The power to make orders under subsection (3) above shall be exercisable by statutory instrument subject to annulment in pursuance of a resolution of either House of Parliament.

[This section is printed as amended by the *Criminal Justice Act* 1987, Sched. 2, the *Police Act* 1996, Sched. 7, the *Police Act* 1997, Sched. 9, the *Immigration and Asylum Act* 1999, s.164, the *Police Reform Act* 2002, Sched. 7, the *Extradition Act* 2003, s.190, the *Anti social Behaviour Act* 2003, s.86 and Sched. 3, the *Asylum and Immigration (Treatment of Claimants, etc.) Act* 2004, s.7, the *Serious Organised Crime and Police Act* 2005, s.140(5) and Scheds 4 and 17, the *Constitutional Reform Act* 2005, Sched. 9, the *Violent Crime Reduction Act* 2006, Sched. 3, and the *Serious Crime Act* 2007, s.74(2)(g) and Sched. 8. The insertion of s.3(2)(fa), (fd) and (fe) by the *Violent Crime Reduction Act* 2006, ss.7 and 8, has effect only in relation to proceedings in magistrates' courts in the local justice areas of Birmingham, Bristol, Burnley, Cardiff, Central and South West Staffordshire, City of London, City of Salford, City of Westminster, Corby, Coventry District, Denbighshire, Doncaster, East Berkshire, East Dorset, East Kent, Fenland, Fylde Coast, Grimsby and Cleethorpes, Gwent, Hackney and Tower Hamlets, Halton, Hammersmith and Fulham and Kensington and Chelsea, Hartlepool, Hull and Holderness, Lambeth and Southwark, Leicester,Lincoln District, Manchester City, Mansfield, Merthyr Tydfil, Newcastle-upon-Tyne District, North East Derbyshire and Dales, North East Suffolk, North Kent, North Staffordshire, North Tyneside District, Northampton, Nottingham, Pendle and Rossendale, Plymouth District, Reading, Sedgemoor, South Devon, South East Hampshire, Southampton, Southern Derbyshire, Sussex (Central), Teesside, Wakefield, West Cornwall, and West Hertfordshire: *Violent Crime Reduction Act 2006 (Commencement No. 8) Order* 2010 (S.I. 2010 No. 469) and *Violent Crime Reduction Act 2006 (Commencement No. 9) Order* 2010 (S.I. 2010 No. 2541) .]

Interpretation of Part I

4–13 **15.**—(2) For the purposes of this Part, proceedings in relation to an offence are instituted—

(a) where a justice of the peace issues a summons under section 1 of the *Magistrates' Courts Act* 1980, when the information for the offence is laid before him;

(b) where a justice of the peace issues a warrant for the arrest of any person under that section, when the information for the offence is laid before him;

(ba) where a public prosecutor issues a written charge and requisition for the offence, when the written charge and requisition are issued;

(c) where a person is charged with the offence after being taken into custody without a warrant, when he is informed of the particulars of the charge;

(d) where a bill of indictment is preferred under section 2 of the *Administration of Justice (Miscellaneous Provisions) Act* 1933 in a case falling within paragraph (b) of subsection (2) of that section, when the bill of indictment is preferred before the court;

and where the application of this subsection would result in there being more than one time for the institution of the proceedings, they shall be taken to have been instituted at the earliest of those times.

(3) For the purposes of this Part, references to the conduct of any proceedings include references to the proceedings being discontinued and to the taking of any steps (including the bringing of appeals and making of representations in respect of applications for bail) which may be taken in relation to them.

(4) For the purposes of sections 3(2)(b), 5, 6, 7(1) and 7A of this Act, binding over proceedings shall be taken to be criminal proceedings.

(5) For the purposes of section 5 of this Act, proceedings begun by summons issued under section 3 of the *Obscene Publications Act* 1959 (forfeiture of obscene articles) shall be taken to be criminal proceedings.

[This section is printed as amended by the *Criminal Justice Act* 2003, Sched. 36, and the *Criminal Justice and Immigration Act* 2008, s.55(6).]

(c) *Specified police forces*

4–14 The effect of s.3(2)(a) and (3) is to require the DPP to take over all the prosecution of certain offences instituted by police forces maintained under the *Police Act* 1996 or otherwise specified in an order made by the Secretary of State. Police forces maintained under the 1996 Act are listed in Sched. 2 to that Act; and various other forces have been specified by the Secretary of State in the *Prosecution of Offences Act 1985 (Specified Police Forces) Order* 1985 (S.I. 1985 No. 1956).

(d) *Specified proceedings*

4–15 The DPP has no duty to take over proceedings instituted by police forces for offences which have been specified in an order made by the Attorney General. The *Prosecution of Offences Act 1985 (Specified Proceedings) Order* 1999 (S.I. 1999 No. 904) is an order made for that purpose, and it specifies proceedings for the following offences:

1) Fixed penalty offences within the meaning of s.51(1) of the *Road Traffic Offenders Act* 1988.
2) Offences under s.29(1) of the *Vehicle Excise and Registration Act* 1994.
3) Offences under ss.17(2), 18(3), 24(3), 26(1) and (2), 29, 31(1), 42(b), 47(1), 87(2), 143, 164(6) and (9), 165(3) and (6), 168 and 172(3) of the *Road Traffic Act* 1988.
4) All offences under the *Road Traffic Regulation Act* 1984, other than those under ss.35A(2), 43(5) and (12), 47(3), 52(1), 108(3), 115(1) and (2), 116(1) and 129(3) or those mentioned in paragraph 1, *ante*.
5) Offences in connection with contravention of the *Royal and Other Open Spaces Regulations* 1997, reg.3(9)(a) (involving a pedal cycle) and 3(9)(b) and 4(27) and, (28) and (30).

The offences cease to be "specified proceedings" once a summons has been served unless the necessary documents to enable the case to be dealt with on a written plea of guilty are also served on the offender with the summons. Proceedings also cease to be specified once the court starts to receive evidence but information provided to the court where a written plea of guilty has been entered is not treated as evidence for these purposes.

In practice this means that the court may deal with "specified proceedings" where written pleas are received to the listed offences in the absence of the CPS. The court will be assisted by the presence of a representative of the relevant police force.

(e) *DPPs duties in respect of SOCA prosecutions*

Section 38 of the *Serious Organised Crime and Police Act* 2005 makes special provision for the prosecution of offences investigated by the Serious Organised Crime Agency. Under s.5 of the 2005 Act, SOCA has the power to institute criminal proceedings in England and Wales. It is not a police force, however, for the purposes of s.3(2) of the 1985 Act; and the DPP is accordingly under no duty under that section to take over proceedings instituted by it. Under s.38 the DPP is empowered to institute and conduct proceedings arising out of a criminal investigation by SOCA in respect of a "non-designated" offence, and required to take over the conduct of criminal proceedings instituted by SOCA in respect of such an offence. The section confers corresponding powers and duties on the Director of the Revenue and Customs Prosecution Office in relation to "designated" offences. **4–16**

(3) Crown Prosecutors and Chief Crown Prosecutors

The DPP may designate any member of the CPS who has a general qualification (within the meaning of s.71 of the *Courts and Legal Services Act* 1990) as a Crown Prosecutor: s.1(3). Every Crown Prosecutor has all the powers of the DPP as to the institution and conduct of proceedings, but shall exercise those powers under the direction of the DPP: s.1(6). This gives to every Crown Prosecutor the equivalent power of the DPP to initiate prosecutions and to the DPP the power to assist and control Crown Prosecutors by issuing directions, usually upon policy: *R. v. Crown Court at Liverpool, ex p. Bray* [1987] Crim.L.R. 51, DC. **4–17**

(4) Agent Prosecutors

Prosecution of Offences Act 1985, s.5

Conduct of prosecutions on behalf of the Service

5.—(1) The Director may at any time appoint a person who has a general qualification (within the meaning of section 71 of the *Courts and Legal Services Act* 1990) to institute or take over the conduct of such criminal proceedings or extradition proceedings as the Director may assign to him. **4–18**

(2) Any person conducting proceedings assigned to him under this section shall have all

the powers of a Crown Prosecutor but shall exercise those powers subject to any instructions given to him by a Crown Prosecutor.

[This section is printed as amended by the *Courts and Legal Services Act* 1990, Sched. 10, and the *Extradition Act* 2003, s.190.]

4–19 This section allows agents to act for the CPS. The agent must be a barrister or solicitor from a list approved by the CPS. Individual cases will then be sent to the agent or they may be instructed to deal with all cases listed in the Court on any particular day. The agent will only act in the case in accordance with instructions from the CPS.

(5) Associate Prosecutors (formerly known as Designated Caseworkers, DCWs)

(a) *Legislation*

Prosecution of Offences Act 1985, s.7A

Powers of non-legal staff

4–20 **7A.**—(1) The Director may designate, for the purposes of this section, members of the staff of the Crown Prosecution Service who are not Crown Prosecutors.

(2) Subject to such exceptions (if any) as may be specified in the designation, a person so designated shall have such of the following as may be so specified, namely—

(a) the powers and rights of a Crown Prosecutor in relation to—

(i) applications for, or relating to, bail in criminal proceedings;

(ii) The conduct of criminal proceedings in magistrates' courts other than trials of offences triable either way or offences which are punishable with imprisonment in the case of persons aged 21 or over;

(iii) the conduct of applications or other proceedings relating to preventative civil orders;

(iv) the conduct of proceedings (other than criminal proceedings) in, or in connection with, the discharge of functions assigned to the Director under section 3(2)(g) above.

(b) any powers of a Crown Prosecutor that do not involve the exercise of such rights of audience as are mentioned in paragraph (a) above but are exercisable in relation to the conduct of—

(i) criminal proceedings in magistrates' courts, or

(ii) applications or proceedings falling within paragraph (a)(iii) or (iv).

(3) A person so designated shall exercise any such powers subject to instructions given to him by the Director.

(4) Any such instructions may be given so as to apply generally.

(5) In this section—

"bail in criminal proceedings" has the same meaning as in the *Bail Act* 1976 (see section 1 of that Act);

"preventative civil orders" means —

(a) orders within section 3(2)(fa) to (fe) above;

(b) orders under section 5 or 5A of the *Protection from Harassment Act* 1997 (restraining orders); or

(c) orders under section 8 [or 8A] of the *Crime and Disorder Act* 1998 (parenting orders).

(5A) For the purposes of this section a trial begins with the opening of the prosecution case after the entry of a plea of not guilty and ends with the conviction or acquittal of the accused.

(6) [*Repealed.*]

(7) Details of the following for any year, namely—

(a) the criteria applied by the Director in determining whether to designate persons under this section;

(b) the training undergone by persons so designated; and

(c) any general instructions given by the Director under subsection (4) above, shall be set out in the Director's report undersection 9 of this Act for that year.

(8) As from 1 May 2011 nothing in this section confers on persons designated under this section—

(a) any rights of audience, or

(b) any right to conduct litigation,

for the purposes of Part 3 of the *Legal Services Act* 2007 (reserved legal activities).

(9) As from that date the following provisions of that Act accordingly do not apply to persons designated under this section—

(a) paragraph 1(3) of Schedule 3 (exemption for persons with statutory rights of audience), and

(b) paragraph 2(3) of that Schedule (exemption for persons with statutory right to conduct litigation).

(10) The Attorney General may by order make such modifications in the application of any enactment (including this section) in relation to persons designated under this section as the Attorney General considers appropriate in consequence of, or in connection with, the matters provided for by subsections (8) and (9).

(11) The Attorney General may also by order amend subsection (2)(a)(ii) so as to omit the words "or offences which are punishable with imprisonment in the case of persons aged 21 or over".

(12) The power to make an order under subsection (10) or (11) is exercisable by statutory instrument, but a statutory instrument containing such an order may not be made unless a draft of the instrument has been laid before, and approved by a resolution of, each House of Parliament.

[This section was inserted by the *Courts and Legal Services Act* 1990, s.114. It is printed as amended by the *Crime and Disorder Act* 1998, s.53, the *Criminal Justice Act* 2003, s.331 and Sched. 36, and the *Criminal Justice and Immigration Act* 2008, ss.55 and 149 and Sched. 28. As from a day to be appointed, the words in square brackets in subs. (5) are to be inserted by the *Crime and Security Act* 2010, s.41(6).]

(b) *Scope of powers exercisable by Associate Prosecutors in magistrates' courts*

The effect of s.7A(3) and (4) is that designated non-legal staff may only exercise the powers and rights of Crown Prosecutors set out in s.7(2) subject to instructions given by the DPP. With effect from July 28, 2008, new instructions to "Associate Prosecutors" (APs) have been issued for that purpose. **4–21**

Instructions issued by the Director of Public Prosecutions to Associate Prosecutors of the Crown Prosecution Service Pursuant to s.7A of the Prosecution of Offences Act 1985

1. *Introduction*

1.1 These instructions are issued by the Director of Public Prosecutions pursuant to sections 7A(3) and (4) of the *Prosecution of Offences Act* 1985 which apply generally to CPS non legal employees designated by the Director in accordance with section 7A(1) of the Act. **4–22**

1.2 They will take effect on 23 February 2009.

1.3 A non-legal employee designated in accordance with section 7A(1) will be referred to in these instructions as an Associate Prosecutor (AP).

1.4 These instructions apply whether an AP has been designated prior to the date specified in paragraph 1.2, upon that date, or subsequently.

1.5 Upon these instructions taking effect in accordance with paragraph 1.1, all previous instructions issued to APs pursuant to section 7A(3) and (4) of the Act, and set out in the appropriate Annex of the Director's annual report to the Attorney General in accordance with section 7A(7)(c) of the Act, will cease to have effect.

1.6 The Director may from time to time issue guidance to Chief Crown Prosecutors on the implementation of these instructions, and dealing with related matters including procedures for supervision of APs and training requirements relevant to certain duties.

1.7 Nothing in these instructions prevents an AP from reminding a court of its duties and powers in relation to any proceedings (including sentencing).

2. The statutory powers under s.7A

4–23 2.1 Subject to any exceptions or limitations contained within these instructions, section 7A, as amended, confers on APs the powers and rights of audience of a Crown Prosecutor in relation to:

(i) Bail applications;

(ii) the conduct of criminal proceedings in the magistrates' courts (including the youth court) other than trials of either way offences tried summarily or offences punishable with a term of imprisonment;

(iii) the conduct of applications or other proceedings relating to preventative civil orders;

(iv) the conduct of proceedings (other than criminal proceedings) in connection with the discharge of the functions assigned to the Director by the Attorney General; and

(v) any other powers of a Crown Prosecutor not involving the exercise of rights of audience in relation to the conduct of proceedings falling within (ii), (iii) and (iv) above.

2.2 Section 7A does not give APs power to institute or commence criminal proceedings.

3. Powers and rights of audience

4–24 3.1 Subject to the exceptions or limitations specified in Schedules 1 to 5 and completion of the approved AP training, all APs will exercise the statutory powers under section 7A.

Bail applications (paragraph 2.1(i) above)

4–25 Bail applications include a defendant's application for bail, or application in relation to bail (including proceedings for breach and variation) in the Crown Court or the magistrates' court, subject to the exceptions listed in Schedule 1.

Conduct of criminal proceedings (paragraph 2.1(ii) above)

4–26 3.3 The powers and rights of audience in relation to the conduct of criminal proceedings relate to all stages of the proceedings in magistrates' courts after a person has been charged. However the power to conduct trials is restricted to trials of non-imprisonable summary offences.

3.4 In applying these instructions a "trial" is defined in section 7A(5A) of the Act as beginning with the opening of the prosecution case after a not guilty plea and ends with the conviction or acquittal of the accused.

3.5 APs exercise these powers and rights of audience on the instructions of a Crown Prosecutor and do not have a power of review under the Code for Crown Prosecutors for this purpose, except in accordance with paragraph 3.14 below.

3.6 APs are not designated to exercise the powers and rights of audience of Crown Prosecutors in the magistrates' court (including the youth court) in relation to the proceedings specified in Schedule 2.

Preventative Civil Orders (paragraph 2.1(iii) above)

4–27 3.7 APs are designated to conduct applications or other proceedings relating to those Preventative Civil Orders (PCOs) set out in paragraph 3.8 below. The conduct of proceedings that APs may undertake varies according to the legislative requirements of the particular PCO. This gives APs, where the legislation applies, authority to conduct an application for an order, or adduce further evidence, or apply for the variation or discharge of an order.

3.8 PCOs relate only to the following:

(i) Anti-Social Behaviour Order - the conduct of applications for orders made after a verdict or finding; variation and discharge of such orders.

(ii) Football Banning Order—the conduct of applications on complaint or after a verdict or finding; to adduce and lead further evidence where appropriate; and to appeal against the refusal of a court to impose such an order.

(iii) Drinking Banning Order (to come into force on a day to be appointed)—the conduct of applications for orders made after a verdict or finding; variation and discharge of such orders.

(iv) Parenting Orders—a duty to assist the court on request.

(v) Restraining Orders—in relation to orders made after a verdict or finding to adduce and lead to further evidence; and to apply for a variation or discharge of such an order. In relation to orders on acquittal to adduce and lead to further evidence; and to apply for a variation or discharge of such an order.

3.9 A breach of a PCO is a criminal offence. Each PCO carries a different penalty. APs have power to deal with breaches subject to Schedule 2 and 4 below.

3.10 APs shall only exercise the powers and rights of audience as specified in Schedule 3.

Functions assigned by the Attorney General to the Director (paragraph 2.1(iv) above)

3.11 The Attorney General has assigned to the Director the following functions: **4–28**

(i) applications for warrants of further detention under section 43(1) of the Police and Criminal Evidence Act 1984 and their extension under section 44 of that Act;

(ii) applications by other countries for extradition of persons in the UK;

(iii) conduct of proceedings relating to case stated and *habeas corpus*;

(iv) conduct of proceedings under section 2 of the *Dogs Act* 1871 instituted by a police force (dangerous dogs that may be destroyed); and

(v) applications for removal of driving disqualifications under section 42 *Road Traffic Offenders Act* 1988.

3.12 APs are designated to conduct proceedings only in relation to paragraphs 3.11 (iv) and (v) above, (proceedings under section 2 of the *Dogs Act* 1871 and those under section 42 of the *Road Traffic Offenders Act* 1988).

Powers not involving rights of audience (paragraph 2.1 (v) above)

3.13 The powers of a Crown Prosecutor that do not involve rights of audience relate to all other criminal proceedings conducted in the magistrates' court. **4–29**

3.14 APs shall only review magistrates' court cases which are straight forward and which involve no difficult technical issues, or other complication of fact or law. Consistent with that principle, the power to review and determine such proceedings shall only be exercised in accordance with Schedule 4.

Schedule 1

APs are not designated to conduct bail applications (including any variations, breaches and appeals) in the following matters. **4–30**

1. Bail applications in the Crown Court.
2. Bail applications in youth courts.
3. Bail applications in relation to youths charged with an adult in the magistrates' courts or a youth appearing alone in the magistrates' courts.

Schedule 2

Otherwise than as provided for in Schedule 5 APs are not currently designated to exercise the powers and rights of audience of Crown Prosecutors in the magistrates' court (including the youth court) for the following proceedings. **4–31**

1. Trials relating to summary only non-imprisonable offences. Summary trials relating to either way offences and those punishable with a term of imprisonment are excluded from s.7A of the Act.
2. Post conviction hearings commonly known as '*Newton* Hearings'.
3. Hearings in relation to committal proceedings where there is consideration of the evidence (s.6(1) of the Magistrates' Courts Act 1980).
4. Matters that involve obligatory driving disqualification where evidence will be called in respect of 'special reasons' as to why the court should not impose disqualification.

Schedule 3

APs shall only exercise the powers and rights of audience of Crown Prosecutors in relation to preventative civil orders in the following circumstances. **4–32**

APs shall only conduct proceedings for PCOs where the conditions in (i) and (ii) both apply. The conditions are:

(i) Instructions have been given by a Crown Prosecutor in relation to the application, variation, or discharge or in adducing or leading further evidence, where applicable: and

(ii) The proceedings are not contested.

Schedule 4

4–33 APs shall only exercise the powers of a Crown Prosecutor (including the power to review and determine criminal proceedings) in the following circumstances.

1. To review summary or either way offences only where:

—the defendant is an adult; and the matter is summary-only or considered to be suitable for summary disposal; and a guilty plea is reasonably expected; or (if otherwise) the offence is a minor road traffic offence, provided the defendant is not a youth. a guilty plea may reasonably be expected where the suspect has made a clear and unambiguous admission to the offence to be proved and has said nothing that could be used as a possible defence;

or

—Though the suspect has made no admission in interview (either because he made no comment, or because he was not interviewed at all, but has not at any time denied the offence or otherwise indicated that the charge will be contested at court) the commission of the offence and the identification of the offender can be established by good quality evidence (e.g. of a police officer or another reliable independent witness) or the suspect can be seen clearly committing the offence on a good quality visual recording.

2. To amend a charge or summons where the amendment is minor, for example:

—an error as to the value of any property; the date upon which an offence took place; the venue for the offence; the description of any relevant object. 3. To withdraw a charge or summons where:

—a road traffic offence involves the production of documents by the defendant (otherwise than in specified proceedings), and the defendant has produced the relevant documents to the court's Police Liaison Officer or other police officer; and the AP is satisfied that the charge or summons is no longer sustainable.

Schedule 5

4–34 1. The following provisions of these instructions do not apply to those members of staff designated under Section 7A(1) of the *Prosecution of Offences Act* 1985 who have been appointed as Level 2 Associate Prosecutors:

(i) Schedule 2, paragraph 1 (Trials relating to summary only non-imprisonable offences).

(ii) Schedule 2, paragraph 2 (*Newton* Hearings in relation to summary only non-imprisonable offences only).

(iii) Schedule 2, paragraph 4 ("special reasons hearings").

(iv) Schedule 3, paragraph (ii) (thus allowing Level 2 Associate Prosecutors to conduct contested PCOs)

2. Level 2 Associate Prosecutors will be able to exercise the powers contained in Schedule 4 (2) and (3) to amend a charge or summons, or to withdraw a road traffic offence requiring the production of documents during the course of a trial.

3. Level 2 Associate Prosecutors have the following additional powers also exercisable during the course of prosecuting a trial:

(i) To withdraw or offer no evidence or no further evidence in relation to any charge where:

—they form the opinion that there is no longer sufficient evidence to support the charge and the trial will continue in relation to other charge(s) which are before the court.

C. PROSECUTION OF OFFENCES BY PARTIES OTHER THAN THE CPS

(1) General

Prosecution of Offences Act 1985, ss.6 and 7(4)

Prosecutions instituted and conducted otherwise than by the Service

6.—(1) Subject to subsection (2) below, nothing in this Part shall preclude any person from instituting any criminal proceedings or conducting any criminal proceedings to which the Director's duty to take over the conduct of proceedings does not apply. **4–35**

(2) Where criminal proceedings are instituted in circumstances in which the Director is not under a duty to take over their conduct, he may nevertheless do so at any stage.

Delivery of recognizances, etc., to Director

7.—(4) It shall be the duty of the designated officer for every magistrates' court to send to the Director, in accordance with the regulations, a copy of the information and of any depositions and other documents relating to any case in which— **4–36**

(a) a prosecution for an offence before the magistrates' court is withdrawn or is not proceeded with within a reasonable time;

(b) the Director does not have the conduct of the proceedings; and

(c) there is some ground for suspecting that there is no satisfactory reason for the withdrawal or failure to proceed.

[This section is printed as amended by the *Courts Act* 2003, Sched. 8. There are no regulations supplemental to the section, following the revocation of the previously existing regulations by of the *Prosecution of Offences (Revocation) Regulations* 1997 (S.I. 1997 No. 739).]

Section 6(1) expressly preserves the rights of a private citizens and public authorities other than the CPS and the police to institute and conduct criminal prosecutions.

Where a private prosecution has been instituted but the DPP intervenes and takes over conduct of the proceedings under s.6(2), he is entitled to adopt a policy whereby he applies the evidential and public interest stages in the Code for Crown Prosecutors issued under s.10 and, if he concluded that there was no realistic prospect of conviction, discontinue the proceedings: see *R. (Gujra) v. CPS*, 175 J.P. 161, DC (not following the *obiter* view of Laws L.J. to the contrary in *R. v. DPP, ex p. Duckenfield* [2000] 1 W.L.R. 55, DC).

(2) Other public prosecuting authorities

Serious Fraud Office

Section 1 of the *Criminal Justice Act* 1987 establishes the Serious Fraud Office; makes provision for the appointment of the Director of the SFO, who is to discharge his functions under the superintendence of the Attorney General; confers a power on the director to investigate any suspected offence which appears to him on reasonable grounds to involve serious or complex fraud; and confers powers on the director to institute and have the conduct of any criminal proceedings which appear to him to relate to such fraud, and take over the conduct of any such proceedings at any stage. As to the scope of these provisions, see *R. (Bermingham) v. Director of the SFO* [2006] 3 All E.R. 239, DC. **4–37**

Revenue and Customs Prosecution Office

Section 34 *et seq.* of the *Commissioners for Revenue and Customs Act* 2005 make provision relating to the prosecution of revenue and customs offences. Section 34 establishes the office of Director of Revenue and Customs Prosecutions and provides that the Director and his staff are together to be referred to as the revenue and customs **4–38**

Prosecutions Office. Section 35 confers a power on the director to institute and conduct criminal proceedings relating to a criminal investigation by the Revenue and Customs (*i.e.* the Commissioners of Revenue and Customs, Revenue and Customs officers, and persons acting on their behalf); and requires him to take over the conduct of criminal proceedings instituted by the Revenue and Customs.

4–39 At the present time the office of Director of the RCPO is held by the DPP. Thus although the CPS and RCPO are distinct statutory entities, as a matter of administrative convenience they are in effect incorporated within the same organisation.

Local authorities

4–40 Local authorities derive powers to prosecute offences from the following sources: (i) where the offence is committed in their area, under the specific offence-creating statute or statutory instrument; (ii) where the offence is not committed in their area, by delegation from the local authority in whose area the offence was committed, (see s.101 of the *Local Government Act* 1972; and (iii) more generally under s.222 of the *Local Government Act* 1972), which provides that, where a local authority considers it expedient for the promotion or protection of the interests of the inhabitants of its area, it may prosecute any legal proceedings. The words of s.222 are extremely wide and there was no warrant for limiting their meaning: *R. v. Jarrett and Steward,* unreported, January 30, 1997, CA. Where a local authority purporting to act under s.222 sought to commence a prosecution by laying an information, it was unnecessary to produce a written record to show that the relevant official had specifically considered that the test in the section was satisfied: *R. v. Richards* [1999] Crim.L.R. 598, CA. However, where a local authority sought to prosecute an individual in respect of acts or omissions outside of its own area, but in order to promote or protect the interests of the inhabitants of its own area, it would be wiser to enter into an agreement (under s.101) with the local authority in which the acts or omissions occurred before laying the information; and in the rare cases where s.222 was sought to be relied upon in that situation, although not specifically required in law, the local authority would be wise to record the decision to engage the section, and the reasons why it was considered to apply: *R. (Donnachie) v. Cardiff Magistrates' Court,* unreported, March 16, 2009, DC ([2009] EWHC 489 (Admin.)). In *Monks v. Northamptonshire DC*, 166 J.P. 592, QBD, it was held that a local authority could, under s.222, institute proceedings in its own name, rather than in the name of a particular official. Section 4 of the *Road Traffic Offenders Act* 1988 specifies a number of road traffic offences in respect of which proceedings may be instituted by a local authority. In *Middlesbrough BC v. Safeer* [2002] 1 Cr.App.R. 23, DC, it was held that s.4 of the 1988 Act did not have the effect of precluding a local authority from instituting proceedings for a road traffic offence not specified in that section under s.222 of the 1972 Act.

Other public authorities

4–41 Various other enactments confer specific powers on different public authorities to institute and conduct criminal proceedings. As to the extent to which express statutory words are necessary, see *R. (Securiplan plc) v. Security Industry Authority* [2009] 2 All E.R. 211, DC, where the Security Industry Authority was held to be competent to prosecute offences under the *Private Security Industry Act* 2001 by virtue of s.1(3) of the Act, which conferred on the authority a power to do "anything" it considered was "calculated to facilitate or is incidental or conducive to, the carrying out of its functions".

Further, where a public authority is expressly empowered by statute to prosecute particular offences, as a body corporate with legal personality, it would also enjoy the general common law right to bring a private prosecution in respect of other offences unless expressly excluded from doing so by statute: see *R. v. Rollins; R. v. McInerney* [2011] 1 Cr.App.R. 4, SC.

(3) Private prosecutions

4–42 The right of the private citizen to institute and conduct a criminal prosecution is a historical right originating in the earliest days of the legal process. It has been described as a "useful constitutional safeguard against capricious, corrupt or biased failure or refusal of those authorities to prosecute offenders against the criminal law": *per* Lord Diplock in *Gouriet v. Union of Post Office Workers* [1978] A.C. 435, HL. Despite the existence of the right, it is subject to a number of procedural constraints. The DPP will not be acting ultra vires if he exercises the power under s.6(2) to take over the conduct of proceedings instituted by a private prosecutor and then discontinues them under s.23 or otherwise withdraws or offers no evidence: see, *mutatis mutandis*, *Turner v. DPP*, 68 Cr.App.R. 70, DC; and *Raymond v. Att.-Gen.* [1982] Q.B. 839, DC.

As to whether it will be an abuse of process to bring a private prosecution against a person who has already received a police caution, see *Hayter v. L.* [1998] 1 W.L.R. 854, DC, and *Jones v. Whalley* [2007] A.C. 63, HL (*post*, Ch.8).

A private prosecution may be stayed as an abuse of process where the court's conscience is offended by the fact that the prosecutor has contributed by their own conduct to creating the circumstances in which the offence was alleged to have been committed: *R. (Dacre) v. Westminster Magistrates' Court* [2009] 1 Cr.App.R. 6, DC.

In *R. v. Belmarsh Magistrates' Court, ex p. Watts* [1999] 2 Cr.App.R. 188, DC, it was said that a private prosecutor was still a prosecutor, and hence subject to the same obligations as a minister of justice as are the public prosecuting authorities. However, in *Ewing v. Davis* [2007] 1 W.L.R. 3223, QBD (Mitting J.), it was held that the right to institute a private prosecution is not constrained by a requirement that the prosecution must be in the public interest and not conducted merely in order to pursue an individual grievance (*cf.* the criteria for the institution of a public prosecution, *post*). In so concluding, his Lordship observed that statutory provisions entitling the state to interfere with a private prosecution were to be found in the powers of the DPP to take over and discontinue a prosecution (*ibid.*), and the power of the Attorney-General to restrict vexatious prosecutions by seeking a criminal proceedings order from the High Court under the *Senior Courts Act* 1981, s.42. Additional constraints on the right to institute a private prosecution to which his Lordship did not refer lie in the power of the Attorney-General to terminate proceedings on indictment by entering a *nolle prosequi*; and the possibility that the institution or carrying on of a prosecution is prohibited without the consent of the Attorney-General or the DPP (as to which, see *post*). Furthermore, there is also the possibility that a summons will not issue upon the laying of an information (as to which, see *post*). This latter factor will assume greater significance as a constraint on the right to institute a private prosecution when the written charging and requisitioning procedure is brought into force in full (as to which see *post*), since the same constraint will no longer apply to the institution of public prosecutions.

(4) Responsibility for conduct of prosecutions where multiple proceedings instituted

With many bodies authorised under statute to conduct prosecutions, and the possibility that a private prosecutor might also institute proceedings, there are occasions when issues may arise over who should take responsibility for a prosecution. **4–43**

Where a person other than a police officer arrests a suspect and takes him to the police station to be charged by a custody officer, it does not follow from the fact the suspect is charged by the custody officer that the proceedings are "instituted on behalf of a police force" within s.3(2)(a) of the *Prosecution of Offences Act* 1985 so that the DPP is bound to take over conduct of the proceedings; the right to prosecute was not surrendered by the person who effected the arrest simply because the police formally charged the suspect; a prosecution could only be said to have been instituted on behalf of a police force if a police force had investigated the matter, arrested the suspect and brought him to custody: *R. v. Stafford Magistrates' Court, ex p. Commissioners of Customs and Excise* [1991] 2 Q.B. 339, DC; and *R. (Hunt) v. Criminal Cases Review Commission* [2001] Q.B. 1108, DC.

4–44 In *R. v. Tower Bridge Metropolitan Stipendiary Magistrate, ex p. Chaudhry* [1994] Q.B. 340, DC, the Court considered the propriety of a private individual applying to take out a prosecution when proceedings had already been instituted by the CPS. The defendant was summoned by the CPS for an offence of driving without due care following an incident which resulted in a fatal accident. The mother of the motor cyclist who was killed applied to the magistrates' court for a summons against the defendant for causing death by dangerous driving. The court refused to issue the summons. On appeal the Divisional Court held that the magistrate was right to have regard to all relevant circumstances, including the fact that the CPS had already taken out a prosecution, when considering whether to issue a summons. In the absence of special circumstances, such as apparent bad faith on the part of the prosecutor, the Court said that magistrates should be slow to issue a private summons when the defendant was already subject to informations laid by the Crown.

In *R. (Charlson) v. Guildford Magistrates' Court* [2007] R.T.R. 1, QBD, Silber J., explained that what had been said in *ex p. Chaudhry* applied to the special situation where the public prosecuting authorities have already brought a prosecution in respect of the same matter and that prosecution was still pending. Where, however, the public prosecuting authority had previously commenced a prosecution in respect of the matter but had subsequently discontinued it, since a private prosecution does not need to satisfy the evidential or public interest tests applicable to a public prosecution, it was quite proper for magistrates to issue a summons for a private prosecution without requiring special circumstances. In deciding whether to issue a summons for a private prosecution in this latter situation, the magistrates should ascertain, (a) whether the allegation is an offence known to law and, if so, whether the ingredients of the offence are *prima facie* present, (b) whether any time-limit for prosecution operates as a bar to the issue of the summons, (c) whether the court has jurisdiction, (d) whether the informant has the necessary authority to prosecute, and (e) any other relevant facts.

D. DECISION TO PROSECUTE

(1) DPP's duty to prepare a Code for Crown Prosecutors

Prosecution of Offences Act 1985, s.10

Guidelines for Crown Prosecutors

4–45 **10.**—(1) The Director shall issue a Code for Crown Prosecutors giving guidance on general principles to be applied by them—

(a) in determining, in any case—

(i) whether proceedings for an offence should be instituted or, where proceedings have been instituted, whether they should be discontinued; or

(ii) what charges should be preferred; and

(b) in considering, in any case, representations to be made by them to any magistrates' court about the mode of trial suitable for that case.

(2) The Director may from time to time make alterations in the Code.

(3) The provisions of the Code shall be set out in the Director's report under section 9 of this Act for the year in which the Code is issued; and any alteration in the Code shall be set out in his report under that section for the year in which the alteration is made.

(2) The Code

(a) *Introduction*

4–46 The sixth edition of the code was issued in February 2010 and is set out in full at Appendix E. It applies to Crown Prosecutors, prosecutors who are members of the RCPO; associate prosecutors who are designated under s.7A of the *Prosecution of Offences Act* 1985 and who exercise their powers in accordance with the instructions issued by the DPP; and other members of the RCPO who are designated by the DPP in his capacity as the Director of the Revenue and Customs Prosecutions under s.39 of the *Commissioners for Revenue and Customs Act* 2005.

It has been held to be artificial to distinguish between the decision to prosecute and the decision to divert from prosecution, to which end reference should also be made to the DPP's guidance on conditional cautioning and the Code of Practice on Conditional Cautioning issued by the Secretary of State: *R. (Guest) v. DPP* [2009] 2 Cr.App.R. 26, DC; and para. 3.1. **4–47**

Ordinarily, the decision should be made in accordance with the "Full Code Test". In limited circumstances, where it is proposed to keep the suspect in custody after charge, but the evidence required to apply the "Full Code Test" is not yet available, the "Threshold Test" applies: para. 3.4. Where the "Threshold Test" has been applied, the case must thereafter be reviewed in accordance with the full code test as soon as reasonably practicable: para. 5.13

(b) *The "Full Code Test"*

The "Full Code Test" sets out two stages in the decision: the "evidential stage" and the "public interest stage": para. 4.1. Where the full code test applies, a prosecution will only be started or continued when the case has passed both the evidential and public interest stages: para. 3.4. **4–48**

The evidential stage

The public prosecutor must be satisfied on an objective basis that there is enough evidence to provide a "realistic prospect of conviction" in light of what the defence may be and how that is likely to affect the prosecution case; this is a question of whether the tribunal of fact, properly directed in accordance with the law, is more likely than not to convict the defendant of the charge alleged (paras 4.5 and 4.6). Consideration must be given to whether the evidence can be used and is reliable (para. 4.7). **4–49**

Whether there is a "realistic prospect of conviction" should be decided on a "merits based" approach, where the public prosecutor imagines himself to be the fact finder and asks himself, whether, on balance, the evidence is sufficient to merit a conviction, taking into account what he knows about the defence case, rather than a predictive "bookmaker's" approach, based on past experience of similar cases; questions of how a jury are likely to see a case are not relevant at this stage but at a later stage, under the public interest test: *R. (B.) v. DPP* [2009] 1 Cr.App.R. 38, DC. **4–50**

Where it was alleged that a number of offenders had committed an offence according to joint enterprise principles, the extent to which it would be necessary for a crown prosecutor to inquire into the roles played by each potential defendant would vary according (*inter alia*) to the size of the group, the nature of the offending and the extent to which it was possible to separate out the actions of each participant; and, in such a case, a prosecutor was entitled, where appropriate, to base a decision to charge on the totality of the offending, in which all were involved to a greater or lesser extent: *R. (A.) v. South Yorkshire Police and CPS*, 171 J.P. 465, DC.

The public interest stage

This stage recognises that there exists no rule of law that requires suspected criminal offences automatically to be the subject of prosecution: para. 4.10. However, a prosecution will usually take place unless there are public interest factors tending against prosecution which clearly outweigh those tending in favour, or it appears more appropriate in all the circumstances of the case to divert the person from prosecution: para. 4.11, 4.12. Diversion from prosecution is dealt with in Pt 7: see *post*, §§ 4–117 *et seq*. As to the relationship between the code and the other guidance on diversion, see *R. (Guest) v. DPP* (*ante*, § 4–30). **4–51**

The Code lists at paras 4.16 and 4.17 some of the common factors which weigh both in favour of and against public prosecution. These must be balanced carefully and fairly, and by making an overall assessment rather than simply adding up the factors on each side: paras 4.13–4.15.

4–52 Guidance is given as to the relevance of any views expressed by the victim or the victim's family: see paras 4.18–4.20. As to this and the positive obligation to provide protection against serious assaults arising under Art. 3 of the European Convention on Human Rights (prohibition on torture and inhuman or degrading treatment), see *R. (B.) v. DPP, ibid*, where it was said that a decision not to prosecute an offence of wounding with intent to cause grievous bodily harm was not reasonably defensible where it had been based on a belief that the alleged victim's mental disability would make his identification of the prospective defendant unreliable; the decision humiliated the alleged victim, caused him to feel that he was being treated as a second class citizen and increased his sense of vulnerability and of being beyond the protection of the law.

Crown Prosecutors should have regard to the specific CPS guidance in addition to the Code for Crown Prosecutors when deciding whether it is in the public interest to prosecute (or continue to prosecute) certain offences where it is possible that the potential (or actual) defendant is a victim of human trafficking. As to this generally, and as to the powers of the court to stay a prosecution where the guidance had not been applied correctly or at all, see *R. v. O.*, *The Times*, October 2, 2008, CA; and *R. v. M. (L.), B. (M.) and G. (D.); R. v. Tabot; R. v. Tijani* [2011] 1 Cr.App.R. 12, CA.

(c) *The "Threshold Test"*

4–53 The threshold test may be applied only if the prosecutor is satisfied that all of the following conditions are met: (a) there is insufficient evidence to apply the full code; (b) there are reasonable grounds for believing that further evidence will become available within a reasonable period; (c) the seriousness or circumstances of the case justifies the making of an immediate charging decision; and (d) there are continuing substantial and proper grounds to object to bail being granted to the suspect (para. 5.3). Application of the threshold test requires the prosecutor to be satisfied both that there is at least a reasonable suspicion that the person to be charged has committed the offence (see paras 5.6 to 5.8) and that there are reasonable grounds for believing that the continuing investigation will provide further evidence, within a reasonable period of time, so that all the evidence taken together is capable of establishing a realistic prospect of conviction in accordance with the Full Code Test (see paras 5.9 to 5.12). The Full Code Test must be applied as soon as is reasonably practicable and in any event before the expiry of any applicable custody time limit or extended custody time limit (para. 5.13).

(3) Challenging the decision to prosecute

4–54 The decision as to whether a public prosecution should be instituted or continued involves an exercise of discretion. Although the scope of the discretion is broad, decisions not to institute a public prosecution, or to discontinue a prosecution, are susceptible to judicial review despite the possibility that an aggrieved person might institute a private prosecution: *R. v. Commissioner of Police of the Metropolis, ex p. Blackburn* [1968] 2 Q.B. 118, DC; *R. v. General Council of the Bar, ex p. Percival* [1991] 1 Q.B. 212, DC; *R. v. DPP, ex p. C.* [1995] 1 Cr.App.R. 136, DC. The power of review will be sparingly exercised in such cases, however, although the standard is not set too high: *R. v. DPP, ex p. Manning* [2001] Q.B. 330, DC. Grounds for ordering reconsideration of a decision not to prosecute may exist if it has been demonstrated, on an objective appraisal of the case, that a serious point or serious points supporting a prosecution have not been considered, or that, in a significant area, a conclusion as to what evidence is available to support a prosecution is irrational; but the points must have such force that it would be seriously arguable that the decision would otherwise be different had they been considered properly: *R. (Dennis) v. DPP* [2007] 2 *Archbold News* 3, DC. For a Commonwealth perspective on whether a public prosecutor who exercises the discretion to prosecute in favour of not bringing a prosecution may be guilty of an offence of doing an act tending or intended to pervert the course of justice, see *mutatis mutandis Beaudry v. R.*, 216 C.C.C. (3d) 353, Supreme Court of Canada.

As to the rule of law implications and the width of the discretion where a public prosecutor making a decision to prosecute or continue a prosecution is subjected to a threat, see *R. (Corner House Research) v. Director of the Serious Fraud Office, The Times*, July 31, 2008, HL.

In principle, decisions to institute or continue a prosecution are also susceptible to judicial review, provided that the decision had been made regardless of, or clearly contrary to, a settled policy which had been formulated in the public interest, such as a policy of cautioning juveniles: *R. v. Chief Constable of the Kent County Constabulary, ex p. L. (a minor)* [1993] 1 All ER 756, DC (*cf. R. (S.) v. DPP*, unreported, June 28, 2006, DC); *R. v. Inland Revenue Commissioners, ex p. Mead* [1993] 1 All ER 772, DC. However, a decision to prosecute for an offence would not be unlawful if it was outwith a policy that no one was to be prosecuted for a particular offence in the absence of certain aggravating circumstances; in such a case, it would be the policy itself that was unlawful: *R. (Mondelly) v. Commissoner of Police for the Metropolis*, 171 J.P. 121, DC (but *cf. R. v. Adaway*, 168 J.P. 645, CA). The threshold which must be crossed before the power of review will be exercised is higher than in cases where a decision not to prosecute is challenged, and the remedy will generally not be available unless there was dishonesty or *mala fides* on the part of the prosecutor, or an exceptional circumstance: *R. v. DPP, ex p. Kebilene* [2000] 2 A.C. 326, HL. This is because the complaint will be capable of being dealt with in the trial process (such as by an application for a stay of the proceedings as an abuse of process): *Sharma v. Brown-Antoine* [2007] 1 W.L.R. 780, PC.

The discretion to investigate an offence is even more open-ended than the decision to prosecute: *R. (Bermingham) v. Director of the Serious Fraud Office* [2006] 3 All E.R. 239, DC; *R. (C.) v. Chief Constable of A and A magistrates' court*, unreported, September 29, 2006, QBD (Underhill J.) ([2006] EWHC 2352 Admin.).

In *R. (A.) v. South Yorkshire Police and Crown Prosecution Service*, 171 J.P. 465, DC, it was held that the High Court would only interfere (and even then only on a discretionary basis) with a decision to prosecute a juvenile instead of giving a reprimand or warning under the *Crime and Disorder Act* 1998, s.65 (as to which see Ch.25 *post*), if it was clearly established that the decision had come about as a result of an irrational departure from the guidance issued under s.65 of the 1998 Act.

E. Powers and Duties of the Prosecution

The Prosecutor has the duty of prosecuting the case at court, taking it through the preliminary stages of pre-trial hearings to calling evidence at trial and assisting with information at time of sentence. Full consideration of the duties are covered in the relevant sections, see Chs 8 and 10. **4–55**

F. Cases where Consent to Prosecute is Required

Prosecution of Offences Act 1985, s.25

Consents to prosecutions etc.

25.—(1) This section applies to any enactment which prohibits the institution or carrying on of proceedings for any offence except— **4–56**

(a) with the consent (however expressed) of a Law Officer of the Crown or the Director; or

(b) where the proceedings are instituted or carried on by or on behalf of a Law Officer of the Crown or the Director;

and so applies whether or not there are other exceptions to the prohibition (and in particular whether or not the consent is an alternative to the consent of any other authority or person).

(2) An enactment to which this section applies—

(a) shall not prevent the arrest without warrant, or the issue or execution of a warrant for the arrest, of a person for any offence, or the remand in custody or on bail of a person charged with any offence; and

(b) shall be subject to any enactment concerning the apprehension or detention of children or young persons.

(3) In this section "enactment" includes any provision having effect under or by virtue of any Act; and this section applies to enactments whenever passed or made.

Whereas the clear purpose of s.25(2) is to enable the arrest, charging and remand in custody or bail of a person against whom proceedings may have been commenced without the consent of the Attorney General or DPP having first been obtained, any prohibition in an enactment on the "institution or carrying on of proceedings" without the relevant consent applied at the point at which the person who had been arrested and charged with such an offence was brought to court and the charge was entered in the court register: *R. v. Lambert* [2009] 2 Cr.App.R. 32, CA.

Failure to obtain consent

4–57 Various enactments prohibit the institution or carrying on of proceedings for an offence unless consent has been obtained. One purpose (at least) of a requirement for consent is to remove the absolute right of private prosecution which would otherwise exist and thereby to restrict prosecution of certain offences to public prosecutors unless consent is obtained: *R. (Islamic Human Rights Commission) v. Civil Aviation Authority* [2007] A.C.D. 5, QBD (Ouseley J.).

The traditional view was that where consent to prosecute is required and that consent is not given at all, the proceedings will be a nullity: *R. v. Angel*, 52 Cr.App.R. 280, CA, and *R. v. Pearce*, 72 Cr.App.R. 295, CA. Whether those decisions continue to represent the state of the law will now depend on the proper application of the approach to procedural irregularities identified in *R. v. Soneji* [2006] 2 Cr.App.R. 340, HL (for further discussion in relation to this approach, see § 7–10 *et seq., post*). For the avoidance of doubt, the proceedings will not be a nullity where consent of the DPP is expressly required but given by a Crown Prosecutor; or where consent of the Attorney-General is required and given by the Solicitor-General: see respectively the *Prosecution of Offences Act* 1985, s.1(7), and the *Law Officers Act* 1997, s.1.

Given the purpose of the requirement for consent, it is submitted that the proper application of the *Soneji* approach will be that, as a rule of thumb, the proceedings will be a nullity where consent of the Attorney-General or the DPP is required and a private prosecutor institutes proceedings but does not obtain consent. Likewise, it is submitted that the proceedings will be a nullity where consent of the Attorney-General is required and a Crown Prosecutor or the DPP institutes proceedings but does not obtain consent. More difficult questions may arise where, for example, the Attorney-General gives consent to private prosecutor in a case where consent of the DPP is required; or where consent of the Director of Revenue and Customs Prosecutions is required and consent is given by the DPP.

As to the situation where consent is required but not obtained until after the proceeding have been instituted, see *R. v. D.* [2007] Crim.L.R. 240, Crown Court at Lewes, where H.J.J. Richard Brown purported to apply the decision in *Soneji* (by applying the now somewhat discredited explanation of *Soneji* proffered in *R. v. Ashton*; *R. v. Draz*; *R. v. O'Reilly* [2006] 2 Cr.App.R. 15, CA) and held that the proceedings in such a situation would not be a nullity and should not be stayed. The correctness of this decision may be open to question given the need for stricter application of *Soneji* identified in *R. v. Clarke and McDaid* [2008] 1 W.L.R. 338, HL: see *post* § 7–10.

As to the situation where there is statutory conflict as to whether consent to institute proceedings was required, see *R. (Uberoi) v. City of Westminster Magistrates' Court* [2009] Crim.L.R. 445, DC, where it was held that notwithstanding that s.61(3) of the *Criminal Justice Act* 1993 prohibited institution of proceedings for insider dealing offences under Pt V of that Act except by or with the consent of the Secretary of State or the DPP, the effect of s.402(1) of the *Financial Services and Markets Act* 2000 ("... the Authority may institute proceedings for an offence under—(a) Pt V of the *Criminal Justice Act* 1993 (insider dealing)") was that the Financial Services Authority could institute proceedings under Pt V of the 1993 Act without obtaining the consent required by s.61(2) of the 1993 Act.

DPP's consent

Where consent of the DPP is required, it will be sufficient for consent to have been given by a Crown Prosecutor: see the *Prosecution of Offences Act* 1985, s.1(7), which deems such consent to be consent of the DPP. In this regard, there is no requirement for express written consent of the Crown Prosecutor; all that is required is that he or she established that the consent requirement was considered when making the decision to prosecute: *R. v. Jackson* [1997] Crim.L.R. 293, CA. There may be scope for application of this approach to the situation where a Crown Prosecutor establishes that he or she considered the requirement for consent when deciding whether or not a suspect should be charged by a police officer. **4–58**

Attorney-General's consent

A requirement for consent of the Attorney-General to be given will be satisfied by consent given by the Solicitor-General: see the *Law Officers Act* 1997, s.1. **4–59**

Revenue and Customs offences

Proceedings under the customs and excise Acts may only be instituted by or with the consent of the Director of Revenue and Customs Prosecutions, or by order of, or with the consent of, the Commissioners for Her Majesty's Revenue and Customs (*Customs and Excise Management Act* 1979, s.145(1)); but consent is unnecessary in relation to proceedings instituted by a Law Officer of the Crown: s.145(5). Where a person has been detained in respect of an offence for which consent is required it is unnecessary to obtain the consent before he is brought before a court: s.145(6). It should be noted that the Commissioners for *Revenue and Customs Act* 2005 does not contain any provision analogous to s.1(7) of the *Prosecution of Offences Act* 1985, from which it follows, it is submitted, that (depending on the proper application of the *Soneji* approach) proceedings may be a nullity where consent of the Director of Revenue and Customs is required and consent is given by a Revenue and Customs Prosecutor. **4–60**

Evidence of consent

Prosecution of Offences Act 1985, s.26

Consents to be admissible in evidence

26. Any document purporting to be the consent of a Law Officer of the Crown, the Director or a Crown Prosecutor for, or to— **4–61**

(a) the institution of any criminal proceedings; or

(b) the institution of criminal proceedings in any particular form;

and to be signed by a Law Officer of the Crown, the Director or, as the case may be, a Crown Prosecutor shall be admissible as *prima facie* evidence without further proof.

The consent will need to be produced in court following the first appearance but it is not required for the preliminary actions of arrest and charge. **4–62**

Most cases requiring consent are serious in nature so will usually not give rise to summonses being issued; but where authority to prosecute is required, the person before whom an information is laid should be satisfied that such authority has been obtained before issuing the summons.

The relevant consent to prosecute is proved by the production of a document that meets the requirements of s.26. At the hearing it will be presumed that authority was given and the prosecutor need not take any further steps unless the defence objects. Such an objection should be made before the close of the prosecution case. In the case of *Price v. Humphries* [1958] 2 Q.B. 353, DC, the court held that proof of consent was a formal matter and the prosecution was to be allowed to re-open it's case to produce the consent when late objection to the failure to produce it was taken by the defence.

If the defence requests proof of compliance with s.26 the prosecution must produce evidence that they have satisfied the statutory requirements as to consent. If such evidence is not forthcoming the justices are entitled to hold that there is no case to answer: *Anderton v. Frost* [1984] R.T.R. 106, DC, where computer generated informations named the Chief Constable as the informant the court held that the CPS had to prove in each case that the Chief Constable himself either laid the information or else had given written authority in each individual case to the officers concerned.

4–63 The court has to decide what evidence it would wish to hear to be able to determine whether the consent was properly given and certified. It would appear difficult to challenge the validity of a certificate without challenging the "*bona fides*" of the officer or process concerned.

III. AGAINST WHOM PROCEEDINGS MAY BE BROUGHT

4–64 The jurisdiction of magistrates' courts arises in respect of "offences": see the *Magistrates' Courts Act* 1980, s.2 (*ante*, § 2–42). Offence creating statutes tend to use the form of words, "a person commits an offence"; and the jurisdiction of the magistrates' court to issue process and deal with charges arises in respect of a "person". Subject to the appearance of a contrary intention, the word "person" in a statute or subordinate legislation is to be construed as including a body of persons corporate or unincorporated: *Interpretation Act* 1978, ss.5 and 11, and Scheds 1 and 2.

4–65 As to whether a partnership is a body of persons corporate in respect of which there is no contrary intention, see *R. v. W. Stevenson & Sons (a Partnership); R. v.Bick* [2008] 2 Cr.App.R. 14, CA, where it was said that there was no basis for suggesting that provisions of a criminal statute or statutory instrument are not permitted by law or are incapable of being effective where they confer liability on a partnership as an entity independent from the partners. As to whether an unincorporated association is a body of persons corporate in respect of which there is no contrary intention, see *R. v. R.L. and J.F.* [2008] 9 Archbold News 2, CA, where it was said that although several statutes made specific provision for the criminal liability of unincorporated associations, there was no general proposition that the absence of any such provision in an offence creating statute or statutory instrument signalled an intention that an unincorporated association could not be guilty of an offence under the statute or statutory instrument; but that this conclusion may not apply in relation to common law offences or offences involving any element of *mens rea*.

IV. INSTITUTION OF PROCEEDINGS

A. GENERAL

4–66 Generally speaking criminal proceedings against an individual (whether they are ultimately to be dealt with by a magistrates' court or in the Crown Court) are commenced by a procedure whereby the accused is informed of the allegation against him and then compelled to attend a magistrates' court to answer it. This procedure exists in three separate forms. First, the accused can be charged by the police and either produced before the court in custody or bailed to attend court at a time in the future. Secondly, a prosecutor can issue a written charge accompanied by a requisition requiring the defendant to appear before the court on a particular day. Thirdly, the prosecutor can lay an information to obtain either issue of a summons requiring the accused to attend court on a fixed day or issue of an arrest warrant empowering a constable to arrest the accused and produce him before the court. Commencement of proceedings in the Crown Court by application to a judge of the High Court for a voluntary bill of indictment is outside the scope of this work.

B. The Information or Charge

(1) Meaning of the "information" or "charge"

The criminal jurisdiction of the magistrates' courts to proceed to summary trial is founded on the laying of an information (see s.9(1) of the *Magistrates' Court Act* 1981 (*post*, § 8–73)); it does not depend on the issue of any summons or warrant which followed the laying of the information: *R. v. Manchester Stipendiary Magistrate, ex p. Hill* [1983] 1 A.C. 328, HL. It follows that there is an important distinction between that which founds the jurisdiction of the court ("the information") and the proceeding adopted to compel the appearance of the accused ("the process"). **4–67**

An "information" is nothing more than what the word imports, namely the statement by which the magistrate is informed of the offence, and it need not be in writing unless statute otherwise requires (*R. v. Hughes* (1879) J.P. 556, CCR); it may be made orally or in writing, but it must be designed for the purpose of initiating criminal proceedings, *i.e.* a deliberate act which commences in the conventional sense a prosecution which ultimately will have the effect of bringing an offence and offender before the court (*Schiavo v. Anderton* [1987] Q.B. 20, DC).

Where a defendant is charged with an offence at the police station, the "information" is laid before the magistrates' court at the latest when the charge is read in open court, and in practice, often earlier when, no doubt, the clerk to the justices, or his or her subordinate, is informed by the police of the charge which it is proposed to bring against the defendant later that morning: *R. v. Manchester Stipendiary Magistrate, ex p. Hill* [1983] 1 A.C. 328, HL. Where proceedings are commenced by way of a written charge, s.30(5)(a) of the *Criminal Justice Act* 2003 (*post*, § 4–104) provides that any reference to an "information" in other enactments is to be read as including a reference to a "written charge". It is submitted that this provision was unnecessary, since a written charge informs the court of the offence charged and that by itself makes it an "information" (for the avoidance of doubt, the same argument cannot be deployed in relation to the difference between a "summons" and a "requisition"). Whether or not that argument is correct, there is no practical difference between an "information" or a "charge" (whether a written charge or a charge at the police station); the "charge" is the "information".

(2) Laying the information

The laying of an information is an administrative act performed by the prosecutor and it may be done by the prosecutor in person or by his counsel or solicitor or other person authorised in that behalf. The information is laid when it is received at the office of clerk to the justices in the relevant area: *R. v. Manchester Stipendiary Magistrate, ex p. Hill* [1983] 1 AC 328, HL. **4–68**

An information may not be laid by an unincorporated association such as a police force because the definition of "person" in the *Interpretation Act* 1978 as "a body of persons whether corporate or unincorporated" was not intended to apply to the laying of informations: *Rubin v. DPP* [1990] 2 Q.B. 80, DC. In that case an information purported to have been laid by the Thames Valley Police. Watkins L.J. rejected the argument that "the police" could be regarded as the prosecutor. He said:

> "When the police bring a prosecution it has to be commenced by an information which has been laid by a member of the force; that is to say, by that member who reported the offence and the person accused of committing it or by the chief constable himself of some other member of the force authorised by him to lay an information."

In this particular case, the information was held not to be invalid because the identity of the informant was easily discovered and the defendant had not been misled.

In *Ealing Justices ex p. Dixon* [1990] 2 Q.B. 91, DC, Woolf L.J. observed that it was preferable for an individual to lay an information even when the prosecutor was essentially an organisation such as the Federation Against Copyright Theft.

As to the point at which the information is laid, see *post* § 4–60 *et seq.*

(3) Form and content of the information

(a) *General*

4–69 An information or complaint must comply with the requirements of Pt 7 of the *Criminal Procedure Rules* 2011 (Appendix G). It need not be in writing or on oath unless specifically required to be so by statute. The court should be informed of the precise nature of the offence alleged, including details of the date and place of the offence, the activity which is alleged to amount to an offence and the provision of statute (or common law) which makes the conduct an offence.

(b) *Rule against duplicity*

4–70 Simply stated, the rule against duplicity prohibits the court from proceeding to the trial of an information which charges more than one offence. However, r. 7.3(2) of the *Criminal Procedure Rules* 2011 permits more than one incident of the commission of the offence being included in the allegation if those incidents taken together amount to a course of conduct having regard to the time, place or purpose of commission: see Appendix G. In practice therefore, whilst the rule against duplicity is easy to state, it is difficult to apply particularly in terms of determining what amounts to one offence.

4–71 An information alleging that a person did "unlawfully assault and batter" another would be bad for duplicity, because assault and battery are separate and distinct offences: *DPP v. Taylor* [1992] 1 Q.B. 645, DC. However, an information will not be bad for duplicity if it alleges one activity even if that activity involves more than one act: *Ware v. Fox; Fox v. Dingley* [1967] 1 W.L.R. 379, DC; *Jemmison v. Priddle* [1972] 1 Q.B. 489, DC. This approach was approved and explained by Lord Morris of Borth-y-Gest in *DPP v. Merriman* [1973] A.C. 584, HL, in the following *dictum*:

> "If A attacks B and, in doing so, stabs B five times with a knife, has A committed one offence or five? If A in the dwelling-house of B steals ten different chattels, some perhaps from one rooms and some perhaps from others, has he committed one offence or several? ... In my view, such questions when they are asked are best answered by applying a common sense approach and by deciding what is fair in the circumstances. No precise formula can usefully be laid down, but . . . it will often be legitimate to bring a single charge in respect of what might be called one activity even though that activity may involve more than one act."

Thus no duplicity arose where a defendant had been convicted on two charges of theft and the evidence in relation to each charge revealed that he had stolen a number of separate items from different departments in a store (*R. v. Wilson*, 69 Cr.App.R. 83, CA); where a defendant was convicted on an information alleging the killing of two deer seconds apart (*Jemmison v. Priddle*, *ante*); where the defendant was charged in a single information with driving without due care and attention in relation to two separately observed incidents occurring two miles apart (*Horrix v. Mallam*, 148 J.P. 30, DC); and where an information charged the unlawful felling of a number of trees even though the felling had taken place over a number of days and there was a possibility of the existence of different defences in relation to different trees (*Cullen v. Jardine* [1985] Crim.L.R. 668, DC). However, in *Amos v. DPP* [1988] R.T.R. 198, DC, it was observed that "a bus driver who curses at a passenger with a cigarette in his mouth and refuses to divulge his destination at the same time is not involved in one activity but in three separate activities of cursing, smoking and refusing to divulge"; and that such conduct could not be charged in a single information. The court said that the rule against duplicity was designed to counter a true risk that there may be confusion in the presenting and meeting of charges which are mixed up and uncertain. To similar effect, the court in *Ministry of Agriculture, Fisheries & Food v. Nunn Corn (1987) Ltd* [1990] Crim.L.R. 268, DC, described the decision in *Cullen v. Jardine, ante*, as the "high water mark" of what does not amount to duplicity, and emphasised that the rule was one of elementary fairness and that its purpose was to enable the defendant to know the case he had to meet, such as when making submissions of no case to answer or pleas in mitigation.

An extension of the concept of a single activity is the principle that an information will not be duplicitous if it discloses a "continuous offence". The following *dictum* of Lord Diplock in *DPP v. Merriman, ante*, has been relied on in support of the principle: **4–72**

> "Where a number of acts of a similar nature committed by one or more defendants were connected with one another, in the time and place of their commission or by their common purpose, in such a way that they could fairly be regarded as forming part of the same transaction or criminal enterprise, it was the practice, as early as the eighteenth century, to charge them in a single count of an indictment."

The principle was applied in *DPP v. McCabe*, 157 J.P. 443, DC, where it was held to have been appropriate to charge one offence of theft of 76 library books that were found together in the defendant's home and which must have taken from one or more of 32 different branches of a library owned by the same local authority. In *DPP v. Barton*, 165 J.P. 779, DC, the court, making express reference to the concept of acts forming part of the same criminal enterprise, held that 94 identical thefts of small sums of money committed by an employee from her place of work over a period of a year could be properly be charged in a single information alleging theft of the total amount between the start and finish dates. Each of the individual thefts were identified in a schedule, which particularised every date on which money was stolen and the amount involved. Whilst each line of the schedule could itself have given rise to a separate information, the court held that the charge in a single information was not duplicitous because the defendant did not have different defences in relation to different thefts and because it would have been "oppressive" to have 94 separate informations. The *Barton* approach was expressly approved by Lord Woolf C.J. in *R. v. Tovey* ; *R. v. Smith* [2005] 2 Cr.App.R.(S.) 100, CA, subject to the caveat that it should not be stretched further to cases where the evidence for the prosecution and the defence raises different issues in relation to the different acts alleged.

A further and related aspect of the concept of a single activity is the "general deficiency" principle where a closely linked series of offences may be charged together in a single information because no particulars of the individual offences could be given: *R. v. Cain and others* [1983] Crim.L.R. 802, CA. The rationale underlying cases of this type is that a charge alleging a general deficiency should be permitted because it was otherwise impossible to identify the individual offences. Thus in *R. v. Tomlin* [1954] 2 Q.B. 274, CCA, where a stock take at a shop revealed a cash deficiency since the previous stock-taking, a single count in an indictment alleging embezzlement of the aggregate amount on a day between the two stock takings was held to be maintainable. **4–73**

Particular care is required where offences are expressed in statute as disjunctive activities. Informations in such cases must be drafted carefully to identify the precise offence alleged to have been committed. In *Mallon v. Allon* [1964] 1 Q.B. 385, DC, the manager of a licensed betting office had been convicted on an information which alleged that he had unlawfully admitted a person under the age of 18 and allowed him to remain contrary to s.5 of, and para. 2 of Sched. 2 to the *Betting and Gaming Act* 1960; the information was held to be duplicitous because s.5 of the Act created a single offence of contravening a rule in the schedule, yet the information alleged that two offences had been committed by the two separate activities of admitting and allowing to remain. The care required in relation to such offences will be all the more necessary where the penalty depends on the nature in which the offence was committed. **4–74**

The rule against duplicity does not apply where two offences are set out in a single **4–75** document: r. 7.3(2); and a single document may contain a preamble containing particulars common to a number of otherwise separate allegations: *Shah v. Swallow* [1984] 1 W.L.R. 886, HL.

If it appears to the court at any stage in a trial that the information is duplicitous the court must ask the prosecutor to elect which offence he wished the court to proceed on. Where an election is made, the other offence must be struck out of the information and the court must then proceed to try the information afresh (possibly after adjournment if unfair prejudice has been occasioned to the defendant). Failure by the prosecutor to make the election will result in the information being dismissed: *Fox v. Dingley*; *Ware v. Fox* [1967] 1 W.L.R. 379, DC.

(c) *Statement of offence*

4–76 See *Criminal Procedure Rules* 2011, r. 7.2 in Appendix G–23.

4–77 Under Art. 6(3) of the European Convention on Human Rights every person charged with an offence has the right to be informed promptly, in a language that he understands, and in detail, of the nature and cause of the accusation. The purpose of this right is to provide the accused with the information needed to prepare a defence. Thus the information required must be more specific than the grounds of arrest required under Art. 5(2) of the Convention.

The information must give sufficient particulars of the offence being charged which includes details of the legislative provisions, *i.e.* the Act, Sched., regulations or rules which create the offence; reasonable information about the nature of the charge and elements of the offence alleged to have been committed and clear information about the place and date of the alleged offence: *Atterton v. Brown* [1945] K.B. 122, DC; *Stephenson v. Johnson* [1954] 1 W.L.R. 375, DC; *R. v. Abergavenny J, ex p. Barratt* [1994] R.T.R. 98, DC.

In *Dacre Son & Hartley Ltd v. North Yorkshire Trading Standards*, 169 J.P. 59, DC, it was held that when a challenge was made to the adequacy of particulars or a defect in the information, the critical issue was whether the defendant was prejudiced by the way in which the information was worded. The court said in this instance, the defendant was clear what the case was against him because advanced information had been served and no prejudice was caused. If, however, critical aspects of the prosecution case that should have been revealed in the information in advance of the trial only become clear for the first time during the trial, then the position might well be different. The detail required in an information is both offence and fact dependent; a decision as to the adequacy of the particulars will therefore depend on the precise nature of the offence charged and the factual allegations upon which the charge depends. This approach was confirmed in the case of *Nash v. Birmingham Crown Court*, 169 J.P. 157, DC, where it was held that a defendant was entitled to know from the details of a summons what specific act or omission he was charged with. Here the summons alleged causing suffering to animals without specifying the conduct that amounted to the cruelty. Simply alleging causing suffering was held not to provide sufficient information. However, it was also held that since further information was given in time to the defendant this cured the defect.

A magistrate may not reconsider an application which has already been rejected by a fellow magistrate if there has been no material change to the substance of the information: *R. v. Worthing JJ, ex p. Norvell* [1981] 1 W.L.R. 413, DC.

(d) *Joint offenders*

4–78 An information may charge two or more defendants with having jointly committed an offence: *R. v. Lipscombe, ex p. Biggins* (1862) 26 J.P. 244.

C. Time-Limit for Laying the Information or Charge

(1) The time limit

Magistrates' Courts Act 1980, s.127

Limitation of time.

127.—(1) Except as otherwise expressly provided by any enactment and subject to subsection (2) below, a magistrates' court shall not try an information or hear a complaint unless the information was laid, or the complaint made, within 6 months from the time when the offence was committed, or the matter of complaint arose. **4–79**

(2) Nothing in—

(a) subsection (1) above; or

(b) subject to subsection (4) below, any other enactment (however framed or worded) which, as regards any offence to which it applies, would but for this section impose a time-limit on the power of a magistrates' court to try an information summarily or impose a limitation on the time for taking summary proceedings,

shall apply in relation to any indictable offence.

(3) Without prejudice to the generality of paragraph (b) of subsection (2) above, that paragraph includes enactments which impose a time-limit that applies only in certain circumstances (for example, where the proceedings are not instituted by or with the consent of the Director of Public Prosecutions or some other specified authority).

(4) Where, as regards any indictable offence, there is imposed by any enactment (however framed or worked, and whether falling within subsection (2) (b) above or not) a limitation on the time for taking proceedings on indictment for that offence no summary proceedings for that offence shall be taken after the latest time for taking proceedings on indictment.

The time limit in s.127 applies only to summary offences and does not apply to summary trial of offences triable either way; s.127(2) excludes the time limit from applying to an "indictable offence", which is defined in Sched. 1 to the *Interpretation Act* 1978 as including either way offences: *Kemp v. Liebherr-GB Ltd* [1987] 1 All E.R. 885, DC. As to construing the word "information" to include a written charge, see s.30(5)(a) of the *Criminal Justice Act* 2003. The purpose of the time limit is to ensure that summary offences are charged and tried as soon as reasonably practicable after their commission: *R. v. Newcastle upon Tyne JJ., ex p. John Bryce (Contractors) Ltd* [1976] R.T.R. 325, DC; *R. v. Scunthorpe JJ., ex p. McPhee and Gallagher*, 162, J.P. 635, DC. **4–80**

Save where there has been such delay in the commencement of proceedings as to give rise to an abuse of process (as to which see Ch.8, *post*) or the statute creating the offence provides otherwise, a prosecution in respect of an indictable offence may at common law be commenced at any length of time after commission of the offence.

(2) Laying the information

As to the formalities in relation to the laying of an information, see *post*. **4–81**

(3) Computation of time

(a) *Date of the offence and the intervening period*

The day of the offence is excluded from the computation but the day on which the prosecution begins is included: *Radcliffe v. Bartholomew* [1892] 1 Q.B. 161, DC; *Stewart v. Chapman* [1951] 2 K.B. 792, DC; *Marren v. Dawson Bentley & Co Ltd* [1961] 2 Q.B. 135, Assizes (Havers J.); *Verderers of the New Forest v. Young* [2005] A.C.D. 22, DC. **4–82**

It is not an essential characteristic of a criminal offence that any prohibited act or omission, in order to constitute a single offence, should take place once and for all on a single day; it may take place, whether continuously or intermittently, over a period of time: *Hodgetts v. Chiltern District Council* [1983] 2 A.C. 120, HL. Where the offence is a "continuing offence", it is only complete when the last act is committed, from which it follows that the information will be laid within the six month time limit in s.127 so long as at least one of the incidents relied on occurred within the time limit: *DPP v. Baker*, 169 J.P. 140, DC. A month means a calendar month: *Interpretation Act* 1978, Sched. 1.

For periods calculated in months, the period ends at midnight on the day in the subsequent month that bears the same number as the day of the earlier month or the preceding number if no such number appears in the subsequent month: *Dodds v. Walker* [1981] 1 W.L.R. 1027, HL; *Chief Constable of Merseyside v Reynolds* [2005] A.C.D. 44, DC.

(b) *When the information is laid*

4–83 The information is laid and time stops running when the information is *received* at the office of the justices' clerk; receipt of the information is a "ministerial" act that can be performed by any member of staff without need for it to be considered personally by the justices' clerk: *R. v. Manchester Stipendiary Magistrate, ex p. Hill* [1983] 1 A.C. 328, HL. Where proceedings are instituted by the informant inputting details of the alleged offence into a computer system according to which the details are simultaneously entered on to a computer at the magistrates' court, the information is laid at that moment, even if it is not printed out at the court until a later date: *R. v. Pontypridd Juvenile Court, ex p. B*, 153 J.P. 213, DC; but where the system operates in such a way that the informant can add to or correct the details, and then "validate" them once he considers that all the necessary details to constitute an information are included, the information is laid at the point of validation: *Atkinson v. DPP*, 168 J.P. 472, DC. Where proceedings are instituted by the laying of an information sent by fax, the point at which the information is properly to be regarded as laid is the point at which the fax is retrievable, whether or not in fact retrieved; whether the fax is retrievable is a matter to be established by inference or otherwise; and in the absence of any contrary evidence, fax headers and transmission sheets are capable of establishing the necessary facts: *Rockall v. Department for Environment, Food and Rural Affairs* [2007] 1 W.L.R. 2666, DC.

Where a person is arrested for an offence and duly charged at the police station and brought before (or bailed to appear before) a magistrates' court, the information is laid before the magistrates' court at the latest when the charge is read in open court, and in practice often earlier when the clerk to the justices or his assistant is informed by the police of the charge which it is proposed to bring against the defendant: *R. v. Manchester Stipendiary Magistrate, ex p. Hill, ibid.* Whereas s.30(5)(a) of the *Criminal Justice Act* 2003 construes the laying of an information so as to include the laying of a written charge, it is submitted that the *ex p. Hill* approach should also apply to written charges; thus a written charge will only be laid only when it is received by the court named in the requisition (*i.e.* when the clerk to the justices or his assistant is informed by the prosecutor of the charge or else when the charge is read out in open court), but not merely when it is received by the person charged.

Cf. the approach of the Criminal Procedure Rules Committee in r. 2.1(11) and Pt 7 (starting a prosecution in a magistrates' court) (see Appendix G), which appears to proceed on the basis that a prosecution is commenced by way of a written charge or an oral charge at the police station when the written charge is issued by the prosecutor or when the defendant is formally informed by a police officer that he has been charged with the offence.

Where an information is laid within the time limit, but for want of service of a summons, a fresh information is laid outside the time limit, there is no jurisdiction to proceed to summary trial on the fresh information: *R. v. Network Sites Ltd, ex p. London Borough of Havering* [1997] Crim.L.R. 595, DC. However, in that situation it is unnecessary to lay a fresh information, since more than one summons may issue from the first information laid within the time limit: *Ex p. Fielding*, 25 J.P. 759, DC; and *R. v. Clerkenwell Magistrate' Court, ex p. Ewing, The Times*, June 3, 1987, DC.

(c) *Doubt as to whether information laid within time-limit*

Where it is unclear whether an information has been laid within the requisite time, the defendant is entitled to the benefit of the doubt (*Lloyd v. Young* [1963] Crim.L.R. 703, DC); and the court will only have jurisdiction to try the information if it is proved to the criminal standard of proof that the information was laid within the time limit (*Atkinson v. DPP*, 168 J.P. 472, DC). There is no power to re-open a case following a mistaken ruling on the expiration of time limits: *Verderers of the New Forest v. Young* [2005] A.C.D. 22, DC. **4–84**

Part I

(4) Amendment of information outside of time limit

Where an information is laid within the limit, it may be amended outside the time limit so as to allege a different and summary offence, provided that the new offence relates to the "same misdoing" (*e.g.* substitution of charges of theft and common assault in place of charge of robbery) and that the amendment is in the interests of justice: *R. v. Scunthorpe JJ., ex p. McPhee and Gallagher*, 162 J.P. 635, DC. **4–85**

The phrase "same misdoing" should not be construed too narrowly and it means that the new offence should arise out of the same (or substantially the same) facts as gave rise to the original offence: *ibid*. Whether two offences relate to the same misdoing is a fact-specific question and should not be determined by other decided cases on the same two offences: *Williams v. DPP*, unreported, July 24, 2009, DC ([2009] EWHC 2354 (Admin.)). An allegation of attempt is the same misdoing as the full offence: *R. (James) v. DPP*, 168 J.P. 596, QBD (Mitting J.).

It has been held not to be in the interests of justice to permit amendment after the time-limit in the following circumstances: where the new offence is more serious (*ex p. McPhee and Gallagher, ibid.*), particularly where the accused is rendered liable to imprisonment when he had not been so liable before (*Shaw v. DPP*, 171 J.P. 254, DC); where different statutory defences arose (*R. (DPP) v. Everest, ibid.*); where an adjournment would become necessary, given that the purpose of the time-limit in s.127 was that summary offences should be tried as soon as reasonably practicable after their commission (*ex p. McPhee and Gallagher, ibid.*); where the information was drafted in such a way that it would impossible to understand from it precisely what offence was alleged (*R. v. Thames Magistrates' Court, ex p. Stevens*, 164 J.P. 233, DC); where an unrepresented and absent defendant was not given advance notice (*Shaw v. DPP, ibid*); or where there had been a fundamental failure on the part of the prosecutor during the proceedings properly to comply with its case management duties (*Williams v. DPP, ibid.*).

However, the interests of justice will be unaffected merely through delay by a prosecutor before the application to amend is made, unless there will be some prejudice to the accused (*R. (CPS) v. Gloucester JJ.*, 172 J.P. 506, DC); or by virtue of being deprived of the opportunity to plead guilty at the first opportunity (*R. (James) v. DPP, ibid.*). The amendment may be made as late as the conclusion of the evidence, provided that no prejudice is caused to the defendant (as by depriving him of the opportunity of putting his case in an appropriate way): *ibid*.

Where an information alleging the commission of a "continuing offence" is laid outside the time limit, but part of the alleged offending occurred within the time limit, amendment of the information is permissible after the expiry of the time limit so as to allege a date within the time limit, provided that this could be done without unfairness: *R. v. Blackburn JJ., ex p. Holmes*, 164 J.P. 163, DC.

An information cannot be amended after the expiration of the time limit so as to substitute a subsidiary company for its parent company (*i.e.* a separate legal entity) since this would amount to the preferment of a charge against a new defendant outside the time limit; but it is permissible simply to correct a misdescription of the company originally charged: *Sainsbury's Supermarkets Ltd and J. Sainsbury plc v. Plymouth Magistrates' Court*, 170 J.P. 690, DC.

(5) Time limits in other enactments

4–86 In accordance with the opening words of s.127(1), various other enactments which create offences provide different time limits to the six-month period specified in s.127. A typical form of words used in such statutes is to prohibit the institution of a prosecution after the expiry of a specified period "from its discovery by the prosecutor". For this purpose, the relevant "discovery" is one which gives rise to a reasonable belief that an offence has been committed: *Tesco Stores Ltd v. London Borough of Harrow*, 167 J.P. 657, DC (approved in *R. v. Gale*, 169 J.P. 166, CA, where the accused had been placed under observation after information had been received that he was operating an unlicensed slaughterhouse, and several days later his premises were entered and slaughtered animals were discovered; "discovery" of the offence was the date when the premises had been entered, since before that date there was evidence giving rise to suspicion but not knowledge of the "material facts which would found the offence"). Where the enactment further specifies the prosecuting authority responsible for enforcing the enactment, the "prosecutor" is the authority itself, rather than the individual who lays the information; and the authority, as prosecutor, will have the necessary knowledge when its officials, whose knowledge is attributable it, have the necessary knowledge: *R. (Donnachie) v. Cardiff Magistrates' Court* [2008] R.T.R. 2, DC.

Where a statute disapplied s.127(1) of the *Magistrates' Courts Act* 1980 and provided that proceedings for an offence might be brought within a fixed period "from the date on which evidence sufficient in the opinion of the prosecutor to warrant the proceedings came to his knowledge", and that "a certificate signed by or on behalf of the prosecutor and stating the date on which evidence sufficient in his opinion to warrant the proceedings came to his knowledge shall be conclusive evidence of that fact", the certificate would normally be determinative of the issue of when the relevant period began to run, such that a court could not go behind it save where it was inaccurate on its face or fraud could be shown; but a certificate would be invalid if it stated merely that the proceedings had been brought within the specified period after "the date on which evidence sufficient in the opinion of the prosecutor came to his knowledge" and did not recite the actual date on which sufficient evidence came to the knowledge of the prosecutor: *Burwell v. DPP*, 173 J.P. 351, DC. See also *Azham v. Epping Forest DC*, unreported, October 14, 2009, DC.

Although prosecutors are not entitled to shuffle papers between officers or sit on information so as to extend a time-limit, there is no principle of law that knowledge in a prosecutor begins immediately when any employee of that prosecutor has the relevant information; there is a degree of judgment involved in bringing a prosecution, and knowledge involves an opportunity for those with appropriate skills to consider whether there is sufficient information to justify a prosecution: *RSPCA v. Johnson*, unreported, October 16, 2009, DC ([2009] EWHC 2702 (Admin.)).

D. CHARGING OF OFFENCES AT THE POLICE STATION

(1) General

4–87 In criminal proceedings, a person suspected of committing an offence may attend voluntarily at a police station or he may be arrested and taken to a police station. Once arrested, suspects may be detained for investigations to be carried out to determine if there is sufficient evidence to bring a charge. Those charged with an offence are either then bailed from the police station to attend at court or are brought to court in custody. The charge sheet which accompanies them gives information about the defendant, including his name, address, date of birth and ethnic origin together with details of the offence, the time of charge and release and any bail conditions.

4–88 The process of charging offences and the powers and duties of police officers to charge offenders are found in the *Police and Criminal Evidence Act* 1984. Under s.66 of this Act, codes of practice have been drawn up which set out procedures to be followed during investigations.

Paragraphs 16.1 *et seq.* of the Code of Practice for the Detention, Treatment and Questioning of Persons by Police Officers ("Code C") make provision in connection with the charging of suspects at the police station: see Appendix A.

Once a custody officer has charged a suspect the prosecution commences. The Director of Public Prosecutions will take over the proceedings from the police unless that responsibility is assigned to another person (*Prosecution of Offences Act* 1985, s.6).

4–89 Where a person other than a police officer investigated the matter, arrested the suspect and brought him to the police station to be charged by a custody officer, the fact the custody officer is a police officer does not require the DPP to take over conduct of the proceedings; the prosecutor is the person who brought the suspect to the police station: see *ante*, § 4–43.

(2) Duties of the custody officer before charge

Police and Criminal Evidence Act 1984, ss.37–37D

Duties of custody officer before charge

4–90 **37.**—(1) Where—

(a) a person is arrested for an offence—

(i) without a warrant; or

(ii) under a warrant not endorsed for bail,

the custody officer at each police station where he is detained after his arrest shall determine whether he has before him sufficient evidence to charge that person with the offence for which he was arrested and may detain him at the police station for such period as is necessary to enable him to do so.

(2) If the custody officer determines that he does not have such evidence before him, the person arrested shall be released either on bail or without bail, unless the custody officer has reasonable grounds for believing that his detention without being charged is necessary to secure or preserve evidence relating to an offence for which he is under arrest or to obtain such evidence by questioning him.

(3) If the custody officer has reasonable grounds for so believing, he may authorise the person arrested to be kept in police detention.

(4) Where a custody officer authorises a person who has not been charged to be kept in police detention, he shall, as soon as is practicable, make a written record of the grounds for the detention.

(5) Subject to subsection (6) below, the written record shall be made in the presence of the person arrested who shall at that time be informed by the custody officer of the grounds for his detention.

(6) Subsection (5) above shall not apply where the person arrested is, at the time when the written record is made—

(a) incapable of understanding what is said to him;

(b) violent or likely to become violent; or

(c) in urgent need of medical attention.

(7) Subject to section 41(7) below, if the custody officer determines that he has before him sufficient evidence to charge the person arrested with the offence for which he was arrested, the person arrested—

(a) shall be—

(i) released without charge and on bail, or

(ii) kept in police detention,

for the purpose of enabling the Director of Public Prosecutions to make a decision under section 37B below,

(b) shall be released without charge and on bail but not for that purpose,.

(c) shall be released without charge and without bail, or

(d) shall be charged.

(7A) The decision as to how a person is to be dealt with under subsection (7) above shall be that of the custody officer.

(7B) Where a person is dealt with under subsection (7)(a) above, it shall be the duty of the custody officer to inform him that he is being released, or (as the case may be) detained, to enable the Director of Public Prosecutions to make a decision under section 37B below.

(8) Where—

(a) a person is released under subsection (7)(b) or (c) above; and

(b) at the time of his release a decision whether he should be prosecuted for the offence for which he was arrested has not been taken,

it shall be the duty of the custody officer so to inform him.

(8A) Subsection (8B) applies if the offence for which the person is arrested is one in relation to which a sample could be taken under section 63B below and the custody officer—

(a) is required in pursuance of subsection (2) above to release the person arrested and decides to release him on bail, or

(b) decides in pursuance of subsection (7)(a) or (b) above to release the person without charge and on bail.

(8B) The detention of the person may be continued to enable a sample to be taken under section 63B, but this subsection does not permit a person to be detained for a period of more than 24 hours after the relevant time.

(9) If the person arrested is not in a fit state to be dealt with under subsection (7) above, he may be kept in police detention until he is.

(10) The duty imposed on the custody officer under subsection (1) above shall be carried out by him as soon as practicable after the person arrested arrives at the police station or, in the case of a person arrested at the police station, as soon as practicable after the arrest.

(15) In this Part of this Act—

"arrested juvenile" means a person arrested with or without a warrant who appears to be under the age of 17;

"endorsed for bail" means endorsed with a direction for bail in accordance with section 117(2) of the *Magistrates' Courts Act* 1980.

[This section is printed as amended by the *Children Act* 1989, Sched. 15, the *Criminal Justice Act* 1991, s.72 and Sched. 13, the *Criminal Justice and Public Order Act* 1994, s.29(1) and Sched. 11, the *Criminal Justice Act* 2003, Sched. 2, the *Drugs Act* 2005, Sched. 1, and the *Police and Justice Act* 2006, s.11, and Sched. 14.]

Guidance

4–91 **37A.**—(1) The Director of Public Prosecutions may issue guidance—

(a) for the purpose of enabling custody officers to decide how persons should be dealt with under section 37(7) above or 37C(2) or 37CA(2) below, and

(b) as to the information to be sent to the Director of Public Prosecutions under section 37B(1) below.

(2) The Director of Public Prosecutions may from time to time revise guidance issued under this section.

(3) Custody officers are to have regard to guidance under this section in deciding how persons should be dealt with under section 37(7) above or 37C(2) or 37CA(2) below.

(4) A report under section 9 of the *Prosecution of Offences Act* 1985 (report by DPP to Attorney General) must set out the provisions of any guidance issued, and any revisions to guidance made, in the year to which the report relates.

(5) The Director of Public Prosecutions must publish in such manner as he thinks fit—

(a) any guidance issued under this section, and

(b) any revisions made to such guidance.

(6) Guidance under this section may make different provision for different cases, circumstances or areas.

Consultation with the Director of Public Prosecutions

4–92 **37B.**—(1) Where a person is dealt with under section 37(7)(a) above, an officer involved in the investigation of the offence shall, as soon as is practicable, send to the Director of Public Prosecutions such information as may be specified in guidance under section 37A above.

(2) The Director of Public Prosecutions shall decide whether there is sufficient evidence to charge the person with an offence.

(3) If he decides that there is sufficient evidence to charge the person with an offence, he shall decide—

(a) whether or not the person should be charged and, if so, the offence with which he should be charged, and

(b) whether or not the person should be given a caution and, if so, the offence in respect of which he should be given a caution.

(4) The Director of Public Prosecutions shall give notice of his decision to an officer involved in the investigation of the offence.

(4A) Notice under subsection (4) above shall be in writing, but in the case of a person kept in police detention under section 37(7)(a) above it may be given orally in the first instance and confirmed in writing subsequently.

(5) If his decision is—

(a) that there is not sufficient evidence to charge the person with an offence, or

(b) that there is sufficient evidence to charge the person with an offence but that the person should not be charged with an offence or given a caution in respect of an offence,

a custody officer shall give the person notice in writing that he is not to be prosecuted.

(6) If the decision of the Director of Public Prosecutions is that the person should be charged with an offence, or given a caution in respect of an offence, the person shall be charged or cautioned accordingly.

(7) But if his decision is that the person should be given a caution in respect of the offence and it proves not to be possible to give the person such a caution, he shall instead be charged with the offence.

(8) For the purposes of this section, a person is to be charged with an offence either—

(a) when he is in police detention at a police station (whether because he has returned to answer bail, because he is detained under section 37(7)(a) above or for some other reason), or

(b) in accordance with section 29 of the *Criminal Justice Act* 2003.

(9) In this section "caution" includes—

(a) a conditional caution within the meaning of Part 3 of the *Criminal Justice Act* 2003, and

(b) a warning or reprimand under section 65 of the *Crime and Disorder Act* 1998.

Breach of bail following release under section 37(7)(a)

37C.—(1) This section applies where— **4–93**

(a) a person released on bail under section 37(7)(a) above or subsection (2)(b) below is arrested under section 46A below in respect of that bail, and

(b) at the time of his detention following that arrest at the police station mentioned in section 46A(2) below, notice under section 37B(4) above has not been given.

(2) The person arrested—

(a) shall be charged, or

(b) shall be released without charge, either on bail or without bail.

(3) The decision as to how a person is to be dealt with under subsection (2) above shall be that of a custody officer.

(4) A person released on bail under subsection (2)(b) above shall be released on bail subject to the same conditions (if any) which applied immediately before his arrest.

Breach of bail following release under section 37(7)(b)

37CA.—(1) This section applies where a person released on bail under section 37(7)(b) above or subsection (2)(b) below— **4–94**

(a) is arrested under section 46A below in respect of that bail,

(b) is being detained following that arrest at the police station mentioned in section 46A(2) below.

(2) The person arrested—

(a) shall be charged, or

(b) shall be released without charge, either on bail or without bail.

(3) The decision as to how a person is to be dealt with under subsection (2) above shall be that of a custody officer.

(4) A person released on bail under subsection (2)(b) above shall be released on bail subject to the same conditions (if any) which applied immediately before his arrest.

Release on bail under section 37: further provision

37D.—(1) Where a person is released on bail under section 37(7), 37C(2)(b) or 37CA(2)(b) **4–95**

above, a custody officer may subsequently appoint a different time, or an additional time, at which the person is to attend at the police station to answer bail.

(2) The custody officer shall give the person notice in writing of the exercise of the power under subsection (1).

(3) The exercise of the power under subsection (1) shall not affect the conditions (if any) to which bail is subject.

(4) Where a person released on bail under section 37(7)(a) or 37C(2)(b) above returns to a police station to answer bail or is otherwise in police detention at a police station, he may be kept in police detention to enable him to be dealt with in accordance with section 37B or 37C above or to enable the power under subsection (1) above to be exercised.

(4A) Where a person released on bail under section 37(7)(b) or 37CA(2)(b) above returns to a police station to answer bail or is otherwise in police detention at a police station, he may be kept in police detention to enable him to be dealt with in accordance with section 37CA above or to enable the power under subsection (1) above to be exercised.

(5) If the person mentioned in subsection (4) or (4A) above is not in a fit state to enable him to be dealt with as mentioned in that subsection or to enable the power under subsection (1) above to be exercised, he may be kept in police detention until he is.

(6) Where a person is kept in police detention by virtue of subsection (4), (4A) or (5) above, section 37(1) to (3) and (7) above (and section 40(8) below so far as it relates to section 37(1) to (3)) shall not apply to the offence in connection with which he was released on bail under section 37(7), 37C(2)(b) or 37CA(2)(b) above.

[Sections 37A, 37B, 37C and 37D were inserted by the *Criminal Justice Act* 2003, Sched. 2. They are printed as amended by the *Police and Justice Act* 2006, s.11 and Scheds 6 and 14. Section 37CA was inserted by the *Police and Justice Act* 2006, Sched. 6.]

4–96 The purpose behind the amendments made to the charging regime in *PACE* 1984 by the *Criminal Justice Act* 2003 was to involve the Crown Prosecution Service at an earlier stage of a prosecution. Under s.37(7)(a), a custody officer may detain or release a person on bail in order to consult with the DPP as to whether that person should be charged. Sections 37A and 37B which have been inserted into *PACE* 1984 provide for the DPP to issue guidance on the exercise of the power to bail pending consultation and also allow for the DPP to consider the sufficiency of the evidence and advise on any charge or caution, including a conditional caution.

Such guidance has been issued by the DPP and it is crucial to the operation of the charging regime. In particular, the guidance provides that in most cases a Crown Prosecutor will be responsible for the decision to charge and the specifying or drafting of the charges.

The custody officer is not obliged to investigate the lawfulness of the arrest before charging a suspect: *DPP v. L* [1999] Crim.L.R. 752, DC; and see *Al-Fayed v. Metropolitan Police Commissioner* [2005] 1 *Archbold News* 2, CA.

The periods of detention are specified in the Act. Even if there is not sufficient evidence to charge, detention may be ordered to protect evidence or elicit evidence by further questioning. Once the decision is made that there is sufficient evidence the suspect must be charged or released without charge, although he can at this stage be bailed to return to the police station at a later date whilst inquiries are still ongoing.

4–97 The custody officer has power to grant unconditional or conditional bail under s.47 of *PACE* 1984 when exercising his power to release suspects under s.38. The provisions of the *Bail Act* 1976 apply, see Ch.5. The officer may impose similar conditions of bail as the court except those requiring residence in a bail hostel, co-operation with report writers or attendance at lawyers interviews. The officer may also entertain applications to vary bail conditions made by him. Section 41(7) limits the time of detention without charge to 24 hours initially. The suspect, if not charged must then be released on bail or he may be released from detention with no direction about bail and therefore no legal duty to return to the police station. The period of detention may also be extended. When a person fails to answer police bail he may be arrested without a warrant: *PACE* 1984, ss.37C, 37D and 46A.

Charging of offences by the Director of Revenue and Customs Prosecutions

Schedule 3 to the *Commissioners for Revenue and Customs Act* 2005 applies ss.37 to 37B of the 1984 Act to persons arrested following a criminal investigation by HM Revenue and Customs, as if references to the DPP were references to the Director of Revenue and Customs Prosecutions. Further, the *Police and Criminal Evidence Act 1984 (Application to Revenue and Customs) Order* 2007 (S.I. 2007 No. 3175) applies certain provisions of the 1984 Act, subject to specified modifications, to relevant investigations conducted by officers of Revenue and Customs and to persons detained by such officers. A relevant investigation is a criminal investigation by such an officer which relates to a matter in respect of which HM Revenue and Customs has functions, apart from certain specified former Inland Revenue matters. Art. 3(1) stipulates that the provisions of the Act listed in Sched. 1 to the order, which relate to investigations conducted by police officers or to persons detained by the police, shall apply to relevant investigations conducted by officers of Revenue and Customs and to persons detained by such officers. So far as the charging of offenders is concerned, Arts 9 and 10 of the order respectively modify ss.35 (designated police stations) and 36 of the 1984 Act (custody officers at police stations), so that offices of Revenue and Customs may be designated for the purposes of detaining arrested persons, and so that custody officers may be appointed at such places. Schedule 1 to the order lists (*inter alia*) s.37 of the Act. One effect of the order, therefore, is (in conjunction with Sched. 3 to 2005 Act) to apply the charging regime in s.37 to custody officers at revenue and customs offices. **4–98**

(3) Duties of custody officer after charge

Police and Criminal Evidence Act 1984, s.38

Duties of custody officer after charge

38.—(1) Where a person arrested for an offence otherwise than under a warrant endorsed for bail is charged with an offence, the custody officer shall, subject to section 25 of the *Criminal Justice and Public Order Act* 1994, order his release from police detention, either on bail or without bail, unless— **4–99**

(a) if the person arrested is not an arrested juvenile—

(i) his name or address cannot be ascertained or the custody officer has reasonable grounds for doubting whether a name or address furnished by him as his name or address is his real name or address;

(ii) the custody officer has reasonable grounds for believing that the person arrested will fail to appear in court to answer to bail;

(iii) in the case of a person arrested for an imprisonable offence, the custody officer has reasonable grounds for believing that the detention of the person arrested is necessary to prevent him from committing an offence;

(iiia) in a case where a sample may be taken from the person under section 63B below, the custody officer has reasonable grounds for believing that the detention of the person is necessary to enable the sample to be taken from him;

(iv) in the case of a person arrested for an offence which is not an imprisonable offence, the custody officer has reasonable grounds for believing that the detention of the person arrested is necessary to prevent him from causing physical injury to any other person or from causing loss of or damage to property;

(v) the custody officer has reasonable grounds for believing that the detention of the person arrested is necessary to prevent him from interfering with the administration of justice or with the investigation of offences or of a particular offence; or

(vi) the custody officer has reasonable grounds for believing that the detention of the person arrested is necessary for his own protection;

(b) if he is an arrested juvenile—

(i) any of the requirements of paragraph (a) above is satisfied (but, in the case of paragraph (a)(iiia) above, only if the arrested juvenile has attained the minimum age); or

(ii) the custody officer has reasonable grounds for believing that he ought to be detained in his own interests.

(2) If the release of a person arrested is not required by subsection (1) above, the custody officer may authorise him to be kept in police detention but may not authorise a person to be kept in police detention by virtue of subsection (1)(a)(iiia) after the end of the period of six hours beginning when he was charged with the offence.

(2A) The custody officer, in taking the decisions required by subsection (1)(a) and (b) above (except (a)(i) and (vi) and (b)(ii)), shall have regard to the same considerations as those which a court is required to have regard to in taking the corresponding decisions under paragraph 2(1) of Part I of Schedule 1 to the *Bail Act* 1976 (disregarding paragraph 2(2) of that Part).

(3) Where a custody officer authorises a person who has been charged to be kept in police detention, he shall, as soon as practicable, make a written record of the grounds for the detention.

(4) Subject to subsection (5) below, the written record shall be made in the presence of the person charged who shall at that time be informed by the custody officer of the grounds for his detention.

(5) Subsection (4) above shall not apply where the person charged is, at the time when the written record is made—

(a) incapable of understanding what is said to him;
(b) violent or likely to become violent; or
(c) in urgent need of medical attention.

(6) Where a custody officer authorises an arrested juvenile to be kept in police detention under subsection (1) above, the custody officer shall, unless he certifies—

(a) that, by reason of such circumstances as are specified in the certificate, it is impracticable for him to do so; or
(b) in the case of an arrested juvenile who has attained the age of 12 years, that no secure accommodation is available and that keeping him in other local authority accommodation would not be adequate to protect the public from serious harm from him,

secure that the arrested juvenile is moved to local authority accommodation.

(6A) In this section—

"local authority accommodation" means accommodation provided by or on behalf of a local authority (within the meaning of the *Children Act* 1989);
"minimum age" means the age specified in section 63B(3)(b) below.
"secure accommodation" means accommodation provided for the purpose of restricting liberty;
"sexual offence" means an offence specified in Part 2 of Schedule 15 to the *Criminal Justice Act* 2003;
"violent offence"means murder or an offence specified in Part 1 of that Schedule.

and any reference, in relation to an arrested juvenile charged with a violent or sexual offence, to protecting the public from serious harm from him shall be construed as a reference to protecting members of the public from death or serious personal injury, whether physical or psychological, occasioned by further such offences committed by him.

(6B) Where an arrested juvenile is moved to local authority accommodation under subsection (6) above, it shall be lawful for any person acting on behalf of the authority to detain him.

(7) A certificate made under subsection (6) above in respect of an arrested juvenile shall be produced to the court before which he is first brought thereafter.

(7A) In this section "imprisonable offence" has the same meaning as in Schedule 1 to the *Bail Act* 1976.

(8) In this Part of this Act "local authority" has the same meaning as in the *Children Act* 1989.

[This section is printed as amended by the *Children Act* 1989, Sched. 13, the *Criminal Justice Act* 1991, s.59, the *Criminal Justice and Public Order Act* 1994, ss.24 and 28 and Sched. 10, the *Criminal Justice and Court Services Act* 2000, s.57, the *Powers of Criminal Courts (Sentencing) Act* 2000, Sched. 9, the *Criminal Justice Act* 2003, s.5 and Scheds 32 and 36, and the *Drugs Act* 2005, Sched. 1.]

Once a suspect is charged the custody sergeant will decide whether to detain him in custody to appear at court or to release him on bail with or without conditions for appearance at court at a later date. The custody sergeant is bound by the provisions of the *Bail Act* 1976, see Ch.5. **4–100**

The custody officer may order detention for six hours if any of the conditions in s.38(1) are met. This now includes the power to detain to conduct a drugs test under s.63B of *PACE* 1984.

Section 25 of the *Criminal Justice and Public Order Act* 1994 applies in cases of murder, attempted murder, manslaughter, rape and attempted rape, if the defendant has previously been convicted of any such offence or culpable homicide and in the case of culpable homicide. On its face, the section appears to provide that bail should only be granted if there are exceptional circumstances to justify it. However, in *R. (O.) v. Crown Court at Harrow* [2007] 1 A.C. 249, HL, it was held that the subsection merely served as a reminder of the risks normally posed by defendants to whom it applied; it had no substantive effect upon the way in which bail applications should be determined under the *Bail Act* 1976.

Section 63B of *PACE* 1984 gives power for samples to be taken from a person in police detention for the purpose of ascertaining whether the person has a Class A drug in his body. A period of six hours is deemed sufficient time to arrange for the sample to be taken. **4–101**

Young persons may also be detained but the police have an over-riding duty to transfer young persons aged between 10 and 17 to local authority accommodation. In *R. (M.) v. Gateshead Metropolitan Borough Council* [2006] Q.B. 650, CA, it was held that where a local authority received a request from the police under subs. (6) to receive a juvenile whom a custody officer had authorised under subs. (1) to be kept in police detention, the authority was under a duty, pursuant to s.21(2) of the *Children Act* 1989, to provide accommodation in response to such request, regardless of whether or not the juvenile was within in its area at the time of the request; however, there was no absolute duty to provide secure accommodation where such accommodation was requested, merely a duty to provide accommodation.

Pursuant to para. 16 of Code C of the Codes of Practice, when a person is charged with an offence at a police station he must be cautioned and given written notice of the charge, which shows the particulars of the offence stated in simple language and the precise offence in law with which he is charged.

(4) Detention after charge

Police and Criminal Evidence Act 1984, s.46

Detention after charge

46.—(1) Where a person— **4–102**

(a) is charged with an offence; and

(b) after being charged—

(i) is kept in police detention; or

(ii) is detained by a local authority in pursuance of arrangements made under section 38(6) above,

he shall be brought before a magistrates' court in accordance with the provisions of this section.

(2) If he is to be brought before a magistrates' court in the local justice area in which the police station at which he was charged is situated, he shall be brought before such a court as soon as is practicable and in any event not later than the first sitting after he is charged with the offence.

(3) If no magistrates' court in that area is due to sit either on the day on which he is charged or on the next day, the custody officer for the police station at which he was charged shall inform the designated officer for the area that there is a person in the area to whom subsection (2) above applies.

(4) If the person charged is to be brought before a magistrates' court in a local justice

area other than that in which the police station at which he was charged is situated, he shall be removed to that area as soon as is practicable and brought before such a court as soon as is practicable after his arrival in the area and in any event not later than the first sitting of a magistrates' court in that area after his arrival in the area.

(5) If no magistrates' court in that area is due to sit either on the day on which he arrives in the area or on the next day—

(a) he shall be taken to a police station in the area; and

(b) the custody officer at that station shall inform the designated officer for the area that there is a person in the area to whom subsection (4) applies.

(6) Subject to subsection (8) below, where the designated officer for a local justice area has been informed—

(a) under subsection (3) above that there is a person in the area to whom subsection (2) above applies; or

(b) under subsection (5) above that there is a person in the area to whom subsection (4) above applies,

the designated officer shall arrange for a magistrates' court to sit not later than the day next following the relevant day.

(7) In this section "the relevant day"—

(a) in relation to a person who is to be brought before a magistrates' court in the local justice area in which the police station at which he was charged is situated, means the day on which he was charged; and

(b) in relation to a person who is to be brought before a magistrates' court for any other local justice area, means the day on which he arrives in the area.

(8) Where the day next following the relevant day is Christmas Day, Good Friday or a Sunday, the duty of the designated officer under subsection (6) above is a duty to arrange for a magistrates' court to sit not later than the first day after the relevant day which is not one of those days.

(9) Nothing in this section requires a person who is in hospital to be brought before a court if he is not well enough.

[This section is printed as amended by the *Courts Act* 2003, Sched. 8.]

4–103 The police have a duty under this section to produce a defendant from custody to court as soon as practicable after charge. Most magistrates' courts are open from Monday to Friday so defendants can be produced either on the day of charge or the following day. Many courts are also open on Saturdays and Bank Holidays and on those days may deal with work for other courts in their area that are not open. It is not lawful for a policy to be promoted by a body responsible for running the magistrates court to restrict the convening of courts to weekdays only: *R. v. Avon Magistrates' Courts Committee, ex p. Broome* [1988] 1 W.L.R. 1246, DC.

Under the *Courts Act* 2003, s.30, the Lord Chancellor may give directions as to the days and times when a magistrates' court may sit and they may be directed to sit on any day at any time. See Ch.2.

E. WRITTEN CHARGING AND REQUISITIONING

(1) General

4–104 As from a day to be appointed, the institution of all public prosecutions will be governed by a new procedure. This will replace the laying of informations (other than by charging at the police station) and issue of summonses with a process under which the public prosecutor may issue a "written charge" which charges the person with an offence. The written charge must be accompanied by the issue of a "requisition" which requires the person to appear before a magistrates' court to answer the written charge. The new procedure is not in force generally, but is being piloted on a limited basis in a number of magistrates' courts sitting at specified locations: see *post*. When the new procedure is brought into force in full, public prosecutors will no longer have the power to lay an information for the purpose of obtaining the issue of a summons. However, the power of a public prosecutor to lay an information in order to obtain an arrest warrant is retained. The new procedure does not apply to criminal proceedings instituted by private prosecutors, which will continue to be instituted by the laying of an information and the issue of a summons.

(2) Legislation

Criminal Justice Act 2003, ss.29 and 30

New method of instituting proceedings

[29.—(1) A public prosecutor may institute criminal proceedings against a person by issuing a document (a "written charge") which charges the person with an offence. **4–105**

(2) Where a public prosecutor issues a written charge, it must at the same time issue a document (a "requisition") which requires the person to appear before a magistrates' court to answer the written charge.

(3) The written charge and requisition must be served on the person concerned, and a copy of both must be served on the court named in the requisition.

(4) In consequence of subsections (1) to (3), a public prosecutor is not to have the power to lay an information for the purpose of obtaining the issue of a summons under section 1 of the *Magistrates' Courts Act* 1980.

(5) In this section "public prosecutor" means—

(a) a police force or a person authorised by a police force to institute criminal proceedings,

(b) the Director of the Serious Fraud Office or a person authorised by him to institute criminal proceedings,

(c) the Director of Public Prosecutions or a person authorised by him to institute criminal proceedings,

(ca) the Director of Revenue and Customs Prosecutions or a person authorised by him to institute criminal proceedings,

(cb) the Director General of the Serious Organised Crime Agency or a person authorised by him to institute criminal proceedings,

(d) the Attorney General or a person authorised by him to institute criminal proceedings,

(e) a Secretary of State or a person authorised by a Secretary of State to institute criminal proceedings,

(f) the Commissioners for Her Majesty's Revenue and Customs or a person authorised by them to institute criminal proceedings,

(g) […], or

(h) a person specified in an order made by the Secretary of State for the purposes of this section or a person authorised by such a person to institute criminal proceedings.

(6) In subsection (5) "police force" has the meaning given by section 3(3) of the *Prosecution of Offences Act* 1985.]

[This section is printed as amended by the *Serious Organised Crime and Police Act* 2005, Sched. 4, and the *Commissioners for Revenue and Customs Act* 2005, s.50 and Sched. 4. It is not in force generally, but subss. (1) to (3), (5) and (6) have been brought into force for the purposes of a pilot scheme in a number of magistrates' courts sitting at specified locations: see *post*.]

Further provision about new method

[30.—(1), (2) (power to make *Criminal Procedure Rules*) **4–106**

(3) (repealed)

(4) Nothing in section 29 affects—

(a) the power of a public prosecutor to lay an information for the purpose of obtaining the issue of a warrant under section 1 of the *Magistrates' Courts Act* 1980,

(b) the power of a person who is not a public prosecutor to lay an information for the purpose of obtaining the issue of a summons or warrant under section 1 of that Act, or

(c) any power to charge a person with an offence whilst he is in custody.

(5) Except where the context otherwise requires, in any enactment contained in an Act passed before this Act—

(a) any reference (however expressed) which is or includes a reference to an information within the meaning of section 1 of the *Magistrates' Courts Act* 1980 (or to the laying of such an information) is to be read as including a reference to a written charge (or to the issue of a written charge),

(b) any reference (however expressed) which is or includes a reference to a summons under section 1 of the *Magistrates' Courts Act* 1980 (or to a justice of the peace issuing such a summons) is to be read as including a reference to a requisition (or to a public prosecutor issuing a requisition).

(6) Subsection (5) does not apply to section 1 of the *Magistrates' Courts Act* 1980.

(7) The reference in subsection (5) to an enactment contained in an Act passed before this Act includes a reference to an enactment contained in that Act as a result of an amendment to that Act made by this Act or by any other Act passed in the same Session as this Act.

(8) In this section "public prosecutor", "requisition" and "written charge" have the same meaning as in section 29].

[This section is printed as amended by the *Courts Act 2003 (Consequential Amendments) Order* 2004 (S.I. 2004 No. 2035). It is not in force generally, but it has been brought into force for the purposes of a pilot scheme in a number of specified magistrates' courts: see *post*.]

(3) Piloting of new procedure in magistrates' courts sitting at specified locations

4–107 The *Criminal Justice Act 2003 (Commencement No. 16) Order* 2007 (S.I. 2007 No. 1999), the *Criminal Justice Act 2003 (Commencement No. 21) Order* 2008 (S.I. 2008 No. 1424), the *Criminal Justice Act 2003 (Commencement No. 23) Order* 2009 (S.I. 2009 No. 2879) and the *Criminal Justice Act 2003 (Commencement No. 25) Order* 2010 (S.I. 2010 No. 3005) brought ss.29(1) to (3), (5), (6) and 30 into force for the purposes of a pilot scheme. The provisions have effect only for the purposes of:

(a) criminal proceedings instituted by a public prosecutor within the meaning of s.29(5)(a) in a magistrates' court sitting at or in: Barking, Bexley, Brent, Brentford, Bromley, Chester, City of Westminster, Coalville, Crewe, Croydon, Essex, Feltham, Gloucestershire, Harrow, Havering, Hendon, Knowsley, Loughborough, Macclesfield, Melton, Northwich, Oakham, Redbridge, Richmond, Runcorn, St Helens, Southwestern, Waltham Forest, Warrington, Widnes, Wimbledon; and

(b) criminal proceedings instituted by a public prosecutor within the meaning of s.29(5)(e) who is authorised to do so for the purposes of s.49 of the *Vehicle Excise and Registration Act* 1994 (authorised persons) anywhere in England and Wales, and (ii) on behalf of the Vehicle Operator Services Agency.

(c) criminal proceedings instituted by a public prosecutor within the meaning of s.29(5)(e) where they are instituted by the Secretary of State for Work and Pensions or the Secretary of State for Health anywhere in England and Wales.

It is to be noted that s.29(4) has not been brought into force as part of the pilot scheme; and it follows that the public prosecutors to whom the pilot scheme applies are not prohibited from instituting proceedings by the laying of an information to obtain the issue of a summons.

(4) Form, content and service of written charge and requisition

4–108 As to the form and content of written charges and requisitions, see Pt 7 of the *Criminal Procedure Rules* 2011 (Appendix G) and *ante*, §§ 4–47 *et seq.*, as to the form and content of the information.

As to the service of a written charge or requisition throughout the United Kingdom, see the *Criminal Law Act* 1977, s.39(1) (*post*), and Pt 4 of the *Criminal Procedure*

Rules 2011 (Appendix G). As to the service of a written charge or requisition overseas, the provisions in ss.3 and 4 of the *Crime (International Co-operation) Act* 2003 (see *post*) as to the service of "process" overseas do not apply. Whereas "process" is defined in s.51(3) of that Act as any summons or order issued by a court, including a document issued by a court or a prosecuting authority outside the United Kingdom, a written charge and/ or requisition is issued by a *prosecutor* not a *court* and does not fall within this definition (notwithstanding the effect of s.30(5) of the *Criminal Justice Act* 2003). Service of written charges and requisitions overseas is governed by ss.4A and 4B of the *Crime (International Co-operation) Act* 2003, which have not been brought into force for any purpose and do not therefore apply to the pilot scheme referred to *ante*.

Part I

F. Laying of Information to Obtain Issue of Summons or Warrant of Arrest

(1) Introduction

Until the commencement of the written charging and requisitioning procedure under ss.29 and 30 of the *Criminal Justice Act* 2003, public and private prosecutors may institute prosecutions by laying an information in order to obtain a summons or warrant requiring or compelling the person to appear before the court. Once the new provisions are brought into force, only private prosecutors will be able to use this procedure to institute proceedings. The power to obtain a warrant will remain exercisable by both public and private prosecutors when the written charging and requisitioning procedure is brought into force. **4–109**

(2) Discretion to issue summonses and warrants

Magistrates' Courts Act 1980, s.1

Issue of summons to accused or warrant for his arrest

1.—(1) On an information being laid before a justice of the peace that a person has, or is suspected of having committed an offence, the justice may issue— **4–110**

(a) a summons directed to that person requiring him to appear before a magistrates' court to answer the information, or

(b) a warrant to arrest that person and bring him before a magistrates' court.

(2) [*Repealed by the* Courts Act *2003*].

(3) No warrant shall be issued under this section unless the information is in writing.

(4) No warrant shall be issued under this section for the arrest of any person who has attained the age of 18 unless—

(a) the offence to which the warrant relates is an indictable offence or is punishable with imprisonment,or

(b) the person's address is not sufficiently established for a summons to be served on him.

(5) [*Repealed by the* Courts Act *2003*].

(6) Where the offence charged is an indictable offence, a warrant under this section may be issued at any time notwithstanding that a summons has previously been issued.

(7) A justice of the peace may issue a summons or warrant under this section upon an information being laid before him notwithstanding any enactment requiring the information to be laid before two or more justices.

(8) [*Repealed by the* Courts Act *2003*].

[This section is printed as amended by the *Criminal Justice Act* 1991, Sched. 8, the *Courts Act* 2003, s.43 and Sched. 10, and the *Criminal Justice Act* 2003, Sched. 36. As from a day to be appointed, the *Criminal Justice Act* 2003, Sched. 36, will make further amendments to subs. (3) and (6) and will insert new subs. (6A) and (7A), the effect being to make provision in connection with written charges and requisitions.]

General considerations

Before a summons or warrant is issued, the information must be laid before a magis- **4–111** trate and he must go through the judicial exercise of deciding whether a summons or warrant ought to be issued or not; if a magistrate authorises the issue of a summons or warrant without applying his mind to the information then he is guilty of dereliction of duty: *R. v. Brentford Justices, ex p. Catlin* [1975] Q.B. 455, DC.

A summons (but not a warrant) may be issued by a justices' clerk or an assistant clerk who has been specifically authorised by the justices' clerk for that purpose: see the *Justices Clerks Rules* 2005 (S.I. 2005 No. 545), rr. 2, 3, Sched., para. 2 (*post*, § 7–130).

Summonses or warrants will not lawfully issue where they are processed by administrators in the justices' clerks office; but batches of informations having similar characteristics may be assembled and placed before a single magistrate or clerk and authority can then be given for others to affix the signature of the person who has considered the informations and authorised the issue of the summonses; and the task of signing them can be vicariously performed by the use of a facsimile signature on a rubber stamp: *Gateshead JJ., ex. Tesco Stores Ltd* [1981] Q.B. 470 DC.

Exercise of the discretion

4–112 Given the discretionary nature of the power, no exhaustive catalogue of matters to which consideration should be given can be laid down, but the magistrate must satisfy himself that it is a proper case in which to issue a summons or warrant and he should at the very least ascertain (i) that the allegation is of an offence known to the law and if so that the essential ingredients of the offence are *prima facie* present, (ii) that the offence alleged is not "out of time", (iii) that the court has jurisdiction, and (iv) that the informant has the necessary authority to prosecute: *R. v. West London JJ., ex p. Klahn* [1979] 1 W.L.R. 933, DC; *R. v. Highbury Corner Magistrates' Court, ex p. Tawfick* [1994] C.O.D. 106, DC.

The magistrate or clerk may also refuse to issue a summons or warrant if to do so would be vexatious or oppressive: *ex p. Klahn* (*ibid.*); *ex p. Tawfick* (*ibid.*); *R. v. Belmarsh JJ., ex p., Watts* [1999] Cr. App. R. 188, DC; and *R. (DPP) v. Taylor* [2005] A.C.D. 23, QBD (Mitting J.). However, there is no requirement that the magistrate or clerk must satisfy himself that this would not be case before issuing the summons or warrant, the protection for the proposed defendant being the court's jurisdiction to dismiss or stay the proceedings in due course as an abuse of process; but if a magistrate or clerk was aware that an individual informant was one who had been plaguing the court with vexatious informations, he could and probably should act upon that knowledge; and equally, if he felt unease about any aspect of an information, it would be open to him to make inquiries and to discover whether there was any basis for that unease: *R. v. Bradford JJ., ex p. Sykes and Shoesmith*, 163 J.P. 224, DC.

Delay in the laying of an information, even though strictly within the time limits, is a factor which may be taken into account, and a magistrate or clerk may legitimately inquire into delay before issuing or refusing to issue a summons: *R. v. Medway JJ., ex p. Department of Health and Social Security*, 150 J.P. 401, DC. Justices may also consider the previous history of the matter, particularly if there has been a previous summons which was later withdrawn: *R. v. Grays JJ, ex p. Low* [1990] 1 Q.B. 54, DC.

The discretion to issue the summons or warrant is not unfettered and unlimited, however; the general principle is that a summons or warrant ought to issue pursuant to informations which, *prima facie*, were properly laid, unless there were compelling reasons not to do so, most obviously if an abuse of process or impropriety was involved; it was not the function of the magistrates' court at that stage to decide how the matter could thereafter be most fairly tried or dealt with (by choosing which offences should proceed); and that was especially so as it simply could not be known at that stage what course the proceedings would take or what stance the defendant in question would take: *R. (Mayor and Burgesses of London Borough of Newham) v. Stratford Magistrates' Court*, 168 J.P. 658, QBD (Davis J.).

There is no invariable requirement that a private prosecutor applying for a summons or warrant must first have taken the matter to the police, although in a particular case it may be a relevant circumstance; thus a magistrate's decision to refuse to issue process for that reason alone without considering the whole of the relevant circumstances and without informing himself of all relevant facts would be a flawed exercise of the discretion: *Barry v. Birmingham Magistrates' Court* [2010] 1 Cr.App.R. 13, DC.

Hearing the proposed defendant

In the overwhelming majority of cases the magistrate will not need to consider material beyond that provided by the informant; and so generally speaking, the proposed defendant has no right to be heard until the summons has been issued, although the magistrate has a residual discretion to hear him if necessary for the purpose of reaching the decision: *R. v. West London JJ., ex p. Klahn* [1979] 1 W.L.R. 933, DC. There will be rare or exceptional cases where a hearing should be convened before the summons is issued, however as where the "alarm bells" were ringing that the allegations were vexatious or oppressive (see *R. (Swindon B.C.) v. Swindon JJ.*, unreported, July 30, 2004, DC ([2004] EWHC 2239(Admin))). See also r. 7.4 of the *Criminal Procedure Rules* 2011 (Appendix G). **4–113**

Warrant or summons

A warrant should not be issued initially for a minor offence: s.1(4). A warrant will not issue where a summons would be equally effectual, except in cases of a very serious nature: *O'Brien v. Brabner*, 49 J.P.N. 227. **4–114**

Miscellaneous considerations

It may be doubtful whether it is proper for justices to decide, as a matter of discretion, to entertain a second application on exactly the same material as has been considered by other justices of the same bench: *R. v. Worthing Justices, ex p. Norvell* [1981] 1 W.L.R. 413, D.C. **4–115**

(3) Effect of defective information, summons or warrant

Magistrates' Courts Act 1980, s.123

Defect in process

123.—(1) No objection shall be allowed to any information or complaint, or to any summons or warrant to procure the presence of the defendant, for any defect in it in substance or in form, or for any variance between it and the evidence adduced on behalf of the prosecutor or complainant at the hearing of the information or complaint. **4–116**

(2) If it appears to a magistrates' court that any variance between a summons or warrant and the evidence adduced on behalf of the prosecutor or complainant is such that the defendant has been misled by the variance, the court shall, on the application of the defendant, adjourn the hearing.

An irregularity or illegality in the mode of bringing a defendant before the court, if not objected to at the hearing, does not invalidate the conviction: *Gray v. Customs Commissioners*, 48 J.P. 343, DC. **4–117**

Although no objection is allowed to any information or complaint, or to any summons or warrant, for any defect in its substance or form, if the magistrate considers that any variance between a summons or warrant and the evidence adduced on behalf of the prosecutor or complainant is such that the defendant has been misled by that variance, the court must on the application of the defendant, adjourn the hearing. The effect of s.123(2) is that a summons can be amended: *Meek v. Powell* [1952] 1 K.B. 164, DC.

The amendment of an information by a magistrates' court is subject to judicial review and is liable to be quashed: *R. v. Greater Manchester JJ, ex p. Aldi GmbH & Co KG*, 159 J.P. 717, DC; *Marco (Croydon) Ltd v. Metropolitan Police* [1984] R.T.R. 24, DC.

A summons may be amended even if by the time the case comes before the court and the application to amend is made, the six months' time limit for laying an information in s.127 of the *Magistrates' Courts Act* 1980 has expired: *R. v. Newcastle JJ, ex p. Bryce* [1976] R.T.R. 325, DC; *R. v. Sandwell J, ex p. West Midlands Passenger Transport Board* [1979] Crim.L.R. 56, DC.

4–118 The Divisional Court in *R. v. Scunthorpe JJ, ex p. McPhee*, 162 J.P. 635, DC, enunciated the principles. The defendant was charged with robbery and it was held that the CPS could amend the charges to common assault and theft despite the fact that the six-month time limit in respect of the assault charge had expired. The Court held that the proper test was whether the new offences arose from the same or substantially the same facts and if they did, then the charges could be amended, having regard to the interests of justice and in particular the defendant's interest and the purpose of the time limit. See also *R. v. Blackburn JJ, ex p. Holmes*, 164 J.P. 163, DC; *R. v. Thames Magistrates' Court, ex p. Stevens*, 164 J.P. 233, DC; *R. (DPP) v. Everest*, 169 J.P. 345, QBD; and *cf. Sainsbury's Supermarkets Ltd and J. Sainsbury plc v. Plymouth Magistrates' Court*, 170 J.P. 690, DC.

The power of the magistrates to allow an application to amend and information was considered in *R. (James) v. DPP*, 168 J.P. 596, QBD. The defendant was charged with supplying a Class B drug contrary to s.4(1) of the *Misuse of Drugs Act* 1971. At the close of the defence case, a submission was made that the evidence did not make out the offence of supplying but only amounted to an attempt to supply. The prosecution then made application under s.123(1) to amend the information to charge the offence of attempting to supply a drug contrary to the *Criminal Attempts Act* 1981. The defendant objected to any amendment on the grounds that it was a major change with a different offence charged under a different statute. The magistrates allowed the amendment. On appeal by the defendant, the court held that the magistrates were acting within their powers under s.123 to amend the information. The wording of the section was very wide and there is no authority indicating the existence of any restriction on an amendment that resulted in a different offence under a different act of parliament being substituted. The main issue was to consider whether any injustice or prejudice would be caused to the defendant by such an amendment. In this case the defendant had suffered no prejudice. This case asserts the wide scope of s.123 and indicates that in the magistrates' court as in the Crown Court there is an extensive discretion to amend an information. It would appear to allow for the prosecution to see what offence is made out in the evidence and then apply to amend the charge to fit it with the only proviso being that the defendant must not be prejudiced thereby and would be entitled to an adjournment to address the changes if that is required in the interests of justice.

The power to amend and adjourn under s.123(2) is available until the case is ended and the magistrates are "*functus officio*", so it is possible for a case to be adjourned after conviction and the charge amended before sentence: see *Allan v. Wiseman* [1975] Crim.L.R. 37, DC, where the defendant's name was amended on the charge after conviction but before the case was ended.

(4) Service of summons out of time after failure to prove service by post

Magistrates' Courts Act 1980, s.47

Service of summons out of time after failure to prove service by post

4–119 **47.** Where any enactment requires, expressly or by implication, that a summons in respect of an offence shall be issued or served within a specified period after the commission of the offence, and service of the summons may under rules of court be effected by post, then, if under the rules service of the summons is not treated as proved, but it is shown that a letter containing the summons was posted at such time as to enable it to be delivered in the ordinary course of post within that period, a second summons may be issued on the same information; and the enactment shall have effect, in relation to that summons, as if the specified period were a period running from the return day of the original summons.

[This section is printed as amended by the *Courts Act* 2003, s.109(1), Sched. 8, para. 207].

(5) Validity of summons or warrant on death or cessation of office of justice of the peace

Magistrates' Courts Act 1980, s.124

Process valid notwithstanding death, etc., of justice

124. A warrant or summons issued by a justice of the peace shall not cease to have effect by reason of his death or his ceasing to be a justice. **4–120**

(6) Service of summons, written charge or requisition throughout the UK

(a) *General*

Criminal Law Act 1977, s.39(1)

Service of summonses and citation throughout United Kingdom

39.—(1) The following documents, namely— **4–121**

(a) a summons requiring a person charged with an offence to appear before a court in England or Wales,

(b) a written charge (within the meaning of section 29 of the *Criminal Justice Act* 2003) charging a person with an offence,

(c) a requisition (within the meaning of that section) requiring a person charged with an offence to appear before a court in England or Wales, and

(d) any other document which, by virtue of any enactment, may or must be served on a person with, or at the same time as, a document mentioned in paragraph (a), (b) or (c) above, may, in such manner as may be prescribed by rules of court, be served on him in Scotland or Northern Ireland.

[This section is printed as amended by the *Criminal Justice Act* 2003, s.331 and Sched. 36, para. 6].

(b) *Criminal Procedure Rules*

See *Criminal Procedure Rules* 2011, Pt 4, in Appendix G–14 *et seq.* A summons or requisition may only be served on an individual by: (a) handing it to him in person; or (b) leaving it at, or sending it to by first class post, an address (i) where it is reasonably believed that the individual will receive it, or (ii) which is the office of the individual's legal representative. Modified versions of the same requirements apply to the service of summonses or requisitions on corporations. **4–122**

If a person voluntarily attends the court, that attendance cures any want of process or any irregularity in service: *Hughes* (1879) L.R. 4 Q.B.D. 614, CCR. However where a person attends before a magistrate to draw attention to the irregularity and then withdraws from the case such conduct does not amount to an appearance so as to waive irregularity in service: *Pearks, Gunston & Tee Ltd v. Richardson* [1902] 1 K.B. 91, DC. Where the person appears before the magistrates' court he should be informed of the irregularity or omission and of the right to object because without that knowledge there can be no waiver: *R. v. Essex Justices, ex p. Perkins* [1927] 2 K.B. 475, DC. **4–123**

(7) Service of summons written charge or requisition overseas

Crime (International Co-operation) Act 2003, ss.3, 4, [4A, 4B] and 51(3)

General requirements for service of process

3.—(1) This section applies to any process issued or made for the purposes of criminal proceedings by a court in England and Wales or Northern Ireland. **4–124**

(2) The process may be issued or made in spite of the fact that the person on whom it is to be served is outside the United Kingdom.

(3) Where the process is to be served outside the United Kingdom and the person at whose request it is issued or made believes that the person on whom it is to be served does not understand English, he must—

(a) inform the court of that fact, and

(b) provide the court with a copy of the process, or of so much of it as is material, translated into an appropriate language.

(4) Process served outside the United Kingdom requiring a person to appear as a party or attend as a witness—

(a) must not include notice of a penalty,

(b) must be accompanied by a notice giving any information required to be given by rules of court.

(5) If process requiring a person to appear as a party or attend as a witness is served outside the United Kingdom, no obligation to comply with the process under the law of the part of the United Kingdom in which the process is issued or made is imposed by virtue of the service.

(6) Accordingly, failure to comply with the process does not constitute contempt of court and is not a ground for issuing a warrant to secure the attendance of the person in question.

(7) But the process may subsequently be served on the person in question in the United Kingdom (with the usual consequences for non-compliance).

Service of process otherwise than by post

4–125 **4.**—(1) Process to which section 3 applies may, instead of being served by post, be served on a person outside the United Kingdom in accordance with arrangements made by the Secretary of State.

(2) But where the person is in a participating country, the process may be served in accordance with those arrangements only if one of the following conditions is met.

(3) The conditions are—

(a) that the correct address of the person is unknown,

(b) that it has not been possible to serve the process by post,

(c) that there are good reasons for thinking that service by post will not be effective or is inappropriate.

[General requirements for service of written charge or requisition

4–126 **4A.**—(1) This section applies to the following documents issued for the purposes of criminal proceedings in England and Wales by a prosecutor—

(a) a written charge (within the meaning of section 29 of the *Criminal Justice Act* 2003),

(b) a requisition (within the meaning of that section).

(2) The written charge or requisition may be issued in spite of the fact that the person on whom it is to be served is outside the United Kingdom.

(3) Where the written charge or requisition is to be served outside the United Kingdom and the prosecutor believes that the person on whom it is to be served does not understand English, the written charge or requisition must be accompanied by a translation of it in an appropriate language.

(4) A written charge or requisition served outside the United Kingdom must be accompanied by a notice giving any information required to be given by rules of court.

(5) If a requisition is served outside the United Kingdom, no obligation under the law of England and Wales to comply with the requisition is imposed by virtue of the service.

(6) Accordingly, failure to comply with the requisition is not a ground for issuing a warrant to secure the attendance of the person in question.

(7) But the requisition may subsequently be served on the person in question in the United Kingdom (with the usual consequences for non-compliance).

Service of written charge or requisition otherwise than by post

4–127 **4B.**—(1) A written charge or requisition to which section 4A applies may, instead of being served by post, be served on a person outside the United Kingdom in accordance with arrangements made by the Secretary of State.

(2) But where the person is in a participating country, the written charge or requisition may be served in accordance with those arrangements only if one of the following conditions is met.

(3) The conditions are—

(a) that the correct address of the person is unknown,

(b) that it has not been possible to serve the written charge or requisition by post,

(c) that there are good reasons for thinking that service by post will not be effective or is inappropriate.]

[As from a day to be appointed, ss.4A and 4B are inserted by the *Criminal Justice Act* 2003, s.331 and Sched. 36, para. 36. No such day has been appointed.]

General interpretation

51.—(3) In this Part, "process", in relation to England and Wales and Northern Ireland, means any summons or order issued or made by a court and includes— **4–128**

(a) any other document issued or made by a court for service on parties or witnesses,

(b) any document issued by a prosecuting authority outside the United Kingdom for the purposes of criminal proceedings.

See *Criminal Procedure Rules* 2011, r. 32.1 (Appendix G), for the form and content of the notice which, under s.3(4)(b), must accompany process served outside the United Kingdom requiring a person to appear as a party or attend as a witness. In particular, the notice must state that the person required by the process to appear as a party or attend as a witness can obtain information about his rights in connection therewith from the prosecuting authority which requested the process to be served (or in the case of a private prosecution, the court by which the process is served); and give particulars about that authority: r. 32.1(2), (3). The particulars which must be given are the name and contact details of the prosecuting authority (or court) and the name and contact details of a person who can provide information about the rights of the person concerned: r. 32.1(4). The justices' clerk must send, together with any process served outside the United Kingdom, any translation which is provided under s.3(3)(b) of the Act, any translation of the information required to be given by this rule which is provided to him: r. 32.1(5). **4–129**

(8) Failure to answer summons or requisition

Where a person summonsed to appear before a magistrates' court fails to answer a the summons or requisition, he is not guilty of failing to surrender to bail (*Bail Act* 1976, s.6(1) and (2)), for the obvious reason that he was not on bail; but a person who has knowledge of the summons and had intended to fail to answer it may be guilty of contempt of court: see *R. v. Noble, The Times*, July 21, 2008, CA. The remedy (and means of compelling the person's attendance before the court) upon failure to answer a summons (whether he knew of it or not) is to issue a warrant of arrest (backed for bail or not). **4–130**

Magistrates' Courts Act 1980, s.13

Non-appearance of accused: issue of warrant

13.—(1) Subject to the provisions of this section, where the court, instead of proceeding in the absence of the accused, adjourns or further adjourns the trial, the court may, issue a warrant for his arrest. **4–131**

(2) Where a summons has been issued, the court shall not issue a warrant under this section unless the condition in subsection (2A) below or that in subsection (2B) below is fulfilled.

(2A) The condition in this subsection is that it is proved to the satisfaction of the court, on oath or in such other manner as may be prescribed, that the summons was served on the accused within what appears to the court to be a reasonable time before the trial or adjourned trial.

(2B) The condition in this subsection is that—

(a) the adjournment now being made is a second or subsequent adjournment of the trial.

(b) the accused was present on the last (or only) occasion when the trial was adjourned, and

(c) on that occasion the court determined the time for the hearing at which the adjournment is now being made.

(3) A warrant for the arrest of any person who has attained the age of 18 shall not be issued under this section unless—

(a) the offence to which the warrant relates is punishable with imprisonment, or

(b) the court, having convicted the accused, proposes to impose a disqualification on him.

(3A) A warrant for the arrest of any person who has not attained the age of 18 shall not be issued under this section unless—

(a) the offence to which the warrant relates is punishable in the case of a person who has attained the age of 18, with imprisonment, or

(b) the court, having convicted the accused, proposes to impose a disqualification on him.

(4) This section shall not apply to an adjournment on the occasion of the accused's conviction in his absence under subsection (5) of section 12 above or to an adjournment required by subsection (9) of that section.

[This section is printed as amended by the *Criminal Procedure and Investigations Act* 1996, s.48, the *Magistrates' Courts (Procedure) Act* 1998, s.3, and the *Criminal Justice Act* 2003, s.31 and Sched. 37 and the *Criminal Justice and Immigration Act* 2008, s.54 and Sched. 28.]

4–132 The requirement for the information to be substantiated on oath is removed. The new requirement is substituted that the offence is punishable with imprisonment for a person who has attained the age of 18.

This section gives power for the court to issue a warrant during the proceedings if the defendant fails to attend at court. It is most commonly used in road traffic matters. In such cases the court will first ensure that the summons has been properly served and that the defendant has had reasonable time to attend at court. If so satisfied the court may then proceed with the case in the absence of the defendant. If the case is proved the court may wish to disqualify the defendant from driving. If the court does not wish to disqualify and sentence him in absence the case may be adjourned and a notice sent to the defendant requiring him to attend. If he fails to attend after the adjournment notice is sent a warrant may be issued under this section. A warrant may also issue after a written plea of guilty has been received and the court wishes to impose a disqualification in the defendant's presence.

The court will need to consider whether a s.13 warrant should be backed for bail and will take into account the defendants attendance record and the gravity of the offence: *Magistrates' Courts Act* 1980, s.117.

(9) Force and execution of warrant

4–133 A warrant of arrest remains in force until it is executed or withdrawn or it ceases to have effect, and it may be executed throughout England and Wales, Scotland, Northern Ireland, the Isle of Mann and the Channel Islands.

Magistrates' Courts Act 1980, s.125(1)–(2)

Warrants

4–134 **125.**—(1) A warrant of arrest issued by a justice of the peace shall remain in force until it is executed or withdrawn or it ceases to have effect in accordance with rules of court.

(2) A warrant of arrest, warrant of commitment, warrant of detention, warrant of distress [warrant of control] or search warrant issued by a justice of the peace may be executed anywhere in England and Wales by any person to whom it is directed or by any constable acting within his police area.

This subsection does not apply to a warrant of commitment or a warrant of distress issued under Part VI of the General Rate Act *1967.*

[This section is printed as amended by the *Police and Criminal Evidence Act* 1984, s.33, the *Criminal Justice Act* 1988, s.65(1), the *Access to Justice Act* 1999, ss.95(1), 97(4), 106, Sched. 15, and the *Courts Act* 2003, s.109(1) and Sched. 8. As from a day or days to be appointed, the words in square brackets in subs (2) are to be replaced by those which follow in square brackets; and those which follow subs (2) are to be repealed: *Tribunals, Courts and Enforcement Act* 2007, s.62(3) and Sched. 13.]

Part I

Magistrates' Courts Act 1980, s.126

Execution of certain warrants outside England and Wales

126. Sections 13(1) and (2) of the *Indictable Offences Act* 1848 (which relate, among other things, to the execution in Scotland, Northern Ireland, the Isle of Man and the Channel Islands of warrants of arrest for the offences referred to in those sections) shall, so far as applicable, apply to— **4–135**

(a) warrants of arrest issued under section 1 above for offences other than indictable offences;
(b) warrants of arrest issued under section 13 above;
(c) warrants of arrest issued under section 97 above other than warrants issued in bastardy proceedings to arrest a witness;
(cc) warrants of arrest issued under section 97A above;
(d) warrants of commitment issued under this Act;
(e) warrants of arrest issued under paragraph 4 of Schedule 3 to the *Crime and Disorder Act* 1998; and
(f) warrants of arrest issued under paragraph 3(2) of Schedule 1 to the *Powers of Criminal Courts (Sentencing) Act* 2000 (offender referred to court by youth offender panel).

[This section is printed as amended by the *Crime and Disorder Act* 1998, ss.119 and 120 and Sched. 8, the *Youth Justice and Criminal Evidence Act* 1999, s.67 and Scheds 4 and 6, the *Powers of Criminal Courts (Sentencing) Act* 2000, s.165 and Sched. 9, and the *Courts Act* 2003, s.109(1) and Sched. 8.]

Indictable Offences Act 1848, s.13

13. If any person against whom a warrant shall be issued in England or Wales, by any justice of the peace, or by any judge of her Majesty's Court of Queen's Bench, or the Crown Court for any indictable offence, shall escape, go into, reside, or be, or be supposed or suspected to be, in any of the Isles of Man, Guernsey, Jersey, Alderney, or Sark, it shall be lawful for any officer within the district into which such accused person shall escape or go, or where he shall reside or be, or be supposed or suspected to be, who shall have jurisdiction to issue any warrant or process in the nature of a warrant for the apprehension of offenders within such district, to indorse (K.) such warrant in the manner herein-before mentioned, or to the like effect; or if any person against whom any warrant, or process in the nature of a warrant, shall be issued in any of the isles aforesaid shall escape, go into, reside, or be, or be supposed or suspected to be, in England or Wales, it shall be lawful for any justice of the peace in England and Wales to indorse (K.) such warrant or process in manner herein-before mentioned; and every such warrant or process so indorsed shall be a sufficient authority to the person or persons bringing the same, and to all persons to whom the same respectively was originally directed, and also to all constables and peace officers in the county, district, or jurisdiction within which such warrant or process shall be so indorsed, to execute the same within the county, district, or place where the justice or officer indorsing the same is acting or has jurisdiction, and to convey such offender, when apprehended, into the county or district wherein the justice or person who issued such warrant or process is acting or has jurisdiction, and carry him before such justice or person, or before some other justice or person within the same county or district who shall have jurisdiction to commit such offender to prison for trial, and such justice or person may thereupon proceed in such and the same manner as if the said offender had been apprehended in England or Wales or (as the case may be) within his jurisdiction. **4–136**

[This section is printed as amended by the *Statute Law Revision Act* 1891, the the-*Courts Act* 1971, s.56 and Sched. 8, and the *Courts Act* 2003, s.109 and Sched. 8.]

Criminal Justice and Public Order Act 1994, s.136

Execution of warrants

4–137 **136.**—(1) A warrant issued in England, Wales or Northern Ireland for the arrest of a person charged with an offence may (without any endorsement) be executed in Scotland by any constable of any police force of the country of issue or of the country of execution, or by a constable appointed under section 53 of the *British Transport Commission Act* 1949, as well as by any other persons within the directions in the warrant.

(2) A warrant issued in—

(a) Scotland; or

(b) Northern Ireland,

for the arrest of a person charged with an offence may (without any endorsement) be executed in England or Wales by any constable of any police force of the country of issue or of the country of execution, or by a constable appointed under section 53 of the *British Transport Commission Act* 1949, as well as by any other persons within the directions in the warrant.

(3) A warrant issued in—

(a) England or Wales; or

(b) Scotland,

for the arrest of a person charged with an offence may (without any endorsement) be executed in Northern Ireland by any constable of any police force of the country of issue or of the country of execution as well as by any other persons within the directions in the warrant.

(4) A person arrested in pursuance of a warrant shall be taken, as soon as reasonably practicable, to any place to which he is committed by, or may be conveyed under, the warrant.

(5) A constable executing a warrant—

(a) under subsection (1), (2)(b) or (3)(a) of this section may use reasonable force and shall have the powers of search conferred by section 139;

(b) under subsection (2)(a) or (3)(b) of this section shall have the same powers and duties, and the person arrested the same rights, as they would have had if execution had been in Scotland by a constable of a police force in Scotland.

(6) Any other person within the directions in a warrant executing that warrant under this section shall have the same powers and duties, and the person arrested the same rights, as they would have had if execution had been in the country of issue by the person within those directions.

(7) This section applies as respects—

(a) a warrant of commitment and a warrant to arrest a witness issued by a judicial authority in England, Wales or Northern Ireland as it applies to a warrant for arrest; and

(b) a warrant for committal, a warrant to imprison (or to apprehend and imprison) and a warrant to arrest a witness issued by a judicial authority in Scotland as it applies to a warrant for arrest.

(7A) This section applies as respects a warrant issued under paragraph 3(2) of Schedule 1 to the *Powers of Criminal Courts (Sentencing) Act* 2000 (warrant for arrest of offender referred back to court by youth offender panel) as it applies to a warrant issued in England or Wales for the arrest of a person charged with an offence,

(8) In this section "judicial authority" means any justice of the peace or the judge of any court exercising jurisdiction in criminal proceedings; and any reference to a part of the United Kingdom in which a warrant may be executed includes a reference to the adjacent sea and other waters within the seaward limits of the territorial sea.

(9) Powers under this section and sections 137 to 139 may be exercised by an officer of Revenue and Customs in accordance with section 87 of the *Finance Act* 2007.

[This section is printed as amended by the *Youth Justice and Criminal Evidence Act* 1999, s.67 and Sched. 4, the *Powers of Criminal Courts (Sentencing) Act* 2000, s.165 and Sched. 9, the *Anti-terrorism, Crime and Security Act* 2001, s.101 and Sched. 7, and the *Finance Act* 2007, s.87.]

(10) Statutory declarations

4–138 The court may not always issue a warrant for the arrest of a defendant who fails to attend court. There is a discretion for the court to proceed with the case in the absence of the defendant under s.11 of the *Magistrates' Courts Act* 1980. The Act provides a safeguard for the absent defendant by allowing for proceedings commenced by way of summons to be invalidated when the defendant makes and serves a statutory declaration to the effect that he did not attend court because he was unaware of the court hearing date.

Magistrates' Courts Act 1980, s.14

Proceedings invalid where accused did not know of them

14.—(1) Where a summons has been issued under section 1 above and a magistrates' court has begun to try the information to which the summons relates, then, if— **4–139**

(a) the accused, at any time during or after the trial, makes a statutory declaration that he did not know of the summons or the proceedings until a date specified in the declaration, being a date after the court has begun to try the information; and

(b) within 21 days of that date the declaration is served on the designated officer for the court,

without prejudice to the validity of the information, the summons and all subsequent proceedings shall be void.

(2) For the purposes of subsection (1) above a statutory declaration shall be deemed to be duly served on the designated officer if it is delivered to him, or left at his office, or is sent in a registered letter or by the recorded delivery service addressed to him at his office.

(3) If on the application of the accused it appears to a magistrates' court (which for this purpose may be composed of a single justice) that it was not reasonable to expect the accused to serve such a statutory declaration as is mentioned in subsection (1) above within the period allowed by that subsection, the court may accept service of such a declaration by the accused after that period has expired; and a statutory declaration accepted under this subsection shall be deemed to have been served as required by that subsection.

(4) Where any proceedings have become void by virtue of subsection (1) above, the information shall not be tried again by any of the same justices.

[This section is printed as amended by the *Courts Act* 2003, Sched. 8.]

In proceedings in the magistrates' court, particularly those commenced by way of summons, the prosecution may present the case in the absence of the defendant if the court is satisfied that the summons has been properly served. **4–140**

Many cases are dealt with in this way, *e.g.* road traffic cases, but caution must be exercised and the seriousness of the offence will be taken into account. The prosecution evidence is heard, which usually consists of statements from prosecution witnesses which have been served under s.9 of the *Criminal Justice Act* 1967 and the court will go on to acquit or convict the defendant. If convicted, an adjournment notice may be sent to the defendant requiring his presence for sentencing and if he fails to answer to the notice a warrant may be issued for his arrest. The court may also proceed to sentence in absence.

The first a defendant may know about the proceedings is when an adjournment notice or notice of fine is received or a warrant is executed. It is then open to the defendant to make a statutory declaration under this section that he knew nothing of the proceedings and if that declaration is served on the court then the proceedings are invalidated. The additional requirement is that the declaration should be served on the court within 21 days of the date when the proceedings first came to the notice of the defendant but the court does have a discretion to accept service outside of the 21-day limit if it is not reasonable to expect the defendant to serve the declaration within that time.

Defendants will often make such declarations at court but it is possible for them to be made before a solicitor, etc. It is not necessary for the declaration to be made before the court where the proceedings took place but this will often be the case.

The effect of accepting service of the declaration is that the summons and all proceedings based on it will be void but the information is not affected: *Singh v. DPP* [1999] R.T.R. 424, DC. The Court will expunge the conviction and penalty from the records. **4–141**

The Prosecution has the right to re-institute proceedings using the original information and if present in court at the time when the statutory declaration is made and served, application may be made by the prosecution to re-issue the summons immediately and serve it personally on the defendant. Proceedings will then start again but must be tried before a fresh bench.

A defendant who knowingly and wilfully makes a false statement relating to his knowledge of the proceedings under this section may be prosecuted for perjury under s.5 of the *Perjury Act* 1911 and the applicant will be given a warning to this effect when the declaration is made.

V. ALTERNATIVES TO PROSECUTION (DIVERSION)

A. INTRODUCTION

4–142 Both the full code test and the threshold test in the Code for Crown Prosecutors require consideration to be given to (a) the sufficiency of evidence in the case and (b) whether prosecution is in the public interest. The public interest does not automatically require a prosecution (para. 4.10); but a prosecution will usually take place unless there are public interest factors tending against prosecution which clearly outweigh those in favour, or it appears more appropriate in the circumstances of the case to "divert the person from prosecution" (para. 4.12). Accordingly, paras 7.1 to 7.8 of the code provide that when making the decision to prosecute consideration should be given to the alternatives to prosecution (including suitable rehabilitative, reparative and restorative justice processes): see Appendix E–10 *et seq*.

It is wholly artificial to distinguish between the decision not to prosecute and the decision to divert from prosecution: see *R. (Guest) v. DPP*, *post*, § 4–123.

See *R. (R.) v. Durham Constabulary and another* [2005] 1 W.L.R. 1184, HL, as authority for a proposition that measures diverting a person from prosecution do not ordinarily amount to a "criminal charge" for the purposes of Art. 6 of the European Convention on Human Rights where they only culminate in measures of a preventative, curative, rehabilitative or welfare-promoting kind and do not expose the subject of the charge to the possibility of punishment, whether in the event punishment is imposed or not. Whether penalty notices or conditional cautions with "financial penalty" conditions constitute a "criminal charge" remains to be decided.

As to the application of the principles of *autrefois convict* where a person has been diverted from prosecution, see *DPP v. Alexander*, 174 J.P. 519, DC (*autrefois convict* has no application in relation to a caution).

B. CHILDREN AND YOUNG PERSONS

(1) General

4–143 Section 44 of the *Children and Young Persons Act* 1933 (*post*, § 25–3) requires courts to have regard to the welfare of a child or young person; and s.37 of the *Crime And Disorder Act* 1998 (*post*, § 25–2) requires all persons and bodies carrying out functions in relation to the youth justice system to have regard to the principle aim of the system, which is the prevention of offending by children and young persons. To that end paras 8.8 and 8.9 of the code require crown prosecutors to consider the interests of a youth when deciding whether prosecution is in the public interest.

(2) Reprimands and warning

4–144 Sections 65 and 66 of the *Crime and Disorder Act* 1998 set out a statutory diversion scheme of reprimanding and warning children and young persons. As to this, see *post*, §§ 25–12 *et seq*.

Reprimanding or warning a youth (including the decision to do so) under s.65 of the

1998 does not involve the determination of a "criminal charge" in respect of which the right to a fair trial under Art. 6 of the European Convention on Human Rights would otherwise be engaged: *R. (R.) v. Durham Constabulary and another* [2005] 1 W.L.R. 1184, HL. The purpose of ss.65 and 66 is not a system of criminal trial and punishment administered by policemen but is aimed to keep first-time young offenders out of court while seeking to prevent future offending in their own interests and that of society: *R. (R.) v. Durham Constabulary and another, ibid., R. (on the application of F.) v. Crown Prosecution Service and Chief Constable of Merseyside Police*, 168 J.P. 93, DC.

In *R. (A.) v. South Yorkshire Police and CPS*, 171 J.P. 465, DC, it was held that the High Court would only interfere (and even then only on a discretionary basis) with a decision to prosecute a juvenile instead of giving a reprimand or warning under the *Crime and Disorder Act* 1998, s.65, if it was clearly established that the decision had come about as a result of an irrational departure from the guidance issued under s.65 of the 1998 Act. A crown prosecutor could legitimately decide that the combination of the seriousness of an offence and the public interest warranted prosecution, despite the fact that the particular circumstances of the offence would normally, in accordance with the guidance issued under s.65, be such as to justify only a final warning; and an expression of willingness on the part of a crown prosecutor to recommend that a final warning should be administered will not give rise to a legitimate expectation that a final warning would in fact be administered: *D. and B. v. Commissioner of Police for the Metropolis, Crown Prosecution Service, Croydon JJ.* [2008] A.C.D. 47, DC.

Although the code for crown prosecutors requires consideration to be given to the interests of a child or young person when deciding whether it was in the public interest to prosecute, there was no requirement that the crown prosecutor should obtain risk assessments from the youth offending services or that he should contact the potential defendant's school: *R. (A.) v. South Yorkshire Police and CPS, ibid.*

(3) Youth conditional cautions

The *Criminal Justice and Immigration Act* 2008, s.48 and Sched. 9, insert new ss.66A to 66H in the *Crime and Disorder Act* 1998 setting out a scheme of "youth conditional cautions". **4–145**

C. MENTALLY DISORDERED PERSONS

Paragraph 4.17(g) of the code lists amongst the public interest factors which militate against prosecution the fact that the defendant is or was at the time of the offence "suffering from significant mental or physical ill health". In such cases crown prosecutors are required to balance the desirability of diverting the defendant from prosecution against the need to safeguard the general public: *ibid*. Diversion of mentally disordered persons generally consists of cautioning and/ or admission to hospital or support in the community. See Home Office Circulars 66/90 (Provision for Mentally Disordered Offenders) and 12/95 (Mentally Disordered Offenders Inter-Agency Working): § 28–4, *post*. **4–146**

D. CAUTIONING OF ADULTS

(1) General

Cautions are alternatives to prosecution available in respect of adult offenders. Cautions are generally administered by police officers and are available in two forms: the simple caution and the conditional caution. **4–147**

(2) Simple cautions

The principles governing simple cautions are set out in Home Office Circular 16/2008. Simple cautions are non-statutory disposals for adult offenders which may be used **4–148** for disposing of offences when specified public interest and eligibility criteria are met: they should be used for low-level offending and only in exceptional circumstances to deal with more serious offences (paras 2, 3). With the introduction of the statutory charging scheme, decisions to issue simple cautions must be made in accordance with the DPP's Guidance on Charging: the police retain the authority to issue a simple caution in all cases other than cases involving indictable-only offences (which must be referred to the CPS for a decision and which may otherwise be deemed not to have been properly administered).

Home Office Circular 16/2008, paras 9 to 17

Criteria for a Simple Caution

4–149 **9.** When deciding if a simple caution is appropriate, a police officer must answer the following questions:

— Has the suspect made a clear and reliable admission of the offence either verbally or in writing? (See also paragraph 16 for what constitutes a clear and reliable admission and paragraphs 18 and 19 for recording an admission.)

— Is there a realistic prospect of conviction if the offender were to be prosecuted in line with the Code for Crown Prosecutors, "The Full Code Test"? (A clear, reliable admission of the offence, corroborated by some other material and significant evidential fact will be sufficient evidence to provide a realistic prospect of conviction.)

— Is it in the public interest to use a simple caution as the means of disposal? Officers should take into account the public interest factors set out in the Code for Crown Prosecutors, "The Full Code Test", in particular the seriousness of the offence.

— Is the suspect 18 years of age or older at the time the caution is to be administered? Where a suspect is under 18, a reprimand or warning would be the equivalent disposal, as per the *Crime and Disorder Act* 1998. Guidance may be found in Final Warning Scheme: Guidance for Police and Youth Offending Teams.

— Is a simple caution appropriate to the offence and the offender? (With reference to ACPO's Gravity Factors Matrix and the offender's criminal history.)

10. If all of the above requirements are met, the offence may be suitable for disposal by simple caution.

11. If the offence is indictable-only, the case must be referred to the CPS for a decision. In exceptional circumstances, a simple caution may still be an appropriate disposal. But generally the more serious the offence, the more likely a prosecution will be required.

12. There are a range of out-of-court disposals available to the police (and CPS). See Out-of-court disposals for adults - a guide to alternatives to prosecution for further information. A decision to administer a simple caution needs to be taken in the context of all possible out-of-court disposals, particularly the conditional caution.

Aggravating or mitigating factors

13. There may be aggravating or mitigating factors in the course of an offence which will either increase or decrease its seriousness. The ACPO Gravity Factors Matrix assists officers in deciding whether or not a simple caution remains the most appropriate disposal with these factors in mind.

14. Officers should use it to determine the seriousness of the offence. This is initially determined on a scale between 1 and 4, with 1 being the least serious.

15. If there are any aggravating or mitigating factors, then the seriousness of the case will either increase or decrease by one level. The seriousness of an offence may only increase or decrease by one level, regardless of the number of aggravating/mitigating factors. If there is one of each (aggravating and mitigating), they simply cancel each other out.

Circumstances where a simple caution cannot be considered

16. A simple caution will not be appropriate:

— Where a person has not made a clear and reliable admission of the offence or has otherwise raised a defence. This includes occasions where intent is denied, there are doubts about their mental health or intellectual capacity, or where a statutory defence is offered. An admission which may be qualified - where, for example, an offender commits an offence while under the influence of alcohol and cannot remember the full circumstances, but evidence of involvement is agreed either through supporting witness evidence or other evidence (such as CCTV) - may be considered a full and frank admission if all evidence is accepted by the offender.

— If someone refuses to accept it.

17. In addition, a simple caution cannot be viewed as an appropriate method of disposing of offences committed by serving prisoners or those subject to prison recall. It is also not appropriate to use a simple caution when the offender was on court bail or subject to a court order at the time of the commission of the offence. In general, it would be more appropriate to prosecute in these cases (or for such offences to be taken into consideration in relation to any other ongoing prosecution of that offender—see CPS guidance on Offences to be taken into consideration (TICs)).

— Is there sufficient evidence of the suspect's guilt to meet the threshold test (as outlined in the Director's Guidance)?

— Is the offence indictable only (and the available evidence meets the threshold test)? If the answer is 'yes', this disposal option must be referred to a crown prosecutor.

— Has the suspect made a clear and reliable admission of the offence (either verbally or in writing)? An admission of the offence, corroborated by some other material and significant evidential fact will be sufficient evidence to provide a realistic prospect of conviction. This corroboration could be obtained from information in the crime report or obtained during the course of the investigation. A simple caution will not be appropriate where a person has not made a clear and reliable admission of the offence (for example if intent is denied or there are doubts about their mental health or intellectual capacity, or where a statutory defence is offered).

— Is it in the public interest to use a simple caution as the appropriate means of disposal? Officers should take into account the public interest principles set out in the Code for Crown Prosecutors.

— Is the suspect 18 years or over? Where a suspect is under 18, a reprimand or final warning would be the equivalent disposal.

If all the above requirements are met, the officer must consider whether the seriousness of the offence makes it appropriate for disposal by a simple caution.

(3) Conditional cautions

(a) *Introduction*

Part 3 of the *Criminal Justice Act* 2003 sets out an enhanced statutory cautioning scheme whereby a caution with specific conditions attached (at present designed to facilitate rehabilitation of the suspect and/ or ensure that he makes reparation for the offence) may be administered where a prosecutor has concluded both that there is sufficient evidence to charge the suspect with the offence and that a conditional caution is appropriate, and the suspect both admits the offence and agrees to the caution: ss.22 and 23. Where the suspect fails to comply with the conditions, the conditional caution ceases to have effect and the suspect is liable to be prosecuted for the original offence (with the conditional caution, including the admission that the offence was committed, being admissible as evidence at any trial): s.24. There is a power of arrest without warrant where there are reasonable grounds for believing that there has been a failure to comply with the conditions: s.24A. **4–150**

As from a day or days to be appointed, the *Police and Justice Act* 2006 amends the conditional cautioning regime by including punitive conditions (including the payment of a financial penalty) amongst those which may be attached.

Conditional cautions are intended to be a swift and effective means of dealing with straightforward cases where the offender is willing to admit the offence and to agree to comply with specified conditions; the disposal should only be used where it provides an appropriate and proportionate response to the offending behaviour: DPP's guidance on conditional cautioning (see *post*).

It is wholly artificial to distinguish between the decision not to prosecute and the decision to administer a conditional caution; when making the decision proper regard should therefore be had to the Code for Crown Prosecutors, the DPP's guidance on conditional cautions, and the Secretary of State's Code of Practice on conditional cautions; by Pt 3 of the 2003 Act Parliament had decided to place very considerable responsibility on the CPS; a decision to offer a conditional caution effectively bypassed the court and meant that someone who was guilty of committing a criminal offence was not prosecuted, did not appear before the court and was not sentenced by the court; the importance of taking the decision conscientiously should not be overstated, the effect on the victim and the damage to the criminal justice system being self-evident if the decision was taken without proper regard to the relevant guidance: *R. (Guest) v. DPP*, [2009] 4 Archbold News 2, DC.

(b) *When a conditional caution may be given*

Criminal Justice Act 2003, ss.22, 23 and 27

Conditional cautions

4–151 **22.**—(1) An authorised person may give a conditional caution to a person aged 18 or over ("the offender") if each of the five requirements in section 23 is satisfied.

(2) In this Part "conditional caution" means a caution which is given in respect of an offence committed by the offender and which has conditions attached to it with which the offender must comply.

(3) *The conditions which may be attached to such a caution are those which have either or both of the following objects—*

(a) *facilitating the rehabilitation of the offender,*

(b) *ensuring that he makes reparation for the offence.*

[(3) The conditions which may be attached to such a caution are those which have one or more of the following objects—

(a) facilitating the rehabilitation of the offender;

(b) ensuring that the offender makes reparation for the offence;

(c) punishing the offender.]

[(3A) The conditions which may be attached to a conditional caution include—

(a) (subject to section 23A) a condition that the offender pay a financial penalty;

(b) a condition that the offender attend at a specified place at specified times.

"Specified" means specified by a relevant prosecutor.

(3B) Conditions attached by virtue of subsection (3A)(b) may not require the offender to attend for more than 20 hours in total, not including any attendance required by conditions attached for the purpose of facilitating the offender's rehabilitation.

(3C) The Secretary of State may by order amend subsection (3B) by substituting a different figure.]

(4) In this Part "authorised person" means—

(a) a constable,

(b) an investigating officer, or

(c) a person authorised by a relevant prosecutor for the purposes of this section.

[As from a day or days to be appointed, subs. (3) as set out in italics is to be replaced by the subs. (3) set out in square brackets, and subs. (3A) to (3C) are to be inserted: *Police and Justice Act* 2006, s.17(1) to (3). The substitution of subs. (3) has been brought into force for the limited purposes of a pilot scheme only in relation to the police areas of Cambridgeshire, Merseyside and Norfolk, immediately before July 8, 2009: *Police and Justice Act 2006 (Commencement No. 11) Order* 2009 (S.I. 2009 No. 1679).]

The five requirements

4–152 **23.**—(1) The first requirement is that the authorised person has evidence that the offender has committed an offence.

(2) The second requirement is that a relevant prosecutor decides—

(a) that there is sufficient evidence to charge the offender with the offence, and

(b) that a conditional caution should be given to the offender in respect of the offence.

(3) The third requirement is that the offender admits to the authorised person that he committed the offence.

(4) The fourth requirement is that the authorised person explains the effect of the

conditional caution to the offender and warns him that failure to comply with any of the conditions attached to the caution may result in his being prosecuted for the offence.

(5) The fifth requirement is that the offender signs a document which contains—

(a) details of the offence,

(b) an admission by him that he committed the offence,

(c) his consent to being given the conditional caution, and

(d) the conditions attached to the caution.

Interpretation of Part 3

27. In this Part— **4–153**

"authorised person" has the meaning given by section 22(4),

"conditional caution" has the meaning given by section 22(2),

"investigating officer" means an officer of Revenue and Customs, appointed in accordance with section 2(1) of the *Commissioners for Revenue and Customs Act* 2005, or a person designated as an investigating officer under section 38 of the *Police Reform Act* 2002,

"the offender" has the meaning given by section 22(1),

"relevant prosecutor" means—

(a) the Attorney General,

(ba) the Director of Revenue and Customs Prosecutions,

(b) the Director of the Serious Fraud Office

(c) the Director of Public Prosecutions,

(d) a Secretary of State,

(e), (f) *repealed*],

(g) a person who is specified in an order made by the Secretary of State as being a relevant prosecutor for the purposes of this Part.

[This section is printed as amended by the *Commissioners for Revenue and Customs Act* 2005, s.50(6), and Sched. 4.]

(c) *Financial penalties*

As from a day to be appointed, the conditional cautioning scheme is to be amended by the *Police and Justice Act* 2006 by the insertion of a new s.23A (together with amendment of s.22(3), *ante*) so that a financial penalty may be attached as a condition of a conditional caution. **4–154**

Criminal Justice Act 2003, s.23A

Financial penalties

[23A.—(1) A condition that the offender pay a financial penalty (a "financial penalty condition") may not be attached to a conditional caution given in respect of an offence unless the offence is one that is prescribed, or of a description prescribed, in an order made by the Secretary of State. **4–155**

(2) An order under subsection (1) must prescribe, in respect of each offence or description of offence in the order, the maximum amount of the penalty that may be specified under subsection (5)(a).

(3) The amount that may be prescribed in respect of any offence must not exceed—

(a) one quarter of the amount of the maximum fine for which a person is liable on summary conviction of the offence, or

(b) £250,

whichever is the lower.

(4) The Secretary of State may by order amend subsection (3) by—

(a) substituting a different fraction in paragraph (a);

(b) substituting a different figure in paragraph (b).

(5) Where a financial penalty condition is attached to a conditional caution, a relevant prosecutor must also specify—

(a) the amount of the penalty,

(b) the person to whom the financial penalty is to be paid and how it may be paid.

(6) To comply with the condition, the offender must pay the penalty in accordance with the provision specified under subsection (5)(b).

(6A) Where a financial penalty is (in accordance with the provision specified under subsection (5)(b)) paid to a person other than a designated officer for a local justice area, the person to whom it is paid must give the payment to such an officer.]

[This section is printed as amended by the *Criminal Justice and Immigration Act* 2008, Sched. 26. The new s.23A is to be inserted in the 2003 Act as from a day or days to be appointed. The insertion has been brought into force for the limited purposes of a pilot scheme only in relation to the police areas of Cambridgeshire, Merseyside and Norfolk, immediately before July 8, 2009: *Police and Justice Act 2006 (Commencement No. 11) Order* 2009 (S.I. 2009 No. 1679)].

(d) *Variation of conditions*

Variation of conditions

4–156 **23B.**—(1) A relevant prosecutor may, with the consent of the offender, vary the conditions attached to a conditional caution by—

(a) modifying or omitting any of the conditions;

(b) adding a condition.

[This section was inserted by the *Criminal Justice and Immigration Act* 2008, Sched. 26.]

(e) *Failure to comply with conditions*

Criminal Justice Act 2003, ss.24 and 24A

Failure to comply with conditions

4–157 **24.**—(1) If the offender fails, without reasonable excuse, to comply with any of the conditions attached to the conditional caution, criminal proceedings may be instituted against the person for the offence in question.

(2) The document mentioned in section 23(5) is to be admissible in such proceedings.

(3) Where such proceedings are instituted, the conditional caution is to cease to have effect.

Arrest for failure to comply

4–158 **24A.**—(1) If a constable has reasonable grounds for believing that the offender has failed, without reasonable excuse, to comply with any of the conditions attached to the conditional caution, he may arrest him without warrant.

(2) A person arrested under this section must be—

(a) charged with the offence in question,

(b) released without charge and on bail to enable a decision to be made as to whether he should be charged with the offence, or

(c) released without charge and without bail (with or without any variation in the conditions attached to the caution).

(3) Subsection (2) also applies in the case of—

(a) a person who, having been released on bail under subsection (2)(b), returns to a police station to answer bail or is otherwise in police detention at a police station;

(b) a person who, having been released on bail under section 30A of the 1984 Act (bail elsewhere than at police station) as applied by section 24B below, attends at a police station to answer bail or is otherwise in police detention at a police station;

(c) a person who is arrested under section 30D or 46A of the 1984 Act (power of arrest for failure to answer to police bail) as applied by section 24B below.

(4) Where a person is released under subsection (2)(b), the custody officer must inform him that he is being released to enable a decision to be made as to whether he should be charged with the offence in question.

(5) A person arrested under this section, or any other person in whose case subsection (2) applies, may be kept in police detention—

(a) to enable him to be dealt with in accordance with that subsection, or

(b) where applicable, to enable the power under section 37D(1) of the 1984 Act (power of custody officer to appoint a different or additional time for answering to police bail), as applied by section 24B below, to be exercised.

If the person is not in a fit state to enable him to be so dealt with, or to enable that power to be exercised, he may be kept in police detention until he is.

(6) The power under subsection (5)(a) includes power to keep the person in police detention if it is necessary to do so for the purpose of investigating whether he has failed, without reasonable excuse, to comply with any of the conditions attached to the conditional caution.

(7) Subsection (2) must be complied with as soon as practicable after the person arrested arrives at the police station or, in the case of a person arrested at the police station, as soon as practicable after the arrest.

(8) Subsection (2) does not require a person who—

(a) falls within subsection (3)(a) or (b), and

(b) is in police detention in relation to a matter other than the conditional caution,

to be released if he is liable to be kept in detention in relation to that other matter.

(9) In this Part—

"the 1984 Act" means the *Police and Criminal Evidence Act* 1984;

"police detention" has the same meaning as in the 1984 Act (see section 118(2) of that Act).

[This section was inserted by the *Police and Justice Act* 2006, s.18(1). It applies in respect of any failure to comply occurring on or after June 29, 2007: 2006 Act, s.18(2) and *Police and Justice Act 2006 (Commencement No. 3) Order* 2007 (S.I. 2007 No. 1614).]

Section 24B of the Act (inserted in the same manner and from the same date as s.24A) modifies various provisions of the *Police and Criminal Evidence Act* 1984 in relation to persons arrested under s.24A.

(e) *Code of practice and DPP's guidance*

Section 25 of the *Criminal Justice Act* 2003 requires the Secretary of State to issue a code of practice in relation to conditional cautions. A code made under this section and entitled "Revised Code of Practice for Conditional Cautions-Adults" was brought into effect on January 26, 2010, by the *Criminal Justice Act 2003 (Conditional Cautions: Code of Practice) Order* 2010 (S.I. 2010 No. 133) (replacing the previous code brought into effect by S.I. 2004 No. 1683). For the full text of the code, see *http://www.officialdocuments.gov.uk/document/other/9789999098144/9789999098144.pdf*. **4–159**

Additionally, the DPP has issued guidance under s.37A of the *Police and Criminal Evidence Act* 1984 entitled, "The Director's Guidance on Adult Conditional Cautions". The sixth edition of the guidance was published in January 2010 and is set out in full at *http://www.cps.gov.uk/publications/directors_guidance/adult_conditional_cautions.html*. **4–160**

E. PENALTY NOTICES

(1) On the spot penalties for disorderly behaviour

(a) *Introduction*

Chapter 1 of Pt 1 (ss.1–11) of the *Criminal Justice and Police Act* 2001 sets out a scheme whereby police officers may give on the spot penalties to persons responsible for disorderly behaviour. The scheme operates by the giving of a penalty notice to the person alleged to have committed the offence, who may discharge liability to be convicted of the offence by paying the sum referred to in the penalty notice. **4–161**

By virtue of Sched. 3 to the *Police Reform Act* 2002, police community support officers may also give on the spot penalties under the 2001 Act.

(b) *"Penalty offences"*

Criminal Justice and Police Act 2001, s.1(1)

Offences leading to penalties on the spot

4–162 **1.**—(1) For the purposes of this Chapter "penalty offence" means an offence committed under any of the provisions mentioned in the first column of the following Table and described, in general terms, in the second column:

Offence creating provision	**Description of offence**
Section 12 of the *Licensing Act* 1872	Being drunk in a highway, other public place or licensed premises
Section 80 of the *Explosives Act* 1875	Throwing fireworks in a thoroughfare
Section 55 of the *British Transport Commission Act* 1949	Trespassing on a railway
Section 56 of the *British Transport Commission Act* 1949	Throwing stones etc. at trains or other things on railways
Section 91 of the *Criminal Justice Act* 1967	Disorderly behaviour while drunk in a public place
Section 5(2) of the *Criminal Law Act* 1967	Wasting police time or giving false report
Section 1 of the *Theft Act* 1968	Theft
Section 1(1) of the *Criminal Damage Act* 1971	Destroying or damaging property
Section 5(2) of the *Misuse of Drugs Act* 1971 so far as relating to the following— (a) cannabinol, (b) cannabinol derivatives (within the meaning of Part 4 of Schedule 2 to that Act), (c) cannabis or cannabis resin (within the meaning of that Act), (d) any stereoisomeric form of a substance specified in any of paragraphs (a) to (c), (e) any ester or ether of a substance specified in paragraph (a) or (b), (f) any salt of a substance specified in paragraphs (a) to (e), (g) any preparation or other product containing a substance or product specified in any of paragraphs (a) to (f), not being a preparation falling within paragraph 6 of Part 1 of Schedule 2 to that Act.	Possession of cannabis
Section 5 of the *Public Order Act* 1986	Behaviour likely to cause harassment, alarm or distress
Section 87 of the *Environmental Protection Act* 1990	Depositing and leaving litter
Section 12 of this Act	Consumption of alcohol in designated public place
Section 127(2) of the *Communications Act* 2003	Using public electronic communications network in order to cause annoyance, inconvenience or needless anxiety
Section 11 of the *Fireworks Act* 2003	Contravention of a prohibition or failure to comply with a requirement imposed by or under fireworks regulations or making false statements

Section 141 of the *Licensing Act* 2003	Sale of alcohol to a person who is drunk
Section 146(1) and (3) of the *Licensing Act* 2003	Sale of alcohol to children
Section 149 of the *Licensing Act* 2003	Purchase of alcohol by or on behalf of children
Section 149(4) of the *Licensing Act* 2003	Buying or attempting to buy alcohol for consumption on licensed premises, etc by child
Section 150 of the *Licensing Act* 2003	Consumption of alcohol by children or allowing such consumption
Section 151 of the *Licensing Act* 2003	Delivering alcohol to children or allowing such delivery
Section 49 of the *Fire and Rescue Services Act* 2004	Knowingly giving a false alarm of fire.

This section is printed as amended by the *Criminal Justice and Police Act 2001 (Amendment) Order* 2002 (S.I. 2002 No. 1934), the *Fireworks Act* 2003, s.15, the *Communications Act* 2003, s.406 and Scheds 17 to 19, the *Fire and Rescue Services Act* 2004, ss.53(1), 54, Scheds 1 and 2, the *Criminal Justice and Police Act 2001 (Amendment) and the Police Reform Act 2002 (Modification) Order* 2004 (S.I. 2004 No. 2540), the *Criminal Justice and Police Act 2001 (Amendment) Order* 2005 (S.I. 2005 No. 1090), the *Licensing Act 2003 (Consequential Amendments) Order* 2005 (S.I. 2005 No. 3048) and the *Criminal Justice and Police Act 2001 (Amendment) Order* 2009 (S.I. 2009 No. 110)].

(c) *Penalty notices*

Criminal Justice and Police Act 2001, s.2

Penalty notices

2.—(1) A constable who has reason to believe that a person aged 10 or over has committed a penalty offence may give him a penalty notice in respect of the offence. **4–163**

(2) Unless the notice is given in a police station, the constable giving it must be in uniform.

(3) At a police station, a penalty notice may be given only by an authorised constable.

(4) In this Chapter "penalty notice" means a notice offering the opportunity, by paying a penalty in accordance with this Chapter, to discharge any liability to be convicted of the offence to which the notice relates.

(5) "Authorised constable" means a constable authorised, on behalf of the chief officer of police for the area in which the police station is situated, to give penalty notices.

(6) to (9) *[Power of Secretary of State to amend age in subsection (1)].*

[This section is printed as amended by the *Anti-social Behaviour Act* 2003, s.87, and the *Penalties for Disorderly Behaviour (Amendment of Minimum Age) Order* 2004 (S.I. 2004 No. 3166).]

The *Penalties for Disorderly Behaviour (Amendment of Minimum Age) Order* 2004 (S.I. 2004 No. 3166) makes special provision in relation to the giving of penalty notices to persons under the age of 16. The parent or guardian of the young person must be notified of the giving of the penalty notice: Art. 3(1). The notification must be in writing and it must include a copy of the penalty notice (Art. 3(2)); and it must be served within 28 days of the giving of the penalty notice (Art. 3(4)). Service may be effected personally or by first class post: Art. 3(3). Art. 4 makes provision for the original notification under Art. 3 to be cancelled and for notification to be given to somebody else where it becomes apparent that the notification should have been served on some other parent or guardian, or that the person on whom the notification was served is not a parent or guardian of the young person. Where the parent or guardian has properly been notified of the giving of the penalty notice, he or she is liable to pay the penalty: Art. 5.

Section 3(1) to (2A) of the 2001 Act makes provision for the amount of the penalty to be specified by order made by the Secretary of State. Pursuant to those subsections, amounts are specified in the *Penalties for Disorderly Behaviour (Amount of Penalty) Order* 2002 (S.I. 2002 No. 1837) (as amended by S.I. 2003 No. 2155, S.I. 2004 No. 316, S.I. 2004 No. 2468, S.I. 2004 No. 3167, S.I. 2004 No. 3371, S.I. 2005 No. 3048 S.I. 2009 No. 83).

(d) *Effect of penalty notice and restriction on proceedings where penalty notice given*

Criminal Justice and Police Act 2001, ss.4, 5

Effect of penalty notice

4–164 **4.**—(1) This section applies if a penalty notice is given to a person ("A") under section 2.

(2) If A asks to be tried for the alleged offence, proceedings may be brought against him.

(3) Such a request must be made by a notice given by A—

(a) in the manner specified in the penalty notice; and

(b) before the end of the period of suspended enforcement (as to which see section 5).

(4) A request which is made in accordance with subsection (3) is referred to in this Chapter as a "request to be tried".

(5) If, by the end of the suspended enforcement period—

(a) the penalty has not been paid in accordance with this Chapter, and

(b) A has not made a request to be tried,

a sum equal to one and a half times the amount of the penalty may be registered under section 8 for enforcement against A as a fine.

General restriction on proceedings

4–165 **5.**—(1) Proceedings for the offence to which a penalty notice relates may not be brought until the end of the period of 21 days beginning with the date on which the notice was given ("the suspended enforcement period").

(2) If the penalty is paid before the end of the suspended enforcement period, no proceedings may be brought for the offence.

(3) Subsection (1) does not apply if the person to whom the penalty notice was given has made a request to be tried.

4–166 The issue or acceptance of a penalty notice under the scheme set out in Ch.1 of Pt 1 of the *Criminal Justice and Police Act* 2001 does not constitute a conviction, an admission of guilt or any proof that a crime has been committed; as such penalty notices for disorder are in this respect quite distinct from cautions: *R. v. Hamer* [2011] 1 Cr.App.R. 3, CA. However, where a person is issued with a fixed penalty notice in respect of one offence under s.2 of the *Criminal Justice and Police Act* 2001, payment of the penalty does not relieve him of any possible further proceedings if subsequently it becomes apparent that a more serious offence, and in particular a non-penalty offence, was in fact committed during the course of the incident that gave rise to the issuing of the penalty notice; no reasonable expectation of non-prosecution could be said to arise and instituting proceedings in such circumstances involved no improper escalation of charge: *R. v. Gore and Maher* [2009] 2 Cr.App.R. 27, CA.

(e) *Guidance*

4–167 Section 6 of the *Criminal Justice and Police Act* 2001 confers a power on the Secretary of State to issue guidance in relation to the giving of penalty notices for disorder. Guidance was issued under that section in March 2005, and supplemented by additional guidance in relation to offences committed by young people aged between 16 and 17 (July 2005), offences committed by young people aged between 10 and 15 (October 2005), and use of the powers by community support officers. For the full text of the guidance documents, see *http://www.police.homeoffice.gov.uk/publications/operational-policing/penalty-notices-guidance/?view=Standard=657593*.

With effect from July 16, 2009, Ministry of Justice Circular 2009/04 sets out revised guidance on the use of the penalty notice scheme as a means to deal with offences of retail theft and criminal damage.

With effect from July 23, 2009, Ministry of Justice Circular 2009/05 sets out self-standing guidance on the use of penalty notices as a means to deal with adult offenders in possession of cannabis and its derivatives for personal use.

(2) On the spot penalties for other offences

Part III (ss.51–90) of the *Road Traffic Offenders Act* 1988 makes special provision as to the giving of fixed penalty notices in respect of road traffic offences. Schedule 3 to the Act sets out the offences to which the scheme applies. See *Wilkinson's Road Traffic Offences*, 17–01 *et seq.*, A19.119 *et seq.*, and A19.247. **4–168**

Various other on the spot penalty schemes exist in connection with environmental offences: see the *Refuse Disposal (Amenity) Act* 1978, ss.1–2C (abandoning of vehicles); the *Control of Pollution (Amendment) Act* 1989 (failure to produce authority to transport controlled waste), the *Environmental Protection Act* 1990, ss.29–78 (waste on land) and 86– 98 (leaving of litter); the *Noise Act* 1996, ss.1– 9 (emission of noise from dwelling above permitted level following service of warning notice); the *Anti-social Behaviour Act* 2003, ss.43–47 (graffiti and fly-posting); and the *Clean Neighbourhoods and Environment Act* 2005, ss.55–67 (control of dogs). Ancillary matters in connection with those provisions are set out in the *Environmental Offences (Fixed Penalties) (Miscellaneous Provisions) Regulations* 2007 (S.I. 2007 No. 175).

F. Regulatory Enforcement and Sanctions

Part 3 (ss.36-71) of the *Regulatory Enforcement and Sanctions Act* 2008 introduces a scheme for the imposition and enforcement of civil sanctions in relation to certain regulatory offences. Various regulatory bodies (expressly excluding the Crown Prosecution Service and the police) are empowered under the scheme (once regulations have been made by a relevant Secretary of State) to impose "fixed monetary penalties" (a requirement to pay the regulator a penalty of a prescribed amount), "discretionary requirements" (a requirement to pay a variable monetary penalty or a requirement to take steps to secure that an offence does not continue or recur or to restore the position to what it would have been had the offence not been committed), "stop notices" (a prohibition on carrying on an activity until the person has taken the steps specified in the notice) and "enforcement undertakings" (an undertaking to take certain actions) in lieu of prosecution for the offence. **4–169**

G. Cannabis Warnings

The Association of Chief Police Officers has issuedrevised guidance (dated January 28, 2009) on possession of cannabis for personal use, which takes into account the re-classification of cannabis as a Class B drug as from January 26, 2009. The cannabis warning cannot be given in respect of an offender aged 17 and under, and is distinct from a warning under s.65 of the *Crime and Disorder Act* 1998: para. 3.2. **4–170**

The guidance should only be applied in respect of non-vulnerable individuals in possession of small quantities of cannabis consistent with personal use, who are aged 18 or over, are capable of understanding the significance of the questions put to them and are not under the influence of drink of drugs at the time, who admit the offence, and whose personal details have been satisfactorily verified: para. 3.1.

Where the guidance applies, the expectation is that a cannabis warning will be given where the following conditions are satisfied: (i) there is no previous record of a cannabis warning being given to the offender; (ii) he has not previously been given a penalty notice for disorder; (iii) he has no previous convictions; (iv) he is not known locally as being a persistent offender; (iv) there are no aggravating factors; and (v) he is compliant with the procedure: paras 2.1 and 3.1.1. Aggravating factors include that the cannabis was smoked in a public place or view, that the circumstances are part of a local policing problem or community concern (*e.g.* fear of anti-social behaviour associated with use of cannabis), that there is a particular risk to young persons: paras 2.2.1 to 2.2.3. Other relevant factors include the impact the warning will have on the offender, his understanding of the seriousness of the offence, whether he will benefit from and take heed of the warning, and whether there is evidence that shows that he has little regard for the law: para. 2.2.5.

If the offender has already received a cannabis warning since January 26, 2009, a penalty notice for disorder should be issued or there should be an arrest: para. 3.1. Cannabis warnings qualify as a "sanction detection": para. 3.4.

H. BINDING OVER TO KEEP THE PEACE

4–171 Magistrates' courts have inherent and statutory powers to bind persons over to keep the peace or to be of good behaviour: see *post*, §§ 16–345 and 23–249 *et seq*. Exercise of the power does not depend on conviction; and where criminal proceedings have been instituted, the prosecutor may invite the court to bind the defendant over as an alternative to prosecution (generally once a decision has been made to offer no evidence).

Proceedings instituted by a police force for a person to be bound over under the *Magistrates' Courts Act* 1980, s.115, must be taken over by the DPP: *Prosecution of Offences Act* 1980, s.3(2)(c).

As to procedural and practical matters in connection with binding over, see the *Consolidated Criminal Practice Direction*, paras III.31.1 to III.31.18 (Appendix F–45 *et seq.*).

CHAPTER 5

BAIL

I. INTRODUCTION

Cases in the magistrates' court are not always concluded at the first hearing. The *Magistrates' Courts Act* 1980 confers powers of adjournment in several different circumstances and also gives the court power on adjournment to remand the accused either in custody or on bail during the period of any adjournment: s.128 of the *Magistrates' Courts Act* 1980. **5–1**

Any decision to remand a person in criminal proceedings must be made in accordance with the provisions of the *Bail Act* 1976. The Act has been extensively amended by the *Magistrates' Courts Act* 1980, the *Criminal Justice Acts* of 1988 and 1991, the *Criminal Justice and Public Order Act* 1994 and the *Crime and Disorder Act* 1998. It is also amended by the *Criminal Justice Act* 2003, ss.13–21. Further amendments have been made by s.51 and Sched. 11 and s.52 and Sched. 12 of the *Criminal Justice and Immigration Act* 2008.

In addition the *Criminal Procedure Rules* 2011 Pt 19 covers applications made under the *Bail Act* 1976.

Under the *Bail Act* 1976 there is a general presumption that bail will be granted: s.4(1). Bail can only be withheld if the exceptions to bail, listed in Sched. 1 to the Act, apply. When the court finds the exceptions to apply they must explain their reasons. The question of bail must be considered every time that an accused person appears before the court: s.4(2). When the accused appears in answer to bail or is brought before the court in custody and the case is to be adjourned, the court will invite the prosecution to make representations on bail. The prosecution may object to bail and explain the reasons why (Sched. 1 exceptions) or propose conditional or unconditional **5–2** bail. The defence may then make an application for bail, arguing that either the exceptions are not made out or that the objections can be addressed by the imposition of conditions. The court has an inquisitorial role in bail proceedings and may ask questions of both parties to ensure that it has the required information to enable a proper decision on bail to be made. Also, notwithstanding any agreement reached by the prosecution and defence, it is the decision of the court whether bail should be granted and with what conditions.

The fact that the prosecutor cannot give rise to an expectation on behalf of the defendant that he will get bail at court was confirmed in *R. (on the application of Burns) v. Woolwich Crown Court* [2010] EWHC 129 (Admin). The defendant was charged with offences of fraud, blackmail and possession of criminal property. No objections were made to bail at the magistrates' court and he was granted conditional bail by the court. At a Crown Court hearing full details of the defendant and the offences were asked about and the Crown Court indicated the issue of bail would be reconsidered at which stage the prosecution did object to bail which was then refused.

The Crown Court said, having heard all the information about the charges and in addition that the defendant was liable to be arrested for further offences arising out of the discovery of large amounts of cash deposited in his bank account, that a change of circumstances had arisen requiring reconsideration of bail. This decision was appealed on the basis that the Crown Court was not entitled to look again at bail as there had been no relevant change in circumstances. It was argued that the decision was irrational and also went against a legitimate expectation that bail would be granted as throughout the proceedings the prosecution had never objected to bail until the intervention of the Crown Court. It was held that there was a change of circumstances since the defendant was to be charged with new offences; that the decision was rational and within the *Bail Act* criteria and that the prosecution cannot give any expectation of bail as that decision was for the court not the prosecution.

The Crown Prosecution Service has issued guidance to prosecutors deprecating the practice of requesting "technical" bail for defendants already in custody on other matters. This approach had developed on the basis of administrative convenience and the saving of transport costs from custody. The new guidance makes it clear that the provisions of the *Bail Act* apply to each and every hearing and if exceptions to the right to unconditional bail exist then bail should be opposed despite the fact that the defendant is already in custody. The avoidance of remands on technical bail prevents a situation arising where a defendant may be released unexpectedly from a custodial remand being left only on unconditional bail for charges where a remand in custody or with conditions of bail may have been imposed had it not been for the fact that he was already held in custody.

The presumption of bail has been affected by the *Criminal Justice and Public Order Act* 1994 which requires that in respect of some specified serious offences, bail shall only be granted if there are exceptional circumstances to justify it.

The *Bail Act* 1976 must be applied so as to be compatible with art. 5 of the European Convention on Human Rights which secures the right to liberty. No person shall be deprived of their liberty save in specified circumstances and in accordance with a procedure prescribed by law. Article 5(1)(c) allows for detention in order to bring a person before a competent legal authority on reasonable suspicion of having committed a crime.

The balance between the art. 5 right to liberty and detention in custody pending trial must be considered according to the special features of each case. Pre-trial detention must not exceed a reasonable time. There must always be a reasonable suspicion that the detained person has committed an offence but as time goes on, that alone no longer suffices. The prosecution must also demonstrate "special diligence"in their conduct of the case and ensure that detention is of a reasonable period. Regard will be had to the complexity of the case and the justification for delay. But where a defendant also contributed substantially to the delay by his own actions there was no breach of art. 5: *O'Dowd v.UK* [2010] ECHR 1324.

Coroners and Justice Act 2009 s.115

Bail decisions in murder cases to be made by Crown Court judge

115.—(1) A person charged with murder may not be granted bail except by order of a judge of the Crown Court. 5–2a

(2) Subsections (3) and (4) apply where a person appears or is brought before a magistrates' court charged with murder.

(3) A judge of the Crown Court must make a decision about bail in respect of the person as soon as reasonably practicable and, in any event, within the period of 48 hours beginning with the day after the day on which the person appears or is brought before the magistrates' court.

(4) The magistrates' court must, if necessary for the purposes of subsection (3), commit the person to custody to be brought before a judge of the Crown Court.

(5) For the purposes of subsections (3) and (4), it is immaterial whether the magistrates' court—

(a) sends the person to the Crown Court for trial, or

(b) adjourns proceedings under section 52(5) of the *Crime and Disorder Act* 1998 (c.37) and remands the person.

(6) In this section a reference to a person charged with murder includes a person charged with murder and one or more other offences.

(7) For the purposes of subsection (3), when calculating the period of 48 hours Saturdays, Sundays, Christmas Day, Good Friday and bank holidays are to be excluded.

[This section came into force on February 1, 2010 by virtue of the *Coroners and Justice Act 2009 (Commencement No.3 and Transitional Provision) Order* 2010 (S.I. 2010 No. 145)].

The *Coroners and Justice Act* 2009 removes from the magistrates' court the power to make decisions on bail for defendants charged with murder. Such cases must now be sent to the Crown Court in custody to be heard by a Crown Court judge within 48 hours. This provision came into effect on February 1, 2010. The section is offence specific and does not apply to attempted murder or other homicides. It applies in both the adult and youth courts.

Interim guidance on the practical arrangements for the listing of such cases at the Crown Court was issued by the Senior Presiding Judge on March 2, 2010. Where there is unlikely to be a substantive application for bail within the 48 hours it is anticipated that the magistrates court will not consider it necessary for the defendant to be produced before the Crown Court under s.115(4) so the decision on bail may be made in his absence. Where there is likely to be an application or where the defendant is unrepresented, a direction for production of the defendant before the Crown Court will be necessary.

Any breach of bail granted by the Crown Court must be dealt with at the Crown Court in accordance with s.7(4) and (8) of the *Bail Act* 1976 as amended. See § 5–83.

In relation to bail decisions, the European Court has said domestic courts must, "examine all the facts arguing for and against the existence of a genuine requirement of public interest justifying ... a departure from the rule of respect for individual liberty and set them out in their decisions on applications for release": *Wemhoff v. Germany* [1979] 1 E.H.R.R. 55. 5–3

Case law also requires that the court must consider if there are "relevant and sufficient reasons" to justify detention and these reasons must be given: *Letellier v. France* [1992] 14 E.H.R.R. 83. This was held to require the exercise of a judicial discretion in reaching bail decisions which cannot be restricted by law: *CC v. UK* (1999) E.H.R.L.R. 210.

In *Gault v. UK*, [2007] All E.R. (D) 297 the European Court held that there must be clarity in the reasons given for refusing bail. The defendant faced trial for a third time on a charge of murder. Bail was withheld for the reason that the further trial would take place promptly and because of fears of absconding. The defendant had previously been on bail during the proceedings and had answered her bail in the past so it was held that the reasons given were not sufficient. See also *R. (Fergus) v. Southampton Crown Court* [2008] EWHC 3273.

II. COURT BAIL

A. GENERAL RIGHT TO BAIL

Bail Act 1976, s.1

Meaning of "bail in criminal proceedings"

5–4 **1.**—(1) In this Act "bail in criminal proceedings" means—

(a) bail grantable in or in connection with proceedings for an offence to a person who is accused or convicted of the offence, or

(b) bail grantable in connection with an offence to a person who is under arrest for the offence or for whose arrest for the offence a warrant (endorsed for bail) is being issued.

(2) In this Act "bail" means bail grantable under the law (including common law) for the time being in force.

(3) Except as provided by section 13(3) of this Act, this section does not apply to bail in or in connection with proceedings outside England and Wales.

(4) Repealed.

(5) This section applies—

(a) Whether the offence was committed in England or Wales or elsewhere, and

(b) whether it is an offence under the law of England and Wales, or of any other country or territory.

(6) Bail in criminal proceedings shall be granted (and in particular shall be granted unconditionally or conditionally) in accordance with this Act.

[This section is reprinted as amended by the *Criminal Justice and Public Order Act* 1994, Sched. 11, para. 2.]

Bail Act 1976, s.2

Other definitions

5–5 **2.**—(1) In this Act, unless the context otherwise requires, "conviction" includes—

(a) a finding of guilt,

(b) a finding that a person is not guilty by reason of insanity,

(c) a finding under section 11(1) of the *Powers of Criminal Courts (Sentencing) Act* 2000 (remand for medical examination) that the person in question did the act or made the omission charged, and

(d) a conviction of an offence for which an order is made discharging the offender absolutely or conditionally,

and "convicted" shall be construed accordingly.

(2) In this Act, unless the context otherwise requires—

"bail hostel" means premises for the accommodation of persons remanded on bail,

"child" means a person under the age of fourteen,

"court" includes a judge of a court, or a justice of the peace and, in the case of a specified court, includes a judge or (as the case may be) justice having powers to act in connection with proceedings before that court,

"Courts-Martial Appeal rules" means rules made under section 49 of the *Courts-Martial (Appeals) Act* 1968,

"offence" includes an alleged offence,

"probation hostel" means premises for the accommodation of persons who may be required to reside there by a community order under section 177 of the *Criminal Justice Act* 2003,

"proceedings against a fugitive offender" means proceedings under the *Extradition Act* 1989 or section 2(1) or 4(3) of the *Backing of Warrants (Republic of Ireland) Act* 1965, "surrender to custody" means, in relation to a person released on bail, surrendering himself into the custody of the court or of the constable (according to the requirements of the grant of bail) at the time and place for the time being appointed for him to do so,

"vary", in relation to bail, means imposing further conditions after bail is granted, or varying or rescinding conditions,

"young person" means a person who has attained the age of fourteen and is under the age of seventeen.

(3) Where an enactment (whenever passed) which relates to bail in criminal proceedings refers to the person bailed appearing before a court it is to be construed unless the context otherwise requires as referring to his surrendering himself into the custody of the court.

(4) Any reference in this Act to any other enactment is a reference thereto as amended, and includes a reference thereto as extended or applied, by or under any other enactment, including this Act.

[This section is reprinted as amended by the *Powers of Criminal Courts (Sentencing) Act* 2000, Sched. 9, para. (3)(b) the *Courts Act* 2003, Sched. 10 and the *Criminal Justice Act* 2003, Sched. 32.]

The definition of the term "surrender to custody" has been considered in case law. **5–6**
Attendance by a defendant at court and "overtly subjecting himself to the court's directions" by appearance at an arraignment in the Crown Court was held to be a surrender to custody sufficient to relieve a surety of his obligations: *Central Criminal Court, ex p. Guney* [1995] 2 All E.R. 577 (Bingham L.J. dissenting). Reporting to a court official in accordance with published instructions was held to be a surrender to custody for the purposes of s.2(2) so that no offence was committed under s.6 of failing to surrender but departure from court later in the morning and without waiting for the case to be called on did engage the powers of s.7 and a warrant for arrest could be issued. Once a defendant has surrendered he is under an implied obligation not to leave the court without consent and court officials would be wise to make it clear that a person who reports to them must not leave the court without being given permission to do so: *DPP v. Richards* [1988] Q.B. 701. The question of whether a person has surrendered to custody depends on the facts of the case and not the precise nature of the constraints placed upon them. The fact that there are no security officers or gaolers present in court to restrain the defendant physically does not mean that a defendant cannot surrender to custody. A defendant who left the court after being sentenced to imprisonment rather than wait for the security officers to arrive was held to be unlawfully at large. The argument that he had never surrendered to custody because there was no person there to whose direct control he could submit and so he could not be at large was dismissed by the court on appeal: *Rumble (Jonathan Mark)* (2003) 167 JP 205.

Simply arriving at court at the time and place directed is not sufficient. There must be some statement or conduct signifying an indication of acceptance of the court's control: *Reader* (1987) 84 Cr.App.R. 294

Bail Act 1976, s.3

General provisions

3.—(1) A person granted bail in criminal proceedings shall be under a duty to surrender to custody, and that duty is enforceable in accordance with section 6 of this Act. **5–7**

(2) No recognizance for his surrender to custody shall be taken from him.

(3) Except as provided by this section—

(a) no security for his surrender to custody shall be taken from him,

(b) he shall not be required to provide a surety or sureties for his surrender to custody, and

(c) no other requirement shall be imposed on him as a condition of bail.

(4) He may be required, before release on bail, to provide a surety or sureties to secure his surrender to custody.

(5) He may be required, before release on bail, to give security for his surrender to custody.

The security may be given by him or on his behalf.

(6) He may be required to comply, before release on bail or later, with such requirements as appear to the court to be necessary—

(a) to secure that he surrenders to custody,

(b) to secure that he does not commit an offence while on bail,

(c) to secure that he does not interfere with witnesses or otherwise obstruct the course of justice whether in relation to himself or any other person,

(ca) for his own protection or, if he is a child or young person, for his own welfare or in his own interests,

(d) to secure that he makes himself available for the purpose of enabling inquiries or a report to be made to assist the court in dealing with him for the offence.

(e) to secure that before the time appointed for him to surrender to custody, he attends an interview with an authorised advocate or authorised litigator, as defined by section 119(1) of the *Courts and Legal Services Act* 1990;

and, in any Act, "the normal powers to impose conditions of bail" means the powers to impose conditions under paragraph (a), (b), (c) or (ca) above.

(6ZAA) The requirements which may be imposed under subsection (6) include electronic monitoring requirements.

The imposition of electronic monitoring requirements is subject to section 3AA (in the case of a child or young person), section 3AB (in the case of other persons) and section 3AC (in all cases).

(6ZAB) In this section and sections 3AA to 3AC "electronic monitoring requirements" means requirements imposed for the purpose of securing the electronic monitoring of a person's compliance with any other requirement imposed on him as a condition of bail.

(6ZA) Where he is required under subsection (6) above to reside in a bail hostel or probation hostel, he may also be required to comply with the rules of the hostel.

(6A) In the case of a person accused of murder the court granting bail shall, unless it considers that satisfactory reports on his mental condition have already been obtained, impose as conditions of bail—

(a) a requirement that the accused shall undergo examination by two medical practitioners, for the purpose of enabling such reports to be prepared; and

(b) a requirement that he shall for that purpose attend such an institution or place as the court directs and comply with any other directions which may be given to him for that purpose by either of those practitioners.

(6B) Of the medical practitioners referred to in subsection (6A) above at least one shall be practitioner approved for the purposes of section 12 of the *Mental Health Act* 1983.

(6C) Subsection (6D) below applies where—

(a) the court has been notified by the Secretary of State that arrangements for conducting a relevant assessment or, as the case may be, providing relevant follow-up have been made for the local justice area in which it appears to the court that the person referred to in subsection (6D) would reside if granted bail; and

(b) the notice has not been withdrawn.

(6D) In the case of a person ("P")—

(a) in relation to whom paragraphs (a) to (c) of paragraph 6B(1) of Part 1 of Schedule 1 to this Act apply (including where P is a person to whom the provisions of Part 1A of Schedule 1 apply) ;

(b) who, after analysis of the sample referred to in paragraph (b) of that paragraph, has been offered a relevant assessment or, if a relevant assessment has been carried out, has had relevant follow-up proposed to him; and

(c) who has agreed to undergo the relevant assessment or, as the case may be, to participate in the relevant follow-up,

the court, if it grants bail, shall impose as a condition of bail that P both undergo the relevant assessment and participate in any relevant follow-up proposed to him or, if a relevant assessment has been carried out, that P participate in the relevant follow-up.

(6E) In subsections (6C) and (6D) above—

(a) "relevant assessment" means an assessment conducted by a suitably qualified person of whether P is dependent upon or has a propensity to misuse any specified Class A drugs;

(b) "relevant follow-up" means, in a case where the person who conducted the relevant assessment believes P to have such a dependency or propensity, such further assessment, and such assistance or treatment (or both) in connection with the dependency or propensity, as the person who conducted the relevant assessment (or conducts any later assessment) considers to be appropriate in P's case,

and in paragraph (a) above "Class A drug" and "misuse" have the same meaning as in the *Misuse of Drugs Act* 1971, and "specified" (in relation to a Class A drug) has the same meaning as in Part 3 of the *Criminal Justice and Court Services Act* 2000.

(6F) In subsection (6E)(a) above, "suitably qualified person" means a person who has such qualifications or experience as are from time to time specified by the Secretary of State for the purposes of this subsection.

(7) If a parent or guardian of a child or young person consents to be surety for the child or young person for the purposes of this subsection, the parent or guardian may be required to secure that the child or young person complies with any requirement imposed on him by virtue of subsection (6), (6ZAA) or (6A) above, but—

(a) no requirement shall be imposed on the parent or the guardian of a young person by virtue of this subsection where it appears that the young person will attain the age of seventeen before the time to be appointed for him to surrender to custody; and

(b) the parent or guardian shall not be required to secure compliance with any requirement to which his consent does not extend and shall not, in respect of those requirements to which his consent does extend, be bound in a sum greater than £50.

(8) Where a court has granted bail in criminal proceedings that court or, where that court has sent a person on bail to the Crown Court for trial or to be sentenced or otherwise dealt with, that court or the Crown Court may on application—

(a) by or on behalf of the person to whom bail was granted, or

(b) by the prosecutor or a constable,

vary the conditions of bail or impose conditions in respect of bail which has been granted unconditionally.

(8A) Where a notice of transfer is given under a relevant transfer provision, subsection (8) above shall have effect in relation to a person in relation to whose case the notice is given as if he has been committed on bail on the Crown Court for trial.

(8B) Subsection (8) above applies where a court has sent a person on bail to the Crown Court for trial under section 51 of the *Crime and Disorder Act* 1998 as it applies where a court has committed a person on bail to the Crown Court for trial.

(9) This section is subject to subsection (3) of section 11 of the *Powers of Criminal Courts (Sentencing) Act* 2000 (conditions of bail on remand for medical examination). (10) This section is subject, in its application to bail granted by a constable, to section 3A of this Act.

(10) In subsection (8A) above "relevant transfer provision" means—

(a) section 4 of the *Criminal Justice Act* 1987, or

(b) section 53 of the *Criminal Justice Act* 1991.

[This section is printed as amended by the *Criminal Justice and Police Act* 2001, s.131(3); the *Criminal Justice Act* 2003 ss.13 and 19 and the *Criminal Justice and Immigration Act* 2008 s.52 and Sched. 12 and Sched. 11.]

For the definition of failing to surrender, see *ante*, § 5–6. Section 6 provides for the **5–8**
offence of failing to surrender to custody. Under s.3 pre or post-release requirements or conditions may be attached to bail.

Securities and sureties are pre-release conditions. A security is a sum of money or other valuable that the person bailed must deposit with the court before he can be released on bail. The asset will be returned when the case is completed but will be forfeited if the defendant fails to answer his bail: *Bail Act* 1976, s.5. It is easier for a court to accept cash or some other asset that is realisable and not affected by rights of third parties. A security may be deposited by the defendant or someone else on his behalf. Where a defendant deposited the title deeds to his house the court was not obliged to notify his mother who had a registered charge on the property but the security could only extend to the amount of the son's beneficial interest in the house: *R. (Stevens) v. Truro Magistrates' Court* [2002] 1 W.L.R. 144.

A surety is provided by someone other than the defendant. The surety enters into an undertaking that if the defendant fails to surrender to custody the surety will then forfeit the amount of money in which he has stood as surety and if the money cannot be paid the surety may be committed to prison in default: *Bail Act* 1976, s.8; *Magistrates' Courts Act* 1980, s.120. A surety may be taken in court or elsewhere, *e.g.* at a police station. The surety may agree to stand as surety until the next appointed court date or it may be made to be continuous to a certain event, *e.g.* committal to the Crown Court or first appearance at the Crown Court. A continuous surety is not obliged to attend at court in all the interim hearings for his surety to be taken again provided that the date to which he has agreed to stand as surety is clear.

Where the defendant is a child or young person and a parent or guardian stands as surety, the court may require the parent or guardian to ensure that the child or young person complies with any condition imposed: *Bail Act* 1976, s.3(7), *ante*. A condition under s.3(7) can only be imposed with the parent or guardian's consent and the surety may not exceed £50.

5–9 In all cases where bail is granted, whether the offence involved is imprisonable or non-imprisonable, the power to impose conditions under s.3 applies. Bail can only be withheld and a person remanded in custody on the grounds set out in the *Bail Act* 1976 (Scheds 1 and 2) which differ in relation to imprisonable and non-imprisonable offences. Refusal to consent to a condition of bail is not an exception to the right to bail in either case so a defendant cannot be remanded in custody for that reason: *Bournemouth Justices, ex p. Cross, Griffen and Pamment*, (1989) 89 Cr.App.R. 90.

Sections 3(3)(c) and (6) restrict the conditions that may be imposed where bail is granted.

When considering the imposition of conditions the court does not have to be satisfied that there are substantial grounds for believing that the instances listed in s.3(6) would occur. It is sufficient if the court "perceived a real and not fanciful risk" that the defendant may not surrender to custody, or may commit offences or interfere with witnesses or obstruct justice or not attend for reports or interviews. Conditions may then be necessary to address the risk. The test is more rigorous when the defendant is being refused bail and deprived of his liberty: *Mansfield Justices, ex p. Sharkey* [1985] 1 Q.B. 613.

Section 3 was amended by the *Criminal Justice Act* 2003, s.19 which provides for further powers in relation to drug users. The court may withhold bail from defendants unless they consent to undergo assessments for drugs and participate in follow-up treatment during the period of the remand. The amendments came into force in April 2004 but are dependent on appropriate facilities being available.

Bail may be refused to an offender aged 18 or over who is charged with an imprisonable offence if the following conditions are fulfilled:

a) A drug test taken under s.63B of *PACE* 1984 or s.161 of the *Criminal Justice Act* 2003 shows the presence in his body of a specified Class A drug.
b) Either the offence is one under s.5(2) or (3) of the *Misuse of Drugs Act* 1971 (possession or possession with intent to supply) and relates to a specified Class A drug OR the court is satisfied there are substantial grounds for believing that misuse of a specified Class A drug caused or contributed to the offence or the offence was motivated by drug misuse.
c) The offender has refused to undergo assessment and/or follow up treatment offered consequent to the drug tests.

All assessments are carried out by qualified and trained personnel. The Class A drugs are specified by order by the Secretary of State for the Home Office and listed in Sched. 2, Pt 1 of the *Misuse of Drugs Act* 1971.

Where the defendant agrees to the assessment and follow up treatment the court may grant bail but a condition must be imposed that the assessment and treatment be undertaken.

5–10 Section 3A of the *Bail Act* 1976 relates to the granting of bail by the custody officer at a police station and gives the power to impose conditions on police bail. Conditions can only be imposed by the police where they appear necessary in order to prevent a failure to surrender, or the commission of further offences or the interference with witnesses or the obstruction of justice. Police bail cannot include a requirement to reside at a bail hostel or electronic monitoring. See § 5–107.

Section 3AA of the *Bail Act* 1976 covers the electronic monitoring of compliance with bail conditions for children and young persons, see Ch.26.

Bail Act 1976, s.3AB

Conditions for the imposition of electronic monitoring requirements: other persons

3AB.—(1) A court may not impose electronic monitoring requirements on a person who has attained the age of seventeen unless each of the following conditions is met.

(2) The first condition is that the court is satisfied that without the electronic monitoring requirements the person would not be granted bail.

(3) The second condition is that the court is satisfied that the necessary provision for dealing with the person concerned can be made under arrangements for the electronic monitoring of persons released on bail that are currently available in each local justice area which is a relevant area.

(4) If the person is aged seventeen, the third condition is that a youth offending team has informed the court that in its opinion the imposition of electronic monitoring requirements will be suitable in his case.

[This section is printed as inserted by s.51 and Sched. 11 of the *Criminal Justice and Immigration Act* 2008.]

Electronic monitoring: general provisions

3AC.—(1) Where a court imposes electronic monitoring requirements as a condition of bail, the requirements must include provision for making a person responsible for the monitoring.

(2) A person may not be made responsible for the electronic monitoring of a person on bail unless he is of a description specified in an order made by the Secretary of State.

(3) The Secretary of State may make rules for regulating—

(a) the electronic monitoring of persons on bail;

(b) without prejudice to the generality of paragraph (a), the functions of persons made responsible for such monitoring.

(4) The rules may make different provision for different cases.

(5) Any power of the Secretary of State to make an order or rules under this section is exercisable by statutory instrument.

(6) A statutory instrument containing rules under this section shall be subject to annulment in pursuance of a resolution of either House of Parliament.

(7) For the purposes of section 3AA or 3AB a local justice area is a relevant area in relation to a proposed electronic monitoring requirement if the court considers that it will not be practicable to secure the electronic monitoring in question unless electronic monitoring arrangements are available in that area.

(8) Nothing in sections 3, 3AA or 3AB is to be taken to require the Secretary of State to ensure that arrangements are made for the electronic monitoring of persons released on bail.

[This section was inserted by s.51 and Sched. 11 of the *Criminal Justice and Immigration Act* 2008.]

The court must make a person responsible for the monitoring of an electronic curfew (which will usually be a named company) and the Secretary of State may make rules regulating the electronic monitoring. The *Bail (Electronic Monitoring of Requirements) (Responsible Officer) Order* 2008 (S.I. 2008 No.2713) names employees of Serco Ltd and G4S as the responsible officers for the relevant areas listed in the Schedules to the Order. Under s.3(6) of the *Bail Act* 1976 the court still retains the power to impose a condition of bail of a "doorstep" curfew as opposed to an electronically monitored curfew. The person bailed is required to stay indoors during the set hours with an additional requirement to present himself at the doorstep of the relevant premises when required to do so by a police officer to prove that he is observing the curfew. It is important to distinguish between these two types of curfew condition because it is only in the case of electronically monitored curfews that time spent on curfew can be taken into account by way of credit towards to any eventual custodial sentence imposed under the *Criminal Justice Act* 2003, s.240A.

In *Barrett* [2009] EWCA Crim 2213, it was confirmed that there is no obligation to give credit for time spent on bail with a curfew where it had not been electronically monitored. Although the argument to give some credit was appealing the court held that the statutory provisions did not allow for it.

The *Remand on Bail (Disapplication of Credit Period) Rules* 2008 (S.I. 2008 No.2793) are designed to prevent the double counting of credit periods under these provisions. See §§ 5–43 and 23–145.

Bail Act 1976, s.4

General right to bail of accused persons and others

5–11 **4.**—(1) A person to whom this section applies shall be granted bail except as provided in Schedule 1 to this Act.

(2) This section applies to a person who is accused of an offence when—

(a) he appears or is brought before a magistrates' court or the Crown Court in the course of or in connection with proceedings for the offence, or

(b) he applies to a court for bail or for a variation of the conditions of bail in connection with the proceedings.

This subsection does not apply as respects proceedings on or after a person's conviction of the offence or proceedings against a fugitive offender for the offence.

(3) This section also applies to a person who, having been convicted of an offence, appears or is brought before a magistrates' court or the Crown Court to be dealt with under–

(a) Part 2 of Schedule 3 to the *Powers of Criminal Courts (Sentencing) Act* 2000 (breach of certain youth community orders); or

(b) Part 2 of Schedule 8 to the *Criminal Justice Act* 2003 (breach of requirement of community order).

(4) This section also applies to a person who has been convicted of an offence and whose case is adjourned by the court for the purpose of enabling inquiries or a report to be made to assist the court in dealing with him for the offence.

(5) Schedule 1 to this Act also has effect as respects conditions of bail for a person to whom this section applies.

(6) In Schedule 1 to this Act "the defendant" means a person to whom this section applies and any reference to a defendant whose case is adjourned for inquiries or a report is a reference to a person to whom this section applies by virtue of subsection (4) above.

(7) This section is subject to section 41 of the *Magistrates' Courts Act* 1980 (restriction of bail by magistrates' court in cases of treason).

(8) This section is subject to section 25 of the *Criminal Justice and Public Order Act* 1994 (exclusion of bail in cases of homicide and rape).

(9) In taking any decisions required by Part I or II of Schedule 1 to this Act, the considerations to which the court is to have regard include, so far as relevant, any misuse of controlled drugs by the defendant ("controlled drugs" and "misuse" having the same meanings as in the *Misuse of Drugs Act* 1971).

[This section is reprinted as amended by the *Criminal Justice and Court Services Act* 2000, s.58 and the *Criminal Justice Act* 2003.]

5–12 Section 4 of the *Bail Act* 1976 creates a general right to bail for persons charged with an offence. A court must grant bail to any person accused of an offence or brought before a court for breach of a requirement of probation or community service order, if none of the exceptions specified in Sched. 1 applies. Sched. 1 is divided into Pt 1 which deals with imprisonable offences and Pt II which covers non-imprisonable offences. The exceptions to bail are listed in the Schedule—see para. 5–35. Where the defendant has previously been remanded in custody by the court, consideration must be given to whether bail should be granted on each occasion that the defendant is brought before the court regardless of whether the defendant makes an application: *Bail Act* 1976, Sched. 1, Pt IIA. This ensures that there is the periodic review of detention as required under art. 5 ECHR.

Section 4(1) does not apply once a person has been convicted of an offence. An appellant seeking bail pending the outcome of an appeal has no right to bail under this section. Section 4(1) does not apply to offenders who have been committed to the Crown Court for sentencing following conviction in the magistrates' court. In these situations a magistrate has the power to grant bail but the decision is entirely at the discretion of the court and there is no initial presumption either way. The *Bail Act* 1976 applies to offenders brought before the court in respect of any breach of a requirement of community penalties under the *Criminal Justice Act* 1991, Sched. 2, Pt 2. A convicted person has the right to bail if the case is adjourned for the purpose of obtaining reports but under para. 7, Sched. 1, Pt I of the *Bail Act* 1976 there is an additional exception to the right to bail; the defendant need not be granted bail where it appears to the court that it would be impracticable to complete inquiries or make a report without keeping the defendant in custody.

Where a drugs test is carried out by the police under s.63B *PACE* 1984, the result of the test is relevant to a bail decision under s.4(9). The misuse of drugs may give rise to a fear of commission of further offences to feed the drug habit or failure to attend if affected by taking drugs.

Criminal Justice and Public Order Act 1994, s.25

No bail for defendants charged with or convicted of homicide or rape after previous conviction of such offences.

25.—(1) A person who in any proceedings has been charged with or convicted of an offence to which this section applies in circumstances to which it applies shall be granted bail in those proceedings only if the court or, as the case may be, the constable considering the grant of bail is satisfied that there are exceptional circumstances which justify it. **5–13**

(2) This section applies, subject to subsection (3) below, to the following offences, that is to say—

(a) murder;

(b) attempted murder;

(c) manslaughter;

(d) rape under the law of Scotland or Northern Ireland;

(e) an offence under section 1 of the *Sexual Offences Act* 1956 (rape);

(f) an offence under section 1 of the *Sexual Offences Act* 2003 (rape);

(g) an offence under section 2 of that Act (assault by penetration);

(h) an offence under section 4 of that Act (causing a person to engage in sexual activity without consent), where the activity caused involved penetration within subsection (4)(a) to (d) of that section;

(i) an offence under section 5 of that Act (rape of a child under 13);

(j) an offence under section 6 of that Act (assault of a child under 13 by penetration);

(k) an offence under section 8 of that Act (causing or inciting a child under 13 to engage in sexual activity), where an activity involving penetration within subsection (3)(a) to (d) of that section was caused;

(l) an offence under section 30 of that Act (sexual activity with a person with a mental disorder impeding choice), where the touching involved penetration within subsection (3)(a) to (d) of that section;

(m) an offence under section 31 of that Act (causing or inciting a person, with a mental disorder impeding choice, to engage in sexual activity), where an activity involving penetration within subsection (3)(a) to (d) of that section was caused;

(n) an attempt to commit an offence within any of paragraphs (d) to (m).

(3) This section applies to a person charged with or convicted of any such offence only if he has been previously convicted by or before a court in any part of the United Kingdom of any such offence or of culpable homicide and, in the case of a previous conviction of manslaughter or of culpable homicide, if he was then sentenced to imprisonment or, if he was then a child or young person, to long-term detention under any of the relevant enactments.

(4) This section applies whether or not an appeal is pending against conviction or sentence.

(5) In this section—

"conviction" includes—

(a) a finding that a person is not guilty by reason of insanity;

(b) a finding under section 4A(3) of the *Criminal Procedure (Insanity) Act* 1964 (cases of unfitness to plead) that a person did the act or made the omission charged against him; and

(c) a conviction of an offence for which an order is made discharging the offender absolutely or conditionally;

and "convicted" shall be construed accordingly; and

"the relevant enactments" means—

(a) as respects England and Wales, section 91 of the *Powers of Criminal Courts (Sentencing) Act* 2000;

(b) as respects Scotland, sections 205(1) to (3) and 208 of the *Criminal Procedure (Scotland) Act* 1995;

(c) as respects Northern Ireland, section 73(2) of the *Children and Young Persons Act (Northern Ireland)* 1968.

(6) This section does not apply in relation to proceedings instituted before its commencement.

[This section is printed as amended by the *Criminal Justice Act* 2003, Sched. 32.]

5–14 Section 25 of the *Criminal Justice and Public Order Act* 1994 removes the presumption of bail in the case of persons who have been charged with or convicted of murder, attempted murder, manslaughter, rape or attempted rape and who have previously been convicted of any such offences as described in subs. (3). Then bail shall only be granted if the court or constable is satisfied that there are exceptional circumstances which justify it.

5–15 In *Ilijokov v. Bulgaria* [2001] 7 *Archbold News* 1, the European Court of Human Rights held that a provision making pre-trial custody the rule for defendants charged with offences of a specified level of seriousness, except where there was not even a theoretical possibility of absconding, commission of further offences or interference with witnesses violated art. 5(3) of the Convention, because it is for the state to satisfy the court that there are relevant and sufficient reasons for withholding bail. The "exceptional circumstances" referred to in s.25 of the *Criminal Justice and Public Order Act* 1994 preserve a sufficient discretion to ensure that art. 5 is not violated.

Bail Act 1976, s.5

Supplementary provisions about decisions on bail

5–16 5.—(1) Subject to subsection (2) below, where—

(a) a court or constable grants bail in criminal proceedings, or

(b) a court withholds bail in criminal proceedings from a person to whom section 4 of this act applies, or

(c) a court, officer of a court or constable appoints a time or place or appoints a different time or place for a person granted bail in criminal proceedings to surrender to custody, or

(d) a court or constable varies any conditions of bail or imposes conditions in respect of bail in criminal proceedings,

that court, officer or constable shall make a record of the decision in the prescribed manner and containing the prescribed particulars and, if requested to do so by the person in relation to whom the decision was taken, shall cause him to be given a copy of the record of the decision as soon as practicable after the record is made.

(2) Where bail in criminal proceedings is granted by endorsing a warrant of arrest for bail the constable who releases on bail the person arrested shall make the record required by subsection (1) above instead of the judge or justice who issued the warrant.

(2A) Where a magistrates' court or the Crown Court grants bail in criminal proceedings to a person to whom section 4 of this Act applies after hearing representations from the prosecutor in favour of withholding bail, then the court shall give reasons for granting bail.

(2B) A court which is by virtue of subsection (2A) above required to give reasons for its decision shall include a note of those reasons in the record of its decision and, if requested to do so by the prosecutor, shall cause the prosecutor to be given a copy of the record of the decision as soon as practicable after the record is made.

(3) Where a magistrates' court or the Crown Court—

(a) withholds bail in criminal proceedings, or

(b) imposes conditions in granting bail in criminal proceedings, or

(c) varies any conditions of bail or imposes conditions in respect of bail in criminal proceedings,

and does so in relation to a person to whom section 4 of this Act applies, then the court shall, with a view to enabling him to consider making an application in the matter to another court, give reasons for withholding bail or for imposing or varying the conditions.

(4) A court which is by virtue of subsection (3) above required to give reasons for its decision shall include a note of those reasons in the record of its decision and shall (except in a case where, by virtue of subsection (5) below, this need not be done) give a copy of that note to the person in relation to whom the decision was taken.

(5) The Crown Court need not give a copy of the note of the reasons for its decision to the person in relation to whom the decision was taken where that person is represented by counsel or a solicitor unless his counsel or solicitor requests the court to do so.

(6) Where a magistrates' court withholds bail in criminal proceedings from a person who is not represented by counsel or a solicitor, the court shall—

(a) if it is committing him for trial to the Crown Court or if it issues a certificate under subsection (6A) below, inform him that he may apply to the High Court or to the Crown Court to be granted bail;

(b) in any other case, inform him that he may apply to the High Court for that purpose.

(6A) Where in criminal proceedings—

(a) a magistrates' court remands a person in custody under section 11 of the *Powers of Criminal Courts (Sentencing) Act* 2000 (remand for medical examination) or any of the following provisions of the *Magistrates' Courts Act* 1980—

(i) section 5 (adjournment of inquiry into offence);

(ii) section 10 (adjournment of trial); or

(iii) section 18 (initial procedure on information against adult for offence triable either way),

after hearing full argument on an application for bail from him; and

(b) either—

(i) it has not previously heard such argument on an application for bail from him in those proceedings; or

(ii) it has previously heard full argument from him on such an application but it is satisfied that there has been a change in his circumstances or that new considerations have been placed before it,

it shall be the duty of the court to issue a certificate in the prescribed form that they heard full argument on his application for bail before they refused the application.

(6B) Where the court issues a certificate under subsection (6A) above in a case to which paragraph (b)(ii) of that subsection applies, it shall state in the certificate the nature of the change of circumstances or the new considerations which caused it to hear a further fully argued bail application.

(6C) Where a court issues a certificate under subection (6A) above it shall cause the person to whom it refuses bail to be given a copy of the certificate.

(7) Where a person has given security in pursuance of section 3(5) above and a court is satisfied that he failed to surrender to custody then, unless it appears that he had reasonable cause for his failure, the court may order the forfeiture of the security.

(8) If a court orders the forfeiture of a security under subsection (7) above, the court may declare that the forfeiture extends to such amount less than the full value of the security as it thinks fit to order.

(8A) An order under subsection (7) above shall, unless previously revoked, have effect at the end of twenty-one days beginning with the day on which it is made.

(8B) A court which has ordered the forfeiture of a security under subsection (7) above may, if satisfied on an application made by or on behalf of the person who gave it that he did after all have reasonable cause for his failure to surrender to custody, by order remit the forfeiture or declare that it extends to such amount less than the full value of the security as it thinks fit to order.

(8C) An application under subsection (8B) above may be made before or after the order for forfeiture has taken effect, but shall not be entertained unless the court is satisfied that the prosecution was given reasonable notice of the applicant's intention to make it.

(9) A security which has been ordered to be forfeited by a court under subsection (7) above shall, to the extent of the forfeiture—

(a) if it consists of money, be accounted for and paid in the same manner as a fine imposed by that court would be;

(b) if it does not consist of money, be enforced by such magistrates' court as may be specified in the order.

(9A) Where an order is made under subsection (8B) above after the order for forfeiture of the security in question has taken effect, any money which would have fallen to be repaid or paid over to the person who gave the security if the order under subsection (8B) had been made before the order for forfeiture took effect shall be repaid or paid over to him.

(10) In this section "prescribed" means, in relation to the decision of a court or an officer of a court, prescribed by Civil Procedure Rules, Courts-Martial Appeal Rules or Criminal Procedure Rules as the case requires or, in relation to a decision of a constable, prescribed by direction of the Secretary of State.

(11) This section is subject, in its application to bail granted by a constable, to section 5A of this Act.

[This section is reprinted as amended by the *Criminal Justice and Police Act* 2001, s.129(1) and the *Courts Act* 2003, Sched. 8.]

5–17 Under this section the court will provide a written bail notice to the defendant. It includes details of exceptions found and reasons given for the decision and standard requirements of conditional bail to be deleted or amended as appropriate. There is also a duty on the court under s.5(2A) to give written reasons in cases where bail is granted after the prosecution has objected to bail. The provision of reasons enables the parties affected to consider fully the basis of an appeal.

At the first hearing at which the defendant is a person to whom s.4 applies, the court shall grant the defendant bail unless one of the exceptions under Pt I or II of Sched. 1 applies. If the prosecution make representations against the grant of bail the defendant may support the application for bail with any argument in fact or law. The court must consider the question of bail regardless of whether the defendant makes an application for bail and must record reasons if the remand is to be in custody.

If bail is refused at the first hearing, the court is still bound to consider the question of bail at each subsequent hearing. An application for further remand in custody in the absence of the defendant and with his consent under s.128(3A) of the *Magistrates' Courts Act* 1980 is not a hearing for this purpose. Section 4 does not apply in such a case because the defendant does not appear, is not brought before the court and makes no application for bail: *Dover and East Kent Justices, ex p. Dean* [1992] Crim.L.R. 33, DC.

5–18 After the first hearing at which the defendant is denied bail the defendant may support one more application for bail with any argument in fact or law, whether or not the argument has been raised previously. The purpose of the legislation is to provide for any argument being advanced on two occasions as of right, and at the second hearing the court is obliged to consider the matter *de novo*.

This is not always the effect of the legislation. Sometimes when a defendant faces a serious charge and is brought to court in custody there may be any number of reasons why a bail application is not made on the first appearance. When the defendant next appears before the court, an application for bail may be made and any argument raised as of right. If bail is withheld once more at the second hearing the defendant has no right to raise the same arguments again at later hearings, in effect depriving the defendant of the intended right to have two attempts at contesting the objections to bail made by the prosecution. If no application is made at the first hearing after that at which the court decided not to grant the defendant bail, the *Bail Act* 1976, para. 2 of Pt IIA, Sched. 1 does not apply so as to confer a right to make an application at subsequent hearings based on the same arguments of fact and law. The defendant always has the right to make an application for bail but whether the court is bound to entertain the application is a different question. There must be some material change of circumstance to warrant repeated applications: *R. v. Dover and East Kent Justices, ex p. Dean* (*ante*). Part IIA, para. 3 provides that where a person has been remanded in custody then at subsequent hearings the court need not hear arguments as to fact or law which it has heard previously. This implies that it has a discretion to do so. On that basis the court should not hear arguments as to fact or law which it has heard previously unless there has been such a change of circumstances as might justify a different decision. To do so would be to act in an appellate capacity which would be inappropriate: *Slough Justices, ex p. Duncan*, (1982) 75 Cr.App.R. 384, DC.

But in *R. (on the application of B) v. Brent Youth Court* 2010] EWHC 1893 (Admin) it was held that there was no need for a "change of circumstances" as such to justify a renewed application for bail and "new considerations"not put before the court previously may found a further application. It was said that the court always retains a discretion to re-consider bail and in the case of a young person the welfare principle of s.44 of the *Children and Young Persons Act* 1933 requires the court to consider hearing a further bail application even in the absence of any change of circumstances or fresh considerations. This case seems to indicate that when a court refuses to exercise its discretion to hear the same argument again it must give reasons for that approach.

Where the court decides that a defendant should be remanded in custody because it has not been practicable to obtain sufficient information to consider a bail application, this does not amount to a decision to refuse bail within the meaning of para. 1 of Pt IIA: *Calder Justices, ex p. Kennedy* [1992] Crim.L.R. 496.

The passage of time may require a court to hear further bail applications to ensure **5–19** that the defendant's rights under art. 5 are reviewed regularly: *Neumeister v. Austria (No.1)* (1979–80) 1 E.H.R.R. 91.

Under s.5(6A) a certificate that a full bail argument has taken place must be issued when the court remands a defendant in custody following the first full bail application. Such a certificate must also be issued if a further full bail application is allowed because of a change in circumstances or the identification of new considerations and the defendant is again remanded in custody. The certificate can be provided immediately and is often incorporated in the printed bail notice given to the defendant. The purpose of the certificate is to form the basis of an appeal against the bail decision to the Crown Court and to confirm that all avenues of argument in the magistrates' court have been exhausted.

A security can be imposed as a condition of bail: s.3. Section 5 provides for the procedure to be followed if the defendant fails to answer his bail. The order of forfeiture only takes effect after 21 days and in the meantime the court may serve a notice of forfeiture on the person who deposited the security whether that be the defendant or someone else on his behalf so they may make representations.

B. BAIL FOLLOWING ADJOURNMENT

Magistrates' Courts Act 1980, ss.5; 6(3), (4)

Adjournment of inquiry

5.—(1) A magistrates' court may, before beginning to inquire into an offence as examining **5–20** justices, or at any time during the inquiry, adjourn the hearing, and if it does so shall remand the accused.

(2) The court shall when adjourning fix the time and place at which the hearing is to be resumed; and the time fixed shall be that at which the accused is required to appear or be brought before the court in pursuance of the remand or would be required to be brought before the court but for section 128(3A) below.

Discharge or committal for trial

6.—(3) Subject to section 4 of the *Bail Act* 1976 and section 41 below, the court may commit **5–21** a person for trial—

(a) in custody, that is to say, by committing him to custody there to be safely kept until delivered in due course of law, or

(b) on bail in accordance with the *Bail Act* 1976, that is to say, by directing him to appear before the Crown Court for trial;

and where his release on bail is conditional on his providing one or more surety or sureties and, in accordance with section 8(3) of the *Bail Act* 1976, the court fixes the amount in which the surety is to be bound with a view to his entering into his recognizance subsequently in accordance with subsections (4) and (5) or (6) of that section the court shall in the meantime commit the accused to custody in accordance with paragraph (a) of this subsection.

(4) Where the court has committed a person to custody in accordance with paragraph (a) of subsection (3) above, then, if that person is in custody for no other cause, the court may, at any time before his first appearance before the Crown Court, grant him bail in accordance with the *Bail Act* 1976 subject to a duty to appear before the Crown Court for trial.

Crime and Disorder Act 1998, s.52

Provisions supplementing section 51

5–22 **52.**—(1) Subject to section 4 of the *Bail Act* 1976, section 41 of the 1980 Act, regulations under section 22 of the 1985 Act and section 25 of the 1994 Act, the court may send a person for trial under section 51 above—

(a) in custody, that is to say, by committing him to custody there to be safely kept until delivered in due course of law; or

(b) on bail in accordance with the *Bail Act* 1976, that is to say, by directing him to appear before the Crown Court for trial.

(2) Where—

(a) the person's release on bail under subsection (1)(b) above is conditional on his providing one or more sureties; and

(b) in accordance with subsection (3) of section 8 of the *Bail Act* 1976, the court fixes the amount in which a surety is to be bound with a view to his entering into his recognisance subsequently in accordance with subsections (4) and (5) or (6) of that section,

the court shall in the meantime make an order such as is mentioned in subsection (1)(a) above.

(3) The court shall treat as an indictable offence for the purposes of section 51 above an offence which is mentioned in the first column of Schedule 2 to the 1980 Act (offences for which the value involved is relevant to the mode of trial) unless it is clear to the court, having regard to any representations made by the prosecutor or the accused, that the value involved does not exceed the relevant sum.

(4) In subsection (3) above "the value involved" and "the relevant sum" have the same meanings as in section 22 of the 1980 Act (certain offences triable either way to be tried summarily if value involved is small).

(5) A magistrates' court may adjourn any proceedings under section 51 above, and if it does so shall remand the accused.

(6) Schedule 3 to this Act (which makes further provision in relation to persons sent to the Crown Court for trial under section 51 above) shall have effect.

5–23 Where a magistrates' court commits a person for trial in the Crown Court on bail the bail ceases when the defendant surrenders to the Crown Court. If the Crown Court releases the defendant on bail, it must consider the suitability of any conditions afresh: *Kent Crown Court, ex p. Jodka* (1997) 161 J.P. 638, DC.

5–24 Committal for trial is not necessarily a new circumstance which entitles the defendant to make a new bail application. In *Slough Justices, ex p. Duncan* [1981] Q.B. 451 it was stated that new arguments in favour of bail may be advanced upon committal for trial because the strength of the prosecution case at the committal hearing may be better assessed.

5–25 If after committal for trial but before arraignment at the Crown Court there is an application to vary the conditions of bail, the magistrates' court has concurrent jurisdiction with the Crown Court to hear and determine the application: *Lincoln Magistrates' Court, ex p. Mawer* (1996) 160 J.P. 219.

The magistrates' court also has power to commit a defendant to the Crown Court for sentence under the *Powers of Criminal Courts (Sentencing) Act* 2000, ss.3 and 6 (see

Pt IV on Sentencing). The court has power to commit either on bail or in custody. Upon committal for sentence the usual practice should be to commit the defendant in custody only if he has been in custody prior to the committal hearing: *Rafferty* [1999] 1 Cr.App.R. 235, CA. In the judgment Thomas J. said—

> "In the usual case where a person who has been on bail pleads guilty at the plea before venue, the usual practice should be to continue bail, even if it is anticipated that a custodial sentence will be imposed by the Crown Court,unless there are good reasons for remanding the defendant in custody".

The encouragement to a defendant to plead guilty at the earliest opportunity is not then affected by a fear of being remanded into custody.

Part I

Magistrates' Courts Act 1980, ss.10, 17C, 18(4), (5)

Adjournment of trial

10.—(1) A magistrates' court may at any time, whether before or after beginning to try an information, adjourn the trial, and may do so, notwithstanding anything in this Act, when composed of a single justice. **5-26**

(2) The court may when adjourning either fix the time and place at which the trial is to be resumed, or, unless it remands the accused, leave the time and place to be determined later by the court; but the trial shall not be resumed at that time and place unless the court is satisfied that the parties have had adequate notice thereof.

(3) A magistrates' court may, for the purpose of enabling inquiries to be made or of determining the most suitable method of dealing with the case, exercise its power to adjourn after convicting the accused and before sentencing him or otherwise dealing with him; but, if it does so, the adjournment shall not be for more than 4 weeks at a time unless the court remands the accused in custody and, where it so remands him, the adjournment shall not be for more than 3 weeks at a time.

(3A) A youth court shall not be required to adjourn any proceedings for an offence at any stage by reason only of the fact—

(a) that the court commits the accused for trial for another offence; or

(b) that the accused is charged with another offence.

(4) On adjourning the trial of an information the court may remand the accused and, where the accused has attained the age of 18 years, shall do so if the offence is triable either way and—

(a) on the occasion on which the accused first appeared, or was brought, before the court to answer to the information he was in custody or, having been released on bail, surrendered to the custody of the court; or

(b) the accused has been remanded at any time in the course of proceedings on the information;

and, where the court remands the accused, the time fixed for the resumption of the trial shall be that at which he is required to appear or be brought before the court in pursuance of the remand or would be required to be brought before the court but for section 128(3A) below.

Intention as to plea adjournment

17C. A magistrates' court proceeding under section 17A or 17B above may adjourn the proceedings at any time, and on doing so on any occasion when the accused is present may remand the accused, and shall remand him if— **5-27**

(a) on the occasion on which he first appeared, or was brought, before the court to answer to the information he was in custody or, having been released on bail, surrendered to the custody of the court; or

(b) he has been remanded at any time in the course of proceedings on the information;

and where the court remands the accused, the time fixed for the resumption of proceedings shall be that at which he is required to appear or be brought before the court in pursuance of the remand or would be required to be brought before the court but for section 128(3A) below.

Initial procedure on information against adult for offence triable either way

18.—(4) A magistrates' court proceeding under sections 19 to 23 below may adjourn the proceedings at any time, and on doing so on any occasion when the accused is present may remand the accused, and shall remand him if— **5-28**

(a) on the occasion on which he first appeared, or was brought, before the court to answer to the information he was in custody or, having been released on bail, surrendered to the custody of the court; or

(b) he has been remanded at any time in the course of proceedings on the information;

and where the court remands the accused, the time fixed for the resumption of the proceedings shall be that at which he is required to appear or be brought before the court in pursuance of the remand or would be required to be brought before the court but for section 128(3A) below.

(5) The functions of a magistrates' court under sections 19 to 23 below may be discharged by a single justice, but the foregoing provision shall not be taken to authorise the summary trial of an information by a magistrates' court composed of less than two justices.

C. BAIL PENDING AN APPEAL

Magistrates' Courts Act 1980, s.113

Bail on appeal or case stated

5–29 **113.**—(1) Where a person has given notice of appeal to the Crown Court against the decision of a magistrates' court or has applied to a magistrates' court to state a case for the opinion of the High Court, then, if he is in custody, the magistrates' court may, subject to section 25 of the *Criminal Justice and Public Order Act* 1994 grant him bail.

(2) If a person is granted bail under subsection (1) above, the time and place at which he is to appear (except in the event of the determination in respect of which the case is stated being reversed by the High Court) shall be—

(a) if he has given notice of appeal, the Crown Court at the time appointed for the hearing of the appeal;

(b) if he has applied for the statement of a case, the magistrates' court at such time within 10 days after the judgment of the High Court has been given as may be specified by the magistrates' court;

and any recognizance that may be taken from him or from any surety for him shall be conditioned accordingly.

(3) Subsection (1) above shall not apply where the accused has been committed to the Crown Court for sentence under section 3 of the *Powers of Criminal Courts (Sentencing) Act* 2000.

(4) Section 37(6) of the *Criminal Justice Act* 1948 (which relates to the currency of a sentence while a person is released on bail by the High Court) shall apply to a person released on bail by a magistrates' court under this section pending the hearing of a case stated as it applies to a person released on bail by the High Court under section 22 of the *Criminal Justice Act* 1967.

5–30 The court may be reluctant to grant the appellant bail pending appeal where a custodial sentence has been imposed following conviction. Bail would only be appropriate in the most exceptional circumstances, *e.g.* if there was a strong likelihood of success of an appeal or that a sentence would have been served by the time the appeal would be heard: *Watton* (1979) 68 Cr.App.R. 293.

D. BAIL ON ARREST

Magistrates' Courts Act 1980, s.43

Bail on arrest

5–31 **43.**—(1) Where a person has been granted bail under Part IV of the *Police and Criminal Evidence Act* 1984 subject to a duty to appear before a magistrates' court, the court before which he is to appear may appoint a later time as the time at which he is to appear and may enlarge the recognizances of any sureties for him at that time.

(2) The recognizance of any surety for any person granted bail subject to a duty to attend at a police station may be enforced as if it were conditioned for his appearance before a magistrates' court acting in the local justice area in which the police station named in the recognizance is situated.

E. BAIL WHERE APPEARANCE BEFORE CROWN COURT CONTEMPLATED

Magistrates' Courts Act 1980, s.43A

Functions of magistrates' court where a person in custody is brought before it with a view to his appearance before the Crown Court

43A.—(1) Where a person in custody in pursuance of a warrant issued by the Crown Court with a view to his appearance before the Crown Court is brought before a magistrates' court in pursuance of section 81(5) of the *Supreme Court Act* 1981— **5–32**

(a) the magistrates' court shall commit him in custody or release him on bail until he can be brought or appear before the Crown Court at the time and place appointed by the Crown Court;

(b) if the warrant is endorsed for bail, but the person in custody is unable to satisfy the conditions endorsed, the magistrates' court may vary those conditions, if satisfied that it is proper to do so.

(2) A magistrates' court shall have jurisdiction under subsection (1) whether or not the offence was committed, or the arrest was made, within the court's area.

A person arrested on a Crown Court or "Bench" warrant may be brought before a magistrates' court usually on a Saturday or other day when the Crown Court is closed. The case may be adjourned to the next convenient date at the Crown Court with the defendant remanded on bail or in custody. **5–33**

III. PRINCIPLES FOR GRANTING/DENYING BAIL

(1) Statutory grounds for refusal

Section 4 of the *Bail Act* 1976 is subject to the First Schedule to the Act, which sets out the reasons why a defendant need not be granted bail. Part 1 applies to imprisonable offences, and Pt II to non-imprisonable offences. **5–34**

The *Criminal Justice and Immigration Act* 2008, amended Sched. 1 to the *Bail Act* 1976 by inserting a new Pt 1A which provides that certain exceptions to the right to bail now apply to all summary offences whether imprisonable or not. Previously the exceptions to bail in respect of non-imprisonable summary offences were restricted so that bail was more likely to be granted. The amendments now ensure that bail is also more likely to be granted in cases that may carry imprisonment provided that they are summary only charges. Other amendments also reflect the position with respect to defendants under the age of 18 charged with an offence of causing criminal damage. In the adult court the value of the damage done dictates whether the offence is summary only or triable either way. With respect to young offenders the mode of trial provisions do not apply, so the offence could not be defined as summary only. Section 9A inserted into the Act imposes a duty on a magistrates' court considering whether to withhold or grant bail in such a case to consider the value involved in the offence. If it is less than £5,000 the offence will be triable summarily only and the court shall make a determination to that effect so the new provisions of Pt 1A of the Bail Act will apply.

Part 1 of Sched. 1 to the *Bail Act* 1976 was amended by the*Coroners and Justice Act* 2009, s.114 with effect from February 1, 2010 with the insertion of a new para. 6ZA which applies only to murder cases in respect of which the magistrates' court no longer has power to grant bail.

Bail Act 1976, Sched. 1

SCHEDULE 1

PERSONS ENTITLED TO BAIL: SUPPLEMENTARY PROVISIONS

PART I

Defendants Accused or Convicted of Imprisonable Offences

Defendants to whom Part I applies

1.—(1) The following provisions of this Part of this Schedule apply to the defendant if— **5–35**

(a) the offence or one of the offences of which he is accused or convicted in the proceedings is punishable with imprisonment, or

(b) his extradition is sought in respect of an offence.

(2) But those provisions do not apply by virtue of sub-paragraph (1)(a) if the offence, or each of the offences punishable with imprisonment, is—

(a) a summary offence; or

(b) an offence mentioned in Schedule 2 to the *Magistrates' Courts Act* 1980 (offences for which the value involved is relevant to the mode of trial) in relation to which—

(i) a determination has been made under section 22(2) of that Act (certain either way offences to be tried summarily if value involved is less than the relevant sum) that it is clear that the value does not exceed the relevant sum for the purposes of that section; or

(ii) a determination has been made under section 9A(4) of this Act to the same effect.

Exceptions to right to bail

2.—(1) The defendant need not be granted bail if the court is satisfied that there are substantial grounds for believing that the defendant, if released on bail (whether subject to conditions or not) would—

(a) fail to surrender to custody, or

(b) commit an offence while on bail, or

(c) interfere with witnesses or otherwise obstruct the course of justice, whether in relation to himself or any other person.

(2) Where the defendant falls within one or more of paragraphs 2A, 6 and 6B of this Part of this Schedule, this paragraph shall not apply unless—

(a) where the defendant falls within paragraph 2A, the court is satisfied as mentioned in sub-paragraph (1) of that paragraph;

(b) where the defendant falls within paragraph 6, the court is satisfied as mentioned in sub-paragraph (1) of that paragraph;

(c) where the defendant falls within paragraph 6B, the court is satisfied as mentioned in paragraph 6A of this Part of this Schedule or paragraph 6A does not apply by virtue of paragraph 6C of this Part of this Schedule.

2A.—(1) The defendant need not be granted bail if—

(a) the offence is an indictable offence or an offence triable either way; and

(b) it appears to the court that he was on bail in criminal proceedings on the date of the offence.

[2A.—(1) If the defendant falls within this paragraph he may not be granted bail unless the court is satisfied that there is no significant risk of his committing an offence while on bail (whether subject to conditions or not).

(2) The defendant falls within this paragraph if—

(a) he is aged 18 or over, and

(b) it appears to the court that he was on bail in criminal proceedings on the date of the offence.]

2B. The defendant need not be granted bail in connection with extradition proceedings if—

(a) the conduct constituting the offence would, if carried out by the defendant in England and Wales, constitute an indictable offence or an offence triable either way; and

(b) it appears to the court that the defendant was on bail on the date of the offence.

3. The defendant need not be granted bail if the court is satisfied that the defendant should be kept in custody for his own protection or, if he is a child or young person, for his own welfare.

4. The defendant need not be granted bail if he is in custody in pursuance of the sentence of a court or of any authority acting under any of the Services Acts.

5. The defendant need not be granted bail where the court is satisfied that it has not been practicable to obtain sufficient information for the purpose of taking the decisions required by this Part of this Schedule for want of time since the institution of the proceedings against him.

6. The defendant need not be granted bail if, having been released on bail in or in con-

nection with the proceedings for the offence or the extradition proceedings, he has been arrested in pursuance of section 7 of this Act.

[6.—(1) If the defendant falls within this paragraph, he may not be granted bail unless the court is satisfied that there is no significant risk that, if released on bail (whether subject to conditions or not), he would fail to surrender to custody.

(2) Subject to sub-paragraph (3) below, the defendant falls within this paragraph if–

(a) he is aged 18 or over, and

(b) it appears to the court that, having been released on bail in or in connection with the proceedings for the offence, he failed to surrender to custody.

(3) Where it appears to the court that the defendant had reasonable cause for his failure to surrender to custody, he does not fall within this paragraph unless it also appears to the court that he failed to surrender to custody at the appointed place as soon as reasonably practicable after the appointed time.

(4) For the purposes of sub-paragraph (3) above, a failure to give to the defendant a copy of the record of the decision to grant him bail shall not constitute a reasonable cause for his failure to surrender to custody.]

(6ZA) If the defendant is charged with murder, the defendant may not be granted bail unless the court is of the opinion that there is no significant risk of the defendant committing, while on bail, an offence that would, or would be likely to, cause physical or mental injury to any person other than the defendant.

Exception applicable to drug users in certain areas

6A. Subject to paragraph 6C below, a defendant who falls within paragraph 6B below may not be granted bail unless the court is satisfied that there is no significant risk of his committing an offence while on bail (whether subject to conditions or not).

6B.—(1) A defendant falls within this paragraph if—

(a) he is aged 18 or over;

(b) a sample taken—

(i) under section 63B of the *Police and Criminal Evidence Act* 1984 (testing for presence of Class A drugs) in connection with the offence; or

(ii) under section 161 of the *Criminal Justice Act* 2003 (drug testing after conviction of an offence but before sentence),

has revealed the presence in his body of a specified Class A drug;

(c) either the offence is one under section 5(2) or (3) of the *Misuse of Drugs Act* 1971 and relates to a specified Class A drug, or the court is satisfied that there are substantial grounds for believing—

(i) that misuse by him of any specified Class A drug caused or contributed to the offence; or

(ii) (even if it did not) that the offence was motivated wholly or partly by his intended misuse of such a drug; and

(d) the condition set out in sub-paragraph (2) below is satisfied or (if the court is considering on a second or subsequent occasion whether or not to grant bail) has been, and continues to be, satisfied.

(2) The condition referred to is that after the taking and analysis of the sample—

(a) a relevant assessment has been offered to the defendant but he does not agree to undergo it; or

(b) he has undergone a relevant assessment, and relevant follow-up has been proposed to him, but he does not agree to participate in it.

(3) In this paragraph and paragraph 6C below—

(a) "Class A drug" and "misuse" have the same meaning as in the *Misuse of Drugs Act* 1971;

(b) "relevant assessment" and "relevant follow-up" have the meaning given by section 3(6E) of this Act;

(c) "specified" (in relation to a Class A drug) has the same meaning as in Part 3 of the *Criminal Justice and Court Services Act* 2000.

6C. Paragraph 6A above does not apply unless—

(a) the court has been notified by the Secretary of State that arrangements for conducting a relevant assessment or, as the case may be, providing relevant follow-up have been made for the local justice area in which it appears to the court that the defendant would reside if granted bail; and

(b) the notice has not been withdrawn.

Exception applicable only to defendant whose case is adjourned for inquiries or a report

7. Where his case is adjourned for inquiries or a report, the defendant need not be granted bail if it appears to the court that it would be impracticable to complete the inquiries or make the report without keeping the defendant in custody.

Restrictions of conditions of bail

8.—(1) Subject to sub-paragraph (3) below, where the defendant is granted bail, no conditions shall be imposed under subsections (4) to (7) (except subsections (6)(d) or (e)) of section 3 of this Act unless it appears to the court that it is necessary to do so—

(a) for the purpose of preventing the occurrence of any of the events mentioned in paragraph 2(1) of this Part of this Schedule or

(b) for the defendant's own protection or, if he is a child or young person, for his own welfare or in his own interests

(1A) No condition shall be imposed under section 3(6)(d) of this Act unless it appears to be necessary to do so for the purpose of enabling inquiries or a report to be made.

(2) Sub-paragraphs (1) and (1A) above also apply on any application to the court to vary the conditions of bail or to impose conditions in respect of bail which has been granted unconditionally.

(3) The restriction imposed by sub-paragraph (1A) above shall not apply to the conditions required to be imposed under section 3(6A) of this Act or operate to override the direction in section 11(3) of the *Powers of Criminal Courts (Sentencing) Act* 2000 to a magistrates' court to impose conditions of bail under section 3(6)(d) of this Act of the description specified in the said section 11(3) in the circumstances so specified.

Decisions under paragraph 2

9. In taking the decisions required by paragraph 2(1), or in deciding whether it is satisfied as mentioned in paragraph 2A(1), 6(1) or *6A* of this Part of this Schedule, the court shall have regard to such of the following considerations as appear to it to be relevant, that is to say—

(a) the nature and seriousness of the offence or default (and the probable method of dealing with the defendant for it),

(b) the character, antecedents, associations and community ties of the defendant,

(c) the defendant's record as respects the fulfilment of his obligations under previous grants of bail in criminal proceedings,

(d) except in the case of a defendant whose case is adjourned for inquiries or a report, the strength of the evidence of his having committed the offence or having defaulted,

(e) if the court is satisfied that there are substantial grounds for believing that the defendant, if released on bail (whether subject to conditions or not), would commit an offence while on bail, the risk that the defendant may do so by engaging in conduct that would, or would be likely to, cause physical or mental injury to any person other than the defendant.

as well as to any others which appear to be relevant.

[9AA.—(1) This paragraph applies if—

(a) the defendant is under the age of 18, and

(b) it appears to the court that he was on bail in criminal proceedings on the date of the offence.

(2) In deciding for the purposes of paragraph 2(1) of this Part of this Schedule whether it is satisfied that there are substantial grounds for believing that the defendant, if released on bail (whether subject to conditions or not), would commit an offence while on bail, the court shall give particular weight to the fact that the defendant was on bail in criminal proceedings on the date of the offence.

9AB.—(1) Subject to sub-paragraph (2) below, this paragraph applies if—

(a) the defendant is under the age of 18, and

(b) it appears to the court that, having been released on bail in or in connection with the proceedings for the offence, he failed to surrender to custody.

(2) Where it appears to the court that the defendant had reasonable cause for his failure to surrender to custody, this paragraph does not apply unless it also appears to the court that he failed to surrender to custody at the appointed place as soon as reasonably practicable after the appointed time.

(3) In deciding for the purposes of paragraph 2(1) of this Part of this Schedule whether it is satisfied that there are substantial grounds for believing that the defendant, if released on bail (whether subject to conditions or not), would fail to surrender to custody the court shall give particular weight to—

(a) where the defendant did not have reasonable cause for his failure to surrender to custody, the fact that he failed to surrender to custody, or

(b) where he did have reasonable cause for his failure to surrender to custody, the fact that he failed to surrender to custody at the appointed place as soon as reasonably practicable after the appointed time.

(4) For the purposes of this paragraph, a failure to give to the defendant a copy of the record of the decision to grant him bail shall not constitute a reasonable cause for his failure to surrender to custody.]

9B. Where the court is considering exercising the power conferred by section 128A of the *Magistrates' Courts Act* 1980 (power to remand in custody for more than 8 clear days), it shall have regard to the total length of time which the accused would spend in custody if it were to exercise the power.

PART 1A

Defendants Accused or Convicted of Imprisonable Offences to which Part 1 does not apply

Defendants to whom Part 1A applies

1. Subject to sub-para.(2), the following provisions of this Part apply to the defendant if—

(a) the offence or one of the offences of which he is accused or convicted is punishable with imprisonment, but

(b) Part 1 does not apply to him by virtue of paragraph 1(2) of that Part.

Exceptions to right to bail

2. The defendant need not be granted bail if—

(a) it appears to the court that, having been previously granted bail in criminal proceedings, he has failed to surrender to custody in accordance with his obligations under the grant of bail; and

(b) the court believes, in view of that failure, that the defendant, if released on bail (whether subject to conditions or not) would fail to surrender to custody.

3. The defendant need not be granted bail if—

(a) it appears to the court that the defendant was on bail in criminal proceedings on the date of the offence; and

(b) the court is satisfied that there are substantial grounds for believing that the defendant, if released on bail (whether subject to conditions or not) would commit an offence while on bail.

4. The defendant need not be granted bail if the court is satisfied that there are substantial grounds for believing that the defendant, if released on bail (whether subject to conditions or not), would commit an offence while on bail by engaging in conduct that would, or would be likely to, cause—

(a) physical or mental injury to any person other than the defendant; or

(b) any person other than the defendant to fear physical or mental injury.

5. The defendant need not be granted bail if the court is satisfied that the defendant should be kept in custody for his own protection or, if he is a child or young person, for his own welfare.

6. The defendant need not be granted bail if he is in custody in pursuance of a sentence of a court or a sentence imposed by an officer under the *Armed Forces Act* 2006.

7. The defendant need not be granted bail if —

(a) having been released on bail in or in connection with the proceedings for the offence, he has been arrested in pursuance of section 7 of this Act; and

(b) the court is satisfied that there are substantial grounds for believing that the defendant, if released on bail (whether subject to conditions or not) would fail to surrender to custody, commit an offence while on bail or interfere with witnesses or otherwise obstruct the course of justice (whether in relation to himself or any other person).

8. The defendant need not be granted bail where the court is satisfied that it has not

been practicable to obtain sufficient information for the purpose of taking the decisions required by this Part of this Schedule for want of time since the institution of the proceedings against him.

Application of paragraphs 6A to 6C of Part 1

9. Paragraphs 6A to 6C of Part 1 (exception applicable to drug users in certain areas and related provisions) apply to a defendant to whom this Part applies as they apply to a defendant to whom that Part applies.

Bail decisions relating to persons aged under 18 who are accused of offences mentioned in Schedule 2 to the Magistrates' Courts Act 1980

9A.—(1) This section applies whenever—

(a) a magistrates' court is considering whether to withhold or grant bail in relation to a person aged under 18 who is accused of a scheduled offence; and

(b) the trial of that offence has not begun.

(2) The court shall, before deciding whether to withhold or grant bail, consider whether, having regard to any representations made by the prosecutor or the accused person, the value involved does not exceed the relevant sum for the purposes of section 22.

(3) The duty in subsection (2) does not apply in relation to an offence if—

(a) a determination under subsection (4) has already been made in relation to that offence; or

(b) the accused person is, in relation to any other offence of which he is accused which is not a scheduled offence, a person to whom Part 1 of Schedule 1 to this Act applies.

(4) If where the duty in subsection (2) applies it appears to the court clear that, for the offence in question, the amount involved does not exceed the relevant sum, the court shall make a determination to that effect.

(5) In this section—

(a) "relevant sum" has the same meaning as in section 22(1) of the Magistrates' Courts Act 1980 (certain either way offences to be tried summarily if value involved is less than the relevant sum);

(b) "scheduled offence" means an offence mentioned in Schedule 2 to that Act (offences for which the value involved is relevant to the mode of trial); and

(c) "the value involved" is to be construed in accordance with section 22(10) to (12) of that Act."

PART II

DEFENDANTS ACCUSED OR CONVICTED OF NON-IMPRISONABLE OFFENCES

Defendants to whom Part II applies

5–36 1. Where the offence or every offence of which the defendant is accused or convicted in the proceedings is one which is not punishable with imprisonment the following provisions of this Part of this Schedule apply.

Exceptions to right to bail

2. The defendant need not be granted bail if—

(a) it appears to the court that, having been previously granted bail in criminal proceedings, he has failed to surrender to custody in accordance with his obligations under the grant of bail; and

(b) the court believes, in view of that failure, that the defendant, if released on bail (whether subject to conditions or not) would fail to surrender to custody.

3. The defendant need not be granted bail if the court is satisfied that the defendant should be kept in custody for his own protection or, if he is a child or young person, for his own welfare.

4. The defendant need not be granted bail if he is in custody in pursuance of the sentence of a court or of any authority acting under any of the Services Acts.

5. The defendant need not be granted bail if—

(a) having been released on bail in or in connection with the proceedings for the offence, he has been arrested in pursuance of section 7 of this Act, and

(b) the court is satisfied that there are substantial grounds for believing that the defendant, if released on bail (whether subject to conditions or not) would fail to surrender to custody, commit an offence on bail or interfere with witnesses or otherwise obstruct the court of justice whether in relation to himself or any other person.

PART IIA

DECISIONS WHERE BAIL REFUSED ON PREVIOUS HEARING

1. If the court decides not to grant the defendant bail, it is the court's duty to consider, at each subsequent hearing while the defendant is a person to whom s.4 above applies and remains in custody, whether he ought to be granted bail. **5–37**

2. At the first hearing after that at which the court decided not to grant the defendant bail he may support an application for bail with any argument as to fact or law that he desires (whether or not he has advanced that argument previously).

3. At subsequent hearings the court need not hear arguments as to fact or law which its has heard previously.

[This Sched. is printed as amended by the *Criminal Justice Act* 2003, ss.13, 20 and ss.14 and 15 which came into force (partially) on January 1, 2007: *Criminal Justice Act 2003 (Commencement No.14 and Transitional Provision) Order* 2006 (S.I. 2006 No.3217). The paragraphs printed in square brackets are the new provisions which apply only to offences carrying life imprisonment. The Schedule is also amended by the *Criminal Justice and Immigration Act* 2008 s.52 and Sch. 12 which came into force on July 14, 2008: *Criminal Justice and Immigration Act* 2008 (Commencement No.2 and Transitional and Saving Provisions) Order 2008 (S.I. 2008 No.1586) and the *Coroners and Justice Act* 2009 s.114 which came into force on February 1, 2010: *Coroners and Justice Act 2009 (Commencement No.3 and Transitional Provision) Order* 2010 (S.I. 2010 No. 145).]

Considerations on the granting of bail

Bail need not be granted if there are substantial grounds for believing that the defendant would fail to surrender to custody, commit an offence whilst on bail or interfere with witnesses or otherwise obstruct the course of justice. The test for withholding bail is more rigorous than the test for imposing conditions on bail. The court need not be satisfied that the consequences in para. 2(a)–(c) would actually occur if bail were to be granted. It has to be satisfied that there are substantial grounds for believing that they would occur. However, it is not enough for the court to have a subjective belief that there is a risk of one or more of the events in para. 2 occurring: *Mansfield Justices, ex p. Sharkey* [1985] Q.B. 613. **5–38**

Express consideration must be given to any safeguards offered by the defence aimed at addressing the risks giving rise to exceptions to bail. The court is obliged to demonstrate that any proposals put forward have been properly considered to a sufficient and appropriate degree in making any decision on bail, but more so when serious charges are faced. *R. (on the application of Bailey) v. Central Criminal Court* [2010] EWHC 667.

Consideration has been given in European case law to the reasons why a person may be refused bail and be deprived of his liberty. Substantial grounds for believing a person may fail to surrender to custody are sufficient grounds but the court has said that there must be "a whole set of circumstances …..which give reason to suppose that the consequences and hazards of flight will seem to him to be a lesser evil than continued imprisonment": *Stogmuller v. Austria* (1969) 1 E.H.R.R. 155. It has also been indicated that the aspects of the individual case must be taken into account which include,"the character of the person involved, his morals, his home, his occupation, his assets, his family ties and all kinds of links with the country in which he is being prosecuted.": *Neumeister v. Austria* (1968) 1 E.H.R.R. 91.

5–39 The severity of the potential sentence alone cannot of itself justify the refusal of bail. There have to exist other grounds that give rise to the belief that the accused may abscond: *Letellier v. France* (1992) 14 E.H.R.R. 83; *W v. Switzerland* (1993) 17 E.H.R.R. 60; *Mansur v. Turkey* 20 E.H.R.R. 535. In *R. (Thompson) v. Central Criminal Court* [2005] EWHC 2345 it was held that a defendant charged with a serious offence and liable to a severe penalty may be considered likely to abscond if granted bail. If conditions cannot safely eliminate such a risk the court may refuse bail but the decision must be based on all relevant factors specific to the individual and the case and clear and explicit reasons for refusal of bail must be given by the court. See also *Hurnam v. State of Mauritius* [2006] 1 W.L.R. 857.

In relation to the commission of further offences it has been held that this may amount to "good and sufficient reason" and detention may be justified to prevent crime: *Matznetter v. Austria* (1969) 1 E.H.R.R. 198. Detention may also be justified for the preservation of public order where in offences of particular gravity there are substantial grounds to believe that public disorder may result from the accused's release: *Letellier v. France*.

Schedule 1 to the *Bail Act* is printed here as amended by s.14 and 15(1) and (2) of the *Criminal Justice Act* 2003 which were brought into force partially on January 1, 2007 by the *Criminal Justice Act 2003 (Commencement No.14 and Transitional Provision) Order* 2006 (S.I. 2006 No.3217). At this stage the statutory instrument makes it clear that the amendments only apply to offences which carry life imprisonment. The amendments are printed in square brackets. The existing wording of the Schedule still applies to all other offences.

The test has been changed where the court considers bail for a person charged with a relevant offence who has committed an offence whilst on bail or who has failed to surrender to bail during the proceedings. Where the defendant is 18 years or over and it appears to the court that he committed the offence whilst on bail then bail may not be granted unless the court is satisfied that there is no significant risk of his committing an offence if granted bail. Similarly, for a defendant aged 18 or over, where it appears that he was released on bail for the offence and failed to surrender to custody during the proceedings then bail may not be granted unless the court is satisfied that there is no significant risk of his failing to surrender to custody again if released on bail. If the court finds there was a reasonable cause for the failure to surrender then these provisions only apply if it appears to the court that the defendant failed to surrender to custody as soon as reasonably practicable after the appointed time. Failure to be provided with a copy of the bail record sheet cannot be a reasonable cause for failing to surrender at the appointed time.

Slightly different and less stringent provisions apply to youths. For defendants under the age of 18 the court must give "particular weight" to the fact that a defendant was on bail at the time when it appears to the court that he committed the offence in order to determine whether there are substantial grounds to believe that the defendant would commit offences if released on bail. Where a defendant aged under 18 has failed to surrender to bail previously then also "particular weight" must be given to that fact in determining whether there are substantial grounds to believe that he would fail to surrender in future if granted bail.

These amendments come into force on January 1, 2007 but only apply to offences carrying life imprisonment. In respect of s.14 which relates to offences committed on bail it applies only to offences committed on or after that date. For s.15 which covers failure to answer bail it applies where there has been a failure to surrender to bail in the proceedings on or after January 1, 2007. The provisions apply only to court bail and not to bail granted by the police.

These amendments provide a further refinement to the application of the *Bail Act* and are designed to ensure that compliance with ECHR is beyond dispute. Under the provisions of para. 2A of Sched. 1 which continue to apply to indictable or either way offences that do not attract a sentence of life imprisonment, bail need not be granted if it appears to the court that the defendant was on bail in criminal proceedings on the date of the offence. There is no qualification to that discretion. By the amendments of s.14 the presumption of bail is affected so that the defendant may not be granted bail if he was on bail at the date of the offence unless the court is satisfied there is no significant risk of further offences whilst on bail. The terminology "significant risk" differs from the substantial grounds referred to in para. 2(1) of the Schedule and appears to be a higher test. The "significant risk" test also applies in cases where the defendant appears to have failed to answer his bail in the proceedings and the amendments of s.15 also affect the presumption of bail so that the defendant may not be granted bail where he has failed to answer bail in the proceedings before. With respect to youths the test is not quite so high as "particular weight" is to be given to these aspects of the situation in order to determine whether there are substantial grounds for believing the defendant would commit offences or fail to answer his bail. The determination of significant risk does not apply to youths but the fact of offences being committed on bail in the past and a history of failing to answer bail in the proceedings would apparently contribute heavily to finding substantial grounds to believe that this would happen again in future if bail were granted.

As to the fear of interference with witnesses or the obstruction of justice, the court has indicated that a generalised risk that this might occur is not sufficient. A specific risk must be identifiable and supported by evidence: *Clooth v. Belgium* (1991) 14 E.H.R.R. 717. The risk may involve the interference with witnesses, warning suspects or destroying evidence: *Wemhoff v. Germany* (1979) 1 E.H.R.R. 55.

The court must have regard to the four considerations of para. 9, Sched. 1 as well as others that appear relevant. The desirability of a medical examination of a defendant charged with murder was held to be a relevant consideration which may amount to an exception to bail: *Vernege* [1982] 1 All E.R. 403. **5–40**

The prosecution, when making representations about bail must ensure that relevant reasons are brought to the attention of the court. Previous convictions are relevant and where the accused has a criminal record, a copy may be handed to the court, but as far as possible detailed oral reference to it should be avoided: *Dyson* 29 Cr.App.R. 104. Sight of the record disqualifies the court from hearing any subsequent trial as the *Magistrates' Courts Act* 1980 provides that a magistrate shall not participate in trying the issue of a defendant's guilt on the summary trial of an information if in the course of the same proceedings, for the purpose of deciding whether the defendant should have bail, he or she has been informed of any previous convictions: *Magistrates' Courts Act* 1980, s.42. This section will be repealed by the *Criminal Justice Act* 2003, s.41 and Sched. 3.

The Schedule prescribes a different approach for imprisonable and non-imprisonable offences. For the latter, the exceptions to bail are more limited. The *Criminal Justice and Immigration Act* 2008 also distinguished between imprisonable offences which are summary only and those that are not. Again the exceptions to bail in relation to summary only imprisonable offences are more limited. In addition to those exceptions listed in Pt II of the Schedule for non-imprisonable offences, if the offence is imprisonable but summary only the further exceptions to bail are that the instant offence was committed whilst on bail and there are substantial grounds for believing that further offences would be committed were the defendant to be released on bail; that there are substantial grounds to believe that the defendant if granted bail would commit an offence which would involve physical or mental injury to any other person or would cause any other person to fear physical or mental injury and bail may also be refused if there is insufficient information available to enable the court to make a bail decision.

IV. CONDITIONS OF BAIL

(1) Bail Act 1976, Sched. 1, para. 8

Paragraph 8 gives the power to impose conditions on bail. Section 3 of the *Bail Act* 1976 sets out the types of conditions which may be attached to the grant of bail in criminal proceedings. When bail is granted to a person to whom s.4 applies, no condition **5–41** may be attached unless it is considered necessary for the purpose of preventing absconding, the commission of an offence on bail or interference with witnesses or the obstruction of justice, or for the purpose of obtaining medical or other reports.

Pre-release

5–42 1. To provide a security or sureties (see *post*, for details). The imposition of sureties and securities has been considered by the European Court which held that the figure set must take account of the means of the accused who deposits a security or the third person if standing as a surety. The relationship between the accused and the surety should also be considered: *Wemhoff v. Germany* (*ante*); *Neumeister v. Austria*, (*ante*).

2. To surrender a passport to the police. The surrender of a passport or other travel documents and indeed driving documents was held by the European Court to be proportional: *Stogmuller v. Austria*, (*ante*). It is not appropriate for such documents to be surrendered to the magistrates' court as there is no procedure for the retention or disposal of such items.

Post-release

5–43 1. A condition of residence to live and sleep each night at a fixed, approved address. This may stipulate residence at a bail or other type of hostel. The court should be assured that the address is suitable and in the case of hostels, a place should formally be confirmed by the appropriate authorities. It is also usual for a further condition to be attached when directing residence at a hostel that the rules and regulations of the hostel must be observed. The European Court has approved the proportionality of a condition of residence: *Schmid v. Austria* [1985] 44 D.R. 195. The National Offender Management Service has introduced a bail accommodation support service which has been contracted out to private suppliers. The contractors may provide accommodation in cases where bail may be refused mainly because of the lack of a suitable address. Accommodation will be in houses and flats within the community and the person bailed will have to keep appointments with the support service on a weekly basis when help will be given to find permanent accommodation, etc. The service is aimed at low risk offenders. Availability of the support service will be indicated to the court through a bail information report from prison or probation. Rule 19.27 of the *Criminal Procedure Rules* 2011 applies to bail granted subject to accommodation or support requirements provided by, or on behalf of, a local authority. Under the rule the court has a duty to inform the service provider of the details of the defendant and the offence and also to give details of the accommodation or support requirement and other bail conditions and the return date to court. The defendant must be notified by the court of the name and contact details of the service provider and the address where he must reside under the requirement. Any subsequent changes to the requirement or bail conditions or the date must also be notified by the court to the service provider. See Appendix G. Rule 19.25 of the *Criminal Procedure Rules* 2011 puts a requirement on the defendant to inform the prosecutor of the details of any proposed address put forward as a condition of residence. The information must be conveyed as soon as practicable and any change of the address must also be notified. There is also a requirement on the prosecutor to help the court assess the suitability of the proposed address. This gives legislative effect to the well-established court practice of asking the police or prosecution to check suggested addresses when bail applications are being made. See Appendix G.

2. A curfew may be imposed ordering the defendant to stay indoors at a specified address during specified hours. Whether any such condition is necessary to protect the public, (*i.e.* proportional) is a question of fact for each case. *R. (CPS) v. Chorley Justices* [2002] EWHC 2162.

Part I

The *Bail Act* 1976 ss.3AB and 3AC provide for electronic monitoring of curfews and set out the pre-conditions for imposition; see § 5–10. Rule 19.26 of the *Criminal Procedure Rules* 2011 applies to bail granted subject to a condition of electronic curfew. The court is under a duty to notify those responsible for monitoring the curfew of the details of the defendant, the offence and the specific requirements of the curfew. The court must also provide the defendant with the name of those responsible for monitoring the curfew and their contact details. The court must also notify those responsible for monitoring the curfew of any subsequent changes or variations to the curfew. The court still retains the power under s.3(6) of the *Bail Act* 1976 to require a "doorstep" condition that the person bailed present himself at the doorstep of the premises named during the hours of a curfew if a police officer so demands to prove that he is staying indoors and abiding by the curfew. It is important to distinguish between the different nature of the curfew conditions because the time spent on remand subject to an electronically monitored curfew must be taken into account when calculating the period to be served of any subsequent sentence of imprisonment. A curfew period of at least nine hours counts as a half day spent in custody and credit for that time must be given unless there is good reason to disallow it. See § 23–145 *et seq*. This credit is not given to any curfew which is not electronically monitored.

3. The accused may be directed to report to a police station in person on specific days and at specific times. His attendance will be noted. It is advisable to check that the police station is at a convenient location for the accused and that it is open at the relevant times.
4. A condition of non-contact may be made in relation to specific persons who should be named. This condition is common in charges involving violence where the alleged victim may be named but it may also relate to other witnesses or co-defendants. Direct and indirect contact which may be prohibited includes the use of the internet, mobile phones and texting either by the accused or someone else on his behalf.
5. The accused may be prohibited from going to certain specified areas. This could cover a specific address where an offence was said to have occurred or where the alleged victim lives. It could also cover a wider area, such as a shopping centre or the London Tube system where the offence is one that is habitually committed in those places. The area prohibited must be clearly identified and measurements are sometimes used, (*e.g.* not to go within 100 metres of ...) and exceptions can be made to the exclusion by permitting appearances at court or solicitors if located within the prohibited area. If a defendant is excluded from his place of residence the condition may be expressed to allow one visit accompanied by a police officer to collect personal effects.
6. The accused may be required to attend at all appointments and to co-operate with all directions given for the preparation of reports.

The court and the police should ensure that the defendant is able to comply with any **5–44**
condition they intend to impose under section 3(6) and that such conditions are clearly expressed, proportional and enforceable. The list above is far from exhaustive and the court and police have a wide discretion to devise and impose such conditions as appear necessary. Any conditions must be designed to address the real risks of failing to surrender, committing further offences, obstructing justice or interfering with witnesses or failing to attend for interviews. The European Court has said that equal care must be taken in fixing appropriate bail conditions as in deciding on continued detention: *Iwanczuk v. Poland* (2004) 38 E.H.R.R. 8.

In deciding on conditions the court is entitled to use its knowledge of local events and conditions. In *Mansfield Justices, ex p. Sharkey* [1985] Q.B. 613, Lord Lane said that:

"The question the justices should ask themselves is a simple one; 'Is this condition necessary for the prevention of the commission of an offence when on bail?' They are not obliged to have substantial grounds. It is enough if they perceive a real and not a fanciful risk of the offence being committed. Thus, section 3(6) and paragraph 8 give the court a wide discretion to inquire whether the condition is necessary."

5–45 The defendants were arrested on suspicion of public order offences allegedly committed during the miners' strike of 1984–85. The court was entitled to impose conditions of bail not to picket except in respect of their own pits. The court was not obliged to have substantial grounds for believing that a repetition of the defendant's conduct would occur. That perception could be based on knowledge of what was happening in the pits in the area.

5–46 Conditions on bail may be imposed in respect of offences which are not punishable by imprisonment. In *Bournemouth Magistrates' Court, ex p. Cross* [1989] Crim.L.R. 207, the defendant was in the habit of protesting at fox hunt meets. He was bailed in respect of a public order offence arising from such a protest on the condition that he did not attend another hunt meeting before his next court appearance. The Divisional Court held that the condition had been validly imposed as the magistrates had considered that it was necessary to prevent the commission of further offences.

(2) Sureties

5–47 A person who stands surety enters into a recognisance to pay a fixed sum of money if the defendant fails to attend court.

Bail Act 1976, s.8

Bail with sureties

5–48 **8.**—(1) This section applies where a person is granted bail in criminal proceedings on condition that he provides one or more surety or sureties for the purpose of securing that he surrenders to custody.

(2) In considering the suitability for that purpose of a proposed surety, regard may be had (amongst other things) to—

(a) the surety's financial resources;

(b) his character and any previous convictions of his; and

(c) his proximity (whether in point of kinship, place of residence or otherwise) to the person for whom he is to be surety.

(3) Where a court grants a person bail in criminal proceedings on such a condition but is unable to release him because no surety or no suitable surety is available, the court shall fix the amount in which the surety is to be bound and subsections (4) and (5) below, or in a case where the proposed surety resides in Scotland subsection (6) below, shall apply for the purpose of enabling the recognizance of the surety to be entered into subsequently.

(4) Where this subsection applies the recognizance of the surety may be entered into before such of the following persons or descriptions of persons as the court may by order specify or, if it makes no such order, before any of the following persons, that is to say—

(a) where the decision is taken by a magistrates' court, before a justice of the peace, a justices' clerk or a police officer who either is of the rank of inspector or above or is in charge of a police station or, if *Criminal Procedure Rules* so provide, by a person of such other description as is specified in the rules;

(b) where the decision is taken by the Crown Court, before any of the persons specified in paragraph (a) above or, if *Criminal Procedure Rules* so provide, by a person of such other description as is specified in the rules;

(c) where the decision is taken by the High Court or the Court of Appeal, before any of the persons specified in paragraph (a) above or, if *Civil Procedure Rules* or *Criminal Procedure Rules* so provide, by a person of such other description as is specified in the rules;

(d) where the decision is taken by the Courts-Martial Appeal Court, before any of the persons specified in paragraph (a) above or, if *Courts-Martial Appeal rules* so provide, by a person of such other description as is specified in the rules;

and *Civil Procedure Rules*, *Criminal Procedure Rules* or *Courts-Martial Appeal rules* may also prescribe the manner in which a recognizance which is to be entered into before such a person is to be entered into and the persons by whom and the manner in which the recognizance may be enforced.

(5) Where a surety seeks to enter into his recognizance before any person in accordance with subsection (4) above but that person declines to take his recognizance because he is not satisfied of the surety's suitability, the surety may apply to—

(a) the court which fixed the amount of the recognizance in which the surety was to be bound, or

(b) a magistrates' court,

for that court to take his recognizance and that court shall, if satisfied of his suitability, take his recognizance.

(6) Where this subsection applies, the court, if satisfied of the suitability of the proposed surety, may direct that arrangements be made for the recognizance of the surety to be entered into in Scotland before any constable, within the meaning of the *Police (Scotland) Act* 1967, having charge at any police office or station in like manner as the recognizance would be entered into in England or Wales.

(7) Where, in pursuance of subsection (4) or (6) above, a recognizance is entered into otherwise than before the court that fixed the amount of the recognizance, the same consequences shall follow as if it had been entered into before that court.

[This section is printed as amended by the *Courts Act* 2003, Scheds 8 and 10.]

The obligation of a surety extends only to securing the defendant's attendance at court. A surety is not responsible for preventing any other defaults while the defendant is on bail. A surety should only be required where there is a risk that the defendant will fail to surrender to custody. **5–49**

A surety may be taken in court by the magistrates or out of court by a legal adviser or other person to whom the justices' clerk has delegated the power. A surety may also be taken at a police station by a police officer of the rank of inspector or above or by a prison governor if the accused is in prison: *Magistrates' Courts Rules* 1981, r.86. The procedure adopted will depend on the gravity of the charge and the amount of surety fixed by the court. The person taking the surety will investigate the matters listed in s.8(2) and production of bank statements, savings accounts and payslips may be required as evidence of financial resources. The nature of the relationship between the surety and the defendant must also be inquired into so the court may be satisfied of the extent of the influence the surety holds over the defendant. The nature of the responsibility that is being assumed must also be explained to the surety. The surety has a personal duty to ensure that the defendant surrenders to custody at the time and place specified. If the defendant fails to surrender the amount of the recognisance fixed or some of it may be ordered to be paid. If the money is not paid immediately or within a time set, the surety can be committed to prison in default of payment.

The defendant's representative has a particular responsibility to ensure that a surety would be able to meet his or her financial obligations before being tendered to the court: *Birmingham Crown Court, ex p. Rashid Ali* [1999] Crim.L.R. 504.

Bail Act 1976, s.9

Offence of agreeing to indemnify sureties in criminal proceedings

9.—(1) If a person agrees with another to indemnify that other against any liability which that other may incur as a surety to secure the surrender to custody of a person accused or convicted of or under arrest for an offence, he and that other person shall be guilty of an offence. **5–50**

(2) An offence under subsection (1) above is committed whether the agreement is made before or after the person to be indemnified becomes a surety and whether or not he becomes a surety and whether the agreement contemplates compensation in money or in money's worth.

(3) Where a magistrates' court convicts a person of an offence under subsection (1) above the court may, if it thinks—

(a) that the circumstances of the offence are such that greater punishment should be inflicted for that offence than the court has power to inflict, or

(b) in a case where it sends that person for trial to the Crown Court for another offence, that it would be appropriate for him to be dealt with for the offence under subsection (1) above by the court before which he is tried for the other offence,

commit him in custody or on bail to the Crown Court for sentence.

(4) A person guilty of an offence under subsection (1) above shall be liable—

(a) on summary conviction, to imprisonment for a term not exceeding 3 months or to a fine not exceeding £400 or to both; or

(b) on conviction on indictment or if sentenced by the Crown Court on committal for sentence under subsection (3) above, to imprisonment for a term not exceeding 12 months or to a fine or to both.

(5) No proceedings for an offence under subsection (1) above shall be instituted except by or with the consent of the Director of Public Prosecutions.

Magistrates' Courts Act 1980, s.119

Postponement of taking recognizance

5–51 **119.**—(1) Where a magistrates' court has power to take any recognizance, the court may, instead of taking it, fix the amount in which the principal and his sureties, if any, are to be bound; and thereafter the recognizance may be taken by any such person as may be prescribed.

(2) Where, in pursuance of this section, a recognizance is entered into otherwise than before the court that fixed the amount of it, the same consequences shall follow as if it had been entered into before that court; and references in this or any other Act to the court before which a recognizance was entered into shall be construed accordingly.

(3) Nothing in this section shall enable a magistrates' court to alter the amount of a recognizance fixed by the High Court or the Crown Court.

5–52 *Criminal Procedure Rules* 2011, r.19.5 in Appendix G explain the requirements to be complied with before a person subject to a surety may be released.

(3) Security

5–53 A person granted bail may be required to give security for his or her surrender to custody: *Bail Act* 1976, s.3(5). In *Truro Magistrates' Court, ex p. Stevens* [2002] 1 W.L.R. 144, DC, the court held that although Parliament had not limited the type of security which might be given under s.3(5) what was envisaged was the lodging of some asset, in cash or in kind, which could be readily forfeited on the defendant's non-appearance. However, the security could be given in less simple form if the justice of the case demanded it and it could be readily forfeited in the event of non-appearance without disputes with third parties. While it was permissible for a third party to make an asset available as security for the defendant, where a court failed to make clear the extent to which a third party's interest in registered land belonging to the defendant was the subject of the security, the security was to be interpreted as extending only to the defendant's beneficial interest.

5–54 *Criminal Procedure Rules* 2011, r.19.4 in Appendix G enables the court to give directions as to how a requirement of bail such as a surety shall be complied with.

(4) Application to vary conditions of bail

5–55 Under s.3(8)(a) of the *Bail Act* 1976, (see § 5–7) where bail has been granted subject to conditions, the magistrates' court may, on application by the person granted bail or the prosecutor or constable vary the conditions of bail or impose conditions in respect of the bail already granted. Notice of the application must be given so that both the defendant and the prosecution can make representations. The defendant is not bound to appear and simple variations can be made in the absence of the defendant. The court is under no duty to notify a surety of any application to vary bail conditions particularly when the surety is expressed to be continuous as the surety should keep himself informed of the bail position. Any ignorance of the variation may be taken into account when the court considers forfeiting the surety: *Wells Street Magistrates' Court, ex p. Albanese* [1982] Q.B. 333. When the defendant has been committed to the Crown

Court from the magistrates' court on bail then once he has surrendered to the Crown Court, that court is seised of all bail matters and any application to vary must be made to the Crown Court: *Lincoln Magistrates' Court, ex p. Mawer* (1996) 160 J.P. 219.

Rule 19.1 of the *Criminal Procedure Rules* 2011 applies to all applications to vary bail conditions not just police bail and requires that advance notice must be given explaining the changes sought, including any change of residence and the reasons for the application.

V. APPEAL AND RECONSIDERATION

A. GENERAL

The defence and the prosecution have the right to challenge bail decisions made by both the police and the court. **5–56**

A defendant detained by the police must be produced at a court as soon as is practicable after charge and then application for bail may be made to the court. If a defendant is remanded in custody by the court he has a right of appeal and may apply for bail to the Crown Court.

When the police impose conditions on bail the defendant may appeal to the magistrates' court for the conditions to be removed or varied. Where conditions are imposed by the magistrates' court, application may be made to the court to vary them or an appeal against certain conditions may be made to the Crown Court.

The prosecution may appeal to the Crown Court against a decision to grant bail where it was opposed. If fresh information comes to light the prosecution may also apply to the magistrates' court for a decision to grant bail to be reconsidered.

B. APPEAL TO MAGISTRATES' COURT IN RESPECT OF POLICE BAIL

Magistrates' Courts Act 1980, s.43B

Power to grant bail where police bail has been granted

43B.—(1) Where a custody officer— **5–57**

(a) grants bail to any person under Part IV of the *Police and Criminal Evidence Act* 1984 in criminal proceedings and imposes conditions, or

(b) varies, in relation to any person, conditions of bail in criminal proceedings under section 3(8) of the *Bail Act* 1976

a magistrates' court may, on application by or on behalf of that person, grant bail or vary the conditions.

(2) On an application under subsection (1) the court, if it grants bail and imposes conditions or if it varies the conditions, may impose more onerous conditions.

(3) On determining an application under subsection (1) the court shall remand the applicant, in custody or on bail in accordance with the determination, and, where the court withholds bail or grants bail the grant of bail made by the custody officer shall lapse.

(4) In this section "bail in criminal proceedings" and "vary" have the same meanings as they have in the *Bail Act* 1976.

Criminal Procedure Rules 2011, r.19.1 in Appendix G sets out the procedure. **5–58**

Section 43B effectively allows for an appeal to the magistrates' court against a decision of a police officer to grant or vary conditional bail. A person aggrieved by any requirements imposed by the custody officer may apply to the court but the court then has the power to impose more onerous conditions or to remand the applicant in custody as well as to accede to the requested variation. The decision of the court overrides the decision of the officer. The procedure is set down in r.19.1 which requires the application to be heard within 72 hours with the prosecution and sureties being given notice of the date and time of hearing. **5–59**

The procedure to be adopted when application is made to a court to vary police bail was considered in *R. (On the application of Ajaib) v. Birmingham Magistrates'*

Court [2009] EWHC 2127 (Admin). An appeal was made against the refusal of a court to vary bail conditions imposed by the police. The court had heard from the officer in the case that the appellant was said to be liquidating his assets with a view to leaving the country and on this information a condition was imposed to address the fear of failure to answer bail. This decision was appealed as being unfair and in breach of arts 5, 6 and 8 ECHR. It was contended on appeal that disclosure should have been ordered to clarify the origin and source of this information before any decision was made. On appeal it was held that no human rights had been breached and as these were pre-charge proceedings the *Criminal Procedure Rules*, especially those relating to disclosure, did not apply. It was open to the court to rely on this information given by the officer and the appellant's rights were not infringed as he had the opportunity to give evidence himself and to challenge the information.

C. APPEAL TO THE HIGH COURT

5–60 The *Criminal Justice Act* 2003, s.17 abolished the High Court's jurisdiction in respect of magistrates' court bail where it duplicates that of the Crown Court.

D. APPLICATION TO THE CROWN COURT BY DEFENDANT

Supreme Court Act 1981, s.81(1)(g); (1J)

Bail

5–61 **81.**—(1) The Crown Court may, subject to section 25 of the *Criminal Justice and Public Order Act* 1994, grant bail to any person—

(g) who has been remanded in custody by a magistrates' court on adjourning a case under section 11 of the *Powers of Criminal Courts (Sentencing) Act* 2000 (remand for medical examination) or—

(i) section 5 (adjournment of inquiry into offence);
(ii) section 10 (adjournment of trial); or
(iii) section 18 (initial procedure on information against adult for offence triable either way);

and the time during which a person is released on bail under any provision of this subsection shall not count as part of any term of imprisonment or detention under his sentence.

(1J) The Crown Court may only grant bail to a person under subsection (1)(g) if the magistrates' court which remanded him in custody has certified under section 5(6A)of the *Bail Act* 1976 that it heard full argument on his application for bail before it refused the application.

[This section is printed omitting paras (1)(a)–(f), (1A)–(1I), (2)–(7) which are not relevant to the Magistrates' Court.]

5–62 The defendant has a right to apply to the Crown Court for bail, when remanded in custody, and against conditions imposed on bail.

Criminal Justice Act 2003, s.16

Appeal to Crown Court

5–63 **16.**—(1) This section applies where a magistrates' court grants bail to a person ("the person concerned") on adjourning a case under—

(a) section 10 of the *Magistrates' Courts Act* 1980 (adjournment of trial),
(b) section 17C of that Act (intention as to plea: adjournment),
(c) section 18 of that Act (initial procedure on information against adult for offence triable either way),
(d) section 24C of that Act (intention as to plea by child or young person: adjournment),
(e) section 52(5) of the *Crime and Disorder Act* 1998 (adjournment of proceedings under section 51 etc), or
(f) section 11 of the *Powers of Criminal Courts (Sentencing) Act* 2000 (remand for medical examination).

(2) Subject to the following provisions of this section, the person concerned may appeal to the Crown Court against any condition of bail falling within subsection (3).

(3) A condition of bail falls within this subsection if it is a requirement—

(a) that the person concerned resides away from a particular place or area,

(b) that the person concerned resides at a particular place other than a bail hostel,

(c) for the provision of a surety or sureties or the giving of a security,

(d) that the person concerned remains indoors between certain hours,

(e) imposed under section 3(6ZAA) of the 1976 Act (requirements with respect to electronic monitoring), or

(f) the person concerned makes no contact with another person.

(4) An appeal under this section may not be brought unless subsection (5) or (6) applies.

(5) This subsection applies if an application to the magistrates' court under section 3(8)(a) of the 1976 Act (application by or on behalf of person granted bail) was made and determined before the appeal was brought.

(6) This subsection applies if an application to the magistrates' court—

(a) under section 3(8)(b) of the 1976 Act (application by constable or prosecutor), or

(b) under section 5B(1) of that Act (application by prosecutor),

was made and determined before the appeal was brought.

(7) On an appeal under this section the Crown Court may vary the conditions of bail.

(8) Where the Crown Court determines an appeal under this section, the person concerned may not bring any further appeal under this section in respect of the conditions of bail unless an application or a further application to the magistrates' court under section 3(8)(a) of the 1976 Act is made and determined after the appeal.

This provision gives a power to appeal to the Crown Court against certain conditions **5–64** of bail relating to residence away from a particular place or area or residence other than at a bail hostel; the provision of a surety or security; a curfew; electronic tagging or non-contact. Such an appeal can only be made where application to vary has already been made and refused at the magistrates' court.

For full certificates of bail see s.5, *ante* § 5–16.

E. APPEAL TO THE CROWN COURT BY PROSECUTION

Bail (Amendment) Act 1993, s.1

Prosecution right of appeal

1.—(1) Where a magistrates' court grants bail to a person who is charged with or convicted of **5–65** an offence punishable by imprisonment, the prosecution may appeal to a judge of the Crown Court against the granting of bail.

(2) Subsection (1) above applies only where the prosecution is conducted—

(a) by or on behalf of the Director of Public Prosecutions; or

(b) by a person who falls within such class or description of person as may be prescribed for the purposes of this section by order made by the Secretary of State.

(3) Such an appeal may be made only if—

(a) the prosecution made representations that bail should not be granted; and

(b) the representations were made before it was granted.

(4) In the event of the prosecution wishing to exercise the right of appeal set out in subsection (1) above, oral notice of appeal shall be given to the magistrates' court at the conclusion of the proceedings in which such bail has been granted and before the release from custody of the person concerned.

(5) Written notice of appeal shall thereafter be served on the magistrates' court and the person concerned within two hours of the conclusion of such proceedings.

(6) Upon receipt from the prosecution of oral notice of appeal from its decision to grant bail the magistrates' court shall remand in custody the person concerned, until the appeal is determined or otherwise disposed of.

(7) Where the prosecution fails, within the period of two hours mentioned in subsection (5) above, to serve one or both of the notices required by that subsection, the appeal shall be deemed to have been disposed of.

(8) The hearing of an appeal under subsection (1) above against a decision of the magistrates' court to grant bail shall be commenced within forty-eight hours, excluding weekends and any public holiday (that is to say, Christmas Day, Good Friday or a bank holiday), from the date on which oral notice of appeal is given.

(9) At the hearing of any appeal by the prosecution under this section, such appeal shall be by way of re-hearing, and the judge hearing any such appeal may remand the person concerned in custody or may grant bail subject to such conditions (if any) as he thinks fit.

(10) In relation to a child or young person (within the meaning of the *Children and Young Persons Act* 1969)—

(a) the reference in subsection (1) above to an offence punishable by imprisonment is to be read as a reference to an offence which would be so punishable in the case of an adult; and

(b) the reference in subsection (6) above to remand in custody is to be read subject to the provisions of section 23 of the Act of 1969 (remands to local authority accommodation).

(11) The power to make an order under subsection (2) above shall be exercisable by statutory instrument and any instrument shall be subject to annulment in pursuance of a resolution of either House of Parliament.

[This section is printed as amended by the *Criminal Justice Act* 2003, s.18.]

5–66 See *Criminal Procedure Rules* 2011, r.19.16 in Appendix G sets out the procedure.

5–67 The prescribed prosecutors under s.1(2)(b) are the Serious Fraud Office, the Trade and Industry Department, HM Customs and Revenue, Secretary of State for Social Security and the Post Office: *Bail (Amendment) Act 1993 (Prescription of Prosecuting Authorities) Order* 1994 (S.I. 1994 No.1438).

The prosecution has the right in the specified cases to appeal against a grant of bail when bail was originally opposed. The requirement that the offence carries a minimum sentence of five years imprisonment was removed by the *Criminal Justice Act* 2003, s.18 which requires only that the offence be imprisonable. Under s.5(2A), the court has a duty to provide written reasons when bail is granted after the prosecution has objected to bail which assists in the formulation of any subsequent appeal by the prosecution.

5–68 The requirement that oral notice of appeal be given to the magistrates' court "at the conclusion of the proceedings" was satisfied where notice was given five minutes after the case had been dealt with when the legal adviser was still at court although the magistrates had left the building: *Isleworth Crown Court, ex p. Clark* [1998] 1 Cr.App.R. 257. The hearing must be commenced within 48 hours of the end of the day on which oral notice of appeal is given: *Middlesex Guildhall Crown Court, ex p. Okoli* [2000] 1 Cr.App.R. 1.

5–69 Where a defendant who had been granted bail challenged the service of the written notice of appeal because it was not served within two hours of the oral notice he claimed that the appeal should be deemed disposed of under s.1(7). The court held, dismissing the appeal, that the prosecutor had used all due diligence to try and serve the notice and the failure to do so was due to circumstances beyond his control. The notice was served only three minutes late and as oral notice had been given the appellant was not prejudiced by this delay: *R. (Jeffrey) v. Warwick Crown Court;* [2003] Crim.L.R. 190.

F. RECONSIDERATION

Bail Act 1976, s.5B

Reconsideration of decisions granting bail

5–70 **5B.**—(1) Where a magistrates' court has granted bail in criminal proceedings in connection with an offence, or proceedings for an offence, to which this section applies or a constable has granted bail in criminal proceedings in connection with proceedings for such an offence, that court or the appropriate court in relation to the constable may, on application by the prosecutor for the decision to be reconsidered,—

(a) vary the conditions of bail,

(b) impose conditions in respect of bail which has been granted unconditionally, or

(c) withhold bail.

(2) The offences to which this section applies are offences triable on indictment and offences triable either way.

(3) No application for the reconsideration of a decision under this section shall be made unless it is based on information which was not available to the court or constable when the decision was taken.

(4) Whether or not the person to whom the application relates appears before it, the magistrates' court shall take the decision in accordance with section 4(1) (and Schedule 1) of this Act.

(5) Where the decision of the court on a reconsideration under this section is to withhold bail from the person to whom it was originally granted the court shall—

(a) if that person is before the court, remand him in custody, and

(b) if that person is not before the court, order him to surrender himself forthwith into the custody of the court.

(6) Where a person surrenders himself into the custody of the court in compliance with an order under subsection (5) above, the court shall remand him in custody.

(7) A person who has been ordered to surrender to custody under subsection (5) above may be arrested without warrant by a constable if he fails without reasonable cause to surrender to custody in accordance with the order.

(8) A person arrested in pursuance of subsection (7) above shall be brought as soon as practicable, and in any event within 24 hours after his arrest, before a justice of the peace and the justice shall remand him in custody.

In reckoning for the purposes of this subsection any period of 24 hours, no account shall be taken of Christmas Day, Good Friday or any Sunday.

(8A) Where the court, on a reconsideration under this section, refuses to withhold bail from a relevant person after hearing representations from the prosecutor in favour of withholding bail, then the court shall give reasons for refusing to withhold bail.

(8B) In subsection (8A) above, "relevant person" means a person to whom section 4(1) (and Schedule 1) of this Act is applicable in accordance with subsection (4) above.

(8C) A court which is by virtue of subsection (8A) above required to give reasons for its decision shall include a note of those reasons in any record of its decision and, if requested to do so by the prosecutor, shall cause the prosecutor to be given a copy of any such record as soon as practicable after the record is made.

(9) Criminal Procedure rules shall include provision—

(a) requiring notice of an application under this section and of the grounds for it to be given to the person affected, including notice of the powers available to the court under it;

(b) for securing that any representations made by the person affected (whether in writing or orally) are considered by the court before making its decision; and

(c) designating the court which is the appropriate court in relation to the decision of any constable to grant bail.

[This section is reprinted as amended by the *Criminal Justice and Police Act* 2001, s.129(3) and the *Courts Act* 2003, Scheds 8 and 10 which came into force on April 4, 2005.]

See *Criminal Procedure Rules* 2011, r.19.2 in Appendix G sets out the procedure. **5–71**

The prosecutor may apply to the magistrates' court to for bail to be reconsidered **5–72**
when new information comes to light affecting the original bail decision made either by the police or the court. This right does not apply to summary only offences.

It is envisaged that the defendant may be enjoying bail and the prosecutor discovers information not available earlier on the basis of which concerns arise about bail. The application must be heard within 72 hours, with notice being sent to the person affected, the prosecution and any surety. The case can then be dealt with before the scheduled adjourned date.

The court may decide a reconsideration application regardless of whether the accused appears before the court. When the court decides to withhold bail, the defendant may be arrested without a warrant and remanded in custody.

A magistrate is entitled to refuse bail notwithstanding that at the previous hearing unconditional bail had been granted. Where there had been no subsequent changes in the circumstances, but the court requested and obtained further information from the prosecutor at the second hearing which was not sought at the previous hearing the court's decision to refuse bail was upheld: *Tower Bridge Magistrates' Court, ex p. Gilbert* (1988) 152 J.P. 307.

VI. ABSCONDING AND BREACH OF BAIL CONDITIONS

A. OFFENCE OF ABSCONDING WHILE ON BAIL

Bail Act 1976, s.6

Offence of absconding by person released on bail

5–73 **6.**—(1) If a person who has been released on bail in criminal proceedings fails without reasonable cause to surrender to custody he shall be guilty of an offence.

(2) If a person who—

(a) has been released on bail in criminal proceedings, and

(b) having reasonable cause therefor, has failed to surrender to custody,

fails to surrender to custody at the appointed place as soon after the appointed time as is reasonably practicable he shall be guilty of an offence.

(3) It shall be for the accused to prove that he had reasonable cause for his failure to surrender to custody.

(4) A failure to give to a person granted bail in criminal proceedings a copy of the record of the decision shall not constitute a reasonable cause for that person's failure to surrender to custody.

(5) An offence under subsection (1) or (2) above shall be punishable either on summary conviction or as if it were a criminal contempt of court.

(6) Where a magistrates' court convicts a person of an offence under subsection (1) or (2) above the court may, if it thinks—

(a) that the circumstances of the offence are such that greater punishment should be inflicted for that offence than the court has power to inflict, or

(b) in a case where it commits that person for trial to the Crown Court for another offence, that it would be appropriate for him to be dealt with for the offence under subsection (1) or (2) above by the court before which he is tried for the other offence,

commit him in custody or on bail to the Crown Court for sentence.

(7) A person who is convicted summarily of an offence under subsection (1) or (2) above and is not committed to the Crown Court for sentence shall be liable to imprisonment for a term not exceeding 3 months or to a fine not exceeding level 5 on the standard scale or to both and a person who is so committed for sentence or is dealt with as for such a contempt shall be liable to imprisonment for a term not exceeding 12 months or to a fine or to both.

(8) In any proceedings for an offence under subsection (1) or (2) above a document purporting to be a copy of the part of the prescribed record which relates to the time and place appointed for the person specified in the record to surrender to custody and to be duly certified to be a true copy of that part of the record shall be evidence of the time and place appointed for that person to surrender to custody.

(9) For the purposes of subsection (8) above—

(a) "the prescribed record" means the record of the decision of the court, officer or constable made in pursuance of section 5(1) of this Act;

(b) the copy of the prescribed record is duly certified if it is certified by the appropriate officer of the court or, as the case may be, by the constable who took the decision or a constable designated for the purpose by the officer in charge of the police station from which the person to whom the record relates was released;

(c) "the appropriate officer" of the court is—

(i) in the case of a magistrates' court, the designated officer for the Court;

(10) Section 127 of the *Magistrates' Courts Act* 1980 shall not apply in relation to an offence under subsection (1) or (2) above.

(11) Where a person has been released on bail in criminal proceedings and that bail was granted by a constable, a magistrates' court shall not try that person for an offence under subsection (1) or (2) above in relation to that bail (the "relevant offence") unless either or both of subsection (12) and (13) below applies.

(12) This subsection applies if an information is laid for the relevant offence within 6 months from the time of the commission of the offence.

(13) This subsection applies if an information is laid for the relevant offence no later than 3 months from the time of the occurrence of the first of the events mentioned in subsection (14) below to occur after the commission of the relevant offence.

(14) Those events are—

(a) the person surrenders to custody at the appointed place;

(b) the person is arrested, or attends at a police station, in connection with the relevant offence or the offence for which he was granted bail;

(c) the person appears or is brought before a court in connection with the relevant offence or the offence for which he was granted bail.

[This section is reprinted as amended by the *Access to Justice Act* 1999, Sched. 13, para. 89, the *Criminal Justice Act* 2003 s.15(3), and the *Courts Act* 2003, Sched. 8.]

Under s.3(1) of the *Bail Act* 1976, a person granted bail in criminal proceedings is under a duty to surrender to custody. That duty is enforceable under s.6 of the Act. If a person released on bail fails without reasonable cause to surrender to custody he is guilty of an offence under s.6. Although "surrender to custody" means surrender "at the time and place for the time being appointed for him to do so" the *de minimis* rule should be applied if a defendant is only marginally late. Being seven minutes late was held not to constitute an offence under s.6: *Gateshead Justices, ex p. Usher* [1981] Crim.L.R. 491, DC. **5–74**

In *Scott* (2008) 172 JP 149, the case of *Usher* was referred to as not a very satisfactory authority which should not be taken as establishing any general principle in bail cases about the effect of the *de minimis* principle. The defendant arrived over half an hour late for his case because he overslept. His conviction for failure to answer his bail was appealed on the basis that he was only marginally late. On appeal it was held that the proper construction of the act must mean that the surrender is "at the appointed time- "and does not allow any identified further margin. The mere fact of being only slightly late cannot afford a defence. There does remain a discretion in the court as to whether to put the bail charge but the exercise of that discretion will only be interfered with on appeal if it is shown to be *Wednesbury* unreasonable and the cases where the late arrival is so truly marginal that it would be unreasonable to pursue it would be rare.

The obligation of a person on bail is to comply with the directions of the court. Once a person has reported as instructed to the appropriate court official he has surrendered to custody and is under an implied obligation not to leave without consent. If the defendant leaves he is liable to be arrested under s.7(2) although no offence under s.6 may have been committed: *DPP v. Richards* [1988] Q.B. 701.

What amounts to "a reasonable cause" is a matter of fact in each case. A mistake about the date due to an administrative blunder by solicitors did not provide a reasonable excuse but was relevant for mitigation: *Laidlaw v. Atkinson*, *The Times*, August 2, 1986. Whether a mistake by a solicitor, such as giving the defendant the wrong date, amounts to a reasonable excuse is a question of fact to be decided in all the circumstances of the particular case: *Liverpool City J.J., ex p. Santos*, *The Times*, January 23, 1997, DC.

There are two offences under the section: **5–75**

1) It is an offence to fail to surrender without reasonable cause; and
2) It is an offence to fail to surrender as soon as is reasonably practicable after having had reasonable cause for failing to surrender initially.

The second limb of the section covers the situation of a defendant who may be too ill to attend as originally expected and so has reasonable cause for not coming to court but then fails to contact the court or surrender himself as soon as he has recovered.

The burden of proving the reasonable cause rests with the defendant to the civil standard of balance of probabilities: *Carr Briant* [1943] K.B. 607.

The court will deal with an absconder as a summary offence. There is no power to commit a bail offence to the Crown Court for trial because it is not an either way offence. The power to commit to the Crown Court only applies after conviction. In *Schiavo v. Anderton* [1987] Q.B. 20, DC, the defendant was granted bail in the magistrates' court pending summary trial but failed to answer bail. When he was brought before the court two years later on a warrant, he pleaded guilty to absconding and was committed to the Crown Court for sentence. In the Crown Court he argued that the magistrates' court had had no jurisdiction to try the matter, since no information had been laid within six months of the offences. The Divisional Court held that no information need be laid; the court heard the proceedings of its own motion and that the matter could be tried only by the court which granted bail.

The *Consolidated Criminal Practice Directions* gives detailed directions on bail and the failure to surrender, see Appendix F.

When a defendant fails to answer his bail, in the absence of any explanation the court will issue a warrant under s.7. When the warrant has been executed and the defendant appears before the court, it will be considered whether an offence under s.6 should be put. If the defendant is on police bail and failed to surrender to custody at his first court appearance the prosecutor will decide whether to initiate proceedings. An information must be laid within six months' of the offence or three months of the surrender to custody, arrest, or court appearance. Where the defendant fails to answer court bail, the court may initiate proceedings by its own motion at any time and the six month time-limit does not apply. The court will be invited to take proceedings by the prosecutor, if proceedings are considered appropriate: see also *Murphy v. DPP* [1990] 2 All E.R. 390; *Teeside Magistrates' Court, ex p. Bujnowski* [1997] Crim.L.R. 51.

5–76 Whether or not a warrant of arrest has been issued or executed, the question of proceedings regarding a possible failure to surrender will be dealt with by the Crown Prosecution Service whose discretion to invite the court to proceed is unfettered: *France v. Dewsbury Magistrates' Court* (1987) 152 J.P. 301. The court must give the defendant an opportunity to explain his failure to surrender and also to make submissions before sentence: *Davis (Seaton Roy)* (1989) 8 Cr.App.R. 64, CA; *Woods* (1986) 11 Cr.App.R. 551, CA. The fact that a defendant has been acquitted of the principal offence does not affect his criminality in relation to any offence under the *Bail Act* 1976: *Clarke* [2000] 1 Cr.App.R. 173. In *Cockburn-Smith* [2009] 2 Cr.App.R.(S.) 20. a sentence of 3 months imprisonment for absconding from bail when a warrant had been outstanding for 2 years was upheld even though the substantive charges had not been proceeded with.

The court also has the power to commit the defendant to the Crown Court for sentence on a bail offence if they consider their powers of sentencing to be insufficient or if the defendant has other related matters which are being committed for trial.

5–77 The Magistrates' Court Sentencing Guidelines cover the offences under both s.6(1) and (2) of the *Bail Act* 1976. In the magistrates' court the sentence is a maximum of three months' imprisonment or a fine at level 5.

The guidelines say that on assessing seriousness the court must consider the offender's culpability and the harm that is caused or is intended to be caused or could forseeably have been caused by the offence. Offences under s.6(2) where there originally was a reasonable excuse for non-attendance are likely to be less serious on this basis.

Culpability is measured according to the reason for non-attendance. This can range from forgetfulness or fear of the outcome of a case to deliberate disregard of the bail requirement. The offender who seeks to disrupt the system to his own advantage may be treated more seriously than a person who simply gives no thought to the consequences of his actions.

5–78 The harm caused is the delay, distress and inconvenience to individual victims and witnesses and also the unnecessary drain on police, defence and court resources with the resultant waste of public money. There is also the wider negative impact on public confidence in the justice system when bailed defendants ignore their duty to appear at court. The guideline goes into some detail in considering the varying degrees of harm caused, depending at what stage and in what circumstances the non-attendance occurs. A failure to surrender to police bail may give rise to less serious harm than a failure to answer court bail but the sentencing approach is the same. It is stated that the seriousness of the original offence may be relevant, especially where it is a violent or sexual offence which may have repercussions for public safety if the witnesses or others are caused fear or distress by any failure of the offender to answer bail. However, if the offender is acquitted on the original offence this does not automatically reduce the seriousness of the bail offence.

The aggravating factors are;-

Repeated previous convictions for bail offending; the offender's absence causing a lengthy delay to the administration of justice (although the period of time for which a defendant has been absent may aggravate an offence, the harm caused by even a short absence must be considered. Arriving at court a few hours late may cause a trial to be aborted and witnesses may be required to attend again at court with the attendant distress and inconvenience) and a determined attempt to avoid the jurisdiction of the court by going abroad or changing identity or appearance.

A mitigating factor is a prompt, voluntary surrender as this can save police time and may indicate remorse. The harm done must still be considered as must the stage at which the defendant surrendered. **5–79**

There are other factors which provide mitigation but do not amount to a defence, such as where there is a genuine misunderstanding rather than just a mistake on the part of the defendant. Also if there has been a failure to comprehend the requirements or significance of bail because a defendant has literacy or language problems the court must inquire whether such difficulties were apparent when bail was granted and what efforts were made to check on the defendant's understanding of the bail obligations. Where the offender is the sole or primary carer for dependants and unable to leave them unattended that may amount to personal mitigation. A disorganised or chaotic lifestyle caused by alcohol or drug addiction may in certain circumstances amount to personal mitigation but it cannot reduce the seriousness of the offence.

Bail offences should be dealt with as soon as practicable and it is not necessary to adjourn the case over with any substantive charge. The factors to be considered are how soon the main charge is expected to be concluded; how serious that offence is and what penalty is likely to be imposed in respect of it together with any other relevant circumstances. The recommendation is that any bail offence should be dealt with on first appearance after arrest or surrender unless an adjournment is needed for the production of evidence such as medical certificates etc. Then following plea or conviction, sentence should be imposed as soon as possible. It is also relevant to consider whether the offender will be on bail or in custody for the main charge because if the defendant is in custody the options for sentence are limited whereas community orders or a suspended sentence with requirements would be possible for offenders on bail. It is recognized that in some cases it will be more appropriate to deal with all offences including the bail offence together so that the totality of criminality is properly reflected within the proper sentence range. The power to commit a bail offence for sentence to the Crown Court is also a relevant consideration.

The guidelines state that any custodial sentences should be consecutive unless that would be disproportionate. **5–80**

It is pointed out that the court has power to proceed in absence when bail is not answered and this may lead to a reduction in the harm caused but does not affect culpability. The *Magistrates' Court Sentencing Guidelines 2008* are set out as follows.

STARTING POINTS AND SENTENCE RANGE
(BASED ON A FIRST TIME OFFENDER PLEADING NOT GUILTY)

5–81

Examples of nature of activity	Starting point	Range
Surrenders late on day but case proceeds as planned	Band A fine	Band A fine to Band B fine
Negligent or non-deliberate failure to attend causing delay and/or interference with the administration of justice	Band C fine	Band B fine to medium level community order
Deliberate failure to attend causing delay and/or interference with the administration of justice	14 days custody	Low level community order to 10 weeks custody

AGGRAVATING AND MITIGATING FACTORS

5–82

Factors indicating higher culpability	**Factors indicating lower culpability**
1. Serious attempts to evade justice 2. Determined attempt seriously to undermine the course of justice 3. Previous relevant convictions and/or breach of court orders or police bail	1. Misunderstanding 2. Failure to comprehend bail significance or requirements 3. Caring responsibilities
Factor indicating greater degree of harm	**Factor indicating lesser degree of harm**
1. Lengthy absence	1. Prompt voluntary surrender

B. LIABILITY TO ARREST

Bail Act 1976, s.7

Liability to arrest for absconding or breaking conditions of bail.

7.—(1) If a person who has been released on bail in criminal proceedings and is under a duty to surrender into the custody of a court fails to surrender to custody at the time appointed for him to do so the court may issue a warrant for his arrest. **5–83**

(1A) Subsection (1B) applies if—

(a) a person has been released on bail in connection with extradition proceedings,

(b) the person is under a duty to surrender into the custody of a constable, and

(c) the person fails to surrender to custody at the time appointed for him to do so.

(1B) A magistrates' court may issue a warrant for the person's arrest.

(2) If a person who has been released on bail in criminal proceedings absents himself from the court at any time after he has surrendered into the custody of the court and before the court is ready to begin or to resume the hearing of the proceedings, the court may issue a warrant for his arrest; but no warrant shall be issued under this subsection where that person is absent in accordance with leave given to him by or on behalf of the court.

(3) A person who has been released on bail in criminal proceedings and is under a duty to surrender into the custody of a court may be arrested without warrant by a constable—

(a) if the constable has reasonable grounds for believing that that person is not likely to surrender to custody;

(b) if the constable has reasonable grounds for believing that that person is likely to break any of the conditions of his bail or has reasonable grounds for suspecting that that person has broken any of those conditions; or

(c) in a case where that person was released on bail with one or more surety or sureties, if a surety notifies a constable in writing that that person is unlikely to surrender to custody and that for that reason the surety wishes to be relieved of his obligations as a surety.

(4) a person arrested in pursuance of subsection (3) above—

(a) shall, except where he was arrested within 24 hours of the time appointed for him to surrender to custody, be brought as soon as practicable and in any event within 24 hours after his arrest before a justice of the peace ; and

(b) in the said excepted case shall be brought before the court at which he was to have surrendered to custody.

(4A) A person who has been released on bail in connection with extradition proceedings and is under a duty to surrender into the custody of a constable may be arrested without warrant by a constable on any of the grounds set out in paragraphs (a) to (c) of subsection (3).

(4B) A person arrested in pursuance of subsection (4A) above shall be brought as soon as practicable and in any event within 24 hours after his arrest before a justice of the peace for the petty sessions area in which he was arrested.

(5) A justice of the peace before whom a person is brought under subsection (4) or (4B) above may, subject to subsection (6) below, if of the opinion that that person—

(a) is not likely to surrender to custody, or

(b) has broken or is likely to break any condition of his bail, remand him in custody or commit him to custody, as the case may require, or alternatively, grant him bail subject to the same or to different conditions, but if not of that opinion shall grant him bail subject to the same conditions (if any) as were originally imposed.

(6) Where the person so brought before the justice is a child or young person and the justice does not grant him bail, subsection (5) above shall have effect subject to the provisions of section 23 of the *Children and Young Persons Act* 1969 (remands to the care of local authorities).

(7) In reckoning for the purposes of this section any period of 24 hours, no account shall be taken of Christmas Day, Good Friday or any Sunday.

(8) In the case of a person charged with murder or with murder and one or more other offences—

(a) subsections (4) and (5) have effect as if for "justice of the peace" there were substituted "judge of the Crown Court",

(b) subsection (6) has effect as if for "justice" (in both places) there were substituted "judge", and

(c) subsection (7) has effect, for the purposes of subsection (4), as if at the end there were added ", Saturday or bank holiday."

[This section is printed as amended by the*Criminal Law Act* 1977, Sched.12, the *Courts Act* 2003 Sched. 10 and the *Coroners and Justice Act* 2009 Sched. 21(7) para. 74(b) which came into force on February 1, 2010]

This section has been amended to recognise the fact that decisions on bail can only be made by the Crown Court as regards any defendant charged with murder as a result of amendments made by the *Coroners and Justice Act* 2009 s.115. Any defendant charged with murder and in breach of bail will have to be produced before the Crown Court as the magistrates' court no longer has power to deal with such cases.

5–84 Where the accused fails to surrender to custody in answer to his or her bail, the court may issue a warrant of arrest. Alternatively the court may adjourn and enlarge the defendant's bail under s.129 of the *Magistrates' Courts Act* 1980 but only if it is satisfied that there is a good reason for the defendant's non-attendance or attendance has been excused by the court.

Where a suspect is bailed from a police station pursuant to s.37(2) of the *Police and Criminal Evidence Act* 1984 and fails to attend the police station on a prescribed subsequent date he may be arrested without warrant: *Police and Criminal Evidence Act* 1984, s.46A.

5–85 A defendant may also be arrested by an officer without a warrant under s.7(3), *ante*. The usual reason for arrest is a breach of a bail condition. The arrested person may be brought either before the court to which he should have surrendered if arrested within 24 hours of his scheduled appearance or before any court. The time limit requires the arrested person to be produced at a court within 24 hours of his arrest. Where an arrested person is not brought before a court within 24 hours he has an absolute right to be released from custody. Bringing the defendant within the precincts or to the cells of a magistrates' court is not sufficient for this purpose; the defendant must actually appear before the magistrates: *Governor of Glen Parva Young Offenders Institution, ex p. G (a minor)* [1998] 2 Cr.App.R. 349. Once the defendant has been brought before the court, the hearing can then be adjourned to later in the day to be dealt with by a different bench: *R. (Hussain) v. Derby Magistrates' Court* [2001] 1 W.L.R. 2454.

In *R. (on the application of Culley) v.Dorchester Crown Court* (2007) 171 JP 373 the extent of the 24 hour time limit in s.7(4)(a) was considered. The defendant had been arrested for being in breach of bail conditions and was brought before the Crown Court where his trial was due to take place the next day. The judge adjourned the case overnight partly to allow evidence to be provided by the defendant relating to the alleged breach. On appeal it was held that the time limits of s.7 are strict and once the 24 hours from arrest have elapsed the court no longer has jurisdiction. The court's subsequent decision to remand the defendant into custody was invalid. The investigation and decision-making by the court had to be completed within the 24 hours. This case demonstrates that not only must the police be speedy in producing defendants in breach of bail at court and the gaolers ensure that they are produced before the court without delay but also the court must keep an eye on the clock as the case is dealt with. If deliberations are not completed within time the court no longer has jurisdiction.

When a person arrested under s.7 is brought before the magistrates' court he must be dealt with according to s.7(5). The magistrate has no power to commit the defendant to the Crown Court for a decision on the breach to be made there even when the original bail was granted by the Crown Court: *Teeside Magistrates' Court, ex p. Ellison* (2001) 165 J.P. 355, DC.

In *Liverpool City Justices, ex p. DPP* (1993) 95 Cr.App.R. 222, DC, detailed consideration was given to the operation of s.7.

— The section contemplates the constable who has arrested the person bailed bringing him before the court and stating the grounds for believing that the defendant has broken or is likely to break a condition of his bail; this may well involve the giving of "hearsay" evidence. **5–86**

— Even where the defendant disputes the ground on which he was arrested, there is no necessity for the giving of evidence on oath or providing an opportunity to the person arrested, or his lawyer to cross-examine, or give evidence himself. Nevertheless the court must give the defendant an opportunity to respond to what the constable alleges.

— The court has no power to adjourn the proceedings, but must consider on the material before it whether it is able to form one of the opinions set out in s.7(5) and if it does so, go on to decide whether to remand the defendant in custody or on bail on the same or more stringent conditions. **5–87**

— If the court feels unable to form one of the opinions set out in s.7(5) it must order the person concerned to be released on bail on the same terms as were originally imposed.

— Proceedings under s.7(5) do not preclude the defendant who has been remanded in custody from making an application for bail to the magistrates' court, Crown Court or to a judge as appropriate. The presumption in favour of granting bail under s.4 of the Act will be subject not only to the exceptions to the right to bail in Pt 1, para. 2 of Sched. 1 to the Act but also to the exception in para 6 of that Sched..

Where a person is arrested pursuant to s.7(3) the procedure contained in s.7(5) does not involve the determination of a criminal charge within the meaning of art. 6(1) of the European Convention on Human Rights. **5–88**

In *Havering Magistrates' Court, ex p. DPP* [2001] 1 W.L.R. 805, the DPP applied for judicial review of a decision of justices that proceedings brought against the defendant under the *Bail Act* 1976, s.7(5) should be withdrawn. The justices had found that oral evidence was necessary to show that the defendant had acted in breach of the conditions. The issue before the court related to the compatibility of the procedures under s.7(5) and Sched. 1, Pt I, para. 6 of the Act with the right to a fair trial and the right to liberty and security guaranteed under the *Human Rights Act* 1998, Sched. 1, Pt I, arts 6 and 5 respectively. The court held that since s.7 made provision for a means of achieving the purposes for which bail conditions were imposed, liability for detention under s.7 derived from the charge that a defendant faced as a means of securing those purposes and did not equate to the facing of a criminal charge. It followed that art. 6 did not have any direct relevance. The procedures would not breach art. 5 provided that the court evaluated the material presented in the context of the consequences to a defendant and, in particular, took account of the fact that where hearsay evidence was relied on, it had not been subject to cross-examination. This approach was confirmed in *R. (on the application of Thomas) v. Greenwich Magistrates Court* [2009] Crim.L.R. 800, where it was said such hearsay material was not affected by the hearsay provisions of the *Criminal Justice Act* 2003. A defendant should be given a fair opportunity to comment on the material upon which the proceedings were based. The court is not limited under art. 5 to only considering evidence that was admissible in the strict sense. The facts upon which the decision was based did not need to be proved to the criminal standard of proof. See also *Wirral Borough Magistrates' Court, ex p. McKeown* [2001] 2 Cr.App.R. 2, DC.

In *West London Magistrates' Court, ex p. Vickers* [2004] Crim.L.R. 63, the defendant sought judicial review of the magistrates' decision to remand him in custody following a finding that he had broken conditions of his bail. He argued that the magistrates had been wrong to hold that reasonable excuse was not a defence to an allegation of breaking a bail condition. He submitted that the words "without reasonable cause" should be read into the *Bail Act* 1976, s.7(5) otherwise the provision would be incompatible with the *Human Rights Act* 1998, Sched. 1 Pt I, art.5. The application was refused on the basis that when magistrates were considering whether there had been a breach of a condition of bail under s.7(5), they had a duty to act fairly and give the bailed person the opportunity of responding to the allegation. However, they did not have to consider whether the defendant had a reasonable excuse for breaking the relevant condition. When, having satisfied themselves that a breach of condition had occurred, the magistrates were considering whether to admit the bailed person to bail again or remand him in custody, they should take into account the reasons for the breach, at which point issues relating to reasonable excuse might arise. Provided that the magistrates followed the procedure set out in *Havering Magistrates' Court, ex p. DPP* there would be no breach of art. 5.

C. CONSEQUENCES FOR SURETIES

Magistrates' Courts Act 1980, s.120

Forfeiture of recognizance

5–89 **120.**—(1) This section applies where—

(a) a recognizance to keep the peace or to be of good behaviour has been entered into before a magistrates' court; or

(b) any recognizance is conditioned for the appearance of a person before a magistrates' court, or for his doing any other thing connected with a proceeding before a magistrates' court.

(1A) If, in the case of a recognizance which is conditioned for the appearance of an accused before a magistrates' court, the accused fails to appear in accordance with the condition, the court shall—

(a) declare the recognizance to be forfeited;

(b) issue a summons directed to each person bound by the recognizance as surety, requiring him to appear before the court on a date specified in the summons to show cause why he should not be adjudged to pay the sum in which he is bound;

and on that date the court may proceed in the absence of any surety if it is satisfied that he has been served with the summons.

(2) If, in any other case falling within subsection (1) above, the recognizance appears to the magistrates' court to be forfeited, the court may—

(a) declare the recognizance to be forfeited; and

(b) adjudge each person bound by it, whether as principal or surety, to pay the sum in which he is bound;

but in a case falling within subsection (1)(a) above, the court shall not declare the recognizance to be forfeited except by order made on complaint.

(3) The court which declares the recognizance to be forfeited may, instead of adjudging any person to pay the whole sum in which he is bound, adjudge him to pay part only of the sum or remit the sum.

(4) Payment of any sum adjudged to be paid under this section, including any costs awarded against the defendant, may be enforced, and any such sum shall be applied, as if it were a fine and as if the adjudication were a summary conviction of an offence not punishable with imprisonment and so much of section 85(1) above as empowers a court to remit fines shall not apply to the sum but so much thereof as relates to remission after a term of imprisonment has been imposed shall so apply; but at any time before the issue of a warrant of commitment to enforce payment of the sum, or before the sale of goods under a warrant of distress to satisfy the sum, the court may remit the whole or any part of the sum either absolutely or on such conditions as the court thinks just.

(5) A recognizance such as is mentioned in this section shall not be enforced otherwise than in accordance with this section, and accordingly shall not be transmitted to the Crown Court nor shall its forfeiture be certified to that Court.

5–90 Where a defendant who is on conditional bail with a condition of a surety fails to appear the court must declare the recognisance (the amount of money fixed) forfeit and then issue a summons to the surety requiring appearance before the court to show "just cause" as to why the sum required should not be paid. The court may order that the recognisance be paid in full, or a lesser amount may be ordered reflecting the circumstances of the case. It is also open to the court to remit the recognisance in full and order that nothing be paid. If the recognisance cannot be paid the surety can be given time to pay and a period of imprisonment may be fixed in default of payment.

The power to declare a recognisance to be forfeited is strictly dependant on there being a breach of the condition of the recognisance; a mere breach of a condition of bail by the defendant provides no basis for declaring the recognisance to be forfeited: *Bow Street Magistrates' Court, ex p. Hart* [2002] 1 W.L.R. 1242, DC.

The burden of persuading the court that a recognisance should not be paid is upon the surety. The court must hear such evidence and argument as the surety wishes to put forward. The onus on the surety of showing that the full amount should not be lost is a heavy one: *Uxbridge Justices, ex p. Heward-Mills* [1983] 1 W.L.R. 56. An application to forfeit a surety is a civil proceeding and the standard of proof is the ordinary civil standard on the balance of probabilities: *Marlow Justices, ex p. O'Sullivan* [1984] Q.B. 381, DC.

Lack of culpability on the part of the surety is not, of itself, a ground for holding that the recognisance should not be paid: *Crown Court at Warwick, ex p. Smalley* (1987) 84 Cr.App.R. 51. In *Maidstone Crown Court, ex p. Lever and Connell* [1996] 1 Cr.App.R. 524 the Court of Appeal (Criminal Division) reviewed the principles which govern the forfeiture of a recognisance. The applicants provided sureties of £19,000 and £40,000 for the defendant who failed to attend his trial in the Crown Court. When, in breach of his bail, the accused failed to report to the police station one evening, the local police did not inform anyone, not even the police officer in charge of the case. Two days later one surety discovered that the accused had not been at home for two nights and telephoned the other surety and the police. At first instance the judge found that there was no culpability in either surety and that the police were negligent but nonetheless ordered forfeiture of £16,000 and £35,000 respectively. The Divisional Court then refused their application for judicial review. The Court of Appeal said:

> "The general principle is that the purpose of a recognisance is to bring the defendant to court for trial. The basis for estreatment is not as a matter of punishment of the surety, but because he has failed to fulfil the obligation which he undertook. The starting point on the failure to bring a defendant to court is the forfeiture of the full recognisance. The right to estreat is triggered by the non-attendance of the defendant at court. It is for the surety to establish to the satisfaction of the trial court that there are grounds upon which the court may remit for forfeiture part or, wholly exceptionally, the whole recognisance. The presence or absence of culpability is a factor but the absence of culpability, as found in this case by the judge, is not in itself a reason to reduce or set aside the obligation entered into by the surety to pay in the event of a failure to bring the defendant to court. The court may, in the exercise of a wide discretion, decide it would be fair and just to estreat some or all of the recognisance."

Any reduction in the amount of the recognisance should be confined to the really deserving cases and any reduction should be regarded as the exception rather than the rule.

This may be contrasted with the decision in *Southampton Justices, ex p. Green* [1976] Q.B. 11 where it was held that the magistrates had wrongly failed to consider the applicant's culpability. The statement in this case that the recognisance should be remitted in full if the surety used all due diligence and efforts to secure the appearance has been considered in later case law.

The court's approach was explained again in *Horseferry Stipendiary Magistrate, ex p. Pearson* [1976] 1 W.L.R. 511. The court should approach the question for forfeiture "on the footing that the surety has seriously entered into a serious obligation and ought to pay the amount which he or she has promised unless there are circumstances in the case, relating either to means or culpability, which make it fair and just to pay a smaller sum." In this case the surety made serious efforts to get something done when she feared that the accused would abscond which the court on appeal said had not been taken into account when the recognisance was forfeited. **5–91**

In a later case it was repeated that it might be proper to remit the recognisance entirely where the surety acted with all due diligence and made every effort to secure the appearance of the accused: *Waltham Forest Justices, ex p. Parfrey* (1980) 2 Cr.App.R.(S.) 208.

The presumption has been said to be that the whole of the recognisance should be estreated in "normal cases" but the fact that a defendant had attended at all preliminary and committal hearings and had initially arrived at the Crown Court for his trial before absconding in the middle of the day meant that the case was not normal and the blameworthiness of the surety should have been assessed on that basis: *Crown Court at York, ex p. Coleman and How* (1988) 86 Cr.App.R. 151.

5–92 By contrast in another case the court said that the purpose of the surety is to force the defendant to surrender to the court. If the defendant fails to do so, the recognisance should be paid and the surety cannot escape liability by showing he has no means nor that it was not his fault that the defendant did not attend: *Southampton Justices, ex p. Corker* (1976) 120 S.J. 214.

The case law indicates that each case should be dealt with on its merits and there is a wide discretion to remit the recognisance taking into account culpability and means.

Sureties should always be notified when a hearing date was fixed and if no date was fixed, they should be informed of the dates between which the case was likely to be listed. Ignorance of the date would not always be an answer to proceedings for forfeiture: *Reading Crown Court, ex p. Bello* (1991) 92 Cr.App.R. 303, CA (Civ. Div). An order for forfeiture was described as "premature"when the question had been considered in advance of a fixed date for trial. The defendant had gone abroad in breach of his bail conditions. The matter should have been considered once it was known that he would not appear to stand trial: *Inner London Crown Court, ex p. Springall* (1987) 85 Cr.App.R. 214, DC

5–93 References in the authorities to consideration of means implies that the court should consider the surety's ability to pay and the consequences to the surety of ordering payment in an amount which would inevitably lead to imprisonment for default. There may be cases where the culpability of the surety is so great that an amount may be estreated that he cannot afford thereby making a prison sentence likely: *Crown Court of Wood Green, ex p. Howe* (1991) 93 Cr.App.R. 213, DC

It is relevant for the court in deciding whether to exercise its power under s.120(4) to remit the whole or any part of a sum to consider the potential impact of making payment not just on the surety but others as well: *Leicestershire Sipendiary Magistrate, ex p. Kaur* (2000) 164 J.P. 127, DC.

When a surety is concerned that the defendant will abscond, he may notify the police in writing of that fact and that he wishes to be relieved of his obligation as a surety under s.7(3)(c). On receipt of such notice the police may then arrest the defendant. A surety is not automatically relieved of his duty by contacting the police to convey his concerns but the court should take into account the efforts made to secure attendance and means of the surety when any forfeiture is considered: *Crown Court at Ipswich, ex p. Reddington* [1981] Crim.L.R. 618. If a surety does wish to withdraw, the proper procedure appears to be that an application to vary bail should be made under s.3(8) but as such application can only be made by the prosecution or defence this seems to require that the defendant would need to be before the court when the application was made: *Crown Court at Wood Green, ex p. Howe* [1992] 3 All E.R. 366. When a surety was unrepresented the court should assist by explaining the relevant principles in ordinary language and giving the surety an opportunity to call evidence and advance arguments: *Uxbridge Justices, ex p. Heward-Mills* [1983] 1 W.L.R. 56, DC. Representation by the Criminal Defence Service or the Community Legal Service is not available to an unrepresented surety: *Access to Justice Act* 1999, s.12(2); *The Chief Clerk of Maidstone Crown Court, ex p. Clark* [1995] 2 Cr.App.R. 617, DC.

VII. REMANDS

(1) Introduction

5–94 A court may adjourn a case and remand the defendant in custody or bail. Under the

Magistrates' Courts Act 1980, time limits are set on the period of remand. Before conviction when the defendant is remanded in custody the limits are as follows—

1. three days in custody to a Police Constable;
2. eight clear days in custody to prison;
3. 28 clear days in custody to prison where the next stage of the proceedings is fixed to occur within that time and the accused at the time of remand is before the court and has previously been remanded in custody by the court in the proceedings;
4. 28 clear days in custody to prison if the defendant is already serving a custodial sentence;
5. 28 clear days in custody to prison where the defendant consents to remands in future in custody in his absence for a maximum of three adjournments of eight clear days. The defendant must be produced in court on the fourth adjournment which will usually be 28 days later.

After conviction a defendant can be remanded into custody for a maximum of three weeks.

Where a defendant is granted bail before conviction the case can be adjourned for any period of time taking into account the interests of justice and the need to ensure a speedy trial. After conviction the time limit on adjournments on bail is four weeks.

(2) Adjournments and remands

Magistrates' Courts Act 1980, s.128

Remand in custody or on bail

128.—(1) Where a magistrates' court has power to remand any person, then, subject to section 4 of the *Bail Act* 1976 and to any other enactment modifying that power, the court may— **5–95**

(a) remand him in custody, that is to say, commit him to custody to be brought before the court, subject to subsection (3A) below, at the end of the period of remand or at such earlier time as the court may require; or

(b) where it is inquiring into or trying an offence alleged to have been committed by that person or has convicted him of an offence, remand him on bail in accordance with the *Bail Act* 1976, that is to say, by directing him to appear as provided in subsection (4) below; or

(c) except in a case falling within paragraph (b) above, remand him on bail by taking from him a recognizance (with or without sureties) conditioned as provided in that subsection;

and may, in a case falling within paragraph (c) above, instead of taking recognizances in accordance with that paragraph, fix the amount of the recognizances with a view to their being taken subsequently in accordance with section 119 above.

(1A) Where—

(a) on adjourning a case under section 5, 10(1), 17C, or 18(4) above the court proposes to remand or further remand a person in custody; and

(b) he is before the court; and

(d) he is legally represented in that court,

it shall be the duty of the court—

(i) to explain the effect of subsections (3A) and (3B) below to him in ordinary language; and

(ii) to inform him in ordinary language that, notwithstanding the procedure for a remand without his being brought before a court, he would be brought before a court for the hearing and determination of at least every fourth application for his remand, and of every application for his remand heard at a time when it appeared to the court that he had no legal representative acting for him in the case.

(1B) For the purposes of subsection (1A) above a person is to be treated as legally represented in a court if, but only if, he has the assistance of a legal representative to represent him in the proceedings in that court.

(1C) After explaining to an accused as provided by subsection (1A) above the court shall ask him whether he consents to hearing and determination of such applications in his absence.

(2) Where the court fixes the amount of a recognizance under subsection (1) above or section 8(3) of the *Bail Act* 1976 with a view to its being taken subsequently the court shall in the meantime commit the person so remanded to custody in accordance with paragraph (a) of the said subsection (1).

(3) Where a person is brought before the court after remand, the court may further remand him.

(3A) Subject to subsection (3B) below, where a person has been remanded in custody and the remand was not a remand under section 128A below for a period exceeding 8 clear days, the court may further remand him (otherwise than in the exercise of the power conferred by that section) on an adjournment under section 5, 10(1), 17C or 18(4) above without his being brought before it if it is satisfied—

(a) that he gave his consent, either in response to a question under subsection (1C) above or otherwise, to the hearing and determination in his absence of any application for his remand on an adjournment of the case under any of those provisions; and

(b) that he has not by virtue of this subsection been remanded without being brought before the court on more than two such applications immediately preceding the application which the court is hearing; and

(c) that he has not withdrawn his consent to their being so heard and determined.

(3B) The court may not exercise the power conferred by subsection (3A) above if it appears to the court, on an application for a further remand being made to it, that the person to whom the application relates has no legal representative acting for him in the case (whether present in court or not).

(3C) Where—

(a) a person has been remanded in custody on an adjournment of a case under section 5, 10(1), 17C or 18(4) above; and

(b) an application is subsequently made for his further remand on such an adjournment; and

(c) he is not brought before the court which hears and determines the application; and

(d) that court is not satisfied as mentioned in subsection (3A) above,

the court shall adjourn the case and remand him in custody for the period for which it stands adjourned.

(3D) An adjournment under subsection (3C) above shall be for the shortest period that appears to the court to make it possible for the accused to be brought before it.

(3E) Where—

(a) on an adjournment of a case under section 5, 10(1), 17C or 18(4) above a person has been remanded in custody without being brought before the court; and

(b) it subsequently appears—

(i) to the court which remanded him in custody; or

(ii) to an alternate magistrates' court to which he is remanded under section 130 below,

that he ought not to have been remanded in custody in his absence, the court shall require him to be brought before it at the earliest time that appears to the court to be possible.

(4) Where a person is remanded on bail under subsection (1) above the court may, where it remands him on bail in accordance with the *Bail Act* 1976 direct him to appear or, in any other case, direct that his recognizance be conditioned for his appearance—

(a) before that court at the end of the period of remand; or

(b) at every time and place to which during the course of the proceedings the hearing may be from time to time adjourned;

and, where it remands him on bail conditionally on his providing a surety during an inquiry into an offence alleged to have been committed by him, may direct that the recognizance of the surety be conditioned to secure that the person so bailed appears—

(d) at every time and place to which during the course of the proceedings the hearing may be from time to time adjourned and also before the Crown Court in the event of the person so bailed being committed for trial there.

(5) Where a person is directed to appear or a recognizance is conditioned for a person's

appearance in accordance with paragraph (b) or (c) of subsection (4) above, the fixing at any time of the time for him next to appear shall be deemed to be a remand; but nothing in this subsection or subsection (4) above shall deprive the court of power at any subsequent hearing to remand him afresh.

(6) Subject to the provisions of sections 128A and 129 below, a magistrates' court shall not remand a person for a period exceeding 8 clear days, except that—

(a) if the court remands him on bail, it may remand him for a longer period if he and the other party consent;

(b) where the court adjourns a trial under section 10(3) above or section 11 of the *Powers of Criminal Courts (Sentencing) Act* 2000, the court may remand him for the period of the adjournment;

(c) where a person is charged with an offence triable either way, then, if it falls to the court to try the case summarily but the court is not at the time so constituted, and sitting in such a place, as will enable it to proceed with the trial, the court may remand him until the next occasion on which it will be practicable for the court to be so constituted, and to sit in such a place, as aforesaid, notwithstanding that the remand is for a period exceeding 8 clear days.

(7) A magistrates' court having power to remand a person in custody may, if the remand is for a period not exceeding 3 clear days, commit him to detention at a police station.

(8) Where a person is committed to detention at a police station under subsection (7) above—

(a) he shall not be kept in such detention unless there is a need for him to be so detained for the purposes of inquiries into other offences;

(b) if kept in such detention, he shall be brought back before the magistrates' court which committed him as soon as that need ceases;

(c) he shall be treated as a person in police detention to whom the duties under section 39 of the *Police and Criminal Evidence Act* 1984 (responsibilities in relation to persons detained) relate;

(d) his detention shall be subject to periodic review at the times set out in section 40 of that Act (review of police detention).

The direction to appear does not put an unconditional duty on a prison governor to **5–96**
produce any prisoner from custody who is on bail for other offences. A formal production order is required under s.29 of the *Criminal Justice Act* 1961 and a request to produce a prisoner at court must not be unreasonably refused: *Governor of Brixton Prison, ex p. Walsh* [1985] A.C. 154. It is usually the responsibility of the Crown Prosecution Service to arrange for such orders.

The computation of eight clear days is calculated by counting eight days intervening between the date of appearance and the day when the defendant will be brought before the court again.

When a defendant is remanded on conditional bail with a surety he will only be released once the surety is taken. If no surety is provided, the defendant must be produced from custody after eight days: *Criminal Procedure Rules* 2011, r.18.13 in Appendix G.

Section 10(3) of the *MCA* 1980 provides that after conviction the court may adjourn **5–97**
a case for inquiries or to determine the most suitable method of dealing with the case either for three weeks if the defendant is in custody or four weeks if he is on bail. Section 11 of the *PCC(S)A* 2000 allows for an adjournment for three weeks in custody or four weeks on bail for medical examination after conviction or when the court is satisfied that a defendant did the act or omission.

A defendant may be remanded in custody for a period exceeding eight clear days where he is legally represented and consents to remands in his absence. The safeguards are that the procedure and the defendant's rights must be clearly explained to him and his consent must be freely given whilst he has the benefit of legal representation and advice. The consent may be given to the maximum of the fourth adjournment after the first appearance and then on that occasion the defendant must be produced. The defendant may withdraw his consent at any time and the case will be re-listed.

Police detention for an adult is for a maximum of three days but for a child or young person it is 24 hours: *Children and Young Persons Act* 1969, s.23. Police detention to inquire into "other offences" is not to be given a restricted meaning but includes other offences that are related to those with which the defendant has already been charged: *Bailey and Smith* (1993) 97 Cr.App.R. 365.

Magistrates' Courts Act 1980, s.128A(2), (3)

Remands in custody for more than eight days

5–98 **128A.**—(2) A magistrates' court may remand the accused in custody for a period exceeding 8 clear days if—

(a) it has previously remanded him in custody for the same offence; and
(b) he is before the court,

but only if, after affording the parties an opportunity to make representations, it has set a date on which it expects that it will be possible for the next stage in the proceedings, other than a hearing relating to a further remand in custody or on bail, to take place, and only—

(i) for a period ending not later than that date; or
(ii) for a period of 28 clear days,

whichever is the less.

(3) Nothing in this section affects the right of the accused to apply for bail during the period of the remand.

5–99 This applies on a second appearance in custody when a remand can then be for up to 28 days in custody if a specific event such as a committal or trial will occur on the next date. It does not apply to interim adjournment dates.

Magistrates' Courts Act 1980, s.129

Further remand

5–100 **129.**—(1) If a magistrates' court is satisfied that any person who has been remanded is unable by reason of illness or accident to appear or be brought before the court at the expiration of the period for which he was remanded, the court may, in his absence, remand him for a further time; and section 128(6) above shall not apply.

(2) Notwithstanding anything in section 128(1) above, the power of a court under subsection (1) above to remand a person on bail for a further time—

(a) where he was granted bail in criminal proceedings, includes power to enlarge the recognizance of any surety for him to a later time;
(b) where he was granted bail otherwise than in criminal proceedings, may be exercised by enlarging his recognizance and those of any sureties for him to a later time.

(3) Where a person remanded on bail is bound to appear before a magistrates' court at any time and the court has no power to remand him under subsection (1) above, the court may in his absence—

(a) where he was granted bail in criminal proceedings, appoint a later time as the time at which he is to appear and enlarge the recognizances of any sureties for him to that time;
(b) where he was granted bail otherwise than in criminal proceedings, enlarge his recognizance and those of any sureties for him to a later time;

and the appointment of the time or the enlargement of his recognizance shall be deemed to be a further remand.

(4) Where a magistrates' court commits a person for trial on bail and the recognizance of any surety for him has been conditioned in accordance with paragraph (a) of subsection (4) of section 128 above the court may, in the absence of the surety, enlarge his recognizance so that he is bound to secure that the person so committed for trial appears also before the Crown Court.

5–101 A remand in absence under this section applies equally to defendants in custody or on bail where the defendant does not appear before the court because of illness or accident. The court must have been given solid grounds to found a reliable opinion relating to the illness or accident: *Liverpool City Justices, ex p. Grogan* [1991] 155 J.P. 450.

Magistrates' Courts Act 1980, s.130

Transfer of remand hearings

130.—(1) A magistrates' court adjourning a case under section 5, 10(1), 17C or 18(4) above, and remanding the accused in custody, may, if he has attained the age of 17, order that he be brought up for any subsequent remands before an alternate magistrates' court nearer to the prison where he is to be confined while on remand. **5–102**

(2) The order shall require the accused to be brought before the alternate court at the end of the period of remand or at such earlier time as the alternate court may require.

(3) While the order is in force, the alternate court shall, to the exclusion of the court which made the order, have all the powers in relation to further remand (whether in custody or on bail) and the grant of a right to representation funded by the Legal Services Commission as part of the Criminal Defence Service which that court would have had but for the order.

(4) The alternate court may, on remanding the accused in custody, require him to be brought before the court which made the order at the end of the period of remand or at such earlier time as that court may require; and, if the alternate court does so, or the accused is released on bail, the order under subsection (1) above shall cease to be in force.

(4A) Where a magistrates' court is satisfied as mentioned in section 128(3A) above—

(a) subsection (1) above shall have effect as if for the words "he be brought up for any subsequent remands before" there were substituted the words "applications for any subsequent remands be made to";

(b) subsection (2) above shall have effect as if for the words "the accused to be brought before" there were substituted the words "an application for a further remand to be made to" and

(c) subsection (4) above shall have effect as if for the words "him to be brought before" there were substituted the words "an application for a further remand to be made to".

(5) Schedule 5 to this Act shall have effect to supplement this section.

Magistrates' Courts Act 1980, s.131(1)–(2)

Remand of accused already in custody

131.—(1) When a magistrates' court remands an accused person in custody and he is already detained under a custodial sentence, the period for which he is remanded may be up to 28 clear days. **5–103**

(2) But the court shall inquire as to the expected date of his release from that detention; and if it appears that it will be before 28 clear days have expired, he shall not be remanded in custody for more than 8 clear days or (if longer) a period ending with that date.

VIII. POLICE BAIL

The police may bail a defendant pending an attendance or return to the police station or an appearance at court. There are no statutory time limits. Sections 47 (*post*) and 34 of the *Police and Criminal Evidence Act* 1984 have been amended by the *Police (Detention and Bail) Act* 2011 to address the difficulties that arose in the case of *R. (on the application of Chief Constable of Greater Manchester Police) v. Salford Magistrates' Court and Paul Hookway* [2011] EWHC 1578 (Admin). In that case, the statutory scheme was interpreted to prevent police from seeking a warrant of further detention in respect of a suspect who had been released on bail after initial detention but in respect of whom the full period allowed for detention before charge had not expired. The amendments to the act now disapply any such time limit to time spent on bail. The act has retrospective effect. **5–104**

Police and Criminal Evidence Act, s.38

Duties of custody officer after charge.

38.—(1) Where a person arrested for an offence otherwise than under a warrant endorsed for bail is charged with an offence, the custody officer shall, subject to section 25 of the *Criminal* **5–105**

Justice and Public Order Act 1994, order his release from police detention, either on bail or without bail, unless—

(a) if the person arrested is not an arrested juvenile—

(i) his name or address cannot be ascertained or the custody officer has reasonable grounds for doubting whether a name or address furnished by him as his name or address is his real name or address;

(ii) the custody officer has reasonable grounds for believing that the person arrested will fail to appear in court to answer to bail;

(iii) in the case of a person arrested for an imprisonable offence, the custody officer has reasonable grounds for believing that the detention of the person arrested is necessary to prevent him from committing an offence;

(iiia) except in a case where (by virtue of subsection (9) of section 63B below) that section does not apply, the custody officer has reasonable grounds for believing that the detention of the person is necessary to enable a sample to be taken from him under that section;

(iv) in the case of a person arrested for an offence which is not an imprisonable offence, the custody officer has reasonable grounds for believing that the detention of the person arrested is necessary to prevent him from causing physical injury to any other person or from causing loss of or damage to property;

(v) the custody officer has reasonable grounds for believing that the detention of the person arrested is necessary to prevent him from interfering with the administration of justice or with the investigation of offences or of a particular offence; or

(vi) the custody officer has reasonable grounds for believing that the detention of the person arrested is necessary for his own protection;

(b) if he is an arrested juvenile—

(i) any of the requirements of paragraph (a) above is satisfied (but, in the case of paragraph (a)(iiia) above, only if the arrested juvenile has attained the minimum age); or

(ii) the custody officer has reasonable grounds for believing that he ought to be detained in his own interests.

(2) If the release of a person arrested is not required by subsection (1) above, the custody officer may authorise him to be kept in police detention but may not authorise a person to be kept in police detention by virtue of subsection (1)(a)(iiia) after the end of the period of six hours beginning when he was charged with the offence.

(2A) The custody officer, in taking the decisions required by subsection (1)(a) and (b) above (except (a)(i) and (vi) and (b)(ii)), shall have regard to the same considerations as those which a court is required to have regard to in taking the corresponding decisions under paragraph 2(1) of Part I of Schedule 1 to the *Bail Act* 1976 (disregarding paragraph 2(2) of that Part).

(3) Where a custody officer authorises a person who has been charged to be kept in police detention, he shall, as soon as practicable, make a written record of the grounds for the detention.

(4) Subject to subsection (5) below, the written record shall be made in the presence of the person charged who shall at that time be informed by the custody officer of the grounds for his detention.

(5) Subsection (4) above shall not apply where the person charged is, at the time when the written record is made—

(a) incapable of understanding what is said to him;

(b) violent or likely to become violent; or

(c) in urgent need of medical attention.

(6) Where a custody officer authorises an arrested juvenile to be kept in police detention under subsection (1) above, the custody officer shall, unless he certifies—

(a) that, by reason of such circumstances as are specified in the certificate, it is impracticable for him to do so; or

(b) in the case of an arrested juvenile who has attained the age of 12 years, that no secure accommodation is available and that keeping him in other local authority accommodation would not be adequate to protect the public from serious harm from him, secure that the arrested juvenile is moved to local authority accommodation.

(6A) In this section—

"local authority accommodation" means accommodation provided by or on behalf of a local authority (within the meaning of the *Children Act* 1989);

"minimum age" means the age specified in section 63B(3) below;

"secure accommodation" means accommodation provided for the purpose of restricting liberty;

"sexual offence" and "violent offence" have the same meanings as in Part I of the *Criminal Justice Act* 1991 the *Powers of Criminal Courts (Sentencing) Act* 2000;

and any reference, in relation to an arrested juvenile charged with a violent or sexual offence, to protecting the public from serious harm from him shall be construed as a reference to protecting members of the public from death or serious personal injury, whether physical or psychological, occasioned by further such offences committed by him.

(6B) Where an arrested juvenile is moved to local authority accommodation under subsection (6) above, it shall be lawful for any person acting on behalf of the authority to detain him.

(7) A certificate made under subsection (6) abovein respect of an arrested juvenile shall be produced to the court before which he is first brought thereafter.

(7A) In this section "imprisonable offence" has the same meaning as in Schedule 1 to the *Bail Act* 1976.

(8) In this Part of this Act "local authority" has the same meaning as in the *Children and Young Persons Act* 1969.

[This section is reprinted as amended by the *Criminal Justice and Court Services Act* 2000, s.57(3)(b) and the *Criminal Justice Act* 2003, s.5(2)(b).]

Police and Criminal Evidence Act 1984, s.47

Bail after arrest

47.—(1) Subject to subsection (2) below, a release on bail of a person under this Part of this Act shall be a release on bail granted in accordance with sections 3, 3A, 5 and 5A of the *Bail Act* 1976 as they apply to bail granted by a constable. **5–106**

(1A) The normal powers to impose conditions of bail shall be available to him where a custody officer releases a person on bail under section 38(1) above (including that subsection as applied by section 40(10) above) but not in any other cases.

In this subsection, "the normal powers to impose conditions of bail" has the meaning given in section 3(6) of the *Bail Act* 1976.

(2) Nothing in the *Bail Act* 1976 shall prevent the re-arrest without warrant of a person released on bail subject to a duty to attend at a police station if new evidence justifying a further arrest has come to light since his release.

(3) Subject to subsections (3A) and (4) below, in this Part of this Act references to "bail" are references to bail subject to a duty—

(a) to appear before a magistrates' court at such time and such place; or

(b) to attend at such police station at such time,

as the custody officer may appoint.

(3A) Where a custody officer grants bail to a person subject to a duty to appear before a magistrates' court, he shall appoint for the appearance—

(a) a date which is not later than the first sitting of the court after the person is charged with the offence; or

(b) where he is informed by the designated officer for the relevant local justice area that the appearance cannot be accommodated until a later date, that later date.

(4) Where a custody officer has granted bail to a person subject to a duty to appear at a police station, the custody officer may give notice in writing to that person that his attendance at the police station is not required.

(6) Where a person who has been granted bail and either has attended at the police station in accordance with the grant of bail or has been arrested under section 46A above is detained at a police station, any time during which he was in police detention prior to being granted bail shall be included as part of any period which falls to be calculated under this Part of this Act and any time during which he was on bail shall not be so included.

(7) Where a person who was released on bail subject to a duty to attend at a police station is re-arrested, the provisions of this Part of this Act shall apply to him as they apply to a person arrested for the first time; but this subsection does not apply to a person who is arrested under section 46A above or has attended a police station in accordance with the grant of bail (and who accordingly is deemed by section 34(7) above to have been arrested for an offence).

(8) [Amendments to *MCA* 1980].

[This section is printed as amended by the *Police (Detention and Bail) Act* 2011 with effect from July 12, 2011 and retrospectively.]

Bail Act 1976, s.3A

Conditions of bail in case of police bail

5–107 **3A.**—(1) Section 3 of this Act applies, in relation to bail granted by a custody officer under Part IV of the *Police and Criminal Evidence Act* 1984 in cases where the normal powers to impose conditions of bail are available to him, subject to the following modifications.

(2) Subsection (6) does not authorise the imposition of a requirement to reside in a bail hostel or any requirement under paragraph (d) or (e).

(3) Subsections (6ZAA), (6ZA), (6A) and (6F) shall be omitted.

(4) For subsection (8), substitute the following—

"(8) Where a custody officer has granted bail in criminal proceedings he or another custody officer serving at the same police station may, at the request of the person to whom it was granted, vary the conditions of bail; and in doing so he may impose conditions or more onerous conditions.".

(5) Where a constable grants bail to a person no conditions shall be imposed under subsections (4), (5), (6) or (7) of section 3 of this Act unless it appears to the constable that it is necessary to do so

(a) for the purposes of preventing that person from failing to surrender to custody, or

(b) for the purposes of preventing that person from committing an offence while on bail, or

(c) for the purposes of preventing that person from interfering with witnesses or otherwise obstructing the course of justice, whether in relation to himself or any other person or

(d) for that person's own protection or, if he is a child or young person, for his own welfare or in his own interests.

(6) Subsection (5) above also applies on any request to a custody officer under subsection (8) of section 3 of this Act to vary the conditions of bail.

[This section is printed as amended by the *Criminal Justice Act* 2003.]

Bail Act 1976, s.5A

Supplementary provisions in cases of police bail.

5–108 **5A.**—(1) Section 5 of this Act applies, in relation to bail granted by a custody officer under Part IV of the *Police and Criminal Evidence Act* 1984 in cases where the normal powers to impose conditions of bail are available to him, subject to the following modifications.

(1A) Subsections (2A) and (2B) shall be omitted.

(2) For subsection (3) substitute the following—

"(3) Where a custody officer, in relation to any person,—

(a) imposes conditions in granting bail in criminal proceedings, or

(b) varies any conditions of bail or imposes conditions in respect of bail in criminal proceedings,

the custody officer shall, with a view to enabling that person to consider requesting him or another custody officer, or making an application to a magistrates' court, to vary the conditions, give reasons for imposing or varying the conditions.".

(3) For subsection (4) substitute the following—

"(4) A custody officer who is by virtue of subsection (3) above required to give reasons for his decision shall include a note of those reasons in the custody record and shall give a copy of that note to the person in relation to whom the decision was taken.".

(4) Subsections (5) and (6) shall be omitted.

A custody officer who grants bail subject to conditions including a surety or security or varies the conditions of bail must give reasons and make a record of the decision, but there is no obligation to give reasons for the withholding of bail: *Bail Act* 1976, ss.5 and 5A. Part 19 of the *Criminal Procedure Rules* 2011 applies to the procedure for various applications relating to police bail, see Appendix G. **5–109**

IX. WARRANTS WITH AND WITHOUT BAIL

When a warrant of arrest is issued by the court, consideration must be given as to whether the warrant should be backed for bail or not. The decision will depend on the nature and gravity of the offence charged and the defendant's bail history. **5–110**

Magistrates' Courts Act 1980, s.117

Warrant endorsed for bail

117.—(1) A justice of the peace on issuing a warrant for the arrest of any person may grant him bail by endorsing the warrant for bail, that is to say, by endorsing the warrant with a direction in accordance with subsection (2) below. **5–111**

(2) A direction for bail endorsed on a warrant under subsection (1) above shall—

(a) in the case of bail in criminal proceedings, state that the person arrested is to be released on bail subject to a duty to appear before such magistrates' court and at such time as may be specified in the endorsement;

(b) ...(civil proceedings)

and the endorsement shall fix the amounts in which any sureties and, in a case falling within paragraph (b) above, that person is or are to be bound.

(3) Where a warrant has been endorsed for bail under subsection (1) above—

(a) where the person arrested is to be released on bail on his entering into a recognizance without sureties, it shall not be necessary to take him to a police station, but if he is so taken, he shall be released from custody on his entering into the recognizance; and

(b) where he is to be released on his entering into a recognizance with sureties, he shall be taken to a police station on his arrest, and the custody officer there shall (subject to his approving any surety tendered in compliance with the endorsement) release him from custody as directed in the endorsement.

X. CUSTODY TIME LIMITS

Introduction

The *Magistrates' Courts Act* 1980 and other enactments provide for limits on the periods of time for which a person may be remanded, either in custody or on bail. Custody time limits also apply, which dictate the length of time over which a person may be remanded in custody during the progress of a criminal case. The limits are designed to ensure that where a defendant is in custody, the case will be expedited. If there is any delay the defendant may be released from custody for further adjournments. The custody time limit for cases tried summarily is 56 days from first appearance to trial and for cases going to the Crown Court, the limit is 70 days from first appearance to committal. Application may be made for the limits to be extended in specific circumstances. Time limits do not apply to defendants remanded on bail but all cases must be dealt with expeditiously in accordance with the *Criminal Procedure Rules* 2011. **5–112**

Prosecution of Offences Act 1985, s.22

Power of Secretary of State to set time limits in relation to preliminary stages of criminal proceedings

5–113 **22.**—(1) The Secretary of State may by regulations make provision, with respect to any specified preliminary stage of proceedings for an offence, as to the maximum period—

(a) to be allowed to the prosecution to complete that stage;

(b) during which the accused may, while awaiting completion of that stage, be—

(i) in the custody of a magistrates' court; or

(ii) in the custody of the Crown Court;

in relation to that offence.

(2) The regulations may, in particular—

(a) be made so as to apply only in relation to proceedings instituted in specified areas, or proceedings of, or against persons of, specified classes or descriptions;

(b) make different provision with respect to proceedings instituted in different areas, or different provision with respect to proceedings of, or against persons of, different classes or descriptions;

(c) make such provision with respect to the procedure to be followed in criminal proceedings as the Secretary of State considers appropriate in consequence of any other provision of the regulations;

(d) provide for the *Magistrates' Courts Act* 1980 and the *Bail Act* 1976 to apply in relation to cases to which custody or overall time limits apply subject to such modifications as may be specified (being modifications which the Secretary of State considers necessary in consequence of any provision made by the regulations); and

(e) make such transitional provision in relation to proceedings instituted before the commencement of any provision of the regulations as the Secretary of State considers appropriate.

(3) The appropriate court may, at any time before the expiry of a time limit imposed by the regulations, extend, or further extend, that limit; but the court shall not do so unless it is satisfied—

(a) that the need for the extension is due to—

(i) the illness or absence of the accused, a necessary witness, a judge or a magistrate;

(ii) a postponement which is occasioned by the ordering by the court of separate trials in the case of two or more accused or two or more offences; or

(iii) some other good and sufficient cause; and

(b) that the prosecution has acted with all due diligence and expedition.

(4) Where, in relation to any proceedings for an offence, an overall time limit has expired before the completion of the stage of the proceedings to which the limit applies the appropriate court shall stay the proceedings.

(5) Where—

(a) a person escapes from the custody of a magistrates' court or the Crown Court before the expiry of a custody time limit which applies in his case; or

(b) a person who has been released on bail in consequence of the expiry of a custody time limit—

(i) fails to surrender himself into the custody of the court at the appointed time; or

(ii) is arrested by a constable on a ground mentioned in section 7(3)(b) of the *Bail Act* 1976 (breach, or likely breach, of conditions of bail);

the regulations shall, so far as they provide for any custody time limit in relation to the preliminary stage in question, be disregarded.

(6) Subsection (6A) below applies where—

(a) a person escapes from the custody of a magistrates' court or the Crown Court; or

(b) a person who has been released on bail fails to surrender himself into the custody of the court at the appointed time;

and is accordingly unlawfully at large for any period.

(6A) The following, namely—

(a) the period for which the person is unlawfully at large; and

(b) such additional period (if any) as the appropriate court may direct, having regard to the disruption of the prosecution occasioned by—

(i) the person's escape or failure to surrender; and

(ii) the length of the period mentioned in paragraph (a) above,

shall be disregarded, so far as the offence in question is concerned, for the purposes of the overall time limit which applies in his case in relation to the stage which the proceedings have reached at the time of the escape or, as the case may be, at the appointed time.

(7) Where a magistrates' court decides to extend, or further extend, a custody or overall time limit or to give a direction under subsection (6A) above, the accused may appeal against the decision to the Crown Court.

(8) Where a magistrates' court refuses to extend, or further extend, a custody or overall time limit, or to give a direction under subsection (6A) above, the prosecution may appeal against the refusal to the Crown Court.

(9) An appeal under subsection (8) above may not be commenced after the expiry of the limit in question; but where such an appeal is commenced before the expiry of the limit the limit shall be deemed not to have expired before the determination or abandonment of the appeal.

(10) Where a person is convicted of an offence in any proceedings, the exercise, in relation to any preliminary stage of those proceedings, of the power conferred by subsection (3) above shall not be called into question in any appeal against that conviction.

(11) In this section—

"appropriate court" means—

(a) where the accused has been committed for trial, sent for trial under section 51 of the *Crime and Disorder Act* 1998 or indicted for the offence, the Crown Court; and

(b) in any other case, the magistrates' court specified in the summons or warrant in question or, where the accused has already appeared or been brought before a magistrates' court, a magistrates' court for the same area;

"custody" includes local authority accommodation to which a person is remanded or committed by virtue of section 23 of the *Children and Young Persons Act* 1969, and references to a person being committed to custody shall be construed accordingly;

"custody of the Crown Court" includes custody to which a person is committed in pursuance of—

(a) section 6 of the *Magistrates' Courts Act* 1980 (magistrates' court committing accused for trial); or

(b) section 43A of that Act (magistrates' court dealing with a person brought before it following his arrest in pursuance of a warrant issued by the Crown Court); or

(c) section 5(3)(a) of the *Criminal Justice Act* 1987 (custody after transfer order in fraud case); or

(d) paragraph 2(1)(a) of Schedule 6 to the *Criminal Justice Act* 1991 (custody after transfer order in certain cases involving children).

"custody of a magistrates' court" means custody to which a person is committed in pursuance of section 128 of the *Magistrates' Courts Act* 1980 (remand);

"custody time limit" means a time limit imposed by regulations made under subsection (1)(b) above or, where any such limit has been extended by a court under subsection (3) above, the limit as so extended;

"preliminary stage", in relation to any proceedings, does not include any stage after the start of the trial (within the meaning given by subsections (11A) and (11B) below);

"overall time limit" means a time limit imposed by regulations made under subsection (1)(a) above or, where any such limit has been extended by a court under subsection (3) above, the limit as so extended; and

"specified" means specified in the regulations.

(11A) For the purposes of this section, the start of a trial on indictment shall be taken to occur when a jury is sworn to consider the issue of guilt or fitness to plead or, if the court accepts a plea of guilty before a jury is sworn, when that plea is accepted but this is subject to section 8 of the *Criminal Justice Act* 1987 and section 30 of the *Criminal Procedure and Investigations Act* 1996 (preparatory hearings).

(11ZA) For the purposes of this section, proceedings for an offence shall be taken to begin when the accused is charged with the offence or, as the case may be, an information is laid charging him with the offence.

(11B) For the purposes of this section, the start of a summary trial shall be taken to occur—

(a) when the court begins to hear evidence for the prosecution at the trial or to consider whether to exercise its power under section 37(3) of the *Mental Health Act* 1983 (power to make hospital order without convicting the accused), or

(b) if the court accepts a plea of guilty without proceeding as mentioned above, when that plea is accepted.

(12) For the purposes of the application of any custody time limit in relation to a person who is in the custody of a magistrates' court or the Crown Court—

(a) all periods during which he is in the custody of a magistrates' court in respect of the same offence shall be aggregated and treated as a single continuous period; and

(b) all periods during which he is in the custody of the Crown Court in respect of the same offence shall be aggregated and treated similarly.

(13) For the purposes of section 29(3) of the *Supreme Court Act* 1981 (High Court to have power to make prerogative orders in relation to jurisdiction of Crown Court in matters which do not relate to trial on indictment) the jurisdiction conferred on the Crown Court by this section shall be taken to be part of its jurisdiction in matters other than those relating to trial on indictment.

Prosecution of Offences (Custody Time Limits) (Amendment) Regulations 1989 (S.I. 1989 No. 767)

5–114 **1.**—(1) These *Regulations* may be cited as the *Prosecution of Offences (Custody Time Limits) (Amendment) Regulations* 1989.

(2) In these *Regulations* "the principal regulations" means the *Prosecution of Offences (Custody Time Limits) Regulations* 1987 and references to a notice of transfer are references to a notice given under section 4 of the *Criminal Justice Act* 1987.

(3) These *Regulations* shall come into force on 1st June 1989, but—

(a) regulations 2 and 4(a) shall not apply in relation to proceedings for an offence instituted before that date except where—

(i) the accused is committed for trial in the Crown Court, or

(ii) notice of transfer is given in respect of the case, or

(iii) a bill of indictment is preferred against the accused under section 2(2)(b) of the *Administration of Justice (Miscellaneous Provisions) Act* 1933,

on or after that date; and

(b) regulations 3 and 4(b) shall not apply in relation to proceedings for an offence instituted before that date.

Prosecution of Offences (Custody Time Limits) Regulations 1987, regs. 4, 7

Custody time limits in magistrates' courts

5–115 **4.**—(1) The maximum period during which a person accused of an indictable offence other than treason may be in the custody of a magistrates' court in relation to that offence while awaiting completion of any preliminary stage of the proceedings specified in the following provisions of this Regulation shall be as stated in those provisions.

(2) Except as provided in paragraph (3) below, in the case of an offence triable either way the maximum period of custody between the accused's first appearance and the start of summary trial or, as the case may be, the time when the court decides whether or not to commit the accused to the Crown Court for trial shall be 70 days.

(3) In the case of an offence triable either way if, before the expiry of 56 days following the day of the accused's first appearance, the court decides to proceed to summary trial in pursuance of sections 19 to 24 of the 1980 Act the maximum period of custody between the accused's first appearance and the start of the summary trial shall be 56 days.

(4) In the case of an offence triable on indictment exclusively the maximum period of custody between the accused's first appearance and the time when the court decides whether or not to commit the accused to the Crown Court for trial, shall be 70 days.

(4A) In the case of a summary offence, the maximum period of custody beginning with the date of the accused's first appearance and ending with the date of the start of the summary trial shall be 56 days.

(5) The foregoing provisions of this regulation shall have effect as if any reference therein to the time when the court decides whether or not to commit the accused to the Crown Court for trial were a reference—

(a) where a court proceeds to inquire into an information as examining justices in pursuance of section 6(1) of the 1980 Act, to the time when it begins to hear evidence for the prosecution at the inquiry;

(b) where a notice has been given under section 4(1)(c) of the *Criminal Justice Act* 1987 (in these *Regulations* referred to as a "notice of transfer"), to the date on which notice of transfer was given.

Application for extension of custody time limit

7.—(1) An application to a court for the extension or further extension of a custody time limit under section 22(3) of the 1985 Act may be made orally or in writing. **5–116**

(2) Subject to paragraphs (3) and (4) below the prosecution shall—

(a) not less than 5 days before making such an application in the Crown Court; and

(b) not less than 2 days before making such an application in a magistrates' court,

give notice in writing to the accused or his representative and to the proper officer of the court stating that it intends to make such an application.

(2A) In paragraph (2) above, "the proper officer of the court" means in relation to an application in the Crown Court the appropriate officer of the court and in relation to an application in a magistrates' court the clerk of the court.

(3) It shall not be necessary for the prosecution to comply with paragraph (2) above if the accused or his representative has informed the prosecution that he does not require such notice.

(4) If the court is satisfied that it is not practicable in all the circumstances for the prosecution to comply with paragraph (2) above, the court may direct that the prosecution need not comply with that paragraph or that the minimum period of notice required by that paragraph to be given shall be such lesser minimum period as the court may specify.

The period of custody begins at the close of the day during which the defendant was first remanded and expires at midnight on the relevant day. The relevant day is that prescribed by reg. 4 of the *Prosecution of Offences (Custody Time Limits) Regulations* 1987: *Governor of Canterbury Prison, ex p. Craig* [1991] 2 Q.B. 195; (1990) 91 Cr.App.R. 7. Once the limit has expired it is the duty of the court and not a prison governor to direct the release on bail of the defendant: *Olotu v. Home Office* [1997] 1 All E.R. 385. **5–117**

The relevant limits are prescribed in r. 4 (*ante*) as 56 days in the case of summary or either way offences to be dealt with by way of summary trial and 70 days for either way or indictable offences that are to be committed to the Crown Court for trial. Application may be made to extend the time limits under s.22(3) and reg. 7. The requirement on the prosecution to give two days notice of an application has been held to be directory only and not mandatory, so the court retains the power to extend the time limit at any time before it expires: *Governor of Canterbury prison, ex p. Craig* [1991] 2 Q.B. 195; (1990) 91 Cr.App.R. 7.

Once a custody time limit has expired and the prosecution have failed to obtain an extension of time the court has no power to extend time and bail must be granted: *Sheffield Justices, ex p. Turner* [1991] 2 W.L.R. 987

Before the court will direct an extension of the time limit it must be satisfied on the balance of probabilities that the conditions of s.22(3) are met. Guidance on the approach to be taken by the courts was given in *Crown Court at Manchester, ex p. MacDonald* [1999] 1 All E.R. 805. It is recognised that there are an infinite number of matters that might amount to "good and sufficient cause". Lack of court time, listing difficulties because of the size and complexity of a case and the unavailability of a senior judge or any judge to hear the case have all been held to amount to "good and sufficient cause": *Re C* (2000) 164 J.P. 693; *R. (Eliot) v. Crown Court at Reading* [2002] 1 Cr.App.R. 3; *Central Criminal Court, ex p. Abu-Wardeh* [1997] 1 All E.R. 159; *Crown Court at Norwich, ex p. Cox* (1993) 97 Cr.App.R. 145; (1993) 157 J.P. 593. The seriousness of the offence and shortness of the extension sought do not qualify: *Governor of Winchester Prison, ex p. Roddie* [1991] 2 All E.R. 931. **5–118**

In *R. (Bannister) v. Crown Court at Guildford* [2004] EWHC 221, the court took a more robust view and held that the chronic lack of resources which led to an inability to list an "utterly routine" case did not amount to "good and sufficient cause". The court said that positive judicial intervention at listing stage was to be encouraged to ensure that the time limits were observed. This approach was approved in the case of *R. (Miah) v. Snaresbrook Crown Court* [2006] EWHC 2873 where listing difficulties due to the normal pressure of work were held not to constitute "good and sufficient cause" for extending the time limits. There had to be some exceptional circumstances.

The difficulties over listing at the Crown Court and the consequent delays to trials continue to exercise the Appeal Court. In *Kalonji v.Wood Green Crown Court* (2008) ACD 11, the custody time limits expired in a Crown Court trial and so were extended by about 13 weeks to the date of trial. The "good and sufficient cause" for the extension was found to be the inability of the court to list the trial any earlier. This decision was appealed by the defendants as not falling within the requirements of s.22 of the *Prosecution of Offences Act* 1985. The case was not difficult or overly lengthy and the only reason for the delay was the listing difficulty. Reference was made to the case of *Crown Court at Manchester* (*ex parte*) *McDonald* (*supra*) where it was said that listing difficulties did not amount to good and sufficient cause. The prosecution referred to the case of *Gibson* (see below) and it was this approach that was preferred by the court and on appeal it was held that it cannot be ignored that available resources are limited or that occasions will occur when pressure on courts is more intense than usual. It is important that courts and parties strive to overcome difficulties and if no efforts are made, that may debar courts from extending the time limits but judges are not entitled to ignore availability of resources. In the instant case the judge had identified that the closure of Middlesex Guildhall and the loss of seven courts there had added to the pressure on resources and increased the workload by 117 per cent. These were held to be exceptional circumstances and the decision of the judge to extend the time limits was not unreasonable. This approach was adopted in *Polat and others v Wood Green Crown Court* [2007] EWHC 2885 when a similar argument came before the High Court. It was said that listing officers cannot be expected to be constantly checking on whether cases can be moved and there is no requirement for specific inquiries to be made in respect of each and every case. The judge had in mind the difficulties in London and had reasonably taken those into account in deciding to extend the time limits without requiring the listing officer to come and report to him. The appeal court took the opportunity to make observations regarding the necessity of all parties keeping to timetables so that if an earlier trial date becomes available it may be taken advantage of and also said that the issue of custody time limits should be addressed as soon as the trial date is set. Although *Kalonji* governs the position for now and in the immediate future, it was hoped that those responsible for the provision of resources in the London area would address the situation.

In assessing "good and sufficient cause" considerations relating to bail are not relevant and extending the limit for the protection of the public could not of itself amount to "good and sufficient cause": *Sheffield Crown Court, ex p. Headley* [2000] 2 Cr.App.R. 1; *R. (Eliot) v. Crown Court at Reading*. But see *Crown Court at Luton, ex p. Neaves* [1993] 157 J.P. 80 where it was held that an extension for the protection of an individual member of the public from violence was justified.

5–119 With regard to the condition of "due diligence and expedition", the court will require such diligence and expedition as would be expected from a competent prosecutor who is alert to his duty. It is an objective test: *Crown Court at Manchester, ex p. MacDonald* (*ante*); *Governor of Winchester prison, ex p. Roddie* (*ante*). When assessing whether due diligence has been used the limits set are to be seen not as a target but a maximum period of time and the prosecution must ensure that the evidence and papers are served on the defence within a reasonable time to permit them to be properly considered by the time of committal: *Crown Court at Norwich, ex p. Parker* (1993) 96 Cr.App.R. 68. The prosecution also had to expedite the case to allow for a contested rather than uncontested committal within the 70-day limit: *Leeds Crown Court, ex p.*

Briggs [1998] 2 Cr.App.R. 424. Once the prosecution judge that a piece of evidence is likely to be important, it has a duty to ensure that the evidence reaches the defence swiftly. A case has to be advanced as to why there was a delay in delivering evidence: *Central Criminal Court, ex p. Behbehani* [1994] Crim.L.R. 352; *R. (Smith) v. Woolwich Crown Court* [2002] Crim.L.R. 915. In *R. (Thomas); R. (Stubbs) v. Central Criminal Court* (2007) 1 Cr.App.R. 7 the defendants were charged with attempted murder and firearms offences. The Crown Court extended the custody time limits for three months. The defence challenged this extension and referred to earlier delay by the prosecution which they submitted indicated that the prosecution had not acted with due diligence and expedition. It was held on appeal that when the court considers an application to extend custody time limits it must look at the circumstances that led to the need for an extension. The defence could not effectively use the same argument again in respect of delay in the past and seek to appeal an earlier decision. The court may take an overall view so that previous delay in the case could be relevant but only if it was the root cause of the reason for seeking a further extension. In this case the appeal was dismissed as the court found there were additional different reasons for the prosecution to seek extensions and the due diligence test was met.

In *R. (Gibson and Gibson) v. Winchester Crown Court* [2004] 1 W.L.R. 1623, it was held by the court that if "good and sufficient cause" were found, the fact that the prosecution had failed to act with due diligence may be irrelevant as the need for the extension may not be directly referable to their failure. The Court also commented that availability of resources could not be ignored but all relevant considerations must be taken into account when deciding on an extension.

The period before charge should not be taken into account in deciding whether the prosecution has acted with all due diligence and expedition. Delays in arrest and charge may be relevant to the argument as to whether "good and sufficient cause"for the extension of time exists but the due diligence and expedition test applies only to the time after charge. *R. (on the application of the CPS) v. Ipswich Crown Court* [2010] EWHC 1515(Admin).

When extending the time limits it is important that the defendant should understand without a doubt why his liberty is being restricted. The application must be clear and understandable and the defendant must be given an opportunity to object and make representations. The order of the court must be clear, detailed and properly recorded: *Re Ward, Ward and Bond* [1991] Crim.L.R. 558.

The procedure in such applications is informal and art. 6 is not engaged because it **5–120** does not involve the trial of a criminal charge. Formal rules of evidence do not apply but the defendant must be allowed to question any areas of the application as he wishes: *Wildman v. DPP* [2001] Crim.L.R. 565. Where a defendant is charged with various offences at different times, each offence attracts its own custody time limit: *Wirral District Magistrates' Court, ex p. Meikle* [1990] 154 J.P. 1035. A new custody time limit then runs from the date of the new charge but it could amount to an abuse of process by the prosecution if the new charges were preferred solely for the purpose of defeating the custody time limits: *Waltham Forest Magistrates, ex p. Lee and Lee* (1993) 97 Cr.App.R. 287; *Wolverhampton Magistrates, ex p. Uppal* [1995] 159 J.P. 86.

The commencement of a new custody time limit with every new charge does not infringe the right to liberty under art. 5 ECHR. In *Crown Court at Leeds, ex p. Wardle* [2001] 2 Cr.App.R. 20, the defendant was charged originally with murder but the CPS substituted a charge of manslaughter at a later date. It was argued by the defence that new custody time limits did not attach to the new charge which was expressly or impliedly included in the original murder charge. It was also claimed that the detention was therefore in breach of art. 5 ECHR. It was held that a requirement on the magistrates' court to enquire into whether a new charge also constituted one of the potential offences for which a defendant might be convicted on the original charge would place an undue burden on the examining justices. Accordingly, each fresh and different offence charged did give rise to a new custody limit. No breach of art. 5 was found in view of the fact that the proceedings were both lawful and the consequences of the restriction imposed sufficiently accessible. Whilst there was always a risk that the custody time limit might be extended as a result of an arbitrary decision by the prosecution, that risk was subject to judicial control by the court.

More than one application can be made to extend time limits provided the application is made during the currency of the initial time limit or the time limit as extended by the court. This was confirmed in *R. (Haque) v. Central Criminal Court* (2004) Crim L.R. 298. The court also said that the "root and principal cause" of the need for the extension must be looked at rather than whether the prosecution had contributed to that need.

Chapter 6

DISCLOSURE

I. INTRODUCTION

Historically there has been no obligation on the defence to give the court or the prosecution advance warning of any evidence that it may seek to adduce at the trial other than via a summons or complaint, which contains information about the alleged offence; this absence of obligation being a natural consequence of the rule that it is for the prosecution to prove the case against the accused. There has also been little formal legal requirement for the prosecution to give notice of its evidence pre-trial. However, the position is becoming more formalised and the law has reached a position where it imposes limited and varying obligations on both sides to reveal its case to the other before the trial. It is plain from the steer of both legislative and judicial policy that the obligations on the defence to disclose its case pre-trial will become ever more onerous and expansive. A major aim of the *Criminal Procedure Rules* 2011 is to encourage courts at every level to oblige both prosecution and defence to identify all issues of dispute and significance at a pre-trial stage. See *Jisl and Tekin*, *The Times*, April 19, 2004, CA at [113]–[121]. **6–1**

II. OBLIGATIONS TO DISCLOSE EVIDENCE PRE-TRIAL

A. Obligations Common to Both Parties

(1) Obligation to disclose evidence to be adduced in writing

The effect of the *Criminal Justice Act* 1967, s.9, is to require any party proposing to tender a *written statement* from a witness in evidence to serve to statement upon the other side at least seven days before the evidence is adduced. After the statement has been served the other party can prevent the evidence being adduced in written form by **6–2** giving notice, within seven days of receipt of the statement, to the party that served the statement. The statement is only admissible if it complies with the requirements particularised in s.9 and therefore it is good practise for all witness statements to be drawn up in the approved form, so that the written document may be used in evidence if the need should arise. Provided no party objects, any statement which complies with the formalities of s.9 may be read in evidence even though less than seven days' notice has been given.

Criminal Justice Act 1967, s.9

Proof by written statement

6–3 **9.**—(1) In any criminal proceedings, *other than committal proceedings*, a written statement by any person shall, if such of the conditions mentioned in the next following subsection as are applicable are satisfied, be admissible as evidence to the like extent as oral evidence to the like effect by that person.

(2) The said conditions are—

(a) the statement purports to be signed by the person who made it;

(b) the statement contains a declaration by that person to the effect that it is true to the best of his knowledge and belief and that he made the statement knowing that, if it were tendered in evidence, he would be liable to prosecution if he wilfully stated in it anything which he knew to be false or did not believe to be true;

(c) before the hearing at which the statement is tendered in evidence, a copy of the statement is served, by or on behalf of the party proposing to tender it, on each of the other parties to the proceedings; and

(d) none of the other parties or their solicitors, within seven days from the service of the copy of the statement, serves a notice on the party so proposing objecting to the statement being tendered in evidence under this section:

Provided that the conditions mentioned in paragraphs (c) and (d) of this subsection shall not apply if the parties agree before or during the hearing that the statement shall be so tendered.

(3) The following provisions shall also have effect in relation to any written statement tendered in evidence under this section, that is to say—

(a) if the statement is made by a person under the age of eighteen, it shall give his age;

(b) if it is made by a person who cannot read it, it shall be read to him before he signs it and shall be accompanied by a declaration by the person who so read the statement to the effect that it was so read; and

(c) if it refers to any other document as an exhibit, the copy served on any other party to the proceedings under paragraph (c) of the last foregoing subsection shall be accompanied by a copy of that document or by such information as may be necessary in order to enable the party on whom it is served to inspect that document or a copy thereof.

(4) Notwithstanding that a written statement made by any person may be admissible as evidence by virtue of this section—

(a) the party by whom or on whose behalf a copy of the statement was served may call that person to give evidence; and

(b) the court may, of its own motion or on the application of any party to the proceedings, require that person to attend before the court and give evidence.

(5) An application under paragraph (b) of the last foregoing subsection to a court other than a magistrates' court may be made before the hearing and on any such application the powers of the court shall be exercisable *by a puisne judge of the High Court, a Circuit judge or Recorder sitting alone* [by any of the following sitting alone—

(a) a puisne judge of the High Court;

(b) a Circuit judge;

(c) a District Judge (Magistrates' Courts);

(d) a Recorder.]

(6) So much of any statement as is admitted in evidence by virtue of this section shall, unless the court otherwise directs, be read aloud at the hearing and where the court so directs an account shall be given orally of so much of any statement as is not read aloud.

(7) Any document or object referred to as an exhibit and identified in a written statement tendered in evidence under this section shall be treated as if it had been produced as an exhibit and identified in court by the maker of the statement.

(8) A document required by this section to be served on any person may be served—
(a) by delivering it to him or to his solicitor; or
(b) by addressing it to him and leaving it at his usual or last known place of abode or place of business or by addressing it to his solicitor and leaving it at his office; or
(c) by sending it in a registered letter or by the recorded delivery service or by first class post addressed to him at his usual or last known place of abode or place of business or addressed to his solicitor at his office; or
(d) in the case of a body corporate, by delivering it to the secretary or clerk of the body at its registered or principal office or sending it in a registered letter or by the recorded delivery service or by first class post addressed to the Secretary or clerk of that body at that office; and in paragraph (d) of this subsection references to the secretary, in relation to a limited liability partnership, are to any designated member of the limited liability partnership.

[This section is printed as amended by the *Criminal Procedure and Investigations Act* 1996, s.69, and the *Limited Liability Partnerships Regulations* 2001 (S.I. 2001 No. 1090). As from a day or days to be appointed, a new subs. (3A) is inserted by the *Children and Young Persons Act* 1969, Sched. 5 (not set out above). As from a further day to be appointed, the italicised words in subs. (1) are repealed by the *Criminal Justice Act* 2003, Sched. 7. As from a further day to be appointed, the italicised words in subs. (5) are replaced by to the words which follow in square brackets: *Courts Act* 2003, Sched. 4.]

The contents of a statement tendered under this section are not deemed to be **6–4** conclusive proof of any matter stated and are to be treated in the same way as if the maker of the statement had given evidence in accordance with his statement at the trial; the provision is a valuable one designed to save expense and trouble in many instances, but where evidence is central to the issues of the case, prosecutors should give very careful consideration as to whether or not they call the actual witnesses so that the proper impact of that evidence can be made upon the court: *Lister v. Quaife* [1983] 1 W.L.R. 48, DC.

The requirements of the section should be complied with strictly, failing which the statement will be inadmissible: see *Patterson v. DPP* [1990] RTR 329, DC (declaration stating that the statement consisted of six pages when in fact it contained eight). However, the declaration referred to in subs. (2)(b), as distinct from the statement itself, need not be signed, and may be placed at the heading of the statement before the body of evidence begins: *Chapman v. Ingleton*, 57 Cr.App.R. 476, DC.

The word "statement" in the section is a reference to the assertion of the facts in the body of the document; there is no requirement that an identical document should be served on the defence; and provided that the statements were identical, there is no requirement that the document served on the defence should (a) have a copy of the signature of the witness, (b) have the same date as the original, or (c) correctly identify in the declaration the number of pages in the document: *Wood v. DPP*, 174 J.P. 562, QBD (Mitting J.).

(2) Obligation to disclose expert evidence

The combined effect of rr.1.2 and 3.3 (duty of parties to conduct case in accordance **6–5** with overriding objective and to assist court to further it by actively managing case) of the *Criminal Procedure Rules* 2011 (Appendix G–1a, G–5) has been construed to amount to an obligation to notify the court and the other parties at the earliest practicable moment if it is intended, or may be intended, to adduce expert evidence: *Ensor* [2010] 1 Cr.App.R. 18, CA. Rule 33.4(1) expressly requires a party who wishes to introduce expert evidence to serve it as soon as practicable (and in any event together with any application in support of which that party relies on the evidence) on the court officer and each other party; and, if another party so requires, to provide copies of (or a reasonable opportunity to inspect) records of examinations, measurements, tests or experiments carried out by the expert in reaching his opinion (see Appendix G–194). Drafts of an expert's reports are privileged and are not disclosable by virtue of an obligation under the rules to give notice: see *Jackson v. Marley Davenport Ltd* [2004] 1 W.L.R. 2926.

6–6 Rule 33.4(2) prohibits a party who fails to comply with the requirements in r.33.4(1) from introducing the evidence unless every other party agrees or the court gives permission. Insofar as that rule appears to operate as an exclusionary rule of evidence, see the discussion as to the limits of the *vires* of the *Criminal Procedure Rules* generally at § 7–3, *post*. See also the judgment of Laws L.J. in *R. (Kelly) v. Warley Magistrates' Court* [2008] 1 Cr.App.R. 14, DC at [33], as authority for a proposition that any sanction imposed by rules of court must be proportionate, must provide for no more than might reasonably be required for the proper working of the case management code (here as to disclosure of expert evidence), and must be of a procedural nature only and not purport to change the laws of evidence. However, decisions of trial courts not to allow a party to introduce expert evidence for failure to comply with the requirements have been upheld. Thus in *Ensor*, *ibid.*, it was held that the trial judge had been entitled to refuse to permit expert evidence to be called where the conduct of the defence (by failing totally to comply with either the spirit or the letter of the predecessor to r.33.4 and by failing until the end of the prosecution case to inform the prosecution that expert evidence might be adduced) amounted to a "deliberate tactical ploy" and "nothing less than an attempt to ambush the prosecution"; and in *Writtle v. DPP*, 173 J.P. 224, DC, the justices' refusal to admit an expert's report was upheld in circumstances where some weeks following the adjourning of a trial part heard at the end of the prosecution case the defence had served an expert report on the prosecution which dealt with matters on which a prosecution witness had already given evidence.

As to disclosure (as unused material) of material connected with an expert's report, see *post*, § 6–65.

B. Obligations on the Defence

6–7 Rules 3.2 and 3.3 of the *Criminal Procedure Rules* 2011 (Appendix G–4, G–5) have been construed to give rise to a duty on the defence, even in a relatively straightforward trial in the magistrates' court, to make its defence and the issues it raises clear to the prosecution and to the court at an early stage, at the latest before the prosecution closes its case: see *Malcolm v. DPP* [2007] 2 Cr.App.R. 1, DC; and *Writtle v. DPP*, 173 J.P. 224, DC. In practice, upon a case being set down for summary trial (*i.e.* at the first appearance and when a not guilty plea is entered), the defendant will be asked to identify the issues which will arise in the trial: see the revised case management form issued by the Criminal Procedure Rule Committee: *post* § 7–138; and see also *R. (Firth) v. Epping Magistrates' Court*, unreported, February 3, 2011, DC ([2011] EWHC 388 (Admin.)), as to admissions by or on behalf of an accused in the case management form being used as evidence against him in the proceedings (the case management form being endorsed to say that the defence was self defence when subsequently the prosecution was put to proof as to the defendant's presence implicitly admitting presence at the scene of the alleged offence. The admission on the form was properly held to be relied upon as evidence of presence).

C. Obligations on the Prosecution to Disclose Initial Details (Formerly Advanced Information) and Evidence

(1) Power to make rules requiring the prosecution to furnish information relating to facts and matters of which he proposes to adduce evidence

Criminal Law Act 1977, s.48

Power to make rules as to furnishing of information by prosecutor in criminal proceedings

6–8 **48.**—(1) Criminal Procedure Rules may make, with respect to proceedings against any person for a prescribed offence or an offence of any prescribed class, provision—

(a) for requiring the prosecutor to do such things as may be prescribed for the purpose of securing that the accused or a person representing him is furnished with, or can obtain, advance information concerning all, or any prescribed class of, the facts and matters of which the prosecutor proposes to adduce evidence; and

(b) for requiring a magistrates' court, if satisfied that any requirement imposed by virtue of paragraph (a) above has not been complied with, to adjourn the proceedings pending compliance with that requirement unless the court is satisfied that the conduct of the case for the accused will not be substantially prejudiced by non-compliance with the requirement.

(2) Rules made by virtue of subsection (1)(a) above—

(a) may require the prosecutor to do as provided in the rules either—

(i) in all cases; or

(ii) only if so requested by or on behalf of the accused;

(b) may exempt facts and matters of any prescribed description from any requirement imposed by the rules, and may make the opinion of the prosecutor material for the purposes of any such exemption; and

(c) may make different provision with respect to different offences or offences of different classes.

(3) It shall not be open to a person convicted of an offence to appeal against the conviction on the ground that a requirement imposed by virtue of subsection (1) above was not complied with by the prosecutor.

[This section is printed as amended by the *Magistrates' Courts Act* 1980, s.154 and Sched. 7, and the *Courts Act* 2003, s.109 and Sched. 8.]

(2) Initial details rules (formerly advance information rules)

General

As from April 6, 2009, the *Criminal Procedure (Amendment No. 2) Rules* 2008 (S.I. 2008 No. 3269) substituted a new Pt 21 in the *Criminal Procedure Rules* 2005. The new Pt 21 was re-enacted in the *Criminal Procedure Rules* 2011 and is set out in full at Appendix G–134. **6–9**

The new rules replaced the previous "advanced information" rules with a new duty requiring the prosecution to disclose "initial details" the accused. Unlike the old advance information rules (which applied only in relation to either way offences), the initial details must be disclosed in respect of both summary only and either way offences.

Disclosure of initial details under the new rules is not conditional upon a request being made by the accused (as it was under the old advanced information rules), but is framed in mandatory terms. **6–10**

Power to direct that advance information rules to continue to apply

Whilst the new Pt 21 applies generally as from April 6, 2009, particular courts may direct that, for a specified period, the new Pt 21 will not apply to any case in that court or to any specified category of case: r.21.1(2). If such a direction is given, the rules in the previous Pt 21 (advance information) continue to apply (for which see Pt 21 as described at §§ 6–13 *et seq.* of the 2009 main work and set out in Appendix G thereto), from which it may follow that the new regime would not apply to summary only offences. **6–11**

When the initial details must be disclosed

The prosecutor must provide the "initial details" of the prosecution case by serving those details on the court officer and making them available to the accused at or before the beginning of the day of the "first hearing": see r.21.2 (*cf.* the old rules, which required advance information to be disclosed only where requested by the accused). As to the meaning of the "first hearing", there is no definition provided, but it is submitted that this must mean the day on which the defendant first appears before the court in relation to the offence, whether when produced in custody from the police station for the **6–12** first time or pursuant to a warrant, or when answering a summons, requisition or police bail.

Content of initial details

6–13 Rule 21.3 prescribes the content of the initial details. The prosecution must supply a summary of the evidence on which the case will be based, or any statement, document or extract setting out facts or other matters on which that case will be based, or any combination of such a summary, statement, document or extract. The initial details must also include the defendant's previous convictions.

It should be noted, however, that there is no equivalent to the old r.21.3(3), which expressly required the prosecutor also to provide copies of, or an opportunity to inspect, "documents" referred to in written statements or the summary. To that end, it is unclear to what extent the principle in *Calderdale Magistrates Court, ex p. Donahue and Cutler* [2001] Crim.L.R. 141, DC (adjournment granted to allow defendant to view video constituting the identification evidence in the case and referred to in the advance information), will continue to apply.

As to the meaning of "documents", existing authorities may continue to assist. In *ex p. Donahue and Cutler* the point was not decided, but it had been common ground between the parties that the video was a "document". *Cf. R. (DPP) v. Croydon Magistrates' Court* [2001] Crim.L.R. 980, DC (reference in a case summary to results of DNA samples did not amount to reference to a document and the prosecution was not obliged to provide further documentary information about the DNA profiling at that stage of the proceedings) and *Dunmow Justices, ex p. Nash*, 157 J.P. 1153, DC (in a prosecution in respect of possession of allegedly pornographic material, there was no need to serve copies of videos themselves where there was sufficient description of the kind of pornography present in videos in the material already provided).

No power to withhold initial details

6–14 The new Pt 21 does not contain an equivalent to the old r.21.4, which permitted the withholding of advance information where there was a risk of witness intimidation or interference with the course of justice. To some extent this risk is now mitigated by the possibility of a witness anonymity order under Pt 3 of the *Coroners and Justice Act* 2009.

Adjournments where initial details not disclosed

6–15 There is no express presumption (or any power at all) in the new Pt 21 to adjourn where the prosecution fails to provide the initial details (*cf.* r.21.6 in the old rules, which required the court to adjourn unless conduct of the case for the accused would not be substantially prejudiced by the non-compliance).

However, it may be that such a power was unnecessary in view of the court's discretionary powers to adjourn the plea before venue procedure, determination of mode of trial (allocation), and summary trial of an information, under the *Magistrates' Courts Act* 1980, ss.17C, 18(4) and 10 (see *post*, §§ 7–31, 7–36 and 7–160). Exercise of those discretions where there has been a failure to provide initial details should, it is submitted, be in accordance with general principles (for which see *post*, § 7–155), textured further by consideration of the mandatory nature of the requirement to provide initial details. Accordingly, the court should adjourn, it is submitted, unless proceeding without initial details would not prejudice the accused. As to whether *Calderdale Magistrates Court, ex p. Donahue and Cutler* [2001] Crim.L.R. 141, DC, will continue to require an adjournment where a "document" referred to in a summary (*e.g.* CCTV) is not disclosed with the initial details remains to be seen: see *ante*, § 6–13.

Given the interaction between the statutory regime as a matter of primary legislation and Pt 21 of the rules as a matter of delegated legislation, proceeding notwithstanding non-compliance with the mandatory requirement to disclose initial details cannot, it is submitted, of itself invalidate the subsequent proceedings. See also s.48(3) of the *Criminal Law Act* 1977 (*ante*).

Abuse of process where initial details not disclosed

There is authority for a proposition that there is no power to stay a prosecution as an abuse of process on the ground that the prosecution have failed to comply with their obligations under Pt 21: see *R. (P.(A.), D.(M.) and S.(J.)) v. Leeds Youth Court*, 165 J.P. 684, DC (a case on the advance information rules). However, that decision was made without reference to the earlier decision of *King v. Kucharz*, 153 J.P. 336, DC, where it had been said that failure to comply with the advanced information rules could, in an exceptional case, give rise to an abuse. See also *Willesden JJ., ex p Clemmings*, 87 Cr.App.R. 280, DC, where it was said that in cases of continued default, the court will be entitled to form the opinion that enough is enough and to stay the proceedings as an abuse of process for want of prosecution. It is submitted that the proper understanding of these authorities is that mere failure to comply with Pt 21 will not, of itself, give rise to an abuse, the proper remedy being to adjourn; but if in the face of continued failure to comply there has been such a delay in the prosecution of the case as to render the proceedings an abuse, then the court will be entitled to stay the proceedings according to ordinary abuse of process principles (as to which, see Ch.8). *Cf. R. v. O.*, unreported, September 27, 2007, CA ([2007] EWCA Crim. 3483), a case in relation to abuse on grounds of failure to serve unused material. **6–16**

Effect of service of initial details

The provision of initial details by way of witness statements is equivalent to the service of witness statements in the Crown Court, with the result that at that stage the prosecution's discretion as to which witnesses should be called at trial is fettered and they ought normally to call any witness whose evidence was capable of belief: *Haringey Justices ex p. DPP* [1996] Q.B. 351, DC. **6–17**

(3) Further duties on the prosecutor to serve evidence on the accused in advance of summary trial

General

Whereas the duty of the prosecution to serve initial details under Pt 21 of the *Criminal Procedure Rules* 2011 will be discharged by provision of a summary of the evidence on which the case will be based, there is no statutory provision requiring the prosecution to disclose to the defence the evidence on which it is proposed to rely at summary trial. There is authority for a proposition that no such general or absolute obligation arises at common law or under art. 6 of the European Convention on Human Rights, the proper course where the defence are taken by surprise being to seek an adjournment: see *Kingston-upon-Hull JJ., ex p. McCann*, 155 J.P. 569, DC; and *Stratford JJ., ex p. Imbert* [1999] 2 Cr.App.R. 276, DC. **6–18**

It is submitted, however, that those authorities no longer accurately represent the law in view of the developing body of law concerning the principles of natural justice and culminating in the decision in *Filmer v. DPP* [2007] RTR 28, DC, to the effect that there is an obligation on the prosecution at common law to disclose its case to the defendant before summary trial.

Principles of natural justice

Criminal proceedings should not proceed by way of ambush, and this is a principle which applies equally to the prosecution as to the defence: *Hawkes v. DPP*, unreported, November 5, 2005, QBD (Newman J.) ([2005] EWCA 3046, Admin). It is elementary that if a charge is being made against a person, he must be given a fair chance of meeting it; that often means he must be given documents necessary for the purpose: *HM Coroner at Hammersmith ex p. Peach* [1980] Q.B. 211, DC. Any practice which leads to the withholding of material until the day of any judicial hearing is calculated to be to the significant disadvantage of the party from whom they have been withheld; the argument that any injustice can be cured by the grant of an adjournment is nothing to the point and will involve extra costs and delay; when the straightforward step can be taken **6–19** of making available to a party material which, it is conceded he will be entitled to receive in any event, it makes no sense at all to say that he must wait and take his chance with obtaining an adjournment of the hearing: *Criminal Injuries Compensation Board, ex p. Leatherland*, unreported, July 2, 2000, QBD (Turner J.). See also *R. (Bentley) v. HM Coroner District of Avon*, 166 J.P. 297, QBD (Sullivan J.).

Although there is no relevant rule which requires evidence to be served in writing in advance, necessity and fairness require that the prosecution must normally serve written versions of the evidence they propose to adduce in sufficient time before the hearing to enable the defendant fairly to deal with it; generally speaking it will be wrong to decide that it will be fair for the defendant to have short adjournments during the hearing to consider how to deal with evidence as it emerges: *R. (Cleary) v. Highbury Corner Magistrates' Court (Practice Note)* [2007] 1 W.L.R. 1272, DC (decided in the context of closure of premises order under the *Anti-Social Behaviour Act* 2003).

There is no inflexible or standard disclosure obligation which applies to the prosecution (in relation to their own case) before a summary trial, the extent of the disclosure necessary to ensure a fair trial depending on the evidence and the issues in the case; but in relation to both trials on indictment and summary trials, the prosecution case must be revealed in sufficient detail to enable the defendant properly to prepare his defence: *Filmer v. DPP* [2007] R.T.R. 28, DC (concluding that the precise wording or content of disclosed statements, exhibits or other documentation does not limit what questions the prosecution may ask of their witnesses or the evidence they may introduce; provided that the natural justice requirements of the case are not breached, supplementary questions may be asked and areas may be explored in greater detail than revealed in the disclosed material).

See also *Thames Magistrates' Court, ex p. Polemis* [1974] 1 W.L.R. 1371, DC, and the quotation therefrom set out at § 7–162, *post*.

Attorney General's Guidelines

6–20 In *ex p. McCann*, *ibid.*, the court had advised that prosecutors should adopt a policy of disclosing to the defence the material upon which they intend to rely, save where it was necessary to limit the extent of disclosure (as where prosecution witnesses may be at risk of reprisal). To that end, para. 57 of the *Attorney-General's Guidelines on Disclosure* instructs prosecutors to provide to the defence all evidence upon which the Crown proposes to rely in a summary trial in sufficient time properly to consider it before it is called: see Appendix G–19.

III. DISCLOSURE OF PROSECUTION MATERIAL WHICH IS NOT RELIED UPON AS EVIDENCE (UNUSED MATERIAL): PART 1 OF THE CRIMINAL PROCEDURE AND INVESTIGATIONS ACT 1996

A. GENERAL

6–21 In relation to offences into which a criminal investigation was commenced on or after April 4, 2005, the duties and responsibilities of parties with regard to disclosure are now governed by Pts I and II of the *Criminal Procedure and Investigations Act* 1996, as amended by the *Criminal Justice Act* 2003.

Part I (ss.1-21) has created a staged approach (initial prosecution disclosure (formerly primary disclosure), defence disclosure, continual review by the prosecution (formerly secondary disclosure)). Part II (ss.22-27) provides for a code of practice for regulating action the police must take in recording and retaining material obtained in the course of a criminal investigation and revealing it to the prosecution for a decision on disclosure. A revised code of practice, taking account of the amendments made by the 2003 Act, was brought into operation on April 4, 2005 (see *post*, §§ 6–99 *et seq.*, and Appendix B).

The Attorney-General issued new guidelines on disclosure of information in criminal proceedings, also taking the 2003 Act amendments into account, in April 2005 (see *passim* in this Chapter and Appendix C–1 *et seq.*). A protocol for the provision of advance information (sic.), prosecution evidence and disclosure of unused material in the magistrates' court was published under the auspices of the Court of Appeal on May 12, 2006, which protocol was effective only at four pilot sites in England and Wales but it was expressly stated therein that it was expected that courts and practitioners in all areas would use and refer to the document for guidance. Additionally, the Crown Prosecution Service issued a disclosure manual in April 2005 designed to assist prosecutors and police officers to fulfill their disclosure duties consistently and effectively.

For the full text of the protocol, see: *http://old.judiciary.gov.uk/docs/judgments__guidance/protocols/mags__courts__%20disclosure.pdf*; and for the full text of the disclosure manual, see: *www.cps.gov.uk/legal/section 20/chapter__a.html*).

B. THE EUROPEAN CONVENTION

Article 6(1) of the European Convention on Human Rights requires that the prosecution authorities should disclose to the accused all material evidence in their possession for or against the accused; it is a fundamental aspect of the right to a fair trial that criminal proceedings should be adversarial and that there should be equality of arms between the prosecution and defence: see *Edwards v. UK*, 15 E.H.R.R. 417, ECtHR; *Rowe and Davis v. UK*, 30 E.H.R.R. 1, ECtHR; *Jasper v. UK*, 30 E.H.R.R. 441, ECtHR. These authorities have been interpreted as meaning that art. 6(1) requires the Crown to disclose to the defence any material of which it is aware which would tend either to materially weaken the prosecution case or materially strengthen the case for the defence: see *Holland v. H.M. Advocate*, *The Times*, June 1, 2005, PC; *Sinclair v. H.M. Advocate*, *The Times*, June 1, 2005, PC; *McDonald v. H.M. Advocate*, *The Times*, November 5, 2008, PC; *Allison v. H.M. Advocate*, unreported, February 10, 2010, SC ([2010] UKSC 6). Only such measures restricting the right of the defence to disclosure which are strictly necessary are permissible: *Rowe and Davies v. UK*, *ibid.*, especially paras 60–62. **6–22**

C. SURVIVING AT COMMON LAW

General

The effect of s.1 of the *Criminal Procedure and Investigations Act* 1996 (see *post*, §§ 6–29 *et seq.*) is that the disclosure regime in Pt 1 of the Act is not triggered in the following stages of proceedings: between arrest and being charged with a summary offence; between arrest and being committed, sent or transferred to the Crown Court for trial; where a defendant pleads guilty to an offence; and arguably where a person is summonsed in relation to an offence and the court proceeds to summary trial. In *DPP, ex p. Lee* [1999] 2 Cr.App.R. 304, DC, it was said that whereas s.21(1) of the Act provides that "Where this Part applies" the common law rules relating to disclosure of material by the prosecutor do not apply, it follows that the Act does not purport to abolish the common law where the Act does not apply; but the scope of the surviving common law was limited, since the purpose of the Act would be undermined if the surviving common law rules exceeded the scope of the disclosure regime in the statute; the prosecutor should therefore ask himself what if any immediate disclosure justice and fairness required him to make in the particular circumstances of the case, and he should always be alive to the need to make advance disclosure of material of which he is aware (either from his consideration of the papers or because his attention has been drawn to it by the defence): see *DPP, ex p. Lee* [1999] 2 Cr.App.R. 304, DC. The same approach was applied in *R. (Johnson) v. Stratford Magistrates' Court*, unreported, February 12, 2003, DC ([2003] EWHC 353 (Admin.)), where the court concluded that, irrespective of whether the Act applied if proceedings were commenced by the obtaining of a summons (see *post*, § 6–28), the common law obligation of disclosure was sufficient to require disclosure of unused material if the Act did not apply. These principles have been adopted in the *Attorney-General's Guidelines on Disclosure*: see Appendix C–18. **6–23**

Pre-interview disclosure

6–24 Police officers conducting an interview with a suspect are under a duty not to mislead him, but there is no duty to reveal the entirety of their hand before the interview: see *Imran and Hussain* [1997] Crim.L.R. 754, CA (no duty to reveal video recording of offence); and *R. v. A.*, unreported, November 12, 2009, CA ([2009] EWCA Crim. 2571) (no duty to disclose that description given by complainant in a rape case did not match appearance of suspect, or that there was DNA evidence linking suspect to complainant).

Pre-committal, sending or transfer disclosure

6–25 In *ex p. Lee* (*ibid.*), the court identified the following examples of material which might fall to be disclosed prior to committal (and by analogy sending or transfer): (a) previous convictions of a complainant or deceased if that information could reasonably be expected to assist the defence when applying for bail; (b) material which might enable a defendant to make a pre-committal, sending or transfer application to stay the proceedings as an abuse of process; (c) material which might enable a defendant to submit that he should only be committed for trial on a lesser charge, or perhaps that he should not be committed for trial at all; and (d) material which would enable the defendant and his legal advisors to make preparations for trial which might be significantly less effective if disclosure was delayed (*e.g.* names of eye witnesses who the prosecution do not intend to use).

Material relevant to sentence and Newton hearings

6–26 Paragraph 58 of the *Attorney-General's Guidelines on Disclosure* requires prosecutors to consider disclosing in the interests of justice any material which is relevant to sentence: see Appendix C–20. It is submitted that particular consideration should be given to this requirement where a guilty plea is entered but the case proceeds to a *Newton* hearing.

Disclosure post-conviction

6–27 Paragraph 59 of the *Guidelines* require prosecutors to disclose to the defence material which comes to light after the conclusion of the proceedings and which casts doubt on the safety of the conviction: see Appendix C–21; and see also *Makin* (2004) 148 S.J. 821, CA.

6–28 Paragraph 55 of the Attorney General's Guidelines on Disclosure advises prosecutors to make disclosure before initial disclosure if this is in the interests of justice and fairness. See Appendix C–18.

The prosecution's obligation of disclosure at common law is sufficient to require disclosure even where proceedings were instituted by summons for a speeding offence: *R. (Johnson) v. Stratford Magistrates' Court, ex p. Johnson*, unreported, February 12, 2003, DC ([2003] EWHC 353, Admin). The applicant argued the magistrate was incorrect in construing s.1 of the *Criminal Procedure and Investigations Act* 1996 as meaning that it did not apply to proceedings instituted by way of summons. The Divisional Court considered that it was unnecessary to determine the scope of s.1 of the 1996 Act because the prosecution's obligation of disclosure at common law was sufficient to require disclosure in the case.

D. When the Act Applies to Magistrates' Courts Proceedings

Criminal Procedure and Investigations Act 1996, ss.1–2

Application of this Part

6–29 **1.**—(1) This Part applies where—

(a) a person is charged with a summary offence in respect of which a court proceeds to summary trial and in respect of which he pleads not guilty,

(b) a person who has attained the age of 18 is charged with an offence which is triable either way, in respect of which a court proceeds to summary trial and in respect of which he pleads not guilty, or

(c) a person under the age of 18 is charged with an indictable offence in respect of which a court proceeds to summary trial and in respect of which he pleads not guilty.

(2) (*Applies only in relation to trial on indictment*)

(3) This Part applies in relation to alleged offences into which no criminal investigation has begun before the appointed day.

(4) For the purposes of this section a criminal investigation is an investigation which police officers or other persons have a duty to conduct with a view to it being ascertained—

(a) whether a person should be charged with an offence, or

(b) whether a person charged with an offence is guilty of it.

(5) The reference in subsection (3) to the appointed day is to such day as is appointed for the purposes of this Part by the Secretary of State by order.

[This section is printed as amended by the *Crime and Disorder Act* 1998, s.119 and Sched. 8. As from a day to be appointed, a new subs. (6) is to be inserted by the *Sexual Offences (Protected Material) Act* 1997, s.9 (not set out in this work). Amendments to subs. (2) by the *Criminal Justice Act* 2003, s.41 and Sched. 3, are not relevant to this work.]

General interpretation

2.—(1) References to the accused are to the person mentioned in section 1(1) or (2). **6–30**

(2) Where there is more than one accused in any proceedings this Part applies separately in relation to each of the accused.

(3) References to the prosecutor are to any person acting as prosecutor, whether an individual or a body.

(4) References to material are to material of all kinds, and in particular include references to—

(a) information, and

(b) objects of all descriptions.

(5) References to recording information are to putting it in a durable or retrievable form (such as writing or tape).

(6) This section applies for the purposes of this Part.

General

The prosecutor's duty to disclose unused material applies when the accused pleads not guilty and the court proceeds to summary trial. The defence is not entitled to disclosure where the accused has pleaded guilty or where the accused has been committed for sentence to the Crown Court following a plea in the magistrates' court. It would appear, therefore, that the provisions of Pt 1 of the Act do not apply to *Newton* hearings and, it is submitted, the common law obligations must therefore apply (see also para. 58 of the Attorney-General's guidelines). The disclosure obligations do not apply to the pre-committal stage. **6–31**

"Charged" with an offence

As to whether a person is "charged" with an offence where an information is laid and a summons or warrant issues under s.1 of the *Magistrates' Courts Act* 1980 to secure his attendance before the court, the point was raised in *R. (Johnson) v. Stratford Magistrates' Court*, unreported, February 12, 2003, DC ([2003] EWHC 353, Admin.), but the court concluded that it was unnecessary to adjudicate on it as, in any event, the common law obligation of disclosure (as to which, see *ante*, §§ 6–21 *et seq.*) was more than sufficient to deal with the circumstances of the particular case. *Cf. R. (Salubi) v. Bow Street Magistrates' Court* [2002] 2 Cr.App.R. 40, DC, where "charged" with an offence within the meaning of s.51 of the *Crime and Disorder Act* 1998 (determining when a case would be sent to the Crown Court for trial) was construed to include proceedings commenced by the laying of an information. **6–32**

The appointed day

The appointed day for the purposes of subs. (3) is April 1, 1997: *Criminal Procedure* **6–33** *and Investigations Act 1996 (Appointed Day No. 3) Order* 1997 (S.I. 1997 No. 682). A "criminal investigation" within the meaning of subs. (3) may begin before the actual commission of the offence, from which it follows that there may be cases where Pt I of the Act does not apply even though the offence was committed after the appointed day: *Uxbridge Magistrates' Court, ex p. Patel*; *City of London Magistrates' Court, ex p. Cropper*, 164 J.P. 209, DC (not following *Norfolk Stipendiary Magistrate, ex p. Keable* [1998] Crim.L.R. 510, DC).

Private prosecutors

6–34 The definition of a "prosecutor" in s.2(3) is apt to include a private prosecutor (who is subject to the same "minister of justice" obligations as the public prosecuting authorities): *Belmarsh Magistrates' Court, ex p. Watts* [1999] 2 Cr.App.R. 188, DC; *R. (Dacre and Associated Newspapers) v. City of Westminster Magistrates' Court* [2009] 1 Cr.App.R. 6, DC.

E. PROSECUTION DUTY OF INITIAL DISCLOSURE

Criminal Procedure and Investigations Act 1996, ss.3–4

Initial duty of prosecutor to disclose

6–35 **3.**—(1) The prosecutor must—

(a) disclose to the accused any prosecution material which has not previously been disclosed to the accused and which might reasonably be considered capable of undermining the case for the prosecution against the accused or of assisting the case for the accused, or

(b) give to the accused a written statement that there is no material of a description mentioned in paragraph (a).

(2) For the purposes of this section prosecution material is material—

(a) which is in the prosecutor's possession, and came into his possession in connection with the case for the prosecution against the accused, or

(b) which, in pursuance of a code operative under Part II, he has inspected in connection with the case for the prosecution against the accused.

(3) Where material consists of information which has been recorded in any form the prosecutor discloses it for the purposes of this section—

(a) by securing that a copy is made of it and that the copy is given to the accused, or

(b) if in the prosecutor's opinion that is not practicable or not desirable, by allowing the accused to inspect it at a reasonable time and a reasonable place or by taking steps to secure that he is allowed to do so;

and a copy may be in such form as the prosecutor thinks fit and need not be in the same form as that in which the information has already been recorded.

(4) Where material consists of information which has not been recorded the prosecutor discloses it for the purposes of this section by securing that it is recorded in such form as he thinks fit and—

(a) by securing that a copy is made of it and that the copy is given to the accused, or

(b) if in the prosecutor's opinion that is not practicable or not desirable, by allowing the accused to inspect it at a reasonable time and a reasonable place or by taking steps to secure that he is allowed to do so.

(5) Where material does not consist of information the prosecutor discloses it for the purposes of this section by allowing the accused to inspect it at a reasonable time and a reasonable place or by taking steps to secure that he is allowed to do so.

(6) Material must not be disclosed under this section to the extent that the court, on an application by the prosecutor, concludes it is not in the public interest to disclose it and orders accordingly.

(7) Material must not be disclosed under this section to the extent that it is material the disclosure of which is prohibited by section 17 of the *Regulation of Investigatory Powers Act* 2000.

(8) The prosecutor must act under this section during the period which, by virtue of section 12, is the relevant period for this section.

[This section is printed as amended by the *Regulation of Investigatory Powers Act* 2000, s.82 and Sched. 4, and the *Criminal Justice Act* 2003, ss.32 and 331 and Sched. 36.]

Initial duty to disclose: further provisions

4.—(1) This section applies where— **6–36**

(a) the prosecutor acts under section 3, and

(b) before so doing he was given a document in pursuance of provision included, by virtue of section 24(3), in a code operative under Part II.

(2) In such a case the prosecutor must give the document to the accused at the same time as the prosecutor acts under section 3.

[This section is printed as amended by the *Criminal Justice Act* 2003, s.331 and Sched. 36.]

As to the nature of the duty under s.3(1)(a), see *post*, §§ 6–56 *et seq*. As to the time limit for compliance with that duty, see *post*, §§ 6–70 *et seq*. As to withholding material in the public interest under s.3(6), see *post*, §§ 6–76 *et seq*. **6–37**

For the purposes of s.4(1)(b), the effect of s.24(3) and paras 6.2 and 6.3 of the Disclosure Code of Practice (see Appendix B–7) is that a schedule (referred to in practice as an "MG6C") must be prepared for the prosecutor listing all non-sensitive material which has been retained during the investigation and which does not form part of the prosecution case. It is only where the prosecutor has this schedule in his possession when initial disclosure occurs that it must be sent to the accused at the same time under s.4; where the prosecutor complies with s.3(1) but does not at the same time provide the schedule under s.4 because it has not been provided to him, the duty of initial disclosure will have been discharged and the schedule can be served subsequently: see *DPP v. Wood*; *DPP v. McGillicuddy*, 170 J.P. 177, DC. **6–38**

F. The Defence Statement and Identity of Defence Witnesses

(1) Introduction

In cases to be tried summarily, the accused is under no obligation to provide a defence statement or notice of alibi. Compulsory disclosure by the accused only arises where the case is to be tried on indictment and even then does not have to be undertaken until the case has been committed, sent or transferred for trial. An accused, therefore, must choose whether to serve a defence statement or not. Section 6 of the *Criminal Procedure and Investigations Act* 1996 addresses the situation of such voluntary disclosure. **6–39**

Whether or not an accused serves a defence statement, he must, however, give notice to both the court and the prosecutor of whether he intends to call any persons (other than himself) as witnesses at the trial and, if so, details of the identities of those persons: see s.6C.

As from a day or days to be appointed, the *Criminal Justice Act* 2003 inserts further provisions in the 1996 Act, setting out an enhanced defence disclosure requirement which require the accused to give notification of updated disclosure (new s.6B) and the names of experts instructed (new s.6D). No such day or days have been appointed.

(2) Current requirements as to the defence statements

Criminal Procedure and Investigations Act 1996, ss.6A, 6E

Voluntary disclosure by accused

6.—(1) This section applies where— **6–40**

(a) this Part applies by virtue of section 1(1), and

(b) the prosecutor complies with section 3 or purports to comply with it.

(2) The accused—

(a) may give a defence statement to the prosecutor, and
(b) if he does so, must also give such a statement to the court.

(3) [*repealed*]

(4) If the accused gives a defence statement under this section he must give it during the period which, by virtue of section 12 is the relevant period for this section.

[This section is printed as amended by the *Criminal Justice Act* 2003, s.331 and Sched. 36.]

Contents of defence statement

6–41 **6A.**—(1) For the purposes of this Part a defence statement is a written statement—

(a) setting out the nature of the accused's defence, including any particular defences on which he intends to rely,
(b) indicating the matters of fact on which he takes issue with the prosecution,
(c) setting out, in the case of each such matter, why he takes issue with the prosecution, and
(ca) setting out particulars of the matters of fact on which he intends to rely for the purposes of his defence,
(d) indicating any point of law (including any point as to the admissibility of evidence or an abuse of process) which he wishes to take, and any authority on which he intends to rely for that purpose.

(2) A defence statement that discloses an alibi must give particulars of it, including—

(a) the name, address and date of birth of any witness the accused believes is able to give evidence in support of the alibi, or as many of those details as are known to the accused when the statement is given;
(b) any information in the accused's possession which might be of material assistance in identifying or finding any such witness in whose case any of the details mentioned in paragraph (a) are not known to the accused when the statement is given.

(3) For the purposes of this section evidence in support of an alibi is evidence tending to show that by reason of the presence of the accused at a particular place or in a particular area at a particular time he was not, or was unlikely to have been, at the place where the offence is alleged to have been committed at the time of its alleged commission.

(4) The Secretary of State may by regulations make provision as to the details of the matters that, by virtue of subsection (1), are to be included in defence statements.

[This section was inserted by the *Criminal Justice Act* 2003, s.33. It is printed as amended by the *Criminal Justice and Immigration Act* 2008, s.60(1). That amendment was brought into effect on November 3, 2008, by the *Criminal Justice and Immigration Act 2008 (Commencement No. 3 and Transitional Provisions) Order* 2008 (S.I. 2008 No. 2712). Pursuant to Article 3 of that order, the amendment has no effect: (i) in relation to offences into which a criminal investigation within the meaning of s.1(4) of the *Criminal Procedure and Investigations Act* 1996, has begun, in England and Wales, before April 4, 2005; and (ii) in relation to a case to which Pt 1 of the 1996 Act applies by virtue of s.1(1) or (2) of that Act before November 3, 2008.]

Disclosure by accused: further provisions

6–42 **6E.**—(1) Where an accused's solicitor purports to give on behalf of the accused—

(a) a defence statement under section 5, 6 or 6B, or
(b) a statement of the kind mentioned in section 6B(4),

the statement shall, unless the contrary is proved, be deemed to be given with the authority of the accused.

(2) If it appears to the judge at a pre-trial hearing that an accused has failed to comply fully with section 5, 6B or 6C, so that there is a possibility of comment being made or inferences drawn under section 11(5), he shall warn the accused accordingly.

(3) In subsection (2) "pre-trial hearing" has the same meaning as in Part 4 (see section 39).

(4)–(6) (*Apply only in relation to trial on indictment*).

[This section was inserted by the *Criminal Justice Act* 2003, s.36.]

General

The effect of s.6 and 11(3) (*post*, § 10–146) of the Act is that service of a defence statement is voluntary in a case which proceeds to summary trial; and so no adverse inference may be drawn where a defence statement is not served (as distinct from an inadequate defence statement or late defence statement). In so far as it was said in *Essa* [2009] 5 *Archbold News* 2, CA, that no lawyer should properly advise his client not to serve a defence statement, those comments were made in the specific context of the mandatory requirement (under s.5) to serve a defence statement for the purposes of trial on indictment and plainly have no application to the voluntary provision in s.6. **6–43**

The significance of a defence statement in summary proceedings is (a) that it may identify material which falls to be disclosed by the prosecution in accordance with the continuing duty of disclosure under s.7A (*post*, § 6–52), and (b) that an application for specific disclosure under s.8 (*post*, § 6–54) cannot be made unless and until a defence statement has been served.

As to the requirements of s.6A, an accused is not required to incriminate himself, merely to disclose what is to happen at trial; where he intends to put forward no positive case, and not to take issue with any matters of fact advanced by the prosecution, the defence statement must say that he does not admit the offence (or the relevant part of it), that he calls upon the prosecution to prove it, and that he advances no positive case; if, however, the possibility is to be raised distinctly in the trial that the prosecution may be wrong as to a factual matter, that must be set out in the defence statement: *Rochford* [2011] 1 Cr.App.R. 11, CA.

Whilst it is good practice for a defence statement to be signed by the accused (*Wheeler* [2001] 1 Cr.App.R. 10, CA), a judge has no power to issue a direction requiring a defence statement to be signed (*Maidstone Crown Court, ex p. Sullivan* [2002] 1 Cr.App.R. 31, DC); and, in any event, s.6E deems (unless the contrary is proved) a defence statement to have been given with the authority of the accused. As to cross-service of defence statements between co-accused, see *post*, § 6–64.

Consequences of inadequate and late defence statements

The effect of s.11(3)(b) (*post*, § 10–146) is that an adverse inference may be drawn against an accused who (inter alia) serves a defence statement and then relies at trial on a matter not set out as required by s.6A; but a court has no power to order an accused to comply with the requirements in s.6A and then punish disobedience as contempt (*Rochford, ibid.*) or to prevent an accused from calling an alibi witness who has not been disclosed in a defence statement (*R. (Tinnion) v. Reading Crown Court* 174 J.P. 36, DC). However, the provisions of s.11 do not prohibit a party from cross-examining an accused on deficiencies in a defence statement (*Tibbs* [2004] 2 Cr.App.R. 309, CA); but no such use should be made of a defence statement if the accused denies knowledge of it and it cannot be shown that he knew of its contents:*R. v. V.* (2005) 149 S.J. 301, CA. As to the relationship between the right to a fair trial and s.11, see *Essa, ibid.* **6–44**

As to the consequences of service of a defence statement after expiry of the time-limit prescribed by s.12 (*post*, § 6–68), see s.11(3)(a) (*post*, § 10–146).

Advocates' duties in relation to defence statements

As to the duties of counsel in relation to the preparation of a defence statement, see the guidance issued by the Bar Standards Board (dated March 9, 2011). **6–45**

Criminal Procedure Rules and time-limits

For procedural requirements in connection with service of a defence statement, see r.22.4 of the*Criminal Procedure Rules* 2011 (Appendix G–140c). As to the time-limit for service of the defence statement, see *post*, § 6–72. **6–46**

(3) Notice of intention to call defence witnesses

Criminal Procedure and Investigations Act 1996, s.6C

Notification of intention to call defence witnesses

6–47 **6C.**—(1) The accused must give to the court and the prosecutor a notice indicating whether he intends to call any persons (other than himself) as witnesses at his trial and, if so—

(a) giving the name, address and date of birth of each such proposed witness, or as many of those details as are known to the accused when the notice is given;

(b) providing any information in the accused's possession which might be of material assistance in identifying or finding any such proposed witness in whose case any of the details mentioned in paragraph (a) are not known to the accused when the notice is given.

(2) Details do not have to be given under this section to the extent that they have already been given under section 6A(2).

(3) The accused must give a notice under this section during the period which, by virtue of section 12, is the relevant period for this section.

(4) If, following the giving of a notice under this section, the accused—

(a) decides to call a person (other than himself) who is not included in the notice as a proposed witness, or decides not to call a person who is so included, or

(b) discovers any information which, under subsection (1), he would have had to include in the notice if he had been aware of it when giving the notice,

he must give an appropriately amended notice to the court and the prosecutor.

[This section was inserted by the *Criminal Justice Act* 2003, s.34, with effect from May 1, 2010: *Criminal Justice Act 2003 (Commencement No. 24 and Transitional Provisions) Order* 2010 (S.I. 2010 No. 1183). It has no effect in relation to a case to which Pt 1 of the 1996 Act applies by virtue of s.1(1) or (2) of that Act before that date.]

6–48 As to the time limit for compliance with the duty under this section, see *post* §§ 6-72. As to arranging and conducting interviews of witnesses notified by the accused under this section, see the *Criminal Procedure and Investigations Act 1996 (Code of Practice for Interviews of Witnesses Notified by Accused) Order* 2010 (S.I. 2010 No. 1223).

For procedural requirements in connection with service of a defence witness notice, see r.22.4 of the *Criminal Procedure Rules* 2011 (Appendix G-140c). The Law Society has issued a Practice Note (dated January 27, 2011) setting out a solicitor's duties to his client and any witness where a requirement to give notice under this section arises.

(4) Enhanced defence disclosure regime (not yet in force)

6–49 As from a day or days to be appointed, the *Criminal Justice Act* 2003 inserts new ss.6B (updated disclosure by the accused), ss.6D (notification of names of experts instructed by accused). No such day or days have been appointed. The sections are reproduced below in anticipation of their implementation.

Criminal Procedure and Investigations Act 1996, ss.6B, 6D

[Updated disclosure by accused

6–50 **6B.**—(1) Where the accused has, before the beginning of the relevant period for this section, given a defence statement under section 5 or 6, he must during that period give to the court and the prosecutor either—

(a) a defence statement under this section (an "updated defence statement"), or

(b) a statement of the kind mentioned in subsection (4).

(2) The relevant period for this section is determined under section 12.

(3) An updated defence statement must comply with the requirements imposed by or under section 6A by reference to the state of affairs at the time when the statement is given.

(4) Instead of an updated defence statement, the accused may give a written statement stating that he has no changes to make to the defence statement which was given under section 5 or 6.

(5) Where there are other accused in the proceedings and the court so orders, the accused must also give either an updated defence statement or a statement of the kind mentioned in subsection (4), within such period as may be specified by the court, to each other accused so specified.

(6) The court may make an order under subsection (5) either of its own motion or on the application of any party.

Notification of names of experts instructed by accused

6D.—(1) If the accused instructs a person with a view to his providing any expert opinion for possible use as evidence at the trial of the accused, he must give to the court and the prosecutor a notice specifying the person's name and address. **6–51**

(2) A notice does not have to be given under this section specifying the name and address of a person whose name and address have already been given under section 6C.

(3) A notice under this section must be given during the period which, by virtue of section 12, is the relevant period for this section.]

G. CONTINUING DUTY OF PROSECUTION DISCLOSURE

Criminal Procedure and Investigations Act 1996, s.7A

Continuing duty of prosecutor to disclose

7A.—(1) This section applies at all times— **6–52**

(a) after the prosecutor has complied with section 3 or purported to comply with it, and

(b) before the accused is acquitted or convicted or the prosecutor decides not to proceed with the case concerned.

(2) The prosecutor must keep under review the question whether at any given time (and, in particular, following the giving of a defence statement) there is prosecution material which—

(a) might reasonably be considered capable of undermining the case for the prosecution against the accused or of assisting the case for the accused, and

(b) has not been disclosed to the accused.

(3) If at any time there is any such material as is mentioned in subsection (2) the prosecutor must disclose it to the accused as soon as is reasonably practicable (or within the period mentioned in subsection (5)(a), where that applies).

(4) In applying subsection (2) by reference to any given time the state of affairs at that time (including the case for the prosecution as it stands at that time) must be taken into account.

(5) Where the accused gives a defence statement under section 5, 6 or 6B—

(a) if as a result of that statement the prosecutor is required by this section to make any disclosure, or further disclosure, he must do so during the period which, by virtue of section 12, is the relevant period for this section;

(b) if the prosecutor considers that he is not so required, he must during that period give to the accused a written statement to that effect.

(6) For the purposes of this section prosecution material is material—

(a) which is in the prosecutor's possession and came into his possession in connection with the case for the prosecution against the accused, or

(b) which, in pursuance of a code operative under Part 2, he has inspected in connection with the case for the prosecution against the accused.

(7) Subsections (3) to (5) of section 3 (method by which prosecutor discloses) apply for the purposes of this section as they apply for the purposes of that.

(8) Material must not be disclosed under this section to the extent that the court, on an application by the prosecutor, concludes it is not in the public interest to disclose it and orders accordingly.

(9) Material must not be disclosed under this section to the extent that it is material the disclosure of which is prohibited by section 17 of the *Regulation of Investigatory Powers Act* 2000.

[This section was inserted by the *Criminal Justice Act* 2003, s.37.]

As to the nature of the duty under s.7A(2), see *post*, §§ 6–56 *et seq.* As to the time **6–53** limit for compliance with that duty, see *post*, §§ 6–70 *et seq*. As to withholding material in the public interest under s.7A(8), see *post*, §§ 6–76 *et seq*.

H. DEFENCE APPLICATIONS FOR PROSECUTION DISCLOSURE

Criminal Procedure and Investigations Act 1996, s.8

Application by accused for disclosure

6–54 **8.**—(1) This section applies where the accused has given a defence statement under section 5, 6 or 6B and the prosecutor has complied with section 7A(5) or has purported to comply with it or has failed to comply with it.

(2) If the accused has at any time reasonable cause to believe that there is prosecution material which is required by section 7A to be disclosed to him and has not been, he may apply to the court for an order requiring the prosecutor to disclose it to him.

(3) For the purposes of this section prosecution material is material—

(a) which is in the prosecutor's possession and came into his possession in connection with the case for the prosecution against the accused.

(b) which, in pursuance of a code operative under Part II, he has inspected in connection with the case for the prosecution against the accused, or

(c) which falls within subsection (4).

(4) Material falls within this subsection if in pursuance of a code operative under Part II the prosecutor must, if he asks for the material, be given a copy of it or be allowed to inspect it in connection with the case for the prosecution against the accused.

(5) Material must not be disclosed under this section to the extent that the court, on an application by the prosecutor, concludes it is not in the public interest to disclose it and orders accordingly.

(6) Material must not be disclosed under this section to the extent that[it is material the disclosure of which is prohibited by section 17 of the *Regulation of Investigatory Powers Act* 2000.

[This section is printed as amended by the *Criminal Justice Act* 2003, s.38.]

6–55 In *DPP v. Wood*; *DPP v. McGillicuddy*, 170 J.P. 177, DC, it was said that where a defence statement was served late, the accused was nevertheless entitled to make an application under s.8 for further disclosure by the prosecutor. It was also said that where the material in respect of which disclosure was sought was in possession of a third party and had never come into possession of the "prosecutor", a s.8 application could not be made in respect of the material; but if the prosecution took the view that a third party has material which might be disclosable if they were in possession of it, steps should be taken to obtain it, if necessary by seeking a witness summons (as to which see *post*).

For procedural requirements in connection with s.8 applications, see r.22.5 of the *Criminal Procedure Rules* 2011 (Appendix G–140d).

I. NATURE OF THE DUTIES OF INITIAL AND CONTINUING DISCLOSURE

General

6–56 Whether material falls to be disclosed under s.3 or 7A of the *Criminal Procedure and Investigations Act* 1996 is a matter to be determined by the prosecutor, the court having no power to make an order as to the extent of any disclosure under those sections; the power of the court to order disclosure of material falling within s.3(1)(a) or 7A(2) arises only where a proper application is made by the accused under s.8: see *R. v. M.*, unreported, November 4, 2003, CA ([2003] EWCA Crim. 3764).

In determining whether material falls within s.3(1)(a) or 7A(2) the following guidance was given by the House of Lords in *R. v. H.* [2004] 2 A.C. 134:

> [35] If material does not weaken the prosecution case or strengthen that of the defendant, there is no requirement to disclose it. For this purpose the parties' respective cases should not be restrictively analysed. But they must be carefully analysed, to ascertain the specific facts the prosecution seek to establish and the specific grounds on which the charges are resisted. The

> trial process is not well served if the defence are permitted to make general and unspecified allegations and then seek far-reaching disclosure in the hope that material may turn up to make them good. Neutral material or material damaging to the defendant need not be disclosed and should not be brought to the attention of the court. Only in truly borderline cases should the prosecution seek a judicial ruling on the disclosability of material in its hands. If the material contains information which the prosecution would prefer that the defendant did not have, on forensic as opposed to public interest grounds, that will suggest that the material is disclosable.

Otherwise disclosable material should not be withheld because the prosecutor considers that the accused is unlikely to use it during the trial (*Hilton*, unreported, February 27, 2003, CA ([2003] EWCA Crim. 761)); but disclosure should not be made of everything available regardless of any conceivable relevance: *R. v. M.*, *ibid.*

The test should be applied on a "thinking" basis, with all those involved having a proper understanding of what is relevant; it is the task of the prosecuting lawyer to identify the issues in the case, and the disclosure officer should act under his guidance; if there are difficulties with disclosure, it is essential that the court is closely involved in their resolution, ensuring that the prosecution perform their duties; the court will have a clear view of the issues and be astute to see that disclosure in respect of those issues is properly carried out and abusive requests or procedures do not develop: *Olu, Wilson and Brooks*, 175 J.P. 1, CA.

The duties under ss.3(1)(a) and 7A(2) would not appear to require the prosecutor to comb through all material in his possession for the purposes of investigating all possible lines of defence, on the look-out for anything which might assist the defence; the duties required him to be alert to examine and re-examine his case in the light of known and emerging lines of defence and to disclose any disclosable material of which he was aware or became aware while carrying out that duty: *McDonald v. H.M. Advocate*, *The Times*, November 5, 2008, PC (a Scottish appeal decided in relation to the duty under art. 6 of the European Convention on Human Rights).

Withholding material in the public interest

As to the powers of the court under ss.3(6), 7A(8) and 8(5) to order that otherwise disclosable material may be withheld on the basis that it is not in the public interest to disclose it, see *post*, §§ 6–76 *et seq*. **6–57**

Third party disclosure and overseas material

As to disclosure obligations in relation to material in the possession of third parties and overseas authorities, see *post*, § 6–74. **6–58**

Attorney General's Guidelines

Paragraphs 8 to 14 and 17 to 19 of the *Attorney General's Guidelines on Disclosure* set out guidance in relation to what material falls within ss.3(1)(a) and 7A(2). Prosecutors are only expected to anticipate what material might weaken their case or strengthen the defence in light of information available at the time of the disclosure decision, which may include information revealed during questioning: para. 9. Generally, material falling within ss.3(1)(a) or 7A(2) will include anything tending to show a fact inconsistent with the elements of the case that must be proved by the prosecution; this may be by the use to be made of it in cross-examination, its capacity to support submissions that could lead to the exclusion of evidence, a stay of proceedings, or a finding that any public authority had acted incompatibly with the accused's rights under the ECHR, or by its capacity to suggest an explanation or partial explanation of the accused's actions; but the disclosure should not support speculative arguments or permit the manufacture of defences: paras 10, 11. **6–59**

Examples of material falling within ss.3(1)(a) or 7A(2) are: (i) any material casting doubt upon the accuracy of any prosecution evidence; (ii) any material which may point to another person, whether charged or not (including a co-accused) having involvement in the commission of the offence; (iii) any material which may cast doubt upon the reliability of a confession; (iv) any material that might go to the credibility of a prosecution witness; (v) any material that might support a defence that is either raised by the defence or apparent from the prosecution papers; (vi) any material which may have a bearing on the admissibility of any prosecution evidence: para. 12. Prosecutors should bear in mind that an item of material by itself may not fall within ss.3(1)(a) or 7A(2), but the combined effect of several items together may do so: para. 13. Material relating to the accused's mental or physical health, intellectual capacity or ill treatment in custody is likely to be disclosable: para. 14.

Bad character of prosecution witnesses

6–60 Most authorities on this issue have concerned the question of whether a conviction is unsafe as a result of non-disclosure of the material (it being assumed that the material was disclosable): see *Vasiliou* [2000] Crim.L.R. 845; *Eccleston*, unreported, July 1, 2001, CA ([2001] EWCA Crim. 1626); *Underwood* [2003] 6 *Archbold News* 1, CA; *McCartney, Hamlett and ors* [2003] 6 *Archbold News* 2, CA.

The Supreme Court and Privy Council have considered the issue more generally in the context of the application of art. 6(1) of the ECHR as a matter of Scots law. It is submitted that these authorities are highly persuasive as to the interpretation of the scope of ss.3(1) and 7A(2) given the similarity of the obligation arising under art. 6(1) (as to which see *ante*, § 6–22) with those provisions. Thus in *Holland v. H.M. Advocate*, *The Times*, June 1, 2005, PC, where it was said that (i) an accused, and his legal advisers, were entitled to information about the previous convictions of any witnesses who were to give evidence at the trial, such information being likely to be of material assistance to the proper preparation or presentation of the defence; additionally disclosure of the material ensured that the accused's right to equality of arms would be respected; and (ii) as to outstanding criminal charges against a prosecution witness, there was no good reason for the prosecution not to disclose such information, even where no decision had been made whether to charge the witness; but there is no general duty to search for outstanding charges and if prosecution officials were asked about a particular witness, they need only take such steps to search for any outstanding charges as were appropriate, having regard to any indications given in the defence request. However, there is no absolute rule that the complete criminal history of a prosecution witness must be disclosed; disclosure of such material engaged the right of the witness under art. 8 of the ECHR and would be incompatible with that right unless the interference could be justified under art. 8(2); but the balance would fall firmly in favour of disclosure to the accused where the information could be used for a legitimate attack on the credibility or character of the witness, in which case it would be relevant to the accused's defence and interference with the art. 8 right of the witness would be justified as being necessary to secure the accused's right to a fair trial; the decision as to what should be disclosed is for the prosecution, but a generous view should be taken without adopting a test which excluded everything to which objection might possibly be taken on the ground that it was not relevant; in case of dispute, the issue should be referred to the judge for decision and the prosecution should place the previous conviction(s) before the judge with a brief indication, agreed with the defence, of the matter about which the witness is expected to give evidence: *H.M. Advocate v. Murtagh*, unreported, August 3, 2009, PC. ([2009] UKPC 36). It is submitted that it is implicit in this approach that bad character of a prosecution witness will fall within s.3(1)(a) or 7A(2) where a legitimate application could be made by the accused under s.100 of the *Criminal Justice Act* 2003 (bad character being important explanatory evidence or evidence having substantial probative value in relation to a matter in issue in the proceedings).

Where pivotal evidence comes from a man with a known prison record, the prosecution should at an early stage equip themselves with his prison records; not only might they include matters prejudicial to their case and disclosable to the defence, but they might find their own case strengthened: *McCartney and Hamlett* [2003] 6 Archbold News 2, CA.

Previous statements of prosecution witnesses

6–61 A previous statement of a prosecution witness which would have be likely to undermine the integrity of that witness and or others should be disclosed: see *Kelly (deceased)*; *Connolly (deceased)* (2003) 147 S.J. 1276, CA (not decided in the context of the 1996 Act). See also *Swash v. DPP*, unreported, March 4, 2009, DC ([2009] EWHC 803 (Admin.)).

In cases which are dependant on eye-witness evidence, what a witness says when first seen, even informally, is often the most reliable; all contacts, notes of conversations and draft statements should therefore be obtained (where available) and scheduled and disclosed at the outset (either as used or unused material): *Olu, Wilson and Brooks*, 175 J.P. 1, CA.

Reward paid to prosecution witness or co-defendant

Information as to the reward to be paid, after the trial, to a registered police informant who was a prosecution witness, or to a co-defendant giving evidence for the prosecution, has been held to fall within s.3(1)(a) or 7A(2): *Allan* [2005] Crim.L.R. 716, CA; *Smith* [2004] 8 Archbold News 1, CA. **6–62**

Witnesses not relied on by the prosecution

The identity of persons who might have witnessed an incident giving rise to criminal charges is material capable of undermining the prosecution case or supporting the defence case: *Heggart* [2001] 4 *Archbold News* 2, CA. Under the old common law disclosure rules this applied to the details of a witness who had given a statement but whom the prosecution had decided not to call on the basis that the witness was regarded as unworthy of belief: see *Mills and Poole* [1998] A.C. 382, HL. The duty of disclosure under s.3(1)(a) and 7A(2) also extends to the telephone numbers of the makers of 999 calls, such that a general practice of non-disclosure of the identity of persons making 999 calls could not be justified; there was no basis in the ordinary course of events for any expectation of confidentiality on the part of the caller, although in an individual case the particular facts may give rise to a possible argument of an expectation of confidentiality: *Heggart, ibid.* **6–63**

Co-accused's defence statement

A co-accused's defence statement is "prosecution material" within the meaning of s.3(2) and 7A(2), so that a duty to disclose it will arise where it is reasonably considered capable of capable of undermining the case for the prosecution against the accused or of assisting the case for the accused: *Cairns, Zaidi and Chaudhary* [2003] 1 Cr.App.R. 38, CA. Although that case was concerned with "cut throat" defences, it is submitted that the principle should apply more generally, as where an admission by a co-accused undermines the prosecution case against the accused. **6–64**

Expert evidence

Where a case involves issues on which there is expert evidence, it is of great importance that there is full disclosure at the outset of the information provided to the expert when instructed and the expert's working papers: *Olu, Wilson and Brooks*, 175 J.P. 1, CA. **6–65**

Consequences of inadequate disclosure

Where the prosecution had failed to disclose matters which ought to have been disclosed, the imperatives of justice would require an adjournment of the trial unless there would be no prejudice to the defence: *S. v. DPP*, 170 J.P. 707, DC; *Swash v. DPP*, unreported, March 4, 2009, DC ([2009] EWHC 803 (Admin.)). Where there is no prejudice to the defence and the trial proceeds, given the risk that the tribunal of fact might otherwise regard cross-examination designed to elicit the defects and failures in disclosure as an effort to draw attention away from the real issues, it should be explained to them that the inadequate disclosure by the prosecution was inherently unfair, created unjustified pressure on the defence team struggling with the difficult task of defending and could deprive the defendant of a proper opportunity of presenting his case: *Kenedy*, unreported, October 9, 2008, CA ([2008] EWCA Crim. 2817). Where it becomes appar- **6–66** ent after a trial that the prosecution had failed adequately to comply with the duty to disclose unused material, the mere fact that the material satisfied the test for disclosure does not decide the question of whether the additional material, if available at trial, might reasonably have affected the decision of the tribunal to convict (not least because any potential assistance that the material gives the defence may be greatly outweighed by the help it gives the prosecution case); the question has to be decided by consideration of the overall impact of the additional material on the case: see *Kenedy*, unreported, October 9, 2008, CA ([2008] EWCA Crim. 2817); and *Pomfrett*, unreported, October 8, 2009, CA ([2009] EWCA Crim. 1939).

Serious instances of non-disclosure may give rise to applications to stay the proceedings as an abuse of process: see Ch.8.

J. DISCLOSURE TIME LIMITS

(1) Legislation

Criminal Procedure and Investigations Act 1996, ss.10, 12, 13

Prosecutor's failure to observe time limits

6–67 **10.**—(1) This section applies if the prosecutor—

(a) purports to act under section 3 after the end of the period which, by virtue of section 12, is the relevant period for section 3, or

(b) purports to act under section 7A(5) after the end of the period which, by virtue of section 12, is the relevant period for section 7A.

(2) Subject to subsection (3) the failure to act during the period concerned does not on its own constitute grounds for staying the proceedings for abuse of process.

(3) Subsection (2) does not prevent the failure constituting such grounds if it involves such delay by the prosecutor that the accused is denied a fair trial.

[This section is printed as amended by the *Criminal Justice Act* 2003, s.331 and Sched. 36.]

Time limits

6–68 **12.**—(1) This section has effect for the purpose of determining the relevant period for sections 3, 5, 6, 6B, 6C and 7A(5).

(2) Subject to subsection (3), the relevant period is a period beginning and ending with such days as the Secretary of State prescribes by regulations for the purposes of the section concerned.

(3) The regulations may do one or more of the following—

(a) provide that the relevant period for any section shall if the court so orders be extended (or further extended) by so many days as the court specifies;

(b) provide that the court may only make such an order if an application is made by a prescribed person and if any other prescribed conditions are fulfilled;

(c) provide that an application may only be made if prescribed conditions are fulfilled;

(d) provide that the number of days by which a period may be extended shall be entirely at the court's discretion;

(e) provide that the number of days by which a period may be extended shall not exceed a prescribed number;

(f) provide that there shall be no limit on the number of applications that may be made to extend a period;

(g) provide that no more than a prescribed number of applications may be made to extend a period;

and references to the relevant period for a section shall be construed accordingly.

(4) Conditions mentioned in subsection (3) may be framed by reference to such factors as the Secretary of State thinks fit.

(5) Without prejudice to the generality of subsection (4), so far as the relevant period for section 3 or 7A(5) is concerned—

(a) conditions may be framed by reference to the nature or volume of the material concerned;

(b) the nature of material may be defined by reference to the prosecutor's belief that the question of non-disclosure on grounds of public interest may arise.

(6) In subsection (3) "prescribed" means prescribed byregulations under this section.

Time limits: transitional

13.—(1) As regards a case in relation to which no regulations under section 12 have come into force for the purposes of section 3, section 3(8) shall have effect as if it read— **6–69**

"(8) The prosecutor must act under this section as soon as is reasonably practicable after—

(a) *the accused pleads not guilty (where this Part applies by virtue of section 1(1)),*

(b) *the accused is committed for trial (where this Part applies by virtue of section 1(2)(a)),*

(c) *the proceedings are transferred (where this Part applies by virtue of section 1(2)(b) or (c)),*

(ca) copies of the documents containing the evidence on which the charge or charges are based are served on the accused (where this Part applies by virtue of section 1(2)(cc)),

(d) the count is included in the indictment (where this Part applies by virtue of section 1(2)(d)), or

(e) the bill of indictment is preferred (where this Part applies by virtue of section 1(2)(e) or (f))."

(2) As regards a case in relation to which no regulations under section 12 have come into force for the purposes of section 7A, section 7A(5) shall have effect as if—

(a) in paragraph (a) for the words from "during the period" to the end, and

(b) in paragraph (b) for "during that period",

there were substituted "as soon as is reasonably practicable after the accused gives the statement in question".

[This section is printed as amended by the *Crime and Disorder Act* 1998, s.119 and Sched. 8; the *Access to Justice Act* 1999, s.67(2); and the *Criminal Justice Act* 2003, s.331 and Sched. 36. As from a day or days to be appointed, the section is further amended by the 2003 Act, s.41 and Sched. 3, which repeal subss. (a) to (c) of the modified s.3(8).]

(2) Time-limits for prosecution compliance with duties of initial and continuing disclosure

No regulations have been made by the Secretary of State in relation to disclosure by the prosecution under ss.3 (initial duty of disclosure) and 7(5) (continuing duty of disclosure following service of defence statement). Accordingly, the prosecution must comply with the duties arising under those provisions as soon as reasonably practicable: s.13. **6–70**

It should be noted, however, that by virtue of the *Consolidated Criminal Practice Direction*, para. V.56.2 and the relevant form in Annex E (see Appendix F), various time limits are set out as part of the case management timetable. **6–71**

(3) Time-limit for service of defence statement and notice of intention to call defence witnesses

The *Criminal Procedure and Investigations Act 1996 (Defence Disclosure Time Limits) Regulations* 2011 (S.I. 2011 No. 209) prescribe the time-limit for voluntary service of a defence statement and mandatory service of a defence witness notice. The regulations came into force on February 28, 2011; but they have no effect in relation to any case where the court proceeds to summary trial if the accused was charged with the offence before that date: see reg. 4 (*post*) and s.1(1) of the 1996 Act (*ante*, § 6–29). As to the purpose of the regulations, see Ministry of Justice Circular 2011/02. For the regulations applying before the commencement date, see the 2011 edition of this work. **6–72**

Where the prosecutor serves a written statement that there is no material to be disclosed pursuant to the duty of initial disclosure under s.3, and then on a subsequent date serves the schedule of unused material, time runs for the purposes of service of the defence statement from the date of service of the written statement, not from the service of the schedule: *DPP v. Wood*; *DPP v. McGillicuddy*, 170 J.P 177, DC. As to the consequences of late service of a defence statement or defence witness notice, see s.11(4) of the 1996 Act (*post*, § 10–146) and *ante*, § 6–66.

Criminal Procedure and Investigations Act 1996 (Defence Disclosure Time Limits) Regulations 2011 (S.I. 2011 No. 209)

Citation, commencement, extent and interpretation

6–73 **1.**—(1) These Regulations—

(a) may be cited as the *Criminal Procedure and Investigations Act 1996 (Defence Disclosure Time Limits) Regulations* 2011;

(b) come into force on 28th February 2011; and

(c) extend to England and Wales only.

(2) In these Regulations, a reference to a section or Part is a reference to a section or Part of the *Criminal Procedure and Investigations Act* 1996.

Prescribed period for disclosure by the accused

2.—(1) The relevant period for section 5 (compulsory disclosure), section 6 (voluntary disclosure) and section 6C (notification of intention to call defence witnesses) begins with the day on which the prosecutor complies or purports to comply with section 3 (initial duty of the prosecutor to disclose).

(2) In a case where Part 1 applies by virtue of section 1(1) (application of Part 1 in respect of summary proceedings), the relevant period for section 6 and section 6C expires at the end of 14 days beginning with the first day of the relevant period.

(3) In a case where Part 1 applies by virtue of section 1(2) (application of Part 1 in respect of Crown Court proceedings), the relevant period for section 5 and section 6C expires at the end of 28 days beginning with the first day of the relevant period.

(4) Where the relevant period would expire on a Saturday, Sunday, Christmas Day, Good Friday or any day that under the *Banking and Financial Dealings Act* 1971 is a bank holiday in England and Wales, the relevant period is treated as expiring on the next day that is not one of those days.

(5) Paragraphs (2) and (3) are subject to regulation 3.

Power to extend

3.—(1) The court may by order extend (or further extend) the relevant period by so many days as it specifies.

(2) The court may only make such an order—

(a) on an application by the accused; and

(b) if it is satisfied that it would be unreasonable to require the accused to give a defence statement under section 5 or section 6, or give notice under section 6C, as the case may be, within the relevant period.

(3) Such an application must—

(a) be made within the relevant period;

(b) specify the grounds on which it is made; and

(c) state the number of days by which the accused wishes the relevant period to be extended.

(4) There is no limit on the number of applications that may be made under paragraph (2)(a).

Revocation

4. The *Criminal Procedure and Investigations Act 1996 (Defence Disclosure Time Limits) Regulations* 1997 and the *Criminal Procedure and Investigations Act 1996 (Notification of Intention to Call Defence Witnesses) (Time Limits) Regulations* 2010 are revoked, but that revocation shall not have effect in relation to a case to which Part 1 applies before the coming into force of these Regulations.

K. THIRD PARTY DISCLOSURE

General

Where material is sought from a third party who is under no duty to disclose it, production of the material may be compelled by obtaining a summons under s.97 of the *Magistrates' Courts Act* 1980: see *post*, §§ 9–1 *et seq*. For the procedure to be followed when a summons is sought under that provision, see Pt 28 of the *Criminal Procedure Rules* 2011 (Appendix G–160 *et seq*.). Those rules were precipitated by the decision in *R. (T.B.) v. Stafford Crown Court* [2006] 2 Cr.App.R. 34, DC, where it was said that the rights of a third party under art. 8 of the European Convention on Human Rights would be engaged by an application for a witness summons. **6–74**

Whether a duty of the prosecutor to obtain third party material

Material in the hands of a third party is not material in the hands of the prosecutor and is not, therefore, "prosecution material" for the purposes of s.3(1), 7A(2) or 8(2) of the *Criminal Procedure and Investigations Act* 1996; accordingly, there is no duty to disclose it and no power to order disclosure arising under provisions of the Act: see *R. (Johnson) v. Stratford Magistrates' Court*, unreported, February 12, 2003, DC ([2003] EWHC 353 (Admin.)); and*DPP v. Wood; DPP v. McGillicuddy*, 170 J.P 177, DC. However, the Crown (whether investigator or prosecutor) has a duty to pursue reasonable lines of inquiry in relation to material that may be held by third parties, and, if it appears that there is material that might reasonably be considered capable of undermining the prosecution case or of assisting the case for the accused, to take reasonable steps to obtain it: *Alibhai* [2004] 5 Archbold News 1, CA; *DPP v. Wood; DPP v. McGillicuddy, ibid.*; *Flook* [2010] 1 Cr.App.R. 30, CA. See also paras 47-54 of the *Attorney General's Guidelines on Disclosure* (Appendix C-16 *et seq.*); and*Brushett* [2001] Crim.L.R. 471, CA (case of childhood sexual abuse with numerous complainants), *McCartney and Hamlett* [2003] 6 Archbold News 2, CA (pivotal prosecution witness a man with a known prison record). If necessary, the prosecutor should seek a summons under s.97 of the *Magistrates' Courts Act* 1980 in order to obtain the material: see *DPP v. Wood; DPP v. McGillicuddy, ibid.*; and para. 52 of the *Attorney General's Guidelines*. **6–75**

The obligation of the Crown to pursue reasonable lines of inquiry extends to material that may be held in states outside the European Union; if it appears that there is disclosable material in such a state, the Crown must take reasonable steps to obtain it, whether informally or under the *Crime (International Co-operation) Act* 2003 and international conventions; if the prosecution are not permitted by the third party to disclose everything that they know, that must be made clear to the court so that it can consider what to do: *Flook, ibid.*

L. PUBLIC INTEREST IMMUNITY

(1) Introduction

Whereas ss.3(6), 7A(8) and 8(5) confer a power on the court to order that otherwise disclosable material may be withheld, this power is intended for those circumstances which may arise in which material held by the prosecution and tending to undermine the prosecution or assist the defence cannot be disclosed to the defence, fully or even at all, without risk of serious prejudice to an important public interest; in such circumstances some derogation from the golden rule of full disclosure may be justified but such derogation must always be the minimum derogation necessary to protect the public interest in question and must never imperil the overall fairness of the trial: *R. v. H.* [2004] 2 A.C. 134, HL. **6–76**

(2) Categories of Public Interest Immunity

General

The categories of public interest are not closed, and must alter from time to time **6–77** whether by restriction or extension as social conditions and social legislation develop: *D. v. NSPCC* [1978] A.C. 171, HL; *Chief Constable of the West Midlands Police, ex p. Wiley* [1995] 1 A.C. 274, HL. Nevertheless, the following examples of sensitive material are given in the code of practice under Pt II of the *Criminal Procedure and Investigations Act* 1996, para. 6.1:

— material relating to national security;
— material received from the intelligence and security agencies;
— material relating to intelligence from foreign sources which reveals sensitive intelligence gathering methods;
— material given in confidence;
— material relating to the identity or activities of informants, or undercover police officers, or witnesses, or other persons supplying information to the police who may be in danger if their identities are revealed;
— material revealing the location of any premises or other place used for police surveillance, or the identity of any person allowing a police officer to use them for surveillance;
— material revealing, either directly or indirectly, techniques and methods relied upon by a police officer in the course of a criminal investigation, for example covert surveillance techniques, or other methods of detecting crime;
— material whose disclosure might facilitate the commission of other offences or hinder the prevention and detection of crime;
— material upon the strength of which search warrants were obtained;
— material containing details of persons taking part in identification parades;
— material supplied to an investigator during a criminal investigation which has been generated by an official of a body concerned with the regulation or supervision of bodies corporate or of persons engaged in financial activities, or which has been generated by a person retained by such a body;
— material supplied to an investigator during a criminal investigation which relates to a child or young person and which has been generated by a local authority social services department, an area child protection committee or other party contacted by an investigator during the investigation;
— material relating to the private life of a witness.

Material relating to informants

6–78 Courts must scrutinisewith great care applications by the defence for disclosure of details about informants and adopt a robust approach in declining to order disclosure when they were not justified (*Turner* [1995] 2 Cr.App.R. 94, CA); but where a participating informant is a prosecution witness called at trial, it is extremely likely that his status will have to be disclosed (*Patel* [2002] Crim.L.R. 304, CA; *Early* [2003] 1 Cr.App.R. 19, CA).

Material relating to observation posts

6–79 Public interest immunity protects the identity of a person who has allowed his premises to be used for surveillance, the location of the premises and any other information which might reveal his identity: *Rankine* [1986] Q.B. 861, CA. However, information which can be revealed without disclosing the identity of the occupier should be disclosed unless public interest immunity can be justified on some other ground: *Johnson (Kenneth)*, 88 Cr.App.R. 131; *Grimes* [1994] Crim.L.R. 213. For guidance in relation to prosecution applications to withhold material falling in this category, see *Johnson, ibid.*

Material generated by financial regulators

6–80 The mere fact that information or documents have come into possession of a government department as a result of the exercise by it of statutory powers to obtain information or documents does not prohibit their disclosure in the absence of a statutory prohibition thereon: *Norwich Pharmacal Co. v. Customs and Excise Commrs* [1974] A.C. 133, HL.

Material relating to children and young persons generated by social services

Various categories of documents and records maintained by social services and organisations such as the NSPCC in relation to children and young persons are subject to public interest immunity, in view of the particular circumstances of the welfare of the child and the risk that frankness would be imperiled if such records were liable to be disclosed: *Re D. (Infants)* [1970] 1 W.L.R. 599, CA (Civ. Div.); *D. v. NSPCC* [1978] A.C. 171, H.L; *Re M. (A Minor) (Disclosure)* [1990] 2 F.L.R. 36, CA (Civ. Div.). **6–81**

Identity of prosecution witnesses

As to the withholding of details leading to the identification of prosecution witnesses, see Pt 3 of the *Coroners and Justice Act* 2009 (anonymity in investigations). **6–82**

Material in relation to sexual offences

As from a day or days to be appointed, the *Sexual Offences (Protected Material) Act* 1997 makes provision limiting access by defendants and others to certain categories of material disclosed by the prosecution in connection with particular sexual and other offences. **6–83**

(3) The decision as to non-disclosure

(a) *The issue to be determined*

Sections 3(6), 7A(8) and 8(5) of the Criminal Procedure and Investigations Act 1996 each provide that material otherwise satisfying the criteria for disclosure must not be disclosed to the extent that the court, on an application by the prosecutor, concludes that it is not in the public interest to disclose it and orders accordingly. In *R. v. H.* [2004] 2 A.C. 134, HL, their Lordships set out (at [36], [37]) the following principles to be applied where an application is made for an order under those subsections: **6–84**

> [36]. When any issue of derogation from the golden rule of full disclosure comes before it, the court must address a series of questions:
>
> (1) What is the material which the prosecution seek to withhold? This must be considered by the court in detail.
>
> (2) Is the material such as may weaken the prosecution case or strengthen that of the defence? If No, disclosure should not be ordered. If Yes, full disclosure should (subject to (3), (4) and (5) below) be ordered.
>
> (3) Is there a real risk of serious prejudice to an important public interest (and, if so, what) if full disclosure of the material is ordered? If No, full disclosure should be ordered.
>
> (4) If the answer to (2) and (3) is Yes, can the defendant's interest be protected without disclosure or disclosure be ordered to an extent or in a way which will give adequate protection to the public interest in question and also afford adequate protection to the interests of the defence? This question requires the court to consider, with specific reference to the material which the prosecution seek to withhold and the facts of the case and the defence as disclosed, whether the prosecution should formally admit what the defence seek to establish or whether disclosure short of full disclosure may be ordered. This may be done in appropriate cases by the preparation of summaries or extracts of evidence, or the provision of documents in an edited or anonymised form, provided the documents supplied are in each instance approved by the judge. In appropriate cases the appointment of special counsel may be a necessary step to ensure that the contentions of the prosecution are tested and the interests of the defendant protected (as to the appointment of special counsel, see post, § 12-85). In cases of exceptional difficulty the court may require the appointment of special counsel to ensure a correct answer to questions (2) and (3) as well as (4).
>
> (5) Do the measures proposed in answer to (4) represent the minimum derogation necessary to protect the public interest in question? If No, the court should order such greater disclosure as will represent the minimum derogation from the golden rule of full disclosure.
>
> (6) If limited disclosure is ordered pursuant to (4) or (5), may the effect be to render the trial process, viewed as a whole, unfair to the defendant? If Yes, then fuller disclosure

should be ordered even if this leads or may lead the prosecution to discontinue the proceedings so as to avoid having to make disclosure.

(7) If the answer to (6) when first given is No, does that remain the correct answer as the trial unfolds, evidence is adduced and the defence advanced?

It is important that the answer to (6) should not be treated as a final, once-and-for-all, answer but as a provisional answer which the court must keep under review.

[37]. Throughout his or her consideration of any disclosure issue the trial judge must bear constantly in mind the overriding principles referred to in this opinion. In applying them, the judge should involve the defence to the maximum extent possible without disclosing that which the general interest requires to be protected but taking full account of the specific defence which is relied on. There will be very few cases indeed in which some measure of disclosure to the defence will not be possible, even if this is confined to the fact that an ex parte application is to be made. If even that information is withheld and if the material to be withheld is of significant help to the defendant, there must be a very serious question whether the prosecution should proceed, since special counsel, even if appointed, cannot then receive any instructions from the defence at all.

6–85 In order to make a decision as to non-disclosure, the court must necessarily study the material in respect of which the claim of public interest immunity is made: *ibid.* Great caution is necessary and there should be the most searching investigation by the police, by prosecuting authorities and by the courts of the facts relating to matters in respect of which public interest immunity is claimed, coupled with the most searching consideration of their possible relevance in light of whatever defence is being advanced: *West,* 69 J.C.L 309, CA.

6–86 Where an application for non-disclosure is made in a magistrates' court before the bench which will subsequently hear the trial to which the material relates, there will be no requirement for the court to recuse itself on grounds of bias provided that the public interest immunity application is confined, as it should be, to material which undermines the prosecution case or strengthens that of the defence (in which case the bench will not be alerted to material damaging to the defendant); the court's duty of continuing review would ordinarily militate in favour of continuing the proceedings before the court which determined the public interest immunity application: *R. v. H.* [2004] 2 A.C. 134, HL (considering *Stipendiary Magistrate for Norfolk, ex p Taylor*, 161 J.P. 773, DC, and *R. (DPP) v. Acton Youth Court* [2001] 1 WLR 1828, DC; and observing that if a case raises complex and contentious public interest immunity issues, and the court has discretion to commit the case to the Crown Court for trial, the magistrates' court should carefully consider whether those issues are best resolved in the Crown Court).

In exceptional cases, where the court is satisfied that no other course will adequately meet the overriding requirement of fairness to the defendant, it may be necessary to appoint an approved advocate as special counsel to advance arguments on behalf of the accused during the public interest immunity hearing; but the occasions on which it will be appropriate to appoint special counsel in the magistrates' court will be even rarer than in the Crown Court: *R. v. H., ibid.*

(b) *Procedure*

6–87 Rule 22.3 of the *Criminal Procedure Rules* 2011 sets out the procedure to be followed where an application is made for an order under s.3(6), 7A(8) or 8(5) of the *CPIA* 1996: see Appendix G–140b). The general rule is that the accused will have notice of the application, and an opportunity to make representations before further representations are made by the prosecutor in the absence of the defendant: *Davis, Johnson and Rowe*, 97 Cr.App.R. 110, CA.

(3) Review of orders for non-disclosure

Criminal Procedure and Investigations Act 1996, ss.14, 16

Public interest: review for summary trials

6–88 **14.**—(1) This section applies where this Part applies by virtue of section 1(1),

(2) At any time—

(a) after a court makes an order under section 3(6), 7A(8)) or 8(5), and

(b) before the accused is acquitted or convicted or the prosecutor decides not to proceed with the case concerned,

the accused may apply to the court for a review of the question whether it is still not in the public interest to disclose material affected by its order.

(3) In such a case the court must review that question, and if it concludes that it is in the public interest to disclose material to any extent—

(a) it shall so order, and

(b) it shall take such steps as are reasonable to inform the prosecutor of its order.

(4) Where the prosecutor is informed of an order made under subsection (3) he must act accordingly having regard to the provisions of this Part (unless he decides not to proceed with the case concerned).

[This section is printed as amended by the *Criminal Justice Act* 2003, s.331 and Sched. 36.]

For procedural provisions in connection with this section, see r.22.6 of the *Criminal Procedure Rules* 2011 (Appendix G-140e, *post*). **6–89**

(4) Rights of third parties to be heard

Applications: opportunity to be heard

16. Where— **6–90**

(a) an application is made under section 3(6), 7A(8), 8(5), 14(2) or 15(4),

(b) a person claiming to have an interest in the material applies to be heard by the court, and

(c) he shows that he was involved (whether alone or with others and whether directly or indirectly) in the prosecutor's attention being brought to the material,

the court must not make an order under section 3(6), 7A(8), 8(5), 14(3) or 15(5) (as the case may be) unless the person applying under paragraph (b) has been given an opportunity to be heard.

[This section is printed as amended by the *Criminal Justice Act* 2003, s.331 and Sched. 36.]

M. CONFIDENTIALITY OF DISCLOSED MATERIAL

Criminal Procedure and Investigations Act 1996, s.17–18

Confidentiality of disclosed information

17.—(1) If the accused is given or allowed to inspect a document or other object under— **6–91**

(a) section 3, 4, 7A, 14 or 15, or

(b) an order under section 8,

then, subject to subsections (2) to (4), he must not use or disclose it or any information recorded in it.

(2) The accused may use or disclose the object or information—

(a) in connection with the proceedings for whose purposes he was given the object or allowed to inspect it,

(b) with a view to the taking of further criminal proceedings (for instance, by way of appeal) with regard to the matter giving rise to the proceedings mentioned in paragraph (a), or

(c) in connection with the proceedings first mentioned in paragraph (b).

(3) The accused may use or disclose—

(a) the object to the extent that it has been displayed to the public in open court, or

(b) the information to the extent that it has been communicated to the public in open court;

but the preceding provisions of this subsection do not apply if the object is displayed or the information is communicated in proceedings to deal with a contempt of court under section 18.

(4) If—

(a) the accused applies to the court for an order granting permission to use or disclose the object or information, and

(b) the court makes such an order,

the accused may use or disclose the object or information for the purpose and to the extent specified by the court.

(5) An application under subsection (4) may be made and dealt with at any time, and in particular after the accused has been acquitted or convicted or the prosecutor has decided not to proceed with the case concerned: but this is subject to rules made by virtue of section 19(2).

(6) Where—

(a) an application is made under subsection (4), and

(b) the prosecutor or a person claiming to have an interest in the object or information applies to be heard by the court,

the court must not make an order granting permission unless the person applying under paragraph (b) has been given an opportunity to be heard.

(7) References in this section to the court are to—

(a) a magistrates' court, where this Part applies by virtue of section 1(1);

(b) the Crown Court, where this Part applies by virtue of section 1(2).

(8) Nothing in this section affects any other restriction or prohibition on the use or disclosure of an object or information, whether the restriction or prohibition arises under an enactment (whenever passed) or otherwise.

[This section is printed as amended by the *Criminal Justice Act* 2003, s.331 and Sched. 36.]

Confidentiality: contravention

6–92 **18.**—(1) It is a contempt of court for a person knowingly to use or disclose an object or information recorded in it if the use or disclosure is in contravention of section 17.

(2) The following courts have jurisdiction to deal with a person who is guilty of a contempt under this section—

(a) a magistrates' court, where this Part applies by virtue of section 1(1),

(b) the Crown Court, where this Part applies by virtue of section 1(2).

(3) A person who is guilty of a contempt under this section may be dealt with as follows—

(a) a magistrates' court may commit him to custody for a specified period not exceeding six months or impose on him a fine not exceeding £5,000 or both;

(b) the Crown Court may commit him to custody for a specified period not exceeding two years or impose a fine on him or both.

(4) If—

(a) a person is guilty of a contempt under this section, and

(b) the object concerned is in his possession,

the court finding him guilty may order that the object shall be forfeited and dealt with in such manner as the court may order.

(5) The power of the court under subsection (4) includes power to order the object to be destroyed or to be given to the prosecutor or to be placed in his custody for such period as the court may specify.

(6) If—

(a) the court proposes to make an order under subsection (4), and

(b) the person found guilty, or any other person claiming to have an interest in the object, applies to be heard by the court,

the court must not make the order unless the applicant has been given an opportunity to be heard.

(7) If—

(a) a person is guilty of a contempt under this section and

(b) a copy of the object concerned is in his possession,

the court finding him guilty may order that the copy shall be forfeited and dealt with in such manner as the court may order.

(8) Subsections (5) and (6) apply for the purposes of subsection (7) as they apply for the purposes of subsection (4), but as if references to the object were references to the copy.

(9) An object or information shall be inadmissible as evidence in civil proceedings if to adduce it would in the opinion of the court be likely to constitute a contempt under this

section and "the court" here means the court before which the civil proceedings are being taken.

(10) The powers of a magistrates' court under this section may be exercised either of the court's own motion or by order on complaint.

6–93 Rules 22.7 and 22.8 of the *Criminal Procedure Rules* 2011 make ancillary provision in connection with matters arising under ss.17 and 18 of the *Criminal Procedure and Investigations Act* 1996: see Appendix G. See also Pt 62, which makes provision in connection with contempt proceedings.

IV. DISCLOSURE CODE OF PRACTICE: PT II OF THE CRIMINAL PROCEDURE AND INVESTIGATIONS ACT 1996

(a) *Introduction*

6–94 Part II (ss.22–27) of the *Criminal Procedure and Investigations Act* 1996 makes provision as to the making of a code of practice in relation to the collection, recording and retention of "material" during a "criminal investigation".

(b) *"Material" and "criminal investigation"*

Criminal Procedure and Investigations Act 1996, s.22

Introduction

6–95 **22.**—(1) For the purposes of this Part a criminal investigation is an investigation conducted by police officers with a view to it being ascertained—

(a) whether a person should be charged with an offence, or

(b) whether a person charged with an offence is guilty of it.

(2) In this Part references to material are to material of all kinds, and in particular include references to—

(a) information, and

(b) objects of all descriptions.

(3) In this Part references to recording information are to putting it in a durable or retrievable form (such as writing or tape).

6–96 Where the arrest and charge of a person does not involve any deliberation on the part of the police officers concerned (as where a person is arrested by a police officer for allegedly committing an offence in the sight of the officer and then taken to a police station and charged with the offence), there is no "investigation" within the meaning of subs. (1): *DPP v. Metten*, unreported, January 22, 1999, DC.

(c) *Duty to prepare code of practice*

Criminal Procedure and Investigations Act 1996, s.23

Code of practice

6–97 **23.**—(1) The Secretary of State shall prepare a code of practice containing provisions designed to secure—

(a) that where a criminal investigation is conducted all reasonable steps are taken for the purposes of the investigation and, in particular, all reasonable lines of inquiry are pursued;

(b) that information which is obtained in the course of a criminal investigation and may be relevant to the investigation is recorded;

(c) that any record of such information is retained;

(d) that any other material which is obtained in the course of a criminal investigation and may be relevant to the investigation is retained;

(e) that information falling within paragraph (b) and material falling within paragraph (d) is revealed to a person who is involved in the prosecution of criminal proceedings arising out of or relating to the investigation and who is identified in accordance with prescribed provisions;

(f) that where such a person inspects information or other material in pursuance of a requirement that it be revealed to him, and he requests that it be disclosed to the accused, the accused is allowed to inspect it or is given a copy of it;

(g) that where such a person is given a document indicating the nature of information or other material in pursuance of a requirement that it be revealed to him, and he requests that it be disclosed to the accused, the accused is allowed to inspect it or is given a copy of it;

(h) that the person who is to allow the accused to inspect information or other material or to give him a copy of it shall decide which of those (inspecting or giving a copy) is appropriate;

(i) that where the accused is allowed to inspect material as mentioned in paragraph (f) or (g) and he requests a copy, he is given one unless the person allowing the inspection is of opinion that it is not practicable or not desirable to give him one;

(j) that a person mentioned in paragraph (e) is given a written statement that prescribed activities which the code requires have been carried out.

(2) The code may include provision—

(a) that a police officer identified in accordance with prescribed provisions must carry out a prescribed activity which the code requires;

(b) that a police officer so identified must take steps to secure the carrying out by a person (whether or not a police officer) of a prescribed activity which the code requires;

(c) that a duty must be discharged by different people in succession in prescribed circumstances (as where a person dies or retires).

(3) The code may include provision about the form in which information is to be recorded.

(4) The code may include provision about the manner in which and the period for which—

(a) a record of information is to be retained, and

(b) any other material is to be retained;

and if a person is charged with an offence the period may extend beyond a conviction or an acquittal.

(5) The code may include provision about the time when, the form in which, the way in which, and the extent to which, information or any other material is to be revealed to the person mentioned in subsection (1)(e).

(6) The code must be so framed that it does not apply to material intercepted in obedience to a warrant issued under section 2 of the *Interception of Communications Act* 1985 or under the authority of an interception warrant under section 5 of the *Regulation of Investigatory Powers Act* 2000.

(7) The code may—

(a) make different provision in relation to different cases or descriptions of case;

(b) contain exceptions as regards prescribed cases or descriptions of case.

(8) In this section "prescribed" means prescribed by the code.

[This section is printed as amended by the *Regulation of Investigatory Powers Act* 2000, s.82(1), Sched. 4.]

6–98 Section 24 gives examples of the kinds of provision that may be included in the code by virtue of s.23(5). Section 25 makes provision as to the operation and revision of the code. In particular, the code of practice is to be brought into force by order of the Secretary of State, but only after it has been laid before both House of Parliament: s.25(2).

(d) *The code*

6–99 The most recent code was brought into force on April 4, 2005: *Criminal Procedure and Investigations Act 1996 (Code of Practice) Order* 2005 (S.I. 2005 No. 985). It is set out in full at Appendix B.

(e) *Effect of the code*

Criminal Procedure and Investigations Act 1996, s.26

Effect of code

26.—(1) A person other than a police officer who is charged with the duty of conducting an investigation with a view to it being ascertained— **6–100**

(a) whether a person should be charged with an offence, or

(b) whether a person charged with an offence is guilty of it,

shall in discharging that duty have regard to any relevant provision of a code which would apply if the investigation were conducted by police officers.

(2) A failure—

(a) by a police officer to comply with any provision of a code for the time being in operation by virtue of an order under section 25, or

(b) by a person to comply with subsection (1),

shall not in itself render him liable to any criminal or civil proceedings.

(3) In all criminal and civil proceedings a code in operation at any time by virtue of an order under section 25 shall be admissible in evidence.

(4) If it appears to a court or tribunal conducting criminal or civil proceedings that—

(a) any provision of a code in operation at any time by virtue of an order under section 25, or

(b) any failure mentioned in subsection (2)(a) or (b),

is relevant to any question arising in the proceedings, the provision or failure shall be taken into account in deciding the question.

CHAPTER 7

PRE-TRIAL PROCEDURE

I. INTRODUCTION

Some cases heard at the magistrates' court are concluded at the first listing but others require more time for preparation and so will be adjourned. Cases are treated differently according to the plea to be tendered. When a not guilty plea is expected then preliminary steps will be taken at the first court appearance to prepare for trial. Pre-trial proceedings consist of considering legal representation, taking a plea and giving directions relating to trial issues and disclosure, *etc*. For guilty pleas, the expectation is that the case will be dealt with on the first listing. **7–1**

II. GENERAL PRINCIPLES OF CASE MANAGEMENT

A. CRIMINAL PROCEDURE RULES AND THE DUTIES OF ACTIVE CASE MANAGEMENT

(1) Introduction

7–2 The *Criminal Procedure Rules* 2011 (S.I. 2011 No. 1709) prescribe a procedural code for the management of the progression of criminal cases through the courts (*i.e.* from first appearance through to final disposal). Many of the rules are expressed in wide ranging terms, and it is important to bear in mind the true purpose for which they were intended when considering how the rules are to be applied.

(2) Rule making powers (vires) and the nature of rules of court

7–3 Sections 68 to 74 of the *Courts Act* 2003 provide a statutory framework for the making of "Criminal Procedure Rules". The general rule making power (*vires*) is in s.69, which provides that the rules are to made by the Criminal Procedure Rules Committee and that they are to be in the form of rules of court governing "practice and procedure" to be followed in the criminal courts (including magistrates' courts). It should be noted, however, that the rule making power is not located solely in s.68 nor in the *Courts Act* 2003. Various other statutes dealing with matters of criminal procedure require Criminal Procedure Rules to make provision in connection with the operation of the statutory procedure. For example, s.30(1) of the *Criminal Justice Act* 2003 provides that "Criminal Procedure Rules" may make provision "as to the form, content, recording, authentication and service of written charges or requisitions" and "such other provision in relation to written charges or requisitions as appears ... to be necessary or expedient.". Any power to make Criminal Procedure Rules is to be exercised with a view to securing that "the criminal justice system is accessible, fair and efficient" and "that the rules are both simple and simply expressed": s.68(4).

A further point to be made in relation to the rule making power of the Criminal Procedure Rules Committee is that unlike the provisions as to the making of Family Procedure Rules and Civil Procedure Rules, there is no provision for the modification of the law of evidence: see for comparison s.76(3) of the *Courts Act* 2003 (Family Procedure Rules) and para. 4 of Sched. 1 to the *Civil Procedure Act* 1997 (Civil Procedure Rules). It is submitted that this was deliberate on the part of Parliament in that criminal evidence is a matter not suitable to be left to a delegated rule committee.

It is submitted that as rules of court, Criminal Procedure Rules cannot extend the jurisdiction of the court from that which the law provides; they merely give directions as to how the existing jurisdiction should be exercised: see *Capewell v. Revenue and Customs Commissioners and another* [2007] 1 W.L.R. 397, HL; and *Jaffray and others v. Society of Lloyd's (Practice Note)* [2008] 1 W.L.R. 75, CA (Civ. Div.).

See also *R. (Kelly) v. Warley Magistrates' Court* [2008] 1 Cr.App.R. 14, DC at [31]–[33], as authority for a proposition that any sanction for failure to comply with a requirement arising under the rules must be proportionate and should provide for no more than might reasonably be required for the proper working of the procedural case management code; case management rules governing the procedure for adducing evidence (as opposed to amounting to a rule of evidence) will properly be within the vires of the rules, provided they are not open-ended but are coloured and confined by moderate procedural sanctions for breach. *Cf. Musone* [2007] 2 Cr.App.R. 29, CA, where the overriding objective in the rules was applied in such a way as to create an exclusionary rule of evidence where a defendant had failed to give notice of an intention to adduce evidence of bad character of a co-defendant. It is submitted that any such power (*i.e.* a power to prohibit a party from giving relevant and probative evidence) is not properly within the vires of the rules. Following the decision in *Kelly* the *Criminal Procedure (Amendment No. 3) Rules* 2007 (S.I. 2007 No. 3662) (re-enacted in the

Criminal Procedure Rules 2011) amended the case management code in Pt 3 of the rules by introducing r.3.5(6) making clear the powers of the court where a party had failed to comply with a rule or direction of the court.

(3) The rules

The *Criminal Procedure Rules* 2005 (S.I. 2005 No. 384) came into force on April 4, 2005. They replaced but also consolidated existing rules with additional provisions setting out the overriding objective and a new code for case management. A series of amendments were then made to the rules (see S.I. 2006 No. 353, S.I. 2006 No. 2636, S.I. 2007 No. 699, S.I. 2007 No. 2317, S.I. 2007 No. 3662, S.I. 2008 No. 2076, S.I. 2008 No. 3269, S.I. 2009 No. 2087), which were then consolidated with further amendments into the *Criminal Procedure Rules* 2011 (S.I. 2011 No. 1709) with effect from April 5, 2010. Those rules were then further amended by S.I. 2010 No. 1921 and S.I. 2010 No. 3026. The rules were then further amended and consolidated into the *Criminal Procedure Rules* 2011(S.I. 2011 No. 1709). The rules (as amended) are set out in Appendix G. **7–4**

The overriding objective

The overriding objective is that criminal cases be dealt with justly and the rules indicate how this is to be achieved. For example dealing with a case justly includes acquitting the innocent and convicting the guilty, dealing with both parties fairly, recognising the defendant's rights and respecting the interests of witnesses and other third parties and keeping them informed of the progress of the case. In addition the case must be dealt with "efficiently and expeditiously". Appropriate information must be made available to the court on considering bail or sentence and the complexity, gravity and consequences of the case for the defendant and others as well as the needs of other cases must all be taken into account. **7–5**

The case management duty of the court

The court has a general duty to further the overriding objective. All participants in a case have a duty under the rules to prepare and conduct the case in accordance with the overriding objective and to comply with not only the rules, but also any relevant practice directions and specific court directions. In addition they have a duty to let the court know of any significant failure of compliance which might lead to the case not being dealt with justly. This duty extends to anyone involved in a case so could include witnesses and particularly expert witnesses whose unavailability can occasionally cause delay. **7–6**

The rules also include principles relating to case management designed to secure that cases are dealt with "efficiently and expeditiously". The court and the parties have a duty to manage cases actively and the court may give directions to ensure that cases proceed swiftly. A new role of a case progression officer is introduced and the court and all parties must each nominate an individual to take responsibility for progressing the case through the system. Wide powers of general case management are conferred on the court together with a system of forms and records to help monitor the process. The court also has power to require the parties to provide a certificate of readiness to ensure that trials proceed on the hearing date.

Under r.3.2(1) the court has a duty to manage cases actively and r.3.2(2)(f) requires the court to discourage delay and avoid unnecessary hearings. Under r.3.8 the court has to give directions to ensure that cases are concluded as soon as possible. This includes the duty to set a timetable and to give directions to expedite progress. The Criminal Procedure Rule Committee has issued a revised case management form for use in preparation for trial in magistrates' courts under r.3.11(1): see *post*, § 7–139.

The rationale behind the principle of case management was identified in *Jisl and*

Tekin, The Times, April 19, 2004, CA, as the problem that resources are limited, so that the proper use of court time requires judicial management and control; whilst the defendant is entitled to a fair trial and the prosecution is equally entitled to a reasonable opportunity to present the evidence against the defendant, it is not a concomitant of the entitlement to a fair trial that either or both sides are further entitled to take as much time as they like, or for that matter, as long as counsel and solicitors or the defendants themselves think appropriate. In *Chaaban* [2003] Crim.L.R. 658, CA, it was explained that one of the most important functions of a judge was management of the trial process; to perform that function the judge had to strike a fair balance between the interests of the defendant, the prosecution, the complainant, every witness, the tribunal of fact, and the community's interest that justice should be done without unnecessary delay. In *Phillips* [2007] 5 *Archbold News* 2, CA, it was said that active hands-on case management, both pre-trial and during trial, is an essential part of a judge's task, and judges should be robust when making case management decisions; parties who are ordered to take steps by the court must take them and it is the duty of case progression officers for both parties to ensure that there is compliance. However, the duty of the judge to manage the trial process and to be robust in doing so must be exercised with courtesy to counsel; discourtesy by a judge may affect confidence in the trial process: *Hare*; *Sullivan, The Times*, December 9, 2004, CA.

In *Penner, The Times*, June 3, 2010, CA, it was said that where it occurs to an advocate that he has failed properly to identify the issues in the case at an early stage, it is his duty to alert the court before continuing and to ask how to proceed; it is no longer possible to attempt to ambush the prosecution with a submission of no case to answer.

B. CONSOLIDATED CRIMINAL PRACTICE DIRECTION

7–7 Section 74 of the *Courts Act* 2003 confers power on the Lord Chief Justice, with the concurrence of the Lord Chancellor, to give directions as to the practice and procedure of the criminal courts. That power may be exercised by a person other than the Lord Chief Justice with the approval of the Lord Chief Justice and the Lord Chancellor: s.74(2). The *Consolidated Criminal Practice Direction* is made in accordance with that power and it sets out directions across a broad range of issues. So far as relevant to this work, Pt I sets out directions of general application; Pt III sets out further directions applying in the Crown Court and magistrates' courts; and Pt V sets out further directions applying in the magistrates' courts. Annexes D and E prescribe a series of forms which supplement the *Criminal Procedure Rules* 2011. Certain of those forms are intended to apply case progression timetables by specifying certain standard directions which apply to a case when a procedural step is taken (particularly when a case is sent, committed or transferred to the Crown Court, or when a case is listed for summary trial).

Relevant extracts of the practice direction are set out at Appendix F.

C. CRIMINAL JUSTICE—SIMPLE, SPEEDY, SUMMARY (CJSSS)

7–8 The "*Criminal Justice - Simple, Speedy, Summary*" (CJSSS) programme has put an onus on the courts to reduce unnecessary hearings and progress cases faster. The programme has no legal basis, but originates in a policy document published by what was then the Department of Constitutional Affairs: "*Delivering Simple, Speedy, Summary Justice*" (DCA 37/06) (July 2006). It was initially piloted in four magistrates' courts (Thames, Camberwell, Coventry and West Cumbria) and was implemented nationally during 2007 and 2008. The programme has now effectively been absorbed within the Criminal Case Management Framework (see *post*), but in practice it is still referred to as "CJSSS".

The purpose of the programme is to ensure that the prosecution is ready so that the first hearing can be effective and proportionate; that the level of information is appropriate and sufficient for the type of charge, expectation of plea and court decisions; and that all appropriate information is given to the defence and the court so that the defence can be ready to ensure that the first hearing is effective.

At the first hearing, the judiciary will ensure that issues are identified and the defendant will be expected to enter a plea. A copy of the full file of the evidence or the initial details will be made available to the court at 9.00am, and the papers will be read by the legal adviser or the district judge. If a guilty plea is entered, sentencing will take place on the same day where possible; and if a not guilty plea is entered, an effective trial date will be fixed within four to six weeks. If the matter has to be adjourned without a plea being taken, the reasons for the adjournment will be noted by the chairman or the district judge.

From first hearing to trial, the programme will ensure that the case management regime is appropriate to the seriousness of the case; that pre-trial reviews will be conducted only exceptionally; that case progression will take place outside the courtroom; that interim hearings will take place only where necessary; and that trials proceed where appropriate on the appointed day in the absence of the defendant where there is a failure to appear. The parties will be assumed to be aware of the requirements imposed on them by the *Criminal Procedure Rules*. Only tailor-made directions to the particular case will be provided in writing. Certificates of trial readiness will not be required; instead the parties will be required to certify if the trial will not be ready to proceed as soon as they become aware of that fact.

Following a pilot scheme at Balham Youth Court, a ministerial commitment was given to extend the CJSSS programme to all youth courts throughout England and Wales by the end of December 2008.

D. Criminal Case Management Framework (CCMF)

The Criminal Case Management Framework (CCMF) is a guide for participants involved in criminal case management to help them to prepare and conduct cases in compliance with the *Criminal Procedure Rules* so that each case is brought to a fair conclusion as quickly as possible. The third edition of the framework incorporates practical improvements arising from the *Criminal Justice Simple Speedy Summary* (CJSSS) programme. Part 1 of the framework (published July 26, 2007) deals with the entire process for adult cases in the magistrates' courts, from pre-charge activity through to conclusion of the case. Part 2 (published on January 18, 2008) covers the process for adult cases in the Crown Court (including appeals from magistrates' courts). The framework does not cover cases involving offenders under the age of 18 years. A separate youth framework is to be issued in due course. **7–9**

It is submitted that it is important when interpreting and applying both CJSSS and the CCMF to have regard to the rule of law and to bear in mind that neither scheme has any force of law but results essentially from an interpretation of the Criminal Procedure Rules proffered by an executive branch of the government (*i.e.* the Office of Criminal Justice Reform).

Relevant extracts of framework are set out at Appendix I.

E. Dealing with Procedural Irregularities

Procedural irregularities may arise as a case progresses through the court in the form of a failure to comply with a rule of procedure. For example, s.17A of the *Magistrates' Courts Act* 1980 requires the accused to be present in court (other than in cases of disorderly behaviour) during the plea before venue procedure. Where a court fails to comply with such a requirement, issues will arise as to whether subsequent steps taken by the court are within its jurisdiction. **7–10**

The answer to this question depends on the consequences of non-compliance, and posing the question whether Parliament can fairly be taken to have intended total invalidity: *Attorney General's Reference (No. 3of 1999)* [2001] 2 A.C. 91, HL. In *Soneji* [2006] 1 A.C. 340, the House of Lords adopted the approach formulated by the *High Court of Australia in Project Blue Sky Inc v. Australian Broadcasting Authority*, 194 C.L.R. 355, namely that the court should ask whether it was a purpose of the legislation that an act done in breach of the provision should be invalid, having regard to the language of the relevant provision and the scope and object of the whole statute. In a subsequent series of joined cases (*Ashton*; *Draz*; *O'Reilly* [2006] 2 Cr.App.R. 15), the Court of Appeal set out the test in *Soneji* but then applied the logic of the overriding objective in the *Criminal Procedure Rules* and concluded that result of *Soneji* was that the prevailing approach to litigation was to avoid determining cases on technicalities (when they did not result in real prejudice and injustice) but instead to ensure that they were decided fairly on their merits.

However, in *Clarke and McDaid* [2008] 1 W.L.R. 338, the House of Lords explained that the decision in *Soneji* was valuable and salutary, but the effect of the sea-change which it wrought had been exaggerated and it did not warrant the jettisoning of all rules affecting procedure irrespective of their effect. The proper approach identified in *Soneji* was for a judge confronted by a procedural irregularity to ask "whether it was the purpose of the legislation that any act done in breach of the provision should be invalid" and the decision to be made was therefore to be expressed rather differently to the explanation given in *Ashton et al.* Lord Bingham explained that, "Technicality is always distasteful when it appears to contradict the merits of a case. But the duty of the court is to apply the law, which is sometimes technical, and it may be thought that if the state exercises its coercive power to put a citizen on trial for serious crime a certain degree of formality is not out of place."

It is submitted that the proper understanding of the rejection of *Ashton et al.* in *Clarke and McDaid* was that too much focus in *Ashton et al.* (particularly in the way the Court of Appeal had purported to apply its own test) had been placed on the question of whether the accused would be prejudiced by proceeding notwithstanding the procedural failure. The proper approach, it is submitted, is simply to apply *Project Blue Sky* by conducting a purposive interpretation of the legislation (which necessarily involves a detailed and difficult examination of the history, origin and purpose of the provision read in the context of the legislation as a whole, rather than a mere construction of the discrete provision). If that examination leads to the conclusion that Parliament intended that the court should have no jurisdiction following the procedural failure, then questions of prejudice to the accused are irrelevant because any further proceedings are invalid; prejudice to the accused only becomes relevant if Parliament intended the court to retain jurisdiction notwithstanding the procedural failure.

III. THE FIRST HEARING

(1) General

7–11 Some cases heard at the magistrates' court are concluded at the first listing but others require more time for preparation and so will be adjourned. Cases are treated differently according to the plea to be tendered.

When a not guilty plea is expected then preliminary steps will be taken at the first court appearance to prepare for trial, including the question of legal representation as one of the first considerations. Pre-trial proceedings consist of considering legal representation, taking a plea and giving directions relating to trial issues and disclosure etc. Where the accused is before the court in relation an offence triable only on indictment or either way, the expectation is that plea before venue, mode of trial and sending or transfer to the Crown Court (where applicable) will take place at the first hearing. In practice an adjournment will be necessary before a case can be committed to the Crown Court for trial.

For guilty pleas the expectation is that the case will be dealt with on first appearance.

(2) Early Administrative Hearings

Crime and Disorder Act 1998, s.50

Early administrative hearings

7–12 **50.**—(1) Where a person ("the accused") has been charged with an offence at a police station, the magistrates' court before whom he appears or is brought for the first time in relation to the charge may, *unless the accused falls to be dealt with under section 51 below,* consist of a single justice.

(2) At a hearing conducted by a single justice under this section the accused shall be asked whether he wishes to be granted a right to representation funded by the Legal Services Commission as part of the Criminal Defence Service.

(2A) Where the accused wishes to be granted such a right, the Legal Services Commission shall decide whether or not to grant him that right.

(3) At such a hearing the single justice—

(a) may exercise, subject to subsection (2) above, such of his powers as a single justice as he thinks fit; and

(b) on adjourning the hearing, may remand the accused in custody or on bail.

(4) This section applies in relation to a justices' clerk as it applies in relation to a single justice; but nothing in subsection (3)(b) above authorises such a clerk to remand the accused in custody or, without the consent of the prosecutor and the accused, to remand the accused on bail on conditions other than those (if any) previously imposed.

(4A) A hearing conducted by a single justice under this section may be—

(a) adjourned to enable the decision mentioned in subsection (2A) above to be taken, and

(b) subsequently resumed by a single justice.

[This section is printed as amended by the *Access to Justice Act* 1999, Sched. 15, and the *Criminal Defence Service (Representation Orders and Consequential Amendments) Regulations* 2006 (S.I. 2006 No. 2493). As from a day to be appointed, the words in italics in subs (1) are to be repealed by the *Criminal Justice Act* 2003, Scheds 3 and 37.]

Police and Criminal Evidence Act 1984, s.47A

Early administrative hearings conducted by justices' clerks

47A. Where a person has been charged with an offence at a police station, any requirement imposed under this Part for the person to appear or be brought before a magistrates' court shall be taken to be satisfied if the person appears or is brought before a justices' clerk in order for the clerk to conduct a hearing under section 50 of the *Crime and Disorder Act* 1998 (early administrative hearings). **7–13**

[This section was inserted by the *Crime and Disorder Act* 1998, Sched. 8. It is printed as amended by the *Courts Act* 2003, Sched. 8.]

Where a defendant is charged at a police station the custody officer may grant him bail to appear at a magistrates' court: *Police and Criminal Evidence Act* 1984, s.47. The police and local court will have in place an arrangement for the listing of such cases and the intention is for them to be dealt with expeditiously and certainly within a matter of days: *Crime and Disorder Act* 1998, s.46. The prosecutor will attend at the police station the day before the cases are due to be heard to review the files and to assess whether there is likely to be a guilty or not guilty plea. If the offence is admitted on the police files, an early first hearing will take place at court in anticipation of a guilty plea. These cases may be prosecuted by an associate prosecutor (AP) from the Crown Prosecution Service and must be heard before a bench of magistrates or a district judge. The AP has limited rights of audience. In all other cases, the matter will be listed as an early administrative hearing. These cases can be dealt with by a magistrate sitting alone or by the justices' clerk or a member of the court staff to whom the justices' clerk has delegated the relevant powers. Usually the delegation will be to legal advisers. The powers of the justices' clerk in early administrative hearings are limited by s.50(4) and (4A). **7–14**

(3) Practical considerations

As to the objectives and expectations of the parties at the first hearing, see Ch. 3 of the Criminal Case Management Framework (Appendix I). **7–15**

IV. CLASSIFICATION OF OFFENCES BY MODE OF TRIAL

(1) Introduction

7–16 The scheme of the *Magistrates' Courts Act* 1980 preserves the classification of offences introduced by the *Criminal Law Act* 1977, namely into offences which are triable: (a) only on indictment; (b) only summarily; and (c) either way. Definitions for these classifications are set out in Sched. 1 to the *Interpretation Act* 1978 (*post*, § 7–18). To some extent these classifications are blurred by the powers of the Crown Court to deal with summary only offences under ss.40 and 41 of the *Criminal Justice Act* 1988 (*post*, §§ 7–97 *et seq*.), and the special procedure under s.22 of the *Magistrates' Courts Act* 1980 (*post*, §§ 7–60 *et seq*) which requires summary trial of certain either way offences where the value involved is small.

Where an adult is brought before a magistrates' court upon an information being laid, this classification will affect where the matter is dealt with both in respect of the appropriate venue for trial and sentencing powers. Different considerations arise in respect of persons appearing before the youth court, as to which see *post*, §§ 25–25 *et seq*).

In general, the classification of an offence will be prescribed by the statute creating it, normally the description of the nature of the penalty on conviction. Thus an offence will be indictable only if the statute prescribes only a penalty on conviction on indictment; an offence will be triable either way if the statute prescribes penalties for both conviction on indictment and on summary conviction; and an offence will be summary only if the statute prescribes on a penalty only on summary conviction. Offences created by the common law are in general triable only on indictment. This is subject, however, to the *Magistrates' Courts Act* 1980, s.17 and Sched. 1, which classifies as triable either way certain statutory offences for which only a penalty on indictment is prescribed on conviction on indictment, and certain common law offences.

(2) Statutory definitions

Interpretation Act 1978, s.5

Definitions

7–17 **5.** In any Act, unless the contrary intention appears, words and expressions listed in Sched. 1 to this Act are to be construed according to that Schedule.

Interpretation Act 1978, Sched. 1 (extract)

Construction of certain expressions relating to offences

7–18 **1.** In relation to England and Wales—

(a) "indictable offence" means an offence which, if committed by an adult, is triable on indictment, whether it is exclusively so triable or triable either way;

(b) "summary offence" means an offence which, if committed by an adult, is triable only summarily;

(c) "offence triable either way" means an offence, other than an offence triable on indictment only by virtue of Part V of the*Criminal Justice Act* 1988 which, if committed by an adult, is triable either on indictment or summarily;

and the terms "indictable", "summary" and "triable either way", in their application to offences, are to be construed accordingly.

In the above definitions references to the way or ways in which an offence is triable are to be construed without regard to the effect, if any, of s.22 of the *Magistrates' Courts Act* 1980 on the mode of trial in a particular case.

(3) Offences specially classified as triable either way

Magistrates Courts Act 1980, s.17

Certain offences triable either way

7–19 **17.**—(1) The offences listed in Schedule 1 to this Act shall be triable either way.

(2) Subsection (1) above is without prejudice to any other enactment by virtue of which any offence is triable either way.

Magistrates Courts Act 1980, Sched. 1

1. Offences at common law of public nuisance. 7–20

1A. An offence at common law of outraging public decency.

3. Offences consisting in contravention of section 13 of the *Statutory Declarations Act* 1835 (administration by a person of an oath etc. touching matters in which he has no jurisdiction).

4. Offences under section 36 of the *Malicious Damage Act* 1861 (obstructing engines or carriages on railways).

5. Offences under the following provisions of the *Offences against the Person Act* 1861—
   (a) section 16 (threats to kill);
   (b) section 20 (inflicting bodily injury, with or without a weapon);
   (c) section 26 (not providing apprentices or servants with food etc.);
   (d) section 27 (abandoning or exposing child);
   (e) section 34 (doing or omitting to do anything so as to endanger railway passengers);
   (f) section 36 (assaulting a clergyman at a place of worship etc);
   (g) section 38 (assault with intent to resist apprehension);
   (h) section 47 (assault occasioning bodily harm);
   (i) section 57 (bigamy);
   (j) section 60 (concealing the birth of a child).

6. Offences under section 20 of the *Telegraph Act* 1868 (disclosing or intercepting messages).

7. Offences under section 13 of the *Debtors Act* 1869 (transactions intended to defraud creditors).

8. Offences under section 5 of the *Public Stores Act* 1875 (obliteration of marks with intent to conceal).

9. Offences under section 12 of the *Corn Returns Act* 1882 (false returns).

11. Offences under section 3 of the *Submarine Telegraph Act* 1885 (damaging submarine cables).

12. Offences under section 13 of the *Stamp Duties Management Act* 1891 (offences in relation to dies and stamps).

13. Offences under section 8(2) of the *Cremation Act* 1902 (making false representations etc. with a view to procuring the burning of any human remains).
   All offences under the *Perjury Act* 1911 except offences under—
   (a) section 1 (perjury in judicial proceedings);
   (b) section 3 (false statements etc. with reference to marriage);
   (c) section 4 (false statements etc. as to births or deaths).

16. Offences under section 17 of the *Deeds of Arrangement Act* 1914 (trustee making preferential payments).

18. Offences under section 8(2) of the *Census Act* 1920 (disclosing census information).

19. Offences under section 36 of the *Criminal Justice Act* 1925 (forgery of passports etc.).

20. Offences under section 11 of the *Agricultural Credits Act* 1928 (frauds by farmers).

26. The following offences under the *Criminal Law Act* 1967—
   (a) offences under section 4(1) (assisting offenders); and
   (b) offences under section 5(1) (concealing arrestable offences and giving false information), where the offence to which they relate is triable either way.

28. All indictable offences under the *Theft Act* 1968 except—
   (a) robbery, aggravated burglary, blackmail and assault with intent to rob;
   (b) burglary comprising the commission of, or an intention to commit, an offence which is triable only on indictment;
   (c) burglary in a dwelling if any person in the dwelling was subjected to violence or the threat of violence.

29. Offences under the following provisions of the *Criminal Damage Act* 1971—
—section 1(1) (destroying or damaging property);
—section 1(1) and (3) (arson);
—section 2 (threats to destroy or damage property);
—section 3 (possessing anything with intent to destroy or damage property).

30. Offences in relation to stamps issued for the purpose of national insurance under the provisions of any enactments as applied to those stamps.

31. Uttering any forged document the forgery of which is an offence listed in this Schedule

33. Aiding, abetting, counselling or procuring the commission of any offence listed in the preceding paragraphs of this Schedule except paragraph 26.

[This schedule is printed as amended by the *Criminal Attempts Act* 1981, s.10, the *Wages Act* 1986, s.32 and Sched. 5, the *Criminal Justice Act* 1988, ss.123 and 170, and Scheds 8 and 16, the *Electricity Act* 1989, s.112 and Scheds 17 and 18, the *Statute Law (Repeals) Act* 1989, s.1 and Sched. 1, the *Housing (Consequential Provisions) Act* 1985, ss.3 and 5 and Scheds 1 and 4, the *Postal Services Act 2000 (Consequential Modifications No. 1) Order* 2001 (S.I. 2001 No. 1149), Sched. 2, the *Criminal Justice Act* 2003, s.320, the *Sexual Offences Act* 2003, Sched. 7, the *Serious Crime Act* 2007, s.92 and Sched. 14, and the *Statute Law (Repeals) Act* 2008, s.1 and Sched. 1.]

V. PLEA BEFORE VENUE AND MODE OF TRIAL (ALLOCATION) PROCEDURE IN RESPECT OF EITHER WAY OFFENCES WHERE ACCUSED AN ADULT

A. INTRODUCTION

7–21 When a person who has attained the age of 18 is charged or summoned to appear at the magistrates' court the details of the charge will be recorded on the charge sheet or the summons. The classification of the offence must then be ascertained so that the defendant can be advised of the correct procedure that applies in his case. Where the offence is triable either way, the court is required to proceed under ss.17A–22 of the *Magistrates' Courts Act* 1980.

7–22 Sections 17A–C provide for the "plea before venue" procedure. A defendant facing an either way offence will be asked by the court at the earliest opportunity if he is prepared to give an indication of his plea. The indication will be that he will plead guilty or not guilty, or he has a right to give no indication of plea. If there is an indication of a guilty plea the court may then proceed as if he had been convicted of the offence and consider sentence. The court may also commit the defendant to the Crown Court for sentence if it is of the opinion that the powers of sentencing in the magistrates' court are not sufficient. If a not guilty plea is indicated or no indication of plea is given then the court must adopt the "mode of trial" procedure to decide where the case shall be tried. Sections 18–23 set out the procedure to be followed. The prosecution is first invited to make representations as to where it considers it is most suitable for the matter to be tried. The defence will then be asked if it has any representations to make as to whether the magistrates' court or Crown Court would be a more suitable venue. Having heard the representations the court will then decide whether the charge is more suitable for summary trial or trial on indictment. In making this decision the court will take into account the powers of sentencing available in the magistrates' court and will consider whether, were there to be a conviction on the charge those powers would be sufficient. In making this decision the court is aided by the *Magistrate's Court Sentencing Guidelines* issued by the Sentencing Council. If the court is of the opinion that on conviction of the offence a greater sentence might have to be imposed than it has power to inflict then the court will decline jurisdiction and direct that the case be dealt with at the Crown Court. The defendant is bound by this decision.

If the court is of the opinion that the case is suitable for summary trial because the powers of the magistrate' court would be sufficient then the defendant is asked whether he would consent to summary trial. If he does not consent to summary trial he will be tried at the Crown Court by judge and jury. He may then consent to summary trial or elect to be tried at the Crown Court by a jury. The right to jury trial cannot be denied to a defendant.

Section 25 allows for a change of election so that a summary trial may be changed into a committal for trial or vice versa.

These provisions apply only to adults aged 18 and over. The mode of trial procedure in the youth court is dealt with in s.24 of the *Magistrates' Courts Act* 1980, see *post*, § 25–25. **7–23**

As from a day to be appointed, the *Criminal Justice Act* 2003, s.41 and Sched. 3, will replace the mode of trial procedure with a new procedure of "allocation" of cases. A decision will still be made as to whether the case is more suitable for summary trial or trial on indictment and "allocation guidelines" will be issued under the Act. Various other amendments are also made, including a power for the court to give an indication of sentence to a defendant before he decides whether to consent to summary trial. The new provisions are reproduced along side existing mode of trial provisions in anticipation of their implementation.

B. PLEA BEFORE VENUE

(1) Intention as to plea in presence of accused

Magistrates' Courts Act 1980, s.17A

Initial procedure: accused to indicate intention as to plea

17A—(1) This section shall have effect where a person who has attained the age of 18 years appears or is brought before a magistrates' court on an information charging him with an offence triable either way. **7–24**

(2) Everything that the court is required to do under the following provisions of this section must be done with the accused present in court.

(3) The court shall cause the charge to be written down, if this has not already been done, and to be read to the accused.

(4) The court shall then explain to the accused in ordinary language that he may indicate whether (if the offence were to proceed to trial) he would plead guilty or not guilty, and that if he indicates that he would plead guilty—

(a) the court must proceed as mentioned in subsection (6) below; and

(b) *he may be committed for sentence to the Crown Court under section 3 of the* Powers of Criminal Courts (Sentencing) Act *2000 if the court is of such opinion as is mentioned in subsection (2) of that section* [he may (unless section 17D(2) below were to apply) be committed for sentence to the Crown Court under section 3 or (if applicable) 3A of the *Powers of Criminal Courts (Sentencing) Act* 2000 if the court is of such opinion as is mentioned in subsection (2) of the applicable section].

(5) The court shall then ask the accused whether (if the offence were to proceed to trial) he would plead guilty or not guilty.

(6) If the accused indicates that he would plead guilty the court shall proceed as if—

(a) the proceedings constituted from the beginning the summary trial of the information; and

(b) section 9(1) above was complied with and he pleaded guilty under it.

(7) If the accused indicates that he would plead not guilty section 18(1) below shall apply.

(8) If the accused in fact fails to indicate how he would plead, for the purposes of this section and section 18(1) below he shall be taken to indicate that he would plead not guilty.

(9) Subject to subsection (6) above, the following shall not for any purpose be taken to constitute the taking of a plea—

(a) asking the accused under this section whether (if the offence were to proceed to trial) he would plead guilty or not guilty;

(b) an indication by the accused under this section of how he would plead.

[(10) If in respect of the offence the court receives a notice under section 51B or 51C of the *Crime and Disorder Act* 1998 (which relate to serious or complex fraud cases and to certain cases involving children respectively), the preceding provisions of this section and the provisions of section 17B below shall not apply, and the court shall proceed in relation to the offence in accordance with section 51 or, as the case may be, section 51A of that Act.]

[This section was inserted by the *Criminal Procedure and Investigations Act* 1996. It is printed as amended by the *Powers of Criminal Courts (Sentencing) Act* 2000, Sched. 9. As from a day or days to be appointed, the words in italics in subs. (4)(b) will be substituted for those set out in square brackets and subs. 10 will be inserted: *Criminal Justice Act* 2003, Sched. 3, as amended by the *Criminal Justice and Immigration Act* 2008, Sched. 13.]

Explaining the procedure to the accused

7–25 Once the either way charge has been written down and read to the accused in accordance with s.17A(3), subs. (4) requires the court to explain the procedure to the accused "in ordinary language". By a circular letter dated September 30, 1997, to Justices' Clerks from the Judicial Studies Board, the following form of words (approved in *Southampton Magistrates' Court, ex p. Sansome* [1999] 1 Cr.App.R.(S.), DC) have been suggested for this purpose—

> "For this charge you may be tried either in the magistrates' court or by a jury in the Crown Court. First however this court must ask you whether, if the case proceeds to trial, you would plead guilty or not guilty. Before you answer that I want to explain what will happen then. If you say that you would plead guilty, the court will hear the prosecution case against you, listen to your mitigation and formally find you guilty. The court will then decide what sentence it thinks you should receive. Do you understand? (*If yes, say*) If the court believes that you deserve greater punishment than this court can give (or if you have to be sent to the Crown Court to be tried on a related charge) it will send you to the Crown Court to be sentenced. Otherwise you will be sentenced here. If you do not indicate a guilty plea the court will decide whether to send you to the Crown Court for trial Do you understand that or do you want anything to be explained further? (*Unless repeated or further explanation is required say*) Then if the charge against you was to go to trial, would you plead guilty or not guilty."

Committal to the Crown Court for sentence following indication of intention to plead guilty

7–26 For detailed commentary the powers of the court to commit to the Crown Court for sentence under the *Powers of Criminal Courts (Sentencing) Act* 2000, ss.3 to 6, see *post*, §§ 23–112 *et seq*.

Where an indication of an intention to plead guilty has been given under s.17A, the court should not commit for sentence on the ground that the offence is one which otherwise would have been deemed suitable for trial on indictment, but should do so only if the statutory criteria in ss.3 to 6 of the 2000 Act are satisfied; in a clear case, the court should be prepared to commit for sentence without hearing mitigation or obtaining a pre-sentence report, but the accused should be given an opportunity to address the court on the matter and the prosecution a right of reply; if the decision as to adequacy of sentencing powers depends on the resolution of a Newton hearing, such hearing should be conducted: *Warley Magistrates' Court, ex p. DPP* [1998] 2 Cr.App.R. 307, DC.

As to the reduction in sentence for guilty plea during the plea before venue procedure, an accused is entitled to a greater discount for an indication of a guilty plea during the plea before venue procedure than if the case was committed to the Crown Court for trial and he pleaded guilty at the first hearing in that court: see Annex 1 to the Sentencing Guidelines Council guideline on reduction in sentence for a guilty plea. See also *Rafferty* [1999] 1 Cr.App.R. 235, CA, and *Barber* [2002] 1 Cr.App.R.(S.) 548, CA. Appropriate allowance for the reduction should be made when deciding whether to commit for sentence; and if the court decides that its own powers of sentence are adequate only by virtue of the discount for the plea, it should say so: *Warley Magistrates' Court, ex p. DPP* (*ibid.*).

As to whether the committal for sentence following a plea of guilty at the plea before venue procedure should be on bail or in custody, it will not be usual to alter the position existing before the plea was entered; unless there are good reasons for remanding the defendant in custody, where the accused was previously on bail, the usual practice should be to continue bail, even if it is anticipated that a custodial sentence will be imposed by the Crown Court: *Raffery* [1999] 1 Cr.App.R. 235, CA.

Procedure for offences triable either way where value involved is small

The special procedure in relation to mode of trial for certain offences where the value involved is small as provided for by the *Magistrates' Courts Act* 1980, s.22 and Sched. 2 (*post* § 7–58, § 7–62), prevails over the plea before venue procedure in s.17A; accordingly, upon on an indication of a guilty plea for a "scheduled offence" to which s.22 applies, if the value of the damage does not exceed the "prescribed sum", the court has no power to commit for sentence under s.3 of the *Powers of Criminal Courts (Sentencing) Act* 2000: *Kelly* [2001] R.T.R. 5, CA. As from a day to be appointed, the *Criminal Justice Act* 2003, Sched. 3, inserts new s.17D in the 1980 Act making express provision in this respect. No such day has been appointed. **7–27**

Adjournment of the plea before venue procedure

As to the specific power to adjourn the plea before venue procedure, see *post*, § 7–31. **7–28**

Provision of initial details (formerly advance information) before plea before venue procedure

Part 21 of the *Criminal Procedure Rules* 2011 (Appendix G) places the prosecution under a duty to disclose to the accused and the court "initial details" of the prosecution case when the accused first appears before the court. The new rules in Pt 21 replace the old "advance information" rules, which required disclosure of information as to the prosecution case only for the purposes of the plea before venue and mode of trial procedures. The new rules do not contain an equivalent to the power in the old rules to adjourn where there has been a failure to disclose the necessary information. For a discussion as to adjournments in the face of non-compliance with the duty to provide initial details generally, and as to whether the principle in *Calderdale Magistrates' Court, ex p. Donahue and Cutler* [2001] Crim.L.R. 141, DC (requirement to adjourn where "document" referred to in summary, *e.g.* CCTV, not disclosed), will continue to apply, see *ante*, §§ 6–13 *et seq.* **7–29**

(2) Intention as to plea when the accused is absent

Magistrates' Courts Act 1980, ss.17B

Intention as to plea: absence of accused

17B.—(1) This section shall have effect where— **7–30**

(a) a person who has attained the age of 18 years appears or is brought before a magistrates' court on an information charging him with an offence triable either way.

(b) the accused is represented by a legal representative,

(c) the court considers that by reason of the accused's disorderly conduct before the court it is not practicable for proceedings under section 17A above to be conducted in his presence, and

(d) the court considers that it should proceed in the absence of the accused.

(2) In such a case—

(a) the court shall cause the charge to be written down, if this has not already been done, and to be read to the representative;

(b) the court shall ask the representative whether (if the offence were to proceed to trial) the accused would plead guilty or not guilty;

(c) if the representative indicates that the accused would plead guilty the court shall proceed as if the proceedings constituted from the beginning the summary trial of the information, and as if section 9(1) above was complied with and the accused pleaded guilty under it;

(d) if the representative indicates that the accused would plead not guilty section 18(1) below shall apply.

(3) If the representative in fact fails to indicate how the accused would plead, for the purposes of this section and section 18(1) below he shall be taken to indicate that the accused would plead not guilty.

(4) Subject to subsection (2)(c) above, the following shall not for any purpose be taken to constitute the taking of a plea—

(a) asking the representative under this section whether (if the offence were to proceed to trial) the accused would plead guilty or not guilty;

(b) an indication by the representative under this section of how the accused would plead.

[This section was inserted by the *Criminal Procedure and Investigations Act* 1996.]

(3) Adjournment of plea before venue procedure

Magistrates' Courts Act 1980, s.17C

Intention as to plea adjournment

7–31 **17C.** A magistrates' court proceeding under section 17A or 17B above may adjourn the proceedings at any time, and on doing so on any occasion when the accused is present may remand the accused, and shall remand him if—

(a) on the occasion on which he first appeared, or was brought, before the court to answer to the information he was in custody or, having been released on bail, surrendered to the custody of the court; or

(b) he has been remanded at any time in the course of proceedings on the information;

and where the court remands the accused, the time fixed for the resumption of proceedings shall be that at which he is required to appear or be brought before the court in pursuance of the remand or would be required to be brought before the court but for section 128(3A) below.

[This section was inserted by the *Criminal Procedure and Investigations Act* 1996.]

7–32 As to adjournments generally, see *post*, §§ 7–154 *et seq*.

(4) Special procedure for offences triable either way where value involved is small (not brought into force)

Magistrates' Courts Act 1980, s.17D

Maximum penalty under section 17A(6) or 17B(2)(c) for certain offences

7–33 **[17D.**—(1) If—

(a) the offence is a scheduled offence (as defined in section 22(1) below);

(b) the court proceeds in relation to the offence in accordance with section 17A(6) or 17B(2)(c) above; and

(c) the court convicts the accused of the offence,

the court shall consider whether, having regard to any representations made by him or by the prosecutor, the value involved (as defined in section 22(10) below) appears to the court to exceed the relevant sum (as specified for the purposes of section 22 below).

(2) If it appears to the court clear that the value involved does not exceed the relevant sum, or it appears to the court for any reason not clear whether the value involved does or does not exceed the relevant sum—

(a) subject to subsection (4) below, the court shall not have power to impose on the accused in respect of the offence a sentence in excess of the limits mentioned in section 33(1)(a) below; and

(b) sections 3 and 4 of the *Powers of Criminal Courts (Sentencing) Act* 2000 shall not apply as regards that offence.

(3) *Subsections (9) to (12) of section 22* below shall apply for the purposes of this section as they apply for the purposes of that section (reading the reference to subsection (1) in section 22(9) as a reference to subsection (1) of this section).

(4) Subsection (2)(a) above does not apply to an offence under section 12A of the *Theft Act* 1968 (aggravated vehicle-taking).]

[As from a day to be appointed, this section is to be inserted by the *Criminal Justice Act* 2003, Sched. 3]

For s.22 of the 1980 Act and associated provisions, see *post*, §§ 7-60 *et seq.* **7-34**

(5) Power of single justice to conduct plea before venue procedure (not brought into force)

Magistrates' Courts Act 1980, s.17E

Functions under sections 17A to 17D capable of exercise by single justice

[17E.—(1) The functions of a magistrates' court under sections 17A to 17D above may be **7-35**
discharged by a single justice.

(2) Subsection (1) above shall not be taken as authorising—

(a) the summary trial of an information (otherwise than in accordance with section 17A(6) or 17B(2)(c) above); or

(b) the imposition of a sentence,

by a magistrates' court composed of fewer than two justices.]

[As from a day to be appointed, this section is to be inserted by the *Criminal Justice Act* 2003, Sched. 3.]

C. MODE OF TRIAL PROCEDURE (ALLOCATION)

(1) Initial procedure

Magistrates' Courts Act 1980, s.18

Initial procedure on information against adult for offence triable either way

18.—(1) Sections 19 to 23 below shall have effect where a person who has attained the age of **7-36**
18 years appears or is brought before a magistrates' court on an information charging him with an offence triable either way and—

(a) he indicates under section 17A above that (if the offence were to proceed to trial) he would plead not guilty, or

(b) his representative indicates under section 17B above that (if the offence were to proceed to trial) he would plead not guilty.

(2) Without prejudice to section 11(1) above, everything that the court is required to do under sections 19 to 22 below must be done before any evidence is called and, subject to subsection (3) below and section 23 below, with the accused present in court.

(3) The court may proceed in the absence of the accused in accordance with such of the provisions of sections 19 to 22 below as are applicable in the circumstances if the court considers that by reason of his disorderly conduct before the court it is not practicable for the proceedings to be conducted in his presence; and subsections (3) to (5) of section 23 below, so far as applicable, shall have effect in relation to proceedings conducted in the absence of the accused by virtue of this subsection (references in those subsections to the person representing the accused being for this purpose read as references to the person, if any, representing him).

(4) A magistrates' court proceeding under sections 19 to 23 below may adjourn the proceedings at any time, and on doing so on any occasion when the accused is present may remand the accused, and shall remand him if—

(a) on the occasion on which he first appeared, or was brought, before the court to answer to the information he was in custody or, having been released on bail, surrendered to the custody of the court; or

(b) he has been remanded at any time in the course of proceedings on the information;

and where the court remands the accused, the time fixed for the resumption of the proceedings shall be that at which he is required to appear or be brought before the court in pursuance of the remand or would be required to be brought before the court but for section 128(3A) below.

(5) The functions of a magistrates' court under subsections 19 to 23 below may be discharged by a single justice, *but the foregoing provision shall not be taken to authorise the summary trial of an information by a magistrates' court composed of less than two justices* [but this subsection shall not be taken as authorising—

(a) the summary trial of an information (otherwise than in accordance with section 20(7) below); or

(b) the imposition of a sentence,

by a magistrates' court comprised of fewer than two justices.]

[This section is printed as amended by the *Criminal Justice Act* 1982, Sched. 9, the *Criminal Justice Act* 1991, Sched. 8, and the *Criminal Procedure and Investigations Act* 1996, s.49. As from a day to be appointed, the words in italics in subs. (5) will be substituted by those set out in square brackets.]

General

7–37 Subject to very limited exceptions (see *post*), the mode of trial procedure in ss.18 to 23 has been described "mandatory" in nature, so that failing to conduct it will render the subsequent proceedings a nullity, even if the accused consented to summary trial: *Tottenham JJ., ex p. Arthurs Transport Services* [1981] Crim.L.R. 180, DC. Whether this will continue to be the case in light of the decision of the House of Lords in *Soneji* [2006] 1 A.C. 340, which removed the distinction between mandatory and directory requirements, has not been considered judicially. As to the effect of *Soneji*, see *ante*, § 7–10 *et seq*.

Age of the accused

7–38 The date on which the accused must have attained the age of 18 for the purposes of s.18(1) is the date on which the court proceeds to determine mode of trial; it is not the occasion when the defendant committed the offence or first appeared before the youth court to answer the information: *Islington North Juvenile Court, ex p. Daley* [1983] 1 A.C. 347, HL. Where the accused has not attained the age of 18 and the youth court has proceeded under s.24 (see *post*, § 25–25) and made a decision as to mode of trial under that section, the fact that the defendant then attains the age of 18 before any trial in the youth court actually takes place does not trigger the procedure under ss.18 to 23: *Nottingham JJ., ex p. Taylor* [1992] 1 Q.B. 557, DC. The taking of a plea from a defendant who is under the age of 18 amounts to a decision as to mode of trial: *West London JJ., ex p. Siley-Winditt* [2000] Crim.L.R. 926, DC.

Accused suffering from mental illness

7–39 In "very rare" cases (and usually with the consent of those acting for the accused), the court may proceed under s.37(3) of the *Mental Health Act* 1983 (power to make hospital order without convicting accused (*post*, § 28–20)) without conducting the mode of trial procedure in ss.18 to 23 of the 1980 Act: see *Lincoln (Kesteven) JJ., ex p. O'Connor* [1983] 1 W.L.R. 335, DC. It should be noted that in that case the court had begun the mode of trial of procedure and had determined that the case was suitable for summary trial, but the accused, by reason of his mental disorder, neither understood his right to elect trial by jury nor was capable of making such a decision.

Relationship with power to transfer case to the Crown Court

A notice of transfer under s.4 of the *Criminal Justice Act* 1987 or s.53 of the *Criminal Justice Act* 1991 may precede the magistrates' court's determination of mode of trial under ss.18 to 23 so as to remove the obligation to conduct that procedure, but it may not reverse it; once the accused has consented to summary trial under s.20, service a notice of transfer will have no effect: *Fareham Youth Court and Morey, ex p. CPS*, 163 J.P. 812, DC. **7–40**

Proceedings conducted by the Attorney-General, Solicitor-General or DPP

Where the prosecution is being carried on by the Attorney-General, Solicitor-General or DPP, the mode of trial procedure does not apply if an application is made by him for the offence to be tried on indictment: see s.19(4) post (not re-enacted in the s.19 substituted as from a day to be appointed by the *Criminal Justice Act* 2003). **7–41**

Proceeding in the absence of the accused

See s.23, *post* § 7–69. **7–42**

(2) Decision as to mode of trial (allocation)

Magistrates' Courts Act 1980, s.19

Court to begin by considering which mode of trial appears more suitable

19.—(1) *The court shall consider whether, having regard to the matters mentioned in subsection (3) below and any representations made by the prosecutor or the accused, the offence appears to the court more suitable for summary trial or for trial on indictment.* **7–43**

(2) *Before so considering, the court—*

(a) *[repealed]*

(b) *shall afford first the prosecutor and then the accused an opportunity to make representations as to which mode of trial would be more suitable.*

(3) *The matters to which the court is to have regard under subsection (1) above are the nature of the case; whether the circumstances make the offence one of serious character; whether the punishment which a magistrates' court would have power to inflict for it would be adequate; and any other circumstances which appear to the court to make it more suitable for the offence to be tried in one way rather than the other.*

(4) *If the prosecution is being carried on by the Attorney General, the Solicitor General or the Director of Public Prosecutions and he applies for the offence to be tried on indictment, the preceding provisions of this section and sections 20 and 21 below shall not apply, and the court shall proceed to inquire into the information as examining justices.*

(5) *The power of the Director of Public Prosecutions under subsection (4) above to apply for an offence to be tried on indictment shall not be exercised except with the consent of the Attorney General.*

Decision as to allocation

[19.—(1) The court shall decide whether the offence appears to it more suitable for summary trial or for trial on indictment.

(2) Before making a decision under this section, the court—

(a) shall give the prosecution an opportunity to inform the court of the accused's previous convictions (if any); and

(b) shall give the prosecution and the accused an opportunity to make representations as to whether summary trial or trial on indictment would be more suitable.

(3) In making a decision under this section, the court shall consider—

(a) whether the sentence which a magistrates' court would have power to impose for the offence would be adequate; and

(b) any representations made by the prosecution or the accused under subsection (2)(b) above, and shall have regard to any allocation guidelines (or revised allocation guidelines) issued as definitive guidelines under section 122 of the *Coroners and Justice Act* 2009.

(4) Where—

(a) the accused is charged with two or more offences; and

(b) it appears to the court that the charges for the offences could be joined in the same indictment or that the offences arise out of the same or connected circumstances,

subsection (3)(a) above shall have effect as if references to the sentence which a magistrates' court would have power to impose for the offence were a reference to the maximum aggregate sentence which a magistrates' court would have power to impose for all of the offences taken together.

(5) In this section any reference to a previous conviction is a reference to—

(a) a previous conviction by a court in the United Kingdom;

(aa) a previous conviction by a court in another member State of a relevant offence under the law of that State; or

(b) *a previous finding of guilt in—*

(i) *any proceedings under the* Army Act *1955, the* Air Force Act *1955 or the* Naval Discipline Act 1957 *(whether before a court-martial or any other court or person authorised under any of those Acts to award a punishment in respect of any offence); or*

(ii) *any proceedings before a Standing Civilian Court*

[(b) a previous conviction of a service offence within the meaning of the *Armed Forces Act* 2006 ("conviction" here including anything that under section 376(1) and (2) of that Act is to be treated as a conviction)].

(5A) For the purposes of subsection (5)(aa) an offence is "relevant" if the offence would constitute an offence under the law of any part of the United Kingdom if it were done in that part at the time when the allocation decision is made.

(6) If, in respect of the offence, the court receives a notice under section 51B or 51C of the *Crime and Disorder Act* 1998 (which relate to serious or complex fraud cases and to certain cases involving children respectively), the preceding provisions of this section and sections 20, 20A and 21 below shall not apply, and the court shall proceed in relation to the offence in accordance with section 51(1) of that Act.]

[The italicised section is printed as amended by the *Prosecution of Offences Act* 1985, Sched. 1, and the *Criminal Procedure and Investigations Act* 1996, s.49. As from a day to be appointed, a new s.19 (set out in square brackets) will be substituted for the original section: *Criminal Justice Act* 2003, Sched. 3 (as amended by the *Coroners and Justice Act* 2009, Scheds 17, 21, 23). As from a further day to be appointed, subs. (5)(b) in the substituted section will be amended by the *Armed Forces Act* 2006, Sched. 16 (the italicised text being replaced by that subsequently set out in square brackets).]

General

7–44 The mode of trial procedure allows for either the court or the defendant to decide that trial at the Crown Court would be most suitable. In the majority of cases the court will hear representations from the prosecution and the defence and then the court will decide on suitability. The court must have regard to the matters mentioned in subs (3). The decision is made on the basis of the facts of the case as outlined by the prosecution and the nature and seriousness of the offence must be made out. The court must consider whether its powers of sentencing would be sufficient in view of the information that it has received from the prosecution. Regard may also be had to other circumstances affecting the suitability of the case to be tried one way or the other. The question of plea or the strength of the evidence is not relevant in defence representations because at this stage the court is only concerned with trying to ensure that serious cases are dealt with by the Crown Court. The gravity of the offence will be assessed not on the basis of evidence but on the assertions made by the prosecution.

National Mode of Trial Guidelines

7–45 The most recent version of the National Mode of Trial Guidelines are incorporated in the *Consolidated Criminal Practice Direction* at V.51 (Appendix F). The guidelines provide guidance not direction and to that end each case should be considered individually and on its own particular facts: see para. V.51.1 and *Derby JJ., ex p. DPP*, *The Times*, August 17, 1999, DC.

To the extent that paras V.51.4 to V.51.18 of the *Consolidated Criminal Practice Direction* (Appendix F) set out specific guidance in relation to particular offences, this has been superseded by the Magistrates' Courts Sentencing Guidelines: see *post*.

For reasons given *post*, it is submitted, however, that the general observations at para. V.51.3 remain relevant. Read in conjunction with the Magistrates' Courts Sentencing Guidelines they are as follows:

—the court should never make its decision on the grounds of convenience or expedition;

—the court should assume for the purpose of deciding mode of trial that the prosecution version of the facts is correct;

—the fact that the offences are alleged to be specimens is a relevant consideration; the fact that the defendant will be asking for other offences to be taken into consideration, if convicted, is not;

—where cases involve complex questions of fact or difficult questions of law, including difficult issues of disclosure of sensitive material, the court should consider committal for trial;

—where two or more defendants are jointly charged with an offence each has an individual right to elect his mode of trial;

—in general, except where otherwise stated, either way offences should be tried summarily unless the court considers that on the application of sentencing guidelines to the particular its sentencing powers are insufficient;

—the court should also consider its power to commit an offender for sentence under ss.3 and 4 of the *Powers of Criminal Courts (Sentencing) Act* 2000, if information emerges during the course of the hearing which leads it to conclude that the offence is so serious, or the offender such a risk to the public, that its powers to sentence him are inadequate. This means that committal for sentence is no longer determined by reference to the character and antecedents of the offender.

Sentencing and allocation guidelines

The Magistrates' Courts Sentencing Guidelines apply to all relevant cases appearing for mode of trial (allocation) or for sentence on or after August 4, 2008. The specific offence guidelines, which are set out throughout this work as relevant to the particular offence, operate as a guide to the level of sentence on conviction after trial and indicate where the case should be committed to the Crown Court. For the avoidance of doubt, although those guidelines were issued by the Sentencing Guidelines Council ("SGC") prior to the abolition of that body and establishment of the new Sentencing Council for England and Wales by the *Coroners and Justice Act* 2009, existing definitive guidelines issued by the SGC have effect as if made by the new Sentencing Council: 2009 Act, Sched. 22, para. 28; and *Coroners and Justice Act 2009 (Commencement No. 4, Transitional and Saving Provisions) Order* 2010 (S.I. 2010 No. 816), art. 7(1). Insofar as the guidelines are expressly said to supersede the National Mode of Trial Guidelines as set out in Pt V.51 of the *Consolidated Criminal Practice Direction* in relation to the offences contained within the guidelines, it is submitted that the general mode of trial considerations set out in paras V.51.2 and V.51.3 (see Appendix F–47) will remain relevant until superseded by definitive allocation guidelines. **7–46**

Although there is no reference to a duty to consider sentencing guidelines when determining mode of trial (allocation) in either version of s.19 (currently in force or to be brought into force), s.125(1)(b) of the *Coroners and Justice Act* 2009 provides that a court must, unless satisfied that it would be contrary to the interests of justice to do so, "follow" any relevant sentencing guideline when exercising any function relating to the sentencing of offenders. *Cf.* the duty under s.172(1)(b) of the *Criminal Justice Act* 2003 to "have regard" to any relevant sentencing guideline. The repeal of s.172 of the 2003 Act has no effect where a court is exercising any function relating to the sentencing of offenders in respect of an offence committed before April 6, 2010: S.I. 2010 No. 816, art. 7(2).

It is not open to a court to disregard a guideline, but a guideline need not always be followed: *Oosthuizen* [2006] 1 Cr.App.R.(S.) 73, CA. Courts are not obliged slavishly to follow them and are entitled to deviate from them when satisfied there is good reason to do so (*Wilson* [2008] 1 Cr.App.R.(S.) 90, CA), particularly where the facts of the case diminish its seriousness in comparison to the norm (*Att.-Gen.'s Reference (No. 8of 2007) (R. v. Krivec)* [2008] 1 Cr.App.R.(S.) 1, CA). Guidelines should not to be used or approached as if each offence can be put into fixed and inflexible compartments; assessing the seriousness of an offence involves a broad judgment of overall criminality: *Herbert, Harris, Hulme (Joseph), Hulme (Danny) and Mallett, The Times*, November 24, 2008, CA. Reasons should be given as to why a guideline has not been followed: *Bowering* [2006] 2 Cr.App. R.(S.) 10, CA. Those authorities were all decided in relation to the duty under s.172 of the 2003 Act and may not apply in the same way to s.125 of the 2009 given the different natures of the duties.

To date, no definitive allocation guidelines have been issued for the purposes of the new s.19(3). Draft allocation guidelines have been issued (reproduced at Appendix H); but see *Doidge, The Times*, March 10, 2005, CA; *Lloyd, The Times*, March 26, 2007, CA; *Abbas* [2009] R.T.R. 3, CA, as authorities for a proposition that it is not appropriate to have regard to draft guidelines unless and until they become definitive.

Accused's previous convictions

7–47 The previous convictions or good character of the accused are irrelevant to the mode of trial decision and the court should neither hear nor take into account any such information: *Colchester JJ., ex p. North East Essex Building Co. Ltd* [1977] 1 W.L.R. 1109, DC; *Hammersmith Juvenile Court, ex p. O.*, 86 Cr. App. R. 343, DC. *Cf.* s.19(2) of the *Magistrates' Courts Act* 1980, as substituted by the *Criminal Justice Act* 2003 on a day to be appointed.

Election by co-accused

7–48 Where more than one accused appear jointly charged with an offence triable either way, the fact that one of them indicates that he will elect trial on indictment does not make summary trial unsuitable in respect of each defendant; each accused has the individual right to elect his mode of trial, irrespective of the election made by his co-accused: *Bentwood JJ., ex p. Nicholls* [1992] 1 A.C. 1, HL; *Bradford Magistrates' Court, ex p. Grant*, 163 J.P. 717, DC; *Ipswich JJ., ex p. Callaghan*, 159 J.P. 748, DC. There is no requirement that co-accused jointly charged should be before the Crown Court together: *West Norfolk JJ., ex p. McMullen*, 157 J.P. 461, DC. Once the court has indicated that the case is suitable for summary trial and one accused elects trial on indictment, the mode of trial decision cannot be changed at the request of the prosecutor for the purposes of ensuring that all accused should be committed to the Crown Court: *Wigan Magistrates' Court, ex p. Layland* [1995] Crim.L.R. 892, DC.

Other relevant circumstances

7–49 The fact that it may be more "convenient and expeditious" to deal with serious offences summarily is not relevant to the decision as to mode of trial and cannot amount to a reason for accepting jurisdiction: *Norfolk JJ., ex p. DPP* [1950] 2 K.B. 558, DC, *Coe*, 53 Cr.App.R. 66, CA.

The complexity and sensitivity of the case may make it desirable for the matter to be dealt with on indictment: see *Horseferry Road Magistrates' Court, ex p. K.* [1997] Q.B. 23, DC (possible defence of insanity), and *Bromley JJ., ex p. Smith and Wilkins; Wells Street Stipendiary Magistrate, ex p. King* [1995] 2 Cr.App.R. 285, DC (contested issues as to the disclosure of sensitive material foreseen); but issues as to non-disclosure of material on the grounds of public interest immunity should not invariably lead to the conclusion that jurisdiction should be declined (*Stipendiary Magistrate for Norfolk, ex p. Taylor*, 161 J.P. 773, DC).

Re-visiting the decision as to mode of trial

The decision as to mode of trial may be revisited once the court has begun to try an information summarily or has begun to inquire into the information as examining justices: s.25 (*post*, § 7–71). Aside from that power, there is no inherent jurisdiction to reconsider mode of trial (*R. (DPP) v. Camberwell Green Youth Court*, 168 J.P. 157, DC) and it is neither open to a second bench to revisit the decision made by a previous bench (*Liverpool JJ. ex p. CPS*, 90 Cr.App.R. 261, DC) nor open to the prosecution to seek to persuade the court to revisit the question for the purposes of ensuring that jointly charged accused are dealt with together where one of them has elected trial on indictment (*Wigan Magistrates' Court, ex p. Layland* [1995] Crim.L.R. 892, DC). *Cf.* the different position in relation to re-election by an accused: *post*, § 7–54. **7–50**

(3) Procedure where summary trial appears more suitable

Magistrates' Courts Act 1980, s.20

Procedure where summary trial appears more suitable

20.—(1) *If, where the court has considered as required by section 19(1) above, it appears to the court that the offence is more suitable for summary trial, the following provisions of this section shall apply (unless excluded by section 23 below).* **7–51**

(2) *The court shall explain to the accused in ordinary language—*

(a) *that it appears to the court more suitable for him to be tried summarily for the offence, and that he can either consent to be so tried or, if he wishes, be tried by a jury; and*

(b) *that if he is tried summarily and is convicted by the court, he may be committed for sentence to the Crown Court under section 3 of the* Powers of Criminal Courts (Sentencing) Act *2000 if the convicting court, is of such opinion as is mentioned in subsection (2) of that section.*

(3) *After explaining to the accused as provided by subsection (2) above the court shall ask him whether he consents to be tried summarily or wishes to be tried by a jury, and—*

(a) *if he consents to be tried summarily, shall proceed to the summary trial of the information;*

(b) *if he does not so consent, shall proceed to inquire into the information as examining justices.*

[Procedure where summary trial appears more suitable

20.—(1) If the court decides under section 19 above that the offence appears to it more suitable for summary trial, the following provisions of this section shall apply (unless they are excluded by section 23 below).

(2) The court shall explain to the accused in ordinary language—

(a) that it appears to the court more suitable for him to be tried summarily for the offence;

(b) that he can either consent to be so tried or, if he wishes, be tried on indictment; and

(c) that if he is tried summarily and is convicted by the court, he may be committed for sentence to the Crown Court under section 3 or (if applicable) section 3A of the *Powers of Criminal Courts (Sentencing) Act* 2000 if the court is of such opinion as is mentioned in subsection (2) of the applicable section.

(3) The accused may then request an indication ("an indication of sentence") of whether

a custodial sentence or non-custodial sentence would be more likely to be imposed if he were to be tried summarily for the offence and to plead guilty.

(4) If the accused requests an indication of sentence, the court may, but need not, give such an indication.

(5) If the accused requests and the court gives an indication of sentence, the court shall ask the accused whether he wishes, on the basis of the indication, to reconsider the indication of plea which was given, or is taken to have been given, under section 17A or 17B above.

(6) If the accused indicates that he wishes to reconsider the indication under section 17A or 17B above, the court shall ask the accused whether (if the offence were to proceed to trial) he would plead guilty or not guilty.

(7) If the accused indicates that he would plead guilty the court shall proceed as if—

(a) the proceedings constituted from that time the summary trial of the information; and

(b) section 9(1) above were complied with and he pleaded guilty under it.

(8) Subsection (9) below applies where—

(a) the court does not give an indication of sentence (whether because the accused does not request one or because the court does not agree to give one);

(b) the accused either—

(i) does not indicate, in accordance with subsection (5) above, that he wishes; or

(ii) indicates, in accordance with subsection (5) above, that he does not wish, to reconsider the indication of plea under section 17A or 17B above; or

(c) the accused does not indicate, in accordance with subsection (6) above, that he would plead guilty.

(9) The court shall ask the accused whether he consents to be tried summarily or wishes to be tried on indictment and—

(a) if he consents to be tried summarily, shall proceed to the summary trial of the information; and

(b) if he does not so consent, shall proceed in relation to the offence in accordance with section 51(1) of the *Crime and Disorder Act* 1998.

Procedure where summary trial appears more suitable: supplementary

20A.—(1) Where the case is dealt with in accordance with section 20(7) above, no court (whether a magistrates' court or not) may impose a custodial sentence for the offence unless such a sentence was indicated in the indication of sentence referred to in section 20 above.

(2) Subsection (1) above is subject to sections 3A(4), 4(8) and 5(3) of the *Powers of Criminal Courts (Sentencing) Act* 2000.

(3) Except as provided in subsection (1) above—

(a) an indication of sentence shall not be binding on any court (whether a magistrates' court or not); and

(b) no sentence may be challenged or be the subject of appeal in any court on the ground that it is not consistent with an indication of sentence.

(4) Subject to section 20(7) above, the following shall not for any purpose be taken to constitute the taking of a plea—

(a) asking the accused under section 20 above whether (if the offence were to proceed to trial) he would plead guilty or not guilty; or

(b) an indication by the accused under that section of how he would plead.

(5) Where the court gives an indication of sentence under section 20 above, it shall cause each such indication to be entered in the register.

(6) In this section and in section 20 above, references to a custodial sentence are to a custodial sentence within the meaning of section 76 of the *Powers of Criminal Courts (Sentencing) Act* 2000, and references to a non-custodial sentence shall be construed accordingly.]

[The text set out in italics is the original text of s.20, printed as amended by the *Criminal Justice Act* 1991, Sched. 11, and the *Powers of Criminal Courts (Sentencing) Act* 2000, Sched. 9. As from a day to be appointed, the *Criminal Justice Act* 2003, Sched. 3 (as amended by the *Criminal Justice and Immigration Act* 2008, Sched. 13), substitutes new ss.20 and 20A (the text set out in square brackets).]

General

Under the present s.20, after considering the representations of the prosecution and defence, the court may decide that the case is suitable for summary trial on the basis that if there were to be a conviction the powers of sentencing in the magistrates' court would be sufficient. The defendant must then be asked if he consents to summary trial. He is not bound to do so and there is a right to jury trial. The legal adviser will put the election to the defendant and will explain the procedure and his rights. **7–52**

Part I

Explaining the procedure to the accused

Once the court has determined that the offence is more suitable for summary trial and the accused is present in court, s.20(2) requires the court to explain in "ordinary language" that he may either consent to summary trial or elect trial by jury but that if he consents to summary trial the court may nevertheless commit him to the Crown Court for sentence if he is convicted. By a circular letter dated September 30, 1997, to Justices' Clerks from the Judicial Studies Board, the following form of words (approved in *Southampton Magistrates' Court, ex p. Sansome* [1999] 1 Cr.App.R.(S.), DC) have been suggested for this purpose— **7–53**

> "It appears to this court more suitable for you to be tried here. You may now consent to be tried by this court, but if you wish, you may choose to be tried by a jury instead. If you are tried by this court and are found guilty, this court may still send you to the Crown Court for sentence if it is of the opinion that greater punishment should be inflicted for the offence than it has power to impose. Do you wish to be tried by this court or do you wish to be tried by a jury?"

Discretion to permit accused to re-elect mode of trial

Although the procedure in s.20 envisages that the court shall proceed to summary trial or committal proceedings (sending to the Crown Court once committal proceedings are abolished) as the case may be after the accused has been asked whether he consents to be tried summarily or wishes to be tried on indictment, the court nevertheless has a discretion to permit re-election by the accused depending on the broad justice of the situation: *Craske, ex p. Metropolitan Police Commissioner* [1957] 2 Q.B. 591, DC; *Southampton City Justices, ex p. Briggs* [1972] 1 W.L.R. 277, DC; *Birmingham JJ., ex p. Hodgson*, 81 Cr.App.R 231, DC. This is separate and distinct from the power to switch from summary trial to committal proceedings and vice versa under s.22, which is concerned only with reconsideration of mode of trial. The discretion, it is submitted, is equivalent to permitting an accused to change his plea from guilty to not guilty. **7–54**

Relevant to a proper exercise of the discretion will be questions concerning whether (a) the accused's rights as to the modes of trial open to him had been fully explained to him, (b) he had understood them, (c) he had voluntarily consented to be tried summarily, and (d) there were unusual, difficult or grave features in the facts of the case which made it one of a serious character: *Lambeth Metropolitan Stipendiary Magistrate, ex p. Wright* [1974] Crim.L.R. 444, DC. The central factor to which attention should be paid should be the state of mind of the accused at the time he made his election, *viz.* whether he properly understood the nature and significance of the choice which was put to him; if it is demonstrated that he did not understand the nature and significance of his choice, then it is as if he had never made it: *Birmingham JJ., ex p. Hodgson*, 81 Cr.App.R. 231, DC. The other vital factor is that an accused is not lightly to be deprived of a right to trial by jury; the fact that the court faced with the application may take the view that the case is more suitable for summary trial or that it was capable of dealing with the particular difficulties in the case, are not factors which should tell against the application: *ibid* and *Highbury Corner Metropolitan Stipendiary Magistrate, ex p. Weekes* [1985] Q.B. 1147, DC.

The fact that the accused was not represented at the time of the election will not of itself require the court to permit re-election: *Lambeth Metropolitan Stipendiary Mag-* **7–55** *istrate, ex p. Wright* [1974] Crim.L.R. 444, DC. Further, provided that the court is satisfied that the accused's choice was an informed one, the fact the accused has become dissatisfied with the advice given to him by his former solicitors is not a relevant consideration: *Bourne JJ., ex p. Cope*, 153 J.P. 161, DC.

Where the accused has been permitted to vacate a plea of guilty given during the plea before venue procedure and then enters a plea of not guilty, he must be given the right to consider whether he wishes to elect trial by jury (*Bow Street Magistrates' Court, ex p. Welcome*, 156 J.P. 609, DC); but where an accused's plea is vacated and he consents to summary trial but then seeks re-election, the court will be entitled in the exercise of the discretion to permit re-election to have regard to the fact that allowing every litigant to vacillate from one view to another indefinitely would disrupt the procedures of the courts and delay the trial of other persons: *West Bromwich JJ., ex p. Pearson* [1981] Crim.L.R. 709, DC.

Given the pressure on the Crown Court and the desirability that all proper cases should be tried summarily, there may be very many cases in which an accused, particularly if unrepresented, had elected to be tried on indictment but thereafter, on a proper consideration of the prosecution evidence, it would be right for his advisers to ask the court to allow him to change his election and to proceed with the case summarily: *Warrington JJ., ex p. McDonagh* [1981] Crim.L.R. 629, DC (although upholding on the facts a decision not to permit the accused to consent to summary trial where he had had engaged in "something very close to sharp practice" by electing trial on indictment to obtain a committal bundle and then having done so sought to re-elect to be tried summarily).

Upon an application for re-election being made, the court should hear evidence from the defendant and, if differently constituted to that before which the original election was made, from the court clerk who was then present: *Forest Magistrates' Court, ex p. Spicer*, 153 J.P. 81, DC.

Election by co-accused

7–56 Where more than one accused appear jointly charged with an offence triable either way and one of them elects trial on indictment, the court has no power to commit to the Crown Court for trial any other accused who has consented to summary trial: *Bentwood JJ., ex p. Nicholls* [1992] 1 A.C. 1, HL; *Ipswich JJ., ex p. Callaghan*, 159 J.P. 748, DC; *Bradford Magistrates' Court, ex p. Grant*, 159 J.P. 717, DC. There is no requirement that co-accused jointly charged should be before the Crown Court together: *West Norfolk JJ., ex p. McMullen*, 157 J.P. 461, DC. Where there have been different elections by co-accused, the prosecution cannot invite the court to reconsider mode of trial with a view to ensuring that all accused are committed to the Crown Court for trial: *Wigan Magistrates' Court, ex p. Layland* [1995] Crim.L.R. 892, DC.

Preferment of further charges following election to adjust mode of trial

7–57 Once mode of trial has been determined (and if available to him the accused has made his election), the prosecution may thereafter seek to dictate the mode of trial by discontinuing the offence in respect of which the decision was made and then laying a new information alleging a summary only or indictable only offence (as the case may be). Such applications by prosecutors are not of themselves an abuse of process or otherwise impermissible, it being a matter of prosecutorial discretion as to which charges are preferred; but they must be subjected to particular scrutiny to ensure (a) that the course proposed is "proper and appropriate" in light of the facts disclosed about the alleged offence, and (b) that there is no bad faith on the part of the prosecutor or unfairness to the accused: see *Canterbury and St Augustine JJ., ex p. Klisiak* [1982] Q.B. 398, DC; *Redbridge JJ. and Fox, ex p. Whitehouse*, 94 Cr.App.R. 332, DC; *Liverpool Stipendiary Magistrate, ex p. Ellison* [1990] R.T.R 220, DC; *Sheffield JJ., ex p. DPP*

[1993] Crim.L.R. 136, DC; *Barking JJ., ex p. DPP* [1993] C.O.D. 108, DC. Regard should also be had to the wider picture, including the promptness of the application and considerations of the good administration of justice; prosecutors should not therefore assume that the substitution can be made at any stage of the proceedings virtually as of right: see *DPP v. Hammerton* [2010] Q.B. 79, QBD (Davis J.) (justices had exercised their discretion properly by refusing to allow an application to substitute a summary only offence made on day listed for committal for trial in circumstances where no committal bundle had been prepared and the prosecution had already proceeded to trial against co-defendants in the youth court on the more serious charge). The law is to some extent unclear as to what amounts to bad faith on the part of the prosecutor so as to make the substitution impermissible: compare *ex p. Whitehouse* (prosecutor should not be allowed improperly to frustrate the earlier decision as to mode of trial) with *ex p. Ellison* (prosecutor's motive for substitution of charges is irrelevant even if it was precisely to deprive the accused of his right to jury trial)). It is clear, however, that there will be no prejudice to the accused simply because he has been deprived his right to trial by jury or to consent to summary trial: see *ex p. Klisiak*.

In so far as the court has no means of control over the process by which proceedings for new offences are commenced where the accused is charged at the police station or there is a written charge by the prosecutor, it is submitted that the court's powers to stay an information as an abuse of process will be exercisable, to which end the principles derived from the authorities, *ante*, will be relevant. As to the magistrates court's abuse of process powers in respect of an indictable only offence which would otherwise be sent forthwith to the Crown Court under s.51 of the *Crime and Disorder Act* 1998, see *R. (Salubi) v. Bow Street Magistrates' Court* [2002] 2 Cr.App.R. 40, DC (*post*, § 7–84).

(4) Procedure where trial on indictment appears more suitable

Magistrates' Courts Act 1980, s.21

Procedure where trial on indictment appears more suitable

21. *If, where the court has considered as required by section 19(1) above, it appears to the court that the offence is more suitable for trial on indictment, the court shall tell the accused that the court has decided that it is more suitable for him to be tried for the offence by a jury, and shall proceed to inquire into the information as examining justices.* **7–58**

[Procedure where trial on indictment appears more suitable

21. If the court decides under section 19 above that the offence appears to it more suitable for trial on indictment, the court shall tell the accused that the court has decided that it is more suitable for him to be tried on indictment, and shall proceed in relation to the offence in accordance with section 51(1) of the *Crime and Disorder Act* 1998.]

[The text set out in italics is the original text of s.21. As from a day to be appointed, the *Criminal Justice Act* 2003, Sched. 3, will substitute a new section (the text set out in square brackets).]

Once the court has declined jurisdiction the defendant has no right to be put to his election. The decision of the court overrides any wish he may have to consent to summary trial and committal to the Crown Court will take place. In some cases, a defendant will indicate a guilty plea to a serious charge which, had it been contested would have been considered more suitable to be tried at the Crown Court at the mode of trial stage. On an early guilty plea the court may not decline jurisdiction but the court may still send the defendant to the Crown Court for sentence if the magistrates' courts powers of sentencing are not sufficient. The defendant meanwhile will benefit at the Crown Court from a greater reduction in his sentence to give credit for his pleading guilty at the earliest opportunity. **7–59**

If an earlier court has declined summary jurisdiction a later court cannot hear representations and agree to summary trial: *Liverpool Justices, ex p. CPS*, 90 Cr.App.R. 261, DC.

(5) Special procedure for offences triable either way where value involved is small

Magistrates' Courts Act 1980, s.22 and 33

Certain offences triable either way to be tried summarily if value involved is small

7–60 **22.**—(1) If the offence charged by the information is one of those mentioned in the first column of Schedule 2 to this Act (in this section referred to as "scheduled offences") then, the court shall, before proceeding in accordance with section 19 above, consider whether, having regard to any representations made by the prosecutor or the accused, the value involved (as defined in subsection (10) below) appears to the court to exceed the relevant sum.

For the purposes of this section the relevant sum is £5,000.

(2) If, where subsection (1) above applies, it appears to the court clear that, for the offence charged, the value involved does not exceed the relevant sum, the court shall proceed as if the offence were triable only summarily, and sections 19 to 21 above shall not apply.

(3) If, where subsection (1) above applies, it appears to the court clear that, for the offence charged, the value involved exceeds the relevant sum, the court shall thereupon proceed in accordance with section 19 above in the ordinary way without further regard to the provisions of this section.

(4) If, where subsection (1) above applies, it appears to the court for any reason not clear whether, for the offence charged, the value involved does or does not exceed the relevant sum, the provisions of subsections (5) and (6) below shall apply.

(5) The court shall cause the charge to be written down, if this has not already been done, and read to the accused, and shall explain to him in ordinary language—

(a) that he can, if he wishes, consent to be tried summarily for the offence and that if he consents to be so tried, he will definitely be tried in that way; and

(b) that if he is tried summarily and is convicted by the court, his liability to imprisonment or a fine will be limited as provided in section 33 below.

(6) After explaining to the accused as provided by subsection (5) above the court shall ask him whether he consents to be tried summarily and—

(a) if he so consents, shall proceed in accordance with subsection (2) above as if that subsection applied;

(b) if he does not so consent, shall proceed in accordance with subsection (3) above as if that subsection applied.

(7) [*repealed*]

(8) Where a person is convicted by a magistrates' court of a scheduled offence, it shall not be open to him to appeal to the Crown Court against the conviction on the ground that the convicting court's decision as to the value involved was mistaken.

(9) If, where subsection (1) above applies, the offence charged is one with which the accused is charged jointly with a person who has not attained the age of 18, the reference in that subsection to any representations made by the accused shall be read as including any representations made by the person under 18.

(10) In this section "the value involved", in relation to any scheduled offence, means the value indicated in the second column of Schedule 2 to this Act, measured as indicated in the third column of that Schedule; and in that Schedule "the material time" means the time of the alleged offence.

(11) Where—

(a) the accused is charged on the same occasion with two or more scheduled offences and it appears to the court that they constitute or form part of a series of two or more offences of the same or a similar character; or

(b) the offence charged consists in incitement to commit two or more scheduled offences,

this section shall have effect as if any reference in it to the value involved were a reference to the aggregate of the values involved.

(12) Subsection (8) of section 12A of the *Theft Act* 1968 (which determines when a vehicle is recovered) shall apply for the purposes of paragraph 3 of Schedule 2 to this Act as it applies for the purposes of that section.

[This section is printed as amended by the *Criminal Justice Act* 1988, s.38 and Sched. 16, the *Criminal Justice Act* 1991, Sched. 8, the *Aggravated Vehicle-Taking*

Act 1992, s.2, and the *Criminal Justice and Public Order Act* 1994, s.46 and Sched. 11. In subs (11)(b), the reference to incitement has effect as a reference to conduct amounting to the offences in relation to encouraging or assisting crime in Pt 7 of the *Serious Crime Act* 2007: see s.63(1) and Sched. 6 to the 2007 Act.]

Maximum penalties on summary conviction in pursuance of section 22

33.—(1) Where in pursuance of subsection (2) of section 22 above a magistrates' court proceeds to the summary trial of an information, then, if the accused is summarily convicted of the offence **7–61**

(a) subject to subsection (3) below the court shall not have power to impose on him in respect of that offence imprisonment for more than *3 months* [51 weeks] or a fine greater than level 4 on the standard scale; and

(b) section 3 of the *Powers of Criminal Courts (Sentencing) Act* 2000 (committal to Crown Court for sentence) shall not apply as regards that offence.

(2) In subsection (1) above "fine" includes a pecuniary penalty but does not include pecuniary forfeiture or pecuniary compensation.

(3) Paragraph (a) of subsection (1) above does not apply to an offence under section 12A of the *Theft Act* 1968 (aggravated vehicle-taking).

[This section is printed as amended by the *Aggravated Vehicle-Taking Act* 1992, s.2, the *Criminal Justice Act* 1991, s.17 and Sched. 4, and the *Powers of Criminal Courts (Sentencing) Act* 2000, s.165 and Sched. 9. As from a day or days to be appointed, the words in italics are to be repealed and the words in square brackets inserted: *Criminal Justice Act* 2003, s.304 and Sched 32. The prospective amendments (never brought into force) made by s.41 and Sched. 3 to the 2003 Act were repealed by the *Criminal Justice and Immigration Act* 2008, ss.53 and 149, and Scheds 13 and 28.]

Magistrates' Courts Act 1980, Sched. 2

Section 22 SCHEDULE 2

OFFENCES FOR WHICH THE VALUE INVOLVED IS RELEVANT TO THE MODE OF TRIAL

7–62

Offence	*Value involved*	*How measured*
1. Offences under section 1 of the *Criminal Damage Act* 1971 (destroying or damaging property), excluding any offence committed by destroying or damaging property by fire	As regards property alleged to have been destroyed, its value.	What the property would probably have cost to buy in the open market at the material time.
	As regards property alleged to have been damaged, the value of the alleged damage.	(a) If immediately after the material time the damage was capable of repair— (i) what would probably then have been the market price for the repair of the damage, or (ii) what the property alleged to have been damaged would probably have cost to buy in the open market at the material time, whichever is the less; or (b) if immediately after the material time the damage was beyond repair, what the said property would probably have cost to buy in the open market at the material time.

Offence	*Value involved*	*How measured*
2. The following offences, namely— (a) aiding, abetting, counselling or procuring the commission of any offence mentioned in paragraph 1 above; (b) attempting to commit any offence so mentioned; and (c) inciting another to commit any offence so mentioned.	The value indicated in paragraph 1 above for the offence alleged to have been aided, abetted, counselled or procured, or attempted or incited.	As for the corresponding entry in paragraph 1 above.
3. Offences under section 12A of the *Theft Act* 1968 (aggravated vehicle-taking) where no allegation is made under subsection (1)(b) other than of damage, whether to the vehicle or other property or both.	The total value of the damage alleged to have been caused.	(1) In the case of damage to any property other than the vehicle involved in the offence, as for the corresponding entry in paragraph 1 above, substituting a reference to the time of the accident concerned for any reference to the material time. (2) In the case of damage to the vehicle involved in the offence— (a) if immediately after the vehicle was recovered the damage was capable of repair— (i) what would probably then have been the market price for the repair of the damage, or (ii) what the vehicle would probably have cost to buy in the open market immediately before it was unlawfully taken, whichever is the less; or (b) if immediately after the vehicle was recovered the damage was beyond repair, what the vehicle would probably have cost to buy in the open market immediately before it was unlawfully taken.

[This schedule is printed as amended by the *Aggravated Vehicle-Taking Act* 1992, s.2. In para. 2, the reference to incitement has effect as a reference to conduct amounting to the offences in relation to encouraging or assisting crime in Pt 7 of the *Serious Crime Act* 2007: see s.63(1) and Sched. 6 of the 2007 Act.]

General

The provisions in s.22 have been described as "mandatory" in nature: *Braden*, 87 Cr.App.R 289, CA. 7–63

In so far as Sched. 2 refers to criminal damage under s.1 of the *Criminal Damage Act* 1971 (excluding any offence committed by destroying or damaging property by fire), this is to be treated as applying only the offence contrary to subs. (1) and does not apply to offences under subs. (2) and (3) of criminal damage with intent to endanger life, etc., or arson: *Burt*, 161 J.P. 77, CA.

The provisions in s.22 do not apply to conspiracy to commit criminal damage, which is an indictable only offence contrary to s.1(1) of the *Criminal Law Act* 1977 and is neither contrary to s.1 of the *Criminal Damage Act* 1971 nor expressly referred to in para. 2 of Sched. 2: *Ward and others* [1997] 1 Cr.App.R.(S.) 442, CA.

Notwithstanding that the effect of s.22 is procedurally to make the offences to which it applies triable only summarily, those offences retain their classification as offences triable either way: *Considine*, 70 Cr.App.R. 239, CA; *Fennell* [2000] 1 W.L.R. 2011, CA; *Alden* [2002] 2 Cr.App.R.(S.) 326, CA.

The procedure provided by s.22 prevails over the plea before venue procedure 7–64
provided for by s.17A; accordingly, upon on an indication of a guilty plea for a "scheduled offence" to which s.22 applies, if the value of the damage does not exceed the "prescribed sum", the court has no power to commit for sentence under s.3 of the *Powers of Criminal Courts (Sentencing) Act* 2000: *Kelly* [2001] R.T.R. 5, CA.

Determining the "value involved"

The "value involved" is to be calculated by reference to the open market replacement 7–65
cost where the property has been damaged beyond repair and does not extend to include consequential loss; where, therefore, the actual value of damage done to a GM maize crop was £750 but consequential loss to research was over £5,000, the value involved did not exceed the prescribed sum and the court should proceed as if the offence was triable summarily: *Colchester Magistrates' Court, ex p. Abbott*, 165 J.P. 386, DC. *Cf. R. (DPP) v. Prestatyn Magistrates' Court* [2002] Crim.L.R. 924, DC, where there was damage to an experimental crop of GM maize with significant investment costs and which had not been marketed; in those circumstances, where the value was unclear, the court was entitled to take the view that the charge remained triable either way.

It is unnecessary for the court to hear evidence as to the value of the property in 7–66
question unless it wished to do so; "representations" (as referred to in subs. (1)) as to value may consist of submissions, assertions of fact and the production of documents: *Canterbury and St Augustine JJ., ex p. Klisiak* [1982] Q.B. 398, DC.

As to the approach to be adopted where the damage is caused by a number of individuals collectively, it was said *obiter* in *Brentwood JJ, ex p. Nicholls* [1992] 1 A.C. 1, HL, that the procedure in subs. (4) to (6) refers to accused persons individually and not to accused persons collectively. See also *Salisbury Magistrates' Court, ex p. Mastin*, 84 Cr.App.R. 248, DC.

Series of offences of same or similar character

If the offences are committed in different places and involve different types of prop- 7–67
erty they may be too remote to form part of a series of offences of the same or similar character within the meaning of s.22(11): see *Braden*, 152 J.P. 92, CA (damage to vehicle and then to a police cell an hour later were too remote). See also *Hatfield JJ., ex p Castle* [1981] 1 W.L.R. 217, DC.

Miscellaneous

The special procedure in s.22 may be conducted by a court comprised of a single 7–68 justice of the peace: see s.18(5) (*ante*, § 7–36). As to the powers to proceed under s.22 in the absence of the accused or to issue a summons or warrant to secure his attendance, see ss.23 and 26.

(6) Power to proceed in the absence of the accused or issue summons or warrant to secure his attendance

Magistrates' Courts Act 1980, ss.23 and 26

Power of court, with consent of legally represented accused, to proceed in his absence

7–69 **23.**—(1) Where—

(a) the accused is represented by a legal representative who in his absence signifies to the court the accused's consent to the proceedings for determining how he is to be tried for the offence being conducted in his absence; and

(b) the court is satisfied that there is good reason for proceeding in the absence of the accused,

the following provisions of this section shall apply.

(2) Subject to the following provisions of this section, the court may proceed in the absence of the accused in accordance with such of the provisions of sections 19 to 22 above as are applicable in the circumstances.

(3) If, in a case where subsection (1) of section 22 above applies, it appears to the court as mentioned in subsection (4) of that section, subsections (5) and (6) of that section shall not apply and the court—

(a) if the accused's consent to be tried summarily has been or is signified by the person representing him, shall proceed in accordance with subsection (2) of that section as if that subsection applied; or

(b) if that consent has not been and is not so signified, shall proceed in accordance with subsection (3) of that section as if that subsection applied.

(4) *If, where the court has considered as required by section 19(1) above, it appears to the court that the offence is more suitable for summary trial then* [If the court decides under section 19 above that the offence appears to it more suitable for summary trial then]—

(a) if the accused's consent to be tried summarily has been or is signified by the person representing him, section 20 above shall not apply, and the court shall proceed to the summary trial of the information; or

(b) if that consent has not been and is not so signified, section 20 above shall not apply and the court shall proceed *to inquire into the information as examining justices and may adjourn the hearing without remanding the accused* [in relation to the offence in accordance with section 51(1) of the *Crime and Disorder Act* 1998].

(5) *If, where the court has considered as required by section 19(1) above, it appears to the court that the offence is more suitable for trial on indictment, section 21 above shall not apply, and the court shall proceed to inquire into the information as examining justices and may adjourn the hearing without remanding the accused.*

[(5) If the court decides under section 19 above that the offence appears to it more suitable for trial on indictment, section 21 above shall not apply and the court shall proceed in relation to the offence in accordance with section 51(1) of the *Crime and Disorder Act* 1998.]

[This section is printed as amended by the *Courts and Legal Services Act* 1990, Sched. 18. As from a day or days to be appointed, the words in italics will be substituted by those set out in square brackets: *Criminal Justice Act* 2003, Sched. 3 (as amended by the *Criminal Justice and Immigration Act* 2008, Sched. 13]).

Power to issue summons to accused in certain circumstances

7–70 **26.**—(1) *Where—*

(a) *in the circumstances mentioned in section 23(1)(a) above the court is not satisfied that there is good reason for proceeding in the absence of the accused; or*

(b) *subsection 4(b) or (5) of section 23 or subsection (2) or (6) of section 25 above applies, and the court adjourns the hearing in pursuance of that subsection without remanding the accused, the justice or any of the justices of which the court is composed may issue a summons directed to the accused requiring his presence before the court.*

(2) *If the accused is not present at the time and place appointed—*

(a) *in a case within subsection (1)(a) above, for the proceedings under section 19(1) or 22(1) above, as the case may be; or*

(b) *in a case within subsection (1)(b) above, for the resumption of the hearing, the court may issue a warrant for his arrest.*

[Power to issue summons to accused in certain circumstances

26.—(1) Where, in the circumstances mentioned in section 23(1)(a) above, the court is not satisfied that there is good reason for proceeding in the absence of the accused, the justice or any of the justices of which the court is composed may issue a summons directed to the accused requiring his presence before the court.

(2) In a case within subsection (1) above, if the accused is not present at the time and place appointed for the proceedings under section 19 or section 22(1) above, the court may issue a warrant for his arrest.]

[The text set in italics is the original text of s.26. As from a day to be appointed, the *Criminal Justice Act* 2003, s.41 and Sched. 3, will substitute a new section (the text set out in square brackets).]

(7) Power to reconsider mode of trial (allocation)

Magistrates' Courts Act 1980, s.25

Power to change from summary trial to committal proceedings, and vice versa

25.—(1) Subsections (2) to (4) [(2D)] below shall have effect where a person who has attained the age of 18 years appears or is brought before a magistrates' court on an information charging him with an offence triable either way. **7–71**

(2) *Where the court has (otherwise than in pursuance of section 22(2) above) begun to try the information summarily, the court may, at any time before the conclusion of the evidence for the prosecution, discontinue the summary trial and proceed to inquire into the information as examining justices and, on doing so, shall adjourn the hearing.*

[(2) Where the court is required under section 20(9) above to proceed to the summary trial of the information, the prosecution may apply to the court for the offence to be tried on indictment instead.

(2A) An application under subsection (2) above—

(a) must be made before the summary trial begins; and

(b) must be dealt with by the court before any other application or issue in relation to the summary trial is dealt with.

(2B) The court may grant an application under subsection (2) above but only if it is satisfied that the sentence which a magistrates' court would have power to impose for the offence would be inadequate.

(2C) Where—

(a) the accused is charged on the same occasion with two or more offences; and

(b) it appears to the court that they constitute or form part of a series of two or more offences of the same or a similar character,

subsection (2B) above shall have effect as if references to the sentence which a magistrates' court would have power to impose for the offence were a reference to the maximum aggregate sentence which a magistrates' court would have power to impose for all of the offences taken together.

(2D) Where the court grants an application under subsection (2) above, it shall proceed in relation to the offence in accordance with section 51(1) of the *Crime and Disorder Act* 1998.]

(3) *Where the court has begun to inquire into the information as examining justices, then, if at any time during the inquiry it appears to the court, having regard to any representations made in the presence of the accused by the prosecutor, or made by the accused, and to the nature of the case, that the offence is after all more suitable for summary trial, the court may, after doing as provided in subsection (4) below, ask the accused whether he consents to be tried summarily and, if he so consents, may subject to subsection (3A) below proceed to try the information summarily;*

(3A) *Where the prosecution is being carried on by the Attorney General or the Solicitor General, the court shall not exercise the power conferred by subsection (3) above without his consent and, where the prosecution is being carried on by the Director of Public Prosecutions, shall not exercise that power if the Attorney General directs that it should not be exercised.*

(4) *Before asking the accused under subsection (3) above whether he consents to be tried summarily, the court shall in ordinary language—*

(a) *explain to him that it appears to the court more suitable for him to be tried summarily for the offence, but that this can only be done if he consents to be so tried; and*

(b) *unless it has already done so, explain to him, as provided in section 20(2)(b) above, about the court's power to commit to the Crown Court for sentence.*

(5) *Where a person under the age of 18 years appears or is brought before a magistrates' court on an information charging him with an indictable offence other than homicide, and the court—*

(a) *has begun to try the information summarily on the footing that the case does not fall within paragraph (a) or (b) of section 24(1) above and must therefore be tried summarily, as required by the said section 24(1); or*

(b) *has begun to inquire into the case as examining justices on the footing that the case does so fall,*

subsection (6) or (7) below, as the case may be, shall have effect.

(6) *If, in a case falling within subsection (5)(a) above, it appears to the court at any time before the conclusion of the evidence for the prosecution that the case is after all one which under the said section 24(1) ought not to be tried summarily, the court may discontinue the summary trial and proceed to inquire into the information as examining justices and, on doing so, shall adjourn the hearing.*

(7) *If, in a case falling within subsection (5)(b) above, it appears to the court at any time during the inquiry that the case is after all one which under the said section 24(1) ought to be tried summarily, the court may proceed to try the information summarily.*

(8) *If the court adjourns the hearing under subsection (2) or (6) above it may (if it thinks fit) do so without remanding the accused.*

[This section is printed as amended by the *Prosecution of Offences Act* 1985, Scheds 1 and 2, the *Criminal Justice Act* 1991, Sched. 8, the *Criminal Procedure and Investigations Act* 1996, Sched. 1, and the *Criminal Justice Act* 2003, s.42. As from a day or days to be appointed, the *Criminal Justice Act* 2003, Sched. 3, will substitute for the italicised text, the text in square brackets.]

General

7–72 After the court has begun a summary trial or a committal, s.25 confers a discretion on the court to change the procedure and switch from hearing a summary trial to inquiring into the offence as examining justices or to discontinue a committal and (with the accused's consent) proceed to hear a summary trial of the charge. The decision will be made subject to the evidence that has been called, representations made and the nature of the case. These factors may mean that a less serious case becomes more serious or a case first believed to be serious enough to warrant committal is shown to be less serious. The intention is that the court should keep the mode of trial under continuous review.

Aside from the power in s.25, there is no inherent jurisdiction to reconsider mode of trial: *Liverpool JJ., ex p. CPS*, 90 Cr.App.R. 261, DC; *R. (DPP) v. Camberwell Green Youth Court*, 168 J.P. 157, DC; *R. (C.) v. Grimsby and Cleethorpes Magistrates' Court*, 168 J.P. 569, DC. This is so even where further indictable matters arising out of the same incident had been brought against the accused and the court wishes to commit all matters together: *St Helen's Magistrates' Court, ex p. Critchley*, 152 J.P. 102, DC.

Where a number of accused are jointly charged and some have elected trial on indictment, but others have consented to summary trial, s.25 may not be used as a means to ensure that there is only one trial and that all accused are tried on indictment:

Bentwood JJ., ex p. Nicholls [1992] 1 A.C. 1, HL; *Bradford Magistrates' Court, ex p. Grant*, 163 J.P. 717, DC; *Ipswich JJ., ex p. Callaghan*, 159 J.P. 748, DC; *West Norfolk JJ., ex p. McMullen*, 157 J.P. 461, DC.

Once the amendments to s.25 made by the *Criminal Justice Act* 2003 are brought into force, the power in s.25 will be limited to switching from summary trial to sending for trial under s.51 of the *Crime and Disorder Act* 1998 (consequent upon the abolition of committal proceedings) and will only be available where, before the summary trial begins, an application is made by the prosecution that the case should be tried on indictment instead. Any such application must be dealt with before the trial begins and before any other application or issue in relation to the summary trial is dealt with. Whether the court will grant the application appears to be discretionary and will depend on whether (and only whether) its sentencing powers are inadequate. In view of this discretion, it is submitted that there will be cases where the court will not allow the application, notwithstanding that further examination shows that the previous decision as to mode of trial was wrong.

Part I

"Begun to try the information summarily"

The power to switch from summary trial to committal proceedings in the current version of s.25 in force does not become available until the court has "begun to try the information summarily", which is the actual process of determining guilt or innocence: *Horseferry Road Magistrates' Court, ex p. K.* [1997] Q.B. 23, DC. It will not have begun merely because the accused had consented to summary trial (*Southend JJ., ex p. Wood*, 152 J.P. 97, DC) or where the court took a deposition from a prosecution witness but did not allow any cross-examination (*Birmingham Stipendiary Magistrate, ex p. Webb*, 95 Cr.App.R. 75, DC). Something more than a plea of guilty is required, but it is unnecessary for the process of giving evidence actually to have begun; there are a number of possible circumstances in which, after a plea of not guilty and before the commencement of the evidence, it would become apparent that the court has embarked upon the process of determining the guilt or innocence of the accused and thus has "begun" the trial in question; and whilst it was neither necessary nor appropriate to enumerate them, one such possible circumstance could arise where the defence made and the court considered preliminary submissions of law having a direct and immediate bearing on the conduct and content of the process of determining the guilt or innocence of the accused: *Horseferry Road Magistrates' Court, ex p. K., ibid.* (expressly rejecting the *obiter* view in *Hammersmith Juvenile Court, ex p. O.*, 86 Cr.App.R. 343, DC, that the process began with the "not guilty" plea). **7–73**

The power in s.25(2) is only available during a trial; it is not available where there has been a plea of guilty to the information, there being nothing to try so that the court has not at any stage "begun to try the information summarily"; in those circumstances the only power available to the court is to commit for sentence: *Dudley JJ., ex p. Gillard* [1986] A.C. 442, HL. The same applies where there is a plea of guilty but the factual basis thereof is disputed so that a Newton hearing is required: *Telford Magistrates' Court, ex p. Darlington*, 87 Cr.App.R. 194, DC.

"Conclusion of the evidence for the prosecution"

Where the court has heard the evidence in the trial but the bench is unable to agree on a verdict and adjourns for a rehearing, the evidence for the prosecution is not concluded: *Coventry JJ., ex p. Wilson* [1981] Crim.L.R. 787, DC. **7–74**

Exercise of the discretion

A magistrates' court must exercise the discretion conferred by s.25 in a lawful manner: *H. v. Balham Youth Court*, 168 J.P. 177, DC. The discretion may be exercised where there has been a "change of circumstance", which includes not only the emer- **7–75** gence of new material in the course of the evidence, but also cases where, as the evidence unfolds, the manner in which it is presented by the witness or witnesses is, of itself, of a nature which justifies the conclusion that the original decision as to mode of trial is no longer appropriate: *R. (K.) v. Leeds Youth Court*, 165 J.P. 694, DC. Exercise of the power is not fettered by the previous decision as to mode of trial which a subsequent examination showed to be wrong: *R. (R.) v. Manchester City Youth Court*, 170 J.P. 217, QBD (Ouseley J.). The court may be under a duty to exercise the discretion even in the absence of any representations on the issue from either party: *H. v. Balham Youth Court, ibid*. (where the more serious of two charges had been dropped and it should have appeared to the court that the case was one which ought to be tried summarily).

VI. SENDING, TRANSFERRING AND COMMITTING CASES TO THE CROWN COURT

A. GENERAL

7–76 An adult magistrates' court has no jurisdiction to proceed to summary trial of (a) indictable only offences, (b) serious fraud offences and certain offences involving children, or (c) either way offences where the court has declined jurisdiction to deal with the matter or where the defendant has elected to be tried at the Crown Court. All such offences may only be tried on indictment at the Crown Court.

At present (save with a minor exception), once preliminary matters have been concluded in the magistrates' court:

(a) indictable only offences are *sent* to the Crown Court (*Crime and Disorder Act* 1998, s.51);

(b) serious fraud offences and certain offences involving children are *transferred* to the Crown Court (*Criminal Justice Act* 1987, ss.4–5, and *Criminal Justice Act* 1991, s.53); and

(c) either way offences where there has been a not guilty plea or no indication as to plea and the court has declined jurisdiction to deal with the matter or the defendant has elected to be tried at the Crown Court are *committed* to the Crown Court (*Magistrates' Courts Act* 1980, s.5–8).

(d) certain summary only offences may be *committed to or otherwise dealt with by* the Crown Court with related either way offences committed under s.6 of the 1980 Act (*Criminal Justice Act* 1988, ss.40 and 41); and

(e) either way offences and related summary offences may be *committed for sentence* to the Crown Court where the accused has pleaded guilty to, or been convicted after summary trial of, an information (*Powers of Criminal Courts (Sentencing) Act* 2000, ss.3 to 6 (*post*, §§ 23–112 *et seq.*).

As from a day to be appointed, however, the *Criminal Justice Act* 2003, s.41 and Sched. 3, will abolish the existing sending, transfer and committal for trial procedures and replace them with a single enhanced regime under new ss.51 to 51E of the *Crime and Disorder Act* 1998, whereby the case will be sent to the Crown Court.

This new regime has been brought into force partially, but only to the very limited extent that a magistrates' court must send a child who has been charged with a "specified offence" (within the meaning of s.24 of the *Criminal Justice Act* 2003) if it "appears" to the court that the criteria for imposing a sentence of detention for public protection or an extended sentence of detention would be met.

B. SENDING CASES TO THE CROWN COURT

(1) The current regime

Crime and Disorder Act 1998, s.51

No committal proceedings for indictable-only offence

51.—(1) *Where an adult appears or is brought before a magistrates' court ("the court") charged with an offence triable only on indictment ("the indictable-only offence"), the court shall send him forthwith to the Crown Court for trial—* **7–77**

(a) *for that offence, and*

(b) *for any either-way or summary offence with which he is charged which fulfils the requisite conditions (as set out in subsection (11) below).*

(2) *Where an adult who has been sent for trial under subsection (1) above subsequently appears or is brought before a magistrates' court charged with an either-way or summary offence which fulfils the requisite conditions, the court may send him forthwith to the Crown Court for trial for the either-way or summary offence.*

(3) *Where—*

(a) *the court sends an adult for trial under subsection (1) above;*

(b) *another adult appears or is brought before the court on the same or a subsequent occasion charged jointly with him with an either-way offence; and*

(c) *that offence appears to the court to be related to the indictable-only offence,*

the court shall where it is the same occasion, and may where it is a subsequent occasion, send the other adult forthwith to the Crown Court for trial for the either-way offence.

(4) *Where a court sends an adult for trial under subsection (3) above, it shall at the same time send him to the Crown Court for trial for any either-way or summary offence with which he is charged which fulfils the requisite conditions.*

(5) *Where—*

(a) *the court sends an adult for trial under subsection (1) or (3) above; and*

(b) *a child or young person appears or is brought before the court on the same or a subsequent occasion charged jointly with the adult with an indictable offence for which the adult is sent for trial,*

the court shall, if it considers it necessary in the interests of justice to do so, send the child or young person forthwith to the Crown Court for trial for the indictable offence.

(6) *Where a court sends a child or young person for trial under subsection (5) above, it may at the same time send him to the Crown Court for trial for any either-way or summary offence with which he is charged which fulfils the requisite conditions.*

(7) *The court shall specify in a notice the offence or offences for which a person is sent for trial under this section and the place at which he is to be tried; and a copy of the notice shall be served on the accused and given to the Crown Court sitting at that place.*

(8) *In a case where there is more than one indictable-only offence and the court includes an either-way or a summary offence in the notice under subsection (7) above, the court shall specify in that notice the indictable-only offence to which the either-way offence or, as the case may be, the summary offence appears to the court to be related.*

(9) *The trial of the information charging any summary offence for which a person is sent for trial under this section shall be treated as if the court had adjourned it under section 10 of the 1980 Act and had not fixed the time and place for its resumption.*

(10) *In selecting the place of trial for the purpose of subsection (7) above, the court shall have regard to—*

(a) *the convenience of the defence, the prosecution and the witnesses;*

(b) *the desirability of expediting the trial; and*

(c) *any direction given by or on behalf of the Lord Chief Justice with the concurrence of the Lord Chancellor under section 75(1) of the* Senior Courts Act *1981.*

(11) *An offence fulfils the requisite conditions if—*

(a) *if appears to the court to be related to the indictable-only offence; and*

(b) *in the case of a summary offence, it is punishable with imprisonment or involves obligatory or discretionary disqualification from driving.*

(12) *For the purposes of this section—*

(a) *"adult" means a person aged 18 or over, and references to an adult include references to a corporation;*

(b) *"either-way offence" means an offence which, if committed by an adult, is triable either on indictment or summarily;*

(c) *an either-way offence is related to an indictable-only offence if the charge for the either-way offence could be joined in the same indictment as the charge for the indictable-only offence;*

(d) *a summary offence is related to an indictable-only offence if it arises out of circumstances which are the same as or connected with those giving rise to the indictable-only offence.*

[The *Criminal Justice Act* 2003, Sched. 3, substitutes new ss.51 to 51E (*post*) in place of this section. The substitution of new s.51A (except subs. (3)(a) to (c)) was effected as from April 4, 2005, by the *Criminal Justice Act 2003 (Commencement No. 8and Transitional and Saving Provisions Order* 2005 (S.I. 2005 No. 950), as was the substitution of new ss.51D and 51E (but only insofar as they apply to cases sent under s.51A(3)(d)). In all other respects, the remaining sections and subsections are to be substituted as from a day or days to be appointed. The section is printed as amended by the *Constitutional Reform Act* 2005, Sched. 11.]

(2) The new regime (only partially in force)

Sending cases to the Crown Court: adults

7–78 **[51.**—(1) Where an adult appears or is brought before a magistrates' court ("the court") charged with an offence and any of the conditions mentioned in subsection (2) below is satisfied, the court shall send him forthwith to the Crown Court for trial for the offence.

(2) Those conditions are—

(a) that the offence is an offence triable only on indictment other than one in respect of which notice has been given under section 51B or 51C below;

(b) that the offence is an either-way offence and the court is required under section 20(9)(b), 21, 23(4)(b) or (5) or 25(2D) of the *Magistrates' Courts Act* 1980 to proceed in relation to the offence in accordance with subsection (1) above;

(c) that notice is given to the court under section 51B or 51C below in respect of the offence.

(3) Where the court sends an adult for trial under subsection (1) above, it shall at the same time send him to the Crown Court for trial for any either-way or summary offence with which he is charged and which—

(a) (if it is an either-way offence) appears to the court to be related to the offence mentioned in subsection (1) above; or

(b) (if it is a summary offence) appears to the court to be related to the offence mentioned in subsection (1) above or to the either-way offence, and which fulfils the requisite condition (as defined in subsection (11) below).

(4) Where an adult who has been sent for trial under subsection (1) above subsequently appears or is brought before a magistrates' court charged with an either-way or summary offence which—

(a) appears to the court to be related to the offence mentioned in subsection (1) above; and

(b) (in the case of a summary offence) fulfils the requisite condition,

the court may send him forthwith to the Crown Court for trial for the either-way or summary offence.

(5) Where—

(a) the court sends an adult ("A") for trial under subsection (1) or (3) above;

(b) another adult appears or is brought before the court on the same or a subsequent occasion charged jointly with A with an either-way offence; and

(c) that offence appears to the court to be related to an offence for which A was sent for trial under subsection (1) or (3) above,

the court shall where it is the same occasion, and may where it is a subsequent occasion, send the other adult forthwith to the Crown Court for trial for the either-way offence.

(6) Where the court sends an adult for trial under subsection (5) above, it shall at the same time send him to the Crown Court for trial for any either-way or summary offence with which he is charged and which—

(a) (if it is an either-way offence) appears to the court to be related to the offence for which he is sent for trial; and

(b) (if it is a summary offence) appears to the court to be related to the offence for which he is sent for trial or to the either-way offence, and which fulfils the requisite condition.

(7) Where—

(a) the court sends an adult ("A") for trial under subsection (1), (3) or (5) above; and

(b) a child or young person appears or is brought before the court on the same or a subsequent occasion charged jointly with A with an indictable offence for which A is sent for trial under subsection (1), (3) or (5) above, or an indictable offence which appears to the court to be related to that offence,

the court shall, if it considers it necessary in the interests of justice to do so, send the child or young person forthwith to the Crown Court for trial for the indictable offence.

(8) Where the court sends a child or young person for trial under subsection (7) above, it may at the same time send him to the Crown Court for trial for any indictable or summary offence with which he is charged and which—

(a) (if it is an indictable offence) appears to the court to be related to the offence for which he is sent for trial; and

(b) (if it is a summary offence) appears to the court to be related to the offence for which he is sent for trial or to the indictable offence, and which fulfils the requisite condition.

(9) Subsections (7) and (8) above are subject to sections 24A and 24B of the *Magistrates' Courts Act* 1980 (which provide for certain cases involving children and young persons to be tried summarily).

(10) The trial of the information charging any summary offence for which a person is sent for trial under this section shall be treated as if the court had adjourned it under section 10 of the 1980 Act and had not fixed the time and place for its resumption.

(11) A summary offence fulfils the requisite condition if it is punishable with imprisonment or involves obligatory or discretionary disqualification from driving.

(12) In the case of an adult charged with an offence—

(a) if the offence satisfies paragraph (c) of subsection (2) above, the offence shall be dealt with under subsection (1) above and not under any other provision of this section or section 51A below;

(b) subject to paragraph (a) above, if the offence is one in respect of which the court is required to, or would decide to, send the adult to the Crown Court under—

(i) subsection (5) above; or

(ii) subsection (6) of section 51A below,

the offence shall be dealt with under that subsection and not under any other provision of this section or section 51A below.

(13) The functions of a magistrates' court under this section, and its related functions under section 51D below, may be discharged by a single justice.]

[As noted, *ante*, this section is to be substituted as from a day to be appointed.]

Sending cases to the Crown Court: children and young persons

51A.—(1) This section is subject to sections 24A and 24B of the *Magistrates' Courts Act* 1980 (which provide for certain offences involving children or young persons to be tried summarily). **7–79**

(2) Where a child or young person appears or is brought before a magistrates' court ("the court") charged with an offence and any of the conditions mentioned in subsection (3) below is satisfied, the court shall send him forthwith to the Crown Court for trial for the offence.

(3) Those conditions are—

[(a) that the offence falls within subsection (12) below;

(b) that the offence is such as is mentioned in subsection (1) of section 91 of the *Powers of Criminal Courts (Sentencing) Act* 2000 (other than one mentioned in paragraph (d) below in relation to which it appears to the court as mentioned there) and the court considers that if he is found guilty of the offence it ought to be possible to sentence him in pursuance of subsection (3) of that section;

(c) that notice is given to the court under section 51B or 51C below in respect of the offence;]

(d) that the offence is a specified offence (within the meaning of section 224 of the *Criminal Justice Act* 2003) and it appears to the court that if he is found guilty of the offence the criteria for the imposition of a sentence under section 226(3) or 228(2) of that Act would be met.

(4) Where the court sends a child or young person for trial under subsection (2) above, it may at the same time send him to the Crown Court for trial for any indictable or summary offence with which he is charged and which—

(a) (if it is an indictable offence) appears to the court to be related to the offence mentioned in subsection (2) above; or

(b) (if it is a summary offence) appears to the court to be related to the offence mentioned in subsection (2) above or to the indictable offence, and which fulfils the requisite condition (as defined in subsection (9) below).

(5) Where a child or young person who has been sent for trial under subsection (2) above subsequently appears or is brought before a magistrates' court charged with an indictable or summary offence which—

(a) appears to the court to be related to the offence mentioned in subsection (2) above; and

(b) (in the case of a summary offence) fulfils the requisite condition,

the court may send him forthwith to the Crown Court for trial for the indictable or summary offence.

(6) Where—

(a) the court sends a child or young person ("C") for trial under subsection (2) or (4) above; and

(b) an adult appears or is brought before the court on the same or a subsequent occasion charged jointly with C with an either-way offence for which C is sent for trial under subsection (2) or (4) above, or an either-way offence which appears to the court to be related to that offence,

the court shall where it is the same occasion, and may where it is a subsequent occasion, send the adult forthwith to the Crown Court for trial for the either-way offence.

(7) Where the court sends an adult for trial under subsection (6) above, it shall at the same time send him to the Crown Court for trial for any either-way or summary offence with which he is charged and which—

(a) (if it is an either-way offence) appears to the court to be related to the offence for which he was sent for trial; and

(b) (if it is a summary offence) appears to the court to be related to the offence for which he was sent for trial or to the either-way offence, and which fulfils the requisite condition.

(8) The trial of the information charging any summary offence for which a person is sent for trial under this section shall be treated as if the court had adjourned it under section 10 of the 1980 Act and had not fixed the time and place for its resumption.

(9) A summary offence fulfils the requisite condition if it is punishable with imprisonment or involves obligatory or discretionary disqualification from driving.

(10) In the case of a child or young person charged with an offence—

(a) if the offence satisfies any of the conditions in subsection (3) above, the offence shall be dealt with under subsection (2) above and not under any other provision of this section or section 51 above;

(b) subject to paragraph (a) above, if the offence is one in respect of which the requirements of subsection (7) of section 51 above for sending the child or young person to the Crown Court are satisfied, the offence shall be dealt with under that subsection and not under any other provision of this section or section 51 above.

(11) The functions of a magistrates' court under this section, and its related functions under section 51D below, may be discharged by a single justice.

(12) An offence falls within this subsection if—

(a) it is an offence of homicide;

(b) each of the requirements of section 51A(1) of the *Firearms Act* 1968 would be satisfied with respect to—

(i) the offence; and

(ii) the person charged with it,

if he were convicted of the offence; or

(c) section 29(3) of the *Violent Crime Reduction Act* 2006 (minimum sentences in certain cases of using someone to mind a weapon) would apply if he were convicted of the offence.

[This section is printed as amended by the *Violent Crime Reduction Act* 2006, Sched. 1. As noted *ante*, this section (other than the text set out in square brackets in subs. (3)) was brought into force as from April 4, 2005. The text set out in square brackets in subs. (3) is to be brought into force as from a day to be appointed.]

Notices in serious or complex fraud cases

[51B.—(1) A notice may be given by a designated authority under this section in respect of an indictable offence if the authority is of the opinion that the evidence of the offence charged— **7–80**

(a) is sufficient for the person charged to be put on trial for the offence; and

(b) reveals a case of fraud of such seriousness or complexity that it is appropriate that the management of the case should without delay be taken over by the Crown Court.

(2) That opinion must be certified by the designated authority in the notice.

(3) The notice must also specify the proposed place of trial, and in selecting that place the designated authority must have regard to the same matters as are specified in paragraphs (a) to (c) of section 51D(4) below.

(4) A notice under this section must be given to the magistrates' court at which the person charged appears or before which he is brought.

(5) Such a notice must be given to the magistrates' court before any summary trial begins.

(6) The effect of such a notice is that the functions of the magistrates' court cease in relation to the case, except—

(a) for the purposes of section 51D below;

(b) as provided by paragraph 2 of Schedule 3 to the *Access to Justice Act* 1999; and

(c) as provided by section 52 below.

(7) The functions of a designated authority under this section may be exercised by an officer of the authority acting on behalf of the authority.

(8) A decision to give a notice under this section shall not be subject to appeal or liable to be questioned in any court (whether a magistrates' court or not).

(9) In this section "designated authority" means—

(a) the Director of Public Prosecutions;

(b) the Director of the Serious Fraud Office;

(c) the Commissioners for Her Majesty's Revenue and Customs;

(d) ...; or

(e) the Secretary of State.]

[This section is printed as amended by the *Commissioners for Revenue and Customs Act* 2005, s.50. As noted above at § 7–77 under the italicised text of the original s.51, this section is to be substituted as from a day to be appointed.]

Notices in certain cases involving children

[51C.—(1) A notice may be given by the Director of Public Prosecutions under this section in respect of an offence falling within subsection (3) below if he is of the opinion— **7–81**

(a) that the evidence of the offence would be sufficient for the person charged to be put on trial for the offence;

(b) that a child would be called as a witness at the trial; and

(c) that, for the purpose of avoiding any prejudice to the welfare of the child, the case should be taken over and proceeded with without delay by the Crown Court.

(2) That opinion must be certified by the Director of Public Prosecutions in the notice.

(3) This subsection applies to an offence—

(a) which involves an assault on, or injury or a threat of injury to, a person;

(b) under section 1 of the *Children and Young Persons Act* 1933 (cruelty to persons under 16);

(c) under the *Sexual Offences Act* 1956, the *Protection of Children Act* 1978 or the *Sexual Offences Act* 2003;

(d) of kidnapping or false imprisonment, or an offence under section 1 or 2 of the *Child Abduction Act* 1984;

(e) which consists of attempting or conspiring to commit, or of aiding, abetting, counselling, procuring or inciting the commission of, an offence falling within paragraph (a), (b), (c) or (d) above.

(4) Subsections (4), (5) and (6) of section 51B above apply for the purposes of this section as they apply for the purposes of that.

(5) The functions of the Director of Public Prosecutions under this section may be exercised by an officer acting on behalf of the Director.

(6) A decision to give a notice under this section shall not be subject to appeal or liable to be questioned in any court (whether a magistrates' court or not).

(7) In this section "child" means—

(a) a person who is under the age of 17; or

(b) any person of whom a video recording (as defined in section 63(1) of the *Youth Justice and Criminal Evidence Act* 1999) was made when he was under the age of 17 with a view to its admission as his evidence in chief in the trial referred to in subsection (1) above.]

[As noted, *ante*, this section is to be substituted as from a day to be appointed.]

Notice of offence and place of trial

7–82 **51D.**—(1) The court shall specify in a notice—

(a) the offence or offences for which a person is sent for trial under section 51 or 51A above; and

(b) the place at which he is to be tried (which, if a notice has been given under section 51B above, must be the place specified in that notice).

(2) A copy of the notice shall be served on the accused and given to the Crown Court sitting at that place.

(3) In a case where a person is sent for trial under section 51 or 51A above for more than one offence, the court shall specify in that notice, for each offence—

(a) the subsection under which the person is so sent; and

(b) if applicable, the offence to which that offence appears to the court to be related.

(4) Where the court selects the place of trial for the purposes of subsection (1) above, it shall have regard to—

(a) the convenience of the defence, the prosecution and the witnesses;

(b) the desirability of expediting the trial; and

(c) any direction given by or on behalf of the Lord Chief Justice with the concurrence of the Lord Chancellor under section 75(1) of the *Senior Courts Act* 1981.

[As noted, *ante*, this section is in force only to the extent that it applies where a case is sent under s.51A(3)(d). For all other purposes, it is to be brought into force as from a day or days to be appointed. The section is printed as amended by the *Constitutional Reform Act* 2005, Sched. 11.]

Interpretation of sections 50A to 51D

7–83 **51E.** For the purposes of sections 50A to 51D above—

(a) "adult" means a person aged 18 or over, and references to an adult include a corporation;

(b) "either-way offence" means an offence triable either way;

(c) an either-way offence is related to an indictable offence if the charge for the either-way offence could be joined in the same indictment as the charge for the indictable offence;

(d) a summary offence is related to an indictable offence if it arises out of circumstances which are the same as or connected with those giving rise to the indictable offence."

[As noted, *ante*, this section is in force only to the extent that it applies where a case is sent under s.51A(3)(d). For all other purposes, it is to be brought into force as from a day or days to be appointed.]

(3) Interpretation

The word "charged" does not just mean offences charged at the police station or by the laying of an information but includes charges preferred at or after the first court appearance: *R. (Salubi) v. Bow Street Magistrates' Court* [2002] 2 Cr.App.R. 40, DC. The fact that a magistrates' court has a duty under s.51(1) to send an indictable-only case to the Crown Court "forthwith" does not necessarily preclude it from exercising its jurisdiction to stay the proceedings as an abuse of process in an appropriate case, but such a case would be very rare; the onus is on the defence to establish bad faith or serious misconduct (incorrect procedure based on lack of judgment is not sufficient) and in most cases the Crown Court is likely to be better equipped to make such value judgments; instances of possible bad faith might be the addition of an unmeritorious indictable only charge in the late stages of committal proceedings for either-way offences, solely with the object of overcoming custody time limits or of overcoming evidential difficulties that would otherwise delay or defeat a committal: *ibid.*; and *R. (Craik, Chief Constable of Northumbria Police) v. Newcastle upon Tyne Magistrates Court* [2010] 5 *Archbold Review* 2, DC (where proceedings, in the form of a private prosecution of a chief constable for an offence of false imprisonment, were said to be hopelessly misconceived both in law and in fact such that pursuit of them, having absolutely no foundation in fact was, as a matter of law, on that ground alone and without the need to establish any other vitiating feature, both vexatious and an abuse of process). **7–84**

Summary trial of an offence that is triable on indictment only is a nullity. The case must be dealt with at the Crown Court: *West* [1964] 1 Q.B. 15, CA.

(4) Practical considerations

(a) *Criminal Procedure Rules*

Part 12 of the *Criminal Procedure Rules* 2011 sets out a series of rules in connection with sending of cases to the Crown Court: see Appendix G. **7–85**

(b) *Consolidated Criminal Practice Direction*

See paras V.56.1 and V.56.3 to V.56.5 of the *Consolidated Criminal Practice Direction* (Appendix F). **7–86**

By virtue of para. V.56.3 and Annex E, the following standard directions for case progression apply where a case is sent to the Crown Court under section 51 of the *Crime and Disorder Act* 1998.

Consolidated Criminal Practice Direction, Annex E, Case Management Form - Directions for Case Sent to the Crown Court

ACTION	TIME LIMITS	DIRECTIONS
1	Cust: 50 days after sent Bail: 70 days after sent	Prosecution to serve draft indictment, case papers and primary or initial disclosure.
2	14 days after Action 1	Defence to notify prosecution of witness requirements Prosecution to serve any application for hearsay or defendant's bad character. Defence to serve: (i) defence statement (including any alibi details) or notification of guilty plea; (ii) any application for hearsay/bad character; (iii) any notice of application to dismiss charges.

ACTION	TIME LIMITS	DIRECTIONS
3	28 days after Action 1	Prosecution to serve final draft indictment and any special measures applications. Defence to serve any application under section 41 of the *Youth Justice and Criminal Evidence Act* 1999.
4	14 days after Action 2	Prosecution to serve responses to hearsay/ bad character/ dismissal of charges applications. Defence to serve response to hearsay/bad character application by prosecution.
5	14 days after Action 3	Defence to serve response to any prosecution application for special measures. Prosecution and defence to notify Crown Court of names of trial advocate and time estimate. Defence to notify Crown Court of non-availability of expert witnesses, with reasons. Witness Care Unit to notify Crown Court and prosecution of dates when witnesses required by defence are unavailable, with reasons.

(c) *Criminal Case Management Framework*

7–87 As to the objectives and expectations of the parties where a case is sent for trial under s.51 of the *Crime and Disorder Act* 1998, see Ch. 6 of the Criminal Case Management Framework (Appendix I).

C. TRANSFER OF CASES TO THE CROWN COURT

(1) General

7–88 Cases of serious fraud or offences involving children may be transferred to the Crown Court to prevent unnecessary delay.

As to the relationship between service of a notice of transfer and the plea before venue and mode of trial procedures under ss.17A to 23 of the *Magistrates' Courts Act* 1980, see *Fareham Youth Court and Morey, ex p. CPS*, 163 J.P. 812, DC (*ante*, § 7–40).

(2) Transfer of serious fraud cases

Criminal Justice Act 1987, ss.4–5

Notices of transfer and designated authorities

7–89 **4.**—(1) *If—*

(a) *a person has been charged with an indictable offence; and*

(b) *in the opinion of an authority designated by subsection (2) below or of one of such an authority's officers acting on the authority's behalf the evidence of the offence charged—*

(i) *would be sufficient for the person charged to be committed for trial; and*

(ii) *reveals a case of fraud of such seriousness or complexity that it is appropriate that the management of the case should without delay be taken over by the Crown Court; and*

(c) *before the magistrates' court in whose jurisdiction the offence has been charged begins to inquire into the case as examining justices the authority or one of the authority's officers acting on the authority's behalf gives the court a notice (in this Act referred to as a "notice of transfer") certifying that opinion.*

the functions of the magistrates' court shall cease in relation to the case, except as provided by section 5(3), (7A) and (8) below and by paragraph 2 of Schedule 3 to the Access to Justice Act *1999.*

(2) *The authorities mentioned in subsection (1) above (in this Act referred to as "designated authorities") are—*

(a) *the Director of Public Prosecutions;*

(b) *the Director of the Serious Fraud Office;*

(c) *the Commissioners of Revenue and Customs;*

(d) *...; and*

(e) *the Secretary of State.*

(3) *A designated authority's decision to give notice of transfer shall not be subject to appeal or liable to be questioned in any court.*

(4) *This section and sections 5 and 6 below shall not apply in any case in which section 51 of the* Crime and Disorder Act *1998 (no committal proceedings for indictable-only offences) applies.*

[This section is printed as amended by the *Criminal Justice Act* 1988, s.114, the *Legal Aid Act* 1988, Sched. 5, the *Criminal Justice and Public Order Act* 1994, Sched. 9, the *Crime and Disorder Act* 1998, Sched. 8, the *Access to Justice Act* 1999, Sched. 4, and the *Commissioners for Revenue and Customs Act* 2005, s.50. As from a day to be appointed, the whole section is to be repealed by the *Criminal Justice Act* 2003, Sched. 3, and replaced by the new scheme of sending for trial under ss.51 to 51E of the *Crime and Disorder Act* 1998 (*ante*, §§ 7–77 *et seq.*).]

Notices of transfer—procedure

5.—(1) *A notice of transfer shall specify the proposed place of trial and in selecting that place the designated authority shall have regard to the considerations to which section 7 of the* Magistrates' Courts Act *1980 requires a magistrates' court committing a person for trial to have regard when selecting the place at which he is to be tried.* **7–90**

(2) *A notice of transfer shall specify the charge or charges to which it relates and include or be accompanied by such additional matter as regulations under subsection (9) below may require.*

(3) *If a magistrates' court has remanded a person to whom a notice of transfer relates in custody, it shall have power, subject to section 4 of the* Bail Act *1976 and regulations under section 22 of the* Prosecution of Offences Act *1985—*

(a) *to order that he shall be safely kept in custody until delivered in due course of law; or*

(b) *to release him on bail in accordance with the* Bail Act *1976, that is to say, by directing him to appear before the Crown Court for trial;*

and where his release on bail is conditional on his providing one or more surety or sureties and, in accordance with section 8(3) of the Bail Act *1976, the court fixes the amount in which the surety is to be bound with a view to his entering into his recognizance subsequently in accordance with subsections (4) and (5) or (6) of that section, the court shall in the meantime make an order such as is mentioned in paragraph (a) of this subsection.*

(4) *If the conditions specified in subsection (5) below are satisfied, a court may exercise the powers conferred by subsection (3) above in relation to a person charged without his being brought before it in any case in which by virtue of section 128(3A) of the* Magistrates' Courts Act *1980 it would have power further to remand him on an adjournment such as is mentioned in that subsection.*

(5) *The conditions mentioned in subsection (4) above are—*

(a) *that the person in question has given his written consent to the powers conferred by subsection (3) above being exercised without his being brought before the court; and*

(b) *that the court is satisfied that, when he gave his consent, he knew that the notice of transfer had been issued.*

(6) *Where notice of transfer is given after a person to whom it relates has been remanded on bail to appear before a magistrates' court on an appointed day, the requirement that he shall so appear shall cease on the giving of the notice, unless the notice states that it is to continue.*

(7) *Where the requirement that a person to whom the notice of transfer relates shall appear before a magistrates' court ceases by virtue of subsection (6) above, it shall be his duty to appear before the Crown Court at the place specified by the notice of transfer as the proposed*

place of trial or at any place substituted for it by a direction under section 76 of the Senior Courts Act *1981.*

(7A) *If the notice states that the requirement is to continue, when a person to whom the notice relates appears before the magistrates' court, the court shall have—*

(a) *the powers and duty conferred on a magistrates' court by subsection (3) above, but subject as there provided; and*

(b) *power to enlarge, in the surety's absence, a recognizance conditioned in accordance with section 128(4)(a) of the* Magistrates' Courts Act *1980 so that the surety is bound to secure that the person charged appears also before the Crown Court.*

(8) *For the purposes of the* Criminal Procedure (Attendance of Witnesses) Act *1965—*

(a) *any magistrates' court for the petty sessions area for which the court from which a case was transferred sits shall be treated as examining magistrates; and*

(b) *a person indicated in the notice of transfer as a proposed witness; shall be treated as a person who has been examined by the court.*

(9) *The Attorney General—*

(a) *shall by regulations make provision requiring the giving of a copy of a notice of transfer, together with copies of the documents containing the evidence (including oral evidence) on which any charge to which it relates is based—*

(i) *to any person to whom the notice of transfer relates; and*

(ii) *to the Crown Court sitting at the place specified by the notice of transfer as the proposed place of trial; and*

(b) *may by regulations make such further provision in relation to notices of transfer, including provision as to the duties of a designated authority in relation to such notices, as appears to him to be appropriate.*

(9A) *Regulations under subsection (9)(a) above may provide that there shall be no requirement for copies of documents to accompany the copy of the notice of transfer if they are referred to, in documents sent with the notice of transfer, as having already been supplied.*

(10) *The power to make regulations conferred by subsection (9) above shall be exercisable by statutory instrument subject to annulment in pursuance of a resolution of either House of Parliament.*

(11) *Any such regulations may make different provision with respect to different cases or classes of case.*

[This section is printed as amended by the *Criminal Justice Act* 1988, s.144, and the *Criminal Procedure and Investigations Act* 1996, s.45 and the *Constitutional Reform Act* 2005, Sched. 11. The whole section is to be repealed by the *Criminal Justice Act* 2003, Sched. 3, as from a day to be appointed, and replaced by the new scheme of sending for trial under ss.51 to 51E of the *Crime and Disorder Act* 1998 (*ante*, §§ 7–77 *et seq.*).]

7–91 The *Criminal Justice Act 1987 (Notice of Transfer) Regulations* 1988 (S.I. 1988 No. 1691) (made under s.5(9) of the 1987 Act) prescribe standard forms (set out in the schedule to the regulations) in which the notice of transfer must be given; and require copies of the notice to be given to the defendant, the Crown Court and to any person who has custody of a person to whom the notice relates. The regulations have been amended by S.I. 1997 No. 737 and S.I. 2001 No. 444.

(3) Transfer of certain cases involving children

Criminal Justice Act 1991, s.53

Notices of transfer in certain cases involving children

7–92 **53.**—(1) *If a person has been charged with an offence to which section 32(2) of the 1988 Act applies (sexual offences and offences involving violence or cruelty) and the Director of Public Prosecutions is of the opinion—*

(a) *that the evidence of the offence would be sufficient for the person charged to be committed for trial;*

(b) *that a child who is alleged—*

(i) *to be a person against whom the offence was committed; or*

(ii) *to have witnessed the commission of the offence,*
will be called as a witness at the trial; and

(c) *that, for the purpose of avoiding any prejudice to the welfare of the child, the case should be taken over and proceeded with without delay by the Crown Court,*

a notice ("notice of transfer") certifying that opinion may be given by or on behalf of the Director to the magistrates' court in whose jurisdiction the offence has been charged.

(2) *A notice of transfer shall be given before the magistrates' court begins to inquire into the case as examining justices.*

(3) *On the giving of a notice of transfer the functions of the magistrates' court shall cease in relation to the case except as provided by paragraphs 2 and 3 of Schedule 6 to this Act or by paragraph 2 of Schedule 3 to the* Access to Justice Act *1999.*

(4) *The decision to give a notice of transfer shall not be subject to appeal or liable to be questioned in any court.*

(5) *Schedule 6 to this Act (which makes further provision in relation to notices of transfer) shall have effect.*

(6) *In this section "child" means a person who—*

(a) *in the case of an offence falling within section 32(2)(a) or (b) of the 1988 Act, is under fourteen years of age or, if he was under that age when any such video recording as is mentioned in section 32A(2) of that Act was made in respect of him, is under fifteen years of age; or*

(b) *in the case of an offence falling within section 32(2)(c) of that Act, is under seventeen years of age or, if he was under that age when any such video recording was made in respect of him, is under eighteen years of age.*

(7) *Any reference in subsection (6) above to an offence falling within paragraph (a), (b) or (c) of section 32(2) of that Act includes a reference to an offence which consists of attempting or conspiring to commit, or of aiding, abetting, counselling, procuring or inciting the commission of, an offence falling within that paragraph.*

(8) *This section shall not apply in any case in which section 51 of the* Crime and Disorder Act *1998 (no committal proceedings for indictable-only offences) applies.*

[This section is printed as amended by the *Criminal Justice and Public Order Act* 1994, Sched. 9, the *Crime and Disorder Act* 1998, Sched. 8, and the *Access to Justice Act* 1999, Sched. 4. As from a day to be appointed, the whole section is to be repealed by the *Criminal Justice Act* 2003, Sched. 3, and replaced by the new scheme of sending for trial under ss.51 to 51E of the *Crime and Disorder Act* 1998 (*ante*, §§ 7–77 *et seq.*). In subs. (7), the reference to incitement has effect as a reference to conduct amounting to the offences in relation to encouraging or assisting crime in Pt 7 of the *Serious Crime Act* 2007: see s.63(1) and Sched. 6 of the 2007 Act.]

(4) Practical considerations

(a) *Criminal Procedure Rules*

Part 11 of the *Criminal Procedure Rules* 2011 sets out a series of rules in connection with sending of cases to the Crown Court: see Appendix G. **7–93**

(b) *Consolidated Criminal Practice Direction*

See paras V.56.1 and V.56.3 to V.56.5 of the *Consolidated Criminal Practice Direction* (Appendix F). Annex E does not contain a form setting out standard directions applicable where a case is transferred to the Crown Court. **7–94**

(c) *Criminal Case Management Framework*

As to the objectives and expectations of the parties where a case is transferred to the Crown Court, see Ch. 6 of the Criminal Case Management Framework (Appendix I). **7–95**

D. Committal of Summary Offences

(1) Introduction

Normally summary only offences will be tried by the magistrates' court and the ques- **7–96** tion of mode of trial does not arise. The *Criminal Justice Act* 1988 makes provision for certain summary offences to be dealt with at the Crown Court but only if there is some evident connection between the either way offence that is being committed and the summary offence which justifies the offences being dealt with together. The powers are included in ss.40 and 41.

(2) Joinder of certain summary offences in an indictment

Criminal Justice Act 1988, s.40

Power to join in indictment count for common assault etc.

7–97 **40.**—(1) A count charging a person with a summary offence to which this section applies may be included in an indictment if the charge—

(a) is founded on the same facts or evidence as a count charging an indictable offence; or

(b) is part of a series of offences of the same or similar character as an indictable offence which is also charged,

but only if (in either case) the facts or evidence relating to the offence *were disclosed to a magistrates' court inquiring into the offence as examining justices or* are disclosed by material which, in pursuance of regulations made under paragraph 1 of Schedule 3 to the *Crime and Disorder Act* 1998 (procedure where person sent for trial under section 51 [or 51A]), has been served on the person charged.

(2) Where a count charging an offence to which this section applies is included in an indictment, the offence shall be tried in the same manner as if it were an indictable offence; but the Crown Court may only deal with the offender in respect of it in a manner in which a magistrates' court could have dealt with him.

(3) The offences to which this section applies are—

(a) common assault;

(aa) an offence under section 90(1) of the *Criminal Justice Act* 1991 (assaulting a prisoner custody officer);

(ab) an offence under section 13(1) of the *Criminal Justice and Public Order Act* 1994 (assaulting a secure training centre custody officer);

(b) an offence under section 12(1) of the *Theft Act* 1968 (taking motor vehicle or other conveyance without authority etc.);

(c) an offence under section 103(1)(b) of the *Road Traffic Act* 1988 (driving a motor vehicle while disqualified);

(d) an offence mentioned in the first column of Schedule 2 to the *Magistrates' Courts Act* 1980 (criminal damage etc.) which would otherwise be triable only summarily by virtue of section 22(2) of that Act; and

(e) any summary offence specified under subsection (4) below.

(4) The Secretary of State may by order made by statutory instrument specify for the purposes of this section any summary offence which is punishable with imprisonment or involves obligatory or discretionary disqualification from driving.

(5) A statutory instrument containing an order under this section shall be subject to annulment in pursuance of a resolution of either House of Parliament.

[This section is printed as amended by the *Road Traffic (Consequential Provisions) Act* 1988, Sched. 3, the *Criminal Justice and Public Order Act* 1994, Sched. 9, the *Criminal Procedure and Investigations Act* 1996, Sched. 1, and the *Crime and Disorder Act* 1998, Sched. 8. As from a day to be appointed, the *Criminal Justice Act* 2003, Scheds 3 and 37, repeal the words in italics in subs.(1) and insert the words in square brackets. As from May 9, 2005, the *Criminal Justice Act 2003 (Commencement No. 9) Order* 2005 (S.I. 2005 No. 1267) brought the insertion of the words in square brackets into force for the limited purpose of cases sent for trial under s.51A(3)(d) of the *Crime and Disorder Act* 1998 (*ante*, § 7–79).]

General

7–98 Section 40 is a procedural provision enabling the joinder in an indictment in certain circumstances of a count charging a summary offence together with a count validly charging an indictable offence: *Plant* [2008] 2 Cr.App.R. 27, CA. Since it was always the intention of Parliament that summary offences should be tried by magistrates, the language of s.40 ought not to be strained in its application to defeat that intention: *Smith (B.P.)* [1997] 1 Cr.App.R. 390, CA. A conviction on an offence misjoined in breach of s.40(1) will be a nullity (*Callaghan*, 94 Cr.App.R. 226, CA) as will a conviction for an offence not specified in s.40(3) purportedly joined under subs. (1) (*Ashton; Draz; O'Reilly* [2006] 2 Cr.App.R. 15, CA).

The power in s.40 only applies where there has been a committal for trial or a sending for trial pursuant to s.51 of the *Crime and Disorder Act* 1998; it does not permit the inclusion of a count charging such an offence in an indictment where there has been a transfer for trial under s.4 of the *Criminal Justice Act* 1987 or s.53 of the *Criminal Justice Act* 1991: *T. and K.* [2001] 1 Cr.App.R. 32, CA.

The offences which may be joined

The reference to "common assault" in s.40(3) includes an offence of battery: *Lynsey* **7-99** [1995] 2 Cr. App. R. 667, CA.

No order has been made by the Secretary of State under s.40(4) specifying further offences to which the section applies.

Nature of the connection between the summary only and indictable offence

There must be an appropriate nexus between the summary offence proposed to be **7-100** joined under s.40 and the indictable offence in the indictment; it will not be sufficient if the only connection is with another summary offence that is itself validly joined: *Callaghan*, 94 Cr.App.R. 226, CA.

The phrase "founded on the same facts or evidence" within s.40(1)(a) refers to a sufficient factual or evidential overlap to make it both just and convenient for the summary only offence and the indictable offence to be tried together, and would certainly apply where the evidence of facts going to establish the summary offence would be admissible as part of the narrative leading up to the commission of the indictable offence: *Cox* [2001] 5 *Archbold News* 2, CA. Thus, a charge of driving whilst disqualified was properly joined to a charge of witness intimidation where the latter offence arose from threats made to the arresting officer (*ibid.*); a charge of taking a conveyance without authority was founded on the same facts as an offence of robbery where those offences formed part of a continuous series of events during an evening of criminality (*Simon* [1992] Crim.L.R. 444, CA (see the transcript)); a charge of driving whilst disqualified was founded on the same facts or evidence as a charge of possession of an offensive weapon, where the weapon had been found in a motor car that was being driven by the disqualified driver (*Bird* [1995] Crim.L.R. 745, CA).

As to whether the two offences "form part of a series of offences of the same or similar character", see *Smith (B.P.)* [1997] 1 Cr.App.R. 390, CA (driving a conveyance taken without authority and driving whilst disqualified on the same date not properly joined to an offence of dangerous driving more than a month later) and *Lewis*, 95 Cr.App.R. 131, CA (common assault on police officer at police station not properly joined with threats to kill former girlfriend and her cohabitee).

Offences of criminal damage etc otherwise triable only summarily

The limited sentencing powers in s.33 of the *Magistrates' Courts Act* 1980 do not **7-101** apply where an offence to which s.22 of that Act would otherwise apply is included in an indictment under s.40 of the *Criminal Justice Act* 1988: see *Fennell* [2000] 2 Cr.App.R. 310, CA, and *Alden* [2002] 2 Cr.App.R. 326, CA.

(3) Power of Crown Court to deal with summary offence where person committed for either way offence

Criminal Justice Act 1988, s.41

Power of Crown Court to deal with summary offence where person committed for either way offence

7–102 **41.**—(1) *Where a magistrates' court commits a person to the Crown Court for trial on indictment for an offence triable either way or a number of such offences, it may also commit him for trial for any summary offence with which he is charged and which—*

(a) *is punishable with imprisonment or involves obligatory or discretionary disqualification from driving; and*

(b) *arises out of circumstances which appear to the court to be the same as or connected with those giving rise to the offence, or one of the offences, triable either way,*

whether or not evidence relating to that summary offence appears on the depositions or written statements in the case; and the trial of the information charging the summary offence shall then be treated as if the magistrates' court had adjourned it under section 10 of the Magistrates' Courts Act *1980 and had not fixed the time and place for its resumption.*

(2) *Where a magistrates' court commits a person to the Crown Court for trial on indictment for a number of offences triable either way and exercises the power conferred by subsection (1) above in respect of a summary offence, the magistrates' court shall give the Crown Court and the person who is committed for trial a notice stating which of the offences triable either way appears to the court to arise out of circumstances which are the same as or connected with those giving rise to the summary offence.*

(3) *A magistrates' court's decision to exercise the power conferred by subsection (1) above shall not be subject to appeal or liable to be questioned in any court.*

(4) *The committal of a person under this section in respect of an offence to which section 40 above applies shall not preclude the exercise in relation to the offence of the power conferred by that section; but where he is tried on indictment for such an offence, the functions of the Crown Court under this section in relation to the offence shall cease.*

(4A) *The committal of a person under this section in respect of an offence to which section 40 above applies shall not prevent him being found guilty of that offence under section 6(3) of the* Criminal Law Act *1967 (alternative verdicts on trial on indictment); but where he is convicted under that provision of such an offence, the functions of the Crown Court under this section in relation to the offence shall cease.*

(5) *If he is convicted on the indictment, the Crown Court shall consider whether the conditions specified in subsection (1) above were satisfied.*

(6) *If it considers that they were satisfied, it shall state to him the substance of the summary offence and ask him whether he pleads guilty or not guilty.*

(7) *If he pleads guilty, the Crown Court shall convict him, but may deal with him in respect of that offence only in a manner in which a magistrates' court could have dealt with him.*

(8) *If he does not plead guilty, the Crown Court may try him for the offence, but may deal with him only in a manner in which a magistrates' court could have dealt with him.*

(9) [*Repealed*]

(10) *The Crown Court shall inform the designated officer for the magistrates' court of the outcome of any proceedings under this section.*

(11) *Where the Court of Appeal allows an appeal against conviction of an offence triable either way which arose out of circumstances which were the same as or connected with those giving rise to a summary offence of which the appellant was convicted under this section—*

(a) *it shall set aside his conviction of the summary offence and give the designated officer for the magistrates' court notice that it has done so; and*

(b) *it may direct that no further proceedings in relation to the offence are to be undertaken;*

and the proceedings before the Crown Court in relation to the offence shall thereafter be disregarded for all purposes.

(12) *A notice under subsection (11) above shall include particulars of any direction given under paragraph (b) of that subsection in relation to the offence.*

(13) [*Repealed*].

[This section is re-printed as amended by the *Access to Justice Act* 1999, Scheds 13 and 15, and the *Courts Act* 2003, Scheds 8 and 10. As from a day or days to be appointed, the *Domestic Violence Crime and Victims Act* 2004, Sched. 10, inserts subs. (4A). The whole section is due to be repealed by the *Criminal Justice Act* 2003, Scheds 3 and 37, as from a day to be appointed.]

Section 41 provides for the magistrates' court which commits a person to the Crown Court for trial on an either way matter under s.6 of the *Magistrates' Courts Act* 1980 to also commit for trial certain summary offences with which he is charged. The summary offence must be punishable with imprisonment or carry a disqualification from driving. It must also arise out of the same circumstances as the indictable offence. **7–103**

The summary offence must be charged from the outset rather than added to the indictment as under s.40 but evidence relating to it does not need to have been disclosed in the committal papers. The court will adjourn the summary offence 'sine die' (without a date being fixed) and await the outcome of the Crown Court proceedings. A notice must be served on the Crown Court and defence identifying the either way offence to which the summary offence is linked.

The section does not apply to cases sent under s.51 or 51A of the *Crime and Disorder Act* 1998 or cases transferred under the *Criminal Justice Act* 1987 or the *Criminal Justice Act* 1991.

The Crown Court can only deal with a summary offence under this section when there is a conviction on an indictable offence and a guilty plea to the summary offence. On conviction, the sentences available are those of the magistrates' court and the observations about s.22 and the categorisation of criminal damage offences apply equally under this section as they do under s.40. If the defendant is acquitted of the linked indictable offence or pleads not guilty to the summary offence the powers of the Crown Court cease. The Crown Court may then dismiss the case under s.41(9) or send the case back to the magistrates' court for trial. **7–104**

In *Foote*, 94 Cr.App.R. 82, CA, a defendant was committed to the Crown Court for trial on a charge of reckless driving and was also committed under s.41 for on a charge of careless driving. At the Crown Court his plea of guilty to the lesser charge was accepted by the prosecution and the Crown Court proceeded to sentence him. It was held that the conviction and sentence at the Crown Court was a nullity. The case should have been remitted to the magistrates' court where it was deemed to have been adjourned and it should be dealt with there. The provisions of s.41 relating to the conviction of a summary charge on the indictment also applies to charges properly included on the indictment under s.40. Where a defendant pleaded guilty at the Crown Court to an offence of driving whilst disqualified which was a summary only offence which had been included on the indictment under s.40 with a charge of possessing an offensive weapon it was held that the Crown Court could impose a sentence even though the indictable offence was not proceeded with because there was a conviction on the indictment: *Bird*, *ante*.

E. Committal of Either Way Offences For Trial to the Crown Court

(1) Introduction

Criminal offences are categorised into three types according to the seriousness of the offence. The gravity of the offence is marked by the length of sentence that can be imposed. The powers of the magistrates' courts are limited to six months' imprisonment or a fine of £5,000 for as single offence. Where there are two or more either way offences the total sentencing powers of the court are increased to 12 months' imprisonment as a maximum. Less serious offences are classified as summary only. The most serious offences are triable on indictment only and must be dealt with at the Crown Court. In between are the either way offences which can be tried at the magistrates' court or the Crown Court. These are offences that cover a wide range of criminal conduct and aggravating features could affect the seriousness of the offence so that Crown Court trial is more suitable with the added sentencing powers of that court. **7–105**

Summary offences must normally be dealt with in the magistrates' court (but see *Criminal Justice Act* 1988, ss.40 and 41). Either way offences may be tried either at the magistrates' court or the Crown Court. The mode of trial procedure is described *ante*: ss.17A–25. Where the case is to be dealt with at the Crown Court it must be committed under *Magistrates' Courts Act* 1980, ss.6(1) or 6(2). Indictable only charges cannot be dealt with at the magistrates' court and are sent to the Crown Court under s.51 of the *Crime and Disorder Act* 1998. By s.41 and Sched. 3 of the *Criminal Justice Act* 2003, commitals will be abolished and all indictable only and either way cases that have been allocated for Crown Court trial will be sent to the Crown Court under the new scheme set out in ss.51 to 51E of the *Crime and Disorder Act* 1998 (*ante*, §§ 7–77 *et seq.*).]

A case can also be brought before the Crown Court by applying for a voluntary bill of indictment which is done directly to the Crown Court: *Administration of Justice (Miscellaneous Provisions) Act* 1933, s.2. This procedure involves no proceedings before a magistrates' court and, accordingly, is outside the scope of this work.

(2) General nature of committal proceedings

7–106 The court, when committing a case for trial is referred to in statute as "examining justices". Its role is to inquire into the charge and decide whether there is sufficient evidence to put the defendant on trial before a jury. If there is, the case is committed. If not, the case is discharged. The prosecution will prepare the committal documents which will consist of written statements from witnesses, depositions, documents and exhibits. Prior to the committal, a copy of all the papers must be served on the defence who will then review the evidence and decide whether to seek a committal without consideration of the evidence (s.6(2)) or request a contested committal on the basis that there is no case to answer that could be put before a jury: s.6(1).

Standard guidelines are applied locally for the preparation of committal bundles, usually six weeks for cases in custody and eight weeks for those on bail. The original papers will be served on the court to be forwarded to the Crown Court on committal.

Magistrates' Courts Act 1980, s.4

General nature of committal proceedings

7–107 **4.**—(1) *The functions of examining justices may be discharged by a single justice.*

(2) *Examining justices shall sit in open court except where any enactment contains an express provision to the contrary and except where it appears to them as respects the whole or any part of committal proceedings that the ends of justice would not be served by their sitting in open court.*

(3) *Subject to subsection (4) below, evidence tendered before examining justices shall be tendered in the presence of the accused.*

(4) *Examining justices may allow evidence to be tendered before them in the absence of the accused if—*

(a) *they consider that by reason of his disorderly conduct before them it is not practicable for the evidence to be tendered in his presence, or*

(b) *he cannot be present for reasons of health but is represented by a legal representative and has consented to the evidence being tendered in his absence.*

[This section is printed as amended by the *Courts and Legal Services Act* 1990, Sched. 18, and the *Criminal Procedure and Investigations Act* 1996, Sched. 1. As from a day to be appointed, the whole section is to be repealed by the *Criminal Justice Act* 2003, Sched. 37.]

7–108 A committal can be heard by a single magistrate. The rule is for the committal to take place in open court. An exception to this is when a defendant is charged under the *Official Secrets Act* 1920. The presence of the accused at committal may be excused if he is behaving in a disorderly manner or if he is unwell and he may then be represented through his lawyer. This section relates only to the process of the committal when the evidence is considered by the court and not to the actual act of committal itself. The evidence must comply with the requirements of *Magistrates' Courts Act* 1980, ss.5A–5F.

Part I

(3) Evidence at committal proceedings

Magistrates' Courts Act 1980, ss.5A, 5B

Evidence which is admissible

5A.—(1) *Evidence falling within subsection (2) below, and only that evidence, shall be admissible by a magistrates' court inquiring into an offence as examining justices.* **7–109**

(2) *Evidence falls within this subsection if it—*

(a) *is tendered by or on behalf of the prosecutor, and*

(b) *falls within subsection (3) below.*

(3) *The following evidence falls within this subsection—*

(a) *written statements complying with section 5B below;*

(b) *the documents or other exhibits (if any) referred to in such statements;*

(c) *depositions complying with section 5C below;*

(d) *the documents or other exhibits (if any) referred to in such depositions;*

(e) *statements complying with section 5D below;*

(f) *documents falling within section 5E below.*

(4) *In this section "document" means anything in which information of any description is recorded.*

[Sections 5A to 5F were inserted by the *Criminal Procedure and Investigations Act* 1996, Sched. 1. As from a day to be appointed, they are to be repealed by the *Criminal Justice Act* 2003, Sched. 3, and replaced by the scheme of sending to the Crown Court under ss.51 to 51E of the *Crime and Disorder Act* 1998 (*ante*, §§ 7–77 *et seq.*).]

Written statements

5B.—(1) *For the purposes of section 5A above a written statement complies with this section if—* **7–110**

(a) *the conditions falling within subsection (2) below are met, and*

(b) *such of the conditions falling within subsection (3) below as apply are met.*

(2) *The conditions falling within this subsection are that—*

(a) *the statement purports to be signed by the person who made it;*

(b) *the statement contains a declaration by that person to the effect that it is true to the best of his knowledge and belief and that he made the statement knowing that, if it were tendered in evidence, he would be liable to prosecution if he wilfully stated in it anything which he knew to be false or did not believe to be true;*

(c) *before the statement is tendered in evidence a copy of the statement is given, by or on behalf of the prosecutor, to each of the other parties to the proceedings.*

(3) *The conditions falling within this subsection are that—*

(a) *if the statement is made by a person under 18 years old, it gives his age;*

(b) *if it is made by a person who cannot read it, it is read to him before he signs it and is accompanied by a declaration by the person who so read the statement to the effect that it was so read;*

(c) *if it refers to any other document as an exhibit, the copy given to any other party to the proceedings under subsection (2)(c) above is accompanied by a copy of that document or by such information as may be necessary to enable the party to whom it is given to inspect that document or a copy of it.*

(4) *So much of any statement as is admitted in evidence by virtue of this section shall, unless the court commits the accused for trial by virtue of section 6(2) below or the court otherwise directs, be read aloud at the hearing; and where the court so directs an account shall be given orally of so much of any statement as is not read aloud.*

(5) *Any document or other object referred to as an exhibit and identified in a statement admitted in evidence by virtue of this section shall be treated as if it had been produced as an exhibit and identified in court by the maker of the statement.*

(6) *In this section "document" means anything in which information of any description is recorded.*

[Sections 5A to 5F were inserted by the *Criminal Procedure and Investigations Act* 1996, Sched. 1. As from a day to be appointed, they are to be repealed by the *Criminal*

Justice Act 2003, Sched. 3, and replaced by the scheme of sending to the Crown Court under ss.51 to 51E of the *Crime and Disorder Act* 1998 (*ante*, §§ 7–77 *et seq.*).]

7–111 Any statement must be that of the witness. If the witness does not speak English his statement must be recorded in the language in which it was made and signed by him and not written in English by an interpreter. The correct procedure is for the interpreter to provide a written translation of the statement which is then produced as an exhibit: *Raynor*, 165 J.P. 149, CA.

Magistrates' Courts Act 1980, s.5C

Depositions

7–112 **5C.**—(1) *For the purposes of section 5A above a deposition complies with this section if—*

(a) *a copy of it is sent to the prosecutor under section 97A(9) below,*

(b) *the condition falling within subsection (2) below is met, and*

(c) *the condition falling within subsection (3) below is met, in a case where it applies.*

(2) *The condition falling within this subsection is that before the magistrates' court begins to inquire into the offence concerned as examining justices a copy of the deposition is given, by or on behalf of the prosecutor, to each of the other parties to the proceedings.*

(3) *The condition falling within this subsection is that, if the deposition refers to any other document as an exhibit, the copy given to any other party to the proceedings under subsection (2) above is accompanied by a copy of that document or by such information as may be necessary to enable the party to whom it is given to inspect that document or a copy of it.*

(4) *So much of any deposition as is admitted in evidence by virtue of this section shall, unless the court commits the accused for trial by virtue of section 6(2) below or the court otherwise directs, be read aloud at the hearing; and where the court so directs an account shall be given orally of so much of any deposition as is not read aloud.*

(5) *Any document or other object referred to as an exhibit and identified in a deposition admitted in evidence by virtue of this section shall be treated as if it had been produced as an exhibit and identified in court by the person whose evidence is taken as the deposition.*

(6) *In this section "document" means anything in which information of any description is recorded.*

[Sections 5A to 5F were inserted by the *Criminal Procedure and Investigations Act* 1996, Sched. 1. As from a day to be appointed, they are to be repealed by the *Criminal Justice Act* 2003, Sched. 3, and replaced by the scheme of sending to the Crown Court under ss.51 to 51E of the *Crime and Disorder Act* 1998 (*ante*, §§ 7–77 *et seq.*).]

7–113 Depositions cover situations where a witness will not provide a statement voluntarily under ss.5B. The witness may be summonsed or brought before the court by warrant and then the evidence will be taken before the court in the form of a deposition: *Magistrates' Courts Act* 1980, s.97A.

Magistrates' Courts Act 1980, s.5D

Statements

7–114 **5D.**—(1) *For the purposes of section 5A above a statement complies with this section if the conditions falling within subsections (2) to (4) below are met.*

(2) *The condition falling within this subsection is that, before the committal proceedings begin, the prosecutor notifies the magistrates' court and each of the other parties to the proceedings that he believes—*

(a) *that the statement might by virtue of section 23 or 24 of the* Criminal Justice Act *1988 (statements in certain documents) be admissible as evidence if the case came to trial, and*

(b) *that the statement would not be admissible as evidence otherwise than by virtue of section 23 or 24 of that Act if the case came to trial.*

(3) *The condition falling within this subsection is that—*

(a) *the prosecutor's belief is based on information available to him at the time he makes the notification,*

(b) *he has reasonable grounds for his belief, and*

(c) *he gives the reasons for his belief when he makes the notification.*

(4) *The condition falling within this subsection is that when the court or a party is notified as mentioned in subsection (2) above a copy of the statement is given, by or on behalf of the prosecutor, to the court or the party concerned.*

(5) *So much of any statement as is in writing and is admitted in evidence by virtue of this section shall, unless the court commits the accused for trial by virtue of section 6(2) below or the court otherwise directs, be read aloud at the hearing; and where the court so directs an account shall be given orally of so much of any statement as is not read aloud.*

[Sections 5A to 5F were inserted by the *Criminal Procedure and Investigations Act* 1996, Sched. 1. As from a day to be appointed, they are to be repealed by the *Criminal Justice Act* 2003, Sched. 3, and replaced by the scheme of sending to the Crown Court under ss.51 to 51E of the *Crime and Disorder Act* 1998 (*ante*, §§ 7–77 *et seq.*).]

These statements are those to which ss.23 and 24 of the *Criminal Justice Act* 1988 apply. But see *R. (CPS) v. City of London Magistrates' Court, The Times*, April 17, 2006, DC where it was noted that these sections have been repealed by the *Criminal Justice Act* 2003. In this case the court indicated that s.5D is now "otiose" as a result of the hearsay provisions of the *Criminal Justice Act* 2003. However, s.5D has yet to be repealed. It may be that the section can still apply but all reference to the repealed ss.23 and 24 should be read as applying to the hearsay sections of the *Criminal Justice Act* 2003 (see *post*, § 10–66). **7–115**

Magistrates' Courts Act 1980, ss.5E, 5F

Other documents

5E.—(1) *The following documents fall within this section—* **7–116**

(a) *any document which by virtue of any enactment is evidence in proceedings before a magistrates' court inquiring into an offence as examining justices;*

(b) *any document which by virtue of any enactment is admissible, or may be used, or is to be admitted or received, in or as evidence in such proceedings;*

(c) *any document which by virtue of any enactment may be considered in such proceedings;*

(d) *any document whose production constitutes proof in such proceedings by virtue of any enactment;*

(e) *any document by the production of which evidence may be given in such proceedings by virtue of any enactment.*

(2) *In subsection (1) above—*

(a) *references to evidence include references to prima facie evidence;*

(b) *references to any enactment include references to any provision of this Act.*

(3) *So much of any document as is admitted in evidence by virtue of this section shall, unless the court commits the accused for trial by virtue of section 6(2) below or the court otherwise directs, be read aloud at the hearing; and where the court so directs an account shall be given orally of so much of any document as is not read aloud.*

(4) *In this section "document" means anything in which information of any description is recorded.*

[Sections 5A to 5F were inserted by the *Criminal Procedure and Investigations Act* 1996, Sched. 1. As from a day to be appointed, they are repealed by the *Criminal Justice Act* 2003, Sched. 3, and replaced by the scheme of sending to the Crown Court under ss.51 to 51E of the *Crime and Disorder Act* 1998 (*ante*, §§ 7–77 *et seq.*).]

Proof by production of copy

5F.—(1) *Where a statement, deposition or document is admissible in evidence by virtue of section 5B, 5C, 5D or 5E above it may be proved by the production of—* **7–117**

(a) *the statement, deposition or document, or*

(b) *a copy of it or the material part of it.*

(2) *Subsection (1)(b) above applies whether or not the statement, deposition or document is still in existence.*

(3) *It is immaterial for the purposes of this section how many removes there are between a copy and the original.*

(4) *In this section "copy", in relation to a statement, deposition or document, means anything onto which information recorded in the statement, deposition or document has been copied, by whatever means and whether directly or indirectly."*

[Sections 5A to 5F were inserted by the *Criminal Procedure and Investigations Act* 1996, Sched. 1. As from a day to be appointed, they are repealed by the *Criminal Justice Act* 2003, Sched. 3, and replaced by the scheme of sending to the Crown Court under ss.51 to 51E of the *Crime and Disorder Act* 1998 (*ante*, §§ 7–77 *et seq.*).]

(4) Decision to discharge or commit

Magistrates' Courts Act 1980, s.6

Discharge or committal for trial

7–118 **6.**—(1) *A magistrates' court inquiring into an offence as examining justices shall on consideration of the evidence—*

(a) *commit the accused for trial if it is of opinion that there is sufficient evidence to put him on trial by jury for any indictable offence;*

(b) *discharge him if it is not of that opinion and he is in custody for no other cause than the offence under inquiry;*

but the preceding provisions of this subsection have effect subject to the provisions of this and any other Act relating to the summary trial of indictable offences.

(2) *If a magistrates' court inquiring into an offence as examining justices is satisfied that all the evidence tendered by or on behalf of the prosecutor falls within section 5A(3) above, it may commit the accused for trial for the offence without consideration of the contents of any statements, depositions or other documents, and without consideration of any exhibits which are not documents, unless—*

(a) *the accused or one of the accused has no legal representative acting for him in the case, or*

(b) *a legal representative for the accused or one of the accused, as the case may be, has requested the court to consider a submission that there is insufficient evidence to put that accused on trial by jury for the offence;*

and subsection (1) above shall not apply to a committal for trial under this subsection.

(3) *Subject to section 4 of the* Bail Act *1976 and section 41 below, the court may commit a person for trial—*

(a) *in custody, that is to say, by committing him to custody there to be safety kept until delivered in due course of law, or*

(b) *on bail in accordance with the* Bail Act *1976, that is to say, by directing him to appear before the Crown Court for trial;*

and where his release on bail is conditional on his providing one or more surety or sureties and, in accordance with section 8(3) of the Bail Act *1976, the court fixes the amount in which the surety is to be bound with a view to his entering into his recognizance subsequently in accordance with subsections (4) and (5) or (6) of that section the court shall in the meantime commit the accused to custody in accordance with paragraph (a) of this subsection.*

(4) *Where the court has committed a person to custody in accordance with paragraph (a) of subsection (3) above, then, if that person is in custody for no other cause, the court may, at any time before his first appearance before the Crown Court, grant him bail in accordance with the* Bail Act *1976 subject to a duty to appear before the Crown Court for trial.*

(5) *Where a magistrates' court acting as examining justices commits any person for trial or determines to discharge him, the designated officer the court shall, on the day on which the committal proceedings are concluded or the next day, cause to be displayed in a part of the court house to which the public have access a notice—*

(a) *in either case giving that person's name, address, and age (if known);*

(b) *in a case where the court so commits him, stating the charge or charges on which he is committed and the court to which he is committed;*

(c) *in a case where the court determines to discharge him, describing the offence charged and stating that it has so determined;*

but this subsection shall have effect subject to section 4 of the Sexual Offences (Amendment) Act *1976 (anonymity of complainant in rape etc. cases).*

(6) *A notice displayed in pursuance of subsection (5) above shall not contain the name or*

address of any person under the age of 18 years unless the justices in question have stated that in their opinion he would be mentioned in the notice apart from the preceding provisions of this subsection and should be mentioned in it for the purpose of avoiding injustice to him.

[This section is printed as amended by the *Criminal Justice Act* 1988, Sched. 15, the *Criminal Justice Act* 1991, Sched. 8, the *Criminal Procedure and Investigations Act* 1996, Sched. 1, and the *Courts Act* 2003, Sched. 8. As from a day to be appointed, the whole section is to be repealed by the *Criminal Justice Act* 2003, Sched. 3.]

Only an either way offence can be committed to the Crown Court for trial under this **7–119** section. The court does not sit as "examining justices" when it is dealing with a summary only matter. The committal of such an offence is a nullity: *Bannister v. Clarke* [1920] 3 K.B. 598, DC. But see the *Criminal Justice Act* 1988, ss.40 and 41, *ante* §§ 7–97 *et seq.*

There are two types of committal. Under subs. (2) the court need not consider the evidence contained in the prosecution statements, etc. if it is satisfied that all such documentation complies with the admissibility requirements of s.5A. Under subs. (2)(a) and (b), the court has to consider the evidence if the defendant is unrepresented or if he wishes to make a submission that there is not sufficient evidence in the prosecution case to put him on trial before a jury. The procedure in connection with the two different committals is set out in the *Criminal Procedure Rules* 2011, rr.10.2 and 10.3 (Appendix G.). A contested committal takes place on the basis of the written statements and no live witnesses will be called.

In the committal without consideration of the evidence the defence admits that there is sufficient evidence on the face of the statements for the case to go to trial. If no admission is forthcoming the evidence will be read out to the court and the committal will only take place if the court is of the opinion that there is sufficient evidence to put the defendant on trial. For a committal under s.6(2) to be valid, all that is necessary is that the magistrates' court is satisfied that all the evidence tendered by the prosecution falls within s.5A(3) of the 1980 Act and that no submission of no case is made; the mere fact that a statement essential to support the charge is omitted from the papers will not invalidate the committal: *Harding* [1998] Crim.L.R. 877, CA.

The function of committal proceedings is to ensure that no person should stand trial unless a *prima facie* case is made out. The onus of making out the case is on the prosecution: *Epping and Harlow Justices, ex p. Massaro* [1973] Q.B. 433, DC.

The test to be applied is whether there is any evidence that the crime alleged has been committed by the defendant and if there is, whether that evidence is such that a jury, properly directed could convict on it: *Galbraith* [1981] 1 W.L.R. 1039, CA.

The prosecution has a discretion as to which witnesses to rely on and need only bring **7–120** evidence of a prima facie case, not one beyond reasonable doubt. Failure to include the statement of any specific witness is not a breach of natural justice but the prosecution is subject to a duty to be fair and not to mislead the court: *Wilkinson v. DPP*, 162 J.P. 591, DC.

The court must be satisfied that the evidence tendered is admissible. Where the committal was based on transcripts of police interviews of co-defendants who implicated the defendant this was held to be inadmissible as it did not comply with section 5A. This was a procedural defect that could not be remedied and the committal was quashed: *Bedwellty Justices, ex p. Williams* [1997] A.C. 225, HL.

But it is not the role of the court to assess the weight of evidence and rule on its admissibility. Where the evidence is legally admissible the case should be committed as the discretion to reject the evidence rests with the trial judge: *Horsham Justices, ex p. Bukhari*, 74 Cr.App.R. 291, DC.

The court may commit on any indictable offence that is made out in the evidence. It **7–121** is not restricted to finding sufficient evidence for the offence formally charged. If the court contemplates committing on a lesser charge, it should allow legal representatives to address them and it is bad practice for the prosecution to invite the court to commit on charges made out after the substantive matter has been discharged: *Gloucester Magistrates' Court, ex p. Chung*, 153 J.P. 75, DC.

If the court is not of the opinion that there is sufficient evidence it will discharge the defendant. The prosecution may later charge the defendant again if more evidence comes to light and seek committal once more. There is no question of *autrefois acquit* arising as the case has not been tried on its merits. The court may entertain charges which have been discharged before but repeated use of the committal procedure may be vexatious or amount to an abuse of process: *Manchester City Justices, ex p. Snelson*, 66 Cr.App.R. 44, DC.

Section 4 allows for the committal proceedings to take place in the absence of the accused in certain circumstances. Section 6 provides for the court to commit the accused for trial and the *Criminal Procedure Rules* 2011 require that the charge be read to the accused. There is no reference to procedure in the absence of the defendant. It has been held that this does not preclude the court from committing a person in absence. Where the defendant was absent through ill health, but was represented the appeal court said that the provisions of s.4(4) of the *Magistrates' Courts Act* 1980 and s.122 (representation through lawyer) allowed the court to proceed in the absence of the accused as there were no statutory provisions to the contrary: *Liverpool Street Magistrates' Court, ex p. Quantrell* [1999] 2 Cr.App.R. 24, DC. See also *Bow Street Magistrates' Court, ex p. Government of Germany* [1998] Q.B. 556, DC.

7–122 In some committals there is a good deal of paperwork to be considered by the court. It is acceptable for the documents in the case to be lodged with the court in advance so that there may be an opportunity to read and digest the evidence. That this is done with out the defence consenting is immaterial. Copies of the statements have to be served on the court in any event under the *Criminal Procedure Rules* 2011, r.27.1 (Appendix G–158): *Colchester Stipendiary Magistrate, ex p. Beck* [1979] Q.B. 674, DC.

(5) Discharge or committal without consideration of evidence

7–123 See *Criminal Procedure Rules* 2011, r.10.2 in Appendix G.

7–124 See *Criminal Procedure Rules* 2011, r.10.3 in Appendix G.

(6) Reminder to defendant

7–125 On committal the defendant must be advised that live witnesses will not be called at the Crown Court trial unless he requests that they attend.

7–126 See *Criminal Procedure Rules* 2011, r.10.4 in Appendix G.

7–127 Where a defendant is charged with an offence involving a death the court has a duty to inform the coroner of the charge and proceedings. The coroner is responsible for an inquest: *Coroner's Act* 1988, s.17.

(7) Place of trial

Magistrates' Courts Act 1980, s.7

Place of trial on indictment

7–128 **7.** *—A magistrates' court committing a person for trial shall specify the place at which he is to be tried, and in selecting that place shall have regard to—*

(a) *the convenience of the defence, the prosecution and the witnesses,*
(b) *the expediting of the trial, and*
(c) *any direction given by or on behalf of the Lord Chief Justice with the concurrence of the Lord Chancellor under section 4(5) of the* Courts Act *1971.*

[As from a day to be appointed, this section is repealed by the *Criminal Justice Act* 2003, Scheds 3 and 37.]

7–129 The court will select the appropriate Crown Court according to its location and the directions in the *Consolidated Criminal Practice Directions* (see Appendix F) which allocate types of cases to different tiers of the Crown Court based on the seriousness of the offence. The case will be adjourned to a fixed date where a Plea and Case Management Hearing will take place. The Crown Court provides the appropriate dates. The Crown Court may change the venue once the case has been committed.

(8) Reporting restrictions

Magistrates' Courts Act 1980, s.8

Restrictions on reports of committal proceedings

8.—(1) *Except as provided by subsections (2), (3) and (8) below, it shall not be lawful to publish in Great Britain a written report, or to include in a relevant programme for reception in Great Britain a report, of any committal proceedings in England and Wales containing any matter other than that permitted by subsection (4) below.* **7–130**

(2) *Subject to subsection (2A) below a magistrates' court shall, on an application for the purpose made with reference to any committal proceedings by the accused or one of the accused, as the case may be, order that subsection (1) above shall not apply to reports of those proceedings.*

(2A) *Where in the case of two or more accused one of them objects to the making on an order under subsection (2) above, the court shall make the order if, and only if, it is satisfied, after hearing the representations of the accused, that it is in the interests of justice to do so.*

(2B) *An order under subsection (2) above shall not apply to reports of proceedings under subsection (2A) above, but any decisions of the court to make or not to make such an order may be contained in reports published or included in a relevant programme before the time authorised by subsection (3) below.*

(3) *It shall not be unlawful under this section to publish or include in a relevant programme a report of committal proceedings containing any matter other than that permitted by subsection (4) below—*

(a) *where the magistrates' court determines not to commit the accused, or determines to commit none of the accused, for trial, after it so determines;*

(b) *where the court commits the accused or any of the accused for trial, after the conclusion of his trial or, as the case may be, the trial of the last to be tried;*

and where at any time during the inquiry the court proceeds to try summarily the case of one or more of the accused under section 25(3) or (7) below, while committing the other accused or one or more of the other accused for trial, it shall not be unlawful under this section to publish or include in a relevant programme as part of a report of the summary trial, after the court determines to proceed as aforesaid, a report of so much of the committal proceedings containing any such matter as takes place before the determination.

(4) *The following matters may be contained in a report of committal proceedings published or included in a relevant programme without an order under subsection (2) above before the time authorised by subsection (3) above, that is to say—*

(a) *the identity of the court and the names of the examining justices;*

(b) *the names, addresses and occupations of the parties and witnesses and the ages of the accused and witnesses;*

(c) *the offence or offences, or a summary of them, with which the accused is or are charged;*

(d) *the names of the legal representatives engaged in the proceedings;*

(e) *any decision of the court to commit the accused or any of the accused for trial, and any decision of the court on the disposal of the case of any accused not committed;*

(f) *where the court commits the accused or any of the accused for trial, the charge or charges, or a summary of them, on which he is committed and the court to which he is committed;*

(g) *where the committal proceedings are adjourned, the date and place to which they are adjourned;*

(h) *any arrangements as to bail on committal or adjournment;*

(i) *whether a right to representation funded by the Legal Services Commission as part of the Criminal Defence Service was granted to the accused or any of the accused.*

(5) *If a report is published or included in a relevant programme in contravention of this section, the following persons, that is to say—*

(a) *in the case of a publication of a written report as part of a newspaper or periodical, any proprietor, editor or publisher of the newspaper or periodical;*
(b) *in the case of a publication of a written report otherwise than as part of a newspaper or periodical, the person who publishes it;*
(c) *in the case of the inclusion of a report in a relevant programme, any body corporate which provides the service in which the programme is included and any person having functions in relation to the programme corresponding to those of an editor of a newspaper,*

shall be liable on summary conviction to a fine not exceeding level 5 on the standard scale.

(6) *Proceedings for an offence under this section shall not, in England and Wales, be instituted otherwise than by or with the consent of the Attorney-General.*

(7) *Subsection (1) above shall be in addition to, and not in derogation from, the provisions of any other enactment with respect to the publication of reports and proceedings of magistrates' and other courts.*

(8) *For the purposes of this section committal proceedings shall, in relation to an information charging an indictable offence, be deemed to include any proceedings in the magistrates' court before the court proceeds to inquire into the information as examining justices; but where a magistrates' court which has begun to try an information summarily discontinues the summary trial in pursuance of section 25(2) or (6) below and proceeds to inquire into the information as examining justices, that circumstance shall not make it unlawful under this section for a report of any proceedings on the information which was published or included in a relevant programme before the court determined to proceed as aforesaid to have been so published or included in a relevant programme.*

(9) [*Repealed*]

(10) *In this section—*

"publish", in relation to a report, means publish the report, either by itself or as part of a newspaper or periodical, for distribution to the public.

"relevant programme" means a programme included in a programme service (within the meaning of the Broadcasting Act *1990).*

[This section is printed as amended by the *Contempt of Court Act* 1981, s.4, the *Criminal Justice (Amendment) Act* 1981, s.1, the *Criminal Justice Act* 1982, the *Broadcasting Act* 1990, Sched. 20, the *Courts and Legal Services Act* 1990, Sched. 18, and the *Access to Justice Act* 1999, Sched. 24. As from a day to be appointed, the whole section is to be repealed by the *Criminal Justice Act* 2003, Scheds 3 and 37.]

7–131 See the *Criminal Procedure Rules* 2011, r.10.1 in Appendix G–47.

7–132 Although committal proceedings must normally take place in open court (s.4) reporting restrictions automatically apply under s.8 and the effect of this must be explained to the defendant personally if he is present.

Application can be made for the restrictions to be lifted. If there is only one defendant the court shall lift the restrictions but if there are two or more defendants and not all of them wish to have the restrictions lifted then the court has to exercise its discretion in the interests of justice.

Subsection (4) lists the information that is not covered by the restrictions and basic details of this nature may be included in a report. Breach of the restrictions is a summary offence under subs. (5).

Before the court makes an order for the lifting of reporting restrictions at committal all the defendants must be present and be given an opportunity to make representations. The lifting of restrictions in a case of murder without hearing submissions from all the defendants was held to be in breach of natural justice: *Wirral District Magistrates' Court, ex p. Meikle* [1991] C.O.D. 2, DC.

Only where a very strong case is made out should the court lift restrictions when not all the accused wish to have them lifted. The interests of justice test was not met when one defendant wanted to lift the restrictions to publicise "sharp practice" by the police: *Leeds Justices, ex p. Sykes*, 76 Cr.App.R. 129, DC.

7–133 Application can be made at any time in the proceedings and before the committal begins. Where a defendant faced several charges and there were several defendants, an application to lift the restrictions was dealt with at the preliminary stage. The case then led to several different sets of committal proceedings. The order made at the start of the initial committal was held to apply to all the committals in which the defendant was later involved. The appeal court did advise that the court should be precise about the extent and effect of the order: *Magistrates' Courts Act* 1980, s.8(8); *Bow Street Magistrates, ex p. Kray* [1969] 1 Q.B. 473, DC.

Section 4(2) of the *Contempt of Court Act* 1981 also applies to committals. The restrictions are imposed in different situations and for different purposes; that is where the publication of committal proceedings was prejudicial to the defendant's interests and where publication of proceedings, whether or not prejudicial to the defendant would be a contempt. A defendant applied for reporting restrictions to be lifted but later on in the committal the court made an order under s.4 of the *Contempt of Court Act* 1981 and re-imposed reporting restrictions. A journalist challenged this decision and the court held that the words "any other proceedings pending or imminent" in s.4(2) included potential proceedings in the Crown Court and so did apply: *Horsham Justices, ex p. Farquharson* [1982] Q.B. 762, DC and CA (Civ.Div).

(9) Committal of corporation

Magistrates' Courts Act 1980, Sched. 3, paras 1–3(1)

1.—(1) A magistrates' court may commit a corporation for trial by an order in writing empowering the prosecutor to prefer a bill of indictment in respect of the offence named in the order. **7–134**

(2) An order under this paragraph shall not prohibit the inclusion in the bill of indictment of counts that under section 2 of the *Administration of Justice (Miscellaneous Provisions) Act* 1933 may be included in the bill in substitution for, or in addition to, counts charging the offence named in the order.

2. A representative may on behalf of a corporation—

(a) *make before examining justices such representations as could be made by an accused who is not a corporation;*

(b) consent to the corporation being tried summarily;

(c) enter a plea of guilty or not guilty on the trial by a magistrates' court of an information.

3.—(1) Where a representative appears, any requirement of this Act that anything shall be done in the presence of the accused, or shall be read or said to the accused, shall be construed as a requirement that that thing shall be done in the presence of the representative or read or said to the representative.

[The preceding paragraphs are printed as amended by the *Criminal Procedure and Investigations Act* 1996, Sched. 1. As from a day to be appointed, the words in italics in para. (2)(a) will be repealed by the *Criminal Justice Act* 2003, Scheds 3 and 37.]

The act of committal of a corporation is the oral determination by court, which will not be invalidated if the court subsequently uses the wrong form for the purposes of para. 1(1): *Nelson Group Services (Maintenance) Ltd* [1999] 1 W.L.R. 1526, CA.

(10) Practical considerations

(a) *Criminal Procedure Rules*

Part 10 of the *Criminal Procedure Rules* 2011 sets out a series of rules in connection with committal of cases to the Crown Court under s.6 of the *Magistrates' Courts Act* 1980: see Appendix G. **7–135**

(b) *Consolidated Criminal Practice Direction*

See paragraphs V.56.1 and V.56.3 to V.56.5 of the *Consolidated Criminal Practice Direction* (Appendix F). **7–136**

By virtue of para. V.56.3 and Annex E, the following standard directions for case progression apply where a case is committed to the Crown Court under s.6 of the *Magistrates' Courts Act* 1980.

Consolidated Criminal Practice Direction, Annex E, Case Management Form—Directions for Case Sent to the Crown Court

ACTION	TIME LIMITS	DIRECTIONS
1	Date committed	Prosecution to serve provisional draft indictment, if not already done.
2	14 days after Action 1	Prosecution to serve primary or initial disclosure. Defence to notify prosecution of witness requirements. Prosecution to serve any application for hearsay or defendant's bad character.
3	28 days after Action 1	Prosecution to serve final draft indictment and any special measures applications. Defence to serve any application under section 41 of the *Youth Justice and Criminal Evidence Act* 1999.
4	14 days after Action 2	Defence to serve: (i) defence statement (including any alibi details) or notification of guilty plea; (ii) any application for hearsay/bad character; (iii) response to hearsay/bad character application by prosecution.
5	14 days after Action 3	Defence to serve response to any prosecution application for special measures. Prosecution and defence to notify Crown Court of names of trial advocate and time estimate. Defence to notify Crown Court of non-availability of expert witnesses, with reasons. Witness Care Unit to notify Crown Court and prosecution of dates when witnesses required by defence are unavailable, with reasons.
6	14 Days after Action 4	Prosecution to serve responses to hearsay/ bad character.

(c) *Criminal Case Management Framework*

7–137 As to the objectives and expectations of the parties where a case is sent for trial under s.51 of the *Crime and Disorder Act* 1998, see Ch. 6 of the Criminal Case Management Framework (Appendix I).

VII. PREPARATION FOR SUMMARY TRIAL

(1) General

7–138 Once a plea of not guilty has been entered and the case is to proceed to summary trial, an adjournment will be necessary in order for the parties to prepare for the trial (see *Thames Magistrates' Court, ex p. Polemis* [1974] 1 W.L.R. 1371, DC (*post*, § 7–162)).

The Criminal Procedure Rule Committee has issued a revised case management form for use in preparation for trial in magistrates' courts under r.3.11(1) of the *Criminal Procedure Rules* 2011 (S.I. 2011 No. 1709). The form was authorised for use with effect from October 3, 2011. Its purpose is to assist the parties and the court to comply with their respective obligations under Pts 1 and 3 of the 2011 Rules, but it is the duty of the court to decide whether, and how, the form is to be used in any given case, or category of case. The form is divided into four parts. Part 1 is for completion by the prosecution, and requires prosecution details and case management information to be provided, together with the details of any directions that are to be requested by the prosecution. Part 2 is the equivalent for the defence, and includes questions as to whether the defendant has been advised that credit will be given for a plea and that a trial may be conducted in his absence if he fails to appear. Part 3 requires (a) each party to provide details about the witnesses they propose to call, and (b) the court to specify whether the attendance of specified prosecution witnesses is justified. Part 4 requires the court to record its directions for trial. Standard case preparation time-limits are set out on page 6 of the form (see *post*, § 7–139).

Additionally, there are guidance notes appended to the form. Part A sets out as follows how it is expected that the form will be used in practice: (a) as a general rule, the form is for use in any case to be tried in a magistrates' court in which a not guilty plea is entered; (b) where the prosecutor anticipates such a plea then, unless otherwise directed by the court, he should complete Parts 1 and 3 and serve it on the defendant with the initial details of the prosecution case, or as soon as possible thereafter (and in any event before first hearing); and (c) before (or if the court allows, during) the first hearing the defendant must complete Parts 2 and 3 unless the court otherwise directs. The notes also give guidance on adapting the procedure for completion of the form where a defendant is unrepresented or a prosecutor has not anticipated a not guilty plea.

The form and guidance notes are set out in full at: *http://www.justice.gov.uk/criminal/procrules_fin/index.htm*.

As to the use in evidence of matters stated in the case management form by, or on behalf of, an accused, for the purposes of trial and committal proceedings, see *R. (Firth) v. Epping Magistrates' Court*, unreported, February 3, 2011, DC ([2011] EWHC 388 (Admin.)), where an admission by an agent entered on the form was held to be admissible as evidence.

Although in general unnecessary hearings are to be avoided, in some cases, a case management hearing or pre-trial review will be necessary before the trial to resolve pre-trial preparation issues; and in other cases it may be necessary for the court to conduct a pre-trial hearing to make a binding pre-trial ruling under s.8A of the *Magistrates' Courts Act* 1980 (see *post*, § 7–192) in relation to issues of law (*e.g.* abuse of process or ambit of a criminal offence) and/ or admissibility of evidence (*e.g.* bad character or hearsay). Where a case management hearing or pre-trial review is held, it is the obligation of any party, prior to the hearing, carefully to look at the papers so as to apprise the court of the issues; such hearings are not exercises in formality, but are the proper occasion for each of the parties carefully to examine its case and for the justices, or their clerks, to subject the case to scrutiny so that the trial can take place efficiently by concentrating on the identified issues and the evidence needed in respect of them; if an oversight occurs, the relevant party must apply immediately to the court rather than leaving the issue unresolved until the trial, particularly in a busy court where it may be that resources do not permit an adjourned trial to take place for some time: *Williams v. DPP*, unreported, July 24, 2009, DC ([2009] EWHC 2354 (Admin)).

(2) Consolidated Criminal Practice Direction

The following revised standard case preparation time limits apply where a case is listed for summary trial (see Page 6 of the revised case management form issued by the Criminal Procedure Rule Committee, *ante*, § 7–138). **7–139**

Consolidated Criminal Practice Direction, Annex E, Case Management Form - Standard case preparation time limits

*The court can vary any of these time limits. Time limits marked * are not prescribed by rules. The total time needed to comply with all these time limits is 6 weeks (9 weeks if paragraph m applies).*

Written admissions (*Criminal Procedure Rules* 2011, r.37.6; *Criminal Justice Act* 1967, s.10)

a. The parties must serve any written admissions of agreed facts within **14 days**.*

Defence statement (*Criminal Procedure Rules* 2011, r.22.4; *Criminal Procedure and Investigations Act* 1996, s.6)

b. Any defence statement must be served within **14 days** of the prosecutor completing or purporting to complete initial disclosure.

Defence witnesses (*Criminal Procedure and Investigations Act* 1996, s.6C)

c. Defence witness names, etc. must be notified within **14 days** of the prosecutor completing or purporting to complete initial disclosure.

Application for disclosure (*Criminal Procedure Rules* 2011, rr.22.2 & 22.5; *Criminal Procedure and Investigations Act* 1996, s.8)

d. The defendant must serve any application for prosecution disclosure when serving any defence statement.*

e. The prosecutor must serve any representations in response within **14 days** after that.

Witness statements (*Criminal Procedure Rules* 2011, r.27.4; *Criminal Justice Act* 1967, s.9)

f. The defendant must serve any defence witness statement to be read at trial at least 14 days before the trial.*

g. Any objection to a witness statement being read at trial must be made within 7 days of service of the statement. *This does not apply to the statements listed in paragraph 10.1.*

Measures to assist a witness or defendant to give evidence (*Criminal Procedure Rules* 2011, rr.29.3, 29.13, 29.17, 29.22, 29.26)

h. Any [further] application for special or other measures must be served within **14 days.**

i. Any representations in response must be served within **14 days after that.**

Cross-examination where defendant not represented (*Criminal Procedure Rules* 2011, rr.31.1, 31.4)

j. The defendant must serve notice of any representative appointed to cross-examine within **7 days.**

k. The prosecutor must serve any application to prohibit cross-examination by the defendant in person as soon as reasonably practicable.

l. Any representations in response must be served within **14 days after that.**

Expert evidence (*Criminal Procedure Rules* 2011, rr.33.4, 33.6)

m. If either party relies on expert evidence, the directions below apply.
   (i) The expert's report must be served within **28 days.***
   (ii) A party who wants that expert to attend the trial must give notice within **7 days after (i).***
   (iii) A party who relies on expert evidence in response must serve it within **14 days after (ii).***
   (iv) There must be a meeting of experts under rule 33.6 within **14 days after (iii).***
   (v) The parties must notify the court **immediately after (iv)** if the length of the trial is affected by the outcome of the meeting.*

Hearsay evidence (*Criminal Procedure Rules* 2011, rr.34.2, 34.3)

n. The prosecutor must serve any notice to introduce hearsay evidence within **14 days.**

o. The defendant must serve any notice to introduce hearsay evidence as soon as reasonably practicable.

p. Any application to determine an objection to hearsay evidence must be served within **14 days of service** of the notice or evidence.

Bad character evidence (*Criminal Procedure Rules* 2011, rr.35.2, 35.3, 35.4)

q. The prosecutor must serve any notice to introduce evidence of the defendant's bad character within **14 days.**

r. Any application to determine an objection to that notice must be served within **14 days after that.**

s. Any application to introduce evidence of a non-defendant's bad character must be served within **14 days** of prosecution disclosure.

t. Any notice of objection to that evidence must be served within **14 days after that.**

Previous sexual behaviour evidence (*Criminal Procedure Rules* 2011, rr.36.2, 36.3, 36.4. 36.5)

u. The defendant must serve any application for permission to introduce evidence of a complainant's previous sexual behaviour within **28 days** of prosecution disclosure.

v. The prosecutor must serve any representations in response within **14 days after that.**

Point of law (*Criminal Procedure Rules* 2011, rr.3.3, 3.9)

w. Any skeleton argument must be served at least **14 days before the trial.***

x. Any skeleton argument in reply must be served within **7 days after that.***

Trial readiness (*Criminal Procedure Rules* 2011, rr.3.3, 3.9)

y. The parties must certify readiness for trial at least **14 days before the trial**, confirming which witnesses will give evidence in person and the trial time estimate.*

(3) Criminal Case Management Framework

As to the objectives and expectations of the parties where a case is listed for summary trial, see Ch. 4 of the Criminal Case Management Framework (Appendix I). **7–140**

VIII. SPECIFIC CASE MANAGEMENT POWERS

A. POWERS EXERCISABLE BY SINGLE JUSTICE

Crime and Disorder Act 1998, s.49

Powers of magistrates' courts exercisable by single justice etc.

49.—(1) The following powers of a magistrates' court for any area may be exercised by a single justice of the peace for that area, namely— **7–141**

(a) to extend bail or to impose or vary conditions of bail;

(b) to mark an information as withdrawn;

(c) to dismiss an information, or to discharge an accused in respect of an information, where no evidence is offered by the prosecution;

(d) to make an order for the payment of defence costs out of central funds;

(e) to request a pre-sentence report following a plea of guilty and, for that purpose, to give an indication of the seriousness of the offence;

(f) to request a medical report and, for that purpose, to remand the accused in custody or on bail;

(g) to remit an offender to another court for sentence;

(h) where a person has been granted police bail to appear at a magistrates' court, to appoint an earlier time for his appearance;

(i) to extend, with the consent of the accused, a custody time limit or an overall time limit;

(j) [*Repealed*];

(k) where an accused has been convicted of an offence, to order him to produce his driving licence;

(l) to give a direction prohibiting the publication of matters disclosed or exempted from disclosure in court;

(m) to give, vary or revoke directions for the conduct of a trial, including directions as to the following matters, namely—

(i) the timetable for the proceedings;

(ii) the attendance of the parties;

(iii) the service of documents (including summaries of any legal arguments relied on by the parties);

(iv) the manner in which evidence is to be given; and

(n) to give, vary or revoke orders for separate or joint trials in the case of two or more accused or two or more informations.

(2) Criminal Procedure Rules may, subject to subsection (3) below, provide that any of the things which, by virtue of subsection (1) above, are authorised to be done by a single justice of the peace for any area may, subject to any specified restrictions or conditions, be done by a justices' clerk for that area.

(3) Criminal Procedure Rules which make such provision as is mentioned in subsection (2) above shall not authorise a justices' clerk—

(a) without the consent of the prosecutor and the accused, to extend bail on conditions other than those (if any) previously imposed, or to impose or vary conditions of bail;

(b) to give an indication of the seriousness of an offence for the purposes of a pre-sentence report;

(c) to remand the accused in custody for the purposes of a medical report or, without the consent of the prosecutor and the accused, to remand the accused on bail for those purposes on conditions other than those (if any) previously imposed;

(d) to give a direction prohibiting the publication of matters disclosed or exempted from disclosure in court; or

(e) without the consent of the parties, to give, vary or revoke orders for separate or joint trials in the case of two or more accused or two or more informations.

(4) Before making any Criminal Procedure Rules which make such provision as is mentioned in subsection (2) above in relation to any area, the Criminal Procedure Rule Committee shall consult justices of the peace and justices' clerks for that area.

(5) In this section and section 50 below "justices' clerk" has the same meaning as in section 144 of the 1980 Act.

[This section is printed as amended by the *Access to Justice Act* 1999, Sched. 15, and the *Courts Act 2003 (Consequential Amendments) Order* 2004 (S.I. 2004 No. 2035).]

A single justice of the peace is also entitled to conduct the mode of trial procedure in relation to adult defendants under ss.19 to 23 of the *Magistrates' Courts Act* 1980 (including the special procedure in s.22 where the value involved is small): s.18(5) (*ante*, § 7–36).

As from a day to be appointed, a single justice will be entitled to conduct the plea before procedure under ss.17A to 17D: see s.17E (*ante*, § 7–35). No such day has been appointed.

B. POWERS EXERCISABLE BY JUSTICES' CLERKS AND THEIR ASSISTANTS

Justices' Clerks Rules 2005 (S.I. 2005 No. 545), rr. 2, 3

7–142 **2.** The things specified in Schedules 1 and 2 to these Rules, being authorised to be done by, to or before a single justice of the peace, may be done by, to or before a justices' clerk.

7–143 **3.**—(1) The things specified in paragraphs 1 to 36 of Schedule 1 and paragraphs 1 to 7 of Schedule 2 to these Rules, being authorised to be done by, to or before a justices' clerk, may be done by, to or before an assistant clerk, provided that that person has been specifically authorised by the justices' clerk for that purpose, and any reference in the Schedule to a justices' clerk shall be taken to include such a person.

(2) The powers authorised to be exercised by a justices' clerk at an early administrative hearing under section 50 of the *Crime and Disorder Act* 1998 may be exercised instead by an assistant clerk who has been specifically authorised by the justices' clerk for that purpose.

(3) Any authorisation by the justices' clerk under paragraph (1) or (2) above shall be recorded in writing at the time the authority is given or as soon as practicable thereafter.

[These rules are printed as amended by the *Justices' Clerks (Amendment) Rules* 2011 (S.I. 2011 No. 633).]

Justices' Clerks Rules 2005 (S.I. 2005 No. 545), Sched. 1

7–144 1. The laying of an information or the making of a complaint, other than an information or complaint substantiated on oath.

2. The issue of any summons, including a witness summons.

3. The issue of a warrant of arrest, whether or not endorsed for bail, for failure to surrender to the court, where there is no objection on behalf of the accused.

4. The marking of an information as withdrawn.

5. The dismissing of an information, or the discharging of an accused in respect of an information, or the discharging of an accused in respect of an information, where no evidence is offered by the prosecution.

6. The making of an order for the payment of defence costs out of central funds.

7. The adjournment of the hearing of a complaint if the parties to the complaint consent to the complaint being adjourned.

8. The extending of bail on the same conditions as those (if any) previously imposed, or, with the consent of the prosecutor and the accused, the imposing or varying of conditions of bail.

9. The further adjournment of criminal proceedings with the consent of the prosecutor and the accused, if but only if,

(a) the accused, not having been remanded on the previous adjournment, is not remanded on the further adjournment; or

(b) the accused, having been remanded on bail on the previous adjournment, is remanded on bail on the like terms and conditions, or, with the consent of the prosecutor and the accused, on other terms and conditions.

10.—(1) The further adjournment of criminal proceedings, where there has been no objection by the prosecutor, where the accused, having been remanded on bail on the previous adjournment, is remanded on bail on the like terms and conditions in his absence.

(2) The remand of the accused on bail in his absence at the time of further adjourning the proceedings in pursuance of sub-paragraph (1) above.

11.—(1) The appointment of a later time at which a person, who has been granted bail under the *Police and Criminal Evidence Act* 1984 subject to a duty to appear before a magistrates' court, is to appear, and the enlargement of any sureties for that person at that time, in accordance with section 43(1) of the *Magistrates' Courts Act* 1980, provided there is no objection by the prosecutor.

(2) Where a person has been granted police bail to appear at a magistrates' court, the appointment of an earlier time for his appearance.

12. The committal of a person for trial on bail in accordance with section 6(2) and (3)(b) of the *Magistrates' Courts Act* 1980 where, having been remanded on bail on the previous adjournment, he is released on bail on the like terms and conditions.

13. [*Omitted*].

14. The asking of an accused whether he pleads guilty or not guilty to a charge, after having stated to him the substance of the information laid against him.

15. The fixing or setting aside of a date, time and place for the trial of an information.

16. The making of a direction in accordance with rule 93A(7) or (8) of the *Magistrates' Courts Rules* 1981.

17. The giving, variation or revocation of directions for the conduct of a criminal trial, including directions as to the following matters, namely—

the timetable for proceedings;

the attendance of the parties;

the service of documents (including summaries of any legal arguments relied on by the parties);

the manner in which evidence is to be given.

18. With the consent of the parties, the giving, variation or revocation of orders for separate or joint trials in the case of two or more accused or two or more informations.

19. The extension, with the consent of the accused, of an overall time limit under section 22 of the *Prosecution of Offences Act* 1985.

Sentences, etc.

20. The request of a pre-sentence report following a plea of guilty.

21. The request of a medical report and, for that purpose, the remand of an accused on bail on the same conditions as those (if any) previously imposed, or, with the consent of the prosecutor and the accused, on other conditions.

22. The remitting of an offender to another court for sentence.

23. Where an accused has been convicted of an offence, the making of an order for him to produce his driving licence.

24. The giving of consent for another magistrates' court to deal with an offender for an earlier offence in respect of which, after the offender had attained the age of eighteen

years, a court had made an order for conditional discharge, where the justices' clerk is the clerk of the court which made the order, or in the case of a community rehabilitation order, of that court or the supervising court.

25. The amending, in accordance with paragraph 15 of Schedule 3 to the *Powers of Criminal Courts (Sentencing) Act* 2000, of a community rehabilitation order or community punishment order by substituting for the local justice area specified in the order the other area in which the offender proposes to reside or is residing.

26. The varying, in accordance with paragraph 5(1) of Schedule 5 to the *Powers of Criminal Courts (Sentencing) Act* 2000, of an attendance centre order by—

(a) varying the day or hour specified in the order for the offender's first attendance at the relevant attendance centre; or

(b) substituting for the relevant attendance centre an attendance centre which the justices' clerk is satisfied is reasonably accessible to the offender, having regard to his age, the means of access available to him and any other circumstances.

27. The signing of a certificate given to the Crown Court under paragraph 4(6) of Schedule 3 to the *Powers of Criminal Courts (Sentencing) Act* 2000 as to non-compliance with a community order.

28. The acceptance under section 14 of the *Magistrates' Courts Act* 1980 of service of such a statutory declaration as is mentioned in subsection (3) of that section.

Fines

29. The issue of a warrant of distress.

30. The allowing of further time for payment of a sum enforceable by a magistrates' court.

31. The varying of the number of instalments payable, the amount of any instalment payable and the date on which any instalment becomes payable where a magistrates' court has ordered that a sum adjudged to be paid shall be paid by instalments.

32. The making of a transfer of fine order under section 89 of the *Magistrates' Courts Act* 1980.

33. The making of an order before an enquiry into the means of a person under section 82 of the *Magistrates' Courts Act* 1980 that that person shall furnish to the court a statement of his means under section 84 of that Act.

34. The fixing under section 86(3) of the *Magistrates' Courts Act* 1980 of a later day in substitution for a day previously fixed for the appearance of an offender to enable an enquiry into his means to be made under section 82 of that Act or to enable a hearing required by section 82(5) of that Act to be held.

35. The making or withdrawal of an application to the Secretary of State, pursuant to the *Fines (Deductions from Income Support) Regulations* 1992, for deductions to be made from an offender's income support.

36. The doing of such other things as are required or permitted to be done by a magistrates' court under the *Fines (Deductions from Income Support) Regulations* 1992.

[This schedule is printed as amended by the *Criminal Defence Service (Representation Orders and Consequential Amendments) Regulations* 2006 (S.I. 2006 No. 2493) [and the *Justices' Clerks (Amendment) Rules* 2011 (S.I. 2011 No. 633)].]

C. PRELIMINARY, SENTENCING AND OTHER HEARINGS BY VIDEO LINK

(1) Introduction

7–145 Section 45 of the *Police and Justice Act* 2006 replaced s.57 of the *Crime and Disorder Act* 1998 (which provided for an accused's attendance at a preliminary hearing by "live link" where he was in custody in a prison or other institution) with a new Pt 3A (ss.57A–57E) so as to permit in certain circumstances the use of live links at both "preliminary" and "sentencing" hearings (defined in s.57A(3)), including where the accused is in police custody.

The provisions have since been amended by the *Coroners and Justice Act* 2009.

(2) Interpretation

Crime and Disorder Act 1998, s.57A

Introductory

57A.—(1) This Part— 7–146

(a) applies to preliminary hearings and sentencing hearings in the course of proceedings for an offence and enforcement hearings relating to confiscation orders; and

(b) enables the court in the circumstances provided for in sections 57B, 57C, 57E and 57F to direct the use of a live link for securing the accused's attendance at a hearing to which this Part applies.

(2) The accused is to be treated as present in court when, by virtue of a live link direction under this Part, he attends a hearing through a live link.

(3) In this Part—

"confiscation order" means an order made under—

(a) section 71 of the *Criminal Justice Act* 1988;

(b) section 2 of the *Drug Trafficking Act* 1994; or

(c) section 6 of the *Proceeds of Crime Act* 2002;

"custody"—

(a) includes local authority accommodation to which a person is remanded or committed by virtue of section 23 of the *Children and Young Persons Act* 1969; but

(b) does not include police detention;

"enforcement hearing" means a hearing under section 82 of the *Magistrates' Courts Act* 1980 to consider the issuing of a warrant of committal or to inquire into a person's means;

"live link" means an arrangement by which a person (when not in the place where the hearing is being held) is able to see and hear, and to be seen and heard by, the court during a hearing (and for this purpose any impairment of eyesight or hearing is to be disregarded);

"police detention" has the meaning given by section 118(2) of the *Police and Criminal Evidence Act* 1984;

"preliminary hearing" means a hearing in the proceedings held before the start of the trial (within the meaning of subsection (11A) or (11B) of section 22 of the 1985 Act) including, in the case of proceedings in the Crown Court, a preparatory hearing held under—

(a) section 7 of the *Criminal Justice Act* 1987 (cases of serious or complex fraud); or

(b) section 29 of the *Criminal Procedure and Investigations Act* 1996 (other serious, complex or lengthy cases);

"sentencing hearing" means any hearing following conviction which is held for the purpose of—

(a) proceedings relating to the giving or rescinding of a direction under section 57E;

(b) proceedings (in a magistrates' court) relating to committal to the Crown Court for sentencing; or

(c) sentencing the offender or determining how the court should deal with him in respect of the offence.

[This section is printed as amended by the *Coroners and Justice Act* 2009, s.109(2).]

(3) Live link at preliminary hearings where accused is in custody other than at the police station

Crime and Disorder Act 1998, s.57B

Use of live link at preliminary hearings where accused is in custody

57B.—(1) This section applies in relation to a preliminary hearing in a magistrates' court or the Crown Court. 7–147

(2) Where it appears to the court before which the preliminary hearing is to take place that the accused is likely to be held in custody during the hearing, the court may give a live link direction under this section in relation to the attendance of the accused at the hearing.

(3) A live link direction under this section is a direction requiring the accused, if he is being held in custody during the hearing, to attend it through a live link from the place at which he is being held.

(4) If a hearing takes place in relation to the giving or rescinding of such a direction, the court may require or permit a person attending the hearing to do so through a live link.

(5) The court shall not give or rescind such a direction (whether at a hearing or otherwise) unless the parties to the proceedings have been given the opportunity to make representations.

(6) If in a case where it has power to do so a magistrates' court decides not to give a live link direction under this section, it must—

(a) state in open court its reasons for not doing so; and

(b) cause those reasons to be entered in the register of its proceedings.

(7) The following functions of a magistrates' court under this section may be discharged by a single justice—

(a) giving a live link direction under this section;

(b) rescinding a live link direction before a preliminary hearing begins; and

(c) requiring or permitting a person to attend by live link a hearing about a matter within paragraph (a) or (b).

[This section is printed as amended by the *Coroners and Justice Act* 2009, s.106(2).]

(4) Live link at preliminary hearings where the accused is in custody at the police station

Crime and Disorder Act 1998, s.57C

Use of live link at preliminary hearings where accused is at police station

7–148 **57C.**—(1) This section applies in relation to a preliminary hearing in a magistrates' court.

(2) Where subsection (3) or (4) applies to the accused, the court may give a live link direction in relation to his attendance at the preliminary hearing.

(3) This subsection applies to the accused if—

(a) he is in police detention at a police station in connection with the offence; and

(b) it appears to the court that he is likely to remain at that station in police detention until the beginning of the preliminary hearing.

(4) This subsection applies to the accused if he is at a police station in answer to live link bail in connection with the offence.

(5) A live link direction under this section is a direction requiring the accused to attend the preliminary hearing through a live link from the police station.

(6) But a direction given in relation to an accused to whom subsection (3) applies has no effect if he does not remain in police detention at the police station until the beginning of the preliminary hearing.

(6A) A live link direction under this section may not be given unless the court is satisfied that it is not contrary to the interests of justice to give the direction.

(7) (Repealed).

(8) A magistrates' court may rescind a live link direction under this section at any time during a hearing to which it relates.

(9) A magistrates' court may require or permit—

(a) (repealed)

(b) any party to the proceedings who wishes to make representations in relation to the giving or rescission of a live link direction under this section to do so through a live link.

(10) Where a live link direction under this section is given in relation to an accused person who is answering to live link bail he is to be treated as having surrendered to the custody of the court (as from the time when the direction is given).

(11) In this section, "live link bail" means bail granted under Part 4 of the *Police and Criminal Evidence Act* 1984 subject to the duty mentioned in section 47(3)(b) of that Act.

[This section is printed as amended by the *Coroners and Justice Act* 2009, s.106(3) and Sched. 23, Pt 3.]

Piloting of s.57C in courts sitting at specified locations

The *Police and Justice Act 2006 (Commencement No. 2, Transitional and Saving Provisions) Order* 2007 (S.I. 2007 No. 709) and the *Police and Justice Act 2006 (Commencement No. 10) Order* 2008 (S.I. 2008 No. 2785) brought s.57C into force in various pilot local justice areas in London and Kent: **7–149**

(i) In London: Barking and Dagenham, Barnet, Bexley, Brent, Bromley, Camden and Islington, City of London, City of Westminster, Croydon, Ealing, Enfield, Greenwich and Lewisham, Hackney and Tower Hamlets, Hammersmith and Fulham and Kensington and Chelsea, Haringey, Harrow Gore, Havering, Hillingdon, Hounslow, Kingston-upon-Thames, Lambeth and Southwark, Merton, Newham, Redbridge, Richmond-upon-Thames, Sutton, Waltham Forest, and Wandsworth.

(ii) In Kent: Central Kent, East Kent and North Kent.

The amendments made to s.57C by the *Coroners and Justice Act* 2009 have been brought into force in the same pilot local justice areas: see the *Coroners and Justice Act 2009 (Commencement No. 1and Transitional Provisions) Order* 2009 (S.I. 2009 No. 3253) and the *Coroners and Justice Act 2009 (Commencement No. 4, Transitional and Saving Provisions) Order* 2010 (S.I. 2010 No. 816).

(5) Live link sentencing hearing continuing after conviction of accused at live link preliminary hearing from custody or the police station

Crime and Disorder Act 1998, s.57D

Continued use of live link for sentencing hearing following a preliminary hearing

57D.—(1) Subsection (2) applies where— **7–150**

(a) a live link direction under section 57B or 57C is in force;

(b) the accused is attending a preliminary hearing through a live link by virtue of the direction;

(c) the court convicts him of the offence in the course of that hearing (whether by virtue of a guilty plea or an indication of an intention to plead guilty); and

(d) the court proposes to continue the hearing as a sentencing hearing in relation to the offence.

(2) The accused may continue to attend through the live link by virtue of the direction if—

(a) the hearing is continued as a sentencing hearing in relation to the offence;

(b) (repealed); and

(c) the court is satisfied that the accused continuing to attend through the live link is not contrary to the interests of justice.

(3) But the accused may not give oral evidence through the live link during a continued hearing under subsection (2) unless—

(a) (repealed)

(b) the court is satisfied that it is not contrary to the interests of justice for him to give it in that way.

[This section is printed as amended by the *Coroners and Justice Act* 2009, s.106(4) and Sched. 23, Pt 3.]

(6) Live link sentencing hearing where accused convicted at other hearings

Crime and Disorder Act 1998, s.57E

Use of live link in sentencing hearings

57E.—(1) This section applies where the accused is convicted of the offence. **7–151**

(2) If it appears to the court by or before which the accused is convicted that it is likely that he will be held in custody during any sentencing hearing for the offence, the court may give a live link direction under this section in relation to that hearing.

(3) A live link direction under this section is a direction requiring the accused, if he is being held in custody during the hearing, to attend it through a live link from the place at which he is being held.

(4) Such a direction—

(a) may be given by the court of its own motion or on an application by a party; and

(b) may be given in relation to all subsequent sentencing hearings before the court or to such hearing or hearings as may be specified or described in the direction.

(5) The court may not give such a direction unless—

(a) (repealed)

(b) the court is satisfied that it is not contrary to the interests of justice to give the direction.

(6) The court may rescind such a direction at any time before or during a hearing to which it relates if it appears to the court to be in the interests of justice to do so (but this does not affect the court's power to give a further live link direction in relation to the offender).

The court may exercise this power of its own motion or on an application by a party.

(7) The offender may not give oral evidence while attending a hearing through a live link by virtue of this section unless—

(a) (repealed)

(b) the court is satisfied that it is not contrary to the interests of justice for him to give it in that way.

(8) The court must—

(a) state in open court its reasons for refusing an application for, or for the rescission of, a live link direction under this section; and

(b) if it is a magistrates' court, cause those reasons to be entered in the register of its proceedings.

[This section is printed as amended by the *Coroners and Justice Act* 2009, s.106(5) and Sched. 23, Pt 3.]

(7) Use of live link in certain enforcement hearings

Crime and Disorder Act 1998, s.57F

7–152 **57F.**—(1) This section applies where—

(a) a confiscation order is made against a person; and

(b) the amount required to be paid under the order is not paid when it is required to be paid.

(2) If it appears to the court before which an enforcement hearing relating to the confiscation order is to take place that it is likely that the person will be held in custody at the time of the hearing, the court may give a live link direction under this section in relation to that hearing.

(3) A live link direction under this section is a direction requiring the person, if the person is being held in custody at the time of the hearing, to attend it through a live link from the place at which the person is being held.

(4) Such a direction—

(a) may be given by the court of its own motion or on an application by a party; and

(b) may be given in relation to all subsequent enforcement hearings before the court or to such hearing or hearings as may be specified or described in the direction.

(5) The court may rescind a live link direction under this section at any time before or during a hearing to which it relates.

(6) The court may not give or rescind a live link direction under this section (whether at a hearing or otherwise) unless the parties to the proceedings have been given the opportunity to make representations.

(7) If a hearing takes place in relation to the giving or rescinding of such a direction, the court may require or permit any party to the proceedings who wishes to make representations in relation to the giving or rescission of a live link direction under this section to do so through a live link.

(8) The person may not give oral evidence while attending a hearing through a live link by virtue of this section unless the court is satisfied that it is not contrary to the interests of justice for the person to give it that way.

(9) If in a case where it has power to do so a court decides not to give a live link direction under this section, it must—

(a) state in open court its reasons for not doing so; and

(b) cause those reasons to be entered in the register of its proceedings.

(10) The following functions of a magistrates' court under this section may be discharged by a single justice—

(a) giving a live link direction under this section;

(b) rescinding a live link direction before a preliminary hearing begins; and

(c) requiring or permitting a person to attend by live link a hearing about a matter within paragraph (a) or (b).

[This section was inserted by the *Coroners and Justice Act* 2009, s.109(1).]

(8) Live link in extradition hearings

The *Policing and Crime Act* 2009, s.78, inserted new ss.206A to 206C in the *Extradition Act* 2003, which make provision for the use of live link in certain hearings under Pts 1 and 2 of the 2003 Act. **7–153**

D. ADJOURNMENTS

(1) Introduction

Not all cases will be concluded at the first hearing and requests for adjournment will be made to the court, which has a discretion (derived under specific provisions of the *Magistrates' Courts Act* 1980) whether to grant an adjournment or not. The party applying for the adjournment should explain the reasons why the case cannot proceed and the issues that need to be addressed with further time. Both parties may require an adjournment in the early stages of a case but the court must always consider the reasons for putting a case off and must make its decision taking into account the interests of justice. The court may require to know the history of the case and whether adjournments have been granted before and the reasons for them. These details should be available from the court file and will be recounted in open court by the legal adviser. The court should make clear the expectations for progress at the next hearing. **7–154**

(2) General principles

Under r. 3.2(1) of the *Criminal Procedure Rules* 2011 the court has a duty to manage cases actively. Rule 3.2(2)(f) requires the court to discourage delay and avoid unnecessary hearings; and r.3.8 requires the court to give directions to ensure that cases are concluded as soon as possible. This includes a duty to set a timetable and to give directions to expedite progress. However, although justices have a wide discretion in relation to matters of case management, and whilst the efficient dispatch of court business has to be considered when exercising the discretion, an adjournment must be granted where the imperatives of justice so require: *S. v. DPP*, 170 J.P. 707, DC. Further, there is a duty to hear submissions in support of an application for an adjournment despite the fact that there was a fixed expectation that the case would proceed: *Bradford Justices, ex p. Wilkinson*, 91 Cr.App.R. 390, DC. **7–155**

In *CPS v. Picton*, 170 J.P. 567, DC, Jack J. conducted a review of the authorities relating to the exercise of the discretion to adjourn proceedings and set out (at [9]) the following factors to be considered:

"(a) A decision whether to adjourn is a decision within the discretion of the trial court. An appellate court will interfere only if very clear grounds for doing so are shown.

(b) Magistrates should pay great attention to the need for expedition in the prosecution of criminal proceedings; delays are scandalous; they bring the law into disrepute; summary justice should be speedy justice; an application for an adjournment should be rigorously scrutinised.

(c) Where an adjournment is sought by the prosecution, magistrates must consider both the interest of the defendant in getting the matter dealt with, and the interest of the public that criminal charges should be adjudicated upon, and the guilty convicted as well as the innocent acquitted. With a more serious charge the public interest that there be a trial will carry greater weight.

(d) Where an adjournment is sought by the accused, the magistrates must consider whether, if it is not granted, he will be able fully to present his defence and, if he will not be able to do so, the degree to which his ability to do so is compromised.

(e) In considering the competing interests of the parties the magistrates should examine the likely consequences of the proposed adjournment, in particular its likely length, and the need to decide the facts while recollections are fresh.

(f) The reason that the adjournment is required should be examined and, if it arises through the fault of the party asking for the adjournment, that is a factor against granting the adjournment, carrying weight in accordance with the gravity of the fault. If that party was not at fault, that may favour an adjournment. Likewise if the party opposing the adjournment has been at fault, that will favour an adjournment.

(g) The magistrates should take appropriate account of the history of the case, and whether there have been earlier adjournments and at whose request and why.

(h) Lastly, of course the factors to be considered cannot be comprehensively stated but depend upon the particular circumstances of each case, and they will often overlap. The court's duty is to do justice between the parties in the circumstances as they have arisen."

Although *CPS v. Picton* was concerned with the question of whether a trial should be adjourned, the approach laid out has expressly been applied to the question of whether committal proceedings should be adjourned: *R. (Khan) v. Waltham Forest Magistrates' Court*, unreported, July 3, 2007, DC ([2007] EWHC 1801, Admin.). It is submitted that as a general principle, the test should be applied whenever an adjournment is sought.

Implicit in the test formulated by Jack J. are the basic principles (a) that where an adjournment is sought by the prosecution, justices must balance the interests of society that the guilty should be convicted with the interests of the accused in having to attend court unnecessarily (see *Aberdare Justices, ex p. DPP*, 155 J.P. 324, DC); and (b) that where an adjournment is sought by the defence, generally if there is a risk of unfairness to the accused, then the adjournment should be granted (see *Kingston-upon-Hull Justices, ex p. McCann*, 155 J.P. 569, DC).

An application to adjourn essentially involves an exercise of a judicial discretion; accordingly, whilst the delegated powers in the Schedule to the *Justices' Clerks Rules* 2005 (S.I. 2005 No. 545) (*ante*, § 7–144) permit a justice's clerk or a duly authorised assistant to sanction the adjournment of a case where both parties agree, it does not follow that the clerk or assistant can refuse to grant an adjournment where there is no agreement between the parties; the proper procedure in those circumstances should be for the application for the adjournment to be heard by the court in advance of the hearing which is sought to be adjourned: see *R. (DPP) v. Lancaster Youth Court*, 174 J.P. 320 QBD (Foskett J.) ([2010] EWHC 662 (Admin.)).

As to reconsideration of a decision concerning an adjournment, it is necessary for the efficacious administration of justice to take a strict approach to the power of a lower court to revisit an earlier decision; but there must be some power to do so in the interests of justice, which power would arise where there had been a change of relevant circumstances, or where a relevant circumstance had not been drawn to the attention of the first bench:*R. (DPP) v. Acton Youth Court* [2002] Crim.L.R. 75, DC. For this purpose, the parameters of the interests of justice test are now measured not simply by changed circumstances but by reference to the overriding objective in the *Criminal Procedure Rules* 2011: *Jones v. South East Surrey Local Justice Area*, 174 J.P. 342, DC (concluding that it had been open to the justices, where a prosecution application for an adjournment of a summary trial fixed for the following day had been refused, to grant a fresh application for an adjournment where they were told that the true reason for the non-availability of crucial evidence was police inefficiency rather than the inefficiency of the prosecuting authority; furthermore it was relevant that the decision was being revisited promptly and that the alleged offence was still relatively recent).

As to the way in which an appeal against a decision concerning an adjournment should be brought in the High Court (including on an interlocutory basis), see *Balogun v. DPP (Practice Note)* [2010] 1 W.L.R. 1915, DC. Where it was observed that an application for judicial review of such a decision may be appropriate.

(3) Adjournment of plea before venue and determination of mode of trial (allocation)

For the discretionary power to adjourn the plea before venue procedure, see s.17C of the *Magistrates' Courts Act* 1980. **7–156**

For the discretionary power to adjourn determination of mode of trial (allocation), see s.18(4) of the 1980 Act.

The requirement to adjourn where the prosecution has failed to serve advance information (now initial details) has not been reproduced in the new Pt 21 of the *Criminal Procedure Rules* 2011. As to the effect of this omission, see *ante*, § 6–13.

(4) Adjournment of sending of a case to the Crown Court

Section 52(5) of the *Crime and Disorder Act* 1998 confers a discretion on a magistrates' court to adjourn the sending of a case to the Crown Court under s.51 or 51A. It is submitted that this discretion should be exercised only sparingly, given that both s.51 and 51A require the case to be sent to the Crown Court "forthwith". **7–157**

(5) Adjournment of committal proceedings

(a) *Legislation*

Magistrates' Courts Act 1980, s.5

Adjournment of inquiry

5.—(1) *A magistrates' court may, before beginning to inquire into an offence as examining justices, or at any time during the inquiry, adjourn the hearing, and if it does so shall remand the accused* **7–158**

(2) *The court shall when adjourning fix the time and place at which the hearing is to be resumed; and the time fixed shall be that at which the accused is required to appear or be brought before the court in pursuance of the remand or would be required to be brought before the court but for section 128(3A) below.*

[This section is printed as amended by the *Criminal Justice Act* 1982, Sched. 9. As from a day to be appointed, the whole section will be repealed by the *Criminal Justice Act* 2003, Scheds 3 and 37.]

(b) *Approach*

In *R. (Khan) v. Waltham Forest Magistrates' Court*, unreported, July 3, 2007, DC ([2007] EWHC 1801 (Admin.)), the Divisional Court commented on a proposition that it was almost invariable that a first prosecution application to adjourn committal proceedings until another day would be granted unless cogent arguments were raised by the defence. The court said that each case should be considered on its merits; and that there should be no policy of nodding through prosecution applications for adjournments in circumstances where there had been some form of administrative failure which meant that the Crown was not ready to proceed on any given day. Any policy of a "free" adjournment in those circumstances would be utterly unacceptable and entirely contrary to the overriding objective set out in the *Criminal Procedure Rules* 2011, Appendix G; and it would be wrong and unlawful to allow a policy to develop at any mag- **7–159** istrates' court which would encourage or condition the prosecution to think that there would be no difficulty in gaining an adjournment of the case on at least one occasion through administrative failure or inefficiency on its part. Where adjournment of committal proceedings was sought on that ground, each of the parties should consider the duty under r.3.3 of the *Criminal Procedure Rules* actively to assist the court in the fulfilment of its own duty to further the overriding objective by actively managing the case. This required the parties to put their heads together and adopt some pragmatic solution, such as adjourning the hearing to later on the same day to see whether the committal could take place at that time. If the prosecution did not volunteer such a course, it would be incumbent upon the defence to seek to make matters work properly by raising that suggestion; and it would be incumbent upon the court, as the manager of the process, of its own initiative, to consider whether such an avenue was worth exploring and to make an order, if necessary. The mere claim by one party that something cannot conveniently be done could not be a trump card. Notwithstanding the force of these comments, on the particular facts of the case the Divisional Court concluded that the justices had been acting within the limits of their discretion by adjourning for seven days in the face of the particular administrative failure.

(5) Adjournment of trial

(a) *Legislation*

Magistrates' Courts Act 1980, s.10

Adjournment of trial

7–160 **10.**—(1) A magistrates' court may at any time, whether before or after beginning to try an information, adjourn the trial, and may do so, notwithstanding anything in this Act, when composed of a single justice.

(2) The court may when adjourning either fix the time and place at which the trial is to be resumed, or, unless it remands the accused, leave the time and place to be determined later by the court; but the trial shall not be resumed at that time and place unless the court is satisfied that the parties have had adequate notice thereof.

(3) A magistrates' court may, for the purpose of enabling inquiries to be made or of determining the most suitable method of dealing with the case, exercise its power to adjourn after convicting the accused and before sentencing him or otherwise dealing with him; but, if it does so, the adjournment shall not be for more than 4 weeks at a time unless the court remands the accused in custody and, where it so remands him, the adjournment shall not be for more than 3 weeks at a time.

(3A) A youth court shall not be required to adjourn any proceedings for an offence at any stage by reason only of the fact—

(a) that the court commits the accused for trial for another offence; or

(b) that the accused is charged with another offence.

(4) On adjourning the trial of an information the court may remand the accused and, where the accused has attained the age of 18 years, shall do so if the offence is triable either way and—

(a) on the occasion on which the accused first appeared, or was brought, before the court to answer to the information he was in custody or, having been released on bail, surrendered to the custody of the court; or

(b) the accused has been remanded at any time in the course of proceedings on the information;

and, where the court remands the accused, the time fixed for the resumption of the trial shall be that at which he is required to appear or be brought before the court in pursuance of the remand or would be required to be brought before the court but for section 128(3A) below.

(b) *General principles*

7–161 For the general approach to the question of whether a trial should be adjourned, see *CPS v. Picton* (*ante*). As Jack J. expressly recognised at point (h), the factors to be considered cannot be comprehensively stated but depend upon the particular circumstances of each case.

Where an accused has been compelled to appear before a court by the institution of proceedings and all pre-trial formalities (*e.g.* determination of mode of trial) have been complied with so that that the next stage of the proceedings is summary trial, the *Magistrates' Courts Act* 1980 makes no provision requiring the trial to be adjourned to a different date. Theoretically, therefore, the Act envisages the possibility that the trial could take place at the first appearance. In practice, however, trials are adjourned under section 10 at the first appearance, on the basis that either the prosecution or the defence (or both) will not be ready to proceed at the first appearance.

More difficult questions arise where a trial has been adjourned at the first appearance and then listed for a particular date, but one or other of the parties then seeks an adjournment under section 10 of the trial fixed for that date. As to this see *R. (DPP) v. North East Hertfordshire JJ. and Simpole*, 172 J.P. 193, DC, where it was said that the fundamental issue with which a court must grapple upon an application to adjourn a trial is that of justice to all those involved, which requires a balance to be struck between the interests of the defendant (including his legitimate expectation that his case will be dealt with promptly) and the general public interest in prosecuting and convicting offenders. A decision under s.10 would be flawed where the only factor considered was the need for proceedings to be conducted expeditiously, without enquiring as to the next available trial date and without considering the history of the matter, the extent to which the trial would be delayed and the extent to which that would prejudice the other party: *R. (Nadour) v. Chester Magistrates' Court*, unreported, June 11, 2009, DC ([2009] EWHC 1505 (Admin.)).

(c) *Adequate time and facilities for preparation of defence case*

The requirement under art. 6(3)(b) of the ECHR that a defendant should have "adequate time and facilities" for the preparation of his defence runs parallel to the notion of natural justice in the common law. In *Thames Magistrates' Court, ex p. Polemis* [1974] 1 W.L.R. 1371, DC, a summons was served and listed for trial on the same day. Quashing the refusal of the justices to grant an adjournment, Lord Widgery C.J. explained that: **7–162**

> "To start with nothing is clearer today than that a breach of the rules of natural justice is said to occur if a party to proceedings, and more especially the defendant in a criminal case, is not given a reasonable chance to present his case. It is so elementary and so basic it hardly needs to be said. But of the versions of breach of the rules of natural justice with which in this court we are dealing constantly, perhaps the most common today is the allegation that the defence were prejudiced because they were not given a fair and reasonable opportunity to present their case to the court, and of course the opportunity to present a case to the court is not confined to being given an opportunity to stand up and say what you want to say; it necessarily extends to a reasonable opportunity to prepare your case before you are called upon to present it. A mere allocation of court time is of no value if the party in question is deprived of the opportunity of getting his tackle in order and being able to present his case in the fullest sense."

The time that is adequate will vary depending on the complexity of the case: *X. v. Austria* (1979) 15 D.R. 160, ECtHR, and *Perez Mahia v. Spain*, 9 E.H.R.R. 91, ECtHR.

The situation may well be different if there is a change of lawyers at a late stage and if instructions are only taken on the day of trial an adjournment may be required: *Goddi v. Italy*, 6 E.H.R.R. 457, ECtHR. However in *Ulcay and Toygun* [2008] 1 All E.R. 547, CA, detailed consideration was given to the situation where an advocate has been instructed late in a case and has not had sufficient time to prepare. As to whether the advocate should withdraw in this situation and leave the defendant unrepresented, and as to whether the court has any power to compel the advocate to stay where the advocate indicates that he or she intends to withdraw, see § 8–133, *post* (and as to wasted costs see § 29–48, *post*). As to whether the court should grant an adjournment, and if so for how long, in order to accommodate the advocate, it was said that the responsibility was vested in the court without exceptions and that the rules of the legal professions had to defer to and be consistent with that principle. Where on the day of trial there is a late amendment of the charge or charges arising out of the same or substantially the same facts as the original case, the defendant must be given time to consider his position; but that time should be measured in minutes and there should not be an adjournment to another day, unless there were compelling reasons: *Williams v. DPP*, unreported, July 24, 2009, DC ([2009] EWHC 2354 (Admin)).

(d) *Non-disclosure by the prosecution*

7–163 The same principle of natural justice applies (for the same reason, *i.e.* because the defence will be unable to prepare for trial) where the prosecution have failed to disclose the statements of the witnesses to be called at trial. Whilst the prosecution is under no statutory duty to disclose witness statements before trial, it will generally speaking be wrong for the court to proceed on the basis that it would be fair for the claimant to have short adjournments during the hearing to consider how to deal with evidence as it emerged; the proper course will be to grant an adjournment: see *R. (Cleary) v. Highbury Corner Magistrates' Court (Practice Note)* [2007] 1 W.L.R. 1272, DC (applied to the context of criminal proceedings in *Filmer v. DPP* [2007] R.T.R. 28, DC). Where the defence are taken by surprise by late service of prosecution evidence, see *Kingston-upon-Hull JJ., ex p. McCann*, 155 J.P. 569, DC, as authority for a proposition that the proper course should be to grant an adjournment. To similar effect, see *S. v. DPP*, 170 J.P. 707, DC, where it was said that the imperatives of justice would require an adjournment where the prosecution had failed to disclose matters which ought to have been disclosed, unless there would be no prejudice to the defence. See also *Phillips* [2007] 5 *Archbold News* 2, CA, where it was said that although judges should be robust when making case management decisions, where there had been a failure by the prosecution to comply with a series of orders to make disclosure of specified material, it would have been better for the judge to have granted the defence more time, rather than insist that the trial proceed on time. See also *Swash v. DPP*, unreported, March 4, 2009, DC ([2009] EWHC 803 (Admin.)).

(e) *Prosecution not ready to proceed*

7–164 Prosecution applications for an adjournment should not unreasonably be refused; but rigorous scrutiny must be given to the reasons why adjournment is sought and a full explanation must be sought. Where the prosecution are the authors of their own misfortune by failing properly to prepare for trial (*e.g.* by failing to warn witnesses), adjournments should not be granted easily and where they are granted the court must be careful to give full and cogent reasons: *Essen v. DPP*, unreported, May 12, 2005, DC.

(f) *Non-attendance of prosecution witnesses*

7–165 It is submitted that for the purposes of applying the test set out in *CPS v. Picton* (*ante*) when a prosecution witness fails to attend, it will be material whether or not the witness has been warned to attend (and thus whether the prosecuting authority is at fault); and if so, whether or not that witness is a civilian. If, for example, a constable has been warned to attend, but fails to appear without any (or any satisfactory) explanation, then that will be a factor militating against the granting of the adjournment (subject, of course, to consideration of the other factors set out in *Picton*). See *R. (Visvaratnam) v. Brent Magistrates' Court*, 174 J.P. 61, DC (overturning a decision to adjourn) for robust observations that the prosecution must not think that they are always allowed at least one application to adjourn a case and that the sooner the prosecution realised that they could not rely on their own serious failures to warn witnesses of trial dates, the sooner efficiency in the magistrates' courts would be improved. However, see *Aberdare Justices, ex p. DPP*, 155 J.P. 324, DC, where it was said that if a police officer is unavoidably required at a Crown Court or other superior court on the day of trial, justices should look favourably at the prosecution application to adjourn.

Where a prosecution witness is absent without good reason, the prosecutor should be given a reasonable period in which to make enquiries: *Swansea Justices, ex p. DPP*, 154 J.P. 709, DC.

In *Picton* itself, the trial had been listed to start at 10am but the prosecution witnesses had erroneously been warned to attend at 2.00pm (at which time the court would be dealing with a different trial). The next available date for the trial if an adjournment were to be granted would be more than a year after the alleged offence and nearly a year after the defendant had first been produced before the court. Having formulated the test set out above, Jack J. concluded that by refusing to accede to an application by the prosecution to adjourn the case until 2.00pm or another day, the justices had been acting within the limits of the discretion conferred on them. *Cf. R. (DPP) v. North East Hertfordshire JJ. and Simpole*, 172 J.P. 193, DC, where a refusal to adjourn a trial for driving with excess alcohol was held to be irrational and perverse in circumstances where a crucial civilian witness (who had attended on a previous occasion and had co-operated throughout) had failed to attend (she lived 65 miles away, wintry conditions had closed her children's school and she had no alternative childcare), the case was 10 months old, and there had been one previous abortive hearing which had been the fault of neither party; neither the prosecution nor the witness could be said to have been at fault and the only reason given by the justices was that adjournment was not in the interests of justice in light of "the history of the matter".

In *DPP v. Birmingham Magistrates' Court*, unreported, July 29, 2003, DC ([2003] EWHC 2352, Admin) a complainant in an assault charge failed to attend at trial because she had been the victim of another unrelated serious attack just prior to the hearing. The prosecution requested an adjournment on the grounds that the witness was too ill to attend but did not disclose the full details of why this was so. On appeal, the court held that the failure to attend in this case was of secondary importance. Once it was accepted that a complainant through an unexpected event that was no fault of her own was not fit to attend, there was an extremely powerful argument for an adjournment and as there was no history of delay in the case, the argument for an adjournment became unanswerable.

In *R. (CPS) v. Uxbridge Magistrates' Court*, 171 J.P. 279, DC, the complainant in respect of an allegation of domestic violence had not attended court on the day fixed for summary trial (which was the first date on which the case had been fixed for trial) because she had been compulsorily detained in a psychiatric unit. The High Court held that justices had been acting within their discretion by refusing a prosecution application to adjourn the trial, even though the prosecution had had no reason to suppose she would not attend (the defendant being the only person before the court who had known of her compulsory admission to hospital) and there was no suggestion that the defendant would be prejudiced if an adjournment were granted. However, the court said that the position would have been different had the consequence of refusal been the inevitable collapse of the prosecution, as there was a strong public interest in the prosecution continuing (there being scope in the particular case for the missing witness's statement to be admitted under s.116(1) and (2)(b) of the *Criminal Justice Act* 2003 (witness unfit)).

(g) *Absent defendant*

Where a defendant fails to appear, the question whether the matter should be **7-166**
adjourned will depend on whether it is legitimate in the circumstances to proceed in his absence: as to which see *post*. If it is not legitimate to proceed in his absence, then plainly the trial must be adjourned until such time when his attendance can be secured.

(h) *Expert witnesses*

A court confronted by an application to adjourn proceedings so that an expert can be **7-167**
instructed is entitled to weigh against the general desirability of the applicant having the advantage of expert opinion, the reason for his failure to have such evidence already: *R.*

(Lappin) v. H.M. Customs and Excise [2004] A.C.D. 48, QBD (Goldring J.). In that case it was said that persistent failure to instruct expert, notwithstanding the timetable for doing so, justified refusal of an application to adjourn a two-day appeal to the Crown Court which had been set down months in advance.

(i) *Defendant unfit or unwell*

7–168 In general where an accused is unfit to attend trial, and such unfitness is supported by medical evidence, an adjournment should be granted to enable him to attend: *Bolton Justices, ex p. Merna*, 155 J.P. 612, DC.

It would take a very strong case before it would be appropriate to refuse an application for an adjournment on the basis that the defendant had gone through a severe trauma shortly before the date of the hearing; facing court proceedings was an ordeal of itself, and there would be a clear risk of prejudice to a defendant who was forced to give evidence when his mind might not be on the issues that mattered: *R. (Costello) v. North East Essex Magistrates*, 171 J.P. 153, QBD (Collins J.).

(j) *Non-attendance of defence witnesses*

7–169 An accused may not receive a fair trial if an independent witness is unavoidably absent: *Hereford Magistrates' Court, ex p. Rowlands and Ingram*, 161 J.P. 258, DC.

(k) *"Ambush tactics"*

7–170 Pursuant to the modern approach to summary justice brought about by the *Criminal Procedure Rules*, each party must identify the real issues in the case and at once inform the court and all other parties of any significant failure by another party to take a procedural step; defendants can no longer expect to benefit by taking ambush points, failing to co-operate, and failing to identify what matters are in issue at an early stage; and where one party is ambushed by another (*e.g.* where crucial issues in a trial are identified for the first time in a closing argument) an adjournment may be necessary to allow the other party to deal with it: *R. (DPP) v. Chorley JJ.*, unreported, June 8, 2006, DC; *Robinson v. Abergavenny Magistrates' Court*; *Fine v. Same* [2007] L.S. Gazette, September 20, 30, DC; *R. (Lawson) v. Stafford Magistrates' Court* [2007] L.S. Gazette, October 18, 26, DC; and *R. (Taylor) v. Southampton Magistrates' Court*, 173 J.P. 17, DC (where a "technical point" as to the sufficiency of the evidence had been taken for the first time during closing submissions for the accused and no positive case in that respect had been advanced during the trial). The principle that trials by ambush were no longer to take place applies as much to the prosecution as it does to the defence: *Williams v. DPP*, unreported, July 24, 2009, DC ([2009] EWHC 2354 (Admin)). Defence advocates should no longer rely on the decision in *R. (DPP) v. Cheshire JJ.*, unreported, March 7, 2002, DC ([2002] EWHC 466, Admin.) (where it had been said that there is no obligation in a summary trial to make known to the prosecution in advance what the defence was going to be, it being for the prosecution to be in a position to deal with whatever defence arose) when resisting prosecution applications to adjourn in these circumstances; but this was not to be taken as a licence to the prosecution to fail to attend to the necessity of proving their case or as absolving the court from the responsibility of subjecting prosecution applications to adjourn to close scrutiny; the mere fact of the procedural failing should not be determinative of the application to adjourn: *Robinson v. Abergavenny Magistrates' Court*; *Fine v. Same* (*ibid.*).

It is submitted, however, that there is a limit on the extent to which these authorities apply; plainly there is no requirement on the accused to inform the prosecutor how to prosecute the case against him, and it is submitted that on a prosecution application to adjourn in these circumstances proper regard should be had to the reasons why the prosecution had failed, for example, to obtain evidence to prove an essential and obvious plank of its case.

(l) *Consequences of refusal of prosecution application to adjourn*

7–171 The power of a magistrates' court to dismiss an information derives principally from s.9(2) of the *Magistrates' Courts Act* 1980 (*post*, § 8–1), which provides that a court shall dismiss an information only "after hearing the evidence of the parties". If a prosecution application to adjourn is refused, and the prosecution do not intend to discontinue the proceedings, the justices have no power simply to dismiss the information; the prosecutor should therefore be invited to present any evidence he wishes: *Harrington v. Roots*, 149 J.P. 211, DC.

It follows that where, for example, there have been a number of earlier adjournments and a final prosecution application is refused, the justices have no power to dismiss an information simply because they are of the view that it would be unjust for the prosecution to continue (*Birmingham Justices, ex p. Lamb* [1983] 1 W.L.R. 339, DC); or for "want of prosecution" (*Crawley Justices, ex p. DPP* [1990] R.T.R. 374, DC); or because it is suspected that a fair trial might not be possible (*Dorchester Magistrates' Court, ex p. DPP*, 154 J.P. 211, DC). The power available to the justices in those circumstance would be to stay the proceedings as an abuse of process, where it would be appropriate to do so (as to which, see Ch. 8, *post*). As to the power to dismiss an information where the prosecutor fails to appear, however, see *post*.

Part I

(m) *Miscellaneous considerations*

The provisions of s.10 allow a court to adjourn a case for re-trial before a different bench: *Ripon Liberty JJ., ex p. Bugg*, 155 J.P. 213, DC; *R. (Kendall) v. Selby Magistrates' Court*, unreported, November 13, 2003, DC ([2003] EWHC 2909, Admin). **7–172**

It is an improper exercise of the discretion under s.10 to adjourn a trial to a later date for the sole reason that a new statutory provision would be in force on the later date; although a defendant might not have an inalienable right or entitlement to be tried on the law as it stood on the day which happened to be fixed for his trial, it was a principle of the rule of law that courts applied the law as it existed and to grant an adjournment in such circumstances would therefore be to fail to apply the law as it existed on the date fixed for trial: *Walsall JJ., ex p. W.* [1990] 1 Q.B. 253, DC.

Where a bench of two justices were unable to reach either of those two decisions, they were under a duty to adjourn the matter to be reheard by a bench of three justices: *Redbridge Magistrates' Court, ex p. Ram* [1992] Q.B. 384, DC.

Where an application for an adjournment in such circumstances has been refused, then a second application may only be made where there has been a change of circumstances; an adjournment should not therefore be granted by a second bench where an earlier bench had concluded (*e.g.* at a pre-trial review) that insufficient reasons were put forward in support of an application to adjourn, and no different reasons were then put forward in support of an application made to the second bench: *R. (Watson) v. Dartford Magistrates' Court*, unreported, May 12, 2005, DC ([2005] EWHC 905, Admin).

(6) Adjournment of sentencing decision

Section 10(3) of the *Magistrates' Courts Act* 1980 permits the court after convicting the accused and before sentencing him or otherwise dealing with him to adjourn for the purpose of enabling inquiries to be made or of determining the most suitable method of dealing with the case. Such adjournments are not to exceed four weeks at a time if the accused is on bail, and three weeks at a time where the accused is in custody. **7–173**

For the avoidance of doubt, s.10(3) applies whether the accused has been convicted after trial or whether he has pleaded guilty. Such is the effect of s.9(3) of the 1980 Act, which provides that if the accused pleads guilty, the court may "convict" him without hearing evidence.

See generally *post*, §§ 22–36.

E. PROCEEDING WHERE A PARTY FAILS TO APPEAR

(1) General

Magistrates' Courts Act 1980, s.122

Appearance by counsel or solicitor

7–174 **122.**—(1) A party to any proceedings before a magistrates' court may be represented by a legal representative.

(2) Subject to subsection (3) below, an absent party so represented shall be deemed not to be absent.

(3) Appearance of a party by a legal representative shall not satisfy any provision of any enactment or any condition of a recognizance expressly requiring his presence.

[This section is printed as amended by the *Courts and Legal Services Act* 1990, s.125(3) and Sched. 18, para. 25(3)(b).]

(2) The accused

(a) *Legislation*

Magistrates' Courts Act 1980, s.11

Non-appearance of accused: general provisions

7–175 **11.**—(1) Subject to the provisions of this Act, where at the time and place appointed for the trial or adjourned trial of an information the prosecutor appears but the accused does not—

(a) if the accused is under 18 years of age, the court may proceed in his absence; and

(b) if the accused has attained the age of 18 years, the court shall proceed in his absence

unless it appears to the court to be contrary to the interests of justice to do so. This is subject to subsections (2), (2A), (3) and (4).

(2) Where a summons has been issued, the court shall not begin to try the information in the absence of the accused unless either it is proved to the satisfaction of the court, on oath or in such other manner as may be prescribed, that the summons was served on the accused within what appears to the court to be a reasonable time before the trial or adjourned trial or the accused has appeared on a previous occasion to answer to the information.

(2A) The court shall not proceed in the absence of the accused if it considers that there is an acceptable reason for his failure to appear.

(3) In proceedings to which this subsection applies, the court shall not in a person's absence sentence him to imprisonment or detention in a young offender institution or make a detention and training order or an order under para. 8(2)(a) or (b) of Schedule 12 to the *Criminal Justice Act* 2003 that a suspended sentence passed on him shall take effect.

(3A) But where a sentence or order of a kind mentioned in subsection (3) is imposed or given in the absence of the offender, the offender must be brought before the court before being taken to a prison or other institution to begin serving his sentence (and the sentence or order is not to be regarded as taking effect until he is brought before the court).

(4) In proceedings to which this subsection applies, the court shall not in a person's absence impose any disqualification on him, except on resumption of the hearing after an adjournment under section 10(3) above; and where a trial is adjourned in pursuance of this subsection the notice required by section 10(2) above shall include notice of the reason for the adjournment.

(5) Subsections (3) and (4) apply to—

(a) proceedings instituted by an information, where a summons has been issued; and

(b) proceedings instituted by a written charge.

(6) Nothing in this section requires the court to enquire into the reasons for the accused's failure to appear before deciding whether to proceed in his absence.

(7) The court shall state in open court its reasons for not proceeding under this section

in the absence of an accused who has attained the age of 18 years; and the court shall cause those reasons to be entered in its register of proceedings.

[This section is printed as amended by the *Criminal Justice Act* 1988, Sched. 8, the *Criminal Justice and Public Order Act* 1994, Sched. 10, the *Crime and Disorder Act* 1998, Sched. 8, the *Powers of Criminal Courts (Sentencing) Act* 2000, Sched. 9, the *Criminal Justice and Courts Services Act* 2000, Scheds 7 and 8, the *Criminal Justice Act* 2003, Sched. 32 and the *Criminal Justice and Immigration Act* 2008, s.54.]

(b) *General principles*

Section 11(1) confers a power on the magistrates' court to proceed to the trial of an information where the accused does not attend. In the case of an accused under the age of 18, there is an open ended discretion conferred on the court, whereas in the case of an accused aged 18 or over there is a presumption that the trial will proceed in his absence unless it appears to the court to be contrary to the interests of justice to do so or the court considers that there is an acceptable reason for the accused's absence. Plainly, therefore, the court should be more likely to adjourn where an accused under the age of 18 fails to appear than in the case of an accused aged 18 or over. It is further submitted that the existing authorities will continue to guide magistrates' courts as to when it will be appropriate to proceed in the absence of the accused: if the accused's absence is properly to be described as "involuntary" then there will an acceptable reason for his absence (and in any event it will not be in the interests of justice to proceed without him); and if the accused's absence is properly to be described as "voluntary" but in the particular circumstances of the case the trial would be unfair without him present (so that the conviction would necessarily be unsafe) then it will not be in the interests of justice to proceed (although see also what was said in *Shirzadeh*, *post*, as to the possibility of re-opening the case and the automatic right of appeal to the Crown Court). Consideration of exercise of the discretion to proceed in the absence of the accused was given by the Court of Appeal in *Hayward*; *Jones*; *Purvis* [2001] Q.B. 862 and then on appeal to the House of Lords in *Jones* [2003] 1 A.C. 1. The following list of factors were identified by the Court of Appeal and then modified to an extent by the House of Lords as being relevant when deciding whether to proceed in the absence of the accused: **7–176**

1. The nature and circumstances of the defendant's behaviour in absenting him or herself from the trial or disrupting it, and in particular whether the behaviour was voluntary and so plainly waived the right to be present;
2. Whether an adjournment would resolve the matter;
3. The likely length of such an adjournment;
4. Whether the defendant, though absent, wished to be represented or had waived his or her right to representation;
5. Whether the defendant's representatives were able to receive instructions from him or her and the extent to which they could present the defence;
6. The extent of the disadvantage to the defendant in not being able to present his or her account of events;
7. The risk of the jury reaching an improper conclusion about the absence of the defendant;
8. The general public interest that a trial should take place within a reasonable time;
9. The effect of the delay on the memories of the witnesses;
10. Where there was more than one defendant, and not all had absconded, the undesirability of having separate trials.

Those principles were set out in relation to trial on indictment, but they have expressly been applied and adopted for the purposes of summary trial: see *Shirzadeh v. Maidstone Magistrates' Court*, unreported, August 21, 2003, DC ([2003] EWHC 2216, Admin); and *R. (Morsby) v. Tower Bridge Magistrates' Court*, 172 J.P. 155, DC. In *Shirzadeh* the Divisional Court concluded that additional factors to those listed in *Jones* (*ante*) applied in the magistrates' and youth courts. These were:

1. There was less risk from either a trained lay justice or a district judge (as opposed to a jury) drawing an impermissible inference from a defendant's absence;
2. The finder of fact (being the lay justices or district judge) could ask its own questions and test the evidence of prosecution witnesses;
3. A defendant had a right under s.142 of the *Magistrates' Courts Act* 1980 to have the case re-opened;
4. A defendant in summary proceedings had an automatic right of appeal to the Crown Court by way of a full re-hearing of the evidence.

Nevertheless, in *R. (Neil Webb-Johnson) v. DPP*, unreported, December 8, 2005, QBD (Gibbs J.) ([2005] EWHC 3123 (Admin.)), *Morsby*, and *M. v. Burnley, Pendle and Rossendale Magistrates' Court*, unreported, October 14, 2009, QBD (Langstaff J.) ([2009] EWHC 2874 (Admin.)), it was said that it was inconceivable that any different standard should apply to trials in the youth court or magistrates' court than should apply to trial on indictment.

In *O'Hare* [2006] Crim.L.R. 950, CA, it was said that, in order for an accused to be taken to have waived his right to be present at his trial, it must be proved that he knew of, or was indifferent to, the consequences of being tried in his absence and without legal representation (*i.e.* where his absence can properly be described as being "involuntary"); and an incontrovertible means by which this would be proved would be where a court had given a direction to the accused when granting bail explaining the consequences of non-attendance at trial, and had then provided him with a written statement to the same effect.

See also the *Consolidated Criminal Practice Directions* (Appendix F).

See *R. (Morsby) v. Tower Bridge Magistrates' Court* (*ibid.*), as authority for a proposition that the general approach to the question of whether to proceed in the absence of the accused is that where there is some fault on the part of a defendant which led to his absence, that will often be relevant (but not by itself determinative) to the court's decision; but it would normally be in the interests of justice for a defendant to be able to defend himself, and unless the evidence indicated that his absence from trial was deliberate and voluntary, an adjournment would normally be the appropriate course. A decision to proceed in the absence of an accused would be flawed where no enquiry was made as to the accused's absence and no consideration was given to whether the matter should be adjourned: see *James v. Tower Bridge Magistrates' Court*, unreported, June 9, 2009, DC ([2009] EWHC 1500 (Admin.)).

(c) *Defendant in custody and not produced*

7–177 Arrest and detention by the police preventing a defendant from attending his trial is not voluntary absence and the court was criticised for proceeding in absence in those circumstances: *R. (R.) v. Thames Youth Court*, 166 J.P. 613, QBD.

In *R. (Morsby) v. Tower Bridge Magistrates' Court* (*ante*), the defendant had pleaded not guilty to an offence and was bailed to attend for trial. Subsequently, he was arrested in respect of a separate offence and was remanded in custody; but on the date ultimately fixed for trial in relation to the original charge, he was not produced from custody and was convicted in his absence. When the reason for his absence became apparent, he was produced and an application was made under to reopen the case under s.142(2) of the *Magistrates' Courts Act* 1980 (see Ch.11, *post*). Refusing the application, the district judge had concluded that the fault was on the part of the defendant, since he could have obtained the court's address through the solicitors acting for him in respect of the subsequent offence or the gaolers. The Divisional Court said that there where there was some fault on the part of a defendant which led to his absence at trial, that might often be relevant (but not by itself determinative) to the court's decision whether it was in the interests of justice to make a direction under s.142(2); but it would normally be in the interests of justice for a defendant to be able to defend himself, and unless the evidence indicated that his absence from trial was deliberate and voluntary, a re-hearing would normally be the appropriate course. To the same effect, see also *Hodges*, unreported, January 16, 2008, CA ([2008] EWCA Crim 620).

In *Amrouchi*, unreported, November 22, 2007, CA ([2007] EWCA Crim. 3019), it was observed that where a defendant refused to leave prison to be transported to court for his trial, the power in the *Crime (Sentences) Act* 1997, Sched. 1, to invite the Secretary of State to direct the prison service to bring the defendant to court could not be invoked to compel the defendant's attendance; the power did not operate where the prison service was otherwise willing to produce the defendant, from which it followed that the existence of the power was not a matter to be taken into account by a court when deciding to proceed in the defendant's absence. However, the court said (in relation to trial on indictment) that, in this kind of situation, the proper course was to adjourn for 24 hours and to ensure that an explicit warning was delivered to the defendant that his trial was going to take place without him if he was not there tomorrow morning. Such a warning could be delivered in a number of ways; and whilst the judge would need to satisfy himself that it had been delivered, it would suffice for the court to require only written confirmation from the prison, rather than to hear evidence from the prison officer who had delivered the message or the prison governor.

Cf. Balham Youth Court, ex p. K., The Independent, December 20, 1999, DC, where it was said that neither a children's home where a young offender was living, nor a social services department that had assumed responsibility for him were responsible for his appearance at court (declining to grant judicial review of a refusal by justices to set aside the applicant's conviction after he had been convicted in his absence having twice failed to appear, although he had been notified of the dates).

(d) *Defendant unwell or otherwise incapacitated*

The discretion to commence a trial in the absence of a defendant should be exercised **7–178** with the utmost care and caution; if the absence of the defendant is attributable to involuntary illness or incapacity it would very rarely, if ever, be right to exercise the discretion in favour of commencing the trial, at any rate unless the defendant is represented and asks that the trial should begin: *Jones* [2003] 1 A.C. 1, HL. In general where an accused is unfit to attend trial, and such unfitness is supported by medical evidence, an adjournment should be granted to enable him to attend. Where a defendant's legal representative has reason to believe that the accused is unfit and has been attended by a medical practitioner, the general practice is to obtain from the doctor, wherever possible in writing, something which can be handed to the court and in the majority of cases that will suffice to secure the necessary adjournment; but it would be unrealistic to ignore the fact that defendants may seek to defer the date of trial and may resort to a variety of expedients to that end, including the production of spurious or unconvincing medical excuses for non-attendance. Accordingly, the court is not obliged to accept any excuse proffered and if the court suspects the grounds to be spurious or believes them to be inadequate, it should ordinarily express its doubts and thereby give the defendant an opportunity to seek to resolve the doubts (*e.g.* by calling for better evidence, requiring further inquiries to be made or adopting any other expedient steps fair to both parties): *Bolton Justices, ex p. Merna*, 155 J.P. 612, DC.

As to the relevance of the fact that defendant was unrepresented (as where his legal representatives have withdrawn), see also *R. (Neil Webb-Johnson) v. DPP*, unreported, December 8, 2005, QBD (Gibbs J.) ([2005] EWHC 3123 (Admin.)).

Cf. Ealing Magistrates' Court, ex p. Burgess, 165 J.P. 82, DC, where it was said that in cases of continued absence the court would be entitled eventually to conclude "enough is enough" when confronted by the latest of a series of applications to adjourn based on ill-health rather than to postpone the trial indefinitely. It is submitted, however, that this decision should be placed in its proper context. First, it was decided before the decision of the House of Lords in *Jones* and arguably it no longer represents the proper understanding of the law (even with the additional factors in *Shirzadeh* taken into account). Secondly, it is also important to bear in mind that on the facts of the case, there was evidence that the defendant had been attending other magistrates' courts on a regular basis to conduct a series of proceedings as prosecutor of a series of private prosecutions and there was voluminous correspondence from the accused on the court file which tended to undermine his medical diagnosis.

(e) *Unruly or disorderly behaviour by accused*

7–179 Although it is a serious matter for an accused to be excluded from proceedings, particularly where he would be likely to give evidence or may be entitled to give evidence on crucial matters, there must come a point at which an accused's (even an unrepresented accused's) disruption to the proceedings means that the judge has no choice but to exclude the person concerned from those proceedings and to continue with the trial in his absence: see *R. (Ezeugo) v. Hendon Magistrates' Court*, unreported, March 1, 2010, QBD (Nicol J.) ([2010] EWHC 516 (Admin.)). Where, however, an accused attended court for his trial and wished to give evidence, but was excluded from court premises by a member of court security following an incident of disorderly behaviour, his absence could not properly be regarded as "voluntary"; whilst the exclusion from the premises was a consequence of disorderly behaviour on his part and was in that sense his own fault, that was not the same as saying that it was his choice: *R. (Davies) v. Solihull JJ.*, unreported, April 23, 2008, DC ([2008] EWHC 1157 (Admin.)).

(f) *Withdrawal of legal representative where a party fails to appear*

7–180 A solicitor's decision to withdraw from a trial rather than to continue after the defendant had voluntarily absented himself is not be "unreasonable" within the meaning of s.19A(3) of the *Prosecution of Offences Act* 1985 where it could not be inferred that the defendant had expected his legal representatives to continue to represent him in his absence and where the solicitor genuinely believed that it would not be in the defendant's best interests to continue to represent him; the responsibility for deciding whether a trial should continue in a defendant's absence was that of the trial judge, but the judge should not assume, when making a decision to proceed, that legal representation would continue; fundamental questions of trust between lawyers and litigants arise when a defendant absents himself (as do practical questions as to the conduct of the trial), and the role of the independent professional representative in the administration of justice must be borne in mind together with the need not to undermine it by illegitimate pressures: *Re Boodhoo* [2007] 1 Cr.App.R. 32, CA.

(g) Duties of defence advocate where trial proceeds in absence of defendant

7–181 Where an accused has absconded but remains in contact with his lawyers and is then tried in his absence in circumstances where his advocate has not withdrawn, the advocate is not limited to acting on instructions received before the date when the defendant absconded; if there were to be a principle that the advocate were not permitted to take into account fresh instructions received from the absent accused, it would increase unnecessarily the possibility of error or oversight against which legal representation provided a valuable safeguard; and it could also prevent the advocate from being able to deal effectively with new evidence or new issues, even where the absent defendant had valid points to make in relation to them; but it would always be important for the judge to keep an eye on the overall fairness of the proceedings and to exercise his discretion appropriately to prevent any unfair manipulation of the process by an absent defendant, particularly to the disadvantage of any co-defendants: *Pomfrett*, unreported, October 8, 2009, CA ([2009] EWCA Crim. 1939).

(3) The prosecution

Magistrates' Courts Act 1980, s.15

Non-appearance of prosecutor

7–182 **15.**—(1) Where at the time and place appointed for the trial or adjourned trial of an information the accused appears or is brought before the court and the prosecutor does not appear, the court may dismiss the information or, if evidence has been received on a previous occasion, proceed in the absence of the prosecutor.

(2) Where, instead of dismissing the information or proceeding in the absence of the prosecutor, the court adjourns the trial, it shall not remand the accused in custody unless he has been brought from custody or cannot be remanded on bail by reason of his failure to find sureties.

A prosecutor is not absent if he is represented by counsel or solicitor: *Magistrates' Courts Act* 1980, s.122. The prosecutor may be absent if he is physically not present in court or if, although present he is not able to prosecute the case because he does not have the file. **7–183**

It is apparent from case law that the appeal courts frown upon the use of the power in this section as a punitive measure. In *DPP v. Shuttleworth*, 166 J.P. 417, DC, a defendant indicated she would plead guilty but the prosecutor could not proceed with the case because he did not have the file. The court purported to dismiss the charge. It was held on appeal that there was a want of prosecution because the file was not available but the purpose of the hearing was for plea and not for trial. The choice for the court in view of the guilty plea was to adjourn the case or proceed without the information from the file. The dismissal of the case was a punitive measure against the CPS which was not a proper exercise of the courts discretion. Costs penalties were available for that and the court failed to have regard to public interests including those of the defendant and victim.

It is not reasonable to use this power to punish a prosecutor for late attendance without taking into account all the circumstances. Where the CPS were told by the court that a trial was not in the court list and that the court was not sitting, the court acted unreasonably in dismissing the charge since the reason for the non-attendance was because the CPS had been misinformed. On discovering the mistake, a prosecutor contacted the court to say he was on his way. The court did not wait for him to arrive but dismissed the charge apparently as a means of punishing the prosecutor for perceived inefficiency which was held to be an improper exercise of its power: *Hendon Justices, ex p. DPP* [1994] Q.B. 167, DC; and see *R. (CPS) v. Portsmouth Crown Court* [2004] Crim.L.R. 224, DC. **7–184**

The overall consideration is one of fairness, and it is not fair for a court to dismiss an information on a peremptory basis by virtue of the failure of the prosecution to attend: *London Borough of Bromley v. Bromley Magistrates' Court,* 175 J.P. 179, DC (where it was said to be unreasonable to exercise the discretion in circumstances where the case was heard at short notice on execution of a warrant for the defendant's arrest and the prosecutor had been informed at short notice and could not have anticipated the hearing).

Another device resorted to occasionally by the court is to direct a change of plea from guilty to not guilty so that a charge may be dismissed in the absence of the prosecutor.

The mere fact that a case could be dismissed for want of prosecution is not a good reason to allow a change of plea: *Uxbridge Justices, ex p. Smith* [1977] R.T.R. 93, DC. Allowing a change of plea in order to exercise the discretion to dismiss was held to be in breach of natural justice as the discretion should not be exercised in order to discipline the prosecution: *Sutton Justices, ex p. DPP*, 95 Cr.App.R. 180, DC.

(4) Non-appearance of both parties

Magistrates' Courts Act 1980, s.16

Non-appearance of both parties

16. Subject to section 11(3) and (4) and to section 12 above, where at the time and place appointed for the trial or adjourned trial of an information neither the prosecutor nor the accused appears, the court may dismiss the information or, if evidence has been received on a previous occasion, proceed in their absence. **7–185**

7–186 The circumstances in which the court would proceed in the absence of both the prosecutor and defendant are very limited. It may not do so when the presence of the defendant is required for the imposition of custodial sentences and for disqualification in certain circumstances under s.11, of the *Magistrates' Courts' Act* 1980.

The prosecutor and defendant may not be present when a case is dealt with under s.12 of the 1980 Act which provides for cases to be heard in absence when a written plea of guilty has been received by the court.

(5) Death of the defendant

7–187 The court may receive information that the defendant has died. In such circumstances in the magistrates' court there is no legal requirement for strict proof of this fact. The court may require that a death certificate be produced or the case may be adjourned for the prosecution to investigate the veracity of the report. The prosecution will then make the appropriate application to withdraw the proceedings or offer no evidence with the court register being marked that the defendant is "deceased".

F. TRANSFER OF PROCEEDINGS TO DIFFERENT MAGISTRATES' COURT

(1) Transfer of remand hearings

7–188 Where the court adjourns a case under s.5, 10(1), 17C or 18(4) of the *Magistrates' Courts Act* 1980 and remands into custody an accused who has attained the age of 17, the court may order that he is to be brought up for any subsequent remands before an alternative magistrates' court nearer to the prison to which he is remanded: see s.130 of the 1980 Act (*ante*, § 5–102).

(2) Transfer of trial or committal

Magistrates' Courts Act 1980, s.27A

Power to transfer criminal proceedings

7–189 **27A.**—(1) Where a person appears or is brought before a magistrates' court—

(a) to be tried by the court for an offence, or

(b) for the court to inquire into the offence as examining justices,

the court may transfer the matter to another magistrates' court.

(2) The court may transfer the matter before or after beginning the trial or inquiry.

(3) But if the court transfers the matter after it has begun to hear the evidence and the parties, the court to which the matter is transferred must begin hearing the evidence and the parties again.

(4) The power of the court under this section to transfer any matter must be exercised in accordance with any directions given under section 30(3) of the *Courts Act* 2003.

[This section was inserted by the *Courts Act* 2003, s.46.]

(3) Transfer for sentence

Powers of Criminal Courts (Sentencing) Act 2000 s.10

Power of magistrates' court to remit case to another magistrates' court for sentence

7–190 **10.**—(1) Where a person aged 18 or over ("the offender") has been convicted by a magistrates' court ("the convicting court") of an offence to which this section applies ("the instant offence") and—

(a) it appears to the convicting court that some other magistrates' court ("the other court") has convicted him of another such offence in respect of which the other court has neither passed sentence on him nor committed him to the Crown Court for sentence nor dealt with him in any other way, and

(b) the other court consents to his being remitted under this section to the other court, the convicting court may remit him to the other court to be dealt with in respect of the instant offence by the other court instead of by the convicting court.

(2) This section applies to—

(a) any offence punishable with imprisonment; and

(b) any offence in respect of which the convicting court has a power or duty to order the offender to be disqualified under section 34, 35 or 36 of the *Road Traffic Offenders Act* 1988 (disqualification for certain motoring offences).

(3) Where the convicting court remits the offender to the other court under this section, it shall adjourn the trial of the information charging him with the instant offence, and—

(a) section 128 of the *Magistrates' Court Act* 1980 (remand in custody or on bail) and all other enactments, whenever passed, relating to remand or the granting of bail in criminal proceedings shall have effect, in relation to the convicting court's power or duty to remand the offender on that adjournment, as if any reference to the court to or before which the person remanded is to be brought or appear after remand were a reference to the court to which he is being remitted; and

(b) subject to subsection (7) below, the other court may deal with the case in any way in which it would have power to deal with it if all proceedings relating to the instant offence which took place before the convicting court had taken place before the other court.

(4) The power conferred on the other court by subsection (3)(b) above includes, where applicable, the power to remit the offender under this section to another magistrates' court in respect of the instant offence.

(5) Where the convicting court has remitted the offender under this section to the other court, the other court may remit him back to the convicting court; and the provisions of subsections (3) and (4) above (so far as applicable) shall apply with the necessary modifications in relation to any remission under this subsection.

(6) The offender, if remitted under this section, shall have no right of appeal against the order of remission (but without prejudice to any right of appeal against any other order made in respect of the instant offence by the court to which he is remitted).

(7) Nothing in this section shall preclude the convicting court from making any order which it has power to make under section 148 below (restitution orders) by virtue of the offender's conviction of the instant offence.

(8) In this section—

(a) "conviction" includes a finding under section 11(1) below (remand for medical examination) that the person in question did the act or made the omission charged, and "convicted" shall be construed accordingly;

(b) "enactment" includes an enactment contained in any order, regulation or other instrument having effect by virtue of an Act; and

(c) "bail in criminal proceedings" has the same meaning as in the *Bail Act* 1976.

G. POWER TO MAKE PRE-TRIAL RULINGS

(1) Introduction

Sections 8A to 8D of the *Magistrates Courts' Act* 1980 (inserted by the *Courts Act* 2003) allow binding rulings of law to be made at pre-trial hearings. The power may be exercised following a not guilty plea up to the commencement of the trial, and may be used in relation to issues of law and admissibility of evidence. The power is intended to assist in ensuring more efficient preparation of cases for trial. There is no specific right of appeal against a pre-trial ruling, although it would seem that such rulings may be amenable to judicial review. There is also a power to vary a pre-trial ruling on application by a party to the case (where there has been a material change of circumstances) or where it is in the interests of justice: s.8B(3); as to the exercise of this power, see *R. (CPS) v. Gloucester JJ.*, 172 J.P. 506, DC (*post*, § 7–194). **7–191**

(2) Power to make pre-trial rulings

Magistrates' Courts 1980, s.8A

Power to make rulings at pre-trial hearing

8A.—(1) For the purposes of this section a hearing is a pre-trial hearing if— **7–192**

(a) it relates to an information—
(i) which is to be tried summarily, and
(ii) to which the accused has pleaded not guilty, and
(b) it takes place before the start of the trial.

(2) For the purposes of subsection (1)(b), the start of a summary trial occurs when the court begins—
(a) to hear evidence from the prosecution at the trial, or
(b) to consider whether to exercise its power under section 37(3) of the *Mental Health Act* 1983 (power to make hospital order without convicting the accused).

(3) At a pre-trial hearing, a magistrates' court may make a ruling as to any matter mentioned in subsection (4) if—
(a) the condition in subsection (5) is met,
(b) the court has given the parties an opportunity to be heard, and
(c) it appears to the court that it is in the interests of justice to make the ruling.

(4) The matters are—
(a) any question as to the admissibility of evidence;
(b) any other question of law relating to the case.

(5) The condition is that, if the accused is not legally represented—
(a) the court must ask whether he wishes to be granted a right to representation funded by the Legal Services Commission as part of the Criminal Defence Service, and
(b) if he does, the Legal Services Commission must decide whether or not to grant him that right.

(6) A ruling may be made under this section—
(a) on an application by a party to the case, or
(b) of the court's own motion.

(7) For the purposes of this section and section 8B, references to the prosecutor are to any person acting as prosecutor, whether an individual or body.

[This section is printed as amended by the *Criminal Defence Service (Representation Orders and Consequential Amendments) Regulations* 2006 (S.I. 2006 No. 2493), reg. 7.]

(3) Effect of pre-trial rulings and power to discharge

Magistrates' Courts Act 1980, s.8B

Effect of rulings at pre-trial hearing

7–193 **8B.**—(1) Subject to subsections (3) and (6), a ruling under section 8A has binding effect from the time it is made until the case against the accused or, if there is more than one, against each of them, is disposed of.

(2) The case against an accused is disposed of if—
(a) he is acquitted or convicted,
(b) the prosecutor decides not to proceed with the case against him, or
(c) the information is dismissed.

(3) A magistrates' court may discharge or vary (or further vary) a ruling under section 8A if—
(a) the condition in section 8A(5) is met,
(b) the court has given the parties an opportunity to be heard, and
(c) it appears to the court that it is in the interests of justice to do so.

(4) The court may act under subsection (3)—
(a) on an application by a party to the case, or
(b) of its own motion.

(5) No application may be made under subsection (4)(a) unless there has been a material change of circumstances since the ruling was made or, if a previous application has been made, since the application (or last application) was made.

(6) A ruling under section 8A is discharged in relation to an accused if—
(a) the magistrates' court commits or sends him to the Crown Court for trial for the offence charged in the information, or

(b) a count charging him with the offence is included in an indictment by virtue of section 40 of the *Criminal Justice Act* 1988.

Varying or discharging the pre-trial ruling

It will not be "in the interests of justice" for the court to annul or discharge its own earlier ruling without there being some compelling reason, such as changed circumstances, or fresh evidence, so to do; one bench cannot set aside a previous bench's ruling under s.8B because on the same material it thought it would reach a different conclusion: *R. (CPS) v. Gloucester JJ*, 172 J.P. 506, DC. **7–194**

As to the meaning of a "material change of circumstances" in subs (5), this has been held to include the situation where, six days before the anticipated trial date, the court had made a ruling that the statement of an absent prosecution witness could be read under s.116(1) and (2)(e) of the *Criminal Justice Act* 2003 (witness abroad and not reasonably practicable to secure his attendance) but where the trial did not in the event take place until four months later; the period of delay before the actual trial date was such that it had been open to the prosecution to make enquiries of the witness, to ascertain whether there was any time in the proximate future when she might otherwise be in, or could come to, the UK or otherwise discover what could be done to secure the evidence other than by the use of s.116: see *Brett v. DPP*, 173 J.P. 274, DC.

(3) Reporting restrictions

Magistrates' Courts Act 1980, ss.8C, 8D

Restrictions on reporting

8C.—(1) Except as provided by this section no report of matters falling within subsection (2) may be published in England and Wales. **7–195**

(2) The following matters fall within this subsection—

(a) a ruling under section 8A;

(b) proceedings on an application for a ruling under section 8A;

(c) an order under section 8B that a ruling under section 8A be discharged, varied or further varied;

(d) proceedings on an application under section 8B for a ruling under section 8A to be discharged, varied or further varied.

(3) A magistrates' court dealing with any matter falling within subsection (2) may order that subsection (1) does not apply, or does not apply to a specified extent, to a report of the matter.

(4) Where there is only one accused and he objects to the making of an order under subsection (3)—

(a) the court may make the order if (and only if) satisfied after hearing the representations of the accused that it is in the interests of justice to do so, and

(b) if the order is made, it shall not apply to the extent that a report deals with any such objection or representations.

(5) Where there are two or more accused and one or more of them objects to the making of an order under subsection (3)—

(a) the court may make the order if (and only if) satisfied after hearing the representations of each of the accused that it is in the interests of justice to do so, and

(b) if the order is made, it shall not apply to the extent that a report deals with any such objection or representations.

(6) Subsection (1) does not apply to the publication of a report of matters after the case against the accused or, if more than one, against each of them, is disposed of.

(7) Subsection (1) does not apply to a report which contains only one or more of the following matters—

(a) the identity of the court and the names of the justices;

(b) the names, ages, home addresses and occupations of the accused and witnesses;

(c) the offence or offences, or a summary of them, with which the accused or any of the accused are charged;

(d) the names of counsel and solicitors in the proceedings;

(e) where the proceedings are adjourned, the date and place to which they are adjourned;

(f) any arrangements as to bail;

(g) whether a right to representation funded by the Legal Services Commission as part of the Criminal Defence Service was granted to the accused or any of the accused.

(8) The addresses that may be included in a report by virtue of subsection (7) are addresses—

(a) at any relevant time, and

(b) at the time of their inclusion in the publication.

(9) In subsection (8), "relevant time" means a time when events giving rise to the charges to which the proceedings relate are alleged to have occurred.

(10) Nothing in this section affects any prohibition or restriction imposed by virtue of any other enactment on the publication of a report of any matter.

(11) In this section and in section 8D—

(a) references to publication of a report of matters falling within subsection (2)—

(i) include references to inclusion of those matters in any speech, writing, relevant programme or other communication in whatever form which is addressed to the public at large or any section of the public (and for this purpose every relevant programme is to be taken to be so addressed), but

(ii) do not include references to inclusion of those matters in a document prepared for use in particular legal proceedings;

(b) "relevant programme" means a programme included in a programme service, within the meaning of the *Broadcasting Act* 1990.

Offences in connection with reporting

7–196 **8D.**—(1) If a report is published in contravention of section 8C each of the following persons is guilty of an offence—

(a) in the case of a publication of a report as part of a newspaper or periodical, any proprietor, editor or publisher of the newspaper or periodical;

(b) in the case of the inclusion of a report in a relevant programme, any body corporate which is engaged in providing the service in which the programme is included and any person having functions in relation to the programme corresponding to those of an editor of a newspaper;

(c) in the case of any other publication, any person publishing it.

(2) If an offence under this section committed by a body corporate is proved—

(a) to have been committed with the consent or connivance of, or

(b) to be attributable to any neglect on the part of,

an officer, the officer as well as the body corporate is guilty of the offence and liable to be proceeded against and punished accordingly.

(3) In subsection (2), "officer" means a director, manager, secretary or other similar officer of the body, or a person purporting to act in any such capacity.

(4) If the affairs of a body corporate are managed by its members, "director" in subsection (3) means a member of that body.

(5) A person guilty of an offence under this section is liable on summary conviction to a fine of an amount not exceeding level 5 on the standard scale.

(6) Proceedings for an offence under this section may not be instituted otherwise than by or with the consent of the Attorney General.

H. SUMMARY TRIAL OF MULTIPLE INFORMATIONS

(1) Decision as to Separate or Joint Trials of Informations

7–197 A defendant appearing before the magistrates' court may be charged with several offences arising from one incident or may face further charges concerning unrelated matters. The court must then decide whether to try the cases together or whether separate trials are required. Similarly there may be several co-accused charged with joint offences who may wish to be tried separately. The main issue for the court is to consider the interests of justice and whether a trial will be fair in compliance with art. 6 of the ECHR. Different charges being tried together may result in prejudice being caused to the defence.

In *Chief Constable of Norfolk v. Clayton* [1983] 2 A.C. 473, HL, the circumstances in which the court may hear and determine separate informations were reviewed. If in each case the facts are connected, then if the court thinks fit they can be heard together. Before embarking on a joint trial, the court should seek the consent of both the prosecution and the defence. If consent is not forthcoming the court should consider submissions and rule as they think fit in the interests of justice. The fact that the defence does not consent to joint trials is an important factor but does not deprive the court of its discretion to order joint trials. See also *Camberwell Green Stipendiary Magistrate, ex p. Martin* [2001] A.C.D. 8, DC.

When the prosecution and defence agree to separate trials, the court may still order joint trial but the court should be slow to reach such a conclusion: *Highbury Corner Magistrates' Court, ex p. McGinley*, 150 J.P. 257, DC. Where a defendant applies for a separate trial because an essential part of his defence consists of an attack on his co-defendant it remained a matter for the discretion of the court whether to allow separate trials: *Grondkowski* [1946] K.B. 369, CA. Separate representation may be granted which would protect the interests of the defendant.

Defendants jointly charged will appear in the dock together and may be jointly or **7–198** separately represented. The practice of putting in the dock defendants who are not jointly charged and who have been arrested at different times and places is discouraged as it gives the impression of "group justice": *Mansfield Justices, ex p. Sharkey* [1985] Q.B. 613, DC.

It was held that under no circumstances may a court order that a summons and cross-summons should be heard together. Although in many cases joint trials were appropriate the court identified added difficulties with the conduct of such a case which made joint trial inappropriate: *Epsom Justices, ex p. Gibbons* [1984] Q.B. 574, DC.

If the informations are to be tried separately the question that then arises is whether the same bench should hear all the cases. It is a matter of discretion for the bench to decide whether it should try all the charges or whether they should be adjourned to different days before different benches. The court must apply its mind judicially to ensure there is no likelihood of bias. Where a court decided to proceed with hearing six sets of offences against a defendant no bias was apparent because the exercise of the discretion was plainly reviewed after hearing each batch of charges: *Sandwich Justices, ex p. Berry*, 74 Cr.App.R. 132, DC.

Joint trials either of co-defendants or of several charges may give rise to an appear- **7–199** ance of bias. The test to be applied is whether a reasonable and fair-minded person, knowing all the facts, would have a reasonable suspicion that a fair trial would not be possible. That some unrelated charges are all included on the same charge sheet was held not to be improper and did not give rise to bias: *Weston-super-Mare Justices, ex p. Shaw* [1987] Q.B. 640, DC. But disclosing on the register sheets all charges pending against a defendant could give rise to the appearance of bias and was wrong in law as it did not comply with r.66 of the *Magistrates' Courts Rules* 1981 (now see r.6.1 of the *Criminal Procedure Rules* 2011 (Appendix G): *Liverpool City Justices, ex p. Topping*, 79 Cr.App.R. 170, DC.

Where a number of cases involving separate defendants have a common factual issue, the magistrates' court has a discretion to hear all the cases at the same time, without making the defendants co-defendants; to adopt such an approach, the court must separate out the evidence in each case, and permit no cross-examination of witnesses on factual issues where those issues related to one particular case: *Skinner v. DPP* [2005] R.T.R. 17, DC.

(2) Alternative charges

The magistrates' court has no inherent power to convict on a lesser offence rather **7–200** than the one charged in a summary trial. The proper procedure is for the prosecution to charge offences in the alternative. This can be done either right from the start at charge or an alternative offence can be preferred during the course of the proceedings.

When an alternative charge is brought the defence has a right to an adjournment to consider it. It is a matter for the prosecution which charge to prefer. Where a defendant was charged with assault occasioning actual bodily harm the prosecution preferred an alternative charge of common assault. The defendant said this was an abuse of process because the prosecution wanted to deprive him of his right to jury trial. The motive for choosing a particular charge was held irrelevant in the absence of bad faith: *Sheffield Justices, ex p. DPP* [1993] Crim.L.R. 136, DC; *Canterbury and St Augustine Justices, ex p. Klisiak* [1982] Q.B. 398, DC.

In *R. (CPS) v. Blaydon Youth Court*, 168 J.P. 638, DC, at trial the defendant was charged with a racially aggravated offence under s.4A of the *Public Order Act* 1986 and also with the same offence but not aggravated. The prosecution said that the charges were in the alternative and a joint trial on both charges was held. The defendant neither objected nor consented at the time but the court took the view that the charges were duplicitous. At the Divisional Court it was held that the court was wrong and that there could be a joint trial of two informations. Where the charges arose from the same facts it would be inconvenient and expensive for them to be tried separately and it was not against the interests of justice for them to be tried together. The proper course if there was a conviction on the more serious offence would be to adjourn the remaining offence generally so it would remain as a charge if there were a successful appeal against conviction on the other offence. This case confirms that alternative verdicts are available in the magistrates'court provided alternative charges are brought.

7–201 Where an accused has been tried upon two informations laid in the alternative and convicted on one of them, s.9(2) of the *Magistrates' Courts Act* 1980 prevents the justices from dismissing the alternative on which the accused was not convicted; in those circumstances the proper course is for the prosecution to withdraw the remaining charge: *DPP v. Gane* [1991] Crim.L.R. 711, DC. *Cf. Clarke v. CPS*, unreported, July 18, 2007, DC ([2007] EWHC 2228 (Admin.)), where it was observed that whereas a magistrates' court seemingly has no power to leave a charge on the file not to be proceeded without the leave of the court, it might be possible to achieve an equivalent result in relation to the non-conviction alternative by staying a prosecution on that charge.

IX. TERMINATION OF PROCEEDINGS

(1) Introduction

7–202 After the defendant has been charged, the prosecution may decide that it will not proceed. The case may then be dealt with in one of three ways; withdrawal, no evidence offered, or discontinuance.

(2) Withdrawal of summons

7–203 The court has power to grant an application to withdraw a summons without an adjudication being made. There is no requirement for the matter to be put and a plea to be entered: *Redbridge Justices, ex p. Sainty* [1981] R.T.R. 13, DC.

The withdrawal of a summons is not the equivalent to an acquittal and so will not act as a bar on the issue of a further summons in respect of the same charge where there has been no adjudication on the merits of the case: *Grays Justices, ex p. Low* [1990] 1 Q.B. 54, DC; *London Borough of Islington v. Michaelides* [2001] Crim.L.R. 843, DC.

(3) Offering no evidence

7–204 Once the accused has entered a plea of not guilty to the information, it is no longer possible for the prosecution to ask for the matter to be withdrawn. The prosecution may offer no evidence and the case will be dismissed under s.9 of the *Magistrates' Courts Act* 1980. The charge cannot then be revived.

Where an accused has been lawfully acquitted by a magistrates' court of competent jurisdiction acting within its jurisdiction, he cannot be prosecuted again for the same offence, even if the acquittal resulted from the prosecution not offering any evidence: *Pressick* [1978] Crim.L.R. 377, CA; *Swansea Justices, ex p. Purvis*, 145 J.P. 252, DC. If the prosecution are of the view that the case is too weak to proceed, and that they would not resist a submission of no case to answer, they may nonetheless allow the proceedings to continue and to leave it to the judge to decide whether or not there is a case to answer; but it would be preferable for them to abandon the prosecution; and if the matter is allowed to proceed to a submission of no case to answer and it is ruled that there is a case to answer, it will be too late for the prosecution to abandon the case subsequently (although there is no obligation to cross-examine defence witnesses or to make a closing speech): *R. v. O.* [1999] 1 *Archbold News* 2, CA.

Where two separate prosecuting authorities instituted proceedings against a defendant for the same offence and one authority then withdrew the summons (and the court file was marked as "no evidence offered") on the basis that another separate prosecuting agency had laid identical charges, but that other prosecuting authority then offered no evidence against the defendant for entirely unconnected reasons, the court had no power to set aside the first prosecutor's withdrawal under s.142 of the *Magistrates' Courts Act* 1980) or pursuant to the common law: *R. (Green and Green Scaffolding Ltd) v. Staines Magistrates' Court*, 172 J.P. 353, DC.

(4) Statutory discontinuance

Prosecution of Offences Act 1985, s.23

Discontinuance of proceedings in magistrates' courts

23—(1) Where the Director of Public Prosecutions has the conduct of proceedings for an offence, this section applies in relation to the preliminary stages of those proceedings. **7–205**

(2) In this section, "preliminary stage" in relation to proceedings for an offence does not include—

(a) *in the case of a summary offence, any stage of the proceedings after the court has begun to hear evidence for the prosecution at the trial;*

[(a) any stage of the proceedings after the court has begun to hear evidence for the prosecution at a summary trial of the offence; or]

(b) *in the case of an indictable offence, any stage of the proceedings after—*

(i) *the accused has been committed for trial; or*

(ii) *the court has begun to hear evidence for the prosecution at a summary trial of the offence;*

[(b) any stage of the proceedings after the accused has been sent for trial for the offence.]

(c) *in the case of any offence, any stage of the proceedings after the accused has been sent for trial under section 51 of the* Crime and Disorder Act *1998 (no committal proceedings for indictable-only and related offences).*

(3) Where, at any time during the preliminary stages of the proceedings, the Director gives notice under this section to the designated officer for the court that he does not want the proceedings to continue, they shall be discontinued with effect from the giving of that notice but may be revived by notice given by the accused under subsection (7) below.

(4) Where, in the case of a person charged with an offence after being taken into custody without a warrant, the Director gives him notice, at a time when no magistrates' court has been informed of the charge, that the proceedings against him are discontinued, they shall be discontinued with effect from the giving of that notice.

(5) The Director shall, in any notice given under subsection (3) above, give reasons for not wanting the proceedings to continue.

(6) On giving any notice under subsection (3) above the Director shall inform the accused of the notice and of the accused's right to require the proceedings to be continued; but the Director shall not be obliged to give the accused any indication of his reasons for not wanting the proceedings to continue.

(7) Where the Director has given notice under subsection (3) above, the accused shall, if he wants the proceedings to continue, give notice to that effect to the designated officer for the court within the prescribed period; and where notice is so given the proceedings shall continue as if no notice had been given by the Director under subsection (3) above.

(8) Where the designated officer for the court has been so notified by the accused he shall inform the Director.

(9) The discontinuance of any proceedings by virtue of this section shall not prevent the institution of fresh proceedings in respect of the same offence.

(10) In this section "prescribed" means prescribed by Criminal Procedure Rules.

[This section is printed as amended by the *Crime and Disorder Act* 1998, Sched. 8, and the *Courts Act* 2003, Sched. 8. The *Criminal Justice Act* 2003, Sched. 3, substitutes for the words set out in italics in subs. (2), the words which are set out in square brackets. That amendment was brought into force as from May 9, 2005, by the *Criminal Justice Act 2003 (Commencement No. 9) Order* 2005 (S.I. 2005 No. 1267), only for the purposes of cases sent to the Crown Court under s.51A(3)(d) of the 1998 Act. For all other purposes, the amendment is to be brought into force as from a day to be appointed.]

7–206 A notice of discontinuance may be served by the prosecution on the court and the defence during the preliminary stages of a case. The preliminary stages are defined in subs. (2). A case cannot be discontinued after a case has begun with prosecution evidence being heard in a summary trial or after an indictable case has been committed or sent to the Crown Court.

The defendant may require the proceedings to continue. He is also entitled to apply for costs after a discontinuance.

The prosecution may recharge the offence after a discontinuance.

This power does not affect the right of the prosecution to withdraw or offer no evidence in a case: *Cooke v. DPP and Brent Justices*, 156 J.P. 497, DC.

The *Commissioners for Revenue and Customs Act* 2005, s.36(3), and the *Serious Organised Crime and Police Act* 2005, s.38(5), apply s.23 of the 1985 Act (with necessary modifications) to proceedings conducted by the Director of the Revenue and Customs Prosecutions Office.

Part II

Summary Trial

Chapter 8

SUMMARY TRIAL

I. HEARING IN OPEN COURT

A. GENERAL PRINCIPLE

8–1 Magistrates' Courts have a statutory duty to sit in open court: *Magistrates' Courts Act* 1980, s.121(4); *Criminal Procedure Rules*, r.37.2 (see appendix G *post* § G–224). This means that proceedings must be held in public, evidence must be communicated publicly, and fair, accurate and contemporaneous media reporting of proceedings should not be prevented by any action of the court unless strictly necessary. Unless there are exceptional circumstances laid down by statute law and/or common law, the court must not order or allow the exclusion of the press or public from court for any part of the proceedings, permit the withholding of information from the open court proceedings, or impose permanent or temporary bans on reporting of the proceedings or any part of them including anything that prevents the proper identification, by name and address, of those appearing or mentioned in the course of proceedings. In *Att.-Gen. v. Leveller Magazine Ltd* [1979] A.C. 440 Lord Diplock stated:

> "The application of this principle of open justice has two aspects: as respects proceedings in the court itself it requires that they should be held in open court to which the press and public are admitted and that, in criminal cases at any rate, all evidence communicated to the court is communicated publicly. As respects the publication to a wider public of fair and accurate reports of proceedings that have taken place in court the principle requires that nothing should be done to discourage this."

ECHR, Art. 6(1) provides an entitlement to a "public hearing", subject to certain limited exceptions. It allows public scrutiny, guarantees a fair trial and maintains public confidence: *Pretto v. Italy*, 6 E.H.R.R. 182 at para. 21; *Stefanelli v. San Marino* (2001) 33 E.H.R.R. 16. The public and press must be admitted to the courtroom and evidence must be given publicly. Access by the press is particularly important; publicity contributes to the achievement of the aim of Art. 6(1), namely a fair trial: *Axen v. Germany*, 6 E.H.R.R. 195.

If evidence is not given orally but by way of statement this is read aloud either fully or in summary: *Criminal Justice Act* 1967, s.9(6). Matters of plea and sentence should be dealt with in open court, save exceptionally, and any communication between a party and a court must be communicated to the other parties: *Bowers* [2006] EWCA Crim 1433. This was a case where counsel for two defendants had acted upon a misunderstanding as to an indication of sentence as a result of a message conveyed by a court official rather than the judge, and without bringing it to the notice of the court or the prosecution; the defendants could not rely upon such information and therefore could not complain when their sentences were longer than they had understood to have been indicated by the judge. The imposition of sentence is part of a criminal trial and ought in any ordinary case to take place in public at a hearing at which the defendant is entitled to be present and represented and able to participate: *Hammond v. Secretary of State for the Home Department*, [2006] 1 A.C. 603. Likewise, a bail application should be heard in public unless there are sound reasons for not doing so: *R (Malik) v. CCC*, [2007] 1 W.L.R. 2455.

8–2 The principle of open justice requires that, unless the circumstances are highly exceptional, justice must be administered in public. Nevertheless, even this fundamental principle is subject to a number of recognised exceptions both at common law and within Art.6 itself. The absence of discretion to allow an oral hearing has been held not incompatible with Art 6(1): *Re A* [2006] 2 Cr.App.R. 2 (distinguishing *Hammond ante*). Case management powers enabled a judge to deal with issues preliminary to a trial by way of written submissions and to limit the length of those submissions. A judge is not bound to allow oral submissions: *R. v. K.* [2006] Crim.L.R. 1012; it is submitted that this is equally true in the magistrates' courts.

B. CLOSED COURT IN THE INTERESTS OF JUSTICE

8–3 Although proceedings in the courts in England and Wales are normally conducted in public, the courts have inherent jurisdiction to sit in camera if that is necessary for the due administration of justice. In *Scott v. Scott*, [1913] A.C. 417, Lord Loreburn said, at p.446:

> ". . . in all cases where the public has been excluded with admitted propriety the underlying principle, as it seems to me, is that the administration of justice would be rendered impracticable by their presence, whether because the case could not be effectively tried, or the parties entitled to justice would be reasonably deterred from seeking it at the hands of the court."

In *Att.-Gen. v. Leveller Magazine Ltd* (*ante*) Lord Diplock made clear that in order for a court to exercise its inherent jurisdiction to depart from the principle of open justice it must be satisfied that the hearing of the case in public would frustrate or render impracticable the administration of justice, and that the test is one of necessity:

> "However, since the purpose of the general rule is to serve the ends of justice it may be necessary to depart from it where the nature or circumstances of the particular proceeding are such that the application of the general rule in its entirety would frustrate or render impracticable the administration of justice or would damage some other public interest for whose protection Parliament has made some statutory derogation from the rule. Apart from statutory exceptions, however, where a court in the exercise of its inherent power to control the conduct of the proceedings before it departs in any way from the general rule, the departure is justified to the extent and to no more than the extent that the court reasonably believes to be necessary in order to serve the ends of justice."

Part II

Whilst a magistrates' court has the power to exclude the press and the public, it is undesirable that, save where statute otherwise provides, any part of proceedings in a magistrates' court should be heard in camera unless there are compelling reasons, the existence of which will be rare: *Malvern Justices, ex p. Evans*, [1988] Q.B. 540, 87 Cr.App.R. 19. Where a court in the exercise of its inherent power to control its own proceedings departs in any way from the general rule that proceedings in court should be held in open court with the press and public admitted, the departure is justified only to the extent that the court reasonably believes it to be necessary in order to serve the ends of justice. The burden lies on those seeking to displace the application of the general rule in a particular case to make out that the general rule must of necessity be superseded. The matter does not rest in the discretion of the judge as to what is expedient; the judge must treat it as a matter of principle, turning not on convenience but on necessity: *Reigate Justices, ex p. Argus Newspapers*, 5 Cr.App.R.(S.).

The court's ability to admit the public and representatives of the media may be limited by the physical constraints of the courtroom, the number of seats, the undesirability of allowing people to stand, and the need to ensure that people are safe. In *Denbigh Justices, ex p. Williams and Evans* [1974] Q.B. 759, the court stated at 765 that:

> "The injunction to the presiding judge or magistrate is: do your best to enable the public to come in and see what is happening, having a proper common sense regard for the facilities available and the facility for keeping order, security and the like . . . the presence of absence of the press is a vital factor in deciding whether a particular hearing was or was not in open court. I find it difficult to imagine a case which can be said to be held publicly if the press have been actively excluded. On the other hand, the fact that the press is present is not conclusive the other way . . ."

The presence of large numbers in a court room may inhibit a reluctant witness and the general power to restrict access in the interests of the administration of justice may be used in such circumstances, but sensitively and reluctantly: *R. (CPS) v. Bolton Magistrates' Court* [2004] 1 Cr.App.R. 33. A judge who formed the view that, in a trial for murder, a witness's protestation that she would not give evidence unless the public gallery was cleared was genuine, was entitled to exclude the public provided that he concluded that it was strictly necessary for him to do so. Despite the general principle that a criminal trial should take place in public, it was recognised that a more fundamental principle was that justice should be done: *Richards (Randall)* [1999] Crim.L.R. 764. It is submitted that in balancing the principles that on the one hand justice should be done and on the other, it should be seen to be done, in magistrates' courts both the nature of the offences prosecuted, and the widespread availability of special measures for witnesses, suggest that the decision in *Richards* will have little application to a witness giving evidence in a summary trial in a magistrates' court. As special measures are not available to the accused, were the court to find that, like the witness in the *Richards* case, the accused would choose not to give evidence at all rather than give evidence in public, this might deprive a defendant of a genuine choice whether or not to give evidence in his own defence to the detriment of the fair trial process: *R. (S) v. Waltham Forest Youth Court* [2004] 2 Cr.App.R. 21.

8–4 Generally no distinction should be drawn between exclusion of the press and the public. There may be situations, however, where such a distinction may be necessary to ensure that justice can be done without a completely closed hearing. Where the court is satisfied that an important prosecution witness would refuse to give evidence unless the public were not permitted in court, it is entitled to close the court to the general public but with members of the press remaining: *Richards ante*. Protection of public decency is not a sufficient reason to justify excluding the public from court: *Scott v. Scott ante*. The public has no right to see exhibits, particularly if the exhibit is an obscene film, but it might want to know the type of films involved. If a judge excludes the general public when such films are shown, the press should normally be permitted to remain so that they can provide the public with information upon which to base opinions, *Waterfield*, 60 Cr.App.R. 296.

The principle of open justice in criminal proceedings does not extend to a right for the public or the press to inspect or demand the disclosure of documents or other exhibits placed before the court. However, the presentation of written material to the court in the form of skeleton arguments which judges and magistrates consider in private was the subject of a note of caution from Lord Scarman in *Home Office v. Harman* [1983] 1 A.C. 280 at 316 when he said that that:

> "When public policy in the administration of justice is considered, public knowledge of the evidence and the arguments of the parties is certainly as important as expedition: and, if the price of expedition is to be the silent reading by the judge before or at trial of relevant documents, it is arguable that expedition will not always be consistent with justice being seen to be done."

Lord Bingham C.J. later considered this warning when he explained in *SmithKline Beecham Biologicals S.A. v. Connaught Laboratories* [1999] 4 All E.R. 498 at 511–512 that:

> "Since the date when Lord Scarman expressed doubt in Home Office v Harman as to whether expedition would always be consistent with open justice, the practices of counsel preparing skeleton arguments, chronologies and reading guides, and of judges pre-reading documents (including witness statements) out of court, have become much more common. These means of saving time in court are now not merely permitted, but are positively required, by practice directions. The result is that a case may be heard in such a way that even an intelligent and well-informed member of the public, present throughout every hearing in open court, would be unable to obtain a full understanding of the documentary evidence and the arguments on which the case was to be decided. In such circumstances, there may be some degree of unreality in the proposition that the material documents in the case have (in practice as well as in theory) passed into the public domain. That is a matter which gives rise to concern. In some cases (especially cases of obvious and genuine public interest) the judge may in the interests of open justice permit or even require a fuller oral opening, and fuller reading of crucial documents, than would be necessary if economy and efficiency were the only considerations. In all cases the judge's judgment (delivered orally in open court, or handed down in open court in written form with copies available for the press and public) should provide a coherent summary of the issues, the evidence and the reasons for the decision."

The issue of access of the press to skeleton arguments was considered in the context of criminal appeals in *Howell* [2003] EWCA Crim 486 when, at the conclusion of the hearing, a request had been received from a member of the press who had been present in court to be granted access to written skeleton arguments presented by counsel for the parties. Judge L.J. giving the judgment of the court stressed the distinction between on the one hand words written on paper which "the court stated that they would be regarded as if they had been advanced orally in court" and, on the other hand written material which would not normally have been dealt with orally and which is not to be disclosed.

> ". . . the principle of open justice leads inexorably to the conclusion that written skeleton arguments, or those parts of the skeleton arguments adopted by the counsel and treated by the court as forming parts of his oral submissions, should be disclosed if and when a request to do so is received."

However, in circumstances where all the issues relied upon were fully set out in the oral submissions of counsel in open court, every member of the public and press was able to hear the exposition of all the issues in great detail, and there was nothing relied upon and contained in the skeleton arguments which was not repeated orally in open court, disclosure to the press of court documents was not required: *R. (Guardian News & Media Ltd) v. City of Westminster Magistrates' Court* [2010] EWHC 3376 (Admin). This case also made clear that s.32(1) of the *Freedom of Information Act* 2000 provides an exemption from the provisions of the Act for a document filed with, or otherwise placed in the custody of, a court for the purposes of proceedings in a particular cause or matter.

In a case where the offender had significant intellectual disadvantages and mental health problems such that he had a limited ability to concentrate and to understand what was going on, the sentencing judge had been perfectly entitled to tailor his sentencing remarks accordingly. However, he should have reduced his remarks to writing before passing sentence, and read them out in open court at the same time as passing sentence, rather than handing them over a few days later; the defendant need not have remained in court whilst the reasons were read, unless he wanted to do so. Sentencing decisions, or the reasons for them, must not be announced behind closed doors: *F.* [2010] EWCA Crim 350.

The risk of financial damage, or damage to reputation or goodwill, resulting from the institution of proceedings concerning a person's business is not a valid reason for departing from the principle that proceedings should be heard in open court: *Dover Justices, ex p. Dover DC*, 156 J.P. 433; the only question for a tribunal to ask itself when considering the exclusion was whether it believed it to be reasonably necessary in order to serve the ends of justice. There is no power to exclude the press or the public because of the intimate or embarrassing nature of the evidence: *Chancellor of Chichester Consistory Court, ex p. News Group Newspapers Ltd* [1992] C.O.D. 48. In *Reigate Justices, ante*, the court was asked to sit in camera to hear certain facts in mitigation relating to assistance the defendant had previously given to the police as an informant; it was held that if the court could avoid going into camera by allowing facts in mitigation to be put into writing, that was a better course to take (see *post* § 22–85). **8–5**

It may also be necessary to protect a witness's right to life under art. 2 ECHR: *Lord Saville of Newdigate, ex p. A.* [2000] 1 W.L.R. 1855. This case concerned the anonymity of soldiers giving evidence to the "Bloody Sunday" tribunal in Northern Ireland and their fear of reprisal. The court has to balance the conflicting interests of the defendant and any witness.

Even when it is claimed that the safety of the witness is at stake the court should consider whether he can be adequately protected by means which are less drastic than total exclusion of the public, for example the making of an order prohibiting the publication of a person's name under s.11 of the *Contempt of Court Act* 1981 or by using a letter to designate his name and the use of screens: *Lord Saville of Newdigate, ex p.A, ante*. See *post*, § 9–26, and in particular witness anonymity orders.

A court cannot make an order to protect the children of a defendant where there is no statutory power to do so: *Croydon Crown Court ex. p. Trinity Mirror Plc* [2008] Q.B. 770. In this case Sir Igor Judge, P, giving the judgment of the Court of Appeal constituted by five judges, said that everyone appreciates the risk that innocent children may suffer prejudice and damage when a parent is convicted of a serious offence. If the court were to make an order to protect the rights of a defendant's children under

ECHR art. 8, it would be countenancing a substantial erosion of the principle of open justice, to the overwhelming disadvantage of public confidence in the criminal justice system, the free reporting of criminal trials and the proper identification of those convicted and sentenced in them. Such an order cannot begin to be contemplated unless the circumstances are properly described as exceptional (see *post* § 8–19).

When a court considers excluding the public it should draw a distinction between matters which should never meet the public eye and matters where, if publicity were to be given before the conclusion of the trial or related proceedings, it would give rise to a substantial risk of prejudice to the administration of justice. In the latter situation the risk of prejudice can often be dealt with by an order under s.4(2) of the *Contempt of Court Act* 1981 or the postponing of a press report: *Crook*, 93 Cr.App.R. 17 (see *post* § 8–17 *et seq.*).

Applications to sit in camera

8–6 The term in camera covers situations where the court sits in the absence of the press and public. The court may exclude the press and the public during the application itself and will do so if it is intimated that the administration of justice could be prejudiced by the reasons for the application being stated in open court. Once it is clear that justice will not be prejudiced the court will open the courtroom again and will summarise what has occurred whilst in camera. If the court decides to sit in camera for all or part of the hearing itself, it will open the court to announce that fact and give general reasons for so doing: *Tower Bridge J.J., ex.p. Osborne*, 88 Cr.App.R. 28.

Generally a defendant and his advocate must not be excluded from a hearing in camera nor should restrictions be placed on an advocate as to what he may disclose to his client or his instructing solicitor if there is one: *Preston* [1994] 2 A.C. 130, 98 Cr.App.R. 405.

8–7 Where the disclosure of certain matters might be against the public interest because it might compromise state security or the proper functioning of a public service, the prosecutor will claim immunity from disclosure. Difficulties may arise where public interest immunity is sought by the prosecution and an application is made to hear arguments regarding disclosure in the absence of the defendant and his advocate. In most cases the defence will be given notice of an application and may make representations. There will be a few highly sensitive cases, however, where the defendant and his advocate will be excluded. The court, in dealing with such an exceptional application, may consider the appointment of special independent counsel to take part in the proceedings but that is a course of last resort as it presents its own difficulties such as ethical problems with the taking of full instructions and the usual client/counsel relationship. The cardinal and overriding requirement is that of a fair trial: *H and C* [2004] 2 A.C. 134, [2004] 2 Cr.App.R. 10 (see Public interest immunity, *ante*, § 6–76 and *post*, § 8–107).

C. STATUTORY EXCEPTIONS

8–8 The general rule that a summary trial must be held in open court is subject to several statutory exceptions.

Children and Young Persons Act 1933, ss.36–37

Prohibition against children being present in court during the trial of other persons

8–9 **36.** No child (other than an infant in arms) shall be permitted to be present in court during the trial of any other person charged with an offence, or during any proceedings preliminary thereto, except during such time as his presence is required as a witness or otherwise for the purposes of justice or while the court consents to his presence; and any child present in court when under this section he is not to be permitted to be so shall be ordered to be removed …

Power to clear court while child or young person is giving evidence in certain cases

8–10 **37.**—(1) Where, in any proceedings in relation to an offence against, or any conduct contrary to, decency or morality, a person who, in the opinion of the court, is a child or young person is called as a witness, the court may direct that all or any persons, not being members or officers of the court or parties to the case, their counsel or solicitors, or persons otherwise directly concerned in the case, be excluded from the court during the taking of the evidence of that witness:

Provided that nothing in this section shall authorise the exclusion of bona fide representatives of a newspaper or news agency.

(2) The powers conferred on a court by this section shall be in addition and without prejudice to any other powers of the court to hear proceedings in camera.

Children under fourteen years of age (other than babies) are generally excluded **8–11** from court although application may be made to the court to allow such a child to be present. This sometimes happens when a defendant's child cannot be looked after elsewhere. It may also happen when a party of schoolchildren wish to visit the court. Each application will be dealt with on its merits and will, amongst other matters, depend upon the nature of the court proceedings. The court may also clear the court where a child is giving evidence.

Official Secrets Act 1920, s.8

Provisions as to trial and punishment of offences

8.—(4) In addition and without prejudice to any powers which a court may possess to order **8–12** the exclusion of the public from any proceedings if, in the course of proceedings before a court against any person for an offence under the principal Act or this Act or the proceedings on appeal, or in the course of the trial of a person for felony or misdemeanour under the principal Act or this Act, application is made by the prosecution, on the ground that the publication of any evidence to be given or of any statement to be made in the course of the proceedings would be prejudicial to the national safety, that all or any portion of the public shall be excluded during any part of the hearing, the court may make an order to that effect, but the passing of sentence shall in any case take place in public.

Although cases under this Act are finalised in the Crown Court there may be in- **8–13** stances where, *e.g.* on a bail application the prosecution will make use of this section.

Youth Justice and Criminal Evidence Act 1999

An application may be made under s.25 of the *Youth Justice and Criminal Evi-* **8–14** *dence Act* 1999 for a special measures direction providing for the exclusion from the court of specified persons during a witness's evidence in proceedings for a sexual offence, or where there are reasonable grounds for believing that someone other than the accused has sought, or will seek, to intimidate the witness in connection with testifying in the proceedings (see *post* § 9–46). The persons who may be excluded do not include the accused, legal representatives acting in the proceedings, or any interpreter or other person assisting the witness. Any direction under this provision providing for the exclusion of representatives of news gathering or reporting organisations must be expressed not to apply to one named individual who has been nominated on behalf of one or more such organisations, unless no such nomination has been made.

Where the defendant is accused of a sexual offence, an application may be made under s.41 of the *Youth Justice and Criminal Evidence Act* 1999 for leave to adduce evidence or to cross-examine the complaint about their sexual behaviour; s.43 provides that such an application shall be heard in private. The reasons for any decision on a s.41 application must be given in open court and entered in the court register (see *post* § 9–105 *et seq.*).

An application under s.46 *Youth Justice and Criminal Evidence Act* 1999, to restrict **8–15** the reporting of a witness's particulars, need not identify the witness by name and date of birth where the applicant can show that there is a good reason for not providing such details in order to protect the true identity of the witness: *Criminal Procedure Rules*, r.16.1 (see Appendix G *post* § G–73) and the prescribed form in the *Consolidated Criminal Practice Direction* (*http://www.justice.gov.uk/criminal/procrules_fin/docs/*

Part II

f17page1-2.pdf). The court may determine the application without a hearing, but it also has power to hear and take into account representations made to it by any person who in the court's view has a legitimate interest in the application before it: r.16.7 (see *post* § 8–29).

D. PUBLICITY

Contempt of Court Act 1981, ss.1, 2, 4, and 11

The strict liability rule

8–16 **1.** In this Act "the strict liability rule" means the rule of law whereby conduct may be treated as a contempt of court as tending to interfere with the course of justice in particular legal proceedings regardless of intent to do so.

Limitation of scope of strict liability

2.—(1) The strict liability rule applies only in relation to publications, and for this purpose "publication" includes any speech, writing, programme included in a cable programme service or other communication in whatever form, which is addressed to the public at large or any section of the public.

(2) The strict liability rule applies only to a publication which creates a substantial risk that the course of justice in the proceedings in question will be seriously impeded or prejudiced.

(3) The strict liability rule applies to a publication only if the proceedings in question are active within the meaning of this section at the time of the publication

Contemporary reports of proceedings

8–17 **4.**—(1) Subject to this section a person is not guilty of contempt of court under the strict liability rule in respect of a fair and accurate report of legal proceedings held in public, published contemporaneously and in good faith.

(2) In any such proceedings the court may, where it appears to be necessary for avoiding a substantial risk of prejudice to the administration of justice in those proceedings, or in any other proceedings pending or imminent, order that the publication of any report of the proceedings, or any part of the proceedings, be postponed for such period as the court thinks necessary for that purpose.

(3) For the purposes of subsection (1) of this section a report of proceedings shall be treated as published contemporaneously—

(a) in the case of a report of which publication is postponed pursuant to an order under subsection (2) of this section, if published as soon as practicable after that order expires;

(b) in the case of a report of committal proceedings of which publication is permitted by virtue only of subsection (3) of section 8 of the *Magistrates' Courts Act* 1980, if published as soon as practicable after publication is so permitted.

Publication of matters exempted from disclosure in court

8–18 **11.** In any case where a court (having power to do so) allows a name or other matter to be withheld from the public in proceedings before the court, the court may give such directions prohibiting the publication of that name or matter in connection with the proceedings as appear to the court to be necessary for the purpose for which it was so withheld.

The press plays an important part in keeping the public informed of court proceedings and it is important that reports are fair and accurate. Adverse publicity may give rise to a breach of art. 6(1) of the European Convention on Human Rights and may constitute grounds for a stay of the proceedings.

It is a contempt of court under the "strict liability rule"in s.2(2) of the *Contempt of Court Act* 1981 to publish anything relating to court proceedings that creates a substantial risk that the course of justice in the proceedings in question will be seriously impeded or prejudiced. Section 2 will be enforced by the courts on an application by the Attorney General: see *Att. Gen. v. Associated Newspapers Ltd.* [2011] EWHC 418 (Admin). However, s.4(1) provides an exception to the strict liability rule in respect of a fair and accurate report of legal proceedings held in public, published contemporaneously and in good faith. Section 4(2) enables a court to order the postponement of any reporting of its proceedings that would otherwise fall within s.4(1), where there is a substantial risk of prejudice to the administration of justice in those proceedings or other proceedings. It is clear however that the section only permits postponement and the need for postponement cannot subsist beyond the end of the proceedings in question. A trial judge's order under s.4(2) which was expressed at the end of the trial to be "with indefinite effect", did not fall within the jurisdiction conferred by the section: *Re The Times Newspapers Ltd* [2008] 1 Cr.App.R. 16.

Section 11 does not give the court power to restrict publicity of proceedings; it applies where a power to withhold a name or other matter already exists, and enables the court to issue directions prohibiting the publication of that name or matter in connection with the proceedings, as appear to the court to be necessary for the purpose for which it was so withheld. It follows that where the court has power to restrict publicity under its inherent jurisdiction, or by virtue of some statutory exception to the general principle of open justice, it can support that power with an appropriate order under s.11.

The power under s.4(2) of the *Contempt of Court Act* 1981 is to be exercised in accordance with the statutory criteria and should only be used where there is a substantial risk of prejudice to the administration of justice. Section 4(2) may not be used where the court is concerned merely for the welfare of the defendant: *Re MGN Ltd's Application*, [2011] EWCA Crim 100, see the comments of Lord Judge, C.J. at para. 22:

> "Without minimising the burdens and difficulties faced by witnesses, the use of section 4(2) of the 1981 Act for the purposes of alleviating the difficulties of giving evidence, even if evidence has to be given in more than one trial, is rarely appropriate. Of course, if the conditions for an order under section 4(2) are established in the case of a particular witness or witnesses so that the order is justified in accordance with principle, then the order should be made. But in essence the protection of witnesses is more appropriately secured by statutory measures designed for the purpose, such as section 39 of the *Children and Young Persons Act* 1933, or sections 23–30 of the *Youth Justice and Criminal Evidence Act* 1999, or any further legislation designed to enable witnesses to give of their best."

In the *MGN* case the court approved the three stage test set out by the Court of Appeal in *The Telegraph Group plc*, [2001] 1 W.L.R. 1983 in the judgment of Longman, L.J. at p.1991:

> (1) The first question is whether reporting would give rise to a "not insubstantial" risk of prejudice to the administration of justice in the relevant proceedings. If not, that will be the end of the matter.
>
> (2) If such a risk is perceived to exist, then the second question arises: would a s.4(2) order eliminate it? If not, obviously there could be no necessity to impose such a ban. Again, that would be the end of the matter. On the other hand, even if the judge is satisfied that an order would achieve the objective, he or she would still have to consider whether the risk could satisfactorily be overcome by some less restrictive means. If so, it could not be said to be "necessary" to take the more drastic approach: see *Ex p Central Television plc* [1991] 1 W.L.R. 4, 8 d-g per Lord Lane CJ.
>
> (3) Suppose that the judge concludes that there is indeed no other way of eliminating the perceived risk of prejudice; it still does not follow *necessarily* that an order has to be made. The judge may still have to ask whether the degree of risk contemplated should be regarded as tolerable in the sense of being "the lesser of two evils". It is at this stage that value judgments may have to be made as to the priority between "competing public interests": see *Ex p The Telegraph plc* [1993] 1 W.L.R. 980, 986 b-c."

In the *MGN* case, Lord Judge (at para. 14) highlighted the need for care to avoid confusing the senses in which the word "necessary" is used in the legislation:

> "Adapting Viscount Falkland's famous aphorism, the court's approach should be that, unless it is necessary to impose an order, it is necessary not to impose one; and if it is necessary to impose an order at all, it must go no further than necessary. In summary, an order under section 4(2) of the 1981 Act should be regarded as a last resort."

Further guidance on restricting publication of court proceedings was given by the Court of Appeal in *Legal Aid Board, ex p. Kaim Todner* [1999] Q.B. 966. Lord Woolf M.R. commented at page 977:

> "In deciding whether to accede to an application for protection from disclosure of the proceedings it is appropriate to take into account the extent of the interference with the general rule which is involved. If the interference is for a limited period that is less objectionable than a restriction on disclosure which is permanent. If the restriction relates only to the identity of a witness or a party this is less objectionable than a restriction which involves proceedings being conducted in whole or in part behind closed doors. The nature of the proceedings is also relevant. If the application relates to an interlocutory application this is a less significant intrusion into the general rule than interfering with the public nature of the trial. Interlocutory hearings are normally of no interest to anyone other than the parties ... If proceedings are ex parte and involve serious allegations being made against another party who has no notice of those allegations, the interests of justice may require non-disclosure until such a time as a party against whom the allegations are made can be heard."

All orders made under s.4(2) must be formulated in precise terms having regard to the decision in *Horsham Justices ex p. Farquharson* [1982] Q.B. 762, 76 Cr.App.R. 87. An order must state: (a) its precise scope, (b) the time at which it shall cease to have effect, if appropriate, and (c) the specific purpose of making the order; see the *Consolidated Criminal Practice Direction*, para. I.3 (see Appendix F *post* § F–5).

The importance of the safeguard of the application of strict liability rule under section 2 has been emphasised as a reason for not imposing reporting restrictions. In *R. v. B* [2007] H.R.L.R. 1, Sir Igor Judge, P emphasised this when he said, at para. 25:

> "... responsibility for avoiding the publication of material which may prejudice the outcome of a trial rests fairly and squarely on those responsible for the publication. In our view, broadcasting authorities and newspaper editors should be trusted to fulfil their responsibilities accurately to inform the public of court proceedings, and to exercise sensible judgment about the publication of comment which may interfere with the administration of justice. They have access to the best legal advice; they have their own personal judgments to make. The risk of being in contempt of court for damaging the interests of justice is not one which any responsible editor would wish to take. In itself that is an important safeguard, and it should not be overlooked simply because there are occasions when there is widespread and ill-judged publicity in some parts of the media."

Sir Igor Judge went on to describe as a "second safeguard", the "passionate and profound belief" on the part of juries in the right of a defendant to be given a fair trial; juries follow the directions given to them by the judge that they must focus exclusively on the evidence and ignore anything they may have heard or read out of court.

A court has no common law power to make an order postponing the publication of a report of proceedings conducted in open court; any such powers must be conferred by legislation: *Independent Publishing Co. Ltd. v. Attorney General of Trinidad and Tobago* [2005] 1 A.C. 190. Likewise, a court cannot make a direction under s.11 prohibiting publication of a name where that name has not first been withheld from the public: *Arundel Justices, ex p. Westminster Press Ltd* [1985] 1 W.L.R. 708. In this case the name of an individual was mentioned in open court before the court made a direction withholding it; it was held that (a point of construction of s.11) in order for the court to have power to prohibit the publication of a name it must first allow that name to be withheld from the public in the court proceedings. However, in a trial of offences under the *Official Secrets Act* 1989, a question and answer were inadvertently given in open court which should have formed part of the in camera evidence. The Court of Appeal held that the question and answer fell within the category of evidence that the judge had ordered should be withheld from the public by his ruling under s.8(4) of the *Official Secrets Act* and it was open to him to make an order under s.11 of the *Contempt of Court Act* that embraced the question and answer, notwithstanding that the question and answer had, by mistake, been heard in public: *Times Newspapers Ltd. v. R.* (*ante*).

A court may only make an order to the effect that the identity of a defendant shall be withheld from the public where it is satisfied either that the administration of justice would be seriously affected were the order not to be made, or that there would be a real and immediate risk to the life of the person whose identity it was sought to protect, such that ECHR, art. 2 was engaged: *Re The Times Newspapers Ltd and another* [2009] 1 W.L.R. 1015. However, magistrates were right to refuse to make orders preventing the press from publishing the home addresses of two senior police officers charged with offences of misconduct in a public office: *R. (Harper and Johncox) v. Aldershot Magistrates' Court*, 174 J.P. 410. The officers concerned had been responsible for the investigation and prosecution of serious crimes for over 25 years and it was said that publication of their addresses would put them and their families at risk. Both officers had been involved in covert operations, and in one case the officer and his family were placed in witness protection for a period of 18 months following his involvement in the investigation and prosecution of a serious crime. However, the Divisional Court was told that withholding the officers' addresses would serve no practical purpose as it had been possible to find their addresses on the Internet within five minutes at a cost of £4.95. The court held that art. 2 was not engaged and that, if a risk to the officers did exist, it would not be enhanced by the publication of their addresses.

In a series of more recent cases the House of Lords, and subsequently the Supreme **8–19**
Court, has considered the problem of balancing an individual's rights to privacy under ECHR, art. 8, against the rights of the media under art. 10 to freedom of expression. In *Re S. (a child) (Identification: Restriction on Publication)* [2005] 1 A.C. 593, the defendant had been charged with the murder of her child. The guardian, acting for another of the defendant's children, applied to the High Court for an order preventing the publication of the defendant's identity in order to protect the privacy of the child who was not involved in the proceedings. The child's right to private and family life under art. 8 of the Convention was in conflict with the right of the press to freedom of expression under art. 10. The House of Lords held that neither article had precedence over the other. In such a case it was necessary for the court to focus on the comparative importance of the specific rights claimed in the individual case, taking into account the justifications for interfering or restricting each right. Finally, the proportionality test must be applied to each of the conflicting rights; described by Lord Steyn as "the ultimate balancing test". Applying these principles, their lordships held that the interference with the child's art. 8 rights, albeit distressing, was indirect. By contrast, the art. 10 rights at issue concerned the freedom of the press to report proceedings at criminal trials, which was a valuable check on the criminal process and promoted public confidence in the administration of justice. The guardian's application was therefore refused.

The issue of conflicting rights under the ECHR was considered once again by the House of Lords in *Re British Broadcasting Corporation: Att.-Gen.'s Reference (No.3 of 1999)* [2010] 1 A.C. 145. In this case D had been acquitted of offences, including rape, in circumstances in which it might be possible for him to be retried for the offences; the BBC applied to lift an anonymity order so that it might broadcast a television programme suggesting that at least close consideration was warranted of the possibility of a retrial of D. A balance had to be struck between D's art. 8 rights to respect for his private life, and the presumption of innocence in art. 6(2) on the one hand, and the broadcaster's art. 10 rights to freedom of expression and communication, on the other. Their lordships concluded that there was no sensible risk of the proposed broadcast compromising the fairness of any possible retrial of D; striking of the balance between the competing rights was to be approached on the basis that the media should be free to exercise their own judgment in the presentation of journalistic material and that publication of D's identity pursued a legitimate aim. It was held that the benefits which would be achieved by publication were proportionate to the harm which might be done by the interference with D's art. 8 rights, and that the balance fell in favour of the BBC's right to free expression.

The conflict between art. 8 and art. 10 rights was again considered, this time by the Supreme Court, in *re Guardian News and Media Ltd* [2010] 2 A.C. 697. In this case a number of individuals were alleged, based upon undisclosed information in the possession of the security service, to be Al-Qaida facilitators; their assets were subject to a freezing order made under terrorism legislation. Those subject to the orders argued that publication of their names would seriously affect their article 8 rights to private life because of the impact on their reputation within the community. It was held that there was a powerful general interest in identifying the parties in any report of the proceedings as there was a legitimate public interest in the publication of a full account of a matter of public concern; where the publication concerns a question "of general interest", art. 10(2) scarcely leaves any room for restrictions on freedom of expression. In giving the judgment of the court, Lord Rodger commented on the practice of anonymity orders being made by consent of both parties without the court considering in any detail what is the basis or justification for the order, and approved the warning given by Sir Christopher Staughton in *Westminster City Council, ex p. P* (1998) 31 H.L.R. 154 that "when both sides agreed that information should be kept from the public, that was when the court had to be most vigilant".

8–20 Representatives of the press may address the court before an order is made: *Clerkenwell Magistrates' Court, ex p. Telegraph Plc* [1993] Q.B. 462; see also Consolidated Criminal Practice Direction, para. I.3.2 (see Appendix F *post* § F–5). In *Tower Bridge Magistrates' Court, ex p. Osborne*, 88 Cr.App.R. 28, it was held that it is generally necessary for magistrates, when hearing an application to restrict publicity in a case, to hear the reasons for the application in camera. If the court decides that there is substance to the application, it may continue to sit in camera to determine the application and afterwards in open court to announce its decision. If the court decides, having heard the reasons for the application, that those reasons have no substance, it should return to open court, announce accordingly and proceed with the substantive proceedings in the normal way.

Where automatic reporting restrictions provide protection it is generally not necessary to impose additional discretionary restrictions.

The *Consolidated Criminal Practice Direction*, para. I.3 (see Appendix F *post* § F–5), gives specific directions to courts dealing with applications for reporting restrictions. Paragraph I.3.3 directs that a permanent record of such orders is kept, and that an order is formulated in precise terms having regard to the decision in *Horsham Justices, ex p. Farquharson* (*ante*, see § 8–18). The order must be committed to writing either by the judge or magistrate personally, or by the clerk of the court under the judge's or magistrates' directions. Courts are expected to give notice to the press in some form that an order has been made.

Further guidance to courts, practitioners, and the media is available in the form of a guide to reporting restrictions in the criminal courts, published by the Judicial Studies Board, the Newspaper Society, the Society of Editors, and Times Newspapers Ltd. The guide includes a useful checklist providing a structured approach for magistrates and judges, and is available on-line from the Judicial Communications Office at: *http://www.judiciary.gov.uk/Resources/JCO/Documents/Guidance/crown_court_reporting_restrictions_021009.pdf*.

The general right to contemporaneous publication of fair and accurate reports of legal proceedings under s.4(1) is subject to several statutory restrictions in the magistrates' courts; these relate to committal proceedings, youths, certain adult witnesses, rape cases, and derogatory assertions made in mitigating statements (see *post* § 8–21 *et seq.*). For the provisions relating to youth courts see *post*, § 25–8—25–9.

Magistrates' Courts Act 1980, s.8

Restrictions on reports of committal proceedings

8–21 **8.**—(1) Except as provided by subsections (2), (3) and (8) below, it shall not be lawful to publish in Great Britain a written report, or to include in a relevant programme for reception in Great Britain a report, of any committal proceedings in England and Wales containing any matter other than that permitted by subsection (4) below.

(2) Subject to subsection (2A) below a magistrates' court shall, on an application for the

purpose made with reference to any committal proceedings by the accused or one of the accused, as the case may be, order that subsection (1) above shall not apply to reports of those proceedings.

(2A) Where in the case of two or more accused one of them objects to the making on an order under subsection (2) above, the court shall make the order if, and only if, it is satisfied, after hearing the representations of the accused, that it is in the interests of justice to do so.

(2B) An order under subsection (2) above shall not apply to reports of proceedings under subsection (2A) above, but any decisions of the court to make or not to make such an order may be contained in reports published or included in a relevant programme before the time authorised by subsection (3) below.

(3) It shall not be unlawful under this section to publish or include in a relevant programme a report of committal proceedings containing any matter other than that permitted by subsection (4) below—

(a) where the magistrates' court determines not to commit the accused, or determines to commit none of the accused, for trial, after it so determines;

(b) where the court commits the accused or any of the accused for trial, after the conclusion of his trial or, as the case may be, the trial of the last to be tried;

and where at any time during the inquiry the court proceeds to try summarily the case of one or more of the accused under section 25(3) or (7) below, while committing the other accused or one or more of the other accused for trial, it shall not be unlawful under this section to publish or include in a relevant programme as part of a report of the summary trial, after the court determines to proceed as aforesaid, a report of so much of the committal proceedings containing any such matter as takes place before the determination.

(4) The following matters may be contained in a report of committal proceedings published or included in a relevant programme without an order under subsection (2) above before the time authorised by subsection (3) above, that is to say—

(a) the identity of the court and the names of the examining justices;

(b) the names, addresses and occupations of the parties and witnesses and the ages of the accused and witnesses;

(c) the offence or offences, or a summary of them, with which the accused is or are charged;

(d) the names of the legal representatives engaged in the proceedings;

(e) any decision of the court to commit the accused or any of the accused for trial, and any decision of the court on the disposal of the case of any accused not committed;

(f) where the court commits the accused or any of the accused for trial, the charge or charges, or a summary of them, on which he is committed and the court to which he is committed;

(g) where the committal proceedings are adjourned, the date and place to which they are adjourned;

(h) any arrangements as to bail on committal or adjournment;

(i) whether a right to representation funded by the Legal Services Commission as part of the Criminal Defence Service was granted to the accused or any of the accused.

(5) If a report is published or included in a relevant programme in contravention of this section, the following persons, that is to say—

(a) in the case of a publication of a written report as part of a newspaper or periodical, any proprietor, editor or publisher of the newspaper or periodical;

(b) in the case of a publication of a written report otherwise than as part of a newspaper or periodical, the person who publishes it;

(c) in the case of the inclusion of a report in a relevant programme, any body corporate which provides the service in which the programme is included and any person having functions in relation to the programme corresponding to those of an editor of a newspaper,

shall be liable on summary conviction to a fine not exceeding level 5 on the standard scale.

(6) Proceedings for an offence under this section shall not, in England and Wales, be instituted otherwise than by or with the consent of the Attorney-General.

(7) Subsection (1) above shall be in addition to, and not in derogation from, the provisions of any other enactment with respect to the publication of reports and proceedings of magistrates' and other courts.

(8) For the purposes of this section committal proceedings shall, in relation to an information charging an indictable offence, be deemed to include any proceedings in the magistrates' court before the court proceeds to inquire into the information as examining justices; but where a magistrates' court which has begun to try an information summarily discontinues the summary trial in pursuance of section 25(2) or (6) below and proceeds to inquire into the information as examining justices, that circumstance shall not make it unlawful under this section for a report of any proceedings on the information which was published or included in a relevant programme before the court determined to proceed as aforesaid to have been so published or included in a relevant programme.

(10) In this section—

"publish", in relation to a report, means publish the report, either by itself or as part of a newspaper or periodical, for distribution to the public.

"relevant programme" means a programme included in a programme service (within the meaning of the *Broadcasting Act* 1990).

8–22 Upon a proper construction of s.8(2A), when an application is made for the lifting of reporting restrictions in a case involving a number of accused, all must be present and allowed to be heard before the application is determined: *Wirral Magistrates Court Ex p. Meikle* (1990) 154 J.P. 1035. Since s.8(1) provides that committal proceedings should not be reported, in cases with two or more defendants, where one of the defendants applies to lift reporting restrictions under s.8(2A) and his co-defendant objects on the ground that the publicity might prejudice his trial, magistrates should only grant the application where a "powerful case" has been made out: *Leeds Justices, ex p. Sykes*, 76 Cr.App.R 129. The Criminal Procedure Rules require that an explanation is given to the defendant of the reporting restrictions imposed by section 8, and of his right to apply to have them removed: see r.10.1 (see Appendix G *post* § G–47).

Children and Young Persons Act 1933, s.39

Power to prohibit publication of certain matter in newspapers

8–23 **39.**—(1) In relation to any proceedings in any court [...], the court may direct that—

(a) no newspaper report of the proceedings shall reveal the name, address or school, or include any particulars calculated to lead to the identification, of any child or young person concerned in the proceedings, either as being the person [by or against] or in respect of whom the proceedings are taken, or as being a witness therein:

(b) no picture shall be published in any newspaper as being or including a picture of any child or young person so concerned in the proceedings as aforesaid;

except in so far (if at all) as may be permitted by the direction of the court.

(2) Any person who publishes any matter in contravention of any such direction shall on summary conviction be liable in respect of each offence to a fine not exceeding [level 5 on the standard scale].

[This section is reprinted as amended by the *Children and Young Persons Act* 1963, ss.57(1), 64 and Sched. 5, and the *Criminal Justice Act* 1982, ss.38, 46.]

8–24 This section has subsequently been applied with the necessary modifications to sound and television broadcast by s.57(4) of the *Children and Young Persons Act* 1963. An order under s.39 is a discretionary order which may be made in any court and is generally made of the court's own motion. It is different from the general prohibition in the *Children and Young Persons Act* 1933, s.49, which applies to youth courts, where the presumption is plainly against the naming of children and young people. In *Crawford v. CPS* (2008) 172 J.P. 273 Thomas L.J. emphasised that orders are not to be made as a matter of routine. Before imposing such orders a balancing exercise should be carried out of matters relating to the public interest, after submissions made by the parties and members of the press.

The words "any proceedings" in that subsection do not mean "any proceedings anywhere"; they mean any proceedings in the court that is making the order: *Lee (Anthony William) (a minor)*, 96 Cr.App.R. 188. In this case it was also said that there was nothing in s.39 to suggest that a direction would only be given, or if given, would only be discharged, in rare and exceptional cases. There must be good reason for making an order under s.39, just as there must be good reason for lifting the restriction on publicity of proceedings in the youth court under s.39 of the Act, namely, to avoid injustice to the child. This proposition was endorsed in *Central Criminal Court* [2001] 1 Cr.App.R. 2, a case concerning a judge's decision to lift restrictions imposed by s.39. It was said that the fact that a youth was being tried with an adult was not a conclusive factor in favour of lifting reporting restrictions, any more than the youth's age would be a conclusive factor in the other direction. A similar issue had come before the Divisional Court two years earlier in *Central Criminal Court, ex p. S.* (1999) 163 J.P. 776. This case involved a decision by the same judge sitting at the CCC to lift reporting decisions. Upholding the judge's decision, the Divisional Court commented that in deciding whether to make a s.39 order, the weight which the court would attach to the various factors might be different at differing stages of the proceedings. After an accused person had been convicted of an offence, it might be appropriate to place greater weight on the interest of the public knowing the identity of those who had committed serious crimes.

Part II

The principles to be applied in deciding whether or not to make a s.9 order were also considered by Elias, J. when giving his judgment in the Administrative Court in *R. (T.) v. St Albans Crown Court* [2002] EWHC 1129 (Admin). He commented that:

> "However, it would equally be a mistake to assume that the effect of these decisions is that it is only in exceptional circumstances that a section 39 direction can be made. There is a balancing exercise that has to be carried out in all cases where there is conflict between the public interest in disclosure and the welfare of the young person which may require anonymity. In carrying out that task, it is, in my view, incumbent on the court carefully to weigh the conflicting considerations... Whilst the court plainly does not have to refer to every factor which may weigh in favour of a section 39 direction being made, it is necessary, in my view, that it should briefly summarise the principal factors weighing in favour, even if the decision finally is that these factors are outweighed by the public interest in disclosure. In this connection, it is pertinent to bear in mind section 44 of the *Children and Young Person's Act*. This provides: '*Every court, in dealing with a child or young person who is brought before it, either as an offender or otherwise, shall have regard to the welfare of the child or young person.*' This is a mandatory obligation."

Elias, J. went on to cite the judgement of Simon Brown L.J. in *Winchester Crown Court, ex p. B* [2000] 1 Cr.App.R. 11; this was a case that was, in part, subsequently overruled, but not in a way that affected the observations set out below:

> "The principles to be distilled from the various authorities can, I think, fairly be summarised in this way (and substantially I use the language of the earlier judgments):
>
> (i) In deciding whether to impose or thereafter to lift reporting restrictions, the court will consider whether there are good reasons for naming the defendant.
>
> (ii) In reaching that decision, the court will give considerable weight to the age of the offender and the potential damage to any young person of public identification as a criminal before the offender has the benefit or burden of adulthood.
>
> (iii) By virtue of section 44 of the 1933 Act, the Court must 'have regard to the welfare of the child or young person'.
>
> (iv) The prospect of being named in court with the accompanying disgrace is a powerful deterrent and the naming of a defendant in the context of his punishment serves as a deterrent to others. These deterrents are proper objectives for the court to seek.
>
> (v) There is strong public interest in open justice and in the public knowing as much as possible about what has happened in court, including the identity of those who have committed crime.
>
> (vi) The weight to be attributed to the different factors may shift at different stages of the proceedings, and, in particular, after the defendant has been found, or pleads, guilty and is sentenced. It may then be appropriate to place greater weight on the interest of the public in knowing the identity of those who have committed crimes, particularly serious and detestable crimes.
>
> (vii) The fact that an appeal has been made may be a material consideration."

The principles would apply in the case of a youth being tried with an adult in the magistrates' court.

Embarrassment is an unfortunate consequence of a parent's criminal conviction and it is not appropriate to restrict publicity of the identity of a victim or defendant on the grounds that it would lead to the identification of his or her child where the child is not a witness or otherwise concerned in the proceedings: *Re. S* [2005] 1 A.C. 593. A court must also balance competing Convention rights and it is appropriate to begin by acknowledging the force of the argument for unrestricted publicity of proceedings in a criminal trial (see § 8–19 *ante*).

An order need not be made during the course of the proceedings to which it relates; it may be made at any time: *Harrow Crown Court, ex p. Perkins; Cardiff Crown Court, ex p. M. (a minor)* (1998) 162 J.P. 527, DC. In that case an order of Cardiff Crown Court under s.39 made on Monday July 7, in relation to proceedings concluded on Friday July 4, was upheld. The court accepted that normally a direction would be made when the case was first listed and in the absence of such a direction, publicity might make it inappropriate to make a direction at a later stage. The making of a direction is not an integral part of the trial process and there is no reason in law why a direction cannot be made in relation to proceedings which have been concluded at an earlier date. The amount of publicity would be a relevant factor in determining whether to make a direction or not.

Applications for Anti-Social Behaviour Orders are heard before a magistrates' court rather than a youth court, and there is no automatic prohibition on publishing details of any child or young person who is the subject of an application. Applications for an order restricting publicity can be made under s.39, and each application must be considered on its merits. The factors and principles to be taken into account in determining applications under s.39 generally, were identified by the Administrative Court in *R. (T.) v. St Albans Crown Court* (*ante*), but the case specifically concerned an application for a s.39 order where an ASBO was being sought; Elias J. gave the following guidance:

> "In my judgment, where an anti-social behaviour order has been imposed, that is a factor which reinforces, and in some cases may strongly reinforce, the general public interest in the public disclosure of court proceedings. There are two reasons for this. First, disclosure of the identity of the individuals may well assist in making an order efficacious. If persons in the community are aware that the order has been made against specified individuals, then it must improve the prospect of that order being effectively enforced. Any subsequent breach is more likely to be reported back to the authorities. Second, the very purpose of these orders is to protect the public from individuals who have committed conduct or behaviour which is wholly unacceptable and of an anti-social nature. The public has a particular interest in knowing who in its midst has been responsible for such outrageous behaviour... I do not accept that the consequence of this is that in every case it raises a presumption in favour of refusing to make a section 39 direction. It is a weighty factor to be taken into consideration against upholding any claim for anonymity, but, in my judgment, it is not helpful in a case of this kind to talk about presumptions one way or another. In each case there will be a wide variety of factors which will have to be considered, and in each case the balance has to be struck between the desirability of public disclosure on the one hand and the need to protect the welfare of the individual at trial on the other after a full appreciation of the relevant considerations."

This approach was specifically endorsed by Harrison J. when giving judgment in the Administrative Court in *R (Keating) v. Knowsley MBC*, (2004) 168 J.P. 461, a case concerning interim ASBOs. Setting aside the magistrates' decision to refuse to make a s.39 order, Harrison J. emphasised the importance of taking into account the interim nature of the proceedings:

> "I do not go so far as to say. . . that a section 39 order should be the norm in the case of applications for interim ASBOs because the very nature of the allegations of antisocial behaviour reinforce the importance of the public interest in public disclosure. But I do say that the interim nature of the proceedings, which do not involve any finding on the allegations, is a very

important consideration to put into the balance so that it can be balanced against the undoubtedly important consideration that the justices did take into account relating to publicity assisting in the effectiveness of enforcing the interim order."

In youth courts (in relation to ASBOs on conviction and to breaches of ASBOs generally), s.141 of the *Serious Organised Crime and Police Act* 2005 disapplies, the automatic restrictions on publicity that apply in the youth court by virtue of s.49 of the *Children and Young Persons Act* 1933.

Where the alleged victim is a ward of court, it is for the court in the criminal proceedings, not the wardship judge, to make any orders restraining reporting of the criminal trial. The guardian will provide the prosecution with the material necessary to make the application. In *R. (a minor) (Wardship: restriction on publication)* [1994] 3 W.L.R. 36, the defendant applied for an order on the basis that he might feel inhibited in presenting his defence as he apprehended that it would lead to publicity harmful to his child and perhaps weaken his position in the wardship proceedings. **8–25**

Although *Central Criminal Court, ex p. Crook, ante*, suggested a formal procedure for reducing orders under s.39 to writing by means of a pro forma, the normal practice in the magistrates' court is for the order to be written in precise terms in accordance with the section in the court register. The order must be confined to the wording of the section; there is no scope for extending restrictions: *R. (Gazette Media Co Ltd) v. Teeside Crown Court* [2005] E.M.L.R. 34. Vague restrictions may cause a prosecution for contravening such an order under s.39(2) to founder: *Briffett and Bradshaw v. DPP* (2002) 166 J.P. 66. **8–26**

There is no power to prohibit the publication of the name of a defendant who is not a child or young person although this may be the unintentional result of such an order. Where this is likely, the court may hear representations on the identification of particular details: *Southwark Crown Court, ex p. Godwin* [1992] Q.B. 190; 94 Cr.App.R. 34.

In *Tyne Tees Television Ltd, The Times*, October 20, 1997 the Court of Appeal considered that where there has been an alleged breach of an order under s.39, the better course is to report the matter for consideration as to whether there should be a prosecution for the specific summary offence under s.39(2) rather than deal with the matter as an alleged contempt of court. The court declined to rule whether contempt proceedings would ever be appropriate in view of the specific statutory offence.

Section 44 of the *Youth Justice and Criminal Evidence Act* 1999 is not yet in force. It provides that the reporting of a crime before proceedings commence, where a person under the age of 18 is a victim or a potential witness or defendant, is prohibited where it may lead to his identification. The court may lift the restriction if it is satisfied that it is in the interests of justice to do so. **8–27**

Section 45 of the *Youth Justice and Criminal Evidence Act* 1999 is not yet in force. This provision gives the court power to restrict reporting in relation to a witness or defendant under the age of 18. This section will supersede s.39 of the *Children and Young Persons Act* 1933, *ante*. **8–28**

Youth Justice and Criminal Evidence Act 1999, s.46

Power to restrict reports about certain adult witness in criminal proceedings

46.—(1) This section applies where— **8–29**

(a) in any criminal proceedings in any court (other than a service court) in England and Wales or Northern Ireland, or

(b) in any proceedings (whether in the United Kingdom or elsewhere) in any service court,

a party to the proceedings makes an application for the court to give a reporting direction in relation to a witness in the proceedings (other than the accused) who has attained the age of 18.

In this section "reporting direction" has the meaning given by subsection (6).

(2) If the court determines—

(a) that the witness is eligible for protection, and

(b) that giving a reporting direction in relation to the witness is likely to improve—

(i) the quality of evidence given by the witness, or

(ii) the level of co-operation given by the witness to any party to the proceedings in connection with that party's preparation of its case,

the court may give a reporting direction in relation to the witness.

(3) For the purposes of this section a witness is eligible for protection if the court is satisfied—

(a) that the quality of evidence given by the witness, or

(b) the level of co-operation given by the witness to any party to the proceedings in connection with that party's preparation of its case,

is likely to be diminished by reason of fear or distress on the part of the witness in connection with being identified by members of the public as a witness in the proceedings.

(4) In determining whether a witness is eligible for protection the court must take into account, in particular—

(a) the nature and alleged circumstances of the offence to which the proceedings relate;

(b) the age of the witness;

(c) such of the following matters as appear to the court to be relevant, namely—

(i) the social and cultural background and ethnic origins of the witness,

(ii) the domestic and employment circumstances of the witness, and

(iii) any religious beliefs or political opinions of the witness;

(d) any behaviour towards the witness on the part of—

(i) the accused,

(ii) members of the family or associates of the accused, or

(iii) any other person who is likely to be an accused or a witness in the proceedings.

(5) In determining that question the court must in addition consider any views expressed by the witness.

(6) For the purposes of this section a reporting direction in relation to a witness is a direction that no matter relating to the witness shall during the witness's lifetime be included in any publication if it is likely to lead members of the public to identify him as being a witness in the proceedings.

(7) The matters relating to a witness in relation to which the restrictions imposed by a reporting direction apply (if their inclusion in any publication is likely to have the result mentioned in subsection (6)) include in particular—

(a) the witness's name,

(b) the witness's address,

(c) the identity of any educational establishment attended by the witness,

(d) the identity of any place of work, and

(e) any still or moving picture of the witness.

(8) In determining whether to give a reporting direction the court shall consider—

(a) whether it would be in the interests of justice to do so, and

(b) the public interest in avoiding the imposition of a substantial and unreasonable restriction on the reporting of the proceedings.

(9) The court or an appellate court may by direction ("an excepting direction") dispense, to any extent specified in the excepting direction, with the restrictions imposed by a reporting direction if—

(a) it is satisfied that it is necessary in the interests of justice to do so, or

(b) it is satisfied—

(i) that the effect of those restrictions is to impose a substantial and unreasonable restriction on the reporting of the proceedings, and

(ii) that it is in the public interest to remove or relax that restriction;

but no excepting direction shall be given under paragraph (b) by reason only of the fact that the proceedings have been determined in any way or have been abandoned.

(10) A reporting direction may be revoked by the court or an appellate court.

(11) An excepting direction—

(a) may be given at the time the reporting direction is given or subsequently; and

(b) may be varied or revoked by the court or an appellate court.

(12) In this section—

(a) "appellate court", in relation to any proceedings in a court, means a court dealing with an appeal (including an appeal by way of case stated) arising out of the proceedings or with any further appeal;
(b) references to the quality of a witness's evidence are to its quality in terms of completeness, coherence and accuracy (and for this purpose "coherence" refers to a witness's ability in giving evidence to give answers which address the questions put to the witness and can be understood both individually and collectively);
(c) references to the preparation of the case of a party to any proceedings include, where the party is the prosecution, the carrying out of investigations into any offence at any time charged in the proceedings.

The court has the power to restrict reports about an adult witness' evidence if it believes that the witness is afraid or distressed about being identified and as a result the quality of the evidence that the witness would give or the witness' co-operation is likely to be diminished. The court will take into account the nature of the offence, the age, social, cultural background and ethnic origins, domestic and employment circumstances, religious or political beliefs of the witness and any behaviour of the defendant, his family and friends or other witnesses towards the witness. The court will also want to be satisfied that the order is likely to improve the quality of the evidence or the witness' co-operation. The court will take the witness' views into account. **8–30**

The *Criminal Procedure Rules* 2011 provide for applications in respect of s.46: rr. 16.1–16.8. See Appendix G–73—G–81. **8–31**

Part II

Youth Justice and Criminal Evidence Act 1999, s.47

Restrictions on reporting directions under Chapter I or II

47.—(1) Except as provided by this section, no publication shall include a report of a matter falling within subsection (2). **8–32**

(2) The matters falling within this subsection are—
(a) a direction under section 19 or 36 or an order discharging, or (in the case of a direction under section 19) varying, such a direction;
(b) proceedings—
(i) on an application for such a direction or order, or
(ii) where the court acts of its own motion to determine whether to give or make any such direction or order.

(3) The court dealing with a matter falling within subsection (2) may order that subsection (1) is not to apply, or is not to apply to a specified extent, to a report of that matter.

(4) Where—
(a) there is only one accused in the relevant proceedings, and
(b) he objects to the making of an order under subsection (3),
the court shall make the order if (and only if) satisfied after hearing the representations of the accused that it is in the interests of justice to do so; and if the order is made it shall not apply to the extent that a report deals with any such objections or representations.

(5) Where—
(a) there are two or more accused in the relevant proceedings, and
(b) one or more of them object to the making of an order under subsection (3),
the court shall make the order if (and only if) satisfied after hearing the representations of each of the accused that it is in the interests of justice to do so; and if the order is made it shall not apply to the extent that a report deals with any such objections or representations.

(6) Subsection (1) does not apply to the inclusion in a publication of a report of matters after the relevant proceedings are either—
(a) determined (by acquittal, conviction or otherwise), or
(b) abandoned,
in relation to the accused or (if there is more than one) in relation to each of the accused.

(7) In this section "the relevant proceedings" means the proceedings to which any such direction as is mentioned in subsection (2) relates or would relate.

(8) Nothing in this section affects any prohibition or restriction by virtue of any other enactment on the inclusion of matter in a publication.

The reporting of a direction in relation to special measures or prohibiting cross ex- **8–33** amination of a particular witness or an order varying or discharging such a direction is prohibited unless the court directs otherwise. If the court is minded to allow publication it shall hear the objections or representations of any defendant and must only make the order if it is in the interests of justice and to the extent that the report deals with the objections or representations.

Youth Justice and Criminal Evidence Act 1999, s.49

Offences under Chapter IV

8–34 **49.**—(1) This section applies if a publication—

(a) includes any matter in contravention of section 44(2) or of a direction under section 45(3) or 46(2); or

(b) includes a report in contravention of section 47.

(2) Where the publication is a newspaper or periodical, any proprietor, any editor and any publisher of the newspaper or periodical is guilty of an offence.

(3) Where the publication is a relevant programme—

(a) any body corporate or Scottish partnership engaged in providing the programme service in which the programme is included, and

(b) any person having functions in relation to the programme corresponding to those of an editor of a newspaper,

is guilty of an offence.

(4) In the case of any other publication, any person publishing it is guilty of an offence.

(5) A person guilty of an offence under this section is liable on summary conviction to a fine not exceeding level 5 on the standard scale.

(6) Proceedings for an offence under this section in respect of a publication falling within subsection (1)(b) may not be instituted—

(a) in England and Wales otherwise than by or with the consent of the Attorney General, or

(b) in Northern Ireland otherwise than by or with the consent of the Attorney General for Northern Ireland.

8–35 In *T. v. DPP; North East Press Ltd* (2004) 168 J.P. 194, the defendant had attained the age of 18 during the course of proceedings against him in the youth court. It was held that the restriction applies only for so long as the person concerned continues to be a child or young person.

Youth Justice and Criminal Evidence Act 1999, s.52

Decisions as to public interest for purposes of Chapter IV

8–36 **52.**—(1) Where for the purposes of any provision of this Chapter it falls to a court to determine whether anything is (or, as the case may be, was) in the public interest, the court must have regard, in particular, to the matters referred to in subsection (2) (so far as relevant).

(2) Those matters are—

(a) the interest in each of the following—

(i) the open reporting of crime,

(ii) the open reporting of matters relating to human health or safety, and

(iii) the prevention and exposure of miscarriages of justice;

(b) the welfare of any person in relation to whom the relevant restrictions imposed by or under this Chapter apply or would apply (or, as the case may be, applied); and

(c) any views expressed—

(i) by an appropriate person on behalf of a person within paragraph (b) who is under the age of 16 ("the protected person"), or

(ii) by a person within that paragraph who has attained that age.

(3) In subsection (2) "an appropriate person", in relation to the protected person, has the same meaning as it has for the purposes of section 50.

Sexual Offences (Amendment) Act 1992, ss.1–4

Anonymity of victims of certain offences

8–37 **1.**—(1) Where an allegation has been made that an offence to which this Act applies has been committed against a person, no matter relating to that person shall during that person's lifetime be included in any publication if it is likely to lead members of the public to identify that person as the person against whom the offence is alleged to have been committed.

(2) Where a person is accused of an offence to which this Act applies, no matter likely to lead members of the public to identify a person as the person against whom the offence is alleged to have been committed ("the complainant") shall during the complainant's lifetime be included in any publication.

(3) This section—

(a) does not apply in relation to a person by virtue of subsection (1) at any time after a person has been accused of the offence, and

(b) in its application in relation to a person by virtue of subsection (2), has effect subject to any direction given under section 3.

(3A) The matters relating to a person in relation to which the restrictions imposed by subsection (1) or (2) apply (if their inclusion in any publication is likely to have the result mentioned in that subsection) include in particular—

(a) the person's name,

(b) the person's address,

(c) the identity of any school or other educational establishment attended by the person,

(d) the identity of any place of work, and

(e) any still or moving picture of the person.

(4) Nothing in this section prohibits the inclusion in a publication of matter consisting only of a report of criminal proceedings other than proceedings at, or intended to lead to, or on an appeal arising out of, a trial at which the accused is charged with the offence.

Offences to which this Act applies

2.—(1) This Act applies to the following offences against the law of England and Wales— **8–38**

(aa) rape;

(ab) burglary with intent to rape;

(a) any offence under any of the provisions of the *Sexual Offences Act* 1956 mentioned in subsection (2);

(b) any offence under section 128 of the *Mental Health Act* 1959 (intercourse with mentally handicapped person by hospital staff etc.);

(c) any offence under section 1 of the *Indecency with Children Act* 1960 (indecent conduct towards young child);

(d) any offence under section 54 of the *Criminal Law Act* 1977 (incitement by man of his grand-daughter, daughter or sister under the age of 16 to commit incest with him);

(da) any offence under any of the provisions of Part 1 of the *Sexual Offences Act* 2003 except section 64, 65, 69 or 71;

(e) any attempt to commit any of the offences mentioned in paragraphs (aa) to (da);

(f) any conspiracy to commit any of those offences;

(g) any incitement of another to commit any of those offences;

(h) aiding, abetting, counselling or procuring the commission of any of the offences mentioned in paragraphs (aa) to (e) and (g).

(2) The provisions of the Act of 1956 are—

(a) section 2 (procurement of a woman by threats);

(b) section 3 (procurement of a woman by false pretences);

(c) section 4 (administering drugs to obtain intercourse with a woman);

(d) section 5 (intercourse with a girl under the age of 13);

(e) section 6 (intercourse with a girl between the ages of 13 and 16);

(f) section 7 (intercourse with a mentally handicapped person);

(g) section 9 (procurement of a mentally handicapped person);

(h) section 10 (incest by a man);

(i) section 11 (incest by a woman);

(j) section 12 (buggery);

(k) section 14 (indecent assault on a woman);

(l) section 15 (indecent assault on a man);

(m) section 16 (assault with intent to commit buggery);
(n) section 17 (abduction of woman by force).

(3) This Act applies to the following offences against the law of Northern Ireland—

(a) rape;
(b) burglary with intent to rape;
(c) any offence under any of the following provisions of the *Offences against the Person Act* 1861—
(i) section 52 (indecent assault on a female);
(ii) section 53 so far as it relates to abduction of a woman against her will;
(iii) section 61 (buggery);
(iv) section 62 (attempt to commit buggery, assault with intent to commit buggery or indecent assault on a male);
(d) any offence under any of the following provisions of the *Criminal Law Amendment Act* 1885—
(i) section 3 (procuring unlawful carnal knowledge of woman by threats, false pretences or administering drugs);
(ii) section 4 (unlawful carnal knowledge, or attempted unlawful carnal knowledge, of a girl under 14);
(iii) section 5 (unlawful carnal knowledge of a girl under 17);
(e) any offence under any of the following provisions of the *Punishment of Incest Act* 1908—
(i) section 1 (incest, attempted incest by males);
(ii) section 2 (incest by females over 16);
(f) any offence under section 22 of the *Children and Young Persons Act (Northern Ireland)* 1968 (indecent conduct towards child);
(g) any offence under Article 9 of the Criminal Justice (Northern Ireland) Order 1980 (inciting girl under 16 to have incestuous sexual intercourse);
(h) any offence under any of the following provisions of the *Mental Health (Northern Ireland) Order* 1986—
(i) Article 122(1)(a) (unlawful sexual intercourse with a woman suffering from severe mental handicap);
(ii) Article 122(1)(b) (procuring a woman suffering from severe mental handicap to have unlawful sexual intercourse);
(iii) Article 123 (unlawful sexual intercourse by hospital staff, etc. with a person receiving treatment for mental disorder);
(ha) any offence under any of sections 15 to 21, 47 to 53, 57 to 59, 66, 67, 70 and 72 of the *Sexual Offences Act* 2003;
(i) any attempt to commit any of the offences mentioned in paragraphs (a) to (ha);
(j) any conspiracy to commit any of those offences;
(k) any incitement of another to commit any of those offences;
(l) aiding, abetting, counselling or procuring the commission of any of the offences mentioned in paragraphs (a) to (i) and (k).

(4) This Act applies to an offence under section 42 of the *Armed Forces Act* 2006 if the corresponding offence under the law of England and Wales (within the meaning given by that section) is an offence within a paragraph of subsection (1) above.

Power to displace section 1

8–39 **3.**—(1) If, before the commencement of a trial at which a person is charged with an offence to which this Act applies, he or another person against whom the complainant may be expected to give evidence at the trial, applies to the judge for a direction under this subsection and satisfies the judge—

(a) that the direction is required for the purpose of inducing persons who are likely to be needed as witnesses at the trial to come forward; and
(b) that the conduct of the applicant's defence at the trial is likely to be substantially prejudiced if the direction is not given,

the judge shall direct that section 1 shall not, by virtue of the accusation alleging the offence in question, apply in relation to the complainant.

(2) If at a trial the judge is satisfied—

(a) that the effect of section 1 is to impose a substantial and unreasonable restriction upon the reporting of proceedings at the trial, and

(b) that it is in the public interest to remove or relax the restriction,

he shall direct that that section shall not apply to such matter as is specified in the direction.

(3) A direction shall not be given under subsection (2) by reason only of the outcome of the trial.

(4) If a person who has been convicted of an offence and has given notice of appeal against the conviction, or notice of an application for leave so to appeal, applies to the appellate court for a direction under this subsection and satisfies the court—

(a) that the direction is required for the purpose of obtaining evidence in support of the appeal; and

(b) that the applicant is likely to suffer substantial injustice if the direction is not given,

the court shall direct that section 1 shall not, by virtue of an accusation which alleges an offence to which this Act applies and is specified in the direction, apply in relation to a complainant so specified.

(5) A direction given under any provision of this section does not affect the operation of section 1 at any time before the direction is given.

(6) In subsections (1) and (2), "judge" means —

(a) in the case of an offence which is to be tried summarily or for which the mode of trial has not been determined, any justice of the peace; and

(b) in any other case, any judge of the Crown Court in England and Wales.

(6A) In its application to Northern Ireland, this section has effect as if—

(a) in subsections (1) and (2) for any reference to the judge there were substituted a reference to the court; and

(b) subsection (6) were omitted.

(6B) Where a person is charged with an offence to which this Act applies by virtue of section 2(4), this section applies as if—

(a) in subsections (1) and (2) for any reference to the judge there were substituted a reference to the court; and

(b) subsections (6) and (6A) were omitted.

(7) If, after the commencement of a trial at which a person is charged with an offence to which this Act applies, a new trial of the person for that offence is ordered, the commencement of any previous trial shall be disregarded for the purposes of subsection (1).

Special rules for cases of incest or buggery

4.—(1) In this section— **8–40**

"section 10 offence" means an offence under section 10 of the *Sexual Offences Act* 1956 (incest by a man) or an attempt to commit that offence;

"section 11 offence" means an offence under section 11 of that Act (incest by a woman) or an attempt to commit that offence;

"section 12 offence" means an offence under section 12 of that Act (buggery) or an attempt to commit that offence.

(2) Section 1 does not apply to a woman against whom a section 10 offence is alleged to have been committed if she is accused of having committed a section 11 offence against the man who is alleged to have committed the section 10 offence against her.

(3) Section 1 does not apply to a man against whom a section 11 offence is alleged to have been committed if he is accused of having committed a section 10 offence against the woman who is alleged to have committed the section 11 offence against him.

(4) Section 1 does not apply to a person against whom a section 12 offence is alleged to have been committed if that person is accused of having committed a section 12 offence against the person who is alleged to have committed the section 12 offence against him.

(5) Subsection (2) does not affect the operation of this Act in relation to anything done at any time before the woman is accused.

(6) Subsection (3) does not affect the operation of this Act in relation to anything done at any time before the man is accused.

(7) Subsection (4) does not affect the operation of this Act in relation to anything done at any time before the person mentioned first in that subsection is accused.

(8) In its application to Northern Ireland, this section has effect as if—

(a) subsection (1) were omitted;

(b) for references to a section 10 offence there were substituted references to an of-

Part II

fence under section 1 of the *Punishment of Incest Act* 1908 (incest by a man) or an attempt to commit that offence;

(c) for references to a section 11 offence there were substituted references to an offence under section 2 of that Act (incest by a woman) or an attempt to commit that offence; and

(d) for references to a section 12 offence there were substituted references to an offence under section 61 of the *Offences against the Person Act* 1861 (buggery) or an attempt to commit that offence.

Sexual Offences (Amendment) Act 1992, s.6

Interpretation etc.

8–41 **6.**—(1) In this Act—

"complainant" has the meaning given in section 1(2);

"picture" includes a likeness however produced;

"publication" includes any speech, writing, relevant programme or other communication in whatever form, which is addressed to the public at large or any section of the public (and for this purpose every relevant programme shall be taken to be so addressed), but does not include an indictment or other document prepared for use in particular legal proceedings;

"relevant programme" means a programme included in a programme service, within the meaning of the *Broadcasting Act* 1990;

(1A) Section 48 of the *Armed Forces Act* 2006 (attempts, conspiracy, incitement and aiding and abetting outside England and Wales) applies for the purposes of this Act as if the reference in subsection (3)(b) of that section to any of the following provisions of that Act were a reference to any provision of this Act.

(2) For the purposes of this Act—

(a) where it is alleged that an offence to which this Act applies has been committed, the fact that any person has consented to an act which, on any prosecution for that offence, would fall to be proved by the prosecution, does not prevent that person from being regarded as a person against whom the alleged offence was committed; and

(b) where a person is accused of an offence of incest or buggery, the other party to the act in question shall be taken to be a person against whom the offence was committed even though he consented to that act.

(2A) For the purposes of this Act, where it is alleged or there is an accusation—

(a) that an offence of conspiracy or incitement of another to commit an offence mentioned in section 2(1)(aa) to (d) or (3)(a) to (h) has been committed, or

(b) that an offence of aiding, abetting, counselling or procuring the commission of an offence of incitement of another to commit an offence mentioned in section 2(1)(aa) to (d) or (3)(a) to (h) has been committed,

the person against whom the substantive offence is alleged to have been intended to be committed shall be regarded as the person against whom the conspiracy or incitement is alleged to have been committed.

In this subsection, "the substantive offence" means the offence to which the alleged conspiracy or incitement related.

(3) For the purposes of this Act, a person is accused of an offence, other than an offence under section 42 of the *Armed Forces Act* 2006, if—

(a) an information is laid, or (in Northern Ireland) a complaint is made, alleging that he has committed the offence,

(b) he appears before a court charged with the offence,

(c) a court before which he is appearing commits him for trial on a new charge alleging the offence, or

(d) a bill of indictment charging him with the offence is preferred before a court in which he may lawfully be indicted for the offence,

and references in subsection (2A) and in section 3 to an accusation alleging an offence shall be construed accordingly.

(3A) For the purposes of this Act, a person is accused of an offence under section 42 of the *Armed Forces Act* 2006 if he is charged (under Part 5 of that Act) with the offence, and references in section 3 to an accusation alleging an offence shall be construed accordingly.

(4) Nothing in this Act affects any prohibition or restriction imposed by virtue of any other enactment upon a publication or upon matter included in a relevant programme.

It has been held that legislation preventing the publication of information likely to lead members of the public to identify a child victim of alleged gross indecency is not disproportionate or in breach of the right of freedom of expression: *O'Riordan v. DPP*, *The Times*, May 31, 2005; [2005] EWHC 1240. **8–42**

Criminal Procedure and Investigations Act 1996, ss.58–61

Orders in respect of certain assertions

58.—(1) This section applies where a person has been convicted of an offence and a speech in mitigation is made by him or on his behalf before— **8–43**

(a) a court determining what sentence should be passed on him in respect of the offence, or

(b) a magistrates' court determining whether he should be committed to the Crown Court for sentence.

(2) This section also applies where a sentence has been passed on a person in respect of an offence and a submission relating to the sentence is made by him or on his behalf before—

(a) a court hearing an appeal against or reviewing the sentence, or

(b) a court determining whether to grant leave to appeal against the sentence.

(3) Where it appears to the court that there is a real possibility that an order under subsection (8) will be made in relation to the assertion, the court may make an order under subsection (7) in relation to the assertion.

(4) Where there are substantial grounds for believing—

(a) that an assertion forming part of the speech or submission is derogatory to a person's character (for instance, because it suggests that his conduct is or has been criminal, immoral or improper), and

(b) that the assertion is false or that the facts asserted are irrelevant to the sentence,

the court may make an order under subsection (8) in relation to the assertion.

(5) An order under subsection (7) or (8) must not be made in relation to an assertion if it appears to the court that the assertion was previously made—

(a) at the trial at which the person was convicted of the offence, or

(b) during any other proceedings relating to the offence.

(6) Section 59 has effect where a court makes an order under subsection (7) or (8).

(7) An order under this subsection—

(a) may be made at any time before the court has made a determination with regard to sentencing;

(b) may be revoked at any time by the court;

(c) subject to paragraph (b), shall cease to have effect when the court makes a determination with regard to sentencing.

(8) An order under this subsection—

(a) may be made at any time before the court has made a determination with regard to sentencing, but only if it is made as soon as is reasonably practicable after the making of the determination;

(b) may be revoked at any time by the court;

(c) subject to paragraph (b), shall cease to have effect at the end of the period of 12 months beginning with the day on which it is made;

(d) may be made whether or not an order has been made under subsection (7) with regard to the case concerned.

(9) For the purposes of subsection (7) and (8) the court makes a determination with regard to sentencing—

(a) when it determines what sentence should be passed (where this section applies by virtue of subsection (1)(a);

(b) when it determines whether the person should be committed to the Crown Court for sentence (where this section applies by virtue of subsection (1)(b));

(c) when it determines what the sentence should be (where this section applies by virtue of subsection (2)(a));

Part II

(d) when it determines whether to grant leave to appeal (where this section applies by virtue of subsection (2)(b).

Restriction on reporting of assertions

8–44 **59.**—(1) Where a court makes an order under section 58(7) or (8) in relation to any assertion, at any time when the order has effect the assertion must not—

(a) be published in Great Britain in a written publication available to the public, or

(b) be included in a relevant programme for reception in Great Britain.

(2) In this section—

"relevant programme" means a programme included in a programme service, within the meaning of the *Broadcasting Act* 1990;

"written publication" includes a film, a soundtrack and any other record in permanent form but does not include an indictment or other document prepared for use in particular legal proceedings.

(3) For the purposes of this section an assertion is published or included in a programme if the material published or included—

(a) names the person about whom the assertion is made or, without naming him, contains enough to make it likely that members of the public will identify him as the person about whom it is made, and

(b) reproduces the actual wording of the matter asserted or contains its substance.

Reporting of assertions: offences

8–45 **60.**—(1) If an assertion is published or included in a relevant programme in contravention of section 59, each of the following persons is guilty of an offence—

(a) in the case of publication in a newspaper or periodical, any proprietor, any editor and any publisher of the newspaper or periodical;

(b) in the case of publication in any other form, the person publishing the assertion;

(c) in the case of an assertion included in a relevant programme, any body corporate engaged in providing the service in which the programme is included and any person having functions in relation to the programme corresponding to those of an editor of a newspaper.

(2) A person guilty of an offence under this section is liable on summary conviction to a fine of an amount not exceeding level 5 on the standard scale.

(3) Where a person is charged with an offence under this section it is a defence to prove that at the time of the alleged offence—

(a) he was not aware, and neither suspected nor had reason to suspect, that an order under section 58(7) or (8) had effect at that time, or

(b) he was not aware, and neither suspected nor had reason to suspect, that the publication or programme in question was of, or (as the case may be) included, the assertion in question.

(4) Where an offence under this section committed by a body corporate is proved to have been committed with the consent or connivance of, or to be attributable to any neglect on the part of—

(a) a director, manager, secretary or other similar officer of the body corporate, or

(b) a person purporting to act in any such capacity,

he as well as the body, corporate is guilty of the offence and liable to be proceeded against and punished accordingly.

(5) In relation to a body corporate whose affairs are managed by its members "director" in subsection (4) means a member of the body corporate.

(6) Subsections (2) and (3) of section 59 apply for the purposes of this section as they apply for the purposes of that.

Reporting of assertions: commencement and supplementary

8–46 **61.**—(1) Section 58 applies where the offence mentioned in subsection (1) or (2) of that section is committed on or after the appointed day.

(2) The reference in subsection (1) to the appointed day is to such day as is appointed for the purposes of this section by the Secretary of State by order.

(3) Nothing in section 58 or 59 affects any prohibition or restriction imposed by virtue of any other enactment on a publication or on matter included in a programme.

(4) [*Repealed.*]
(5) [*Repealed.*]
(6) In section 159 of the *Criminal Justice Act* 1988 (appeal to Court of Appeal against orders restricting reports etc.) in subsection (1) the following paragraph shall be inserted after paragraph (a)—

"(aa) an order made by the Crown Court under section 58(7) or (8) of the *Criminal Procedure and Investigations Act* 1996 of the *Criminal Procedure and Investigations Act* 1996 in a case where the Court has convicted a person on a trial on indictment;".

When a plea in mitigation is made to the court the defendant or his representative may try to minimise his offending behaviour by making remarks about the victim's character suggesting that the victim's conduct has been immoral, improper or criminal. If the court finds that there are substantial grounds for believing that the assertion is derogatory and that either it is false or irrelevant to the sentence, it can make a s.58 order. An interim order may be made as soon as the assertion has been made but only if there is a real possibility that a final order will be made. A final order may be made before sentence is passed or afterwards. If it is made after sentence it must be made as soon as is reasonably practicable. The effect of such an order is to bar publication of the assertion which is the subject of the order. An order cannot be made if it appears that the assertion has previously been made at the trial or during any other proceedings in relation to the offence. **8–47**

An interim order will cease when the defendant is sentenced. A final order continues until it is either revoked by the court or at the end of twelve months beginning on the day on which it is made.

For the purposes of s.61(1) where an offence is committed over a period of more than one day, or at some time during a period of more than one day, it must be taken to be committed on the last of the days in the period: *Criminal Procedure and Investigations Act* 1996, s.75(2), (3).

Reporting of magistrates' names

The names of district judges and magistrates do not routinely appear on court lists. An application may be made for the disclosure of such names to the legal adviser in court or after the hearing to the justices' clerk. In *Felixstowe Justices, ex p. Leigh* [1987] Q.B. 582, 84 Cr.App.R. 327, Watkins, L.J. said: **8–48**

"There is, in my view, no such person known to the law as the anonymous J.P. I do not for one moment suggest that the right to know involves the disclosure of any more than the name of a justice. No one can demand the address and still less the telephone number of a justice of the peace. Moreover, a clerk to justices would, it seems to me, act with justification in refusing during and after a hearing to give the name of one of the justices to a person who the clerk reasonably believes requires that information solely for a mischievous purpose. Save for such considerations as that, I would hold that the bona fide inquirer is entitled to know the name of a justice who is sitting or who has sat upon a case recently heard."

It is submitted that this decision is unaffected by the provisions of the *Freedom of Information Act* 2000, because this Act does not require the disclosure of sensitive personal information.

Photographs

Criminal Justice Act 1925, s.41

Prohibition on taking photographs, &c., in court

41.—(1) No person shall— **8–49**

(a) take or attempt to take in any court any photograph, or with a view to publication make or attempt to make in any court any portrait or sketch, of any person, being a judge of the court or a juror or a witness in or a party to any proceedings before the court, whether civil or criminal; or

(b) publish any photograph, portrait or sketch taken or made in contravention of the foregoing provisions of this section or any reproduction thereof;

and if any person acts in contravention of this section be shall, on summary conviction, be liable in respect of each offence to a fine not exceeding fifty pounds.

(2) For the purposes of this section—

(a) the expression "court" means any court of justice, including the court of a coroner:

(b) the expression "Judge" includes […], registrar, magistrate, justice and coroner:

(c) a photograph, portrait or sketch shall be deemed to be a photograph, portrait or sketch taken or made in court if it is taken or made in the court-room or in the building or in the precincts of the building in which the court is held, or if it is a photograph, portrait or sketch taken or made of the person while he is entering or leaving the court-room or any such building or precincts as aforesaid.

8–50 The issue here is one of identification of people. It is intended to ensure a fair trial. It is not a general prohibition on taking photographs of the court building. Neither does it prevent an artist who has sat in court and observed the proceedings from producing a sketch thereafter so long as the sketching does not take place within the prohibited areas. A person who has taken photographs by means of a mobile telephone can also be dealt with for criminal contempt of court: *D. (Vincent)* [2004] EWCA Crim 1271. The Court of Appeal stated it was concerned about the possibilities of intimidation. The taking of photographs in this way "has the potential to gravely prejudice the administration of criminal justice".

The precincts of the building could be taken to mean any area surrounding the courthouse a photograph of which would identify a person as being linked with that courthouse.

The filming of a defendant in the cell area of a magistrates' court for the purpose of having the film compared with a picture taken by CCTV of a person committing a robbery was held to be unlawful as being in breach of this prohibition: *Loveridge, Lee and Loveridge* [2001] 2 Cr.App.R. 29, CA.

Tape recordings

Contempt of Court Act 1981, s.9

Use of tape recorders

8–51 **9.**—(1) Subject to subsection (4) below, it is a contempt of court—

(a) to use in court, or bring into court for use, any tape recorder or other instrument for recording sound, except with the leave of the court;

(b) to publish a recording of legal proceedings made by means of any such instrument, or any recording derived directly or indirectly from it, by playing it in the hearing of the public or any section of the public, or to dispose of it or any recording so derived, with a view to such publication;

(c) to use any such recording in contravention of any conditions of leave granted under paragraph (a).

(2) Leave under paragraph (a) of subsection (1) may be granted or refused at the discretion of the court, and if granted may be granted subject to such conditions as the court thinks proper with respect to the use of any recording made pursuant to the leave; and where leave has been granted the court may at the like discretion withdraw or amend it either generally or in relation to any particular part of the proceedings.

(3) Without prejudice to any other power to deal with an act of contempt under paragraph (a) of subsection (1), the court may order the instrument, or any recording made with it, or both, to be forfeited; and any object so forfeited shall (unless the court otherwise determines on application by a person appearing to be the owner) be sold or otherwise disposed of in such manner as the court may direct.

(4) This section does not apply to the making or use of sound recordings for purposes

of official transcripts of proceedings.

The *Consolidated Criminal Practice Direction*, para. I.2 in Appendix F–4 gives guidance on the exercise of the court's discretion stating that reasonable need; the risk of briefing witnesses out of court and distraction or disturbance by the use of the recorder, may be of relevance. **8–52**

Live, text based communications in court

Lord Judge, C.J. has issued guidance on the use of live, text based communications in court: *Interim Practice Guidance: The Use of Live Text-Based Forms of Communication (Including Twitter) from Court for the Purposes of Fair and Accurate Reporting* [2011] 1 Cr.App.R. 23. There is no statutory prohibition on the use of live, text-based communications (*e.g.* mobile email, social media (including Twitter) and internet enabled laptops) in open court. The court may either of its own motion, or following a formal application or informal request, permit live, text-based communications from court. In deciding whether to grant such permission, and to whom it should be granted, the paramount question will be whether allowing such communications may lead to an interference with the proper administration of justice. The use of an unobtrusive, hand-held, virtually silent piece of modern equipment for the purposes of simultaneous reporting of proceedings to the outside world as they unfold in court is generally unlikely to interfere with the proper administration of justice. Any danger is likely to be most acute in the context of criminal trials where, for example, witnesses who are out of court may be informed of what has already happened in court, or where information posted on Twitter about inadmissible evidence may influence members of a jury. Permission to use live, text-based communications may be withdrawn if court proceedings are adversely affected, and it may be necessary for the judge to limit such communications to representatives of the media for journalistic purposes and to disallow their use by the general public, because, for example, of the potential for electronic interference with the court's own sound recording equipment, or because the widespread use of such devices in court may be distracting. **8–53**

Part II

II. LANGUAGE

A. GENERAL

Court proceedings are ordinarily conducted in English: see *Re Trepca Mines* [1960] 1 W.L.R. 24. **8–54**

B. INTERPRETERS

Interpreters are used for witnesses and defendants where they do not understand English. In accordance with art. 6(3) ECHR, *ante*, where a defendant does not understand the English language or does not understand it sufficiently to follow court proceedings the evidence at trial should be translated to him. Similarly where the defendant is deaf, mute or both the court must ensure that proper means are taken to communicate to the defendant the case made against him and to enable him to make an answer to it. Sign language may be used or the evidence could be reduced to writing. The assistance of an interpreter is within the court's discretion and the court can itself assess whether a witness needs an interpreter. A court can determine the need by assessing the limits of the witness's comprehension and fluency when the evidence is given: *Sharma* [2006] 2 Cr.App.R.(S.) 63, CA. It has been held that where the indication of the need for an interpreter arose only during the defence case and that there had been no prejudice to the defendant the court's refusal to appoint an interpreter did not render the trial unfair: *Wei Hai Restaurant Ltd v. Kingston upon Hull City Council* (2002) 166 J.P. 185, DC. **8–55**

Where the difficulty in interpretation was such as to make it impossible for a witness's evidence to be tested by cross-examination, the conviction was quashed: *Imrie*, 12 Cr.App.R. 282

It is important that the interpreter is someone who can be expected to interpret impartially. In *Mitchell* (1970) 114 S.J. 86, it was held that the employment of an interpreter who was a waiter at the restaurant where offences were alleged to have been committed was irregular; an interpreter who could have no bias was necessary

8–56 In *West London Youth Court, ex p. N.* [2000] 1 W.L.R. 2368, the police interviewed the 11-year-old defendant who spoke only Bosnian Romany. A relative, acting as the appropriate adult, was used for the second limb of a double interpretation process consisting of interpretation from one language into a second language, and then from the second language into a third language. There were no competent or qualified interpreters from Bosnian Romany in the United Kingdom who could act as interpreters in the criminal proceedings and the designated interpreter did not have a high enough level of understanding to meet the needs of the case. The process of double translation was ruled unlawful by the magistrates' court. On review, the Divisional Court held that double interpretation was acceptable and a necessary method of interpretation during both interview and trial on the condition that it had been impossible to find an interpreter who spoke fluently both in English and in a language in which the defendant was fluent. Both interpreters have to be suitably qualified and wholly impartial. It is not sufficient to use an appropriate adult for one limb; they are not impartial as their function is to assist the person questioned. It is important to ensure a proper, mutual understanding between the defendant and the interpreter, between the two interpreters and their common language, and also to ensure that the second interpreter was fluent in the English language. The onus is on the court to ensure that the defendant is fully able to participate in the proceedings even where the defendant's lawyer is content to make do with an inadequate interpreter: *Cuscani v. UK*, (2003) 36 E.H.R.R. 2.

8–57 Evidence from a police officer as to what the defendant had said during an interview, as related to the officer by an interpreter, is hearsay; the only valid witness is the interpreter: *Attard* 43 Cr.App.R. 90. If the interpreter used at the police station is to be called as a prosecution witness, a separate interpreter should be used for the court.

Interpreters are paid fees by the court. The right to free interpretation is unqualified. A convicted person cannot therefore be ordered to pay the costs of an interpreter: *Luedicke, Belkacem and Koc v. Germany* (1979–80) 2 E.H.R.R. 149. The fees include travelling time but not travelling expenses. The latter may be claimed separately.

C. COURTS IN WALES AND MONMOUTHSHIRE

Welsh Language Act 1993, ss.22, 24

Use of Welsh in legal proceedings

8–58 **22.**—(1) In any legal proceedings in Wales the Welsh language may be spoken by any party, witness or other person who desires to use it, subject in the case of proceedings in a court other than a magistrates' court to such prior notice as may be required by rules of court; and any necessary provision for interpretation shall be made accordingly.

(2) Any power to make rules of court includes power to make provision as to the use, in proceedings in or having a connection with Wales, of documents in the Welsh language.

Provision of interpreters

8–59 **24.** Lord Chancellor may make rules as to the provision and employment of interpreters of the Welsh and English languages for the purposes of proceedings before courts in Wales.

(2) The interpreters shall be paid, out of the same fund as the expenses of the court are payable, such remuneration in respect of their services as the Lord Chancellor may determine.

(3) The Lord Chancellor's powers under this section shall be exercised with the consent of the Treasury.

8–60 The *Consolidated Criminal Practice Direction*, paras III.22 and 23 applies, see Appendix F. The purpose of the direction is to give effect to the *Welsh Language Act* 1993 which provides for equal status for Welsh and English in Wales. Legal representatives are under a duty to inform the court where Welsh will be used so that appropriate listing arrangements can be made.

III. REPRESENTATION OF THE DEFENDANT

A. LEGAL REPRESENTATION

Magistrates' Courts Act 1980, s.122

Appearance by counsel or solicitor

122.—(1) A party to any proceedings before a magistrates' court may be represented by [a legal representative]. **8–61**

(2) Subject to subsection (3) below, an absent party so represented shall be deemed not to be absent.

(3) Appearance of a party by [a legal representative] shall not satisfy any provision of any enactment or any condition of a recognizance expressly requiring his presence.

[This section is reprinted as amended by the *Courts and Legal Services Act* 1990, s.125(3), Sched. 18, para. 25(3)(b).]

As to rights of audience see *ante*, § 2–32.

Article 6(3) ECHR, *ante*, guarantees the right to legal representation. The provision of legal aid is subject to the means of the defendant and confined to cases where the interests of justice require it: see *post*, § 29–31.

A defendant is entitled to be represented by a lawyer of his choosing if it is reasonably practicable. It is not an absolute right although his choice should be respected: *Goddi v. Italy* (1984) 6 E.H.R.R. 457. The overriding consideration is the requirements of justice, for both prosecution and defence, in the circumstances of the case: *R. v. De Oliveira* [1997] Crim.L.R. 600, CA. It will depend not only on the defendant's choice but on the availability of the advocate, a suitably equipped court, witnesses as well as the time scale of the case. Where an advocate withdraws because of professional reasons or is dismissed by his client, the court has a discretion to grant an adjournment so that a new advocate can be instructed. It is not appropriate for the court to seek an explanation for the withdrawal or dismissal. The court is, however, entitled to take into account the likelihood that another advocate would suffer the same fate as the original, the interests of witnesses and of the public. Additional matters to consider are the stage that the trial has reached and the apparent ability of the defendant to conduct his or her own case: *Al-Zubeidi* [1999] Crim.L.R. 906, CA. The defendant is always at liberty to ask the court's permission to conduct his own defence: *Lyons* 68 Cr.App.R. 104, CA.

There is no significant prejudice to a trial where a legal adviser has been replaced during the trial and has not had the opportunity to observe witnesses; the adviser can consult with the defendant and the previous legal adviser: *Gibson v. HM Advocate* [2008] HCJAC 52.

The wrongful denial of the defendant's right to legal representation is likely to result in the quashing of the conviction: *Kingston* (1948) 32 Cr.App.R. 183, CA; *Harris* [1985] Crim.L.R. 244, CA.

B. RIGHT TO CONDUCT OWN DEFENCE

A defendant has the right to conduct his own defence with or without the services of a solicitor: *Woodward* [1944] K.B. 118; *De Courcy*, 48 Cr.App.R. 323 An unrepresented defendant cannot, however, rely on the disadvantages of lack of representation to support an argument that there was inequality of arms at trial to render the conviction unsafe: *Van Geyseghem v. Belgium*, (2001) 35 E.H.R.R. 24. **8–62**

In magistrates' courts many defendants represent themselves and the legal adviser has a specific duty to assist by putting questions to witnesses on the defendant's behalf. For a more detailed commentary on the role of the legal adviser in assisting an unrepresented defendant, see *post* § 8–134 *et seq.*

8–63 The more serious the charge, the more complex the case and the greater the potential for penalty, the more likely it is that representation will be needed to ensure a fair trial: *Hinds v. Att.-Gen. of Barbados* [2002] 2 W.L.R. 470, PC. A court may place reasonable restrictions on the right of a defendant to appear without a lawyer in a complex case: *Croissant v. Germany*, 16 E.H.R.R. 135; *Philis v. Greece*, 25 E.H.R.R. 417. There are also restrictions on the right to cross-examine witnesses: *Youth Justice and Criminal Evidence Act* 1999, s.36.

C. McKenzie Friends

8–64 Although a defendant may not be represented by someone who does not have a right of audience, he may apply to the court to have with him a "friend" who will assist him by taking notes, prompting, and quietly giving advice: *McKenzie v. McKenzie* (1970) 3 W.L.R. 472. In *Leicester City Justices, ex p. Barrow* [1991] 2 Q.B. 260 it was confirmed that the right does not go beyond assistance. A McKenzie friend has personally no rights over and above any other member of the public; it is the party seeking to use the McKenzie friend who has the right to request this assistance.

A McKenzie friend has no right to be an advocate and the court has discretion to exclude a person from acting as a McKenzie friend. However, there must be some justification established if a person is not to have the benefit of the assistance of another person, or some evidence that that person has previously acted inappropriately or is acting inappropriately at the hearing which makes it reasonable for the court to deprive the litigant of the assistance which would otherwise be provided: *Bow County Court* [1999] 1 W.L.R. 1807.

The Master of the Rolls and the President of the Family Division have jointly issued guidance on the use of McKenzie Friends: *Practice Note (McKenzie Friends: Civil and Family Courts)* [2010] 1 W.L.R. 1881. In essence a Mackenzie friend may provide moral support, takes notes, help with case papers, quietly give advice on points of law or procedure, issues that the person may wish to raise with the court and questions that may be put to witness. A McKenzie friend has no right to act on behalf of the person he assists, is not entitled to address the court, ask questions of witnesses or manage a case out of court or act as a person's agent, for example, signing papers.

D. Representation of a Corporate Defendant

Magistrates' Courts Act 1980, Sched. 3, paras 2–3

8–65 2. A representative may on behalf of a corporation—

(a) make before examining justices such representations as could be made by an accused who is not a corporation;

(b) consent to the corporation being tried summarily;

(c) enter a plea of guilty or not guilty on the trial by a magistrates' court of an information.

3.—(1) Where a representative appears, any requirement of this Act that anything shall be done in the presence of the accused, or shall be read or said to the accused, shall be construed as a requirement that that thing shall be done in the presence of the representative or read or said to the representative.

(2) Where a representative does not appear, any such requirement, and any requirement that the consent of the accused shall be obtained for summary trial, shall not apply.

[This Sched. is reprinted as amended by *Criminal Procedure and Investigations Act* 1996, Sched. 1, para. 13.]

8–66 A company may be represented by an appointed lawyer, a director or the secretary. It is advisable for a solicitor to be appointed by the company's representative: *Birming-*

ham and Gloucester Railway Co, TRe LCC and London Tramways Co; *Manchester Corp* and *Ascanio Puck & Co and Paice* (1912) 76 J.P. 487. It is usual to request the completion of a form in the following words:

X Co.

I appoint .... to represent the company in the above case

Signed A.B. Director/Secretary

This also applies to unincorporated bodies: *Companies Act* 2006, s.1130.

IV. PLEA

A. GENERAL

The first stage in a summary trial is for the court through the legal adviser to read the information to the defendant and ask him whether he pleads guilty or not guilty. **8–67**

Magistrates' Courts Act 1980, s.9

Procedure on trial

9.—(1) On the summary trial of an information, the court shall, if the accused appears, state to him the substance of the information and ask him whether he pleads guilty or not guilty. **8–68**

(2) The court, after hearing the evidence and the parties, shall convict the accused or dismiss the information.

(3) If the accused pleads guilty, the court may convict him without hearing evidence.

See *Criminal Procedure Rules*, r.37.2(2) in Appendix § G–224. The expectation under the Rules is that cases are concluded as soon as possible. **8–69**

In December 2009 the Senior Presiding Judge issued a reminder to all members of the judiciary that the word "must" in the *Criminal Procedure Rules R3.8* means must and that exceptions to the rule requiring the pleas to be taken are rare and must be strictly justified. This obligation does not depend on the extent of advance information, service of evidence, disclosure of unused material or the grant of legal aid. The court should also pass sentence the same day if at all possible.

The defendant, unless it is a company, should be asked personally to plead even where he is represented; *R. v. Wakefield Justices, ex.p. Butterworth* [1970] 1 All E.R. 1181. Where a defendant does not attend court but is represented, he is deemed to be present under *Magistrates' Courts Act* 1980, s.122. In those circumstances the court may allow the advocate to enter a plea of guilty on the defendant's behalf. **8–70**

B. PLEA OF GUILTY

If the defendant pleads guilty to an information the court may convict the defendant without hearing any evidence. The prosecution will read out the facts in open court: The *Consolidated Criminal Practice Direction*, para. III.26, in Appendix F. In the absence of a guilty plea, the court is under a duty to hear evidence and either convict the defendant or dismiss the information: *Magistrates' Courts Act* 1980, s.9(2). The plea of guilty must be unequivocal: *R. v. Tottenham Justices, ex p. Rubens* [1970] 1 All E.R. 879. Where the defendant is unrepresented the legal adviser will ensure that he understands the elements of the offence, especially if the facts suggest that he has a defence: *Griffiths*, 23 Cr.App.R. 153, CA; *R. v. Blandford Justices, ex p. G (an infant)*, *ante*. **8–71**

Where the defendant unequivocally admits the essential ingredients of an offence but disputes various facts, the court should hear evidence on the facts disputed, make findings and proceed to sentence; it should not direct that pleas of not guilty are entered: *R. v. Telford Justices, ex p. Darlington* (1988) 87 Cr.App.R. 194. On the other hand, where a court receives facts in mitigation which are inconsistent with a guilty plea that plea must be considered equivocal and a plea of not guilty entered: *R. v. Durham*

Quarter Sessions, ex p. Virgo [1952] 2 Q.B. 1. A court may allow a guilty plea to be withdrawn if it becomes apparent that a defendant did not appreciate the elements of the offence or where the prosecution facts do not add up to the offence charged; such a situation should be rare, for it is unlikely to arise where a defendant is represented and, where he is not, it is the duty of the court to make sure that the nature of the offence is made clear to him before a plea of guilty is accepted; in this case it was held incredible that the defendants did not understand the offence of dangerous driving thinking that instead they had been charged with nuisance: *Revitt v. DPP* [2006] 1.W.L.R. 3172.

8–72 Pleas which are entered under duress may also be covered by the rule that the plea must be unequivocal: *R. v. Huntingdon Crown Court, ex p. Jordan* [1981] Q.B. 857. In that case, the defendant pleaded guilty to theft in the magistrates' court where she was jointly charged with her husband. She appealed against conviction to the Crown Court, on the ground that both the offence and the plea were made under the duress of her husband. The judge ruled that the defendant's plea had been unequivocal and that the court has no jurisdiction to entertain the appeal. On application for judicial review it was held that the Crown Court had jurisdiction to inquire into an allegedly equivocal plea and to remit the matter to the magistrates if satisfied that the plea was equivocal. That jurisdiction extended to cases where an apparently unequivocal plea was entered under duress and was in fact a nullity.

Where the defendant wishes to plead guilty but there is a substantial dispute between the prosecution and defence version of events, the court should conduct a *Newton* hearing: *Newton* (1982) 77 Cr.App.R. 13; *Williams* (1983) 5 Cr.App.R. 134. The procedure will follow that of a trial and the parties will be able to call witnesses. The court will then decide the facts upon which it proposes to sentence (see *post* § 22–54).

A court is entitled to reject the basis of a guilty plea, without holding a *Newton* hearing, if it is manifestly absurd: *Taylor* [2007] Crim.L.R. 491.

Criminal Justice Act 1925, s.33

Procedure on charge of offence against corporation

8–73 **33.**—(1) [*repealed*]

(2) [*repealed*]

(3) On arrangement of a corporation, the corporation may enter in writing by its representative a plea of guilty or not guilty, and if either the corporation does not appear by a representative or, though it does so appear, fails to enter as aforesaid any plea, the court shall order a plea of not guilty to be entered and the trial shall proceed as though the corporation had duly entered a plea of not guilty.

(4) Provision may be made by rules under the *Indictments Act* 1915 with respect to the service on any corporation charged with an indictable offence of any documents requiring to be served in connection with the proceedings.

(5) [*repealed*]

(6) In this section the expression "representative" in relation to a corporation means a person duly appointed by the corporation to represent it for the purpose of doing any act or thing which the representative of a corporation is by this section authorized to do, but a person so appointed shall not, by virtue only of being so appointed, be qualified to act on behalf of the corporation before any court for any other purpose.

A representative for the purposes of this section need not be appointed under the seal of the corporation, and a statement in writing purporting to be signed by a managing director of the corporation, or by any person (by whatever name called) having, or being one of the persons having, the management of the affairs of the corporation, to the effect that the person named in the statement has been appointed as the representative of the corporation for the purposes of this section shall be admissible without further proof as prima facie evidence that that person has been so appointed.

8–74 Where a company via its representative (see *ante*) fails to appear the court will enter a not guilty plea and will hear the evidence.

C. PLEA OF GUILTY BY POST

Magistrates' Courts Act 1980, s.12

Non-appearance of accused; plea of guilty

12.—(1) This section shall apply where— 8–75

(a) a summons has been issued requiring a person to appear before a magistrates' court, other than a youth court, to answer to an information for a summary offence, not being—

(i) an offence for which the accused is liable to be sentenced to be imprisoned for a term exceeding 3 months; or

(ii) an offence specified in an order made by the Secretary of State by statutory instrument; and

(b) the designated officer for the court is notified by or on behalf of the prosecutor that the documents mentioned in subsection (3) below have been served upon the accused with the summons.

(2) The reference in subsection (1)(a) above to the issue of a summons requiring a person to appear before a magistrates' court other than a youth court includes a reference to the issue of a summons requiring a person who has attained the age of 16 at the time when it is issued to appear before a youth court.

(3) The documents referred to in subsection (1)(b) above are—

(a) a notice containing such statement of the effect of this section as may be prescribed;

(b) either of the following, namely—

(i) a concise statement of such facts relating to the charge as will be placed before the court by the prosecutor if the accused pleads guilty without appearing before the court, or

(ii) a copy of such written statement or statements complying with subsections (2)(a) and (b) and (3) of section 9 of the *Criminal Justice Act* 1967 (proof by written statement) as will be so placed in those circumstances; and

(c) if any information relating to the accused will or may, in those circumstances, be placed before the court by or on behalf of the prosecutor, a notice containing or describing that information.

(4) Where the designated officer for the court receives a notification in writing purporting to be given by the accused or by a legal representative acting on his behalf that the accused desires to plead guilty without appearing before the court—

(a) the designated officer for the court shall inform the prosecutor of the receipt of the notification; and

(b) the following provisions of this section shall apply:

(5) If at the time and place appointed for the trial or adjourned trial of the information—

(a) the accused does not appear; and

(b) it is proved to the satisfaction of the court, on oath or in such manner as may be prescribed, that the documents mentioned in subsection (3) above have been served upon the accused with the summons,

the court may, subject to section 11(3) and (4) above and subsections (6) to (8) below, proceed to hear and dispose of the case in the absence of the accused, whether or not the prosecutor is also absent, in like manner as if both parties had appeared and the accused had pleaded guilty.

(6) If at any time before the hearing the designated officer for the court receives an indication in writing purporting to be given by or on behalf of the accused that he wishes to withdraw the notification—

(a) the designated officer for the court shall inform the prosecutor of the withdrawal; and

(b) the court shall deal with the information as if the notification had not been given.

(7) Before accepting the plea of guilty and convicting the accused under subsection (5) above, the court shall cause the following to be read out before the court by the clerk of the court, namely—

(a) in a case where a statement of facts as mentioned in subsection (3)(b)(i) above was served on the accused with the summons, that statement;

(aa) in a case where a statement or statements as mentioned in subsection (3)(b)(ii) above was served on the accused with the summons and the court does not otherwise direct, that statement or those statements;

(b) any information contained in a notice so served, and any information described in such a notice and produced by or on behalf of the prosecutor;

(c) the notification under subsection (4) above; and

(d) any submission received with the notification which the accused wishes to be brought to the attention of the court with a view to mitigation of sentence.

(7A) Where the court gives a direction under subsection (7)(aa) above the court shall cause an account to be given orally before the court by the clerk of the court of so much of any statement as is not read aloud.

(7B) Whether or not a direction under paragraph (aa) of subsection (7) above is given in relation to any statement served as mentioned in that paragraph the court need not cause to be read out the declaration required by section 9(2)(b) of the *Criminal Justice Act* 1967.

(8) If the court proceeds under subsection (5) above to hear and dispose of the case in the absence of the accused, the court shall not permit—

(a) any other statement with respect to any facts relating to the offence charged; or

(b) any other information relating to the accused,

to be made or placed before the court by or on behalf of the prosecutor except on a resumption of the trial after an adjournment under section 10(3) above.

(9) If the court decides not to proceed under subsection (5) above to hear and dispose of the case in the absence of the accused, it shall adjourn or further adjourn the trial for the purpose of dealing with the information as if the notification under subsection (4) above had not been given.

(10) In relation to an adjournment on the occasion of the accused's conviction in his absence under subsection (5) above or to an adjournment required by subsection (9) above, the notice required by section 10(2) above shall include notice of the reason for the adjournment.

(11) No notice shall be required by section 10(2) above in relation to an adjournment—

(a) which is for not more than 4 weeks; and

(b) the purpose of which is to enable the court to proceed under subsection (5) above at a later time.

(12) No order shall be made under subsection (1) above unless a draft of the order has been laid before and approved by resolution of each House of Parliament.

(13) Any such document as is mentioned in subsection (3) above may be served in Scotland with a summons which is so served under the *Summary Jurisdiction (Process) Act* 1881.

Magistrates' Courts Act 1980, Sched. 3, para. 4

8–76 4.—(1) Notification or intimation for the purposes of subsections (2) and (3) of section 12 above may be given on behalf of a corporation by a director or the secretary of the corporation; and those subsections shall apply in relation to a notification or intimation purporting to be so given as they apply to a notification or intimation purporting to be given by an individual accused.

(2) In this paragraph "director", in relation to a corporation which is established by or under any enactment for the purpose of carrying on under national ownership any industry or part of an industry or undertaking and whose affairs are managed by the members thereof, means a member of that corporation.

8–77 The defendant may enter a plea of guilty by post if the conditions in s.12 of the *Magistrates' Courts Act* 1980 are met. Provided that the court receives the defendant's notification of a guilty plea by post before the hearing date, it does not matter that it was received after the return date specified in the summons: *Norham and Islandshire Justices* [1961] 1 W.L.R. 364. If there are several summonses it is essential that the defendant makes it clear to which one he is pleading guilty: *Burnham Bucks Justices, ex p. Ansorge* [1959] 1 W.L.R. 1041. If the offence is endorsable or disqualifiable, the defendant must also send his driving licence and a statement of his date of birth and his (or her) sex: *Road Traffic Offenders Act* 1988, s.8.

The defendant may withdraw a plea of guilty by post at any time before the hearing by giving the court written notice: *Magistrates' Courts Act* 1980, s.12(6); see also the-*Criminal Procedure Rules*, r.37.8– (3) in Appendix G *post* § G–229a. The court has jurisdiction at the hearing to allow a change of plea so that a defendant who has earlier pleaded guilty by post may contest the matter: *Bristol Justices, ex p. Sawyers* [1988] Crim.L.R. 754. In *Rymer v. DPP* [2011] 1 W.L.R. 188, the defendant pleaded guilty by post to a requisition requiring him to answer the written charge that he used a hand-held mobile phone whilst driving. The magistrates accepted his plea and adjourned the case as they were considering imposing a disqualification from driving. At the adjourned hearing his solicitor sought to change the defendant's plea to not guilty on the basis that he had an automatic right to do so under s.12(6). He argued that, at the earlier hearing, the court had not proceeded under s.12(5) to "hear and dispose of the case", but instead proceeded to exercise its power to adjourn under s.12(9) and therefore, under the provisions of that section, the guilty plea was to be regarded as not having been entered. The Divisional Court dismissed this argument; the magistrates had adjourned sentence having accepted a guilty plea and convicted the defendant. The words in s.12(9), "as if the notification of the written guilty plea had not been given", had no application, and the defendant's guilty pleas, and his consequent convictions, did not fall away when the justices adjourned his case. It followed that his ability to change his plea was at the discretion of the justices.

The notification of the guilty plea, the statement of facts served by the prosecution or the written statement under the *Criminal Justice Act* 1967, s.9 and any statements submitted in mitigation must be read out by the legal adviser in open court. Failure to do so will render the proceedings a nullity: *Oldham Justices, ex p. Morrissey* [1959] 1 W.L.R. 58; *Epping and Ongar Justices, ex p. Breach* [1987] R.T.R. 233. Such a defect cannot be remedied by s.142(2) of the *Magistrates' Courts Act* 1980 (see *post* § 11–1) because the defendant has not been found guilty but has simply notified his or her intention to plead guilty. The prosecution may serve a fresh summons upon the original information: *Epping and Ongar Justices, ante*.

The court has a residual discretion to decide that the case is not suitable to be dealt with by way of a plea of guilty by post. The court may adjourn the matter for the defendant to appear. The notice of adjournment sent to the defendant must specify the reason for the adjournment: *Mason* [1965] 2 All E.R. 308.

Magistrates' Courts Act 1980, s.12A

Application of section 12 where accused appears

12A.—(1) Where the designated officer has received such a notification as is mentioned in subsection (4) of section 12 above but the accused nevertheless appears before the court at the time and place appointed for the trial or adjourned trial, the court may, if he consents, proceed under subsection (5) of that section as if he were absent. **8–78**

(2) Where the designated officer has not received such a notification and the accused appears before the court at that time and place and informs the court that he desires to plead guilty, the court may, if he consents, proceed under section 12(5) above as if he were absent and the designated officer had received such a notification.

(3) For the purposes of subsections (1) and (2) above, subsections (6) to (11) of section 12 above shall apply with the modifications mentioned in subsection (4) or, as the case may be, subsection (5) below.

(4) The modifications for the purposes of subsection (1) above are that—

(a) before accepting the plea of guilty and convicting the accused under subsection (5) of section 12 above, the court shall afford the accused an opportunity to make an oral submission with a view to mitigation of sentence; and

(b) where he makes such a submission, subsection (7)(d) of that section shall not apply.

(5) The modifications for the purposes of subsection (2) above are that—

(a) subsection (6) of section 12 above shall apply as if any reference to the notification under subsection (4) of that section were a reference to the consent under subsection (2) above;

(b) subsection (7)(c) and (d) of that section shall not apply; and

(c) before accepting the plea of guilty and convicting the accused under subsection (5) of that section, the court shall afford the accused an opportunity to make an oral submission with a view to mitigation of sentence.

8–79 Sometimes a defendant will appear in court despite having sent a written plea of guilty by post. In those circumstances, the legal adviser will ask the defendant whether he wishes the guilty plea to stand and, if so, the written plea of guilty procedure will be followed save that the defendant will be offered an opportunity to address the court personally.

D. PLEA OF NOT GUILTY

8–80 Where the defendant pleads not guilty the court will proceed to trial. The case will generally be adjourned to a date when the witnesses can attend and which, within a reasonable timescale, is convenient to the parties. Courts should make clear to all defendants that if they fail to attend a trial it is likely that the court will proceed in absence and possibly without legal representation: *O'Hare* [2006] Crim.L.R. 950. Where a defendant is absent on the occasion of an adjournment the court must give him notice in writing of the trial date, place and time: *Criminal Procedure Rules*, r.37.11–(3) (Appendix G *post* § G–229d).

The court is under a duty, and the parties must assist, to manage the case so that it proceeds to trial on the date allocated. This will involve the early identification of the issues, the needs of witnesses, the making of appropriate orders and timetabling the case. The emphasis is on discouraging delay, avoiding unnecessary adjournments ensuring that the evidence is presented at trial in the shortest and most clear way and that only those witnesses who are really needed in relation to genuinely disputed, relevant issues should be required to attend the trial. The court and each party will nominate a case progression officer whose responsibility it is to progress the case, monitor any directions made and keep the court informed of progress. The responsibility must be exercised in a proactive rather than a reactive way, responding promptly to communications from other parties: *Criminal Procedure Rules*, r.3.1 *et seq.* (Appendix G *post* § G–3 to G–13). The court may adjourn the case to a specific case management hearing where trial readiness is assessed and further directions may be given. Immediately prior to entering a not guilty plea, the parties will have been expected to have completed the case management form prescribed in the Consolidated Criminal Practice Direction: *Criminal Procedure Rules*, r.3.11–(1) (Appendix G *post* § G–13).

The form may be found at: *http://www.justice.gov.uk/criminal/procrules_fin/docs/crimpr-2010-part3-magistrates-courts-prep-for-trial-form-Aug2010.pdf*.

The defendant is obliged to give advance notice of the names and certain details of his intended witnesses to the court and to the prosecutor: Criminal Procedure and Investigations Act 1996, s.6C (see *ante* § 6–47). The defence must normally do this within 14 days of the prosecutor serving initial disclosure: *Criminal Procedure and Investigations Act 1996 (Defence Disclosure Time Limits) Regulations* 2011, reg.2(2). The notice must give the name, address and date of birth of each such witness, or as many of those details as are known to the defendant when the notice is given, and, where any of those details are not known, provide any information in the defendant's possession which might be of material assistance in identifying or finding any such witness: see *Criminal Procedure Rules*, r.22.4 (Appendix G *post* § G–140c); the form of the defence witness notice is prescribed by the Consolidated Criminal Practice Direction. If the defence fail to comply with these requirements the prosecution may comment upon this at trial, and the court may draw such inferences as appear proper in deciding whether the defendant is guilty: *Criminal Procedure and Investigations Act* 1996, s.11 (see *post* § 10–146).

As to the principles and procedures for dealing with applications for the adjournment of trial, see *ante* § 7–154 *et seq.*

Where the defendant fails to attend on the date set for his trial, in the case of a defendant over the age of 18, there is a presumption that the court will proceed in his absence unless it appears to the court to be contrary to the interests of justice to do so; if the accused is under 18 the court has a discretion to proceed in his absence: *Magistrates' Courts Act* 1980, s.11. For a detailed commentary on s.11 see *ante* § 7–175 *et seq*. See also the *Consolidated Criminal Practice Direction* para. I.13.17 *et seq.* (*post* § F–18).

If the defendant has been excluded from the building because of his behaviour in the waiting area, he should be brought into court at the start of the trial and warned that he will he excluded from his trial if he disrupts proceedings: *R. (Davies) v. Solihull Justices* [2008] EWHC 1157 (Admin). A trial, even for a serious matter, may proceed in the absence of the accused and without him being represented: *Smith (Henry Lee)* [2007] Crim.L.R. 325. In this case the defendant was being tried at the Crown Court in respect of an allegation of unlawful wounding. He had dismissed his defence team and, when refused an application to transfer his representation order to another firm, he refused to co-operate, and refused to leave his cell. It was held that the judge had been left with no option but to proceed with the trial in the absence of the defendant.

Part II

E. FAILURE TO PLEAD

Where the defendant fails to plead to the information, the court will hear the evi- **8–81**
dence in accordance with s.9(2) of the *Magistrates' Courts Act* 1980 as if there had been a plea of not guilty.

F. CHANGE OF PLEA

A defendant may apply to withdraw a plea of guilty but must do so as soon as **8–82**
practicable after making his decision: *Criminal Procedure Rules*, r.37.9; Appendix G § G–229b *post*. It may only be done before the final disposal of the case whether by sentence or otherwise. The Rule puts the onus on the defendant to make the application and requires it be made in writing unless the court dispenses with that requirement. The defendant's written application must set out the reasons why it would be unjust for the plea to remain, indicate the evidence the defendant wishes to call, identify any proposed witness and, where a defendant is or has been represented, indicate whether legal professional privilege is waived. This application must be served on the prosecutor and the court.

The discretion to allow a defendant to vacate a plea of guilty must be exercised sparingly and circumspectly: *Sorhaindo* [2006] EWCA Crim 1429. This was a case in which the exercise of discretion on the part of the judge was said to have been flawed because he had failed to give weight to the fact that S had pleaded guilty on the basis of wrong advice. By contrast, where the defendant had experienced criminal lawyers who well understood that he should not plead guilty without truly being prepared to admit to each of the ingredients of the offence, the court upheld a judge's decision to refuse to allow a change of plea: *Kidd (Stephen Brian)* [2010] EWCA Crim 954.

If, after an unequivocal plea of guilty had been made, it became apparent that the defendant had not appreciated the elements of the offence to which he was pleading guilty, it was likely to be appropriate to permit him to withdraw his plea. Such a situation should be rare, for it was unlikely to arise where the defendant was represented and, where he was not, it was the duty of the court to make sure that the nature of the offence was made clear to him before a guilty plea was accepted. The onus lay on a party seeking to vacate a guilty plea to demonstrate that justice required that that should be permitted: *Revill v. DPP* [2007] 1 Cr App.R. 19. There is no automatic rule that a defendant who was unrepresented when the plea was entered is entitled to change the plea upon subsequently obtaining legal representation in the period before sentencing: *South Tameside Magistrates' Court, ex p. Rowland* [1983] 3 All E.R. 689.

Where the defendant is represented and it becomes apparent that the advocate has advised the defendant to plead guilty under a mistaken view of the nature of the charge, the court should consider whether a change of plea should be allowed on the basis of equivocality: *P. Foster (Haulage) Ltd v. Roberts* [1978] 2 All E.R. 751.

A guilty plea could only found a conviction and bring to an end the presumption of innocence where it was unequivocal. However, where a defendant made an unequivocal plea of guilty which the court accepted, the defendant was thereupon "proved guilty according to law" within the meaning of art. 6(2) of the European Convention on Human Rights: *Revitt v. DPP, ante*.

8–83 Where a plea of guilty is withdrawn, evidence of that plea as a confession of fact is admissible at the trial. The court should, however, carefully balance the probative value of such evidence against its prejudicial nature and will not normally admit it: *Rimmer* [1972] 1 W.L.R. 268.

Where a defendant changes his plea from not guilty to guilty, it is improper for the court to inquire into the defendant's reasons or motives for the change of plea unless the new plea is equivocal: *Eccles Justices, ex p. Fitzpatrick*, 89 Cr.App.R. 324.

The case of *Bow Street Magistrates' Court, ex p. Welcombe* (1992) 156 J.P. 609 is authority for saying that upon a change of plea, where the offence is triable either way, the court should proceed to allow the defendant to consider whether to consent to summary trial. This case was heard before the plea before venue procedure was introduced. It is submitted that the same principles should now apply.

8–84 Once the court has pronounced sentence it is *functus officio* and the conviction recorded upon the plea of guilty can be challenged only by way of appeal to the Crown Court. Where it is clear that a mistake has arisen, however, the court may consider its powers under s.142(2) of the *Magistrates' Courts Act* 1980 (see *post* § 11–1 *et seq.*).

Similarly, if a plea of guilty is unequivocal the court should not make use of section 142 to allow it to be withdrawn in order to substitute a plea of not guilty: *Croydon Youth Court, ex p. DPP* [1997] 2 Cr.App.R. 411.

V. PRELIMINARY ISSUES

A. GENERAL

8–85 The *Criminal Procedure Rules*, r.37.3–37.6, set out the order of evidence and speeches in a summary trial: (Appendix G *post* § G–225—G–228). The *Rules* are designed to ensure that, so far as is possible, preliminary matters have been raised, and where possible determined, in advance of the trial date; these issues may include any amendment to the charge or information, fitness to plead, pleas of *autrefois acquit* or convict, abuse of process, and any issues of public interest immunity. Courts are also enjoined by the *Rules* to determine applications relating to the admissibility of evidence as preliminary points prior to any trial, and are given powers to make such determinations without a hearing, although it is the general practice of magistrates' courts to list such applications for a hearing.

The *Criminal Procedure Rules* also give courts powers to give directions relating to the conduct of the trial itself, and require courts to consider setting a timetable for the trial: r.3.10 (Appendix G *post* § G–12). In timetabling the trial, courts have power to require the parties to identify which witnesses are to be called, and to give directions as to the order in which those witnesses will give evidence, and the duration of any examination and cross-examination; time limits can also be set for any opening or closing speeches.

A magistrates' court determines its own procedure within statutory restraints: *Epping and Ongar Justices, ex p. Manby* [1986] Crim L.R. 555. Where there has been a procedural failure in the exercise of a statutory power the court should first ask itself whether the intention of the legislature was that any act done following that procedural failure should be invalid. This has been held to be a better approach that concentrating on whether a provision was mandatory or directory: *Soneji* [2006] 1 A.C. 340. The concept was enunciated in more colourful terms in *Soneji* by Lord Rodger of Earlsferry:

"If your young daughter wants to go out with friends for the evening and you agree, but tell her that she must be home by 23.00, she is under a duty to return by then. But this does not mean that her duty is to return by then or not at all. Rather, even if she fails to meet your deadline, she still remains under a duty to return home. On the other hand, if you contract with a conjuror to perform at your daughter's birthday party, you want the conjuror and his tricks only for the party. His duty is accordingly limited to performing at the party held on your daughter's birthday and, if he fails to turn up, he cannot discharge the duty later."

However, the House of Lords has more recently expressed caution over what Lord Bingham described as the "sea change wrought by" the decision in *Soneji*. In *Clarke and McDaid* [2008] 2 Cr.App.R. 2, Lord Bingham commented:

"Technicality is always distasteful when it appears to contradict the merits of a case. But the duty of the court is to apply the law, which is sometimes technical, and it may be thought that if the state exercises its coercive power to put a citizen on trial for serious crime a certain degree of formality is not out of place."

For a more detailed commentary on dealing with procedural irregularities see *ante* § 7–10.

B. FITNESS TO PLEAD

Unlike the Crown Court, there is no specific procedure in the magistrates' courts for determining a person's fitness to plead. The court may, if the offence is triable either way, commit him to the Crown Court to have the question of fitness determined by a jury. The procedure to be followed by magistrates' courts when dealing with such issues is provided for by a combination of s.37(3) of the *Mental Health Act* 1983 (see *post* § 28–20), used in conjunction with s.1(1) of the *Powers of Criminal Courts (Sentencing) Act* 2000 (see *post* § 23-1). Those sections provide a complete framework for the determination by the magistrates' court, itself a creature of statute, of all issues that arise in cases of defendants who are, or might be, mentally ill or suffering from severe mental impairment in the context of offences which are triable only summarily: *R. (P) v. Barking Youth Court* [2002] 2 Cr.App.R. 19. **8–86**

The defence of insanity can be relied upon in the magistrates' court. In contrast to the position in the Crown Court, there is no "special verdict" available in the magistrates' court and if the defence of insanity is established, the defendant must be acquitted, and it is not possible to revert to the procedure under s.37(3). However, there is no entitlement to a trial of the issue of insanity. If it is clear that it is a possibility, the magistrates' court should invite submissions upon the course to be adopted. In particular, careful consideration must be given to any reason advanced as to why the issue of insanity should be tried. Such an application should be resolved having regard to the interests of justice. Even if an order under s.37(3) is likely, an accused is entitled to a full consideration of whether there should be a trial of the issue of insanity: *R. (Surat Singh) v.Stratford Magistrates' Court* [2008] 1 Cr.App.R. 2. This was a case in which the defendant had pleaded not guilty to assault; although he formally admitted the facts, he sought to advance a defence of insanity. A psychiatric report indicated that at the time of the offence the defendant suffered from a defect of reason from a disease of the mind as not to know the nature and quality of his act. It was not suggested that the defendant was unfit to stand trial. The District Judge declined to consider the defence of insanity, and adjourned the trial for a second psychiatric report to be prepared under s.11(1) of the *Powers of Criminal Courts (Sentencing) Act* 2000 with a view to proceeding under s.37(3) of the *Mental Health Act* 1983; the Divisional Court upheld this decision.

The usual procedure is that, if the defendant is thought to be suffering from a mental disability, the court or the defence will request psychiatric reports. Many magistrates' courts have an on site facility to produce such reports. The prosecutor may, in the light of such a report, decide not to proceed with the charge. Alternatively, the court may hear evidence and, having satisfied itself that the defendant did the act or made an omission but without convicting him, make an order under s.37 of the *Mental Health Act* 1983.

In proceedings against co-defendants, if one of the defendants were to become "unfit", the trial of the issue of his guilt would come to an end, but the proceedings can continue in order to determine as a fact, whether he had committed the actus reus: *R. v. B* [2009] 1 Cr.App.R. 19.

For a more detailed commentary on dealing with mentally disordered offenders, see *post*—Ch.28.

C. AUTREFOIS ACQUIT AND AUTREFOIS CONVICT

8–87 A person cannot be tried for an offence if he or she has previously been acquitted or convicted of the same, or substantially the same, offence: *Connelly v. DPP* [1964] A.C. 1254. There is no special procedure in the magistrates' courts for pleading *autrefois acquit* or *autrefois convict*; an actual plea of *autrefois acquit* or *autrefois convict* can only be raised at a trial on indictment. Although the pleas cannot be entered in a magistrates' court, the principles giving rise to such pleas are the same as in the *Crown Court: DPP v. Porthouse*, 89 Cr.App.R. 21. In that case May, L.J. summarised what those principles are:

> "The rules of *autrefois convict* and acquit are rooted in *nemo debet bis vexari*. A defendant is twice-vexed only when he was in peril of a valid conviction upon his first trial. Accordingly *autrefois convict* is not available unless the first trial was before a lawfully constituted court, having jurisdiction in the matter, and trying an offence known to the law in accordance with law. An acquitted defendant has been at peril if he has been at risk of such a conviction."

The defendant, however, has the burden of proving on the balance of probabilities that there has been a previous conviction or acquittal on the merits: *Coughlan and Young*, 63 Cr.App.R. 33.

For a plea of *autrefois acquit* to succeed the defendant must have been put in genuine jeopardy at an earlier hearing: *Dabhade* [1993] Q.B. 329, 96 Cr.App.R. 146. There must have been a hearing on the merits: *Pressick* [1978] Crim.L.R. 377. A procedural irregularity resulting in an acquittal is not sufficient to put a defendant in jeopardy: *Williams v. DPP*, 93 Cr.App.R. 319; neither is the situation where a defendant has been charged and acquitted of an offence unknown to law: *DPP v. Porthouse* (*ante*). The withdrawal of a summons does not equate with an acquittal: *Grays Justices, ex p. Low* [1990] 1 Q.B. 54, 88 Cr.App.R. 291.

The Special Immigration Appeals Commission (SIAC) is not a "competent" court for the purposes of criminal proceedings and therefore a defendant in criminal proceedings cannot avail himself of the double jeopardy rule on the grounds that he has been detained by SIAC on substantially the same or overlapping set of facts i.e. terrorism; the court is not deciding the same issue and he is not in jeopardy of a conviction; both sets of proceedings must be criminal: *R. v. K, B and A* [2007] 2 Cr.App.R. 15. Punishable acts of importing and exporting the same drug prosecuted in different Schengen signatory states are to be considered the same acts: *Van Straaten v. Netherlands*, [2006] All ER (D) 142 (Sep); see also *Gasparini* [2007] 1 C.M.L.R. 12. It is not the legal classification but the nature of the acts which matters: *Van Esbroeck* [2006] 3 C.M.L.R. 6. A person should not be tried for offences on an ascending scale of seriousness: *Beedie* [1997] 2 Cr.App.R. 167. In such circumstances the defendant may also plead *autrefois acquit* or *autrefois convict*.

In *CPS v. Tweddell* [2001] A.C.D. 83, it was held that there could be no abuse in merely pursuing criminal proceedings based upon the same facts as had been the subject matter of a contempt hearing. In this case the defendant had been sentenced to three months' imprisonment in contempt proceedings, but the Divisional Court observed that contempt proceedings and criminal proceedings had different purposes.

8–88 Where a prosecutor has been properly asked to choose upon which information to proceed, the plea of *autrefois acquit* cannot be raised. If a charge is summarily dismissed because the prosecution recognises the difficulties which exist in prosecuting that charge, and a new charge is substituted, a plea of *autrefois acquit* on the first charge cannot be made: *Broadbent v. High* [1985] R.T.R. 359. If there has been an acquittal of a lesser offence which contains the same ingredients of a greater offence the defendant cannot be convicted in a subsequent trial of the greater offence because the conviction would effectively reverse the acquittal for the lesser offence. A defendant could still be found guilty of the full offence, however, if he was acquitted of an attempt to commit that offence: *Velasquez* [1996] 1 Cr.App.R. 155.

A note of judicial caution has been expressed about the practice in magistrates' court of dismissing a charge on which a decision has been made not to proceed, before having heard and disposed of another charge, founded on the same facts. In *Porthouse* (*ante*) May, L.J. commented that magistrates should be "very careful about the procedural steps they take in these and similar circumstances". In making this comment, May, L.J. was reflecting the comments made by Watkins, L.J. in *Broadbent v. High* (*ante*) when he said:

> "It would of course have been preferable had the justices stayed their hand with regard to the first information until they had heard the evidence on the second information and adjudicated upon it. . . . As to whether they had, procedurally, acted prudently: it seems to me that justices must beware not to deal with an information on which it has been decided not to proceed until the information which is to be heard has been heard and disposed of."

Part II

This problem was illustrated in *R. (A.) v. South Staffordshire Magistrates' Court*, (2007) 171 J.P. 36. In this case the defendant appeared before the youth court and was charged with assault occasioning actual bodily harm contrary to s.47 of the *Offences Against the Person Act* 1861. The CPS subsequently preferred a charge of causing grievous bodily harm contrary to s.20 of that Act, and offered no evidence in relation to the initial charge under s.47; that charge was formally dismissed. However, during the trial of the matter the CPS indicated that it would withdraw the s.20 charge if the defendant pleaded guilty to a charge under s.47. The defendant entered a guilty plea and then argued that the s.47 allegation against him had been disposed of when the court formally dismissed that charge at the earlier hearing, and that he was entitled to rely on the doctrine of *autrefois acquit*. It was held by the Divisional Court that the *Magistrates' Courts Act* 1980, s.27, which provided that the dismissal of an information would have the same effect as an acquittal on indictment, entitled the defendant to claim *autrefois acquit*.

If the court acquits when acting outside its jurisdiction a plea of autrefois acquit can- **8–89**
not be made: *West* [1964] 1 Q.B. 15, 46 Cr.App.R. 296. In this case the magistrates had purported to dismiss a charge which was triable on indictment only.

Where an information had been dismissed for want of prosecution and duplicate proceedings started, the plea of *autrefois acquit* was not open to the defendant nor were the proceedings per se an abuse of the process: *Willesden Justices, ex p. Clemmings*, 87 Cr.App.R. 280.

The principles of autrefois convict and autrefois acquit apply only where there has been a finding by a court of guilt or innocence. Where a defendant is cautioned for an offence, notwithstanding that it will only be administered if the accused admits his guilt, since a caution is not a conviction the defence of autrefois convict is not available: *DPP v. Alexander:* [2011] 1 W.L.R. 653. However, where criminal conduct has been the subject of an agreed caution it may constitute an abuse of the process of the court, absent good reason, for it to be the subject of a subsequent prosecution (see *post* § 8–93 and 8–94).

D. ABUSE OF PROCESS

The general principles

The court will refuse to allow the prosecution to proceed where it considers that the **8–90**
prosecution amounts to an abuse of the process of the court. However, the power to

stop a prosecution should only be used in most exceptional circumstances: *DPP v. Humphrys* [1977] A.C. 1, 63 Cr.App.R. 95; *Oxford City Justices, ex p. Smith*, 75 Cr.App.R. 200. In *Derby Crown Court, ex p. Brooks*, 80 Cr.App.R. 164, Sir Roger Ormrod, giving the judgment of the Court, said:

"The power to stop a prosecution arises only when it is an abuse of the process of the court. It may be an abuse of process if either (a) the prosecution have manipulated or misused the process of the court so as to deprive the defendant of a protection provided by the law or to take unfair advantage of a technicality, or (b) on the balance of probability, the defendant has been, or will be, prejudiced in the preparation or conduct of his defence by delay on the part of the prosecution which is unjustifiable. . . . The ultimate objective of this discretionary power is to ensure that there should be a fair trial accordingly to law, which involves fairness both to the defendant and the prosecution"

What constitutes an abuse of process was summarised in the judgement of Sir John Dyson SCJ in the Supreme Court's decision in *Maxwell* [2010] UKSC 48, 13:

"It is well established that the court has the power to stay proceedings in two categories of case, namely (i) where it will be impossible to give the accused a fair trial, and (ii) where it offends the court's sense of justice and propriety to be asked to try the accused in the particular circumstances of the case. In the first category of case, if the court concludes that an accused cannot receive a fair trial, it will stay the proceedings without more. No question of the balancing of competing interests arises. In the second category of case, the court is concerned to protect the integrity of the criminal justice system. Here a stay will be granted where the court concludes that in all the circumstances a trial will 'offend the court's sense of justice and propriety' (per Lord Lowry in *R. v. Horseferry Road Magistrates' Court, Ex p Bennett* [1994] 1 AC 42, 74G) or will 'undermine public confidence in the criminal justice system and bring it into disrepute' (per Lord Steyn in *R. v. Latif* [1996] 1 W.L.R. 104, 112F)."

8–91 However, the jurisdiction exercised by magistrates to deal with issues of abuse of process is strictly confined to matters directly affecting the fairness of the trial of the particular accused with whom they are dealing, and does not extend to the wider supervisory jurisdiction for upholding the rule of law that is vested in the High Court: *Horseferry Road Magistrates' Court, Ex p. Bennett* [1994] 1 A.C. 42, 98 Cr.App.R. 114. Where a question arises as to the deliberate abuse of the court's procedures, the magistrates should adjourn the matter so that an application can be made to the Divisional Court. Where a defendant seeks to establish that the second limb of the abuse of process test applies, it is essential that this is identified at an early point in proceedings. Either the proceedings can be adjourned pending a decision of the High Court, or judicial review sought of the decision to prosecute. A pragmatic step would be for a magistrates' court to make findings of fact that might be determinative of a prosecution before the question of abuse of process was addressed: *Nembhard v. DPP*, [2009] EWHC 194 (Admin), [2009] All E.R. (D) 145 (Jan).

The second limb of the abuse of process test was discussed by the House of Lords in *Latif* [1996] 2 Cr.App.R. 92, and Lord Steyn observed:

""The law is settled. Weighing countervailing considerations of policy and justice, it is for the judge in the exercise of his discretion to decide whether there has been an abuse of process, which amounts to an affront to the public conscience and requires the criminal proceedings to be stayed: *R. v. Horseferry Road Magistrates' Court, ex parte Bennett* (1994) 98 Cr.App.R. 114, [1994] 1 A.C. 42. *Bennett* was a case where a stay was appropriate because a defendant had been forcibly abducted and brought to this country to face trial in disregard of extradition laws. The speeches in *Bennett* conclusively establish that proceedings may be stayed in the exercise of the judge's discretion not only where a fair trial is impossible but also where it would be contrary to the public interest in the integrity of the criminal justice system that a trial should take place. An infinite variety of cases could arise. General guidance as to how the discretion should be exercised in particular circumstances will not be useful. But it is possible to say that in a case such as the present the judge must weigh in the balance the public interest in ensuring that those that are charged with grave crimes should be tried and the competing public interest in not conveying the impression that the court will adopt the approach that the end justifies any means."

Lord Steyn's comments were echoed by Lord Dyson in the decision of the Privy

Council in *Warren v. Attorney General of Jersey* [2011] UKPC 10:

"But rigid classifications are undesirable. It is clear from Latif. . . . that the balance must always be struck between the public interest in ensuring that those who are accused of serious crimes should be tried and the competing public interest in ensuring that executive misconduct does not undermine public confidence in the criminal justice system and bring it into disrepute."

Although it is not possible to apply rigid classifications of the type of case falling within the second category of abuse of process cases, there are some instances where courts will generally conclude that the balance described by Lord Steyn favours a stay. Examples include unlawful abduction cases: *Ex p Bennett* (*ante*); entrapment cases, *Looseley* [2002] 1 Cr.App.R. 29; and cases which involve the breach of an assurance that there will be no prosecution in particular circumstances such as those that occurred in *Croydon Justices, ex p Dean* [1993] Q.B. 769, [1994] 98 Cr.App.R. 76 (see *post* § 8–93).

The burden of proof

The onus is on the accused to show, on a balance of probabilities, that a fair trial is no longer possible: *Telford Justices, ex p. Badhan*, [1991] 2 Q.B. 78. Where the defence alleges *mala fides* by the prosecutor there is a heavy burden on them to prove this: *Great Yarmouth Magistrates, ex p. Thomas* [1992] Crim.L.R. 116. In the context of delay, it was held in *Tan v. Cameron* [1992] 2 A.C. 205, that to be granted a stay the defendant must show on the balance of probabilities that owing to the delay he would suffer such prejudice as to deny him a fair trial, which would render the continuance of the prosecution a abuse of the process of the court; the burden of demonstrating this was a heavy one and remained throughout on the defendant. **8–92**

The court must determine an application to stay proceedings for an abuse of process on the material provided by both the prosecution and defence. In *Clerkenwell Magistrates' Court, ex p. Bell*, 155 J.P. 669, the defendant argued that the proceedings should be stayed because they had been so delayed that he could not receive a fair trial. The magistrate heard evidence from a police officer explaining the delay, but declined to hear the defendant. The Divisional Court held that the refusal to hear the defendant's evidence constituted a breach of natural justice because any possible prejudice to him by reason of the delay was a relevant matter for the magistrate to consider.

Decisions to prosecute

In *ex p Dean* (*ante*), the prosecution of a person who had received a promise from the police during a murder enquiry that he would not be prosecuted for his involvement in the matter was held to be capable of being an abuse of the process of the court notwithstanding the absence of bad faith on the part of the police. In that case the court concluded that the police had told the applicant that he would not be prosecuted and, having particular regard to his age (17), it was held to be an abuse of process for him to be prosecuted subsequently; the justices ought to have treated the case as one of abuse of process and enabled an application to have been made to the Divisional Court rather than continue with committal proceedings. Some emphasis has subsequently been placed upon the fact that in *ex p Dean*, after the defendant had been given assurances that he would not be prosecuted, he volunteered information in circumstances where he was neither under caution nor acting with the benefit of legal advice, and he acted to his detriment. It does not follow that in every case where a defendant is given such an assurance, that subsequent prosecution will be held in be a abuse of process. In *Abu Hamza* [2007] Q.B. 659, [2007] 1 Cr.App.R. 27, Lord Phillips, C.J. said: **8–93**

"Circumstances can exist where it will be an abuse of process to prosecute a man for conduct in respect of which he has been given an assurance that no prosecution will be brought. It is by no means easy to define a test for those circumstances, other than to say that they must be such as to render the proposed prosecution an affront to justice. The judge expressed reservations as to the extent to which one can apply the common law principle of "legitimate expectation" in this field, and we share those reservations. That principle usually applies to the expectation

Part II

generated in respect of the exercise of an administrative discretion by or on behalf of the person whose duty it is to exercise that discretion. The duty to prosecute offenders cannot be treated as an administrative discretion, for it is usually in the public interest that those who are reasonably suspected of criminal conduct should be brought to trial. Only in rare circumstances will it be offensive to justice to give effect to this public interest."

In *R. (Guest) v. Director of Public Prosecutions* [2009] 2 Cr.App.R. 26, the Divisional Court quashed a decision to offer an offender a conditional caution for a serious assault, and doubted whether it would be possible to argue that any subsequent prosecution would be an abuse of process based upon the proposition that the original offer of a conditional caution constituted an undertaking not to prosecute the offender. It was pointed out that, unlike the situation in *ex p Dean*, the defendant had not acted to his detriment as a result of the initial decision to offer a conditional caution. Likewise, a private prosecution is not automatically an abuse of process where a defendant has already received a police caution: *Hayter v. L.* [1998] 1 W.L.R. 854. It could, however, be an abuse of process where a person had agreed to a caution on the assurance that he would not have to go before a criminal court: *Jones v. Whalley* [2006] 3 W.L.R. 179.

The underlying principle is that it is for prosecutors to decide when to prosecute a case. In *Wandsworth LBC v. Rashid*, 173 J.P. 547, it was held that the magistrates' finding that it would have been reasonable for the local authority to take another course of action other than prosecution did not necessarily lead to a conclusion that the decision to prosecute amounted to an abuse of process. The local authority was not required to go through each of the other possible courses of action in order to justify the lawfulness of its decision to prosecute. It was only when an abuse was plainly shown that a court should intervene. It was also held in that case that magistrates should only take into account the evidence available to the prosecuting authority when the information was laid. In *R. v. B, P, and C* [2010] 2 Cr.App.R. 35, it was held that a judge had no power at common law to halt proceedings simply because he did not believe that they were appropriately brought; the *Criminal Procedure Rules* did not expressly or by implication include a power to alter that position.

8–94 However there is a limited category of cases in which the courts appear to have been more interventionist in relation to decisions to prosecute. On occasion courts have required departures from a prosecutor's policy in relation to criminal proceedings to be justified, particularly in relation to the prosecution of children and young persons. In *R. (Mondelly) v. Commissioner of Police of the Metropolis*, 171 J.P. 121, Moses, L.J. commented that where the courts have intervened in such decisions, they have done so with reluctance, "ever mindful of the need not to interfere with operational decisions by those best placed to meet the demands of the practical application of the criminal law". In Chief Constable of the *Kent County Constabulary ex p. L (a minor)* [1991] 93 Cr.App.R. 416, Watkins, L.J. concluded that:

> "In respect of juveniles, the discretion of the CPS to continue or discontinue criminal proceedings is reviewable by this court but only where it can be demonstrated that the decision was made regardless of or clearly contrary to a settled policy at the Director of Public Prosecutions evolved in the public interest, for example the policy of cautioning juveniles, a policy which the CPS are bound to apply where appropriate to the exercise of their discretion to continue or discontinue criminal proceedings. But I envisage that it would be only rarely that a defendant could succeed in showing that a decision was fatally flawed in such a manner as that."

In *Jones v. DPP* [2011] EWHC 50 (Admin), the Divisional Court rejected the defendant's claim that his prosecution for exceeding the speed limit should be stayed as it was in breach of a prosecuting authority's clear and settled policy not to enforce the speed limit on a particular stretch of road, in circumstances where the policy was itself based upon a misinterpretation of the law in relation to road signage. The court concluded that, contrary to the defendant's assertions, right thinking people would conclude that in those circumstances a decision not to prosecute would bring the administration of justice into disrepute.

In *Bloomfield* [1997] 1 Cr.App.R. 135at a plea and directions hearing in the Crown Court, prosecuting counsel indicated to defence counsel that the prosecution wished to offer no evidence because it was accepted that the defendant had been the victim of a set-up. The prosecution subsequently altered its position, and decided to continue with the prosecution. The Court of Appeal held that whether or not there was a prejudice to the defendant it would bring the administration of justice into disrepute to allow the Crown to revoke the original decision without any reason being given as to what was wrong with it. Staughton L.J., giving the judgment of the court, said:

> "The statement of the prosecution that they would offer no evidence at the next hearing was not merely a statement made to the defendant or to his legal representative. It was made coram judice, in the presence of the judge. It seems to us that whether or not there was prejudice it would bring the administration of justice into disrepute if the Crown Prosecution Service were able to treat the court as if it were at its beck and call, free to tell it one day that it was not going to prosecute and another day that it was."

In *R. (H) v. Guildford Youth Court* [2008] EWHC 506 (Admin), H applied for judicial review of a decision of the youth court to refuse to stay a prosecution against him for an offence of grievous bodily harm. During police interview H had admitted the offence and it had been indicated that the matter would be dealt with by way of a final warning. However, the matter was subsequently referred to the CPS and he was charged. H contended that the decision to prosecute was an abuse of process as he had a legitimate expectation that the matter would be dealt with by way of a final warning. The Administrative Court (Silber, J.) held that the fact that a promise was made by an officer of the State, namely the police officer who was at that stage in charge of deciding whether or not to prosecute, is something that there is a clear public interest in upholding. He said that the argument that a distinguishing feature in this case might be the seriousness of the charge was not a valid factor. In reaching his decision in this appeal, the judge placed some emphasis on the fact that there had not been an adequate explanation given to justify the decision of the CPS. It is submitted that this decision may be limited to the particular facts in that case.

Part II

Vexatious proceedings

However, in *Belmarsh Magistrates Court, ex p. Watts* [1999] 2 Cr.App.R. 188, the **8–95** Divisional Court held that as a magistrate had jurisdiction to refuse to issue a summons that was vexatious, he also had jurisdiction to stay proceedings on such a summons at a later stage. This decision was applied in *R. (Craik, Chief Constable of Northumbria) v. Newcastle Upon Tyne Magistrates' Court* [2010] A.C.D. 55, where it was held that a district judge could, and should, have refused to issue the summons against a chief constable in circumstances where the proceedings against him were hopelessly misconceived and, therefore, vexatious and an abuse of process. The Divisional Court went on to comment that, having issued the summons, the district judge could, and should, have exercised his discretion to stay the proceedings. Whether or not there was bad faith, to pursue a case that was hopelessly misconceived, vexatious and an abuse of process, was to be guilty of the kind of serious misconduct that "amply merited, indeed required", the exercise by the magistrates' court of its power to stay proceedings as an abuse of process.

Likewise, an attempt to prefer fresh charges against a defendant based on similar charges already rejected in old-style committal proceedings is vexatious and frivolous and an abuse of process: *Horsham Justices, ex p. Reeves*, 75 Cr.App.R. 236.

Effective participation in proceedings

In *R. (P) v. West London Youth Court* [2006] 1 Cr.App.R. 25, the defendant ap- **8–96** plied to stay proceedings for abuse of process on the basis that his intellectual capacity was such that he could not effectively participate in the proceedings in accordance with the requirements of the right to a fair trial under ECHR art. 6. It was held that a fair trial could be achieved since the youth court is a specialist court designed and adapted for hearing cases where young people are charged with criminal offences. Specialist judges with the requisite training sit in the youth court, and they have experience in dealing with the kind of problems presented by young people whose intellectual capacity might be more limited. It was emphasised that the judge hearing the trial had a continuing jurisdiction to stay proceedings for abuse of process if it became apparent during the course of the hearing that the defendant was unable effectively to participate. This was said to be a better course than staying a prosecution at the outset.

In *R. (C) v. Sevenoaks Youth Court* [2010] 1 All E.R. 735, C had serious psychological problems and a psychologist reported to the court that although C understood the charges against him, the nature of his plea, and that he was fit for trial, he would have great difficulty with the trial process itself as his ability to concentrate, assimilate large amounts of information, and challenge the evidence, would be limited. The Divisional Court held that although a youth court had no statutory power to appoint an intermediary, it did have a duty, both under the common law and in seeking to achieve the overriding objective as set out in the *Criminal Procedure Rules*, to appoint an intermediary if such an appointment was necessary to ensure a young defendant received a fair trial and could participate effectively.

In *DPP v. P* [2008] 1 W.L.R. 1005, P applied for proceedings before a youth court to be stayed as an abuse of process on the ground that his intellectual capacity was such that he could not participate effectively in the proceedings. The previous year, unrelated criminal proceedings brought against P in the Crown Court were stayed on the ground that he was unfit to plead. The Divisional Court held that although the youth court had an inherent jurisdiction to stay proceedings as an abuse of process at any stage, it was only in exceptional cases that a stay should be granted on the ground of a child defendant's capacity, before any evidence was heard. Giving the judgment of the court, Smith, L.J. said that medical evidence would rarely provide the whole answer to the question of whether a child ought to be tried, and should in most cases be considered as part of the evidence in the case rather than as the sole evidence on a freestanding application for a stay. He went on to say that if, at any stage, the court decided to halt the trial on the ground that the child was not able to participate effectively in it, it should consider exercising its discretion to inquire into whether he had done the act alleged with a view to the possibility of exercising its power under s.37(3) of the *Mental Health Act* 1983 to make a hospital order without convicting him. He said that such a fact-finding inquiry was protective rather than criminal in nature, and did not therefore engage the child's rights under ECHR art. 6, and the fact that he could not take an effective part in it did not render it unfair. It was also said that the fact that the Crown Court had previously determined that the defendant was unfit to plead did not mean that it was an abuse of process to try a defendant for subsequent criminal acts; questions about a child's capacity were essentially factual, to be determined on the basis of all the information available at the time of the decision.

Delay

8–97 In order to stay proceedings on the grounds of delay, the court must be satisfied that the delay is such that either a fair hearing is no longer possible, or it is for any compelling reason unfair to try the defendant. Even where the delay can be said to be unjustifiable, the imposition of a permanent stay should be the exception rather than the rule: *Att.-Gen.'s Reference (No.1 of 1990)* [1992] Q.B. 630, 95 Cr.App.R. 296. In that case the Court of Appeal went on to explain that it would be still more rare that a stay can be properly imposed in the absence of any fault on the part of the complainant or prosecution. Delay due merely to the complexity of the case, or contributed to by the actions of the defendant himself, should never be the foundation for a stay. No stay should be imposed unless the defendant can show that, on the balance of probabilities, due to delay he would suffer serious prejudice to the extent that no fair trial could be held, *i.e.*, that the continuance of the prosecution amounted to a misuse of the process of the court. The Court emphasised the exceptional nature of the jurisdiction (to stay proceedings on the ground of delay), and said that a stay will not be the appropriate course if the unfairness can be cured by exercise of the court's discretion within the trial process. Where a court refuses a stay on such grounds, the appropriate procedure is for the trial to proceed in accordance with that ruling and, if necessary, the point should be argued as part of any subsequent appeal; proceedings should not generally be further delayed in order to seek an interlocutory ruling on the point.

If through the action or inaction of a public authority, a criminal charge was not determined within a reasonable time there was necessarily a breach of the defendant's rights under ECHR art. 6(1) for which he was entitled, pursuant to s.8(1) of the *Human Rights Act* 1998, to a remedy: the appropriate remedy would depend on the nature of the breach and all the circumstances: *Att.-Gen.'s Reference (No.2 of 2001)* [2004] 2 A.C. 72, [2004] 1 Cr.App.R. 25. In that case the House of Lords held (Lords Hope and Rogers dissenting) that the public interest in the final determination of criminal charges required that charges should not be stayed or dismissed if any lesser remedy would be just and proportionate in all the circumstances; such remedies might include a declaration, a reduction of sentence or compensation, all of which fall short of a stay. The category of cases in which it might be unfair to try a defendant includes cases of bad faith, unlawfulness and executive manipulation, but is not confined to such cases; such cases will be "exceptional". **8–98**

This approach has been followed in other jurisdictions. In *Williams* [2009] 2 N.Z.L.R. 750 Supreme Court of NZ, it was held that a stay is neither a mandatory nor a usual remedy; a stay is likely to be the correct remedy only if the delay has been egregious, or there has been prosecutorial misconduct, or a sanction is required against a prosecutor who does not proceed promptly to trial after being directed by a court to do so.

Giving the leading judgment of the House of Lords in *Att.-Gen.'s Reference (No.2 of 2001) (ante)*, Lord Bingham discussed the power of a court to stay proceedings on the ground of delay, and sought to place the exercise of this power in the context of Convention jurisprudence. He said that in determining whether to impose a stay, the court should not be concerned so much with the reasonable time requirement, as with the ECHR art. 6 fair trial guarantee.

> "If the court were satisfied, before an impending trial, that the prosecution had been guilty of serious delay such as to cause serious prejudice to the accused, to the point that no fair trial could be held, or if the authorities were shown to have acted in such a way as to render any trial of the defendant unfair in the circumstances, further proceedings would be restrained as an abuse of the court's process by imposition of a stay: *Attorney-General's Reference (No 1 of 1990)* (1992) 95 Cr.App.R 296, [1992] 1 Q.B. 630; *R. v. Horseferry Road Magistrates' Court, Ex p. Bennett* (1994) 98 Cr.App.R. 114. If such abuse were shown after the trial, any resulting conviction would be quashed. Such is the rule in domestic law, and it is uncontroversial. It is consistent with the Convention. But it rests, in Convention terms, on the fair trial guarantee and not on the reasonable time requirement."

The House of Lords also confirmed that in considering whether a criminal charge has been determined within a reasonable time for the purposes of art. 6, the relevant time will normally start to run from the date when the defendant is charged by the police or served with a summons. Any period prior to a formal charge may be considered if the defendant has during that period been substantially affected by the conduct of the prosecution but time would not ordinarily run until after a suspect had been interviewed under caution. Arrest would not ordinarily mark the beginning of the period but an official indication that a person would be reported with a view to prosecution might do so. The interviewing of a person for the purposes of a regulatory inquiry would not meet the test: *Fayed v. UK* (1994) 18 E.H.R.R. 393. **8–99**

The Court of Appeal has also commented upon the practice of submitting an application for a stay of proceedings on the ground of abuse of process in prosecutions involving allegations of sexual abuse that is alleged to have occurred many years earlier. In *Smolinski* [2004] 2 Cr.App.R. 40, Lord Woolf, C.J. said that it would not always be appropriate to make such an application, and that it was to be discouraged, as unless the case was exceptional, the application would be unsuccessful. If such an application is to be made in such circumstances, it is preferable to do so after the evidence had been called.

In *Dyer v. Watson* [2004] 1 A.C. 379, the Privy Council considered the effect of delay in criminal proceedings. It held that the threshold of proving that a trial has not occurred within a reasonable time is a high one. If the period which has elapsed is one which, on its face, gives rise to real concern, it is necessary to look into the detailed circumstances of the particular case and it must be possible to justify any lapse of time which appears to be excessive. Regard must be had to the complexity of the case, the conduct of the defendant and the manner in which the case has been dealt with by the prosecution and the courts. There is no general obligation on a prosecutor to act with all due expedition and diligence but a marked lack of expedition if unjustified would indicate a breach of the reasonable time requirement. A decision on delay is a judicial assessment dependant on judgement rather than on any conclusion as to facts based on evidence so the use of the phrases burden and standard of proof are potentially misleading. The correct approach is to bear in mind the following principles:

(i) even where delay was unjustifiable, a permanent stay should be the exception rather than the rule;

(ii) where there was no fault on the part of the complainant or the prosecution, it would be very rare for a stay to be granted;

(iii) no stay should be granted in the absence of serious prejudice to the defence so that no fair trial could be held;

(iv) when assessing possible serious prejudice, the judge should bear in mind his or her power to regulate the admissibility of evidence and that the trial process itself should ensure that all relevant factual issues arising from delay would be placed before the jury for their consideration in accordance with appropriate directions from the judge; and

(v) if, having considered all those factors, a judge's assessment was that a fair trial would be possible, a stay should not be granted: *R. v. S* [2006] 2 Cr.App.R. 23.

These principles were endorsed by the Court of Appeal in *MacKreth* [2010] Crim.L.R. 226.

In *Department of Work and Pensions v. Courts and Costello* [2006] EWHC 1156(Admin), the defendants had admitted in interviews to making false representations in order to obtain benefits. There had then been a delay of more than a year before informations were laid in respect of those offences. The Divisional Court set aside the decisions of the magistrates to stay the prosecutions; it was said that a court should exercise its discretion to stay proceedings with great caution and only in exceptional cases. The power to stay proceedings was not to be used to punish the prosecution for delay; the issue is whether a fair trial can take place and magistrates must give reasons to indicate that they have considered factors such as the decline in witness memory or the death of witnesses. Where charges had been preferred seven years after the incident and documents that were part of the material by which the victim's credibility could be assessed had gone missing the trial should be stayed: *Ali v. CPS* [2007] EWCA Crim 691.

8–100 The discretionary decision whether or not to stay proceedings as an abuse of process because of delay is an exercise in judicial assessment dependent on judgment rather than on any conclusion as to fact based on evidence. It is, therefore, potentially misleading to apply to the exercise of that discretion, the language of burden and standard of proof, which is more applicable to an evidence-based fact-finding process: *R.. v. S (SP)* [2006] 2 Cr.App.R. 23.

In considering whether it was appropriate to stay proceedings on the grounds of delay, it is relevant to look at the whole picture, including the merits of the defendant's case but at end the question is whether he can have a fair hearing: *Rose v. DPP* [2010] R.T.R. 25. This case was one of several involving somewhat technical challenges to the type approval of breathalyser machines used in police stations. Expert witnesses were involved in the many cases in the magistrates' courts and the Crown Court litigating the issue, and trial and appeal dates became increasingly difficult to arrange due to lack of witness availability. Although the delay in that case was described by the court as, "on the face of it, scandalous", the question of whether a fair trial was still possible was the key factor and it was said that the court had to guard against complex but bad points extending litigation and enabling an application on the basis of abuse for delay being made. Waller, L.J. commented:

> ". . . overall, the picture is one of a defendant, like many others breathalysed, fighting a trial over many days taking a number of technical points, losing and then as appellant taking any point however unarguable and not resisting indeed acquiescing in delays in the appellate procedure. But the important point is that he could also still have a fair hearing in relation to the points he took."

Delay can also apply to enforcement proceedings: *R. (on the application of Flaherty) v. City of Westminster Magistrates' Court* [2008] EWHC 2589 (Admin). In that case the Divisional Court said that a district judge had been wrong to refuse to stay proceedings where there had been a two year period of inactivity on the part of the enforcement authorities. Moses, L.J. explained:

> "Thus, on the one hand, Mr Flaherty has a continuing liability to satisfy the confiscation order of which he has been aware from the time when the order was first imposed in 1997. The passage of time has not prejudiced him in any way in resisting the order or being able to advance such arguments as he can in relation either to an appeal or a certificate of inadequacy. However, it is plain as a matter of principle that enforcement proceedings must be brought within a reasonable time. . . . Since part of the purpose of the proceedings is, as I have said, to maintain the integrity of the system for collection of confiscation orders made by the Crown Court, and thus vindicate part of the system of criminal punishment and penalties imposed by the Crown Court, all the more important it is that the Enforcement Agency should pursue that purpose with vigour and within a reasonable period. In the instant case, in my judgment, the period which elapsed between 2004 and 2006 was inexcusable and runs counter to the whole purpose for which such an order was sought. It reveals an insouciant attitude by the Enforcement Agency to that which they were required to pursue, for which no proper explanation has ever been given."

The inquiry into an offence does not begin merely by the hearing of submissions as **8–101** to abuse of process relating to the transfer of proceedings to another court. The inquiry into the offence begins only with the calling of witnesses, the opening of the prosecution case or some other pertinent step: *Worcester Magistrates' Court, ex p. Bell* (1992) 157 JP 921. In that case Rose, L.J. explained the position of examining magistrates, faced with an application to stay proceedings as an abuse of process:

> "Equally, as it seems to me, magistrates are not, by hearing submissions on abuse of process, inquiring into an offence: for the question of whether a fair trial can be held by reason of abuse of process is a quite separate question from whether, if it can, the strength of the evidence justifies committal for trial. I see nothing inconsistent with any of the statutory provisions to which I have referred in holding that in carrying out those two functions, both of which are functions of their role as examining justices, the magistrates are doing anything inappropriate."

Failure to obtain / preserve evidence

A further feature of cases involving a delay in bringing proceedings is that they **8–102** sometimes involve the loss of evidence relating to the offence, to the prejudice of the defendant. In *R. v. T.* [2000] Crim.L.R. 832, a conviction for serious sexual offences against children after complaints that had been delayed for thirteen years was quashed where the file and all papers had been routinely destroyed after three years, and with it the evidence of the only contemporaneous complaint, and that evidence lay at the heart of the questions of credibility on which the case turned. The Court of Appeal concluded that this was something that no direction of law or control over the evidence could rectify, and a stay should have been granted. By contrast, in *McNamara and Mcnamara* [1998] Crim.L.R. 278, where a book which was to be exhibited by the prosecution had been lost, the Court of Appeal concluded that the fact of the loss was no more than an indication of poor management of exhibits, and it deprived the prosecution witnesses of their contemporaneous record. It had not been deliberately destroyed, and the loss could not have been a detriment to the defence; there were no grounds for a stay.

In *McKeon v. DPP* [2008] R.T.R. 14, a police officer, when using a Lion Intoxyliser to take evidential breath specimens at a police station, failed to retain the Intoxyliser mouthpiece used by the defendant despite the requirement to do so. The defendant argued that this prejudiced his right to a fair trial as it might have been shown to be defective and the cause of his failure to provide a satisfactory specimen of breath. The Divisional Court held that the defendant had not been disadvantaged by the absence of the mouthpiece. The police officer had seen that the mouthpiece was working properly, combined with the fact that the defendant blew into it for very short periods, the reason for which, on his evidence, was that he had a chest complaint; the court said that it readily understood why the justices concluded that there had been no disadvantage to the defendant.

There is no automatic requirement on the prosecution to retain CCTV evidence where it potentially records the administering of a warning of prosecution when asking for a sample of blood in excess alcohol cases under s.7(7) *Road Traffic Act* 1988: *Morris v. DPP* (2009) 173 J.P. 41.

8–103 A number of cases have dealt with problems that have arisen as a result of failure obtain evidence. In *Lamont* [2010] EWCA Crim 2144, the Court of Appeal considered a case involving an allegation of rape; the defendant's case was that the complainant had sought to make sexual advances towards him and that he had rejected them. In the course of his interview, the defendant urged the police on a number of occasions to obtain telephone records from his phone, as well as those of the complainant, as he alleged that she had made many calls and sent lots of text messages to him. The police initially took no action but the investigation was reopened some years later following another similar allegation. The police accepted that it would have been possible to obtain the phone records, but they had not done so. The defendant argued that the proceedings should be stayed. Elias, L.J. giving the judgment of the Court of Appeal said:

> "In this context it is in our view important to bear in mind two points which were emphasised by this court in Ebrahim. First, the discretionary power to ensure fairness means fairness to both the defendant and to the prosecution. It is important that the guilty are convicted as well as the innocent acquitted. Second, there will frequently be holes in the prosecution case which may result from some failing by the prosecution. Typically, for example, it may be a failure to recover CCTV material which would have been available had steps been taken at the appropriate time."

The Court of Appeal approved an earlier decision of the Divisional Court in *R. (Ebrahim) v. Feltham Magistrates' Court*; *Mouat v. DPP* [2001] 2 Cr.App.R. 23, and in particular the principles set out in that case for determining whether a stay should be granted where the prosecution has failed to preserve evidence.

(1) Was the prosecution in breach of a duty in failing to obtain evidence? In determining that question regard should be had to the Code of Practice applicable to prosecuting authorities and the Attorney General's guidelines. If there is no breach of duty, then the question of stay will not arise.
(2) If the prosecution is in breach of duty, have they acted in bad faith or otherwise in serious default of their duty? If so, then the prosecution should be stayed on that ground alone, irrespective of whether a fair trial would be possible. In these very exceptional cases it is not so much that the defendant cannot receive a fair trial but that it would be unfair to subject him to a trial at all.
(3) Absent bad faith or serious default, there should only be a stay if there is such serious prejudice to the defendant that a fair trial cannot be guaranteed.
(4) In most cases, the difficulty arising from the lack of evidence can be dealt with by an appropriate direction in the trial process itself. It is only in exceptional circumstances that a stay is likely to be appropriate.

The *Ebrahim* and *Mouat* cases both related to the obliteration of video evidence. Giving the judgment of the Divisional Court, Brookes, L.J. said:

> "It must be remembered that it is a commonplace in criminal trials for a defendant to rely on

"holes" in the prosecution case, for example, a failure to take fingerprints or a failure to submit evidential material to forensic examination. If, in such a case, there is sufficient credible evidence, apart from the missing evidence, which, if believed, would justify a safe conviction, then a trial should proceed, leaving the defendant to seek to persuade the jury or magistrates not to convict because evidence which might otherwise have been available was not before the court through no fault of his. Often the absence of a video film or fingerprints or DNA material is likely to hamper the prosecution as much as the defence."

The Divisional court concluded that the trial process itself is equipped to deal with the bulk of complaints on which applications for a stay are founded.

Manipulation or misuse of the process of court

An abuse of process may arise where illegal conduct on the part of the police or prosecutor is so grave as to threaten or undermine the rule of law. In *Grant* [2005] 2 Cr.App.R. 28, the Court of Appeal held that deliberate interference by police with a detained suspect's right to the confidence of privileged communication with his solicitor by eavesdropping and taping a conversation justified a stay of proceedings notwithstanding the absence of prejudice. However, the correctness of the decision in *Grant* has subsequently been doubted by the Supreme Court in *Maxwell* (*ante*), and the Privy Council in *Warren v. Attorney General of Jersey* (*ante*). The jurisdiction exercised by magistrates to deal with issues of abuse of process is strictly confined to matters directly affecting the fairness of the trial of the particular accused and does not extend to the wider supervisory jurisdiction for upholding the rule of law that is vested in the High Court: *Horseferry Road Magistrates' Court, ex p. Bennett* (*ante*). **8–104**

In *Rotherham Justices, ex p. Brough* [1991] Crim.L.R. 522, the prosecution had deliberately taken steps to ensure that a defendant who was charged with an offence that would be triable only on indictment in the case of an adult did not appear before the court until he had reached the age where the justices ceased to have a discretion whether or not to deal with it themselves. Although the court viewed the procedure as incorrect, it was held not to amount to an abuse of process because, on the facts the conduct of the prosecution showed at most a lack of judgment rather than misconduct or *mala fides*. There was no prejudice to the defendant because the delay involved had been minimal, the justices would probably have committed the case to the Crown Court anyway, and in the event of conviction the judge would undoubtedly take account of the defendant's age at the time of the offence and the circumstances of the committal.

R. (Hussain) v. Peterborough Magistrates' Court (2007) 171 JP 339, a legal adviser, who had earlier been involved in a pre-trial hearing, had intervened in court shortly after the case had begun, suggesting that, on the authorities, the defendant had no case to answer. When the prosecutor had found another authority the case had been adjourned. Subsequently the prosecutor had complained about the legal adviser's intervention and on the adjourned hearing a different legal adviser was in court. The defendant alleged that the legal adviser had been moved off the case as a result of the complaints and the way that the prosecution had gone about objecting was an abuse of process. The Divisional Court concluded that there was no intention on the part of prosecuting counsel to bring about the result that there be a different legal adviser at the renewed trial hearing, and that there was no intentional manipulation of the court's procedures. It was also said that the change in legal adviser did not have any impact on any previous ruling or decision previously given. The court said that it would be untenable to argue that whenever the CPS corresponds with the court with regard to an ongoing case without notifying the defendant, and the communication has (even if not intended) some effect on the conduct of that case, that this will in all circumstances be such an abuse as to require the court to intervene and stay the proceedings.

Where one magistrate had considered and ruled on the question of whether a summons should be issued and had come to the conclusion that it should not be issued, if the matter was subsequently taken before a different magistrate, it was a requirement that the different magistrate be told what the first magistrate had decided. Any other **8–105** course of action was a clear abuse of the process of the court: *Gleaves v. Insall*; *Dore v. Insall*; *Bolton v. Insall*; *Gleaves v.Insall* [1999] 2 Cr.App.R. 466.

8–106 The mere presence of an indirect or improper motive in launching a prosecution does not necessarily vitiate it and a court should be slow to halt such a prosecution in the case of mixed motives unless the conduct is truly oppressive: *R. (Dacre) v. Westminster Magistrates' Court* [2009] 1 Cr.App.R. 6. This was an application by the mother of a child for a summons against a newspaper and an editor under the *Children Act* 1989, s.97 in relation to an unpublished article which was likely to identify the child. The applicants argued for a stay of proceedings on the grounds that the case was being brought not only for punishment but to publicise the message of Fathers4Justice with which she was involved. On appeal the proceedings were stayed as the mother had been prepared to be interviewed about her involvement with Fathers4Justice and had provided material willingly and deliberately which would lead to the identification of the child.

Laying additional charges following a committal for sentence is not an abuse of process: *DPP v. B* [2008] EWHC 201 (Admin). The defendant had been committed on a charge of indecent assault on a female and at the Crown Court the judge had made it plain that he was of the opinion that this charge did not reflect the criminality in question and as a result a further seventeen counts of indecent assault were preferred. The Divisional Court upheld the intervention of the judge as being proper and expected to ensure that such charges were brought as to enable an appropriate sentence to be passed.

Where a summary trial is adjourned part-heard before the conclusion of the case for the prosecution and, at the adjourned hearing, the prosecution proposed to call a witness whom they had not intended to call at the original hearing but of whose existence they had always been aware, any objection based on an assertion that an unfair advantage had been taken should be dealt with by reference to s.78 of the *Police and Criminal Evidence Act* 1984, and not as an abuse of process.

It is an abuse of process for the prosecution, upon realising, after the magistrates had retired to consider sentence, that the charge was punishable only by way of fine, to invite the magistrates back into court, and then invite them to substitute a charge in respect of the same facts which carried the possibility of a custodial sentence: *Harlow Magistrates Court, ex p. O'Farrell* [2000] Crim.L.R. 589.

E. PUBLIC INTEREST IMMUNITY

8–107 The prosecution has the duty generally to disclose voluntarily all unused material to the defence if it has some bearing on the offences charged and the surrounding circumstances of the case. Sections 3(6), 7A(8), and 8(5) of the *Criminal Procedure and Investigations Act* 1996 (see *ante*, § 6–35, § 6–52, § 6–54) provide that, on the application of the prosecutor, the court may give a direction that it is not in the public interest to disclose material that would otherwise have to be disclosed. Where public interest immunity is relied upon to justify non-disclosure the prosecution should, whenever possible, give notice to the defence that application is being made for a ruling by the court, indicating at least the category of the material held see*Criminal Procedure Rules*, r.22.3 (Appendix G *post* § G–140b); the defence will then have the opportunity to make representations to the court. Where disclosure of the category of the material would in effect reveal that which the prosecution claimed should not in the public interest be revealed, the prosecution should notify the defence that an application is to be made to the court, but the category need not be specified and the application should be made ex parte. Where the court considers that the normal inter partes procedure ought to have been followed, it will order that this must happen, but otherwise it will rule on the ex parte application. In a highly exceptional case, where to reveal even the fact that an ex parte application is to be made could stultify the application, the prosecution can apply ex parte, without notice to the defence, and where the court considers that notice of the application should have been given to the defence or that the normal inter partes procedure should have been adopted, it will order that this must happen. A ruling in favour of non-disclosure before the hearing of the case is not necessarily final; the court should continue to monitor the issue of disclosure throughout the hearing and, on a change of view, should notify the prosecution, who would then have to determine whether to disclose, or to offer no further evidence: *Criminal Procedure and Investigations Act* 1996, s.14 (see *ante*, § 6–88); *Criminal Procedure Rules*, r.22.6 (Appendix G *post* § G–140e).

Although such applications are not common in the magistrates' court, they are sometimes made in cases involving informers, or to protect the occupiers of premises used during surveillance operations. It prevents material from being disclosed by the prosecution to the defence where the public interest in non-disclosure outweighs the public interest that, in the interests of justice, the courts should have the fullest possible access to all relevant material. Where disclosure is ordered the prosecution may decide not to proceed with the case.

Part II

The anonymity of informers has been upheld in several cases: *Savage v. Chief Constable of Hampshire* [1997] 1 W.L.R. 1061. Those who allow premises to be used for police surveillance have been protected: *Johnson*, 88 Cr.App.R. 131. Information upon which search warrants have been issued, as well as reports from the police to the DPP, have also been protected through non-disclosure: *Taylor v. Anderton (Police Complaints Authority Intervening)* [1995] 1 W.L.R. 447.

In *Rowe and Davis v. UK* (2000) 30 E.H.R.R. 1, the court stated that it is a **8–108**
fundamental aspect of the right to a fair trial that criminal proceedings should be adversarial and that there should be equality of arms between the prosecution and defence. The right to an adversarial trial means, in a criminal case, that the prosecution and defence must be given the opportunity to have knowledge of and comment on the observations filed and the evidence adduced by the other party. The court went on to state that courts have to weigh national security and the need to protect witnesses at risk of reprisals and keep secret police methods of investigation of crime against the interest of the accused.

In the leading case on public interest immunity, *R. v. H and C* [2004] 2 A.C. 134 **8–109**
the House of Lords confirmed that in cases where public interest immunity was argued, some derogation from the rule of full disclosure might be justified but it had to be the minimum necessary to protect the public interest in question. In appropriate cases, the appointment of special counsel might be a necessary step to ensure that the contentions of the prosecution were tested and the interests of the defendant protected: (for a detailed commentary on this case see *ante*, § 6–84).

In *R. v. H and C* (*ante*) Lord Bingham gave specific guidance in relation to magis- **8–110**
trates' courts:

> "The relevant principles had been correctly applied in *R. (DPP) v. Acton Youth Court* [2001] 1 W.L.R. 1828). If public interest immunity applications were confined, as they should be, to material undermining the prosecution case or strengthening that of the defence, the bench would not be alerted to material damaging to the defendant. If it was, the principles governing the court's decision whether to recuse itself were the same as in the case of any other tribunal of fact, but the court's duty of continuing review ordinarily militated in favour of continuing proceedings before the court which determined the immunity application. If a case raised complex and contentious immunity issues, and the court had discretion to send the case to the crown court for trial, the magistrates court should carefully consider whether those issues were best resolved at the crown court. The occasions when it would be appropriate to appoint special counsel in the magistrates court would be even rarer than in the crown court."

R (DPP) v. Acton Youth Court [2001] 1 W.L.R. 1828 concerned a case in the youth court where a district judge who had ruled on an application for public interest immunity recused himself from sitting on the trial. It was held that a judge who conducted a trial, whether a magistrate or a district judge, had final responsibility for ensuring justice at that trial. It was said that where there had been an ex parte application for non-disclosure on the ground of public interest immunity, justice could best be achieved by the same tribunal then conducting the trial since, if anything unforeseen then occurred, it would be in a position to protect the defendant; this must be especially true given the court's continuing duty to review PII rulings on the application of the defence under s.14 of the *Criminal Procedure and Investigations Act* 1996 (see *ante*, § 6–88). Unless there are special circumstances, the fact that magistrates and district judges are judges of both fact and law should not prevent them from conducting a trial after they had made an interlocutory ruling.

Where the government is a party to litigation, it has a high duty to assist the court with full and accurate explanations of all the facts relevant to the issue that the court must decide; the complete integrity of PII certificates and the schedules attached to them, signed by ministers of the Crown, is essential as the courts must be able to have complete confidence in their credibility and reliability. Where it appears that a court has been misled or may have been misled, it should be notified immediately that there is a possible problem and that the matter is under investigation: *R. (Al-Sweady and others) v. Secretary of State for Defence* [2009] EWHC 1687 (Admin). This judgement, given following a stay of judicial review proceedings, warned courts to approach the content of PII certificates and schedules issued by the Ministry of Defence with caution until such time as the Ministry could demonstrate that its procedures had eliminated the risk of serious errors occurring.

Court should not generally redact sensitive sections from their written reasons or judgments; even within the small number of permissible exceptions, such as material excluded from disclosure on established public interest immunity principles, any disapplication of the principle of open justice had to be rigidly contained: *R. (Mohamed) v. Secretary of State for Foreign and Commonwealth Affairs (No.2) (Guardian News and Media Ltd and others intervening)* [2011] Q.B. 218.

For a more detailed commentary on public interest immunity see *ante*, § 6–76 *et seq.*

F. HANDCUFFS IN COURT

8–111 The right to a fair and impartial trial as required by *ECHR*, art. 6 may be prejudiced if the defendant appears in court restrained by handcuffs; it may also amount to degrading treatment and infringe *ECHR*, art. 3. Handcuffs may be used but only after an application to the court made by the CPS or the prison escort and dock security contractors. It must be shown that there are reasonable grounds to believe that there is a risk of escape or violence: *Cambridgeshire Justices ex p. Peacock*, 161 J.P. 113. The application must be heard *inter partes*, if necessary in a closed court; *Rollinson*, 161 J.P. 107. In *Horden* [2009] 2 Cr.App.R. 24, the Court of Appeal said that physical restraint should be ordered only when truly necessary. Unless there is sufficient reason, which usually means a real risk of either violence or escape, a defendant ought not to be visibly restrained by handcuffs or otherwise, either in the dock or in the witness box. Even if there is some relevant risk, alternative forms of avoiding it ought to be investigated before resort was made to visible restraint. A secure dock, the interposition of prison officers between defendants or either side of a single defendant, and police officers inside or outside the courtroom, are all alternatives which are routinely employed. In an extreme case, authorisation can be sought from the Senior Presiding Judge for armed officers to be in the court building.

[The next paragraph is § 8–113.]

VI. THE PROSECUTION CASE

A. PROSECUTION OPENING SPEECH

8–113 The prosecutor's opening speech sets the parameters of the case. It succinctly outlines and sometimes analyses the facts upon which the prosecution relies. It must be borne in mind that the judiciary in the magistrates' courts do not need the same sort of explanations as a jury in the crown court. They will, however, appreciate the scene being set for the evidence to follow. The prosecutor is under no obligation to open its case and in many simple cases chooses not to do so.

Where a case has been adjourned part heard and the court has difficulty in remembering the evidence it may allow the prosecutor to open his case again on the adjourned hearing so that he may remind the court of the evidence given. In those circumstances, the defence advocate should also be allowed to address the court: *L. and B. v. DPP* [1998] 2 Cr.App.R. 69.

B. Rule Requiring Prosecution to Call all its Evidence before the Close of the Case

The general rule is that the prosecution must call all the evidence on which it intends to rely before the close of its case: *Pilcher*, 60 Cr.App.R. 1. The court has a discretion, however, in the interests of justice, to allow the prosecution to call evidence after it has closed its case and before the court considers its decision. In *Tuck v. Vehicle Inspectorate* [2004] EWHC 728 (Q.B.), Mackay J., giving judgment in the Divisional Court, set out the principles, derived from a series of authorities, which should be applied by courts considering prosecution applications to re-open their case: **8–114**

Part II

"(1) The discretion to allow the case to be re-opened is not limited to matters arising ex improviso or mere technicalities, but is a more "general discretion" (see Kennedy L.J.: *Jolly v. DPP* 31st March 2000, unreported).

(2) The exercise of this discretion should not be interfered with by a higher court unless its exercise was wrong in principle or perverse (*R. v. Tate* [1997] RTR 17 at 22C).

(3) The general rule remains that the prosecution must finish its case once and for all (*R. v. Pilcher*, 60 Cr.App.R. 1 at 5) and the test to be applied is narrower than consideration of whether the additional evidence would be of value to the tribunal (loc cit). The discretion will only be exercised "on the rarest of occasions" (*R. v. Francis* 91 Cr.App.R. 271 at 175).

(4) The discretion must be exercised carefully having regard to the need to be fair to the defendant (*Matthews v Morris* [1981] JP 262), and giving consideration to the question of whether any prejudice to the defendant will be caused (*Tate* at 23C).

(5) The courts have in the past differed as to whether the mere loss of a tactical advantage can constitute such prejudice. The defendant, having spotted and drawn attention to a gap in the case by way of submission, as to which he could have remained silent, and taken advantage of that gap at the close of the evidence, was thought in *R. v. Munnery* [1992] 94 Cr.App.R. 164 at 172 to be an important consideration. However, later cases take a discernibly different approach. A different view was expressed in *Khatibi v. DPP* [2004] EWCA 83 Admin at 25 to 26 and in *Leeson* [2000] RTR 385 and 391F–G.

(6) Criminal procedure while adversarial is not a game (see *Leeson* (loc cit), *Hughes v DPP* [2003] EWHC Admin 2470), and the overall interests of justice include giving effect to the requirement that a prosecution should not fail through inefficiency, carelessness or oversight (Leeson).

(7) Of particular significance is the consideration of whether there is any risk of prejudice to the defendant (see *Jolly* and *Tate*)."

Although it was suggested in *Tuck* that the discretion to allow the prosecution to re-open their case should be used on the rarest of occasions, there has since been positive encouragement to magistrates' courts to exercise this discretion in cases where "ambush" defences are employed. In *Malcolm v. DPP* [2007] 2 Cr.App.R. 1, it was held that magistrates had been entitled to use their discretion to receive further evidence to remedy a deficiency in the prosecution case, notwithstanding the fact that they had already retired, returned to the court room and had been part way through giving their decision. In this case a technical point, which had never been put to any of the witnesses, was raised for the first time in the closing speech of the defence counsel; when the magistrates returned and started to give their decision, the prosecution applied to re-open their case. Giving the leading judgment in the Divisional Court, Stanley Burnton J., expressed himself in robust terms:

". . . the obligation of the prosecution to prove its case in its entirety before closing its case, and certainly before the end of the final speech for the defence, had an anachronistic, and obsolete, ring. Criminal trials are no longer to be treated as a game, in which each move is final and any omission by the prosecution leads to its failure. It is the duty of the defence to make its defence and the issues it raises clear to the prosecution and to the court at an early stage. That duty is implicit in r.3.3 of the *Criminal Procedure Rules* 2005, which requires the parties actively to assist the exercise by the court of its case management powers, the exercise of which requires early identification of the real issues. Even in a relatively straightforward trial such as the present, in the magistrates' court (where there is not yet any requirement of a defence statement or a pre-trial review), it is the duty of the defence to make the real issues clear at the latest before the prosecution closes its case."

Maurice Kay, L.J., agreed, and added that he considered the case to be one where the defence had sought to ambush the prosecution and commended the magistrates for "refusing to succumb to this kind of forensic legerdemain".

In *R. (on the application of Lawson) v. Stafford Magistrates' Court* [2007] EWHC 2490(Admin), it was held that where a driver on trial for speeding, had identified two purportedly crucial issues for the first time during his closing argument, *i.e.* signage of a temporary 30 m.p.h. limit and regulatory compliance, magistrates were entitled to adjourn the trial to allow the prosecution to adduce further evidence.

A somewhat different view was taken by Bean J., sitting as a single judge in the Administrative Court, *R. (Traves) v. DPP*, 169 J.P. 421. In this case the defendant had been charged with driving whilst disqualified and the fact that he was disqualified from driving was not contested. After the magistrates had retired to consider their decision is was noticed that the prosecution had not adduced evidence that the defendant was disqualified; the magistrates allowed an application to admit this evidence. Bean J. relying on the decision of the Divisional Court in *Webb v. Leadbetter* [1966] 1 W.L.R. 245, and on the decision in *Jolly v. DPP* (*ante*) concluded that the magistrates discretion to allow the prosecution to re-open its case does not extend beyond the point where the defence close their case and the magistrates retire to consider their decision. In the subsequent decision of the Divisional Court in *Malcolm v. DPP* (*ante*) it is suggested that *Webb v. Leadbetter* was decided at a time when the rules of criminal procedure were very different, and that *Traves* was wrongly decided.

8–115 In *Matthews v. Morris* [1981] Crim.L.R. 495 the Divisional Court held that the magistrates were correct to have allowed the prosecution to reopen its case to tender a statement which by mistake had not been tendered as part of the prosecution case, but which had been served on the defendant under the *Criminal Justice Act* 1967, s.9. No injustice had been caused to the defendant by the admission of the evidence.

In *Doran* (1972) 56 Cr.App.R. 429 the judge allowed the prosecution to call two witnesses after the close of its case. The witnesses were members of the public who had been present at the trial and realised during the course of the defence case that they could give evidence.

8–116 If further evidence is to be called the court should ensure that proper notice of it has been given to the defendant. The prosecution should serve the evidence by way of notice and the court should grant an adjournment if necessary: *Dartey* (1987) 84 Cr.App.R. 352.

C. DUTY OF PROSECUTION IN CALLING WITNESSES

8–117 The prosecution must serve copies of the statements of the witnesses upon whom it intends to rely as part of the prosecution case. The prosecution retains discretion to call those witnesses, or to tender them for cross-examination, but that discretion must be exercised in a manner which is calculated to further the interests of justice and, at the same time, be fair to the defence. If the prosecution acts improperly in not calling a witness, it is open to the court to invite the prosecutor to tender the witness and, if he refuses, to call the witness itself for cross-examination by the defence: *Wellingborough Justices, ex p. Francois*, 158 J.P. 813.

Generally the prosecution ought to call or offer to call all the witnesses who give direct evidence of the primary facts of the case, unless for good reason, it regards the witnesses' evidence as unworthy of belief. In the case of *Oliva*, 49 Cr.App.R. 298, Lord Parker C.J. said at 309–310:

> "The prosecution does not, of course, put forward every witness as a witness of truth, but where the witness's evidence is capable of belief, then it is their duty, well recognised, that he should be called, even though the evidence that he is going to give is inconsistent with the case sought to be proved. Their discretion must be exercised in a manner which is calculated to further the interests of justice, and at the same time be fair to the defence. If the prosecution appear to be exercising that discretion improperly, it is open to the judge of trial to interfere and in his discretion in turn to invite the prosecution to call a particular witness, and, if they refuse, there is the ultimate sanction in the judge himself calling that witness."

The principles to be applied in deciding which witnesses the prosecution must call were summarised as follows by Kennedy, L.J. in *R. v. Russell-Jones* [1995] 1 Cr.App.R. 538.

(1) Generally speaking the prosecution must have at court all the witnesses whose statements have been served as witnesses on whom the prosecution intend to rely, if the defence want those witnesses to attend. In deciding which statements to serve, the prosecution has an unfettered discretion, but must normally disclose material statements not served.

(2) The prosecution enjoy a discretion whether to call, or tender, any witness it requires to attend, but the discretion is not unfettered.

(3) The first principle which limits this discretion is that it must be exercised in the interests of justice, so as to promote a fair trial: see Lord Parker C.J. *Oliva* (*ante*).

(4) The next principle is that the prosecution ought normally to call or offer to call all the witnesses who give direct evidence of the primary facts of the case, unless for good reason, the prosecutor regards a witness's evidence as unworthy of belief. In most cases the court should have available all of that evidence, which the prosecution, when serving statements, considered to be material, even if there are inconsistencies between one witness and another. The defence cannot always be expected to call for themselves witnesses of the primary facts whom the prosecution has discarded. The evidence they may give, albeit at variance with other evidence called by the Crown, may well be detrimental to the defence case. If what a witness of the primary facts has to say is properly regarded by the prosecution as being incapable of belief, or as some of the authorities say 'incredible,' then his evidence cannot help the court assess the overall picture of the crucial events, hence, it is not unfair that he is not called.

(5) It is for the prosecution to decide which witnesses give direct evidence of the primary facts of the case. A prosecutor may reasonably take the view that what a particular witness has to say is at best marginal.

(6) The prosecutor is also the primary judge of whether or not a witness to the material events is incredible, or unworthy of belief. It goes without saying that he could not properly condemn a witness as incredible merely because, for example, he gives an account at variance with that of a larger number of witnesses, and one which is less favourable to the prosecution case than that of the others.

(7) A prosecutor properly exercising his discretion is not therefore obliged to proffer a witness merely in order to give the defence material with which to attack the credit of other witnesses on whom the Crown relies.

In *Haringey Justices, ex p. DPP* [1996] 2 W.L.R. 114 the prosecution decided not **8–118**
to call a police officer who had been suspended from duty. The defence wished the officer to be present. The court invited the prosecution to call the witness and when the prosecution declined to do so, dismissed the case on the ground that it was an abuse of process. It was held that the court could not force the prosecution to call the witness but it could call the witness itself rather than dismiss the case.

The prosecution must take all reasonable steps to secure the attendance of each of its witnesses at trial, including the making of an application for a summons or warrant (see *post* § 9–1 *et seq.*). If, however, despite such steps, it has proved impossible to have the witnesses present, the court might in its discretion permit the trial to proceed, provided no injustice would be done: *Cavanagh and Shaw*, 56 Cr.App.R. 407. In that case, the witness was out of the country and there was no information as to when he would be back. The court, in exercising its discretion, should consider the desire of the defence to call the witness if the prosecution did not, the extent to which the evidence would help the defence, the chances of securing the attendance of the witness in a reasonable time, whether delay would result in other witnesses not being available, and the willingness of the prosecution to proceed.

If the court has set a timetable for the trial, the prosecution must call its witnesses in the order set out in the court's directions: *Criminal Procedure Rules*, r.3.10 (Appendix G *post* § G–12); see also *ante*, § 8–85. In the absence of such a timetable, the prosecutor has discretion as to the order in which witnesses should be called. Any witness should remain outside the courtroom until called unless the witness is an expert who may need to hear the evidence because his opinion is based on the facts. This is a rule of practice not law: *Bexley Justices, ex p. King* [1980] R.T.R. 49; *Moore v. Registrar of Lambeth County Court* [1969] 1 W.L.R. 141.

D. NO CASE TO ANSWER

8–119 The *Criminal Procedure Rules*, r.37.3–(3)(c), provide that at the conclusion of the prosecution case, on the defendant's application or on its own initiative, the court may acquit the defendant on the ground that the prosecution evidence is insufficient for any reasonable court properly to convict, but that it must not do so unless the prosecutor has had an opportunity to make representations (Appendix G *post* § G–225). The finding of a case to answer requires a determination of law separate from a finding of guilt; a decision to acquit where, after finding a case to answer, the defendant called no evidence, is based on factual evidence and may not be perverse: *DPP v. Uddin* [2006] EWHC 1523.

In *Galbraith*, 73 Cr.App.R. 124, CA the Court of Appeal set out the test to be applied in the Crown Court. Lord Lane C.J. stated at 127 that:

> "(1) If there is no evidence that the crime alleged has been committed by the defendant there is no difficulty—the judge will stop the case. (2) The difficulty arises where there is some evidence but it is of a tenuous character, for example, because of inherent weakness or vagueness or because it is inconsistent with other evidence. (a) Where the judge concludes that the prosecution evidence, taken at its highest, is such that a jury properly directed could not properly convict on it, it is his duty, on a submission being made, to stop the case. (b) Where however the prosecution evidence is such that its strength or weakness depends on the view to be taken of a witness's reliability, or other matters which are generally speaking within the province of the jury and where on one possible view of the facts there *is* evidence on which the jury could properly come to the conclusion that the defendant is guilty, then the judge should allow the matter to be tried by the jury."

This test is also used in the magistrates' courts. The court is entitled to dismiss a case of its own motion. If it proposes to do so, however, it must first allow submissions to be made by the parties: *DPP v. Cosier* [2000] C.O.D. 284. Issues relating to the credibility of witnesses, except in the clearest of cases, do not normally result in a finding that there is no prima facie case; they are usually left to be determined at the trial: *Barking and Dagenham Justices, ex p. DPP*, 159 J.P. 373.

Where reliance has been placed by the prosecution on circumstantial evidence the proper approach is to determine whether a reasonable jury properly directed would be entitled to draw an adverse inference from the combination of factual circumstances by dismissing other possible explanations in relation to that evidence: *Jabber* [2006] EWCA Crim 2694. In *London Borough of Haringey v. Tshilumbe*, 174 J.P. 41, a senior environmental health practitioner for the local authority had affixed a hygiene emergency prohibition notice to T's premises. After the notice was affixed he returned to the premises and found a group of individuals sitting at a table eating food from plates and drinking from cans. It was alleged that T had failed to comply with the notice as he had continued to operate the premises as a food business. The magistrates held that T had no case to answer as the local authority had produced no evidence that the food and drink that were on the table had been provided to the occupants of the premises by T in the course of a food business. It was held that justices had been wrong to find that there was no case to answer; it could be inferred from the circumstances that the premises were being used for a food business and the defendant should have explained himself at trial. Strong circumstantial evidence may be sufficient for the court to find a case to answer: *Danells* [2006] EWCA Crim 628.

It is wrong to ambush the prosecution by a submission of no case to answer after raising a new issue in cross-examination; case issues must be identified and examined carefully at the plea and case management hearing: *Penner* [2010] Crim.L.R. 936.

There is no power to find that there is no case to answer before the conclusion of the prosecution case: *R. v. N Ltd* [2009] 1 Cr.App.R. 3.

In *Pydar Justices, ex p. Foster*, 160 J.P. 87, evidence of the defendant's intoximeter **8–120**
reading had been handed to the prosecutor by the police officer in court and the case was then closed, but the defendant had submitted there was no case to answer because the reading had not been produced in evidence. His application for review was dismissed because an exhibit was available for the court to examine whenever it wished and, as the justices had jurisdiction over it, it was for the defence to lay the foundations for their submissions through cross-examination or by calling evidence. Defence counsel should not wait to point out the exhibit, and then submit that there was no case to answer.

Where both the parties and the justices agree that a mistake has been made, it should be rectified immediately without the cost and delay of an appeal. Thus, where magistrates had announced that they we re acceding to a submission of no case to answer and gave their reasons, and the prosecution immediately drew their attention to an error in their reasons which was accepted by the defence, the magistrates were right to reverse their decision: *Steward v. DPP*, [2004] 1 W.L.R. 592.

In *Gleeson* [2004] 1 Cr.App.R. 29, Auld, L.J. stated that a criminal trial is not a game; its object is to ensure that the guilty are convicted and the innocent acquitted. It is contrary to defence counsel's professional duty and not in the legitimate interests of the defendant to take advantage of procedural errors made by the prosecution in delaying identifying those errors at issue in the case until the last possible moment. It is wrong to wait to make a submission of no case on an unanswerable legal challenge rather than point out a prosecution error earlier.

There is no obligation on the court to give reasons for rejecting a submission of no **8–121**
case to answer: *Moran v. DPP*, 166 J.P. 467.

Where a magistrates' court finds that there is no case to answer in a matter where it would have been open to the court to consider an alternative verdict at the conclusion of the trial, the court has jurisdiction to continue to consider the lesser offence: *R. (H) v. Liverpool City Youth Court* [2001] Crim.L.R. 487. In this case the court found no case to answer on a charge of aggravated vehicle taking, but concluded that it was open to it to continue to hear the matter on the basis of the lesser offence of taking a motor vehicle without consent. Likewise, where magistrates dismissed a charge of dangerous driving on the basis that there was no case to answer, they ought to have considered the alternative offence of careless driving: *DPP v. Smith* [2002] Crim.L.R. 970.

VII. THE DEFENCE CASE

A. REPRESENTATION

It is for the defendant to decide whether or not to be represented by a solicitor or **8–122**
counsel. For a more detailed commentary on defence representation, including the use of a McKenzie friend, see *ante* § 8–64 *et seq*.

B. SEQUENCE OF THE DEFENCE EVIDENCE

8–123 At the conclusion of the prosecution case the defendant may give evidence and call witnesses: r 37.3 *Criminal Procedure Rules* (see *post* § G–225).

The defendant is not obliged to give evidence at trial or to call any witnesses. He may no longer make an unsworn statement from the dock.

A defendant has the right to explain his story, however improbable, without being subjected to the bench's unnecessary interruptions, sarcasm or hostility; magistrates may clarify ambiguities and the answers given but must not cross-examine, especially during examination-in-chief, or comment on evidence while it is being given: *Michel v. R.*, [2010] 1 Cr.App.R. 24. In *R. v. Perren* [2009] EWCA Crim 348 the Court of Appeal set aside a conviction where a judge had asked a large number of questions which were of the nature of hostile cross-examination. On repeated occasions while the appellant was in the witness box he had asked questions which the Court of Appeal said were designed not to elucidate the appellant's evidence but to discredit it.

8–124 The court has a discretionary power to allow the defendant to be recalled to give evidence after the conclusion of the defence evidence, but a defendant may only be recalled to deal with matters that have arisen since he gave evidence if he could not reasonably have anticipated them, and if it appears to be in the interests of justice. It will be only in the most exceptional circumstances in which the interests of justice might require a court to permit a defendant to be recalled so that he might contradict his earlier evidence, and advance a new version of events, where that version was available to him when he was first in the witness box: *Ikram* [2008] 2 Cr.App.R. 24.

Such exceptional circumstances were held to exist in *Reid* [2010] EWCA Crim 1478, where a co-defendant had originally given an account incriminating his co-accused, had conducted his case consistently with that account up to the point of giving evidence, and then gave evidence supportive of his co-accused's defence of self-defence. In cross-examination he denied being intimidated by his co-accused but, after closing speeches, he applied to be recalled to revert to his original account on the ground that he had actually been intimidated by his co-accused. The Court of Appeal commented that this was not a case of a defendant seeking to give an entirely new account after having heard what a co-defendant had said; what he was seeking to do was to resolve the contradiction in the accounts he had given and to explain it. The court also said that it was not necessarily in his interest to revert to his original account and so this was not a tactical decision.

Criminal Justice Act 1982, s.72

Abolition of right of accused to make unsworn statement

8–125 **72.**—(1) Subject to subsections (2) and (3) below, in any criminal proceedings the accused shall not be entitled to make a statement without being sworn, and accordingly, if he gives evidence, he shall do so (subject to sections 55 and 56 of the *Youth Justice and Criminal Evidence Act* 1999) on oath and be liable to cross-examination; but this section shall not affect the right of the accused, if not represented by counsel or a solicitor, to address the court or jury otherwise than on oath on any matter on which, if he were so represented, counsel or a solicitor could address the court or jury on his behalf.

(2) Nothing in subsection (1) above shall prevent the accused making a statement without being sworn—

(a) if it is one which he is required by law to make personally; or

(b) if he makes it by way of mitigation before the court passes sentence upon him.

Criminal Evidence Act 1898, s.1

Competency of witnesses in criminal cases.

8–126 **1.**—(1) A person charged in criminal proceedings shall not be called as a witness in the proceedings except upon his own application.

(2) Subject to section 101 of the *Criminal Justice Act* 2003 (admissibility of evidence of

defendant's bad character), a person charged in criminal proceedings who is called as a witness in the proceedings may be asked any question in cross-examination notwithstanding that it would tend to criminate him as to any offence with which he is charged in the proceedings.

(3) [...]

(4) Every person charged in criminal proceedings who is called as a witness in the proceedings shall, unless otherwise ordered by the court, give his evidence from the witness box or other place from which the other witnesses give their evidence.

In *Farnham Justices, ex p. Gibson* [1991] R.T.R. 309 a policy requiring a defendant to give evidence from the dock, not from the witness box, was declared unlawful. At his trial for driving with excess breath-alcohol and for failing to stop after an accident, the defendant was compelled by the justices, as a matter of policy, to give his evidence from the dock, not from the witness box as the other witnesses had done. The defendant argued that the policy requiring him to give evidence from the dock was unlawful in the light of the *Criminal Evidence Act* 1898, s.1(4). It was held that the justices, in exceptional circumstances, could deny a person the right to give evidence from the witness box but that right could only be denied by reason of misconduct or some other specific consideration. By being compelled to give evidence from the dock, the defendant was adversely treated compared to the other witnesses and justice was not seen to be done. **8–127**

If the defendant chooses to testify he must do so on oath and is liable to be cross-examined by both the advocate for the prosecution and for any co-defendants: *Hilton* [1972] 1 Q.B. 421. Subject to any application to admit bad character evidence against the defendant, he cannot be cross-examined as to previous convictions or as to his character (see *post* § 10–107 *et seq.*).

Criminal Justice and Public Order Act 1994, s.35

Effect of accused's silence at trial

35.—(1) At the trial of any person for an offence, subsections (2) and (3) below apply unless— **8–128**

(a) the accused's guilt is not in issue; or

(b) it appears to the court that the physical or mental condition of the accused makes it undesirable for him to give evidence;

but subsection (2) below does not apply if, at the conclusion of the evidence for the prosecution, his legal representative informs the court that the accused will give evidence or, where he is unrepresented, the court ascertains from him that he will give evidence.

(2) Where this subsection applies, the court shall, at the conclusion of the evidence for the prosecution, satisfy itself (in the case of proceedings on indictment, in the presence of the jury) that the accused is aware that the stage has been reached at which evidence can be given for the defence and that he can, if he wishes, give evidence and that, if he chooses not to give evidence, or having been sworn, without good cause refuses to answer any question, it will be permissible for the court or jury to draw such inferences as appear proper from his failure to give evidence or his refusal, without good cause, to answer any question.

(3) Where this subsection applies, the court or jury, in determining whether the accused is guilty of the offence charged, may draw such inferences as appear proper from the failure of the accused to give evidence or his refusal, without good cause, to answer any question.

(4) This section does not render the accused compellable to give evidence on his own behalf, and he shall accordingly not be guilty of contempt of court by reason of a failure to do so.

(5) For the purposes of this section a person who, having been sworn, refuses to answer any question shall be taken to do so without good cause unless—

(a) he is entitled to refuse to answer the question by virtue of any enactment, whenever passed or made, or on the ground of privilege; or

(b) the court in the exercise of its general discretion excuses him from answering it.

[...]

(7) This section applies—

(a) in relation to proceedings on indictment for an offence, only if the person charged with the offence is arraigned on or after the commencement of this section;

(b) in relation to proceedings in a magistrates' court, only if the time when the court begins to receive evidence in the proceedings falls after the commencement of this section.

8–129 Section 35 of the *Criminal Justice and Public Order Act* 1994 (see § 10–141, *post*) provides that the court is under a duty to warn the defendant that it may draw inferences should he choose not to give evidence; such inferences may only be drawn in a case where the defendant is present. The *Consolidated Criminal Practice Direction*, para. IV.44, although applying to Crown Courts, is generally used by magistrates' courts. Where the defendant is represented, the representative should inform the court as to whether the defendant intends to give evidence. If the defendant intends to give evidence the case should proceed in the normal way. If the representative states that his client does not wish to give evidence, he should be asked whether he has advised his client of the provisions of the section. The formula to be used is set out in para. IV.44.3 of the *Practice Direction*, and may be adapted for use in the magistrates' courts as follows:

> "Have you advised your client that the stage has now been reached at which he may give evidence and, if he chooses not to do so or, having been sworn, without good cause refuses to answer any question, the magistrates may draw such inferences as appear proper from his failure to do so?"

In the case of an unrepresented defendant, the court has a duty under s.35(2) of the Act to satisfy itself that the defendant is aware of the provisions. The legal adviser will give a warning using the wording set out in para. IV.44.5, once again with suitable adaptations:

> "You have heard the evidence against you. Now is the time for you to make your defence. You may give evidence on oath, and be cross-examined like any other witness. If you do not give evidence or, having been sworn, without good cause refuse to answer any question the magistrates may draw such inferences as appear proper. That means they may hold it against you. You may also call any witness or witnesses whom you have arranged to attend court. Afterwards you may also, if you wish, address the magistrates by arguing your case from the dock. But you cannot at that stage give evidence. Do you now intend to give evidence?"

Police and Criminal Evidence Act 1984, s.79

Time for taking accused's evidence

8–130 **79.** If at the trial of any person for an offence—

(a) the defence intends to call two or more witnesses to the facts of the case; and

(b) those witnesses include the accused,

the accused shall be called before the other witness or witnesses unless the court in its discretion otherwise directs.

8–131 Where there are co-defendants it is usual for the first charged or named on the court list to give evidence first.

C. ROLE OF LEGAL REPRESENTATIVES

8–132 Barristers and solicitors are officers of the court and should not mislead it in any way. They have a duty to draw the court's attention to the law and that includes guideline cases on sentencing: *Att.-Gen.'s Reference (No.52 of 2003)* [2004] Crim.L.R. 306. The court, on the other hand, must not ask advocates questions which might compromise them in any way, *e.g.* a court should ask an advocate whether he has seen a list of previous convictions relating to his client not whether he has agreed them. It is the duty of a defence advocate to put his client's case to the court.

The following statement of principles which governs the conduct of defence counsel was made by the Chairman of the Bar following the rejection of complaints about defence counsel's conduct in *McFadden* (1976) 62 Cr.App.R. 187:

> "It is the duty of counsel when defending an accused on a criminal charge to present to the court, fearlessly and without regard to his personal interests, the defence of that accused. It is

> not his function to determine the truth or falsity of that defence, nor should he permit his personal opinion of that defence to influence his conduct of it. No counsel may refuse to defence because of his opinion of the character of the accused nor of the crime charged. That is a cardinal rule of the Bar ... Counsel also has a duty to the court and to the public. This duty includes the clear presentation of the issues and the avoidance of waste of time, repetition and prolixity. In the conduct of every case counsel must be mindful of this public responsibility."

The remarks made in *Att.-Gen.'s Reference (No.52 of 2003) ante*, also apply. It is the duty of defence counsel to put the defendant's case whether or not he intends to call evidence in support of it; the fact that a defendant does not call evidence should be recorded by counsel in writing, along with a brief summary of the reasons for that decision and if possible endorsed by the defendant: *Ebanks v. R.* [2006] 1 W.L.R. 1827. Sir Igor Judge observed in *Ulcay* [2008] 1 Cr.App.R. 27 that the correct meaning of "acting on instructions" is sometimes misunderstood. The following propositions can be extracted: **8–133**

1. Neither the client nor the solicitor is entitled to direct counsel as to how the case should be constructed.
2. The client's "instructions" encompass whatever the client facing a criminal charge asserts to be true about the allegations and that is the case that the advocate should advance.
3. There are some decisions which can be made only by the defendant, following professional advice from counsel, *i.e.* the plea and the decision as to whether to give evidence or not.
4. Counsel should not seek to challenge evidence which has been accepted to be true on a basis of facts which are agreed or described by the defendant, just because the defendant or instructing solicitor wishes him to do so.
5. The duty imposed by the *Criminal Defence Service (General) (No.2) Regulations* 2001 (SI 2001 No.1437) reg.16(2)(a) to provide details of the nature of the duty requiring counsel to withdraw or detail the nature of the breakdown, does not impinge confidentiality nor oblige counsel to continue to act when he has made a professional judgement for compelling reasons to withdraw
6. The absence of sufficient time to prepare a case does not enable counsel to refuse to conduct it. It does not classify as an exception to the "cab-rank" rule. Counsel is expected to "soldier on".

Where a court proceeds in the absence of the defendant his counsel should conduct the case as though he were present and must be allowed to cross-examine witnesses: *Kepple* [2007] EWCA Crim 1339.

D. UNREPRESENTED DEFENDANT

In magistrates' courts many defendants represent themselves and the legal adviser has a specific duty to assist a defendant who is not represented: *Criminal Procedure Rules*, r.37.14–(3)(a) (see Appendix G, *post* § G–229g). Where the defendant is not represented, the legal adviser may ask any question necessary in the defendant's interests: *CPR*, r.37.4–(5) (see *post* § G–226). However, this duty to assist unrepresented parties to present their case includes a duty do so without appearing to become an advocate for the party concerned: *Consolidated Criminal Practice Direction*, para. V.55.9 (see Appendix F *post* § F–70). In general neither the court nor the legal adviser should take an active part in the proceedings except to clear up ambiguities in the evidence: *Simms v. Moore* [1970] 2 Q.B. 327, 54 Cr.App.R. 347. A legal adviser is no more entitled to step into the arena and conduct a litigant's case for him than is a magistrate himself; it is important in the interests of justice that the legal adviser should not give the appearance of seeking himself to conduct the case of either party, or to limit the way in which that case is conducted: *Hobby v. Hobby* [1954] 1 W.L.R. 1020. **8–134**

The legal adviser will explain the nature of the charge, the consequences of not giving evidence (*Criminal Justice and Public Order Act* 1994, s.35, *ante*), and will assist **8–135** the defendant in turning the statements he makes about his defence into questions which can be put to witnesses. Care is needed where the defendant makes a statement which is not evidence but is merely an aid to the legal adviser in assisting to draft questions; magistrates must not make a finding of fact on such a statement or admission made: *Haringey LBC v. Tshilumbe ante*. The legal adviser is also under a duty to ensure that an unrepresented defendant understands evidential issues and that he is not prejudiced by conduct which might put his or her bad character in evidence. If such a course is anticipated by the nature of the questions asked by the defendant in person, the prosecution should ask for an adjournment so that the legal adviser may explain to the defendant the risk of pursuing such a line of questioning: *Weston-Super-Mare Justices, ex p. Townsend*, 132 J.P. 526.

Where a district judge is assisted by a court associate rather than a legal adviser, it is submitted that the duty of the court to assist any unrepresented litigant, without giving the appearance of entering into the arena, applies to the district judge. Where the defendant makes character an issue in the case, particular care will be needed because the district judge may not know whether the defendant is of good character.

E. Rebuttal of Evidence

8–136 At the conclusion of the defence case the prosecution may call rebuttal evidence. This evidence should be confined to a matter which arises unexpectedly in the course of the defence case: *Whelan* (1881) 14 Cox C.C. 595; *Price v. Humphries* [1958] 2 Q.B. 353. In *Owen* [1952] 2 Q.B. 362 the prosecution was allowed to call evidence in order to rebut a matter which it could not have foreseen. Whether a matter is reasonably foreseeable is a matter for the court to determine in the circumstances of the case: *Mendy* (1977) 64 Cr.App.R. 4. The court has a discretion to allow evidence which is not strictly of a rebutting nature. This could also extend to calling evidence to rebut assertions made by a co-defendant.

F. Viewing the Scene of the Crime

8–137 The court may be invited to view the scene of an alleged offence. A view of the scene is part and parcel of a trial. It is part of the evidence in the case. It is akin to real evidence and it is in substitution or supplemental to plans and photographs. If the court agrees to view the scene, then both prosecution and defence should be present or be given the opportunity to be present. The view should take place before the conclusion of the evidence so that both parties have the opportunity of commenting on it: *Parry v. Boyle*, 83 Cr.App.R. 310. The defendant, even when he is legally represented, should be allowed to be present as the view is part of the trial process. Failure to allow the defendant to attend a view is contrary to the fairness of the proceedings: *Ely Justices, ex p. Burgess*, 157 J.P. 484. In this case the prosecutor travelled to view the scene in a car with the magistrates and their clerk and returned to court in the car with the magistrates alone. It was held that these travel arrangements gave the appearance of unfairness.

It is critical before any court embarks upon a view that there is absolute clarity about precisely what is to happen on such a view, about who is to stand in what position, about what (if any) objects should be placed in a specific position and about who will do what. None of this should happen at the scene of a view, which should be conducted without discussion: *M v. DPP* [2009] 2 Cr.App.R. 12.

If a magistrate attends the scene of an alleged offence unofficially during an adjournment it does not necessarily mean that an irregularity has occurred. If the parties allow the trial to continue with the knowledge that an unofficial view has occurred and no prejudice is alleged, then the conviction is unlikely to be quashed on that basis: *Telfer and Telfer v. DPP* (1996) 160 J.P. 512.

Where a court has decided that an organised view would be impracticable, it is not appropriate for a magistrate to conduct a private view, take photographs of the site or carry out experiments in relation to the site: *R. (Broxbourne Borough Council) v. North and East Hertfordshire Magistrates' Court* [2009] N.P.C. 60.

G. Closing Speech

The prosecution's right to make a closing speech, without the court's permission, is restricted by the provisions of s.2 of the *Criminal Procedure Act* 1865, and by s.3 of the *Criminal Evidence Act* 1898. The 1865 Act in essence provides that, if the defendant calls no evidence, the prosecution may only make a closing speech if the defendant is represented. The 1898 Act provides that the fact that an unrepresented defendant gives evidence, does not confer on the prosecution a right to a closing speech. These provisions have been distilled in the *Criminal Procedure Rules*, r.37.3–(3)(g) (see *post* § G–225); the prosecution may make final representations where the defendant is legally represented, or where he has introduced evidence other than his own. In *Bryant* [1979] Q.B. 108, 67 Cr.App.R. 157, Lane, L.J. emphasised that the right of the prosecution to make a closing speech where the defendant, although represented, gives no evidence and calls none, should only rarely be exercised, save possibly in a long and complex case. **8–138**

The position is more complicated where there are co-defendants, one of whom is not represented, or where one of the co-defendants neither gives nor calls any evidence. The general right of reply enjoyed by the prosecution in these circumstances, must be exercised with discretion. Where the evidence called by one defendant does not affect the case of the other, the prosecution's closing speech ought to be confined to the case of the defendant who called the evidence: *Trevelli*, 15 Cox C.C. 289. An example of this would be where a co-defendant calls evidence of an alibi that relates solely to his case.

The defendant is entitled to make any final representations in support of his case after any closing speech by the prosecution. The defendant may address the court on both facts and law; where the defendant raises an issue of law, the practice is that the court will permit the prosecution to reply on the law only. Where the prosecution replies the defendant will have a further opportunity to argue his case.

It is general practice for the legal adviser to advise magistrates in open court so that the legal representatives know the exact basis of the advice. No advice should be offered by a legal adviser, provisional or otherwise, on sentence until the magistrates have returned to court, announced their decision on conviction, heard about the accused's antecedents and listened to counsel's submissions. Legal advisers should only attend upon the bench when called upon to do so, and then only to assist with matters arising at that stage; they should ensure that any list of the defendant's antecedent history is left elsewhere when retiring to give the justices legal advice during any part of the trial process: *R. (Murchison) v. Southend Magistrates' Court*, 170 J.P. 230.

VIII. THE DECISION

A. Alternative Verdicts

Section 9(2) of the *Magistrates' Courts Act* 1980, requires the court either to convict or acquit the defendant. A magistrates' court has no power to return a verdict of not guilty as charged in the information but guilty of a lesser offence. There are two statutory exceptions: **8–139**

Road Traffic Offenders Act 1988, s.24(1)–(3)

Alternative verdicts: general

24.—(1) Where— **8–140**

(a) a person charged with an offence under a provision of the *Road Traffic Act* 1988 specified in the first column of the Table below (where the general nature of the offences is also indicated) is found not guilty of that offence, but

(b) the allegations in the indictment or information (or in Scotland complaint) amount to or include an allegation of an offence under one or more of the provisions specified in the corresponding entry in the second column,

he may be convicted of that offence or of one or more of those offences.

(2) Where the offence with which a person is charged is an offence under section 3A of the *Road Traffic Act* 1988, subsection (1) above shall not authorise his conviction of any offence of attempting to drive.

(3) Where a person is charged with having committed an offence under section 4(1) or 5(1)(a) of the *Road Traffic Act* 1988 by driving a vehicle, he may be convicted of having committed an offence under the provision in question by attempting to drive.

Offence charged	***Alternative***
Section 1 (causing death by dangerous driving)	Section 2 (dangerous driving) Section 3 (careless, and inconsiderate, driving)
Section 2 (dangerous driving)	Section 3 (careless, and inconsiderate, driving)
Section 2B (causing death by careless, or inconsiderate, driving)	Section 3 (careless, and inconsiderate, driving)
Section 3A (causing death by careless driving when under influence of drink or drugs)	[Section 2B (causing death by careless, or inconsiderate, driving)] Section 3 (careless, and inconsiderate, driving) Section 4(1) (driving when unfit to drive through drink or drugs) Section 5(1)(a) (driving with excess alcohol in breath, blood or urine) Section 7(6) (failing to provide specimen) Section 7A(6) (failing to give permission for laboratory test)
Section 4(1) (driving or attempting to drive when unfit to drive through drink or drugs)	Section 4(2) (being in charge of a vehicle when unfit to drive through drink or drugs)
Section 5(1)(a) (driving or attempting to drive with excess alcohol in breath, blood or urine)	Section 5(1)(b) (being in charge of a vehicle with excess alcohol in breath, blood or urine)
Section 28 (dangerous cycling)	Section 29 (careless, and inconsiderate, cycling)

Theft Act 1968, s.12A(5)

Aggravated vehicle-taking

8–141 **12A.**—(5) If a person who is charged with an offence under this section is found not guilty of that offence but it is proved that he committed a basic offence, he may be convicted of the basic offence.

8–142 Where, on a submission of no case to answer, the court dismisses an offence where it would have been open to the court to consider an alternative verdict at the conclusion of the trial, the court has jurisdiction to continue to consider the lesser offence: *DPP v. Smith*, *ante* (concerning s.24); *R. (H) v. Liverpool City Youth Court*, *ante* (concerning s.12A).

Where an information charges an attempt but the evidence establishes the full offence, the court may convict the defendant of the attempt: *Webley v. Buxton* [1977] Q.B. 481.

There is no objection in principle to hearing alternative charges, arising from the same facts, in the same trial. *R. (CPS) v. Blaydon Youth Court*, 168 J.P. 638. Where there is a conviction on both charges, it might be appropriate to impose no separate penalty on the lesser offence. In *DPP v. Gane*, 155 J.P. 846, the defendant pleaded not guilty to charges of driving with excess alcohol, and of being in charge of a vehicle with excess alcohol; the magistrates convicted on the first charge but dismissed the second on the basis that they were alternative charges and that it would be oppressive to convict on both matters. On appeal by the CPS, the Divisional Court held that prosecution should have been invited to indicate whether they wished to pursue the alternative charge. If the prosecution did not wish to pursue the charge it would then have been appropriate for the justices to dismiss it. Alternatively, if the prosecution want to preserve their position pending any possible appeal, the magistrates could either adjourn the matter sine die, or convict of the lesser offence and impose no separate penalty.

Decision Making Process

Magistrates are under a duty to reach a decision and a mandatory order will be granted against them if they do not: *Bridgend Justices, ex p. Randall* [1975] Crim.L.R. 287; *Bromley Justices, ex p. Haymills (Contractors) Ltd*, 148 J.P. 363. If three magistrates are unable to reach a decision on the issue of guilt then the prosecution has failed to prove its case and the proper decision is one of not guilty. **8–142a**

A bench of magistrates reaches its decisions by majority and that is the reason for securing an odd number of magistrates on the bench: *Barnsley v. Marsh* [1947] K.B. 672. There is no casting vote procedure. If magistrates are evenly numbered and equally divided, it will be necessary for the case to be adjourned for rehearing before a differently constituted court of three magistrates: *Redbridge Justices, ex p. Ram* [1992] Q.B. 384, [1992] 94 Cr.App.R. 127.

If magistrates, in considering the verdict, wish to have their memories of the evidence refreshed, then the legal adviser will remind them of what has been said. In *Hulme* [2007] 1 Cr.App.R. 26, where a witness had given oral evidence but a previous inconsistent statement was admitted as evidence, the witness having been treated as hostile, it was decided that a jury should not have access to the statement itself when considering verdict as they would apply a disproportionate weight to the documentary account as opposed to the oral evidence. In a magistrates' court, however, the judiciary are judges of fact and law and the legal adviser would give clear guidance on the appropriate use of the statement. The court may use its local knowledge when deciding a question of fact, however, where justices do use their own local knowledge they should make that known to the parties and give the parties an opportunity to comment: *Bowman v. DPP* [1991] R.T.R. 263; *Norbrook Laboratories (GB) Ltd v. Health & Safety Executive* [1998] E.H.L.R. 207. The fact that magistrates become aware of previous convictions after verdict has been decided but before it has been announced in court does not invalidate the decision: *R. (Murchison) v. Southend Magistrates' Court, ante*.

The court is not obliged to give detailed reasons for its decision: *Brent Justices, ex p. McGowan* (2002) 166 J.P. 29. It is unnecessary for reasons to be elaborate or in the form of a judgement reciting the charges, the evidence and the findings of fact. The essence of the exercise is to inform the defendant why he has been found guilty. This can be done in a few simple sentences.

Reasons should be clear however, and should cover matters which have been raised and why they have been rejected: *Weightman v. DPP* [2007] R.T.R. 45. In that case the Crown Court dealing with an appeal from a magistrates' court, had not given any finding on the statutory defence which had been raised. This case followed the case of *Pullum v. CPS* [2000] C.O.D. 206, an appeal from the magistrates' court to the Crown Court, in which it had been stated that the minimum that a defendant was entitled to was a clear statement as to what evidence the court had accepted. In that case, Lord Bingham, C.J. cited with approval the judgment of Pill, J. sitting in the Divisional Court in *Harrow Crown Court, ex p. Dave*, 99 Cr.App.R. 114 when he gave the following guidance:

"The Crown Court judge giving the decision of the court upon an appeal must say enough to demonstrate that the court has identified the main contentious issues in the case and how it has resolved each of them. In the present case the issues were of fact and not of law. Elaborate reasoning was not required. . . The reasoning required will depend upon the circumstances. In some cases the bald statement that the evidence of a particular witness is accepted may be sufficient ... The appellant was entitled to know the basis upon which the prosecution case had been accepted by the court... A refusal to give reasons may amount to the denial of natural justice."

It is submitted that the same guidance would apply to magistrates giving their decision, and a failure to give reasons, however brief, might constitute a breach of the fair trial requirement under ECHR art. 6.

It is also essential that a court does not give the impression, by the choice of words used, that it has not applied the correct criminal standard of proof: *Ukpabi v. DPP* [2008] EWHC 952 (Admin).

CHAPTER 9

WITNESSES

I. SECURING THE ATTENDANCE OF WITNESSES

A. SUMMONSES AND WARRANTS

Magistrates' Courts Act 1980, s.97

Summons to witness and warrant for his arrest

9–1 **97.**—(1) Where a justice of the peace is satisfied that—

(a) any person in England or Wales is likely to be able to give material evidence, or produce any document or thing likely to be material evidence, at the summary trial of an information or hearing of a complaint by a magistrates' court, and

(b) it is in the interests of justice to issue a summons under this subsection to secure the attendance of that person to give evidence or produce the document or thing,

the justice shall issue a summons directed to that person requiring him to attend before the court at the time and place appointed in the summons to give evidence or to produce the document or thing.

(2) If a justice of the peace is satisfied by evidence on oath of the matters mentioned in subsection (1) above, and also that it is probable that a summons under that subsection would not procure the attendance of the person in question, the justice may instead of issuing a summons issue a warrant to arrest that person and bring him before such a court as aforesaid at a time and place specified in the warrant; but a warrant shall not be issued under this subsection where the attendance is required for the hearing of a complaint.

(2A) A summons may also be issued under subsection (1) above if the justice is satisfied that the person in question is outside the British Islands but no warrant shall be issued under subsection (2) above unless the justice is satisfied by evidence on oath that the person in question is in England or Wales.

(2B) A justice may refuse to issue a summons under subsection (1) above in relation to the summary trial of an information if he is not satisfied that an application for the summons was made by a party to the case as soon as reasonably practicable after the accused pleaded not guilty.

(2C) In relation to the summary trial of an information, subsection (2) above shall have effect as if the reference to the matters mentioned in subsection (1) above included a reference to the matter mentioned in subsection (2B) above.

(3) On the failure of any person to attend before a magistrates' court in answer to a summons under this section, if—

(a) the court is satisfied by evidence on oath that he is likely to be able to give material evidence or produce any document or thing likely to be material evidence in the proceedings; and

(b) it is proved on oath, or in such other manner as may be prescribed, that he has been duly served with the summons, and that a reasonable sum has been paid or tendered to him for costs and expenses; and

(c) it appears to the court that there is no just excuse for the failure,

the court may issue a warrant to arrest him and bring him before the court at a time and place specified in the warrant.

(4) If any person attending or brought before a magistrates' court refuses without just excuse to be sworn or give evidence, or to produce any document or thing, the court may commit him to custody until the expiration of such period not exceeding one month as may be specified in the warrant or until he sooner gives evidence or produces the document or thing or impose on him a fine not exceeding £2,500 or both.

(5) A fine imposed under subsection (4) above shall be deemed, for the purposes of any enactment, to be a sum adjudged to be paid by a conviction.

[This section is printed as amended by the *Serious Organised Crime and Police Act* 2005, s.169(2).]

9–2 The court may issue a summons or a warrant to secure the attendance of a witness. The test for issuing a summons has been amended by the *Serious Organised Crime and Police Act* 2005. The court no longer has to be satisfied that a witness will not voluntarily attend court or produce a document or something else which is likely to be material evidence. The court may issue a summons if it is in the interests of justice and the court is satisfied with regard to the material evidence criteria. It is important that if the court is to serve the summons "conduct money", *i.e.* sufficient money to enable the witness to attend court is deposited with the court.

The *Criminal Procedure Rules* 2011, r. 28.2 as amended by the *Criminal Procedure (Amendment) Rules* 2007 in Appendix G provide for a hearing to be in private unless the court otherwise directs. The applicant may make an application orally unless the court directs that it be in writing or it is an application usually known as third party disclosure, *i.e.* where the witness is asked to produce a document or thing (other than a banker's book) or where he is asked to give evidence about a confidential matter. The applicant must identify the witness; explain what evidence the proposed witness can give or produce, why the evidence is likely to be material and why it would be in the interests of justice to issue the summons. Where an application must be made in writing it must be in the proper form. Documents sought must be identified with sufficient certainty so as to leave no doubt in the mind of the person to whom the summons is addressed as to what to bring to court: *Tajik Aluminium Plant v. (1) Hydro Aluminium AS; (2) Abdukadir Ganievich Ermatov; (3) Alexander Shushko; (4) Avaz Nazarov; (5) Ashton Investments Ltd* [2005] EWCA Civ 1218. **9–3**

Part II

The application must be served on the proposed witness, unless the court otherwise directs and, if the court directs, on the person to whom the proposed evidence relates and any other person the court directs. Service can be effected abroad although there is no sanction for non-compliance: *Crime (International Co-operation) Act* 2003, s.3. The court will not issue a summons where the application is required to be in writing unless anyone served has had fourteen days in which to make representation on the application or whether there should be a hearing before the summons is issued. The court must also be satisfied that it has been able to take adequate account of the duties and rights including confidentiality of the proposed witness and any other person to whom the evidence relates. Where a person objects to the production of a document on the ground that it is not likely to be material evidence or, if it were, the right of confidentiality would outweigh the issue of a summons, the court may require the document to be made available for the court to assess, with the help of the proposed witness or his representative or the person or his representative to whom the document relates.

It must be remembered that the provisions for disclosure are not directed to creating duties for third parties to follow; the duties are created in respect of material that the prosecution or police have and which the prosecution has inspected: *DPP v. Wood* [2006] EWHC 32. The Attorney General's Guidelines on Disclosure at Appendix C–17 direct the prosecution to take appropriate steps to obtain material in the hands of third parties which might reasonably be considered capable of undermining the prosecution case or assisting the defence. It is for the prosecution to determine what is deemed to be appropriate in the circumstances of each case; in an extreme case it might be so unfair to proceed in the absence of the third party material that the case should not proceed: *Alibhai* [2004] EWCA Crim 681. Where material comes into the hands of the prosecution then the third party must be consulted before disclosure takes place.

If a party refuses to supply the information the prosecution will consider applying for a witness summons. The applicant must then show that the likely evidence is material to the case: *R. v. Peterborough Magistrates' Court, ex p. Willis* (1987) 151 J.P. 785. It will be material if it is relevant to the case: *R. v. Reading J.J., ex. p. Berkshire County Council* [1996] 1 Cr.App.R. 239, DC. In this case a summons was held to be improper where it had been issued to test whether files held by the Director of Social Services in respect of a fifteen-year-old boy who was a victim of an alleged assault by police officers might offer any relevant or important information. It is improper to use the witness summons procedure to obtain discovery or to require production of documents at a hearing when they are not likely to be material evidence but their presence in court is desired for cross-examination purposes (in this case many documents relating to the Lion Intoximeter device): *R. v. Skegness Magistrates' Court ex p. Cardy* [1985] R.T.R. 49. The applicant must also show that the evidence is admissible. Where there is a suggestion that information about bad character, for example, is available then, it is submitted, the applicant must show through which gateway it will be adduced. If the material is not *prima facie* admissible the summons is likely to be set aside: *R. v. Cheltenham J.J., ex.p. Secretary of State for Trade* [1977] 1 W.L.R. 95, DC. That case involved transcripts and material obtained during an investigation which were to be used for the purposes of cross-examination only to contradict what witnesses might say. It was said that even if the documents were material, they should not be produced because the public interest in maintaining sources of information in respect of an inquiry of the kind carried out under section 165 of the *Companies Act* 1948 would outweigh the private disadvantage of non-disclosure. In *R. v. Derby Magistrates' Court, ex p. B.* [1996] A.C. 487 it was said that documents had to be admissible *per se* and a summons was not appropriate to obtain discovery of documents which might, or might not be, upon examination, admissible. Production of documents should not be ordered where they are likely merely to afford or assist a relevant line of inquiry or challenge: *H. (L.), Re* [1997] 1 Cr.App.R. 176. A court should not issue a witness summons to produce evidence where evidence had then to be given by expert witnesses as to its admissibility: *R. (Cunliffe) v. West London Magistrates' Court* [2006] EWHC 2081. In that case it was held that the summons for complete unedited settings of a breath test machine, engineers' reports, calibration/service sheets and the engineer's standing operating procedures had been wrongly issued.

A court must also be satisfied that the issue of a summons is in the public interest and this is where issues of confidentiality and Article 8 ECHR arise with respect to personal records, such as school, social service, income tax or medical records. It has been accepted that medical records are private and confidential: *Campbell v. MGN Ltd* [2004] 2 A.C. 457 at para. 145 and that includes psychiatric medical notes: *Ashworth Hospital Authority v. MGN* [2002] UKHL 29 at para. 63. In *R. (Axon) v. Secretary of State for Health* [2006] 2 W.L.R. 1130 it was said that the duty of confidence owed by a medical professional to a competent young person is a high one which should not be overridden except for a very powerful reason. In order to order disclosure, therefore, a court must be satisfied that it is proportionate and necessary to prevent crime or protect the rights and freedom of others, *i.e.* ensuring a fair trial. In *Re M., (a minor) (Disclosure of Material)* [1990] 2 F.L.R. 36 the court was of the opinion that social work reports prepared in circumstances concerning the welfare of children were subject to a special form of immunity and disclosure could only be justified in the circumstances of a particular case. Documents relating to family proceedings and filed with the court cannot be disclosed to anyone without the leave of the court: *Family Proceedings Rules* 1991, r. 4.23.

A summons should not be refused where the preconditions are satisfied and where it is crucial to the applicant's case: *R. v. Bradford JJ. ex p. Wilkinson* [1990] 1 W.L.R. 692.

A court must carry out a balancing exercise, having regard to the weight of the public interest in non-disclosure and the importance of the documents to the defence. If the material might prove a person's innocence or avoid a miscarriage of justice, the balance should come down resoundingly in favour of disclosure: *Keane* [1994] 1 W.L.R. 746. A court must ensure that a defendant is not disadvantaged by a refusal to allow him to gather necessary evidence: *D.* [2006] EWCA Crim 2600. In that case the defendant had been charged with grievous bodily harm and sought to adduce evidence of the victim's bad character, including behaviour at school and college, a previous altercation between him and the defendant and an attack on a co-defendant. Evidence of the assault was allowed but not the disclosure of school records of pupils who had made complaints against the victim. On appeal it was held that, in view of the public interest in preserving the confidentiality of school records and Art. 8 rights of those involved, the names of those involved, in so far as they were children, should not be disclosed but it was also held that the defendant had been disadvantaged as the evidence was relevant to the defendant's state of mind at the time and a simple admission by the prosecution that the defendant knew of the victim's reputation for bullying would have sufficed. It is the duty of the prosecution to co-operate in ensuring that a defendant has a fair trial.

It was said in *Rothon v. DPP* [2006] All E.R. (D) 367 that where evidence in an intoximeter case was accepted from an expert that the device was working correctly the magistrates should have ordered disclosure of the records relating to that device so that the defendant could cross-examine properly.

A summons may be withdrawn on application by the original applicant, the witness if he was not aware of the application and cannot give or produce material evidence or the person to whom the evidence relates if he was unaware of the application and the evidence is not likely to be material or even if it is, his rights or those of the witness outweigh the reasons for the issue of the summons: *Criminal Procedure Rules* 2011, r. 28.7.

Formal service of a witness summons is not required provided its existence is distinctly brought to the attention of the witness; in issuing a warrant for the arrest of the witness who has failed to answer the summons a court should, where it believes that the witness will voluntarily attend or accompany police officers to court, back the warrant for bail or direct that it should be executed at court: *R. v. Popat* (2009) 172 J.P. 24.

See *Criminal Procedure Rules* 2011, r. 28 in Appendix G. **9–4**

B. CASE MANAGEMENT DUTIES IN RELATION TO WITNESSES

The *Criminal Procedure Rules*, in force since 2005, and accompanying statutory **9–4a** measures, make important provision *inter alia* for the attendance and needs of witnesses. The then senior Presideing Judge, Leveson L.J., said in December 2009, "*It is important to note that all participants in criminal cases including magistrates, District Judges and Justices Clerks* ***must*** *follow and apply the Criminal Procedure Rules. The Rules are not mere guidance. Compliance is compulsory. The word* ***must*** *in the Rules means* ***must***". The text of the Rules is to be found at Appendix G.

Any person involved in any way with a criminal case is a participant in its conduct for the purposes of the Rules (Rule 1.2(2)).

Failure to comply with the Rules may result in sanctions.

The overriding objective of the new code is that criminal cases be dealt with justly (Rule 1.1(1)).

Dealing with a criminal case justly includes respecting the interests of the witnesses and victims (Rule 1.1(2)(d)).

For a fuller account of the Rules and how they relate to witnesses—see § 7–3 *et seq.*

The requirement to identify witnesses in Rule 3.10(c) is also statutory. See *Criminal Procedure and Investigations Act* 1996, s.6C which is inserted into that Act by s.34 of the *Criminal Justice Act* 2003. The section is reproduced at § 6–47, above.

II. SWEARING OF A WITNESS

A. GENERAL

Unless a particular statute allows unsworn evidence, all evidence given before a magistrates' court will be given on oath: *Magistrates' Courts Act* 1980, s.98. A child's evidence will be given unsworn but witnesses aged 14 years or over must give evidence on oath: *Sharman* [1998] 1 Cr.App.R. 406; *Youth Justice and Criminal Evidence Act* 1999, s.55(2)(a). **9–5**

B. FORM OF OATH

Oaths Act 1978, s.1

Manner of administration of oaths

1.—(1) Any oath may be administered and taken in England, Wales or Northern Ireland in the following form and manner— **9–6**

The person taking the oath shall hold the New Testament, or, in the case of a Jew, the Old

Testament, in his uplifted hand, and shall say or repeat after the officer administering the oath the words "I swear by Almighty God that ...", followed by the words of the oath prescribed by law.

(2) The officer shall (unless the person about to take the oath voluntarily objects thereto, or is physically incapable of so taking the oath) administer the oath in the form and manner aforesaid without question.

(3) In the case of a person who is neither a Christian nor a Jew, the oath shall be administered in any lawful manner.

(4) In this section "officer" means any person duly authorised to administer oaths.

9–7 Magistrates' courts have facilities to administer the oath in accordance with most religions and will ask a witness outside of court how he wishes to be sworn so that the oath taking in court proceeds in a proper manner.

The purpose of taking an oath is that it should be binding on a witness's conscience. The question whether a witness who is neither a Christian nor a Jew has been lawfully sworn depends on whether the oath appears to the court to be binding on the conscience of the witness and whether the witness himself considers his conscience bound. If a Muslim takes the oath using the New Testament he could still be lawfully sworn. The question of whether an oath is lawfully administered does not depend on what may be the considerable intricacies of the particular religion adhered to by the witness: *Kemble* [1990] 1 W.L.R. 1111.

It is not usual to ask whether someone objects to taking the oath. A witness is asked to choose between the oath and affirmation.

C. AFFIRMATION

Oaths Act 1978, ss.5–6

Making of solemn affirmations

9–8 **5.**—(1) Any person who objects to being sworn shall be permitted to make his solemn affirmation instead of taking an oath.

(2) Subsection (1) above shall apply in relation to a person to whom it is not reasonably practicable without inconvenience or delay to administer an oath in the manner appropriate to his religious belief as it applies in relation to a person objecting to be sworn.

(3) A person who may be permitted under subsection (2) above to make his solemn affirmation may also be required to do so.

(4) A solemn affirmation shall be of the same force and effect as an oath.

Form of affirmation

9–9 **6.**—(1) Subject to subsection (2) below, every affirmation shall be as follows—

"I ... do solemnly, sincerely and truly declare and affirm,"

and then proceed with the words of the oath prescribed by law, omitting any words of imprecation or calling to witness.

(2) Every affirmation in writing shall commence—

"I ... do solemnly and sincerely affirm,"

and the form in lieu of jurat shall be "Affirmed at ... this ... day of ... 19..., Before me."

D. UNSWORN TESTIMONY

Youth Justice and Criminal Evidence Act 1999, ss.55–57

Determining whether witness to be sworn

9–10 **55.**—(1) Any question whether a witness in criminal proceedings may be sworn for the purpose of giving evidence on oath, whether raised—

(a) by a party to the proceedings, or
(b) by the court of its own motion,

shall be determined by the court in accordance with this section.

(2) The witness may not be sworn for that purpose unless—

(a) he has attained the age of 14, and

(b) he has a sufficient appreciation of the solemnity of the occasion and of the particular responsibility to tell the truth which is involved in taking an oath.

(3) The witness shall, if he is able to give intelligible testimony, be presumed to have a sufficient appreciation of those matters if no evidence tending to show the contrary is adduced (by any party).

(4) If any such evidence is adduced, it is for the party seeking to have the witness sworn to satisfy the court that, on a balance of probabilities, the witness has attained the age of 14 and has a sufficient appreciation of the matters mentioned in subsection (2)(b).

(5) Any proceedings held for the determination of the question mentioned in subsection (1) shall take place in the absence of the jury (if there is one).

(6) Expert evidence may be received on the question.

(7) Any questioning of the witness (where the court considers that necessary) shall be conducted by the court in the presence of the parties.

(8) For the purposes of this section a person is able to give intelligible testimony if he is able to—

(a) understand questions put to him as a witness, and

(b) give answers to them which can be understood.

Reception of unsworn evidence

56.—(1) Subsections (2) and (3) apply to a person (of any age) who— **9–11**

(a) is competent to give evidence in criminal proceedings, but

(b) (by virtue of section 55(2)) is not permitted to be sworn for the purpose of giving evidence on oath in such proceedings.

(2) The evidence in criminal proceedings of a person to whom this subsection applies shall be given unsworn.

(3) A deposition of unsworn evidence given by a person to whom this subsection applies may be taken for the purposes of criminal proceedings as if that evidence had been given on oath.

(4) A court in criminal proceedings shall accordingly receive in evidence any evidence given unsworn in pursuance of subsection (2) or (3).

(5) Where a person ("the witness") who is competent to give evidence in criminal proceedings gives evidence in such proceedings unsworn, no conviction, verdict or finding in those proceedings shall be taken to be unsafe for the purposes of any of sections 2(1), 13(1) and 16(1) of the *Criminal Appeal Act* 1968 (grounds for allowing appeals) by reason only that it appears to the Court of Appeal that the witness was a person falling within section 55(2) (and should accordingly have given his evidence on oath).

Penalty for giving false unsworn evidence

57.—(1) This section applies where a person gives unsworn evidence in criminal proceedings in pursuance of section 56(2) or (3). **9–12**

(2) If such a person wilfully gives false evidence in such circumstances that, had the evidence been given on oath, he would have been guilty of perjury, he shall be guilty of an offence and liable on summary conviction to—

(a) imprisonment for a term not exceeding 6 months, or

(b) a fine not exceeding £1,000,

or both.

(3) In relation to a person under the age of 14, subsection (2) shall have effect as if for the words following "on summary conviction" there were substituted "to a fine not exceeding £250".

A witness may not take the oath unless he is fourteen years old. He must also appreciate the solemnity of the occasion and the responsibility to tell the truth. This may be ascertained from the fact that he is able to give an intelligent explanation of what has happened. It is for the party calling the witness to satisfy the court of those matters on a balance of probabilities and, in certain circumstances, expert evidence may be received. If it is found that he is incapable of giving sworn evidence then his evidence will be taken unsworn. **9–13**

III. COMPETENCE AND COMPELLABILITY

A. GENERAL

9–14 A witness is competent if he can lawfully give evidence and compellable if he can be lawfully required to give evidence.

Youth Justice and Criminal Evidence Act 1999, s.53

Competence of witnesses to give evidence

9–15 **53.**—(1) At every stage in criminal proceedings all persons are (whatever their age) competent to give evidence.

(2) Subsection (1) has effect subject to subsections (3) and (4).

(3) A person is not competent to give evidence in criminal proceedings if it appears to the court that he is not a person who is able to—

(a) understand questions put to him as a witness, and

(b) give answers to them which can be understood.

(4) A person charged in criminal proceedings is not competent to give evidence in the proceedings for the prosecution (whether he is the only person, or is one of two or more persons, charged in the proceedings).

(5) In subsection (4) the reference to a person charged in criminal proceedings does not include a person who is not, or is no longer, liable to be convicted of any offence in the proceedings (whether as a result of pleading guilty or for any other reason).

B. DETERMINING COMPETENCY

9–16 The general rule that all persons are competent to give evidence at every stage in criminal proceedings is subject to a test of competence contained in the *Youth Justice and Criminal Evidence Act* 1999, s.54.

Youth Justice and Criminal Evidence Act 1999, s.54

Determining competence of witnesses

9–17 **54.**—(1) Any question whether a witness in criminal proceedings is competent to give evidence in the proceedings, whether raised—

(a) by a party to the proceedings, or

(b) by the court of its own motion,

shall be determined by the court in accordance with this section.

(2) It is for the party calling the witness to satisfy the court that, on a balance of probabilities, the witness is competent to give evidence in the proceedings.

(3) In determining the question mentioned in subsection (1) the court shall treat the witness as having the benefit of any directions under section 19 which the court has given, or proposes to give, in relation to the witness.

(5) Expert evidence may be received on the question.

(6) Any questioning of the witness (where the court considers that necessary) shall be conducted by the court in the presence of the parties.

9–18 Any objection to a witness's competency must be made before he is sworn or gives evidence: *Hampshire* [1996] Q.B.1; [1995] 2 Cr.App.R. 319, CA. In *Yacoob* (1981) 72 Cr.App.R. 313, CA, the court said that the beginning of the trial was the appropriate time for determining competence and compellability of prosecution witnesses. If, prior to the hearing, an objection has been raised with the prosecution then the evidence to be given by that witness should not be referred to in the opening speech.

C. CHILDREN

9–19 All persons of whatever age are competent to give evidence: s.53(1), *ante*. The evidence of a child will be received unless it appears to the court that the child is incapable of giving intelligible testimony; that is evidence which is capable of being understood:

Hampshire [1996] Q.B. 1. The procedure of determining intelligible testimony is the same for children as for adults: s.55. The issue of competence should be dealt with as early as possible, not as an act of "ratification" after the evidence has been given. It is not an issue to be resolved in response to an adversarial examination and cross-examination but is a matter for the court to decide having heard the child in person. In *G. v. DPP* [1998] Q.B. 919 it was held that the test is within the competence of the court and there is no need for expert evidence unless there are special circumstances, *e.g.* where a child is mentally handicapped. *R. v. MacPherson* [2006] 1 Cr.App.R. 30 reviewed the position of child witnesses. If a child can only understand and communicate in a way only his parent can understand, he may not be competent as a witness but if a child can understand questions put to him in simple English, and is able to give answers the court can understand, he should be allowed to give evidence. This was taken further in *R. v. Barker* [2010] EWCA Crim 4, where, in the case of a four-year-old child deemed to be competent, the Court of Appeal held that whenever the competency question is addressed, what is required is not the exercise of a discretion but the making of a judgement of whether the witness fulfils the statutory criteria. The approach must be child specific: (i) although the chronological age of the child will inevitably help to inform the judicial decision, in the end it is a decision about the individual child and his competence to give evidence in the particular trial; (ii) although due allowance must be made in the trial process for the fact that the witness is a child, none of the characteristics of childhood and none of the special measures which apply to a child's evidence carry with them the implicit stigma that children should be deemed in advance to be somehow less reliable than adults; (iii) at the stage when the question of competency is determined the court is not deciding whether a witness will or will not tell the truth or give accurate evidence. Provided the witness is competent, the weight to be attached to the evidence is for the court to decide having heard the evidence; (iv) the competency test is not failed because the forensic techniques of the advocate or the process of the court have to be adapted to enable the child to give best evidence of which he is capable; (v) comment on the evidence including comment which may bear unfavourably on the credibility of the child, should be addressed after the child has finished giving evidence. Generally speaking it is the legal adviser who will talk to the child, ask if he knows why he is there and from simple questions find out whether he understands what telling the truth means.

The fact that a child under ten years of age cannot be prosecuted for the offence of wilfully giving false evidence contrary to the *Youth Justice and Criminal Evidence Act* 1999, s.57 is not a reason for excluding the unsworn evidence of a competent child: *N.* (1992) 95 Cr.App.R. 256. It is essential that a very young child is interviewed as soon as possible after the event complained of and that the trial takes place very soon thereafter: *P.* [2006] EWCA Crim 3. The evidence of a child witness may be contaminated where the child says that his mother told him what to say: *C.* [2006] 1 W.L.R. 2994; . Where there is a video interview it is appropriate for a court to take the view that the child is competent and allow evidence in chief and cross-examination to take place and then revisit the question of competence: *R. v. MacPherson*, *ante*; *R. v. Powell* [2006] 1 Cr.App.R. 31. The court must be aware, in the case of a very young child, that there is a risk that, because of age, recollection may not be accurate when a long period of time has elapsed between the alleged commission of the offence and the trial: *R. v. Malicki* [2009] EWCA Crim 365.

The case of *Barker*, *ante* concluded that the decisions in *Powell and Maliki (ante)* should not be understood to establish as a matter of principle that where the complainant is a young child, delay which does not constitute an abuse of process within well understood principles, can give rise to some special form of defence, or that, if it does not, a submission based on "unfairness" under s.78 *Police and Criminal Evidence Act* 1984 is bound to succeed, or that there is some kind of unspecified limitation period.

The *Consolidated Criminal Practice Direction*, para. I.5, in Appendix F–7 applies to wards of court.

D. MENTALLY DISORDERED PERSONS

A witness who is prevented from giving rational testimony by reason of mental illness **9–20** or drunkenness is not competent. Where a witness appears to be unable to give intelligible testimony by reason of mental illness or intoxication, the court should ascertain whether the witness is capable of understanding the questions put to him or to give answers which can be understood pursuant to the provisions of ss.54–57 of the *Youth Justice and Criminal Evidence Act* 1999. This may be done by calling expert evidence, see *Hill* (1851) 2 Den. 254; *Dunning* [1965] Crim.L.R. 372. The worth of the evidence will ultimately be a matter for the court. In cases of mental illness this will depend on degree. In *Hill*, *ante*, the circumstances were such that the proper course was to reject the evidence.

E. THE ACCUSED

Criminal Evidence Act 1898, s.1

Competency of witnesses in criminal cases

9–21 **1.**—(1) A person charged in criminal proceedings shall not be called as a witness in the proceedings except upon his own application.

(2) Subject to section 101 of the *Criminal Justice Act* 2003 (admissibility of evidence of defendant's bad character), a person charged in criminal proceedings who is called as a witness in the proceedings may be asked any question in cross-examination notwithstanding that it would tend to criminate him as to any offence with which he is charged in the proceedings.

(3) […]

(4) Every person charged in criminal proceedings who is called as a witness in the proceedings shall, unless otherwise ordered by the court, give his evidence from the witness box or other place from which the other witnesses give their evidence.

[This section is printed as amended by *Criminal Justice Act* 2003, Sched. 37.]

9–22 The defendant is not a compellable witness for the prosecution: *Rhodes* [1899] 1 Q.B. 77 and a defendant cannot be compelled to give evidence against a co-defendant: *Payne* L.R. 1 C.C.R. 349; *Grant*, 30 Cr.App.R. 99; *Sharrock* (1948) 32 Cr.App.R. 124.

A defendant who has pleaded guilty is not a "person charged" within the meaning of section 1 of the 1898 Act because he is not concerned in any issue before the judge of fact. A defendant who has pleaded guilty is therefore competent and compellable to give evidence for a co-defendant: *Boal* [1965] 1 Q.B. 402. A plea of guilty by a co-defendant is not evidence against the defendant: *Smith* (1984) 148 J.P. 215.

A co-defendant who has been acquitted is not a "person charged" within the *Criminal Evidence Act* 1898, s.1, and is therefore compellable as a witness: *Conti* (1974) 58 Cr.App.R. 387, CA. Those concerned with the charge should not be called by the prosecution: *Pipe* (1967) 51 Cr.App.R. 17. The prosecution may, however, call an accomplice who is to be charged and tried separately: *Palmer* (1994) 99 Cr.App.R. 83.

The defendant is a competent witness for himself. He is not, however, a compellable witness for the defence: *Criminal Evidence Act* 1898, s.1(1). An acquitted person called by the defendant may be cross-examined by a co-defendant.

A defendant who gives evidence for a co-defendant is liable to be cross-examined on the issue of his own guilt: *Rowland* [1910] 1 K.B. 458. If a defendant refuses to answer questions incriminating other persons, the court is not bound to receive his or her evidence: *Minihane* 16 Cr.App.R. 38.

F. THE DEFENDANT'S SPOUSE

Police and Criminal Evidence Act 1984, s.80

Competence and compellability of the defendant's spouse

9–23 **80.**—(2) In any proceedings the wife or husband of a person charged in the proceedings shall, subject to subsection (4) below, be compellable to give evidence on behalf of that person.

(2A) In any proceedings the wife or husband of a person charged in the proceedings shall, subject to subsection (4) below, be compellable—

(a) to give evidence on behalf of any other person charged in the proceedings but only in respect of any specified offence with which that other person is charged; or

(b) to give evidence for the prosecution but only in respect of any specified offence with which any person is charged in the proceedings.

(3) In relation to the wife or husband of a person charged in any proceedings, an offence is a specified offence for the purposes of subsection (2A) above if—

(a) it involves an assault on, or injury or a threat of injury to, the wife or husband or a person who was at the material time under the age of 16;

(b) it is a sexual offence alleged to have been committed in respect of a person who was at the material time under that age; or

(c) it consists of attempting or conspiring to commit, or of aiding, abetting, counselling, procuring or inciting the commission of, an offence falling within paragraph (a) or (b) above.

(4) No person who is charged in any proceedings shall be compellable by virtue of subsection (2) or (2A) above to give evidence in the proceedings.

(4A) References in this section to a person charged in any proceedings do not include a person who is not, or is no longer, liable to be convicted of any offence in the proceedings (whether as a result of pleading guilty or for any other reason).

(5) In any proceedings a person who has been but is no longer married to the accused shall be compellable to give evidence as if that person and the accused had never been married.

(6) Where in any proceedings the age of any person at any time is material for the purposes of subsection (3) above, his age at the material time shall for the purposes of that provision be deemed to be or to have been that which appears to the court to be or to have been his age at that time.

(7) In subsection (3)(b) above "sexual-offence" means an offence under the *Sexual Offences Act* 1956, the *Indecency with Children Act* 1960, the *Sexual Offences Act* 1967, section 54 of the *Criminal Law Act* 1977 or the *Protection of Children Act* 1978.

(8) […]

(9) Section 1(d) of the *Criminal Evidence Act* 1898 (communications between husband and wife) and section 43(1) of the *Matrimonial Causes Act* 1965 (evidence as to marital intercourse) shall cease to have effect.

A spouse is competent to give evidence against a defendant but is only compellable in the terms of the statute. Compelling a wife to give evidence is not the same thing as permitting another witness to give evidence of a voluntary statement made by a wife in the past: *R. v. L* 2 Cr.App.R. 18 where, in a case of child abuse, a statement made by the wife to the police was admitted unders.114 of the *Criminal Justice Act* 2003 despite the fact that she did not want to give evidence. The Court of Appeal decided that whether such a statement should be admitted was a matter for each individual case, that there was no obligation on the police to warn a wife that she was not compellable as that could inhibit the investigation of a crime although a warning might well assist a court to find that a statement had been made voluntarily. **9–24**

Section 80 does not apply to the defendant's unmarried partner: *Pearce* [2002] 1 Cr.App.R. 39, CA. Although the compellability of a family member to give evidence against another might conflict with the right to family life under Art. 8 of the European Convention on Human Rights the interference may be justified under Art. 8(2) as necessary in a democratic society for the prevention of crime.

The position of a wife of a second polygamous marriage is no different from that of a woman who has not gone through a marriage ceremony at all or who has gone through a ceremony which was invalid: *Yacoob* (1981) 72 Cr.App.R. 313, CA; *Khan* (1987) 84 Cr.App.R. 44, CA.

The prosecution has a duty to disclose to the defence that a spouse has informed the prosecutor outside the court that he does not wish to give evidence against his spouse and that the statement given to the police is inaccurate: *R. v. Birmingham Justices, ex p. Shields*, *The Times*, August 3, 1994, CA. The prosecution must also inform the court so that the spouse can be warned that he need not give evidence. Once a spouse has started to give evidence he must complete it and may be treated as a hostile witness if he shows an unwillingness to continue: *Pitt* [1983] Q.B. 25.

The failure of a spouse to give evidence should not be subject to comment by the prosecution: s.80A of the *Police and Criminal Evidence Act* 1984.

G. OTHER WITNESSES

9–25 The sovereign is a competent but not compellable witness. Foreign heads of state, diplomatic and consular staff, members of the family of a diplomatic agent, members of the administrative and technical staff of a diplomatic mission and members of their families, persons connected with consular posts and members of staff of international organisations enjoy total or partial immunity from compellability to give evidence.

See *Diplomatic Privileges Act* 1964, s.1(1), Sched. 1, Arts 1, 30, 37, 38(2) and 39; *State Immunity Act* 1978, s.14; and the *International Organisations Act* 1968, s.5.

High Court judges and those of inferior courts are not compellable witnesses: *Warren v. Warren* [1997] 1 F.C.R. 237, CA. Magistrates and their legal advisers, however, are compellable: *Re McC (a minor)* [1985] A.C. 528.

IV. THE PROTECTION OF WITNESSES

A. GENERAL

9–26 Generally witnesses give their evidence in open court and with their identity disclosed. There may be circumstances, however, where they will either give evidence anonymously or where measures may be taken by the court to assist them. The *Youth Justice and Criminal Evidence Act* 1999 post provides for special measures to be taken for the protection of vulnerable witnesses and these measures may include screening witnesses from the defendant, giving evidence by live link, video-recorded evidence in chief and cross-examination, examination of a witness through an intermediary, protection from cross-examination by a defendant in person and restrictions on the type of questions asked. In 2002 the Home Office published Achieving Best Evidence in Criminal Proceedings: Guidance for Vulnerable or Intimidated Witnesses, including Children *www.homeoffice.gov.uk* which describes good practice in such matters. The Judicial Studies Board has also published guidance for the judiciary and legal staff in magistrates' courts: *www.jsboard.co.uk*. It recommends that:

1. cases involving child or vulnerable or intimidated witnesses are identified and their needs assessed;
2. cases are given an early trial date where double listing is avoided;
3. applications for special measures are made in a timely manner;
4. witnesses are provided with adequate pre-trial information, including the "Young Witness Pack", "Going to Court" DVD and visits where appropriate;
5. video recorded evidence is seen by the witness before the trial;
6. all playback equipment is checked for compatibility and good working order before the day of the trial;
7. witnesses are separated from the other side at court;
8. waiting times on the day are minimised and every effort is made to make the trial effective;
9. appropriate introductions are given to child or vulnerable witnesses before they give their evidence;
10. inappropriate cross-examination is controlled and questioning that lacks relevance, is repetitive, oppressive or intimidating is ruled out in accordance with the court's overriding duty to deal with cases justly;
11. witnesses receive a simple "thank-you" after giving their evidence.

Lord Carswell in *R. v. Davis* (2008) 3 W.L.R. 125 outlined the following propositions gleaned from domestic authorities:

(a) there is a presumption in favour of open justice and confrontation of a defendant by his accuser;
(b) it is possible to allow departures from the basic rule of open justice, to some extent, but a clear case of necessity should be made out;
(c) the court should be sufficiently satisfied that the witness's reluctance to give evidence in the ordinary manner is genuine and that the extent of his or her fear justifies a degree of anonymity;
(d) anonymising expedients may include the withholding of the witness's name and address, screening of the witness from the defendant and the public, screening from the defendant's legal advisers, disguising of the witness's voice from the defendant and public and disguising the witness's voice from the legal advisers;
(e) the more of these expedients the court might consider adopting, the stronger the case must be for invading the principle of open justice. Determination of the question depends upon balancing to ensure that the trial continues to be fair;
(f) an important consideration is the relative importance of the witness's testimony in the prosecution case. If it constitutes the sole or decisive evidence against the defendant, anonymising which prevents or unduly hinders the defendant and his advisers from taking steps to undermine the credit of the witness is most likely to operate unfairly. It is a question of fact in any given case what, if any, measures would be compatible with sufficient fairness of the trial. Courts trying criminal cases should not be over-ready to resort to such measures. As a general rule it is unlikely that the trial will be fair if a very substantial degree of anonymising evidence is permitted where the testimony of the witnesses concerned constitutes the sole or decisive evidence implicating the defendant.

As a result of this judgment the government swiftly drew up the *Criminal Evidence (Witness Anonymity) Act* 2008 now superceded in the *Coroners and Justice Act* 2009. The Act provides for the court to make orders securing the anonymity of witnesses in criminal proceedings see 9–56a *post*. **9–27**

In determining whether to order special measures and in considering the type of measure the court will balance the right of a defendant to have a normal hearing where the witness gives evidence openly in his presence and the need to protect the witness "in the interests, not only of the child witness but also of justice, to ensure that the witness will be able to give evidence and give evidence unaffected by the stress of appearing in court itself": *R. (DPP) v. Redbridge Youth Court*; *R. (L.) v. Bicester Youth Court* [2001] EWHC Admin 209. When used the court will direct itself that the special measures are there to assist witnesses in giving evidence and are in no way prejudicial to the defendant.

Where a defendant has learning difficulties the court may assist him in giving his evidence through either an interpreter, reading a defence statement and allowing leading questions: *R. v. H. (Special Measures), The Times*, April 15, 2003.

The decision as to whether a witness may give evidence without being identified is a matter for the court's discretion: *Taylor* [1995] Crim.L.R. 253. The factors for the court to consider when exercising that discretion are:

1. Whether there are real grounds for fear of the consequences if evidence were given and the identity of the witness were revealed;
2. The evidence must be sufficiently relevant and important to make it unfair for the prosecution to proceed without that evidence;
3. The prosecution must satisfy the court that the creditworthiness of the witness has been fully investigated;
4. There must be no undue prejudice to the defendant; and
5. The court must balance the need for protection of the witness against the unfairness or the appearance of unfairness to the defendant.

In order to come to a decision the court ought to be told that a witness will refuse to give evidence unless the court exercises its discretion in favour of a particular measure: *R. (DPP) v. West London Youth Court* [2005] EWHC 2834. In that case the prosecution withdrew the case where an undercover officer was not allowed to give evidence behind a screen.

B. SPECIAL MEASURES

Youth Justice and Criminal Evidence Act 1999, s.16

Witnesses eligible for assistance on grounds of age or incapacity

9–28 **16.**—(1) For the purposes of this Chapter a witness in criminal proceedings (other than the accused) is eligible for assistance by virtue of this section—

(a) if under the age of 18 at the time of the hearing; or

(b) if the court considers that the quality of evidence given by the witness is likely to be diminished by reason of any circumstances falling within subsection (2).

(2) The circumstances falling within this subsection are—

(a) that the witness—

(i) suffers from mental disorder within the meaning of the *Mental Health Act* 1983, or

(ii) otherwise has a significant impairment of intelligence and social functioning;

(b) that the witness has a physical disability or is suffering from a physical disorder.

(3) In subsection (1)(a) "the time of the hearing", in relation to a witness, means the time when it falls to the court to make a determination for the purposes of section 19(2) in relation to the witness.

(4) In determining whether a witness falls within subsection (1)(b) the court must consider any views expressed by the witness.

(5) In this Chapter references to the quality of a witness's evidence are to its quality in terms of completeness, coherence and accuracy; and for this purpose "coherence" refers to a witness's ability in giving evidence to give answers which address the questions put to the witness and can be understood both individually and collectively.

[This section is printed as amended by the *Coroners and Justice Act* 2009, s.98, which came into force on June 27, 2011, S.I. 2011 No. 1452.]

9–29 There is a strong presumption in favour of the use of special measures.

Youth Justice and Criminal Evidence Act 1999, s.17

Witnesses eligible for assistance on grounds of fear or distress about testifying

9–30 **17.**—(1) For the purposes of this Chapter a witness in criminal proceedings (other than the accused) is eligible for assistance by virtue of this subsection if the court is satisfied that the quality of evidence given by the witness is likely to be diminished by reason of fear or distress on the part of the witness in connection with testifying in the proceedings.

(2) In determining whether a witness falls within subsection (1) the court must take into account, in particular—

(a) the nature and alleged circumstances of the offence to which the proceedings relate;

(b) the age of the witness;

(c) such of the following matters as appear to the court to be relevant, namely—

(i) the social and cultural background and ethnic origins of the witness,

(ii) the domestic and employment circumstances of the witness, and

(iii) any religious beliefs or political opinions of the witness;

(d) any behaviour towards the witness on the part of—

(i) the accused,

(ii) members of the family or associates of the accused, or

(iii) any other person who is likely to be an accused or a witness in the proceedings.

(3) In determining that question the court must in addition consider any views expressed by the witness.

(4) Where the complainant in respect of a sexual offence is a witness in proceedings relating to that offence (or to that offence and any other offences), the witness is eligible for assistance in relation to those proceedings by virtue of this subsection unless the witness has informed the court of the witness' wish not to be so eligible by virtue of this subsection.

(5) A witness in proceedings relating to a relevant offence (or to a relevant offence and any other offences) is eligible for assistance in relation to those proceedings by virtue of this subsection unless the witness has informed the court of the witness's wish not to be so eligible by virtue of this subsection.

(6) For the purposes of subsection (5) an offence is a relevant offence if it is an offence described in Schedule 1A.

(7) The Secretary of State may by order amend Schedule 1A.

[This section is printed as amended by the *Coroners and Justice Act* 2009, s.99 which came into force on June 27, 2011, S.I. 2011 No. 1452.]

Youth Justice And Criminal Evidence Act 1999, Sched. 1A

SCHEDULE 1A

RELEVANT OFFENCES FOR THE PURPOSES OF SECTION 17

Murder and manslaughter

1 Murder in a case where it is alleged that a firearm or knife was used to cause the death in question.

2 Manslaughter in a case where it is alleged that a firearm or knife was used to cause the death in question.

3 Murder or manslaughter in a case (other than a case falling within paragraph 1 or 2) where it is alleged that—

(a) the accused was carrying a firearm or knife at any time during the commission of the offence, and

(b) a person other than the accused knew or believed at any time during the commission of the offence that the accused was carrying a firearm or knife.

Offences against the Person Act 1861 (c. 100)

4 An offence under section 18 of the *Offences against the Person Act* 1861 (wounding with intent to cause grievous bodily harm etc) in a case where it is alleged that a firearm or knife was used to cause the wound or harm in question.

5 An offence under section 20 of that Act (malicious wounding) in a case where it is alleged that a firearm or knife was used to cause the wound or inflict the harm in question.

6 An offence under section 38 of that Act (assault with intent to resist arrest) in a case where it is alleged that a firearm or knife was used to carry out the assault in question.

7 An offence under section 47 of the *Offences against the Person Act* 1861 (assault occasioning actual bodily harm) in a case where it is alleged that a firearm or knife was used to inflict the harm in question.

8 An offence under section 18, 20, 38 or 47 of the *Offences against the Person Act* 1861 in a case (other than a case falling within any of paragraphs 4 to 7) where it is alleged that—

(a) the accused was carrying a firearm or knife at any time during the commission of the offence, and

(b) a person other than the accused knew or believed at any time during the commission of the offence that the accused was carrying a firearm or knife.

Prevention of Crime Act 1953 (c. 14)

9 An offence under section 1 of the *Prevention of Crime Act* 1953 (having an offensive weapon in a public place).

Firearms Act 1968 (c. 27)

10 An offence under section 1 of the *Firearms Act* 1968 (requirement of firearm certificate).

11 An offence under section 2(1) of that Act (possession etc of a shotgun without a certificate).

12 An offence under section 3 of that Act (business and other transactions with firearms and ammunition).

13 An offence under section 4 of that Act (conversion of weapons).

14 An offence under section 5(1) of that Act (weapons subject to general prohibition).

15 An offence under section 5(1A) of that Act (ammunition subject to general prohibition).

16 An offence under section 16 of that Act (possession with intent to injure).

17 An offence under section 16A of that Act (possession with intent to cause fear of violence).

18 An offence under section 17 of that Act (use of firearm to resist arrest).

19 An offence under section 18 of that Act (carrying firearm with criminal intent).

20 An offence under section 19 of that Act (carrying firearm in a public place).

21 An offence under section 20 of that Act (trespassing with firearm).

22 An offence under section 21 of that Act (possession of firearms by person previously convicted of crime).

23 An offence under section 21A of that Act (firing an air weapon beyond premises).

24 An offence under section 24A of that Act (supplying imitation firearms to minors).

Criminal Justice Act 1988 (c. 33)

25 An offence under section 139 of the *Criminal Justice Act* 1988 (having article with blade or point in public place).

26 An offence under section 139A of that Act (having article with blade or point (or offensive weapon) on school premises).

Violent Crime Reduction Act 2006 (c. 38)

27 An offence under section 28 of the *Violent Crime Reduction Act* 2006 (using someone to mind a weapon).

28 An offence under section 32 of that Act (sales of air weapons by way of trade or business to be face to face).

29 An offence under section 36 of that Act (manufacture, import and sale of realistic imitation firearms).

General

30 A reference in any of paragraphs 1 to 8 to an offence ("offence A") includes—

(a) a reference to an attempt to commit offence A in a case where it is alleged that it was attempted to commit offence A in the manner or circumstances described in that paragraph,

(b) a reference to a conspiracy to commit offence A in a case where it is alleged that the conspiracy was to commit offence A in the manner or circumstances described in that paragraph,

(c) a reference to an offence under Part 2 of the *Serious Crime Act* 2007 in relation to which offence A is the offence (or one of the offences) which the person intended or believed would be committed in a case where it is alleged that the person intended or believed offence A would be committed in the manner or circumstances described in that paragraph, and

(d) a reference to aiding, abetting, counselling or procuring the commission of offence A in a case where it is alleged that offence A was committed, or the act or omission charged in respect of offence A was done or made, in the manner or circumstances described in that paragraph.

31 A reference in any of paragraphs 9 to 29 to an offence ("offence A") includes—

(a) a reference to an attempt to commit offence A,

(b) a reference to a conspiracy to commit offence A,

(c) a reference to an offence under Part 2 of the *Serious Crime Act* 2007 in relation to which offence A is the offence (or one of the offences) which the person intended or believed would be committed, and

(d) a reference to aiding, abetting, counselling or procuring the commission of offence A.

Interpretation

32 In this Schedule—

"firearm" has the meaning given by section 57 of the *Firearms Act* 1968;

"knife" has the meaning given by section 10 of the *Knives Act* 1997.

Special measures directions may apply to certain witnesses but not to all witnesses in a case: *Brown* ; [2004] Crim.L.R. 1034. **9–31**

Youth Justice and Criminal Evidence Act 1999, s.18–21

Special measures available to eligible witnesses

18.—(1) For the purposes of this Chapter— **9–32**

(a) the provision which may be made by a special measures direction by virtue of each of sections 23 to 30 is a special measure available in relation to a witness eligible for assistance by virtue of section 16; and

(b) the provision which may be made by such a direction by virtue of each of sections 23 to 28 is a special measure available in relation to a witness eligible for assistance by virtue of section 17;

but this subsection has effect subject to subsection (2).

(2) Where (apart from this subsection) a special measure would, in accordance with subsection (1)(a) or (b), be available in relation to a witness in any proceedings, it shall not be taken by a court to be available in relation to the witness unless—

(a) the court has been notified by the Secretary of State that relevant arrangements may be made available in the area in which it appears to the court that the proceedings will take place, and

(b) the notice has not been withdrawn.

(3) In subsection (2) "relevant arrangements" means arrangements for implementing the measure in question which cover the witness and the proceedings in question.

(4) The withdrawal of a notice under that subsection relating to a special measure shall not affect the availability of that measure in relation to a witness if a special measures direction providing for that measure to apply to the witness's evidence has been made by the court before the notice is withdrawn.

(5) The Secretary of State may by order make such amendments of this Chapter as he considers appropriate for altering the special measures which, in accordance with subsection (1)(a) or (b), are available in relation to a witness eligible for assistance by virtue of section 16 or (as the case may be) section 17, whether—

(a) by modifying the provisions relating to any measure for the time being available in relation to such a witness,

(b) by the addition—

(i) (with or without modifications) of any measure which is for the time being available in relation to a witness eligible for assistance by virtue of the other of those sections, or

(ii) of any new measure, or

(c) by the removal of any measure.

Special measures direction relating to eligible witness

19.—(1) This section applies where in any criminal proceedings— **9–33**

(a) a party to the proceedings makes an application for the court to give a direction under this section in relation to a witness in the proceedings other than the accused, or

(b) the court of its own motion raises the issue whether such a direction should be given.

(2) Where the court determines that the witness is eligible for assistance by virtue of section 16 or 17, the court must then—

(a) determine whether any of the special measures available in relation to the witness (or any combination of them) would, in its opinion, be likely to improve the quality of evidence given by the witness; and

(b) if so—

(i) determine which of those measures (or combination of them) would, in its opinion, be likely to maximise so far as practicable the quality of such evidence; and

(ii) give a direction under this section providing for the measure or measures so determined to apply to evidence given by the witness.

(3) In determining for the purposes of this Chapter whether any special measure or measures would or would not be likely to improve, or to maximise so far as practicable, the quality of evidence given by the witness, the court must consider all the circumstances of the case, including in particular—

(a) any views expressed by the witness; and

(b) whether the measures or measures must tend to inhibit such evidence being effectively tested by a party to the proceedings.

(4) A special measures direction must specify particulars of the provision made by the direction in respect of each special measure which is to apply to the witness's evidence.

(5) In this Chapter "special measures direction" means a direction under this section.

(6) Nothing in this Chapter is to be regarded as affecting any power of a court to make an order or give leave of any description (in the exercise of its inherent jurisdiction or otherwise)—

(a) in relation to a witness who is not an eligible witness, or

(b) in relation to an eligible witness where (as, for example, in a case where a foreign language interpreter is to be provided) the order is made or the leave is given otherwise than by reason of the fact that the witness is an eligible witness.

Further provisions about directions: general

9–34 **20.**—(1) Subject to subsection (2) and section 21(8), a special measures direction has binding effect from the time it is made until the proceedings for the purposes of which it is made are either—

(a) determined (by acquittal, conviction or otherwise), or

(b) abandoned,

in relation to the accused or (if there is more than one) in relation to each of the accused.

(2) The court may discharge or vary (or further vary) a special measures direction if it appears to the court to be in the interests of justice to do so, and may do so either—

(a) on an application made by a party to the proceedings, if there has been a material change of circumstances since the relevant time, or

(b) of its own motion.

(3) In subsection (2) "the relevant time" means —

(a) the time when the direction was given, or

(b) if a previous application has been made under that subsection, the time when the application (or last application) was made.

(4) Nothing in section 24(2) and (3), 27(4) to (7) or 28(4) to (6) is to be regarded as affecting the power of the court to vary or discharge a special measures direction under subsection (2).

(5) The court must state in open court its reasons for—

(a) giving or varying,

(b) refusing an application for, or for the variation or discharge of, or

(c) discharging,

a special measures direction and, if it is a magistrates' court, must cause them to be entered in the register of its proceedings.

(6) Rules of court may make provision—

(a) for uncontested applications to be determined by the court without a hearing;

(b) for preventing the renewal of an unsuccessful application for a special measures direction except where there has been a material change of circumstances;

(c) for expert evidence to be given in connection with an application for, or for varying or discharging, such a direction;

(d) for the manner in which confidential or sensitive information is to be treated in connection with such an application and in particular as to its being disclosed to, or withheld from, a party to the proceedings.

Special provisions relating to child witnesses.

9–35 **21.**—(1) For the purposes of this section—

(a) a witness in criminal proceedings is a "child witness" if he is an eligible witness by reason of section 16(1)(a) (whether or not he is an eligible witness by reason of any other provision of section 16 or 17); and

[*Repealed*...]

(c) a "relevant recording", in relation to a child witness, is a video recording of an interview of the witness made with a view to its admission as evidence in chief of the witness.

(2) Where the court, in making a determination for the purposes of section 19(2), determines that a witness in criminal proceedings is a child witness, the court must—

(a) first have regard to subsections (3) to [(4C)] below; and

(b) then have regard to section 19(2);

and for the purposes of section 19(2), as it then applies to the witness, any special measures required to be applied in relation to him by virtue of this section shall be treated as if they were measures determined by the court, pursuant to section 19(2)(a) and (b)(i), to be ones that (whether on their own or with any other special measures) would be likely to maximise, so far as practicable, the quality of his evidence.

(3) The primary rule in the case of a child witness is that the court must give a special measures direction in relation to the witness which complies with the following requirements—

(a) it must provide for any relevant recording to be admitted under section 27 (video recorded evidence in chief); and

(b) it must provide for any evidence given by the witness in the proceedings which is not given by means of a video recording (whether in chief or otherwise) to be given by means of a live link in accordance with section 24.

(4) The primary rule is subject to the following limitations—

(a) the requirement contained in subsection (3)(a) or (b) has effect subject to the availability (within the meaning of section 18(2)) of the special measure in question in relation to the witness;

(b) the requirement contained in subsection (3)(a) also has effect subject to section 27(2);

(ba) if the witness informs the court of the witness's wish that the rule should not apply or should apply only in part, the rule does not apply to the extent that the court is satisfied that not complying with the rule would not diminish the quality of the witness's evidence; and

(c) the rule does not apply to the extent that the court is satisfied that compliance with it would not be likely to maximise the quality of the witness's evidence so far as practicable (whether because the application to that evidence of one or more other special measures available in relation to the witness would have that result or for any other reason).

(4A) Where as a consequence of all or part of the primary rule being disapplied under subsection (4)(ba) a witness's evidence or any part of it would fall to be given as testimony in court, the court must give a special measures direction making such provision as is described in section 23 for the evidence or that part of it.

(4B) The requirement in subsection (4A) is subject to the following limitations—

(a) if the witness informs the court of the witness's wish that the requirement in subsection (4A) should not apply, the requirement does not apply to the extent that the court is satisfied that not complying with it would not diminish the quality of the witness's evidence; and

(b) the requirement does not apply to the extent that the court is satisfied that making such a provision would not be likely to maximise the quality of the witness's evidence so far as practicable (whether because the application to that evidence of one or more other special measures available in relation to the witness would have that result or for any other reason).

(4C) In making a decision under subsection (4)(ba) or (4B)(a), the court must take into account the following factors (and any others it considers relevant)—

(a) the age and maturity of the witness;

(b) the ability of the witness to understand the consequences of giving evidence otherwise than in accordance with the requirements in subsection (3) or (as the case may be) in accordance with the requirement in subsection (4A);

(c) the relationship (if any) between the witness and the accused;

(d) the witness's social and cultural background and ethnic origins;
(e) the nature and alleged circumstances of the offence to which the proceedings relate.

(8) Where a special measures direction is given in relation to a child witness who is an eligible witness by reason only of section 16(1)(a), then—

(a) subject to subsection (9) below, and
(b) except where the witness has already begun to give evidence in the proceedings,

the direction shall cease to have effect at the time when the witness attains the age of 18.

(9) Where a special measures direction is given in relation to a child witness who is an eligible witness by reason only of section 16(1)(a) and—

(a) the direction provides—
   (i) for any relevant recording to be admitted under section 27 as evidence in chief of the witness, or
   (ii) for the special measure available under section 28 to apply in relation to the witness, and
(b) if it provides for that special measure to so apply, the witness is still under the age of 18 when the video recording is made for the purposes of section 28,

then, so far as it provides as mentioned in paragraph (a)(i) or (ii) above, the direction shall continue to have effect in accordance with section 20(1) even though the witness subsequently attains that age.

[This section is printed as amended by the *Coroners and Justice Act* 2009 c. 25, s.100 and Schedule 23 with effect from June 27, 2011: S.I. 2011 No. 1452.]

All children are on an equal footing and a child may opt out of giving evidence by a combination of video-recorded evidence-in-chief and live link, provided the court is satisfied, after taking into account certain factors i.e. the age and maturity of the witness, his ability to understand the consequences of giving evidence, the relationship, if any, between the witness and defendant, that the quality of the evidence would not be diminished.

The framework of special measures for young people has been amended by provisions of the *Coroners and Justice Act* 2009 with effect from June 27, 2011. The age for protection is raised to 18 and automatic eligibility applies where the offence charged is one which involves weapons.

9–36 Cases are often transferred to adjacent courthouses where facilities exist. Safeguards in relation to video-recorded evidence in chief are contained in s.27(2).

Youth Justice and Criminal Evidence Act 1999, ss.22–23

Extension of provisions of section 21 to certain witnesses over 18

9–37 **22.**—(1) For the purposes of this section—

(a) a witness in criminal proceedings (other than the accused) is a "qualifying witness" if he—
   (i) is not an eligible witness at the time of the hearing (as defined by section 16(3)), but
   (ii) was under the age of 18 when a relevant recording was made; and
(c) a "relevant recording", in relation to a witness, is a video recording of an interview of the witness made with a view to its admission as evidence in chief of the witness.

(2) Subsections (2) to (4) and (4C) of section 21 so far as relating to the giving of a direction complying with the requirement contained in section 21(3)(a), apply to a qualifying witness in respect of the relevant recording as they apply to a child witness (within the meaning of that section).

[This section is printed as amended by the *Coroners and Justice Act* 2009, s.98 with effect from June 27, 2011: S.I. 2011 No. 1452.]

Screening witness from accused

9–38 **23.**—(1) A special measures direction may provide for the witness, while giving testimony or being sworn in court, to be prevented by means of a screen or other arrangement from seeing the accused.

(2) But the screen or other arrangement must not prevent the witness from being able to see, and to be seen by—

(a) the judge or justices (or both) and the jury (if there is one);

(b) legal representatives acting in the proceedings; and

(c) any interpreter or other person appointed (in pursuance of the direction or otherwise) to assist the witness.

(3) Where two or more legal representatives are acting for a party to the proceedings, subsection (2)(b) is to be regarded as satisfied in relation to those representatives if the witness is able at all material times to see and be seen by at least one of them.

A child may opt out of this requirement subject to the agreement of the court.

See *Criminal Procedure Rules* 2011, r. 29 in Appendix G. **9–39**

An application for a special measures direction may be made by the parties or the court may give a direction of its own motion. Special measures are available to a court when brought into force despite the fact that the court has not been notified: *R. v. R.* [2008] 2 Cr.App.R. 10. The court must be satisfied that either the witness is a child or the quality of evidence is likely to be impaired without a direction. In the latter case quality may be impaired on the grounds of mental or physical disability, impairment of intelligence, fear or distress. **9–40**

An application must be made on a prescribed form sent to the court and copied to the other parties within 14 days of a plea of not guilty or within 28 days of a defendant's first appearance if before the youth court. These time limits may be extended upon application with good reason: Time limits are discretionary not mandatory and it is for the court to determine whether any undue prejudice has been caused to a defendant by granting a late application: *Brown, ante.*

An unopposed application may be determined by a single justice. Where the application is opposed there must be a hearing of which all parties must receive notice as they have a right to attend and be heard. The court must give notice of its decision to the parties together with reasons

Upon a change of circumstances an application may be renewed, varied, or discharged. **9–41**

In *KL and LAK v. DPP* (2002) 166 J.P. 369, QBD, the precaution of bringing a screen into court before an application was concluded was confirmed to be a sensible course of action and could not suggest that the magistrates had pre-judged the issue. Section 23 requires that the witness be prevented from seeing the accused. There is no requirement that the defendant should not be able to see the witness. This may prove difficult in practice because of courtroom layout. In *DJX* (1990) 91 Cr.App.R. 36, screens were placed between a child witness and the defendants. It was said that the necessity of trying to ensure that the children gave evidence without intimidation outweighed any possible prejudice to the defendants. **9–42**

In *X.* (1990) 91 Cr.App.R. 36, CA where a screen was used and social workers had been permitted to sit alongside the child witnesses when they gave evidence, the Court of Appeal stated that to have anyone sitting alongside a witness was a course of conduct that had to be undertaken with considerable care and the court had to be astute to ensure that nothing improper occurred and no undue encouragement was given to the witness. The *Consolidated Criminal Practice Direction*, para. III.29 (see Appendix F) gives guidance on the use of a witness supporter. It states that the supporter should be independent, have no previous knowledge or personal involvement in the case and should be suitably trained. An usher should be available to assist.

Any special measures direction does not affect common law or statutory rules governing the admissibility of evidence: *R. (CPS) v. Brentford Youth Court* [2003] EWHC 2409; (2003) 167 J.P. 614.

Youth Justice and Criminal Evidence Act 1999, s.24

Evidence by live link

24.—(1) A special measures direction may provide for the witness to give evidence by means of a live link. **9–43**

(1A) Such a direction may also provide for a specified person to accompany the witness while the witness is giving evidence by live link.

(1B) In determining who may accompany the witness, the count must have regard to the wishes of the witness.

(2) Where a direction provides for the witness to give evidence by means of a live link, the witness may not give evidence in any other way without the permission of the court.

(3) The court may give permission for the purposes of subsection (2) if it appears to the court to be in the interests of justice to do so, and may do so either—

(a) on an application by a party to the proceedings, if there has been a material change of circumstances since the relevant time, or

(b) of its own motion.

(4) In subsection (3) "the relevant time" means —

(a) the time when the direction was given, or

(b) if a previous application has been made under that subsection, the time when the application (or last application) was made.

(5) Where in proceedings before a magistrates' court—

(a) evidence is to be given by means of a live link in accordance with a special measures direction, but

(b) suitable facilities for receiving such evidence are not available at any petty-sessional court-house in which that court can (apart from this subsection) lawfully sit,

the court may sit for the purposes of the whole or any part of those proceedings at a place where such facilities are available and which has been appointed for the purposes of this subsection by the justices acting for the petty sessions area for which the court acts.

(6) A place appointed under subsection (5) may be outside the petty sessions area for which it is appointed; but (if so) it is to be regarded as being in that area for the purpose of the jurisdiction of the justices acting for that area.

(7) In this section "petty-sessional court-house" has the same meaning as in the [1980 c. 43.]*Magistrates' Courts Act* 1980 and "petty sessions area" has the same meaning as in the [1997 c. 25.] Justices of the *Peace Act* 1997.

(8) In this Chapter "live link" means a live television link or other arrangement whereby a witness, while absent from the courtroom or other place where the proceedings are being held, is able to see and hear a person there and to be seen and heard by the persons specified in section 23(2)(a) to (c).

[This section is printed as amended by the *Coroners and Justice Act* 2009, s.102 with effect from June 27, 2011, S.I. 2011 No. 1452.]

Where a court makes a direction allowing a witness to give evidence by live link, it may also direct that a specified person may accompany the witness while giving evidence; in determining who that person should be the court must have regard to the wishes of the witness.

9–44 See *Criminal Procedure Rules* 2011, r. 29.10 in Appendix G–176a.

[The next paragraph is § 9–46.]

Youth Justice and Criminal Evidence Act 1999, s.25

Evidence given in private

9–46 **25.**—(1) A special measures direction may provide for the exclusion from the court, during the giving of the witness's evidence, of persons of any description specified in the direction.

(2) The persons who may be so excluded do not include—

(a) the accused,

(b) legal representatives acting in the proceedings, or

(c) any interpreter or other person appointed (in pursuance of the direction or otherwise) to assist the witness.

(3) A special measures direction providing for representatives of news gathering or reporting organisations to be so excluded shall be expressed not to apply to one named person who—

(a) is a representative of such an organisation, and

(b) has been nominated for the purpose by one or more such organisations, unless it appears to the court that no such nomination has been made.

(4) A special measures direction may only provide for the exclusion of persons under this section where—

(a) the proceedings relate to a sexual offence; or

(b) it appears to the court that there are reasonable grounds for believing that any person other than the accused has sought, or will seek, to intimidate the witness in connection with testifying in the proceedings.

(5) Any proceedings from which persons are excluded under this section (whether or not those persons include representatives of news gathering or reporting organisations) shall nevertheless be taken to be held in public for the purposes of any privilege or exemption from liability available in respect of fair, accurate and contemporaneous reports of legal proceedings held in public.

Criminal Justice Act 2003, Pt 8 (ss.51–53, 55–56)

PART 8

LIVE LINKS

Live links in criminal proceedings

51.—(1) A witness (other than the defendant) may, if the court so directs, give evidence through a live link in the following criminal proceedings. **9–47**

(2) They are—

(a) a summary trial,

(b) an appeal to the Crown Court arising out of such a trial,

(c) a trial on indictment,

(d) an appeal to the criminal division of the Court of Appeal,

(e) the hearing of a reference under section 9 or 11 of the *Criminal Appeal Act* 1995,

(f) a hearing before a magistrates' court or the Crown Court which is held after the defendant has entered a plea of guilty, and

(g) a hearing before the Court of Appeal under section 80 of this Act.

(3) A direction may be given under this section—

(a) on an application by a party to the proceedings, or

(b) of the court's own motion.

(4) But a direction may not be given under this section unless—

(a) the court is satisfied that it is in the interests of the efficient or effective administration of justice for the person concerned to give evidence in the proceedings through a live link,

(b) it has been notified by the Secretary of State that suitable facilities for receiving evidence through a live link are available in the area in which it appears to the court that the proceedings will take place, and

(c) that notification has not been withdrawn.

(5) The withdrawal of such a notification is not to affect a direction given under this section before that withdrawal.

(6) In deciding whether to give a direction under this section the court must consider all the circumstances of the case.

(7) Those circumstances include in particular—

(a) the availability of the witness,

(b) the need for the witness to attend in person,

(c) the importance of the witness's evidence to the proceedings,

(d) the views of the witness,

(e) the suitability of the facilities at the place where the witness would give evidence through a live link,

(f) whether a direction might tend to inhibit any party to the proceedings from effectively testing the witness's evidence.

(8) The court must state in open court its reasons for refusing an application for a direction under this section and, if it is a magistrates' court, must cause them to be entered in the register of its proceedings.

Effect of, and rescission of, direction

9–48 **52.**—(1) Subsection (2) applies where the court gives a direction under section 51 for a person to give evidence through a live link in particular proceedings.

(2) The person concerned may not give evidence in those proceedings after the direction is given otherwise than through a live link (but this is subject to the following provisions of this section).

(3) The court may rescind a direction under section 51 if it appears to the court to be in the interests of justice to do so.

(4) Where it does so, the person concerned shall cease to be able to give evidence in the proceedings through a live link, but this does not prevent the court from giving a further direction under section 51 in relation to him.

(5) A direction under section 51 may be rescinded under subsection (3)—

(a) on an application by a party to the proceedings, or

(b) of the court's own motion.

(6) But an application may not be made under subsection (5)(a) unless there has been a material change of circumstances since the direction was given.

(7) The court must state in open court its reasons—

(a) for rescinding a direction under section 51, or

(b) for refusing an application to rescind such a direction,

and, if it is a magistrates' court, must cause them to be entered in the register of its proceedings.

Magistrates' courts permitted to sit at other locations

9–49 **53.**—(1) This section applies where—

(a) a magistrates' court is minded to give a direction under section 51 for evidence to be given through a live link in proceedings before the court, and

(b) suitable facilities for receiving such evidence are not available at any petty-sessional court-house in which the court can (apart from subsection (2)) lawfully sit.

(2) The court may sit for the purposes of the whole or any part of the proceedings at any place at which such facilities are available and which has been appointed for the purposes of this section by the justices acting for the petty sessions area for which the court acts.

(3) A place appointed under subsection (2) may be outside the petty sessions area for which it is appointed; but (if so) it shall be deemed to be in that area for the purpose of the jurisdiction of the justices acting for that area.

Rules of court

9–50 **55.**—(1) [Criminal Procedure Rules] may make such provision as appears to the [Criminal Procedure Rule Committee] to be necessary or expedient for the purposes of this Part.

(2) [Criminal Procedure Rules] may in particular make provision—

(a) as to the procedure to be followed in connection with applications under section 51 or 52, and

(b) as to the arrangements or safeguards to be put in place in connection with the operation of live links.

(3) The provision which may be made by virtue of subsection (2)(a) includes provision—

(a) for uncontested applications to be determined by the court without a hearing,

(b) for preventing the renewal of an unsuccessful application under section 51 unless there has been a material change of circumstances,

(c) for the manner in which confidential or sensitive information is to be treated in connection with an application under section 51 or 52 and in particular as to its being disclosed to, or withheld from, a party to the proceedings.

(4) Nothing in this section is to be taken as affecting the generality of any enactment conferring power to make [Criminal Procedure Rules].

[This section is printed as amended by transitional provisions specified in the *Courts Act 2003 (Consequential Amendments) Order* 2004 (S.I. 2004 No. 2035), Art.2 and Sched. 1, para. 47.]

Interpretation of Part 8

9–51 **56.**—(1) In this Part—

"legal representative" means an authorised advocate or authorised litigator (as defined by section 119(1) of the *Courts and Legal Services Act* 1990),

"petty-sessional court-house" has the same meaning as in the *Magistrates*' Courts Act 1980,

"petty sessions area" has the same meaning as in the *Justices of the Peace Act* 1997,

"rules of court" means Magistrates' Courts Rules, Crown Court Rules or Criminal Appeal Rules,

"witness", in relation to any criminal proceedings, means a person called, or proposed to be called, to give evidence in the proceedings.

(2) In this Part "live link" means a live television link or other arrangement by which a witness, while at a place in the United Kingdom which is outside the building where the proceedings are being held, is able to see and hear a person at the place where the proceedings are being held and to be seen and heard by the following persons.

(3) They are—

(a) the defendant or defendants,

(b) the judge or justices (or both) and the jury (if there is one),

(c) legal representatives acting in the proceedings, and

(d) any interpreter or other person appointed by the court to assist the witness.

(4) The extent (if any) to which a person is unable to see or hear by reason of any impairment of eyesight or hearing is to be disregarded for the purposes of subsection (2).

(5) Nothing in this Part is to be regarded as affecting any power of a court—

(a) to make an order, give directions or give leave of any description in relation to any witness (including the defendant or defendants), or

(b) to exclude evidence at its discretion (whether by preventing questions being put or otherwise).

These measures are available to all vulnerable witnesses in summary trials. They **9–52** should be made in a timely manner as it is important that witnesses know from an early stage how they are going to give evidence. Special measures have been held to be compatible with the ECHR: *R. (D.) v. Camberwell Green Youth Court* 4; [2005] 1 W.L.R. 393; [2005] Crim.L.R. 497. The case considered six defendants who were all charged with offences of robbery or assault, and were all aged 16 or under. In applications for judicial review of the decisions to make special measures directions under the 1999 Act, it was submitted that as s.21(5) required the court to give a special measures direction in relation to the evidence of a child witness in need of special protection, the court was deprived of any power to consider whether the restriction on the rights of the defendant was necessary or in the interests of justice and thus the provision was incompatible with Art. 6 of the European Convention on Human Rights.

The House of Lords held that it is not unjust for evidence to be given by live link and video where there is no reason to think that the child in question would be upset, traumatised, or intimidated by giving evidence in open court. The Convention does not guarantee a confrontation face to face. The court doubted, however, the decision in *R. (S.) v. Waltham Forest Youth Court*, *ante*, that there was no inherent power to allow a defendant to give evidence by live link. The situation of witnesses and defendants are different and it would be very rarely that a defendant would give evidence that way but he might, *e.g.* where he was very young and was too terrified to give evidence in the presence of a co-accused.

Since this case live links have been brought in for vulnerable defendants' evidence from January 15, 2007: *Police and Justice Act* 2006, s.47 (see *Police and Justice Act 2006 (Commencement No. 1 Transitional and Savings Provisions) Order* 2006 (S.I. 2006 No. 3364).

[The next paragraph is § 9–54.]

Live link directions

33A.—(1) This section applies to any proceedings (whether in a magistrates' court or before **9–54** the Crown Court) against a person for an offence.

(2) The court may, on the application of the accused, give a live link direction if it is satisfied—

(a) that the conditions in subsection (4) or, as the case may be, subsection (5) are met in relation to the accused, and

(b) that it is in the interests of justice for the accused to give evidence through a live link.

(3) A live link direction is a direction that any oral evidence to be given before the court by the accused is to be given through a live link.

(4) Where the accused is aged under 18 when the application is made, the conditions are that—

(a) his ability to participate effectively in the proceedings as a witness giving oral evidence in court is compromised by his level of intellectual ability or social functioning, and

(b) use of a live link would enable him to participate more effectively in the proceedings as a witness (whether by improving the quality of his evidence or otherwise).

(5) Where the accused has attained the age of 18 at that time, the conditions are that—

(a) he suffers from a mental disorder (within the meaning of the *Mental Health Act* 1983) or otherwise has a significant impairment of intelligence and social function,

(b) he is for that reason unable to participate effectively in the proceedings as a witness giving oral evidence in court, and

(c) use of a live link would enable him to participate more effectively in the proceedings as a witness (whether by improving the quality of his evidence or otherwise).

(6) While a live link direction has effect the accused may not give oral evidence before the court in the proceedings otherwise than through a live link.

(7) The court may discharge a live link direction at any time before or during any hearing to which it applies if it appears to the court to be in the interests of justice to do so (but this does not affect the power to give a further live link direction in relation to the accused). The court may exercise this power of its own motion or on an application by a party.

(8) The court must state in open court its reasons for—

(a) giving or discharging a live link direction, or

(b) refusing an application for or for the discharge of a live link direction,

and, if it is a magistrates' court, it must cause those reasons to be entered in the register of its proceedings.

9–55 An intermediary may be used where certain vulnerable defendants i.e. those under 18 years of age whose ability to communicate effectively is compromised by their level of intellectual ability or social functioning or those over 18 years who (a) suffer from a mental disorder or have a significant impairment of intelligence and social function and (b) are for that reason unable to participate effectively in the proceedings as a witness. The court must be able to see and hear the examination and to communicate with the intermediary. The court may discharge or vary an intermediary direction at any time if it appears to be necessary to do so in order to ensure that the defendant receives a fair trial and provided it states in open court its reasons for so doing.

Saving

9–56 **33C.**— Nothing in this Chapter affects—

(a) any power of a court to make an order, give directions or give leave of any description in relation to any witness (including an accused), or

(b) the operation of any rule of law relating to evidence in criminal proceedings."

C. WITNESS ANONYMITY

Coroners and Justice Act 2009, ss.86–93

Witness anonymity orders

9–56a **86.**—(1) In this Chapter a "witness anonymity order" is an order made by a court that requires such specified measures to be taken in relation to a witness in criminal proceedings as the court considers appropriate to ensure that the identity of the witness is not disclosed in or in connection with the proceedings.

(2) The kinds of measures that may be required to be taken in relation to a witness include measures for securing one or more of the following—

(a) that the witness's name and other identifying details may be—

(i) withheld;

(ii) removed from materials disclosed to any party to the proceedings;

(b) that the witness may use a pseudonym;

(c) that the witness is not asked questions of any specified description that might lead to the identification of the witness;

(d) that the witness is screened to any specified extent;

(e) that the witness's voice is subjected to modulation to any specified extent.

(3) Subsection (2) does not affect the generality of subsection (1).

(4) Nothing in this section authorises the court to require—

(a) the witness to be screened to such an extent that the witness cannot be seen by—

(i) the judge or other members of the court (if any), or

(ii) the jury (if there is one);

(b) the witness's voice to be modulated to such an extent that the witness's natural voice cannot be heard by any persons within paragraph (a)(i) or (ii).

(5) In this section "specified" means specified in the witness anonymity order concerned.

Applications

87.—(1) An application for a witness anonymity order to be made in relation to a witness in criminal proceedings may be made to the court by the prosecutor or the defendant.

(2) Where an application is made by the prosecutor, the prosecutor—

(a) must (unless the court directs otherwise) inform the court of the identity of the witness, but

(b) is not required to disclose in connection with the application—

(i) the identity of the witness, or

(ii) any information that might enable the witness to be identified, to any other party to the proceedings or his or her legal representatives.

(3) Where an application is made by the defendant, the defendant—

(a) must inform the court and the prosecutor of the identity of the witness, but

(b) (if there is more than one defendant) is not required to disclose in connection with the application—

(i) the identity of the witness, or

(ii) any information that might enable the witness to be identified, to any other defendant or his or her legal representatives.

(4) Accordingly, where the prosecutor or the defendant proposes to make an application under this section in respect of a witness, any relevant material which is disclosed by or on behalf of that party before the determination of the application may be disclosed in such a way as to prevent—

(a) the identity of the witness, or

(b) any information that might enable the witness to be identified, from being disclosed except as required by subsection (2)(a) or (3)(a).

(5) "Relevant material" means any document or other material which falls to be disclosed, or is sought to be relied on, by or on behalf of the party concerned in connection with the proceedings or proceedings preliminary to them.

(6) The court must give every party to the proceedings the opportunity to be heard on an application under this section.

(7) But subsection (6) does not prevent the court from hearing one or more parties in the absence of a defendant and his or her legal representatives, if it appears to the court to be appropriate to do so in the circumstances of the case.

(8) Nothing in this section is to be taken as restricting any power to make rules of court.

Conditions for making order

88.—(1) This section applies where an application is made for a witness anonymity order to be made in relation to a witness in criminal proceedings.

(2) The court may make such an order only if it is satisfied that Conditions A to C below are met.

(3) Condition A is that the proposed order is necessary—

(a) in order to protect the safety of the witness or another person or to prevent any serious damage to property, or

(b) in order to prevent real harm to the public interest (whether affecting the carrying on of any activities in the public interest or the safety of a person involved in carrying on such activities, or otherwise).

(4) Condition B is that, having regard to all the circumstances, the effect of the proposed order would be consistent with the defendant receiving a fair trial.

(5) Condition C is that the importance of the witness's testimony is such that in the interests of justice the witness ought to testify and—

(a) the witness would not testify if the proposed order were not made, or

(b) there would be real harm to the public interest if the witness were to testify without the proposed order being made.

(6) In determining whether the proposed order is necessary for the purpose mentioned in subsection (3)(a), the court must have regard (in particular) to any reasonable fear on the part of the witness—

(a) that the witness or another person would suffer death or injury, or

(b) that there would be serious damage to property, if the witness were to be identified.

Relevant considerations

89.—(1) When deciding whether Conditions A to C in section 88 are met in the case of an application for a witness anonymity order, the court must have regard to—

(a) the considerations mentioned in subsection (2) below, and

(b) such other matters as the court considers relevant.

(2) The considerations are—

(a) the general right of a defendant in criminal proceedings to know the identity of a witness in the proceedings;

(b) the extent to which the credibility of the witness concerned would be a relevant factor when the weight of his or her evidence comes to be assessed;

(c) whether evidence given by the witness might be the sole or decisive evidence implicating the defendant;

(d) whether the witness's evidence could be properly tested (whether on grounds of credibility or otherwise) without his or her identity being disclosed;

(e) whether there is any reason to believe that the witness—

(i) has a tendency to be dishonest, or

(ii) has any motive to be dishonest in the circumstances of the case, having regard (in particular) to any previous convictions of the witness and to any relationship between the witness and the defendant or any associates of the defendant;

(f) whether it would be reasonably practicable to protect the witness by any means other than by making a witness anonymity order specifying the measures that are under consideration by the court

Discharge or variation of order

91.—(1) A court that has made a witness anonymity order in relation to any criminal proceedings may in those proceedings subsequently discharge or vary (or further vary) the order if it appears to the court to be appropriate to do so in view of the provisions of sections 88 and 89 that apply to the making of an order.

(2) The court may do so—

(a) on an application made by a party to the proceedings if there has been a material change of circumstances since the relevant time, or

(b) on its own initiative.

(3) The court must give every party to the proceedings the opportunity to be heard—

(a) before determining an application made to it under subsection (2);

(b) before discharging or varying the order on its own initiative.

(4) But subsection (3) does not prevent the court hearing one or more of the parties to the proceedings in the absence of a defendant in the proceedings and his or her legal representatives, if it appears to the court to be appropriate to do so in the circumstances of the case.

(5) "The relevant time" means—

(a) the time when the order was made, or

(b) if a previous application has been made under subsection (2), the time when the application (or the last application) was made.

Discharge or variation after proceedings

92.—(1) This section applies if—

(a) a court has made a witness anonymity order in relation to a witness in criminal proceedings ("the old proceedings"), and

(b) the old proceedings have come to an end.

(2) The court that made the order may discharge or vary (or further vary) the order if it appears to the court to be appropriate to do so in view of—

(a) the provisions of sections 88 and 89 that apply to the making of a witness anonymity order, and

(b) such other matters as the court considers relevant.

(3) The court may do so—

(a) on an application made by a party to the old proceedings if there has been a material change of circumstances since the relevant time, or

(b) on an application made by the witness if there has been a material change of circumstances since the relevant time.

(4) The court may not determine an application made to it under subsection (3) unless in the case of each of the parties to the old proceedings and the witness—

(a) it has given the person the opportunity to be heard, or

(b) it is satisfied that it is not reasonably practicable to communicate with the person.

(5) Subsection (4) does not prevent the court hearing one or more of the persons mentioned in that subsection in the absence of a person who was a defendant in the old proceedings and that person's legal representatives, if it appears to the court to be appropriate to do so in the circumstances of the case.

(6) "The relevant time" means—

(a) the time when the old proceedings came to an end, or

(b) if a previous application has been made under subsection (3), the time when the application (or the last application) was made.

A magistrates' court can make an order: s.12(2)(a) and such an order may be discharged or varied subsequently on an application made by a party or on the court's own initiative. The magistrates' court, in hearing the evidence of the witness, must be careful to ensure that the fact that an order is in existence does not prejudice the defendant. The grant of anonymity must satisfy ECHR principles including a witness's right to security of person Art.5, the right to a fair trial Art.6 and a witness's right to respect for private life: Art.8.

The explanatory notes to the Bill envisaged the application being made *ex parte* by the prosecution with the defence making representations at a later *inter partes* hearing. Prosecution and defence applications are treated in different ways. The prosecution is not required to disclose the identity to any other party but the defence must disclose the identity of a defence witness to the prosecution although not to any other defendant. Each party must inform the court of the witness's identity but in a prosecution application the court may direct that it should not be informed of the identity of the witness. Consideration should be given to Art 6(3)(d) ECHR that a defendant has a right "to obtain the examination of witnesses on his behalf under the same conditions as witnesses against him". See *Criminal Procedure Rules* 2011, r.29.

An anonymity order is a special measure of last practicable resort, and witness relocation can only be a practicable alternative in the rarest of circumstances. Nothing in the Act diminishes the overriding responsibility of the court to ensure that proceedings are conducted fairly. Conditions A, B and C in s.4 have to be met before an anonymity order can be made. Condition A is not fulfilled unless the order is necessary, among other things, for the protection of the safety of the witness and prevention of real harm to the public interest. In respect of police witnesses, particularly those working undercover, there may be sound, operational reasons for maintaining anonymity and a court will normally be entitled to follow the unequivocal assertion by an undercover police officer that without such an order he will not be prepared to testify. The court must also consider the protection of the interests of the defendant who is normally entitled to know the identity of the witness who incriminates him. The court is also required to decide whether the evidence is the sole or decisive evidence; if it is then Condition B relating to the fairness of the trial may be harder to satisfy. The court must also have regard to the number of anonymous witnesses and the possibility of collusion. This Act together with the *Criminal Justice Act* 2003 and the common law do not allow a court to extend witness orders to permit anonymous hearsay evidence: *R. v. Mayers* [2008] EWCA Crim 1418.

Guidance was given in the case of *R. v. Chisholm* [2010] EWCA Crim 258 where witnesses had given evidence in closed proceedings after witness anonymity orders had been made and where a special advocate had been appointed for the defendant. It was said that the provisions of the Act would be unworkable if fairness required the disclosure of all material relied upon in support of the making of an anonymity order. Protection was given to the defendant by the appointment of special counsel and the written reasons for the orders which were susceptible to review; The reference in s.88(3) to "safety" is not limited to objective consideration of the actual physical safety of the witness; it is enough that the witness believes himself to be in peril.

It is important that eye witnesses should testify and whilst the calling of anonymous witnesses must not become a routine event, witness anonymity orders should not be confined to cases of terrorism or gangland killings. The intimidation of witnesses has become a feature of contemporary life: *R. v. Powar* [2009] 2 Cr.App.R. 8.

The 2009 Act which came into force on January 1, 2010 will also apply to applications to vary or discharge orders made before December 31, 2008.

9–56b The *Consolidated Criminal Practice Direction (Amendment No.24)* [2010] Cr.App.R. 39(6) contains up-to-date references to Part 29 of the *Criminal Procedure Rules* and substitutes new forms for use in making an application for these orders.

V. METHODS OF GIVING ORAL TESTIMONY

A. VIDEO RECORDING

Youth Justice and Criminal Evidence Act 1999, s.27

Video recorded evidence in chief

9–57 **27.**—(1) A special measures direction may provide for a video recording of an interview of the witness to be admitted as evidence in chief of the witness.

(2) A special measures direction may, however, not provide for a video recording, or a part of such a recording, to be admitted under this section if the court is of the opinion, having regard to all the circumstances of the case, that in the interests of justice the recording, or that part of it, should not be so admitted.

(3) In considering for the purposes of subsection (2) whether any part of a recording should not be admitted under this section, the court must consider whether any prejudice to the accused which might result from that part being so admitted is outweighed by the desirability of showing the whole, or substantially the whole, of the recorded interview.

(4) Where a special measures direction provides for a recording to be admitted under this section, the court may nevertheless subsequently direct that it is not to be so admitted if—

(a) it appears to the court that—

(i) the witness will not be available for cross-examination (whether conducted in the ordinary way or in accordance with any such direction), and

(ii) the parties to the proceedings have not agreed that there is no need for the witness to be so available; or

(b) any rules of court requiring disclosure of the circumstances in which the recording was made have not been complied with to the satisfaction of the court.

(5) Where a recording is admitted under this section—

(a) the witness must be called by the party tendering it in evidence, unless—
(i) a special measures direction provides for the witness's evidence on cross-examination to be given otherwise than by testimony in court, or
(ii) the parties to the proceedings have agreed as mentioned in subsection (4)(a)(ii); and
(b) the witness may not without the permission of the court give evidence in chief otherwise than by means of the recording as to any matter which, in the opinion of the court, is dealt with in the witness's recorded testimony.

(6) Where in accordance with subsection (2) a special measures direction provides for part only of a recording to be admitted under this section, references in subsections (4) and (5) to the recording or to the witness's recorded testimony are references to the part of the recording or testimony which is to be so admitted.

(7) The court may give permission for the purposes of subsection (5)(b) if it appears to the court to be in the interests of justice to do so, and may do so either—
(a) on an application by a party to the proceedings, or
(b) of its own motion.

(8) [Omitted]

(9) The court may, in giving permission for the purposes of subsection (5)(b), direct that the evidence in question is to be given by the witness by means of a live link; and, if the court so directs, subsections (5) to (7) of section 24 shall apply in relation to that evidence as they apply in relation to evidence which is to be given in accordance with a special measures direction.

(9A) If the court directs under subsection (9) that evidence is to be given by live link it may also make such provision in that direction as it could make under section 24(1A) in a special measures direction.

(10) A magistrates' court inquiring into an offence as examining justices under section 6 of the [1980 c. 43.] *Magistrates' Courts Act* 1980 may consider any video recording in relation to which it is proposed to apply for a special measures direction providing for it to be admitted at the trial in accordance with this section.

(11) Nothing in this section affects the admissibility of any video recording which would be admissible apart from this section.

[This section is printed as amended by the *Coroners and Justice Act* 2009, s.102 with effect from June 27, 2011, S.I. 2011 No. 1452.]

Video-recorded evidence in chief is currently available for child witnesses in cases of violence or threats of violence, sexual offences, kidnapping, abduction and cruelty. **9–58**

In *R. (CPS, Harrow) v. Brentford Youth Court* [2003] EWHC 2409, Admin, the word "desirability" in s.27(3) was considered in the context of the inadmissibility of evidence. The legislative purpose of s.27(3) was said to be (i) to resolve in favour of video evidence its question of relative worth in relation to live evidence and (ii) to tackle the problem of the unusual case in which the evidence of a child or disabled person could not be given without referring to inadmissible matters. In that circumstance if the evidence could not be understood without the whole of it being played, and it was desirable that the whole should be played then the court should direct itself to ignore the inadmissible matters.

In *G. v. DPP* [1997] 2 Cr.App.R. 78, DC the court held that failure to comply with the earlier *Memorandum of Good Practice* was a matter to be taken into account by a court in deciding whether to exercise its discretion to refuse to admit the recording. The decision should not depend so much on the nature and extent of any breaches, as on whether the passages tainted by the breaches are confirmed by other untainted passages or are corroborated by independent evidence. **9–59**

In *D. and S.* (2002) 166 J.P. 792, CA it was held that a failure to comply with the Home Office and Department of Health Memorandum of Good Practice did not *per se* render the complainant's video evidence inadmissible. The correct test for determining the admissibility of video-recorded evidence of a child is that provided in *Hanton* [2005] EWCA Crim 2009 of whether a reasonable jury properly directed can be sure that the witness has given a credible and accurate account on the video tape, notwithstanding any breaches of the relevant guidance for conducting interviews. It is possible for a court to consider other evidence that might corroborate the video evidence, but such consideration should be undertaken with considerable care: *K.* [2006] 2 Cr.App.R. 10.

Where a court with good reason receives transcripts of video evidence, the court must take care to examine the video as shown, not least because of the demeanour of the witness in giving evidence: *R. v. Popescu* [2010] EWCA Crim 1230.

Youth Justice and Criminal Evidence Act 1999, s.28

Video recorded cross-examination or re-examination

9–60 **28.**—(1) Where a special measures direction provides for a video recording to be admitted under section 27 as evidence in chief of the witness, the direction may also provide—

(a) for any cross-examination of the witness, and any re-examination, to be recorded by means of a video recording; and

(b) for such a recording to be admitted, so far as it relates to any such cross-examination or re-examination, as evidence of the witness under cross-examination or on re-examination, as the case may be.

(2) Such a recording must be made in the presence of such persons as rules of court or the direction may provide and in the absence of the accused, but in circumstances in which—

(a) the judge or justices (or both) and legal representatives acting in the proceedings are able to see and hear the examination of the witness and to communicate with the persons in whose presence the recording is being made, and

(b) the accused is able to see and hear any such examination and to communicate with any legal representative acting for him.

(3) Where two or more legal representatives are acting for a party to the proceedings, subsection (2)(a) and (b) are to be regarded as satisfied in relation to those representatives if at all material times they are satisfied in relation to at least one of them.

(4) Where a special measures direction provides for a recording to be admitted under this section, the court may nevertheless subsequently direct that it is not to be so admitted if any requirement of subsection (2) or rules of court or the direction has not been complied with to the satisfaction of the court.

(5) Where in pursuance of subsection (1) a recording has been made of any examination of the witness, the witness may not be subsequently cross-examined or re-examined in respect of any evidence given by the witness in the proceedings (whether in any recording admissible under section 27 or this section or otherwise than in such a recording) unless the court gives a further special measures direction making such provision as is mentioned in subsection (1)(a) and (b) in relation to any subsequent cross-examination, and re-examination, of the witness.

(6) The court may only give such a further direction if it appears to the court—

(a) that the proposed cross-examination is sought by a party to the proceedings as a result of that party having become aware, since the time when the original recording was made in pursuance of subsection (1), of a matter which that party could not with reasonable diligence have ascertained by then, or

(b) that for any other reason it is in the interests of justice to give the further direction.

(7) Nothing in this section shall be read as applying in relation to any cross-examination of the witness by the accused in person (in a case where the accused is to be able to conduct any such cross-examination).

[This section is not in force.]

Criminal Justice Act 2003, ss.137–138, 140

Evidence by video recording

9–61 **137.**—(1) This section applies where—

(a) a person is called as a witness in proceedings for an offence triable only on indictment, or for a prescribed offence triable either way,

(b) the person claims to have witnessed (whether visually or in any other way)—

(i) events alleged by the prosecution to include conduct constituting the offence or part of the offence, or

(ii) events closely connected with such events,

(c) he has previously given an account of the events in question (whether in response to questions asked or otherwise),

(d) the account was given at a time when those events were fresh in the person's memory (or would have been, assuming the truth of the claim mentioned in paragraph (b)),

(e) a video recording was made of the account,

(f) the court has made a direction that the recording should be admitted as evidence in chief of the witness, and the direction has not been rescinded, and

(g) the recording is played in the proceedings in accordance with the direction.

(2) If, or to the extent that, the witness in his oral evidence in the proceedings asserts the truth of the statements made by him in the recorded account, they shall be treated as if made by him in that evidence.

(3) A direction under subsection (1)(f)—

(a) may not be made in relation to a recorded account given by the defendant;

(b) may be made only if it appears to the court that—

(i) the witness's recollection of the events in question is likely to have been significantly better when he gave the recorded account than it will be when he gives oral evidence in the proceedings, and

(ii) it is in the interests of justice for the recording to be admitted, having regard in particular to the matters mentioned in subsection (4).

(4) Those matters are—

(a) the interval between the time of the events in question and the time when the recorded account was made;

(b) any other factors that might affect the reliability of what the witness said in that account;

(c) the quality of the recording;

(d) any views of the witness as to whether his evidence in chief should be given orally or by means of the recording.

(5) For the purposes of subsection (2) it does not matter if the statements in the recorded account were not made on oath.

(6) In this section "prescribed" means of a description specified in an order made by the Secretary of State.

[Section 137 is not yet in force.]

Video evidence: further provisions

138.—(1) [Repealed] 9–62

(2) The reference in subsection (1)(f) of section 137 to the admission of a recording includes a reference to the admission of part of the recording; and references in that section and this one to the video recording or to the witness's recorded account shall, where appropriate, be read accordingly.

(3) In considering whether any part of a recording should be not admitted under section 137, the court must consider—

(a) whether admitting that part would carry a risk of prejudice to the defendant, and

(b) if so, whether the interests of justice nevertheless require it to be admitted in view of the desirability of showing the whole, or substantially the whole, of the recorded interview.

(4) A court may not make a direction under section 137(1)(f) in relation to any proceedings unless—

(a) the Secretary of State has notified the court that arrangements can be made, in the area in which it appears to the court that the proceedings will take place, for implementing directions under that section, and

(b) the notice has not been withdrawn.

(5) Nothing in section 137 affects the admissibility of any video recording which would be admissible apart from that section.

[This section is printed as amended by the *Coroners and Justice Act* 2009, s.111 with effect from June 27, 2011, S.I. 2011 No. 1452.]

Interpretation of Chapter 3

9–63 **140.** In this Chapter—

"criminal proceedings" means criminal proceedings in relation to which the strict rules of evidence apply;

"defendant", in relation to criminal proceedings, means a person charged with an offence in those proceedings;

"document" means anything in which information of any description is recorded, but not including any recording of sounds or moving images;

"oral evidence" includes evidence which, by reason of any disability, disorder or other impairment, a person called as a witness gives in writing or by signs or by way of any device;

"video recording" means any recording, on any medium, from which a moving image may by any means be produced, and includes the accompanying sound-track.

B. INTERMEDIARY

Youth Justice and Criminal Evidence Act 1999, s.29

Examination of witness through intermediary

9–64 **29.**—(1) A special measures direction may provide for any examination of the witness (however and wherever conducted) to be conducted through an interpreter or other person approved by the court for the purposes of this section ("an intermediary").

(2) The function of an intermediary is to communicate—

(a) to the witness, questions put to the witness, and

(b) to any person asking such questions, the answers given by the witness in reply to them,

and to explain such questions or answers so far as necessary to enable them to be understood by the witness or person in question.

(3) Any examination of the witness in pursuance of subsection (1) must take place in the presence of such persons as rules of court or the direction may provide, but in circumstances in which—

(a) the judge or justices (or both) and legal representatives acting in the proceedings are able to see and hear the examination of the witness and to communicate with the intermediary, and

(b) (except in the case of a video recorded examination) the jury (if there is one) are able to see and hear the examination of the witness.

(4) Where two or more legal representatives are acting for a party to the proceedings, subsection (3)(a) is to be regarded as satisfied in relation to those representatives if at all material times it is satisfied in relation to at least one of them.

(5) A person may not act as an intermediary in a particular case except after making a declaration, in such form as may be prescribed by rules of court, that he will faithfully perform his function as intermediary.

(6) Subsection (1) does not apply to an interview of the witness which is recorded by means of a video recording with a view to its admission as evidence in chief of the witness; but a special measures direction may provide for such a recording to be admitted under section 27 if the interview was conducted through an intermediary and—

(a) that person complied with subsection (5) before the interview began, and

(b) the court's approval for the purposes of this section is given before the direction is given.

(7) Section 1 of the *Perjury Act* 1911 (perjury) shall apply in relation to a person acting as an intermediary as it applies in relation to a person lawfully sworn as an interpreter in a judicial proceeding; and for this purpose, where a person acts as an intermediary in any proceeding which is not a judicial proceeding for the purposes of that section, that proceeding shall be taken to be part of the judicial proceeding in which the witness's evidence is given.

9–65 Where provision is made for examination of a witness via a live link to be made through an intermediary the witness shall be accompanied at the link only by the intermediary and such others as may be acceptable to the court: *Criminal Procedure Rules* 2011, r. 29.10. This is currently available in pilot areas only.

See *Criminal Procedure Rules* 2011, r. 29.10 in Appendix G–176a. **9–66**

Intermediaries

Section 29 makes provision for a vulnerable witness for the prosecution or defence to give evidence with the assistance of an intermediary. There is no definition of this term and the court will approach each application to appoint such a person on the basis of the need identified. Section 18 of the *Youth Justice and Criminal Evidence Act* 1999 limits the availability of intermediaries to witnesses eligible for special measures on the grounds of age or incapacity under s.16 of that Act. A national list of approved intermediaries is maintained, although any person with the appropriate experience may be approved by the court. In practise, if the witness is for the prosecution the police and CPS will implement the steps set out in the Intermediary Procedural Guidance Manual. In addition guidance to prosecutors is set out in the Crown Prosecution Service Intermediary Special Measure Protocol updated in August 2010. Once an intermediary has been engaged he or she will meet the vulnerable witness and carry out an assessment. A note, which is disclosable, should be made at this meeting. The purpose of the meeting is to assess whether the witness requires assistance during the investigation, if ongoing, and at court. If it is decided that the assistance of an intermediary is desirable, the assessment may form the basis of a report to the court. **9–66a**

Part II

An application for the use of an intermediary at trial, like all special measures applications, should comply with rule 29.3 of the *Criminal Procedure Rules*. The application may seek the court's retrospective approval for the use of an intermediary during a video recorded interview when an application is being made for the recording to be admitted as the witness' evidence in chief.

Prior to the witness giving evidence the court may be asked to hold a "ground rules" hearing. Although there is no provision in the *Criminal Procedure Rules*, the protocol referred to above suggests that such a hearing should be attended by the intermediary, the prosecutor, the magistrates or judge and the trial advocates.

At the ground rules hearing, the court will wish to discuss and agree the most effective way to question a witness. This includes how the intermediary should signal that he or she wishes to intervene, how to indicate that a break is required and whether visual aids or other resources for communication should be used. The issues to be discussed will depend on all the circumstances of the case and no exhaustive list can be formulated.

Function of Intermediaries

Section 29 of the *Youth and Criminal Justice Act* 1999 provides directly for the use of an intermediary for examination of the witness in court. The function of an intermediary is to communicate to the witness questions put to the witness and to any person asking such questions, the answers given by the witness in reply. The intermediary may explain questions and answers so far as necessary to enable questions and answers to be understood: s.29(2). **9–66b**

The intermediary must make a declaration that he or she will faithfully perform the function of intermediary (s.29(5)) not only before the witness gives evidence in court but also before the commencement of a video recorded interview with the witness. This is so even if the intermediary is the same on both occasions. The terms of the declaration are set out at rule 29.7 of the *Criminal Procedure Rules* 2011.

The function of an intermediary is not to act on behalf of the prosecutor, the defence or the witness. Nor is the intermediary an investigator, expert witness, advocate for the witness or appropriate adult.

Intermediaries to Assist the Defendant

The words "other than the accused" in s.16(1) of the *Youth Justice and Criminal* **9–66c**

Evidence Act 1999 (*ante* § 9–28) were thought to exclude a successful application for special measures on behalf of a defendant. In *R. (S) v. Waltham Forest Youth Court* [2004] EWHC 715 (Admin), the court concluded that there was no statutory authority to allow a youth who was a defendant to give evidence by video link pursuant to S 24 of that Act (see § 9–43) because the special measures allowed by statute applied only to witnesses. However, in *C v. Sevenoaks Youth Court* [2009] EWHC 3088 (Admin) Sullivan J identified inherent powers in the youth court which were unaffected by the 1999 Act to assist a defendant to give best quality evidence by the use of special measures. C was aged 12 and to be tried for robbery. Before trial he was examined by a chartered clinical psychologist who reported that he suffered from a learning disability, possibly within the range of "exceptionally low". He had a long standing diagnosis of ADHD and suffered from a personality disorder known as Oppositional Defiance Disorder. He presented with many of the symptoms of Asperger's Syndrome. Nonetheless he was fit to plead and stand trial provided there were regular breaks and simple language was used. A doctor also reported that C might be assisted in following the proceedings if the court appointed an intermediary. The case proceeded with the agreement of prosecution and defence, that an intermediary was required to ensure a fair trial.

Reviewing the authorities including *R. v. H* [2003] EWCA Crim 1209, *SC v. UK* (2005) 40 EHRR 10, *R. (D) v. Camberwell Green Youth Court* 2005 UKHL 4 and *R. (P) v. West London Youth Court* [2006] 1 W.L.R. 1219, the court concluded that jurisdiction to provide special measures derived from the youth court's inherent power and duty to ensure a fair trial under the Rules and Article 6 of the Convention. Guidance on the role of the intermediary both before and during trial is to be found at paragraph 17 of the judgement. In particular "C must know the intermediary and have confidence in him or her. Such trust will not be established if their first meeting is on the morning of the trial".

The judgement does not refer to the particular duty of a youth court under s.44 of the *Children and Young Persons Act* 1933 to address the welfare of a young person, and therefore, it may be that the same inherent powers will apply in the magistrates' court to adult defendants.

The *Coroners and Justice Act* 2009 makes provision by s.104 to add a statutory power to appoint an intermediary to assist a qualifying defendant, by inserting ss.33BA and 33BB into the *Youth Justice and Criminal Evidence Act* 1999. The new section applies to a defendant of any age although the requirements differ according to whether the defendant is under or over 18 when the application for special measures is made. Section 33BA(5) provides that a defendant under 18 may qualify for an intermediary, if the accused's ability to participate effectively in the proceedings as a witness giving oral evidence in court is compromised by his level of intellectual ability or social functioning. Section 33BA(6) provides that if the defendant is over 18 the conditions are that he suffers from a mental disorder (within the meaning of the *Mental Health Act* 1983) or otherwise has a significant impairment of intelligence and social function, and he is for that reason unable to participate effectively in the proceedings as a witness giving oral evidence in court.

Section 33BB sets out the court's powers of variation or discharge of an order made under S33BA. A magistrate' court must give reasons for varying or discharging an order and cause those reasons to be entered in the register of its proceedings.

***Note.* Section 104 of the *Coroners and Justice Act* 2009 is not yet in force and no commencement date has been fixed.**

Until s.104 is in force, the power to appoint an intermediary will fall under the court's inherent jurisdiction as identified in *C v. Sevenoaks Youth Court*, above. The regime envisaged by the judgement in this case appears to go beyond the assistance provided for by statute, the latter being limited to "any examination of the accused to be conducted through an intermediary" and therefore to proceedings in court.

Youth Justice and Criminal Evidence Act 1999, ss.30–33

Aids to communication

9–67 **30.** A special measures direction may provide for the witness, while giving evidence (whether by testimony in court or otherwise), to be provided with such device as the court considers appropriate with a view to enabling questions or answers to be communicated to or by the witness despite any disability or disorder or other impairment which the witness has or suffers from.

Status of evidence given under Chapter I

31.—(1) Subsections (2) to (4) apply to a statement made by a witness in criminal proceedings which, in accordance with a special measures direction, is not made by the witness in direct oral testimony in court but forms part of the witness's evidence in those proceedings. **9–68**

(2) The statement shall be treated as if made by the witness in direct oral testimony in court; and accordingly—

(a) it is admissible evidence of any fact of which such testimony from the witness would be admissible;

(b) it is not capable of corroborating any other evidence given by the witness.

(3) Subsection (2) applies to a statement admitted under section 27 or 28 which is not made by the witness on oath even though it would have been required to be made on oath if made by the witness in direct oral testimony in court.

(4) In estimating the weight (if any) to be attached to the statement, the court must have regard to all the circumstances from which an inference can reasonably be drawn (as to the accuracy of the statement or otherwise).

(5) Nothing in this Chapter (apart from subsection (3)) affects the operation of any rule of law relating to evidence in criminal proceedings.

(6) Where any statement made by a person on oath in any proceeding which is not a judicial proceeding for the purposes of section 1 of the *Perjury Act* 1911 (perjury) is received in evidence in pursuance of a special measures direction, that proceeding shall be taken for the purposes of that section to be part of the judicial proceeding in which the statement is so received in evidence.

(7) Where in any proceeding which is not a judicial proceeding for the purposes of that Act—

(a) a person wilfully makes a false statement otherwise than on oath which is subsequently received in evidence in pursuance of a special measures direction, and

(b) the statement is made in such circumstances that had it been given on oath in any such judicial proceeding that person would have been guilty of perjury,

he shall be guilty of an offence and liable to any punishment which might be imposed on conviction of an offence under section 57(2) (giving of false unsworn evidence in criminal proceedings).

(8) In this section "statement" includes any representation of fact, whether made in words or otherwise.

Warning to jury

32. Where on a trial on indictment evidence has been given in accordance with a special measures direction, the judge must give the jury such warning (if any) as the judge considers necessary to ensure that the fact that the direction was given in relation to the witness does not prejudice the accused. **9–69**

Interpretation etc. of Chapter I

33.—(1) In this Chapter— **9–70**

"eligible witness" means a witness eligible for assistance by virtue of section 16 or 17;

"live link" has the meaning given by section 24(8);

"quality", in relation to the evidence of a witness, shall be construed in accordance with section 16(5);

"special measures direction" means (in accordance with section 19(5)) a direction under section 19.

(2) In this Chapter references to the special measures available in relation to a witness shall be construed in accordance with section 18.

(3) In this Chapter references to a person being able to see or hear, or be seen or heard by, another person are to be read as not applying to the extent that either of them is unable to see or hear by reason of any impairment of eyesight or hearing.

(4) In the case of any proceedings in which there is more than one accused—

(a) any reference to the accused in sections 23 to 28 may be taken by a court, in connection with the giving of a special measures direction, as a reference to all or any of the accused, as the court may determine, and

(b) any such direction may be given on the basis of any such determination.

C. WITNESS OVERSEAS

9–71 Section 32 of the *Criminal Justice Act* 1988 allows witnesses who are overseas to give evidence by video link. It applies to certain offences only and because of this there is no provision for magistrates other than youth courts to hear evidence from witnesses overseas in this manner.

Evidence by telephone link. The use of a telephone to receive evidence in a criminal trial is not authorised by statute and there is no precedent for such a course. The Convention on Mutual Assistance in Criminal Matters 2000 (OJ2000/C197/3) was implemented by the *Crime (International Co-operation) Act* 2003 so as to continue the common law tradition that evidence must be given by a witness in person unless the provisions enabling hearsay evidence to be given apply or where the evidence may be given by video link. Sections 30 and 31 of the 2003 Act enable witnesses present in the United Kingdom to give evidence in a foreign court by telephone or television link, but witnesses located abroad may give evidence in a court in the United Kingdom by television link but not by telephone: *Criminal Justice Act* 1988 s.32, *R. v. Diane* (2010) 2 Cr.App.R.(S.) 1 (1), CA

VI. WRITTEN EVIDENCE AT SUMMARY TRIAL

A. STATEMENTS

Criminal Justice Act 1967, s.9

Proof by written statement

9–72 **9.**—(1) In any criminal proceedings, other than committal proceedings, a written statement by any person shall, if such of the conditions mentioned in the next following subsection as are applicable are satisfied, be admissible as evidence to the like extent as oral evidence to the like effect by that person.

(2) The said conditions are—

(a) the statement purports to be signed by the person who made it;

(b) the statement contains a declaration by that person to the effect that it is true to the best of his knowledge and belief and that he made the statement knowing that, if it were tendered in evidence, he would be liable to prosecution if he wilfully stated in it anything which he knew to be false or did not believe to be true;

(c) before the hearing at which the statement is tendered in evidence, a copy of the statement is served, by or on behalf of the party proposing to tender it, on each of the other parties to the proceedings; and

(d) none of the other parties or their solicitors, within seven days from the service of the copy of the statement, serves a notice on the party so proposing objecting to the statement being tendered in evidence under this section:

Provided that the conditions mentioned in paragraphs (c) and (d) of this subsection shall not apply if the parties agree before or during the hearing that the statement shall be so tendered.

(3) The following provisions shall also have effect in relation to any written statement tendered in evidence under this section, that is to say—

(a) if the statement is made by a person under the age of eighteen, it shall give his age;

(b) if it is made by a person who cannot read it, it shall be read to him before he signs it and shall be accompanied by a declaration by the person who so read the statement to the effect that it was so read; and

(c) if it refers to any other document as an exhibit, the copy served on any other party to the proceedings under paragraph (c) of the last foregoing subsection shall be accompanied by a copy of that document or by such information as may be necessary in order to enable the party on whom it is served to inspect that document or a copy thereof.

(4) Notwithstanding that a written statement made by any person may be admissible as evidence by virtue of this section—

(a) the party by whom or on whose behalf a copy of the statement was served may call that person to give evidence; and

(b) the court may, of its own motion or on the application of any party to the proceedings, require that person to attend before the court and give evidence.

(5) An application under paragraph (b) of the last foregoing subsection to a court other than a magistrates' court may be made before the hearing and on any such application the powers of the court shall be exercisable by a puisne judge of the High Court, a Circuit judge or Recorder sitting alone.

(6) So much of any statement as is admitted in evidence by virtue of this section shall, unless the court otherwise directs, be read aloud at the hearing and where the court so directs an account shall be given orally of so much of any statement as is not read aloud.

(7) Any document or object referred to as an exhibit and identified in a written statement tendered in evidence under this section shall be treated as if it had been produced as an exhibit and identified in court by the maker of the statement.

(8) A document required by this section to be served on any person may be served—

(a) by delivering it to him or to his solicitor; or

(b) by addressing it to him and leaving it at his usual or last known place of abode or place of business or by addressing it to his solicitor and leaving it at his office; or

(c) by sending it in a registered letter or by the recorded delivery service or by first class post addressed to him at his usual or last known place of abode or place of business or addressed to his solicitor at his office; or

(d) in the case of a body corporate, by delivering it to the secretary or clerk of the body at its registered or principal office or sending it in a registered letter or by the recorded delivery service or by first class post addressed to the Secretary or clerk of that body at that office; and in paragraph (d) of this subsection references to the secretary, in relation to a limited liability partnership, are to any designated member of the limited liability partnership.

The principle that it is no longer acceptable for defence advocates to seek to take advantage of prosecution errors by deliberately delaying identification of an issue of fact or law until the last possible moment applies equally where a statement has been served under s.9 even where it is a case before the youth court: *R. (P.) v. South and South East Hampshire Youth Court*, unreported, April 14, 2005. In this case the defence took a point on what was contained in the statement when it had not asked for the witness to attend and give evidence. The court used its discretion to adjourn the proceedings so that, in the interests of justice, the witness could be called. There must be strict compliance with the requirements of this section and the *Criminal Procedure Rules* 2011 otherwise the statement will be inadmissible: *Paterson v. DPP* [1990] Crim.L.R. 651. The Practice Direction provides a precedent of a notice for the prosecution to send to the defendant when it wants to tender a statement in evidence under s.9. A statement admitted in evidence pursuant to s.9 is not taken to be conclusive evidence. It will be treated as if the maker had given oral evidence and appropriate weight will be given to it. Where the evidence is crucial to the case it is desirable for the witness to be called in person: *Lister v. Quaife* (1982) 75 Cr.App.R. 313; [1983] 1 W.L.R. 48. **9–73**

A statement may be edited where there is irrelevant, inadmissible or prejudicial material or several statements may be reduced to one statement: see *Consolidation Criminal Practice Direction* para. III.24 (see Appendix F).

An analyst's statement may be served under s.16 of the *Road Traffic Act* 1988 where different rules of service apply than to a s.9 statement, *i.e.* it must be served personally, by registered post or by recorded delivery and at least seven days before a hearing: *DPP v. Stephens* [2006] EWHC 1860. Section 16(1) is permissive rather than an exclusive stipulation as to how an analyst's evidence can be adduced. It does not stipulate the only manner in which evidence of analysis can be given. It authorises the use of a certificate where the analyst is authorised within the meaning of s.16(7). A blood sample analysis can also be given by means of a s.9 statement, by an analyst who is not such an "authorised analyst":*R. (on the application of CPS) v. Sedgemoor Justices* [2007] EWHC 1803 (Admin). It may, in relation the to the service of a statement under the *Road Traffic Offenders Act* 1988, s.20(8) the service was rejected where the statement was of such poor quality that it could not be used: *Griffiths v. DPP* [2007] EWHC 619, Admin.

B. ADMISSION OF FACTS

Criminal Justice Act 1967, s.10

Proof by formal admission

9–74 **10.**—(1) Subject to the provisions of this section, any fact of which oral evidence may be given in any criminal proceedings may be admitted for the purpose of those proceedings by or on behalf of the prosecutor or defendant, and the admission by any party of any such fact under this section shall as against that party be conclusive evidence in those proceedings of the fact admitted.

(2) An admission under this section—

(a) may be made before or at the proceedings;

(b) if made otherwise than in court, shall be in writing;

(c) if made in writing by an individual, shall purport to be signed by the person making it and, if so made by a body corporate, shall purport to be signed by a director or manager, or the secretary or clerk, or some other similar officer of the body corporate;

(d) if made on behalf of a defendant who is an individual, shall be made by his counsel or solicitor;

(e) if made at any state before the trial by a defendant who is an individual, must be approved by his counsel or solicitor (whether at the time it was made or subsequently) before or at the proceedings in question.

(3) An admission under this section for the purpose of proceedings relating to any matter shall be treated as an admission for the purpose of any subsequent criminal proceedings relating to that matter (including any appeal or retrial).

(4) An admission under this section may with the leave of the court be withdrawn in the proceedings for the purpose of which it is made or any subsequent criminal proceedings relating to the same matter.

9–75 Where a fact is admitted orally in court by or on behalf of the prosecutor or defendant, the fact admitted will be written down and signed by or on behalf of the party making the admission: *Criminal Procedure Rules* 2011, r. 37.4. See Appendix G–225. A form is usually available at court for this purpose.

Leave to withdraw an admission is unlikely to be given under s.10(4) without cogent evidence that the admissions were made by reason of mistake or misunderstanding: *Kolton* [2000] Crim.L.R. 761.

VII. EXAMINATION IN CHIEF

A. GENERAL

9–76 After the witness has been sworn or has affirmed the party who calls the witness, either in person or through a legal representative, will ask him questions to adduce relevant and admissible evidence which is supportive of the party's case. No time limits are set for the examination or cross-examination of witnesses. Where counsel indulges in prolix and repetitious questioning however, the court is entitled and obliged to impose reasonable time limits to ensure fair and sensible trial management: *Butt* [2005] EWCA Crim 805.

9–76a A magistrates' local court legal adviser is entitled to assist an unrepresented defendant to put his case as effectively as he can by speaking to him to discover the general nature of his case and establish what questions might properly be put to other witnesses. The answer can be converted into a question for the witness. However, if that procedure is not followed then what the defendant tells the legal advisor is not evidence in the case and magistrates were wrong to make a finding of fact based solely on what had been said between the defendant and the legal advisor, where no evidence to justify that finding had been called: *London Borough of Haringey v. Tshilumbe*, 174 J.P. 41, DC.

B. IDENTIFICATION OF THE WITNESS

The witness will be asked to state his full name. A witness is only asked for his address in exceptional circumstances and if it is relevant to an issue at trial. He may be asked for his occupation and if he is, it is not considered objectionable: *D.S.* [1999] Crim.L.R. 911, CA. **9–77**

Concern has been expressed about hearing evidence from a female witness whose face is veiled for religious purposes and whose expression is invisible. The senior Presiding Judge gave guidance to magistrates in a letter dated July 31, 2007. He stated that the:

> "assessment of evidence is based upon a number of different factors. Responses, behaviour and the manner in which a person delivers his or her evidence can be affected by a range of matters including social and cultural background or ethnicity, or the effects of injury or any disability. If in the light of the nature of the case, the potential evidence and the prevailing circumstances, any one of the magistrates is of the view that he or she may be disadvantaged in assessing the witness, then the magistrates should retire and discuss the most appropriate course of action. This is not to be decided on a majority decision because each magistrate must be faithful to his or her oath. If, following discussion, the question of a veil remains a matter for concern, such a course of action may well include asking the defendant or witness to remove that part of the veil which covers her face and to consider what might be done to facilitate a resolution to the difficulty."

Reasons for removal should be fully explained *i.e.*

> "that the role of the magistrates is to weigh and evaluate the evidence presented in court and that, in order to make that evaluation, magistrates draw of the full range of information available to them. This includes the oral evidence of witnesses whether called by the prosecution or defence. The evaluation also involves, to some extent, an assessment of the way in which the person gives that evidence, how each responds or reacts to questions or even to other people in court while the way in which evidence is given may only be part of the assessment, in certain cases they may feel that they cannot be assured that they can provide a fair and just assessment of all the evidence without seeing the defendant/witness's face during the course of the hearing, thereby creating disadvantage. It would need to be made clear that, whilst demeanour and facial expressions will not be allowed to over-influence the consideration given to any case, those features would usually be available to assist magistrates when weighing up the evidence. Once the person concerned has been informed about any perceived difficulties, it must then be left to the woman concerned to decide how she then wants to proceed. The Equal Treatment Bench Book suggests that "one option might be to allow a short adjournment to enable the woman concerned to seek guidance or advice or possibly to enable her to attend court differently attired or perhaps for the court to be cleared of anyone other than those directly involved in the case". A further option might be to offer the use of a screen. If the defendant/witness does not wish to remove that part of the veil which covers her face, this will be accepted by the magistrates, but it should be confirmed that the reason for the request to remove has been explained. . .. . . and that the person understands the reason for the concern."

C. LEADING QUESTIONS

Witnesses should not be asked leading questions in examination in chief unless they relate to formal or introductory matters or facts which are not in dispute: *Robinson* (1897) 61 J.P. 520. A leading question is one which suggests the desired answer or assumes the existence of a disputed fact. If a person or object is to be identified in court a leading question may be used: *Watson* (1817) 2 Stark 116. **9–78**

Whereas answers to leading questions are admissible, the weight of the evidence is reduced: *Wilson* 9 Cr.App.R. 124, CCA; *Moor v. Moor* [1954] 1 W.L.R. 927. In certain circumstances the court, in the interests of justice, may use its discretion to allow such questions. In *ex p. Bottomley* [1909] 2 K.B. 14, a magistrate died in the course of proceedings. When a witness was recalled before a new magistrate, a leading question was allowed to elicit whether a deposition represented the evidence already given.

Where a witness gives evidence of a fact and another witness is called in order to con-

Part II

tradict him, the latter may be asked directly whether that fact ever took place: *Courteen v. Touse* (1807) 1 Camp. 43. Leading questions may also be asked when a witness has been classified as hostile: see *post*.

D. REFRESHING MEMORY

Criminal Justice Act 2003, s.139

Use of documents to refresh memory

9–79 **139.**—(1) A person giving oral evidence in criminal proceedings about any matter may, at any stage in the course of doing so, refresh his memory of it from a document made or verified by him at an earlier time if—

(a) he states in his oral evidence that the document records his recollection of the matter at that earlier time, and

(b) his recollection of the matter is likely to have been significantly better at that time than it is at the time of his oral evidence.

(2) Where—

(a) a person giving oral evidence in criminal proceedings about any matter has previously given an oral account, of which a sound recording was made, and he states in that evidence that the account represented his recollection of the matter at that time,

(b) his recollection of the matter is likely to have been significantly better at the time of the previous account than it is at the time of his oral evidence, and

(c) a transcript has been made of the sound recording,

he may, at any stage in the course of giving his evidence, refresh his memory of the matter from that transcript.

9–80 A witness may refresh his memory from a document made or checked earlier if he states that it records his recollection at that time and at that time his recollection is likely to have been significantly better than the present. He may also, in similar circumstances, refer to a manuscript of a sound recording. It is entirely within the discretion of the court to assess whether the conditions in s.139(1) have been met:*R. v. Mangena*, 174 J.P. 67, CA.This case also establishes that the objection that a witness cannot be allowed to refresh his memory because he has not stumbled is one that is misconceived. The document is an *aide-memoire* and will not amount to corroboration: *Virgo* (1978) 67 Cr.App.R. 323, CA. The document does not have to have been made contemporaneously and it could have been written by someone else so long as it has been checked and verified by the witness. Under the previous law, a copy of a document might not be used where the original no longer existed and the witness had no independent recollection of the facts: *Harvey* (1869) 11 Cox 546. If a copy had been made or verified at the time it would have been admissible: *Burton v. Plummer* (1834) 2 A.&E. 341. It is submitted that the document may be inspected: *Senat v. Senat* [1965] P.172. The witness may be cross-examined on the document.

E. PREVIOUS CONSISTENT STATEMENTS

9–81 Such statements (sometimes called self serving statements) are now dealt with under s.120 of the *Criminal Justice Act* 2003.

Criminal Justice Act 2003, s.120

Other previous statements of witnesses

9–82 **120.**—(1) This section applies where a person (the witness) is called to give evidence in criminal proceedings.

(2) If a previous statement by the witness is admitted as evidence to rebut a suggestion that his oral evidence has been fabricated, that statement is admissible as evidence of any matter stated of which oral evidence by the witness would be admissible.

(3) A statement made by the witness in a document—

(a) which is used by him to refresh his memory while giving evidence,

(b) on which he is cross-examined, and
(c) which as a consequence is received in evidence in the proceedings,

is admissible as evidence of any matter stated of which oral evidence by him would be admissible.

(4) A previous statement by the witness is admissible as evidence of any matter stated of which oral evidence by him would be admissible, if—

(a) any of the following three conditions is satisfied, and
(b) while giving evidence the witness indicates that to the best of his belief he made the statement, and that to the best of his belief it states the truth.

(5) The first condition is that the statement identifies or describes a person, object or place.

(6) The second condition is that the statement was made by the witness when the matters stated were fresh in his memory but he does not remember them, and cannot reasonably be expected to remember them, well enough to give oral evidence of them in the proceedings.

(7) The third condition is that—

(a) the witness claims to be a person against whom an offence has been committed,
(b) the offence is one to which the proceedings relate,
(c) the statement consists of a complaint made by the witness (whether to a person in authority or not) about conduct which would, if proved, constitute the offence or part of the offence,
(d) the complaint was made as soon as could reasonably be expected after the alleged conduct,
(e) the complaint was not made as a result of a threat or a promise, and
(f) before the statement is adduced the witness gives oral evidence in connection with its subject matter.

(8) For the purposes of subsection (7) the fact that the complaint was elicited (for example, by a leading question) is irrelevant unless a threat or a promise was involved.

With the exception of section 120(7) these provisions apply to anyone who gives evidence including a defendant where oral evidence is given and a suggestion is made that the evidence has been fabricated. A previous statement can then be introduced to rebut that suggestion. It is admissible as evidence of the matter stated. The previous statement might have been given orally or in a document. It might be a witness statement, a statement under caution, an officer's notebook, letter or an oral complaint made to someone else. Where the previous statement is in a document that document will become evidence: see previous case law: *Owen v. Edwards* (1983) 77 Cr.App.R. 191, DC; *Sekhon* (1987) 85 Cr.App.R. 19, CA; *M.* [1999] 1.W.L.R. 307. **9–83**

It has always been the view that evidence of identification was strengthened if it could be shown that soon after the commission of the offence the witness saw and recognized the defendant: *Fannon* (1922) 22 S.R. (NSW) 427; *Christie* [1914] A.C. 545. A photofit portrait may be introduced as it was in *Cook* [1987] Q.B. 417 and a police artist's impression in *Smith* [1976] Crim.L.R. 511. Section 120(5) extends identification to an object or place. This will include the identification of a motor vehicle and/or index number.

Recent complaints of victims extends beyond the former rule of recent complaints in sexual cases: s.120(7). They may be made as soon as they could reasonably be expected and that too is different from the previous qualification of first reasonable opportunity: see *Valentine* [1996] 2.Cr.App.R. 213 where the character of the complainant, the relationship to the person to whom the complaint was made and the relationship to the person the complainant had the opportunity to complain to but chose not to were taken into account.

The previous statement will not be an independent confirmation of the person's evidence: see *Wright* (1990) 90 Cr.App.R. 91; *Islam* [1999] 1 Cr.App.R. 22; *N.K.* [1999] Crim.L.R. 980.

F. Unfavourable and Hostile Witnesses

If a witness does not come up to proof he is regarded as unfavourable. In such a sit- **9–84** uation the party is only able to call another witness to prove what the unfavourable witness failed to establish: *Ewer v. Ambrose* (1825) 3 B. & C. 746. Where two equally credible witnesses contradict each other, in *Sumner and Leivesley v. John Brown & Co* (1909) 25 T.L.R. 745 it was said that the party calling them is not entitled to accredit one and discredit the other. In *Brent* [1973] Crim.L.R. 295 it was said that that case does not apply to criminal proceedings because the prosecution has a duty to call all relevant evidence.

Criminal Procedure Act 1865, s.3

How far witness may be discredited by the party producing

9–85 **3.** A party producing a witness shall not be allowed to impeach his credit by general evidence of bad character; but he may, in case the witness shall in the opinion of the judge prove adverse, contradict him by other evidence, or, by leave of the judge, prove that he has made at other times a statement inconsistent with his present testimony; but before such last-mentioned proof can be given the circumstances of the supposed statement, sufficient to designate the particular occasion, must be mentioned to the witness, and he must be asked whether or not he has made such statement.

9–86 A hostile witness is much more than an unfavourable witness. Hostility is defined as an unwillingness to tell the truth of what happened and is determined by the court's considering the witness's demeanour and answers, if any. It is the court's determination and it is within the court's discretion to allow a party to cross-examine its own witness and that means allowing leading questions and questions on previous inconsistent statements *Booth* (1982) 74 Cr.App.R. 123: *Booth* (1982) 74 Cr.App.R. 123, CA; *Rice v. Howard* (1886) 26 Q.B.D. 681; *Honeyghon and Sayles* [1999] Crim.L.R. 221, CA. The court should also consider allowing the witness to refresh his memory from a witness statement: *Maw* [1994] Crim.L.R. 841, CA. A witness who is mute of malice can be held to be hostile: *R. v. Thompson* [1916] 64 Cr.App.R. 96.

Once a witness has been treated as hostile, his evidence must be approached with caution, even if in the event he does not prove hostile because he adopts his previous statement: *R. v. Greene* [2009] EWCA Crim 2282.

9–87 The court must have regard to what is likely to happen if the witness is confronted with a previous statement, and to the possibility of serious prejudice and lack of credibility if a damaging statement is elicited. Where a witness is cross-examined on his previous inconsistent statement, the statement does not become evidence of the facts stated in it: *Dibble*, 1 Cr.App.R. 155; *R. v. Norton and Driver (No. 1)* [1987] Crim.L.R. 687. When a hostile witness admits making an unsworn statement but later states on oath, that the contents are untrue, the statement should not be exhibited and the effect is to render the evidence of the witness negligible: *Harris* [1927] 2 K.B. 587; 20 Cr.App.R. 144. Where a hostile witness admits that he has been threatened and the earlier statement was in fact true the court, if it believes the witness, may take that evidence into account.

If the witness adopts the statement it becomes evidence even if credibility is in issue: *R. v. Allen, Sampson and Howlett*, November 10, 2000, unreported. If the witness does not adopt the statement then the evidence only casts doubt on the credibility of the witness: *R. v. Golder* [1961] 45 Cr.App.R. 5. A court must treat any evidence given by a hostile witness incriminating the defendant with caution: *R. v. Ugorji* 9 *Archbold News* 3, CA.

9–88 A witness may be treated as hostile at any stage of his evidence, including re-examination: *Powell* [1985] Crim.L.R. 592, CA. There are now numerous cases in which the Court of Appeal has endorsed the use of s.119 *Criminal Justice Act* 2003 *post* without declaring a witness hostile and where there is compliance with the section's conditions: see *R. v. Gibbons* (2009) 173 J.P. 260.

VIII. CROSS EXAMINATION

A. GENERAL

A sworn witness is liable to be cross-examined by the other party or anyone else having a legitimate interest: *Bingham and Cooke* [1999] 1 W.L.R. 598. It is not necessary for the witness to have been examined-in-chief before being cross-examined. Sometimes a witness may be tendered as a witness simply for the purpose of being cross-examined. **9–89**

A defendant has the right to cross-examine a co-defendant regardless of whether or not the co-defendant has given evidence against the defendant: *Hadwen* [1902] 1 K.B. 882; *Paul* [1920] 2 K.B. 183; *Hilton* [1972] 1 Q.B. 421; *Murdoch v. Taylor* [1965] A.C. 574.

The Crown need not call a witness on whom the Crown did not rely, merely so that the defendant could put the defence case in cross-examination: *Bradish & Hall* [2004] EWCA Crim 1340.

B. FORM OF QUESTIONING

Cross-examination should be conducted with restraint and with the courtesy and consideration which a witness is entitled to expect in a court of law: *Mechanical and General Inventions Co Ltd v. Austin* [1935] A.C. 346. Questions should be framed to elicit answers as to matters of fact: see *Randall v. The Queen* [2002] 1 W.L.R. 2237. Leading questions may be used: *Parkin v. Moon* (1836) 7 C. & P. 409. **9–90**

Cross-examination is not confined to the issues that were raised in evidence in chief, however, questions must relate either to the issues in the case or to the credibility of the witness: *Treacey* [1944] 2 All E.R. 229. Questions may also be asked to elicit how evidence has been obtained: *Att.-Gen.'s Reference (No. 5 of 2002)* [2004] UKHL 40. In that case, questions were allowed to investigate whether intercept material relied on by the Crown had been obtained by tapping a private as opposed to a public telecommunications system.

A witness may not be asked about inadmissible evidence: *Thompson* [1912] 3 K.B. 19; *Treacy* (*ante*); *Rice* [1963] 1 Q.B. 857. A defendant may, however, be cross-examined by a co-defendant as to the contents of an inadmissible statement made by the defendant if he or she gives evidence which is inconsistent with the statement: *Rowson* 80 Cr.App.R. 218; *Lui Mei Lin v. R.* [1989] 2 W.L.R. 175.

If a party intends to call evidence to contradict that given by the witness, the party should put his version of events to the witness in cross-examination so that the witness may explain the contradiction: *Brown v. Dunn* (1869) 6 R. 67; *Hart* 23 Cr.App.R. 202. **9–91**

The court does not have to accept the evidence of a witness just because it has not been challenged: *O'Connell v. Adams* [1973] R.T.R. 150. This was confirmed in *R. (Wilkinson) v. DPP* (2003) 167 J.P. 229, QBD, where Burton J. stated that it is the professional obligation of an advocate acting for the defence to put to prosecution witnesses conflicts between the defence case and the evidence given by the prosecution witness in question in order to give the prosecution witness an opportunity to comment on what is put: whether it is the possibility of a mistake or whether the prosecution witness is lying, whether his recollection is incorrect, whether he has been confused or whatever. The position in relation to the defence case is somewhat different. By the time the defence comes to give evidence, the prosecution evidence has been given, the defence is aware of what evidence has been given and is able, therefore, in chief, to ask witnesses whether or not they agree with the prosecution evidence and to comment on it. It is nonetheless the professional duty of the advocate acting for the defence to make it clear what evidence is rejected or disputed.

The court should disallow questions which are irrelevant or vexatious and keep cross-examination to the points in issue: *Kalia* 60 Cr.App.R. 200; *Simmonds* [1969] 1 Q.B. 685; *Maynard* 69 Cr.App.R. 309. It is the duty of the legal adviser to assist an unrepresented defendant in putting succinct questions to witnesses. Where the offence **9–92** is of a sexual nature and the defendant is unrepresented, the court is under a duty to protect the complainant from intimidation or abuse by the manner of the defendant's questioning: *Brown* [1998] 2 Cr.App.R. 364.

For restrictions on cross-examination of such witnesses, see *post*, § 9–95.

Where more than one defendant is being tried and each is defended by different legal representatives, the rule is that in the absence of agreement between the representatives the court will call upon them to cross-examine in the order in which the names of the defendants appear on the court list.

C. THE DUTY OF LEGAL REPRESENTATIVES

9–93 The duties of counsel in conducting cross-examination are contained in the Code of Conduct for the Bar of England and Wales, pronouncements made to the profession by or on behalf of the Bar Council and judicial statements.

In *O'Neill* 34 Cr.App.R. 105 Lord Goddard C.J. stated:

> "In this case a violent attack was made on the police. It was suggested that they had done improper things ...The applicants had the opportunity of going into the box at the trial and explaining and supporting what they had instructed their counsel to say. They did not dare go into the box and therefore counsel, who knew they were not going into the box, ought not to have made these suggestions against the police ... It is ... entirely wrong to make such suggestions as were made in this case, namely that the police beat the prisoners until they made confessions, and then, when there is the chance for the prisoners to substantiate what has been said by going into the box, for counsel not to call them ..."

9–94 This was endorsed in *Callaghan* (1979) 69 Cr.App.R. 88, CA. The effect of such comments is that the defendant may be forced to relinquish the right to refuse to give evidence: see *ante*.

Where a client requires police evidence to be challenged in the manner considered in *O'Neill* and *Callaghan* but refuses to give evidence because of his bad record, it is an advocate's duty to warn his client that the court will probably view the failure to give evidence adversely.

D. RESTRICTIONS ON CROSS EXAMINATION

9–95 Generally, the defendant is entitled to cross-examine in person any witness called by the prosecution. This rule is subject to the common law and statutory exceptions.

9–96 In *Brown (Milton)* [1998] 2 Cr.App.R. 364, the Court of Appeal stated that a trial is not fair if an unrepresented defendant gains an advantage he would not have otherwise have had by abusing the rules in relation to relevance and repetition when cross-examining. While it was vital that the judge did his utmost to ensure that such a defendant received a fair trial and was seen by the jury to have done so, the judge was also under a duty to protect the interests of other parties to the proceedings, particularly witnesses who were required to describe a traumatic incident which was alleged to have occurred. In those circumstances, it was preferable for the judge to meet with the defendant in the jury's absence to discuss the nature of the evidence the defendant wished to elicit from the complainant and from any defence witnesses.

In the magistrates' courts the duty to elicit the nature of the evidence lies with the legal adviser.

Youth Justice and Criminal Evidence Act 1999, s.34

Complainants in proceedings for sexual offences

9–97 **34.** No person charged with a sexual offence may in any criminal proceedings cross— examine in person a witness who is the complainant, either—

(a) in connection with that offence, or

(b) in connection with any other offence (of whatever nature) with which that person is charged in the proceedings.

There is no power to appoint counsel to cross-examine on a defendant's behalf where the defendant is prohibited under s.34(a): *Smith* [2004] EWCA Crim 2414. **9–98**

Youth Justice and Criminal Evidence Act 1999, ss.35–38

Child complainants and other child witnesses

35.—(1) No person charged with an offence to which this section applies may in any criminal proceedings cross-examine in person a protected witness, either— **9–99**

(a) in connection with that offence, or
(b) in connection with any other offence (of whatever nature) with which that person is charged in the proceedings.

(2) For the purposes of subsection (1) a "protected witness" is a witness who—

(a) either is the complainant or is alleged to have been a witness to the commission of the offence to which this section applies, and
(b) either is a child or falls to be cross-examined after giving evidence in chief (whether wholly or in part)—
(i) by means of a video recording made (for the purposes of section 27) at a time when the witness was a child, or
(ii) in any other way at any such time.

(3) The offences to which this section applies are—

(a) any offence under—
(iva) any of sections 33–36 of the *Sexual Offences Act* 1956.
(v) the *Protection of Children Act* 1978; or
(vi) Part 1 of the *Sexual Offences Act* 2003 [or any relevant superseded enactment]
(b) kidnapping, false imprisonment or an offence under section 1 or 2 of the *Child Abduction Act* 1984;
(c) any offence under section 1 of the *Children and Young Persons Act* 1933;
(d) any offence (not within any of the preceding paragraphs) which involves an assault on, or injury or a threat of injury to, any person.

(3A) In subsection (3)(a)(vi) "relevant superseded enactment" means—

(a) any of sections 1 to 32 of the *Sexual Offences Act* 1956,
(b) the *Indecency with Children Act* 1960,
(c) the *Sexual Offences Act* 1967,
(d) section 54 of the *Criminal Law Act* 1977.

(4) In this section "child" means—

(a) where the offence falls within subsection (3)(a), a person under the age of 18; or
(b) where the offence falls within subsection (3)(b), (c) or (d), a person under the age of 14.

(5) For the purposes of this section "witness" includes a witness who is charged with an offence in the proceedings.

[This section is printed as amended by the *Criminal Justice and Immigration Act* 2008 and the *Coroners and Justice Act* 2009 s.105.]

A child is defined here as a person under 17 years of age.

Direction prohibiting accused from cross-examining particular witness

36.—(1) This section applies where, in a case where neither of sections 34 and 35 operates to prevent an accused in any criminal proceedings from cross— examining a witness in person— **9–100**

(a) the prosecutor makes an application for the court to give a direction under this section in relation to the witness, or
(b) the court of its own motion raises the issue whether such a direction should be given.

(2) If it appears to the court—

(a) that the quality of evidence given by the witness on cross-examination—
(i) is likely to be diminished if the cross-examination (or further cross-examination) is conducted by the accused in person, and

(ii) would be likely to be improved if a direction were given under this section, and

(b) that it would not be contrary to the interests of justice to give such a direction,

the court may give a direction prohibiting the accused from cross-examining (or further cross-examining) the witness in person.

(3) In determining whether subsection (2)(a) applies in the case of a witness the court must have regard, in particular, to—

(a) any views expressed by the witness as to whether or not the witness is content to be cross-examined by the accused in person;

(b) the nature of the questions likely to be asked, having regard to the issues in the proceedings and the defence case advanced so far (if any);

(c) any behaviour on the part of the accused at any stage of the proceedings, both generally and in relation to the witness;

(d) any relationship (of whatever nature) between the witness and the accused;

(e) whether any person (other than the accused) is or has at any time been charged in the proceedings with a sexual offence or an offence to which section 35 applies, and (if so) whether section 34 or 35 operates or would have operated to prevent that person from cross-examining the witness in person;

(f) any direction under section 19 which the court has given, or proposes to give, in relation to the witness.

(4) For the purposes of this section—

(a) "witness", in relation to an accused, does not include any other person who is charged with an offence in the proceedings; and

(b) any reference to the quality of a witness's evidence shall be construed in accordance with section 16(5).

Further provisions about directions under 36

9–101 **37.**—(1) Subject to subsection (2), a direction has binding effect from the time it is made until the witness to whom it applies is discharged.

In this section "direction" means a direction under section 36.

(2) The court may discharge a direction if it appears to the court to be in the interests of justice to do so, and may do so either—

(a) on an application made by a party to the proceedings, if there has been a material change of circumstances since the relevant time, or

(b) of its own motion.

(3) In subsection (2) "the relevant time" means—

(a) the time when the direction was given, or

(b) if a previous application has been made under that subsection, the time when the application (or last application) was made.

(4) The court must state in open court its reasons for—

(a) giving, or

(b) refusing an application for, or for the discharge of, or

(c) discharging,

a direction and, if it is a magistrates' court, must cause them to be entered in the register of its proceedings.

(5) Rules of court may make provision—

(a) for uncontested applications to be determined by the court without a hearing;

(b) for preventing the renewal of an unsuccessful application for a direction except where there has been a material change of circumstances;

(c) for expert evidence to be given in connection with an application for, or for discharging, a direction;

(d) for the manner in which confidential or sensitive information is to be treated in connection with such an application and in particular as to its being disclosed to, or withheld from, a party to the proceedings.

9–102 An application by the prosecutor for the court to give a direction under s.36 must be sent to the court and every other party to the proceedings stating why, in his opinion, the evidence given by the witness is likely to be diminished if cross-examination is undertaken by the accused in person and why the evidence would be improved if a direction were given; *Criminal Procedure Rules* 2011, r. 31.1. See Appendix G–178..

Defence representation for purposes of cross-examination

38.—(1) This section applies where an accused is prevented from cross-examining a witness in person by virtue of section 34, 35 or 36. **9–103**

(2) Where it appears to the court that this section applies, it must—

(a) invite the accused to arrange for a legal representative to act for him for the purpose of cross-examining the witness; and

(b) require the accused to notify the court, by the end of such period as it may specify, whether a legal representative is to act for him for that purpose.

(3) If by the end of the period mentioned in subsection (2)(b) either—

(a) the accused has notified the court that no legal representative is to act for him for the purpose of cross-examining the witness, or

(b) no notification has been received by the court and it appears to the court that no legal representative is to so act,

the court must consider whether it is necessary in the interests of justice for the witness to be cross-examined by a legal representative appointed to represent the interests of the accused.

(4) If the court decides that it is necessary in the interests of justice for the witness to be so cross-examined, the court must appoint a qualified legal representative (chosen by the court) to cross-examine the witness in the interests of the accused.

(5) A person so appointed shall not be responsible to the accused.

(6) Rules of court may make provision—

(a) as to the time when, and the manner in which, subsection (2) is to be complied with;

(b) in connection with the appointment of a legal representative under subsection (4), and in particular for securing that a person so appointed is provided with evidence or other material relating to the proceedings.

(7) Rules of court made in pursuance of subsection (6)(b) may make provision for the application, with such modifications as are specified in the rules, of any of the provisions of—

(a) Part I of the *Criminal Procedure and Investigations Act* 1996 (disclosure of material in connection with criminal proceedings), or

(b) the *Sexual Offences (Protected Material) Act* 1997.

(8) For the purposes of this section—

(a) any reference to cross-examination includes (in a case where a direction is given under section 36 after the accused has begun cross-examining the witness) a reference to further cross-examination; and

(b) "qualified legal representative" means a legal representative who has a right of audience (within the meaning of the *Courts and Legal Services Act* 1990) in relation to the proceedings before the court.

The court may direct, in particular cases, that a defendant may not cross-examine a child or a complainant in proceedings for a sexual offence. It may also prevent cross-examination in person of any other witness if the quality of the evidence is likely to be diminished in those circumstances and that it would be improved if a direction were given and it is in the interests of justice. **9–104**

The court will invite the defendant to be represented for the purposes of cross-examination and, in the event that the defendant chooses not to be, will arrange representation for him.

Youth Justice and Criminal Evidence Act 1999, ss.41–43

Restriction on evidence or questions about complainant's sexual history

41.—(1) If at a trial a person is charged with a sexual offence, then, except with the leave of the court— **9–105**

(a) no evidence may be adduced, and

(b) no question may be asked in cross-examination,

by or on behalf of any accused at the trial, about any sexual behaviour of the complainant.

(2) The court may give leave in relation to any evidence or question only on an application made by or on behalf of an accused, and may not give such leave unless it is satisfied—

(a) that subsection (3) or (5) applies, and

(b) that a refusal of leave might have the result of rendering unsafe a conclusion of the jury or (as the case may be) the court on any relevant issue in the case.

(3) This subsection applies if the evidence or question relates to a relevant issue in the case and either—

(a) that issue is not an issue of consent; or

(b) it is an issue of consent and the sexual behaviour of the complainant to which the evidence or question relates is alleged to have taken place at or about the same time as the event which is the subject matter of the charge against the accused; or

(c) it is an issue of consent and the sexual behaviour of the complainant to which the evidence or question relates is alleged to have been, in any respect, so similar—

(i) to any sexual behaviour of the complainant which (according to evidence adduced or to be adduced by or on behalf of the accused) took place as part of the event which is the subject matter of the charge against the accused, or

(ii) to any other sexual behaviour of the complainant which (according to such evidence) took place at or about the same time as that event,

that the similarity cannot reasonably be explained as a coincidence.

(4) For the purposes of subsection (3) no evidence or question shall be regarded as relating to a relevant issue in the case if it appears to the court to be reasonable to assume that the purpose (or main purpose) for which it would be adduced or asked is to establish or elicit material for impugning the credibility of the complainant as a witness.

(5) This subsection applies if the evidence or question—

(a) relates to any evidence adduced by the prosecution about any sexual behaviour of the complainant; and

(b) in the opinion of the court, would go no further than is necessary to enable the evidence adduced by the prosecution to be rebutted or explained by or on behalf of the accused.

(6) For the purposes of subsections (3) and (5) the evidence or question must relate to a specific instance (or specific instances) of alleged sexual behaviour on the part of the complainant (and accordingly nothing in those subsections is capable of applying in relation to the evidence or question to the extent that it does not so relate).

(7) Where this section applies in relation to a trial by virtue of the fact that one or more of a number of persons charged in the proceedings is or are charged with a sexual offence—

(a) it shall cease to apply in relation to the trial if the prosecutor decides not to proceed with the case against that person or those persons in respect of that charge; but

(b) it shall not cease to do so in the event of that person or those persons pleading guilty to, or being convicted of, that charge.

(8) Nothing in this section authorises any evidence to be adduced or any question to be asked which cannot be adduced or asked apart from this section.

Interpretation and application of section 41

9–106 **42.**—(1) In section 41—

(a) "relevant issue in the case" means any issue falling to be proved by the prosecution or defence in the trial of the accused;

(b) "issue of consent" means any issue whether the complainant in fact consented to the conduct constituting the offence with which the accused is charged (and accordingly does not include any issue as to the belief of the accused that the complainant so consented);

(c) "sexual behaviour" means any sexual behaviour or other sexual experience, whether or not involving any accused or other person, but excluding (except in section 41(3)(c)(i) and (5)(a)) anything alleged to have taken place as part of the event which is the subject matter of the charge against the accused; and

(d) subject to any order made under subsection (2), "sexual offence" shall be construed in accordance with section 62.

(2) The Secretary of State may by order make such provision as he considers appropriate for adding or removing, for the purposes of section 41, any offence to or from the offences which are sexual offences for the purposes of this Act by virtue of section 62.

(3) Section 41 applies in relation to the following proceedings as it applies to a trial, namely—

(a) proceedings before a magistrates' court inquiring into an offence as examining justices,

(b) the hearing of an application under paragraph 5(1) of Schedule 6 to the *Criminal Justice Act* 1991 (application to dismiss charge following notice of transfer of case to Crown Court),

(c) the hearing of an application under paragraph 2(1) of Schedule 3 to the *Crime and Disorder Act* 1998 (application to dismiss charge by person sent for trial under section 51 of that Act),

(d) any hearing held, between conviction and sentencing, for the purpose of determining matters relevant to the court's decision as to how the accused is to be dealt with, and

(e) the hearing of an appeal,

and references (in section 41 or this section) to with an offence accordingly include a person convicted of an offence.

Procedure on applications under section 41

43.—(1) An application for leave shall be heard in private and in the absence of the complainant. **9–107**

In this section "leave" means leave under section 41.

(2) Where such an application has been determined, the court must state in open court (but in the absence of the jury, if there is one)—

(a) its reasons for giving, or refusing, leave, and

(b) if it gives leave, the extent to which evidence may be adduced or questions asked in pursuance of the leave,

and, if it is a magistrates' court, must cause those matters to be entered in the register of its proceedings.

(3) Rules of court may make provision—

(a) requiring applications for leave to specify, in relation to each item of evidence or question to which they relate, particulars of the grounds on which it is asserted that leave should be given by virtue of subsection (3) or (5) of section 41;

(b) enabling the court to request a party to the proceedings to provide the court with information which it considers would assist it in determining an application for leave;

(c) for the manner in which confidential or sensitive information is to be treated in connection with such an application, and in particular as to its being disclosed to, or withheld from, parties to the proceedings.

The purpose of s.41 is to protect complainants from being subjected to unnecessary and embarrassing cross-examination. It is aimed not at preserving the sexual reputation of a complainant but at protecting her from having to relive previous experiences and ordeals except for those permitted by a judge's ruling: *Abdelrahman* [2005] EWCA Crim 1367. Section 41(2) does not require the court to give leave, it merely gives the court a discretion to grant leave: *Mokrecovas* [2002] 1 Cr.App.R. 20, CA. Questions relating to a complainant's failure to complain about alleged sexual assaults or about telling lies about those matters are not automatically excluded: *B.T.* [2002] 1 Cr.App.R. 254. **9–108**

It applies to the trial of sexual offences committed before the *Criminal Justice Act* 2003 came into force: *R. v. C* [2008] 1 Cr.App.R. 22. It does not apply to evidence provided by a prosecution witness who is not the complainant under cross-examination by the defence: *R. v. Hamadi* [2007] EWCA Crim. 3048.

An application will be heard "in camera" with the reasons for any ruling being given in open court and entered in the court's register.

The section itself has been held to be incompatible with ECHR in that it renders inadmissible evidence which might be relevant to the charge concerned. The court will have to decide whether the evidence and the questioning in relation to it is so relevant that to exclude it would endanger a fair trial: *A. (No. 2)* [2002] 1 A.C. 45. In that case, which concerned the issue of consent, Lord Hope gave examples of what might fall within s.41(3)(a):

- — Honest belief in consent;
- — Bias on the part of the complainant against the accused or a motive to fabricate the evidence;
- — An alternative explanation for the physical conditions on which the prosecution relies;
- — The detail of the complainant's account (especially where the complainant is young) must have come from other sexual activity which provides an explanation for knowledge of that activity.

9–109 In *R.T.*; *M.H.* [2002] 1 W.L.R. 632, CA it was held that, for the purposes of s.41, a distinction is to be drawn between questions about sexual behaviour itself and questions concerning statements about such behaviour by the complainant, even if the questions concerned the credibility of the complainant they were not automatically barred by s.41. Where the issue at trial is consent, a defendant is allowed to cross-examine the complainant on what she said to him at the time even if it reveals that she is a virgin: *Soroya* [2006] All E.R. (D) 151. At a trial of a defendant charged with sexual offences it is permitted to question the victim about her previous sexual behaviour but only if the principal purpose is to strengthen the defence case and not if it is merely to impugn the victim's credibility: *Martin* [2004] EWCA Crim 916; [2004] 2 Cr.App.R. 22. Once the criteria for the admissibility of evidence are established, all the evidence relevant to the issues can be adduced: *F.* [2005] EWCA Crim 493; [2005] 1 W.L.R. 2848. It was said that although s.41(4) prevents the deployment of evidence "relating to a relevant issue in the case" where the purpose is to impugn the credibility of the complainant, in one sense, any evidence which directly challenged the evidence of the complainant or sought to demonstrate a malicious motive, involved an attack on credibility. It did not necessarily follow that, merely because cross-examination might impugn credibility, that that was its main purpose. A court must be careful not to impose such significant limits on the examination of a critical issue that a defendant is deprived of worthwhile support for his defence.

A statement by a woman that she had a loving and devoted relationship with a man is not to be adjudged as a lie merely because she had a sexual relationship with another man and if it does contain a lie it is comparatively insignificant and is not a matter about which questions should be permitted: *R. v. Winter* [2008] EWCA Crim. 3.

Other restrictions

9–110 A witness may not be cross-examined if he has not been sworn and has been called merely to produce a document: *Sumners v. Moseley* (1834) 2 Cr. & M. 477. A witness who is called by mistake where matters are not within his knowledge is not liable to be cross-examined, provided that the mistake is discovered after the witness has been sworn but before examination in chief: *Wood v. Mackinson* (1840) 2 Mood. & R. 273. A witness called by the court may only be cross-examined with leave of the court. Leave should be given if the witness's evidence has been adverse to either party: *Coulson v. Disborough* [1894] 2 Q.B. 316; *Cliburn* (1898) 62 J.P. 232.

E. PREVIOUS INCONSISTENT STATEMENTS

Criminal Procedure Act 1865, ss.4–5

As to proof of contradictory statements of adverse witness

9–111 **4.** If a witness, upon cross-examination as to a former statement made by him relative to the subject matter of the indictment or proceeding, and inconsistent with his present testimony, does not distinctly admit that he has made such statement, proof may be given that he did in fact make it; but before such proof can be given the circumstances of the supposed statement, sufficient to designate the particular occasion, must be mentioned to the witness, and he must be asked whether or not he has made such statement.

Cross-examinations as to previous statements in writing

5. A witness may be cross-examined as to previous statements made by him in writing, or reduced into writing, relative to the subject matter of the indictment or proceeding, without such writing being shown to him; but if it is intended to contradict such witness by the writing, his attention must, before such contradictory proof can be given, be called to those parts of the writing which are to be used for the purpose of so contradicting him: **9–112**

Provided always, that it shall be competent for the judge, at any time during the trial, to require the production of the writing for his inspection, and he may thereupon make such use of it for the purposes of the trial as he may think fit.

A witness may, when giving evidence, make a statement which contradicts what the witness has said before thus undermining the witness in a material particular or credibility. It usually happens in cross-examination. The inconsistency should be put to the witness so that he has a chance of stating which facts are true. If the witness denies the statement evidence may be called to show that he did make the statement. **9–113**

In *Derby Magistrates' Court, ex p. B.* [1996] A.C. 487, HL, it was said that s.4 applies to written as well as oral statements.

Part II

Criminal Justice Act 2003, s.119

119.—(1) If in criminal proceedings a person gives oral evidence and— **9–114**

(a) he admits making a previous inconsistent statement, or

(b) a previous inconsistent statement made by him is proved by virtue of section 3, 4 or 5 of the *Criminal Procedure Act* 1865,

the statement is admissible as evidence of any matter stated of which oral evidence by him would be admissible.

(2) If in criminal proceedings evidence of an inconsistent statement by any person is given under section 124(2)(c), the statement is admissible as evidence of any matter stated in it of which oral evidence by that person would be admissible.

Where a witness does not come up to proof a party may seek to introduce a previous statement as evidence. This is more likely to be done by the prosecution when trying to prove particular facts especially in domestic violence cases. **9–115**

It is for the court to determine whether the statement relates to the subject matter of the proceedings: *Bashir* (1970) 54 Cr.App.R. 1. **9–116**

In *Clarke and Hewins* [1999] *Archbold News* 2, CA, it was stated that when a witness is cross-examined on a previous statement, the questioning should be selective and done with precision; it is inappropriate to read long extracts from the statement and then merely to ask one or two short questions; such a method lengthens the proceedings, makes cross-examination difficult to follow and creates the risk that the witness's evidence will become confused with what was said on the previous occasion. The statement need not be shown to the witness but it must be available in court even if the advocate does not intend to use it: *Anderson* 21 Cr.App.R. 178. The witness's answers may not be contradicted by putting the document in evidence unless the witness has been shown the document and has been given the opportunity of explaining its contents.

A previous inconsistent statement may now prove the truth of what is stated i.e. what a witness has said earlier and what he says on oath are both capable of providing evidence of the truth of what happened. The court must evaluate the evidence: *Joyce* [2005] EWCA Crim 1785; see also *Read* [2005] EWCA Crim 3292. See *post*, § 10–78. It must judge the extent and importance of any inconsistency and in weighing the evidence where a previous statement is exculpatory of a defendant, it is sufficient for a court to conclude that it might be true rather than it was true: *R. v. Billingham* [2009] EWCA Crim 19. **9–117**

F. CROSS EXAMINATION AS TO CREDIBILITY

The credibility of a witness depends on: (a) his knowledge of the facts to which he **9–118** testifies; (b) independence; (c) integrity; (d) veracity; and (e) being bound to speak the truth either on oath or by affirmation. Questions may be put to a witness in relation to any improper conduct of which he may be guilty in order to show that the witness should not be believed: *Edwards* 93 Cr.App.R. 48.

A witness can be compelled to answer questions about his credibility: *Cundell v. Pratt* (1827) M. & M. 108. The court has a discretion to direct that a witness should not answer where the court is of the opinion that an answer verifying the truth of the matter suggested would not in fact affect the credibility of the witness: *Sweet-Escott* 55 Cr.App.R. 316. In *Malik* [2000] 2 Cr.App.R. 8, CA, cross-examination of a police officer whose evidence in a previous case had been disbelieved resulting in an acquittal was allowed even though the misconduct alleged was of a different nature from that alleged in the earlier case. Cross-examination has been allowed as to credibility on a pre trial letter between a defendant's solicitors and CPS stating the defendant's willingness to plead guilty to a lesser offence: *Hayes* ; [2005] 1 Cr.App.R. 33.

A witness may not be asked to draw an inference of fact which is discreditable to him: *Bernard* (1858) 1 F. & F. 240. A witness may not be asked questions about his religious beliefs for the purposes of discrediting him: *Darby v. Ouseley* (1856) 1 H. & N. 1.

9–119 Where particular allegations of misconduct are put to a witness, it is not open to the party calling the witness to call evidence of the good character of the witness for the purpose of rebutting the allegations. The character of the witness not being itself in issue, such evidence is excluded on the grounds of being collateral: *Hamilton*, *The Times*, July 25, 1998; *Beard* [1998] Crim.L.R. 585, CA, see also para. 10–110, *post*.

Witnesses may be called to speak about a witness's general character, although not in relation to any particular offence of which he may be guilty: *Watson* (1817) 32 St. Tr. 1. Evidence is not admissible to contradict answers given on cross-examination as to credit: *Mendy* 64 Cr.App.R. 4, CA. The following instances are, however, exceptions and the list is not closed.

Bias

9–120 Facts showing that a witness is biased in relation to the party calling him may be elicited in cross-examination and, if denied, independently proved. *Att.-Gen v. Hitchcock* (1847) 1 Ex. 91; *Denley* [1970] Crim.L.R. 583; *Phillips* 26 Cr.App.R. 17; *Mendy* 64 Cr.App.R. 4.

In *Busby* 75 Cr.App.R. 79, police officers were cross-examined to the effect that they had fabricated statements attributed to the defendant and indicative of his guilt and had threatened a potential defence witness to stop him from giving evidence. The judge ruled that the defence could not call that potential witness to give evidence that he had been threatened by the police officers because it would go solely to their credibility. The Court of Appeal held that the judge had been incorrect because, if the allegations were true, it showed that the police were prepared to go to improper lengths to secure a conviction, which would have supported the defence case that the statements attributed to the defendant had been fabricated.

In *Funderburk* 90 Cr.App.R. 466; [1990] 1 W.L.R. 587 it was said that the decision in *Busby* provided an exception to the general rule. In *Edwards* [1991] 1 W.L.R. 207, however, it was said that *Busby* related to the question of bias. Cross-examination is permissible to show that a witness was biased.

Medical issues

9–121 It is admissible to show that a witness suffers from a disease, defect or abnormality of mind which affects the reliability of his evidence: *Toohey v. Metropolitan Police Commissioner* [1965] A.C. 595, HL.

Evidence is not admissible to contradict answers given by a witness to questions put in cross-examination which concern collateral matters, *i.e.* matters which go to credit but not the facts in issue: *Palmer v. Trower* (1852) 8 Exch 247.

G. CROSS EXAMINATION OF THE DEFENDANT

Criminal Evidence Act 1898, s.1

Competency of witnesses in criminal cases

1.—(1) A person charged in criminal proceedings shall not be called as a witness in the proceedings except upon his own application. **9–122**

(2) A person charged in criminal proceedings who is called as a witness in the proceedings may be asked any question in cross-examination notwithstanding that it would tend to criminate him as to any offence with which he is charged in the proceedings.

(3) A person charged in criminal proceedings who is called as a witness in the proceedings shall not be asked, and if asked shall not be required to answer, any question tending to show that he has committed or been convicted of or been charged with any offence other than one with which he is then charged, or is of bad character, unless—

(i) the proof that he has committed or been convicted of such other offence is admissible evidence to show that he is guilty of an offence with which he is then charged; or

(ii) he has personally or by his advocate asked questions of the witnesses for the prosecution with a view to establish his own good character, or has given evidence of his good character, or the nature or conduct of the defence is such as to involve imputations on the character of the prosecutor or the witnesses for the prosecution, or the deceased victim of the alleged crime; or

(iii) he has given evidence against any other person charged in the same proceedings.

(4) Every person charged in criminal proceedings who is called as a witness in the proceedings shall, unless otherwise ordered by the court, give his evidence from the witness box or other place from which the other witnesses give their evidence.

[This section is reprinted as amended by the *Youth Justice and Criminal Evidence Act* 1999, Sched. 4, para. 1.]

If the defendant admits his guilt in the witness box, the prosecution is still entitled to elicit evidence which incriminates co-defendants: *Paul and McFarlane* [1920] 2 K.B. 193; *O'Neill* [1969] Crim.L.R. 260, CA. **9–123**

See *post*, §§ 10–129. **9–124**

H. RE-EXAMINATION

After cross-examination a witness may be re-examined by the party who called him. Unless the court gives leave, questions in re-examination are confined to matters arising out of cross-examination. **9–125**

It is unclear whether a hostile witness may be re-examined after cross-examination: *Booth*, *ante*; *Wong* [1986] Crim.L.R. 683. In the latter case the prosecution was allowed to treat a witness as hostile and to examine him on previous inconsistent statements and following cross-examination by the defence, was allowed to re-examine the witness but only upon completely and genuinely new matters which had arisen from defence cross-examination where those matters were defined beforehand.

A witness may be treated as hostile during re-examination when he has shown hostility to the party calling him during cross-examination: *Powell* [1985] Crim.L.R. 592. In *Norton and Driver* [1987] Crim.L.R. 687 a prosecution witness said that he could not remember incidents relating to the offence charged, however, during cross-examination he gave evidence exculpating the defendants. The prosecution was permitted to treat him as hostile during re-examination.

IX. RECALL OF A WITNESS

Once a party has closed his case, further evidence other than rebuttal evidence may not be called: *Criminal Procedure Rules* 2011, r. 37.3, see Appendix G–225. The court **9–126** has a discretion to re-open a case at any time before final adjudication and this is not confined to technicalities. As a general rule and in the absence of special circumstances, magistrates should not allow evidence to be called once they have retired: *Webb v. Leadbetter* [1996] 2 All E.R. 114. In *MacDonald v. Skelt* [1985] R.T.R. 321 it had been argued that there was no case to answer as there was insufficient evidence to show that the blood specimen taken from the defendant and then analysed by the scientific officer were one and the same. The magistrates allowed the prosecutor to re-open its case and this was upheld. In that case it was said to be relevant that the defence had not taken any point about the sample during the prosecution evidence. The court should look carefully at the interests of justice and the risk of any prejudice to the defendant: *Jolly v. DPP* [2000] Crim.L.R. 471; *Cook v. DPP* [2001] Crim.L.R. 321. In *Malcolm v. DPP* (*ante*) it was said that what are special circumstances justifying permitting the prosecution to re-open its case varies from time to time. Courts must take the overall objective of criminal procedure in the *Criminal Procedure Rules* 2011, r. 1.1 into account. The magistrates were upheld in allowing evidence to be called after they had retired and had partially announced their decision.

X. ILLNESS OR DEATH OF A WITNESS

9–127 If a witness becomes incapable of giving further evidence the court may allow the trial to continue on the basis of the evidence already given: *Stretton* 86 Cr.App.R. 7, CA. The evidence of such a witness remains admissible although little weight may attach to it: *Doolin* 1 Jebb CC 123. For the introduction of statements see *post*, § 10–72.

A defendant will not be allowed a second bite of the cherry by being recalled to give evidence contradicting earlier testimony: *R. v. Ikram and another* [2009] 1 W.L.R. 1419, CA. However, there may be exceptional circumstances which permit such a course. In *R. v. Reid, The Times*, July 19, 2010, CA there was an evidential basis for believing that intimidation may have occurred.

XI. THE POWER OF THE COURT TO CALL WITNESSES

9–128 The court has a residuary discretion to call witnesses where either party has not called them. The discretion should be exercised sparingly and in the interests of justice and fairness: *Grafton* [1992] 3 W.L.R. 532.

This discretion may not usually be exercised after the defence has closed its case, nor after the magistrates have retired to deliberate: *Webb v. Leadbetter* [1966] 1 W.L.R. 245. Once the justices have retired to consider their verdict further evidence should only be called in exceptional circumstances: *French Dairies (Sevenoaks) Ltd v. Davis* [1973] Crim.L.R. 630; *Phelan v. Back* (1972) 56 Cr.App.R. 257.

In *Haringey Justices, exp. DPP* [1996] 2 W.L.R. 114, the defendant was charged with threatening behaviour and assaulting a police officer following an attack on two officers. One police officer was subsequently suspended following accusations concerning his honesty on an unrelated matter. The CPS, in accordance with its policy of not calling suspended officers if it could be avoided, gave notice that it would not be calling the suspended officer, and refused the defendant's request to tender him for cross examination. The justices dismissed the case on the grounds that it was an abuse of process, and the CPS sought judicial review of that decision. The application was granted on the basis that the prosecution has an unfettered discretion as to which witnesses to call. Where there were special reasons for not calling an important witness these should be disclosed to the defence and where the prosecution chose not to call a witness whose evidence was central to the case, and the justices were satisfied that the interests of justice required he be called, they should so rule. If the prosecution refused to call the witness the justices could do so.

It is highly undesirable for a judge or magistrate to cross-examine an unrepresented defendant in such a way as to appear to be siding with the prosecution: *Jahree v. State of Mauritius* [2005] 1 W.L.R. 1952.

The court's permission is required before the prosecution or defence may question a witness called by the court. **9–129**

The court has the power to recall a witness at any stage of the trial to put such questions as may be required in the interests of justice: *Sullivan* [1923] 1 K.B. 47.

The court may also question witnesses during the course of their examination by counsel, however, it should not actively interfere with counsel's examination: *Leggatt* [1970] 1 Q.B. 67; *Hulusi and Purvis* (1974) 58 Cr.App.R. 378. Questions should be for clarification purposes only.

XII. EXHIBITS

Where a witness produces an exhibit, the court will list the exhibit and identify it by name and number, *e.g.* where Ann Smith produces an exhibit it becomes AS1. **9–130**

At the conclusion of the case, the exhibits are generally not retained by the court but are returned to the producing party who then signs for them. The court may retain documentary exhibits.

XIII. WITNESS COACHING

Witness training for criminal trials is prohibited. That does not, however, preclude pre-trial familiarisation which does not involve discussions about proposed or intended evidence: *Momodou* [2005] 2 All E.R. 571. **9–131**

Chapter 10

EVIDENCE

I. INTRODUCTION

Evidence is what the court will hear to determine the facts in issue. It may comprise the testimony of witnesses either oral or by statement, documents, real evidence, *i.e.* exhibits and admissions. It may be direct evidence, *i.e.* what the witness saw or heard or it may be indirect in the form of hearsay (what the witness heard from someone else) or in the form of evidence of surrounding circumstances from which inferences may be drawn. A court must not consider material not produced in court as evidence. Downloading and discussing legal material from the internet, which has not been debated in court, is contrary to basic principles of justice: *Marshall and Crump* [2007] EWCA Crim 35, (2007) 151 S.J.L.B. 122. The rules of evidence provide a framework for deciding whether evidence is admissible or not. **10–1**

The role of the judiciary in magistrates' courts

10–2 In magistrates' courts, the judiciary decides both law and fact and will, therefore, determine the admissibility of evidence. On questions of law, including the law of evidence, it is accepted that magistrates should accept the advice of the legal adviser. District Judges (Magistrates' Courts) may also seek the advice of the legal adviser. Where the court decides that evidence is inadmissible it will put that evidence out of its mind when determining the facts in issue.

The judiciary should keep interventions to a minimum but may clarify evidence if an answer is ambiguous or inaudible and to curb repetition and irrelevance.

Facts in issue

10–3 The facts in issue are: (a) the facts which the prosecution bears the burden of proving or disproving in order to establish the guilt of the defendant; and (b) the facts which the defendant bears the burden of proving in order to succeed in his defence. Where the defendant has pleaded not guilty then "everything is in issue and the prosecution has to prove the whole of its case, including the identity of the accused, the nature of the act and the existence of any necessary knowledge or intent": *Sims* [1946] K.B. 531 at 539.

Circumstantial Evidence

10–4 Circumstantial evidence has been defined as "... evidence of surrounding circumstances which, by undesigned coincidence, is capable of proving a proposition with the accuracy of mathematics"; Lord Hewart CJ in *Taylor, Weaver and Donovan*, 21 Cr.App.R. 20 at 21, CCA.

Lord Normand in *Teper v. R.* [1952] A.C. 480 at 489, PC, stated in relation to circumstantial evidence that:

> "It must always be narrowly examined, if only because evidence of this kind may be fabricated to cast suspicion on another. . .. It is also necessary before drawing the inference of the accused's guilt from circumstantial evidence to be sure that there are no other co-existing circumstances which would weaken or destroy the inference."

On the other hand it has been said that circumstantial evidence is often the best evidence. It is no derogation of evidence to say that it is circumstantial: *Taylor, Weaver and Donovan*.

Relevance

10–5 Evidence is relevant if it is logically probative or disprobative of a matter which must be proved: *DPP v. Kilbourne* [1973] A.C. 729. Evidence is admissible only where it is relevant and this depends on the individual circumstances of each particular case. For example, hearsay evidence is not admissible under the hearsay provisions of the *Criminal Justice Act* 2003 if it is not relevant: *T* [2007] 1 Cr.App.R 4. Similarly, where evidence of misconduct does not amount to evidence of bad character for the purposes of the bad character provisions of the 2003 Act, the admissibility of such evidence is governed by the common law test of relevance: *Mullings* [2010] EWCA Crim 2820. Where the offence is one of strict liability, evidence of motive, intention or knowledge is irrelevant and therefore inadmissible: *Sandhu* [1997] Crim.L.R. 288; *Byrne* [2002] 2 Cr.App.R. 311.

Formal admissions

10–6 Section 10 of the *Criminal Justice Act* 1967 provides for a party to admit certain facts and that formal admission becomes conclusive evidence of those facts. Section 10 is reproduced at § 9–74, above.

II. BURDEN AND STANDARD OF PROOF

10–7 In criminal trials the legal burden of proving the guilt of the defendant is on the prosecution and remains so throughout the trial: *Woolmington v. DPP* [1935] A.C. 462; *Hunt* [1987] A.C. 352. Where the prosecution bears the legal burden of proof the standard of proof is the criminal standard of proof, namely proof beyond reasonable doubt: *Woolmington*. This does not mean proof beyond a shadow of doubt. It is less than absolute certainty. In *Walters* [1969] 2 A.C. 26 the words referring to a jury "satisfied so they are sure" were approved. Being sure of a defendant's guilt was the preferred description in *Majid* [2009] EWCA Crim 2563 where it was felt that beyond reasonable doubt can lead to confusion.

The judiciary must be careful in the use of words on conviction, for example, the words "on balance" have led to the dismissal of a case on appeal on the grounds that the choice of words could have created, in the mind of the informed bystander, the impression that the court had employed the wrong test: *R. (on the application of Ahmed) v. Bradford Magistrates' Court* [2008] EWHC 2934 (Admin).

On a breach of community order the prosecution is obliged to prove each element to the criminal standard including that the defendant is the person named in the order breached; an inference may be drawn from the court's having the name and address and the fact that the name is slightly unusual unless there is evidence to the contrary: *West Yorkshire Probation Board v. Boulter*; [2006] 1 W.L.R. 232. The burden of proving that a defendant has not acted with reasonable excuse when breaching an Anti Social Behaviour Order rests on the prosecution: *Charles* [2010] 1 Cr.App.R.2 as is the case with the breach of a non-molestation order: *Richards* [2010] EWCA Crim 835.

Part II

The criminal standard of proof is normally applicable where the prosecution bears the burden of proving that evidence is admissible: *Ewing*, 77 Cr.App.R. 47. In relation to the issue of the competence of witnesses, however, including that of the makers of hearsay statements, statute has provided that the lower balance of probabilities standard will apply to both prosecution and defence: *Youth Justice and Criminal Evidence Act* 1999, s.54(2); *Criminal Justice Act* 2003, s.123(4)(c). Where the defence bears the legal burden of proving that evidence is admissible, the standard of proof is proof on the balance of probabilities;*Mattey and Queeley* [1995] 2 Cr.App.R. 409.

Where the prosecution bears the legal burden of disproving a defence relied upon by the accused (which is normally the case) but the defence goes beyond a mere denial of an element of the prosecution case and raises a new issue, the defence may be said to bear the evidential burden of adducing evidence to raise the defence, following which it must be disproved by the prosecution to the criminal standard of proof. An example is provided by the defence of self defence in relation to which if the evidence before the court leaves it in doubt as regards self defence then the accused is not guilty: *Lobell* [1957] 1 Q.B. 547.

Exceptionally, the defence may bear the legal burden of proving a defence. Where this is the case, the standard of proof is proof on the balance of probabilities: *Carr-Briant* [1943] K.B. 607; 29 Cr.App.R. 76. The only common law defence which imposes a legal burden of proof on the defence is the defence of insanity:*M'Naghten's Case* (1843) 10 Cl & Fin 200. Statue may impose a legal burden of proof on the accused either expressly or by implication. So far as summary trial is concerned, the nature of those circumstances in which statute may impose a legal burden of proof upon the accused is governed by s.101 of the *Magistrates' Courts Act* 1980.

Magistrates' Courts Act 1980, s.101

Onus of proving exceptions, etc

101. Where the defendant to an information or complaint relies for his defence on any exception, exemption, proviso, excuse or qualification, whether or not it accompanies the description of the offence or matter of complaint in the enactment creating the offence or on which the complaint is founded, the burden of proving the exception, exemption, proviso, excuse or qualification shall be on him; and this notwithstanding that the information or complaint contains an allegation negativing the exception, exemption, proviso, excuse or qualification. **10-8**

In the case of driving without a licence, *e.g.* it is for the driver to prove that he has a **10-9** current driving licence: *John v. Humphreys* [1955] 1 W.L.R. 325. The same applies to driving without insurance: *Williams v. Russell* (1933) 149 L.T. 190; *Philcox v. Carberry* [1960] Crim.L.R. 563.

In *Gatland v. Metropolitan Police Commissioner* [1968] 2 Q.B. 279, the defendant had been charged with leaving a skip on a road contrary to the *Highways Act* 1959, which provided that "if a person, without lawful authority or excuse, deposits anything whatsoever on a highway ... that person shall be guilty of an offence". It was held that the prosecution had to prove that the skip had been deposited on the highway but that the defendant had to prove lawful authority or excuse.

10–10 In*Hunt* [1987] A.C. 352, which concerned a common law rule that equates with that to be found in s.101 of the 1980 Act, the House of Lords indicated that where a linguistic construction of the legislation did not indicate clearly on whom the burden of proof should be, the court might look to other considerations to determine the intention of Parliament. Each case turns on its own construction of the particular legislation, but a court should be slow to infer that Parliament intended to impose an onerous duty on the defendant to prove his innocence in a criminal case. In that case it was held that it was for the prosecution to prove that the compound in the defendant's possession contained morphine contrary to the *Misuse of Drugs Act* 1971. The defendant would have had difficulty in proving that there was either no morphine or that the level was within the permissible level as he had no ready access to scientific facilities for analysis.

10–11 The imposition of a legal burden of proof upon the defence is capable of resulting in a violation of the presumption of innocence guaranteed by art. 6(2) of the European Convention on Human Rights. Thus, where a statutory provision expressly or implicitly imposes a legal burden of proof upon the defence, the court may be required to read the provision down under s.3(1) of the *Human Rights Act* 1998 such that it merely imposes an evidential burden on the defence. In such circumstances, if evidence has been adduced to raise the defence, the legal burden of disproving the defence beyond reasonable doubt must be discharged by the prosecution.

In *DPP, ex p. Kebilene* [2000] 2 A.C. 326, HL the court advised that in order to establish whether a statutory reverse burden provision is vulnerable to challenge under art. 6(2) it is necessary to determine its nature and whether it is an evidential burden requiring a defendant to adduce sufficient evidence to raise an issue or whether it is a persuasive burden requiring him to prove a fact essential to his guilt or innocence. A mandatory presumption of guilt would not necessarily be incompatible so long as it was confined within reasonable limits. In order to decide reasonableness in that context three questions should be asked:

1. What does the prosecution have to prove in order to transfer the onus to the defence?
2. Does the burden on the defendant relate to something which is likely to be difficult for him to prove or is it within his knowledge or to which he has ready access?
3. What is the nature of the threat faced by society which the provision is designed to combat?

10–12 In *Lambert* [2001] 3 W.L.R. 206 the House of Lords applied these principles to s.28(2) and (3) of the *Misuse of Drugs Act* 1971 which created "knowledge" defences to charges of possession. It was decided that the provisions could be read down under s.3(1) of the *Human Rights Act* 1998 as imposing an evidential burden only. In this particular case, once the defendant raised the issue of knowledge, it was for the prosecution to prove the requisite knowledge beyond reasonable doubt. This was followed in *M* [2007] EWCA Crim 3228.

In *Johnstone* [2003] 1 W.L.R. 1736, an offence under the *Trade Marks Act* 1994, the legal burden was said to have passed to the defendant. Lord Nicholls stated that:

> "The extent and nature of the factual matters required to be proved by the accused, and their importance relative to the matters required to be proved by the prosecution, have to be taken into account. So also does the extent to which the burden on the accused relates to

facts which, if they exist, are readily provable by him as matters within his own knowledge or to which he has ready access."

In *Att.-Gen.'s Reference (No. 4 of 2002); Sheldrake v. DPP* [2005] 1 A.C. 264 the House of Lords decided that the justifiability and fairness of provisions which imposed a burden of proof on a defendant in a criminal trial have to be judged in the particular context of each case. In this case it was held that s.5(2) of the *Road Traffic Act* 1988 imposed a legal burden on the defendant to prove that there was no likelihood of his driving a vehicle while over the prescribed limit of alcohol and that this was not unreasonable as this was a matter which was so closely conditioned by his own knowledge and state of mind at the time as to make it more appropriate for him to prove on the balance of probabilities. The provisions of s.11(2) of the *Terrorism Act* 2000, however, were read down so as to impose an evidential burden, as a legal burden, although clearly intended by Parliament, was not a proportionate and justifiable response to the activities threatened by a banned organisation.

The reasons given for this conclusion were that: (1) since an innocent person might fall within s.11(1) there would be a clear breach of the presumption of innocence and a real risk of unfair conviction. A defendant who tried and failed to establish a defence might be convicted on the basis of conduct which was non-criminal at the date of commission; (2) it might be impossible for a defendant to show that he had not taken part in the organisation's activities at any time while it was proscribed—there would be no records or documents he could produce and others were unlikely to testify on his behalf; (3) the subsection provides no flexibility and no room to exercise a discretion and if the defendant could not prove the matters in s.11(2) the court would have no choice but to convict; (4) the potential consequences for a defendant of failing to establish a defence were severe; (5) while security considerations had always to carry weight, they did not absolve member states from their duty to ensure that basic standards were observed; and (6) little significance could be attached to the requirement that the DPP had to give his consent to a prosecution.

In *R. (Grundy & Co Excavations Ltd) v. Halton Division Magistrates' Court*, **10–13** 167 J.P. 387, it was held, in relation to the offence of felling trees without a licence under the *Forestry Act* 1967, that the onus of proving an exception, i.e. that a licence was either in existence or was unnecessary was on the defence, and that whilst this derogated from the presumption of innocence in art. 6(2) it was justified as necessary and proportionate. Similarly, in *DPP v. Barker* [2004] EWHC 2502 (Admin), in the context of a charge of driving whilst disqualified, it was said that where a defendant relies on the exemption in s.37(3) of the *Road Traffic Act* 1988 the burden is on the driver to show not only that he had been driving but also that he had a provisional licence and had complied with its conditions. Again, the effect of s.101 of the 1980 Act was to impose the legal burden of proving the exemption on the accused and again its imposition upon the accused was proportionate.

Subsequently it has been held that the burden of proof on the defendant under s.2 of the *Asylum and Immigration (Treatment of Claimants etc) Act* 2004 is a legal burden on the balance of probabilities and compatible with ECHR as the defendant is likely to have the information required: *Navabi* [2005] EWCA Crim 2865. It has also been held that where a defendant seeks to rely on the statutory defence under s.31(1) of the *Immigration and Asylum Act* 1999 the evidential burden on proving refugee status is on the defendant whereas so far as the other matters in s.31(1) are concerned the legal burden is on the defendant on a balance of probabilities and the imposition of a legal burden of proof on the defence is proportionate: *Makuwa*; [2006] 2 Cr.App.R. 11.

Section 444(1A) of the *Education Act* 1996 provides that the offence is created if the parent knows that his child is failing to attend regularly and fails without reasonable justification to cause him to do so, and an evidential burden is created by that provision. If there is a failure to attend and if no material is laid before the court which could support a case that there was a reasonable justification, the court would be bound to convict; but once material is put before the court which could constitute a reasonable justification, then the court must consider it and may only convict if it is satisfied to the criminal standard that there was no reasonable justification. Reasonable justification does not mean that all possible avenues for ensuring regular schooling have been pursued. *R. (P.) v. Liverpool City Magistrates' Court* [2006] EWHC 887, Admin; [2006] A.C.D. 73.

Where a defendant is charged with acquisition and possession of criminal property under s.329(a) and (c) of the *Proceeds of Crime Act* 2002 and raises the defence of having provided adequate payment for it there is an evidential burden on the defendant. Section 101 of the 1980 Act did not impose legal burden of proof on the accused, but if it did the imposition of a legal burden of proof on the accused was too great an intrusion into the presumption of innocence: *Hogan v. DPP (theft of scaffolding), The Times*, February 28, 2007. In *Keogh* [2007] 2 Cr.App.R. 9 it was held that the reverse burden contained in the *Official Secrets Act* 1989, ss.2(3) and 3(4) was incompatible with the *Human Rights Act* as the *Official Secrets Act* could operate effectively without it.

The statutory defence under s.208(1)(c) of the *Insolvency Act* 1986 imposes a legal rather than an evidential burden; a person faces punishment under that section because he has failed to do what the law requires him to do i.e. to deliver up books and papers in the course of the winding up of a company and the reason for non-delivery is more in the knowledge of the defendant than within the knowledge of the prosecution thus the court did not read the provision down as merely imposing an evidential burden on the defence: *R. (Griffin) v. Richmond Magistrates' Court* [2008] 1 Cr.App.R. 37.

A legal burden on a defendant to show he is qualified under the *Immigration and Asylum Act* 1999 in a prosecution under s.91 is justified as it is not onerous and the defendant has access to the necessary information to establish his qualification: *Clarke* [2008] EWCA Crim 893.

There is no legal burden on the defence to prove the exemptions set out in Sched. 1 to the *Hunting Act* 2004, although there is an evidential burden on a defendant to adduce an evidential case which raises an issue whether the activity is exempt; this was the position under s.101 of the 1980 Act, though the Court would have had to read the 2004 Act down had this been necessary: *DPP v. Wright The Times* February 17, 2009.

Where a defendant is charged under s.57(1) *Terrorism Act* 2000 with possessing an article in circumstances giving rise to a reasonable suspicion that the possession is for a terrorist purpose and the prosecution proves all the elements of the offence beyond reasonable doubt, but the defendant adduces evidence to suggest otherwise, then, by virtue of s.118(2) the defence under s.57(2) is made out unless the prosecution proves, beyond reasonable doubt, that the defence is not made out: *R. v. G* [2009] 2 W.L.R. 724. Section 118(2) expressly imposes an evidential burden on the defence.

Section 2 of the *Public Bodies Corrupt Practices Act* 1889 should be read down under s.3(1) of the *Human Rights Act* 1998 such that it merely imposes an evidential burden on the defence. Whilst this removes the express statutory purpose of s.2, the imposition of a legal burden of proof upon the defence by s.2 now that the courts can draw inferences from silence under provisions of the *Criminal Justice and Public Order Act* 1994 is unnecessary, unreasonable and disproportionate: *Webster* [2011] 1 Cr.App.R. 16.

Where the court is considering whether to exclude evidence under s.78 *Police and Criminal Evidence Act* 1984, the burden of proof on the defence and prosecution is neutral *i.e* s.78 does not impose a burden of proof on any party: *Governor of Brixton Prison, ex p Saifi* [2001] 1 W.L.R. 1134.

III. PRESUMPTIONS

10–14 A court may be required to make assumptions and those may relate to law or fact.

A. PRESUMPTIONS OF FACT

10–15 These are inferences which the court may draw from the facts which are established, but it is not obliged to draw.

For example where a defendant charged with handling stolen goods is found to be in possession of those goods without any explanation, this circumstantial evidence may give rise to a provisional conclusion that the defendant is the handler of those goods.

B. PRESUMPTIONS OF LAW

Presumptions of law may be rebuttable or irrebutable. Some presumptions do not depend upon proof of a basic fact, for example, the presumptions of innocence and sanity. Others depend upon proof of a basic fact **10–16**

A presumption would be irrebuttable where on the proof or admission of a basic or primary fact, another fact could not be rebutted, *e.g.* if a court were satisfied that a child appearing before it were nine years of age then, under s.50 of the *Children and Young Persons Act* 1933, "it shall be conclusively presumed that no child under the age of 10 years can be guilty of an offence". See *Walters v. Lunt* [1951] 2 All E.R. 645.

Most presumptions of law, however, are rebuttable, *i.e.* upon proof of the basic fact (if required) evidence can be brought to show that the presumption is incorrect.

In some cases a rebuttable presumption of law imposes a legal burden of proof which must be satisfied to the requisite standard of proof in order to rebut the presumption whereas some presumptions merely impose an evidential burden. For example, the presumption that a machine was working properly may be rebutted by merely adducing evidence to the contrary: *Tingle, Jacobs and Co v. Kennedy* [1964] 1 W.L.R. 638. In contrast, in order to rebut the presumption, created by s.74(3) of the*Police and Criminal Evidence Act* 1984, that the defendant committed an offence of which he was convicted, the Court of Appeal has held that the defence must prove on the balance of probabilities that the defendant did not commit the offence: *Watson* [2006] EWCA Crim 2308. Similarly, in *Miell*, [2008] 1 Cr.App.R. 23, the Court of Appeal treated s.74(3) as shifting the burden of proof onto the accused. In *C* [2011] 1 Cr.App.R. 17, however, the Court of Appeal, without reference to *Watson*, referred, at p.225, to s.74(3) as creating an "evidential presumption" and indicated that "... if the defendant does adduce evidence to demonstrate that he is not guilty of the offence, it remains open to the Crown then to call evidence to rebut the denial".

Even where a presumption imposes a legal burden of proof, if the imposition of a legal burden of proof upon the defence would give rise to a violation of art. 6(2) of the European Convention of Human Rights it may be necessary to read down the relevant statutory provision under s.3(1) of the *Human Rights Act* 1998, in line with the principles that were considered at §§ 10–11 to 10–12 above, such that it merely imposes an evidential burden.

It can be presumed that a police officer has been lawfully appointed: *Gordon* (1789) 1 Leach 515, that a solicitor has been admitted; *Berryman v. Wise* (1791) 4 Term. Rep. 366, that a limited company has been incorporated: *Langton* (1876) 2 Q.B.D. 296, or that a police officer requiring a breath test was in uniform: *Gage v. Jones* [1983] R.T.R. 508. A document can be presumed to have been made on the date it bears, and a signed deed to have been sealed and delivered: *Hall v. Bainbridge and Enderby* [1848] 12 Q.B. 699 (although a deed no longer needs to be sealed). Evidence of a ceremony of marriage presumes a valid marriage: *Mahadervan v. Mahadervan* [1964] P. 233. The procedure laid down for the preparation of kits used in the taking of blood samples from motorists stopped on suspicion of excess alcohol can be presumed to have been carried out correctly unless there is something in the matter before the court to suggest the contrary: *Carter v. DPP* [2006] EWHC 3328. **10–17**

IV. DOCUMENTARY EVIDENCE

A. GENERAL

Statements contained in documents are subject to the general rules of the admissibility of evidence, particularly those relating to hearsay and opinion. Moreover issues of **10–18** privilege may also arise. These matters are considered below but two issues arise for present consideration: (a) how may the document be proved, and (b) what use may be made of its contents. It is only in relation to the second issue that the rule of hearsay arises. In that case the purpose for which the document is tendered must be identified; see *post*, § 10–75.

B. PUBLIC DOCUMENTS

10–19 Generally it is unnecessary to produce the original of any document made by a public officer. Special provisions are made for the production of public documents such as Acts of Parliament, byelaws, judgments, treaties, previous convictions, court registers, marriage or death certificates etc. These can be regarded as falling within an exception to the hearsay rule and can prove the facts stated therein: *Sturla v. Freccia* (1880) 5 App. Cas. 623, HL; *Wilton & Co v. Phillips* [1903] T.L.R. 390. The relevant exception to the hearsay rule was preserved by s.118 of *Criminal Justice Act* 2003, which is reproduced at § 10–58, below.

Evidence Act 1845, ss.1, 3

Certain documents to be received in evidence without proof of seal or signature, &c. of person signing the same

10–20 **1.** Whenever by any Act now in force or hereafter to be in force any certificate, official or public document, or document or proceeding of any corporation or joint stock or other company, or any certified copy of any document, bye law, entry in any register or other book, or of any other proceeding, shall be receivable in evidence of any particular in any court of justice, or before any legal tribunal, or either House of Parliament, or any committee of either House, or in any judicial proceeding, the same shall respectively be admitted in evidence, provided they respectively purport to be sealed or impressed with a stamp or sealed and signed, or signed alone, as required, or impressed with a stamp and signed, as directed by the respective Acts made or to be hereafter made, without any proof of the seal or stamp, where a seal or stamp is necessary, or of the signature or of the official character of the person appearing to have signed the same, and without any further proof thereof, in every case in which the original record could have been received in evidence.

Copies of private Acts, printed by Queen's printer, journals of Parliament, and proclamations, admissible as evidence

10–21 **3.** All copies of private and local and personal Acts of Parliament not public Acts, if purporting to be printed by the Queen's printers, and all copies of the journals of either House of Parliament, and of royal proclamations, purporting to be printed by the printers to the crown or by the printers to either House of Parliament, or by any or either of them, shall be admitted as evidence thereof by all courts, judges, justices, and others without any proof being given that such copies were so printed.

Documentary Evidence Act 1882, s.2

Documents printed under superintendence of Stationery Office receivable in evidence

10–22 **2.** Where any enactment, whether passed before or after the passing of this Act, provides that a copy of any Act of Parliament, proclamation, order, regulation, rule, warrant, circular, list, gazette, or document shall be conclusive evidence, or be evidence, or have any other effect, when purporting to be printed by the Government Printer, or the Queen's Printer, or the Queen's Printer for Scotland, or a printer authorised by Her Majesty, or otherwise under Her Majesty's authority, whatever may be the precise expression used, such copy shall also be conclusive evidence, or evidence, or have the said effect (as the case may be) if it purports to be printed under the superintendence or authority of Her Majesty's Stationery Office.

Documentary Evidence Act 1868, ss.2, 3, 5 and 6

Mode of proving certain documents

10–23 **2.** Prima facie evidence of any proclamation, order, or regulation issued before or after the passing of this Act by Her Majesty, or by the Privy Council, also of any proclamation, order, or regulation issued before or after the passing of this Act by or under the authority of any such department of the Government or officer or office-holder in the Scottish Administration as is mentioned in the first column of the schedule hereto, may be given in all courts of justice, and in all legal proceedings whatsoever, in all or any of the modes herein-after mentioned; that is to say:

(1) By the production of a copy of the Gazette purporting to contain such proclamation, order, or regulation.

(2) By the production of a copy of such proclamation, order, or regulation, purporting to be printed by the Government printer, or, where the question arises in a court in any British colony or possession, of a copy purporting to be printed under the authority of the legislature of such British colony or possession.

(3) By the production, in the case of any proclamation, order or regulation issued by Her Majesty or by the Privy Council, of a copy or extract purporting to be certified to be true by the clerk of the Privy Council, or by any one of the lords or others of the Privy Council, and, in the case of any proclamation, order, or regulation issued by or under the authority of any of the said departments or officers or office-holders, by the production of a copy or extract purporting to be certified to be true by the person or persons specified in the second column of the said schedule in connexion with such department or officer or office-holder.

Any copy or extract made in pursuance of this Act may be in print or in writing, or partly in print and partly in writing.

No proof shall be required of the handwriting or official position of any person certifying, in pursuance of this Act, to the truth of any copy of or extract from any proclamation, order, or regulation.

Act to be in force in colonies

3. Subject to any law that may be from time to time made by the legislature of any British colony or possession, this Act shall be in force in every such colony and possession. **10–24**

Definition of terms

5. The following words shall in this Act have the meaning herein-after assigned to them, unless there is something in the context repugnant to such construction; (that is to say), **10–25**

"British colony and possession" shall for the purposes of this Act include the Channel Islands, the Isle of Man ... and all other Her Majesty's dominions.

"Legislature" shall signify any authority, other than the Imperial Parliament or Her Majesty in Council, competent to make laws for any colony or possession.

"Privy Council" shall include Her Majesty in Council and the lords and others of Her Majesty's Privy Council, or any of them, and any committee of the Privy Council that is not specially named in the schedule hereto.

"Government printer" shall mean and include the printer to Her Majesty, the Queen's Printer for Scotland, and any printer purporting to be the printer authorized to print the statutes, ordinances, acts of state, or other public acts of the legislature of any British colony or possession, or otherwise to be the Government printer of such colony or possession.

"Gazette" shall include the London Gazette, the Edinburgh Gazette, and the Belfast Gazette, or any of such Gazettes.

" office-holder in the Scottish Administration" has the same meaning as in the Scotland Act 1998.

Act to be cumulative

6. The provisions of this Act shall be deemed to be in addition to, and not in derogation of, any powers of proving documents given by any existing statute, or existing at common law. **10–26**

In *Clarke* [1969] 2 Q.B. 91 the Court of Appeal said that the word "order" in the 1868 Act should be given a wide meaning, covering "any executive act of government performed by the bringing into existence of a public document for the purposes of giving effect to an Act of Parliament". It held that the *Breath Test (Approval) (No. 1) Order* 1968, although not a statutory instrument, was an order within the meaning of the Act. **10–27**

Evidence Act 1851, s.7

Foreign and colonial acts of state, judgments, etc.provable by certified copies, without proof of seal or signature or judicial character of person signing the same

10–28 **7.** All proclamations, treaties, and other acts of state of any foreign state or of any British colony, and all judgments, decrees, orders, and other judicial proceedings of any court of justice in any foreign state or in any British colony, and all affidavits, pleadings, and other legal documents filed or deposited in any such court, may be proved in any court of justice, or before any person having by law or by consent of parties authority to hear, receive, and examine evidence, either by examined copies or by copies authenticated as herein-after mentioned; that is to say, if the document sought to be proved be a proclamation, treaty, or other act of state, the authenticated copy to be admissible in evidence must purport to be sealed with the seal of the foreign state or British colony to which the original document belongs; and if the document sought to be proved be a judgment, decree, order, or other judicial proceeding of any foreign or colonial court, or an affidavit, pleading, or other legal document filed or deposited in any such court, the authenticated copy to be admissible in evidence must purport either to be sealed with the seal of the foreign or colonial court to which the original document belongs, or, in the event of such court having no seal, to be signed by the judge, or, if there be more than one judge, by any one of the judges of the said court, and such judge shall attach to his signature a statement in writing on the said copy that the court whereof he is a judge has no seal; but if any of the aforesaid authenticated copies shall purport to be sealed or signed as hereinbefore respectively directed, the same shall respectively be admitted in evidence in every case in which the original document could have been received in evidence, without any proof of the seal where a seal is necessary, or of the signature, or of the truth of the statement attached thereto, where such signature and statement are necessary, or of the judicial character of the person appearing to have made such signature and statement.

Authenticated or examined copies may be used to prove foreign law or judgments.

Births and Deaths Registration Act 1953, s.34

Entry in register as evidence of birth or death

10–29 **34.**—(1) The following provisions of this section shall have effect in relation to entries in registers under this Act or any enactment repealed by this Act.

(2) An entry or a certified copy of an entry of a birth or death in a register, or in a certified copy of a register, shall not be evidence of the birth or death unless the entry purports to be signed by some person professing to be the informant and to be such a person as might be required or permitted by law at the date of the entry to give to the registrar information concerning that birth or death:

Provided that this subsection shall not apply—

(a) in relation to an entry of a birth which, not being an entry signed by a person professing to be a superintendent registrar, purports to have been made with the authority of the Registrar General; or

(b) in relation to an entry of a death which purports to have been made upon a certificate from a coroner; or

(c) in relation to an entry of a birth or death which purports to have been made in pursuance of the enactments with respect to the registration of births and deaths at sea;

(d) in relation to the re-registration of a birth under section (5) of this Act.

(3) Where more than three months have intervened between the date of the birth of any child or the date when any living new-born child or still-born child was found exposed and the date of the registration of the birth of that child, the entry or a certified copy of the entry of the birth of the child in the register, or in a certified copy of the register, shall not be evidence of the birth unless—

(a) if it appears that not more than twelve months have so intervened, the entry purports either to be signed by the superintendent registrar as well as by the registrar or to have been made with the authority of the Registrar General;

(b) if more than twelve months have so intervened, the entry purports to have been made with the authority of the Registrar General:

Provided that this subsection shall not apply in any case where the original entry in the register was made before the first day of January, eighteen hundred and seventy-five.

(4) Where more than twelve months have intervened between the date of the death or of the finding of the dead body of any person and the date of the registration of that person's death, the entry or a certified copy of the entry of the death in the register, or in a certified copy of the register, shall not be evidence of the death unless the entry purports to have been made with the authority of the Registrar General:

Provided that this subsection shall not apply in any case where the original entry in the register was made before the first day of January, eighteen hundred and seventy-five.

(5) A certified copy of an entry in a register or in a certified copy of a register shall be deemed to be a true copy notwithstanding that it is made on a form different from that on which the original entry was made if any differences in the column headings under which the particulars appear in the original entry and the copy respectively are differences of form only and not of substance.

(6) The Registrar General shall cause any certified copy of an entry given in the General Register Office to be sealed or stamped with the seal of that Office; and, subject to the foregoing provisions of this section, any certified copy of an entry purporting to be sealed or stamped with the said seal shall be received as evidence of the birth or death to which it relates without any further or other proof of the entry, and no certified copy purporting to have been given in the said Office shall be of any force or effect unless it is sealed or stamped as aforesaid.

Part II

Local Government Act 1972, s.238

Evidence of byelaws

238. The production of a printed copy of a byelaw purporting to be made by a local authority, the Greater London Authority, an Integrated Transport Authority for an integrated transport area in England or a combined authority upon which is endorsed a certificate purporting to be signed by the proper officer of the authority stating— **10–30**

(a) that the byelaw was made by the authority;

(b) that the copy is a true copy of the byelaw;

(c) that on a specified date the byelaw was confirmed by the authority named in the certificate or, as the case may require, was sent to the Secretary of State and has not been disallowed;

(d) the date, if any, fixed by the confirming authority for the coming into operation of the byelaw;

shall be prima facie evidence of the facts stated in the certificate, and without proof of the handwriting or official position of any person purporting to sign the certificate.

[This section is printed as amended by the *Greater London Act (Miscellaneous Amendments) (No.2) Order 2011* and the *Local Democracy, Economic Developments and Construction Act* 2009, Sched. 6.]

Public Records Act 1958, s.9

Legal validity of public records and authenticated copies

9.—(1) The legal validity of any record shall not be affected by its removal under the provisions of this Act, or of the *Public Record Office Act*s 1838 to 1898, or by any provisions in those Acts with respect to its legal custody. **10–31**

(2) A copy of or extract from a public record in the Public Record Office purporting to be examined and certified as true and authentic by the proper officer and to be sealed or stamped with the seal of the Public Record Office shall be admissible as evidence in any proceedings without any further or other proof thereof if the original record would have been admissible as evidence in those proceedings.

(3) An electronic copy of or extract from a public record in the Public Record Office which—

(a) purports to have been examined and certified as true and authentic by the proper officer; and

(b) appears on a website purporting to be one maintained by or on behalf of the Public Record Office,;

shall, when viewed on that website, be admissible as evidence in any proceedings without further or other proof if the original record would have been admissible as evidence in those proceedings.

(4) In this section any reference to the proper officer is a reference to the Keeper of Public Records or any other officer of the Public Record Office authorised in that behalf by the Keeper of Public Records, and, in the case of copies and extracts made before the commencement of this Act, the deputy keeper of the records or any assistant record keeper appointed under the *Public Record Office Act* 1838.

Criminal Procedure Rules 2011, r.5.7

Proof of proceedings in magistrates' court

10–32 **5.7** The register of a magistrates' court, or an extract from the register certified by the magistrates' court officer as a true extract, shall be available for admission in any legal proceedings as evidence of the proceedings of the court entered in the register.

This rule was amended by the *Criminal Procedure (Amendment) Rules* 2010 (by substituting the words "available for admission" for the word "admissible") for the purpose of making clear that that the rule is a rule of procedure rather than a rule of evidence.

Police and Criminal Evidence Act 1984, ss.73–75

Proof of convictions and acquittals

10–33 **73.**—(1) Where in any proceedings the fact that a person has in the United Kingdom been convicted or acquitted of an offence otherwise than by a Service court is admissible in evidence, it may be proved by producing a certificate of conviction or, as the case may be, of acquittal relating to that offence, and proving that the person named in the certificate as having been convicted or acquitted of the offence is the person whose conviction or acquittal of the offence is to be proved.

(2) For the purposes of this section a certificate of conviction or of acquittal—

(a) shall, as regards a conviction or acquittal on indictment, consist of a certificate, signed by the proper officer of the court where the conviction or acquittal took place, giving the substance and effect (omitting the formal parts) of the indictment and of the conviction or acquittal; and

(b) shall, as regards a conviction or acquittal on a summary trial, consist of a copy of the conviction or of the dismissal of the information, signed by the proper officer of the court where the conviction or acquittal took place or by the proper officer of the court, if any, to which a memorandum of the conviction or acquittal was sent;

and a document purporting to be a duly signed certificate of conviction or acquittal under this section shall be taken to be such a certificate unless the contrary is proved.

(3) In subsection (2) above "proper officer" means—

(a) in relation to a magistrates' court in England and Wales, the designated officer for the court; and

(b) in relation to any other court, the clerk of the court, his deputy or any other person having custody of the court record.

(4) The method of proving a conviction or acquittal authorised by this section shall be in addition to and not to the exclusion of any other authorised manner of proving a conviction or acquittal.

[This section is printed as amended by the *Access to Justice Act* 1999, s.90(1) and Sched. 13, para. 12 by the *Courts Act* 2003, Sched. 8 para. 285 and by the *Coroners and Justice Act* 2009 Sched. 17, para. 13.]

See *Criminal Procedure Rules* 2011, r. 6.4 in Appendix G–32.

10–34 Section 73 does not apply to foreign convictions which may, however, be proved under s.7 of the *Evidence Act* 1851: *Kordasinski* [2006] EWCA Crim 2984. Section 73 was amended in August 2010 to make it applicable to convictions in EU member states but this is subject to transitional provisions to be found in Pt 5 of Sched. 22 to the *Coroners and Justice Act* 2009.

Conviction as evidence of commission of offence

10–35 **74.**—(1) In any proceedings the fact that a person other than the accused has been convicted of an offence by or before any court in the United Kingdom or by a Service court outside the United Kingdom shall be admissible in evidence for the purpose of proving, that that person committed that offence, where evidence of his having done so is admissible, whether or not any other evidence of his having committed that offence is given.

(2) In any proceedings in which by virtue of this section a person other than the accused is proved to have been convicted of an offence by or before any court in the United Kingdom or by a Service court outside the United Kingdom, he shall be taken to have committed that offence unless the contrary is proved.

(3) In any proceedings where evidence is admissible of the fact that the accused has committed an offence, if the accused is proved to have been convicted of the offence—

(a) by or before any court in the United Kingdom; or

(b) by a Service court outside the United Kingdom,

he shall be taken to have committed that offence unless the contrary is proved.

(4) Nothing in this section shall prejudice—

(a) the admissibility in evidence of any conviction which would be admissible apart from this section; or

(b) the operation of any enactment whereby a conviction or a finding of fact in any proceedings is for the purposes of any other proceedings made conclusive evidence of any fact.

[This section is printed as amended by the *Criminal Justice Act* 2003, Sched. 36(5), para. 85(2) and Sched. 37(5), para. 1 and by the *Coroners and Justice Act* 2009, Sched. 17, paras. 14(2)–(4) by virtue of the *Coroners and Justice Act* 2009 (Commencement No.5) Order 2010 (S.I. 2010 No. 1858) which came into effect on August 15, 2010.]

Section 74(1)

It seems that s.74(1) can apply either where evidence of a previous conviction is admissible under s.100 *Criminal Justice Act* 2003, which is considered at § 10–107, below, or where evidence of a previous conviction does not amount to evidence of bad character, due to the operation of s.98(a) of the 2003 Act, which is considered at § 10–105, below. Admissibility under s.74(1) is subject to the exercise of the court's exclusionary discretion under s.78 *Police and Criminal Evidence Act* 1984: Robertson & Golder [1987] Q.B. 920. In relation to the operation of the presumption created by s.74(2) it is submitted that the better view is that where this operates against the accused it, like that created by s.74(3), which is considered immediately below, merely imposes an evidential burden upon the accused.

It seems that s.74(3) can apply either where the accused's previous conviction amounts to evidence of the accused's bad character and is admissible under s.101 of the *Criminal Justice Act* 2003, [see § 10–110, below] or, as in *Watson* [2006] EWCA Crim 2308, where the accused's previous conviction does not amount to evidence of bad character and is admissible at common law. The nature of the rebuttable presumption of law created by s.74(3) of the 1984 Act was considered at § 10–16, above. It appears that the effect of s.74(3) is that where evidence of the defendant's previous conviction is admitted, if the accused merely denies that he committed the offence of which he was previously convicted this does not require the prosecution to adduce evidence in rebuttal and that the defendant will need to provide a detailed defence statement identifying the case he will advance to discharge the evidential burden that s.74(3) imposes upon him:*C* [2011] 1 Cr.App.R. 17.

Due to the operation of s.75(4), which is considered at § 10–36, below, s.74 does not apply to a conviction that has been quashed as such a conviction is not subsisting.

Provisions supplementary to section 74

75.—(1) Where evidence that a person has been convicted of an offence is admissible by virtue of section 74 above, then without prejudice to the reception of any other admissible evidence for the purpose of identifying the facts on which the conviction was based— **10–36**

(a) the contents of any document which is admissible as evidence of the conviction; and

(b) the contents of the information, complaint, indictment or charge-sheet on which the person in question was convicted, shall be admissible in evidence for that purpose.

(2) Where in any proceedings the contents of any document are admissible in evidence by virtue of subsection (1) above, a copy of that document, or of the material part of it, purporting to be certified or otherwise authenticated by or on behalf of the court or authority having custody of that document shall be admissible in evidence and shall be taken to be a true copy of that document or part unless the contrary is shown.

(3) Nothing in any of the following—

(a) Section 14 of the *Powers of Criminal Courts (Sentencing) Act* 2000 (under which a conviction leading to probation or discharge is to be disregarded except as mentioned in that section);

(aa) section 187 of the *Armed Forces Act* 2006 (which makes similar provision in respect of service convictions);

(b) section 247 of the *Criminal Procedure (Scotland) Act* 1995 (which makes similar provision in respect of convictions on indictment in Scotland); and

(c) section 8 of the *Probation Act* (Northern Ireland) 1950 (which corresponds to section 13 of the *Powers of Criminal Courts Act* 1973) or any legislation which is in force in Northern Ireland for the time being and corresponds to that section

shall affect the operation of section 74 above; and for the purposes of that section any order made by a court of summary jurisdiction in Scotland under section 182 or section 183 of the said Act of 1975 shall be treated as a conviction.

(4) Nothing in section 74 above shall be construed as rendering admissible in any proceedings evidence of any conviction other than a subsisting one.

[This section is printed as amended by the *PCC(S)A* 2000, s.165(1) and Sched. 9, para. 98 and by *Armed Forces Act* 2006 Sched. 16, para. 103 and by *Coroners and Justice Act* 2009, Sched. 17, para. 15, by virtue of the *Coroners and Justice Act* 2009 (Commencement No.5) Order, Statutory Instrument 1858 of 2010 with effect from August 15, 2010.]

10–37 Section 75 does not apply to foreign convictions which may, however, be proved under s.7 of the *Evidence Act* 1851: *Kordasinski* [2006] EWCA Crim 2984. Section 75 was amended in August 2010 to make it applicable to convictions in EU member states but this is subject to transitional provisions to be found in Pt 5 of Sched. 22 to the *Coroners and Justice Act* 2009.

There are other official documents which are not admissible or do not constitute *prima facie* evidence, *e.g*. circulars from government departments: *Peagram v. Peagram* [1926] 2 K.B. 165, a motor vehicle registration book is not evidence as to its contents: *Sealby* [1965] 1 All E.R. 701, and regimental records: *Andrews v. Cordiner* [1947] 1 All E.R. 777.

C. PRIVATE DOCUMENTS

10–38 Usually the original must be produced but secondary evidence may be given where:

— the other party has the evidence and refuses to produce it after proper notice (a defendant is not generally required to produce evidence against himself): *Sanders* [1919] 1 K.B. 550; *Worsenham* (1701) 1 Ld. Raym. 705; *Stokes v. Grosvenor Hotel Co* [1897] 2 Q.B. 124;

— a third person has the document and refuses to produce it, *e.g*. because of privilege;

— the original is lost or destroyed: *Wayte* (1982) 76 Cr.App.R. 110;

— the original is not physically or conveniently removable or may not be lawfully moved: *Owner v. Bee Hive Spinning Co Ltd* [1914] 1 K.B. 105.

D. PROOF

(1) Legislation

Criminal Justice Act 2003, s.133

Proof of statements in documents

133. Where a statement in a document is admissible as evidence in criminal proceedings, the statement may be proved by producing either— **10–39**

(a) the document, or

(b) (whether or not the document exists) a copy of the document or of the material part of it,

authenticated in whatever way the court may approve.

Where s.133 is inapplicable, recourse can be had to the common law principles that were considered at § 10–38, above.

(2) Procedure

A witness who has attested a document may be called to prove it. A document which is more that 20 years old and comes from proper custody, however, is presumed to have been duly executed. **10–40**

(3) Handwriting

Handwriting may be proved by someone who has knowledge of the handwriting: *McCartney and Hansen* (1928) 20 Cr.App.R. 179; *O'Brien* (1911) 7 Cr.App.R. 29. **10–41**

(4) Bankers books

An entry in a banker's book may be proved by a copy produced by a witness in person or by affidavit and examined as correct as being one of the ordinary books of the bank which is in that bank's custody or control and has been made in the usual course of business, *Bankers' Books Evidence Act* 1879, ss.3–5. **10–42**

(5) Microfilm

Police and Criminal Evidence Act 1984, s.71

Microfilm copies

71. In any proceedings the contents of a document may (whether or not the document is still in existence) be proved by the production of an enlargement of a microfilm copy of that document or of the material part of it, authenticated in such manner as the court may approve. **10–43**

Where the proceedings concerned are proceedings before a magistrates' court inquiring into an offence as examining justices this section shall have effect with the omission of the words "authenticated in such manner as the court may approve".

[This section is reprinted as amended by the *Criminal Procedure and Investigation Act* 1996, s.47, Sched. 1, para. 24.]

(6) Representations made other than by a person

Criminal Justice Act 2003, s.129

This section, which is potentially applicable to printouts etc produced by computers, is reproduced at § 10–84, below. **10–44**

(7) Tape, video and DVD recordings

These are treated in the same way as other documents. So long as a tape recording is **10–45** proved to be accurate and authentic it is admissible: *Ali (Maqsud)* [1966] 1 Q.B. 688; *Robson* (1972) 56 Cr.App.R. 450. Normally a summary is available to the court and the tape is made an exhibit. A video/DVD is generally shown in court.

(8) Photographs and sketches

10–46 A photograph or sketch is admissible provided it is verified on oath by a person able to speak to its accuracy, not necessarily the photographer: *Tolson* (1864) 4 F. & F. 103; *Mille v. Lamson*, *The Times*, October 29, 1892.

Sketches are now capable of falling within the ambit of the hearsay rule due to the operation of s.115(2) of the *Criminal Justice Act* 2003, which is reproduced at § 10–57, below.

(9) Certificates and statutory declarations

10–47 Various matters are by statute provable by certificate.

Criminal Justice Act 1948, s.41

Evidence by certificate

10–48 **41.**—(1) In any criminal proceedings, a certificate purporting to be signed by a constable, or by a person having the prescribed qualifications, and certifying that a plan or drawing exhibited thereto is a plan or drawing made by him of the place or object specified in the certificate, and that the plan or drawing is correctly drawn to a scale so specified, shall be evidence of the relative position of the things shown on the plan or drawing.

(4) Nothing in this section shall be deemed to make a certificate admissible as evidence in proceedings for an offence except in a case where and to the extent to which oral evidence to the like effect would have been admissible in those proceedings.

(5) Nothing in this section shall be deemed to make a certificate admissible as evidence in proceedings for any offence—

(a) unless a copy thereof has, not less than seven days before the hearing of trial, been served in the prescribed manner on the person charged with the offence; or

(b) if that person, not later than three days before the hearing or trial or within such further time as the court may in special circumstances allow, serves notice in the prescribed from and manner on the prosecutor requiring the attendance at the trial of the person who signed the certificate

(5A) Where the proceedings mentioned in subsection (1) above are proceedings before a magistrates' court inquiring into an offence as examining justices this section shall have effect with the omission of—

(a) subsection (4), and

(b) in subsection (5), paragraph (b) and the word "or" immediately preceding it.

(6) In this section the expression "prescribed" means prescribed by rules made by the Secretary of State.

Evidence by Certificate Rules 1961 (S.I. 1962 No. 2319), rr.1–3

10–49 **1.** The prescribed qualifications for the purpose of subsection (1) of section forty-one of the *Criminal Justice Act*, 1948 (which relates to the admissibility of certified plans and drawings in criminal proceedings), shall be—

(a) registration as an architect under the Architects (Registration) Acts, 1931 to 1938, or

(b) membership of any of the following bodies, that is to say, the Royal Institution of Chartered Surveyors, the Institution of Civil Engineers, the Institution of Municipal Engineers and the Land Agents Society.

10–50 **2.** A certificate under subsection (1) of section two hundred and forty-two of the *Road Traffic Act*, 1960, shall be in the form numbered 1 in the Schedule hereto or in a form to the like effect and a notice under paragraph (b) of subsection (3) of that section or under paragraph (b) of subsection (5) of section forty-one of the *Criminal Justice Act*, 1948, shall be in the form numbered 2 in the Schedule hereto or in a form to the like effect.

3. Any certificate or other document required to be served by subsection (3) of the said section two hundred and forty-two or by subsection (5) of the said section forty-one shall be served in the following manner, that is to say— **10–51**

(a) where the person to be served is a corporation, by addressing it to the corporation and leaving it at, or sending it by registered post or by the recorded delivery service to, the registered office of the corporation or, if there be no such office, its principal office or place at which it conducts its business;

(b) in any other case, by delivering it personally to the person to be served or by addressing it to him and leaving it at, or sending it by registered post or by the recorded delivery service to, his last or usual place of abode or place of business.

V. PHYSICAL OBJECTS

Material objects are produced as exhibits by the person who found them. **10–52**

The prosecution is not obliged to place every item of physical evidence before the court: *Hocking v. Ahlquist Brothers Ltd* [1944] K.B. 120. Where original exhibits are not available, photographs of them may be admitted as secondary evidence: *Uxbridge Justices, ex p. Sofaer* (1987) 85 Cr.App.R. 367.

VI. JUDICIAL NOTICE

Courts may take judicial notice of matters which are so notorious, or clearly established, or susceptible of demonstration by reference to readily obtainable and authoritative source that evidence of their existence is unnecessary: *Mullen v. Hackney LBC* [1997] 1 W.L.R. 1103, CA (Civ. Div.). **10–53**

The court in *Commonwealth Shipping Representative v. Peninsular and Oriental Branch Service* [1923] A.C. 191 at 212 said that:

> Judicial notice refers to facts, which a judge can be called upon to receive and to act upon, either from his general knowledge of them, or from inquiries to be made by himself for his own information from sources to which it is proper for him to refer.

Examples of such matters are: Rain falls: *Fay v. Prentice* (1845) 14 L.J.C. 298; butterfly knives are offensive weapons made or adapted for use for causing injury: *DPP v. Hynde* [1998] Crim.L.R. 72.

When a court takes judicial notice of a fact it finds that the fact exists although its existence has not been established by evidence. The court should be cautious in treating a factual conclusion as obvious even though the person in the street would unhesitatingly hold it to be so: *Carter v. Eastbourne BC* (2000) 164 J.P. 273, DC.

Although the court may, in arriving at its decision, use general information and a knowledge of the common affairs of life which people of ordinary intelligence possess, it may not act on its own private knowledge or belief regarding the facts of the particular case: *Sutton* (1816) 4 M & S 532; *Ingram v. Percival* [1969] 1 Q.B. 548, DC. In *Wetherall v. Harrison* [1976] Q.B. 773, DC, it was held that it was proper for a magistrate with specialised knowledge of the circumstances forming the background to a particular case to draw upon that knowledge in interpreting the evidence, but improper in effect to give evidence to himself and the other justices which is at variance with the evidence given, for it would offend the fundamental principle that evidence should be given in the presence of the parties and be subject to cross-examination. Magistrates are entitled to rely on knowledge of the area in concluding that residents are likely to be caused nuisance by practice of kerb-crawling: *Paul v. DPP* (1990) 90 Cr.App.R. 173, DC. **10–54**

The judiciary in magistrates' courts must be circumspect in their use of local knowledge and inform the parties when reliance is being placed upon local knowledge. It must be within reasonable limits: *Keane v. Mount Vernon Colliery Co Ltd* [1933] A.C. 309 and should be of a general nature, not the type of knowledge that may be varied by the individual characteristics of a particular case: *Reynolds v. Llanelly Associated Tinplate Co Ltd* [1948] 1 All E.R. 140. Justices are encouraged to use their common sense and general local knowledge: *Hughes v. DPP* [2003] EWHC Admin 2470. In *Bowman v. DPP* [1990] Crim.L.R. 600, DC, the defendant was charged with driving in a public place having consumed excess alcohol contrary to the *Road Traffic Act* 1972, s.6. The issue was whether the car park was a public place. There was evidence that there were other cars in the car park and that there was no barrier present at the time. The magistrates, using their own local knowledge of the car park, found that the car park was a public place and convicted. On appeal it was held that the magistrates were entitled to find as they did on the basis of the evidence before them and their own local knowledge of the area. Where magistrates do use their own local knowledge they should make that known to the parties and give the parties an opportunity to comment.

10–55 In *Norbrook Laboratories (G.B.) Ltd v. Health and Safety Executive, The Times*, February 23, 1998, DC, it was held that an appeal against a conviction under health and safety at work legislation would be allowed where magistrates had failed to inform the parties to the case that they were bringing their own local knowledge to bear in reaching a decision. Although it was perfectly legitimate for local knowledge to be relied upon by magistrates, both defence and prosecution should be informed so that they might be afforded an opportunity to comment upon the knowledge the magistrates claimed to have.

As lay magistrates are not legally qualified, they are in a unique position compared to judges. In *Wetherall v. Harrison* [1976] Q.B. 773, the question was whether the defendant had a reasonable excuse for failing to give a blood sample. The defendant said that he had had a fit but the prosecution alleged that it had not been genuine. One of the magistrates was a medical practitioner and gave his professional opinion to the other magistrates, who drew on their wartime experience of inoculations and the fear that they could create in certain cases. The Divisional Court held that magistrates lack the ability to exclude certain factors from their consideration. If a magistrate is a specialist, such as a doctor, it is not possible for him to approach the case as if he did not have that expertise and it would be a bad thing if that were required. One of the advantages of magistrates is the varied experience that they bring to the magistrates' courts. Although it would be wrong for the magistrate to give evidence personally, he can employ basic knowledge to the benefit of the other magistrates in considering and weighing the evidence.

Every statute passed since 1850 is a public Act to be judicially noted unless the contrary is expressly provided: *Interpretation Act* 1978, s.3, Sched. 2, para. 2. See *Pillai v. Mudanayaka* [1953] A.C. 514, PC.

Evidence Act 1845, s.2

Courts, &c. to take judicial notice of signature of equity or common law judges, &c.

10–56 **2.** All courts, judges, justices, masters in chancery, masters of courts, commissioners judicially acting, and other judicial officers, shall henceforth take judicial notice of the signature of any of the equity or common law judges of the superior courts at the Royal Courts of Justice], provided such signature be attached or appended to any decree, order, certificate, or other judicial or official document.

VII. HEARSAY

A. GENERAL

10–57 Hearsay evidence in criminal proceedings is now governed by Pt 2 of Ch.II of the *Criminal Justice Act* 2003. The provisions apply to all trials taking place after the commencement of the Act even where a preparatory hearing has taken place before: *H.* [2005] EWCA Crim 2083; [2006] 1 Cr.App.R. 4 They apply to trials and committal proceedings: *R. (CPS) v. City of London Magistrates' Court, The Times*, April 17, 2006 as well as to proceedings to determine whether a person under a disability did the act or made the omission in the offence with which he was charged: *Chal* [2008] 1

Cr.App.R.18. They abolish the common law rules save for those expressly preserved by s.118

In the context of confiscation proceedings, if the admissibility of hearsay evidence is important and is in dispute, the hearsay provisions of the *Criminal Justice Act* 2003 apply by analogy, though in many cases the real issue will be the weight of the evidence, in which case the hearsay provisions of the 2003 Act again provide valuable guidance-:*Cliptson* [2011] EWCA Crim 446.

The nature of hearsay evidence

The 2003 Act does not contain a general definition of hearsay evidence but a definition can effectively be obtained from ss.114(1) and 115.

Criminal Justice Act 2003, s.114

Admissibility of hearsay evidence

114.—(1) In criminal proceedings a statement not made in oral evidence in the proceedings is admissible as evidence of any matter stated if, but only if—

(a) any provision of this Chapter or any other statutory provision makes it admissible,
(b) any rule of law preserved by section 118 makes it admissible,
(c) all parties to the proceedings agree to it being admissible, or
(d) the court is satisfied that it is in the interests of justice for it to be admissible.

(2) In deciding whether a statement not made in oral evidence should be admitted under subsection (1)(d), the court must have regard to the following factors (and to any others it considers relevant)—

(a) how much probative value the statement has (assuming it to be true) in relation to a matter in issue in the proceedings, or how valuable it is for the understanding of other evidence in the case;
(b) what other evidence has been, or can be, given on the matter or evidence mentioned in paragraph (a);
(c) how important the matter or evidence mentioned in paragraph (a) is in the context of the case as a whole;
(d) the circumstances in which the statement was made;
(e) how reliable the maker of the statement appears to be;
(f) how reliable the evidence of the making of the statement appears to be;
(g) whether oral evidence of the matter stated can be given and, if not, why it cannot;
(h) the amount of difficulty involved in challenging the statement;
(i) the extent to which that difficulty would be likely to prejudice the party facing it.

(3) Nothing in this Chapter affects the exclusion of evidence of a statement on grounds other than the fact that it is a statement not made in oral evidence in the proceedings.

Criminal Justice Act 2003, s.115

Statements and matters stated

115.—(1) In this Chapter references to a statement or to a matter stated are to be read as follows.

(2) A statement is any representation of fact or opinion made by a person by whatever means; and it includes a representation made in a sketch, photofit or other pictorial form.

(3) A matter stated is one to which this Chapter applies if (and only if) the purpose, or one of the purposes, of the person making the statement appears to the court to have been—

(a) to cause another person to believe the matter, or
(b) to cause another person to act or a machine to operate on the basis that the matter is as stated.

The effect of s.114(1) and s.115 as to the nature of hearsay evidence in criminal proceedings appears to be that a statement that was not made in oral evidence in the proceedings falls within the ambit of the hearsay rule if it is relied on as evidence of a matter stated but only if the purpose (or at least one of the purposes) of the person who made the statement was either to cause another person to believe the matter stated or was to cause another person to act or a machine to operate on the basis that the matter is as stated. Thus, the Court of Appeal in *Chrysostomou* [2010] EWCA Crim 1403 indicated that there are three preliminary questions that must be asked whenever evidence, which is not in the form of oral evidence in the proceedings, is sought to be admitted. Is the proposed evidence relevant? If so, is it a statement within the meaning of s.115(2) *Criminal Justice Act* 2003? If so, is the purpose for which the statement is to be adduced in evidence to prove a "matter stated" as defined by s.115(3)? If the purpose of adducing evidence is not to prove a "matter stated" the 2003 Act has no application.

Thus, due to the operation of s.115(3)(a), statements written in a private diary which the maker did not intend anyone else to read and, which were, thus, not made for the purpose of causing another person to believe the matter stated, do not fall within the ambit of the hearsay rule but may be admissible as "direct evidence": *N* [2006] EWCA Crim 3309; *Knight* [2007] EWCA Crim 3027. Equally, again due to the operation of s.115(3), text messages, sought to be admitted as evidence of an implied assertion, are not hearsay and, subject to any other objections as to admissibility, can be admitted: *Chrysostomou* [2010] EWCA Crim 1403 (though contrast *Chrysostomou* with the previous decision of the Court of Appeal in *Leonard* [2009] EWCA Crim 1251). Similarly, where letters that had been written to the defendant were adduced in evidence because they implied that the accused belonged to or was associated with a particular gang, the Court of Appeal accepted that it was arguable that the statements were not hearsay evidence: *Mullings* [2010] EWCA Crim 2820. Conversely, the Court of Appeal held that a statement made to a person for the purpose of causing the person to look after a bag for the defendant was a hearsay statement due to the operation of s.115(3)(b) (*Walker* [2007] EWCA Crim 1698).

In *Toussaint-Collins* [2009] EWCA Crim 316, the Court of Appeal held that a letter written to the defendant prior to the murder with which the accused was charged did not fall within the ambit of the hearsay rule because the prosecution had not relied upon the letter as evidence of the matter stated but, rather, had relied upon it as evidence of its effect on the defendant's state of mind.

A consequence of the definition of "statement" in s.115(2) is that a representation of fact or opinion that was not made by a person cannot be a hearsay statement. Where, however, a representation of fact that was not made by a person depends on its accuracy on information that a person supplied, the accuracy requirement imposed by s.129 of the 2003 Act, which is reproduced at § 10–85, below, will be applicable. Thus, for example, it is submitted that the s.129 requirement would be applicable where a printout of fields from a computer database is tendered in evidence.

Case law of the European Court of Rights provides authority for the proposition that where a conviction is based solely or decisively on hearsay evidence and the defence have no opportunity to examine the maker of the hearsay statement this will result in a violation of art. 6(3)(d) of the European Convention on Human Rights which guarantees the defendant the right "... to examine or have examined witnesses against him ...": *Al-Khawaja v. United Kingdom* (2009) 49 E.H.R.R. 1. In *Horncastle* [2010] 2 A.C. 273, however, the Supreme Court, doubting whether the European Court of Human Rights had fully appreciated the English Law hearsay regime, held that if the court complies with the provisions of the 2003 Act, including the admissibility conditions in ss.116 and 117 and the safeguards that are contained in ss.124, 125 and 126, the defendant can have a fair trial even though the case against him is wholly or substantially based on such evidence.

B. ADMISSIBILITY AT COMMON LAW

Criminal Justice Act 2003, s.118

Preservation of certain common law categories of admissibility

10–58 **118.**—(1) The following rules of law are preserved.

1. *Public information etc.*

Any rule of law under which in criminal proceedings—

(a) published works dealing with matters of a public nature (such as histories, scientific works, dictionaries and maps) are admissible as evidence of facts of a public nature stated in them,

(b) public documents (such as public registers, and returns made under public authority with respect to matters of public interest) are admissible as evidence of facts stated in them,

(c) records (such as the records of certain courts, treaties, Crown grants, pardons and commissions) are admissible as evidence of facts stated in them, or

(d) evidence relating to a person's age or date or place of birth may be given by a person without personal knowledge of the matter.

2. *Reputation as to character*

Any rule of law under which in criminal proceedings evidence of a person's reputation is admissible for the purpose of proving his good or bad character.

Note

The rule is preserved only so far as it allows the court to treat such evidence as proving the matter concerned.

3. *Reputation or family tradition*

Any rule of law under which in criminal proceedings evidence of reputation or family tradition is admissible for the purpose of proving or disproving—

(a) pedigree or the existence of a marriage,

(b) the existence of any public or general right, or

(c) the identity of any person or thing.

Note

The rule is preserved only so far as it allows the court to treat such evidence as proving or disproving the matter concerned.

4. *Res gestae*

Any rule of law under which in criminal proceedings a statement is admissible as evidence of any matter stated if—

(a) the statement was made by a person so emotionally overpowered by an event that the possibility of concoction or distortion can be disregarded,

(b) the statement accompanied an act which can be properly evaluated as evidence only if considered in conjunction with the statement, or

(c) the statement relates to a physical sensation or a mental state (such as intention or emotion).

5. *Confessions etc*

Any rule of law relating to the admissibility of confessions or mixed statements in criminal proceedings.

6. *Admissions by agents etc*

Any rule of law under which in criminal proceedings—

(a) an admission made by an agent of a defendant is admissible against the defendant as evidence of any matter stated, or

(b) a statement made by a person to whom a defendant refers a person for information is admissible against the defendant as evidence of any matter stated.

7. *Common enterprise*

Any rule of law under which in criminal proceedings a statement made by a party to a common enterprise is admissible against another party to the enterprise as evidence of any matter stated.

8. *Expert evidence*

Any rule of law under which in criminal proceedings an expert witness may draw on the body of expertise relevant to his field.

(2) With the exception of the rules preserved by this section, the common law rules governing the admissibility of hearsay evidence in criminal proceedings are abolished.

Where a statement is admissible under an exception to the rule against hearsay, it is admissible as evidence of the matters stated. The common law hearsay exceptions that s.118 of the *Criminal Justice Act* 2003 preserves are admissible under s.114(1)(b). **10–59**

Confessions

10–60 As to the admissibility of confessions, see *post* § 10–123.

Public documents

10–61 Where the defendant was charged with breaching the conditions of the licence on which he had been released from prison the Divisional Court held that the licence was admissible under the rule preserved by s.118(1) 1 (b): *West Midlands Probation Board v. French* [2009] 1 Cr.App.R. 29.

Reputation as evidence of identity

10–62 Where an identification witness had only become aware of the defendant's surname in consequence of hearsay statements made to the witness subsequent to the commission of the offence, Hughes L.J., with reference to s.118(1) 3 (c), recognised at para. 8 that: "... the attribution of the surname by reputation is and always has been an exception to the rule against hearsay": *Phillips* [2010] EWCA Crim 378.

Statements falling within the res gestae principle

10–63 A statement that was made by a person who was so emotionally overpowered by an event that the possibility of concoction or distortion can be disregarded is admissible under the rule of law preserved by s.118 (1) 4 (a). In *Nye and Loan* 66 Cr.App.R. 252, CA, the statement of the victim of an assault which had taken place during an altercation after a road traffic accident, identifying one of the appellants as the assailant, was admitted. The statement had been made to a police officer shortly after the event. The Court of Appeal said it was difficult to imagine a more spontaneous identification.

10–64 The case of *Andrews* [1987] A.C. 281 set guidelines for the admissibility of *res gestae* under the rule preserved by s.118(1) 4(a).

> "1. The primary question which the judge must ask himself is—can the possibility of concoction or distortion be disregarded?
> 2. To answer that question the judge must first consider the circumstances in which the particular statement was made, in order to satisfy himself that the event was so unusual or startling or dramatic as to dominate the thoughts of the victim, so that his utterance was an instinctive reaction to that event thus giving no real opportunity for reasoned reflection. In such a situation the judge would be entitled to conclude that the involvement or the pressure of the event would exclude the possibility of concoction or distortion, providing that the statement was made in conditions of approximate but not exact contemporaneity.
> 3. in order for the statement to be sufficiently 'spontaneous' it must be so closely associated with the event which has excited the statement, that it can be fairly stated that the mind of the declarant was still dominated by the event. Thus the judge must be satisfied that the event, which provided the trigger mechanism for the statement, was still operative. The fact that the statement was made in answer to a question is but one factor to consider under this heading.
> 4.Quite apart from the time factor, there may be special features in the case, which relate to the possibility of concoction or distortion ... The judge must be satisfied that the circumstances were such that having regard to the special feature of malice there was no possibility of any concoction or distortion to the advantage of the maker or the disadvantage of the accused
> 5.As to the possibility of error in the facts narrated in the statement, if only the ordinary fallibility of human recollection is relied upon, this goes to the weight to be attached to and not to the admissibility of the statement ... However ... here there may be special features that may give rise to the possibility of error. In the instant case there was evidence that the deceased had drunk to excess.... Another example would be where the identification was made in circumstances of particular difficulty or where the declarant suffered from defective eyesight. In such circumstances the trial judge must consider whether he can exclude the possibility of error."

Admissions by agents

The defendant's counsel made an admission on the defendant's behalf at a case management hearing. The case progression form was admissible in committal proceedings under a rule preserved by s.118(1) 6: *Firth v. Epping Magistrates' Court* [2011] EWHC 388 (Admin). **10–65**

C. ADMISSIBILITY BY AGREEMENT OR UNDER STATUTE

Hearsay may be admissible under s.114(1)(a) of the *Criminal Justice Act* 2003 under a statutory provision, whether or not the provision is contained in the 2003 Act, under s.114(1)(c) by agreement between the parties and under s.114(1)(d) in the interests of justice. **10–66**

Pre-trial notice requirements and admissibility by agreement

Pre-trial notice requirements which are applicable where a party wishes to adduce hearsay evidence under s.114(1)(d), s.116 or s.121 are contained in Pt 34 of the *Criminal Procedure Rules* 2011, which can be found at G-199 to G 203, below. Where a party serves notice and no other party applies to the court to object to the introduction of the hearsay evidence, r.34.4(2) provides that the court will treat the hearsay evidence as admissible by agreement: hearsay may be admissible by agreement under s.114(1)(c) of the 2003 Act. **10–67**

Part II

The meaning of agreement was considered in *Emlyn Williams t/a Williams of Porthmadog v. Vehicle and Operator Services Agency* [2008] EWHC 849 (Admin). It does not necessarily require some contract law analysis of "offer" and "acceptance", nor does it require some formal recording of the position by the court, nor does it necessarily require express agreement between the parties in all circumstances. In the absence of objection or submission, the tribunal may infer that there is no objection to the admissibility of the statement and thus that there is agreement to its admissibility. Admissibility depends on the circumstances. If a defendant is unrepresented then it would be very difficult for such an inference to be drawn. More recently, the Court of Appeal has indicated with regard to the admission of hearsay by agreement that it is:

> "... essential ... that the court is informed at the outset of the trial what has been agreed and how the advocates propose the agreed evidence is to be placed before the jury. If an agreement is made during the trial, then the judge should be told immediately after the agreement. This is in the interests of good trial management ..."
>
> *R. v. J* [2010] 2 Cr.App.R. 2at para. 21.

Anonymous witnesses

The courts do not possess the power to admit anonymous hearsay evidence: *Mayers* [2009] 1 Cr.App.R. 30; *Ford* [2010] EWCA Crim 2250. Thus, the evidence of anonymous witnesses is not admissible under s.114(1)(d) or s.116; rather the prosecution must disclose the name of the person who made the hearsay statement both to the court and to the defence: *Mayers*. Indeed, where the prosecution themselves do not know the identity of the anonymous maker of a hearsay statement, the hearsay evidence will not be admissible under s.114(1)(d) or s.116: *Ford*. **10–68**

The admission of hearsay in the interests of justice

The court, having regard to the factors specified by s.114(2) of the *Criminal Justice Act* 2003 and to any other relevant factors, may admit hearsay evidence under s.114(1)(d) if the court is satisfied that it is in the interests of justice for the evidence to be admissible. These provisions were reproduced at § 10–57, above. The factors that s.114(2) specifically requires the court to have regard to when considering whether the admission of hearsay evidence is in the interests of justice are: **10–69**

— its probative value to matters in issue or its value to the understanding of other evidence;
— what other evidence has or can be given on the matter;
— the importance of the matter or the other evidence which needs to be understood;
— the circumstances in which it was made;
— the reliability of its maker;
— the reliability of the making of the statement;
— whether oral evidence can be given and, if not, why not;
— difficulties in challenging the statement;
— the extent that those difficulties would prejudice the defendant.

Section 114(1)(d) is available for all types of hearsay so in the case of an out of court statement contained in, or associated with, a confession, by another it was said that s.118(1) para. 5 does not exclude the application of s.114(1)(d): *R. v. Y* [2008] 1 Cr.App.R. 34.

When determining the admissibility of hearsay under s.114(1)(d) it is wrong for the prosecution to have the advantage of relying on material unavailable to the defence and submitted in a PII application: *Ali v. Revenue and Customs Prosecutions Office* (2008) 172 J.P. 516..

The words "must have regard to" in s.114(2) do not impose an obligation to reach a conclusion on all nine of the factors identified before determining whether to admit hearsay evidence; the court is merely required to consider those factors plus any others that the judge considers to be relevant and exercise judgment in the light of them: *Taylor* [2006] 2 Cr.App.R. 14.

10–70 The governing feature of s.114(1)(d) is whether it is in the interests of justice to admit hearsay evidence. That does not mean whether it is in the interest of the defendant, but whether it is in the interest of arriving at the right conclusion, though the court may apply a less exacting test on a defence application than on one by the Crown: *Marsh* [2008] EWCA Crim 1816. The interests of justice, under s.114(1)(d) include the public interest in crimes being tried as well as the interests of the accused; where at a retrial, a witness, who was paralysed, incapable of facial expression, and had at the first trial given his evidence by pointing to letters on an alphabet board, refused to attend, the record of his evidence at the first trial was properly admitted: *Sadiq and Hussein* (2009)173 J P 471.

The nature of those circumstances in which the hearsay evidence of a witness who is available to testify should be admitted under s.114(1)(d) in circumstances in which the evidence is not admissible under s.116 of the 2003 Act are limited, otherwise s.116 itself and the statutory scheme as a whole would be undermined: *Freeman* [2010] EWCA Crim 1197. Thus, it seems that where the requirements of s.116 are not satisfied, the mere fact that a witness is reluctant to testify will rarely justify the admission of significant and prejudicial hearsay evidence under s.114(1)(d): *Z* [2009] 1 Cr App R 34; *Freeman* [2010] EWCA Crim 1197. Thus, where the hearsay of an important eleven-year-old witness whom the defence wished to cross-examine was admitted under s.114(1)(d) because his parents did not believe that it was in his interests to testify, the Court of Appeal held that the evidence should not have been admitted: *Williams* [2007] EWCA Crim 211. Equally, where the hearsay of a sexual offence complainant had been admitted under s.114(1)(d) because she was pregnant and would have been required to cancel her holiday plans, the Court of Appeal, recognising that the prosecution had been at fault in giving the complainant very little notice of the trial date, held that the hearsay evidence should not have been admitted.

Where there are cogent reasons for its admission in the interests of justice, hearsay evidence may be admitted under s.114(1)(d) even though the evidence is not admissible under s.116: *ED* [2010] EWCA Crim 1213. Thus, where the defendant's wife had made a statement to the police incriminating the defendant but could not be compelled to testify at the defendant's trial and was not willing to do so, the Court of Appeal held that the judge had been entitled to admit her police statement under s.114(1)(d): *L* [2008] 2 Cr.App.R. 18. Equally, where the accused did not appear on the day of the trial, the Court of Appeal held that the judge had been entitled to admit his witness statement under s.114(1)(d) because his evidence related to an uncontentious matter: *Adams* [2008] 1 Cr.App.R. 35. Again, the Court of Appeal held that the judge had been entitled to admit hearsay evidence under s.114(1)(d) in circumstances in which the maker of the hearsay statement was a serving prisoner who refused to testify: *Musone* [2007] 2 Cr.App.R. 29. The Court of Appeal in *ED*, at para. 17, regarded these latter three cases as providing examples of "... occasions when evidence, which cannot be given orally for reasons other than those provided for by s.116, may be admitted" and, at para. 21, was "aware of other circumstances in which evidence has been admitted under s.114(1)(d) when its purpose has been to fill a continuity gap or similar."

Evidence of a statement made by a co-defendant to a third party was admitted under s.114(1)(d) in the context of proceedings for conspiracy to supply a class A drug. The judge had not been required to consider s.116 before admitting the evidence under s.114(1)(d) because the case concerned a remark made by a co-defendant whereas *Z* had concerned a statement made by a person who said that the appellant had raped and abused her and who was alive and could have testified: *O'Connor* [2010] EWCA Crim 2287.

Part II

A key factor under s.114(2) is the reliability of the person who made the hearsay statement as challenging the veracity of a witness who is called to prove a hearsay statement does not present the special difficulties that are associated with challenging the veracity of an absent witness.

Marsh [2008] EWCA Crim 1816. Evidence of a statement made by a prisoner in which it was stated that another prisoner had told him that he had set up the defendant was not admitted as it was impossible to evaluate the veracity of the former prisoner's evidence.

A court must give sufficient weight to the prejudicial effect that the inability to challenge evidence might have on the defence case: *McEwan v. DPP* [2007] EWHC 740, Admin. In this case the evidence admitted was that of a youth who had stated that he had seen the defendant scratch a car and his was the only eye-witness account. The witness had not attended court because of an illness and medical evidence indicated that the stress of attending court might be detrimental to his wellbeing. The magistrates had unduly focused on the probative value of the evidence and had failed properly to address the fact that this evidence was the crux of the prosecution case. The remaining evidence was circumstantial. The finding that the witness was not fit to attend court was not warranted on the medical evidence.

Where evidence of a previous conviction is admissible but the defendant refuses to make an admission as to the circumstances of the conviction, a document summarising the prosecution case, the facts admitted by the defendant and the manner in which the case had been left to the jury by the judge can be admitted under s.114(1)(d) via the interests of justice test to prove the similarity between that offence and the present offence: *Steen* [2008] 2 Cr.App.R. 380(26), C.A.

Even if there is a possibility that a witness might be hostile, it is important to consider the witness's availability before admitting a statement under s.114(1)(d) as it may be in the interest of justice that a witness is called: *Khan (Mohammed)* [2009] EWCA Crim 86.

The party wishing to introduce hearsay evidence must give notice. See *Criminal Procedure Rules* 2011, r.34(2)–(5) in Appendix G-200—G-206. **10–71**

Unavailability of witnesses

Criminal Justice Act 2003, s.116

116.—(1) In criminal proceedings a statement not made in oral evidence in the proceedings is admissible as evidence of any matter stated if— **10–72**

(a) oral evidence given in the proceedings by the person who made the statement would be admissible as evidence of that matter,

(b) the person who made the statement (the relevant person) is identified to the court's satisfaction, and

(c) any of the five conditions mentioned in subsection (2) is satisfied.

(2) The conditions are—

(a) that the relevant person is dead;

(b) that the relevant person is unfit to be a witness because of his bodily or mental condition;

(c) that the relevant person is outside the United Kingdom and it is not reasonably practicable to secure his attendance;

(d) that the relevant person cannot be found although such steps as it is reasonably practicable to take to find him have been taken;

(e) that through fear the relevant person does not give (or does not continue to give) oral evidence in the proceedings, either at all or in connection with the subject matter of the statement, and the court gives leave for the statement to be given in evidence.

(3) For the purposes of subsection (2)(e) "fear" is to be widely construed and (for example) includes fear of the death or injury of another person or of financial loss.

(4) Leave may be given under subsection (2)(e) only if the court considers that the statement ought to be admitted in the interests of justice, having regard—

(a) to the statement's contents,

(b) to any risk that its admission or exclusion will result in unfairness to any party to the proceedings (and in particular to how difficult it will be to challenge the statement if the relevant person does not give oral evidence),

(c) in appropriate cases, to the fact that a direction under section 19 of the *Youth Justice and Criminal Evidence Act* 1999 (c. 23) (special measures for the giving of evidence by fearful witnesses etc) could be made in relation to the relevant person, and

(d) to any other relevant circumstances.

(5) A condition set out in any paragraph of subsection (2) which is in fact satisfied is to be treated as not satisfied if it is shown that the circumstances described in that paragraph are caused—

(a) by the person in support of whose case it is sought to give the statement in evidence, or

(b) by a person acting on his behalf,

In order to prevent the relevant person giving oral evidence in the proceedings (whether at all or in connection with the subject matter of the statement).

10–73 Where a person is dead; mentally or physically unfit; outside the UK and it is not practicable for him to attend; unable to be found or afraid, then his statement may be admissible if his oral evidence would have been admissible and his identity is confirmed. In the case of fear, the court must also give leave: s.116(4). For evidence to be admissible under s.116 it has to be logically probative of a fact in issue between the parties, *i.e.* it must be relevant: *T.* [2007] 1 Cr.App.R. 4. In this case it was held to be wrong to submit a statement of another person who had admitted acts of sexual abuse against the victim where the only purpose for adducing this evidence was "oath helping" and it was admitted simply to support the credibility of the witness.

As was seen in § 10–70, above, the evidence of a reluctant witness should not normally be admitted under s.114(1)(d) if it is not admissible under s.116.

10–74 Where the prosecution wish to adduce hearsay under s.116, the admission of such evidence is subject to the exercise of the court's exclusionary discretion under s.78 *Police and Criminal Evidence Act* 1978, which is preserved by s.126(2)(a) of the *Criminal Justice Act* 2003; useful guidance on the exercise of the s.78 discretion in this context being provided by the factors identified in s.114(2) of the 2003 Act: *Cole and Keet* [2008] 1 Cr.App.R. 5; *Gian v. Crown Prosecution Service* [2009] EWCA Crim 2553.

When the prosecution wish to adduce hearsay evidence under s.116, the prosecution bears the burden of proving to the criminal standard of proof, i.e. proof beyond reasonable doubt, that the s.116 admissibility conditions are satisfied: *Lyons* [2010] EWCA Crim 2029. Thus, whilst the hearsay evidence of a witness who deliberately absents himself from the trial may be admissible under s.116(2)(d), the approach that the court adopts before concluding that the requirements of s.116(2)(d) have been satisfied must be stringent. Where the defence wish to adduce hearsay evidence under s.116 and are, thus, required to establish that the s.116 admissibility conditions are satisfied, it seems that the requisite standard of proof will be proof on the balance of probabilities: *Mattey and Queeley* [1995] 2 Cr.App.R. 409. As regards s.116(5), it is suggested that the burden imposed by that subsection must be discharged by the party who objects to the admission of the hearsay evidence.

In *R. (Meredith) v. Harwich Magistrates' Court* [2006] EWHC 3336, the witness had a long history of anxiety and panic attacks and the prospect of giving evidence had brought about a recurrence; her medical practitioner had certified that it would be better if she did not give evidence. It was held that the statement of the doctor was insufficient to prove the unfitness and as the evidence was so important the case ought to have been adjourned to explore other means of assisting the witness, *e.g.* video link.

Where a witness had been sectioned on the day of the trial and the prosecution had made arrangements to obtain a written statement from a doctor, the magistrates should not have refused the prosecution's application to adduce the witness' hearsay evidence under s.116 without waiting for the doctor's written statement to arrive: *R. (on the application of Crown Prosecution Service) v. Uxbridge Magistrates Court* [2007] EWHC 205 (Admin).

Whether it is not reasonably practicable to secure a witness' attendance for the purposes of s.116(2)(c) depends on the steps that the party who sought to secure the witness' attendance took or failed to take; the court must also consider whether to exercise its exclusionary discretion under s.78 of the *Police and Criminal Evidence Act* 1984: *C and K:* [2006] EWCA Crim 19. Where a witness had given the police a video recorded interview but was located in Jamaica by the time of the murder trial to which his evidence related, the judge, having received evidence from a police officer who had spoken to the witness by telephone and been informed that the witness' father would not allow him to testify by video link, admitted the witness' evidence under s.116 and declined to exclude it under s.78 of the 1984 Act. The Court of Appeal upheld the judge's decision: *Bailey* [2008] EWCA Crim 817.

In *Hurst* [1995] 1 Cr.App.R. 82, it was said that the words "reasonably practicable" involve a consideration of the normal steps which would be taken to secure the attendance of a witness; and the qualification of reasonableness includes other circumstances such as the costs and steps which may be available to secure the witness's attendance. Normal steps are the reasonable steps which a party would take, having regard to the means and resources available: *Maloney* [1994] Crim.L.R. 525.

The right to confrontation is a long standing right of common law, subsequently recognised by ECHR art. 6 and must only be departed from in the limited circumstances prescribed by the *Criminal Justice Act*. All possible efforts must be made to get a witness to court and this must start with a witness being given all possible support and being made to understand the importance of the citizen's duty to give evidence: *R. v. T* (2009) 173 J.P. 425. This was a case under s.116(2)(e) where the witness was afraid. The principles laid down however are equally applicable to applications under (d) *i.e.* that in order to consider an application there must either be an agreed statement of the facts or there must be a finding upon evidence of the steps taken to find the witness. It is then that the court can establish whether steps such as are reasonably practicable have been taken.

There is no distinction between "cannot be found" and "cannot be contacted"; the issue is whether reasonable steps have been taken to find the witness. It is insufficient merely to leave a message on the witness's telephone the night before the trial. Once there is doubt that a person has received the message, a visit to his home/work address should take place or at least a telephone call to those places: *Adams* [2008] 1 Cr.App.R. 35.

Part II

The hearsay evidence of a witness who deliberately absents himself from a trial may be admissible under s.116(2)(d) if the court is satisfied that "such steps as it is reasonably practicable to take to find him have been taken", which means, in the case of a prosecution witness that the police must be

> "... scrupulous in not only tracing witnesses but keeping in contact with them and ensuring that they understand the importance of giving evidence, supported as they should be by those whose responsibility it is to take care for the welfare and confidence of prospective witnesses."

Lyons [2010] EWCA Crim 2029 at para. 17 with reference to *Adams* [2008] 1 Cr.App.R 35 at para. 13

A judge had been entitled to admit a witness statement even though the witness was the only witness to the alleged arson where reasonable steps had been taken to bring the witness to court and he had not attended court, not wanting to be considered a "grass" as there was other strong evidence: *Little* [2008] EWCA Crim 690.

In order to decide whether it is practicable for a witness to attend, a court must take into account the importance of the evidence, prejudice to the defence and the expense and inconvenience occasioned by the witness's attendance: *Castillo* [1996] 1 Cr.App.R. 438; *French* (1993) 97 Cr.App.R. 421; *Gonzales* (1993) 96 Cr.App.R. 399. In *Sawoniuk, ante*, elderly witnesses were brought from Poland because of the nature of the crime.

So far as s.116(2)(e) is concerned, where a witness is being subjected to subtle intimidation from a defendant, a court has to perform a balancing exercise between a subjective assessment of fear and an objective assessment of fairness in deciding whether a statement should be admitted under s.116: *Doherty* (2007) 171 J.P. 79. In *H., A., The Times*, July 6, 2001, a kidnapping case, it was held that a witness's fear is to be assessed by reference to the time at which he is expected to give evidence. In that case, the witness's fear was held to be out of date as the indication was that he was afraid some weeks prior to the trial. A stringent approach should be taken particularly if the evidence was critical to the outcome of the case. A victim's state of mind has to be assessed against the history of the case: *Boulton* [2007] EWCA Crim 942. In this domestic violence case, threats against the victim and her financial resources were considered to be evidence in relation to her "fear". It has been said that before admitting statements a court would be ill advised to seek to test the basis of a fear as it would undermine the very purpose that s.116 set out to achieve; fear is to be widely construed: *Davies* [2006] EWCA Crim 2643; (2006) 150 S.J.L.B. 1288

A witness's statement can be read when there is a fear of reprisals even where she has been inconsistent between the making of the statement and the trial; inconsistency does not necessarily undermine a conclusion of fear: *Kelly* [2007] EWCA Crim 1715. In domestic violence cases a prosecutor must rely on direct evidence where it is not in the interests of justice to admit hearsay evidence of the witness's initial complaint: *K December* 18, 2007 unreported *ante*. Where a witness is reluctant to give evidence against someone with whom the witness may still be living the prosecutor must assess what evidence can be given. In this case there was evidence of the call to police, the fact that it was from a woman, and her address. What was said did not matter although it could have been relied on as *res gestae*. There was direct evidence of police officers who had seen injuries to the witness's face. That could have amounted to a *prima facie* case.

Before granting an application a court should be informed of any, and if so, what efforts have been made to alleviate the fears, for example, witness protection or screens at court.

Business and other documents

Criminal Justice Act 2003, s.117

Business and other documents

10–75 **117.**—(1) In criminal proceedings a statement contained in a document is admissible as evidence of any matter stated if—

(a) oral evidence given in the proceedings would be admissible as evidence of that matter,

(b) the requirements of subsection (2) are satisfied, and

(c) the requirements of subsection (5) are satisfied, in a case where subsection (4) requires them to be.

(2) The requirements of this subsection are satisfied if—

(a) the document or the part containing the statement was created or received by a person in the course of a trade, business, profession or other occupation, or as the holder of a paid or unpaid office,

(b) the person who supplied the information contained in the statement (the relevant person) had or may reasonably be supposed to have had personal knowledge of the matters dealt with, and

(c) each person (if any) through whom the information was supplied from the relevant person to the person mentioned in paragraph (a) received the information in the course of a trade, business, profession or other occupation, or as the holder of a paid or unpaid office.

(3) The persons mentioned in paragraphs (a) and (b) of subsection (2) may be the same person.

(4) The additional requirements of subsection (5) must be satisfied if the statement— **10–76**

(a) was prepared for the purposes of pending or contemplated criminal proceedings, or for a criminal investigation, but

(b) was not obtained pursuant to a request under section 7 of the *Crime (International Co-operation) Act* 2003 or an order under paragraph 6 of Schedule 13 to the *Criminal Justice Act* 1988 (which relate to overseas evidence).

(5) The requirements of this subsection are satisfied if—

(a) any of the five conditions mentioned in section 116(2) is satisfied (absence of relevant person etc), or

(b) the relevant person cannot reasonably be expected to have any recollection of the matters dealt with in the statement (having regard to the length of time since he supplied the information and all other circumstances).

(6) A statement is not admissible under this section if the court makes a direction to that effect under subsection (7).

(7) The court may make a direction under this subsection if satisfied that the statement's reliability as evidence for the purpose for which it is tendered is doubtful in view of—

(a) its contents,

(b) the source of the information contained in it,

(c) the way in which or the circumstances in which the information was supplied or received, or

(d) the way in which or the circumstances in which the document concerned was created or received.

Documents include "anything in which information of any description is recorded", s.134(1). **10–77**

Statements in documents are admissible under s.117 if:

— created or received in the course of a business *etc*.; and

— the person supplying the information had personal knowledge; and

— each person handling the information received it in the course of a business etc.; and

— oral evidence of the fact would have been admissible; and

— (where the document was made for criminal proceedings or an investigation in UK) the maker is dead, physically or mentally unfit, outside UK and impracticable for him to attend, unable to be found or afraid or he cannot be expected to have any recollection.

A label on a container identifying the name of the person whose blood it contained was admissible under the old law as it was said that a court could infer that it was prepared by a police officer in the normal course of his duties: *Khatibi v. DPP* (2004) 168 J.P. 361.

Records concerning use of a mobile telephone were admissible under s.117 even though they were unaccompanied by a statement from the telephone company, though the Court of Appeal doubted whether they should have fallen within the hearsay rule at all as they were, very arguably, not statements made by a person (in which case, see § 10–57, above, though the Court of Appeal did not refer to s.129 of the 2003 Act): *O'Connor* [2010] EWCA Crim 2287.

Section 117 could not be relied upon to justify the admission of a computerised police record providing short statements of the facts of the convictions and the methods used to commit those previous offences because the information in the document was not supplied by the person with personal knowledge: *Humphris* (2005) 169 J.P. 441; see also *Burns (Bad character), post*. A police log noting the registration details of the defendant's vehicle left on the windscreen of the damaged vehicle was not admissible as a business document under s.117 because the person who communicated the information to the police did not have personal knowledge of the facts and had not received it in the course of the trade, business, etc but was admissible hearsay under s.114(2): *Maher v. DPP, ante*.

In *Wellington v. DPP* [2007] EWCA Crim 1116 a PNC printout was admitted containing a list of aliases, one of which was the name which the defendant had given when stopped. It was said that it was an inescapable inference that the police officer supplying the information of aliases "had or could reasonably be supposed to have had personal knowledge" of the fact that the alias in question had been used and it could be inferred that any intermediaries had received the information in the course of a trade, business etc. Although he could be expected to recall that aliases were used he could not be expected to recall details of those aliases.

A statement of a scene of the crimes officer relating to fingerprints found on a window at the scene of a burglary five years previously can be admitted under s.117; the officer cannot be expected to remember the answers to questions he would have been asked under cross-examination i.e. the way the window opened and whether there were fingerprints or smudges elsewhere: *Kamuhuza*, 173 J.P. 55, CA.

The court may direct that a statement is not admissible under s.117 if it believes that its reliability is doubtful: s.117(7).

Criminal Justice Act 2003, ss.119–120

Inconsistent statements

10–78 **119.**—(1) If in criminal proceedings a person gives oral evidence and—

(a) he admits making a previous inconsistent statement, or

(b) a previous inconsistent statement made by him is proved by virtue of section 3, 4 or 5 the *Criminal Procedure Act* 1865,

the statement is admissible as evidence of any matter stated of which oral evidence by him would be admissible.

(2) If in criminal proceedings evidence of an inconsistent statement by any person is given under section 124(2)(c), the statement is admissible as evidence of any matter stated in it of which oral evidence by that person would be admissible.

10–79 Section 119 of the 2003 Act is applicable where a previous inconsistent statement made by a witness is adduced in evidence (see §§ 9–84 to 9–88 and 9–111 to 9–117, above).

When considering the exercise of the exclusionary discretion conferred upon the court by s.78 of the *Police and Criminal Evidence Act* 1984 in the context of a prosecution application to adduce hearsay evidence under s.119 of the 2003 Act, the court may be "greatly helped" by s.114(2) of the *Criminal Justice Act* 2003, which was considered at § 10–68, above: *Bennett* [2008] EWCA Crim 248.

Where evidence of a previous inconsistent statement is admitted for the prosecution under s.119 the court appears to have three options, if they believe that the witness made the statement. As the Court of Appeal put it in *Joyce* [2005] EWCA Crim 1785 at paras 29–30, in approving the directions that the trial judge had given in that case:

> "First, they might accept the police statement by each of the witnesses, if sure that it was true and accurate. Secondly, they might accept what each witness said in his or her evidence, if sure that he or she was telling the truth..."

The judge went on:

> "The third possibility is, given the inconsistencies between the earlier statements and their evidence in court yesterday, you may take the view you cannot rely on any of that witness' evidence and you may choose to ignore completely what that witness has said."

Where, however, a previous inconsistent statement is exculpatory of the accused, it is unnecessary for the court to be sure that it is true before relying on it. Rather, "Where the previous statement is exculpatory of the defendant, it is sufficient for the jury to conclude that it may be true ...": *Billingham* [2009] EWCA Crim 19 at para. 68.

Other previous statements of witnesses

120.—(1) This section applies where a person (the witness) is called to give evidence in criminal proceedings. **10–80**

(2) If a previous statement by the witness is admitted as evidence to rebut a suggestion that his oral evidence has been fabricated, that statement is admissible as evidence of any matter stated of which oral evidence by the witness would be admissible.

(3) A statement made by the witness in a document—

(a) which is used by him to refresh his memory while giving evidence,

(b) on which he is cross-examined, and

(c) which as a consequence is received in evidence in the proceedings,

is admissible as evidence of any matter stated of which oral evidence by him would be admissible.

(4) A previous statement by the witness is admissible as evidence of any matter stated of which oral evidence by him would be admissible, if—

(a) any of the following three conditions is satisfied, and

(b) while giving evidence the witness indicates that to the best of his belief he made the statement, and that to the best of his belief it states the truth.

(5) The first condition is that the statement identifies or describes a person, object or place.

(6) The second condition is that the statement was made by the witness when the matters stated were fresh in his memory but he does not remember them, and cannot reasonably be expected to remember them, well enough to give oral evidence of them in the proceedings.

(7) The third condition is that—

(a) the witness claims to be a person against whom an offence has been committed,

(b) the offence is one to which the proceedings relate,

(c) the statement consists of a complaint made by the witness (whether to a person in authority or not) about conduct which would, if proved, constitute the offence or part of the offence,

(e) the complaint was not made as a result of a threat or a promise, and

(f) before the statement is adduced the witness gives oral evidence in connection with its subject matter.

(8) For the purposes of subsection (7) the fact that the complaint was elicited (for example, by a leading question) is irrelevant unless a threat or a promise was involved.

Where evidence of a previous consistent statement made by a witness is admissible, s.120 renders such evidence admissible as evidence of the matters stated. Where such evidence is tendered by the prosecution, however, its admissibility will be subject to the exercise of the court's exclusionary discretion under s.78 of the *Police and Criminal Evidence Act* 1984: *Athwal* [2009] EWCA Crim 789. **10–81**

Where a previous consistent statement is admitted under s.120(2) in rebuttal of an allegation of recent fabrication it is now admitted as evidence of the matters stated under the hearsay regime created by the *Criminal Justice Act* 2003: *Athwal* [2009] EWCA Crim 789.

Safeguards and Supplementary provisions

The 2003 Act contains a number of safeguards and supplementary provisions relating to hearsay evidence.

Criminal Justice Act 2003, s.121

Additional requirement for admissibility of multiple hearsay

121.—(1) A hearsay statement is not admissible to prove the fact that an earlier hearsay statement was made unless—

(a) either of the statements is admissible under section 117, 119 or 120,

(b) all parties to the proceedings so agree, or

(c) the court is satisfied that the value of the evidence in question, taking into account how reliable the statements appear to be, is so high that the interests of justice require the later statement to be admissible for that purpose.

(2) In this section "hearsay statement" means a statement, not made in oral evidence, that is relied on as evidence of a matter stated in it.

Section 121 imposes an additional requirement where a party wishes to adduce multiple hearsay, *i.e.* where a party wishes to adduce evidence of a hearsay statement to prove that an earlier hearsay statement was made.

When the court is required to consider the admissibility of multiple hearsay under s.121, it appears that the approach that the court should consider is whether hearsay exceptions apply to all of the relevant statements and should not merely consider s.121: *Walker* [2007] EWCA Crim 1698. In this case a witness' hearsay evidence of what an accomplice has told him the defendant has said was held to be properly admitted as evidence.

In relation to the s.121(1)(c) interests of justice test, it seems that this "imposes a higher threshold" than s.114(1)(d), which was considered at § 10–68, above: Walker at para. 33. It seems, however, that when the court is applying the s.121(1)(c) interests of justice test, the court may have recourse to the factors identified by s.114(2): *Musone* [2007] 2 Cr.App.R. 29; *Maher v. DPP* [2006] EWHC 1271 (Admin).

Criminal Justice Act 2003, ss.123 124, 126, 129

Capability to make statement

10–82 **123.**—(1) Nothing in section 116, 119 or 120 makes a statement admissible as evidence if it was made by a person who did not have the required capability at the time when he made the statement.

(2) Nothing in section 117 makes a statement admissible as evidence if any person who, in order for the requirements of section 117(2) to be satisfied, must at any time have supplied or received the information concerned or created or received the document or part concerned—

(a) did not have the required capability at that time, or

(b) cannot be identified but cannot reasonably be assumed to have had the required capability at that time.

(3) For the purposes of this section a person has the required capability if he is capable of—

(a) understanding questions put to him about the matters stated, and

(b) giving answers to such questions which can be understood.

(4) Where by reason of this section there is an issue as to whether a person had the required capability when he made a statement—

(a) proceedings held for the determination of the issue must take place in the absence of the jury (if there is one);

(b) in determining the issue the court may receive expert evidence and evidence from any person to whom the statement in question was made;

(c) the burden of proof on the issue lies on the party seeking to adduce the statement, and the standard of proof is the balance of probabilities.

The effect of s.123 is, essentially, that where the maker of a hearsay statement would not have been competent to give evidence in criminal proceedings at the time when the statement was made, the statement will not be admissible under ss.116, 190 or 120 of the *Criminal Justice Act* 2003, s.123 makes similar provision in relation to the admissibility of hearsay evidence under s.117.

Section 123 does not prevent the admission of hearsay evidence under s.114(1)(d) of the 2003 Act. In *J* [2009] EWCA Crim 1869, evidence of statements made by a small child was admitted under s.114(1)(d) in circumstances in which it was not disputed that, being two and a half years old, she was too young to testify.

Credibility

124.—(1) This section applies if in criminal proceedings— **10–83**

(a) a statement not made in oral evidence in the proceedings is admitted as evidence of a matter stated, and

(b) the maker of the statement does not give oral evidence in connection with the subject matter of the statement.

(2) In such a case—

(a) any evidence which (if he had given such evidence) would have been admissible as relevant to his credibility as a witness is so admissible in the proceedings;

(b) evidence may with the court's leave be given of any matter which (if he had given such evidence) could have been put to him in cross-examination as relevant to his credibility as a witness but of which evidence could not have been adduced by the cross-examining party;

(c) evidence tending to prove that he made (at whatever time) any other statement inconsistent with the statement admitted as evidence is admissible for the purpose of showing that he contradicted himself.

(3) If as a result of evidence admitted under this section an allegation is made against the maker of a statement, the court may permit a party to lead additional evidence of such description as the court may specify for the purposes of denying or answering the allegation.

(4) In the case of a statement in a document which is admitted as evidence under section 117 each person who, in order for the statement to be admissible, must have supplied or received the information concerned or created or received the document or part concerned is to be treated as the maker of the statement for the purposes of subsections (1) to (3) above.

Court's general discretion to exclude evidence

126.—(1) In criminal proceedings the court may refuse to admit a statement as evidence of a matter stated if— **10–84**

(a) the statement was made otherwise than in oral evidence in the proceedings, and

(b) the court is satisfied that the case for excluding the statement, taking account of the danger that to admit it would result in undue waste of time, substantially outweighs the case for admitting it, taking account of the value of the evidence.

(2) Nothing in this Chapter prejudices—

(a) any power of a court to exclude evidence under section 78 of the *Police and Criminal Evidence Act* 1984 (exclusion of unfair evidence), or

(b) any other power of a court to exclude evidence at its discretion (whether by preventing questions from being put or otherwise).

In *Horncastle* [2010] 2 A.C. 273 Lord Phillips, at para. 36, indicated that:

"S.126 preserves the general power of the judge (which existed at common law and is enshrined in s.78 of the *Police and Criminal Evidence Act* 1984) to exclude any evidence relied upon by the Crown (but not by a defendant) if its admission would have such an adverse effect on the fairness of the trial that it ought not to be admitted; the section adds a further obligation upon the judge to exclude hearsay evidence if its admission would generate satellite disputes which would cause an undue waste of time such as to outweigh the case for admitting it."

Representations other than by a person

129.—(1) Where a representation of any fact— **10–85**

(a) is made otherwise than by a person, but

(b) depends for its accuracy on information supplied (directly or indirectly) by a person,

the representation is not admissible in criminal proceedings as evidence of the fact unless it is proved that the information was accurate.

(2) Subsection (1) does not affect the operation of the presumption that a mechanical device has been properly set or calibrated.

10–86 The purpose of this section is to provide that, where a representation of fact made by a machine is based on information supplied by a human, the statement will be admissible only if it is proved that the information is accurate (see § 10–57, above). Section 129(2) preserves the common law presumption that a mechanical device is in proper working order.

VIII. IDENTIFICATION EVIDENCE

A. GENERAL

10–87 The question whether identification is in dispute must be considered at the time of the investigation, not subsequently in the light of evidence given at trial: *Lambert* [2004] EWCA Crim 154. Identification, where a person disputes that he is the person who was previously convicted of an offence, according to *Derwentside Magistrates' Court ex p. Heaviside* [1996] R.T.R. 384 can be proved in two stages:

(1) the production of the certificate of conviction; and

(2) proof to the criminal standard that the person to whom that relates is the accused.

That case went on to state that there was no defined method of proving the second part and gave three examples—admission, fingerprint or by witnesses. Those examples are not exhaustive; statements can also be used: *Derwentside Magistrates' Court ex p. Swift and R. v. Sunderland Justices ex p. Bate* [1997] R.T.R. 89; *DPP v. Mooney* [1997] R.T.R. 434. This issue often arises when the charge is one of disqualified driving as the disqualification will arise from conviction.

It will normally be possible to establish a *prima facie* case on the basis of the consistency of details between the accused and the person named in the memorandum of conviction: *Pattison v. DPP* [2006] 2 All E.R. 317. The cases establish the following principles:

(a) the prosecution must prove to the criminal standard of proof that the person accused was a disqualified driver;

(b) any admissible means may prove that the driver was disqualified;

(c) it is an essential element of the prosecution case that the accused is proved to the criminal standard to be the person named in the certificate where that certificate is relied upon;

(d) the three clear ways in which identity can be proved are set out in *Heaviside*;

(e) there is no prescribed way in which identity must be proved;

(f) where there is no evidence contradicting a prima facie case, the evidence will be sufficient for the court to convict;

(g) failure by the accused to give any contradictory evidence in rebuttal will be a matter for the court to take into account.

The defendant's representative may be called to testify as to what happened in the courtroom and this is not considered to be breach of legal privilege: *R. (Howe) v. South Durham Magistrates' Court* [2005] R.T.R 4. In *West Yorkshire Probation Board v. Boulter, ante*, it was said that the court is entitled to draw an inference that it is the same person if the name, address and date of birth coincide. Whether an inference is sufficient will depend on the facts of the particular case; see also *Burns* [2006] 1 W.L.R. 1273.

Where the identity of the defendant is in issue the prosecution must call identification evidence. Code D of the Police Code of Practice issued under the *Police and Criminal Evidence Act* 1984 applies: see Appendix A.

The House of Lords held in *Forbes* [2001] 1 A.C. 473 that in the case of a disputed identification, the police must hold an identification parade if the suspect consents unless one of the savings made by Code D applies or a parade would be futile because the witness makes it plain that he cannot identify the culprit or can only identify his clothing; or where the case is one of "pure recognition" of someone well known to the victim; or there exists "other exceptional circumstances". In *H.* (2003) 147 S.J.L.B. 237, a recognition case, the Court of Appeal held that Code D now requires an ID parade where a dispute as to identity might reasonably be expected. There is no need for an identification parade when the defendant and the victim are known to each other: In *Harris* (2003) 147 S.J. 237 it was held that an identification procedure should have been held where the witness had not seen the sixteen-year-old defendant for two years.

If a witness can only say that an offender was wearing certain clothing, there is no need for an identification parade as it serves no useful purpose: *Marsh v. DPP* [2007] Crim L.R. 162, [2006] EWHC 1525.

When a witness has failed to make a positive identification in an identification parade the witness may still be called as a witness to describe the offender and what had occurred on the identification parade: *George* [2003] Crim.L.R. 282.

Where a witness notices that the offender has a particular distinguishing feature (in this case, two tattoos on the defendant's neck) an identification procedure is of no value if, either the feature is visible and none of the other participants has such a feature or the feature is concealed but none of the other participants has the corresponding part of his body concealed: *Pecco* [2010] EWCA Crim 972.

The fact that a police officer conducting an identification procedure does not follow the procedure laid down does not automatically make the identification evidence inadmissible: *Hedge and another* [2010] EWCA Crim 2252.

Where there is a breach of Code D this will not automatically result in the exclusion of identification evidence; the issue will be one for the court to consider in the exercise of its exclusionary discretion under s.78 of the *Police and Criminal Evidence Act* 1984 and if the court admits the evidence it should take the breach into account when determining the weight of the hearsay evidence: *Forbes* [2001] 1 A.C. 473.

Where a victim had identified the defendant in the street by twice being driven past **10–88** him by the police, the second identification during which police officers had stood by the defendant did not breach the PACE Codes of Practice as it was one continuous identification: *B. v. DPP* [2006] EWHC 660.

There is no contamination of an identification where witnesses attending a police station for an identification parade had sat in the same waiting room as the defendant but had said that they had paid no attention to him: *Banks* [2005] EWCA Crim 1858 . There is no contamination where a witness makes an identikit picture, has not recognised the person from a photograph but then identifies the defendant at a confrontation at the defendant's home and subsequently makes a dock identification: *Stock* [2008] EWCA Crim 1862. The issue can still be one of identification where a defendant had said that he was on the other side of the road from that where the offence occurred and an identification parade should be held: *M.*, unreported, October 13, 2005, CA.

In summary road traffic proceedings, it is permissible for the prosecution to seek and **10–89** rely upon a dock identification of the defendant in circumstances where there has been no prior notification that identity is in issue. It is not a violation of the right to a fair trial for the court to expect, and in that sense require, an accused person to indicate prior to trial that identification is in issue: see *Karia v. DPP* (2002) 166 J.P. 753, QBD and *Barnes v. Chief Constable of Durham* [1997] 2 Cr.App.R. 505; *Holland v. HM Advocate* [2005] UKPC D1. A witness can identify the person in the dock where an out-of-court identification has taken place on a previous occasion: *Christie* [1914] A.C. 545. It can also take place where a defendant has refused to take part in an identification parade: *John* [1973] Crim.L.R. 113.

Where a police officer, a passenger in a police car, saw the driver of another car, for between one and two seconds, purported to recognise him (but without remembering his name) and, within forty minutes had picked out a photograph of the defendant kept at the police station and was then able to name him as a man with whom he had been at close quarters for a total of eight hours seven weeks earlier, where the driver of the police car had also picked out a photograph of the defendant and where both officers had subsequently identified the defendant in video identification procedures then, the court can take the identification into account despite the brevity of the observations remembering that police officers are trained observers; evidence of previous convictions was also allowed in that it supported the correctness of the identification: *Spittle* [2009] R.T.R. 159, CA.

10–90 The *Att.-Gen.'s Reference (No. 2 of 2002)* [2003] 1 Cr.App.R. 21, CA, gave at least four circumstances where the court can conclude that the defendant is shown on a photographic image from the scene of the crime:

1. where the photographic image was sufficiently clear it could be compared to the defendant in the dock;
2. where the witness knew then defendant sufficiently well to recognise him as the offender depicted in the photograph image, he could give evidence of that;
3. where a witness did not know the defendant but had spent a substantial time viewing and analysing the photographic images from the scene and had therefore acquired special knowledge, he could give evidence of identification based upon a comparison between those images and a reasonably contemporary photograph of the defendant, provided the images and the photograph were available to the jury; or
4. a suitably qualified expert with facial mapping skills could give opinion evidence of identification from a comparison between images from the scene, whether expertly enhanced or not, and a reasonably contemporary photograph of the defendant, provided both were available to the court.

Where photographs have been shown to a victim of those whose names have been given to him as his assailants and he then identifies the same persons in a later identification parade, a court should direct itself of the potential dangers of such an identification, that the victim had identified those on the photographs rather than identifying them as assailants: *I.* [2007] 2 Cr.App.R.24.

In *Chaney* [2009] 1 Cr.App.R. 35 evidence of recognition was allowed where a police officer had received still photographs from CCTV via an email transmission suggesting that the person was the defendant and had confirmed that fact.

The safeguards recommended in *Smith* [2009] 1 Cr.App.R.36, namely that a police officer's initial reactions to viewing a CCTV, what it was about the image that triggered the recognition, failure to pick out anybody, any doubts, were set out and available for scrutiny, do not have any application to a case where a police officer has been shown CCTV footage, having been told that it was thought the offender could be seen on the recording, where he was thus expecting to see the offender and where he identified the offender as the defendant, although when giving evidence, he was unable to say what it was about the image which led him to conclude that it was the defendant: *Tucker* [2009] Crim.L.R. 441, CA.

Evidence of reputation for the purpose of proving the identity of a person is a common law exception to the rule against hearsay and is preserved by s.118 (1) ante so where a witness claimed to recognise an assailant as someone whom he saw a couple of times a day over the course of a week before the incident, that he spoke in a Liverpool accent and was nicknamed "Scouse" and belonged to a particular military unit, the fact that he only learnt the assailant's name as a result of being told it subsequent to the assault did not make that evidence hearsay: *Phillips*, 174 J.P.169.

10–91 When identity is in issue the court will follow the *Turnbull* guidelines: *Turnbull* [1977] Q.B. 244; (1976) 63 Cr.App.R. 132.

1. whenever the case against an accused depends wholly or substantially on the accuracy of one or more identifications of the accused which the defence alleges to be mistaken, there is a special need for caution before convicting the accused on those identifications;
2. the circumstances in which the identification by each witness came to be made

should be examined closely. How long did the witness have the accused under observation? At what distance? In what light? Was the observation impeded in any way, for example, by passing traffic or a press of people? Had the witness ever seen the accused before? How often? If only occasionally, had he any special reason to remember? How long elapsed between the original observation and the subsequent identification to the police? Was there any material discrepancy between the description of the accused given to the police by the witness when first seen by him and the actual appearance of the defendant?

3. any special weaknesses in the identification evidence should be considered.
4. If the quality of the identification evidence is poor and there is no supporting evidence there will be no case for the defendant to answer.

The guidelines are for all cases where identification is in dispute and are not limited to "fleeting glance" cases: *B.* [2004] EWCA Crim 1481. Even where an eyewitness recognises an accused the court should remind itself of the *Turnbull* direction: *Capron* [2006] UKPC 34. In that case the Privy Council deprecated the use of the phrase "exceptional circumstances" to describe the circumstances where the main issue was witness credibility. To determine whether a *Turnbull* direction is necessary each case must turn on its own merits. In *Giga* [2007] Crim.L.R. 571 (CA (Crim Div)) it was stated that there is no need for the court to consider *Turnbull* where, in a recognition case and witnesses are being questioned as to credibility, there is an entire sequence of events rather than a "fleeting glance" scenario or single observation; the first question is whether a witness is honest and if so, whether a mistake has been made.

Where the identification of a defendant's companion is unchallenged the court need not take into account the guidelines: *Bath* [1990] Crim.L.R. 716, CA.

The identification of a motor car is a different matter and need not be approached with special caution: *Hampton, Brown* (2004) 148 S.J.L.B. 973.

Clothing may also be the subject of identification: *Hickin* [1996] Crim.L.R. 584, CA.

The court has discretion to exclude evidence of identification at a confrontation: *Lamb* (1980) 71 Cr.App.R 198, CA. An identification by video (CCTV) recording has been said to be analogous to a street identification: *Jones (M.A.)* (1994) 158 J.P. 293. The use of unmasked images bearing little resemblance to the defendant in age and appearance, where a witness is unable to make an identification from images which masked differently in appearance, in video identification procedures is unlawful: *Marcus* [2004] EWCA Crim 3387. There are cases in which it is appropriate to admit facial mapping evidence even when Code D has been breached by failure to hold an identification parade: *Tobin (William Donald)* [2004] EWCA Crim 1081.

Recognition may be more reliable than identification of a stranger but even then mistakes may be made by close friends and relatives. **10–92**

All these matters relate to the quality of the identification evidence. Where the quality is poor and there is no supporting evidence, the court should find that there is no case to answer: *Fergus (Ivan)* (1994) 98 Cr.App.R. 313, CA. Identification by more than one witness is a factor influencing the quality of the evidence, *i.e.* one witness might support another: *Weeder* (1980) 71 Cr.App.R. 228, CA; *Tyler* (1993) 96 Cr.App.R. 332, CA.

In *Bentley* [1991] Crim.L.R. 620, CA. Lord Lane C.V.J. reminded the court of the expression "I could have sworn it was you" used by people who had thought that they had seen someone in the street only to discover that they were wrong. Care must be taken to ensure that identification by a name is from the witness's own knowledge. The court is entitled to take into account that police officers are trained in observation: *Ramsden* [1991] Crim.L.R. 295, CA; *Tyler, ante*; *Powell v. DPP* [1992] R.T.R. 270. Previous convictions introduced under the bad character provisions can be taken into account when considering whether the identification of a defendant is correct; they are there to assist rather than bolster a poor identification: *Blake* [2006] EWCA Crim 871.

Where a court uses its own eyes to compare CCTV images with a defendant in the dock, it should be aware of the risk of mistaken identification and of the need to exercise particular care: *Ali* [2009] Crim.L.R. 40, CA.

If the witness' credibility is in issue as well as the accuracy of the identification evidence the court should first consider the issue of credibility and then, if satisfied as to credibility, should then consider accuracy in line with the *Turnbull* guidelines: *Campbell* [2010] UKPC 26.

Fingerprints etc.

10–93 A person may be identified by fingerprints alone *Castleton* 3 Cr.App.R. 74, CCA. The prosecution must show that the fingerprints taken from the scene of the crime match those on the fingerprint form, and also identify the fingerprints on the form. Strict proof is required: *Chappell v. DPP* (1989) 89 Cr.App.R. 82, DC. Guidance was given in *Buckley* (1999) 163 J.P. 561. Rose L.J. stated that whether fingerprint evidence was admissible as a matter of law tending to prove guilt would depend on: (1) the experience and expertise of the witness; (2) the number of similar ridge characteristics (if there were fewer than eight admission would be unlikely); (3) whether there are dissimilar characteristics; (4) size of print relied on; and (5) quality and clarity of print.

Strict proof is also required for palm and ear prints. The weight to be attached to such evidence is a matter for the court: *Dallagher* [2003] 1 Cr.App.R. 12. Ear-print comparison is capable of providing information that could identify a person where small anatomical features such as notches, nodules or creases in the ear structure can be identified and matched. It is still possible to make a match from the main cartilaginous folds but there is less confidence because of the ear's flexibility: *Kempster* [2008] 2 Cr.App.R. 19.

For voice identification, see *O'Doherty* [2002] Crim.L.R. 761. The key to admissibility of evidence from a lay listener in voice recognition cases is the degree of familiarity of the witness with the suspect's voice and the amount of time spent in contact with the defendant is very relevant to the issue of familiarity: *Flynn and anr.* [2008] 2 Cr.App.R. 20. There is a danger of misidentification, more so where any recording is poor. When the process of obtaining such evidence is embarked upon by police officers it is vital that the process as well as the date and time spent by the police officer compiling a transcript is properly recorded. Before attempting the exercise a police officer should not be supplied with a copy of the transcript bearing another officer's annotations of whom he believed to be speaking. It is highly desirable that such an exercise should be carried out by someone other than the officer investigating the offence.

Whilst in appropriate circumstances an expert's opinion on footwear can go further than merely stating that the mark could or could not have been made by the shoe, the opinion must not be based upon a mathematical formula and the expert must make clear that the opinion is subjective and is based on the expert's experience; using the word "scientific" is wrong as it could give an impression of a degree of precision and objectivity that is not present: *T* [2011] 1 Cr.App.R. 9.

DNA profiles

10–94 Where the perpetrator of a crime leaves a stain of blood or semen at the scene it may prove possible to extract sufficient sections of DNA to enable a comparison to be drawn with the same sections extracted for a sample of blood taken from the defendant. A DNA profile is not unique; it establishes probabilities. Specific guidance is found in *Doheny* [1997] 1 Cr.App.R. 369. There must be continuity of evidence: *Philips*, unreported, August 25, 2004; *R. (S.) v. Chief Constable of South Yorkshire* [2004] 1 W.L.R. 2194.

If the quantity of DNA that can be analysed is above the stochastic threshold low template DNA can be used to obtain profiles capable of reliable interpretation: *Reed* [2010] 1 Cr.App.R. 23.

Moreover, in some circumstances reliable results may be obtained from amounts below the stochastic threshold: *Broughton* [2010] EWCA Crim 549; *C* [2010] EWCA Crim 2578.

It is not proper for an advocate to make an application under s.78 to exclude an expert's evidence regarding DNA without a statement from a duly qualified expert regarding the shortcomings of the Crown's expert and the reasons for asserting that those shortcomings fundamentally undermined the reliability of the DNA evidence; prior to the production of such a statement the defence expert should first have set out his reasoning in a witness statement and the court, under r.33.6 of the *Criminal Procedure Rules* 2011, should have ordered the prosecution and defence experts to provide a reasoned statement on the matters on which they agree and disagree: *C* [2010] EWCA Crim 2578.

B. OPINION

(1) General

The general rule is that opinion evidence is inadmissible but exceptions include reputation, non-expert opinion and expert opinion. **10–95**

Evidence of reputation

Evidence of reputation is admissible in criminal proceedings to prove pedigree or the existence of a marriage, the existence of public or general rights or the identity of a person or thing: *Criminal Justice Act* 2003, s.118(1) 3. Evidence of reputation may also be admissible to prove good or bad character: *Criminal Justice Act* 2003, s.118(1) 2. Section 118 is reproduced at § 10–58, above. **10–96**

(3) Non-expert opinion

Evidence of the opinion of a witness who is not an expert may be admissible if made as a way of conveying relevant facts perceived by the witness: *Johnson* [1994] Crim LR 376; *Tagg* [2001] EWCA Crim 1230. For example, a witness may give evidence of his opinion of the age of a person: *Cox* [1898] 1 Q.B. 179 (a "young woman"), *Wallworth v. Balmer* [1966] 1 W.L.R. 16 ("a child of about five"); that defendant was drunk, *Davies*, 46 Cr.App.R. 292; or that a voice on a tape recording was that of a man that the witness had spoken to during a car journey, *Robb* (1991) 93 Cr.App.R. 161. **10–97**

(4) Expert opinion

Expert opinion is admissible in criminal proceedings provided both that it is relevant and that it provides information that is likely to be outside the experience and knowledge of the court; if the court can form its own conclusions on the facts without expert assistance, however, then expert evidence is unnecessary: *Turner* [1975] Q.B.834. In *Turner*, psychiatric evidence of the likelihood of someone reacting as the defendant had done was rejected. **10–98**

It is for the court to determine a witness's competence to give expert evidence having regard to qualifications, study and experience (in some fields, such as handwriting and facial mapping, a witness may be competent to give expert evidence in the absence of qualifications and study provided that the witness has obtained the requisite expertise via practical experience): *Silverlock* [1894] 2 Q.B. 766; *Stockwell* (1993) 97 Cr.App.R. 260.

Lack of independence on the part of an expert witness (*e.g.* the fact that an expert witness called by the prosecution was employed by the victim of the offence with which the defendant was charged) does not render the witness' evidence inadmissible but is a factor that the court should take into account when assessing the weight of the witness' evidence: *Stubbs* [2006] EWCA Crim 2312; *Leo Sawrij v. North Cumbria Magistrates' Court* [2010] 1 Cr.App.R. 304.

In general, the reliability of a new technique relied upon by an expert goes to the weight of the evidence rather than to its admissibility, but there may be circumstances in which the witness' techniques are "... insufficiently recognised within his profession for him to be properly qualified to give expert evidence ..." or in which the evidence is "... so lacking in "prima facie reliability" that it has no probative force or its probative force is too slight to influence a decision ..." and the court may find it necessary to exclude unreliable expert evidence tendered by the Crown in the exercise of its exclusionary discretion under s.78 *Police and Criminal Evidence Act* 1984: *Luttrell* [2004] 2 Cr.App.R. 31 at paras. 35-36. When attempting to distinguish reliable expert evidence from unreliable expert evidence, the court should consider factors such as whether an expert assumes the role of an advocate, whether he steps outside his area of expertise, whether he is able to point to a recognised, peer-reviewed, source for his opinion and whether his clinical experience is up-to-date and equal to that of others whose opinions he seeks to contradict: *Henderson, Butler, Oyediran* [2010] 2 Cr.App.R. 24.

Expert opinion should not be based on a mathematical formula if the field of expertise (*e.g.* examination of footwear marks) is one in relation to which the available data does not justify this and such expert evidence should not be described as "scientific": *T* [2011] 1 Cr.App.R. 9. Where photographic comparison experts give evidence of similarities or dissimilarities between a questioned photograph and a known person, an expert may express a conclusion as to the significance of his findings and can do so by the use of conventional expressions arranged in a hierarchy e.g. "lends support/lends powerful support" but not numbers lest they give the impression of an established, measurable scale: *Atkins* (2009) 173 J.P. 529.

Rule 33.7 of the *Criminal Procedure Rules* 2011 (see Appendix G–197) empowers the court to direct that co-defendants who wish to adduce expert evidence in relation to an issue do so via a single joint expert.

The fact that an expert witness may have been discredited (having been convicted of perjury in relation to qualifications) goes to the weight of the evidence, not its admissibility: *Bates v. Chief Constable of Avon and Somerset Police and Bristol Magistrates' Court* (2009) 173 JP 313 and see, also, *Noye* [2011] EWCA Crim 650. In *R. (on the application of Doughty) v. Ely Magistrates' Court* [2008] EWHC 522 (Admin) where it was ruled that a former transport police officer did not have sufficient knowledge and expertise in a speeding trial to be an expert it was said that in order to determine whether a witness was an "expert" a court cannot rely on matters that go to the weight of the witness's evidence *i.e.* whether he was a good witness or whether his report was accurate. It has to be determined by reference to the specific issues to which the evidence relates and on the basis of the specific information available as to the witness's knowledge and expertise. In this case the fact that the witness, a retired police officer had not operated the speeding device since 1999 did not negative his expertise nor did the fact that he had not attended training courses as this was because they were not available to him being only open to law enforcement agencies.

An expert is now permitted to give his opinion on what has been called the "ultimate issue" that is the very issue to be determined by the court, for example on whether the defendant is suffering from diminished responsibility. The ultimate issue is, however, for the tribunal of fact to decide and the court is not bound to accept the expert's opinion: *Stockwell* (1993) 97 Cr.App.R. 260, CA, where the facial mapping expert was allowed to say that he thought photographs strongly supported the view that the defendant was the robber. Special caution is required both in fields where scientific knowledge may be incomplete and where expert opinion evidence is not just relied upon as additional material to support a prosecution but is fundamental to it: *Holdsworth* [2008] EWCA Crim 971. In some circumstances a prosecution should not proceed if the case depends on a serious disagreement between reputable experts but normally it will be for the court to evaluate the expert evidence: *Cannings* [2004] 2 Cr.App.R. 63; *Kai-Whitewind* [2005] 2 Cr.App.R. 31.

When faced with conflicting expert evidence the court can make use of rule 33.6 of the *Criminal Procedure Rules* 2011 to direct pre-hearing discussion between the experts (See Appendix G–196): *Henderson* [2010] 2 Cr.App.R. 24.

In *Jeffries* [1997] Crim.L.R. 819, it was held that a police officer was able to give evidence as to the values and prices of drugs in order that the jury may interpret lists found at the defendant's premises but the officer could not express an opinion that the lists related to the sale of drugs because that would amount to a statement that the defendant was guilty of the offence charged.

Lip reading evidence from a video is a species of real evidence and is admissible; in each case it depends on factors such as the quality of the video and the skill of the interpreting witness and caution must be exercised because errors can occur: *Luttrell* [2004] 2 Cr.App.R. 31.

Expert opinion must be based on admissible evidence of the primary facts, not upon inadmissible hearsay: *Jackson* [1996] 2 Cr.App.R. 420. The primary facts may be proved by the expert, if the expert has knowledge of them, by the evidence of another witness (as in *Mason*, 7 Cr.App.R. 67), by admissible hearsay evidence (see, for example, s.127 of the *Criminal Justice Act* 2003 at § 10–102, below) or by evidence produced by machines (as in *Golizadeh* [1995] Crim LR 232). Under a rule preserved by s.118(1) 8 of the *Criminal Justice Act* 2003 (which was reproduced at § 10–58, above), expert witnesses may refer not only to their own research, tests and experiments but also to works of authority, learned articles, research papers and other similar materials written by others and forming part of the general body of knowledge falling within their field of expertise: *Davie v. Magistrates of Edinburgh*, 1953 S.C. 34; *Seyfang v. J.D. Searle & Co* [1973] Q.B. 148;*H. v. Schering Chemicals Ltd* [1983] 1 W.L.R. 143; *Abadom*, 76 Cr.App.Rep 48 . In forming their opinions experts may also rely upon unpublished papers and upon their expertise: *Weller* [2010] EWCA Crim 1085. This rule does not, however, apply to non-expert witnesses. In *Edwards* [2001] All E.R. (D) 271 the question was whether ecstasy tablets found in the defendant's possession were for personal consumption or supply. The prosecution and defence sought to call persons neither of whom had formal medical or toxicological training to give evidence based on their experience rather than on statistical surveys or reports as to the personal consumption rates of ecstasy tablet users. It was held that the trial judge had properly excluded their evidence as inadmissible hearsay. 10–99

Part II

Rule 33.3 of the*Criminal Procedure Rules* 2011 (see Appendix G–193) requires an expert witness to set out in his expert's report:

— details of his qualifications, experience and accreditation;
— details of the literature or other information that the expert relied on;
— set out the substance of all facts given to the expert which are material to the expert's opinion or on which that opinion is based
— indicate which of the facts stated in the report are within the expert's knowledge;
— indicate who carried out examinations, measurements, tests or experiments which the expert used for the report, give the qualifications, experience and accreditation of such persons, indicate whether the expert supervised them and summarise the findings on which the expert relies
— if there is a range of opinion on the matters dealt with in the report, summarise the range of opinion and give reasons for the expert's opinion;
— if the expert cannot give an unqualified opinion, state the qualification;
— contain a summary of the expert's conclusions;
— contain a statement that the expert understands his duty to the court, has complied with it
— and will continue to do so; and
— contain a declaration of truth.

Rule 33.4 (see Appendix G–194) lays down requirements concerning the service of expert evidence; non-compliance with these service requirements means that the expert evidence admissible will not be admissible unless either the parties all agree to its admission or the court gives permission for it to be admitted (the court is empowered to vary time limits by rule 33.9, which is reproduced at G–198a). Rule 33.5 (see Appendix G–195) provides that where a party serves an expert's report either on another party or on the court, the party who served the report must inform the expert of this at once.

Expert medical evidence as to the weight to be attached to a witness's evidence is admissible even where no physical examination of the witness has been carried out if it demonstrates some form of abnormality relevant to the reliability of a defendant's confession or evidence: *Pinfold* [2004] 2 Cr.App.R. 5. The ability of a witness to remember facts is normally within the experience of the court. It would be extremely rare for an expert to have to give evidence on possible unreliability: *S* [2007] 2 All E.R. 974. In that case an expert was said to be able to give evidence of childhood amnesia only where it was relevant and admissible and in a case where a witness described an incident of an early event in an unrealistic amount of detail.

10–100 In the shaken baby syndrome co-joined cases: *Harris (Lorraine)* [2005] EWCA Crim 1980; [2006] 1 Cr.App.R. 5 the Court of Appeal refused to give fresh guidance on expert evidence. It referred to the cases of *Bonython* [1984] 38 S.A.S.R. 45 and *Clarke* [1985] 2 Cr.App.R. 425 and went on to say that developments in scientific thinking should not be kept from the court simply because they remain at the stage of hypothesis. Courts were to be reminded of the obligations of an expert witness summarised in *Ikarian Reefer* [1993] 2 Lloyds Rep. 68:

(1) expert evidence presented to the court should be and seen to be the independent product of the expert uninfluenced as to form or content by the exigencies of legislation;
(2) an expert witness should provide independent assistance to the court by way of objective unbiased opinion in relation to matters within his expertise . . . [he] should never assume the role of advocate;
(3) an expert witness should state the facts or assumptions on which his opinion is based. He should not omit to consider material facts which detract from his concluded opinion;
(4) an expert should make it clear when a particular question or issue falls outside his expertise;
(5) if an expert's opinion is not properly researched because he considers that insufficient data is available then this must be stated with an indication that the opinion is no more than a provisional one;
(6) if after exchange of reports, an expert witness changes his view on material matters, such change of view should be communicated to the other side without delay and when appropriate to the court.

Further guidance on specific factors to be included in an expert report was given in *Bowman* [2006] 2 Cr.App.R. 3:

(a) details of the expert's academic record and professional qualifications, range of experience and any limitations on expertise;
(b) the substance of the instructions received, questions upon which an opinion was sought, the materials provided and considered and the information or assumptions that were material to the opinions expressed;
(c) information about who carried out measurements and tests, the methodology, and whether they were supervised by the expert;
(d) where there was a range of opinion in the matters dealt with in the report, a summary of the range of opinion and the reasons for the opinion given. In that connection any material facts or matters that detracted from the expert's opinion and any points that should fairly be made against any opinions expressed should be set out;
(e) relevant extracts of literature or other material that might assist the court;
(f) a statement that the expert had complied with his duty to the court to provide independent assistance by way of objective unbiased opinion, and an acknowledgement that the expert would inform all parties and where appropriate the court if his opinion changed on any material issue;
(g) the same guidelines should be followed in any supplemental report.

Rule 33.2 of the*Criminal Procedure Rules* 2011 (see Appendix G–192, below) makes provision concerning the duties of expert witnesses in criminal proceedings and makes clear that the duty of an expert witness to give objective unbiased opinion on matters within his expertise overrides the expert's obligations to the person instructing or paying him and includes an obligation to inform the parties and the court if his opinion changes from that in a report that has been served in evidence or given in a statement.

It is the duty of an expert instructed by the prosecution to act in the interests of justice: *Ward* (1993) 96 Cr.App.R. 1, CA. If a prosecution expert has carried out a test which casts doubt on his opinion, or if such a test has been carried out in his laboratory and is known to him, the expert is under a duty to disclose this to the prosecutor instructing him, who in turn has a duty to disclose it to the defence.

Even where, as a matter of scientific certainty, it is not possible to rule out a proposition consistent with innocence a court may still convict where it is sure, on the whole of the evidence, of guilt: *Gian and Mohd-Yusoff v. Crown Prosecution Service, ante.*

Criminal Justice Act 1988, s.30

Expert reports

30.—(1) An expert report shall be admissible as evidence in criminal proceedings, whether or not the person making it attends to give oral evidence in those proceedings. **10–101**

(2) If it is proposed that the person making the report shall not give oral evidence, the report shall only be admissible with the leave of the court.

(3) For the purpose of determining whether to give leave the court shall have regard—

(a) to the contents of the report;

(b) to the reasons why it is proposed that the person making the report shall not give oral evidence;

(c) to any risk, having regard in particular to whether it is likely to be possible to controvert statements in the report if the person making it does not attend to give oral evidence in the proceedings, that its admission or exclusion will result in unfairness to the accused or, if there is more than one, to any of them; and

(d) to any other circumstances that appear to the court to be relevant.

(4) An expert report, when admitted, shall be evidence of any fact or opinion of which the person making it could have given oral evidence.

(4A) Where the proceedings mentioned in subsection (1) above are proceedings before a magistrates' court inquiring into an offence as examining justices this section shall have effect with the omission of—

(a) in subsection (1) the words "whether or not the person making it attends to give oral evidence in those proceedings", and

(b) subsections (2) to (4).

(5) In this section "expert report" means a written report by a person dealing wholly or mainly with matters on which he is (or would if living be) qualified to give expert evidence.

This section allows for the receipt of reports whether or not the expert gives oral evidence though, in the latter case, the leave of the court is required.

C. EXPERT EVIDENCE / OPINION PREPARATORY WORK

Criminal Justice Act 2003, s.127

Expert evidence: preparatory work

127.—(1) This section applies if— **10–102**

(a) a statement has been prepared for the purposes of criminal proceedings,

(b) the person who prepared the statement had or may reasonably be supposed to have had personal knowledge of the matters stated,

(c) notice is given under the appropriate rules that another person (the expert) will in evidence given in the proceedings orally or under section 9 of the *Criminal Justice Act* 1967 (c. 80) base an opinion or inference on the statement, and

(d) the notice gives the name of the person who prepared the statement and the nature of the matters stated.

(2) In evidence given in the proceedings the expert may base an opinion or inference on the statement.

(3) If evidence based on the statement is given under subsection (2) the statement is to be treated as evidence of what it states.

(4) This section does not apply if the court, on an application by a party to the proceedings, orders that it is not in the interests of justice that it should apply.

(5) The matters to be considered by the court in deciding whether to make an order under subsection (4) include—

(a) the expense of calling as a witness the person who prepared the statement;

(b) whether relevant evidence could be given by that person which could not be given by the expert;

(c) whether that person can reasonably be expected to remember the matters stated well enough to give oral evidence of them.

(6) Subsections (1) to (5) apply to a statement prepared for the purposes of a criminal investigation as they apply to a statement prepared for the purposes of criminal proceedings, and in such a case references to the proceedings are to criminal proceedings arising from the investigation.

(7) Criminal Procedure Rules made by virtue of—

(a) section 81 of the Police and *Criminal Evidence Act* 1984 (advance notice of expert evidence in Crown Court), or

(b) section 20(3) of the*Criminal Procedure and Investigations Act* 1996 (c. 25) (advance notice of expert evidence in magistrates' courts).

[This section is printed as amended by the *Courts Act 2003 (Consequential Amendments) Order* 2004.]

This section creates a hearsay exception which permits an expert witness to bases his opinion upon a statement prepared by a person who may reasonably be supposed to have personal knowledge of the matters stated provided that pre-trial notice requirements are complied with and subject to the possibility that the court, upon application by a party, may order that it is not in the interests of justice for the section to apply.

IX. CHARACTER

A. GOOD CHARACTER

10–103 A defendant may call evidence of his good character, *i.e.* his general reputation: *Rowton* (1865) Le. & Ca. 520. Such evidence is relevant to a defendant's credibility and to whether it is likely that he committed the offence with which he is charged. The calling of such evidence may have implications—see § 10–120, below.

Where a defendant is of good character the court should direct itself on its relevance to credibility where the defendant gives evidence or has made pre trial statements and should direct itself on its relevance to propensity whether or not he gave evidence or made pre trial statements: *Vye* 97 Cr.App.R. 134.

Where a defendant has previous convictions or has been shown to have committed offences of which he has never been convicted the court possesses discretion to treat the defendant as being of good character (*e.g.* if the convictions are old or are of no relevance to the offence with which the defendant is charged) but, equally, the court possesses discretion to modify the *Vye* direction or even not to give itself one or both limbs of the *Vye* direction: *Gray* [2004] 2 Cr.App.R. 30. The discretion also exists where the accused's convictions are spent: *Nye* (1982) 75 Cr.App.R. 247; *Morris* [2004] EWCA Crim 2907. A caution may, in appropriate circumstances, prevent a defendant from being considered as of good character, but, again, the matter is one that falls within the court's discretion: *Maillet* [2005] EWCA Crim 3159. Where, however, the defendant denies that he committed the offence in respect of which he admitted the caution, he will be entitled to a full good character direction if the court decides that he did not commit the offence: *Olu* [2010] EWCA Crim 2975. A defendant of good character is still entitled to the benefit of the *Vye* direction even though his co-defendant is of bad character: *Vye*.

Where there is evidence of bad character (in this case, previous tax enquiries where the charges were cheating the Revenue and false accounting) yet the defendant has no previous convictions, which would normally entitle him to a good character direction, then the court should remind itself that the defendant has no previous convictions but ultimately it is for the court to decide what counts with it more, the absence of previous convictions or the evidence of bad character; if the former then that should be taken into account in favour of the defendant, and, if the latter take it into account against him: *Doncaster* [2008] EWCA Crim.5.

B. BAD CHARACTER

The *Criminal Justice Act* 2003 makes statutory provision for the admission of evidence of bad character through gateways for both defendants and non-defendants although they are different in each case. The common law rules which formerly governed the admissibility of such evidence were abolished by s.99 of the 2003 Act: *Bradley* [2005] 1 Cr.App.R.24, which also made clear that the provisions apply after December 15, 2004. The bad character provisions of the 2003 Act are also applicable in the context of proceedings under s. 4A *Criminal Procedure (Insanity) Act* 1964: *Creed* [2011] EWCA Crim 144, although that Act applies only in the Crown Court. **10–104**

In the magistrates' court the judiciary are judges of both fact and law and will therefore have to decide initially whether the bad character evidence can be admitted and then what relevance and weight it has.

Part 35 of the *Criminal Procedure Rules* 2011, see G-207 to G-212, makes provision for the giving of notice, and objections thereto, where a party to criminal proceedings wishes to adduce evidence of the bad character either of a defendant or of a non-defendant. Whilst the rules do not make express provision concerning the consequences of a failure to give notice (r.35.6 does empower the court to vary the requirements of Pt 35), s.111(4) of the 2003 Act does empower the court the take such a failure into account when considering the exercise of its powers in relation to costs. Moreover, the Court of Appeal has held, in the context of a defence application to adduce evidence of the bad character of a co-defendant, that the court does possess discretion to exclude evidence of bad character in the context of such a failure, though their Lordships indicated that it would be rare for the court to do so if the evidence possessed substantial probative value: *Musone* [2007] 2 Cr.App.R. 29. The Court of Appeal has also recognised in the context of a defence failure to give such notice that since, under the Criminal Procedure Rules, there is discretion to allow bad character evidence to be adduced, despite notice not having been given, by permitting notice to be given orally or in a different form from that prescribed, and there is power to shorten time for it, it must be implicit in that power to shorten time that it can be shortened to any degree, and thus dispensed with: *Lawson* [2007] 1 Cr.App.R. 11.

In *Jarvis* [2008] EWCA Crim 488 it was said a court is not bound to admit evidence on a late application, in this case after the defendant's evidence in chief. Whilst there is no general discretion to refuse a co-accused leave to admit admissible evidence against another on the ground of prejudicial effect outweighing the probative value; and the discretion to exclude evidence under s.101(3) does not apply to evidence admitted under gateway (e) (which is considered at § 10–117, below), there is a wide discretion as to whether to allow an application to be made at a late stage. If the application would produce unfairness then the court has ample power to refuse the application and whether it would refuse would depend on the facts of the particular case. Where a co-defendant gives evidence of bad character of the defendant without prior notice and without any application to admit, the court, before deciding whether to exclude the evidence or not, is entitled to ask itself what decision it would have made had the application been made and whether it is relevant to that co-defendant's defence and has substantial probative value: *Ramirez* [2010] Crim.L.R. 235, CA.

In the context of case law concerning the consequences of failure to give notice of bad character evidence on the part of the prosecution, it has been recognised that two of the key considerations are whether there is a good explanation of the failure to give notice within the time limit and whether the opposing party has suffered any prejudice: *R. (Robinson) v. Sutton Coldfield Magistrates' Court* [2006] 2 Cr.App.R. 13. In the case of *Hassan* [2007] EWCA Crim 1287 although notice was late the matter of a previous conviction had been raised in interview and it was said that the defendant could plainly have been expected to know the position. Where the prosecution fails to comply with the notice requirements, applying orally, almost at the close of the prosecution case, the evidence is not to be allowed: *Urushadze* [2008] EWCA Crim 2498.

Where a defendant wishes to challenge evidence of his bad character that takes the form of a conviction or a caution, the defendant should give notice of the challenge under rule 35.3(4)(b) of the *Criminal Procedure Rules* 2011: *Olu* [2010] EWCA Crim 2975.

The Court of Appeal has indicated that it will not interfere with a ruling concerning the admissibility of evidence of bad character unless it "... is plainly wrong or discretion has been exercised unreasonably in the *Wednesbury* sense: *McKenzie* [2008] RTR 22 at para. 28. So far as the proof of previous convictions is concerned, see § 10–35, above.

Criminal Justice Act 2003, s.98

"Bad character"

10–105 **98.** References in this Chapter to evidence of a person's "bad character" are to evidence of, or of a disposition towards, misconduct on his part, other than evidence which—

(a) has to do with the alleged facts of the offence with which the defendant is charged, or

(b) is evidence of misconduct in connection with the investigation or prosecution of that offence.

10–106 Misconduct means the commission of an offence or other reprehensible behaviour: *Criminal Justice Act* 2003, s.112. It is a very wide definition. Reprehensible is defined in the Oxford dictionary as blameworthy, deserving of censure or rebuke. Shouting at a partner and becoming aggressive when failing to take medication for paranoid schizophrenia, in the context of a case of murdering a friend, was held not to be reprehensible behaviour: *Osbourne* [2007] EWCA Crim 481.

Evidence of bad character in the form of evidence of the commission of an offence will commonly take the form of evidence of a previous conviction, but evidence that the accused committed an offence of which he was never convicted, or indeed with which he was never charged, can also fall within the definition of bad character: *S* [2006] 2 Cr.App.R. 23 (evidence of a caution).

The s. 98 definition of bad character also encompasses evidence of a disposition towards misconduct

Section 98(a) and (b) remove certain forms of misconduct from the definition of bad character. Where evidence of misconduct does not amount to evidence of bad character its admissibility is not governed by the gateways created by ss.100 and 101 of the 2003 Act but, rather, is governed by the common law test of relevance subject, where the evidence is tendered by the prosecution, to the exercise of the court's exclusionary discretion under s.78 *Police and Criminal Evidence Act* 1984: *Weir* [2006] 1 Cr.App.R. 19; *Mullings* [2010] EWCA Crim 2820.

Section 98(a) removes evidence of misconduct from the definition of bad character where it "has to do with the alleged facts of the offence with which the defendant is charged". It seems that this will be the case where, "... there is some nexus in time between the offence with which the defendant is charged and the evidence of misconduct which the prosecution seek to adduce": *Tirnaveanu* [2007] EWCA Crim 1239 at para. 23. In *Mullings* at para. 32 the Court of Appeal indicated that:

> "One of the purposes of the bad character provisions in the *Criminal Justice Act* 2003 is to bring within their scope evidence of extraneous misconduct or disposition towards misconduct so as to subject it to the rigour of analysis for relevance and purpose under the

> s.101 gateways. The wider s.98(a) is construed, and the wider the embrace of evidence which 'has to do' with the facts of the alleged offence, the less effective the statutory purpose becomes. In our view, the narrower interpretation of s.98(a) is to be preferred. A close temporal connection between the event, evidence of which it is sought to adduce, and the "alleged facts of the offence" is required before it can be said that the event "has to do with" those alleged facts."

For example, in *Machado* (2006) 170 J.P 400, the judge wrongly held that the defendant could not give evidence that the complainant had offered to supply drugs on the basis that the evidence was inadmissible evidence of bad character because, since the offer was part of the very circumstances in which the alleged crime occurred, the evidence did not amount to evidence of bad character due to the operation of s.98(a). Equally, where the defendant is charged with driving while disqualified, evidence of his having been disqualified at the material time falls within the exclusion in s.98(a): *Director of Public Prosecutions v. Agyemang* (2009) 173 J.P. 487.

Where the accused is charged with several offences in the same proceedings, s.112(2) provides that the bad character provisions have effect as if each offence were charged in separate proceedings. This means that when a defendant is charged with a number of offences the court must approach the matter on the basis that, when considering offence one, offences two and three are charged in separate proceedings, etc. All evidence of the defendant's misconduct that does not have to do with the alleged facts of offence one will amount to evidence of bad character so far as offence one is concerned and, thus, unless evidence relating to other offences with which the accused is charged also has to do with the alleged facts of offence one (see, for example, *Watson* [2006] EWCA Crim 2308 in which a conviction based on the alleged facts of the offence with which the accused was charged did not amount to evidence of bad character in a retrial), the potential cross-admissibility of such evidence as evidence in relation to offence one will be governed by the gateways created by s.101 of the 2003 Act. Thus, for example, in *Chopra* [2007] 1 Cr.App.R. 16, where the accused was charged with three counts of indecent assault relating to three different complainants, the Court of Appeal held that the admissibility of each count as evidence in relation to the others was governed by the bad character provisions of the 2003 Act, the evidence being cross-admissible under s.101(1)(d), which is considered below. In *Freeman* [2009] 1 Cr.App.R.11, the Court of Appeal indicated that whether or not such evidence is capable of establishing a propensity to commit offences of the kind with which the defendant is charged on the part of the defendant, it may still be cross-admissible if, for example, in consequence of similarities between the evidence relating to each offence, it is capable of increasing the likelihood that the other allegations are true or if, for example, it provides strong evidence that the offences were all committed by the same person.

When the court is considering the cross-admissibility of evidence of bad character, or indeed, in general, when the court is considering the relevance or probative value of evidence of bad character for the purposes of the bad character provisions of the 2003 Act, s.109 requires the court to assume that the evidence of bad character is true unless it appears from material before the court that no court or jury could reasonably find it to be true. Thus, where the defendant alleges that several complainants have colluded in the allegations against him, the issue of collusion will not go to the admissibility of the evidence of bad character if no court or jury could reasonably find it to be true but if evidence of bad character is admitted in the context of allegations of collusion the court should ignore the bad character evidence unless they are sure that the complainants did not collude: *Lamb* [2007] EWCA Crim 1766.

Section 109 does not apply where the court was required to determine the admissibility of allegations in police records because the material did not amount to "evidence" that the witnesses did the alleged acts: *Braithwaite* [2010] 2 Cr.App.R. 18.

Section 98(b) removes evidence of misconduct in connection with the investigation or prosecution of the offence with which the defendant is charged from the definition of bad character.

In many instances especially where notice under the *Criminal Procedure Rules* has been waived the court will hear all the evidence before deciding to admit or exclude. If it decides to exclude then it must put all matters out of its mind.

Criminal Justice Act 2003, s.100

Non-defendant's bad character

10–107 **100.**—(1) In criminal proceedings evidence of the bad character of a person other than the defendant is admissible if and only if—

(a) it is important explanatory evidence,

(b) it has substantial probative value in relation to a matter which—

(i) is a matter in issue in the proceedings, and

(ii) is of substantial importance in the context of the case as a whole, or

(c) all parties to the proceedings agree to the evidence being admissible.

(2) For the purposes of subsection (1)(a) evidence is important explanatory evidence if—

(a) without it, the court or jury would find it impossible or difficult properly to understand other evidence in the case, and

(b) its value for understanding the case as a whole is substantial.

(3) In assessing the probative value of evidence for the purposes of subsection (1)(b) the court must have regard to the following factors (and to any others it considers relevant)—

(a) the nature and number of the events, or other things, to which the evidence relates;

(b) when those events or things are alleged to have happened or existed;

(c) where—

(i) the evidence is evidence of a person's misconduct, and

(ii) it is suggested that the evidence has probative value by reason of similarity between that misconduct and other alleged misconduct,

the nature and extent of the similarities and the dissimilarities between each of the alleged instances of misconduct;

(d) where—

(i) the evidence is evidence of a person's misconduct,

(ii) it is suggested that that person is also responsible for the misconduct charged, and

(iii) the identity of the person responsible for the misconduct charged is disputed,

the extent to which the evidence shows or tends to show that the same person was responsible each time.

(4) Except where subsection (1)(c) applies, evidence of the bad character of a person other than the defendant must not be given without leave of the court.

10–108 Section 100 creates three gateways under which evidence of a non-defendant's bad character may be admissible, namely:

— where it is important explanatory evidence

— where it has substantial probative value in relation to a matter in issue in the proceedings which is of substantial importance in the context of the case as a whole or

— by agreement between all the parties.

Other than where the evidence is admitted by agreement, the leave of the court is required, though it seems that this leave requirement does not give the court power to exclude evidence of bad character which is admissible under section 100 but, rather, that its effect is that evidence of a witness' bad character cannot be adduced under s.100 by any means, including via cross-examination, unless leave is first obtained: *Braithwaite* [2010] 2 Cr.App.R. 18.

Evidence of bad character is important explanatory evidence for the purposes of s.100(1)(a) if the court would find it impossible or difficult properly to understand other evidence in the case without it and it has substantial value for understanding the case as a whole. For example, it seems that evidence of a witness' bad character may amount to important explanatory evidence if it is capable of exposing the witness' motive: *Miller* [2010] 2 Cr.App.R.19.

Section 100(3)(a)-(b) provide that when the court is assessing the probative value of evidence for the purposes of s.100(1)(b) the court should always consider, as well as any other relevant factors, both the nature and number of the events/things to which the evidence relates and when the events/things allegedly happened or existed. Guidance as to the approach that the court should take in circumstances in which a party wishes to adduce evidence of a witness' convictions under s.100(1)(b) for the purpose of discrediting the witness was provided by the Court of Appeal in *Brewster* [2010] 2 Cr.App.R.20 at para. 23.

> "The first question for the trial judge under s.100(1)(b) is whether creditworthiness is a matter in issue which is of substantial importance in the context of the case as a whole. This is a significant hurdle. Just because a witness has convictions does not mean that the opposing party is entitled to attack the witness' credibility. If it is shown that creditworthiness is an issue of substantial importance, the second question is whether the bad character relied upon is of substantial probative value in relation to that issue. Whether convictions have persuasive value on the issue of creditworthiness will, it seems to us, depend principally on the nature, number and age, of the convictions. However, we do not consider that the conviction must, in order to qualify for admission in evidence, demonstrate any tendency towards dishonesty or untruthfulness. The question is whether a fair-minded tribunal would regard them as affecting the worth of the witness' evidence."

Their Lordships in Brewster, at para. 21, agreed with the commentary of Professor Spencer from the second edition of his work '*Evidence and Bad Character*' published in 2009:

> "... the purpose of s.100 was to remove from the criminal trial the right to introduce by cross-examination old or irrelevant or trivial behaviour in an attempt unfairly to diminish in the eyes of the tribunal of fact the standing of the witness, or to permit unsubstantiated attacks on credit."

Evidence of bad character may also be adduced under s.100(1)(b) for purposes other than that of discrediting a witness. For example, in *S* [2006] 2 Cr.App. R. 31 it was relevant as evidence of the complainant's propensity to act dishonestly in circumstances in which the defendant, charged with indecent assault, claimed that the complainant had agreed in sexual activity for an agreed payment and had then threatened to accuse the defendant of rape if he did not give her more money and had tried to take his gold chain.

Section 100(3)(c) provides that where it is suggested that evidence of a person's misconduct has probative value by reason of similarity between it and other misconduct, an additional factor that the court should consider when assessing the probative value of the evidence of bad character for the purposes of s.101(1)(b) is the nature and extent of the similarities and dissimilarities between the alleged instances of misconduct.

Section 100(3)(d) provides that where it is suggested that the person is also responsible for the misconduct with which the defendant is charged and the identity of the person responsible for that misconduct is in dispute, an additional factor that the court should consider when assessing the probative value of the evidence of bad character for the purposes of s.101(1)(b) is the extent to which the evidence tends to show that the same person was responsible each time.

Section 112(1) provides that "important matter" means a matter of substantial importance in the context of the case as a whole.

The word "substantial" in the context of s.100 means that the evidence concerned **10–109** has something more than trivial probative value but not necessarily conclusive probative value: *R. v. S* [2009] EWCA Crim 2457.

Police crime reports relating to unsubstantiated allegations made against prosecution witnesses are of insufficient probative value to be admissible as evidence of the witnesses' bad character: *Braithwaite* [2010] EWCA Crim 1082.

Cross-examination of a witness with a view to eliciting evidence as to his bad character should only be permitted in limited circumstances where the cross-examining party is not in a position, or would not be permitted, to prove the matter in the event of a denial by the witness: *Miller* [2010] 2. Cr.App.R. 9. The ambit of permissible cross examination is determined by the ambit of the evidence that would be permitted.

Defendant's bad character

Criminal Justice Act 2003, ss.101–106

Defendant's bad character

10–110 **101.**—(1) In criminal proceedings evidence of the defendant's bad character is admissible if, but only if—

(a) all parties to the proceedings agree to the evidence being admissible,

(b) the evidence is adduced by the defendant himself or is given in answer to a question asked by him in cross-examination and intended to elicit it,

(c) it is important explanatory evidence,

(d) it is relevant to an important matter in issue between the defendant and the prosecution,

(e) it has substantial probative value in relation to an important matter in issue between the defendant and a co-defendant,

(f) it is evidence to correct a false impression given by the defendant, or

(g) the defendant has made an attack on another person's character.

(2) Sections 102 to 106 contain provision supplementing subsection (1).

(3) The court must not admit evidence under subsection (1)(d) or (g) if, on an application by the defendant to exclude it, it appears to the court that the admission of the evidence wouldhave such an adverse effect on the fairness of the proceedings that the court ought not to admit it.

(4) On an application to exclude evidence under subsection (3) the court must have regard, in particular, to the length of time between the matters to which that evidence relates and the matters which form the subject of the offence charged.

Section 101 creates seven gateways under which evidence the defendant's bad character may be admissible, namely:

— where all parties agree to its admission;
— where the evidence is adduced by the defendant, including via a question asked during cross-examination which was intended to elicit it;
— where the evidence is important explanatory evidence;
— where the evidence is relevant to an important matter in issue between the defendant and the prosecution;
— where the evidence has substantial probative value in relation to an important matter in issue between the defendant and a co-defendant;
— where the evidence is evidence to correct a false impression that the defendant has given; or
— where the defendant has attacked another person's character.

When evidence of the accused's bad character is admitted under any of the gateways created by s.101 of the 2003 Act, the evidence may be used for any purpose for which it is relevant as s.101 only deals with the admissibility of evidence of the accused's bad character, not with the relevance or weight of such evidence if it is admitted: *Edwards and Rowlands* [2006] 2 Cr.App.R. 4.

Once evidence of the defendant's bad character has been admitted through one of the gateways created by s.101 of the 2003 Act it is then up to the court to attach significance to it in any respect to which it is relevant: *Campbell* [2007] 2 Cr.App.R. 28. The degree of significance to be attached to previous convictions is likely to depend upon such variables as their number, their similarity to the offence charged and how recently they were incurred, and the nature of the defence. In considering the inference to be drawn from bad character the distinction between propensity to offend and credibility is said to be unrealistic. If a court learns that a defendant has shown a propensity to commit criminal acts it may well conclude that it is more likely that he is guilty and that he is less likely to be telling the truth when he says that he is not. A propensity for untruthfulness will not of itself go far towards the establishing of a criminal offence. A defendant who has committed a criminal offence may well be prepared to lie about it, even if he has not shown a propensity for lying whereas a defendant who has not committed the offence charged will be likely to tell the truth, even if he has shown a propensity for telling lies. Fundamentally, the court should not attach too much weight to evidence of the defendant's bad character and should not convict the defendant merely in consequence of his bad character.

As was seen at § 10–35, above, the effect of s.74(3) *Police and Criminal Evidence Act* 1984 is that where evidence of the defendant's previous conviction is admitted, if the accused merely denies that he committed the offence of which he was previously convicted this does not require the prosecution to adduce evidence in rebuttal and that the defendant will need to provide a detailed defence statement identifying the case he will advance to discharge the evidential burden that s.74(3) imposes upon him: *C* [2011] 1 Cr.App.R. 17.

Where evidence of the accused's bad character that does not take the form of a previous conviction is admitted, the court should only consider the significance of the evidence of bad character if sure that the evidence is true: *Lowe* [2007] EWCA Crim 3047. Before admitting evidence of bad character that does not take the form of a previous conviction, however, the court should remember that in the absence of a conviction, proof of alleged bad character required the court to try satellite issues which make the trial longer and more expensive, complicate the issues and distract the attention of the court from the important issues:*McKenzie* [2008] RTR 22. If allegations of misconduct are few in number they may fail to show propensity even if true but the greater the number of allegations, the greater the risk of the trial's losing its focus. If the allegations of prior misconduct have not given rise to criminal investigation then the evidence is likely to be stale and incomplete. The defendant may also be prejudiced for lapse of time and inability to pinpoint details to challenge the evidence. Any applications must be approached with caution.

Where the defendant committed, or allegedly committed, the offence with which he is charged when he was aged 21 or over, the effect of s.108(2) of the 2003 Act is that evidence of convictions for offences he committed when he was under the age of 14 is only admissible either if both offences are triable only on indictment or if the interests of justice require the admission of the evidence.

So far as the admission of evidence of the defendant's bad character by agreement under s.101(1)(a) is concerned, the Court of Appeal in *J* [2010] 2 Cr.App.R. 2 at para. 21 indicated that,

> "it is … essential, where hearsay or bad character evidence will be put before the jury … that the court is informed at the outset of the trial what has been agreed and how the advocates propose that the agreed evidence is to be placed before the jury. If an agreement is made during the trial, then the judge should be told immediately after the agreement. This is in the interests of good trial management …

Although evidence can be admitted by agreement of the parties, disclosure of bad character evidence contained in social services files through the hearsay provisions should only be introduced in evidence with the leave of the court because they are generally subject to public interest immunity: *J* (see above).

Where the defendant wishes to adduce evidence of his own bad character under s.101(1)(b), the court cannot refuse such an application: *Edwards and Rowlands* [2006] 2 Cr.App.R. 4. Where the defendant does adduce evidence of his own bad character under section 101(1)(b), the evidence may be used for any purpose for which it is relevant; indeed, as was indicated above, this is true of all the s.101 gateways: *Edwards and Rowlands*

Whilst the Court of Appeal has recognised on a number of occasions that it is arguable that the court's exclusionary discretion under s.78 *Police and Criminal Evidence Act* 1984 should not be applicable where evidence of the defendant's bad character is admissible for the prosecution under a s.101 gateway (on the basis that Parliament has expressly made two of the gateways subject to the s.101(3) fairness test which is virtually identical to the s.78 test) in practice it seems that the s.78 discretion is available in such circumstances (see, for example: *Highton* [2006] 1 Cr.App.R.7; *Weir* [2006] 1 Cr.App.R. 19; *Tirnaveanu* [2007] 2 Cr.App. R. 23).

10–111 A distinction must be drawn between admissibility of bad character which depends on getting through one of the gateways and the use to which it is put once admitted. The use to which it can be put depends on its relevance rather than upon the gateway through which it is admitted: *Highton*; [2005] 1 W.L.R. 3472. Here evidence had been admitted as a result of an attack on another person's character and was used to show the propensity to commit offences of the kind with which the defendant was charged. A protection would be found in s.101(3) and in addition s.78 of the *Police and Criminal Evidence Act* 1984.

Important explanatory evidence

10–112 **102.** For the purposes of section 101(1)(c) evidence is important explanatory evidence if—

(a) without it, the court or jury would find it impossible or difficult properly to understand other evidence in the case, and

(b) its value for understanding the case as a whole is substantial.

10–113 Evidence of bad character is important explanatory evidence for the purposes of s.101(1)(c) if the court would find it impossible or difficult properly to understand other evidence in the case without it and it has substantial value for understanding the case as a whole. For example, where the defendant was charged with the murder of his ex-wife, the judge admitted evidence of his aggressive and threatening behaviour towards both her and towards men with whom she had formed relationships under s.101(1)(c) and the Court of Appeal upheld the judge's decision: *Barron* [2010] EWCA Crim 2950.

The Court of Appeal has indicated that evidence of propensity should not be permitted to "slide in" under s.101(1)(c) rather than having to satisfy the more stringent requirements imposed by s.101(3) and s.103(3), which are considered below: *Davis* [2009] 2 Cr.App.R. 17. In this murder trial the defendant relied on the defence of provocation; he had admitted killing his partner after she had said she had had an affair and was leaving him and taking his son. Evidence from a former girlfriend of their relationship twenty years previously and the fact that he was jealous, controlling, had accused her of having an affair and threatened to kill her was admitted as important explanatory evidence. The judge, in summing up, however, had referred to the evidence as evidence of propensity for jealousy and aggression. The Court of Appeal found that the jury, who had received evidence about the current relationship, would not have found it impossible or difficult to properly understand other evidence without hearing from that former girlfriend.

There is a potential overlap between s.101(1)(c) and s.98(a), which was considered at § 10–106, above. The Court of Appeal has agreed with Professor Spencer (see Spencer "*Evidence of Bad Characte*r" 2009) however, that whether evidence of the accused's misconduct is admitted as important explanatory evidence under s.101(1)(c) or is admitted as evidence which has to do with the alleged facts of the offence with which the accused is charged, due to the operation of s.98(a), is a matter of which is of no significance: *Tirnaveanu* [2007] 2 Cr.App.R. 23.

Matter in issue between the defendant and the prosecution

10–114 **103.**—(1) For the purposes of section 101(1)(d) the matters in issue between the defendant and the prosecution include—

(a) the question whether the defendant has a propensity to commit offences of the kind with which he is charged, except where his having such a propensity makes it no more likely that he is guilty of the offence;

(b) the question whether the defendant has a propensity to be untruthful, except where it is not suggested that the defendant's case is untruthful in any respect.

(2) Where subsection (1)(a) applies, a defendant's propensity to commit offences of the

kind with which he is charged may (without prejudice to any other way of doing so) be established by evidence that he has been convicted of—

(a) an offence of the same description as the one with which he is charged, or

(b) an offence of the same category as the one with which he is charged.

(3) Subsection (2) does not apply in the case of a particular defendant if the court is satisfied, by reason of the length of time since the conviction or for any other reason, that it would be unjust for it to apply in his case.

(4) For the purposes of subsection (2)—

(a) two offences are of the same description as each other if the statement of the offence in a written charge or indictment would, in each case, be in the same terms;

(b) two offences are of the same category as each other if they belong to the same category of offences prescribed for the purposes of this section by an order made by the Secretary of State.

(5) A category prescribed by an order under subsection (4)(b) must consist of offences of the same type.

(6) Only prosecution evidence is admissible under section 101(1)(d).

(7) Where—

(a) a defendant has been convicted of an offence under the law of any country outside England and Wales ("the previous offence"), and

(b) the previous offence would constitute an offence under the law of England and Wales ("the corresponding offence") if it were done in England and Wales at the time of the trial for the offence with which the defendant is now charged ("the current offence"),

subsection (8) applies for the purpose of determining if the previous offence and the current offence are of the same description or category.

(8) For the purposes of subsection (2)—

(a) the previous offence is of the same description as the current offence if the corresponding offence is of that same description, as set out in subsection (4)(a);

(b) the previous offence is of the same category as the current offence if the current offence and the corresponding offence belong to the same category of offences prescribed as mentioned in subsection (4)(b).

(9) For the purposes of subsection (10) "foreign service offence" means an offence which—

(a) was the subject of proceedings under the service law of a country outside the United Kingdom, and

(b) would constitute an offence under the law of England and Wales or a service offence ("the corresponding domestic offence") if it were done in England and Wales by a member of Her Majesty's forces at the time of the trial for the offence with which the defendant is now charged ("the current offence").

(10) Where a defendant has been found guilty of a foreign service offence ("the previous service offence"), for the purposes of subsection (2)—

(a) the previous service offence is an offence of the same description as the current offence if the corresponding domestic offence is of that same description, as set out in subsection (4)(a);

(b) the previous service offence is an offence of the same category as the current offence if the current offence and the corresponding domestic offence belong to the same category of offences prescribed as mentioned in subsection (4)(b).

(11) In this section—

"Her Majesty's forces" has the same meaning as in the *Armed Forces Act* 2006;

"service law", in relation to a country outside the United Kingdom, means the law governing all or any of the naval, military or air forces of that country."

[This section is printed as amended by the *Coroners and Justice Act* 2009, Sched. 17, para. 1(2).]

The gateway created by s.101(1)(d) applies where the prosecution wishes to adduce evidence of the defendant's bad character on the basis that it is relevant to an important matter in issue between the defendant and the prosecution, s.103(6) providing that only prosecution evidence is admissible under this gateway. Section 112(1) provides that **10–115**

Part II

"important matter" means a matter of substantial importance in the context of the case as a whole."

Section 103(1) makes clear that the matters to which evidence adduced under s.101(1)(d) may be relevant may include both the defendants propensity to commit offences of the kind with which he is charged and the defendant's propensity to be untruthful. Section 103(1) also provides, however, that evidence may not be adduced under s.101(1)(d) for the former purpose if the existence of such a propensity makes it no more likely that the accused is guilty of the offence with which he is charged and that evidence may not be adduced under s.101(1)(d) for the latter purpose if it is not suggested that the defendant's case is untruthful. Where it is relevant to an important matter in issue between the defendant and the prosecution, however, evidence of the defendant's bad character may be admissible under s.101(1)(d) for purposes other than that of establishing the defendant's propensity to commit offences of the kind with which he is charged or his propensity to be untruthful. Thus, for example, as was seen at § 10–106, above, where the defendant is charged with several offences in the same proceedings, evidence of his bad character may be cross-admissible under s.101(1)(d) if it is capable of increasing the likelihood that the other allegations are true or if it provides strong evidence that the offences were all committed by the same person: *Freeman* [2009] 1 Cr.App.R. 11.

The admissibility of evidence of the defendant's bad character under s.101(1)(d) is subject to s.101(3). Section 101(3) provides that the court must not admit evidence of bad character either under s.101(1)(d) or under s.101(1)(g) if, on an application by the defendant to have the evidence excluded, it appears to the court that its admission would have such an adverse effect on the fairness of the proceedings that it ought not to be admitted, s.101(4) directing the court, on an application under s.101(3), to pay particular regard to the length of time between the matters to which the evidence of the defendant's bad character relates and the matters that form the subject of the offence with which the defendant is charged.

Section 103(2) provides that the defendant's propensity to commit offences of the kind with which he is charged may be established both via a conviction for "an offence of the same description" as the offence with which the defendant is charged and via a conviction for "an offence of the same category as the offence with which the defendant is charged, though s.103(2) makes clear that these two methods of establishing the defendant's propensity to commit offences do not prevent the use of other methods for that purpose. Essentially, a conviction is a conviction for an offence of the same description if it is a conviction for the same offence with which the accused is now charged and a conviction is a conviction for an offence of the same category if both offences fall within a category prescribed by the Secretary of State: s.103(4). Currently, the Secretary of State had only prescribed two categories, namely, the "theft category" and the sexual offences (persons under the age of 16) category": *Criminal Justice Act 2003 (Categories of Offences) Order* 2004 (S.I. 2004 No. 3346).

Section 103(2) *Criminal Justice Act* 2003 provides permissive and simple ways of establishing propensity; where they do not apply, propensity may still be established by other means; a defendant's propensity to conspire to commit burglary can be proved by evidence of his having committed substantive burglaries notwithstanding that conspiracy to burgle and burglary are neither of the same description as each other nor of the same category as each other: *Johnson* [2009] EWCA Crim 649.

Where evidence of bad character takes the form of a conviction for an offence of the same description or for an offence of the same category, the effect of s.103(3) is that s.103(2) will not apply if, whether by reason of the length of time since the conviction or for any other reason, it would be unjust for it to apply.

The fact that a conviction is not for an offence of the same description or of the same category does not prevent it from being admissible under ss.101(1)(d): *Hanson* [2005] 2 Cr.App.R. 21. Thus, for example, evidence of the defendant's convictions for non-fatal offences against the person was properly admitted as evidence of his propensity to drunken violence: *Slack* [2010] EWCA Crim 1149. Indeed, evidence of a defendant's bad character may be admissible under s.101(1)(d) even though it does not take the form of a previous conviction. For example, it might be proved by evidence relating to other offences with which the accused is charged in the proceedings (*Freeman*) or by cautions or offences taken into consideration on sentence (*Weir* [2006] 1 Cr.App.R. 19). Equally, the fact that the accused has a conviction for an offence of the same description or of the same category does not automatically mean that it will be admissible (*Hanson*); this will only be the case if the test imposed by s.101(1)(d) is satisfied and admissibility will also be subject to s.101(3) and s.103(3). Thus, a single previous conviction for an offence of the same description or category will often not show propensity to commit offences of the kind with which the defendant is charged but it might do so, where, e.g. it shows a tendency to unusual behaviour or where its circumstances (perhaps via striking similarity or perhaps via a *modus operandi* which shares significant features with the offence with which the accused is charged) demonstrates probative force: *Hanson*. Equally, their Lordships in *Hanson* recognised that admitting old convictions is likely to have an adverse effect on the fairness of the proceedings unless they either share a special feature with the offence with which the defendant is charged or show a continuing propensity; the date of commission of an offence, rather than the date of conviction, being the more significant of the two for this purpose. For example, where a judge admitted evidence of a single conviction for robbery in a robbery trial in circumstances in which the facts of the conviction displayed no similarities with the facts of the offence with which the defendant was charged, the Court of Appeal quashed the accused's conviction: *Long* [2006] EWCA Crim 578. Similarly, the Court of Appeal held that a single twenty-year-old conviction for possessing a sawn off shotgun without a certificate was not capable of establishing a propensity on the part of the accused to commit firearms offences: *M* [2007] Crim.L.R. 637. In contrast, a one-year-old single conviction for common assault was held to be admissible on a charge of assault occasioning actual bodily harm where the earlier offence, like that with which the defendant was now charged, involved the defendant voluntarily joining a bullying group attack on a single victim: *Upson* [2009] EWCA Crim 99. Equally, the Court of Appeal held that evidence of two previous convictions for indecent assault both of which were more than thirty years old had properly been admitted in consequence of similarities between their facts and those of the sexual assault with which the defendant was charged: *Sully* (2007) 151 S.J.L.B. 1564.

Care must be taken in introducing a mass of prejudicial and largely irrelevant material to show propensity, *i.e.* documents relating to unpaid parking fines, county court judgments etc in relation to charges of making untrue statements for the purpose of obtaining passports: *Eyidah* [2010] EWCA Crim 987.

Where an admission contained in a caution is admitted as evidence of propensity but the accused challenges whether the caution offence occurred, a court should direct itself on bad character if it finds that the caution offence did occur and good character if it finds that it did not occur: *Olu* [2010] EWCA Crim 2975.

It was said in *Hanson*, *ante*, that where the prosecution seeks to adduce evidence of previous convictions to establish a defendant's propensity to commit offences of the kind with which he is charged there were essentially three questions to be considered:

(i) Did the history of his convictions establish a propensity to commit offences of the kind charged?

(ii) Did that propensity make it more likely that the defendant had committed the offence charged?

(iii) Was it unjust to rely on the convictions of the same description or category; and, in any event, would the proceedings be unfair if they were admitted?

Where a defendant is charged with sexual activity with a child and says it was an accident, evidence of one similar incident 11 years previous was properly admitted as evidence of propensity: *R. v. Woodhouse* (2009) 173 J.P. 337, CA.

A judge properly admitted evidence of a former long term partner to be adduced under s.101(1)(d), to establish a propensity to commit an offence of the kind charged:

Williams [2006] EWCA Crim 2052. This was a murder case where the evidence was of attempts to strangle.

Where the prosecution seeks to adduce evidence of the circumstances of a previous conviction rather than the fact of conviction in order to show propensity to commit offences of the kind with which the accused is charged the circumstances should normally be agreed and put before the court by admission: *Hanson*. A statement or oral evidence of the complainant relating to the previous conviction is not to be demanded lightly. A statement by a police officer drawn from police records is insufficient: *Humphris*, *ante*.

Where there is a dispute between the prosecution and defence on the facts supporting the previous convictions it is not enough for the prosecution to rely on the police national computer. Evidence should be adduced from the complainant, although there is a need for caution, as the defendant might have been sentenced on a different basis to that advanced by the complainant. Care also has to be taken to avoid satellite issues arising: *Ainscough* (2006) 170 J.P. 517.

Where a description of an offender is based on the evidence of one witness only, a court should consider whether a previous conviction might render the evidence unbalanced: *Upson* (2009) 173 C.L.& J. 143. The more recent and similar the previous convictions, the more powerfully they might indicate a relevant propensity: *Eastlake (Nicky)* [2007] EWCA Crim 603.

In sexual offences, a single previous conviction is admissible for the purposes of showing propensity only if the circumstances were such that it has some probative force by reason of similarity to the offence charged: *Clements* [2009] EWCA Crim 2726.

The s.101(1)(d) test is one of relevance: *Bullen* [2008] 2 Cr.App.R. 9. Here the issue at trial was one of intent; propensity to violence was not relevant and so there was a lack of focus as to why the previous convictions were being put in as evidence as the convictions were for offences where specific intent did not have to be proved. The mere fact that the prosecution chooses to rely on bad character evidence which it had previously decided not to make the subject of a criminal charge cannot of itself have such an adverse effect on the fairness of the proceedings that the court should not admit it: *Ngyuen* [2008] 2 Cr.App.R. 9.

10–116 Section 103(2) does not permit all convictions to be introduced. The greater the similarity between the offences, the more probative value the previous convictions would have; this need not be striking similarity but there must be some degree of similarity: *Tully*, [2006] EWCA Crim 2270, in which numerous previous convictions should not have been admitted because they had little probative value and were prejudicial. A single speeding conviction (53mph in a 40mph limit) was not admitted to show propensity on a charge of causing death by dangerous driving: *Whitehead*, [2007] EWCA Crim 2078.

It is a matter for a court to decide whether it can determine propensity at the time of committing an offence by reference to offences committed thereafter: *Adenusi* [2006] EWCA Crim 1059; [2006] Crim.L.R. 929.

In a case of murder, evidence of bad character was held to be relevant and admissible to show a propensity to use knives in a violent manner: *Lamb* [2006] All E.R. (D) 333. Previous convictions for criminal offences involving street violence were admitted to show propensity on charges of grievous and actual bodily harm where the attack took place in a street: *Eastlake*; (2007) 151 S.J.L.B. 258.

Rap lyrics relating to violence and composed by the defendant three months before an assault were evidence of bad character and were admissible under s.101(1)(d) to counter the defendant's innocent explanation of why he was at the scene of the crime: *Saleem* [2007] EWCA Crim 1923. Where the prosecution wishes to rely on previous convictions as evidence of propensity to commit offences of the kind with which the accused is charged, it is good practice for details of those convictions to be available but full details are not required in every case: *Lamaletie* (2008) 172 J.P. 249.

In *Hanson*, *ante*, it was said that previous convictions, whether for dishonesty or otherwise, are likely to be capable of showing a propensity to be untruthful only where in the case being tried, truthfulness is an issue and, in the earlier cases, either there was a plea of not guilty and the defendant had given an account which had not been believed or the way in which the offence was committed showed a propensity for untruthfulness, *e.g.* by the making of false representation.

A propensity for untruthfulness is not restricted to past untruthfulness as a witness: *Jarvis* [2008] EWCA Crim 488 (CA (Crim Div))

Matter in issue between the defendant and a co-defendant

104.—(1) Evidence which is relevant to the question whether the defendant has a propensity to be untruthful is admissible on that basis under section 101(1)(e) only if the nature or conduct of his defence is such as to undermine the co-defendant's defence. **10–117**

(2) Only evidence—

(a) which is to be (or has been) adduced by the co-defendant, or

(b) which a witness is to be invited to give (or has given) in cross-examination by the co-defendant,

is admissible under section 101(1)(e).

The gateway created by s.101(1)(e) applies where evidence of the defendant's bad character has substantial probative value in relation to an important matter in issue between the defendant and a co-defendant, s.104(2) providing that only defence evidence (*i.e.* evidence adduced by the co-defendant or which a witness was invited to give during cross-examination thereby) is admissible under this gateway. Section 112(1) provides that "important matter" means a matter of substantial importance in the context of the case as a whole."

In relation to the issue of the defendant's propensity to be untruthful, evidence of the defendant's bad character is only admissible under the gateway created by s.101(1)(e) if the nature or conduct of the defendant's defence is such as to undermine the co-defendant's defence. A defendant who is defending himself against the evidence of a person whose history of criminal behaviour or other misconduct is such as to be capable of showing him to be unscrupulous and/or otherwise unreliable should be enabled to present that history to the court for its evaluation of the evidence of the witness, to ascertain whether he is telling the truth or not. That may be shown by conduct ranging from large-scale drug or people trafficking to housebreaking or criminal violence. Whether in a particular case it has substantive probative value is a matter for the court: *Lawson* [2007] 1 Cr.App.R. 11. In that case cross-examination of a co-defendant on his previous conviction for assault was allowed in the context of a manslaughter trial in which the co-defendants were trying to incriminate each other; the conviction was capable of having substantial probative value in relation to the important issue of who was telling the truth and the evidence of the co-defendant whose conviction was admitted undermined that of the other co-defendant.

Evidence of a co-defendant's bad character may also be admissible under s.101(1)(e) for purposes other than that of establishing another co-defendant's propensity to be untruthful. A co-defendant's convictions for non-fatal offences against the person and affray were admitted under s.101(1)(e), where each co-defendant claimed that he had not been involved in the attack that the case concerned and claimed that the other had been involved, as evidence that the relevant co-defendant was more likely to have been involved in the attack; *McLean* [2005] 1 W.L.R. 1524.

Once evidence is admissible under s.101(1)(e) there is no power to exclude on the basis of unfairness; the court only possesses discretion to exclude such evidence where there is a failure to comply with the notice requirements of the *Criminal Procedure Rules*: *Musone*, [2007] 2 Cr.App.R. 29 (see § 10–104, above). **10–118**

Evidence to correct a false impression

105.—(1) For the purposes of section 101(1)(f)— **10–119**

(a) the defendant gives a false impression if he is responsible for the making of an express or implied assertion which is apt to give the court or jury a false or misleading impression about the defendant;

(b) evidence to correct such an impression is evidence which has probative value in correcting it.

(2) A defendant is treated as being responsible for the making of an assertion if—

(a) the assertion is made by the defendant in the proceedings (whether or not in evidence given by him),

(b) the assertion was made by the defendant—

(i) on being questioned under caution, before charge, about the offence with which he is charged, or

(ii) on being charged with the offence or officially informed that he might be prosecuted for it,

and evidence of the assertion is given in the proceedings,

(c) the assertion is made by a witness called by the defendant,

(d) the assertion is made by any witness in cross-examination in response to a question asked by the defendant that is intended to elicit it, or is likely to do so, or

(e) the assertion was made by any person out of court, and the defendant adduces evidence of it in the proceedings.

(3) A defendant who would otherwise be treated as responsible for the making of an assertion shall not be so treated if, or to the extent that, he withdraws it or disassociates himself from it.

(4) Where it appears to the court that a defendant, by means of his conduct (other than the giving of evidence) in the proceedings, is seeking to give the court or jury an impression about himself that is false or misleading, the court may if it appears just to do so treat the defendant as being responsible for the making of an assertion which is apt to give that impression.

(5) In subsection (4) "conduct" includes appearance or dress.

(6) Evidence is admissible under section 101(1)(f) only if it goes no further than is necessary to correct the false impression.

(7) Only prosecution evidence is admissible under section 101(1)(f).

The s.101(1)(f) gateway applies where evidence of bad character is tendered to correct a false impression given by the defendant, s.105(7) providing that only prosecution evidence is admissible under this gateway. Thus, in accordance with s.105, where the defendant, in adducing evidence of his good character by any of the various methods specified by s.105(2) is responsible for the making of an express or implied assertion which is apt to give the court a false or misleading impression about him, evidence of his bad character may be adduced to correct the false impression provided that the evidence has probative value in correcting the false impression and that the evidence goes no further than is necessary to correct the false impression, though the defendant may avoid the consequences of s.101(f) by withdrawing or disassociating himself from such an assertion For example, where a defendant who was charged with fraudulent evasion of the prohibition on the importation of goods, namely cocaine and had a spent conviction for theft gave the impression that she was a hard-working, truthful, church-going individual, the Court of Appeal held that the impression that she had given had been a false impression and that the conviction had properly been admitted to correct it: *Amponsah* [2005] EWCA Crim 2993. The methods via which the s.101(1)(f) gateway may be activated include both the giving of a false impression during the trial itself and its giving during the investigative process, *i.e.* where evidence of a statement made by the defendant to the police is given in court (see s.105(2)).

In *Weir* [2006] 1 Cr.App.R. 19 at para. 43, the Court of Appeal accepted that "... a simple denial of the offence or offences alleged cannot, for the purposes of s.101(1)(f), be treated as a false impression given by the defendant". Moreover, in *Iqbal* [2006] EWCA Crim 1302 at para. 16, the Court of Appeal indicated that:

> "Even if what is contained in a defence case statement can amount to an assertion made by a defendant in the proceedings, the document in reality is setting out the contentions of the defence in relation to a fundamental issue in the case, the nature of his defence and the matters of fact upon which he takes issue. This, in the court's judgment, is not an impression about him, let alone a false or misleading one without begging the very question which the jury would have to determine."

Here, the defendant, charged with possession of a Class A drug with intent to supply, had three convictions for possession of heroin and his defence statement had given an innocent explanation for the presence of his DNA on a package containing heroin.

Where this appears just, s.105(4),(5) permit the court to treat the defendant as being responsible for making an assertion which is apt to give the court a false or misleading impression about him via his conduct, including his appearance or dress.

The admissibility and significance of evidence of the accused's good character was considered at § 10–103, above.

Giving a false impression includes appearance or dress: s.105(5) could cover someone who wears, *e.g.* the clothes of a priest. Under s.106(2), evidence of an interview with police (in this case Dutch police) where admissions had been made to being involved with the supply of drugs can be admitted to correct a false impression where a defendant says he had never been involved in drug supply: *Spartley*, [2007] EWCA Crim 1789. **10–120**

Where an application was based on an answer given by a defendant in cross-examination," I am not that type of person", the application should have been refused where the question was in two parts, in consequence of which it was not possible to be sure as to which part the answer related: *Good,* 173 J.P. 1, CA

Only prosecution evidence may be admitted under s.101(1)(f) and (g); the mere fact that the material is contained in a statement made by a prosecution witness does not make it prosecution evidence: *Assani* [2009] Crim.L.R. 514, CA. In that case it was also decided that where a defendant has elicited evidence of a non violent character it was wrong to allow cross-examination [in order to correct a false impression] on a 13-year-old incident where it was alleged that the defendant, then aged 14, had been violent.

Attack on another person's character

106.—(1) For the purposes of section 101(1)(g) a defendant makes an attack on another person's character if— **10–121**

(a) he adduces evidence attacking the other person's character,

(b) he (or any legal representative appointed under section 38(4) of the *Youth Justice and Criminal Evidence Act* 1999 to cross-examine a witness in his interests) asks questions in cross-examination that are intended to elicit such evidence, or are likely to do so, or

(c) evidence is given of an imputation about the other person made by the defendant—

(i) on being questioned under caution, before charge, about the offence with which he is charged, or

(ii) on being charged with the offence or officially informed that he might be prosecuted for it.

(2) In subsection (1) "evidence attacking the other person's character" means evidence to the effect that the other person—

(a) has committed an offence (whether a different offence from the one with which the defendant is charged or the same one), or

(b) has behaved, or is disposed to behave, in a reprehensible way;

and "imputation about the other person" means an assertion to that effect.

(3) Only prosecution evidence is admissible under section 101(1)(g).

The gateway created by s.101(1)(g), applies where the defendant attacks another person's character (see s.106(2)) via any of the methods specified by s.106(1), s.106(3) providing that only prosecution evidence is admissible under this gateway.

Section 106 makes it clear that the s.101(1)(g) gateway may be triggered by an attack either during the course of the trial or during the investigative process. Where an attack is made during the investigation it is essential that evidence of what was said is given at the trial before evidence of the bad character of the defendant is admitted under s.101(1)(f): *Lamaletie* [2008] EWCA Crim 314. Like s.101(1)(d), which was considered at § 10–115, above, s.101(1)(9) is also subject to the operation of s.101(3) fairness test. In the case of *Nelson* [2006] All E.R.(D) 290 the defendant, in interview, had attacked the character of another, a neighbour, by stating that the neighbour was a user of class A **10–122**

Part II

drugs and a liar. The substance of the defence was that the victim had conspired with the neighbour to fabricate the allegations of assault. The neighbour was not called to give evidence. It was said that the attack was capable of triggering the gateway but that it would be improper for the prosecution to adduce evidence which was not relevant to a matter is issue merely to trigger the gateway.

A court may allow evidence of a defendant's previous convictions for possession of a bladed article where he attacks the character of the victims by suggesting that they started the violence and colluded in their accounts: *R. v. O* (2009) 173 J.P. 616.

It was said in *Williams* [2007] EWCA Crim 1951 that a court was correct to conclude that an attack on prosecution witnesses was being made when the defendant, in examination in chief, accused them of collusion and "setting him up" even though it had been argued earlier that the issue of a police conspiracy had been raised in the defence case statement but the judge had ruled at that stage that the evidence was too prejudicial to be admitted. The court ruled that s.101(1)(g) was brought into operation as the allegation made by the defendant when he testified went further than the defence case statement.

Where a 61-year-old defendant had been charged with burglary and had stated that he had entered an aviary to release wild birds which were being kept unlawfully, that was an attack on another person's character and the defendant's previous convictions for burglary were allowed to be put in as evidence: *Hearne* 173 J.P. 97, CA.

Where a defendant gives evidence that the complainant is a Class A drug user that is an "attack" on her character within s.101(1)(g): *Chrysostomou* [2010] EWCA Crim 1403. The Court of Appeal held, however, that the evidence of the defendant's bad character, namely evidence that the defendant was capable of providing class A drugs, should have been excluded under s.101(3) because the prosecution had not asserted that the defendant had sold drugs to the complainant (the charges were possessing an imitation firearm with intent to cause fear of violence and with putting a person in fear of violence by harassment) and admitting the evidence to help the jury decide whether they believed the defendant's evidence was "too flimsy a basis" to justify its admission in the circumstances.

X. UNFAIRLY OR ILLEGALLY OBTAINED EVIDENCE

A. CONFESSIONS

Police and Criminal Evidence Act 1984, ss.76–76A

Confessions

10–123 **76.**—(1) In any proceedings a confession made by an accused person may be given in evidence against him in so far as it is relevant to any matter in issue in the proceedings and is not excluded by the court in pursuance of this section.

(2) If, in any proceedings where the prosecution proposes to give in evidence a confession made by an accused person, it is represented to the court that the confession was or may have been obtained—

(a) by oppression of the person who made it; or

(b) in consequence of anything said or done which was likely, in the circumstances existing at the time, to render unreliable any confession which might be made by him in consequence thereof.

the court shall not allow the confession to be given in evidence against him except in so far as the prosecution proves to the court beyond reasonable doubt that the confession (notwithstanding that it may be true) was not obtained as aforesaid.

(3) In any proceedings where the prosecution proposes to give in evidence a confession made by an accused person, the court may of its own motion require the prosecution, as a condition of allowing it to do so, to prove that the confession was not obtained as mentioned in subsection (2) above.

(4) The fact that a confession is wholly or partly excluded in pursuance of this section shall not affect the admissibility in evidence—

(a) of any facts discovered as a result of the confession; or
(b) where the confession is relevant as showing that the accused speaks, writes or expresses himself in a particular way, of so much of the confession as is necessary to show that he does so.

(5) Evidence that a fact to which this subsection applies was discovered as a result of a statement made by an accused person shall not be admissible unless evidence of how it was discovered is given by him or on his behalf.

(6) Subsection (5) above applies—
(a) to any fact discovered as a result of a confession which is wholly excluded in pursuance of this section; and
(b) to any fact discovered as a result of a confession which is partly so excluded, if the fact is discovered as a result of the excluded part of the confession.

(7) Nothing in Part VII of this Act shall prejudice the admissibility of a confession made by an accused person.

(8) In this section "oppression" includes torture, inhuman or degrading treatment, and the use or threat of violence (whether or not amounting to torture).

(9) Where the proceedings mentioned in subsection (1) above are proceedings before a magistrates' court inquiring into an offence as examining justices this section shall have effect with the omission of—
(a) in subsection (1) the words "and is not excluded by the court in pursuance of this section", and
(b) subsections (2) to (6) and (8).

The method by which evidence is obtained is irrelevant to its admissibility as a matter **10–124** of law, although criminal courts do posses discretion at common law to exclude admissible evidence to prevent unfairness to the defendant: *Kuruma v. R.* [1955] A.C. 197. Confessions are the exception as s.76 of the Act does potentially render them inadmissible as a matter of law if obtained in contravention of s.76(2). There is also a general discretion to exclude evidence which may render the trial unfair under s.78 of the 1984 Act, in addition to the common law disclosure which is preserved by s.82(3) *PACE* 1984, see § 10–130. Where an objection to evidence is based on s.76, the court shall not admit the confession unless it is satisfied beyond reasonable doubt that it was not obtained by oppression or by words or conduct likely to render it unreliable: *Police and Criminal Evidence Act* 1984, s.76(2). The court must determine the question as soon as it is raised and, if it is necessary to hear evidence, to do so upon a *voire dire*: *Liverpool Juvenile Court, ex p. R.* [1988] Q.B. 1.

A confession is defined as any statement wholly or partly adverse to the person who made it, whether made to a person in authority or not and whether made in words or otherwise: s.82(1) then, a mixed statement, which is partly exculpatory and partly inculpatory, is a confession. A confession does not include a statement intended by the maker to be exculpatory or neutral and which appears to be so on its face, but which becomes damaging to him at trial, because, for example its contents could then be shown to be evasive or false or inconsistent with the maker's evidence on oath: *Hasan* [2005] 2 W.L.R. 709. It can be made to a police officer or to someone else, in court, at a police station or anywhere else. It may be in writing, spoken or in other circumstances. Where a probation officer is involved in the preparation of a report caution should be exercised. The court must bear in mind the difference between an interview with a police officer with its protection and that with a probation officer who needs frank disclosure for the preparation of a report: *Elleray* [2003] 2 Cr.App.R. 11, CA.

A confession can include, for example, as well as one made during a police interview:

- A self incriminating telephone call from a defendant resulting from a cooperative conversation: *De Silva* [2003] Crim.L.R. 474.
- A confession made in court at a previous trial: *McGregor* [1968] 1 Q.B. 371.
- Conduct: *Parkes* 64 Cr.App.R. 25 where when asked by the mother of a girl why he had stabbed her and being threatened with being held until the police arrived, the defendant remained silent but brought out a knife.
- In mitigation (via his solicitor): *Turner* (1975) 61 Cr.App.R. 67. Pre-trial admis-

sions in a case progression form are admissible as evidence in committal proceedings: *R. (on the application of Firth) v. Epping Magistrates' Court* [2011] EWHC 388(Admin).

- An unsigned form under s.172(2) of the *Road Traffic Act* 1988 where there is sufficient evidence that the defendant completed it: *Mawdsley v. Chief Constable of Cheshire Constabulary; Yorke v. Same* [2004] 1 All E.R. 58.

Guidance on assessing the admissibility of confessions on the basis of unreliability under s.76(2)(b) was given in *Barry* (1991) 95 Cr.App.R. 384 where the defendant had confessed to a charge of international fraud because he desperately wanted bail as he feared his wife would gain custody of their child. It said that the court must (i) identify everything said and done from the date of arrest to interview; (ii) look at what has been said or done, against the background circumstances and ask whether it is likely to render any confession unreliable; (iii) decide whether the prosecution has proved beyond reasonable doubt that the confession has not been made as a result of things said or done; (iv) if there has been a breach of the PACE code, is the confession likely to be reliable; (v) if the confession has been made in consequence of things said or done. The court must not consider whether the statement is true or not: *Mushtaz (Ashfaq Ahmed)* [2005] 2 Cr.App.R.32.

Whilst a confession is only admissible against it's maker, if the case against a defendant in a joint trial depends on the prosecution's proving the guilt of a co-defendant (and the evidence against the co-defendant consists solely of his own out of court confession) then that confession will be admissible against the defendant but only in so far as it goes to prove the co-defendant's guilt: *Hayter* [2005] UKHL 6. A defendant may adopt a confession made by someone else in line with the principles in *Christie* [1914] A.C. 545. Where a co-accused has pleaded guilty and does not stand trial with a defendant, the co-accused's confession cannot be used as evidence at that defendant's trial under this section.

Disciplinary interviews were admitted in *Welcher* [2007] EWCA Crim 480. The defendant was charged with conspiracy to corrupt and conspiracy to defraud in relation to bribes taken as an employee. Once the matter had come to light the defendant had been subject to disciplinary interviews within the workplace, admitted the matters and was dismissed for gross misconduct. During the trial he gave accounts consistent with the police interview but inconsistent with the disciplinary interview which were then admitted as evidence of the defendant's untruthfulness.

In *Fulling* [1987] Q.B. 426 it was held that "oppression" was to be given its ordinary dictionary meaning. In this case the defendant confessed when told that her lover had been having an affair with the woman in the next cell. Lord Lane said " it is hard to envisage any circumstances in which oppression would not entail some impropriety on the part of the interrogator". In making a judgement about what is oppressive or likely to make a confession unreliable, the court may have regard to the character and experience of the suspect: *Seelig* 94 Cr.App.R. 17, CA. See, also, the statutory definition of oppression in s.76(8), above.

Hostile and aggressive questioning which puts pressure on a defendant will not necessarily render the confession unreliable. The length of the interviews and the nature of the questioning are the important considerations: *L.* [1994] Crim.L.R. 839, CA.

10–125 Raised police voices are not necessarily oppressive: *Heaton* [1993] Crim.L.R. 593, but where shouting amounts to bullying and intimidation it will be: *Paris* (1993) 97 Cr.App.R. 99. Not all breaches of the Code of Practice will amount to oppression: *Parker* [1995] Crim.L.R. 233. In *Parker* the Court of Appeal also indicated that there must be at least a possible casual link between the oppression and the confession. In appropriate circumstances a failure to caution may render a confession unreliable: *Doolan* [1988] Crim.L.R. 747, CA.

The denial of access to a solicitor led to inadmissibility under s.76(2)(b) in *McGovern* (1991) 92 Cr.App.R. 228, CA but not in *Alladice* (1988) 87 Cr.App.R. 380. A cofession may also be excluded under s.78 of the 1984 Act, which is considered at § 10–130, below, but the breach of requirements of PACE or the codes must be significant and substantial: *Keenan* (1990) 90 Cr.App.R. 1; *Absolam* (1989) 88 Cr.App.R. 332; *Canale* (1990) 91 Cr.App.R. 1. Proper advice from a solicitor will rarely provide a basis for excluding a confession and things said or done by the defendant himself do not fall within s.76(2)(b): *Wahab* [2003] 1 Cr.App.R. 15, CA, but interjections from a legal representative during interview have made a confession unreliable: *M*, [2000] 8 *Archbold News* 2, CA.

The court may take into account the defendant's mental condition under s.76(2)(b); police misconduct not being required: *Walker* [1998] Crim.L.R. 211, CA. For expert evidence to be admissible the disorder must be of a type which might render a confession unrealistic and the disorder must be a significant deviation from the norm: *O'Brien* [2000] Crim.L.R. 676, CA; see also *Everett* [1988] Crim.L.R. 826.

Unreliable means "cannot be relied upon as being the truth": *Crampton* (1991) 92 Cr.App.R. 369, CA. Expert evidence concerning the phenomenon of false confessions and the circumstances in which research has shown that a vulnerable individual, after a prolonged period of questioning, might give a coerced compliant confession is admissible: *Blackburn* [2005] 2 Cr.App.R. 30. If the court concludes that what was said and done is likely to make any confession unreliable then it must not be admitted; the question is not whether the specific confession is reliable: *Kenny* [1994] Crim.L.R. 284, CA. Facts discovered as a result of an inadmissible confession can be introduced: s.76(4).

Part II

Counsel's statement, on the basis of documents or a proof of evidence in his possession at the time of speaking, that a confession was or may have been obtained by oppression of the defendant or in consequence of anything said or done which was likely, in the circumstances existing at the time, to have rendered unreliable any confession that the defendant might have made in consequence of the confession, is a "representation" for the purposes of s.76(2) *Police and Criminal Evidence Act* 1984 and the allegations should be tested before a confession is considered admissible and even if neither the prosecution or the defence ask for a *voir dire* the court of its own motion should require the prosecution to prove that the confession is admissible: *Dhorajiwala* [2010] 2 Cr.App.R.21.

In *Gonzales v. Folkestone Magistrates' Court* [2010] EWHC 3428 (Admin) the Divisional Court held that the prosecution should have adduced evidence of a mixed statement that the defendant had made; the defendant had not been entitled to adduce evidence of it because it was self-serving and the magistrates might not have convicted the defendant had they been aware of the statement.

Police and Criminal Evidence Act 1984, s.77

Confessions by mentally handicapped persons

77.—(1) Without prejudice to the general duty of the court at a trial on indictment to direct the jury on any matter on which it appears to the court appropriate to do so, where at such a trial— **10–126**

(a) the case against the accused depends wholly or substantially on a confession by him; and

(b) the court is satisfied—

(i) that he is mentally handicapped; and

(ii) that the confession was not made in the presence of an independent person,

the court shall warn the jury that there is special need for caution before convicting the accused in reliance on the confession, and shall explain that the need arises because of the circumstances mentioned in paragraphs (a) and (b) above.

(2) In any case where at the summary trial of a person for an offence it appears to the court that a warning under subsection (1) above would be required if the trial were on indictment, the court shall treat the case as one in which there is a special need for caution before convicting the accused on his confession.

(3) In this section—

"independent person" does not include a police officer or a person employed for, or engaged on, police purposes;

"mentally handicapped", in relation to a person, means that he is in a state of arrested or incomplete development of mind which includes significant impairment of intelligence and social functioning; and

"police purposes" has the meaning assigned to it by section 101(2) of the *Police Act* 1996.

[This section is reprinted as amended by the *Summary Appeal Court (Navy) Rules* 2000, Sched. 3(III), para. 18(d).]

10–127 A solicitor can be an "independent person" even though he is not an "appropriate adult": *Lewis (M.)* [1996] Crim.L.R. 260, CA.

10–128 For the s.77 warning requirement to apply, the case against the accused must substantially depend upon the confession and the accused must be mentally handicapped: *Scott* [2010] EWCA Crim 321. If the only evidence against the defendant is a confession to which s.77 applies there may be no case for the defendant to answer: see *MacKenzie* (1993) 96 Cr.App.R. 98.

Criminal Justice Act 2003, s.128

Confessions

10–129 **128.**—(1) In the *Police and Criminal Evidence Act* 1984 (c. 60) the following section is inserted after section 76—

Confessions may be given in evidence for co-accused

"76A.—(1) In any proceedings a confession made by an accused person may be given in evidence for another person charged in the same proceedings (a co-accused) in so far as it is relevant to any matter in issue in the proceedings and is not excluded by the court in pursuance of this section.

(2) If, in any proceedings where a co-accused proposes to give in evidence a confession made by an accused person, it is represented to the court that the confession was or may have been obtained—

(a) by oppression of the person who made it; or

(b) in consequence of anything said or done which was likely, in the circumstances existing at the time, to render unreliable any confession which might be made by him in consequence thereof,

the court shall not allow the confession to be given in evidence for the co-accused except in so far as it is proved to the court on the balance of probabilities that the confession (notwithstanding that it may be true) was not so obtained.

(3) Before allowing a confession made by an accused person to be given in evidence for a co-accused in any proceedings, the court may of its own motion require the fact that the confession was not obtained as mentioned in subsection (2) above to be proved in the proceedings on the balance of probabilities.

(4) The fact that a confession is wholly or partly excluded in pursuance of this section shall not affect the admissibility in evidence—

(a) of any facts discovered as a result of the confession; or

(b) where the confession is relevant as showing that the accused speaks, writes or expresses himself in a particular way, of so much of the confession as is necessary to show that he does so.

(5) Evidence that a fact to which this subsection applies was discovered as a result of a statement made by an accused person shall not be admissible unless evidence of how it was discovered is given by him or on his behalf.

(6) Subsection (5) above applies—

(a) to any fact discovered as a result of a confession which is wholly excluded in pursuance of this section; and

(b) to any fact discovered as a result of a confession which is partly so excluded, if the fact is discovered as a result of the excluded part of the confession.

(7) In this section "oppression" includes torture, inhuman or degrading treatment, and the use or threat of violence (whether or not amounting to torture)."

(2) Subject to subsection (1), nothing in this Chapter makes a confession by a defendant

admissible if it would not be admissible under section 76 of the *Police and Criminal Evidence Act* 1984.

(3) In subsection (2) "confession" has the meaning given by section 82 of that Act.

Section 76A is virtually identical to s.76 except that s.76A applies when a defendant wishes to adduce evidence of a co-defendant's confessions and the requisite standard of proof under s.76A(2) is proof on the balance of probabilities not proof beyond reasonable doubt.

A vacated plea of guilty and the written basis for it is a confession for the purposes of s.76A: *Johnson* [2007] EWCA Crim. 1651. Where a confession which is admitted under s.76A in the defence of a defendant incriminates co-defendants, s.76A does not make the confession admissible evidence against the others: *Ibrahim* [2008] 2 Cr.App.R. 23. It seems, however, that a confession admitted under s.76A may be relied on as evidence of it's maker's guilt: *L* [2011] EWCA Crim 649.

Where a co-accused has pleaded guilty and does not stand trial with a defendant, the co-accused's confession cannot be used as evidence at that defendant's trial under s.76A: *Finch* [2007] EWCA Crim 36. In this case the confession was not admitted under s.114(1)(d) as hearsay evidence as it was not in the interests of justice so to do. Under s.114(1)(d), a judge permitted a co-defendant to adduce evidence of a confession made by a third party which exculpated him but incriminated another co-defendant: *Lamb* [2006] EWCA Crim 3347.

B. UNFAIR EVIDENCE

Police and Criminal Evidence Act 1984, s.78

Exclusion of unfair evidence

78.—(1) In any proceedings the court may refuse to allow evidence on which the prosecution proposes to rely to be given if it appears to the court that, having regard to all the circumstances, including the circumstances in which the evidence was obtained, the admission of the evidence would have such an adverse effect on the fairness of the proceedings that the court ought not to admit it. **10–130**

(2) Nothing in this section shall prejudice any rule of law requiring a court to exclude evidence.

(3) This section shall not apply in the case of proceedings before a magistrates' court inquiring into an offences as examining justices.

Whilst the criminal courts normally rely upon the s.78 exclusionary discretion, their, arguably more limited, common law discretion to exclude evidence tendered by the prosecution in criminal proceedings is preserved by s.82(3) of the 1984 Act which provides as follows:

Part VIII—interpretation

82.—(3) Nothing in this Part of this Act shall prejudice any power of a court to exclude evidence (whether by preventing questions from being put or otherwise) at its discretion.

Section 78 empowers the court to exclude evidence tendered by the prosecution the admission of which in the circumstances would have such an adverse effect on the fairness of the proceedings that it ought not to be admitted. The circumstances include those in which the evidence was obtained. The section can be relied upon to exclude any prosecution evidence, *e.g.* confessions, hearsay evidence, evidence of bad character and identification evidence. **10–131**

Where there had been a failure to caution the defendant who had made a statement that had been very damaging to his defence case, the statement should have been excluded under s.78: *Miller* [2007] EWCA Crim 1891. Where there was a deliberate breach of requirements of Code D relating to the conduct of a video identification procedure which was blatantly unfair to the defendant, identification evidence should have been excluded under s.78: *Marcus* [2005] Crim.L.R. 384.

Several breaches of Code C by a young and inexperienced police officer who had not acted in bad faith which were not significant and substantial did not result in the exclusion of statements made by the defendant under s.78: *Skrzypiec v. CPS Essex-Southwest Team* [2010] EWHC 1418 (Admin). A judge properly admitted evidence of remarks made by the defendant prior to his "no comment interview" even though there had been significant breaches of Code C; it would have been unreasonable to exclude the evidence and give a "synthetic direction" about a no-comment interview and the judge directed the jury in relation to the breach: *Heera* [2010] EWCA Crim 177.

A court was wrong to exclude evidence of analysis of a breath specimen obtained under s.7 *Road Traffic Act* 1988 under s.78 where a roadside specimen had not been taken for lack of equipment; s.78 is not to be used as a punishment but to determine whether the evidence to be admitted would have such an adverse effect on the fairness of the proceedings that it should not be admitted: *R. (CPS) v. Wolverhampton Magistrates' Court* [2010] 1 *Archbold Review* 1, D.C.

The admission of lawfully authorised covert surveillance of a defendant in prison was not unfair under s.78 and the evidence was admissible: *Kelly, ante*.

10–132 The concept of the burden of proof has no part to play in the exercise of the s.78 discretion: *Govenor of Brixton prison, ex parte Saif* [2001] 4 All E.R. 168.

Exclusion is not automatic where there has been a breach of the PACE Act or the Codes of practice *Walsh* (1989) 91 Cr.App.R. 161. Case law has suggested that the breach should be significant and substantial before discretion is exercised: *Absalom* 88 Cr.App.R. 332. In *Stewart* [1995] Crim.L.R. 500, CA it was pointed out that it was the nature and not the number of breaches that was the important factor.

There is no requirement of bad faith on the part of police officers before evidence is excluded although case law in breath test cases suggests that evidence will not be excluded unless there is bad faith: *Matto v. Wolverhampton Crown Court* [1987] R.T.R. 337, DC; *Fox v. Chief Constable of Gwent* [1986] A.C. 281, HL. In other cases bad faith means that evidence is usually excluded: *Alladice* 87 Cr.App.R. 380, CA. Good faith, on the other hand, will not excuse serious breaches: *Samuel* [1988] Q.B. 615.

Although entrapment does not *per se* afford a defence to a criminal charge, proceedings may be stayed or evidence may be excluded under s.78: *Sang* [1980] A.C. 402. In *Smurthwaite; Gill* (1994) 98 Cr.App.R. 437, CA, it was said that the following factors but not an exhaustive list ought to be considered: was the officer acting as an agent provocateur in the sense that he was enticing the defendant to commit an offence he would not otherwise have committed? What was the nature of any entrapment? Does the evidence consist of admissions to a completed offence, or does it consist of the actual commission of the offence? How active or passive was the officer's role in obtaining the evidence? Was there an unassailable record of what occurred, or was it strongly corroborated? Had the undercover officer abused his role to ask questions which ought properly to have been asked as a police officer and in accordance with the codes? In *Loosely; Att.-Gen.'s Reference (No. 3 of 2000)* [2002] 1 Cr.App.R. 29, it was held that the appropriate remedy would be staying the prosecution as an abuse of process rather than excluding evidence; but the use of a covert operation may affect the admissibility of particular pieces of evidence and in such circumstances s.78 would apply.

Before a court admits statements made during compulsory disclosure in divorce proceedings, it must determine whether their admission would render the trial unfair and, in so doing, it must consider the nature of the compulsion applied, the nature of the evidence obtained by means of it, the social need which the admission is intended to meet and whether the admission is proportionate; the public interest in prosecuting crime is sufficient to outweigh the public interest in the settlement of disputes and it follows that admissions made in the course of "without prejudice" negotiations will not be inadmissible simply by virtue of the fact that they were made during such negotiations but may be excluded under s.78: *R. v. K* [2010] 1 Cr.App.R. 3.

C. ADMISSIONS

10–133 An admission made in the course of judicial proceedings, whether at an earlier stage of proceedings for the same offence or in separate proceedings will come within the definition of "confession" in s.82(1) of the *Police and Criminal Evidence Act* 1984. The *Fraud Act*, s.13, similar to s.31 of the *Theft Act* 1968, protects a person from incriminating himself for the purposes of offences under the Act (and related offences) but a person is still obliged to co-operate with civil proceedings relating to property.

Fraud Act 2006, s.13

Evidence

13.—(1) A person is not to be excused from— 10–134

(a) answering any question put to him in proceedings relating to property, or

(b) complying with any order made in proceedings relating to property, on the ground that doing so may incriminate him or his spouse or civil partner of an offence under this Act or a related offence.

(2) But, in proceedings for an offence under this Act or a related offence, a statement or admission made by the person in—

(a) answering such a question, or

(b) complying with such an order,

is not admissible in evidence against him or (unless they married or became civil partners after the making of the statement or admission) his spouse or civil partner.

(3) "Proceedings relating to property" means any proceedings for—

(a) the recovery or administration of any property,

(b) the execution of a trust, or

(c) an account of any property or dealings with property,

and "property" means money or other property whether real or personal (including things in action and other intangible property).

(4) "Related offence" means—

(a) conspiracy to defraud;

(b) any other offence involving any form of fraudulent conduct or purpose.

Admissions by a person in a former trial or enquiry are excluded by certain statutes, *e.g.* the *Explosive Substances Act* 1883, s.6(2) 10–135

An admission made during the course of a trial is admissible in the event of a retrial: *McGregor* [1968] 1 Q.B. 372.

"Related offence" is wide enough to include a money laundering offence contrary to s.328 *Proceeds of Crime Act* 2002: *B.T.A. Bank J.S.C v. Ablyazov and ors, The Times*, November 12, 2009, CA.

XI. ADVERSE INFERENCES

At common law, under a rule preserved by ss.34(5), 36(6) and 37(5) of the *Criminal Justice and Public Order Act* 1994, a statement made in the presence of the defendant, which accuses him of having committed a crime, upon an occasion which may be expected reasonably to call for some explanation or denial, is not evidence against him of the facts stated, unless by his words, actions, conduct or demeanour he accepts it; *Christie* [1914] A.C. 545. 10–136

Before admitting a prejudicial statement made in the defendant's presence to which he does not demur, the court must consider whether the defendant's reaction (or lack of reaction) to that statement is potentially relevant: *Osborne* [2005] EWCA Crim 2826. Where it is alleged that a defendant, by his conduct, acquiesces in and adopts a statement the three questions that arise are:

1) Can the court conclude that the defendant adopted the statement in question?
2) If so, is it of sufficient relevance to justify its introduction as evidence?
3) If so, would the admission have such an adverse effect on the fairness of the proceedings that it should not be admitted?

In that case, a verbal exchange had taken place between a group of youths, one of whom was the defendant and an Asian male following which a fight ensued and the

Asian youth died. Two days later, the defendant was asked, "What did you hit him for? I bet he ain't done nothing to you," whereupon one of the youths in the defendant's group said, "Of course we don't like Asian people. They stink. Why do they come over to our country?" The defendant said nothing. The evidence demonstrated that the defendant was hostile to the deceased and was admitted but it had no bearing on the issue of intent.

Evidence can only be admissible under this common law rule if the defendant was speaking on even terms with the person who made the statement: *Parkes v. R* [1976] 1 W.L.R 1251.

Criminal Justice and Public Order Act 1994, s.34

Effect of accused's failure to mention facts when questioned or charged.

10–137 **34.**—(1) Where, in any proceedings against a person for an offence, evidence is given that the accused—

(a) at any time before he was charged with the offence, on being questioned under caution by a constable trying to discover whether or by whom the offence had been committed, failed to mention any fact relied on in his defence in those proceedings; or

(b) on being charged with the offence or officially informed that he might be prosecuted for it, failed to mention any such fact,

being a fact which in the circumstances existing at the time the accused could reasonably have been expected to mention when so questioned, charged or informed, as the case may be, subsection (2) below applies.

(2) Where this subsection applies—

(a) a magistrates' court inquiring into the offence as examining justices;

(b) a judge, in deciding whether to grant an application made by the accused under—

(i) section 6 of the *Criminal Justice Act* 1987 (application for dismissal of charge of serious fraud in respect of which notice of transfer has been given under section 4 of that Act; or

(ii) paragraph 5 of Schedule 6 to the *Criminal Justice Act* 1991 (application for dismissal of charge of violent or sexual offence involving child in respect of which notice of transfer has been given under section 53 of that Act);

(c) the court, in determining whether there is a case to answer; and

(d) the court or jury, in determining whether the accused is guilty of the offence charged,

may draw such inferences from the failure as appear proper.

(2A) Where the accused was at an authorised place of detention at the time of the failure, subsections (1) and (2) above do not apply if he had not been allowed an opportunity to consult a solicitor prior to being questioned, charged or informed as mentioned in subsection (1) above.

(3) Subject to any directions by the court, evidence tending to establish the failure may be given before or after evidence tending to establish the fact which the accused is alleged to have failed to mention.

(4) This section applies in relation to questioning by persons (other than constables) charged with the duty of investigating offences or charging offenders as it applies in relation to questioning by constables; and in subsection (1) above "officially informed" means informed by a constable or any such person.

(5) This section does not—

(a) prejudice the admissibility in evidence of the silence or other reaction of the accused in the face of anything said in his presence relating to the conduct in respect of which he is charged, in so far as evidence thereof would be admissible apart from this section; or

(b) preclude the drawing of any inference from any such silence or other reaction of the accused which could properly be drawn apart from this section.

(6) This section does not apply in relation to a failure to mention a fact if the failure occurred before the commencement of this section.

[This section is reprinted as amended by the *Youth Justice and Criminal Evidence Act* 1999, s.58(2). Subsection 2A is not yet in force.]

The European Court has confirmed that the right to silence is not an absolute right but is at the heart of the notion of a fair trial. Caution must therefore be exercised before drawing adverse inferences. In *Averill v. UK* (2001) 31 E.H.R.R. 839, it was said that the extent to which adverse inferences may be drawn in this context should be limited. In *Argent* [1997] 2 Cr.App.R. 27, Lord Bingham defined the six conditions which had to be met before adverse inferences could be drawn: **10–138**

— proceedings for an offence must be in existence;
— failure to answer must have occurred before charge;
— failure to answer must have occurred during questioning under caution by a police officer or relevant person;
— the questioning was intended to discover whether or by whom the offence was committed;
— the failure had to be with regard to the mention of a fact which was then relied upon in the proceedings; and
— the fact concerned and the one which the defendant had failed to mention must have been one which he could reasonably have been expected to mention at the time of questioning, given the circumstances of the interview.

The significance of s.34 is not whether an offender is silent in interview, but whether he relies at trial on something that should have been said at interview. The question is not whether it is reasonable to rely on it, but whether the defendant could reasonably have been expected to say in interview what he says at the trial. There may be cases where a defendant has a good reason to rely on a solicitor's advice that he should not comment e.g. if he were vulnerable and had difficulty in getting his answers across: *Essa* [2009] EWCA Crim 43

In *Brizzalari* [2004] EWCA Crim 310, the Court of Appeal discouraged prosecutors from too readily seeking to activate the provisions under s.34 unless the merits of the individual case required that that should be done. This was confirmed in: *Maguire* (2008) 172 J.P. 417. An adverse inference should not be drawn from a defendant's refusal to leave a police cell in order to be interviewed: *Johnson, Hind* [2005] EWCA Crim 971.

In *Condron and Condron* [1997] 1 Cr.App.R. 185, it was said that legal advice to remain silence cannot of itself prevent an adverse inference being drawn. The defendant and his solicitor may have to state the basis or the reason for the advice given. There may be good reason for such advice. The European Court of Human Rights found that there had been a violation of art. 6(1) on the ground that an adverse inference could have been drawn even if satisfied that it was for good reason. It therefore said that where silence cannot be attributed to a defendant's having no answer, or none that would stand up in cross-examination, no adverse inference should be drawn. The reason for the silence, if proffered, and its plausibility should be taken into account: *Condron v. UK* [2000] Crim.L.R. 679. **10–139**

In *Roble* [1997] Crim.L.R. 449, CA it was suggested that good reasons might be that the interviewing officer had not disclosed the nature of the case or the offence or the evidence was so complex or old that an immediate response cannot be given; see also *Beard* [2002] Crim.L.R. 684, CA. In *Howell* [2003] EWCA Crim 1169, it was also said that the kind of circumstances which may most likely justify silence are ill health, in particular mental disability, confusion, shock, intoxication, inability to recollect events without documents to hand or speaking to others. There must always be soundly based reasons for silence.

A court should not draw inferences where it believes that the defendant genuinely and reasonably relied on the advice of his solicitor: *Beckles* [2005] 1 W.L.R. 2829. In *Hoare* [2005] 1 W.L.R. 1804 it was said that ultimately the question is whether "regardless of advice, genuinely given and genuinely accepted, an accused has remained silent not because of that advice but because he had no or no satisfactory explanation to give".

The court may draw inferences upon a submission of no case to answer: s.34(2)(c) but s.38(3) states that a case to answer shall not be based solely on an adverse inference. In *Hart and McLean* [1998] 6 *Archbold News* 1, it was said that this could apply where the defence is putting a positive case which might include documentation.

10–140 In *Webber* [2004] 1 Cr.App.R. 40, it was held that a positive suggestion put to a witness by or on behalf of a defendant might amount to a fact relied on in his defence even if that suggestion was not adopted by the witness. The word "fact" should be given a wide meaning. It covers any fact in issue and which was put forward as part of the defence case. A defendant relies on a fact not only when he has given or adduced evidence of it but also when his advocate put a specific and positive case to prosecution witnesses.

Where, in interview, a defendant has read a prepared statement a court must compare what was said in that statement with the evidence given in court; it should also explore why any fresh facts are being put forward at that stage in order to establish whether the defendant has relied on a fact that he failed to mention when questioned and which is one that he could reasonably have been expected to mention: *T v. DPP* (2007) 171 JP Reports 605. Where it is explained that there is forensic evidence and fingerprint evidence, a person can reasonably be expected to mention facts on which he will later rely: *Esimu* [2007] EWCA Crim.1380. In that case the defendant's fingerprints had been found on the rear of a stolen car's number plates. After a "no comment" interview he had said at trial that his fingerprints could have been there when he had valeted the car. The argument put forward was that this explanation was not fact but a hypothesis. It was held that this explanation was based on facts and therefore could be expected to be mentioned in interview.

Although there is a growing practice for suspects to make a no comment interview and then give a prepared statement such a practice could prove dangerous for a defendant if he omitted something significant; it also does not grant automatic immunity from the drawing of adverse inferences: *Mohammad* June 12, 2009 unreported.

Where a defendant merely reveals that he was silent on legal advice this does not give rise to a waiver of legal professional privilege but where a defendant discloses the reasons for the legal advice that he received at the police station this may result in a waiver of legal professional privilege: *Condron* [1997] 1 Cr.App.R 185; *Bowden* [1999] 2 Cr.App.R. 176. Where a defendant has not waived privilege, the defendant should not be asked during cross-examination either whether he told his solicitor the facts that he now relies on in court or whether he is willing to waive privilege; if the defendant is asked such a question the court must inform the defendant that he is not required to answer it: *Seaton* [2011] 1 Cr.App.R. 2. In order to rebut a suggestion of recent fabrication, however, the defendant is entitled to waive privilege and disclose to the court that he did mention the relevant facts to his solicitor: *Seaton*. Where a defendant does waive privilege for either of these purposes, this does not give rise to a waiver of privilege in all communications with his solicitor and may not give rise to a waiver of privilege in relation to everything he discussed with his solicitor on the relevant occasion; "The test is fairness and/or the avoidance of a misleading impression": *Seaton* at para. 43. There is also a waiver of legal professional privilege if, when the police were interviewing the defendant, the defendant or his solicitor revealed the reasons why the solicitor advised the defendant to be silent to the police: *Bowden* (above).

Section 38(3) of the 1984 Act provides that person cannot be convicted solely on an inference under s.34 and if a person is convicted mainly on such an inference it seems that this will result in a violation of art. 6 of the European Convention on Human Rights: *Murray v. UK* (1996) 22 E.H.R.R. 29.

The protection given by s.34(2A) re the absence of an opportunity to consult a solicitor involves the dis-application of the adverse inferences provision in s.34; it does not however render inadmissible the answers given by a detainee during questioning: *Ibrahim & Ors* [2008] 4 All E.R. 208.

Criminal Justice and Public Order Act 1994, s.35

Effect of accused's silence at trial

10–141 **35.**—(1) At the trial of any person for an offence, subsections (2) and (3) below apply unless—

(a) the accused's guilt is not in issue; or

(b) it appears to the court that the physical or mental condition of the accused makes it undesirable for him to give evidence;

but subsection (2) below does not apply if, at the conclusion of the evidence for the prosecution, his legal representative informs the court that the accused will give evidence or, where he is unrepresented, the court ascertains from him that he will give evidence.

(2) Where this subsection applies, the court shall, at the conclusion of the evidence for the prosecution, satisfy itself (in the case of proceedings on indictment, in the presence of the jury) that the accused is aware that the stage has been reached at which evidence can be given for the defence and that he can, if he wishes, give evidence and that, if he chooses not to give evidence, or having been sworn, without good cause refuses to answer any question, it will be permissible for the court or jury to draw such inferences as appear proper from his failure to give evidence or his refusal, without good cause, to answer any question.

(3) Where this subsection applies, the court or jury, in determining whether the accused is guilty of the offence charged, may draw such inferences as appear proper from the failure of the accused to give evidence or his refusal, without good cause, to answer any question.

(4) This section does not render the accused compellable to give evidence on his own behalf, and he shall accordingly not be guilty of contempt of court by reason of a failure to do so.

(5) For the purposes of this section a person who, having been sworn, refuses to answer any question shall be taken to do so without good cause unless—

(a) he is entitled to refuse to answer the question by virtue of any enactment, whenever passed or made, or on the ground of privilege; or

(b) the court in the exercise of its general discretion excuses him from answering it.

[repealed]

(7) This section applies—

(a) in relation to proceedings on indictment for an offence, only if the person charged with the offence is arraigned on or after the commencement of this section;

(b) in relation to proceedings in a magistrates' court, only if the time when the court begins to receive evidence in the proceedings falls after the commencement of this section.

[This section is reprinted as amended by the *Crime and Disorder Act* 1998, Sched. 10, para. 1.]

Under s.35 the court may potentially draw an inference either where the defendant fails to testify or where the defendant refuses to answer a question during cross-examination. The court may not draw an inference from the defendant's failure to testify, however, if there is evidence of a physical or mental condition that makes it undesirable for the defendant to testify: *Friend* [1997] 1 W.L.R. 1433; *Kavanagh* [2005] EWHC 820 (Admin). The court may not draw an inference from the refusal of the defendant to answer a question if he has "good cause" for the failure; i.e., if he is entitled to refuse to answer by virtue of an Act of Parliament or a claim of privilege or the court excuses him from answering in the exercise of its discretion (see s.35(5)). The court cannot draw an inference under s.35 when deciding whether there is no case for the defendant to answer and the court should not draw an inference under s.35 unless it is sure that the defendant's silence, "... can only sensibly be attributed to the defendant's having no answer or none that would stand up to cross-examination ...": *Cowan* [1996] 1 Cr.App.R. 1 at p.7. **10–142**

An adverse inference may be drawn in a trial in the absence of a defendant who is a co-defendant but no adverse inference may be drawn on account of his absence: *Hamidi and Cherazi* [2010] Crim.L.R. 578. In this case it was held that the non-application of s.35 to a co-defendant who failed to attend at his trial did not make it unfair to apply the section to other co-defendants present who chose not to give evidence.

Section 38(3) of the Act prohibits a conviction on an inference alone. In *Murray v. UK* (1996) 22 E.H.R.R. 29, it was said that it would be incompatible with the rights of the defendant to base a conviction solely or mainly on his silence or on a refusal to answer questions or give evidence himself. A defendant does not need to give evidence where the prosecution case is weak. The principle in *Murray* was confirmed in *Beccles v. UK* (2002) 36 E.H.R.R. 162; see also *Milford* [2001] Crim.L.R. 330; *Chenia* [2003] 2 Cr.App.R. 6.

An adverse inference may be drawn where a defendant chooses not to be present at his trial despite being fit to attend and as a consequence does not give evidence; where he cannot remember the events there is nothing to stop him from giving evidence of that: *Charisma*, 173 J.P.633, CA. Where a person suffers from alcohol dependency syndrome he can still give relevant evidence to the effect that he suffers from that condition and the degree of impairment of his mental responsibility; adverse inferences may be drawn in the circumstance where he chooses not to give evidence: *Barry* [2010] 1 Cr.App.R. 32.

A psychiatric report which says no more than that a defendant would have difficulty in giving evidence and that the strain of doing so "could" adversely affect his mental health without saying anything about how the experience might adversely affect his health, is not evidence that it is undesirable for a defendant to give evidence and therefore adverse inferences from a failure to give evidence may be drawn: *Ensor*, *ante*.

Criminal Justice and Public Order Act 1994, ss.36–37

Effect of accused's failure or refusal to account for objects, substances or marks

10–143 **36.**—(1) Where—

(a) a person is arrested by a constable, and there is—

(i) on his person; or

(ii) in or on his clothing or footwear; or

(iii) otherwise in his possession; or

(iv) in any place in which he is at the time of his arrest,

any object, substance or mark, or there is any mark on any such object; and

(b) that or another constable investigating the case reasonably believes that the presence of the object, substance or mark may be attributable to the participation of the person arrested in the commission of an offence specified by the constable; and

(c) the constable informs the person arrested that he so believes, and requests him to account for the presence of the object, substance or mark; and

(d) the person fails or refuses to do so,

then if, in any proceedings against the person for the offence so specified, evidence of those matters is given, subsection (2) below applies.

(2) Where this subsection applies—

(a) a magistrates' court inquiring into the offence as examining justices;

(b) a judge, in deciding whether to grant an application made by the accused under—

(i) section 6 of the *Criminal Justice Act* 1987 (application for dismissal of charge of serious fraud in respect of which notice of transfer has been given under section 4 of that Act); or

(ii) paragraph 5 of Schedule 6 to the *Criminal Justice Act* 1991 (application for dismissal of charge of violent or sexual offence involving child in respect of which notice of transfer has been given under section 53 of that Act);

(c) the court, in determining whether there is a case to answer; and

(d) the court or jury, in determining whether the accused is guilty of the offence charged,

may draw such inferences from the failure or refusal as appear proper.

(3) Subsections (1) and (2) above apply to the condition of clothing or footwear as they apply to a substance or mark thereon.

(4) Subsections (1) and (2) above do not apply unless the accused was told in ordinary language by the constable when making the request mentioned in subsection (1)(c) above what the effect of this section would be if he failed or refused to comply with the request.

(4A) Where the accused was at an authorised place of detention at the time of the failure or refusal, subsections (1) and (2) above do not apply if he had not been allowed an opportunity to consult a solicitor prior to the request being made.

(5) This section applies in relation to officers of customs and excise as it applies in relation to constables.

(6) This section does not preclude the drawing of any inference from a failure or refusal of the accused to account for the presence of an object, substance or mark or from the condition of clothing or footwear which could properly be drawn apart from this section.

(7) This section does not apply in relation to a failure or refusal which occurred before the commencement of this section.

Effect of accused's failure or refusal to account for presence at a particular place

37.—(1) Where— **10–144**

(a) a person arrested by a constable was found by him at a place at or about the time the offence for which he was arrested is alleged to have been committed; and

(b) that or another constable investigating the offence reasonably believes that the presence of the person at that place and at that time may be attributable to his participation in the commission of the offence; and

(c) the constable informs the person that he so believes, and requests him to account for that presence; and

(d) the person fails or refuses to do so,

then if, in any proceedings against the person for the offence, evidence of those matters is given, subsection (2) below applies.

(2) Where this subsection applies—

(a) a magistrates' court inquiring into the offence as examining justices;.

(b) a judge, in deciding whether to grant an application made by the accused under—

(i) section 6 of the *Criminal Justice Act* 1987 (application for dismissal of charge of serious fraud in respect of which notice of transfer has been given under section 4 of that Act); or

(ii) paragraph 5 of Schedule 6 to the *Criminal Justice Act* 1991 (application for dismissal of charge of violent or sexual offence involving child in respect of which notice of transfer has been given under section 53 of that Act);

(c) the court, in determining whether there is a case to answer; and

(d) the court or jury, in determining whether the accused is guilty of the offence charged,

may draw such inferences from the failure or refusal as appear proper.

(3) Subsections (1) and (2) do not apply unless the accused was told in ordinary language by the constable when making the request mentioned in subsection (1)(c) above what the effect of this section would be if he failed or refused to comply with the request.

(3A) Where the accused was at an authorised place of detention at the time of the failure or refusal, subsections (1) and (2) do not apply if he had not been allowed an opportunity to consult a solicitor prior to the request being made.

(4) This section applies in relation to officers of customs and excise as it applies in relation to constables.

(5) This section does not preclude the drawing of any inference from a failure or refusal of the accused to account for his presence at a place which could properly be drawn apart from this section.

(6) This section does not apply in relation to a failure or refusal which occurred before the commencement of this section.

The significance of s.36 and s.37 is that whilst they are narrower in focus than s.34, **10–145** which was considered at § 10–137, above, unlike s.34, they are potentially applicable even though the defendant is not relying on a fact in his defence that he failed to mention when questioned under caution or charged. Both sections are only applicable if the police gave the defendant the special warning required by s.37(3) of the 1994 Act and Code C para. 10.11. A court must be satisfied that a defendant has failed to account for the relevant matter before drawing proper inferences: *Compton* [2002] All E.R. 149.

Section 38(3) of the 1984 Act provides that person cannot be convicted solely on an inference under s.36 or s.37 and if a person is convicted mainly on such an inference it seems that this will result in a violation of art. 6 of the European Convention on Human Rights: *Murray v. UK* (1996) 22 E.H.R.R. 29.

Criminal Procedure and Investigations Act 1996, s.11

Faults in disclosure by accused

10–146 [**11.**—(1) This section applies in the three cases set out in subsections (2), (3) and (4).

(2) The first case is where section 5 applies and the accused—

(a) fails to give an initial defence statement,

(b) gives an initial defence statement but does so after the end of the period which, by virtue of section 12, is the relevant period for section 5,

(c) is required by section 6B to give either an updated defence statement or a statement of the kind mentioned in subsection (4) of that section but fails to do so,

(d) gives an updated defence statement or a statement of the kind mentioned in section 6B(4) but does so after the end of the period which, by virtue of section 12, is the relevant period for section 6B,

(e) sets out inconsistent defences in his defence statement, or

(f) at his trial—

(i) puts forward a defence which was not mentioned in his defence statement or is different from any defence set out in that statement,

(ii) relies on a matter which, in breach of the requirements imposed by or under section 6A, was not mentioned in his defence statement,

(iii) adduces evidence in support of an alibi without having given particulars of the alibi in his defence statement, or

(iv) calls a witness to give evidence in support of an alibi without having complied with section 6A(2)(a) or (b) as regards the witness in his defence statement.

(3) The second case is where section 6 applies, the accused gives an initial defence statement, and the accused—

(a) gives the initial defence statement after the end of the period which, by virtue of section 12, is the relevant period for section 6, or

(b) does any of the things mentioned in paragraphs (c) to (f) of subsection (2).

(5) Where this section applies—

(a) the court or any other party may make such comment as appears appropriate;

(b) the court or jury may draw such inferences as appear proper in deciding whether the accused is guilty of the offence concerned.

(6) Where—

(a) this section applies by virtue of subsection (2)(f)(ii) (including that provision as it applies by virtue of subsection (3)(b)), and

(b) the matter which was not mentioned is a point of law (including any point as to the admissibility of evidence or an abuse of process) or an authority,

comment by another party under subsection (5)(a) may be made only with the leave of the court.

(8) Where the accused puts forward a defence which is different from any defence set out in his defence statement, in doing anything under subsection (5) or in deciding whether to do anything under it the court shall have regard—

(a) to the extent of the differences in the defences, and

(b) to whether there is any justification for it.

(9) Where the accused calls a witness whom he has failed to include, or to identify adequately, in a witness notice, in doing anything under subsection (5) or in deciding whether to do anything under it the court shall have regard to whether there is any justification for the failure.

(10) A person shall not be convicted of an offence solely on an inference drawn under subsection (5).

(12) In this section—

(a) "initial defence statement" means a defence statement given under section 5 or 6;

(b) "updated defence statement" means a defence statement given under section 6B;

(c) a reference simply to an accused's "defence statement" is a reference—

(i) where he has given only an initial defence statement, to that statement;

(ii) where he has given both an initial and an updated defence statement, to the updated defence statement;

(iii) where he has given both an initial defence statement and a statement of the kind mentioned in section 6B(4), to the initial defence statement;

(d) a reference to evidence in support of an alibi shall be construed in accordance with section 6A(3);
(e) "witness notice" means a notice given under section 6C.]

Where a defence statement is discretionary and one is served out of time or sets out inconsistent defences or at trial the defendant puts forward a new defence, relies on a matter which is not included in the statement or calls an alibi witness not mentioned in the defence statement, adverse inferences may be drawn by the court and there may be comments by the other party: s.11(5) of the *Criminal Procedure and Investigations Act* 1996, as amended. **10-147**

XII. PRIVILEGE

A. GENERAL

A witness may refuse to produce documentary evidence or give oral testimony on the ground that the information sought is privileged. In respect of documents he also is protected from giving oral evidence as to their content, or his knowledge or belief founded thereupon. Privilege entitles a party not to answer a question or produce a document. It is not concerned with its admissibility, which depends upon its relevance: *Governor of Pentonville Prison, ex p. Osman* (1990) 90 Cr.App.R. 281, DC. **10-148**

Courts may order disclosure of confidential but not privileged information: *Manchester Crown Court, ex p. Rogers* [1999] 4 All E.R. 35.

Part II

B. LEGAL PROFESSIONAL PRIVILEGE

The right to consult legal advisers without fear of the communication's being revealed is a fundamental condition on which the administration of justice rests: *Derby Magistrates' Court, ex p. B.* [1996] A.C. 487, HL. The first limb of legal professional privilege, namely legal advice privilege, covers confidential written or oral communications made between a professional legal adviser and his client or any person representing the client in connection with the giving of legal advice to the client for the purpose of giving or obtaining legal advice: *Balabel v. Air India* [1988] Ch.317. The second limb, know as litigation privilege, includes communications between the professional adviser, and/or the client and any other person for the purposes of litigation: *Waugh v. British Railways Board* [1980] A.C. 521. **10-149**

The privilege also attaches to an interpreter who attends a confidential conference between solicitor and client: *Bozkurt v. Thames Magistrates' Court* [2002] R.T.R. 246. In *R. (Howe) v. South Durham Magistrates' Court* [2005] R.T.R. 4, it was held that it is not a breach of legal professional privilege for the defendant's solicitor to be summoned to give evidence at his trial for allegedly driving whilst disqualified where no other means or proving disqualification is available. **10-150**

The privilege does not extend to communications which are made for the purposes of obtaining advice on the commission of a future crime or which are themselves part of a crime: *Cox and Railton* (1884) 14 Q.B.D. 153. Documents or information obtained in contravention of domestic or foreign law cannot be privileged: *Dubai Aluminium Co Ltd v. Al-Alwai* [1999] 1 W.L.R. 1964, QBD. There must be *prima facie* evidence that it was the client's intention to obtain advice in furtherance of his criminal purposes: *O'Rourke v. Darbishire* [1920] A.C. 581, HL. In deciding whether a document came into existence in furtherance of a crime the court may be entitled to look at the document itself: *Governor of Pentonville Prison, ex p. Osman, ante*.

A document does not become privileged simply by being handed to a lawyer. A solicitor who holds a document for or relating to his or her client can assert in respect of its seizure no greater authority than the client possesses: *Peterborough Justices, ex p. Hicks* [1977] 1 W.L.R. 1371, DC. If an unprivileged document in counsel's possession is called for in court, it must be produced: *Bursill v. Tanner* (1885) 16 Q.B.D. 1. Privilege does not attach to documents obtained by a client or his legal adviser for the purpose of litigation unless the document has been created for the purpose of litigation: *Ventouris v. Mountain* [1991] 1 W.L.R. 607, CA (Civ. Div.). Copies of non-privileged documents are privileged only if: (a) the copy was made for the purpose of litigation; and (b) the original document is not and has not at any time been in the control of the party claiming privilege: *The Palermo* (1884) L.R. 9 P.D. 6; *Watson v. Cammel Laird & Co Ltd* [1959] 1 W.L.R. 702, CA. Copy documents sent to a lawyer for legal advice do not thereby become privileged where the original in the hands of the maker of the copy is not privileged: *Dubai Bank Ltd v. Galadari* [1990] Ch. 98, CA (Civ. Div.).

10–151 Privilege does not extend to protect material in the hands of a solicitor from being disclosed where there is independent and free-standing evidence of a plot to pervert the course of justice: *Hallinan, Blackburn, Gittings & Nott (a firm) v. Middlesex Crown Court* [2005] 1 W.L.R. 766.

If a prosecutor comes into possession of material in respect of which the defence can justifiably claim legal professional privilege (and that claim is either conceded or upheld) the defence may contend that the way in which the material came into the possession of the prosecutor needs to be investigated and/or the disclosure of that material has so prejudiced the conduct of the defence that the case should not proceed. The prosecutor's duty, in those circumstances, is to explain to the court, either by calling evidence or from uncontested statements of fact, how he came into possession of the material and what use he has made of it, failing which the court may infer that a) he has obtained it by improper means, and/or b) his use of it will unfairly prejudice the defendant. The defence may also wish to call evidence. The court will then be in a position, in any abuse argument, to decide what course of action to take: *R. (Customs and Excise Commissioners) v. Nottingham Magistrates' Court* [2004] EWHC 1922. Legal professional privilege is inapplicable once the material is in the hands of the prosecution and, thus, the matter will be one for the court to consider in the exercise of its exclusionary discretion under s.78 *Police and Criminal Evidence Act* 1984: *Willis* [2004] EWCA Crim 3472, CA.

10–152 Where the selection of documents copied or assembled by a solicitor betrays the trend of the advice given to his client, the documents so selected are privileged: *Lyell v. Kennedy (No.3)* (1884) 27 Ch.D 1.

Translations of documents should be treated in the same way as copies: *Sumitomo Corporation v. Credit Lyonnais Rouse Ltd* [2002] 1 W.L.R. 479, CA (Civ. Div.).

A document or communication is always privileged once it becomes privileged: *Calcraft v. Guest* [1898] 1 Q.B. 759. Legal professional privilege must be upheld in the public interest, even where the witness no longer has any recognisable interest in preserving the confidentiality: *Derby Magistrates' Court, ex p. B.* [1996] A.C. 487, HL.

10–153 Where the expert's opinion is to an extent based on privileged material, the opinion itself is also privileged. Consequently the defence can object if the prosecution seeks to elicit evidence from an expert who has been abandoned and not relied upon by the defence: see *Davies* (2002) 166 J.P. 243, CA. A person interviewed by a doctor at the instigation of his own lawyers for the purpose of his defence is entitled to assume that what he says to the doctor has the same status as communications with his lawyers. Both the interview and the opinion based upon it are privileged: *Davies*, *ante*. An expert's opinion on DNA is privileged where it is based upon a blood sample taken form the defendant and sent to the expert by his solicitors in contemplation of criminal proceedings because the blood sample itself is an item subject to the legal professional privilege within the meaning of the *Police and Criminal Evidence Act* 1984, s.10: *R.* [1995] 1 Cr.App.R. 183, CA.

The *Regulation of Investigatory Powers Act* 2000 Pt II allows "directed" covert surveillance of interviews at prisons and police stations normally subject to privilege; the authorisation required is the same as that for "intrusive surveillance" within the Act but until an order is made it is unlawful: *McE v. Prison Service of Northern Ireland* [2009] 2 W.L.R. 782.

An appropriate adult is not subject to legal privilege but the presence of an appropriate adult during a conversation between an accused and his solicitor does not stop that conversation being subject to legal professional privilege: *A Local Authority v. B* [2009] 1 F.L.R. 289, Fam.Div.

C. PRIVILEGE AGAINST SELF-INCRIMINATION

Basically, a witness is entitled to rely upon the privilege against self-incrimination so as to object to answering a question if answering the question would tend to expose the witness to criminal proceedings, to proceedings for the recovery of a penalty (*e.g.* a tax penalty) or to a forfeiture: *Blunt v. Park Lane Hotel Ltd* [1942] 2 KB 253. The risk of exposure to liability for a debt, or to some other form of civil suit, does not give rise to the privilege: *Witnesses Act* 1806, s.1. **10–154**

Although it has been held that a witness must object personally on oath: *Downie v. Coe*, *The Times*, November 28, 1997, it is the legal adviser who will normally warn of self incrimination so that the court may rule on whether the witness has to answer the question or not. If the witness is wrongly compelled to answer and the defendant is convicted, the defendant cannot use the witness's compulsion to answer as a ground for appeal: *Kinglake* (1870) 11 Cox 499.

If the witness does not object, his replies once given will be admissible evidence in any proceedings brought against him: *Sloggett* (1865) Dears 656. If the witness objects but is compelled to answer the answers are not admissible in evidence in later proceedings: *Garbett* (1847) 1 Den 236.

There must be reasonable grounds for claiming the privilege and the danger must be real and appreciable: *Boyes* (1861) 1 B. & S. 311.

The privilege may be expressly removed by statute. Statutory exceptions include the *Criminal Evidence Act* 1898, s.1(e) and the *Theft Act* 1968, s.31. See *Khan v. Khan* [1982] 1 W.L.R. 513 in respect of the *Theft Act* 1968.

In *Saunders* [1996] 1 Cr.App.R. 463 the Court of Appeal rejected an argument that the trial judge should have excluded the transcript of interviews with DTI inspectors because the questioning under s.434 of the *Companies Act* 1985 was outside the safeguards of an interview under caution and the defendants were deprived of their protection against self-incrimination. Lord Taylor C.J. said that Parliament's intention was clear in s.434(5) and it could not be right for a judge to exercise his or her discretion to exclude evidence of interviews simply on the basis that Parliament ought not to countenance the possibility of self-incrimination. The European Court of Human Rights held that Saunders had been denied a fair trial because the use of statements obtained from him by the DTI inspectors amounted to an unjustifiable infringement of the right to silence and the right not to incriminate oneself: *Saunders v. UK* (1997) 23 E.H.R.R. 313. The court said that the question whether the use made by the prosecution of the statements obtained by the inspectors amounted to such an infringement must be examined in the light of all the circumstances in particular whether the applicant had been subject to compulsion to give principles of a fair procedure inherent in art. 6(1). Subsequently, a variety of statutes which remove the privilege were amended by the *Criminal Justice Act* 2003 so as to provide an alternative protection prevent the use of compelled answers in criminal proceedings. The admission of compelled answers will not violate art. 6 where the provision is a proportionate response to a serious social problem: *DPP v. Wilson* [2002] R.T.R. 37. See *ante*, § 10–134 for the impact of s.13 of the *Fraud Act* 2006. **10–155**

The privilege relates to any risk of prosecution under English law: *Den Norske Bank ASA v. Antonatos*, *ante*. No privilege arises where matters are covered by a pardon: *Boyes* (1861) 1 B. & S. 311, by undertakings and immunities from prosecution given by the DPP, or where the risk relates to liability for debt in civil proceedings. The privilege does not extend to incrimination under foreign law however the court has a discretion to excuse a witness from giving evidence or producing documents which may so incriminate him: *Brannigan v. Davidson* [1997] A.C. 238, PC. A remote possibility of prosecution is not enough. The danger must be "real and appreciable, with reference to the **10–156** ordinary operation of law and in the ordinary course of things": *Boyes, ante*. Provided that the risk of proceedings being taken against the witness is real and not remote or insubstantial, the witness does not have to show that proceedings are likely or could probably be taken against him: *Re Westinghouse Electric Corp* [1977] 3 All E.R. 703.

Privilege against self-incrimination is not an absolute right. *Saunders* above recognised the distinction between admissions obtained in breach of a defendant's right to silence and pre-existing material obtained by the use of statutory powers. Thus, in recognition of the fact that the art. 6 privilege does not encompass the latter, the statutory protection inserted into various statutes by the *Criminal Justice Act* 2003 only protected the former: see for a more recent example, s.13(2) of the *Fraud Act* 2006 at § 10–134, above. There is no privilege in material recovered from a computer and showing objectionable images of children where the search had been conducted under intellectual property proceedings; the material can quite properly be referred to the police: *C PLC v. P; W v. P* [2007] 3 W.L.R. 437. The case of *O'Halloran and Francis v. United Kingdom* [2007] Crim.L.R. 897, a case relating to the failure to identify the driver of a motor vehicle under section 172 of the *Road Traffic Act* 1988, confirmed that cases of direct compulsion do not necessarily lead to a violation of ECHR. To decide whether there has been a violation account must be taken of (a) the direct nature of the compulsion, (b) whether the compulsion is part of a regulatory scheme that fairly imposes obligations on drivers in order to promote safety on roads, (c) whether the information required is simple, specific and restricted fact of who was driving rather than a general account of movements or answers to wide-ranging questions, (d) whether the offence contains a safeguard in the form of a defence of due diligence and (e) that the identity of the driver was only one element in the offence needing to be proved. In *Jalloh v. Germany, ante*, a case involving evidential material held inside the defendant's body and his refusal to give it up through the taking of medication, it was said that the rationale is to "respect the will of the defendant. . ..not to be compelled to provide a statement" and whether a violation took place depends on factors such as "the weight of public interest in the investigation and punishment of the offence at issue"

The principle that evidence existing independently of the will of the subject does not normally engage the privilege against self-incrimination is clearly established. Where an offender is served with a notice under s.49 of the *Regulation of Investigatory Powers Act* 2000 requiring him to disclose the password or keys to encrypted files he cannot rely on the privilege as a reason for failure to comply; it will only apply if the data itself contains incriminating evidence, in which case the exclusion of incriminating evidence under s.78 *Police and Criminal Evidence Act* 1984 may be appropriate as, if the data is incriminating, the offender's knowledge of the key may be incriminating: *R. v. S* [2009] 1 All E.R. 716.

In a civil case concerning a production order for the disclosure of material for a book for the purposes of a terrorist investigation guidance was given on what should be taken into account in deciding whether a person should be required to disclose information where to do so would risk infringing the privilege: *R. (on the application of Malik) v. Manchester Crown Court* [2008] 4 All E.R. 403. The correct approach was said to be:

(i) the court should attach considerable weight to the nature of the Convention right interfered with when an application is made against a journalist
(ii) the proportionality of any proposed order should be measured and justified against that weight and
(iii) a person who applies for an order should provide a clear and compelling case in justification of it.

The Divisonal Court regarded the issue of whether the English Law of Privilege attaches to pre-existing documents as on that needed to be resolved by the House of Lords (now by the Supreme Court).

D. CONFIDENTIAL COMMUNICATIONS

10–157 No legal privilege arises out of the relationship between doctor and patient: *Mc-*

Donald [1991] Crim.L.R. 122, CA. It does not arise between journalist and informer: *Att.-Gen. v. Mulholland and Foster* [1963] 2 Q.B. 477. See, however, the *Contempt of Court Act* 1981, s.10. The position of priest and penitent has not been authoritively decided but the tendency of judicial dicta is that while in strict law the privilege does not exist, a minister of religion should not be required to give evidence as to a confession made to him: *Griffin* (1853) 6 Cox 219; *Hay* (1896) 2 F. & F. 4. Legal professional privilege does not attach to communications between an accountant and the accountant's client, even where the accountant is providing legal advice: *R. (on the application of Prudential Plc) v. Special Commission of Income Tax* [2011] 2 W.L.R. 50.

The court has a discretion to excuse a witness from answering a question where to do so would involve a breach of confidence. In *Hunter v. Mann* [1974] Q.B. 767, 59 Cr.App.R 37, DC, Lord Widgery C.J. said (*obiter*):

> "If a doctor, giving evidence ... is asked a question which he finds embarrassing because it involves him talking about things which he would normally regard as confidential, he can seek the protection of the judge and ask the judge if it is necessary for him to answer. The judge, by virtue of the overriding discretion to control his court which all English judges have, can, if he thinks fit, tell the doctor that he need not answer the question. Whether or not the judge would take that line, of course, depends largely on the importance of the potential answer to the issues being tried."

Before compelling disclosure, the court should be satisfied that the potential answer is relevant and will serve a useful purpose in relation to the proceedings, and then weigh the conflicting interests to determine whether confidentiality should be overridden or respected: *Att.-Gen. v. Mulholland and Foster, ante*.

The *Police and Criminal Evidence Act* 1984 imposed restrictions on the extent to which access may be obtained to confidential information for the purposes of a criminal investigation: *PACE* 1984, ss.8–13.

Alternative Business Structures are due to come into operation in autumn 2011. Where an alternative business structure provides services to a client via a non-legal adviser who acts at the direction and under the supervision of a legal adviser, s.190 of the *Legal Services Act* 2007 makes provision for legal professional privilege to attach to communications with the client.

XIII. CORROBORATION

Corroboration is evidence which supports a witness's testimony. Where one piece of evidence confirms and supports another, corroboration takes place if both pieces of evidence are accepted by the tribunal of fact. **10–158**

A definition of corroboration was found in *Baskerville* [1916] 2 K.B. 658. Lord Reid said at 667:

> "Evidence in corroboration must be independent testimony which affects the accused by connecting or tending to connect him with the crime. In other words, it must be evidence which implicates him, that is, which confirms in some material particular not only the evidence that the crime has been committed, but also that the prisoner committed it. The test applicable to determine the nature and extent of the corroboration is thus the same whether the case falls within the rule of practice at common law or within that class of offences for which corroboration is required by statute."

In general there is no requirement for corroboration. Some statutes, however, do require corroboration. In the magistrates' courts this applies to speeding offences: *Road Traffic Regulation Act* 1984, s.89(2). Apart from those rare circumstances in which the law requires corroboration, in certain cases it was formerly considered dangerous to convict on the evidence of a single person unless the court was convinced of the guilt of the defendant:

— evidence of a complaint in any allegation of a sexual offence;
— evidence of an accomplice when called by the prosecutor;
— evidence of children.

10–159 Legislation has abolished the requirement to warn juries of the danger in the above cases: *Criminal Justice Act* 1988, s.34(2) and *Criminal Justice and Public Order Act* 1994, s.32(1). A judge now possesses discretion to warn the jury of the danger of relying on the evidence of an unreliable witness and, where appropriate, to advise the jury to look for supporting evidence, but such warnings should only be given where there is an evidential basis for regarding the witness as being unreliable: *Makanjuola* [1995] 1 W.L.R. 1348; *Easton* [1995] 2 Cr.App.R 469.

In the magistrates' courts, the judiciary will exercise caution in convicting without supporting evidence if, for example, a witness is shown to have lied, to have made previous false complaints, is of bad character, is a co-defendant, bears the defendant a grudge or has an improper motive: *Makanjuola*; *Muncaster* [1999] Crim.L.R. 409.

XIV. PROCEDURE FOR CHALLENGING ADMISSIBILITY

10–160 Since the judiciary in magistrates' courts are judges of both fact and law they must rule on the admissibility of evidence and decide the question of the defendant's guilt. If they rule evidence inadmissible they must ignore that evidence when deciding whether to convict or acquit the defendant.

The magistrates' court has an overall responsibility for ensuring that the defendant receives a fair trial according to law: *Sang, ante*. It should not wait for an objection to be taken to the admissibility of evidence but should itself stop questions likely to elicit such evidence: *Ellis* [1910] 2 K.B. 746; *Stirland v. DPP* [1944] A.C. 315.

The point at which the magistrates' court should rule upon a question of admissibility is a matter for its discretion: *F. (an infant) v. Chief Constable of Kent* [1982] Crim.L.R. 682. The Divisional Court held that a trial within a trial is not an appropriate procedure in the magistrates' court. This is because the purpose of a *voire dire* is to allow the judge to determine a question of law in the absence of the jury. Incidental matters, such as the admissibility of evidence, should be decided as separate issues from that of guilt.

10–161 In *Epping and Ongar Justices, ex p. Manby* [1986] Crim.L.R. 555, the defendant had been charged with driving an overweight vehicle. The prosecution relied upon a police officer's certificate that the defendant had admitted responsibility for the vehicle pursuant to the *Road Traffic Act* 1972, s.181. The defendant's solicitor wished to challenge the admissibility of the certificate but did not require the officer to be called to give evidence. The justices refused to hear evidence from the defendant on the point as a preliminary issue and proceeded with the prosecution case. No defence evidence was called. The application for review of the decision to refuse to decide the issue of admissibility as a preliminary issue was dismissed since, within statutory restraints, justices determine their own procedure. Since the defendant had not required the officer to be called, the justices were entitled to accept the prosecution evidence as providing a *prima facie* case on the point.

It has also been said, however, that the court should not rule on the admissibility of evidence until the evidence has been tendered and objection taken: *Sang* 69 Cr.App.R. 282; *Williams v. Mohamed* [1977] R.T.R. 12.

Where an application is made under s.78, a magistrates' court has a discretion either to deal with the application by way of a *voire dire* when it arises or to leave the decision until the end of the hearing when all the evidence has been heard. The aim should always be to secure a trial which is fair to both sides: *Vel v. Owen* [1987] Crim.L.R. 496, DC. In *Halawa v. Federation Against Copyright Theft* [1995] 1 Cr.App.R. 21, DC, the court said:

— A proper understanding of what is fair will lead in some cases to the conclusion that, if the defendant wishes to proceed by way of a *voire dire*, he or she should be allowed to do so because, unless there is good reason to take a different course, he or she should have the opportunity to secure the exclusion of unfair evidence before he or she decides whether to give evidence. If he or she is unfairly denied that opportunity, the right to silence is impaired.

— If the application is made as alternative to a submission under s.76 of the 1984 Act, it should be examined at the same time in accordance with the procedure set out in *Liverpool Juvenile Court, ex p. R* [1988] Q.B. 1.

— If the point is raised only under s.78 in most cases the better course will be for the whole of the prosecution case to be heard, including the disputed evidence, before any *voire dire* is held.

— In order to decide which course to take, the court may ask the defence the extent of the issues to be address by the defendant's evidence on the *voire dire*. If the issues are limited to the circumstances in which the evidence was obtained, there would in most cases be no apparent reason why the defendant should be heard as on a *voire dire*. If however the defendant intends to contradict some part of the prosecution's account of "all the circumstances" it would be open to the court to conclude that the proceedings on the *voire dire* might be protracted and would introduce issues which would have to be re-examined in the remaining stages of the trial if a *prima facie* case is held to be established, in which case the securing of a fair trial to both sides would not require a *voire dire*. For this purpose the court would be entitled to take account of the nature and extent of the cross-examination of the prosecution witnesses for an understanding of the extent of any dispute as to "all the circumstances".

Where the court is determining the admissibility of a confession under s.76 of the *Police and Criminal Evidence Act* 1984 then it has been held that admissibility should be determined by way of *voire dire*: *Liverpool Juvenile Court, ex p. R.* [1988] Q.B. 1. Section 76(2) of the same Act provides that if it is represented that the confession has or may have been obtained in either of the two ways set out in that subsection, the court shall not allow it to be given in evidence except insofar as the prosecution proves beyond reasonable doubt that it was not so obtained. Section 76(2) accordingly obliges a magistrates' court to hold a trial within a trial in such cases. This rule also applies to committal proceedings: *Oxford City Justices, ex p. Berry* [1988] Q.B. 507.

If an application to exclude evidence is made under s.78 of the *Police and Criminal Evidence Act* 1984 the court is not obliged to hold a trial within a trial: *Vel v. Owen* [1987] Crim.L.R. 496. The defendant has no right to have the admissibility of evidence determined under s.78 in advance of evidence being given because the court under s.78 has a discretion to exclude evidence if it would bear unfairly on the proceedings and there is no burden on the prosecution to disprove unfairness. **10–162**

The court does not have the power to delegate the function of determining the admissibility of evidence to another bench: *Ormskirk Justices, ex p. Davies* (1994) 158 J.P. 1145. After the court rules that evidence is inadmissible, it must then ignore that evidence when determining the issue of guilt. If a court hears of a defendant's convictions or pending charges, it may be necessary to adjourn the case to be heard by another bench. In *Liverpool Justices, ex p. Topping* (1983) 76 Cr.App.R. 170 the court said that the test in such circumstances is "would a reasonable and fair-minded person sitting in court and knowing all the relevant facts have a reasonable suspicion that a fair trial for the [defendant] was not possible?"

The court may reverse a previous decision as to inadmissibility provided that there is good reason to do so and that no injustice is caused. Such reversals should, however, be exceptional: *Faversham and Sittingbourne Justices,ex p. Stickings* (1996) 160 J.P. 801.

There is no need for evidence to be repeated after the question of admissibility has been determined: *F. (an infant) v. Chief Constable of Kent, ante*.

The jury does not have the power to [illegible] the function of determining the admissibility or otherwise [illegible] [illegible] [illegible] [illegible] [illegible] [illegible] [illegible] [illegible] [illegible] the [illegible] [illegible] [illegible] [illegible] [illegible] that [illegible] [illegible] the [illegible] [illegible] [illegible] [illegible] the issue of [illegible] [illegible] [illegible] [illegible] [illegible] [illegible] [illegible] [illegible] to adjourn the case to be [illegible] a reasonable [illegible] [illegible] [illegible] [illegible] [illegible] [illegible] [illegible] [illegible].

CHAPTER 11

CHALLENGING DECISIONS

I. RE-OPENING A CASE

Magistrates' Courts Act 1980, s.142

Power of magistrates' court to re-open cases to rectify mistakes etc.

142.—(1) A magistrates' court may vary or rescind a sentence or other order imposed or made by it when dealing with an offender if it appears to the court to be in the interests of justice to do so, and it is hereby declared that this power extends to replacing a sentence or order which for any reason appears to be invalid by another which the court has power to impose or make. **11–1**

(1A) The power conferred on a magistrates' court by subsection (1) above shall not be exercisable in relation to any sentence or order imposed or made by it when dealing with an offender if—

(a) the Crown Court has determined an appeal against—

(i) that sentence or order;

(ii) the conviction in respect of which that sentence or order was imposed or made; or

(iii) any other sentence or order imposed or made by the magistrates' court when dealing with the offender in respect of that conviction (including a sentence or order replaced by that sentence or order); or

(b) the High Court has determined a case stated for the opinion of that court on any question arising in any proceeding leading to or resulting from the imposition or making of the sentence or order.

(2) Where a person is convicted by a magistrates' court and it subsequently appears to the court that it would be in the interests of justice that the case should be heard again by different justices, the court may so direct.

(2A) The power conferred on a magistrates' court by subsection (2) above shall not be exercisable in relation to a conviction if—

(a) the Crown Court has determined an appeal against—

(i) the conviction; or

(ii) any sentence or order imposed or made by the magistrates' court when dealing with the offender in respect of the conviction; or

(b) the High Court has determined a case stated for the opinion of that court on any question arising in any proceeding leading to or resulting from the conviction.

(3) Where a court gives a direction under subsection (2) above—

(a) the conviction and any sentence or other order imposed or made in consequence thereof shall be of no effect; and

(b) section 10(4) above shall apply as if the trial of the person in question had been adjourned.

[(4) ...repealed]

(5) Where a sentence or order is varied under subsection (1) above, the sentence or other order, as so varied, shall take effect from the beginning of the day on which it was originally imposed or made, unless the court otherwise directs.

11–2 Section 142 of the *Magistrates' Courts Act* 1980 is a provision which on first reading appears to confer a wide discretion upon the magistrates' court to re-open cases in the interests of justice, but it has been more narrowly interpreted by the Divisional Court in a number of cvases. In *Croydon Youth Court, ex p. DPP* [1997] 2 Cr.App.R. 411, McCowan L.J., giving the judgment of the Divisional Court said:

> "In my judgment the purpose of section 142(2) is accurately described in the heading as a "Power to rectify mistakes". It is generally and correctly regarded as a slip rule. Miss Markus places great reliance on the fact that those words in the heading are followed by "etc.". But in my judgment that cannot extend the power given beyond a situation akin to mistake."

In *R. (Holme) v. Liverpool Magistrates' Court* [2005] A.C.D. 37, Colins J., sitting in the Divisional Court considered the Croydon Youth Court decision and commented that the case indicated that the power under s.142 is to be used "in a relatively limited situation, namely one which is akin to mistake or, as the court says, the slip rule." The decisions in *Holme* and *Croydon Youth Court*, were considered again by the Divisional Court in *Zykin v. CPS*, 173 J.P. 361; Bean J. commented:

> "It is clear to us from the *Croydon* case and the *Holme* case that section 142 does not confer a wide and general power on a Magistrates' Court to re-open a previous decision on the grounds that it is in the interests of justice to do so."

The matter has most recently been considered by the Divisional Court in *R. (Trigger) v. Northampton Magistrates' Court*, 175 J.P. 101. In that case Ramsey J. expressed himself in less cautious terms regarding the use of s.142:

> "On the wording of section 142 itself there is no express limitation on the exercise by the court of what is expressed as a wide power to vary or rescind a sentence or other order imposed or made by it when dealing with an offender, except that it must be "in the interests of justice". The title to the section refers to the power being one "to rectify mistakes etc". Whilst *Croydon Magistrates Court*, *Holme* and *Zykin* all refer to the section being used to rectify mistakes and there is no doubt that this is the most likely reason for exercising the power under section 142, the wording of the section does not lead to the conclusion that it could not be used in other circumstances. So far as the time for the exercise of the power is concerned, equally there is now no limit on the time within which it can be exercised."

It is submitted that the more cautious approach reflects the nature of the cases that the Divisional Court was considering. In the *Croydon Youth Court* case, the defendant sought to re-open a decision where an unequivocal plea of guilty had been entered. Likewise, *Zykin* concerned an application to reopen a previous decision of a magistrates' court imposing a default sentence against Z for non-compliance with a confiscation order. It was held that this would be an improper use of the power; one magistrates' court cannot in effect sit as an appellate court from the decision of a differently constituted magistrates' court.

Holme and *Trigger* both concerned cases where magistrates' courts sought to increase sentences after a considerable lapse of time. The Divisional Court has placed some emphasis upon the importance of magistrates' courts using the discretion to re-open cases in a way that takes account of the principle of finality in sentencing. This principle was expressed in the decision of the House of Lords in *Secretary of State for the Home Department, ex p. Pierson* [1998] A.C. 539; it is a general principle of the common law that a lawful sentence pronounced by a judge may not retrospectively be increased. In *Trigger* the Divisional Court said that although s.142 gives magistrates jurisdiction to vary or rescind a sentence so as to impose a sentence that could have been imposed at the date of the original sentence, it must be borne in mind that it would not usually be in the interests of justice to increase a sentence imposed earlier unless the power is exercised speedily after the date of the original sentence.

The test to be applied in considering applications under s.142 is an "interests of justice" test. In *R. (Blick) v. Doncaster Magistrates' Court* (2008) 172 J.P. 651 a district judge refused to re-open a conviction where the adjournment notice giving the date for the defendant's trial had been sent to an old address in circumstances where the defendant had failed to notify the court of the new address. The Divisional Court criticised the district judge for applying as the primary test the question of whether the defendant had acted with "due diligence"; it was said that the inconvenience to the court could never outweigh the interests of justice.

By contrast, in *Newport Justices, ex p. Carey*, 160 J.P. 613 the Divisional Court held that magistrates had been right to refuse to set aside a conviction imposed in the absence of the defendant. The Court held that in exercising their broad discretion under the 1980 Act, the justices were not depriving C of his right of appeal to the Crown Court; his absence was entirely his own fault, and the decision reflected the inconvenience caused to witnesses by his non-attendance coupled with a desire to show the limit of the court's patience.

Section 142 refers to the courts powers when dealing with "an offender"; it follows that the power does not extend to a case in which the defendant has been acquitted, or where the charges have been withdrawn: *Coles v. East Penwith Justices,* 162 J.P. 353; *R. (Green & Green Scaffolding Ltd) v. Staines Magistrates' Court*, 172 J.P. 353 In *R. (O) v. Stratford Youth Court*, 168 J.P. 469 the CPS did not have their witnesses and applied for, but were refused, an adjournment; no evidence was offered and the case was dismissed. A few minutes later it was discovered that the witnesses were in fact present, and the magistrates purported to set aside their decision to dismiss the case. The Divisional Court held that they had neither the power under s.142 to set aside this conviction, nor an inherent power to correct the mistake.

In *Thames Magistrates Court, ex p. Ramadan* [1999] 1 Cr.App.R. 386, the magistrates' court had made a hospital order but had omitted to ensure that there was a vacancy, and the hospital refused to admit the defendant; the magistrates rescinded the hospital order. The Divisional Court held that the court was entitled to re-open the case and that the terms of s.142(1) were wide enough to encompass a person who had been dealt with under s.37(3) of the *Mental Health Act* 1983. This decision was followed in *R. (Bartram) v. Southend Magistrates' Court* [2004] EWHC 2691 where the Divisional Court suggested (*obiter*) that it had been open to the district judge in that case to set aside a decision to proceed under s.37(3). **11–3**

A court may review orders including the issue of a warrant for overnight detention under s.136 of the *Magistrates' Courts Act* 1980 following non-payment of a fine, provided that there was information indicating that the interests of justice required intervention: *Sheffield City Justices, ex p. Foster, The Times*, November 2, 1999.

11–4 Section 142, as originally enacted, provided that a decision could only be re-opened within 28 days, but the provision was subsequently amended so that there is no time limit for making an application. Mere delay in making an application is not a ground for refusing the application, however it is a factor for the court to take into account along with all other relevant circumstances: *Ealing Justices, ex p. Sahota*, 162 J.P. 73. In this case Garland J., giving the leading judgment in the Divisional Court, observed:

> ". . . we do wish to add (and to add with emphasis) that the repeal of the old 28 day time limit should not be taken as a licence to delay applications of this sort indefinitely, perhaps until papers have been lost or memories have faded, and an adherence to the appeal time limit as a guideline would be a very salutary thing. Delay in matters of this sort is always harmful, memories fade, records may be lost and the essence of doing justice is that it should be done expeditiously."

This decision has subsequently been followed by the Administrative Court in *R. (Dunlop) v. DPP* [2004] EWHC 225, where it was said that it was insufficient for magistrates, in refusing to re-open a case, simply to state that the delay in making the application had been excessive. More substantial reasoning than this has to be given, and it is important that the court identifies the sort of problems that demonstrate that the delay means that the matter cannot properly and fairly be re-opened; magistrates should show through their reasons that they have taken into account relevant and material considerations when arriving at a decision.

11–5 The court must exercise its discretion judicially. The late arrival at court of a defendant is not by itself a proper ground for refusing to re-open a decision: *Camberwell Green Magistrates' Court, ex p. Ibrahim*, 148 J.P. 400. Neither is it proper to refuse where a defendant fails to attend a trial on a summary matter because he has been remanded in custody on more serious matters and had not communicated that fact to the court or to prison officers; standards of justice should not be lowered by the lack of seriousness of the charge: *R. (Morsby) v. Tower Bridge Magistrates' Court*, 172 J.P. 155.

It is expected that a person submitting an appeal to the Crown Court against the decision of a magistrates' court, should consider whether it is an appropriate case in which to apply to the magistrates' court to set aside their decision. The notice of appeal form states: "Under section 142 of the *Magistrates' Courts Act* 1980, in some cases a magistrates' court can reopen a conviction, sentence or other order and make a fresh decision. Have you asked the magistrates' court to reconsider your case?". It may be appropriate to apply to have case re-opened where, for example, a defendant has been convicted in his absence of an offence of using a motor vehicle without insurance, and he has a valid certificate of insurance which covers his use of the vehicle; in such a case there will be a considerable saving of time and expense if the case is dealt with under the s.142 procedure rather than by of an appeal.

It is also appropriate, where the defendant did not know of proceedings until after the court begins to try the matter, for the defendant to make a statutory declaration pursuant to s.14 of the *Magistrates' Courts Act* 1980 (see *post* § 4–139 *et seq.*). Applications under this section must be made within strict time limits.

II. APPEAL TO CROWN COURT

A. GENERAL

Magistrates' Courts Act 1980, s.108

Right of appeal to the Crown Court

11–6 **108.**—(1) A person convicted by a magistrates' court may appeal to the Crown Court—

(a) if he pleaded guilty, against his sentence;

(b) if he did not, against the conviction or sentence.

(1A) [Section 14 of the *Powers of Criminal Courts (Sentencing) Act* 2000] (under which a conviction of an offence for which an order for conditional or absolute discharge is made is deemed not to be a conviction except for certain purposes) shall not prevent an appeal under this Act, whether against conviction or otherwise.

(2) A person sentenced by a magistrates' court for an offence in respect of which an order for conditional discharge has been previously made may appeal to the Crown Court against the sentence.

(3) In this section "sentence" includes any order made on conviction by a magistrates' court, not being—.

(a) ...

(b) an order for the payment of costs;

(c) an order under section 37(1) of the *Animal Welfare Act* 2006 (which enables a court to order the destruction of an animal); or

(d) an order made in pursuance of any enactment under which the court has no discretion as to the making of the order or its terms

and also includes a declaration of relevance, within the meaning of section 23 of the *Football Spectators Act* 1989.

(4) Subsection (3)(d) above does not prevent an appeal against a surcharge imposed under section 161A of the *Criminal Justice Act* 2003.

[This section is reprinted as amended by the *Powers of Criminal Courts (Sentencing) Act* 2000, Sched. 9, para. 71.]

Where a defendant pleads guilty he may only appeal against the sentence imposed. **11–7**
Where a defendant pleads not guilty he may appeal against both conviction and sentence. Appeals by young persons against conviction and/or sentence in the youth court are governed by these provisions, since youth courts are magistrates' courts: *Magistrates' Courts Act* 1980, ss.148, 152; *Children and Young Persons Act* 1933, ss.45, 46 and the *Powers of Criminal Courts (Sentencing) Act* 2000, s.137.

The correct route of appeal against both conviction and sentence for contempt of a magistrates' court is to the Crown Court under the *Contempt of Court Act* 1981, s.12(5): *Haw v. Westminster Magistrates' Court* [2008] Q.B. 888. Where it is appropriate a decision of a magistrates' court on a contempt issue under s.12 may be appealed by way of case stated under s.111 *Magistrates' Courts Act* 1980 Act or challenged in judicial review proceedings.

B. AGAINST CONVICTION

A plea of guilty in the magistrates' court usually means that the defendant cannot ap- **11–8**
peal against conviction to the Crown Court: *Magistrates' Courts Act* 1980, s.108. In *Birmingham Crown Court, ex p. Sharma* [1988] Crim.L.R. 741 the defendant pleaded guilty by post to failing to stop at a traffic light and driving without insurance. He sought leave to appeal to the Crown Court out of time against conviction on the grounds that he had not intended to plead guilty to driving without insurance, and had in fact been insured. On review of the decision to refuse leave it was held that the defendant was not within any exception to the rule that a plea of guilty in the magistrates' court was final. It made no difference that he had pleaded guilty by post.

The Crown Court has no jurisdiction to entertain an application to set aside the conviction or remit the case to the magistrates simply because the defendant has subsequently regretted pleading guilty and thinks that he has an arguable defence: *Marylebone Justices, ex p. Westminster City Council* [1971] 1 W.L.R. 567.

The Crown Court has a limited jurisdiction to hear appeals against conviction where the defendant has pleaded guilty. This will arise when there has been an equivocal plea or where a plea has been made under duress: *Durham Quarter Sessions, ex p. Virgo* [1952] 2 Q.B. 1; *Huntingdon Crown Court, ex p. Jordan* [1981] Q.B. 857. For an appeal against conviction to proceed on the basis that a guilty plea was tendered following erroneous legal advice, that advice must go to the heart of the plea so that the plea of guilty was not a true acknowledgement of guilt: *Saik*, [2004] EWCA Crim 2936 (a case which was subsequently overruled by the House of Lords, but on unrelated grounds).

11–9 If a defendant pleads guilty and is committed to the Crown Court for sentence, the Crown Court has a discretion to re-open a plea and remit the case to the magistrates' court if it considers it just to do so: *Inner London Crown Court, ex p. Sloper*, 69 Cr.App.R. 1.

Where it is argued on appeal to the Crown Court that a guilty plea entered in the magistrates' court was equivocal, provided that a proper inquiry into the issue of plea is made at the Crown Court, it may direct a re-hearing at the magistrates' court: *Plymouth Justices, ex p. Hart* [1986] Q.B. 950, 83 Cr.App.R. 81. The enquiry into the equivocality of the plea will require accounts of what happened at the hearing in the magistrates' court, and the magistrates and their legal adviser may be asked by the Crown Court to supply statements detailing what took place in the magistrates' court, in order to assist that enquiry.

The Crown Court must make proper inquiry as to what happened in the magistrates' court before considering remitting the case: *Marylebone Justices, ex p. Westminster City Council, ante*. It is not under such a duty, however, unless something indicates that the magistrates should have considered permitting a change of plea: *Coventry Crown Court, ex p. Manson*, 67 Cr.App.R. 315.

Where equivocality of plea is raised on appeal, the Crown Court should first decide if there is prima facie evidence of equivocality. If there is, it should request evidence from the bench, the legal adviser, or both. Only if it is then satisfied that the plea was equivocal should the case be remitted back for a fresh plea to be taken: *Rochdale Justices, ex p. Allwork*, 73 Cr.App.R. 319.

11–10 If the Crown Court finds the defendant not guilty of the offence charged, it may not convict the defendant of an attempt to commit the offence as that was not within the powers of the magistrates' court: *R. v. Manchester Crown Court, ex p. Hill* (1985) 149 J.P.N. 29.

C. AGAINST SENTENCE

11–11 There is no appeal against the making of a costs order, the destruction of an animal or a non-discretionary order.

Where a defendant appeals against a sentence imposed by a magistrates' court, the Crown Court should not review the decision reached by the magistrates but should carry out a complete rehearing of the issues and form an independent view, on all the evidence, of the correct sentence: *Swindon Crown Court, ex p. Murray* (1998) 162 J.P. 36.

The Crown Court is not bound by findings of fact made by a magistrates' court in a way that could limit its sentencing powers. Where a defendant appeals against sentence to the Crown Court, the court is entitled to decide the appeal on a different factual basis from that accepted by the magistrates' court. Where the Crown Court rejects the view taken by the magistrates' court, the court should make the position plain to the appellant and give him an opportunity, under the *Newton* principle, to challenge the factual basis adopted by the court: *Bussey v. DPP* [1999] 1 Cr.App.R.(S.) 125.

11–12 The Crown Court has no power to order that the sentence, which was the subject of the appeal, should be consecutive to a sentence passed after the justices had imposed the sentence in question: *Portsmouth Crown Court, ex p. Ballard* (1990) 154 J.P. 109.

A Crown Court, when dealing with an appeal against sentence, should have regard to what had occurred in the magistrates' court even though the appeal was by way of rehearing. In *Isleworth Crown Court, ex p. Irvin* [1992] R.T.R. 281, the magistrates' court adjourned the matter for reports and made it clear that they were not considering a custodial sentence if the reports were favourable; he was subsequently given a custodial sentence and appealed against the decision to the Crown Court. In such circumstances it was held that where the reports are favourable then the Crown Court may not impose or uphold a custodial sentence.

There is no right to appeal against committal to the Crown Court for sentencing: *London Sessions, ex p. Rogers* [1951] 2 K.B. 74.

D. AGAINST BINDING OVER ORDER

Magistrates' Courts (Appeals from Binding Over Orders) Act 1956, s.1

Right of appeal to quarter sessions

1.—(1) Where, under the *Justices of the Peace Act* 1361, or otherwise, a person is ordered by a magistrates' court (as defined in the *Magistrates' Courts Act* 1980) to enter into a recognisance with or without sureties to keep the peace or to be of good behaviour, he may appeal to [the Crown Court] **11–13**

(2) In the case of an appeal under this section—

(a) the other party to the proceedings which were the occasion of the making of the order shall be the respondent to the appeal;

(b) [...] in relation to an appellant in custody for failure to comply with the order, so much of section [twenty-two of the *Criminal Justice Act* 1967], as relates to the release of convicted persons from custody pending an appeal to [the Crown Court] shall, with the necessary adaptations, apply as if the appeal were an appeal against a conviction.

(3) Nothing in this section shall apply in relation to any order an appeal from which lies to [the Crown Court] apart from the provisions of this section.

(4) This section shall not apply to any order made before the expiration of a period of one month beginning with the date of the passing of this Act.

An appeal against a binding over order is by way of rehearing. Unless the appellant admits the facts upon which the order was based, sworn evidence must be adduced and will be open to cross-examination: *Shaw v. Hamilton*, 75 Cr.App.R. 288. **11–14**

E. CONSTITUTION OF CROWN COURT ON APPEAL

Senior Courts Act 1981, ss.73, 74

General provisions

73.—(1) Subject to the provisions of section 8(1)(c), 74 and 75(2) as respects courts comprising justices of the peace, all proceedings in the Crown Court shall be heard and disposed of before a single judge of that court. **11–15**

(2) Rules of court may authorise or require a judge of the High Court, Circuit judge or Recorder, in such circumstances as are specified by the rules, at any stage to continue with any proceedings with a court from which any one or more of the justices initially constituting the court has withdrawn, or is absent for any reason.

(3) Where a judge of the High Court, Circuit judge or Recorder sits with justices of the peace he shall preside, and—

(a) the decision of the Crown Court may be a majority decision; and

(b) if the members of the court are equally divided, the judge of the High Court, Circuit judge or Recorder shall have a second and casting vote.

Appeals and committals for sentence

74.—(1) On any hearing by the Crown Court—

(a) of any appeal;

the Crown Court shall consist of a judge of the High Court or a Circuit judge or a Recorder who, subject to the following provisions of this section, shall sit with not less than two nor more than four justices of the peace.

(2) Rules of Court may, with respect to hearings falling within subsection (1)—

(a) prescribe the number of justices of the peace constituting the court (within the limits mentioned in that subsection); and

(b) prescribe the qualifications to be possessed by any such justices of the peace;

and the rules may make different provision for different descriptions of cases, different places of sitting or other different circumstances.

(3) Rules of Court may authorise or require a judge of the High Court, Circuit judge or Recorder, in such circumstances as are specified by the rules, to enter on, or at any stage to continue with, any proceedings with a court not comprising the justices required by subsections (1) and (2).

(4) The Lord Chancellor may from time to time, having regard to the number of justices, or the number of justices with any prescribed qualifications, available for service in the Crown Court, give directions providing that, in such descriptions of proceedings as may be specified by the Lord Chancellor, the provisions of subsections (1) and (2) shall not apply.

(5) Directions under subsection (4) may frame descriptions of proceedings by reference to the place of trial, or by reference to the time of trial, or in any other way.

(5A) Before exercising any functions under subsection (4), the Lord Chancellor must consult the Lord Chief Justice.

(6) No decision of the Crown Court shall be questioned on the ground that the court was not constituted as required by or under subsections (1) and (2) unless objection was taken by or on behalf of a party to the proceedings not later than the time when the proceedings were entered on, or when the alleged irregularity began.

(7) Rules of Court may make provision as to the circumstances in which—

(a) a person concerned with a decision appealed against is to be disqualified from hearing the appeal;

(b) ...

(c) proceedings on the hearing of an appeal are to be valid notwithstanding that any person taking part in them is disqualified.

(8) The Lord Chief Justice may nominate a judicial office holder (as defined in section 109(4) of the *Constitutional Reform Act* 2005) to exercise his functions under this section.

11–16 The composition of the Crown Court is also prescribed in the *Criminal Procedure Rules*, r.63.10 (see Appendix G *post* § G–308a). On an appeal to the Crown Court a judge will sit with magistrates who have not adjudicated at the hearing in the magistrates' court. On the hearing of an appeal from a youth court, a judge will sit with two magistrates each of whom is a member of a youth panel, and who are chosen so that the court includes a man and a woman. Dispensations relating to the required constitution of the appeal bench apply in certain circumstances.

F. PROCEDURE

11–17 The procedure to be followed on appeal to the Crown Court is set out in Pt 63 of the *Criminal Procedure Rules*: see Appendix G *post* § G–300 *et seq*. The form of notice of appeal is prescribed by the *Consolidated Criminal Practice Direction*: see *http://www.justice.gov.uk/guidance/courts-and-tribunals/courts/procedure-rules/criminal/docs/f141page1-2.pdf*.

11–18 A notice of appeal to the Crown Court must be given in writing within 21 days of the adjudication. A magistrates' court will accept notice of appeal out of time and will forward it to the Crown Court while at the same time notifying the appellant that it is out of time. The Crown Court should give brief reasons to the appellant of any refusal of an extension: *Re Worth (application for judicial review)* 10 Fam. Law 54. The Crown Court will give notice of any hearings and any decisions made, including a decision to allow an appeal to be submitted out of time, to the parties: *Criminal Procedure Rules*, r.63.7 (see *post* § G–306). The appeal will be by way of a rehearing: *Senior Courts Act* 1981, s.79(3). The Crown Court and the parties to the appeal have the same case management responsibilities as any court of trial: *Criminal Procedure Rules*, r.3.10 (see *post* § G–12).

The Crown Court may deal with a procedural irregularity that occurred in the magistrates' court: *Teeside Magistrates' Court, ex p. Bujnowski*, 161 J.P. 302. In that case, it was held that, on appeal against conviction for failing to surrender to bail, the Crown Court had jurisdiction to determine the matter on the basis that the magistrates had acted in breach of the relevant practice direction, and that the Crown Court judge should not have directed that the matter proceed by way of judicial review.

Where a defendant appeals to the Crown Court against conviction, the justices' clerk is not under a duty to provide the defendant with any notes of evidence. There is no rule at common law which entitles the defendant to a copy of the legal adviser's notes and the Criminal Procedure Rules do not require the magistrates' court to send any notes of evidence to the Crown Court when a defendant appeals against conviction. However, justices' clerks should give sympathetic consideration to requests for a copy of the notes of evidence where the defendant identifies a proper reason for requiring the note: *Clerk to Highbury Justices, ex p. Hussein*, 84 Cr.App.R. 112. The position on appeal is in contradistinction to the requirement to send the Crown Court a copy of any note of evidence in the case of a defendant committed for sentence: *Criminal Procedure Rules* r.42.10.–(2)(a)(iv) (see *post* § G–263i). **11–19**

A Crown Court judge giving the decision of the court on an appeal must give reasons for the court's decision: *Weightman v. DPP* [2007] R.T.R. 45. This case followed the case of *Pullum v. CPS* [2000] C.O.D. 206, in which it had been stated that the minimum that a defendant was entitled to was a clear statement as to what evidence the court had accepted. In that case, Lord Bingham, C.J. cited with approval the judgment of Pill, J. sitting in the Divisional Court in *Harrow Crown Court, ex p. Dave*, 99 Cr.App.R. 114 when he gave the following guidance:

> "The Crown Court judge giving the decision of the court upon an appeal must say enough to demonstrate that the court has identified the main contentious issues in the case and how it has resolved each of them. In the present case the issues were of fact and not of law. Elaborate reasoning was not required ... The reasoning required will depend upon the circumstances. In some cases the bald statement that the evidence of a particular witness is accepted may be sufficient ... The appellant was entitled to know the basis upon which the prosecution case had been accepted by the court ... A refusal to give reasons may amount to the denial of natural justice."

In order to reassure an appellant that there has been no subsequent rationalisation of a decision, reasons for any ruling should be given contemporaneously. Reasons will enable a defendant to understand the findings and to consider whether there are grounds for a further appeal to the Divisional Court by way of case stated: *Snaresbrook Crown Court, ex p. Input Management Ltd* (1999) 163 J.P. 533. The failure to provide reasons is not always fatal to the Crown Court's decision since the reasons may be obvious, the decision is simple or the subject matter of the appeal is unimportant: *Kingston Crown Court, ex p. Bell* (2000) 164 J.P. 633.

G. POWERS OF CROWN COURT ON APPEAL

Senior Courts Act 1981, s.48

Appeals to Crown Court

48.—(1) The Crown Court may, in the course of hearing any appeal, correct any error or mistake in the order or judgment incorporating the decision which is the subject of the appeal. **11–20**

(2) On the termination of the hearing of an appeal the Crown Court—

(a) may confirm, reverse or vary the decision appealed against any part of the decision appealed against, including a determination not to impose a separate penalty in respect of an offence; or

(b) may remit the matter with its opinion thereon to the authority whose decision is appealed against; or

(c) may make such other order in the matter as the court thinks just, and by such order exercise any power which the said authority might have exercised.

(3) Subsection (2) has effect subject to any enactment relating to any such appeal which expressly limits or restricts the powers of the court on the appeal.

(4) [Subject to section 11(6) of the *Criminal Appeal Act* 1995, if] the appeal is against a conviction or a sentence, the preceding provisions of this section shall be construed as including power to award any punishment, whether more or less severe than that awarded by the magistrates' court whose decision is appealed against, if that is a punishment which that magistrates' court might have awarded.

(5) This section applies whether or not the appeal is against the whole of the decision.

(6) In this section "sentence" includes any order made by a court when dealing with an offender, including—

(a) a hospital order under Part III of the *Mental Health Act* 1983, with or without a restriction order, and an interim hospital order under that Act; and

(b) a recommendation for deportation made when dealing with an offender.

(7) The fact that an appeal is pending against an interim hospital order under the said Act of 1983 shall not affect the power of the magistrates' court that made it to renew or terminate the order or to deal with the appellant on its termination; and where the Crown Court quashes such an order but does not pass any sentence or make any other order in its place the Court may direct the appellant to be kept in custody or released on bail pending his being dealt with by that magistrates' court.

(8) Where the Crown Court makes an interim hospital order by virtue of subsection (2)—

(a) the power of renewing or terminating the order and of dealing with the appellant on its termination shall be exercisable by the magistrates' court whose decision is appealed against and not by the Crown Court; and

(b) that magistrates' court shall be treated for the purposes of section 38(7) of the said Act of 1983 (absconding offenders) as the court that made the order.

[This section is reprinted as amended by the *Criminal Appeal Act* 1995, Sched. 2, para. 14 and the *Criminal Justice Act* 1988, s.156.]

11–21 Although magistrates' courts have a discretion to amend an information before conviction, the Crown Court hearing an appeal against that conviction does not enjoy that power: *Swansea Crown Court, ex p. Stacey* [1990] R.T.R. 183. However, the Crown Court dealing with an appeal may still have jurisdiction to proceed on a defective information without amendment by virtue of s.123 of the Magistrates' Courts Act 1980 (see *post* § 4–116). Where a defendant was convicted by a magistrates' court on an amended information and appealed to the Crown Court, it was held that the Crown Court was required to re-hear the case on the information in its amended and not in its original form, and could not hear an appeal against the decision to amend the information: *Fairgrieve v. Newman*, 82 Cr.App.R. 60.

It should be noted that as an appeal to the Crown Court is by way of a rehearing, and the Crown Court can impose any sentence that it was open to the magistrates' court to impose; it follows that the Crown Court may impose a more punitive sentence.

H. ABANDONMENT OF APPEAL

Magistrates' Courts Act 1980, s.109

Abandonment of appeal

11–22 **109.**—(1) Where notice to abandon an appeal has been duly given by the appellant—

(a) the court against whose decision the appeal was brought may issue process for enforcing that decision, subject to anything already suffered or done under it by the appellant; and

(b) the said court may, on the application of the other party to the appeal, order the appellant to pay to that party such costs as appear to the court to be just and reasonable in respect of expenses properly incurred by that party in connection with the appeal before notice of the abandonment was given to that party.

(2) In this section "appeal" means an appeal from a magistrates' court to the Crown Court, and the reference to a notice to abandon an appeal is a reference to a notice shown to the satisfaction of the magistrates' court to have been given in accordance with rules of court.

11–23 An appeal may be abandoned by giving notice in writing to the Crown Court, every other party, and to the magistrates' court: *Criminal Procedure Rules*, r.63.8 (see *post* § G–307). The form of the notice is prescribed by the Consolidated Criminal Practice Direction: see *http://www.justice.gov.uk/guidance/courts-and-tribunals/courts/procedure -rules/criminal/docs/f142page1.pdf*. The magistrates' court's decision may then be enforced.

If the appellant fails to attend the Crown Court hearing but has not given notice of withdrawal then the Crown Court is entitled to hear the appeal in his absence as it is a rehearing: *Guildford Crown Court, ex p. Brewer*, 87 Cr.App.R. 265.

Where a person appealing to the Crown Court is represented at the hearing by counsel there is no obligation upon him to be present in person: *Croydon Crown Court, ex p. Clair*, 83 Cr.App.R. 202. Where neither party appears the court should dismiss the appeal.

I. ENFORCEMENT OF CROWN COURT ORDERS ON APPEAL

Magistrates' Courts Act 1980, s.110

Enforcement of decision of the Crown Court

110. After the determination by the Crown Court of an appeal from a magistrates' court the decision appealed against as confirmed or varied by the Crown Court, or any decision of the Crown Court substituted for the decision appealed against, may, without prejudice to the powers of the Crown Court to enforce the decision, be enforced— **11–24**

(a) by the issue by the court by which the decision appealed against was given of any process that it could have issued if it had decided the case as the Crown Court decided it;

(b) so far as the nature of any process already issued to enforce the decision appealed against permits, by that process;

and the decision of the Crown Court shall have effect as if it had been made by the magistrates' court against whose decision the appeal is brought.

[This section is reprinted as amended by the *Access to Justice Act* 1999, Sched. 4, para. 22.]

Any order made by the Crown Court on appeal may be enforced by the magistrates' court. **11–25**

III. APPEAL BY WAY OF CASE STATED

A. APPLICATION TO STATE A CASE

Magistrates' Courts Act 1980, s.111

Statement of case by magistrates' court

111.—(1) Any person who was a party to any proceeding before a magistrates' court or is aggrieved by the conviction, order, determination or other proceeding of the court may question the proceeding on the ground that it is wrong in law or is in excess of jurisdiction by applying to the justices composing the court to state a case for the opinion of the High Court on the question of law or jurisdiction involved; but a person shall not make an application under this section in respect of a decision against which he has a right of appeal to the High Court or which by virtue of any enactment passed after 31st December 1879 is final. **11–26**

(2) An application under subsection (1) above shall be made within 21 days after the day on which the decision of the magistrates' court was given.

(3) For the purpose of subsection (2) above, the day on which the decision of the magistrates' court is given shall, where the court has adjourned the trial of an information after conviction, be the day on which the court sentences or otherwise deals with the offender.

(4) On the making of an application under this section in respect of a decision any right of the applicant to appeal against the decision to the Crown Court shall cease.

(5) If the justices are of opinion that an application under this section is frivolous, they may refuse to state a case, and, if the applicant so requires, shall give him a certificate stating that the application has been refused; but the justices shall not refuse to state a case if the application is made by or under the direction of the Attorney General.

(6) Where justices refuse to state a case, the High Court may, on the application of the person who applied for the case to be stated, make an order of mandamus requiring the justices to state a case.

11–27 If a party is aggrieved by a magistrates' courts' finding of fact the proper course is to appeal to the Crown Court; issues of fact should not be appealed by way of case stated: *James v. Chief Constable of Kent, The Times*, June 7, 1986. If a person wishes to complain about the harshness of the sentence passed, the appeal should also be to the Crown Court, despite the risk that the Crown Court might take a decision to his disadvantage: *Tucker v. DPP*, 13 Cr.App.R.(S.) 495; *Ealing Justices* [1994] R.T.R. 195; *Allen v. West Yorkshire Probation Service*, 165 J.P. 313.

It is highly probable that the High Court does not have power to extend the 21 day limit within which a party must apply to the court to state a case: *Chief Constable of Cleveland v. Vaughan* [2009] EWHC 2831 (Admin); *Michael v. Gowland* [1977] 1 W.L.R. 296. Where an application to state a case was made in time, but there was a delay in issuing the case whilst the applicant sought authority to enter into a recognisance to state a case, the time limits for the case stated to be issued were directory, not mandatory, and therefore the Divisional Court has jurisdiction to entertain the case: *Parsons v. F.W. Woolworth and Co Ltd* [1980] 1 W.L.R. 1472. Substantial compliance with the rules regulating applications to justices to state a case may suffice although the letter of the rules is not complied with: *Croydon Justices, ex p. Lefore Holdings Ltd* [1980] 1 W.L.R. 1465.

Where the final determination is a decision on an application for costs the 21-day time limit starts to run from the date of the decision on costs: *Liverpool City Council v. Worthington, The Times*, June 16, 1998.

The case must be concluded before the magistrates' court may state a case: *Streames v. Copping* [1985] Q.B. 920; *Loade v. DPP* [1990] 1 Q.B. 1052. There is no jurisdiction to state a case in respect of interlocutory matters: *Greater Manchester Justices, ex p. Aldi GmbH and Co KG*, 159 J.P. 717. This was confirmed in *Gillan v. DPP* [2007] 2 Cr.App.R. 12, where it said that the proper course, depending on the circumstances, was judicial review. Where a magistrate decides a preliminary issue as to jurisdiction that is a final decision and can be challenged by way of case stated: *Clerkenwell Metropolitan Stipendiary Magistrate ex p. DPP* [1984] Q.B. 821; *R. (Donnachie) v. Cardiff Magistrates' Court* [2007] 1 W.L.R. 3085. Neither mistakes of law in committal proceedings nor the decision of committal itself can be challenged by way of case stated: *Dewing v. Cummings* [1971] R.T.R. 1295.

The time limits for an application for a case stated do not run until sentence has been concluded. A case must identify the question of law to be determined, and that question might be whether there was sufficient evidence for the court to be entitled to find the applicant guilty; to ask a discrete series of evidential questions is incorrect: *R. (McCombie) v.Liverpool City Magistrates' Court* [2009] EWHC 2881 (Admin). The *Criminal Procedure Rules* require that where one of the questions on which the opinion of the High Court is sought is whether there was evidence on which the magistrates' court could come to its decision, the particular finding of fact made by the magistrates' court which it is claimed cannot be supported by the evidence must be specified in the application. (r.64.1.(2) and r.64.5(2) see *post* § G–309 and § G–313).

11–28 If a magistrates' court considers that the application to state a case is frivolous it may refuse to state a case and must certify that fact to the applicant: *Magistrates' Courts Act* 1980, s.111(5). The leading case giving guidance on what is meant by the word "frivolous" in this context, is *Mildenhall Magistrates' Court, ex p. Forest Heath DC* (1997) 161 J.P. 401; a decision of the Court of Appeal. Lord Bingham, C.J. defined the word as follows:

> "... the court considers the application to be futile, misconceived, hopeless or academic. That is not a conclusion to which justices to whom an application to state a case is made will often or lightly come. It is not a conclusion to which they can properly come simply because they consider their decision to be right or immune from challenge. Still less is it a conclusion to which they can properly come out of a desire to obstruct a challenge to their decision or out of misplaced amour propre. But there are cases in which justices can properly form an opinion that an application is frivolous. Where they do, it will be very helpful to indicate, however briefly, why they form that opinion."

A court requested to state a case should not speculate on what may be behind the application, and it should not point out to an applicant that he could have appealed to the Crown Court: *R (McCombie) v. Liverpool City Magistrates' Court, ante*. The form of the certificate of refusal to state a case is not prescribed. The form set out below, or one to similar affect, may be used.

.... **Local Justice Area**

BETWEEN **Appellant**

And

Respondent

Certificate of Refusal to State a Case for the Opinion of the High Court

On the ...... an information was laid by ...... against ...... that [state offence] and we/I [convicted him] and ordered that ....

The appellant being aggrieved by the determination as being wrong in law (and/or in excess of jurisdiction) has applied to us/me to state a case for the opinion of the High Court, the question(s) being that ....

We are/I am of the opinion that the application is frivolous and refuse to state a case because: ....

Date

Signed

.... District Judge/JP/Justices' Clerk (on behalf of the Justices adjudicating)

If a court refuses to state a case then the applicant may apply for judicial review and seek a mandatory order to compel the stating of a case: *R. v. Blackfriars Crown Court, ex p. Sunworld Ltd* [2000] 1 W.L.R. 2102. In that case the court gave some guidance on the approach for the Divisional Court. The aggrieved party should immediately apply for permission to bring an application for judicial review. If the court has already given a reasoned judgment which contains all the necessary factual findings and has explained why it has refused to state a case in a manner which clearly raises the true point of law in question, the single judge should grant permission for judicial review which challenges the order in question. It may be possible then to proceed immediately to a substantive determination of the merits however this will depend on whether the interested parties are represented and prepared and on the availability of court time: *Thames Magistrates' Court, ex p. Levy, The Times*, July 17, 1997. Where the case is factually complex, an order will be made for a case to be stated, thereby bringing the facts before the court: *Felixstowe Justices*, 72 Cr.App.R. 131. **11–29**

If the court refuses to state a case having been ordered to do so following judicial review, the members of the court may be liable to pay costs: *Huntingdon Magistrates' Court, ex p. Percy*, [1994] C.O.D. 323; *Aldershot Justices, ex p. Rushmoor BC (No.2)* [1996] C.O.D. 280. However, these cases must now be read subject to the provisions s.34 of the *Courts Act* 2003, which provides indemnity from any order for costs for justices and justices' clerks.

The High Court will adopt the same approach on appeals by way of case stated on a point of law, as the Court of Appeal adopt when considering a trial judge's exercise of judgment, namely only to interfere with the judge's ruling if it was *Wednesbury* irrational or perverse: *H v. DPP* [2007] EWHC 2192 (Admin).

Magistrates' Courts Act 1980, ss.112, 114

Effect of decisions made on case stated or on appeal

112.—(1) Any conviction, order, determination or other proceeding of a magistrates' court varied by the High Court on an appeal by case stated, and any judgment or order of the High Court on such an appeal, may be enforced as if it were a decision of the magistrates' court from which the appeal was brought. **11–30**

Part II

(2) Any order, determination or other proceeding of a magistrates' court varied by a county court on an appeal under section 111A, and any judgment or order of a county court on such an appeal, may be enforced as if it were a decision of the magistrates' court from which the appeal was brought.]

Recognizances and fees on case stated

11–31 **114.** Justices to whom application has been made to state a case for the opinion of the High Court on any proceeding of a magistrates' court shall not be required to state the case until the applicant has entered into a recognizance, with or without sureties, before the magistrates' court, conditioned to prosecute the appeal without delay and to submit to the judgment of the High Court and pay such costs as that Court may award; and (except in any criminal matter) a justices' clerk shall not be required to deliver the case to the applicant until the applicant has paid the fees payable for the case and for the recognizances to the designated officer for the court.

[This section is reprinted as amended by the *Access to Justice Act* 1999, Sched. 13, para. 113.]

11–32 A magistrates' court may make the stating of a case conditional on the applicant's entering into a recognisance in order to discourage the waste of resources and to ensure that the applicant fully intends to pursue his claim. However, where magistrates are considering a requirement for a recognizance, they must have regard to the means of the appellant in fixing the amount, and in deciding whether or not to require a recognizance at all: *Newcastle upon Tyne Justices, ex p. Skinner*, 84 Cr.App.R. 311.

The form of recognizance is prescribed by the *Consolidated Criminal Practice Direction*: see *http://www.justice.gov.uk/guidance/courts-and-tribunals/courts/procedure-rules/criminal/docs/f63page1.pdf*.

Constitution of High Court

11–33 An appeal by way of case stated in a criminal cause or matter will be assigned either to a single judge sitting in the Administrative Court, or to at least two judges sitting in a Divisional Court of the Queen's Bench Division. Appeals by way of case stated in a criminal cause or matter, whether from the Crown Court or from a magistrates court are more often listed in the Divisional Court. If the opinion of a two-judge court is divided then the appeal fails: *Flanagan v. Shaw* [1920] 3 K.B. 96.

B. PROCEDURE

11–34 The procedure for making an application under s.111 is contained in Pt 64 of the *Criminal Procedure Rules*: see Appendix G *post* § G–309 *et seq.*

11–35 The above rules outline the exact procedure and timetables to be followed in an application to state a case. A case stated should be succinct. It is usual for the court to draft its own case but there is no reason why the court could not invite the parties to submit the first draft, indicating any areas of disagreement: *Vehicle Inspectorate v. George Jenkins Transport Ltd* [2003] EWHC 2879, Admin where the following guidelines were given:

(1) Where there are a number of informations raising the same question, the case does not need to set out the detail of each information where nothing turns on the differences between them; the details of one or two informations will suffice.
(2) The case should set out the facts as found or accepted for the purposes of the ruling, with reference to any relevant documents.
(3) The case should then set out, in summary form, the submissions made on each side.
(4) The court's conclusions on matters in issue and questions for consideration should be set out.
(5) The court, if minded to state a case, may invite the advocates for the parties to submit a first draft, indicating any areas of disagreement.

The question stated for the High Court should be one the answer to which will resolve the issue in dispute: *Corcoran v. Anderton* (1980) 71 Cr.App.R. 104. It should be drafted as simply as possible and directed to the crucial issues upon which the case turns. Further observations were given in *Oladimeji v. DPP* [2006] EWHC 1199 by Keene L.J. who criticised the way the case was set out. The case had given a summary of the evidence and had not separated out the findings of fact from the evidence; there was no numbering of paragraphs and the questions were largely those of fact not law, e.g.: "Were we right to conclude that there was no evidence to support Dr X's conclusion that...?". He said that those concerned with drafting the case stated had paid little or no attention to the *Criminal Procedure Rules*:

> "Those provisions derive from the fact that the function of this court ... is to determine whether the decision of the justices is 'wrong in law or is in excess of jurisdiction' ... This court is consequently only concerned with the state of the evidence in so far as it is said that the findings of fact made by them demonstrate an error of law or jurisdiction ... The justices should decline to pose questions for this court unless those questions are ones of law ... The weight to be attached to particular pieces of evidence is a matter for the justices. Only if no reasonable Bench could have reached the finding in question will that finding produce an error of law or an *ultra vires* act. If a defendant believes that the justices have arrived at a finding for which there was evidence but at which he contends they should not have arrived (for example, because it was against the weight of the evidence) his remedy lies in an appeal to the Crown Court."

Where a document forms a material part of the case stated, either the original document, or a copy, should be appended: *Gainster v. Marlow* [1984] Q.B. 218, 78 Cr.App.R. 156. It is not permissible to refer to material at the case stated hearing which does not appear in the case stated itself; the proper time to insert that material is at the representations stage prior to the case being stated: *DSG Retail v. Stockton on Tees Borough Council* [2007] A.C.D. 38. An appeal by way of case stated is freestanding and depends only upon the facts found by the lower court. It is therefore impermissible for reference to be made to further material outside the record provided by the case stated. If a party to an appeal considers that the stated case omits relevant matters he should seek to have the case supplemented either by agreement or by application to the High Court: *M v. DPP* [2009] 2 Cr.App.R. 12.

The form of the case stated is prescribed by the *Consolidated Criminal Practice Direction*: see *http://www.justice.gov.uk/guidance/courts-and-tribunals/courts/procedure-rules/criminal/docs/f64page1-2.pdf*. **11–36**

The *Criminal Procedure Rules*, r.46.4 provide for the extension of the normal time limits by a magistrates' court (see *post* § G–312). However, where the timetable has not been met the court is obliged to furnish a statement of delay and the reasons for it. The form set out below, or one to similar affect, may be used.

.... **Local Justice Area**

BETWEEN **Appellant**

And

Respondent

Certificate of Refusal to State a Case for the Opinion of the High Court

On the ...... an information was laid by ...... against ...... that [state offence] and we/I [convicted him] and ordered that ....

The appellant being aggrieved by the determination as being wrong in law (and/or in excess of jurisdiction) has applied to us/me to state a case for the opinion of the High Court, the question(s) being that ....

The reason(s) for the delay in submitting the case is/are as follow:

. . ..

Date
Signed
.... District Judge (Magistrates' Court) / Justices of the Peace / Justices' Clerk (on behalf of the Justices adjudicating)

The appellant may withdraw the appeal by way of case stated without having to obtain the leave of the court: *Collett v. Broomsgrove DC* (1996) 160 J.P. 593.

Upon an application being made to a magistrates' court to state a case the applicant loses the right to appeal to the Crown Court: *Magistrates' Courts Act* 1980, s.111(4). This rule is still effective even if the application to state a case does not arrive within the statutory twenty one days, provided that it was made within the prescribed time and would have in the normal course of events arrived within the prescribed time: *P. and M. Supplies (Essex) Ltd v. Hackney LBC* (1990) 154 J.P. 814.

C. POWERS OF HIGH COURT ON CASE STATED

Senior Courts Act 1981, s.28A

Proceedings on case stated by magistrates' court or Crown Court

11–37 **28A.**—(1) This section applies where a case is stated for the opinion of the High Court—

(a) by a magistrates' court under section 111 of the *Magistrates' Courts Act* 1980; or

(b) by the Crown Court under section 28(1) of this Act.

(2) The High Court may, if it thinks fit, cause the case to be sent back for amendment and, where it does so, the case shall be amended accordingly.

(3) The High Court shall hear and determine the question arising on the case (or the case as amended) and shall—

(a) reverse, affirm or amend the determination in respect of which the case has been stated; or

(b) remit the matter to the magistrates' court, or the Crown Court, with the opinion of the High Court,

and may make such other order in relation to the matter (including as to costs) as it thinks fit.

(4) Except as provided by the *Administration of Justice Act* 1960 (right of appeal to Supreme Court in criminal cases), a decision of the High Court under this section is final.

[This section is reprinted as amended by the *Access to Justice Act* 1999, s.61.]

11–38 The appeal takes the form of legal argument and no evidence is called. The Divisional Court is confined to the facts set out in the case: *Skipaway Ltd v. Environment Agency* [2006] Env. L.R. 41. If an omission occurs a party may seek to have the case supplemented by agreement or by way of an application to amend: *DSG Retail Ltd. v. Stockton on Tees B.C, ante*; *M v. DPP ante*. Small facts may, however, be rectified at the hearing: *Russell v. DPP* [2006] EWHC 3054. On an appeal by way of case stated, the High Court cannot refuse to determine a pure point of law simply because that point of law was only first appreciated after the conviction of the defendant: *Whitehead v. Haines* [1965] 1 Q.B. 200. The High Court has the power to order a rehearing but only where there can still be a fair trial: *Griffith v. Jenkins* [1992] 2 A.C. 76; 95 Cr.App.R. 35. In this case the offences were relatively minor and, by the time the matter had been determined by the House of Lords, three years had passed since the commission of the offences; their lordships declined to order the retrial of the wrongly acquitted defendants.

IV. JUDICIAL REVIEW

A. GENERAL

11–39 Judicial review is the process by which the High Court exercises its supervisory jurisdiction over proceedings and decisions of courts and bodies or persons who are charged with the performance of public acts and duties. It is confined to questions of legality; whether an inferior court has exceeded its powers, committed an error of law, committed a breach of the rules of natural justice, reached a decision which no reasonable court could have reached, or abused its powers. It is the most appropriate procedure for challenging a magistrates' court decision, where the issue is the extent of that court's jurisdiction: *North Essex Justices, ex p. Lloyd* [2001] 2 Cr.App.R.(S.) 15. This case concerned the application of the magistrates' court's power to commit a defendant to the Crown court for sentence; Lord Woolf C.J. gave the following advice:

> "A case stated for appeal is very useful and valuable when the magistrates have determined facts. It is a useful vehicle for them to record their findings of fact. But in a case where the issue is of the sort that exists here as to the extent of their jurisdiction to commit for sentence, an application for judicial review is the most convenient procedure and it is the procedure which should ordinarily be used. It has the advantage, first of all, that it saves the cumbersome procedure of appealing by way of case stated; and secondly, it has the advantage that the matter comes before a judge of the High Court who decides whether or not to give permission to apply for judicial review. That avoids this Court being troubled with cases which lack merit. It also provides assistance to the applicant because at relatively modest cost he knows whether or not he has an arguable case."

Judicial review is concerned not with the decision but with the decision-making process: *Chief Constable of North Wales v. Evans* [1982] 1 W.L.R. 1155.

The proceedings in the magistrates' court must be complete before the Administrative Court will consider a quashing order: *R. (Hoar-Stevens) v. Richmond Upon Thames Magistrates' Court* [2003] EWHC 2660. The case concerned the adequacy of disclosure of material to the defence. The court stated that it was of the utmost importance that the course of a criminal trial in the magistrates' court should not be punctuated by applications for adjournments to test a ruling in the Divisional Court, especially when in reality if the case proceeded, the ruling might turn out to be of little or no importance. That was so, even where there was an important substantive point which arose during a trial. The proper course was to proceed to the end of the trial in the lower court and then to test the matter, almost certainly by way of case stated.

Any decision, before trial, to refuse bail was amenable to judicial review but, following the abolition of the High Court's concurrent jurisdiction to determine bail applications, it is only in exceptional cases that a decision would be reviewed: *R. (Shergill) v. Harrow Crown Court* [2005] EWHC 648.

Judicial review has been used to set aside a refusal to adjourn a case where the decision was irrational and as a result a fair trial might not take place: *R. (Costello) v. North East Essex Magistrates*, 171 J.P. 153. In this case an adjournment of a trial had been sought because the defendant was in an emotional state arising from the attempted suicide of his son the day before. Even though the general rule is that it is necessary in almost every case to wait until the end of the case before seeking the opinion of the High Court, and that the most appropriate way of challenge is by case stated where the facts will be before the High Court, Judicial Review may be heard in relation to whether an adjournment has been properly granted where there are no facts to be found before a point can be authoritatively resolved and reasons for the adjournment or refusal have been given: *R. (CPS) v. Sedgemoor Justices* [2007] EWHC 1803 (Admin). However, in that case the Divisional Court said that the decision ought not to be taken as any encouragement to a party to a magistrates' court case to embark on a similar interlocutory challenge. Permission to bring judicial review is likely to be refused if misconceived applications are made at an interlocutory stage. Permission had been granted here because (a) the refusal of the application and the remittal of the matter back to the magistrates' court would have led to yet more expense and delay; (b) the magistrates' ruling in that case, being in effect a terminating one, would have led to an acquittal as an inevitable result; (c) it was not a case in which it was necessary to have the facts found in order for the point to be authoritatively resolved, and (d) the magistrates' reasons were fully stated in a letter from their clerk.

The court may not necessarily intervene even if there is some element of unfairness. The unfairness must be such, and to such an extent, that the court should intervene and that will depend on the facts of the particular case: *R. (Hussain) v. Peterborough Magistrates' Court*, 171 J.P. 339.

It is a general rule that one Bench of magistrates should not act as an appeal over another. It is not in the interests of justice for the same court to feel free to annul or discharge its own earlier ruling without there being some compelling reason, such as changed circumstances or fresh evidence to do so: *R. (CPS) v. Gloucester Justices & Loveridge*, 172 J.P. 506. In this case a deputy district judge purported to set aside a previous bench's ruling because, on the same material, he would have reached a different conclusion.

Where case stated is available it is the preferred procedure: *Oldbury Justices, ex p. Smith*, 159 J.P. 316. That is not to say that judicial review cannot be used: *Hereford Magistrates' Court, ex p. Rowlands* [1998] Q.B. 110, [1997] 2 Cr.App.R. 340. In *Morpeth Ward Justices, ex p. Ward*, 95 Cr.App.R. 215, it was stated that where the identification of facts as found is critical to challenging the decision, the better course is to appeal by way of case stated.

Applications for judicial review are made in accordance with the procedures set out in the *Senior Courts Act* 1981, ss.29 and 31 and Pt 54 of the *Civil Procedure Rules*. Oral evidence is not normally given, and in so far as there is a factual dispute between the parties, the court is ordinarily obliged to resolve them in favour of the defendant; human rights cases, however, tend to be fact specific and cross-examination is appropriate where there are "hard-edged" questions of fact to resolve and in such cases proper disclosure must be made: *R. (Al-Sweady) v. Secretary of State for Defence* [2010] H.R.L.R. 2.

B. PROCEDURE FOR BRINGING CLAIM

Senior Courts Act 1981, s.29

Mandatory, prohibiting and quashing orders]

11–40 **29.**—(1) The orders of mandamus, prohibition and certiorari shall be known instead as mandatory, prohibiting and quashing orders respectively.

(1A) The High Court shall have jurisdiction to make mandatory, prohibiting and quashing orders in those classes of case in which, immediately before 1st May 2004, it had jurisdiction to make orders of mandamus, prohibition and certiorari respectively.

(2) Every such order shall be final, subject to any right of appeal therefrom.

(3) In relation to the jurisdiction of the Crown Court, other than its jurisdiction in matters relating to trial on indictment, the High Court shall have all such jurisdiction to make mandatory, prohibiting or quashing order as the High Court possesses in relation to the jurisdiction of an inferior court.

(3A) The High Court shall have no jurisdiction to make orders of mandamus, prohibition or certiorari in relation to the jurisdiction of a court-martial in matters relating to—

(a) trial by Court Martial for an offence, or

(b) appeals from a Service Civilian Court;

(4) The power of the High Court under any enactment to require justices of the peace or a judge or officer of a county court to do any act relating to the duties of their respective offices, or to require a magistrates' court to state a case for the opinion of the High Court, in any case where the High Court formerly had by virtue of any enactment jurisdiction to make a rule absolute, or an order, for any of those purposes, shall be exercisable by mandatory order.

(5) In any statutory provision—

(a) references to mandamus or to a writ or order of mandamus shall be read as references to a mandatory order;

(b) references to prohibition or to a writ or order of prohibition shall be read as references to a prohibiting order;

(c) references to certiorari or to a writ or order of certiorari shall be read as references to a quashing order; and

(d) references to the issue or award of a writ of mandamus, prohibition or certiorari shall be read as references to the making of the corresponding mandatory, prohibiting or quashing order.

(6) In subsection (3) the reference to the Crown Court's jurisdiction in matters relating to trial on indictment does not include its jurisdiction relating to orders under section 17 of the *Access to Justice Act* 1999.

[This section is reprinted as amended by the *Armed Forces Act* 2006, Sched. 16 para. 93, and the *Civil Procedure (Modification of Supreme Court Act 1981) Order* 2004 (S.I. 2004 No. 1033), art. 3.] **11–41**

By virtue of an amendment to s.29(1) of the *Senior Courts Act* 1981, the names of mandamus, prohibition and certiorari were changed to mandatory order, prohibiting order and quashing order respectively. **11–42**

Senior Courts Act 1981, s.31

Application for judicial review

31.—(1) An application to the High Court for one or more of the following forms of relief, namely— **11–43**

(a) a mandatory, prohibiting or quashing order;

(b) a declaration or injunction under subsection (2); or

(c) an injunction under section 30 restraining a person not entitled to do so from acting in an office to which that section applies,

shall be made in accordance with rules of court by a procedure to be known as an application for judicial review.

(2) A declaration may be made or an injunction granted under this subsection in any case where an application for judicial review, seeking that relief, has been made and the High Court considers that, having regard to—

(a) the nature of the matters in respect of which relief may be granted by mandatory, prohibiting or quashing orders;

(b) the nature of the persons and bodies against whom relief may be granted by such orders; and

(c) all the circumstances of the case,

it would be just and convenient for the declaration to be made or the injunction to be granted, as the case may be.

(3) No application for judicial review shall be made unless the leave of the High Court has been obtained in accordance with rules of court; and the court shall not grant leave to make such an application unless it considers that the applicant has a sufficient interest in the matter to which the application relates.

(4) On an application for judicial review the High Court may award to the applicant damages, restitution or the recovery of a sum due if—

(a) the application includes a claim for such an award arising from any matter to which the application relates; and

(b) the court is satisfied that such an award would have been made if the claim had been made in an action begun by the applicant at the time of making the application

(5) If, on an application for judicial review, the High Court quashes the decision to which the application relates, it may in addition—

(a) remit the matter to the court, tribunal or authority which made the decision, with a direction to reconsider the matter and reach a decision in accordance with the findings of the High Court, or

(b) substitute its own decision for the decision in question.

(5A) But the power conferred by subsection (5)(b) is exercisable only if—

(a) the decision in question was made by a court or tribunal,

(b) the decision is quashed on the ground that there has been an error of law, and

(c) without the error, there would have been only one decision which the court or tribunal could have reached.

(5B) Unless the High Court otherwise directs, a decision substituted by it under subsection (5)(b) has effect as if it were a decision of the relevant court or tribunal.

(6) Where the High Court considers that there has been undue delay in making an application for judicial review, the court may refuse to grant—

(a) leave for the making of the application; or

(b) any relief sought on the application,

if it considers that the granting of the relief sought would be likely to cause substantial hardship to, or substantially prejudice the rights of, any person or would be detrimental to good administration.

(7) Subsection (6) is without prejudice to any enactment or rule of court which has the effect of limiting the time within which an application for judicial review may be made.

11–44 The procedure for seeking permission to apply for judicial review is very fully set out in Pt 54 of the *Civil Procedure Rules*: *http://www.justice.gov.uk/guidance/courts-and-tribunals/courts/procedure-rules/civil/contents/parts/part54.htm#IDAQCP2B*.

11–45 The *Civil Procedure Rules*, the Civil Court Practice Directions, and the forms to be used are all available on-line at: *http://www.justice.gov.uk/guidance/courts-and-tribunals/ courts/procedure-rules/civil/menus/rules.htm*.

11–46 Upon receipt of a claim form, a party must acknowledge it within the required timescale. Failure to do so may result in not being able to take part in the hearing which decides whether to give the applicant permission to proceed with the judicial review. As permission is often refused where sufficient information is given by both parties for an initial view to be taken on the merits of the claim, a party on whom a claim form is served must act swiftly. In any event, the position with regard to costs at a full hearing needs to be borne in mind. Applications for permission are usually dealt with without a hearing.

C. Response to Claim

11–47 Upon receipt of a claim for judicial review, the defendant or interested party must file an acknowledgment of service in the relevant practice form not more than 14 days after service of the claim form, unless a different timescale has been directed. The form to be used to acknowledge service is available on-line at: *http://www.hmcourts-service.gov.uk/courtfinder/forms/N462_web_0109.pdf*.

11–48 Magistrates' courts must acknowledge service of the claim form and in doing so the court is permitted to make a submission using the form specified in § 11–47. It is usual for the court to indicate in any submission that the justices or the district judge will neither attend nor be represented in the proceedings. It is prudent to include within any submission a reference to s.34 of the *Courts Act* 2003 regarding costs.

A judge, in granting permission in the Administrative Court, will sometimes indicate that an order can be made on the written submissions, and that the court should consider signing a consent order; courts should be in a position to respond quickly to any application for a consent order.

In exceptional cases, a magistrates' court which is in the position of having to respond to a claim may be represented by the Treasury Solicitor.

D. Leave to Proceed

11–49 Section 31(3) of the *Senior Courts Act* 1981 requires that an applicant for judicial review obtain leave from the High Court before bringing an application.

11–50 The claim form seeking permission for a judicial review must include a detailed statement of the claimant's grounds for bringing the claim, a statement of the facts relied on, and any application for directions. In addition, the claim form must be accompanied by any written evidence in support of the claim, a copy of any order that the claimant seeks to have quashed, an approved copy of the reasons for reaching that decision, copies of any documents on which the claimant proposes to rely, copies of any relevant statutory material, and a list of essential documents for advance reading by the court (with page references to the passages relied on): see Practice Direction 54A—Judicial Review *http://www.justice.gov.uk/guidance/courts-and-tribunals/courts/procedure-rules/civil/contents/practice_directions/pd_part54a.htm#IDAFEKAC*.

E. HEARING

The court will generally, in the first instance, consider the question of permission without a hearing. Neither the defendant nor any other interested party need attend a hearing on the question of permission unless the court directs otherwise; if any party does attend a hearing, the court will not generally make an order for costs against the claimant. **11–51**

Where permission to proceed is given the court may also give directions which may include a stay of proceedings to which the claim relates, and directions requiring the proceedings to be heard by a Divisional Court. Within 35 days after service of the order giving permission, a defendant and any other person served with the claim form who wishes to contest the claim, or to support it on additional grounds, must file and serve detailed grounds for contesting the claim, or supporting it on additional grounds, and any written evidence.

An expedited hearing may be sought, in appropriate circumstances, by completing form N463—Application for Urgent Consideration: *R. (DPP) v. Camberwell Youth Court*, 168 J.P. 481. **11–52**

F. STANDING

The High Court will not grant leave to bring a claim for judicial review unless it considers that the applicant has a sufficient interest in the matter to which the application relates. **11–53**

Where one of the parties seeks permission to bring an application for judicial review in criminal proceedings, all parties to those proceedings must be named in the claim form as interested parties, and served with the claim form; the court will generally be named as the defendant.

G. GROUNDS FOR REVIEW

Lord Diplock in the case of *CCSU v. Minister for the Civil Service* [1985] A.C. 374 outlined the main grounds for review: **11–54**

— Illegality—has the decision maker understood the law, acted outside the law, or in excess of jurisdiction? For example, *Croydon Youth Court ex p DPP* [1997] 2 Cr.App.R. 411, where it was held that a magistrates' court had no power to use s.142(2) (*ante*) to allow the defendant to re-open his unequivocal guilty plea.

— Procedural impropriety—failure to observe procedural rules, basic rules of natural justice, or a failure to act with procedural fairness, *Warley Magistrates' Court ex p DPP* [1998] 2 Cr.App.R. 307.

— Irrationality—"*Wednesbury* unreasonableness", *i.e.* a decision which is so outrageous in its defiance of logic or of accepted moral standards that no sensible person who had applied his mind to the question to be decided could have arrived at it: *Associated Picture Houses Ltd v. Wednesbury Corp* [1948] 1 K.B. 223.

The Divisional Court may intervene if police procedures are shown to be manifestly producing a result which induces a plea of guilty where there may be a defence: *Bolton Magistrates' Court, ex p. Scally* [1991] 1 Q.B. 537. In this case the defendants applied to have their convictions for drink driving quashed. They had been arrested on suspicion of drink driving and when blood tests had revealed excessive alcohol levels they had been obliged to plead guilty. That the swabs used were impregnated with alcohol was not known at the time by the CPS, the magistrates or the defendants. It was held that the prosecutor had unwittingly corrupted the process leading to conviction in a way which was detrimental to the defendants because it left them with no choice but to plead guilty and denied them a complete defence. The police had failed in their duty to exercise care when supplying blood-sampling kits. The prosecution case was tantamount to "fraud, collusion or perjury" and the convictions were quashed. **11–55**

A quashing order was primarily a remedy sought on account of an error of the part of the court, but where the way in which the investigation process was conducted by the police vitiated the defendant's plea in the magistrates' court, an order could be granted quashing the conviction: *Kingston-Upon-Thames Justices, ex p. Khana* [1986] R.T.R. 364.

It is a denial of natural justice for a prosecutor to fail to disclose witnesses' statements favourable to the defence: *Leyland Justices, ex p. Hawthorn* [1979] Q.B. 283, 68 Cr.App.R. 269. It was held that although justices themselves had not been in error, a quashing order could be granted to quash the conviction.

A party who had lost his opportunity to be heard through the negligence of his solicitors could not complain that he had been the victim of procedural impropriety or that he had been denied natural justice: *Home Secretary, ex p. Al- Mehdawi* [1990] 1 A.C. 876.

11–56 The jurisdiction of the Divisional Court to quash convictions following a plea of guilty is confined to cases where the plea was obtained by fraud, collusion or perjury on the part of the prosecution: *Burton-Upon-Trent Justices, ex p. Woolley* [1995] R.T.R. 139.

H. REVIEW OF COMMITTAL PROCEEDINGS

11–57 These proceedings are now rare. It is not the practice of the Divisional Court to review committal proceedings which have not been concluded: *Wells Street Stipendiary Magistrate, ex p. Seillon*, 69 Cr.App.R. 77; *Horsham Justices, ex p. Bukhari*, 74 Cr.App.R. 291.

Judicial review lies in respect of committal proceedings where there has been a procedural flaw: *Oxford City Justices, ex p. Berry* [1988] Q.B. 507; 85 Cr.App.R. 89. A court will not grant an order to quash a committal on the grounds of inadmissibility or insufficiency of evidence. A defendant cannot argue on an application for judicial review that, but for the failure of the examining magistrates to exclude evidence against him, there would have been no evidence upon which he could be committed for trial: *Nottingham City Justices, ex p. McLaughlin* [1992] C.O.D. 397.

In *Bedwellty Justices, ex parte Williams* [1997] A.C. 225, [1996] 2 Cr.App.R. 594, the House of Lords held that a committal for trial was liable to be quashed in judicial review proceedings where there had been a procedural error by the magistrates' court, but that the Administrative Court would be slow to interfere on a complaint that evidence had been admissible but insufficient; this is more appropriately dealt with at trial. However, it was said that although a quashing order was at the discretion of the court, it would normally follow where there had been no admissible evidence before the magistrates' court of the defendant's guilt, or where the committal had been so influenced by inadmissible evidence as to amount to an irregularity having substantial adverse consequences for the defendant.

The remedy is discretionary, and is unlikely to be granted if the defendant's own conduct has contributed to the procedural failure or if an application to quash the indictment is an adequate alternative remedy.

I. REMEDIES

11–58 The most common remedy sought by way of judicial review is the quashing order where the defendant seeks to have the conviction quashed. Where the High Court quashes an order on the grounds that it was wrong in law and that without that error there would have been only one decision the magistrates' court could have made, it may also either remit the matter to the magistrates' court with a direction to reconsider the matter and reach a decision in accordance with the High Court's findings, or the High Court may substitute its own decision for the decision in question: *Senior Courts Act* 1981, s.31(5) and s.31(5A).

11–59 The court's powers in respect of quashing orders are set out in the *Civil Procedure Rules*, Pt 54, r.54.19.

Remedies in judicial review are discretionary. In deciding whether to grant a remedy the court will take into account a variety of factors including waiver, bad faith, the premature nature of the application, the absence of any injustice, and whether the decision would have been the same regardless of the error. **11–60**

In *Hereford Magistrates' Court, ex p. Rowlands* [1998] Q.B. 110, [1997] 2 Cr.App.R. 340, Lord Bingham C.J. confirmed the court's supervisory jurisdiction over magistrates' courts as a guarantee of the integrity of proceedings in those courts which ensures that high standards of procedural fairness and impartiality are maintained. He outlined the approach of the court: **11–61**

> "First, leave to move should not be granted unless the applicant advances an apparently plausible complaint which, if made good, might arguably be held to vitiate the proceedings in the magistrates court. Immaterial and minor deviations from best practice would not have that effect, and the court should be respectful of discretionary decisions of magistrates' courts as of all other courts. This court should be generally slow to intervene, and should do so only where good (or arguably good) grounds for doing so are shown. Secondly, the decision whether or not to grant relief by way of judicial review is always, in the end, a discretionary one. Many factors may properly influence the exercise of discretion, and it would be both foolish and impossible to seek to anticipate them all. The need for an applicant to make full disclosure of all matters relevant to the exercise of discretion should require no emphasis. We do not, however, consider that the existence of a right of appeal to the Crown Court, particularly if unexercised, should ordinarily weigh against the grant of leave to move for judicial review, or the grant of substantive relief, in a proper case."

In *DPP, ex p. Kebilene* [1999] 3 W.L.R. 175, Lord Bingham C.J. also said: **11–62**

> "Where the grant of leave to move judicial review would delay or obstruct the conduct of criminal proceedings which ought, in the public interest, to be resolved with all appropriate expedition, the court will always scrutinise the application with greatest care, both to satisfy itself that there are sound reasons for making the application and satisfy itself that there are no discretionary grounds (such as delay or the availability of alternative remedies or vexatious conduct by the applicant) which should lead it to refuse leave. The court would be very slow to intervene where the applicant's complaint is one that can be met by appropriate orders or directions in the criminal proceedings …"

V. SUSPENDING DECISIONS PENDING OUTCOME

A. BAIL

Magistrates' Courts Act 1980, s.113

Bail on appeal or case stated

113.—(1) Where a person has given notice of appeal to the Crown Court against the decision of a magistrates' court or has applied to a magistrates' court to state a case for the opinion of the High Court, then, if he is in custody, the magistrates' court may, subject to section 25 of the *Criminal Justice and Public Order Act* 1994 grant him bail. **11–63**

(2) If a person is granted bail under subsection (1) above, the time and place at which he is to appear (except in the event of the determination in respect of which the case is stated being reversed by the High Court) shall be—

(a) if he has given notice of appeal, the Crown Court at the time appointed for the hearing of the appeal;

(b) if he has applied for the statement of a case, the magistrates' court at such time within 10 days after the judgment of the High Court has been given as may be specified by the magistrates' court;

and any recognizance that may be taken from him or from any surety for him shall be conditioned accordingly.

(3) Subsection (1) above shall not apply where the accused has been committed to the Crown Court for sentence under [sentence 37] [above or section 3 of the *Powers of Criminal Court (Sentencing) Act* 2000].

(4) Section 37(6) of the *Criminal Justice Act* 1948 (which relates to the currency of a sentence while a person is released on bail by the High Court) shall apply to a person released on bail by a magistrates' court under this section pending the hearing of a case stated as it applies to a person released on bail by the High Court under section 22 of the *Criminal Justice Act* 1967.

[This section is reprinted as amended by *Powers of Criminal Courts (Sentencing) Act* 2000, Sched. 9, para. 72.]

11–64 A magistrates' court has the power to grant bail where the defendant, being in custody, challenges its decision by way of appeal or case stated. It does not, however, have the power to grant bail where the challenge is by way of judicial review.

B. SENTENCE

11–65 A sentence is in force and enforceable once it has been passed. The lodging of an appeal against conviction does not prevent the sentence from being enforced: *Greater Manchester Probation Service v. Bent*, 160 J.P. 297. There is statutory provision for the suspension of a driving disqualification pending appeal—see *Road Traffic Offenders Act* 1988, s.39, (*post* § 17–200).

VI. CHALLENGING BAIL DECISIONS

A. DECISIONS TO REFUSE BAIL OR TO IMPOSE CONDITIONS ON BAIL

11–66 The defendant who is refused bail by the magistrates' court, has a right to apply to the Crown Court for bail: s.81 of the *Senior Courts Act* 1981 (see *ante*, § 5–61). An application may only be made to the Crown Court if the magistrates' court has issued a certificate pursuant to s.5(6A) of the *Bail Act* 1976, that it has heard a full bail argument.

Where a magistrates' courts grants bail subject to conditions, the defendant may appeal against the imposition of those conditions where they relate to residence away from a place or area, residence at a place other than a bail hostel, the provision of sureties or security for bail, the imposition of a curfew, the electronic monitoring of a curfew, or a contact with another person: *Criminal Justice Act* 2003, s.16 (see *ante*. § 5–63). The appeal may only been made where an application has already been made to the magistrates' court to vary the conditions of bail, and the application has been refused.

B. DECISIONS TO GRANT BAIL

11–67 Where a magistrates' court grants bail to a defendant charged with an imprisonable offence, the prosecution may appeal to the Crown Court against the decision to grant bail: *Bail (Amendment) Act* 1993, s.1 (see *ante*, § 5–65). Only prosecutors who are specified by the *Bail (Amendment) Act 1993 (Prescription of Prosecuting Authorities) Order* 1994, may exercise a right of appeal under this provision.

The procedure to be followed is set out in the *Criminal Procedure Rules*, r.19.16 (see *post*, § G–126).

For a more detailed commentary on this provision see *ante*. § 5–67 *et seq.*

Part III

Specific Offences

Chapter 12

GENERAL PRINCIPLES

I. ACTUS REUS

(1) General

The *actus reus* consists of the prohibited conduct which forms the basis of the relevant offence. In the majority of cases, this conduct must be voluntary. It is possible to commit an offence through involuntary conduct, such as where the prohibited act consists of a state of affairs, as was the case in *Winzar v. Chief Constable of Kent, The Times*, March 28, 1983, where the relevant offence was "being found drunk on a highway" contrary to the *Licensing Act* 1872, s.12. It was held that the defendant fell within s.12 of the *Licensing Act* 1872 if he was on the highway and was "perceived to be drunk", notwithstanding that his presence there was momentary and not of his own volition. **12–1**

There is no liability for a failure to do something, unless the law imposes some specific duty upon the individual to act. Specific statutory duties are imposed in the context of many regulatory offences, such as the *Companies Act* 1985, which imposes a positive duty on a company to keep accounting records, or the *Water Resources Act* 1991 which makes it an offence to cause or knowingly permit any poisonous, noxious or polluting matter or any solid waste matter to enter any controlled waters. Other statutes make it a criminal offence to fail to disclose certain information. The *Terrorism Act* 2000, s.19 makes it an offence to fail to disclose a belief or suspicion that another person has committed an offence connected with terrorism and ss.330, 331 and 332 of the *Proceeds of Crime Act* 2002 create offences of failing to disclose possible money laundering activities.

Liability for omissions may also stem from the existence of a special relationship between the victim and the accused, which creates a duty to act on the part of the accused. There exist various situations where such a duty of care will arise.

(2) Duty arising from the assumption of care or control of children

12–2 The *Children and Young Persons Act* 1933, s.1 creates the offence of wilful neglect and imposes a duty on parents and those who are legally responsible for children to provide or obtain adequate food, clothing and medical care for the child.

(3) Duty arising from the assumption of care for another

12–3 A person who voluntarily assumes the care and responsibility for another person, that other being incapable of caring for himself, may incur a duty to discharge that undertaking. In *Stone (John Edward)* [1977] Q.B. 354, CA, the accused's sister came to live with him and his mistress. The sister was suffering from anorexia, and became unable to care for herself. The accused did not call for medical assistance and left her to die from atoxemia spreading from infected bed scores, prolonged immobilisation and lack of food. Both the accused and his mistress were convicted of manslaughter. The Court of Appeal upheld their convictions, holding that as they had taken the sister into their home, they had assumed a duty of care towards her and had been grossly negligent in the performance of that duty.

(4) Duty arising from contract

12–4 A duty to act may arise from the existence of a contract requiring some conduct from the defendant. In *Pittwood* [1902] 19 T.L.R. 37, the accused was employed to operate a level crossing on a railway. He failed to close the crossing gates when a train was signalled, causing a cart which was crossing when the train came through to be struck leading to the death of one of the carters. The accused was convicted of gross negligent manslaughter, his duty to act arising from the contract with his employers, which required him to discharge his duty as a level crossing operator appropriately.

(5) Duty arising from the fact that the accused creates the relevant danger

12–5 In *Miller* [1983] 2 A.C. 161, HL, Lord Diplock stated (at 176):

> "I see no rational ground for excluding from conduct capable of giving rise to criminal liability, conduct which consists of failing to take measures that lie within one's power to counteract a danger that one has oneself created, if at the time of such conduct one's state of mind is such as constitutes a necessary ingredient of the offence."

(6) Duty arising from the doctor patient/relationship

12–6 If a doctor or medical staff refuse to treat a patient who has withheld his consent to treatment, they will not be guilty of failing to discharge their duty to provide medical care for their patients: *Re C. (Adult: Refusal of Treatment)* [1994] 1 W.L.R. 290.

The doctor's duty towards his patient does not however require him to keep the patient alive at all costs. In *Airedale NHS Trust v. Bland* [1993] A.C. 789, HL, a patient in a persistent vegetative state was able to breathe normally, but was only sustained by the administration of food being fed through tubes. The House of Lords held that this treatment could be withdrawn, as a large body of informed and responsible medical opinion was of the view that existence in the persistent vegetative state was not a benefit to the patient. Hence the principle of the sanctity of life, which is not absolute, was not violated by ceasing to give medical treatment and care involving invasive manipulation of the patient's body, to which he had not consented and which conferred no benefit upon him. Lord Goff made a vital distinction between acts and omissions in this context, stating that:

> "…the law draws a crucial distinction between cases in which a doctor decides not to provide, or to continue to provide, for his patient treatment or care which could or might prolong his life, and those in which he decides, for example by administering a lethal drug, actively to bring his patient's life to an end. As I have already indicated, the former may be lawful, either

> because the doctor is giving effect to his patient's wishes by withholding the treatment or care, or even in certain circumstances in which [on principles which I shall describe] the patient is incapacitated from stating whether or not he gives his consent. But it is not lawful for a doctor to administer a drug to his patient to bring about his death, even though that course is prompted by a humanitarian desire to end his suffering, however great that suffering may be...So to act is to cross the Rubicon which runs between on the one hand the care of the living patient and on the other hand euthanasia—actively causing his death to avoid or to end his suffering." (at 865)

Certain offences cannot be based on omissions. In *Ahmad* [1987] 84 Cr.App.R. 64, CA, it was held that the words "does acts" in the *Protection from Eviction Act* 1977 mean that the offence may not be committed by omission. However, the offence of committing acts of gross indecency with a child may be committed by omission: in *Speck* (1977) 65 Cr.App.R. 161, an eight-year-old girl had placed her hand on the accused's trousers over his penis. The accused failed to move her hand, and was convicted of committing acts of gross indecency, his liability hinging on his failure to remove her hand. This would seem to be inconsistent with the view that references to acts exclude omissions, though Ashworth (*Principles of Criminal Law*, 4th edn, 2003) suggests that the case may also be viewed as involving an invitation on the part of the accused (constituted by his inactivity in failing to remove the girl's hand) which can be characterised as an act for the purposes of the offence. **12–7**

II. CAUSATION

(1) General

Causation is relevant to the commission of result crimes (those crimes which require a specific consequence to flow from the prohibited act, (*e.g.* theft)). These crimes are distinguished from what are termed "conduct" crimes, whose *actus reus* consists in the doing of the prohibited act, rather than in the consequences flowing from the commission of this act, (*e.g.* rape). For a defendant to be guilty of a result crime, a factual link must first be established between the defendant's conduct and the result he is alleged to have caused. **12–8**

Once this factual link has been established, the prosecution must then prove that the defendant's conduct was a legal cause of the result alleged to be a consequence of the defendant's actions. For a factual cause to also be a legal cause it must be an "operating and substantial" cause of the consequence in issue: *Smith* [1959] 2 Q.B. 35, CA. The following principles are relevant to the determination of legal causation. They are largely distilled from principles developed in homicide cases, though it may be worth considering the rather different application of the rules of causation in relation to crimes of strict liability or negligence, where considerations of the defendant's culpability in bringing about the prescribed result are less potent. For example, in *Empress Car Co (Abertillery) Ltd v. National Rivers Authority* [1999] 2 A.C. 22, HL, the defendant company maintained a diesel tank in a yard. This tank was tampered with by an unknown person, causing the contents of the tank to pass into a nearby river. The House of Lords held that if a necessary additional condition of the actual escape was the act of a third party or a natural event, the justices should consider whether that act or event should be regarded as a matter of ordinary occurrence, which would not negative the effect of the defendant's act, or something extraordinary, leaving open a finding that the defendant did not cause the pollution. Only if the escape could be regarded as something extraordinary would the defendant company escape liability. The issue of culpability was treated as irrelevant to determination of the issue of causation. This approach is in stark contrast to consideration of causation in homicide cases, where the distinction between "but for" and legal causation is used to avoid the conviction of the "morally innocent". Such considerations may be less prevalent in the context of statutory offences, and a different approach may be taken. See also *Express Ltd v. Environment Agency (t/a Express Dairies Distribution)* [2005] 1 W.L.R. 223, where the licensee of a dairy depot had been transferring cream from a tanker to another vehicle and an accident had resulted in the spillage of 10 litres of cream, some of which had escaped into the controlled waters of a local brook. An analysis of the brook had found there was potential for harm. The licensee had pleaded guilty to an offence contrary to s.85(1) of the Act and the owner was charged under s.217(3) of the Act. The owner, the appellant, submitted that as there was no statutory duty to carry out a risk assessment in respect of activities carried out on its premises, therefore it had not defaulted, and that despite the obvious discolouration of the water in the brook, the cream had not caused any harm, therefore it could not be said to have polluted the brook. The QBD dismissed the appeal. Section 85(1) of the Act required every person not to cause or knowingly permit polluting matter to enter controlled waters, which put the owner under an obligation to act. The owner had failed to carry out a risk assessment, which might have prevented the pollution from occurring. That constituted a default, contrary to s.217(3) of the Act, which gave rise to the offence committed by the licensee. Where a landowner allowed an operation on his land that could give rise to a risk of pollution, then, in order not to fall foul of s.85(1) of the Act, the landowner was to carry out a risk assessment and respond to what that assessment revealed. The wording of s.85(1) of the Act did not expressly state nor imply that harm had to be caused in order for the release of a pollutant into a controlled waterway to be an offence contrary to that section. It was sufficient that the pollutant, in this case cream, stained or tainted the water.

(2) The defendant's act must be more than a minimal cause of the result

12–9 In *Cato* [1976] 62 Cr.App.R. 41, CA, Lord Widgery C.J., looking at the ingredients of the offence of manslaughter stated that:

> "As a matter of law, it was sufficient if the prosecution could establish that it (the defendant's act) was *a* cause, provided it was a cause outside the *de minimis* range, and effectively bearing upon the acceleration of the moment of the victim's death."

In *Notman* [1994] Crim. L.R. 518, CA, it was held that the expression "a substantial cause" was convenient to indicate that the cause must have been more than just de minimis and avoids the necessity to go into the details of legal causation and remoteness. This approach was also applied in the context of road traffic offences in *Hennigan* [1971] 3 All E.R. 133, CA, where the defendant's conviction for death caused by dangerous driving was upheld, the Court holding that there was nothing in section 1 of the *Road Traffic Act* 1960 which required the manner of the driving to be a substantial or major cause of death. So long as the dangerous driving was a cause and something more than *de minimis*, the statute would operate.

However, indirect causes of the proscribed result may constitute legal causation. In *McKechnie* [1992] 94 Cr.App.R. 51, CA, the defendants attacked the victim, causing serious head injuries. The victim also had a duodenal ulcer, which could not be operated on due to the head injuries inflicted by the defendants. The victim then died when this ulcer burst. The Court of Appeal upheld the manslaughter conviction, despite the fact that the injuries inflicted were not in themselves the cause of the victim's death. In *Miller* [1992] 95 Cr.App.R. 421 it was held that to establish that property has been obtained by deception it is not necessary to isolate the moment when the money or other property is handed over to see whether at that time the lies told operated to deceive the victim. If on the evidence as a whole it can legitimately be said that the various deceptions alleged in the indictment were the cause of the money being handed over it is, or may be, irrelevant that at the final moment the victim suspected or even believed that he or she had been swindled.

(3) The "eggshell skull" rule

12–10 In *Blaue* [1975] 1 W.L.R. 1411, CA, Lawton L.J. stated that:

> "It has long been the policy of the law that those who use violence on other people must take

their victims as they find them. This in our judgment means the whole man, not just the physical man."

Hence a defendant who stabbed a woman, who then refused to have a blood transfusion due to her faith, was properly convicted of manslaughter, despite the fact that a blood transfusion would have saved the victim's life.

(4) Novus actus interveniens

An intervening act will absolve the defendant from any kind of responsibility for the result caused. The intervening act may be the act of a third party, and act of the victim or an unforeseeable natural event (sometimes called "act of God"). **12–11**

(5) Acts of third parties

Unforeseeable acts

The intervention of a third party may break the chain of causation if the intervention is free, deliberate and informed: *Pagett* [1983] 76 Cr.App.R. 279, CA. In *Pagett*, the defendant shot at police officers who were attempting to arrest him. He had with him his girlfriend, and against her will used her body to shield him from any retaliation by the officers. The officers returned the appellant's fire and as a result the girl was killed. The Court upheld the defendant's manslaughter conviction, holding that the police's actions had not broken the chain of causation between the defendant's act and the victim's death because their action had been a reasonable act performed for the purpose of self-preservation, as well as in the execution of their legal duty to arrest the defendant. **12–12**

(6) Medical intervention

Negligent medical treatment will only break the chain of causation where it was so independent of the defendant's acts and in itself so potent in causing death that they regarded the contribution made by the defendants acts as insignificant: *Cheshire* [1991] 93 Cr.App.R. 251, CA, (medical complications following from the treatment for gunshot wounds leading to the death of the victim). In *Cheshire, ante*, Beldham L.J. concluded that: **12–13**

> "...when the victim of a criminal attack is treated for wounds or injuries by doctors or other medical staff attempting to repair the harm done, it will only be in the most extraordinary and unusual case that such treatment can be said to be so independent of the acts of the accused that it could be regarded in law as the cause of the victim's death to the exclusion of the accused's acts." (at 257)
>
> "In a case in which the jury have to consider whether negligence in the treatment of injuries inflicted by the accused was the cause of death we think it is sufficient for the judge to tell the jury that they must be satisfied that the Crown have proved that the acts of the accused caused the death of the deceased adding that the accused's acts need not be the sole cause or even the main cause of death it being sufficient that his acts contributed significantly to that result. Even though negligence in the treatment of the victim was the immediate cause of his death, the jury should not regard it as excluding the responsibility of the accused unless the negligent treatment was so independent of his acts, and in itself so potent in causing death, that they regard the contribution made by his acts as insignificant." (at 258)

(7) Acts of the victim

The victim's own act can be said to break the chain of causation between the defendant's act and the result caused. In *Roberts* (1972) 56 Cr.App.R. 95, CA, the victim had jumped from a moving car because the defendant had assaulted and threatened her. The appellant was convicted of assault occasioning actual bodily harm. Stephenson L.J. stated: **12–14**

> "The test is: Was it the natural result of what the alleged assailant said and did, in the sense that it was something that could reasonably have been foreseen as the consequences of what he was saying or doing? As it was put in one of the old cases, it had got to be shown to be his

> act, and if of course the victim does something so 'daft,' in the words of the appellant in this case, or so unexpected, not that this particular assailant did not actually foresee it but that no reasonable man could be expected to foresee it, then it is only in a very remote and unreal sense a consequence of his assault, it is really occasioned by a voluntary act on the part of the victim which could not reasonably be foreseen and which breaks the chain of causation between the assault and the harm or injury." (at 102)

In *Williams* [1992] 1 W.L.R. 380, CA, the victim had been killed when he jumped from a car driven by the defendants after they had threatened him. The Court of Appeal quashed the defendants' conviction for manslaughter, stating that the defendants would only be guilty if the victim's response was proportionate to the threat issued, in that it was within the ambit of reasonableness and not so daft as to amount to his own voluntary act which would constitute a *novus actus interveniens*. When considering whether the victim acted reasonably, the judge/jury must consider "any particular characteristics of the victim and the fact that in the agony of the moment he may act without thought or deliberation."

12–15 The question of what could reasonably be foreseen by the defendant provides an objective test: *Marjoram* [2000] Crim. L.R. 372, CA. The defendant, aged 16, was among a group of people who broke into the victim's hostel room, whereupon she fell or jumped into the street and was seriously injured. The defendant appealed against his conviction for grievous bodily harm, contending that in directing the jury on foreseeability, the judge had failed properly to direct the jury that they should consider it in terms of a person of the same age and sex as the defendant involved in similar circumstances. The Court dismissed his appeal holding that the test of causation was objective. The 'reasonable man' would have foreseen the victim's conduct as a natural result of the defendant's actions.

(8) Unforeseeable natural events

12–16 In *Southern Water Authority v. Pegrum* [1989] Crim. L.R. 442, it was held that when deciding whether an intervening cause constitutes a defence, the question is whether the intervening cause was of so powerful a nature that the conduct of the defendant was not a cause at all, but was merely part of the surrounding circumstances.

III. MENS REA

A. GENERAL

12–17 Once the prosecution have established that the defendant committed the *actus reus* of the relevant offence, it must then be proved that the defendant did so with the relevant *mens rea*, *i.e.* that he had the guilty mind necessary for the commission of the offence. Different offences require different mental elements. A fault element may also be applied differently in relation to different offences, hence whilst the most commonly found mental elements can be here outlined for the sake of exposition, it is necessary to bear in mind that their application will vary.

B. SPECIFIC REQUIREMENTS AS TO STATE OF MIND

(1) "With intent to"

12–18 The leading cases on intention arise out of convictions for murder; however the relevant principles are of general application: *per* Lord Bridge in *Moloney* [1985] A.C. 905, HL. The relevant cases are *Moloney* (*ante*); *Hancock and Shankland* [1986] A.C. 455, HL; *Nedrick* 83 Cr.App.R. 267, CA, and *Woolin* [1999] 1 A.C. 82, HL.

In *Nedrick* (1986), *ante*, Lord Lane C.J. stated:

> "When determining whether the defendant had the necessary intent, it may therefore be helpful for a jury to ask themselves two questions: [1] How probable was the consequence which resulted from the defendant's voluntary act? [2] Did he foresee that consequence?

If he did not appreciate that death or really serious harm was likely to result from his act, he cannot have intended to bring it about. If he did, but thought that the risk to which he was exposing the person killed was only slight, then it may be easy for the jury to conclude that he did not intend to bring about that result. On the other hand, if the jury are satisfied that at the material time the defendant recognised that death or serious harm would be virtually certain (barring some unforeseen intervention) to result from his voluntary act, then that is a fact from which they may find it easy to infer that he intended to kill or do serious bodily harm, even though he may not have had any desire to achieve that result." (at 270)

Woollin, *ante*, concerned the death of a three-month old baby, as a result of his being thrown against a wall. The House of Lords held that, where the charge is murder, in the rare cases where the simple direction is not enough, the jury should be directed that they are not entitled to infer the necessary intention, unless they feel sure that death or serious bodily harm was a virtual certainty (barring some unforeseen intervention) as a result of the defendant's actions, and the defendant appreciated that such was the case. The decision was one for the jury to reach upon a consideration of all the evidence. The use of the phrase "virtual certainty" was not confined to cases where the evidence of intent was limited to actions of the accused and the consequences of those actions. If the principles gleaned from these murder cases can be extrapolated to all offences, then it seems appropriate to conclude that, ordinarily, the issue of intention is one to be left to common sense. 12–19

(2) "Unlawfully"

This means without lawful justification or excuse such as self-defence. 12–20

(3) "Maliciously"

This mental requirement appears in the *Offences Against the Person Act* 1861. It is established that malice in the sense of ill-will is not required, rather the word requires either actual intention to cause the relevant harm or foresight of the risk of causing that particular kind of harm: *Cunningham* [1957] 2 Q.B. 296, CCA. This decision was upheld in *Savage, Parmenter* [1992] 1 A.C. 699, HL. 12–21

(4) "Wilfully"

In *Sheppard* [1981] A.C. 394, HL, Lord Diplock stated that the proper direction to be given to a jury on a charge of wilful neglect of a child under s.1 of the *Children and Young Persons Act* 1933 by failing to provide adequate medical aid is that the jury must be satisfied (1) that the child did in fact need medical aid at the time at which the parent is charged with failing to provide it, the *actus reus*; and (2) either that the parent was aware at that time that the child's health might be at risk if it was not provided with medical aid or that the parent's unawareness of this fact was due to his not caring whether his child's health was at risk or not. 12–22

(5) "Knowingly"

This requires the prosecution to prove that the defendant knew of all the material circumstances of the offence. In *Dunne* (1998) 162 J.P. 399, CA, the offender was convicted of being knowingly concerned in the fraudulent evasion of a prohibition on the importation of goods contrary to s.170(2) of the *Customs and Excise Management Act* 1979 after being arrested on his arrival in the UK by customs officers who suspected that videos in his possession, which the defendant referred to as "blue movies", were obscene. He appealed against conviction, contending that a person could not "know" whether an article he was importing was such as would tend to deprave and corrupt within the meaning of the *Obscene Publications Act* 1959, s.1(1) until a jury had found that it was. The Court dismissed his appeal, holding that "knowingly", in the offence of being knowingly concerned in the fraudulent evasion of a prohibition on the importation of an obscene article, was to be construed as emphasising the requirement of *mens* 12–23 *rea*. Whilst a defendant who believed that the obscene videos he was importing were actually videos of sporting events should not be convicted, a defendant who was aware of the true nature of the goods would be liable to conviction if the jury determined that the material fell within the 1959 Act, s.1(1). As the defendant was aware of the nature of the videos and had conceded that they were obscene, there was no basis upon which the defendant could claim that his conviction was unsafe.

(6) "Recklessly"

12–24 Prior to the decision in *G.* [2003] 3 W.L.R. 1060, HL, the concept of recklessness in the criminal law was variable according to the substantive offence charged. The decisions in *Caldwell* [1982] A.C 341 (criminal damage) and *Lawrence* [1982] A.C. 510 (causing death by reckless driving) introduced the concept of objective recklessness, departing from the prior view expressed in *Cunningham* [1957] 2 Q.B. 396, CCA, that recklessness necessarily imparted some degree of subjective fault on the part of the defendant. In *G.* [2003] 3 W.L.R. 1060, two children, one aged 11 and the other 12, set fire to newspapers with a lighter and threw some of the papers under a large plastic wheelie-bin, which was in the yard behind a shop. They then left, and the resulting fire caused approximately £1 million worth of damage. It was accepted that neither boy appreciated that there was any risk of the fire spreading in the way that it did. They were convicted of arson, contrary to s.1 of the *Criminal Damage Act* 1971, the judge having ruled that he was bound to direct the jury in accordance with *Caldwell*, *ante*. The House of Lords quashed their convictions, and overruled the majority decision of the House of Lords in *Caldwell*. Lord Bingham first looked to the legislative background of the *Criminal Damage Act* 1971, and stated that:

> "[T]he starting point is to ascertain what Parliament meant by 'reckless' in 1971...section 1 as enacted followed, subject to an immaterial addition, the draft proposed by the Law Commission. It cannot be supposed that by 'reckless' Parliament meant anything different from the Law Commission. The Law Commission's meaning was made plain both in its report [Law Com No. 29] and in Working Paper No 23 which preceded it. These materials [not, it would seem, placed before the House in *Caldwell*] reveal a very plain intention to replace the old-fashioned and misleading expression 'maliciously' by the more familiar expression 'reckless' but to give the latter expression the meaning which *Cunningham* [1957] 2 All E.R. 412, [1957] 2 Q.B. 396 and Professor Kenny had given to the former. In treating this authority as irrelevant to the construction of 'reckless' the majority fell into understandable but clearly demonstrable error. No relevant change in the mens rea necessary for proof of the offence was intended, and in holding otherwise the majority misconstrued section 1 of the Act." (at para. 29)

12–25 He then went on to examine reasons justifying a departure from the decision established in *Caldwell*:

> "First, it is a salutary principle that conviction of serious crime should depend on proof not simply that the defendant caused [by act or omission] an injurious result to another but that his state of mind when so acting was culpable...But it is not clearly blameworthy to do something involving a risk of injury to another if [for reasons other than self-induced intoxication [see *DPP v. Majewski* [1976] 2 All E.R. 142, [1977] A.C. 443] one genuinely does not perceive the risk. Such a person may fairly be accused of stupidity or lack of imagination, but neither of those failings should expose him to conviction of serious crime or the risk of punishment." (at para. 32)
>
> "Secondly...the model direction formulated by Lord Diplock is capable of leading to obvious unfairness...It is neither moral nor just to convict a defendant [least of all a child] on the strength of what someone else would have apprehended if the defendant himself had no such apprehension. Nor, the defendant having been convicted, is the problem cured by imposition of a nominal penalty." (at para. 33)
>
> "Thirdly, I do not think the criticism of *Caldwell* expressed by academics, judges and practitioners should be ignored. A decision is not, of course, to be overruled or departed from simply because it meets with disfavour in the learned journals. But a decision which attracts reasoned and outspoken criticism by the leading scholars of the day, respected as authorities in the field, must command attention..." (at para. 34)

> "Fourthly, the majority's interpretation of 'reckless' in s 1 of the 1971 Act was, as already shown, a misinterpretation. If it were a misinterpretation that offended no principle and gave rise to no injustice there would be strong grounds for adhering to the misinterpretation and leaving Parliament to correct it if it chose. But this misinterpretation is offensive to principle and is apt to cause injustice. That being so, the need to correct the misinterpretation is compelling." (at para. 35)

The reasoning of Lord Bingham was accepted by the majority of the House, and the concept of recklessness is now restored to the situation before *Caldwell*. The defendant will now be judged to have acted recklessly with respect to (1) a circumstance when he was aware of a risk that it existed or would exist; (2) a result when he was aware of a risk that it would occur; and it was, in the circumstances known to him, unreasonable to take the risk. This is the definition recommended by the Law Commission in the Draft Criminal Code of 1989 (Law Com. No. 177). **12–26**

In *Brady* [2006] EWCA Crim 2413, CA, the Court of Appeal reaffirmed the subjective approach to recklessness in *G.* [2003] 3 W.L.R. 1060. The appellant appealed against his conviction for inflicting grievous bodily harm. He had perched on a low railing above a dance floor having consumed considerable quantities of alcohol and drugs. He lost his balance, fell backwards and landed on the victim, causing her severe injury. The appellant maintained that the injuries were caused by accident rather than any deliberate act on his part and appealed on the basis that the judge failed to direct the jury that the Crown had to establish that the appellant foresaw an obvious and significant risk of injury to another by his actions, or would have done had he been sober, and that the jury properly directed would not have convicted him on the basis that he jumped off the balcony railing, and that the act of falling was not deliberate but accidental and the physical act that caused injury was not a direct assault, absent which there could be no conviction for inflicting grievous bodily harm.

Allowing the appeal, the court held that the judge had wrongly directed the jury that there was only one issue for it to decide, namely recklessness. Whilst there could be an infliction of grievous bodily harm without an assault being committed, in view of deficiencies in the summing up, it was not necessary to come to a view on whether there was deliberate non-accidental conduct on the appellant's part that inflicted grievous bodily harm on the victim. The court doubted whether it was made sufficiently clear to the jury that the test of recklessness was not objective and the question of recklessness was very different depending on which version of events the jury accepted. There was a possibility that the jury had found the appellant guilty of inflicting grievous bodily harm because they concluded he had behaved stupidly and was guilty of causing the victim to suffer grave injuries. This raised the possibility that the jury had convicted on a false basis. The court further stated that since *G.*, above, directions on recklessness must qualify the word "risk" by the words "obvious and significant"; without such qualification any directions on recklessness would be fundamentally flawed.

(7) "Dishonesty"

See exposition in relation to the offence of theft at *post*, § 15–4. **12–27**

(8) "Causes"

The general rule applicable to a statutory offence of causing another person to do a prohibited act is that the offence is only committed if the accused contemplated or desired that the act would ensue and was done on his express or implied authority or as a result of him exercising control or influence over the other person: *Att.-Gen of Hong Kong v. Tse Hung-Lit* [1986] A.C. 876, PC. **12–28**

Where a statute prohibits the causing of a particular result, the word "causes" is to be given a common sense meaning, and does not imply either knowledge or negligence: *Alphacell v. Woodward* [1972] A.C. 824, HL. In *Environmental Agency v. Empress Car Co (Abertillery) Ltd* [1999] 2 A.C. 22, HL, it was held that on a prosecution for causing pollution under s.85(1) of the *Water Resources Act* 1991 it was necessary to identify what the defendant was alleged to have done to cause the pollution. The prosecution need not prove that the defendant did something which was the immediate cause of the pollution and when the prosecution had identified some act done by the defendant the justices had to decide whether it caused the pollution. If a necessary additional condition of the actual escape was the act of a third party or a natural event, the justices should consider whether that act or event should be regarded as a matter of ordinary occurrence, which would not negative the effect of the defendant's act, or something extraordinary, leaving open a finding that the defendant did not cause the pollution; that the distinction between ordinary and extraordinary was one of fact and degree to which the justices had to apply their common sense and knowledge of what occurred in the locality but see *ante*, § 12–8, on causation.

(9) "Negligently"

12–29 An example of negligence being the relevant mental state for the commission of an offence can be found in s.3 of the *Road Traffic Act* 1988, which creates the offence of driving without due care and attention. Negligence imports an objective standard for behaviour, which does not vary according to the characteristics of the individual offender.

Certain statutes provide a defence of mistaken belief on reasonable grounds. Thus, s.1 of the *Protection from Eviction Act* 1977 makes it an offence for any person to unlawfully deprive a residential occupier of his occupation of the premises or any part thereof, unless he proves that he believed, and had reasonable cause to believe, that the residential occupier had ceased to reside in the premises. In *Phekoo* [1981] 1 W.L.R. 1117, CA, it was held that there must be a reasonable basis for the asserted belief on behalf of a person charged with an offence under s.1 of the *Protection from Eviction Act* 1977 that the persons he attempts to evict are not residential occupiers of the premises in question. In *King* [1964] 1 Q.B. 285, CA, it was held that an honest belief on reasonable grounds as to the invalidity of a previous marriage, just as an honest belief on reasonable grounds that the spouse is dead, were good defences to a charge of bigamy.

The reasonableness of the defendant's belief will not always be relevant. Where the relevant statute does not indicate that a belief held by a defendant has to be reasonable, the court is to assume that Parliament did not intend to impart any requirement of reasonableness into the belief providing the basis for a defence. In *B. v. DPP* [2000] 2 W.L.R. 452, HL, the defendant, aged 15, had repeatedly asked a girl, aged 13, who was sitting next to him on a bus to perform oral sex with him. He was charged with inciting a girl under the age of 14 to commit an act of gross indecency with him, contrary to s.1(1) of the *Indecency with Children Act* 1960. It was accepted that he had honestly believed that the girl was over the age of 14, and the justices were asked to rule whether his state of mind could constitute a defence to the charge. The justices ruled that it could not, and he changed his plea to guilty. No finding was made as to whether he had had reasonable grounds for his belief. His conviction was quashed by the House of Lords: *mens rea* was an essential element of every criminal offence unless Parliament expressly or by necessary implication provided to the contrary and, on a true construction of s.1(1) of the Act of 1960 in its statutory context, Parliament had not so provided in respect of the age ingredient of the offence. It was therefore necessary for the prosecution to prove the absence of a genuine belief on the part of the defendant, for which he did not have to have had reasonable grounds, that the victim had been 14 or over. See also *K.* [2002] 1 A.C. 462 and *Kumar* [2005] 1 W.L.R. 1352; [2005] 1 Cr.App.R. 34; [2005] Crim. L.R. 470 (where it was held that on a charge under s.12 of the *Sexual Offences Act* 1956, the defendant was entitled to raise the defence that he had believed that the complainant had attained the age of 16).

(10) "Strict liability"

12–30 In *Deyami* [2007] EWCA Crim 2060, CA, the appellants appealed against a decision that the offence of possessing a prohibited weapon contrary to the *Firearms Act* 1968, s.5(1)(b) was one of strict liability. The appellants had been found with an electrical stun gun after being stopped and searched and claimed they had believed it to be a torch. The judge found that although the appellants did not know it was a stun gun, the offence was one of strict liability. The appellants then pleaded guilty. Appealing against their conviction, they submitted that the statutory provisions should not be read as imposing strict liability and that that interpretation was supported by Art. 6 and Art. 7 of the European Convention on Human Rights 1950.

Dismissing the appeal, the Court held that in order to establish the offence under s.5 of the 1968 Act, the prosecution merely had to prove possession of the object in question and that the object was a firearm or other weapon prohibited by the 1968 Act. It was not necessary to prove that the defendant either knew or could have known it was a weapon prohibited by the 1968 Act, and a defendant would not have a defence if he did not know the "nature" of the object. The Court stated that previous decisions had taken a restrictive approach to the meaning of possession under the 1968 Act, and what had been described as a "halfway house" under which a defendant would be allowed to assert that although he or she was physically in possession of the object, he or she was ignorant of its nature, had been rejected. The Court further held that an offence of strict liability did not infringe Art. 6(2) of the 1950 Convention, and that legislation that created an absolute offence was not, in itself, capable of infringing Art. 6(1) or Art. 6(2). Article 6 did not guarantee any particular content of civil rights and had nothing to say about the content of the law creating an offence, though it could affect any evidential presumptions or statutory defences. In the instant case, Art. 7 did not add anything to Art. 6.

[The next paragraph is § 12–32.]

(11) "Transferred malice"

If a person by mistake, or, *e.g.* bad aim causes injury to a person or property other **12–32**
than the person or property which he intended to attack, he is guilty of a crime to the same degree as if he had achieved his object: *Latimer* [1886] 17 QBD 359. The harm caused must be of the same kind as the harm intended: *Pembliton* [1874] L.R. C.C.R. 119.

IV. ACCESSORIAL LIABILITY

(1) Legislation

Magistrates Courts Act 1980, s.44

Aiders and abettors

44.—(1) A person who aids, abets, counsels or procures the commission by another person of **12–33**
a summary offence shall be guilty of the like offence and may be tried [whether or not he is charged as a principal] either by a court having jurisdiction to try that other person or by a court having by virtue of his own offence jurisdiction to try him.

(2) Any offence consisting in aiding, abetting, counselling or procuring the commission of an offence triable either way [other than an offence listed in Schedule 1 to this Act] shall by virtue of this subsection be triable either way.

The words "aids, abets, counsels or procures" should be given their ordinary meaning. The use of four words suggests that there is a difference between the words for if there were none, Parliament would be wasting time in using four words where two or three would do: *Att.-Gen.'s Reference (No. 1 of 1975)* [1975] Q.B. 773, CA.

(a) *Aiders and abettors*

The words "aiding and abetting" can include acts committed before the commission **12–34** of the *actus reus* of the offence. In *Blakely v. DPP* [1991] R.T.R. 405, DC, McCullough J. said, at 411, that there are many accessories before the fact of whose activity none of the words 'counselling, procuring and commanding' would seem to be apt; whilst the words aiding and abetting would seem more appropriate to describe such activity. In *National Coal Board v. Gamble* [1959] 1 Q.B. 11; 42 Cr.App.R. 240, DC, the defendant's conviction for aiding and abetting the driving of an overweight lorry was upheld; the servant had loaded coal onto the lorry of the principal knowing that this load had rendered the lorry overweight and that the driver intended to take it onto the highway and complete the sale of the coal, thus facilitating the commission of the offence.

To establish aiding and abetting, it must be proved that the defendant intended to encourage, and *wilfully* encouraged the crime committed. Mere continued voluntary presence at the scene of the commission of a crime does not of itself necessarily amount to encouragement; but the fact that a person was voluntarily and purposely present witnessing the commission of a crime, and offered no opposition to it, though he might reasonably be expected to prevent and had the power so to do, or at least to express his dissent, might in some circumstances afford cogent evidence upon which to justify finding that he wilfully encouraged, and so aided and abetted; but this is a question of fact: *Clarkson* 55 Cr.App.R. 445, Ct-MAC. Knowledge of the principal's offence, plus an ability to control his actions, coupled with a deliberate decision not to exercise such control may constitute aiding and abetting: *J.F. Alford Transport Ltd* [1997] 2 Cr.App.R. 326, CA. See also *Nedrick-Smith v. DPP* [2006] EWHC 3015, QBD at § 13–18.

A person may be an aider and abettor even though his age or sex renders him incapable of being a principal: *Eldershaw* [1828] 3 C. & P. 396. A person protected by the offence in question cannot be convicted for aiding and abetting the person who committed the offence against them: *Tyrell* [1894] 1 Q.B. 710, CCR (unlawful sexual intercourse with a girl under 16); *Whitehouse* [1977] Q.B. 868; 65 Cr.App.R. 33, CA (girl under 16 cannot aid and abet incest by her father).

(b) *Joint enterprise*

12–35 Where two of more persons embark on a joint enterprise, each is responsible for acts done within the scope of that joint enterprise. This shared liability ends when a party to the joint enterprise goes beyond what was agreed as part of the common enterprise. It is for the tribunal of fact to decide whether what was done could be construed as being within the joint enterprise or whether it exceeded it: *Anderson and Morris* [1966] 1 Q.B. 110, CCA; *Lovesey and Peterson* [1970] 1 Q.B. 352, CA; *Powell, English* [1999] 1 A.C. 1, HL.

Where the principal does an act which was within the joint enterprise yet with an intent which was outside the contemplation of the other participants to the joint enterprise, the accessory will not escape all liability, and may be found guilty of the degree of offence appropriate to the intention with which he acted: *Gilmour* [2000] 2 Cr.App.R. 407 (an appellant who foresaw that the principals would carry out the act of throwing a petrol bomb into a house, but did not realise that in doing so they intended to kill or do grievous bodily harm to the occupants, would be guilty of manslaughter).

(c) *Counsellors and procurers*

12–36 The word "counsel" does not imply any causal connection with the offence; the essential elements are that there should be counselling, and the principal offence should be committed by the person counselled acting within the scope of his authority and not by accident: *Calhaem* [1985] Q.B. 808, CA.

As regards procurement, in *Att.-Gen.'s Reference (No. 1 of 1975)* [1975] Q.B. 773, CA, it was held that:

> "To procure means to produce by endeavour. You procure a thing by setting out to see that it happens and taking the appropriate steps to produce that happening. We think that there are plenty of instances in which a person may be said to procure the commission of a crime by another even though there is no sort of conspiracy between the two, even though there is

no attempt at agreement or discussion as to the form which the offence should take." (at 779).

With procurement, there must be a causal link between what the accessory did and the commission of the offence. In *Att.-Gen.'s Reference (No.1 of 1975)* [1975] Q.B. 773, CA, the defendant had surreptitiously laced with spirits the drinks of a motorist whom she knew was about to drive home. This led to the motorist driving home while the alcohol concentration in his blood was above the prescribed limit contrary to s.6(1) of the *Road Traffic Act* 1972 and, following the motorist's conviction of this offence, the defendant was convicted as having procured the commission of the motorists' offence due to the fact that there was a causal link between the defendant's act and the offence by the motorist who would not have committed it otherwise. **12–37**

(d) *Agents provocateurs*

Whilst the defendant who would not have committed an offence but for the activity of an agent provocateur will have no defence, the question here is whether the agent provocateur may himself be prosecuted. The following principles may be deduced from the relevant authorities: it is unlawful for a police officer to counsel or procure the commission of an offence which would otherwise not take place, but it may be proper for a police officer to take part in, or to encourage an informer to take part in, an offence which is already "laid on" solely for the purpose of apprehending the offenders: *Birtles* 53 Cr.App.R. 469, CA; *McCann* 56 Cr.App.R. 359, CA; *Clarke (D.G.)* 80 Cr.App.R. 344, CA. **12–38**

(e) *Withdrawal*

A secondary party may be able to escape liability for aiding, abetting, counselling or procuring an offence if he makes an effective withdrawal before the offence is actually committed. In *Whitefield* 79 Cr.App.R. 36, CA it was held that if a person has counselled another to commit a crime, he may escape liability by withdrawal before the crime is committed, but it is not sufficient that he should merely repent or change his mind. If his participation is confined to advice or encouragement, he must at least communicate his change of mind to the other, and the communication must be such as will serve unequivocal notice upon the other party to the common unlawful cause that if he proceeds upon it he does so without the aid and assistance of those who withdraw. **12–39**

In *Bryce* [2004] 2 Cr.App.R. 35, it was held that, in the absence of some overwhelming supervening event, only an act taken by D which amounted to the countermanding of his earlier assistance and a withdrawal from the common purpose would suffice to avoid liability. Repentance alone unsupported by action taken to demonstrate withdrawal would be insufficient. If D had the necessary mens rea at the time of the act of assistance the fact that his mind was innocent at the time when the crime was committed was no defence (paras 75–76).

In *Robinson* [2000] 5 *Archbold News* 2, CA, it was said that only exceptionally can a person withdraw from a crime he has initiated. To do so, he must communicate his withdrawal in order to give the principal[s] the opportunity to desist rather than complete the crime. This communication is even necessary in the context of spontaneous violence, where the accessory will only be excused from not giving such an opportunity to desist if it is not practicable or reasonable so to communicate, an example of such circumstances being found in *Mitchell and King* 163 J.P. 75, CA, where the accused had thrown down his weapon and moved away before the final and fatal blows were struck.

(f) *Acquittal of principal*

A secondary party may be convicted of an offence where the actual perpetrator of the *actus reus* of the substantive offence is either acquitted or convicted of a lesser offence. The secondary party may be convicted of the offence for which the principal is acquitted where there is evidence against the secondary party that may not be admitted against the principal: *Humphreys and Turner* [1965] 3 All E.R. 689, or where there is insuf- **12–40** ficient evidence that the person charged as a principal was in fact involved in the offence: *Davis* [1977] Crim. L.R. 542, CA.

The secondary party may also be convicted where the principal has some defence that does not benefit the secondary party: *Bourne* 36 Cr.App.R. 125, CCA; *Cogan and Leek* [1976] 1 Q.B. 217, CA; *DPP v. K and B* [1997] 1 Cr.App.R. 36, DC. In *Pickford* [1995] 1 Cr.App.R. 420, CA, it was said, *obiter* that the decisions in *Bourne* and *Cogan and Leek* do not support the proposition that where the principal offender lacks all legal capacity to commit the crime in question another may nevertheless be guilty of aiding and abetting him. They were rather cases in which the person who had committed the acts said to constitute the principal offence was fully capable in law of committing that offence but had a complete defence on the facts.

(2) Mental element of accessories

12–41 There are two parts to the mental element:

(i) The accessory must intend to aid, abet, counsel or procure: *Lynch v. DPP for Northern Ireland* [1975] A.C. 653, HL; *Powell, English* [1999] 1 A.C. 1, HL (where it was held that a secondary party is guilty of murder if he participates in a joint venture, realising (but without agreeing thereto) that in the course thereof the principal might use force with intent to kill or cause grievous bodily harm, and the principal does so. The secondary party has lent himself to the enterprise and by doing so, has given assistance and encouragement to the principal in carrying out an enterprise which the secondary party realises may involve murder).

This approach should be adopted in relation to all charges against defendants accused of aiding and abetting the commission of a crime, whatever the crime alleged. Where the defendant is alleged to have counselled or procured the commission of the relevant offence it seems that it is necessary to prove that the defendant intended that the offence or an offence of the same type should be committed: *Ferguson v. Weaving* [1951] 1 K.B. 814, at 819; *Att.-Gen.'s Reference (No 1 of 1975)* [1975] Q.B. 773, CA and *Blakely v. DPP* [1991] R.T.R. 405, DC.

(ii) The secondary party must also know of the essential matters that constitute the offence: *per* Lord Goddard C.J. in *Johnson v. Youden* [1950] 1 K.B. 544, at 546. This is so even where the principal's offence is one of strict liability. In *Smith v. Mellors* [1987] 84 Cr.App.R. 279, DC, both defendants were charged under s.6(1) of the *Road Traffic Act* 1972, for driving with excess alcohol (now s.5(1)(a) of the *RTA* 1988). As it could not be determined who was the driver and who was the passenger, it was held that there was no case to answer, as for the purposes of the strict liability offence under s.6(1), for the secondary party to be convicted, it would be necessary to prove that he knew that the principal was driving with excess alcohol. As it could not be determined who was the driver and who the passenger, the question of knowledge could not be addressed.

Reform

12–42 On May 10, 2007, the Law Commission published a final report, *Participating in Crime* (Cm. 7084). This report concerns the reform of the current law of accessorial liability and accompanies the previous report *Assisting and Encouraging Crime* (LC 300) whose proposals for the reform of the offence of incitement were adopted in the *Serious Crime Bill* 2007. In brief, the report recommends the retention of accessorial liability, but recommends its scope be restricted to those who a) assist offenders *intending* that the principal's offence be carried out, or b) are part of a joint venture and forsee the principal's offence being committed as a possible result of the joint venture. The report includes a draft Bill containing proposals for reform, but at the time of writing, these proposals have not yet been adopted.

V. ASSISTING OFFENDERS

(1) Legislation

Criminal Law Act 1967, s.4

Penalties for assisting offenders

4.—(1) Where a person has committed a relevant offence, any other person who, knowing or believing him to be guilty of the offence or of some other relevant offence, does without lawful authority or reasonable excuse any act with intent to impede his apprehension or prosecution shall be guilty of an offence. **12–43**

(1A) In this section and section 5 below 'relevant offence' means—

(a) an offence for which the sentence is fixed by law,

(b) an offence for which a person of 18 years or over (not previously convicted) may be sentenced to imprisonment for a term of five years (or might be so sentenced but for the restrictions imposed by section 33 of the Magistrates' Courts Act 1980).

(2) If on the trial of an indictment for [a relevant offence] the jury are satisfied that the offence charged (or some other offence of which the accused might on that charge be found guilty) was committed, but find the accused not guilty of it, they may find him guilty of any offence under subsection (1) above of which they are satisfied that he is guilty in relation to the offence charged (or that other offence).

(3) A person committing an offence under subsection (1) above with intent to impede another person's apprehension or prosecution shall on conviction on indictment be liable to imprisonment according to the gravity of the other person's offence, as follows—

(a) if that offence is one for which the sentence is fixed by law, he shall be liable to imprisonment for not more than ten years;

(b) if it is one for which a person [not previously convicted] may be sentenced to imprisonment for a term of fourteen years, he shall be liable to imprisonment for not more than seven years;

(c) if it is not one included above but is one for which a person [not previously convicted] may be sentenced to imprisonment for a term of ten years, he shall be liable to imprisonment for not more than five years;

(d) in any other case, he shall be liable to imprisonment for not more than three years.

(4) No proceedings shall be instituted for an offence under subsection (1) above except by or with the consent of the Director of Public Prosecutions:

[This section is printed as amended by the *Serious Organised Crime and Police Act* 2005, Sched. 7(3), para. 40(2)(6).]

(2) Proof of guilt

Proof of the other person's guilt is essential to proof of the commission of this offence. However, it is not necessary that the principal offender has been convicted of the relevant offence: *Donald and Donald* 83 Cr.App.R. 49, CA. There can be no charge of attempting to commit an offence under s.4 of the *CLA* 1967: *Criminal Attempts Act* 1981, s.1(4). **12–44**

As the language of s.4(1) of the 1967 Act refers to the commission of the relevant offence by the principal offender, not his conviction, the commission of the relevant offence by the principal offender may be established in the case of the person assisting, even though it has not been established against the principal. In *Zaman* [2010] EWCA Crim 209, CA, the appellant had pleaded guilty to assisting an offender in an offence of conspiracy to be concerned in the supply of heroin. Although the principal offender was subsequently acquitted of that conspiracy, the Court of Appeal held that the appellant's unequivocal guilty plea had relieved the Crown of the need for any further proof that the principal had committed the relevant offence.

The policy of this section is that those who assist offenders do so at their peril, the punishment being directly related to the nature of the principal offence rather than the knowledge of the defendant. The defendant must however know or positively believe in the guilt of the person convicted, and mere suspicion as to guilt will be insufficient. The statute does not however require that the defendant knew of the particular offence that the assisted person had committed, though the defendant's state of mind may be a relevant factor in mitigation: *Morgan (M.M.)* [1972] 1 Q.B. 436, CA. The defendant does not have to be proved to have known the identity of the principal offender: *Brindley and Long* [1971] 2 Q.B. 300, CA.

VI. INCHOATE OFFENCES

A. STATUTORY CONSPIRACY

12–45 The *Criminal Law Act* 1977 replaced common law conspiracy with a statutory offence, preserving only common law conspiracy to defraud, and conspiracy to do acts tending to corrupt public morals or outrage public decency. Conspiracy is triable only on indictment and is hence outside the scope of this work.

B. ATTEMPT

(1) Definition

Criminal Attempts Act 1981, ss. 1-4

Attempting to commit an offence.

12–46 **1.**—(1) If, with intent to commit an offence to which this section applies, a person does an act which is more than merely preparatory to the commission of the offence, he is guilty of attempting to commit the offence.

(1A) Subject to section 8 of the *Computer Misuse Act* 1990 (relevance of external law), if this subsection applies to an act, what the person doing it had in view shall be treated as an offence to which this section applies.

(1B) Subsection (1A) above applies to an act if—

(a) it is done in England and Wales; and

(b) it would fall within subsection (1) above as more than merely preparatory to the commission of an offence under section 3 of the *Computer Misuse Act* 1990 but for the fact that the offence, if completed, would not be an offence triable in England and Wales.

(2) A person may be guilty of attempting to commit an offence to which this section applies even though the facts are such that the commission of the offence is impossible.

(3) In any case where—

(a) apart from this subsection a person's intention would not be regarded as having amounted to an intent to commit an offence; but

(b) if the facts of the case had been as he believed them to be, his intention would be so regarded, then, for the purposes of subsection (1) above, he shall be regarded as having had an intent to commit that offence.

(4) This section applies to any offence which, if it were completed, would be triable in England and Wales as an indictable offence, other than—

(a) conspiracy (at common law or under section 1 of the *Criminal Law Act* 1977 or any other enactment);

(b) aiding, abetting, counselling, procuring or suborning the commission of an offence;

(ba) an offence under section 2(1) of the *Suicide Act* 1961 (c. 60) (encouraging or assisting suicide);

(c) offences under section 4(1) (assisting offenders) or 5(1) (accepting or agreeing to accept consideration for not disclosing information about an arrestable offence) of the *Criminal Law Act* 1967.

[Section printed as amended by the *Coroners and Justice Act* 2009, Sched. 21(2) para. 58]

Extended jurisdiction in relation to certain attempts

1A.—(1) If this section applies to an act, what the person doing the act had in view shall be treated as an offence to which section 1(1) above applies. **12–47**

(2) This section applies to an act if—

(a) it is done in England and Wales, and

(b) it would fall within section 1(1) above as more than merely preparatory to the commission of a Group A offence but for the fact that that offence, if completed, would not be an offence triable in England and Wales.

(3) In this section "Group A offence" has the same meaning as in Part 1 of the *Criminal Justice Act* 1993.

(4) Subsection (1) above is subject to the provisions of section 6 of the Act of 1993 [relevance of external law].

(5) Where a person does any act to which this section applies, the offence which he commits shall for all purposes be treated as the offence of attempting to commit the relevant Group A offence.

Application of procedural and other provisions to offences under s.1

2.—(1) Any provision to which this section applies shall have effect with respect to an offence under section 1 above of attempting to commit an offence as it has effect with respect to the offence attempted. **12–48**

(2) This section applies to provisions of any of the following descriptions made by or under any enactment (whenever passed)—

(a) provisions whereby proceedings may not be instituted or carried on otherwise than by, or on behalf or with the consent of, any person (including any provisions which also make other exceptions to the prohibition);

(b) provisions conferring power to institute proceedings;

(c) provisions as to the venue of proceedings;

(d) provisions whereby proceedings may not be instituted after the expiration of a time limit;

(e) provisions conferring a power of arrest or search;

(f) provisions conferring a power of seizure and detention of property;

(g) provisions whereby a person may not be convicted [or committed for trial] on the uncorroborated evidence of one witness (including any provision requiring the evidence of not less than two credible witnesses);

(h) provisions conferring a power of forfeiture, including any power to deal with anything liable to be forfeited;

(i) provisions whereby, if an offence committed by a body corporate is proved to have been committed with the consent or connivance of another person, that person also is guilty of the offence.

Offences of attempt under other enactments

3.—(1) Subsections (2) to (5) below shall have effect, subject to subsection (6) below and to any inconsistent provision in any other enactment, for the purpose of determining whether a person is guilty of an attempt under a special statutory provision. **12–49**

(2) For the purposes of this Act an attempt under a special statutory provision is an offence which—

(a) is created by an enactment other than section 1 above, including an enactment passed after this Act; and

(b) is expressed as an offence of attempting to commit another offence (in this section referred to as "the relevant full offence").

(3) A person is guilty of an attempt under a special statutory provision if, with intent to commit the relevant full offence, he does an act which is more than merely preparatory to the commission of that offence.

(4) A person may be guilty of an attempt under a special statutory provision even though the facts are such that the commission of the relevant full offence is impossible.

(5) In any case where—

(a) apart from this subsection a person's intention would not be regarded as having amounted to an intent to commit the relevant full offence; but

(b) if the facts of the case had been as he believed them to be, his intention would be so regarded,

Part III

then, for the purposes of subsection (3) above, he shall be regarded as having had an intent to commit that offence.

(6) Subsections (2) to (5) above shall not have effect in relation to an act done before the commencement of this Act.

(2) Allocation

Trial and penalties

12–50 **4.**—(1) A person guilty by virtue of section 1 above of attempting to commit an offence shall—

(a) if the offence attempted is murder or any other offence the sentence for which is fixed by law, be liable on conviction on indictment to imprisonment for life; and

(b) if the offence attempted is indictable but does not fall within paragraph (a) above, be liable on conviction on indictment to any penalty to which he would have been liable on conviction on indictment of that offence; and

(c) if the offence attempted is triable either way, be liable on summary conviction to any penalty to which he would have been liable on summary conviction of that offence.

(2) In any case in which a court may proceed to summary trial of an information charging a person with an offence and an information charging him with an offence under section 1 above of attempting to commit it or an attempt under a special statutory provision, the court may, without his consent, try the informations together.

(3) Where, in proceedings against a person for an offence under section 1 above, there is evidence sufficient in law to support a finding that he did an act falling within subsection (1) of that section, the question whether or not his act fell within that subsection is a question of fact.

(4) Where, in proceedings against a person for an attempt under a special statutory provision, there is evidence sufficient in law to support a finding that he did an act falling within subsection (3) of section 3 above, the question whether or not his act fell within that subsection is a question of fact.

(5) Subsection (1) above shall have effect—

(a) subject to section 37 of and Schedule 2 to the *Sexual Offences Act* 1956 [mode of trial of and penalties for attempts to commit certain offences under that Act]; and

(b) notwithstanding anything—

(i) in section 32(1) [no limit to fine on conviction on indictment] of the *Criminal Law Act* 1977; or

(ii) in section 78(1) and (2) [maximum of six months' imprisonment on summary conviction unless express provision made to the contrary] of the *Powers of Criminal Courts (Sentencing) Act* 2000.

12–51 An offence which is triable only summarily may not be the subject of a criminal attempt under s.1 of the 1981 Act, however, provisions creating summary offences will sometimes create corresponding offences of attempt. Such offences are within the scope of s.3 of the 1981 Act which provides that attempts created by special statutory provision shall be governed by the same rules as those contained in subs. 1(1) to (3) of the 1981 Act.

(3) Elements of the offence

"More than merely preparatory"

12–52 The words should be given their natural and ordinary meaning: *Jones* 91 Cr.App.R. 351, CA. In *Geddes* [1996] Crim. L.R. 894, CA, it was held that there was no clear delineation between acts amounting to an attempt and those which were merely preparatory and each case depends upon its facts. For an offence to be committed under section 1 the defendant must have moved from the stage of planning and preparation to implementing his intention. In *Qadir and Khan* [1998] Crim. L.R. 828, CA, the court stated that "attempt begins at the moment when the defendant embarks upon the crime proper, as opposed to taking steps rightly regarded as merely preparatory."

Expressing an intention to drive a motor vehicle after consuming in excess of the prescribed limit, and then opening the door to the vehicle in furtherance of that intention does not amount to acts more than merely preparatory to the act of driving the vehicle: *Mason v. DPP* [2009] EWHC 2198. The appellant had been convicted of attempting to drive a motor vehicle under the influence of excess alcohol. He had reported to the police that his car had been stolen at knifepoint whilst he opened his car door intending to drive home. The police, detecting alcohol on his breath, arrested and breathalysed him. The alcohol level in his breath was almost twice the legal limit. The appellant admitted his intention to drive home knowing he was possibly over the legal limit. Quashing his conviction, the Divisional Court stated that the appellant could not be said to have embarked on the "crime proper" until he did something that was part of the actual process of putting the car in motion, such as turning on the engine. Starting to open the car door was not such an act. Although the appellant had the necessary *mens rea*, *mens rea* absent sufficient *actus reus* was not enough to constitute guilt.

"With intent to commit an offence"

In *Mohan* (1974) 60 Cr.App.R. 272, CA, in relation to the necessary mental element for criminal attempts at common law, James L.J. stated that: **12–53**

> "The bounds are presently set requiring proof of specific intent, a decision to bring about, in so far as it lies within the accused's power, the commission of the offence which it is alleged the accused attempted to commit, no matter whether the accused desired that consequence of his act or not." (p.278)

This was approved in *Pearman* (1985) 80 Cr.App.R. 259, CA. Hence, it must ordinarily be proved that the defendant acted with a specific intent to commit the particular crime attempted, even if the necessary *mens rea* for the particular crime falls below this high threshold.

However, whilst intent is required as to the consequences of the prohibited act, the Court of Appeal has held that something less may be sufficient in terms of the circumstances surrounding the offence. In *Att.-Gen.'s Reference (No. 3 of 1992)* 98 Cr.App.R. 383, CA, the defendant had thrown a petrol bomb at the victim but it smashed into a wall. The Court of Appeal considered whether he could be convicted of attempting to commit aggravated criminal damage, contrary to s.1(2) of the *Criminal Damage Act* 1971. The Court of Appeal held that the substantive offence would be committed if the defendant had a specific intent to cause damage by fire to property and was mentally reckless whether the life of another would thus be endangered. Hence it was possible to convict of attempt if the prosecution proved that the respondents, in that state of mind, intended to damage property by throwing a bomb at it. **12–54**

Attempting the impossible

Following the decision in *Shivpuri* [1987] A.C. 1, HL, a defendant may be guilty of an attempt, notwithstanding that the commission of the actual offence was impossible. In *Shivpuri*, applying the language of s.1 of the *Criminal Attempts Act* 1981 to the facts of the case (attempted drugs importation) Lord Bridge stated: **12–55**

> "[T]he first question to be asked is whether the appellant intended to commit the offences of being knowingly concerned in dealing with and harbouring drugs of Class A or Class B with intent to evade the prohibition on their importation. Translated into more homely language the question may be rephrased, without in any way altering its legal significance, in the following terms: did the appellant intend to receive and store (harbour) and in due course pass on to third parties (deal with) packages of heroin or cannabis which he knew had been smuggled into England from India? The answer is plainly yes, he did. Next, did he in relation to each offence, do an act which was more than merely preparatory to the commission of the offence? (at 19)
>
> ... Here then is the nub of the matter. Does the 'act which is more than merely preparatory

Part III

to the commission of the offence' in section 1 (1) of the Act of 1981 (the *actus reus* of the statutory offence of attempt) require any more than an act which is more than merely preparatory to the commission of the offence which the defendant intended to commit? Section 1 (2) must surely indicate a negative answer; if it were otherwise, whenever the facts were such that the commission of the actual offence was impossible, it would be impossible to prove an act more than merely preparatory to the commission of that offence and subsections (1) and (2) would contradict each other." (at 20)

12–56 A defendant who is not mistaken as to the facts, but who erroneously believes that his actions amount to a criminal office may not be convicted of a criminal attempt. Section 1(2) does not apply in relation to such cases.

(4) Jurisdiction

12–57 The general rule is that if the completed offence would be triable in England and Wales, and attempt to commit it will be so triable: see s.1(1) and (4) of the 1981 Act.

Reform

12–58 On December 10, 2009 the Law Commission published their final report on Conspiracy and Attempts. The report includes a draft Conspiracy and Attempts Bill. The consultation paper preceding the final report had proposed that the offence of attempt should be repealed and replaced by two new offences of attempt and criminal preparation. The final report does not recommend such reform. The recommendations pertaining to attempt in the final report would permit conviction for attempted murder if a person deliberately failed to discharge a legal duty to another person with the intention of killing that person; ensure that a person can be convicted of attempt if their intention to commit an offence was contingent on a condition; and clarify the fault element which needs to be proved for a person to be guilty of attempt. The report can be found in full at *http://www.lawcom.gov.uk/index.htm*.

C. INCITEMENT

(1) General

12–59 Section 59 of the *Serious Crime Act* 2007 came into force on October 1, 2008, abolishing the common law offence of incitement.

Sections 44–55 of the *Serious Crime Act* 2007 came into force on October 1, 2008. Sections 44, 45 and 46 create three new offences: intentionally encouraging or assisting an offence (s.44), encouraging or assisting an offence believing it will be committed (s.45) and encouraging or assisting offences believing one or more will be committed (section 46). The s.46 offence is triable on indictment only and hence outside the scope of this work: *Serious Crime Act* 2007, s.55.

Section 47 of the *Serious Crime Act* 2007 sets out provisions relating to proving the offences created by ss.44, 45 and 46.

All these provisions were brought into force by the *Serious Crime Act 2007 (Commencement No. 3) Order* 2008 (S.I. 2008 No. 2054).

Serious Crime Act 2007, s.47

Proving an offence under this Part

12–60 **47.**—(1) Sections 44, 45 and 46 are to be read in accordance with this section.

(2) If it is alleged under section 44(1)(b) that a person (D) intended to encourage or assist the commission of an offence, it is sufficient to prove that he intended to encourage or assist the doing of an act which would amount to the commission of that offence.

(3) If it is alleged under section 45(b) that a person (D) believed that an offence would be committed and that his act would encourage or assist its commission, it is sufficient to prove that he believed—

(a) that an act would be done which would amount to the commission of that offence; and

(b) that his act would encourage or assist the doing of that act.

(4) [relevant to section 46]

(5) In proving for the purposes of this section whether an act is one which, if done, would amount to the commission of an offence—

(a) if the offence is one requiring proof of fault, it must be proved that—

(i) D believed that, were the act to be done, it would be done with that fault;

(ii) D was reckless as to whether or not it would be done with that fault; or

(iii) D's state of mind was such that, were he to do it, it would be done with that fault; and

(b) if the offence is one requiring proof of particular circumstances or consequences (or both), it must be proved that—

(i) D believed that, were the act to be done, it would be done in those circumstances or with those consequences; or

(ii) D was reckless as to whether or not it would be done in those circumstances or with those consequences.

(6) For the purposes of subsection (5)(a)(iii), D is to be assumed to be able to do the act in question.

(7) In the case of an offence under section 44—

(a) subsection (5)(b)(i) is to be read as if the reference to "D believed" were a reference to "D intended or believed"; but

(b) D is not to be taken to have intended that an act would be done in particular circumstances or with particular consequences merely because its being done in those circumstances or with those consequences was a foreseeable consequence of his act of encouragement or assistance.

(8) Reference in this section to the doing of an act includes reference to—

(a) a failure to act;

(b) the continuation of an act that has already begun;

(c) an attempt to do an act (except an act amounting to the commission of the offence of attempting to commit another offence).

(9) In the remaining provisions of this Part (unless otherwise provided) a reference to the anticipated offence is—

(a) in relation to an offence under section 44, a reference to the offence mentioned in subsection (2); and

(b) in relation to an offence under section 45, a reference to the offence mentioned in subsection (3).

Section 49 of the *Serious Crime Act* 2007 sets out supplemental provisions relating to the offences under sections 44, 45 and 46.

Serious Crime Act 2007, s.49

Supplemental provisions

49.—(1) A person may commit an offence under this Part whether or not any offence capable of being encouraged or assisted by his act is committed. **12–61**

(2) If a person's act is capable of encouraging or assisting the commission of a number of offences—

(a) section 44 applies separately in relation to each offence that he intends to encourage or assist to be committed; and

(b) section 45 applies separately in relation to each offence that he believes will be encouraged or assisted to be committed.

(3) A person may, in relation to the same act, commit an offence under more than one provision of this Part.

(4) In reckoning whether—

(a) for the purposes of section 45, an act is capable of encouraging or assisting the commission of an offence; or

(b) for the purposes of section 46, an act is capable of encouraging or assisting the commission of one or more of a number of offences; offences under this Part and listed offences are to be disregarded.

(5) "Listed offence" means—

(a) in England and Wales, an offence listed in Part 1, 2 or 3 of Schedule 3; and

(b) in Northern Ireland, an offence listed in Part 1, 4 or 5 of that Schedule.

(6) The Secretary of State may by order amend Schedule 3.

(7) For the purposes of sections 45(b)(i) and 46(1)(b)(i) it is sufficient for the person concerned to believe that the offence (or one or more of the offences) will be committed

Section 52 of the *Serious Crime Act* 2007 concerns the jurisdiction of the s.44, 45 and 46 offences.

Serious Crime Act 2007, s.52

Jurisdiction

12–62 **52.**—(1) If a person (D) knows or believes that what he anticipates might take place wholly or partly in England or Wales, he may be guilty of an offence under section 44, 45 or 46 no matter where he was at any relevant time.

(2) If it is not proved that D knows or believes that what he anticipates might take place wholly or partly in England or Wales, he is not guilty of an offence under section 44, 45 or 46 unless paragraph 1, 2 or 3 of Schedule 4 applies.

(3) A reference in this section (and in any of those paragraphs) to what D anticipates is to be read as follows—

(a) in relation to an offence under section 44 or 45, it refers to the act which would amount to the commission of the anticipated offence;

(b) in relation to an offence under section 46, it refers to an act which would amount to the commission of any of the offences specified in the indictment.

(4) In their application to Northern Ireland, this section and Schedule 4 have effect as if references to—

(a) England or Wales; and

(b) England and Wales;

were references to Northern Ireland.

(5) Nothing in this section or Schedule 4 restricts the operation of any enactment by virtue of which an act constituting an offence under this Part is triable under the law of England and Wales or Northern Ireland.

VII. INTENTIONALLY ENCOURAGING OR ASSISTING AN OFFENCE

(1) Definition

Serious Crime Act 2007, s.44

Intentionally encouraging or assisting an offence

12–63 **44.**—(1) A person commits an offence if—

(a) he does an act capable of encouraging or assisting the commission of an offence; and

(b) he intends to encourage or assist its commission.

(2) But he is not to be taken to have intended to encourage or assist the commission of an offence merely because such encouragement or assistance was a foreseeable consequence of his act.

(2) Allocation

12–64 The offence is triable in the same way as the offence assisted or encouraged: *Serious Crime Act* 2007, s.55.

(3) Elements of the offence

12–65 The prosecution must prove that the defendant:

— Did an act capable of encouraging or assisting the commission of an offence; and

— They intended to encourage or assist its commission, though such intention is not to be found merely because such encouragement or assistance was a foreseeable consequence of their act.

If it is alleged under s.44(1)(b) that the defendant intended to encourage or assist the commission of an offence, it is sufficient to prove that he intended to encourage or assist the doing of an act which would amount to the commission of an offence: *Serious Crime Act* 2007, s.47(2).

In proving whether an act is one which, if done, would amount to the commission of an offence, if the offence is one requiring proof of fault, it must be proved that:

- The defendant believed that, were the act to be done, it would be done with that fault or
- The defendant was reckless as to whether or not it would be done with that fault; or
- The defendant's state of mind was such that, were he to do it, it would be done with that fault: *Serious Crime Act* 2007, s.47(5).

If the offence is one requiring proof of particular circumstances or consequences (or both), it must be proved that:

- The defendant believed that were the act to be done, it would be done in those circumstances or with those consequences; or
- They were reckless as to whether or not it would be done in those circumstances or with those consequences: *Serious Crime Act* 2007, s.47(5).

Reference to the doing of an act includes:

- A failure to act
- The continuation of an act that has already begun
- An attempt to do an act (except an act amounting to the commission of the offence of attempting to commit another offence): *Serious Crime Act* 2007, s.47(8).

Reference to the anticipated offence is a reference to the offence mentioned in subs (2): *Serious Crime Act* 2007, s.47(9)(a).

A person may commit an offence under s.44 whether or not any offence capable of being encouraged or assisted is committed: *Serious Crime Act* 2007, s.49(1).

If a person's act is capable of encouraging or assisting the commission of a number of offences, s.44 applies separately in relation to each offence they intend to encourage or assist: *Serious Crime Act* 2007, s.49(2).

The same act may be a basis for an offence under more than one provision of Pt 2: *Serious Crime Act* 2007, s.49(3).

(4) Statutory defence

Sections 50 and 51 of the *Serious Crime Act* 2007 set out two defences that apply to the s.44 offence. Section 50 provides a defence of acting reasonably and s.51 creates a defence relating to protective offences where the person encouraging or assisting the protective offence falls within the category of persons protected. **12–66**

Serious Crime Act 2007, s.50

Defence of acting reasonably

50.—(1) A person is not guilty of an offence under this Part if he proves—

(a) that he knew certain circumstances existed; and

(b) that it was reasonable for him to act as he did in those circumstances.

(2) A person is not guilty of an offence under this Part if he proves—

(a) that he believed certain circumstances to exist;

(b) that his belief was reasonable; and

(c) that it was reasonable for him to act as he did in the circumstances as he believed them to be.

(3) Factors to be considered in determining whether it was reasonable for a person to act as he did include—

(a) the seriousness of the anticipated offence (or, in the case of an offence under s.46, the offences specified in the indictment);

(b) any purpose for which he claims to have been acting;

(c) any authority by which he claims to have been acting.

Serious Crime Act 2007, s.51

Protective offences: victims not liable

12–67 **51.**—(1) In the case of protective offences, a person does not commit an offence under this Part by reference to such an offence if—

(a) he falls within the protected category; and

(b) he is the person in respect of whom the protective offence was committed or would have been if it had been committed.

(2) "Protective offence" means an offence that exists (wholly or in part) for the protection of a particular category of persons ("the protected category").

VIII. ENCOURAGING OR ASSISTING AN OFFENCE BELIEVING IT WILL BE COMMITTED

(1) Definition

Serious Crime Act 2007, s.45

Encouraging or assisting an offence believing it will be committed

12–68 **45.** A person commits an offence if—

(a) he does an act capable of encouraging or assisting the commission of an offence; and

(b) he believes—

(i) that the offence will be committed; and

(ii) that his act will encourage or assist its commission.

(2) Allocation

12–69 The offence is triable in the same way as the offence assisted or encouraged: *Serious Crime Act* 2007, s.55.

(3) Elements of the offence

12–70 The prosecution must prove that the defendant:

— Did an act capable of encouraging or assisting the commission of an offence; and

— Believed that the offence would be committed; and

— Believed that their act would encourage or assist its commission.

If it is alleged under s.45(b) that the defendant believed that an offence would be committed and that his act would encourage or assist its commission, it is sufficient to prove that the defendant believed an act would be done which would amount to the commission of that offence and their act would encourage or assist the doing of that act: *Serious Crime Act* 2007, s.47(3).

In proving whether an act is one which, if done, would amount to the commission of an offence, if the offence is one requiring proof of fault, it must be proved that:

— The defendant believed that, were the act to be done, it would be done with that fault or

— The defendant was reckless as to whether or not it would be done with that fault; or

— The defendant's state of mind was such that, were he to do it, it would be done with that fault: *Serious Crime Act* 2007, s.47(5).

If the offence is one requiring proof of particular circumstances or consequences (or both), it must be proved that:

— The defendant believed that were the act to be done, it would be done in those circumstances or with those consequences; or

— They were reckless as to whether or not it would be done in those circumstances or with those consequences: *Serious Crime Act* 2007, s.47(5).

Reference to the doing of an act includes:

— A failure to act

— The continuation of an act that has already begun

— An attempt to do an act (except an act amounting to the commission of the offence of attempting to commit another offence): *Serious Crime Act* 2007, s.47(8).

Reference to the anticipated offence is a reference to the offence mentioned in subs (3): *Serious Crime Act* 2007, s.47(9)(b).

If a person's act is capable of encouraging or assisting the commission of a number of offences s.45 applies separately in relation to each offence that he believes will be encouraged or assisted to be committed: *Serious Crime Act* 2007, s.49(2)(b).

A person may, in relation to the same act, commit an offence under more than one provision of this Part: *Serious Crime Act* 2007, s.49(3).

In reckoning whether an act is capable of encouraging or assisting the commission of an offence, offences under Pt 2 and "listed offences" are to be disregarded: *Serious Crime Act* 2007, s.49(4). In England and Wales, a "listed offence" in one listed in Pt 1, 2 or 3 of Sched. 3 to the *Serious Crime Act* 2007, and in Northern Ireland, a "listed offence" is one listed in Pt 1, 4 or 5 of that Schedule: *Serious Crime Act* 2007, s.49(5).

For the purposes of ss.45(b)(i) it is sufficient for the defendant to believe that the offence (or one or more of the offences) will be committed if certain conditions are met: *Serious Crime Act* 2007, s.49(7).

(4) Statutory defence

Sections 50 and 51 of the *Serious Crime Act* 2007 apply to the s.45 offence. Section 50 provides a defence of acting reasonably and s.51 creates a defence relating to protective offences where the person encouraging or assisting the protective offence falls within the category of persons protected. **12–71**

Part III

Serious Crime Act 2007, s.50

Defence of acting reasonably

50.—(1) A person is not guilty of an offence under this Part if he proves— **12–72**

(a) that he knew certain circumstances existed; and

(b) that it was reasonable for him to act as he did in those circumstances.

(2) A person is not guilty of an offence under this Part if he proves—

(a) that he believed certain circumstances to exist;

(b) that his belief was reasonable; and

(c) that it was reasonable for him to act as he did in the circumstances as he believed them to be.

(3) Factors to be considered in determining whether it was reasonable for a person to act as he did include—

(a) the seriousness of the anticipated offence (or, in the case of an offence under section 46, the offences specified in the indictment);

(b) any purpose for which he claims to have been acting;

(c) any authority by which he claims to have been acting.

Serious Crime Act 2007, s.51

Protective offences: victims not liable

51.—(1) In the case of protective offences, a person does not commit an offence under this Part by reference to such an offence if— **12–73**

(a) he falls within the protected category; and

(b) he is the person in respect of whom the protective offence was committed or would have been if it had been committed.

(2) "Protective offence" means an offence that exists (wholly or in part) for the protection of a particular category of persons ("the protected category").

Sexual Offences (Conspiracy and Incitement) Act 1996 ss.2–3

Incitement to commit certain sexual acts outside the United Kingdom.

12–74 **2.**—(1) This section applies where—

(a) any act done by a person in England and Wales would amount to the offence of incitement to commit a listed sexual offence but for the fact that what he had in view would not be an offence triable in England and Wales,

(b) the whole or part of what he had in view was intended to take place in a country or territory outside the United Kingdom, and

(c) what he had in view would involve the commission of an offence under the law in force in that country or territory.

(2) Where this section applies—

(a) what he had in view is to be treated as that listed sexual offence for the purposes of any charge of incitement brought in respect of that act, and

(b) any such charge is accordingly triable in England and Wales.

(3) Any act done by means of a message (however communicated) is to be treated as done in England and Wales if the message is sent or received in England and Wales.

[This section is printed as amended by the *Serious Crime Act* 2007, Sched. 6(2), para. 60, and the *Serious Crime Act 2007 (Commencement No. 3) Order* 2008, S.I. 2008 No. 2054, with effect from October 1, 2008.]

Sections 1 and 2: supplementary

12–75 **3.**—(1) Conduct punishable under the law in force in any country or territory is an offence under that law for the purposes of section 2 however it is described in that law.

(2) Subject to subsection (3), a condition in section 2(1)(c) is to be taken to be satisfied unless, not later than rules of court may provide, the defence serve on the prosecution a notice—

(a) stating that, on the facts as alleged with respect to what the accused had in view, the condition is not in their opinion satisfied,

(b) showing their grounds for that opinion, and

(c) requiring the prosecution to show that it is satisfied.

(3) […]

(4) The court, if it thinks fit, may permit the defence to require the prosecution to show that the condition is satisfied without the prior service of a notice under subsection (2).

(5) In the Crown Court the question whether the condition is satisfied is to be decided by the judge alone.

(6) In any proceedings in respect of any offence triable by virtue of section 2 it is immaterial to guilt whether or not the accused was a British citizen at the time of any act or other event proof of which is required for conviction of the offence.

(7) […]

(8) References to an offence of incitement to commit a listed sexual offence include an offence triable in England and Wales as such an incitement by virtue of section 2 [without prejudice to subsection (2) of that section].

(9) Subsection (8) applies to references in any enactment, instrument or document [except those in section 2 of this Act and in Part I of the *Criminal Law Act* 1977].

Sexual Offences (Conspiracy and Incitement) Act 1996, Sched. 1

SCHEDULE 1

LISTED SEXUAL OFFENCES

England and Wales

12–76 1.—(1) In relation to England and Wales, the following are listed sexual offences:

(a) [*repealed by* Sexual Offences Act *2003, s.140 and Sched. 7*];

(b) an offence under any of sections 1 to 12, 14 and 15 to 26 of the *Sexual Offences Act* 2003.

(2) Sub-paragraph (1)(b) does not apply where the victim of the offence has attained the age of sixteen years.

2. [*Northern Ireland.*]

[The Schedule is printed as amended by the *Sexual Offences Act* 2003, s.139, and Sched. 6, para. 35.]

IX. GENERAL DEFENCES

A. INTRODUCTION

Defences can be loosely categorised as those that involve a denial of the necessary *mens rea*, and those that do not deny any of the components of the offence, but which claim that there was some reason for the defendant's conduct that will operate to justify or excuse his offending behaviour. **12–77**

B. DEFENCES DENYING MENS REA

(1) Infancy

Crime and Disorder Act 1998, s.34

Abolition of rebuttable presumption that a child is doli incapax

34. The rebuttable presumption of criminal law that a child aged 10 or over is incapable of committing an offence is hereby abolished. **12–78**

Following enactment of this section (September 30, 1998) the law relating to the culpability of juveniles can be summarised as follows: **12–79**

Children aged under 10 are not responsible in criminal law.

Children aged 10–14 are no longer presumed to be incapable of criminal responsibility. The child's age may, however, be a relevant factor in determining the reasonableness of his actions (where such a factor is relevant.)

In *T* [2009] UKHL 20, HL, the appellant appealed against the Court of Appeal's decision that s.34 of the *Crime and Disorder Act* 1998 had abolished the defence of *doli incapax*. The appellant, who was aged 12 at the time of the offences, had been convicted on 12 counts of causing or inciting a child under 13 to engage in sexual activity. He had pleaded guilty after the trial judge ruled that the defence of *doli incapax* was not available to him. The Court of Appeal determined that the concept of *doli incapax* as a defence was not separate from the rebuttable presumption which had been abolished under s.34, and concluded that s.34 had therefore abolished the defence of *doli incapax*. The issue for determination in the instant appeal was whether s.34 had abolished the defence of *doli incapax* altogether in the case of a child aged between 10 and 14 years, or whether it merely abolished the presumption that a child had that defence, leaving it open to that child to prove that, at the material time, he was *doli incapax*.

Dismissing the appeal, the House of Lords held that when s.34 was read in isolation, its meaning was ambiguous in that it used "*doli incapax*" in the heading and then, in the section itself, referred to the rebuttable presumption that a child aged 10 or over was "incapable of committing an offence". The appeal could not therefore be decided through consideration of the language of s.34 alone. The House of Lords therefore looked at the mischief s.34 was designed to obviate. The House of Lords also had regard to the fact that, although they were different things, the defence of *doli incapax* and the rebuttable presumption had, in recent times, always coexisted. Ministerial statements in Parliament showed that an amendment designed to reverse the presumption rather than abolish it had twice been moved by Lord Goodhart Q.C., on the premise that the clause, as drafted, would abolish the defence of *doli incapax*. The Consultation Paper and the White Paper that preceded the legislation also stressed what was meant by the abolition of the presumption of *doli incapax*. Therefore, in using the language of s.34, Parliament intended to abolish both the presumption and the defence, and accordingly the trial judge and the Court of Appeal were correct to hold that s.34 abolished the defence of *doli incapax*.

(2) Insanity and automatism

12–80 Insanity is dealt with in Ch.28.

Involuntary acts will not attract the sanction of the criminal law, hence a defendant who committed the prohibited act in a state of automatism will have a defence. The relationship between insanity and automatism has been considered in numerous cases:

12–81 In *Quick* [1973] Q.B. 910, CA, the accused was diabetic and raised the defence of automatism due to an imbalance of insulin, which he was taking on prescription. The Court of Appeal held that as the defendant's mental condition stemmed from the use of insulin, rather than his diabetes, his condition stemmed from an external factor, rather than a bodily disorder, hence the defence of automatism should have been available.

In *Bailey* 77 Cr.App.R. 76, CA, the defendant had assaulted his victim during a period of loss of consciousness caused by hypoglaecemia because of his failure to take sufficient food following his last dose of insulin. The Court of Appeal held that self-induced automatism, other than that due to intoxication from alcohol or drugs, may provide a defence to crimes of basic intent. The question in each case will be whether the prosecution have proved the necessary element of recklessness. For example in cases of assault, if the accused knows that his actions or inaction are likely to make him aggressive, unpredictable or uncontrolled with the result that he may cause some injury to others and he persists in the action or takes no remedial action when he knows it is required, it will then be open to the jury to find that he was reckless.

12–82 In *Hennessy* 89 Cr.App.R. 10, CA, the defendant was an insulin dependent diabetic and the offences with which he was charged were committed at a time when he had not taken insulin or eaten for several days and was in a hyperglycaemic state. The relevant question was whether the defendant's state was caused by disease or by some external factor. Hyperglycaemia caused by an inherent defect and not corrected by insulin was a disease and any malfunction of the mind thus caused might fall within the *M'Naghten Rules*. However, the stress, anxiety and depression suffered by the appellant could be the result of the operation of external factors; but not in themselves separately or together external factors of the kind capable in law of causing or contributing to a state of automatism. They constituted a state of mind which was prone to recur and lacked the feature of novelty or accident, hence the defence of automatism should not have been available to the defendant.

12–83 However, in *Roach* [2002] 3 *Archbold News* 1, CA; [2001] EWCA Crim 2698, it was held that the defence of automatism should have been left to the jury. The legal definition of automatism allows that if external factors (taking of prescription drugs and drink) are operative on an underlying condition ("mixed personality disorder") which would not otherwise produce a state of automatism, then the defence should be left to the jury.

12–84 In *Burgess* (1991) 93 Cr.App.R. 41, CA, the defendant was sleepwalking at the time of commission of the charged offence and alleged non-insane automatism as his defence. The Court of Appeal held that on the question of automatism the judge had to decide, first, whether a proper evidential foundation for the defence of automatism had been laid; and, secondly, whether the evidence showed the case to be one of insane automatism falling within the *M'Naghten Rules*, or one of non-insane automatism. The Court held that sleepwalking was an abnormality or disorder, albeit transitory, due to an internal factor, whether functional or organic. It was a disorder or abnormality which might recur, though the possibility of it recurring in the form of serious violence was unlikely. It therefore amounted to a disease of the mind and the trial judge was correct in ruling that the medical evidence adduced amounted to evidence of insanity within the *M'Naghten Rules*.

(3) Intoxication

Introduction

Different rules apply depending on whether the intoxication is voluntary or involuntary. The intoxication will be classed as voluntary where the defendant knowingly takes alcohol or other intoxicating drugs (except when he acts under medical supervision or direction.) A defendant who drinks a spiked drink will be treated as being involuntarily intoxicated. A defendant who forms the *mens rea* required for the crime will not be able to rely on his intoxication as a defence, be that intoxication voluntary or involuntary: *Kingston* (1994) 99 Cr.App.R. 286, HL. **12–85**

As regards intoxicating drugs, in *Bailey* (1983) 77 Cr.App.R. 76, CA, the Court of Appeal stated that for crimes of basic intent, intoxication due to voluntary consumption of dangerous drugs could not amount to a defence as recklessness will suffice for the *mens rea* of the offence, and such recklessness can be found in the decision to consume dangerous drugs. However, in the context of non-dangerous drugs, such as insulin taken by a diabetic, such recklessness cannot be so easily found as whilst "It is common knowledge that those who take alcohol to excess or certain sorts of drugs may become aggressive or do dangerous or unpredictable things … the same cannot be said without more of a man who fails to take food after an insulin injection. If he does appreciate the risk that such a failure may lead to aggressive, unpredictable and uncontrollable conduct and he nevertheless deliberately runs the risk or otherwise disregards it, this will amount to recklessness"; *per* Griffiths L.J. (at 80). In *Hardie* 80 Cr.App.R. 157, CA, the defendant, charged with an offence under the *Criminal Damage Act* 1971, had taken a number of valium tablets (prescribed for someone else). The Court of Appeal held that this did not necessarily amount to voluntary intoxication, Parker L.J stating that:

> "…if the effect of a drug is merely soporific or sedative the taking of it, even in some excessive quantity, cannot in the ordinary way raise a *conclusive* presumption against the admission of proof of intoxication for the purpose of disproving *mens rea* in ordinary crimes, such as would be the case with alcoholic intoxication or incapacity or automatism resulting from the self-administration of dangerous drugs." (at 160)

The relevant question was whether the taking of the drug itself was reckless, which would provide the necessary *mens rea* of the offence. **12–86**

Voluntary intoxication

Voluntary intoxication may negate the *mens rea* requirements of crimes of specific intent. The exact meaning of this phrase, and whether the lines between crimes of specific and crimes of basic intent are clearly made out is not beyond dispute. Broadly speaking, crimes of specific intent are those for which only intention will suffice as the necessary mental element. The Court of Appeal considered the distinction between crimes of basic intent and crimes of specific intent in *Heard* [2007] EWCA Crim 125, CA, defining, *obiter*, crimes of specific intent as those which require proof of purpose, or consequence. In this case, the appellant was convicted of sexual assault contrary to s.3 of the *Sexual Offences Act* 2003. Counsel for the appellant argued that the appellant's voluntary intoxication prevented him from having an intention to touch the victim (the offence under s.3 requires an "intentional touching"). Referring to *DPP v. Majewski* (see *post*) the Court held that it had never been the case that voluntary intoxication could prevent a defendant forming an intention to touch, and that the *Sexual Offences Act* 2003 did not alter this position. Lord Justice Hughes, *obiter*, cast doubt on the notion that offences could be neatly separated into crimes of specific intent and crimes of basic intent, stating: "it should not be supposed that every offence can be categorised simply as either one of specific intent or of basic intent. So to categorise an offence may conceal the truth that different elements of it may require proof of different states of mind." (para. 30) **12–87**

Lord Justice Hughes went on to discuss the distinction between specific and basic intent:

> "It is necessary to go back to *Majewski* in order to see the basis for the distinction there upheld between crimes of basic and of specific intent. It is to be found most clearly in the speech of Lord Simon, at pages 478B to 479B. Lord Simon's analysis had been foreshadowed in his speech in *DPP v. Morgan* [1976] A.C. 182, 216 (dissenting in the result), which analysis was cited and approved in *Majewski* by Lord Elwyn-Jones (at 471). It was that crimes of specific intent are those where the offence requires proof of purpose or consequence, which are not confined to, but amongst which are included, those where the purpose goes beyond the actus reus (sometimes referred to as cases of 'ulterior intent'). By that test, element (a) (the touching) in sexual assault contrary to section 3 of the *Sexual Offences Act* 2003 is an element requiring no more than basic intent. It follows that voluntary intoxication cannot be relied upon to negate that intent" (para. 31).

However, Lord Justice Hughes also recognised that the decision as to whether a crime was one of specific or basic intent, and thus whether voluntary intoxication may be relied upon to negative intention "involves a great deal of policy" and "common sense" (para. 32).

In *Sheehan and Moore* 60 Cr.App.R. 308, Geoffrey Lane L.J. stated:

> "in cases where drunkenness and its possible effect upon the defendant's *mens rea* is an issue, we think that the proper direction to a jury is, first, to warn them that the mere fact that the defendant's mind was affected by drink so that he acted in a way in which he would not have done had he been sober does not assist him at all, provided that the necessary intention was there. A drunken intent is nevertheless an intent.
>
> Secondly, and subject to this, the jury should merely be instructed to have regard to all the evidence, including that relating to drink, to draw such inferences as they think proper from the evidence, and on that basis to ask themselves whether they feel sure that at the material time the defendant had the requisite intent." (at 312)

In *Alden and Jones* [2001] 5 *Archbold News* 3, Ct-MAC, the court said that so far as the question of alcohol and specific intent was concerned, the crucial question where there is evidence of the consumption by the defendant of a substantial quantity of drink is whether there is an issue as to the defendant's formation of specific intent by reason of the alcohol which he has taken and that the necessary pre-requisite to a direction of the kind identified in *Sheehan v. Moore*, *ante*, is that there must be an issue as to the effect of drunkenness upon the defendant's state of mind.

12–88 Where the prosecution has to prove recklessness, *G.* [2004] 1 Cr.App.R. 21, HL, preserves the position whereby the voluntarily intoxicated defendant cannot rely on his intoxication to assert that he did not appreciate the consequences of his actions. Although the House of Lords overruled *Caldwell* as regards the definition of recklessness for the purposes of s.1 of the *Criminal Damage Act* 1971, holding that "a person acts recklessly within the meaning of s.1 of the 1971 Act with respect to (i) a circumstance when he is aware of a risk that it exists or will exist; (ii) a result when he is aware of a risk that it will occur; and it is, in the circumstances known to him, unreasonable to take the risk", the House held that it was not blameworthy to do something involving a risk of injury to another if (for reasons other than self-induced intoxication) one genuinely did not perceive the risk. The subjective view of recklessness is also adopted in cases involving malicious wounding and assault. In such cases, the fact that the accused was unaware of the relevant risk due to the effect of alcohol will not avail him, provided that the risk is one he would have been aware of had he been sober: *Aitken* 95 Cr.App.R. 304, Ct-MAC; *Richardson and Irwin* [1999] 1 Cr.App.R. 392, CA.

12–89 When the question of drunkenness arises, it is not a question of the capacity of the defendant to form the particular intent which is in issue; what is in issue is simply whether he did form such an intent: *Garlick* 72 Cr.App.R. 291, CA.

In *DPP v. Majewski* (1977) A.C. 443, HL, the appellant had been convicted of assaults occasioning actual bodily harm and assaults on police officers in the execution of their duty. His defence was that by reason of drugs voluntarily taken he did not know what he was doing. The House of Lords held that as regards crimes of basic intent, where the necessary mental element is recklessness, or in the context of assault, foresight that the accused actions would cause another person to have apprehension of immediate and unlawful violence, or would possibly have such a consequence, a voluntarily intoxicated defendant will not be able to assert that due to the intoxication he was senseless and therefore had neither recklessness nor intent as regards the *actus reus* of the offence. Lord Elwyn-Jones L.C. stated:

> "If a man of his own volition takes a substance which causes him to cast off the restraints of reason and conscience, no wrong is done to him by holding him answerable criminally for any injury he may do while in that condition. His course of conduct in reducing himself by drugs and drink to that condition in my view supplies the evidence of *mens rea*, of guilty mind certainly sufficient for crimes of basic intent. It is a reckless course of conduct and recklessness is enough to constitute the necessary *mens rea* in assault cases ... The drunkenness is itself an intrinsic, an integral part of the crime, the other part being the evidence of the unlawful use of force against the victim. Together they add up to criminal recklessness. On this I adopt the conclusion of Stroud in (1920) 36 L.Q.R. at p. 273 ... By allowing himself to get drunk and thereby putting himself in such a condition as to be no longer amenable to the law's commands, a man shows such regardlessness as amounts to *mens rea* for the purpose of all ordinary crimes." (at 464–475)

And at 475:

> "My noble and learned friends and I think it may be helpful if we give the following indication of the general lines on which in our view the jury should be directed as to the effect upon the criminal responsibility of the accused of drink or drugs or both, whenever death or physical injury to another person results from something done by the accused for which there is no legal justification and the offence with which the accused is charged is manslaughter or assault at common law or the statutory offence of unlawful wounding under section 20, or of assault occasioning actual bodily harm under section 47 of the *Offences against the Person Act* 1861.
>
> In the case of these offences it is no excuse in law that, because of drink or drugs which the accused himself had taken knowingly and willingly, he had deprived himself of the ability to exercise self-control, to realise the possible consequences of what he was doing, or even to be conscious that he was doing it. As in the instant case, the jury may be properly instructed that they "can ignore the subject of drink or drugs as being in any way a defence" to charges of this character."

Thus for crimes where recklessness is the sufficient *mens rea*, voluntary intoxication **12–90** will not afford an defence. These crimes would seem to include (for the purposes of the magistrates' courts) common assault, assault occasioning actual bodily harm, assault on a police officer in the execution of his duty, malicious wounding against s.20 of the *Offences Against the Person Act* 1861, taking a conveyance without the owner's authority contrary to s.12(1) of the *Theft Act* 1968, arson or criminal damage contrary to s.1(1) of the *Criminal Damage Act* 1971 if recklessness is charged, arson or criminal damage contrary to s.1(2) of the *Criminal Damage Act* 1971 if recklessness is alleged.

DPP v. Majewski was approved in *G., ante*.

(4) Consent

For some offences (common assault) it is necessary for the prosecution to prove **12–91** absence of consent. For other, more serious, offences, consent will be no defence in the absence of good reason. Properly conducted games and sports, lawful chastisement, reasonable surgical interference, dangerous exhibitions may constitute good reason: *Att.-Gen.'s Reference (No. 6 of 1980)* [1981] Q.B. 715; sado-masochistic pleasure does not constitute good reason: according to the majority of the HL in *Brown* [1994] 1 A.C. 212, upheld by the ECHR in *Laskey, Jaggard and Brown v. UK* 24 E.H.R.R. 39. *Brown* was distinguished in *Wilson* [1996] 2 Cr.App.R. 241, but followed in *Emmett*, *The Times*, October 15, 1999; [1999] 8 *Archbold News* 4, where "high-risk" sexual activity had resulted on one occasion in haemorrhages to the victim's eyes and bruising to her neck caused by asphyxiation, and on another in burns to her breast. The Court of Appeal upheld D's conviction.

More recently, in *Barnes* [2005] 1 W.L.R. 910; [2005] 1 Cr.App.R. 30, D appealed against his conviction under s.20 of the *Offences against the Person Act* 1861. The CA held that the prosecution of those who inflicted injury on another in the course of a sporting event was reserved for those situations where the conduct was sufficiently grave to be properly categorised as criminal. Where injuries were sustained in the course of contact sports, such as football, public policy limited the availability of the defence of consent to situations where there had been implicit consent to what had occurred. Whether conduct reached the required threshold to be criminal would depend on all the circumstances. The fact that the play had been within the rules and practice of the game and had not gone beyond it would be a firm indication that what had occurred was not criminal. However, in highly competitive sports, where conduct outside the rules could be expected to occur in the heat of the moment, such conduct might not reach the threshold level required for it to be criminal. That level was an objective one which would be determined by the type of sport, the level at which it was played, the nature of the act, the degree of force used, the extent of the risk of injury and D's state of mind.

Fraud does not necessarily vitiate consent: *Richardson* [1998] 2 Cr.App.R. 200 (victim did not know that dentist was suspended from practice: no assault), but see also *Cort* [2004] 1 Cr.App.R. 18, where D induced women waiting at bus stops to accept a lift by falsely pretending that the bus had broken down, the CA upheld convictions for kidnapping. In *Konzani* [2005] 2 Cr.App.R. 14 the CA held that, in the context of inflicting HIV by sexual intercourse (s.20 of the *Offences against the Person Act* 1861), there was a critical distinction between taking a risk as to the various potentially adverse and possibly problematic consequences of unprotected consensual sexual intercourse, and the giving of informed consent to the risk of infection with a fatal disease. For consent to the risk of contracting HIV to provide a defence, the consent had to be an informed consent. Where consent provided a defence to an offence against the person, it was generally the case that an honest belief in consent would also provide a defence. However, in the circumstances, the defendant's honest belief had to be concomitant with the consent which provided a defence. Unless the consent would provide a defence, an honest belief in it would not assist a defendant. In *Dica* [2005] EWCA Crim 2304 the CA held that it was bound by its own decision in the first appeal (*Dica* [2004] Q.B. 1257) but certified a question of public importance, namely, "in what circumstances, if any, may a defendant who knows or believes he is infected with a serious sexually transmitted infection and recklessly transmits it to another through consensual sexual activity be convicted of an offence of inflicting grievous bodily harm contrary to the *Offences against the Person Act* 1861, s.20." Leave to appeal to the HL was refused by both the CA and HL.

Consent to an assault is not to be implied in the case of an assault on a teacher at a school for children with special needs: *H v Crown Prosecution Service* [2010] EWHC 1374 (Admin). In this case, the appellant appealed by way of case stated against a decision of a youth court to convict him of two counts of common assault carried out on one of his teachers. The appellant had been a pupil at a school specialising in the education of children with emotional, behavioural and social needs and suffered from ADHD and conduct disorder. The court was required to determine whether a person who was employed to teach at a school for children with special needs, including behavioural problems, impliedly consented to the use of violence against them. Dismissing the appeal, the court stated that neither as a matter of new analysis nor legal policy could it be said that consent to assault should be implied to a teacher at a school specialising in the education of children with special educational needs. There was little, if any, similarity to conduct in sports cases where there were comprehensive rules governing instances of inappropriate conduct and reciprocity as between players that assaults would not be tolerated. If the situation were treated as being analogous then there would be a case that dinner ladies, support staff and other students would also be taken to have impliedly consented, opening the floodgates to litigation. Accordingly, there was no good reason to deprive the teacher of his right to complain to the police on the basis that he must be taken to have consented to the type of assault suffered.

For theft, it is not necessary to prove that the victim did not consent: see § 15–6. For consent in relation to offences under the *Sexual Offences Act* 2003, see §§ 14–79 – 14–82.

(5) Mistake of fact

Since the decision in *Tolson* (1889) L.R. 23 QBD 168 it has been an accepted principle that mistake of fact, in the sense of a belief in circumstances which, if true would make the defendant's conduct innocent, is a defence to some, but not all criminal charges. The QBD (Crown Cases Reserved) in *Tolson* held that it was a good defence to a charge of bigamy that the accused believed on reasonable grounds, that the first spouse was dead. **12–92**

Mistake negativing ingredient of offence

In *Williams (G.)* 78 Cr.App.R. 276, CA, the decision in *Morgan* [1976] A.C. 182, HL, was applied to a case of assault occasioning actual bodily harm. One of the elements of this offence is that the accused was acting unlawfully, *i.e.* not acting in self-defence, in the defence of others or for the prevention of crime. The prosecution must establish that the accused was aware of the unlawful nature of his actions. Hence if the accused establishes that he believed in facts which would, were they true, have rendered his conduct lawful, the prosecution have failed to prove their case. The reasonableness of the defendant's belief was only relevant to the question of determining whether he did in fact hold that belief. *Williams* was applied in the cases of *Jones (Terence)* 83 Cr.App.R. 375, CA and *Blackburn v. Bowering* (1994) 1 W.L.R. 1324, CA (Civ Div) Note the presumptions in the *Sexual Offences Act* 2003 with the effect that *Morgan* no longer applies to sexual offences: see *post*, § 14–79. **12–93**

Mistake not negativing ingredient of offence

In *Tolson, ante,* where the defendant was charged with bigamy, her belief that her first spouse was dead provided her with a defence as it was found to be based on reasonable grounds. *Tolson* was applied in *Albert v. Lavin* (1981) 72 Cr.App.R. 178, DC to a charge of assaulting a police constable in the execution of his duty. It was held that a mistaken belief that the victim was not a police constable would not avail the defendant if there were no reasonable grounds for such a belief. In *Phekoo* 73 Cr.App.R. 107, it was held that the offence under s.1(3) of the *Protection from Eviction Act* 1977 was not an absolute offence, and that it had to be proved that the defendant intended to harass someone he knew or believed to be a residential occupier, rather than a squatter. The defendant would be entitled to be acquitted if his belief that the person was not a residential occupier was based on reasonable grounds. **12–94**

The distinction between mistakes which negative an element of the offence and those that do not has been blurred by the decision of the House of Lords in *B. (a minor) v. DPP* [2000] 2 A.C. 428. The defendant was charged with an offence contrary to s.1 of the *Indecency with Children Act* 1960, which provided that a person "who commits an act of gross indecency with or towards a child under the age of fourteen (subsequently amended to 16) is guilty of an offence." The House of Lords held that if the defendant honestly believed that the child was 14 or over, he would not be guilty of the offence. The reasonableness of that belief was not relevant.

Mistake is not an available defence as regards offences of strict liability, which carry no requirement of *mens rea*. In *Howells* [1977] Q.B. 614, 65 Cr.App.R. 86, CA, it was held that an honest and reasonable belief that a firearm was an antique, and therefore exempt from the *Firearms Act* 1968 was no defence. See also *Bradish* [1990] 1 Q.B. 981.

Mistake of law

An honest and reasonable belief that an action is not criminal is no defence, though it may afford considerable mitigation: *Johnson v. Youden* [1950] 1 K.B. 544 at 546. **12–95**

Part III

A mistake as to the civil law may have the effect of negativing *mens rea*. For example, s.2(1)(a) of the *Theft Act* 1968 provides that a person's conduct will not be regarded as dishonest if he appropriates the property in the belief that he has in law the right to deprive the other of it, on behalf of himself or of a third person. In *Smith* [1974] Q.B. 354; 58 Cr.App.R. 320, CA it was held that mistaken belief as to ownership of property is a defence to a charge of criminal damage. As regards alleged contravention of a statutory instrument, s.3(2) of the *Statutory Instruments Act* 1946 provides:

> "In any proceedings against any person for an offence consisting of a contravention of any such statutory instrument, it shall be a defence to prove that the instrument had not been issued by or under the authority of His Majesty's Stationery Office at the date of the alleged contravention unless it is proved that at that date reasonable steps had been taken for the purpose of bringing the purport of the instrument to the notice of the public, or of persons likely to be affected by it, or of the person charged."

C. DEFENCES CLAIMING CONDUCT WAS EXCUSABLE OR JUSTIFIED

(1) Duress

12–96 In *Lynch v. DPP for Northern Ireland* [1975] A.C. 653, HL, Lord Simon stated that "Where so little is clear, this at least seems to be established: that the type of threat which affords a defence must be one of human physical harm (including, possibly, imprisonment), so that threat of injury to property is not enough" (at 686). The threat may relate to a person for whose safety the defendant would have reasonably regarded himself as responsible: *Wright* [2000] Crim. L.R. 510, CA. In *Howe* [1987] A.C. 417, HL, it was held that the relevant test whether a person when charged with a criminal offence was acting under duress is an objective, not subjective, one. This test could be stated as; was the threat was so grave as to cause a person of reasonable firmness, sharing the characteristics of the defendant, to act as he did?

The question of what are the relevant characteristics to which the court should have regard was considered in *Bowen* [1996] 2 Cr.App.R. 157, CA. Stewart-Smith L.J. stated that the following principles apply:

> "(1) The mere fact that the accused is more pliable, vulnerable, timid or susceptible to threats than a normal person are not characteristics with which it is legitimate to invest the reasonable/ordinary person for the purpose of considering the objective test.
>
> (2) The defendant may be in a category of persons who the jury may think less able to resist pressure than people not within that category. Obvious examples are age, where a young person may well not be so robust as a mature one; possibly sex, though many women would doubtless consider they had as much moral courage to resist pressure as men; pregnancy, where there is added fear for the unborn child; serious physical disability, which may inhibit self protection; recognised mental illness or psychiatric condition, such as post traumatic stress disorder leading to learned helplessness.
>
> (3) Characteristics which may be relevant in considering provocation, because they relate to the nature of the provocation, itself will not necessarily be relevant in cases of duress. Thus homosexuality may be relevant to provocation if the provocative words or conduct are related to this characteristic; it cannot be relevant in duress, since there is no reason to think that homosexuals are less robust in resisting threats of the kind that are relevant in duress cases.
>
> (4) Characteristics due to self-induced abuse, such as alcohol, drugs or glue-sniffing, cannot be relevant.
>
> (5) Psychiatric evidence may be admissible to show that the accused is suffering from some mental illness, mental impairment or recognised psychiatric condition provided persons generally suffering from such condition may be more susceptible to pressure and threats and thus to assist the jury in deciding whether a reasonable person suffering from such a condition might have been impelled to act as the defendant did. It is not admissible simply to show that in the doctor's opinion an accused, who is not suffering from such illness or condition, is especially timid, suggestible or vulnerable to pressure and threats. Nor is medical opinion admissible to bolster or support the credibility of the accused." (at 166–167)

12–97 The threat must have been effective when the crime was committed, but it is not fatal to the defence if the threat is not of immediate injury in the event of non-compliance: *Hudson and Taylor* [1971] 2 Q.B. 202, CA; *Abdul-Hussain* [1999] Crim. L.R. 570, CA. The defendant must avail himself of an opportunity which was reasonably open to him to render the threat ineffective. If he does not, the threat will no longer operate as a defence.

The defence of duress will be excluded where as a result of the defendant's voluntary association with others he foresaw or ought reasonably to have foreseen the risk of being subjected to any compulsion by threats of violence. There does not need to be foresight of coercion to commit crimes of the kind with which the defendant was charged: *Hasan* [2005] 2 A.C. 467, HL. This case overruled the previous decision of the CA in *Baker and Ward* [1999] 2 Cr.App.R. 355 which had held that the defence of duress would be excluded where the defendant had foreseen that they may be coerced to commit crimes of the kind with which they were charged. **12–98**

In *Hasan* [2005] 2 A.C. 467, HL, the defendant was convicted of burglary. He had raised the defence of duress, claiming that a drug dealer with a reputation for violence had threatened that he and his family would be harmed if he did not carry out the burglary. The dealer was the boyfriend of his employer, who ran an escort agency and was involved in prostitution. The Crown appealed against the Court of Appeal's decision that the defendant's conviction was unsafe, submitting that the defence of duress was excluded when as a result of the accused's voluntary association with others he foresaw or should have foreseen the risk of being subjected to any compulsion by threats of violence. The defendant submitted that duress should only be excluded if he had actually foreseen the risk of being compelled to commit criminal offences of the type actually committed. Allowing the appeal, the House of Lords stated that policy pointed towards an objective test of what the defendant, placed as he was and knowing what he did, ought reasonably to have foreseen. The policy of the law had to be to discourage association with known criminals, and it should be slow to excuse the criminal conduct of those who did so. (N.B. Lord Bingham, with whom three other Law Lords agreed, suggested that the defence is excluded when as a result of the defendant's voluntary association with others engaged in criminal activity, he foresaw or ought reasonably to have foreseen the risk of being subjected to any compulsion by threats of violence; Lady Hale, dissenting on this point, concluded that the defence should only be excluded when the defendant foresaw the risk of being subjected to compulsion to commit criminal offences.)

In *Ali* [2008] EWCA Crim 716, CA, the appellant had been convicted of robbery. He had submitted that he had been acting under duress when he carried out the robbery, and that he was responding to threats issued by another person. The appellant submitted he did not know this person was a criminal when he first met him. The judge had directed the jury that 'the defence of duress does not apply … if the defendant chooses voluntarily to associate with others where he ought to foresee that he might be subjected to compulsion by threats of violence … . If you choose to join very bad company, such bad company that you can foresee that you are going to be liable to threats of some kind to do things, then you cannot complain and say I was forced to do them when you had voluntarily associated with those people'. The appellant submitted this gave the jury the impression that the appellant could not rely on duress if it was the result of threats made by persons of "bad company". The appellant further submitted that the judge failed to direct the jury that duress is not available as a defence if, but only if, the accused voluntarily associates with others who the accused knows are engaged in criminal activity. Dismissing the appeal, the Court held that as the judge had made clear that duress was unavailable where the defendant ought to foresee that he might be subjected to compulsion by threats of violence, there was no misdirection.

In *Hussain* [2008] EWCA Crim 1117, CA, the appellant appealed against his conviction for attempted robbery. He worked in the building where the offence was committed. His colleague came from the building basement at closing time, armed with a knife, and tied up another member of staff. The victim was able to contact her manager and the police were notified; foiling the robbery. The prosecution alleged that the ap-

Part III

pellant and his colleague had devised the plan together. The appellant claimed he was acting under duress, and said his colleague had a reputation for violence. To support this, he applied to admit under the *Criminal Justice Act* 2003 s.101(1)(c) or s.101(1)(e) the fact that his colleague had previously been charged with murder. Although he had been charged with murder, he was convicted of causing actual bodily harm. The judge refused to admit the evidence. The appellant submitted that the judge had erred in declining to admit the evidence as this prevented him fully developing the defence of duress. Dismissing the appeal, the Court of Appeal stated the appellant was entitled to give evidence of what he believed his colleague had done in the past, and what he believed he was capable of doing to advance his defence of duress. If there was evidence that that belief had some foundation in fact, it could also be adduced, however, a mere unproven charge could not be evidence of bad character. If the judge had been asked to admit evidence of what the appellant believed about his colleague, and to admit evidence that he had been tried for murder on the basis that there was some foundation for his belief, the evidence would have been relevant and ought to have been admitted. The evidence the appellant sought to adduce was admissible but not through the bad character provisions. To that extent, evidence that ought to have been admitted was not. However, the excluded evidence would not have made a difference to the defence as the appellant had had ample opportunity to go to the authorities to avoid being compelled to commit the offence. Instead he had continued to associate with his colleague. It was obvious that the plan required his assistance and he ought to have foreseen that he would come under pressure to assist his colleague. The defence of duress could therefore not have succeeded.

(2) Necessity/duress of circumstances

12–99 In *Shayler* [2001] 1 W.L.R. 2206, CA, Lord Woolf C.J. stated that "the distinction between duress of circumstances and necessity has, correctly, been by and large ignored or blurred by the courts...the law has tended to treat duress of circumstances and necessity as one and the same." (at para. 55) He then approved the statement in *Archbold Crown* at § 17–124 that:

> "There has in recent years developed the expression 'duress of circumstances'. The use of the word 'duress' in this contest is misleading. Duress, whether in criminal law or civil law, suggests pressure being brought to bear by one person on another person to persuade that other person to do something which he is unwilling to do. 'Duress of circumstances' has nothing to do with one person being told to commit a crime 'or else': it relates to a situation where a person is driven to commit a crime by force of circumstances. Accordingly, duress of circumstances is more conveniently dealt with under the heading of 'necessity' ... Indeed, it may be that duress, strictly so called, should itself be regarded as a form of the defence of necessity: see *per* Lord Hailsham L.C. in *Howe* and others..."

Stephen, *Digest of the Criminal Law*, p. 9, stated that an act which would otherwise be a crime may in some cases be excused if the defendant can show that:

(a) it was done only to avoid consequences which could not otherwise be avoided and which if they had followed, would have inflicted upon him, or upon others whom he was bound to protect, inevitable and irreparable evil;
(b) that no more was done than was reasonably necessary for that purpose; and
(c) that the evil inflicted by it was not disproportionate to the evil avoided.

This statement was approved by Brooke L.J. in *A. (Children) (Conjoined Twins: Surgical Separation), Re* [2001] Fam. 147, HL, where he concluded that the separation of conjoined twins to save the life of one twin, whilst entailing death for the other would satisfy Stephen's three criteria, and was hence appropriate (at p. 204). Each of the three judges in *Re A.* stressed the unique nature of the case, and, as *Archbold Crown* notes at § 17–128, it would seem that the defence would only succeed where the inevitable consequence of taking no action would have been the death of two individuals, whereas the consequence of the defendant taking action was to save the life of one of those individuals, albeit at the cost of accelerating the death of the other. As Ward

L.J. stated (at p. 204):

"[I]t is important to restate the unique circumstances for which this case is authority. They are that it must be impossible to preserve the life of X without bringing about the death of Y, that Y by his or her very continued existence will inevitably bring about the death of X within a short period of time, and that X is capable of living an independent life but Y is incapable under any circumstances, including all forms of medical intervention, of viable independent existence. As I said at the beginning of this judgment, this is a very unique case."

In *Conway* (1989) Q.B. 290, the Court of Appeal concluded that: **12–100**

"necessity can only be a defence to a charge of reckless driving where the facts establish 'duress of circumstances,' ...i.e., where the defendant was constrained by circumstances to drive as he did to avoid death or serious bodily harm to himself or some other person... Whether 'duress of circumstances' is called 'duress' or 'necessity' does not matter." [at p. 164]

Conway was applied in *Martin* (1989) 88 Cr.App.R. 343, CA where Simon Brown J. stated: **12–101**

"The principles may be summarised thus: first, English law does, in extreme circumstances, recognise a defence of necessity. Most commonly this defence arises as duress, that is, pressure on the accused's will from the wrongful threats or violence of another. Equally however it can arise from other objective dangers threatening the accused or others. Arising thus it is conveniently called 'duress of circumstances'.

Second, the defence is available only if, from an objective standpoint, the accused can be said to be acting reasonably and proportionately in order to avoid a threat of death or serious injury.

Third, assuming the defence to be open to the accused on his account of the facts, the issue should be left to the jury, who should be directed to determine these two questions: first, was the accused, or may he have been, impelled to act as he did because as a result of what he reasonably believed to be the situation he had good cause to fear that otherwise death or serious physical injury would result second, if so, would a sober person of reasonable firmness, sharing the characteristics of the accused, have responded to that situation by acting as the accused acted? If the answer to both those questions was Yes, then the jury would acquit the defence of necessity would have been established." [at pp.345–346]

In *DPP v. Bell* (1992) R.T.R. 335, DC, the defendant was charged with driving after consuming alcohol in excess of the prescribed limit. He had been out drinking with friends, and it had always been the plan that he would drive home. However, the Crown Court had found as a fact that the defendant was at the time of driving in terror of being caused serious personal injury. They had hence upheld the defendant's plea of duress and quashed the conviction imposed by the justices. The question for the opinion of the High Court was whether, given the defendant's intention to drive anyway, the Crown Court was correct to accept that the defence of duress of circumstance applied to the defendant's driving away from the car park on account of the threatened violence. The DC held that as the Crown Court had accepted that the defendant drove off in terror, the question of the relevance of the fact that the duress may not have been the *sine qua non* of the defendant's conduct was not a question forming part of the case stated.

The applicability of necessity as a defence to a charges under ss.1 and 4 of the *Official Secrets Act* 1989 was examined in *Shayler* [2001] 1 W.L.R. 2206, CA. The Court of Appeal held that the defence of necessity was available to such charges, though in the instant case there were a number of difficulties relating to the establishment of the defence. The Court therefore concluded that there was no necessity or duress as those words are ordinarily understood (the HL rejected a further appeal on other grounds). In *Jones* [2006] UKHL 16, the House of Lords held, unanimously, in the context of trials of protestors against the war on Iraq, that even if the Government had committed the international law crime of aggression in preparing to make war on Iraq, this did not justify the defendants otherwise unlawful conduct. (The HL dealt less specifically with the defence of necessity than had the CA at *Jones* [2005] Q.B. 259; [2004] 3 W.L.R. 1362; [2005] 1 Cr.App.R. 12). **12–102**

(3) Self-defence/protection of private property

Section 3 of the *Criminal Law Act* 1967 provides that 'a person may use such force **12–103**

Part III

as is reasonable in the circumstances in the prevention of crime, or in effecting or assisting in the lawful arrest of offenders or suspected offenders or of persons unlawfully at large.'

In *Beckford v. The Queen* [1988] A.C. 130, Lord Griffiths stated:

> "The common law recognises that there are many circumstances in which one person may inflict violence upon another without committing a crime, as for instance, in sporting contests, surgical operations or in the most extreme example judicial execution. The common law has always recognised as one of these circumstances the right of a person to protect himself from attack and to act in the defence of others and if necessary to inflict violence on another in so doing. If no more force is used than is reasonable to repel the attack such force is not unlawful and no crime is committed. Furthermore a man about to be attacked does not have to wait for his assailant to strike the first blow or fire the first shot; circumstances may justify a pre-emptive strike." (at p.144)

He then referred to the speech of Lord Lane C.J. in *Williams (Gladstone)* (1984) 78 Cr.App.R. 276, which he stated as giving the correct definition of the English law of self-defence: Lord Lane said:

> "In a case of self-defence, where self-defence or the prevention of crime is concerned, if the jury came to the conclusion that the defendant believed, or may have believed, that he was being attacked or that a crime was being committed, and that force was necessary to protect himself or to prevent the crime, then the prosecution have not proved their case. If however the defendant's alleged belief was mistaken and if the mistake was an unreasonable one, that may be a powerful reason for coming to the conclusion that the belief was not honestly held and should be rejected. Even if the jury come to the conclusion that the mistake was an unreasonable one, if the defendant may genuinely have been labouring under it, he is entitled to rely upon it." (at p.281)

Criminal Law Act 1967

Use of force in making arrest, etc.

12–104 **3.**—(1) A person may use such force as is reasonable in the circumstances in the prevention of crime, or in effecting or assisting in the lawful arrest of offenders or suspected offenders or of persons unlawfully at large.

(2) Subsection (1) above shall replace the rules of the common law on the question when force used for a purpose mentioned in the subsection is justified

12–105 The *Criminal Justice and Immigration Act* 2008 aims to clarify the existing law on self-defence. The Act received royal assent on May 8, 2008, and s.76, which concerns self-defence, came into force on July 14, 2008: *Criminal Justice and Immigration Act 2008 (Commencement No. 2 and Transitional and Saving Provisions) Order* 2008 (S.I. 2008 No. 1586)

Section 76 provides that when considering whether the degree of force used in self-defence was reasonable, the defendant's actions are to be judged by reference to the circumstances as they believed them to be, and the defendant can rely on genuine, if mistaken beliefs, regardless of whether their mistake was reasonable, unless the mistake is attributable to voluntary intoxication. The section further provides that the degree of force used by the defendant should not be regarded as reasonable if it was disproportionate. In considering this issue, it should be remembered that a person acting for a legitimate purpose may not be able to weigh to a nicety the exact measure of any necessary action; and evidence of a person's having only done what they honestly and instinctively thought was necessary for a legitimate purpose constitutes strong evidence that only reasonable action was taken for that purpose.

Section 76 of the *Criminal Justice and Immigration Act* 2008 does not alter the previously existing law. It is not the law that where a defendant had either started the fight with the victim, or entered it willingly, that would always and inevitably be a bar to self-defence arising. Self-defence could arise in the case of the original aggressor, but only where the violence offered by the victim was so out of proportion to what the original aggressor did that the roles were effectively reversed. It is not the law that if a defendant set out to provoke another to punch him, and succeeded, then the defendant is entitled to punch the other person. Underlying the law of self-defence is the common-sense morality that what is not unlawful is force which was reasonably necessary: *Keane (Daniel), McGrath (Katherine Rosa)* [2010] EWCA Crim 2514, CA.

Criminal Justice and Immigration Act 2008, s.76

Reasonable force for purposes of self-defence etc.

76.—(1) This section applies where in proceedings for an offence— **12–106**

(a) an issue arises as to whether a person charged with the offence ("D") is entitled to rely on a defence within subsection (2), and

(b) the question arises whether the degree of force used by D against a person ("V") was reasonable in the circumstances.

(2) The defences are—

(a) the common law defence of self-defence; and

(b) the defences provided by section 3(1) of the *Criminal Law Act* 1967 (c. 58) or section 3(1) of the *Criminal Law Act* (Northern Ireland) 1967 (c. 18 (N.I.)) (use of force in prevention of crime or making arrest).

(3) The question whether the degree of force used by D was reasonable in the circumstances is to be decided by reference to the circumstances as D believed them to be, and subsections (4) to (8) also apply in connection with deciding that question.

(4) If D claims to have held a particular belief as regards the existence of any circumstances—

(a) the reasonableness or otherwise of that belief is relevant to the question whether D genuinely held it; but

(b) if it is determined that D did genuinely hold it, D is entitled to rely on it for the purposes of subsection (3), whether or not—

(i) it was mistaken, or

(ii) (if it was mistaken) the mistake was a reasonable one to have made.

(5) But subsection (4)(b) does not enable D to rely on any mistaken belief attributable to intoxication that was voluntarily induced.

(6) The degree of force used by D is not to be regarded as having been reasonable in the circumstances as D believed them to be if it was disproportionate in those circumstances.

(7) In deciding the question mentioned in subsection (3) the following considerations are to be taken into account (so far as relevant in the circumstances of the case)—

(a) that a person acting for a legitimate purpose may not be able to weigh to a nicety the exact measure of any necessary action; and

(b) that evidence of a person's having only done what the person honestly and instinctively thought was necessary for a legitimate purpose constitutes strong evidence that only reasonable action was taken by that person for that purpose.

(8) Subsection (7) is not to be read as preventing other matters from being taken into account where they are relevant to deciding the question mentioned in subsection (3).

(9) This section is intended to clarify the operation of the existing defences mentioned in subsection (2).

(10) In this section—

(a) "legitimate purpose" means—

(i) the purpose of self-defence under the common law, or

(ii) the prevention of crime or effecting or assisting in the lawful arrest of persons mentioned in the provisions referred to in subsection (2)(b);

(b) references to self-defence include acting in defence of another person; and

(c) references to the degree of force used are to the type and amount of force used.

The defence of self defence has involves both a subjective and an objective matters. First, the use of force must be considered in light of the situation that the accused perceived to exist. It must then be asked whether the defendant's use of force in this situation was reasonable. In *Duffy v. Chief Constable of Cleveland* [2007] EWHC 3169, DC, the Court held that a judge had erred in convicting a man of affray because she failed to consider the subjective element of self-defence. The appellant visited a restaurant, and found out that a man with whom he had previously had a violent

Part III

confrontation was upstairs. The appellant approached this man, who had been drinking heavily, and they began shouting at each other. The police were called, and the two men were fighting when the police arrived. The appellant claimed that the other man initiated the fight and he had been acting in self-defence. The judge found that by the time the police arrived, it was no longer reasonable or necessary for either man to continue fighting and the defendant's actions could not be considered as self-defence. Allowing the appeal, the court held that there was nothing to indicate the judge had applied her mind to the facts as they were perceived to be by the defendant at the time of the incident. Had the judge had regard to the subjective element of self-defence she would have at least summarised what the defendant had to say about his continued use of violence, but there was a very real possibility that she adopted a purely objective approach to the issue.

An accused who misjudges the degree of force required and who uses force that is seen as excessive will be deprived of the defence: *Palmer v. The Queen* [1971] A.C. 814. When deciding whether a defendant has used reasonable force in self defence it is not appropriate, save in exceptional circumstances which would make the evidence especially probative, to take into account whether they were suffering from some psychiatric condition: *Martin* [2001] EWCA Crim 2245.

It is not for the defendant to set the standard of reasonable force in his own mind; rather the jury, considering all the circumstances but not the psychiatric condition, must set the standards of reasonableness in considering the individual case: *Canns* [2005] EWCA Crim 2264, CA.

An accused who mistakenly believes that he is being attacked can still rely on the defence of self-defence. In *Williams* (1984) 78 Cr.App.R. 276, the Court held that the accused's mistake in believing that he was being attacked does not need to be a reasonable one. This subjective approach to mistake will not pertain where the defendant's mistake is due to his own voluntary intoxication: *O'Grady* [1987] Q.B. 995, CA. *O'Grady* was followed in *O'Connor* [1991] Crim. L.R. 135 and *Hatton* [2005] EWCA Crim 2951, CA.

Where the accused's mistake is that he believed there were no circumstances warranting the use of force in self defence when in fact there were, the defence of self defence will be unavailable: *Dadson* (1850) 2 Den CC 35. There is no distinction to be drawn between the use of excessive force in self-defence and the use of excessive force in the prevention of crime or in arresting an offender: *Clegg* [1995] 1 A.C. 482, HL.

12–107 It is a principle of common law that a person may use such force to defend his property or the property of others from attack or the threat of imminent attack. The court should ask whether:

(i) the use of force was reasonable to defend property from actual or imminent damage which constituted or could constitute an unlawful or criminal act;

(ii) on the facts as the defendant considered them to be, whether objectively the force used was no more than reasonable in all the circumstances, given the beliefs.

See *DPP v. Bayer* [2004] 1 W.L.R. 2856, (sowing of genetically modified maize not unlawful so defence of defence of property not available to those charged with aggravated trespass contrary to s.68 of the *Criminal Justice and Public Order Act* 1994).

In *Salih* [2007] EWCA Crim 2750, CA, the appellant appealed against his conviction for possession of a firearm contrary to s.16 of the *Firearms Act* 1968. The appellant, who owned a shop, had been found by police with a loaded pistol in his pocket, and was charged with possession of a firearm with intent to endanger life. The prosecution alleged that the appellant had the pistol because he was dealing in guns and had armed himself for protection. The appellant claimed the gun had belonged to his father in law and had been in the shop for many years. He claimed he had intended to hand it to police during a gun amnesty, but had put it in his pocket when a young man entered his shop; he said he had no intent in respect of the weapon. The appellant submitted that the trial judge ought to have made it clear to the jury that if he had the gun for use in lawful self-defence he would not have been guilty of the charge otherwise persons lawfully in possession of a shotgun who accepted they might use it should armed robbers attack their home would be guilty of the same offence. The Crown argued that in order to establish his defence, the appellant would need to show fear of an imminent attack in circumstances where he would be acting in lawful self-defence if he used the firearm. Dismissing the appeal, the Court held that the effectiveness of legislation to prevent the carrying of firearms or offensive weapons would be seriously impaired if anyone who reasonably feared they might at some time be unlawfully attacked was allowed to carry a weapon. If, at the moment when the defendant was alleged to be in possession of a firearm, he was anticipating an imminent attack and was carrying the weapon for his own defence against a specific danger, that might be different. There was a distinction to be drawn between an individual arming themselves with an offensive weapon and those concerned with security and law enforcement. The public policy reasons which prohibited a person from possessing a firearm with intent to endanger life, even though they might only use the firearm in lawful self-defence, would not apply to a person in lawful possession of a firearm whose intent was to use it for purposes other than to endanger life, even though they might have the conditional intention to use it should they be attacked.

It might be open to the owner of a vehicle, in the last resort and when all reasonably practicable alternatives had failed, forcibly to remove an individual who had entered his vehicle without permission and who refused to leave it. However, where an individual had entered the car as a passenger, at the invitation of the car owner, on the basis that they mutually understood that when their dealings were completed she would be driven back in the car from whence she had come, the use of force to remove her at the driver's unilateral whim was unlawful: *Burns (Paul)* [2010] EWCA Crim 1023, CA.

In this case, the appellant appealed against his conviction for assault occasioning actual bodily harm. He picked up the complainant, a prostitute, in a town centre. He drove to a secluded area, stopped the car and, after changing his mind about the transaction, asked her to get out of the car. When she refused, he forcefully ejected her. She asked to be driven back to the pick-up point, and he pushed her away and drove off without her.The judge directed the jury that the appellant had not been entitled to use force to eject her from the car and that provided they were satisfied that the complainant had sustained actual bodily harm at the appellant's hands then, as a matter of law, the force used by him was unlawful. The appellant submitted that that direction had not been correct.

Dismissing his appeal, the Court of Appeal stated that the appellant had acted neither in self-defence nor in defence of anyone else, he had not acted to prevent a crime, nor had he acted in defence of property. He had not acted for any of the purposes envisaged by the *Criminal Law Act* 1967 or the *Criminal Damage Act* 1971, or by the well established common law defences to allegations of violence which would otherwise be criminal, such as participation in sports involving an element of violence. His activities could amount to self-help, as action to recover exclusive possession and occupation of his car, however common law had always been reluctant to extend the ambit of self-help to situations which could culminate in violence. A request to extend the very limited circumstances in which self-help might be used to justify activity which would otherwise constitute a violent offence had to be subjected to the closest possible scrutiny. In any event, the resort to self-help was not justified because the appellant could have regained exclusive possession of his vehicle without the use of force by driving the complainant back to the starting point.

(4) Marital coercion

Criminal Justice Act 1925, s.47

Abolition of presumption of coercion of married woman by husband

47. Any presumption of law that an offence committed by a wife in the presence of her **12–108**

husband is committed under the coercion of the husband is hereby abolished, but on a charge against a wife for any offence other than treason or murder it shall be a good defence to prove that the offence was committed in the presence of, and under the coercion of, the husband.

12–109 Coercion was defined in *DPP for Northern Ireland v. Lynch* [1975] A.C. 653 as an external force which cannot be resisted and which impels its subject to act otherwise than he would wish, *per* Lord Simon.

In *Shortland* [1996] 1 Cr.App.R. 116, CA it was held that to establish the defence of marital coercion under s.47 of the *Criminal Justice Act* 1925, a jury had to be satisfied, on the balance of probabilities, that the will of the defendant wife was so overborne by the wishes of her husband that she had been forced to participate unwillingly. That defence did not necessarily require proof of physical force or the threat of physical force. To succeed, the woman has to prove, on the balance of probabilities that her will was so overborne by the wishes of her husband that she had been forced to participate in the unlawful conduct unwillingly.

Chapter 13

OFFENCES OF VIOLENCE

I. DANGEROUS OFFENDERS AND VIOLENT CRIME

Dangerous offenders

The *Criminal Justice Act* 2003, ss.225–228, provides for sentences of imprisonment to be imposed for public protection and for extended sentences. Such sentences can be passed in respect of offenders aged 18 or over who are convicted of certain violent or sexual offences. The offences are specified in Sched. 15 of the Act and they are serious specified offences if they carry a maximum sentence of life imprisonment or a determinate sentence of at least 10 years (s.224). The specified offences in this chapter are assault occasioning actual bodily harm; malicious wounding or inflicting grievous **13–1** bodily harm; racially or religiously aggravated assaults; assault with intent to resist arrest; abandonment of children under two; putting people in fear of violence and the racially or religiously aggravated offence of that nature. Child cruelty and making threats to kill are serious specified offences. See also Ch. 23—Sentencing.

II. ASSAULT

13–2 On March 16, 2011, the Sentencing Council published a new Guideline on assault offences for judges and magistrates. The new Guideline comes into effect on June 13, 2011 and applies to all offenders aged 18 and over who are sentenced on or after that date, regardless of the date of the offence. For youths charged with these offences, reference should be made to the "Overarching Principles Sentencing Youths" Guideline. The Guideline provides specific guidelines to both the Magistrates Court and the Crown Court. The Guidelines applicable to the Magistrates Court cover the offences of inflicting grievous bodily harm/unlawful wounding contrary to section 20 of the *Offences Against the Person Act* 1861, assault occasioning actual bodily harm contrary to section 47 of the *Offences Against the Person Act* 1861, assault with intent to resist arrest contrary to section 38 of the *Offences Against the Person Act* 1861, assault on a police constable in the execution of his duty contrary to section 89 of the *Police Act* 1996 and common assault, contrary to section 39 of the *Criminal Justice Act 1988. The Guideline is available from the Sentencing Council's website http://www.sentencingcouncil.org.uk/index.htm. For the guidelines pertaining to each offence, see the relevant offence sections below.*

A. ASSAULT AND BATTERY

(1) Definition

Criminal Justice Act 1988, s.39

Common assault and battery to be summary offences

13–3 **39.** Common assault and battery shall be summary offences and a person guilty of either of them shall be liable to a fine not exceeding level 5 on the standard scale, to imprisonment for a term not exceeding six months, or to both.

(2) Allocation

13–4 Common assault and battery are triable summarily. The *Crime and Disorder Act* 1998 (see § 13–24, *post*) created an aggravated form of this offence, committed when an attack is motivated by racial or religious hostility, which is triable either way.

(3) Elements of the offence

13–5 An assault occurs when the defendant intentionally or recklessly causes another to apprehend immediate unlawful violence: *Burstow* [1998] A.C. 147, HL. It is the causing of another to apprehend violence, regardless of whether any violence is used, which defines an assault. An assault can also be committed by words alone: in *Ireland* [1998] A.C. 147, HL, the defendant was convicted of assault occasioning actual bodily harm after making repeated silent phone calls to three women.

A battery is committed when a person intentionally or recklessly applies unlawful force to the complainant. Spitting on another person constitutes a battery: *Lynsey* [1995] 3 All E.R. 654, CA. The battery does not need to be directly inflicted by the defendant, and can be delivered through an instrument: in *DPP v. K* [1990] 1 W.L.R. 1067, QBD, the defendant was found guilty of assault after he placed sulphuric acid in a hand dryer which sprayed over the next user causing scarring to their face.

The *mens rea* for assault and battery may consist either of intention to apply physical force, or recklessness: *Venna* [1976] Q.B. 421. A single information which includes both assault and battery is bad for duplicity and where the allegation is that the defendant intentionally or recklessly applied unlawful force to the complainant then the information should allege "assault by beating": *Norman* [1994] Crim.L.R 518.

In *McMillan v. CPS*, 172 J.P. 485, DC, it was held that a police officer who had physically escorted a woman from a garden to a public footpath after finding her shouting and swearing in a drunken state had been acting within the bounds of what was generally acceptable in the ordinary conduct of daily life and was therefore not guilty of assault. The police officer found the appellant in the garden of her daughter's house shouting and swearing. Another officer advised her to leave but she continued to shout and swear. The police officer then took the appellant by the arm and led her down some steps to a public path. The appellant continued to shout and argue and was arrested. At the appellant's trial for being drunk and disorderly in a public place, the magistrates' court considered whether the officer acted lawfully in leading her from the garden to the path. The magistrates held there had been no assault. The appellant appealed by way of case stated, alleging that the officer had assaulted her and her disorderly behaviour was that of the victim of a continuing assault against which she was entitled to protest. The Divisional Court held that common sense compelled the answer that the police office had not assaulted the appellant. The magistrates were satisfied the officer had made the pragmatic decision not to arrest the appellant in the garden and instead negotiate a conclusion to matters that would be in the appellant's interests. The magistrates found that the officer had taken the appellant by the arm so that he could speak to her in the street, and rejected any suggestion that she was removed to a public place to justify an arrest for an offence with a public place requirement. The officer, thinking of the steepness of the steps, had wanted to steady the appellant, and could properly be said to have acted in accordance with generally acceptable standards of conduct.

Part III

(4) Sentence

When tried summarily, the maximum sentence for this offence is imprisonment for a term not exceeding six months, a fine not exceeding level 5 on the standard scale, or both. After commencement of the relevant provisions, the maximum custodial sentence in a magistrates' court will be 12 months imprisonment: *Criminal Justice Act* 2003, ss.154 and 282. The Sentencing Council issued a definitive guideline on assault applicable from June 13, 2011. **13–6**

The Sentencing Guideline on Common Assault (2011) states that the court should first determine the offence category by reference to the table below: **13–7**

Category 1	Greater harm (injury or fear of injury must normally be present) and higher culpability
Category 2	Greater harm (injury or fear of injury must normally be present) and lower culpability or lesser harm and higher culpability
Category 3	Lesser harm and lower culpability

The court should determine the offender's culpability and the harm caused, or intended, by reference only to the factors below. These factors are described as "the principal factual elements of the offence" and should determine the offence category.

Factors indicating higher culpability	Factors indicating lower culpability
Statutory aggravating factors: • Offence motivated by, or demonstrating, hostility to the victim based on his or her sexual orientation (or presumed sexual orientation) • Offence motivated by or demonstrating hostility to the victim based on the victim's disability (or presumed disability) Other aggravating factors: • Significant degree of premeditation • Threatened or actual use of weapon or weapon equivalent (for example, shod foot, headbutting, use of acid, use of animal) • Intention to commit more serious harm than actually resulted from the offence • Deliberately causes more harm than is necessary for commission of offence • Deliberate targeting of vulnerable victim • Leading role in group or gang • Offence motivated by, or demonstrating, hostility based on the victim's age, sex, gender identity (or presumed gender identity)	• Subordinate role in a group or gang • A greater degree of provocation than normally expected • Lack of premeditation • Mental disorder or learning disability, where linked to commission of the offence • Excessive self-defence
Factors indicating greater harm	**Factors indicating lesser harm**
• Injury or fear of injury which is serious in the context of the offence (must normally be present) • Victim is particularly vulnerable because of personal circumstances • Sustained or repeated assault on the same victim	• Injury which is less serious in the context of the offence

Having determined the offence category, the court should then use the corresponding starting points to reach a sentence within the category range below. The starting point applies to all offenders irrespective of plea or previous convictions. A case of particular gravity, reflected by multiple features of culpability in step one, could merit upward adjustment from the starting point before further adjustment for aggravating or mitigating features.

Offence Category	Starting Point (applicable to all offenders)	Category Range (applicable to all offenders)
Category 1	High level community order	Low level community order – 26 weeks custody

Category 2	Medium level community order	Band A fine – High level community order
Category 3	Band A fine	Discharge – Band C fine

The court should determine the offender's culpability and the harm caused, or intended, by reference only to the factors below. These factors are described as "the principal factual elements of the offence" and should determine the offence category.

When sentencing category 1 offences, the court should also consider the custody threshold as follows:

1) Has the custody threshold been passed?
2) If so, is it unavoidable that a custodial sentence be imposed?
3) If so, can that sentence be suspended?

When sentencing category 2 offences, the court should also consider the community order threshold as follows:

1) Has the community order threshold been passed?

Factors increasing seriousness	Factors reducing seriousness or reflecting personal mitigation
Statutory aggravating factors: • Previous convictions, having regard to i) the nature of the offence to which the conviction relates and its relevance to the current offence; and ii) the time that has elapsed since the conviction • Offence committed whilst on bail Other aggravating factors: • Location of the offence • Timing of the offence • Ongoing effect upon the victim • Offence committed against those working in the public sector or providing a service to the public • Presence of others including relatives, especially children or partner of the victim • Gratuitous degradation of victim • In domestic violence cases, victim forced to leave their home. • Failure to comply with current court orders • Offence committed whilst on licence • An attempt to conceal or dispose of evidence • Failure to respond to warnings or concerns expressed by others about the offender's behaviour • Commission of offence whilst under the influence of alcohol or drugs • Abuse of power and/or position of trust • Exploiting contact arrangements with a child to commit an offence • Established evidence of community impact • Any steps taken to prevent the victim reporting the incident, obtaining assistance and/or from assisting or supporting the prosecution • Offences taken into consideration (TICs)	• No previous convictions or no relevant/recent convictions • Single blow • Remorse • Good character and/or exemplary conduct • Determination and or/demonstration of steps taken to address addiction or offending behaviour • Serious medical conditions requiring urgent, intensive or long-term treatment • Isolated incident • Age and/or lack of maturity where it affects the responsibility of the offender • Lapse of time since the offence where this is not the fault of the offender. • Mental disorder or learning disability where **not** linked to the commission of the offence • Sole or primary carer for dependent relatives.

When dealing with an offence under section 29 of the *Crime and Disorder Act* 1998, the court should determine the appropriate sentence for the offence without taking account of the element of aggravation and then make an addition to the sentence, considering the level of aggravation involved. It may be appropriate to move outside the identified category range, taking into account the increased statutory maximum.

Having determined the appropriate sentence, the court should then consider the following issues:

> *1. Any other factors which indicate a reduction, such as assistance to the prosecution.*
> The court should take into account any rule of law by virtue of which an offender may receive a discounted sentence in consequence of assistance given (or offered) to the prosecutor or investigator.
> *2. Reduction for guilty pleas*
> The court should take account of any potential reduction for a guilty plea in accordance with section 144 of the *Criminal Justice Act* 2003 and the Guilty Plea guideline.
> *3. Dangerousness*
> Inflicting grievous bodily harm/Unlawful wounding and racially/religiously aggravated GBH/Unlawful wounding are specified offences within the meaning of Chapter 5 of the *Criminal Justice Act* 2003. The court should consider whether having regard to the criteria contained in that Chapter it would be appropriate to award an extended sentence.
> *4. Totality principle*
> If sentencing an offender for more than one offence, or where the offender is already serving a sentence, consider whether the total sentence is just and proportionate to the offending behaviour.
> *5. Compensation and ancillary orders*
> In all cases, the court should consider whether to make compensation and/or other ancillary orders.
> *6. Reasons*
> Section 174 of the *Criminal Justice Act* 2003 imposes a duty to give reasons for, and explain the effect of, the sentence.
> *7. Consideration for remand time*
> Sentencers should take into consideration any remand time served in relation to the final sentence. The court should consider whether to give credit for time spent on remand in custody

Offences committed in a domestic context

The *Magistrates Court Sentencing Guidelines* (2008) provide that when sentencing an offence committed in a domestic context, the Court should refer to the Sentencing Guidelines Council's definitive guideline *Overarching Principles: Domestic Violence*, published December 2006. The guideline emphasises that: **13–8**

- as a starting point for sentence, offences committed in a domestic context should be regarded as no less serious than offences committed in a non-domestic context;
- many offences of violence in a domestic context are dealt with in a magistrates' court as an offence of common assault or assault occasioning actual bodily harm because the injuries sustained are relatively minor. Offences involving serious violence will warrant a custodial sentence in the majority of cases;
- a number of aggravating factors may commonly arise by virtue of the offence being committed in a domestic context (see list below);
- since domestic violence takes place within the context of a current or past relationship, the history of the relationship will often be relevant in assessing the gravity of the offence. A court is entitled to take into account anything occurring within the relationship as a whole, which may reveal relevant aggravating or mitigating factors;

- in respect of an offence of violence in a domestic context, an offender's good character in relation to conduct outside the home should generally be of no relevance where there is a proven pattern of behaviour;
- assertions that the offence has been provoked by conduct of the victim need to be treated with great care, both in determining whether they have a factual basis and in considering whether the circumstances of the alleged conduct amounts to provocation sufficient to mitigate the seriousness of the offence;
- where the custody threshold is only just crossed, so that if a custodial sentence is imposed it will be a short sentence, the court will wish to consider whether the better option is a suspended sentence order or a community order, including in either case a requirement to attend an accredited domestic violence programme. Such an option will only be appropriate where the court is satisfied that the offender genuinely intends to reform his or her behaviour and that there is a real prospect of rehabilitation being successful. Such a situation is unlikely to arise where there has been a pattern of abuse.

Wishes of the victim

13–9 The Sentencing Guidelines Council's definitive guideline *Overarching Principles: Domestic Violence* (2007) provides that as a matter of general principle, a sentence imposed for an offence of violence should be determined by the seriousness of the offence, not the expressed wishes of the victim. However, there may be circumstances in which the court can properly mitigate a sentence to give effect to the expressed wish of the victim that the relationship be permitted to continue. The court must be confident that such a wish is genuine, and that giving effect to it will not expose the victim to a real risk of further violence. Critical conditions are likely to be the seriousness of the offence and the history of the relationship. It is vitally important that the court has up-to-date information in a pre-sentence report and victim personal statement.

Either the offender or the victim (or both) may ask the court to take into consideration the interests of any children and to impose a less severe sentence. The court will wish to have regard not only to the effect on the children if the relationship is disrupted but also to the likely effect on the children of any further incidents of domestic violence.

Aggravating factors

13–10

Factors indicating higher culpability
1. Abuse of trust and abuse of power
2. Using contact arrangements with a child to instigate an offence
3. Proven history of violence or threats by the offender in a domestic setting
4. History of disobedience to court orders

Factors indicating greater degree of harm
1. Victim is particularly vulnerable
2. Impact on children

Racial or religious aggravation and aggravation related to disability or sexual orientation

13–11 Section 145 of the *Criminal Justice Act* 2003 provides that the court must regard racial or religious aggravation as an aggravating factor. The court should not treat an offence as racially or religiously aggravated for the purposes of s.145 where a racially or religiously aggravated form of the offence was charged but resulted in an acquittal. The court should not normally treat an offence as racially or religiously aggravated if a racially or religiously aggravated form of the offence was available but was not charged.

Section 146 of the *Criminal Justice Act* 2003 provides that the court must treat as an aggravating factor the fact that:

(a) an offender demonstrated hostility towards the victim based on his or her sexual orientation or disability (or presumed sexual orientation or disability); or

(b) the offence was motivated by hostility towards persons who are of a particular sexual orientation or who have a particular disability.

A court should not conclude that offending involved aggravation related to race, religion, disability or sexual orientation without first putting the offender on notice and allowing him or her to challenge the allegation. When sentencing any offence where such aggravation is found to be present, the following approach should be followed.

- sentencers should first determine the appropriate sentence, leaving aside the element of aggravation related to race, religion, disability or sexual orientation but taking into account all other aggravating or mitigating factors;
- the sentence should then be increased to take account of the aggravation related to race, religion, disability or sexual orientation;
- the increase may mean that a more onerous penalty of the same type is appropriate, or that the threshold for a more severe type of sentence is passed;
- the sentencer must state in open court that the offence was aggravated by reason of race, religion, disability or sexual orientation;
- the sentencer should state what the sentence would have been without that element of aggravation.

The extent to which the sentence is increased will depend on the seriousness of the aggravation. The following factors could be taken as indicating a high level of aggravation:

(a) *Offender's intention*

- the element of aggravation based on race, religion, disability or sexual orientation was planned; 13–12
- the offence was part of a pattern of offending by the offender;
- the offender was a member of, or was associated with, a group promoting hostility based on race, religion, disability or sexual orientation;
- the incident was deliberately set up to be offensive or humiliating to the victim or to the group of which the victim is a member.

(b) *Impact on the victim or others*

- the offence was committed in the victim's home; 13–13
- the victim was providing a service to the public;
- the timing or location of the offence was calculated to maximise the harm or distress it caused;
- the expressions of hostility were repeated or prolonged;
- the offence caused fear and distress throughout a local community or more widely;
- the offence caused particular distress to the victim and/or the victim's family.

The aggravation may be regarded as less serious if:

- it was limited in scope or duration;
- the offence was not motivated by hostility on the basis of race, religion, disability or sexual orientation, and the element of hostility or abuse was minor or incidental.

Racial or religious aggravation cannot be used as an aggravating factor by the sentencer when sentencing for the basic offence of common assault. Where there is evidence that the offence was racially or religiously motivated, the aggravated form of the offence should be charged. See *post*, § 13–24. 13–14

Violence between motorists will in the vast majority of cases lead to custodial sentences: *Fenton* (1994) 15. Cr.App.R.(S.) 682. In the course of a dispute with another motorist, the offender pushed the other motorist in the chest. His sentence of fourteen days' imprisonment was reduced to seven.

Part III

The trend in sentencing for violence between motorists has recognised the increase in the number and severity of incidents. In *Sharpe* [2000] 1 Cr.App.R.(S.) 1 it was stated that custody in such cases is almost inevitable and that, where any significant injury was caused, the period would be more likely to be measured in months than in weeks.

A similar principle applies within the context of sporting fixtures. Whilst some level of physical contact is to be expected, nonetheless violence beyond that will often merit a custodial sentence. In *Thelwell* [2004] EWCA Crim 208, during a football match, the defendant punched another player in the mouth and then on the back of the neck causing tenderness and pain. He then headbutted the same victim but without breaking the victim's nose. He was convicted of two charges of common assault. Concurrent sentences of one month and three months respectively were upheld on appeal as "deserved and correct".

B. ASSAULT OCCASIONING ACTUAL BODILY HARM

(1) Definition

Offences against the Person Act 1861, s.47

Assault occasioning bodily harm. Common assault

13–15 **47.** Whosoever shall be convicted upon an indictment of any assault occasioning actual bodily harm shall be liable ... to imprisonment for not more than five years.

13–16 As regards the racially or religiously aggravated form of this offence created by the *Crime and Disorder Act* 1998, s.29, see *post*, § 13–24.

(2) Allocation

13–17 The offence is triable either way. For guidance as to mode of trial, see *Consolidated Criminal Practice Direction* (2002), Appendix F–54.

Due to the fact that the seriousness of this offence can differ depending on the circumstances, it is of particular importance that the magistrates hear the facts before making a decision as to whether to accept jurisdiction.

(3) Elements of the offence

13–18 There must be an assault or battery (see *ante*, § 13–5) which causes some bodily harm. The harm caused may be a direct or indirect consequence of the assault or battery. The harm caused must be something which the defendant could reasonably have foreseen as the consequence of what he was saying or doing towards the complainant: *Roberts* 56 Cr.App.R. 95, CA. Evidence of external bodily injury, or a break in or bruise to the surface of the skin is not required. In *DPP v. Smith* [2006] 1 W.L.R. 1571, QBD, the Court held that a person's hair is part of the human body intrinsic to each individual, and even if, medically and scientifically, the hair above the surface of the scalp was dead tissue, it remained part of the body and fell within the meaning of "bodily" in the phrase "actual bodily harm", thus the cutting off of a substantial part of a person's hair, without that person's consent in the course of an assault could amount to actual bodily harm. The injury need not be permanent, but must be more than merely transient or trifling: *Donovan* [1934] 2 K.B 498.

The *actus reus* of the offence may be established where someone, by act or word or a combination of the two, creates a danger and thereby exposes another to a reasonably foreseeable risk of injury that materialised: *DPP v. Santana-Bermudez* [2004] Crim. L.R. 471, DC. In this case, a police officer was injured by a hypodermic needle when conducting a search of the defendant. The Divisional Court held that the *actus reus* of the offence could be established by the defendant's assurances before the search commenced that he was not carrying needles or sharps. Whilst this decision may be followed, it should not be regarded as authoritative as the respondent did not make representations at the hearing.

The actual bodily harm may consist of psychiatric injury but emotional distress or panic are insufficient: *Ireland* [1998] A.C. 147, HL. If the prosecution alleges that the actual bodily harm was psychiatric injury then it should be proved by expert evidence: *Chan-Fook* 99 Cr.App.R. 147, CA. Psychological injury not amounting to recognisable psychiatric illness does not fall within the ambit of bodily harm: *D.* [2006] EWCA Crim 1139, CA. In this case the defendant's wife had committed suicide and he had been indicted for his wife's manslaughter and the infliction upon her of grievous bodily harm. Two of the three psychiatric experts giving evidence were unable to make a "psychiatric diagnosis" although they believed the wife had sustained "psychological injury" and the defendant's treatment of her would have impacted on her "psychological functioning". The judge recorded that the prosecution case depended on the submission that "psychological injury, without any recognised psychiatric illness" was capable of being "bodily harm" within the meaning of the *Offences against the Person Act* 1861 and accordingly there was no basis on which a reasonable jury, properly directed, could convict the defendant. The Crown disputed this, submitting that there was no difference between a medically diagnosed psychological condition and a medically diagnosed psychiatric condition brought about by psychological factors. Upholding the judge's ruling, the Court of Appeal stated that adhering to the principle of recognisable psychiatric illness allowed the issue to be clearly understood, allowing those advising to approach cases with an appropriate degree of certainty.

A defendant can be criminally liable for an offence of assault if they do not enter the premises where an assault takes place, do not strike a blow forming part of the assault and do not provide any active encouragement to those engaged in the assault: *Nedrick-Smith v. DPP* [2006] EWHC 3015, QBD. In this case the appellant appealed against her conviction for assault occasioning actual bodily harm. She had driven three women to the victim's house and then watched the three women assault the victim. The appellant knew that there had been a recent incident between the victim and one of the women involved in the assault, that there remained ill-feeling between these women, and that the purpose of the visit was to sort this matter out. The Divisional Court upheld her conviction, stating that the appellant was:

> "a party to driving a car to the premises of the victim with the object of sorting things out. She knew of the incident the week before. She foresaw that violence might take place and she aided the possible attack by driving the other girls there. Far from withdrawing when she saw that violence was taking place, she came up to the house and watched them, doing nothing to stop the violence. Those facts support both a finding that she was an aider and abetter and that she was a party to a joint enterprise". (*per* Lord Justice Waller, para. 15).

The *mens rea* is the same as for common assault and battery, see § 13–8, above.

(4) Sentence

When tried summarily, the maximum sentence for this offence is imprisonment for a **13–19** term not exceeding six months, a fine not exceeding level 5 on the standard scale, or both. After commencement of the relevant provisions, the maximum custodial sentence in a magistrates' court will be 12 months imprisonment: *Criminal Justice Act* 2003, ss.154 and 282. The Sentencing Council has issued a definitive Guideline for assault occasioning actual bodily harm which applies from June 13, 2011.

The Sentencing Guideline on assault occasionaing actual bodily harm (2011) states **13–20** that the court should first determine the offence category by reference to the table below:

Category 1	Greater harm (serious injury must normally be present) and higher culpability
Category 2	Greater harm (serious injury must normally be present) and lower culpability or lesser harm and higher culpability

Category 3	Lesser harm and lower culpability

The court should determine the offender's culpability and the harm caused, or intended, by reference only to the factors below. These factors are described as "the principal factual elements of the offence" and should determine the offence category.

Factors indicating higher culpability	**Factors indicating lower culpability**
Statutory aggravating factors: • Offence motivated by, or demonstrating, hostility to the victim based on his or her sexual orientation (or presumed sexual orientation) • Offence motivated by, or demonstrating, hostility to the victim based on the victim's disability (or presumed disability) Other aggravating factors: • A significant degree of premeditation • Use of weapon or weapon equivalent (for example, shod foot, headbutting, use of acid, use of animal) • Intention to commit more serious harm than actually resulted from the offence • Deliberately causes more harm than is necessary for commission of offence • Deliberate targeting of vulnerable victim • Leading role in group or gang • Offence motivated by, or demonstrating, hostility based on the victim's age, sex, gender identity (or presumed gender identity)	• Subordinate role in a group or gang • A greater degree of provocation than normally expected • Lack of premeditation • Mental disorder or learning disability, where linked to commission of the offence • Excessive self defence
Factors indicating greater harm	**Factors indicating lesser harm**
• Injury (which includes disease transmission and/or psychological harm) which is serious in the context of the offence (must normally be present) • Victim is particularly vulnerable because of personal circumstances • Sustained or repeated assault on the same victim	• Injury which is less serious in the context of the offence

Having determined the offence category, the court should then use the corresponding starting points to reach a sentence within the category range below. The starting point applies to all offenders irrespective of plea or previous convictions. A case of particular gravity, reflected by multiple features of culpability in step one, could merit upward adjustment from the starting point before further adjustment for aggravating or mitigating features.

Offence Category	Starting Point (applicable to all offenders)	Category Range (applicable to all offenders)
Category 1	Crown Court	Crown Court
Category 2	26 weeks' custody	Low level community order – Crown Court (51 weeks' custody)
Category 3	Medium level community order	Band A fine – High level community order

See § 13–9 for the non-exhaustive list of aggravating factors and factors reducing seriousness or reflecting mitigation, which must be referred to in identifying the starting point for sentence. Section 29 of the *Crime and Disorder Act* 1998 and the seven listed further issues must also be considered.

Offences committed in a domestic context

13–21 The *Magistrates Court Sentencing Guidelines* (2008) provide that when sentencing an offence committed in a domestic context, the Court should refer to the Sentencing Guidelines Council's definitive guideline *Overarching Principles: Domestic Violence*, published December 2006. See *ante*, § 13–8.

In *Southworth* [2009] EWCA Crim 147, CA, the appellant pleaded guilty to a charge of assault occasioning actual bodily harm and was sentenced to 12 months' imprisonment. The appellant had punched his partner following a domestic argument, knocking her to the floor and knocking out two of her teeth. Dismissing his appeal against sentence, the Court held that even on the basis that the appellant had acted recklessly, the sentence was not manifestly excessive.

Racial or religious aggravation and aggravation related to disability or sexual orientation

13–22 See *ante*, § 13–11.

13–23 In *Marangwanda (Peace)* [2009] EWCA Crim 60, CA, the appellant appealed against a sentence of two years' imprisonment imposed concurrently on two counts of causing grievous bodily harm. The appellant had moved in with a woman and her two daughters who were aged four and six. He had been diagnosed with gonorrhoea, and the daughters then both contracted the disease. He pleaded guilty to causing grievous bodily harm on the basis that he had had no sexual contact with the daughters, but rather the disease had been passed through regular contact. The appellant had written a letter to the court expressing his remorse, and a pre-sentence report stated he accepted responsibility and had passed on the disease through poor personal hygiene. The appellant was recommended for deportation, prevented from working with children and made the subject of a sexual offences prevention order. Allowing his appeal, the Court of Appeal stated the sentence had to reflect the appellant's basis of plea as well as the fact that the disease had been passed on to young children through reckless acts. It was a difficult balancing exercise but the sentence was manifestly excessive, and would be reduced to twelve months' imprisonment on each count concurrent. As the sentence no longer exceeded 12 months, the order preventing the appellant from working with children was no longer valid. Transmitting gonorrhoea was serious sexual harm. Any person who cared for young children and was prepared to act recklessly should receive a sexual offences prevention order. The recommendation for deportation remained.

13–24 In *Porter* [2002] EWCA Crim 2124, the offender became involved in a scuffle in a public house, during which he threw a glass bottle at a barman's head, causing much blood loss and the need for three stitches. Sentencing him to eight months' imprisonment, the judge emphasised the common nature of such offences, committed by men of otherwise good character, and the obligation of the courts to discourage such behaviour. See also *Audit* (1994) 15 Cr.App.R.(S.) 36.

A sentence of four months' imprisonment was appropriate for an offender who had fractured someone's nose in the course of an altercation in a taxi queue: *Marples* (1998) 1 Cr.App.R.(S.) 335.

Custodial sentences will almost always be appropriate where the assault on a police constable causes actual bodily harm: *Roughsedge (Att.-Gen.'s Reference (No. 7 of 1993))* [1994] R.T.R. 322. A sentence of nine months' imprisonment was appropriate where the offender headbutted a police officer, chipping his tooth and splitting his lip: *Broyd* [2002] 1 Cr.App.R.(S.) 47, CA. Persons in positions of authority may also expect the protection of the courts, hence violence towards public transport employees will be met by immediate prison sentences: *Tremlett* (1983) 5 Cr.App.R.(S.) 199, as will violence towards traffic wardens: *Charlton* (1995) 16 Cr.App.R.(S.) 703. A sentence of nine months' imprisonment was imposed on an offender convicted of assaulting a schoolteacher: *Byrne* [2000] 1 Cr.App.R.(S.) 282. Heavier sentences will also be passed when the victim of the assault is a hospital worker: *Eastwood* [2002] 2 Cr.App.R.(S.) 72 (offender who assaulted a nurse sentenced to 15 months' imprisonment, Mitchell J. saying that "if drunks assault staff in hospitals, leniency is the last thing they should expect.")

Equally, prisoners are entitled to the protection of the courts, and prison officers who assault inmates can expect heavy sentences. In *Fryer* [2002] 2 Cr.App.R.(S). 122, three prison officers who brutally assaulted an inmate were sentenced to either three or four years' imprisonment. Newman J. described such conduct as going beyond a breach of trust in respect of the individual prisoner concerned, being rather a breach of trust to society generally.

In *Cotterill* [2007] EWCA Crim 526; [2007] 2 Cr.App.R.(S.) 64, CA the appellant, a semi-professional footballer who had punched an opponent in the course of a game, causing a fracture of the jaw, appealed against his sentence of four months' imprisonment. The Court dismissed his appeal, stating that the fact that this was a match between professional footballers was significant, and the attack on the victim caused serious injury at a critical time in his career, which must have brought his whole career as a professional footballer into doubt. Furthermore, professional footballers were role models whose behaviour was frequently replicated by others.

In *Abbas* [2009] EWCA Crim 1386, CA, the appellant had been convicted of assault occasioning actual bodily harm. He had drunkenly barged into a group of people, which included the victim, outside a bar. When someone asked him to apologise, he punched the victim in the face, knocking him to the ground. The victim lost consciousness when his head hit the pavement and sustained significant cuts and bruises to his head and one eye. The appellant appealed against his sentence of two years' imprisonment. Allowing his appeal, the Court of Appeal held that although the Sentencing Guideline Council's guideline on assault prescribes a sentencing range of 12 to 36 weeks' custody where there is pre-meditated, minor non-permanent injury occasioned by a defendant of previous good character, and although this was not a case of pre-meditated violence, but rather a drunken over-reaction to events, the offence called for a sentence considerably in excess of 36 weeks due to the appellant's previous conviction for an offence committed in almost identical circumstances, the fact that the instant offence was committed whilst on bail for that offence, and the fact that the victim had been knocked unconscious, which might foreseeably have had much more serious consequences. When assessing seriousness, the general principles section in the sentencing guidelines provided that harm included the harm actually caused and any harm the offence was intended to cause or might foreseeably have caused. Taking account of the appellant's good behaviour when not in drink, the appropriate sentence was 15 months' imprisonment.

In *Coggin* [2009] EWCA Crim 2790, CA, the appellant appealed against his sentence of six months' imprisonment following conviction of a single count of assault occasioning actual bodily harm. The appellant was playing in a football game, and had punched the victim, a player on the opposing team, at least five times to his head. The victim sustained a 1.5 cm gash to his forehead, swelling to the upper lip and bruising to his left eyebrow and jaw. The gash required four sutures and left a small permanent scar. Allowing the appeal, the Court considered the relevant sentencing guidelines, and stated that this case did not fall neatly into the lowest level of offence as it was a sustained attack leading to some permanent injury, albeit a relatively minor scar. The assault being a sustained attack on a much smaller man who was not attempting to defend himself by any form of retaliation was a significant aggravating factor to which had to be added the presence of a small permanent scar. A starting point of six months' imprisonment was therefore not manifestly excessive. The appellant also suffered from Crohn's disease, which the Court accepted would greatly increase the hardship of a custodial sentence. The Court held that given the appellant's medical condition, although a custodial sentence was an appropriate starting point, the appropriate sentence would be three months' imprisonment.

C. WOUNDING OR INFLICTING GRIEVOUS BODILY HARM

(1) Definition

Offences against the Person Act 1861, s.20

Inflicting bodily injury, with or without weapon

20. Whosoever shall unlawfully and maliciously wound or inflict any grievous bodily harm upon any other person, either with or without any weapon or instrument, shall be guilty of an offence, and being convicted thereof shall be liable to imprisonment for not more than five years **13–25**

As to the racially aggravated version of this offence created by the *Crime and Disorder Act* 1998, s.20, see *ante*, § 13–24.

(2) Allocation

Both the basic and the religiously or racially aggravated form of the offence are triable either way. **13–26**

For guidance as to mode of trial, see *post*, the *Consolidated Criminal Practice Direction* (2002), App. F, para. V.51.

(3) Elements of the offence

For harm to amount to a "wound" the continuity of the skin must be broken: *Wood* 1 Mood. 278. A wound is not simply a break in the surface of the skin: *Morris* [2005] EWCA Crim 609, CA. In this case, the victim of an assault had suffered bruising to his head, bleeding around his ear and swelling to his head. The judge had directed the jury that a wound was very simply a break to the surface of the skin. Upholding the appellant's appeal, the Court of Appeal held that that direction was wrong and that the correct direction was "a break in the continuity of the whole skin". **13–27**

The words "grievous bodily harm" should be given their ordinary and natural meaning of "really serious harm": *Smith* [1961] A.C. 290. There may therefore be grievous bodily harm where there is no wound for the purposes of s.20. Serious psychiatric injury may amount to "grievous bodily harm": *Ireland* [1998] A.C. 147, HL.

To "inflict" grievous bodily harm it is not necessary to apply physical violence directly or indirectly to the victim: *Burstow* [1997] 1 Cr.App.R. 144, CA. In this case, the Court held that grievous bodily harm could be inflicted through the making of silent phone calls.

The prosecution does not have to prove the defendant intended or foresaw that his act would cause grievous bodily harm or wounding; it is sufficient that the defendant intended or foresaw that his act would cause physical harm to some person, albeit only of a minor character: *Savage* [1992] 1 A.C. 699, HL. See also *DPP v. W* [2006] EWHC 92, QBD, Admin. The word "maliciously" adds no meaning over and above the requirement for recklessness (in the subjective sense): *Mowatt* [1968] 1 Q.B. 421, CA.

13–28 On the issue of whether consent is relevant where the victim is caused to contract HIV by the defendant see, *Dica* [2005] EWCA Crim 2304.

(4) Sentence

13–29 When tried summarily, the maximum sentence for this offence is imprisonment for a term not exceeding six months, a fine not exceeding level 5 on the standard scale, or both. After commencement of the relevant provisions, the maximum custodial sentence in a magistrates' court will be 12 months imprisonment: *Criminal Justice Act* 2003, ss.154 and 282. The Sentencing Council issued a definitive guideline which applies to the offence of inflicting grievous bodily harm or unlawful wounding and comes into effect for all offences sentenced on and after June 13, 2011.

13–30 The Sentencing Guideline on inflicting grievous bodily harm, or unlawful wounding (2011) states that the court should first determine the offence category by reference to the table below:

Category 1	Greater harm (serious injury must normally be present) and higher culpability
Category 2	Greater harm (serious injury must normally be present) and lower culpability or lesser harm and higher culpability
Category 3	Lesser harm and lower culpability

The court should determine the offender's culpability and the harm caused, or intended, by reference only to the factors below. These factors are described as "the principal factual elements of the offence" and should determine the offence category.

Factors indicating higher culpability	Factors indicating lower culpability
Statutory aggravating factors: • Offence motivated by, or demonstrating, hostility to the victim based on his or her sexual orientation (or presumed sexual orientation) • Offence motivated by, or demonstrating hostility to the victim based on the victim's disability (or presumed disability) Other aggravating factors: • A significant degree of premeditation • Use of weapon or weapon equivalent (for example, shod foot, headbutting, use of acid, use of animal) • Intention to commit more serious harm than actually resulted from the offence • Deliberately causes more harm than is necessary for commission of offence • Deliberate targeting of vulnerable victim • Leading role in group or gang • Offence motivated by, or demonstrating, hostility based on the victim's age, sex, gender identity (or presumed gender identity)	• Subordinate role in a group or gang • A greater degree of provocation than normally expected • Lack of premeditation • Mental disorder or learning disability, where linked to commission of the offence • Excessive self defence
Factors indicating greater harm	**Factors indicating lesser harm**
• Injury (which includes disease transmission and/or psychological harm) which is serious in the context of the offence (must normally be present) • Victim is particularly vulnerable because of personal circumstances • Sustained or repeated assault on the same victim	• Injury which is less serious in the context of the offence

Having determined the offence category, the court should then use the corresponding starting points to reach a sentence within the category range below. The starting point applies to all offenders irrespective of plea or previous convictions. A case of particular gravity, reflected by multiple features of culpability in step one, could merit upward adjustment from the starting point before further adjustment for aggravating or mitigating features.

Offence category	Starting Point (Applicable to all offenders)	Category Range (Applicable to all offenders)
Category 1	Crown Court	Crown Court

Category 2	Crown Court	Crown Court
Category 3	High level community order	Low level community order – Crown Court (51 weeks' custody)

See § 13–9 for the non-exhaustive list of aggravating factors and factors reducing seriousness or reflecting mitigation, which must be referred to in identifying the starting point for sentence. Section 29 of the *Crime and Disorder Act* 1998 and the seven listed further issues must also be considered.

Offences committed in a domestic context

13–31 The Magistrates Court Sentencing Guidelines (2008) provide that when sentencing an offence committed in a domestic context, the Court should refer to the Sentencing Guidelines Council's definitive guideline *Overarching Principles: Domestic Violence*, published December 2006. See *ante*, § 13–8.

In *Howard* [2009] EWCA Crim 1984, CA, the Court discussed the meaning of "particularly grave injury" in the context of the Sentencing Guidelines Council guideline on sentencing offences under s.20 of the *Offences Against the Person Act* 1861. The appellant had been convicted of inflicting grievous bodily harm and sentenced to 18 months' imprisonment. The appellant had twice pushed the victim, who had attempted to intervene in an argument in a pub. The latter push caused the victim to fall through some patio doors and break his hip. The Court of Appeal stated that although the broken hip was a serious injury, it could not be described as particularly serious by the standards of grievous bodily harm generally. The appropriate starting point for the offence would therefore be six months' imprisonment. The aggravating factors (namely the fact that the victim was entirely innocent, that he was pushed twice with considerable violence, and that the second push resulted in a serious injury to a man of 63) made a sentence of nine months' imprisonment, the maximum recommended by the guideline, appropriate.

In *Singh* [2009] EWCA Crim 2782, CA, the appellant appealed against his sentence of 10 months' imprisonment for a conviction of inflicting grievous bodily harm. The victim worked with the appellant. The victim had been dismissed, and asked the appellant what had happened, which led to an argument following which the appellant hit the victim's hand with a pole, causing a fracture. Allowing his appeal, The Court held that the appellant was an individual of mature years and good character and the injuries were not particularly serious. A sentence of four months' imprisonment would be appropriate.

In *Shannon* [2008] EWCA Crim 2131, CA, the appellant had pleaded guilty to inflicting grievous bodily harm and sentenced to 12 months' imprisonment. Both the appellant and victim were in a bar and had both been drinking. The appellant punched the victim without any provocation, causing a broken jaw and a cracked tooth needing surgery. Substituting a sentence of eight months' imprisonment, the Court stated that although by the standard of offences of grievous bodily harm generally, the injury caused was not particularly grave, it did not follow that the case fell into the lowest category of the guidelines. The case was within the category of "premeditated assault where no weapon has been used". The appropriate starting point after a full trial would have been about 12 months' imprisonment. As the appellant pleaded guilty at the earliest opportunity the appropriate sentence would be eight months' imprisonment.

Racial or religious aggravation and aggravation related to disability or sexual orientation

13–32 See *ante*, § 13–11.

13–33 In *Rogers* (1993) 15 Cr.App.R.(S.) 393, the offender head-butted an opponent during a football match, causing a fracture. Given the defendant's good character and likely effect of a long custodial sentence, the original sentence of nine months' imprisonment was reduced on appeal to four months. See also *Moss* [2000] 1 Cr.App.R.(S.) 307 for injuries inflicted in the course of a rugby match and *Thelwell* (*ante*) for injuries inflicted in the course of a football match.

In *Clare* [2002] 2 Cr.App.R.(S.) 97, Aikens J. issued guidelines on the correct sentencing approach when the attack involves a single blow leading to injury to the victim. The first relevant factor is the strength of the blow that has been imposed. The second relevant factor is the consequence to the victim. In *Clare*, the blow was described as obviously hard as the victim lost consciousness, with the consequence of two injuries and the need for at least one operation to treat the injuries. A sentence of eighteen months' imprisonment was imposed. **13-34**

The use of a weapon is likely to necessitate a custodial sentence beyond the sentencing powers of the magistrates. In *Robertson* [1998] 1 Cr.App.R.(S.) 21, the offender attacked a man in a public house by thrusting a beer glass into his face. His sentence of two and a half years' imprisonment was reduced to two years on appeal. In *Simpson* [1998] 1 Cr.App.R.(S.) 197 an unprovoked attack with a chisel resulted in four years' imprisonment.

Where an attack involves grievous bodily harm, an immediate custodial sentence will almost always be appropriate, and the courts will impose significant penalties on those committing offences against those performing a service for the public: *Olawale Olawo* [2008] EWCA Crim 528, CA. In this case, a sentence of 20 months imprisonment imposed on an individual of good character, in stable employment and described as a "family man", who recklessly inflicted grievous bodily harm would be manifestly excessive. The judge sentencing the appellant made reference to a consultative document relating to sentencing guidelines for the particular type of offence and had sentenced the appellant on the basis that his assault was a "pre-meditated assault or spontaneous assault where a weapon had been used" which required a starting point of 18 months custody. The consultative document later became a definitive set of guidelines that bore significant differences from the consultative document. The Court of Appeal held that the judge had erred when reasoning that the offence was a "pre-meditated assault or spontaneous assault where a weapon had been used"; this error led him to adopt too high a starting point. The appellant was of good character and was reckless in carrying the victim out of his house and allowing him to fall to the ground. He was in stable employment and a family man. However, he did not have the benefit of a guilty plea. There was a serious aggravating feature in that the victim was a certified enforcement officer and the sentencing guidelines contained a general aggravating factor where an offence was "committed against those working in the public sector or providing a service to the public". Certified officers like the victim performed duties essential for the administration of justice and were vulnerable to attack. To protect them, the courts had to impose significant penalties on those who assaulted them.

D. RACIALLY OR RELIGIOUSLY AGGRAVATED OFFENCES

(1) Definition

Crime and Disorder Act 1998, s.29

Racially or religiously aggravated assaults

29.—(1) A person is guilty of an offence under this section if he commits— **13-35**

(a) an offence under section 20 of the *Offences Against the Person Act* 1861 (malicious wounding or grievous bodily harm);

(b) an offence under section 47 of that Act (actual bodily harm); or

(c) common assault, which is racially or religiously aggravated for the purposes of this section.

(2) A person guilty of an offence falling within subsection (1)(a) or (b) above shall be liable

Part III

(a) on summary conviction, to imprisonment for a term not exceeding six months or to a fine not exceeding the statutory maximum, or to both;

(b) on conviction on indictment, to imprisonment for a term not exceeding seven years or to a fine, or to both.

(3) A person guilty of an offence falling within subsection (1)(c) above shall be liable—

(a) on summary conviction, to imprisonment for a term not exceeding six months or to a fine not exceeding the statutory maximum, or to both;

(b) on conviction on indictment, to imprisonment for a term not exceeding two years or to a fine, or to both.

[The words "or religiously" were inserted by the *Anti-Terrorism, Crime and Security Act* 2001, s.39(5) and (6)(a). This amendment has no effect in relation to anything done before it came into effect, December 14, 2001: s.42.]

(2) Allocation

13–36 Offences contrary to s.29 are triable either way.

(3) Elements of the offence

Crime and Disorder Act 1998, s.28

Meaning of "racially or religiously aggravated"

13–37 **28.**—(1) An offence is racially or religiously aggravated for the purposes of sections 29 to 32 below if—

(a) at the time of committing the offence, or immediately before or after doing so, the offender demonstrates towards the victim of the offence hostility based on the victim's membership (or presumed membership) of a racial or religious group; or

(b) the offence is motivated (wholly or partly) by hostility towards members of a racial or religious group based on their membership of that group.

(2) In subsection (1)(a) above—

"membership", in relation to a racial or religious group, includes association with members of that group;

"presumed" means presumed by the offender.

(3) It is immaterial for the purposes of paragraph (a) or (b) of subsection (1) above whether or not the offender's hostility is also based, to any extent, on any other factor not mentioned in that paragraph.

(4) In this section "racial group" means a group of persons defined by reference to race, colour, nationality (including citizenship) or ethnic or national origins.

(5) In this section "religious group" means a group of persons defined by reference to religious belief or lack of religious belief.

Whilst the legislation refers to a racial group, this does not mean that a purely inclusive definition of those words should be adopted. The size of the group is immaterial and words or actions can be directed to large or small groups irrespective of origin: *DPP v. M.* [2004] 1 W.L.R. 2758, QBD. An offence may not be racially aggravated pursuant to the *Crime and Disorder Act* 1998, s.28(1)(b) where the offence is not motivated by hostility towards members of a racial group, but rather by hostility toward an individual victim: *DPP v. Howard* [2008] EWHC 608, see *post*, § 13–111.

The definition of a racial group in s.28(4) of the *Crime and Disorder Act* 1998 goes beyond groups defined by their colour, race or ethnic origin. It encompasses both nationality (including citizenship) and national origins: *R. v. Rogers* [2007] UKHL 8; [2007] 2 A.C. 62, HL. Under s.28(1) the victim might be presumed by the offender to be a member of the hated group even if he was not. Section 28(2) provides that membership of a group included association with members of that group. Under s.28(3), the fact that the offender's hostility was based on other factors as well as racism or xenophobia was immaterial. The essence of the aggravated versions of the relevant offences was the denial of equal respect and dignity to people who were seen as "other", which was more deeply hurtful, damaging and disrespectful to the victims than the simple versions of the offences. Furthermore, this denial was more damaging to the community as a whole, by denying acceptance to members of certain groups, not for their own sake, but for the sake of something they could do nothing about: *Rogers* [2007] UKHL 8; [2007] 2 A.C. 62, HL.

Hostility may be demonstrated at the time, or immediately before or after, the offence was committed: *Rogers* [2007] UKHL 8; [2007] 2 A.C. 62, HL. The word "immediately" in section 28(1)(a) of the Act qualifies both the words "before" and "after" in the section; hostility therefore has to be demonstrated immediately in either case. Hostility can be demonstrated even if the victim was absent, as long as it occurs in the immediate context of the substantive offence: *Parry v. DPP* [2005] A.C.D. 64, CA.

No subjective intent is required under s.28(1)(a); the test is objective and all that must be shown is the demonstration of racial hostility. Under s.28(1)(b) the motivation behind the behaviour had to be proved: *R. (on the application of Jones) v. Bedfordshire and Mid Bedfordshire Magistrates Court* [2010] EWHC 523 (Admin).

Section 28 (1)(a) is directed not so much as to words, as to the hostility demonstrated towards a victim with the relevant racist or religious connotations: *Babbs* [2007] EWCA Crim 2737, CA. In this case the appellant had described the victim and his companion as "foreign fuckers" during a confrontation, and then physically assaulted the victim during a second confrontation that occurred between five and 15 minutes later. The Court held that the earlier words were capable of colouring the later confrontation, and that hostility based upon race was evinced over a continuing period from the moment the words were first used to the moment it exploded into the later violence. The jury were thus entitled to find that the hostility shown later was based upon the victim being foreign.

Hostility demonstrated to foreigners because they were foreign could be just as objectionable as hostility based on a more limited racial characteristic: *Rogers* [2005] EWCA Crim 2863, CA. Whether using the word "immigrant" is capable of demonstrating hostility based on the victim's membership (or perceived membership) of a racial group as defined by the *Crime and Disorder Act* 1998, s.28(4) is a question of fact: *Att.-Gens Reference (No. 4 of 2004)* [2005] 1 W.L.R. 2810, CA. In this case, the CA held that it was for the jury to decide whether a defendant's use of the term "immigrant doctor" was an allegation of non-Britishness or part of a demonstration by the defendant of hostility to the victim within the terms of s.28(1)(a) because she perceived his non-Britishness to derive from his race, colour, nationality or ethnic or national origins.

It does not matter whether the hostility displayed is partly racial and partly directed **13–38**
at a general class of individuals; it is sufficient if the hostility is in part racial: *Johnson v. DPP* [2008] EWHC 509 (Admin), DC. In this case, the appellant appealed by way of case stated against his conviction for a racially aggravated public order offence. The appellant, who was black, had been involved in an altercation with two parking attendants who were white. He told them "this is our patch not yours" and "you don't belong here" and said "why don't you get up … with your white uncles and aunties". The magistrates' court found him guilty of an offence under section 5 of the *Public Order Act* 1986 and concluded that the offence was racially aggravated, contrary to the *Crime and Disorder Act* 1998, s.31. The appellant argued that the mere fact that reference was made to the colour of the parking attendants and to leaving the black community alone was not sufficient to constitute racial hostility.

Dismissing his appeal, the Court stated that there had been a proper evidential basis for the Crown Court to find that the appellant's words had demonstrated a racial hostility at least in part, and it was accordingly entitled to find that he had committed a racially aggravated public order offence. The appellant's language made it clear that he was talking in racial terms. The words used were capable of demonstrating racial hostility and it did not matter whether the hostility displayed was partly racial and partly directed at a general class of individuals; it was sufficient that the hostility was in part racial.

(4) Sentence

13–39 When tried summarily the maximum penalty for these offences is six months' imprisonment, a fine not exceeding the statutory maximum or both: s.29(2) and (3). After commencement of the relevant provisions, the maximum custodial sentence in a magistrates' court will be 12 months' imprisonment: *Criminal Justice Act* 2003, ss.154 and 282.

The *Magistrates Court Sentencing Guidelines* (2008) address the specific racially or religiously aggravated offences under the *Crime and Disorder Act* 1998 on the same page as the "basic offence"; the starting points and ranges indicated on the guideline therefore relate to the 'basic' (non-aggravated) offence. The increase for the element of racial or religious aggravation may result in a sentence above the range; this will not constitute a departure from the guideline for which reasons must be given.

A court should not conclude that offending involved aggravation related to race or religion without first putting the offender on notice and allowing him or her to challenge the allegation.

Guidance as to the correct sentencing approach was given in *Saunders* [2000] 2 Cr.App.R.(S.) 71, where the Court of Appeal advised the sentencing court to first consider the appropriate sentence for the offence in the absence of racial aggravation, and then add a further term for the racial element, so the total term reflects the overall criminality. Even if the basic offence would not have crossed the custody threshold, the element of racial aggravation may well result in the custody threshold being passed. Relevant factors when determining sentence would be the nature of the hostile demonstration, whether by language, gestures or weapons; its length, whether isolated repeated or persistent; its location, whether public or private; the number both of those demonstrating and those demonstrated against; and the presence or absence of other features. A discount will be appropriate for, amongst other things, genuine remorse, a plea of guilty and previous good character.

13–40 In *Kelly and Donnelly* [2001] 2 Cr.App.R.(S.) 73, factors seriously aggravating the racial element of the offence in terms of the offender's intention were identified as planning by the offender, the offence being part of a pattern of racist offending by the offender, membership of a group promoting racist activities and the deliberate setting up of the victim for the purpose of humiliating him or being offensive towards him.

Factors aggravating the offence in terms of its impact on the victim include the offence taking place at the victims home; the victim being particularly vulnerable or providing a service to the public; the timing and location of the offence being such as to maximise the harm or distress it caused; the expressions of racial hostility being repeated or prolonged; fear and distress being caused throughout a particular community and particular distress being caused to the victim or the victim's family.

In *Beglin* [2003] 1 Cr.App.R.(S.) 21 the approach in *Saunders* and *Kelly and Donnelly* of demarcating the sentence appropriate for the basic form of the offence and then indicating the addition for the racially aggravated element was affirmed. In the case of a racially aggravated common assault, a sentence of four months' imprisonment was held to be sufficient for the basic form of the offence, hence a sentence of 12 months' imprisonment in total was too long. A sentence of eight months' imprisonment was substituted, with four months being the appropriate sentence for both the basic part of the offence and the addition for the racial element.

In some cases, the racial aggravation will be so inherent and integral to the offence itself that it will not be possible to assess the overall criminality involved in a discrete way. In such cases, the court must assess the seriousness of the offence as a whole: *Fitzgerald* [2003] 1 Cr.App.R.(S.) 74, CA. In this case, the appellant swore and addressed deeply distressing racial abuse and obscenities to an officer during the course of arrest. A sentence of 10 months' imprisonment was imposed, Burnton J. stating that the offender's history, which showed repeated offences against the police, did not aggravate the present offence, yet was significant as to its context and background, and provided grounds for distinguishing the case from authorities such as *Kelly and Donnelly* [2001] 2 Cr.App.R.(S.) 341.

Where an assault itself is not such as to justify a custodial sentence, and it is the racial aggravation that makes a custodial sentence appropriate, the correct sentencing approach is to treat the appropriate custodial sentence for the assault itself as a notional, or very short one, and then to decide the appropriate uplift for the element of racial aggravation: *Slater* [2005] EWCA Crim 2882, CA.

E. ASSAULT WITH INTENT TO RESIST OR PREVENT ARREST

(1) Definition

Offences against the Person Act 1861, s.38

Assault with intent to commit felony, or on peace officers &c.

38. Whosoever [...] shall assault any person with intent to resist or prevent the lawful apprehension or detainer of himself or of any other person for any offence, shall be guilty of a misdemeanour, and being convicted thereof shall be liable, at the discretion of the court, to be imprisoned for any term not exceeding two years, [...] **13–41**

[This section is printed as amended by the *Police Act* 1964, Sched. 10, Pt I; the *Criminal Law Act* 1967, Sched. 3, Pt III and the *Criminal Justice Act* 1948, s.1(2).]

(2) Allocation

This offence is triable either way. **13–42**

(3) Elements of the offence

The prosecution must prove: **13–43**

— an assault, see *ante*, § 13–5;

— that the person assaulted had the right to apprehend or detain the defendant: see *Self* 95 Cr.App.R. 42;

— an intention to resist or prevent the lawful apprehension or detainer of the defendant or another person.

(4) Sentence

The Sentencing Council has issued a definitive guideline on assault which includes offences of assault with intent to resist or prevent arrest and applies from June 13, 2011. **13–44**

The Sentencing Guideline on assault with intent to resist or prevent arrest (2011) states that the court should first determine the offence category by reference to the table below: **13–45**

Category 1	Greater harm and higher culpability
Category 2	Greater harm and lower culpability or lesser harm and higher culpability
Category 3	Lesser harm and lower culpability

The court should determine the offender's culpability and the harm caused, or intended, by reference only to the factors below. These factors are described as "the principal factual elements of the offence" and should determine the offence category.

Factors indicating higher culpability	**Factors indicating lower culpability**
Statutory aggravating factors: • Offence racially or religiously aggravated • Offence motivated by, or demonstrating, hostility to the victim based on his or her sexual orientation (or presumed sexual orientation) • Offence motivated by or demonstrating hostility to the victim based on the victim's disability (or presumed disability) Other aggravating factors: • A significant degree of premeditation • Use of weapon or weapon equivalent (for example, shod foot, headbutting, use of acid, use of animal) • Intention to commit more serious harm than actually resulted from the offence • Deliberately causes more harm than is necessary for commission of offence • Leading role in group or gang • Offence motivated by, or demonstrating, hostility based on the victim's age, sex, gender identity (or presumed gender identity)	• Subordinate role in a group or gang • Lack of premeditation • Mental disorder or learning disability, where linked to commission of the offence
Factors indicating greater harm	**Factors indicating lesser harm**
• Sustained or repeated assault on the same victim	• Injury which is less serious in the context of the offence

Having determined the offence category, the court should then use the corresponding starting points to reach a sentence within the category range below. The starting point applies to all offenders irrespective of plea or previous convictions. A case of particular gravity, reflected by multiple features of culpability in step one, could merit upward adjustment from the starting point before further adjustment for aggravating or mitigating features.

Offence Category	**Starting Point (applicable to all offenders)**	**Category Range (applicable to all offenders)**
Category 1	26 weeks' custody	12 weeks' custody – Crown Court (51 weeks' custody)
Category 2	Medium level community order	Low level community order – High level community order
Category 3	Band B fine	Band A fine – Band C fine

The court should determine the offender's culpability and the harm caused, or intended, by reference only to the factors below. These factors are described as "the principal factual elements of the offence" and should determine the offence category.

When sentencing category 1 offences, the court should also consider the custody threshold as follows:

1) Has the custody threshold been passed?
2) If so, is it unavoidable that a custodial sentence be imposed?
3) If so, can that sentence be suspended?

Factors increasing seriousness	**Factors reducing seriousness or reflecting personal mitigation**
Statutory aggravating factors: • Previous convictions, having regard to i) the nature of the offence to which the conviction relates and its relevance to the current offence; and ii) the time that has elapsed since the conviction • Offence committed whilst on bail Other aggravating factors: • Location of the offence • Timing of the offence • Ongoing effect upon the victim • Gratuitous degradation of victim • Failure to comply with current court orders • Offence committed whilst on licence • An attempt to conceal or dispose of evidence • Failure to respond to warnings or concerns expressed by others about the offender's behaviour • Commission of offence whilst under the influence of alcohol or drugs • Established evidence of community impact • Any steps taken to prevent the victim reporting the incident, obtaining assistance and/or from assisting or supporting the prosecution • Offences taken into consideration (TICs)	• No previous convictions or no relevant/recent convictions • Single blow • Remorse • Good character and/or exemplary conduct • Determination and or/demonstration of steps taken to address addiction or offending behaviour • Serious medical conditions requiring urgent, intensive or long-term treatment • Isolated incident • Age and/or lack of maturity where it affects the responsibility of the offender • Lapse of time since the offence where this is not the fault of the offender. • Mental disorder or learning disability where **not** linked to the commission of the offence • Sole or primary carer for dependent relatives.

The court should then consider the seven listed issues as set out at *ante*, § 13–7.

F. ASSAULT ON CONSTABLE IN EXECUTION OF DUTY

(1) Definition

Police Act 1996, s.89(1), (3)–(6)

Assaults on constables

89.—(1) Any person who assaults a constable in the execution of his duty, or a person assist- **13–46**

ing a constable in the execution of his duty, shall be guilty of an offence and liable on summary conviction to imprisonment for a term not exceeding six months or to a fine not exceeding level 5 on the standard scale, or to both.

(3) This section also applies to a constable who is a member of a police force maintained in Scotland or Northern Ireland when he is executing a warrant or otherwise acting in England or Wales, by virtue of any enactment conferring powers on him in England and Wales.

(4) In this section references to a person assisting a constable in the execution of his duty include references to any person who is neither a constable nor in the company of a constable but who—

(a) is a member of an international joint investigation team that is led by a member of a police force; and

(b) is carrying out his functions as a member of that team.

(5) In this section 'international joint investigation team' means any investigation team formed in accordance with—

(a) any framework decision on joint investigation teams adopted under Article 34 of the Treaty on European Union;

(b) the Convention on Mutual Assistance in Criminal Matters between the Member States of the European Union, and the Protocol to that Convention, established in accordance with that Article of that Treaty; or

(c) any international agreement to which the United Kingdom is a party and which is specified for the purposes of this section in an order made by the Secretary of State.

(6) A statutory instrument containing an order under subsection (5) shall be subject to annulment in pursuance of a resolution of either House of Parliament.

[This section is printed as amended by the *Serious Organised Crime and Police Act* 2005, Sched. 17(2), para. 1.]

(2) Allocation

13–47 This offence is triable summarily: *Police Act* 1996, s.89(1).

(3) Elements of the offence

13–48 The prosecution must prove:

— an assault, see *ante*, § 13–5;

— of a constable;

— in the execution of his duty.

Assault

13–49 Charges under s.89 necessarily include the offence of common assault, however magistrates' courts do not have the power to convict for included offences. Therefore, where there is doubt concerning whether the constable was acting in execution of their duty it may be advisable to draft alternative charges: *Bentley v. Brudzinski* 75 Cr.App.R. 217, DC; *Kerr v. DPP* [1995] Crim. L.R. 394, or proceed with a charge of common assault: *C. v. DPP* [2003] EWHC 2780.

Where justices had found that a defendant had bitten the hand of a police officer, yet had rejected the prosecution case that the bite had been deliberate and intentional, it was open to them to convict the defendant of an assault on the basis of recklessness as when the defendant brought the policeman's hand to his mouth in the course of a struggle to avoid recapture, justices were entitled to find that there was a clearly foreseeable risk, taken by the defendant, of contact with the defendant's teeth as he shouted and struggled: *D. v. DPP* [2005] Crim. L.R. 962; [2005] EWHC 967, QBD.

Constable

13–50 It is not necessary for the prosecution to prove that the defendant knew that the person assaulted was a police constable or in the execution of his duty, though a mistake of fact (a belief that the person was not a constable) may be a defence.

Execution of duty

The general powers, duties and responsibilities of police officers are governed by the *Police Act* 1996. Powers concerning the stopping and searching of persons or vehicles, the seizure of articles, entering premises with or without search warrants and the arrest and detention of persons are largely contained in the *Police and Criminal Evidence Act* 1984. See Ch. 1. **13–51**

Whether the detention of a citizen by a police officer short of arrest is unlawful is a question of fact which depends on the circumstances proceeding it and the degree of force used: *Bentley v. Brudzinski* 75 Cr.App.R. 217, DC; *Mepstead v. DPP* (1996) 160 J.P.N. 448, DC. Not every interference with a citizen's liberty will amount to a course of conduct sufficient to take the constable outside the execution of their duty: *Donnelly v. Jackman*, 54 Cr.App.R. 229, DC.

An officer will not be considered to be acting within the execution of their duty when they fail to adduce any evidence establishing that an arrest and subsequent search of the individual's property was lawful: *R. (Odewale) v. DPP* 2000 WL 33148750, DC. See also *Kynaston v. DPP* 87 Cr.App.R. 200, DC (attempting to arrest individuals when police officers knew a robbery had been committed, desired to arrest a known person and communicated that intention to those they were trying to arrest judged to be action within the scope of the officers' duty). **13–52**

Where a person has been arrested whilst impeding the arrest of a third party, for the second arrest to be lawful, it must be shown that the first arrest was lawful: *Riley v. DPP* 91 Cr.App.R. 14, DC. A police officer may exceed their powers even though they are acting in good faith: *C. v. DPP* [2003] EWHC 2780, DC (failure to explain the reasons for restraining a 16-year-old girl to her boyfriend, coupled with a failure to allow the girl to explain her conduct sufficed to remove the officer's actions from the scope of his duty).

In *Baker v. Crown Prosecution Service* [2009] EWHC 299 (Admin), the appellant appealed by way of case stated against a decision of a magistrates' court to convict her of the offence of assaulting a police constable in the execution of his duty. A police officer had been sent to an address following a report that the appellant had "gone berserk" with a knife. The officer entered the house without asking for permission. He said in evidence that he did so for the purpose of saving life or limb pursuant to the *Police and Criminal Evidence Act* 1984, s.17(1)(e). He saw the appellant sitting on the floor with blood on her clothes, and asked where the knife was but she gave no response. At that point, other police officers had arrived on the scene, including a female officer. The officer stated he wished to search the appellant to see if she had the knife. He told her to stand up and began to approach her, but she lunged forward and starting shouting. The female officer took hold of her arm to stop her from falling but the appellant struck her, and then the first police officer, who said that he ceased to be concerned about life or limb when the appellant stood up and it was clear she did not have the knife. Another officer said no search had taken place, and that there had been no chance to confirm whether the appellant had a knife before the assault occurred. The magistrates found the appellant guilty, holding that the actions of the police from the entry into her property up until her arrest had been carried out in pursuance of its powers under the Act. The appellant submitted that the police officer had not been executing his duty when she struck him as he did not have authority to search her, and he had not informed her of the reason he had entered the premises.

Dismissing the appeal, the court stated it was clear that no search of the appellant had taken place before the assault occurred. The appellant had not seemed to rely on her argument that there was an obligation on the police officer to inform her of the reason for exercising his power to enter the premises in front of the magistrates. Further, it was not subject to any finding made by the magistrates, and was not one of the matters covered by the case stated. Accordingly, each of the grounds advanced by the appellant had to be rejected. The Court went on to make statements regarding the scope of s.17(1)(e) and s.17(4) of the *Police and Criminal Evidence Act* 1984: (1) A police constable entering and searching premises for the purposes of saving life or limb pursuant to the powers under the Act could enter without the permission of the occupant. The purpose of the provision was that entry would be allowed without permission: there would be no point if consent were required; (2) The words "saving life or limb" were wide enough to cover saving someone from themselves as well as saving someone from a third party; (3) Although it was desirable for an officer to give reasons for exercising his powers of entry, there was no hard and fast rule to that effect. There was no need for an officer to give an occupant any such explanation where it was impossible, impracticable or undesirable. In the instant case, it was clear that the fear that the appellant would use the knife justified the decision not to explain to her why entry had been obtained; (4) Once a police constable had located an occupant, he was entitled, under s.17(4), to carry out a search to the extent that was reasonably required for the purpose for which the power of entry was exercised. In the instant case, as the reason for entry was the danger to life or limb posed by the knife, the powers granted to the police included a search for that knife. The conduct of the police was therefore entirely lawful under s.17(1), and the appellant's assault was accordingly an assault on a police constable in the execution of his duty.

13–53 Where a police officer restrained a person, but did not at that time intend or purport to arrest him, he was committing an assault, even if an arrest would have been justified: *Wood v. DPP* [2008] EWHC 1056 (Admin), DC. In this case, three police officers had attended a wine bar to find a customer who had allegedly smashed an ashtray. The appellant fitted the description of this person, and one of the police officers took hold of him by the arm and asked if he was the person they were looking for. The appellant said he was not. Another police officer then took hold of the appellant's other arm. Other people then left the wine bar and said the appellant was the person the police were looking for. By that time the appellant was trying to pull away from the police officers, and in the struggle, he assaulted two of them. Owing to his behaviour, the appellant was not informed of the reasons for his arrest at that time but was told as soon as reasonably practicable thereafter. One of the police officers said at trial that when the appellant came out of the wine bar he could not arrest him as he was not sure who he was, although he thought he was the person they were looking for. He said that he took hold of his arm to detain him to confirm who he was and when other people said he was this person, his belief crystallised and gave him reasonable grounds to arrest the appellant. The appellant submitted that the court could not conclude that the distinction made by the officer in his evidence between detaining the appellant and arresting him was mere semantics. The DPP argued that the officer had reasonable grounds for suspecting that criminal damage had been committed, and the appellant was the person who had committed it.

Allowing the appeal, the Court stated that the officer did not intend or purport to arrest the appellant when he restrained him and at no stage in the struggle which resulted did he say that he was arresting the appellant. Had he or either of the other officers done so, before the appellant struggled in order to obtain his release, the position would have been different. But the facts found did not support such a conclusion. The convictions were quashed.

When the police received an emergency call giving them reason to believe that a child was at risk at a property, they were fully entitled, as an exercise of their discretion under s.17(1)(e) of the *Police and Criminal Evidence Act* 1984, to enter on to that property without a warrant to investigate. Their presence on the property concerned will therefore be lawful. The police will also not be acting outside the scope of their duty when they arrest an individual on the basis of abundant evidence indicating that there had been a breach of the peace, and that another breach was imminent. Where it was not practicable for an officer to inform a detainee of the reason for his arrest, the arrest should be maintained until it was possible to inform him of the reason. But any delay in informing the detainee of the reason for his arrest could not retrospectively render unlawful his correct and lawful arrest by the officer for breach of the peace: *Blench v. DPP* [2004] EWHC 2717, QBD.

In *Syed v. DPP* [2010] EWHC 81 (Admin), the appellant appealed by way of case stated against his conviction for assaulting a constable in the execution of his duty. Two police officers had attended his house following a report of a disturbance. When they arrived there was no sign of a disturbance. The appellant told them that he had been arguing with his brother and behaved in an evasive way. The officers explained they had a right to enter the premises without a warrant pursuant to the *Police and Criminal Evidence Act* 1984, s.17(1)(e) if they were in fear for the welfare of persons within the house. The appellant did not accept this, and spat in one officer's face and headbutted the other. The question for the High Court was whether the magistrates had properly concluded that the police were acting in the execution of their duty when they purported to act under s.17(1)(e). Allowing the appeal, the Court held that it was plain from the wording of s.17(1)(e) that Parliament had intended that the right of entry by force without warrant to be limited to cases where it was apprehended something serious was otherwise likely to occur or had occurred on the premises. That included a degree of apprehension of some serious injury to an individual therein. The test applied in the instant case was not sufficient to justify an entry within the terms of s.17(1)(e).

Where a police officer makes an unlawful arrest, any other officer who goes to assist him will also be acting outside the execution of his duty. The person being arrested and any third parties seeking to prevent the unlawful arrest will be entitled to use reasonable force in resisting their attempts to effect the arrest: *Cumberbatch v. Crown Prosecution Service*; *Ali v. DPP* [2009] EWHC 3353 (Admin) .

Police officers may still be acting in the execution of their duty in arresting someone they believed to be committing an offence under s.5 of the *Public Order (Amendment) Act* 1996 even though the prosecution may fail to prove that the individual arrested had committed this offence; the issue is whether it was reasonable for the arresting officers to suspect that the individual's conduct would cause someone to feel alarm or distress: *Burrell v. CPS* [2005] EWHC 786, QBD.

Where police officers are contemplating a search within the meaning of s.2(2) of the *Police and Criminal Evidence Act* 1984, they are required to comply with s.2(3) of that Act. The strict requirements of the Act and the Codes have to be complied with prior to an intended search notwithstanding that the person apprehending the suspect was obviously a police officer and that that officer had genuine concerns about another officer's safety: *Bonner v. DPP* [2004] EWHC 2415.

A conviction for assaulting a police officer in the execution of his duty could not stand where the officer had exercised his powers unlawfully by arresting the defendant for a purported actual breach of the peace in the absence of any violent conduct: *Hawkes v. DPP*, *The Times*, November 29, 2005.

The test of whether an individual has revoked an implied license for police officers to enter their property is objective: *R. (Fullard) v. Woking Magistrates' Court* [2005] EWHC 2922, QBD. Furthermore, if implied permission to be on the premises is revoked, the person concerned has to be given a reasonable opportunity to leave: *ibid.*

(4) Sentence

The maximum sentence for this offence is imprisonment for a term not exceeding six **13–54**
months, a fine not exceeding level 5 on the standard scale, or both. The Sentencing Council has issued a definitive guideline on assault which includes the offence of assault on a constable in the execution of his duty and applies to all offences sentenced on or after June 13, 2011.

[The next paragraph is § 13–56.]

The Sentencing Guideline on assault on a constable in the execution of his duty **13–56**

Part III

(2011) states that the court should first determine the offence category by reference to the table below:

Category 1	Greater harm and higher culpability
Category 2	Greater harm and lower culpability or lesser harm and higher culpability
Category 3	Lesser harm and lower culpability

The court should determine the offender's culpability and the harm caused, or intended, by reference only to the factors below. These factors are described as "the principal factual elements of the offence" and should determine the offence category.

Factors indicating higher culpability	**Factors indicating lower culpability**
Statutory aggravating factors: • Offence racially or religiously aggravated • Offence motivated by, or demonstrating, hostility to the victim based on his or her sexual orientation (or presumed sexual orientation • Offence motivated by or demonstrating hostility to the victim based on the victim's disability (or presumed disability) Other aggravating factors: • A significant degree of premeditation • Use of weapon or weapon equivalent (for example, shod foot, headbutting, use of acid, use of animal) • Intention to commit more serious harm than actually resulted from the offence • Deliberately causes more harm than is necessary for commission of offence • Leading role in group or gang • Offence motivated by, or demonstrating, hostility based on the victim's age, sex, gender identity (or presumed gender identity)	• Subordinate role in a group or gang • Lack of premeditation • Mental disorder or learning disability, where linked to commission of the offence
Factors indicating greater harm • Sustained or repeated assault on the same victim	**Factors indicating lesser harm** • Injury which is less serious in the context of the offence

Having determined the offence category, the court should then use the corresponding starting points to reach a sentence within the category range below. The starting point applies to all offenders irrespective of plea or previous convictions. A case of particular gravity, reflected by multiple features of culpability in step one, could merit upward adjustment from the starting point before further adjustment for aggravating or mitigating features.

Offence Category	Starting Point (applicable to all offenders)	Category Range (applicable to all offenders)
Category 1	12 weeks' custody	Low level community order – 26 weeks' custody
Category 2	Medium level community order	Low level community order – High level community order
Category 3	Band B fine	Band A fine – Band C fine

See *ante*, § 13–7 for the aggravating factors and factors reducing seriousness or reflecting personal mitigation which must be referred to in identifying the starting point for sentence.

Having determined the appropriate sentence, the court should then consider the seven listed issues as set out at § 13–7, *ante*.

G. Resisting or Wilfully Obstructing Constable

(1) Definition

Police Act 1996, s.89(2)

Assaults on constables

89.—(2) Any person who resists or wilfully obstructs a constable in the execution of his duty, or a person assisting a constable in the execution of his duty, shall be guilty of an offence and liable on summary conviction to imprisonment for a term not exceeding one month or to a fine not exceeding level 3 on the standard scale, or to both. **13–57**

(2) Allocation

This offence is triable summarily: *Police Act* 1996, s.89(2). **13–58**

(3) Elements of the offence

The prosecution must prove that the defendant: **13–59**
— resisted or wilfully obstructed
— a constable, or a person assisting a constable
— in the execution of his duty.

Obstruction

Obstruction is defined as making it more difficult for a police officer to carry out his duty: *Hinchcliffe v. Sheldon* [1955] 1 W.L.R. 1207. **13–60**

Consequently, resisting an unlawful arrest will not amount to obstruction: *Edwards v. DPP* (1993) 97 Cr.App.R 301. In *Redmond-Bate v. DPP* (1999) 163 J.P. 789, the appellant was one of a group of women preachers who had been arrested on the steps of a cathedral by a constable fearing a breach of the peace following the reaction of some members of the crowd who had gathered to listen. As the actions of the police officer in arresting the appellant were not reasonable, there being no reason to suspect a breach of the peace, the Court of Appeal held that the constable was acting unlawfully when he attempted to arrest her, and she could not be said to be obstructing him in the execution of his duty when she resisted arrest.

A police officer carrying out a drugs search under s.23 of the *Misuse of Drugs Act* 1971 who fails to take reasonable steps to give the individual being searched his name, the police station to which he was attached and the nature of the search, will not be acting in the execution of his duty as the failure to give his name means that the search will have been carried out in breach of s.2 of the *Police and Criminal Evidence Act* 1984: *R. v. Bristol* [2007] EWCA Crim 3214, CA. In this case, the police officer had seen the appellant in the street and asked him to open his mouth. He saw what he believed to be a wrap of drugs, and then physically intervened to prevent the appellant from swallowing and instructed him to "spit it out". The Court of Appeal held that the officer had not taken reasonable steps to give the required information as all he had to do was state his name, the police station, "drugs search" and "spit it out" in order to comply with the procedures. There was no need for the officer to have said more than that but Parliament intended that at least that minimum was required. The requirements of s.2 of *PACE* 1984 were clear and there was no evidence that it would have been difficult for the officer to say the words required of him.

In *Green v. Moore* [1982] Q.B. 1044, it was held that it is an obstruction of a constable in the execution of his duty, to warn someone so that he may postpone the commission of a crime. Although the net result was the prevention of a crime, liability hinged on the defendant's *mens rea* and the question of whether the defendant's intention was to assist the potential criminals or to assist the police.

Where a driver warned other drivers as to the presence of a speed trap set up by a police officer on a road, the actus reus of the offence under s.89(2) will only be established where it is proved that the drivers warned were, or were likely to be, exceeding the speed limit at the location of the speed trap: *DPP v. Glendinning*, *Daily Telegraph*, October 27, 2005, DC.

Running away to avoid apprehension after being approached by police officers is capable of amounting to an offence under s.89(2): *Sekfali v. DPP* (2006) 170 J.P. 393, QBD.

13–61 The obstruction must also be wilful. Hence making the police officers task more difficult by genuinely trying to offer assistance will not found a charge under this section: *Wilmott v. Atack* [1977] Q.B. 498.

A solicitor who attempts to interview witnesses for the purpose of preparing the defence of his client in criminal proceedings and in so doing acts against the instruction of a police officer, is not thereby guilty of obstructing the officer: *Connolly v. Dale* [1996] 1 Cr.App.R. 200.

Execution of duty

13–62 If a constable is acting unlawfully then he is not acting in the course of his duty and the person who obstructs a constable not acting in accordance with his duty cannot be guilty of an offence: *Edwards v. DPP* (1993) 97 Cr.App.R. 301.

Where a police officer has ample grounds to justify making an arrest, their conduct will not be rendered unlawful by them not formally using the word "arrest" until investigations into the conduct justifying the arrest are completed: *Fiak (Engin)* [2005] EWCA Crim 2381, CA.

(4) Sentence

13–63 The *Magistrates' Court Sentencing Guidelines* (2008) follow the Guidance on Assault and other offences against the person issued by the Sentencing Guidelines Council on February 28, 2008. When tried summarily, the maximum sentence for this offence is a fine not exceeding level 3 on the standard scale, one month's imprisonment or both. For general sentencing factors set out in the *Magistrates' Court Sentencing Guidelines* (2008) see Ch. 23, *post*. The *Magistrates' Court Sentencing Guidelines* (2008) provide the following guidelines for cases of resisting of wilfully obstructing a constable.

STARTING POINT AND RANGE OF SENTENCE

(BASED ON A FIRST TIME OFFENDER PLEADING NOT GUILTY)

Examples of nature of activity	Starting Point	Range
Failure to move when required to do so	Band A fine	Conditional discharge to band B fine
Attempt to prevent arrest or other lawful police action; or giving false details	Band B fine	Band A fine to band C fine
Several people attempting to prevent arrest or other lawful police action	Low level community order	Band C fine to medium level community order

AGGRAVATING AND MITIGATING FACTORS

Factors indicating higher culpability	Factors indicating lower culpability
1. Premeditated action	1. Genuine mistake or misjudgement
2. Aggressive words/threats	2. Brief incident
3. Aggressive group action	

H. OBSTRUCTION OF EMERGENCY WORKERS

(1) Definition

Emergency Workers (Obstruction) Act 2006, ss.1–4

Obstructing or hindering certain emergency workers responding to emergency circumstances

1.—(1) A person who without reasonable excuse obstructs or hinders another while that other person is, in a capacity mentioned in subsection (2) below, responding to emergency circumstances, commits an offence. **13–64**

(2) The capacity referred to in subsection (1) above is—

(a) that of a person employed by a fire and rescue authority in England and Wales;

(b) in relation to England and Wales, that of a person (other than a person falling within paragraph (a)) whose duties as an employee or as a servant of the Crown involve—

(i) extinguishing fires; or

(ii) protecting life and property in the event of a fire;

(c) that of a person employed by a relevant NHS body in the provision of ambulance services (including air ambulance services), or of a person providing such services pursuant to arrangements made by, or at the request of, a relevant NHS body;

(d) that of a person providing services for the transport of organs, blood, equipment or personnel pursuant to arrangements made by, or at the request of, a relevant NHS body;

(e) that of a member of Her Majesty's Coastguard;

(f) that of a member of the crew of a vessel operated by—
(i) the Royal National Lifeboat Institution, or
(ii) any other person or organisation operating a vessel for the purpose of providing a rescue service, or a person who musters the crew of such a vessel or attends to its launch or recovery.

(3) For the purposes of this section and section 2 of this Act, a person is responding to emergency circumstances if the person—
(a) is going anywhere for the purpose of dealing with emergency circumstances occurring there; or
(b) is dealing with emergency circumstances or preparing to do so.

(4) For the purposes of this Act, circumstances are "emergency" circumstances if they are present or imminent and—
(a) are causing or are likely to cause—
(i) serious injury to or the serious illness (including mental illness) of a person;
(ii) serious harm to the environment (including the life and health of plants and animals);
(iii) serious harm to any building or other property; or
(iv) a worsening of any such injury, illness or harm; or
(b) are likely to cause the death of a person.

(5) In subsection (2) above "relevant NHS body" means—
(a) in relation to England and Wales, an NHS foundation trust, National Health Service trust, Special Health Authority, Primary Care Trust or Local Health Board;
(b) in relation to Northern Ireland, a Health and Social Services trust or Health and Social Services Board.

Obstructing or hindering persons assisting emergency workers

13–65 **2.**—(1) A person who without reasonable excuse obstructs or hinders another in the circumstances described in subsection (2) below commits an offence.

(2) Those circumstances are where the person being obstructed or hindered is assisting another while that other person is, in a capacity mentioned in section 1(2) of this Act, responding to emergency circumstances.

Provisions supplementary to sections 1 and 2

13–66 **3.**—(1) A person may be convicted of the offence under section 1 or 2 of this Act notwithstanding that it is—
(a) effected by means other than physical means; or
(b) effected by action directed only at any vehicle, vessel, apparatus, equipment or other thing or any animal used or to be used by a person referred to in that section.

(2) For the purposes of section 1 or 2 of this Act, circumstances to which a person is responding are to be taken to be emergency circumstances if the person believes and has reasonable grounds for believing they are or may be emergency circumstances.

Penalties

13–67 **4.** A person guilty of an offence under this Act is liable on summary conviction to a fine not exceeding level 5 on the standard scale.

(2) Allocation

13–68 The offences are triable summarily: s.1(4).

(3) Elements of the offence

13–69 The *Emergency Workers (Obstruction) Act* 2006 creates two offences of obstructing or hindering certain emergency workers and obstructing those assisting certain emergency workers. The Act came into force on February 20, 2007. The Prosecution must prove that:

— The defendant, without reasonable excuse;
— Obstructed or hindered;

— A person acting in one of the capacities listed in the *Emergency Workers (Obstruction) Act* 2006, s.1(2); or a person assisting someone acting in such a capacity;
— While that person was responding to emergency circumstances (defined in the *Emergency Workers (Obstruction) Act* 2006, s.3(2)).

(4) Sentence

The maximum penalty for each offence is a fine not exceeding level 5 on the standard scale: s.3. **13–70**

For general sentencing factors set out in the *Magistrates' Court Sentencing Guidelines* (2008) see Ch. 23, *post*.

III. OFFENCES INVOLVING CHILDREN

A. ABANDONMENT OF CHILDREN UNDER TWO

(1) Definition

Offences Against the Person Act 1861, s.27

Exposing children whereby life is endangered

27. Whosoever shall unlawfully abandon or expose any child, being under the age of two years, whereby the life of such child shall be endangered, or the health of such child shall have been or shall be likely to be permanently injured, shall be guilty of a misdemeanor, and being convicted thereof shall be liable to imprisonment for a term not exceeding five years. **13–71**

(2) Allocation

This offence is triable either way. **13–72**

(3) Elements of the offence

The prosecution must prove that: **13–73**
— the defendant wilfully abandoned or exposed the child;
— that the child was then under two;
— that its life was thereby endangered or its health was likely to be permanently injured.

(4) Sentence

When tried summarily, the maximum penalty is six months' imprisonment, a fine not exceeding the statutory maximum or both. After commencement of the relevant provisions, the maximum custodial sentence in a magistrates' court will be 12 months' imprisonment: *Criminal Justice Act* 2003, ss.154 and 282. **13–74**

For general sentencing factors set out in the *Magistrates' Court Sentencing Guidelines* (2008) see Ch. 23, *post*.

B. CHILD CRUELTY

(1) Definition

Children and Young Persons Act 1933, s.1

Cruelty to persons under sixteen

1.—(1) If any person who has attained the age of sixteen years and has responsibility for any child or young person under that age, wilfully assaults, ill-treated, neglects, abandons, or exposes **13–75**

Part III

him, or causes or procures him to be assaulted, ill-treated, neglected, abandoned, or exposed, in a manner likely to cause him unnecessary suffering or injury to health (including injury to or loss of sight, or hearing, or limb, or organ of the body, and any mental derangement), that person shall be guilty of a misdemeanour, and shall be liable—

(a) on conviction on indictment, to a fine or alternatively, or in addition thereto, to imprisonment for any term not exceeding ten years;

(b) on summary conviction, to a fine not exceeding £400 pounds, or alternatively, or in addition thereto, to imprisonment for any term not exceeding six months.

(2) For the purposes of this section—

(a) a parent or other person legally liable to maintain a child or young person, or the legal guardian of a child or young person, shall be deemed to have neglected him in a manner likely to cause injury to his health if he has failed to provide adequate food, clothing, medical aid or lodging for him, or if, having been unable otherwise to provide such food, clothing, medical aid or lodging, he has failed to take steps to procure it to be provided under the enactments applicable in that behalf;

(b) where it is proved that the death of an infant under three years of age was caused by suffocation (not being suffocation caused by disease or the presence of any foreign body in the throat or air passages of the infant) while the infant was in bed with some other person who has attained the age of sixteen years, that other person shall, if he was, when he went to bed, under the influence of drink, be deemed to have neglected the infant in a manner likely to cause injury to its health.

(3) A person may be convicted of an offence under this section—

(a) notwithstanding that actual suffering or injury to health, or the likelihood of actual suffering or injury to health, was obviated by the action of another person;

(b) notwithstanding the death of the child or young person in question.

[This section is printed as amended by the *Children Act* 2004, Sched. 5.]

(2) Allocation

13–76 This offence is triable either way, when tried summarily, the *Children and Young Persons Act* 1933, s.14 has effect.

It is usual, unless one of the following factors is present, to try this offence summarily:

— neglect over a long period of time, even where the injury may not be substantial;
— injuries that exhibit a sadistic nature;
— where substantial injury is caused.

Children and Young Persons Act 1933, s.14

Mode of charging offences and limitation of time

13–77 **14.**—(1) Where a person is charged with committing any of the offences mentioned in the First Schedule to this Act in respect of two or more children or young persons, the same information or summons may charge the offence in respect of all or any of them, but the person charged shall not, if he is summarily convicted, be liable to a separate penalty in respect of each child or young person except upon separate information.

(2) The same information or summons may charge him with the offences of assault, ill-treatment, neglect, abandonment, or exposure, together or separately, and may charge him with committing all or any of those offences in a manner likely to cause unnecessary suffering or injury to health, alternatively or together, but when those offences are charged together the person charged shall not, if he is summarily convicted, be liable to a separate penalty for each.

(4) When any offence mentioned in the First Schedule to this Act charged against any person is a continuous offence, it shall not be necessary to specify in the information, summons, or indictment, the date of the acts constituting the offence.

(3) Elements of the offence

13–78 The prosecution must prove that:

— the defendant is 16 or over;
— he had responsibility for the child (under 16);
— he acts wilfully: see *Shepherd* [1981] A.C. 394;
— he assaults, ill-treats, neglects, etc. in a manner likely to cause unnecessary suffering or injury to health.

It is no mitigation that motivation of the defendant was a deluded belief that the child was possessed by spirits; such motivation did not reduce the culpability of such offences: *Pinto*, *The Times*, March 17, 2006, CA.

It is not necessary to prove that the defendant knows the consequences of their actions, or intends to harm the victim; the offence is established where the defendant knows there was some risk of injury to the victim: *Turner* [2008] EWCA Crim 272, CA. In this case, the appellant appealed against their conviction under s.1 of the *Children and Young Persons Act* 1933. The victim was the appellant's daughter, who had suffered from fainting and convulsions since 2001. The victim had been prescribed medication for this condition, however her symptom's persisted, and following a referral to her local hospital, a consultant recommended her medication be gradually reduced and then stopped. However, the appellant did not adhere to these recommendations, and continued with the previous medication, causing a severe deterioration in the victim's health. The appellant appealed against her conviction on the grounds that she had not known the consequences of continuing to administer the drug and had not intended to harm the victim. Dismissing her appeal, the Court of Appeal held that for a conviction under s.1, it was sufficient that the appellant knew there was some injury or risk of injury to the victim's health.

In *D.* [2008] EWCA Crim 2360, CA, the appellant appealed against her conviction of child cruelty. The appellant and her husband were the adoptive parents of the victim, a two-and-a-half year old girl. They had taken the victim to hospital with serious head injuries. A paediatric radiologist gave evidence that although it was possible that the injuries were accidental, they were more likely to have been non-accidental and caused by shaking. The appellant and her husband denied causing the injuries, the appellant claiming the victim had hurt herself through a fall. The Crown's case was that either one or both were responsible. The appellant was convicted of causing or procuring the victim to be wilfully assaulted or ill-treated in a manner likely to cause her unnecessary suffering or injury to her health. The appellant appealed, submitting that the judge had failed to direct the jury that any wilful assault had to be carried out in a manner likely to cause unnecessary suffering or injury to the victim's health and failed to give any sufficient direction to the jury on whether the acts relied on were "wilful" Dismissing the appeal, the Court of Appeal stated the question whether an assault was in a manner likely to cause unnecessary suffering was an objective one. The judge had failed to direct the jury as to the *actus reus* and that failure was without justification. Moreover, he should have directed the jury that they had to be sure that any assault or ill-treatment was done "wilfully", explaining the meaning of that word. However, had the judge directed the jury that they must be satisfied that the assault had been committed in a manner likely to cause her unnecessary suffering or injury to her health, given the gravity of the victim's injuries there was no doubt that the jury would have convicted. In terms of *mens rea*, the jury rejected the defence case of accident. If the appellant's counsel's suggestion that she might have shaken the victim in circumstances that did not indicate either that she intended her to undergo unnecessary suffering or injury to her health, or that she was reckless in that regard been a realistic possibility, the judge's failure to direct the jury as to the meaning of "wilfully" would have rendered the conviction unsafe. It was not, however, a realistic possibility. The appellant's case was that the victim had been injured in a fall; there was no evidence that she had shaken the victim in an innocent but misguided attempt to help her; and there was no evidence from which such a conclusion could reasonably be inferred. The failure to direct the jury as to the meaning of "wilfully" did not, therefore, render the appellant's conviction unsafe.

(4) Sentence

The *Magistrates' Court Sentencing Guidelines* (2008) follow the Guidance on As- **13–79** sault and other offences against the person issued by the Sentencing Guidelines Council on February 28, 2008. When tried summarily, the maximum sentence for this offence is imprisonment for a term not exceeding six months, a fine not exceeding level 5 on the standard scale, or both. After commencement of the relevant provisions, the maximum custodial sentence in a magistrates' court will be 12 months imprisonment: *Criminal Justice Act* 2003, ss.154 and 282. For general sentencing factors set out in the *Magistrates' Court Sentencing Guidelines* (2008) see Ch. 23, *post*. The *Magistrates' Court Sentencing Guidelines* (2008) provide the following guidelines for cases of child cruelty.

Key Factors

13–80 (a) The same starting point and sentencing range is proposed for offences which might fall into the four categories (assault; ill-treatment or neglect; abandonment; and failure to protect). These are designed to take into account the fact that the victim is particularly vulnerable, assuming an abuse of trust or power and the likelihood of psychological harm, and designed to reflect the seriousness with which society as a whole regards these offences.

(b) As noted above, the starting points have been calculated to reflect the likelihood of psychological harm and this cannot be treated as an aggravating factor. Where there is an especially serious physical or psychological effect on the victim, even if unintended, this should increase sentence.

(c) The normal sentencing starting point for an offence of child cruelty should be a custodial sentence. The length of that sentence will be influenced by the circumstances in which the offence took place.

(d) However, in considering whether a custodial sentence is the most appropriate disposal, the court should take into account any available information concerning the future care of the child.

(e) Where the offender is the sole or primary carer of the victim or other dependants, this potentially should be taken into account for sentencing purposes, regardless of whether the offender is male or female. In such cases, an immediate custodial sentence may not be appropriate.

(f) The most relevant areas of personal mitigation are likely to be:

- Mental illness/depression
- Inability to cope with the pressures of parenthood
- Lack of support
- Sleep deprivation
- Offender dominated by an abusive or stronger partner
- Extreme behavioural difficulties in the child, often coupled with a lack of support
- Inability to secure assistance or support services in spite of every effort having been made by the offender

Some of the factors identified above, in particular sleep deprivation, lack of support and an inability to cope, could be regarded as an inherent part of caring for children, especially when a child is very young and could be put forward as mitigation by most carers charged with an offence of child cruelty. It follows that, before being accepted as mitigation, there must be evidence that these factors were present to a high degree and had an identifiable and significant impact on the offender's behaviour.

STARTING POINT AND RANGE OF SENTENCE

(BASED ON A FIRST TIME OFFENDER PLEADING NOT GUILTY)

Examples of nature of activity	**Starting Point**	**Range**
(i) Short term neglect or ill-treatment. (ii) Single incident of short-term abandonment. (iii) Failure to protect a child from any of the above.	12 weeks custody	Low level community order to 26 weeks custody
(i) Assault(s) resulting in injuries consistent with actual bodily harm. (ii) More than one incident of neglect or ill-treatment (but not amounting to long-term behaviour). (iii) Single incident of long-term abandonment OR regular incidents of short-term abandonment (the longer the period of long-term abandonment or the greater the number of incidents of short-term abandonment) the more serious the offence). (iv) Failure to protect a child from any of the above.	Crown Court	26 weeks custody to Crown Court

Part III

Examples of nature of activity	Starting Point	Range
(i) Series of assaults: (ii) Protracted neglect or ill-treatment; (iii) Serious cruelty over a period of time; (iv) Failure to protect a child from any of the above.	Crown Court	Crown Court

AGGRAVATING AND MITIGATING FACTORS

Factors indicating higher culpability	Factors indicating lower culpability
1. Targeting one particular child from the family. 2. Sadistic behaviour. 3. Threats to prevent the victim from reporting the offence. 4. Deliberate concealment of the victim from the authorities. 5. Failure to seek medical help.	1. Seeking medical help or bringing the situation to the notice of the authorities.

In *Weaver* [1998] 2 Cr.App.R.(S.) 56, a sentence of six years' imprisonment for neglect of a child by its mother which resulted in the death of the child was reduced to three years' imprisonment, and a sentence of three years' imprisonment for neglect of a child causing death by its father was reduced to two years' imprisonment. The mother pleaded guilty on the basis that she had failed to ensure that the child was adequately nourished, that she had failed to get medical attention when the child required it, that she had failed to keep the flat where they lived sufficiently clean, and that she had assaulted the child by slapping his thigh. The father pleaded guilty on the basis that he had failed to notice the child's declining condition and to ensure that something was done about it.

In *Harvey* [1987] 9 Cr.App.R.(S.) 524, a mother was convicted of four counts of cruelty to her children. The offender was frequently drunk and smoking cannabis; the family's living accommodation was not kept clean, pornographic material was left about, and the children were told about the appellant's sexual activities; the children were not kept clean and in some cases were denied affection. In one case the appellant failed to arrange medical attention when it was necessary. A sentence of nine months' imprisonment was upheld. A sentence of eight months' imprisonment was appropriate for a mother who has held an iron to the leg of her four-year-old son, despite the Court finding that the mother was an "inadequate young woman" (*per* Forbes, J.) who suffered considerable stress and isolation as a result of bringing up four small children: *Potova* [2004] 2 Cr.App.R.(S.) 32, CA.

In *Melanie O.* [2006] EWCA Crim 1158; [2007] 1 Cr.App.R.(S.) 15, CA, a sentence of fifteen months' imprisonment for neglect of three young children by allowing them to be outside unsupervised and inadequately clothed in cold weather was varied to six months. The Court of Appeal acknowledged that the appellant's addiction to crack cocaine was the root of the offences and stated that every alternative to custody had been explored before the original sentencing hearing. The Court further stated that the facts of the case involved only one incident, rather than a course of neglect, and there was no element of violence or injury to the children and no emotional or sexual abuse. The Court of Appeal described the case as on the cusp of the custody threshold, but found that the sentencing judge had no option but to pass a custodial sentence in view of the appellant's response to efforts by the probation service to consider alternatives to custody. However, a sentence of six months' imprisonment on each count concurrent would be appropriate.

A sentence of nine months' imprisonment was held to be appropriate in an offence involving a "total abdication of maternal instincts" rather than "deliberate cruelty": *Beese* [2007] EWCA Crim 2649, CA. In this case, the appellant was found to have neglected her two sons, who were aged three and two. The appellant's neighbour had visited her home and seen absolute squalor. The appellant had previously asked her neighbour to look after her children and on January 4, 2007 she asked her neighbour to do so again, promising to return four days later. The appellant did not return and was found by the police on January 27. Going to the appellant's house, the neighbour found the home to be in an even worse state than it had been before. The author of the pre-sentence report commented that the appellant displayed few maternal instincts and little empathy or concern for her children. Reducing the original sentence of 14 months' imprisonment to nine months' imprisonment, the Court of Appeal stated that this was not a case in which there had been deliberate cruelty; there had, however, been a total abdication of maternal instincts and it was only through the good luck of having such a good neighbour that the children did not suffer a more disastrous fate.

In *Pounder* [2007] EWCA Crim 1852, CA, the appellant appealed against a sentence of seven months' imprisonment following his pleas of guilty to six counts of cruelty by neglect to six children. The appellant accepted that for a period of three months he had failed to ensure that the children were supplied with sufficient bedding, to ensure that their hygiene was acceptable, to provide sufficient toys and means of mental stimulation and to provide sufficient help for his wife to care for the children when she was suffering mental health problems. The appellant had significant mitigation including the fact that he had a good employment record, and had worked in the same job for 20 years. Allowing his appeal, the Court of Appeal stated that punishment of the appellant was not merited at all; it was a case that required leniency and mercy. There was no deliberate assault of the children, merely low-grade neglect characterised by a general failure of care causing the children to cease to thrive and fail to meet developmental milestones. The appellant required help and assistance. The sentences were quashed and a probation order to run for 12 months was substituted.

In *Z* [2008] EWCA Crim 2847, CA, the appellant appealed against a sentence of 26 weeks' imprisonment, suspended for one year, imposed for cruelty to a person under 16. The appellant was a devout Shia Muslim. Whilst attending a religious festival he permitted his sons, aged 15 and 13, to use a zanjeer (a wooden handled instrument with lightweight curved blades) resulting in them sustaining cuts to their backs. The manager of the mosque had ruled that those under 16 were not allowed to use the zanjeer. Dismissing the appeal, the Court held that the judge was faced with a notoriously difficult sentencing exercise and reached a conclusion that could not be faulted. The appellant had ignored advice from mosque elders and his sons caused damage to themselves whilst under his supervision. Those circumstances did pass the custody threshold.

In *Hallmark* [2009] EWCA Crim 1180, CA, the Attorney General referred as unduly lenient a community order made up of a two-year supervision requirement, a prohibited activity requirement and a 250-hour unpaid work requirement imposed on the offender for assault and child cruelty. The offender had committed habitual acts of

Part III

violence against two of his children and his stepdaughter. The offender pleaded guilty to the offences on a limited basis and received the full discount for his plea. The Attorney General argued that the judge erred in not imposing an immediate term of imprisonment. The Court held that the sentence was unduly lenient but it was not varied. The offences involved chastisement rather than sadism, or violence for its own sake, and there was no serious cruelty. However, the offences were not isolated and attributable to the offender's repeated loss of temper. A starting point of immediate custody would be appropriate. The sentence was therefore wrong. However, as the sentence had been designed to engage the offender and encourage different behaviour and was working, it was not in the public interest to pass a different sentence.

13–81 The act of failing to seek medical assistance can amount to neglect for the purposes of a charge under this section. In *S.* [1999] 1 Cr.App.R.(S.) 67, the offence was made out by the failure to seek medical help, and a sentence of four months imprisonment was imposed. In *Laut* [2002] 2 Cr.App.R.(S.) 7, the offender's child fell whilst holding the door of the washing machine closed on his mother's instructions. The offender had been warned on a previous occasion that such conduct was likely to result in injury to the child. The Court stated that its normal practice was not to impose a custodial sentence for a single, albeit wilful act of neglect. However, given the prior warning, the offender's conduct could be classed as a case of serious neglect and hence a sentence of imprisonment was justified. Her original sentence of four months' imprisonment was, however, reduced to 12 weeks.

13–82 The approach to sentencing for offences of child cruelty which involve violence to young children was again considered by the Court of Appeal in two cases. In *Att.-Gen.'s Reference (No. 81 of 2004)* [2004] EWCA Crim 3315, the Court allowed an appeal against the imposition of a community rehabilitation order where the basis of the charge was the deliberate manhandling of a child aged 23 months. Although the offender had been suffering from post-traumatic stress following two serious assaults, "the only sentence that was appropriate ... was an immediate custodial sentence". A sentence of 18 months' imprisonment was substituted.

In *Faruk Ahmed* [2003] 1 Cr.App.R.(S.) 40, the position was set out as "infants are entitled to care at the hands of those who, despite stresses and strains, can contain their temper and control unwelcome impulses. For an attack upon a child, custody will almost always be inevitable" (*per* Rafferty J. at para. 11 of his judgment).

C. CHILD ABDUCTION

(1) Definition

Child Abduction Act 1984, ss.1–2

Offence of abduction of child by parent, etc.

13–83 **1.**—(1) Subject to subsections (5) and (8) below, a person connected with a child under the age of sixteen commits an offence if he takes or sends the child out of the United Kingdom without the appropriate consent.

(2) A person is connected with a child for the purposes of this section if—

(a) he is a parent of the child; or

(b) in the case of a child whose parents were not married to each other at the time of his birth, there are reasonable grounds for believing that he is the father of the child; or

(c) he is a guardian of the child; or

(ca) he is a special guardian of the child; or

(d) he is a person in whose favour a residence order is in force with respect to the child; or

(e) he has custody of the child.

(3) In this section "the appropriate consent", in relation to a child, means—

(a) the consent of each of the following—

(i) the child's mother;

(ii) the child's father, if he has parental responsibility for him;
(iii) any guardian of the child;
(iiia) any special guardian of the child;
(iv) any person in whose favour a residence order is in force with respect to the child;
(v) any person who has custody of the child; or
(b) the leave of the court granted under or by virtue of any provision of Part II of the *Children Act* 1989; or
(c) if any person has custody of the child, the leave of the court which awarded custody to him.

(4) A person does not commit an offence under this section by taking or sending a child out of the United Kingdom without obtaining the appropriate consent if— **13–84**

(a) he is a person in whose favour there is a residence order in force with respect to the child, and he takes or sends the child out of the United Kingdom for a period of less than one month; or
(b) he is a special guardian of the child and he takes or sends the child out of the United Kingdom for a period of less than three months.

(4A) [...]

(5) A person does not commit an offence under this section by doing anything without the consent of another person whose consent is required under the foregoing provisions if—

(a) he does it in the belief that the other person—
(i) has consented; or
(ii) would consent if he was aware of all the relevant circumstances; or
(b) he has taken all reasonable steps to communicate with the other person but has been unable to communicate with him; or
(c) the other person has unreasonably refused to consent.

(5A) Subsection (5)(c) above does not apply if—

(a) the person who refused to consent is a person—
(i) in whose favour there is a residence order in force with respect to the child;
(ia) who is a special guardian of the child; or
(ii) who has custody of the child; or
(b) the person taking or sending the child out of the United Kingdom is, by so acting, in breach of an order made by a court in the United Kingdom.

(6) Where, in proceedings for an offence under this section, there is sufficient evidence to raise an issue as to the application of subsection (5) above, it shall be for the prosecution to prove that that subsection does not apply.

(7) For the purposes of this section—

(a) "guardian of a child", "special guardian", "residence order" and "parental responsibility" have the same meaning as in the *Children Act* 1989; and
(b) a person shall be treated as having custody of a child if there is in force an order of a court in the United Kingdom awarding him (whether solely or jointly with another person) custody, legal custody or care and control of the child.

(8) This section shall have effect subject to the provisions of the Schedule to this Act in relation to a child who is in the care of a local authority detained in a place of safety, remanded to a local authority accommodation or the subject of proceedings or an order relating to adoption.

[This section is printed as amended by the *Adoption and Children Act* 2002, Sched. 3.]

Offence of abduction of child by other persons

2.—(1) Subject to subsection (3) below, a person, other than one mentioned in subsection (2) below. commits an offence if, without lawful authority or reasonable excuse, he takes or detains a child under the age of sixteen— **13–85**

(a) so as to remove him from the lawful control of any person having lawful control of the child; or

(b) so as to keep him out of the lawful control of any person entitled to lawful control of the child.

[(2) The persons are—

(a) where the father and mother of the child in question were married to each other at the time of his birth, the child's father and mother;

(b) where the father and mother of the child in question were not married to each other at the time of his birth, the child's mother; and

(c) any other person mentioned in section 1(2)(c) to (e) above.

(3) In proceedings against any person for an offence under this section, it shall be a defence for that person to prove—

(a) where the father and mother of the child in question were not married to each other at the time of his birth—

(i) that he is the child's father; or

(ii) that, at the time of the alleged offence, he believed, on reasonable grounds, that he was the child's father; or

(b) that, at the time of the alleged offence, he believed that the child had attained the age of sixteen.

(2) Allocation

13–86 The offence under s.1 is triable either way. The consent of the DPP is required before a prosecution under s.1 of the Act can be brought: *Child Abduction Act* 1984, s.(4)(1).

The offence under s.2 is also triable either way, though there is no need to obtain the DPP's consent before a prosecution can proceed.

(3) Elements of the offence

13–87 The prosecution must prove that:

— the defendant caused the child to accompany him;

— the child was thus removed from the control of his lawful guardian;

— that the child is under 16;

— the defendant intended to keep the child.

An offence under s.2(1)(a) of the *Child Abduction Act* 1984 requires that at the time when the child was taken or detained he was in the lawful control of someone: *Foster v. DPP* [2005] 1 W.L.R. 1400. A defendant who believes that a child is over 16 will have a defence to a charge under s.2 of the 1984 Act: *ibid*.

(4) Sentence

13–88 The maximum penalty is six months' imprisonment, a fine not exceeding level five on the standard scale or both. After commencement of the relevant provisions, the maximum custodial sentence in a magistrates' court will be 12 months' imprisonment: *Criminal Justice Act* 2003, ss.154 and 282.

For general sentencing factors set out in the *Magistrates' Court Sentencing Guidelines* (2008) see Ch. 23, *post*.

A sentence of 16 months' imprisonment for an offence of child abduction will not be manifestly excessive where there had been a degree of planning and the offender had not acted in the best interests of the child or assisted the police with their enquiries: *R. v. M.* [2008] EWCA Crim 313.

IV. HARASSMENT OFFENCES

A. HARASSMENT

(1) Definition

Protection from Harassment Act 1997, ss.1–2

Prohibition of harassment

1.—(1) A person must not pursue a course of conduct— **13–89**

(a) which amounts to harassment of another, and

(b) which he knows or ought to know amounts to harassment of the other.

(1A) A person must not pursue a course of conduct—

(a) which involves harassment of two or more persons, and

(b) which he knows or ought to know involves harassment of those persons, and

(c) by which he intends to persuade any person (whether or not one of those mentioned above)—

(i) not to do something that he is entitled or required to do, or

(ii) to do something that he is not under any obligation to do;

(2) For the purposes of this section, the person whose course of conduct is in question ought to know that it amounts to or involves harassment of another if a reasonable person in possession of the same information would think the course of conduct amounted to or involved harassment of the other.

(3) Subsection (1) or subsection (1A) does not apply to a course of conduct if the person who pursued it shows—

(a) that it was pursued for the purpose of preventing or detecting crime,

(b) that it was pursued under any enactment or rule of law or to comply with any condition or requirement imposed by any person under any enactment, or

(c) that in the particular circumstances the pursuit of the course of conduct was reasonable.

Offence of harassment

2.—(1) A person who pursues a course of conduct in breach of section 1 or (1A) is guilty of an offence. **13–90**

(2) A person guilty of an offence under this section is liable on summary conviction to imprisonment for a term not exceeding six months, or a fine not exceeding level 5 on the standard scale, or both.

[This section is printed as amended by the *Serious Organised Crime and Police Act* 2005, s.125.]

For the racially or religiously aggravated form of this offence, see *post*, § 13–107: *Crime and Disorder Act* 1998, s.32.

(2) Allocation

The basic form of the offence is triable summarily only: s.2(2). The racially or religiously aggravated form of the offence is triable either way. **13–91**

(3) Elements of the offence

Protection from Harassment Act 1997, s.7

Interpretation of this group of sections

7.—(1) This section applies for the interpretation of sections 1 to 5A. **13–92**

(2) References to harassing a person include alarming the person or causing the person distress.

(3) A "course of conduct" must involve—

(a) in the case of conduct in relation to a single person (see section 1(1)), conduct on at least two occasions in relation to that person, or

(b) in the case of conduct in relation to two or more persons (see section 1(1A)), conduct on at least one occasion in relation to each of those persons.

(3A) A person's conduct on any occasion shall be taken, if aided, abetted, counselled or procured by another—

(a) to be conduct on that occasion of the other (as well as conduct of the person whose conduct it is); and

(b) to be conduct in relation to which the other's knowledge and purpose, and what he ought to have known, are the same as they were in relation to what was contemplated or reasonably foreseeable at the time of the aiding, abetting, counselling or procuring.

(4) "Conduct" includes speech.

(5) References to a person, in the context of the harassment of a person, are references to a person who is an individual.

[This section is printed as amended by the *Domestic Violence, Crime and Victims Act* 2004, Sched. 10.]

13–93 The prosecution must prove:

— a course of conduct

— which amounts to harassment of another and

— the defendant knows, or ought to have known that this conduct amounted to harassment of another and

— the conduct was not pursued for the purpose of preventing or detecting crime, OR pursued under any enactment or rule of law OR reasonable.

Course of conduct

13–94 Proof of two incidents can establish the offence, yet the fewer the occasions and the wider they are spread the less likely they are to result in a finding of harassment: *Lau v. DPP* (2000) 1 F.L.R. 799. The stalking type of behaviour at which this Act was intended was miles away from a prosecution based on two incidents six months apart between two people who were partners and lived together: *Hills* [2001] 1 F.L.R. 580, CA.

Three threatening and abusive telephone calls made consecutively can amount to a course of conduct, even though the victim listened to all three messages together, and was hence only distressed on one occasion: *Kelly v. DPP* (2002) 166 J.P. 621.

Where the course of conduct lasted two years and eight months, s.127 of the *Magistrates' Courts Act* 1980 is not violated so long as at least one incident occurred within the six month limitation period. Evidence prior to the six-month limitation period could be admitted as highly relevant background evidence: *DPP v. Baker* (2005) 169 J.P.N. 78.

In *Buckley and Smith* [2008] EWHC 136 (Admin), DC; the Court considered whether a series of events amounted to a "course of conduct" within s.2. In March 2005, the former partner of one of the appellants committed suicide. The appellant blamed the victims for the death. In May, another appellant approached one of the victims and told them they would face the mafia should the death be proven to be their fault. About three weeks later, the first appellant stopped her car alongside the same victim at a set of traffic lights, and said, "you're fucking dead". In November, at the graveside of the deceased, the other appellant said words to the effect of, "your mother's dead", to the victims. Following that comment, the victims returned to their car, and drove away. The first appellant pursued the victims' car in her car, and when the victims arrived at the car park of a public house, one of the appellants took the keys from the ignition of the victims' car and another appellant threw gravel towards the car. Intimidatory comments were also made. The appellants were charged with offences of harassment under s.2. At trial, the judge held that the events between May and November 2005 could constitute a "course of conduct" for the purposes of s.2 of the Act. The appellants were accordingly convicted of offences of harassment, and appealed by way of case stated.

Dismissing the appeal, the Court held that the conduct in the period between May and November 2005 could not be regarded as one continuous episode of intimidation; rather, there had been a number of distinct episodes which amounted to a 'course of conduct' for the purposes of convicting under s.2 of the Act.

Being continually abusive to someone coming within the abuser's vicinity amounts to a course of conduct, even if the victim chose to come within the abuser's vicinity: *James v. Crown Prosecution Service* [2009] EWHC 2925 (Admin). In this case, the appellant appealed by way of case stated against the Crown Court's decision that the necessary elements of the offence of harassment were made out. The appellant had been receiving care from his local authority. He had telephoned them on three occasions to complain. On two occasions, the care team manager returned his calls and the appellant swore, shouted and was verbally abusive. The appellant was arrested and convicted of an offence of harassment under the *Protection from Harassment Act* 1997 s.2(1). The appellant argued he had not pursued a course of conduct as the calls had been made by the care services manager and he had not carried out a positive action himself. Dismissing his appeal, the Court held that s.7(3)(a) of the Act defined a course of conduct as conduct in relation to a person. The fact that the appellant had not made the telephone calls himself was irrelevant. He had known the recipient was obliged to return his calls. Even if the calls had not been directly initiated by the appellant, if an individual was continually abusive to someone who came within his vicinity that would still amount to a course of conduct, even if the victim chose to come within his vicinity.

If the facts of another, separately charged, offence are to be relied on as constituting a course of conduct that should be made clear to a defendant so that any issues of unfairness can be dealt with. As a general proposition, facts of other, separately charged, offences as might be found proved, whether they led to a conviction or not, are capable of forming part of a course of conduct amounting to harassment. However, where the specific facts of offences charged led to a conviction, and where that conviction could make the difference between a course of conduct short of harassment, and a course of conduct constituting harassment, it was oppressive and unfair for those facts in effect to lead to a second conviction: *Jones v Director of Public Prosecutions* [2010] EWHC 523 (Admin). **13–95**

In *Curtis (James Daniel)* [2010] EWCA Crim 123, CA, the appellant appealed against his convictions for putting a person in fear of violence by harassment contrary to the *Protection from Harassment Act* 1997, s.4(1) and for causing danger to road users. He was in a volatile relationship with the complainant, who complained of six incidents occurring over nine months. Most of the incidents were assaults. The complainant admitted she had behaved aggressively during some of these incidents. In one incident, the appellant pull the handbrake of a car the complainant was driving, causing it to skid (this incident forms the basis of the count of causing danger to road users). The appellant argued this did not amount to an offence under s.4(1) of the 1997 Act, and that had the case been stopped, it would have been necessary to discharge the jury on the causing danger to road users count because they had heard evidence unrelated to that count which may have unfairly prejudiced him. **13–96**

Allowing the appeal, the court held that harassment was tormenting a person by subjecting them to constant interference or intimidation. The conduct had to be oppressive, unreasonable and unacceptable to a degree that would sustain criminal liability. It also had to be calculated to produce the consequences set out in s.7 of the 1997 Act. Although the appellant's conduct had been deplorable and the incidents had been far from trivial, it could not be concluded that, in the course of a volatile relationship where there had been aggression on both sides, the six incidents over a nine-month period amounted to a course of conduct amounting to harassment within the meaning of the Act.

Harassment

Unreasonable and oppressive conduct pursed in the context of acrimonious divorce **13–97**

Part III

proceedings is capable of amounting to harassment: *Crawford v. CPS* [2008] EWHC 148 (Admin), QBD. In this case, the appellant had written a letter to the firm of solicitors for whom his wife worked alleging serious professional misconduct against his wife and another solicitor in her firm with whom she was having an affair and then further corresponded with the firm on the subject of his wife's conduct. The appellant also observed his former matrimonial home where his wife lived with their two children, followed his wife and made comments to a different man with whom she was involved, and took photographs of them together in her home. Dismissing the appellant's appeal against conviction under s.2 of the *Protection from Harassment Act* 1997, the Crown Court held that it was satisfied that the course of conduct pursued by the appellant in his correspondence with his wife's firm, his observations of his matrimonial home and his taking of photographs was unreasonable and amounted to harassment. The appellant appealed to the High Court, contending that the Crown Court had not given proper reasons in its judgment and had approached its findings on credibility with a subconscious bias against him. Dismissing this appeal, the High Court stated that the Crown Court had reflected a balanced and measured approach in its assessment of the respective credibility of the witnesses and had not displayed a subconscious bias against the appellant. The Crown Court had erred in deciding that the appellant's correspondence with his wife's firm of solicitors amounted to harassment as, although it undoubtedly caused distress, it was reasonable given that it made allegations of professional misconduct against one of the firm's solicitors. The other conduct pursued by the appellant was undoubtedly unreasonable and oppressive and the Crown Court was entitled to find that that conduct amounted to harassment.

In *Singh v. Bhakar and Bhakar* (2006) 150 S.J. 112, Nottingham County Court, the court found that conduct by the mother-in-law of a devout Sikh (who was living with her husband's family) which included forcing her to depart from Sikh practice, having to do excessive and pointless housework, controlling her contact with her family and isolating her generally was more than enough to amount to harassment within ss.1 and 7 of the *Protection from Harassment Act* 1997.

In *DPP v. Hardy* [2008] EWHC 2874 (Admin) the appellant DPP appealed against a decision of a magistrates' court that there was no case to answer in respect of a charge brought against the respondent under the *Protection from Harassment Act* 1997. A business owner ran a small company and had an emergency telephone line. The respondent used this line to telephone the business owner, saying they wanted to discuss their partner's recent unsuccessful interview with the company. The respondent said they would not discuss this matter due to data protection concerns and put the phone down. The respondent then rang incessantly for an hour and a half. During one call, they said they would continue phoning until the business owner spoke to them. During another call, they mentioned the home address and birthday of the business owner and their son's home address. The phonecalls ceased when the business owner's son contacted the respondent. At trial, the magistrates held that no reasonable tribunal properly directed might convict the respondent and therefore there was no case to answer. They found that the pursuit of the course of conduct in the case was reasonable within s.1(3) of the 1997 Act and therefore did not amount to the harassment of another. Allowing the appeal, the Court of Appeal held that a course of conduct that might begin with a legitimate enquiry might become harassment by reason of persistence and the manner of its being pursued. There was evidence of numerous phone calls made to a small business within an hour and a half, the caller said they would persist until they was spoken to and said they had the recipient's personal details. Such conduct was capable of amounting to harassment. There was a prima facie case, and no reasonable bench could have found otherwise.

Lawful conduct

13–98 Conduct in contravention of an injunction designed to prevent it will not be judged to be reasonable for the purposes of s.1(3)(c) of the *Protection from Harassment Act* 1997: *DPP v. Selvanayagam, The Times*, June 23, 1999, DC.

Where the course of conduct lasted two years and eight months, s.127 of the *Magistrates' Courts Act* 1980 is not violated so long as at least one incident occurred within the six-month limitation period. Evidence prior to the six-month limitation period could be admitted as "highly relevant" background evidence: *DPP v. Baker* (2005) 169 J.P.N. 78. **13–99**

(4) Sentence

The *Magistrates' Court Sentencing Guidelines* (2008) follow the Guidance on assaults on children and cruelty to a child issued by the Sentencing Guidelines Council on February 28, 2008. When tried summarily, the maximum sentence for the offences of causing harassment and causing racially or religiously aggravated harassment is imprisonment for a term not exceeding six months, a fine not exceeding level 5 on the standard scale, or both. After commencement of the relevant provisions, the maximum custodial sentence in a magistrates' court will be 12 months imprisonment: *Criminal Justice Act* 2003, ss.154 and 282. For general sentencing factors set out in the *Magistrates' Court Sentencing Guidelines* (2008) see Ch. 23, *post*. The *Magistrates' Court Sentencing Guidelines* (2008) provide the following guidelines for offences of harassment under ss.1 and 2 of the 1997 Act. **13–100**

Examples of nature of activity	Starting Point	Range
Small number of incidents	Medium level community order	Band C fine to high level community order
Constant contact at night, trying to come into workplace or home, involving others	6 weeks custody	Medium level community order to 12 weeks custody
Threatening violence, taking personal photographs, sending offensive material	18 weeks custody	12 to 26 weeks custody

AGGRAVATING AND MITIGATING FACTORS

Factors indicating higher culpability	Factors indicating lower culpability
1. Planning 2. Offender ignores obvious distress 3. Offender involves others 4. Using contact arrangements with a child to instigate offence	1. Limited understanding of effect on victim 2. Initial provocation

Factors indicating greater degree of harm	
1. Victim needs medical help/counselling 2. Action over long period 3. Children frightened 4. Use or distribution of photographs	

Racially or religiously aggravated harassment

13–101 See the *Magistrates' Court Sentencing Guidelines* (2008) paras. 3–9, *ante*.

Offences committed in a domestic context

13–102 The *Magistrates' Court Sentencing Guidelines* (2008) provide that when sentencing an offence committed in a domestic context, the Court should refer to the Sentencing Guidelines Council's definitive guideline *Overarching Principles: Domestic Violence*, published December 2006. See § 13–8, *ante*.

As regards the racially or religiously aggravated form of the offence, when tried summarily the maximum penalty is six months' imprisonment, a fine not exceeding the statutory maximum or both. After commencement of the relevant provisions, the maximum custodial sentence in a magistrates' court will be 12 months' imprisonment: *Criminal Justice Act* 2003, ss.154 and 282.

In *Wells* [2006] EWCA Crim 610, CA, a sentence of 12 months' imprisonment was held appropriate for an offence of racially aggravated harassment where the offender had sent four voicemail messages to a neighbour in which he described her, among other things, as a "Jewish cunt bitch". The victim was left feeling shaken and scared to live at her home address. The Court of Appeal stated that the offence was extremely unpleasant, and its effect on the victim should not be overlooked. However, given the appellant's early guilty plea and the comparatively short duration of the offence, a sentence of 15 months was too long, and a sentence of 12 months' imprisonment was appropriate. The court may also make a restraining order: under s.5 or s.32(7).

Protection from Harassment Act 1997 s.3A

Injunctions to protect persons from harassment within section 1(1A)

13–103 **3A.**—(1) This section applies where there is an actual or apprehended breach of section 1(1A) by any person ("the relevant person").

(2) In such a case—

(a) any person who is or may be a victim of the course of conduct in question, or

(b) any person who is or may be a person falling within section 1(1A)(c), may apply to the High Court or a county court for an injunction restraining the relevant person from pursuing any conduct which amounts to harassment in relation to any person or persons mentioned or described in the injunction.

(3) Section 3(3) to (9) apply in relation to an injunction granted under subsection (2) above as they apply in relation to an injunction granted as mentioned in section 3(3)(a).

Protection from Harassment Act 1997 s.5

Restraining orders on conviction.

13–104 **5.**—(1) A court sentencing or otherwise dealing with a person ("the defendant") convicted of an offence may (as well as sentencing him or dealing with him in any other way) make an order under this section.

(2) The order may, for the purpose of protecting the victim or victims of the offence, or any other person mentioned in the order, from conduct which—

(a) amounts to harassment, or

(b) will cause a fear of violence,

prohibit the defendant from doing anything described in the order.

(3) The order may have effect for a specified period or until further order.

(3A) In proceedings under this section both the prosecution and the defence may lead, as further evidence, any evidence that would be admissible in proceedings for an injunction under section 3.

(4) The prosecutor, the defendant or any other person mentioned in the order may apply to the court which made the order for it to be varied or discharged by a further order.

(4A) Any person mentioned in the order is entitled to be heard on the hearing of an application under subsection (4).

(5) If without reasonable excuse the defendant does anything which he is prohibited from doing by an order under this section, he is guilty of an offence.

(6) A person guilty of an offence under this section is liable—

(a) on conviction on indictment, to imprisonment for a term not exceeding five years, or a fine, or both, or

(b) on summary conviction, to imprisonment for a term not exceeding six months, or a fine not exceeding the statutory maximum, or both.

(7) A court dealing with a person for an offence under this section may vary or discharge the order in question by a further order

[This section is printed as amended by the *Domestic Violence, Crime and Victims Act* 2004, Sched. 10.]

Part III

Protection from Harassment Act 1997, s.5A

Protection from Harassment Act 1997, s.5A Restraining orders on acquittal

5A.—(1) A court before which a person ("the defendant") is acquitted of an offence may, if it considers it necessary to do so to protect a person from harassment by the defendant, make an order prohibiting the defendant from doing anything described in the order. **13–105**

(2) Subsections (3) to (7) of section 5 apply to an order under this section as they apply to an order under that one.

(3) Where the Court of Appeal allow an appeal against conviction they may remit the case to the Crown Court to consider whether to proceed under this section.

(4) Where—

(a) the Crown Court allows an appeal against conviction, or

(b) a case is remitted to the Crown Court under subsection (3), the reference in subsection (1) to a court before which a person is acquitted of an offence is to be read as referring to that court.

(5) A person made subject to an order under this section has the same right of appeal against the order as if—

(a) he had been convicted of the offence in question before the court which made the order, and

(b) the order had been made under section 5.

[This section was added by the *Domestic Violence, Crime and Victims Act* 2004, s.12(5), which came into force on September 30, 2009: *Domestic Violence, Crime and Victims Act 2004 (Commencement No. 11) Order* 2009 (S.I. 2009 No. 2051) Art. 2(a).]

B. PUTTING PEOPLE IN FEAR OF VIOLENCE

(1) Definition

Protection from Harassment Act 1997, s.4

Putting people in fear of violence

4.—(1) A person whose course of conduct causes another to fear, on at least two occasions, **13–106**

that violence will be used against him is guilty of an offence if he knows or ought to know that his course of conduct will cause the other so to fear on each of those occasions.

(2) For the purposes of this section, the person whose course of conduct is in question ought to know that it will cause another to fear that violence will be used against him on any occasion if a reasonable person in possession of the same information would think the course of conduct would cause the other so to fear on that occasion.

(3) It is a defence for a person charged with an offence under this section to show that—

(a) his course of conduct was pursued for the purpose of preventing or detecting crime,

(b) his course of conduct was pursued under any enactment or rule of law or to comply with any condition or requirement imposed by any person under any enactment, or

(c) the pursuit of his course of conduct was reasonable for the protection of himself or another or for the protection of his or another's property.

(4) A person guilty of an offence under this section is liable—

(a) on conviction on indictment, to imprisonment for a term not exceeding five years, or a fine, or both, or

(b) on summary conviction, to imprisonment for a term not exceeding six months, or a fine not exceeding the statutory maximum, or both.

(5) If on the trial on indictment of a person charged with an offence under this section the jury find him not guilty of the offence charged, they may find him guilty of an offence under section 2

(6) The Crown Court has the same powers and duties in relation to a person who is by virtue of subsection (5) convicted before it of an offence under section 2 as a magistrates' court would have on convicting him of the offence.

Crime and Disorder Act 1998, s.32

Racially or religiously aggravated harassment etc.

13–107 **32.**—(1) A person is guilty of an offence under this section if he commits—

(a) an offence under section 2 of the *Protection from Harassment Act* 1997 (offence of harassment); or

(b) an offence under section 4 of that Act (putting people in fear of violence), which is racially or religiously aggravated for the purposes of this section.

(3) A person guilty of an offence falling within subsection (1)(a) above shall be liable—

(a) on summary conviction, to imprisonment for a term not exceeding six months or to a fine not exceeding the statutory maximum, or to both;

(b) on conviction on indictment, to imprisonment for a term not exceeding two years or to a fine, or to both.

(4) A person guilty of an offence falling within subsection (1)(b) above shall be liable—

(a) on summary conviction, to imprisonment for a term not exceeding six months or to a fine not exceeding the statutory maximum, or to both;

(b) on conviction on indictment, to imprisonment for a term not exceeding seven years or to a fine, or to both.

(2) Allocation

13–108 Both forms of the offence are triable either way: *Protection from Harassment Act* 1997, s.4(4) and *Crime and Disorder Act* 1998, s.32(4).

In general, summary trial is appropriate except where one or more of the following factors is present:

— racial motivation,

— a course of conduct over a long period of time,

— where the victim was particularly vulnerable.

(3) Elements of the offence

13–109 The prosecution must prove:

— a course of conduct which causes another to fear, on at least two occasions, violence against him;
— that the defendant knew or ought to have known that his course of conduct would have caused fear or each occasion.

Fear of violence

Two threats to burn down a victim's house can amount to a course of conduct putting the victim in fear of violence even where the victim was not unduly concerned by the first threat: *A. v. DPP* [2004] EWHC 2454 (Admin). In this case the appellant had threatened to burn down his victim's house on two occasions. At trial the victim had conceded that she had not been "unduly concerned" by the first threat, yet the magistrates found that as a result of the second threat, the victim had come to believe that the earlier threat would be used against her and that the appellant's conduct on the two separate occasions had caused the victim to fear that violence would be used against her. The appellant submitted that the victim had only been in fear of violence on the last occasion when he had threatened to burn down her house, thus there had been no course of conduct, and it had not been open to the magistrates to convict. Dismissing his appeal, the Court of Appeal held that as the magistrates had found as a fact that the victim had felt threatened and intimidated on both occasions they were entitled to conclude that the two incidents constituted a course of conduct which had put the victim in fear of violence. **13–110**

When considering whether a victim was not giving oral evidence through fear in accordance with the *Criminal Justice Act* 2003, s.116, the victim's state of mind had to be assessed against the history of the case: *Boulton* [2007] EWCA Crim 942. In this case, the appellant appealed against his convictions for rape, false imprisonment and putting people in fear of violence contrary to the *Protection from Harassment Act* 1997, s.4. The victim alleged that the appellant had beaten and raped her on several occasions and that whilst he was in custody awaiting trial, he and another person had made threats to her and other witnesses in order for them to retract their evidence. Consequently she was offered full witness protection and witnesses alleged that the appellant had offered a reward for information as to the victim's location. The victim explained prior to trial that she did not wish to give evidence against the appellant due to the threats to herself, her friends and her family and she deliberately concealed her whereabouts and did not attend to give evidence at trial. The trial judge allowed her evidence to be read to the jury in accordance with s.116 of the *Criminal Justice Act* 2003. The appellant appealed against conviction, submitting that the victim had rather failed to give evidence because of an unwillingness to submit to the trauma of giving evidence against him. Dismissing this appeal, the Court stated that it may have been the case that the victim had the additional reason for not giving evidence that was suggested by the appellant. However it was clear during the period that she was in witness protection that the appellant was trying to find the victim and was using threats and his financial resources to try to stop her giving evidence. The victim's state of mind had to be assessed against the full history of the case, and there was ample evidence of the victim's continuing fear of what might happen to her if she gave evidence.

Racially or religiously aggravated harassment

An offence may not be racially aggravated pursuant to the *Crime and Disorder Act* 1998, s.28(1)(b) where the offence is not motivated by hostility towards members of a racial group, but rather by hostility toward an individual victim: *DPP v. Howard* [2008] EWHC 608. In this case, the defendant was charged with the offence of using threatening, abusive or insulting words or behaviour within the hearing or sight of a person likely to be caused harassment, alarm or distress contrary to the *Public Order Act* 1986, s.5, having chanted "I'd rather be a Paki than a cop" at the victim. He had been charged six months previously under the same provision for another incident also **13–111**

Part III

involving the victim. The magistrates concluded that there was insufficient evidence on which they could be satisfied that s.28 of the 1998 Act had been made out as the evidence showed that the defendant's hostility was motivated only by his intense dislike of the victim. Dismissing the DPP's appeal, the Court of Appeal stated that whilst choice of words might indeed demonstrate hostility and choice of such words might indeed demonstrate that the motivation for an offence was, at least in part, hostility toward a racial group in this case there was an abundance of evidence that the sole motivation for the defendant's chanting was his hostility toward the victim, evidenced by his previous conviction for a similar offence.

See also *ante*, § 13–92 for interpretation provisions.

(4) Sentence

13–112 The *Magistrates' Court Sentencing Guidelines* (2008) follow the Guidance on Assault and other offences against the person issued by the Sentencing Guidelines Council on February 28, 2008. When tried summarily, the maximum sentence for the offence of putting people in fear of violence and the racially or religiously aggravated offence of putting people in fear of violence is imprisonment for a term not exceeding six months, a fine not exceeding level 5 on the standard scale, or both. After commencement of the relevant provisions, the maximum custodial sentence in a magistrates' court will be 12 months imprisonment: *Criminal Justice Act* 2003, ss.154 and 282. The court may also impose a restraining order upon an offender convicted of an assault under s.4: *Protection from Harassment Act* 1997, s.5. For general sentencing factors set out in the *Magistrates' Court Sentencing Guidelines* (2008) see Ch. 23, *post*. The *Magistrates' Court Sentencing Guidelines* (2008) provide the following guidelines for offences of putting people in fear of violence.

STARTING POINT AND RANGE OF SENTENCE

(BASED ON A FIRST TIME OFFENDER PLEADING NOT GUILTY)

Examples of nature of activity	**Starting Point**	**Range**
A pattern of two or more incidents of unwanted contact	6 weeks custody	High level community order to 18 weeks custody
Deliberate threats, persistent action over a longer period; or Intention to cause fear of violence	18 weeks custody	12 weeks custody to Crown Court
Sexual threats, vulnerable person targeted	Crown Court	Crown Court

AGGRAVATING AND MITIGATING FACTORS

Factors indicating higher culpability	**Factors indicating lower culpability**
1. Planning 2. Offender ignores obvious distress 3. Visits in person to victim's home or workplace 4. Offender involves others 5. Using contact arrangements with a child to instigate offence	1. Limited understanding of effect on victim 2. Initial provocation
Factors indicating greater degree of harm 1. Victim needs medical help/counselling 2. Physical violence used 3. Victim aware that offender has history of using violence 4. Grossly violent or offensive material sent 5. Children frightened 6. Evidence that victim changed lifestyle to avoid contact	

Racially or religiously aggravated harassment putting a person in fear of violence

See the *Magistrates' Court Sentencing Guidelines* (2008) paras. 3–9, *ante*. **13–113**

Offences committed in a domestic context

The *Magistrates' Court Sentencing Guidelines* (2008) provide that when sentencing an offence committed in a domestic context, the Court should refer to the Sentencing Guidelines Council's definitive guideline *Overarching Principles: Domestic Violence*, published December 2006. See § 13–8, *ante*. **13–114**

As regards the racially or religiously aggravated form of the offence, when tried summarily the maximum penalty is six months' imprisonment, a fine not exceeding the statutory maximum or both. After commencement of the relevant provisions, the maximum custodial sentence in a magistrates' court will be 12 months' imprisonment: *Criminal Justice Act* 2003, ss.154 and 282. **13–115**

The *Magistrates Courts' Sentencing Guidelines* provide the same guideline as for the basic form of the offence.

Where the offender has previously breached a court order or has been convicted for

Part III

the same offence previously, it is usual for the magistrates to commit for sentence: *Liddle* [2000] 1 Cr.App.R.(S.) 131.

A restraining order may be granted in respect of a conviction under this section subject to the usual requirements for an order of this type. Breach of a restraining order without reasonable excuse is an offence punishable by imprisonment: s.5.

C. DIRECTIONS STOPPING HARASSMENT

(1) Definition

Criminal Justice and Police Act 2001, s.42

Police directions stopping the harassment etc of

13–116 **42.**—(1) Subject to the following provisions of this section, a constable who is at the scene may give a direction under this section to any person if—

(a) that person is present outside or in the vicinity of any premises that are used by any individual ("the resident") as his dwelling;

(b) that constable believes, on reasonable grounds, that that person is present there for the purpose (by his presence or otherwise) of representing to the resident or another individual (whether or not one who uses the premises as his dwelling), or of persuading the resident or such another individual—

(c) that constable also believes, on reasonable grounds, that the presence of that person (either alone or together with that of any other persons who are also present)—

(i) amounts to, or is likely to result in, the harassment of the resident; or

(ii) is likely to cause alarm or distress to the resident.

(2) A direction under this section is a direction requiring the person to whom it is given to do all such things as the constable giving it may specify as the things he considers necessary to prevent one or both of the following—

(a) the harassment of the resident; or

(b) the causing of any alarm or distress to the resident.

(3) A direction under this section may be given orally; and where a constable is entitled to give a direction under this section to each of several persons outside, or in the vicinity of, any premises, he may give that direction to those persons by notifying them of his requirements either individually or all together.

(4) The requirements that may be imposed by a direction under this section include—

(a) a requirement to leave the vicinity of the premises in question, and

(b) a requirement to leave that vicinity and not to return to it within such period as the constable may specify, not being longer than 3 months;

and (in either case) the requirement to leave the vicinity may be to do so immediately or after a specified period of time.

(5) A direction under this section may make exceptions to any requirement imposed by the direction, and may make any such exception subject to such conditions as the constable giving the direction thinks fit; and those conditions may include—

(a) conditions as to the distance from the premises in question at which, or otherwise as to the location where, persons who do not leave their vicinity must remain; and

(b) conditions as to the number or identity of the persons who are authorised by the exception to remain in the vicinity of those premises.

(6) The power of a constable to give a direction under this section shall not include—

(a) any power to give a direction at any time when there is a more senior-ranking police officer at the scene; or

(b) any power to direct a person to refrain from conduct that is lawful under section 220 of the *Trade Union and Labour Relations (Consolidation) Act* 1992 (c. 52) (right peacefully to picket a work place); but it shall include power to vary or withdraw a direction previously given under this section.

(7) Any person who knowingly fails to comply with a requirement in a direction given to him under this section (other than a requirement under subsection (4)(b)) shall be guilty of an offence and liable, on summary conviction, to imprisonment for a term not exceeding three months or to a fine not exceeding level 4 on the standard scale, or to both.

(7A) Any person to whom a constable has given a direction including a requirement under subsection (4)(b) commits an offence if he—

(a) returns to the vicinity of the premises in question within the period specified in the direction beginning with the date on which the direction is given; and

(b) does so for the purpose described in subsection (1)(b).

(7B) A person guilty of an offence under subsection (7A) shall be liable, on summary conviction, to imprisonment for a term not exceeding 51 weeks or to a fine not exceeding level 4 on the standard scale, or to both.

(7C) In relation to an offence committed before the commencement of section 281(5) of the *Criminal Justice Act* 2003 (alteration of penalties for summary offences), the reference in subsection (7B) to 51 weeks is to be read as a reference to 6 months;

(9) In this section "dwelling" has the same meaning as in Part 1 of the *Public Order Act* 1986 (c. 64).

[This section is printed as amended by the *Serious Organised Crime and Police Act* 2005, Sched. 15.]

(2) Allocation

Both offences in this section are triable summarily only: s.42(7), 42(7B). **13–117**

(3) Elements of the offence

There are two offences; failure to comply with a direction and returning to the vicinity to harass. In respect of each the prosecution must prove: **13–118**

— A direction was issued by a constable
— The nature of the requirements of the direction
— That the direction was communicated to the individuals or a group
— That the defendant knowingly failed to comply with a requirement in the direction OR in the case of an offence under section 42(4)(b) that the defendant returned to the vicinity within the prohibited period in order to harass.

A direction cannot be made when there is peaceful picketing in furtherance of a trade dispute.

(4) Sentence

For the offence of knowingly failing to comply with a direction the sentence is a period of imprisonment up to three months or a fine up to level 4. **13–119**

For general sentencing factors set out in the *Magistrates' Court Sentencing Guidelines* (2008) see Ch. 23, *post*.

For the offence of returning to the vicinity the sentence is a period of imprisonment up to 51 weeks or a fine up to level 4.

D. HARASSMENT IN THE HOME

(1) Definitions

Criminal Justice and Police Act 2001, s.42A

Offence of harassment etc. of a person in his home

42A.—(1) A person commits an offence if— **13–120**

(a) that person is present outside or in the vicinity of any premises that are used by any individual ("the resident") as his dwelling;

(b) that person is present there for the purpose (by his presence or otherwise) of representing to the resident or another individual (whether or not one who uses the premises as his dwelling), or ofpersuading the resident or such another individual—

(i) that he should not do something that he is entitled or required to do; or

(ii) that he should do something that he is not under any obligation to do;

(c) that person—

(i) intends his presence to amount to the harassment of, or to cause alarm or distress to, the resident; or

(ii) knows or ought to know that his presence is likely to result in the harassment of, or to cause alarm or distress to, the resident; and

(d) the presence of that person—

(i) amounts to the harassment of, or causes alarm or distress to, any person falling within subsection (2); or

(ii) is likely to result in the harassment of, or to cause alarm or distress to, any such person.

(2) A person falls within this subsection if he is—

(a) the resident,

(b) a person in the resident's dwelling, or

(c) a person in another dwelling in the vicinity of the resident's dwelling.

(3) The references in subsection (1)(c) and (d) to a person's presence are references to his presence either alone or together with that of any other persons who are also present.

(4) For the purposes of this section a person (A) ought to know that his presence is likely to result in the harassment of, or to cause alarm or distress to, a resident if a reasonable person in possession of the same information would think that A's presence was likely to have that effect.

(5) A person guilty of an offence under this section shall be liable, on summary conviction, to imprisonment for a term not exceeding 51 weeks or to a fine not exceeding level 4 on the standard scale, or to both.

(6) In relation to an offence committed before the commencement of section 281(5) of the *Criminal Justice Act* 2003 (alteration of penalties for summary offences), the reference in subsection (5) to 51 weeks is to be read as a reference to 6 months.

(7) In this section "dwelling" has the same meaning as in Part 1 of the *Public Order Act* 1986.

[This section is printed as inserted by the *Serious Organised Crime and Police Act* 2005, s.126.]

(2) Allocation

13–121 The offence is triable summarily: s.42A(5).

(3) Elements of the offence

13–122 The prosecution must prove that:

— Premises are the dwelling of any individual (the resident)

— The defendant is outside or in the vicinity of the dwelling

— His purpose (by his presence or otherwise) is to represent to or persuade the resident or any individual not to do something he is entitled or required to do OR to do something he is not obliged to do

AND

The defendant intends his presence to amount to harassment alarm or distress to the resident AND

The presence of the defendant amounts to or is likely to cause harassment alarm or distress to the resident or any person in the dwelling or any person in the vicinity of the resident's dwelling.

(4) Sentence

13–123 The maximum sentence is 51 weeks' imprisonment or a fine up to level 4: s.42A(5).

For general sentencing factors set out in the *Magistrates' Court Sentencing Guidelines* (2008) see Ch. 23, *post*.

E. THREATS TO KILL

(a) *Definition*

Offences Against the Person Act 1861, s.16

Threats to kill

16. A person who without lawful excuse makes to another a threat, intending that that other would fear it would be carried out, to kill that other or a third person shall be guilty of an offence and liable on conviction on indictment to imprisonment for a term not exceeding ten years. **13–124**

(b) *Procedure*

This offence is triable either way. **13–125**

(c) *Elements of the offence*

"Maliciously" means wilfully or intentionally and without lawful excuse. In *Solanke* [1970] 1 W.L.R. 1, CA, the appellant sent a letter threatening to murder his wife to his probation officer. The Court of Appeal upheld his conviction under s.16, holding that that so long as the sender of a letter acts intentionally with full knowledge of its contents and without lawful excuse, he does so "maliciously" and it is unnecessary to look for an ulterior evil motive. Implied threats can amount to a threat to kill: *Solanke*, *ibid*. Evidence of a previous assault is admissible as tending to prove that the accused intended his victim to take the threat seriously: *Williams* (1987) 84 Cr.App.R. 299, CA. **13–126**

It is the person to whom the threat is made that must believe that the threat will be carried out, not the person to be killed. A threat to a pregnant woman to kill her unborn baby before its birth will not fall under s.16, as a foetus in utero is not a person distinct from its mother; there is thus no threat to kill a third person contrary to section 16: *Tait* [1990] 1 Q.B. 290, CA. However, it would seem that a threat to kill a child after its birth at a time when it was still a foetus was an offence under s.16: *Tait*, *ibid*.

The prosecution must prove that there was no lawful excuse. A lawful excuse could exist if a threat to kill was made for the prevention of crime or self-defence, provided that it was reasonable in the circumstances to make such a threat: *Cousins* [1982] Q.B. 526, CA.

(d) *Sentence*

As threatening to kill is a serious specified offence for the purposes of ss.225–229 of the *Criminal Justice Act* 2003, a court should consider whether to commit the offender to the Crown Court for sentence. **13–127**

For general sentencing factors set out in the *Magistrates' Court Sentencing Guidelines* (2008) see Ch. 23, *post*. The *Magistrates' Court Sentencing Guidelines* (2008) provide the following guidelines for offences of making threats to kill.

Part III

STARTING POINT AND RANGE OF SENTENCE

(BASED ON A FIRST TIME OFFENDER PLEADING NOT GUILTY)

Examples of nature of activity	Starting Point	Range
One threat uttered in the heat of the moment, no more than fleeting impact on victim	Medium level community order	Low level community order to high level community order
Single calculated threat or victim fears that threat will be carried out	12 weeks custody	6 to 26 weeks custody
Repeated threats or visible weapon	Crown Court	Crown Court

AGGRAVATING AND MITIGATING FACTORS

Factors indicating higher culpability	Factors indicating lower culpability
1. Planning 2. Offender deliberately isolates victim 3. Group action 4. Threat directed at victim because of job 5. History of antagonism towards victim	1. Provocation
Factors indicating greater degree of harm 1. Vulnerable victim 2. Victim needs medical help/counselling	

Offences committed in a domestic context

13–128 The *Magistrates' Court Sentencing Guidelines* (2008) provide that when sentencing an offence committed in a domestic context, the Court should refer to the Sentencing Guidelines Council's definitive guideline *Overarching Principles: Domestic Violence*, published December 2006. See § 13–8, *ante*.

In *Hull* (1992) 13 Cr.App.R.(S.) 223 the Court of Appeal recognised the breadth of circumstances in which threats to kill may be made, and provided guidance on factors to take into consideration when sentencing. Lord Justice Bedlam stated:

> "threats to kill are made in many differing circumstances. It is the circumstances and the effect which the threat has, whether they are really intended to be carried out and the surrounding facts which determine the sentence which is appropriate in a given case. Sometimes

> threats are made by a person who is under emotional stress or a person suffering from depression. Sometimes it is clear that the threat is an idle threat, and is realised by the victim to be an idle threat. Sometimes the threat is accompanied by the flourish of a weapon which adds to the effect it had on the victim. Sometimes, after the threat, remorse is expressed. All these are circumstances which the court takes into account."

Choudhury [1997] 2 Cr.App.R.(S.) 300, CA gives an example of a less serious offence under s.16. The offender had been arrested for a public order offence, and after being released on bail, sat on a wall outside the police station. When the officers left the police station the appellant shouted at one of them "you're a dead man". The appellant then addressed the officer in Punjabi, which the officer understood, threatening to kill him and his family. The Court of Appeal held that this was not the most serious of its kind and a sentence of two years' imprisonment would be appropriate.

In *Williams* [2006] EWCA Crim 2565 the appellant had been drinking heavily all day and got into an argument with a passer-by. The passer-by threatened the appellant, who then lost his temper, and began searching for knives in his former partner's home to attack the victim. This frightened his former partner so much that she locked all the doors and windows of the house to prevent him leaving, and called the police. When the police arrested the appellant, he said "you better get my right name for that, I was going to stab him. Good job you showed up or I'd be banged up for murder." He later said he had been wound up by the passer-by and had no intention of carrying out the threats and he was acting in bravado. The Court of Appeal reduced his sentence of three years' imprisonment to two years, after finding that the passer-by played a significant part in bringing about the loss of self-control, and never took these threats seriously, however much they were to be deplored.

In *S.M.* [2003] EWCA Crim 2683, CA, a sentence of three years' imprisonment was held appropriate where a father claimed to be taking his child to school, yet took her on a long journey, during which he made phonecalls to the child's mother stating he would only return the child if the mother agreed to meet him, and made statements which the court found to be calculated to convince the mother that the threat to the child was real and imminent. The threat lasted from 10.40 when the child was taken to 14.50 when the appellant was arrested. The victim had no doubt that this was a real threat and had contacted the police. The Court of Appeal held that the fact that the threat was elliptical made it no less convincing, and upon arrest there was no display of remorse, the father offering a false exculpatory account for his actions.

In *Pooley* [2008] the appellant appealed against a sentence of three-and-a-half years' imprisonment for making threats to kill and affray. The victim was walking with her mother and boyfriend when the appellant waved a knife in front of her. The appellant then cornered the victim, held the knife to her throat and threatened to kill her. The police arrived and defused the situation. The appellant pleaded guilty at the first opportunity. He was taking anti-depressants and had problems with his use of alcohol, which he expressed willingness to address. He presented several references from employers that spoke very highly of him, and had written a long letter of apology to the victim. A pre-sentence report stated he had a low risk of re-offending, a medium risk of harm to others and a high risk to himself. The appellant submitted that the sentence was manifestly excessive given his good character and remorse and the fact that he pleaded guilty and the event was unlikely to reoccur. Allowing the appeal, the Court of Appeal stated that the offence clearly passed the custody threshold. However, the offence lacked some aggravating features of offences of making threats to kill. It was not a campaign but a single occasion and the appellant was of previous good character. That would not normally be regarded too highly but in the exceptional circumstances and in the light of the exceptional mitigation, the appellant's sentence was reduced to two years and nine months' imprisonment.

Part III

F. BREACH OF A NON-MOLESTATION ORDER

(1) Definitions

Family Law Act 1996, s.42A

Offence of breaching non-molestation order

13–129 **42A.**—(1) A person who without reasonable excuse does anything that he is prohibited from doing by a non-molestation order is guilty of an offence.

(2) In the case of a non-molestation order made by virtue of section 45(1), a person can be guilty of an offence under this section only in respect of conduct engaged in at a time when he was aware of the existence of the order.

(3) Where a person is convicted of an offence under this section in respect of any conduct, that conduct is not punishable as a contempt of court.

(4) A person cannot be convicted of an offence under this section in respect of any conduct which has been punished as a contempt of court.

(5) A person guilty of an offence under this section is liable—

(a) on conviction on indictment, to imprisonment for a term not exceeding five years, or a fine, or both;

(b) on summary conviction, to imprisonment for a term not exceeding 12 months, or a fine not exceeding the statutory maximum, or both.

(6) A reference in any enactment to proceedings under this Part, or to an order under this Part, does not include a reference to proceedings for an offence under this section or to an order made in such proceedings.

"Enactment" includes an enactment contained in subordinate legislation within the meaning of the *Interpretation Act* 1978 (c. 30).

[Section 1 of the *Domestic Violence Crime and Victims Act* 2004 came into force on July 1, 2007. This section inserts a s.42A into the *Family Law Act* 1996].

(2) Allocation

13–130 The offence is triable either way: s.42A(5).

(3) Elements of the offence

13–131 The prosecution must prove that the defendant:

— without reasonable excuse,

— did anything they were prohibited from doing by a non-molestation order.

The burden of proving that the defendant had no reasonable excuse for breaching a non-molestation order lies with the prosecution: *Richards* [2010] EWCA Crim 835.

(4) Sentence

13–132 On summary conviction the maximum penalty is imprisonment for a term not exceeding 12 months or a fine not exceeding the statutory maximum or both.

The *Magistrates Court Sentencing Guidelines* (2008) state that where the conduct is particularly serious, it would normally be charged as a separate offence. The starting points in the guideline are based on the premise that the activity has either been prosecuted separately as an offence or is not of a character sufficient to justify prosecution of it as an offence in its own right. For general sentencing factors set out in the *Magistrates' Court Sentencing Guidelines* (2008) see Ch. 23, *post*. The *Magistrates' Court Sentencing Guidelines* (2008) provide the following guidelines for the offence of breach of a non-molestation order.

Examples of nature of activity	Starting Point	Range
Single breach involving no/minimal direct contact	Low level community order	Band C fine to medium level community order
More than one breach involving no/minimal contact or some direct contact	Medium level community order	Low level community order to high level community order
Single breach involving some violence and/or significant physical or psychological harm to the victim	18 weeks custody	13 to 26 weeks custody
More than one breach involving some violence and/or significant physical or psychological harm to the victim	Crown Court	26 weeks custody to Crown Court
Breach (whether one or more) involving significant physical violence and significant physical or psychological harm to the victim	Crown Court	Crown Court

AGGRAVATING AND MITIGATING FACTORS

Factors indicating higher culpability	Factors indicating lower culpability
1. Proven history of violence or threats by the offender 2. Using contact arrangements with a child to instigate offence 3. Offence is a further breach, following earlier breach proceedings 4. Offender has history of disobedience to court orders 5. Breach committed immediately or shortly after order made	1. Breach occurred after long period of compliance 2. Victim initiated contact
Factors indicating greater degree of harm 1. Victim is particularly vulnerable 2. Impact on children 3. Victim is forced to leave home	

Part III

Offences committed in a domestic context

13–133 The *Magistrates' Court Sentencing Guidelines* (2008) provide that when sentencing an offence committed in a domestic context, the Court should refer to the Sentencing Guidelines Council's definitive guideline *Overarching Principles: Domestic Violence*, published December 2006. See § 13–8, *ante*.

V. OFFENCES CONNECTED WITH OFFENSIVE WEAPONS

A. SALES OF AIR WEAPONS

(1) Definition

Violent Crime Reduction Act 2006, s.32

Sales of air weapons by way of trade or business to be face to face

13–134 **32.**—(1) This section applies where a person sells an air weapon by way of trade or business to an individual in Great Britain who is not registered as a firearms dealer.

(2) A person is guilty of an offence if, for the purposes of the sale, he transfers possession of the air weapon to the buyer otherwise than at a time when both—

(a) the buyer, and

(b) either the seller or a representative of his, are present in person.

(3) The reference in subsection (2) to a representative of the seller is a reference to—

(a) a person who is employed by the seller in his business as a registered firearms dealer;

(b) a registered firearms dealer who has been authorised by the seller to act on his behalf in relation to the sale; or

(c) a person who is employed by a person falling within paragraph (b) in his business as a registered firearms dealer.

(4) A person guilty of an offence under this section shall be liable—

(a) on summary conviction in England and Wales, to imprisonment for a term not exceeding 51 weeks or to a fine not exceeding level 5 on the standard scale, or to both; and

(b) on summary conviction in Scotland, to imprisonment for a term not exceeding 12 months or to a fine not exceeding level 5 on the standard scale, or to both.

(5) In relation to an offence committed before the commencement of section 281(5) of the *Criminal Justice Act* 2003, the reference in subsection (4)(a) of this section to 51 weeks is to be read as a reference to 6 months.

(2) Allocation

13–135 The offence is triable summarily: s.32(4).

(3) Sentence

13–136 The offence carries a maximum penalty of imprisonment for a term not exceeding six months or to a fine not exceeding level 5 on the standard scale, or to both. On commencement of the relevant provisions the maximum custodial sentence will be 51 weeks: *Criminal Justice Act* 2003, s.281(5). For general sentencing factors set out in the *Magistrates' Court Sentencing Guidelines* (2008) see Ch. 23, *post*.

B. FIRING AN AIR WEAPON

(1) Definition

Firearms Act 1968, s.21A

13–137 **21A.**—(1) A person commits an offence if—

(a) he has with him an air weapon on any premises; and

(b) he uses it for firing a missile beyond those premises.

(2) In proceedings against a person for an offence under this section it shall be a defence for him to show that the only premises into or across which the missile was fired were premises the occupier of which had consented to the firing of the missile (whether specifically or by way of a general consent).

(2) Allocation

The offence is triable summarily only. 13–138

(3) Sentence

The offence carries a maximum penalty of a fine not exceeding level 3 on the standard scale. The court may also order forfeiture or disposal of any firearm or ammunition found in the offender's possession or any air weapons or ammunition in respect of which the offence was committed (*Firearms Act* 1968, Sched. 6 as amended). For general sentencing factors set out in the *Magistrates' Court Sentencing Guidelines* (2008) see Ch. 23, *post*. 13–139

C. SUPPLYING IMITATION FIREARMS

(1) Definition

Firearms Act 1968, s.24A

Supplying imitation firearms to minors

24A.—(1) is an offence for a person under the age of eighteen to purchase an imitation firearm. 13–140

(2) It is an offence to sell an imitation firearm to a person under the age of eighteen.

(3) In proceedings for an offence under subsection (2) it is a defence to show that the person charged with the offence—

(a) believed the other person to be aged eighteen or over; and

(b) had reasonable ground for that belief.

(4) For the purposes of this section a person shall be taken to have shown the matters specified in subsection (3) if—

(a) sufficient evidence of those matters is adduced to raise an issue with respect to them; and

(b) the contrary is not proved beyond a reasonable doubt.

[This section is printed as inserted by the *Violent Crime Reduction Act* 2006, s.4D which came into force on October 1, 2007.]

(2) Allocation

The offence is triable summarily only. 13–141

(3) Sentence

The offence carries a maximum penalty of imprisonment for a term not exceeding six months or a fine on level 5 on the standard scale, or both (*Firearms Act* 1968, Sched. 6 as amended). On commencement of the relevant provisions, the maximum custodial sentence in a magistrates' court will be 51 weeks' imprisonment: *Criminal Justice Act* 2003, s.281(5). For general sentencing factors set out in the *Magistrates' Court Sentencing Guidelines* (2008) see Ch. 23, *post*. 13–142

D. OFFENCES UNDER THE FIREARMS ACT 1968

The mode of trial, maximum sentences, and powers of courts with respect to offences created by the *Firearms Act* 1968 are set out in Sched. 6 to that Act [See *Violent Crime* 13–143

Part III

Reduction Act 2005 (Commencement No. 1) Order 2007 (S.I. 2007 No. 74) and *VCRA (Commencement Order No. 2) Order* 2007 (S.I. 2007 No. 858).]

Section 51 SCHEDULE 6

PROSECUTION AND PUNISHMENT OF OFFENCES

PART I

TABLE OF PUNISHMENTS

13–144

Section of this Act creating offence	General nature of offence	Mode of prosecution	Punishment	Additional provisions
Section 1(1)	Possessing etc. firearm or ammunition without firearm certificate.	(a) Summary	6 months or a fine of the prescribed sum;or both	
		(b) On indictment	(i) where the offence is committed in an aggravated form within the meaning of section 4(4) of this Act, 7 years, or a fine; or both, (ii) in any other case, 5 years or a fine; or both.	Paragraph 1 of Part II of this Schedule applies.
Section 1(2)	Non-compliance with condition of firearm certificate.	Summary	6 months or a fine of level 5 on the standard scale; or both.	Paragraph 1 of Part II of this Schedule applies.
Section 2(1)	Possessing, etc., shot gun without shot gun certificate.	(a) Summary.	6 months or the statutory maximum or both.	Paragraph 1 of Part II of this Schedule applies.
		(b) On indictment.	3 years 5 years or a fine; or both.	
Section 2(2)	Non-compliance with condition of shot gun certificate.	Summary	6 months or a fine of level 5 on the standard scale; or both.	Paragraph 1 of Part II of this Schedule applies.
Section 3(1)	Trading in firearms without being registered as firearms dealer.	(a) Summary	6 months or a fine of the prescribed sum or both.	
		(b) On indictment	5 years or a fine; or both.	
Section 3(2)	Selling firearms to person without a certificate.	(a) Summary	6 months or a fine of the prescribed sum; or both.	

Section of this Act creating offence	General nature of offence	Mode of prosecution	Punishment	Additional provisions
		(b) On indictment	5 years or a fine; or both.	
Section 3(3)	Repairing, testing etc. firearm for person without a certificate.	(a) Summary	6 months or a fine of the prescribed sum; or both.	
		(b) On indictment	5 years or a fine; or both.	
Section 3(5)	Falsifying certificate, etc., with view to acquisition of firearm.	(a) Summary	6 months or a fine of the prescribed sum; or both.	
		(b) On indictment	5 years or a fine; or both	
Section 3(6)	Pawnbroker taking firearm in pawn.	Summary	3 months or a fine of level 3 on the standard scale; or both.	
Section 4(1) (3)	Shortening a shot gun; conversion of firearms.	(a) Summary	6 months or a fine of the prescribed sum; or both.	
		(b) On indictment	7 years or a fine; or both.	
		(b) On indictment	10 years or a fine; or both.	
Section 5(1)(a), (ab), (aba), (ac), (ad), (ae), (af) or (c)	Possessing or distributing prohibited weapons or ammunition.	On indictment	10 years or a fine, or both.	
Section 5(1)(b)	Possessing or distributing prohibited weapon designed for discharge of noxious liquid etc.	(a) Summary	6 months or a fine of the statutory maximum, or both.	
		(b) On indictment	10 years or a fine or both.	
Section 5(1A)(a)	Possessing or distributing firearm disguised as other object.	On indictment	10 years or a fine, or both.	
Section 5(1A)(b), (c), (d), (e), (f) or (g)	Possessing or distributing other prohibited weapons.	(a) Summary	6 months or a fine of the statutory maximum, or both.	

Part III

Section of this Act creating offence	General nature of offence	Mode of prosecution	Punishment	Additional provisions
		(b) On indictment	10 years or a fine, or both.	
Section 5(5)	Non-compliance with condition of Secretary of State authority.	Summary	6 months or a fine of level 5 on the standard scale; or both.	
Section 5(6)	Non-compliance with requirements to surrender authority to possess, etc., prohibited weapon or ammunition.	Summary	A fine of level 3 on the standard scale.	
Section 6(3)	Contravention of order under s. 6 (or corresponding Northern Irish order) restricting removal of arms.	Summary	3 months or, for each firearm or parcel of ammunition in respect of which the offence is committed, a fine of level 3 on the standard scale or both.	Paragraph 2 of Part II of this Schedule applies.
Section 7(2)	Making false statement in order to obtain police permit.	Summary	6 months or a fine of level 5 on the standard scale; or both.	
Section 9(3)	Making false statement in order to obtain permit for auction of firearms, etc.	Summary	6 months or a fine not exceeding level 5 on the standard scale; or both.	
		(b) On indictment	3 years or a fine; or both.	
Section 13(2)	Making false statement in order to obtain permit for removal of signalling apparatus.	Summary	6 months or a fine of level 5 on the standard scale; or both.	
Section 16	Possession of firearm with intent to endanger life or injure property.	On indictment	life imprisonment or a fine; or, both.	
Section 16A	Possession of firearm with intent to cause fear of violence.	On indictment	10 years or a fine; or both.	

Section of this Act creating offence	General nature of offence	Mode of prosecution	Punishment	Additional provisions
Section 17(1)	Use of firearms to resist arrest.	On indictment	life imprisonment or a fine; or, both.	Paragraphs 3 to 5 of Part II of this Schedule apply.
Section 17(2)	Possessing firearms while committing an offence specified in Schedule 1 or, in Scotland, an offence specified in Schedule 2.	On indictment	Life imprisonment or a fine; or, both.	Paragraphs 3 and 6 of Part II of this Schedule apply.
Section 18(1)	Carrying firearms or imitation firearms with intent commit indictable offence (or, in Scotland, an offence specified in Schedule 2) or to resist arrest.	On indictment	Life imprisonment; or a fine; or, both.	
Section 19	Carrying firearm or imitation firearm in public place.	(a) Summary except if the firearm is a firearm specified in section 5(1)(a), (ab), (aba), (ac), (ad), (ae) or (af) or section 5(1A)(a) of this Act.	6 months or a fine of the prescribed sum; or both.	
		(b) On indictment (but not in the case of an imitation firearm or if the firearm is an air weapon).	7 years (i) if the weapon is an imitation firearm, 12 months or a fine, or both; (ii) in any other case, 7 years or a fine, or both.	

Part III

Section of this Act creating offence	General nature of offence	Mode of prosecution	Punishment	Additional provisions
Section 20(1)	Trespassing with firearm or imitation firearm in a building.	(a) Summary except if the firearm is a firearm specified in section 5(1)(a), (ab), (aba), (ac), (ad), (ae) or (af) or section 5(1A)(a) of this Act.	6 months or a fine of the prescribed sum; or both.	
		(b) On indictment (but not in the case of an imitation firearm or if the firearm is an air weapon).	5 years or a fine; or both.	
Section 20(2)	Trespassing with firearm or imitation firearm on land.	Summary	3 months or a fine of level 4 on the standard scale; or both.	
Section 21(4)	Contravention of provisions denying firearms to ex-prisoners and the like.	(a) Summary	6 months or a fine of the prescribed sum; or both.	
		(b) On indictment	5 years of a fine; or both.	
Section 21(5)	Supplying firearms to person denied them under section 21.	(a) Summary	6 months or a fine of the prescribed sum; or both.	
		(b) On indictment.	5 years or a fine; or both.	
Section 21A	Person making improper use of air weapon.	Summary	A fine of level 3 on the standard scale.	Paragraphs 7 and 8 of Part II of this Schedule apply.

Section of this Act creating offence	General nature of offence	Mode of prosecution	Punishment	Additional provisions
Section 22(1)	Person under 18 acquiring firearm	Summary	(i) where the offence is committed by a person aged 17 in relation to a firearm other than an air weapon or ammunition other than ammunition for an air weapon, 3 months or a fine of level 5 on the standard scale; or both; (ii) in any other case, 6 months or a fine of level 5 on the standard scale; or both.	
Section 22(1A)	Person under 18 using certificated firearm for unauthorised purpose.	Summary	3 months or a fine of level 5 on the standard scale; or both.	
Section 22(2)	Person under 14 having firearms in his possession without lawful authority.	Summary	6 months or a fine of level 5 on the standard scale; or both.	
Section 22(3)	Person under 15 having with him a shot gun without adult supervision.	Summary	A fine of level 3 on the standard scale.	Paragraph 8 of Part II of this Schedule applies.
Section 22(4)	Person under 17 18 having with him an air weapon or ammunition therefor.	Summary	A fine of level 3 on the standard scale.	Paragraphs 7 and 8 of Part II of this Schedule apply.
Section 23(1)	17 Person supervising a person under 18 and allowing him to make improper use of air weapon.	Summary	A fine of level 3 on the standard scale.	Paragraphs 7 and 8 of Part II of this Schedule apply.
Section 23(4)	Person under 17 making improper use of air weapon on private premises.	Summary	A fine of level 3 on the standard scale.	Paragraphs 7 and 8 of Part II of this Schedule apply.

Part III

Section of this Act creating offence	General nature of offence	Mode of prosecution	Punishment	Additional provisions
Section 24(1)	Selling or letting on hire a firearm to a person under 18.	Summary	(i) where the offence is committed in relation to a person aged 17 and in relation to a firearm other than an air weapon or ammunition other than ammunition for an air weapon, 3 months or a fine of level 5 on the standard scale; or both; (ii) in any other case, 6 months or a fine of level 5 on the standard scale; or both.	
Section 24(2)	Supplying firearm or ammunition (being of a kind to which section 1 of this Act applies) to person under 14.	Summary	6 months or a fine of level 5 on the standard scale; or both.	
Section 24(3)	Making gift of shot gun to person under 15.	Summary	A fine of level 3 on the standard scale.	Paragraphs 9 of Part II of this Schedule applies.
Section 24(4)	Supplying air weapon to person under 1718.	Summary	A fine of level 3 on the standard scale.	Paragraphs 7 and 8 of Part II of this Schedule apply.
Section 24ZA(1)	Failing to prevent minors from having air weapons.	Summary	A fine of level 3 on the standard scale.	Paragraphs 7 and 8 of Part II of this Schedule apply.
Section 24A(1) or (2)	Acquisition by a minor of an imitation firearm and supplying him.	Summary	In England and Wales, 51 weeks or a fine of level 5 on the standard scale, or both. In Scotland, 6 months, or a fine of level 5 on the standard scale, or both.	—
Section 25	Supplying firearm to person drunk or insane.	Summary	3 months or a fine of level 3 on the standard scale; or both.	

Section of this Act creating offence	General nature of offence	Mode of prosecution	Punishment	Additional provisions
Section 26(5)Section 28A(7)	Making false statement in order to procure grant or renewal of a firearm or shot gun certificate.	Summary	6 months or a fine of level 5 on the standard scale; or both.	
Section 29(3)	Making false statement in order to procure variation of a firearm certificate.	Summary	6 months or a fine of level 5 on the standard scale; or both.	
Section 30(4)Section 30D(3)	Failing to surrender certificate on revocation.	Summary	A fine of level 3 on the standard scale.	
Section 32B(5)	Failure to surrender expired European firearms pass.	Summary	A fine of level 3 on the standard scale.	
Section 32C(6)	Failure to produce European firearms pass or Article 7 authority for variation or cancellation etc.; failure to notify loss or theft of firearm identified in pass or to produce pass for endorsement.	Summary	3 months or a fine of level 5 on the standard scale; or both.	
Section 38(8)	Failure to surrender certificate of registration or register of transactions on removal of firearms dealer's name from from register.	Summary	A fine of level 3 on the standard scale.	
Section 39(1)	Making false statement in order to secure registration or entry in register of a place of business.	Summary	6 months or a fine of level 5 on the standard scale; or both.	

Part III

Section of this Act creating offence	General nature of offence	Mode of prosecution	Punishment	Additional provisions
Section 39(2)	Registered firearms dealer having place of business not entered in the register.	Summary	6 months or a fine of level 5 on the standard scale; or both.	
Section 39(3)	Non-compliance with condition of registration.	Summary	6 months or a fine of level 5 on the standard scale; or both.	
Section 40(5)	Non-compliance by firearms dealer with provisions as to register of transactions; making false entry in register.	Summary	6 months or a fine of level 5 on the standard scale; or both.	
Section 42A	Failure to report transaction authorised by visitor's shot gun permit.	Summary	3 months or a fine of level 5 on the standard scale; or both.	
Section 46	Obstructing constable or civilian officer in exercise of search powers.	Summary	6 months or a fine of level 5 on the standard scale; or both.	
Section 47(2)	Failure to hand over firearm or ammunition on demand by constable.	Summary	3 months, or a fine of level 4 on the standard scale; or both.	
Section 48(3)	Failure to comply with requirement of a constable that a person shall declare his name and address.	Summary	A fine of level 3 on the standard scale.	
Section 48(4)	Failure to produce firearms pass issued in another member State.	Summary	A fine of level 3 on the standard scale.	

Section of this Act creating offence	General nature of offence	Mode of prosecution	Punishment	Additional provisions
Section 49(3)	Failure to give constable facilities for examination of firearms in transit, or to produce papers.	Summary	3 months or, for each firearm or parcel of ammunition in respect of which the offence is committed, a fine of level 3 on the standard scale; or both.	Paragraph 2 of Part II of this Schedule applies.
Section 52(2)(c)	Failure to surrender firearm or shot gun certificate cancelled by court on conviction.	Summary	A fine of level 3 on the standard scale.	

[This section is printed as amended by the *Firearms (Amendment) Regulations* 2010 (S.I. 2010 No. 1759), regulation 2(7)(a) and (b),which came into force on July 28, 2010.]

PART II

SUPPLEMENTARY PROVISIONS AS TO TRIAL AND PUNISHMENT OF OFFENCES

2. In the case of an offence against s.6(3) or 49(3) of this Act, the court before which the offender is convicted may, if the offender is the owner of the firearms or ammunition, make such order as to the forfeiture of the firearms or ammunition as the court thinks fit.

(1) Where in England or Wales a person who has attained the age of seventeen is charged before a magistrates' court with an offence triable either way listed in [Schedule 1 to the *Magistrates' Courts Act* 1980 ('the listed offence') and is also charged before that court with an offence under section 17(1) or (2) of this Act, the following provisions of this paragraph shall apply.

(2) Subject to the following sub-paragraph the court shall proceed as if the listed offence were triable only on indictment and [sections 18 to 23 of the said Act of 1980 (procedure for determining mode of trial of offences triable either way) shall not apply in relation to that offence.

(3) If the court determines not to commit the accused for trial in respect of the offence under section 17(1) or (2), or if proceedings before the court for that offence are otherwise discontinued, the preceding sub-paragraph shall cease to apply as from the time when this occurs and—

(a) if at that time the court has not yet begun to inquire into the listed offence as examining justices, the court shall, in the case of the listed offence, proceed in the ordinary way in accordance with; but

(b) if at that time the court has begun so to inquire into the listed offence, those sections shall continue not to apply and the court shall proceed with its inquiry into that offence as examining justices, but shall have power in accordance with [section 25(3) and (4) of the said Act of 1980 to change to summary trial with the accused's consent.

4. Where a person commits an offence under section 17(1) of this Act in respect of the lawful arrest or detention of himself for any other offence committed by him, he shall be liable to the penalty provided by Part I of this Schedule in addition to any penalty to which he may be sentenced for the other offence.

5. If on the trial of a person for an offence under section 17(1) of this Act the jury are not satisfied that he is guilty of that offence but are satisfied that he is guilty of an offence under section 17(2), the jury may find him guilty of the offence under section 17(2) and he shall then be punishable accordingly.

6. The punishment to which a person is liable for an offence under section 17(2) of this Act shall be in addition to any punishment to which he may be liable for the offence first referred to in section 17(2).

7. The court by which a person is convicted of an offence under section 21A, 22(4) or 23(1) of this Act may make such order as it thinks fit as to the forfeiture or disposal of the air weapons or ammunition in respect of which the offence was committed.

8. The court by which a person is convicted of an offence under section 21A, 22(3) or (4), or 23(1) may make such order as it thinks fit as to the forfeiture or disposal of any firearm or ammunition found in his possession.

9. The court by which a person is convicted of an offence under section 24(3) of this Act may make such order as it thinks fit as to the forfeiture or disposal of the shot gun or ammunition in respect of which the offence was committed.

[This Sched. is printed as amended by the *Anti-Social Behaviour Act* 2003, s.38 and by the *Violent Crime Reduction Act* 2006, s.30(4). The amendments of VCRA are printed in square brackets. They came into force on April 6, 2007. See the *Violent Crime Reduction Act (Commencement Order No. 2)* 2007 (S.I. 2007 No. 858).]

Note that after the commencement of the relevant provisions, the maximum custodial sentence in a magistrates' court will be 12 months' imprisonment: *Criminal Justice Act* 2003, ss.154 and 282.

E. FAILURE TO POSSESS OR TO PURCHASE A FIREARM OR SHOTGUN CERTIFICATE

(1) Definition

Firearms Act 1968, ss.1–2

Requirement of firearms certificate

13–146 **1.**—(1) Subject to any exemption under this Act, it is an offence for a person—

(a) to have in his possession, or to purchase or acquire, a firearm to which this section applies without holding a firearm certificate in force at the time, or otherwise than as authorised by such a certificate;

(b) to have in his possession, or to purchase or acquire, any ammunition to which this section applies without holding a firearm certificate in force at the time, or otherwise than as authorised by such a certificate, or in quantities in excess of those so authorised.

(2) It is an offence for a person to fail to comply with a condition subject to which a firearm certificate is held by him.

(3) This section applies to every firearm except—

(a) a shot gun within the meaning of this Act, that is to say a smooth-bore gun (not being an air gun) which—

(i) has a barrel not less than 24 inches in length and does not have any barrel with a bore exceeding 2 inches in diameter;

(ii) either has no magazine or has a non-detachable magazine incapable of holding more than two cartridges; and

(iii) is not a revolver gun; and

(b) an air weapon (that is to say, an air rifle, air gun or air pistol[which does not fall within section 5(1) and which is]1 not of a type declared by rules made by the Secretary of State under section 53 of this Act to be specially dangerous).

(3A) A gun which has been adapted to have such a magazine as is mentioned in subsection (3)(a)(ii) above shall not be regarded as falling within that provision unless the magazine bears a mark approved by the Secretary of State for denoting that fact and that mark has been made, and the adaptation has been certified in writing as having been carried out in a manner approved by him, either by one of the two companies mentioned in section 58(1) of this Act or by such other person as may be approved by him for that purpose.

(4) This section applies to any ammunition for a firearm, except the following articles, namely:—

(a) cartridges containing five or more shot, none of which exceeds 36 inch in diameter;

(b) ammunition for an air gun, air rifle or air pistol; and

(c) blank cartridges not more than one inch in diameter measured immediately in front of the rim or cannelure of the base of the cartridge.

Requirement of certificate for possession of shot guns

2.—(1) Subject to any exemption under this Act, it is an offence for a person to have in his possession, or to purchase or acquire, a short gun without holding a certificate under this Act authorising him to possess shot guns.

(2) It is an offence for a person to fail to comply with a condition subject to which a shot gun certificate is held by him.

(2) Allocation

These offences are triable either way. **13–147**

(3) Elements of the offence

The prosecution must prove that the defendant: **13–148**

— possesses or purchases or acquires a firearm OR any ammunition OR shotgun,

— without a certificate or other authority.

This is an absolute offence: see *Waller* [1991] Crim. L.R. 381 where the Court of Appeal upheld the conviction of a defendant in possession of his friend's bag which he did not realise contained a firearm: *Steele* [1993] Crim. L.R. 298. An honest and reasonable belief that a certificate was not required is no defence: *Howells* [1977] Q.B. 614.

"Firearm" or "shotgun" are defined in s.1(3) and 1(3A), *ante*.

(4) Sentence

On summary conviction, the sentence can be six months imprisonment or a fine of the prescribed sum. On commencement of the relevant provisions, the maximum custodial sentence in a magistrates' court will be 12 months' imprisonment: *Criminal Justice Act* 2003, ss.154 and 282. For general sentencing factors set out in the *Magistrates' Court Sentencing Guidelines* (2008) see Ch. 23, *post*. **13–149**

F. FAILURE TO COMPLY WITH CONDITION OF FIREARM OR SHOTGUN CERTIFICATE

(1) Definition

Firearms Act 1968, s.1(2)

Requirement of firearms certificate

1.—(2) It is an offence for a person to fail to comply with a condition subject to which a firearm certificate is held by him. **13–150**

(2) Procedure

This offence is summary only. **13–151**

(3) Sentence

The maximum sentence for this offence is six months' imprisonment or a fine of level 5. For general sentencing factors set out in the *Magistrates' Court Sentencing Guidelines* (2008) see Ch. 23, *post*. **13–152**

G. CARRYING A FIREARM IN A PUBLIC PLACE

(1) Definition

Firearms Act 1968, s.19

Carrying firearm in a public place

13–153 **19.** A person commits an offence if, without lawful authority or reasonable excuse (the proof whereof lies on him) he has with him in a public place

(a) a loaded shot gun,
(b) an air weapon (whether loaded or not),
(c) any other firearm (whether loaded or not) together with ammunition suitable for use in that firearm, or
(d) an imitation firearm.

(2) Allocation

13–154 This offence is triable either way, unless the firearm is an air weapon, in which case it is triable summarily only: s.51 and Sched. 6.

(3) Elements of the offence

13–155 The prosecution must prove that the defendant:

— has the firearm with him,
— in a public place,
— without lawful authority or reasonable excuse (the proof of this lies on the defendant).

"Shotgun" is defined in s.1(3), *ante*.

"Imitation firearm": in *Bentham* [2005] 1 W.L.R. 1057 D had been convicted of possessing an imitation firearm during the course of a robbery contrary to the *Firearms Act* 1968, s.17(2). He had put his fingers inside his jacket during a robbery so as to give the appearance of having a gun. In dismissing his appeal, the Court of Appeal had found that it did not matter whether the item was made of plastic, wood, or simply anorak fabric stiffened by a finger, if in the opinion of the jury at the relevant time, it had the appearance of a firearm. The House of Lords unanimously allowed the appeal. The definition of "imitation firearm" in s.57(4) of the Act meant that the offence in s.17(2) of the Act required an accused to be carrying a "thing" that was separate and distinct from himself and therefore capable of being possessed. An unsevered hand or finger was part of oneself and therefore could not be "possessed". Parliament had not created an offence of falsely pretending to have a firearm and although a purposive construction could have a valuable role where the meaning of a statutory provision was doubtful, it could not be relied upon to create an offence that Parliament had not created. The Court of Appeal had erred in attaching importance to the impression made on the victim when deciding the issue of possession.

(4) Sentence

13–156 On summary conviction, the sentence is a maximum period of imprisonment of six months or a fine of the prescribed sum. On commencement of the relevant provisions, the maximum custodial sentence in a magistrates' court will be 12 months imprisonment: *Criminal Justice Act* 2003, ss.154 and 282. For general sentencing factors set out in the *Magistrates' Court Sentencing Guidelines* (2008) see Ch. 23, *post*.

STARTING POINT AND RANGE OF SENTENCE
(BASED ON A FIRST TIME OFFENDER PLEADING NOT GUILTY)

Examples of nature of activity	**Starting Point**	**Range**
Carrying an unloaded air weapon	Low level community order	Band B fine to medium level community order
Carrying loaded air weapon/ imitation firearm/ unloaded shotgun without ammunition	High level community order	Medium level community order to 26 weeks custody (air weapon) Medium level community order to Crown Court (imitation firearm, unloaded shotgun)
Carrying loaded shotgun/carrying shotgun or any other firearm together with ammunition for it	Crown Court	Crown Court

AGGRAVATING AND MITIGATING FACTORS

Factors indicating higher culpability	**Factors indicating lower culpability**
1.Brandishing the firearm 2.Carrying firearm in a busy place 3.Planned illegal use	1.Firearm not in sight 2.No intention to use firearm 3.Firearm to be used for lawful purpose (not amounting to a defence)
Factors indicating greater degree of harm 1.Person or people put in fear 2.Offender participating in a violent incident	

For sentence guidance, see *Avis* [1998] 1 Cr.App.R. 420.

In *McCabe* [2009] EWCA Crim 1007, CA, the appellant had been sentenced to a term of 30 months' imprisonment for possession of an imitation firearm in a public place. He had entered a supermarket, under the influence of drink or drugs or both. While he was buying cigarettes, he produced what appeared to be a black handgun and placed it onto the supermarket counter. He did not use the gun in any way and paid

Part III

for his cigarettes. However, witnesses were extremely frightened. Allowing his appeal, the Court had regard to the fact that the offence was a frightening one for members of the public who were present and did not know the firearm was an imitation. The appellant also had a very significant criminal record. Mitigating factors were the fact that he did not use the gun for any unlawful purpose, and his early guilty plea. The appropriate sentence after a trial in this case would have been nine months' imprisonment, therefore allowing for the appellant's guilty plea, a sentence of six months' imprisonment would be appropriate.

13–157 Section 46 of the *Crime and Security Act* 2010 came into force on February 10, 2011. Section 46 inserts a new s.24ZA into the *Firearms Act* 1968, making it an offence for a person in possession of an air weapon to fail to take reasonable precautions to prevent someone under the age of 18 gaining unauthorised access to it.

Firearms Act 1968, s.24ZA

Failing to prevent minors from having air weapons

13–158 **24ZA.**—(1) It is an offence for a person in possession of an air weapon to fail to take reasonable precautions to prevent any person under the age of eighteen from having the weapon with him.

(2) Subsection (1) does not apply where by virtue of section 23 of this Act the person under the age of eighteen is not prohibited from having the weapon with him.

(3) In proceedings for an offence under subsection (1) it is a defence to show that the person charged with the offence—

(a) believed the other person to be aged eighteen or over; and

(b) had reasonable ground for that belief.

(4) For the purposes of this section a person shall be taken to have shown the matters specified in subsection (3) if—

(a) sufficient evidence of those matters is adduced to raise an issue with respect to them; and

(b) the contrary is not proved beyond a reasonable doubt.

[This section is printed as inserted by the *Crime and Security Act* 2010, s.46(2).]

This offence is triable summarily only: see *ante*, § 13–144.

The offence does not apply where a young person is permitted to have an air weapon under one of the exceptions set out in s.23 of the *Firearms Act* 1968.

Firearms Act 1968, s.23

Exceptions from s.22(4)

13–159 **23.**—(1) It is not an offence under section 22(4) of this Act for a person to have with him an air weapon or ammunition while he is under the supervision of a person of or over the age of twenty-one; but where a person has with him an air weapon on any premises in circumstances where he would be prohibited from having it with him but for this subsection, it is an offence for the person under whose supervision he is to allow him to use it for firing any missile beyond those premises.

(1A) In proceedings against a person for an offence under subsection (1) it shall be a defence for him to show that the only premises into or across which the missile was fired were premises the occupier of which had consented to the firing of the missile (whether specifically or by way of a general consent).

(2) It is not an offence under section 22(4) of this Act for a person to have with him an air weapon or ammunition at a time when—

(a) being a member of a rifle club or miniature rifle club for the time being approved by the Secretary of State for the purposes of this section or section 15 of the *Firearms (Amendment) Act* 1988, he is engaged as such a member in connection with target shooting; or

(b) he is using the weapon or ammunition at a shooting gallery where the only firearms used are either air weapons or miniature rifles not exceeding .23 inch calibre.

(3) It is not an offence under section 22(4) of this Act for a person of or over the age of fourteen to have with him an air weapon or ammunition on private premises with the consent of the occupier.

H. POSSESSION OF OFFENSIVE WEAPONS

(1) Definition

Prevention of Crime Act 1953, s.1

Prohibition of the carrying of offensive weapons without lawful authority or reasonable excuse

1.—(1) Any person who without lawful authority or reasonable excuse, the proof whereof shall lie on him, has with him in any public place any offensive weapon shall be guilty of an offence, and shall be liable. **13–160**

(a) on summary conviction, to imprisonment for a term not exceeding six months or a fine not exceeding the prescribed sum or both;

(b) on conviction on indictment, to imprisonment for a term not exceeding two years or a fine, or both.

(2) Where any person is convicted of an offence under subsection (1) of this section the court may make an order for the forfeiture or disposal of any weapon in respect of which the offence was committed.

(3) [...]

(4) In this section "public place" includes any highway and any other premises or place to which at the material time the public have or are permitted to have access, whether on payment or otherwise; and "offensive weapon" means any article made or adapted for use for causing injury to the person, or intended by the person having it with him for such use by him.

(2) Allocation

This offence is triable either way. **13–161**

(3) Elements of the Offence

The prosecution must prove that: **13–162**

— the defendant had an offensive weapon,

— in his possession,

— in a public place,

— without lawful authority or reasonable excuse.

"Has with him"

The words "has with him in a public place" mean "knowingly has with him in any public place" it being for the prosecution to prove knowledge: *Cugullere* 45 Cr.App.R. 108, CCA. Once a person has something knowingly, he continues to have it until he does something to rid himself of it: *McCalla* 87 Cr.App.R. 372, CA. In *Glidewell* 163 J.P. 557, CA, it was held that forgetfulness could be a reasonable excuse; the defendant being a taxi driver who had not placed the relevant items in his car and who had intended to clear them out. The words "has with him" also denote something more than mere possession of the article: *McCalla* (*ante*) and *Daubney* (2000) 164 J.P. 519, CA. **13–163**

Where a person uses an article offensively in a public place, the offensive use of the article is not conclusive of the question whether he had it with him as an offensive weapon within s.1(1): *Jura* [1954] 1 Q.B. 503, CA; *Veasey* [1999] Crim. L.R. 158, CA, (motorist assaulting horsewoman with Krooklock not necessarily guilty under s.1(1)); *C. v. DPP* [2002] Crim. L.R. 322, QBD (dog lead not an offensive weapon where its use on police officers was immediately preceded by detaching the lead from the dog.)

"Public place"

13–164 The definition in s.1(4) is the same as that in the *Firearms Act* 1968, the *Public Order Act* 1936 and the *Criminal Law Act* 1967. In *Knox v. Anderton* (1983) 76 Cr.App.R. 156, QBD the Divisional Court held that the justices were entitled to find that premises where there are no barriers or notices restricting access, such as the upper landing of a block of flats which could be entered by members of the public without hindrance, were a public place. Where access to the landing of a block of flats is restricted and can only be gained through the use of a key, security code, tenant's intercom or caretaker, the landing will not be classified as a public place, access being dependant on the consent of the occupiers of the flats: *Williams v. DPP* (1992) 95 Cr.App.R. 415.

"Offensive weapon"

13–165 In *Simpson (C.)* 78 Cr.App.R.115, CA, the Court identified three categories of offensive weapon:

(a) those made for use for causing injury to the person, that is a weapon that is offensive *per se*,

(b) those adapted for causing injury to the person, such as a bottle deliberately broken in order that the jagged end may be inserted into the victim's face, and;

(c) an object not so made or adapted, but one which the person carrying intends to use for the purpose of causing injury to the person.

In the first two categories, the prosecution does not have to establish that the defendant had the weapon with him for the purpose of inflicting injury.

In *R.* [2008] 1 Cr.App.R. 26, CA, the Court of Appeal held that a "sand glove" was capable of being an "offensive weapon". The Crown had appealed against a ruling that terminated proceedings against the respondent, who had been in possession of a pair of "sand gloves". At trial, the Crown had argued that the gloves were an offensive weapon *per se* and not on an alternative basis that they were carried with the intention of causing injury. At the close of the Crown's evidence, the recorder withdrew the case from the jury, stating that the gloves were not weapons *per se* and that, despite the evidence adduced by the Crown, they were nevertheless gloves. The Crown submitted that the recorder had erred in concluding that there was no basis upon which the gloves could be considered an offensive weapon since that was a decision for the jury. Allowing the appeal, the Court stated that the issue in the case was whether the Crown could establish that the gloves were made or adapted for use as a weapon. The court had had the benefit of examining the gloves and it was noticeable that they were very heavy. There was material consisting of the evidence of the nature of the gloves and the evidence of the internet advertisement from which a reasonable jury could infer that the gloves had been made for use as a weapon. Accordingly, the recorder had erred in withdrawing the case from the jury and it was in the interests of justice to order a fresh trial.

An object which is a flick-knife and a lighter is an offensive weapon under the *Prevention of Crime Act* 1953. Having a dual purpose did not mean the item ceased to be a flick knife: *Vasili (Temis)* [2011] EWCA Crim 615.

"Offensive per se"

13–166 In *Simpson* (*ante*) Lord Lane C.J. gave as instances of weapons offensive *per se* a bayonet, a stiletto or a handgun. Weapons which are manufactured for an innocent purpose are not offensive *per se*: *Petrie* (1961) 45 Cr.App.R. 72, CA (razor). Where there is doubt as to whether a weapon is an offensive weapon *per se*, the deciders of fact must have their attention drawn to the statutory definition, but determining whether any weapon is an offensive weapon is a matter of fact: *Williamson* (1978) 67 Cr.App.R. 35, CA.

"Adapted for use"

13–167 Whether an article falls into this category is a question of fact for the justices. Examples of weapons adapted for use include a bottle deliberately broken to attack the victim: *Simpson* (*ante*) and a potato with a razor blade inserted into it: *Williamson* (*ante*).

In *R. (Sills) v. DPP*, 171 J.P. 201, QBD, it was held that justices had been entitled to find, in the circumstances of the case, that the butt end of a pool cue, unscrewed from its other end as designed, had been "adapted for use for causing injury".

"Intended for use for causing injury"

Intention to use the weapon to cause injury must be proved for such an article to be categorised as an offensive weapon. It is for the prosecution to prove the element of intention: *Petrie* (1961) 1 W.L.R. 358. In *Patterson v. Block* (1984) 81 L.S. Gaz. 2458, DC, the Court held that justices were entitled to find the requisite intention where the defendant had with him a lock knife for the purposes of self defence. **13–168**

"Without lawful authority or reasonable excuse"

The burden of establishing lawful authority or reasonable excuse rests on the defendant. In *Bryan v. Mott* (1975) 62 Cr.App.R. 71, the Divisional Court held that the reference to lawful authority applies to those people who from time to time carry an offensive weapon as a matter of duty, for example a soldier with his rifle and a police officer with his truncheon. **13–169**

It can be a reasonable excuse for having an offensive weapon in a public place that the carrier was anticipating imminent attack and was carrying the weapon for his own personal defence (see *Evans v. Hughes* 56 Cr.App.R. 813, DC). This can be the position even in circumstances where the defendant has knowingly put himself in a position where he might be attacked, having left his home to follow a notorious trouble-maker who had been throwing stones at his car and house: *Archbold*, 171 J.P. 664, CA.

The application of the excuse of self defence was explained by Lord Widgery C.J. in *Evans v. Hughes*, above, where he said:

> "It may be a reasonable excuse for the carrying of an offensive weapon that the carrier is in anticipation of imminent attack and is carrying it for his own personal defence, but what is abundantly clear to my mind is that this Act never intended to sanction the permanent or constant carriage of an offensive weapon merely because of some constant or enduring supposed or actual threat or danger to the carrier."

(4) Sentence

When tried summarily, the maximum penalty for this offence is a term of imprisonment not exceeding six months, a fine not exceeding the prescribed sum or both. On commencement of the relevant provisions, the maximum custodial sentence in a magistrates' court will be 12 months' imprisonment: *Criminal Justice Act* 2003, ss.154 and 282. For general sentencing factors set out in the *Magistrates' Court Sentencing Guidelines* (2008) see Ch. 23, *post*. **13–170**

The Magistrates' Court Sentencing Guidelines (2008) provide the following guidance on sentence for this offence:

When tried summarily, the maximum penalty for this offence is imprisonment for a term not exceeding six months, a fine of the prescribed sum or both: s.139(6)(a). On commencement of the relevant provisions, the maximum custodial sentence in a magistrates' court will be 12 months' imprisonment: *Criminal Justice Act* 2003, ss.154 and 282. For general sentencing factors set out in the Magistrates' Court Sentencing Guidelines (2008) see Ch. 23, *post*.

The *Magistrates' Court Sentencing Guidelines* (2008) are based on the Court of Appeal's decision in *Celaire and Poulton* [2003] 1 Cr.App.R.(S.) 116 and state that the following factors should be taken into consideration when sentencing for this offence:

Key Factors

(a) Concurrent sentences may be appropriate if the weapons offence is ancillary to a **13–171**

Part III

more serious offence; consecutive sentences may be appropriate if the offences are distinct and independent.

(b) When assessing offence seriousness, consider the offender's intention, the circumstances of the offence and the nature of the weapon involved.

(c) Some weapons are inherently more dangerous than others but the nature of the weapon is not the primary determinant of offence seriousness. A relatively less dangerous weapon, such as a billiard cue or knuckle-duster, may be used to create fear and such an offence may be at least as serious as one in which a more obviously dangerous weapon, such as a knife or an acid spray, is being carried for self-defence or where no actual attempt has been made by the offender to use it.

(d) Nevertheless, the fact that the offender was carrying a weapon which is offensive *per se* may shed light on his or her intentions.

STARTING POINT AND RANGE OF SENTENCE

(BASED ON A FIRST TIME OFFENDER PLEADING NOT GUILTY)

Examples of nature of activity	**Starting Point**	**Range**
Weapon not used to threaten or cause fear	High level community order	Band C fine to 12 weeks custody
Weapon not used to threaten or cause fear but offence committed in dangerous circumstances	6 weeks custody	High level community order to Crown Court
Weapon used to threaten or cause fear and offence committed in dangerous circumstances	Crown Court	Crown Court

AGGRAVATING AND MITIGATING FACTORS

Factors indicating higher culpability	**Factors indicating lower culpability**
1. Particularly dangerous weapon 2. Specifically planned use of weapon to commit violence, threaten violence or intimidate 3. Offence motivated by hostility towards minority individual or group 4. Offender under influence of drink or drugs 5. Offender operating in group or gang	1. Weapon carried only on temporary basis 2. Original possession legitimate e.g. in course of trade or business
Factors indicating greater degree of harm 1. Offence committed at school, hospital or other place where vulnerable persons may be present 2. Offence committed on premises where people carrying out public services 3. Offence committed on or outside licensed premises 4. Offence committed on public transport 5. Offence committed at large public gathering, especially where there may be risk of disorder	

A sentence of six months' imprisonment was held appropriate where the offender was convicted of possessing an offensive weapon (vegetable knife) and held two previous convictions for the same offence: *Shorter* (1988) 10 Cr.App.R.(S.) 4. In *Simpson* (1992) 13 Cr.App.R.(S.) 665, the offender was found in possession of an unopened flick knife with a three inch blade. He was sentenced to nine months' imprisonment. *Simpson* was distinguished in *Norman* (1995) 16 Cr.App.R.(S.) 848.

In *Poulton* [2002] EWCA Crim 2487, CA, the Court of Appeal stated that in ascertaining the seriousness of an offence involving offensive weapons, it was necessary to consider the intention behind the offence, the circumstances in which it was committed, and the nature of the weapon involved. There were three factors in relation to intention which could aggravate the offence, namely (1) if it had been planned that the weapon would be used to commit violence or threaten others; (2) if hostility to a minority group motivated the offence, and (3) if the offender was under the influence of alcohol or drugs whilst in possession of the weapon. The circumstances of the offence would be aggravated by the offence being committed in a vulnerable place, such as a school or hospital, or at a large public gathering or on public transport or in licensed premises. Some weapons were more dangerous than others but the nature of the weapon would not be the main determinant of the offence, given that a less dangerous weapon such as a knuckle duster could be used to create fear and such an offence may be as serious as that involving a more obviously dangerous weapon. A defendant's intention could be gauged if the weapon he was carrying had been adapted in such a way as to cause serious injury. The offence was mitigated if the weapon was only carried on a temporary basis. Further mitigation could be provided by personal factors, cooperation with the police and a timely guilty plea.

In *Povey* [2008] EWCA Crim 1261, CA, the appellants sought leave to appeal against sentences imposed on them following their convictions for various offences involving the possession of knives and offensive weapons. In the course of his judgment, Sir Igor Judge stated that offences of carrying an offensive weapon or knife were reaching epidemic proportions and sentencers had to have in the forefront of their thinking that sentences for such offences should focus on the reduction of crime, including reduction by deterrence, and the protection of the public, whatever other considerations might arise in the individual case. Even if an offender did no more than carry a weapon, the court, when considering the seriousness of the offence, had to bear in mind the harm which the weapon might foreseeably have caused. Conditions were much more grave than they were when guidance was given in *Poulton*, above. That increased gravity, together with the sentencing considerations identified above, had clearly to be borne in mind when applying that guidance. Further, any relevant guidance from the Sentencing Guidelines Council to magistrates had normally to be applied at the most severe end of the appropriate range of sentences.

On August 1, 2008, the Sentencing Guidelines Council, following *Povey*, above, issued an additional note on knife crime to accompany the *Magistrates' Court Sentencing Guidelines* (2008) on sentencing offenders found in possession of a bladed article or offensive weapon. The note states that the guideline is not limited to possession of knives.

The note states that the guideline has been strengthened from the previous Court of Appeal guideline and is likely to result in many more offences (committed by adult offenders) crossing the custody threshold. The note reiterates the approach of the Court of Appeal in *Povey*, above, which emphasised the recent escalation in offences of this kind and the importance, for the time being, of courts focusing on the purposes of sentencing of reduction of crime (including its reduction by deterrence) and the protection of the public. The note also reiterates Sir Igor Judge's statement in *Povey* that the *Magistrates' Court Sentencing Guidelines* guideline should normally be applied at the most severe end of the appropriate range to reflect current prevalence concerns, which is likely to lead to more cases being sentenced in the Crown Court. The note states that when the current concerns have been overcome, courts will be notified that the approach should return to the guideline as published.

The note further states how the Guideline should be applied following *Povey*:

The guideline provides three categories of seriousness:

- **level 1** is for the situation where a person has a weapon or bladed article, is not in a "dangerous circumstance" and the weapon or bladed article is not used to threaten or to cause fear; in those circumstances:
    - — applying *Povey*, where the offensive weapon is a knife the starting point would be close to 12 weeks custody for a first time adult offender who has pleaded not guilty;

— in relation to an offensive weapon other than a knife, the starting point for a first time adult offender who has pleaded not guilty is a high level community order.

- **level 2** is for the situation where a weapon is in the possession of the offender in "dangerous circumstances" but is not used to threaten or to cause fear; in those circumstances:
  — applying *Povey*, where the offensive weapon is a knife the starting point for a first time adult offender who has pleaded not guilty is committal to the Crown Court and, therefore, a custodial sentence in excess of 6 months;
  — in relation to an offensive weapon other than a knife, the starting point for a first time adult offender who has pleaded not guilty is a custodial sentence of 6 weeks.
- **level 3** is for the situation where a weapon is used in dangerous circumstances to threaten or cause fear; in those circumstances, both the starting point and range for a first time adult offender who has pleaded not guilty are for sentencing in the Crown Court and, therefore, in excess of 6 months custody.

  "Dangerous circumstances" has not been judicially defined but was used in the previous Court of Appeal guideline judgment in *Poulton*, *ante*. In relation to a knife, a circumstance is likely to be dangerous if there is a real possibility that it could be used.

The Guidelines and the Note can be found at *www.sentencing-guidelines.gov.uk*.

I. Having a Bladed Article in a Public Place

(1) Definition

Criminal Justice Act 1988, s.139

139.—(1) Subject to subsections (4) and (5) below, any person who has an article to which this section applies with him in a public place shall be guilty of an offence. **13–172**

(2) Subject to subsection (3) below, this section applies to any article which has a blade or is sharply pointed except a folding pocketknife.

(3) This section applies to a folding pocketknife if the cutting edge of its blade exceeds 3 inches.

(4) It shall be a defence for a person charged with an offence under this section to prove that he had good reason or lawful authority for having the article with him in a public place.

(5) Without prejudice to the generality of subsection (4) above, it shall be a defence for a person charged with an offence under this section to prove that he had the article with him.

(a) for use at work;

(b) for religious reasons; or

(c) as part of any national costume.

(6) A person guilty of an offence under subsection (1) above shall be liable

(a) on summary conviction, to imprisonment for a term not exceeding six months, or a fine not exceeding the statutory maximum, or both;

(b) on conviction on indictment, to imprisonment for a term not exceeding four years, or a fine, or both.

(7) In this section "public place" includes any place to which at the material time the public have or are permitted access, whether on payment or otherwise.

(8) This section shall not have effect in relation to anything done before it comes into force.

[This section is printed as amended by the *Violent Crime Reduction Act* 2006, s.42.]

(2) Allocation

This offence is triable either way. **13–173**

(3) Elements of the offence

13–174 The prosecution must prove that:

— the defendant had in his possession, in a public place,

— a bladed article, or article that was sharply pointed (folding pocketknifes being an exception under this section).

A lock-knife will not be classified as a folding pocketknife because it is not immediately foldable at all times: *Deegan* [1998] 2 Cr.App.R. 121, CA. "Blade": see *Brooker v. DPP* (2005) 169 J.P. 368; (2005) 169 J.P.N. 497. B had with him in a public place a blade from a butter knife which was 10cm long and had no handle, sharp edge or point. He appealed by way of case stated from the magistrates' decision that the butter knife constituted a blade and came within the ambit of s.139 of the 1988 Act. QBD (Admin) held that whilst a sharp blade or pointed article was the paradigm case to which s.139 of the 1988 Act was directed, the words of the Act were unqualified, and there was no rule that only sharp blades were caught: *Davis* [1998] Crim. L.R. 564 considered (concerning a screwdriver). It would create a great mischief if the Act was construed so as to invite argument, in case after case, as to whether or not the object in question was sharp. Section 139 of the 1988 Act was not enacted to fill a lacuna in the 1953 Act. The new provision was intended to complement the old.

The words "has with him in a public place" means "knowingly has with him": *Jolie* [2003] EWCA Crim 1543, CA. In this case, the defendant appealed against his conviction for having a knife with him in a public place without good reason. Police had stopped the appellant in his brother's girlfriend's car and found a pair of scissors on the driver's seat and a kitchen knife under the seat. The appellant admitted the knife was his and that he used it to start the car as he had lost the car keys. The appellant said the knife had been mislaid and that the pair of scissors were used to start the car instead.

Allowing the appeal, the Court of Appeal found that the judge had failed to adequately clarify the legal issues involved. The issue of possession was difficult because the appellant had alleged that the knife had not been under his control when it was placed under the driver's seat, as it was his brother and his girlfriend who had been using the car when the knife was mislaid and they had obtained the scissors to use instead of the knife to start the car. The question of possession had to be dealt with first because only if possession was established would the jury have to decide whether the appellant had had, on the balance of probabilities, a good reason for having the knife in a public place. Forgetfulness in itself did not amount to a good reason, but forgetfulness coupled with another reason might afford a good reason.

The meaning of the phrases "good reason" and "for use at work" is to be determined by the jury, or justices when the offence is tried summarily: *Manning* [1998] Crim. L.R. 198.

(4) Defence

13–175 It shall be a defence for the accused to prove that he had the article with him for use at work, for religious reasons or as part of any national costume: *Criminal Justice Act* 1988, s.139(4) and (5).

It could amount to a good reason if an appellant was carrying a knife for his own protection and that he could show on the balance of probabilities that he was in fear of an imminent attack: *McAuley* [2009] EWCA Crim 2130, CA.

In *Chahal v. DPP* [2010] EWHC 439 (Admin), the appellant appealed by way of case stated against a decision of a magistrates' court convicting him of possession of a bladed article in a public place. The appellant had been searched by two police officers on patrol and found to have a lock knife. He maintained he used the knife at work but a police check found he was unemployed. He was charged with being in possession of a bladed article in a public place contrary to the *Criminal Justice Act* 1988 s.139(1) and argued at trial that he had a defence under s.139(4) of the Act as he used the knife at a business run by his uncle; he had worn a jacket at work due to cold temperatures and that he left the knife in a pocket and forgotten about it. The magistrates' court found that as the appellant's work was "casual" and that at the time he did not need to use the knife on a regular basis, he did not have a defence under s.139(4). Allowing his appeal, the Court held that the magistrates' court had fallen into error by considering that the "casual" nature of the appellant's work was a relevant consideration when it was irrelevant.

(5) Sentence

When tried summarily, the maximum penalty for this offence is imprisonment for a term not exceeding six months, a fine of the prescribed sum or both: s.139(6)(a). On commencement of the relevant provisions, the maximum custodial sentence in a magistrates' court will be 12 months' imprisonment: *Criminal Justice Act* 2003, ss.154 and 282. For general sentencing factors set out in the *Magistrates' Court Sentencing Guidelines* (2008) see Ch. 23, *post*. **13–176**

The *Magistrates' Courts Sentencing Guidelines* (2008) are the same as for offensive weapons; see § 13–171 *ante*.

In *Wall* [2009] EWCA Crim 826, CA, the applicant applied for permission to appeal against a total sentence of three years' imprisonment imposed following his pleas of guilty to three offences of threatening behaviour, possession of a bladed article and failing to surrender to bail. The applicant had made unprovoked threats to a fellow train passenger. He was also in possession of a Stanley knife blade during the incident, but he did not use it, and its existence was only discovered when he told police officers that he had it. The applicant argued that the judge had given insufficient weight to his guilty plea and the fact that he had stayed out of trouble since his arrest, and had given too much weight to his possession of the blade and to the threats uttered in the presence of the police officers.

Refusing his application, the Court held that whilst the three-year sentence was undoubtedly severe, those who carried knives on trains could expect to receive severe sentences. Every knife or weapon carried in the street represented a public danger and it was in the public interest that such crime had to be confronted and stopped. Whatever other considerations might arise in an individual case, sentencing courts had to focus on the reduction of crime, including its reduction by deterrence, and the protection of the public. Even if the offender did no more than carry the weapon, the court had to bear in mind the harm that the weapon might foreseeably have caused. The message was stark; carrying a knife in a public place was a serious offence and was to be treated with the seriousness it deserved.

J. HAVING AN ARTICLE WITH A BLADE OR A POINT (OR OFFENSIVE WEAPON) ON SCHOOL PREMISES

(1) Definition

Criminal Justice Act 1988, s.139A

Offence of having article with blade or point (or offensive weapon) on school premises

139A.—(1) Any person who has an article to which section 139 of this Act applies with him on school premises shall be guilty of an offence. **13–177**

(2) Any person who has an offensive weapon within the meaning of section 1 of the *Prevention of Crime Act* 1953 with him on school premises shall be guilty of an offence.

(3) It shall be a defence for a person charged with an offence under subsection (1) or (2) above to prove that he had good reason or lawful authority for having the article or weapon with him on the premises in question.

(4) Without prejudice to the generality of subsection (3) above, it shall be a defence for a person charged with an offence under subsection (1) or (2) above to prove that he had the article or weapon in question with him.

(a) for use at work,

Part III

(b) for educational purposes,
(c) for religious reasons, or
(d) as part of any national costume.

(5) A person guilty of an offence.

(a) under subsection (1) above shall be liable.
  (i) on summary conviction to imprisonment for a term not exceeding six months, or a fine not exceeding the statutory maximum, or both;
  (ii) on conviction on indictment, to imprisonment for a term not exceeding four years, or a fine, or both;
(b) under subsection (2) above shall be liable.
  (i) on summary conviction, to imprisonment for a term not exceeding six months, or a fine not exceeding the statutory maximum, or both;
  (ii) on conviction on indictment, to imprisonment for a term not exceeding four years, or a fine, or both.

(6) In this section and section 139B, "school premises" means land used for the purposes of a school excluding any land occupied solely as a dwelling by a person employed at the school; and "school" has the meaning given by section 4 of the *Education Act* 1996

(7) [Northern Ireland]

[This section is printed as amended by the *Violent Crime Reduction Act* 2006, s.42.]

(2) Allocation

13–178 This offence is triable either way.

(3) Elements of the offence

13–179 The prosecution must prove:

— the defendant had an article to which s.139 of the *Criminal Justice Act* 1988 applies with him on school premises, OR
— the defendant had an offensive weapon within the meaning of s.1 of the *Prevention of Crime Act* 1953 with him on school premises.

For the meanings of "has with him", "for good reason" and "for use at work", see § 13–174, *ante*.

(4) Defence

13–180 The defendant will have a defence if he can prove that he was carrying the article in question on the relevant premises for use at work, for educational purposes, for religious reasons or as part of any national costume: *Criminal Justice Act* 1988, s.139A(4).

Sentence

13–181 When tried summarily, the offences carry a maximum punishment of six months' imprisonment, a fine not exceeding the statutory maximum or both: *Criminal Justice Act* 1988, s.139A(5). On commencement of the relevant provisions, the maximum custodial sentence in a magistrates' court will be 12 months' imprisonment: *Criminal Justice Act* 2003, ss.154 and 282. For general sentencing factors set out in the *Magistrates' Court Sentencing Guidelines* (2008) see Ch. 23, *post*.

K. OFFENCES UNDER THE KNIVES ACT 1997

(1) Definition

Knives Act 1997, ss.1–2

Unlawful marketing of knives

13–182 **1.**—(1) A person is guilty of an offence if he markets a knife in a way which.

(a) indicates, or suggests, that it is suitable for combat; or

(b) is otherwise likely to stimulate or encourage violent behaviour involving the use of the knife as a weapon.

(2) "Suitable for combat" and "violent behaviour" are defined in section 10.

(3) For the purposes of this Act, an indication or suggestion that a knife is suitable for combat may, in particular, be given or made by a name or description.

(a) applied to the knife;

(b) on the knife or on any packaging in which it is contained; or

(c) included in any advertisement which, expressly or by implication, relates to the knife.

(4)

(a) he sells or hires it;

(b) he offers, or exposes, it for sale or hire; or

(c) he has it in his possession for the purpose of sale or hire.

(5) A person who is guilty of an offence under this section is liable.

(a) on summary conviction to imprisonment for a term not exceeding six months or to a fine not exceeding the statutory maximum, or to both;

(b) on conviction on indictment to imprisonment for a term not exceeding two years or to a fine, or to both.

Publications

2.—(1) A person is guilty of an offence if he publishes any written, pictorial or other material in connection with the marketing of any knife and that material.

(a) indicates, or suggests, that the knife is suitable for combat; or

(b) is otherwise likely to stimulate or encourage violent behaviour involving the use of the knife as a weapon.

(2) A person who is guilty of an offence under this section is liable.

(a) on summary conviction to imprisonment for a term not exceeding six months or to a fine not exceeding the statutory maximum, or to both;

(b) on conviction on indictment to imprisonment for a term not exceeding two years or to a fine, or to both.

(2) Allocation

These offences are triable either way. **13–183**

(3) Elements of the offence

Regarding the offence of unlawful marketing of knives, the prosecution must establish that: **13–184**

— the defendant sold or hired, offered or exposed for sale or hire or had in his possession for the purpose of sale or hire a knife and,

— the manner in which he so marketed the knife indicates, or suggests that it is suitable for combat OR,

— is otherwise likely to stimulate or encourage violent behaviour involving the use of the knife as a weapon.

Regarding the offence of unlawful publication of materials in connection with the marketing of knives, the prosecution must prove that:

— the defendant published any written, pictorial or other material in connection with the marketing of any knife AND

— that material suggests that the knife is suitable for combat, OR

— is likely to stimulate or encourage violent behaviour involving the use of the knife as a weapon.

Knives Act 1997, s.10

Interpretation

10.— In this Act "the court" means. **13–185**

(a) in relation to England and Wales or Northern Ireland, the Crown Court or a magistrate's court;

Part III

(b) in relation to Scotland, the sheriff;

"knife" means an instrument which has a blade or is sharply pointed;

"marketing" and related expressions are to be read with section 1(4);

"publication" includes a publication in electronic form and, in the case of a publication which is, or may be, produced from electronic data, any medium on which the data are stored;

"suitable for combat" means suitable for use as a weapon for inflicting injury on a person or causing a person to fear injury;

"violent behaviour" means an unlawful act inflicting injury on a person or causing a person to fear injury.

(4) Defences

Knives Act 1997, ss.3–4

Exempt trades

13–186 **3.**—(1) It is a defence for a person charged with an offence under section 1 to prove that—

(a) the knife was marketed—

(i) for use by the armed forces of any country;

(ii) as an antique or curio; or

(iii) as falling within such other category (if any) as may be prescribed;

(b) it was reasonable for the knife to be marketed in that way; and

(c) there were no reasonable grounds for suspecting that a person into whose possession the knife might come in consequence of the way in which it was marketed would use it for an unlawful purpose.

(2) It is a defence for a person charged with an offence under section 2 to prove that—

(a) the material was published in connection with marketing a knife—

(i) for use by the armed forces of any country;

(ii) as an antique or curio; or

(iii) as falling within such other category (if any) as may be prescribed;

(b) it was reasonable for the knife to be marketed in that way; and

(c) there were no reasonable grounds for suspecting that a person into whose possession the knife might come in consequence of the publishing of the material would use it for an unlawful purpose.

(3) In this section "prescribed" means prescribed by regulations made by the Secretary of State.

Other defences

13–187 **4.**—(1) It is a defence for a person charged with an offence under section 1 to prove that he did not know or suspect, and had no reasonable grounds for suspecting, that the way in which the knife was marketed.

(a) amounted to an indication or suggestion that the knife was suitable for combat; or

(b) was likely to stimulate or encourage violent behaviour involving the use of the knife as a weapon.

(2) It is a defence for a person charged with an offence under section 2 to prove that he did not know or suspect, and had no reasonable grounds for suspecting, that the material

(a) amounted to an indication or suggestion that the knife was suitable for combat; or

(b) was likely to stimulate or encourage violent behaviour involving the use of the knife as a weapon.

(3) It is a defence for a person charged with an offence under section 1 or 2 to prove that he took all reasonable precautions and exercised all due diligence to avoid committing the offence

(5) Sentence

13–188 When tried summarily, the maximum penalty is six months' imprisonment, a fine not exceeding the prescribed sum, or both: s.1(5)(a) and s.2(2)(a). On commencement of the relevant provisions, the maximum custodial sentence in a magistrates' court will be 12 months' imprisonment: *Criminal Justice Act* 2003, ss.154 and 282. For general sentencing factors set out in the *Magistrates' Court Sentencing Guidelines* (2008) see Ch. 23, *post*.

L. SALE OF KNIVES TO PERSONS UNDER 18

(1) Definition

Criminal Justice Act 1988, s.141A

Sale of knives and certain articles with blade or point to persons under eighteen

141A.—(1) Any person who sells to a person under the age of eighteen years an article to which this section applies shall be guilty of an offence and liable on summary conviction to imprisonment for a term not exceeding six months, or a fine not exceeding level 5 on the standard scale, or both. **13–189**

(2) Subject to subsection (3) below, this section applies to.

(a) any knife, knife blade or razor blade,

(b) any axe, and

(c) any other article which has a blade or which is sharply pointed and which is made or adapted for use for causing injury to the person.

(3) This section does not apply to any article described in.

(a) section 1 of the *Restriction of Offensive Weapons Act* 1959.

(b) an order made under section 141(2) of this Act, or

(c) an order made by the Secretary of State under this section.

(4) It shall be a defence for a person charged with an offence under subsection (1) above to prove that he took all reasonable precautions and exercised all due diligence to avoid the commission of the offence.

(5) The power to make an order under this section shall be exercisable by statutory instrument which shall be subject to annulment in pursuance of a resolution of either House of Parliament.

[This section is printed as amended by the *Violent Crime Reduction Act* 2006, s.43 which came into force on October 1, 2007.]

(2) Allocation

This offence is triable summarily. **13–190**

(3) Elements of the offence

The prosecution must prove that: **13–191**

— the defendant sold to a person under the age of 18,

— any knife, knife blade or razor blade, any axe or any other article which has a blade or which is sharply pointed and which is made or adapted for use for causing injury to the person.

A grapefruit knife is a knife for the purposes of the offence of selling a knife to a person under the age of 16 contrary to the *Criminal Justice Act* 1988, s.141A: *R. (on the application of Windsor and Maidenhead RLBC) v East Berkshire Justices* [2010] EWHC 3020 (Admin). The knife in question had a blade just over four inches in length, with a pointed end, serrations along half the length of both edges and a curved profile.

(4) Defence

It will be a defence for the accused to establish that he took all reasonable precautions and exercised all due diligence to avoid the commission of the offence. **13–192**

In *Enfield LBC v. Argos Ltd* [2008] EWHC 2597, DC, the appellant local authority appealed by way of case stated against a decision of a magistrates' court to acquit the respondent company of an offence contrary to s.141A of the *Criminal Justice Act* 1988. A company employee had sold a knife set to a 15-year-old boy who was assisting trading standards officers. The company was then charged with an offence contrary to s.141A of the 1988 Act. The magistrates' court found that the company had a clear system to avoid unlawful sales of knives to under-age purchasers that used till bulletins highlighting such sales and staff training. The magistrates' court concluded that the company could rely on the defence under s.141A(4) of the 1988 Act as it had taken all reasonable precautions and exercised all due diligence to avoid the commission of the offence. The magistrates' court had only considered what occurred at the till and not the period between the transaction at the till and the handing over of goods to the purchaser. The questions for the High Court were whether (i) the magistrates' court was entitled in all the circumstances to consider only what happened at the till and not consider what happened between the transaction at the till and the handing over of the goods to the purchaser; (ii) the magistrates' court was entitled to find that the company had exercised all due diligence and taken all reasonable precautions to prevent the commission of the offence in question in circumstances where they lacked a documented policy of refusing sales to persons a specified age above the minimum, without appropriate identification (though they had subsequently introduced such a precaution).

Dismissing the appeal, the Court of Appeal stated that the information laid against the company and the conduct of the prosecution had focused on the transaction at the till and accordingly the magistrates' court was entitled to consider only what happened at the till, rather than what happened between the transaction at the till and the handing over of the goods to the purchaser. Whether the company had taken all reasonable precautions and had exercised all due diligence to avoid the commission of the offence was an issue of fact for the magistrates' court to determine. It could not be said that on the evidence before it the magistrates' court had reached a decision that was not open to it.

The statutory defence under s.141A(4) of the *Criminal Justice Act* 1988 requires proof of two elements: the taking of all reasonable precautions and the exercise of all due diligence. These are cumulative requirements, although circumstances may arise where they overlap: *Croydon LBC v. Pinch a Pound (UK) Ltd* [2010] EWHC 3283 (Admin).

(5) Sentence

13–193 The maximum penalty for this offence is imprisonment for a term not exceeding six months, a fine not exceeding the level five on the standard scale or both. On commencement of the relevant provisions, the maximum custodial sentence in a magistrates' court will be 12 months' imprisonment: *Criminal Justice Act* 2003, ss.154 and 282. For general sentencing factors set out in the *Magistrates' Court Sentencing Guidelines* (2008) see Ch. 23, *post*.

M. OFFENCES RELATING TO THE MANUFACTURE OF OFFENSIVE WEAPONS

(1) General

13–194 The following four offences are all triable summarily only. They concern the manufacture, sale or hire of dangerous weapons, the manufacture, sale and hire of offensive weapons, the sale and letting of a crossbow to a person under 18, and the purchase and hiring of a crossbow by a person under 18.

(2) Legislation

Restriction of Offensive Weapons Act 1959, s.1

Penalties for offences in connection with dangerous weapons

13–195 **1.**—(1) Any person who manufactures, sells or hires or offers for sale or hire, or exposes or has in his possession for the purpose of sale or hire or lends to gives to any other person.

(a) any knife which has a blade which opens automatically by hand pressure applied to a button, spring or other device in or attached to the handle of the knife, sometimes known as a 'flick knife' or 'flick gun'; or

(b) any knife which has a blade which is released from the handle or sheath thereof by the force of gravity or the application of centrifugal force and which, when released, is locked in place by means of a button, spring, lever, or other device, sometimes known as a 'gravity knife', shall be guilty of an offence and shall be liable on summary conviction in the case of a first offence to imprisonment for a term not exceeding three months or to a fine not exceeding fifty pounds or to both such imprisonment and fine, and in the case of a second or subsequent offence to imprisonment for a term not exceeding six months or to a fine not exceeding two hundred pounds or to both such imprisonment and fine.

(2) The importation of any such knife as is described in the foregoing subsection is hereby prohibited.

Criminal Justice Act 1988, s.141

Offensive weapons

141.—(1) Any person who manufactures, sells or hires or offers for sale or hire, exposes or has in his possession for the purpose of sale or hire, or lends or gives to any other person, a weapon to which this section applies shall be guilty of an offence and liable on summary conviction to imprisonment for a term not exceeding six months or to a fine not exceeding level 5 on the standard scale or both. **13–196**

(2) The Secretary of State may by order made by statutory instrument direct that this section shall apply to any description of weapon specified in the order except—

(a) any weapon subject to the *Firearms Act* 1968; and

(b) crossbows.

(4) The importation of a weapon to which this section applies is hereby prohibited.

(5) It shall be a defence for any person charged in respect of any conduct of his relating to a weapon to which this section applies—

(a) with an offence under subsection (1) above; or

(b) with an offence under section 50(2) or (3) of the *Customs and Excise Management Act* 1979 (improper importation),

to [show] that his conduct was only for the purposes of functions carried out on behalf of the Crown or of a visiting force.

(6) In this section the reference to the Crown includes the Crown in right of Her Majesty's Government in Northern Ireland; and"visiting force" means any body, contingent or detachment of the forces of a country—

(a) mentioned in subsection (1)(a) of section 1 of the Visiting Forces Act 1952; or

(b) designated for the purposes of any provision of that Act by Order in Council under subsection (2) of that section, which is present in the United Kingdom (including United Kingdom territorial waters) or in any place to which subsection (7) below applies on the invitation of Her Majesty's Government in the United Kingdom

(7) This subsection applies to any place on, under or above an installation in a designated area within the meaning of section 1(7) of the *Continental Shelf Act* 1964 or any waters within 500 metres of such an installation.

(8) It shall be a defence for any person charged in respect of any conduct of his relating to a weapon to which this section applies—

(a) with an offence under subsection (1) above; or

(b) with an offence under section 50(2) or (3) of the *Customs and Excise Management Act* 1979,

to [show] that the conduct in question was only for the purposes of making the weapon available to a museum or gallery to which this subsection applies.

(9) If a person acting on behalf of a museum or gallery to which subsection (8) above applies is charged with hiring or lending a weapon to which this section applies, it shall be a defence for him to [show] that he had reasonable grounds for believing that the person to whom he lent or hired it would use it only for cultural, artistic or educational purposes.

(10) Subsection (8) above applies to a museum or gallery only if it does not distribute profits.

Part III

(11) In this section "museum or gallery" includes any institution which has as its purpose, or one of its purposes, the preservation, display and interpretation of material of historical, artistic or scientific interest and gives the public access to it.

(11A) It shall be a defence for a person charged in respect of conduct of his relating to a weapon to which this section applies–

(a) with an offence under subsection (1) above, or

(b) with an offence under section 50(2) or (3) of the *Customs and Excise Management Act* 1979,

to show that his conduct was for the purpose only of making the weapon in question available for one or more of the purposes specified in subsection (11B).

(11B) Those purposes are–

(a) the purposes of theatrical performances and of rehearsals for such performances;

(b) the production of films (within the meaning of Part 1 of the *Copyright, Designs and Patents Act* 1988 — see section 5B of that Act);

(c) the production of television programmes (within the meaning of the *Communications Act* 2003 — see section 405(1) of that Act).

(11C) For the purposes of this section a person shall be taken to have shown a matter specified in subsection (5), (8), (9) or (11A) if–

(a) sufficient evidence of that matter is adduced to raise an issue with respect to it; and

(b) the contrary is not proved beyond a reasonable doubt.

(11D) The Secretary of State may by order made by statutory instrument–

(a) provide for exceptions and exemptions from the offence under subsection (1) above or from the prohibition in subsection (4) above; and

(b) provide for it to be a defence in proceedings for such an offence, or for an offence under section 50(2) or (3) of the *Customs and Excise Management Act* 1979, to show the matters specified or described in the order.

(11E) A statutory instrument containing an order under this section shall not be made unless a draft of the instrument has been laid before Parliament and approved by a resolution of each House.

(12) This section shall not have effect in relation to anything done before it comes into force.

This section applies to weapons listed by the Secretary of State in an order, and must not include any weapon subject to the *Firearms Act* 1968, or crossbows. The order currently in force is the *Criminal Justice Act 1988 (Offensive Weapons) Order* 1988 (S.I. 1988 No. 2019). See also the *Criminal Justice Act 1988 (Offensive Weapons) Order* 2002 (S.I. 2002 No. 1668) which adds the disguised knife to the list of specified weapons outlined in the 1988 Order, and the *Criminal Justice Act 1988 (Offensive Weapons) (Amendment) Order* 2008 (S.I. 2008 No. 973) which adds swords with a curved blade, (or samurai swords) to the list with effect from April 6, 2008. See also the *Criminal Justice Act 1988 (Offensive Weapons) (Amendment No. 2) Order* 2008 (S.I. 2008 No. 2039) which amends the 1988 Order to provide a defence for weapons made before 1954 or made at any other time according to traditional methods of making swords by hand, and for conduct with the sole purpose of making the weapon available for use in religious ceremonies with effect from August 1, 2008).

Crossbows Act 1987, ss.1–3

Sale and letting on hire

13–197 **1.** A person who sells or lets on hire a crossbow or a part of a crossbow to a person under the age of eighteen is guilty of an offence, unless he believes him to be eighteen years of age or older and has reasonable ground for the belief.

Purchase and hiring

13–198 **2.** A person under the age of eighteen who buys or hires a crossbow or a part of a crossbow is guilty of an offence.

Possession

13–199 **3.** A person under the age of eighteen who has with him—

(a) a crossbow which is capable of discharging a missile, or
(b) parts of a crossbow which together (and without any other parts) can be assembled to form a crossbow capable of discharging a missile, is guilty of an offence, unless he is under the supervision of a person who is twenty one years of age or older.

(3) Sentence

A person guilty of an offence under s.1 of the *Restriction of Offensive Weapons Act* 1959 is liable, in the case of a first offence, to imprisonment up to three months or to a fine of up to £50, or both; in the case of a subsequent offence, the maximum is six months' imprisonment or a fine of £200, or both. The maximum penalty for an offence under s.141 of the *Criminal Justice Act* 1988 is six months' imprisonment or a fine not exceeding level 5 on the standard scale, or both. For general sentencing factors set out in the *Magistrates' Court Sentencing Guidelines* (2008) see Ch. 23, *post*. **13–200**

A person guilty of an offence under s.1 of the *Crossbows Act* 1987 is liable to imprisonment for a term not exceeding six months, to a fine not exceeding level five on the standard scale, or to both. The court may also make a forfeiture order regarding any crossbow or part of a crossbow in respect of which the offence was committed: s.6(1) and (3). A person guilty of an offence under s.2 is liable to a fine not exceeding level three on the standard scale. The court may also make a forfeiture order regarding any crossbow or part of a crossbow in respect of which the offence was committed: s.6(2) and (3). Note that, on commencement of the relevant provisions, the maximum custodial sentence in a magistrates' court will be 12 months' imprisonment: *Criminal Justice Act* 2003, ss.154 and 282. For general sentencing factors set out in the *Magistrates' Court Sentencing Guidelines* (2008) see Ch. 23, *post*.

Chapter 14

SEXUAL OFFENCES

Part III

I. SEXUAL OFFENCES

Introduction—the old and new law

The *Sexual Offences Act* 2003 substantially reformed the law relating to sexual offences. It came into force on May 1, 2004 and created many new offences. The new offences are dealt with in §§ 14–78 *et seq., post*. Whilst the 2003 Act did not repeal all earlier legislation in this area, most of the old legislation was either repealed or amended. As the old offences may still be the subject of proceedings in the courts, they are dealt with in this chapter but readers are urged to bear in mind that many "old" offences were repealed on May 1, 2004 and therefore can only be used to prosecute offences committed before that date. **14–1**

In May 2007, the Sentencing Guidelines Council issued a definitive guideline which applies to all the offences covered by the *Sexual Offences Act* 2003 and other sexual offences. These guidelines are incorporated into the Magistrates' Courts Sentencing Guidelines as updated in 2008. The guidelines are included in this Chapter and the starting points and sentencing range are referred to for each relevant offence.

II. OFFENCES PRIOR TO THE INTRODUCTION OF THE SEXUAL OFFENCES ACT 2003

A. SEXUAL INTERCOURSE WITH A GIRL UNDER SIXTEEN

(1) Definition

Sexual Offences Act 1956, s.6

Intercourse with girl between thirteen and sixteen

6.—(1) It is an offence, subject to the exceptions mentioned in this section, for a man to have unlawful sexual intercourse with a girl under the age of sixteen. **14–2**

(2) Where a marriage is invalid under section two of the *Marriage Act* 1949, or section one of the *Age of Marriage Act* 1929 (the wife being a girl under the age of sixteen), the invalidity does not make the husband guilty of an offence under this section because he has sexual intercourse with her, if he believes her to be his wife and has reasonable cause for the belief.

(3) A man is not guilty of an offence under this section because he has unlawful sexual intercourse with a girl under the age of sixteen, if he is under the age of twenty-four and has not previously been charged with a like offence, and he believes her to be of the age of sixteen or over and has reasonable cause for the belief.

In this subsection, "a like offence" means an offence under this section or an attempt to commit one, or an offence under paragraph (1) of section five of the *Criminal Law Amendment Act* 1885 (the provision replaced for England and Wales by this Section).

[This section is printed as amended by the *CLA* 1967, s.10(1) and Sched. 2, para. 14. It was repealed by the *Sexual Offences Act* 2003, Sched. 7, on May 1, 2004.]

Section 6 applies to sexual intercourse with a girl aged 13 or over but under 16.

(2) Allocation

This offence is triable either way. The *Consolidated Criminal Practice Direction* (see §§ F-55–F-56) provides that cases of unlawful sexual intercourse should be tried summarily unless the court considers that one or more of the following features are present and that its sentencing powers are insufficient: **14–3**

(a) wide disparity of age;

(b) breach of position of trust;

(c) the victim is particularly vulnerable.

(3) Sentence

When tried summarily, the maximum penalty for this offence is six months' imprison- **14–4** ment, a fine not exceeding the statutory maximum or both: *Sexual Offences Act* 1956, s.37 and Sched. 2; *Magistrates' Courts Act* 1980, s.32.

In *Taylor*, 64 Cr.App.R 182, CA the Court laid down guidelines for sentencing people convicted of this offence. Lawton L.J. referred to the wide spectrum of guilt covered by the offence known as having unlawful sexual intercourse with a girl under the age of sixteen. He distinguished cases of "virtuous friendship" between two people of a similar age and the case where the man in a supervisory capacity sets out deliberately to seduce a girl under the age of 16 who is in his charge. In the first type of case it would be inappropriate to pass sentences of a punitive nature. As regards the second a sentence near the maximum allowed by law would be appropriate. In between there are many degrees of guilt. Lawton L.J. gave the example of a common type of offender being the youth who picks up a girl of loose morals at a dance, takes her out into the local park and, behind the bushes, has sexual intercourse with her. That is the kind of offence that would normally be dealt with by a fine.

A case at the bottom end of the scale was *Cooke* (1979) 1 Cr App.R.(S.) 325. The offender pleaded guilty to one act of unlawful sexual intercourse with a girl aged 14 years and 10 months who was sexually experienced and looked older than her true age. A sentence of six months' imprisonment was substituted for the original sentence of nine months' imprisonment. In *Wood* (1990) 12 Cr.App.R.(S.) 129, the offender admitted unlawful sexual intercourse with the 15-year-old daughter of the woman he had been living with for a number of years. He was sentenced to nine months' imprisonment. In *Wong* [2001] All E.R. 162 the offender pleaded guilty on the basis that the girl instigated the offence and he admitted being reckless as to whether the girl was 15 or 16. He was sentenced to three months' imprisonment.

In *Att.-Gen.'s Reference (No. 80 of 2000)* [2001] 2 Cr.App.R.(S.) 12, the Attorney General sought leave to refer a sentence of 100 hours' community service imposed for one offence of indecent assault and four offences of unlawful sexual intercourse on account of it being unduly lenient. The victim was 13-years-old when they began a consensual sexual relationship. The sentence was held to be too lenient and a period of imprisonment of at least 12 months' should have been imposed.

In *Reeves* [2002] 1 Cr.App.R.(S.) 15 the Court of Appeal held that a sentence of two years' imprisonment imposed for indecently assaulting a 15-year-old girl should be reduced to 18 months to provide the offender with a discount for his plea of guilty.

In *Cronshaw* [2005] 1 Cr.App.R.(S.) 89, earlier authorities were reviewed and guidance given on sentencing a defendant who has been convicted of both unlawful sexual intercourse and indecent assault. Where the indecent assaults are no more than unlawful sexual intercourse, the maximum penalty that should be imposed is two years, *i.e.* the maximum penalty for unlawful sexual intercourse (and not 10 years, the maximum penalty for indecent assault).

See also *O'Grady* (1978) 66 Cr.App.R.(S.) 279 and *Harding* (1979) 1 Cr.App.R.(S.) 160.

B. GROSS INDECENCY

(1) Definition

Sexual Offences Act 1956, s.13

Indecency between men

14–5 **13.** It is an offence for a man to commit an act of gross indecency with another man otherwise than in the circumstances described below, whether in public or private, or to be a party to the commission by a man of an act of gross indecency with another man, or to procedure the commission by a man of an act of gross indecency with another man.

The circumstances referred to above are that the man is under the age of sixteen and the other man has attained that age.

[This section is printed as amended by the *Sexual Offences (Amendment) Act* 2000, s.2(2)(a) and (b) and was repealed by the *Sexual Offences Act* 2003, Sched. 7, para. 1 on May 1, 2004.]

Gross Indecency is no longer an offence when committed in private by two consenting persons over the age of sixteen: *Sexual Offences Act* 1967, ss.1 and 4(3). Sections 1 and 4 of the *Sexual Offences Act* 1967 are repealed by the *Sexual Offences Act* 2003, Sched. 7. **14–6**

In *ADT v. UK* (2001) 31 E.H.R.R. 33, the European Court of Human Rights held unanimously that the very existence of legislation relating to gross indecency between two men was in breach of Art. 8. It follows that charges should no longer be brought for buggery or gross indecency between consenting adults, even if those offences were committed prior to the implementation of the *Sexual Offences Act* 2003.

In *X. v. Y. (Employment: Sex offender)* [2004] UKHRR 1172, the appellant had been cautioned for an offence of gross indecency committed in a public lavatory. This was conduct which occurred in a public place and which constituted a criminal offence by virtue of the fact that it took place in public, as it did not take place in the "private life" of the participants Art. 8 was not engaged. The fact that one of them wished to keep the matter private did not make it part of his private life or deprive it of its public character; a criminal offence was normally a matter for legitimate concern to the public.

(2) Allocation

This offence is triable either way. Proceedings may not be instituted after the expiration of 12 months since the commission of the offence: *Sexual Offences Act* 1967, s.7. Where either man was under 16 years of age at the time of the offence, proceedings may not be instituted without the consent of the DPP: *SOA* 1967, s.8. **14–7**

(3) Elements of the offence

There is no need for physical contact between the men, but both must participate. **14–8**

(4) Sentence

When tried summarily, the maximum penalty for this offence is six months imprisonment, a fine not exceeding the statutory maximum or both: *SOA* 1956, Sched. 2. **14–9**

The guideline judgment for this offence is *Morgan and Dockerty* [1979] Crim.L.R. 60 where Lawton L.J. stated that in general, first time offenders using public lavatories and behaving in this sort of way in them do not get sent to prison. They are generally fined. The offenders' sentences of three months and six weeks' imprisonment were varied to fines of £100 and £50 respectively.

In *Clayton* (1981) 3 Cr.App.R.(S.) 67 the offenders were sentenced to four months' imprisonment, recommended in one case for deportation. These sentences were replaced with fines of £50 on appeal, Eastham J. describing the original sentences as excessive, and stating that the appropriate penalty for men of hitherto good character should be a financial penalty.

C. PERMITTING GIRLS TO USE PREMISES FOR UNLAWFUL SEXUAL INTERCOURSE

(1) Definition

Sexual Offences Act 1956, s.26

Permitting girl between thirteen and sixteen to use premises for intercourse

26. It is an offence for a person who is the owner or occupier of any premises, or who has, or acts or assists in, the management or control of any premises, to induce or knowingly suffer a girl under the age of sixteen, to resort to or be on those premises for the purposes of having unlawful sexual intercourse with men or with a particular man. **14–10**

Part III

[Repealed by the *Sexual Offences Act* 2003, Sched. 7, on May 1, 2004.]

(2) Allocation

14–11 This offence is triable either way.

(3) Sentence

14–12 When tried summarily, the maximum penalty for this offence is six months' imprisonment, a fine not exceeding the statutory maximum or both: *Sexual Offences Act* 1956, s.37 and Sched. 2 and *Magistrates' Courts Act* 1980, s.32.

D. INDECENT ASSAULT

(1) Definition

Sexual Offences Act 1956, ss.14–15

Indecent assault on a woman

14–13 **14.**—(1) It is an offence, subject to the exception mentioned in subsection (3) of this section, for a person to make an indecent assault on a woman.

(2) A girl under the age of sixteen cannot in law give any consent which would prevent an act being an assault for the purposes of this section.

(3) Where a marriage is invalid under section two of the *Marriage Act* 1949, or section one of the *Age of Marriage Act* 1929 (the wife being a girl under the age of sixteen), the invalidity does not make the husband guilty of any offence under this section by reason of her incapacity to consent while under that age, if he believes her to be his wife and has reasonable cause for the belief.

(4) A woman who is a defective cannot in law give any consent which would prevent an act being an assault for the purposes of this section, but a person is only to be treated as guilty of an indecent assault on a defective by reasons of that incapacity to consent, if that person knew or had reason to suspect her to be a defective.

Indecent assault on a man

14–14 **15.**—(1) It is an offence for a person to make an indecent assault on a man.

(2) A boy under the age of sixteen cannot in law give any consent which would Prevent an act being an assault for the purposes of this section.

(3) A man who is a defective cannot in law give any consent which would prevent an act being an assault for the purposes of this section, but a persons is only to be treated as guilty of an indecent assault on a defective by reason of that incapacity to consent, if that person knew or had reason to suspect him to be a defective

[Sections 14 and 15 were repealed by the *Sexual Offences Act* 2003, Sched. 7, on May 1, 2004.]

(2) Allocation

14–15 This offence is triable either way. The *Consolidated Criminal Practice Direction* (see §§ F–55–F–56) provides that cases of unlawful sexual intercourse should be tried summarily unless the court considers that one or more of the following features is present and that its sentencing powers are insufficient:

(a) substantial disparity in age between victim and defendant, and the assault is more than trivial;
(b) violence or threats of violence;
(c) relationship of trust and responsibility between defendant and victim;
(d) several similar offences and the assault more than trivial;
(e) the victim is particularly vulnerable
(f) serious nature of the assault.

Cases that have been held suitable for summary disposal include *Tanyildiz* [1998] 1

Cr.App.R.(S.) 362 and *Yazbek* [1998] 1 Cr.App.R.(S.) 406 (both concerning indecent assaults on underground trains).

(3) Elements of the offence

For a full analysis of the offences of indecent assault, see *Court* [1989] A.C. 28, HL (which will not apply to offences under the *Sexual Offences Act* 2003). **14–16**

(4) Sentence

When tried summarily, an offence under sections 14 or 15 carries a maximum penalty of six months' imprisonment, a fine not exceeding the statutory maximum or both: *Sexual Offences Act* 1956, s.37 and Sched. 2. **14–17**

The Magistrates' Association advised that if the victim is a young girl the case ought to go to the Crown Court if the indecency is serious. Any suggestion of attempted penetration or use of force also indicates that the matter should be sent to the Crown Court for sentence. If there is any suggestion that the defendant is not of full adult capacity, it may be appropriate for sentence at summary level. Where the victim is an adolescent girl who "consents", consideration should be given to sending the matter to the Crown Court for sentence where there are features such as digital interference or oral sex: *Pickup* (1993) 14 Cr.App.R.(S.) 271, CA. (It should be noted that oral sex would now constitute rape).

In *Tanyildz* (1998) 1 Cr.App.R.(S.) 362, the offender assaulted a woman on an underground train by pushing his erect penis against her on three occasions. He was sentenced to three months' imprisonment. See also *Townsend* (1994) 16 Cr.App.R.(S.) 553, CA, three months' imprisonment where the offender indecently assaulted female passenger on underground train.

The fact that the assault constitutes a breach of trust may result in a higher penalty. **14–18**
In *Att.-Gen.'s Reference (No. 25 of 1997) (Williams)* [1998] 1 Cr.App.R.(S.) 310, CA, the offender was a shop keeper who indecently assaulted a 15-year-old girl working at his shop on a work placement. His sentence of fines totalling £500 was varied to eight months' imprisonment by the Court of Appeal, the Court stating that this was a campaign of sexual harassment towards a girl in relation to whom he was in a position of trust. In *Owen* [2001] All E.R. (D) 96 (August) the offender pleaded guilty to indecently assaulting three girls aged 12 or 14 who stayed overnight with his daughter at parties at which he supplied alcohol. He was sentenced to four months' imprisonment in respect of each offence, to be served consecutively; the Court emphasising that the offences were sordid, and involved some deliberation as the offender had engineered the parties and excessive drinking. He had also acted in breach of trust. See *Att.-Gen.'s Reference (No. 70 of 2003)* [2004] 2 Cr.App.R.(S.) 49 for guidance on the circumstances in which a community sentence may be merited for an indecent assault.

E. LIVING ON THE EARNINGS OF PROSTITUTION

(1) Definition

Sexual Offences Act 1956, s.30

Man living on earnings of prostitution

30.—(1) It is an offence for a man knowingly to live wholly or in part on the earnings of prostitution. **14–19**

(2) For the purposes of this section a man who lives with or is habitually in the company of a prostitute, or who exercises control, direction or influence over a prostitute's movements in a way which shows he is aiding, abetting or compelling her prostitution with others, shall be presumed to be knowingly living on the earnings of prostitution, unless he proves the contrary.

[Repealed by the *Sexual Offences Act* 2003, Sched. 7, on May 1, 2004.]

(2) Allocation

14–20 This offence is triable either way: *Sexual Offences Act* 1956, s.37(2).

(3) Elements of the offence

14–21 The presumptions raised in section 30(2) are raised on proof that:

— the accused was living with the prostitute;

— he was habitually at the material time in her company;

— he exercised control, direction or influence over her movements in a way which showed him to be aiding or abetting her prostitution.

It is then presumed that he is living on immoral earnings and that he is doing so knowingly.

(4) Sentence

14–22 When tried summarily, the maximum penalty for this offence is six months' imprisonment, a fine not exceeding the statutory maximum or both: *Sexual Offences Act* 1956, s.37 and Sched. 2.

Sentencing guidance is given in *Farrugia* (1979) 69 Cr.App.R. 108, Lawton L.J. seeing the presence or absence of coercion as a crucial factor in the sentencing decision. In the absence of any evidence of coercion, whether physical or mental, or of corruption, the old maximum of two years' imprisonment was described as adequate. Anything exceeding two years should be reserved for a case where there is an element of coercion or there is strong evidence of corruption. Where the offender is running a business of encouraging prostitution, and the circumstances are such that he can be said to be living wholly or in part on the earnings of prostitution, the Court should keep in mind the desirability of taking the profit out of such a way of life.

In *Powell* [2001] 1 Cr.App.R.(S.) 76 the offender's sentence of five years' imprisonment following his conviction for living on the earnings of prostitution was upheld. The victim had been ordered to work as a prostitute by the offender and she agreed because she was scared of him. It was held that five years' imprisonment was not inappropriate where coercion and corruption was evidenced.

Where the prostitute is carrying on her own business without coercion or corruption by the offender a more lenient approach will be taken: *Charlery* (1988) 10 Cr.App.R.(S.) 53, a sentence of four months' imprisonment plus a fine of £1,500 was imposed.

F. WOMAN EXERCISING CONTROL OVER PROSTITUTE

(1) Definition

Sexual Offences Act 1956, s.31

Woman exercising control over prostitute

14–23 **31.** It is an offence for a woman for purposes of gain to exercise control, direction or influence over a prostitute's movements in a way which shows she is aiding, abetting or compelling her prostitution.

[Repealed by the *Sexual Offences Act* 2003, Sched. 7, on May 1, 2004.]

(2) Allocation

14–24 This offence is triable either way: *Sexual Offences Act* 1956, s.37(2) and Sched. 2, para. 1.

(3) Sentence

14–25 When tried summarily, the maximum penalty for this offence is six months' imprisonment, a fine not exceeding the statutory maximum or both: *Sexual Offences Act* 1956, s.37 and Sched. 2.

G. Solicitation for Immoral Purposes

(1) Definition

Sexual Offences Act 1956, s.32

Solicitation by men

32. It is an offence for a man persistently to solicit or importune in a public place for immoral purposes. **14–26**

[Repealed by the *Sexual Offences Act* 2003, Sched. 7, on May 1, 2004.]

(2) Allocation

This offence is triable either way. **14–27**

(3) Elements of the offence

Two separate acts of importuning in the period constitute "persistently". An immoral purpose has to be some kind of sexual activity. **14–28**

(4) Sentence

When tried summarily, the maximum penalty for this offence is six months' imprisonment, a fine not exceeding the statutory maximum or both: *Sexual Offences Act* 1956, s.37(3) and Sched. 2, para. 32 and *Magistrates' Courts Act* 1980, ss.32, 34(3)(a). **14–29**

H. Keeping a Brothel

(1) Definition

Those offences contained in ss.33–36 of the 1956 Act were not repealed by the 2003 Act. Section 36 was amended so as to make no distinction between male and female prostitution and s.33A was inserted. **14–30**

Sexual Offences Act 1956, ss.33–36

Keeping a brothel

33. It is an offence for a person to keep a brothel, or to manage, or act or assist in the management of, a brothel. **14–31**

Keeping a brothel used for prostitution

33A.—(1) It is an offence for a person to keep, or to manage, or act or assist in the management of, a brothel to which people resort for practices involving prostitution (whether or not also for other practices). **14–32**

(2) In this section "prostitution" has the meaning given by section 51(2) of the *Sexual Offences Act* 2003.

Landlord letting premises for use as brothel

34. It is an offence for the lessor or landlord of any premises or his agent to let the whole or part of the premises with the knowledge that it is to be used, in whole or in part, as a brothel, or, where the whole or part of the premises is used as a brothel, to be wilfully a party to that use continuing. **14–33**

Tenant permitting premises to be used as brothel

35.—(1) It is an offence for the tenant or occupier, or person in charge, of any premises knowingly to permit the whole or part of the premises to be used as a brothel. **14–34**

(2) Where the tenant or occupier of any premises is convicted of knowingly permitting the whole or part of the premises to be used as a brothel, the First Schedule to this Act shall apply to enlarge the rights of the lessor or landlord with respect to the assignment or determination of the lease or other contract under which the premises are held by the person convicted.

(3) Where the tenant or occupier of any premises is so convicted, and either—

(a) the lessor or landlord, after having the conviction brought to his notice, fails or failed to exercise his statutory rights in relation to the lease or contract under which the premises are or were held by the person convicted; or

(b) The lessor or landlord, after exercising his statutory rights so as to determine that lease or contract, grants or granted a new lease or enters or entered into a new contract of tenancy of the premises to, with or for the benefit of the same person, without having all reasonable provisions to prevent the recurrence of the offence inserted in the new lease or contract;

then, if subsequently an offence under this section is committed in respect of the premises during the subsistence of the lease or contract referred to in paragraph (a) of this subsection or (where paragraph (b) applies) during the subsistence of the new lease or contract, the lessor or landlord shall be deemed to be a party to that offence unless he shows that he took all reasonable steps to prevent the recurrence of the offence.

References in this subsection to the statutory rights of a lessor or landlord refer to his rights under the First Schedule to this Act.

Tenant permitting premises to be used for prostitution

14–35 **36.** It is an offence for the tenant or occupier of any premises knowingly to permit the whole or part of the premises to be used for the purposes of habitual prostitution (whether any prostitute involved is male or female).

[These sections are printed as amended by *Sexual Offences Act* 2003. Section 33A was added by the *Sexual Offences Act* 2003, s.55.]

Sexual Offences Act 1967, s.6

6. Premises shall be treated for purposes of sections 33 to 35 of the Act of 1956 as a brothel if people resort to it for the purpose of lewd homosexual practices in circumstances in which resort thereto for lewd heterosexual practices would have led to its being treated as a brothel for the purposes of those sections.

(2) Allocation

14–36 These offences are triable summarily only: *Sexual Offences Act* 1956, s.37 and Sched. 2, except for the offence created by s.33A, which is triable either way.

(3) Elements of the offence

14–37 A brothel is a place where people of opposite sexes are allowed to resort for sexual intercourse, whether the women are common prostitutes or not: *Winter v. Woolfe* [1931] 1 K.B. 549. A place which is used by one woman for the purposes of her own prostitution is not a brothel: *Stevens v. Christy* (1987) 85 Cr.App.R. 249.

Therefore a person does not keep a brothel unless he/she is aware that the premises are being used by more than one prostitute for the purposes of prostitution.

It is not necessary to prove that normal sexual intercourse was offered on the premises to succeed in classifying a premises as a brothel, it will suffice to prove that more than one woman offered herself as a participant in physical acts of indecency for the gratification of men: *Kelly v. Purvis* [1983] Q.B. 663.

It is not necessary that a person charged with assisting the management of a brothel exercises control over the management of the brothel. That would be acting in the management of a brothel. The question of assisting in the management of a brothel is a question of fact: *Jones v. DPP* (1992) 96 Cr.App.R. 130.

(4) Sentence

14–38 For each section, the first commission of the offence carries a maximum penalty of three months' imprisonment, a fine not exceeding level three on the standard scale or both. For each section, for every offence committed after the first offence, the maximum penalty is six months' imprisonment, a fine not exceeding level five on the standard scale or both: *Sexual Offences Act* 1956, s.37 and Sched. 2.

Upon summary conviction the maximum sentence for the s.33A offence is six months' imprisonment and/or a fine. After commencement of the relevant provisions, the maximum custodial sentence in a magistrates' court will be 12 months' imprisonment: *Criminal Justice Act* 2003, ss.154 and 282.

In *Ramaj and Atesogullari* [2006] 2 Cr.App.R.(S.) 83, the appellants, a 22-year-old and a 19-year-old of previous good character were sentenced to 18 months' imprisonment (amongst other sentences) for keeping a brothel contrary to s.33A. The operation was amateurish and operable for only four days. The sentence was reduced to three months' imprisonment (*Rousseau* [2003] 1 Cr.App.R.(S.) 15 and *Middleton* [2005] 1 Cr.App.R.(S.) 42 were considered).

When tried on indictment the maximum penalty is seven years' imprisonment.

See also *Bao* [2008] 2. Cr.App.R.(S.) 61and *Moir* [2008] 2 Cr.App.R.(S) 242 both of which were prior to the implementation of the new guidelines. In *Baker and Griffiths* [2008] 2 Cr.App.R.(S.) 416, decided after implementation of the Sentencing Guidelines, the defendants were involved in the running of two brothels, the first brothel for 10 months and the second for four months. The first defendant was 57 and of good character the second was 52 and had unrelated convictions, they pleaded guilty on the first day of trial. The first defendant owned the two premises; he paid for advertising, provided condoms and oversaw the running of the brothel. The second defendant initially helped out and then took over the running of the second brothel. The prostitutes were all professional and there was no evidence of threats or coercion. On appeal the sentence of D1 was reduced from 18 months imprisonment to nine months imprisonment and the sentence of D2 was reduced from 10 months imprisonment to five months imprisonment. The Court took into particular consideration the fact that there was an absence of coercion or corruption in the recruitment and control of the prostitutes, the small scale of operation, lack of sophistication and the guilty pleas.

In *Shi and Yang* [2009] 1 Cr.App.R.(S.) 484, D1 who was 26, with leave to enter the country and of good character and D2 who was 34, an illegal immigrant and of good character, ran a brothel for four months in a rented property and with advertisements being placed in a local paper. D1 visited the premises from time to time to check on its management; D2 had introduced undercover officers who visited the premises to a prostitute and admitted to working as one herself over a two week period; D1 considered he had done nothing wrong; on pleas of guilty to keeping a brothel used for prostitution and possession of criminal property, sentences of 21 months' (D1) and 15 months' imprisonment (D2) were too high, but recommendations for deportation upheld; considering the Sentencing Guidelines Council's definitive guideline, D1 fell just into the top bracket and D2 fell into the second bracket, having looked at the facts, the guideline and the mitigation, 16 months (D1) and 10 months (D2) substituted; as to deportation, the offences were serious and both offenders were involved in a commercial enterprise that encouraged the influx of illegal immigrants and thrived on their exploitation, extracting substantial profit for the organisers.

Part III

STARTING POINTS AND SENTENCING RANGES (BASED ON A FIRST TIME OFFENDER AFTER TRIAL):

14–39

Examples of nature of activity	Starting Point	Range
Involvement of the offender was minimal	Medium level community order	Band C fine to high level community order
Offender is the keeper of the brothel and is personally involved in its management	Crown Court	26 weeks to Crown Court
Offender is the keeper of a brothel and has made substantial profits in the region of £5000 and upwards	Crown Court	Crown Court

OFFENCE SERIOUSNESS (CULPABILITY AND HARM)

Factors indicating higher culpability	Factors indicating lower culpability
1. Background of threats, intimidation or coercion 2. Large-scale commercial operation 3. Personal involvement in the prostitution of others 4. Abduction or detention 5. Financial or other gain	1. Using employment as a route out of prostitution and not actively involved in exploitation 2. Coercion by a third party

I. LOITERING OR SOLICITING FOR THE PURPOSE OF PROSTITUTION

(1) Definition

Street Offences Act 1959, ss.1 and 1A

Loitering or soliciting for purposes of prostitution

14–40 **1.**—(1) It shall be an offence for a person (whether male or female) persistently to loiter or solicit in a street or public place for the purpose of prostitution.

(2) A person guilty of an offence under this section shall be liable on summary conviction to a fine of an amount not exceeding level 2 on the standard scale, or, for an offence committed after a previous conviction, to a fine of an amount not exceeding level 3 on that scale.

(2A) The court may deal with a person convicted of an offence under this section by making an order requiring the offender to attend three meetings with the person for the time being specified in the order ("the supervisor") or with such other person as the supervisor may direct.

(2B) The purpose of an order under subsection (2A) is to assist the offender, through attendance at those meetings, to—

(a) address the causes of the conduct constituting the offence, and

(b) find ways to cease engaging in such conduct in the future.

(2C) Where the court is dealing with an offender who is already subject to an order under subsection (2A), the court may not make a further order under that subsection unless it first revokes the existing order.

(2D) If the court makes an order under subsection (2A) it may not impose any other penalty in respect of the offence.

(4) For the purposes of this section

(a) conduct is persistent if it takes place on two or more occasions in any period of three months;

(b) any reference to a person loitering or soliciting for the purposes of prostitution is a reference to a person loitering or soliciting for the purposes of offering services as a prostitute;

(c) "street" includes any bridge, road, lane, footway, subway, square, court, alley or passage, whether a thoroughfare or not, which is for the time being open to the public; and the doorways and entrances of premises abutting on a street (as hereinbefore defined), and any ground adjoining and open to a street, shall be treated as forming part of the street.

[This section is printed as amended by the *Criminal Justice Act* 1982, s.1(2), the *Sexual Offences Act* 2003, Sched. 1, the *Serious Organised Crime and Police Act* 2005, Sched. 17 and the *Policing and Crime Act* 2009, ss.16 and 17 with effect from April 1, 2010.]

Part III

Orders under section 1(2A): supplementary

1A.—(1) This section applies to an order under section 1(2A).

(2) The order may not be made unless a suitable person has agreed to act as supervisor in relation to the offender.

(3) In subsection (2) "suitable person" means a person appearing to the court to have appropriate qualifications or experience for helping the offender to make the best use of the meetings for the purpose mentioned in section 1(2B).

(4) The order must specify—

(a) a date (not more than six months after the date of the order) by which the meetings required by the order must take place;

(b) the local justice area in which the offender resides or will reside while the order is in force.

(5) The supervisor must determine—

(a) the times of the meetings required by the order and their duration, and

(b) the places at which they are held.

(6) The supervisor must—

(a) make any arrangements that are necessary to enable the meetings required by the order to take place; and

(b) once the order has been complied with, notify the court which made the order of that fact.

(7) The court making the order must provide copies of it to the offender and the supervisor.

(8) Subsection (9) applies where—

(a) the order is made by the Crown Court, or

(b) the order is made by a magistrates' court but specifies a local justice area for which the court making the order does not act.

(9) The court must provide to a magistrates' court acting for the local justice area specified in the order—

(a) a copy of the order, and

(b) any documents and information relating to the case that it considers likely to be of assistance to that court in the exercise of any functions in relation to the order.

(10) The order ceases to be in force (unless revoked earlier under section 1(2C) or under the Schedule to this Act)—

(a) at the end of the day on which the supervisor notifies the court that the order has been complied with, or

(b) at the end of the day specified in the order under subsection (4)(a),

whichever first occurs.

(11) The Schedule to this Act (which relates to failure to comply with orders under section 1(2A) and to the revocation or amendment of such orders) has effect.

[This section was inserted by the *Policing and Crime Act* 2009, s.17 with effect from April 1, 2010.]

(2) Allocation

14–41 This offence is triable summarily: *Street Offences Act* 1959, s.1(2).

(3) Elements of the offence

14–42 This section applies regardless of the gender of the prostitute.

The person does not have to be present in the public place to which they project their solicitous efforts, yet they must be physically present to solicit. An advertisement displaying services will not suffice: *Weisz v. Monahan* [1962] 1 W.L.R. 262.

"Public place" is not defined in section 1 and is a question of fact for the magistrates.

(4) Sentence

14–43 The first offence under this section carries a maximum penalty of a fine not exceeding level two on the standard scale. Each offence after that conviction carries a maximum penalty of a fine not exceeding level three on the standard scale: *Street Offences Act* 1959, s.1(2). The *Policing and Crime Act* 2009 inserted section 1A into the Act to allow for the court, instead of sentencing a defendant for this offence, to impose an "engagement and support order". This is designed to rehabilitate rather than punish so that re-offending might be prevented. It requires a "suitable person" to be available to act as a supervisor. A new Schedule has also been inserted into the Act which applies to breaches, revocation and amendments of the orders.

J. INDECENCY WITH CHILDREN

(1) Definition

Indecency with Children Act 1960, s.1

Indecent conduct towards young child

14–44 **1.**—(1) Any person who commits an act of gross indecency with or towards a child under the age of sixteen or who incites a child under that age to such an act with him or another, shall be liable on conviction on indictment to imprisonment for a term not exceeding ten years, or on summary conviction to imprisonment for a term not exceeding six months, to a fine not exceeding the prescribed sum, or to both.

(2) [...]

(3) References in the *Children and Young Persons Act* 1933 to the offences mentioned in the First Schedule to that Act shall include offences under this section.

(4) Offences under this section shall be deemed to be offences against the person for the purpose of section three of the *Visiting Forces Act* 1952 (which restricts the trial by United Kingdom courts of offenders connected with visiting forces).

[This section is repealed by the *Sexual Offences Act* 2003, Sched. 7, on May 1, 2004.]

(2) Allocation

This offence is triable either way: s.1(1). 14–45

(3) Elements of the offence

There must be an act, but allowing a child to continue an activity may constitute an act. 14–46

(4) Sentence

When tried summarily, the maximum penalty for this offence is imprisonment for a term not exceeding six months, a fine not exceeding £400 or both: s.1(1). 14–47

K. MISCELLANEOUS OFFENCES

(1) Outraging public decency

(a) *Definition*

The common law offence of outraging public decency makes it an offence to do an act of a lewd, obscene or disgusting nature in public which outrages public decency. 14–48

(b) *Allocation*

The offence is triable either way. (See s.320 of the *Criminal Justice Act* 2003.) 14–49

(c) *Elements*

The prosecution must prove behaviour that is 14–50
— lewd;
— obscene;
— disgusting;
— committed in a public place;
— which outrages public decency.

Many of the offences under the *Sexual Offences Act* 2003 automatically fall within this description such as exposure (s.66), voyeurism (s.67) and sexual activity in a public lavatory (s.71). The common law may be reserved for serious examples of such activity or other types of behaviour with sexual connotations which does not amount to an offence under the Act.

Obscene

Obscenity was referred to in *Stanley* [1965] 2 Q.B. 327 as being something that offended against the recognized standards of propriety, indecent being at the lower end of the scale and obscene at the upper end of the scale. 14–51

Disgusting

In *Choi* [1999] EWCA Crim 1279 where the defendant filmed a woman urinating in a public toilet, the word disgusting was held to cover an act that "filled the onlooker with loathing or extreme distaste or caused the onlooker extreme annoyance". 14–52

Public Place

The offence must be committed in a public place where members of the public might witness it. There is a common law rule that at least two members of the public must witness or be in a position to witness the act. In *Hamilton* [2007] EWCA Crim 2062 the de- 14–53

Part III

fendant hid a camera in his bag and put it on the floor in a shop in order to film up women's skirts. It was held that the way the filming was done was capable of being seen in the shop even if no-one had actually seen it and the conviction was upheld. But in *Rose v DPP* [2006] EWHC 852 a conviction was quashed for a couple who performed a sex act in the public foyer of a bank after midnight. The offence only came to light when the manageress watched CCTV of the area the next day. It was held this had not been witnessed by two people so the offence was not made out. See also *F* [2010] EWCA Crim 2243.

It is sufficient for the only two witnesses to be police officers: *Mayling* [1963] 2 Q.B. 717 . In *Walker* [1996] 1 Cr.App.R. 111 the appellant invited two young girls into his home and exposed himself to them in his living room. It was held this was not a public place and as there was no risk of his conduct being witnessed by the general public the offence was not made out. However, the offence is committed if the indecent act occurred in a private place but was still capable of being seen by members of the public.

Outraging Public decency

14–54 To outrage public decency the act must be such that ordinary members of the public are outraged. In *Knuller (Publishing, Printing and Promoting Ltd) v DPP* [1973] A.C. 435 it was said that indecency includes anything which an ordinary decent man or woman would find to be shocking, disgusting and revolting. To be outraged is to be utterly disgusted which was a strong word going beyond simply being shocked. Having sex in a public place has been held to amount to the offence: *Curran* [1998] EWCA Crim 3048. There need be no intention to outrage public decency, a deliberate act suffices: *Gibson and Sylveire* [1990] 91 Cr.App.R. 341.

(c) *Sentence*

14–55 When tried summarily the maximum sentence is six months imprisonment or a fine not exceeding the statutory maximum. After commencement of the relevant provisions, the maximum custodial sentence will be 12 months imprisonment in the magistrates' court: *Criminal Justice Act* 2003, ss.154 and 282.

There are no Guidelines on sentence but reference may be had to the equivalent charges in the *Sexual Offences Act* 2003. In *Cosco* [2005] 2 Cr.App.R.(S.) 405 a case dealt with for offences committed before the Act came into force but sentenced after it, a sentence of 4 and a half years was reduced to 18 months imprisonment on a man who had exposed himself three times on a beach frequented by children. He had 13 previous convictions for offences of a similar nature. The guidelines for exposure and the maximum sentence for that offence were considered. See also *Miah* [2006] EWCA Crim 132 and *Birch* [2007] EWCA Crim 1008.

(2) Abuse of a position of trust

(a) *Definition*

Sexual Offences (Amendment) Act 2000, s.3

Abuse of position of trust

14–56 **3.**—(1) Subject to subsections (2) and (3) below, it shall be an offence for a person aged 18 or over—

(a) to have sexual intercourse (whether vaginal or anal) with a person under that age; or

(b) to engage in any other sexual activity with or directed towards such a person,

if (in either case) he is in a position of trust in relation to that person.

(2) Where a person ("A") is charged with an offence under this section of having sexual intercourse with, or engaging in any other sexual activity with or directed towards, another person ("B"), it shall be a defence for A to prove that, at the time of the intercourse or activity—

(a) he did not know, and could not reasonably have been expected to know, that B was under 18;
(b) he did not know, and could not reasonably have been expected to know, that B was a person in relation to whom he was in a position of trust; or
(c) he was lawfully married to or in civil partnership with B.

(3) It shall not be an offence under this section for a person ("A") to have sexual intercourse with, or engage in any other sexual activity with or directed towards, another person ("B") if immediately before the commencement of this Act—
(a) A was in a position of trust in relation to B; and
(b) a sexual relationship existed between them.

(4) A person guilty of an offence under this section shall be liable—
(a) on summary conviction, to imprisonment for a term not exceeding six months, or to a fine not exceeding the statutory maximum, or to both;
(b) on conviction on indictment, to imprisonment for a term not exceeding five years, or to a fine, or to both.

[Repealed by the *Sexual Offences Act* 2003, Sched. 7 on May 1, 2004. This section is printed as amended by the *Civil Partnership Act* 2004, s.261(2), Sched. 28, Pt 4, para. 62.]

(b) *Allocation*

This offence is triable either way: s.3(4). **14–57**

(c) *Elements of the offence*

Sexual Offences (Amendment) Act 2000, ss.3(5), 4

3.—(5) In this section, "sexual activity"— **14–58**
(a) does not include any activity which a reasonable person would regard as sexual only with knowledge of the intentions, motives or feelings of the parties; but
(b) subject to that, means any activity which such a person would regard as sexual in all the circumstances.

Part III

Meaning of "position of trust"

4.—(1) For the purposes of section 3 above, a person aged 18 or over ("A") is in a position of trust in relation to a person under that age ("B") if any of the four conditions set out below, or any condition specified in an order made by the Secretary of State by statutory instrument, is fulfilled. **14–59**

(2) The first condition is that A looks after persons under 18 who are detained in an institution by virtue of an order of a court or under an enactment, and B is so detained in that institution.

(3) The second condition is that A looks after persons under 18 who are resident in a home or other place in which—
(a) accommodation and maintenance are provided by an authority under section 23(2) of the *Children Act* 1989 or Article 27(2) of the *Children (Northern Ireland) Order* 1995;
(b) accommodation is provided by a voluntary organisation under section 59(1) of that Act or Article 75(1) of that Order; or
(c) accommodation is provided by an authority under section 26(1) of the *Children (Scotland) Act* 1995,

and B is resident, and is so provided with accommodation and maintenance or accommodation, in that place.

(4) The third condition is that A looks after persons under 18 who are accommodated and cared for in an institution which is—
(a) a hospital;
(b) a residential care home, nursing home, mental nursing home or private hospital;
(bb) "care home service" has the meaning given by section 2(3) of the *Regulation of Care (Scotland) Act* 2001 (asp 8);
(c) a community home, voluntary home, children's home or residential establishment; or

(d) a home provided under section 82(5) of the *Children Act* 1989,
and B is accommodated and cared for in that institution.

(5) The fourth condition is that A looks after persons under 18 who are receiving full-time education at an educational institution, and B is receiving such education at that institution.

(6) No order shall be made under subsection (1) above unless a draft of the order has been laid before and approved by a resolution of each House of Parliament.

(7) A person looks after persons under 18 for the purposes of this section if he is regularly involved in caring for, training, supervising or being in sole charge of such persons.

(8) For the purposes of this section a person receives full-time education at an educational institution if—

(a) he is registered or otherwise enrolled as a full-time pupil or student at the institution; or

(b) he receives education at the institution under arrangements with another educational institution at which he is so registered or otherwise enrolled.

(9) In this section, except where the context otherwise requires—

"authority" means

(a) in relation to Great Britain, a local authority; and

(b) in relation to Northern Ireland, an authority within the meaning given by Article 2(2) of the *Children (Northern Ireland) Order* 1995;

"care home service" has the meaning given by section 2(3) of the *Regulation of Care (Scotland) Act* 2001 (asp 8);]

"children's home" has—

(a) in relation to England and Wales, the meaning which would be given by subsection (3) of section 63 of the *Children Act* 1989 if the reference in paragraph (a) of that subsection to more than three children were a reference to one or more children; and

(b) in relation to Northern Ireland, the meaning which would be given by Article 90(1) of the *Children (Northern Ireland) Order* 1995 if, in Article 91(2) of that Order, paragraphs (f) and (g) and the words after paragraph (h) were omitted;

"community home" has the meaning given by section 53(1) of the *Children Act* 1989;

"hospital" has—

(a) in relation to England and Wales, the meaning given by section 128(1) of the *National Health Service Act* 1977;

(b) in relation to Scotland, the meaning given by section 108(1) of the *National Health Service (Scotland) Act* 1978; and

(c) in relation to Northern Ireland, the meaning given by Article 2(2) of the *Health and Personal Social Services (Northern Ireland) Order* 1972;

"mental nursing home" has, in relation to England and Wales, the meaning given by section 22(1) of the *Registered Homes Act* 1984;

"nursing home" —

(a) in relation to England and Wales, has the meaning given by section 21(1) of the *Registered Homes Act* 1984;

(b) in relation to Scotland, means a nursing home registered under section 1 of the *Nursing Homes Registration (Scotland) Act* 1938; and

(c) in relation to Northern Ireland, has the meaning given by Article 16(1) of the *Registered Homes (Northern Ireland) Order* 1992;

"private hospital" —

(a) in relation to Scotland, means "private psychiatric hospital" within the meaning of section 77(1) of the *Regulation of Care (Scotland) Act* 2001 (asp 8); and

(b) in relation to Northern Ireland, the meaning given by Article 90(2) of the *Mental Health (Northern Ireland) Order* 1986;

"residential care home" —

(a) in relation to England and Wales, has the meaning given by section 1(2) of the *Registered Homes Act* 1984;

(b) in relation to Scotland, means an establishment in respect of which a person is registered under section 62 or 63 of the *Social Work (Scotland) Act* 1968; and

(c) in relation to Northern Ireland, has the meaning given by Article 3(1) of the *Registered Homes (Northern Ireland) Order* 1992;

"residential establishment" has the meaning given by section 93(1) of the *Children (Scotland) Act* 1995 as the meaning of that expression in relation to a place in Scotland;

"voluntary home" has—

(a) in relation to England and Wales, the meaning given by section 60(3) of the *Children Act* 1989; and

(b) in relation to Northern Ireland, the meaning given by Article 74(1) of the *Children (Northern Ireland) Order* 1995.

[This section is printed as amended by the *Regulation of Care (Scotland) Act* 2001, s.79, Sched. 3, para. 25.]

(d) *Sentence*

When tried summarily, the maximum penalty for this offence is six months' imprisonment, a fine not exceeding the statutory maximum or both: s.3(4). **14–60**

[The next paragraph is § 14–62.]

(3) Possession of indecent photographs of children

(a) *Definition*

Criminal Justice Act 1988, ss.160, 160A

Possession of indecent photograph of child

160.—(1) Subject to section 160A it is an offence for a person to have any indecent photograph or pseudo-photograph of a child in his possession. **14–62**

(2) Where a person is charged with an offence under subsection (1) above, it shall be a defence for him to prove—

(a) that he had a legitimate reason for having the photograph or pseudo-photograph in his possession; or

(b) that he had not himself seen the photograph or pseudo-photograph and did not know, nor had any cause to suspect, it to be indecent; or

(c) that the photograph or pseudo-photograph was sent to him without any prior request made by him or on his behalf and that he did not keep it for an unreasonable time.

(2A) A person shall be liable on conviction on indictment of an offence under this section to imprisonment for a term not exceeding five years or a fine, or both

(3) A person shall be liable on summary conviction of an offence under this section to imprisonment for a term not exceeding six months or a fine not exceeding level 5 on the standard scale, or both.

(4) Sections 1(3), 2(3), 3 and 7 of the *Protection of Children Act* 1978 shall have effect as if any reference in them to that Act included a reference to this section.

[This section is printed as amended and repealed in part by the *CJPOA* 1994, ss.84(4)(a) and (b), 86(1) and 168(3) and Sched. 11; and the *CJCSA* 2000, s.41(3) (insertion of subs. (2A)). The amendment effected by the 2000 Act came into force on January 11, 2001: *Criminal Justice and Court Services Act 2000 (Commencement No. 1) Order* 2000 (S.I. 2000 No. 3302). There is no transitional provision in the statute or the commencement order. The combined effect of s.3 of the *Human Rights Act* 1998 and Art. 7 of the European Convention will, however, be such as to require that the increase in penalty should apply only to offences committed on or after the commencement date.]

Marriage and other relationships

160A.—(1) This section applies where, in proceedings for an offence under section 160 relating to an indecent photograph or pseudo-photograph of a child, the defendant proves that the **14–63**

photograph or pseudo-photograph was of the child aged 16 or over, and that at the time of the offence charged the child and he—

(a) were married or civil partners of each other, or

(b) lived together as partners in an enduring family relationship.

(2) This section also applies where, in proceedings for an offence under section 160 relating to an indecent photograph or pseudo-photograph of a child, the defendant proves that the photograph or pseudo-photograph was of the child aged 16 or over, and that at the time when he obtained it the child and he–

(a) were married or civil partners of each other, or

(b) lived together as partners in an enduring family relationship.

(3) This section applies whether the photograph or pseudo-photograph showed the child alone or with the defendant, but not if it showed any other person.

(4) If sufficient evidence is adduced to raise an issue as to whether the child consented to the photograph or pseudo-photograph being in the defendant's possession, or as to whether the defendant reasonably believed that the child so consented, the defendant is not guilty of the offence unless it is proved that the child did not so consent and that the defendant did not reasonably believe that the child so consented.

[This section is printed as amended by the *Sexual Offences Act* 2003, s.45, the *Civil Partnership Act* 2004, Sched. 27 and the *Coroners and Justice Act* 2009, s.69.]

(b) *Allocation*

14–64 This offence is triable either way: s.160(2A) and (3).

(c) *Elements of the offence*

14–65 The offence of possession is not committed unless the defendant knows he has the photographs in his possession: *Atkins v. DPP* [2000] 2 All E.R. 425, DC.

In the case of deleted computer images contained on the hard drive of a computer, if a person could not retrieve or gain access to an image without the use of specialist forensic techniques to which he did not have access, then he no longer has custody or control of them within the meaning of the section: *Porter* [2006] 2 Cr.App.R. 25. See *Stamford* and *Owen* for the test of indecency (§ 14–73).

In *Collier* [2005] 1 W.L.R. 843, where the defendant was charged with possessing indecent photographs of a child, it was held that the defence as set in s.160(2) of the *Criminal Justice Act* 2003 could be relied upon where the defendant suspected that the image was of an indecent nature, but had no cause to suspect that it was of a child.

Section 160A provides a "marriage defence".

(d) *Sentence*

14–66 When tried summarily, the maximum penalty for this offence is imprisonment for a term not exceeding six months, a fine not exceeding level five on the standard scale, or both: s.160(3). After commencement of the relevant provisions, the maximum custodial sentence in a magistrates' court will be 12 months' imprisonment: *Criminal Justice Act* 2003, ss.154 and 282.

Starting points and sentencing ranges: See table below at § 14–74 in respect of offences contrary to *Protection of Children Act* 1978, s.1.

Aggravating and mitigating factors: See table below at § 14–74 in respect of offences contrary to *Protection of Children Act* 1978, s.1.

The leading authority on sentencing for offences relating to the possession of child pornography was *Oliver* [2003] 1 Cr.App.R. 28. The Magistrates Courts Sentencing Guidelines are based on that case. In sentencing two factors need to be taken into consideration: the nature of the material and the extent of the offender's involvement with it. The material should be graded into levels.

Level 1	images depicting erotic posing with no sexual activity
Level 2	non-penetrative sexual activity between children or solo masturbation
Level 3	non-penetrative sexual activity between adults and children
Level 4	penetrative sexual activity involving a child or children, or both children and adults
Level 5	sadism or penetration of or by an animal

Aggravating features include the proximity to the sexual abuse; commercial activity; wide-scale distribution even for little or no profit; original films or photographs are more serious than downloads; to actually download an image rather than just view it on the internet is more serious. In cases on the cusp of the custody threshold suitability for treatment should be considered. A fine would normally be appropriate where the offender was in possession of material solely for his own use and the material was no more than a small quantity of level 1 material. A community sentence may be appropriate in a case of possession of a large amount of level (i) material, and/or a small amount of level 2 material, provided it has not been distributed. Simple possession of a large amount of level 2 or a small amount of level 3 material will usually result in a sentence of up to six months' imprisonment. Showing or distributing a large amount of level 2 or a small amount of level 3 material, or possessing a small amount of level 4 or 5 material may result in a sentence of up to 12 months' imprisonment.

In *Gardner* [2006] EWCA Crim 2439, the Court of Appeal considered *Oliver* (*ante*) in which it was said "some, but not much, weight should be attached to good character". The appellant in this case was a soldier who in mitigation asserted positive good character. The court held that it was impossible to believe that such an assertion was not relevant to mitigation and suspended an immediate sentence of nine months' imprisonment.

Part III

(4) Indecent photographs of children

(a) *Definition*

Protection of Children Act 1978, ss.1–1B

Indecent photographs of children

1.—(1) Subject to sections 1A and 1B it is an offence for a person— **14–67**

(a) to take, or permit to be taken or to make, any indecent photograph or pseudo-photograph of a child; or

(b) to distribute or show such indecent photographs or pseudo-photographs; or

(c) to have in his possession such indecent photographs or pseudo- photographs, with a view to their being distributed or shown by himself or others; or

(d) to publish or cause to be published any advertisement likely to be understood as conveying that the advertiser distributes or shows such indecent photographs or pseudo-photographs, or intends to do so.

(2) For purposes of this Act, a person is to be regarded as distributing an indecent photograph or pseudo-photograph if he parts with possession of it to, or exposes or offers it for acquisition by, another person.

(3) Proceedings for an offence under this Act shall not be instituted except by or with the consent of the Director of Public Prosecutions.

(4) Where a person is charged with an offence under subsection (1)(b) or (c), it shall be a defence for him to prove—

(a) that he had a legitimate reason for distributing or showing the photographs or pseudo-photographs or (as the case may be) having them in his possession; or

(b) that he had not himself seen the photographs or pseudo-photographs and did not know, nor had any cause to suspect, them to be indecent.

(5) References in the *Children and Young Persons Act* 1933 (except in sections 15 and 99') to the offences mentioned in Schedule 1 to that Act shall include an offence under subsection (1)(a) above.

Marriage and other relationships

14-68 **1A.**—(1) This section applies where, in proceedings for an offence under section 1(1)(a) of taking or making an indecent photograph or pseudo-photograph of a child, or for an offence under section 1(1)(b) or (c) relating to an indecent photograph or pseudo-photograph of a child, the defendant proves that the photograph or pseudo-photograph was of the child aged 16 or over, and that at the time of the offence charged the child and he—

(a) were married, or civil partners of each other, or

(b) lived together as partners in an enduring family relationship.

(2) Subsections (5) and (6) also apply where, in proceedings for an offence under section 1(1)(b) or (c) relating to an indecent photograph of a child, the defendant proves that the photograph or pseudo-photograph was of the child aged 16 or over, and that at the time when he obtained it the child and he—

(a) were married, or civil partners of each other, or

(b) lived together as partners in an enduring family relationship.

(3) This section applies whether the photograph [or pseudo-photograph] showed the child alone or with the defendant, but not if it showed any other person.

(4) In the case of an offence under section 1(1)(a), if sufficient evidence is adduced to raise an issue as to whether the child consented to the photograph or pseudo-photograph being taken or made, or as to whether the defendant reasonably believed that the child so consented, the defendant is not guilty of the offence unless it is proved that the child did not so consent and that the defendant did not reasonably believe that the child so consented.

(5) In the case of an offence under section 1(1)(b), the defendant is not guilty of the offence unless it is proved that the showing or distributing was to a person other than the child.

(6) In the case of an offence under section 1(1)(c), if sufficient evidence is adduced to raise an issue both—

(a) as to whether the child consented to the photograph or pseudo-photograph being in the defendant's possession, or as to whether the defendant reasonably believed that the child so consented, and

(b) as to whether the defendant had the photograph or pseudo-photograph in his possession with a view to its being distributed or shown to anyone other than the child,

the defendant is not guilty of the offence unless it is proved either that the child did not so consent and that the defendant did not reasonably believe that the child so consented, or that the defendant had the photograph or pseudo-photograph in his possession with a view to its being distributed or shown to a person other than the child.

Exception for criminal proceedings, investigations etc.

14-69 **1B.**—(1) In proceedings for an offence under section 1(1)(a) of making an indecent photograph or pseudo-photograph of a child, the defendant is not guilty of the offence if he proves that—

(a) it was necessary for him to make the photograph or pseudo-photograph for the purposes of the prevention, detection or investigation of crime, or for the purposes of criminal proceedings, in any part of the world,

(b) at the time of the offence charged he was a member of the Security Service, and it was necessary for him to make the photograph or pseudo-photograph for the exercise of any of the functions of the Service, or

(c) at the time of the offence charged he was a member of GCHQ, and it was necessary for him to make the photograph or pseudo-photograph for the exercise of any of the functions of GCHQ.

(2) In this section "GCHQ" has the same meaning as in the *Intelligence Services Act* 1994.

[Sections 1, 1A and 1B are printed as amended and repealed in part by the *CJPOA* 1994, ss.84(2), 168(3), Sched. 11 and the *Civil Partnership Act* 2004, Sched. 27, para. 60, which came into force on December 5, 2005 and the *Coroners and Justice Act* 2009, s.69(1).]

The 1978 legislation was not repealed but was amended by the 2003 Act, s.45 so as to extend the protection to children aged 16 and 17. A marriage defence is also included at section 1A. The marriage defence applies provided the defendant and the subject were married at the time of the offence charged. The photograph must show the subject alone or with the defendant, but not any third party, and must be of the subject aged 16 or over.

In terms of consent, where the charge is one of taking a photo, the evidential burden lies on the defendant to show that the subject consented or, the defendant reasonably believed that to be so. It is then for the prosecution to rebut that. Where the charge is under section 1(1)(c) the prosecution must prove absence of consent.

Protection of Children Act 1978, ss.4, 5

Entry, search and seizure

4.—(1) The following applies where a justice of the peace is satisfied by information on oath, laid by or on behalf of the Director of Public Prosecutions or by a constable, that there is reasonable ground for suspecting that, in any premises, there is an indecent photograph or pseudo-photography of a child. **14–70**

(2) The justice may issue a warrant under his hand authorising any constable to enter (if need be by force) and search the premises, and to seize and remove any articles which he believes (with reasonable cause) to be or include indecent photographs or pseudo-photographs of children.

Forfeiture

5. The Schedule to this Act makes provision about the forfeiture of indecent photographs and pseudo-photographs. **14–71**

[This section is printed as amended and repealed in part by the *CJA* 1988, s.170(1) and Sched. 15, paras 61 and 62; the *CJPOA* 1994, s.168(1), (2) and Sched. 9, para. 23, and Sched. 10, para. 37; the *Courts Act* 2003, Sched. 8, paras 199(3) and para. 200; the *Criminal Justice Act* 1988, s.170(1), Sched. 15, paras 60, 61; the *Criminal Justice and Public Order Act* 1994, s.168(2), Sched. 10, para. 37(3); and the *Police and Justice Act* 2006, s.39.

Part III

(b) *Allocation*

This offence is triable either way: *Protection of Children Act* 1978, s.6(1). **14–72**

Proceedings may not be instituted without the consent of the DPP. The extra-territorial jurisdiction provisions of the*Sexual Offences Act* 2003 apply.

(c) *Elements of the offence*

Protection of Children Act 1978, s.7

Interpretation.

7.—(1) The following subsections apply for the interpretation of this Act. **14–73**

(2) References to an indecent photograph include an indecent film, a copy of an indecent photograph or film, and an indecent photograph comprised in a film.

(3) Photographs (including those comprised in a film) shall, if they show children and are indecent, be treated for all purposes of this Act as indecent photographs of children and so as respects pseudo-photographs.

(4) References to a photograph include—

(a) the negative as well as the positive version; and

(b) data stored on a computer disc or by other electronic means which is capable of conversion into a photograph.

(4A) References to a photograph also include—

(a) a tracing or other image, whether made by electronic or other means (of whatever nature)—

(i) which is not itself a photograph or pseudo-photograph, but

(ii) which is derived from the whole or part of a photograph or pseudo-photograph (or a combination of either or both); and

(b) data stored on a computer disc or by other electronic means which is capable of conversion into an image within paragraph (a); and subsection (8) applies in relation to such an image as it applies in relation to a pseudo-photograph.

(5) "Film" includes any form of video-recording.

(6) "Child", subject to subsection (8), means a person under the age of 18.

(7) "Pseudo-photograph" means an image, whether made by computer-graphics or otherwise howsoever, which appears to be a photograph.

(8) If the impression conveyed by a pseudo-photograph is that the person shown is a child, the pseudo-photograph shall be treated for all purposes of this Act as showing a child and so shall a pseudo-photograph where the predominant impression conveyed is that the person shown is a child notwithstanding that some of the physical characteristics shown are those of an adult.

(9) References to an indecent pseudo-photograph include—

(a) a copy of an indecent pseudo-photograph; and

(b) data stored on a computer disc or by other electronic means which is capable of conversion into an indecent pseudo-photograph.

[This section is printed as amended by the *Criminal Justice and Public Order Act* 1994, s.84, the *Sexual Offences Act* 2003, s.45 and the *Criminal Justice and Immigration Act* 2008, s.69.]

Section 7 of the *Protection of Children Act* 1978 gives the definition of "photograph" and "pseudo-photograph" to include any derivatives of photographs or pseudo-photographs, including line-traced and computer traced images, such as pencil-traced images using tracing paper, computer traced images of photographs or pseudo-photographs taken on mobile phones or images manipulated from photographs or pseudo-photographs using computer software. In such cases, the prosecution will have to show that the image or tracing has been derived from an indecent photograph or pseudo-photograph of a child or a combination of both.

In deciding whether the photograph is indecent, the test to be applied is the recognised standard of propriety: *Stamford* [1972] 2. Q.B. 391. In a case of "taking", the circumstances and motivation of the taker of the photograph may be relevant as to whether his taking was accidental or intentional; it would not be relevant for determining whether the photograph was indecent: *Graham-Kerr* (1989) 88 Cr.App.R. 302, CA and *Smethurst* [2002] 1 Cr.App.R. 6, CA. In determining whether the photograph is indecent the age of the child is of relevance: *Owen* (1988) 86 Cr.App.R. 291, CA.

Opening an email attachment of an indecent photograph may constitute "making" the photograph or pseudo-photograph if at the time it was opened, the individual did so intentionally and with the knowledge that what he was "making" was, or was likely to be an indecent image of a child. The same would apply to downloading an image from the internet to a computer screen. It is not necessary to prove in either scenario that the individual intended to save the image: *Bowden* [2000] 1 Cr.App.R. 438; *Atkins v. DPP* [2000] 2 Cr.App.R. 248, DC.

Responding to an advertisement offering to supply indecent photographs of children by placing an order may amount to an offence of inciting the commission of an offence of distribution of indecent photographs of children, contrary to s.1(1)(b), or an attempt if the order was never received. Likewise, the supplier would be guilty of an offence of distribution as distinct from an offence relating to the advertisement: *Goldman* [2001] Crim.L.R. 822, CA; see also, *R. (O.)* [2004] Crim.L.R. 948, DC.

Where indecent photographs of a child were stored in a shared folder, the offence of possessing indecent photographs of a child with a view to distributing them would be made out if the intention in storing them in a shared folder was in order for other users to have access to them: *Dooley* [2006] 1 W.L.R. 775.

In *Collier* [2005] 1 W.L.R. 843, where the defendant was charged with possessing indecent photographs of a child, it was held that the defence as set in s.160(2) of the *Criminal Justice Act* 2003 could be relied upon where the defendant suspected that the image was of an indecent nature, but had no cause to suspect that it was of a child.

In *Price* [2006] EWCA Crim 3363, it was held that the offence under s.1(1)(b) of the 1978 Act is one of strict liability, subject to the defence set out in s.1(4).

(d) *Sentence*

When tried summarily, the maximum penalty for this offence is imprisonment for a term not exceeding six months, a fine not exceeding the prescribed sum or both: *Protection of Children Act* 1978, s.6(3). After commencement of the relevant provisions, the maximum custodial sentence in a magistrates' court will be 12 months' imprisonment: *Criminal Justice Act* 2003, ss.154 and 282. In accordance with s.80 and Sched. 3 to the *Sexual Offences Act* 2003, automatic notification requirements apply upon conviction to an offender aged 18 or over where the offence involved photographs of children aged under 16. **14–74**

STARTING POINTS AND SENTENCING RANGES: (BASED ON A FIRST TIME OFFENDER AFTER TRIAL)

Examples of nature of activity	**Starting Point**	**Range**
Possession of a large amount of level 1 material and/or no more than a small amount of level 2, and the material is for personal use and has not been distributed or shown to others	Medium level community order	Band C fine to high level community order
Offender in possession of a large amount of material at level 2 or a small amount at level 3 Offender has shown or distributed material at level 1 on a limited scale Offender has exchanged images at level 1 or 2 with other collectors, but with no element of financial gain	12 weeks custody	4–26 weeks custody

Part III

Examples of nature of activity	Starting Point	Range
Possession of a large quantity of level 3 material for personal use Possession of a small number of images at level 4 or 5 Large number of level 2 images shown or distributed Small number of level 3 images shown or distributed	26 weeks custody	4 weeks custody—Crown Court
Possession of a large quantity of level 4 or 5 material for personal use only Large number of level 3 images shown or distributed	Crown Court	26 weeks custody—Crown Court
Offender traded material at levels 1–3 Level 4 or 5 images shown or distributed Offender involved in the production of material of any level	Crown Court	Crown Court

OFFENCE SERIOUSNESS (CULPABILITY AND HARM)

Factors indicating higher culpability	**Factors indicating lower culpability**
1. Collection is systematically stored or organized, indicating a sophisticated approach to trading or a high level of personal interest. 2. Use of drugs, alcohol or other substance to facilitate the offence of making or taking 3. Background of intimidation or coercion 4. Threats to prevent victim reporting the activity 5. Threats to disclose victim's activity to friends/relatives 6. Financial or other gain **Factors indicating greater degree of harm** 1. Images shown or distributed to others, especially children 2. Images stored, made available or distributed in such a way that they can be inadvertently accessed by others	1. A few images held solely for personal use 2. Images viewed but not stored 3. A few images held solely for personal use and it is established that the subject is aged 16 or 17 and that he or she was consenting

In *Toomer* [2001] 2 Cr.App.R.(S.) 8, the Court of Appeal issued guidance on sentencing under this section, Kennedy L.J. stating that: **14–75**

> "First, sentences up to statutory maximum should be imposed where there is a contested case, and there is evidence of commercial or large scale exploitation, and the amount of material is significant, especially if the offender has previous convictions.
> Secondly, non-custodial disposals should normally be reserved for isolated offences where the amount of material is very small, and it is for personal use, or use within a very restricted circle, as for example by passing it to one other recipient, when there is no commercial element and the defendant has pleaded guilty and is a first offender. Thirdly, where between those two extremes a particular case falls, will depend on the circumstances, and in particular on, first of all, the quality and nature of the material and the quantity thereof, and whether there is any element of exploitation or commercial gain.
> Thirdly, whether the offence is simply one of making; that is to say, in most cases downloading and saving or also involves distribution and, if so, to what extent there has been distribution, whether it has been by e-mail to a single specified recipient, or whether the distribution has been significantly more widespread.
> Fourthly, the character of the defendant is an important factor, and also the effect of the conviction upon the individual.
> Finally, it is of great importance to consider whether there has been a plea of guilty coupled with co-operation from the outset in the investigation."

14–76 In *Jefferson* [2001] EWCA Crim 1278, the offender, 56, was a man of good character who admitted downloading indecent images of children. The images were for his own use and he said he did not know such action was a crime. His appeal against a sentence of three months' imprisonment was allowed, the Court stating that a fine would have been the appropriate penalty, however, as he had served four weeks of his prison sentence he was conditionally discharged. Aggravating factors will include the degree of obscenity involved in the image, the age and number of children involved, whether the children were of one or both sexes and the nature of the conduct to which they were subjected or in which they are depicted as taking part: *Allison* [2001] EWCA Crim 1971 (six months' imprisonment where offender pleaded guilty to distributing indecent photographs or pseudo indecent photographs of children). In *Sturgess* [2010] EWCA Crim 2550 the defendant was convicted of 12 counts of voyeurism and three of taking indecent photographs of a child. He had been taking video films of guests staying in his holiday-let property by using concealed cameras. Three of the photographs were of teenage girls. It was held that the offences were extremely grave so that a sentence of two years' imprisonment for the taking of the photographs and six months consecutive for the voyeurism was upheld.

(5) Extreme Pornography

Criminal Justice and Immigration Act 2008, ss.63, 64, 65, 66, 67

Possession of extreme pornographic images

14–77 **63.**—(1) It is an offence for a person to be in possession of an extreme pornographic image.

(2) An "extreme pornographic image" is an image which is both—

(a) pornographic, and

(b) an extreme image.

(3) An image is "pornographic" if it is of such a nature that it must reasonably be assumed to have been produced solely or principally for the purpose of sexual arousal.

(4) Where (as found in the person's possession) an image forms part of a series of images, the question whether the image is of such a nature as is mentioned in subsection (3) is to be determined by reference to—

(a) the image itself, and

(b) (if the series of images is such as to be capable of providing a context for the image) the context in which it occurs in the series of images.

(5) So, for example, where—

(a) an image forms an integral part of a narrative constituted by a series of images, and

(b) having regard to those images as a whole, they are not of such a nature that they must reasonably be assumed to have been produced solely or principally for the purpose of sexual arousal,

the image may, by virtue of being part of that narrative, be found not to be pornographic, even though it might have been found to be pornographic if taken by itself.

(6) An "extreme image" is an image which—

(a) falls within subsection (7), and

(b) is grossly offensive, disgusting or otherwise of an obscene character.

(7) An image falls within this subsection if it portrays, in an explicit and realistic way, any of the following—

(a) an act which threatens a person's life,

(b) an act which results, or is likely to result, in serious injury to a person's anus, breasts or genitals,

(c) an act which involves sexual interference with a human corpse, or

(d) a person performing an act of intercourse or oral sex with an animal (whether dead or alive),

and a reasonable person looking at the image would think that any such person or animal was real.

(8) In this section "image" means—

(a) a moving or still image (produced by any means); or

(b) data (stored by any means) which is capable of conversion into an image within paragraph (a).

(9) In this section references to a part of the body include references to a part surgically constructed (in particular through gender reassignment surgery).

(10) Proceedings for an offence under this section may not be instituted—

(a) in England and Wales, except by or with the consent of the Director of Public Prosecutions; or

(b) in Northern Ireland, except by or with the consent of the Director of Public Prosecutions for Northern Ireland.

Exclusion of classified films etc.

64.—(1) Section 63 does not apply to excluded images.

(2) An "excluded image" is an image which forms part of a series of images contained in a recording of the whole or part of a classified work.

(3) But such an image is not an "excluded image" if—

(a) it is contained in a recording of an extract from a classified work, and

(b) it is of such a nature that it must reasonably be assumed to have been extracted (whether with or without other images) solely or principally for the purpose of sexual arousal.

(4) Where an extracted image is one of a series of images contained in the recording, the question whether the image is of such a nature as is mentioned in subsection (3)(b) is to be determined by reference to—

(a) the image itself, and

(b) (if the series of images is such as to be capable of providing a context for the image) the context in which it occurs in the series of images;

and section 63(5) applies in connection with determining that question as it applies in connection with determining whether an image is pornographic.

(5) In determining for the purposes of this section whether a recording is a recording of the whole or part of a classified work, any alteration attributable to—

(a) a defect caused for technical reasons or by inadvertence on the part of any person, or

(b) the inclusion in the recording of any extraneous material (such as advertisements),

is to be disregarded.

(6) Nothing in this section is to be taken as affecting any duty of a designated authority to have regard to section 63 (along with other enactments creating criminal offences) in determining whether a video work is suitable for a classification certificate to be issued in respect of it.

(7) In this section—

"classified work" means (subject to subsection (8)) a video work in respect of which a classification certificate has been issued by a designated authority (whether before or after the commencement of this section);

"classification certificate" and "video work" have the same meanings as in the *Video Recordings Act* 1984 (c. 39);

"designated authority" means an authority which has been designated by the Secretary of State under section 4 of that Act;

"extract" includes an extract consisting of a single image;

"image" and "pornographic" have the same meanings as in section 63;

"recording" means any disc, tape or other device capable of storing data electronically and from which images may be produced (by any means).

(8) Section 22(3) of the *Video Recordings Act* 1984 (effect of alterations) applies for the purposes of this section as it applies for the purposes of that Act.

Defences: general

65.—(1) Where a person is charged with an offence under section 63, it is a defence for the person to prove any of the matters mentioned in subsection (2).

(2) The matters are—

Part III

(a) that the person had a legitimate reason for being in possession of the image concerned;

(b) that the person had not seen the image concerned and did not know, nor had any cause to suspect, it to be an extreme pornographic image;

(i) was sent the image concerned without any prior request having been made by or on behalf of the person, and

(ii) did not keep it for an unreasonable time.

(3) In this section "extreme pornographic image" and "image" have the same meanings as in section 63.

Defence: participation in consensual acts

66.—(1) This section applies where—

(a) a person ("D") is charged with an offence under section 63, and

(b) the offence relates to an image that portrays an act or acts within paragraphs (a) to (c) (but none within paragraph (d)) of subsection (7) of that section.

(2) It is a defence for D to prove—

(a) that D directly participated in the act or any of the acts portrayed, and

(b) that the act or acts did not involve the infliction of any non-consensual harm on any person, and

(c) if the image portrays an act within section 63(7)(c), that what is portrayed as a human corpse was not in fact a corpse.

(3) For the purposes of this section harm inflicted on a person is "non-consensual" harm if—

(a) the harm is of such a nature that the person cannot, in law, consent to it being inflicted on himself or herself; or

(b) where the person can, in law, consent to it being so inflicted, the person does not in fact consent to it being so inflicted.

Penalties etc. for possession of extreme pornographic images

67.—(1) This section has effect where a person is guilty of an offence under section 63.

(2) Except where subsection (3) applies to the offence, the offender is liable—

(a) on summary conviction, to imprisonment for a term not exceeding the relevant period or a fine not exceeding the statutory maximum or both;

(b) on conviction on indictment, to imprisonment for a term not exceeding 3 years or a fine or both.

(3) If the offence relates to an image that does not portray any act within section 63(7)(a) or (b), the offender is liable—

(a) on summary conviction, to imprisonment for a term not exceeding the relevant period or a fine not exceeding the statutory maximum or both;

(b) on conviction on indictment, to imprisonment for a term not exceeding 2 years or a fine or both.

(4) In subsection (2)(a) or (3)(a) "the relevant period" means—

(a) in relation to England and Wales, 12 months;

(b) in relation to Northern Ireland, 6 months.

Sections 63 to 68 of the *Criminal Justice and Immigration Act* 2008 create a new offence of being in possession of extreme pornographic images. Section 63(3) defines an image as "pornographic" if it is of such a nature that it must reasonably be assumed to have been produced solely or principally for the purposes of sexual arousal. If it is part of a series of images in determining whether the image is "pornographic" within the meaning of s.3 reference should be made to the context of the images (s.63(4)). Section 63(8) defines an "image" as moving or still (produced by any means) or data (stored by any means) which is capable of conversion into an image. An extreme image is defined as "grossly offensive, disgusting or otherwise of an obscene character" s.63(3) and if it portrays, in an explicit and realistic way, any of the acts listed in s.63(7).

In *Ping Chen Cheung* [2009] EWCA Crim 2965 it was held that the prosecution only have to prove physical possession of the images of extreme pornography and not that the nature of the images was known. The defendant had to prove on the balance of probabilities that he had not seen the images and neither knew or had cause to suspect they were extreme pornographic images. The statutory defence was available under s.65(1). In this case the defendant was found in possession of hundreds of DVDs, 8 of which concerned bestiality. It was held the prosecution only had to prove he was in possession of these DVDs and not that he knew the nature of the images concerned.

III. THE SEXUAL OFFENCES ACT 2003

A. INTRODUCTION

The *Sexual Offences Act* 2003 came into force on May 1, 2004. **14–78**

The Act re-codifies many existing offences and creates a number of new ones. The case law that follows emanates from offences charged under the previous legislation but remains valid nonetheless. All of the offences created in the 2003 Act are either triable either way or only on indictment, save for the single exception of the new offence of sexual activity in a public lavatory, which is triable only in the magistrates' court (see *post*, § 14–275). One feature of the Act is that it creates some widely defined offences with considerable overlap, thus placing considerable reliance on prosecutorial discretion. In July 2004, the Crown Prosecution Service produced guidance as to which offence should be charged under the new Act, and on priority between charging options. Additional information as to relevant considerations of prosecutors when charging can be found at *www.cps.gov.uk/legal*. The Sentencing Guidelines Council has issued a revised *Magistrates' Court Sentencing Guidelines* which will apply to sentencing decisions on or after August 4, 2008. These should be read in conjunction with the definitive guideline in relation to offences under the *Sexual Offences Act* 2003 published by the Sentencing Guidelines Council in April 2007. These guidelines are available from *www.sentencing-guideline.gov.uk*. Where the sexual offence has been committed in a domestic context reference should also be made to the Sentencing Council's guideline "Overarching Principles: Domestic Violence", published in December 2006.

Section 72 of the *Sexual Offences Act* 2003 (as amended by s.72 of the *Criminal Justice and Immigration Act* 2008) allows for the prosecution of sexual offences against children committed abroad. A British national or resident of the UK who travels abroad to commit sexual offences against children, regardless of whether their actions amount to a criminal offence in the country concerned, is liable to prosecution.

B. CONSENT—SS.74 TO 76

The legislation brings with it statutory provisions regarding consent contained in ss.74–76. The redefinition of consent is one of the most radical innovations in the 2003 Act. The decision in *DPP v. Morgan* [1976] A.C. 182 is replaced by the statutory definition. Under the new law the prosecution must prove that B (the complainant) did not consent and that A (the defendant) did not reasonably believe that B was consenting. An honest but unreasonable belief as to the consent of the complainant will no longer entitle the defendant to an acquittal. In determining whether the defendant's belief in consent is reasonable, the court will need to have regard to all the circumstances at the time in question, including any steps the defendant may have taken to establish that the complainant did consent to the sexual activity. The statute introduces both conclusive presumptions about consent (s.76) and "rebuttable" evidential presumptions about consent: s.75. **14–79**

Sexual Offences Act 2003, ss.74–76

"Consent"

74. For the purposes of this Part, a person consents if he agrees by choice, and has the freedom and capacity to make that choice. **14–80**

Evidential presumptions about consent

75.—(1) If in proceedings for an offence to which this section applies it is proved— **14–81**

Part III

(a) that the defendant did the relevant act,

(b) that any of the circumstances specified in subsection (2) existed, and

(c) that the defendant knew that those circumstances existed,

the complainant is to be taken not to have consented to the relevant act unless sufficient evidence is adduced to raise an issue as to whether he consented, and the defendant is to be taken not to have reasonably believed that the complainant consented unless sufficient evidence is adduced to raise an issue as to whether he reasonably believed it.

(2) The circumstances are that—

(a) any person was, at the time of the relevant act or immediately before it began, using violence against the complainant or causing the complainant to fear that immediate violence would be used against him;

(b) any person was, at the time of the relevant act or immediately before it began, causing the complainant to fear that violence was being used, or that immediate violence would be used, against another person;

(c) the complainant was, and the defendant was not, unlawfully detained at the time of the relevant act;

(d) the complainant was asleep or otherwise unconscious at the time of the relevant act;

(e) because of the complainant's physical disability, the complainant would not have been able at the time of the relevant act to communicate to the defendant whether the complainant consented;

(f) any person had administered to or caused to be taken by the complainant, without the complainant's consent, a substance which, having regard to when it was administered or taken, was capable of causing or enabling the complainant to be stupefied or overpowered at the time of the relevant act.

(3) In subsection (2)(a) and (b), the reference to the time immediately before the relevant act began is, in the case of an act which is one of a continuous series of sexual activities, a reference to the time immediately before the first sexual activity began.

Conclusive presumptions about consent

14–82 **76.**—(1) If in proceedings for an offence to which this section applies it is proved that the defendant did the relevant act and that any of the circumstances specified in subsection (2) existed, it is to be conclusively presumed—

(a) that the complainant did not consent to the relevant act, and

(b) that the defendant did not believe that the complainant consented to the relevant act.

(2) The circumstances are that—

(a) the defendant intentionally deceived the complainant as to the nature or purpose of the relevant act;

(b) the defendant intentionally induced the complainant to consent to the relevant act by impersonating a person known personally to the complainant.

C. SEXUAL ACTIVITY AND GENERAL INTERPRETATION

Sexual Offences Act 2003, ss.78 and 79

"Sexual"

14–83 **78.** For the purposes of this Part (except section 71), penetration, touching or any other activity is sexual if a reasonable person would consider that—

(a) whatever its circumstances or any person's purpose in relation to it, it is because of its nature sexual, or

(b) because of its nature it may be sexual and because of its circumstances or the purpose of any person in relation to it (or both) it is sexual.

Part 1: general interpretation

14–84 **79.**—(1) The following apply for the purposes of this Part.

(2) Penetration is a continuing act from entry to withdrawal.

(3) References to a part of the body include references to a part surgically constructed (in particular, through gender reassignment surgery).

(4) "Image" means a moving or still image and includes an image produced by any means and, where the context permits, a three-dimensional image.

(5) References to an image of a person include references to an image of an imaginary person.

(6) "Mental disorder" has the meaning given by section 1 of the *Mental Health Act* 1983 (c. 20).

(7) References to observation (however expressed) are to observation whether direct or by looking at an image.

(8) Touching includes touching—

(a) with any part of the body,

(b) with anything else,

(c) through anything, and in particular includes touching amounting to penetration.

(9) "Vagina" includes vulva.

(10) In relation to an animal, references to the vagina or anus include references to any similar part.

IV. OFFENCES UNDER THE SEXUAL OFFENCES ACT 2003

A. RAPE AND ASSAULT BY PENETRATION

(1) Definition

Sexual Offences Act 2003, ss.1 and 2

Rape

1.—(1) A person (A) commits an offence if— **14–85**

(a) he intentionally penetrates the vagina, anus or mouth of another person (B) with his penis,

(b) B does not consent to the penetration, and

(c) A does not reasonably believe that B consents.

(2) Whether a belief is reasonable is to be determined having regard to all the circumstances, including any steps A has taken to ascertain whether B consents.

(3) Sections 75 and 76 apply to an offence under this section.

(4) A person guilty of an offence under this section is liable, on conviction on indictment, to imprisonment for life.

Assault by penetration

2.—(1) A person (A) commits an offence if—

(a) he intentionally penetrates the vagina or anus of another person (B) with a part of his body or anything else:

(b) the penetration is sexual;

(c) B does not consent to the penetration, and

(d) A does not reasonably believe that B consents.

(2) Whether a belief is reasonable is to be determined having regard to all the circumstances, including any steps A has taken to ascertain whether B consents.

(3) Sections 75 and 76 apply to an offence under this section.

(4) A person guilty of an offence under this section is liable, on conviction on indictment, to imprisonment for life.

(2) Allocation

These offences are triable only on indictment. **14–86**

(3) Sentence

The maximum sentence is life imprisonment. An offender convicted of this offence is **14–87** automatically subject to notification requirements *SOA* 2003, s.80. See § 14–281.

In *Att.-Gen.'s Reference (No. 104 of 2004)* [2005] 1 Cr.App.R.(S.) 117 and *Min-*

shull [2004] EWCA Crim 2673, both concerning digital penetration, the Court of Appeal indicated that previous decisions regarding the level of sentence appropriate for indecent assault involving digital penetration could no longer be regarded as authoritative given the maximum sentence under s.2 of the *Sexual Offences Act* 2003 of life imprisonment. Sentences would be at a higher level than was previously appropriate for an offence of indecent assault.

In *Child* [2006] 1 Cr.App.R.(S.) 122 the appellant pleaded guilty to assault by penetration. The appellant had spent the evening socialising with the complainant and her boyfriend at a mutual friends' home. Later that evening they all went to sleep on a mattress in an upstairs room. In the night the complainant awoke to find the appellant had two fingers in her vagina. He also licked her. The complainant immediately raised the alarm and the appellant was removed from the house. The Court of Appeal considered the *Att.-Gen's Reference (No. 104 of 2004)*, see *ante*. The appeal was allowed in that the sentence of three years' imprisonment was substituted for two and a half years' imprisonment.

P. (John James) [2009] 1 Cr.App.R.(S.) 247 — the appellant pleaded guilty to assault by penetration of his two-year-old step-granddaughter by digitally penetrating her. He also took some indecent photographs of her and of the assault. Held: that a sentence of six years imprisonment was too high. Whilst the judge could not be criticised for choosing the first sentencing category, insufficient discount was given from the range to reflect the fact that there was minimal penetration (with a finger) and to avoid the anomaly of the sentence being on a par with rape. A starting point of seven and half years had been appropriate, taking into account discount for a plea, five years substituted.

B. SEXUAL ASSAULT

(1) Definition

Sexual Offences Act 2003, s.3

Sexual assault

14–88 **3.**—(1) A person (A) commits an offence if—

(a) he intentionally touches another person (B),

(b) the touching is sexual,

(c) B does not consent to the touching, and

(d) A does not reasonably believe that B consents.

(2) Whether a belief is reasonable is to be determined having regard to all the circumstances, including any steps A has taken to ascertain whether B consents.

(3) Sections 75 and 76 apply to an offence under this section.

(4) A person guilty of an offence under this section is liable—

(a) on summary conviction, to imprisonment for a term not exceeding 6 months or a fine not exceeding the statutory maximum or both;

(b) on conviction on indictment, to imprisonment for a term not exceeding 10 years.

(2) Allocation

14–89 This offence is triable either way. See Appendix F–57 for mode of trial guidelines.

(3) Elements of the offence

14–90 See *ante*, §§ 14–80–14–84 regarding consent and the definition of "touching".

Where the victim is under 13, there is no "reasonable belief in consent" defence.

In *H.* [2005] 2 Cr.App.R. 9, the Court ruled that where a man had grabbed at the trousers of a female complainant, shortly after asking her "Do you fancy a shag?", the touching was "sexual" for the purposes of s.79(8) and the behaviour amounted to a s.3 offence. The Court set out the correct approach where an activity may be sexual. There are two distinct questions which should be considered: first, whether the touching could, because of its nature, be sexual, and secondly, whether because of the circumstances or the purpose of any person in relation to it, it was sexual.

In *Heard* [2007] 1 Cr.App.R. 37 a man was charged with an offence contrary to s.3. He sought to rely on self-induced intoxication as defence, namely that he was unable to form the specific or purposive intent required to intentionally touch someone. The Court of Appeal held, that despite "intentional touching" being an element of the offence which has to be proved this was not a crime of specific intent, a defendant therefore could not rely on self-induced intoxication as a defence.

(4) Sentence

Upon summary conviction the maximum sentence is six months' imprisonment. After commencement of the relevant provisions, the maximum custodial sentence in a magistrates' court is 12 months' imprisonment: *Criminal Justice Act* 2003, ss.154 and 282. In accordance with s.80 of, and Sched. 3 to, the *Sexual Offences Act* 2003, automatic notification requirements apply upon conviction to an offender aged 18 or over where the victim was under 18; or a term of imprisonment or a community sentence of at least 12 months is imposed. See § 14–281. **14–91**

STARTING POINT AND RANGE (BASED ON A FIRST TIME OFFENDER AFTER TRIAL):

Type/nature of activity	Starting points	Sentencing ranges
Contact between naked genitalia of offender and naked genitalia, face or mouth of the victim	5 years custody if the victim is under 13 3 years custody if the victim is aged 13 or over	4–8 years custody 2–5 years custody
Contact between part of offender's body (other than the genitalia) with part of the victim's body (other than the genitalia)	26 weeks custody if the victim is under 13 Community order if the victim is aged 13 or over	4 weeks to 18 months custody An appropriate non-custodial sentence (community order or fine)

Part III

Contact between naked genitalia of offender and another part of victim's body. Contact with genitalia of victim by offender using part of his or her body other than the genitalia, or an object	2 years custody if the victim is under 13 12 months cutody if the victim is aged 13 or over	1–4 years custody 2 years custody
Contact between either the clothed genitalia of offender and naked genitalia of victim or naked genitalia of offender and clothed genitalia of victim		

AGGRAVATING AND MITIGATING CIRCUMSTANCES

Additional aggravating factors	**Additional mitigating factos**
1. Offender ejaculated or caused victim to ejaculate 2. Background of intimidation or coercion 3. Use of drugs, alcohol or other substance to facilitate the offence 4. Threats to prevent the victim reporting the incident 5. Abduction or detention 6. Offender aware that he or she is suffering from a sexually transmitted infection 7. Physical harm caused 8. Prolonged activity or contact	*Where the victim is aged 16 or over* Victim engaged in consensual sexual activity with the offender on the same occasion and immediately before the offence *Where the victim is under 16* Sexual activity between two children (one of whom is the offender) was mutually agreed and experimental Reasonable belief (by a young offender) that the victim was aged 16 or over Youth and immaturity of the offender Minimal or fleeting contact

Where the touching is brief and takes place over clothing, recent decisions of the Court of Appeal would suggest that the magistrates' court's sentencing powers are sufficient.

In *Gledhill* [2005] EWCA Crim 290, the appellant, aged 41, pleaded guilty to one count of sexual assault. He had approached the 17-year-old victim on the street twice and touched her upper leg and groin area over her trousers. He admitted the offence in interview. He had one similar previous conviction dating from 1981, but was otherwise of good character. The Court of Appeal took account of the strong mitigation available and the Pre-Sentence Report, which suggested that he would be susceptible to one-on-one treatment. The sentence of imprisonment was substituted with a three year community rehabilitation order.

In *Elvidge* [2005] EWCA Crim 1194, the Court of Appeal allowed an appeal against a sentence of eight months' imprisonment for an offence under section 3. The appellant had placed his hand on the complainant's seat in a pub, so that when she returned to her seat and sat down his hand went between her legs and touched her genitals over her trousers. The appellant was found guilty after trial, but had no previous convictions for sexual offences. The appeal was allowed in that a sentence of three months' imprisonment was substituted.

In *Mazzon* [2005] EWCA Crim 1702, the 23-year-old victim was followed into her hotel, at night, by the appellant who pushed her against a wall and touched her breast whilst his penis was exposed—his fly was undone. The appellant was 40-years-old and effectively of good character. The Court of Appeal was referred to *Jolil* [2003] EWCA Crim 3395 and *Hayworth* [2004] EWCA Crim 2243. The appeal was allowed in that six months' imprisonment was substituted for the original sentence of 15 months.

In *Bamonadio* [2005] EWCA Crim 3355, a sentence of six months' imprisonment was upheld where the appellant had rubbed himself against a 16-year-old girl, tried to kiss her, and pulled down her top to touch her breasts whilst attempting to pull her into an alleyway.

In *Wain* [2005] EWCA Crim 3488, the Court of Appeal considered the sentence for an offence contrary to s.7 of the Act (complainant under 13). The appellant had, whilst lying on the floor in a drunken stupor, opened the front of his trousers and grabbed the hand of an 11-year-old girl pulling it towards his crotch. He pleaded guilty at the magistrates' court; he had no previous convictions for sexual offences. The court substituted a three year community order with supervision requirements in order to reduce the risk of re-offending, but noted that a custodial sentence of around six months could well have been appropriate.

In *DPP v. Clutterbuck* [2007] 2 Cr.App.R.(S.) 16 the DPP appealed by way of case stated against the decision of a magistrates' court to sentence the respondent to a community order of less than 12 months, the impact of which meant that the respondent would be subject to a shorter period of registration on the sex offenders register, and would not be able to complete the full sex offenders programme which it was contended by probation would require a 24-month period. The questions posed for the High Court were (i) in light of the DPP's representations regarding how the court should approach sentencing, whether the decision of the court to impose a community order of less than 12 months was correct in law; (ii) the court should reconsider the length of the community order to enable a sex offenders' programme to be completed. Dismissing the appeal it was held that, the magistrates' had not erred in law, they had taken into consideration the effect the community order would have on the respondents' liberty, his previous good character and the pre-sentence report. In all the circumstances the community order of 11 months was appropriate.

In *Piper* [2008] 1 Cr.App.R.(S.) 545, the defendant aged 63 and of good character placed an advertisement looking for women "willing to flaunt it" and interested in earning £2,400 for six days work. A number of women responded and attended an interview in a hotel room. The defendant had a hidden video camera. He told them the job entailed posing with cars. They were asked to take their clothes off save for their underwear and then pose. He then measured them during which he was "careless with his hands". Seven women complained. He pleaded guilty to the seven counts of sexual assault at the first opportunity and was sentenced to 12 months' imprisonment concurrent on each count. Upholding the sentences the Court of Appeal said the offence involved planning, organisation, the women had not consented to being filmed or being touched, the whole interview process was a charade.

In *Att.-Gen.'s Reference (No. 70 of 2008) (R. v. W.), The Times*, February 2, 2009, CA, it was stated that in cases of serious sexual assault, the age of the offender or the age of the offence could be mitigation although, in many cases, they would not receive much weight, especially if the offender had pressurised his/her victims into silence; but those matters did not cease to be factors which could form part of the mitigation, and they were not always of comparatively little weight.

In *S. (Luke)* [2009] 1 Cr.App.R.(S.) 86, the appellant, aged 12 at the time of the offence, appealed against a sentence of four years detention. The appellant had knocked on the door of the 75-year-old victim who mistakenly invited him in. The appellant asked her what kind of underwear she was wearing, unzipped her dressing gown, touched her indecently and then exposed himself to her. The victim was taken to hospital, where an ulcer she had not known about burst and she suffered a heart attack which led to her death 10 days later. The appellant pleaded guilty, the Court of Appeal stated that whilst a custodial sentence upon a boy of 13 would not necessarily be wrong for an offence of sexual assault, there was significant mitigation, the appellant's childhood home had been "indescribably bad". A three year supervision order with specified treatment and programme requirements substituted.

C. CAUSING A PERSON TO ENGAGE IN SEXUAL ACTIVITY WITHOUT CONSENT

(1) Definition

Sexual Offences Act 2003, s.4

Causing a person to engage in sexual activity without consent

14–92 **4.**—(1) A person (A) commits an offence if—

(a) he intentionally causes another person (B) to engage in an activity,

(b) the activity is sexual,

(c) B does not consent to engaging in the activity, and

(d) A does not reasonably believe that B consents.

(2) Whether a belief is reasonable is to be determined having regard to all the circumstances, including any steps A has taken to ascertain whether B consents.

(3) Sections 75 and 76 apply to an offence under this section.

(4) A person guilty of an offence under this section, if the activity caused involved—

(a) penetration of B's anus or vagina,

(b) penetration of B's mouth with a person's penis,

(c) penetration of a person's anus or vagina with a part of B's body or by B with anything else, or

(d) penetration of a person's mouth with B's penis,

is liable, on conviction on indictment, to imprisonment for life.

(5) Unless subsection (4) applies, a person guilty of an offence under this section is liable—

(a) on summary conviction, to imprisonment for a term not exceeding 6 months or to a fine not exceeding the statutory maximum or both;

(b) on conviction on indictment, to imprisonment for a term not exceeding 10 years.

14–93 See *ante*, §§ 14–81–14–82, regarding ss.75 and 76.

(2) Allocation

14–94 This offence is triable either way, unless s.4(4) applies when it is indictable only.

(3) Sentence

14–95 The maximum sentence is one of six months' imprisonment if tried summarily, and/or a fine. After commencement of the relevant provisions, the maximum custodial sentence in a magistrates' court will be 12 months' imprisonment: *Criminal Justice Act* 2003, ss.154 and 282. An offender convicted of this offence is automatically subject to notification requirements *SOA* 2003, s.80. See § 14–281.

STARTING POINT AND RANGE (BASED ON A FIRST TIME OFFENDER AFTER TRIAL):

Type/nature of activity	Starting Point	Range
Penetration with any one of the following aggravating factors: abduction or detention; offender aware that he or she is suffering from a sexually transmitted infection; more than one offender acting together; abuse of trust; offence motivated by prejudice (race, religion, sexual orientation, physical disability); sustained attack	13 years custody if the victim is a child under 13 or a person with a mental disorder 10 years custody if the victim is 13 or over but under 16 8 years custody if the victim is 16 or over	11–17 years custody 8–13 years custody 6–11 years custody
Single offence of penetration of/by single offender with no aggravating or mitigating factors	7 years custody if the victim is a child under 13 or a person with a mental disorder 5 years custody if the victim is 13 or over but under 16 3 years custody if the victim is 16 or over	5–10 years custody 4–8 years custody 2–5 years custody
Contact between naked genitalia of offender and naked genitalia of victim, or causing two or more victims to engage in such activity with each other, or causing victim to masturbate him/herself	5 years custody if the victim is a child under 13 or a person with a mental disorder 3 years custody	4–8 years custody 2–5 years custody

Type/nature of activity	Starting Point	Range
Contact between naked genitalia of offender and another part of victim's body, or causing two or more victims to engage in such activity with each other Contact with the naked genitalia of victim by offender using part of the body other then the genitalia or an object, or causing two or more victims to engage in such activity with each other Contact between either the clothed genitalia of offender and naked genitalia of victim, between naked genitalia of offender and clothed genitalia of victim, or causing two or more victims to engage in such activity with each other	2 years custody if the victim is a child under 13 or a person with a mental disorder 12 months custody	1–4 years custody 26 weeks–2 years custody
Contact between part of offender's body (other than the genitalia) with part of victim's body (other than genitalia)	26 weeks custody if the victim is a child under 13 or a person with a mental disorder Community order	4 weeks–18 months custody An appropriate non-custodial sentence

AGGRAVATING AND MITIGATING FACTORS:

Additional aggravating factors	Additional mitigating factors
1. Offender ejaculated or caused victim to ejaculate 2. History of intimidation or coercion 3. Use of drugs, alcohol or other substance to facilitate the offence 4. Threats to prevent victim reporting the incident 5. Abduction or detention 6. Offender aware that he or she is suffering from a sexually transmitted infection	

V. CHILD SEX OFFENCES UNDER THE SEXUAL OFFENCES ACT 2003

A. INTRODUCTION

Relevant age provisions

Child sex offences are those in which the complainant is under the age of 16. There are now statutory provisions with respect to the relevance of the complainant's age. Sections 5 and 6 of the Act provide for offences of rape and assault by penetration of a child under the age of 13 where consent is irrelevant. These offences are triable on indictment only. **14–96**

Proving age and defences

The prosecution is required to prove that the child is under 16. In cases where the defendant claims to have believed that the child was 16 or over, it will be for the prosecution to prove that he did not believe this or that his belief was not reasonably held. This provision as to mistaken belief in age does not apply where the child is under 13. **14–97**

General sentencing provisions

The maximum sentence where an offender aged 18 or over is convicted summarily of a child sex offence is six months' imprisonment or a fine not exceeding the statutory maximum or both. After commencement of the relevant provisions, the maximum custodial sentence in a magistrates' court will be 12 months' imprisonment: *Criminal Justice Act* 2003, ss.154 and 282. **14–98**

Section 13 of the Act also provides that any of the child sex offences in ss.9 to 12 can be committed by a person under the age of 18, in which case the maximum sentence is reduced to five years' custody. Such offences would normally, of course, be tried in the youth court but the power to commit such offence to the Crown Court as grave crimes is preserved by the amendment to s.91 of *PCC(S)A* 2000 contained in Sched. 6, para. 13(2) to the *Sexual Offences Act* 2003.

In *Corran* [2005] 2 Cr.App.R.(S.) 73 the Court of Appeal, presided over by the Vice-President of the Criminal Division, Rose L.J., considered sentences in respect of sexual offences committed against children. Although the judgment is principally concerned with rape of a child under 13 (an indictable only offence), the Court gave guidance that the same considerations, *i.e.* the defendant's age in relation to the complainant's age, the nature of the relationship of those involved, their character and maturity, remorse, the use of contraception, and the consequences for the complainant, should be taken into account when sentencing for offences under ss.9 and 10 of the Act.

In *Ismail* [2005] 2 Cr.App.R.(S.) 88, the Court of Appeal held that for offences which appear to have had a significant impact on the victim it is essential for sentencing judges to have victim impact statements, especially where a sexual offence has been committed against a young victim, so that that impact can be taken into account when determining the appropriate sentence.

B. SEXUAL ASSAULT OF A CHILD UNDER 13

(1) Definition

Sexual Offences Act 2003, s.7

Sexual assault of a child under 13

14–99 **7.**—(1) A person commits an offence if—

(a) he intentionally touches another person,

(b) the touching is sexual, and

(c) the other person is under 13.

(2) A person guilty of an offence under this section is liable—

(a) on summary conviction, to imprisonment for a term not exceeding 6 months or a fine not exceeding the statutory maximum or both;

(b) on conviction on indictment, to imprisonment for a term not exceeding 14 years.

(2) Allocation

14–100 This offence is triable either way.

(3) Elements

14–101 Consent and belief that the complainant was older are irrelevant.

(4) Sentence

14–102 When tried summarily the maximum sentence is six months imprisonment or a fine not exceeding the statutory maximum. After commencement of the relevant provisions, the maximum custodial sentence will be 12 months imprisonment in the magistrates' court: *Criminal Justice Act* 2003, ss.154 and 282. For the sentencing guidelines see *ante*, § 14–91.

C. CAUSING OR INCITING A CHILD UNDER 13 TO ENGAGE IN SEXUAL ACTIVITY

(1) Definition

Sexual Offences Act 2003, s.8

Causing or inciting a child under 13 to engage in sexual activity

14–103 **8.**—(1) A person commits an offence if—

(a) he intentionally causes or incites another person (B) to engage in an activity,

(b) the activity is sexual, and

(c) B is under 13.

(2) A person guilty of an offence under this section, if the activity caused or incited involved—

(a) penetration of B's anus or vagina,

(b) penetration of B's mouth with a person's penis,

(c) penetration of a person's anus or vagina with a part of B's body or by B with anything else, or

(d) penetration of a person's mouth with B's penis, is liable, on conviction on indictment, to imprisonment for life.

(3) Unless subsection (2) applies, a person guilty of an offence under this section is liable—

(a) on summary conviction, to imprisonment for a term not exceeding 6 months or to a fine not exceeding the statutory maximum or both;

(b) on conviction on indictment, to imprisonment for a term not exceeding 14 years.

(2) Allocation

These offences are triable either way except in the case of s.8 where if subs.(2) applies the offence is triable on indictment only. **14–104**

(3) Elements

The prosecution must prove that the defendant **14–105**

— intentionally

— caused or incited

— another person

— to engage in sexual activity

— proof is required of the complainant's age.

In *Grout* [2011] EWCA Crim 299 the court stressed the importance of the prosecution specifying which of the four different offences created by section 8 was being charged. In this case the parties had met at a church group and became friends. The appellant was eight years older than the 12-year-old female complainant. They communicated largely by computer and text messages but gradually the messages from the appellant became sexual in nature. This led the complainant, after a request from him, to pull back her jumper and reveal her bra-strap over the webcam. He was charged under s.8. In their judgment the court referred to there being four offences under the section which were two of causing or inciting penetrative activity and two of causing or inciting non-penetrative activity. Here the charge was general. The court pointed out that the charge was directed to the complainant being caused or incited to engage in sexual activity, not the defendant. Activity is not defined but was held to cover conversations or texts or MSN messages, depending on the circumstances. The activity had to be sexual according to the definition in *H* (above). The conviction was held to be unsafe in view of the lack of specificity in the charges and failure to give proper directions to the jury about the meaning of sexual activity.

(4) Sentence

When tried summarily the maximum sentence is 6 months imprisonment or a fine not exceeding the statutory maximum. After commencement of the relevant provisions, the maximum custodial sentence will be 12 months imprisonment in the magistrates' court: *Criminal Justice Act* 2003, ss.154 and 282. For the sentencing guidelines see *ante*, § 14–95. **14–106**

D. SEXUAL ACTIVITY WITH A CHILD

(1) Definition

Sexual Offences Act 2003, s.9

Sexual activity with a child

14–107 **9.**—(1) A person aged 18 or over (A) commits an offence if—

(a) he intentionally touches another person (B),

(b) the touching is sexual, and

(c) either—

(i) B is under 16 and A does not reasonably believe that B is 16 or over, or

(ii) B is under 13.

(2) A person guilty of an offence under this section, if the touching involved—

(a) penetration of B's anus or vagina with a part of A's body or anything else,

(b) penetration of B's mouth with A's penis,

(c) penetration of A's anus or vagina with a part of B's body, or

(d) penetration of A's mouth with B's penis,

is liable, on conviction on indictment, to imprisonment for a term not exceeding 14 years.

(3) Unless subsection (2) applies, a person guilty of an offence under this section is liable—

(a) on summary conviction, to imprisonment for a term not exceeding 6 months or to a fine not exceeding the statutory maximum or both;

(b) on conviction on indictment, to imprisonment for a term not exceeding 14 years.

(2) Allocation

14–108 The offence is triable either way unless s.9(2) applies.

(3) Elements of the offence

14–109 Touching is defined in s.79(8) of the Act (see *ante*, § 14–84).

It is a defence if the accused reasonably believed the complainant to be 16 or over. This defence does not apply if the complainant is under 13 years old.

(4) Sentence

14–110 The maximum sentence is six months' imprisonment and/or a fine when tried summarily. After commencement of the relevant provisions, the maximum custodial sentence in a magistrates' court will be 12 months' imprisonment: *Criminal Justice Act* 2003, ss.154 and 282. An offender convicted of this offence is automatically subject to notification requirements: *SOA* 2003, s.80. See § 14–281.

STARTING POINT AND RANGE (BASED ON FIRST TIME OFFENDER AFTER TRIAL):

Type/nature of activity	Starting Point	Range
Penile penetration of the vagina, anus or mouth or penetration of the vagina or anus with another body part or an object	4 years custody	3–7 years custody
Contact between naked genitalia of offender and naked genitalia or another part of victim's body, particularly face or mouth	2 years custody	1–4 years custody
Contact between naked genitalia of offender or victim and clothed genitalia of victim or offender or contact with naked genitalia of victim by offender using part of his or her body other than the genitalia or an object	12 months custody	26 weeks–2 years custody
Contact between part of offender's body (other than the genitalia) with part of the victim's body (other than the genitalia)	Community order	An appropriate non-custodial sentence (community order or fine)

Part III

AGGRAVATING AND MITIGATING FACTORS:

Additional aggravating factors	**Additional mitigating factors**
1. Offender ejaculated or caused victim to ejaculate 2. Threats to prevent victim reporting the incident 3. Offender aware that he or she is suffering from a sexually transmitted infection	1. Offender intervenes to prevent incited offence from taking place 2. Small disparity in age between the offender and victim

In *Couch* [2005] EWCA Crim 1309, the Court of Appeal substituted a sentence of four months' detention for an offence under this section in a case involving an 18-year-old appellant and a 14-year-old complainant. After a family gathering involving heavy drinking, the complainant had consented to sexual touching, oral sex and some penile penetration. The complainant had made it clear that she was consenting from the outset of the investigation. The appellant pleaded guilty. The Court of Appeal relied upon Rose L.J.'s comments in *Corran* [2005] 2 Cr.App.R.(S.) 73 to the effect that where everyone is young and everyone consents, a very short period of custody is likely to suffice for a teenager.

In *Att.-Gen.'s Reference (No. 59 of 2006), Re (Nelson Doe)* [2006] EWCA Crim 2096, a sentence of 51 weeks' imprisonment suspended for two years was held to be unduly lenient, despite early guilty pleas in a case where the defendant had developed a sexual relationship with a 14-year-old. The aggravating features of a breach of a position of trust—he was considered a father figure to her and had a close relationship with her family and the recurring nature of the offence meant a sentence of 51 weeks' imprisonment could not be justified. Taking into account the double jeopardy rule the court imposed a sentence of 18 months' immediate imprisonment.

In *Held* [2007] 1 Cr.App.R.(S.) 24 the Court of Appeal upheld a sentence of 12 months' imprisonment, following a guilty plea to three counts of sexual activity with a child. A 41-year-old woman of previous good character, had developed an inappropriate relationship with a 14-year-old girl, who was a friend of her daughters and whom she coached as a member of a football team. The sexual activity had included kissing her breasts, touching over clothing and partial digital penetration of her vagina. The Court of Appeal reiterated that when adults are placed in a position of trust in relation to children which they abuse, the punishment is likely to be significant.

In *Att.-Gen.'s Reference (No. 29 of 2008) (R. v. Dixon)* [2009]1 Cr.App.R.(S.) 86, CA, the appellant met the victim in an internet chat room, where they exchanged sexually explicit emails. He initially believed her to have been 20 although by the time of their meeting in person he knew she was 11. All the sexual activity took place with the full consent and encouragement of the child. A community order with supervision requirements for three years was unduly lenient; two years' imprisonment was substituted.

E. Causing or Inciting a Child to Engage in Sexual Activity

(1) Definition

Sexual Offences Act 2003, s.10

Causing or inciting a child to engage in sexual activity

10.—(1) A person aged 18 or over (A) commits an offence if— **14–111**

(a) he intentionally causes or incites another person (B) to engage in an activity,

(b) the activity is sexual, and

(c) either–

(i) B is under 16 and A does not reasonably believe that B is 16 or over, or

(ii) B is under 13.

(2) A person guilty of an offence under this section, if the activity caused or incited involved–

(a) penetration of B's anus or vagina,

(b) penetration of B's mouth with a person's penis,

(c) penetration of a person's anus or vagina with a part of B's body or by B with anything else, or

(d) penetration of a person's mouth with B's penis,

is liable, on conviction on indictment, to imprisonment for a term not exceeding 14 years.

(3) Unless subsection (2) applies, a person guilty of an offence under this section is liable—

(a) on summary conviction, to imprisonment for a term not exceeding 6 months or to a fine not exceeding the statutory maximum or both;

(b) on conviction on indictment, to imprisonment for a term not exceeding 14 years.

(2) Allocation

These offences are triable either way unless s.10(2) or s.8(2) applies. **14–112**

(3) Sentence

The maximum sentence is six months' imprisonment and/or a fine when tried summarily. After the commencement of the relevant provisions, the maximum custodial sentence in a magistrates' court will be 12 months' imprisonment: *Criminal Justice Act* 2003, ss.154 and 282. See *Corran, ante* at § 14–98. An offender convicted of this offence is automatically subject to notification requirements *SOA* 2003; s.80. See *post*, § 14–281. **14–113**

Starting point and range (based on a first time offender after trial): See table above at § 14–110 re Sexual Activity with a child contrary to *Sexual Offences Act* 2003, s.9.

F. Engaging in Sexual Activity in the Presence of a Child

(1) Definition

Sexual Offences Act 2003, s.11

Engaging in sexual activity in the presence of a child

11.—(1) A person aged 18 or over (A) commits an offence if— **14–114**

(a) he intentionally engages in an activity,

(b) the activity is sexual,

(c) for the purpose of obtaining sexual gratification, he engages in it—

(i) when another person (B) is present or is in a place from which A can be observed, and

(ii) knowing or believing that B is aware, or intending that B should be aware, that he is engaging in it, and

(d) either—

(i) B is under 16 and A does not reasonably believe that B is 16 or over, or

Part III

(ii) B is under 13.

(2) A person guilty of an offence under this section is liable—

(a) on summary conviction, to imprisonment for a term not exceeding 6 months or a fine not exceeding the statutory maximum or both;

(b) on conviction on indictment, to imprisonment for a term not exceeding 10 years.

(2) Allocation

14–115 This offence is triable either way.

(3) Sentence

14–116 The maximum sentence is six months' imprisonment and/or a fine when tried summarily. After the commencement of the relevant provisions, the maximum custodial sentence in a magistrates' court will be 12 months' imprisonment: *Criminal Justice Act* 2003, ss.154 and 282. An offender convicted of this offence is automatically subject to notification requirements; *SOA* 2003, s.80. See *post*, § 14–281.

STARTING POINT AND RANGE (BASED ON A FIRST TIME OFFENDER AFTER TRIAL):

Type/nature of activity	**Starting Point**	**Range**
Consensual intercourse or other forms of consensual penetration	2 years custody	1–4 years custody
Masturbation (of oneself or another person)	18 months custody	12 months–2 years 6 months custody
Consensual sexual touching involving naked genitalia	12 months custody	26 weeks–18 months custody
Consensual sexual touching of naked body parts but not involving naked genitalia	26 weeks custody	4 weeks–18 months custody

AGGRAVATING AND MITIGATING FACTORS:

Additional aggravating factors	**Additional mitigating factors**
1. Background of intimidation or coercion 2. Use of drugs, alcohol or other substance to facilitate the offence 3. Threats to prevent victim reporting the incident 4. Abduction or detention	

In *W&T* [2005] EWCA Crim 2448 the Court of Appeal substituted sentences of six months' imprisonment for the 12-month sentences originally imposed. The appellants were a couple who pleaded guilty. The woman's nine-year-old daughter had taken photographs of the couple having sexual intercourse. The judge made a finding of fact that the photographs were posed. The appellants were of previous good character and were assessed as not posing a risk to children in general. It was noted that only an immediate custodial sentence was appropriate.

In *Abbondandolo* [2008] 2 Cr.App.R.(S.) 119, the defendant communicated over the internet with two cousins, a girl and a boy, who were staying together, aged 12 and 13 respectively. When he tried to get the girl to engage in sexual activity over a webcam as well as trying to get her phone number, she refused. When the defendant came on the webcam they realised he was older than he had claimed. He, in fact, was 34-years-old. The mother of the boy was told. Later that week, when the defendant came back on line, the children told the boy's mother, who was then able to see the defendant, whilst communicating with someone else, expose his penis and start to masturbate. She took photographs and contacted the police. The defendant, of previous good character, made full admissions and pleaded guilty. On arrest he was also found to have in his possession 48 indecent photographs and an indecent video. He was sentenced to 12 months imprisonment in respect of the offence of engaging in sexual activity in the presence of a child. He received consecutive sentences of three months imprisonment for the offences of making and possessing indecent photographs of a child. The Court of Appeal upheld the sentences.

In *Brown* [2011] 1 Cr.App.R.(S.) 38 the appellant was convicted of two charges of attempting to engage in a sexual activity in the presence of a child. He masturbated over a webcam when he thought he was being watched by a 14-year-old girl. In fact it was an under cover police officer. The 15 month sentence was upheld on appeal. The court said that the guidelines applied to a single offence and here were two and although the offences were technical attempts the fact that the observer was actually an adult was not something that could benefit the appellant.

G. Causing a Child to Watch a Sexual Act

(1) Definition

Sexual Offences Act 2003, s.12

Causing a child to watch a sexual act

12.—(1) A person aged 18 or over (A) commits an offence if— **14–117**

(a) for the purpose of obtaining sexual gratification, he intentionally causes another person (B) to watch a third person engaging in an activity, or to look at an image of any person engaging in an activity,

(b) the activity is sexual, and

(c) either—

(i) B is under 16 and A does not reasonably believe that B is 16 or over, or

(ii) B is under 13.

(2) A person guilty of an offence under this section is liable—

(a) on summary conviction, to imprisonment for a term not exceeding 6 months or a fine not exceeding the statutory maximum or both;

(b) on conviction on indictment, to imprisonment for a term not exceeding 10 years.

(2) Allocation

This offence is triable either way. **14–118**

(3) Elements of the offence

It is an element of the offence that the defendant caused the child to watch the sexual act for the purpose of obtaining sexual gratification; the sexual gratification need not be immediate, it can be long-term, short-term, immediate or deferred: *Abdullahi* [2007] 1 Cr.App.R. 14. **14–119**

In *JTB* [2009] UKHL 20, the appellant pleaded guilty to twelve counts of offences of causing or inciting a child under 13 to engage in sexual activity contrary to section 13(1) of the *Sexual Offences Act* 2003. The victims of this activity were young boys and the activity included anal penetration with the penis, oral sex and masturbation. At the time of the activity the appellant was 12 years of age. In interview he admitted the activity but said that he had not thought that what he was doing was wrong. The House of Lords dismissed the appeal on the basis that *doli incapax* did not exist as a defence.

(4) Sentence

14–120 The maximum sentence is six months' imprisonment and/or a fine when tried summarily. After commencement of the relevant provisions, the maximum custodial sentence in a magistrates' court will be 12 months' imprisonment: *Criminal Justice Act* 2003, ss.154 and 282. An offender convicted of this offence is automatically subject to notification requirements: *SOA* 2003, s.80.

STARTING POINTS AND SENTENCING RANGE (BASED ON A FIRST TIME OFFENDER AFTER TRIAL):

Type/nature of activity	Starting Point	Range
Live sexual activity	18 months custody	12 months–2 years custody
Moving or still images of people engaged in sexual activity involving penetration	32 weeks custody	26 weeks–12 months custody
Moving or still images of people engaged in sexual activity other than penetration	Community order	Community order–26 weeks custody

AGGRAVATING AND MITIGATING FACTORS:

Additional aggravating factors	Additional mitigating factors
1. Background of intimidation or coercion 2. Use of drugs, alcohol or other substance to facilitate the offence 3. Threats to prevent victim reporting the incident 4. Abduction or detention 5. Images of violent activity	1. Small disparity in age between victim and offender

In *Corran*, (*ante*) at § 14–98, it was suggested that the age and character of the child and the defendant, the nature of the act, the number of incidents, the impact on the child, remorse, and future risk were all relevant considerations when sentencing for offences under ss.11 and 12.

H. CHILD SEX OFFENCES COMMITTED BY CHILDREN OR YOUNG PERSONS

(1) Definition

Sexual Offences Act 2003, s.13

Child sexual offence committed by children or young persons

13.—(1) A person under 18 commits an offence if he does anything which would be an offence under any of sections 9 to 12 if he were aged 18. **14–121**

(2) A person guilty of an offence under this section is liable—

(a) on summary conviction, to imprisonment for a term not exceeding 6 months or a fine not exceeding the statutory maximum or both;

(b) on conviction on indictment, to imprisonment for a term not exceeding 5 years.

(2) Allocation

The offence is triable either way. In *(G)* 171 J.P. 445, DC the issue of mode of trial of children and young persons was addressed. The allegation contrary to s.13 of the *Sexual Offences Act* 2003, was that a group of 13–14 year-old boys and girls (all of good character) were alleged to have sexually assaulted a 13-year-old at a party where they had all had too much to drink. The sexual assault involved being grabbed when she went to the toilet, pushed to the floor, had her trousers and knickers removed, breast felt over clothing and something inserted into her vagina which she believed to be a vibrator. The decision to commit for trial to the Crown Court under s.24 of *Magistrates Courts Act* 1980 was held to be manifestly wrong and was quashed as there was no real possibility that a sentence of detention for more than two years would be appropriate. **14–122**

(3) Sentence

The maximum sentence on summary conviction is six months detention and/or a fine. An offender convicted of this offence is subject to notification requirements if sentenced to at least 12 months detention: *SOA* 2003, s.80. See § 14–281. **14–123**

I. ARRANGING OR FACILITATING A CHILD SEX OFFENCE

(1) Definition

Sexual Offences Act 2003, s.14

Arranging or facilitating commission of a child sex offence

14.—(1) A person commits an offence if— **14–124**

(a) he intentionally arranges or facilitates something that he intends to do, intends another person to do, or believes that another person will do, in any part of the world, and

(b) doing it will involve the commission of an offence under any of sections 9 to 13.

(2) A person does not commit an offence under this section if—

(a) he arranges or facilitates something that he believes another person will do, but that he does not intend to do or intend another person to do, and

(b) any offence within subsection (1)(b) would be an offence against a child for whose protection he acts.

(3) For the purposes of subsection (2), a person acts for the protection of a child if he acts for the purpose of—

(a) protecting the child from sexually transmitted infection,

(b) protecting the physical safety of the child,

(c) preventing the child from becoming pregnant, or

(d) promoting the child's emotional well-being by the giving of advice,

and not for the purpose of obtaining sexual gratification or for the purpose of causing or encouraging the activity constituting the offence within subsection (1)(b) or the child's participation in it.

(4) A person guilty of an offence under this section is liable—

(a) on summary conviction, to imprisonment for a term not exceeding 6 months or a fine not exceeding the statutory maximum or both;

(b) on conviction on indictment, to imprisonment for a term not exceeding 14 years.

Section 14 was designed to impose criminal liability on preparatory acts and does not limit the stage at which criminal liability is imposed as to what would be regarded as an attempt, but widened liability to steps taken with the requisite criminal intent by way of preparation. It did not require an agreement or arrangement and did not require the consent or acquiescence of anyone else. *R* [2009] 1 W.L.R. 713

(2) Defence

14–125 The defence to this offence is afforded to anyone who acts to protect the physical safety or emotional wellbeing of a child. It covers anyone providing contraception, contraceptive or family planning advice, and advice or guidance in sexual matters, including doctors, nurses, family planning clinic staff, teachers, magazine or newspaper columnists, parents and other relatives or friends. The test is that the actions were designed to protect the child and were not perpetrated for the purpose of obtaining sexual gratification.

In *Robson* [2009] EWCA Crim 1472, the appellant was convicted of attempting to arrange the commission of a child sex offence. The appellant asked a prostitute if she knew of any prostitutes aged about 12 and then followed this up with two text messages to the prostitute asking whether she was able to arrange contact with a 12-year-old and whether the 12-year-old would be prepared to "go with a dog". It had been open to a jury to find that his oral request and texts, taken together, were more than merely preparatory and, therefore, amounted to an attempt. Had the prostitute agreed to what the offender was seeking, there would have been an arrangement, and the full offence would have been committed.

(3) Allocation

14–126 This offence is triable either way.

(4) Sentence

14–127 The maximum sentence is six months' imprisonment if tried summarily. After commencement of the relevant provisions, the maximum custodial sentence in a magistrates' court will be 12 months' imprisonment: *Criminal Justice Act* 2003, ss.154 and 282. An offence contrary to s.14 is a "lifestyle offence" within the *Proceeds of Crime Act* 2002, Sched. 2, in respect of which a financial reporting order may be made under the *Serious Organised Crime and Police Act* 2005, s.76. An offender convicted of this offence is automatically subject to notification requirements: *SOA* 2003, s.80.

STARTING POINTS AND RANGES (BASED ON A FIRST TIME OFFENDER AFTER TRIAL):

Type/nature of activity	**Starting points and sentencing ranges**
Where the activity is arranged or facilitated as part of a commercial enterprise, even if the offender is under 18	As this offence is primarily aimed at persons organizing the commission of relevant sexual offences for gain, and sometimes across international borders, this is the most likely aggravating factor. Starting points and sentencing ranges should be increased above those for the relevant substantive offence under sections 9–13
Basic offence as defined in the *SOA* 2003 assuming no aggravating or mitigating factors	The starting point and sentencing range should be commensurate with that for the relevant substantive offence under sections 9–13

AGGRAVATING AND MITIGATING FACTORS:

Additional aggravating factors	**Additional mitigating factors**
1. Background of intimidation or coercion 2. Use of drugs, alcohol or other substance to facilitate the offence 3. Threats to prevent victim reporting the incident 4. Abduction or detention 5. Number of victims involved	

In *Harrison* [2005] EWCA Crim 3458, the Court of Appeal considered the appropriate sentence for an offence contrary to s.14 of the Act. Amongst other offences, the appellant had pleaded guilty to inciting a 14-year-old girl to engage in masturbation whilst on the telephone with him. The basis of plea stated that there was never to be a meeting between the appellant and the victim. The appellant was a man of good character except for a caution in 2001 for masturbation in a public place. The court substituted a sentence of 18 months' imprisonment for the 27 months originally imposed, and ordered that it run concurrently to the sentences for offences involving indecent photographs of children imposed in respect of other counts.

J. MEETING A CHILD FOLLOWING SEXUAL GROOMING

(1) Definition

Sexual Offences Act 2003, s.15

Meeting a child following sexual grooming etc.

14–128 **15.**—(1) A person aged 18 or over (A) commits an offence if—

(a) A has met or communicated with another person (B) on at least two occasions and subsequently—

(i) A intentionally meets B,

(ii) A travels with the intention of meeting B in any part of the world or arranges to meet B in any part of the world, or

(iii) B travels with the intention of meeting A in any part of the world,

(b) A intends to do anything to or in respect of B, during or after the meeting mentioned in paragraph (a)(i) to (iii) and in any part of the world, which if done will involve the commission by A of a relevant offence,

(c) B is under 16, and

(d) A does not reasonably believe that B is 16 or over.

(2) In subsection (1)—

(a) the reference to A having met or communicated with B is a reference to A having met B in any part of the world or having communicated with B by any means from, to or in any part of the world;

(b) "relevant offence" means—

(i) an offence under this Part,

(ii) an offence within any of paragraphs 61 to 92 of Schedule 3, or

(iii) anything done outside England and Wales and Northern Ireland which is not an offence within sub-paragraph (i) or (ii) but would be an offence within sub-paragraph (i) if done in England and Wales.

(3) In this section as it applies to Northern Ireland—

(a) subsection (1) has effect with the substitution of "17" for "16" in both places;

(b) subsection (2)(b)(iii) has effect with the substitution of "sub-paragraph (ii) if done in Northern Ireland" for "sub-paragraph (i) if done in England and Wales".

(4) A person guilty of an offence under this section is liable—

(a) on summary conviction, to imprisonment for a term not exceeding 6 months or a fine not exceeding the statutory maximum or both;

(b) on conviction on indictment, to imprisonment for a term not exceeding 10 years.

[This section is printed as amended by the *Criminal Justice and Immigration Act* 2008, Sched. 15.]

14–129 Note that this offence enables charges to be brought before any other substantive offence takes place.

(2) Allocation

14–130 This offence is triable either way.

(3) Elements

14–131 In *G.* [2011] Crim.L.R. 339 the court said that the purpose of s.15 was to penalise those who used a relationship as a platform to launch sexual offending. The defendant was a friend of the family of a 12-year-old girl. He contacted her and arranged to collect her from school. He took her home and no other adult was there. The child's mother returned home and found the girl in a state of undress and the defendant hiding under the child's bed. The court said for grooming there needed to be only two prior meetings or communications which did not need to be sexual in nature. However, for the offence to be committed, the sexual intention did have to be contemporaneous with an intention to meet. Where advantage was taken of a situation that arose without the previous intent the offence may not be made out.

(4) Sentence

14–132 The maximum sentence is six months' imprisonment if tried summarily. After commencement of the relevant provisions, the maximum custodial sentence in a magistrates' court will be 12 months' imprisonment: *Criminal Justice Act* 2003, ss.154 and 282. An offender convicted of this offence is automatically subject to notification requirements: *SOA* 2003, s.80.

See *post*, § 14–281.

STARTING POINTS AND SENTENCING RANGES:

Type/nature of activity	Starting Point	Range
Where the intent is to commit an assault by penetration or rape	4 years custody if the victim is under 13 2 years custody if the victim is 13 or over but under 16	3–7 years custody 1–4 years custody
Where the intent is to coerce the child into sexual activity	2 years custody if the victim is under 13 18 months custody if the victim is 13 or over but under 16	1–4 years custody 12 months–2 years 6 months custody

AGGRAVATING AND MITIGATING FACTORS:

Additional aggravating factors	Additional mitigating factors
1. Background of intimidation or coercion 2. Use of drugs, alcohol or other substance to facilitate the offence 3. Offender aware that he or she is suffering from a sexually transmitted infection 4. Abduction or detention	

K. ABUSE OF A POSITION OF TRUST

(1) Definition

14–133 The abuse of trust offences are identical to the child sex offences at ss.9 to 12 inasmuch as they cover sexual activity of the same nature, but they are committed in circumstances where a breach of trust by the offender is an inherent element of the offence.

The complainant must be under 18 for the offences above to be properly charged.

Sexual Offences Act 2003, ss.16–19

Abuse of position of trust: sexual activity with a child

14–134 **16.**—(1) A person aged 18 or over (A) commits an offence if—

(a) he intentionally touches another person (B),

(b) the touching is sexual,

(c) A is in a position of trust in relation to B,

(d) where subsection (2) applies, A knows or could reasonably be expected to know of the circumstances by virtue of which he is in a position of trust in relation to B, and

(e) either—

(i) B is under 18 and A does not reasonably believe that B is 18 or over, or

(ii) B is under 13.

(2) This subsection applies where A—

(a) is in a position of trust in relation to B by virtue of circumstances within section 21(2), (3), (4) or (5), and

(b) is not in such a position of trust by virtue of other circumstances.

(3) Where in proceedings for an offence under this section it is proved that the other person was under 18, the defendant is to be taken not to have reasonably believed that that person was 18 or over unless sufficient evidence is adduced to raise an issue as to whether he reasonably believed it.

(4) Where in proceedings for an offence under this section—

(a) it is proved that the defendant was in a position of trust in relation to the other person by virtue of circumstances within section 21(2), (3), (4) or (5), and

(b) it is not proved that he was in such a position of trust by virtue of other circumstances,

it is to be taken that the defendant knew or could reasonably have been expected to know of the circumstances by virtue of which he was in such a position of trust unless sufficient evidence is adduced to raise an issue as to whether he knew or could reasonably have been expected to know of those circumstances.

(5) A person guilty of an offence under this section is liable—

(a) on summary conviction, to imprisonment for a term not exceeding 6 months or a fine not exceeding the statutory maximum or both;

(b) on conviction on indictment, to imprisonment for a term not exceeding 5 years.

Abuse of position of trust: causing or inciting a child to engage in sexual activity

14–135 **17.**—(1) A person aged 18 or over (A) commits an offence if—

(a) he intentionally causes or incites another person (B) to engage in an activity,

(b) the activity is sexual,

(c) A is in a position of trust in relation to B,

(d) where subsection (2) applies, A knows or could reasonably be expected to know of the circumstances by virtue of which he is in a position of trust in relation to B, and

(e) either—

(i) B is under 18 and A does not reasonably believe that B is 18 or over, or

(ii) B is under 13.

(2) This subsection applies where A—

(a) is in a position of trust in relation to B by virtue of circumstances within section 21(2), (3), (4) or (5), and

(b) is not in such a position of trust by virtue of other circumstances.

(3) Where in proceedings for an offence under this section it is proved that the other person was under 18, the defendant is to be taken not to have reasonably believed that that person was 18 or over unless sufficient evidence is adduced to raise an issue as to whether he reasonably believed it.

(4) Where in proceedings for an offence under this section—

(a) it is proved that the defendant was in a position of trust in relation to the other person by virtue of circumstances within section 21(2), (3), (4) or (5), and

(b) it is not proved that he was in such a position of trust by virtue of other circumstances, it is to be taken that the defendant knew or could reasonably have been expected to know of the circumstances by virtue of which he was in such a position of trust unless sufficient evidence is adduced to raise an issue as to whether he knew or could reasonably have been expected to know of those circumstances.

(5) A person guilty of an offence under this section is liable—

(a) on summary conviction, to imprisonment for a term not exceeding 6 months or a fine not exceeding the statutory maximum or both;

(b) on conviction on indictment, to imprisonment for a term not exceeding 5 years.

Abuse of position of trust: sexual activity in the presence of a child

18.—(1) A person aged 18 or over (A) commits an offence if— **14–136**

(a) he intentionally engages in an activity,

(b) the activity is sexual,

(c) for the purpose of obtaining sexual gratification, he engages in it—

(i) when another person (B) is present or is in a place from which A can be observed, and

(ii) knowing or believing that B is aware, or intending that B should be aware, that he is engaging in it,

(d) A is in a position of trust in relation to B,

(e) where subsection (2) applies, A knows or could reasonably be expected to know of the circumstances by virtue of which he is in a position of trust in relation to B, and

(f) either—

(i) B is under 18 and A does not reasonably believe that B is 18 or over, or

(ii) B is under 13.

(2) This subsection applies where A—

(a) is in a position of trust in relation to B by virtue of circumstances within section 21(2), (3), (4) or (5), and

(b) is not in such a position of trust by virtue of other circumstances.

(3) Where in proceedings for an offence under this section it is proved that the other person was under 18, the defendant is to be taken not to have reasonably believed that that person was 18 or over unless sufficient evidence is adduced to raise an issue as to whether he reasonably believed it.

(4) Where in proceedings for an offence under this section—

(a) it is proved that the defendant was in a position of trust in relation to the other person by virtue of circumstances within section 21(2), (3), (4) or (5), and

(b) it is not proved that he was in such a position of trust by virtue of other circumstances,

it is to be taken that the defendant knew or could reasonably have been expected to know of the circumstances by virtue of which he was in such a position of trust unless sufficient evidence is adduced to raise an issue as to whether he knew or could reasonably have been expected to know of those circumstances.

(5) A person guilty of an offence under this section is liable—

(a) on summary conviction, to imprisonment for a term not exceeding 6 months or a fine not exceeding the statutory maximum or both;

(b) on conviction on indictment, to imprisonment for a term not exceeding 5 years.

Abuse of position of trust: causing a child to watch a sexual act

19.—(1) A person aged 18 or over (A) commits an offence if— **14–137**

(a) for the purpose of obtaining sexual gratification, he intentionally causes another person (B) to watch a third person engaging in an activity, or to look at an image of any person engaging in an activity,

(b) the activity is sexual,

(c) A is in a position of trust in relation to B,

(d) where subsection (2) applies, A knows or could reasonably be expected to know of the circumstances by virtue of which he is in a position of trust in relation to B, and

(e) either—

(i) B is under 18 and A does not reasonably believe that B is 18 or over, or

Part III

(ii) B is under 13.

(2) This subsection applies where A—

(a) is in a position of trust in relation to B by virtue of circumstances within section 21(2), (3), (4) or (5), and

(b) is not in such a position of trust by virtue of other circumstances.

(3) Where in proceedings for an offence under this section it is proved that the other person was under 18, the defendant is to be taken not to have reasonably believed that that person was 18 or over unless sufficient evidence is adduced to raise an issue as to whether he reasonably believed it.

(4) Where in proceedings for an offence under this section—

(a) it is proved that the defendant was in a position of trust in relation to the other person by virtue of circumstances within section 21(2), (3), (4) or (5), and

(b) it is not proved that he was in such a position of trust by virtue of other circumstances,

it is to be taken that the defendant knew or could reasonably have been expected to know of the circumstances by virtue of which he was in such a position of trust unless sufficient evidence is adduced to raise an issue as to whether he knew or could reasonably have been expected to know of those circumstances.

(5) A person guilty of an offence under this section is liable—

(a) on summary conviction, to imprisonment for a term not exceeding 6 months or a fine not exceeding the statutory maximum or both;

(b) on conviction on indictment, to imprisonment for a term not exceeding 5 years.

(2) Elements of the offence

Position of trust

Sexual Offences Act 2003, ss.21–22

Positions of trust

14–138 **21.**—(1) For the purposes of sections 16 to 19, a person (A) is in a position of trust in relation to another person (B) if—

(a) any of the following subsections applies, or

(b) any condition specified in an order made by the Secretary of State is met.

(2) This subsection applies if A looks after persons under 18 who are detained in an institution by virtue of a court order or under an enactment, and B is so detained in that institution.

(3) This subsection applies if A looks after persons under 18 who are resident in a home or other place in which—

(a) accommodation and maintenance are provided by an authority under section 23(2) of the *Children Act* 1989 (c. 41) or Article 27(2) of the *Children (Northern Ireland) Order* 1995 (S.I. 1995 No. 755 (N.I. 2)), or

(b) accommodation is provided by a voluntary organisation under section 59(1) of that Act,

and B is resident, and is so provided with accommodation and maintenance or accommodation, in that place.

(4) This subsection applies if A looks after persons under 18 who are accommodated and cared for in one of the following institutions—

(a) a hospital,

(b) in Wales an independent clinic,

(c) a care home, residential care home or private hospital,

(d) a community home, voluntary home or children's home,

(e) a home provided under section 82(5) of the *Children Act* 1989, or

(f) a residential family centre

and B is accommodated and cared for in that institution.

(5) This subsection applies if A looks after persons under 18 who are receiving education at an educational institution and B is receiving, and A is not receiving, education at that institution.

(6) … [*Northern Ireland.*]

(7) This subsection applies if A is engaged in the provision of services under, or pursuant to anything done under—

(a) sections 8 to 10 of the *Employment and Training Act* 1973 (c. 50), or

(b) section 68, 70(1)(b) or 74 of the *Education and Skills Act* 2008,

and, in that capacity, looks after B on an individual basis.

(8) This subsection applies if A regularly has unsupervised contact with B (whether face to face or by any other means)—

(a) in the exercise of functions of a local authority under section 20 or 21 of the *Children Act* 1989 (c. 41),

(9) This subsection applies if A, as a person who is to report to the court under section 7 of the *Children Act* 1989 on matters relating to the welfare of B, regularly has unsupervised contact with B (whether face to face or by any other means).

(10) This subsection applies if A is a personal adviser appointed for B under—

(a) section 23B(2) of, or paragraph 19C of Schedule 2 to, the *Children Act* 1989,

and, in that capacity, looks after B on an individual basis.

(11) This subsection applies if—

(a) B is subject to a care order, a supervision order or an education supervision order, and

(b) in the exercise of functions conferred by virtue of the order on an authorised person or the authority designated by the order, A looks after B on an individual basis.

(12) This subsection applies if A—

(a) is an officer of the Service appointed for B under section 41(1) of the *Children Act* 1989,

(b) is appointed a children's guardian of B under rule 6 or rule 18 of the *Adoption Rules* 1984 (S.I. 1984 No. 265), or

(c) is appointed to be the guardian ad litem of B under rule 9.5 of the *Family Proceedings Rules* 1991 (S. I. 1991/1247),

and, in that capacity, regularly has unsupervised contact with B (whether face to face or by any other means).

(13) This subsection applies if—

(a) B is subject to requirements imposed by or under an enactment on his release from detention for a criminal offence, or is subject to requirements imposed by a court order made in criminal proceedings, and

(b) A looks after B on an individual basis in pursuance of the requirements.

[This section is printed as amended by the *Education and Skills Act* 2008, s.169, Sched. 1, Pt 1, para. 81.]

Positions of trust: interpretation

22.—(1) The following provisions apply for the purposes of section 21. **14–139**

(2) Subject to subsection (3), a person looks after persons under 18 if he is regularly involved in caring for, training, supervising or being in sole charge of such persons.

(3) A person (A) looks after another person (B) on an individual basis if—

(a) A is regularly involved in caring for, training or supervising B, and

(b) in the course of his involvement, A regularly has unsupervised contact with B (whether face to face or by any other means).

(4) A person receives education at an educational institution if—

(a) he is registered or otherwise enrolled as a pupil or student at the institution, or

(b) he receives education at the institution under arrangements with another educational institution at which he is so registered or otherwise enrolled.

(5) In section 21—

"authority"–

(a) in relation to England and Wales, means a local authority;

(b) in relation to Northern Ireland, has the meaning given by Article 2(2) of the *Children (Northern Ireland) Order* 1995 (S.I. 1995/755 (N.I. 2));

"care home" means an establishment which is a care home for the purposes of the Care Standards Act 2000;

"care order" has–

(a) in relation to England and Wales, the same meaning as in the *Children Act* 1989 and

(b) in relation to Northern Ireland, the same meaning as in the *Children (Northern Ireland) Order* 1995;

"children's home" has–

(a) in relation to England and Wales, the meaning given by section 1 of the *Care Standards Act* 2000, and

(b) in relation to Northern Ireland, the meaning that would be given by Article 9 of the *Health and Personal Social Services (Quality, Improvement and Regulation) (Northern Ireland) Order* 2003 (S.I. 2003/431 (N.I. 9)) ("the 2003 Order") if in paragraph (4) of that Article sub-paragraphs (d), (f) and (g) were omitted;

"community home" has the meaning given by section 53 of the *Children Act* 1989;

"education supervision order" has–

(a) in relation to England and Wales, the meaning given by section 36 of the *Children Act* 1989, and

(b) in relation to Northern Ireland, the meaning given by Article 49(1) of the *Children (Northern Ireland) Order* 1995;

"hospital" means—

(a) a hospital as defined by section 275 of the *National Health Service Act* 2006, or section 206 of the *National Health Service (Wales) Act* 2006; or

(b) any other establishment—

(i) in England, in which any of the services listed in subsection (6) are provided; and

(ii) in Wales, which is a hospital within the meaning given by section 2(3) of the *Care Standards Act* 2000;

"independent clinic" has–

(a) the meaning given by section 2 of the *Care Standards Act* 2000;

(b) in relation to Northern Ireland, the meaning given by Article 2(2) of the 2003 Order;

"private hospital" has the meaning given by Article 90(2) of the *Mental Health (Northern Ireland) Order* 1986 (S.I. 1986/595 (N.I. 4));

"residential care home" means an establishment which is a residential care home for the purposes of the 2003 Order;

"residential family centre" has the meaning given by section 22 of the *Health and Personal Social Services Act (Northern Ireland)* 2001 (c. 3);

"supervision order" has–

(a) in relation to England and Wales, the meaning given by section 31(11) of the *Children Act* 1989 (c. 41), and

(b) in relation to Northern Ireland, the meaning given by Article 49(1) of the *Children (Northern Ireland) Order* 1995 (S.I. 1995/ 755 (N.I. 2);

"voluntary home" has–

(a) in relation to England and Wales, the meaning given by section 60(3) of the *Children Act* 1989, and

(b) in relation to Northern Ireland, the meaning given by Article 74(1) of the *Children (Northern Ireland) Order* 1995.

(6) The services referred to in paragraph (b)(i) of the definition of "hospital" are as follows—

(a) medical treatment under anaesthesia or intravenously administered sedation;

(b) dental treatment under general anaesthesia;

(c) obstetric services and, in connection with childbirth, medical services;

(d) termination of pregnancies;

(e) cosmetic surgery, other than—

(i) ear and body piercing;

(ii) tattooing;

(iii) the subcutaneous injection of a substance or substances into the skin for cosmetic purposes; or

(iv) the removal of hair roots or small blemishes on the skin by the application of heat using an electric current.

[This section is printed as amended by the *Health and Social Care Act 2008 (Consequential Amendments No 2) Order* 2010 (S.I. 2010 No. 813).]

Consent

The offences are drafted so as to protect all children under 18, but they are primarily intended to be charged in relation to victims who are over the age of consent and where the sexual activity would not be an offence save for the abuse of trust. Any sexual activity involving a child under 16 is unlawful and one of the generic child sex offences or offences against a child under 13 should be charged. The breach of trust will be an aggravating factor for sentencing purposes. Sections 6 to 19 apply regardless of consent between the parties. Importantly, therefore, the normal age of consent at 16 will not apply to offences under these sections. **14–140**

Statutory defences

There are a number of specific defences to the offences within these sections. **14–141**

Where the complainant is over 16 at the time of the conduct and:

(i) the parties are lawfully married at the time of the offence (s.23); and

(ii) a lawful sexual relationship existed between the parties immediately before the position of trust arose (s.24);

no offence will have been committed. There is an evidential burden on the defendant to prove that either of these circumstances existed at the time of the offence.

The *Civil Partnership Act* 2004 extended the marriage exceptions in the *Sexual Offences Act* 2003 to include "civil partnerships" as defined.

The age of the complainant at the time of the offence

If the child is between 13 and 18 at the time of the offence the prosecution must prove that the defendant did not reasonably believe that the child was over 18. **14–142**

It will be taken that the defendant did not reasonably believe that the complainant was aged 18 or over, unless he can raise significant evidence to the contrary. This presumption does not apply where the defendant looks after the complainant in one of the following settings:

(a) the complainant is detained by virtue of a court order or enactment;

(b) the complainant is in a hospital, independent clinic, care home or residential family centre;

(c) the complainant is receiving education at an educational institution and the defendant is not receiving education at that institution;

and the defendant looks after the complainant in a caring or training role.

Knowledge of the position of trust

If the defendant looks after the complainant in one of the scenarios (a) to (c), *ante*, there will be a presumption that the defendant knew or could reasonably have been expected to know of the position of trust unless he can raise significant evidence to the contrary. **14–143**

(3) Sentence

In respect of each offence the maximum sentence upon summary conviction is six months' imprisonment and/or a fine. After commencement of the relevant provisions, the maximum custodial sentence in a magistrates' court will be 12 months' imprisonment: *Criminal Justice Act* 2003, ss.154 and 282. An offender convicted of these offences is automatically subject to notification requirements: *SOA* 2003, s.80. **14–144**

Abuse of trust: sexual activity with a child (section 16) and Abuse of position of trust: Causing or inciting a child to engage in sexual activity (section 17)

14–145 The starting points shown below are intended to be used only in relation to victims aged 16 or 17. Where the victim is a child under 16, one of the child sex offences in ss.9 to 13 should normally be charged.

STARTING POINTS AND SENTENCING RANGES: (BASED ON A FIRST TIME OFFENDER AFTER TRIAL)

Type/nature of activity	Starting Point	Range
Penile penetration of the vagina, anus or mouth or penetration of the vagina or anus with another body part or an object	18 months custody	12 months–2 years 6 months
Other forms of non-penetrative activity	26 weeks custody	4 weeks–18 months custody
Contact between part of offender's body (other than the genitalia) with part of the victim's body (other than the genitalia)	Community order	An appropriate non-custodial sentence

AGGRAVATING AND MITIGATING FACTORS:

Additional aggravating factors	Additional mitigating factors
1. Background of intimidation or coercion 2. Offender ejaculated or caused the victim to ejaculate 3. Use of drugs, alcohol or other substance to facilitate the offence. 4. Offender aware that he or she is suffering from a sexually transmitted infection	1. Small disparity in age between victim and offender 2. Relationship of genuine affection 3. No element of corruption

In *Howell* [2007] EWCA Crim 1863, a 34-year-old music teacher of previous good character was convicted after trial of an offence contrary to s.17 of the *Sexual Offences Act* 2003. He sent suggestive and inappropriate text messages to a sixth form pupil (17-year-old) over a four month period. The pupil reported that the text messages made him feel uncomfortable but not particularly traumatised. The sentence of 12 months imprisonment was reduced to six months on appeal.

In *Wilson (Daniel Rushton)* [2008] 1 Cr.App.R.(S.) 542 the defendant was a student teacher (aged 31) with no previous convictions. He pleaded guilty to a s.17 offence, having conducted a "full consensual sexual relationship" with a 17-year-old pupil. He was sentenced to 10 months imprisonment. Whilst he had breached the trust placed in him by his employers, he was not a sexual predator, he had not corrupted the pupil—she was already sexually experienced. He had allowed himself to get involved with her. He had lost his career, would never work with children again and was at the time of appeal in a relationship with a mature woman. The Court held that while the guidelines suggested a starting point of 18 months imprisonment, judges are not obliged to slavishly follow the guidelines, but can deviate from them when the facts require it. His sentence was reduced from 10 months to six months imprisonment.

Abuse of trust: sexual activity in the presence of a child (section 18)

STARTING POINTS AND SENTENCING RANGES: (BASED ON FIRST TIME OFFENDER AFTER TRIAL)

14–146

Type/nature of activity	Starting Point	Range
Consensual intercourse or other forms of consensual penetration	2 years custody	1–4 years custody
Masturbation (of oneself or another person)	18 months custody	12 months–2 years 6 months custody
Consensual sexual touching involving naked genitalia	12 months custody	26 weeks–2 years custody
Consensual sexual touching of naked body parts but not involving naked genitalia	26 weeks custody	4 weeks–18 months custody

AGGRAVATING AND MITIGATING FACTORS:

Additional aggravating factors	Additional mitigating factors
1. Background of intimidation or coercion 2. Use of drugs, alcohol or other substance to facilitate the offence 3. Threats to prevent victim reporting the incident. 4. Abduction or detention	

Abuse of trust: causing a child to watch a sexual act (section 19)

STARTING POINTS AND SENTENCING RANGES: (BASED ON FIRST TIME OFFENDER AFTER TRIAL)

14–147

Type/nature of activity	Starting Point	Range
Live sexual activity	18 months custody	12 months–2 years custody
Moving or still images of people engaged in sexual activity involving penetration	32 weeks custody	26 weeks–12 months custody
Moving or still images of people engaging in sexual activity other than penetration	Community order	Community order–26 weeks custody

AGGRAVATING AND MITIGATING FACTORS:

Additional aggravating factors	Additional mitigating factors
1. Background of intimidation or coercion 2. Use of drugs, alcohol or other substance to facilitate the offence 3. Threats to prevent the victim reporting the incident 4. Abduction or detention 5. Images of violent activity	1. Small disparity in age between victim and offender

Some relationships caught within the scope of these offences, although unlawful, will be wholly consensual. The length of time over which a relationship has been sustained and the proximity in age between the parties could point to a relationship borne out of genuine affection. Each case must be considered carefully on its own facts.

VI. FAMILIAL SEXUAL OFFENCES UNDER THE SEXUAL OFFENCES ACT 2003

A. DEFINITION OF A FAMILY RELATIONSHIP

Sexual Offences Act 2003, s.27

Family relationships

27.—(1) The relation of one person (A) to another (B) is within this section if— **14–148**

(a) it is within any of subsections (2) to (4), or

(b) it would be within one of those subsections but for section 39 of the *Adoption Act* 1976 or section 67 of the *Adoption and Children Act* 2002 (status conferred by adoption).

(2) The relation of A to B is within this subsection if—

(a) one of them is the other's parent, grandparent, brother, sister, half-brother, half-sister, aunt or uncle, or

(b) A is or has been B's foster parent.

(3) The relation of A to B is within this subsection if A and B live or have lived in the same household, or A is or has been regularly involved in caring for, training, supervising or being in sole charge of B, and—

(a) one of them is or has been the other's step-parent,

(b) A and B are cousins,

(c) one of them is or has been the other's stepbrother or stepsister, or

(d) the parent or present or former foster parent of one of them is or has been the other's foster parent.

(4) The relation of A to B is within this subsection if—

(a) A and B live in the same household, and

(b) A is regularly involved in caring for, training, supervising or being in sole charge of B.

(5) For the purposes of this section—

(a) "aunt" means the sister or half-sister of a person's parent, and "uncle" has a corresponding meaning;

Part III

(b) "cousin" means the child of an aunt or uncle;
(c) a person is a child's foster parent if—
 (i) he is a person with whom the child has been placed under section 22C of the *Children Act* 1989 in a placement falling within subsection (6)(a) or (b) of that section (placement with local authority foster parent),
 (ia) he is a person with whom the child has been placed under section 59(1)(a) of that Act (placement by voluntary organisation),
 (ii) he fosters the child privately, within the meaning given by section 66(1)(b) of that Act;
(d) a person is another's partner (whether they are of different sexes or the same sex) if they live together as partners in an enduring family relationship;
(e) "step-parent" includes a parent's partner and "stepbrother" and "stepsister" include the child of a parent's partner.

[This section is printed as amended by the *Children and Young Persons Act* 2008, s.8(2), Sched. 1, para. 16.]

14–149 Subsections (3), (4) and (5) of s.27 set out the different circumstances in which a family relationship between the defendant and the complainant will exist.

B. RELEVANCE OF AGE

14–150 Where the complainant is under 13, the offences are ones of strict liability. If the complainant is between 13 and 18, the defendant will have the evidential burden of showing that he reasonably believed that the complainant was over 18.

C. STATUTORY DEFENCES

(1) Marriage exception

14–151 The marriage defence applies where the complainant was aged 16 or over at the time of the alleged offence.

The *Civil Partnership Act* 2004 extended the marriage exceptions in the *Sexual Offences Act* 2003 to include "civil partnerships" as defined.

(2) Knowledge of the family relationship

14–152 There is an evidential burden on the defendant to prove that he did not know and could not reasonably have been expected to know that a familial relationship existed.

D. SEXUAL ACTIVITY WITH A FAMILY MEMBER

(1) Definition

Sexual Offences Act 2003, s.25

Sexual activity with a child family member

14–153 **25.**—(1) A person (A) commits an offence if—
(a) he intentionally touches another person (B),
(b) the touching is sexual,
(c) the relation of A to B is within section 27,
(d) A knows or could reasonably be expected to know that his relation to B is of a description falling within that section, and
(e) either—
 (i) B is under 18 and A does not reasonably believe that B is 18 or over, or
 (ii) B is under 13.

(2) Where in proceedings for an offence under this section it is proved that the other person was under 18, the defendant is to be taken not to have reasonably believed that that person was 18 or over unless sufficient evidence is adduced to raise an issue as to whether he reasonably believed it.

(3) Where in proceedings for an offence under this section it is proved that the relation of the defendant to the other person was of a description falling within section 27, it is to be taken that the defendant knew or could reasonably have been expected to know that his relation to the other person was of that description unless sufficient evidence is adduced to raise an issue as to whether he knew or could reasonably have been expected to know that it was.

(4) A person guilty of an offence under this section, if aged 18 or over at the time of the offence, is liable—

(a) where subsection (6) applies, on conviction on indictment to imprisonment for a term not exceeding 14 years;

(b) in any other case—

(i) on summary conviction, to imprisonment for a term not exceeding 6 months or a fine not exceeding the statutory maximum or both;

(ii) on conviction on indictment, to imprisonment for a term not exceeding 14 years.

(5) Unless subsection (4) applies, a person guilty of an offence under this section is liable—

(a) on summary conviction, to imprisonment for a term not exceeding 6 months or a fine not exceeding the statutory maximum or both;

(b) on conviction on indictment, to imprisonment for a term not exceeding 5 years.

(6) This subsection applies where the touching involved—

(a) penetration of B's anus or vagina with a part of A's body or anything else,

(b) penetration of B's mouth with A's penis,

(c) penetration of A's anus or vagina with a part of B's body, or

(d) penetration of A's mouth with B's penis.

Touching is defined in s.79(8), see *ante*, § 14–84.

(2) Allocation

This offence is triable either way unless s.25(4)(a) and (6) apply. **14–154**

(3) Sentence

Upon summary conviction the maximum sentence is six months' imprisonment. After commencement of the relevant provisions, the maximum custodial sentence in a magistrates' court will be 12 months' imprisonment: *Criminal Justice Act* 2003, ss.154 and 282. **14–155**

The table below sets out sentencing guidance for use in cases where;

(a) the victim is 13 or over but under 16, regardless of the familial relationship with the offender;

(b) the victim is 16 or 17 but the sexual relationship commenced when the victim was under 16; or

(c) the victim is aged 16 or 17 and the offender is a blood relative.

STARTING POINTS AND SENTENCING RANGES: (BASED ON FIRST TIME OFFENDER AFTER TRIAL)

Examples of nature of activity	**Starting Point**	**Range**
Penile penetration of the vagina, anus, or mouth or penetration of the vagina or anus with another body part or an object	5 years custody	4–8 years custody
Contact between naked genitalia of offender and naked genitalia of victim	4 years custody	3–7 years custody
Contact between naked genitalia of offender or victim and clothed genitalia of the victim or offender Contact between naked genitalia of victim by another part of the offender's body or an object, or between the naked genitalia of offender and another part of victim's body	18 months custody	12 months–2 years 6 months custody
Contact between part of the offender's body (other than the genitalia) with part of the victim's body (other than the genitalia)	Community order	An appropriate non-custodial sentence

The table below sets out sentencing guidance for use in cases where the victim was aged 16 or 17 when the sexual relationship commenced and the relationship is only unlawful because of the abuse of trust implicit in the offence.

Examples of nature of activity	Starting Point	Range
Penile penetration of the vagina, anus or mouth or penetration of the vagina or anus with another body part of an object	2 years custody	1–4 years custody
Any other form of non-penetrative sexual activity involving the naked contact between the offender and victim	12 months custody	26 weeks–2 years custody
Contact between clothed part of the offender's body (other than the genitalia) with clothed part of victim's body (other than the genitalia)	Community order	An appropriate non-custodial sentence

AGGRAVATING AND MITIGATING FACTORS:

Additional aggravating factors	Additional mitigating factors
1. Background of intimidation or coercion 2. Use of drugs, alcohol or other substance 3. Threats deterring the victim reporting the incident 4. Offender aware that he or she is suffering from a sexually transmitted infection 5. Closeness of familial relationship	1. Small disparity in age between victim and offender

Where the victim of a familial child sex offence is aged 16 or 17 when the sexual activity is commenced and the sexual relationship is unlawful only because it takes place within a familial setting, the starting points for sentencing should be in line with those for the generic abuse of trust offences.

In *Thomas* [2006] 1 Cr.App.R.(S.) 101 the Court of Appeal held that categorising the seriousness of an offence contrary to s.25 according to the particular type of relationship between the parties, *i.e.* incest/sexual intercourse with a child in foster care, etc. was not entirely appropriate. The seriousness of the offence lay in the abuse of the relationship with a child. The court in sentencing should take into consideration the age of the parties (the younger the child and the greater the gap in ages the more serious the offence), the extent and nature of the sexual activity and the number of occasions upon which it occurred.

E. INCITING A CHILD FAMILY MEMBER TO ENGAGE IN SEXUAL ACTIVITY

(1) Definition

Sexual Offences Act 2003, s.26

Inciting a child family member to engage in sexual activity

14–156 **26.**—(1) A person (A) commits an offence if—

(a) he intentionally incites another person (B) to touch, or allow himself to be touched by, A,

(b) the touching is sexual,

(c) the relation of A to B is within section 27,

(d) A knows or could reasonably be expected to know that his relation to B is of a description falling within that section, and

(e) either—

(i) B is under 18 and A does not reasonably believe that B is 18 or over, or

(ii) B is under 13.

(2) Where in proceedings for an offence under this section it is proved that the other person was under 18, the defendant is to be taken not to have reasonably believed that that person was 18 or over unless sufficient evidence is adduced to raise an issue as to whether he reasonably believed it.

(3) Where in proceedings for an offence under this section it is proved that the relation of the defendant to the other person was of a description falling within section 27, it is to be taken that the defendant knew or could reasonably have been expected to know that his relation to the other person was of that description unless sufficient evidence is adduced to raise an issue as to whether he knew or could reasonably have been expected to know that it was.

(4) A person guilty of an offence under this section, if he was aged 18 or over at the time of the offence, is liable—

(a) where subsection (6) applies, on conviction on indictment to imprisonment for a term not exceeding 14 years;

(b) in any other case—

(i) on summary conviction, to imprisonment for a term not exceeding 6 months or a fine not exceeding the statutory maximum or both;

(ii) on conviction on indictment, to imprisonment for a term not exceeding 14 years.

(5) Unless subsection (4) applies, a person guilty of an offence under this section is liable—

(a) on summary conviction, to imprisonment for a term not exceeding 6 months or a fine not exceeding the statutory maximum or both;

(b) on conviction on indictment, to imprisonment for a term not exceeding 5 years.

(6) This subsection applies where the touching to which the incitement related involved—

(a) penetration of B's anus or vagina with a part of A's body or anything else,

(b) penetration of B's mouth with A's penis,

(c) penetration of A's anus or vagina with a part of B's body, or

(d) penetration of A's mouth with B's penis.

(2) Allocation

14–157 This offence is triable either way unless s.26(4)(A) and (6) apply.

(3) Sentence

14–158 Upon summary conviction the maximum sentence is six months' imprisonment and/or a fine. After commencement of the relevant provisions, the maximum custodial sentence in a magistrates' court will be 12 months' imprisonment: *Criminal Justice Act* 2003, ss.154 and 282. An offender convicted of this offence is automatically subject to notification requirements: *SOA* 2003, s.80.

Starting points and sentencing ranges: See table above at § 14–155 in respect of offences contrary to s.25.

Aggravating and mitigating factors: See table above at § 14–155 in respect of offences contrary to s.25.

In *R.* [2005] EWCA Crim 1296 the Court held that there was nothing wrong in principle in passing a custodial sentence for this offence. The court reduced the sentence to one of six months' imprisonment plus a 12-month extended licence where the appellant had asked his 12-year-old step-daughter if he could perform a sexual act on her. It should be noted that this case was tried on indictment.

F. Sex with an Adult Relative

The act defines two offences, one of penetration and the other of another consenting to the complainant penetrating them. **14–159**

(1) Definition

Sexual Offences Act 2003, ss.64, 65

Sex with an adult relative: penetration

64.—(1) A person aged 16 or over (A) (subject to subsection (3A)) commits an offence if— **14–160**

(a) he intentionally penetrates another person's vagina or anus with a part of his body or anything else, or penetrates another person's mouth with his penis,

(b) the penetration is sexual,

(c) the other person (B) is aged 18 or over,

(d) A is related to B in a way mentioned in subsection (2), and

(e) A knows or could reasonably be expected to know that he is related to B in that way.

(2) The ways that A may be related to B are as parent, grandparent, child, grandchild, brother, sister, half-brother, half-sister, uncle, aunt, nephew or niece.

(3) In subsection (2)—

(za) "parent" includes an adoptive parent;

(zb) "child" includes an adopted person within the meaning of Chapter 4 of Part 1 of the *Adoption and Children Act* 2002;

(a) "uncle" means the brother of a person's parent, and "aunt" has a corresponding meaning;

(b) "nephew" means the child of a person's brother or sister, and "niece" has a corresponding meaning.

(3A) Where subsection (1) applies in a case where A is related to B as Bs child by virtue of subsection (3)(zb), A does not commit an offence under this section unless A is 18 or over.

(4) Where in proceedings for an offence under this section it is proved that the defendant was related to the other person in any of those ways, it is to be taken that the defendant knew or could reasonably have been expected to know that he was related in that way unless sufficient evidence is adduced to raise an issue as to whether he knew or could reasonably have been expected to know that he was.

(5) A person guilty of an offence under this section is liable—

(a) on summary conviction, to imprisonment for a term not exceeding 6 months or a fine not exceeding the statutory maximum or both;

(b) on conviction on indictment, to imprisonment for a term not exceeding 2 years.

(6) Nothing in

(a) section 47 of the *Adoption Act* 1976 (which disapplies the status provisions in section 39 of that Act for the purposes of this section in relation to adoptions before 30 December 2005), or

(b) section 74 of the *Adoption and Children Act* 2002 (which disapplies the status provisions in section 67 of that Act for those purposes in relation to adoptions on or after that date),

is to be read as preventing the application of section 39 of the *Adoption Act* 1976 or section 67 of the *Adoption and Children Act* 2002 for the purposes of subsection (3)(za) and (zb) above.

[This section is printed as amended by the *Criminal Justice and Immigration Act* 2008, s.73, and Sched. 15, para. 1.]

Sex with an adult relative: consenting to penetration

14–161 **65.**—(1) A person aged 16 or over (A) (subject to subsection (3A)) commits an offence if—

(a) another person (B) penetrates A's vagina or anus with a part of B's body or anything else, or penetrates A's mouth with B's penis,

(b) A consents to the penetration,

(c) the penetration is sexual,

(d) B is aged 18 or over,

(e) A is related to B in a way mentioned in subsection (2), and

(f) A knows or could reasonably be expected to know that he is related to B in that way.

(2) The ways that A may be related to B are as parent, grandparent, child, grandchild, brother, sister, half-brother, half-sister, uncle, aunt, nephew or niece.

(3) In subsection (2)—

(za) "parent" includes an adoptive parent;

(zb) "child" includes an adopted person within the meaning of Chapter 4 of Part 1 of the *Adoption and Children Act* 2002;

(a) "uncle" means the brother of a person's parent, and "aunt" has a corresponding meaning;

(b) "nephew" means the child of a person's brother or sister, and "niece" has a corresponding meaning.

(3A) Where subsection (1) applies in a case where A is related to B as Bs child by virtue of subsection (3)(zb), A does not commit an offence under this section unless A is 18 or over.

(4) Where in proceedings for an offence under this section it is proved that the defendant was related to the other person in any of those ways, it is to be taken that the defendant knew or could reasonably have been expected to know that he was related in that way unless sufficient evidence is adduced to raise an issue as to whether he knew or could reasonably have been expected to know that he was.

(5) A person guilty of an offence under this section is liable—

(a) on summary conviction, to imprisonment for a term not exceeding 6 months or a fine not exceeding the statutory maximum or both;

(b) on conviction on indictment, to imprisonment for a term not exceeding 2 years.

(6) Nothing in

(a) section 47 of the *Adoption Act* 1976 (which disapplies the status provisions in section 39 of that Act for the purposes of this section in relation to adoptions before 30 December 2005), or

(b) section 74 of the *Adoption and Children Act* 2002 (which disapplies the status provisions in section 67 of that Act for those purposes in relation to adoptions on or after that date),

is to be read as preventing the application of section 39 of the *Adoption Act* 1976 or section 67 of the *Adoption and Children Act* 2002 for the purposes of subsection (3)(za) and (zb) above.

[This section is printed as amended by the *Criminal Justice and Immigration Act* 2008, s.73, and Sched. 15, para. 1.]

(2) Allocation

14–162 Both of these offences are triable either way.

(3) Statutory defences

14–163 It is a defence to both offences that the offender was unaware of the blood relationship, unless it is proved that he or she could reasonably have been expected to be aware of it: ss.64(9) and 65(4).

(4) Sentence

14–164 Upon summary conviction the maximum sentence is six months' imprisonment and/or a fine. After commencement of the relevant provisions, the maximum custodial sentence in a magistrates' court will be 12 months' imprisonment: *Criminal Justice Act* 2003, ss.154 and 282. An offender convicted of these offences is automatically subject to notification requirements: *SOA* 2003, s.80. See *post*, § 14–281.

Sex with an adult relative: penetration (section 64) and sex with an adult relative: consenting to penetration (section 65)

STARTING POINTS AND SENTENCING RANGES: (BASED ON FIRST TIME OFFENDER AFTER TRIAL)

14–165

Type/nature of activity	Starting Point	Range
Where there is evidence of long term grooming that took place at a time when the person being groomed was under 18	12 months custody if offender is 18 or over	26 weeks–2 years custody
Where there is evidence of grooming of one party by the other at a time when both parties were over the age of 18	Community order	An appropriate non-custodial sentence
Sexual penetration with no aggravating factors	Community order	An appropriate non-custodial sentence

AGGRAVATING AND MITIGATING FACTORS:

Additional aggravating factors	Additional mitigating factors
1. Background of intimidation or coercion 2. Use of drugs, alcohol or other substance to facilitate the offence 3. Threats to prevent the victim reporting the incident 4. Evidence of long-term grooming 5. Offender aware that he or she is suffering from a sexually transmitted infection 6. Where there is evidence that no effort was made to avoid pregnancy or the sexually transmitted infection	1. Small disparity in age between victim and offender 2. Relationship of genuine affection

Where the offence involves no harm to a victim (other than the offensiveness of the conduct to society at large), the starting point for sentencing should normally be a community order.

VII. OFFENCES AGAINST PERSONS WITH MENTAL DISORDERS UNDER THE SEXUAL OFFENCES ACT 2003

A. MENTAL DISORDER

14–166 The Act changed significantly the previous legislation in this area which required the victim to be deemed "defective" and prosecutions could only be brought with the consent of the DPP.

14–167 Section 79(6) of the Act refers to the meaning of "mental disorder" being that defined in s.1 of the *Mental Health Act* 1983.

Mental Health Act 1983, s.1

Application of Act: "mental disorder"

14–168 **1.**—(1) The provisions of this Act shall have effect with respect to the reception, care and treatment of mentally disordered patients, the management of their property and other related matters.

(2) In this Act—

"mental disorder" means any disorder or disability of mind and "mentally disordered" shall be construed accordingly;

and other expressions shall have the meanings assigned to them in section 145 below.

(2A) But a person with learning disability shall not be considered by reason of that disability to be—

(a) suffering from mental disorder for the purposes of the provisions mentioned in subsection (2B) below; or

(b) requiring treatment in hospital for mental disorder for the purposes of sections 17E and 50 to 53 below,

unless that disability is associated with abnormally aggressive or seriously irresponsible conduct on his part.

(2B) The provisions are—

(a) sections 3, 7, 17A, 20 and 20A below;

(b) sections 35 to 38, 45A, 47, 48 and 51 below; and

(c) section 72(1)(b) and (c) and (4) below.

(3) Dependence on alcohol or drugs is not considered to be a disorder or disability of the mind for the purposes of subsection (2) above.

(4) In subsection (2A) above, "learning disability" means a state of arrested or incomplete development of the mind which includes significant impairment of intelligence and social functioning.

[This section is printed as amended by the *Mental Health Act* 2007, Ch. 12, Pt 1.]

B. SEXUAL ACTIVITY WITH A PERSON WITH A MENTAL DISORDER IMPEDING CHOICE AND CAUSING OR INCITING A PERSON WITH A MENTAL DISORDER IMPEDING CHOICE TO ENGAGE IN SEXUAL ACTIVITY

The offences in ss.30 to 32 relate to persons whose mental functioning is so impaired at the time of the sexual activity that they are deemed to be "unable to refuse" either because of, or for a reason relating to, their mental disorder. Examples of activity covered include where D causes X to have sex with him / D causes X to undress for him for sexual gratification / D causes X to have sex with D's friend. **14–169**

In *C* [2010] 1 Cr.App.R. 7— the House of Lords reversed a decision of the Court of Appeal and confirmed that where B is "unable to refuse" sexual activity if "(a) he lacks the capacity to choose whether to agree to the touching, or (b) he is unable to communicate to such a choice to A", it is not necessary to establish that the complainant was physically unable to communicate by reason of his mental disorder; provided the inability to communicate was the result of, or related to, a disorder or disability of the mind. There was no warrant in the Act for limiting it to a physical inability to communicate.

Section 31 "inciting", is included to cover scenarios where the actual act does not take place.

The definition of being "unable to refuse" is contained in subsection (2) of sections 30 to 33, and is only relevant to these offences. The complainant is unable to refuse if—

(a) he lacks the capacity to choose whether to agree to the touching (whether because he lacks sufficient understanding of the nature or reasonably foreseeable consequences of what is being done, or for any other reason); or

(b) he is unable to communicate such a choice to the defendant.

(1) Definition

Sexual Offences Act 2003, s.30

Sexual activity with a person with a mental disorder impeding choice

30.—(1) A person (A) commits an offence if— **14–170**

(a) he intentionally touches another person (B),

(b) the touching is sexual,

(c) B is unable to refuse because of or for a reason related to a mental disorder, and

(d) A knows or could reasonably be expected to know that B has a mental disorder and that because of it or for a reason related to it B is likely to be unable to refuse.

(2) B is unable to refuse if—

Part III

(a) he lacks the capacity to choose whether to agree to the touching (whether because he lacks sufficient understanding of the nature or reasonably foreseeable consequences of what is being done, or for any other reason), or
(b) he is unable to communicate such a choice to A.

(3) A person guilty of an offence under this section, if the touching involved—
(a) penetration of B's anus or vagina with a part of A's body or anything else,
(b) penetration of B's mouth with A's penis,
(c) penetration of A's anus or vagina with a part of B's body, or
(d) penetration of A's mouth with B's penis,
is liable, on conviction on indictment, to imprisonment for life.

(4) Unless subsection (3) applies, a person guilty of an offence under this section is liable—
(a) on summary conviction, to imprisonment for a term not exceeding 6 months or to a fine not exceeding the statutory maximum or both;
(b) on conviction on indictment, to imprisonment for a term not exceeding 14 years.

Causing or inciting a person, with a mental disorder impeding choice, to engage in sexual activity

14–171 **31.**—(1) A person (A) commits an offence if—
(a) he intentionally causes or incites another person (B) to engage in an activity,
(b) the activity is sexual,
(c) B is unable to refuse because of or for a reason related to a mental disorder, and
(d) A knows or could reasonably be expected to know that B has a mental disorder and that because of it or for a reason related to it B is likely to be unable to refuse.

(2) B is unable to refuse if—
(a) he lacks the capacity to choose whether to agree to engaging in the activity caused or incited (whether because he lacks sufficient understanding of the nature or reasonably foreseeable consequences of the activity, or for any other reason), or
(b) he is unable to communicate such a choice to A.

(3) A person guilty of an offence under this section, if the activity caused or incited involved—
(a) penetration of B's anus or vagina,
(b) penetration of B's mouth with a person's penis,
(c) penetration of a person's anus or vagina with a part of B's body or by B with anything else, or
(d) penetration of a person's mouth with B's penis,
is liable, on conviction on indictment, to imprisonment for life.

(4) Unless subsection (3) applies, a person guilty of an offence under this section is liable—
(a) on summary conviction, to imprisonment for a term not exceeding 6 months or to a fine not exceeding the statutory maximum or both;
(b) on conviction on indictment, to imprisonment for a term not exceeding 14 years.

(2) Allocation

14–172 These offences are triable either way unless ss.30(3) or 31(3) apply.

(3) Elements of the offence

14–173 In *Hulme v. DPP* [2006] EWHC 1347 it was held that a woman suffering with cerebral palsy with a mental age well below her chronological 27 years, although she was able to speak she was not able to communicate her choice of whether to agree to sexual touching within the meaning of s.30(2) and was therefore "unable to refuse because of or for a reason related to a mental disorder" (s.30(1)(c)).

A person is unable to refuse sexual touching because of or for a reason related to a mental disorder within subsection (1) "if … he lacks the capacity to choose whether to agree to the touching (whether because he lacks sufficient understanding of the nature of reasonably forseeable consequences of what is being done, or for any other reason)" (s.30(2)(a)). For the purposes of this section, the effect of a mental disorder would have to be severe for it to be such as to render the person unable to choose to submit to sexual activity, notwithstanding that he understood the nature of the activity; an acute episode of a mental disorder that resulted in the inability to make a rational decision might do so, but an irrational fear that prevented the exercise of choice could not be equated to a lack of capacity to choose, which could not be "person specific" or even "situation specific": *C.* (above).

(4) Sentence

Upon summary conviction the maximum sentence is six months' imprisonment. After commencement of the relevant provisions, the maximum custodial sentence in a magistrates' court will be 12 months' imprisonment: *Criminal Justice Act* 2003, ss.154 and 282. An offender convicted of these offences is automatically subject to notification requirements: *SOA* 2003, s.80. See *post*, § 14–281. **14–174**

Sexual activity with a person with a mental disorder impeding choice (section 30)

STARTING POINTS AND SENTENCING RANGES: (BASED ON FIRST TIME OFFENDER AFTER TRIAL)

14–175

Type/nature of activity	Starting Point	Range
Contact between naked genitalia of offender and another part of victim's body or naked genitalia of victim by offender using part of his or her body other than the genitalia	15 months custody	36 weeks–3 years custody
Contact between clothed genitalia of offender and naked genitalia of victim or naked genitalia of offender and clothed genitalia of victim		

Type/nature of activity	Starting Point	Range
Contact between part of offender's body (other than the genitalia) with parts of victim's body (other than the genitalia)	26 weeks custody	4 weeks–18 months custody

AGGRAVATING AND MITIGATING FACTORS:

Additional aggravating factors	Additional mitigating factors
1. Background of intimidation or coercion 2. Offender ejaculated or caused the victim to ejaculate 3. Use of drugs, alcohol or other substance to facilitate the offence 4. Threats to prevent the victim reporting the incident 5. Abduction or detention 6. Offender aware that he or she is suffering from a sexually transmitted infection	1. Relationship of genuine affection 2. Offender had a mental disorder at the time of the offence that significantly affected his or her culpability.

In *D. (Donald David)* [2005] EWCA Crim 1459, the 74-year-old appellant had pleaded guilty to an offence under section 30. The complainant was his partner's grand-daughter, aged 25 but with a mental age of between four and eight years old. The appellant had previously been cautioned for indecently assaulting the complainant, and was charged after being found with his hand down her trousers and between her legs. He denied digital penetration in an accepted basis of plea. The Court of Appeal regarded the matter as a gross breach of trust, but found there were exceptional circumstances and reduced the custodial element of the sentence to six months but maintained the extended licence period of two years and nine months. In *Johnson* [2010] EWCA Crim 2082 a six year sentence was reduced to five on appeal on a 76-year-old man who had a sexual relationship with a 42-year-old autistic woman whom he met as a community driver. The reduction was allowed on the basis of his age and his genuine affection for the victim.

Causing or inciting a person with a mental disorder impeding choice to engage in sexual activity (section 31)

See table at § 14–95, *ante*.

In *Jones* [2006] 2 Cr.App.R.(S.) 18, CA, the appellant was convicted of an offence under section 31. The complainant was a 19-year-old who suffered from Down's syndrome. He had the mental age of a five-year-old. The appellant was seen in the toilets of a public house with his hand on the complainant's shoulder and his penis exposed. A psychiatrist concluded that the complainant did not have the capacity to consent to sexual activity. The appellant was apprehended at the scene and badly beaten by the family. The Court of Appeal held that the general considerations set out in *Milberry and Others* [2003] 2 Cr.App.R.(S.) 31, in relation to the level of culpability of the offender and the level of risk posed by the offender to society also applied to sexual offences other than rape. Also that offences of this kind, depending on the facts, could be commensurate in terms of seriousness to offences against children. The appellant was treated as a man of good character. The appeal was allowed in that the sentence of three years' imprisonment was reduced to 15 months' imprisonment.

In *Att.-Gen.'s Reference (No. 106 of 2005), Re (Hunter)* [2006] 2 Cr.App.R.(S.) 78, a two year community rehabilitation order with a condition of residence at a probation hostel for six months was upheld on appeal. The defendant, a 45-year-old man, pleaded guilty to having unprotected sexual intercourse and oral sex with a 17-year-old girl with learning difficulties, whilst her mother had left her in his care. The complainant had indicated consent and did not appear to be either physically or psychologically affected. The conduct had stopped prior to it being discovered.

C. Engaging in Sexual Activity in the Presence of a Person with a Mental Disorder Impeding Choice

(1) Definition

Sexual Offences Act 2003, s.32

Engaging in sexual activity in the presence of a person with a mental disorder impeding choice

32.—(1) A person (A) commits an offence if— **14–177**

(a) he intentionally engages in an activity,

(b) the activity is sexual,

(c) for the purpose of obtaining sexual gratification, he engages in it—

(i) when another person (B) is present or is in a place from which A can be observed, and

(ii) knowing or believing that B is aware, or intending that B should be aware, that he is engaging in it,

(d) B is unable to refuse because of or for a reason related to a mental disorder, and

(e) A knows or could reasonably be expected to know that B has a mental disorder and that because of it or for a reason related to it B is likely to be unable to refuse.

(2) B is unable to refuse if—

(a) he lacks the capacity to choose whether to agree to being present (whether because he lacks sufficient understanding of the nature of the activity, or for any other reason), or

(b) he is unable to communicate such a choice to A.

(3) A person guilty of an offence under this section is liable—

(a) on summary conviction, to imprisonment for a term not exceeding 6 months or a fine not exceeding the statutory maximum or both;

(b) on conviction on indictment, to imprisonment for a term not exceeding 10 years.

(2) Allocation

This offence is triable either way. **14–178**

(3) Elements of the offence

This offence occurs where the defendant engages in sexual activity with another in **14–179**

Part III

the presence of the complainant with a mental disorder for the purpose of sexual gratification. The defendant must know or believe that the complainant is aware of the activity or intends them to be aware of it.

This offence can also include situations where the defendant commits a sexual act that does not involve a third party, for example where he engages in self-masturbation. Offences under this section can be committed either in the physical presence of the complainant or in a place from which the defendant can be observed by the complainant, *e.g.* via a webcam.

(4) Sentence

14–180 Upon summary conviction the maximum sentence is six months' imprisonment. After commencement of the relevant provisions, the maximum custodial sentence in a magistrates' court will be 12 months' imprisonment: *Criminal Justice Act* 2003, ss.154 and 282. An offender convicted of this offence is automatically subject to notification requirements: *SOA* 2003, s.80. See *post*, § 14–281.

See table at § 14–116 for Guidelines.

D. CAUSING A PERSON WITH A MENTAL DISORDER TO WATCH A SEXUAL ACT

(1) Definition

Sexual Offences Act 2003, s.33

Causing a person, with a mental disorder impeding choice, to watch a sexual act

14–181 **33.**—(1) A person (A) commits an offence if—

(a) for the purpose of obtaining sexual gratification, he intentionally causes another person (B) to watch a third person engaging in an activity, or to look at an image of any person engaging in an activity,

(b) the activity is sexual,

(c) B is unable to refuse because of or for a reason related to a mental disorder, and

(d) A knows or could reasonably be expected to know that B has a mental disorder and that because of it or for a reason related to it B is likely to be unable to refuse.

(2) B is unable to refuse if—

(a) he lacks the capacity to choose whether to agree to watching or looking (whether because he lacks sufficient understanding of the nature of the activity, or for any other reason), or

(b) he is unable to communicate such a choice to A.

(3) A person guilty of an offence under this section is liable—

(a) on summary conviction, to imprisonment for a term not exceeding 6 months or a fine not exceeding the statutory maximum or both;

(b) on conviction on indictment, to imprisonment for a term not exceeding 10 years.

Sexual Offences Act 2003, s.79(5)

Part 1: general interpretation

14–182 **79.**—(5) References to an image of a person include references to an image of an imaginary person.

Note that the defendant must know or be reasonably expected to know that the complainant has a mental disorder and is unable to consent.

(2) Allocation

14–183 This offence is triable either way.

(3) Sentence

14–184 Upon summary conviction the maximum sentence is six months' imprisonment. After commencement of the relevant provisions, the maximum custodial sentence in a magistrates' court will be 12 months' imprisonment: *Criminal Justice Act* 2003, ss.154 and 282. An offender convicted of these offences is automatically subject to notification requirements: *SOA* 2003, s.80. See *post*, § 14–281.

See table at § 14–120 for Guidelines.

E. PROCURING SEXUAL ACTIVITY WITH A PERSON WITH A MENTAL DISORDER

The offences in ss.34 to 37 relate to persons who have a mental disorder where their agreement to sexual activity is secured through inducement, threat (*e.g.* harm to complainant or someone complainant knows) or deception (*e.g.* complainant will get into trouble by not engaging in this activity). 14–185

(1) Definition

Sexual Offences Act 2003, s.34

Inducement, threat or deception to procure sexual activity with a person with a mental disorder

34.—(1) A person (A) commits an offence if— 14–186

(a) with the agreement of another person (B) he intentionally touches that person,

(b) the touching is sexual,

(c) A obtains B's agreement by means of an inducement offered or given, a threat made or a deception practised by A for that purpose,

(d) B has a mental disorder, and

(e) A knows or could reasonably be expected to know that B has a mental disorder.

(2) A person guilty of an offence under this section, if the touching involved—

(a) penetration of B's anus or vagina with a part of A's body or anything else,

(b) penetration of B's mouth with A's penis,

(c) penetration of A's anus or vagina with a part of B's body, or

(d) penetration of A's mouth with B's penis,

is liable, on conviction on indictment, to imprisonment for life.

(3) Unless subsection (2) applies, a person guilty of an offence under this section is liable—

(a) on summary conviction, to imprisonment for a term not exceeding 6 months or a fine not exceeding the statutory maximum or both;

(b) on conviction on indictment, to imprisonment for a term not exceeding 14 years.

(2) Allocation

This offence is triable either way unless s.34(2) applies. 14–187

(3) Sentence

Upon summary conviction the maximum sentence is six months' imprisonment. After commencement of the relevant provisions, the maximum custodial sentence in a magistrates' court will be 12 months' imprisonment: *Criminal Justice Act* 2003, ss.154 and 282. An offender convicted of these offences is automatically subject to notification requirements: *SOA* 2003, s.80. See *post*, § 14–281. 14–188

See table at § 14–175 for Guidelines.

F. CAUSING A PERSON WITH A MENTAL DISORDER TO ENGAGE IN OR AGREE TO ENGAGE IN SEXUAL ACTIVITY BY INDUCEMENT, THREAT OR DECEPTION

(1) Definition

Sexual Offences Act 2003, s.35

Causing a person with a mental disorder to engage in or agree to engage in sexual activity by inducement, threat or deception

35.—(1) A person (A) commits an offence if— 14–189

(a) by means of an inducement offered or given, a threat made or a deception practised by him for this purpose, he intentionally causes another person (B) to engage in, or to agree to engage in, an activity,
(b) the activity is sexual,
(c) B has a mental disorder, and
(d) A knows or could reasonably be expected to know that B has a mental disorder.

(2) A person guilty of an offence under this section, if the activity caused or agreed to involved—
(a) penetration of B's anus or vagina,
(b) penetration of B's mouth with a person's penis,
(c) penetration of a person's anus or vagina with a part of B's body or by B with anything else, or
(d) penetration of a person's mouth with B's penis,

is liable, on conviction on indictment, to imprisonment for life.

(3) Unless subsection (2) applies, a person guilty of an offence under this section is liable—
(a) on summary conviction, to imprisonment for a term not exceeding 6 months or a fine not exceeding the statutory maximum or both;
(b) on conviction on indictment, to imprisonment for a term not exceeding 14 years.

(2) Allocation

14–190 This offence is triable either way unless section 35(2) applies.

(3) Sentence

14–191 Upon summary conviction the maximum sentence is six months imprisonment or a fine. After commencement of the relevant provisions, the maximum custodial sentence will be 12 months imprisonment in the magistrates' court: *Criminal Justice Act* 2003, ss.154 and 282. An offender convicted of this offence is automatically subject to notification requirements: *SOA* 2003, s.80.

See *ante*, § 14–175 for sentencing guidelines.

G. ENGAGING IN SEXUAL ACTIVITY IN THE PRESENCE, PROCURED BY INDUCEMENT, THREAT OR DECEPTION, OF A PERSON WITH A MENTAL DISORDER

(1) Definition

Sexual Offences Act 2003, s.36

Engaging in sexual activity in the presence, procured by inducement, threat or deception, of a person with a mental disorder

14–192 **36.**—(1) A person (A) commits an offence if—
(a) he intentionally engages in an activity,
(b) the activity is sexual,
(c) for the purpose of obtaining sexual gratification, he engages in it—
(i) when another person (B) is present or is in a place from which A can be observed, and
(ii) knowing or believing that B is aware, or intending that B should be aware, that he is engaging in it,
(d) B agrees to be present or in the place referred to in paragraph (c)(i) because of an inducement offered or given, a threat made or a deception practised by A for the purpose of obtaining that agreement,
(e) B has a mental disorder, and
(f) A knows or could reasonably be expected to know that B has a mental disorder.

(2) A person guilty of an offence under this section is liable—
(a) on summary conviction, to imprisonment for a term not exceeding 6 months or a fine not exceeding the statutory maximum or both;

(b) on conviction on indictment, to imprisonment for a term not exceeding 10 years.

(2) Allocation

This offence is triable either way. **14–193**

(3) Sentence

Upon summary conviction the maximum sentence is six months' imprisonment. After commencement of the relevant provisions the maximum custodial sentence in a magistrates' court will be 12 months' imprisonment: *Criminal Justice Act* 2003, ss.154 and 282. An offender convicted of this offence is automatically subject to notification requirements: *SOA* 2003, s.80. See *post*, § 14–281. **14–194**

STARTING POINTS AND SENTENCING RANGES: (BASED ON FIRST TIME OFFENDER AFTER TRIAL)

Type/nature of activity	Starting Point	Range
Consensual intercourse or other forms of consensual penetration	2 years custody	1–4 years custody
Masturbation (of oneself or anther person)	18 months custody	12 months–2 years 6 months custody
Consensual sexual touching involving naked genitalia	12 months custody	26 weeks–2 years custody
Consensual sexual touching of naked body parts but not involving naked genitalia	26 weeks custody	4 weeks–18 months custody

AGGRAVATING AND MITIGATING FACTORS:

Additional aggravating factors	Additional mitigating factors
1. Background of intimidation or coercion 2. Use of drugs, alcohol or other substance to facilitate the offence 3. Threats to prevent victim reporting the incident 4. Abduction or detention	

Part III

H. CAUSING A PERSON WITH A MENTAL DISORDER TO WATCH A SEXUAL ACT BY INDUCEMENT, THREAT OR DECEPTION

(1) Definition

Sexual Offences Act 2003, s.37

Causing a person with a mental disorder to watch a sexual act by inducement, threat or deception

14–195 **37.**—(1) A person (A) commits an offence if—

(a) for the purpose of obtaining sexual gratification, he intentionally causes another person (B) to watch a third person engaging in an activity, or to look at an image of any person engaging in an activity,

(b) the activity is sexual,

(c) B agrees to watch or look because of an inducement offered or given, a threat made or a deception practised by A for the purpose of obtaining that agreement,

(d) B has a mental disorder, and

(e) A knows or could reasonably be expected to know that B has a mental disorder.

(2) A person guilty of an offence under this section is liable—

(a) on summary conviction, to imprisonment for a term not exceeding 6 months or a fine not exceeding the statutory maximum or both;

(b) on conviction on indictment, to imprisonment for a term not exceeding 10 years.

(2) Allocation

14–196 This offence is triable either way.

(3) Sentence

14–197 Upon summary conviction the maximum sentence is six months' imprisonment. After commencement of the relevant provisions, the maximum custodial sentence in a magistrates' court will be 12 months' imprisonment: *Criminal Justice Act* 2003, ss.154 and 282. An offender convicted of this offence is automatically subject to notification requirements: *SOA* 2003, s.80. See *post*, § 14–281.

STARTING POINTS AND SENTENCING RANGES: (BASED ON FIRST TIME OFFENDER AFTER TRIAL)

Type/nature of activity	Starting Point	Range
Live sexual activity	18 months custody	12 months–2 years custody
Moving or still images of people engaged in sexual activity involving penetration	32 weeks custody	26 weeks–12 months custody
Moving or still images of people engaging in sexual activity other than penetration	Community order	Community order–26 weeks custody

AGGRAVATING AND MITIGATING FACTORS:

Additional aggravating factors	Additional mitigating factors
1. Background of intimidation or coercion 2. Use of drugs, alcohol or other substance to facilitate the offence 3. Threats to prevent victim reporting the incident 4. Abduction or detention 5. Images of violent activity	

I. CARE WORKERS

The Act creates separate offences that can be committed by the mentally disordered person's care worker. Section 42 defines what a care worker is for the purposes of the offences created in ss.38 to 41. **14–198**

The offences in ss.38 to 41 relate to persons who have a mental disorder regardless of their ability to choose whether or not to take part in sexual activity, whose actions may be influenced by their familiarity with, or dependence upon, a care worker. Therefore, within this close relationship, the existence of a mental disorder is sufficient in establishing that aspect of the offence and further, it is no defence to say that the complainant consented to the act.

Each offence that falls under this section must be read with reference to the following definitions and defences.

(1) Care worker definition

Sexual Offences Act 2003, s.42

Care workers: interpretation

42.—(1) For the purposes of sections 38 to 41, a person (A) is involved in the care of another person (B) in a way that falls within this section if any of subsections (2) to (4) applies. **14–199**

(2) This subsection applies if—

(a) B is accommodated and cared for in a care home, community home, voluntary home or children's home, and

(b) A has functions to perform in the home in the course of employment which have brought him or are likely to bring him into regular face to face contact with B.

(3) This subsection applies if B is a patient for whom services are provided—

(a) by a National Health Service body or an independent medical agency;

(b) in an independent hospital; or

(c) in Wales, in an independent clinic,

and A has functions to perform for the body or agency or in the hospital or clinic in the course of employment which have brought A or are likely to bring A into regular face to face contact with B.

(4) This subsection applies if A—

(a) is, whether or not in the course of employment, a provider of care, assistance or services to B in connection with B's mental disorder, and

(b) as such, has had or is likely to have regular face to face contact with B.

(5) In this section—

"care home" means an establishment which is a care home for the purposes of the *Care Standards Act* 2000;

"children's home" has the meaning given by section 1 of that Act;

"community home" has the meaning given by section 53 of the *Children Act* 1989 (c. 41);

"employment" means any employment, whether paid or unpaid and whether under a contract of service or apprenticeship, under a contract for services, or otherwise than under a contract;

"independent clinic" has the meaning given by section 2 of the *Care Standards Act* 2000;

"independent hospital"—

(a) in England, means—

(i) a hospital as defined by section 275 of the *National Health Service Act* 2006 that is not a health service hospital as defined by that section; or

(ii) any other establishment in which any of the services listed in section 22(6) are provided and which is not a health service hospital as so defined; and

(b) in Wales, has the meaning given by section 2 of the *Care Standards Act* 2000;

"independent medical agency" means an undertaking (not being an independent hospital, or in Wales an independent clinic) which consists of or includes the provision of services by medical practitioners;

"National Health Service body" means–

(a) a [Local Health Board]

(b) a National Health Service trust,

(c) a Primary Care Trust, or

(d) a Special Health Authority;

"voluntary home" has the meaning given by section 60(3) of the *Children Act* 1989.

(6) In subsection (5), in the definition of "independent medical agency", "undertaking" includes any business or profession and—

(a) in relation to a public or local authority, includes the exercise of any functions of that authority; and

(b) in relation to any other body of persons, whether corporate or unincorporate, includes any of the activities of that body.

[This section is printed as amended by the *Health and Social Care Act* 2008 (Consequential Amendments No. 2) Order 2008 (S.I. 2008 No. 813).]

(2) Defence: awareness of condition

14–200 There is an evidential burden on the defendant to prove that he did not know and could not reasonably have been expected to know that the complainant had a mental disorder. If this evidential burden is discharged, it is then for the Prosecution to prove that he could reasonably be expected to know about the condition.

The relevant provisions are contained in subection (2) of the relevant sections providing for the offences.

(3) Marriage exception

Sexual Offences Act 2003, s.43

Sections 38 to 41: exception for spouses and civil partners

14–201 **43.**—(1) Conduct by a person (A) which would otherwise be an offence under any of sections 38 to 41 against another person (B) is not an offence under that section if at the time—

(a) B is 16 or over, and

(b) A and B are lawfully married or civil partners of each other.

(2) In proceedings for such an offence it is for the defendant to prove that A and B were married lawfully at the time, or civil partners of each other.

[This section is printed as amended by the *Civil Partnership Act* 2004, Sched. 27, para. 175.]

(4) Existing sexual relationship

The pre-existing sexual relationship defence provides that any lawful sexual relationship that existed *immediately before* the care relationship will not be criminalised as a result of the relationship of care. 14–202

Sexual Offences Act 2003, s.44

Sections 38 to 41: sexual relationships which pre-date care relationships

44.—(1) Conduct by a person (A) which would otherwise be an offence under any of sections 38 to 41 against another person (B) is not an offence under that section if, immediately before A became involved in B's care in a way that falls within section 42, a sexual relationship existed between A and B. 14–203

(2) Subsection (1) does not apply if at that time sexual intercourse between A and B would have been unlawful.

(3) In proceedings for an offence under any of sections 38 to 41 it is for the defendant to prove that such a relationship existed at that time.

J. CARE WORKERS—SEXUAL ACTIVITY WITH A PERSON WITH A MENTAL DISORDER

(1) Definition

Sexual Offences Act 2003, s.38

Care workers: sexual activity with a person with a mental disorder

38.—(1) A person (A) commits an offence if— 14–204

(a) he intentionally touches another person (B),
(b) the touching is sexual,
(c) B has a mental disorder,
(d) A knows or could reasonably be expected to know that B has a mental disorder, and
(e) A is involved in B's care in a way that falls within section 42.

(2) Where in proceedings for an offence under this section it is proved that the other person had a mental disorder, it is to be taken that the defendant knew or could reasonably have been expected to know that that person had a mental disorder unless sufficient evidence is adduced to raise an issue as to whether he knew or could reasonably have been expected to know it.

(3) A person guilty of an offence under this section, if the touching involved—

(a) penetration of B's anus or vagina with a part of A's body or anything else,
(b) penetration of B's mouth with A's penis,
(c) penetration of A's anus or vagina with a part of B's body, or
(d) penetration of A's mouth with B's penis,

is liable, on conviction on indictment, to imprisonment for a term not exceeding 14 years.

(4) Unless subsection (3) applies, a person guilty of an offence under this section is liable—

(a) on summary conviction, to imprisonment for a term not exceeding 6 months or a fine not exceeding the statutory maximum or both;
(b) on conviction on indictment, to imprisonment for a term not exceeding 10 years.

(2) Allocation

This offence is triable either way, unless s.38(3) applies. 14–205

(3) Sentence

Upon summary conviction the maximum sentence is six months' imprisonment. After commencement of the relevant provisions, the maximum custodial sentence in a magistrates' court will be 12 months' imprisonment: *Criminal Justice Act* 2003, ss.154 and 282. 14–206

Part III

STARTING POINTS AND SENTENCING RANGES: (BASED ON FIRST TIME OFFENDER AFTER TRIAL)

Examples of nature of activity	Starting Point	Range
Basic offence of sexual activity involving penetration, assuming no aggravating or mitigating factors	3 years custody	2–5 years custody
Other forms of non-penetrative activity	12 months custody	26 weeks–2 years custody
Naked contact between part of the offender's body with part of the victim's body	Community order	An appropriate non-custodial sentence

AGGRAVATING AND MITIGATING FACTORS:

Additional aggravating factors	Additional mitigating factors
1. History of intimidation 2. Use of drugs, alcohol or other substance to facilitate the offence 3. Threats to prevent victim reporting the incident 4. Abduction or detention 5. Offender aware that he or she is suffering from a sexually transmitted infection	1. Relationship of genuine affection

K. CARE WORKERS—CAUSING OR INCITING SEXUAL ACTIVITY

(1) Definition

Sexual Offences Act 2003, s.39

Care workers: causing or inciting sexual activity

14–207 **39.**—(1) A person (A) commits an offence if—

(a) he intentionally causes or incites another person (B) to engage in an activity,

(b) the activity is sexual,

(c) B has a mental disorder,

(d) A knows or could reasonably be expected to know that B has a mental disorder, and

(e) A is involved in B's care in a way that falls within section 42.

(2) Where in proceedings for an offence under this section it is proved that the other person had a mental disorder, it is to be taken that the defendant knew or could reasonably have been expected to know that that person had a mental disorder unless sufficient evidence is adduced to raise an issue as to whether he knew or could reasonably have been expected to know it.

(3) A person guilty of an offence under this section, if the activity caused or incited involved—

(a) penetration of B's anus or vagina,
(b) penetration of B's mouth with a person's penis,
(c) penetration of a person's anus or vagina with a part of B's body or by B with anything else, or
(d) penetration of a person's mouth with B's penis,

is liable, on conviction on indictment, to imprisonment for a term not exceeding 14 years.

(4) Unless subsection (3) applies, a person guilty of an offence under this section is liable—

(a) on summary conviction, to imprisonment for a term not exceeding 6 months or a fine not exceeding the statutory maximum or both;
(b) on conviction on indictment, to imprisonment for a term not exceeding 10 years.

(2) Allocation

This offence is triable either way unless s.39(3) applies. **14–208**

(3) Sentence

Upon summary conviction the maximum sentence is six months' imprisonment. After commencement of the relevant provisions, the maximum custodial sentence in a magistrates' court will be 12 months' imprisonment: *Criminal Justice Act* 2003, ss.154 and 282. **14–209**

See table at § 14–206 for Guidelines.

L. CARE WORKERS—SEXUAL ACTIVITY IN THE PRESENCE OF A PERSON WITH A MENTAL DISORDER

(1) Definition

Sexual Offences Act 2003, s.40

Care workers: sexual activity in the presence of a person with a mental disorder

40.—(1) A person (A) commits an offence if— **14–210**

(a) he intentionally engages in an activity,
(b) the activity is sexual,
(c) for the purpose of obtaining sexual gratification, he engages in it—
  (i) when another person (B) is present or is in a place from which A can be observed, and
  (ii) knowing or believing that B is aware, or intending that B should be aware, that he is engaging in it,
(d) B has a mental disorder,
(e) A knows or could reasonably be expected to know that B has a mental disorder, and
(f) A is involved in B's care in a way that falls within section 42.

(2) Where in proceedings for an offence under this section it is proved that the other person had a mental disorder, it is to be taken that the defendant knew or could reasonably have been expected to know that that person had a mental disorder unless sufficient evidence is adduced to raise an issue as to whether he knew or could reasonably have been expected to know it.

(3) A person guilty of an offence under this section is liable—

(a) on summary conviction, to imprisonment for a term not exceeding 6 months or a fine not exceeding the statutory maximum or both;
(b) on conviction on indictment, to imprisonment for a term not exceeding 7 years.

Part III

(2) Allocation

14–211 This offence is triable either way.

(3) Sentence

14–212 Upon summary conviction the maximum sentence is six months' imprisonment. After commencement of the relevant provisions, the maximum custodial sentence in a magistrates' court will be 12 months' imprisonment: *Criminal Justice Act* 2003, ss.154 and 282.

See table at § 14–194 for Guidelines.

M. Care Workers—Causing a Person with a Mental Disorder to Watch a Sexual Act

(1) Definition

Sexual Offences Act 2003, s.41

Care workers: causing a person with a mental disorder to watch a sexual act

14–213 **41.**—(1) A person (A) commits an offence if—

(a) for the purpose of obtaining sexual gratification, he intentionally causes another person (B) to watch a third person engaging in an activity, or to look at an image of any person engaging in an activity,

(b) the activity is sexual,

(c) B has a mental disorder,

(d) A knows or could reasonably be expected to know that B has a mental disorder, and

(e) A is involved in B's care in a way that falls within section 42.

(2) Where in proceedings for an offence under this section it is proved that the other person had a mental disorder, it is to be taken that the defendant knew or could reasonably have been expected to know that that person had a mental disorder unless sufficient evidence is adduced to raise an issue as to whether he knew or could reasonably have been expected to know it.

(3) A person guilty of an offence under this section is liable—

(a) on summary conviction, to imprisonment for a term not exceeding 6 months or a fine not exceeding the statutory maximum or both;

(b) on conviction on indictment, to imprisonment for a term not exceeding 7 years.

(2) Allocation

14–214 This offence is triable either way.

(3) Sentence

14–215 Upon summary conviction the maximum sentence is six months' imprisonment. After commencement of the relevant provisions, the maximum custodial sentence in a magistrates' court will be 12 months' imprisonment: *Criminal Justice Act* 2003, ss.154 and 282.

See table at § 14–197 for Guidelines.

VIII. PROSTITUTION, EXPLOITATION AND PORNOGRAPHY OFFENCES

A. PAYING FOR THE SEXUAL SERVICES OF A CHILD

(1) Definition

Sexual Offences Act 2003, s.47

Paying for sexual services of a child

47.—(1) A person (A) commits an offence if— **14–216**

(a) he intentionally obtains for himself the sexual services of another person (B),

(b) before obtaining those services, he has made or promised payment for those services to B or a third person, or knows that another person has made or promised such a payment, and

(c) either—

(i) B is under 18, and A does not reasonably believe that B is 18 or over, or

(ii) B is under 13.

(2) In this section, "payment" means any financial advantage, including the discharge of an obligation to pay or the provision of goods or services (including sexual services) gratuitously or at a discount.

(3) A person guilty of an offence under this section against a person under 13, where subsection (6) applies, is liable on conviction on indictment to imprisonment for life.

(4) Unless subsection (3) applies, a person guilty of an offence under this section against a person under 16 is liable—

(a) where subsection (6) applies, on conviction on indictment, to imprisonment for a term not exceeding 14 years;

(b) in any other case—

(i) on summary conviction, to imprisonment for a term not exceeding 6 months or a fine not exceeding the statutory maximum or both;

(ii) on conviction on indictment, to imprisonment for a term not exceeding 14 years.

(5) Unless subsection (3) or (4) applies, a person guilty of an offence under this section is liable—

(a) on summary conviction, to imprisonment for a term not exceeding 6 months or a fine not exceeding the statutory maximum or both;

(b) on conviction on indictment, to imprisonment for a term not exceeding 7 years.

(6) This subsection applies where the offence involved—

(a) penetration of B's anus or vagina with a part of A's body or anything else,

(b) penetration of B's mouth with A's penis,

(c) penetration of A's anus or vagina with a part of B's body or by B with anything else, or

(d) penetration of A's mouth with B's penis.

(7) In the application of this section to Northern Ireland, subsection (4) has effect with the substitution of "17" for "16".

(2) Allocation

This offence is triable either way unless s.47(3), (4)(A) or (6) apply. **14–217**

(3) Elements of the offence

If the child is aged between 13 and 17 and the defendant raises the issue that they believed that child was over 18, it is for the prosecution to prove that this belief was not reasonably held. **14–218**

Where a child is under 13, there is no issue as to the defendant's belief; this element of the offence will have been committed.

(4) Sentence

Upon summary conviction the maximum sentence is six months' imprisonment. Af- **14–219**

Part III

ter commencement of the relevant provisions, the maximum custodial sentence in a magistrates' court will be 12 months' imprisonment: *Criminal Justice Act* 2003, ss.154 and 282. An offender convicted of this offence is automatically subject to notification requirements: *SOA* 2003, s.80. See *post*, § 14–281.

STARTING POINTS AND SENTENCING RANGES: (BASED ON FIRST TIME OFFENDER AFTER TRIAL)

Examples of nature of activity	**Starting Point**	**Range**
History of paying for penetrative sex with children under 18	If the victim is under 13, the offence of "rape of a child under 13' "or "assault of a child under 13 by penetration" would normally be charged. Any commercial element to the offence and any history of repeat offending would be aggravating factors. However, if this offence is charged – 15 years custody	13–19 years custody
	7 years custody if the victim is 13 or over but under 16	5–10 years custody
	3 years custody if the victim is aged 16 or 17	2–5 years custody

Examples of nature of activity	Starting Point	Range
Penile penetration of the vagina, anus or mouth or penetration of the vagina or anus with another body part or an object	If the victim is under 13, the offence of "rape of a child under 13" or "assault of a child under 13 by penetration" would normally be charged. Any commercial element to the offence would be an aggravating factor. However, if this offence is charged – 12 years custody	4–8 years custody
	5 years custody if the victim is 13 or over but under 16	4–8 years custody
	2 years custody if the victim is aged 16 or 17	1–4 years custody
Sexual touching falling short of penetration	If the victim is under the offence of "sexual assault of a child under 13" would normally be charged. Any commercial element to the offence would be an aggravating factor. However, if this offence is charged – 5 years custody	4–8 years custody
	4 years custody if the victim is 13 or over but under 16	3–7 years custody
	12 months custody if the victim is aged 16 or 17	26 weeks–2 years custody

Part III

AGGRAVATING AND MITIGATING FACTORS:

Additional aggravating factors	Additional mitigating factors
1. Use of drugs, alcohol or other substance to secure the victim's compliance 2. Threats to prevent victim reporting the incident 3. Abduction or detention 4. Threats to disclose victim's activity to friends or relatives 5. Offender aware that he or she is suffering from a sexually transmitted infection	

B. CAUSING OR INCITING CHILD PROSTITUTION OR PORNOGRAPHY

(1) Definition

Sexual Offences Act 2003, s.48

Causing or inciting child prostitution or pornography

14–220 **48.**—(1) A person (A) commits an offence if—

(a) he intentionally causes or incites another person (B) to become a prostitute, or to be involved in pornography, in any part of the world, and

(b) either—

(i) B is under 18, and A does not reasonably believe that B is 18 or over, or

(ii) B is under 13.

(2) A person guilty of an offence under this section is liable—

(a) on summary conviction, to imprisonment for a term not exceeding 6 months or a fine not exceeding the statutory maximum or both;

(b) on conviction on indictment, to imprisonment for a term not exceeding 14 years.

(2) Allocation

14–221 This offence is triable either way.

(3) Elements of the offence

Sexual Offences Act 2003, s.51

Sections 48 to 50: interpretation

14–222 **51.**—(1) For the purposes of sections 48 to 50, a person is involved in pornography if an indecent image of that person is recorded; and similar expressions, and "pornography", are to be interpreted accordingly.

(2) In those sections "prostitute" means a person (A) who, on at least one occasion and whether or not compelled to do so, offers or provides sexual services to another person in return for payment or a promise of payment to A or a third person; and "prostitution" is to be interpreted accordingly.

(3) In subsection (2), "payment" means any financial advantage, including the discharge of an obligation to pay or the provision of goods or services (including sexual services) gratuitously or at a discount.

This section defines what is meant by "pornography" and "prostitute" and "payment".

If the child is aged between 13 and 17 and the defendant raises the issue that he believed that child was over 18, it is for the prosecution to prove that this belief was not reasonably held.

Where a child is under 13, there is no issue as to the defendant's belief; this element of the offence will have been committed.

If the child is aged between 13 and 17 and the defendant raises the issue that they believed the child was over 18, it is for the prosecution to prove that this belief was not reasonably held. Where the child is under 13, there is no issue as to the defendant's belief.

(4) Sentence

Upon summary conviction the maximum sentence is six months' imprisonment. After commencement of the relevant provisions, the maximum custodial sentence in a magistrates' court will be 12 months' imprisonment: *Criminal Justice Act* 2003, ss.154 and 282. An offender convicted of this offence is automatically subject to notification requirements: *SOA* 2003, s.80. See *post*, § 14–281. **14–223**

There may be cases where a custodial sentence within the jurisdiction of the magistrates court may be appropriate, although such offences will normally be dealt with in the Crown Court.

STARTING POINTS AND SENTENCING RANGES:

Type/nature of activity	Starting Point	Range
Penetrative activity Organised commercial exploitation	If the victim is under 13, the offence of "causing or inciting a child under 13 to engage in sexual activity" would normally be charged. The commercial element of the offence would be an aggravating factor, However if this offence is charged–10 years custody.	8–13 years custody
	8 years custody if the victim is 13 or over but under 16	6–11 years custody
	4 years custody if the victim is aged 16 or 17	3–7 years custody

Type/nature of activity	Starting Point	Range
Penetrative activity Offender's involvement is minimal and not perpetrated for gain	If the victim is under 13, the offence of "causing or inciting a child under 13 to engage in sexual activity" would normally be charged. The commercial element of the offence would be an aggravating factor. However, if this offence is charged–8 years custody	6–11 years custody
	5 years custody if the victim is 13 or over but under 16	4–8 years custody
	2 years custody if the victim is aged 16 or 17	1–4 years custody
Non-penetrative activity Offender's involvement is minimal and not perpetrated for gain	If the victim is under 13, the offence of "causing or inciting a child under 13 to engage in sexual activity" would normally be charged. The commercial element would be an aggravating factor. However if this offence is charged–6 years custody	4–9 years custody
	3 years custody if the victim is aged 13 or over but under 16	2–5 years custody
	12 months custody if the victim is aged 16 or 17	26 weeks–2 years custody

Type/nature of activity	Starting Point	Range
Non-penetrative activity Organised commercial exploitation	If the victim is under 13, the offence of "causing or inciting a child under 13 to engage in sexual activity" would normally be charged. The commercial element of the offence would be an aggravating factor. However if this offence is charged–8 years custody	6–11 years custody
	6 years custody if the victim is aged 13 or over but under 16	4–9 years custody
	3 years custody if the victim is aged 16 or 17	26 weeks–2 years custody

OFFENCE SERIOUSNESS (CULPABILITY AND HARM)

Factors indicating higher culpability	Factors indicating lower culpability
1. Background of threats or intimidation 2. Large scale commercial operation 3. Use of drugs, alcohol or other substance to secure the victim's compliance 4. Forcing a victim to violate another person 5. Abduction or detention 6. Victim has been manipulated into physical and emotional dependence on the offender 7. Threats to prevent victim reporting the activity 8. Threats to disclose victim's activity to friends or relatives 9. Images distributed to other children or persons known to the victim 10. Financial or other gain **Factors indicating greater degree of harm** 1. Induced dependency on drugs 2. Victim has been manipulated into physical and emotional dependence on offender 3. Storing, making available or distributing images in such a way that they can be inadvertently accessed by others	1. Offender also being controlled in prostitution or pornography and subject to threats or intimidation.

C. SOLICITING

(1) Definition

Sexual Offences Act 2003, s.51A

Soliciting

51A.—(1) It is an offence for a person in a street or public place to solicit another (B) for the purpose of obtaining B's sexual services as a prostitute. **14–224**

(2) The reference to a person in a street or public place includes a person in a vehicle in a street or public place.

(3) A person guilty of an offence under this section is liable on summary conviction to a fine not exceeding level 3 on the standard scale

(4) In this section "street" has the meaning given by section 1(4) of the *Street Offences Act* 1959.

[This section was inserted by the *Policing and Crime Act* 2009, s.19. Section 51A came into force on April 1, 2010: *Policing and Crime Act 2009 (Commencement No. 4) Order* 2010 (S.I. 2010 No. 507).]

(2) Allocation

This offence is triable summarily only. **14–225**

(3) Elements

The prosecution must prove that the defendant **14–226**

— solicited another person

— for the purpose of obtaining that persons sexual services as a prostitute.

The offence is gender neutral. It also applies specifically to a person who solicits in public from a motor vehicle thereby covering kerb-crawling.

Prostitute is defined in s.51(2).

(4) Sentence

The sentence is a fine only not exceeding level 3 presently set at £1,000: s.51A(3). **14–227**

D. PROSTITUTION FOR GAIN

(1) Definition

Sexual Offences Act 2003, s.52(1)

Causing or inciting prostitution for gain

52.—(1) A person commits an offence if— **14–228**

(a) he intentionally causes or incites another person to become a prostitute in any part of the world, and

(b) he does so for or in the expectation of gain for himself or a third person.

(2) A person guilty of an offence under this section is liable—

(a) on summary conviction, to imprisonment for a term not exceeding 6 months or a fine not exceeding the statutory maximum or both;

(b) on conviction on indictment, to imprisonment for a term not exceeding 7 years.

Sexual Offences Act 2003, s.53A

Paying for sexual services of a prostitute subjected to force etc.

53A.—(1) A person (A) commits an offence if — **14–228a**

(a) A makes or promises payment for the sexual services of a prostitute (B),

(b) a third person (C) has engaged in exploitative conduct of a kind likely to induce or encourage B to provide the sexual services for which A has made or promised payment, and

(c) C engaged in that conduct for or in the expectation of gain for C or another person (apart from A or B).

(2) The following are irrelevant—

(a) where in the world the sexual services are to be provided and whether those services are provided,

(b) whether A is, or ought to be, aware that C has engaged in exploitative conduct.

(3) C engages in exploitative conduct if—

(a) C uses force, threats (whether or not relating to violence) or any other form of coercion, or

(b) C practises any form of deception.

(4) A person guilty of an offence under this section is liable on summary conviction to a fine not exceeding level 3 on the standard scale.

[This section was inserted by the*Policing and Crime Act* 2009, s.14. Section 53A came into force on April 1, 2010; *Policing and Crime Act 2009 (Commencement No. 4) Order* 2010 (S.I. 2010 No. 507).]

(2) Allocation

14–229 This offence under s.52 is triable either way. The offence under s.53A is triable summarily only.

(3) Elements of the offence

Sexual Offences Act 2003, s.54

Sections 51A–53A: interpretation

14–230 **54.**—(1) In sections 52, 53 and 53A, "gain" means—

(a) any financial advantage, including the discharge of an obligation to pay or the provision of goods or services (including sexual services) gratuitously or at a discount; or

(b) the goodwill of any person which is or appears likely, in time, to bring financial advantage.

(2) In sections 51A, 52 and 53A "prostitute" and "prostitution" have the meaning given by section 51(2).

(3) In section 53A "payment" has the meaning given by section 51(3).

[This section is printed as amended by amended by the *Policing and Crime Act* 2009, s.112, Sched. 7, para. 24.]

[The next paragraph is § 14–232.]

(4) Sentence

14–232 Upon summary conviction of a s.52 offence, the maximum sentence is six months' imprisonment and /or a level 5 fine. After commencement of the relevant provisions, the maximum custodial sentence in a magistrates' court will be 12 months' imprisonment: *Criminal Justice Act* 2003, ss.154 and 282. An offence contrary to section 52(1) is a "lifestyle offence" within the *Proceeds of Crime Act* 2002, Sched. 2, in respect of which a financial reporting order may be made under the *Serious Organised Crime and Police Act* 2005, s.76.

The offence under s.53A carries a sentence of a fine only.

STARTING POINTS AND SENTENCING RANGES: (BASED ON FIRST TIME OFFENDER AFTER TRIAL)

Examples of nature of activity	Starting Point	Range
Evidence of physical and/or mental coercion	Crown Court	Crown Court
No coercion or corruption, but the offender is closely involved in the victim's prostitution	Crown Court	26 weeks to Crown Court
No evidence that the victim was physically coerced or corrupted, and the involvement of the offender was minimal	Community order medium level	Band C fine to high level community order

OFFENCE SERIOUSNESS (CULPABILITY AND HARM)

Factors indicating higher culpability	Factors indicating lower culpability
1. Background of threats, intimidation or coercion 2. Large scale commercial operation 3. Substantial gain (in the region of £5000 and upwards) 4. Use of drugs, alcohol or other substance to secure the victim's compliance 5. Abduction or detention 6. Threats to prevent victim reporting the activity 7. Threats to disclose victim's activity to friends or relatives. **Factors indicating greater degree of harm** 1. Induced dependency on drugs	1. Offender also being controlled in prostitution and subject to threats or intimidation

E. CONTROLLING PROSTITUTION FOR A GAIN

(1) Definition

Sexual Offences Act 2003, s.53

Controlling prostitution for gain

14–233 **53.**—(1) A person commits an offence if—

(a) he intentionally controls any of the activities of another person relating to that person's prostitution in any part of the world, and

(b) he does so for or in the expectation of gain for himself or a third person.

(2) A person guilty of an offence under this section is liable—

(a) on summary conviction, to imprisonment for a term not exceeding 6 months or a fine not exceeding the statutory maximum or both;

(b) on conviction on indictment, to imprisonment for a term not exceeding 7 years.

14–234 Gain is defined in section 54, *ante*. See § 14–230.

(2) Allocation

14–235 This offence is triable either way.

(3) Elements

14–236 In *Massey* [2008] 1 W.L.R. 937, the meaning of "control" was considered. The defendant had lived with the complainant for 10 years, during which time she had also worked as a prostitute. When the relationship ended the defendant forced the complainant to work as a prostitute and kept all her earnings. He had been violent towards her. She had worked as a prostitute out of fear. The judge at first instance directed the jury that "control" required that the complainant had acted under compulsion but did not require that the defendant had forced the complainant into prostitution. The Court of Appeal in dismissing the appeal against conviction said "control" includes but is not limited to one who forces another to carry out an activity. It is an ordinary English word, it is enough that a person instructs or directs another to carry out a particular activity or do it in a particular way. There is a wide variety of possible circumstances in which a person may exert "control" over another, for example, the use or threat of force, emotional blackmail or financial reward.

(4) Sentence

14–237 Upon summary conviction the maximum sentence is six months' imprisonment and/or a fine. After commencement of the relevant provisions, the maximum custodial sentence in a magistrates' court will be 12 months' imprisonment: *Criminal Justice Act* 2003, ss.154 and 282. An offence contrary to s.53 is a "lifestyle offence" within the *Proceeds of Crime Act* 2002, Sched. 2, in respect of which a financial reporting order may be made under the *Serious Organised Crime and Police Act* 2005, s.76.

See table at § 14–232 for Guidelines.

F. CONTROLLING A CHILD PROSTITUTE OR A CHILD INVOLVED IN PORNOGRAPHY

(1) Definition

Sexual Offences Act 2003, s.49

Controlling a child prostitute or a child involved in pornography

14–238 **49.**—(1) A person (A) commits an offence if—

(a) he intentionally controls any of the activities of another person (B) relating to B's prostitution or involvement in pornography in any part of the world, and

(b) either—

(i) B is under 18, and A does not reasonably believe that B is 18 or over, or

(ii) B is under 13.

(2) A person guilty of an offence under this section is liable—

(a) on summary conviction, to imprisonment for a term not exceeding 6 months or a fine not exceeding the statutory maximum or both;

(b) on conviction on indictment, to imprisonment for a term not exceeding 14 years.

(2) Allocation

This offence is triable either way. **14–239**

(3) Elements of the offence

If the child is aged between 13 and 17 and the defendant raises the issue that they believed that child was over 18, it is for the prosecution to prove that this belief was not reasonably held. **14–240**

Where a child is under 13, there is no issue as to the defendant's belief; this element of the offence will have been committed.

In *Massey* [2008] 1 W.L.R. 937, "control" included, but was not limited to, individuals who forced another to carry out a relevant activity. It could be exercised in a variety of ways including physical violence and emotional blackmail. However, if, for example, a group of young women were recruited overseas and put to work as prostitutes in the United Kingdom, the Crown would not have to prove that there was an absence of free will to show that there was control of the women for gain. Therefore control should be given its ordinary dictionary meaning as directing an activity. It did not, in the strict sense need the Crown to demonstrate that an individual was coerced, compelled or forced to work, although such things would undoubtedly be forms of control.

(4) Sentence

Upon summary conviction the maximum sentence is six months' imprisonment. After commencement of the relevant provisions, the maximum custodial sentence in a magistrates' court will be 12 months' imprisonment: *Criminal Justice Act* 2003, ss.154 and 282. An offender convicted of this offence is automatically subject to notification requirements: *SOA* 2003, s.80. **14–241**

There may be cases where a custodial sentence within the jurisdiction of the magistrates court may be appropriate.

See table at § 14–223 for Guidelines.

Part III

G. Arranging or Facilitating Child Prostitution or Pornography

(1) Definition

Sexual Offences Act 2003, s.50

Arranging or facilitating child prostitution or pornography

50.—(1) A person (A) commits an offence if— **14–242**

(a) he intentionally arranges or facilitates the prostitution or involvement in pornography in any part of the world of another person (B), and

(b) either—

(i) B is under 18, and A does not reasonably believe that B is 18 or over, or

(ii) B is under 13.

(2) A person guilty of an offence under this section is liable—

(a) on summary conviction, to imprisonment for a term not exceeding 6 months or a fine not exceeding the statutory maximum or both;

(b) on conviction on indictment, to imprisonment for a term not exceeding 14 years.

(2) Allocation

14–243 This offence is triable either way.

(2) Elements of the offence

14–244 If the child is aged between 13 and 17 and the defendant raises the issue that they believed that child was over 18, it is for the prosecution to prove that this belief was not reasonably held.

Where a child is under 13, there is no issue as to the defendant's belief; this element of the offence will have been committed.

(4) Sentence

14–245 Upon summary conviction the maximum sentence is six months' imprisonment. After commencement of the relevant provisions, the maximum custodial sentence in a magistrates' court will be 12 months' imprisonment: *Criminal Justice Act* 2003, ss.154 and 282. An offender convicted if this offence is automatically subject to notification requirements: *SOA* 2003, s.80.

See table at § 14–223 for Guidelines.

H. TRAFFICKING INTO, WITHIN AND OUT OF THE UK FOR SEXUAL EXPLOITATION

(1) Definition

Sexual Offences Act 2003, ss.57, 58, 59

Trafficking into the UK for sexual exploitation

14–246 **57.**—(1) A person commits an offence if he intentionally arranges or facilitates the arrival in, or the entry into, the United Kingdom of another person (B) and either—

(a) he intends to do anything to or in respect of B, after B's arrival but in any part of the world, which if done will involve the commission of a relevant offence, or

(b) he believes that another person is likely to do something to or in respect of B, after B's arrival but in any part of the world, which if done will involve the commission of a relevant offence.

(2) A person guilty of an offence under this section is liable—

(a) on summary conviction, to imprisonment for a term not exceeding 6 months or a fine not exceeding the statutory maximum or both;

(b) on conviction on indictment, to imprisonment for a term not exceeding 14 years.

[This section is printed as amended by the *UK Borders Act* 2007.]

Trafficking within the UK for sexual exploitation

14–247 **58.**—(1) A person commits an offence if he intentionally arranges or facilitates travel within the United Kingdom by another person (B) and either—

(a) he intends to do anything to or in respect of B, during or after the journey and in any part of the world, which if done will involve the commission of a relevant offence, or

(b) he believes that another person is likely to do something to or in respect of B, during or after the journey and in any part of the world, which if done will involve the commission of a relevant offence.

(2) A person guilty of an offence under this section is liable—

(a) on summary conviction, to imprisonment for a term not exceeding 6 months or a fine not exceeding the statutory maximum or both;

(b) on conviction on indictment, to imprisonment for a term not exceeding 14 years.

Trafficking out of the UK for sexual exploitation

59.—(1) A person commits an offence if he intentionally arranges or facilitates the departure from the United Kingdom of another person (B) and either— **14–248**

(a) he intends to do anything to or in respect of B, after B's departure but in any part of the world, which if done will involve the commission of a relevant offence, or

(b) he believes that another person is likely to do something to or in respect of B, after B's departure but in any part of the world, which if done will involve the commission of a relevant offence.

(2) A person guilty of an offence under this section is liable—

(a) on summary conviction, to imprisonment for a term not exceeding 6 months or a fine not exceeding the statutory maximum or both;

(b) on conviction on indictment, to imprisonment for a term not exceeding 14 years.

(2) Allocation

These offences are triable either way. **14–249**

(3) Elements of the offence

Sexual Offences Act 2003, s.60

Sections 57 to 59: interpretation and jurisdiction

60.—(1) In sections 57 to 59, "relevant offence" means— **14–250**

(a) an offence under this Part,

(b) an offence under section 1(1)(a) of the *Protection of Children Act* 1978 (c. 37),

(c) an offence listed in Schedule 1 to the *Criminal Justice (Children) (Northern Ireland) Order* 1998 (S.I. 1998 No. 1504 (N.I. 9)),

(d) an offence under Article 3(1)(a) of the *Protection of Children (Northern Ireland) Order* 1978 (S.I. 1978 No. 1047 (N.I. 17)), or

(e) anything done outside England and Wales and Northern Ireland which is not an offence within any of paragraphs (a) to (d) but would be if done in England and Wales or Northern Ireland.

(2) Sections 57 to 59 apply to anything done whether inside or outside the United Kingdom.

[Repealed by s.31(4) of the *UK Borders Act* 2007.]

The provisions defining a relevant offence are set out at section 60(1) of the Act. Section 60 further considers issues of jurisdiction.

(4) Sentence

Upon summary conviction the maximum sentence is six months' imprisonment and/or a fine. After commencement of the relevant provisions, the maximum custodial sentence in a magistrates' court will be 12 months' imprisonment: *Criminal Justice Act* 2003, ss.154 and 282. **14–251**

Part III

STARTING POINTS AND SENTENCING RANGES: (BASED ON FIRST TIME OFFENDER AFTER TRIAL)

Type/nature of activity	Starting Point	Range
Involvement at any level in any stage of the trafficking operation where there was no coercion of the victim	2 years custody	1–4 years custody
Involvement at any level in any stage of the trafficking operation where the victim was co-erced.	6 years custody	4–9 years custody

AGGRAVATING AND MITIGATING FACTORS:

Additional aggravating factors	Additional mitigating factors
1. Large scale commercial operation 2. High degree of planning or sophistication 3. Large number of people trafficked 4. Substantial financial (in the region of £5000 and upwards) or other gain 5. Fraud 6. Financial extortion of the victim 7. Deception 8. Use of force, threats of force or other forms of coercion 9. Threats against victim or members of victim's family 10. Abduction or detention 11. Restriction of victim's liberty 12. Inhumane treatment 13. Confiscation of victim's passport	1. Coercion of the offender by a third party 2. No evidence of personal gain 3. Limited involvement

In *Maka* [2006] 2 Cr.App.R.(S.) 14 the Court of Appeal approved a total sentence of 18 years' imprisonment for four offences under s.58(1) and one offence under s.57(1) committed by a man with no previous convictions where the victim was a 15-year-old Lithuanian girl.

In *Ramaj and Atesogullari* [2006] 2 Cr.App.R.(S.) 83 a sentence of 10 years' imprisonment was reduced on appeal to five years' imprisonment. The appellant was 19-years-old and of previous good character; he was the principal involved in bringing an 18-year-old girl into the UK from Lithuania. The complainant whilst naïve was not an unwilling participant, she was put to work in a brothel and worked there for two days.

See *Makai* [2008] 1 Cr.App.R.(S.) 423 as an example of sentencing for trafficking for sexual exploitation post implementation of the SGC Guideline. A custodial sentence was reduced because there was no evidence of coercion or involvement in prostitution.

IX. MISCELLANEOUS OFFENCES UNDER THE SEXUAL OFFENCES ACT 2003

A. ADMINISTERING A SUBSTANCE WITH INTENT

(1) Definition

Sexual Offences Act 2003, s.61

Administering a substance with intent

61.—(1) A person commits an offence if he intentionally administers a substance to, or causes a substance to be taken by, another person (B)— **14–252**

(a) knowing that B does not consent, and

(b) with the intention of stupefying or overpowering B, so as to enable any person to engage in a sexual activity that involves B.

(2) A person guilty of an offence under this section is liable—

(a) on summary conviction, to imprisonment for a term not exceeding 6 months or a fine not exceeding the statutory maximum or both;

(b) on conviction on indictment, to imprisonment for a term not exceeding 10 years.

(2) Allocation

This offence is triable either way. **14–253**

(3) Sentence

Upon summary conviction the maximum sentence is six months' imprisonment and/or a fine. After commencement of the relevant provisions, the maximum custodial sentence in a magistrates' court will be 12 months' imprisonment: *Criminal Justice Act* 2003, ss.154 and 282. Custodial sentences of less than 12 months will consist of a custody plus order. An offender convicted of this offence is automatically subject to notification requirements: *SOA* 2003, s.80. See *post*, § 14–281. **14–254**

STARTING POINTS AND SENTENCING RANGES: (BASED ON FIRST TIME OFFENDER AFTER TRIAL)

Type/nature of activity	Starting Point	Range
If intended offence is rape or assault by penetration	8 years custody if the victim is under 13 6 years custody otherwise	6–9 years custody 4–9 years custody
If intended offence is any sexual offence other than rape or assault by penetration	6 years custody if the victim is under 13 4 years custody otherwise	4–9 years custody 3–7 years custody

AGGRAVATING AND MITIGATING FACTORS:

Additional aggravating factors	Additional mitigating factors
1. Threats to prevent the victim reporting an offence 2. Abduction or detention 3. Offender aware that he or she or the person planning to commit the sexual offence is suffering from a sexually transmitted infection 4. Targeting of the victim	1. Offender intervenes to prevent intended sexual offence from taking place

B. COMMITTING AN OFFENCE WITH INTENT TO COMMIT A SEXUAL OFFENCE

(1) Definition

Sexual Offences Act 2003, s.62

Committing an offence with intent to commit a sexual offence

14–255 **62.**—(1) A person commits an offence under this section if he commits any offence with the intention of committing a relevant sexual offence.

(2) In this section, "relevant sexual offence" means any offence under this Part (including an offence of aiding, abetting, counselling or procuring such an offence).

(3) A person guilty of an offence under this section is liable on conviction on indictment, where the offence is committed by kidnapping or false imprisonment, to imprisonment for life.

(4) Unless subsection (3) applies, a person guilty of an offence under this section is liable—

(a) on summary conviction, to imprisonment for a term not exceeding 6 months or a fine not exceeding the statutory maximum or both;

(b) on conviction on indictment, to imprisonment for a term not exceeding 10 years.

In section 62(2) "this part" refers to Pt I of the *Sexual Offences Act* 2003, *i.e.* the part creating substantive offences, and therefore excludes notification and orders covered in Pt II.

(2) Allocation

This offence is triable either way, except where the offence is committed by kidnapping or false imprisonment, and then the offence is indictable only. 14–256

(3) Sentence

Upon summary conviction the maximum sentence is six months' imprisonment and/or a fine. After commencement of the relevant provisions the maximum custodial sentence in a magistrates' court will be 12 months' imprisonment: *Criminal Justice Act* 2003, ss.154 and 282. 14–257

STARTING POINTS AND SENTENCING RANGES:

Type/nature of activity	Starting points and sentencing ranges
Any offence committed with intent to commit a sexual offence *e.g.* assault	The starting point and sentencing range should be commensurate with that for the preliminary offence actually committed, but with an enhancement to reflect the intention to commit a sexual offence. The enhancement will need to be varied depending on the nature and seriousness of the intended sexual offence, but 2 years is suggested as a suitable enhancement where the intent was to commit rape or an assault by penetration

AGGRAVATING AND MITIGATING FACTORS:

Additional aggravating factors	Additional mitigating factors
1. Use of drugs, alcohol or other substance to facilitate the offence. 2. Offender aware that he or she is suffering from a sexually transmitted infection (where the intended offence would have involved penile penetration)	1. Offender decides of his own volition not to proceed with the intended sexual offence 2. Incident of brief duration

The case of *Wisniewski* [2005] 2 Cr.App.R.(S.) 39 sets out, in relation to battery with intent, the factors that should be taken into account by sentencers. These are: (a) the method and degree of force used; (b) the nature and extent of the indecency

Part III

perpetrated or intended; (c) the degree of harm to the victim; (d) the nature and general circumstances of the attack including the time, the place and level of risk posed by the offender; (e) good character, which affords only limited mitigation.

C. TRESPASS WITH INTENT TO COMMIT A SEXUAL OFFENCE

(1) Definition

Sexual Offences Act 2003, s.63

Trespass with intent to commit a sexual offence

14–258 **63.**—(1) A person commits an offence if—

(a) he is a trespasser on any premises,

(b) he intends to commit a relevant sexual offence on the premises, and

(c) he knows that, or is reckless as to whether, he is a trespasser.

(2) In this section—

"premises" includes a structure or part of a structure;

"relevant sexual offence" has the same meaning as in section 62;

"structure" includes a tent, vehicle or vessel or other temporary or movable structure.

(3) A person guilty of an offence under this section is liable—

(a) on summary conviction, to imprisonment for a term not exceeding 6 months or a fine not exceeding the statutory maximum or both;

(b) on conviction on indictment, to imprisonment for a term not exceeding 10 years.

(2) Allocation

14–259 This offence is triable either way.

(3) Sentence

14–260 Upon summary conviction the maximum sentence is six months' imprisonment and/or a fine. After commencement of the relevant provisions, the maximum custodial sentence in a magistrates' court will be 12 months' imprisonment: *Criminal Justice Act* 2003, ss.154 and 282. An offender convicted of this offence is automatically subject to notification requirements: *SOA* 2003, s.80. See *post*, § 14–281.

STARTING POINTS AND SENTENCING RANGES: (BASED ON FIRST TIME OFFENDER AFTER TRIAL)

Type/nature of activity	Starting Point	Range
The intention is to commit rape or an assault by penetration	4 years custody	3–7 years custody
The intended sexual offence is other than rape or assault by penetration	2 years custody	1–4 years custody

AGGRAVATING AND MITIGATING FACTORS:

Additional aggravating factors	Additional mitigating factors
1. Offender aware that he or she is suffering from a sexually transmitted infection (where intended offence would have involved penile penetration) 2. Targeting of a vulnerable victim 3. Significant impact on persons present in the premises	1. Offender decides of his or her own volition not to commit the intended sexual offence

D. EXPOSURE

(1) Definition

Sexual Offences Act 2003, s.66

Exposure

66.—(1) A person commits an offence if— 14–261

(a) he intentionally exposes his genitals, and

(b) he intends that someone will see them and be caused alarm or distress.

(2) A person guilty of an offence under this section is liable—

(a) on summary conviction, to imprisonment for a term not exceeding 6 months or a fine not exceeding the statutory maximum or both;

(b) on conviction on indictment, to imprisonment for a term not exceeding 2 years.

(2) Allocation

This offence is triable either way. 14–262

(3) Sentence

Upon summary conviction the maximum sentence is six months' imprisonment and/or a fine. After the commencement of the relevant provisions, the maximum custodial sentence in a magistrates' court will be 12 months' imprisonment: *Criminal Justice Act* 2003, ss.154 and 282. A person convicted of this offence is subject to notification requirements: *SOA* 2003, s.80. See *post*, § 14–281. 14–263

Part III

STARTING POINTS AND SENTENCING RANGES: (BASED ON FIRST TIME OFFENDER AFTER TRIAL)

Examples of nature of activity	**Starting Point**	**Range**
Repeat offender — two or more aggravating factors	12 weeks' custody	6 weeks to Crown Court
Basic offence as defined in the *SOA* 2003, assuming no aggravating or mitigating factors	Community order	An appropriate non-custodial sentence

OFFENCE SERIOUSNESS (CULPABILITY AND HARM)

Factors indicating higher culpability
1. Threats to prevent the victim reporting an offence
2. Intimidating behaviour/threats of violence
Factor indicating greater degree of harm
1. Victim is a child

In *Mailer* [2006] 2 Cr.App.R.(S). 84 the appellant a 26-year-old with numerous previous convictions for like offences pleaded guilty to two offences of exposing his penis and masturbating on a bus whilst sitting next to a young woman. He was subject to a community rehabilitation order for similar offending at the time. The court upheld a sentence of six months' imprisonment with an order that the existing community sentence continue.

In *Bell* [2008] 2 Cr.App.R.(S.) 337, a 25-year-old with no previous convictions pleaded guilty to five counts of exposure contrary to s.66. On the five occasions each victim was alone walking either in an alleyway, by a park or along a road. On one occasion the defendant was reported to have an erect penis. Two of the victims were aged 15. He was sentenced to nine months imprisonment concurrent on each count. Under the SGC Guidelines the appropriate sentence where no aggravating factors were present was a community order unless it was a repeat offence. The defendant was a first time offender. The sentence was quashed and a community order with a two year supervision requirement was substituted. See also *Hawkins* [2007] EWCA Crim 2221.

In *Lam-Callinan* [2010] 1 Cr.App.R. 49 an appeal was lodged against a 15 month custodial sentence imposed concurrently for seven charges of exposure. The appellant was a learning mentor at a school and had exposed himself over a period of 18 months to female members of staff. On appeal the sentence was reduced to nine months. The court said custody was inevitable, especially for repeat offending but as there were no previous convictions for similar offences and as the maximum sentence was 2 years, the sentence was reduced.

In *Pennant* [2011] 1 Cr.App.R. 92 a two year sentence of detention for two offences of exposure was reduced on appeal to 12 months. The appellant had exposed himself and masturbated in front of teenage girls. He had seven previous convictions for exposure and was aged 20. Referring to the guidelines the court said custody was inevitable with the masturbation and targetting of young girls being aggravating factors but insufficient credit had been given for the guilty pleas.

E. VOYEURISM

(1) Definition

Sexual Offences Act 2003, ss.67, 68

Voyeurism

67.—(1) A person commits an offence if— 14–264

(a) for the purpose of obtaining sexual gratification, he observes another person doing a private act, and

(b) he knows that the other person does not consent to being observed for his sexual gratification.

(2) A person commits an offence if—

(a) he operates equipment with the intention of enabling another person to observe, for the purpose of obtaining sexual gratification, a third person (B) doing a private act, and

(b) he knows that B does not consent to his operating equipment with that intention.

(3) A person commits an offence if—

(a) he records another person (B) doing a private act,

(b) he does so with the intention that he or a third person will, for the purpose of obtaining sexual gratification, look at an image of B doing the act, and

(c) he knows that B does not consent to his recording the act with that intention.

(4) A person commits an offence if he instals equipment, or constructs or adapts a structure or part of a structure, with the intention of enabling himself or another person to commit an offence under subsection (1).

(5) A person guilty of an offence under this section is liable—

(a) on summary conviction, to imprisonment for a term not exceeding 6 months or a fine not exceeding the statutory maximum or both;

(b) on conviction on indictment, to imprisonment for a term not exceeding 2 years.

Voyeurism: interpretation

68.—(1) For the purposes of section 67, a person is doing a private act if the person is in a place which, in the circumstances, would reasonably be expected to provide privacy, and— 14–265

(a) the person's genitals, buttocks or breasts are exposed or covered only with underwear,

(b) the person is using a lavatory, or

(c) the person is doing a sexual act that is not of a kind ordinarily done in public.

(2) In section 67, "structure" includes a tent, vehicle or vessel or other temporary or movable structure.

(2) Allocation

This offence is triable either way. 14–266

(3) Elements of the offence

The reference to "breasts" in s.68(1)(a) does not include a man's breasts: *Bassett*, [2009] 1 W.L.R. 1032. 14–267

(4) Sentence

Upon summary conviction the maximum sentence is six months' imprisonment and/or a fine. After the commencement of the relevant provisions, the maximum custodial sentence in a magistrates' court will be 12 months' imprisonment: *Criminal Justice Act* 2003, ss.154 and 282. In accordance with s.80 of, and Sched. 3 to the *Sexual Offences Act* 2003, automatic notification requirements apply upon conviction. See *post*, § 14–281. 14–268

STARTING POINTS AND SENTENCING RANGES: (BASED ON FIRST TIME OFFENDER AFTER TRIAL)

Examples of nature of activity	**Starting Point**	**Range**
Offence with serious aggravating factors such as recording sexual activity and placing it on a website or circulating it for commercial gain.	Crown Court	26 weeks to Crown Court
Offence with aggravating factors such as recording sexual activity and showing it to others	26 weeks custody	4 weeks to 18 months custody
Basic offence as defined in the *SOA* 2003, assuming no aggravating or mitigating factors, *e.g.* the offender spies through a hole he or she has made in a changing room wall	Community order	An appropriate non-custodial sentence

OFFENCE SERIOUSNESS — (CULPABILITY AND HARM)

Factors indicating higher culpability	Additional mitigating factors
1. Threats to prevent the victim reporting an offence 2. Recording activity and circulating pictures / videos 3. Circulating pictures or videos for commercial gain – particularly if victim is vulnerable, *e.g.* a child or person with a mental or physical disorder **Factor indicating greater degree of harm** 1. Distress to victim, *e.g.* where the pictures/videos are circulated to people known to the victim	

A pre sentence report identifying sexually deviant tendencies and whether an offender would benefit from participation in a programme designed to address those tendencies should be obtained.

In *I.P.* [2005] 1 Cr.App.R.(S.) 102 the Court ruled that a custodial sentence was not justified on the facts of the case: the offender had recorded an adult stepdaughter in the shower, and he had not shown his video recording to anyone else. The appropriate sentence was held to be a community sentence.

P. (*ante*) was considered by the Court of Appeal in *Turner* [2006] 2 Cr.App.R.(S). 51, when it substituted a sentence of nine months' imprisonment for an offence contrary to s.67(3). The appellant, who was a man of good character and worked as the manager of a gym, had recorded video images of women showering and using sun beds in the gym. He pleaded guilty to three offences and asked for a fourth to be taken into consideration. The court stated that in this case the abuse of a position of trust took it over the custody threshold, although it was made clear that this was not to be taken as a guideline for all cases involving an abuse of trust, and treatment in the community may in particular circumstances be appropriate.

In *McCann* [2007] 1 Cr.App.R.(S.) 4 the appellant, a 28-year-old serving police officer of previous good character, obtained a surveillance camera and hid it in the bathroom of a neighbour whilst a guest at her home. The camera was discovered and attempts were made to retrieve it. There was no evidence that any footage had actually been obtained. The appellant was convicted and sentenced to six months' imprisonment. The Court of Appeal considered *I.P.* and *Turner* and held that whilst a breach of trust should not necessarily result in a custodial sentence, in this case the appellant was a serving police officer, there was a breach of trust and no guilty plea; the custody threshold had been passed. The appeal was allowed in that the sentence was reduced to 90 days' imprisonment.

In *Hodgson* [2009] 1 Cr.App.R.(S.) 145, a 44-year-old of good character installed a camera in the ladies lavatories at his place of work which transmitted images to the men's lavatories. The case did not fall neatly into category one or two of the sentencing guidelines. It was more serious than the 'basic' offence due to its ongoing nature, sophistication of technology and elements of planning and pre-meditation but did not include the aggravating features of recording or distribution. The sentence of 20 weeks was quashed, a community rehabilitation order was substituted with a three year supervision period and 60 days in a community sex offender programme.

F. INTERCOURSE WITH AN ANIMAL

(1) Definition

Sexual Offences Act 2003, s.69

Intercourse with an animal

14–269 **69.**—(1) A person commits an offence if—

(a) he intentionally performs an act of penetration with his penis,

(b) what is penetrated is the vagina or anus of a living animal, and

(c) he knows that, or is reckless as to whether, that is what is penetrated.

(2) A person (A) commits an offence if—

(a) A intentionally causes, or allows, A's vagina or anus to be penetrated,

(b) the penetration is by the penis of a living animal, and

(c) A knows that, or is reckless as to whether, that is what A is being penetrated by.

(3) A person guilty of an offence under this section is liable—

(a) on summary conviction, to imprisonment for a term not exceeding 6 months or a fine not exceeding the statutory maximum or both;

(b) on conviction on indictment, to imprisonment for a term not exceeding 2 years.

(2) Allocation

14–270 This offence is triable either way.

(3) Sentence

14–271 Upon summary conviction the maximum sentence is six months' imprisonment and/or a fine. After commencement of the relevant provisions, the maximum custodial sentence in a magistrates' court will be 12 months' imprisonment: *Criminal Justice Act* 2003, ss.154 and 282. An offender convicted of this offence is automatically subject to notification requirements: *SOA* 2003, s.80.

STARTING POINTS AND SENTENCING RANGES:

Type/nature of activity	Starting Point	Range
Basic offence as defined in the *SOA* 2003, assuming no aggravating or mitigating factors	Community order	An appropriate non-custodial sentence

AGGRAVATING AND MITIGATING FACTORS:

Additional aggravating factors	Additional mitigating factors
1. Recording activity and/or circulating pictures or videos	1. Symptom of isolation rather than depravity

G. SEXUAL PENETRATION OF A CORPSE

(1) Definition

Sexual Offences Act 2003, s.70

Sexual penetration of a corpse

70.—(1) A person commits an offence if— **14–272**

(a) he intentionally performs an act of penetration with a part of his body or anything else,

(b) what is penetrated is a part of the body of a dead person,

(c) he knows that, or is reckless as to whether, that is what is penetrated, and

(d) the penetration is sexual.

(2) A person guilty of an offence under this section is liable–

(a) on summary conviction, to imprisonment for a term not exceeding 6 months or a fine not exceeding the statutory maximum or both;

(b) on conviction on indictment, to imprisonment for a term not exceeding 2 years.

(2) Allocation

This offence is triable either way. **14–273**

(3) Sentence

Upon summary conviction the maximum sentence is six months' imprisonment and/or a fine. After commencement of the relevant provisions, the maximum custodial sentence in a magistrates' court will be 12 months' imprisonment: *Criminal Justice Act* 2003, ss.154 and 282. An offender convicted of this offence is automatically subject to notification requirements: *SOA* 2003, s.80. See *post*, § 14–281. **14–274**

STARTING POINTS AND SENTENCING RANGES: (BASED ON FIRST TIME OFFENDER AFTER TRIAL)

Type/nature of activity	Starting Point	Range
Repeat offending and /or aggravating factors	26 weeks custody	4 weeks–18 months custody
Basic offence as defined in the *SOA* 2003, assuming no aggravating or mitigating factors	Community order	An appropriate non-custodial sentence

Part III

AGGRAVATING AND MITIGATING FACTORS:

Additional aggravating factors	Additional mitigating factors
1. Distress caused to relatives or friends of the deceased 2. Physical damage caused to body of the deceased 3. The corpse was that of a child 4. The offence was committed in a funeral home or mortuary	

H. SEXUAL ACTIVITY IN A PUBLIC LAVATORY

(1) Definition

Sexual Offences Act 2003, s.71

Sexual activity in a public lavatory

14–275 **71.**—(1) A person commits an offence if—

(a) he is in a lavatory to which the public or a section of the public has or is permitted to have access, whether on payment or otherwise,

(b) he intentionally engages in an activity, and,

(c) the activity is sexual.

(2) For the purposes of this section, an activity is sexual if a reasonable person would, in all the circumstances but regardless of any person's purpose, consider it to be sexual.

(3) A person guilty of an offence under this section is liable on summary conviction, to imprisonment for a term not exceeding 6 months or a fine not exceeding level 5 on the standard scale or both.

(2) Allocation

14–276 This offence is triable summarily only.

(3) Sentence

14–277 The maximum custodial sentence is six months imprisonment and or a fine.

STARTING POINTS AND SENTENCING RANGES:

Type/nature of activity	Starting Point	Range
Repeat offending and/or aggravating features	Low level community order	Band C fine to medium level community order
Basic offence as defined in the *SOA* 2003, assuming no aggravating or mitigating factors	Band C fine	Band C fine

OFFENCE SERIOUSNESS (CULPABILITY AND HARM)

Factors indicating higher culpability	
1. Intimidating behaviour / threats of violence to member(s) of the public 2. Blatant behaviour	

I. TERRITORIAL AND EXTRA-TERRITORIAL JURISDICTION

The jurisdiction of the courts in respect of certain sexual offences has been through a series of changes. It is important to ensure when dealing with a case that falls into this category that the correct legislation has been applied. Each of the new provisions does not have retrospective effect. **14–278**

Section 7 of the *Sex Offenders Act* 1997, which came into force on September 1, 1997 initially dealt with the jurisdiction to try in England and Wales certain sexual offences committed abroad. The section was repealed and replaced with the original *Sexual Offences Act* 2003, s.72 which came into force on May 1, 2004. This section has now been heavily amended by *Criminal Justice and Immigration Act* 2008, s.72 with effect from July 14, 2008.

(1) Definition

Sexual Offences Act 2003, s.72

Offences outside the United Kingdom

72.—(1) If— **14–279**

(a) a United Kingdom national does an act in a country outside the United Kingdom, and

(b) the act, if done in England and Wales or Northern Ireland, would constitute a sexual offence to which this section applies,

the United Kingdom national is guilty in that part of the United Kingdom of that sexual offence.

(2) If—

(a) a United Kingdom resident does an act in a country outside the United Kingdom,

(b) the act constitutes an offence under the law in force in that country, and

(c) the act, if done in England and Wales or Northern Ireland, would constitute a sexual offence to which this section applies,

the United Kingdom resident is guilty in that part of the United Kingdom of that sexual offence.

(3) If—

(a) a person does an act in a country outside the United Kingdom at a time when the person was not a United Kingdom national or a United Kingdom resident,

(b) the act constituted an offence under the law in force in that country,

(c) the act, if done in England and Wales or Northern Ireland, would have constituted a sexual offence to which this section applies, and

(d) the person meets the residence or nationality condition at the relevant time,

proceedings may be brought against the person in that part of the United Kingdom for that sexual offence as if the person had done the act there.

(4) The person meets the residence or nationality condition at the relevant time if the person is a United Kingdom national or a United Kingdom resident at the time when the proceedings are brought.

(5) An act punishable under the law in force in any country constitutes an offence under that law for the purposes of subsections (2) and (3) however it is described in that law.

(6) The condition in subsection (2)(b) or (3)(b) is to be taken to be met unless, not later than rules of court may provide, the defendant serves on the prosecution a notice—

(a) stating that, on the facts as alleged with respect to the act in question, the condition is not in the defendant's opinion met,

(b) showing the grounds for that opinion, and

(c) requiring the prosecution to prove that it is met.

(7) But the court, if it thinks fit, may permit the defendant to require the prosecution to prove that the condition is met without service of a notice under subsection (6).

(8) In the Crown Court the question whether the condition is met is to be decided by the judge alone.

(9) In this section—

"country" includes territory;

"United Kingdom national" means an individual who is—

(a) a British citizen, a British overseas territories citizen, a British National (Overseas) or a British Overseas citizen;

(b) a person who under the *British Nationality Act* 1981 is a British subject; or

(c) a British protected person within the meaning of that Act;

"United Kingdom resident" means an individual who is resident in the United Kingdom.

(10) Schedule 2 lists the sexual offences to which this section applies."

Sexual Offences Act 2003, Sched. 2, para. 1

14–280 **1.** In relation to England and Wales the following are sexual offences to which section 72 applies—

(a) an offence under any of sections 5 to 19, 25 and 26 and 47 to 50;

(b) an offence under any of sections 1 to 4, 30 to 41 and 61 where the victim of the offence was under 18 at the time of the offence;

(c) an offence under section 62 or 63 where the intended offence was an offence against a person under 18;

(d) an offence under—

(i) section 1 of the *Protection of Children Act* 1978 (indecent photographs of children), or

(ii) section 160 of the *Criminal Justice Act* 1988 (possession of indecent photograph of a child).

[This section is printed as amended by s.72(1) of the *Criminal Justice and Immigration Act* 2008.]

The main difference between the old s.72 and the new section are as follows;

— It is no longer limited to offences against children under the age of 16.

— Where the offence falls into the non-consensual category, *e.g.* rape, child prostitution, the new age limit is 18.

— By virtue of s.72(1), a UK National is now capable of being prosecuted in this country for an act which may not have been offence in the country in which it was committed. For example a UK national who has consensual sexual activity with a child under 16 outside the UK may be prosecuted in this jurisdiction even though the act would not be an offence in the country in which it was committed.

X. ANCILLARY ORDERS

A. SEX OFFENDERS' REGISTER: NOTIFICATION REQUIREMENTS

(1) Definition

Sexual Offences Act 2003, s.80

Persons becoming subject to notification requirements(1)

14–281 **80.**—(1) A person is subject to the notification requirements of this Part for the period set out in section 82 ("the notification period") if–

(a) he is convicted of an offence listed in Schedule 3;
(b) he is found not guilty of such an offence by reason of insanity;
(c) he is found to be under a disability and to have done the act charged against him in respect of such an offence; or
(d) in England and Wales or Northern Ireland, he is cautioned in respect of such an offence.

(2) A person for the time being subject to the notification requirements of this Part is referred to in this Part as a "relevant offender".

Notification is mandatory and follows automatically if the offender has committed an offence listed in Sched. 3 to the *Sexual Offences Act* 2003. The requirements, set out in Pt 2 of the Act, oblige the offender to furnish the police with the following information within three days of the relevant conviction, finding or caution: name (and any aliases), date of birth, national insurance number, home address and any other address at which he regularly resides or stays and other information, as prescribed by the Secretary of State. The Secretary of State may amend the frequency with which relevant offenders without a sole or main residence in the United Kingdom are required to notify their details to the police (s.142 of the *Criminal Justice and Immigration Act* 2008). Subsequent changes to these details must also be notified to the police.

The table below sets out the thresholds which must be met before an offender becomes subject to the notification requirements of Pt 2 of the *Sexual Offences Act* 2003.

It must be made clear by the sentencing bench that the duration of the community sentence is for 12 months or more in order to render the defendant liable to the notification requirements: *Odman* [2005] 5 *Archbold News* 3, CA. (Community sentence comprising a community order with an unpaid work requirement of 80 hours held not to be a "community sentence of at least 12 months" within Sched. 3 to the *Sexual Offences Act* 2003 as in accordance with s.200(3) of the *Criminal Justice Act* 2003, a community order with a singular requirement of unpaid work only remains in force until the work has been completed.)

Part III

Sexual Offences Act 2003, s.82

The notification period

82.—(1) The notification period for a person within section 80(1) or *81(1)* is the period in the second column of the following Table opposite the description that applies to him. **14–282**

THRESHOLDS AS TO NOTIFICATION REQUIREMENTS

Offence	**Threshold to registration in Sched. 3**
Intercourse with a girl under 16 (s.6 *SOA* 1956)	Automatic registration where the offender is 20 or above
Gross indecency (s.13 *SOA* 1956)	Where the offender is 20 or above and the victim or (as the case may be) other party was under 18

Offence	Threshold to registration in Sched. 3
Indecent assault on a woman (s.14 *SOA* 1956)	Where: • the victim or (as the case may be) other party was under 18; or • the offender, in respect of the offence or finding, is or has been sentenced to imprisonment for a term of at least 30 months; or • admitted to a hospital subject to a restriction order.
Indecent assault on a man (s.15 *SOA* 1956)	Where: • the victim or (as the case may be) other party was under 18; or • the offender, in respect of the offence or finding, is or has been sentenced to imprisonment for a term of at least 30 months; or • admitted to a hospital subject to a restriction order.
Indecent conduct towards young child (s.1 *ICA* 1960)	Automatic registration
Indecent photographs of children (s.1 *POCA 1978*)	Where the offender is under 18: 12 months imprisonment Where the offender is 18 or above: Automatic registration
Possession of indecent photograph of a child (s.160 *CJA* 1988)	Where the indecent photographs or pseudo-photographs showed persons under 16 and: • the conviction, finding or caution was before the commencement of this Part, or • the offender was 18 or over, or • the offender is sentenced to imprisonment for a term of at least 12 months.
Abuse of position of trust (s.3 *SO(A)A* 2000)	Automatic registration where the offender is 20 or above

Offence	**Threshold to registration in Sched. 3**
Sexual assault (s.3 *SOA* 2003)	Where the offender is under 18: 12 months imprisonment Where the offender is 18 or above and: • The victim was under 18; or • The offender receives a prison sentence; or • Is detained in a hospital; or • Is made the subject of a community sentence for at least 12 months
Causing sexual activity without consent (s.4 *SOA* 2003)	Automatic registration
Child sex offences committed by adults (ss.9–12 *SOA* 2003)	Automatic registration
Arranging or facilitating the commission of a child sex offence (s.14 *SOA* 2003)	Where the offender is under 18: 12 months imprisonment Where the offender is 18 or above: Automatic registration
Meeting a child following sexual grooming (s.15 *SOA* 2003)	Automatic registration
Abuse of a position of trust (ss.16–19 *SOA* 2003)	Where the offender: • Receives a prison sentence; or • Is detained in a hospital; or • Is made the subject of a community sentence for at least 12 months
Familial child sex offences (ss.25–26 *SOA 2004*)	Where the offender is under 18: 12 months imprisonment Where the offender is 18 or above: Automatic registration
Offences against persons with a mental disorder (ss.30–37 *SOA* 2003)	Automatic registration
Care worker offences (ss.28–41 *SOA* 2003)	Where the offender is under 18:12 months imprisonment Where the offender is 18 or above and: • Receives a prison sentence; or • Is detained in a hospital; or • Is made the subject of a community sentence for at least 12 months

Part III

Offence	**Threshold to registration in Sched. 3**
Paying for the sexual services of a child (s.47 *SOA* 2003)	Where the victim was under 16: • And the offender was under 18, 12 months imprisonment • And the offender was 18 or above, automatic registration
Causing or inciting child prostitution or pornography (s.48 *SOA* 2003)	Where the offender is under 18: 12 months imprisonment Where the offender is 18 or above: Automatic registration
Administering a substance with intent (s.61 *SOA* 2003)	Automatic registration
Committing an offence, or trespassing, with intent to commit a sexual offence (ss.62–63 *SOA* 2003)	Where the offender is under 18: 12 months imprisonment Where the offender is 18 or above and: • The victim was under 18; or • The offender receives a prison sentence; or • Is detained in a hospital; or • Is made the subject of a community sentence for at least 12 months
Sex with an adult relative (ss.64–65 *SOA* 2003)	Where the offender is under 18: 12 months imprisonment Where the offender is 18 or above: • Receives a prison sentence; or • Is detained in a hospital
Exposure (s.66 *SOA* 2003)	Where the offender is under 18: 12 months imprisonment Where the offender is 18 or above and: • The victim was under 18; or • The offender receives a prison sentence; or • Is detained in a hospital; or • Is made the subject of a community sentence for at least 12 months

Offence	Threshold to registration in Sched. 3
Voyeurism (s.67 *SOA* 2003)	Where the offender is under 18: 12 months imprisonment Where the offender is 18 or above and: • The victim was under 18; or • The offender receives a prison sentence; or • Is detained in a hospital; or • Is made the subject of a community sentence for at least 12 months
Intercourse with an animal (s.69 *SOA* 2003) or sexual penetration of a corpse (s.70 *SOA* 2003)	Where the offender is under 18: 12 months imprisonment Where the offender is 18 or above and: • Receives a prison sentence or • Is detained in a hospital

(2) Length of notification period

The requirements are not an additional form of punishment and should not be taken into account when determining the sentence to be passed for an offence (*Att.-Gen's Reference (No. 50 of 1997)* [1998] 2 Cr.App.R.(S.) 155). The provisions of the 2003 Act are, in principle, automatic and do not require the sentencer to make reference to them. However it is good practice to state in open court that the offence is one to which the notification requirements of the *Sexual Offences Act* 2003 applies and to explain to the defendant the nature and effect of the requirements. **14–283**

Where the defendant is under the age of 18 the court may make a parental direction, transferring the obligations which would otherwise be imposed on the defendant to the parent, until the defendant attains the age of 18 or for such shorter period as the court directs.

The length of the notification period depends on the sentence that is imposed.

LENGTH OF NOTIFICATION PERIODS

14–284

Description of relevant offender	Notification period
A person sentenced to imprisonment for life or a term of 30 months or more, or admitted to a hospital subject to a restriction order	Indefinite period
A person sentenced to imprisonment for a term of more than six months but less than 30 months	10 years

A person sentenced to imprisonment for a term of six months or less or admitted to hospital without being subject to a restriction order	7 years
A person cautioned	2 years
A person conditionally discharged	The period of the conditional discharge
A person of any other description (sentenced to a community penalty or fine)	5 years

The notification periods apply to sentences of detention in a young offender's institution the same way as they do to imprisonment. If the offender is a youth however, the notification period will be half of the requirements referred to in the table above.

For the purposes of determining the notification period where consecutive terms of imprisonment have been imposed, the sentence is deemed to be equal to the aggregate of those terms.

In *F.* [2009] 2 Cr.App.R.(S.) 68, the appellant aged 11 at the time of the offences appealed against a total sentence of 30 months' detention imposed following his convictions on two counts of rape of a child under 13, three counts of causing or inciting a child under 13 to engage in sexual activity and one count of sexual assault on a child under 13 against his 6-year-old neighbour. The consequence of the length of his sentence was that he was required to comply with the notification provisions for an indefinite period. If his sentence had been less than 30 months' detention, the notification period would have been five years. An appeal against sentence had already been dismissed on the basis that it was neither wrong in principle nor manifestly excessive. During an application for judicial review in relation to the instant case, the Divisional Court had held that the provisions of Pt 2 of the Act, particularly when they related to sentences imposed on young persons, were not in conformity with the requirements of the European Convention on Human Rights Art. 8 because the consequence of the cut-off period of 30 months produced disproportionate notification requirements.

The appeal was dismissed on the basis that the courts were the determining body as to appropriate sentences and, as a matter of principle, should not reduce a sentence to limit the extent of an obligation to register. The decision of the Divisional Court was based on the premise that, particularly in relation to juveniles, there should be an opportunity for the offender to establish that he, or she, no longer presented the sort of risk which justified a notification requirement remaining in place. It was disproportionately harsh for a child of 11 who had committed offences such as those in the instant case to be subject to the notification requirements for the rest of his or her life without the opportunity for review. The decision was subsequently upheld by the Supreme Court, see [2011] 1 A.C. 331.

(3) Failure to comply with notification requirements / supplying false information

(a) *Definition*

Sexual Offences Act 2003, s.91

Offences relating to notification

91.—(1) A person commits an offence if he— 14–285

(a) fails, without reasonable excuse, to comply with section 83(1), 84(1), 84(4)(b), 85(1), 87(4) or 89(2)(b) or any requirement imposed by regulations made under section 86(1); or

(b) notifies to the police, in purported compliance with section 83(1), 84(1) or 85(1) or any requirement imposed by regulations made under section 86(1), any information which he knows to be false.

(2) A person guilty of an offence under this section is liable—

(a) on summary conviction, to imprisonment for a term not exceeding 6 months or a fine not exceeding the statutory maximum or both;

(b) on conviction on indictment, to imprisonment for a term not exceeding 5 years.

(3) A person commits an offence under paragraph (a) of subsection (1) on the day on which he first fails, without reasonable excuse, to comply with section 83(1), 84(1) or 85(1) or a requirement imposed by regulations made under section 86(1), and continues to commit it throughout any period during which the failure continues; but a person must not be prosecuted under subsection (1) more than once in respect of the same failure.

(4) Proceedings for an offence under this section may be commenced in any court having jurisdiction in any place where the person charged with the offence resides or is found.

(b) *Allocation*

These offences are triable either way. 14–286

(c) *Sentence*

The maximum sentence when tried summarily is a level 5 fine and / or 6 months imprisonment. 14–287

The starting points set out in the table below are from the Magistrates' Courts sentencing guidelines.

STARTING POINTS AND SENTENCING RANGES: (BASED ON A FIRST TIME OFFENDER AFTER TRIAL)

Examples of nature of activity	Starting Point	Range
Negligent or inadvertent failure to comply with requirements	Medium level community order	Band C fine to high level community order
Deliberate failure to comply with requirements OR Supply of information known to be false	6 weeks custody	High level community order to 26 weeks custody

Examples of nature of activity	Starting Point	Range
Conduct as described in box above AND Long period of non-compliance OR Attempts to avoid detection	18 weeks custody	6 weeks custody to Crown Court

OFFENCE SERIOUSNESS (CULPABILITY AND HARM)

Factor indicating higher culpability	Factor indicating lower culpability
1. Long period of non-compliance (where not in the examples above) **Factor indicating degree of harm** 1. Alarm or distress caused to victim 2. Particularly serious original offence	1. Genuine misunderstanding

In *Grosvenor* [2010] 2 Cr.App.R.(S.) 100 there was an appeal against a sentence of 6 months imprisonment for breach of a notification order. The appellant had refused to live at a probation hostel and did not notify police of his address. He said he was of no fixed abode and so had no address to notify. On appeal the court said the sentencing range of 4–6 months was only appropriate where there were no aggravating factors. A sexual predator who deliberately flouts an order or breaches it repeatedly must expect a longer sentence. It was said that living rough is not necessarily a mitigating factor.

B. NOTIFICATION ORDER

Sexual Offences Act 2003, s.97

Notification orders: applications and grounds

14–288 **97.**—(1) A chief officer of police may, by complaint to any magistrates' court whose commission area includes any part of his police area, apply for an order under this section (a "notification order") in respect of a person ("the defendant") if—

(a) it appears to him that the following three conditions are met with respect to the defendant, and

(b) the defendant resides in his police area or the chief officer believes that the defendant is in, or is intending to come to, his police area.

(2) The first condition is that under the law in force in a country outside the United Kingdom—

(a) he has been convicted of a relevant offence (whether or not he has been punished for it),

(b) a court exercising jurisdiction under that law has made in respect of a relevant offence a finding equivalent to a finding that he is not guilty by reason of insanity,

(c) such a court has made in respect of a relevant offence a finding equivalent to a finding that he is under a disability and did the act charged against him in respect of the offence, or

(d) he has been cautioned in respect of a relevant offence.

(3) The second condition is that—

(a) the first condition is met because of a conviction, finding or caution which occurred on or after 1st September 1997,

(b) the first condition is met because of a conviction or finding which occurred before that date, but the person was dealt with in respect of the offence or finding on or after that date, or has yet to be dealt with in respect of it, or

(c) the first condition is met because of a conviction or finding which occurred before that date, but on that date the person was, in respect of the offence or finding, subject under the law in force in the country concerned to detention, supervision or any other disposal equivalent to any of those mentioned in section 81(3) (read with sections 81(6) and 131).

(4) The third condition is that the period set out in section 82 (as modified by subsections (2) and (3) of section 98) in respect of the relevant offence has not expired.

(5) If on the application it is proved that the conditions in subsections (2) to (4) are met, the court must make a notification order.

(6) In this section and section 98, "relevant offence" has the meaning given by section 99.

Where an offender has been dealt with for a relevant offence (see table of relevant offences above) by a court in an overseas jurisdiction, a notification order may be sought. This imposes the sex offender registration requirements on offenders living in the UK, who have been convicted of sexual offences overseas. **14–289**

Such an order can be sought by way of complaint on application to the Magistrates Court by a chief police officer.

C. SEXUAL OFFENCES PREVENTION ORDER

(1) Definition

Sexual Offences Act 2003, s.104

Sexual offences prevention orders: applications and grounds

104.—(1) A court may make an order under this section in respect of a person ("the defendant") where any of subsections (2) to (4) applies to the defendant and— **14–290**

(a) where subsection (4) applies, it is satisfied that the defendant's behaviour since the appropriate date makes it necessary to make such an order, for the purpose of protecting the public or any particular members of the public from serious sexual harm from the defendant;

(b) in any other case, it is satisfied that it is necessary to make such an order, for the purpose of protecting the public or any particular members of the public from serious sexual harm from the defendant.

(2) This subsection applies to the defendant where the court deals with him in respect of an offence listed in Schedule 3 or 5.

(3) This subsection applies to the defendant where the court deals with him in respect of a finding—

(a) that he is not guilty of an offence listed in Schedule 3 or 5 by reason of insanity, or

(b) that he is under a disability and has done the act charged against him in respect of such an offence.

(4) This subsection applies to the defendant where—

(a) an application under subsection (5) has been made to the court in respect of him, and

(b) on the application, it is proved that he is a qualifying offender.

(5) A chief officer of police may by complaint to a magistrates' court apply for an order under this section in respect of a person who resides in his police area or who the chief officer believes is in, or is intending to come to, his police area if it appears to the chief officer that—

(a) the person is a qualifying offender, and

(b) the person has since the appropriate date acted in such a way as to give reasonable cause to believe that it is necessary for such an order to be made.

Part III

(6) An application under subsection (5) may be made to any magistrates' court whose commission area includes—

(a) any part of the applicant's police area, or

(b) any place where it is alleged that the person acted in a way mentioned in subsection (5)(b).

[This section is printed as amended by s.141 of the *Criminal Justice and Immigration Act* 2008.]

Sexual Offences act 2003, s.106

Section 104: supplemental

14–291 **106.**—(1) In this Part, "sexual offences prevention order" means an order under section 104 or 105.

(2) Subsections (3) to (8) apply for the purposes of section 104.

(3) "Protecting the public or any particular members of the public from serious sexual harm from the defendant" means protecting the public in the United Kingdom or any particular members of that public from serious physical or psychological harm, caused by the defendant committing one or more offences listed in Schedule 3.

(4) Acts, behaviour, convictions and findings include those occurring before the commencement of this Part.

(5) "Qualifying offender" means a person within subsection (6) or (7).

(6) A person is within this subsection if, whether before or after the commencement of this Part, he—

(a) has been convicted of an offence listed in Schedule 3 (other than at paragraph 60) or in Schedule 5,

(b) has been found not guilty of such an offence by reason of insanity,

(c) has been found to be under a disability and to have done the act charged against him in respect of such an offence, or

(d) in England and Wales or Northern Ireland, has been cautioned in respect of such an offence.

(7) A person is within this subsection if, under the law in force in a country outside the United Kingdom and whether before or after the commencement of this Part—

(a) he has been convicted of a relevant offence (whether or not he has been punished for it),

(b) a court exercising jurisdiction under that law has made in respect of a relevant offence a finding equivalent to a finding that he is not guilty by reason of insanity,

(c) such a court has made in respect of a relevant offence a finding equivalent to a finding that he is under a disability and did the act charged against him in respect of the offence, or

(d) he has been cautioned in respect of a relevant offence.

(8) "Appropriate date", in relation to a qualifying offender, means the date or (as the case may be) the first date on which he was convicted, found or cautioned as mentioned in subsection (6) or (7).

(9) In subsection (7), "relevant offence" means an act which—

(a) constituted an offence under the law in force in the country concerned, and

(b) would have constituted an offence listed in Schedule 3 (other than at paragraph 60) or in Schedule 5 if it had been done in any part of the United Kingdom.

(10) An act punishable under the law in force in a country outside the United Kingdom constitutes an offence under that law for the purposes of subsection (9), however it is described in that law.

(11) Subject to subsection (12), on an application under section 104(5) the condition in subsection (9)(b) (where relevant) is to be taken as met unless, not later than rules of court may provide, the defendant serves on the applicant a notice—

(a) stating that, on the facts as alleged with respect to the act concerned, the condition is not in his opinion met,

(b) showing his grounds for that opinion, and

(c) requiring the applicant to prove that the condition is met.

(12) The court, if it thinks fit, may permit the defendant to require the applicant to prove that the condition is met without service of a notice under subsection (11).

(13) Subsection (14) applies for the purposes of section 104 and this section in their application in relation to England and Wales or Northern Ireland.

(14) In construing any reference to an offence listed in Schedule 3, any condition subject to which an offence is so listed that relates—

(a) to the way in which the defendant is dealt with in respect of an offence so listed or a relevant finding (as defined by section 132(9)), or

(b) to the age of any person,

is to be disregarded.

Sexual Offences Act 2003, s.107

SOPOs: effect

107.—(1) A sexual offences prevention order— **14–292**

(a) prohibits the defendant from doing anything described in the order, and

(b) has effect for a fixed period (not less than 5 years) specified in the order or until further order.

(2) The only prohibitions that may be included in the order are those necessary for the purpose of protecting the public or any particular members of the public from serious sexual harm from the defendant.

(3) Where—

(a) an order is made in respect of a defendant who was a relevant offender immediately before the making of the order, and

(b) the defendant would (apart from this subsection) cease to be subject to the notification requirements of this Part while the order (as renewed from time to time) has effect,

the defendant remains subject to the notification requirements.

(4) Where an order is made in respect of a defendant who was not a relevant offender immediately before the making of the order—

(a) the order causes the defendant to become subject to the notification requirements of this Part from the making of the order until the order (as renewed from time to time) ceases to have effect, and

(b) this Part applies to the defendant, subject to the modification set out in subsection (5).

(5) The "relevant date" is the date of service of the order.

(6) Where a court makes a sexual offences prevention order in relation to a person already subject to such an order (whether made by that court or another), the earlier order ceases to have effect.

(7) Section 106(3) applies for the purposes of this section and section 108.

A court has a duty to consider making a sexual offences prevention order (it is not a mandatory order) if: **14–293**

— the offence is one listed in Scheds 3 or 5 to the *Sexual Offences Act* 2003;

— it is satisfied that it is necessary to make such an order for the purpose of protecting the public or any particular members of the public from serious sexual harm from the defendant.

Such an order can be made either at the point of sentence or, by way of application to the magistrate's court in respect of a person who has previously been convicted of a sexual offence where that person's behaviour suggests the possibility of re-offending.

(2) Elements

Serious sexual harm is interpreted as serious physical or psychological harm caused by the offender committing an offence listed in Sched. 3 to the *Sexual Offences Act* 2003. Focus is on the risk of further offending. The court has to conduct a risk assessment and to satisfy itself that it is necessary, rather than just "desirable", to make an order because of the likelihood of the defendant committing further, relevant offences. In *B v. Chief Constable of the Avon and Somerset Constabulary* [2001] 1 All E.R. 562, DC) it was held that magistrates are not obliged to apply the criminal standard of proof however, a bare balance of probability is not to be applied; the civil standard to apply **14–294**

Part III

should for all practical purposes be indistinguishable from the criminal standard and should be applied with the strictness appropriate to the seriousness of the matters to be proved and the implications of proving them.

In *Chief Constable of Cleveland Police v. Haggas* [2010] 3 All E.R. 506—the case of *B v. Chief Constable of Avon and Somerset Constabulary* [2001] 1 W.L.R. 340 was considered and applied namely, that in reality it meant that it was necessary to establish to the criminal standard what the respondent was alleged to have done.

The fact that a defendant did not satisfy the requirements of Chapter 5 of Pt 12 of the *Criminal Justice Act* 2003 (the dangerous offender provisions), does not prevent the imposition of a sexual offences prevention order, the two tests are different. There is no requirement for the purposes of a sexual offender prevention order that there is a "significant" risk of serious harm. Furthermore, "serious sexual harm" for the purposes of section 104 is defined as "serious physical or psychological harm" as distinct from death or serious personal injury as is required under the dangerousness provisions. See *Rampley* [2007] 1 Cr.App.R.(S.) 87, CA and *Richards* [2007] 1 Cr.App.R.(S.) 120, CA.

If it is proved that the defendant's behaviour since the appropriate date makes it necessary to make such an order, the court may make an order prohibiting the defendant from doing anything described in the order. The prohibitions imposed must not be wider than necessary for the purpose of protecting the public from serious harm (*B v. Chief Constable of the Avon and Somerset Constabulary* [2001] 1 All E.R. 562, DC). The order may include only negative prohibitions; there is no power to impose positive obligations.

Where a child may in the future wish to have contact with the defendant the order should allow for the jurisdiction of the family court to be invoked, *e.g.* "shall not, without the order of a judge exercising jurisdiction under the *Children Act* 1989, communicate or seek to communicate, whether directly or indirectly with [XXX] whilst he/she remains under 16 years of age": *D (Sexual offences prevention order)* [2006] 1 W.L.R. 1088, CA.

In *D* [2006] 2 Cr.App.R.(S.) 204 the defendant had committed a series of sexual offences against his daughter when she was aged between 10–13. The judge imposed a sexual offences prevention order prohibiting the offender from contacting his son. Although his son had not been a victim of the offending it was found that he had suffered psychological harm as a result and would do again in the future if further offences were committed. The Court of Appeal upheld the order.

In *Smith* [2009] 2 Cr.App.R.(S.) 110 the appellant pleaded guilty to four charges of making an indecent photograph or pseudo photograph of a child. The four images were DVDs ranging between levels 3–5. All depicted young teenage girls. One of the terms of the sexual offences prevention order prohibited the offender from denying police officers access to his home in order to check that other prohibitions in the order relating to access and use of the internet were being complied with. The court held that such a term of a sexual offences prevention order was not objectionable in principle under s.107(2), but neither was it justifiable on the facts of the case. This was not the sort of case in which the nature of the offending was such that it was necessary to monitor the offender's compliance by such an intrusive condition.

In *Hemsley* [2010] 3 All E.R. 965 a SOPO was quashed because the terms were held to be too wide. The court said it was essential that such an order is clear and capable of being complied with and free of the real risk of unintentional breach. The order prohibited the use or possession of any computer unless a constable was permitted to enter the premises to examine and if necessary remove the computer. This was held to involve the co-operation of third parties which might not easily be secured. In addition it could limit his employment abilities and so was too wide. Similarly in *Mortimer* [2010] EWCA Crim 1303 an order which prohibited the appellant from having in his possession, without permission, any photograph of a child under 16 and various prohibitions on possession or use of computers, internet accounts and mobile phones was held to be oppressive, disproportionate and almost impossible to police and so the order was amended on appeal. See also *Brown* [2011] EWCA Crim 1223 where the court said it was not adequate to draw up wide terms and then rely on the good sense of the prosecutors only to take action when they saw fit.

In *Hoath and Standage* [2011] EWCA Crim 274 it was confirmed that there is a right of appeal to the Court of Appeal where the Crown Court has refused to vary a SOPO. The importance of taking care over the form and wording of such orders was emphasised.

(3) Duration of order

It is not appropriate for any sentence passed for the primary offence to be reduced in order to limit the extent of an offender's obligation to register under the *Sexual Offences Act* 2003. **14–295**

A sexual offences prevention order has effect for a fixed period of not more than five years. During the time that such order is in force, the notification requirements under Pt 2 of the *Sexual Offences Act* 2003 shall have effect. There are provisions for the variation, renewal and discharge of such orders set out in ss.108 and 110. **14–296**

(4) Breach of Sexual Offences Prevention Order

(a) *Definition*

Sexual Offences Act 2003, s.113

Offence: breach of SOPO or interim SOPO

113.—(1) A person commits an offence if, without reasonable excuse, he does anything which he is prohibited from doing by— **14–297**

(a) a sexual offences prevention order;
(b) an interim sexual offences prevention order;
(c) an order under section 5A of the *Sex Offenders Act* 1997 (c. 51) (restraining orders);
(d) an order under section 2, 2A or 20 of the *Crime and Disorder Act* 1998 (sex offender orders and interim orders made in England and Wales and in Scotland);
(e) an order under Article 6 or 6A of the *Criminal Justice (Northern Ireland) Order* 1998 (S.I. 1998/2839 (N.I. 20)) (sex offender orders and interim orders made in Northern Ireland).

(2) A person guilty of an offence under this section is liable—

(a) on summary conviction, to imprisonment for a term not exceeding 6 months or a fine not exceeding the statutory maximum or both;
(b) on conviction on indictment, to imprisonment for a term not exceeding 5 years.

(3) Where a person is convicted of an offence under this section, it is not open to the court by or before which he is convicted to make, in respect of the offence, an order for conditional discharge or, in Scotland, a community payback order.

(b) *Allocation*

This offence is triable either way. **14–298**

(c) *Sentence*

Failure to comply with a sexual offences prevention order without reasonable excuse is punishable on summary conviction to a maximum of six months imprisonment and / or a fine; on indictment to maximum of five years' imprisonment. Section 113 prevents the imposition of a conditional discharge. **14–299**

In *Fenton* [2007] 1 Cr.App.R.(S.) 97, CA, it was held that where the breach does not involve any real or obvious risk to the section of the public sought to be protected by the order then a community penalty would be an appropriate sentence. Where there are repeated breaches of any order a custodial sentence may be appropriate. Where the person or persons sought to be protected are as a result of the breach, put at a real and obvious risk then the breach should be treated more seriously.

A two year custodial sentence was upheld in respect of a conviction for breaching a SOPO on seven occasions. It was held to be a persistent and deliberate breach of an order by way of the appellant having or seeking contact with two 16 year-old-boys. Although there had been no further sexual offending, over 16 months the appellant had extensive contact with the boys which was a calculated defiance of the court order justifying a lengthy custodial sentence: *Byrne* [2010] 1 Cr.App.R.(S.) 65.

D. RISK OF SEXUAL HARM ORDER

(1) Definition

Sexual Offences Act 2003, s.123

Risk of sexual harm orders: applications, grounds and effect

14–300 **123.**—(1) A chief officer of police may by complaint to a magistrates' court apply for an order under this section (a "risk of sexual harm order") in respect of a person aged 18 or over ("the defendant") who resides in his police area or who the chief officer believes is in, or is intending to come to, his police area if it appears to the chief officer that—

(a) the defendant has on at least two occasions, whether before or after the commencement of this Part, done an act within subsection (3), and

(b) as a result of those acts, there is reasonable cause to believe that it is necessary for such an order to be made.

(2) An application under subsection (1) may be made to any magistrates' court whose commission area includes—

(a) any part of the applicant's police area, or

(b) any place where it is alleged that the defendant acted in a way mentioned in subsection (1)(a).

(3) The acts are—

(a) engaging in sexual activity involving a child or in the presence of a child;

(b) causing or inciting a child to watch a person engaging in sexual activity or to look at a moving or still image that is sexual;

(c) giving a child anything that relates to sexual activity or contains a reference to such activity;

(d) communicating with a child, where any part of the communication is sexual.

(4) On the application, the court may make a risk of sexual harm order if it is satisfied that—

(a) the defendant has on at least two occasions, whether before or after the commencement of this section, done an act within subsection (3); and

(b) it is necessary to make such an order, for the purpose of protecting children generally or any child from harm from the defendant.

(5) Such an order—

(a) prohibits the defendant from doing anything described in the order;

(b) has effect for a fixed period (not less than 2 years) specified in the order or until further order.

(6) The only prohibitions that may be imposed are those necessary for the purpose of protecting children generally or any child from harm from the defendant.

(7) Where a court makes a risk of sexual harm order in relation to a person already subject to such an order (whether made by that court or another), the earlier order ceases to have effect.

(2) Elements

Sexual Offences Act 2003, s.124

Section 123: interpretation

14–301 **124.**—(1) Subsections (2) to (7) apply for the purposes of section 123.

(2) "Protecting children generally or any child from harm from the defendant" means protecting children generally or any child from physical or psychological harm, caused by the defendant doing acts within section 123(3).

(3) "Child" means a person under 16.

(4) "Image" means an image produced by any means, whether of a real or imaginary subject.

(5) "Sexual activity" means an activity that a reasonable person would, in all the circumstances but regardless of any person's purpose, consider to be sexual.

(6) A communication is sexual if—

(a) any part of it relates to sexual activity, or

(b) a reasonable person would, in all the circumstances but regardless of any person's purpose, consider that any part of the communication is sexual.

(7) An image is sexual if—

(a) any part of it relates to sexual activity, or

(b) a reasonable person would, in all the circumstances but regardless of any person's purpose, consider that any part of the image is sexual.

(8) In this section, as it applies to Northern Ireland, subsection (3) has effect with the substitution of "17" for "16".

A risk of sexual harm order may be applied for by a chief police officer if a defendant has on at least two occasions: **14–302**

— engaged in sexual activity involving a child or in the presence of a child;

— caused or incited a child to watch a person engaging in sexual activity or to look at a moving or still image that is sexual;

— given a child anything that relates to sexual activity or contains a reference to such activity;

— communicated with a child, where any part of the communication is sexual;

and as a result of those acts, there is reasonable cause to believe that it is necessary for such an order to be made.

The court may make a risk of sexual harm order if it is satisfied that the defendant has on at least two occasions done one of the above acts and it is necessary to make such an order, for the purpose of protecting children generally or any child from harm from the defendant.

A risk of sexual harm order prohibits the defendant from doing anything described in the order. Prohibitions in the order must not be wider than are necessary for protecting children generally or any child from harm from the defendant.

(3) Length of order

Sexual Offences Act 2003, s.126

Interim RSHOs

126.—(1) This section applies where an application for a risk of sexual harm order ("the main application") has not been determined. **14–303**

(2) An application for an order under this section ("an interim risk of sexual harm order")—

(a) may be made by the complaint by which the main application is made, or

(b) if the main application has been made, may be made by the person who has made that application, by complaint to the court to which that application has been made.

(3) The court may, if it considers it just to do so, make an interim risk of sexual harm order, prohibiting the defendant from doing anything described in the order.

(4) Such an order—

(a) has effect only for a fixed period, specified in the order;

(b) ceases to have effect, if it has not already done so, on the determination of the main application.

(5) The applicant or the defendant may by complaint apply to the court that made the interim risk of sexual harm order for the order to be varied, renewed or discharged.

A full order may be set for a fixed period which must be more than two years or until further order. It is also possible to make an interim hearing pending a full hearing and a fixed period must be set whilst the case is adjourned to a date for hearing.

(4) Breach of a Risk of Sexual Harm Order

(a) *Definition*

Sexual Offences Act 2003, s.128

Offence: breach of RSHO or interim RSHO

14–304 **128.**—(1) A person commits an offence if, without reasonable excuse, he does anything which he is prohibited from doing by—

(a) a risk of sexual harm order; or

(b) an interim risk of sexual harm order.

(1A) In subsection (1) and, accordingly, in section 129(5) the references to a risk of sexual harm order and to an interim risk of sexual harm order include references, respectively—

(a) to an order under section 2 of the *Protection of Children and Prevention of Sexual Offences (Scotland) Act 2005* (RSHOs in Scotland); and

(b) to an order under section 5 of that Act (interim RSHOs in Scotland);

and, for the purposes of this section, prohibitions imposed by an order made in one part of the United Kingdom apply (unless expressly confined to particular localities) throughout that and every other part of the United Kingdom.

(2) A person guilty of an offence under this section is liable—

(a) on summary conviction, to imprisonment for a term not exceeding 6 months or a fine not exceeding the statutory maximum or both;

(b) on conviction on indictment, to imprisonment for a term not exceeding 5 years.

(3) Where a person is convicted of an offence under this section, it is not open to the court by or before which he is convicted to make, in respect of the offence, an order for conditional discharge.

[This section is printed as amended by the *Violent Crime Reduction Act* 2006.]

(b) *Allocation*

14–305 This offence is triable either way.

(c) *Sentence*

14–306 On summary conviction, the maximum sentence is six months imprisonment and/or fine at level 5.

E. FOREIGN TRAVEL ORDER

(1) Definition

Sexual Offences Act 2003, ss.114, 117

Foreign travel orders: applications and grounds

14–307 **114.**—(1) A chief officer of police may by complaint to a magistrates' court apply for an order under this section (a "foreign travel order") in respect of a person ("the defendant") who resides in his police area or who the chief officer believes is in or is intending to come to his police area if it appears to the chief officer that—

(a) the defendant is a qualifying offender, and

(b) the defendant has since the appropriate date acted in such a way as to give reasonable cause to believe that it is necessary for such an order to be made.

(2) An application under subsection (1) may be made to any magistrates' court whose commission area includes any part of the applicant's police area.

(3) On the application, the court may make a foreign travel order if it is satisfied that—

(a) the defendant is a qualifying offender, and

(b) the defendant's behaviour since the appropriate date makes it necessary to make such an order, for the purpose of protecting children generally or any child from serious sexual harm from the defendant outside the United Kingdom.

Foreign travel orders: effect

117.—(1) A foreign travel order has effect for a fixed period of not more than 5 years, specified in the order. **14–308**

(2) The order prohibits the defendant from doing whichever of the following is specified in the order—

(a) travelling to any country outside the United Kingdom named or described in the order,

(b) travelling to any country outside the United Kingdom other than a country named or described in the order, or

(c) travelling to any country outside the United Kingdom.

(3) The only prohibitions that may be included in the order are those necessary for the purpose of protecting children generally or any child from serious sexual harm from the defendant outside the United Kingdom.

(4) If at any time while an order (as renewed from time to time) has effect a defendant is not a relevant offender, the order causes him to be subject to the requirements imposed by regulations made under section 86(1) (and for these purposes the defendant is to be treated as if he were a relevant offender).

(5) Where a court makes a foreign travel order in relation to a person already subject to such an order (whether made by that court or another), the earlier order ceases to have effect.

(6) Section 115(2) applies for the purposes of this section and section 118.

A foreign travel order prohibits the defendant from travelling outside the United Kingdom for a fixed period not exceeding 5 years. An application cane be made by a chief police officer to the magistrate's court.

[The next paragraph is § 14–310.]

(2) Elements

Sexual Offences Act 2003, ss.115, 116

Section 114: interpretation

115.—(1) Subsections (2) to (5) apply for the purposes of section 114. **14–310**

(2) "Protecting children generally or any child from serious sexual harm from the defendant outside the United Kingdom" means protecting persons under 16 generally or any particular person under 18 from serious physical or psychological harm caused by the defendant doing, outside the United Kingdom, anything which would constitute an offence listed in Schedule 3 if done in any part of the United Kingdom.

(3) Acts and behaviour include those occurring before the commencement of this Part.

(4) "Qualifying offender" has the meaning given by section 116.

(5) "Appropriate date", in relation to a qualifying offender, means the date or (as the case may be) the first date on which he was convicted, found or cautioned as mentioned in subsection (1) or (3) of section 116.

(6) *Applies to N. Ireland*

Section 114: qualifying offenders

116.—(1) A person is a qualifying offender for the purposes of section 114 if, whether before or after the commencement of this Part, he— **14–311**

(a) has been convicted of an offence within subsection (2),

(b) has been found not guilty of such an offence by reason of insanity,

(c) has been found to be under a disability and to have done the act charged against him in respect of such an offence, or

(d) in England and Wales or Northern Ireland, has been cautioned in respect of such an offence.

(2) The offences are—

(a) an offence within any of paragraphs 13 to 15, 44 to 46, 77, 78 and 82 of Schedule 3;

Part III

(b) an offence within paragraph 31 of that Schedule, if the intended offence was an offence against a person under 18;

(c) an offence within paragraph 93 or 93A of that Schedule, if—

(i) the corresponding civil offence is an offence within any of paragraphs 13 to 15 of that Schedule;

(ii) the corresponding civil offence is an offence within paragraph 31 of that Schedule, and the intended offence was an offence against a person under 18; or

(iii) the corresponding civil offence is an offence within any of paragraphs 1 to 12, 16 to 30 and 32 to 35 of that Schedule, and the victim of the offence was under 18 at the time of the offence.

(d) an offence within any other paragraph of that Schedule, if the victim of the offence was under 18 at the time of the offence.

(2A) In subsection (2)(c) references to the corresponding civil offence are to be read, in relation to an offence within paragraph 93A of Schedule 3, as references to the corresponding offence under the law of England and Wales.

(3) A person is also a qualifying offender for the purposes of section 114 if, under the law in force in a country outside the United Kingdom and whether before or after the commencement of this Part—

(a) he has been convicted of a relevant offence (whether or not he has been punished for it),

(b) a court exercising jurisdiction under that law has made in respect of a relevant offence a finding equivalent to a finding that he is not guilty by reason of insanity,

(c) such a court has made in respect of a relevant offence a finding equivalent to a finding that he is under a disability and did the act charged against him in respect of the offence, or

(d) he has been cautioned in respect of a relevant offence.

(4) In subsection (3), "relevant offence" means an act which—

(a) constituted an offence under the law in force in the country concerned, and

(b) would have constituted an offence within subsection (2) if it had been done in any part of the United Kingdom.

(5) An act punishable under the law in force in a country outside the United Kingdom constitutes an offence under that law for the purposes of subsection (4), however it is described in that law.

(6) Subject to subsection (7), on an application under section 114 the condition in subsection (4)(b) above (where relevant) is to be taken as met unless, not later than rules of court may provide, the defendant serves on the applicant a notice—

(a) stating that, on the facts as alleged with respect to the act concerned, the condition is not in his opinion met,

(b) showing his grounds for that opinion, and

(c) requiring the applicant to prove that the condition is met.

(7) The court, if it thinks fit, may permit the defendant to require the applicant to prove that the condition is met without service of a notice under subsection (6).

14–312 For any such prohibition on travel the defendant must be a qualifying offender as set out in s.116 which refers to offences in Sched. 3 and must have acted in such a way as to give reasonable cause to believe that it is necessary for such an order to be made. The purpose of such an order is to protect children generally, or a particular child from serious sexual harm from the defendant outside the United Kingdom and must be deemed necessary by virtue of the defendant's behaviour.

(3) Breach of a Foreign Travel Order

(a) *Definition*

Sexual Offences Act 2003, s.122

Offence: breach of foreign travel order

14–313 **122.**—(1) A person commits an offence if, without reasonable excuse, he does anything which he is prohibited from doing by a foreign travel order.

(1A) A person commits an offence if, without reasonable excuse, the person fails to comply with a requirement under section 117A(2).

(2) A person guilty of an offence under this section is liable—

(a) on summary conviction, to imprisonment for a term not exceeding 6 months or a fine not exceeding the statutory maximum or both;

(b) on conviction on indictment, to imprisonment for a term not exceeding 5 years.

(3) Where a person is convicted of an offence under this section, it is not open to the court by or before which he is convicted to make, in respect of the offence, an order for conditional discharge (or, in Scotland, a probation order).

[This section is printed as amended by the *Violent Crime Reduction Act* 2006 and the *Policing and Crime Act* 2009, s.25(3).]

(b) *Allocation*

This offence is triable either way. **14–314**

(c) *Sentence*

The maximum sentence for breach of a foreign travel order on summary conviction is six months imprisonment and/or a fine at level 5. **14–315**

F. FINANCIAL ORDERS

Compensation Order

In all cases where the commission of an offence has resulted in injury, loss or damage the court must consider compensation. In cases involving sexual offences this can be a particularly sensitive issue. The Sentencing Guidelines Council definitive guideline Sexual Offences Act 2003 emphasises that compensation should benefit, not inflict further harm on, the victim. Any financial recompense from the offender for a sexual offence may cause the victim additional humiliation, degradation and distress. It is important that the views of the victim are sought before such an order is made. Whilst the making of an order in such cases has not been held to be improper in principle, the Court of Appeal has stated that it would be inappropriate to make a compensation order in a modest amount to a small child who has been sexually abused and which is capable of being misconstrued by the general public (*Att.-Gen's Reference (No. 35 of 1994)* 16 Cr.App.R.(S.) 635, CA; *Att.-Gen's Reference (No. 50 of 2003)* [2004] 2 Cr.App.R.(S.) 254, CA). **14–316**

The Magistrates' Court Sentencing Guidelines provide the following as suggested starting points, based on the Criminal Injuries Compensation Authority tariff:

STARTING POINTS FOR COMPENSATION

Sexual abuse of adult	Non-penetrative indecent physical acts over clothing	£1,000
	Non-penetrative indecent act(s) under clothing	£2,000

Sexual abuse of child (under 18)	Non-penetrative indecent physical act(s) over clothing	£1,000
	Non-penetrative frequent assaults over clothing or non-penetrative indecent act under clothing	£2,000
	Repetitive indecent acts under clothing	£3,300

G. COMMUNITY ORDERS

(1) Sex Offender Treatment Programme

14–317 Whenever a court imposes a community order for a sexual offence, it should consider imposing a requirement to attend a sex offender's treatment programme. Such programmes are in fact available both in prison and in the community; however participation is only mandatory when imposed as part of a requirement of a community order. Programmes are available for both male and female offenders. Most programmes are only available to those who are given lengthy community orders (normally two years) but can be available for those sentenced to shorter periods. Where such a recommendation is made in a pre-sentence report the courts' attention should be drawn to the length of community order required for such a programme to be completed, its availability to the offender and the courses content, it being in the public interest to help the offender recognise and control any sexually deviant tendencies. See §§ 23–66 *et seq*.

(2) Curfews

14–318 A curfew requirement can also be considered by the court, assisted by electronic monitoring. Such a requirement could prevent an offender from leaving their property during the school run. A curfew requirement can be for between 2 to 12 hours per day and last for up to a maximum of six months. See §§ 23–70 *et seq*.

Chapter 15

PROPERTY OFFENCES

Part III

I. OFFENCES UNDER THE THEFT ACTS 1968 AND 1978

A. Theft

(1) Definition

Theft Act 1968, s.1

Basic definition of theft

15–1 **1.**—(1) A person is guilty of theft if he dishonestly appropriates property belonging to another with the intention of permanently depriving the other of it; and "thief" and "steal" shall be construed accordingly.

(2) It is immaterial whether the appropriation is made with a view to gain, or is made for the thief's own benefit.

(3) The five following sections of this Act shall have effect as regards the interpretation and operation of this section (and, except as otherwise provided by this Act, shall apply only for purposes of this section).

(2) Allocation

15–2 Theft is triable either way: *Magistrates' Courts Act* 1980, s.17(1) and Sched. 1. The *Consolidated Criminal Practice Direction*, Pt V.51.7 *(Mode of Trial)* states that theft should be tried summarily unless one of the aggravating features is present and sentencing powers are insufficient. See Appendix F–49.

(3) Elements of the offence

15–3 The prosecution must prove that the defendant:
— dishonestly;
— appropriated;
— property;
— belonging to another;
— with the intention of permanently depriving the other of that property.

Dishonestly

Theft Act 1968, s.2

"Dishonestly"

15–4 **2.**—(1) A person's appropriation of property belonging to another is not to be regarded as dishonest—

(a) if he appropriates the property in the belief that he has in law the right to deprive the other of it, on behalf of himself or of a third person; or

(b) if he appropriates the property in the belief that he would have the other's consent if the other knew of the appropriation and the circumstances of it; or

(c) (except where the property came to him as trustee or personal representative) if he appropriates the property in the belief that the person to whom the property belongs cannot be discovered by taking reasonable steps.

(2) A person's appropriation of property belonging to another may be dishonest notwithstanding that he is willing to pay for the property.

The test of dishonestly is that contained in *Feely* [1973] Q.B. 530 and *Ghosh* [1982] Q.B. 1053; 75 Cr.App.R. 154, CA. The relevant test is to consider the conduct of the defendant by the standards of reasonable and honest people. If the conduct is not found dishonest by these standards then the prosecution will fail. If the conduct is found to be dishonest, the next stage is to consider whether the defendant himself realised that his conduct was dishonest by those standards. If so, then the defendant will be held to have been acting dishonestly. The second question need only be considered when the defendant raises this issue: *Price* (1990) 90 Cr.App.R. 409.

In *DPP v. Gohill and others* [2007] EWHC 239 (Admin), the Divisional Court found that a magistrates court's decision to acquit individuals who allowed customers of a tool hire company to hire equipment without making a payment of theft and false accounting on the grounds that the individuals' actions were not dishonest by the standards of reasonable and honest people was perverse. The defendant worked for company that hired equipment to members. The company policy was that if hired equipment was returned to the store within two hours of being hired, namely because the equipment was faulty or because incorrect equipment had been chosen, no fee was charged. The defendant had allowed customers to return working and correctly chosen equipment to be returned within two hours; customers returning such goods usually tipped the defendant £5 or £10. The defendant then altered the computer records so that no hire charge was applicable. The defendants accepted that the equipment belonged to the company and that they had acted contrary to company procedure but asserted that they had acted to promote the business and in the interests of customer care so that the company benefited "in the long run". The magistrates' court acquitted the defendants on the basis that on the standards of reasonable and honest people they had not acted dishonestly. Allowing the DPP's appeal, the Court held that the magistrates' court's decision was perverse, stating that it was completely inappropriate to find that the defendants had not acted dishonestly when they allowed customers to receive equipment for hire from a hire company without those customers making a payment, especially where the company's procedure did not allow any alternative for the return of equipment other than for two particular reasons. The matter was remitted for the court to determine the matter under the second stage of the test elucidated in *Ghosh*, above.

Claim of right

Section 2(1) offers three occasions when the defendant's appropriation is not to be considered as dishonest. To come within the terms of s.2(1)(a) the defendant must believe that in law he had the right to deprive the other of his property: *Bernard* 26 Cr.App.R. 137, CCA. It does not matter that there is no basis in law for such a belief: *Bernard*, *ante*, though belief in a moral right is no defence: *Harris v. Harrison* [1963] Crim.L.R. 497, DC. **15–5**

Appropriates

Theft Act 1968, s.3

"Appropriates"

3.—(1) Any assumption by a person of the rights of an owner amounts to an appropriation, and this includes, where he has come by the property (innocently or not) without stealing it, any later assumption of a right to it by keeping or dealing with it as owner. **15–6**

(2) Where property or a right or interest in property is or purports to be transferred for value to a person acting in good faith, no later assumption by him of rights which he believed himself to be acquiring shall, by reason of any defect in the transferor's title, amount to theft of the property.

15–7 Appropriation will be established by the assumption of any of the owner's rights in the goods in question. It is not necessary to show assumption of all of the owner's rights: *Morris* [1984] A.C. 320, HL. It is not necessary to show that the appropriation was without the consent of the owner: *Lawrence v. Metropolitan Police Commissioner* [1972] A.C. 626, HL; *DPP v. Gomez* [1993] A.C. 442, HL; *Hinks* [2001] 2 A.C. 241.

Class A drugs unlawfully in an individual's possession constitute property that is capable of being appropriated: *Smith (Michael Andrew)* [2011] EWCA Crim 66.

Gifts

15–8 Following the majority decision of the House of Lords in *Hinks* [2001] 2 A.C. 241, HL, it is now established that where the defence to a charge of theft is that the property is question was given as a gift, the question of the belief in the owner's consent to the giving of the gift is only relevant to the question of dishonesty. Hence the acquisition of indefeasible title to property is capable of amounting to an appropriation of property belonging to another for the purposes of the offence of theft.

Property

Theft Act 1968, s.4

"Property"

15–9 **4.**—(1) "Property" includes money and all other property, real or personal, including things in action and other intangible property.

(2) A person cannot steal land, or things forming part of land and severed from it by him or by his directions, except in the following cases, that is to say—

(a) when he is a trustee or personal representative, or is authorised by power of attorney, or as liquidator of a company, or otherwise, to sell or dispose of land belonging to another, and he appropriates the land or anything forming part of it by dealing with it in breach of the confidence reposed in him; or

(b) when he is not in possession of the land and appropriates anything forming part of the land by severing it or causing it to be severed, or after it has been severed; or

(c) when, being in possession of the land under a tenancy, he appropriates the whole or part of any fixture or structure let to be used with the land.

For purposes of this subsection "land" does not include incorporeal hereditaments; "tenancy" means a tenancy for years or any less period and includes an agreement for such a tenancy, but a person who after the end of a tenancy remains in possession as statutory tenant or otherwise is to be treated as having possession under the tenancy, and "let" shall be construed accordingly.

(3) A person who picks mushrooms growing wild on any land, or who picks flowers, fruit or foliage from a plant growing wild on any land, does not (although not in possession of the land) steal what he picks, unless he does it for reward or for sale or other commercial purpose.

For purposes of this subsection "mushroom" includes any fungus, and "plant" includes any shrub or tree.

(4) Wild creatures, tamed or untamed, shall be regarded as property; but a person cannot steal a wild creature not tamed nor ordinarily kept in captivity, or the carcass of any such creature, unless either it has been reduced into possession by or on behalf of another person and possession of it has not since been lost or abandoned, or another person is in course of reducing it into possession.

Things or choses in action

15–10 A chose in action is a right over property which can only be claimed or enforced by action, rather than by taking physical possession. A debt owed by a bank to a customer is a chose in action and can hence be appropriated. In *Kohn* 69 Cr.App.R. 395, CA, the defendant drew cheques on the account of a company of which he was a director for the benefit of various third parties. However, the cheques were intended for the benefit of the defendant, who was charged with theft of the chose in action (being the debt owed by the bank to the company) and theft of the cheque (being the property of the company). Where the account was in credit, or within the agreed overdraft limit (where the bank had an obligation to honour the cheques drawn) it was held that the defendant had appropriated a chose in action. Where the account was beyond the agreed overdraft limit (where the bank had no such obligation to honour the cheques drawn) it was held that there could be no appropriation as there was no chose in action.

Intangible property

Confidential information *per se* will not be classed as property for the purposes of s.4(1): *Oxford v. Moss* 68 Cr.App.R. 183, DC. In *Att.-Gen. for Hong Kong v. Nai-Keung* (1987) 1 W.L.R. 1339, PC, export quotas which were transferable for value on a temporary or permanent basis were held to be property within the meaning of a provision identically worded to s.4(1) of the 1968 Act. **15–11**

Belonging to another

Theft Act 1968, s.5

"Belonging to another"

5.—(1) Property shall be regarded as belonging to any person having possession or control of it, or having in it any proprietary right or interest (not being an equitable interest arising only from an agreement to transfer or grant an interest). **15–12**

(2) Where property is subject to a trust, the persons to whom it belongs shall be regarded as including any person having a right to enforce the trust, and an intention to defeat the trust shall be regarded accordingly as an intention to deprive of the property any person having that right.

(3) Where a person receives property from or on account of another, and is under an obligation to the other to retain and deal with that property or its proceeds in a particular way, the property or proceeds shall be regarded (as against him) as belonging to the other.

(4) Where a person gets property by another's mistake, and is under an obligation to make restoration (in whole or in part) of the property or its proceeds or of the value thereof, then to the extent of that obligation the property or proceeds shall be regarded (as against him) as belonging to the person entitled to restoration, and an intention not to make restoration shall be regarded accordingly as an intention to deprive that person of the property or proceeds.

(5) Property of a corporation sole shall be regarded as belonging to the corporation notwithstanding a vacancy in the corporation.

Property will belong to any person who has possession or control of it, or any proprietary right or interest in it, other than an equitable proprietary interest arising from an agreement to transfer or grant an interest. Train tickets purchased from travellers and then sold on will be deemed to remain the property of the train company who issued the tickets, as they retain a proprietary interest in the tickets after their purchase by a customer. Buying and then selling on such tickets will constitute theft: *Marshall* [1998] 2 Cr.App.R. 282, CA. **15–13**

A company partner, who has a proprietary interest in the shares of the company may steal such shares as the other partners also have a proprietary interest in the shares: *Bonner* (1970) 1 W.L.R. 838.

Things which have been abandoned are not capable of being stolen: *White* 7 Cr.App.R. 266, CCA.

As regards s.5(3) the "obligation" must be a legal one, as opposed to a social or moral one: *Gilks* 56 Cr.App.R. 734, CA; *Klineberg and Marsden* [1999] 1 Cr.App.R. 427, CA. The obligation must also be one of which the defendant was aware: *Wills* 92 Cr.App.R. 297, CA. As regards s.5(4) the obligation to make restoration of another's property acquired by mistake, must be a legal one: *Gilks* (*ante*).

In *R. (on the application of Ricketts) v Basildon Magistrates' Court* [2010] EWHC 2358 (Admin), the claimant had taken items from outside charity shops and from bins placed at the rear of a charity shop and admitted he had taken them to sell. At the committal hearing the magistrates' court rejected his submission that it could not properly be concluded on the evidence that the property belonged to either of the shops and that therefore an essential ingredient of the offence of theft had not been made out. The claimant contended that there was insufficient evidence for it to be open to the magistrates' court to conclude that the property "belonged to another" for the purposes of the *Theft Act* 1968 s.1(1) as the only inference open to it had been that would-be donors had abandoned their property.

Refusing his application, the court held that the magistrates' court had been entitled to infer that people deposited the items outside the shop intending to give to the charity. It was also permissible to infer that the shop would have either kept and resold those items or disposed of them; in either event, they still would have come within its possession and control and it would have had a proprietary right in them. It had not been open to the magistrates' court to infer that when appropriation occurred, the charity had a proprietary interest or taken possession or control of the items simply because they had been left close to the shop. However, it had been open to the court to infer that the items were not abandoned. The donor intended the items to be a gift and attempted to effect delivery. Delivery would be complete when the shop took possession. Until then, the donor would have relinquished possession but not ownership. It would therefore have been more appropriate to charge the claimant with stealing property belonging to persons unknown, but it was immaterial that he had been charged with appropriating items belonging to the charity. Regarding the items placed in bins at the rear of the charity shop, it would be open to a court to infer that donors had placed the items in the bin for the charity or that charity employees had placed them there for disposal. Either way, the charity was in possession of the items at the time of appropriation.

With the intention of permanently depriving the other of it

Theft Act 1968, s.6

"With the intention of permanently depriving the other of it"

15–14 **6.**—(1) A person appropriating property belonging to another without meaning the other permanently to lose the thing itself is nevertheless to be regarded as having the intention of permanently depriving the other of it if his intention is to treat the thing as his own to dispose of regardless of the other's rights; and a borrowing or lending of it may amount to so treating it if, but only if, the borrowing or lending is for a period and in circumstances making it equivalent to an outright taking or disposal.

(2) Without prejudice to the generality of subsection (1) above, where a person, having possession or control (lawfully or not) of property belonging to another, parts with the property under a condition as to its return which he may not be able to perform, this (if done for purposes of his own and without the other's authority) amounts to treating the property as his own to dispose of regardless of the other's rights.

15–15 In *Fernandes* [1996] 1 Cr.App.R. 175, CA, the Court held that s.6 should not be given a restrictive interpretation, and that the critical notion is whether the "defendant intended to treat the thing as his own to dispose of regardless of the other's rights". The second limb of subs (1) and (2) are to be construed as illustrations of this general principle.

A conditional appropriation will not suffice to establish the offence of theft: *Easom* [1971] 2 Q.B. 315, CA.

In *Raphael* [2008] EWCA Crim 1014, CA, both appellants had been convicted of conspiracy to rob and one appellant had been convicted of murder. They had posed as potential buyers of cars and arranged to meet the first victim to examine their car. The victim was struck over the head, pulled from the car and the car was stolen. The appellants later contacted the victim, and said he could buy his car back for a sum of money. During a second robbery, the victim was stabbed and died of his injuries. At trial the judge rejected the appellants' submission that there was no case to answer in relation to the first robbery. The appellants submitted that the judge was wrong in this ruling as, at most, the evidence showed that the extent of any agreement between them was that the victim's car would be returned to him in exchange for money. **15–16**

Dismissing their appeal, the Court of Appeal held that there was ample evidence for the jury to be invited to consider whether the appellants had agreed to rob the victim. Whilst the victim was offered the opportunity to buy back his car, that did not prevent the jury from finding an intention to permanently deprive him of it. The *Theft Act* 1968, s.6 specified that the *mens rea* for theft included an intention on the part of the taker "to treat the thing as his own to dispose of regardless of the other's rights". There was clearly such an intention in the instant case as an offer was made to the victim to sell the car back to him subject to a condition inconsistent with his right to possession of his own property.

In *Mitchell* [2008] EWCA Crim 850, CA, the defendant had been convicted of robbery. He and three others had crashed their vehicle after being pursued by police officers. They then approached the victim, who was sitting in her husband's car, smashed the car windows, pulled her out, and drove off with the car, which they subsequently abandoned. At trial, the prosecution relied on s.6(1) of the *Theft Act* 1968. There was evidence that after abandoning the first car, the defendant and others had taken a red car which they later abandoned, and then taken another car, which they later burnt. At the close of the prosecution case, defence counsel submitted that there was no case to answer as there was insufficient evidence to found an offence of robbery pursuant to s.6(1) of the 1968 Act. The judge rejected this submission, finding that the taking, using, and abandoning of the vehicle was evidence capable of amounting to an intention to dispose of property regardless of the owner's rights pursuant to s.6(1) of the 1968 Act. The defendant was convicted and appealed against conviction, submitting that the judge had erred in rejecting the submission of no case to answer as he had had no intention to treat the car as his own regardless of the owner's right, as evidenced by him only driving the car for a few miles before abandoning it.

Allowing the appeal, the Court of Appeal held that settled law demonstrated that the purpose of s.6 of the 1968 Act was not to greatly widen the requirement, pursuant to s.1, to permanently deprive the other of property. It provided a broader definition of that intention to deal with a small number of difficult cases, so that even if there was no intention permanently to deprive, nevertheless, something equivalent could be obtained through the intention to treat the thing as his own and to dispose of the owner's right. "Borrowing or lending" an article could only be deemed by s.6(1) to amount to an "intention of permanently depriving" the owner of the article if the intention of the borrower or lender was to return the property to the owner in such a changed state that it had lost all its practical value.

The facts of the instant case did not support a case of theft or of robbery as the victim's vehicle had been taken for use as a getaway car. The obvious inference to be drawn was that the defendant had needed another vehicle. The fact that the taking of the two other vehicles could not be prosecuted as a case of theft demonstrated that the taking of the victim's car could not be regarded as a case of theft of robbery. None of the authorities extended the scope of section 6 to a case, however violent, of taking a car for its brief use before abandoning it.

(4) Sentence

When tried summarily the maximum penalty for theft is imprisonment for a term **15–17**

Part III

not exceeding six months or a fine not exceeding the statutory maximum, or both (*TA* 1968, s.1(7)). After commencement of the relevant provisions, the maximum custodial sentence in a magistrates' court will be 12 months' imprisonment: *Criminal Justice Act* 2003, ss.154 and 282.

15–18 On January 5, 2009, the Sentencing Guidelines Council issued a final guideline on sentencing for theft and for burglary of a building other than a dwelling. The guideline applies to the sentencing of offenders convicted of theft or burglary in a building other than a dwelling who are sentenced on or after January 5, 2009. For the guideline in full, see *http://www.sentencing-guidelines.gov.uk/*.

The forms of theft and burglary covered by the guideline are:

- theft in breach of trust;
- theft in a dwelling;
- theft from the person;
- theft from a shop;
- burglary in a building other than a dwelling.

The Guideline states principles relevant to the assessment of seriousness that will be relevant to all five offences.

Assessing seriousness

The seriousness of the offence is to be determined by assessing the culpability of the offender and any harm which the offence caused, was intended to cause or might foreseeably have caused.

Culpability and harm

The culpability of the offender is the initial factor in determining offence seriousness. It is an essential element of the offences addressed in the guideline that the offender acted dishonestly. This requires that:

- the conduct was dishonest according to ordinary standards of reasonable and honest people; and
- the offender knew that the conduct was by those standards dishonest.

An offender convicted of these offences will have demonstrated a high level of culpability.

The precise level of culpability will vary according to factors such as the offender's motivation, whether the offence was planned or spontaneous and whether the offender was in a position of trust. An offence will be aggravated where there is evidence of planning.

The starting points and sentencing ranges in the guideline are based on the assumption that the offender was motivated by greed or a desire to live beyond his or her means. To avoid double counting, such a motivation should not be treated as a factor that increases culpability. Where an offence of theft is motivated by an intention to cause harm, or out of revenge, this will aggravate the offence.

When assessing the harm caused by theft and burglary in a building other than a dwelling offences, the starting point should be the loss suffered by the victim. In general, the greater the loss, the more serious the offence. However, the monetary value of the loss may not reflect the full extent of the harm caused by the offence. The court should also take into account the impact of the offence on the victim (which may be significantly greater than the monetary value of the loss; this may be particularly important where the value of the loss is high in proportion to the victim's financial circumstances even though relatively low in absolute terms), any harm to persons other than the direct victim, and any harm in the form of public concern or erosion of public confidence.

In some theft and burglary in a building other than a dwelling cases, the harm that results from an offence may be greater than the harm intended by the offender. In others, the offender may have intended more harm than actually results.

Aggravating and mitigating factors

The most common factors that are likely to aggravate an offence of theft or burglary in a building other than a dwelling are:

Factors indicating higher culpability

- planning of an offence;
- offenders operating in groups or gangs; and
- deliberate targeting of vulnerable victims.

Factors indicating a more than usually serious degree of harm

- victim is particularly vulnerable;
- high level of gain from the offence; and
- high value (including sentimental value) of property to the victim or substantial consequential loss.

The Council identified aggravating factors in addition to those from the general list that may be of particular relevance to the individual offences (see below). The Council did not identify any additional offence mitigating factors pertinent to the offences in this guideline.

Personal mitigation

The Council identified the following matters of personal mitigation that might apply to the offences contained in this guideline.

(a) Return of stolen property

Whether and the degree to which the return of stolen property constitutes a matter of personal mitigation will depend on an assessment of the circumstances and, in particular, the voluntariness and timeliness of the return.

(b) Impact on sentence of offender's dependency

Many offenders convicted of acquisitive crimes are motivated by an addiction, often to drugs, alcohol or gambling. This does not mitigate the seriousness of the offence, but an offender's dependency may properly influence the type of sentence imposed. In particular, it may sometimes be appropriate to impose:

- a drug rehabilitation requirement (which can be part of a community order within all the community sentencing bands from low to high seriousness); or
- an alcohol treatment requirement (for dependent drinkers); or
- an activity or supervision requirement including alcohol specific information, advice and support (for harmful and hazardous drinkers) as part of a community order or a suspended sentence order in an attempt to break the cycle of addiction and offending, even if an immediate custodial sentence would otherwise be warranted.

(c) Offender motivated by desperation or need

The fact that an offence has been committed in desperation or need arising from particular hardship may count as personal mitigation in exceptional circumstances.

Ancillary and other orders

Restitution order

Under s.148 of the *Powers of Criminal Courts (Sentencing) Act* 2000, a court may order that stolen goods be restored to the victim or that a sum not exceeding the value of the goods be paid to the victim from money taken out of the offender's possession at the time of apprehension. Further, on the application of the victim, the court may order that other goods representing the proceeds of disposal or realisation of the stolen goods be transferred to the victim. Where the stolen property cannot be traced or the offender is not in possession of sufficient money at the time of apprehension, a restitution order will not be available and a compensation order should be considered instead.

A restitution order should not normally impact on or influence the choice of sentence as the offender has no control over the making of the order.

Compensation order

Under s.130 of the *Powers of Criminal Courts (Sentencing) Act* 2000, the court must consider making a compensation order in any case where an offence has resulted in personal injury, loss or damage. Compensation can either be a sentence in its own right or an ancillary order.

Compensation should benefit, not inflict further harm on, the victim. A victim may or may not want compensation from the offender and assumptions should not be made either way. If the victim does not want compensation, this should be made known to the court and respected. In cases where it is difficult to ascertain the full amount of the loss suffered by the victim, consideration should be given to making a compensation order for an amount representing the agreed or likely loss. Where relevant information is not immediately available, it may be appropriate to grant an adjournment for it to be obtained. When imposed as an ancillary order, a compensation order normally should not impact on or influence the choice of sentence. However, in cases where the court considers that it is appropriate to impose both a fine and compensation order and the offender has insufficient means to pay both, priority must be given to the compensation order.

Where an offender has acted (as opposed to offered) to free assets in order to pay compensation, this is akin to making voluntary restitution and may be regarded as personal mitigation.

Confiscation order

Where there is evidence in a case before the Crown Court that the offender has benefited financially from his or her offending, the court must, in accordance with the *Proceeds of Crime Act* 2002, consider whether to make a confiscation order. A magistrates' court may commit the offender to the Crown Court for sentence with a view to such an order being made.

Deprivation order

Under s.143 of the *Powers of Criminal Courts (Sentencing) Act* 2000, a court may deprive an offender of property used or intended to be used to commit or facilitate the commission of an offence.

Where the property has an "innocent use" but can also be used to commit or facilitate the commission of an offence, a deprivation order must be taken into account when considering whether the overall penalty is commensurate with the seriousness of the offence. However, where the property can be used only for the purpose of crime, a deprivation order should not be taken into account when determining the appropriate sentence.

Offence Guidelines

Theft in breach of trust

Factors to take into consideration

15–19 The following starting points and sentencing ranges are for a first time offender aged 18 or over who pleaded not guilty.

In relation to harm, in general, the greater the loss, the more serious the offence. However, this is subject to the considerations set out in the rest of this paragraph. The guideline is based on the monetary value of the amount involved but the monetary value may not reflect the full extent of the harm caused by the offence. The court should also take into account the impact of the offence on the victim (which may be significantly greater than the monetary value of the loss; this may be particularly important where the value of the loss is high in proportion to the victim's financial circumstances even though relatively low in absolute terms), any harm to persons other than the direct victim, and any harm in the form of public concern or erosion of public confidence.

In general terms, the seriousness of the offence will increase in line with the level of trust breached. The extent to which the nature and degree of trust placed in an offender should be regarded as increasing seriousness will depend on a careful assessment of the circumstances of each individual case, including the type and terms of the relationship between the offender and victim.

The concept of breach of trust for the purposes of the offence of theft is wide. It includes not only employer/employee relationships and those between a professional adviser and client, but also extends more generally to relationships in which the offender was in a position of authority in relation to the victim, or one whereby they would be expected to have a duty to protect the interests of the victim, such as medical, social or care workers.

Thefts by offenders in whom a high degree of trust has been placed should generally attract higher sentences than thefts of similar amounts by offenders in whom a lower degree of trust is vested. The targeting of a vulnerable victim by an offender through a relationship or position of trust will indicate a higher level of culpability.

When assessing the seriousness of an offence, a court must always have regard to the full list of aggravating and mitigating factors in the Sentencing Guidelines Council guideline Overarching Principles: Seriousness. Additional aggravating factors likely to be particularly relevant to this type of theft are:

(i) Long course of offending

Offending carried out over a period of months or years represents a sustained and deliberate course of conduct and should be regarded as increasing an offender's culpability. Offending over an extended period may also result in greater harm to the victim in terms of financial loss and/or distress.

(ii) Suspicion deliberately thrown on others

Where an offender has taken positive steps to incriminate another, either at the time of committing the offence or subsequently, this should be regarded as an aggravating factor.

Additional matters of personal mitigation may be:

(i) Inappropriate degree of trust or responsibility

The fact that an offender succumbed to temptation having been placed in a position of trust or given responsibility to an inappropriate degree may be regarded as personal mitigation.

(ii) Cessation of offending

The fact that an offender voluntarily ceased offending before being discovered does not reduce the seriousness of the offence. However, if the claim to have stopped offending is genuine, it may constitute personal mitigation, particularly if it is evidence of remorse.

(iii) Reporting an undiscovered offence

Where an offender brings the offending to the attention of his or her employer or the authorities, this may be treated as personal mitigation. In many cases of theft in breach of trust, termination of an offender's employment will be a natural consequence of committing the offence. Other than in the most exceptional of circumstances, loss of employment and any consequential hardship should not constitute personal mitigation.

Where a court is satisfied that a custodial sentence of 12 months or less is appropriate for an offence of theft in breach of trust, consideration should be given to whether that sentence can be suspended in accordance with the criteria in the Sentencing Guidelines Council guideline *New Sentences: Criminal Justice Act 2003*. A suspended sentence order may be particularly appropriate where this would allow for reparation to be made either to the victim or to the community at large.

Theft in breach of trust

THEFT ACT 1968 (SECTION 1)

MAXIMUM PENALTY: 7 YEARS IMPRISONMENT

Examples of nature of activity	Starting Point	Range
Theft of £125,000 or more or Theft of £20,000 or more in breach of a high degree of trust	3 years custody	2-6 years custody
Theft of £20,000 or more but less than £125,000 or Theft of £2,000 or more but less than £20,000 in breach of a high degree of trust	2 years custody	12 months-3 years custody
Theft of £2,000 or more but less than £20,000 or Theft of less than £2,000 in breach of a high degree of trust	18 weeks custody	Community order (HIGH)-12 months custody
Theft of less than £2,000	Community order (MEDIUM)	Fine-26 weeks custody

ADDITIONAL AGGRAVATING FACTORS

1. Long course of offending 2. Suspicion deliberately thrown on others 3. Offender motivated by intention to cause harm or out of revenge

Theft in a dwelling

Factors to take into consideration

The following starting points and sentencing ranges are for a first time offender aged 18 or over who pleaded not guilty.

The category of theft in a dwelling covers the situation where a theft is committed by an offender who is present in a dwelling with the authority of the owner or occupier.

Examples include thefts by lodgers or visitors to the victim's residence, such as friends, relatives or sales people. Such offences involve a violation of the privacy of the victim's home and constitute an abuse of the victim's trust. Where an offender enters a dwelling as a trespasser in order to commit theft, his or her conduct will generally constitute the more serious offence of burglary; this guideline does not apply where the offender has been convicted of burglary.

A "vulnerable victim" is a person targeted by the offender because it is anticipated that he or she is unlikely or unable to resist the theft. The exploitation of a vulnerable victim indicates a high level of culpability and will influence the category of seriousness into which the offence falls.

The guideline is based on the assumption that most thefts in a dwelling do not involve property of high monetary value or of high value to the victim. Where the property stolen is of high monetary value or of high value (including sentimental value) to the victim, the appropriate sentence may be beyond the range into which the offence otherwise would fall. For the purpose of this form of theft, property worth more than £2,000 should generally be regarded as being of "high monetary value", although this will depend on an assessment of all the circumstances of the particular case.

A sentence beyond the range into which the offence otherwise would fall may also be appropriate where the effect on the victim is particularly severe or where substantial consequential loss results (such as where the theft of equipment causes serious disruption to the victim's life or business).

When assessing the seriousness of an offence, a court must always have regard to the full list of aggravating and mitigating factors in the Sentencing Guidelines Council guideline *Overarching Principles: Seriousness*. Identified below are additional aggravating factors likely to be particularly relevant to this type of theft:

(i) Confrontation with the victim

Where there is intimidation and/or a face-to-face confrontation between the offender and victim, this should be regarded as an aggravating factor. Where the victim is a "vulnerable victim", the use of intimidation will influence the category of seriousness into which the offence falls.

(ii) Use of force, or threat of force

Generally, where theft in a dwelling is accompanied by force or the threat of force, it will constitute the more serious offence of robbery. However, there may be some cases involving force which are charged as theft in a dwelling, perhaps where the force was used after the theft had taken place. In such cases, an offender can be sentenced only for the offence of which he or she is convicted and the court is bound by the maximum penalty for that offence. At the same time, the court must have regard to all the circumstances of the case when determining the appropriate sentence. Where the victim as a "vulnerable victim" the use or threat of force will influence the category of seriousness into which the offence falls. In other cases, it may be an aggravating factor.

(iii) Use of deception

Where an offender has deceived or tricked the victim in order to gain entry, for example by falsely claiming to be a meter reader, this should be regarded as an aggravating factor. Where the victim is a "vulnerable victim", the use of deception will influence the category of seriousness into which the offence falls.

(iv) Taking steps to prevent the victim reporting the crime or seeking help Where an offender takes steps to prevent the victim from reporting the offence or seeking help, such as by damaging a telephone, this should be regarded as increasing offence seriousness.

Where the effect on the victim is particularly severe, the stolen property is of high value, or substantial consequential loss results, a sentence higher than the range into which the offence otherwise would fall may be appropriate.

Theft in a dwelling

THEFT ACT 1968 (SECTION 1)
MAXIMUM PENALTY: 7 YEARS IMPRISONMENT

Examples of nature of activity	Starting Point	Range
Theft from a vulnerable victim involving intimidation or the use or threat of force (falling short of robbery) or the use of deception	18 months custody	12 months-3 years custody
Theft from a vulnerable victim	18 months custody	Community order (HIGH)-12 months custody
Theft in a dwelling not involving vulnerable victim	Community order (MEDIUM)	Fine-18 weeks custody

ADDITIONAL AGGRAVATING FACTORS

1. Offender motivated by intention to cause harm or out of revenge
2. Intimidation or face-to-face confrontation with victim [except where this raises the offence into a higher sentencing range]
3. Use of force, or threat of force, against victim (not amounting to robbery) [except where this raises the offence into a higher sentencing range]
4. Use of deception [except where this raises the offence into a higher sentencing range]
5. Offender takes steps to prevent the victim from reporting the crime or seeking help

Theft from the person

Factors to take into consideration

The following starting points and sentencing ranges are for a first time offender aged 18 or over who pleaded not guilty. While in some cases the conduct may be similar, this guideline does not apply where the offender has been convicted of robbery; sentencers should instead refer to the Sentencing Guidelines Council guideline on robbery.

Theft from the person may encompass conduct such as "pick-pocketing", where the victim is unaware that the property is being stolen, as well as the snatching of handbags, wallets, jewellery and mobile telephones from the victim's possession or from the vicinity of the victim. Where there is evidence of planning, that will be an aggravating factor. This may, for example, be demonstrated where tourists are targeted because of their unfamiliarity with an area or because of a perception that they will not be available to give evidence if a case proceeds to trial. The offence constitutes an invasion of the victim's privacy and may cause the victim to experience distress, fear and inconvenience either during or after the event.

For the purpose of this guideline, a "vulnerable victim" is a person targeted by the offender because it is anticipated that he or she is unlikely or unable to resist the theft. Young or elderly persons or those with disabilities may fall into this category. The exploitation of a vulnerable victim indicates a high level of culpability and will influence the category of seriousness into which the offence falls.

The guideline is based on the assumption that most thefts from the person do not involve property of high monetary value or of high value to the victim. Where the property stolen is of high monetary value or of high value (including sentimental value) to the victim, the appropriate sentence may be beyond the range into which the offence otherwise would fall. For the purpose of this form of theft, "high monetary value" is defined as more than £2,000.

A sentence beyond the range into which the offence otherwise would fall may also be appropriate where the effect on the victim is particularly severe or where substantial consequential loss results (such as where the theft of equipment causes serious disruption to the victim's life or business).

When assessing the seriousness of an offence, a court must always have regard to the full list of aggravating and mitigating factors in the Sentencing Guidelines Council guideline *Overarching Principles: Seriousness*. Additional aggravating factors likely to be particularly relevant to this type of theft are:

(i) Confrontation with the victim

Where there is intimidation and/or a face-to-face confrontation between the offender and victim, this should be regarded as an aggravating factor. Where the victim is a "vulnerable victim", the use of intimidation will influence the category of seriousness into which the offence falls.

(ii) Use of force, or threat of force

Where the offender uses or threatens to use force to commit the theft, the conduct may constitute the more serious offence of robbery. However, there may be some cases involving force which are charged as theft from the person. In such cases, an offender can be sentenced only for the offence of which he or she is convicted and the court is bound by the maximum penalty for that offence. At the same time, the court must have regard to all the circumstances of the case when determining the appropriate sentence. Where the victim is a "vulnerable victim", the use or threat of force will influence the category of seriousness into which the offence falls. In other cases, it may be an aggravating factor.

(iii) High level of inconvenience caused to victim

The theft of some items, such as house keys and credit cards, may cause a particularly high level of distress and inconvenience to victims and this should be regarded as an aggravating factor. Tourists are vulnerable as a target for thefts from the person (not least because it may be perceived that they will not be available to give evidence) and may experience greater distress and inconvenience than others in arranging the replacement of documents, cash and cards. Such factors should be taken into account as increasing the seriousness of the offence.

Previous authorities have expressed concern about the prevalence of theft against the person and the associated need for deterrence, particularly in relation to pick-pocketing. The Sentencing Guidelines Council guideline *Overarching Principles: Seriousness* sets out the approach which should be adopted when considering issues of local prevalence.

Further, national prevalence should not be used by sentencers to justify including a deterrent element in sentences as this is already taken into account in Council guidelines.

Theft from the person

THEFT ACT 1968 (SECTION 1)

MAXIMUM PENALTY: 7 YEARS IMPRISONMENT

Where the effect on the victim is particularly severe, the stolen property is of high value or substantial consequential loss results, a sentence higher than the range into which the offence otherwise would fall may be appropriate.

Examples of nature of activity	Starting Point	Range
Theft from a vulnerable victim involving intimidation or the use or threat of force (falling short of robbery)	18 months custody	12 months-3 years custody
Theft from a vulnerable victim	18 weeks custody	Community order (HIGH)-12 months custody
Theft from the person not involving vulnerable victim	Community order (MEDIUM)	Fine-18 weeks custody

ADDITIONAL AGGRAVATING FACTORS

1. Offender motivated by intention to cause harm or out of revenge
2. Intimidation or face-to-face confrontation with victim [except where this raises the offence into a higher sentencing range]
3. Use of force, or threat of force, against victim (not amounting to robbery) [except where this raises the offence into a higher sentencing range]
4. High level of inconvenience caused to victim, e.g. replacing house keys, credit cards etc.

Theft from a shop

Factors to take into consideration

The following starting points and sentencing ranges are for a first time offender aged 18 or over who pleaded not guilty.

The circumstances of this offence can vary significantly. At the least serious end of the scale are thefts involving low value goods, no (or little) planning and no violence or damage; a non-custodial sentence will usually be appropriate for a first time offender. At the higher end of the spectrum are thefts involving organised gangs or groups or the threat or use of force and a custodial starting point will usually be appropriate.

When assessing the level of harm, the circumstances of the retailer are a proper consideration; a greater level of harm may be caused where the theft is against a small retailer.

Retailers may suffer additional loss as a result of this type of offending such as the cost of preventative security measures, higher insurance premiums and time spent by staff dealing with the prosecution of offenders. However, the seriousness of an individual case must be judged on its own dimension of harm and culpability and the sentence on an individual offender should not be increased to reflect the harm caused to retailers in general by the totality of this type of offending.

In accordance with s.143(2) of the *Criminal Justice Act* 2003, any recent previous convictions for theft and dishonesty offences will need to be taken into account in sentencing. Where an offender demonstrates a level of "persistent" or "seriously persistent" offending, the community and custody thresholds may be crossed even though the other characteristics of the offence would otherwise warrant a lesser sentence.

When assessing the seriousness of an offence, a court must always have regard to the full list of aggravating and mitigating factors in the sentencing Guidelines Council guideline *Overarching Principles: Seriousness*.

The guideline on Seriousness identifies high value as an aggravating factor in property offences. In cases of theft from a shop, theft of high value goods may be associated with other aggravating factors such as the degree of planning, professionalism and/or operating in a group, and care will need to be taken to avoid double counting. Deliberately targeting high value goods will always make an offence more serious.

Additional aggravating factors particularly relevant to this type of theft include:

(i) Involving a child

Where a child accompanies an offender during the offence, it will be an aggravating factor if the child is involved in, or is likely to be aware of, the theft or could be influenced or distressed by it. However, the mere presence of a child does not make the offence more serious.

(ii) Offender subject to a banning order

The fact that an offender is subject to a banning order that includes the store in which the offence is committed is an aggravating factor. Breach of any type of order (for example a civil banning order or a shop imposed ban) will aggravate to the same degree. However, where an offender is being sentenced also for breach, care must be taken to ensure that there is no double counting.

(iii) Intimidation, threat or use of force and additional damage to property.

Generally, where theft from a shop is accompanied by force or the threat of force, it will be appropriate to charge the offender with the more serious offence of robbery. However, there may be some cases involving force which are charged as theft from a shop. In such cases, an offender can be sentenced only for the offence of which he or she is convicted and the court is bound by the maximum penalty for that offence. At the same time, the court must have regard to all the circumstances of the case when determining the appropriate sentence. This may result in sentencers concluding that the offending was aggravated by the use or threat of force and that a more severe sentence is warranted. Any additional damage to property (for example caused when an offender is tackled or detained) also aggravates the seriousness of the offence.

Theft from a shop

THEFT ACT 1968 (SECTION 1)

MAXIMUM PENALTY: 7 YEARS IMPRISONMENT

Examples of nature of activity	**Starting Point**	**Range**
Organised gang/group and Intimidation or the use or threat of force (short of robbery)	12 months custody	36 weeks-4 years custody
Significant intimidation or threats or Use of force resulting in slight injury or Very high level of planning or Significant related damage	6 weeks custody	Community order (HIGH)-36 weeks custody
Low level intimidation or threats or Some planning e.g. a session of stealing on the same day or going equipped or Some related damage	Community order (LOW)	Fine-Community order (MEDIUM)

Examples of nature of activity	Starting Point	Range
Little or no planning or sophistication and Goods stolen of low value	Fine	Conditional discharge-Community order (LOW)

ADDITIONAL AGGRAVATING FACTORS

1. Child accompanying offender is involved in or aware of theft
2. Offender is subject to a banning order that includes the store targeted
3. Offender motivated by intention to cause harm or out of revenge
4. Professional offending
5. Victim particularly vulnerable (e.g. small independent shop)
6. Offender targeted high value goods

In *Kinloch* [2009] EWCA Crim 1356, CA, the appellant pleaded guilty to theft, and was sentenced to 16 months' imprisonment. He had worked for his employer, which ran public houses, for several years, and confessed to having stolen more than £20,000 from the company in the space of a fortnight. He told the police that he had gone away for a few days and on his return £2,400 was missing. The appellant had previously been in trouble for taking money from the company, and he was thus worried about his position. He decided to use the money still in the public house to gamble, aiming to recoup the missing £2,400. Using online facilities he gambled, and lost, all this money. Substituting a sentence of 9 months' imprisonment, the Court of Appeal referred to the Sentencing Guidelines Council's guideline on theft in breach of trust and stated that the appellant would not fall into the category of theft involving breach of a high degree of trust. The case fell within the category of theft of £2,000 to £20,000.

In *Graham* [2009] EWCA Crim 611, CA, the appellant had pleaded guilty to three offences of theft and been sentenced to 8 months' imprisonment on each concurrent with two offences of theft taken into consideration. As part of his job, the appellant had access to sites where there were large quantities of old rail. The appellant had offered this old rail to someone from a haulage company on the understanding that the proceeds from sale of the old rail could be split. The value of the stolen metal amounted to somewhere in the region of £18,300. Substituting a sentence of 6 months' imprisonment for each offence, to run concurrently, the Court had regard to the aggravating features of the case (namely the abuse of a position of trust, the fact that the offences were the appellant's idea, the fact that the thefts were organised by him and that he profited significantly from them). However, the appellant was entitled to full discount for his pleas of guilty and his acceptance of guilt at an early stage, and there was substantial mitigation in the context of previous good character of a very positive kind.

In *De Weever* [2009] EWCA Crim 803, CA, the appellant had pleaded guilty to an offence of theft, and sentenced to 18 months' imprisonment (less 132 days spent in custody on remand). The appellant had stolen the victim's purse from her bag after pushing her as she boarded a train. Substituting a sentence of 10 months' imprisonment, the Court had regard to the Sentencing Guidelines Council's guideline on sentencing offences of theft from the person and held that the sentencing judge's decision to consider the victim to be a vulnerable person was wrong. The victim had been targeted because she was carrying a bag which permitted the appellant to steal without her realising, not because she was of an age, or suffering from a disability, that made

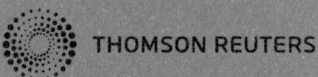

her vulnerable. The appropriate starting point would therefore be a medium level community order with a range from a fine to 18 weeks in custody. The Court identified aggravating features of the offence (the offence planning and highly professional manner in which the offence was carried out; the use of force, inconvenience to the victim and the appellant's previous convictions for similar offences). These aggravating factors took the sentence out of the lower bracket in the sentencing guideline and into the bracket above it, which gave a starting point of 12 months' imprisonment. The only mitigation was the appellant's last minute guilty plea, which made a total sentence of 10 months' imprisonment (less the 132 days spent on remand) appropriate.

B. BURGLARY

(1) Definition

Theft Act 1968, s.9

Burglary

9.—(1) A person is guilty of burglary if— **15–20**

(a) he enters any building or part of a building as a trespasser and with intent to commit any such offence as is mentioned in subsection (2) below; or

(b) having entered any building or part of a building as a trespasser he steals or attempts to steal anything in the building or that part of it or inflicts or attempts to inflict on any person therein any grievous bodily harm.

(2) The offences referred to in subsection (1)(a) above are offences of stealing anything in the building or part of a building in question, of inflicting on any person therein any grievous bodily harm therein, and of doing unlawful damage to the building or anything therein.

(3) A person guilty of burglary shall on conviction on indictment be liable to imprisonment for a term not exceeding—

(a) where the offence was committed in respect of a building or part of a building which is a dwelling, fourteen years;

(b) in any other case, ten years.

(4) References in subsections (1) and (2) above to a building, and the reference in subsection (3) above to a building which is a dwelling, shall apply also to an inhabited vehicle or vessel, and shall apply to any such vehicle or vessel at times when the person having a habitation in it is not there as well as at times when he is.

[This section is printed as amended by the *Sexual Offences Act* 2003, Sched. 7.]

(2) Allocation

Burglary is triable either way: *MCA* 1980, s.17 and Sched.1, para. 28. Burglary will be triable on indictment only if (i) the burglary comprises the commission of, or an intention to commit an offence which is triable only on indictment: *MCA* 1980, Sched. 1, para. 28(b) or (ii) if the burglary is in a dwelling house and any person in the dwelling was subjected to violence or the threat of violence, the offence is triable only on indictment: *MCA* 1980, Sched. 1, para. 28(c). **15–21**

The *Consolidated Criminal Practice Direction* Pt V.51.65 and 6 [2002] 1 W.L.R. 2870 *(Mode of Trial)* gives separate guidelines for burglary of a dwelling house and burglary of a non-dwelling. See Appendix F–49 and F–50.

The *Powers of Criminal Courts (Sentencing) Act* 2000 provides that the court must impose a minimum custodial sentence of three years where an offender aged 18 or over is convicted of a third "domestic burglary" where all of the three domestic burglaries were committed on or after November 30, 1999 and where the circumstances of the offence or the offender do not state that it would be unjust in all the circumstances to impose such a penalty: *PCC(S)A* 2000, s.111. Section 111(4) provides that where a person is charged with a domestic burglary which would be triable either way, and the circumstances are such that, if he were convicted of the burglary, he could be sentenced **15–22**

Part III

for it under subs (2) *ante*, the burglary shall be triable only on indictment. The Court will rely on the prosecution to provide appropriate information relating to the defendant's previous convictions to identify whether the charge is indictable only or not, and this must be clarified before mode of trial is considered.

(3) Elements of the offence

15–23 The prosecution must prove that:

— the defendant entered a building or part of a building;

— with the intention to steal anything in the building or part of the building in question OR with the intention to inflict on any person in the building grievous bodily harm OR of doing unlawful damage to the building or anything therein;

OR

— the defendant had entered a building as a trespasser; and

he then stole or attempted to steal anything in the building;

OR

he inflicted or attempted to inflict upon any person therein grievous bodily harm.

The building

15–24 The word "building" is to be treated as an ordinary word of the English language and its meaning is a question of fact not law: *Brutus v. Cozens* [1973] A.C. 854, HL.

Entry as a trespasser

15–25 The definition of trespass is that used in the law of tort; *i.e.* any intentional, reckless or negligent entry into a building which is in the possession of another person who does not consent to the entry. The defendant must intend, or be reckless as to the facts which make the entry a trespass: *Collins* [1973] Q.B. 100, CA.

The entry

15–26 In *Collins* (*ante*) Lord Edmund-Davies said the entry in question had to be "effective and substantial." In *Brown (V.)* [1985] Crim.L.R. 212, CA, the Court held that a man who had both feet on the ground outside a shop "entered" it when he leant through a broken window with the upper half of his body.

(4) Sentence

15–27 The maximum sentence varies depending on whether the burglary is of a dwelling or non-dwelling.

(a) *Burglary of a dwelling*

15–28 The maximum penalty for burglary of a building or part of a building which is a dwelling is 14 years' imprisonment on indictment, six months or a fine not exceeding the statutory maximum or both summarily (*TA* 1968, s.9(4)). After commencement of the relevant provisions, the maximum custodial sentence in a magistrates' court will be 12 months' imprisonment: *Criminal Justice Act* 2003, ss.154 and 282.

The *Magistrates Courts Sentencing Guidelines* (2008) follow the guidance issued by the Court of Appeal in *McInerney and Keating* [2002] EWCA Crim 3003.

Key Factors

15–29 (a) Even where the custody threshold is passed, consider whether a community order is appropriate (*McInerney and Keating*).

(b) Cases in the Crown Court category may be suitable for a community order (see note (a) above), but should nevertheless be committed to the Crown Court for trial/sentence so that any breach of order can be sentenced within the powers of that Court.

(c) For attempted burglary or burglary under s.9(1)(a) of the *Theft Act* 1968, it is the offender's intention that will determine which of the three categories opposite the offence falls into, not the fact that nothing was stolen.

Relevant convictions that will aggravate offence seriousness in accordance with s.143(2) of the *Criminal Justice Act* 2003 may include convictions for both property and violent offences.

STARTING POINT AND SENTENCING RANGES

(BASED ON A FIRST TIME OFFENDER AFTER TRIAL)

Examples of nature of activity	**Starting Point**	**Range**
Unforced entry and low value theft with no aggravating features	Medium level community order	Low level community order to 12 weeks custody
Forced entry, goods stolen not high value, no aggravating features	12 weeks custody	High level community order to Crown Court
Goods stolen high value or any aggravating feature present	Crown Court	Crown Court

AGGRAVATING AND MITIGATING FACTORS

Factors indicating higher culpability	**Factors indicating lower culpability**
1. Ransacking property 2. Professionalism 3. Victim deliberately targeted e.g. out of spite 4. Housebreaking implements or weapons carried	1. Offender played only a minor role in the burglary 2. Offence committed on impulse
Factors indicating greater degree of harm 1. Occupier at home or returns home while offender present 2. Goods stolen of sentimental value	**Factor indicating lesser degree of harm** 1. No damage or disturbance to property

Part III

On January 16, 2009, the Court of Appeal gave further guidance on sentencing of offences of domestic burglary in the case of *Saw and others* [2009] EWCA Crim 1, CA. The Sentencing Guidelines Council then issued a note describing the key elements in that judgment in the light of the guideline in the *Magistrates' Court Sentencing Guidelines* (2008), which are based on the guideline cases of *McInerney* [2002] EWCA Crim 3003, CA.

The note provides the following key points regarding approach to sentencing. For the note in full, see *http://www.sentencing-guidelines.gov.uk*.

1. The aim of the judgment is to achieve consistency of approach, clearly recognising the seriousness of this offence - not only is it an offence against property but it is also an offence against the person. Particular focus is required on the impact of the offence on those living in the burgled house; sentences should reflect the level of harmful consequences even when not intended by the offender.
2. The sentence must reflect the criminality of the offender. Previous convictions and the record of an offender are of more significance than in the case of some other crimes. Burglary of a dwelling should be treated as more serious when committed by an offender with previous convictions for relevant dishonesty than an identical offence committed by a first offender.
3. The judgment states that it does not add anything to the *Magistrates' Court Sentencing Guidelines*, emphasising the importance of addressing the aggravating and mitigating factors referred to in the judgment. The *Magistrates' Court Sentencing Guidelines* currently provide for committal to the Crown Court where an aggravating feature is present and sentence within the powers of the Crown Court is included within the range in some other circumstances.
4. A non-exhaustive list of aggravating and mitigating features commonly encountered in burglary is provided in the judgment; this is more extensive than the list in the *Magistrates' Court Sentencing Guidelines* derived from *McInerney* (see below) The importance of the aggravating features derives from the increase in the impact of the offence that results from them, or from the increase in the culpability of the offender that they demonstrate, or from a combination of the two.

Aggravating and Mitigating Features (not exhaustive)

Aggravating features:

- the use or threat of force on or against the victim (NB: this would make the offence triable on indictment only),
- trauma to the victim beyond that normally associated with this type of offence,
- pre-meditation and professional planning or organisation, such as by offenders working in groups or when housebreaking implements are carried,
- vandalism of the premises burgled,
- deliberate targeting of any vulnerable victim,
- deliberate targeting of any victim,
- the presence of the occupier whether at night or during the day,
- high economic or sentimental value of the property stolen or damaged,
- offence committed on bail or shortly after imposition of a non-custodial sentence,
- two or more burglaries of homes rather than a single offence,
- the offender's previous convictions.

Mitigating features:

- nothing, or only property of very low value is taken,
- offender played a minor part in the burglary, and treated by others in group as if he were on the fringes,
- exploited by others,
- offence committed on impulse,

- age and state of health (mental and physical),
- good character,
- evidence of genuine regret and remorse,
- ready co-operation with the police,
- positive response to previous sentences.

The note sets out the following categories of seriousness, based on the Magistrates' Court Sentencing Guidelines (2008):

Category 1 - Offences likely to be able to be sentenced within the jurisdiction of a magistrates' court (when committed by a first time offender) are those where the entry to the premises was unforced, the property stolen of low value and there were no aggravating features; the starting point is a community sentence. In determining whether an aggravating feature was present, the court should refer to the list set out in *Saw and others*.

Category 2 - Where the entry was forced, the goods were not of high value, and there were no aggravating features, the sentencing range commences within the jurisdiction of a magistrates' court but ends within the jurisdiction of the Crown Court; the starting point is 12 weeks custody. In determining whether an aggravating feature was present, the court should refer to the list set out in *Saw and others*.

Although *Saw and others* requires particular focus on the impact of the offence on the victim, it confirms that a low level burglary with minimal loss and minimal damage and without raised culpability or raised impact, committed by a first time offender, may be dealt with by way of a community order rather than an immediate custodial penalty.

Category 3 – An offence would be expected to be committed to the Crown Court where the goods stolen were of high value or any aggravating feature was present. *Saw and others* provides that the court must address the overall criminality of the offender (in the light of previous convictions) and the impact of the offence on the victim(s):

- where there is limited raised culpability and/or impact, it is likely that the sentence will be within a general range of 9 to18 months custody; a shorter sentence (including the making of a community order) may be appropriate where it is established that the offender played a subsidiary role or was exploited by other offenders;
- where there is seriously raised culpability and/or serious impact, the starting point should be a custodial sentence in excess of 18 months; a community order should be considered only in the most extreme and exceptional circumstances.

Where a case otherwise appropriate for sentence in the Crown Court is, on its own particular facts likely to attract a community order, it should nonetheless be sentenced in the Crown Court so that any sanction for non-compliance can be imposed with the powers of that court rather than within the more limited powers of a magistrates' court.

The note also provides that magistrates should consult their legal adviser for guidance.

In *Saw and others* [2009] EWCA Crim 1, CA, five of the appellants applied for permission to appeal against their sentences, and the sixth appellant appealed against his sentence for burglary of occupied domestic premises. The sixth appellant was a heroin user and had been in a residential area at night. He stole from a garage and attempted to get into two different houses. At least one householder had confronted him. He then rang the bell of another house that was occupied by a very elderly man, who used a wheelchair and was dependent on the help of his neighbours. He was in bed and opened the door by remote control. The appellant entered and went through his belongings for several minutes, despite the occupant shouting at him to get out. The appellant left empty-handed, and was later arrested. He asked for the three earlier offences to be taken into account and intended to plead guilty, but absconded before the hearing. He was re-arrested and pleaded guilty. He had previous convictions for cheating and stealing from elderly householders, and had received custodial sentences. He

Part III

had also been convicted of a further theft from a house about a month before the offences in question, but had received a conditional discharge. Due to his postponing his guilty plea, he did not receive a full discount for it and received a sentence of five years' imprisonment.

The Court of Appeal refused the applications of the first five appellants and held that the burglary committed by the sixth appellant was most serious and had considerable impact on the victim. It was an aggravating feature that the appellant had been undeterred by his previous confrontation with at least one local resident that evening. There was no evidence that he deliberately targeted the victim's home due to his vulnerability, but once inside he had taken advantage of the victim's immobility and continued his attempts to steal in his full view. It took place in the middle of the night. If the appellant's later claim that his conduct was due to the adverse affect of a mixture of drugs was true, that only made the matter worse for the victim. All that could be said in the appellant's favour was that he did not touch or threaten the victim. However, the experience had reinforced the victim's sense of how vulnerable they were and would remain an alarming shadow over their life. Shorter sentences of imprisonment had failed to deter the appellant from preying on householders, especially the elderly. He had a significant history of relevant, persistent and recent offending against vulnerable victims. The judge's sentence was therefore severe but not manifestly excessive.

The Lord Chief Justice commented that "*R v McInerney*: *R v Keating* used the expression 'starting point' in a sense different from that which has since become conventional. It is nowadays used to identify a notional point within a broad range, from which the sentence should be increased or decreased to allow for aggravating or mitigating features, rather than the lowest point in the range. It was for this reason that the decision may have been understood to suggest that the normal sentence even for a repeat offender should be non-custodial. Furthermore, the concept of the 'first time burglar' was itself problematic, not least because what was described as the 'standard' burglary assumed that the defendant had already been convicted of burglary on previous occasions. The division of the aggravating features into higher and medium level was also insufficiently flexible in practice, and the omission of potentially aggravating but unspecified features from what appeared to be a comprehensive list meant that, on occasions, the defendant's true criminality was not fully addressed" (at paragraph 4).

The Court stated that the guidance in *McInerney* had proved difficult to apply, and offered fresh guidance pending definitive guidance on the subject of domestic burglary that might be issued by the Sentencing Guidelines Council. The starting point was always that burglary of a home was a serious criminal offence, following *Brewster* [1998] 1 Cr.App.R. 220, CA. The sense of disturbance and distress suffered by the homeowner was not quantifiable in bare economic terms. Therefore in the sentencing decision particular focus is required on the impact of the offence on those living in the burgled house. Whether or not the dwelling house burglar has any specific intention to cause harm, he runs the risk that the victim or victims may suffer serious adverse consequences. Where this happens, sentences should be reflective even of unintended consequences.

The court provided a non-exhaustive list of aggravating features commonly encountered in burglary cases. It was artificial and unhelpful to make a distinction between high-level and medium-level aggravating features, as *McInerney*, above, had done. The question to be answered was where a particular aggravating feature should be placed on the scale. The culpability of an offender was not diminished merely because it was the common characteristic of many burglaries that the offender had previous convictions. On the contrary, an offender's record was of more significance in the case of domestic burglary than in some other crimes, following *Brewster*, above. Therefore, consistently with s.143(2) of the *Criminal Justice Act* 2003, even what had previously been described as a "standard" burglary was, and should be treated as, more serious when committed by a defendant with previous convictions for relevant dishonesty than an identical offence committed by a first time offender.

All the aggravating features required the court to address two specific features that might be present in every dwelling house burglary: first, the overall criminality of the offender, in the light of his previous convictions, and second, the true impact of the offence on the victims.

In *McInerney* [2003] Crim.L.R. 209, CA the court stated that cases in which a court would previously have been looking to starting points of up to 18 months' imprisonment may now be dealt with by the imposition of a community sentence. If and only if the court is satisfied that the offender has demonstrated by his or her behaviour that punishment in the community was not practicable should the court resort to a custodial sentence. Where a custodial sentence is necessary, it should be no longer than necessary. Aggravating and mitigating features would alter the appropriate starting point. High level aggravating features included the use or threat of force, injury or especially traumatic effect on the victim, professional planning, vandalism, racially aggravated offences or the deliberate targeting of a vulnerable victim. Medium level aggravating features included the theft of high value goods, burglars working as a group and the victim being at home during the commission of the offence. Mitigating features included the crime being a first offence, nothing or low value property being stolen, the fact that an offender played only a minor part in the offence, the impulsive nature of the crime, the fact that no property was damaged and the entering of an early guilty plea.

Whilst the decision in *Saw* [2009] EWCA Crim 1, CA, stressed the impact of burglary on home-owners, the courts may, in certain circumstances, take a lenient approach to sentence, especially in the case of a young offender or a first offender, or an offender who had reached a critical stage in his life with a real prospect of turning his back on crime: *Martin* [2009] EWCA Crim 1963, CA. In this case, the appellant appealed against a sentence of 16 months' detention in a young offender institution following his guilty plea to an offence of burglary. The appellant had burgled an isolated family home, taking property worth approximately £12,000. Prior to his conviction, he had received a suspended sentence order for two other burglaries, with eight matters of burglary or attempted burglary taken into consideration, but the appellant had not requested that this burglary be taken into consideration. He had no previous convictions prior to the suspended sentence order. Allowing his appeal, the Court held that the appellant's genuine attempt to break the cycle of offending was a factor which the court should set against the aggravating features of the case. The appellant was 19 years old, in good employment, had very favourable references, had complied with the suspended sentence order and had a very low risk of re-offending. The sentence was quashed and a sentence of 6 months' detention in a young offender institution was substituted. The revocation of the suspended sentence order was confirmed.

Part III

(b) *Burglary of a non-dwelling*

As regards burglary of a non-dwelling, when tried summarily, the maximum penalty is six months' imprisonment or a fine not exceeding the statutory maximum or both: *Theft Act* 1968, s.9(4). **15–30**

For general sentencing factors set out in the *Magistrates' Court Sentencing Guidelines* (2008) see Ch. 23, *post*.

On January 5, 2009, the Sentencing Guidelines Council issued a final guideline on sentencing for theft and for burglary of building other than a dwelling. For general factors relevant to sentencing for offences of burglary, see 15–17, above. The guideline applies to the sentencing of offenders convicted of burglary in a building other than a dwelling who are sentenced on or after January 5, 2009. For the guideline in full, see *http://www.sentencing-guidelines.gov.uk/*.

Burglary in a building other than a dwelling

Factors to take into consideration

The following starting points and sentencing ranges are for a first time offender aged 18 or over who pleaded not guilty.

Section 9 of the *Theft Act* 1968 provides that the offence of burglary can be committed in a number of ways. This guideline is concerned solely with burglary committed in a building other than a dwelling and is limited to situations in which an offender enters a building as a trespasser with intent to steal or, having entered a building as a trespasser, actually goes on to steal.

The seriousness of individual instances of this offence can vary significantly. At the lower end are cases of opportunistic offending by a single offender where there was no forced entry, no damage caused and nothing stolen. Towards the other end of the spectrum are cases involving significant planning and professionalism, multiple offenders going equipped with implements to facilitate the commission of the offence, targeting of particular premises and the theft of property or cash or damage and consequential losses of a significant value. In these circumstances, a sentence in excess of seven years imprisonment may be appropriate.

In relation to harm, the greater the loss, the more serious the offence. However, the monetary value of the loss may not reflect the full extent of the harm caused by the offence. The court should also take into account the impact of the offence on the victim (which may be significantly greater than the monetary value of the loss; this may be particularly important where the value of the loss is high in proportion to the victim's financial circumstances even though relatively low in absolute terms), any harm to persons other than the direct victim, and any harm in the form of public concern or erosion of public confidence.

When assessing the seriousness of an offence, the courts must always have regard to the full list of aggravating and mitigating factors in the Sentencing Guidelines Council guideline *Overarching Principles: Seriousness*. The following factors from the general list may be particularly relevant:

- deliberate and gratuitous violence or damage to property, over and above what is needed to carry out the offence;
- abuse of a position of trust.

Additional aggravating factors which may be relevant to this offence are:

(i) Targeting premises

Some offenders deliberately target premises because high value, often easily disposable, property is likely to be found there. This is an aggravating factor as it indicates a degree of professionalism and organisation in the offending, as well as an intention to derive a high level of gain. Community premises, including schools, clubrooms, places of worship and doctors' surgeries, may be particular targets. Burglaries of such premises may result in a higher than usual degree of harm in terms of, for example, the inconvenience caused by the theft of the property and this should be regarded as an aggravating factor. Premises which have been burgled on a prior occasion are also sometimes targeted, often on the assumption that security is weak or that goods stolen in the earlier burglary will have been replaced. This indicates planning, organisation and professionalism and, therefore, should be regarded as increasing the offender's culpability. Repeat victimisation may also increase the harm caused by the offence in terms of distress, inconvenience and expense to the victim.

(ii) Possession of a weapon

In cases where it is not clear whether the offender was in possession of a weapon at the time of entry into the building (which may fulfill the requirements for a more serious charge of aggravated burglary), an additional charge of possession of an offensive weapon may be before the court. If however, an offender found with a weapon is charged solely with burglary, possession of that weapon may be regarded as an aggravating factor, subject to the overriding principle that an offender can be sentenced only for the offence of which he or she has been convicted.

Burglary in a building other than a dwelling

Where the effect on the victim is particularly severe, the goods are of particularly high value, the cost of damage or consequential losses is significant, or there is evidence of a professional burglary and/or significant planning, a sentence of more than seven years custody may be appropriate.

THEFT ACT 1968 (SECTION 9)

MAXIMUM PENALTY: 10 YEARS IMPRISONMENT

Examples of nature of activity	Starting Point	Range
Burglary involving goods valued at £20,000 or more	2 years custody	12 months-7 years custody
Burglary involving goods valued at £2,000 or more but less than £20,000	18 weeks custody	Community order (HIGH)-12 months custody
Burglary involving goods valued at less than £2,000	Community order (MEDIUM)	Fine-26 weeks custody

ADDITIONAL AGGRAVATING FACTORS

1. Targeting premises containing property of high value
2. Targeting vulnerable community premises
3. Targeting premises which have been burgled on prior occasion(s)
4. Possession of a weapon (where this is not charged separately)

C. REMOVAL OF ARTICLES FROM PLACES OPEN TO THE PUBLIC

(1) Definition

Theft Act 1968, s.11

Removal of articles from places open to the public

11.—(1) Subject to subsections (2) and (3) below, where the public have access to a building in order to view the building or part of it, or a collection or part of a collection housed in it, any person who without lawful authority removes from the building or its grounds the whole or part of any article displayed or kept for display to the public in the building or that part of it or in its grounds shall be guilty of an offence. **15–31**

For this purpose "collection" includes a collection got together for a temporary purpose, but references in this section to a collection do not apply to a collection made or exhibited for the purpose of effecting sales or other commercial dealings.

(2) It is immaterial for purposes of subsection (1) above, that the public's access to a building is limited to a particular period or particular occasion; but where anything removed from a building or its grounds is there otherwise than as forming part of, or being on loan for exhibition with, a collection intended for permanent exhibition to the public, the person removing it does not thereby commit an offence under this section unless he removes it on a day when the public have access to the building as mentioned in subsection (1) above.

(3) A person does not commit an offence under this section if he believes that he has lawful authority for the removal of the thing in question or that he would have it if the person entitled to give it knew of the removal and the circumstances of it.

(2) Allocation

15–32 Removal of an article from a place open to the public is triable either way: *MCA* 1980, s.17 and Sched. 1, para. 28.

(3) Elements of the offence

15–33 The prosecution must prove that:

- — the defendant had access to a building to view it or any part of it, or to view a collection or part of a collection housed there; and
- — he removed from the building or its grounds the whole or part of any article displayed or kept in the building for display to the public;
- — without lawful authority.

The words "a collection intended for permanent exhibition to the public" mean simply a collection intended to be permanently available for exhibition to the public, for example, a local authority's settled practice of periodically displaying to the public at the gallery the pictures in their permanent collection: *Durkin* [1973] 1 Q.B. 786, CA.

(4) Statutory defence under s.11(3)

15–34 Where the defendant raises the issue of whether he believed he had lawful authority for the removal of the articles concerned, or that he would have had, had the person entitled to authorise the removal known of the removal and its attendant circumstances, the burden is on the prosecution to establish the defendant's bad faith.

(5) Sentence

15–35 The maximum penalty when tried on indictment is five years imprisonment (*TA* 1968, s.11(4)). When tried summarily, the maximum penalty is six months' imprisonment and/or a fine not exceeding the statutory maximum. After commencement of the relevant provisions, the maximum custodial sentence in a magistrates' court will be 12 months' imprisonment: *Criminal Justice Act* 2003, ss.154 and 282.

For general sentencing factors set out in the *Magistrates' Court Sentencing Guidelines* (2008) see Ch. 23, *post*.

D. TAKING A CONVEYANCE WITHOUT AUTHORITY

(1) Definition

Theft Act 1968, s.12(1)–(4C)

Taking motor vehicle or other conveyance without authority

15–36 **12.**—(1) Subject to subsections (5) and (6) below, a person shall be guilty of an offence if, without having the consent of the owner or other lawful authority, he takes any conveyance for his own or another's use or, knowing that any conveyance has been taken without such authority, drives it or allows himself to be carried in or on it.

(2) A person guilty of an offence under subsection (1) above shall be liable on summary conviction to a fine not exceeding level 5 on the standard scale, to imprisonment for a term not exceeding six months, or to both.

(3) [...]

(4) If on the trial of an indictment for theft the jury are not satisfied that the accused committed theft, but it is proved that the accused committed an offence under subsection (1) above, the jury may find him guilty of the offence under subsection (1).

and if he is found guilty of it, he shall be liable as he would have been liable under subsection (2) above on summary conviction.

(4A) Proceedings for an offence under subsection (1) above (but not proceedings of a kind falling within subsection (4) above) in relation to a mechanically propelled vehicle—

(a) shall not be commenced after the end of the period of three years beginning with the day on which the offence was committed; but

(b) subject to that, may be commenced at any time within the period of six months beginning with the relevant day.

(4B) In subsection (4A)(b) above "the relevant day" means—

(a) in the case of a prosecution for an offence under subsection (1) above by a public prosecutor, the day on which sufficient evidence to justify the proceedings came to the knowledge of any person responsible for deciding whether to commence any such prosecution;

(b) in the case of a prosecution for an offence under subsection (1) above which is commenced by a person other than a public prosecutor after the discontinuance of a prosecution falling within paragraph (a) above which relates to the same facts, the day on which sufficient evidence to justify the proceedings came to the knowledge of the person who has decided to commence the prosecution or (if later) the discontinuance of the other prosecution;

(c) in the case of any other prosecution for an offence under subsection (1) above, the day on which sufficient evidence to justify the proceedings came to the knowledge of the person who has decided to commence the prosecution.

(4C) For the purposes of subsection (4A)(b) above a certificate of a person responsible for deciding whether to commence a prosecution of a kind mentioned in subsection (4B)(a) above as to the date on which such evidence as is mentioned in the certificate came to the knowledge of any person responsible for deciding whether to commence any such prosecution shall be conclusive evidence of that fact.

[Subsections (4A) to (4C) apply only in relation to offences committed on or after their commencement (October 1, 2001): s.37(2).]

(2) Allocation

This offence is triable summarily. However, an offence under s.12 may be included in an indictment for another offence in the circumstances set out in the *Criminal Justice Act* 1988, s.40. See *ante*, § 7–88. **15–37**

(3) Elements of the offence

The prosecution must prove that: **15–38**

— the defendant took any conveyance for his own or another's use;

— without having the consent of the owner, or lawful authority;

OR

— the defendant allowed himself to be carried in, or drove himself, any conveyance;

— which had, to the defendant's knowledge, been taken without the owner's consent or other lawful authority.

(4) Statutory defence

Theft Act 1968, s.12(5)–(7)

Taking motor vehicle or other conveyance without authority

12.—(5) Subsection (1) above shall not apply in relation to pedal cycles; but, subject to subsection (6) below, a person who, without having the consent of the owner or other lawful authority, takes a pedal cycle for his own or another's use, or rides a pedal cycle knowing it to have been taken without such authority, shall on summary conviction be liable to a fine not exceeding level 3 on the standard scale **15–39**

(6) A person does not commit an offence under this section by anything done in the belief that he has lawful authority to do it or that he would have the owner's consent if the owner knew of his doing it and the circumstances of it.

(7) For purposes of this section—

(a) "conveyance" means any conveyance constructed or adapted for the carriage of a person or persons whether by land, water or air, except that it does not include a conveyance constructed or adapted for use only under the control of a person not carried in or on it, and "drive" shall be construed accordingly; and

(b) "owner", in relation to a conveyance which is the subject of a hiring agreement or hire-purchase agreement, means the person in possession of the conveyance under that agreement.

15–40 Where the defendant raises the issue of whether he believed he had lawful authority for the taking of the conveyance the burden is on the prosecution to establish the defendant's bad faith.

(5) Sentence

15–41 The maximum penalty for taking a conveyance without authority is six months' imprisonment and/or a fine not exceeding level 5 on the standard scale (s.12(2)). If the offence is committed or attempted in relation to a motor vehicle, there is discretionary disqualification (*Road Traffic Offenders Act* 1988, Sched. 2). After commencement of the relevant provisions, the maximum custodial sentence in a magistrates' court will be 12 months: *Criminal Justice Act* 2003, ss.181, 280–282 (see Ch. 23, *post*.).

For general sentencing factors set out in the *Magistrates' Court Sentencing Guidelines* (2008) see Ch. 23, *post*. The *Magistrates' Court Sentencing Guidelines* (2008) provide the following guidelines for the offence of taking a conveyance without authority.

STARTING POINT AND SENTENCING RANGES

(BASED ON A FIRST TIME OFFENDER AFTER TRIAL)

Examples of nature of activity	**Starting Point**	**Range**
Exceeding authorised use of e.g. employer's or relative's vehicle; retention of hire car beyond return date	Low level community order	Band B fine to medium level community order
As above with damage caused to lock/ignition; or stranger's vehicle involved but no damage caused	Medium level community order	Low level community order to high level community order
Taking vehicle from private premises; Causing damage to e.g. lock/ignition of stranger's vehicle	High level community order	Medium level community order to 26 weeks custody

AGGRAVATING AND MITIGATING FACTORS

Factors indicating greater degree of harm	Factor indicating lower culpability
1. Vehicle later burnt	1. Misunderstanding with owner
2. Vehicle belonging to elderly/disabled person	**Factor indicating lesser degree of harm**
3. Emergency services vehicle	1. Offender voluntarily returned vehicle to owner
4. Medium to large goods vehicle	
5. Passengers carried	

A custodial sentence may be imposed where the offence forms part of a series of offences arising out of the same circumstances: in *Jeary* (1986) 8 Cr.App.R.(S.) 491 a sentence of four months' detention was deemed appropriate when the offender stole vehicles, drove them around a city at high speed, eventually colliding head on leaving one car damaged beyond repair. The offender later stated that the cars had been taken for "a bit of fun" and pleaded guilty to two counts of occasioning actual bodily harm, two counts of taking a conveyance, two counts of theft as well as asking two other offences to be taken into consideration. In the view of the Court, these were serious offences involving taking vehicles and deliberately destroying them, and custody was fully merited. **15–42**

In *Ahmad (Asif)* (1992) 12 Cr.App.R.(S.) 212, CA, the offender pleaded guilty to taking a conveyance without authority, reckless driving and driving while disqualified. A sentence of 200 hours' community service and a compensation order was upheld.

E. AGGRAVATED VEHICLE TAKING

(1) Definition

Theft Act 1968, s.12A(1)–(3)

Aggravated vehicle-taking

12A.—(1) Subject to subsection (3) below, a person is guilty of aggravated taking of a vehicle if— **15–43**

(a) he commits an offence under section 12(1) above (in this section referred to as a "basic offence") in relation to a mechanically propelled vehicle; and

(b) it is proved that, at any time after the vehicle was unlawfully taken (whether by him or another) and before it was recovered, the vehicle was driven, or injury or damage was caused, in one or more of the circumstances set out in paragraphs (a) to (d) of subsection (2) below.

(2) The circumstances referred to in subsection (1)(b) above are—

(a) that the vehicle was driven dangerously on a road or other public place;

(b) that, owing to the driving of the vehicle, an accident occurred by which injury was caused to any person;

(c) that, owing to the driving of the vehicle, an accident occurred by which damage was caused to any property, other than the vehicle;

(d) that damage was caused to the vehicle.

(3) A person is not guilty of an offence under this section if he proves that, as regards any such proven driving, injury or damage as is referred to in subsection (1)(b) above, either—

(a) the driving, accident or damage referred to in subsection (2) above occurred before he committed the basic offence; or

(b) he was neither in nor on nor in the immediate vicinity of the vehicle when that driving, accident or damage occurred.

(2) Allocation

15–44 This offence is triable either way. However, where the only allegation is of damage to the vehicle or other property or both and the total value of the damage alleged to have been caused is less than the relevant sum, *i.e.* £5,000, the offender has no right to elect trial on indictment: *MCA* 1980, ss.22 and 33 and Sched. 2.

If a person charged with the offence under section 12A is found not guilty of that offence, he may still be found guilty of the basic form of the offence: s.12A(5) of the *TA* 1968. This section applies to trial in the magistrates' court as much as to trial in the Crown Court: *R. (H.) v. Liverpool Youth Court* [2001] Crim.L.R. 487.

(3) Elements of the offence

15–45 The prosecution must prove that:

— the defendant committed an offence under s.12(1) of the *Theft Act* 1968;

— in relation to a mechanically propelled vehicle;

— and injury or damage was caused at any time between the taking of the vehicle and its recovery;

— when the vehicle was being driven dangerously on a road or other public place; OR

— when an accident occurred which caused injury and was due to the driving of the vehicle; OR

— when an accident occurred which caused damage to any property other than the vehicle and was due to the driving of the vehicle; OR

— damage was caused to the vehicle.

Theft Act 1968, s.12A(7), (8)

Aggravated vehicle-taking

15–46 **12A.**—(7) For the purposes of this section a vehicle is driven dangerously if—

(a) it is driven in a way which falls far below what would be expected of a competent and careful driver; and

(b) it would be obvious to a competent and careful driver that driving the vehicle in that way would be dangerous.

(8) For the purposes of this section a vehicle is recovered when it is restored to its owner or to other lawful possession or custody; and in this subsection "owner" has the same meaning as in section 12 above.

(4) Statutory defence in s.12A(3)

15–47 A person will not be guilty of an offence under this section if he proves that, as regards any such proven driving, injury or damage as is referred to in subs (1)(b) either the driving, accident or damage referred to in subs (2), *ante*, occurred before he committed the basic offence or he was neither in nor on nor in the immediate vicinity of the vehicle when that driving, accident or damage occurred.

(5) Sentence

15–48 The maximum penalty on summary conviction is a term of imprisonment not exceeding six months or a fine not exceeding the statutory maximum or both. Section 33(1) of the *Magistrates' Courts Act* 1980 reducing the maximum sentence to three months for offences of criminal damage where the value is under £5,000 does not apply to the offence of aggravated vehicle taking: s.33(3) of the *Magistrates' Courts Act* 1980. After commencement of the relevant provisions, the maximum custodial sentence in a magistrates' court will be 12 months' imprisonment: *Criminal Justice Act* 2003, ss.154 and 282.

This section carries obligatory disqualification and endorsement (3 to 11 points): *Road Traffic Offenders Act* 1988, ss.28, 34, 44, 96 and 97 and Sched. 2, Pt II. The fact that the defendant did not drive the vehicle during the commission of the offence is not a reason to avoid obligatory disqualification (*Road Traffic Offenders Act* 1988, s.34).

Damage caused to property other than the vehicle in accident or damage caused to the vehicle

The *Magistrates Courts Sentencing Guidelines* (2008) provide that when sentencing this offence, the court must endorse and disqualify for at least 12 months. The court must disqualify for at least two years if offender has had two or more disqualifications for periods of 56 days or more in preceding three years. If there is a delay in sentencing after conviction, consider interim disqualification. **15–49**

For general sentencing factors set out in the *Magistrates Courts Sentencing Guidelines* (2008) see Ch. 23, *post*. The *Magistrates Courts Sentencing Guidelines* (2008) provide the following guidelines for the offence of aggravated vehicle taking.

STARTING POINT AND SENTENCING RANGES

(BASED ON A FIRST TIME OFFENDER AFTER TRIAL)

Examples of nature of activity	**Starting Point**	**Range**
Exceeding authorised use of e.g. employer's or relative's vehicle; retention of hire car beyond return date; minor damage to taken vehicle	Medium level community order	Low level community order to high level community order
Greater damage to taken vehicle and/or moderate damage to another vehicle and/or property	High level community order	Medium level community order to 12 weeks custody
Vehicle taken as part of burglary or from private premises; severe damage	18 weeks custody	12 to 26 weeks custody (Crown Court if damage over £5,000)

Part III

AGGRAVATING AND MITIGATING FACTORS

Factors indicating higher culpability	Factors indicating lower culpability
1. Vehicle deliberately Damaged/destroyed 2. Offender under influence of alcohol/drugs	1. Misunderstanding with owner 2. Damage resulting from actions of another (where this does not provide a defence)
Factors indicating greater degree of harm 1. Passenger(s) carried 2. Vehicle belonging to elderly or disabled person 3. Emergency services vehicle 4. Medium to large goods vehicle 5. Damage caused in moving traffic accident	

Dangerous driving or accident causing injury

STARTING POINT AND SENTENCING RANGES

(BASED ON A FIRST TIME OFFENDER AFTER TRIAL)

15–50

Examples of nature of activity	Starting Point	Range
Taken vehicle involved in single incident of bad driving where little or no damage or risk of personal injury	High level community order	Medium level community order to 12 weeks custody
Taken vehicle involved in incident(s) involving excessive speed or showing off, especially on busy roads or in built-up area	18 weeks custody	12 to 26 weeks custody

Examples of nature of activity	Starting Point	Range
Taken vehicle involved in prolonged bad driving involving deliberate disregard for safety of others	Crown Court	Crown Court

AGGRAVATING AND MITIGATING FACTORS

Factors indicating higher culpability	Factors indicating lower culpability
1. Disregarding warnings of others 2. Evidence of alcohol or drugs 3. Carrying out other tasks while driving 4. Carrying passengers or heavy load 5. Tiredness 6. Trying to avoid arrest 7. Aggressive driving, such as driving much too close to vehicle in front, inappropriate attempts to overtake, or cutting in after overtaking	Nil.

In *Bird* (1993) 14 Cr.App.R.(S.) 343, CA, Lord Taylor C.J. stated that the aggravating features of this offence will be primarily the overall culpability of the driving; how bad it was and for how long, and to a lesser extent, how much injury or damage, or both was caused. Drink would affect the culpability of the driving, but where it had played a large part it would usually be the subject of another charge. A guilty plea will be a mitigating feature if made with contrition, though the youth of the offender will be less significant in mitigation as the Act is aimed at young offenders.

In *Clifford* [2007] EWCA Crim 2442, CA, a sentence of six months' imprisonment was held to be appropriate in the case of a 43-year-old man of good character who had pleaded guilty to aggravated vehicle-taking. Although his decision to drive had led to the death of a seven-year-old boy, the Court held that the offence lacked aggravating features. The appellant held a provisional licence and took his partner's car for a drive whilst she was asleep. During the drive, he knocked down a seven-year-old boy, who died from his injuries. There was no suggestion that the appellant's driving had caused or contributed to the accident. The appellant did not stop after the accident but later went to the local police station stating that he thought that he had hit something. Sentencing him to two year's imprisonment, the sentencing judge took into account the appellant's guilty plea, the remorse that he had shown, his good character and the fact that the car belonged to him and his partner. The appellant argued that the sentence

Part III

imposed was too long, having regard to the mitigating features and the lack of any aggravating features other than the initial failure to stop. Allowing his appeal and substituting a sentence of six month's imprisonment, the Court of Appeal stated that no sentence would be adequate to reflect the loss of a child to those who loved him. That child's death would not have occurred were it not for the appellant's commission of the offence. However, the sentence was far too long.

See also *Timothy* (1995) 16 Cr.App.R.(S.) 1028 and *Frostick* [1998] 1 Cr.App.R.(S.) 257.

F. TAKING OR RIDING A PEDAL CYCLE WITHOUT AUTHORITY

(1) Definition

Theft Act 1968, s.12

Taking motor vehicle or other conveyance without authority

15-51 **12.**—(5) Subsection (1) above shall not apply in relation to pedal cycles; but, subject to subsection (6) below, a person who, without having the consent of the owner or other lawful authority, takes a pedal cycle for his own or another's use, or rides a pedal cycle knowing it to have been taken without such authority, shall on summary conviction be liable to a fine not exceeding level 3 on the standard scale

(6) A person does not commit an offence under this section by anything done in the belief that he has lawful authority to do it or that he would have the owner's consent if the owner knew of his doing it and the circumstances of it.

(2) Allocation

15-52 This offence is triable summarily only: s.12(6).

(3) Elements of the offence

15-53 The prosecution must prove that:

— the defendant took a pedal cycle for his own or another's use;

— without the consent of the owner or other lawful authority;

OR

— the defendant rode a pedal cycle knowing it to have been taken without the consent of the owner or other lawful authority.

The owner of the pedal cycle does not need to be identified; if the offender admits that he did not have the owner's consent, the court is entitled to find that the prosecution had made out a case to answer as it is entitled to infer that the bicycle had an owner: *Sturrock v. DPP* (1996) R.T.R. 216.

(4) Sentence

15-54 The maximum penalty is a fine not exceeding level 3 on the standard scale: *Theft Act* 1968, s.12(5).

For general sentencing factors set out in the *Magistrates' Court Sentencing Guidelines* (2008) see Ch. 23, *post*.

G. ABSTRACTING ELECTRICITY

(1) Definition

Theft Act 1968, s.13

Abstracting of electricity

15-55 **13.** A person who dishonestly uses without due authority, or dishonestly causes to be wasted or diverted, any electricity shall on conviction on indictment be liable to imprisonment for a term not exceeding five years.

(2) Allocation

Abstracting electricity is triable either way: *MCA* 1980, s.17 and Sched. 1, para. 28. **15–56**

(3) Elements of the offence

The prosecution must prove that: **15–57**

— the defendant dishonestly, or without due authority;
— used any electricity; OR
— caused any electricity to be wasted or diverted.

"Dishonesty" has the same meaning in this context as it does in the context of the offence of theft.

In *McCreadie and Tume* 96 Cr.App.R. 143, CA, it was held that the offence does not require tampering with the electricity meter. It is sufficient to prove that electricity was used without the authority of the electricity supplier by a person who had no intention of paying for it.

(4) Sentence

When tried summarily, the maximum sentence is six months' imprisonment, a fine **15–58** not exceeding the statutory maximum or both: *Theft Act* 1968, s.13. After commencement of the relevant provisions, the maximum custodial sentence in a magistrates' court will be 12 months' imprisonment: *Criminal Justice Act* 2003, ss.154 and 282.

The *Magistrates Courts Sentencing Guidelines* (2008) provide the following key factors a court must consider when sentencing for this offence:

Key Factors

(a) The starting points and sentencing ranges in this guideline are based on **15–59** the assumption that the offender was motivated by greed or a desire to live beyond his or her means. To avoid double counting, such a motivation should not be treated as a factor that increases culpability.

(b) When assessing the harm caused by this offence, the starting point should be the loss suffered by the victim. In general, the greater the loss, the more serious the offence. However, the monetary value of the loss may not reflect the full extent of the harm caused by the offence. The court should also take into account the impact of the offence on the victim, any harm to persons other than the direct victim, and any harm in the form of public alarm or erosion of public confidence.

(c) The following matters of personal mitigation may be relevant to this offence:

(i) *Offender motivated by desperation or need*
The fact that an offence has been committed in desperation or need arising from particular hardship may count as personal mitigation in exceptional circumstances.

(ii) *Voluntary restitution*
Whether and the degree to which payment for stolen electricity constitutes a matter of personal mitigation will depend on an assessment of the circumstances and, in particular, the voluntariness and timeliness of the payment.

(iii) *Impact on sentence of offender's dependency*
Many offenders convicted of acquisitive crimes are motivated by an addiction, often to drugs, alcohol or gambling. This does not mitigate the seriousness of the offence, but an offender's dependency may properly influence the type of sentence imposed. In particular, it may sometimes be appropriate to impose a drug rehabilitation requirement or an alcohol treatment requirement as part of a community order or a suspended sentence order in an at-

tempt to break the cycle of addiction and offending, even if an immediate custodial sentence would otherwise be warranted.

STARTING POINT AND SENTENCING RANGES

(BASED ON A FIRST TIME OFFENDER AFTER TRIAL)

Examples of nature of activity	**Starting Point**	**Range**
Where the offence results in substantial commercial gain, a custodial sentence may be appropriate		
Offence involving evidence of planning and indication that the offending was intended to be continuing, such as using a device to interfere with the electricity meter or re-wiring to by-pass the meter	Medium level community order	Band A fine to high level community order

AGGRAVATING OR MITIGATING FACTORS

Factor indicating greater degree of harm	
1. Risk of danger caused to property and/or life	

In *Hodkinson* (1980) 2 Cr.App.R.(S.) 331, CA, the offender had fitted a device to the electricity meter at his home, causing the meter to give a false reading. A sentence of one month's imprisonment and a fine of £750 was upheld, the necessity for deterrent sentences being emphasised.

See also *Western* (1987) 9 Cr.App.R.(S.) 6 and *Wright* (1981) 3 Cr.App.R.(S.) 242.

H. FALSE ACCOUNTING

(1) Definition

Theft Act 1968, s.17(1)

False accounting

17.—(1) Where a person dishonestly, with a view to gain for himself or another or with intent to cause loss to another,— **15–60**

(a) destroys, defaces, conceals or falsifies any account or any record or document made or required for any accounting purpose; or

(b) in furnishing information for any purpose produces or makes use of any account, or any such record or document as aforesaid, which to his knowledge is or may be misleading, false or deceptive in a material particular;

he shall, on conviction on indictment, be liable to imprisonment for a term not exceeding seven years.

(2) Procedure

The offence is triable either way (*MCA* 1980, s.17 and Sched. 1, para. 28). For guidance as to when summary trial of fraud cases is appropriate, see *Consolidated Criminal Practice Direction*, Pt V.51.7, Appendix F–51. **15–61**

(3) Elements of the offence

The prosecution must prove that; **15–62**

— the defendant dishonestly,

— with a view to gain for himself or another or with intent to cause loss to another,

— destroyed, defaced, concealed or falsified any account or any record or document made or required for any accounting purpose; OR

— in furnishing information for any purpose, produced or makes use of any account, or any such record or document as aforesaid, which to his knowledge was or may have been misleading, false or deceptive in a material particular.

Theft Act 1968, s.17(2)

False accounting

17.—(2) For purposes of this section a person who makes or concurs in making in an account or other document an entry which is or may be misleading, false or deceptive in a material particular, or who omits or concurs in omitting a material particular from an account or other document, is to be treated as falsifying the account or document. **15–63**

An omission will be 'material' if it had the effect that the document was liable to mislead in a significant way, and that would depend on the nature of the document and the context: *Lancaster* [2010] EWCA Crim 370. In this case the appellant appealed against his conviction for offences of false accounting and of dishonesty. He had filled out claim forms for housing benefit and council tax benefit claiming he and his wife were neither employed nor self-employed, but on one form he claimed his wife usually did 40 hours per week of unpaid work. On one form he said that they used their home for business. The prosecution's case was that they had run a substantial web design business from their home. The particulars of the alleged offences under section 17 were expressed in terms of misrepresentation by material omissions. The appellant submitted that the judge had misdirected the jury on the issue of what was a material particular. Dismissing the appeal, the Court held that in a non-disclosure case, the omission would be material if it had the effect that the document was liable to mislead in a significant way. Whether the omission was significant would depend on the nature of the document and the context. In the instant case, it was plain beyond doubt that the information provided by the appellant was materially misleading on the facts known to him.

Giving a false name and employment details on mortgage application forms constitutes furnishing false information in a document required for an accounting purpose, contrary to the *Theft Act* 1968, section 17(1)(b): *O, H* [2010] EWCA Crim 2233, CA.

(4) Sentence

15–64 When tried summarily, the maximum penalty is six months' imprisonment, a fine not exceeding the statutory maximum or both.

The Sentencing Guidelines Council guideline on *Sentencing for Fraud—statutory offences*, issued on October 13, 2009, states that false accounting under s.17 of the *Theft Act* 1968 may be sentenced as a type of confidence fraud; as fraud involving banking and insurance fraud; as obtaining credit through fraud; as benefit fraud or as revenue fraud (against HM Revenue and Customs). The Sentencing Guidelines Council's guideline on these types of fraud is considered at 15–112, below.

In *Kefford* [2002] 2 Cr.App.R.(S.) 106, CA, Lord Woolf issued guidance for sentencing in the context of economic crimes, stating that when the offender was of previous good character alternative sentences to imprisonment could be an appropriate punishment. In view of the overcrowded prison system a sentence of imprisonment should only be imposed when necessary and only for as long as necessary. A starting point of 18 months following guilty pleas for theft and false accounting was held to be excessive, and the sentence was reduced to four months, with 12 months being the appropriate starting point.

In *Spencer* [2002] EWCA Crim 2196, CA (Crim. Div.) a sentence of 18 months' imprisonment concurrent on each of six counts of false accounting was reduced to a sentence of six months' imprisonment. The appellant was of previous good character, and evidence suggested she had been initially forced to make the fraudulent claims by a violent partner. The Court of Appeal affirmed the propriety of taking into consideration the Lord Chief Justice's comments in *Kefford* (*ante*) about prison overcrowding.

In *Postle* [2007] EWCA Crim 2542, CA, the Court of Appeal held that a sentence of 18 months' imprisonment imposed following guilty pleas to one count of false accounting and five counts of theft was not manifestly excessive in circumstances where the offender had caused significant losses to her employer that threatened the future of the company. The appellant was manager of a travel agency, and was appointed as company secretary. Over two years, she obtained holidays for nothing, stole cash and covered up her actions by falsifying records and undercharging holidays to generate business that would cover up her theft. After pleading guilty at the first available opportunity, she accepted that she had obtained a benefit of £10,000, and caused losses to the company in the region of £250,000, which left the future of the company in doubt. In mitigation, the appellant relied on her early guilty plea, the value of the personal gain, and the fact that she was of previous good character, posed a low risk of re-offending, was married with two children and had committed no offence whilst on bail. The sentencing judge passed concurrent sentences of 18 months' imprisonment on each count, stating that she had committed a massive breach of trust and deliberately created a state of chaos and confusion to mask her activity.

The appellant submitted that the sentence was manifestly excessive. She contended that, apart from the mitigation, the case of *Clark* (1998) 2 Cr.App.R. 13 (see § 15–19, above) showed a range of sentences up to 21 months after trial for thefts of less than £17,500. She argued that she had been employed as a clerk, rather than a bank manager, accountant or solicitor. Whilst the period of offending was fairly long, she had been trying to cover up what had gone before. She had lost her good character and job, the business continued to trade and the other employees retained their jobs. The appellant also contended that the judge could only sentence on the money she had taken, not the loss to the company, and whilst that loss was a relevant factor, it did not move the case outside the guideline figures. Dismissing her appeal, the Court referred to the man hours involved in investigating the offence due to the complexity of the accounting trail, the significant loss of £250,000 and the fact that the offence involved a breach of trust in circumstances which were bound to have a significant impact, not only on the travel agency, but also on the employees whose trust had been betrayed. The sentences were therefore not manifestly excessive.

For general sentencing factors set out in the *Magistrates' Court Sentencing Guidelines* (2008) see Ch. 23, *post*.

See also *Smith* (1994) 15 Cr.App.R.(S.) 145. **15–65**

I. FALSE STATEMENTS BY OFFICERS OF A COMPANY OR ASSOCIATION

(1) Definition

Theft Act 1968, s.19(1)

False statements by company directors, etc.

19.—(1) Where an officer of a body corporate or unincorporated association (or person purporting to act as such), with intent to deceive members or creditors of the body corporate or association about its affairs, publishes or concurs in publishing a written statement or account which to his knowledge is or may be misleading, false or deceptive in a material particular, he shall on conviction on indictment be liable to imprisonment for a term not exceeding seven years. **15–66**

(2) Allocation

The offence is triable either way (*MCA* 1980, s.17 and Sched. 1, para. 28) For guidance as to when summary trial of fraud cases is appropriate, see Appendix F–51. **15–67**

(3) Elements of the offence

The prosecution must prove that: **15–68**

- the defendant was the officer of a body corporate or unincorporated association, or was purporting to act as such, and;
- with intent to deceive members or creditors of the body corporate or association about its affairs, he;
- published or concurred in publishing a written statement or account which;
- to his knowledge was or might have been misleading, false or deceptive in a material particular.

Theft Act 1968, s.19(2)–(3)

False statements by company directors, etc.

19.—(2) For purposes of this section a person who has entered into a security for the benefit of a body corporate or association is to be treated as a creditor of it. **15–69**

(3) Where the affairs of a body corporate or association are managed by its members, this section shall apply to any statement which a member publishes or concurs in publishing in connection with his functions of management as if he were an officer of the body corporate or association.

(4) Sentence

When tried summarily, the maximum penalty is six months' imprisonment, a fine not exceeding the statutory maximum or both. After commencement of the relevant provisions, the maximum custodial sentence in a magistrates' court is 12 months' imprisonment: *Criminal Justice Act* 2003, ss.154 and 282. **15–70**

For general sentencing factors set out in the *Magistrates' Court Sentencing Guidelines* (2008) see Ch. 23, *post*.

For sentencing guidelines in fraud cases generally, see § 15–105, *post*.

J. SUPPRESSION OF DOCUMENTS

(1) Definition

Theft Act 1968, s.20(1), (3)

Suppression, etc. of documents

15–71 **20.**—(1) A person who dishonestly, with a view to gain for himself or another or with intent to cause loss to another, destroys, defaces or conceals any valuable security, any will or other testamentary document or any original document of or belonging to, or filed or deposited in, any court of justice or any government department shall on conviction on indictment be liable to imprisonment for a term not exceeding seven years.

(3) For purposes of this section "valuable security" means any document creating, transferring, surrendering or releasing any right to, in or over property, or authorising the payment of money or delivery of any property, or evidencing the creation, transfer, surrender or release of any such right, or the payment of money or delivery of any property, or the satisfaction of any obligation.

[This section is printed as amended by the *Fraud Act* 2006.]

(2) Allocation

15–72 This offence is triable either way (*MCA* 1980, s.17 and Sched. 1, para. 28). For guidance as to when summary trial of fraud cases is appropriate, see Appendix F–51.

(3) Elements of the offence

15–73 The prosecution must prove that:

— the defendant dishonestly,

— with a view to gain for himself or another OR with intent to cause loss to another,

— destroyed, defaced or concealed,

— any valuable security, any will or other testamentary document or any original document of or belonging to, or filed or deposited in any court of justice or any government department.

(4) Sentence

15–74 When tried summarily the maximum penalty for this offence is six months' imprisonment, a fine not exceeding statutory maximum or both. After commencement of the relevant provisions, the maximum custodial sentence in a magistrates' court will be 12 months' imprisonment: *Criminal Justice Act* 2003, ss.154 and 282.

For general sentencing factors set out in the *Magistrates' Court Sentencing Guidelines* (2008) see Ch. 23, *post*.

K. HANDLING STOLEN GOODS

(1) Definition

Theft Act 1968, s.22

Handling stolen goods

15–75 **22.**—(1) A person handles stolen goods if (otherwise than in the course of the stealing) knowing or believing them to be stolen goods he dishonestly receives the goods, or dishonestly undertakes or assists in their retention, removal, disposal or realisation by or for the benefit of another person, or if he arranges to do so.

(2) A person guilty of handling stolen goods shall on conviction on indictment be liable to imprisonment for a term not exceeding fourteen years.

(2) Allocation

15–76 This offence is triable either way (*MCA* 1980, s.17 and Sched. 1, para. 28). The

Consolidated Criminal Practice Direction, para. V.51.8 provides that cases of handling should be tried summarily unless the court considers that one or more of several features are present and that its sentencing powers are insufficient. See Appendix F–52.

(3) Elements of the offence

The prosecution must prove that: 15–77

— the defendant dishonestly,
— received OR undertook or assisted in the retention, removal, disposal or realisation by or for the benefit of another person, OR arranged to so undertake or assist, of,
— goods which he knew or believed to be stolen,
— otherwise than in the course of stealing them.

Stolen goods

The term "goods" is defined in s.34(2)(b) of the 1968 Act as including money and every other description of property except land, and things severed from the land by stealing. The fact that the goods are stolen may be proved by the thief or by circumstantial evidence. 15–78

Handling

Handling is proved by establishing that the defendant either received the goods, or arranged to do so, or undertook or assisted in their retention, removal, disposal or realisation by or for the benefit of another person, or arranged to do so. 15–79

In *Frost* (1964) 48 Cr.App.R. 284, CCA it was held that for a defendant to be convicted of receiving, it must be established that he took possession or control of the property, either jointly or exclusively. The requirement that control is taken of the goods means that proof that the defendant physically handled the goods will not suffice.

Where a person is charged with undertaking or assisting etc, there is no need to prove possession or control. In *Bloxham* (1983) 1 A.C. 109, HL, the HL examined the ambit of the second limb of the offence established by s.22(1) and concluded that the second limb creates a second offence that can be committed in a number of ways, the activities envisaged by the section being retention, removal, disposal and realisation. Lord Bridge stated:

> "The offence can be committed in relation to any one of these activities in one or other of two ways. First, the offender may himself undertake the activity *for the benefit of* another person. Secondly, the activity may be undertaken by another person and the offender may assist him. Of course, if the thief or an original receiver and his friend act together in, say, removing the stolen goods, the friend may be committing the offence in both ways. But this does not invalidate the analysis and if the analysis holds good, it must follow, I think, that the category of other persons contemplated by the subsection is subject to the same limitations in whichever way the offence is committed." 15–80

The words "or if he arranges to do so" apply to both limbs of section 22(1).

Dishonestly

The relevant test if that established by the case of *Ghosh*, see *ante*, § 15–4. 15–81

The defendant's knowledge or belief that the goods were stolen at the material time may be established by the direct evidence of the principal offender or circumstantially. This question is subjective, and it is not enough that the goods were handled in circumstances that would put the reasonable man on inquiry. Suspicion that the goods were stolen, even coupled with the fact that the defendant shut his eyes to the circumstances, is not enough, although those matters may be taken into account: *Moys* 79 Cr.App.R. 72, CA.

Proof of guilty knowledge by evidence of the possession of other stolen property by previous conviction

Theft Act 1968, s.27(3), (5)

Evidence and procedure on charge of theft or handling stolen goods

15–82 **27.**—(3) Where a person is being proceeded against for handling stolen goods (but not for any offence other than handling stolen goods), then at any stage of the proceedings, if evidence has been given of his having or arranging to have in his possession the goods the subject of the charge, or of his undertaking or assisting in, or arranging to undertake or assist in, their retention, removal, disposal or realisation, the following evidence shall be admissible for the purpose of proving that he knew or believed the goods to be stolen goods—

(a) evidence that he has had in his possession, or has undertaken or assisted in the retention, removal, disposal or realisation of, stolen goods from any theft taking place not earlier than twelve months before the offence charged; and

(b) (provided that seven days' notice in writing has been given to him of the intention to prove the conviction)

evidence that he has within the five years preceding the date of the offence charged been convicted of theft or of handling stolen goods.

(5) This section is to be construed in accordance with section 24 of this Act; and in subsection (3)(b) above the reference to handling stolen goods shall include any corresponding offence committed before the commencement of this Act.

(4) Sentence

15–83 When tried summarily the maximum penalty for this offence is six months' imprisonment, a fine not exceeding the statutory maximum or both. After commencement of the relevant provisions, the maximum custodial sentence in a magistrates' court will be 12 months' imprisonment: *Criminal Justice Act* 2003, ss.154 and 282.

For general sentencing factors set out in the *Magistrates' Court Sentencing Guidelines* (2008) see Ch. 23, *post*. The *Magistrates Courts Sentencing Guidelines* (2008) follow the guidance issued by the Court of Appeal *R. v. Webbe and others* [2001] EWCA Crim 1217.

STARTING POINT AND SENTENCING RANGES

(BASED ON A FIRST TIME OFFENDER AFTER TRIAL)

Examples of nature of activity	**Starting Point**	**Range**
Property worth less than £1,000 acquired for offender's own use	Band B fine	Band B fine to low level community order

Examples of nature of activity	**Starting Point**	**Range**
Property worth less than £1,000 acquired for re-sale; or Property worth more than £1,000 acquired for offender's own use; or Presence of at least one aggravating factor listed below – regardless of value	Medium level community order	Low level community order to 12 weeks custody Note: the custody threshold is likely to be passed if the offender has a record of dishonesty offences
Sophisticated offending; or Presence of at least two aggravating factors listed below	12 weeks custody	6 weeks custody to Crown Court
Offence committed in context of a business; or Offender acts as organiser/distributor of proceeds of crime; or Offender makes self available to other criminals as willing to handle the proceeds of thefts or burglaries; or Offending highly organised, professional; or Particularly serious original offence, such as armed robbery	Crown Court	Crown Court

Part III

AGGRAVATING AND MITIGATING FACTORS

Factors indicating higher culpability	Factors indicating lower culpability
1. Closeness of offender to primary offence. Closeness may be geographical, arising from presence at or near the primary offence when it was committed, or temporal, where the handler instigated or encouraged the primary offence beforehand, or, soon after, provided a safe haven or route for disposal. 2. High level of profit made or expected by offender **Factors indicating greater degree of harm** 1. Seriousness of the primary offence, including domestic burglary 2. High value of goods to victim, including sentimental value 3. Threats of violence or abuse of power by offender over others, such as an adult commissioning criminal activity by children, or a drug dealer pressurising addicts to steal in order to pay for their habit	1. Little or no benefit to offender 2. Voluntary restitution to victim **Factor indicating lower degree of harm** 1. Low value of goods

15–84 In *Webbe* [2002] 1 Cr.App.R.(S.) 22, the Court of Appeal considered guidelines for sentencing in cases of handling stolen goods proposed by the Sentencing Advisory Panel. The Court agreed with the panel's view that the handler's advance knowledge of the original offence was an important question; where the handler had knowledge of the original offence, the seriousness of the handling was inevitably linked to the seriousness of the original offence. The replacement value of the goods involved a helpful indication of the seriousness of the offence, although not the determining factor. Other factors identified as relevant considerations were the level of sophistication of the handler; the ultimate destination of the goods; the criminal origin of the goods; the impact on the victim; the level of profit made or expected by the handler and the precise role played by the handler. The Court also held that handling cases at or towards the lower end of the scale were characterised by the handler having no connection with the original offence; an absence of sophistication on the part of the handler;

the less serious nature of the original offence; the relatively low value of goods and the absence of any significant profit.

Aggravating factors include: closeness of the handler to the primary offence; particular seriousness in the primary offence; high value of goods to the loser, including sentimental value; the fact that the goods were the proceeds of a domestic burglary; sophistication in relation to the handling; a high level of profit made or expected by the handler; the provision by the handler of a regular outlet for the stolen goods. Threats of violence or abuse of power by the handler over others, for example an adult commissioning criminal activity by children or a drug dealer pressurising addicts to steal to pay for their habit and the commission of an offence while on bail are aggravating factors.

Mitigating factors include the low monetary value of goods; the fact that the offence was a one-off offence committed by an otherwise honest defendant; the fact that there was little no benefit to the defendant and the fact that voluntary restitution had been made. The Court also agreed that other mitigating factors included personal mitigation; ready co-operation with the police and a timely plea of guilty. Previous convictions were relevant. In *Wilson* (1980) 2 Cr.App.R.(S.) 196, the offender, a man of good character pleaded guilty to handling stolen caravans worth some £4,500. The Court of Appeal stated that imprisonment was the only way of dealing with these offences since the property was of considerable value. However, for a man in the appellant's position a short immediate sentence of imprisonment, perhaps coupled with a fine, was likely to have the deterrent effect desired. The offender was sentenced to two months' imprisonment. See also *Raper* [2003] EWCA Crim 1860.

In *Allan* [2007] EWCA Crim 2459, CA, the Court of Appeal held that a sentence of 22 weeks' imprisonment imposed on a 19-year-old offender following his guilty plea to an offence of handling stolen goods was manifestly excessive. The appellant had given a co-defendant, who worked for the DVLA, details of a stolen car; the co-defendant then provided the appellant with a tax disc for the vehicle. The appellant initially pleaded not guilty, but then changed his plea on the basis that he had not kept the tax disc for himself. The appellant was aged 19 at the time of the offence, in full-time work and at the time of sentencing, had one previous conviction for an offence of theft committed after the instant offence. The sentencing judge accepted the offence was an isolated incident, treated the appellant as of good character, accepted that the guilty plea was entered as soon as the Crown indicated it would be satisfactory, and took the appellant's employment into account. However, the judge did not agree that the appellant was several steps back from handling the car himself, and considered that he had pleaded "at the court door". He found the matter so serious that only a custodial sentence was justified and passed a sentence of 22 weeks' imprisonment. The appellant submitted that the sentence was manifestly excessive. The single aggravating factor was that the tax disc was for a stolen car of high value that had been taken from outside a dwelling. Against this there were a series of mitigating factors: the appellant was far removed from any direct involvement in the theft of the car and had made no financial gain from receiving the tax disc. The Court of Appeal held that custody could and should have been avoided, and that the mitigating factors justified a non-custodial disposal. As the appellant had served the equivalent of 50 days of his sentence, the custodial sentence was replaced with a conditional discharge of two years.

L. RETAINING A WRONGFUL CREDIT

(1) Definition

Theft Act 1968, s.24A

Dishonestly retaining a wrongful credit

24A.—(1) A person is guilty of an offence if— **15–85**

(a) a wrongful credit has been made to an account kept by him or in respect of which he has any right or interest;

(b) he knows or believes that the credit is wrongful; and

(c) he dishonestly fails to take such steps as are reasonable in the circumstances to secure that the credit is cancelled.

(2) References to a credit are to a credit of an amount of money.

(2A) A credit to an account is wrongful to the extent that it derives from—

(a) theft;

(b) blackmail;

(c) fraud (contrary to section 1 of the *Fraud Act* 2006); or

(d) stolen goods.

(5) In determining whether a credit to an account is wrongful, it is immaterial (in particular) whether the account is overdrawn before or after the credit is made.

(6) A person guilty of an offence under this section shall be liable on conviction on indictment to imprisonment for a term not exceeding ten years.

(7) Subsection (8) below applies for purposes of provisions of this Act relating to stolen goods (including subsection (2A) above).

(8) References to stolen goods include money which is dishonestly withdrawn from an account to which a wrongful credit has been made, but only to the extent that the money derives from the credit.

(9) "Account" means an account kept with—

(a) a bank;

(b) a person carrying on a business which falls within subsection (10) below; or

(c) an issuer of electronic money (as defined for the purposes of Part 2 of the *Financial Services and Markets Act* 2000).

(10) A business falls within this subsection if—

(a) in the course of the business money received by way of deposit is lent to others; or

(b) any other activity of the business is financed, wholly or to any material extent, out of the capital of or the interest on money received by way of deposit.

(11) References in subsection (10) above to a deposit must be read with—

(a) section 22 of the *Financial Services and Markets Act* 2000;

(b) any relevant order under that section; and

(c) Schedule 2 to that Act;

but any restriction on the meaning of deposit which arises from the identity of the person making it is to be disregarded.

(12) For the purposes of subsection (10) above—

(a) all the activities which a person carries on by way of business shall be regarded as a single business carried on by him; and

(b) "money" includes money expressed in a currency other than sterling.

[This section is printed as amended by the *Fraud Act* 2006, Sched. 1, para. 7.]

(2) Allocation

15–86 This offence is triable either way (*MCA* 1980, s.17 and Sched. 1, para. 28).

(3) Elements of the offence

15–87 The prosecution must prove that:

— a wrongful credit was made to an account kept by the defendant, or to an account in respect of which he had any right or interest, and

— the defendant knew or believed that the credit was wrongful, and

— he dishonestly,

— failed to take such steps as were reasonable in the circumstances to secure that the credit is cancelled.

Theft Act 1968, s.24A(2)–(9)

Dishonestly retaining a wrongful credit

15–88 **24A.**—(2) References to a credit are to a credit of an amount of money.

(3) A credit to an account is wrongful if it is the credit side of a money transfer obtained contrary to section 15A of this Act.

(4) A credit to an account is also wrongful to the extent that it derives from—

(a) theft;

(b) an offence under section 15A of this Act;

(c) blackmail; or

(d) stolen goods.

(5) In determining whether a credit to an account is wrongful, it is immaterial (in particular) whether the account is overdrawn before or after the credit is made.

(6) A person guilty of an offence under this section shall be liable on conviction on indictment to imprisonment for a term not exceeding ten years.

(7) Subsection (8) below applies for purposes of provisions of this Act relating to stolen goods (including subsection (4) above).

(8) References to stolen goods include money which is dishonestly withdrawn from an account to which a wrongful credit has been made, but only to the extent that the money derives from the credit.

(9) In this section "account" and "money" shall be construed in accordance with section 15B of this Act.

(4) Sentence

When tried summarily, the maximum penalty is six months' imprisonment, a fine not exceeding the statutory maximum or both. After commencement of the relevant provisions, the maximum custodial sentence in a magistrates' court will be 12 months' imprisonment: *Criminal Justice Act* 2003, ss.154 and 282. **15–89**

For general sentencing factors set out in the *Magistrates' Court Sentencing Guidelines* (2008) see Ch. 23, *post*.

Part III

M. ADVERTISING REWARDS FOR RETURN OF GOODS STOLEN OR LOST

(1) Definition

Theft Act 1968, s.23

Advertising rewards for return of goods stolen or lost

23. Where any public advertisement of a reward for the return of any goods which have been stolen or lost uses any words to the effect that no questions will be asked, or that the person producing the goods will be safe from apprehension or inquiry, or that any money paid for the purchase of the goods or advanced by way of loan on them will be repaid, the person advertising the reward and any person who prints or publishes the advertisement shall on summary conviction be liable to a fine not exceeding level 3 on the standard scale. **15–90**

(2) Allocation

This offence is triable summarily only: *Theft Act* 1968, s.23. **15–91**

(3) Elements of the offence

The prosecution must prove that: **15–92**

— the defendant advertised a reward for the return of any goods stolen or lost, or printed or published such an advertisement, and

— the advertisement used words to the effect that no questions will be asked, or that the person producing the goods will be safe from apprehension or inquiry or that any money paid for the purchase of the goods or advanced by way of loan will be repaid.

The offence is one of strict liability; publishing an advert for the return of goods for a reward stating that no questions would be asked will establish the offence. *Mens rea* does not need to be proved: *Denham v. Scott* (1983) 77 Cr.App.R. 210. **15–93**

(4) Sentence

15–94 The maximum penalty for this offence is a fine not exceeding level three on the standard scale: *Theft Act* 1968, s.23.

For general sentencing factors set out in the *Magistrates' Court Sentencing Guidelines* (2008) see Ch. 23, *post*.

N. GOING EQUIPPED

(1) Definition

Theft Act 1968, s.25(1), (3)–(5)

Going equipped for stealing, etc.

15–95 **25.**—(1) A person shall be guilty of an offence if, when not at his place of abode, he has with him any article for use in the course of or in connection with any burglary, theft or cheat.

(2) [indictment only]

(3) Where a person is charged with an offence under this section, proof that he had with him any article made or adapted for use in committing a burglary, theft or cheat shall be evidence that he had it with him for such use.

(5) For purposes of this section an offence under section 12(1) of this Act of taking a conveyance shall be treated as theft.

[This section is printed as amended by the *Fraud Act* 2006, Sched. 1, para. 8.]

(2) Allocation

15–96 This offence is triable either way: *MCA* 1980, s.17 and Sched. 1, para. 28.

(3) Elements of the offence

15–97 The prosecution must prove that:

— the defendant was not at his place of abode; and

— he had with him any article for use in the course of or in connection with any burglary or theft.

(4) Sentence

15–98 When tried summarily, the maximum penalty for this offence is six months' imprisonment, a fine not exceeding the statutory maximum or both. After commencement of the relevant provisions, the maximum custodial sentence in a magistrates' court will be 12 months' imprisonment: *Criminal Justice Act* 2003, ss.154 and 282. For general sentencing factors set out in the *Magistrates' Court Sentencing Guidelines* (2008) see Ch. 23, *post*. The *Magistrates Courts Sentencing Guidelines* (2008) provide that the court may disqualify if offence committed with reference to theft or taking of motor vehicles (no points available).

STARTING POINT AND SENTENCING RANGES

(BASED ON A FIRST TIME OFFENDER AFTER TRIAL)

Examples of nature of activity	Starting Point	Range
Possession of items for theft from shop or of vehicle	Medium level community order	Band C fine to high level community order
Possession of items for burglary, robbery	High level community order	Medium level community order to Crown Court

AGGRAVATING AND MITIGATING FACTORS

Factors indicating higher culpability	
1. Circumstances suggest offender equipped for particularly serious offence	
2. Items to conceal identity	

In *Ferry and Wynn* [1997] 2 Cr.App.R.(S.) 42 a sentence of 12 months' imprisonment for going equipped to steal from telephone boxes was upheld by the Court of Appeal. The offenders were in possession of a cordless drill and other tools, and a map indicating the location of other telephone boxes. A custodial sentence was held to be justified as the offences involved a sustained enterprise to break into telephone boxes in rural areas, and could not be compared with a single attack on a telephone box in an urban area.

O. MAKING OFF WITHOUT PAYMENT

(1) Definition

Theft Act 1978, s.3

Making off without payment

3.—(1) Subject to subsection (3) below, a person who, knowing that payment on the spot for any goods supplied or service done is required or expected from him, dishonestly makes off without having paid as required or expected and with intent to avoid payment of the amount due shall be guilty of an offence. **15–99**

(2) For purposes of this section "payment on the spot" includes payment at the time of collecting goods on which work has been done or in respect of which service has been provided.

(3) Subsection (1) above shall not apply where the supply of the goods or the doing of the service is contrary to law, or where the service done is such that payment is not legally enforceable.

[This section is printed as amended by the *Serious Organised Crime and Police Act* 2005, Sched. 17, para. 1.]

(2) Allocation

15–100 This offence is triable either way (*Theft Act* 1978, s.4(1)). For guidance as to when the offence is appropriately tried summarily, see *ante*.

(3) Elements of the offence

15–101 The prosecution must prove that:

— the defendant knew that payment on the spot for any goods supplied or service done was required or expected of him, and
— he dishonestly,
— made off without having paid as required or expected,
— with intent to avoid payment of the amount due.

"Making off" involves a departure from the spot where payment was required: *Brooks* 76 Cr.App.R. 66, CA. In *Allen* (1985) A.C. 1029, HL it was held that the following must be proved to secure a conviction under s.3(1) that the defendant in fact made off without making payment on the spot; (2) the following mental elements—(a) knowledge that payment on the spot was required or expected of him; and (b) dishonesty; and (c) intent to avoid payment of the amount due.

(4) Sentence

15–102 When tried summarily, the maximum penalty is six months' imprisonment, a fine not exceeding the statutory maximum or both. After commencement of the relevant provisions, the maximum custodial sentence in a magistrates' court will be 12 months' imprisonment: *Criminal Justice Act* 2003, ss.154 and 282.

For general sentencing factors set out in the *Magistrates' Court Sentencing Guidelines* (2008) see Ch. 23, *post*. The *Magistrates Courts Sentencing Guidelines* (2008) provide the following key factors a court must consider when sentencing for this offence:

Key factors

15–103 (a) The starting points and sentencing ranges in this guideline are based on the assumption that the offender was motivated by greed or a desire to live beyond his or her means. To avoid double counting, such a motivation should not be treated as a factor that increases culpability.

(b) When assessing the harm caused by this offence, the starting point should be the loss suffered by the victim. In general, the greater the loss, the more serious the offence. However, the monetary value of the loss may not reflect the full extent of the harm caused by the offence. The court should also take into account the impact of the offence on the victim, any harm to persons other than the direct victim, and any harm in the form of public alarm or erosion of public confidence.

(c) The following matters of personal mitigation may be relevant to this offence:

(i) *Offender motivated by desperation or need*
The fact that an offence has been committed in desperation or need arising from particular hardship may count as personal mitigation in exceptional circumstances.

(ii) *Voluntary return of stolen property*
Whether and the degree to which the return of stolen property constitutes a matter of personal mitigation will depend on an assessment of the

circumstances and, in particular, the voluntariness and timeliness of the return.

(iii) *Impact on sentence of offender's dependency*
Many offenders convicted of acquisitive crimes are motivated by an addiction, often to drugs, alcohol or gambling. This does not mitigate the seriousness of the offence, but an offender's dependency may properly influence the type of sentence imposed. In particular, it may sometimes be appropriate to impose a drug rehabilitation requirement or an alcohol treatment requirement as part of a community order or a suspended sentence order in an attempt to break the cycle of addiction and offending, even if an immediate custodial sentence would otherwise be warranted.

STARTING POINT AND SENTENCING RANGES

(BASED ON A FIRST TIME OFFENDER AFTER TRIAL)

Examples of nature of activity	**Starting Point**	**Range**
Single offence committed by an offender acting alone with evidence of little or no planning, goods or services worth less than £200	Band C fine	Band A fine to high level community order
Offence displaying one or more of the following: — offender acting in unison with others — evidence of planning — offence part of a 'spree' — intimidation of victim — goods or services worth £200 or more	Medium level community order	Low level community order to 12 weeks custody

In *Foster* (1994) 15 Cr.App.R.(S.) 340 a sentence of three months' imprisonment was upheld for making off without payment of taxi fares of between £37 and £63. The appellant had previous convictions for conspiracy to burgle and theft, and was subject to a suspended sentence of nine months at the time of the offences. That sentence was activated consecutively, meaning that the total sentence was one of 12 months' imprisonment. **15–104**

II. OFFENCES UNDER THE FRAUD ACT 2006

Introduction

15–105 On October 13, 2009, the Sentencing Guidelines Council published a Final Guideline on *Sentencing for Fraud – statutory offences*. For the guideline in full, see *http://www.sentencing-guidelines.gov.uk/docs/sentencing_for_fraud_statutory_offences.pdf*.

The introduction to the guideline states that since many of the fraud offences are defined broadly (in order to encapsulate a wide range of behaviour), some types of fraudulent activity are capable of leading to conviction for more than one offence; accordingly, the guidelines focus on the type of fraud, rather than the specific conviction offence, in order to establish appropriate sentence levels which take account of the inter-relationship between the offences. The offences are grouped by type as follows:

Confidence fraud

Fraud Act 2006, s.1

Theft Act 1968, s.17

Possessing, making or supplying articles for use in fraud

Fraud Act 2006, ss.1, 6 and 7

Banking and insurance fraud, and obtaining credit through fraud

Fraud Act 2006, s.1

Theft Act 1968, s.17

Benefit fraud

Fraud Act 2006, s.1

Theft Act 1968, s.17

Tax Credits Act 2002, s.35

Social Security Administration Act 1992, ss.111A(1), 111(1A), 111(1B), 111(1D) and 111(1E)

Revenue fraud (against HM Revenue and Customs)

Fraud Act 2006, s.1

Theft Act 1968, s.17

Value Added Tax Act 1994, ss.72(1), 72(3), and 72(8)

Finance Act 2000, s.144

Customs and Excise Management Act 1979, ss.170(1)(a)(i) and (ii), 170(1)(b), 170(2)(a), 170B, 50(1)(a), and 50(2)

The guideline states that the offence of obtaining services dishonestly (contrary to s.11 of the *Fraud Act* 2006) may be committed in circumstances that otherwise could be charged as an offence contrary to s.1 of the Act or may be more akin to the offence under the *Theft Act*. For this reason, it has not been included specifically within any of these guidelines, and one of the following approaches should be used:

1. Where it involves conduct which can be characterised as a fraud offence (such as obtaining credit through fraud or payment card fraud), the court should apply the guideline for the relevant type of fraud; or
2. Where the conduct could be characterised as *making off without payment* (that is, where an offender, knowing that payment on the spot for any goods supplied or service done is required or expected, dishonestly makes off without having paid and with intent to avoid payment), the guideline for that offence in the *Magistrates' Court Sentencing Guidelines* (2008) should be used.

The guideline states that the primary consideration when sentencing fraud offences is the seriousness of the offending behaviour. Sentencers must also have regard to the five purposes of sentencing set out in s.142(1) of the *Criminal Justice Act* 2003; as a general principle, the approach to sentencing types of fraud offence should be the same, regardless of the context within which the offence was committed.

The approach to sentencing, starting points and ranges takes account of the other sanctions and ancillary orders likely to be applied (some of which are mandatory and others discretionary), which may have a significant impact on an offender. The guideline applies to the sentencing of adult offenders only; separate legislative provisions and sentencing principles apply to young offenders.

Assessing seriousness

The court must consider the offender's culpability in committing the offence and any harm that the offence caused, was intended to cause, or might foreseeably have caused. Key considerations are the degree of planning, the determination with which the offender carried out the offence and the value of the money or property involved.

Culpability and harm

The guideline refers to the four levels of culpability set out in the *Overarching Principles: Seriousness* guideline and states that it is a general feature of fraud offences that an offender intended to bring about a gain (whether for the offender or for another person) or to cause a loss, or risk of loss, to another (except VAT fraud, which can be committed recklessly). Fraud offences will therefore generally involve the highest level of culpability. Within that level, culpability will vary according to the offender's motivation, whether the offence was planned or spontaneous and whether the offender was in a position of trust.

Where the offending involves a number of people acting co-operatively, the offence of fraud will be aggravated as it indicates planning or professional activity; it may also increase the degree of loss caused or intended. As a result, it is likely to cause an offence to be in a higher level of seriousness. The role of each offender will therefore be important in determining movement above or below the starting point within the range applicable to that level (see aggravating and mitigating factors below).

The guideline states that fraud is not a victimless crime.

In assessing the harm caused by fraud offences, the primary consideration is the loss to the victim or to the community at large. In some fraud cases, the harm that results from an offence may be greater than the harm intended by the offender. In others, the offender may have intended more harm than actually results. In these situations, the harm caused by the offence should be judged in light of the offender's culpability.

In general terms, the greater the loss, the more serious will be the offence. However, the financial value of the loss may not reflect the full extent of the harm caused by the offence. The court should also take into account:

(a) the impact of the offence on the victim
(b) harm to persons other than the direct victim
(c) erosion of public confidence
(d) any physical harm or risk of physical harm to the direct victim or another person
(e) difference between loss intended and resulting
(f) legitimate entitlement to part or all of the amount obtained

Aggravating factors

Factors indicating higher culpability

Planning of an offence
An intention to commit more serious harm than actually resulted from the offence (including any physical harm or risk of physical harm)
Offenders operating in groups or gangs
"Professional offending"
High level of profit from the offence
An attempt to conceal or dispose of evidence

Deliberate targeting of vulnerable victim(s)
Abuse of a position of trust

Factors indicating a more than usually serious degree of harm

Multiple victims
Victim is particularly vulnerable
High value (including sentimental value) of property to the victim, or substantial consequential loss

The Council identified four factors that are particularly relevant to this type of offending behaviour:

(a) Number involved in the offence and role of offender
(b) Offending carried out over a significant period of time
(c) Use of another person's identity
(d) Offence has a lasting effect on the victim

Mitigating factors

Factors indicating significantly lower culpability:

Mental illness or disability
Youth or age, where it affects the responsibility of the individual defendant
The fact that the offender played only a minor role in the offence

The Council identified three mitigating factors that are particularly relevant to this type of offending:

(a) Peripheral involvement
(b) Behaviour not fraudulent from the outset
(c) Misleading or incomplete advice

Personal mitigation

(a) Voluntary cessation of offending
(b) Complete and unprompted disclosure of the extent of the fraud
(c) Voluntary restitution
(d) Financial pressure

Combining custodial sentences and fines

The guideline states that the issue of whether to impose a fine alongside a custodial sentence may arise when sentencing for fraud offences. If a fine is imposed, further issues arise concerning the impact of the fine on the length of the custodial sentence. In the light of additional powers relating to confiscation and to seizure of assets and the proceeds of crime, a court normally should not impose a fine alongside a custodial sentence. However, exceptionally, it may be appropriate to impose a fine in addition to a custodial sentence where:

(i) a confiscation order is not being contemplated; and
(ii) there is no obvious victim to whom compensation can be awarded; and
(iii) the offender has, or will have, resources from which a fine can be paid.

A court must ensure that the overall sentence remains commensurate with the seriousness of the offence and that the size of the fine does not enable wealthier offenders to "buy themselves out of custody".

Ancillary and other orders

Orders relating to property that either must be considered or are most likely to be imposed in relation to fraud offences are:

(i) Compensation order
(ii) Confiscation order
(iii) Deprivation order
(iv) Restitution order
(v) Disqualification from acting as a company director
(vi) Disqualification from driving
(vii) Financial reporting order
(viii) Serious crime prevention order

Guidelines and approach to sentencing

The guidelines are based on types of conduct reflecting common fraudulent behaviour. Confidence frauds are dealt with as a separate category as is the possession, making or supply of articles for use in fraud.

A further group includes those offences committed against an organisation in either the private or public sector; most commonly, in the public sector these will arise in relation to the tax and benefit system and, in the private sector, in relation to banking and insurance.

Although not intended to be exclusive, each guideline includes examples of the fraudulent activity likely to have taken place. In addition, the guideline refers to the offences under which the activity might be charged and the related legislative provisions.

The starting points and sentencing ranges for banking and insurance fraud, for benefit fraud, and for fraud against HM Revenue and Customs (revenue fraud) are the same since the seriousness of all offences of organisational fraud derives from the extent of the fraudulent activity (culpability) and the financial loss caused or likely to be caused (harm).

Separate guidelines are provided for banking, insurance and credit fraud, benefit fraud and revenue fraud, allowing greater detail of the types of activity and the aggravating or mitigating factors likely to be particularly relevant to be included.

In relation to these types of fraud, the Council considers that there will be few cases where £100,000 or more is obtained in a single fraudulent transaction. Similarly, it is likely that there will be few cases where less than £20,000 is obtained in a professionally planned fraud carried out over a significant period of time or multiple professionally planned frauds. Accordingly, the Council has not proposed starting points and ranges for such frauds. In this chapter, the guidelines on each type of fraud will be considered alongside the individual offences to which they relate.

(1) Definition

Fraud Act 2006, s.1

Fraud

1—(1) A person is guilty of fraud if he is in breach of any of the sections listed in subsection (2) (which provide for different ways of committing the offence). **15–106**

(2) The sections are—

(a) section 2 (fraud by false representation),

(b) section 3 (fraud by failing to disclose information), and

(c) section 4 (fraud by abuse of position).

(3) A person who is guilty of fraud is liable—

(a) on summary conviction, to imprisonment for a term not exceeding 12 months or to a fine not exceeding the statutory maximum (or to both);

(b) on conviction on indictment, to imprisonment for a term not exceeding 10 years or to a fine (or to both).

(4) Subsection (3)(a) applies in relation to Northern Ireland as if the reference to 12 months were a reference to 6 months.

This offence can be committed in any one of three different ways.

B. FRAUD BY FALSE REPRESENTATION

(1) Definition

Fraud Act 2006, s.2

Fraud by false representation

15–107 **2**—(1) A person is in breach of this section if he—

(a) dishonestly makes a false representation, and

(b) intends, by making the representation—

(i) to make a gain for himself or another, or

(ii) to cause loss to another or to expose another to a risk of loss.

(2) A representation is false if—

(a) it is untrue or misleading, and

(b) the person making it knows that it is, or might be, untrue or misleading.

(3) "Representation" means any representation as to fact or law, including a representation as to the state of mind of—

(a) the person making the representation, or

(b) any other person.

(4) A representation may be express or implied.

(5) For the purposes of this section a representation may be regarded as made if it (or anything implying it) is submitted in any form to any system or device designed to receive, convey or respond to communications (with or without human intervention).

(2) Allocation

15–108 The offence is triable either way.

(3) Elements of the offence

15–109 "Dishonestly" will presumably be defined as before: see *Feely* [1973] Q.B. 530 and *Ghosh* [1982] Q.B. 1053 (at § 15–4.).

D must make the representation with the intention of making a gain or causing loss or risk of loss to another. The gain or loss does not actually have to take place. Gain and loss are defined in s.5, *post*.

An offence of fraud is committed where an individual has another person impersonate them for the purposes of sitting a theory driving test: *Idrees v DPP* [2011] EWHC 624 (Admin).

Fraud Act 2006, s.5

"Gain" and "loss"

15–110 **5**—(1) The references to gain and loss in sections 2 to 4 are to be read in accordance with this section.

(2) "Gain" and "loss"—

(a) extend only to gain or loss in money or other property;

(b) include any such gain or loss whether temporary or permanent;

and "property" means any property whether real or personal (including things in action and other intangible property).

(3) "Gain" includes a gain by keeping what one has, as well as a gain by getting what one does not have.

(4) "Loss" includes a loss by not getting what one might get, as well as a loss by parting with what one has.

15–111 "False": see s.2(2). The representation must be untrue or misleading, and D must know that it is or might be untrue or misleading.

"Representation": see s.2(3). A representation is defined as false if it is untrue or misleading and the person making it knows that it is, or might be, untrue or misleading.

It means any representation as to fact or law, including a representation as to a person's state of mind. It may be express or implied. It can be stated in words or communicated by conduct. There is no limitation on the way in which the representation must be expressed. So it could be written or spoken or posted on a website. A representation may also be implied by conduct. Misusing a credit card is clearly caught: by tendering the card, D is falsely representing that he has the authority to use it for that transaction, whether or not the person accepting the card for payment is deceived by the representation. The *Explanatory Notes* state that this offence would also be committed by someone who engages in "phishing": *i.e.* where a person disseminates an email to large groups of people falsely representing that the email has been sent by a legitimate financial institution. The email prompts the reader to provide information such as credit card and bank account numbers so that the "phisher" can gain access to others' assets. The main purpose of s.2(5) is "to ensure that fraud can be committed where a person makes a representation to a machine and a response can be produced without any need for human involvement" (*e.g.* where a person enters a number into a "CHIP and PIN" machine). The Law Commission had concluded that, although it was not clear whether a representation could be made to a machine, such a provision was unnecessary (see para. 8.4 of their report). But s.2(5) is expressed in "fairly general terms", we are told, because it would be artificial to distinguish situations involving modern technology, where it is doubtful whether there has been a "representation", because the only recipient of the false statement is a machine or a piece of software, from other situations not involving modern technology where a false statement is submitted to a system for dealing with communications but is not in fact communicated to a human being, (*e.g.* postal or messenger systems).

(4) Sentence

On summary conviction, the maximum penalty for this offence is imprisonment for a term not exceeding 12 months or a fine not exceeding the statutory maximum (or both). But Sched. 2, para. 1 provides for 12 months to be 6 months pending the increase in sentencing powers in a magistrates' court (section 154 of the *Criminal Justice Act* 2003 has yet to be implemented). **15–112**

The Sentencing Guidelines Council guideline on *Sentencing for Fraud – statutory offences* states that frauds under s.1 of the *Fraud Act* 2006 may be sentenced as confidence frauds; frauds involving the possession, making or supplying articles for use in fraud; banking and insurance fraud, and obtaining credit through fraud; benefit fraud and revenue fraud.

CONFIDENCE FRAUD

Factors to take into consideration

This type of offending involves a victim transferring money and/or property as a result of being deceived or misled by the offender. An example of a simple confidence fraud is a person claiming to be collecting money for charity when, in fact, he or she intends to keep the money. Other examples of common confidence frauds are:

Advance fee frauds—Common advance fee frauds include *lottery/prize draw scams* and *foreign money-making frauds*.

Fraudulent sales of goods and services—These include goods that are never received by the purchaser or are worth less than the seller represents; services that are unnecessary, overpriced or not performed; and investments that are never obtained for the investor or are worth less than the seller represents.

A factor common to many confidence frauds is that the offender targets a vulnerable victim; it is therefore a determinant of seriousness for this type of fraud. An offender is more culpable if he or she deliberately targets a victim who is vulnerable as a result of old age, youth or disability and there is a more than usually serious degree of harm where the victim is particularly vulnerable.

Some victims of advance fee frauds may have personalities which make them "vulnerable in a way and to a degree not typical of the general population" because they fall for scams many times.

As the determinants of seriousness include the "value of property or consequential loss involved", the table provides both a fixed amount (on which the starting point is based) and a band (on which the sentencing range is based). Where the value is larger or smaller than the amount on which the starting point is based, this should lead to upward or downward movement as appropriate. Where the amount the offender intended to obtain cannot be established, the appropriate measure will be the amount that was likely to be achieved in all the circumstances.

A further determinant of seriousness is whether the fraud was a single fraudulent transaction or a multiple fraud. Most confidence frauds will by their nature involve many actual or potential victims and multiple transactions and should be regarded as multiple fraud.

Confidence fraud

Fraud: *Fraud Act* 2006 (s.1)
False accounting: *Theft Act* 1968 (s.17)
Maximum penalty: Fraud, 10 years custody
False accounting, 7 years custody

	Value of property or consequential loss			
Nature of offence	**£500,000 or more Starting point based on: £750,000***	**£100000 or more and less than £500,000 Starting point based on: £300,000***	**£20,000 or more and less than £100,000 Starting point based on: £60,000***	**Less than £20,000 Starting point based on: £10,000***
Large scale advance fee fraud **or** other confidence fraud involving the deliberate targeting of a large number of vulnerable victims	**Starting point**: 6 years custody **Range:** 5-8 years custody	Starting point: 5 years custody **Range**: 4-7 years Custody	**Starting point:** 4 years custody **Range:** 3-6 years custody	**Starting point:** 3 years custody **Range**: 2-5 years custody
Lower scale advance fee fraud **or** other confidence fraud characterised by a degree of planning and/or multiple transactions	**Starting point:** 5 years custody **Range**: 4-7 years custody	**Starting point**: 4 years custody **Range**: 3-6 years custody	**Starting point:** 3 years custody **Range:** 2-5 years custody	**Starting point**: 18 months custody **Range:** 26 weeks-3 years Custody

Single fraudulent transaction confidence fraud involving targeting of a vulnerable victim			**Starting point:** 26 weeks custody **Range:** Community order (HIGH)-18 months custody	**Starting point:** 6 weeks custody **Range:** Community order (MEDIUM)-26 weeks custody
Single fraudulent transaction confidence fraud not targeting a vulnerable victim, and involving no or limited planning			**Starting point:** 12 weeks custody **Range:** Community order (MEDIUM)-36 weeks custody	**Starting point:** Community order (MEDIUM) Range:Fine-6 weeks custody

* Where the actual amount is greater or smaller than the figure on which the starting point is based, that is likely to be one of the factors that will move the sentence within the range.

Additional aggravating factors	**Additional mitigating factors**
1. Number involved in the offence and role of the offender	1. Peripheral involvement
2. Offending carried out over a significant period of time	2. Behaviour not fraudulent from the outset
3. Use of another person's identity	3. Misleading or inaccurate advice
4. Offence has a lasting effect on the victim	

The presence of one or more aggravating factors may indicate a more severe sentence within the suggested range while the presence of one or more mitigating factors may indicate a less severe sentence within the suggested range.

The presence of aggravating or mitigating factors of exceptional significance may indicate that the case should move to a higher or lower level of seriousness.

POSSESSING, MAKING OR SUPPLYING ARTICLES FOR USE IN FRAUD

There are many ways in which offenders may commit this group of offences. "Articles" will include any electronic programs or data stored electronically.

As lists of credit card and bank account details constitute "articles", the making of such lists through certain electronic programmes, which contravenes s.1 of the *Fraud Act* 2006, is also criminalised by s.7 of the same Act. The Council considers that carrying out the following activities should be treated as making articles for use in fraud and sentenced using this guideline, regardless of whether the offence is charged under s.1 or s.7:

> *Phishing* —where an offender sends an email purporting to come from a financial institution, which asks victims to follow a hyperlink to a (false) website and induces them to enter their card or account details;
>
> *Vishing* —where an offender uses an automated telephone system, purporting to be the telephone system of a financial institution, to induce victims to disclose their card or account details;
>
> *Pharming* —where victims intend to visit a financial institution's website but are

redirected to the offender's website (which purports to be the financial institution's website) and induced to enter their card or account details; and

Use of a "Trojan"—where an offender installs a virus on victims' computers to gain access to their card or account details. Often the offender will send an email inducing victims to visit a website, where the virus is automatically downloaded onto their computers.

Making, adapting, supplying or offering to supply computer programmes, emails or websites for the above activities amounts to an offence under s.7 of the *Fraud Act* 2006.

Offenders who possess, make or supply articles for use in fraud intend their actions to lead to a fraud. Such offenders therefore have the highest level of culpability.

There are three types of activity relating to articles for use in fraud: making or adapting, supplying or offering to supply and possession. The guideline does not distinguish between the first two categories; they carry the same maximum penalty and, depending on the sophistication and planning involved and the harm resulting from an offence, they may be equally serious.

The three offences in this group all involve an element of planning (whether by the offender or by another person); the planning of an offence has been identified by the Council as a factor indicating a higher level of culpability and the proposed starting points incorporate this aggravating factor.

In relation to harm, the value of the fraud (either that intended by the offender where that can be ascertained, or that which was likely to be achieved) is not a determinant of seriousness for these offences in the way that it is for other offences of fraud. However, it is a factor that should be taken into account in determining the appropriate sentence within the sentencing range.

Possessing, making or supplying articles for use in fraud

Possession of articles for use in frauds: *Fraud Act* 2006 (s.6)

Making or supplying articles for use in frauds: *Fraud Act* 2006 (s.7)

Fraud: *Fraud Act* 2006 (s.1)

Maximum penalty: Possession of articles for use in frauds, 5 years custody. For both other offences, 10 years custody.

	Type of offence	
Nature of offence	Making or adapting (ss.1 or 7) **or** Supplying or offering to supply (s.7)	Possessing (s.6)
Article(s) intended for use in an extensive and skilfully planned fraud	**Starting point:** 4 years custody **Range:** 2-7 years custody	**Starting point:** 36 weeks custody **Range:** 6 weeks–2 years custody
Article(s) intended for use in a less extensive and less skilfully planned fraud	**Starting point:** 26 weeks custody **Range:** Community order (HIGH)-2 years custody	**Starting point:** Community order (MEDIUM) **Range:** Community order (LOW)-26 weeks custody

Additional aggravating factors	**Additional mitigating factors**
1. Number involved in the offence and role of the offender	1. Peripheral involvement
2. Offending carried out over a significant period of time	
3. Use of another person's identity	

4. Offence has a lasting effect on the victim	

The presence of one or more aggravating factors may indicate a more severe sentence within the suggested range while the presence of one or more mitigating factors may indicate a less severe sentence within the suggested range.

The presence of aggravating or mitigating factors of exceptional significance may indicate that the case should move to a higher or lower level of seriousness.

BANKING AND INSURANCE FRAUD, AND OBTAINING CREDIT THROUGH FRAUD

Types of offending behaviour include:

Payment card and bank account fraud—Frauds involving the use of payment cards and bank accounts include use of another person's card, cloning another person's card, taking over or sending instructions relating to another person's bank or card account, and use of another person's cheque.

Insurance fraud —Fraudulent claims by or against the insurer (claims that are entirely fraudulent and those that are exaggerated through either claiming for injury, loss or damage that did not occur or increasing the value of a genuine claim for injury, loss or damage) and supplier fraud (whereby builders, motor repairers and other trades-people engaged by insurers to repair insured property charge for work that they have not done or inflate the cost of their work).

Obtaining credit through fraud —Obtaining credit through fraud includes the fraudulent obtaining of mortgages, loans, interest free credit, in-store credit, goods or services on a "buy now pay later" basis, car finance, credit cards, store cards, and bank accounts (with overdrafts).

A payment card or bank account fraud is unlikely to be committed in circumstances where the offender's intention was not fraudulent from the outset.

As the determinants of seriousness include the "value of property or consequential loss involved", the table provides both a fixed amount (on which the starting point is based) and a band (on which the sentencing range is based). Where the value is larger or smaller than the amount on which the starting point is based, this should lead to upward or downward movement as appropriate. Where the amount the offender intended to obtain cannot be established, the appropriate measure will be the amount that was likely to be achieved in all the circumstances.

A further determinant of seriousness is whether the fraud was a single fraudulent transaction or a multiple fraud. Where one false declaration or a failure to disclose a change in circumstances results in multiple payments, this should be regarded as multiple fraud.

The maximum penalty for most of the offences covered by this guideline is seven years imprisonment. Where fraud under the 2006 Act is charged and the maximum penalty is 10 years, the proposed sentencing ranges leave headroom for offences involving the most serious frauds to be sentenced outside the range and up to the maximum.

Banking and insurance fraud, and obtaining credit through fraud

Maximum penalty: Fraud (prosecuted under the *Fraud Act* 2006), 10 years custody. For all other offences, seven years custody.

Part III

Nature of offence	£500,000 or more Starting point based on: £750,000*	£100,000 or more and less than £500,000 Starting point based on: £300,000*	£20,000 or more and less than £100,000 Starting point based on: £60,000*	£5,000 or more and less than £20,000 Starting point based on: £12,500*	Less than £5,000 Starting point based on: £2,500*
Fraudulent from the outset, professionally planned **and either** fraud carried out over a significant period of time **or** multiple frauds	**Starting point**: 5 years custody **Range:** 4-7 years custody	**Starting point**: 4 years custody **Range:** 3-5 years custody	**Starting point**: 2 years custody **Range:** 18 months- 3 years custody		
Fraudulent from the outset **and either** fraud carried out over a significant period of time **or** multiple frauds	**Starting point:** 4 years custody **Range:** 3-7 years custody	**Starting point:** 3 years custody **Range:** 2-4 years custody	**Starting point:** 15 months custody **Range:** 18 weeks-30 months custody	**Starting point:** 12 weeks custody **Range:** Community order (HIGH)-12 months custody	**Starting point:** Community order (HIGH) **Range:** Community order (LOW)-6 weeks custody
Not fraudulent from the outset **and either** fraud carried out over a significant period of time **or** multiple frauds	**Starting point:** 3 years custody **Range:** 2-6 years custody	**Starting point**: 2 years custody **Range:** 12 months-3 years custody	**Starting point**: 36 weeks custody **Range:** 12 weeks-18 months custody	**Starting point:** 6 weeks custody **Range:** Community order (MEDIUM)-26 weeks custody	**Starting point:** Community order (MEDIUM) **Range:** Fine-Community order (HIGH)

Single fraudulent transaction, fraudulent from the outset			**Starting point:**26 weeks custody **Range:** 6 weeks-12 months custody	**Starting point:** Community order (HIGH) **Range:** Fine-18 weeks custody	**Starting point:** Community order (LOW) **Range:** Fine-Community order (MEDIUM)
Single fraudulent transaction, not fraudulent from the outset			**Starting point**: 12 weeks custody Range: Community order (MEDIUM) -36 weeks custody	**Starting point:** Community order (MEDIUM) **Range:** Fine-6 weeks custody	**Starting point:** Fine **Range:** Fine-Community order (LOW)

* Where the actual amount is greater or smaller than the figure on which the starting point is based, that is likely to be one of the factors that will move the sentence within the range.

Additional aggravating factors	**Additional mitigating factors**
1. Number involved in the offence and role of the offender	1. Peripheral involvement
2. Use of another person's identity	2. Misleading or incomplete advice

The presence of one or more aggravating factors may indicate a more severe sentence within the suggested range while the presence of one or more mitigating factors may indicate a less severe sentence within the suggested range.

The presence of aggravating or mitigating factors of exceptional significance may indicate that the case should move to a higher or lower level of seriousness.

BENEFIT FRAUD

This guideline is based on an understanding that the prosecutor will generally seek summary trial for appropriate benefit fraud cases involving sums up to £35,000; the Council does not consider that the starting points proposed would interfere with that practice.

The Council's proposals are governed by bands based on amounts of money. The starting point defined at the top of each column relates to the midpoint of each financial band.

As the determinants of seriousness include the "value of property or consequential loss involved", the table provides both a fixed amount (on which the starting point is based) and a band (on which the sentencing range is based). Where the value is larger or smaller than the amount on which the starting point is based, this should lead to upward or downward movement as appropriate. Where the amount the offender intended to obtain cannot be established, the appropriate measure will be the amount that was likely to be achieved in all the circumstances.

A further determinant of seriousness is whether the fraud was a single fraudulent transaction or a multiple fraud. Where one false declaration or a failure to disclose a change in circumstances results in multiple payments, this should be regarded as multiple fraud.

The Council considers it unlikely that more than £100,000 could be obtained in a benefit fraud, unless the offence was professionally planned and either carried out over a significant period of time or through multiple frauds. In addition, it is unlikely that more than £20,000 could be obtained in a single fraudulent transaction benefit fraud. Consequently, the guideline does not provide separately for such circumstances.

The maximum penalty for most of the offences covered by this guideline is seven years imprisonment. Where fraud under the 2006 Act is charged and the maximum penalty is 10 years, the proposed sentencing ranges leave headroom for offences involving the largest scale frauds to be sentenced outside the range and up to the maximum.

Benefit Fraud

Maximum penalty: Fraud (prosecuted under the *Fraud Act* 2006), 10 years custody. For all other offences, seven years custody.

	Amount obtained or intended to be obtained				
Nature of offence	**£500,000 or more Starting point based on: £750,000***	**£100,000 or more and less than £500,000 Starting point based on: £300,000***	**£20,000 or more and less than £100,000 Starting point based on: £60,000***	**£5,000 or more and less than £20,000 Starting point based on: £12,500***	**Less than £5,000 Starting point based on: £2,500***
Fraudulent from the outset, professionally planned **and either** fraud carried out over a significant period of time **or** multiple frauds	**Starting point:** 5 years custody **Range:** 4-7 years custody	**Starting point:** 4 years custody **Range:** 3-5 years custody	**Starting point:** 2 years custody **Range:** 18 months-3 years custody		

Fraudulent from the outset **and either** fraud carried out over a significant period of time **or** multiple frauds	**Starting point:** 4 years custody **Range:** 3-7 years custody	**Starting point:** 3 years custody **Range:** 2-4 years custody	**Starting point:** 15 months custody **Range:** 18 weeks-30 months custody	**Starting point:** 12 weeks custody **Range:** Community order (HIGH)-12 months custody	**Starting point:** Community order (HIGH) **Range:** Community order (LOW)-6 weeks custody
Not fraudulent from the outset **and either** fraud carried out over a significant period of time **or** multiple frauds	**Starting point:** 3 years custody **Range:** 2-6 years custody	Starting point: 2 years custody **Range:** 12 months-3 years custody	**Starting point:** 36 weeks custody **Range:** 12 weeks-18 months custody	**Starting point:** 6 weeks custody **Range:** Community order (MEDIUM) -26 weeks custody	**Starting point:** Community order (MEDIUM) **Range:** Fine-Community order (HIGH)
Single fraudulent transaction, fraudulent from the outset			**Starting point:** 26 weeks custody **Range:** 6 weeks-12 months custody	**Starting point:** Community order (HIGH) **Range:** Fine-18 weeks custody	**Starting point:** Community order (LOW) **Range:** Fine-Community order (MEDIUM)
Single fraudulent transaction, not fraudulent from the outset			**Starting point:** 12 weeks custody **Range:** Community order (MEDIUM) -36 weeks custody	**Starting point:** Community order (MEDIUM) **Range:** Fine-6 weeks custody	**Starting point:** Fine **Range:** Fine-Community order (LOW)

* Where the actual amount is greater or smaller than the figure on which the starting point is based, that is likely to be one of the factors that will move the sentence within the range.

Additional aggravating factors	**Additional mitigating factors**
1. Number involved in the offence and role of the offender	1. Peripheral involvement
2. Use of another person's identity	2. Misleading or incomplete advice

The presence of one or more aggravating factors may indicate a more severe sentence within the suggested range while the presence of one or more mitigating factors may indicate a less severe sentence within the suggested range.

The presence of aggravating or mitigating factors of exceptional significance may indicate that the case should move to a higher or lower level of seriousness.

REVENUE FRAUD (AGAINST HM REVENUE AND CUSTOMS (HMRC))

This type of offending may take many forms, including:

Fraudulent evasion of VAT—this includes situations where a trader does not charge VAT to the customer, situations where a customer pays VAT to the trader but the trader does not pay it to HM Revenue and Customs (HMRC), and so-called "Missing Trader Intra-Community Frauds" (MTIC Frauds) or "Carousel Frauds".

MTIC Frauds— involve traders importing goods from the European Union free from VAT, charging VAT when they sell the goods and then keeping the money rather than paying it to HMRC. Carousel Frauds are MTIC Frauds where the trader sells the goods to another trader who re-exports them and claims back the VAT paid to the first trader from HMRC. Usually the goods are passed along a chain of traders between the missing trader and the broker known as "buffers", in order to disguise the fraudulent nature of the activity. Having been exported by the broker, the goods are typically re-imported by the missing trader and pass through the same circle of transactions again and again in rapid succession.

Fraudulent evasion of income tax—this may be committed by failing to declare earnings in a tax return or by an employer keeping the tax collected from employees rather than paying it to HMRC.

Fraudulent evasion of excise duty—this includes alcohol and tobacco smuggling and the laundering of "red diesel" into diesel engine road fuel.

The Council considers it unlikely that more than £20,000 could be obtained in a single fraudulent transaction against HMRC in circumstances where the offender's intention was not fraudulent from the outset or where the claim was exaggerated. In addition, it is unlikely that more than £100,000 could be obtained in a fraud against HMRC in circumstances where the offender's intention was not fraudulent from the outset.

As in other types of fraud, the fact that the behaviour was not fraudulent from the outset may be a mitigating factor. Although the type of harm is the same since both lead to a loss to HMRC, where payment is sought from HMRC in such circumstances, culpability is likely to be higher. Such offences are therefore likely to be regarded as more serious.

As the determinants of seriousness include the "value of property or consequential loss involved", the table provides both a fixed amount (on which the starting point is based) and a band (on which the sentencing range is based). Where the value is larger or smaller than the amount on which the starting point is based, this should lead to upward or downward movement as appropriate. Where the amount the offender intended to obtain cannot be established, the appropriate measure will be the amount that was likely to be achieved in all the circumstances.

A further determinant of seriousness is whether the fraud was a single fraudulent transaction or a multiple fraud. Where one false declaration or a failure to disclose a change in circumstances results in multiple payments, this should be regarded as multiple fraud.

The maximum penalty for most of the offences covered by this guideline is seven years' imprisonment. Where fraud under the 2006 Act is charged and the maximum penalty is 10 years, the proposed sentencing ranges leave headroom for offences involving multi-million pound frauds to be sentenced outside the range and up to the maximum.

	Amount obtained or intended to be obtained				
Nature of offence	**£500,000 or more Starting point based on: £750,000***	**£100,000 or more and less than £500,000 Starting point based on: £300,000***	**£20,000 or more and less than £100,000 Starting point based on: £60,000***	**£5,000 or more and less than £20,000 Starting point based on: £12,500***	**Less than £5,000 Starting point based on: £2,500***
Fraudulent from the outset, professionally planned **and either** fraud carried out over a significant period of time **or** multiple frauds	**Starting point:** 5 years custody **Range:** 4-7 years custody	**Starting point**: 4 years custody **Range:** 3-5 years custody	**Starting point:** 2 years custody **Range:** 18 months-3 years custody		
Fraudulent from the outset **and either** fraud carried out over a significant period of time **or** multiple frauds	**Starting point:** 4 years custody **Range:** 3-7 years custody	**Starting point:** 3 years custody **Range:** 2-4 years custody	**Starting point:** 15 months custody **Range:** 18 weeks-30 months custody	Starting point: 12 weeks custody **Range:** Community order (HIGH)-12 months custody	**Starting point:** Community order (HIGH) **Range:** Community order (LOW)-6 weeks custody

Part III

Not fraudulent from the outset **and either** fraud carried out over a significant period of time **or** multiple frauds	**Starting point:** 3 years custody **Range**:2-6 years custody	**Starting point:** 2 years custody **Range:**12 months-3 years custody	**Starting point:** 36 weeks custody **Range:** 12 weeks-18 months custody	**Starting point:** 6 weeks custody **Range:** Community order (MEDIUM) -26 weeks custody	**Starting point:** Community order (MEDIUM) **Range:** Fine-Community order (HIGH)
Single fraudulent transaction, fraudulent from the outset			**Starting point:** 26 weeks custody **Range:** 6 weeks-12 months custody	**Starting point:** Community order (HIGH) **Range:** Fine-18 weeks custody	**Starting point:** Community order (LOW) **Range:** Fine-Community order (MEDIUM)
Single fraudulent transaction, not fraudulent from the outset			**Starting point:**12 weeks custody **Range:** Community order (MEDIUM) -36 weeks custody	**Starting point:** Community order (MEDIUM) **Range:** Fine-6 weeks custody	**Starting point:** Fine **Range:** Fine-Community order (LOW)

* Where the actual amount is greater or smaller than the figure on which the starting point is based, that is likely to be one of the factors that will move the sentence within the range.

Additional aggravating factors	Additional mitigating factors
1. Number involved in the offence and role of the offender	1. Peripheral involvement
2. Use of another person's identity	2. Misleading or incomplete advice
3. Making repeated importations, particularly in the face of warnings from the authorities	
4. Dealing in goods with an additional health risk	
5. Disposing of goods to under-aged purchasers	

In *Awosika* [2009] EWCA Crim 625, CA, the appellant had pleaded guilty to an offence of fraud contrary to s.1 of the *Fraud Act* 2006, and was sentenced to 10 months' imprisonment. The appellant was sentenced before the Sentencing Guidelines Council's Final Guideline had been issued. The appellant and a colleague sought to purchase a watch costing £11,480 and attempted to pay with an American Express card in the name of another person. Substituting a sentence of six months' imprisonment, the Court concluded that although an immediate custodial sentence was appropriate, the sentencing judge had adopted too high a starting point. The appellant did have a long record of deception-type offences. The four-year interval between this offence and her previous conviction showed, if anything, the precariousness of any change in her way of life. While there was a degree of pre-planning and the use of another person's identity, this was an attempt to commit a fairly elementary fraud. A sentence of 12 months would have marked the court's duty to honest traders and the appellant's record. Further reduction would be appropriate to reflect recent efforts at reform and the appellant's guilty plea.

In *Peacock* [2009] EWCA Crim 766, CA, the appellant had pleaded guilty to fraud contrary to ss.1 and 2 of the *Fraud Act* 2006 and sentenced to nine months' imprisonment. The appellant was one of a group of people making dishonest representations to the Department of Work and Pensions. He had changed the amount on a cheque for his incapacity benefit from £110.62 to £410.62. The Court held that the sentence of nine months' imprisonment was too long. An appropriate loss of liberty would be three months.

In *Rahman (Mohammed)* [2009] EWCA Crim 1073, CA the appellant appealed against a sentence of 40 weeks' imprisonment suspended for two years following his guilty plea to an offence of fraud. The appellant's co-defendant had been employed by a major chain store and ordered goods from the store using a customer's credit card details. The appellant collected these goods from the store using a false name. Allowing his appeal, the Court stated that the appellant's offence did not involve a breach of trust and did not have the aggravating feature often present in such cases of suspicion being cast on another employee. He had committed a short and unsuccessful act of dishonesty for which a non-custodial sentence was appropriate. The appropriate sentence was a community order with a requirement to perform 125 hours of unpaid work within 12 months.

In *M* [2008] EWCA Crim 2144, CA the appellant, a Zimbabwean national, appealed against a recommendation for their deportation following pleas of guilty to a number of fraud offences. The appellant arrived in the United Kingdom and claimed asylum. This claim and subsequent appeal were refused leaving him unable to formally obtain employment in the UK. He acquired a false passport and used it to try and obtain work through employment agencies and to obtain a bank account and credit. He pleaded guilty to offences of possession of identity documents with intent, fraud by false representation, and possession of articles for the purposes of fraud. A sentence of eight months imprisonment was imposed and the court recommended a deportation order. Allowing his appeal, the Court of Appeal stated the judge had given no reasons why the appellant should be deported. In *Attorney General's Reference (Nos.1 and 6 of 2008)* [2008] EWCA Crim 677 it was deemed absurd to make a deportation order given the policy relating to those whose home country was Zimbabwe. A deportation order was, therefore, neither necessary nor appropriate.

In *McDermott* [2008] EWCA Crim 1713, CA, the appellant appealed against their sentence of 12 months' imprisonment for an offence of fraud by false representation. The appellant had placed two pairs of trousers onto one clothes hanger and taken them into a changing room. He had then returned the hanger to the shop assistant with only one pair of trousers, having placed the other pair in a bag. He later attempted to return and obtain a refund for the hidden pair of trousers. He obtained the refund but was stopped by security guards. Allowing his appeal, the Court considered the facts of the offence, the appellant's plea of guilty and the limited offending (a single offence in respect of which the appellant made no profit) and held the custodial sentence of twelve months was manifestly excessive and substituted a sentence of six months' imprisonment.

For general sentencing factors set out in the *Magistrates' Court Sentencing Guidelines* (2008) see Ch. 23, *post*.

Part III

C. FRAUD BY FAILING TO DISCLOSE INFORMATION

(1) Definition

Fraud Act 2006, s.3

Fraud by failing to disclose information

15–113 3— A person is in breach of this section if he—

(a) dishonestly fails to disclose to another person information which he is under a legal duty to disclose, and

(b) intends, by failing to disclose the information—

(i) to make a gain for himself or another, or

(ii) to cause loss to another or to expose another to a risk of loss.

(2) Allocation

15–114 The offence is triable either way.

(3) Elements of the offence

15–115 "Dishonestly" will presumably be defined as before: see *Feeley* and *Ghosh* (at § 15–4).

D must fail to disclose the information with the intention of making a gain or causing loss or risk of loss to another. The gain or loss does not actually have to take place. Gain and loss are defined in s.5 (see *ante*).

A legal duty to disclose information may include duties under oral contracts as well as written contracts. According to the Law Commission's Report on Fraud (Law Com No. 276, Cm 5560, 2002):

> "7.28. Such a duty may derive from statute (such as the provisions governing company prospectuses), from the fact that the transaction in question is one of the utmost good faith (such as a contract of insurance), from the express or implied terms of a contract, from the custom of a particular trade or market, or from the existence of a fiduciary relationship between the parties (such as that of agent and principal).
>
> 7.29. For this purpose there is a legal duty to disclose information not only if the defendant's failure to disclose it gives the victim a cause of action for damages, but also if the law gives the victim a right to set aside any change in his or her legal position to which he or she may consent as a result of the non-disclosure. For example, a person in a fiduciary position has a duty to disclose material information when entering into a contract with his or her beneficiary, in the sense that a failure to make such disclosure will entitle the beneficiary to rescind the contract and to reclaim any property transferred under it."

The *Explanatory Notes* to the Act suggest that the failure of a solicitor to share vital information with a client within the context of their work relationship, in order to perpetrate a fraud upon that client, would be covered by the section. Similarly, an offence could be committed under this section if a person intentionally failed to disclose information relating to his heart condition when making an application for life insurance.

(4) Sentence

15–116 On summary conviction, the maximum penalty for this offence is imprisonment for a term not exceeding 12 months or a fine not exceeding the statutory maximum (or both). But Sched. 2, para. 1 of the Act provides for 12 months to be 6 months pending the increase in sentencing powers in a magistrates' court (s.154 of the *Criminal Justice Act* 2003 has yet to be implemented).

The Sentencing Guidelines Council guideline on *Sentencing for Fraud—statutory offences* states that frauds under s.1 of the *Fraud Act* 2006 may be sentenced as confidence frauds; frauds involving the possession, making or supplying articles for use in fraud; banking and insurance fraud, and obtaining credit through fraud; benefit fraud and revenue fraud. See 15–112 above, for guidance on factors that should be taken into consideration when sentencing these types of fraud.

For general sentencing factors set out in the *Magistrates' Court Sentencing Guidelines* (2008) see Ch. 23, *post*.

D. FRAUD BY ABUSE OF POSITION

(1) Definition

Fraud Act 2006, s.4

Fraud by abuse of position

4—(1) A person is in breach of this section if he— **15–117**

(a) occupies a position in which he is expected to safeguard, or not to act against, the financial interests of another person,

(b) dishonestly abuses that position, and

(c) intends, by means of the abuse of that position—

(i) to make a gain for himself or another, or

(ii) to cause loss to another or to expose another to a risk of loss.

(2) A person may be regarded as having abused his position even though his conduct consisted of an omission rather than an act.

(2) Allocation

The offence is triable either way. **15–118**

(3) Elements of the offence

"Dishonestly" will presumably be defined as before: see *Feeley* and *Ghosh* (at § 15–4). **15–119**

D must abuse his position with the intention of making a gain or causing loss or risk of loss to another. The gain or loss does not actually have to take place. Gain and loss are defined in s.5 (see *ante*).

D must abuse his position. The Law Commission (Law Com No. 276, Cm 5560, 2002) explained the meaning of "position" (and this is not further clarified in the statute):

> "The necessary relationship will be present between trustee and beneficiary, director and company, professional person and client, agent and principal, employee and employer, or between partners. It may arise otherwise, for example within a family, or in the context of voluntary work, or in any context where the parties are not at arm's length. In nearly all cases where it arises, it will be recognised by the civil law as importing fiduciary duties, and any relationship that is so recognised will suffice. We see no reason, however, why the existence of such duties should be essential. This does not of course mean that it would be entirely a matter for the fact-finders whether the necessary relationship exists. The question whether the particular facts alleged can properly be described as giving rise to that relationship will be an issue capable of being ruled upon by the judge and, if the case goes to the jury, of being the subject of directions." (at para. 7.38)

The term "abuse" is not defined (or as the *Explanatory Notes* put it "not limited by a definition"!). Note that s.4(2) makes clear that the offence can be committed by omission as well as by positive action. The *Explanatory Notes* give the following examples. An employee who fails to take up the chance of a crucial contract in order that an associate or rival company can take it up instead at the expense of the employer, commits an offence under this section. An employee of a software company who uses his position to clone software products with the intention of selling the products on would commit an offence under this section. Or a person who is employed to care for an elderly or disabled person has access to that person's bank account and abuses his position by transferring funds to invest in a high-risk business venture of his own. **15–120**

(4) Sentence

On summary conviction, the maximum penalty for this offence is imprisonment for a **15–121** term not exceeding 12 months or a fine not exceeding the statutory maximum (or both). But Sched. 2, para. 1 of the Act provides for 12 months to be six months pending the increase in sentencing powers in a magistrates' court (s.154 of the *Criminal Justice Act* 2003 has yet to be implemented).

The Sentencing Guidelines Council guideline on *Sentencing for Fraud – statutory offences*, issued on October 13, 2009, describes fraud under s.1 of the *Fraud Act* 2006 as "confidence fraud". The Sentencing Guidelines Council's guideline on sentencing such frauds are considered at 15–112, *above*.

In *Marshall* [2009] EWCA Crim 2076, CA, the appellant appealed against her sentence of 12 months' imprisonment following a guilty plea to an offence of fraud, contrary to ss.1 and 4 of the *Fraud Act* 2006. The appellant was the joint manager of a residential care home which had four residents with severe learning difficulties. The appellant had wrongly withdrawn £7,600 from one of the resident's bank accounts. Dismissing the appeal, the Court held that the appellant's personal circumstances (she had a young child and was currently pregnant) must be set against the theft of £7,000 odd from a vulnerable victim in a gross and even wicked breach of trust over a longish period. The sentence was therefore not in any way excessive.

In *Gayle (Mark Diego)* [2008] EWCA Crim 1344, CA, the appellant appealed against a sentence of eight months' imprisonment imposed for fraud under s.4 of the *Fraud Act* 2006. The appellant was employed by a global shipping company and based at an international airport. He had been asked to move a crate through the airport for a payment of £100, which he accepted. The appellant then sent a crate to New York, certifying it as "known cargo". He did not know what the crate contained and was aware it would not be searched. The crate contained 500 kilos of khat, an illegal substance in the United States. The appellant submitted that his exemplary work record and good character coupled with his having only succumbed on one occasion to a bribe suggested his sentence should have been suspended. Dismissing his appeal, the Court held that people occupying positions such as that of the appellant were very valuable to criminals who wanted to get contraband through security. It was therefore important that people in those positions should be trustworthy and it should be known that people who took bribes must expect to receive an appropriate period of imprisonment.

For general sentencing factors set out in the *Magistrates' Court Sentencing Guidelines* (2008) see Ch. 23, *post*.

E. POSSESSION ETC. OF ARTICLES FOR USE IN FRAUD

(1) Definition

Fraud Act 2006, s.6

Possession etc. of articles for use in frauds

15–122 6—(1) A person is guilty of an offence if he has in his possession or under his control any article for use in the course of or in connection with any fraud.

(2) A person guilty of an offence under this section is liable—

(a) on summary conviction, to imprisonment for a term not exceeding 12 months or to a fine not exceeding the statutory maximum (or to both);

(b) on conviction on indictment, to imprisonment for a term not exceeding 5 years or to a fine (or to both).

(3) Subsection (2)(a) applies in relation to Northern Ireland as if the reference to 12 months were a reference to 6 months.

(2) Allocation

15–123 The offence is triable either way.

(3) Elements of the offence

15–124 This broad preliminary offence is similar to s.25 of the *Theft Act* 1968 (without the need for absence from place of abode). The prosecution must prove that:

— D possessed or controlled the article(s). "Article" is defined in s.8:

Fraud Act 2006, s.8

"Article"

8—(1) For the purposes of— **15–125**

(a) sections 6 and 7, and

(b) the provisions listed in subsection (2), so far as they relate to articles for use in the course of or in connection with fraud,

"article" includes any program or data held in electronic form.

(2) The provisions are—

(a) section 1(7)(b) of the *Police and Criminal Evidence Act* 1984 (c. 60),

(b) section 2(8)(b) of the *Armed Forces Act* 2001 (c. 19), and

(c) Article 3(7)(b) of the *Police and Criminal Evidence (Northern Ireland) Order* 1989 (S.I. 1989/1341 (N.I. 12)) (meaning of "prohibited articles" for the purposes of stop and search powers).

Although not expressly stated, it would appear that D must possess the article for the **15–126** purpose or with the intention of using it in the course of fraud. It is not necessary to prove that he intended to use it in a specific fraud, or that he intended to use it himself: *Ellames* (1974) 60 Cr.App.R. 7.

(4) Sentence

On summary conviction, the maximum penalty for this offence is imprisonment for a **15–127** term not exceeding 12 months or a fine not exceeding the statutory maximum (or both). But Sched. 2, para. 1 of the Act provides for 12 months to be 6 months pending the increase in sentencing powers in a magistrates' court (s.154 of the *Criminal Justice Act* 2003 has yet to be implemented).

The Sentencing Guidelines Council guideline on *Sentencing for Fraud—statutory offences* states that fraud under s.6 of the *Fraud Act* 2006 may be sentenced as frauds involving the possession, making or supplying articles for use in fraud. See 15-109, above, for guidance on factors that should be taken into consideration when sentencing this type of fraud.

In *Mensah-Golo* [2009] EWCA Crim 640, CA, the appellant had pleaded guilty to possessing articles for use in frauds. He was sentenced to 18 months' imprisonment and recommended for deportation. Following a search of the car the appellant was driving when stopped by the police, the police found a bank card in the name of another person, which the appellant claimed belonged to his brother. Upon searching the appellant, the police officers found bank cards in the names of two other people. The police also found a piece of paper with the names, addresses and bank details of various people. The appellant had three previous convictions. Substituting a sentence of 12 months' imprisonment, the Court stated that the culpability of the offender depended on whether the fraud for which the articles were intended to be used was an extensive and skilfully planned one, whether the offender was involved in a professional operation, and how much money was involved. Since three different cards were involved, and the appellant had them to enable the proceeds of fraud to be transferred into those accounts, the case had all the hallmarks of professionalism and would be on the serious side of such cases. However, there was nothing to suggest that the appellant had been involved in the frauds whose proceeds he was being asked, albeit fraudulently, to transfer. The appropriate starting point in this case would be 18 months' imprisonment; as the appellant had pleaded guilty, a sentence of 12 months would be appropriate.

In *Omgbwa* [2009] EWCA Crim 1215, CA, the appellant was convicted of an offence of possessing articles for use in fraud, contrary to s.6(1) of the *Fraud Act* 2006 and sentenced to twelve months' imprisonment. The case involved what was described as a "black money" scam or a "wash wash" fraud. The appellant and his co-accused would coat a genuine bank note with glue and iodine, turning the note black. This note would be shown to a victim, who would then be shown the note being treated with a "special" chemical which washed it clean and made it legal tender. The victim would then be persuaded to buy a pile of similar bank notes and some of the "special" chemical. In reality the black notes would be pieces of blank paper and the chemical would be washing-up liquid. The appellant had been arrested and found to be in possession of some "black money", padding tissue, four bottles of an unknown liquid, some plastic goods, a vial of clear liquid, two pieces of paper cut to the size of a £20 note and a bottle of iodine. Substituting a sentence of eight months' imprisonment, the Court described the significant planning the appellant and his co-accused had engaged in to carry out the offences. However, the sums of money involved in the instant offence were small, and this offence was the appellant's first offence of anything like this nature.

For general sentencing factors set out in the *Magistrates' Court Sentencing Guidelines* (2008) see Ch. 23, *post*.

F. MAKING OR SUPPLYING ARTICLES FOR USE IN FRAUDS

(1) Definition

Fraud Act 2006, s.7

Making or supplying articles for use in frauds

15–128 **7**—(1) A person is guilty of an offence if he makes, adapts, supplies or offers to supply any article—

(a) knowing that it is designed or adapted for use in the course of or in connection with fraud, or

(b) intending it to be used to commit, or assist in the commission of, fraud.

(2) A person guilty of an offence under this section is liable—

(a) on summary conviction, to imprisonment for a term not exceeding 12 months or to a fine not exceeding the statutory maximum (or to both);

(b) on conviction on indictment, to imprisonment for a term not exceeding 10 years or to a fine (or to both).

(3) Subsection (2)(a) applies in relation to Northern Ireland as if the reference to 12 months were a reference to 6 months.

(2) Allocation

15–129 The offence is triable either way.

(3) Elements of the offence

15–130 For this preliminary offence, the prosecution must prove that:

— D makes, adapts, supplies of offers to supply any article. "Article" is defined in s.8 (*ante*) and includes any program or data held in electronic form. The *Explanatory Notes* give the example of someone who makes devices which when attached to electricity meters cause the meter to malfunction.

— D must intend or know that it will be used in connection with fraud. For knowledge, see *ante*, § 12–23.

(4) Sentence

15–131 On summary conviction, the maximum penalty for this offence is imprisonment for a term not exceeding 12 months or a fine not exceeding the statutory maximum (or both). But Sched. 2, para. 1 of the Act provides for 12 months to be 6 months pending the increase in sentencing powers in a magistrates' court (s.154 of the *Criminal Justice Act* 2003 has yet to be implemented).

The Sentencing Guidelines Council guideline on *Sentencing for Fraud – statutory offences* states that fraud under s.7 of the *Fraud Act* 2006 may be sentenced as fraud involving the possession, making or supplying articles for use in fraud. See 15–112, *above*, for guidance on factors that should be taken into consideration when sentencing this type of fraud.

For general sentencing factors set out in the *Magistrates' Court Sentencing Guidelines* (2008) see Ch. 23, *post*.

G. PARTICIPATING IN FRAUDULENT BUSINESS CARRIED ON BY SOLE TRADER ETC.

(1) Definition

Fraud Act 2006, s.9

Participating in fraudulent business carried on by sole trader etc.

9.—(1) A person is guilty of an offence if he is knowingly a party to the carrying on of a business to which this section applies. **15–132**

(2) This section applies to a business which is carried on—

(a) by a person who is outside the reach of section 993 of the *Companies Act* 2006 (offence of fraudulent trading), and

(b) with intent to defraud creditors of any person or for any other fraudulent purpose.

(3) The following are within the reach of that section—

(a) a company (as defined in section 1(1) of the *Companies Act* 2006);

(b) a person to whom that section applies (with or without adaptations or modifications) as if the person were a company;

(c) a person exempted from the application of that section.

(4) [repealed]

(5) "Fraudulent purpose" has the same meaning as in that section.

(6) A person guilty of an offence under this section is liable—

(a) on summary conviction, to imprisonment for a term not exceeding 12 months or to a fine not exceeding the statutory maximum (or to both);

(b) on conviction on indictment, to imprisonment for a term not exceeding 10 years or to a fine (or to both).

(7) Subsection (6)(a) applies in relation to Northern Ireland as if the reference to 12 months were a reference to 6 months.

[Section printed as amended by the *Companies Act 2006 (Consequential Amendments, Transitional Provisions and Savings) Order* 2009 (S.I. 2009 No. 1941) Sched.1 para.257 which came into force on October 1, 2009.]

(2) Allocation

The offence is triable either way. **15–133**

(3) Elements of the offence

This offence is similar to that under the *Companies Act* 1985, s.458, but extends the offence to non-corporate traders. Under s.9, the prosecution must prove: **15–134**

— dishonesty, which will presumably be defined as before: see *Feeley* and *Ghosh* (at § 15–4);

— an intention to defraud;

— that D exercised some kind of controlling or managerial function within the company.

(4) Sentence

On summary conviction, the maximum penalty for this offence is imprisonment for a term not exceeding 12 months or a fine not exceeding the statutory maximum (or both). But Sched. 2, para. 1 of the Act provides for 12 months to be six months pending **15–135** the increase in sentencing powers in a magistrates' court (s.154 of the *Criminal Justice Act* 2003 has yet to be implemented).

The Sentencing Guidelines Council guideline on *Sentencing for Fraud—statutory offences* does not specifically refer to s.9 of the *Fraud Act* 2006. However, as the guideline states it "aims to produce a coherent and consistent approach to sentencing all forms of fraudulent behaviour", it may be assumed that the general guidelines on sentencing offences of fraud in the guideline (see *15-109, above*) may be applied to the offence under s.9 of the *Fraud Act* 2006.

For general sentencing factors set out in the *Magistrates' Court Sentencing Guidelines* (2008) see Ch. 23, *post*.

H. OBTAINING SERVICES DISHONESTLY

(1) Definition

Fraud Act 2006, s.11

Obtaining services dishonestly

15–136 **11**—(1) A person is guilty of an offence under this section if he obtains services for himself or another

(a) by a dishonest act, and

(b) in breach of subsection (2).

(2) A person obtains services in breach of this subsection if—

(a) they are made available on the basis that payment has been, is being or will be made for or in respect of them;

(b) he obtains them without any payment having been made for or in respect of them or without payment having been made in full, and

(c) when he obtains them, he knows—

(i) that they are being made available on the basis described in paragraph (a), or

(ii) that they might be,

but intends that payment will not be made, or will not be made in full.

(3) A person guilty of an offence under this section is liable—

(a) on summary conviction, to imprisonment for a term not exceeding 12 months or to a fine not exceeding the statutory maximum (or to both);

(b) on conviction on indictment, to imprisonment for a term not exceeding 5 years or to a fine (or to both).

(4) Subsection (3)(a) applies in relation to Northern Ireland as if the reference to 12 months were a reference to 6 months.

(2) Allocation

15–137 The offence is triable either way.

(3) Elements of the offence

15–138 This offence replaces the offence under s.1 of the *Theft Act* 1978 (though there is no longer any need for a deception). The prosecution must prove that:

— D dishonestly obtained services from another. The *Explanatory Notes* give the example of someone who attaches a decoder to her TV to enable access to satellite TV channels for which she has no intention of paying;

— knowing that the services are to be paid for or knowing that they might have to be paid for;

— with the intent to avoid payment in whole or in part.

(4) Sentence

15–139 On summary conviction, the maximum penalty for this offence is imprisonment for a term not exceeding 12 months or a fine not exceeding the statutory maximum (or both). But Sched. 2, para. 1 of the Act provides for 12 months to be 6 months pending the increase in sentencing powers in a magistrates' court (s.154 of the *Criminal Justice Act* 2003 has yet to be implemented).

The Sentencing Guidelines Council guideline on *Sentencing for Fraud – statutory offences* states that the offence of obtaining services dishonestly (contrary to s.11 of the *Fraud Act* 2006) may be committed in circumstances that otherwise could be charged as an offence contrary to s.1 of the Act or may be more akin to *making off without payment*. It has therefore not been specifically included in the guideline, and the guideline states that one of the following approaches should be used:

1. Where the offence involves conduct which can be characterised as a fraud offence (such as obtaining credit through fraud or payment card fraud), the court should apply the guideline for the relevant type of fraud; or
2. Where the conduct could be characterised as *making off without payment* (that is, where an offender, knowing that payment on the spot for any goods supplied or service done is required or expected, dishonestly makes off without having paid and with intent to avoid payment), the guideline for that offence in the *Magistrates' Court Sentencing Guidelines* (2008) should be used.

For general sentencing factors set out in the *Magistrates' Court Sentencing Guidelines* (2008) see Ch. 23, *post*.

III. OFFENCES OF FORGERY, PERSONATION AND CHEATING

Part III

A. FORGERY

(1) Definition

Forgery and Counterfeiting Act 1981, s.1

The offence of forgery

1. A person is guilty of forgery if he makes a false instrument, with the intention that he or another shall use it to induce somebody to accept it as genuine, and by reason of so accepting it to do or not to do some act to his own or any other person's prejudice. **15–140**

(2) Allocation

This offence is triable either way: *Forgery and Counterfeiting Act* 1981, s.6. **15–141**

(3) Elements of the offence

The prosecution must prove that: **15–142**

— the defendant made a false instrument,

— with the intention that he or another should use it to induce somebody to accept it as genuine and to hence,

— do or not do some act to his own or another person's prejudice by reason of that acceptance.

The intention required for a charge under s.1 is (a) the intention that the false instrument will be used to induce somebody to accept it as genuine and (b) the intention to induce somebody by reason of so accepting it to do or not do some act to his own or another person's prejudice: *Campbell* 80 Cr.App.R. 47, CA.

Forgery and Counterfeiting Act 1981, ss.8–10

Meaning of "instrument"

8.—(1) Subject to subsection (2) below, in this Part of this Act "instrument" means— **15–143**

(a) any document, whether of a formal or informal character;

(b) any stamp issued or sold by a postal operator;
(c) any Inland Revenue stamp; and
(d) any disc, tape, sound track or other device on or in which information is recorded or stored by mechanical, electronic or other means.

(2) A currency note within the meaning of Part II of this Act is not an instrument for the purposes of this Part of this Act.

(3) A mark denoting payment of postage which a postal operator authorises to be used instead of an adhesive stamp is to be treated for the purposes of this Part of this Act as if it were a stamp issued by the postal operator concerned.

(3A) In this section "postal operator" has the same meaning as in the *Postal Services Act* 2000.

(4) In this Part of this Act "Inland Revenue stamp" means a stamp as defined in section 27 of the *Stamp Duties Management Act* 1891.

Meaning of "false" and "making"

15-144 **9.**—(1) An instrument is false for the purposes of this Part of this Act—
(a) if it purports to have been made in the form in which it is made by a person who did not in fact make it in that form; or
(b) if it purports to have been made in the form in which it is made on the authority of a person who did not in fact authorise its making in that form; or
(c) if it purports to have been made in the terms in which it is made by a person who did not in fact make it in those terms; or
(d) if it purports to have been made in the terms in which it is made on the authority of a person who did not in fact authorise its making in those terms; or
(e) if it purports to have been altered in any respect by a person who did not in fact alter it in that respect; or
(f) if it purports to have been altered in any respect on the authority of a person who did not in fact authorise the alteration in that respect; or
(g) if it purports to have been made or altered on a date on which, or at a place at which, or otherwise in circumstances in which, it was not in fact made or altered; or
(h) if it purports to have been made or altered by an existing person but he did not in fact exist.

(2) A person is to be treated for the purposes of this Part of this Act as making a false instrument if he alters an instrument so as to make it false in any respect (whether or not it is false in some other respect apart from that alteration).

Meaning of "prejudice" and "induce"

15-145 **10.**—(1) Subject to subsections (2) and (4) below, for the purposes of this Part of this Act an act or omission intended to be induced is to a person's prejudice if, and only if, it is one which, if it occurs—
(a) will result—
(i) in his temporary or permanent loss of property; or
(ii) in his being deprived of an opportunity to earn remuneration or greater remuneration; or
(iii) in his being deprived of an opportunity to gain a financial advantage otherwise than by way of remuneration; or
(b) will result in somebody being given an opportunity—
(i) to earn remuneration or greater remuneration from him; or
(ii) to gain a financial advantage from him otherwise than by way of remuneration; or
(c) will be the result of his having accepted a false instrument as genuine, or a copy of a false instrument as a copy of a genuine one, in connection with his performance of any duty.

(2) An act which a person has an enforceable duty to do and an omission to do an act which a person is not entitled to do shall be disregarded for the purposes of this Part of this Act.

(3) In this Part of this Act references to inducing somebody to accept a false instrument as genuine, or a copy of a false instrument as a copy of a genuine one, include references

to inducing a machine to respond to the instrument or copy as if it were a genuine instrument or, as the case may be, a copy of a genuine one.

(4) Where subsection (3) above applies, the act or omission intended to be induced by the machine responding to the instrument or copy shall be treated as an act or omission to a person's prejudice.

(5) In this section "loss" includes not getting what one might get as well as parting with what one has.

Section 31 of the *Immigration and Asylum Act* 1999 provides a defence based on Art. 31(1) of the Refugee Convention for a defendant charged with an offence under this section. **15–146**

Immigration and Asylum Act 1999, s.31

Defences based on Article 31(1) of the Refugee Convention.

31.—(1) It is a defence for a refugee charged with an offence to which this section applies to show that, having come to the United Kingdom directly from a country where his life or freedom was threatened (within the meaning of the Refugee Convention), he— **15–147**

(a) presented himself to the authorities in the United Kingdom without delay;

(b) showed good cause for his illegal entry or presence; and

(c) made a claim for asylum as soon as was reasonably practicable after his arrival in the United Kingdom.

(2) If, in coming from the country where his life or freedom was threatened, the refugee stopped in another country outside the United Kingdom, subsection (1) applies only if he shows that he could not reasonably have expected to be given protection under the Refugee Convention in that other country.

(3) In England and Wales and Northern Ireland the offences to which this section applies are any offence, and any attempt to commit an offence, under—

(a) Part I of the *Forgery and Counterfeiting Act* 1981 (forgery and connected offences);

(aa) section 25(1) or (5) of the *Identity Cards Act* 2006;

(b) section 24A of the 1971 Act (deception); or

(c) section 26(1)(d) of the 1971 Act (falsification of documents).

(4) In Scotland, the offences to which this section applies are those—

(a) of fraud,

(b) of uttering a forged document,

(ba) under section 25(1) or (5) of the *Identity Cards Act* 2006;

(c) under section 24A of the 1971 Act (deception), or

(d) under section 26(1)(d) of the 1971 Act (falsification of documents), and any attempt to commit any of those offences.

(5) A refugee who has made a claim for asylum is not entitled to the defence provided by subsection (1) in relation to any offence committed by him after making that claim.

(6) "Refugee" has the same meaning as it has for the purposes of the Refugee Convention.

(7) If the Secretary of State has refused to grant a claim for asylum made by a person who claims that he has a defence under subsection (1), that person is to be taken not to be a refugee unless he shows that he is.

[This section is printed as amended by the *Identity Cards Act* 2006.]

In *Dast Jerdi (Bakhshi Ali)* [2011] EWCA Crim 365, the Court of Appeal quashed the appellant's conviction for possession of a false identity document under the *Identity Cards Act* 2006 s.25(1)(a) as he had not been advised of the availability of a defence under section 31 of the 1999 Act and the Court determined that such a defence would very probably have succeeded.

Where a defendant raises a defence under s.31(1) of the *Immigration and Asylum Act* 1999 they must adduce sufficient evidence to support their claim to refugee status to raise the issue. The prosecution bears the burden of proving that the defendant is not in fact a refugee. Section 31(1) also imposes a legal burden of proof on the defen- **15–148**

Part III

dant to prove that they presented themselves to the authorities without delay, showed good cause for their illegal entry or presence, and made a claim for asylum as soon as was reasonably practicable. The existence of the reverse burden of proof in s.31(1) does not prevent a defendant receiving a fair trial: *Makuwa (Liliane)* [2006] EWCA Crim 175, CA.

In *H* [2008] EWCA Crim 3117, CA. The appellant appealed against their conviction for possessing a false identity document with intent. The appellant was of Somalian origin and had been arrested on entry to the United Kingdom. Although he subsequently received advice from solicitors, he refused to plead on arraignment. He was given further advice and stated that he accepted he was not the person on the passport he had used to enter the UK, that he had not sought asylum as soon as was reasonably practical and that he could not show a good cause for his illegal entry. He then pleaded guilty on re-arraignment. He submitted that his plea was not a true plea as he never properly admitted his guilt and that his circumstances fell within the defence provided in s.31 of the *Immigration and Asylum Act* 1999.

Allowing his appeal, the Court of Appeal stated that it was reasonably arguable that the appellant had a reasonable prospect of demonstrating that he came directly from a country where his life or freedom was threatened within the meaning of Art. 31 of the Convention relating to the Status of Refugees 1951 (United Nations) and did not stop in another country. The appellant would have had a reasonable prospect of relying on s.31 and defending the charge and he had not been given advice specifically on the meaning of coming directly from a country where his life or freedom was threatened or on the ambit of s.31(2). The safety of the conviction could be considered, notwithstanding the fact that the appellant pleaded guilty and the conviction was quashed. As the appellant had already served his sentence, it was not in the interests of justice to order a retrial.

15–149 Section 31 is not limited to offences attributable to a refugee's illegal entry into or presence in the United Kingdom, but provides immunity from the imposition of criminal penalties for offences attributable to a refugee's attempt to leave the United Kingdom in the continuing course of a flight from persecution even after a short stopover in transit: *R. v. Asfaw* [2008] UKHL 31, HL. The appellant had been convicted of attempting to obtain services by deception. She was an Ethiopian national who intended to travel to the United States on forged documents and seek refugee status there. She arrived in the United Kingdom on a forged passport and passed through immigration. Later that day, she attempted to leave for the United States, and was arrested for using a false passport. She was acquitted of using a false instrument with intent after raising the defence under s.31. She pleaded guilty to attempting to obtain services by deception following the trial judge's ruling that this defence was not available for that offence. The issue for determination by the House of Lords was whether, to the extent that s.31 did not match the protection which the UK was bound to give by the Convention relating to the Status of Refugees 1951 (United Nations) Art. 31, UK domestic law gave the defendant any remedy. The prosecution argued that the offences committed by the appellant fell outside Art. 31 and s.31, because they were committed whilst trying to leave the country and the Art. 31 immunity was limited to offences of entering and being illegally in a country, thus excluding offences committed when leaving an intermediate country to seek asylum elsewhere. The appellant submitted that it was an abuse of the criminal process to prosecute her for attempting to obtain services by deception.

Allowing the appeal, the House of Lords (*per* Lords Bingham, Hope and Carswell; Lords Rodgers and Mance dissenting) held that s.31 should not be read as limited to offences attributable to a refugee's illegal entry into or presence in the UK, but should provide immunity from the imposition of criminal penalties for offences attributable to a refugee's attempt to leave the UK in the continuing course of a flight from persecution even after a short stopover in transit. That interpretation was consistent with the Convention jurisprudence and its humanitarian purpose. The offence of attempting to obtain services by deception, although within Art. 31, was not listed in s.31. That must be regarded as an oversight, not a deliberate omission. If the count was included in the indictment to prevent the appellant from relying on the defence which s.31 would otherwise provide, there would be strong grounds for arguing that that was an abuse of process.

When considering whether a person who had entered the United Kingdom on a false passport was "in transit" within the meaning of section 31 of the *Immigration and Asylum Act* 1999, that phrase had to be given a generous interpretation. The court had to decide, looking at all the circumstances, whether that person was in the United Kingdom in the course of a flight: *SK* [2010] EWCA Crim 1335. In this case, the appellant was a Sri Lankan national who was subject to persecution in Sri Lanka. He arrived in the United Kingdom via Russia and Poland. After staying in the UK for around a month he went to the airport intending to board a flight to Canada, but was detained after presenting a false Norwegian passport. Although he initially raised a defence under section 31 of the *Immigration and Asylum Act* 1999, he changed his plea to one of guilty. He submitted that his appeal should be allowed so that he could enter a plea of not guilty. Dismissing his appeal, the court held that the phrase "in transit" had to be given a generous interpretation and time spent in the intervening country could be much more than the three hours on the facts of *Asfaw*. The question was whether the person was in the course of a flight. In the instant case however, it was clear that the appellant intended to come to the UK to seek asylum and that his decision to go to Canada was during his stay in the UK. On that basis, once in the UK he was no longer in transit.

(4) Sentence

When tried summarily, the maximum penalty for this offence is six months' imprisonment or a fine not exceeding the statutory maximum or both: *Forgery and Counterfeiting Act* 1981, s.6. After commencement of the relevant provisions, the maximum custodial sentence in a magistrates' court will be 12 months' imprisonment: *Criminal Justice Act* 2003, ss.154 and 282. **15–150**

For general sentencing factors set out in the *Magistrates' Court Sentencing Guidelines* (2008) see Ch. 23, *post*.

In *Lincoln* (1994) 15 Cr.App.R.(S.) 333, a husband forged his estranged wife's signature on a contract of sale of house and Land Registry transfer. The original sentence of twelve months' imprisonment for this offence was reduced to six months' imprisonment on appeal. It was held that forgery of documents of title to property must be visited by an immediate custodial sentence in all but the most exceptional circumstances yet in view of the mitigating circumstances, the sentence would be reduced to six months.

In *Dover* (1995) 16 Cr.App.R.(S.) 61, the offender pleaded guilty to two counts of forgery, one of procuring the execution of a valuable security by deception and one of theft. The offender had forged an estimate for the repair of the storm-damaged block of flats that he was responsible for managing, and then kept the difference between the actual cost of repair and the insurance companies' payment for himself. He was sentenced to five months' imprisonment, the court stating "having regard to the breach of trust involved in the offence of theft and the serious nature of the forgeries involving as they do fraud upon an insurance company, five months was, looked at in the round a very lenient sentence."

B. COPYING A FALSE INSTRUMENT

(1) Definition

Forgery and Counterfeiting Act 1981, s.2

The offence of copying a false instrument

2. It is an offence for a person to make a copy of an instrument which is, and which he knows **15–151**

or believes to be, a false instrument, with the intention that he or another shall use it to induce somebody to accept it as a copy of a genuine instrument, and by reason of so accepting it to do or not to do some act to his own or any other person's prejudice.

(2) Allocation

15–152 This offence is triable either way: *Forgery and Counterfeiting Act* 1981, s.6.

(3) Elements of the offence

15–153 The prosecution must prove that:

— the defendant made a copy of an instrument which,

— he knew or believed to be a false instrument, and

— he intended that he or another should use the copy to induce somebody to accept it as a copy of a genuine instrument, and

— to cause that other person to do or not do some act to his or another person's prejudice by reason of so accepting the copy.

For the definition of "instrument", see s.8 of the 1981 Act (*ante*); of "false", s.9 (*ante*) and of "prejudice" or "induce" see s.10 (*ante*). Section 31 of the *Immigration and Asylum Act* 1999 provides a defence based on Art. 31(1) of the Refugee Convention for a defendant charged with an offence under this section, see *ante*, §§ 15–146–15–149.

(4) Sentence

15–154 When tried summarily, the maximum penalty is six months' imprisonment, a fine not exceeding the statutory maximum or both: *Forgery and Counterfeiting Act* 1981, s.6. After commencement of the relevant provisions, the maximum custodial sentence in a magistrates' court will be 12 months' imprisonment: *Criminal Justice Act* 2003, ss.154 and 282.

For general sentencing factors set out in the *Magistrates' Court Sentencing Guidelines* (2008) see Ch. 23, *post*.

C. USING A FALSE INSTRUMENT, USING COPY OF A FALSE INSTRUMENT

(1) Definition

Forgery and Counterfeiting Act 1981, ss.3–4

The offence of using a false instrument

15–155 **3.** It is an offence for a person to use an instrument which is, and which he knows or believes to be, false, with the intention of inducing somebody to accept it as genuine, and by reason of so accepting it to do or not to do some act to his own or any other person's prejudice.

The offence of using a copy of a false instrument

15–156 **4.** It is an offence for a person to use a copy of an instrument which is, and which he knows or believes to be, a false instrument, with the intention of inducing somebody to accept it as a copy of a genuine instrument, and by reason of so accepting it to do or not to do some act to his own or any other person's prejudice.

(2) Allocation

15–157 This offence is triable either way: *Forgery and Counterfeiting Act* 1981, s.6.

(3) Elements of the offence

15–158 The prosecution must prove that either:

— the defendant used an instrument that is, and that he knew or believed to be, false,

— with the intention of inducing somebody to accept it as genuine, and,

— to cause that person to do or not to do some act to his own or any other person's prejudice by reason of so accepting the instrument as genuine;

OR

— the defendant used a copy of an instrument that is, and that he knew or believed to be false,
— with the intention of inducing somebody to accept it as a copy of a genuine instrument and,
— to cause that person to do or not to do some act to his own or any other person's prejudice by reason of so accepting the instrument as a copy of a genuine instrument.

Section 31 of the *Immigration and Asylum Act* 1999 provides a defence based on s.31(1) of the Refugee Convention for a defendant charged with an offence under this section, see *ante*, §§ 15–146–15–149.

The operative deception does not have to be proved "through the mouth" of the person on whom the deception was said to have operated: *Kiernan* [2008] EWCA Crim 972, CA. The appellant appealed against their conviction for obtaining a money transfer by deception. The charge involved obtaining a mortgage with the aid of false documents. The appellant argued that the operative deception had to be proved "through the mouth" of the person on whom the deception allegedly operated, and in the instant case the prosecution had not called the individual at the mortgage company who had acted on the application to give evidence, and instead called a manager who had nothing to do with the case. **15–159**

Dismissing the appeal, the Court of Appeal stated that the law of evidence contained no rule that the effect of a deception could only be proved by the testimony of the person who allegedly acted on the deception. Mortgages were granted by very large companies on a very large scale, deploying more or less fixed and formal procedures. It was simply unreal to suppose that an individual employee of such a company, called months or years after the event, would remember the details of a specific past transaction and the effect of the specific loan application.

Part III

(4) Sentence

When tried summarily, the maximum penalty is six months' imprisonment, a fine not exceeding the statutory maximum or both: *Forgery and Counterfeiting Act* 1981, s.6. After commencement of the relevant provision, the maximum custodial sentence in a magistrates' court will be 12 months' imprisonment: *Criminal Justice Act* 2003, ss.154 and 282. For general sentencing factors set out in the *Magistrates' Court Sentencing Guidelines* (2008) see Ch. 23, *post*. **15–160**

In *Duffy* (1994) 15 Cr.App.R.(S.) 677, the offender pleaded guilty to forgery of a candidate's nomination form in connection with a local election and was sentenced to six months' imprisonment. It was held that the offence here was a technical one. As such, a custodial sentence was unwarranted; a substantial financial penalty would have been appropriate. As the defendant had served a month in custody, an absolute discharge was substituted.

In *Balasubramaniam* [2002] 2 Cr.App.R.(S.) 17, a sentence of 12 months' imprisonment for attempting to use a false passport to travel to Canada to visit the appellant's sick mother was reduced to six months. This was a case where there was a plea of guilty by a person of good character, but it was not an exceptional case where a sentence of less than six months could be justified. There were no aggravating features to justify a sentence in excess of six to nine months. This was not a case of using a false passport for financial gain or to subvert entry requirements or to seek employment in a country that would not otherwise grant admission. The facts placed the particular case at the bottom of the six months to nine months bracket.

In *Daljit Singh* [1999] 1 Cr.App.R.(S.) 490, the offender pleaded guilty before a magistrates' court to using a false passport in order to board a flight to Canada. The Court of Appeal upheld his sentence of eight months' imprisonment. Rose L.J. explaining that for reasons of deterrence "cases involving the use of false passports will almost always merit a significant period of custody."

D. CUSTODY OR CONTROL OF CERTAIN FALSE INSTRUMENTS AND MANUFACTURE, CUSTODY OR CONTROL OF EQUIPMENT OR MATERIALS WITH WHICH SUCH INSTRUMENTS MAY BE MADE

(1) Definition

Forgery and Counterfeiting Act 1981, s.5(1)–(4)

Offences relating to money orders, share certificates, passports, etc.

15–161 **5.**—(1) It is an offence for a person to have in his custody or under his control an instrument to which this section applies which is, and which he knows or believes to be, false, with the intention that he or another shall use it to induce somebody to accept it as genuine, and by reason of so accepting it to do or not to do some act to his own or any other person's prejudice.

(2) It is an offence for a person to have in his custody or under his control, without lawful authority or excuse, an instrument to which this section applies which is, and which he knows or believes to be, false.

(3) It is an offence for a person to make or to have in his custody or under his control a machine or implement, or paper or any other material, which to his knowledge is or has been specially designed or adapted for the making of an instrument to which this section applies, with the intention that he or another shall make an instrument to which this section applies which is false and that he or another shall use the instrument to induce somebody to accept it as genuine, and by reason of so accepting it to do or not to do some act to his own or any other person's prejudice.

(4) It is an offence for a person to make or to have in his custody or under his control any such machine, implement, paper or material, without lawful authority or excuse.

(2) Allocation

15–162 These offences are triable either way: *Forgery and Counterfeiting Act* 1981, s.6.

(3) Elements of the offence

15–163 The prosecution must prove that either:

— the defendant had in his custody or under his control,
— an instrument of the kind listed in s.5(3) of the 1981 Act, which
— he knows or believes to be false,
— with the intention that he or another shall induce somebody to accept it as genuine, and
— cause that person to do or not do some act to his own or another person's prejudice by reason of him accepting the instrument as genuine;

OR

— the defendant had in his custody or under his control,
— an instrument of the kind listed in s.5(3) of the 1981 Act, which
— is, and which he knows to be false,
— without lawful authority or excuse;

OR

— the defendant had in his custody or under his control,
— a machine or implement, or paper or any other material,
— which to his knowledge is or has been designed or adapted for the making of an instrument of the kind listed in s.5(3) of the 1981 Act,
— with the intention that he or another shall make an instrument of the kind listed in s.5(3) of the 1981 Act which is false, and
— that he or another shall use the instruments to induce somebody to accept it as genuine, and

— cause that person to do or not do some act to his own or another person's prejudice by reason of him accepting the instrument as genuine;

OR

— the defendant had in his custody or under his control,
— any such machine, implement, paper or material as described in s.5(3),
— without lawful authority or excuse.

Forgery and Counterfeiting Act 1981, s.5(5), (6)

Offences relating to money orders, share certificates, passports, etc.

5.—(5) The instruments to which this section applies are— **15–164**

(a) money orders;
(b) postal orders;
(c) United Kingdom postage stamps;
(d) Inland Revenue stamps;
(e) share certificates;
(f) passports and documents which can be used instead of passports;
(g) cheques;
(h) travellers' cheques;
(j) cheque cards;
(k) credit cards;
(l) certified copies relating to an entry in a register of births, adoptions, marriages or deaths and issued by the Registrar General, the Registrar General for Northern Ireland, a registration officer or a person lawfully authorised to register marriages; and
(m) certificates relating to entries in such registers.

(6) In subsection (5)(e) above "share certificate" means an instrument entitling or evidencing the title of a person to a share or interest—

(a) in any public stock, annuity, fund or debt of any government or state, including a state which forms part of another state; or
(b) in any stock, fund or debt of a body (whether corporate or unincorporated) established in the United Kingdom or elsewhere.

Section 31 of the *Immigration and Asylum Act* 1999 provides a defence based on 31(1) of the Refugee Convention for a defendant charged with an offence under this section, see *ante*, §§15–146–15–149. **15–165**

(4) Sentence

When tried summarily, the maximum penalty is six months' imprisonment, a fine not exceeding the statutory maximum or both: *Forgery and Counterfeiting Act* 1981, s.6. After commencement of the relevant provisions, the maximum custodial sentence in a magistrates' court will be 12 months' imprisonment: *Criminal Justice Act* 2003, ss.154 and 282. **15–166**

In *Siliavski* [2000] 1 Cr.App.R.(S.) 23, the offender pleaded guilty to possessing forged passports after four forged Greek passports were found concealed in his trousers at Heathrow Airport. He was sentenced to 12 months' imprisonment and recommended for deportation. This sentence was reduced to six months on appeal, the Garland J. drawing a distinction between cases involving use of a false passport and cases involving mere carrying. This distinction was disapproved in *Cheema* [2002] 2 Cr.App.R.(S.) 79, CA. A sentence of three years' imprisonment was substituted for a sentence of four years imprisonment where the offender had been convicted of having custody or control of twelve false passports. Pill L.J. disapproved of lenient treatment in the context of carrying in of false passports and advocated the use of deterrent sentences to stop others "taking part as couriers in a lucrative but obnoxious trade."

In *Kolawole* [2004] EWCA Crim 3047, the Court of Appeal reviewed the authorities on offences of possession of a false instrument contrary to the *Forgery and Counterfeit-*

ing Act 1981 s.3, s.5(1) and s.5(2) and the correct sentencing procedure to be followed. The appellant appealed against a total sentence of 16 months' imprisonment following pleas of guilty to two counts of possession of a false instrument with intent. Following a search of the appellant's car, police officers had discovered a forged Nigerian passport and a stolen British passport. Consecutive sentences of eight months had been passed for each offence. The appellant contended that the sentence was manifestly excessive as it was bad practice to impose consecutive sentences for the possession of two different passports. The Court of Appeal held that the sentence was not manifestly excessive and that a clear distinction was not always drawn between the three different offences commonly charged in relation to false passports under the *Forgery and Counterfeiting Act* 1981 s.3, s.5(1) and s.5(2).

In the present case the appellant was in possession of two false passports with intent contrary to s.5(1) of the Act. The sentence imposed had to reflect that. Further, international events in recent years and increased public concern, which they had generated, justified deterrent sentences. Where one false passport was being used contrary to s.3 of the Act, or was held with the intention of use contrary to s.5(1), the appropriate sentence, even on a plea of guilty by a person of good character, should be in the range of 12 to 18 months.

The Court also disapproved the decision in *Siliavski* [2000] 1 Cr.App.R.(S.) 23, above, stating that it should not be regarded as authoritative as to the level of sentence appropriate for couriers of false passports and that *Cheema* was the more appropriate guide.

In *Koudache* [2005] EWCA Crim 714, CA, the Court of Appeal held that a sentence of two years' imprisonment for two counts of having a false instrument was manifestly excessive given that the offences were not the most serious of their type. The appellant had been found in possession of two forged passports and documents relating to two other false identities. The trial judge considered that there had been the plainest evidence of an offence that was always serious and imposed the maximum available sentence. The Court of Appeal held that the trial judge had erred in imposing the maximum sentence as although the offences were serious, they were not the most serious of their type. An appropriate sentence was 18 months' imprisonment on each count to run concurrently.

In *De Oliveira* [2005] EWCA Crim 3187, CA, the appellant appealed against his sentence of 15 months' imprisonment following his guilty plea to having a false instrument. The appellant, a Brazilian national, had been found in possession of an Italian passport. The passport contained his photograph but had the personal details of someone else and subsequent examination revealed it was a forgery. The recorder considered the guidelines in *Kolawole* [2004] EWCA Crim 3047, CA, when passing sentence. The appellant argued the sentence of 15 months' imprisonment was manifestly excessive considering the maximum sentence for the offence. Allowing the appeal, the Court stated that the appellant had pleaded guilty to an offence contrary to s.5(2) of the 1981 Act for which the maximum sentence was two years' imprisonment. It seemed the recorder had not appreciated the difference in sentences imposed in relation to s.3, s.5(1) and s.5(2) of the 1981 Act, and had imposed too high a sentence. The sentence of 15 months' imprisonment was quashed and replaced by a sentence of eight months.

In *Araujo*, [2006] EWCA Crim 1439, CA, the appellant pleaded guilty to two counts of having a false instrument contrary to s.5(2) of the *Forgery and Counterfeiting Act* 1981. He was sentenced to six months' imprisonment on each count, with the sentences to run consecutively. The appellant argued that the judge erred in principle in passing consecutive sentences where the convictions arose out of a single incident. The Court held that on the facts of this case, possession of two passports in two different names, the imposition of consecutive sentences was not wrong in principle. As the offence was one of simple possession, the Court held that the overall length of sentence was too high and replaced the sentence of 12 months' imprisonment with a sentence of eight months' imprisonment, with four months on one count and four months on the second count running consecutively.

In *Ali* [2009] EWCA Crim 985, the appellant had been convicted of having a false instrument with intent, and obtaining a pecuniary advantage by deception. The Court of Appeal gave guidance on sentencing cases involving false identity documents. The Court stated that save in exceptional circumstances, a custodial sentence is always necessary and that, depending on the facts, the length of sentence should normally be between six months and 18 months. Cases in which false identity documents are obtained by a person who is not permitted to work in this country and who obtains the documents to evade that prohibition are normally dealt with by a sentence at or near the bottom end of the range. See also *Ovieriakhi* (2009) EWCA Crim 452.

For general sentencing factors set out in the *Magistrates' Court Sentencing Guidelines* (2008) see Ch. 23, *post*.

E. COUNTERFEITING NOTES OR COINS

(1) Definition

Forgery and Counterfeiting Act 1981, s.14

Offences of counterfeiting notes and coins

14.—(1) It is an offence for a person to make a counterfeit of a currency note or of a protected coin, intending that he or another shall pass or tender it as genuine. **15–167**

(2) It is an offence for a person to make a counterfeit of a currency note or of a protected coin without lawful authority or excuse.

(2) Allocation

These offences are triable either way: *Forgery and Counterfeiting Act* 1981, s.22. **15–168**

(3) Elements of the offence

The prosecution must prove either that; **15–169**

— the defendant made a counterfeit of a currency note or a protected coin,

— with the intention that he or another should pass or tender it as genuine;

OR

— the defendant made a counterfeit of a currency note or a protected coin,

— without lawful authority or excuse.

Forgery and Counterfeiting Act 1981, s.27

Meaning of "currency note" and "protected coin"

27.—(1) In this Part of this Act— **15–170**

"currency note" means—

(a) any note which—

(i) has been lawfully issued in England and Wales, Scotland, Northern Ireland, any of the Channel Islands, the Isle of Man or the Republic of Ireland; and

(ii) is or has been customarily used as money in the country where it was issued; and

(iii) is payable on demand; or

(b) any note which—

(i) has been lawfully issued in some country other than those mentioned in paragraph (a)(i) above; and

(ii) is customarily used as money in that country; and

"protected coin" means any coin which—

(a) is customarily used as money in any country; or

(b) is specified in an order made by the Treasury for the purposes of this Part of this Act.

(2) The power to make an order conferred on the Treasury by subsection (1) above shall be exercisable by statutory instrument.

(3) A statutory instrument containing such an order shall be laid before Parliament after being made.

15–171 The *Forgery and Counterfeiting (Protected Coins) Order* 1981 (S.I. 1981 No. 1505) specifies the following coins for the purposes of Pt II of the Act:

Sovereign;
Half Sovereign;
Krugerrand;
Any coin denominated as a fraction of a Kruggerand;
Maria-Theresa thaler bearing the date of 1780.

The *Forgery and Counterfeiting (Protected Coins) Order* (1999) (S.I. 1999 No. 2095) specifies any euro coin produced in accordance with Council Regulation No 975/98/EC by or at the instance of a member state which has adopted the single currency, for the purposes of Pt II of the 1981 Act.

Forgery and Counterfeiting Act 1981, s.28

Meaning of "counterfeit"

15–172 **28.**—(1) For the purposes of this Part of this Act a thing is a counterfeit of a currency note or of a protected coin—

(a) if it is not a currency note or a protected coin but resembles a currency note or protected coin (whether on one side only or on both) to such an extent that it is reasonably capable of passing for a currency note or protected coin of that description; or
(b) if it is a currency note or protected coin which has been so altered that it is reasonably capable of passing for a currency note or protected coin of some other description.

(2) For the purposes of this Part of this Act—

(a) a thing consisting of one side only of a currency note, with or without the addition of other material, is a counterfeit of such a note;
(b) a thing consisting—
 (i) of parts of two or more currency notes; or
 (ii) of parts of a currency note, or of parts of two or more currency notes, with the addition of other material,

is capable of being a counterfeit of a currency note.

(3) References in this Part of this Act to passing or tendering a counterfeit of a currency note or a protected coin are not to be construed as confined to passing or tendering it as legal tender.

(4) Sentence

15–173 When tried summarily, offences under both s.14(1) and (2) are punishable by a maximum sentence of six months' imprisonment, a fine not exceeding the statutory maximum or both. After commencement of the relevant provisions, the maximum custodial sentence in a magistrates' court will be 12 months' imprisonment: *Criminal Justice Act* 2003, ss.154 and 282.

In *Howard* (1986) 82 Cr.App.R. 262, CA it was said that where a defendant is convicted of passing counterfeit notes, the issue of which undermines the whole economy of the country, in nearly every case this requires a custodial sentence to punish the wrongdoer and deter him from committing the same sort of offence in the future and to act as a deterrent to others. The offender pleaded guilty to having custody of counterfeit currency (£20 notes) and tendering one such counterfeit note, and was sentenced to concurrent terms of two years' imprisonment. *Howard* was followed in *Luxford* [1996] 1 Cr.App.R.(S.) 186, CA, where the offender pleaded guilty to having custody of a counterfeit currency note and was sentenced to nine months' imprisonment. He appealed against sentence, submitting that the judge gave insufficient credit for a plea of guilty, good character and the pre-sentence report. The court held that whilst the sentence imposed was excessive, a custodial sentence would be an inevitable punishment for this offence. A sentence of four months' imprisonment was substituted. See also *Crick* (1981) 3 Cr.App.R.(S.) 275.

For general sentencing factors set out in the *Magistrates' Court Sentencing Guidelines* (2008) see Ch. 23, *post*.

F. PASSING COUNTERFEIT NOTES AND COINS

(1) Definition

Forgery and Counterfeiting Act 1981, s.15

Offences of passing etc. counterfeit notes and coins

15.—(1) It is an offence for a person— **15–174**

(a) to pass or tender as genuine any thing which is, and which he knows or believes to be, a counterfeit of a currency note or of a protected coin; or

(b) to deliver to another any thing which is, and which he knows or believes to be, such a counterfeit, intending that the person to whom it is delivered or another shall pass or tender it as genuine.

(2) It is an offence for a person to deliver to another, without lawful authority or excuse, any thing which is, and which he knows or believes to be, a counterfeit of a currency note or of a protected coin.

(2) Procedure

These offences are triable either way: *Forgery and Counterfeiting Act* 1981, s.22. **15–175**

(3) Elements of the offence

The prosecution must prove that either: **15–176**

— the defendant passed or tendered;

OR

— delivered to another,

— any thing which is, and which he knows to be a counterfeit of a currency note or a protected coin,

— intending that the person to whom it is delivered shall pass or tender it as genuine;

OR

— the defendant delivered to another,

— without lawful authority or excuse,

— any thing which is, and which he knows to be a counterfeit of a currency note or a protected coin.

For the meaning of "currency note" "protected coin" and "counterfeit" see ss.27 and 28 of the 1981 Act (*ante*).

(4) Sentence

When tried summarily, offences under both ss.14(1) and (2) are punishable by a maximum sentence of six months' imprisonment, a fine not exceeding the statutory maximum or both. After commencement of the relevant provisions, the maximum custodial sentence in a magistrates' court will be 12 months' imprisonment: *Criminal Justice Act* 2003, ss.154 and 282. **15–177**

In *Derbyshire* (1992) 13 Cr.App.R.(S.) 126 the offender pleaded guilty to three counts of delivering counterfeit goods with intent, having bought nine forged notes which he then sold on to three other men. He was sentenced to twelve months' imprisonment. On appeal, it was held that the offences were at or near the bottom of the scale for offences of their type and the appropriate sentence was six months' imprisonment. In *Shah* (1987) 9 Cr.App.R.(S.) 167 the offender was convicted of tendering a counterfeit note. He had attempted to buy a record offering a forged £50 note. The offender claimed he had picked up the note without realising what it was, and there was no other evidence of dealing with counterfeit notes. The Court of Appeal upheld his sentence of twelve months' imprisonment, to be suspended for two years, with a supervision order, Steyn J. stating that in the absence of exceptional circumstances an immediate custodial sentence is necessary in all cases involving the tendering or passing of forged banknotes. A case lying towards the less serious end of the spectrum is *Dickens* (1993) 14 Cr.App.R.(S.) 76. The offender had tendered a counterfeit £20 note in a shop. He admitted that he knew the note was counterfeit, but claimed that he had received it innocently in change for a £50 note, and decided to pass it on. He was sentenced to 12 months' imprisonment. On appeal, the propriety of an immediate custodial sentence was approved, yet 12 months was manifestly excessive, and a sentence of six months was substituted.

In *Wake* (1992) 13 Cr.App.R.(S.) 422, the offender was convicted of two counts of passing a counterfeit note. The Court of Appeal held that although an immediate custodial sentence was entirely appropriate, a sentence of 12 months' imprisonment for this offence was manifestly excessive and a sentence of three months' imprisonment was appropriate. A sentence of four months' imprisonment was imposed where the offender had been in possession of 47 counterfeit £5 notes for 20 minutes after the driver of the car in which he was a passenger gave him them to conceal from the police: *Luxford* [1996] 1 Cr.App.R.(S.) 186, CA.

For general sentencing factors set out in the *Magistrates' Court Sentencing Guidelines* (2008) see Ch. 23, *post*.

G. CUSTODY OR CONTROL OF COUNTERFEITS

(1) Definition

Forgery and Counterfeiting Act 1981, s.16

Offences involving the custody or control of counterfeit notes and coins

15–178 **16.**—(1) It is an offence for a person to have in his custody or under his control any thing which is; and which he knows or believes to be, a counterfeit of a currency note or of a protected coin, intending either to pass or tender it as genuine or to deliver it to another with the intention that he or another shall pass or tender it as genuine.

(2) It is an offence for a person to have in his custody or under his control, without lawful authority or excuse, any thing which is, and which he knows or believes to be, a counterfeit of a currency note or of a protected coin.

(3) It is immaterial for the purposes of subsections (1) and (2) above that a coin or note is not in a fit state to be passed or tendered or that the making or counterfeiting of a coin or note has not been finished or perfected.

(2) Allocation

15–179 These offences are triable either way: *Forgery and Counterfeiting Act* 1981, s.22.

(3) Elements of the offence

15–180 The prosecution must prove that:

— the defendant had in his custody or under his control,
— any thing which was and which he knew or believed to be,
— a counterfeit of a currency note or protected coin,
— intending either to pass or tender it as genuine or to deliver it to another with the intention that he or another shall pass or tender it as genuine;

OR

— the defendant had in his custody or under his control,
— any thing which was and which he knew or believed to be,

— a counterfeit of a currency note or protected coin.

For the meaning of "currency note" "protected coin" and "counterfeit" see *ante*, ss.27 and 28 of the 1981 Act: § 15–160 and § 15–169.

(4) Sentence

When tried summarily, offences under both s.14(1) and (2) are punishable by a maximum sentence of six months' imprisonment, a fine not exceeding the statutory maximum or both. After commencement of the relevant provisions, the maximum custodial sentence in a magistrates' court will be 12 months' imprisonment: *Criminal Justice Act* 2003, ss.154 and 282. **15–181**

In *Torry* (1983) 5 Cr.App.R.(S.) 326, CA, the offender pleaded guilty to one count of handling stolen goods and one of having custody or control of a counterfeit currency note. Forty-six counterfeit £20 had been found at his house, and he received a sentence of eighteen months' imprisonment for possession of the counterfeit notes. This was substituted for a sentence of 12 months on appeal due to the mitigating circumstances of the offender. See also *Carter* (1983) 5 Cr.App.R.(S.) 256.

In cases involving poor quality counterfeit notes and a lack of intention to use them, a community sentence may be appropriate: *Leslie* [2009] EWCA Crim 884, CA. In this case, the appellant had been sentenced to four years' imprisonment following his guilty plea to having custody or control of counterfeit currency contrary to s.16(2) of the *Forgery and Counterfeiting Act* 1981. Police officers had found 15 counterfeit £20 notes following a search of the appellant's car. The serial numbers on all the notes were the same and under ultra violet light there was no watermark. The appellant was initially charged under s.16(1) which involves the element of intention to pass the notes. However, the pleas were accepted to s.16(2), seemingly on the basis that the fakes were so poor that they could not have been passed for profit. Substituting a community order with a requirement for 80 hours of unpaid work, the Court held that the poor quality of the notes and lack of intention to use them made a community penalty appropriate.

For general sentencing factors set out in the *Magistrates' Court Sentencing Guidelines* (2008) see Ch. 23, *post*.

H. MAKING, CUSTODY OR CONTROL OF COUNTERFEITING MATERIALS AND IMPLEMENTS

(1) Definition

Forgery and Counterfeiting Act, s.17

Offences involving the making or custody or control of counterfeiting materials and implements

17.—(1) It is an offence for a person to make, or to have in his custody or under his control, any thing which he intends to use, or to permit any other person to use, for the purpose of making a counterfeit of a currency note or of a protected coin with the intention that it be passed or tendered as genuine. **15–182**

(2) It is an offence for a person without lawful authority or excuse—

(a) to make; or

(b) to have in his custody or under his control,

any thing which, to his knowledge, is or has been specially designed or adapted for the making of a counterfeit of a currency note.

(3) Subject to subsection (4) below, it is an offence for a person to make, or to have in his custody or under his control, any implement which, to his knowledge, is capable of imparting to any thing a resemblance—

(a) to the whole or part of either side of a protected coin; or

(b) to the whole or part of the reverse of the image on either side of a protected coin.

(4) It shall be a defence for a person charged with an offence under subsection (3) above to show—

(a) that he made the implement or, as the case may be, had it in his custody or under his control, with the written consent of the Treasury; or
(b) that he had lawful authority otherwise than by virtue of paragraph (a) above, or a lawful excuse, for making it or having it in his custody or under his control.

(2) Allocation

15–183 These offences are triable either way: *Forgery and Counterfeiting Act* 1981, s.22.

(3) Elements of the offence

15–184 The prosecution must prove that:
— the defendant made, or had in his custody or under his control,
— any thing which he intends to use, or to permit any other person to use, for the purpose of making a counterfeit of a currency note or of a protected coin with,
— with the intention that it be passed or tendered as genuine;
OR
— the defendant made, or had in his custody or under his control,
— any thing which, to his knowledge, had been specially designed or adapted for the making of a counterfeit of a currency note,
— without lawful authority or excuse;
OR
— the defendant made, or had in his custody or control,
— any implement which, to his knowledge was capable of imparting to any thing a resemblance either to the whole or part of a protected coin, or to the whole or part of the reverse of the image on either side of a protected coin, and,
— the defendant did not make the implement or, have it in his custody or under his control with the written consent of the Treasury; or with lawful authority otherwise than by virtue of permission of the Treasury, or lawful excuse.

For the meaning of "currency note" "protected coin" and "counterfeit" see *ante*, ss.27 and 28 of the 1981 Act: § 15–70 and § 15–72.

(4) Sentence

15–185 When tried summarily, offences under both s.17(1) and (2) are punishable by a maximum sentence of six months' imprisonment, a fine not exceeding the statutory maximum or both. After commencement of the relevant provisions, the maximum custodial sentence in a magistrates' court will be 12 months' imprisonment: *Criminal Justice Act* 2003, ss.154 and 282.

For general sentencing factors set out in the *Magistrates' Court Sentencing Guidelines* (2008) see Ch. 23, *post*.

I. REPRODUCING BRITISH CURRENCY

(1) Definition

Forgery and Counterfeiting Act 1981 ss.18(1), 19(1)

The offence of reproducing British currency notes

15–186 **18.**—(1) It is an offence for any person, unless the relevant authority has previously consented in writing, to reproduce on any substance whatsoever, and whether or not on the correct scale, any British currency note or any part of a British currency note.

Offences of making etc. imitation British coins

15–187 **19.**—(1) It is an offence for a person—

(a) to make an imitation British coin in connection with a scheme intended to promote the sale of any product or the making of contracts for the supply of any service; or

(b) to sell or distribute imitation British coins in connection with any such scheme, or to have imitation British coins in his custody or under his control with a view to such sale or distribution,

unless the Treasury have previously consented in writing to the sale or distribution of such imitation British coins in connection with that scheme.

(2) Allocation

These offences are triable either way: *Forgery and Counterfeiting Act* 1981, s.22. **15–188**

(3) Elements of the offence

The prosecution must prove that: **15–189**

— the defendant produced, on any substance, or to any scale whatsoever,
— any British currency note or any part of a British currency note,
— without the written consent of the relevant consenting authority;

OR

— the defendant made an imitation British coin,
— in connection with a scheme intended to promote the sale of any product or the making of contracts for the supply of any service;

OR

— the defendant sold or distributed imitation British coins,
— in connection with a scheme intended to promote the sale of any product or the making of contracts for the supply of any service;

OR

— the defendant had imitation British coins in his custody or control,
— with a view to their sale or distribution,
— without the written consent of the Treasury to such sale or distribution of imitation British coins.

Forgery and Counterfeiting Act 1981, ss.18(2) and 19(2)

The offence of reproducing British currency notes

18.—(2) In this section— **15–190**

"British currency note" means any note which—

(a) has been lawfully issued in England and Wales, Scotland or Northern Ireland; and
(b) is or has been customarily used as money in the country where it was issued; and
(c) is payable on demand; and

"the relevant authority", in relation to a British currency note of any particular description, means the authority empowered by law to issue notes of that description.

Offences of making etc. imitation British coins

19.—(2) In this section— **15–191**

"British coin" means any coin which is legal tender in any part of the United Kingdom; and

"imitation British coin" means any thing which resembles a British coin in shape, size and the substance of which it is made.

(4) Sentence

When tried summarily, offences under both s.14(1) and (2) are punishable by a maximum sentence of six months' imprisonment, a fine not exceeding the statutory maximum or both. After commencement of the relevant provisions, the maximum custodial sentence in a magistrates' court will be 12 months' imprisonment: *Criminal Justice Act* 2003, ss.154 and 282. **15–192**

For general sentencing factors set out in the *Magistrates' Court Sentencing Guidelines* (2008) see Ch. 23, *post*.

Part III

J. PROHIBITION OF IMPORTATION AND EXPORTATION ON COUNTERFEITS

(1) Definition

Forgery and Counterfeiting Act 1981, ss.20–21

Prohibition of importation of counterfeit notes and coins

15–193 **20.** The importation, landing or unloading of a counterfeit of a currency note or of a protected coin without the consent of the Treasury is hereby prohibited.

Prohibition of exportation of counterfeit notes and coins

15–194 **21.**—(1) The exportation of a counterfeit of a currency note or of a protected coin without the consent of the Treasury is hereby prohibited.

(2) A counterfeit of a currency note or of a protected coin which is removed to the Isle of Man from the United Kingdom shall be deemed to be exported from the United Kingdom—

(a) for the purposes of this section; and

(b) for the purposes of the customs and excise Acts, in their application to the prohibition imposed by this section.

(3) [Amends *Isle of Man Act* 1979, s.9(1).]

(2) Procedure

15–195 Sections 20 and 21 do not create offences, rather they impose prohibitions. The relevant offences are those committed under the *Customs and Excise Management Act* 1979, ss.50 and 68. See *post*, §§ 19–17 and 19–25.

IV. MISCELLANEOUS OFFENCES

A. OFFENCES UNDER THE PROCEEDS OF CRIME ACT 2002

(1) Concealing

(a) *Definition*

Proceeds of Crime Act 2002, s.327

Concealing etc

15–196 **327.**—(1) A person commits an offence if he—

(a) conceals criminal property;

(b) disguises criminal property;

(c) converts criminal property;

(d) transfers criminal property;

(e) removes criminal property from England and Wales or from Scotland or from Northern Ireland.

(2) But a person does not commit such an offence if—

(a) he makes an authorised disclosure under section 338 and (if the disclosure is made before he does the act mentioned in subsection (1)) he has the appropriate consent;

(b) he intended to make such a disclosure but had a reasonable excuse for not doing so;

(c) the act he does is done in carrying out a function he has relating to the enforcement of any provision of this Act or of any other enactment relating to criminal conduct or benefit from criminal conduct.

(2A) Nor does a person commit an offence under subsection (1) if—

(a) he knows, or believes on reasonable grounds, that the relevant criminal conduct occurred in a particular country or territory outside the United Kingdom, and

(b) the relevant criminal conduct—
(i) was not, at the time it occurred, unlawful under the criminal law then applying in that country or territory, and
(ii) is not of a description prescribed by an order made by the Secretary of State.

(2B) In subsection (2A) "the relevant criminal conduct" is the criminal conduct by reference to which the property concerned is criminal property.

(2C) A deposit-taking body that does an act mentioned in paragraph (c) or (d) of subsection

(1) does not commit an offence under that subsection if—
(a) it does the act in operating an account maintained with it, and
(b) the value of the criminal property concerned is less than the threshold amount determined under section 339A for the act.

(3) Concealing or disguising criminal property includes concealing or disguising its nature, source, location, disposition, movement or ownership or any rights with respect to it.

(b) *Allocation*

The offence is triable either way: *Proceeds of Crime Act* 2002, s.334. Part 7 of the 2002 Act was brought into force on February 24, 2003 (*Proceeds of Crime Act 2002 (Commencement No. 4, Transitional Provisions and Savings) Order* 2003 (S.I. 2003 No. 120)). The provisions do not apply where the conduct allegedly constituting an offence began before February 24, 2003 and ended on or after that date: *Proceeds of Crime Act 2002 (Commencement No. 4, Transitional Provisions and Savings) Order* 2003 (S.I. 2003 No. 120), art. 3. **15–197**

(c) *Elements of the offence*

The prosecution must prove that: **15–198**

— the defendant concealed, disguised, converted or transferred criminal property;

OR

— removed criminal property from England and Wales, or from Scotland or from Northern Ireland.

"Criminal Property"

Property is criminal property if it constitutes a person's benefit from criminal conduct or it represents such a benefit (in whole or part and whether directly or indirectly), and the alleged offender knows or suspects that it constitutes or represents such a benefit: *Proceeds of Crime Act* 2002, s.340(3). **15–199**

It is immaterial who carried out the conduct, who benefited from it, and whether the conduct occurred before or after the passing of the *Proceeds of Crime Act* 2002: *Proceeds of Crime Act* 2002, s.340(4).

A person benefits from conduct if he obtains property as a result of or in connection with the conduct: *Proceeds of Crime Act* 2002, s.340(5).

If a person obtains a pecuniary advantage as a result of or in connection with conduct, he is to be taken to obtain as a result of or in connection with the conduct a sum of money equal to the value of the pecuniary advantage: *Proceeds of Crime Act* 2002, s.340(6)

References to property or a pecuniary advantage obtained in connection with conduct include references to property or a pecuniary advantage obtained in both that connection and some other: *Proceeds of Crime Act* 2002, s.340(7).

If a person benefits from conduct his benefit is the property obtained as a result of or in connection with the conduct: *Proceeds of Crime Act* 2002, s.340(8).

Property is all property wherever situated and includes money, all forms of property, real or personal, heritable or moveable and things in action and other intangible or incorporeal property:*Proceeds of Crime Act* 2002, s.340(9).

Property is obtained by a person if he obtains an interest in it, and references to an interest, in relation to land in England and Wales or Northern Ireland, are to any legal estate or equitable interest or power. References to an interest, in relation to land in Scotland, are to any estate, interest, servitude or other heritable right in or over land, including a heritable security and references to an interest, in relation to property other than land, include references to a right (including a right to possession): *Proceeds of Crime Act* 2002, s.340(10).

The property concealed, disguised, converted or transferred must have been criminal property at the time that it was concealed, disguised, converted or transferred. In a case of transfer, the offence of transferring criminal property would not be committed if the property was not criminal property at the time of the transfer:*Loizou* [2005] EWCA Crim 1579, CA. It could not be said that property acquired legitimately would become criminal property within s.340 of the 2002 Act, if a person formed a purpose or intention to use it for criminal purposes: *Loizou* [2005] EWCA Crim 1579, CA.

The prosecution do not have to prove only one way by which the relevant property was criminal property and negate all other ways by which the property could be criminal property: *Craig* [2007] EWCA Crim 2913, CA. In this case, the appellant appealed against his convictions for using criminal property, transferring criminal property and possessing criminal property. The prosecution case was that for a year and a half the appellant's admitted use of substantial amounts of cash, cars and other items could not be justified when tax and national insurance records showed he had not been employed or earning during that period, creating the overwhelming inference that his funds were derived from criminal activity. The appellant claimed that he had amassed substantial funds over many years through legitimate work, and accepted he had paid no tax or national insurance on these earnings. The appellant submitted that there were several ways in which his alleged criminal property could be criminal property and the judge should have given a direction in accordance with *Brown* (1984) 1 B.C.C. 98970, CA, that the jury all had to be sure about which of those ways had been proved. The appellant also submitted that the judge's summing up was defective, the defence case was not properly put and his evidence not placed before the jury in a manner enabling it to be understood.

Allowing the appeal, the Court held that it did not have to be shown that the property emanated from a particular crime or a specific type of criminal conduct; the jury only needed to be sure that the property was criminal property. A huge burden would be placed on the prosecution if it had to prove only one way by which the property was criminal property and negate all other ways. However, the judge had failed to properly sum up the defence case for the jury; the summing up had followed no logical pattern and provided no clear idea of what the defence was. The appellant had to deal with detailed cash receipts and withdrawals to demonstrate his possession of large amounts of money was not the result of money laundering; therefore his and his witnesses' evidence was vital to his defence and required a focused exposition in the summing up. Whilst the case against the appellant was strong, he had not received a fair trial; his convictions were therefore quashed and a retrial ordered.

In *NW, SW, RC and CC* [2008] EWCA Crim 2, CA, the Crown appealed against a ruling of no case to answer made in respect of three charges relating to money laundering offences. The crown had alleged that the offences involved the transfer of over £105,000 out of the United Kingdom to Jamaica, all of which represented the proceeds of criminal conduct. At the close of the Crown's case, the judge accepted a defence submission of no case to answer, finding, firstly, that the funds allegedly transferred were not criminal property, as the prosecution had produced no evidence of specific criminal conduct, or even a particular type of criminal conduct, and secondly, that the circumstances surrounding the origin of the transferred funds created a reverse burden of proof upon the defendants explain such funds, which was not a proper way to leave a case to a jury.

Dismissing the appeal, the Court held that under the civil recovery provisions of the 2002 Act there had to be proof of at least the class of offence said to constitute the alleged unlawful conduct. Whilst the criminal provisions of the 2002 Act contained no such express requirement, the linguistic differences were not so pressing as to yield a conclusion that the legislature intended, in the context of criminal measures, to strike the balance between civil rights and the protection of the public at a markedly different place from where it lay in relation to the civil provisions. Parliament could not have intended a state of affairs in which no particulars need be given or proved of a cardinal element in the case, namely, the criminal conduct relied on. It was a requirement of elementary fairness that such particulars be required. The Court further stated that the judge was wrong to characterise the Crown's position as involving a reversal of the burden of proof as the presence of an evidential burden on the defendant to show that an inference based on circumstantial evidence was wrong did not reposition the legal burden of proof

There are two ways in which it might be proven that property derived from crime. One is to show that it derived from conduct of a specific kind and that conduct of that kind was unlawful. The other is to put forward evidence of the circumstances in which the property was handled that gives rise to the irresistible inference that it could only be derived from crime: *Anwoir* [2008] EWCA Crim 1354, CA. In *F* [2008] EWCA Crim 1868, CA, the appellant Revenue and Customs Prosecution Office appealed against a ruling of no case to answer made in favour of the two respondents in respect of charges of being concerned in a money laundering arrangement and transferring criminal property, contrary to ss.327 and 328 of the 2002 Act. One of the respondents had been stopped at an airport and their baggage found to contain £1,184,670, which the respondent alleged was criminal property. The judge accepted the respondent's submission that the appellant had failed to establish at least the type of criminal conduct which had produced the money and therefore had failed to prove that the money was criminal property. The appellant alleged that, following *Anwoir* [2008] (above) it had been entitled to ask the jury to consider evidence of the circumstances in which the property had been handled, from which they could have inferred that the money had been derived from crime. Allowing the appeal, the Court stated that the respondent could rely upon the statement of principle in *Anwoir*, and their failure to point to any particular criminality had not resulted in procedural unfairness.

In *Middleton* [2008] EWCA Crim 233, CA, the appellants appealed against their convictions of converting the proceeds of drug trafficking and converting criminal property contrary to s.327 of the 2002 Act. The case against the appellants was that they had been laundering the proceeds of their own drug trafficking over a number of years through thousands of different transactions (intermingling such transactions with legitimate transactions). The prosecution invited the jury to draw the inference that income that could not be explained was payments relating to drug trafficking. The judge directed the jury that they should not convict unless they were sure that the prosecution had established that the defendants were guilty of at least 80 per cent of the criminality alleged. The respondents argued that the judge's decision to permit the prosecution to proceed was wrong as a matter of principle and had not been saved by his specific direction to the jury.

Dismissing the appeal, the Court held that it was impossible to untangle the appellant's legitimate and illegitimate activity and it would have been unduly oppressive and onerous to have identified each and every individual transaction as separate counts. To have adopted a relatively small number of discrete specimen counts would have caused two problems. First, the judge's powers in sentencing would have been constrained by authority so as to be limited to those specimen counts which had been proved. Second, in any event, the prosecution had been unable to say, of any individual transaction, that the jury could be sure that the money in question derived from drug trafficking. The judge's direction ensured that convictions on each count would reflect that the jury were sure that the appellants were guilty of the criminal activity alleged and on the scale alleged.

Lodging, receiving, retaining and withdrawing money from a bank account might all amount to a conversion: *Fazal* [2009] EWCA Crim 1697, CA. In this case, the appellant appealed against his conviction on seven counts of converting criminal property contrary to the *Proceeds of Crime Act* 2002, s.327(1)(c). Seven deposits had been made into his bank account, which were the proceeds of fraud. The appellant had given his bank details, debit card and PIN to a friend who had needed to use his account to have his wages paid into it. He stated that he did not use the account. Dismissing his appeal, the Court held that each transaction of lodging, receiving, retaining and withdrawing money from a bank account could amount to a conversion. Asking or allowing another person, who might or might not have had the required *mens rea* to make such transactions did not prevent an account owner from converting money through his account. When the money was withdrawn from the appellant's account it was transferred into cash. At each stage the property concerned was passed through the appellant's account, thereby being converted.

(d) *Statutory defence*

15–200 A person will not commit an offence under this section if they have:
- — Made an authorised disclosure under s.338 of the 2002 Act and (if the disclosure is made before he does the act) he has the appropriate consent or;
- — Intended to make such a disclosure but had reasonable cause for not doing so, or;
- — Done the act in order to carry out a function he has relating to the enforcement of any provision of the 2002 Act or any other enactment relating to criminal conduct or benefit from criminal conduct.

A person will not commit an offence under this section if they:
- — Know, or believe on reasonable grounds,
- — That the relevant criminal conduct occurred in a particular country or territory outside the United Kingdom and was not, at the time it occurred, unlawful under the criminal law then applying in that country or territory, nor was it of a description prescribed by an order made by the Secretary of State.

"Appropriate Consent"

Proceeds of Crime Act 2002, ss.335, 336

Appropriate consent

15–201 **335.**—(1) The appropriate consent is—

(a) the consent of a nominated officer to do a prohibited act if an authorised disclosure is made to the nominated officer;

(b) the consent of a constable to do a prohibited act if an authorised disclosure is made to a constable;

(c) the consent of a customs officer to do a prohibited act if an authorised disclosure is made to a customs officer.

(2) A person must be treated as having the appropriate consent if—

(a) he makes an authorised disclosure to a constable or a customs officer, and

(b) the condition in subsection (3) or the condition in subsection (4) is satisfied.

(3) The condition is that before the end of the notice period he does not receive notice from a constable or customs officer that consent to the doing of the act is refused.

(4) The condition is that—

(a) before the end of the notice period he receives notice from a constable or customs officer that consent to the doing of the act is refused, and

(b) the moratorium period has expired.

(5) The notice period is the period of seven working days starting with the first working day after the person makes the disclosure.

(6) The moratorium period is the period of 31 days starting with the day on which the person receives notice that consent to the doing of the act is refused.

(7) A working day is a day other than a Saturday, a Sunday, Christmas Day, Good Friday or a day which is a bank holiday under the Banking and *Financial Dealings Act*

1971 (c. 80) in the part of the United Kingdom in which the person is when he makes the disclosure.

(8) References to a prohibited act are to an act mentioned in section 327(1), 328(1) or 329(1) (as the case may be).

(9) A nominated officer is a person nominated to receive disclosures under section 338.

(10) Subsections (1) to (4) apply for the purposes of this Part.

Nominated officer: consent

336.—(1) A nominated officer must not give the appropriate consent to the doing of a prohibited act unless the condition in subsection (2), the condition in subsection (3) or the condition in subsection (4) is satisfied.

(2) The condition is that—

(a) he makes a disclosure that property is criminal property to a person authorised for the purposes of this Part by the Director General of SOCA, and

(b) such a person gives consent to the doing of the act.

(3) The condition is that—

(a) he makes a disclosure that property is criminal property to a person authorised for the purposes of this Part by the Director General of SOCA, and

(b) before the end of the notice period he does not receive notice from such a person that consent to the doing of the act is refused.

(4) The condition is that—

(a) he makes a disclosure that property is criminal property to a person authorised for the purposes of this Part by the Director General of SOCA,

(b) before the end of the notice period he receives notice from such a person that consent to the doing of the act is refused, and

(c) the moratorium period has expired.

(5) A person who is a nominated officer commits an offence if—

(a) he gives consent to a prohibited act in circumstances where none of the conditions in subsections (2), (3) and (4) is satisfied, and

(b) he knows or suspects that the act is a prohibited act.

(6) A person guilty of such an offence is liable—

(a) on summary conviction, to imprisonment for a term not exceeding six months or to a fine not exceeding the statutory maximum or to both, or

(b) on conviction on indictment, to imprisonment for a term not exceeding five years or to a fine or to both.

(7) The notice period is the period of seven working days starting with the first working day after the nominated officer makes the disclosure.

(8) The moratorium period is the period of 31 days starting with the day on which the nominated officer is given notice that consent to the doing of the act is refused.

(9) A working day is a day other than a Saturday, a Sunday, Christmas Day, Good Friday or a day which is a bank holiday under the Banking and *Financial Dealings Act* 1971 (c. 80) in the part of the United Kingdom in which the nominated officer is when he gives the appropriate consent.

(10) References to a prohibited act are to an act mentioned in section 327(1), 328(1) or 329(1) (as the case may be).

(11) A nominated officer is a person nominated to receive disclosures under section 338.

"Authorised Disclosures"

Proceeds of Crime Act 2002, s.338

Authorised disclosures

338.—(1) For the purposes of this Part a disclosure is authorised if— **15–202**

(a) it is a disclosure to a constable, a customs officer or a nominated officer by the alleged offender that property is criminal property, and

(b) the first, second or third condition set out below is satisfied.

(2) The first condition is that the disclosure is made before the alleged offender does the prohibited act.

(2A) The second condition is that—

(a) the disclosure is made while the alleged offender is doing the prohibited act,

(b) he began to do the act at a time when, because he did not then know or suspect that the property constituted or represented a person's benefit from criminal conduct, the act was not a prohibited act, and

(c) the disclosure is made on his own initiative and as soon as is practicable after he first knows or suspects that the property constitutes or represents a person's benefit from criminal conduct.

(3) The third condition is that—

(a) the disclosure is made after the alleged offender does the prohibited act,

(b) [he has a reasonable excuse]1 for his failure to make the disclosure before he did the act, and

(c) the disclosure is made on his own initiative and as soon as it is practicable for him to make it.

(4) An authorised disclosure is not to be taken to breach any restriction on the disclosure of information (however imposed).

(5) A disclosure to a nominated officer is a disclosure which—

(a) is made to a person nominated by the alleged offender's employer to receive authorised disclosures, and

(b) is made in the course of the alleged offender's employment.

(6) References to the prohibited act are to an act mentioned in section 327(1), 328(1) or 329(1) (as the case may be).

"Deposit-taking bodies"

15–203 A "deposit-taking body" will not commit an offence under this section if:

— It did the act in operating an account maintained with it, and

— The value of the criminal property concerned is less than the threshold amount determined under section 339A of the 2002 Act.

"Deposit-taking body" means a business which engages in the activity of accepting deposits, or the *National Savings Bank: Proceeds of Crime Act* 2002, s.340(14).

Proceeds of Crime Act 2002, s.339A

Threshold amounts

339A.—(1) This section applies for the purposes of sections 327(2C), 328(5) and 329(2C).

(2) The threshold amount for acts done by a deposit-taking body in operating an account is £250 unless a higher amount is specified under the following provisions of this section (in which event it is that higher amount).

(3) An officer of Revenue and Customs, or a constable, may specify the threshold amount for acts done by a deposit-taking body in operating an account—

(a) when he gives consent, or gives notice refusing consent, to the deposit-taking body's doing of an act mentioned in section 327(1), 328(1) or 329(1) in opening, or operating, the account or a related account, or

(b) on a request from the deposit-taking body.

(4) Where the threshold amount for acts done in operating an account is specified under subsection (3) or this subsection, an officer of Revenue and Customs, or a constable, may vary the amount (whether on a request from the deposit-taking body or otherwise) by specifying a different amount.

(5) Different threshold amounts may be specified under subsections (3) and (4) for different acts done in operating the same account.

(6) The amount specified under subsection (3) or (4) as the threshold amount for acts done in operating an account must, when specified, not be less than the amount specified in subsection (2).

(7) The Secretary of State may by order vary the amount for the time being specified in subsection (2).

(8) For the purposes of this section, an account is related to another if each is maintained with the same deposit-taking body and there is a person who, in relation to each account,

is the person or one of the persons entitled to instruct the body as respects the operation of the account.

(e) *Sentence*

When tried summarily, the maximum penalty for this offence is imprisonment for a term not exceeding six months or to a fine not exceeding the statutory maximum or to both: *Proceeds of Crime Act* 2002, s.334. **15–204**

(2) Arranging

(a) *Definition*

Proceeds of Crime Act 2002, s.328

Arrangements

328.—(1) A person commits an offence if he enters into or becomes concerned in an arrangement which he knows or suspects facilitates (by whatever means) the acquisition, retention, use or control of criminal property by or on behalf of another person. **15–205**

(2) But a person does not commit such an offence if—

(a) he makes an authorised disclosure under section 338 and (if the disclosure is made before he does the act mentioned in subsection (1)) he has the appropriate consent;

(b) he intended to make such a disclosure but had a reasonable excuse for not doing so;

(c) the act he does is done in carrying out a function he has relating to the enforcement of any provision of this Act or of any other enactment relating to criminal conduct or benefit from criminal conduct.

(3) Nor does a person commit an offence under subsection (1) if—

(a) he knows, or believes on reasonable grounds, that the relevant criminal conduct occurred in a particular country or territory outside the United Kingdom, and

(b) the relevant criminal conduct—

(i) was not, at the time it occurred, unlawful under the criminal law then applying in that country or territory, and

(ii) is not of a description prescribed by an order made by the Secretary of State.

(4) In subsection (3)"the relevant criminal conduct" is the criminal conduct by reference to which the property concerned is criminal property.

(5) A deposit-taking body that does an act mentioned in subsection (1) does not commit an offence under that subsection if—

(a) it does the act in operating an account maintained with it, and

(b) the arrangement facilitates the acquisition, retention, use or control of criminal property of a value that is less than the threshold amount determined under section 339A for the act.

(b) *Allocation*

The offence is triable either way: *Proceeds of Crime Act* 2002, s.334. Part 7 of the 2002 Act was brought into force on February 24, 2003 (*Proceeds of Crime Act 2002 (Commencement No. 4, Transitional Provisions and Savings) Order* 2003 (S.I. 2003 No. 120)). The provisions do not apply where the conduct allegedly constituting an offence began before February 24, 2003 and ended on or after that date: *Proceeds of Crime Act 2002 (Commencement No. 4, Transitional Provisions and Savings) Order* 2003 (S.I. 2003 No. 120), art. 3. **15–206**

(c) *Elements of the offence*

The prosecution must prove that: **15–207**

— the defendant entered into or became concerned in an arrangement;

— knowing, or suspecting that it facilitates (by whatever means);
— the acquisition, retention, use or control of criminal property by or on behalf of another person

The *Fraud Act* 2006 s.13 had removed the privilege against self-incrimination in respect of an offence under the *Proceeds of Crime Act* 2002 s.328 because an offence under s.328 of the 2002 Act was a "related offence" within the meaning of s.13(4) of the 2006 Act: *JSC BTA Bank v. Ablyazov* [2009] EWCA Civ 1124. The appellant company appealed against a decision that it was not entitled to rely upon the privilege against self-incrimination because an offence under the *Proceeds of Crime Act* 2002 s.328 was a "related offence" within the meaning of the *Fraud Act* 2006 s.13(4). The appellant contended that an offence under s.328 of the 2002 Act fell outside the definition of "related offence" because the court was limited to consideration of the essential character or ingredients of the offence, rather than the particular manner in which it might have been committed, and conduct within the scope of s.328 was not necessarily fraudulent. Dismissing the appeal, the Court held that the matter had to be judged by reference to the essential character of the offence rather than one particular manner of committing it. The important feature of the definition under section 13(4)(b) was that it defined related offence by reference to the quality of the conduct brought within the scope of the charge and not merely by reference to the intention of the alleged offender. Section 13(4)(b) was wide enough to include an offence which charged conduct which had a fraudulent quality, notwithstanding that it had no fraudulent purpose. The judge was therefore correct in concluding that s.328 of the 2002 Act was a related offence for the purposes of s.13 of the 2006 Act.

The natural and ordinary meaning of s.328(1) was that the arrangement to which it referred had to be one which related to property which was criminal property at the time when the arrangement began to operate on it. To say that it extended to property which was originally legitimate but became criminal only as a result of carrying out the arrangement stretched the language of the section beyond its proper limits. An arrangement relating to property which had an independent criminal object might, when carried out, render the subject matter criminal property, but it could not be said that the arrangement applied to property that was already criminal property at the time it began to operate on it: *Geary (Michael)* [2010] EWCA Crim 1925, CA.

In *Akhtar (Urfan)* [2011] EWCA Crim 146, CA, the Court of Appeal held that the appellant, who had knowingly submitted false mortgage applications on behalf of third parties, was not guilty of the offence under section 328 of the *Proceeds of Crime Act* 2002 because when he entered into the relevant arrangements with the mortgage brokers, the property in question was not criminal in the hands of the mortgage company, *Geary (Micheal)* (above) applied.

"Criminal property"

15–208 For the definition of "criminal property", see *Proceeds of Crime Act* 2002, s.340(3)–(10) above.

"Deposit-taking bodies"

15–209 A "deposit-taking" body will not commit an offence under this section if:
— It did the act in operating an account maintained with it, and
— The value of the criminal property concerned is less than the threshold amount determined under section 339A of the 2002 Act.

"Deposit-taking body" means a business which engages in the activity of accepting deposits, or the *National Savings Bank: Proceeds of Crime Act 2002*, s.340(14).

For the relevant threshold amount, see the *Proceeds of Crime Act* 2002, s.339A, *above*.

(d) *Statutory defence*

15–210 A person will not commit an offence under this section if they have:

— made an authorised disclosure under section 338 of the 2002 Act and (if the disclosure is made before he does the act) he had the appropriate consent or;
— intended to make such a disclosure but had reasonable cause for not doing so, or;
— done the act in order to carry out a function he has relating to the enforcement of any provision of the 2002 Act or any other enactment relating to criminal conduct or benefit from criminal conduct.

A person will not commit an offence under this section if they:
— know, or believe on reasonable grounds,
— that the relevant criminal conduct occurred in a particular country or territory outside the United Kingdom and was not, at the time it occurred, unlawful under the criminal law then applying in that country or territory, nor was it of a description prescribed by an order made by the Secretary of State.

For the definition of "appropriate consent" see the *Proceeds of Crime Act* 2002, s.335, above

For the definition of "authorised disclosure" see the *Proceeds of Crime Act* 2002, s.338, above.

(e) *Sentence*

When tried summarily, the maximum penalty for this offence is imprisonment for a term not exceeding six months or to a fine not exceeding the statutory maximum or to both: *Proceeds of Crime Act* 2002, s.334. **15–211**

Part III

(3) Acquisition, use or possession of criminal property

(a) *Definiton*

Proceeds of Crime Act 2002, s.329

Acquisition, use and possession

329.—(1) A person commits an offence if he— **15–212**

(a) acquires criminal property;
(b) uses criminal property;
(c) has possession of criminal property.

(2) But a person does not commit such an offence if—

(a) he makes an authorised disclosure under section 338 and (if the disclosure is made before he does the act mentioned in subsection (1)) he has the appropriate consent;
(b) he intended to make such a disclosure but had a reasonable excuse for not doing so;
(c) he acquired or used or had possession of the property for adequate consideration;
(d) the act he does is done in carrying out a function he has relating to the enforcement of any provision of this Act or of any other enactment relating to criminal conduct or benefit from criminal conduct.

(2A) Nor does a person commit an offence under subsection (1) if—

(a) he knows, or believes on reasonable grounds, that the relevant criminal conduct occurred in a particular country or territory outside the United Kingdom, and
(b) the relevant criminal conduct—
 (i) was not, at the time it occurred, unlawful under the criminal law then applying in that country or territory, and
 (ii) is not of a description prescribed by an order made by the Secretary of State.

(2B) In subsection (2A) "the relevant criminal conduct" is the criminal conduct by reference to which the property concerned is criminal property.

(2C) A deposit-taking body that does an act mentioned in subsection (1) does not commit an offence under that subsection if—

(a) it does the act in operating an account maintained with it, and
(b) the value of the criminal property concerned is less than the threshold amount determined under section 339A for the act.

(3) For the purposes of this section—

(a) a person acquires property for inadequate consideration if the value of the consideration is significantly less than the value of the property;
(b) a person uses or has possession of property for inadequate consideration if the value of the consideration is significantly less than the value of the use or possession;
(c) the provision by a person of goods or services which he knows or suspects may help another to carry out criminal conduct is not consideration.

(b) *Allocation*

15–213 The offence is triable either way: *Proceeds of Crime Act* 2002, s.334. Part 7 of the 2002 Act was brought into force on February 24, 2003 (*Proceeds of Crime Act 2002 (Commencement No. 4, Transitional Provisions and Savings) Order* 2003 (S.I. 2003 No. 120)). The provisions do not apply where the conduct allegedly constituting an offence began before February 24, 2003 and ended on or after that date:*Proceeds of Crime Act 2002 (Commencement No. 4, Transitional Provisions and Savings) Order* 2003 (S.I. 2003 No. 120), art. 3.

(c) *Elements of the offence*

15–214 The prosecution must prove that the defendant acquired, used or had possession of criminal property.

"Criminal Property"

15–215 For the definition of "criminal property", see the *Proceeds of Crime Act* 2002, s.340(3)–(10) above.

Profits made from trading in legitimate goods will not automatically be converted into criminal property by a failure to declare them to the Inland Revenue or the Department of Work and Pensions: *Gabriel* [2006] EWCA Crim 229, CA. In this case, the appellant appealed against her conviction on two counts of possession of criminal property contrary to s.329 of the 2002 Act. The appellant, her husband and her three teenage sons received £500 a week in state benefits. Police officers had searched her house and seized £11,700 in cash. Ten weeks later other officers found a further £6,070 at the family home. The prosecution case was that the money was the result of money laundering; the defence case was that the cash came from savings honestly acquired and winnings from gambling. Although the matter had not been part of the prosecution case, the jury asked the Recorder whether it was a criminal offence to regularly buy and sell goods without making a declaration when claiming benefits or making an income tax return. The Recorder replied that it was if there was dishonesty on the part of the person concerned. The appellant contended that the recorder should have answered that for the purposes of s.329(1)(c) "not necessarily" and the Recorder's wrong answer rendered her convictions unsafe.

Allowing the appeal, the Court of Appeal stated the failure to declare the profits for the purposes of income tax could give rise to a criminal offence but it did not make the trading itself an offence. Whilst benefits obtained on the basis of a false declaration or a failure to disclose a change in circumstances could amount to obtaining a pecuniary advantage under s.340(6) of the 2002 Act, no attempt had been made to prove that the appellant or anyone else in her family had made any false declaration or failed to disclose a change of circumstances. The prosecution case had been one of alleged money laundering, not income tax fraud or benefit fraud. Since it was not known whether the jury had found the appellant guilty on a legitimate basis, her convictions would be quashed.

A person who cheated the Inland Revenue does obtain a pecuniary advantage as a result of criminal conduct within the meaning of s.340(6) of the 2002 Act: *K* [2007] EWCA Crim 491, CA. In this case, the Court had to consider whether the proceeds of cheating the Revenue could amount to "criminal property" within the meaning of the Act where the trade whose profits were liable to income tax or whose turnover was subject to VAT was a legitimate trade. The Court of Appeal held that *Gabriel*, above, did not establish that where money is the takings of a lawful business, it can never be the fruits of criminal conduct. If that were correct, it would mean that the money laundering provisions of the Act could never be invoked in relation to tax evasion where the business concerned was engaged in a lawful trade. It could not have been intended that the money laundering provisions of the Act, particularly those relating to the obtaining of benefit in the form of a pecuniary advantage, should not extend to the fruits of cheating the Revenue. A failure to declare income did not of itself give rise to criminal property and *Gabriel* went no further than meaning that profits from legitimate trading could never, without more, give rise to criminal property.

(d) Statutory defence

A person will not commit an offence under this section if they have: **15–216**

— made an authorised disclosure under section 338 of the 2002 Act and (if the disclosure is made before he does the act) he had the appropriate consent or;
— intended to make such a disclosure but had reasonable cause for not doing so, or
— did the act in order to carry out a function he has relating to the enforcement of any provision of the 2002 Act or any other enactment relating to criminal conduct or benefit from criminal conduct

OR

The defendant:

— acquired, or
— used, or
— had possession of the property
— for adequate consideration;

The defendant:

— knew, or believed on reasonable grounds,
— that the relevant criminal conduct occurred in a particular country or territory outside the United Kingdom, and was not at the time it occurred, unlawful under the criminal law then applying in that country or territory,
— nor was it of a description prescribed by an order made by the Secretary of State.

"Authorised Disclosure"

For the definition of "authorised disclosure" see the *Proceeds of Crime Act* 2002, s.338, *above*. **15–217**

"Appropriate Consent"

For the definition of "appropriate consent" see the *Proceeds of Crime Act* 2002, s.335, *above*. **15–218**

"Adequate consideration"

A person acquires property for inadequate consideration if the value of the consideration is significantly less than the value of the property: *Proceeds of Crime Act* 2002, s.329(3). **15–219**

A person uses or has possession of property for inadequate consideration if the value of the consideration is significantly less than the value of the use or possession: *Proceeds of Crime Act* 2002, s.329(3).

The provision by a person of goods or services which he knows or suspects may help another to carry out criminal conduct is not consideration: Proceeds of Crime Act 2002, s.329(3).

If the property in question was not acquired for inadequate consideration, no offence will be committed, and even if the person knew or suspected the property to be criminal property: *Kausar* [2009] EWCA Crim 2242, CA. In this case, the appellant appealed against a conviction of acquiring criminal property contrary to s.329 of the *Proceeds of Crime Act* 2002. The appellant had applied for a "buy to let" mortgage but the information given on the application form concerning her employment and income was false. The Court was required to determine on appeal whether the property in question had been acquired for inadequate consideration under s.329. Allowing her appeal, the Court stated that the use of "consideration" in criminal statutes was not unusual, and it was difficult to see why Parliament should have used a legal term of art in the 2002 Act if some other meaning was intended. Section 329 made perfect sense if the word was given its normal legal meaning. Given the availability of other offences with which the appellant could have been charged, there was no reason for any unusual meaning to be given to a clearly worded statutory provision. The charge and the undertaking to repay with interest were the consideration for the advance. There was no suggestion that the interest was not at a market rate, or that in any other respect the consideration passing from the appellant was inadequate. Inadequacy of consideration was clearly a separate ingredient of the offence under s.329. The Court added that the appellant should never have been charged with an offence under s.329.

"Deposit-taking bodies"

15–220 A deposit taking body will not commit an offence under this section if:

— it does the act in operating an account maintained with it, and

— the value of the criminal property concerned is less than the threshold amount determined under section 339A of the 2002 Act.

"Deposit-taking body" means a business which engages in the activity of accepting deposits, or the *National Savings Bank: Proceeds of Crime Act 2002*, s.340(14).

For the relevant threshold amount, see the *Proceeds of Crime Act* 2002, section 339A, *above*.

(e) *Sentence*

15–221 When tried summarily, the maximum penalty for this offence is imprisonment for a term not exceeding six months or to a fine not exceeding the statutory maximum or to both: *Proceeds of Crime Act* 2002, s.334.

(4) Failure to disclose: regulated sector

(a) *Definition*

Proceeds of Crime Act 2002, s.330

Failure to disclose: regulated sector

15–222 **330.**—(1) A person commits an offence if the conditions in subsections (2) to (4) are satisfied.

(2) The first condition is that he—

(a) knows or suspects, or

(b) has reasonable grounds for knowing or suspecting, that another person is engaged in money laundering.

(3) The second condition is that the information or other matter—

(a) on which his knowledge or suspicion is based, or
(b) which gives reasonable grounds for such knowledge or suspicion, came to him in the course of a business in the regulated sector.

(3A) The third condition is—
(a) that he can identify the other person mentioned in subsection (2) or the whereabouts of any of the laundered property, or
(b) that he believes, or it is reasonable to expect him to believe, that the information or other matter mentioned in subsection (3) will or may assist in identifying that other person or the whereabouts of any of the laundered property.

(4) The fourth condition is that he does not make the required disclosure to—
(a) a nominated officer, or
(b) a person authorised for the purposes of this Part by the Director General of SOCA, as soon as is practicable after the information or other matter mentioned in subsection (3) comes to him.

(5) The required disclosure is a disclosure of—
(a) the identity of the other person mentioned in subsection (2), if he knows it,
(b) the whereabouts of the laundered property, so far as he knows it, and
(c) the information or other matter mentioned in subsection (3).

(5A) The laundered property is the property forming the subject-matter of the money laundering that he knows or suspects, or has reasonable grounds for knowing or suspecting, that other person to be engaged in.

(6) But he does not commit an offence under this section if—
(a) he has a reasonable excuse for not making the required disclosure,
(b) he is a professional legal adviser or relevant professional adviser and—
(i) if he knows either of the things mentioned in subsection (5)(a) and (b), he knows the thing because of information or other matter that came to him in privileged circumstances, or
(ii) the information or other matter mentioned in subsection (3) came to him in privileged circumstances, or
(c) subsection (7) or (7B) applies to him.

(7) This subsection applies to a person if—
(a) he does not know or suspect that another person is engaged in money laundering, and
(b) he has not been provided by his employer with such training as is specified by the Secretary of State by order for the purposes of this section.

(7A) Nor does a person commit an offence under this section if—
(a) he knows, or believes on reasonable grounds, that the money laundering is occurring in a particular country or territory outside the United Kingdom, and
(b) the money laundering—
(i) is not unlawful under the criminal law applying in that country or territory, and
(ii) is not of a description prescribed in an order made by the Secretary of State.

(7B) This subsection applies to a person if—
(a) he is employed by, or is in partnership with, a professional legal adviser or a relevant professional adviser to provide the adviser with assistance or support,
(b) the information or other matter mentioned in subsection (3) comes to the person in connection with the provision of such assistance or support, and
(c) the information or other matter came to the adviser in privileged circumstances.

(8) In deciding whether a person committed an offence under this section the court must consider whether he followed any relevant guidance which was at the time concerned—
(a) issued by a supervisory authority or any other appropriate body,
(b) approved by the Treasury, and
(c) published in a manner it approved as appropriate in its opinion to bring the guidance to the attention of persons likely to be affected by it.

(9) A disclosure to a nominated officer is a disclosure which—
(a) is made to a person nominated by the alleged offender's employer to receive disclosures under this section, and

Part III

(b) is made in the course of the alleged offender's employment.

(9A) But a disclosure which satisfies paragraphs (a) and (b) of subsection (9) is not to be taken as a disclosure to a nominated officer if the person making the disclosure—

(a) is a professional legal adviser or relevant professional adviser,

(b) makes it for the purpose of obtaining advice about making a disclosure under this section, and

(c) does not intend it to be a disclosure under this section.

(10) Information or other matter comes to a professional legal adviser or relevant professional adviser in privileged circumstances if it is communicated or given to him—

(a) by (or by a representative of) a client of his in connection with the giving by the adviser of legal advice to the client,

(b) by (or by a representative of) a person seeking legal advice from the adviser, or

(c) by a person in connection with legal proceedings or contemplated legal proceedings.

(11) But subsection (10) does not apply to information or other matter which is communicated or given with the intention of furthering a criminal purpose.

(12) Schedule 9 has effect for the purpose of determining what is—

(a) a business in the regulated sector;

(b) a supervisory authority.

(13) An appropriate body is any body which regulates or is representative of any trade, profession, business or employment carried on by the alleged offender.

(14) A relevant professional adviser is an accountant, auditor or tax adviser who is a member of a professional body which is established for accountants, auditors or tax advisers (as the case may be) and which makes provision for—

(a) testing the competence of those seeking admission to membership of such a body as a condition for such admission; and

(b) imposing and maintaining professional and ethical standards for its members, as well as imposing sanctions for non-compliance with those standards.

(b) *Allocation*

15–223 The offence is triable either way: *Proceeds of Crime Act* 2002, s.334. Part 7 of the 2002 Act was brought into force on February 24, 2003 (*Proceeds of Crime Act 2002 (Commencement No. 4, Transitional Provisions and Savings) Order* 2003 (S.I. 2003 No. 120)). The provisions do not apply where the conduct allegedly constituting an offence began before February 24, 2003 and ended on or after that date: *Proceeds of Crime Act 2002 (Commencement No. 4, Transitional Provisions and Savings) Order* 2003 (S.I. 2003 No. 120), art. 3.

(c) *Elements of the offence*

15–224 The Prosecution must prove that the defendant:

— knew, or;

— suspected, or;

— had reasonable grounds for knowing or suspecting;

— that another person is engaged in money laundering and;

— The information on which this suspicion, knowledge or reasonable grounds for such suspicion of knowledge;

— Came to him in the course of a business in the regulated sector and;

— The defendant can identify the other person or the whereabouts of any of the laundered property, or;

— Believes, or it is reasonable to expect him to believe, that the information will or may assist in identifying that other person or the whereabouts of any of the laundered property and;

— The defendant does not make the required disclosure to a nominated officer as soon as is practicable after the information comes to him or;

— The defendant does not make the required disclosure to a person authorised for the purposes of this Part by the Director General of SOCA as soon as is practicable after the information comes to him.

"Required Disclosure"

The required disclosure is a disclosure of the identity of the other person if they know it, the whereabouts of the laundered property, so far as they know it, and the information falling under the section: *Proceeds of Crime Act* 2002, s.330(5). 15–225

(d) *Statutory defence*

A person will not commit an offence under this section if they have a reasonable excuse for not making the required disclosure, or are a professional legal adviser or relevant professional adviser and they know either of the things mentioned in subsection (5)(a) and (b) because of information or other matter that came to them in privileged circumstances, or the information or other matter mentioned in subsection (3) came to him in privileged circumstances, or they do not know or suspect that another person is engaged in money laundering, and they have not been provided by their employer with such training as is specified by the Secretary of State by order for the purposes of this section: *Proceeds of Crime Act* 2002, s.330(6) and (7). 15–226

A person will not commit an offence under this section if they are employed by, or in partnership with, a professional legal adviser or a relevant professional adviser to provide the adviser with assistance or support, the information or other matter mentioned in subsection (3) comes to the person in connection with the provision of such assistance or support, and the information or other matter came to the adviser in privileged circumstances: *Proceeds of Crime Act* 2002, s.330(7B).

A person will not commit an offence under this section if they know, or believes on reasonable grounds, that the money laundering is occurring in a particular country or territory outside the United Kingdom, and the money laundering is not unlawful under the criminal law applying in that country or territory, and is not of a description prescribed in an order made by the Secretary of State: *Proceeds of Crime Act* 2002, s.330(7A).

(e) *Sentence*

When tried summarily, the maximum penalty for this offence is imprisonment for a term not exceeding six months or to a fine not exceeding the statutory maximum or to both: Proceeds of Crime Act 2002, s.334. 15–227

(5) Failure to disclose: nominated officers in the regulated sector

Proceeds of Crime Act 2002, s.331

Failure to disclose: nominated officers in the regulated sector

331.—(1) A person nominated to receive disclosures under section 330 commits an offence if the conditions in subsections (2) to (4) are satisfied. 15–228

(2) The first condition is that he—

(a) knows or suspects, or

(b) has reasonable grounds for knowing or suspecting, that another person is engaged in money laundering.

(3) The second condition is that the information or other matter—

(a) on which his knowledge or suspicion is based, or

(b) which gives reasonable grounds for such knowledge or suspicion, came to him in consequence of a disclosure made under section 330.

(3A) The third condition is—

(a) that he knows the identity of the other person mentioned in subsection (2), or the whereabouts of any of the laundered property, in consequence of a disclosure made under section 330,

(b) that that other person, or the whereabouts of any of the laundered property, can be identified from the information or other matter mentioned in subsection (3), or

(c) that he believes, or it is reasonable to expect him to believe, that the information or other matter will or may assist in identifying that other person or the whereabouts of any of the laundered property.

(4) The fourth condition is that he does not make the required disclosure to a person authorised for the purposes of this Part by the Director General of SOCA as soon as is practicable after the information or other matter mentioned in subsection (3) comes to him.

(5) The required disclosure is a disclosure of—

(a) the identity of the other person mentioned in subsection (2), if disclosed to him under section 330,

(b) the whereabouts of the laundered property, so far as disclosed to him under section 330, and

(c) the information or other matter mentioned in subsection (3).

(5A) The laundered property is the property forming the subject-matter of the money laundering that he knows or suspects, or has reasonable grounds for knowing or suspecting, that other person to be engaged in.

(6) But he does not commit an offence under this section if he has a reasonable excuse for not making the required disclosure.

(6A) Nor does a person commit an offence under this section if—

(a) he knows, or believes on reasonable grounds, that the money laundering is occurring in a particular country or territory outside the United Kingdom, and

(b) the money laundering—

(i) is not unlawful under the criminal law applying in that country or territory, and

(ii) is not of a description prescribed in an order made by the Secretary of State.

(7) In deciding whether a person committed an offence under this section the court must consider whether he followed any relevant guidance which was at the time concerned—

(a) issued by a supervisory authority or any other appropriate body,

(b) approved by the Treasury, and

(c) published in a manner it approved as appropriate in its opinion to bring the guidance to the attention of persons likely to be affected by it.

(8) Schedule 9 has effect for the purpose of determining what is a supervisory authority.

(9) An appropriate body is a body which regulates or is representative of a trade, profession, business or employment.

(a) *Allocation*

15–229 The offence is triable either way: *Proceeds of Crime Act* 2002, s.334. Part 7 of the 2002 Act was brought into force on February 24, 2003 (*Proceeds of Crime Act 2002 (Commencement No. 4, Transitional Provisions and Savings) Order* 2003 (S.I. 2003 No. 120)). The provisions do not apply where the conduct allegedly constituting an offence began before February 24, 2003 and ended on or after that date: *Proceeds of Crime Act 2002 (Commencement No. 4, Transitional Provisions and Savings) Order* 2003 (S.I. 2003 No. 120), art. 3.

(b) *Elements of the offence*

15–230 The Prosecution must prove that the defendant:

— knew, or;

— suspected, or;

— had reasonable grounds for knowing or suspecting;

— that another person is engaged in money laundering and;

— the information on which this suspicion, knowledge or reasonable grounds for such suspicion of knowledge;

— came to him in consequence of a disclosure made under section 330 and;
— the defendant can identify the other person or the whereabouts of any of the laundered property in consequence of a disclosure made under section 330, or;
— the defendant can identify the other person or the whereabouts of any of the laundered property from information obtained in consequence of a disclosure made under section 330, or;
— believes, or it is reasonable to expect him to believe, that the information will or may assist in identifying that other person or the whereabouts of any of the laundered property and;
— the defendant does not make the required disclosure to a person authorised for the purposes of this Part by the Director General of SOCA as soon as is practicable after the information comes to him.

"Required Disclosure"

The required disclosure is a disclosure of the identity of the other person disclosed to them under section 330, the whereabouts of the laundered property, as disclosed to them under section 330, and the information mentioned in s.331(3) that came to him in consequence of a disclosure made under section 33: *Proceeds of Crime Act* 2002, s.331(5). **15–231**

(c) *Statutory defence*

A person will not commit an offence under this section if they have a reasonable excuse for not making the required disclosure or they know, or believes on reasonable grounds, that the money laundering is occurring in a particular country or territory outside the United Kingdom, and the money laundering is not unlawful under the criminal law applying in that country or territory, and is not of a description prescribed in an order made by the Secretary of State: *Proceeds of Crime Act* 2002, s.331(6), (6A). **15–232**

(d) *Sentence*

When tried summarily, the maximum penalty for this offence is imprisonment for a term not exceeding six months or to a fine not exceeding the statutory maximum or to both: *Proceeds of Crime Act* 2002, s.334. **15–233**

(6) Failure to disclose: other nominated officers

(a) *Definition*

Proceeds of Crime Act 2002, s.332

Failure to disclose: other nominated officers

332.—(1) A person nominated to receive disclosures under section 337 or 338 commits an offence if the conditions in subsections (2) to (4) are satisfied. **15–234**

(2) The first condition is that he knows or suspects that another person is engaged in money laundering.

(3) The second condition is that the information or other matter on which his knowledge or suspicion is based came to him in consequence of a disclosure made under the applicable section.

(3A) The third condition is—

(a) that he knows the identity of the other person mentioned in subsection (2), or the whereabouts of any of the laundered property, in consequence of a disclosure made under the applicable section,

(b) that that other person, or the whereabouts of any of the laundered property, can be identified from the information or other matter mentioned in subsection (3), or

(c) that he believes, or it is reasonable to expect him to believe, that the information or other matter will or may assist in identifying that other person or the whereabouts of any of the laundered property.

(4) The fourth condition is that he does not make the required disclosure to a person authorised for the purposes of this Part by the Director General of SOCA as soon as is practicable after the information or other matter mentioned in subsection (3) comes to him.

(5) The required disclosure is a disclosure of—

(a) the identity of the other person mentioned in subsection (2), if disclosed to him under the applicable section,

(b) the whereabouts of the laundered property, so far as disclosed to him under the applicable section, and

(c) the information or other matter mentioned in subsection (3).

(5A) The laundered property is the property forming the subject-matter of the money laundering that he knows or suspects that other person to be engaged in.

(5B) The applicable section is section 337 or, as the case may be, section 338.

(6) But he does not commit an offence under this section if he has a reasonable excuse for not making the required disclosure.

(7) Nor does a person commit an offence under this section if—

(a) he knows, or believes on reasonable grounds, that the money laundering is occurring in a particular country or territory outside the United Kingdom, and

(b) the money laundering—

(i) is not unlawful under the criminal law applying in that country or territory, and

(ii) is not of a description prescribed in an order made by the Secretary of State.

(b) *Allocation*

15–235 The offence is triable either way: *Proceeds of Crime Act* 2002, s.334. Part 7 of the 2002 Act was brought into force on February 24, 2003 (*Proceeds of Crime Act 2002 (Commencement No. 4, Transitional Provisions and Savings) Order* 2003 (S.I. 2003 No. 120)). The provisions do not apply where the conduct allegedly constituting an offence began before February 24, 2003 and ended on or after that date: *Proceeds of Crime Act 2002 (Commencement No. 4, Transitional Provisions and Savings) Order* 2003 (S.I. 2003 No. 120), art. 3.

(c) *Elements of the offence*

15–236 The Prosecution must prove that the defendant:

— Is a person nominated to receive disclosures under section 337 or 338 of the *Proceeds of Crime Act* 2002 and they:

— Knew or suspected that another person was engaged in money laundering and;

— The information or other matter on which their knowledge or suspicion is based came to them in consequence of a disclosure made under the applicable section and;

— They knew the identity of the other person mentioned in s.331(2), or the whereabouts of any of the laundered property, in consequence of a disclosure made under the applicable section or;

— The other person, or the whereabouts of any of the laundered property, can be identified from the information or other matter mentioned in s.331(3), or;

— They believed, or it is reasonable to expect them to believe, that the information or other matter will or may assist in identifying that other person or the whereabouts of any of the laundered property and;

— The defendant did not make the required disclosure to a person authorised for the purposes of this Part by the Director General of SOCA as soon as is practicable after the information or other matter mentioned in s.331(3) came to them.

"Nominated to receive disclosures"

Proceeds of Crime Act 2002, s.337

Protected disclosures

337.—(1) A disclosure which satisfies the following three conditions is not to be taken to breach any restriction on the disclosure of information (however imposed). **15–237**

(2) The first condition is that the information or other matter disclosed came to the person making the disclosure (the discloser) in the course of his trade, profession, business or employment.

(3) The second condition is that the information or other matter—

(a) causes the discloser to know or suspect, or

(b) gives him reasonable grounds for knowing or suspecting,

that another person is engaged in money laundering.

(4) The third condition is that the disclosure is made to a constable, a customs officer or a nominated officer as soon as is practicable after the information or other matter comes to the discloser.

(4A) Where a disclosure consists of a disclosure protected under subsection (1) and a disclosure of either or both of—

(a) the identity of the other person mentioned in subsection (3), and

(b) the whereabouts of property forming the subject-matter of the money laundering that the discloser knows or suspects, or has reasonable grounds for knowing or suspecting, that other person to be engaged in, the disclosure of the thing mentioned in paragraph (a) or (b) (as well as the disclosure protected under subsection (1)) is not to be taken to breach any restriction on the disclosure of information (however imposed).

(5) A disclosure to a nominated officer is a disclosure which—

(a) is made to a person nominated by the discloser's employer to receive disclosures under section 330 or this section, and

(b) is made in the course of the discloser's employment

Proceeds of Crime Act 2002, s.338

Authorised disclosures

338.—(1) For the purposes of this Part a disclosure is authorised if—

(a) it is a disclosure to a constable, a customs officer or a nominated officer by the alleged offender that property is criminal property, and

(b) the first, second or third condition set out below is satisfied.

(2) The first condition is that the disclosure is made before the alleged offender does the prohibited act.

(2A) The second condition is that—

(a) the disclosure is made while the alleged offender is doing the prohibited act,

(b) he began to do the act at a time when, because he did not then know or suspect that the property constituted or represented a person's benefit from criminal conduct, the act was not a prohibited act, and

(c) the disclosure is made on his own initiative and as soon as is practicable after he first knows or suspects that the property constitutes or represents a person's benefit from criminal conduct.

(3) The third condition is that—

(a) the disclosure is made after the alleged offender does the prohibited act,

(b) [he has a reasonable excuse]1 for his failure to make the disclosure before he did the act, and

(c) the disclosure is made on his own initiative and as soon as it is practicable for him to make it.

(4) An authorised disclosure is not to be taken to breach any restriction on the disclosure of information (however imposed).

(5) A disclosure to a nominated officer is a disclosure which—

(a) is made to a person nominated by the alleged offender's employer to receive authorised disclosures, and

(b) is made in the course of the alleged offender's employment.

(6) References to the prohibited act are to an act mentioned in section 327(1), 328(1) or 329(1) (as the case may be).

"Required Disclosure"

15–238 The "required disclosure" is the identity of the other person mentioned in s.332(2), if disclosed to him under the applicable section, the whereabouts of the laundered property, so far as disclosed to him under the applicable section, and the information or other matter mentioned in s.332(3): *Proceeds of Crime Act* 2002, s.332(5).

(d) *Statutory defence*

15–239 A person will not commit an offence under this section if they have a reasonable excuse for not making the required disclosure or they know, or believes on reasonable grounds, that the money laundering is occurring in a particular country or territory outside the United Kingdom, and the money laundering is not unlawful under the criminal law applying in that country or territory, and is not of a description prescribed in an order made by the Secretary of State: *Proceeds of Crime Act* 2002, s.332(6), (7).

(e) *Sentence*

15–240 When tried summarily, the maximum penalty for this offence is imprisonment for a term not exceeding six months or to a fine not exceeding the statutory maximum or to both: *Proceeds of Crime Act* 2002, s.334.

(7) Tipping Off: Regulated Sector

(a) *Definition*

Proceeds of Crime Act 2002, ss.333A–333E

15–241 **333A.**—(1) A person commits an offence if—

(a) the person discloses any matter within subsection (2);

(b) the disclosure is likely to prejudice any investigation that might be conducted following the disclosure referred to in that subsection; and

(c) the information on which the disclosure is based came to the person in the course of a business in the regulated sector.

(2) The matters are that the person or another person has made a disclosure under this Part—

(a) to a constable,

(b) to an officer of Revenue and Customs,

(c) to a nominated officer, or

(d) to a member of staff of the Serious Organised Crime Agency authorised for the purposes of this Part by the Director General of that Agency,

of information that came to that person in the course of a business in the regulated sector.

(3) A person commits an offence if—

(a) the person discloses that an investigation into allegations that an offence under this Part has been committed is being contemplated or is being carried out;

(b) the disclosure is likely to prejudice that investigation; and

(c) the information on which the disclosure is based came to the person in the course of a business in the regulated sector.

(4) A person guilty of an offence under this section is liable—

(a) on summary conviction to imprisonment for a term not exceeding three months, or to a fine not exceeding level 5 on the standard scale, or to both;

(b) on conviction on indictment to imprisonment for a term not exceeding two years, or to a fine, or to both.

(5) This section is subject to—

(a) section 333B (disclosures within an undertaking or group etc),

(b) section 333C (other permitted disclosures between institutions etc), and
(c) section 333D (other permitted disclosures etc).

Disclosures within an undertaking or group etc

333B.—(1) An employee, officer or partner of an undertaking does not commit an offence under section 333A if the disclosure is to an employee, officer or partner of the same undertaking.

(2) A person does not commit an offence under section 333A in respect of a disclosure by a credit institution or a financial institution if—

(a) the disclosure is to a credit institution or a financial institution,
(b) the institution to whom the disclosure is made is situated in an EEA State or in a country or territory imposing equivalent money laundering requirements, and
(c) both the institution making the disclosure and the institution to whom it is made belong to the same group.

(3) In subsection (2) "group" has the same meaning as in Directive 2002/87/EC of the European Parliament and of the Council of 16th December 2002 on the supplementary supervision of credit institutions, insurance undertakings and investment firms in a financial conglomerate.

(4) A professional legal adviser or a relevant professional adviser does not commit an offence under section 333A if—

(a) the disclosure is to professional legal adviser or a relevant professional adviser,
(b) both the person making the disclosure and the person to whom it is made carry on business in an EEA State or in a country or territory imposing equivalent money laundering requirements, and
(c) those persons perform their professional activities within different undertakings that share common ownership, management or control.

Other permitted disclosures between institutions etc

333C.—(1) This section applies to a disclosure—

(a) by a credit institution to another credit institution,
(b) by a financial institution to another financial institution,
(c) by a professional legal adviser to another professional legal adviser, or
(d) by a relevant professional adviser of a particular kind to another relevant professional adviser of the same kind.

(2) A person does not commit an offence under section 333A in respect of a disclosure to which this section applies if—

(a) the disclosure relates to—
 (i) a client or former client of the institution or adviser making the disclosure and the institution or adviser to whom it is made,
 (ii) a transaction involving them both, or
 (iii) the provision of a service involving them both;
(b) the disclosure is for the purpose only of preventing an offence under this Part of this Act;
(c) the institution or adviser to whom the disclosure is made is situated in an EEA State or in a country or territory imposing equivalent money laundering requirements; and
(d) the institution or adviser making the disclosure and the institution or adviser to whom it is made are subject to equivalent duties of professional confidentiality and the protection of personal data (within the meaning of section 1 of the *Data Protection Act* 1998).

Other permitted disclosures etc

333D.—(1) A person does not commit an offence under section 333A if the disclosure is—

(a) to the authority that is the supervisory authority for that person by virtue of the *Money Laundering Regulations* 2007 (S.I. 2007/2157); or
(b) for the purpose of—
 (i) the detection, investigation or prosecution of a criminal offence (whether in the United Kingdom or elsewhere),
 (ii) an investigation under this Act, or

Part III

(iii) the enforcement of any order of a court under this Act.

(2) A professional legal adviser or a relevant professional adviser does not commit an offence under section 333A if the disclosure—

(a) is to the adviser's client, and

(b) is made for the purpose of dissuading the client from engaging in conduct amounting to an offence.

(3) A person does not commit an offence under section 333A(1) if the person does not know or suspect that the disclosure is likely to have the effect mentioned in section 333A(1)(b).

(4) A person does not commit an offence under section 333A(3) if the person does not know or suspect that the disclosure is likely to have the effect mentioned in section 333A(3)(b).

Interpretation of sections 333A to 333D

333E.—(1) For the purposes of sections 333A to 333D, Schedule 9 has effect for determining—

(a) what is a business in the regulated sector, and

(b) what is a supervisory authority.

(2) In those sections—

"credit institution" has the same meaning as in Schedule 9;

"financial institution" means an undertaking that carries on a business in the regulated sector by virtue of any of paragraphs (b) to (i) of paragraph 1(1) of that Schedule.

(3) References in those sections to a disclosure by or to a credit institution or a financial institution include disclosure by or to an employee, officer or partner of the institution acting on its behalf.

(4) For the purposes of those sections a country or territory imposes "equivalent money laundering requirements" if it imposes requirements equivalent to those laid down in Directive 2005/60/EC of the European Parliament and of the Council of 26th October 2005 on the prevention of the use of the financial system for the purpose of money laundering and terrorist financing.

(5) In those sections "relevant professional adviser" means an accountant, auditor or tax adviser who is a member of a professional body which is established for accountants, auditors or tax advisers (as the case may be) and which makes provision for—

(a) testing the competence of those seeking admission to membership of such a body as a condition for such admission; and

(b) imposing and maintaining professional and ethical standards for its members, as well as imposing sanctions for non-compliance with those standards.

(b) *Allocation*

15–242 The offence is triable either way: *Proceeds of Crime Act* 2002, s.334. Part 7 of the 2002 Act was brought into force on February 24, 2003 (*Proceeds of Crime Act 2002 (Commencement No. 4, Transitional Provisions and Savings) Order* 2003 (S.I. 2003 No. 120)). The provisions do not apply where the conduct allegedly constituting an offence began before February 24, 2003 and ended on or after that date: *Proceeds of Crime Act 2002 (Commencement No. 4, Transitional Provisions and Savings) Order* 2003 (S.I. 2003 No. 120), art. 3.

(c) *Elements of the offence*

15–243 Section 333A creates two offences. For the first offence, the prosecution must prove that the defendant:

— Disclosed information that came to that person in the course of a business in the regulated sector;

— To a constable or;

— To an officer of Revenue and Customs or;

— To a nominated officer, or;

— To a member of staff of the Serious Organised Crime Agency authorised for the purposes of this Part by the Director General of that Agency, and;

— The disclosure is likely to prejudice any investigation that might be conducted following the disclosure referred to in that subsection.

For the second offence, the Prosecution must prove that the defendant:

— Disclosed that an investigation into allegations that an offence under Part 7 of the *Proceeds of Crime Act* 2002 has been committed is being contemplated or is being carried out, and;

— The disclosure is likely to prejudice that investigation; and

— The information on which the disclosure is based came to the person in the course of a business in the regulated sector.

(d) *Statutory defence*

Sections 333B–333D set out situations in which persons carrying out the conduct specified in section 333A will not commit an offence. These situations are where: **15–244**

— The disclosure is made by an employee, officer or partner of an undertaking to an employee, officer or partner of the same undertaking: *Proceeds of Crime Act* 2002, s.333B(1).

— The disclosure is made by a credit institution or a financial institution and the disclosure is to a credit institution or a financial institution, the institution to whom the disclosure is made is situated in an EEA State or in a country or territory imposing equivalent money laundering requirements, and both the institution making the disclosure and the institution to whom it is made belong to the same group: *Proceeds of Crime Act* 2002, s.333B(2). sclosure is made by a professional legal adviser or a relevant professional adviser to a professional legal adviser or a relevant professional adviser, both the person making the disclosure and the person to whom it is made carry on business in an EEA State or in a country or territory imposing equivalent money laundering requirements, and those persons perform their professional activities within different undertakings that share common ownership, management or control: *Proceeds of Crime Act* 2002, s.333B(4).

— The disclosure is made by a credit institution to another credit institution, by a financial institution to another financial institution, by a professional legal adviser to another professional legal adviser, or by a relevant professional adviser of a particular kind to another relevant professional adviser of the same kind and the disclosure relates to a client or former client of the institution or adviser making the disclosure and the institution or adviser to whom it is made, a transaction involving them both, or the provision of a service involving them both or the disclosure is for the purpose only of preventing an offence under this Part of this Act: *Proceeds of Crime Act* 2002, s.333C (1), (2).

— The disclosure is made by a credit institution to another credit institution, by a financial institution to another financial institution, by a professional legal adviser to another professional legal adviser, or by a relevant professional adviser of a particular kind to another relevant professional adviser of the same kind and the institution or adviser to whom the disclosure is made is situated in an EEA State or in a country or territory imposing equivalent money laundering requirements; and the institution or adviser making the disclosure and the institution or adviser to whom it is made are subject to equivalent duties of professional confidentiality and the protection of personal data (within the meaning of s.1 of the *Data Protection Act* 1998): *Proceeds of Crime Act* 2002, s.333C(1), (2).

— The disclosure is to the authority that is the supervisory authority for that person by virtue of the *Money Laundering Regulations* 2007 (S.I. 2007 No. 2157); or for the purpose of the detection, investigation or prosecution of a criminal offence (whether in the United Kingdom or elsewhere), an investigation under this Act, or the enforcement of any order of a court under this Act: *Proceeds of Crime Act* 2002, s.333D(1).

— The disclosure is made by a professional legal adviser or a relevant professional adviser and the disclosure is to the adviser's client, and is made for the purpose of dissuading the client from engaging in conduct amounting to an offence: *Proceeds of Crime Act* 2002, s.333D(2).

— The person making the disclosure does not know or suspect that the disclosure is likely to have the effect mentioned in section 333A(1)(b): *Proceeds of Crime Act* 2002, s.333D(3).

— The person making the disclosure does not know or suspect that the disclosure is likely to have the effect mentioned in section 333A(3)(b): *Proceeds of Crime Act* 2002, s.333D(4).

"Business in the regulated sector"

15–245 Section 333E (1) provides that Schedule 9 of the 2002 Act shall apply to determine what is a business in the regulated sector.

Proceeds of Crime Act 2002, Schedule 9, para. 1

1.—(1) A business is in the regulated sector to the extent that it consists of—

(a) the acceptance by a credit institution of deposits or other repayable funds from the public, or the granting by a credit institution of credits for its own account;

(b) the carrying on of one or more of the activities listed in points 2 to 12 and 14 of Annex 1 to the Banking Consolidation Directive by an undertaking other than—

(i) a credit institution; or

(ii) an undertaking whose only listed activity is trading for own account in one or more of the products listed in point 7 of Annex 1 to the Banking Consolidation Directive and which does not act on behalf of a customer (that is, a third party which is not a member of the same group as the undertaking);

(c) the carrying on of activities covered by the Life Assurance Consolidation Directive by an insurance company authorised in accordance with that Directive;

(d) the provision of investment services or the performance of investment activities by a person (other than a person falling within Article 2 of the Markets in Financial Instruments Directive) whose regular occupation or business is the provision to other persons of an investment service or the performance of an investment activity on a professional basis;

(e) the marketing or other offering of units or shares by a collective investment undertaking;

(f) the activities of an insurance intermediary as defined in Article 2(5) of the Insurance Mediation Directive, other than a tied insurance intermediary as mentioned in Article 2(7) of that Directive, in respect of contracts of long-term insurance within the meaning given by article 3(1) of, and Part II of Schedule 1 to, the *Financial Services and Markets Act 2000 (Regulated Activities) Order* 2001;

(g) the carrying on of any of the activities mentioned in paragraphs (b) to (f) by a branch located in an EEA State of a person referred to in those paragraphs (or of an equivalent person in any other State), wherever its head office is located;

(h) the activities of the National Savings Bank;

(i) any activity carried on for the purpose of raising money authorised to be raised under the *National Loans Act* 1968 under the auspices of the Director of Savings;

(j) the carrying on of statutory audit work within the meaning of section 1210 of the *Companies Act* 2006 (meaning of "statutory auditor" etc) by any firm or individual who is a statutory auditor within the meaning of Part 42 of that Act (statutory auditors);

(k) the activities of a person appointed to act as an insolvency practitioner within the meaning of section 388 of the *Insolvency Act* 1986 (meaning of "act as insolvency practitioner") or article 3 of the *Insolvency (Northern Ireland) Order* 1989;

(l) the provision to other persons of accountancy services by a firm or sole practitioner who by way of business provides such services to other persons;

(m) the provision of advice about the tax affairs of other persons by a firm or sole practitioner who by way of business provides advice about the tax affairs of other persons;

(n) the participation in financial or real property transactions concerning—
 (i) the buying and selling of real property (or, in Scotland, heritable property) or business entities;
 (ii) the managing of client money, securities or other assets;
 (iii) the opening or management of bank, savings or securities accounts;
 (iv) the organisation of contributions necessary for the creation, operation or management of companies; or
 (v) the creation, operation or management of trusts, companies or similar structures, by a firm or sole practitioner who by way of business provides legal or notarial services to other persons;
(o) the provision to other persons by way of business by a firm or sole practitioner of any of the services mentioned in sub-paragraph (4);
(p) the carrying on of estate agency work (within the meaning given by section 1 of the *Estate Agents Act* 1979 (estate agency work)) by a firm or a sole practitioner who carries on, or whose employees carry on, such work;
(q) the trading in goods (including dealing as an auctioneer) whenever a transaction involves the receipt of a payment or payments in cash of at least 15,000 euros in total, whether the transaction is executed in a single operation or in several operations which appear to be linked, by a firm or sole trader who by way of business trades in goods;
(r) operating a casino under a casino operating licence (within the meaning given by section 65(2) of the*Gambling Act* 2005 (nature of licence)).

(2) For the purposes of sub-paragraph (1)(a) and (b) "credit institution" means—
(a) a credit institution as defined in Article 4(1)(a) of the Banking Consolidation Directive; or
(b) a branch (within the meaning of Article 4(3) of that Directive) located in an EEA state of an institution falling within paragraph (a) (or of an equivalent institution in any other State) wherever its head office is located.

(3) For the purposes of sub-paragraph (1)(n) a person participates in a transaction by assisting in the planning or execution of the transaction or otherwise acting for or on behalf of a client in the transaction.

(4) The services referred to in sub-paragraph (1)(o) are—
(a) forming companies or other legal persons;
(b) acting, or arranging for another person to act—
 (i) as a director or secretary of a company;
 (ii) as a partner of a partnership; or
 (iii) in a similar position in relation to other legal persons;
(c) providing a registered office, business address, correspondence or administrative address or other related services for a company, partnership or any other legal person or arrangement;
(d) acting, or arranging for another person to act, as—
 (i) a trustee of an express trust or similar legal arrangement; or
 (ii) a nominee shareholder for a person other than a company whose securities are listed on a regulated market.

(5) For the purposes of sub-paragraph (4)(d) "regulated market"—
(a) in relation to any EEA State, has the meaning given by point 14 of Article 4(1) of the Markets in Financial Instruments Directive; and
(b) in relation to any other State, means a regulated financial market which subjects companies whose securities are admitted to trading to disclosure obligations which are contained in international standards and are equivalent to the specified disclosure obligations.

(6) For the purposes of sub-paragraph (5) "the specified disclosure obligations" means disclosure requirements consistent with—
(a) Article 6(1) to (4) of Directive 2003/6/EC of the European Parliament and of the Council of 28th January 2003 on insider dealing and market manipulation;
(b) Articles 3, 5, 7, 8, 10, 14 and 16 of Directive 2003/71/EC of the European Parliament and of the Council of 4th November 2003 on the prospectuses to be published when securities are offered to the public or admitted to trading;
(c) Articles 4 to 6, 14, 16 to 19 and 30 of Directive 2004/109/EC of the European

Parliament and of the Council of 15th December 2004 relating to the harmonisation of transparency requirements in relation to information about issuers whose securities are admitted to trading on a regulated market; or

(d) Community legislation made under the provisions mentioned in paragraphs (a) to (c).

(7) For the purposes of sub-paragraph (1)(j) and (l) to (q) "firm" means any entity, whether or not a legal person, that is not an individual and includes a body corporate and a partnership or other unincorporated association.

(8) For the purposes of sub-paragraph (1)(q) "cash" means notes, coins or travellers' cheques in any currency.

"Supervisory Authority"

15–246 Section 333E (1) provides that Schedule 9 of the 2002 Act shall apply to determine what is a supervisory authority.

Proceeds of Crime Act 2002, Schedule 9, para. 4

4.—(1) The following bodies are supervisory authorities—

(a) the Commissioners for Her Majesty's Revenue and Customs;
(b) the Department of Enterprise, Trade and Investment in Northern Ireland;
(c) the Financial Services Authority;
(d) the Gambling Commission;
(e) the Office of Fair Trading;
(f) the Secretary of State; and
(g) the professional bodies listed in sub-paragraph (2).

(2) The professional bodies referred to in sub-paragraph (1)(g) are—

(a) the Association of Accounting Technicians;
(b) the Association of Chartered Certified Accountants;
(c) the Association of International Accountants;
(d) the Association of Taxation Technicians;
(e) the Chartered Institute of Management Accountants;
(f) the Chartered Institute of Public Finance and Accountancy;
(g) the Chartered Institute of Taxation;
(h) the Council for Licensed Conveyancers;
(i) the Faculty of Advocates;
(j) the Faculty Office of the Archbishop of Canterbury;
(k) the General Council of the Bar;
(l) the General Council of the Bar of Northern Ireland;
(m) the Insolvency Practitioners Association;
(n) the Institute of Certified Bookkeepers;
(o) the Institute of Chartered Accountants in England and Wales;
(p) the Institute of Chartered Accountants in Ireland;
(q) the Institute of Chartered Accountants of Scotland;
(r) the Institute of Financial Accountants;
(s) the International Association of Book-keepers;
(t) the Law Society;
(u) the Law Society for Northern Ireland; and
(v) the Law Society of Scotland.

Protected Disclosures

15–247 Section 337 of the 2002 Act provides that a disclosure that satisfies certain conditions is not to be taken to breach any restriction on the disclosure of information, however that disclosure is imposed. These conditions are that:

— The information or other matter disclosed came to the person making the disclosure in the course of their trade, profession, business or employment and;

— The information or other matter causes the discloser to know or suspect, or gives them reasonable grounds for knowing or suspecting, that another person is engaged in money laundering and;

— The disclosure is made to a constable, a customs officer or a nominated officer as soon as is practicable after the information or other matter comes to the discloser.

Proceeds of Crime Act 2002, s.337

Protected disclosures

337.—(1) A disclosure which satisfies the following three conditions is not to be taken to breach any restriction on the disclosure of information (however imposed).

(2) The first condition is that the information or other matter disclosed came to the person making the disclosure (the discloser) in the course of his trade, profession, business or employment.

(3) The second condition is that the information or other matter—

(a) causes the discloser to know or suspect, or

(b) gives him reasonable grounds for knowing or suspecting,

that another person is engaged in money laundering.

(4) The third condition is that the disclosure is made to a constable, a customs officer or a nominated officer as soon as is practicable after the information or other matter comes to the discloser. (4A) Where a disclosure consists of a disclosure protected under subsection (1) and a disclosure of either or both of—

(a) the identity of the other person mentioned in subsection (3), and

(b) the whereabouts of property forming the subject-matter of the money laundering that the discloser knows or suspects, or has reasonable grounds for knowing or suspecting, that other person to be engaged in, the disclosure of the thing mentioned in paragraph (a) or (b) (as well as the disclosure protected under subsection (1)) is not to be taken to breach any restriction on the disclosure of information (however imposed).

(5) A disclosure to a nominated officer is a disclosure which—

(a) is made to a person nominated by the discloser's employer to receive disclosures under section 330 or this section, and

(b) is made in the course of the discloser's employment.

(e) *Sentence*

When tried summarily, the maximum penalty for this offence is imprisonment for a term not exceeding six months or to a fine not exceeding the statutory maximum or to both: *Proceeds of Crime Act* 2002, s.333A(4). **15–248**

B. OFFENCES UNDER THE IDENTITY DOCUMENTS ACT 2010

(1) Possession of false identity documents

The *Identity Documents Act* 2010 received the Royal Assent on December 21, 2010. **15–249**
Section 1 of this Act repealed the *Identity Cards Act* 2006, and re-enacted sections 25, 26 and 38 of the *Identity Cards Act* 2006 as new provisions of the *Identity Documents Act* 2010. The new provisions are contained in sections 4, 5 and 6 of the *Identity Documents Act* 2010. Only section 6 is of relevance to the Magistrates' Court as offences under ss.4 and 5 are indictable only. The new offences will be charged for offences committed from January 21, 2011.

(a) *Definition*

Identity Documents Act 2010, s.6

Possession of false identity documents etc without reasonable excuse

6.—(1) It is an offence for a person ("P"), without reasonable excuse, to have in P's possession or under P's control— **15–250**

Part III

(a) an identity document that is false,
(b) an identity document that was improperly obtained,
(c) an identity document that relates to someone else,
(d) any apparatus which, to P's knowledge, is or has been specially designed or adapted for the making of false identity documents, or
(e) any article or material which, to P's knowledge, is or has been specially designed or adapted to be used in the making of such documents.

(2) A person guilty of an offence under this section is liable—
(a) on conviction on indictment, to imprisonment for a term not exceeding 2 years or a fine (or both), or
(b) on summary conviction, to imprisonment for a term not exceeding the maximum period or a fine not exceeding the statutory maximum (or both).

(3) In subsection (2)(b) "the maximum period" means—
(a) in England and Wales or Scotland, 12 months, and
(b) in Northern Ireland, 6 months.

(4) In subsection (3)(a) the reference to 12 months in England and Wales is to be read, in relation to an offence committed before the commencement of section 154(1) of the *Criminal Justice Act* 2003, as a reference to 6 months.

[This section was brought into force by section 14(2) of the *Identity Documents Act* 2010.]

Identity Documents Act 2010, s.7

Meaning of "identity document"

15–251 **7.**—(1) For the purposes of sections 4 to 6 "identity document" means any document that is or purports to be—
(a) an immigration document,
(b) a United Kingdom passport (within the meaning of the *Immigration Act* 1971),
(c) a passport issued by or on behalf of the authorities of a country or territory outside the United Kingdom or by or on behalf of an international organisation,
(d) a document that can be used (in some or all circumstances) instead of a passport,
(e) a licence to drive a motor vehicle granted under Part 3 of the *Road Traffic* 1988 or under Part 2 of the *Road Traffic (Northern Ireland) Order* 1981, or
(f) a driving licence issued by or on behalf of the authorities of a country or territory outside the United Kingdom.

(2) In subsection (1)(a) "immigration document" means—
(a) a document used for confirming the right of a person under the EU Treaties in respect of entry or residence in the United Kingdom,
(b) a document that is given in exercise of immigration functions and records information about leave granted to a person to enter or to remain in the United Kingdom, or
(c) a registration card (within the meaning of section 26A of the *Immigration Act* 1971).

(3) In subsection (2)(b) "immigration functions" means functions under the Immigration Acts (within the meaning of the *Asylum and Immigration (Treatment of Claimants, etc.) Act* 2004).

(4) References in subsection (1) to the issue of a document include its renewal, replacement or re-issue (with or without modifications).

(5) In this section "document" includes a stamp or label.

(6) The Secretary of State may by order amend the definition of "identity document".

[This section was brought into force by section 14(2) of the *Identity Documents Act* 2010.]

Identity Documents Act 2010, s.9

Other definitions

15–252 **9.**—(1) "Apparatus" includes any equipment, machinery or device and any wire or cable, together with any software used with it.

(2) In relation to England and Wales and Northern Ireland, an identity document is "false" only if it is false within the meaning of Part 1 of the *Forgery and Counterfeiting Act* 1981 (see section 9(1)).

(3) An identity document was "improperly obtained" if—

(a) false information was provided in, or in connection with, the application for its issue to the person who issued it, or

(b) false information was provided in, or in connection with, an application for its modification to a person entitled to modify it.

(4) In subsection (3)—

(a) "false" information includes information containing any inaccuracy or omission that results in a tendency to mislead,

(b) "information" includes documents (including stamps and labels) and records, and

(c) the "issue" of a document includes its renewal, replacement or re-issue (with or without modifications).

(5) References to the making of a false identity document include the modification of an identity document so that it becomes false.

(6) This section applies for the purposes of sections 4 to 6.

[This section was brought into force by section 14(2) of the *Identity Documents Act* 2010.]

(b) *Allocation*

The offence is triable either way: *Identity Documents Act* 2010 s.6(2), offences under s.4 possession of false identity documents with improper intention are indictable only. **15–253**

(c) *Elements of the offence*

Section 31 of the *Immigration and Asylum Act* 1999 provides a defence based on 31(1) of the Refugee Convention for a defendant charged with an offence under this section, see *ante*, § 15–146. **15–255**

(d) *Sentence*

After commencement of the relevant provisions the maximum custodial sentence in a magistrates' court will be 12 months' imprisonment: s.25(7). The maximum penalty for offences committed before the commencement of s.54(1) of the *Criminal Justice Act* 2003 is imprisonment for a term not exceeding six months or a fine not exceeding the statutory maximum or both: s.125(3)(a). **15–256**

The offence under s.6(2) of the *Identity Documents Act* 2010 is covered in the Magistrates' Courts Sentencing of 2008, which originally applied to offences under the 2006 Act.

STARTING POINT AND SENTENCING RANGES

(BASED ON A FIRST TIME OFFENDER AFTER TRIAL)

Examples of nature of activity	**Starting Point**	**Range**
Single document possessed	Medium level community order	Band C fine to high level community order
Small number of documents, no evidence of dealing	12 weeks custody	6 weeks custody to Crown Court

Part III

Examples of nature of activity	Starting Point	Range
Considerable number of documents possessed, evidence of involvement in larger operation	Crown Court	Crown Court

AGGRAVATING AND MITIGATING FACTORS

Factors indicating a higher culpability	Factors indicating lower culpability
1. Clear knowledge that document is false 2. Number of documents possessed (where not in offence descriptions above) **Factors indicating a greater degree of harm** 1. Group activity 2. Potential impact of use (where not in offence descriptions above)	1. Genuine mistake or ignorance

Under the old law even simple possession would usually justify an immediate custodial sentence notwithstanding a plea of guilty: possession of false documents is a serious matter. Proof or admission of a specified prohibited intent was likely to make the offence more serious, but it might not always be so. It did not follow that it was irrelevant for a sentencer to take into account that no innocent explanation for the possession of the forged document had been volunteered: *Zenasni* [2008] 1 Cr.App.R. 94, CA.

There was held to be no absolute embargo on a judge suspending a sentence of imprisonment for an offence under the old Act if there was proper ground to do so, nor is there any statutory requirement that there should be exceptional circumstances. However, once it is recognised that ordinarily the appropriate sentence for an offence of that kind involves immediate custody, there must be some good reason for the judge to act differently in a particular case, for simple reasons of consistency: *Carneiro* [2008] 1 Cr.App.R. 571, CA. In this case, the Court of Appeal upheld the appellant's sentence of six months' imprisonment, stating the fact that the appellant was not a drain on the economy was a common factor in the case of people who used false documents to obtain employment in order to support themselves while unlawfully in the country. The fact that the work being done was of a lowly nature was what might be expected in such cases. The appellant's personal circumstances were sad, but there was nothing in them which could really merit suspending the sentence on that account alone.

In *Singh (Hardeep)* [2008] EWCA Crim 1546, CA, the appellant had pleaded guilty to possession of a false identity document under s.5(5)(a) of the *Identity Cards Act* 2006 and was sentenced to 12 months' imprisonment and recommended for deportation. He had been stopped by police officers and found with a false passport. He had no previous convictions. On appeal, he argued that the starting point for the sentence was too high and too close to the maximum of two years. The Court of Appeal held that the sentence was excessive, and replaced it with a sentence of eight months.

In *John (Ishmael)* [2008] EWCA Crim 2022, CA the appellant appealed against a sentence of 15 months' imprisonment imposed following pleas of guilty to two offences of possessing false identity documents with intent and one offence of possession of a false identity document. The appellant came to the United Kingdom from Zimbabwe as an asylum seeker. His application for asylum was refused in 2004, after which he was entitled to, but did not claim, asylum support. In 2007 he bought false documentation which he used to gain employment. The pre-sentence report suggested that, despite one previous conviction for threatening and abusive behaviour, there was a low risk of re-offending and recommended a community order with a requirement of supervision and unpaid work. Allowing the appeal, the Court of Appeal stated that whilst the exercise of the judicial quality of mercy was entirely appropriate, a custodial sentence was inevitable where the appellant had worked dishonestly and deliberately not claimed asylum support to hide from the authorities. Given the uncertainty of the appellant's immigration status, however, the sentence imposed was manifestly excessive. A total sentence of eight months was substituted.

In *Thomas*, [2009] EWCA Crim 107, CA, the appellant had pleaded guilty to three offences of possession of a false identity document contrary to s.5(5) of the *Identity Cards Act* 2006 and had been sentenced to eight months' imprisonment for each of the offences, to be served concurrently, as well as being recommended for deportation. The documents that had been found in the appellant's possession were a Nigerian Passport; a provisional United Kingdom driving licence and a false full UK driving licence. The first two documents were wholly genuine but not the appellant's property. She argued that her sentence was manifestly excessive, and more in line with sentences imposed in cases of possession of false documents with intent, rather than offences of simple possession. Two of the documents forming the basis for her convictions were in fact genuine, although not in the appellant's name. There was also no evidence to show that the documents had been used to the applicant's benefit in any particular way. Allowing the appeal, the Court of Appeal considered authorities on sentencing offences of possession of false identity documents with intent which suggest a sub-category of the offence where an offender has entered the country lawfully and then used false identity documents to obtain work, citing the case of *Mutede* [2006] 2 Cr.App.R.(S.) 22, CA, where a sentence of 14 months' imprisonment was reduced in this court to six months following a plea of guilty. The Court also referred to authorities on sentencing cases of simple possession, such as *De Oliveira* [2006] 2 Cr.App.R.(S.) 17, CA (§ 15–166, above) *Araujo* [2006] EWCA Crim 1439, CA (§ 15–166, above); *Singh* [2008] EWCA Crim 1546; and *Zenasni* [2007] EWCA Crim 2165, CA. where pleas of guilty to simple possession resulted in sentences of eight months, eight months and 12 months respectively. The Court stated that a sentence of six months' imprisonment, would appropriately reflect the authorities considered.

The Court also quashed the recommendation for a deportation order, stating that the sentencing judge gave no warning that he was considering making such a recommendation, contrary to the usual practice that has been prevalent since at least the decision in *Nazari* [1980] 2 Cr.App.R.(S.) 848, and *Carmona* [2006] 1 WLR 2264, CA. The Court stated that giving such warning to counsel mitigating in such cases is generally thought to be required, even where the required statutory notice has been served. The Court added that it was also necessary for a sentencing judge to consider and apply the test identified in the Nazari case: whether the offender's continued presence in this country is in fact a potential detriment to the community at large. This has to be done after a full inquiry into all the circumstances. In the instant case, the judge had given no indication in passing sentence as to his reasons for making the recommendation. The court stated that considering the circumstances of the instant case, it was not possible to show the necessary element of detriment to the community had been established. There was no specific offending beyond the possession of the documents, and the applicant was of good character up to the time of these offences. She had been in the country and out of trouble for some 14 years. The recommendation for a deportation order was therefore quashed.

Possession of stolen passports and the theft of passports are serious matters that must be marked with a custodial sentence. However, there is a distinction between those who possess such documents with intent to use them and those who merely have them in their possession: *Mundirwa* [2009] EWCA Crim 521, CA. In this case, the appellants had been sentenced to 12 months' imprisonment for theft of a passport and possession of a false identity document. The first appellant had flown to the United Kingdom from South Africa and claimed asylum. His sister, the second appellant, had travelled on the same flight with her boyfriend. She admitted that she had facilitated the first appellant's entry into the UK using her boyfriend's passport, which she had stolen and given to the first appellant, who admitted having the passport and that it had permitted him to board the plane to enter the UK. The first appellant agreed that he told lies to immigration officers on arrival, but his story that he was seeking refuge from Zimbabwe was accepted and he was granted asylum. The Court of Appeal held that the sentences of 12 months' imprisonment were excessive, and substituted sentences of 6 months' imprisonment.

For general sentencing factors set out in the *Magistrates' Court Sentencing Guidelines* (2008) see Ch.23, *post*.

C. INTERFERENCE WITH VEHICLES

(1) Definition

Criminal Attempts Act 1981 s.9

Interference with vehicles

15–257 **9.**—(1) A person is guilty of the offence of vehicle interference if he interferes with a motor vehicle or trailer or with anything carried in or on a motor vehicle or trailer with the intention that an offence specified in subsection (2) below shall be committed by himself or some other person.

(2) The offences mentioned in subsection (1) above are—

(a) theft of the motor vehicle or trailer or part of it;

(b) theft of anything carried in or on the motor vehicle or trailer; and

(c) an offence under section 12(1) of the *Theft Act* 1968 (taking and driving away without consent);

and, if it is shown that a person offender of an offence under this section intended that one of those offences should be committed, it is immaterial that it cannot be shown which it was.

[This section is printed as amended by the *CJA* 1982, s.46; the *Police and Criminal Evidence Act* 1984, Sched. 7 and the *Road Traffic (Consequential Provisions) Act* 1988, Sched. 3.]

(2) Allocation

15–258 The offence is triable summarily: *Criminal Attempts Act* 1981, s.9(3).

(3) Elements of the offence

15–259 The prosecution must prove that:

— the defendant interfered. Interference is not defined within the Act. In *Reynolds and Warren v. Metropolitan Police* [1982] Crim.L.R.831 it was held that more than looking into vehicles and touching them was necessary to establish interference.

— with a motor vehicle or trailer or with anything carried in or on a motor vehicle or trailer,

— with the intention that one of the following offences should be committed by himself or some other person; theft of the motor vehicle or trailer or part of it; theft of anything carried in or on the motor vehicle or trailer; taking or diving a vehicle away without consent (offence created by s.2(1) of the *Theft Act* 1968).

"Motor vehicle" and "trailer" have the meanings assigned to them by section 185(1) of the *Road Traffic Act* 1988 (s.9(5)).

(4) Sentence

The maximum penalty for this offence is imprisonment for a term not exceeding three months or a fine not exceeding level four on the standard scale or both: *Criminal Attempts Act* 1981, s.9(3). Section 280(2) and Sched. 26, para. 28 of the *Criminal Justice Act* 2003 increases the maximum term to 51 weeks (not yet in force). **15–260**

For general sentencing factors set out in the *Magistrates' Court Sentencing Guidelines* (2008) see Ch. 23, *post*. The *Magistrates Courts Sentencing Guidelines* (2008) provide the following guideline for this offence:

STARTING POINT AND SENTENCING RANGES

(BASED ON A FIRST TIME OFFENDER AFTER TRIAL)

Examples of nature of activity	**Starting Point**	**Range**
Trying door handles; no entry gained to vehicle; no damage caused	Band C fine	Band A fine to low level community order
Entering vehicle, little or no damage caused	Medium level community order	Band C fine to high level community order
Entering vehicle, with damage caused	High level community order	Medium level community order to 12 weeks custody

AGGRAVATING AND MITIGATING FACTORS

Factor indicating higher culpability 1. Targeting vehicle in dark/isolated location **Factors indicating greater degree of harm** 1. Emergency services vehicle 2. Disabled driver's vehicle 3. Part of series	

D. DISHONESTLY OBTAINING ELECTRONIC COMMUNICATIONS SERVICES

(1) Definition

Communications Act 2003, s.125

Dishonestly obtaining electronic communications services

15–261 **125.**—(1) A person who—

(a) dishonestly obtains an electronic communications service, and

(b) does so with intent to avoid payment of a charge applicable to the provision of that service, is guilty of an offence.

(2) It is not an offence under this section to obtain a service mentioned in section 297(1) of the *Copyright, Designs and Patents Act* 1988 (c. 48) (dishonestly obtaining a broadcasting service provided from a place in the UK).

(3) A person guilty of an offence under this section shall be liable—

(a) on summary conviction, to imprisonment for a term not exceeding six months or to a fine not exceeding the statutory maximum, or to both;

(b) on conviction on indictment, to imprisonment for a term not exceeding five years or to a fine, or to both.

(2) Allocation

15–262 This offence is triable either way.

(3) Elements of the offence

15–263 The prosecution must prove that:

— The defendant dishonestly obtained,

— An electronic communications service,

— With the intention to permanently avoid payment of any charge applicable to the provision of that service.

It is not an offence to obtain a service mentioned in s.297(1) of the *Copyright, Designs and Patents Act* 1988 (s.125(2)).

(4) Sentence

15–264 When tried summarily, the maximum penalty for this offence is imprisonment for a term not exceeding six months or a fine not exceeding the statutory maximum or both: s.125(3)(a). After commencement of the relevant provisions the maximum custodial sentence in a magistrates' court will be 12 months' imprisonment: *Criminal Justice Act* 2003, ss.154 and 282.

In *Nadig* (1993) 14 Cr.App.R.(S.) 49, the offenders were seen using a telephone in a public telephone box to make an international call whilst one of the offenders was using a tone-dialling device. Their original sentences of two months' imprisonment, suspended, and a fine of 1,000 pounds each was varied to conditional discharge on appeal, the fact tat they were first time offenders and that this was an isolated offence being significant.

For general sentencing factors set out in the *Magistrates' Court Sentencing Guidelines* (2008) see Ch. 23, *post*.

E. POSSESSION OR SUPPLY OF APPARATUS TO DISHONESTLY OBTAIN ELECTRONIC COMMUNICATION SERVICES

(1) Definition

Communications Act 2003, s.126

Possession or supply of apparatus etc. for contravening s.125

126.—(1) A person is guilty of an offence if, with an intention falling within subsection (3), he has in his possession or under his control anything that may be used— **15–265**

(a) for obtaining an electronic communications service; or

(b) in connection with obtaining such a service.

(2) A person is guilty of an offence if—

(a) he supplies or offers to supply anything which may be used as mentioned in subsection (1); and

(b) he knows or believes that the intentions in relation to that thing of the person to whom it is supplied or offered fall within subsection (3).

(3) A person's intentions fall within this subsection if he intends—

(a) to use the thing to obtain an electronic communications service dishonestly;

(b) to use the thing for a purpose connected with the dishonest obtaining of such a service;

(c) dishonestly to allow the thing to be used to obtain such a service; or

(d) to allow the thing to be used for a purpose connected with the dishonest obtaining of such a service.

(4) An intention does not fall within subsection (3) if it relates exclusively to the obtaining of a service mentioned in section 297(1) of the *Copyright, Designs and Patents Act* 1988 (c. 48).

(5) A person guilty of an offence under this section shall be liable—

(a) on summary conviction, to imprisonment for a term not exceeding six months or to a fine not exceeding the statutory maximum, or to both; and

(b) on conviction on indictment, to imprisonment for a term not exceeding five years or to a fine, or to both.

(6) In this section, references, in the case of a thing used for recording data, to the use of that thing include references to the use of data recorded by it.

(2) Allocation

These offences are triable either way. **15–266**

(3) Elements of the offence

As regards the offence under s.126, (1) the prosecution must prove that: **15–267**

— The defendant had in his possession or under his control,

— anything that may be used for obtaining an electronic communications service, or

— anything that may be used in connection with obtaining such a service.

As regards the offence under s.126, (2) the prosecution must prove that:

— The defendant supplied or offered to supply anything which may be used for obtaining an electronic communications service, or

— in connection with obtaining such a service AND

— The defendant knew or believed that the person to whom the article is supplied intended to use the article to obtain an electronic communications service dishonestly OR

— Intended to use the thing for a purpose connected with the dishonest obtaining of such a service OR

— Intended dishonestly to allow the thing to be used to obtain such a service; or

— Intended to allow the thing to be used for a purpose connected with the dishonest obtaining of such a service.

It is not an offence under s.126(3) to supply or offer to supply an article to someone whose intentions relate exclusively to the obtaining of a service mentioned in s.297(1) of the *Copyright, Designs and Patents Act* 1988: s.126(4).

(4) Sentence

15–268 When tried summarily, the maximum penalty for this offence is imprisonment for a term not exceeding six months or a fine not exceeding the statutory maximum or both: s.125(3)(a). After commencement of the relevant provisions the maximum custodial sentence in a magistrates' court will be 12 months' imprisonment: *Criminal Justice Act* 2003, ss.154 and 282.

In *Stephens* [2002] 2 Cr.App.R.(S) 67, the defendant had modified mobile telephones to enable calls to be made for free. His original sentence of 18 months' imprisonment was reduced to twelve months' imprisonment on appeal. Whilst the offence was held to definitely pass the custody threshold, an appropriate discount for the defendant's guilty plea had to be given.

For general sentencing factors set out in the *Magistrates' Court Sentencing Guidelines* (2008) see Ch. 23, *post*.

F. RE-PROGRAMMING MOBILE TELEPHONES

(1) Definition

Mobile Telephones (Re-programming) Act 2002, s.1

Re-programming mobile telephone etc.

15–269 **1.**—(1) A person commits an offence if—

(a) he changes a unique device identifier, or
(b) he interferes with the operation of a unique device identifier, or
(c) he offers or agrees to change, or interfere with the operation of, a unique device identifier, or
(d) he offers or agrees to arrange for another person to change, or interfere with the operation of, a unique device identifier.

(2) A unique device identifier is an electronic equipment identifier which is unique to a mobile wireless communications device.

(3) But a person does not commit an offence under this section if—

(a) he is the manufacturer of the device, or
(b) he does the act mentioned in subsection (1) with the written consent of the manufacturer of the device.

(4) A person guilty of an offence under this section is liable—

(a) on summary conviction, to imprisonment for a term not exceeding 6 months or to a fine not exceeding the statutory maximum or to both, or
(b) on conviction on indictment, to imprisonment for a term not exceeding 5 years or to a fine or to both.

[This section is printed as amended by the *Violent Crime Reduction Act* 2006, s.62.]

(2) Allocation

15–270 This offence is triable either way.

(3) Elements of the offence

15–271 The prosecution must prove that:

— The defendant changed a unique device identifier OR
— Interfered with the operation of a unique device identifier OR
— Offered or agreed to change, or interfere with the operation of, a unique device identifier, OR

— Offered or agreed to arrange for another person to change, or interfere with the operation of, a unique device identifier.

The manufacturer of the device, or someone acting with the consent of the manufacturer of the device, will not commit an offence under this section if he modifies or changes the device's unique device identifier.

(4) Sentence

When tried summarily, the maximum penalty for this offence is imprisonment for a term not exceeding six months or a fine not exceeding the statutory maximum or both: s.125(3)(a). After commencement of the relevant provisions the maximum custodial sentence in a magistrates' court will be 12 months' imprisonment: *Criminal Justice Act* 2003, ss.154 and 282. **15–272**

For general sentencing factors set out in the *Magistrates' Court Sentencing Guidelines* (2008) see Ch. 23, *post*.

G. POSSESSION OR SUPPLY OF ANYTHING FOR RE-PROGRAMMING MOBILE TELEPHONES

(1) Definition

Mobile Telephones (Re-programming) Act 2002, s.2

Possession or supply of anything for re-programming purposes

2.—(1) A person commits an offence if— **15–273**

(a) he has in his custody or under his control anything which may be used for the purpose of changing or interfering with the operation of a unique device identifier, and

(b) he intends to use the thing unlawfully for that purpose or to allow it to be used unlawfully for that purpose.

(2) A person commits an offence if—

(a) he supplies anything which may be used for the purpose of changing or interfering with the operation of a unique device identifier, and

(b) he knows or believes that the person to whom the thing is supplied intends to use it unlawfully for that purpose or to allow it to be used unlawfully for that purpose.

(3) A person commits an offence if—

(a) he offers to supply anything which may be used for the purpose of changing or interfering with the operation of a unique device identifier, and

(b) he knows or believes that the person to whom the thing is offered intends if it is supplied to him to use it unlawfully for that purpose or to allow it to be used unlawfully for that purpose.

(4) A unique device identifier is an electronic equipment identifier which is unique to a mobile wireless communications device.

(5) A thing is used by a person unlawfully for a purpose if in using it for that purpose he commits an offence under section 1.

(6) A person guilty of an offence under this section is liable—

(a) on summary conviction, to imprisonment for a term not exceeding 6 months or to a fine not exceeding the statutory maximum or to both, or

(b) on conviction on indictment, to imprisonment for a term not exceeding 5 years or to a fine or to both.

(2) Allocation

This offence is triable either way. **15–274**

(3) Elements of the offence

The prosecution must prove that: **15–275**

— The defendant had in his custody or under his control anything which may be used for the purpose of changing or interfering with the operation of a unique device identifier AND
— They intended to use the thing unlawfully for that purpose or to allow it to be used unlawfully for that purpose OR
— The defendant supplied anything which may be used for the purpose of changing or interfering with the operation of a unique device identifier AND
— They knew or believed that the person to whom the thing was supplied intended to use it unlawfully for that purpose or to allow it to be used unlawfully for that purpose OR
— The defendant offered to supply anything which may be used for the purpose of changing or interfering with the operation of a unique device identifier AND
— They knew or believed that the person to whom the thing was offered intended if it was supplied to him, to use it unlawfully for that purpose or to allow it to be used unlawfully for that purpose.

(4) Sentence

15–276 When tried summarily, the maximum penalty for this offence is imprisonment for a term not exceeding six months or a fine not exceeding the statutory maximum or both: s.125(3)(a). After commencement of the relevant provisions the maximum custodial sentence in a magistrates' court will be 12 months' imprisonment: *Criminal Justice Act* 2003, ss.154 and 282.

For general sentencing factors set out in the *Magistrates' Court Sentencing Guidelines* (2008) see Ch. 23, *post*.

H. FRAUDULENT RECEIPT OF PROGRAMMES

(1) Definition

Copyright Designs and Patents Act 1988, s.297

Offence of fraudulently receiving programmes

15–277 **297.**—(1) A person who dishonestly receives a programme included in a broadcasting service provided from a place in the United Kingdom with intent to avoid payment of any charge applicable to the reception of the programme commits an offence and is liable on summary conviction to a fine not exceeding level 5 on the standard scale.

(2) Where an offence under this section committed by a body corporate is proved to have been committed with the consent or connivance of a director, manager, secretary or other similar officer of the body, or a person purporting to act in any such capacity, he as well as the body corporate is guilty of the offence and liable to be proceeded against and punished accordingly. In relation to a body corporate whose affairs are managed by its members "director" means a member of the body corporate.

[This section is printed as amended by the *Copyright and Related Rights Regulations* 2003 (S.I. 2003 No. 2498), reg.32, Sched. 2, para. 1.]

(2) Allocation

15–278 This offence is triable summarily only (s.297(1)).

(3) Elements of the offence

15–279 The prosecution must prove that:
— the defendant dishonestly,
— received a programme included in a broadcasting service provided from a place in the UK,
— with intent to avoid payment of any charge applicable to the reception of the programme.

(4) Sentence

The maximum penalty for this offence is a fine not exceeding level 5 on the standard scale: s.297(1). **15–280**

For general sentencing factors set out in the *Magistrates' Court Sentencing Guidelines* (2008) see Ch. 23, *post*.

I. HARASSMENT OF DEBTORS

(1) Definition

Administration of Justice Act 1970, s.40

Punishment for unlawful harassment of debtors

40.—(1) A person commits an offence if, with the object of coercing another person to pay money claimed from the other as a debt due under a contract, he— **15–281**

(a) harasses the other with demands for payment which, in respect of their frequency or the manner or occasion of making any such demand, or of any threat or publicity by which any demand is accompanied, are calculated to subject him or members of his family or household to alarm, distress or humiliation;

(b) falsely represents, in relation to the money claimed, that criminal proceedings lie for failure to pay it;

(c) falsely represents himself to be authorised in some official capacity to claim or enforce payment; or

(d) utters a document falsely represented by him to have some official character or purporting to have some official character which he knows it has not.

(2) A person may be guilty of an offence by virtue of subsection (1)(a) above if he concerts with others in the taking of such action as is described in that paragraph, notwithstanding that his own course of conduct does not by itself amount to harassment.

(3) Subsection (1)(a) above does not apply to anything done by a person which is reasonable (and otherwise permissible in law) for the purpose—

(a) of securing the discharge of an obligation due, or believed by him to be due, to himself or to persons for whom he acts, or protecting himself or them from future loss; or

(b) of the enforcement of any liability by legal process.

(3A) Subsection (1) above does not apply to anything done by a person to another in circumstances where what is done is a commercial practice within the meaning of the *Consumer Protection from Unfair Trading Regulations* 2008 and the other is a consumer in relation to that practice.

(4) A person guilty of an offence under this section shall be liable on summary conviction to a fine of not more than level 5 on the standard scale.

[This section printed as amended by the *Consumer Protection from Unfair Trading Regulations* 2008 (S.I. 2008 No. 1277).]

(2) Allocation

This offence is triable summarily only (s.40(4)). **15–282**

(3) Elements of the offence

The prosecution must prove that the defendant: **15–283**

— harassed one of his debtors with demands for payment which, in respect of their frequency or the manner or occasion of making any such demand, or of any threat or publicity by which any demand is accompanied, were calculated to subject him or members of his family or household to alarm, distress or humiliation or,

— falsely represented, in relation to the money claimed, that criminal proceedings lay for failure to pay it, or

— falsely represented himself to be authorised in some official capacity to claim or enforce payment; or
— uttered a document falsely represented by him to have some official character or purporting to have some official character which he knows it has not, with
— the object of coercing the debtor to pay money claimed from as a debt due under a contract.

15–284 An agreement for the supply of electricity between a tariff customer and a public electricity supplier under the *Electricity Act* 1989 is not a contract, as the rights and liabilities under this arrangement are governed by statute: *Norweb Plc v. Dixon* [1995] 3 All E.R. 952.

The phrase "calculated to subject" in s.40(1) means "likely to subject" and not "intending to subject": *Norweb Plc v. Dixon* (*ante*).

(4) Sentence

15–285 The maximum penalty for the first commission of this offence is a fine of not more than £100, and on a second or subsequent conviction, a fine of not more than £400: s.40(4).

For general sentencing factors set out in the *Magistrates' Court Sentencing Guidelines* (2008) see Ch. 23, *post*.

V. CRIMINAL DAMAGE AND RELATED OFFENCES

A. CRIMINAL DAMAGE

(1) Definition

Criminal Damage Act 1971, s.1

Destroying or damaging property

15–286 **1.**—(1) A person who without lawful excuse destroys or damages any property belonging to another intending to destroy or damage any such property or being reckless as to whether any such property would be destroyed or damaged shall be guilty of an offence.

(2) A person who without lawful excuse destroys or damages any property, whether belonging to himself or another—

(a) intending to destroy or damage any property or being reckless as to whether any property would be destroyed or damaged; and
(b) intending by the destruction or damage to endanger the life of another or being reckless as to whether the life of another would be thereby endangered;

shall be guilty of an offence.

(3) An offence committed under this section by destroying or damaging property by fire shall be charged as arson.

(2) Allocation

15–287 For the special procedure for criminal damage charges, see *ante*, §§ 7–60–7–68. See also *Drayton* [2005] 169 J.P 593. Where the value of the damage done is under £5,000 and the offence is not one or arson, or one endangering life, the offence is triable summarily only. Otherwise it is triable summarily or on indictment.

(3) Elements of the offence

15–288 The prosecution must prove:
— damage;
— recklessness: see *ante*, §§ 12–24–12–27;
— "Without lawful excuse": s.5(2) and (3) provide a defence.

Criminal Damage Act 1971, s.5

"Without lawful excuse"

5.—(1) This section applies to any offence under section 1(1) above and any offence under section 2 or 3 above other than one involving a threat by the person charged to destroy or damage property in a way which he knows is likely to endanger the life of another or involving an intent by the person charged to use or cause or permit the use of something in his custody or under his control so to destroy or damage property. **15–289**

(2) A person charged with an offence to which this section applies, shall, whether or not he would be treated for the purposes of this Act as having a lawful excuse apart from this subsection, be treated for those purposes as having a lawful excuse—

(a) if at the time of the act or acts alleged to constitute the offence he believed that the person or persons whom he believed to be entitled to consent to the destruction of or damage to the property in question had so consented, or would have so consented to it if he or they had known of the destruction or damage and its circumstances; or

(b) if he destroyed or damaged or threatened to destroy or damage the property in question or, in the case of a charge of an offence under section 3 above, intended to use or cause or permit the use of something to destroy or damage it, in order to protect property belonging to himself or another or a right or interest in property which was or which he believed to be vested in himself or another, and at the time of the act or acts alleged to constitute the offence he believed—

(i) that the property, right or interest was in immediate need of protection; and

(ii) that the means of protection adopted or proposed to be adopted were or would be reasonable having regard to all the circumstances.

(3) For the purposes of this section it is immaterial whether a belief is justified or not if it is honestly held.

(4) For the purposes of subsection (2) above a right or interest in property includes any right or privilege in or over land, whether created by grant, licence or otherwise. This section shall not be construed as casting doubt on any defence recognised by law as a defence to criminal charges.

The fact that a person was intoxicated at the time does not preclude reliance on this defence: *Jaggard v. Dickinson* (1981) 72 Cr.App.R. 33. **15–290**

In *Booth v. CPS* [2006] EWHC 192, QBD the appellant appealed against his conviction for criminal damage pursuant to the *Criminal Damage Act* 1971, ss.1(1) and 4. The appellant, who had been drinking and smoking drugs but was not drunk or incapable, had run into the path of a motor vehicle without looking and had collided with it, damaging the vehicle. The magistrates found that the damage was an obviously foreseeable consequence of the appellant's actions and that he "would have appreciated" the risk. The appellant argued that the magistrates had applied an objective rather than a subjective test as to recklessness and that, if the appellant had appreciated any risk at the time of the incident, it would have been a risk of personal injury and not property damage. The appellant also argued that as he had crossed the road without checking for traffic he was clearly not aware of any risk of damage to vehicles, and he had genuinely had not intended or foreseen the risk of damage. Dismissing the appeal, the Court held that the magistrates had applied the correct test for recklessness. Their use of the words "would have appreciated" was not inconsistent with their finding that the appellant was in fact aware of the risks associated with running into the road, including the risk of property damage. Applying *G.* [2003] UKHL 50, the Court held that the appellant had been aware of such risks, and then put them out of his mind. Although the risk of personal injury would have been uppermost in the appellant's mind, the magistrates were entitled to conclude that the appellant had also appreciated that there was a risk to property inherent in the overall risk of a collision.

In *Unsworth v DPP* [2010] EWHC 3037 (Admin), the appellant had been in dispute with her neighbours concerning their trees. She cut the trees with a saw, causing them significant damage. A magistrates' court found that she had caused criminal damage, and the Crown Court upheld that on the basis that she had not been entitled to the defence under the *Criminal Damage Act* 1971 s.5(2)(b). The court accepted that at the relevant time she had honestly believed that she was protecting a right to light in her kitchen and that she had felt she needed to take immediate action to remedy the situation, but found that there was no evidence on which it could be said that she had believed there was a need to take immediate action. It noted that there were practical and legal steps she could have taken to resolve the dispute, and that the dark kitchen was a relatively minor interference with her enjoyment of her property. The question for determination was whether the court had been justified, in the light of its findings of fact, in holding that the statutory defence had not been established.

Allowing the appeal, the Court held that the first limb of the defence in section 5(2)(b) ("in order to protect property of himself or another"), has both a subjective and an objective aspect. The second limb of the defence, a test of the defendant's belief, is exclusively subjective. The only question on the second limb is honest belief. Whether the belief is reasonable is not of itself determinative of honest belief. It is immaterial whether the belief was justified. Reasonableness is an element of the second limb, not as a criterion to be met in addition to honest belief but as one of the ingredients in honest belief.

(4) Sentence

15–291 The maximum sentence for criminal damage is six months' imprisonment. When the offence is summary only because the value of the damage is below £5,000, the maximum sentence is three months' imprisonment or a fine up to level 4: *Magistrates' Courts Act* 1980, s.33. After commencement of the relevant provisions, the maximum custodial sentence in a magistrates' court will be 12 months' imprisonment: *Criminal Justice Act* 2003, ss.154 and 282.

For general sentencing factors set out in the *Magistrates' Court Sentencing Guidelines* (2008) see Ch. 23, *post*. The *Magistrates Courts Sentencing Guidelines* (2008) provide the following guideline for this offence:

STARTING POINT AND SENTENCING RANGES

(BASED ON A FIRST TIME OFFENDER AFTER TRIAL)

Examples of nature of activity	**Starting Point**	**Range**
Minor damage e.g. breaking small window; small amount of graffiti	Band B fine	Conditional discharge to band C fine
Moderate damage e.g. breaking large plate-glass or shop window; widespread graffiti	Low level community order	Band C fine to medium level community order
Significant damage up to £5,000 e.g. damage caused as part of a spree	High level community order	Medium level community order to 12 weeks custody
Damage between £5,000 and £10,000	12 weeks custody	6 to 26 weeks custody
Damage over £10,000	Crown Court	Crown Court

AGGRAVATING AND MITIGATING FACTORS

Factors indicating higher culpability	Factors indicating lower culpability
1. Revenge attack 2. Targeting vulnerable victim **Factors indicating greater degree of harm** 1. Damage to emergency equipment 2. Damage to public amenity 3. Significant public or private fear caused e.g. in domestic context	1. Damage caused recklessly 2. Provocation

Part III

Offences Committed In A Domestic Context

The *Magistrates Courts Sentencing Guidelines* (2008) provide that when sentencing an offence committed in a domestic context, the Court should refer to the Sentencing Guidelines Council's definitive guideline *Overarching Principles: Domestic Violence*, published December 2006. See § 13–15, *above*.

The *Magistrates Courts Sentencing Guidelines* (2008) provide the following guideline for cases of arson (criminal damage by fire).

STARTING POINT AND SENTENCING RANGES:

(BASED ON A FIRST TIME OFFENDER AFTER TRIAL)

Examples of nature of activity	Starting Point	Range
Minor damage by fire	High level community order	Medium level community order to 12 weeks custody
Moderate damage by fire	12 weeks custody	6 to 26 weeks custody
Significant damage by fire	Crown Court	Crown Court

AGGRAVATING AND MITIGATING FACTORS

Factors indicating higher culpability	Factors indicating lower culpability
1. Revenge attack	1. Damage caused recklessly
Factors indicating greater degree of harm	**Factors indicating lower culpability**
1. Damage to emergency equipment 2. Damage to public amenity 3. Significant public or private fear caused, *e.g.* in domestic context	1. Damage caused recklessly

B. THREATS TO DESTROY OR DAMAGE PROPERTY

(1) Definition

Criminal Damage Act 1971, s.2

Threats to destroy or damage property

15–292 **2.** A person who without lawful excuse makes to another a threat, intending that that other would fear it would be carried out—

(a) to destroy or damage any property belonging to that other or a third person; or

(b) to destroy or damage his own property in a way which he knows is likely to endanger the life of that other or third person;

shall be guilty of an offence.

(2) Allocation

15–293 This offence is triable either way.

(3) Elements of the offence

15–294 For the purposes of s.2(a) it was necessary to ask whether, objectively construed, the words or actions of the accused constituted a threat to destroy or damage the property of another: *Cakmak* [2002] EWCA Crim 500, CA. In this case, six Turkish nationals appealed against convictions for threatening criminal damage contrary to s.2(a) of the *Criminal Damage Act* 1971. The defendants had occupied sections of the London Eye to protest against alleged human rights abuse within Turkey and threatened they would set fire to themselves if an attempt was made to evacuate them. They appealed against conviction, submitting that the trial judge had erred in refusing a submission of no case to answer and misdirected the jury as to what constituted an offence under s.2(a) of the Act. The judge had directed the jury that the essence of the offence was "setting a fire" and that the method by which the fire was started was irrelevant. Allowing the appeal, the Court stated that for the purposes of s.2(a) it was necessary to ask whether, objectively construed, the words or actions of the accused constituted a threat to destroy or damage the property of another. Unlike s.1(1) of the Act, s.2(a) made no reference to recklessness. Whilst the trial judge had failed to approach the issue in that manner, he had been right to conclude there was sufficient prima facie evidence to justify putting the issue to the jury. However, the judge's direction had wrongly implied that the test was whether the defendants had threatened to set fires, be it to themselves or another's property, rather than considering whether there had been a threat to damage the property of another. The verdicts were therefore unsafe.

(4) Sentence

When tried summarily, the maximum sentence for threatening criminal damage is six months' imprisonment. After commencement of the relevant provisions, the maximum custodial sentence in a magistrates' court will be 12 months' imprisonment: *Criminal Justice Act* 2003, ss.154 and 282. **15–295**

For general sentencing factors set out in the *Magistrates' Court Sentencing Guidelines* (2008) see Ch. 23, *post*.

C. Possessing Anything with Intent to Destroy or Damage Property

(1) Definition

Criminal Damage Act 1971, s.3

Possessing anything with intent to destroy or damage property.

3. A person who has anything in his custody or under his control intending without lawful excuse to use it or cause or permit another to use it— **15–296**

(a) to destroy or damage any property belonging to some other person; or

(b) to destroy or damage his own or the user's property in a way which he knows is likely to endanger the life of some other person;

shall be guilty of an offence.

Part III

(2) Allocation

The offence is triable either way. **15–297**

(3) Elements of the offence

The defendant must intend or permit that an article is used for the purpose of destroying or damaging property: it is not enough that they realise that an article may be used for the purpose of destroying or damaging property. That use does not have to be immediate, and intention to use, should it prove necessary, suffices: *Buckingham* (1976) 63 Cr.App.R. 159, CA. The defendant was a squatter, and had been caught carrying tools for breaking into squats. He would not have used them if he could have got in through other means. He was convicted of possessing an article with intent to damage property and appealed, submitting that the judge's direction that provided the intention to use the article for that purpose existed, it did not matter how far in the future the event was going to take place was wrong. The Court of Appeal dismissed his appeal, stating that the offence was aimed at proscribing what was essentially a preparatory act, and intention to use the article however far in the future or a conditional intention was sufficient. **15–298**

(4) Sentence

There are no sentencing guidelines for this offence. When tried summarily, the maximum sentence for criminal damage is six months' imprisonment. After commencement of the relevant provisions, the maximum custodial sentence in a magistrates' court will be 12 months' imprisonment: *Criminal Justice Act* 2003, ss.154 and 282. **15–299**

For general sentencing factors set out in the *Magistrates' Court Sentencing Guidelines* (2008) see Ch. 23, *post*.

D. RACIALLY OR RELIGIOUSLY AGGRAVATED CRIMINAL DAMAGE

(1) Definition

Crime and Disorder Act 1998, s.30

Racially or religiously aggravated criminal damage

15–300 **30.**—(1) A person is guilty of an offence under this section if he commits an offence under section 1(1) of the *Criminal Damage Act* 1971 (destroying or damaging property belonging to another) which is racially or religiously aggravated for the purposes of this section.

(2) A person guilty of an offence under this section shall be liable—

(a) on summary conviction, to imprisonment for a term not exceeding six months or to a fine not exceeding the statutory maximum, or to both;

(b) on conviction on indictment, to imprisonment for a term not exceeding fourteen years or to a fine, or to both.

(3) For the purposes of this section, section 28(1)(a) above shall have effect as if the person to whom the property belongs or is treated as belonging for the purposes of that Act were the victim of the offence.

(2) Allocation

15–301 The offence is triable either way.

(3) Elements of the offence

15–302 On criminal damage, see *ante*, § 15–286; on other racially or religiously aggravated offences, see *ante*, § 13–22—13–24.

(4) Sentence

15–303 A person guilty of an offence under this section shall be liable on summary conviction, to imprisonment for a term not exceeding six months or to a fine not exceeding the statutory maximum, or to both: s.30(2). After commencement of the relevant provisions, the maximum custodial sentence in a magistrates' court will be 12 months' imprisonment: *Criminal Justice Act* 2003, ss.154 and 282.

For general sentencing factors set out in the *Magistrates' Court Sentencing Guidelines* (2008) see see Ch. 23, *post*. The guideline for aggravated criminal damage is the same as the guideline for criminal damage cases. See § 15–291.

See *Saunders* [2000] 1 Cr.App.R. 458 and *Morrison* [2001] 1 Cr.App.R.(S.) 5 for general guidance.

VI. COMPUTER MISUSE

A. UNAUTHORISED ACCESS TO COMPUTER MATERIAL

(1) Definition

Computer Misuse Act 1990, s.1

Unauthorised access to computer material

15–304 **1.**—(1) A person is guilty of an offence if—

(a) he causes a computer to perform any function with intent to secure access to any program or data held in any computer, or to enable any such access to be secured;

(b) the access he intends to secure, or to enable to be secured, is unauthorised; and

(c) he knows at the time when he causes the computer to perform the function that that is the case.

(2) The intent a person has to have to commit an offence under this section need not be directed at—

(a) any particular program or data;
(b) a program or data of any particular kind; or
(c) a program or data held in any particular computer.

(3) A person guilty of an offence under this section shall be liable—

(a) on summary conviction in England and Wales, to imprisonment for a term not exceeding 12 months or to a fine not exceeding the statutory maximum or to both;
(b) on summary conviction in Scotland, to imprisonment for a term not exceeding six months or to a fine not exceeding the statutory maximum or to both;
(c) on conviction on indictment, to imprisonment for a term not exceeding two years or to a fine or to both.

[Section printed as amended by the *Police and Justice Act* 2006, s.35(3) which came into force on October 1, 2008.]

(2) Allocation

This is a summary offence. **15–305**

(3) Elements of the offence

The prosecution must prove: **15–306**

— unauthorised access;
— intent to access a program or data;
— knowledge of lack of authorisation.

In order for a person to commit an offence under s.1(1) of the *Computer Misuse Act* 1990 the computer which the person with the required intent caused to perform any function did not have to be a different computer to the one into which he intended to secure unauthorised access: *Att-Gen's Ref (No. 1 of 1991)* [1992] 3 W.L.R. 432, CA.

The words in s.1(1)(a) "he causes a computer to perform any function with intent to secure access to any program or data held in any computer", should be given their plain and natural meaning to avoid a lacuna in the field of interference with computers and to meet the mischief of industrial espionage or obtaining information as to security details or other confidential information which might be stored on a company's computer. There are no grounds for implying, or importing the word "other" between "any" and "computer", or excepting the computer which was actually used by the offender from the phrase "any computer" at the end of subs (1)(a): *Att-Gen's Ref (No. 1 of 1991)*, above.

(4) Sentence

A person guilty of an offence under this section shall be liable on summary conviction **15–307** to imprisonment for a term not exceeding six months or to a fine not exceeding level 5 on the standard scale or to both. After commencement of the relevant provisions, the maximum custodial sentence in a magistrates' court will be 12 months' imprisonment: *Criminal Justice Act* 2003, ss.154 and 282.

For general sentencing factors set out in the *Magistrates' Court Sentencing Guidelines* (2008) see Ch. 23, *post*.

B. Unauthorised Access with Intent to Commit or Facilitate Commission of Further Offences

(1) Definition

Computer Misuse Act 1990, s.2

Unauthorised access with intent to commit or facilitate commission of further offences

2.—(1) A person is guilty of an offence under this section if he commits an offence under section 1 above ("the unauthorised access offence") with intent— **15–308**

(a) to commit an offence to which this section applies; or

(b) to facilitate the commission of such an offence (whether by himself or by any other person);

and the offence he intends to commit or facilitate is referred to below in this section as the further offence.

(2) This section applies to offences—

(a) for which the sentence is fixed by law; or

(b) for which a person of twenty-one years of age or over (not previously convicted) may be sentenced to imprisonment for a term of five years (or, in England and Wales, might be so sentenced but for the restrictions imposed by section 33 of the *Magistrates' Courts Act* 1980).

(3) It is immaterial for the purposes of this section whether the further offence is to be committed on the same occasion as the unauthorised access offence or on any future occasion.

(4) A person may be guilty of an offence under this section even though the facts are such that the commission of the further offence is impossible.

(5) A person guilty of an offence under this section shall be liable—

(a) on summary conviction, to imprisonment for a term not exceeding six months or to a fine not exceeding the statutory maximum or to both; and

(b) on conviction on indictment, to imprisonment for a term not exceeding five years or to a fine or to both.

(2) Allocation

15–309 This offence is triable either way.

(3) Elements of the offence

15–310 See *ante*, § 15–308. There must also be an intent to commit an offence punishable with a term of five years' imprisonment.

(4) Sentence

15–311 A person guilty of an offence under this section shall be liable on summary conviction, to imprisonment for a term not exceeding six months or to a fine not exceeding the statutory maximum or to both: s.2(5). After commencement of the relevant provisions, the maximum custodial sentence in a magistrates' court will be 12 months' imprisonment: *Criminal Justice Act* 2003, ss.154 and 282.

In *Gray* (2001), unreported, the defendant had pleaded guilty to six counts of offences under s.1 of the *Computer Misuse Act* 1990 and three counts of offences under s.2 of the Act with the related offences of obtaining by deception. In addition the defendant was to be sentenced for two offences of obtaining by deception that had been committed for sentence from the magistrates' court. He had no previous convictions. The first six counts related to the defendant's use of his computer to attack e-commerce sites whose computers used software with an inherent security weakness. The damage to these sites was minimal. The defendant published the credit card details of over 5,400 customers acquired from customer databases on the Internet to expose the security deficiencies of these e-commerce retailers, and deter customers from giving these retailers their credit card details. The other four counts involved using customers' credit cards to pay for website fees. In his sentencing remarks, the trial judge stated that essential seriousness of this case was the great expense and inconvenience caused to the targeted companies, the issuing banks and the credit card holders. Despite some dishonesty, the defendant's motivation had been mainly altruistic. In light of his history, the medical evidence and the pre-sentence report, an immediate sentence of custody would not be appropriate. A three-year community rehabilitation order coupled with psychiatric treatment would be appropriate.

For general sentencing factors set out in the *Magistrates' Court Sentencing Guidelines* (2008) see Ch. 23, *post*.

C. UNAUTHORISED MODIFICATION OF COMPUTER MATERIAL

(1) Definition

Computer Misuse Act 1990, s.3

Unauthorised acts with intent to impair, or with recklessness as to impairing, operation of computer, etc.

3.—(1) A person is guilty of an offence if— **15–312**

(a) he does any unauthorised act in relation to a computer;

(b) at the time when he does the act he knows that it is unauthorised; and

(c) either subsection (2) or subsection (3) below applies.

(2) This subsection applies if the person intends by doing the act—

(a) to impair the operation of any computer;

(b) to prevent or hinder access to any program or data held in any computer;

(c) to impair the operation of any such program or the reliability of any such data; or

(d) to enable any of the things mentioned in paragraphs (a) to (c) above to be done.

(3) This subsection applies if the person is reckless as to whether the act will do any of the things mentioned in paragraphs (a) to (d) of subsection (2) above.

(4) The intention referred to in subsection (2) above, or the recklessness referred to in subsection (3) above, need not relate to—

(a) any particular computer;

(b) any particular program or data; or

(c) a program or data of any particular kind.

(5) In this section—

(a) a reference to doing an act includes a reference to causing an act to be done;

(b) "act" includes a series of acts;

(c) a reference to impairing, preventing or hindering something includes a reference to doing so temporarily.

(6) A person guilty of an offence under this section shall be liable—

(a) on summary conviction in England and Wales, to imprisonment for a term not exceeding 12 months or to a fine not exceeding the statutory maximum or to both;

(b) on summary conviction in Scotland, to imprisonment for a term not exceeding six months or to a fine not exceeding the statutory maximum or to both;

(c) on conviction on indictment, to imprisonment for a term not exceeding 10 years or to a fine or to both.

[Section printed as amended by the *Police and Justice Act* 2006, s.36, which came into force on October 1, 2008.]

(2) Allocation

This offence is triable either way. **15–313**

(3) Elements of the offence

— an act which causes unauthorised modification of the contents of any computer. **15–314**

— an intent to cause a modification: see *ante*, s.3(2).

In *DPP v. Lennon* [2006] EWHC 1201, QBD, the DPP appealed against the decision of a district judge sitting in a youth court that the respondent had no case to answer to a charge of causing an unauthorised modification to the contents of a company's computer. After being dismissed from the company, the respondent had used a program that automatically sent continuous emails to the company's server, which led to the company's server receiving over 500,000 emails. The district judge had held that s.3 was intended to deal with the sending of malicious material such as viruses and Trojan horses rather than email and that as the company's server was configured to receive emails the company had accepted the modification of its computers by the addition of data in the form of emails. Allowing the appeal, the Court stated that it was clear that the emails had resulted in the modification of the data on the company's computers so that the key question was whether the company had consented to that modification. The owner of a computer able to receive emails would ordinarily be taken to have consented to the sending of emails to his computer. However, such implied consent was not without limits, and the consent did not cover emails that had been sent not for the purpose of communication with the owner but to interrupt the proper operation and use of his system. Further, the emails could not be considered on an email-by-email basis but as a whole. It was probable that the response from the company if asked whether it would receive an email from the respondent would differ from its response if asked whether it would receive 500,000 emails from him.

(4) Sentence

15–315 A person guilty of an offence under this section shall be liable on summary conviction, to imprisonment for a term not exceeding six months or to a fine not exceeding the statutory maximum or to both: s.3(7). On commencement of the relevant provisions, the maximum custodial sentence in a magistrates' court will be 12 months' imprisonment: *Criminal Justice Act* 2003, ss.154 and 282.

In *Lindesay* [2001] EWCA Crim 1720, CA, the Court held that a nine-month sentence for causing unauthorised modification of the contents of a computer was not manifestly excessive. The offence should not however be seen as analogous to glassing a man in a pub. In this case, the appellant was a freelance computer consultant who had worked for a firm that maintained websites. The appellant was dismissed in July 2000 and the following August, after a few drinks and acting on impulse, he gained unauthorised access to the websites of three of the firm's clients. He then deleted some of the contents and data on the websites and moved images around, intending to inconvenience the firm. He also sent e-mails to all the customers of one company informing them prices had gone up and to shop elsewhere if they didn't like this. His actions caused considerable inconvenience and expense to the firm and its clients. On arrest the appellant said that he regretted his actions and wanted to apologise to the affected companies. The appellant was sentenced to 9 month's imprisonment, with the judge stating that the offence involved pure and unmitigated revenge analogous to someone shoving a glass in the face of another person in a pub because they did not like their attitude. Dismissing his appeal, the Court stated that the judge had clearly paid attention to the mitigating factors because he had set them out carefully, though the analogy of a glassing attack was not helpful. However, the judge had identified the gravamen of the appellant's criminality, which was that however real the grievance, however impulsive the act of revenge and however inevitable the discovery of his responsibility for these acts, he had used his skill and knowledge of his employer's business to cause a great deal of work, inconvenience and worry to organisations that were entirely innocent. The offences were properly met by an immediate prison sentence to mark the breach of trust and the sentence was not excessive, let alone manifestly excessive.

For general sentencing factors set out in the *Magistrates' Court Sentencing Guidelines* (2008) see Ch.23, *post*.

Chapter 16

PUBLIC ORDER OFFENCES

Part III

I. OFFENCES UNDER THE PUBLIC ORDER ACT 1936

A. PROHIBITION OF UNIFORMS IN CONNECTION WITH POLITICAL OBJECTS

(1) Definition

Public Order Act 1936, s.1(1)

Prohibition of uniforms in connection with political objects

16–1 **1.**—(1) Subject as hereinafter provided, any person who in any public place or at any public meeting wears uniform signifying his association with any political organisation or with the promotion of any political object shall be guilty of an offence:

Provided that, if the chief officer of police is satisfied that the wearing of any such uniform as aforesaid on any ceremonial, anniversary, or other special occasion will not be likely to involve risk of public disorder, he may, with the consent of a Secretary of State, by order permit the wearing of such uniform on that occasion either absolutely or subject to such conditions as may be specified in the order.

(2) Allocation

16–2 This offence is triable summarily. Section 1(2) provides that proceedings may not be instituted without the consent of the Attorney General.

(3) Elements of the offence

16–3 The prosecution must prove that:

— the defendant wore a uniform signifying his association with any political organisation or promotion of any political object,

— in a public place or at a public meeting and,

— the chief officer of police had not, with the consent of the Secretary of State, made an order permitting the wearing of such a uniform.

Any item worn to show mutual association can amount to a "uniform" without proof of its previous use as such. In *O'Moran v. DPP* [1975] Q.B. 864, the Court of Appeal took the view that the wearer's association with a political organisation may be proved either by showing that the uniform has in the past been associated with a political organisation or by proving that the conduct of the wearer on the occasion complained of indicates activity of a political character. The prosecution does not have to specify the particular political organisation.

The terms "meeting", "public meeting" and "public place" are defined in s.9 of the 1936 Act:

Public Order Act 1936, s.9(1)

Interpretation, &c.

16–4 **9.**—(1) In this Act the following expressions have the meanings hereby respectively assigned to them, that is to say—

"Meeting" means a meeting held for the purpose of the discussion of matters of public interest or for the purpose of the expression of views on such matters;

"Public meeting" includes any meeting in a public place and any meeting which the public or any section thereof are permitted to attend, whether on payment or otherwise.

"Public place" includes any highway, or in Scotland any road within the meaning of the *Roads (Scotland) Act* 1984 and any other premises or place to which at the material time the public have or are permitted to have access, whether on payment or otherwise.

In *Marsh v. Arscott* (1982) 75 Cr.App.R. 211, DC, McCullough J. stated that "it is important to have regard to the words 'at the material time' in the definition of 'public place'." The Court held that a shop car park could not amount to a public place at 11.30p.m. on a Saturday night when the shop was closed. Where the public do have access to a given place at the material time, it will be classed as a public place, despite the fact that entry can be refused to certain people: in *Lawrenson v. Oxford* [1982] Crim.L.R. 185, a public house with open doors inviting the public to enter was held to be a public place. A place will still be classed as a public place even where the public are denied access to certain parts, hence in *Cawley v. Frost* (1977) 64 Cr.App.R. 20, a football ground was classed as a public place, with Lord Widgery C.J. stating that "*Prima facie* the whole establishment should be considered and the court should not be deterred ... merely by finding that access to certain portions of the establishment had been denied to the public." remises such as a front garden will not be classed as a public place, as people are only entitled to enter on an individual basis as visitors: *Edwards* (1978) 67 Cr.App.R. 228. **16–5**

(4) Sentence

The maximum penalty is three months or a fine not exceeding level four on the standard scale: *Public Order Act* 1936, s.7(2). Section 280(2) and Sched. 26, para. 8 of the *Criminal Justice Act* 2003 increases the maximum term to 51 weeks (not yet in force). **16–6**

B. PROHIBITION OF QUASI-MILITARY ORGANISATIONS

(1) Definition

Public Order Act 1936, s.2

2.—(1) If the members or adherents of any association of persons, whether incorporated or not, are— **16–7**

(a) organised or trained or equipped for the purposes of enabling them to be employed in usurping the functions of the police or of the armed forces of the Crown; or

(b) organised and trained or organised and equipped either for the purpose of enabling them to be employed for the use or display of physical force in promoting any political object, or in such manner as to arouse reasonable apprehension that they are organised and either trained or equipped for that purpose;

then any person who takes part in the control or management of the association, or in so organising or training as aforesaid any members or adherents thereof, shall be guilty of an offence under this section.

Provided that in any proceedings against a person charged with the offence of taking part in the control or management of such an association as aforesaid it shall be a defence to that charge to prove that he neither consented to nor connived at the organisation, training, or equipment of members or adherents of the association in contravention of the provisions of this section.

(2) No prosecution shall be instituted under this section without the consent of the Attorney-General.

(3) [powers of the High Court]

(4) In any criminal or civil proceedings under this section proof of things done or of words written, spoken or published (whether or not in the presence of any party to the proceedings) by any person taking part in the control or management of an association or in organising, training or equipping members or adherents of an association shall be admissible as evidence of the purposes for which, or the manner in which, members or ad-

herents of the association (whether those persons or others) were organised, or trained, or equipped.

(5) [powers of the High Court]

(6) Nothing in this section shall be construed as prohibiting the employment of a reasonable number of persons as stewards to assist in the preservation of order at any public meeting held upon private premises, or the making of arrangements for that purpose or the instruction of the persons to be so employed in their lawful duties as such stewards, or their being furnished with badges or other distinguishing signs.

(2) Allocation

16–8 This offence is triable either way: *Public Order Act* 1936, s.7(1). Section 2(2) of the 1936 Act establishes that no prosecution shall take place without the consent of the Attorney General.

(3) Elements of the offence

16–9 The prosecution need to prove that:

— the defendant has managed or controlled an association, or has organised or taken part in the organisation or training of an association whose members are,

— organised or trained or equipped for the purposes of enabling them to be employed in usurping the functions of the police or of the armed forces of the Crown,

OR

— organised and trained or organised and equipped either for the purpose of enabling them to be employed for the use or display of physical force in promoting any political object,

OR

— arouse reasonable apprehension that they are organised and either trained or equipped for that purpose.

The fact that there was no evidence of actual attacks or plans for attacks on opponents will not necessarily remove the grounds for "reasonable apprehension" that the association is organised and equipped for the purpose of enabling them to be employed for use or display of physical force in promoting a political object: *Jordan and Tyndall* [1963] Crim.L.R. 124, CCA.

(4) Specific defences

16–10 A specific defence to proceedings brought under this section is established in s.2 of the 1936 Act:

Public Order Act 1936, s.2(1)

Prohibition of quasimilitary organisations

16–11 **2.**—(1) ... Provided that in any proceedings against a person charged with the offence of taking part in the control or management of such an association as aforesaid it shall be a defence to that charge to prove that he neither consented to nor connived at the organisation, training, or equipment of members or adherents of the association in contravention of the provisions of this section.

Public Order Act 1936, s.2(6)

Prohibition of quasimilitary organisations

16–12 **2.**—(6) Nothing in this section shall be construed as prohibiting the employment of a reasonable number of persons as stewards to assist in the preservation of order at any public meeting held upon private premises, or the making of arrangements for that purpose or the instruction of the persons to be so employed in their lawful duties as such stewards, or their being furnished with badges or other distinguishing signs.

(5) Sentence

When tried summarily, the maximum penalty for this offence is six months' imprisonment or a fine not exceeding the prescribed sum or both: *Public Order Act* 1936, s.7(1). On commencement of the relevant provisions, the maximum custodial sentence in a magistrates' court will be 12 months' imprisonment: *Criminal Justice Act* 2003, ss.154 and 282. **16–13**

II. OFFENCES UNDER THE PUBLIC ORDER ACT 1986

A. VIOLENT DISORDER

(1) Definition

Public Order Act 1986, s.2

Violent disorder

2.—(1) Where 3 or more persons who are present together use or threaten unlawful violence and the conduct of them (taken together) is such as would cause a person of reasonable firmness present at the scene to fear for his personal safety, each of the persons using or threatening unlawful violence is guilty of violent disorder. **16–14**

(2) It is immaterial whether or not the 3 or more use or threaten unlawful violence simultaneously.

(3) No person of reasonable firmness need actually be, or be likely to be, present at the scene.

(4) Violent disorder may be committed in private as well as in public places.

(5) A person guilty of violent disorder is liable on conviction on indictment to imprisonment for a term not exceeding 5 years or a fine or both, or on summary conviction to imprisonment for a term not exceeding 6 months or a fine not exceeding the statutory maximum or both.

(2) Allocation

Violent disorder is triable either way, though the *Practice Direction (Criminal Proceedings: Consolidation)*, para. V.51.11 provides that "cases of violent disorder should normally be committed for trial". **16–15**

(3) Elements of the offence

The prosecution need to prove that: **16–16**

— three or more persons who were present together,

— used or threatened unlawful violence and,

— the conduct of them taken together is such as would cause a person of reasonable firmness present at the scene to fear for his personal safety.

"3 or more persons"

As to the requirement that there be three of more persons present together using or threatening unlawful violence before there can be a conviction of anyone, see *Fleming* (1989) 153 J.P. 517 and *Worton* (1989) 154 J.P. 201. See also *Mahroof* (1988) 88 Cr.App.R. 317. If one of more of the named defendants is acquitted due to a lack of *mens rea*, the remaining defendants may be found guilty, even if there are only two of them: *Public Order Act* 1986, s.6(7).

The words "present together" mean no more than being in the same place at the same time. There is no requirement of any degree of co-operation between those who are threatening violence: *R. v. N.W.* [2010] 2 Cr.App.R. 8, CA.

"Use or threaten"

Being part of a group of people following a man for three-quarters of a mile along a **16–17** footpath in the middle of the night is capable of amounting to violent disorder: *Brodie* [2000] Crim.L.R. 775, CA. The Court held that such conduct would involve a considerable implicit menace, amounting to a threat and that a person of reasonable firmness present during and throughout such action would have been put in fear for his or her personal safety. See also *I. v. DPP*; *M. v. DPP*; *H. v. DPP* [2001] 1 Cr.App.R. 251.

"Unlawful violence"

16–18 The defences of self-defence and reasonable defence of others are preserved by the use of the phrase "unlawful violence". Actions no more than necessary to restore the peace are also permissible: *Rothwell and Barton* [1993] Crim.L.R. 626, CA.

(4) Sentence

16–19 When tried summarily the maximum penalty is six months' imprisonment, a fine not exceeding the statutory maximum or both: s.2(5). On commencement of the relevant provisions, the maximum custodial sentence in a magistrates' court will be 12 months' imprisonment: *Criminal Justice Act* 2003 ss.154 and 282.

The *Magistrates' Court Sentencing Guidelines* (2008) state:

> "These offences should normally be dealt with in the Crown Court. However, there may be rare cases involving minor violence or threats of violence leading to no or minor injury, with few people involved and no weapons or missiles, in which a custodial sentence within the jurisdiction of a magistrates' court may be appropriate."

It is not just the precise acts of individuals which matter but also the fact that in taking part in a violent disorder defendants have been part of the whole threatening and alarming activity. In sentencing for public order offences generally the court must have regard to the whole picture. Although what an individual had himself done was relevant, it was simply part of the whole to which he was contributing: *Fox and Hicks* [2006] 1 Cr.App.R.(S.) 17.

In *Tomlinson* (1993) 157 J.P. 695, it was held that the essence of the offence of violent disorder lies in the using of violence in circumstances where so many people were present as to cause or inspire fear in the general public. The offenders' participation in a demonstration against poll tax culminated in fighting and shouting that caused fear amongst the general public. D1 was sentenced to four months' imprisonment, and D2 and D3 were sentenced to six months' imprisonment and youth custody respectively.

The purposes of sentencing in cases of violent disorder are to punish those who inflict violence or who cause fear to the public, or inflict violence on the police, and to deter others from pursuing such conduct. Where wanton and serious violence has been used, it does not matter that its origin was the views of those who were acting from genuinely held political beliefs: *R. v. Alhaddad* [2011] 1 Cr.App.R.(S.) 86, CA.

16–20 In *Shanoor* (1998) 162 J.P. 731, the involvement of the offender in a brawl outside a nightclub was characterised as spontaneous, with no weapon being used and no injury caused. A sentence of six months' imprisonment imposed by the Crown Court was substituted by a short Community Service Order at the Court of Appeal. In *Pickard* (2000) the defendant was sentenced to eighteen months' detention in a young offenders' institution following a guilty plea to violent disorder. His co-defendants (all younger) received non-custodial sentences, however a distinction was drawn in his case due to his age and history of violent offending. As he had engaged in a racially motivated confrontation and had previously failed to respond to community sentences, custody was inevitable, however his sentence was reduced to twelve months on appeal.

B. AFFRAY

(1) Definition

Public Order Act 1986 s.3

Affray

16–21 **3.**—(1) A person is guilty of affray if he uses or threatens unlawful violence towards another and his conduct is such as would cause a person of reasonable firmness present at the scene to fear for his personal safety.

(2) Where 2 or more persons use or threaten the unlawful violence, it is the conduct of them taken together that must be considered for the purposes of subsection (1).

(3) For the purposes of this section a threat cannot be made by the use of words alone.

(4) No person of reasonable firmness need actually be, or be likely to be, present at the scene.

(5) Affray may be committed in private as well as in public places.

(6) [*Repealed*]

(7) A person guilty of affray is liable on conviction on indictment to imprisonment for a term not exceeding 3 years or a fine or both, or on summary conviction to imprisonment for a term not exceeding 6 months or a fine not exceeding the statutory maximum or both.

[This section is printed as amended by the *Serious Organised Crime and Police Act* 2005, ss.111 and 174(2).]

(2) Allocation

Affray is triable either way. The *Practice Direction (Criminal Proceedings: Consolidation)*, para. V.51.11 provides that cases of affray should be tried summarily unless the court consider that one or more of the following features is present in the case and that their sentencing powers are insufficient: **16–22**

(a) Organised violence or use of weapons;

(b) Significant injury or substantial damage;

(c) The offence has clear racial motivation;

(d) An attack upon police officers, ambulance staff, fire-fighters and the like.

Part III

(3) Elements of the offence

The prosecution must prove that: **16–23**

— the defendant has used or threatened unlawful violence towards another, or two or more persons, their conduct being considered together, have used or threatened unlawful violence, and,

— this conduct is such as would cause a person of reasonable firmness present at the scene to fear for his personal safety.

In *Thind* [1999] Crim.L.R. 842, CA, the Court stated that "for an affray to take place there needs to be: (a) the use or threat of violence by the defendant; (b) to another person; which (c) would cause a third person to fear for his or her own safety." What amounts to a threat depends on the facts of each case. In *I. v. DPP, M. v. DPP, H. v. DPP* [2002] 1 A.C. 285, HL, it was held that whilst the mere possession of petrol bombs which were neither brandished nor waved might constitute a threat of unlawful violence for the purposes of an affray under the 1986 Act, the offence required a threat to be directed towards another person present at the scene; where only police officers were present at the scene, no such threat would be made. Making a threat in an aggressive tone of voice is not enough: *Robinson* [1993] Crim.L.R. 581, CA.

The conduct is judged by the standard of the hypothetical person of reasonable firmness, this person does not necessarily have to be at the scene of the offence: *Davison* [1992] Crim.L.R. 31, CA. It is this hypothetical reasonable bystander that has to be put in fear of his safety, not the victim himself: *Sanchez* [1996] Crim.L.R. 572, CA.

The offence is aimed at the protection of a bystander from fear of unlawful violence and is not to be extended so widely as to cover every case of common assault: *R. (Leeson) v. DPP*, 174 J.P. 367, DC ([2010] EWHC 994 (Admin)). In this case, threats were made by the defendant to her partner in the bathroom of their house and it was held that there was no possibility of a hypothetical bystander.

The use of the word "unlawful" means that the defences of self defence, acting in the defence of others etc are all available: see *Rothwell and Barton*, § 16–18, *ante*.

(4) Sentence

16–24 When tried summarily, the maximum penalty is six months' imprisonment, a fine not exceeding the statutory maximum or both: s.3(7). On commencement of the relevant provisions, the maximum custodial sentence in a magistrates' court will be 12 months' imprisonment: *Criminal Justice Act* 2003, ss.154 and 282. Custodial sentences of less than 12 months will consist of a custody plus order (see *post*, Ch.23).

See the *Magistrates' Court Sentencing Guidelines* (2008).

STARTING POINT AND RANGE OF SENTENCE

(BASED ON A FIRST TIME OFFENDER PLEADING NOT GUILTY)

Examples of nature of activity	**Starting Point**	**Range**
Brief offence involving low-level violence, no substantial fear created	Low level community order	Band C fine to medium level community order
Degree of fighting or violence that causes substantial fear	High level community order	Medium level community order to 12 weeks custody
Fight involving a weapon/throwing objects or conduct causing risk of serious injury	18 weeks custody	12 weeks custody to Crown Court

AGGRAVATING AND MITIGATING FACTORS

Factors indicating higher culpability	**Factors indicating lower culpability**
1. Group action 2. Threats 3. Lengthy incident	1. Did not start the trouble 2. Provocation 3. Stopped as soon as the police arrived
Factors indicating a greater degree of harm 1. Vulnerable persons present 2. Injuries caused 3. Damage to property	

In sentencing in cases of affray, and public order offences generally, the court should bear in mind that although what an individual had himself done was of relevance, it was simply part of the whole to which he was contributing: *Fox and Hicks* [2006] 1 Cr.App.R.(S.) 17.

An unprovoked attack in a public place with a racial motive will warrant a deterrent sentence: *M. (Paul Simon) (A Juvenile)* [1998] 2 Cr.App.R.(S.) 398. In *Fox* [1999] 1

Cr.App.R.(S.) 332, the Court of Appeal reduced a sentence of nine months' imprisonment to four months. The offender pleaded guilty to affray, having intervened during the arrest of a friend. A custodial sentence was held to be necessary, though one of four months was appropriate.

In *Charles & Jones* (1989) 11 Cr.App.R.(S.) 125, CA, the offenders, both of previous good character had a fight in a restaurant, following offensive remarks made by a party at another table. The fight involved chairs being broken and used as weapons and some members of the other party were slightly injured. The CA considered a sentence of three months' imprisonment appropriate. In *Grzybowski and Grzybowski* (1994) 15 Cr.App.R.(S.) 139, CA, a gang of youths went to the home of another late at night armed with a piece of wood. One offender broke a window and later put his fist through the window. The householder then squirted the second offender with ammonia, who then ran away. A sentence of 12 months' detention in a young offender institution and 18 months' imprisonment for the older offender was upheld by the CA, who emphasised that "the gravamen of this type of offence was its effect on law-abiding members of the public." See also *Holmes* [1999] 2 Cr.App.R.(S.) 100 and *Oliver* [1999] 1 Cr.App.R.(S.) 394. **16–25**

In *Bradley* [2005] EWCA Crim 1461; [2006] 1 Cr.App.R.(S.) 42 the CA upheld twelve months' detention in a young offender institution imposed on each of three young men and women who took part in an episode of street fighting. The appellants, a man aged 21 and two women aged 19 and 18, each pleaded guilty to affray. None had any serious previous conviction. Following an exchange of words inside a club and outside a chip shop between two groups of young people, arguments and fights developed. The appellants and others armed themselves with various weapons, including bricks and wood. Two benches were thrown at the other youths. The court reminded itself that the maximum sentence for affray was three years. It had been said in *Caird* (1970) 54 Cr.App.R. 499, that any participation, irrespective of its precise form, in an unlawful or riotous assembly derived its gravity from becoming one of those who by weight of numbers pursued a common and unlawful purpose. The CCTV record of the incident showed an episode in which a number of young people of both sexes carried on for a prolonged period sporadic fights with each other on the pavements and road. The behaviour of most of them was fuelled by alcohol. Conduct of this sort was frightening for innocent people walking home at night and a considerable inconvenience to drivers of vehicles on the road. Quelling such incidents took police time and resources. In the court's judgment, the sentences were not excessive. A recent sentencing decision in the context of football violence is *Fox* [2005] EWCA Crim 1122; [2006] 1 Cr.App.R.(S.) 17 where the CA upheld a sentence of 12 months' imprisonment imposed on one appellant, but reduced the sentence on the other to eight months' imprisonment in recognition that he was the only one of the group with no previous convictions.

C. Fear or Provocation of Violence

(1) Definition

Public Order Act 1986, s.4

Fear or provocation of violence

4.—(1) A person is guilty of an offence if he— **16–26**

(a) uses towards another person threatening, abusive or insulting words or behaviour, or

(b) distributes or displays to another person any writing, sign or other visible representation which is threatening, abusive or insulting, with intent to cause that person to believe that immediate unlawful violence will be used against him or another by any person, or to provoke the immediate use of unlawful violence by that person or another,or whereby that person is likely to believe that such violence will be used or it is likely that such violence will be provoked.

(2) An offence under this section may be committed in a public or a private place,

except that no offence is committed where the words or behaviour are used, or the writing, sign or ostensible representation is distributed or displayed, by a person inside a dwelling and the other person is also inside that or another dwelling.

(3) [*Repealed*]

(4) A person guilty of an offence under this section is liable on summary conviction to imprisonment for a term not exceeding 6 months or a fine not exceeding level 5 on the standard scale or both.

[This section is printed as amended by the *Serious Organised Crime and Police Act* 2005, ss.111 and 174(2).]

Crime and Disorder Act, s.28

Meaning of "racially or religiously aggravated"

16–27 **28.**—(1) An offence is racially or religiously aggravated for the purposes of sections 29 to 32 below if—

(a) at the time of committing the offence, or immediately before or after doing so, the offender demonstrates towards the victim of the offence hostility based on the victim's membership (or presumed membership) of a racial or religious group; or

(b) the offence is motivated (wholly or partly) by hostility towards members of a racial or religious group based on their membership of that group.

(2) In subsection (1)(a) above—

"membership", in relation to a racial or religious group, includes association with members of that group;

"presumed" means presumed by the offender.

(3) It is immaterial for the purposes of paragraph (a) or (b) of subsection (1) above whether or not the offender's hostility is also based, to any extent, on any other factor not mentioned in that paragraph.

(4) In this section "racial group" means a group of persons defined by reference to race, colour, nationality (including citizenship) or ethnic or national origins.

[(5) In this section "religious group" means a group of persons defined by reference to religious belief or lack of religious belief.]

The language of the statute should be given a broad and non-technical meaning: *White (Anthony)* [2001] 1 W.L.R. 1352, CA. The fact that a member of the British National Party, who had put up threatening and abusive posters, wanted to recruit new members to the party did not mean that he was not, at the same time, motivated by racial hostility: *Kendall v. South East Magistrates' Court,* 72 J.C.L. 484, DC.

Crime and Disorder Act 1998, s.31

Racially or religiously aggravated public order offences

16–28 **31.**—(1) A person is guilty of an offence under this section if he commits—

(a) an offence under section 4 of the *Public Order Act* 1986 (fear or provocation of violence);

(b) an offence under section 4A of that Act (intentional harassment, alarm or distress); or

(c) an offence under section 5 of that Act (harassment, alarm or distress),

[hich is racially [or religiously] aggravated for the purposes of this section.

(2) [*Repealed*]

(3) [*Repealed*]

(4) A person guilty of an offence falling within subsection (1)(a) or (b) above shall be liable—

(a) on summary conviction, to imprisonment for a term not exceeding six months or to a fine not exceeding the statutory maximum, or to both;

(b) on conviction on indictment, to imprisonment for a term not exceeding two years or to a fine, or to both.

(5) A person guilty of an offence falling within subsection (1)(c) above shall be liable on summary conviction to a fine not exceeding level 4 on the standard scale.

(6) If, on the trial on indictment of a person charged with an offence falling within subsection (1)(a) or (b) above, the jury find him not guilty of the offence charged, they may find him guilty of the basic offence mentioned in that provision.

(7) For the purposes of subsection (1)(c) above, section 28(1)(a) above shall have effect as if the person likely to be caused harassment, alarm or distress were the victim of the offence.

[This section is printed as amended by the *Anti-Terrorism, Crime and Security Act* 2001, ss.39(5), (6), and s.42, and the *Serious Organised Crime and Police Act* 2005, ss.111 and 174(2), Sched. 7, para. 34, and Sched. 17, Pt 2.]

(2) Allocation

The basic form of this offence is triable summarily only: s.4(4). **16–29**

The racially aggravated form of the offence is triable either way: *Crime and Disorder Act* 1998, s.31(4).

(3) Elements of the offence

As regards the basic form of the offence, the prosecution must prove that: **16–30**

— the defendant used threatening, abusive or insulting words or behaviour towards another person OR

— the defendant distributed or displayed to another person any writing, sign or other visible representation which is threatening or abusive or insulting AND

— the defendant intended to cause that person to believe that immediate unlawful violence would be used against him or another by any other person OR

— the defendant intended to provoke the immediate use of unlawful violence by that person or another OR

— the person is likely to believe that unlawful violence will be used or it is likely that such violence will be provoked.

As regards the racially or religiously aggravated form of this offence, the prosecution must prove:

— the defendant committed an offence under section 4 of the *Public Order Act* 1986, and

— the offence was racially or religiously aggravated; *i.e.* that at the time of committing the offence or immediately before or after doing so the offender demonstrated towards the victim hostility based on the victim's membership (or perceived membership) of a racial or religious group OR the offence was motivated, wholly or partly, by hostility towards members of a racial group based on their membership of that racial group.

"Threatening, abusive or insulting"

"Insulting" is to be given its ordinary meaning and the question whether words or behaviour are insulting is a question of fact: *Brutus v. Cozens* (1973) A.C. 854. See *post*, § 16–40. **16–31**

"Likely to"

It is the state of mind of the victim which is crucial, rather than the statistical risk of violence occurring within a short space of time: *DPP v. Ramos* [2000] Crim.L.R. 768, DC. In *Valentine v. DPP* (1997) COD 339, DC, it was held that the defendant's threats caused a woman to fear immediate unlawful violence the next time she went to work, but only because she may have gone to work the same evening that the threat was made. **16–32**

"Uses towards"

The words "used towards" in s.4(1)(a) connote present physical presence, so that the person against whom the words were used must perceive with his own senses the **16–33**

Part III

threatening words and behaviour: *Atkin v. DPP* (1989) 89 Cr.App.R. 199, DC. It was not necessary for the victim to give evidence in court to prove that he did perceive the words or behaviour: *Swanston v. DPP* 161 J.P. 203, DC.

"Immediate unlawful violence"

16–34 The word "immediate" does not mean "instantaneous," but only a relatively short time interval may elapse between the act which is threatening, abusive or insulting and the unlawful violence. "Immediate" connotes proximity in time and proximity in causation; that it is likely that violence will result within a relatively short period of time and without any other intervening occurrence: *Horseferry Road Magistrates Court, ex p. Siadatan* [1991] 1 Q.B. 280, DC.

(4) Sentence

16–35 The maximum penalty for the basic form of the offence is six months' imprisonment, a fine not exceeding level 5 on the standard scale or both: s.4(4). On commencement of the relevant provisions, the maximum custodial sentence in a magistrates' court will be 12 months' imprisonment: *Criminal Justice Act* 2003, ss.154 and 282.

16–36 When tried summarily, the maximum penalty for the aggravated form of the offence is six months' imprisonment, a fine not exceeding the statutory maximum or both: *Crime and Disorder Act* 1998, s.31(4).

See the *Magistrates' Court Sentencing Guidelines* (2008).

STARTING POINT AND RANGE OF SENTENCE

(BASED ON A FIRST TIME OFFENDER PLEADING NOT GUILTY)

Examples of nature of activity	**Starting Point**	**Range**
Fear or threat of low level immediate unlawful violence such as push, shove or spit	Low level community order	Band B fine to medium level community order
Fear or threat of medium level immediate unlawful violence such as punch	High level community order	Low level community order to 12 weeks custody
Fear or threat of high level immediate unlawful violence such as use of weapon, missile thrown, gang involvement	12 weeks custody	6 to 26 weeks custody

AGGRAVATING AND MITIGATING FACTORS

Factors indicating higher culpability	**Factors indicating lower culpability**
1. Planning	1. Impulsive action
2. Offender deliberately isolates victim	2. Short duration
3. Group action	3. Provocation
4. Threat directed at victim because of job	
5. History of antagonism towards victim	
Factors indicating greater degree of harm	
1. Offence committed at school hospital or other place where vulnerable persons may be present	
2. Offence committed on enclosed premises such as public transport	
3. Vulnerable victim	
4. Victim needs medical help/counselling	

If the offender is convicted of the racially or religiously aggravated offence, the sentence should be increased to reflect this element.

In *Saunders* [2000] 2 Cr.App.R.(S.) 71, CA, Rose L.J. issued guidance in relation to racially aggravated assaults and racially aggravated offences more generally. He stated that those who indulge in racially aggravated violence must expect to be punished severely, in order to discourage the repetition of that behaviour by them or others. Relevant factors for the purposes of determining the increase in sentence to reflect the racially or religiously aggravated element of the offence will include the nature of the hostile demonstration, whether by language, gestures or weapons; its length, whether isolated, repeated, or persistent; its location, whether public or private; the number both of those demonstrating and those demonstrated against; and the presence or absence of other features. A discount in the overall sentence will be appropriate in accordance with general sentencing principles for, among other things, genuine remorse, a plea of guilty and previous good character.

In *Miller* [1999] 2 Cr.App.R.(S.) 392, CA the offender was sentenced to 18 months' imprisonment for racially aggravated threatening words and behaviour and to travelling on a railway without a ticket. Although M pleaded guilty, the evidence against him was overwhelming and he had a record of many previous convictions, some of them serious. The sentence was recognised as severe, yet upheld as it needed to be, to reflect public concern about conduct which damaged good racial relations within the community.

D. INTENTIONALLY CAUSING HARASSMENT, ALARM OR DISTRESS

(1) Definition

Public Order Act 1986, s.4A

Intentional harassment, alarm or distress

16–37 **4A.**—(1) A person is guilty of an offence if, with intent to cause a person harassment, alarm or distress, he—

(a) uses threatening, abusive or insulting words or behaviour, or disorderly behaviour, or

(b) displays any writing, sign or ostensible representation which is threatening, abusive or insulting,

thereby causing that or another person harassment, alarm or distress.

(2) An offence under this section may be committed in a public or a private place, except that no offence is committed where the words or behaviour are used, or the writing, sign or ostensible representation is displayed, by a person inside a dwelling and the person who is harassed, alarmed or distressed is also inside that or another dwelling.

(3) It is a defence for the accused to prove—

(a) that he was inside a dwelling and had no reason to believe that the words or behaviour used, or the writing, sign or ostensible representation displayed, would be heard or seen by a person outside that or any other dwelling, or

(b) that his conduct was reasonable.

16–38 For definition of the racially or religiously aggravated form of this offence see *Crime and Disorder Act* 1998, s.31 (§ 16–28, *ante*).

(2) Allocation

16–39 The basic form of this offence is triable summarily only: s.4A(5). The racially aggravated form of the offence is triable either way: *Crime and Disorder Act* 1998, s.31(4). The *Magistrates' Court Sentencing Guidelines* recommend committal for sentence.

(3) Elements of the offence

16–40 As regards the basic form of the offence the prosecution need to prove that:

— the defendant used threatening, abusive or insulting words or behaviour or displayed any writing, sign or ostensible representation which was threatening, abusive or insulting,

— the defendant so behaved with the intention to cause a person harassment, alarm or distress, and,

— the defendant thereby caused that or another person alarm or distress.

As regards the racially aggravated form of the offence the prosecution need to prove that:

— the defendant committed an offence under section 4A of the *Public Order Act* 1986 and

— the offence was racially or religiously aggravated; *i.e.* that at the time of committing the offence or immediately before or after doing so the offender demonstrated towards the victim hostility based on the victim's membership (or perceived membership) of a racial or religious group,

OR

— the offence was motivated, wholly or partly, by hostility towards members of a racial group based on their membership of that racial group.

An intention to cause harassment alarm or distress must be established: *DPP v. Weeks, Independent*, July 17, 2000. Harassment, alarm and distress are to be treated as ordinary words of the English language, the approach of the Court in *Brutus v. Cozens* (1973) A.C. 854, being adopted in this context.

"Distress" requires some degree of emotional disturbance or upset, which, while it need not be grave, should not be trivialised: *R. (R.) v. DPP*, 170 J.P. 661. See also *DPP v. Orum*, 88 Cr.App.R. 261.

There is no rule that the offence cannot be made out if the only person who sees or hears the defendant's conduct is a police officer: *Southard v. DPP*, A.C.D 53, DC.

(4) Specific defence

Section 4A(3) establishes that the accused will have a defence if he can prove that he had no reason to believe that there was any person within hearing or sight who was likely to be caused harassment, alarm or distress, or that he was inside a dwelling and had no reason to believe that the words or behaviour used, or the writing, sign or ostensible representation displayed, would be heard or seen by a person outside that or any other dwelling, or that his conduct was reasonable. **16–41**

For the purposes of s.4A(3) a "dwelling" does not include a police cell: *Francis* [2007] 1 W.L.R. 1021. Nor does it include a communally used laundry room in self-contained flats in sheltered housing: *Le Vine v. DPP,* 174 J.P. 337, DC.

(5) Sentence

The maximum penalty for the basic form of the offence is six months' imprisonment, a fine not exceeding level five on the standard scale or both: s.4A(5). On commencement of the relevant provisions, the maximum custodial sentence in a magistrates' court will be 12 months' imprisonment: *Criminal Justice Act* 2003, ss.154 and 282. **16–42**

When tried summarily, the maximum penalty for the aggravated form of the offence is six months' imprisonment, a fine not exceeding the statutory maximum or both: *Crime and Disorder Act* 1998, s.31(4). **16–43**

See the Magistrates' Court Sentencing Guidelines (2008). **16–44**

STARTING POINT AND RANGE OF SENTENCE

(BASED ON A FIRST TIME OFFENDER PLEADING NOT GUILTY)

Examples of nature of activity	**Starting Point**	**Range**
Threats, abuse or insults made more than once but on same occasion against the same person e.g. while following down the street	Band C fine	Band B fine to low community order
Group action or deliberately planned action against targeted victim	Medium level community order	Low level community order to 12 weeks custody

Part III

Examples of nature of activity	**Starting Point**	**Range**
Weapon brandished or used or threats against vulnerable victim- course of conduct over longer period	12 weeks custody	High level community order to 26 weeks custody

AGGRAVATING AND MITIGATING FACTORS

Factors indicating higher culpability	**Factors indicating lower culpability**
1. High degree of planning	1. Very short period
2. Offender deliberately isolates victim	2. Provocation
Factors indicating greater degree of harm	
1. Offence committed in vicinity of victim's home	
2. Large number of people in vicinity	
3. Actual or potential escalation into violence	
4. Particularly serious impact on victim	

If the offender is convicted of the racially or religiously aggravated offence, the sentence should be increased to reflect this element.

E. HARASSMENT, ALARM OR DISTRESS

(1) Definition

Public Order Act 1986, s.5(1), (2)

Harassment, alarm or distress

16–45 **5.**—(1) A person is guilty of an offence if he—

(a) uses threatening, abusive or insulting words or behaviour, or disorderly behaviour, or

(b) displays any writing, sign or ostensible representation which is threatening, abusive or insulting,

within the hearing or sight of a person likely to be caused harassment, alarm or distress thereby.

(2) An offence under this section may be committed in a public or a private place, except that no offence is committed where the words or behaviour are used, or the writing, sign or ostensible representation is displayed, by a person inside a dwelling and the other person is also inside that or another dwelling.

(3) It is a defence for the accused to prove—

(a) that he had no reason to believe that there was any person within hearing or sight who was likely to be caused harassment, alarm or distress, or

(b) that he was inside a dwelling and had no reason to believe that the words or behaviour used, or the writing, sign or other visible representation displayed, would be heard or seen by a person outside that or any other dwelling, or
(c) that his conduct was reasonable.

For definition of the racially or religiously aggravated form of this offence see the *Crime and Disorder Act* 1998, s.31 (§ 16–28, *ante*). **16–46**

(2) Allocation

Both the basic and the aggravated forms of this offence are triable summarily only. **16–47**

(3) Elements of the offence

As regards the basic form of this offence, the prosecution need to prove that: **16–48**

— the defendant used threatening, abusive or insulting words or behaviour, or disorderly behaviour;

OR

— the defendant displayed any writing sign or ostensible representation which is threatening, abusive or insulting; and

— such conduct took place within the hearing or sight of a person likely to be caused harassment, alarm or distress thereby.

As regards the racially or religiously aggravated form of the offence, the prosecution must prove that:

— the defendant committed an offence under s.4A of the *Public Order Act* 1986; and

— the offence was racially or religiously aggravated; *i.e.* that at the time of committing the offence or immediately before or after doing so the offender demonstrated towards the victim hostility based on the victim's membership (or perceived membership) of a racial or religious group OR the offence was motivated, wholly or partly, by hostility towards members of a racial group based on their membership of that racial group.

"Threatening, abusive or insulting"

In *Vigon v. DPP* (1998) 162 J.P. 115 it was held that that installing a partially hidden video camera in a changing area, so that customers trying on swimwear would be filmed amounted to insulting behaviour, the wording of s.5 not being limited to "rowdy behaviour". **16–49**

In *Hammond v. DPP* [2004] EWHC 69; (2004) 168 J.P. 601, where an evangelical preacher held up a sign saying "Stop immortality; stop homosexuality; stop lesbianism" and was convicted under s.5, the Divisional Court held that interference with D's rights under arts 9 and 10 of the ECHR was justified by the pressing social need to show tolerance to others. It had not been perverse for the magistrates to hold that the words used on the sign were insulting and D had no defence of reasonable conduct.

"Harassment, alarm or distress"

Whether a person is likely to be caused harassment, alarm or distress is a matter of fact to be determined by the magistrates; it is not necessary that the victim's alarm is due to fears for his own personal safety, he could be concerned about the safety of some third party: *Lodge v. DPP*, *The Times*, October 26, 1998. **16–50**

"Distress" requires some degree of emotional disturbance or upset: *R. (R.) v. DPP*, 170 J.P. 661. See also *DPP v. Orum*, 88 Cr.App.R. 261.

"Harassment" can be experienced without emotional disturbance or upset: *Southard v. DPP* [2007] A.C.D. 53, DC. Although the distress or harassment need not be grave, neither should it be trivialised.

"Within sight of a person"

In *Holloway v. DPP* (2005) 169 J.P. 14, D appealed by way of case stated against a **16–51** conviction for the offence of disorderly conduct contrary to the *POA* 1986, s.5. he had used a video recorder to film a group of school children. While doing this, he stood naked in view of the camera whilst the children were in the background some distance away. The D.J. found that anyone seeing D naked would be likely to be caused harassment, alarm or distress, and that D must have been aware of the likely effect of his naked state on others in a public place. The question for the court was whether a person who had not been seen but could have been seen by anybody had committed an offence under s.5. However, the Divisional Court allowed the appeal, stating that s.5 required the insulting words or behaviour to be "within the . . . sight of a person". Those words meant that some person must have actually seen the abusive or insulting words or behaviour. It was not enough that somebody merely might have seen or could possibly have seen that behaviour. If Parliament had intended that an offence under s.5 would have been committed if the offensive behaviour could have seen by somebody, even it not actually seen, then it would have inserted a provision to that effect in s.5. In contrast, a person could be convicted of an offence of affray under s.3 if a notional person would have seen the conduct complained of, but the legislature did not adopt such wording in s.5, indicating that the parliamentary intention was that the two provisions should be construed differently. Furthermore, the view that someone would have committed an offence under s.5(1) if they could have been seen by somebody entailed a rewriting of the section and there was no reason why it should be rewritten or construed in that way.

"Display"

16–52 In *Chappell v. DPP* (1988) 89 Cr.App.R. 82, it was held that dropping letters through a letter box was not an offence under s.5 because the writing of words which were then concealed in an envelope was not a "display" within s.5(1)(b). Where the letter was opened in the absence of the sender it could not be said that the sender "uses ... words or behaviour ... within the hearing or sight of that person" within s.5(1)(a).

Mens rea

16–53 The accused must intend his words, behaviour, representation or sign to be threatening, abusive or insulting, or be aware that they may be threatening, abusive or insulting, or he must intend his behaviour to be, or be aware that it could be disorderly: *Public Order Act* 1986, s.6(4).

(4) Specific defence

16–54 The defence of reasonable conduct under s.5(3) is to be proved objectively: *DPP v. Clarke* (1992) 94 Cr.App.R. 359; (1991) 156 J.P. 267. In *Percy v. DPP* (2002) 166 J.P. 93 the offender had defaced an American flag, and while outside an American airbase she put the flag on the road and trod upon it. The court was asked to consider whether the offender's protest fell within her right to freedom of expression under the *Human Rights Act* 1998. It was held that whilst it had been open to the district judge to find a pressing social need to prevent the denigration of objects of veneration and cultural importance, the next issue to consider was whether the restriction on the offender's freedom of expression through the imposition of a criminal penalty was proportionate. The fact that she could have demonstrated her message by some other means other than defacing the flag was a factor to be taken into account but was only one of a number of factors. Other relevant considerations included whether the accused's behaviour had gone beyond legitimate protest, whether the behaviour had not been part of an open expression on an issue of public interest but had been disproportionate and unreasonable, the knowledge of the accused of the likely effect of his or her conduct upon those who witnessed it and whether the use of a flag had no relevance to the conveying of the message of protest and had been used as a gratuitous and calculated insult.

In *Norwood v. DPP* [2003] EWHC 1564; *The Times*, July 30, 2003 a regional organiser of the British National Party appealed against his conviction for an offence of causing alarm or distress under the *Public Order Act* 1986, s.5(1)(b). He had visibly displayed a poster on the window of his flat bearing the words "Islam out of Britain" with graphic references to the attacks on the World Trade Centre on September 11, 2001. A passer-by complained to the police and the poster was subsequently removed. The trial judge found that the poster was abusive and insulting to Islam and to the followers of that religion. It was likely to cause harassment, alarm or distress and its display was not objectively reasonable within s.5(3)(c) of the 1986 Act. The Court dismissed the appeal. The judge had been right to conclude that the aggravated offence had been made out as N had displayed the poster with the necessary intention. On the face of it the poster was "clearly racially directed and racially insulting" towards those following the Muslim faith and not simply towards the faith itself. The poster was in such a position that it could be seen by, and cause offence to, people passing by N's window. It was not necessary to show that a Muslim had actually seen or been caused offence by the poster. Once the judge had found that N had the state of mind for the offence to be proved, he could not "sensibly" have found that N had acted "reasonably" to bring him within the defence set out in s.5(3) of the 1986 Act. As N's behaviour was not objectively reasonable, his art. 10 rights had not been infringed since it was right in such circumstances that his freedom of expression be curtailed in order to protect the public interest: *Percy v. DPP* (*ante*) applied.

When considering the relationship between s.5 of the *Public Order Act* 1986 and the right to freedom of expression under art. 10 of the European Convention on Human Rights, the principles are, (i) the starting point is the importance of the right to freedom of expression; (ii) it must be recognised that legitimate protest can be offensive at least to some; the right to freedom of expression must extend beyond those who hold popular mainstream views so that minority views can be expressed, even if distasteful; (iii) justification for interference with the right to freedom of expression must be convincingly established; (iv) the justification for invoking the criminal law is the threat to public order so that the context of the particular occasion will be of first importance; (v) the risk of violence by those reacting to the protest is not, without more, determinative, as sometimes protestors are to be protected; however in striking the right balance when determining whether speech is "threatening, abusive or insulting", the focus on minority rights should not result in overlooking the rights of the majority; (vi) the Crown must establish, where there is a *prima facie* case that an offence has been committed, that prosecution is a proportionate response that is necessary for the preservation of public order; (vii) if the line between legitimate freedom of expression and a threat to public order as been crossed, freedom of speech will not have been impaired by ruling out threatening, abusive or insulting speech; (viii) the legislature has entrusted the decision as to whether an offence has been committed to the magistrates' courts; the High Court should not interfere unless the appellant can establish that the decision of the lower court was one it could not properly have reached. Attending a parade held to celebrate the homecoming of British soldiers from Iraq and Afghanistan and shouting "British soldiers burn in hell", "baby killers", "rapists all of you", "terrorists" and "murderers", gave rise to a clear threat to public order, and the magistrates had been entitled to conclude that what was shouted went well beyond legitimate expressions of protest: *Abdul v. DPP* [2011] Crim.L.R. 553, DC ([2011] EWHC 247 (Admin.)).

Whether a visual display is threatening or abusive and likely to cause harassment, alarm or distress is a value judgment. The argument that a poster was displayed simply to promote a political party was not accepted as a defence or reasonable conduct. The words on the poster together with the photograph on it were held to be also motivated by hostility and the racially aggravated form of the offence was made out, *Kendall v. South East Essex Magistrates Court* [2008] EWHC 1848 (Admin).

(5) Sentence

The maximum penalty for the basic form of the offence is a fine not exceeding level three on the standard scale: *Public Order Act* 1986, s.5(6). **16–55**

16–56 The maximum penalty for the aggravated form of the offence is a fine not exceeding level four on the standard scale: *Crime and Disorder Act* 1998, s.31(5).

See the Magistrates' Court Sentencing Guidelines (2008).

STARTING POINT AND RANGE OF SENTENCE

(BASED ON A FIRST TIME OFFENDER PLEADING NOT GUILTY)

Examples of nature of activity	**Starting Point**	**Range**
Shouting, causing disturbance for some minutes	Band A fine	Conditional discharge to band B fine
Substantial disturbance caused	Band B fine	Band A fine to Band C fine

AGGRAVATING AND MITIGATING FACTORS

Factors indicating higher culpability	**Factors indicating lower culpability**
1. Group action 2. Lengthy incident	1. Stopped as soon as police arrived 2. Brief/minor incident 3. Provocation
Factors indicating greater degree of harm 1. Vulnerable person present 2. Offence committed at school, hospital or other place where vulnerable persons may be present 3. victim providing public service	

If the offender is convicted of the racially or religiously aggravated offence, the sentence should be increased to reflect this element.

F. CONTROL OF PROCESSIONS, ASSEMBLIES AND MEETINGS

(1) Notice and conditions relating to public processions

(a) *Definition*

Public Order Act 1986, ss.11, 12

Advance notice of public processions

16–57 **11.**—(1) Written notice shall be given in accordance with this section of any proposal to hold a public procession intended—

(a) to demonstrate support for or opposition to the views or actions of any person or body of persons,

(b) to publicise a cause or campaign, or

(c) to mark or commemorate an event,

unless it is not reasonably practicable to give any advance notice of the procession.

(2) Subsection (1) does not apply where the procession is one commonly or customarily held in the police area (or areas) in which it is proposed to be held or is a funeral procession organised by a funeral director acting in the normal course of his business.

(3) The notice must specify the date when it is intended to hold the procession, the time when it is intended to start it, its proposed route, and the name and address of the person (or of one of the persons) proposing to organise it.

(4) Notice must be delivered to a police station—

(a) in the police area in which it is proposed the procession will start, or

(b) where it is proposed the procession will start in Scotland and cross into England, in the first police area in England on the proposed route.

(5) If delivered not less than 6 clear days before the date when the procession is intended to be held, the notice may be delivered by post by the recorded delivery service; but section 7 of the *Interpretation Act* 1978 (under which a document sent by post is deemed to have been served when posted and to have been delivered in the ordinary course of post) does not apply.

(6) If not delivered in accordance with subsection (5), the notice must be delivered by hand not less than 6 clear days before the date when the procession is intended to be held or, if that is not reasonably practicable, as soon as delivery is reasonably practicable.

(7) Where a public procession is held, each of the persons organising it is guilty of an offence if—

(a) the requirements of this section as to notice have not been satisfied, or

(b) the date when it is held, the time when it starts, or its route, differs from the date, time or route specified in the notice.

(8) It is a defence for the accused to prove that he did not know of, and neither suspected nor had reason to suspect, the failure to satisfy the requirements or (as the case may be) the difference of date, time or route.

(9) To the extent that an alleged offence turns on a difference of date, time or route, it is a defence for the accused to prove that the difference arose from circumstances beyond his control or from something done with the agreement of a police officer or by his direction.

(10) A person guilty of an offence under subsection (7) is liable on summary conviction to a fine not exceeding level 3 on the standard scale.

Imposing conditions on public processions

12.—(1) If the senior police officer, having regard to the time or place at which and the circumstances in which any public procession is being held or is intended to be held and to its route or proposed route, reasonably believes that— **16–58**

(a) it may result in serious public disorder, serious damage to property or serious disruption to the life of the community, or

(b) the purpose of the persons organising it is the intimidation of others with a view to compelling them not to do an act they have a right to do, or to do an act they have a right not to do,

he may give directions imposing on the persons organising or taking part in the procession such conditions as appear to him necessary to prevent such disorder, damage, disruption or intimidation, including conditions as to the route of the procession or prohibiting it from entering any public place specified in the directions.

(2) In subsection (1) "the senior police officer" means—

(a) in relation to a procession being held, or to a procession intended to be held in a case where persons are assembling with a view to taking part in it, the most senior in rank of the police officers present at the scene, and

(b) in relation to a procession intended to be held in a case where paragraph does not apply, the chief officer of police.

(3) A direction given by a chief officer of police by virtue of subsection (2) shall be given in writing.

(4) A person who organises a public procession and knowingly fails to comply with a condition imposed under this section is guilty of an offence, but it is a defence for him to prove that the failure arose from circumstances beyond his control.

(5) A person who takes part in a public procession and knowingly fails to comply with a

condition imposed under this section is guilty of an offence, but it is a defence for him to prove that the failure arose from circumstances beyond his control.

(6) A person who incites another to commit an offence under subsection (5) is guilty of an offence.

(7) A constable in uniform may arrest without warrant anyone he reasonably suspects is committing an offence under subsection (4), (5) or (6).

(8) A person guilty of an offence under subsection (4) is liable on summary conviction to imprisonment for a term not exceeding 3 months or a fine not exceeding level 4 on the standard scale or both.

(9) A person guilty of an offence under subsection (5) is liable on summary conviction to a fine not exceeding level 3 on the standard scale.

(10) A person guilty of an offence under subsection (6) is liable on summary conviction to imprisonment for a term not exceeding 3 months or a fine not exceeding level 4 on the standard scale or both, notwithstanding section 45(3) of the *Magistrates' Courts Act* 1980 (inciter liable to same penalty as incited).

(11) In Scotland this section applies only in relation to a procession being held, and to a procession intended to be held in a case where persons are assembling with a view to taking part in it.

(b) *Allocation*

16–59 Both of these offences are triable summarily only.

(c) *Elements of the offence*

16–60 Regarding the offence of failing to give notice of a public procession, the prosecution must prove that:

— the organiser of a public procession (it not being one to which s.11(2) of the 1986 Act applies) failed to give notice to a police station in the area in which the procession started

OR

— notice having been given to the relevant police station, the date when the procession was held, the time when it started, or its route, differed from the date, time or route specified in the notice.

Regarding the offence of failing to comply with conditions imposed on public processions, the prosecution must prove that:

— an organiser of a public procession knowingly failed to comply with conditions imposed under s.12 of the *Public Order Act* 1986

OR

— a participant in a public procession knowingly failed to comply with conditions imposed under s.12 of the *Public Order Act* 1986

OR

— a person incited another to commit an offence under s.12(5) of the *Public Order Act* 1986.

(d) *Specific defence*

16–61 A defendant will have a defence to a charge under section 11 if he can prove that he did not know of, and neither suspected nor had reason to suspect, the failure to satisfy the requirements or (as the case may be) the difference of date, time or route: *Public Order Act* 1986, s.11(8). A monthly mass cycle ride through London was a commonly and customarily held procession for the purposes of s.11(2) of the 1986 Act, starting from a fixed point though without a fixed route: *R. (Kay) v. Commissioner of Police for the Metropolis* [2008] 1 W.L.R. 2723, HL (overturning the decision of the Court of Appeal).

A defendant will have a defence to a charge under s.12 if he can prove that the failure to comply with a condition imposed was due to circumstances beyond the defendant's control: *Public Order Act* 1986, s.12(5).

(e) *Sentence*

The maximum penalty for both these offences is a fine not exceeding level three on the standard scale. Section 280(2) and Sched. 26, para. 37 of the *Criminal Justice Act* 2003 increases the maximum term in both s.12(8) and s.12(10) from three months to 51 weeks (not yet in force). **16–62**

(2) Contravention of prohibition on a public procession

(a) *Definition*

Public Order Act 1986, s.13

Prohibiting public processions

13.—(1) If at any time the chief officer of police reasonably believes that, because of particular circumstances existing in any district or part of a district, the powers under section 12 will not be sufficient to prevent the holding of public processions in that district or part from resulting in serious public disorder, he shall apply to the council of the district for an order prohibiting for such period not exceeding 3 months as may be specified in the application the holding of all public processions (or of any class of public procession so specified) in the district or part concerned. **16–63**

(2) On receiving such an application, a council may with the consent of the Secretary of State make an order either in the terms of the application or with such modifications as may be approved by the Secretary of State.

(3) Subsection (1) does not apply in the City of London or the metropolitan police district.

(4) If at any time the Commissioner of Police for the City of London or the Commissioner of Police of the Metropolis reasonably believes that, because of particular circumstances existing in his police area or part of it, the powers under section 12will not be sufficient to prevent the holding of public processions in that area or part from resulting in serious public disorder, he may with the consent of the Secretary of State make an order prohibiting for such period not exceeding 3 months as may be specified in the order the holding of all public processions (or of any class of public procession so specified) in the area or part concerned.

(5) An order made under this section may be revoked varied by a subsequent order made in the same way, that is, in accordance with subsections (1) and (2) or subsection (4), as the case may be.

(6) Any order under this section shall, if not made in writing, be recorded in writing as soon as practicable after being made.

(7) A person who organises a public procession the holding of which he knows is prohibited by virtue of an order under this section is guilty of an offence.

(8) A person who takes part in a public procession the holding of which he knows is prohibited by virtue of an order under this section is guilty of an offence.

(9) A person who incites another to commit an offence under subsection (8) is guilty of an offence.

(10) A constable in uniform may arrest without warrant anyone he reasonably suspects is committing an offence under subsection (7), (8) or (9).

(11) A person guilty of an offence under subsection (7) is liable on summary conviction to imprisonment for a term not exceeding 3 months or a fine not exceeding level 4 on the standard scale or both.

(12) A person guilty of an offence under subsection (8) is liable on summary conviction to a fine not exceeding level 3 on the standard scale.

(13) A person guilty of an offence under subsection (9) is liable on summary conviction to imprisonment for a term not exceeding 3 months or a fine not exceeding level 4 on the standard scale or both, notwithstanding section 45(3) of the *Magistrates' Courts Act* 1980.

(b) *Allocation*

An offence under this section is triable summarily only. **16–64**

(c) *Elements of the offence*

The prosecution must prove that: **16–65**

— a person organised a public procession the holding of which he knows to be prohibited under s.13 of the *Public Order Act* 1986,

OR

— a person incited another to commit an offence under s.13(8) of the *Public Order Act* 1986.

(d) *Sentence*

16–66 The maximum penalty for the offence of organising, or inciting the commission of an offence by another is imprisonment for a term not exceeding three months, or a fine not exceeding level four on the standard scale or both. The maximum penalty for the offence of participating in the prohibited procession is a fine not exceeding level three on the standard scale. Section 280(2) and Sched. 26, para. 37 of the *Criminal Justice Act* 2003 increases the maximum term in both s.12(8) and s.12(10) from three months to 51 weeks (not yet in force).

(3) Contravening prohibition on trespassory assemblies

(a) *Definition*

Public Order Act 1986, ss.14, 14A–14C

Imposing conditions on public assemblies

16–67 **14.**—(1) If the senior police officer, having regard to the time or place at which and the circumstances in which any public assembly is being held or is intended to be held, reasonably believes that—

(a) it may result in serious public disorder, serious damage to property or serious disruption to the life of the community, or

(b) the purpose of the persons organising it is the intimidation of others with a view to compelling them not to do an act they have a right to do, or to do an act they have a right not to do,

he may give directions imposing on the persons organising or taking part in the assembly such conditions as to the place at which the assembly may be (or continue to be) held, its maximum duration, or the maximum number of persons who may constitute it, as appear to him necessary to prevent such disorder, damage, disruption or intimidation.

(2) In subsection (1) "the senior police officer" means —

(a) in relation to an assembly being held, the most senior in rank of the police officers present at the scene, and

(b) in relation to an assembly intended to be held, the chief officer of police.

(3) A direction given by a chief officer of police by virtue of subsection (2)(b) shall be given in writing.

(4) A person who organises a public assembly and knowingly fails to comply with a condition imposed under this section is guilty of an offence, but it is a defence for him to prove that the failure arose from circumstances beyond his control.

(5) A person who takes part in a public assembly and knowingly fails to comply with a condition imposed under this section is guilty of an offence, but it is a defence for him to prove that the failure arose from circumstances beyond his control.

(6) A person who incites another to commit an offence under subsection (5) is guilty of an offence.

[...]

(8) A person guilty of an offence under subsection (4) is liable on summary conviction to imprisonment for a term not exceeding 3 months or a fine not exceeding level 4 on the standard scale or both.

(9) A person guilty of an offence under subsection (5) is liable on summary conviction to a fine not exceeding level 3 on the standard scale.

(10) A person guilty of an offence under subsection (6) is liable on summary conviction to imprisonment for a term not exceeding 3 months or a fine not exceeding level 4 on the standard scale or both, notwithstanding section 45(3) of the *Magistrates' Courts Act* 1980.

[This is printed as amended by the *Serious Organised Crime and Police Act* 2005, Sched. 17(2), para. 1.]

Prohibiting trespassory assemblies

14A.—(1) If at any time the chief officer of police reasonably believes that an assembly is intended to be held in any district at a place on land to which the public has no right of access or only a limited right of access and that the assembly— **16–68**

(a) is likely to be held without the permission of the occupier of the land or to conduct itself in such a way as to exceed the limits of any permission of his or the limits of the public's right of access, and

(b) may result—

(i) in serious disruption to the life of the community, or

(ii) where the land, or a building or monument on it, is of historical, architectural, archaeological or scientific importance, in significant damage to the land, building or monument,

he may apply to the council of the district for an order prohibiting for a specified, period the holding of all trespassory assemblies in the district or a part of it, as specified.

(2) On receiving such an application, a council may—

(a) in England and Wales, with the consent of the Secretary of State make an order either in the terms of the application or with such modifications as may be approved by the Secretary of State; or

(b) in Scotland, make an order in the terms of the application.

(3) Subsection (1) does not apply in the City of London or the metropolitan police district.

(4) If at any time the Commissioner of Police for the City of London or the Commissioner of Police of the Metropolis reasonably believes that an assembly is intended to be held at a place on land to which the public has no right of access or only a limited right of access in his police area and that the assembly—

(a) is likely to be held without the permission of the occupier of the land or to conduct itself in such a way as to exceed the limits of any permission of his or the limits of the public's right of access, and

(b) may result—

(i) in serious disruption to the life of the community, or

(ii) where the land, or a building or monument on it, is of historical, architectural, archaeological or scientific importance, in significant damage to the land, building or monument,

he may with the consent of the Secretary of State make an order prohibiting for a specified period the holding of all trespassory assemblies in the area or a part of it, as specified.

(5) An order prohibiting the holding of trespassory assemblies operates to prohibit any assembly which—

(a) is held on land to which the public has no right of access or only a limited right of access, and

(b) takes place in the prohibited circumstances, that is to say, without the permission of the occupier of the land or so as to exceed the limits of any permission of his or the limits of the public's right of access.

(6) No order under this section shall prohibit the holding of assemblies for a period exceeding 4 days or in an area exceeding an area represented by a circle with a radius of 5 miles from a specified centre.

(7) An order made under this section may be revoked varied by a subsequent order made in the same way, that is, in accordance with subsection (1) and (2) or subsection (4), as the case may be.

(8) Any order under this section shall, if not made in writing, be recorded in writing as soon as practicable after being made.

(9) In this section and sections 14B and 14C—

"assembly" means an assembly of 20 or more persons;

"land" means land in the open air;

"limited", in relation to a right of access by the public to land, means that their use of it is restricted to use for a particular purpose (as in the case of a highway or road) or is subject to other restrictions;

Part III

"occupier" means—

(a) in England and Wales, the person entitled to possession of the land by virtue of an estate or interest held by him; or

(b) in Scotland, the person lawfully entitled to natural possession of the land, and in subsections (1) and (4) includes the person reasonably believed by the authority applying for or making the order to be the occupier;

"public" includes a section of the public; and

"specified" means specified in an order under this section.

[(9A) In relation to Scotland, the references in this section to the public's rights (or limited right) of access do not include any right which the public or any member of the public may have by way of access rights within the meaning of the *Land Reform (Scotland) Act* 2003 (asp 2).]

(10) In relation to Scotland, the references in subsection (1) above to a district and to the council of the district shall be construed—

(a) as respects applications before 1st April 1996, as references to the area of a regional or islands authority and to the authority in question; and

(b) as respects applications on and after that date, as references to a local government area and to the council for that area.

(11) In relation to Wales, the references in subsection (1) above to a district and to the council of the district shall be construed, as respects applications on and after 1st April 1996, as references to a county or county borough and to the council for that county or county borough.

Offences in connection with trespassory assemblies and arrest therefore

16–69 **14B.**—(1) A person who organises an assembly the holding of which he knows is prohibited by an order under section 14A is guilty of an offence.

(2) A person who takes part in an assembly which he knows is prohibited by an order under section 14A is guilty of an offence.

(3) In England and Wales, a person who incites another to commit an offence under subsection (2) is guilty of an offence.

(5) A person guilty of an offence under subsection (1) is liable on summary conviction to imprisonment for a term not exceeding 3 months or a fine not exceeding level 4 on the standard scale or both.

(6) A person guilty of an offence under subsection (2) is liable on summary conviction to a fine not exceeding level 3 on the standard scale.

(7) A person guilty of an offence under subsection (3) is liable on summary conviction to imprisonment for a term not exceeding 3 months or a fine not exceeding level 4 on the standard scale or both, notwithstanding section 45(3) of the *Magistrates' Courts Act* 1980.

(8) Subsection (3) above is without prejudice to the application of any principle of Scots Law as respects art and part guilt to such incitement as is mentioned in that subsection.

Stopping persons from proceeding to trespassory assemblies

16–70 **14C.**—(1) If a constable in uniform reasonably believes that a person is on his way to an assembly within the area to which an order under section 14A applies which the constable reasonably believes is likely to be an assembly which is prohibited by that order, he may, subject to subsection (2) below—

(a) stop that person, and

(b) direct him not to proceed in the direction of the assembly.

(2) The power conferred by subsection (1) may only be exercised within the area to which the order applies.

(3) A person who fails to comply with a direction under subsection (1) which he knows has been given to him is guilty of an offence.

(5) A person guilty of an offence under subsection (3) is liable on summary conviction to a fine not exceeding level 3 on the standard scale.

[These sections are printed as amended by the *Serious Organised Crime and Police Act* 2005, Sched. 17(2), para. 1.]

(b) *Allocation*

16–71 The offences under this section are triable summarily only.

(c) *Elements of the offence*

The prosecution must prove that: **16–72**

— a person organised an assembly which he knew was prohibited by an order made under s.14A of the *Public Order Act* 1986,

OR

— a person participated in an assembly which he knew to be prohibited under s.14A of the *Public Order Act* 1986,

OR

— a person incited another to commit an offence under s.14B(2) of the *Public Order Act* 1986.

(d) *Defences*

In *Jones v. DPP* [1999] 2 A.C. 240, the HL (allowing the appeal by a majority) held that there was a public right of peaceful assembly on a public highway and provided those activities are reasonable, they should not constitute a trespass, it being a question of fact and degree for the court of trial to in each case to decide whether the user was reasonable, this right being subject to the requirement that the activity in question does not amount to a public or private nuisance and does not obstruct the highway by unreasonably impeding the primary right of the general public to pass and repass. Although the matter was essentially one to be judged in the light of the particular case, a peaceful assembly which did not obstruct the highway did not necessarily constitute a trespassory assembly so as to constitute the circumstances for an offence within s.14B(2) of the 1986 Act, where an order under s.14A was in force, *per* Lord Hutton. **16–73**

(e) *Sentence*

The maximum penalty for the offence of organising a trespassory assembly, or inciting another to commit an offence under s.14B is imprisonment for a term not exceeding three months or a fine not exceeding level 4 on the standard scale or both. The maximum penalty for the offence of participating in a trespassory assembly is a fine not exceeding level three on the standard scale. Section 280(2) and Sched. 26, para. 37 of the *Criminal Justice Act* 2003 increases the maximum term in ss.14(8), 14(10), 14B(5) and 14B(7) from three months to 51 weeks (not yet in force). **16–74**

(4) Interpretation

Public Order Act 1986, s.16

Interpretation.

16. In this Part— **16–75**

"the City of London" means the City as defined for the purposes of the Acts relating to the City of London police;

"the metropolitan police district" means that district as defined in section 76 of the *London Government Act* 1963;

"public assembly" means an assembly of 2 or more persons in a public place which is wholly or partly open to the air;

"public place" means —

(a) any highway, or in Scotland any road within the meaning of the *Roads (Scotland) Act* 1984, and

(b) any place to which at the material time the public or any section of the public has access, on payment or otherwise, as of right or by virtue of express or implied permission;

"public procession" means a procession in a public place.

Part III

G. ACTS INTENDED OR LIKELY TO STIR UP RACIAL HATRED

(1) Definition

Public Order Act 1986, s.18

Use of words or behaviour or display of written material

16–76 **18.**—(1) A person who uses threatening, abusive or insulting words or behaviour, or displays any written material which is threatening, abusive or insulting, is guilty of an offence if—

(a) he intends thereby to stir up racial hatred, or

(b) having regard to all the circumstances racial hatred is likely to be stirred up thereby.

(2) An offence under this section may be committed in a public or a private place, except that no offence is committed where the words or behaviour are used, or the written material is displayed, by a person inside a dwelling and are not heard or seen except by other persons in that or another dwelling.

(3) [*Repealed*]

(4) In proceedings for an offence under this section it is a defence for the accused to prove that he was inside a dwelling and had no reason to believe that the words or behaviour used, or the written material displayed, would be heard or seen by a person outside that or any other dwelling.

(5) A person who is not shown to have intended to stir up racial hatred is not guilty of an offence under this section if he did not intend his words or behaviour, or the written material, to be, and was not aware that it might be, threatening, abusive or insulting.

(6) This section does not apply to words or behaviour used, or written material displayed, solely for the purpose of being included in a programme included in a programme service.

[This section is printed as amended by the *Broadcasting Act* 1990, s.164(1), (2) and the *Serious Organised Crime and Police Act* 2005 ss.111 and 174(2).]

(2) Allocation

16–77 This offence is triable either way. No proceedings may be instituted without the consent of the Attorney General: *Public Order Act* 1986, s.27(3).

(3) Elements of the offence

16–78 The prosecution must prove that:

— the defendant used threatening, abusive or insulting words or behaviour, or displayed any written material which is threatening, abusive or insulting

AND

— he intended to stir up racial hatred by so doing

OR

— having regard to all the circumstances, racial hatred was likely to be stirred up by his actions.

Public Order Act 1986, ss.17, 26, 29

Meaning of "racial hatred"

16–79 **17.** In this Part "racial hatred" means hatred against a group of persons defined by reference to colour, race, nationality (including citizenship) or ethnic or national origins.

Savings for reports of parliamentary or judicial proceedings

16–80 **26.**—(1) Nothing in this Part applies to a fair and accurate report of proceedings in Parliament or in the Scottish Parliament.

(2) Nothing in this Part applies to a fair and accurate report of proceedings publicly heard before a court or tribunal exercising judicial authority where the report is published contemporaneously with the proceedings or, if it is not reasonably practicable or would be

unlawful to publish a report of them contemporaneously, as soon as publication is reasonably practicable and lawful.

Interpretation

29. In this Part— **16–81**

"distribute", and related expressions, shall be construed in accordance with section 19(3) (written material) and section 21(2) (recordings);

"dwelling" means any structure or part of a structure occupied as a person's home or other living accommodation (whether the occupation is separate or shared with others) but does not include any part not so occupied, and for this purpose "structure" includes a tent, caravan, vehicle, vessel or other temporary or movable structure;

"programme" means any item which is included in a programme service

"programme service" has the same meaning as in the *Broadcasting Act* 1990;

"publish", and related expressions, in relation to written material, shall be construed in accordance with section 19(3)

"racial hatred" has the meaning given by section 17

"recording" has the meaning given by section 21(2) and "play" and "show", and related expressions, in relation to a recording, shall be construed in accordance with that provision;

"written material" includes any sign or ostensible representation.

For the meaning of "threatening, abusive or insulting" see the materials on s.4A of the *Public Order Act* 1986 (§ 16–38, *ante*).

(4) Defences

Section 19(2) establishes a defence for a defendant who did not intend to stir up racial hatred if he can prove that he was not aware of the content of the material and did not suspect, and had no reason to suspect that it was threatening, abusive or insulting. The burden of proof of establishing this defence lies on the accused. **16–82**

The defence in s.26 of the *Public Order Act* 1986 relating to exceptions for reports of Parliamentary and judicial proceedings applies to s.19.

(5) Sentence

When tried summarily, the maximum penalty is six months' imprisonment, a fine not exceeding the statutory maximum or both. The court also has power under s.25 of the 1986 Act to order forfeiture when the offence consists of displaying written material. On commencement of the relevant provisions, the maximum custodial sentence in a magistrates' court will be 12 months' imprisonment: *Criminal Justice Act* 2003, ss.154 and 282. **16–83**

Possession of threatening, abusive or insulting material with a view to publication led to a 12-month custodial sentence in *Gray* [1999] 1 Cr.App.R.(S.) 50, Judge Peter Crawford Q.C. emphasising the grave social damage done by offences and remarks of a racist nature.

H. PUBLISHING OR DISTRIBUTING WRITTEN MATERIAL STIRRING UP RACIAL HATRED

(1) Definition

Public Order Act 1986, s.19

Publishing or distributing written material

19.—(1) A person who publishes or distributes written material which is threatening, abusive or insulting is guilty of an offence if— **16–84**

(a) he intends thereby to stir up racial hatred, or

(b) having regard to all the circumstances racial hatred is likely to be stirred up thereby.

(2) In proceedings for an offence under this section it is a defence for an accused who is not shown to have intended to stir up racial hatred to prove that he was not aware of the content of the material and did not suspect, and had no reason to suspect, that it was threatening, abusive or insulting.

(3) References in this Part to the publication or distribution of written material are to its publication or distribution to the public or a section of the public.

(2) Allocation

16–85 This offence is triable either way. No proceedings may be instituted without the consent of the Attorney General: *Public Order Act* 1986, s.27(3).

(3) Elements of the offence

16–86 The prosecution must prove that:

— the defendant published or distributed written material which is threatening, abusive or insulting, and,

— he intended to stir up racial hatred

OR

— having regard to all the circumstances, racial hatred was likely to be stirred up by such publication or distribution.

For the meaning of "Racial Hatred" see s.17 of the 1986 Act, *ante*. For the meaning of "threatening, abusive or insulting", see § 16–31 and *Brutus v. Cozens* (1973) A.C. 854, *ante*. For the meaning of "written material" see s.29 of the 1986 Act, *ante*.

In*Sheppard and Whittle* [2010] 1 Cr.App.R. 26, CA, it was held in relation to an allegation of "publishing" on the internet, that it must be established that the material was generally accessible to all, or available to, or was placed before or offered to, the public. This may be proved by the evidence of one or more witnesses. There is no need to go further and prove that anybody actually read the material.

(4) Defences

16–87 The defence established by s.26 of the 1986 Act applies to proceedings instituted under this section.

(5) Sentence

16–88 When tried summarily, the maximum penalty is six months' imprisonment, a fine not exceeding the statutory maximum, or both. On commencement of the relevant provisions, the maximum custodial sentence in a magistrates' court will be 12 months' imprisonment: *Criminal Justice Act* 2003, ss.154 and 282.

I. PUBLIC PERFORMANCE, DISTRIBUTION, BROADCASTING AND POSSESSION OF MATERIALS STIRRING UP RACIAL HATRED

(1) Public performance of a play stirring up racial hatred

(a) *Definition*

Public Order Act 1986, s.20(1), (5), (6)

Public performance of play

16–89 **20.**—(1) If a public performance of a play is given which involves the use of threatening, abusive or insulting words or behaviour, any person who presents or directs the performance is guilty of an offence if—

(a) he intends thereby to stir up racial hatred, or

(b) having regard to all the circumstances (and, in particular, taking the performance as a whole) racial hatred is likely to be stirred up thereby.

(5) In this section "play" and "public performance" have the same meaning as in the *Theatres Act* 1968.

(6) The following provisions of the *Theatres Act* 1968 apply in relation to an offence under this section as they apply to an offence under section 2 of that Act—

section 9 (script as evidence of what was performed),
section 10(power to make copies of script),
section 15 (powers of entry and inspection).

(b) *Allocation*

This offence is triable either way. Proceedings may not be instituted without the consent of the Attorney General: *Public Order Act* 1986, s.27. **16–90**

(c) *Elements of the offence*

The prosecution must prove that: **16–91**

— the defendant was the director or presenter of a play involving the use of threatening, abusive or insulting words or behaviour and,
— the play was performed for the public and,
— the defendant intended thereby to stir up racial hatred
OR
— having regard to all the circumstances, racial hatred was likely to be stirred up by the performance of the play.

For the meaning of racial hatred, see s.17 of the 1986 Act, *ante*.

The words "play" and "public performance" have the same meaning as in the *Theatres Act* 1968.

(d) *Sentence*

When tried summarily, the maximum penalty is six months' imprisonment, a fine not exceeding the statutory maximum, or both. On commencement of the relevant provisions, the maximum custodial sentence in a magistrates' court will be 12 months' imprisonment: *Criminal Justice Act* 2003, ss.154 and 282. **16–92**

Theatres Act 1968, s.18(1)

Interpretation

18.—(1) In this Act— **16–93**

"play" means—

(a) any dramatic piece, whether involving improvisation or not, which is given wholly or in part by one or more persons actually present and performing and in which the whole or a major proportion of what is done by the person or persons performing, whether by way of speech, singing or action, involves the playing of a role; and

(b) any ballet given wholly or in part by one or more persons actually present and performing, whether or not it falls within paragraph (a) of this definition;

"public performance" includes any performance in a public place within the meaning of the *Public Order Act* 1936 and any performance which the public or any section thereof are permitted to attend, whether on payment or otherwise;

(e) *Defences*

Public Order Act 1986, s.20(2)–(4)

Public performance of play

20.—(2) If a person presenting or directing the performance is not shown to have intended to stir up racial hatred, it is a defence for him to prove— **16–94**

(a) that he did not know and had no reason to suspect that the performance would involve the use of the offending words or behaviour, or

(b) that he did not know and had no reason to suspect that the offending words or behaviour were threatening, abusive or insulting, or

(c) that he did not know and had no reason to suspect that the circumstances in which the performance would be given would be such that racial hatred would be likely to be stirred up.

(3) This section does not apply to a performance given solely or primarily for one or more of the following purposes—

(a) rehearsal,

(b) making a recording of the performance, or

(c) enabling the performance to be included in a programme service;

but if it is proved that the performance was attended by persons other than those directly connected with the giving of the performance or the doing in relation to it of the things mentioned in paragraph (b) or (c), the performance shall, unless the contrary is shown, be taken not to have been given solely or primarily for the purposes mentioned above.

(4) For the purposes of this section—

(a) a person shall not be treated as presenting a performance of a play by reason only of his taking part in it as a performer,

(b) a person taking part as a performer in a performance directed by another shall be treated as a person who directed the performance if without reasonable excuse he performs otherwise than in accordance with that person's direction, and

(c) a person shall be taken to have directed a performance of a play given under his direction notwithstanding that he was not present during the performance;

and a person shall not be treated as aiding or abetting the commission of an offence under this section by reason only of his taking part in a performance as a performer.

(f) *Sentence*

16–95 When tried summarily, the maximum penalty for an offence under this section is six months' imprisonment, a fine not exceeding the statutory maximum or both: *POA* 1986, s.27(3). On commencement of the relevant provisions, the maximum custodial sentence in a magistrates' court will be 12 months' imprisonment: *Criminal Justice Act* 2003, ss.154 and 282.

(2) Distributing, showing or playing a recording stirring up racial hatred

(a) *Definition*

Public Order Act 1986, s.21

Distributing, showing or playing a recording

16–96 **21.**—(1) A person who distributes, or shows or plays, a recording of visual images or sounds which are threatening, abusive or insulting is guilty of an offence if—

(a) he intends thereby to stir up racial hatred, or

(b) having regard to all the circumstances racial hatred is likely to be stirred up thereby.

(2) In this Part "recording" means any record from which visual images or sounds may, by any means, be reproduced; and references to the distribution, showing or playing of a recording are to its distribution, showing or playing to the public or a section of the public.

(3) In proceedings for an offence under this section it is a defence for an accused who is not shown to have intended to stir up racial hatred to prove that he was not aware of the content of the recording and did not suspect, and had no reason to suspect, that it was threatening, abusive or insulting.

(4) This section does not apply to the showing or playing of a recording solely for the purpose of enabling the recording to be included in a programme service.

(b) *Allocation*

16–97 This offence is triable either way. Proceedings may not be instituted without the consent of the Attorney General: *POA* 1986, s.27(1).

(c) *Elements of the offence*

The prosecution must prove that: **16–98**

— the defendant distributed, showed or played a recording or visual images or sounds and,

— these visual images or sounds were threatening, abusive or insulting and,

— he so acted with the intention to stir up racial hatred

OR

— having regard to all the circumstances, racial hatred was likely to be stirred up by such actions.

For the meaning of "racial hatred" see s.18 of the 1986 Act, *ante*. For the meaning of "threatening, abusive or insulting", see *Brutus v. Cozens, ante*.

(d) *Defence*

A person who is not shown to have intended to stir up racial hatred will have a defence if he can prove that he was not aware of the contents of the recording and he did not suspect, or have any reason to suspect that the recording was threatening, abusive or insulting: *POA* 1986, s.21(2). **16–99**

The defence applying to fair and accurate reports of parliamentary or judicial proceedings is also available: *POA* 1986, s.26.

(e) *Sentence*

When tried summarily, the maximum penalty for this offence is six months' imprisonment, a fine not exceeding the statutory maximum, or both: *POA* 1986, s.27(3). On commencement of the relevant provisions, the maximum custodial sentence in a magistrates' court will be 12 months' imprisonment: *Criminal Justice Act* 2003, ss.154 and 282. **16–100**

(3) Broadcasting a programme stirring up racial hatred

(a) *Definition*

Public Order Act 1986, s.22

Broadcasting or including programme in cable programme service

22.—(1) If a programme involving threatening, abusive or insulting visual images or sounds is included in a programme service, each of the persons mentioned in subsection (2) is guilty of an offence if— **16–101**

(a) he intends thereby to stir up racial hatred, or

(b) having regard to all the circumstances racial hatred is likely to be stirred up thereby.

(2) The persons are—

(a) the person providing the programme service,

(b) any person by whom the programme is produced or directed, and

(c) any person by whom offending words or behaviour are used.

(3) If the person providing the service, or a person by whom the programme was produced or directed, is not shown to have intended to stir up racial hatred, it is a defence for him to prove that—

(a) he did not know and had not reason to suspect that the programme would involve the offending material, and

(b) having regard to the circumstances in which the programme was included in a programme service, it was not reasonably practicable for him to secure the removal of the material.

(4) It is a defence for a person by whom the programme was produced or directed who is not shown to have intended to stir up racial hatred to prove that he did not know and had not reason to suspect—

(a) that the programme would be included in a programme service, or
(b) that the circumstances in which the programme would be so included would be such that racial hatred would be likely to be stirred up.

(5) It is a defence for a person by whom offending words or behaviour were used and who is not shown to have intended to stir up racial hatred to prove that he did not know and had no reason to suspect—

(a) that a programme involving the use of the offending material would be included in a programme service, or
(b) that the circumstances in which a programme involving the use of the offending material would be so included, or in which a programme so included would involve the use of the offending material, would be such that racial hatred would be likely to be stirred up.

(6) A person who is not shown to have intended to stir up racial hatred is not guilty of an offence under this section if he did not know, and had no reason to suspect, that the offending material was threatening, abusive or insulting.

[This section is printed as amended by the *Broadcasting Act* 1990, s.164(3).]

(b) *Allocation*

16–102 This offence is triable either way. Proceedings may not be instituted without the consent of the Attorney General: *POA* 1986, s.27(1).

(c) *Elements of the offence*

16–103 The prosecution must prove that:

— a programme involving threatening, abusive or insulting visual images or sounds was included in a programme service and
— the defendant was either the person providing the programme service, a person by whom the programme is produced or directed or a person by whom offending words and behaviour are used and
— he intended to stir up racial hatred

OR

— having regard to all the circumstances racial hatred is likely to be stirred up by such actions.

For the meaning of "racial hatred" see section 18 of the 1986 Act, *ante*. For the meaning of "threatening, abusive or insulting", see *Brutus v. Cozens, ante*.

(d) *Defence*

16–104 A person providing the service, or directing or producing the programme who is not shown to have intended to stir up racial hatred will have a defence if it can be shown that he did not know and had no reason to suspect that the programme would involve the offending material and having regard to all the circumstances in which the programme was included in the programme service, it was not reasonably practicable for him to secure the removal of the programme from the programme service: *POA* 1986, s.22(3).

A person directing or producing the programme who is shown not to intend to stir up racial hatred will have a defence if it can be shown that he did not know and had no reason to suspect that the programme would be included in the programme service or that the circumstances of the programme's inclusion in the programme service would be such as to stir up racial hatred: *POA* 1986, s.22(4). A person who used offending words or behaviour in the programme who is not shown to have intended to stir up racial hatred will have a defence if he can prove he did not know and had no reason to suspect that the programme involving the offending conduct would be included in the service programme or that the circumstances involving the use of the programme in the service programme would involve the use of the offending material, or that the circumstances in which a programme so included would involve the use of the offending material would be such as to involve the stirring up of racial hatred: *POA* 1986, s.22(5).

A person who is not shown to have intended to stir up racial hatred will not be guilty of an offence if he did not know and had no reason to suspect that the offending material was abusive, threatening or insulting: s.22(6).

(e) *Sentence*

When tried summarily, the maximum penalty for this offence is six months' imprisonment, a fine not exceeding the statutory maximum, or both: *POA* 1986, s.27(3). On commencement of the relevant provisions, the maximum custodial sentence in a magistrates' court will be 12 months' imprisonment: *Criminal Justice Act* 2003, ss.154 and 282. **16–105**

(4) Possession of racially inflammatory material

(a) *Definition*

Public Order Act 1986, s.23

Possession of racially inflammatory material

23.—(1) A person who has in his possession written material which is threatening, abusive or insulting, or a recording of visual images or sounds which are threatening, abusive or insulting, with a view to— **16–106**

(a) in the case of written material, its being displayed, published, distributed, or included in a cable programme service, whether by himself or another, or

(b) in the case of a recording, its being distributed, shown, played, or included in a cable programme service, whether by himself or another,

is guilty of an offence if he intends racial hatred to be stirred up thereby or, having regard to all the circumstances, racial hatred is likely to be stirred up thereby.

(2) For this purpose regard shall be had to such display, publication, distribution, showing, playing, or inclusion in a programme service as he has, or it may reasonably be inferred that he has, in view.

(3) In proceedings for an offence under this section it is a defence for an accused who is not shown to have intended to stir up racial hatred to prove that he was not aware of the content of the written material or recording and did not suspect, and had no reason to suspect, that it was threatening, abusive or insulting.

[This section is printed as amended by the *Broadcasting Act* 1990, s.164(4).]

(b) *Allocation*

This offence is triable either way and requires the consent of the Attorney General before proceedings can be instituted: *POA* 1986, s.27(1). **16–107**

(c) *Elements of the offence*

For the meaning of "racial hatred" see s.18 of the 1986 Act, *ante*. For the meaning of "threatening, abusive or insulting", see *Brutus v. Cozens*, *ante*. "Written material" means any sign or other visible representation: *POA* 1986, s.29. **16–108**

(d) *Defence*

A person who is not shown to have intended to stir up racial hatred will have a defence if he can prove that he was not aware of the content of the written material or recording, and did not suspect and had no reason to suspect that it was threatening, abusive or insulting: *POA* 1986, s.23(3). **16–109**

(e) *Sentence*

When tried summarily this offence carries a maximum penalty of six months' imprisonment, a fine not exceeding the statutory maximum or both: *POA* 1986, s.27(3). **16–110**

Part III

On commencement of the relevant provisions, the maximum custodial sentence in a magistrates' court will be 12 months' imprisonment: *Criminal Justice Act* 2003, ss.154 and 282. Custodial sentences of less than 12 months will consist of a custody plus order (see *post*, Ch.23).

J. ACTS INTENDED TO STIR UP RELIGIOUS HATRED

16–111 As from October 1, 2007, the *Racial and Religious Hatred Act* 2006 inserted new ss.29A to 29N into the *Public Order Act* 1986. The sections came into force in full, save for s.29(B)(3) which was repealed as from May 8, 2008, by the *Criminal Justice and Immigration Act* 2008. As from March 23, 2010, these sections are further amended by the 2008 Act. The general effect is to extend the scope of the provisions so that they encompass hatred on the grounds of sexual orientation, as defined by s.29AB. Other minor amendments effected by the *Criminal Justice and Immigration Act* 2008 came into force on May 8, 2008, including the insertion of s.29JA (whether this was intended must be open to doubt).

(1) Definition

Public Order Act 1986, s.29B

Use of words or behaviour or display of written material or hatred on the grounds of sexual orientation

16–112 **29B.**—(1) A person who uses threatening words or behaviour, or displays any written material which is threatening, is guilty of an offence if he intends thereby to stir up religious hatred or hatred on the grounds of sexual orientation.

(2) An offence under this section may be committed in a public or a private place, except that no offence is committed where the words or behaviour are used, or the written material is displayed, by a person inside a dwelling and are not heard or seen except by other persons in that or another dwelling.

(3) [*Repealed*].

(4) In proceedings for an offence under this section it is a defence for the accused to prove that he was inside a dwelling and had no reason to believe that the words or behaviour used, or the written material displayed, would be heard or seen by a person outside that or any other dwelling.

(5) This section does not apply to words or behaviour used, or written material displayed, solely for the purpose of being included in a programme service.

(2) Allocation

16–113 This offence is triable either way. No proceedings may be instituted without the consent of the Attorney General: *Public Order Act* 1986, s.29L(1).

(3) Elements of the offence

16–114 The prosecution must prove that:

(a) the defendant used threatening words or behaviour, or displayed written material which was threatening,

AND

(b) he intended to stir up religious hatred [or hatred on the grounds of sexual orientation] by doing so.

Public Order Act 1986, ss.29A, 29J, 29K, 29N

Meaning of "religious hatred" and "hatred on the grounds of sexual orientation"

16–115 **29A.** In this Part "religious hatred" means hatred against a group of persons defined by reference to religious belief or lack of religious belief.

16–116 **29AB** —In the Part "hatred on the grounds of sexual orientation" means hatred against a group of persons defined by reference to sexual orientation (whether towards persons of the same sex, the opposite sex or both).

Protection of freedom of expression

29J. Nothing in this Part shall be read or given effect in a way which prohibits or restricts discussion, criticism or expressions of antipathy, dislike, ridicule, insult or abuse of particular religions or the beliefs or practices of their adherents, or of any other belief system or the beliefs or practices of its adherents, or proselytising or urging adherents of a different religion or belief system to cease practising their religion or belief system. **16–117**

Protection of freedom of expression (sexual orientation)

29JA In this Part, for avoidance of doubt, the discussion or criticism of sexual conduct or practices or the urging of persons to refrain from the modify such conduct or practices shall not be taken to itself to be threatening or intended to stir up hatred. **16–118**

Savings for reports of parliamentary or judicial proceedings

29K.—(1) Nothing in this Part applies to a fair and accurate report of proceedings in Parliament, in the Scottish Parliament or in the National Assembly for Wales. **16–119**

(2) Nothing in this Part applies to a fair and accurate report of proceedings publicly heard before a court or tribunal exercising judicial authority where the report is published contemporaneously with the proceedings or, if it is not reasonably practicable or would be unlawful to publish a report of them contemporaneously, as soon as publication is reasonably practicable and lawful.

Interpretation

29N. In this Part— **16–120**

"distribute", and related expressions, shall be construed in accordance with section 29C(2) (written material) and s.29E(2) (recordings);

"dwelling" means any structure or part of a structure occupied as a person's home or other living accommodation (whether the occupation is separate or shared with others) but does not include any part not so occupied, and for this purpose "structure" includes a tent, caravan, vehicle, vessel or other temporary or movable structure;

"hatred on the grounds of sexual orientation" has the meaning given by section 29AB;

"programme" means any item which is included in a programme service;

"programme service" has the same meaning as in the *Broadcasting Act* 1990;

"publish", and related expressions, in relation to written material, shall be construed in accordance with s.29C(2);

"religious hatred" has the meaning given by s.29A;

"recording" has the meaning given by s.29E(2), and "play" and "show", and related expressions, in relation to a recording, shall be construed in accordance with that provision;

"written material" includes any sign or other visible representation.

Part III

(4) Sentence

When tried summarily, the maximum sentence is six months' imprisonment, a fine not exceeding the statutory maximum or both. The court also has power under s.29I of the 1986 Act to order forfeiture where the offence consists of displaying written material, publishing or distributing such material, distributing, showing or playing a recording or possessing inflamatory material. On commencement of the relevant provisions, the maximum custodial sentence in a magistrates' court will be 12 months' imprisonment: *Criminal Justice Act* 2003, ss.154 and 282. Custodial sentences of less than 12 months will consist of a custody plus order (see *post*, Ch.23). **16–121**

K. PUBLISHING OR DISTRIBUTING WRITTEN MATERIAL STIRRING UP RELIGIOUS HATRED

(1) Definition

Public Order Act 1986, s.29C

Publishing or distributing written material

29C.—(1) A person who publishes or distributes written material which is threatening is **16–122**

guilty of an offence if he intends thereby to stir up religious hatred or hatred on the grounds of sexual orientation.

(2) References in this Part to the publication or distribution of written material are to its publication or distribution to the public or a section of the public.

(2) Allocation

16–123 This offence is triable either way. No proceedings may be instituted without the consent of the Attorney General: *Public Order Act* 1986, s.29L(1).

(3) Elements of the offence

16–124 The prosecution must prove that:

(a) the defendant published or distributed to the public or a section of the public written material,

AND

(b) he intended to stir up religious hatred by doing so or hatred on the grounds of sexual orientation.

(4) Sentence

16–125 When tried summarily, the maximum penalty is six months' imprisonment, a fine not exceeding the statutory maximum, or both. On commencement of the relevant provisions, the maximum custodial sentence in a magistrates' court will be 12 months' imprisonment: *Criminal Justice Act* 2003, ss.154 and 282.

L. PUBLIC PERFORMANCE, DISTRIBUTION, BROADCASTING AND POSSESSION OF MATERIALS STIRRING UP RELIGIOUS HATRED

(1) Public performance of a play stirring up religious hatred

(a) *Definition*

Public Order Act 1986, s.29D(1), (4), (5)

Public performance of play

16–126 **29D.**—(1) If a public performance of a play is given which involves the use of threatening words or behaviour, any person who presents or directs the performance is guilty of an offence if he intends thereby to stir up religious hatred or hatred on the grounds of sexual orientation.

(4) In this section "play" and "public performance" have the same meaning as in the *Theatres Act* 1968.

(5) The following provisions of the *Theatres Act* 1968 apply in relation to an offence under this section as they apply to an offence under section 2 of that Act—

section 9 (script as evidence of what was performed),
section 10 (power to make copies of script),
section 15 (powers of entry and inspection).

(b) *Allocation*

16–127 This offence is triable either way. No proceedings may be instituted without the consent of the Attorney General: *Public Order Act* 1986, s.29L(1).

(c) *Elements of the offence*

16–128 The prosecution must prove that:

— the defendant was the presenter or director of a play involving the use of threatening words or behaviour and,

— the play was performed for the public and,

— the defendant intended thereby to stir up religious hatred [or hatred on the grounds of sexual orientation].

The words "play" and "public performance" have the same meaning as in the *Theatres Act* 1968 (see § 16–93, *ante*).

(d) *Sentence*

When tried summarily, the maximum penalty is six months' imprisonment, a fine not exceeding the statutory maximum, or both. On commencement of the relevant provisions, the maximum custodial sentence in the magistrates' court will be 12 months' imprisonment: *Criminal Justice Act* 2003, ss.154 and 282. **16–129**

(e) *Defences*

Public Order Act 1986, s.29D(2), (3)

29D.—(2) This section does not apply to a performance given solely or primarily for one or more of the following purposes— **16–130**

(a) rehearsal,

(b) making a recording of the performance, or

(c) enabling the performance to be included in a programme service;

but if it is proved that the performance was attended by persons other than those directly connected with the giving of the performance or the doing in relation to it of the things mentioned in paragraph (b) or (c), the performance shall, unless the contrary is shown, be taken not to have been given solely or primarily for the purpose mentioned above.

(3) For the purposes of this section—

(a) a person shall not be treated as presenting a performance of a play by reason only of his taking part in it as a performer,

(b) a person taking part as a performer in a performance directed by another shall be treated as a person who directed the performance if without reasonable excuse he performs otherwise than in accordance with that person's direction, and

(c) a person shall be taken to have directed a performance of a play given under his direction notwithstanding that he was not present during the performance;

and a person shall not be treated as aiding or abetting the commission of an offence under this section by reason only of his taking part in a performance as a performer.

Part III

(2) Distributing, showing or playing a recording stirring up religious hatred

(a) *Definition*

Public Order Act 1986, s.29E

Distributing, showing or playing a recording

29E.—(1) A person who distributes, or shows or plays, a recording of visual images or sounds which are threatening is guilty of an offence if he intends thereby to stir up religious hatred or hatred on the grounds of sexual orientation. **16–131**

(2) In this Part "recording" means any record from which visual images or sounds may, by any means, be reproduced; and references to the distribution, showing or playing of a recording are to its distribution, showing or playing to the public or a section of the public.

(3) This section does not apply to the showing or playing of a recording solely for the purpose of enabling the recording to be included in a programme service.

(b) *Allocation*

This offence is triable either way. Proceedings may not be instituted without the consent of the Attorney General: *Public Order Act* 1986, s.29L(1). **16–132**

(c) *Elements of the offence*

The prosecution must prove that: **16–133**

— the defendant distributed, showed or played a recording of visual images or sounds and,
— these visual images or sounds were threatening and,
— he so acted with the intention to stir up religious hatred or hatred on the grounds of sexual orientation.

(d) *Sentence*

16–134 When tried summarily, the maximum penalty for this offence is six months' imprisonment, a fine not exceeding the statutory maximum, or both. On commencement of the relevant provisions, the maximum sentence in a magistrates' court will be 12 months' imprisonment: *Criminal Justice Act* 2003, ss.154 and 282.

(3) Broadcasting a programme stirring up religious hatred

(a) *Definition*

Public Order Act 1986, s.29F

Broadcasting or including programme in programme service

16–135 **29F.**—(1) If a programme involving threatening visual images or sounds is included in a programme service, each of the persons mentioned in subsection (2) is guilty of an offence if he intends thereby to stir up religious hatred or hatred on the grounds of sexual orientation.

(2) The persons are—

(a) the person providing the programme service,

(b) any person by whom the programme is produced or directed, and

(c) any person by whom offending words or behaviour are used.

(b) *Allocation*

16–136 This offence is triable either way. Proceedings may not be instituted without the consent of the Attorney General: *Public Order Act* 1986, s.29L(1).

(c) *Elements of the offence*

16–137 The prosecution must prove that:
— a programme involving threatening visual images or sounds was included in a programme service and,
— the defendant was either the person providing the programme service, a person by whom the programme was produced or directed or a person by whom offending words or behaviour were used and,
— he intended to stir up religious hatred or hatred on the grounds of sexual orientation.

(d) *Sentence*

16–138 When tried summarily, the maximum penalty for this offence is six months' imprisonment, a fine not exceeding the statutory maximum, or both. On commencement of the relevant provisions, the maximum custodial sentence in a magistrates' court will be 12 months' imprisonment: *Criminal Justice Act* 2003, ss.154 and 282. Custodial sentences of less than 12 months will consist of a custody plus order (see *post*, Ch.23).

(4) Possession of religiously inflammatory material

(a) *Definition*

Public Order Act 1986, s.29G

Possession of inflammatory material

16–139 **29G.**—(1) A person who has in his possession written material which is threatening, or a recording of visual images or sounds which are threatening, with a view to—

(a) in the case of written material, its being displayed, published, distributed, or included in a programme service whether by himself or another, or

(b) in the case of a recording, its being distributed, shown, played, or included in a programme service, whether by himself or another,

is guilty of an offence if he intends thereby to stir up religious hatred on the grounds of sexual orientation.

(2) For this purpose regard shall be had to such display, publication, distribution, showing, playing, or inclusion in a programme service as he has, or it may be reasonably be inferred that he has, in view.

(b) *Allocation*

This offence is triable either way. Proceedings may not be instituted without the consent of the Attorney General: *Public Order Act* 1986, s.29L(1). **16–140**

(c) *Elements of the offence*

The prosecution must prove that: **16–141**

— the defendant had in his possession written material or a recording of visual images or sounds which were threatening,

— in the case of written material, with a view to displaying, publishing, distributing or including it in a programme service,

— in the case of a recording, distributing, showing, playing or including it in a programme service and,

— he intends to stir up religious hatred or hatred on the grounds of sexual orientation.

(d) *Sentence*

When tried summarily, the maximum penalty for this offence is six months' imprisonment, a fine not exceeding the statutory maximum, or both. On commencement of the relevant provisions, the maximum custodial sentence in a magistrates' court will be 12 months' imprisonment: *Criminal Justice Act* 2003, ss.154 and 282. **16–142**

Part III

M. Contamination of or Interference with Goods

(1) Definition

Public Order Act 1986, s.38(1)–(3)

Contamination of or interference with goods with intention of causing public alarm or anxiety, etc.

38.—(1) It is an offence for a person, with the intention— **16–143**

(a) of causing public alarm or anxiety, or

(b) of causing injury to members of the public consuming or using the goods, or

(c) of causing economic loss to any person by reason of the goods being shunned by members of the public, or

(d) of causing economic loss to any person by reason of steps taken to avoid any such alarm or anxiety, injury or loss,

to contaminate or interfere with goods, or make it appear that goods have been contaminated or interfered with, or to place goods which have been contaminated or interfered with, or which appear to have been contaminated or interfered with, in a place where goods of that description are consumed, used, sold or otherwise supplied.

(2) It is also an offence for a person, with any such intention as is mentioned in paragraph (a), (c) or (d) of subsection (1), to threaten that he or another will do, or to claim that he or another has done, any of the acts mentioned in that subsection.

(3) It is an offence for a person to be in possession of any of the following articles with a view to the commission of an offence under subsection (1)—

(a) materials to be used for contaminating or interfering with goods or making it appear that goods have been contaminated or interfered with, or

(b) goods which have been contaminated or interfered with, or which appear to have been contaminated or interfered with.

(2) Allocation

16–144 These offences are triable either way: *POA* 1986, s.38(4).

(3) Elements of the offence

16–145 The prosecution must prove that:

— the defendant had the intention of causing public alarm or anxiety

OR

causing injury to members of the public consuming or using the goods OR causing economic loss to any person by reason of the goods being shunned by members of the public OR causing economic loss to any person by reason of steps taken to avoid such anxiety and,

— he contaminated or interfered with goods OR made it appear that goods had been contaminated OR placed goods which had been or appeared to be contaminated or interfered with in a place where goods of that description are sold, used or otherwise supplied,

OR

— he threatened that he or another would do, or claimed that he or another had done, any of the acts mentioned above

OR

— the defendant was in possession of materials to be used for the contamination of or interference with goods or materials used for making it appear that goods have been contaminated or interfered with or the defendant was in possession of goods which have been contaminated or interfered with, or which appear to have been contaminated or interfered with.

Public Order Act 1986, s.38(5), (6)

Contamination of or interference with goods with intention of causing public alarm or anxiety, etc.

16–146 **38.**—(5) In this section "goods" includes substances whether natural or manufactured and whether or not incorporated in or mixed with other goods.

(6) The reference in subsection (2) to a person claiming that certain acts have been committed does not include a person who in good faith reports or warns that such acts have been, or appear to have been, committed.

(4) Sentence

16–147 When tried summarily, the maximum penalty is six months' imprisonment, a fine not exceeding the statutory maximum or both. On commencement of the relevant provisions, the maximum custodial sentence in a magistrates' court will be 12 months' imprisonment: *Criminal Justice Act* 2003, ss.154 and 282.

III. OFFENCES IN CONNECTION WITH SPORTING ACTIVITY

A. FOOTBALL OFFENCES

(1) Definition

Football (Offences) Act 1991, ss.2–4

Throwing of missiles

16–148 **2.** It is an offence for a person at a designated football match to throw anything at or towards—

(a) the playing area, or any area adjacent to the playing area to which spectators are not generally admitted, or

(b) any area in which spectators or other persons are or may be present,

without lawful authority or lawful excuse (which shall be for him to prove).

Indecent or racialist chanting

3.—(1) It is an offence to engage or take part in chanting of an indecent or racialist nature at a designated football match. **16–149**

(2) For this purpose—

(a) "chanting" means the repeated uttering of any words or sounds (whether alone or in concert with one or more others); and

(b) "of a racialist nature" means consisting of or including matter which is threatening, abusive or insulting to a person by reason of his colour, race, nationality (including citizenship) or ethnic or national origins.

Going onto the playing area

4. It is an offence for a person at a designated football match to go onto the playing area, or any area adjacent to the playing area to which spectators are not generally admitted, without lawful authority or lawful excuse (which shall be for him to prove). **16–150**

(2) Allocation

These offences are all triable summarily: *Football (Offences) Act* 1991, s.5(2). **16–151**

(3) Elements of the offence

To establish the offence of throwing of missiles, the prosecution must prove that: **16–152**

— the defendant was at a designated football match and,

— he threw something at or towards the playing area, or any area adjacent to the playing area to which spectators are not normally admitted OR

— he threw something at or towards any area in which spectators or other persons are or may be present without lawful authority or lawful excuse.

To establish the offence of indecent or racialist chanting, the prosecution must prove that:

— the defendant was at a designated football match and,

— he engaged in indecent or racialist chanting.

To establish the offence of going on to the playing area, the prosecution must prove that:

— the defendant was at a designated football match and,

— he went onto the playing area, or onto any area adjacent to the playing area to which spectators are not generally admitted, without lawful authority or lawful excuse.

Football (Offences) Act 1991, s.1

Designated football matches

1.—(1) In this Act a "designated football match" means an association football match designated, or of a description designated, for the purposes of this Act by order of the Secretary of State. **16–153**

Any such order shall be made by statutory instrument which shall be subject to annulment in pursuance of a resolution of either House of Parliament.

(2) References in this Act to things done at a designated football match include anything done at the ground—

(a) within the period beginning two hours before the start of the match or (if earlier) two hours before the time at which it is advertised to start and ending one hour after the end of the match; or

(b) where the match is advertised to start at a particular time on a particular day but does not take place on that day, within the period beginning two hours before and ending one hour after the advertised starting time.

(4) Sentence

16–154 The maximum penalty for these offences is a fine not exceeding level three on the standard scale: *Football (Offences) Act* 1991, s.5(2).

See the Magistrates' Court Sentencing Guidelines (2008).

STARTING POINT AND RANGE OF SENTENCE

(BASED ON A FIRST TIME OFFENDER PLEADING NOT GUILTY)

Examples of nature of activity	**Starting Point**	**Range**
Going onto playing or other prohibited area	Band B fine	Band A fine to band C fine
Throwing missile; indecent or racist chanting	Band C fine	Band C fine

AGGRAVATING AND MITIGATING FACTORS

Factors indicating higher culpability	**Factors indicating greater degree of harm**
1. Inciting others to misbehave 2. Offensive language or behaviour (where not an element of the offence)	1. Missile likely to cause serious injury e.g. coin, glass, bottle, stone.

B. OFFENCES UNDER THE FOOTBALL SPECTATORS ACT 1989

(1) Unauthorised attendance

(a) *Definition*

The Football Spectators Act 1989, s.2

Offences relating to unauthorised attendance at designated football matches

16–155 **2.**—(1) If a person who is not, in relation to the match, an authorised spectator enters or remains on premises as a spectator during a period relevant to a designated football match that person commits an offence and so does a person who attempts to commit an offence under this subsection of entering premises.

(2) Where a person is charged under subsection(1) above with an offence of entering or remaining on premises, and was at the time of the alleged offence not disqualified from being a member of the national football membership scheme, it shall be a defence to prove that he was allowed to enter the premises as a spectator by a person reasonably appearing to him to have lawful authority to do so.

(3) A person guilty of an offence under subsection (1) above shall be liable on summary conviction to imprisonment for a term not exceeding one month or a fine not exceeding level 3 on the standard scale or to both.

(4) A constable who reasonably suspects that a person has committed an offence under subsection (1) above may arrest him without a warrant.

(b) *Allocation*

This offence is triable summarily. 16–156

(c) *Elements of the offence*

The prosecution must prove that: 16–157

— the defendant was not an authorised spectator and

— he entered or remained on premises as a spectator during a designated football match OR

— he attempted to do so.

The *Football Spectators (Prescription) Order* 2000 (S.I. 2000 No. 2126) designates matches for the purposes of this Act.

(d) *Defence*

Where a person was not disqualified from being a member of the national football membership scheme at the time of the alleged offence he shall have a defence if he can prove that he was allowed to enter the premises as a spectator by a person reasonably appearing to him to have lawful authority to do so: *Football Spectators Act* 1989, s.2(3) 16–158

(e) *Sentence*

The maximum penalty is one months' imprisonment, a fine not exceeding the level 3 on the standard scale, or both. Section 280(2) and Sched. 26, para. 41 of the *Criminal Justice Act* 2003 increases the maximum term to 51 weeks (not yet in force). 16–159

(2) Admitting spectators to unlicensed premises

(a) *Definition*

Football Spectators Act 1989, s.9

Offence of admitting spectators to unlicensed premises

9.—1) Subject to subsection (2) below, if persons are admitted as spectators to, or permitted to remain as spectators on, any premises during a period relevant to a designated football match without a licence to admit spectators being in force, any responsible person commits an offence. 16–160

(2) Where a person is charged with an offence under this section it shall be a defence to prove either that the spectators were admitted in an emergency or—

(a) that the spectators were admitted without his consent; and

(b) that he took all reasonable precautions and exercised all due diligence to avoid the commission of such an offence.

(3) A person guilty of an offence under this section shall be liable—

(a) on summary conviction, to a fine not exceeding the statutory maximum; or

(b) on conviction on indictment, to a fine or to imprisonment for a term not exceeding two years, or to both.

(b) *Allocation*

This offence is triable summarily only. 16–161

(c) *Elements of the offence*

The prosecution has to prove that: 16–162

— persons were admitted as spectators, or allowed to remain as spectators to any premises during a period relevant to a designated football match and,

— there was no license to admit spectators in force and,

— the defendant was responsible.

The *Football Spectators (Prescription) Order* 2004 (S.I. 2004 No. 2409) (in force from October 11, 2004) designates matches for the purposes of this Act.

The *Football Spectators (Prescription) Order* 2004 (S.I. 2004 No. 2409) revokes the *Football Spectators (Prescription) Order* 2000 (S.I. 2000 No. 2126), with effect from October 11, 2004. Articles 3 and 4 describe the football matches in England and Wales and outside England and Wales which are regulated football matches for the purposes of Pt II of the 1989 Act. In England and Wales, a regulated match is any match in which either team is a member of the Football League, the Premier League, the Football Conference or the League of Wales, or represents a country or territory. Outside England and Wales, a regulated match is one involving a national team representing England or Wales or a team representing a Football League, Premier League, Football Conference or League of Wales club. Article 5 prescribes the Football Banning Orders Authority (established under the *Police Act* 1996, s.57) as the enforcing authority for the purposes of Pt II of the 1989 Act, and the Chief Executive of the Football Association for the purposes of s.18(1) and (2) of that Act (person to whom a banning order and an order terminating a banning order must be copied).

The relevant licenses are issued by the Football Licensing Authority under the *Football Spectators (Seating) Order* 1994 (S.I. 1994 No. 1666). Section 10(13) of the 1989 Act also creates a summary offence of failing to observe any term or condition of a licence granted to admit spectators to any premises for the purpose of watching any designated football match played there. A defendant accused of such an offence will have a defence if he can prove that the contravention took place without his consent and that he took all precautions and exercised due diligence to avoid the commission of such an offence.

(d) *Defences*

16–163 The defendant will have a defence if he can establish that he admitted the spectators in an emergency that he took all reasonable precautions and exercised all due diligence to avoid the commission of such an offence: *Football Spectators Act* 1989, s.9(2).

(e) *Sentence*

16–164 When tried summarily, the offence under s.9 carries a maximum penalty of a fine not exceeding the statutory maximum.

C. BREACH OF BANNING ORDERS

(1) Definition

Football Spectators Act 1989, ss.14J, 19

Offences

16–165 **14J.**—(1) A person subject to a banning order who fails to comply with—

(a) any requirement imposed by the order, or

(b) any requirement imposed under section 19(2B) or (2C) below,

is guilty of an offence.

(2) A person guilty of an offence under this section is liable on summary conviction to imprisonment for a term not exceeding six months, or a fine not exceeding level 5 on the standard scale, or both.

Functions of enforcing authority and local police

16–166 **19.**—(1) The enforcing authority and the officer responsible for the police station at which he reports initially shall have the following functions as respects any person subject to a banning order.

(2) On a person reporting initially at the police station, the officer responsible for the station may make such requirements of that person as are determined by the enforcing authority to be necessary or expedient for giving effect to the banning order, so far as relating to regulated football matches outside England and Wales.

(2A) If, in connection with any regulated football match outside England and Wales, the enforcing authority is of the opinion that requiring any person subject to a banning order to report is necessary or expedient in order to reduce the likelihood of violence or disorder at or in connection with the match, the authority must give him a notice in writing under subsection (2B) below.

(2B) The notice must require that person—

(a) to report at a police station specified in the notice at the time, or between the times, specified in the notice,

(b) if the match is outside the United Kingdom and the order imposes a requirement as to the surrender by him of his passport, to surrender his passport at a police station specified in the notice at the time, or between the times, specified in the notice,

and may require him to comply with any additional requirements of the order in the manner specified in the notice.

(2C) In the case of any regulated football match, the enforcing authority may by notice in writing require any person subject to a banning order to comply with any additional requirements of the order in the manner specified in the notice.

(2D) The enforcing authority may establish criteria for determining whether any requirement under subsection (2B) or (2C) above ought to be imposed on any person or any class of person.

(2E) A notice under this section—

(a) may not require the person subject to the order to report except in the control period in relation to a regulated football match outside England and Wales or an external tournament,

(b) may not require him to surrender his passport except in the control period in relation to a regulated football match outside the United Kingdom or an external tournament which includes such matches.

(2F) Where a notice under this section requires the person subject to the order to surrender his passport, the passport must be returned to him as soon as reasonably practicable after the end of the control period in question.

(5) The enforcing authority, in exercising their functions under this section, shall have regard to any guidance issued by the Secretary of State under section 21 below.

(6) A person who, without reasonable excuse, fails to comply with any requirement imposed on him under subsection (2) above shall be guilty of an offence.

(7) A person guilty of an offence under subsection (6) above shall be liable on summary conviction to a fine not exceeding level 2 on the standard scale.

(2) Allocation

Breach of any requirement of a Banning Order imposed under s.19(2B) or (2C) is a summary offence: s.14J. **16–167**

Breach of any requirement of a Banning Order imposed under s.19(2) is a summary offence: s.19(6).

(3) Elements of the offence

Football Spectators Act 1989, s.14

Main definitions

14.—(1) This section applies for the purposes of this Part. **16–168**

(2) "Regulated football match" means an association football match (whether in England and Wales or elsewhere) which is a prescribed match or a match of a prescribed description.

(3) "External tournament" means a football competition which includes regulated football matches outside England and Wales.

(4) "Banning order" means an order made by the court under this Part which—

(a) in relation to regulated football matches in England and Wales, prohibits the person who is subject to the order from entering any premises for the purpose of attending such matches, and

(b) in relation to regulated football matches outside England and Wales, requires that person to report at a police station in accordance with this Part.

(5) "Control period", in relation to a regulated football match outside England and Wales, means the period—

(a) beginning five days before the day of the match, and

(b) ending when the match is finished or cancelled.

(6) "Control period", in relation to an external tournament, means any period described in an order made by the Secretary of State—

(a) beginning five days before the day of the first football match outside England and Wales which is included in the tournament, and

(b) ending when the last football match outside England and Wales which is included in the tournament is finished or cancelled, but, for the purposes of paragraph (a), any football match included in the qualifying or pre-qualifying stages of the tournament is to be left out of account.

(7) References to football matches are to football matches played or intended to be played.

(8) "Relevant offence" means an offence to which Schedule 1 to this Act applies.

(4) Sentence

16–169 The offence under s.14J carries a maximum penalty of imprisonment for a term not exceeding six months, or a fine not exceeding level 5 on the standard scale, or both.

On commencement of the relevant provisions, the maximum custodial sentence in a magistrates' court will be 12 months' imprisonment: *Criminal Justice Act* 2003, ss.154 and 282. The offence under s.19(6) carries a maximum penalty of a fine not exceeding level two on the standard scale.

D. TICKET TOUTS

(1) Definition

Criminal Justice and Public Order Act 1994, s.166(1)

Sale of tickets by unauthorised persons

16–170 **166.**—(1) It is an offence for an unauthorised person to sell, or offer or expose for sale, a ticket for a designated football match in any public place or place to which the public has access or, in the course of a trade or business, in any other place.

(2) Allocation

16–171 This offence is triable summarily: *Criminal Justice and Public Order Act* 1994, s.166(3).

(3) Elements of the offence

16–172 The prosecution must prove that:

— the defendant sold, or offered, or exposed for sale,

— a ticket for a designated football match,

— in any public place or place to which the public have access, or any other place in the course of trade or business.

Criminal Justice and Public Order Act 1994, s.166(2)

Sale of tickets by unauthorised persons

16–173 **166.**—(2) For this purpose—

(a) a person is "unauthorised" unless he is authorised in writing to sell tickets for the match by the home club or by the organisers of the match;

(b) a "ticket" means anything which purports to be a ticket; and

(c) a "designated football match" means a football match of a description, or a particular football match, for the time being designated for the purposes of Part I of the *Football Spectators Act* 1989 or which is a regulated football match for the purposes of Part II of that Act.

(4) Sentence

The maximum penalty is a fine not exceeding level five on the standard scale: *Criminal Justice and Public Order Act* 1994, s.166(5). 16–174

E. OFFENCES IN CONNECTION WITH ALCOHOL ON COACHES AND TRAINS

(1) Definition

Sporting Events (Control of Alcohol etc.) Act 1985, s.1(1)–(4)

Offences in connection with alcohol on coaches and trains

1.—(1) This section applies to a vehicle which— 16–175

(a) is a public service vehicle or railway passenger vehicle, and

(b) is being used for the principal purpose of carrying passengers for the whole or part of a journey to or from a designated sporting event.

(2) A person who knowingly causes or permits intoxicating liquor to be carried on a vehicle to which this section applies is guilty of an offence—

(a) if the vehicle is a public service vehicle and he is the operator of the vehicle or the servant or agent of the operator, or

(b) if the vehicle is a hired vehicle and he is the person to whom it is hired or the servant or agent of that person.

(3) A person who has intoxicating liquor in his possession while on a vehicle to which this section applies is guilty of an offence.

(4) A person who is drunk on a vehicle to which this section applies is guilty of an offence.

(2) Allocation

These offences are triable summarily only: *Sporting Events (Control of Alcohol etc.) Act* 1985, s.8. 16–176

(3) Elements of the offence

The prosecution must prove that: 16–177

— the defendant was the operator, or servant or agent of the operator of a public service vehicle or the defendant was the person to whom, or a servant or agent of the person to whom a hired vehicle was hired and,

— the vehicle was being used to carry passengers to of from a designated sporting event and

— the defendant knowingly caused or permitted intoxicating liquor to be carried on to the vehicle OR

— the defendant was a passenger on such a vehicle and he had intoxicating liquor in his possession during a journey to or from a designated sporting event OR

— the defendant was a passenger on such a vehicle and he was drunk during a journey to or from a designated sporting event.

Sporting Events (Control of Alcohol etc.) Act 1985, s.9(3)

Interpretation

9.—(3) "Designated sporting event"— 16–178

(a) means a sporting event or proposed sporting event for the time being designated, or of a class designated, by order made by the Secretary of State, and

(b) includes a designated sporting event within the meaning of Part V of the *Criminal Justice (Scotland) Act* 1980;

and an order under this subsection may apply to events or proposed events outside Great Britain as well as those in England and Wales.

(4) Sentence

Sporting Events (Control of Alcohol etc.) Act 1985, s.8(a)–(c)

Penalties for offences

16–179 **8.** A person guilty of an offence under this Act shall be liable on summary conviction—

(a) in the case of an offence under section 1(2) to a fine not exceeding level 4 on the standard scale,

(b) in the case of an offence under section 1(3) … to a fine not exceeding level 3 on the standard scale or to imprisonment for a term not exceeding three months or both,

(c) in the case of an offence under section 1(4) … to a fine not exceeding level 2 on the standard scale.

Section 280(2) and Sched. 26, para. 36 of the *Criminal Justice Act* 2003 increases the maximum term in s.8(b) to 51 weeks.

F. OFFENCES CONNECTED WITH ALCOHOL, CONTAINERS ETC. AT SPORTS GROUNDS

(1) Definition

Sporting Events (Control of Alcohol etc.) Act 1985, s.2(1)

Offences in connection with alcohol, containers etc. at sports grounds

16–180 **2.**—(1) A person who has alcohol or an article to which this section applies in his possession—

(a) at any time during the period of a designated sporting event when he is in any area of a designated sports ground from which the event may be directly viewed, or

(b) while entering or trying to enter a designated sports ground at any time during the period of a designated sporting event at that ground,

is guilty of an offence.

(1A) Subsection (1)(a) above has effect subject to section 5A(1) of this Act.

(2) A person who is drunk in a designated sports ground at any time during the period of a designated sporting event at that ground or is drunk while entering or trying to enter such a ground at any time during the period of a designated sporting event at that ground is guilty of an offence.

(3) This section applies to any article capable of causing injury to a person struck by it, being—

(a) a bottle, can or other portable container (including such an article when crushed or broken) which—

(i) is for holding any drink, and

(ii) is of a kind which, when empty, is normally discarded or returned to, or left to be recovered by, the supplier, or

(b) part of an article falling within paragraph (a) above;

but does not apply to anything that is for holding any medicinal product (within the meaning of the *Medicines Act* 1968) or any veterinary medicinal product (within the meaning of the *Veterinary Medicines Regulations* 2006).

(2) Allocation

16–181 This offence is triable summarily: *Sporting Events (Control of Alcohol etc.) Act* 1985, s.8.

(3) Elements of the offence

16–182 The prosecution must prove that:

— the defendant was, during the period of a designated sporting event, in any area of a designated sports ground from which this event could be viewed, OR
— the defendant was entering or trying to enter a designated sports ground at any time during the period of a designated sporting event at the ground AND
— he had in his possession intoxicating liquor OR
— he had in his possession a bottle, can or other portable container (including such an article when crushed or broken) which is for holding any drink, and is of a kind which, when empty, is normally discarded or returned to, or left to be recovered by, the supplier, or forms part of such an article. (Note: Bottles/ articles used for holding any medicinal product do not fall under this section.)

Sporting Events (Control of Alcohol etc.) Act 1985, ss.2(3), 9(1)–(4)

2.—(3) This section applies to any article capable of causing injury to a person struck by it, being— **16–183**

(a) a bottle, can or other portable container (including such an article when crushed or broken) which—
(i) is for holding any drink, and
(ii) is of a kind which, when empty, is normally discarded or returned to, or left to be recovered by, the supplier, or
(b) part of an article falling within paragraph (a) above;

but does not apply to anything that is for holding any medicinal product (within the meaning of the *Medicines Act* 1968).

Interpretation

9.—(1) The following provisions shall have effect for the interpretation of this Act. **16–184**

(2) "Designated sports ground" means any place—
(a) used (wholly or partly) for sporting events where accommodation is provided for spectators, and
(b) for the time being designated, or of a class designated, by order made by the Secretary of State; and an order under this subsection may include provision for determining for the purposes of this Act the outer limit of any designated sports ground.

(3) "Designated sporting event" —
(a) means a sporting event or proposed sporting event for the time being designated, or of a class designated, by order made by the Secretary of State, and
(b) includes a designated sporting event within the meaning of Part V of the *Criminal Justice (Scotland) Act* 1980;

and an order under this subsection may apply to events or proposed events outside Great Britain as well as those in England and Wales.

(4) The period of a designated sporting event is the period beginning two hours before the start of the event or (if earlier) two hours before the time at which it is advertised to start and ending one hour after the end of the event, but—
(a) where an event advertised to start at a particular time on a particular day is postponed to a later day, the period includes the period in the day on which it is advertised to take place beginning two hours before and ending one hour after that time, and
(b) where an event advertised to start at a particular time on a particular day does not take place, the period is the period referred to in paragraph (a) above.

(4) Sentence

In the case of an offence under s.2(1) the maximum penalty is a fine not exceeding level three on the standard scale or to imprisonment for a term not exceeding three months or both: *Sporting Events (Control of Alcohol etc.) Act* 1985, s.8(b). Section 280(2) and Sched. 26, para. 36 of the *Criminal Justice Act* 2003 increases the maximum term in s.8(b) to 51 weeks (not yet in force). **16–185**

In the case of an offence under s.2(2) the maximum penalty is a fine not exceeding level two on the standard scale: *Sporting Events (Control of Alcohol etc.) Act* 1985, s.8(c).

See the *Magistrates' Court Sentencing Guidelines* (2008).

STARTING POINT AND RANGE OF SENTENCE

(BASED ON A FIRST TIME OFFENDER PLEADING NOT GUILTY)

Examples of nature of activity	**Starting Point**	**Range**
Being drunk in, or whilst trying to enter ground	Band A fine	Conditional discharge to band B fine
Possession of alcohol whilst entering or trying to enter ground	Band C fine	Band B fine to high level community order

AGGRAVATING AND MITIGATING FACTORS

Factors indicating higher culpability	
1. Possession of large quantity of alcohol	

G. OFFENCE OF PERSISTENTLY POSSESSING ALCOHOL IN A PUBLIC PLACE

(1) Definition

Policing and Crime Act 2009, s.30

Offence of persistently possessing alcohol in a public place

16–186 **30.**—(1) A person under the age of 18 is guilty of an offence if, without reasonable excuse, the person is in possession of alcohol in any relevant place on 3 or more occasions within a period of 12 consecutive months.

(2) "Relevant place", in relation to a person, means—

(a) any public place, other than excluded premises, or

(b) any place, other than a public place, to which the person has unlawfully gained access.

(3) A person guilty of an offence under this section is liable on summary conviction to a fine not exceeding level 2 on the standard scale.

(4) For the purposes of subsection (2) a place is a public place if at the material time the public or any section of the public has access to it, on payment or otherwise, as of right or by virtue of express or implied permission.

(5) In subsection (2) "excluded premises"—

(a) in relation to England and Wales, means—

(i) premises which may by virtue of Part 3 or 5 of the *Licensing Act* 2003 (premises licence or permitted temporary activity) be used for the supply of alcohol,

(ii) premises which by virtue of Part 4 of that Act (club premises certificate) be used for the supply of alcohol to members or guests,

(b) [*Northern Ireland*.]

(6) In this section "alcohol"—

(a) (a) in relation to England and Wales, has the same meaning as in the *Licensing Act* 2003,

(b) [*Northern Ireland.*]

(7) [*Northern Ireland.*]

[This section came into force on January 29, 2010, *Policing and Crime Act 2009 (Commencement No. 3) Order* 2010 S.I. 125.]

(2) Allocation

This offence is triable summarily: *Policing and Crime Act* 2009, s.30(3). **16–187**

(3) Elements of the offence

The prosecution must prove that: **16–188**

- the defendant was under the age of 18,
- the defendant was in possession of alcohol, without a reasonable excuse, on 3 or more occasions within a period of 12 consecutive months,
- the defendant was, on each occasion, in a relevant place.

(4) Sentence

The maximum penalty is a fine not exceeding level two on the standard scale: *Policing and Crime Act* 2009, s.30(3). **16–189**

IV. OFFENCES AFFECTING THE ENJOYMENT OF PROPERTY

A. UNLAWFUL EVICTION AND HARASSMENT OF OCCUPIER

(1) Definition

Protection from Eviction Act 1977, s.1

Unlawful eviction and harassment of occupier

1.—(1) In this section "residential occupier", in relation to any premises, means a person occupying the premises as a residence, whether under a contract or by virtue of any enactment or rule of law giving him the right to remain in occupation or restricting the right of any other person to recover possession of the premises. **16–190**

(2) If any person unlawfully deprives the residential occupier of any premises of his occupation of the premises or any part thereof, or attempts to do so, he shall be guilty of an offence unless he proves that he believed, and had reasonable cause to believe, that the residential occupier had ceased to reside in the premises.

(3) If any person with intent to cause the residential occupier of any premises—

(a) to give up the occupation of the premises or any part thereof; or

(b) to refrain from exercising any right or pursuing any remedy in respect of the premises or part thereof;

does acts likely to interfere with the peace or comfort of the residential occupier or members of his household, or persistently withdraws or withholds services reasonably required for the occupation of the premises as a residence, he shall be guilty of an offence.

(3A) Subject to subsection (3B) below, the landlord of a residential occupier or an agent of the landlord shall be guilty of an offence if—

(a) he does acts likely to interfere with the peace or comfort of the residential occupier or members of his household, or

(b) he persistently withdraws or withholds services reasonably required for the occupation of the premises in question as a residence,

and (in either case) he knows, or has reasonable cause to believe, that that conduct is likely to cause the residential occupier to give up the occupation of the whole or part of the premises or to refrain from exercising any right or pursuing any remedy in respect of the whole or part of the premises.

(3B) A person shall not be guilty of an offence under subsection (3A) above if he proves that he had reasonable grounds for doing the acts or withdrawing or withholding the services in question.

Part III

(3C) In subsection (3A) above "landlord", in relation to a residential occupier of any premises, means the person who, but for—

(a) the residential occupier's right to remain in occupation of the premises, or
(b) a restriction on the person's right to recover possession of the premises,

would be entitled to occupation of the premises and any superior landlord under whom that person derives title.

(4) A person guilty of an offence under this section shall be liable—

(a) on summary conviction, to a fine not exceeding £400 or to imprisonment for a term not exceeding 6 months or to both;
(b) on conviction on indictment, to a fine or to imprisonment for a term not exceeding 2 years or to both.

(5) Nothing in this section shall be taken to prejudice any liability or remedy to which a person guilty of an offence thereunder may be subject in civil proceedings.

(6) Where an offence under this section committed by a body corporate is proved to have been committed with the consent or connivance of, or to be attributable to any neglect on the part of, any director, manager or secretary or other similar officer of the body corporate or any person who was purporting to act in any such capacity, he as well as the body corporate shall be guilty of that offence and shall be liable to be proceeded against and punished accordingly.

(2) Allocation

16–191 These offences are triable either way.

(3) Elements of the offence

16–192 This section creates three offences. As regards the offence of unlawfully depriving the residential occupier of his occupation of the premises, the prosecution must prove that:

— the defendant unlawfully deprived, or attempted to unlawfully deprive, the residential occupier (defined in s.1(1)) of his occupation of the premises; and
— he did not believe, or have reasonable cause to believe that the residential occupier had ceased to reside in the premises.

As regards the offence of doing acts likely to interfere with the peace or comfort of the residential occupier, the prosecution must prove that:

— the defendant intended to cause the residential occupier of any premises to give up his occupation of the premises or to refrain from exercising any right or pursuing any remedy in respect of the premises or part thereof; and
— he did acts likely to interfere with the peace or comfort of the residential occupier or members of his household; OR
— he persistently withdrew or withheld services reasonably required for the occupation of the premises as a residence.

As regards the offence of the landlord or agent of the landlord doings acts likely to interfere with the peace or comfort of the residential occupier, or withholding services, the prosecution must prove that:

— the defendant was the landlord, or agent of the landlord of the premises in question; and
— he did acts likely to interfere with the peace or comfort of the residential occupier or members of his household or persistently withdrew or withheld services reasonably required for the occupation of the premises in question as a residence; and
— he knew, or had reasonable cause to believe that such conduct is likely to cause the residential occupier to give up the occupation of the whole or part of the premises or to refrain from exercising any right or remedy in respect of the whole or part of the premises.

16–193 Whether the defendant believes, or has reasonable cause to believe that the residential occupier had ceased to reside in the premises are questions of fact for the jury (or justices when the offence is tried summarily): *Davidson-Acres* [1980] Crim.L.R. 50, CA.

In *Yuthiwattana* 80 Cr.App.R. 55, CA, the Court held that s.1(2) of the 1977 Act is concerned with eviction. The necessary eviction does not need to be permanent, but cases which would more accurately be described as "locking out" cases, where a person was shut out of premises for a short period of time but was allowed to remain in occupation of the premises would more accurately fall under subs (3).

The offence under subs (3) requires the necessary intention to cause the owner or occupier to give up occupation of the premises or to refrain from exercising any right or pursuing any remedy in respect of the premises. In *AMK (Property Management) Ltd* [1985] Crim.L.R. 600, CA, an appeal was successful because the trial judge had failed to make it clear that intent to cause the occupiers to leave was different from the consequences of building works being carried out being that the occupiers would have to leave. In *Schon v. Camden London Borough Council* (1986) 84 L.G.R. 830, it was held that whilst an intention to persuade the occupier to leave for a limited period of time would not establish an intention to cause her to leave the premises. It would however establish the intent required under the second limb of s.1(3) as it would be an intention to cause the occupier to refrain from exercising her right to live in and be physically present at the premises.

For examples of acts found to be likely to interfere with the peace and comfort of the **16–194**
occupier see *Yuthiwattana, ante*, (failure to provide a front door key as well as entering the occupier's room without permission, removing his record player and records and shouting at him).

(4) Defences

Section 1(2) of the 1977 Act makes it a defence to any eviction offence for the accused **16–195**
to prove that he believed, and had reasonable cause to believe that the residential occupier had ceased to reside in the premises. Section 1(3)(B) also provides a defence to a charge under subs. (3)(B) if the accused can prove that had reasonable grounds for doing the acts or withdrawing or withholding the services in question.

(5) Sentence

When tried summarily, the maximum punishment is a fine not exceeding the **16–196**
prescribed sum, imprisonment for a term not exceeding six months or both: *Protection From Eviction Act* 1977, s.1(4). Note that, on commencement of the relevant provisions, the maximum custodial sentence in a magistrates' court will be 12 months' imprisonment: *Criminal Justice Act* 2003, ss.154 and 282.

In *Pittard* (1994) 15 Cr.App.R.(S.) 108 the accused was convicted of unlawful eviction and interference with the peace and comfort of a residential occupier. He had let a house to a lady as a sole occupier. While she was away, he broke into the house, moved in, changed the locks and upon her return indicated his intention to stay in the house. His original sentence of a £600 in respect of each count and an order to pay £2000 towards the cost of the prosecution was reduced to a fine of £100, the costs order being upheld.

B. USE OR THREAT OF VIOLENCE FOR THE PURPOSES OF SECURING ENTRY TO PREMISES

(1) Definition

Criminal Law Act 1977, s.6(1), (1A), (2), (4)

Violence for securing entry

6.—(1) Subject to the following provisions of this section, any person who, without lawful **16–197**
authority, uses or threatens violence for the purpose of securing entry into any premises for himself or for any other person is guilty of an offence, provided that—

(a) there is someone present on those premises at the time who is opposed to the entry which the violence is intended to secure; and

(b) the person using or threatening the violence knows that that is the case.

(1A) Subsection (1) above does not apply to a person who is a displaced residential occupier or a protected intending occupier of the premises in question or who is acting on behalf of such an occupier; and if the accused adduces sufficient evidence that he was, or was acting on behalf of, such an occupier he shall be presumed to be, or to be acting on behalf of, such an occupier unless the contrary is proved by the prosecution.

(2) Subject to subsection (1A) above, The fact that a person has any interest in or right to possession or occupation of any premises shall not for the purposes of subsection (1) above constitute lawful authority for the use or threat of violence by him or anyone else for the purpose of securing his entry into those premises.

(4) It is immaterial for the purposes of this section—

(a) whether the violence in question is directed against the person or against property; and

(b) whether the entry which the violence is intended to secure is for the purpose of acquiring possession of the premises in question or for any other purpose.

(2) Allocation

16–198 This is offence is triable summarily only: s.6(5).

Violence for securing entry.

6.—(5) A person guilty of an offence under this section shall be liable on summary conviction to imprisonment for a term not exceeding six months or to a fine not exceeding level 5 on the standard scale or to both.

(3) Elements of the offence

16–199 The prosecution must establish that:

— the defendant, without lawful authority, used or threatened violence for the purpose of securing entry into any premises; and

— there is someone present on those premises at the time who is opposed to the entry which the violence is intended to secure; and

— the defendant knew that this was the case.

16–200 It is immaterial whether the violence in question is directed against the person or against property: s.6(4)(a). Likewise, it is immaterial whether the entry which the violence is intended to secure is for the purpose of acquiring possession of the premises in question or for any other purpose: s.6(4)(b).

Key terms are defined in ss.12 and 12A of the 1977 Act.

Criminal Law Act 1977, ss.12, 12A(1)–(7)

Supplementary positions

16–201 **12.**—(1) In this Part of this Act—

(a) "premises" means any building, any part of a building under separate occupation, any land ancillary to a building, the site comprising any building or buildings together with any land ancillary thereto, and (for the purposes only of sections 10 and 11 above) any other place; and

(b) "access" means, in relation to any premises, any part of any site or building within which those premises are situated which constitutes an ordinary means of access to those premises (whether or not that is its sole or primary use).

(2) References in this section to a building shall apply also to any structure other than a movable one, and to any movable structure, vehicle or vessel designed or adapted for use for residential purposes; and for the purposes of subsection (1) above—

(a) part of a building is under separate occupation if anyone is in occupation or entitled to occupation of that part as distinct from the whole; and

(b) land is ancillary to a building if it is adjacent to it and used (or intended for use) in connection with the occupation of that building or any part of it.

(3) Subject to subsection (4) below, any person who was occupying any premises as a residence immediately before being excluded from occupation by anyone who entered

those premises, or any access to those premises, as a trespasser is a displaced residential occupier of the premises for the purposes of this Part of this Act so long as he continues to be excluded from occupation of the premises by the original trespasser or by any subsequent trespasser.

(4) A person who was himself occupying the premises in question as a trespasser immediately before being excluded from occupation shall not by virtue of subsection (3) above be a displaced residential occupier of the premises for the purposes of this Part of this Act.

(5) A person who by virtue of subsection (3) above is a displaced residential occupier of any premises shall be regarded for the purposes of this Part of this Act as a displaced residential occupier also of any access to those premises.

(6) Anyone who enters or is on or in occupation of any premises by virtue of—

(a) any title derived from a trespasser; or

(b) any licence or consent given by a trespasser or by a person deriving title from a trespasser,

shall himself be treated as a trespasser for the purposes of this Part of this Act (without prejudice to whether or not he would be a trespasser apart from this provision); and references in this Part of this Act to a person's entering or being on or occupying any premises as a trespasser shall be construed accordingly.

(7) Anyone who is on any premises as a trespasser shall not cease to be a trespasser for the purposes of this Part of this Act by virtue of being allowed time to leave the premises, nor shall anyone cease to be a displaced residential occupier of any premises by virtue of any such allowance of time to a trespasser.

(7A) Subsection (6) also applies to the Secretary of State if the tenancy or licence is granted by him under Part III of the *Housing Associations Act* 1985.

(8) No rule of law ousting the jurisdiction of magistrates' courts to try offences where a dispute of title to property is involved shall preclude magistrates' courts from trying offences under this Part of this Act.

Protected intending occupiers: supplementary provisions

12A.—(1) For the purposes of this Part of this Act an individual is a protected intending occupier of any premises at any time if at that time he falls within subsection (2), (4) or (6) below. **16–202**

(2) An individual is a protected intending occupier of any premises if—

(a) he has in those premises a freehold interest or a leasehold interest with not less than two years still to run;

(b) he requires the premises for his own occupation as a residence;

(c) he is excluded from occupation of the premises by a person who entered them, or any access to them, as a trespasser; and

(d) he or a person acting on his behalf holds a written statement—

(i) which specifies his interest in the premises;

(ii) which states that he requires the premises for occupation as a residence for himself; and

(iii) with respect to which the requirements in subsection (3) below are fulfilled.

(3) The requirements referred to in subsection (2)(d)(iii) above are—

(a) that the statement is signed by the person whose interest is specified in it in the presence of a justice of the peace or commissioner for oaths; and

(b) that the justice of the peace or commissioner for oaths has subscribed his name as a witness to the signature.

(4) An individual is also a protected intending occupier of any premises if—

(a) he has a tenancy of those premises (other than a tenancy falling within subsection (2)(a) above or (6)(a) below) or a licence to occupy those premises granted by a person with a freehold interest or a leasehold interest with not less than two years still to run in the premises;

(b) he requires the premises for his own occupation as a residence;

(c) he is excluded from occupation of the premises by a person who entered them, or any access to them, as a trespasser; and

(d) he or a person acting on his behalf holds a written statement—

(i) which states that he has been granted a tenancy of those premises or a licence to occupy those premises;

Part III

(ii) which specifies the interest in the premises of the person who granted that tenancy or licence to occupy ("the landlord");

(iii) which states that he requires the premises for occupation as a residence for himself; and

(iv) with respect to which the requirements in subsection (5) below are fulfilled.

(5) The requirements referred to in subsection (4)(d)(iv) above are—

(a) that the statement is signed by the landlord and by the tenant or licensee in the presence of a justice of the peace or commissioner for oaths;

(b) that the justice of the peace or commissioner for oaths has subscribed his name as a witness to the signatures.

(6) An individual is also a protected intending occupier of any premises if—

(a) he has a tenancy of those premises (other than a tenancy falling within subsection (2)(a) or (4)(a) above) or a licence to occupy those premises granted by an authority to which this subsection applies;

(b) he requires the premises for his own occupation as a residence;

(c) he is excluded from occupation of the premises by a person who entered the premises, or any access to them, as a trespasser; and

(d) there has been issued to him by or on behalf of the authority referred to in paragraph (a) above a certificate stating that—

(i) he has been granted a tenancy of those premises or a licence to occupy those premises as a residence by the authority; and

(ii) the authority which granted that tenancy or licence to occupy is one to which this subsection applies, being of a description specified in the certificate.

(7) Subsection (6) above applies to the following authorities—

(a) any body mentioned in section 14 of the *Rent Act* 1977 (landlord's interest belonging to local authority etc.);

(b) the Housing Corporation;

(c) Housing for Wales and;

(d) a registered social landlord within the meaning of the *Housing Act* 1985.

(4) Sentence

16–203 The maximum penalty for this offence is imprisonment for a term not exceeding six months, a fine not exceeding level five on the standard scale or both: *Criminal Law Act* 1977, s.6(5). Note that, on commencement of the relevant provisions, the maximum custodial sentence in a magistrates' court will be 12 months' imprisonment: *Criminal Justice Act* 2003, ss.154 and 282.

C. ADVERSE OCCUPATION OF RESIDENTIAL PREMISES

(1) Definition

Criminal Law Act 1977, s.7(1)–(5), (7)

Adverse occupation of residential premises

16–204 **7.**—(1) Subject to the following provisions of this section and to section 12A(9) below, any person who is on any premises as a trespasser after having entered as such is guilty of an offence if he fails to leave those premises on being required to do so by or on behalf of—

(a) a displaced residential occupier of the premises; or

(b) an individual who is a protected intending occupier of the premises.

(2) In any proceedings for an offence under this section it shall be a defence for the accused to prove that he believed that the person requiring him to leave the premises was not a displaced residential occupier or protected intending occupier of the premises or a person acting on behalf of a displaced residential occupier or protected intending occupier.

(3) In any proceedings for an offence under this section it shall be a defence for the accused to prove—

(a) that the premises in question are or form part of premises used mainly for non-residential purposes; and

(b) that he was not on any part of the premises used wholly or mainly for residential purposes.

(4) Any reference in the preceding provisions of this section to any premises includes a reference to any access to them, whether or not any such access itself constitutes premises, within the meaning of this Part of this Act.

(5) A person guilty of an offence under this section shall be liable on summary conviction to imprisonment for a term not exceeding six months or to a fine not exceeding level 5 on the standard scale or to both.

(7) Section 12 below contains provisions which apply for determining when any person is to be regarded for the purposes of this Part of this Act as a displaced residential occupier of any premises or of any access to any premises and section 12A below contains provisions which apply for determining when any person is to be regarded for the purposes of this Part of this Act as a protected intending occupier of any premises or of any access to any premises.

(2) Allocation

This offence is triable summarily: s.7(5). **16–205**

(3) Elements of the offence

The prosecution must prove that: **16–206**

— the defendant entered the premises as a trespasser; and

— he was asked to leave the premises by a displaced residential occupier of the premises or by an individual who is a protected intending occupier of the premises; and

— he refused to leave.

For the meaning of "displaced residential occupier" and "protected intending occupier" see ss.12 and 12A of the 1977 Act, *ante*.

(4) Sentence

The maximum penalty is imprisonment for a term not exceeding six months, or a fine not exceeding level five on the standard scale or both: s.7(5). **16–207**

D. TRESPASSING DURING THE CURRENCY OF AN INTERIM POSSESSION ORDER

(1) Definition

Criminal Justice and Public Order Act 1994, s.76

Interim possession orders: trespassing during currency of order

76.—(1) This section applies where an interim possession order has been made in respect of any premises and served in accordance with rules of court; and references to "the order" and "the premises" shall be construed accordingly. **16–208**

(2) Subject to subsection (3), a person who is present on the premises as a trespasser at any time during the currency of the order commits an offence.

(3) No offence under subsection (2) is committed by a person if—

(a) he leaves the premises within 24 hours of the time of service of the order and does not return; or

(b) a copy of the order was not fixed to the premises in accordance with rules of court.

(4) A person who was in occupation of the premises at the time of service of the order but leaves them commits an offence if he re-enters the premises as a trespasser or attempts to do so after the expiry of the order but within the period of one year beginning with the day on which it was served.

(5) A person guilty of an offence under this section shall be liable on summary conviction to imprisonment for a term not exceeding six months or a fine not exceeding level 5 on the standard scale or both.

(6) A person who is in occupation of the premises at the time of service of the order shall be treated for the purposes of this section as being present as a trespasser.

(7) A constable in uniform may arrest without a warrant anyone who is, or whom he reasonably suspects to be, guilty of an offence under this section.

(8) In this section—

"interim possession order" has the same meaning as in section 75 above and "rules of court" is to be construed accordingly; and

"premises" has the same meaning as in that section that is to say the same meaning as in Part II of the *Criminal Law Act* 1977 (offences relating to entering and remaining on property).

(2) Allocation

16–209 This offence is triable summarily only: *CJPOA* 1994, s.76(5).

(3) Elements of the offence

16–210 Regarding the offence of trespass, the prosecution must prove that:

— the defendant was present on the premises as a trespasser,

— during the currency of an interim possession order.

Regarding the offence of re-entering premises as a trespasser, the prosecution must prove that:

— the defendant was in occupation of the premises at the time of service of the interim possession order and,

— he then left the premises, and re-entered as a trespasser or attempted to re-enter the premises,

— after the expiry of the order, but within one year of the date on which the order was served.

16–211 "Interim possession order" has the same meaning as in s.75(4) of the 1994 Act namely "an interim possession order made under rules of court for the bringing of summary proceedings for possession of premises which are occupied by trespassers."

By s.75(4) of the 1994 Act "premises" has the same meaning as in Pt II of the *Criminal Law Act* 1977 (offences relating to entering and remaining on property) and "statement" in relation to an interim possession order means any statement, in writing or oral and whether as to fact or belief, made in or for the purpose of the proceedings.

(4) Defence

16–212 The accused will have a defence if he can establish that he left the premises within 24 hours of the time of service of the order and does not return, or a copy of the order was not fixed to the premises in accordance with the rules of court: s.76(3).

(5) Sentence

16–213 The maximum penalty is a term of imprisonment not exceeding six months, a fine not exceeding level 5 on the standard scale or both: *CJPOA* 1994, s.76(5). Note that, after commencement of the relevant provisions, the maximum custodial sentence in a magistrates' court will be 12 months' imprisonment: *Criminal Justice Act* 2003, ss.154 and 282.

E. INTERIM POSSESSION ORDERS: FALSE OR MISLEADING STATEMENTS

(1) Definition

Criminal Justice and Public Order Act 1994, s.75

Interim possession orders: false or misleading statements

16–214 **75.**—(1) A person commits an offence if, for the purpose of obtaining an interim possession order, he—

(a) makes a statement which he knows to be false or misleading in a material particular; or

(b) recklessly makes a statement which is false or misleading in a material particular.

(2) A person commits an offence if, for the purpose of resisting the making of an interim possession order, he—

(a) makes a statement which he knows to be false or misleading in a material particular; or

(b) recklessly makes a statement which is false or misleading in a material particular.

(3) A person guilty of an offence under this section shall be liable—

(a) on conviction on indictment, to imprisonment for a term not exceeding two years or a fine or both;

(b) on summary conviction, to imprisonment for a term not exceeding six months or a fine not exceeding the statutory maximum or both.

(4) In this section—

"interim possession order" means an interim possession order (so entitled) made under rules of court for the bringing of summary proceedings for possession of premises which are occupied by trespassers;

"premises" has the same meaning as in Part II of the *Criminal Law Act* 1977 (offences relating to entering and remaining on property); and

"statement", in relation to an interim possession order, means any statement, in writing or oral and whether as to fact or belief, made in or for the purposes of the proceedings.

(2) Allocation

This offence is triable either way: *CJPOA* 1994, s.75(3). **16–215**

(3) Elements of the offence

The prosecution must prove that: **16–216**

— the defendant knowingly or recklessly made a false or misleading statement,

— for the purpose of obtaining an interim possession order or,

— for the purpose of resisting the making of an interim possession order.

Criminal Justice and Public Order Act, s.75(4)

See § 16–262, *ante*. **16–217**

(4) Sentence

When tried summarily, the maximum penalty is imprisonment for a term not exceeding six months or a fine not exceeding the statutory maximum or both: *CJPOA* 1994, s.75(3). Note that, on commencement of the relevant provisions, the maximum custodial sentence in a magistrates' court will be 12 months' imprisonment: *Criminal Justice Act* 2003, ss.154 and 282. **16–218**

F. Aggravated Trespass

(1) Definition

Criminal Justice and Public Order Act 1994, s.68(1)–(3), (5)

Offence of aggravated trespass

68.—(1) A person commits the offence of aggravated trespass if he trespasses on land and, in relation to any lawful activity which persons are engaging in or are about to engage in on that or adjoining land, does there anything which is intended by him to have the effect— **16–219**

(a) of intimidating those persons or any of them so as to deter them or any of them from engaging in that activity,

(b) of obstructing that activity, or

(c) of disrupting that activity.

(2) Activity on any occasion on the part of a person or persons on land is "lawful" for the purposes of this section if he or they may engage in the activity on the land on that occasion without committing an offence or trespassing on the land.

(3) A person guilty of an offence under this section is liable on summary conviction to imprisonment for a term not exceeding three months or a fine not exceeding level 4 on the standard scale, or both.

(5) In this section "land" does not include—

(a) the highways and roads excluded from the application of section 61 by paragraph (b) of the definition of land in subsection (9) of that section; or

(b) a road within the meaning of the *Roads (Northern Ireland) Order* 1993.

[This section is printed as amended by the *Anti-Social Behaviour Act* 2003 ss.59, 92 and Sched. 3.]

(2) Allocation

16–220 The offence is triable summarily: *CJPOA* 1994, s.68(3).

(3) Elements of the offence

16–221 The prosecution must prove that:

— the defendant trespasses on land and,

— does something which is intended to intimidate, obstruct or disrupt,

— the lawful activities of people on the land.

"Land"

16–222 For the purposes of s.68, "land" includes buildings. Where a defendant was found within a company building, the *Interpretation Act* 1978 was applied which defines "land" as including buildings: *DPP v. Chivers*, [2011] 1 All E.R. 367, DC.

"Lawful activity"

16–223 By s.68(2) an activity is lawful if the persons engaged in it may do so without committing an offence or trespassing on the land. The persons engaged in the lawful activity must be physically present on the land: *Tilly v. DPP* [2002] Crim.L.R. 128. See *ante*, § 12–102 for comments on *Jones* [2005] Q.B. 259 and *Ayliffe v. DPP* [2005] 3 W.L.R. 628; [2005] Crim.L.R. 959.

Disruption

16–224 Where the charge is under s.68(1)(c) an intention to disrupt the lawful activity must be proved, yet actual disruption need not be established. In *Winder v. DPP* (1996) 160 J.P. 713 when trespassers ran towards a hunt without actually disrupting it, the requisite intention to disrupt was found to be present and a charge under s.68(1)(c) could proceed.

(4) Sentence

16–225 The maximum penalty is a term of imprisonment not exceeding three months or a fine not exceeding level four on the standard scale or both: *CJPOA* 1994, s.68(3). Note that, on commencement of the relevant provisions, the maximum custodial sentence in a magistrates' court will be 12 months' imprisonment: *Criminal Justice Act* 2003, ss.154 and 282.

G. FAILURE TO LEAVE OR RE-ENTRY TO LAND AFTER POLICE DIRECTION TO LEAVE

(1) Definition

Criminal Justice and Public Order Act 1994, s.61(4)

Power to remove trespassers on land

61.—(4) If a person knowing that a direction under subsection (1) above has been given which applies to him— **16–226**

(a) fails to leave the land as soon as reasonably practicable, or

(b) having left again enters the land as a trespasser within the period of three months beginning with the day on which the direction was given,

he commits an offence and is liable on summary conviction to imprisonment for a term not exceeding three months or a fine not exceeding level 4 on the standard scale, or both.

(2) Allocation

This offence is triable summarily: *CJPOA* 1994 s.61(4). **16–227**

(3) Elements of the offence

The prosecution must prove that: **16–228**

— the defendant knew that a police direction to leave had been given to him,

— he then failed to leave the land as soon as was practicable or,

— he left the land, and then re-entered as a trespasser within a period of three months from the date on which the direction to leave was given.

A direction to leave must be given before the offence under s.61 can be committed.

Criminal Justice and Public Order Act 1994, s.61(1)

Power to remove trespassers on land

61.—(1) If the senior police officer present at the scene reasonably believes that two or more persons are trespassing on land and are present there with the common purpose of residing there for any period, that reasonable steps have been taken by or on behalf of the occupier to ask them to leave and— **16–229**

(a) that any of those persons has caused damage to the land or to property on the land or used threatening, abusive or insulting words or behaviour towards the occupier, a member of his family or an employee or agent of his, or

(b) that those persons have between them six or more vehicles on the land,

he may direct those persons, or any of them, to leave the land and to remove any vehicles or other property they have with them on the land.

A direction under s.61 cannot be issued until the trespassers have failed to comply with steps taken by the occupier to ask them to leave. *R. (Fuller) v. Chief Constable of Dorset* [2003] Q.B. 480 held that a s.61 direction was invalid when given at the same time as instructions to leave the premises. The purported s.61 notice was also held to be invalid as it required vacation in two days' time, a s.61 notice can only direct immediate vacation of a site. **16–230**

Key terms are defined in s.61(9) of the 1994 Act.

Criminal Justice and Public Order Act 1994, s.61(9), (1)

Power to remove trespassers on land

61.—(9) In this section— **16–231**

"common land" means common land as defined in section 22 of the *Commons Registration Act* 1965;

"commoner" means a person with rights of common as defined in section 22 of the *Commons Registration Act* 1965;

"land" does not include—

(a) buildings other than—

(i) agricultural buildings within the meaning of, in England and Wales, paragraphs 3 to 8 of Schedule 5 to the *Local Government Finance Act* 1988 or, in Scotland, section 7(2) of the *Valuation and Rating (Scotland) Act* 1956, or

(ii) scheduled monuments within the meaning of the *Ancient Monuments and Archaeological Areas Act* 1979;

(b) land forming part of—

(i) a highway unless it falls within the classifications in section 54 of the *Wildlife and Countryside Act* 1981 (footpath, bridleway or byway open to all traffic or road used as a public path) or is a cycle track under the *Highways Act* 1980 or the *Cycle Tracks Act* 1984; or

(ii) a road within the meaning of the *Roads (Scotland) Act* 1984 unless it falls within the definitions in section 151(2)(a)(ii) or (b) (footpaths and cycle tracks) of that Act or is a bridleway within the meaning of section 47 of the *Countryside (Scotland) Act* 1967;

"the local authority", in relation to common land, means any local authority which has powers in relation to the land under section 9 of the *Commons Registration Act* 1965;

"occupier" (and in subsection (8) "the other occupier") means—

(a) in England and Wales, the person entitled to possession of the land by virtue of an estate or interest held by him; and

(b) in Scotland, the person lawfully entitled to natural possession of the land;

"property", in relation to damage to property on land, means—

(a) in England and Wales, property within the meaning of section 10(1) of the *Criminal Damage Act* 1971; and

(b) in Scotland, either—

(i) heritable property other than land; or

(ii) corporeal movable property, and

"damage" includes the deposit of any substance capable of polluting the land;

"trespass" means, in the application of this section—

(a) in England and Wales, subject to the extensions effected by subsection (7) above, trespass as against the occupier of the land;

(b) in Scotland, entering, or as the case may be remaining on, land without lawful authority and without the occupier's consent; and

"trespassing" and "trespasser" shall be construed accordingly;

"vehicle" includes—

(a) any vehicle, whether or not it is in a fit state for use on roads, and includes any chassis or body, with or without wheels, appearing to have formed part of such a vehicle, and any load carried by, and anything attached to, such a vehicle; and

(b) a caravan as defined in section 29(1) of the *Caravan Sites and Control of Development Act* 1960;

and a person may be regarded for the purposes of this section as having a purpose of residing in a place notwithstanding that he has a home elsewhere.

Power to remove trespassers on land

16–232 **61.**—(1) If the senior police officer present at the scene reasonably believes that two or more persons are trespassing on land and are present there with the common purpose of residing there for any period, that reasonable steps have been taken by or on behalf of the occupier to ask them to leave and—

(a) that any of those persons has caused damage to the land or to property on the land or used threatening, abusive or insulting words or behaviour towards the occupier, a member of his family or an employee or agent of his, or

(b) that those persons have between them six or more vehicles on the land,

he may direct those persons, or any of them, to leave the land and to remove any vehicles or other property they have with them on the land.

(4) Defence

16–233 The accused will have a defence if he can show that he was not trespassing on the land, or that he had a reasonable excuse for failing to leave the land as soon as reasonably practicable or, as the case may be, for again entering the land as a trespasser: *CJPOA* 1994, s.61(6).

(5) Sentence

The maximum penalty is imprisonment for a term not exceeding three months or a fine not exceeding level 4 on the standard scale or both: s.61(4). Note that, on commencement of the relevant provisions, the maximum custodial sentence in a magistrates' court will be 12 months' imprisonment: *Criminal Justice Act* 2003, ss.154 and 282. **16–234**

H. FAILURE TO LEAVE LAND OR RE-ENTRY TO LAND: RAVES

(1) Definition

Criminal Justice and Public Order Act 1994, s.63

Powers to remove persons attending or preparing for a rave

63.—(1) This section applies to a gathering on land in the open air of 20 or more persons (whether or not trespassers) at which amplified music is played during the night (with or without intermissions) and is such as, by reason of its loudness and duration and the time at which it is played, is likely to cause serious distress to the inhabitants of the locality; and for this purpose— **16–235**

(a) such a gathering continues during intermissions in the music and, where the gathering extends over several days, throughout the period during which amplified music is played at night (with or without intermissions); and

(b) "music" includes sounds wholly or predominantly characterised by the emission of a succession of repetitive beats.

(1A) This section also applies to a gathering if–

(a) it is a gathering on land of 20 or more persons who are trespassing on the land; and

(b) it would be a gathering of a kind mentioned in subsection (1) above if it took place on land in the open air.

(2) If, as respects any land, a police officer of at least the rank of superintendent reasonably believes that—

(a) two or more persons are making preparations for the holding there of a gathering to which this section applies,

(b) ten or more persons are waiting for such a gathering to begin there, or

(c) ten or more persons are attending such a gathering which is in progress,

he may give a direction that those persons and any other persons who come to prepare or wait for or to attend the gathering are to leave the land and remove any vehicles or other property which they have with them on the land.

(3) A direction under subsection (2) above, if not communicated to the persons referred to in subsection (2) by the police officer giving the direction, may be communicated to them by any constable at the scene.

(4) Persons shall be treated as having had a direction under subsection (2) above communicated to them if reasonable steps have been taken to bring it to their attention.

(5) A direction under subsection (2) above does not apply to an exempt person.

(6) If a person knowing that a direction has been given which applies to him—

(a) fails to leave the land as soon as reasonably practicable, or

(b) having left again enters the land within the period of 7 days beginning with the day on which the direction was given,

he commits an offence and is liable on summary conviction to imprisonment for a term not exceeding three months or a fine not exceeding level 4 on the standard scale, or both.

(7) In proceedings for an offence under this section it is a defence for the accused to show that he had a reasonable excuse for failing to leave the land as soon as reasonably practicable or, as the case may be, for again entering the land.

(8) A constable in uniform who reasonably suspects that a person is committing an offence under this section may arrest him without a warrant.

Part III

(9) This section does not apply—

(a) in England and Wales, to a gathering licensed by an entertainment licence; or

(b) [Scotland]

(10) In this section—

"entertainment licence" means a licence granted by a local authority under—

(a) Schedule 12 to the *London Government Act* 1963;

(b) section 3 of the *Private Places of Entertainment (Licensing) Act* 1967; or

(c) Schedule 1 to the *Local Government (Miscellaneous Provisions) Act* 1982;

"exempt person", in relation to land (or any gathering on land), means the occupier, any member of his family and any employee or agent of his and any person whose home is situated on the land;

"land in the open air" includes a place partly open to the air;

"local authority" means—

(a) in Greater London, a London borough council or the Common Council of the City of London;

(b) in England outside Greater London, a district council or the council of the Isles of Scilly;

(c) in Wales, a county council or county borough council; and

"occupier", "trespasser" and "vehicle" have the same meaning as in section 61.

(11) Until 1st April 1996, in this section "local authority" means, in Wales, a district council.

(2) Allocation

16–236 This offence is triable summarily: *CJPOA* 1994, s.63(6).

(3) Elements of the offence

16–237 The prosecution must prove that:

— the relevant gathering is one to which section 63(1) applies,

— the defendant knew that a police direction to leave had been issued to him, and

— he failed to leave the land as soon as was reasonably practicable or,

— he left the land, and then re-entered as a trespasser within a period of seven days from the date on which the direction to leave was given.

A direction under s.63(2) may be communicated by any constable at the scene (s.63(3)) and persons shall be treated as having had a direction under subs (2) above communicated to them if reasonable steps have been taken to bring it to their attention (s.63(4)).

Section 63(5) establishes that a direction given under subs (2) will not apply to an "exempt person". Such a person is defined by s.63(10) as "the occupier, any member of his family and any employee or agent of his and any person whose home is situated on the land." By s.63(9) the section does not apply to a gathering licensed by an entertainment licence.

(4) Defence

16–238 A person will also have a defence if he can establish that he had a reasonable excuse for failing to leave the land as soon as reasonably practicable or, as the case may be, for again entering the land: s.63(7).

(5) Sentence

16–239 The maximum penalty is imprisonment for a term not exceeding three months or a fine not exceeding level four on the standard scale or both: *CJPOA* 1994, s.63(6).

A forfeiture order may be imposed under s.66(1) of the 1994 Act where a person has been convicted of this offence and the court is satisfied that sound equipment which has been seized from him under s.64(4) or which was in his possession or under his control at the relevant time, has been used at the gathering.

I. UNAUTHORISED CAMPERS: FAILURE TO LEAVE OR RETURNING TO THE LAND

(1) Definition

Criminal Justice and Public Order Act 1994, s.77

Power of local authority to direct unauthorised campers to leave land

77.—(1) If it appears to a local authority that persons are for the time being residing in a vehicle or vehicles within that authority's area— **16–240**

(a) on any land forming part of a highway;

(b) on any other unoccupied land; or

(c) on any occupied land without the consent of the occupier,

the authority may give a direction that those persons and any others with them are to leave the land and remove the vehicle or vehicles and any other property they have with them on the land.

(2) Notice of a direction under subsection (1) must be served on the persons to whom the direction applies, but it shall be sufficient for this purpose for the direction to specify the land and (except where the direction applies to only one person) to be addressed to all occupants of the vehicles on the land, without naming them.

(3) If a person knowing that a direction under subsection (1) above has been given which applies to him—

(a) fails, as soon as practicable, to leave the land or remove from the land any vehicle or other property which is the subject of the direction, or

(b) having removed any such vehicle or property again enters the land with a vehicle within the period of three months beginning with the day on which the direction was given,

he commits an offence and is liable on summary conviction to a fine not exceeding level 3 on the standard scale.

(4) A direction under subsection (1) operates to require persons who re-enter the land within the said period with vehicles or other property to leave and remove the vehicles or other property as it operates in relation to the persons and vehicles or other property on the land when the direction was given.

(5) In proceedings for an offence under this section it is a defence for the accused to show that his failure to leave or to remove the vehicle or other property as soon as practicable or his re-entry with a vehicle was due to illness, mechanical breakdown or other immediate emergency.

(6) In this section—

"land" means land in the open air;

"local authority" means—

(a) in Greater London, a London borough or the Common Council of the City of London;

(b) in England outside Greater London, a county council, a district council or the Council of the Isles of Scilly;

(c) in Wales, a county council or a county borough council;

"occupier" means the person entitled to possession of the land by virtue of an estate or interest held by him;

"vehicle" includes—

(a) any vehicle, whether or not it is in a fit state for use on roads, and includes any body, with or without wheels, appearing to have formed part of such a vehicle, and any load carried by, and anything attached to, such a vehicle; and

(b) a caravan as defined in section 29(1) of the *Caravan Sites and Control of Development Act* 1960;

and a person may be regarded for the purposes of this section as residing on any land notwithstanding that he has a home elsewhere.

(7) Until 1st April 1996, in this section "local authority" means, in Wales, a county council or a district council.

(2) Allocation

This offence is triable summarily only: *CJPOA* 1994, s.77(3). **16–241**

Part III

(3) Elements of the offence

16–242 The prosecution must prove that:

- — the local council issued a direction to leave the land to the defendant and,
- — the defendant failed to leave the land, or remove any vehicle from the land that formed the subject matter of the local council's direction as soon as was reasonably practicable, or
- — the defendant had removed any relevant vehicle or property and then re-entered the land within a period of three months beginning at the date at which the direction was given.

A direction to leave the land must be given before the offence can be committed: *CJPOA* 1994, s.77(1).

(4) Defence

16–243 The accused will have a defence if he can establish that his failure to leave or to remove the vehicle or other property as soon as practicable or his re-entry with a vehicle was due to illness, mechanical breakdown or other immediate emergency: s.77(5).

(5) Sentence

16–244 The maximum penalty is a fine not exceeding level three on the standard scale: *CJPOA* 1994, s.77(3).

J. TRESPASSING WITH FIREARM IN BUILDING OR ON LAND

(1) Definition

Firearms Act 1968, s.20(1), (2)

Trespassing with firearm

16–245 **20.**—(1) A person commits an offence if, while he has a firearm or imitation firearm with him, he enters or is in any building or part of a building as a trespasser and without reasonable excuse (the proof whereof lies on him).

(2) A person commits an offence if, while he has a firearm with him, he enters or is on any land as a trespasser and without reasonable excuse (the proof whereof lies on him).

[This section is printed as amended by the *Firearms (Amendment) Act* 1994, s.2.]

(2) Allocation

16–246 The offence of trespassing with a firearm in a building is triable either way, unless the weapon concerned is an air weapon or an imitation firearm, in which case the offence is summary only. The mode of trial for trespassing on any land with a firearm is summary only.

(3) Elements of the offence

16–247 The prosecution must prove that:

- — the defendant entered any building, part of a building or land as a trespasser and without reasonable excuse and,
- — was carrying a firearm or imitation forearm with him.

The term "firearm" is defined in section 57 of the *Firearms Act* 1968 as a lethal barrelled weapon of any description from which any shot, bullet or other missile can be discharged, and includes:

(a) any prohibited weapon, whether it is such a lethal weapon as aforesaid or not; and

(b) any component part of such a lethal or prohibited weapon; and

(c) any accessory to any such weapon designed or adapted to diminish the noise or flash caused by firing the weapon.

The *Firearms Act* 1968, s.20(3) defines "land" as including land covered by water. The offender must be proved to have the firearm with him, which denotes more than mere possession, and involves a very close physical link and a degree of immediate control over the weapon by the man alleged to have the firearm with him: *Kelt* [1977] 3 All E.R. 1099, CA. **16–248**

(4) Sentence

When tried summarily, the offence of trespassing in a building with a firearm is punishable by a term of imprisonment not exceeding six months or a fine not exceeding the prescribed sum or both. The offence of trespassing with a firearm on any land is punishable with a term of imprisonment not exceeding three months and a fine not exceeding level four on the standard scale. Note that, on commencement of the relevant provisions, the maximum custodial sentence in a magistrates' court will be 12 months' imprisonment: *Criminal Justice Act* 2003, ss.154 and 282. **16–249**

K. TRESPASSING WITH WEAPONS OF OFFENCE

(1) Definition

Criminal Law Act 1977, s.8(1)

Trespassing with a weapon of offence

8.—(1) A person who is on any premises as a trespasser, after having entered as such, is guilty of an offence if, without lawful authority or reasonable excuse, he has with him on the premises any weapon of offence. **16–250**

(2) Allocation

This offence is triable summarily: *CLA* 1977, s.8(3). **16–251**

(3) Elements of the offence

The prosecution must prove that: **16–252**

— the defendant entered and was present on any premises as a trespasser and

— without any lawful authority or reasonable excuse, he had with him on the premises any weapon of offence.

The term "premises" bears the same meaning as it does in *Criminal Law Act* 1977, s.12.

Section 8(2) defines "weapon of offence" as any article made or adapted for causing injury to or incapacitating a person, or intended by the person having it with him for such use.

(4) Sentence

The maximum penalty for this offence is six months' imprisonment, a fine not exceeding level 5 on the standard scale or both: *CLA* 1977, s.8(3). Note that, on commencement of the relevant provisions, the maximum custodial sentence in a magistrates' court will be 12 months' imprisonment: *Criminal Justice Act* 2003, ss.154 and 282. **16–253**

L. OBSTRUCTION OF COURT OFFICERS EXECUTING PROCESS AGAINST UNAUTHORISED OCCUPIERS

(1) Definition

Criminal Law Act 1977, s.10(1)–(3)

Obstruction of enforcement officers and court officers executing High Court or county court process

16–254 **10.**—(1) Without prejudice to section 8(2) of the *Sheriffs Act* 1887 but subject to the following provisions of this section, a person is guilty of an offence if he resists or intentionally obstructs any person who is in fact an officer of a court engaged in executing any process issued by the High Court or by any county court for the purpose of enforcing any judgment or order for the recovery of any premises or for the delivery of possession of any premises.

(2) Subsection (1) above does not apply unless the judgment or order in question was given or made in proceedings brought under any provisions of rules of court applicable only in circumstances where the person claiming possession of any premises alleges that the premises in question are occupied solely by a person or persons (not being a tenant or tenants holding over after the termination of the tenancy) who entered into or remained in occupation of the premises without the licence or consent of the person claiming possession or any predecessor in title of his.

(3) In any proceedings for an offence under this section it shall be a defence for the accused to prove that he believed that the person he was resisting or obstructing was not an officer of a court.

(2) Allocation

16–255 This offence is triable summarily: *CLA* 1977, s.10(4).

(3) Elements of the offence

16–256 The prosecution must prove that:

— the defendant resisted, or intentionally obstructed any officer of the court who,

— was executing any process for the purpose of enforcing any judgement or order for the recovery of premises or the delivery of possession of any premises.

An "officer of the court" is defined as any sheriff, under sheriff, deputy sheriff, bailiff or officer of a sheriff and any bailiff or other person who is an officer of a county court within the meaning of the *County Courts Act* 1959, s.10(6).

For the definition of "premises" see *Criminal Law Act* 1977, s.12.

(4) Defence

16–257 The accused will have a defence if he can prove that he believed that the person he was restricting or obstructing was not an officer of the court: s.10(3).

(5) Sentence

16–258 The maximum penalty for this offence is imprisonment for a term not exceeding six months, a fine not exceeding level five on the standard scale, or both: *CLA* 1977, s.10(4).

Note that, on commencement of the relevant provisions, the maximum custodial sentence in a magistrates' court will be 12 months' imprisonment: *Criminal Justice Act* 2003, ss.154 and 282.

M. Public Order and Conduct in Public Places

(1) Definition

Serious Organised Crime and Police Act 2005, s.128

Offence of trespassing on a designated site

128.—(1) A person commits an offence if he enters, or is on, any designated site in England and Wales or Northern Ireland as a trespasser. **16–259**

(2) A "designated site" means a site—

(a) specified or described (in any way) in an order made by the Secretary of State, and

(b) designated for the purposes of this section by the order.

(3) The Secretary of State may only designate a site for the purposes of this section—

(a) it is comprised in Crown land; or

(b) it is comprised in land belonging to Her Majesty in Her private capacity or to the immediate heir to the Throne in his private capacity; or

(c) it appears to the Secretary of State that it is appropriate to designate the site in the interests of national security.

(4) It is a defence for a person charged with an offence under this section to prove that he did not know, and had no reasonable cause to suspect, that the site in relation to which the offence is alleged to have been committed was a designated site.

(5) […]

(6) […]

(7) For the purposes of this section a person who is on any designated site as a trespasser does not cease to be a trespasser by virtue of being allowed time to leave the site.

(8) In this section—

(a) "site" means the whole or part of any building or buildings, or any land, or both;

(b) "Crown land" means land in which there is a Crown interest or a Duchy interest.

(9) For this purpose—

"Crown interest" means an interest belonging to Her Majesty in right of the Crown, and

"Duchy interest" means an interest belonging to Her Majesty in right of the Duchy of Lancaster or belonging to the Duchy of Cornwall.

(2) Allocation

No proceedings for an offence under this section may be instituted against any person, except by or with the consent of the Attorney General. **16–260**

(3) Sentence

A person guilty of an offence under s.128 is liable on summary conviction to imprisonment for a term not exceeding 51 weeks, or to a fine not exceeding level 5 on the standard scale, or to both. **16–261**

V. MISCELLANEOUS OFFENCES

A. Drunk and Disorderly

(1) Definition

Criminal Justice Act 1967, s.91(1)

Drunkenness in a public place

91.—(1) Any person who in any public place is guilty, while drunk, of disorderly behaviour shall be liable on summary conviction to a fine not exceeding level 3 on the standard scale. **16–262**

The words "may be arrested without warrant by any person" were removed from

Part III

this section by Sched. 17(2) of the *Serious Organised Crime and Police Act* 2005 (from January 1, 2006).

(2) Allocation

16–263 This offence is triable summarily: s.91(1).

The words "may be arrested without warrant by any person" were removed from this section by Sched. 17(2) of the *Serious Organised Crime and Police Act* 2005 (from January 1, 2006).

(3) Elements of the offence

16–264 The prosecution must prove that:

— the defendant was found in a public place whilst drunk and,

— behaving in a disorderly fashion.

"Drunk"

16–265 "Drunk" means the voluntary consumption of intoxicating liquor to an extent which affects steady self-control. It does not apply to a person who is disorderly as a result of sniffing glue: *Neale v. RMJE (a minor)* (1985) 80 Cr.App.R. 20. See also *Carroll v. DPP* , 173 J.P. 285, DC.

"Disorderly"

16–266 The words "disorderly behaviour" should be given their ordinary meaning. Whether a defendant is guilty of such behaviour is a simple question of fact. There is no requirement of *mens rea* at all. What is required is proof that, viewed objectively, the defendant was guilty of disorderly behaviour: *Carroll v. DPP* , 173 J.P. 285, DC. In *H.v. DPP* [2005] EWHC 2459 it was held that an offence under s.91(1) consisted not of being drunk but of being disorderly whilst drunk. It was the disorderly behaviour that entitled police to arrest an individual without a warrant. In the instant case H had committed no disorderly conduct until after his arrest which was unjustified, accordingly no offence under s.91(1) had occurred (but note the amendment to the Act from January 1, 2006).

"Public Place"

16–267 "Public place" includes any highway and any other premises or place which at the material time the public have or are permitted to have access, whether on payment or otherwise: s.91(4). The common parts of a block of flats, access to which is controlled so as to restrict entry to residents, their visitors and tradesmen and others who were there in a private capacity, not as members of the general public, will not be a public place: *Williams v. DPP* (1992) 156 J.P. 804.

(4) Sentence

16–268 The maximum penalty is a fine not exceeding level three on standard scale: s.91(1). See the *Magistrates' Court Sentencing Guidelines* (2008).

STARTING POINT AND RANGE OF SENTENCE
(BASED ON A FIRST TIME OFFENDER PLEADING NOT GUILTY)

Examples of nature of activity	**Starting Point**	**Range**
Shouting, causing disturbance for some minutes	Band A fine	Conditional discharge to Band B fine
Substantial disturbance Caused	Band B fine	Band A fine to Band C fine

AGGRAVATING AND MITIGATING FACTORS

Factors indicating higher culpability	**Factors indicating lower culpability**
1. Offensive words or behaviour involved 2. Lengthy incident 3. Group action	1. Minor and non-threatening 2. Stopped as soon as police arrived
Factors indicating greater degree of harm	
1. Offence committed at school, hospital or other place where vulnerable persons may be present 2. Offence committed on public transport 3. Victim providing public service	

B. BOMB HOAXES

(1) Definition

Criminal Law Act 1977, s.51

Bomb hoaxes

51.—(1) A person who— **16–269**

(a) places any article in any place whatever; or

(b) dispatches any article by post, rail or any other means whatever of sending things from one place to another,

with the intention (in either case) of inducing in some other person a belief that it is likely to explode or ignite and thereby cause personal injury or damage to property is guilty of an offence.

In this subsection "article" includes substance.

(2) A person who communicates any information which he knows or believes to be false to another person with the intention of inducing in him or any other person a false belief that a bomb or other thing liable to explode or ignite is present in any place or location whatever is guilty of an offence.

(3) For a person to be guilty of an offence under subsection (1) or (2) above it is not necessary for him to have any particular person in mind as the person in whom he intends to induce the belief mentioned in that subsection.

(4) A person guilty of an offence under this section shall be liable—

(a) on summary conviction, to imprisonment for a term not exceeding six months or to a fine not exceeding £1,000, or both;

(b) on conviction on indictment, to imprisonment for a term not exceeding seven years.

(2) Allocation

16–270 This offence is triable either way.

(3) Elements of the offence

16–271 The prosecution must prove that:

— the defendant placed any article in any place, or dispatched any article by post, rail or other means of sending things from one place to another and

— he intended to induce a belief in some person that such thing is likely to explode or ignite, thereby causing personal injury or damage to property OR

— the defendant communicated any information that he knows or believes to be false to another person and

— he intended to induce in that, or any other person, a false belief that a bomb or other thing liable to explode or ignite is present in any place or location.

The words "There is a bomb" said to the operator on a 999 call were sufficient to give rise to an offence under s.51(2), a person communicating the false information does not need to specify a "place or location": *Webb, The Times,* June 19, 1995, CA.

(4) Sentence

16–272 When tried summarily, the maximum penalty for this offence is imprisonment for a term not exceeding six months, or a fine not exceeding £1000 or both: s.51(4)(a). Note that, on commencement of the relevant provisions, the maximum custodial sentence in a magistrates' court will be 12 months' imprisonment: *Criminal Justice Act* 2003, ss.154 and 282.

The public and the emergency services need protection from those who potentially cause fear and disruption by bomb hoaxes. Deterrence is of critical importance and it will, accordingly, be rare, if ever, for such an offence to be met with a non-custodial sentence, regardless of personal mitigation: *Philipson* [2008] 2 Cr.App.R.(S.) 110, CA.

C. USE OF NOXIOUS SUBSTANCE OR THINGS TO CAUSE HARM AND INTIMIDATE

(1) Definition

Anti-Terrorism, Crime and Security Act 2001, s.113

Use of noxious substances or things to cause harm and intimidate

16–273 **113.**—(1) A person who takes any action which—

(a) involves the use of a noxious substance or other noxious thing;

(b) has or is likely to have an effect falling within subsection (2); and

(c) is designed to influence the government or to intimidate the public or a section of the public,

is guilty of an offence.

(2) Action has an effect falling within this subsection if it—

(a) causes serious violence against a person anywhere in the world;

(b) causes serious damage to real or personal property anywhere in the world;

(c) endangers human life or creates a serious risk to the health or safety of the public or a section of the public; or

(d) induces in members of the public the fear that the action is likely to endanger their lives or create a serious risk to their health or safety;

but any effect on the person taking the action is to be disregarded.

(3) A person who—

(a) makes a threat that he or another will take any action which constitutes an offence under subsection (1); and

(b) intends thereby to induce in a person anywhere in the world the fear that the threat is likely to be carried out,

is guilty of an offence.

(4) A person guilty of an offence under this section is liable—

(a) on summary conviction, to imprisonment for a term not exceeding six months or a fine not exceeding the statutory maximum (or both); and

(b) on conviction on indictment, to imprisonment for a term not exceeding fourteen years or a fine (or both).

(5) In this section—

"the government" means the government of the United Kingdom, of a part of the United Kingdom or of a country other than the United Kingdom; and

"the public" includes the public of a country other than the United Kingdom.

(2) Allocation

This offence is triable either way. **16–274**

(3) Elements of the offence

Substance includes any biological agent and any other natural or artificial substance (whatever its form, origin or method of production): s.115(1). **16–275**

For a person to be guilty of this offence, it is not necessary for him to have any particular person in mind as the person in whom he intends to induce the belief in question: s.115(2).

(4) Sentence

When tried summarily, the maximum penalty for this offence is imprisonment for a term not exceeding six months, or a fine not exceeding £1000 or both: s.113(4). Note that, on commencement of the relevant provisions, the maximum custodial sentence in a magistrates' court will be 12 months' imprisonment: *Criminal Justice Act* 2003, ss.154 and 282. **16–276**

D. HOAXES INVOLVING NOXIOUS SUBSTANCES OR THINGS

(1) Definition

Anti-Terrorism, Crime and Security Act 2001, s.114

Hoaxes involving noxious substances or things

114.—(1) A person is guilty of an offence if he— **16–277**

(a) places any substance or other thing in any place; or

(b) sends any substance or other thing from one place to another (by post, rail or any other means whatever);

with the intention of inducing in a person anywhere in the world a belief that it is likely to be (or contain) a noxious substance or other noxious thing and thereby endanger human life or create a serious risk to human health.

(2) A person is guilty of an offence if he communicates any information which he knows

or believes to be false with the intention of inducing in a person anywhere in the world a belief that a noxious substance or other noxious thing is likely to be present (whether at the time the information is communicated or later) in any place and thereby endanger human life or create a serious risk to human health.

(3) A person guilty of an offence under this section is liable—

(a) on summary conviction, to imprisonment for a term not exceeding six months or a fine not exceeding the statutory maximum (or both); and

(b) on conviction on indictment, to imprisonment for a term not exceeding seven years or a fine (or both).

(2) Allocation

16–278 This offence is triable either way.

(3) Elements of the offence

16–279 Substance includes any biological agent and any other natural or artificial substance (whatever its form, origin or method of production): see s.115(1).

For a person to be guilty of this offence, it is not necessary for him to have any particular person in mind as the person in whom he intends to induce the belief in question: s.115(2).

(4) Sentence

16–280 When tried summarily, the maximum penalty for this offence is imprisonment for a term not exceeding six months, or a fine not exceeding £1000 or both: s.114(3). Note that, on commencement of the relevant provisions, the maximum custodial sentence in a magistrates' court will be 12 months' imprisonment: *Criminal Justice Act* 2003, ss.154 and 282.

E. INFORMATION ABOUT ACTS OF TERRORISM

(1) Definition

Terrorism Act 2000, s.38B

Information about acts of terrorism

16–281 **38B.**—(1) This section applies where a person has information which he knows or believes might be of material assistance—

(a) in preventing the commission by another person of an act of terrorism, or

(b) in securing the apprehension, prosecution or conviction of another person, in the United Kingdom, for an offence involving the commission, preparation or instigation of an act of terrorism.

(2) The person commits an offence if he does not disclose the information as soon as reasonably practicable in accordance with subsection (3).

(3) Disclosure is in accordance with this subsection if it is made—

(a) in England and Wales, to a constable,

(b) in Scotland, to a constable, or

(c) in Northern Ireland, to a constable or a member of Her Majesty's forces.

(4) It is a defence for a person charged with an offence under subsection (2) to prove that he had a reasonable excuse for not making the disclosure.

(5) A person guilty of an offence under this section shall be liable—

(a) on conviction on indictment, to imprisonment for a term not exceeding five years, or to a fine or to both, or

(b) on summary conviction, to imprisonment for a term not exceeding six months, or to a fine not exceeding the statutory maximum or to both.

(6) Proceedings for an offence under this section may be taken, and the offence may for the purposes of those proceedings be treated as having been committed, in any place where the person to be charged is or has at any time been since he first knew or believed

that the information might be of material assistance as mentioned in subsection (1).

While it is not sufficient for the prosecution to prove that the defendant closed his eyes to the obvious, evidence that he did so because he did not wish to be told the truth is capable of supporting the conclusion that he did either know or believe that information might be of material assistance to the authorities: *Sherif, Mohammed, Abdurahman and Abdullhai, The Times*, February 11, 2009, CA.

(2) Allocation

This offence is triable either way. **16–282**

(3) Sentence

When tried summarily, the maximum penalty for this offence is imprisonment for a term not exceeding six months, or a fine not exceeding £1000 or both: s.38B(5). Note that, on commencement of the relevant provisions, the maximum custodial sentence in a magistrates' court will be 12 months' imprisonment: *Criminal Justice Act* 2003, ss.154 and 282. **16–283**

F. INTIMIDATION OR ANNOYANCE BY VIOLENCE OR OTHERWISE

(1) Definition

Trade Union and Labour Relations (Consolidation) Act 1992, s.241

Intimidation or annoyance by violence or otherwise

241.—(1) A person commits an offence who, with a view to compelling another person to abstain from doing or to do any act which that person has a legal right to do or abstain from doing, wrongfully and without legal authority— **16–284**

(a) uses violence to or intimidates that person or his wife or children, or injures his property,
(b) persistently follows that person about from place to place,
(c) hides any tools, clothes or other property owned or used by that person, or deprives him of or hinders him in the use thereof,
(d) watches or besets the house or other place where that person resides, works, carries on business or happens to be, or the approach to any such house or place, or
(e) follows that person with two or more other persons in a disorderly manner in or through any street or road.

(2) A person guilty of an offence under this section is liable on summary conviction to imprisonment for a term not exceeding six months or a fine not exceeding level 5 on the standard scale, or both.

(3) A constable may arrest without warrant anyone he reasonably suspects is committing an offence under this section.

(2) Allocation

This offence is triable summarily: s.241(2). **16–285**

(3) Elements of the offence

The prosecution must prove that: **16–286**

— the defendant used violence towards, or intimidated, another person, that person's wife or that person's children or the defendant injured that person's property, or
— the defendant wrongfully and without legal authority, persistently followed another person about from place to place, or
— the defendant wrongfully and without legal authority, hid any tools, clothes or other property owned or used by another person or deprived him or hindered him in the use of such items, or

— the defendant wrongfully and without legal authority, watched or beset the house or other place where another person resides, works, carries on business or happens to be, or watched or beset the approach of any such house or place, or

— the defendant wrongfully and without legal authority, followed another person with two or more persons in a disorderly manner in or through any street or road, with

— a view to compelling that other person to abstain from doing or to do any act which that person has a legal right to do or abstain from doing.

Application to peaceful picketing:

Trade Union and Labour Relations (Consolidation) Act 1992, s.220

Peaceful picketing

16–287 **220.**—(1) It is lawful for a person in contemplation or furtherance of a trade dispute to attend—

(a) at or near his own place of work, or

(b) if he is an official of a trade union, at or near the place of work of a member of the union whom he is accompanying and whom he represents,

for the purpose only of peacefully obtaining or communicating information, or peacefully persuading any person to work or abstain from working.

(2) If a person works or normally works—

(a) otherwise than at any one place, or

(b) at a place the location of which is such that attendance there for a purpose mentioned in subsection (1) is impracticable,

his place of work for the purposes of that subsection shall be any premises of his employer from which he works or from which his work is administered.

(3) In the case of a worker not in employment where—

(a) his last employment was terminated in connection with a trade dispute, or

(b) the termination of his employment was one of the circumstances giving rise to a trade dispute,

in relation to that dispute his former place of work shall be treated for the purposes of subsection (1) as being his place of work.

(4) A person who is an official of a trade union by virtue only of having been elected or appointed to be a representative of some of the members of the union shall be regarded for the purposes of subsection (1) as representing only those members; but otherwise an official of a union shall be regarded for those purposes as representing all its members.

16–288 Section 241 may also be applied to the actions of an anti-roads protester: *Todd v. DPP* [1996] Crim.L.R. 344.

(4) Sentence

16–289 The maximum penalty is six months' imprisonment, a fine not exceeding level five on the standard scale or both: s.241(2). Note that, on commencement of the relevant provisions, the maximum custodial sentence in a magistrates' court will be 12 months' imprisonment: *Criminal Justice Act* 2003, ss.154 and 282.

G. PUBLIC NUISANCE

16–290 Public nuisance is an offence at common law, triable either way. When tried summarily, the statutory maxima apply as regards sentencing: see *Magistrates' Courts Act* 1980, s.17(1) and Sched. 1.

A person is guilty of a public nuisance when he (a) does an act not warranted by law, or (b) omits to discharge a legal duty, if the effect of the act or omission is to endanger the life, health, property, morals or comfort of the public, or to obstruct the public in the exercise or enjoyment of rights common to all Her Majesty's subjects: *Stephen's Digest of the Criminal Law* (9th edn, 1900), p.184, definition approved in *Shorrock* [1994] Q.B. 279.

The question of how widely spread a nuisance must be for it to qualify as a public nuisance was addressed in *Att.-Gen. v. PYA Quarries Ltd* [1957] 2 Q.B. 169, CA where it was held that the question whether the local community within the sphere of a neighbourhood comprised a sufficient number of persons to constitute a class of the public was a question of fact in every case.

The mens rea of the offence will be established if the prosecution can show that the defendant knew or ought to have known that as a result of his action, a public nuisance would be committed: *Shorrock* [1994] Q.B. 279, 98 Cr.App.R. 67, CA. In *Goldstein* [2004] 1 Cr.App.R. 27, the CA held that the common law offence of causing a public nuisance had survived the *Human Rights Act* 1998 and was not in breach of arts 7, 8 or 10 of the European Convention on Human Rights since the common law was sufficiently clear to enable a person, with legal advice if necessary, to foresee the consequences that his action might entail and to regulate his behaviour accordingly. **16–291**

H. Breach of the Peace and Powers to bind over

(1) General

Public Order Act 1986, s.40(4)

Amendments, repeals and savings

40.—(4) Nothing in this Act affects the common law powers in England and Wales to deal with or prevent a breach of the peace. **16–292**

In *Howell* [1982] Q.B. 416 it was held that there is a breach of the peace whenever harm is actually done or is likely to be done to a person or in his presence to his property or a person is in fear of being so harmed through an assault, an affray, a riot, unlawful assembly or other disturbance. **16–293**

Part III

(2) Binding over to keep the peace

The magistrates may bind over a person to keep the peace following a complaint (*MCA* 1980, s.115) or by the court's own motion under common law and statutory powers, notably the *Justices of the Peace Act* 1361. **16–294**

When the court is acting of its own motion, it may make a binding over order at any time before the conclusion of criminal proceedings, on withdrawal of the case by the prosecution, on a decision by the prosecution to offer no evidence, on an adjournment, or upon acquittal of the defendant, where the magistrate considers that there might be a breach of the peace in the future.

The person bound over is required to enter into a recognizance in an amount which will be forfeited if he fails to keep the peace for a specified period.

If the person fails, or refuses to enter into a recognisance the magistrates' may order imprisonment. This may be for a maximum of six months or until the person complies with the order: *MCA* 1980, s.115(3). The *PCC(S)A* 2000, s.89 provides that imprisonment cannot be imposed on a person under the age of 21. A person between 18 and 20 who refuses to consent to be bound over may be detained under section 108 of the *PCC(S)A* 2000. A person under the age of 18 may be detained at an attendance centre.

The *PCC(S)A* 2000, s.139(1) establishes the relevant penalties for non-compliance with the terms of the binding over order. The court may forfeit the whole or part of the recognisance in its discretion, allow payment, direct time for payment, direct payment by instalments or reduce or discharge the recognisance. It is not allowed to impose a prison term.

In the magistrates' court, a recognisance can only be declared to be forfeit following an order on complaint: *MCA* 1980, s.20, by virtue of whichever power the bind over was originally imposed.

In *R. (Laporte) v. Chief Constable of Gloucestershire Constabulary* [2004] EWCA Civ 1639 the question arose as to whether the police action [escorting the buses of anti-war protesters back to London] was justifiable as falling within the ambit of action reasonably taken to prevent a breach of the peace:

> ... If the action on the present facts were to be regarded as justified, this would constitute a significant extension of the previously established principles. It would be a development that is more of a leap and a bound than a measured pace forward.
>
> The Defendant contends that all that was involved was requiring the passengers to make the return journey earlier than they would have done otherwise. This description of what was involved in our judgment underestimates the impact of the police action on the passengers' individual rights to freedom of action. We do not consider it necessary to decide that it would never be justifiable for the police to take action of this nature. However, we are satisfied that such action should be very much a matter of last resort and we are not persuaded that there were no less intrusive possible alternative courses of action here.
>
> Thus, it is not suggested in the evidence that the drivers of the coaches, who were professional drivers, had indicated that they were not prepared to obey a lawful order given by the police. They could, in our judgment, have been lawfully ordered not to proceed to the airbase and to leave the area. The coaches could have been followed if this was thought necessary to see whether the order was obeyed. The order could have been backed up by a warning that, if it was not observed, the police would exercise the powers of arrest which would then be available. ... Like the Administrative Court, we regard the actions that did take place as disproportionate and not justifiable at common law ...
>
> In these circumstances ..., we propose to accede to the submissions of the interested police parties that we should not determine further the application of Article 5 to what happened. We leave this to be decided on the facts of the pending case concerning policing of May Day 2001 in which the issue, we understand, will have to be confronted. In our judgment the appeal can be dismissed on the evidence without any further examination of either domestic or ECHR law (paras 53–56).

See also Pt IV on Sentencing.

(3) Demonstrations in vicinity of Parliament

(a) *Definition*

16–295 Sections 132–138 of the *Serious Organised Crime and Police Act* 2005 create new offences in relation to demonstrations in the vicinity of Parliament.

Serious Organised Crime and Police Act 2005, ss.132, 134(7), 135(3)

Demonstrating without authorisation in designated area.

16–296 **132.**—(1) Any person who—

(a) organises a demonstration in a public place in the designated area, or

(b) takes part in a demonstration in a public place in the designated area, or

(c) carries on a demonstration by himself in a public place in the designated area, is guilty of an offence if, when the demonstration starts, authorisation for the demonstration has not been given under section 134(2).

(2) It is a defence for a person accused of an offence under subsection (1) to show that he reasonably believed that authorisation had been given.

(3) Subsection (1) does not apply if the demonstration is—

(a) a public procession of which notice is required to be given under subsection (1) of section 11 of the *Public Order Act* 1986 (c. 64), or of which (by virtue of subsection (2) of that section) notice is not required to be given, or

(b) a public procession for the purposes of section 12 or 13 of that Act.

(4) Subsection (1) also does not apply in relation to any conduct which is lawful under section 220 of the *Trade Union and Labour Relations (Consolidation) Act* 1992 (c. 52).

(5) If subsection (1) does not apply by virtue of subsection (3) or (4), nothing in sections 133 to 136 applies either.

(6) Section 14 of the *Public Order Act* 1986 (imposition of conditions on public assemblies) does not apply in relation to a public assembly which is also a demonstration in a public place in the designated area.

(7) In this section and in sections 133 to 136—

(a) "the designated area" means the area specified in an order under section 138,
(b) "public place" means any highway or any place to which at the material time the public or any section of the public has access, on payment or otherwise, as of right or by virtue of express or implied permission,
(c) references to any person organising a demonstration include a person participating in its organisation,
(d) references to any person organising a demonstration do not include a person carrying on a demonstration by himself,
(e) references to any person or persons taking part in a demonstration (except in subsection (1) of this section) include a person carrying on a demonstration by himself.

Authorisation of demonstrations in designated area

134.—(7) Each person who takes part in or organises a demonstration in the designated area is guilty of an offence if— **16–297**
(a) he knowingly fails to comply with a condition imposed under subsection (3) which is applicable to him (except where it is varied under section 135), or
(b) he knows or should have known that the demonstration is carried on otherwise than in accordance with the particulars set out in the authorisation by virtue of subsection (5).

Supplementary directions

135.—(3) A person taking part in or organising the demonstration who knowingly fails to comply with a condition which is applicable to him and which is imposed or varied by a direction under this section is guilty of an offence. **16–298**

(b) *Allocation*

These offences are summary only. In *R. (Haw) v. Secretary of State for the Home Department* [2005] EWHC 2061; the QBD (Admin) held by a majority that the Act as enacted did not apply to a continuing demonstration that had commenced before s.132(1) of the Act came into force on July 1, 2005. The *Serious Organised Crime and Police Act 2005 (Commencement No. 1, Transitional and Transitory Provisions) Order* 2005 extended the application of s.132(1) so as to criminalise conduct that was not so under the Act. As such the alteration made by the Order was in fact an amendment and ultra vires. It could not be said that Parliament intended the Act to catch continuing demonstrations. **16–299**

(c) *Sentence*

The penalties for offences under ss.132–135 are found in s.136: a person guilty of an offence under s.132(1)(a) is liable on summary conviction to imprisonment for a term not exceeding 51 weeks, to a fine not exceeding level 4 on the standard scale, or to both; a person guilty of an offence under s.132(1)(b) or (c) is liable on summary conviction to a fine not exceeding level 3 on the standard scale; a person guilty of an offence under ss.134(7) or 135(3) is liable on summary conviction— **16–300**
(a) if the offence was in relation to his capacity as organiser of the demonstration, to imprisonment for a term not exceeding 51 weeks, to a fine not exceeding level 4 on the standard scale, or to both,
(b) otherwise, to a fine not exceeding level 3 on the standard scale.

A person who is guilty of the offence of inciting another to—
(a) do anything which would constitute an offence mentioned in subsection (1), (2) or (3), or
(b) fail to do anything where the failure would constitute such an offence, is liable on summary conviction to imprisonment for a term not exceeding 51 weeks, to a fine not exceeding level 4 on the standard scale, or to both, notwithstanding s.45(3) of the *Magistrates' Courts Act* 1980.

Part III

I. RISK OF DISORDER

(1) Definition

Violent Crime Reduction Act 2006, s.27

Directions to individuals who represent a risk of disorder

16–301 **27**—(1) If the test in subsection (2) is satisfied in the case of an individual aged 16 or over who is in a public place, a constable in uniform may give a direction to that individual–

(a) requiring him to leave the locality of that place; and

(b) prohibiting the individual from returning to that locality for such period (not exceeding 48 hours) from the giving of the direction as the constable may specify.

(2) That test is–

(a) that the presence of the individual in that locality is likely, in all the circumstances, to cause or to contribute to the occurrence of alcoholrelated crime or disorder in that locality, or to cause or to contribute to a repetition or continuance there of such crime or disorder; and

(b) that the giving of a direction under this section to that individual is necessary for the purpose of removing or reducing the likelihood of there being such crime or disorder in that locality during the period for which the direction has effect or of there being a repetition or continuance in that locality during that period of such crime or disorder.

(3) A direction under this section–

(a) must be given in writing;

(b) may require the individual to whom it is given to leave the locality in question either immediately or by such time as the constable giving the direction may specify;

(c) must clearly identify the locality to which it relates;

(d) must specify the period for which the individual is prohibited from returning to that locality;

(e) may impose requirements as to the manner in which that individual leaves the locality, including his route; and

(f) may be withdrawn or varied (but not extended so as to apply for a period of more than 48 hours) by a constable.

(4) A constable may not give a direction under this section that prevents the individual to whom it is given–

(a) from having access to a place where he resides;

(b) from attending at any place which he is required to attend for the purposes of any employment of his or of any contract of services to which he is a party;

(c) from attending at any place which he is expected to attend during the period to which the direction applies for the purposes of education or training or for the purpose of receiving medical treatment; or

(d) from attending at any place which he is required to attend by any obligation imposed on him by or under an enactment or by the order of a court or tribunal.

(5) A constable who gives a direction under this section must make a record of–

(a) the terms of the direction and the locality to which it relates;

(b) the individual to whom it is given;

(c) the time at which it is given;

(d) the period during which that individual is required not to return to the locality.

(6) A person who fails to comply with a direction under this section is guilty of an offence and shall be liable, on summary conviction, to a fine not exceeding level 4 on the standard scale.

(7) In section 64A of the *Police and Criminal Evidence Act* 1984 (c. 60) (power to photograph suspects), in subsection (1B), after paragraph (c) insert–

"(ca) given a direction by a constable under section 27 of the *Violent Crime Reduction Act* 2006;".

(8) In this section "public place" means–

(a) a highway; or

(b) any place to which at the material time the public or any section of the public has access, on payment or otherwise, as of right or by virtue of express or implied permission;and for this purpose "place" includes a place on a means of transport.

[This section came into force on August 22, 2007 by virtue of the *Violent Crime Reduction Act 2006 (Commencement No. 3) Order* 2007 (S.I. 2007 No. 2180).]

(2) Allocation

Failure to comply with such a direction is a summary offence. **16–302**

(3) Sentence

The maximum penalty is a fine not exceeding level 4 on the standard scale. **16–303**

J. NUISANCE OR DISTURBANCE ON HOSPITAL PREMISES

(1) Definition

Criminal Justice and Immigration Act 2008, s.119

Offence of causing nuisance or disturbance on NHS premises

119.—(1) A person commits an offence if— **16–304**

(a) the person causes, without reasonable excuse and while on NHS premises, a nuisance or disturbance to an NHS staff member who is working there or is otherwise there in connection with work,

(b) the person refuses, without reasonable excuse, to leave the NHS premises when asked to do so by a constable or an NHS staff member, and

(c) the person is not on the NHS premises for the purpose of obtaining medical advice, treatment or care for himself or herself.

(2) A person who commits an offence under this section is liable on summary conviction to a fine not exceeding level 3 on the standard scale.

(3) For the purposes of this section—

(a) a person ceases to be on NHS premises for the purpose of obtaining medical advice, treatment or care for himself or herself once the person has received the advice, treatment or care, and

(b) a person is not on NHS premises for the purpose of obtaining medical advice, treatment or care for himself or herself if the person has been refused the advice, treatment or care during the last 8 hours.

(4) In this section—

"English NHS premises" means—

(a) any hospital vested in, or managed by, a relevant English NHS body,

(b) any building or other structure, or vehicle, associated with the hospital and situated on hospital grounds (whether or not vested in, or managed by, a relevant English NHS body), and

(c) the hospital grounds,

"hospital grounds" means land in the vicinity of a hospital and associated with it,

"NHS premises" means English NHS premises or Welsh NHS premises,

"NHS staff member" means a person employed by a relevant English NHS body, or a relevant Welsh NHS body, or otherwise working for such a body (whether as or on behalf of a contractor, as a volunteer or otherwise),

"relevant English NHS body" means—

(a) a National Health Service trust (see section 25 of the*National Health Service Act* 2006 (c. 41)), all or most of whose hospitals, establishments and facilities are situated in England,

(b) a Primary Care Trust (see section 18 of that Act), or (c) an NHS foundation trust (see section 30 of that Act),

(c) an NHS foundation trust (see section 30 of that Act),

"relevant Welsh NHS body" means—

(a) a National Health Service trust (see section 18 of the *National Health Service*

(Wales) Act 2006 (c. 42)), all or most of whose hospitals, establishments and facilities are situated in Wales, or

(b) a Local Health Board (see section 11 of that Act),

"vehicle" includes an air ambulance,

"Welsh NHS premises" means—

(a) any hospital vested in, or managed by, a relevant Welsh NHS body,

(b) any building or other structure, or vehicle, associated with the hospital and situated on hospital grounds (whether or not vested in, or managed by, a relevant Welsh NHS body), and

(c) the hospital grounds.

Power to remove person causing nuisance or disturbance

16–305 **120.**—(1) If a constable reasonably suspects that a person is committing or has committed an offence under section 119, the constable may remove the person from the NHS premises concerned.

(2) If an authorised officer reasonably suspects that a person is committing or has committed an offence under section 119, the authorised officer may—

(a) remove the person from the NHS premises concerned, or

(b) authorise an appropriate NHS staff member to do so.

(3) Any person removing another person from NHS premises under this section may use reasonable force (if necessary).

(4) An authorised officer cannot remove a person under this section or authorise another person to do so if the authorised officer has reason to believe that—

(a) the person to be removed requires medical advice, treatment or care for himself or herself, or

(b) the removal of the person would endanger the person's physical or mental health.

(5) In this section—

"appropriate NHS staff member"—

(a) in relation to English NHS premises, means an English NHS staff member, and

(b) in relation to Welsh NHS premises, means a Welsh NHS staff member,

"authorised officer"—

(a) in relation to English NHS premises, means any English NHS staff member authorised by a relevant English NHS body to exercise the powers which are conferred by this section on an authorised officer in respect of English NHS premises, and

(b) in relation to Welsh NHS premises, means any Welsh NHS staff member authorised by a relevant Welsh NHS body to exercise the powers which are conferred by this section on an authorised officer in respect of Welsh NHS premises,

"English NHS staff member" means a person employed by a relevant English NHS body or otherwise working for it (whether as or on behalf of a contractor, as a volunteer or otherwise),

"Welsh NHS staff member" means a person employed by a relevant Welsh NHS body or otherwise working for it (whether as or on behalf of a contractor, as a volunteer or otherwise).

(6) Terms defined in section 119 have the same meaning in this section as in that section.

(2) Allocation

16–306 This offence is triable summarily: s.119(2).

(3) Sentence

16–307 The maximum penalty is a fine not exceeding level 3 on the standard scale.

Chapter 17

ROAD TRAFFIC OFFENCES

I. DEFINITIONS

A. General

Throughout road traffic law, there are a number of words or phrases that recur and which have developed a specialist meaning. The key words that relate to offences covered by this work are set out, *post*, and the key principles that apply to the interpretation is described. For further information, reference should be made to *Wilkinson's Road Traffic Offences*, Ch.1. **17–1**

B. ACCIDENT

17–2 There is no statutory definition of this term in relation to road traffic offences. Although some judicial suggestions have been made, it is recognised that the word is one in common use and, when faced with the issue, a court should ask itself "Would an ordinary man in the circumstances of the case say there had been an accident?": *Chief Constable of West Midlands Police v. Billingham* [1979] R.T.R. 446.

It is clear that it can be the result of a deliberate act. In *Chief Constable of Staffordshire v. Lees* [1981] R.T.R. 506, a defendant deliberately drove at a gate and smashed it. This was a breath test case and the powers of the police constable depended on there having been an accident. The court considered that it would be wrong for those powers to be exercisable where something happened as a result of a careless act but not where there had been a deliberate act. In the civil case of *Charlton v. Fisher* [2001] EWCA Civ 112; [2001] R.T.R. 33, a car was deliberately driven into the rear of another stationary car and a person in that car was injured. In order to be able to claim successfully against the driver's insurance, the injured person had to show there had been an accident and the Court of Appeal considered that there had been.

It is also clear that there does not need to be any contact between vehicles. In the Scottish case of *Bremner v. Westwater* (1993) 1994 S.L.T. 707, the issue arose in the context of whether a notice of intended prosecution, see *post*, § 17–13, was needed. The defendant had driven erratically at night without lights. In overtaking another vehicle, he had caused an oncoming vehicle to brake sharply and drive onto the verge in order to avoid a collision and the overtaken vehicle also had to brake sharply. It was held that this could properly be described as an accident.

C. IN CHARGE OF

17–3 There is no statutory definition of this phrase which is very much a question of fact and degree. The leading case is *DPP v. Watkins* [1989] 2 W.L.R. 966 which identified two classes of cases which could be identified—those cases where the defendant was the owner or otherwise in lawful possession of the vehicle or had recently driven it and those cases where none of those descriptions applied. In the first situation, there would usually be an assumption that he was in charge unless he had given the charge of the vehicle to another person. However, if the defendant adduces sufficient evidence to show that there was no likelihood of him driving the vehicle whilst unfit, the prosecution must also prove that there was a real risk of him driving: *Road Traffic Act* 1988, ss.4(3) or 5(2). The House of Lords has held that, whilst this imposes a legal burden on the defendant, that is not oppressive. Even if the presumption of innocence is infringed, the provision was directed to a legitimate objective, did not go beyond what was necessary and reasonable and was not arbitrary. Accordingly, the provision did not contravene the European Convention on Human Rights: *Sheldrake v. DPP* [2005] 1 A.C. 264; [2005] R.T.R. 2. It is for the prosecution to prove that the defendant was in charge. If that is done, the defence may seek to assert that there was no likelihood of driving whilst unfit through drink or drugs or over the prescribed limit. The way that the statute is drafted has led to misunderstanding of who needs to prove what and in what order. The issue came before the Divisional Court again in *CPS v. Bate* [2004] EWHC 2811. The court had found no case to answer having concluded that the prosecution had to prove that he was in charge of the vehicle where the defendant had put forward reasons why he was in the vehicle. It was patently clear that the defendant was in charge of the vehicle but that he may well have been able to satisfy the court that there was no likelihood of him driving whilst over the limit. It seemed to the Divisional Court that the justices had confused the question of whether the defendant was in charge and whether the statutory defence was open to him. The statutory defence required the defendant to prove (on the balance of probabilities) that there was no likelihood of driving whilst he remained unfit. The justices concluded that the intention of the driver not to drive was sufficient to determine that he was not in charge but, as the Divisional Court stated, it is the likelihood of driving not the intention of the defendant that provides the defence.

The two may be closely related but they are not the same and it is for the defendant to satisfy the court that the defence has been made out.

It is not normally sufficient for the defence to focus on the intent of the driver. There would usually be other compelling circumstantial evidence or expert scientific evidence. In *CPS v. Thompson* [2007] EWHC 1841 Admin; [2008] R.T.R. 5, the defendant was well above the prescribed level and stated that he intended to drive when he felt "alright". He had no way of knowing when his blood/alcohol level would fall below the prescribed limit and there was no scientific evidence of when that point might have been reached. In those circumstances, the acquittal was overturned and the case was remitted to the justices for further consideration.

Where the defendant was not the owner or in lawful possession or had not recently driven the vehicle but was nonetheless sitting in the vehicle or otherwise involved in some way with it, the court will look to see if he was, in practice, voluntarily in control or in such a position that he might be expected to take control imminently—where the defendant was, what he was doing and what his intentions were would all be relevant.

In either class of case the court will need to consider where the defendant was in relation to the vehicle (and, if he was inside, where he was), what he was doing, whether he had a key that fitted the ignition, any evidence showing that the defendant intended to demonstrate his control of the vehicle (whether by driving or in some other way) and, finally, whether anyone else was in or near the vehicle and, if so, for what reason. An unusual application of this principle was seen in *DPP v. Janman* [2004] R.T.R. 31. A person was supervising a provisional licence holder. He had consumed sufficient alcohol to be over the limit and was prosecuted for being "in charge". Although there may be exceptional cases where a supervisor could demonstrate that there was no likelihood of driving the vehicle, that will be a very difficult task for the supervisor. It is of the essence of the role of a supervisor of a provisional licence holder that they must be prepared to intervene when necessary.

Another unusual situation arose in *Mason v. DPP* [2009] EWHC 2198; [2010] R.T.R. 11 (p. 120). The defendant had opened the door of his car when he was approached by a man with a knife who took the keys and the vehicle. On reporting this to the police, it was suspected that he had been drinking and analysis showed he was nearly twice the limit. He was charged both with attempting to drive and with being in charge. He was convicted of attempting to drive and the "in charge" offence was dismissed. On appeal, the conviction was overturned (since the act was not "more than merely preparatory" to committing the offence); however, the court and the defence accepted that the "in charge" offence would have been made out.

D. DRIVE/DRIVER

Almost inevitably, the plain meaning of these words has been stretched to ensure that **17–4**
culpable behaviour is properly brought within the remit of the various offences. That has been less necessary where an alternative of being "in charge" of a vehicle has been available.

The essence of driving is having control over the movement of the vehicle. Key elements can be drawn from the decisions in *MacDonagh* [1974] R.T.R. 372 and *Burgoyne v. Phillips* [1983] R.T.R. 49. This is a question of fact, needing to accord with the ordinary meaning of "driving". It will involve substantial control over the movement and direction of the vehicle. It will probably require the presence of the driver inside the vehicle, at least to some extent, so standing outside pushing the vehicle has not generally been found to be "driving". It may however be "using" or "attempting to drive". In *R. (Traves) v. DPP* [2005] EWHC 1482; (2005) 169 J.P. 421, the appellant was in the driver's seat of his own vehicle which was being towed by another vehicle. The justices accepted that he had been steering and using the brakes to slow the vehicle down for approximately three miles. The issue arose as to whether he was "driving". Upholding the justices' decision that this amounted to "driving", the Divisional Court cited with approval the statement in *Whitfield v. DPP* [1998] Crim.L.R. 349 that "The essence of

Part III

driving is the use of the driver's controls in order to direct the movement, however that movement is produced". Here, movement was produced by the vehicle being towed but the defendant's involvement in both steering and in controlling the movement through the use of the brakes was sufficient.

Issues have also arisen as to when driving stops as there will be times when a person is clearly driving a vehicle even though it is not in motion. Key principles were summarised in *Edkins v. Knowles* [1973] Q.B. 748. There will be interludes in a journey when the vehicle will stop and the questions to be asked will be concerning the purpose and length of the stop and whether the driver left the vehicle. If the journey is continuing and the stop of short duration or because of traffic congestion, then the driving will continue. If the journey has ended then, allowing for a short while to switch the engine off etc. the driving is likely to have come to an end. This may be particularly significant in prosecutions for using a hand held mobile telephone whilst driving. Whilst the purpose of creating the offence is one of road safety, there is no limitation of the definition of "drive" for that offence. However, it can be expected that prosecution will not follow where, although the driving continues, none the less there is no possible adverse effect on road safety, such as when a car is stationary at the roadside or stuck in traffic with no prospect of moving immediately.

17–5 More than one person may be driving the same vehicle. In *Tyler v. Whatmore* [1976] R.T.R. 83, a passenger was leaning across the person in the driving seat with both hands on the wheel and obstructing the view of the person in the driving seat who continued to control the propulsion of the vehicle but could not steer it. Both were driving. However, a passenger who grabbed the steering wheel causing the car to leave the road was not driving: *Jones v. Pratt* [1983] R.T.R. 54.

E. MECHANICALLY PROPELLED VEHICLE

17–6 There are a variety of terms defined in the *Road Traffic Act* 1988 and elsewhere to cover vehicles used on roads. In s.185 of the 1988 Act, a motor vehicle is defined as a "mechanically propelled vehicle intended or adapted for use on roads". There are further definitions of "motor car", "invalid carriage", "motor cycle" etc. which all use the phrase mechanically propelled vehicle.

This is a term which has been judicially considered on many occasions, often turning on whether a vehicle which undoubtedly has been a mechanically propelled vehicle continues to come within that definition even though it is no longer able to be driven. In connection with offences under the *Vehicle Excise and Registration Act* 1994, liability is extended to vehicles that not only are mechanically propelled vehicles but also to ones that have at some stage been a mechanically propelled vehicle s.1(1B).

The test to be applied is set out in *Binks v. Department of the Environment* [1975] R.T.R. 318 as "whether the vehicle has reached such a stage that it can be said that there is no reasonable prospect of the vehicle ever being made mobile again".

F. ROAD OR OTHER PUBLIC PLACE

17–7 There are a range of definitions of "road" for various purposes and it will be a question of fact and degree whether something is a road or other public place in the circumstances of any alleged offence.

In essence, a "road" is a highway and any other road to which the public has access: *Road Traffic Act* 1988, s.192(1). It is a definable way for passage between two points: *Oxford v. Austin* [1981] R.T.R. 416. It will have the physical character of a defined or definable route or way, with ascertained or ascertainable edges, leading from one point to another with the function of serving as a means of access enabling travellers to move from one point to another along that route: *Cutter v. Eagle Star Insurance Co Ltd* [1998] 4 All E.R. 417.

A road to which the public have access is one on which the public generally can be found without having to overcome a physical obstruction or to defy an express or implied prohibition: *Harrison v. Hill*, 1932 J.C. 13. Connotations of public expense in maintaining it should not be imported: *DPP v. Cargo Handling Ltd* [1992] R.T.R. 318.

In *Barrett v. DPP* [2009] EWHC Admin 423; [2010] R.T.R 2, a roadway was inside a caravan park which was situated between a main road and a beach. A public footpath existed commencing at the main road and, in part, following the line of the roadway through the park; that footpath was found to be a "highway" and so, justices found, the roadway was a "road". The defence contended that the caravan park was private and, since there was no right for vehicles to access the beach through the caravan park (and no car park at the beach), was not a place to which the public had access. There appeared to be some confusion about what needed to be proved before the justices but the Divisional Court was clear that it was a "road"; the defendant had followed a route marked on a plan which was a tarmac roadway with defined edges, road markings and signs and in respect of which there was unchallenged evidence that it was used by members of the public as a route to the beach, including those who had no other business in the caravan park. The absence of a beach car park was not significant.

The extent of the definition of "other public place" has often arisen in the context of **17–8** car parks. Provided the public generally could be expected to use the area (even if only for purposes that not every member of the public would choose to avail themselves of) then it is likely to be a public place. Thus, courts have brought within the definition a hospital car park: *DPP v. Greenwood* [1997] C.O.D. 278, an "airside" road at Heathrow Airport: *DPP v. Neville* (1996) 160 J.P. 758, a lane leading from a cross-Channel ferry through the immigration terminal: *DPP v. Coulman* [1993] R.T.R. 230 and a caravan park: *DPP v. Vivier* [1991] 4 All E.R. 18.

G. Using, Causing and Permitting

These terms are commonly used in relation to road traffic offences and their meaning has been developed in attempts to ensure that the purposes of the legislation are achieved. **17–9**

Certain statutory provisions impose absolute liability on the user; for instance, if a vehicle is used and the use is not covered by insurance, the user is generally liable whether or not aware of the absence of insurance cover. The user will be the driver but will also often include a person whose vehicle was being used by another person for his purposes and under his control—often the employer/employee relationship. However, "use" is defined more restrictively where there are alternatives such as "causing" or "permitting" which could be used.

"Causing" unlawful use requires proof of knowledge of the facts making the use unlawful where there is an alternative offence of "using". Where that alternative is not provided, "causing", though it requires a positive act, will not necessarily require knowledge.

"Permitting" unlawful use is less precise than "causing" it. The extent to which **17–10** knowledge is required will vary depending on the offence. For instance, permitting use without insurance will require proof that the use was permitted but not that it was known that the use was uninsured.

For a further exploration of these terms, see *Wilkinson's Road Traffic Offences*, Ch.1.

H. Vehicle

This can have a very wide meaning. In most instances for road traffic offences it is **17–11** used with some other limiting factors, such as "motor vehicle" or "mechanically propelled vehicle" but it will sometimes be used on its own. In those circumstances, the dictionary definition of "a thing used for transporting people or goods on land" becomes relevant.

A bicycle is a vehicle as are trams, trolley buses and horse-drawn carts. In some circumstances, it may include a pram or a pushchair. For instance, one of the occasions in which the obligation to stop after an accident arises is where damage is caused to a vehicle and it is likely that a pram would be a vehicle for those purposes at least.

II. BAD DRIVING

A. GENERAL

17–12 There are two main offences dealt with in magistrates' courts where the issue is whether the standard of driving fell below an acceptable standard. These offences are dangerous driving: *Road Traffic Act* 1988, s.2 and driving without due care and attention or without reasonable consideration for other road users: *Road Traffic Act* 1988, s.3. As well as issues surrounding the assessment of a particular piece of driving, there will be difficult decisions needing to be made on sentencing since the consequences of bad driving do not always correlate with the badness of the driving. Further offences have been created which provide for situations where death arises from driving without due care and attention or following driving by a person disqualified, unlicensed or uninsured. These are either way offences and the provisions are set out at the appropriate place in the text, *post*. The Sentencing Guidelines Council has published definitive guidelines on sentencing for both these offences: *www.sentencingcouncil.judiciary.gov.uk*. In addition, the Crown Prosecution Service has published its policy relating to the prosecution of bad driving: this can be found at *www.cps.gov.uk*. Amongst other things, this explores the boundary between dangerous driving and driving without due care and attention.

B. WARNING OF PROSECUTION

17–13 In order to secure a conviction under either section 2 or 3, the prosecution must have complied with the requirements to give notice of intended prosecution: *Road Traffic Offenders Act* 1988, s.1. The driver must receive warning of prosecution within 14 days of the offence. This warning may be given at the time of the offence, by service of the summons (or copy of a charge sheet) within 14 days of the offence or by the prosecutor sending notice to the driver or the registered keeper of the vehicle within 14 days. Where the notice is by service of the summons, that must take place within the 14 days. Where the notification is by notice, it is only necessary for that to be sent within the 14 days.

One of the methods of service is by first class post; there is a presumption that letters sent by post will be delivered in the "ordinary course of the post", for first class mail that is the second working day after posting. In *Gidden v. Chief Constable of Humberside* [2009] EWHC 2924; [2010] R.T.R. 9 (p.95) a notice was posted which should have arrived within 12 days and so well within the 14-day limit. However, a postal strike occurred and it was accepted that the notice did not arrive until after the 14 days. In relation to service by post using registered post or recorded delivery there is an irrebuttable presumption that service took place when properly posted in time but, in relation to first class post, the presumption is rebuttable, that is, the requirement is deemed to be complied with unless the contrary is proved. As it was accepted that the notice did not arrive within the prescribed time-limit, the conviction was set aside.

Exceptions to this requirement are set out in s.2. They include where, at the time of the offence or immediately after it, an accident occurs owing to the presence on the road of the vehicle in respect of which the offence was committed. By virtue of s.1(3) of the Act, the provisions are deemed to be complied with unless the contrary is proved.

Further consideration has been given to the meaning of "accident" in *Currie* [2007] R.T.R 37. Having been stopped by police officers, the defendant returned to his car whilst the officer talking to him was distracted and started the ignition. The officer shouted at him to stop and ran towards the vehicle; the vehicle lurched forward and the police officer had to put her hands on the bonnet. Another driver blocked the way forward, the officer grabbed hold of the open passenger door and the defendant reversed up the road causing the officer to lose her grip on the door. On two occasions, the offender nearly hit another vehicle. The offender was subsequently prosecuted for dangerous driving and convicted by the Crown Court after a trial. The trial judge had determined that there had been an accident having considered the contested facts. On appeal, it was argued both that the issue was one of fact to be determined by the jury and that it could not be said that there had been an accident. Since the existence of an accident created an exemption from the requirements, the provisions in s.1(3) did not apply (that applies to proving that the requirements of s.1(1) had not been complied with) and the burden of proof was on the prosecution to prove that an accident had occurred. Having reviewed the authorities, the court was clear that the judge was entitled to find that there was an "accident" in these circumstances. It was emphasised that the purpose of the requirements was to draw the attention of a potential defendant to the possibility of prosecution; in circumstances such as these, the events would have been "sufficiently memorable" for that to be unnecessary.

A similarly expansive interpretation of the provisions was applied in *Myers* [2007] R.T.R. 34. Three vehicles were being driven in convoy along a road and aspects of that driving were dangerous. At one point, all the cars dangerously turned around to face the direction from which they had come. As a result, one of those vehicles veered and collided with a parked car. There was no contact between the other two cars and the car involved in the collision which was caused by the manner of the driving of that particular vehicle and the unnecessary use of the handbrake. No warning of prosecution was given and the defendants were prosecuted for dangerous driving. It was argued that the exception did not apply because the accident had not occurred "owing to the presence on a road of the vehicle in respect of which the offence was committed". That argument was rejected in the Crown Court and on appeal. The section required there to be a sufficiently causal link between the offence and the accident that the driver did not need to be warned of the risk of prosecution. In the circumstances of this case, there was a sufficient link and the defendants did not need to be warned.

These decisions appear to be a further manifestation of the low level of tolerance of the courts for unmeritorious technical arguments seeking to avoid conviction where the underlying purpose of the provision has been achieved.

For further information, refer to *Wilkinson's Road Traffic Offences*, Ch.2.

Part III

C. DANGEROUS DRIVING

(1) Definition

Road Traffic Act 1988, s.2

Dangerous driving

2. A person who drives a mechanically propelled vehicle dangerously on a road or other public place is guilty of an offence. **17–14**

(2) What must the prosecution prove?

The elements of this offence that the prosecution must prove are that: **17–15**

— the defendant was the driver;
— the vehicle was being driven;
— the vehicle was a mechanically propelled vehicle;
— the vehicle was being driven dangerously; and
— the vehicle was being driven on a road or other public place.

A defendant who is acquitted of dangerous driving may be found guilty of driving without due care and attention or without reasonable consideration even though no charge has been preferred—see Alternative Verdict, *post*, at § 17–23. **17–16**

For issues of identification, see *ante*, §§ 10–89 *et seq.* in this work. For issues surrounding the meaning of "drive", see *ante*, § 17–4. The phrase "mechanically propelled vehicle" is wider than "vehicle"; again this is more fully explored in § 17–6, *ante*. The phrase "road or other public place" has been subject to detailed consideration; this also is explored more fully in §§ 17–7 and 17–8, *ante*.

(3) Allocation

17–17 Dangerous driving is an either way offence and particular care needs to be taken. In the Crown Court, approximately 2,300 offenders are sentenced each year. About 60 per cent of those convicted receive an immediate custodial sentence with a further 25 per cent receiving a suspended sentence order. About 75 per cent of sentences of immediate custody are for one year or less and about 25 per cent are for six months or less and so within the power of a magistrates' court. In magistrates' courts, approximately 2,000 are sentenced each year. Less than 20 per cent per cent of those convicted receive an immediate custodial sentence and about 50 per cent of those were for three months or less. A further 17 per cent received a suspended sentence order in 2008 whilst over 30 per cent were made subject to a community order.

The mode of trial guidelines in the *Consolidated Criminal Practice Direction*, para. V.51.17 (see Appendix F, F–58) have been replaced by the *Magistrates' Court Sentencing Guidelines* issued by the Sentencing Guidelines Council: see *www.sentencingcouncil.judiciary.gov.uk*. These guidelines provide that the type of case generally suitable for trial in the Crown Court will be those where there is prolonged bad driving involving deliberate disregard for the safety of others or where there is excessive speed or showing off by a disqualified driver, especially if that occurs on a busy road or in a built up area. Lesser situations, (such as single incidents where little or no damage or risk of personal injury but the driver was disqualified or excessive speed or showing off by a driver who was not disqualified) will also be suitable for the Crown Court where the driving occurred whilst the driver was being pursued by the police.

There will be occasions where a difficult choice needs to be made regarding whether to charge this offence and/or one of the offences contained in the *Offences Against the Person Act* 1861 (see *ante*, Ch.13). This may arise from a situation where injury is caused as a result of dangerous driving or it may arise where the vehicle itself is used as the equivalent of a weapon for the purpose of causing injury.

(4) Meaning of "dangerous driving"

17–18 The definition is set out in statute in *Road Traffic Act* 1988, s.2A.

Road Traffic Act 1988, s.2A

Meaning of dangerous driving

17–19 **2A.**—(1) For the purposes of sections 1 and 2 above a person is to be regarded as driving dangerously if (and, subject to subsection (2) below, only if)—

(a) the way he drives falls far below what would be expected of a competent and careful driver, and

(b) it would be obvious to a competent and careful driver that driving in that way would be dangerous.

(2) A person is also to be regarded as driving dangerously for the purposes of sections 1 and 2 above if it would be obvious to a competent and careful driver that driving the vehicle in its current state would be dangerous.

(3) In subsections (1) and (2) above "dangerous" refers to danger either of injury to any person or of serious damage to property; and in determining for the purposes of those subsections what would be expected of, or obvious to, a competent and careful driver in a particular case, regard shall be had not only to the circumstances of which he could be expected to be aware but also to any circumstances shown to have been within the knowledge of the accused.

(4) In determining for the purposes of subsection (2) above the state of a vehicle, regard

may be had to anything attached to or carried on or in it and to the manner in which it is attached or carried.

There are, therefore, two routes by which the offence is committed, one related to the way of driving (s.2A(1)) and one related to the decision to drive the vehicle at all: s.2A(2). The first (and more common) route test has two main parts both of which relate to a "competent and careful driver" and both of which must be proved. **17–20**

The first part requires that the manner of driving falls "far below" that of a competent and careful driver: s.2A(1)(a). (For the lesser offence under s.3 of careless driving, the test is "below" that of a competent and careful driver.) This is an objective test and the authorities indicate that the court should not add in an element that imports to the "competent and careful driver" of the test any of the characteristics of the defendant concerned or what the offender believed the situation to be: *Collins* [1997] R.T.R. 439. The condition of the driver (perhaps that he was intoxicated) is admissible but that condition is not sufficient in itself to prove the offence of dangerous driving: *Webster* [2006] R.T.R. 19.

The second part (s.2A(1)(b)) requires proof that it would have been obvious to a competent and careful driver that driving in the way the defendant drove would be dangerous. Again an objective test and again two main elements, what is meant by "obvious" and what is meant by "dangerous".

In relation to "obvious", a dictionary definition of "seen or realised at first glance, evident" has been used in relation to offences under s.2A(2) and would be equally applicable here. Would it be obvious to the careful and competent driver that driving in this way would be dangerous? In addition, s.2A(3) requires a court to take account not only of what would be obvious to the careful and competent driver but also what was actually known to the defendant. Therefore, if something was known to the driver that would not have been obvious, the standard of driving has to be assessed in the light of that additional knowledge. **17–21**

The Divisional Court has had cause to consider the test for dangerous driving in very unusual circumstances. An advanced police driver chose to test a vehicle newly allocated to him by driving at extremely high speeds in order, it was asserted, to enable him to familiarise himself with the vehicle's handling characteristics. A significant factor in determining whether or not the driving was dangerous was the provision in s.2A(3) of the *Road Traffic Act* 1988 that, in determining what would be expected of, or obvious to, a competent and careful driver regard should be had to "any circumstances shown to be within the knowledge of the accused". In most instances, these would be factors that were adverse to the accused; on this occasion, it was his competence as a grade 1 advanced police driver. The District Judge had concluded that the test of whether the driving was dangerous was an objective one (as it undoubtedly is) and this precluded from the circumstances relevant under s.2A(B) any that reflected the ability or lack of ability of the driver. The Divisional Court disagreed and concluded that these unusual driving skills were relevant to the issue and it was for the tribunal to determine what weight to attach: *Milton v. DPP* [2007] R.T.R. 43.

However, that approach has been found to be wrong. In a further case involving an experienced police driver, the Court of Appeal determined that the approach in *Milton* was "inconsistent with the objective test of the competent and careful driver set out in the statute": *Bannister* [2009] EWCA Crim 1571. To take account of the special skills of a driver would mean that the standard being applied is that of a driver with special skills and not, as the statute specifies, the "competent and careful driver". The special skill (or lack of skill) of a driver is an irrelevant circumstance when a court is considering whether driving is dangerous.

In relation to "dangerous", s.2A(3) is defined as meaning danger of injury to any person or of serious damage to property. The injury may be to any person, including the driver, and there is no limitation on the nature of the injury. However, it is suggested that that injury should be physical injury (as proposed in the Road Traffic Law Review (the North Report) that led to the creation of this offence) but there is no

Part III

requirement that injury should have occurred, just that there was a danger of such injury occurring. In relation to property, there is again no further definition but there is the qualification that the damage must be "serious". Again, it would appear to be quite acceptable for that property to be the mechanically propelled vehicle being driven by the defendant as well as any other property.

The second route by which the offence is committed is by driving a mechanically propelled vehicle when it was obvious that to do so in its current state would be dangerous: s.2A(2). The state of the vehicle includes anything attached to it or carried on it or in it and the manner in which it is attached or carried: s.2A(4). Again the determinant of what is obvious is the careful and competent driver. The test is whether there is evidence that it would be obvious (that is, capable of being seen or realised at first glance, evident) that it would be dangerous (that is, liable to cause injury or serious damage to property) to drive the vehicle in that state. In addition, anything of which the driver was actually aware should be taken into account even where that would not have been obvious to a careful and competent driver: s.2A(3).

17–22 A difficult issue was considered in *Marchant* [2004] 1 All E.R. 1187; [2004] R.T.R. 15. An agricultural vehicle had (as part of its construction) a grab with spikes attached to its front. It was authorised by the Secretary of State for use on public roads. The grab was in the recommended position for use on the roads. Whilst the vehicle was waiting to turn off the road, a motor cyclist ran into it and was killed. The driver was prosecuted for causing death by dangerous driving relying on s.2A(2). Allowing the driver's appeal against conviction, the Court of Appeal (Criminal Division) stated that, whilst there will be cases where it will be appropriate to prosecute those responsible for vehicles in a dangerous condition even where they had been authorised by the Secretary of State, that would be where the driver had manoeuvred the vehicle in a dangerous fashion. Where, as here, the danger was in the design, it is unlikely to be appropriate to prosecute the user at all.

Despite this route being limited in the statute to the defective state of the vehicle, it appears to have been extended to circumstances where it was the "defective" state of the driver that caused the danger. In *Marison* [1997] R.T.R. 457, the driver suffered from diabetes and was aware that there was a real risk that he would suffer a sudden hypoglycaemic attack which would cause him to lose control of the vehicle. He did suffer such an attack resulting in the car crashing into an oncoming vehicle and killing the driver. The Judge drew an analogy with s.2A(2) and this was supported by the Court of Appeal.

Alternative verdict

17–23 A court faced with an offence of dangerous driving and finding the defendant not guilty can instead find the defendant guilty of driving without due care and attention even though no charge has been preferred and even though it would not be possible to lay an information because too much time had elapsed from the date of the offence: *Road Traffic Offenders Act* 1988, s.24.

(5) Penalty

17–24 The maximum sentence at present is two years' imprisonment on indictment and/or an unlimited fine; on summary trial, six months' imprisonment and/or a fine up to level 5. A significant issue is the gap between the maximum custodial sentence for this offence and for causing death by dangerous driving which is 14 years' imprisonment. The same standard of driving may result in death, in very serious injury or in no injury at all and it is these issues that must be grappled with by those having to pass sentence. In December 2009, the Government stated that it intended to seek to increase the maximum to 5 years imprisonment.

Mandatory disqualification and endorsement follows (including an obligation to be re-tested). In the absence of "special reasons", see *post*, at § 17–209, the minimum period of disqualification is 12 months. For more information on disqualification and endorsement generally, see *post*, §§ 17–183 *et seq*.

See also the power to deprive the offender of the vehicle contained in section 143(1), (6) and (7) of the *Powers of Criminal Courts (Sentencing) Act* 2000, see *post*, § 17–212.

(6) Sentence

The *Magistrates' Court Sentencing Guidelines* state aggravating factors that will increase either the culpability of the offender or the level of harm relevant to the seriousness of the offence. Those factors indicating higher culpability are disregarding warnings of others, evidence of alcohol or drugs, carrying out other tasks while driving, carrying passengers or a heavy load, tiredness, aggressive driving (for example, driving much too close to vehicle in front, racing, inappropriate attempts to overtake, or cutting in after overtaking), driving when knowingly suffering from a medical condition which significantly impairs the offender's driving skills and driving a poorly maintained or dangerously loaded vehicle, especially where motivated by commercial concerns. Those factors indicating a greater degree of harm are injury to others and damage to other vehicles or property. Mitigating circumstances include driving in a genuine emergency and speed that was not excessive. **17–25**

If the offence was due to the inexperience of the driver rather than to the driver's irresponsibility, that may also mitigate the seriousness of the offence. This may occur where a driver faced with a choice responds inappropriately because of a lack of experience; in that case culpability will be lower than in other circumstances.

In *Cooksley*; *Stride*; *Cook (Att.-Gen.'s Reference (No.152 of 2002))* [2003] 2 Cr.App.R. 18, (a case of causing death by dangerous driving), the Court emphasised that, although the offence is one which does not require an intention to drive dangerously (or an intention to injure), since the driving has to fall "far below" the standard of driving that would be expected of a competent and careful driver and the driving must be such that it would be obvious to the same competent and careful driver that driving in that way would be dangerous, it will usually be obvious to the offender that the driving was dangerous and he therefore deserves to be punished accordingly.

The courts have demonstrated a readiness to protect people who are particularly vulnerable to the commission of this offence. In *Joseph* [2002] 1 Cr.App.R.(S.) 20, the defendant had deliberately driven at a traffic warden and driven off with him on the bonnet of the vehicle, trying to shake him off. The Court of Appeal endorsed the observations of the sentencing judge that it was the duty of the courts to give protection to traffic wardens and other public servants who were carrying out public duties, and emphasised the propriety of a deterrent custodial sentence. The defendant was sentenced to ten months' imprisonment. Leveson J. stated: **17–26**

> "Parking attendants, in particular, are subject to vilification and abuse if not worse. It is a very real reflection on the hazards of the job that this particular parking attendant felt it appropriate to carry a tape recorder with him to record what happened when confronted by angry motorists. The fact that others have complained about this particular attendant does not take this appellant's position or the character of his driving any further. An immediate custodial sentence, in the form of a deterrent sentence, which inevitably pays less attention to the individual circumstances of the offender was both proper and, in our judgement, inevitable" (at p.75–76)

For "road rage" cases of dangerous driving, where no accident or injury results and there was no consumption of alcohol, but there is evidence to suggest furious driving in temper with an intent of causing fear and possible injury, the appropriate sentencing bracket lies between six and 12 months: *Howells* [2003] 1 Cr.App.R.(S.) 61, CA. **17–27**

Some more recent cases have given examples of approaches to sentencing for this offence.

In *A.*, unreported, July 22, 2004, CA, the two defendants had been "sharing" the driving of a motor car—one had been steering, the other changing the gears—over a

Part III

distance over 20 miles until the car left the road at a bend at 60mph. The car rolled over causing serious injuries to the three other passengers. At the time of the offence, the defendant who had been steering was 17 years old and had no driving experience and the other defendant was 19 years old. Both defendants were of good character. Sentences on each of 18 months' detention (after a guilty plea) were held not to be manifestly excessive.

17–28 In contrast, in *Andrews* (2004) 148 S.J. 1031, the defendant had driven at high speeds, mounted a pavement, failed to stop at junctions and crossed traffic lights at red. In addition he was drunk. On this occasion, a sentence of 10 months' imprisonment (following a guilty plea) was held not to be excessive. Indeed, a custodial sentence was inevitable.

In *Bentley* [2004] EWCA Crim 2162, the defendant was 18 years old at the time of the offence and had passed both ordinary and an advanced driving test. He was of exemplary character and showed a great deal of remorse for the serious injuries that were caused to one of his passengers. He had pleaded guilty at the earliest possible opportunity. The Judge sentenced on the basis that the defendant had been showing off, there having been information from the passengers that he had been driving very fast and swerving the car all over the road from time to time. He had attempted to negotiate a bend at 50mph when the fastest safe speed was 39mph, the car rolled, struck a stone wall and then a tree. The injured passenger had been travelling in the boot area of the hatchback car. Sentence at the Crown Court was to 12 months' detention and disqualification for three years and until an extended re-test had been taken. The Court of Appeal noted the positive good character of the defendant, the fact that the offence was out of character and more a product of irresponsibility than of criminality. Nonetheless, the grave consequences that arose could not be ignored. Although the court considered 12 months to be severe in the light of the plea, the good character, the remorse and the absence of the worst features of dangerous driving, it was not manifestly excessive and was not reduced. These cases appear to indicate the high probability of a custodial sentence especially where serious injury results. This reflects the statement, *ante*, at § 17–25 that, since the driving has to fall "far below" the standard of driving that would be expected, it will usually be obvious that the driving was dangerous.

In *Tomkins* [2004] EWCA Crim 2792, the defendant had committed a series of offences that led to him being sentenced by different magistrates' courts on two occasions in April 2004. The offences included driving whilst disqualified, taking without consent and aggravated vehicle taking. Whilst on bail, he also committed an offence of dangerous driving. Police officers had noticed the defendant in the driver's seat of a stationary car. When they approached him, he pulled away and drove towards them striking one officer who needed hospital treatment but was not seriously injured. The defendant then drove into a road against a "No Entry" sign and collided with an oncoming car causing the driver foot, stomach and knee injuries. He was sentenced to 18 months' imprisonment to run consecutively to a total of 11 months' imprisonment imposed at the April hearings. On appeal, the defence argued that, with a two year maximum sentence, since this was not the worst example of dangerous driving and given the guilty plea and mitigating circumstances, an 18 month sentence was excessive. The Court of Appeal disagreed and upheld the sentence. In *Grover* [2009] EWCA Crim 876 the defendant drove through red lights at 35-40mph in a 30mph zone. He struck a woman who was 8 months pregnant; she suffered multiple injuries including a ruptured placenta which meant that an emergency caesarean section had to be carried out; the child survived. The mother remained in a coma for some time and was not able to see her child for some 2 months and so missed the bonding that would otherwise have occurred; she was unlikely to make a complete recovery from her injuries. The defendant was of previous good character and asserted that he had been dazzled by the sun (a clear, bright, November afternoon) and simply not seen the colour of the traffic lights. He pleaded guilty at the earliest opportunity. The Court of Appeal reduced the sentence from 8 months to 5 months and so within the powers of a magistrates' court. Should

Parliament not choose to increase the maximum sentence, it may be that serious consideration may need to be given to prosecuting this type of use of a motor vehicle under the appropriate offence of assault or causing grievous bodily harm. Examples of such an approach can be found in the following cases. In *Bain* [2005] 2 Cr.App.R.(S.) 53, the defendant was aged 19. In the course of driving dangerously, serious injuries were caused to a passenger in the vehicle that he was driving. He was charged with dangerous driving and with causing grievous bodily harm (s.20). Dangerous driving attracts a maximum of two years' imprisonment, GBH a maximum of five years. The Court of Appeal held that there was nothing wrong in principle in charging such offences even though they arose from the same course of conduct. However, since the offences did arise out of the same course of conduct, concurrent sentences should have been imposed that reflected the totality of the offending conduct. In *Ballard* [2005] 2 Cr.App.R.(S.) 31, a 17-year-old had been charged with gross negligence manslaughter following a course of bad driving in which a person had been killed. This had been done with the express purpose of making available greater powers of sentence than would have been available following conviction of causing death by dangerous driving. That approach (and the subsequent lengthy sentence imposed) was held to be correct.

The level of sentence was considered in *Goldring* [2005] EWCA Crim 2254. The appellant was aged 19 when the offence was committed. Having been disqualified 14 days before the incident (for driving without insurance), he was observed by a police officer sitting at the wheel of a stationary vehicle. The officer attempted to give him a notice but the appellant drove the car, made a U-turn and then drove at the police officer causing him to jump out of the way. No injury was caused and the appellant was arrested five days later at his home. At the Crown Court a sentence of 18 months had been imposed with a further three months consecutive for driving whilst disqualified. On appeal, it was argued that this was a very short lived piece of dangerous driving, no injury was caused and no member of the public was endangered. Since the maximum is two years' imprisonment, this was not serious enough to warrant such a long sentence. Reducing the sentence to 12 months, the Court of Appeal agreed that 18 months was too high.

A useful reminder of the circumstances in which maximum sentences should be considered for offences (such as this one) where there is a relatively low maximum penalty can be found in *Butt* [2006] EWCA Crim 47. The driving consisted of driving on the wrong side of the road whilst trying to evade the police; the driver was the worse for both drink and drugs. Upholding a sentence of 18 months imprisonment (after a guilty plea), the Court of Appeal drew attention to existing guidance on the circumstances in which it is appropriate to use the maximum as a starting point. In *Ambler* [1976] Crim.L.R. 266, it had been emphasised that, whilst the maximum should be passed only for the worst kind of offence, judicial imagination should not be stretched to attempt to identify unlikely examples—"what they should consider is the worst type of offence which comes before the court and ask themselves whether the particular case they are dealing with comes within the broad band of that type. When the maximum sentence is low, the band may be wide" (*per* Lawton L.J.) Although some cases may end with a sentence within the powers of a magistrates' court, it is submitted that all cases involving serious injury should be sentenced in the Crown Court since the level of sentence will only be able to be determined after full inquiry into the relevant circumstances. In *Byrne* [2009] EWCA Crim 1825, the defendant had consumed a quantity of strong lager and brandy and then drove "as if he was on a race track". In due course, the car hit the pavement, went out of control and veered into the path of a car coming in the opposite direction; the estimated speed of the defendant's car before impact was 80mph and he fled the scene before the emergency services arrived although he was found nearby shortly afterwards. The driver of the car that was hit was a 19-year-old woman who suffered severe injuries to her body, particularly severe head injuries. Although the prognosis had been poor, she had made a better than expected recovery; nonetheless the effect on her had been profound and continuing. A passenger in her car has also been injured though suffering relatively minor injuries. There had been a late guilty plea and the sentence of 20 months was upheld with the court remarking on the inadequacy of the current maximum sentence for cases such as this. By contrast, in *Ball* [2009] EWCA Crim 1265, the defendant had overtaken 5 vehicles whilst driving up a hill. He accelerated to 50mph as he approached the brow of the hill and, as he went over the brow, he collided with another vehicle. The driver of that other vehicle suffered serious injuries with continuing mental impairment and scarring. The defendant was aged 17 at the time of the offence. Noting that there had not been a prolonged course of bad driving, the speed limit had not been exceeded and that neither drugs nor alcohol were involved, the Crown Court had been wrong to take the maximum sentence as the starting point; it should have used 18 months as the starting point. That was then reduced to 12 months on account of personal mitigation and the guilty plea.

It may be appropriate to consider consecutive sentences where the driver both drove dangerously and drove with excess alcohol or disqualified. Although the general practice is to impose concurrent sentences where the offences arose from a single incident, nonetheless there is a well recognised practice that, in circumstances such as these, consecutive sentences may be imposed. In *Hardy* [2005] EWCA Crim 3097, the defendant was convicted of dangerous driving, driving whilst disqualified and failing to provide a specimen. Consecutive sentences totalling two years were imposed in the Crown Court. Upholding those sentences and the approach, the Court of Appeal stated that, whilst consecutive sentences would not generally be appropriate where the matters arose out of the same incident "it would be bizarre that this man would in fact have a licence to drive with excess alcohol and while disqualified without any added penalty." An approach that may have less offended general sentencing principle would have been to have treated the alcohol and disqualification as aggravating factors and increased the sentence accordingly; however, the low maximum penalty does not allow that to happen so readily and this is perhaps another example of the problems that arise when maximum sentences are allowed to remain at a level that is too low.

D. CARELESS OR INCONSIDERATE DRIVING

(1) Definition

Road Traffic Act 1988, ss.3, 3ZA

Careless, and inconsiderate, driving

17–29 **3.** If a person drives a mechanically propelled vehicle on a road or other public place without due care and attention, or without reasonable consideration for other persons using the road or place, he is guilty of an offence.

Meaning of careless, or inconsiderate, driving

17–30 **3ZA.**—(1) This section has effect for the purposes of sections 2B and 3 above and section 3A below.

(2) A person is to be regarded as driving without due care and attention if (and only if) the way he drives falls below what would be expected of a competent and careful driver.

(3) In determining for the purposes of subsection (2) above what would be expected of a careful and competent driver in a particular case, regard shall be had not only to the circumstances of which he could be expected to be aware but also to any circumstances shown to have been within the knowledge of the accused.

(4) A person is to be regarded as driving without reasonable consideration for other persons only if those persons are inconvenienced by his driving.

(2) What must the prosecution prove?

17–31 The elements of this offence that the prosecution must prove are that:

— the defendant was the driver;
— the vehicle was being driven;
— the vehicle was a mechanically propelled vehicle;
— the vehicle was being driven on a road or other public place;

— the vehicle was being driven without due care and attention; *or*

— the vehicle was being driven without reasonable consideration for other persons using the road or place.

For issues of identification, see *ante*, §§ 10–89 *et seq.* in this work.

For issues surrounding the meaning of "drive", see *ante*, § 17–4. **17–32**

The phrase "mechanically propelled vehicle" is wider than "vehicle"; again this is more fully explored in § 17–6, *ante*.

The phrase "road or other public place" has been subject to detailed consideration; this also is explored more fully in §§ 17–7 and 17–8, *ante*.

(3) Allocation

These offences are summary only. **17–33**

(4) Standard of driving

Until recently, statute had not assisted in defining the standard of driving for the offences contained in s.3. The standard widely accepted had been that of a reasonable, prudent and competent driver in all the circumstances of the case which had an element to be judged objectively (the reasonable etc. driver) and one to be judged subjectively (the circumstances of the case). However, s.3ZA of the 1988 Act now provides that the standard is that of the "competent and careful" driver in circumstances of which the driver could be expected to be aware or was aware, even if he would not otherwise have been expected to be aware of them. "Reasonable and prudent" is thus replaced by "careful" which may not be too much of a change in practice. The widening of the circumstances to include those of which the driver is aware may be a little more significant. The Crown Prosecution Service has published its policy relating to the prosecution of bad driving: this can be found at *www.cps.gov.uk*. Amongst other things, this explores the type of driving that might constitute careless or inconsiderate driving. Examples of the type of driving that might lead to a charge of careless driving are stated to be overtaking on the inside or driving inappropriately close to another vehicle, inadvertent mistakes such as driving through a red light or emerging from a side road into the path of another vehicle and short distractions such as tuning a car radio, reading a newspaper/map, selecting and lighting a cigarette/cigar/pipe or talking to and looking at a passenger. **17–34**

Examples of the type of driving that might lead to a charge of driving without reasonable consideration are flashing of lights to force other drivers in front to give way, driving that inconveniences other road users or causes unnecessary hazards such as unnecessarily remaining in an overtaking lane, unnecessarily slow driving or braking without good cause, driving with un-dipped headlights which dazzle oncoming drivers or driving through a puddle causing pedestrians to be splashed and misuse of any lane to avoid queuing or gain some other advantage over other drivers. Driving without reasonable consideration is almost always going to be capable of falling within the offence of driving without due care and attention since no reasonable, prudent and competent driver would drive without reasonable consideration for other road users. However, that does not work in reverse since, for the second limb, there must be other persons using the road or other public place whereas that is not necessary for the first limb. It may be that there are now fewer reasons why the second limb should be prosecuted at all.

The cause of the failure to drive at the acceptable standard is not, therefore, relevant to conviction (though it may be to sentence) but how the driver would be expected to conduct himself or herself is to be judged on the basis of the circumstances as they actually were or as the driver could have expected to be aware. There can be some fine judgements as to whether the competent and careful driver of the test would have avoided getting into the situation altogether or whether, accepting that the situation occurred, the actions of the driver have to be tested against this standard. Thus, the fact that the driver is a learner driver or otherwise inexperienced does not affect the assessment of what the standard of driving should be whereas the standard may well vary with the time of day, type of road, or weather conditions. There is no need for anyone to be adversely affected. However, where the allegation is of driving without reasonable consideration, it will be necessary to prove that others have been inconvenienced by the driving: s.3ZA(4).

17–35 It is not unusual for any accident to be observed by no one other than the driver. In those circumstances, the court is entitled to draw inferences from the nature of the circumstances in which the accident occurred to justify finding the offence proved providing the facts are strong enough to enable the court to be satisfied beyond reasonable doubt that the standard of driving was below that required: *Scott v. Warren* [1974] R.T.R. 104. If an explanation (other than a fanciful one) is put forward by the defendant, it is for the prosecution to disprove it: *Spurge* [1961] 2 All E.R. 688.

The Highway Code can be used to assist in understanding what is expected in any given situation. Failure to observe the Code does not of itself prove the case but it will tend to show that the standard of driving was unacceptable.

Once it is proved that the driving fell below the acceptable standard, there are a limited number of defences that have been created—mechanical defect, sudden loss of visibility or sudden illness. The underlying principle is that the driver has been deprived of control of the vehicle by something of which he was not aware. If the driver, without fault, can show that he was deprived of control because of a mechanical defect of which he was unaware and which he could not have discovered by the exercise of reasonable prudence then he ought to be acquitted. Similarly, if he finds himself unexpectedly blinded by headlights or by the sun and an accident occurs before he can stop, that can be a defence. In such circumstances, the competent and careful driver will quickly reduce speed or stop his vehicle but there will be a very short time in which it is accepted that the defence would arise. Finally, sudden illness may again raise a defence providing it could not be anticipated and the reactions of the driver when he became aware of the illness were those of a competent and careful driver. Falling asleep is not sufficient since that could have been anticipated: *Henderson v. Jones* (1955) 119 J.P. 305.

(5) Penalty

17–36 The maximum penalty is a fine of level 5 (£5,000). It is an endorsable offence within the range of 3–9 penalty points and so disqualification may be imposed.

(6) Sentence

17–37 The *Magistrates' Court Sentencing Guidelines* provide aggravating factors that will increase either the culpability of the offender or the level of harm relevant to the seriousness of the offence. Those factors indicating higher culpability are driving at excessive speed, carrying out other tasks while driving, carrying passengers or a heavy load or driving whilst tired. Those factors indicating a greater degree of harm are injury to others, damage to other vehicles or property, high level of traffic or pedestrians in the vicinity and the location of the offence (for example, taking place near a school when children are likely to be present). Mitigating factors include minor risk, inexperience of the driver and a sudden change in road or weather conditions.

The most likely penalty is a fine with penalty points. However, disqualification should be considered where there is a risk of further poor driving. This may be until a further test is passed which will be particularly appropriate where there are concerns about the overall driving ability of the defendant.

STARTING POINT AND RANGE OF SENTENCE

(BASED ON A FIRST TIME OFFENDER PLEADING NOT GUILTY)

Examples of nature of activity	**Starting Point**	**Range**
Momentary lapse of concentration or misjudgement at low speed	Band A fine	Band A fine 3–4 points
Loss of control due to speed, mishandling or insufficient attention to road conditions, or carelessly turning right across on-coming traffic	Band B fine	Band B fine 5–6 points
Overtaking manoeuvre at speed resulting in collision of vehicles, or driving bordering on the dangerous	Band C fine	Band C fine Consider disqualification OR 7–9 points

A court will have to face situations where the seriousness of the result of the bad driving is greatly out of proportion to how bad the driving was—a relatively minor lapse can result in death or very serious injury. For many years, courts have based sentence for this offence primarily on the degree of fault. In *Krawec* (1984) 6 Cr.App.R.(S.) 367, the appellant was convicted of driving without due care and attention on an indictment for causing death by reckless driving. Reducing the fine, Lord Lane C.J. stated that:

> "The unforeseen and unexpected results of the carelessness are not in themselves relevant to penalty. The primary considerations are the quality of the driving, the extent to which the appellant on the particular occasion fell below the standard of the reasonably competent driver; in other words, the degree of carelessness and culpability. The unforeseen consequences may sometimes be relevant to those considerations. In the present case the fact that the appellant failed to see the pedestrian until it was too late and therefore collided with him was plainly a relevant factor. We do not think that the fact that the unfortunate man died was relevant on this charge."

However, that approach has been steadily changing.

In *King* [2001] 2 Cr.App.R.(S.) 114, CA, the appellant was convicted of three offences of driving without due care and attention having been acquitted of three counts of causing death by dangerous driving. He was fined £2,250 and disqualified for a period of three years. Holding that this sentence was too high, the Court of Appeal substituted a fine of £1,500 and disqualification for two years. While culpability remained the primary consideration in sentencing for driving without due care and attention where death had resulted, the sentencing judge was entitled to bear in mind that he was dealing with an offence that had led to death. Mackay J. reviewed the authorities on sentencing in this difficult situation, and stated:

> "The sentencer must still, therefore, make it his primary task to assess culpability, but should not close his eyes to the fact that death has resulted, especially multiple death, where, as here, **17–38**

that was all too readily foreseeable as the consequence of the admitted lack of care in this case."

17–39 However, the maximum penalty remains a fine and that should be capable of being paid within one year. As a result of concerns that the range of offences was not sufficient to enable sentence to be properly imposed where death results from careless or inconsiderate driving, Parliament has created new offences which are set out in the next sections but the above guidance will continue to apply to offences committed before commencement or where serious injury is caused but death does not result.

An example is seen in *Holman* [2010] R.T.R. 23. The defendant had been charged with causing death by dangerous driving arising out of an accident in December 2007. At the Crown Court, he was found not guilty but convicted of careless driving (the offence of causing death by careless driving being not yet in force). The Court emphasised that the approach to calculating the fine was to be that set out in the Sentencing Guidelines with a "very significant uplift for the aggravating feature of the appalling consequence" of the careless driving: Pitchford L.J. at [17].

E. Causing Death by Careless, or Inconsiderate, Driving

(1) Definition

Road Traffic Act 1988, s.2B

Causing death by careless, or inconsiderate, driving

17–40 **2B.** A person who causes the death of another person by driving a mechanically propelled vehicle on a road or other public place without due care and attention, or without reasonable consideration for other persons using the road or place, is guilty of an offence.

(2) What must the prosecution prove?

17–41 The elements of this offence that the prosecution must prove are that:
- — the defendant was the driver;
- — the vehicle was being driven;
- — the vehicle was a mechanically propelled vehicle;
- — the vehicle was being driven on a road or other public place;
- — the vehicle was being driven without due care and attention; *or*
- — the vehicle was being driven without reasonable consideration for other persons using the road or place;
- — the death of another person is caused by that driving.

For issues of identification, see *ante*, §§ 10–89 *et seq.* in this work.

For issues surrounding the meaning of "drive", see *ante*, § 17–4.

The phrase "mechanically propelled vehicle" is wider than "vehicle"; again, this is explored more fully in § 17–6, *ante*.

The phrase "road or other public place" has been subject to detailed consideration; this also is explored more fully in §§ 17–7 and 17–8, *ante*.

(3) Allocation

17–42 This offence is triable either way. It can be expected that most cases will be dealt with in the Crown Court in recognition of the fact that death has occurred.

(4) Standard of driving

17–43 The standard set out in s.3ZA to the 1988 Act (see *ante*) applies also to this offence. The additional factor is that the driving below the requisite standard must have caused the death of a person other than the driver. This will include a person inside the vehicle driven by the defendant.

(5) Penalty

The maximum penalty is imprisonment of 6 months (to be 12 months on implementation of *Criminal Justice Act* 2003, s.154) and/or a fine of level 5 (£5,000) on summary conviction and imprisonment of five years or a fine on indictment. It is an endorsable offence within the range of 3–11 points but one that attracts mandatory disqualification in the absence of special reasons. **17–44**

(6) Sentence

The Sentencing Guidelines Council has published a definitive guideline for this offence which explores the consequences arising from an offence with a very high level of harm and a very low level of culpability. The offence itself has attracted a wide range of both support and criticism. In a debate in the House of Lords, it was said that: **17–45**

> "... it will mean that the families of those killed by careless drivers feel that the law is adequate to deal with the circumstances and that the justice system is on their side so that if, in all the circumstances, a court feels that custody is appropriate, it will be available. Of course, there will be instances—probably the majority—where custody is not considered to be the most appropriate penalty."

However, it is difficult to see how a court could do other than give serious consideration to a custodial sentence where Parliament has prescribed a maximum penalty of five years' imprisonment and the range of potential culpability is narrow. The Council's approach to sentencing identifies three levels of carelessness; the least serious is described as that which arises from momentary inattention with no aggravating factors, the most serious is described as that which falls not far short of dangerous driving and the remainder fall into the middle category. All but the least serious category has a starting point outside the powers of a magistrates' court: *www.sentencingcouncil.judiciary.gov.uk*. Since the aggravating factors include the commission of other offences at the same time (such as driving without insurance or a valid licence as well as those such as taking a vehicle without consent), previous convictions for motoring offences, causing serious injury as well as death, causing the death of more than one person and irresponsible behaviour after the collision, in most circumstances, it is likely that an offence will be sentenced in the Crown Court.

The problems that might be caused in sentencing for this offence are being revealed as cases begin to appear in the courts including the Court of Appeal. In *Larke* [2009] EWCA Crim 870 the defendant was performing a U turn from a lay-by on an A road. She failed to see an oncoming car which swerved and avoided a collision; however, a following motorcyclist was unable to avoid a collision and both he and his passenger (his 11-year-old step-daughter) were killed. The defendant was aged 74 with an unblemished driving record for 50 years; until 4 years before she had worked with adults with learning disabilities including driving them in a minibus. The U turn was a manoeuvre she had often undertaken successfully at this spot. She was genuinely devastated by what she had done. The Crown Court found carelessness of a high order approaching dangerousness and imposed a sentence of 2 years imprisonment; it was recognised that the carelessness was momentary not continuing but also that 2 deaths had been caused. The sentence was above the starting point but well below the top of the range provided in the relevant definitive guideline. The Court of Appeal did not place the offence within a different level of seriousness but noted the early guilty plea, the considerable remorse and the impeccable driving history. In all the circumstances, a custodial sentence was warranted but it could be at the lower end of the range and could be suspended; a sentence of 39 weeks suspended for 12 months was substituted. It appears that the defendant is likely to have spent almost 2 months in custody pending the hearing of the appeal and this may have been a factor in the decision of the Court of Appeal though not overtly referred to. In *Campbell (Karl)* [2010] R.T.R. 27 the defendant, who was aged 19, had been driving a vehicle which emerged from a junction onto a dual carriageway and struck a motor cyclist, who died from his injuries. He claimed to have looked but not seen the motor cyclist, and evidence from his expert suggested that the motor cycle had been travelling at excessive speed. The defendant accepted responsibility for the offence on the basis that he had had an unintentional momentary lapse in concentration. The Judge identified this offence as falling within level 2 of the guidelines and imposed a sentence of 24 weeks' imprisonment, suspended for two years with requirements for two years' supervision and 100 hours' unpaid work. On appeal, the Court of Appeal recognised that it is not an easy task for a judge to apply the categories in the sentencing guidelines. The lowest category concerned momentary inattention with no aggravating features, whilst the highest category involved driving falling not far short of dangerous driving. The second, intermediate, category is a residual category for driving which neither fell just short of dangerous driving nor constituted momentary inattention. That category could include instances of momentary misjudgement; each case would turn on its own facts and had to be viewed objectively in relation to the surrounding circumstances. In this case the judge had not fallen into error in categorising Mr Campbell's driving as falling within the second, intermediate, category in the sentencing guidelines. It was difficult to categorise what had happened as momentary inattention. The motorist had stopped at the junction and looked right, left and right again. He should have seen the motor cyclist. However, it was not clear that the judge had been aware of the defence evidence as to the speed of the motor cyclist. The unresolved issue of speed meant that the defendant's single misjudgement had to be placed at the lower end of the intermediate, second, category of careless driving in the guidelines. In all the circumstances, the level of culpability did not justify a custodial sentence and the sentence was quashed and substituted by a community order with an unpaid work requirement of 100 hours.

Substantial custodial sentences have been imposed in *Shepherd* [2010] EWCA Crim 46; [2010] 2 Cr.App.R.(S.) 54 (where a 4 year sentence was reduced on appeal to 3 years), in *Sims* [2010] EWCA Crim 2721 (where a 16 month sentence was upheld on appeal) and in *Crew* [2010] 2 Cr.App.R.(S.) 23 (where a 14 month sentence was upheld on appeal).

In *Shepherd* the defendant was driving too fast (possibly up to 80mph) on a September evening on a rural road in Cornwall which had a 40mph limit. To his knowledge, the car's anti-skid braking system was faulty; when he braked hard approaching a bend, the back wheels locked and the car swung into the path of an oncoming vehicle—the passenger in that car was killed. There was evidence that the defendant had been warned about his driving 3 days before the accident and had been involved in another incident of bad driving 3 hours before the fatal accident. This was a case that could have been charged as dangerous driving. The defendant was 18 years old and had only recently passed his driving test but had no previous convictions.

In *Sims* the defendant (who had a previous conviction for careless driving arising out of a fatal accident) made a right turn into the path of a motor cyclist who died following the collision.

In *Crew* the defendant was driving a hire car conveying two of his children from Heathrow Airport to Lincolnshire having flown overnight from San Francisco. On a long, straight section of single carriageway, and in good visibility and weather conditions, he collided with a car coming in the opposite direction; it was accepted that the defendant had fallen asleep momentarily. It was agreed that this fell into the most serious category identified in the guidelines. A custodial sentence of this length was considered to be inevitable even though, as stated by the Judge in the Crown Court when imposing sentence, the defendant did "not have a bad driving record in any way, shape or form, is a thoroughly decent man of positive good character", provided excellent testimonials and was a person for whom a sentence of imprisonment would be very hard to bear. At the other end of the spectrum is *Odedora* [2010] 2 Cr.App.R.(S.) 51, again a case arising from a motorist failing to see a motor cyclist when making a right turn. Although sentenced to 4 months imprisonment (following a guilty plea) in the Crown Court, a strongly constituted Court of Appeal considered that this was a matter of momentary inattention with no aggravating factors and that the custody threshold was not crossed. Carefully considering the sentencing guideline, the Court of Appeal noted that the impact of the death is likely to be considerable in every case and that Parliament had provided that sentences should be "in a bracket above careless driving without a fatality"; nonetheless, sentence has to be "matched to the culpability or blameworthiness of the defendant". In two further cases arising from a misjudged right turn, community orders have been imposed. In *Marjoram* [2011] 1 Cr.App.R.(S.) 55, a 34-year-old was driving his coach with 18 elderly passengers on a B road in Suffolk; he pulled into a filter lane governed by Give Way markings with a view to turning right. Believing the road to be clear he moved slowly across the junction without stopping but he had failed to see an approaching car that was being properly driven. He had been a coach driver for some years with an unblemished record. It was accepted that this fell into the lowest category of seriousness and the Court of Appeal replaced the suspended sentence order with a community order; as the defendant had already completed the 300 hours of unpaid work imposed under the SSO no change was made although it was not necessarily accepted to have been an order of the correct length. In *Palmer* [2010] EWCA Crim 1863 the defendant turned right from a main road into a side road across the path of a motor cycle which was being carefully ridden and well illuminated; she was 22 years old with an unblemished driving record and had pleaded guilty at the first opportunity. She received a community order requiring 200 hours of unpaid work. In both cases, attention was drawn to the provision in the sentencing guidelines that: "Where the level of carelessness is low and there are no aggravating factors, even the fact that death was caused is not sufficient to justify a prison sentence" (see *Magistrates' Court Sentencing Guidelines*, p.118, para. (c)).

F. Causing Death by Driving: Unlicensed, Disqualified or Uninsured Drivers

(1) Definition

Road Traffic Act 1988, s.3ZB

3ZB. A person is guilty of an offence under this section if he causes the death of another person by driving a motor vehicle on a road and, at the time when he is driving, the circumstances are such that he is committing an offence under— **17–46**

(a) section 87(1) of this Act (driving otherwise than in accordance with a licence),
(b) section 103(1)(b) of this Act (driving while disqualified), or
(c) section 143 of this Act (using motor vehicle while uninsured or unsecured against third party risks.)

(2) What must the prosecution prove?

The elements of this offence that the prosecution must prove are that: **17–47**

— the defendant was the driver;
— the vehicle was being driven;
— the vehicle was a motor vehicle;
— the vehicle was being driven on a road;
— the driver was committing an offence under section 87(1) *or* s.103(1)(b) *or* s.143;
— the death of another person is caused by that driving.

For issues of identification, see *ante*, §§ 10–89 *et seq.* in this work. For issues surrounding the meaning of "drive", see *ante*, § 17–4.

The phrase "motor vehicle" is different from "mechanically propelled vehicle"; again, this is explored more fully in § 17–6, *ante*.

The meaning of "road" has been subject to detailed consideration; this also is explored more fully in §§ 17–7 and 17–8, *ante*.

Note the exclusion of "other public place" in respect of this offence.

The issue of causation has, inevitably, reached the Court of Appeal and was considered by a strong constitution presided over by Thomas L.J. who gave the judgment of the court. In *Williams* (2010) 174 J.P. 606 the defendant was driving his own car although he was neither licensed nor insured. Early on a February evening, he was driving on a dual carriageway in a town centre within the 30mph speed limit when the victim stepped off the central reservation into his path and was killed; it was accepted that there was "no fault, carelessness or lack of consideration in driving" that could be attributed to the defendant. The defendant was convicted of causing death by driving without insurance and without a licence and sentenced to 9 months imprisonment. On appeal, it was submitted for the defence that the offence could not be committed without some fault of the defendant and that "cause" had to be construed in that way or, if not, that the fact that the defendant was driving had to be shown to be a substantial or major cause of the death. The prosecution submitted that Parliament had clearly intended the contrary. Having reviewed the leading authorities on causation, the Court of Appeal concluded (at para. 14) that "the simple question for the court is whether the death was caused by driving without insurance or without a driving licence". This was inevitable given the other offence of causing death by careless driving which provided a higher maximum penalty for situations where there had been a degree of fault in the driving. The cause must be "more than minute or negligible" but it was not relevant that there could be no civil claim against the defendant. Accordingly, even though the principal cause of the death was the action of the victim in stepping out in front of the car, the defendant was rightly convicted of the offence. However, the sentence of 9 months imprisonment was considered to be too long and was replaced by one of 24 weeks imprisonment.

(3) Allocation

17–48 This offence is triable either way. It can be expected that many cases will be dealt with in the Crown Court in recognition of the fact that death has occurred.

(4) Standard of driving

17–49 The offence is committed where the driving causes death and the offender is not properly licensed, is disqualified or is uninsured. There is unlikely to be an allegation of bad driving because that would have most likely resulted in a prosecution for a different offence.

(5) Penalty

17–50 The maximum penalty is imprisonment of up to six months (to be 12 months on implementation of *Criminal Justice Act* 2003, s.154) and/or a fine of level 5 (£5,000) on summary conviction and imprisonment of two years or a fine on indictment. It is an endorsable offence within the range of 3–11 points but one that attracts mandatory disqualification in the absence of special reasons.

(6) Sentence

17–51 This offence raises difficult issues where the level of harm far exceeds the level of culpability since it must be assumed that the fault of the driver was that of being on the road at all rather than the way in which the vehicle was driven (see *Williams* (2010) 174 J.P. 606 in § 17–47, *ante*). In the Sentencing Guidelines Council Guideline, *Overarching Principles: Seriousness* it is emphasised that, where there is an imbalance between harm and culpability, first consideration is to be given to the level of culpability. Nonetheless, it is clear that courts must now take fully into account the level of harm, particularly where death has resulted. The Sentencing Guidelines Council has published a definitive guideline for this offence which explores the issues arising from an offence where the driver's culpability is to do with the decision to drive rather than to the manner of the driving. It is likely that all offences committed by disqualified drivers will be sentenced in the Crown Court since the guideline provides for a starting point of 12 months imprisonment within a range of 36 weeks to 2 years for a first time offender who has pleaded not guilty. For this offence, in determining whether an offender was a first time offender, the offence which led to the disqualification from driving is ignored. Where the death is caused by a driver who was uninsured or unlicensed, that same starting point and range will apply where 2 or more aggravating factors were present. These are listed as previous convictions for motoring offences, causing serious injury as well as death, causing the death of more than one person and irresponsible behaviour after the collision. Where only one of those factors was present, the starting point will be 26 weeks (the limit for a magistrates' court) within a range of high community order to 36 weeks imprisonment. Where the offender was not a disqualified driver and there are no aggravating factors, the starting point will be a medium level community order and a custodial sentence will be outside the range. In most circumstances, because of the complexities of this offence in terms of sentence, it is likely that an offence will be sentenced in the Crown Court.

G. Failing to Stop after an Accident, Failing to Report an Accident

(1) Definition

Road Traffic Act 1988, s.170

Duty of driver to stop, report accident and give information or documents

170.—(1) This section applies in a case where, owing to the presence of a mechanically propelled vehicle on a road or other public place, an accident occurs by which— **17–52**

(a) personal injury is caused to a person other than the driver of that mechanically propelled vehicle, or

(b) damage is caused—

(i) to a vehicle other than that mechanically propelled vehicle or a trailer drawn by that mechanically propelled vehicle, or

(ii) to an animal other than an animal in or on that mechanically propelled vehicle or a trailer drawn by that mechanically propelled vehicle, or

(iii) to any other property constructed on, fixed to, growing in or otherwise forming part of the land on which the road or place in question is situated or land adjacent to such land.

(2) The driver of the mechanically propelled vehicle must stop and, if required to do so by any person having reasonable grounds for so requiring, give his name and address and also the name and address of the owner and the identification marks of the vehicle.

(3) If for any reason the driver of the mechanically propelled vehicle does not give his name and address under subsection (2) above, he must report the accident.

(4) A person who fails to comply with subsection (2) or (3) above is guilty of an offence.

(5) If, in a case where this section applies by virtue of subsection (1)(a) above, the driver of a motor vehicle does not at the time of the accident produce such a certificate of insurance or security, or other evidence, as is mentioned in section 165(2)(a) of this Act—

(a) to a constable, or

(b) to some person who, having reasonable grounds for so doing, has required him to produce it,

the driver must report the accident and produce such a certificate or other evidence.

This subsection does not apply to the driver of an invalid carriage.

(6) To comply with a duty under this section to report an accident or to produce such a certificate of insurance or security, or other evidence, as is mentioned in section 165(2)(a) of this Act, the driver—

(a) must do so at a police station or to a constable, and

(b) must do so as soon as is reasonably practicable and, in any case, within twenty-four hours of the occurrence of the accident.

(7) A person who fails to comply with a duty under subsection (5) above is guilty of an offence, but he shall not be convicted by reason only of a failure to produce a certificate or other evidence if, within seven days after the occurrence of the accident, the certificate or other evidence is produced at a police station that was specified by him at the time when the accident was reported.

(8) In this section "animal" means horse, cattle, ass, mule, sheep, pig, goat or dog.

(2) What must the prosecution prove?

17–53 The elements of this offence that the prosecution must prove are that:

— an accident occurs;
— the accident was due to the presence of a mechanically propelled vehicle on a road or other public place;
— personal injury or damage was caused; and
— that the driver of the mechanically propelled vehicle failed to fulfil the obligation placed on him to stop and report.

For the meaning of "accident", "mechanically propelled vehicle" and "road or other public place" see *ante*, §§ 17–2 *et seq.*

17–54 The obligation on the driver arises regardless of the responsibility for the accident. Once an accident has occurred as a result of the presence of a mechanically propelled vehicle on a road or other public place and there has been the qualifying injury or damage, then the obligation is on the driver of that vehicle to stop, to give the requisite details on request and, in certain circumstances, to report the accident to the police.

A driver can avoid this responsibility where he proves that he did not know that an accident had occurred. Once the prosecution has proved that an accident has occurred where the obligation arose to stop, in order to avoid responsibility the defendant must prove (on the balance of probabilities) that he was unaware of the accident: *Harding v. Price* [1948] 1 All E.R. 283. The more obvious the accident (noise of impact or damage to defendant's vehicle may be relevant) the more difficult it will be for the defendant to discharge the onus of proof.

(3) Allocation

17–55 These offences are summary only.

(4) Driver

17–56 The accident must arise from the presence of a mechanically propelled vehicle on a road or other public place. The obligations arising under this section fall on the driver of that vehicle. This is a potentially wide definition and there is no requirement to prove that the driver of the vehicle in question caused the accident. However, there must be a direct causal connection between the vehicle and the accident occurring. In *Quelch v. Phipps* [1955] 2 All E.R. 302, an accident occurred when a passenger got off a bus which he thought was slowing down for traffic lights. In fact, those lights had changed to green by the time the bus would have halted and so the driver continued. The driver was unaware of the accident until informed by the conductor at the next stop. Having not exchanged the necessary particulars with the passenger, the driver should have reported the accident. Since the accident happened through the passenger getting out of a motor vehicle on a road, it occurred "owing to the presence of a motor vehicle on a road" and came within the meaning of the section. Since the driver knew of the accident, albeit after the event, he was under an obligation to report it. The obligation to stop and report is designed to ensure that those who suffer as a result of bad driving have enough information to pursue any claims for compensation. A stationary vehicle may lead to liability if parked badly and the bad parking was such as to lead to the accident whereas a properly parked vehicle is unlikely to lead to liability.

(5) Qualifying injury or damage

17–57 For the obligations to arise, there must have been injury or damage. If injury is the basis, the injury must be to a person other than the driver of the mechanically propelled vehicle. So, if *A* and *B* are involved in an accident and *B* is injured but there is no other damage, the obligations to stop and report fall on *A* but not on *B*. This applies equally whether *B* is in the same vehicle as *A* or in a different vehicle.

If damage is the basis, then that damage may be to another vehicle (or trailer), to an animal in that other vehicle or trailer or to property on or close to the road. The types of animal are described in s.170(8) which limits them to any horse, cattle, ass, mule, sheep, pig, goat or dog.

The property has to be constructed on, fixed to, growing in or otherwise forming part of the land in question. It therefore has to have some degree of permanence—something placed temporarily on the land will not be sufficient. **17–58**

(6) Obligation imposed

Where the obligation exists, the driver must stop. He must also give certain details. If he fails to give those details he must provide them to the police within the time specified in the section. **17–59**

It is an absolute obligation to stop. This means to stop and to remain at the scene long enough to allow someone who has the right to do so to require the driver to provide the information that the section obliges him to give: *Lee v. Knapp* [1966] 3 All E.R. 961. This does not have to be an indefinite time, simply something sufficient in the circumstances prevailing at the time. There is no obligation on a driver to go and look for somebody who may be entitled to the information: *Mutton v. Bates (No.1)* [1984] R.T.R. 256. The stopping must be at the scene. Driving on for 80 yards before stopping and returning has been held to be insufficient compliance: *McDermott v. DPP* [1997] R.T.R. 474.

Any person having reasonable grounds for so doing, may require the driver to give his name and address and also the name and address of the owner and the identification marks of the vehicle. The purpose of this is to ensure that anyone who may have a claim against the driver has sufficient information to pursue it. It may be acceptable, therefore, for the address to be one through which the driver can be reached even if not the place where he is currently residing: *DPP v. McCarthy* [1999] R.T.R. 323.

Where personal injury has occurred to another person, if the driver does not produce proof of insurance at the scene to the police or to another person having reasonable grounds for requiring it, he must report the accident and produce the proof: s.170(5). Alternatively, if the proof of insurance is not produced when the accident is reported, that proof must be produced at a police station which must be a station specified by the driver when he reported the accident. **17–60**

If a driver does not give his name and address to anyone (for whatever reason) or produce the insurance certificate where that is required, he must report the accident to the police. He must do this by reporting it to a police station or to a constable as soon as reasonably practicable. Even where it is not reasonably practicable, that time must be within 24 hours of the accident. This obligation arises even where the police were present at the scene and even where, though present, the police did not request information. In *DPP v. Hay* [2006] R.T.R. 3, the defendant was the driver of a car which hit a wall rendering the driver unconscious. The police were quickly on the scene but unable to speak to the driver who remained unconscious. The driver argued successfully before justices that the obligation to stop and report did not arise where the police were on the scene throughout. However, the Divisional Court held that the statutory requirement was plain and there was no exception (express or implied) where the police attended the accident but did not speak to the driver for whatever reason. The case was returned with a direction to convict.

The reporting must be done personally since the requirement is to report "at" a police station or "to" a constable: *Wisdom v. Macdonald* [1983] R.T.R. 186.

(7) Penalties

The maximum penalty for an offence under this section is a fine of level 5 (£5000) and/or six months imprisonment. All offences are endorsable with a range of 5–10 points. Disqualification can be imposed. **17–61**

See also the power to deprive the offender of the vehicle contained in subss. 143(1), (6) and (7) of the *Powers of Criminal Courts (Sentencing) Act* 2000 (see *post*, §§ 17–209 and 23–229 *et seq*.).

(8) Sentence

17–62 This section contains a range of offences with differing levels of seriousness. A court passing sentence will do so against the background of the purpose of the section and the reason why the defendant failed to fulfil his obligation.

The purpose of the offences stems from the recognition that causing an accident will, at the very least, lead to issues of compensating those who have suffered loss as a result and may lead to criminal proceedings. The motivation of the defendant may range from panic or fear for personal safety through to a deliberate attempt to avoid responsibility for a more serious offence, perhaps because the driver suspected that his alcohol level was such that he would be liable for compulsory disqualification.

A defendant may commit an offence in the following ways:

s.170(2)	Failing to stop (but still reporting the accident)
	Stopping but not giving details (but reporting the accident)
	Stopping but not giving details (and not reporting the accident)
	Stopping, giving details but not producing proof of insurance even though personal injury caused to another person
s.170(3)	Not reporting the accident at all
	Reporting the accident but later than permitted
s.170(7)	Failing to produce proof of insurance when required—if it was not produced at the scene of the accident, it should be produced when reporting the accident or within 7 days of reporting it

17–63 The *Magistrates' Court Sentencing Guidelines* provides for three levels of seriousness. Those levels depend either on the extent of damage or injury caused or on the extent to which the offender failed to fulfil the legal obligations placed on a driver. Where both of those elements are found to be present, it can be expected that a sentence towards the higher part of the range will be imposed.

STARTING POINT AND RANGE OF SENTENCE

(BASED ON A FIRST TIME OFFENDER PLEADING NOT GUILTY)

Examples of nature of activity	**Starting Point**	**Range**
Minor damage/injury or stopped at scene but failed to exchange particulars or report	Band B fine	Band B fine 5–6 points
Moderate damage/injury or failed to stop and failed to report	Band C fine	Band C fine 7–8 points Consider disqualification

Examples of nature of activity	Starting Point	Range
Serious damage/injury and/or evidence of bad driving	High level community order	Band C fine to 26 weeks custody Disqualify 6–12 months OR 9–10 points

A number of aggravating and mitigating factors are identified as being particularly relevant to this offence:

AGGRAVATING AND MITIGATING FACTORS

Factors indicating higher culpability	Factors indicating lower culpability
1. Evidence of drink or drugs / evasion of test 2. Knowledge / suspicion that personal injury caused (where not an element of the offence) 3. Leaving injured party at scene 4. Giving false details	1. Believed identity known 2. Genuine fear of retribution 3. Subsequently reported

Although the offences are imprisonable, it is suggested that this power should be used only rarely. Use may be appropriate where the Court considers that the defendant was deliberately trying to evade responsibility for a more serious offence for which he would have received a custodial sentence or where serious injury was caused which could have been better treated if the defendant had stopped.

Disqualification should be considered for the more serious offences though short periods are likely to be sufficient to emphasise the importance of the responsibility placed on drivers. If the offence was accompanied by driving below an acceptable standard, there is likely to be a separate offence. **17–64**

III. ALCOHOL/DRUGS RELATED OFFENCES

This is a highly complex (and much litigated) area of the criminal law. This work sets out the key areas and the key issues. For a more detailed examination, reference should be made to *Wilkinson's Road Traffic Offences*. There are two main offences (those under ss.4 and 5) and then other offences arising from the two stages for producing evidence to assess the amount of alcohol or drugs involved. **17–65**

A. DRIVING ETC. WHILST UNFIT THROUGH ALCOHOL OR DRUGS

(1) Definition

Road Traffic Act 1988, s.4

Driving, or being in charge, when under influence of drink or drugs

4.—(1) A person who, when driving or attempting to drive a mechanically propelled vehicle on a road or other public place, is unfit to drive through drink or drugs is guilty of an offence. **17–66**

(2) Without prejudice to subsection (1) above, a person who, when in charge of a mechanically propelled vehicle which is on a road or other public place, is unfit to drive through drink or drugs is guilty of an offence.

(3) For the purposes of subsection (2) above, a person shall be deemed not to have been in charge of a mechanically propelled vehicle if he proves that at the material time the circumstances were such that there was no likelihood of his driving it so long as he remained unfit to drive through drink or drugs.

(4) The court may, in determining whether there was such a likelihood as is mentioned in subsection (3) above, disregard any injury to him and any damage to the vehicle.

(5) For the purposes of this section, a person shall be taken to be unfit to drive if his ability to drive properly is for the time being impaired.

(2) Allocation

17–67 These offences are summary only.

(3) What must the prosecution prove?

17–68 The prosecution must prove that:

— the defendant:

— drove *or* attempted to drive *or* was in charge of:

— a mechanically propelled vehicle;

— on a road or other public place;

— whilst unfit through drink or drugs.

For issues of identification, see *ante*, §§ 10–89 *et seq.* in this work.

For issues surrounding the meaning of "drive", see *ante*, § 17–4.

The phrase "mechanically propelled vehicle" is wider than "vehicle"; again this is more fully explored in § 17–6, *ante*.

The phrase "road or other public place" has been subject to detailed consideration; this also is explored more fully in §§ 17–7 and 17–8, *ante*.

In order to prove an offence under this section, the prosecution must prove that the defendant was unfit to drive and that that was due to drink or to drugs. To that extent, it is more widely drawn than s.5 which is restricted to alcohol and sets a standard that is capable of precise measurement. Since evidence available to support a charge under s.5 is also admissible under s.4, it is likely that charges under s.4 are more likely to be used where the presence of *alcohol* is not the cause of the unfitness.

A person is unfit to drive if "his ability to drive properly is for the time being impaired": s.4(5). It is the ability to drive *properly* that is impaired not the ability to drive at all. This may be evidenced by the way the vehicle was being driven, or by involvement in an accident where there was nothing that would normally cause such an accident or it may be evidenced by the condition of the defendant. Where alcohol is alleged to be the cause of the unfitness, a certificate of analysis obtained under s.7 of the 1988 Act (see *post*, § 17–96) is admissible and must be taken into account: s.15(2) and (3) of the *Road Traffic Offenders Act* 1988.

17–69 Where drugs are alleged to be the cause of the unfitness, s.11 of the *Road Traffic Act* 1988 defines "drug" as meaning any intoxicant other than alcohol. According to the Oxford Concise Dictionary, "intoxicate" can have three variants—it can mean to cause someone to lose control of their faculties; it can also mean to poison or to excite or exhilarate—presumably it is the first variant that is intended! It is possible that the effect of alcohol could be increased when taken in conjunction with certain drugs and a conviction under s.4 would be appropriate in such circumstances where the combined effect impaired the defendant's ability to drive properly whereas the amount of alcohol on its own may have caused the level in the body to be below the legal limit. Under s.7 of the 1988 Act, the police may require a person to provide samples of breath, blood or urine for analysis in the course of an investigation concerning a possible offence under s.4. A breath test will not disclose useful information about drugs. Where a medical practitioner advises the police officer that the defendant's condition might be due to drugs (and there must be a clear oral statement to that effect by the medical practitioner), the police officer can require the defendant to provide a specimen of blood or urine even if a specimen of breath has already been provided: s.7(3)(c). A certificate of analysis must be taken into account (ss.15 and 16 of the *Road Traffic Offenders Act* 1988) but, in contrast to a certificate relating to alcohol, there is no statutory assumption that the proportion of drug in a specimen is not less than at the time the offence was committed. Since the Act does not provide a level that must be exceeded for an offence under s.4 (as it does for an offence under s.5), it will be for the court to assess whether the defendant was unfit and whether this was due to the presence of the drugs identified in the certificate.

If the defendant wishes to allege that the level in the analysis was caused by consumption of alcohol or drugs after the driving, etc. had ceased but before the sample was provided, then the onus is on the defendant to satisfy the court on the balance of probabilities not only that that happened but also that the amount was sufficient to render the reading invalid as proof that the defendant was unfit at the time of the offence or, in the case of alcohol (see *ante*), above the prescribed limit: s.15(3) of the *Road Traffic Offenders Act* 1988.

Where it is alleged that a person has "attempted" to commit an offence, it seems clear that, even for a statutory, summary only, offence such as those under s.4 or s.5, the prosecution must prove that the defendant has done an act that is "more than merely preparatory" to the commission of the full offence. There is no single definition of where the border falls between an act that is "merely preparatory" and one that is sufficient to found liability for an attempt. As Lord Reid stated in *Haughton* [1975] A.C. 476, there is an immense variety of possible causes and "it must be left to common sense to determine in each case whether the accused has gone beyond mere preparation". In relation to attempts to drive on a road, the boundary was explored again in *Moore v. DPP* [2010] R.T.R. 36. The defendant worked for an establishment with a secure perimeter. He collected his car from within that perimeter and was driving towards the security gate which gave access to the public road. He was stopped shortly before that gate because the security guard suspected that he had consumed sufficient alcohol to be over the legal limit. The defendant sought to avoid conviction for attempting to drive on a public road with excess alcohol by two main arguments—one that, as he was "driving" (albeit not on a public road), he could not be convicted of attempting to drive and the other that his acts were "no more than merely preparatory" and so not sufficient. Both arguments were rejected. The activity of the defendant was sufficiently close to the final act to be properly regarded as part of the execution of the defendant's course of criminal conduct; the fact that there was an intervening factor which prevented the driving on the public road did not prevent the actions of the defendant from being an attempt to drive on a public road.

Part III

(4) Penalties

The maximum penalty for *driving or attempting to drive* is a fine of level 5 (cur- **17–70**
rently £5000) and/or six months' imprisonment. There is a mandatory requirement to disqualify from driving (in the absence of special reasons) for one year (though see *post*, § 17–177 for the circumstances where that minimum is increased). On endorsement only, there will be penalty points of between 3 and 11.

The maximum penalty for *being in charge* is a fine of level 4 (currently £2500) and/or three months' imprisonment. There is a discretionary requirement to disqualify from driving. On endorsement, there will be penalty points of 10.

See also the power to deprive the offender of the vehicle contained in s.143(1), (6) and (7) of the *Powers of Criminal Courts (Sentencing) Act* 2000 (see *post*, §§ 17–212 and 23–204).

(5) Sentence

The primary factor for the court in determining sentence will be the extent of the **17–71**
intoxication. Lower penalties are generally imposed for being in charge than for driving.

Normally, financial penalties are considered sufficient together with the disqualification which is mandatory in the case of driving offences and discretionary for in charge offences.

However, the starting point for a first time offender who has been convicted of driving or attempting to drive whilst unfit after pleading not guilty will be a custodial sentence where there is evidence of a high level of impairment accompanied by one or more of the aggravating factors listed in the guideline (see below). Where convicted of being in charge, a custodial sentence is within the range in such circumstances.

STARTING POINT AND RANGE OF SENTENCE

(BASED ON A FIRST TIME OFFENDER PLEADING NOT GUILTY)

Examples of nature of activity	**Starting point**	**Range**	**Disqualification**	**Disqual. 2nd offence in 10 years**
Evidence of moderate level of impairment and no aggravating factors	Band C fine	Band C fine	12–16 months	36–40 months
Evidence of moderate level of impairment and presence of one or more aggravating factors listed below	Band C fine	Band C fine	17–22 months	36–46 months
Evidence of high level of impairment and no aggravating factors	Medium level community order	Low level community order to high level community order	23–28 months	36–52 months

Examples of nature of activity	Starting point	Range	Disqualification	Disqual. 2nd offence in 10 years
Evidence of high level of impairment and presence of one or more aggravating factors listed below	12 weeks custody	High level community order to 26 weeks custody	29–36 months	36–60 months

AGGRAVATING AND MITIGATING FACTORS

Factors indicating higher culpability	Factors indicating lower culpability
1. LGV, HGV, PSV etc. 2. Poor road or weather conditions 3. Carrying passengers 4. Driving for hire or reward 5. Evidence of unacceptable standard of driving	1. Genuine emergency established * 2. Spiked drinks * 3. Very short distance driven * * even where not amounting to special reasons
Factors indicating greater degree of harm 1. Involved in accident 2. Location e.g. near school 3. High level of traffic or pedestrians in the vicinity	

As will be seen, the assessment of seriousness is based initially on the level of impairment—was that moderate or high?—and then on the presence of aggravating factors. For the "moderate impairment" levels, the presence of aggravating factors is likely to make the greatest difference to the period of disqualification rather than to the level of fine. **17–72**

For "high impairment" levels, the presence of aggravating factors is likely to take the offence across the custody threshold.

A similar approach is adopted in relation to "being in charge" but with lower levels of sentence and a more restricted range of aggravating factors reflecting the characteristics of the offence.

STARTING POINT AND RANGE OF SENTENCE

(BASED ON A FIRST TIME OFFENDER PLEADING NOT GUILTY)

Examples of nature of activity	Starting Point	Range
Evidence of moderate level of impairment and no aggravating factors	Band B fine	Band B fine 10 points
Evidence of moderate level of impairment and presence of one or more aggravating factors listed below	Band B fine	Band B fine 10 points or consider disqualification
Evidence of high level of impairment and no aggravating factors	Band C fine	Band C fine to medium level community order 10 points or consider disqualification
Evidence of high level of impairment and presence of one or more aggravating factors listed below	High level community order	Medium level community order to 12 weeks custody Consider disqualification OR 10 points

AGGRAVATING AND MITIGATING FACTORS

Factors indicating higher culpability	Factor indicating lower culpability
1. LGV, HGV, PSV etc.	1. Low likelihood of driving
2. High likelihood of driving	
3. Driving for hire or reward	

B. DRIVING ETC. WITH EXCESS ALCOHOL IN THE BODY

(1) Definition

Road Traffic Act 1988, s.5

Driving or being in charge of a motor vehicle with alcohol concentration above prescribed limit

17–73 5.—(1) If a person—

(a) drives or attempts to drive a motor vehicle on a road or other public place, or

(b) is in charge of a motor vehicle on a road or other public place,
after consuming so much alcohol that the proportion of it in his breath, blood or urine exceeds the prescribed limit he is guilty of an offence.

(2) It is a defence for a person charged with an offence under subsection (1)(b) above to prove that at the time he is alleged to have committed the offence the circumstances were such that there was no likelihood of his driving the vehicle whilst the proportion of alcohol in his breath, blood or urine remained likely to exceed the prescribed limit.

(3) The court may, in determining whether there was such a likelihood as is mentioned in subsection (2) above, disregard any injury to him and any damage to the vehicle.

(2) Allocation

These offences are summary only. 17–74

(3) What must the prosecution prove?

The prosecution must prove that: 17–75

— the defendant:
— drove *or* attempted to drive *or* was in charge of:
— a mechanically propelled vehicle;
— on a road or other public place;
— after consuming so much alcohol;
— that the proportion in his breath, blood or urine;
— exceeded the prescribed limit.

For issues of identification, see *ante*, §§ 10–89 *et seq.* in this work. 17–76

For issues surrounding the meaning of "drive", see *ante*, § 17–4.

For the approach to an "attempt" to commit this offence, see *ante*, § 17–69.

The phrase "mechanically propelled vehicle" is wider than "vehicle"; again this is more fully explored in § 17–6, *ante*. The phrase "road or other public place" has been subject to detailed consideration; this also is explored more fully in §§ 17–7 and 17–8, *ante*.

"Consuming" has been defined more widely than just "drinking"; entry into the body by other means can also be included: *DPP v. Johnson (David)* [1995] R.T.R. 9.

The proportion of alcohol can be assessed through an analysis of breath or of blood or of urine. This is provided for by s.7—see *post*, § 17–96.

The prescribed limit is set out in s.11(2) of the *Road Traffic Act* 1988. 17–77

In breath, the limit is 35 microgrammes of alcohol in 100 millilitres of breath.

In blood, the limit is 80 milligrammes of alcohol in 100 millilitres of blood.

In urine, the limit is 107 milligrammes of alcohol in 100 millilitres of urine.

This limit must be exceeded before a prosecution can be commenced, *e.g.* the analysis must be at least 81mg in blood, 80 is not sufficient. In practice, in relation to analysis based on breath, the police will normally allow for a margin of error. When machinery was introduced that enabled the proportion of alcohol in breath to be measured, the accompanying Home Office Circular (46/1983) provided for an allowance to be made where the analysis showed that the limit was exceeded by a small amount. This was in recognition both of the similar practice undertaken in laboratory analysis of blood or urine and of the relatively new technology incorporated in those early breath testing machines. The circular provided for prosecution based on an analysis of breath only where the reading was 40 microgrammes or more. The relevant part provides:

> "The reading produced by the calibration check test must fall within 3 micrograms of 35 (*i.e.* within the range 32–38 inclusive) to establish that the instrument is working correctly. To cater for those occasions where the machine may be reading high, albeit within this range, the police will not proceed against offenders with a result of less than 40 micrograms. This will ensure that any offender prosecuted will have a result in excess of the prescribed limit. This allowance is comparable to the allowance currently subtracted from specimens analysed in the laboratory."

Part III

This was subsequently incorporated into the Code of Practice for Crown Prosecutors which provides:

> "In most cases of drink/driving, there will be scientific and/or medical evidence to show that the driver has exceeded the prescribed limit. In such cases a charge under section 5 will be proper.
> Although the prescribed breath alcohol limit is 35 microgrammes, a driver will not be prosecuted under section 5 with a breath alcohol level of less than 40 microgrammes. This is in accordance with the guidelines contained in Home Office Circular 46/1983. That level will usually be taken as that recorded by an evidential breath testing machine or by analysis of a blood/urine sample. However, it may be the level as determined by back calculations."

The allowance in relation to blood or urine will already have been taken into account when the analysis is undertaken.

If a defendant wishes to allege that the analysis showed an excess as a result of alcohol consumed after the driving, etc. had ceased but before the sample was taken, then the defendant must prove (on the balance of probabilities) both that alcohol had been consumed in those circumstances and that the amount would have been sufficient to take the reading over the limit: *Road Traffic Offenders Act* 1988, s.15(3). Unless the effect of the alcohol would have been obvious, expert evidence must be adduced: *DPP v. Dukolli* [2009] EWHC 3097.

There have been continual attempts to evade conviction for these offences by a range of technical arguments calling into question the machines or the process used. Likewise, the appeal courts have continued to decline to accept the arguments put forward.

In *DPP v. Stephens* [2006] EWHC 1860 there were issues about the admissibility of a statement from the doctor and a certificate from an analyst neither of which had been served in accordance with the provisions of s.16 of the *Road Traffic Offenders Act* 1988. The doctor's statement had, however, been properly served as a s.9 statement. The defence successfully sought to exclude both documents because they had not been served properly under the s.16 provisions. The court refused the prosecution application for an adjournment to serve them properly. Allowing the prosecution appeal, the Divisional Court stated that the court had been wrong to exclude the doctor's statement which should have been admissible under s.9 which was not overridden by the s.16 provisions. Whilst the certificate was not admissible, the court was wrong to refuse the prosecution's application for an adjournment. Although an appeal court will only interfere with the exercise of discretion whether to grant an adjournment where it is plain that substantial unfairness will be caused to one of the parties, this was such a situation. The refusal to grant the adjournment was irrational and could not be upheld.

In *Sneyd v. DPP* [2007] R.T.R. 6, the defendant had been one of two drivers stopped whilst driving a car out of the car park of a public house. He confirmed he had been drinking and then provided a positive specimen. That process was challenged by an assertion that the driver should have been cautioned before being asked whether he had been drinking. The Divisional Court rejected that argument—it is not an offence to drink so there was no suspicion that an offence had been committed until after the specimen had been provided. The answer was however adequate to raise a sufficient suspicion to justify the requirement to provide a specimen of breath. Evidence of the subsequent reading of the machine undertaking the analysis of breath was given orally rather than by a printout and there was no evidence that the machine was properly calibrated. The defence argument that this was unacceptable was robustly rejected. There was ample authority that oral evidence could be given and since the evidence that the machine was working properly was sufficiently clear, it followed that the machine was properly calibrated. It was for the defence to raise the issue by cross-examination rather than to assert subsequently that there had been no evidence.

(4) Penalties

17–78 The maximum penalty for *driving or attempting to drive* is a fine of level 5 (currently £5000) and/or six months' imprisonment. There is a mandatory requirement to disqualify from driving (in the absence of special reasons, see *post*, § 17–194) for one year (though see *post*, § 17–177 for circumstances where that minimum is increased). On endorsement only, there will be penalty points of between 3 and 11.

The maximum penalty for *being in charge* is a fine of level 4 (currently £2500) and/or three months' imprisonment. There is a discretionary requirement to disqualify from driving. On endorsement, there will be penalty points of 10.

See also the power to deprive the offender of the vehicle contained in subss. 143(1), (6) and (7) of the *Powers of Criminal Courts (Sentencing) Act* 2000 (see *post*, § 17–209).

(5) Sentence

The *Magistrates' Court Sentencing Guidelines* provide for the approach to sentencing to be based on the level of alcohol. Where the offender is convicted of driving or attempting to drive, the community threshold is identified as being crossed where the level was between 90–119μg and the custody threshold where the level exceeded 120μg. In *Goldsmith (Thomas) v. DPP* [2010] R.T.R 20, it was held that the assumption in s.15(2) of the *Road Traffic Offenders Act* 1988 (that the proportion of alcohol in the breath, blood or urine at the time of the alleged offence was not less than in the specimen) applies only to trials and not to sentence. The complicated facts in this case could (if the assumption applied) have led to a court imposing sentence on the basis of a level of alcohol which was believed to be significantly higher than the actual level at the time the driving took place. Following a detailed analysis, the Divisional Court concluded that the presumption in s.15(2) applied only to trials: "It would be an affront to justice if a sentencer was compelled by reason of a statutory assumption to sentence a convicted defendant on a basis that was not merely known to the sentencer to be false but was known to be falsely adverse to the defendant". The starting point for the extent of disqualification also increases in proportion to the level. The guideline also provides for increasing levels of disqualification where the minimum period is increased to 3 years because of a previous relevant conviction. Courts are encouraged to consider an interim disqualification if there is a delay between conviction and sentencing. **17–79**

Note: the final column below provides guidance regarding the length of disqualification that may be appropriate in cases to which the 3 year minimum applies. The period to be imposed in any individual case will depend on an assessment of all the relevant circumstances, including the length of time since the earlier ban was imposed and the gravity of the current offence.

STARTING POINT AND RANGE OF SENTENCE

(BASED ON A FIRST TIME OFFENDER PLEADING NOT GUILTY)

Level of alcohol: Breath (µg)	**Level of alcohol: Blood (ml)**	**Level of alcohol: Urine (ml)**	**Starting point**	**Range**	**Disqualification**	**Disqual. (2nd offence in 10 years —see note above)**
36–59	81–137	108–183	Band C fine	Band C fine	12–16 months	36–40 months
60–89	138–206	184–274	Band C fine	Band C fine	17–22 months	36–46 months
90–119	207-275	275-366	Medium level community order	Low level community order to high level community order	23–28 months	36–52 months
120–150 and above	276-345 and above	367-459 and above	12 weeks custody	High level community order to 26 weeks custody	29–36 months	36–60 months

AGGRAVATING AND MITIGATING FACTORS

Factors indicating higher culpability	Factors indicating lower culpability
1. LGV, HGV, PSV etc. 2. Poor road or weather conditions 3. Carrying passengers 4. Driving for hire or reward 5. Evidence of unacceptable standard of driving **Factors indicating greater degree of harm** 1. Involved in accident 2. Location e.g. near school 3. High level of traffic or pedestrians in the vicinity	1. Genuine emergency established * 2. Spiked drinks * 3. Very short distance driven * * even where not amounting to special reasons

A similar approach is adopted where the offender is convicted of being "in charge" with the community and custody thresholds being placed at a higher level. Whilst custody is provided in the range for the most serious level of offending, it is not the starting point. It is likely to be crossed, therefore, either when the level of intoxicant was significantly above 150μg or there were aggravating factors, including relevant previous convictions. **17–80**

STARTING POINT AND RANGE OF SENTENCE

(BASED ON A FIRST TIME OFFENDER PLEADING NOT GUILTY)

Level of alcohol: Breath (μg)	Level of alcohol: Blood (ml)	Level of alcohol: Urine (ml)	Starting Point	Range
36–59	81-137	108-183	Band B fine	Band B fine 10 points
60–89	138-206	184-274	Band B fine	Band B fine 10 points OR consider disqualification

Level of alcohol: Breath (μg)	**Level of alcohol: Blood (ml)**	**Level of alcohol: Urine (ml)**	**Starting Point**	**Range**
90–119	207-275	275-366	Band C fine	Band C fine to medium level community order Consider disqualification up to 6 months OR 10 points
120–150 and above	276-345 and above	367-459 and above	Medium level community order	Low level community order to 6 weeks custody Disqualify 6-12 months

AGGRAVATING AND MITIGATING FACTORS

Factors indicating higher culpability	**Factor indicating lower culpability**
1. LGV, HGV, PSV etc. 2. Ability to drive seriously impaired 3. High likelihood of driving 4. Driving for hire or reward	1. Low likelihood of driving

C. FAILURE TO SUPPLY A PRELIMINARY SPECIMEN OF BREATH

(1) Definitions

Road Traffic Act 1988, ss.6–6E

Power to administer preliminary tests

17–81 **6.**—(1) If any of subsections (2) to (5) applies a constable may require a person to cooperate with any one or more preliminary tests administered to the person by that constable or another constable.

(2) This subsection applies if a constable reasonably suspects that the person—

(a) is driving, is attempting to drive or is in charge of a motor vehicle on a road or other public place, and

(b) has alcohol or a drug in his body or is under the influence of a drug.

(3) This subsection applies if a constable reasonably suspects that the person—

(a) has been driving, attempting to drive or in charge of a motor vehicle on a road or other public place while having alcohol or a drug in his body or while unfit to drive because of a drug, and

(b) still has alcohol or a drug in his body or is still under the influence of a drug.

(4) This subsection applies if a constable reasonably suspects that the person—

(a) is or has been driving, attempting to drive or in charge of a motor vehicle on a road or other public place, and

(b) has committed a traffic offence while the vehicle was in motion.

(5) This subsection applies if—

(a) an accident occurs owing to the presence of a motor vehicle on a road or other public place, and

(b) a constable reasonably believes that the person was driving, attempting to drive or in charge of the vehicle at the time of the accident.

(6) A person commits an offence if without reasonable excuse he fails to cooperate with a preliminary test in pursuance of a requirement imposed under this section.

(7) A constable may administer a preliminary test by virtue of any of subsections (2) to (4) only if he is in uniform.

(8) In this section—

(a) a reference to a preliminary test is to any of the tests described in sections 6A to 6C, and

(b) "traffic offence" means an offence under—

(i) a provision of Part II of the *Public Passenger Vehicles Act* 1981,

(ii) a provision of the *Road Traffic Regulation Act* 1984,

(iii) a provision of the *Road Traffic Offenders Act* 1988 other than a provision of Part III, or

(iv) a provision of this Act other than a provision of Part V.

Preliminary breath test

6A.—(1) A preliminary breath test is a procedure whereby the person to whom the test is administered provides a specimen of breath to be used for the purpose of obtaining, by means of a device of a type approved by the Secretary of State, an indication whether the proportion of alcohol in the person's breath or blood is likely to exceed the prescribed limit. **17–82**

(2) A preliminary breath test administered in reliance on section 6(2) to (4) may be administered only at or near the place where the requirement to cooperate with the test is imposed.

(3) A preliminary breath test administered in reliance on section 6(5) may be administered—

(a) at or near the place where the requirement to cooperate with the test is imposed, or

(b) if the constable who imposes the requirement thinks it expedient, at a police station specified by him.

Preliminary impairment test

6B.—(1) A preliminary impairment test is a procedure whereby the constable administering the test— **17–83**

(a) observes the person to whom the test is administered in his performance of tasks specified by the constable, and

(b) makes such other observations of the person's physical state as the constable thinks expedient.

(2) The Secretary of State shall issue (and may from time to time revise) a code of practice about—

(a) the kind of task that may be specified for the purpose of a preliminary impairment test,

(b) the kind of observation of physical state that may be made in the course of a preliminary impairment test,

(c) the manner in which a preliminary impairment test should be administered, and

(d) the inferences that may be drawn from observations made in the course of a preliminary impairment test.

(3) In issuing or revising the code of practice the Secretary of State shall aim to ensure that a preliminary impairment test is designed to indicate—

(a) whether a person is unfit to drive, and

(b) if he is, whether or not his unfitness is likely to be due to drink or drugs.

(4) A preliminary impairment test may be administered—

(a) at or near the place where the requirement to cooperate with the test is imposed, or

(b) if the constable who imposes the requirement thinks it expedient, at a police station specified by him.

(5) A constable administering a preliminary impairment test shall have regard to the code of practice under this section.

(6) A constable may administer a preliminary impairment test only if he is approved for that purpose by the chief officer of the police force to which he belongs.

(7) A code of practice under this section may include provision about—

(a) the giving of approval under subsection (6), and

(b) in particular, the kind of training that a constable should have undergone, or the kind of qualification that a constable should possess, before being approved under that subsection.

Preliminary drug test

17–84 **6C.**—(1) A preliminary drug test is a procedure by which a specimen of sweat or saliva is—

(a) obtained, and

(b) used for the purpose of obtaining, by means of a device of a type approved by the Secretary of State, an indication whether the person to whom the test is administered has a drug in his body.

(2) A preliminary drug test may be administered—

(a) at or near the place where the requirement to cooperate with the test is imposed, or

(b) if the constable who imposes the requirement thinks it expedient, at a police station specified by him.

Arrest

17–85 **6D.**—(1) A constable may arrest a person without warrant if as a result of a preliminary breath test the constable reasonably suspects that the proportion of alcohol in the person's breath or blood exceeds the prescribed limit.

(1A) The fact that specimens of breath have been provided under section 7 of this Act by the person concerned does not prevent subsection (1) above having effect if the constable who imposed on him the requirement to provide the specimens has reasonable cause to believe that the device used to analyse the specimens has not produced a reliable indication of the proportion of alcohol in the breath of the person.

(2) A constable may arrest a person without warrant if—

(a) the person fails to cooperate with a preliminary test in pursuance of a requirement imposed under section 6, and

(b) the constable reasonably suspects that the person has alcohol or a drug in his body or is under the influence of a drug.

(2A) A person arrested under this section may, instead of being taken to a police station, be detained at or near the place where the preliminary test was, or would have been, administered, with a view to imposing on him there a requirement under section 7 of this Act.

(3) A person may not be arrested under this section while at a hospital as a patient.

Power of entry

17–86 **6E.**—(1) A constable may enter any place (using reasonable force if necessary) for the purpose of—

(a) imposing a requirement by virtue of section 6(5) following an accident in a case where the constable reasonably suspects that the accident involved injury of any person, or

(b) arresting a person under section 6D following an accident in a case where the constable reasonably suspects that the accident involved injury of any person.

(2) This section—

(a) does not extend to Scotland, and

(b) is without prejudice to any rule of law or enactment about the right of a constable in Scotland to enter any place.

(2) Allocation

These offences are triable summarily only. **17–87**

(3) What must the prosecution prove?

The prosecution must prove that: **17–88**
— the defendant:
— having been required to provide a breath specimen under this section;
— failed to do so;
— [without reasonable excuse].

For issues of identification, see § 10–89 in this work.

A person commits an offence by failing to provide this preliminary specimen of **17–89** breath without reasonable excuse. The purpose of the test is to obtain an indication whether the proportion of alcohol is likely to exceed the prescribed limit.

The prosecution must prove that the test was lawfully required but was not provided. It is for the defendant to initiate the "reasonable excuse" but, once that is done, it is for the prosecution to negative that defence.

There are a number of elements that must exist before a requirement is lawfully made under this section.

1) The test must be required by a *constable in uniform* where the reason for the requirement is that:
   — the constable has reasonable cause to *suspect* that:
   — a person who is driving/attempting to drive/in charge of:
   — a motor vehicle (*note: not a "mechanically propelled vehicle"*);
   — on a road or other place;
   — either:
      — has alcohol in his body (s.6(2)); or
      — has committed a traffic offence whilst the vehicle was in motion (s.6(4)).

   Similarly where the constable in uniform has reasonable cause to suspect that the person *has been* driving/attempting to drive/in charge of a motor vehicle with adjustments to reflect the fact that the driving, etc. has ceased: s.6(3).
2) The test may be required by a *constable* where the reason for the requirement is that:
   — an accident has occurred:
   — owing to the presence of a motor vehicle on a road or other public place;
   — and the constable has reasonable cause to *believe*;
   — that the person was driving/in charge at the time of the accident (s.6(5)).

The test must be taken at or near the place where the requirement is made save that, **17–90** where the requirement arises from an accident as in 2, *ante*, the constable may require it to be taken at a police station if he thinks fit: s.6A(3). If a person is at a hospital as a patient, the requirement for a breath test may only be made after notice has been given to the medical practitioner in charge of the case. The medical practitioner may object on the grounds that either requiring or taking the test would be prejudicial to the proper care and treatment of the patient; in those circumstances, the requirement may not be made. If a requirement is made, it must be for the taking of this preliminary breath test at the hospital: s.9(1). "Hospital" is defined in s.11(2).

A "constable" is any police officer of whatever rank. The purpose of the requirement **17–91** that the constable be in uniform is to ensure that he is easily identifiable as a police constable. Accordingly, not wearing a helmet but otherwise being in uniform was sufficient: *Wallwork v. Giles* (1969) 114 S.J. 36.

In relation to most circumstances, the constable must have reasonable cause to "suspect" that the qualifying circumstances exist. In relation to the power following an accident, the constable must have reasonable cause to "believe" that a person was the driver etc. The distinction is a matter of degree. It is for the prosecution to prove that the officer had reasonable cause to suspect or believe.

One of the grounds for requiring a test is where there is suspicion that the person has committed a traffic offence whilst the vehicle was in motion. "Traffic offence" is defined in s.6(8) and covers a wide variety of offences.

17–92 The breath test must be taken by means of a device of a type approved by the Secretary of State. A number of Breath Test (Type Approval) Orders have been made, including the Preliminary Breath Test Device Approval 2005. Each device will operate in different ways. In the absence of bad faith, it is not necessary to comply fully with the manufacturer's instructions (see *DPP v. Carey* [1969] 3 All E.R. 1662)—the specimen must be sufficient to enable the test to be carried out and for the objective of the test to be achieved: s.11(3). The validity and reliability of various devices has been much litigated. For a full review of the issues and authorities, see Wilkinson, *Road Traffic Offences*, 24nd edn, para. 4.117ff. The Appeal Courts have become increasingly intolerant of arguments about the validity of devices.

Refusal to take a test is a failure to take the test for the purposes of an offence under section 6 (see s.11(2)). Refusal can be inferred from the actions of the person concerned, such as an attempt to abscond. If a person fails to take the test in a way that complies with s.11(3), he may be arrested if the constable has reasonable cause to suspect that the person has alcohol in his body: s.6D(2). If a person takes the test and the device indicates that the level of alcohol is higher than permitted then that person also will be arrested: s.6(5)(a). A person who is at hospital as a patient may not be arrested under s.6D(3).

Despite this provision, in *DPP v. Wilson* [2009] EWHC Admin 1988 a driver was arrested whilst in hospital where he had been taken after an accident. He had consented to provide a preliminary breath test and that showed a figure in excess of the legal limit. It was accepted on all sides that the arrest was unlawful; the defence argued that the subsequent sample was illegal and should be disregarded. This argument was accepted in the magistrates' court and the defendant acquitted. Allowing the prosecution appeal, the Divisional Court noted that a valid arrest is not a prerequisite for a sample and that, as all the other requisites and procedures had been properly followed, there was no justification for excluding the sample.

The range of reasonable excuses for failing to provide this specimen of breath is limited and largely restricted to circumstances where the person is physically unable to provide sufficient breath in a way that allows the test to be completed. It is not sufficient to assert that no alcohol had been consumed or that the person had not been driving, etc.

In *DPP v. Swan* [2004] EWHC 2432 Admin, the defendant was seen driving, stopped and asked to supply a specimen of breath. He was rude and aggressive and sought to delay providing the specimen of breath. As a consequence, he was handcuffed and arrested before the roadside breathalyser device was made available. It was argued that the offence was not made out because the device had not been proffered to the defendant and this was accepted by the justices. Allowing the prosecutor's appeal, the Court confirmed that it was not necessary for the roadside device to be made available where the driver's conduct showed he was either not willing to provide a specimen or he imposed unacceptable terms on which such a specimen would be provided. In this case, the behaviour of the defendant and delaying tactics clearly amounted to a failure to provide the specimen.

(4) Penalty

17–93 The maximum penalty is a fine of up to level 3 (currently £1000). It is endorsable with 4 penalty points and disqualification is discretionary.

(5) Sentence

The *Magistrates' Court Sentencing Guidelines* provide a starting point at level B (100 per cent of relevant weekly income). The penalty will reflect the fact that refusal to supply this sample does not of itself prevent the gathering of evidence to show whether the principal offence has been committed. **17–94**

D. FAILURE TO SUPPLY A SPECIMEN FOR ANALYSIS

(1) Definition

The requirement to provide for analysis a specimen of breath, blood or urine is the key element in the gaining of evidence to support charges of driving etc. whilst under the influence of alcohol. This includes the offence of causing death by careless driving under the influence of drugs or alcohol. **17–95**

If the specimen is provided, it will show the level of alcohol; if the person fails to provide a specimen without reasonable excuse, an offence is committed under s.7(6) and the maximum penalty is the same as for the substantive offence of which the person would have been liable to have been convicted if the specimen had been provided and the level of alcohol shown to be above the limit.

Road Traffic Act 1988, ss.7–11

Provision of specimen for analysis

7.—(1) In the course of an investigation into whether a person has committed an offence under section 3A, 4 or 5 of this Act a constable may, subject to the following provisions of this section and section 9 of this Act, require him— **17–96**

(a) to provide two specimens of breath for analysis by means of a device of a type approved by the Secretary of State, or

(b) to provide a specimen of blood or urine for a laboratory test

(2) A requirement under this section to provide specimens of breath can only be made—

(a) at a police station,

(b) at a hospital, or

(c) at or near a place where a relevant breath test has been administered to the person concerned or would have been so administered but for his failure to co-operate with it.

(2A) For the purposes of this section "a relevant breath test" is a procedure involving the provision by the person concerned of a specimen of breath to be used for the purpose of obtaining an indication whether the proportion of alcohol in his breath or blood is likely to exceed the prescribed limit.

(2B) A requirement under this section to provide specimens of breath may not be made at or near a place mentioned in subsection (2)(c) above unless the constable making it—

(a) is in uniform, or

(b) has imposed a requirement on the person concerned to co-operate with a relevant breath test in circumstances in which section 6(5) of this Act applies.

(2C) Where a constable has imposed a requirement on the person concerned to co-operate with a relevant breath test at any place, he is entitled to remain at or near that place in order to impose on him there a requirement under this section.

(2D) If a requirement under subsection (1)(a) above has been made at a place other than at a police station, such a requirement may subsequently be made at a police station if (but only if)—

(a) a device or a reliable device of the type mentioned in subsection (1)(a) above was not available at that place or it was for any other reason not practicable to use such a device there, or

(b) the constable who made the previous requirement has reasonable cause to believe that the device used there has not produced a reliable indication of the proportion of alcohol in the breath of the person concerned.

(3) A requirement under this section to provide a specimen of blood or urine can only be made at a police station or at a hospital; and it cannot be made at a police station unless—

(a) the constable making the requirement has reasonable cause to believe that for medical reasons a specimen of breath cannot be provided or should not be required, or

(b) specimens of breath have not been provided elsewhere and at the time the requirement is made a device or a reliable device of the type mentioned in subsection (1)(a) above is not available at the police station or it is then for any other reason not practicable to use such a device there, or

(bb) a device of the type mentioned in subsection (1)(a) above has been used (at the police station or elsewhere) but the constable who required the specimens of breath has reasonable cause to believe that the device has not produced a reliable indication of the proportion of alcohol in the breath of the person concerned, or

(bc) as a result of the administration of a preliminary drug test, the constable making the requirement has reasonable cause to believe that the person required to provide a specimen of blood or urine has a drug in his body, or

(c) the suspected offence is one under section 3A or 4 of this Act and the constable making the requirement has been advised by a medical practitioner that the condition of the person required to provide the specimen might be due to some drug;

but may then be made notwithstanding that the person required to provide the specimen has already provided or been required to provide two specimens of breath.

(4) If the provision of a specimen other than a specimen of breath may be required in pursuance of this section the question whether it is to be a specimen of blood or a specimen of urine and, in the case of a specimen of blood, the question who is to be asked to take it shall be decided (subject to subsection (4A)) by the constable making the requirement.

(4A) Where a constable decides for the purposes of subsection (4) to require the provision of a specimen of blood, there shall be no requirement to provide such a specimen if—

(a) the medical practitioner who is asked to take the specimen is of the opinion that, for medical reasons, it cannot or should not be taken; or

(b) the registered health care professional who is asked to take it is of that opinion and there is no contrary opinion from a medical practitioner;

and, where by virtue of this subsection there can be no requirement to provide a specimen of blood, the constable may require a specimen of urine instead.

(5) A specimen of urine shall be provided within one hour of the requirement for its provision being made and after the provision of a previous specimen of urine.

(6) A person who, without reasonable excuse, fails to provide a specimen when required to do so in pursuance of this section is guilty of an offence.

(7) A constable must, on requiring any person to provide a specimen in pursuance of this section, warn him that a failure to provide it may render him liable to prosecution.

Specimens of blood taken from persons incapable of consenting

17–97 **7A.**—(1) A constable may make a request to a medical practitioner for him to take a specimen of blood from a person ('the person concerned') irrespective of whether that person consents if—

(a) that person is a person from whom the constable would (in the absence of any incapacity of that person and of any objection under section 9) be entitled under section 7 to require the provision of a specimen of blood for a laboratory test;

(b) it appears to that constable that that person has been involved in an accident that constitutes or is comprised in the matter that is under investigation or the circumstances of that matter;

(c) it appears to that constable that that person is or may be incapable (whether or not he has purported to do so) of giving a valid consent to the taking of a specimen of blood; and

(d) it appears to that constable that that person's incapacity is attributable to medical reasons.

(2) A request under this section—

(a) shall not be made to a medical practitioner who for the time being has any responsibility (apart from the request) for the clinical care of the person concerned; and

(b) shall not be made to a medical practitioner other than a police medical practitioner unless—

(i) it is not reasonably practicable for the request to made to a police medical practitioner; or

(ii) it is not reasonably practicable for such a medical practitioner (assuming him to be willing to do so) to take the specimen.

(3) It shall be lawful for a medical practitioner to whom a request is made under this section, if he thinks fit—

(a) to take a specimen of blood from the person concerned irrespective of whether that person consents; and

(b) to provide the sample to a constable.

(4) If a specimen is taken in pursuance of a request under this section, the specimen shall not be subjected to a laboratory test unless the person from whom it was taken—

(a) has been informed that it was taken; and

(b) has been required by a constable to give his permission for a laboratory test of the specimen; and

(c) has given his permission.

(5) A constable must, on requiring a person to give his permission for the purposes of this section for a laboratory test of a specimen, warn that person that a failure to give the permission may render him liable to prosecution.

(6) A person who, without reasonable excuse, fails to give his permission for a laboratory test of a specimen of blood taken from him under this section is guilty of an offence.

(7) In this section 'police medical practitioner' means a medical practitioner who is engaged under any agreement to provide medical services for purposes connected with the activities of a police force.

Choice of specimens of breath

8.—(1) Subject to subsection (2) below, of any two specimens of breath provided by any person in pursuance of section 7 of this Act that with the lower proportion of alcohol in the breath shall be used and the other shall be disregarded. **17–98**

(2) If the specimen with the lower proportion of alcohol contains no more than 50 microgrammes of alcohol in 100 millilitres of breath, the person who provided it may claim that it should be replaced by such specimen as may be required under section 7(4) of this Act and, if he then provides such a specimen, neither specimen of breath shall be used.

(2A) If the person who makes a claim under subsection (2) above was required to provide specimens of breath under section 7 of this Act at or near a place mentioned in subsection (2)(c) of that section, a constable may arrest him without warrant.

(3) The Secretary of State may by regulations substitute another proportion of alcohol in the breath for that specified in subsection (2) above.

Protection for hospital patients

9.—(1) While a person is at a hospital as a patient he shall not be required to co-operate with a preliminary test or to provide a specimen under section 7 of this Act unless the medical practitioner in immediate charge of his case has been notified of the proposal to make the requirement; and— **17–99**

(a) if the requirement is then made, it shall be for co-operation with a test administered, or for the provision of a specimen, at the hospital, but

(b) if the medical practitioner objects on the ground specified in subsection (2) below, the requirement shall not be made.

(1A) While a person is at a hospital as a patient, no specimen of blood shall be taken from him under section 7A of this Act and he shall not be required to give his permission for a laboratory test of a specimen taken under that section unless the medical practitioner in immediate charge of his case—

(a) has been notified of the proposal to take the specimen or to make the requirement; and

(b) has not objected on the ground specified in subsection (2).

(2) The ground on which the medical practitioner may object is—

(a) in a case falling within subsection (1), that the requirement or the provision of the specimen or (if one is required) the warning required by section 7(7) of this Act would be prejudicial to the proper care and treatment of the patient; and

(b) in a case falling within subsection (1A), that the taking of the specimen, the requirement or the warning required by section 7A(5) of this Act would be so prejudicial.

Detention of persons affected by alcohol or a drug

17–100 **10.**—(1) Subject to subsections (2) and (3) below, a person required under section 7 or 7A to provide a specimen of breath, blood or urine may afterwards be detained at a police station (or, if the specimen was provided otherwise than at a police station, arrested and taken to and detained at a police station) if a constable has reasonable grounds for believing that, were that person then driving or attempting to drive a mechanically propelled vehicle on a road, he would commit an offence under section 4 or 5 of this Act.

(2) Subsection (1) above does not apply to the person if it ought reasonably to appear to the constable that there is no likelihood of his driving or attempting to drive a mechanically propelled vehicle whilst his ability to drive properly is impaired or whilst the proportion of alcohol in his breath, blood or urine exceeds the prescribed limit.

(2A) A person who is at a hospital as a patient shall not be arrested and taken from there to a police station in pursuance of this section if it would be prejudicial to his proper care and treatment as a patient.

(3) A constable must consult a medical practitioner on any question arising under this section whether a person's ability to drive properly is or might be impaired through drugs and must act on the medical practitioner's advice.

Interpretation

17–101 **11.**—(1) The following provisions apply for the interpretation of sections 3A to 10 of this Act.

(2) In those sections—

"drug" includes any intoxicant other than alcohol,

"fail" includes refuse,

"hospital" means an institution which provides medical or surgical treatment for in-patients or out-patients,

"the prescribed limit" means, as the case may require—

(a) 35 microgrammes of alcohol in 100 millilitres of breath,

(b) 80 milligrammes of alcohol in 100 millilitres of blood, or

(c) 107 milligrammes of alcohol in 100 millilitres of urine,.

or such other proportion as may be prescribed by regulations made by the Secretary of State

"registered health care professional" means a person (other than a medical practitioner) who is—

(a) a registered nurse; or

(b) a registered member of a health care profession which is designated for the purposes of this paragraph by an order made by the Secretary of State.

(2A) A health care profession is any profession mentioned in section 60(2) of the *Health Act* 1999 (c. 8) other than the profession of practising medicine and the profession of nursing.

(2B) An order under subsection (2) shall be made by statutory instrument; and any such statutory instrument shall be subject to annulment in pursuance of a resolution of either House of Parliament.

(3) A person does not provide a specimen of breath for a preliminary test or for analysis unless the specimen—

(a) is sufficient to enable the test or the analysis to be carried out, and

(b) is provided in such a way as to enable the objective of the test or analysis to be satisfactorily achieved.

(4) A person provides a specimen of blood if and only if—

(a) he consents to the taking of such a specimen from him; and

(b) the specimen is taken from him by a medical practitioner or, if it is taken in a police station, either by a medical practitioner or by a registered health care professional.

(2) Allocation

17–102 These offences are triable summarily only.

(3) What must the prosecution prove?

The prosecution must prove that: **17–103**

— the defendant:

— failed to provide a specimen;

— [without reasonable excuse];

— when required to do so pursuant to section 7.

For issues of identification, see § 10–89.

"Fail" includes "refuse": s.11(2). A specimen of breath must be sufficient to enable the analysis to be carried out and the objective of the analysis to be satisfactorily achieved: s.11(3). A novel point was raised in relation to the meaning of "breath" in *Zafar v. DPP* [2005] R.T.R. 18. The defendant provided specimens of breath at a police station that were found to contain alcohol in excess of the prescribed limit. On appeal against conviction to the Crown Court, he argued that he had consumed only one pint of lager but that he suffered from heartburn which caused an occasional reflux of the stomach contents to the mouth for which he took medicine. Expert evidence was given that demonstrated that the Intoximeter was designed to detect alcohol in deep lung air as opposed to alcohol in the mouth. It also asserted that this particular machine was very poor at detecting mouth alcohol. The Crown Court dismissed the appeal holding that the prosecution was not obliged to show that the reading related to deep lung air. The distinction between that and mouth alcohol was not required by the Act and that "breath" in the statute did not distinguish between the two meanings. The Divisional Court dismissed the further appeal. The main dictionary definition of breath was "air exhaled from anything" and there was nothing in the statute that suggested that any other definition should be used.

The consequences of the decision in *Zafar* were considered in *McNeil v. DPP* [2008] EWHC 1254. The effect of *Zafar* was to curtail the arguments being used to demonstrate that a sample of breath was unreliable because of reflux which, it was alleged, increased the potential amount of alcohol in the reading. In *McNeil v. DPP*, having given two specimens of breath resulting in readings well above the limit, the defendant was asked: "Before you used the instrument, I asked you whether you have brought up anything from your stomach. Have you brought anything up from your stomach since I asked you that question?". The appellant replied that he had. The form then in use said that in these circumstances a reliable indication of the proportion of alcohol in a person's breath may not have been obtained, and it will be usual to proceed to a requirement for blood or urine. The officer conducting the procedure followed the instructions on the form and requested a sample of blood (which provided a reading of 95μg) on the basis of which the defendant was convicted. The conviction was overturned because, on the facts of the case, the cause which the officer thought he had to believe that the breath samples did not give a reliable indication of the proportion of alcohol in the appellant's breath was not in law capable of rendering that indication unreliable. In those circumstances the subsequent request for a blood sample was not one which the officer was entitled to make. This is one of the increasingly rare cases where a technical argument has gone in favour of the defendant (who appeared to have been driving whilst well over the limit) and may well be viewed as a decision on its own facts. Where specimens are provided in a way that does not allow analysis to be undertaken satisfactorily, refusal to provide further specimens likely to contravene the legal requirement. In *Hussain v. DPP* [2008] EWHC 901, a machine would not provide a reading for a second specimen of breath. Later, at another police station, the defendant refused to provide further specimens and was convicted of failing to provide them. Upholding the conviction, the Divisional Court held that the earlier attempt did not provide valid specimens for the purpose of s.11(3) of the 1988 Act and the police officer was entitled to require further specimens to be provided.

Once the possibility of a reasonable excuse is raised by the defence, it is for the prosecution to satisfy the court beyond reasonable doubt that there was no reasonable excuse. In *McKeon v. DPP* [2008] R.T.R. 14, having failed to provide a specimen of **17–104** breath for analysis, the defendant consulted his general practitioner some days later and was referred to a consultant who concluded that the defendant might have a variable airflow obstruction. The consultant gave evidence that the extraordinarily low lung volumes produced at the police station could have resulted from the defendant's airways collapsing, or his being affected by the anxiety and stress of being at a police station, which could be a medical reason for his failure to provide a specimen. In convicting the motorist, the justices stated:

> "We considered that the specimens of breath provided by Mr McKeon at the police station were of such an extraordinarily low volume as not to be explicable by his physical condition, despite the evidence of Dr Costello, and had been given in such a way that they did not comply with the requirements of section 11(3) of the *Road Traffic Act* 1988. We were of the opinion that the appellant had failed to make out a reasonable excuse for his failure to provide a breath specimen in accordance with the requirements of the Act, and accordingly convicted him of the offence."

The conviction was overturned, as the wording used clearly suggested that the justices considered that there was a burden on the appellant to make out, that is to prove, a reasonable excuse for his failure.

Although it is a question of fact whether a defendant has a reasonable excuse, nonetheless it is a question of law as to whether particular circumstances can be a reasonable excuse for failing to provide a specimen. The category has been very narrowly drawn and little can justify failing or refusing to provide a specimen unless it arises out of a physical or mental inability to provide a specimen or a substantial risk to health in its provision: *Lennard* [1973] R.T.R. 252. In *DPP v. Coulter* [2005] EWHC 1533, the defendant was prosecuted for failing to provide a specimen of breath. During the procedure, he had been asked whether he had eaten anything and replied that he might have had a tic-tac. The station procedure general booklet that was being followed said that, if anything had been eaten, there should be a 20 minute wait before the test. The officer conducting the procedure did not wait. It was argued that there should have been a 20 minute wait and the request for a test was therefore unlawful. Dismissing the appeal, the Divisional Court commented that there was no evidence of the effect that a tic-tac would have had on the reading and that there was no suggestion that the failure to provide the specimen had anything to do with the consumption of the tic-tac. The Court quoted with approval part of the judgment in *DPP v. Smith* [2000] R.T.R. 341 in which the Court (though dealing with a different point) had stated:

> "I have examined the forms MG DD/A and B and conclude that they are, in essence, no more than what I would describe as the "plain man's guide" to a simple understanding of the procedures provided by the Act of 1988 to ensure, in a practical way, that those called upon to operate the procedures do not omit a relevant step; that, at stages where there is a choice of steps, they appreciate that such a choice exists; and it also offers quite clearly some common sense guidance as to the way in which choices should be exercised when they fall to be made."

The Court in *Coulter* then concluded that:

> "If there is a failure to follow the guidance, it is possible, in certain circumstances, that that might affect the reliability of a specimen that was in fact provided. There are limited circumstances in which a challenge to the reliability of a specimen that is provided can arise. That, in my view, is not relevant here. No specimen was provided. There was a failure to provide a specimen."

It would seem that a challenge to the procedure can only follow the provision of a specimen not to justify a failure to provide one at all.

The approach where a defendant is seeking to rely on a "reasonable excuse" for failing to provide a specimen for analysis and the basis for that is a medical reason which was not mentioned at the time of the failure was also considered in *Piggott v. DPP* [2008] R.T.R. 16. The fact that the defendant did not mention the medical reason (in this case asthma and hyperventilation syndrome) does not, as a matter of law, preclude a court from finding a "reasonable excuse". However, failure to refer to the medical condition is likely to be taken into account in determining whether it was the medical condition that was the reason why the specimen was refused and will probably lead a court to determine that the failure was not based on a reasonable excuse.

The majority of the circumstances have arisen in connection with specimens of blood. In relation to the provision of specimens of breath, most normal people could do what is required without effort. It will, therefore, require powerful evidence to justify finding a reasonable excuse and courts have been warned not to be gullible: *DPP v. Eddowes* [1991] R.T.R. 35. Most commonly, issues are likely to be raised in the context of the driver suffering from asthma. The statement of the Court of Appeal in *Lennard* that "No excuse can be adjudged a reasonable one unless a person from whom the specimen is required is physically or mentally unable to provide it or the provision of the specimen would entail a substantial risk to his health" has been re-iterated in the context of asthma sufferers in both *Eddowes* [1991] R.T.R. 35 and *DPP v. Curtis* [1993] R.T.R. 72. For a situation where a reasonable excuse was found, see *DPP v. Falzarano* [2001] R.T.R. 14 where evidence was given by her doctor that the driver was subject to panic attacks in stressful situations. A sufficient causative link was found on the facts between the condition and the failure to provide the specimen.

In *Longstaff v. DPP* [2008] R.T.R. 17, the defendant was arrested on suspicion of driving a vehicle after consuming excess alcohol. At the police station he was unable to provide a satisfactory sample of breath and said, "I cannot breathe properly because of my back pain" and the procedure continued. A doctor who examined the defendant with a view to ascertaining whether there was a medical reason for not providing a sample of breath was of the opinion that there was none. The officers did not request the doctor to take a sample of blood or urine and charged the defendant with failing to supply a sample of breath. The defendant was convicted and that verdict was upheld. The Divisional Court confirmed that the question is whether, in fact, the defendant had a reasonable excuse for failing to provide a specimen of breath and that that is for the justices to decide on all the evidence. Having examined a number of propositions advanced by the defence, the Divisional Court stated:

> "... the points sought to be taken by the appellant in this case are utterly without merit and unsustainable. What the appellant has attempted to do, in common with appellants in numerous other cases, is to force the decision-making powers of police officers into a straight jacket which has no basis in the provisions of the statute or established authority. The forensic technique is to seek to refashion the law by reference to the contents of standard forms used by the police. It is a most unattractive development."

In relation to specimens of urine, the obligation is to provide two specimens, the second (which is to be used for analysis) within an hour of the first. A genuine physical inability to provide the second specimen can amount to a reasonable excuse but is likely to be followed by the police utilising the power to require a specimen of blood.

Inability to understand the statutory warning that a person is liable for prosecution **17–105**
for failing to provide a specimen for analysis may amount to a reasonable excuse where that is due to the person's limited command of English. Where it cannot be understood by the defendant because of self induced intoxication, then that cannot be a reasonable excuse.

There is no entitlement to delay the taking of a specimen to any significant extent in order to enable the suspect to receive legal advice: *Campbell v. DPP* [2004] R.T.R. 5; *Kennedy v. DPP* [2004] R.T.R. 6. Similarly, an attempt by the person arrested to impose conditions on his agreement to provide the specimen is unlikely to be successful. In *DPP v. Swan* [2004] EWHC 243 Admin, the defendant was seen driving, stopped and asked to supply a specimen of breath. He was rude and aggressive and sought to delay providing the specimen of breath. As a consequence, he was handcuffed and arrested before the roadside breathalyser device was made available. At the police station, he continued to be rude and abusive and wanted photographs of the injuries to his wrists caused by the handcuffs to be taken before he would supply the specimen, or, at least, a guarantee that they would be taken. The officer in charge refused to give that guarantee, the defendant continued to insist and the breath analysis machine timed out!

The officer took the view that the defendant had refused to supply a specimen and charged him accordingly. Justices dismissed the charge on the basis that the request for photographs to be taken was not an "outrageous condition". The Divisional Court allowed the prosecutor's appeal. There was no threshold for outrageous conditions and, if a matter could not amount to a reasonable excuse for failing to supply a specimen, it was difficult to see how it could be relied on as a basis for saying there had not been a failure to provide the specimen. Whether there is a refusal is a question of fact and reference to the term "outrageous" is unhelpful in interpreting the effect of a condition placed on consent by the driver.

Another in the series of cases where the defendant has sought to obtain legal advice before providing a specimen and then seeks to justify the failure to provide a specimen by reference to the lack of that advice is *Causey v. DPP* (2005) 169 J.P. 331. The court set out a series of principles and emphasised that recourse to the appeal courts on this issue should only be in exceptional cases. The main principles are that there was no general duty on the police to delay taking a specimen pending advice and that specimens must be taken as close as possible to the time of the alleged offence, that it was a question of fact and degree, depending on the circumstances of the case, whether the custody officer had acted without delay and permitted the defendant to consult a solicitor without delay and that, if a custody officer knew that a solicitor was immediately available, the defendant should be allowed to consult before deciding whether or not to provide specimens. However, a solicitor could not have added anything of significance to the information already given to the defendant orally by the custody officer and in the form with which the defendant had been provided.

See also *Gearing v. DPP* [2009] R.T.R. 7 in which it was emphasised that the public interest in the prompt testing at a police station of those who had failed a roadside breath test means that only a very short delay would be permitted to consult a solicitor.

A further example of the tough line taken where a defendant seeks to put forward a reasonable excuse for failing to supply a specimen is *DPP v. Mukandiwa* [2006] R.T.R 24. The defendant put forward his reaction to the sight of blood as a reason to excuse his failure to provide a specimen. He asserted that the sight of blood could drive him into a trance in which he could become violent to himself and to others. This was accepted as a reasonable excuse by a district judge but the Divisional Court held that that was not a conclusion open to the judge on the facts. A distinction was to be drawn between the sight of blood and the taking of it. There was no reason why the defendant should have to see the blood when it was taken.

Another example of robustness from the appeal courts can be seen in *DPP v. Wood; DPP v. McGillicuddy* [2006] EWHC 32; (2006) 170 J.P. 17. The defence had successfully obtained the stay of proceedings as a result of issues regarding disclosure of information relating to the machines used to measure alcohol in breath. The Divisional Court held that those proceedings should not have been stayed. The lawfulness of type approval was not a matter which could be raised as a defence. Where the contention was that the device which was originally type-approved had been altered in such a way as to take it beyond its approval, and disclosure was sought to further that contention, the court would require more than the asserted fact of unapproved modification to justify disclosure. There would have to be some material which explained how the alteration could go to loss of type approval and how disclosure could advance that point. On the facts of the instant case there was no material sufficient to justify the disclosure orders that had been made.

(4) "Required pursuant to s.7"

17–106 There needs to be an investigation into whether a person has committed an offence under s.3A (causing death by careless driving under the influence of drink or drugs), s.4 (driving etc. whilst unfit through drink or drugs) or s.5 (driving etc. with excess alcohol in the body). If there is, a constable may require that person to provide a specimen for analysis. That specimen may consist of two specimens of breath (which will be analysed by a device approved by the Secretary of State) or a specimen of blood or a specimen of urine: s.7(1). The constable requiring the specimen must warn that a failure to provide the specimen may lead to prosecution: s.(7).

Specimens of *breath* can only be required at a police station: s.7(2). There is no obligation that requires the police to explain to a suspect why a breath test cannot be taken in these circumstances other than at a police station. The law does not allow such a test and that is sufficient. Previous conflicting authorities on this point were resolved by the decision in *Jones v. DPP* [2005] R.T.R. 15. Specimens of *blood* or *urine* can only be required at a police station or a hospital: s.7(3). Such a specimen can only be required at a police station in circumstances set out in s.7(3) but, if any of these circumstances exist, the request can be made even if the person has already provided (or been required to provide) two specimens of breath.

Once it is possible to require a specimen of blood or urine, it is for the constable to choose which: s.7(4). Although that is a very wide discretion, it is a statutory discretion and will be reviewed by a Court in accordance with the *Wednesbury* principles. In *Joseph v. DPP* (2004) 168 J.P. 575, the Divisional Court made it clear that, in a s.8(2) case (that is, where the lower of the two specimens contained no more than 50 microgrammes of alcohol in 100 millilitres of breath), there is no ground on which a driver can expect to be asked to indicate whether a sample of blood or of urine is preferred. However, in this case, the defendant genuinely believed that it was against the tenets of his religion to give blood and this was known to the officer before he decided whether to require blood or urine. The officer considered that, in the absence of a medical reason, he could only ask for a specimen of blood in these circumstances. The Court held that this was wrong. Without wishing to imply that the views of the defendant should be sought, where there is no reason for not choosing urine in preference to blood, if a valid reason is put forward why urine should be the choice, the officer must at least consider that reason. If the officer concludes without reason that it should be the method to which the defendant objects, that decision may be categorised as perverse or it may be concluded that the statutory procedure has not been properly completed. **17–107**

Where a driver has provided specimens of breath the lower of which is no more than 50μg in 100ml of breath, the driver may elect to provide a further specimen of blood or urine (the choice of which being for the constable). If the driver makes that election but then subsequently does not provide the specimen, the prosecution should be based on the specimens of breath not on an allegation of failing to provide a specimen for analysis. This position has been emphasised by the Divisional Court following an extensive review of the statutory provisions and the procedural forms: *Persaud v. DPP* [2010] R.T.R. 29.

A different situation arose in *Myles v. DPP* [2004] 2 All E.R. 902; [2005] R.T.R. 1. Here the result of the breath test was unsatisfactory and a police surgeon was called to take a specimen of blood. The defendant refused to give a specimen and was considered by the surgeon to be obstructive. Warned of the consequences of refusal, the defendant maintained that he required legal advice. He was charged with failing to provide the specimen and argued that the evidence of the request for a sample should be disregarded because he had been denied the right to the services of a solicitor. Reviewing domestic and commonwealth authorities, the Court concluded that there was no justification for delaying the completion of the procedures for taking the specimen. This was the clear line of authority.

It is also for the constable to choose who is to be asked to take a sample of blood which may be a medical practitioner or a registered health care professional (as defined in s.11(2)). The person must consent to the taking of blood: s.11(4). The medical practitioner or registered health care professional may form the opinion that the specimen of blood cannot or should not be taken. In those circumstances, the requirement may not be made: s.7(4A). This still leaves the option of breath or urine. If the opinion is that of a registered health care professional, it can be overridden by a medical practitioner: s.7(4A)(b). If the person subject to the requirement is in hospital as a patient, the medical practitioner in immediate charge of the case must be notified. If he objects on the ground that either giving the statutory warning or taking the specimen would be prejudicial to the proper care and treatment of the patient, then the requirement must not be made. If it is made, the specimen must be provided at the hospital and will then be of blood or urine: s.9.

17–108 As stated in § 17–101 *ante*, s.11(4) requires a person to consent to the taking of a specimen of blood. Section 7A, however, provides an additional procedure where a constable considers that the subject of the requirement is incapable (for medical reasons) of giving valid consent. This procedure arises where the subject has been involved in an accident that is part of the matter under investigation and is a person from whom a specimen would normally be requested (subject to the possibility of objection under s.9—prejudicial to the proper care and treatment of the patient). In such circumstances, a constable may request a medical practitioner to take a specimen from the subject. That medical practitioner will not be a medical practitioner who has current responsibility for the clinical care of the subject and will normally be a police medical practitioner (as defined in s.7A(7)) unless it is not reasonably practicable to ask a police medical practitioner or for such a medical practitioner to take the specimen: s.7A(2). A specimen taken in this way may not be sent for analysis until the subject has been told it has been taken and has given his permission for it to be sent for analysis. He must be warned that failure to give permission may render him liable for prosecution. It is an offence to fail to give permission without reasonable excuse.

Where specimens of breath are given, the one with the lower reading is to be used: s.8(1). If that reading is 50 microgrammes or below, the person providing it may claim that it be replaced by such a specimen as may be required under s.7(4) (blood or urine—at the choice of the constable). If that alternative specimen is provided, neither breath specimens may be used: s.8(2).

(5) Penalty (s.7 or s.7A)

17–109 The maximum penalty for *driving or attempting to drive* is a fine of level 5 (currently £5000) and/or six months' imprisonment. There is a mandatory requirement to disqualify from driving (in the absence of special reasons) for one year (though see *post*, § 17–177 for the circumstances where that minimum is increased). On endorsement only, there will be penalty points of between 3 and 11.

The maximum penalty for *being in charge* is a fine of level 4 (currently £2500) and/or three months' imprisonment. There is a discretionary requirement to disqualify from driving. On endorsement, there will be penalty points of 10.

(6) Sentence

17–110 The *Magistrates' Court Sentencing Guidelines* provide for the approach to sentencing to be based initially on whether the refusal or failure to provide the specimen was deliberate. A lower starting point and range is provided where the refusal arose because of an honestly held but unreasonable excuse; where the excuse was reasonable it would found a defence to the charge but that has been tightly constrained. If the refusal or failure was deliberate, there is a higher starting point and range where there is evidence of serious impairment. The guidelines at this level of seriousness are the equivalent of the most serious level of driving (or being in charge) with excess alcohol and so should remove any incentive to refuse a test solely on the grounds that a less severe penalty might follow when the offender is substantially over the limit.

The guideline also provides for increasing periods of disqualification as the offence increases in seriousness; those increases are provided both from the 12 month minimum where there is no previous relevant offence and from the 3 year minimum where there is. If there is a delay between conviction and sentencing, the guideline suggests that consideration should be given to an interim disqualification. Where the offence is based on the offender driving or attempting to drive, the guideline also states that a court should consider offering a drink/drive rehabilitation course. Successful completion of such a course will reduce the length of disqualification to be completed.

Fail to provide specimen for analysis (drive/attempt to drive), Road Traffic Act 1988, s.7(6)

STARTING POINT AND RANGE OF SENTENCE

(BASED ON A FIRST TIME OFFENDER PLEADING NOT GUILTY)

Examples of nature of activity	Starting point	Range	Disqualification	Disqual. (2nd offence in 10 years)
Defendant refused test when had honestly held but unreasonable excuse	Band C fine	Band C fine	12–16 months	36–40 months
Deliberate refusal or deliberate failure	Low level community order	Band C fine to high level community order	17–28 months	36–52 months
Deliberate refusal or deliberate failure where evidence of serious impairment	12 weeks custody	High level community order to 26 weeks custody	29–36 months	36–60 months

AGGRAVATING AND MITIGATING FACTORS

Factors indicating higher culpability	Factors indicating lower culpability
1. Evidence of unacceptable standard of driving 2. LGV, HGV, PSV etc. 3. Obvious state of intoxication 4. Driving for hire or reward	1. Genuine but unsuccessful attempt to provide specimen

Where the failure to provide a specimen arose from being in charge rather than driving or attempting to drive, a separate guideline is provided with lower starting points and ranges. **17–111**

Fail to provide specimen for analysis (in charge), Road Traffic Act 1988, s.7(6)

STARTING POINT AND RANGE OF SENTENCE

(BASED ON A FIRST TIME OFFENDER PLEADING NOT GUILTY)

Examples of nature of activity	**Starting Point**	**Range**
Defendant refused test when had honestly held but unreasonable excuse	Band B fine	Band B fine 10 points
Deliberate refusal or deliberate failure	Band C fine	Band C fine to medium level community order Consider disqualification OR 10 points
Deliberate refusal or deliberate failure where evidence of serious impairment	Medium level community order	Low level community order to 6 weeks custody Disqualify 6 -12 months

AGGRAVATING AND MITIGATING FACTORS

Factors indicating higher culpability	**Factors indicating lower culpability**
1. Obvious state of intoxication 2. LGV, HGV, PSV etc. 3. High likelihood of driving 4. Driving for hire or reward	1. Genuine but unsuccessful attempt to provide specimen 2. Low likelihood of driving

See also the power to deprive the offender of the vehicle contained in s.143(1), (6) and (7) of the *Powers of Criminal Courts (Sentencing) Act* 2000 (see *post*, §§ 17–212 and 23–204).

IV. DISQUALIFICATION OFFENCES

A. DRIVING WHILST DISQUALIFIED; OBTAINING A LICENCE WHILST DISQUALIFIED

17–112 A person may be disqualified from driving in a number of different ways, see *post*, § 17–194. Once disqualified *by a court*, it is an offence either to obtain a licence or to drive a vehicle. Where the disqualification is until a relevant test is passed (see *post*, § 17–197), the disqualified person can drive as a learner driver pending passing that test.

A person who is disqualified from holding a particular licence because of their age (s.102 of the *Road Traffic Act* 1988)—*e.g.* under 16 for a moped, under 17 for a motor bicycle or car—but nonetheless drives a vehicle of the type in question, is liable to be prosecuted for the offence of driving without holding an appropriate licence: *Road Traffic Act* 1988, s.87, see *post*, § 17–142.

Road Traffic Act 1988, s.103

Obtaining licence, or driving, while disqualified

103.—(1) A person is guilty of an offence if, while disqualified for holding or obtaining a licence, he— **17–113**

(a) obtains a licence, or

(b) drives a motor vehicle on a road.

(2) A licence obtained by a person who is disqualified is of no effect (or, where the disqualification relates only to vehicles of a particular class, is of no effect in relation to vehicles of that class).'

(3) A constable in uniform may arrest without warrant any person driving a motor vehicle on a road whom he has reasonable cause to suspect of being disqualified.

(4) Subsections (1) and (3) above do not apply in relation to disqualification by virtue of section 101 of this Act.

(5) Subsections (1)(b) and (3) above do not apply in relation to disqualification by virtue of section 102 of this Act.

(6) In the application of subsections (1) and (3) above to a person whose disqualification is limited to the driving of motor vehicles of a particular class by virtue of—

(a) section 102, 117 or 117A of this Act, or

(b) subsection (9) of section 36 of the *Road Traffic Offenders Act* 1988 (disqualification until test is passed),

the references to disqualification for holding or obtaining a licence and driving motor vehicles are references to disqualification for holding or obtaining a licence to drive and driving motor vehicles of that class.

B. DISQUALIFICATION OF PERSONS UNDER AGE

Road Traffic Act 1988, s.101

Disqualification of persons under age

101.—(1) A person is disqualified for holding or obtaining a licence to drive a motor vehicle of a class specified in the following Table if he is under the age specified in relation to it in the second column of the Table. **17–114**

TABLE

Class of motor vehicle	*Age (in years)*
1. Invalid carriage	16
2. Moped	16
3. Motor bicycle	17
4. Agricultural or forestry tractor	17
5. Small vehicle	17
6. Medium-sized goods vehicle	18
7. Other motor vehicle	21

In relation to certain classes of vehicles and in certain circumstances, different ages apply (see reg.9 of the *Motor Vehicles (Driving Licence) Regulations* 1999 (S.I. 1999 No.2864). These variants are shown in the Table, *post*, against the classes as numbered in the table, *ante*.

TABLE

Class of motor vehicle	*Age (in years)*
3. Certain large motor bicycles	21
4. Certain agricultural or forestry tractors	16
5. Small vehicles driven by certain people	16
6. Heavier medium-sized goods vehicle	21
7. Various other motor vehicles	18

C. DISQUALIFICATION TO PREVENT DUPLICATION OF LICENCES

Road Traffic Act 1988, s.102

Disqualification to prevent duplication of licences

17–115 **102.**—(1) A person is disqualified for obtaining a licence authorising him to drive a motor vehicle of any class so long as he is the holder of another licence authorising him to drive a motor vehicle of that class, whether the licence is suspended or not.

(2) A person is also disqualified for holding or obtaining a licence authorising him to drive a motor vehicle of any class so long as he is authorised by virtue of section 109(1) if this Act to drive a motor vehicle or that of a corresponding class.

(1) What must the prosecution prove?

Obtaining a licence whilst disqualified

17–116 — the defendant was disqualified (other than by age);
— the defendant obtained a licence.

Since it is possible to obtain licences in advance of the commencement date, this offence is committed where a licence is obtained that purports to give authority to drive covering a period while the person to whom it is issued is disqualified.

Driving while disqualified

17–117 The prosecution must prove that:
— the defendant was the driver;
— the defendant was disqualified (other than by age);
— the vehicle was being driven;
— the vehicle was a motor vehicle;
— the vehicle was being driven on a road.

For issues concerning identification, see §§ 10–89 *et seq.* in this work.

For "drive", "motor vehicle" and "road", see *ante*, §§ 17–4 *et seq.* Note that this is an offence committed on a road and not on a road or other public place.

17–118 The obligation is on the prosecution to prove that the defendant was disqualified. For a number of years, imaginative attempts have been made to persuade courts that the prosecution has not satisfied its obligation to prove that the person before the court is the person disqualified from driving. In the case of *Ellis v. Jones* [1973] 2 All E.R. 893, this led the court to describe the defence submission as "… another example of submissions made by advocates for the defence in circumstances which are wholly inappropriate and which give rise to a great deal of waste of time and money". There has to be cogent evidence linking the person who drove the vehicle with the person who had been disqualified. There are many ways in which evidence can be brought to prove this link. In *Derwentside JJ, ex p. Heaviside* [1996] R.T.R. 384, three methods of proof were given—formal admission by the defendant, fingerprints, and then the evidence of the person in court when the defendant was disqualified. This is not an exhaustive list and the court will need to act on any cogent evidence. In *DPP v. Mooney* [1997] R.T.R. 434 the defendant had made admissions to the police (but not the formal admission listed *ante*) and this was held sufficient to support the certificate of conviction recording the order of disqualification. In *Moran v. CPS* (2000) 164 J.P. 562 an admission to the police and confirmation that that admission had been made by the defendant whilst giving evidence in court was held to be sufficient even without a certificate of conviction. In *Pattison v. DPP* [2006] R.T.R. 13; (2006) 170 J.P. 51, the Divisional Court, after an extensive review of the legal provisions and the authorities, concluded that:

> "The principle that emerges from the cases is that it will normally be possible to establish a prima facie case on the basis of consistency of details between the accused and the person named on the memorandum of conviction. If the accused calls no evidence to contradict that prima facie case, it will be open to the court to be satisfied that identity is proved."

The court set out a number of principles able to be extracted from the cases. It emphasised that it was for the prosecution to prove to the criminal standard that the accused was a disqualified driver but that it could do so by any admissible means including a non-formal admission. *Heaviside* identifies three clear ways but there are no prescribed ways. An example of another way is where there is a match between the personal details of the accused and those recorded on the certificate of conviction. Even where the personal details (such as the name) are not uncommon, a match will be sufficient for a prima facie case. In the absence of evidence contradicting this prima facie case, the evidence will be sufficient for the court to find identity proved. If the accused does not give evidence in rebuttal, that is a matter that the court can take into account. If it is proper to do so (and provided a warning has been given), that can also give rise to an adverse inference (*Criminal Justice and Public Order Act* 1994, s.35(2)). Similarly, in *West Yorkshire Probation Board v. Boulter* (2005) 169 J.P. 601, a person subject to a community rehabilitation order was brought before a magistrates' court on a warrant for breaching the order. The proceedings were adjourned. The defendant did not attend subsequent hearings but was legally represented. Justices accepted defence submissions that the prosecution had failed to prove that the person summoned to appear was the person made subject to the order and that the coincidence of names, date of birth and address was insufficient to prove identity beyond reasonable doubt. The Divisional Court upheld the prosecution appeal:

> "When magistrates have evidence that the person before them has the same name, date of birth and address as the person previously convicted, it was open to them to draw an inference that he is the same person. Whether that inference is to be drawn in any particular case depends on all the facts of that case."

Where all three of those personal details coincided, it was to be expected that justices would draw such an inference unless there was some other factor which cast doubt on the inference.

In *R. (Howe) v. South Durham Magistrates' Court* [2005] R.T.R. 4, the prosecution had obtained a witness summons against the solicitor who had represented the defendant in the proceedings in which he had been disqualified asserting that he could give evidence of what transpired in court on that occasion without breaching legal professional privilege. A further complication was that this solicitor was also retained to act for the defendant in the current proceedings. The defendant appealed against the issuing of that summons but that appeal was dismissed. The solicitor was to be asked solely about issues of fact that did not require any breach of privilege, and, although the consequence of the summons would be to deprive the defendant of the services of the solicitor in the current proceedings, the right to a solicitor of one's own choice is not an absolute one.

The extent of the obligation on the prosecution was considered in *DPP v. Barker* [2004] 168 J.P. 617. The defendant had been disqualified for a fixed period and then until he passed an extended driving test. He was found driving after the fixed period was ended and the issue arose as to whether the prosecution need to prove the absence of "L" plates and a supervisor. The Court held that that burden fell on the defendant. This was wholly proportionate and followed the approach set out under earlier provisions in *Scott v. Jelfe* [1974] R.T.R. 256.

17–119 Once it is proved that the defendant was the driver of the motor vehicle on a road at a time when he was disqualified, then it is no defence that the defendant was unaware either of his disqualification or that the disqualification was still in force. This has meant a defendant being convicted even though his driving licence had been returned to him by the licensing authority by mistake: *Bowsher* [1973] R.T.R. 202. Similarly, a defendant was convicted even where he mistakenly believed he was not driving on a "road": *Miller* [1973] R.T.R. 479. Even where a disqualification is subsequently quashed on appeal, a person who drives whilst the disqualification is in force commits the offence under section 103: *Thames Magistrates' Court, ex p. Levy* [1997] T.L.R. 394. A court may suspend a disqualification pending appeal, but, in the absence of such an order, the disqualification applies regardless of the outcome of the appeal.

A person from outside Great Britain can be disqualified by a court and will commit an offence under s.103(1) by driving a motor vehicle on a road while disqualified even though a licence or permit issued by another state is held. Similarly, a person disqualified elsewhere is not necessarily disqualified from driving in this country though he may be committing the offence of driving otherwise than in accordance with a licence; it will depend on the effect of the disqualification as provided for in the law of the country in which it was imposed.

(2) Allocation

17–120 These offences are summary only.

(3) Penalties

17–121 For *driving while disqualified*, the maximum penalty is a fine at level 5 and/or six months' imprisonment or both. It is an endorsable offence requiring six penalty points. Disqualification is discretionary. There is a separate offence of causing death by driving where the driver was unlicensed, disqualified from driving or uninsured, *Road Traffic Act* 1988, s.2B. This is described at § 17–46, *ante*.

For *obtaining a licence while disqualified*, the maximum penalty is a fine of level 3. The offence is not endorsable.

(4) Sentence

17–122 There are different views on the appropriate level of sentence. There are many who consider that this offence is often a flagrant disregard for an order of the court and that imprisonment should be the starting point. Others point to the fact that people committing this offence have not committed a violent offence and, in the absence of any other offences, have not caused damage to other people or to property; accordingly, a non-custodial sentence should usually be appropriate.

There has been a significant change in the imposition of custodial sentences for this offence. In 2002, over 28,000 were sentenced and 46% received an immediate custodial sentence whilst 47% received a community sentence. In 2004 the immediate custody proportion had dropped to 36% and the community sentence proportion increased to 53%. By 2008, the number sentenced had reduced to just over 23,100, the immediate custody rate had dropped to about 30% but the Suspended Sentence Order rate had become about 17% thus providing 47% of cases in which the court had considered that a custodial sentence was unavoidable. The community order rate had dropped to less than 40%.

The approach to sentencing set out in the *Magistrates' Court Sentencing Guidelines* uses the length of time since the disqualification was imposed as a main criterion. Part of the sentence is likely to be an increase in the period of disqualification originally imposed; since disqualifications take effect from the day on which they are imposed, this will arise from a new disqualification including both the outstanding period and a further period. The lowest starting point and range is for those who have completed a period of disqualification but, having also been disqualified until passing a test, have not passed that test.

STARTING POINT AND RANGE OF SENTENCE

(BASED ON A FIRST TIME OFFENDER PLEADING NOT GUILTY)

Examples of nature of activity	**Starting Point**	**Range**
Full period expired but retest not taken	Low level community order	Band C fine to medium level community order 6 points or disqualify for 3–6 months
Lengthy period of ban already served	High level community order	Medium level community order to 12 weeks custody Lengthen disqualification for 6–12 months beyond expiry of current ban
Recently imposed ban	12 weeks custody	High level community order to 26 weeks custody Lengthen disqualification for 12–18 months beyond expiry of current ban

AGGRAVATING AND MITIGATING FACTORS

Factors indicating higher culpability	Factors indicating lower culpability
1. Never passed test 2. Planned long-term evasion 3. Vehicle obtained during ban 4. Driving for remuneration	1. Defendant not present when disqualification imposed and genuine reason why unaware of ban 2. Genuine emergency established
Factors indicating greater degree of harm 1. Distance driven 2. Evidence of associated bad driving 3. Offender caused accident	

The guidelines also remind courts of the power to order that the offender be deprived of the vehicle used to commit the offence.

A manifestation of the concerns about the extent to which persons who are disqualified continue to drive has been seen in the growing use of the imposition of an anti-social behaviour order in addition to the sentence for the offence. The plethora of cases considering the circumstances of the making of such orders (and the approach to sentencing of those who breach them) is covered in more detail in § 23–269, *post*, but there have been some considerations particularly relevant to orders made following conviction for driving whilst disqualified. One of the issues has been the extent to which an ASBO should prohibit something which is already a criminal offence. This is particularly significant where the maximum penalty for the offence is less than for a breach of an ASBO—this is the case for driving whilst disqualified which carries a maximum of six months' imprisonment compared with a maximum of five years for a breach of an ASBO. In *Hall* [2004] EWCA Crim 2671, the defendant had an appalling driving record and had committed other serious offences. The court concluded that the regularity of the defendant's offending demonstrated total disregard for the law and imposed an unlimited ASBO prohibiting the defendant from driving any mechanically propelled vehicle on a public road in the UK without being the holder of a valid driving licence and certificate of insurance. A primary purpose was to increase the sentencing powers of any court faced with dealing with a further offence. Whilst requiring the ASBO to be for a set period, the Court of Appeal considered that the order was not wrong in principle in these circumstances. It was precise and capable of being understood by the appellant.

A different view was taken by a differently constituted court in *Kirby* [2005] EWCA Crim 1228. Again, the defendant had a bad driving record. An ASBO was made for 10 years prohibiting him, *inter alia*, from driving a motor vehicle until the expiry of his period of disqualification. The Court of Appeal doubted whether it was right to impose an order simply in order to increase the maximum penalty available for further offending. There had to be a demonstrable necessity for such an order.

The approach in *Kirby* has been followed in two further cases, *Lawson* [2005] EWCA Crim 1840; [2005] Crim.L.R. 871 and *Williams* [2005] EWCA Crim 1796; (2005) 169 J.P. 588 and has been specifically endorsed by the Court of Appeal following a review of various cases in *Boness* (2005) 169 J.P. 621 (see further § 23–250, *post*). Before an order can be made, the court must be satisfied both that the offender had acted in an anti-social manner and that an order was necessary to protect persons in England and Wales from further anti-social acts from him.

V. REGULATORY OFFENCES

A. USING A MOTOR VEHICLE WITHOUT INSURANCE

(1) Definitions

The requirement for insurance to be obtained to cover some of the adverse consequences of the use of a motor vehicle reflects the need to ensure that the damage caused by a motor vehicle can be financially compensated. In addition, vehicle owners or users can choose to insure against damage to their own vehicle, however caused. Where damage is caused as a result of the use of a motor vehicle and the user is not insured, it may be possible for compensation to be obtained through the Motor Insurers Bureau (MIB): see *Wilkinson's Road Traffic Offences*, Ch.10. **17–123**

The *Disclosure of Vehicle Insurance Regulations* 2005 (S.I. 2005 No.2833) provide for the Motor Insurers' Information Centre to supply information to the Police Information Technology Organisation. This may be used to assist a police officer in deciding whether to use the power under s.165 of the *Road Traffic Act* 1988 to require a person who is (or may have been) driving a vehicle to produce evidence that the use of the vehicle is insured. There is a further power under ss.165A and 165B to seize and retain a vehicle where the evidence is not produced.

The*Motor Vehicles (Electronic Communication of Certificates of Insurance) Order* 2010 (S.I. 2010 No.1117) enables certificates to be "delivered" as required by the statutory provisions where delivered electronically to the policy holder or made available by the insurer on a website. In relation to electronic transmission, it is a prerequisite that the person effecting the policy agreed to that process and that the address to which it is sent is that provided by that person. In relation to availability on a website, there are similar provisions regarding agreement but also an obligation on the insurer to keep the certificate available on the website whilst it remains in force. The section is further amended to allow the insured person to notify surrender of the policy electronically. Consequential changes have been made to s.165 so that the requirement to produce can be met by making available the electronic copy or a printed, legible, copy of it.

Road Traffic Act 1988, ss.143–145, 147–150, 165, 165A–165B

Users of motor vehicles to be insured or secured against third-party risks

143.—(1) Subject to the provisions of this Part of this Act— **17–124**

(a) a person must not use a motor vehicle on a road or other public place unless there is in force in relation to the use of the vehicle by that person such a policy of insurance or such a security in respect of third party risks as complies with the requirements of this Part of this Act, and

(b) a person must not cause or permit any other person to use a motor vehicle on a road or other public place unless there is in force in relation to the use of the vehicle by that other person such a policy of insurance or such a security in respect of third party risks as complies with the requirements of this Part of this Act.

(2) If a person acts in contravention of subsection (1) above he is guilty of an offence.

(3) A person charged with using a motor vehicle in contravention of this section shall not be convicted if he proves—

(a) that the vehicle did not belong to him and was not in his possession under a contract of hiring or of loan,

(b) that he was using the vehicle in the course of his employment, and

(c) that he neither knew nor had reason to believe that there was not in force in relation to the vehicle such a policy of insurance or security as is mentioned in subsection (1) above.

(4) This Part of this Act does not apply to invalid carriages.

Exceptions from requirement of third-party insurance or security

17–125 **144.**—(1) Section 143 of this Act does not apply to a vehicle owned by a person who has deposited and keeps deposited with the Accountant General of the Senior Courts the sum of £500, 000, at a time when the vehicle is being driven under the owner's control.

(1A) [...]

(1B) [...]

(2) Section 143 does not apply—

(a) to a vehicle owned—

(i) by the council of a county or county district in England and Wales the Broads Authority, the Common Council of the City of London, the council of a London borough, a National Park authority, the Inner London Education Authority, the London Fire and Emergency Planning Authority, a [joint waste authority] or a joint authority (other than a police authority) established by Part IV of the *Local Government Act* 1985,

(ii) ... or

(iii) by a joint board or committee in England or Wales, or joint committee in Scotland, which is so constituted as to include among its members representatives of any such council,

at a time when the vehicle is being driven under the owner's control,

(b) to a vehicle owned by a police authority, at a time when it is being driven under the owner's control, or to a vehicle at a time when it is being driven for police purposes by or under the direction of a constable, or by a person employed by a police authority, or

(c) to a vehicle at a time when it is being driven on a journey to or from any place undertaken for salvage purposes pursuant to Part IX of the *Merchant Shipping Act* 1995,

(da) to a vehicle owned by a health service body, as defined in section 60(7) of the *National Health Service and Community Care Act* 1990, by a Primary Care Trust established under section 18 of the *National Health Service Act* 2006 or by a Local Health Board established under section 11 of the *National Health Service (Wales) Act* 2006 or the *National Health Service (Scotland) Act* 1978, at a time when the vehicle is being driven under the owner's control.

(db) to an ambulance owned by a National Health Service trust established under section 25 of the *National Health Service Act* 2006, section 18 of the *National Health Service (Wales) Act* 2006 or the *National Health Service (Scotland) Act* 1978, at a time when a vehicle is being driven under the owner's control

(dc) to an ambulance owned by an NHS Foundation trust at a time when the vehicle is being driven under the owner's control,

(e) to a vehicle which is made available by the Secretary of State, or the Welsh Ministers to any person, body or local authority in pursuance of section 12 or 80 of the *National Health Service Act* 2006 or section 10 or 38 of the National Health Service (Wales) Act 2006 at a time when it is being used in accordance with the terms on which it is so made available,

(f) to a vehicle which is made available by the Secretary of State to any local authority, education authority or voluntary organisation in Scotland in pursuance of section 15 or 16 of the *National Health Service (Scotland) Act* 1978 at a time when it is being used in accordance with the terms on which it is so made available.

(g) to a vehicle owned by the Care Quality Commission, at a time when the vehicle is being driven under the owner's control.

Offence of keeping vehicle which does not meet insurance requirements

17–126 **144A.**—(1) If a motor vehicle registered under the *Vehicle Excise and Registration Act* 1994 does not meet the insurance requirements, the person in whose name the vehicle is registered is guilty of an offence.

(2) For the purposes of this section a vehicle meets the insurance requirements if—

(a) it is covered by a such a policy of insurance or such a security in respect of third party risks as complies with the requirements of this Part of this Act, and

(b) either of the following conditions is satisfied.

(3) The first condition is that the policy or security, or the certificate of insurance or security which relates to it, identifies the vehicle by its registration mark as a vehicle which is covered by the policy or security.

(4) The second condition is that the vehicle is covered by the policy or security because—

(a) the policy or security covers any vehicle, or any vehicle of a particular description, the owner of which is a person named in the policy or security or in the certificate of insurance or security which relates to it, and

(b) the vehicle is owned by that person.

(5) For the purposes of this section a vehicle is covered by a policy of insurance or security if the policy of insurance or security is in force in relation to the use of the vehicle.

Exceptions to section 144A offence

144B.—(1) A person ("the registered keeper") in whose name a vehicle which does not meet the insurance requirements is registered at any particular time ("the relevant time") does not commit an offence under section 144A of this Act at that time if any of the following conditions are satisfied. **17–127**

(2) The first condition is that at the relevant time the vehicle is owned as described—

(a) in subsection (1) of section 144 of this Act, or

(b) in paragraph (a), (b), (da), (db), (dc) or (g) of subsection (2) of that section, (whether or not at the relevant time it is being driven as described in that provision).

(3) The second condition is that at the relevant time the vehicle is owned with the intention that it should be used as described in paragraph (c), (d), (e) or (f) of section 144(2) of this Act.

(4) The third condition is that the registered keeper—

(a) is not at the relevant time the person keeping the vehicle, and

(b) if previously he was the person keeping the vehicle, he has by the relevant time complied with any requirements under subsection (7)(a) below that he is required to have complied with by the relevant or any earlier time.

(5) The fourth condition is that—

(a) the registered keeper is at the relevant time the person keeping the vehicle,

(b) at the relevant time the vehicle is not used on a road or other public place, and

(c) the registered keeper has by the relevant time complied with any requirements under subsection (7)(a) below that he is required to have complied with by the relevant or any earlier time.

(6) The fifth condition is that—

(a) the vehicle has been stolen before the relevant time,

(b) the vehicle has not been recovered by the relevant time, and

(c) any requirements under subsection (7)(b) below that, in connection with the theft, are required to have been complied with by the relevant or any earlier time have been complied with by the relevant time.

(7) Regulations may make provision—

(a) for the purposes of subsection (4)(b) and (5)(c) above, requiring a person in whose name a vehicle is registered to furnish such particulars and make such declarations as may be prescribed, and to do so at such times and in such manner as may be prescribed, and

(b) for the purposes of subsection (6)(c) above, as to the persons to whom, the times at which and the manner in which the theft of a vehicle is to be notified.

(8) Regulations may make provision amending this section for the purpose of providing for further exceptions to section 144A of this Act (or varying or revoking any such further exceptions).

(9) A person accused of an offence under section 144A of this Act is not entitled to the benefit of an exception conferred by or under this section unless evidence is adduced that is sufficient to raise an issue with respect to that exception; but where evidence is so adduced it is for the prosecution to prove beyond reasonable doubt that the exception does not apply.

Requirements in respect of policies of insurance

145.—(1) In order to comply with the requirements of this Part of this Act, a policy of insurance must satisfy the following conditions. **17–128**

(2) The policy must be issued by an authorised insurer.

(3) Subject to subsection (4) below, the policy—

(a) must insure such person, persons or classes of persons as may be specified in the policy in respect of any liability which may be incurred by him or them in respect of the death of or bodily injury to any person or damage to property caused by, or arising out of, the use of the vehicle on a road or other public place in Great Britain, and

(aa) must, in the case of a vehicle normally based in the territory of another member State, insure him or them in respect of any civil liability which may be incurred by him or them as a result of an event related to the use of the vehicle in Great Britain if,—

(i) according to the law of that territory, he or they would be required to be insured in respect of a civil liability which would arise under that law as a result of that event if the place where the vehicle was used when the event occurred were in that territory, and

(ii) the cover required by that law would be higher than that required by paragraph (a) above, and

(b) must, in the case of a vehicle normally based in Great Britain, insure him or them in respect of any liability which may be incurred by him or them in respect of the use of the vehicle and of any trailer, whether or not coupled, in the territory other than Great Britain and Gibraltar of each of the member States of the Communities according to—

(i) the law on compulsory insurance against civil liability in respect of the use of vehicles of the State in whose territory the event giving rise to the liability occurred; or

(ii) if it would give higher cover, the law which would be applicable under this Part of this Act if the place where the vehicle was used when that event occurred were in Great Britain; and

(c) must also insure him or them in respect of any liability which may be incurred by him or them under the provisions of this Part of this Act relating to payment for emergency treatment.

(4) The policy shall not, by virtue of subsection (3)(a) above, be required—

(a) to cover liability in respect of the death, arising out of and in the course of his employment, of a person in the employment of a person insured by the policy or of bodily injury sustained by such a person arising out of and in the course of his employment, or

(b) to provide insurance of more than £1,000,000 in respect of all such liabilities as may be incurred in respect of damage to property caused by, or arising out of, any one accident involving the vehicle, or

(c) to cover liability in respect of damage to the vehicle, or

(d) to cover liability in respect of damage to goods carried for hire or reward in or on the vehicle or in or on any trailer (whether or not coupled) drawn by the vehicle, or

(e) to cover any liability of a person in respect of damage to property in his custody or under his control, or

(f) to cover any contractual liability.

(4A) In the case of a person—

(a) carried in or upon a vehicle, or

(b) entering or getting on to, or alighting from, a vehicle,

the provisions of paragraph (a) of subsection (4) above do not apply unless cover in respect of the liability referred to in that paragraph is in fact provided pursuant to a requirement of the *Employers' Liability (Compulsory Insurance) Act* 1969.

(5) "Authorised insurer" has the same meaning as in section 95.

(6) If any person or body of persons ceases to be a member of the Motor Insurers' Bureau, that person or body shall not by virtue of that cease to be treated as an authorised insurer for the purposes of this Part of this Act—

(a) in relation to any policy issued by the insurer before ceasing to be such a member, or

(b) in relation to any obligation (whether arising before or after the insurer ceased to be such a member) which the insurer may be called upon to meet under or in consequence of any such policy or under section 157 of this Act by virtue of making a payment in pursuance of such an obligation.

Issue and surrender of certificates of insurance and of security

147.—(1) A policy of insurance shall be of no effect for the purposes of this Part of this Act unless and until there is delivered by the insurer to the person by whom the policy is effected a certificate (in this Part of this Act referred to as a "certificate of insurance") in the prescribed form and containing such particulars of any conditions subject to which the policy is issued and of any other matters as may be prescribed. **17–129**

(1A) A certificate of insurance is to be treated for the purposes of this Part of this Act as having been delivered under subsection (1) above to the person by whom the policy is effected if—

(a) it is transmitted electronically by the insurer to the person in accordance with subsection (1B) below, or

(b) it is made available by the insurer to the person on a website in accordance with subsection (1C) below.

(1B) A certificate is transmitted electronically by an insurer to a person in accordance with this subsection if—

(a) on effecting the policy to which the certificate relates, the person agreed to its electronic transmission for the purposes of subsection (1) above, and

(b) the certificate is transmitted by the insurer to an electronic address specified by the person for this purpose.

(1C) A certificate is made available by an insurer to a person on a website in accordance with this subsection if—

(a) on effecting the policy to which the certificate relates, the person agreed to its being made available on a website for the purposes of subsection (1) above,

(b) the insurer makes the certificate available to the person by placing an electronic copy of it on a website, and

(c) the person is notified by the insurer, in a manner agreed by the person, of—

(i) the certificate's presence on the website,

(ii) the address of the website,

(iii) the place on the website where he may access the certificate, and

(iv) how he may access the certificate.

(1D) Where a certificate made available on a website is treated by virtue of subsection (1A)(b) above as having been delivered by an insurer to a person, the insurer must ensure that the certificate remains continuously accessible to the person on the website until the expiry of the last day on which the policy to which it relates has effect.

(1E) For the purposes of subsection (1D) above, a certificate is to be treated as remaining continuously accessible to a person on a website, despite its being temporarily inaccessible to him on the website, if the insurer has taken all reasonable steps to make it continuously accessible to him on the website (including steps to remedy any temporary inaccessibility).

(2) A security shall be of no effect for the purposes of this Part of this Act unless and until there is delivered by the person giving the security to the person to whom it is given a certificate (in this Part of this Act referred to as a "certificate of security") in the prescribed form and containing such particulars of any conditions subject to which the security is issued and of any other matters as may be prescribed.

(3) Different forms and different particulars may be prescribed for the purposes of subsection (1) or (2) above in relation to different cases or circumstances.

(4) Where a certificate has been delivered under this section [, otherwise than as described in subsection (1A)(a) or (b) above,]2 and the policy or security to which it relates is cancelled by mutual consent or by virtue of any provision in the policy or security, the person to whom the certificate was delivered must, within seven days from the taking effect of the cancellation—

(a) surrender the certificate to the person by whom the policy was issued or the security was given, or

(b) if the certificate has been lost or destroyed, make a statutory declaration to that effect.

(4A) Where subsection (4) above applies in respect of a certificate of insurance that has not been lost or destroyed, the person to whom the certificate was delivered—

(a) may, instead of surrendering the certificate under subsection (4)(a) above, transmit to the insurer, by means of an electronic communication to an electronic address specified by the insurer, a statement confirming that the policy to which the certificate relates has ceased to have effect, and

(b) if he does so, is to be treated as having surrendered the certificate.

(4B) Where subsection (4) above applies in respect of a certificate of insurance that has been lost or destroyed, the person to whom the certificate was delivered—

(a) may, instead of making a statutory declaration as described in subsection (4)(b) above, transmit to the insurer, by means of an electronic communication to an electronic address specified by the insurer, a statement confirming that the certificate has been lost or (as applicable) destroyed, and

(b) if he does so, is to be treated as having made a statutory declaration as described in subsection (4)(b) above.

(4C) Subsection (4D) below applies where—

(a) a certificate of insurance is treated, by virtue of subsection (1A) above, as having been delivered to a person under this section, and

(b) the policy to which it relates is cancelled by mutual consent or by virtue of any provision in the policy.

(4D) The person must, within seven days from the taking effect of the cancellation, either—

(a) transmit to the insurer, by means of an electronic communication to an electronic address specified by the insurer, a statement confirming that the policy to which the certificate relates has ceased to have effect, or

(b) deliver to the insurer a legible printed copy of the certificate endorsed with a statement made and signed by him to that effect.

(4E) A person who transmits a statement or delivers a copy of a certificate as described in paragraph (a) or (b) of subsection (4D) above is to be treated as having surrendered the certificate in question.

(4F) In this section, "electronic communication" has the meaning given in the *Electronic Communications Act* 2000.

(5) A person who fails to comply with subsection (4) [or (4D)] above is guilty of an offence.

Avoidance of certain exceptions to policies or securities

17–130 **148.**—(1) Where a certificate of insurance or certificate of security has been delivered under section 147 of this Act to the person by whom a policy has been effected or to whom a security has been given, so much of the policy or security as purports to restrict—

(a) the insurance of the persons insured by the policy, or

(b) the operation of the security,

(as the case may be) by reference to any of the matters mentioned in subsection (2) below shall, as respects such liabilities as are required to be covered by a policy under section 145 of this Act, be of no effect.

(2) Those matters are—

(a) the age or physical or mental condition of persons driving the vehicle,

(b) the condition of the vehicle,

(c) the number of persons that the vehicle carries,

(d) the weight or physical characteristics of the goods that the vehicle carries,

(e) the time at which or the areas within which the vehicle is used,

(f) the horsepower or cylinder capacity or value of the vehicle,

(g) the carrying on the vehicle of any particular apparatus, or

(h) the carrying on the vehicle of any particular means of identification other than any means of identification required to be carried by or under the *Vehicle Excise and Registration Act* 1994.

(3) Nothing in subsection (1) above requires an insurer or the giver of a security to pay any sum in respect of the liability of any person otherwise than in or towards the discharge of that liability.

(4) Any sum paid by an insurer or the giver of a security in or towards the discharge of any liability of any person which is covered by the policy or security by virtue only of subsection (1) above is recoverable by the insurer or giver of the security from that person.

(5) A condition in a policy or security issued or given for the purposes of this Part of this Act providing—

(a) that no liability shall arise under the policy or security, or
(b) that any liability so arising shall cease,

in the event of some specified thing being done or omitted to be done after the happening of the event giving rise to a claim under the policy or security, shall be of no effect in connection with such liabilities as are required to be covered by a policy under section 145 of this Act.

(6) Nothing in subsection (5) above shall be taken to render void any provision in a policy or security requiring the person insured or secured to pay to the insurer or the giver of the security any sums which the latter may have become liable to pay under the policy or security and which have been applied to the satisfaction of the claims of third parties.

(7) Notwithstanding anything in any enactment, a person issuing a policy of insurance under section 145 of this Act shall be liable to indemnify the persons or classes of persons specified in the policy in respect of any liability which the policy purports to cover in the case of those persons or classes of persons.

Avoidance of certain agreements as to liability towards passengers

149.—(1) This section applies where a person uses a motor vehicle in circumstances such that under section 143 of this Act there is required to be in force in relation to his use of it such a policy of insurance or such a security in respect of third-party risks as complies with the requirements of this Part of this Act. **17–131**

(2) If any other person is carried in or upon the vehicle while the user is so using it, any antecedent agreement or understanding between them (whether intended to be legally binding or not) shall be of no effect so far as it purports or might be held—

(a) to negative or restrict any such liability of the user in respect of persons carried in or upon the vehicle as is required by section 145 of this Act to be covered by a policy of insurance, or
(b) to impose any conditions with respect to the enforcement of any such liability of the user.

(3) The fact that a person so carried has willingly accepted as his the risk of negligence on the part of the user shall not be treated as negativing any such liability of the user.

(4) For the purposes of this section—

(a) references to a person being carried in or upon a vehicle include references to a person entering or getting on to, or alighting from, the vehicle, and
(b) the reference to an antecedent agreement is to one made at any time before the liability arose.

Insurance or security in respect of private use of vehicle to cover use under car-sharing arrangements

150.—(1) To the extent that a policy or security issued or given for the purposes of this Part of this Act— **17–132**

(a) restricts the insurance of the persons insured by the policy or the operation of the security (as the case may be) to use of the vehicle for specified purposes (for example, social, domestic and pleasure purposes) of a non-commercial character, or
(b) excludes from that insurance or the operation of the security (as the case may be)—
   (i) use of the vehicle for hire or reward, or
   (ii) business or commercial use of the vehicle, or
   (iii) use of the vehicle for specified purposes of a business or commercial character,

then, for the purposes of that policy or security so far as it relates to such liabilities as are required to be covered by a policy under section 145 of this Act, the use of a vehicle on a journey in the course of which one or more passengers are carried at separate fares shall, if the conditions specified in subsection (2) below are satisfied, be treated as falling within that restriction or as not falling within that exclusion (as the case may be).

(2) The conditions referred to in subsection (1) above are—

(a) the vehicle is not adapted to carry more than eight passengers and is not a motor cycle,
(b) the fare or aggregate of the fares paid in respect of the journey does not exceed

the amount of the running costs of the vehicle for the journey (which for the purposes of this paragraph shall be taken to include an appropriate amount in respect of depreciation and general wear), and

(c) the arrangements for the payment of fares by the passenger or passengers carried at separate fares were made before the journey began.

(3) Subsections (1) and (2) above apply however the restrictions or exclusions described in subsection (1) are framed or worded.

(4) In subsections (1) and (2) above "fare" and "separate fares" have the same meaning as in section 1(4) of the *Public Passenger Vehicles Act* 1981.

Power of constables to obtain names and addresses of drivers and others, and to require production of evidence of insurance or security and test certificates

165.—(1) Any of the following persons—

(a) a person driving a motor vehicle (other than an invalid carriage) on a road, or

(b) a person whom a constable [or vehicle examiner] has reasonable cause to believe to have been the driver of a motor vehicle (other than an invalid carriage) at a time when an accident occurred owing to its presence on a road [or other public place], or

(c) a person whom a constable [or vehicle examiner] has reasonable cause to believe to have committed an offence in relation to the use on a road of a motor vehicle (other than an invalid carriage),

must, on being so required by a constable [or vehicle examiner], give his name and address and the name and address of the owner of the vehicle and produce the following documents for examination.

(2) Those documents are—

(a) the relevant certificate of insurance or certificate of security (within the meaning of Part VI of this Act), or such other evidence that the vehicle is not or was not being driven in contravention of section 143 of this Act as may be prescribed by regulations made by the Secretary of State,

(b) in relation to a vehicle to which section 47 of this Act applies, a test certificate issued in respect of the vehicle as mentioned in subsection (1) of that section, and

(c) in relation to a goods vehicle the use of which on a road without a plating certificate or goods vehicle test certificate is an offence under section 53(1) or (2) of this Act, any such certificate issued in respect of that vehicle or any trailer drawn by it.

(2A) Subsections (2B) and (2C) below apply where a certificate of insurance is treated as having been delivered to a person under section 147(1) of this Act by virtue of section 147(1A) of this Act.

(2B) In the case of a certificate transmitted to a person as described in section 147(1A)(a) of this Act, the person is to be treated for the purposes of this section as producing the relevant certificate of insurance if—

(a) using electronic equipment provided by him or made available to him by the constable or examiner, he provides the constable or examiner with electronic access to a copy of the certificate, or

(b) he produces a legible printed copy of the certificate.

(2C) In the case of a certificate made available to a person as described in section 147(1A)(b) of this Act, the person is to be treated for the purposes of this section as producing the relevant certificate of insurance if—

(a) using electronic equipment provided by him or made available to him by the constable or examiner, he provides the constable or examiner with electronic access on the website in question to a copy of the certificate, or

(b) he produces a legible printed copy of the certificate.

(2D) Nothing in subsection (2B) or (2C) above requires a constable or examiner to provide a person with electronic equipment for the purpose of compliance with a requirement imposed on the person by this section.

(3) Subject to subsection (4) below, a person who fails to comply with a requirement under subsection (1) above is guilty of an offence.

(4) A person shall not be convicted of an offence under [subsection (3)] above by reason only of failure to produce any certificate or other evidence [...] if in proceedings against him for the offence he shows that—

(a) within seven days after the date on which the production of the certificate or other evidence was required it was produced at a police station that was specified by him at the time when its production was required, or

(b) it was produced there as soon as was reasonably practicable, or

(c) it was not reasonably practicable for it to be produced there before the day on which the proceedings were commenced,

and for the purposes of this subsection the laying of the information or, in Scotland, the service of the complaint on the accused shall be treated as the commencement of the proceedings.

(5) A person—

(a) who supervises the holder of a provisional licence granted under Part III of this Act while the holder is driving on a road a motor vehicle (other than an invalid carriage), or

(b) whom a constable [or vehicle examiner] has reasonable cause to believe was supervising the holder of such a licence while driving, at a time when an accident occurred owing to the presence of the vehicle on a road or at a time when an offence is suspected of having been committed by the holder of the provisional licence in relation to the use of the vehicle on a road,

must, on being so required by a constable [or vehicle examiner], give his name and address and the name and address of the owner of the vehicle.

(6) A person who fails to comply with a requirement under subsection (5) above is guilty of an offence.

(7) In this section "owner" in relation to a vehicle which is the subject of a hiring agreement, includes each party to the agreement [...][and "vehicle examiner" means an examiner appointed under section 66A of this Act.]

Power to seize vehicles driven without licence or insurance

165A.—(1) Subsection (5) applies if any of the following conditions is satisfied. 17–133

(2) The first condition is that—

(a) a constable in uniform requires, under section 164, a person to produce his licence and its counterpart for examination,

(b) the person fails to produce them, and

(c) the constable has reasonable grounds for believing that a motor vehicle is or was being driven by the person in contravention of section 87(1).

(3) The second condition is that—

(a) a constable in uniform requires, under section 165, a person to produce evidence that a motor vehicle is not or was not being driven in contravention of section 143,

(b) the person fails to produce such evidence, and

(c) the constable has reasonable grounds for believing that the vehicle is or was being so driven.

(4) The third condition is that—

(a) a constable in uniform requires, under section 163, a person driving a motor vehicle to stop the vehicle,

(b) the person fails to stop the vehicle, or to stop the vehicle long enough, for the constable to make such lawful enquiries as he considers appropriate, and

(c) the constable has reasonable grounds for believing that the vehicle is or was being driven in contravention of section 87(1) or 143.

(5) Where this subsection applies, the constable may—

(a) seize the vehicle in accordance with subsections (6) and (7) and remove it;

(b) enter, for the purpose of exercising a power falling within paragraph (a), any premises (other than a private dwelling house) on which he has reasonable grounds for believing the vehicle to be;

(c) use reasonable force, if necessary, in the exercise of any power conferred by paragraph (a) or (b).

(6) Before seizing the motor vehicle, the constable must warn the person by whom it appears that the vehicle is or was being driven in contravention of section 87(1) or 143 that he will seize it—

(a) in a section 87(1) case, if the person does not produce his licence and its counterpart immediately;

(b) in a section 143 case, if the person does not provide him immediately with evidence that the vehicle is not or was not being driven in contravention of that section.

But the constable is not required to give such a warning if the circumstances make it impracticable for him to do so.

(7) If the constable is unable to seize the vehicle immediately because the person driving the vehicle has failed to stop as requested or has driven off, he may seize it at any time within the period of 24 hours beginning with the time at which the condition in question is first satisfied.

(8) The powers conferred on a constable by this section are exercisable only at a time when regulations under section 165B are in force.

(9) In this section—

(a) a reference to a motor vehicle does not include an invalid carriage;

(b) a reference to evidence that a motor vehicle is not or was not being driven in contravention of section 143 is a reference to a document or other evidence within section 165(2)(a);

(c) "counterpart" and "licence" have the same meanings as in section 164;

(d) "private dwelling house" does not include any garage or other structure occupied with the dwelling house, or any land appurtenant to the dwelling house.

Retention etc. of vehicles seized under section 165A

17–134 **165B.**—(1) The Secretary of State may by regulations make provision as to—

(a) the removal and retention of motor vehicles seized under section 165A; and

(b) the release or disposal of such motor vehicles.

(2) Regulations under subsection (1) may, in particular, make provision—

(a) for the giving of notice of the seizure of a motor vehicle under section 165A to a person who is the registered keeper, the owner or the driver of that vehicle;

(b) for the procedure by which a person who claims to be the registered keeper or the owner of a motor vehicle seized under section 165A may seek to have it released;

(c) for requiring the payment, by the registered keeper, owner or driver of the vehicle, of fees, charges or costs in relation to the removal and retention of such a motor vehicle and to any application for its release;

(d) as to the circumstances in which a motor vehicle seized under section 165A may be disposed of;

(e) as to the destination—

(i) of any fees or charges payable in accordance with the regulations;

(ii) of the proceeds (if any) arising from the disposal of a motor vehicle seized under section 165A;

(f) for the delivery to a local authority, in circumstances prescribed by or determined in accordance with the regulations, of any motor vehicle seized under section 165A.

(3) Regulations under subsection (1) must provide that a person who would otherwise be liable to pay any fee or charge under the regulations is not liable to pay it if—

(a) he was not driving the motor vehicle at the time in question, and

(b) he did not know that the vehicle was being driven at that time, had not consented to its being driven and could not, by the taking of reasonable steps, have prevented it from being driven.

(4) Regulations under subsection (1) may make different provision for different cases.

(5) In this section—

"local authority"—

(a) in relation to England, means—

(i) a county council,

(ii) the council of a district comprised in an area for which there is no county council,

(iii) a London borough council,

(iv) the Common Council of the City of London, or

(v) transport for London;

(b) in relation to Wales, means the council of a county or county borough; and

(c) in relation to Scotland, means a council constituted under section 2 of the *Local Government etc. (Scotland) Act* 1994;

"registered keeper", in relation to a motor vehicle, means the person in whose name the vehicle is registered under the *Vehicle Excise and Registration Act* 1994.

(2) What must the prosecution prove?

For an offence contrary to s.143, the prosecution must prove that the defendant used (or caused or permitted another person to use) a vehicle on a road or other public place. Having done that, it is for the defence to prove (on the balance of probabilities) that the use was covered by insurance or a relevant security. A new offence has been created through the insertion of s.144A to the 1988 Act by s.22 of the *Road Safety Act* 2006. If a registered vehicle does not meet the insurance requirements, the registered owner is guilty of an offence. A series of exceptions are set out in s.144B which incorporates those set out in s.144 but also provides for circumstances where the person shown as the registered owner is no longer the keeper of the vehicle and has complied with notification requirements or where the vehicle has been stolen and notification requirements have again been complied with. **17–135**

A person who is not actually the keeper is exempt provided, if previously the keeper, he has complied with the requisite notification requirements; these are set out in the *Motor Vehicles (Insurance Requirements) Regulations* 2011 (S.I. 2011 No.20), reg.2 and vary depending on whether the vehicle has been sold or transferred in the normal way or for the purpose of destruction or for sending permanently outside Great Britain. There is a further exemption where the registered keeper is the person who keeps the vehicle for these purposes but the vehicle is not used on a road or other public place at the relevant time and the registered keeper has complied with the notification requirements prescribed under reg.3 of the 2011 Regulations (the Statutory Off-Road Notification); that notification requirement is not needed if the vehicle did not have either a licence or a nil licence under the *Vehicle Excise and Registration Act* 1994 on January 31, 1998 and has neither had such a licence nor been kept or used on a public road since then: s.144B(6A) as inserted by reg.5 of the 2011 Regulations. The final exemption is where the vehicle has been stolen and not recovered and the police have been notified of the theft within 14 days of the day on which it came to the notice of the registered keeper: 2011 Regulations, reg.4.

For identification, see *ante*, §§ 10–89 *et seq*. For use and for causing or permitting use, see *ante*, §§ 17–9 and 17–10. For "vehicle", see *ante*, § 17–11 (note the exemption for invalid carriages: s.143(4)). For "road" or "other public place", see *ante*, §§ 17–7 and 17–8.

(3) Allocation

This offence is summary only. Proceedings for an offence must be commenced within six months of the offence coming to the knowledge of the prosecutor providing that is no more than three years from the date the offence was committed. **17–136**

(4) Insurance

The obligation is to be insured against third party risks. The insurance in force may be limited so as to restrict the circumstances in which the vehicle is used; this may be by reference to the purposes for which the vehicle is being used or the person who is using it. It is not possible for the insurance to exclude certain things—see ss.145, 148 and 150. **17–137**

Certain vehicles can be used without insurance, generally vehicles owned and being used for the purposes of specified national or local government functions: s.144. Crown vehicles are also exempt. The situations most commonly encountered are vehicles owned by a County Council at a time when the vehicle is being driven under the control of the owner (s.144(2)(a)) and vehicles owned by a police authority and driven under the control of the authority or any vehicle when it is being driven for police purposes by or under the direction of a constable or employee of a police authority: s.144(2)(b).

To satisfy the provisions of s.143, an insurance policy does not become effective until a certificate is delivered to the person taking out the cover. The certificate must be in the prescribed form. Those issuing the certificate must keep a record and, on request, must give details without charge to the Secretary of State or to any Chief Officer of Police. If a defendant who has lost his copy of the certificate is facing difficulties obtaining a duplicate, a formal police request will need to be complied with by the insurance company.

(5) Defence

17–138 A special defence is provided for those using in the course of their employment vehicles they do not own whilst unaware of the lack of cover: s.143(3).

It is for the defendant to prove (on the balance of probabilities) that:

— the vehicle did not belong to him;

— he was using the vehicle in the course of his employment;

— he did not know (and had no reason to believe) that the vehicle was not insured.

(6) Penalty

17–139 The maximum penalty for an offence contrary to s.143 is a fine up to a maximum of level 5 (£5000). It is an endorsable offence with a range of 6–8 penalty points. Disqualification is discretionary. The maximum penalty for an offence contrary to s.144A is a fine up to a maximum of level 3 (£1,000). It is not endorsable.

(7) Sentence

17–140 The offence can be committed in a very wide range of circumstances from the conscientious individual who (after years of proper insurance) overlooked the need to renew or believed on reasonable (but mistaken) grounds that the use was covered to the individual who deliberately chooses not to insure, probably because he perceives the cost of insurance to be so high and the risk of detection so low that it is a risk worth taking.

The dilemma for a court is that the financial penalty it could legitimately impose on the relatively feckless offender is probably substantially below the annual cost of insurance. However, this is a regulatory offence; the consequence for any victim can be great but it is not in itself an offence that is dangerous or violent.

The sentence is most likely to be a financial penalty. It should be noted that the user may have been offered a fixed penalty and that will have been in the sum of £200 (s.143) or £100 (s.144A).

Since implementation of the relevant provisions in the *Criminal Justice and Immigration Act* 2008, it is no longer possible to impose a community order for this offence. The approach to sentence in the *Magistrates' Court Sentencing Guidelines* is to provide for a single starting point and range of a band C fine—a starting point of 150% of relevant weekly income within a range of 125%–175%. In relation to penalty points and disqualification, 6-12 months disqualification is included where there is evidence of sustained uninsured use and/or involvement in an accident and 7 points to 2 months disqualification where the vehicle was actually being driven when stopped and where there was no evidence that the offender has held insurance. This can be a fine distinction but seems to make it clear that disqualification is an important part of the penalty for this offence. The explanatory material that accompanies the guideline emphasises the important principle that a court may only sentence the offender on the basis of facts either proved or admitted; comparisons with annual rates of insurance will need to be treated with care. That material also states that the court should not be influenced by the level of any fixed penalty that might have been offered since, when imposing sentence, a court is obliged by statute to have regard both to the seriousness of the offence and the financial circumstances of the offender whereas the fixed penalty is a flat rate that takes no account of financial circumstances.

STARTING POINT AND RANGE OF SENTENCE

(BASED ON A FIRST TIME OFFENDER PLEADING NOT GUILTY)

Examples of nature of activity	Starting Point	Range
Using a motor vehicle on a road or other public place without insurance	Band C fine	Band C fine 6 points–12 months disqualification—see notes below

AGGRAVATING AND MITIGATING FACTORS

Factors indicating higher culpability	Factors indicating lower culpability
1. Never passed test 2. Gave false details 3. Driving LGV, HGV, PSV etc. 4. Driving for hire or reward 5. Evidence of sustained uninsured use **Factor indicating greater degree of harm** 1. Involved in accident 2. Accident resulting in injury	1. Responsibility for providing insurance rests with another 2. Genuine misunderstanding 3. Recent failure to renew or failure to transfer vehicle details where insurance was in existence 4. Vehicle not being driven

Notes

Consider range from 7 points–2 months disqualification where vehicle was being driven and no evidence that the offender has held insurance.

Consider disqualification of 6–12 months if evidence of sustained uninsured use and/or involvement in accident.

In addition to a financial penalty, a court may impose a period of disqualification, **17–141** perhaps for a relatively short period depending on the circumstances. However, the recurring dilemma for courts is that the annual cost of insurance can outweigh any financial penalty that can realistically be paid within one year.

B. USING A VEHICLE WITHOUT HOLDING A DRIVING LICENCE

(1) Definition

Road Traffic Act 1988, s.87

Drivers of motor vehicles to have driving licences

87.—(1) It is an offence for a person to drive on a road a motor vehicle of any class otherwise **17–142** than in accordance with a licence authorising him to drive a motor vehicle of that class.

(2) It is an offence for a person to cause or permit another person to drive on a road a motor vehicle of any class otherwise than in accordance with a licence authorising that other person to drive a motor vehicle of that class.

(2) Allocation

17–143 This offence is triable summarily only.

(3) What must the prosecution prove?

17–144
— the defendant
— drove
— on a road
— a motor vehicle

The *defence* must then show (on the balance of probabilities) that that driving was in accordance with a licence granted to the defendant.

For issues of identification, see §§ 10–89 *et seq.* in this work. For issues surrounding the meaning of "drive", see *ante*, § 17–4. The phrase "mechanically propelled vehicle" is wider than "vehicle"; see *ante*, § 17–6. The phrase "road or other public place" has been subject to detailed consideration; see *ante*, §§ 17–7 and 17–8.

17–145 The offence is committed by driving a motor vehicle whilst not holding a licence authorising the use of that type of vehicle. Licences may be restricted by virtue of the type of vehicle able to be used or by the age of the person entitled to use a particular type of vehicle. A full licence will only be issued following the passing of an appropriate test (both theory and practical); in most circumstances, a provisional licence can be issued enabling a person to use a vehicle in controlled circumstances (usually involving supervision by a full licence holder aged over 21).

Different tests are administered for different vehicles; for instance, a person holding a full driving licence authorising the use of a motor car and small goods vehicles will need to pass a separate test before being authorised to drive medium sized goods vehicles or small buses.

All licences have an age restriction; a moped can be used by a person 16 or over, a motor car or motor bicycle by a person aged 17 or over, most HGV licences require the driver to be aged at least 21 (see *ante*, § 17–114, for further detail). Full licences are granted until the age of 70 (except where the presence of disease or disability requires a shorter period). Thereafter, they may be renewed for three year periods. If the licence is issued as a photocard, then that photocard must be surrendered at least every 10 years in order that a more recent photograph can be incorporated.

17–146 A person who drives a motor vehicle whilst under the age at which a licence could be granted (*e.g.* 15-year-old driving a car) commits an offence under this section rather than that of driving whilst disqualified under s.103. Although a person below the set age is disqualified from holding or obtaining a licence (s.101), s.103(4) provides that they do not commit an offence under that section by driving, see *ante*, § 17–113.

The most complex conditions apply to provisional licence holders. In respect of motorcycles, there are limits on the size of the engine in the vehicle which can be used (generally "learner motor cycles") and "L" plates must be displayed. Passengers may not be carried. A person who fails to comply with those obligations commits an offence under this section. In respect of other vehicles, there is a general requirement that provisional licence holders be supervised by a "qualified driver" present in the vehicle. Generally, this will be a full licence holder for that class of vehicle who is over 21 years of age and has held that type of licence for at least three years. Whilst any "qualified driver" can supervise or teach a provisional licence holder, in relation to motor cars instruction for money or money's worth can only be given by a person registered or licensed under Pt V of the *Road Traffic Act* 1988.

There are further extensive provisions governing the entitlement of drivers from abroad—see *Wilkinson's Road Traffic Offences*, Ch.11.

(4) Sentence

The maximum penalty is a fine of level 3 (£1000). The *Magistrates' Court Sentencing Guidelines* provide that the starting point for this offence is a Band A fine (50 per cent of the defendant's relevant weekly income). **17–147**

It will aggravate the seriousness of the offence if no licence has ever been held.

It is endorsable (and thus disqualifiable) in some circumstances with a range of 3–6 penalty points.

The offence is endorsable where the driving did not accord with any licence that could have been granted to the driver. Thus, a full licence holder whose licence had expired but who would have been entitled to have it renewed and who drove a vehicle authorised by that licence would not be subject to endorsement or disqualification. However, a provisional licence holder who fails to display "L" plates or to be properly supervised would be liable to endorsement. Similarly, a person who drives a vehicle for which a licence could not have been issued (*e.g.* a 15-year-old driving a car) is subject to endorsement. Some full licences give provisional entitlement for other classes of vehicle. A person driving a vehicle in circumstances which are only covered by the provisional entitlement who fails to comply with the conditions of the provisional licence will be liable to endorsement.

C. Forgery of Documents

(1) Definition

With the increased emphasis on safety which affects both the testing of vehicles and the licensing of their users, there will be a risk that some will seek to avoid the law by fraudulent means. These sections provide a series of offences designed to penalise those who make misrepresentations (whether or not in documentary form) and those who create documents that are false. **17–148**

In addition, a driving licence (or a document that purports to be such a licence) is an "identity document' within the meaning of s.7 of the *Identity Documents Act* 2010; possession with an "improper intention" of a document that is known to be false or improperly obtained or which relates to someone else is an offence punishable only on indictment with a maximum penalty of 10 years imprisonment and/or an unlimited fine: s.4. An "improper intention" includes an intention to allow it to be used (or to induce its use) in order to establish, ascertain or verify personal information about the defendant or any other person. By s.8, "personal information" includes full name and address. There is a further offence of possessing (without reasonable excuse) such a document which is false, improperly obtained or relating to someone else; this offence does not require knowledge that the document is false etc., and is punishable by a maximum of two years imprisonment and or a fine on indictment, 6 months imprisonment or a level 5 fine on summary conviction: s.6. "False" has the same meaning as in the *Forgery and Counterfeiting Act* 1981. A document is "improperly obtained" if false information was provided to obtain it in its current form (s.9(3)).

The 2010 Act replaced (with some changes) the like named 2006 Act; aspects of those earlier provisions were considered in *Jamalov* [2010] EWCA Crim 309; [2010] 2 Cr.App.R. 4 (p.28). At the scene of a collision, a police officer asked Mr. Jamalov if he had any identification and he produced a forged Czech driving licence. The Court of Appeal agreed that these facts amounted to an offence under what is now s.4. The false document had been produced at the scene of the collision with the purpose of establishing who he was. The court then considered the leading case on false identification documents, *Ovieriakhi* [2009] EWCA Crim 452; [2009] 2 Cr.App.R.(S) 91 (p.607), and also *Zeraj* [2009] EWCA Crim 744, before concluding that the proper sentence for a man who was in possession of a false licence so that he could pretend that he was lawfully entitled to drive is one of four months' imprisonment.

Road Traffic Act 1988, ss.173–174, 176

Forgery of documents, etc

17–149 **173.**—(1) A person who, with intent to deceive—

(a) forges, alters or uses a document or other thing to which this section applies, or

(b) lends to, or allows to be used by, any other person a document or other thing to which this section applies, or

(c) makes or has in his possession any document or other thing so closely resembling a document or other thing to which this section applies as to be calculated to deceive,

is guilty of an offence.

(2) This section applies to the following documents and other things—

(a) any licence under any Part of this Act or, in the case of a licence to drive, any counterpart of such a licence,

(aa) any counterpart of a Northern Ireland licence or Community licence,

(b) any test certificate, goods vehicle test certificate, plating certificate, certificate of conformity or Minister's approval certificate (within the meaning of Part II of this Act),

(c) any certificate required as a condition of any exception prescribed under section 14 of this Act,

(cc) any seal required by regulations made under section 41 of this Act with respect to speed limiters,

(d) any plate containing particulars required to be marked on a vehicle by regulations under section 41 of this Act or containing other particulars required to be marked on a goods vehicle by sections 54 to 58 of this Act or regulations under those sections,

(dd) any document evidencing the appointment of an examiner under section 66A of this Act,

(e) any records required to be kept by virtue of section 74 of this Act,

(f) any document which, in pursuance of section 89(3) of this Act, is issued as evidence of the result of a test of competence to drive,

(ff) any document evidencing the successful completion of a driver training course provided in accordance with regulations under section 99ZA of this Act,

(g) any certificate under section 133A or any badge or certificate prescribed by regulations made by virtue of section 135 of this Act,

(h) any certificate of insurance or certificate of security under Part VI of this Act,

(j) any document produced as evidence of insurance in pursuance of Regulation 6 of the *Motor Vehicles (Compulsory Insurance) (No.2) Regulations* 1973,

(k) any document issued under regulations made by the Secretary of State in pursuance of his power under section 165(2)(a) of this Act to prescribe evidence which may be produced in lieu of a certificate of insurance or a certificate of security,

(l) any international road haulage permit, and

(m) a certificate of the kind referred to in section 34B(1) of the *Road Traffic Offenders Act* 1988, and

(3) In the application of this section to England and Wales "forges" means makes a false document or other thing in order that it may be used as genuine.

(4) In this section "counterpart" and "Community licence" have the same meanings as in Part III of this Act.

False statements and withholding material information

17–150 **174.**—(1) A person who knowingly makes a false statement for the purpose—

(a) of obtaining the grant of a licence under any Part of this Act to himself or any other person, or

(b) of preventing the grant of any such licence, or

(c) of procuring the imposition of a condition or limitation in relation to any such licence, or

(ca) of obtaining a document evidencing the successful completion of a driver training course provided in accordance with regulations under section 99ZA of this Act, or

(d) of securing the entry or retention of the name of any person in the register of approved instructors maintained under Part V of this Act, or

(dd) of obtaining the grant to any person of a certificate under section 133A of this Act, or

(e) of obtaining the grant of an international road haulage permit to himself or any other person,

is guilty of an offence.

(2) A person who, in supplying information or producing documents for the purposes either of sections 53 to 60 and 63 of this Act or of regulations made under sections 49 to 51, 61, 62 and 66(3) of this Act—

(a) makes a statement which he knows to be false in a material particular or recklessly makes a statement which is false in a material particular, or

(b) produces, provides, sends or otherwise makes use of a document which he knows to be false in a material particular or recklessly produces, provides, sends or otherwise makes use of a document which is false in a material particular,

is guilty of an offence.

(3) A person who—

(a) knowingly produces false evidence for the purposes of regulations under section 66(1) of this Act, or

(b) knowingly makes a false statement in a declaration required to be made by the regulations,

is guilty of an offence.

(4) A person who—

(a) wilfully makes a false entry in any record required to be made or kept by regulations under section 74 of this Act, or

(b) with intent to deceive, makes use of any such entry which he knows to be false,

is guilty of an offence.

(5) A person who makes a false statement or withholds any material information for the purpose of obtaining the issue—

(a) of a certificate of insurance or certificate of security under Part VI of this Act, or

(b) of any document issued under regulations made by the Secretary of State in pursuance of his power under section 165(2)(a) of this Act to prescribe evidence which may be produced in lieu of a certificate of insurance or a certificate of security,

is guilty of an offence.

Power to seize articles in respect of which offences under sections 173 to 175 may have been committed

176.—(1) If a constable has reasonable cause to believe that a document produced to him— **17–151**

(a) in pursuance of section 137 of this Act, or

(b) in pursuance of any of the preceding provisions of this Part of this Act,

is a document in relation to which an offence has been committed under section 173, 174 or 175 of this Act or under section 115 of the *Road Traffic Regulation Act* 1984, he may seize the document.

(1A) Where a licence to drive or a counterpart of any such licence or of any Community licence may be seized by a constable under subsection (1) above, he may also seize the counterpart, the licence to drive or the Community licence (as the case may be) produced with it.

(2) When a document is seized under subsection (1) above, the person from whom it was taken shall, unless—

(a) the document has been previously returned to him, or

(b) he has been previously charged with an offence under any of those sections,

be summoned before a magistrates' court or, in Scotland, the sheriff to account for his possession of the document.

(3) The court or sheriff must make such order respecting the disposal of the document and award such costs as the justice of the case may require.

(3A) An order under subsection (3) above respecting the disposal of any such licence or Community licence to drive or a counterpart of any such licence or of a Northern Ireland licence or Community licence may include an order respecting the disposal of any document seized under subsection (1A) above.

(4) If a constable, an examiner appointed under section 66A of this Act has reasonable cause to believe that a document or plate carried on a motor vehicle or by the driver of the vehicle is a document or plate to which this subsection applies, he may seize it.

For the purposes of this subsection the power to seize includes power to detach from a vehicle.

(5) Subsection (4) above applies to a document or plate in relation to which an offence has been committed under sections 173, 174 or 175 of this Act in so far as they apply—

(a) to documents evidencing the appointment of examiners under section 66A of this Act, or

(b) to goods vehicle test certificates, plating certificates, certificates of conformity or Minister's approval certificates (within the meaning of Part II of this Act), or

(c) to plates containing plated particulars (within the meaning of that Part) or containing other particulars required to be marked on goods vehicles by sections 54 to 58 of this Act or regulations made under them, or

(d) to records required to be kept by virtue of section 74 of this Act, or

(e) to international road haulage permits.

(6) When a document or plate is seized under subsection (4) above, either the driver or owner of the vehicle shall, if the document or plate is still detained and neither of them has previously been charged with an offence in relation to the document or plate under section 173, 174 or 175 of this Act, be summoned before a magistrates' court or, in Scotland, the sheriff to account for his possession of, or the presence on the vehicle of, the document or plate.

(7) The court or sheriff must make such order respecting the disposal of the document or plate and award such costs as the justice of the case may require.

(8) In this section "counterpart", "Community licence" and "Northern Ireland licence" have the same meanings as in Part III of this Act.

(2) Allocation

17–152 These offences are triable either way. General mode of trial considerations are listed in the *Consolidated Criminal Practice Direction*. In relation to offences of fraud, there is a presumption towards summary trial (see para. V.51.7: Appendix F, F–49). Factors that might suggest trial on indictment include breach of trust by a person in a position of *substantial* authority or in whom a high degree of trust is placed, conducting (or disguising) the fraud in a sophisticated manner, organised gang and victim particularly vulnerable. These guidelines may be replaced by the National Allocation Guidelines prepared by the Sentencing Guidelines Council once the new allocation procedures are implemented. These guidelines are less related to specific offences. They emphasise that the primary consideration is the adequacy of the sentencing powers of the court taking the prosecution version of events as the basis.

(3) What must the prosecution prove?

17–153 There are a range of elements: in each case there must be an intent to deceive and the offences must be committed in relation to a document or similar to which the section applies—these are listed in s.173(2). Perhaps the most common subjects of the offence are test and insurance certificates but a wide range of other documents are included.

If the document is one to which the section applies and if there is an intent to deceive, an offence is committed either by creating a document intended to deceive or using such a document in one way or another.

(4) Creating a document or other thing

17–154 This can be by forgery, by altering or by creating something that so closely resembles the real thing (without actually copying the real thing) as to be calculated to deceive. "Forges" is defined in s.173(3) as meaning "making … in order that it may be used as genuine".

(5) Using a document etc.

17–155 This can be straightforward use but also includes lending a document or thing to another person (or at least allowing them to use it) or having in your possession a document so closely resembling the real things as to be calculated to deceive.

For an offence of "using" under s.173(1)(a), the use must be of one of the specified documents. If it is a forgery or an altered document, it may be that the prosecution would need to be under s.173(1)(c): see *Holloway v. Brown* [1978] R.T.R. 537. However, that strict interpretation may be less likely now.

(6) Making false statements or withholding material information

It is an offence to make false statements in order to secure one of four effects set out in s.175(1) or in the circumstances set out in s.175(2) or (3) or (5). The prosecution must prove that: **17–156**

— the defendant
— knowingly (or, in relation to s.174(2), recklessly)
— made a false statement
— for one of the specified purposes.

For issues of identification, see *ante*, §§ 10–89 *et seq.*

(7) Issuing false documents

It is also an offence to issue a document of certain specified types in the knowledge that it is false in a material particular. **17–157**

(8) Penalties

Forgery, etc. of documents (under s.173(1)) and making false statements (under s.174) are either way offences. At the Crown Court, they are punishable by up to two years imprisonment and/or an unlimited fine. In a magistrates' court, the maximum punishment is a fine of level 5, and, in respect of s.174, six months' imprisonment increasing to 12 months for offences committed on or after commencement of *Criminal Justice Act* 2003, s.154. The offences are not endorsable. **17–158**

(9) Sentencing

These offences are punishable by imprisonment in the Crown Court only. In most instances, a financial penalty will result but, for the more serious offences, a community order would be appropriate particularly one containing a significant punishment element. Since these are not violent offences, a custodial sentence would only be appropriate where there has been a sophisticated and substantial organisation or a very substantial breach of trust. **17–159**

However, since implementation of the relevant provisions in the *Criminal Justice and Immigration Act* 2008, it is not possible for a magistrates' court to impose a community order for these offences because they are punishable with imprisonment only in the Crown Court. Where a community order is required, the case will need to be sentenced in the Crown Court.

D. TRAFFIC SIGNS

(1) Definition

It is an offence to fail to comply with traffic signs properly placed. This section states the law generally and then deals specifically with the four signs that, on conviction, are endorsable. **17–160**

Road Traffic Act 1988, s.36

Drivers to comply with traffic signs

36.—(1) Where a traffic sign, being a sign— **17–161**

(a) of the prescribed size, colour and type, or

(b) of another character authorised by the Secretary of State under the provisions in that behalf of the *Road Traffic Regulation Act* 1984,

has been lawfully placed on or near a road, a person driving or propelling a vehicle who fails to comply with the indication given by the sign is guilty of an offence.

(2) A traffic sign shall not be treated for the purposes of this section as having been lawfully placed unless either—

(a) the indication given by the sign is an indication of a statutory prohibition, restriction or requirement, or

(b) it is expressly provided by or under any provision of the Traffic Acts that this section shall apply to the sign or to signs of a type of which the sign is one;

and, where the indication mentioned in paragraph (a) of this subsection is of the general nature only of the prohibition, restriction or requirement to which the sign relates, a person shall not be convicted of failure to comply with the indication unless he has failed to comply with the prohibition, restriction or requirement to which the sign relates.

(3) For the purposes of this section a traffic sign placed on or near a road shall be deemed—

(a) to be of the prescribed size, colour and type, or of another character authorised by the Secretary of State under the provisions in that behalf of the *Road Traffic Regulation Act* 1984, and

(b) (subject to subsection (2) above) to have been lawfully so placed,

unless the contrary is proved.

(4) Where a traffic survey of any description is being carried out on or in the vicinity of a road, this section applies to a traffic sign by which a direction is given—

(a) to stop a vehicle,

(b) to make it proceed in, or keep to, a particular line of traffic, or

(c) to proceed to a particular point on or near the road on which the vehicle is being driven or propelled,

being a direction given for the purposes of the survey (but not a direction requiring any person to provide any information for the purposes of the survey).

(5) Regulations made by the Secretary of State for the Environment, Transport and the Regions, the Secretary of State for Wales and the Secretary of State for Scotland acting jointly may specify any traffic sign for the purposes of column 5 of the entry in Schedule 2 to the *Road Traffic Offenders Act* 1988 relating to offences under this section (offences committed by failing to comply with certain signs involve discretionary disqualification).

(2) What the prosecution must prove

17–162 The prosecution must prove that:

— the defendant

— drove or propelled

— a vehicle

— failed to comply with a sign.

Although a sign has to be lawfully placed and to be of a prescribed size etc., there is a presumption that that is the case unless the contrary is proved: s.36(3). Thus it is for the defence to prove (on the balance of probabilities) that a sign was not lawfully placed or was not of the prescribed size, colour, type or character (for more detail, see *Wilkinson*, Pt 2, B57). The Divisional Court gave detailed consideration to the signage indicating a speed limit in *Coombes v. DPP* [2007] R.T.R. 31. In this case, one of the signs at the start of a speed limit had become overgrown and was not visible. The court considered all the relevant obligations regarding the placing and maintenance of such signs. Although allowing the appeal against conviction on a single aspect, the court drew attention to the limits on the obligations of the authority responsible for the signs.

Courts are increasingly reluctant to allow culpable defendants to escape criminal liability on technical grounds that otherwise have no merit.

(3) Allocation

17–163 This offence is summary only.

(4) Sentencing

Contravention of most traffic signs is punishable by a fine only—up to level 3 (£1000). However, in respect of a small number of signs, it is endorsable with three penalty points and thus subject to discretionary disqualification. The relevant signs are traffic lights, pedestrian crossings, double white lines, stop signs. **17–164**

In relation to both endorsable and non-endorsable offences, the *Magistrates' Court Sentencing Guidelines* provides for a starting point of fine band A (50% of relevant weekly income within a range of 25%–75%). The additional punishment will be the imposition of penalty points and the power to disqualify.

E. SPEEDING

(1) Definition

Road Traffic Regulation Act 1984, ss.81, 82, 84–87, 89

General speed limit for restricted roads

81.—(1) It shall not be lawful for a person to drive a motor vehicle on a restricted road at a speed exceeding 30 miles per hour. **17–165**

(2) The Ministers acting jointly may by order made by statutory instrument and approved by a resolution of each House of Parliament increase or reduce the rate of speed fixed by subsection (1) above, either as originally enacted or as varied under this subsection.

What roads are restricted roads

82.—(1) Subject to the provisions of this section and of section 84(3) of this Act, a road is a restricted road for the purposes of section 81 of this Act if— **17–166**

(a) in England and Wales, there is provided on it a system of street lighting furnished by means of lamps placed not more than 200 yards apart;

(b) in Scotland, there is provided on it a system of carriageway lighting furnished by means of lamps placed not more than 185 metres apart and the road is of a classification or type specified for the purposes of this subsection in regulations made by the Secretary of State.

(2) The traffic authority for a road may direct—

(a) that the road which is a restricted road for the purposes of section 81 of this Act shall cease to be a restricted road for those purposes, or

(b) that the road which is not a restricted road for those purposes shall become a restricted road for those purposes.

(3) A special road is not a restricted road for the purposes of section 81 on or after the date declared by the traffic authority, by notice published in the prescribed manner, to be the date on which the special road, or the relevant part of the special road, is open for use as a special road.

Speed limits on roads other than restricted roads

84.—(1) An order made under this subsection as respects any road may prohibit— **17–167**

(a) the driving of motor vehicles on that road at a speed exceeding that specified in the order,

(b) the driving of motor vehicles on that road at a speed exceeding that specified in the order during periods specified in the order, or

(c) the driving of motor vehicles on that road at a speed exceeding the speed for the time being indicated by traffic signs in accordance with the order.

(1A) An order made by virtue of subsection (1)(c) above may—

(a) make provision restricting the speeds that may be indicated by traffic signs or the periods during which the indications may be given, and

(b) provide for the indications to be given only in such circumstances as may be determined by or under the order;

but any such order must comply with regulations made under subsection (1B) below, except where the Secretary of State authorises otherwise in a particular case.

(1B) The Secretary of State may make regulations governing the provision which may be made by orders of local authorities under subsection (1)(c) above, and any such regulations may in particular—

(a) prescribe the circumstances in which speed limits may have effect by virtue of an order,

(b) prescribe the speed limits which may be specified in an order, and

(c) make transitional provision and different provision for different cases.

(2) The power to make an order under subsection (1) is exercisable by the traffic authority, who shall before exercising it in any case give public notice of their intention to do so.

(3) While an order made by virtue of subsection (1)(a) above is in force as respects a road, that road shall not be a restricted road for the purposes of section 81 of this Act.

(4) This section does not apply to any part of a special road which is open for use as a special road.

(5) Section 68(1)(c) of this Act shall apply to any order made under subsection (1) above.

(6) Any reference in a local Act to roads subject to a speed limit shall, unless the contrary intention appears, be treated as not including a reference to roads subject to a speed limit imposed only by virtue of subsection (1)(b) or (c) above.

Traffic signs for indicating speed restrictions

17–168 **85.**—(1) For the purpose of securing that adequate guidance is given to drivers of motor vehicles as to whether any, and if so what, limit of speed is to be observed on any road, it shall be the duty of the Secretary of State, in the case of a road for which he is the traffic authority, to erect and maintain traffic signs in such positions as may be requisite for that purpose.

(2) In the case of any other road, it is the duty of the local traffic authority—

(a) to erect and maintain traffic signs in such positions as may be requisite in order to give effect to general or other directions given by the Secretary of State for the purpose mentioned in subsection (1) above, and

(b) to alter or remove traffic signs as may be requisite in order to give effect to such directions, either in consequence of the making of an order by the Secretary of State or otherwise.

(3) If a local traffic authority makes default in executing any works required for the performance of the duty imposed on them by subsection (2) above, the Secretary of State may himself execute the works; and the expense incurred by him in doing so shall be recoverable by him from the local traffic authority and, in England or Wales, shall be so recoverable summarily as a civil debt.

(4) Where no such system of street or carriageway lighting as is mentioned in section 82(1) is provided on a road, but a limit of speed is to be observed on the road, a person shall not be convicted of driving a motor vehicle on the road at a speed exceeding the limit unless the limit is indicated by means of such traffic signs as are mentioned in subsection (1) or subsection (2) above.

(5) In any proceedings for a contravention of section 81 of this Act, where the proceedings relate to driving on a road provided with such a system of street or carriageway lighting, evidence of the absence of traffic signs displayed in pursuance of this section to indicate that the road is not a restricted road for the purposes of that section shall be evidence that the road is a restricted road for those purposes.

(6) Where by regulations made under section 17(2) of this Act a limit of speed is to be observed, then, if it is to be observed—

(a) on all special roads, or

(b) on all special roads provided for the use of particular classes of traffic, or

(c) on all special roads other than special roads of such description as may be specified in the regulations, or

(d) as mentioned in paragraph (a), (b) or (c) above except for such lengths of special road as may be so specified,

this section shall not apply in relation to that limit (but without prejudice to its application in relation to any lower limit of maximum speed or, as the case may be, any higher limit of minimum speed, required by any such regulations to be observed on any specified length of any specified special road).

(7) The power to give general directions under subsection (2) above shall be exercisable by statutory instrument.

Speed limits for particular classes of vehicles

17–169 **86.**—(1) It shall not be lawful for a person to drive a motor vehicle of any class on a road at a speed greater than the speed specified in Schedule 6 to this Act as the maximum speed in relation to a vehicle of that class.

(2) Subject to subsections (4) and (5) below, the Secretary of State may by regulations vary, subject to such conditions as may be specified in the regulations, the provisions of that Schedule.

(3) Regulations under this section may make different provision as respects the same class of vehicles in different circumstances.

(5) The Secretary of State shall not have power under this section to vary the speed limit imposed by section 81 of this Act.

(6) The Secretary of State shall not have power under this section to impose a speed limit, as respects driving on roads which are not restricted roads for the purposes of section 81 of this Act, on a vehicle which—

(a) is constructed solely for the carriage of passengers and their effects;

(b) is not adapted to carry more than 8 passengers exclusive of the driver;

(c) is neither a heavy motor car nor an invalid carriage;

(d) is not drawing a trailer; and

(e) is fitted with pneumatic tyres on all its wheels.

Exemption of fire brigade, ambulance and police vehicles from speed limits

87.—(1) No statutory provision imposing a speed limit or motor vehicle shall apply to any vehicle on an occasion being used for ambulance or police purposes or for or in connection with the exercise of any function of a related authority (as defined in section 6 of the *Fire (Scotland) Act* 2005 (asp 5)), if the observance of that provision likely to hinder the use of the vehicle for the purpose for which it is being used on that occasion.

(2) Subsection (1) above applies in relation to a vehicle being used—

(a) for Serious Organised Crime Agency purposes, or

(b) for training persons to drive vehicles for use for Serious Organised Crime Agency purposes,

as it applies in relation to a vehicle being used for police purposes.

(3) But (except where it is being used for training the person by whom it is being driven) subsection (1) above does not apply in relation to a vehicle by virtue of subsection (2) above unless it is being driven by a person who has been trained in driving vehicles at high speeds.

[Exemption of fire brigade, ambulance and police vehicles from speed limits [As amended by section 19 of the Road Safety Act 2006 when in force.]]

87.—(1) No statutory provision imposing a speed limit on motor vehicles shall apply to any vehicle on an occasion when— **17–170**

(a) it is being used for fire and rescue authority purposes or for or in connection with the exercise of any function of a relevant authority as defined in section 6 of the *Fire (Scotland) Act 2005*, for ambulance purposes or for police or Serious Organised Crime Agency purposes,

(b) it is being used for other prescribed purposes in such circumstances as may be prescribed, or

(c) it is being used for training persons to drive vehicles for use for any of the purposes mentioned in paragraph (a) or (b) above,

if the observance of that provision would be likely to hinder the use of the vehicle for the purpose for which it is being used on that occasion.

(2) Subsection (1) above does not apply unless the vehicle is being driven by a person who—

(a) has satisfactorily completed a course of training in the driving of vehicles at high speed provided in accordance with regulations under this section, or

(b) is driving the vehicle as part of such a course.

(3) The Secretary of State may by regulations make provision about courses of training in the driving of vehicles at high speed.

(4) The regulations may include—

(a) provision about the nature of courses,

(b) provision for the approval by the Secretary of State of persons providing courses or giving instruction on courses and the withdrawal of approvals (including provision for appeals against refusal and withdrawal of approvals),

(c) provision specifying the maximum fees that a person may be required to pay for a course,
(d) provision for the training or assessment, or the supervision of the training or assessment, of persons providing courses or giving instruction on courses,
(e) provision for the evidencing of the successful completion of courses,
(f) provision authorising the Secretary of State to make available information about persons providing courses or giving instruction on courses, and
(g) provision treating courses of training in the driving of vehicles at high speed which have been completed before the coming into force of the regulations as if they had been provided in accordance with the regulations.

(5) The regulations may include provision for the charging of reasonable fees in respect of any function conferred or imposed on the Secretary of State by the regulations.

(6) The regulations may make different provision—
(a) for different classes of vehicle,
(b) for different descriptions of persons, or
(c) otherwise for different circumstances.]

Speeding offences generally

17–171 **89.**—(1) A person who drives a motor vehicle on a road at a speed exceeding a limit imposed by or under any enactment to which this section applies shall be guilty of an offence.

(2) A person prosecuted for such an offence shall not be liable to be convicted solely on the evidence of one witness to the effect that, in the opinion of the witness, the person prosecuted was driving the vehicle at a speed exceeding a specified limit.

(3) The enactments to which this section applies are—
(a) any enactment contained in this Act except section 17(2);
(b) section 2 of the *Parks Regulation (Amendment) Act* 1926; and
(c) any enactment not contained in this Act, but passed after 1st September 1960, whether before or after the passing of this Act.

(4) If a person who employs other persons to drive motor vehicles on roads publishes or issues any time-table or schedule, or gives any directions, under which any journey, or any stage or part of any journey, is to be completed within some specified time, and it is not practicable in the circumstances of the case for that journey (or that stage or part of it) to be completed in the specified time without the commission of such an offence as is mentioned in subsection (1) above, the publication or issue of the time-table or schedule, or the giving of the directions, may be produced as prima facie evidence that the employer procured or (as the case may be) incited the persons employed by him to drive the vehicles to commit such an offence.

(2) What must the prosecution prove?

17–172 — the defendant
— drove
— a motor vehicle
— on a road (note only "road" not "other public place")
— at a speed
— exceeding a limit imposed by or under an enactment to which this section applies.

(3) Allocation

17–173 This offence is summary only.
A prosecution must be initiated within six months.

(4) Warning of intended prosecution

17–174 By virtue of Sched. 1 to the *Road Traffic Offenders Act* 1988, the prosecution must have complied with the requirements to give notice of intended prosecution: *Road Traffic Offenders Act* 1988, s.1. Unless an accident has occurred of which the driver was aware (*Road Traffic Offenders Act* 1988, s.2(1)), the driver must receive warning of prosecution within 14 days of the offence. This warning may be given at the time of the offence, by service of the summons (or copy of a charge sheet) within 14 days of the offence or by the prosecutor sending notice to the driver or the registered keeper of the vehicle within 14 days. Where the notice is by service of the summons, that must take place within the 14 days. Where the notification is by notice, it is only necessary for that to be sent within the 14 days. However, by virtue of s.2(3) of the Act, failure to comply with these requirements is not to be a bar to conviction where the name and address of the driver or the registered keeper could not have been ascertained by the exercise of reasonable diligence in time to comply with the requirements of the section. Similarly where the accused contributed to the failure by his own conduct—perhaps by leaving the scene or not registering the vehicle correctly.

For further information, refer to *Wilkinson's Road Traffic Offences*, Ch.2: see also § 17–13, *ante*.

(5) Limits and exceptions

Limits can apply to roads or to different types of vehicle and care must be taken regarding both factors. Many prosecutions are under s.89 of the *Road Traffic Regulation Act* 1984 (see *ante*, at § 17–171). In *R. (Harrison) v. Flintshire Magistrates' Court* (2004) 168 J.P. 653, an unusual situation arose which served to emphasise the pragmatic approach of the appeal courts to regulatory provisions. The defendant was prosecuted in the belief that a 30mph limit applied to the road and the information alleged "... contrary to ss.81(1) and 89(1)" of the 1984 Act. It was subsequently discovered that the national speed limit (60mph) applied in which case the information should have alleged "... contrary to ss.84 and 89(1)" of the 1984 Act. The recorded speed was 67mph. The defendant was fined and disqualified. If it was known that the limit was 60mph, it was unlikely that disqualification would have resulted. The Divisional Court declined to overturn the conviction but agreed that sentence should be reconsidered. **17–175**

A further case explored the authority under which a County Council (as a traffic authority) can designate that a road is subject to a 30mph limit. In *DPP v. Evans* [2004] EWHC 2785 Admin, the court had to examine s.82(2)(b) of the 1984 *Act* (see *ante*, § 17–156). This complements the well known provision in s.82(1) that a road is a restricted road for the purposes of s.81 if there is a system of lighting by lamps not more than 200 yards apart. A traffic authority, by s.82(2), may designate that such a road should not be a restricted road or that a road that is not so lit should become a restricted road. In such circumstances, signs need to be displayed of the limit in force: s.85(4). The defence argument that s.82(2) was not a power generally available to a traffic authority but narrow and restricted in application was rebuffed by the Divisional Court.

Although, by s.89(2), the evidence of one witness is not sufficient for the defendant to be convicted, a wide range of devices have been developed for producing supporting evidence ranging from the humble speedometer to sophisticated radar and camera devices.

For a speed limit to be enforceable, certain obligations need to be complied with including the display of signs in certain circumstances. The Divisional Court has taken a robust approach where it is alleged that signs did not exactly comply with the requirements. In *Canadine and others v. DPP* [2007] EWHC 383 signs showing the 20mph limit on Tower Bridge had a 2cm peripheral black border which was alleged to take them outside the requirements. The court held that the border was caused by the casing to the sign and, since that was to the front, could not be said to be part of the background against which the sign was displayed. If the surround had been substantial that might have been significant but here it was effectively invisible to road users. Even if the sign had not been compliant, there was no question of road users being misled and the deviation would have been *de minimis*. This appears to be a further manifestation of the low level of tolerance of the courts for unmeritorious technical arguments seeking to avoid conviction where the underlying purpose of the provision has been achieved.

Another example is *Peake v. DPP* [2010] EWHC 286; [2011] R.T.R. 3; (2010) 174

J.P. 457. The defendant had driven in excess of a 40mph limit on a stretch of road where repeater signs were properly placed. However, it was argued (and agreed in respect of at least one part) that other signage within that particular 40mph zone was not correctly placed and that this invalidated the limit for the whole area. This approach was soundly rejected both by the magistrates' court and the Divisional Court. A further submission that the defendant should avoid liability because he may have accessed the part of the road where he exceeded the limit by means of a road that had been incorrectly signed was also rejected. In response to an attempt by the defendant to rely on a 1967 decision, the Divisional Court stated that "statutory interpretation has progressed since 1967 from a focus on the actual words of the statutory provision to a combination of the actual words of the provision together with its purpose". The purpose of s.85 was stated to be to ensure (so far as possible) that motorists drive at safe speeds, that they are enabled to do so by adequate guidance and that they are penalised only if such guidance is available on the road on which the limit is exceeded. Reference (as in this case) to "zones" or "envelopes" was unhelpful. The Court also emphasised that it is irrelevant whether or not the driver actually knows the speed limit; if the signs are defective, the prosecution cannot rely on the defendant's knowledge and, if they are compliant, the defendant cannot rely on the absence of knowledge.

This decision was further considered and applied rigorously in *Jones v. DPP* (2011) 175 J.P. 129 where the court was concerned to ascertain whether the driver had been given adequate guidance by the time he reached the point on the road where the alleged offence took place. Again, the conviction was upheld.

The principal exemption is contained in s.87 (which is replaced by s.19 of the *Road Safety Act* 2006 when in force). It exempts certain vehicles driven by those who have completed a course of training in driving vehicles at high speed provided in accordance with regulations or who are driving the vehicle as part of such a course. The vehicle must be one being used for fire and rescue authority purposes, for ambulance purposes, for police purposes or for the purposes of the Serious Organised Crime Agency in circumstances where observance of the speed limit would be likely to hinder the use of the vehicle for the purpose for which it is being used on that occasion. It will be for the defence to prove (on the balance of probabilities) the purpose for which the vehicle was being used, the need to drive more quickly than the limit and the qualification of the driver. The vehicle does not have to be an ambulance or a fire engine, *etc*. but it must be being used for the purposes specified and adherence to the speed limit must hinder the use of the vehicle on that occasion. Thus, bringing a human organ from one part of the country to another for use in a transplant operation where speed is of the essence is likely to meet the criteria. The exemption is only from speed limits—there is still the obligation to drive with due care and attention, *etc*.

(6) Penalty

17–176 Exceeding the speed limit is generally subject to a maximum fine of level 3; the exception is where the speed limit exceeded is the overall maximum on a motorway when it becomes level 4 (currently £2,500). The level of financial penalty (and the number of penalty points) will generally vary by reference to the speed and the proportion by which it exceeded the limit. Thus, exceeding a 30mph limit by 15mph will be more serious than exceeding a 60mph limit by the same amount.

The *Magistrates' Court Sentencing Guidelines* sets out three levels of seriousness determined by the degree to which the speed of the vehicle exceeded the limit. Increases in seriousness are reflected in an increase in the fine band and/or in the increase in likelihood or length of disqualification.

STARTING POINT AND RANGE OF SENTENCE

(BASED ON A FIRST TIME OFFENDER PLEADING NOT GUILTY)

Speed limit (mph)	**Recorded speed (mph)**		
20	21-30	31-40	41-50
30	31-40	41-50	51-60
40	41-55	56-65	66-75
50	51-65	66-75	76-85
60	61-80	81-90	91-100
70	71-90	91-100	101-110
Starting point	**Band A fine**	**Band B fine**	**Band B fine**
Range	**Band A fine**	**Band B fine**	**Band B fine**
Points/ disqualification	**3 points**	**4–6 points OR Disqualify 7–28 days**	**Disqualify 7–56 days OR 6 points**

AGGRAVATING AND MITIGATING FACTORS

Factors indicating higher culpability	**Factor indicating lower culpability**
1. Poor road or weather conditions 2. LGV, HGV, PSV etc. 3. Towing caravan / trailer 4. Carrying passengers or heavy load 5. Driving for hire or reward 6. Evidence of unacceptable standard of driving over and above speed **Factors indicating greater degree of harm** 1. Location, e.g. near school 2. High level of traffic or pedestrians in the vicinity	1. Genuine emergency established

Many offences are dealt with by a fixed penalty and, in that case, three penalty points will be endorsed on the licence. If the offender is convicted by a court, there is a range of 3–6 points; again the point in the range will depend mainly on the proportion by which the actual speed exceeded the limit. When in force, the *Road Safety Act 2006*, s.17 changes this range to 2–6. If a fixed penalty would have been offered but for some reason beyond the control of the offender it was not, the court is often inclined to stay with both the financial penalty and the number of penalty points though there will be an obligation to impose the victim surcharge.

Disqualification for relatively short periods will be appropriate where the risks were greater, and is usually considered seriously in any case once a speed limit is exceeded by 30mph.

F. BEING IN PROPER CONTROL OF A VEHICLE

(1) General

17–177 For many years there has been an offence of failing to be in proper control of a vehicle. More recently, this has been complemented by specific provisions relating to the use of a mobile telephone whilst driving. Section 26 of the *Road Safety Act* 2006 introduces a new s.41D to the *Road Traffic Act* 1988 which becomes the provision creating such offences.

Road Traffic Act 1988, s.41D

17–178 **41D.**— A person who contravenes or fails to comply with a construction and use requirement—

(a) as to not driving a motor vehicle in a position which does not give proper control or a full view of the road and traffic ahead, or not causing or permitting the driving of a motor vehicle by another person in such a position, or

(b) as to not driving or supervising the driving of a motor vehicle while using a hand-held mobile telephone or other hand-held interactive communication device, or not causing or permitting the driving of a motor vehicle by another person using such a telephone or other device

is guilty of an offence.

(2) What must the prosecution prove?

17–179 In respect of the part relating to mobile telephones,

— the defendant
— drove (or was supervising the driving)
— a motor vehicle
— whilst using
— a hand held mobile telephone

Where the telephone was not hand held, it is still possible that an offence will be committed under s.41D(a) if it can be shown that the driver was not in proper control of the vehicle. There is no exception provided for this offence but the definition of "driving" is wide (see *ante*, § 17–4). This could mean that the offence would be committed where the vehicle was stationary not just when it was in motion providing the defendant was still "driving" in the technical sense.

(3) Allocation

17–180 This offence is summary only.

(4) Penalty

17–181 The offence is a fixed penalty offence. If prosecuted, an offender will be liable to a maximum penalty of Level 4 (currently £2,500) if committed in respect of a goods vehicle or a vehicle adapted to carry more than 8 eight passengers or to a maximum of Level 3 (currently £1,000) in any other case. Disqualification is discretionary; endorsement is mandatory with three points.

(5) Sentencing

17–182 The *Magistrates' Court Sentencing Guidelines* provides for a starting point of fine band A for use of a mobile phone where the maximum is a level 3 fine.

VI. EFFECT OF PENALTIES

A. GENERAL

Many road traffic offences lead, on conviction, to a requirement that details of the offender be endorsed onto the offender's driving record and/or to the possibility of disqualification from driving. In most cases, disqualification is at the discretion of the court but, in some cases, the court is obliged to disqualify the offender unless there are "special reasons" (see *post*) for not doing so. Similarly, where endorsement is required, it is always mandatory in the absence of "special reasons". There is also the consequential power to deprive an offender of the vehicle used in certain circumstances. **17–183**

B. ENDORSEMENT

Road Traffic Offenders Act 1988, ss.44–48, 28(1)–(6), 30A

Orders for endorsement

44.—(1) Where a person is convicted of an offence involving obligatory endorsement, the court must order there to be endorsed on the counterpart of any licence held by him particulars of the conviction and also— **17–184**

(a) if the court orders him to be disqualified, particulars of the disqualification, or

(b) if the court does not order him to be disqualified—

(i) particulars of the offence, including the date when it was committed, and

(ii) the penalty points to be attributed to the offence.

(2) Where the court does not order the person convicted to be disqualified, it need not make an order under subsection (1) above if for special reasons it thinks fit not to do so.

(3) In relation to Scotland, references in this section to the court include the justice of the peace court.

(3A) Where a person who is not the holder of a licence is convicted of an offence involving obligatory endorsement, subsection (1) above applies as if the reference to the counterpart of any licence held by him were a reference to his driving record.

(4) This section is subject to section 48 of this Act.

Endorsement of driving record in accordance with order

44A.—(1) Where the court orders the endorsement of a person's driving record with any particulars or penalty points it must send notice of the order to the Secretary of State. **17–185**

(2) On receiving the notice, the Secretary of State must endorse those particulars or penalty points on the person's driving record.

(3) A notice sent by the court to the Secretary of State in pursuance of this section must be sent in such manner and to such address and contain such particulars as the Secretary of State may require.

Effect of endorsement of counterparts

45.—(1) An order that any particulars or penalty points are to be endorsed on the counterpart of any licence held by the person convicted shall operate as an order that the counterpart of any licence he may then hold or may subsequently obtain is to be so endorsed until he becomes entitled under subsection (4) below to have a licence issued to him with its counterpart free from the particulars or penalty points. **17–186**

(2) On the issue of a new licence to a person, any particulars or penalty points ordered to be endorsed on the counterpart of any licence held by him shall be entered on the counterpart of the licence unless he has become entitled under subsection (4) below to have a licence issued to him with its counterpart free from those particulars or penalty points.

(3) [...]

(4) A person the counterpart of whose licence has been ordered to be endorsed is entitled to have issued to him with effect from the end of the period for which the endorsement remains effective a new licence with a counterpart free from the endorsement if he applies for a new licence in pursuance of section 97(1) of the *Road Traffic Act* 1988, surrenders any subsisting licence and its counterpart, pays the fee prescribed by regulations under Part III of that Act and satisfies the other requirements of section 97(1).

(5) An endorsement ordered on a person's conviction of an offence remains effective (subject to subsections (6) and (7) below)—

(a) if an order is made for the disqualification of the offender, until four years have elapsed since the conviction, and

(b) if no such order is made, until either—

(i) four years have elapsed since the commission of the offence, or

(ii) an order is made for the disqualification of the offender under section 35 of this Act.

(6) Where the offence was one under section 1 of that Act (causing death by dangerous driving and dangerous driving), the endorsement remains in any case effective until four years have elapsed since the conviction.

(7) Where the offence was one—

(a) under section 3A, 4(1) or 5(1)(a) of that Act (driving offences connected with drink or drugs), or

(b) under section 7(6) of that Act (failing to provide specimen) involving obligatory disqualification, or

(c) under section 7A(6) of that Act (failing to allow a specimen to be subjected to laboratory test),

the endorsement remains effective until eleven years have elapsed since the conviction.

Combination of disqualification and endorsement with probation orders and orders for discharge

17–187 **46.**—(1) Notwithstanding anything in section 14(3) of the *Powers of Criminal Courts (Sentencing) Act* 2000 (conviction of offender discharged to be disregarded for the purposes of enactments relating to disqualification), a court in England and Wales which on convicting a person of an offence involving obligatory or discretionary disqualification makes—

(b) an order discharging him absolutely or conditionally,

may on that occasion also exercise any power conferred, and must also discharge any duty imposed, on the court by sections 34, 35, 36, 44 or 44A of this Act.

(2) A conviction—

(a) in respect of which a court in England and Wales has ordered a person to be disqualified, or

(b) of which particulars have been endorsed on the counterpart of any licence held by him or his driving record,

is to be taken into account, notwithstanding anything in section 14(1) of the *Powers of Criminal Courts (Sentencing) Act* 2000 (conviction of offender discharged to be disregarded for the purpose of subsequent proceedings), in determining his liability to punishment or disqualification for any offence involving obligatory or discretionary disqualification committed subsequently.

(3) Where—

(a) a person is charged in Scotland with an offence involving obligatory or discretionary disqualification, and

(b) the court makes an order in respect of the offence under section 228(probation) or 246(2) or (3) (absolute discharge) of the *Criminal Procedure (Scotland) Act* 1995,

then, for the purposes of sections 34, 35, 36, 44, 45 and 45A of this Act, he shall be treated as if he had been convicted of an offence of the kind in question and section 247 of that Act shall not apply.

Supplementary provisions as to disqualifications and endorsements

17–188 **47.**—(1) In any case where a court exercises its power under section 34, 35 or 44 of this Act not to order any disqualification or endorsement or to order disqualification for a shorter period than would otherwise be required, it must state the grounds for doing so in open court and, if it is a magistrates' court or, in Scotland, a court of summary jurisdiction, must cause them to be entered in the register (in Scotland, record) of its proceedings.

(2) Where a court orders the endorsement of the counterpart of any licence held by a person it may, and where a court orders the holder of a licence to be disqualified for a period of 56 days or more it must, send the licence and its counterpart, on its their being produced to the court, to the Secretary of State; and if the court orders the endorsement but does not send the licence and its counterpart to the Secretary of State it must send him notice of the endorsement.

(2A) Subsection (2) above is subject to section 2(2) of and paragraph 7(2) of Schedule 1 *Road Traffic (New Drivers) Act* 1995 (obligation of court to send licence and its counterpart to the Secretary of State).

(3) Where on an appeal against an order for the endorsement of a licence or the disqualification of a person the appeal is allowed, the court by which the appeal is allowed must send notice of that fact to the Secretary of State.

(4) A notice sent by a court to the Secretary of State in pursuance of this section must be sent in such manner and to such address and contain such particulars as the Secretary of State may determine, and a licence and the counterpart of a licence so sent in pursuance of this section must be sent to such address as the Secretary of State may determine.

Exemption from disqualification and endorsement for certain construction and use offences

48.—(1) Where a person is convicted of an offence under section 40A of the *Road Traffic Act* 1988 (using vehicle in dangerous condition etc) the court must not— **17–189**

(a) order him to be disqualified, or

(b) order any particulars or penalty points to be endorsed on the counterpart of any licence held by him or his driving record,

if he proves that he did not know, and had no reasonable cause to suspect, that the use of the vehicle involved a danger of injury to any person.

(2) Where a person is convicted of an offence under section 41A of the *Road Traffic Act* 1988 (breach of requirement as to brakes, steering-gear or tyres) the court must not—

(a) order him to be disqualified, or

(b) order any particulars or penalty points to be endorsed on the counterpart of any licence held by him or his driving record,

if he proves that he did not know, and had no reasonable cause to suspect, that the facts of the case were such that the offence would be committed.

(3) In relation to licences which came into force before 1st June 1990, the references in subsections (1) and (2) above to the counterpart of a licence shall be construed as references to the licence itself.

Penalty points to be attributed to an offence

28.—(1) Where a person is convicted of an offence involving obligatory endorsement, then, subject to the following provisions of this section, the number of penalty points to be attributed to the offence is— **17–190**

(a) the number shown in relation to the offence in the last column of Part I or Part II of Schedule 2 to this Act, or

(b) where a range of numbers is shown, a number within that range.

(2) Where a person is convicted of an offence committed by aiding, abetting, counselling or procuring, or inciting to the commission of, an offence involving obligatory disqualification, then, subject to the following provisions of this section, the number of penalty points to be attributed to the offence is ten.

(3) For the purposes of sections 57(5), 57A(6), 77(5) and 77A(8) of this Act, the number of penalty points attributed to an offence is—

(a) where both a range of numbers and a number followed by the words "(fixed penalty") is shown in the column of Part 1 of Schedule 2 to this Act in relation to the offence, that number,

(b) where a range of numbers followed by the words "or appropriate penalty points (fixed penalty)" is shown in relation to the offence, the appropriate number of penalty points for the offence, and

(c) where only a range of numbers is shown there in relation to the offence, the lowest number in the range.

(3A) For the purposes of subsection (3)(b), above, the appropriate number of penalty points for an offence is such number of penalty points as the Secretary of State may by order made by statutory instrument prescribe.

(3B) An order made under subsection (3A) above in relation to an offence may make provision for the appropriate number of penalty points for the offence to be different depending on the circumstances, including (in particular)

(a) the nature of contravention or failure constituting the offence,

(b) how serious it is,

(c) the area, or sort of place, where it takes place, and

(d) whether the offender appears to have committed an offence or offences of a description specified in during a period so specified.

(4) Where a person is convicted (whether on the same occasion or not) of two or more offences committed on the same occasion and involving obligatory endorsement, the total number of penalty points to be attributed to them is the number or highest number that would be attributed on a conviction of one of them (so that if the convictions are on different occasions the number of penalty points to be attributed to the offences on the later occasion or occasions shall be restricted accordingly).

(5) In a case where (apart from this subsection) subsection (4) above would apply to two or more offences, the court may if it thinks fit determine that that subsection shall not apply to the offences (or, where three or more offences are concerned, to any one or more of them).

(6) Where a court makes such a determination it shall state its reasons in open court and, if it is a magistrates' court, or in Scotland a court of summary jurisdiction, shall cause them to be entered in the register (in Scotland, record) of its proceedings.

Reduced penalty points for attendance on course

17–191 **30A.**—(1) This section applies where—

(a) a person is convicted of a specified offence by or before a court,

(b) penalty points are to be attributed to the offence and the court does not order him to be disqualified, and

(c) at least seven but no more than eleven penalty points are to be taken into account on the occasion of the conviction.

(2) In this section "specified offence" means—

(a) an offence under section 3 of the *Road Traffic Act* 1988 (careless, and inconsiderate, driving),

(b) an offence under section 36 of that Act (failing to comply with traffic signs),

(c) an offence under section 17(4) of the *Road Traffic Regulation Act* 1984 (use of special road contrary to scheme or regulations), or

(d) an offence under section 89(1) of that Act (exceeding speed limit).

(3) But the Secretary of State may by regulations amend subsection (2) above by adding other offences or removing offences.

(4) Where this section applies, the court may make an order that three of the penalty points attributed to the offence (or all of them if three or fewer are so attributed) shall not be taken into account under section 29(1)(b) of this Act on the occasion of any conviction of an offence after the end of the period of twelve months beginning with the date of the order if, by the relevant date, the offender completes an approved course specified in the order.

(5) In subsection (4) above—

"an approved course" means a course approved by the appropriate national authority for the purposes of this section in relation to the description of offence of which the offender is convicted, and "the relevant date" means such date, no later than ten months after the day on which the order is made, as is specified in the order.

(6) A court shall not make an order under this section in the case of an offender convicted of an offence if—

(a) the offender has, during the period of three years ending with the date on which the offence was committed, committed a specified offence and successfully completed an approved course pursuant to an order made under this section or section 34A of this Act on conviction of that offence, or

(b) the offence was committed during his probationary period.

(7) A court shall not make an order under this section in the case of an offender unless—

(a) the court is satisfied that a place on the course specified in the order will be available for the offender,

(b) the offender appears to the court to be of or over the age of 17,

(c) the court has informed the offender (orally or in writing and in ordinary language) of the effect of the order and of the amount of the fees which he is required to pay for the course and when he must pay them, and

(d) the offender has agreed that the order should be made.

[Introduced by s.34 of the *Road Safety Act* 2006 when in force.]

The offences involving obligatory endorsement are set out in the *Road Traffic Offenders Act* 1988, Sched. 2. Where endorsement is required, it will contain particulars of the conviction, any disqualification or, if no disqualification is imposed, particulars of the offence and the penalty points attributed to the offence. Codes have been allocated to all endorsable offences and to all sentences that could be imposed. **17–192**

The number of penalty points may be fixed by statute or a range may be given (for example, careless driving has a range of 3–9 points) which allows the court to reflect the varying levels of seriousness. When the number of points reaches a particular level (see *post*), the court must disqualify the offender in the absence of "mitigating circumstances" (see *post*).

The requirement is to endorse "any licence held by" the offender. The order must be made whether or not the offender actually holds a licence: see *Road Traffic Offenders Act* 1988, s.45. The licence referred to is one issued under Pt III of the *Road Traffic Act* 1988 (*Road Traffic Act* 1988, s.108) and does not include, *e.g.* international driving permits, foreign driving licences or heavy goods vehicles licences. However, the details need to be notified to the Secretary of State and a record kept. An accumulation of points will still lead to disqualification even though no licence issued under Pt III is ever held.

Where an offender is convicted of more than one offence committed on the same occasion, the court will generally attribute just the highest number of points to be allocated to any one of the offences: *Road Traffic Offenders Act* 1988, s.28(4). Thus, where an offender is convicted of careless driving and of using a vehicle without insurance and the court decides to impose four penalty points for the careless driving and seven penalty points for the no insurance, it will be the 7 points alone that will be endorsed on the licence. However, the court retains the discretion to endorse more than one set of points where it thinks fit (s.28(5)) but must then give its reasons for so doing (s.28(6)). If that was applied to the example, *ante*, the offender would then have 11 points endorsed. Where the court disqualifies the offender, no further penalty points are endorsed either for the offence on which the disqualification is ordered or any other offence of which he is convicted on the same occasion: *Martin v. DPP* [2000] R.T.R. 188. This is also the case where the disqualification is obligatory: *Road Traffic Offenders Act* 1988, s.44(1). **17–193**

In considering what level of points to attribute where a range is prescribed, the court will be primarily concerned with the gravity of the offence—the more serious the offence within its class, the higher the number of points. However, this decision will also be taken within the context of the overall purpose of sentencing in criminal cases which will encompass the need to impose a punishment proportionate to the offence and the need to reduce the likelihood of the offender committing further offences. Since the court will always have the power to disqualify wherever it is required to endorse, there will be no need to increase the penalty points beyond what the offence justifies. However, a court may legitimately take the view that the goal of reducing crime justifies fixing the level of points in a way that leaves the offender in no doubt that a further conviction will lead to disqualification.

C. DISQUALIFICATION

(1) Legislation

Road Traffic Offenders Act 1988, ss.34, 34A, 34D, 35–39, 42, 43, 26, 29,

Disqualification for certain offences

34.—(1) Where a person is convicted of an offence involving obligatory disqualification, the court must order him to be disqualified for such period not less than twelve months as the court thinks fit unless the court for special reasons thinks fit to order him to be disqualified for a shorter period or not to order him to be disqualified. **17–194**

(1A) Where a person is convicted of an offence under section 12A of the *Theft Act* 1968 (aggravated vehicle-taking), the fact that he did not drive the vehicle in question at any particular time or at all shall not be regarded as a special reason for the purposes of subsection (1) above.

(2) Where a person is convicted of an offence involving discretionary disqualification, and either—

(a) the penalty points to be taken into account on that occasion number fewer than twelve, or

(b) the offence is not one involving obligatory endorsement,

the court may order him to be disqualified for such period as the court thinks fit.

(3) Where a person convicted of an offence under any of the following provisions of the *Road Traffic Act* 1988, that is—

(aa) section 3A (causing death by careless driving when under the influence of drink or drugs),

(a) section 4(1) (driving or attempting to drive while unfit),

(b) section 5(1)(a) (driving or attempting to drive with excess alcohol),

(c) section 7(6) (failing to provide a specimen) where that is an offence involving obligatory disqualification,

(d) section 7A(6) (failing to allow a specimen to be subjected to laboratory test) where that is an offence involving obligatory disqualification;

has within the ten years immediately preceding the commission of the offence been convicted of any such offence, subsection (1) above shall apply in relation to him as if the reference to twelve months were a reference to three years.

(4) Subject to subsection (3) above, subsection (1) above shall apply as if the reference to twelve months were a reference to two years—

(a) in relation to a person convicted of—

(i) manslaughter, or in Scotland culpable homicide, or

(ii) an offence under section 1 of the *Road Traffic Act* 1988 (causing death by dangerous driving), or

(iii) an offence under section 3A of that Act (causing death by careless driving while under the influence of drink or drugs), and

(b) in relation to a person on whom more than one disqualification for a fixed period of 56 days or more has been imposed within the three years immediately preceding the commission of the offence.

(4A) For the purposes of subsection (4)(b) above there shall be disregarded any disqualification imposed under section 26 of this Act or section 147 of the *Powers of Criminal Courts (Sentencing) Act* 2000 or section 223A or 436A of the *Criminal Procedure (Scotland) Act* 1975 (offences committed by using vehicles) and any disqualification imposed in respect of an offence of stealing a motor vehicle, an offence under section 12 or 25 of the *Theft Act* 1968, an offence under section 178 of the *Road Traffic Act* 1988, or an attempt to commit such an offence.

(4B) Where a person convicted of an offence under section 40A of the *Road Traffic Act* 1988 (using vehicles in poor condition etc.) has within the three years immediately preceding the commission of the offence been convicted of such offence, subsection (1) above shall apply in relation to him as if the reference to twelve months were a six months.

(5) The preceding provisions of this section shall apply in relation to a conviction of an offence committed by aiding, abetting, counselling or procuring, or inciting to the commission of, an offence involving obligatory disqualification as if the offence were an offence involving discretionary disqualification.

(6) This section is subject to section 48 of this Act.

Reduced disqualification period for attendance on courses

17–195 **34A.**—(1) This section applies where—

(a) a person is convicted of an offence under section 3A (causing death by careless driving when under influence of drink or drugs), 4 (driving or being in charge when under influence of drink or drugs), 5 (driving or being in charge with excess alcohol) or 7 (failing to provide a specimen) of the *Road Traffic Act* 1988, and

(b) the court makes an order under section 34 of this Act disqualifying him for a period of not less than twelve months.

(2) Where this section applies, the court may make an order that the period of disqualification imposed under section 34 shall be reduced if, by a date specified in the or-

der under this section, the offender satisfactorily completes a course approved by the Secretary of State for the purposes of this section and specified in the order.

(3) The reduction made by an order under this section in a period of disqualification imposed under section 34 shall be a period specified in the order of not less than three months and not more than one quarter of the unreduced period (and accordingly where the period imposed under section 34 is twelve months, the reduced period shall be nine months).

(4) The court shall not make an order under this section unless—

(a) it is satisfied that a place on the course specified in the order will be available for the offender,

(b) the offender appears to the court to be of or over the age of 17,

(c) the court has explained the effect of the order to the offender in ordinary language, and has informed him of the amount of the fees for the course and of the requirement that he must pay them before beginning the course, and

(d) the offender has agreed that the order should be made.

(5) The date specified in an order under this section as the latest date for completion of a course must be at least two months before the last day of the period of disqualification as reduced by the order.

(6) An order under this section shall name the petty sessions area (or in Scotland the sheriff court district) in which the offender resides or will reside.

Certificates of completion of courses

34B.—(1) An offender shall be regarded for the purposes of section 34A of this Act as having completed a course satisfactorily if (and only if) a certificate that he has done so is received by the proper officer of the supervising court before the end of the period of disqualification imposed under section 34.

(2) If the certificate referred to in subsection (1) above is received by the proper officer of the supervising court before the end of the period of disqualification imposed under section 34 but after the end of the period as it would have been reduced by the order, the order shall have effect as if the reduced period ended with the day on which the certificate is received by the proper officer.

(3) The certificate referred to in subsection (1) above shall be a certificate in such form, containing such particulars, and given by such person, as may be prescribed by, or determined in accordance with, regulations made by the Secretary of State.

(4) A course organiser shall give the certificate mentioned in subsection (1) above to the offender not later than fourteen days after the date specified in the order as the latest date for completion of the course, unless the offender fails to make due payment of the fees for the course, fails to attend the course in accordance with the organiser's reasonable instructions, or fails to comply with any other reasonable requirements of the organiser.

(5) Where a course organiser decides not to give the certificate mentioned in subsection (1) above, he shall give written notice of his decision to the offender as soon as possible, and in any event not later than fourteen days after the date specified in the order as the latest date for completion of the course.

(6) An offender to whom a notice is given under subsection (5) above may, within such period as may be prescribed by rules of court, apply to the supervising court for a declaration that the course organiser's decision not to give a certificate was contrary to subsection (4) above; and if the court grants the application section 34A of this Act shall have effect as if the certificate had been duly received by the proper officer of the court.

(7) If fourteen days after the date specified in the order as the latest date for completion of the course the course organiser has given neither the certificate mentioned in subsection (1) above nor a notice under subsection (5) above, the offender may, within such period as may be prescribed by rules of court, apply to the supervising court for a declaration that the course organiser is in default; and if the court grants the application section 34A of this Act shall have effect as if the certificate had been duly received by the proper officer of the court.

(8) A notice under subsection (5) above shall specify the ground on which it is given, and the Secretary of State may by regulations make provision as to the form of notices under that subsection and as to the circumstances in which they are to be treated as given.

(9) Where the [proper officer of a court]] receives a certificate of the kind referred to in subsection (1) above, or a court grants an application under subsection (6) or (7) above, the

officer or court must send notice of that fact to the Secretary of State; and the notice must be sent in such manner and to such address, and must contain such particulars, as the Secretary of State may determine.

Provisions supplementary to sections 34A and 34B

34C.—(1) The Secretary of State may issue guidance to course organisers, or to any category of course organiser as to the conduct of courses approved for the purposes of section 34A of this Act; and—

(a) course organisers shall have regard to any guidance given to them under this subsection, and

(b) in determining for the purposes of section 34B(6) whether any instructions or requirements of an organiser were reasonable, a court shall have regard to any guidance given to him under this subsection.

(2) In sections 34A and 34B and this section—

"course organiser", in relation to a course, means the person who, in accordance with regulations made by the Secretary of State, is responsible for giving the certificates mentioned in section 34B(1) in respect of the completion of the course;

"proper officer" means—

(a) in relation to a magistrates' court in England and Wales, the justices' chief executive for the court, and

(b) in relation to a sheriff court in Scotland, the clerk of the court;

"supervising court", in relation to an order under section 34A, means—

(a) in England and Wales, a magistrates' court acting for the petty sessions area named in the order as the area where the offender resides or will reside;

(b) in Scotland, the sheriff court or the justice of the peace court for the district where the offender resides or will reside

(3) Any power to make regulations under section 34B or this section—

(a) includes power to make different provision for different cases, and to make such incidental or supplemental provision as appears to the Secretary of State to be necessary or expedient;

(b) shall be exercisable by statutory instrument, which shall be subject to annulment in pursuance of a resolution of either House of Parliament.

Disqualification for repeated offences

17–196 **35.**—(1) Where—

(a) a person is convicted of an offence to which this subsection applies, and

(b) the penalty points to be taken into account on that occasion number twelve or more,

the court must order him to be disqualified for not less than the minimum period unless the court is satisfied, having regard to all the circumstances, that there are grounds for mitigating the normal consequences of the conviction and thinks fit to order him to be disqualified for a shorter period or not to order him to be disqualified.

(1A) Subsection (1) above applies to—

(a) an offence involving discretionary disqualification and obligatory endorsement, and

(b) an offence involving obligatory disqualification in respect of which no order is made under section 34 of this Act.

(2) The minimum period referred to in subsection (1) above is—

(a) six months if no previous disqualification imposed on the offender is to be taken into account, and

(b) one year if one, and two years if more than one, such disqualification is to be taken into account;

and a previous disqualification imposed on an offender is to be taken into account if it was for a fixed period of 56 days or more and was imposed within the three years immediately preceding the commission of the latest offence in respect of which penalty points are taken into account under section 29 of this Act.

(3) Where an offender is convicted on the same occasion of more than one offence to which subsection (1) above applies—

(a) not more than one disqualification shall be imposed on him under subsection (1) above,

(b) in determining the period of the disqualification the court must take into account all the offences, and

(c) for the purposes of any appeal any disqualification imposed under subsection (1) above shall be treated as an order made on the conviction of each of the offences.

(4) No account is to be taken under subsection (1) above of any of the following circumstances—

(a) any circumstances that are alleged to make the offence or any of the offences not a serious one,

(b) hardship, other than exceptional hardship, or

(c) any circumstances which, within the three years immediately preceding the conviction, have been taken into account under that subsection in ordering the offender to be disqualified for a shorter period or not ordering him to be disqualified.

(5) References in this section to disqualification do not include a disqualification imposed under section 26 of this Act or section 147 of the *Powers of Criminal Courts (Sentencing) Act* 2000 or section 223A or 436A of the *Criminal Procedure (Scotland) Act* 1975 (offences committed by using vehicles) or a disqualification imposed in respect of an offence of stealing a motor vehicle, an offence under section 12 or 25 of the *Theft Act* 1968, an offence under section 178 of the *Road Traffic Act* 1988, or an attempt to commit such an offence.

(5A) The preceding provisions of this section shall apply in relation to a conviction of an offence committed by aiding, abetting, counselling, procuring, or inciting to the commission of, an offence involving obligatory disqualification as if the offence were an offence involving discretionary disqualification.

(6) In relation to Scotland, references in this section to the court include the justice of the peace court.

(7) This section is subject to section 48 of this Act.

[Sections 35A and 35B are inserted by Sched. 16, para. 2 to the *Coroners and Justice Act* 2009 when in force.]

Extension of disqualification where custodial sentence also imposed

35A.—(1) This section applies where a person is convicted in England and Wales of an offence for which the court—

(a) imposes a custodial sentence, and

(b) orders the person to be disqualified under section 34 or 35.

(2) The order under section 34 or 35 must provide for the person to be disqualified for the appropriate extension period, in addition to the discretionary disqualification period.

(3) The discretionary disqualification period is the period for which, in the absence of this section, the court would have disqualified the person under section 34 or 35.

(4) The appropriate extension period is—

(a) where an order under section 82A(2) of the *Powers of Criminal Courts (Sentencing) Act* 2000 (life sentence: determination of tariffs) is made in relation to the custodial sentence, a period equal to the part of the sentence specified in that order;

(b) in the case of a detention and training order under section 100 of that Act (offenders under 18: detention and training orders), a period equal to half the term of that order;

(c) where an order under section 181 of the *Criminal Justice Act* 2003 (prison sentences of less than 12 months) is made in relation to the custodial sentence, a period equal to the custodial period specified pursuant to section 181(3)(a) of that Act less any relevant discount;

(d) where an order under section 183 of that Act (intermittent custody orders) is made in relation to the custodial sentence, a period equal to the number of custodial days specified pursuant to section 183(1)(a) of that Act less any relevant discount;

(e) where section 227 of that Act (extended sentence for certain violent or sexual offences: persons 18 or over) applies in relation to the custodial sentence, a period equal to half the term imposed pursuant to section 227(2C)(a) of that Act calculated after that term has been reduced by any relevant discount;

(f) where section 228 of that Act (extended sentence for certain violent or sexual offences: persons under 18) applies in relation to the custodial sentence, a period equal to half the term imposed pursuant to section 228(2B)(a) of that Act calculated after that term has been reduced by any relevant discount;

(g) where an order under section 269(2) of that Act (determination of minimum term in relation to mandatory life sentence: early release) is made in relation to the custodial sentence, a period equal to the part of the sentence specified in that order;

(h) in any other case, a period equal to half the custodial sentence imposed calculated after that sentence has been reduced by any relevant discount.

(5) If a period determined under subsection (4) includes a fraction of a day, that period is to be rounded up to the nearest number of whole days.

(6) The "relevant discount" is the total number of days to count as time served by virtue of a direction under—

(a) section 240 of the *Criminal Justice Act* 2003 (crediting periods of remand in custody), or

(b) section 240A of that Act (crediting periods of remand on bail).

(7) This section does not apply where—

(a) the custodial sentence was a suspended sentence,

(b) the court has made an order under section 269(4) of the *Criminal Justice Act* 2003 mandatory life sentence: no early release) in relation to the custodial sentence, or

(c) the court has made an order under section 82A(4) of the *Powers of Criminal Courts (Sentencing) Act* 2000 (determination of minimum term in relation to discretionary life sentence: no early release) in relation to the custodial sentence.

(8) Subsection (9) applies where an amending order provides that the proportion of a prisoner's sentence referred to in section 244(3)(a) or 247(2) of the *Criminal Justice Act* 2003 (release of prisoners in certain circumstances) is to be read as a reference to another proportion ("the new proportion").

(9) The Secretary of State may by order—

(a) if the amending order makes provision in respect of section 244(3)(a) of that Act, provide that the proportion specified in subsection (4)(h) of this section is to be read, in the case of a custodial sentence to which the amending order applies, as a reference to the new proportion;

(b) if the amending order makes provision in respect of section 247(2) of that Act, provide that the proportion specified in subsection (4)(e) and (f) of this section is to be read, in the case of a custodial sentence to which the amending order applies, as a reference to the new proportion.

(10) An order under subsection (9) is to be made by statutory instrument and a draft of the statutory instrument containing the order must be laid before, and approved by a resolution of, each House of Parliament.

(11) In this section—

"amending order" means an order under section 267 of the *Criminal Justice Act* 2003 (alteration by order of relevant proportion of sentence);

"custodial sentence" has the meaning given by section 76 of the *Powers of Criminal Courts (Sentencing) Act* 2000;

"suspended sentence" has the meaning given by section 189 of the *Criminal Justice Act* 2003.

Effect of custodial sentence in other cases

35B.—(1) This section applies where a person is convicted in England and Wales of an offence for which a court proposes to order the person to be disqualified under section 34 or 35 and—

(a) the court proposes to impose on the person a custodial sentence (other than a suspended sentence) for another offence, or

(b) at the time of sentencing for the offence, a custodial sentence imposed on the person on an earlier occasion has not expired.

(2) In determining the period for which the person is to be disqualified under section 34 or 35, the court must have regard to the consideration in subsection (3) if and to the extent that it is appropriate to do so.

(3) The consideration is the diminished effect of disqualification as a distinct punishment if the person who is disqualified is also detained in pursuance of a custodial sentence.

either by order remove the disqualification as from such date as may be specified in the order or refuse the application.

(3) No application shall be made under subsection (1) above for the removal of a disqualification before the expiration of whichever is relevant of the following periods from the date of the order by which the disqualification was imposed, that is—

(a) two years, if the disqualification is for less than four years,

(b) one half of the period of disqualification, if it is for less than ten years but not less than four years,

(c) five years in any other case;

and in determining the expiration of the period after which under this subsection a person may apply for the removal of a disqualification, any time after the conviction during which the disqualification was suspended or he was not disqualified shall be disregarded.

(4) Where an application under subsection (1) above is refused, a further application under that subsection shall not be entertained if made within three months after the date of the refusal.

(5) If under this section a court orders a disqualification to be removed, the court—

(a) must—

(i) if particulars of the disqualification were previously endorsed on the counterpart of any licence previously held by the applicant, cause particulars of the order to be endorsed on that counterpart, and

(ii) if particulars of the disqualification were previously endorsed on the driving record of the applicant, send notice of the order to the Secretary of State,

(b) may in any case order the applicant to pay the whole or any part of the costs of the application.

(5A) Subsection (5)(a)(i) above shall apply only where the disqualification was imposed in respect of an offence involving obligatory endorsement; and in any other case the court must send notice of the order made under this section to the Secretary of State.

(5AA) If the disqualification was imposed in respect of an offence involving obligatory endorsement, the Secretary of State must, on receiving notice of an order under subsection (5)(a)(ii) above, make any necessary adjustments to the endorsements on the person's driving record to reflect the order.

(5B) A notice under subsection (5)(a)(ii) or (5A) above must be sent in such manner and to such address, and must contain such particulars, as the Secretary of State may determine.

(6) The preceding provisions of this section shall not apply where the disqualification was imposed by order under section 36(1) of this Act.

Rule for determining end of period of disqualification

43. In determining the expiration of the period for which a person is disqualified by an order of a court made in consequence of a conviction, any time after the conviction during which the disqualification was suspended or he was not disqualified shall be disregarded. **17–202**

Interim disqualification

26.—(1) Where a magistrates' court— **17–203**

(a) commits an offender to the Crown Court under section 6 of the *Powers of Criminal Courts (Sentencing) Act* 2000 or any enactment mentioned in subsection (4) of that section applies, or

(b) remits an offender to another magistrates' court under section 10 of that Act,

to be dealt with for an offence involving obligatory or discretionary disqualification, it may order him to be disqualified until he has been dealt with in respect of the offence.

(2) Where a court in England and Wales—

(a) defers passing sentence on an offender under section 1 of that Act in respect of an offence involving obligatory or discretionary disqualification, or

(b) adjourns after convicting an offender of such an offence but before dealing with him for the offence,

it may order the offender to be disqualified until he has been dealt with in respect of the offence.

(3–5) [Scotland]

(6) Where a court orders a person to be disqualified under this section ("the first order"), no court shall make a further order under this section in respect of the same offence or any offence in respect of which an order could have been made under this section at the time the first order was made.

(7) Where a court makes an order under this section in respect of any person it must—

(a) require him to produce to the court any licence held by him and its counterpart, and

(b) retain the licence and counterpart until it deals with him or (as the case may be) cause them to be sent to the proper officer of the court which is to deal with him.

(7A) In subsection (7) above "proper officer" means—

(a) in relation to a magistrates' court in England and Wales, the designated officer for the court, and

(b) in relation to any other court, the clerk of the court.

(8) If the holder of the licence has not caused it and its counterpart to be delivered, or has not posted them, in accordance with section 7 of this Act and does not produce the licence and counterpart as required under subsection (7) above, then he is guilty of an offence.

(9) Subsection (8) above does not apply to a person who—

(a) satisfies the court that he has applied for a new licence and has not received it, or

(b) surrenders to the court a current receipt for his licence and its counterpart issued under section 56 of this Act, and produces the licence and counterpart to the court immediately on their return.

(10) Where a court makes an order under this section in respect of any person, sections 44(1), 47(2) 91ZA(7) and 91A(5) of this Act shall not apply in relation to the order, but—

(a) the court must send notice of the order to the Secretary of State, and

(b) if the court which deals with the offender determines not to order him to be disqualified under section 34 or 35 of this Act, it must send notice of the determination to the Secretary of State.

(11) A notice sent by a court to the Secretary of State in pursuance of subsection (10) above must be sent in such manner and to such address and contain such particulars as the Secretary of State may determine.

(12) Where on any occasion a court deals with an offender—

(a) for an offence in respect of which an order was made under this section, or

(b) for two or more offences in respect of any of which such an order was made,

any period of disqualification which is on that occasion imposed under section 34 or 35 of this Act shall be treated as reduced by any period during which he was disqualified by reason only of an order made under this section in respect of any of those offences.

(13) Any reference in this or any other Act (including any Act passed after this Act) to the length of a period of disqualification shall, unless the context otherwise requires, be construed as a reference to its length before any reduction under this section.

(14) In relation to licences which came into force before 1st June 1990, the references in this section to counterparts of licences shall be disregarded.

Penalty points to be taken into account on conviction

17–204 **29.**—(1) Where a person is convicted of an offence involving obligatory endorsement, the penalty points to be taken into account on that occasion are (subject to subsection (2) below)—

(a) any that are to be attributed to the offence or offences of which he is convicted, disregarding any offence in respect of which an order under section 34 of this Act is made, and

(b) any that were on a previous occasion ordered to be endorsed on the counterpart of any licence held by him or on his driving record, unless the offender has since that occasion and before the conviction been disqualified under section 35 of this Act.

(2) If any of the offences was committed more than three years before another, the penalty points in respect of that offence shall not be added to those in respect of the other.

(3) In relation to licences which came into force before 1st June 1990, the reference in subsection (1) above to the counterpart of a licence shall be construed as a reference to the licence itself.

(2) Driving licences

17–205 Wherever a court is obliged to endorse details of a conviction on a licence, it may also disqualify the offender from holding or obtaining a licence. A period of disqualification (or the number of penalty points) should not be reduced solely as a result of the reduction in sentence given when a defendant enters a guilty plea. The Sentencing Guidelines Council Guideline *Reduction in Sentence for a Guilty Plea* states that the reduction "has no impact on sentencing decisions in relation to ancillary orders, including orders of disqualification from driving". In those circumstances, neither the length of the disqualification nor the number of penalty points will be affected by the guideline. It is an offence to drive a motor vehicle whilst disqualified by an order of a court, see *ante*, § 17–112.

A disqualification is generally for a prescribed period during which the offender may not lawfully drive any vehicle on a road. The period starts from the moment it is imposed. However, a disqualification may also (or instead) be until the offender has passed a relevant driving test. In those circumstances, the offender may drive as if a provisional licence holder pending the successful taking of the test (though if this order is combined with a disqualification for a fixed period, that period must first expire before the offender can commence to drive as a provisional licence holder): s.37(3) of the *Road Traffic Offenders Act* 1988.

When in force, s.35A (as inserted by the *Coroners and Justice Act* 2009) will require a court imposing both a custodial sentence and disqualification from driving under these provisions to extend the period of disqualification so that the period of disqualification, in effect, starts at the point at which the offender is likely to be released from the custodial sentence. Section 35B applies where a court is imposing the custodial sentence and the disqualification for different offences; in those circumstances the court must consider the diminished effect of the disqualification and may, but is not obliged to, increase the period of disqualification: s.35B(2).

Orders of disqualification may be mandatory or discretionary. Mandatory disqualification follows conviction of "an offence involving obligatory disqualification". In these circumstances, the minimum period of disqualification is 12 months: s.34(1) of the *Road Traffic Offenders Act* 1988. This minimum is extended to two years where the offender has had at least two disqualifications of at least 56 days imposed on him within the three years that preceded the *commission* of the offence currently before the court: s.34(4)(b). The minimum is extended to three years in relation to the obligatorily disqualifiable offences relating to alcohol/drug influenced driving where the offender has been convicted of one of those offences within the 10 years preceding the *commission* of the current offence: s.34(3). The only discretion to not impose this disqualification either at all or for a lesser period arises where the court finds "special reasons" (see *post*). Where the disqualification is for at least 12 months and arises from certain alcohol/drug influenced offences, the court may authorise the period to be reduced if the offender satisfactorily completes a suitable course. The court will specify the extent of the reduction—at least three months but no more than one quarter of the total period: *Road Traffic Offenders Act* 1988, s.34A.

A further circumstance where a court is obliged to disqualify is where the total number of penalty points to be taken into account amounts to at least 12. The court must disqualify for at least six months unless it finds "mitigating circumstances" (see *post*). This period of six months is increased to one year or two years if there are previous disqualifications of at least 56 days imposed in the three years prior to the *commission* of the current offence. The increase to one year follows one such disqualification; the increase to two years follows two or more previous disqualifications. Certain disqualifications do not count for these purposes: s.35(5).

Points on a licence are taken into account and added to those imposed for the current offence. The points on a licence must be in respect of an offence committed within three years (before or after) of the current offence: s.29(2). However, those points will be disregarded if there has been a disqualification under s.35 (totting-up) between the earlier imposition of the points and the commission of the current offence: s.29(1)(b). Other disqualifications (*e.g.* obligatory disqualifications under s.34) do not have the same effect. **17–206**

A different, more stringent, power applies where offences are committed within the first two years after a person first passes a driving test. If six points are acquired for offences committed prior to the end of that two year period, the licence is automatically revoked: *Road Traffic (New Drivers) Act* 1995. This is not a disqualification. A person whose licence is revoked who drives subsequently will not be driving whilst disqualified but may be driving other than in accordance with a licence. They will be able to apply for a further provisional licence and must comply with the conditions until an appropriate test is passed. This requirement is triggered where six points are acquired but not by a court ordered disqualification. Where a young driver is likely to receive sufficient points to trigger this requirement, it is inappropriate for a court to order disqualification simply to avoid the effects of revocation. If a court is considering disqualification from driving because of the nature of the offence or because it is mandatory, it is suggested that it should also give consideration to disqualifying until a test is passed.

Discretionary disqualification can follow commission of an endorsable offence. It may also be imposed on commission of certain other offences that are not endorsable. In those circumstances, there is no minimum period.

Different procedures regarding the retention of the licence by the court apply depending on whether the period of the disqualification is 56 days or more: *Road Traffic Offenders Act* 1988, s.47. Where the period is less than 56 days (or is an interim disqualification under s.29), the licence automatically has effect again at the end of the period: s.37(1A). Otherwise, the licence will be retained by the court and sent to the Secretary of State; the driver will need to apply for its return before the end of the period of disqualification to ensure that it is in his possession when he is entitled to drive again. When a person is disqualified from driving and the licence sent by the Court to the Secretary of State, any vocational licence held also ceases to be effective. Confusions have arisen because vocational licences are not returned automatically since each case will be referred by the DVLA to the Traffic Commissioner for the area in which the defendant resides. In a News Sheet (07/2004), the Justices' Clerks' Society recommends as good practice that, where a Court is aware that a person being disqualified holds a vocational licence (that is, one to drive either a large goods vehicle or a passenger carrying vehicle), a warning should be given to the disqualified person that the return of the vocational licence will not be automatic but subject to the decision of the Traffic Commissioner.

As well as a disqualification for a fixed period (after which the offender can drive as before) the court may impose a disqualification until the offender passes a driving test. This driving test will normally be the usual test of competence to drive but, where the offender is also disqualified under s.35 (totting-up) the test will be an extended one: s.36(4), (5).

A period of disqualification may be reduced following attendance on certain specified courses when imposed for the types of offences set out in s.34A(1) of the *Road Traffic Offenders Act* 1988. This provision will be repealed and replaced by the *Road Safety Act* 2006 when in force and extends to a wider range of offences than previously. It continues to apply to "relevant drink offences". However, it also applies to "specified offences", a category that can be expanded by the Secretary of State by regulations. At present, offences included are those of careless or inconsiderate driving (s.3 of the *Road Traffic Act* 1988), failing to comply with traffic signs (s.36 of the *Road Traffic Offenders Act* 1988), use of special road contrary to scheme or regulations (*Road Traffic Regulation Act* 1984, s.17(4)), and speeding (*Road Traffic Regulation Act* 1984, s.89(1)). Whichever category of offence, the period of disqualification must be at least 12 months and must have been imposed under s.34 of the *Road Traffic Offenders Act* 1988 (that is the normal obligatory or discretionary disqualification provisions) not under the "totting-up" provisions. Amendments in the *Road Safety Act* 2006 (when in force) provide for similar reductions in the number of penalty points imposed. The provisions allow for a reduction of at least three months and not more than one quarter. In practice, it seems that a three month reduction is the most common. The purpose of the reduction is to reward a driver who takes steps to improve their awareness in the expectation that this will enable them to drive in a way that is more likely to be safe. However, it is difficult to see circumstances in which a reduction of more than three months is likely to be justified. By s.34A(8), it is not possible to make an order providing for a reduction in disqualification where an offender has completed an approved course as a result of an offence committed in the three years prior to the current offence or whilst the driver was in the probationary period provided for new drivers. When in force, a new s.34D provides for those convicted of a second relevant drink offence receiving a disqualification of at least two years to be offered a reduced disqualification if they participate successfully in an "alcohol ignition interlock programme". This will allow for a reduction of at least 12 months in (but no more than half of) the period of disqualification.

Interim disqualification

A court which adjourns a case for sentence after conviction or which defers sentence or remits an offender to another court for sentence may impose an interim disqualification in respect of any endorsable offence. This disqualification may not last longer than six months. Any period will be attributed to a disqualification imposed as a sentence. **17–207**

Discretion of the court to disqualify or impose endorsement

Obligatory disqualification or endorsement can only be avoided where a court finds "special reasons" for doing so. Special reasons may reduce a period of disqualification below the minimum set by statute but may not reduce the penalty points below the lower limit fixed—in relation to points, finding special reasons will enable the court to avoid endorsing any points at all. Disqualification under s.35 (totting-up) may only be avoided where a court finds "mitigating circumstances". Even where either is found to exist, the court retains its discretion and may still disqualify or endorse if it thinks fit. Both these terms have been subject to extensive case law. For a full examination of the authorities, see *Wilkinson's Road Traffic Offences*, Ch.21. This is one of the inevitable consequences of courts being subject to mandatory orders—whilst this promotes consistency and reinforces the seriousness of the offences, it also requires an elaborate system to be created to avoid injustice in the small number of unusual cases that inevitably arise. **17–208**

Special reasons

A special reason must be "special to the facts that constitute the offence". It must be one relevant to the offence and not the offender and it must be something that a court ought properly to take into account when passing sentence: *Crossen* [1939] 1 N.I. 106; *Whittal v. Kirby* [1946] 2 All E.R. 552. In *Wickens* (1958) 42 Cr.App.R. 236 the court set out four criteria which have to be satisfied before special reasons can be found to exist. The circumstance put forward must be a mitigating or extenuating circumstance; it must not amount in law to a defence to the charge; it must be something which is directly connected with the offence and it must be something which is proper for the court to take into account when imposing sentence. Courts are generally difficult to persuade that special reasons exist. **17–209**

Given that Parliament has prescribed these orders as part of the penalty for the offences, it seems that the reason has to be outside of the mischief at which the offence is aimed: see *Nicholson v. Brown* [1974] R.T.R. 177.

Thus special reasons have been found where the defendant was coping with a true emergency (though the courts have been very careful about what constitutes such an emergency and examine closely alternative courses of action in the circumstances) or where the driving was for a very short distance. However, courts have been very cautious over accepting the shortness of the distance driven as sufficient by itself for alcohol or drug related offences. In *Chatters v. Burke* [1986] 3 All E.R. 168, seven relevant factors were set out. As well as the distance driven, the court will consider the manner in which it was driven, the state of the vehicle, whether the driver intended to drive fur- **17–210** ther, the road and traffic conditions at the time and the reason for the car being driven. The most important factor will be the extent to which it was possible that danger would be caused through contact with either other road users or with pedestrians. The restrictive approach was again demonstrated in *R. (Khan) v. DPP* [2004] EWHC 2505 Admin. In the early hours of New Year's Day, the defendant arrived home at 2.30 am. His wife (who had driven home) went to bed but he waited up for his sons (aged 14 and 15) to return from a local party. Some time later (when he was already apprehensive because they were later than expected), he received news of a fatal road accident on a nearby road and was made aware that young Asian boys were involved and that they had come from the same party as that attended by his sons. In addition, three years before, the defendant had attended a fatal road traffic accident in which the 19-year-old son of a very close friend had been killed. Fearing that his sons had been killed or injured, the defendant wanted to reach the scene as quickly as possible and drove his car one mile to the scene. There was no evidence of bad driving. He was found to be about 2.5 times over the limit. His wife had not drunk alcohol at all but he did not wait for her and get her to drive. It was found as a fact that he could have walked to the scene in less than 20 minutes. The Justices found that special reasons did not exist and this was upheld by the Divisional Court. Referring to *DPP v. Bristow* [1998] R.T.R. 100 (would a sober, reasonable and responsible friend have advised the appellant not to drive in the circumstances?) and *Taylor v. Rajan* [1974] R.T.R. 304 (was the emergency sufficiently acute to justify the driver taking his car out? Justices to exercise their discretion in favour of the driver only in clear and compelling circumstances), the Divisional Court noted that the defendant was well over the limit and that his wife was perfectly capable of driving if she had been woken. A further example of the restrictive approach to the "emergency" argument can be seen in *DPP v. Harrison* [2007] EWHC 556, Admin. The Divisional Court emphasised the significance of the distance driven (446 yards), the level of alcohol and the alternatives available to the driver and concluded that the justices' decision to find special reasons could not be upheld.

In *Warring Davies v. DPP* [2009] R.T.R. 35, the defendant pleaded guilty to speeding but sought to persuade the court not to endorse his licence on the grounds that he anticipated that he was becoming hypoglycaemic and decided to speed up in order to reach a safe point at which he could take glucose. This was rejected by the Magistrates' Court, the Crown Court and the Divisional Court. Whilst accepting that the onset of a medical condition could amount to a special reason where it caused momentary excess speed or was otherwise reasonable, here the defendant had made a conscious decision to speed up which the court had concluded was not reasonable in the circumstances. Accordingly, the decision of the Crown Court to endorse the licence was upheld.

In the context of offences concerning driving after the consumption of alcohol, the unexpected presence of alcohol may be capable of providing a special reason. This most commonly occurs where it is alleged that a drink has been "laced". The increasingly restrictive approach to assessing the circumstances in which those reasons can be seen demonstrated in *DPP v. Sharma* [2005] R.T.R. 27, although the Divisional Court was not prepared to overturn the magistrates' court on the facts. The defendant went for a drink after work with friends. Unknown to her, a friend added vodka to each of the two drinks that she drank believing that she was travelling home by taxi. Unaware of the additional alcoholic content and not feeling any effect, the defendant drove home, was stopped, breathalysed and found to be over the limit. The justices found that she was unaware of the alcohol that had been added, that she did not display any signs of impairment, that there had been nothing unusual about the manner of her driving and that she would not have been over the limit without the added alcohol. The Divisional Court re-iterated the test set out by the Court of Appeal in *DPP v. O'Connor* [1992] R.T.R. 66 that it is for the motorist whose drink has been "laced" to establish that fact by admissible and relevant evidence and also the fact that he did not know or suspect that the drink had been "laced". Additionally, the driver must establish that he would not have exceeded the prescribed limit without the additional alcohol—expert evidence will often be required. In *Sharma*, the Divisional Court observed that the justices' finding that the defendant was unaware of the additional alcohol was surprising but could not be said to be one to which they were not entitled to come on the evidence that they had heard. A different situation was considered in *Robinson v. DPP* [2004] 168 J.P. 522. The defendant was a Rastafarian who contended that drinking alcohol was contrary to his faith. He stated that he had been to a funeral of a friend and had drunk the punch supplied which he did not expect to be alcoholic. In fact, it contained approximately 28 per cent alcohol. Justices accepted that the defendant had chosen to drink the punch believing it to contain no alcohol but disqualified on the grounds that he had made no inquiries about what it contained. This approach was endorsed by the Divisional Court. The purpose of the legislation is to ensure that people do not drive when they have consumed alcohol sufficient to exceed the prescribed limit. If a driver attends a function at which alcohol is available, he must be able to show that he has done all that could reasonably be expected of him if he is to demonstrate that special reasons exist for mitigating the disqualification required by law. Emphasising the rigour of these provisions and the importance of the public interest, the Court went on to say that, even if the defendant had been told that the punch was non-alcoholic and had no reason to suspect alcohol in his body, then the magistrates, even though finding special reasons to exist, would have been entitled to have imposed the normal statutory period of disqualification because the level was so high (83/100).

It is for the defendant to satisfy the court that the special reason exists.

Mitigating circumstances

The obligation to disqualify a person who collects at least 12 penalty points is capable **17–211** of being avoided only if the court is satisfied, having regard to all the circumstances, that there are grounds for mitigating the normal consequences of the conviction: s.35(1). The narrowness of this is emphasised in s.35(4). This precludes a court from taking into account any of the circumstances that are said to make the offence not serious, of hardship unless it is exceptional and states that nothing may be used to support the finding if it has been taken into account in the three years preceding conviction of the current offence in order to avoid or reduce a disqualification to which a defendant would otherwise have been liable under s.35.

It is for the defendant to satisfy the court that the grounds exist. It is not open to the defendant to argue that any of the offences are not serious; disqualification in these circumstances is designed for situations where a driver repeatedly commits offences that do not in themselves warrant disqualification. The wording of s.34(4)(a) seems clearly to encompass not only the latest offence but also any others that are taken into account. If the defendant wishes to rely on hardship then the court will need to be satisfied that that hardship is exceptional. The hardship may be experienced by someone other than the defendant but it must be more than the ordinary hardship that is likely to be experienced when a person is disqualified from driving. This is a question of fact and degree and no precise guidance is possible save that courts are generally difficult to persuade. If mitigating circumstances are found and the court is prepared to allow them to influence the disqualification, that may lead to a reduction in the minimum period or no disqualification at all. In the absence of mitigating circumstances, a court has no alternative but to disqualify for the minimum period provided by statute in the circumstances of the case.

D. DEPRIVATION OF MOTOR VEHICLE

Powers of Criminal Courts (Sentencing) Act 2000, s.143

Powers to deprive offender of property used etc. for purposes of crime

143.—(1) Where a person is convicted of an offence and the court by or before which he is **17–212** convicted is satisfied that any property which has been lawfully seized from him, or which was in his possession or under his control at the time when he was apprehended for the offence or when a summons in respect of it was issued—

(a) has been used for the purpose of committing, or facilitating the commission of, any offence, or

(b) was intended by him to be used for that purpose,

the court may (subject to subsection (5) below) make an order under this section in respect of that property.

(2) Where a person is convicted of an offence and the offence, or an offence which the court has taken into consideration in determining his sentence, consists of unlawful possession of property which—

(a) has been lawfully seized from him, or

(b) was in his possession or under his control at the time when he was apprehended for the offence of which he has been convicted or when a summons in respect of that offence was issued,

the court may (subject to subsection (5) below) make an order under this section in respect of that property.

(3) An order under this section shall operate to deprive the offender of his rights, if any, in the property to which it relates, and the property shall (if not already in their possession) be taken into the possession of the police.

(4) Any power conferred on a court by subsection (1) or (2) above may be exercised—

(a) whether or not the court also deals with the offender in any other way in respect of the offence of which he has been convicted; and

(b) without regard to any restrictions on forfeiture in any enactment contained in an Act passed before 29th July 1988.

(5) In considering whether to make an order under this section in respect of any property, a court shall have regard—

(a) to the value of the property; and

(b) to the likely financial and other effects on the offender of the making of the order (taken together with any other order that the court contemplates making).

(6) Where a person commits an offence to which this subsection applies by—

(a) driving, attempting to drive, or being in charge of a vehicle, or

(b) failing to comply with a requirement made under section 7 or 7A of the *Road Traffic Act* 1988 (failure to provide specimen for analysis or laboratory test or to give permission for such a test) in the course of an investigation into whether the offender had committed an offence while driving, attempting to drive or being in charge of a vehicle, or

(c) failing, as the driver of a vehicle, to comply with subsection (2) or (3) of section 170 of the *Road Traffic Act* 1988 (duty to stop and give information or report accident),

the vehicle shall be regarded for the purposes of subsection (1) above (and section 144(1)(b) below) as used for the purpose of committing the offence (and for the purpose of committing any offence of aiding, abetting, counselling or procuring the commission of the offence).

(7) Subsection (6) above applies to—

(a) an offence under the *Road Traffic Act* 1988 which is punishable with imprisonment;

(b) an offence of manslaughter; and

(c) an offence under section 35 of the *Offences Against the Person Act* 1861 (wanton and furious driving).

(8) Facilitating the commission of an offence shall be taken for the purposes of subsection (1) above to include the taking of any steps after it has been committed for the purpose of disposing of any property to which it relates or of avoiding apprehension or detection.

17–213 An additional sanction available to a court for some road traffic offences is the power to deprive the offender of the vehicle used while committing the offence. The effect of the order must be proportionate to the offence (s.143(5)) but it is a sanction which may have considerable impact. A motor vehicle used in connection with offences described in this chapter would not automatically fall within the remit of this section since it would not have been used for the purposes set out in s.143(1) nor would it come within s.143(2) which requires the offence to be one of unlawful possession. However, that remit is extended by subss. (6) and (7) to include offences punishable under the *Road*

Traffic Act 1988 by imprisonment which consist of driving, attempting to drive or being in charge of the vehicle, failure to provide a specimen for analysis and failing to stop and report an accident. See *post*, § 23–204.

Chapter 18

OFFENCES INVOLVING DRUGS

I. OFFENCES UNDER THE MISUSE OF DRUGS ACT 1971

A. Prohibition on Importation and Exportation of Controlled Drugs

(1) Definition

Misuse of Drugs Act 1971, s.3

Restriction of importation and exportation of controlled drugs

3.—(1) Subject to subsection (2) below— **18–1**

(a) the importation of a controlled drug; and

(b) the exportation of a controlled drug,

are hereby prohibited.

(2) Subsection (1) above does not apply—

(a) to the importation or exportation of a controlled drug which is for the time being excepted from paragraph (a) or, as the case may be, paragraph (b) of subsection (1) above by regulations under section 7 of this Act; or

(b) to the importation or exportation of a controlled drug under and in accordance with the terms of a licence issued by the Secretary of State and in compliance with any conditions attached thereto.

Section 3 does not create an offence: the offence of evading the prohibitions imposed thereby arises from the combined effect of *Customs and Excise Management Act* 1979, ss.3 and 170—see Ch.19, § 19–48. **18–2**

B. RESTRICTION OF PRODUCTION AND SUPPLY OF CONTROLLED DRUGS

(1) Definition

Misuse of Drugs Act 1971, ss.4, 4A

Restriction of production and supply of controlled drugs

18-3 **4.**—(1) Subject to any regulations under section 7 of this Act for the time being in force, it shall not be lawful for a person—

(a) to produce a controlled drug; or

(b) to supply or offer to supply a controlled drug to another.

(2) Subject to section 28 of this Act, it is an offence for a person—

(a) to produce a controlled drug in contravention of subsection (1) above; or

(b) to be concerned in the production of such a drug in contravention of that subsection by another.

(3) Subject to section 28 of this Act, it is an offence for a person—

(a) to supply or offer to supply a controlled drug to another in contravention of subsection (1) above; or

(b) to be concerned in the supplying of such a drug to another in contravention of that subsection; or

(c) to be concerned in the making to another in contravention of that subsection of an offer to supply such a drug.

Aggravation of offence of supply of controlled drug

18-4 **4A.**—(1) This section applies if—

(a) a court is considering the seriousness of an offence under section 4(3) of this Act, and

(b) at the time the offence was committed the offender had attained the age of 18.

(2) If either of the following conditions is met the court—

(a) must treat the fact that the condition is met as an aggravating factor (that is to say, a factor that increases the seriousness of the offence), and

(b) must state in open court that the offence is so aggravated.

(3) The first condition is that the offence was committed on or in the vicinity of school premises at a relevant time.

(4) The second condition is that in connection with the commission of the offence the offender used a courier who, at the time the offence was committed, was under the age of 18.

(5) In subsection (3), a relevant time is—

(a) any time when the school premises are in use by persons under the age of 18;

(b) one hour before the start and one hour after the end of any such time.

(6) For the purposes of subsection (4), a person uses a courier in connection with an offence under section 4(3) of this Act if he causes or permits another person (the courier)—

(a) to deliver a controlled drug to a third person, or

(b) to deliver a drug related consideration to himself or a third person.

(7) For the purposes of subsection (6), a drug related consideration is a consideration of any description which—

(a) is obtained in connection with the supply of a controlled drug, or

(b) is intended to be used in connection with obtaining a controlled drug.

(8) In this section—

"school premises" means land used for the purposes of a school excluding any land occupied solely as a dwelling by a person employed at the school; and

"school" has the same meaning—

(a) in England and Wales, as in section 4 of the *Education Act* 1996;

(b) in Scotland, as in section 135(1) of the *Education (Scotland) Act* 1980;

(c) in Northern Ireland, as in Article 2(2) of the *Education and Libraries (Northern Ireland) Order* 1986.

Section 4A was inserted by the *Drugs Act* 2005, s.1(1) and came into force on January 1, 2006. It does not apply to offences committed before that date.

(2) Allocation

This offence is triable either way. The *Consolidated Criminal Practice Direction* (2002) provides that cases of supplying Class A drugs should be committed for trial; cases of supplying Class B drugs should be committed for trial unless there is only small-scale supply for no payment. No guidelines are given in relation to Class C drugs. **18–5**

Section 25(4) of the 1971 Act also provides that a magistrates' court in England and Wales may try an information for an offence under the 1971 Act if the information was laid at any time within twelve months from the commission of the offence.

(3) Elements of the offence

Misuse of Drugs Act 1971, s.2 and Sched. 2

Controlled drugs and their classification for purposes of this Act.

2.—(1) In this Act— **18–6**

(a) the expression "controlled drug" means any substance or product for the time being specified in Part I, II, or III of Schedule 2 to this Act; and

(b) the expressions "Class A drug", "Class B drug" and "Class C drug" mean any of the substances and products for the time being specified respectively in Part I, Part II and Part III of that Schedule;

and the provisions of Part IV of that Schedule shall have effect with respect to the meanings of expressions used in that Schedule.

(2) Her Majesty may by Order in Council make such amendments in Schedule 2 to this Act as may be requisite for the purpose of adding any substance or product to, or removing any substance or product from, any of Parts I to III of that Schedule, including amendments for securing that no substance or product is for the time being specified in a particular one of those Parts or for inserting any substance or product into any of those Parts in which no substance or product is for the time being specified.

(3) An Order in Council under this section may amend Part IV of Schedule 2 to this Act, and may do so whether or not it amends any other Part of that Schedule.

(4) An Order in Council under this section may be varied or revoked by a subsequent Order in Council thereunder.

(5) No recommendation shall be made to Her Majesty in Council to make an Order under this section unless a draft of the Order has been laid before Parliament and approved by a resolution of each House of Parliament; and the Secretary of State shall not lay a draft of such an Order before Parliament except after consultation with or on the recommendation of the Advisory Council.

SCHEDULE 2

CONTROLLED DRUGS

PART I

Class A Drugs

1. The following substances and products, namely: **18–7**

Acetorphine.
Alfentanil.
Allylprodine.
Alphacetylmethadol.
Alphameprodine.
Alphamethadol.
Alphaprodine.
Anileridine.
Benzethidine.
Benzylmorphine (3-benzylmorphine).
Betacetylmethadol.
Betameprodine.

Betamethadol.
Betaprodine.
Bezitramide.
Bufotenine.
Carfentanil.
Clonitazene.
Coca leaf.
Cocaine.
Desomorphine.
Dextromoramide.
Diamorphine.
Diampromide.
Diethylthiambutene.
Difenoxin (1-(3-cyano-3,3-diphenylpropyl)-4-phenylpiperidine-4-carboxylic acid).
Dihydrocodeinone *O*-carboxymethyloxime.
Dihydroetorphine.
Dihydromorphine.
Dimenoxadole.
Dimepheptanol.
Dimethylthiambutene.
Dioxaphetyl butyrate.
Diphenoxylate.
Dipipanone.
Drotebanol (3,4-dimethoxy-17-methylmorphinan- 6ß 14-diol).
Ecgonine, and any derivative of ecgonine which is convertible to ecgonine or to cocaine.
Ethylmethylthiambutene.
Eticyclidine.
Etonitazene.
Etorphine.
Etoxeridine.
Etryptamine.
Fentanyl.
Fungus (of any kind) which contains psilocin or an ester of psilocin.
Furethidine.
Hydrocodone.
Hydromorphinol.
Hydromorphone.
Hydroxypethidine.
Isomethadone.
Ketobemidone.
Levomethorphan.
Levomoramide.
Levophenacylmorphan.
Levorphanol.
Lofentanil.
Lysergamide.
Lysergide and other *N*-alkyl derivatives of lysergamide.
Mescaline.
Metazocine.
Methadone.
Methadyl acetate.
Methylamphetamine.
Methyldesorphine.
Methyldihydromorphine (6-methyldihydromorphine).
Metopon.

Morpheridine.
Morphine.
Morphine methobromide, morphine *N*-oxide and other pentavalent nitrogen morphine derivatives.
Myrophine.
Nicomorphine (3,6-dinicotinoylmorphine).
Noracymethadol.
Norlevorphanol.
Normethadone.
Normorphine.
Norpipanone.
Opium, whether raw, prepared or medicinal.
Oxycodone.
Oxymorphone.
Pethidine.
Phenadoxone.
Phenampromide.
Phenazocine.
Phencyclidine.
Phenomorphan.
Phenoperidine.
Piminodine.
Piritramide.
Poppy-straw and concentrate of poppy-straw.
Proheptazine.
Properidine (1-methyl-4-phenylpiperidine-4-carboxylic acid isopropyl ester).
Psilocin.
Racemethorphan.
Racemoramide.
Racemorphan.
Remifentanil.
Rolicyclidine.
Sufentanil.
Tapentadol.
Tenocylidine.
Thebacon.
Thebaine.
Tilidate.
Trimeperidine.
4-Bromo-2,5-dimethoxy-α-methylphenethylamine.
4-Cyano-2-dimethylamino-4,4-diphenylbutane.
4-Cyano-1-methyl-4-phenylpiperidine.
N,N-Diethyltryptamine.
N,N-Dimethyltryptamine.
2,5-Dimethoxy-α 4-dimethylphenethylamine.
N-Hydroxy-tenamphetamine.
1-Methyl-4-phenylpiperidine-4-carboxylic acid.
2-Methyl-3-morpholino-1,1-diphenylpropane-carboxylic acid.
4-Methyl-aminorex.
4-Phenylpiperidine-4-carboxylic acid ethyl ester.

(b) any compound (not being a compound for the time being specified in sub-paragraph (a) above) structurally derived from tryptamine or from a ring-hydroxy tryptamine by substitution at the nitrogen atom of the sidechain with one or more alkyl substituents but no other substituent;

(ba) the following phenethylamine derivatives, namely:—

Allyl(α-methyl-3,4-methylenedioxyphenethyl)amine

Part III

2-Amino-1-(2,5-dimethoxy-4-methylphenyl)ethanol
2-Amino-1-(3,4-dimethoxyphenyl)ethanol
Benzyl(α-methyl-3,4-methylenedioxyphenethyl)amine
4-Bromo-β,2,5-trimethoxyphenethylamine
N-(4-*sec*-Butylthio-2,5-dimethoxyphenethyl)hydroxylamine
Cyclopropylmethyl(α-methyl-3,4-methylenedioxyphenethyl)amine
2-(4,7-Dimethoxy-2,3-dihydro-1*H*-indan-5-yl)ethylamine
2-(4,7-Dimethoxy-2,3-dihydro-1*H*-indan-5-yl)-1-methylethylamine
2-(2,5-Dimethoxy-4-methylphenyl)cyclopropylamine
2-(1,4-Dimethoxy-2-naphthyl)ethylamine
2-(1,4-Dimethoxy-2-naphthyl)-1-methylethylamine
N-(2,5-Dimethoxy-4-propylthiophenethyl)hydroxylamine
2-(1,4-Dimethoxy-5,6,7,8-tetrahydro-2-naphthyl)ethylamine
2-(1,4-Dimethoxy-5,6,7,8-tetrahydro-2-naphthyl)-1-methylethylamine
α,α-Dimethyl-3,4-methylenedioxyphenethylamine
α,α-Dimethyl-3,4-methylenedioxyphenethyl(methyl)amine
Dimethyl(α-methyl-3,4-methylenedioxyphenethyl)amine
N-(4-Ethylthio-2,5-dimethoxyphenethyl)hydroxylamine
4-Iodo-2,5-dimethoxy-α-methylphenethyl(dimethyl)amine
2-(1,4-Methano-5,8-dimethoxy-1,2,3,4-tetrahydro-6-naphthyl)ethylamine
2-(1,4-Methano-5,8-dimethoxy-1,2,3,4-tetrahydro-6-naphthyl)-1-methylethylamine
2-(5-Methoxy-2,2-dimethyl-2,3-dihydrobenzo[*b*]furan-6-yl)-1-methylethylamine
2-Methoxyethyl(α-methyl-3,4-methylenedioxyphenethyl)amine
2-(5-Methoxy-2-methyl-2,3-dihydrobenzo[*b*]furan-6-yl)-1-methylethylamine
β-Methoxy-3,4-methylenedioxyphenethylamine
1-(3,4-Methylenedioxybenzyl)butyl(ethyl)amine
1-(3,4-Methylenedioxybenzyl)butyl(methyl)amine
2-(α-Methyl-3,4-methylenedioxyphenethylamino)ethanol
α-Methyl-3,4-methylenedioxyphenethyl(prop-2-ynyl)amine
N-Methyl-*N*-(α-methyl-3,4-methylenedioxyphenethyl)hydroxylamine
O-Methyl-*N*-(α-methyl-3,4-methylenedioxyphenethyl)hydroxylamine
α-Methyl-4-(methylthio)phenethylamine
β,3,4,5-Tetramethoxyphenethylamine
β,2,5-Trimethoxy-4-methylphenethylamine;

(c) any compound (not being methoxyphenamine or a compound for the time being specified in sub-paragraph (a) above) structurally derived from phenethylamine, an *N*-alkylphenethylamine, α-methylphenethylamine, an *N*-alkyl-α-methyl-phenethylamine, α-ethylphenethylamine, or an *N*-alkyl-α-ethylphenethylamine by substitution in the ring to any extent with alkyl, alkoxy, alkylenedioxy or halide substituents, whether or not further substituted in the ring by one or more other univalent substituents.

(d) any compound (not being a compound for the time being specified in sub-paragraph (a) above structurally derived from fentanyl by modification in any of the following ways, that is to say,

(i) by replacement of the phenyl portion of the phenethyl group by any heteromonocycle whether or not further substituted in the heterocycle;
(ii) by substitution in the phenethyl group with alkyl, alkenyl, alkoxy, hydroxy, halogeno, haloalkyl, amino or nitro groups;
(iii) by substitution in the piperidine ring with alkyl or alkenyl groups;
(iv) by substitution in the aniline ring with alkyl, alkoxy, alkylenedioxy, halogeno or haloalkyl groups;
(v) by substitution at the 4-position of the piperidine ring with any alkoxycarbonyl or alkoxyalkyl or acyloxy group;
(vi) by replacement of the *N*-propionyl group by another acyl group;

(e) any compound (not being a compound for the time being specified in sub-paragraph (a) above) structurally derived from pethidine by modification in any of the following ways, that is to say,

(i) by replacement of the 1-methyl group by an acyl, alkyl whether or not unsaturated, benzyl or phenethyl group, whether or not further substituted;

(ii) by substitution in the piperidine ring with alkyl or alkenyl groups or with a propano bridge, whether or not further substituted;

(iii) by substitution in the 4-phenyl ring with alkyl, alkoxy, aryloxy, halogeno or haloalkyl groups;

(iv) by replacement of the 4-ethoxycarbonyl by any other alkoxycarbonyl or any alkoxyalkyl or acyloxy group;

(v) by formation of an *N*-oxide or of a quaternary base.

2. Any stereoisomeric form of a substance for the time being specified in paragraph 1 above not being dextromethorphan or dextrorphan. **18–8**

3. Any ester or ether of a substance for the time being specified in paragraph 1 or 2 above not being a substance for the time being specified in Part II of this Schedule.

4. Any salt of a substance for the time being specified in any of paragraphs 1 to 3 above.

5. Any preparation or other product containing a substance or product for the time being specified in any of paragraphs 1 to 4 above.

6. Any preparation designed for administration by injection which includes a substance or product for the time being specified in any of paragraphs 1 to 3 of Part II of this Schedule.

PART II

Class B Drugs

1. The following substances and products, namely: **18–9**

(a) Acetyldihydrocodeine.
Amphetamine.
Cannabinol.
Cannabinol derivatives.
Cannabinol and cannabis resin.
Codeine.
Dihydrocodeine.
Ethylmorphine (3-ethylmorphine).
Glutethimide.
Lefetamine.
Mecloqualone.
Methaqualone.
Methcathinone.
α–Methylphenethylhydroxylamine.
Methylphenidate.
Methylphenobarbitone.
Nicocodine.
Nicodicodine (6-nicotinoyldihydrocodeine).
Norcodeine.
Pentazocine.
Phenmetrazine.
Pholcodine.
Propiram.
Zipeprol.

(aa) Any compound (not being bupropion, cathinone, diethylpropion, pyrovalerone or a compound for time being specified in sub-paragraph (a) above) structurally derived from 2–amino–1–phenyl–1–propanone by modification in any of the following ways, that is to say,

(i) by substitution in the phenyl ring to any extent with alkyl, alkoxy, alkylenedioxy, haloalkyl or halide substituents, whether or not further substituted in the phenyl ring by one or moreother univalent substituents;

(ii) by substitution at the 3–position with an alkyl substituent;

Part III

(iii) by substitution at the nitrogen atom with alkyl or dialkyl groups, or by inclusion of the nitrogen atom in a cyclic structure.

(ab) Any compound structurally derived from 2-aminopropan-1-one by substitution at the 1-position with any monocyclic, or fused-polycyclic ring system (not being a phenyl ring or alkylenedioxyphenyl ring system), whether or not the compound is further modified in any of the following ways, that is to say:

(i) by substitution in the ring system to any extent with alkyl, alkoxy, haloalkyl or halide substituents, whether or not further substituted in the ring system by one or more univalent substituents;

(ii) by substitution at the 3-position with an alkyl substituent;

(iii) by substitution at the 2-amino nitrogen atom with alkyl or dialkyl groups, or by inclusion of the 2-amino nitrogen atom in a cyclic structure.

(b) any 5,5 disubstituted barbituric acid.

(c) [2,3–Dihydro–5–methyl–3–(4–morpholinylmethyl)pyrrolo[1, 2, 3–de]–1,4–benzoxazin–6–yl]–1–naphthalenylmethanone.

3–Dimethylheptyl–11–hydroxyhexahydrocannabinol.

[9–Hydroxy–6–methyl–3–[5–phenylpentan–2–yl] oxy–5, 6, 6a, 7, 8, 9, 10, 10a–octahydrophenanthridin–1–yl] acetate.

9-(Hydroxymethyl)–6, 6–dimethyl–3–(2–methyloctan–2–yl)–6a, 7, 10, 10a–tetrahydrobenzo[c]chromen–1–ol.

Nabilone.

Any compound structurally derived from 3–(1–naphthoyl)indole or 1H–indol–3– yl–(1–naphthyl)methane by substitution at the nitrogen atom of the indole ring by alkyl, alkenyl, cycloalkylmethyl, cycloalkylethyl or 2–(4–morpholinyl)ethyl, whether or not further substituted in the indole ring to any extent and whether or not substituted in the naphthyl ring to any extent.

Any compound structurally derived from 3–(1–naphthoyl)pyrrole by substitution at the nitrogen atom of the pyrrole ring by alkyl, alkenyl, cycloalkylmethyl, cycloalkylethyl or 2–(4–morpholinyl)ethyl, whether or not further substituted in the pyrrole ring to any extent and whether or not substituted in the naphthyl ring to any extent.

Any compound structurally derived from 1–(1–naphthylmethyl)indene by substitution at the 3–position of the indene ring by alkyl, alkenyl, cycloalkylmethyl, cycloalkylethyl or 2–(4–morpholinyl)ethyl, whether or not further substituted in the indene ring to any extent and whether or not substituted in the naphthyl ring to any extent.

Any compound structurally derived from 3–phenylacetylindole by substitution at the nitrogen atom of the indole ring with alkyl, alkenyl, cycloalkylmethyl, cycloalkylethyl or 2–(4–morpholinyl)ethyl, whether or not further substituted in the indole ring to any extent and whether or not substituted in the phenyl ring to any extent.

Any compound structurally derived from 2–(3–hydroxycyclohexyl)phenol by substitution at the 5–position of the phenolic ring by alkyl, alkenyl, cycloalkylmethyl, cycloalkylethyl or 2–(4–morpholinyl)ethyl, whether or not further substituted in the cyclohexyl ring to any extent.

18–10 2. Any stereoisomeric form of a substance for the time being specified in para. 1 of this Part of this Schedule.

2A. Any ester or ether of cannabinol or of a cannabinol derivative or of a substance for the time being specified in paragraph 1(c) of this Part of this Schedule.

3. Any salt of a substance for the time being specified in para. 1 or 2 of this Part of this Schedule.

4. Any preparation or other product containing a substance or product for the time being specified in any of paras 1 to 3 of this Part of this Schedule, not being a preparation falling within para. 6 of Pt I of this Schedule.

PART III

Class C Drugs

18–11 1.

(a) The following substances, namely:

Alprazolam.
Amineptine.
Aminorex.
Benzphetamine.
Bromazepam.
Brotizolam.
Buprenorphine.
Camazepam.
Cathine.
Cathinone.
Chlordiazepoxide.
Chlorphentermine.
Clobazam.
Clonazepam.
Clorazepic acid.
Clotiazepam.
Cloxazolam.
Delorazepam.
Dextropropoxyphene.
Diazepam.
Diethylpropion.
Estazolam.
Ethchlorvynol.
Ethinamate.
Ethyl loflazepate.
Fencamfamin.
Fenethylline.
Fenproporex.
Fludiazepam.
Flunitrazepam.
Flurazepam.
Gamma-butyrolactone.
Halazepam.
Haloxazolam.
4-Hydroxy-n-butyric acid.
Ketamine.
Ketazolam.
Ketazolam.
Loprazolam.
Lorazepam.
Lormetazepam.
Mazindol.
Medazepam.
Mefenorex.
Mephentermine.
Meprobamate.
Mesocarb.
Methyprylone.
Midazolam.
Nimetazepam.
Nitrazepam.
Nordazepam.
Oxazepam.
Oxazolam.
Pemoline.
Phendimetrazine.

Part III

Phentermine.
Pinazepam.
Pipradrol.
Prazepam.
Pyrovalerone.
Temazepam.
Tetrazepam.
Triazolam.
N-Ethylamphetamine.
Zolpidem.

(b) 5a-Androstane-3,17-diol.
Androst-4-ene-3,17-diol.
1-Androstenediol.
1-Androstenedione.
4-Androstene-3, 17-dione.
5-Androstenedione.
5-Androstene-3, 17-diol.
Atamestane.
Bolandiol.
Bolasterone.
Bolazine.
Boldenone.
Boldione.
Bolenol.
Bolmantalate.
1,4-Butanediol.
Calusterone.
4-Chloromethandienone.
Clostebol.
Danazol.
Desoxymethyltestosterone
Drostanolone.
Enestebol.
Epitiostanol.
Ethyloestrenol.
Fluoxymesterone.
Formebolone.
Furazabol.
Gestrinone.
3-Hydroxy-5a-androstan-17-one.
Mebolazine.
Mepitiostane.
Mesabolone.
Mestanolone.
Mesterolone.
Methandienone.
Methandriol.
Methenolone.
Methyltestosterone.
Metribolone.
Mibolerone.
Nandrolone.
19-Norandrostenedione.
19-Nor-4-Androstene-3, 17-dione.
19-Nor-5-Androstene-13, 17-diol.
19-Norandrosterone.

Norboletone.
Norclostebol.
Norethandrolone.
19-Noretiocholanolone.
Oripavine.
Ovandrotone.
Oxabolone.
Oxandrolone.
Oxymesterone.
Oxymetholone.
Prasterone.
Propetandrol.
Prostanozol.
Quinbolone.
Roxibolone.
Silandrone.
Stanolone.
Stanozolol.
Stenbolone.
Testosterone.
Tetrahydrogestrinone.
Thiomesterone.
Trenbolone.

(c) any compound (not being Trilostane or a compound for the time being specified in sub-paragraph (b) above) structurally derived from 17-hydroxyandrostan-3-one or from 17-hydroxyestran-3-one by modification in any of the following ways, that is to say,
  (i) by further substitution at position 17 by a methyl or ethyl group;
  (ii) by substitution to any extent at one or more of positions 1, 2, 4, 6, 7, 9, 11 or 16, but at no other position;
  (iii) by unsaturation in the carbocyclic ring system to any extent, provided that there are no more than two ethylenic bonds in any one carbocyclic ring;
  (iv) by fusion of ring A with a heterocyclic system;

(ca) 1–benzylpiperazine or any compound structurally derived from 1– benzylpiperazine or 1–phenylpiperazine by modification in any of the following ways—
  (i) by substitution at the second nitrogen atom of the piperazine ring with alkyl, benzyl, haloalkyl or phenyl groups;
  (ii) by substitution in the aromatic ring to any extent with alkyl, alkoxy, alkylenedioxy, halide or haloalkyl groups.

(d) any substance which is an ester or ether (or, where more than one hydroxyl function is available, both an ester and an ether) of a substance specified in sub-paragraph (b) or described in sub-paragraph (c) above.

(e) Chorionic Gonadotrophin (HCG).
Clenbuterol.
Non-human chorionic gonadotrophin.
Somatotropin.
Somatrem.
Somatropin.
Zeranol.
Zilpaterol.

2. Any stereoisomeric form of a substance for the time being specified in para. 1 of this Part of this Schedule not being phenylpropanolamine. **18–12**

3. Any salt of a substance for the time being specified in para. 1 or 2 of this Part of this Schedule.

4. Any preparation or other product containing a substance for the time being specified in any of paras 1 to 3 of this Part of this Schedule.

PART IV

Meaning of Certain Expressions Used in This Schedule

18–13 For the purposes of this Schedule the following expressions (which are not among those defined in s.37(1) of this Act) have the meanings hereby assigned to them respectively, that is to say—

"cannabinol derivatives" means the following substances, except where contained in cannabis or cannabis resin, namely tetrahydro derivatives of cannabinol and 3-alkyl homologues of cannabinol or of its tetrahydro derivatives;

"coca leaf" means the leaf of any plant of the genus *Erythroxylon* from whose leaves cocaine can be extracted either directly or by chemical transformation;

"concentrate of poppy-straw" means the material produced when poppy-straw has entered into a process for the concentration of its alkaloids;

"medicinal opium" means raw opium which has undergone the process necessary to adapt it for medicinal use in accordance with the requirements of the British Pharmacopoeia, whether it is in the form of powder or is granulated or is in any other form, and whether it is or is not mixed with neutral substances;

"opium poppy" means the plant of the species *Papaver somniferum* L;

"poppy straw" means all parts, except the seeds, of the opium poppy, after mowing;

"raw opium" includes powdered or granulated opium but does not include medicinal opium.

18–14 The prosecution must prove that the drug in question is controlled. Drugs are divided into three classes as listed in Sched. 2 to the Act. Proof that the drug is controlled is provided either by admission or an analyst's certificate. Such a scientific report should identify the drug and level of purity: *Jones (K.)*, 161 J.P. 597, CA.

"Supply" includes distributing (s.37(1)) but the term is not further elaborated by the statute. The word "supply" has to be given its ordinary everyday meaning: *Holmes v. Chief Constable of Merseyside* [1976] Crim. L.R. 125, DC. In *Maginnis* [1987] A.C. 303, HL, the majority opinion drew a distinction between a "custodier" who has the necessary intent to supply when he returns controlled drugs to a person who had deposited them with him and a "depositor" who places the drugs in the temporary possession of the "custodier" without an intention of enabling the "custodier" to use the drugs for his own purposes. Establishing intent to supply does not require the defendant's offer to supply be proved genuine: *Prior* [2004] EWCA Crim 1147. It is neither necessary for the prosecution to establish that the supply was commercial nor to identify the intended recipient: *Ibrahima* [2005] Crim.L.R. 887, CA.

The *Maginnis* meaning of "supply" is to be applied regardless of whether the supplier was in voluntary or "involuntary" possession of the drugs supplied: *Panton, The Times*, March 27, 2001, CA.

Where two people agree to buy drugs for themselves, it is undesirable to charge the one who happens to take physical possession of the drugs with the supply of drugs when he distributes the other's share to him; although technically a supply, it was inevitable that a person convicted on the basis of such distribution would be dealt with as for simple possession: *Denslow* [1998] Crim. L.R. 566, CA.

There is no defence of medical necessity in relation to a charge of possessing cannabis with intent to supply: *Att.-Gen's Reference (No. 2 of 2004)* 2 Cr.App.R. 34, CA.

Misuse of Drugs Act 1971, s.28

Proof of lack of knowledge etc. to be a defence in proceedings for certain offences

18–15 **28.**—(1) This section applies to offences under any of the following provisions of this Act, that is to say section 4(2) and (3), section 5(2) and (3), section 6(2) and section 9.

(2) Subject to subsection (3) below, in any proceedings for an offence to which this section applies it shall be a defence for the accused to prove that he neither knew of nor suspected nor had reason to suspect the existence of some fact alleged by the prosecution which it is necessary for the prosecution to prove if he is to be convicted of the offence charged.

(3) Where in any proceedings for an offence to which this section applies it is necessary, if the accused is to be convicted of the offence charged, for the prosecution to prove that some substance or product involved in the alleged offence was the controlled drug which the prosecution alleges it to have been, and it is proved that the substance or product in question was that controlled drug, the accused—

(a) shall not be acquitted of the offence charged by reason only of proving that he neither knew nor suspected nor had reason to suspect that the substance or product in question was the particular controlled drug alleged; but

(b) shall be acquitted thereof—

(i) if he proves that he neither believed nor suspected nor had reasons to suspect that the substance or product in question was a controlled drug; or

(ii) if he proves that he believed the substance or product in question to be a controlled drug, or a controlled drug of a description, such that, if it had in fact been that controlled drug or a controlled drug of that description, he would not at the material time have been committing any offence to which this section applies.

(4) Nothing in this section shall prejudice any defence which it is open to a person charged with an offence to which this section applies to raise apart from this section.

In order to render it compatible with the presumption of innocence in Art. 6(2) of the ECHR, s.28 is to be read as imposing only an evidential burden, not a persuasive burden, on the accused: *Lambert* [2002] A.C. 545, HL (see *ante*, § 10–11). If sufficient evidence is adduced to raise the issue, it is for the prosecution to show to the criminal standard that the defence is not made out. See also *Choudhury*, unreported, December 18, 2008, CA ([2008] EWCA Crim. 3179).

Part III

(4) Sentence

It is necessary to draw a distinction between the three different classifications of drugs. When tried summarily, an offence under s.4(2) committed in relation to a Class A or B drug carries a maximum penalty of six months' imprisonment, a fine not exceeding the prescribed sum, or both. Commission involving a Class C drug carries a maximum penalty of three months' imprisonment, a fine not exceeding £2,500 or both. An offence under s.4(3), when tried summarily, carries the same maximum penalties as regards each classification of drug: *Misuse of Drugs Act* 1971, s.25 and Sched. 4. After commencement of the relevant provisions, the maximum custodial sentence able to be imposed in a magistrates' court will be 12 months' imprisonment: *Criminal Justice Act* 2003, ss.154 and 282. **18–16**

In relation to the production and supply of Class A drugs, the Magistrates' Court Sentencing Guidelines 2008 state:

> "These offences should normally be dealt with in the Crown Court. However, there may be very rare cases involving non-commercial supply (*e.g.* between equals) of a very small amount (*e.g.* one small wrap or tablet) in which a custodial sentence within the jurisdiction of a magistrates' court may be appropriate."

In the guideline judgment of *Aramah* (1982) 4 Cr.App.R.(S.) 407, Lord Lane C.J. indicated that it would rarely be appropriate for offences involving Class A drugs to be tried summarily, stating: **18–17**

> "Class A drugs and particularly heroin and morphine: It is common knowledge that these are the most dangerous of all the addictive drugs...Consequently, anything which the courts of this country can do by way of deterrent sentences on those found guilty of crimes involving those Class A drugs should be done."

STARTING POINTS AND SENTENCING RANGES

Examples of nature of activity	Starting Point	Range
Sharing minimal quantity between equals on a non-commercial basis, *e.g.* a reefer	Band C fine	Band B fine to low level community order
Small scale retail supply to consumer	High level community order (Class C)	Low level community order to 6 weeks custody (Class C) Medium level community order to 26 weeks custody (Class B)
Any other supply, including small scale supply in prison whether by prisoner or another	Crown Court	Crown Court

AGGRAVATING AND MITIGATING FACTORS

Factors indicating higher culpability 1. offender exercising or acting in position of special responsibility. **Factors indicating greater degree of harm** 1. supply to vulnerable persons including children 2. offence committed on/in vicinity of school premises.	

18–18 The CA decision in *Ronchetti* [1998] 2 Cr.App.R.(S.) 100 gives guidance concerning appropriate penalties for particular quantities of drugs. Lord Justice Rose stated:

> "... we have been invited by the Crown to give some indication for the guidance of judges of first instance, in relation to the sort of level of sentence which is appropriate for importations of the order of 100 kg. In conformity with, but by way of addendum to, *Aramah*, we would suggest that, following a trial, the importation of 100 kg by persons playing more than a subordinate role, should attract a sentence of seven to eight years. In our judgment, 10 years is the appropriate starting point, following a trial, for importations of 500 kg or more, by such persons. Larger importations will, as the authorities show, attract a higher starting point. That starting point should, in our judgment, rise according to the roles played, the weight involved, and all the other circumstances of the case, up to the statutory maximum of 14 years provided by Parliament. The fact that, in a particular case of massive importation, an even greater quantity of the drug might one day have to be dealt with by the courts, is not in itself, in our judgment, a reason for not imposing the maximum sentence where those at the top of an organisation are before the court."

There are offenders who are unemployed addicts, supplying in order to finance their own addiction, who hold no stock of drugs, who have made a few retail supplies of Class A drugs, for example, to undercover police officers. For some such offenders a drug treatment and testing order would be appropriate. In other such cases, generally for a first drug-supply offence, adults, following a trial should be short term prisoners and, following a plea of guilty at the first reasonable opportunity, should be sentenced to a term of the order of two-and-a-half years' imprisonment: *Afonso*; *Sajid*; *Andrews* [2005] 1 Cr.App.R.(S.) 99, CA. In *Evans* (2005) 149 S.J. 1222, the Court of Appeal made it clear that such sentences are appropriate for those with no criminal record. For those with minor convictions for dishonesty or simple possession of drugs, who have not previously served a custodial sentence, sentences between two and two-and-a-half years' imprisonment are appropriate. For those with more serious convictions for dishonesty, minor violence or simple possession of drugs, who have served custodial sentences, three to three-and-a-half years is appropriate. Those with more serious convictions, including drug-supply offences, do not fall into the category of offender identified in *Afonso*.

In *Wijs* [1998] 2 Cr.App.R. 436, a case concerning the importation and possession of amphetamine with intent to supply the Court of Appeal stated that following conviction for importing amphetamine after a contested trial a custodial sentence will almost invariably be called for, save in exceptional circumstances or where the quantity of the drug is so small as to be compatible only with personal consumption by the importer. The ordinary level of sentence on conviction following a contested trial (and on quantities calculated on the basis of 100 per cent pure amphetamine base) should be:

(1) Up to 500 grammes: up to two years' imprisonment;
(2) More than 500 grammes but less than 2.5 kilos: two–four years' imprisonment;
(3) More than 2.5 kilos but less than 10 kilos: four–seven years' imprisonment;
(4) More than 10 kilos but less than 15 kilos: seven–ten years' imprisonment;
(5) More than 15 kilos: upwards of 10 years' imprisonment, subject to the statutory maximum of 14 years' imprisonment.

The level of sentence for the supply and importation of cannabis remained unchanged during the period when it was reclassified as a Class C drug *Lappalainen* [2005] EWCA Crim 1458 (affirming the decision in *Donovan* [2005] 1 Cr.App.R.(S.) 16, CA). As from January 26, 2009, cannabis has once again been classified as a Class B drug.

Limited guidance in relation to sentencing in cases involving ketamine alone was provided in *Johnson* [2010] 2 Cr.App.R.(S.) 24, CA, (12 months' imprisonment for possession with intent of the equivalent of 612 grammes of pure ketamine with a value of £11,000). See also *Dix* [2011] 1 Cr.App.R.(S.) 45, CA.

C. RESTRICTION OF POSSESSION OF CONTROLLED DRUGS

(1) Definition

Misuse of Drugs Act 1971, s.5

Restriction of possession of controlled drugs

5.—(1) Subject to any regulations under section 7 of this Act for the time being in force, it shall not be lawful for a person to have a controlled drug in his possession. **18-19**

(2) Subject to section 28 of this Act and to subsection (4) below, it is an offence for a person to have a controlled drug in his possession in contravention of subsection (1) above.

(3) Subject to section 28 of this Act, it is an offence for a person to have a controlled drug in his possession, whether lawfully or not, with intent to supply it to another in contravention of section 4(1) of this Act.

(4) In any proceedings for an offence under subsection (2) above in which it is proved that the accused had a controlled drug in his possession, it shall be a defence for him to prove—

(a) that, knowing or suspecting it to be a controlled drug, he took possession of it for the purpose of preventing another from committing or continuing to commit an offence in connection with that drug and that as soon as possible after taking possession of it he took all such steps as were reasonably open to him to destroy the drug or to deliver it into the custody of a person lawfully entitled to take custody of it; or

(b) that, knowing or suspecting it to be a controlled drug, he took possession of it for the purpose of delivering it into the custody of a person lawfully entitled to take custody of it and that as soon as possible after taking possession of it he took all such steps as were reasonably open to him to deliver it into the custody of such a person.

(6) Nothing in subsection (4) or (5) above shall prejudice any defence which it is open to a person charged with an offence under this section to raise apart from that subsection.

(2) Allocation

18–20 This offence is triable either way: s.25 and Sched. 4 to the Act.

The *Consolidated Criminal Practice Direction* (2002), para. V.51.15, states that cases of possession of Class A drugs should be committed for trial unless the amount is small and consistent with only personal use; cases of Class B drugs should be committed for trial when the quantity is substantial. See Appendix F, F–57. No guideline is given in relation to Class C drugs.

Section 25(4) of the 1971 Act also provides that a magistrates' court in England and Wales may try an information for an offence under the 1971 Act if the information was laid at any time within twelve months from the commission of the offence.

(3) Elements of the offence

18–21 The specific defence provided by s.28 of the 1971 Act is also available to a charge under this section (see above).

"Possession" is not defined by the statute, save that "things which a person has in his possession shall be taken to include anything subject to his control which is in the custody of another: s.13(3). Possession requires physical custody of the drug and the intention to possess it: *Warner v. MPC* [1969] 2 A.C. 256. A person does not have possession of something which has been put into his pocket or house without his knowledge. But a mistake as to the precise quality of the substance under the defendant's control does not itself prevent him from being in possession (*e.g.* possession of heroin believing it to be cannabis or aspirin): *Searl v. Randolph* [1972] Crim.L.R. 779, DC. If the drugs are contained inside a package or box then the defendant was in possession of the contents; but the defendant was not in possession if the contents were quite different in kind from what he believed them to be: *McNamara* 87 Cr.App.R. 246, CA. Provided physical custody and knowledge can be proved, the quantity of the drug is not relevant to the issue of possession: *Boyesen* [1982] A.C. 768, HL; *DPP v. Brooks* [1974] A.C. 862.

Where a person in possession of drugs intends to supply them only when he arrives in a foreign country, he commits no offence contrary to s.5(3) of the 1971 Act, given that the presumption against extra-territorial effect applies to the prohibition on supply in s.4(1): *Seymour v. The Queen* [2008] 1 A.C. 713, PC. See also *Hussain (Shabbir)* [2010] 2 Cr.App.R. 11, CA.

The intention to supply must be an intention to supply the thing of which the defendant was in possession. Where a defendant had been in possession of immature cannabis plants, which as yet had no useable flowering heads, the intended supply was a supply of the harvested product of the process of cultivation, not as the plants as they existed and were in his possession at the time to which the charge related. That conclusion should not give cause for concern since the core offence in such a case is the production of cannabis: *R. v. Wright* [2011] 5 *Archbold Review* 1, CA ([2011] EWCA Crim. 1180).

(4) Sentence

It is necessary to draw a distinction between the three different classifications of drugs. When tried summarily, the maximum penalty for an offence under s.5(2) as regards a Class A is six months' imprisonment, a fine not exceeding the prescribed sum, or both. As regards a Class B drug, the maximum penalty is three months' imprisonment, a fine of not more than £3,000 or both, and as regards a Class C drug, three months' imprisonment, a fine of not more than £2,500 or both: *Misuse of Drugs Act* 1971, s.25 and Sched. 4. After commencement of the relevant provisions, the maximum custodial sentence in a magistrates' court will be 12 months' imprisonment: *Criminal Justice Act* 2003, ss.154 and 282. **18–22**

In relation to cases of simple possession of Class A drugs, the starting points set out in the table below are based on a first time offender who was convicted after trial; see the *Magistrates' Court Sentencing Guidelines (2008)*.

STARTING POINTS AND SENTENCING RANGES

Examples of nature of activity	**Starting Point**	**Range**
Possession of a very small quantity of the drug *e.g.* one small wrap or tablet	Band C fine	Band B fine to medium level community order
More than a very small quantity of the drug *e.g.* up to six wraps or tablets	Medium level community order	Low level community order to high level community order
Larger amounts	High level community order	Medium level community order to Crown Court
Possession of drug in prison whether by prisoner or another	Crown Court	Crown Court

AGGRAVATING AND MITIGATING FACTORS

Factors indicating higher culpability 1. offender exercising or acting in position of special responsibility. **Factors indicating greater degree of harm** 1. possession of drug in a public place or school.	

However, following the guideline judgement of *Aramah* (1982) 4 Cr.App.R.(S.) 407 offences involving Class A drugs will rarely be tried summarily. **18–23**

Part III

In *Busby* [2000] 1 Cr.App.R.(S.) 279, the offender pleaded guilty to possessing a Class A substance (Ecstasy) and a Class B drug (amphetamine) in each case with intent to supply. He possessed fourteen Ecstasy tablets and four amphetamine tablets. He admitted that he intended to share the drugs with two friends. His sentence was reduced from nine months to six months' imprisonment by the Court of Appeal. The short custodial sentence was explained by the fact that imprisonment sends out a clear message to others who need to hear the consequences of this kind of offence. In *Att.-Gen.'s Reference (No. 20 of 2002)* [2003] 1 Cr.App.R.(S.) 58 the offender pleaded guilty to possessing Ecstasy with intent to supply. He was found with 24 tablets in his car, and 760 tablets in his bedroom. He admitted he had been selling drugs for a year. He was sentenced to a community punishment and rehabilitation order and ordered to pay £200 prosecution costs. On appeal, this sentence was held to be unduly lenient and given that the offender had already completed his community punishment, a sentence of two years imprisonment was substituted, emphasising the need for custodial sentences in such cases. In *Campbell* (1992) 13 Cr.App.R.(S.) 630, the appellant was convicted of possessing a Class A drug, having been found in possession of 106 capsules each containing amphetamine sulphate and a strip of card impregnated with LSD. He was sentenced to 12 months' imprisonment.

Possession of cannabis with intent to supply is an offence which almost inevitably attracts a custodial sentence, even during that period when it was reclassified as a Class C drug. A six-month custodial sentence was appropriate following conviction of possession of cannabis with intent to supply where the offender's involvement in supply was very limited and he was of previous good character: *Donovan* [2004] EWCA Crim 1237, CA, *per* Gloster J.

18–24 In relation to cases of simple possession of Class B and C drugs, the starting points in the table set out below are based on a first time offender who was convicted after trial; see the Magistrates' Court Sentencing Guidelines (2008).

STARTING POINTS AND SENTENCING RANGES

Examples of nature of activity	Starting Point	Range
Possession of a small amount of Class B drug for personal use	Band B fine	Band A fine to low level community order
Possession of large amount if Class B drug for personal use	Band C fine	Band B fine to 12 weeks custody

AGGRAVATING AND MITIGATING FACTORS

Factors indicating higher culpability	Factors indicating lower culpability
1. offender exercising or acting in position of special responsibility. **Factors indicating greater degree of harm** 1. possession of drugs in a public place or school.	1. possession of Class C rather than Class B drug 2. evidence that use was to help cope with a medical condition.

The *Aramah* guidelines indicate that in cases of simple possession of small amounts of cannabis for personal use, a fine will often be the appropriate penalty, unless the history shows a "persistent flouting of the law", which may render a custodial sentence appropriate. **18–25**

In *Gregory* (1993) 14 Cr.App.R.(S.) 403 the offender pleaded guilty to possessing a Class A drug with intent to supply, possessing a Class A drug, possessing a Class B drug, and permitting premises to be used for smoking opium. G was sentenced to six months' imprisonment for possessing heroin with intent to supply, three months for possessing a Class A drug, three months for possessing a Class B drug, all concurrent, and 15 months' consecutive for allowing premises to be used for smoking opium.

The Court of Appeal held that in relation to Class B drugs, it might be appropriate to pass a non-custodial sentence in respect of an offence of this kind, but any criminal conduct which facilitated the use of a Class A drug must be regarded as serious, even without a commercial motive. It was submitted that G had not corrupted those who used his flat, or profited from them but he had provided the venue in which they could take Class A drugs in comparative safety. However, the sentence of 15 months was considered too long and a sentence of six months was substituted, consecutive to the other sentences. **18–26**

In *Doyle* [1996] 1 Cr.App.R.(S.) 449, the offender pleaded guilty to possession of cannabis with intent to supply and simple possession of cannabis. On a search of his premises the police had found a pot containing five grams of cannabis and a further 380 grams hidden in his garden. He was sentenced to six months' imprisonment. In *Busuttill* [2001] EWCA Crim 627, the defendant pleaded guilty to possession of forty packages of cannabis resin with intent to supply, stating that he was storing them for an associate without payment. He was sentenced to six months' imprisonment.

Supplying drugs to a serving prisoner may result in a more severe penalty. In *Doyle* [1998] 1 Cr.App.R.(S.) 79, CA, the defendant smuggled cannabis to her boyfriend who was serving a prison sentence. She was sentenced to twelve months' imprisonment, the Court stating that in view of the pressing nature of the issue of drug culture in prisons, "six months is no longer the tariff for passing drugs to a prisoner."

D. RESTRICTION OF CULTIVATION OF THE CANNABIS PLANT

(1) Definition

Misuse of Drugs Act 1971, s.6

Restriction of cultivation of cannabis plant

6.—(1) Subject to any regulations under section 7 of this Act for the time being in force, it shall not be lawful for a person to cultivate any plant of the genus Cannabis. **18–27**

(2) Subject to section 28 of this Act, it is an offence to cultivate any such plant in contravention of subsection (1) above.

(2) Allocation

18–28 This offence is triable either way. Section 25(4) of the 1971 Act provides that a magistrates' court in England and Wales may try an information for an offence under the 1971 Act if the information was laid at any time within twelve months from the commission of the offence.

(3) Elements of the offence

18–29 The specific defence provided by s.28 of the 1971 Act is also available to a charge under this section, above.

Authorisation of activities otherwise unlawful under ss.3 to 6

Misuse of Drugs Act 1971, s.7

Authorisation of activities otherwise unlawful under foregoing provisions

18–30 **7.**—(1) The Secretary of State may by regulations—

(a) except from section 3(1)(a) or (b), 4(1)(a) or (b) or 5(1) of this Act such controlled drugs as may be specified in the regulations; and

(b) make such other provision as he thinks fit for the purpose of making it lawful for persons to do things which under any of the following provisions of this Act, that is to say sections 4(1), 5(1) and 6(1), it would otherwise be unlawful for them to do.

(2) Without prejudice to the generality of paragraph (b) of subsection (1) above, regulations under that subsection authorising the doing of any such thing as is mentioned in that paragraph may in particular provide for the doing of that thing to be lawful—

(a) if it is done under and in accordance with the terms of a licence or other authority issued by the Secretary of State and in compliance with any conditions attached thereto; or

(b) if it is done in compliance with such conditions as may be prescribed.

(3) Subject to subsection (4) below, the Secretary of State shall so exercise his power to make regulations under subsection (1) above as to secure—

(a) that it is not unlawful under section 4(1) of this Act for a doctor, dentist, veterinary practitioner or veterinary surgeon, acting in his capacity as such, to prescribe, administer, manufacture, compound or supply a controlled drug, or for a pharmacist or a person lawfully conducting a retail pharmacy business, acting in either case in his capacity as such, to manufacture, compound or supply a controlled drug; and

(b) that it is not unlawful under section 5(1) of this Act for a doctor, dentist, veterinary practitioner, veterinary surgeon, pharmacist or person lawfully conducting a retail pharmacy business to have a controlled drug in his possession for the purpose of acting in his capacity as such.

(4) If in the case of any controlled drug the Secretary of State is of the opinion that it is in the public interest—

(a) for production, supply and possession of that drug to be either wholly unlawful or unlawful except for purposes of research or other special purposes; or

(b) for it to be unlawful for practitioners, pharmacists and persons lawfully conducting retail pharmacy businesses to do in relation to that drug any of the things mentioned in subsection (3) above except under a licence or other authority issued by the Secretary of State,

he may by order designate that drug as a drug to which this subsection applies; and while there is in force an order under this subsection designating a controlled drug as one to which this subsection applies, subsection (3) above shall not apply as regards that drug.

(5) Any order under subsection (4) above may be varied or revoked by a subsequent order thereunder.

(6) The power to make orders under subsection (4) above shall be exercisable by statutory instrument, which shall be subject to annulment in pursuance of a resolution of either House of Parliament.

(7) The Secretary of State shall not make any order under subsection (4) above except after consultation with or on the recommendation of the Advisory Council.

(8) References in this section to a person's "doing" things include references to his having things in his possession.

(9) In its application to Northern Ireland this section shall have effect as if for references to the Secretary of State there were substituted references to the Ministry of Home Affairs for Northern Ireland and as if for subsection (6) there were substituted—

"(6) Any order made under subsection (4) above by the Ministry of Home Affairs for Northern Ireland shall be subject to negative resolution within the meaning of section 41(6) of the *Interpretation Act (Northern Ireland)* 1954 as if it were a statutory instrument within the meaning of that Act."

Misuse of Drugs Regulations 2001 (S.I. 2001 No. 3998)

These regulations, made under s.7, make lawful acts that would otherwise be offences **18–31** under the *Misuse of Drugs Act* 1971. They provide for certain exemptions from the provisions of the 1971 Act, and make provision in relation to prescriptions, records and the furnishing of information concerning controlled drugs and for the supervision of the destruction of such drugs.

(4) Sentence

When tried summarily, the maximum penalty for this offence is six months' imprison- **18–32** ment, a fine not exceeding the prescribed sum, or both: s.25 and Sched. 4. After commencement of the relevant provisions, the maximum sentence in a magistrates' court will be 12 months' imprisonment: *Criminal Justice Act* 2003, ss.154 and 282.

The starting points set out in the table below are based on a first time offender who was convicted after trial; see the *Magistrates' Court Sentencing Guidelines (2008)*.

STARTING POINTS AND SENTENCING RANGES

Examples of nature of activity	**Starting Point**	**Range**
Very small scale cultivation For personal use only, *i.e.* one or two plants	Band C fine	Band B fine to low level community order
Small scale cultivation for personal use and non-commercial supply to small circle of friends	High level community order	Medium level community order to 12 weeks custody
Commercial cultivation	Crown Court	Crown Court

Part III

AGGRAVATING AND MITIGATING FACTORS

Factors indicating higher culpability	Factors indicating lower culpability
1. use of sophisticated growing system; use of sophisticated system of concealment 2. persistent use/cultivation of cannabis.	1. evidence drug used to help with a medical condition 2. original planting carried out by others.
Factors indicating greater degree of harm 1. involvement of vulnerable/young persons.	

18–33 When sentencing for an offence contrary to section 6, a court should recognise the distinction between cultivating cannabis for personal use and cultivating with intent to supply: *Herridge* [2005] EWCA Crim 1410, CA. In *Marsland* (1994) 15 Cr.App.R.(S.) 665 the offender pleaded guilty to producing cannabis. Police officers searching the appellant's premises were shown a room in which 22 mature cannabis plants were growing; the room had been adapted for the purpose. A further 55 cannabis plants in various stages of growth were found in other parts of the house. The appellant claimed that he was producing cannabis solely for his own use, and he was sentenced to nine months' imprisonment.

In cases of large scale commercial cultivation of cannabis, sentences with a starting point of three years are appropriate for those acting as "gardeners"; for those acting as "managers" sentences of three to seven years were appropriate depending on the level of involvement and the value of the drugs. "Organisers" should expect six to seven years. Longer sentences may be appropriate for those who control a number of such operations. These starting points take no account of credit for a guilty plea or for personal mitigation: *Xu* [2008] Crim.L.R. 318, CA.

Where the potential yield from a cannabis factory was particularly great a starting point of eight years was held to be appropriate for an offender who was clearly more than a manager, though not an organiser (five-and-a-half years after a guilty plea): *Wong* [2008] 2 Cr.App.R.(S.) 111, CA.

Where the scale of cultivation is smaller than the industrial production considered in *Xu*, but is intensive, well-planned and resourced, likely to include hydroponic cultivation and artificial lighting, with the object of producing flowering tops that are significantly stronger than imported herbal cannabis and are often called "skunk", the appropriate sentencing ranges following conviction are, (i) where the cultivation genuinely involves no element of supply of any kind, nine to 18 months' imprisonment, depending on the size of the operation and the personal history of the offender; (ii) where the cultivation is for the offender's own use and is not a frankly commercial operation for profit, but will involve supply to others, 18 months' to three years' imprisonment; where an individual comes within this range will depend on, *inter alia*, the scale of the cultivation, the investment made, the number of parties involved, the nature of the likely supply (the term "social supply" is of little use for sentencing purposes because it covers a wide range of activity) and the level of any profit element; a previous history of directly similar offending could take the case above this range; (iii) where the cultivation is a frankly commercial one designed with a view to sale for profit, and whether or not the offender may use a limited quantity of the drug himself, the sentence will usually be somewhat below the *Xu* range because of the smaller size of operation, but is likely to be between three and six years: Auton; Hindle; Vincent; Willis [2011] Crim.L.R. 406, 19, CA ([2011] EWCA Crim. 76). The court added that where the cultivation is accompanied by unlawful abstraction of electricity, often on a substantial scale, that will ordinarily be an aggravating factor.

The guidance in *R. v. Xu* does not deal expressly with those who permit their premises to be used for producing a drug, as opposed to those involved in the actual production. The relative culpability of such a person will depend in part upon the degree to which he was aware of the scale of the operation and the extent to which he was benefiting from involvement in that operation: *R. v. Chan* [2011] 1 Cr.App.R.(S.) 98, CA.

The question of whether cannabis was being produced for the defendant's own use for supply to others is capable of being resolved within the sentencing process, if necessary by a *Newton* hearing. It is unnecessary to add a count of possession with intent to supply in order to determine the purpose for which the cannabis was being produced: *R. v. Wright* [2011] 5 *Archbold Review* 1, CA ([2011] EWCA Crim. 1180).

E. OFFENCES COMMITTED BY OCCUPIERS OF PREMISES

(1) Definition

Misuse of Drugs Act 1971, s.8

Occupiers etc. of premises to be punishable for permitting certain activities to take place there

8. A person commits an offence if, being the occupier or concerned in the management of any premises, he knowingly permits or suffers any of the following activities to take place on those premises, that is to say— **18–34**

(a) producing or attempting to produce a controlled drug in contravention of section 4(1) of this Act;

(b) supplying or attempting to supply a controlled drug to another in contravention of section 4(1) of this Act, or offering to supply a controlled drug to another in contravention of section 4(1);

(c) preparing opium for smoking;

(d) smoking cannabis, cannabis resin or prepared opium.

(2) Allocation

This offence is triable either way. **18–35**

Section 25(4) of the 1971 Act also provides that a magistrates' court in England and Wales may try an information for an offence under the 1971 Act if the information was laid at any time within twelve months from the commission of the offence.

(3) Elements of the offence

The word "occupier" includes those with the requisite degree of control to be able to exclude those who might otherwise use the premises for the forbidden purposes. "Permits" involves an unwillingness to prevent the activity which may be inferred from failure to take reasonable steps (judged objectively) to prevent it. **18–36**

(4) Sentence

When tried summarily, and the offence concerns a Class A or B drug, the maximum penalty is six months' imprisonment, a fine not exceeding the prescribed sum, or both. When the offence concerns a Class C drug, the maximum penalty is three months' imprisonment, a fine not exceeding £2,500 or both: s.25 and Sched. 4. After commencement of the relevant provisions the maximum custodial sentence in a magistrates' court will be 12 months' imprisonment: *Criminal Justice Act* 2003, ss.154 and 282. **18–37**

Part III

In *Coulson* [2001] 1 Cr.App.R.(S.) 121, a sentence of 30 months' imprisonment was upheld in the case of an offender who had allowed his premises to be used for supplying heroin. See also *Setchall* [2002] 1 Cr.App.R.(S.) 76.

Permitting a public house to be used for the smoking of cannabis would normally be substantially more serious than permitting a private house to be used for the same purpose, because it involves drug taking effectively in public and in an environment which makes it seem acceptable so that others may be encouraged to share in it and take it up. Equally important, the use of drugs is frequently accompanied by dealing in drugs: *Lunn* [2009] 1 Cr.App.R.(S) 93, CA (30 months' imprisonment upheld for public house manager).

F. OPIUM: PROHIBITED ACTIVITIES

(1) Definition

Misuse of Drugs Act 1971, s.9

Prohibition of certain activities etc. relating to opium

18–38 **9.** Subject to section 28 of this Act, it is an offence for a person—

(a) to smoke or otherwise use prepared opium; or

(b) to frequent a place used for the purpose of opium smoking; or

(c) to have in his possession—

(i) any pipes or other utensils made or adapted for use in connection with the smoking of opium, being pipes or utensils which have been used by him or with his knowledge and permission in that connection or which he intends to use or permit others to use in that connection; or

(ii) any utensils which have been used by him or with his knowledge and permission in connection with the preparation of opium for smoking.

(2) Allocation

18–39 This offence is triable either way.

(3) Elements of the offence

18–40 "Prepared opium" means opium prepared for smoking and includes dross and any other residues remaining after opium has been smoked: *Misuse of Drugs Act* 1971, s.37(1).

(4) Sentence

18–41 When tried summarily, the maximum penalty for this offence is six months' imprisonment, a fine not exceeding the prescribed sum, or both: s.25 and Sched. 4. After commencement of the relevant provisions, the maximum custodial sentence in a magistrates' court will be 12 months' imprisonment: *Criminal Justice Act* 2003, ss.154 and 282.

G. INCITEMENT

Misuse of Drugs Act 1971, s.19

Attempts etc. to commit offences

18–42 **19.** It is an offence for a person to incite another to commit an offence under any other provision of this Act.

18–43 By s.25(3) of, and Sched. 4 to the 1971 Act, the offence of incitement is triable and punishable in the same way as the substantive offence cited.

H. Participation in Offences Outside the United Kingdom

(1) Definition

Misuse of Drugs Act 1971, s.20

Assisting in or inducing commission outside United Kingdom of offence punishable under a corresponding law

20. A person commits an offence if in the United Kingdom he assists in or induces the commission in any place outside the United Kingdom of an offence punishable under the provisions of a corresponding law in force in that place. **18–44**

(2) Allocation

This offence is triable either way. **18–45**

Section 25(4) of the 1971 Act also provides that a magistrates' court in England and Wales may try an information for an offence under the 1971 Act if the information was laid at any time within 12 months from the commission of the offence.

(3) Elements of the offence

"Assisting" is to be construed as an ordinary English word: *Vickers* (1975) 1 W.L.R. 811. **18–46**

"Corresponding law" is defined in s.36 of the 1971 Act:

Misuse of Drugs Act 1971, s.36

Meaning of "corresponding law", and evidence of certain matters by certificate

36.—(1) In this Act the expression "corresponding law" means a law stated in a certificate purporting to be issued by or on behalf of the government of a country outside the United Kingdom to be a law providing for the control and regulation in that country of the production, supply, use, export and import of drugs and other substances in accordance with the provisions of the Single Convention on Narcotic Drugs signed at New York on 30th March 1961 or a law providing for the control and regulation in that country of the production, supply, use, export and import of dangerous or otherwise harmful drugs in pursuance of any treaty, convention or other agreement or arrangement to which the government of that country and Her Majesty's Government in the United Kingdom are for the time being parties. **18–47**

(2) A statement in any such certificate as aforesaid to the effect that any facts constitute an offence against the law mentioned in the certificate shall be evidence, and in Scotland sufficient evidence, of the matters stated.

(4) Sentence

When tried summarily, the maximum penalty for this offence is six months' imprisonment, a fine not exceeding the prescribed sum, or both: s.25 and Sched. 4. After commencement of the relevant provisions, the maximum custodial sentence in a magistrates' court will be 12 months' imprisonment: *Criminal Justice Act* 2003, ss.154 and 282. **18–48**

This is also a drug trafficking offence: *Drug Trafficking Act* 1994, s.1(3)(b). A minimum custodial sentence of seven years applies to the third Class A drug trafficking offence. A forfeiture order or a confiscation order may also be imposed for a drug trafficking offence.

I. Power to Direct Special Precautions at Certain Premises

(1) Definition

Misuse of Drugs Act 1971, s.11

Power to direct special precautions for safe custody of controlled drugs to be taken at certain premises

11.—(1) Without prejudice to any requirement imposed by regulations made in pursuance **18–49**

of section 10(2)(a) of this Act, the Secretary of State may by notice in writing served on the occupier of any premises on which controlled drugs are or are proposed to be kept give directions as to the taking of precautions or further precautions for the safe custody of any controlled drugs of a description specified in the notice which are kept on those premises.

(2) It is an offence to contravene any directions given under subsection (1) above.

(2) Allocation

18–50 This offence is triable either way.

Section 25(4) of the 1971 Act provides that a magistrates' court in England and Wales may try an information for an offence under the 1971 Act if the information was laid at any time within twelve months from the commission of the offence.

(3) Sentence

18–51 When tried summarily, the maximum penalty is six months' imprisonment, a fine not exceeding the prescribed sum, or both. After commencement of the relevant provisions, the maximum custodial sentence in a magistrates' court will be 12 months' imprisonment: *Criminal Justice Act* 2003, ss.154 and 282.

J. DIRECTION RELATING TO PRESCRIBING BY PRACTITIONERS

(1) Definition

Misuse of Drugs Act 1971, s.12–13

Directions prohibiting prescribing, supply etc. of controlled drugs by practitioners etc. convicted of certain offences

18–52 **12.**—(1) Where a person who is a practitioner or pharmacist has after the coming into operation of this subsection been convicted—

(a) of an offence under this Act or under the *Dangerous Drugs Act 1965* or any enactment repealed by that Act; or

(b) of an offence under section 45, 56 or 304 of the *Customs and Excise Act* 1952 or under section 50, 68 or 170 of the *Customs and Excise Management Act* 1979 in connection with a prohibition of or restriction on importation or exportation of a controlled drug having effect by virtue of section 3 of this Act or which has effect by virtue of any provision contained in or repealed by the *Dangerous Drugs Act* 1965;

(c) of an offence under section 12 or 13 of the *Criminal Justice (International Co-operation) Act* 1990;

the Secretary of State may give a direction under subsection (2) below in respect of that person.

(2) A direction under this subsection in respect of a person shall—

(a) if that person is a practitioner, be a direction prohibiting him from having in his possession, prescribing administering, manufacturing, compounding and supplying and from authorising the administration and supply of such controlled drugs as may be specified in the direction;

(b) if that person is a pharmacist, be a direction prohibiting him from having in his possession, manufacturing, compounding and supplying and from supervising and controlling the manufacture, compounding and supply of such controlled drugs as may be specified in the direction.

(3) The Secretary of State may at any time give a direction cancelling or suspending any direction given by him under subsection (2) above, or cancelling any direction of his under this subsection by which a direction so given is suspended.

(4) The Secretary of State shall cause a copy of any direction given by him under this section to be served on the person to whom it applies, and shall cause notice of any such direction to be published in the London, Edinburgh and Belfast Gazettes.

(5) A direction under this section shall take effect when a copy of it is served on the person to whom it applies.

(6) It is an offence to contravene a direction given under subsection (2) above.

Directions prohibiting prescribing, supply etc. of controlled drugs by practitioners in other cases

18–53 **13.**—(1) In the event of a contravention by a doctor of regulations made in pursuance of paragraph (h) or (i) of section 10(2) of this Act, or of the terms of a licence issued under regulations made in pursuance of the said paragraph (i), the Secretary of State may, subject to and in accordance with section 14 of this Act, give a direction in respect of the doctor concerned prohibiting him from prescribing, administering and supplying and from authorising the administration and supply of such controlled drugs as may be specified in the direction.

(2) If the Secretary of State is of the opinion that a practitioner is or has after the coming into operation of this subsection been prescribing, administering or supplying or authorising the administration or supply of any controlled drugs in an irresponsible manner, the Secretary of State may, subject to and in accordance with section 14 or 15 of this Act, give a direction in respect of the practitioner concerned prohibiting him from prescribing, administering and supplying and from authorising the administration and supply of such controlled drugs as may be specified in the direction.

(3) A contravention such as is mentioned in subsection (1) above does not as such constitute an offence, but it is an offence to contravene a direction given under subsection (1) or (2) above.

(2) Allocation

These offences are triable either way: Sched. 4 to the *Misuse of Drugs Act* 1971. **18–54**

(3) Sentence

When tried summarily, if it is a Class A or B drugs involved the maximum sentence is six months' imprisonment or a fine at level 5 or both. If the drug is Class C the maximum period of imprisonment is three months and a fine of £2,500 or both: see Sched. 4. After commencement of the relevant provisions the maximum custodial sentence will be 12 months: see *CJA* 2003, ss.154 and 282. **18–55**

K. FAILURE TO COMPLY WITH NOTICE REQUIRING INFORMATION RELATING TO PRESCRIBING SUPPLY ETC OF DRUGS

(1) Definition

Misuse of Drugs Act 1971, s.17

Power to obtain information from doctors, pharmacists etc. in certain circumstances

17.—(1) If it appears to the Secretary of State that there exists in any area in Great Britain a social problem caused by the extensive misuse of dangerous or otherwise harmful drugs in that area, he may by notice in writing served on any doctor or pharmacist practising in or in the vicinity of that area, or on any person carrying on a retail pharmacy business within the meaning of the *Medicines Act* 1968 at any premises situated in or in the vicinity of that area, require him to furnish to the Secretary of State, with respect to any such drugs specified in the notice and as regards any period so specified, such particulars as may be so specified relating to the quantities in which and the number and frequency of the occasions on which those drugs— **18–56**

(a) in the case of a doctor, were prescribed, administered or supplied by him;

(b) in the case of a pharmacist, were supplied by him; or

(c) in the case of a person carrying on a retail pharmacy business, were supplied in the course of that business at any premises so situated which may be specified in the notice.

(2) A notice under this section may require any such particulars to be furnished in such manner and within such time as may be specified in the notice and, if served on a pharmacist or person carrying on a retail pharmacy business, may require him to furnish the names and addresses of doctors on whose prescriptions any dangerous or otherwise harmful drugs to which the notice relates were supplied, but shall not require any person to furnish any particulars relating to the identity of any person for or to whom any such drug has been prescribed, administered or supplied.

(3) A person commits an offence if without reasonable excuse (proof of which shall lie on him) he fails to comply with any requirement to which he is subject by virtue of subsection (1) above.

(4) A person commits an offence if in purported compliance with a requirement

Part III

imposed under this section he gives any information which he knows to be false in a material particular or recklessly gives any information which is so false.

(5) In its application to Northern Ireland this section shall have effect as if for the references to Great Britain and the Secretary of State there were substituted respectively references to Northern Ireland and the Ministry of Home Affairs for Northern Ireland.

(2) Allocation

18–57 The offence under s.17(3) is triable summarily; the offence under s.17(4) is triable either way: s.25 and Sched. 4.

(3) Sentence

18–58 The maximum penalty for the offence under s.17(3) is a fine not exceeding level three on the standard scale: s.25 and Sched. 4. When tried summarily, the maximum sentence for an offence under s.17(3) will be a custody plus order and for an offence under s.17(4) will be 12 months' imprisonment: *Criminal Justice Act* 2003, ss.154, 181 and 280–282.

L. MISCELLANEOUS OFFENCES

Misuse of Drugs Act 1971, s.18

Miscellaneous offences

18–59 **18.**—(1) It is an offence for a person to contravene any regulations made under this Act other than regulations made in pursuance of section 10(2)(h) or (i).

(2) It is an offence for a person to contravene a condition or other term of a licence issued under section 3 of this Act or of a licence or other authority issued under regulations made under this Act, not being a licence issued under regulations made in pursuance of section 10(2)(i).

(3) A person commits an offence if, in purported compliance with any obligation to give information to which he is subject under or by virtue of regulations made under this Act, he gives any information which he knows to be false in a material particular or recklessly gives any information which is so false.

(4) A person commits an offence if, for the purpose of obtaining, whether for himself or another, the issue or renewal of a licence or other authority under this Act or under any regulations made under this Act, he—

(a) makes any statement or gives any information which he knows to be false in a material particular or recklessly gives any information which is so false; or

(b) produces or otherwise makes use of any book, record or other document which to his knowledge contains any statement or information which he knows to be false in a material particular.

II. MISCELLANEOUS OFFENCES

A. INTOXICATING SUBSTANCES

(1) Definition

Intoxicating Substances (Supply) Act 1985, s.1

Offence of supply of intoxicating substance

18–60 **1.**—(1) It is an offence for a person to supply or offer to supply a substance other than a controlled drug—

(a) to a person under the age of eighteen whom he knows, or has reasonable cause to believe, to be under that age; or

(b) to a person—

(i) who is acting on behalf of a person under that age; and

(ii) whom he knows, or has reasonable cause to believe, to be so acting,

if he knows or has reasonable cause to believe that the substance is, or its fumes are, likely to be inhaled by the person under the age of eighteen for the purpose of causing intoxication.

(2) In proceedings against any person for an offence under subsection (1) above it is a defence for him to show that at the time he made the supply or offer he was under the age of eighteen and was acting otherwise than in the course or furtherance of a business.

(3) A person guilty of an offence under this section shall be liable on summary conviction to imprisonment for a term not exceeding six months or to a fine not exceeding level 5 on the standard scale, or to both.

(4) In this section "controlled drug" has the same meaning as in the *Misuse of Drugs Act* 1971.

(2) Allocation

This offence is triable summarily only: s.1(3). **18–61**

(3) Sentence

The maximum penalty for this offence is six months' imprisonment of a fine not exceeding level five on the standard scale or both: s.1(3). **18–62**

B. Manufacture or Supply of Scheduled Substances

(1) Definition

Criminal Justice (International Co-operation) Act 1990, s.12

Manufacture and supply of scheduled substances

12.—(1) It is an offence for a person— **18–63**

(a) to manufacture a scheduled substance; or

(b) to supply such a substance to another person,

knowing or suspecting that the substance is to be used in or for the unlawful production of a controlled drug.

(1A) A person does not commit an offence under subsection (1) above if he manufactures or, as the case may be, supplies the scheduled substance with the express consent of a constable.

(2) A person guilty of an offence under subsection (1) above is liable—

(a) on summary conviction, to imprisonment for a term not exceeding six months or a fine not exceeding the statutory maximum or both;

(b) on conviction on indictment, to imprisonment for a term not exceeding fourteen years or a fine or both.

(3) In this section "a controlled drug" has the same meaning as in the *Misuse of Drugs Act* 1971 and "unlawful production of a controlled drug" means the production of such a drug which is unlawful by virtue of section 4(1)(a) of that Act.

(4) In this section and elsewhere in this Part of this Act "a scheduled substance" means a substance for the time being specified in Schedule 2 to this Act.

(5) Her Majesty may by Order in Council amend that Schedule (whether by addition, deletion or transfer from one Table to the other) but—

(a) no such Order shall add any substance to the Schedule unless—

(i) it appears to Her Majesty to be frequently used in or for the unlawful production of a controlled drug; or

(ii) it has been added to the Annex to the Vienna Convention under Article 12 of that Convention; and

(b) no such Order shall be made unless a draft of it has been laid before and approved by a resolution of each House of Parliament.

(2) Allocation

This offence is triable either way, though no proceedings may be instituted without **18–64** the consent of the DPP or the Commissioners of Customs and Excise: *Criminal Justice (International Co-operation) Act* 1990, s.21(2)(a).

(3) Elements of the offence

18–65 Schedule 2 to the 1990 Act specifies what shall be classed as a "scheduled substance".

Criminal Justice (International Co-operation) Act 1990, Sched. 2

SCHEDULE 2

SUBSTANCES USEFUL FOR MANUFACTURING CONTROLLED DRUGS

TABLE I

18–66 *N*-Acetylanthranilic Acid
ephedrine
ergometrine
ergotamine
isosafrole
lysergic Acid
3, 4-Methylene-Dioxyphenyl-2-Propanone
norephedrine
1-Phenyl-2-Propanone
piperonal
pseudoephedrine
safrole

The salts of the substances listed in this Table whenever the existence of such salts is possible.

TABLE II

acetic Anhydride
acetone
anthranilic Acid
ethyl Ether
hydrochloric Acid
methyl Ethyl Ketone (also referred to as 2-Butanone or M.E.K.)
phenylacetic Acid
piperidine
potassium Permanganate
sulphuric Acid
toluene

The salts of the substances listed in this Table except hydrochloric acid and sulphuric acid whenever the existence of such salts is possible.

(4) Sentence

18–67 When tried summarily, the maximum sentence is six months' imprisonment, a fine not exceeding the statutory maximum or both: s.12(2). The offence is classed as a drug trafficking offence (*Drug Trafficking Act* 1994, s.1(3)(d)), hence a minimum custodial sentence of seven years must be imposed for the third commission of the third Class A drug trafficking offence. A forfeiture or confiscation order may also be imposed. After commencement of the relevant provisions, the maximum custodial sentence in a magistrates' court will be 12 months' imprisonment: *Criminal Justice Act* 2003, ss.154 and 282.

C. FAILURE TO COMPLY WITH REGULATIONS MADE UNDER CRIMINAL JUSTICE (INTERNATIONAL CO-OPERATION) ACT 1990

(1) Definition

Criminal Justice (International Co-operation) Act 1990, s.13

Regulations about scheduled substances

13.—(1) The Secretary of State may by regulations make provision— **18–68**

(a) imposing requirements as to the documentation of transactions involving scheduled substances;

(b) requiring the keeping of records and the furnishing of information with respect to such substances;

(c) for the inspection of records kept pursuant to the regulations;

(d) for the labelling of consignments of scheduled substances.

(2) Regulations made by virtue of subsection (1)(b) may, in particular, require—

(a) the notification of the proposed exportation of substances specified in Table I in Schedule 2 to this Act to such countries as may be specified in the regulations; and

(b) the production, in such circumstances as may be so specified, of evidence that the required notification has been given;

and for the purposes of section 68 of the *Customs and Excise Management Act* 1979 (offences relating to exportation of prohibited or restricted goods) any such substance shall be deemed to be exported contrary to a restriction for the time being in force with respect to it under this Act if it is exported without the requisite notification having been given.

(3) Regulations under this section may make different provision in relation to the substances specified in Table I and Table II in Schedule 2 to this Act respectively and in relation to different cases or circumstances.

(4) The power to make regulations under this section shall be exercisable by statutory instrument subject to annulment in pursuance of a resolution of either House of Parliament.

(5) Any person who fails to comply with any requirement imposed by the regulations or, in purported compliance with any such requirement, furnishes information which he knows to be false in a material particular or recklessly furnishes information which is false in a material particular is guilty of an offence and liable—

(a) on summary conviction, to imprisonment for a term not exceeding six months or a fine not exceeding the statutory maximum or both;

(b) on conviction on indictment, to imprisonment for a term not exceeding two years or a fine or both.

(6) No information obtained pursuant to the regulations shall be disclosed except for the purposes of criminal proceedings or of proceedings under the provisions of relating to the confiscation of the proceeds of drug trafficking or corresponding provisions in force in Northern Ireland [or of proceedings under Part 2, 3 or 4 of the *Proceeds of Crime Act* 2002.

(2) Allocation

This offence is triable either way: s.13(5). **18–69**

(3) Elements of the offence

The *Controlled Drugs (Substances Useful for Manufacture) Regulations* 1991 (S.I. 1991 No. 1285) have been made in accordance with s.13. **18–70**

Controlled Drugs (Substances Useful for Manufacture) Regulations 1991, regs. 1–7

1.—(1) These Regulations may be cited as the *Controlled Drugs (Substances Useful for Manufacture) Regulations* 1991 and shall come into force on 1st July 1991.

(2) These Regulations are made under section 2(2) of the 1972 Act and section 13 of the 1990 Act, subject to the following exceptions:

Part III

(a) regulations 3 to 6 are made under section 2(2) of the 1972 Act alone; and
(b) regulation 7 is made under section 13 of the 1990 Act alone.

2. In these Regulations:
'the 1972 Act' means the *European Communities Act* 1972;
'the 1979 Act' means the *Customs and Excise Management Act* 1979;
'the 1990 Act' means the *Criminal Justice (International Co-operation) Act* 1990;
'the Community Regulation' means Council Regulation (EEC) No. 3677/90, and 'operator' has the same meaning as in that Regulation.

3. Subject to regulations 4 and 6 below:
(a) the obligations imposed on operators by Articles 2(2) and (3), 4 and 5 of the Community Regulation and by virtue of regulation 5 below shall be treated as if they were requirements imposed on them by regulations made under section 13(1) of the 1990 Act;

4. In Article 4 of the Community Regulation:
(a) the words "the competent authorities of the Member State" shall be taken as a reference to the Secretary of State;

5.—(1) An operator who is concerned in an export, import or transit operation involving a scheduled substance shall ensure that he has the documentation required by Article 2(1) of the Community Regulation.

In this paragraph, "export", "import", "scheduled substance" and "transit" have the same meanings as in the Community Regulation.

(2) The obligations imposed by Article 2(4) of the Community Regulation shall be complied with by the operator mentioned in paragraph (1) of this regulation, and in that Article the words "the competent authorities" shall be taken as a reference to the Secretary of State.

5A.—(1) An operator who is concerned in an export operation involving a scheduled substance in Category 1 of the Annex to the Community Regulation shall ensure that he has the authorisation required by Article 4 of that Regulation.

(2) An operator who is concerned in an export operation involving a scheduled substance in Category 2 of the Annex to the Community Regulation shall ensure that he has such authorisation as is required by Article 5 of that Regulation.

(3) An operator who is concerned in an export operation involving a scheduled substance in Category 3 of the Annex to the Community Regulation shall ensure that he has such authorisation, if any, as is required by Article 5a of that Regulation.

(4) For the purposes of section 68 of the 1979 Act (offences relating to exportation of prohibited or restricted goods) any scheduled substance shall be deemed to be exported contrary to a restriction for the time being in force with respect to it under these Regulations if it is exported without the requisite authorisation having been obtained.

(5) In this regulation, "export" (except where it occurs in paragraph (4) above) and "scheduled substance" have the same meanings as in the Community Regulation, and in Articles 4, 5 and 5a of the Community Regulation the words "the competent authorities" shall be taken as a reference to the Secretary of State.

5B. An operator who fails to comply with any of the requirements imposed by Article 2a of the Community Regulation is guilty of an offence and liable:
(a) on summary conviction, to imprisonment for a term not exceeding 3 months or a fine not exceeding the statutory maximum or both;
(b) on conviction on indictment, to imprisonment for a term not exceeding two years or a fine or both.

5C.—(1) An operator who fails to comply with any of the requirements imposed by virtue of regulation 5A above is guilty of an offence and liable to the same penalties as an operator who is guilty of an offence under regulation 5B above.

(2) The powers conferred by subsection (1) of section 23 of the *Misuse of Drugs Act* 1971 shall be exercisable also for the purposes of the execution of Articles 4, 5 and 5a of the Community Regulation and subsection (3) of that section (excluding paragraph (a)) shall apply also to the offence under paragraph (1) above, taking references in those subsections to controlled drugs as references to scheduled substances within the meaning of the Community Regulation.

5D. Any reference in regulations 5B and 5C above to an operator who fails to comply with the requirements mentioned in those regulations shall include an operator who, in purported compliance with any such requirement:

(a) furnishes information which he knows to be false in a material particular; or

(b) recklessly furnishes information which is false in a material particular.

6. Where a person is convicted of an offence contrary to section 68 of the 1979 Act [as a result of the application of regulation 5A above,] or section 13(5) of the 1990 Act as a result of the application of regulation 3 above:

(a) section 68(1) of the 1979 Act shall have effect as if after the words 'greater' there were added the words 'but not exceeding the statutory maximum';

(b) section 68(3)(a) of the 1979 Act shall have effect as if after the words 'greater' there were added the words 'but not exceeding the statutory maximum', and for the words '6 months' there were substituted the words '3 months';

(c) section 68(3)(b) of the 1979 Act shall have effect as if for the words '7 years' there were substituted the words '2 years';

(d) section 13(5)(a) of the 1990 Act shall have effect as if for the words '6 months' there were substituted the words '3 months'.

7. A person who produces or supplies a scheduled substance specified in Table 1 in Schedule 2 to the 1990 Act shall:

(a) make a record of each quantity of such scheduled substance produced or supplied by him, as the case may be; and

(b) preserve all records made under this regulation for a period of not less than two years from the end of the calendar year in which the production or supply, as the case may be, took place.

In this regulation, 'produce' and 'supply' have the same meanings as in the *Misuse of Drugs Act* 1971.

Part III

(4) Sentence

When tried summarily, the maximum penalty for this offence is six months' imprisonment, a fine not exceeding the statutory maximum or both: s.13(5). After commencement of the relevant provisions, the maximum custodial sentence able to be imposed in a magistrates' court will be 12 months' imprisonment: *Criminal Justice Act* 2003, ss.154 and 282. **18–71**

D. SHIPS USED FOR ILLICIT TRAFFIC

(1) Definition

Criminal Justice (International Co-operation) Act 1990, s.19

Ships used for illicit traffic

19.—(1) This section applies to a British ship, a ship registered in a state other than the United Kingdom which is a party to the Vienna Convention (a 'Convention state') and a ship not registered in any country or territory. **18–72**

(2) A person is guilty of an offence if on a ship to which this sections applies, wherever it may be, he—

(a) has a controlled drug in his possession; or

(b) is in any way knowingly concerned in the carrying or concealing of a controlled drug on the ship,

knowing or having reasonable grounds to suspect that the drug is intended to be imported or has been exported contrary to section 3(1) of the *Misuse of Drugs Act* 1971 or the law of any state other than the United Kingdom.

(3) A certificate purporting to be issued by or on behalf of the government of any state to the effect that the importation or export of a controlled drug is prohibited by the law of that state shall be evidence, and in Scotland sufficient evidence, of the matters stated.

(4) A person guilty of an offence under this section is liable—

(a) in a case where the controlled drug is a Class A drug—

(i) on summary conviction, to imprisonment for a term not exceeding six months or a fine not exceeding the statutory maximum or both;

(ii) on conviction on indictment, to imprisonment for life or a fine or both;

(b) in a case where the controlled drug is a Class B drug—

(i) on summary conviction, to imprisonment for a term not exceeding six months or a fine not exceeding the statutory maximum or both;

(ii) on conviction on indictment, to imprisonment for a term not exceeding fourteen years or a fine or both;

(c) in a case where the controlled drug is a Class C drug—

(i) on summary conviction, to imprisonment for a term not exceeding three months or a fine not exceeding the statutory maximum or both;

(ii) on conviction on indictment, to imprisonment for a term not exceeding five years or a fine or both.

(5) In this section 'a controlled drug' and the references to controlled drugs of a specified Class have the same meaning as in the said Act of 1971; and an offence under this section shall be included in the offences to which section 28 of that Act (defences) applies.

(2) Allocation

18–73 Each offence is triable either way, though the consent of the DPP or the Director of Revenue and Customs Prosecutions: *Criminal Justice (International Co-operation) Act* 1990, s.21(2)(a). The consent of the Secretary of State of the powers conferred by Sched. 3 is required to institute proceedings when the offence is alleged to have been committed outside the landward limits of the territorial sea of the UK on a ship registered in a state which is party to the Vienna Convention. The *Territorial Waters Jurisdiction Act* 1878, s.3 does not apply to these proceedings: *Criminal Justice (International Co-operation) Act* 1990, s.21(3).

(3) Elements of the offence

Criminal Justice (International Co-operation) Act 1990, s.24

Interpretation of Part II

18–74 **24.**—(1) In this Part of this Act—

'British ship' means a ship registered in the United Kingdom or a colony;

'Convention state' has the meaning given in section 19(1) above;

'scheduled substance' has the meaning given in section 12(4) above;

'ship' includes any vessel used in navigation;

'the territorial sea of the United Kingdom' includes the territorial sea adjacent to any of the Channel Islands, the Isle of Man or any colony;

'the Vienna Convention' means the United Nations Convention against Illicit Traffic in Narcotic Drugs and Psychotropic Substances which was signed in Vienna on 20th December 1988.

(2) Any expression used in this Part of this Act which is also used in the *Drug Trafficking Act* 1994 has the same meaning as in that Act and, in section 22(1), "drug trafficking offences" includes drug trafficking offences within the meaning of the *Criminal Justice (Confiscation) (Northern Ireland) Order* 1990.

(3) In relation to Scotland, any expression used in this Part of this Act which is also used in the *Criminal Justice (Scotland) Act* 1987 has the same meaning as in that Act and 'drug trafficking offence' means an offence to which section 1 of that Act relates.

(4) If in any proceedings under this Part of this Act any question arises whether any country or territory is a state or is a party to the Vienna Convention, a certificate issued by or under the authority of the Secretary of State shall be conclusive evidence on that question.

The defence established by s.28 of the *Misuse of Drugs Act* 1971 applies to this section:s.19(5).

(4) Sentence

18–75 Where the offence committed involves a Class A drug, when tried summarily, the maximum penalty is six months' imprisonment, a fine not exceeding the statutory maximum or both: s.19(4)(a).

Where the offence committed involves a Class B drug, when tried summarily, the maximum penalty is six months' imprisonment, a fine not exceeding the statutory maximum or both: s.19(4)(b).

Where the offence committed involves a Class C drug, when tried summarily, the maximum penalty is three months' imprisonment, a fine not exceeding the statutory maximum or both: s.19(4)(c). After commencement of the relevant provisions, the maximum custodial sentence in a magistrates' court will be 12 months' imprisonment: *Criminal Justice Act* 2003, ss.154 and 282.

E. FAILURE TO PROVIDE A SAMPLE AT A POLICE STATION FOR TESTING

(1) Definition

Police and Criminal Evidence Act 1984, ss.63B, 63C

Testing for presence of Class A drugs

63B.—(1) A sample of urine or a non-intimate sample may be taken from a person in police detention for the purpose of ascertaining whether he has any specified Class A drug in his body if **18–76**

(a) either the arrest condition or the charge condition is met;
(b) both the age condition and the request condition are met; and
(c) the notification condition is met in relation to the arrest condition, the charge condition or the age condition (as the case may be).

(1A) The arrest condition is that the person concerned has been arrested for an offence but has not been charged with that offence and either—

(a) the offence is a trigger offence; or
(b) a police officer of at least the rank of inspector has reasonable grounds for suspecting that the misuse by that person of a specified Class A drug caused or contributed to the offence and has authorised the sample to be taken.

(2) The charge condition is either—

(a) that the person concerned has been charged with a trigger offence; or
(b) that the person concerned has been charged with an offence and a police officer of at least the rank of inspector, who has reasonable grounds for suspecting that the misuse by that person of any specified Class A drug caused or contributed to the offence, has authorised the sample to be taken.

(3) The age condition is—

(a) if the arrest condition is met, that the person concerned has attained the age of 18;
(b) if the charge condition is met, that he has attained the age of 14.

(4) The request condition is that a police officer has requested the person concerned to give the sample.

(4A) The notification condition is that—

(a) the relevant chief officer has been notified by the Secretary of State that appropriate arrangements have been made for the police area as a whole, or for the particular police station, in which the person is in police detention, and
(b) the notice has not been withdrawn.

(4B) For the purposes of subsection (4A) above, appropriate arrangements are arrangements for the taking of samples under this section from whichever of the following is specified in the notification—

(a) persons in respect of whom the arrest condition is met;
(b) persons in respect of whom the charge condition is met;
(c) persons who have not attained the age of 18.

(5) Before requesting the person concerned to give a sample, an officer must—

(a) warn him that if, when so requested, he fails without good cause to do so he may be liable to prosecution, and
(b) in a case within subsection (1A)(b) or (2)(b) above, inform him of the giving of the authorisation and of the grounds in question.

(5A) In the case of a person who has not attained the age of 17—

(a) the making of the request under subsection (4) above;

(b) the giving of the warning and (where applicable) the information under subsection (5) above; and

(c) the taking of the sample,

may not take place except in the presence of an appropriate adult.

(5B) If a sample is taken under this section from a person in respect of whom the arrest condition is met no other sample may be taken from him under this section during the same continuous period of detention but—

(a) if the charge condition is also met in respect of him at any time during that period, the sample must be treated as a sample taken by virtue of the fact that the charge condition is met;

(b) the fact that the sample is to be so treated must be recorded in the person's custody record.

(5C) Despite subsection (1)(a) above, a sample may be taken from a person under this section if—

(a) he was arrested for an offence (the first offence),

(b) the arrest condition is met but the charge condition is not met,

(c) before a sample is taken by virtue of subsection (1) above he would (but for his arrest as mentioned in paragraph (d) below) be required to be released from police detention,

(d) he continues to be in police detention by virtue of his having been arrested for an offence not falling within subsection (1A) above, and

(e) the sample is taken before the end of the period of 24 hours starting with the time when his detention by virtue of his arrest for the first offence began.

(5D) A sample must not be taken from a person under this section if he is detained in a police station unless he has been brought before the custody officer.

(6) A sample may be taken under this section only by a person prescribed by regulations made by the Secretary of State by statutory instrument.

No regulations shall be made under this subsection unless a draft has been laid before, and approved by resolution of, each House of Parliament.

(6A) The Secretary of State may by order made by statutory instrument amend—

(a) paragraph (a) of subsection (3) above, by substituting for the age for the time being specified a different age specified in the order, or different ages so specified for different police areas so specified;

(b) paragraph (b) of that subsection, by substituting for the age for the time being specified a different age specified in the order.

(6B) A statutory instrument containing an order under subsection (6A) above shall not be made unless a draft of the instrument has been laid before, and approved by a resolution of, each House of Parliament.

(7) Information obtained from a sample taken under this section may be disclosed—

(a) for the purpose of informing any decision about granting bail in criminal proceedings (within the meaning of the *Bail Act* 1976) to the person concerned;

(aa) for the purpose of informing any decision about the giving of a conditional caution under Part 3 of the *Criminal Justice Act* 2003 to the person concerned;

(b) where the person concerned is in police detention or is remanded in or committed to custody by an order of a court or has been granted such bail, for the purpose of informing any decision about his supervision;

(c) where the person concerned is convicted of an offence, for the purpose of informing any decision about the appropriate sentence to be passed by a court and any decision about his supervision or release;

(ca) for the purpose of an assessment which the person concerned is required to attend by virtue of section 9(2) or 10(2) of the *Drugs Act* 2005;

(cb) for the purpose of proceedings against the person concerned for an offence under section 12(3) or 14(3) of that Act;

(d) for the purpose of ensuring that appropriate advice and treatment is made available to the person concerned.

(8) A person who fails without good cause to give any sample which may be taken from him under this section shall be guilty of an offence.

(10) In this section—

"appropriate adult", in relation to a person who has not attained the age of 17, means—

(a) his parent or guardian or, if he is in the care of a local authority or voluntary organisation, a person representing that authority or organisation; or

(b) a social worker of a local authority social services department; or

(c) if no person falling within paragraph (a) or (b) is available, any responsible person aged 18 or over who is not a police officer or a person employed by the police;

"relevant chief officer" means—

(a) in relation to a police area, the chief officer of police of the police force for that police area; or

(b) in relation to a police station, the chief officer of police of the police force for the police area in which the police station is situated.

[This section is printed as amended by the *Drugs Act* 2005, s.7 and Sched. 2, para. 1.]

Testing for presence of Class A drugs: supplementary

63C.—(1) A person guilty of an offence under section 63B above shall be liable on summary conviction to imprisonment for a term not exceeding three months, or to a fine not exceeding level 4 on the standard scale, or to both. **18–77**

(2) A police officer may give an authorisation under section 63B above orally or in writing but, if he gives it orally, he shall confirm it in writing as soon as is practicable.

(3) If a sample is taken under section 63B above by virtue of an authorisation, the authorisation and the grounds for the suspicion shall be recorded as soon as is practicable after the sample is taken.

(4) If the sample is taken from a person detained at a police station, the matters required to be recorded by subsection (3) above shall be recorded in his custody record.

(5) Subsections (11) and (12) of section 62 above apply for the purposes of section 63B above as they do for the purposes of that section; and section 63B above does not prejudice the generality of sections 62 and 63 above.

(6) In section 63B above—

"Class A drug" and "misuse" have the same meanings as in the *Misuse of Drugs Act* 1971;

"specified" (in relation to a Class A drug) and "trigger offence" have the same meanings as in Part III of the *Criminal Justice and Court Services Act* 2000.

Part III

(2) Allocation

This offence is triable summarily. It was introduced as an amendment to *PACE* 1984 by s.57 of the *Criminal Justice and Court Services Act* 2000. **18–78**

(3) Elements of the offence

Following the amendments introduced by s.7 of the *Drugs Act* 2005, the conditions for testing are as follows: **18–79**

1. The person has been arrested for an offence that is either a trigger offence or a police officer of at least the rank of inspector has reasonable grounds for suspecting that the misuse by that person of a specified Class A drug caused or contributed to the offence and has authorised the sample to be taken (the "arrest condition") OR that the person concerned has been charged with an offence that is either a trigger offence or a police officer of at least the rank of inspector, who has reasonable grounds for suspecting that the misuse by that person of any specified Class A drug caused or contributed to the offence, has authorised the sample to be taken (the "charge condition"); and
2. In the case of a person satisfying the arrest condition, they have reached the age of 18, and in the case of a person satisfying the charge condition, they have reached the age of 14; and

3. The police officer has requested the person to give the sample; and
4. The relevant chief officer has been notified by the Secretary of State that appropriate arrangements for the taking of samples have been made for the police area as a whole, or for the particular police station, in which the person is in police detention, and that notice has not been withdrawn.

The police officer must warn the detainee of the consequences of failing to give a sample, and where an inspector has authorised the sample, the police officer must provide information regarding this authorisation and its grounds: *Police and Criminal Evidence Act* 1984, s.63B(5).

In the case of individuals under 17, an appropriate adult must be present when the request for a sample is made, the warning about the consequences of failing to give a sample or the information required under subs. (5) is given and when the sample is taken: *Police and Criminal Evidence Act* 1984, s.63B(5A).

A sample may also be taken from a person if he was arrested for an offence that satisfies the arrest condition but not the charge condition and before a sample is taken he would, but for his arrest for an offence not falling within subs. (1A), be required to be released from police detention, if the sample is taken within 24 hours of his detention following arrest for the offence that satisfies the arrest conditions: *Police and Criminal Evidence Act* 1984, s.63B(5C).

(4) Sentence

18–80 Maximum penalty is three months' imprisonment, or to fine not exceeding level 4 on the standard scale, or both.

The starting points set out in the table below are based on a first time offender who was convicted after trial; see the *Magistrates' Court Sentencing Guidelines* (2008).

STARTING POINTS AND SENTENCING RANGES

Examples of nature of activity	Starting Point	Range
Refusal to provide sample without good cause when required by police officer	Medium level community order	Band C fine to high level community order

AGGRAVATING AND MITIGATING FACTORS

Factors indicating greater degree of harm	Factors indicating lower culpability
1. threats or abuse to staff.	1. subsequent voluntary contact with drug workers 2. subsequent compliance with testing on arrest/charge.

III. ARREST REFERRAL SCHEMES

18–81 In addition to the sentencing options available for offenders convicted of drug-related offences, arrest referral schemes employ drug workers to make contact with arrestees in police cells and/or magistrates' courts to assess and refer drug-using offenders to treatment services. These schemes offer a good opportunity to identify drug-using offenders and help them reduce their drug use. Involvement is voluntary and is not an alternative to prosecution or due process.

Home Office guidelines specify that all adult arrestees should be offered the opportunity to see an arrest referral worker as part of the custody suite booking-in procedure (Home Office Drugs Prevention Advisory Service (1999) *Drugs interventions in the Criminal Justice System: guidance manual*). Beyond such guidelines, the operation of local schemes has been left broadly to the service providers' discretion. There is therefore considerable variety in practices across areas, and schemes depend on what services are available locally.

The *Drugs Act* 2005 enables police officers to require an individual who has tested positive for Class A drugs at the police station to attend an initial assessment with a suitably qualified person to determine whether they are dependent on or have a propensity to misuse any specified Class A drug; whether they might benefit from further assessment or treatment or to provide advice on what types of treatment are available: *Drugs Act* 2005, s.9.

Section 12 of the *Drugs Act* 2005 makes it an offence to fail to attend this appointment, or fail to stay for the duration of the appointment. This offence is triable summarily and has a maximum penalty of 51 weeks' imprisonment or a fine not exceeding level 4 on the standard scale: *Drugs Act* 2005, s.12(4). The results of these tests may also be used to inform bail decisions.

The starting points set out in the table below are based on a first time offender who was convicted after trial; see the *Magistrates' Sentencing Guidelines* (2008).

STARTING POINTS AND SENTENCING RANGES

Examples of nature of activity	**Starting Point**	**Range**
Failure to attend at the appointed place and time	Medium level community order	Band C fine to high level community order

AGGRAVATING AND MITIGATING FACTORS

Factors indicating greater degree of harm	**Factors indicating lower degree of culpability**
1. threats or abuse to assessor or other staff.	1. offender turns up but at wrong place and time or fails to remain for duration of appointment 2. subsequent voluntary contact to rearrange appointment.

Drugs Act 2005, ss.9, 11–12, 15–19

Initial assessment following testing for presence of Class A drugs

9.—(1) This section applies if— **18–82**

(a) a sample is taken under section 63B of *PACE* (testing for presence of Class A drug) from a person detained at a police station,

(b) an analysis of the sample reveals that a specified Class A drug may be present in the person's body,

(c) the age condition is met, and

(d) the notification condition is met.

(2) A police officer may, at any time before the person is released from detention at the police station, require him to attend an initial assessment and remain for its duration.

(3) An initial assessment is an appointment with a suitably qualified person (an "initial assessor")—

(a) for the purpose of establishing whether the person is dependent upon or has a propensity to misuse any specified Class A drug,

(b) if the initial assessor thinks that he has such a dependency or propensity, for the purpose of establishing whether he might benefit from further assessment, or from assistance or treatment (or both), in connection with the dependency or propensity, and

(c) if the initial assessor thinks that he might benefit from such assistance or treatment (or both), for the purpose of providing him with advice, including an explanation of the types of assistance or treatment (or both) which are available.

(4) The age condition is met if the person has attained the age of 18 or such different age as the Secretary of State may by order made by statutory instrument specify for the purposes of this section.

(5) In relation to a person ("A") who has attained the age of 18, the notification condition is met if—

(a) the relevant chief officer has been notified by the Secretary of State that arrangements for conducting initial assessments for persons who have attained the age of 18 have been made for persons from whom samples have been taken (under section 63B of *PACE*) at the police station in which A is detained, and

(b) the notice has not been withdrawn.

(6) In relation to a person ("C") who is of an age which is less than 18, the notification condition is met if—

(a) the relevant chief officer has been notified by the Secretary of State that arrangements for conducting initial assessments for persons of that age have been made for persons from whom samples have been taken (under section 63B of *PACE*) at the police station in which C is detained, and

(b) the notice has not been withdrawn.

(7) In subsections (5) and (6), "relevant chief officer" means the chief officer of police of the police force for the police area in which the police station is situated.

Requirements under sections 9 and 10: supplemental

18–83 **11.**—(1) This section applies if a person is required to attend an initial assessment and remain for its duration by virtue of section 9(2).

(2) A police officer must—

(a) inform the person of the time when, and the place at which, the initial assessment is to take place, and

(b) explain that this information will be confirmed in writing.

(3) A police officer must warn the person that he may be liable to prosecution if he fails without good cause to attend the initial assessment and remain for its duration.

(4) If the person is also required to attend a follow-up assessment and remain for its duration by virtue of section 10(2), a police officer must also warn the person that he may be liable to prosecution if he fails without good cause to attend the follow-up assessment and remain for its duration.

(5) A police officer must give the person notice in writing which—

(a) confirms that he is required to attend and remain for the duration of an initial assessment or both an initial assessment and a follow-up assessment (as the case may be),

(b) confirms the information given in pursuance of subsection (2), and

(c) repeats the warning given in pursuance of subsection (3) and any warning given in pursuance of subsection (4).

(6) The duties imposed by subsections (2) to (5) must be discharged before the person is released from detention at the police station.

(7) A record must be made, as part of the person's custody record, of—
(a) the requirement imposed on him by virtue of section 9(2),
(b) any requirement imposed on him by virtue of section 10(2),
(c) the information and explanation given to him in pursuance of subsection (2) above,
(d) the warning given to him in pursuance of subsection (3) above and any warning given to him in pursuance of subsection (4) above, and
(e) the notice given to him in pursuance of subsection (5) above.

(8) If a person is given a notice in pursuance of subsection (5), a police officer or a suitably qualified person may give the person a further notice in writing which—
(a) informs the person of any change to the time when, or to the place at which, the initial assessment is to take place, and
(b) repeats the warning given in pursuance of subsection (3) and any warning given in pursuance of subsection (4).

Attendance at initial assessment

12.—(1) This section applies if a person is required to attend an initial assessment and remain for its duration by virtue of section 9(2). **18–84**

(2) The initial assessor must inform a police officer or a police support officer if the person—
(a) fails to attend the initial assessment at the specified time and place, or
(b) attends the assessment at the specified time and place but fails to remain for its duration.

(3) A person is guilty of an offence if without good cause—
(a) he fails to attend an initial assessment at the specified time and place, or
(b) he attends the assessment at the specified time and place but fails to remain for its duration.

(4) A person who is guilty of an offence under subsection (3) is liable on summary conviction to imprisonment for a term not exceeding 51 weeks, or to a fine not exceeding level 4 on the standard scale, or to both.

(5) If a person fails to attend an initial assessment at the specified time and place, any requirement imposed on him by virtue of section 10(2) ceases to have effect.

(6) In this section—
(a) the specified time, in relation to the person concerned, is the time specified in the notice given to him in pursuance of subsection (5) of section 11 or, if a further notice specifying a different time has been given to him in pursuance of subsection (8) of that section, the time specified in that notice, and
(b) the specified place, in relation to the person concerned, is the place specified in the notice given to him in pursuance of subsection (5) of section 11 or, if a further notice specifying a different place has been given to him in pursuance of subsection (8) of that section, the place specified in that notice.

(7) In relation to an offence committed before the commencement of section 281(5) of the *Criminal Justice Act* 2003 (alteration of penalties for summary offences), the reference in subsection (4) to 51 weeks is to be read as a reference to 3 months.

Disclosure of information about assessments

15.—(1) An initial assessor may disclose information obtained as a result of an initial assessment to any of the following— **18–85**
(a) a person who is involved in the conduct of the assessment;
(b) a person who is or may be involved in the conduct of any follow-up assessment.

(2) A follow-up assessor may disclose information obtained as a result of a follow-up assessment to a person who is involved in the conduct of the assessment.

(3) Subject to subsections (1) and (2), information obtained as a result of an initial or a follow-up assessment may not be disclosed by any person without the written consent of the person to whom the assessment relates.

(4) Nothing in this section affects the operation of section 17(4).

Samples submitted for further analysis

16.—(1) A requirement imposed on a person by virtue of section 9(2) or 10(2) ceases to have effect if at any time before he has fully complied with the requirement— **18–86**

Part III

(a) a police officer makes arrangements for a further analysis of the sample taken from him as mentioned in section 9(1)(a), and

(b) the analysis does not reveal that a specified Class A drug was present in the person's body.

(2) If a requirement ceases to have effect by virtue of subsection (1), a police officer must so inform the person concerned.

(3) Nothing in subsection (1) affects the validity of anything done in connection with the requirement before it ceases to have effect.

(4) If a person fails to attend an assessment which he is required to attend by virtue of section 9(2) or fails to remain for the duration of such an assessment but, at any time after his failure, the requirement ceases to have effect by virtue of subsection (1) above—

(a) no proceedings for an offence under section 12(3) may be brought against him, and

(b) if any such proceedings were commenced before the requirement ceased to have effect, those proceedings must be discontinued.

(5) If a person fails to attend an assessment which he is required to attend by virtue of section 10(2) or fails to remain for the duration of such an assessment but, at any time after his failure, the requirement ceases to have effect by virtue of subsection (1) above—

(a) no proceedings for an offence under section 14(3) may be brought against him, and

(b) if any such proceedings were commenced before the requirement ceased to have effect, those proceedings must be discontinued.

Relationship with Bail Act 1976 etc.

18–87 **17.**—(1) A requirement imposed on a person by virtue of section 9(2) or 10(2) ceases to have effect if at any time before he has fully complied with the requirement—

(a) he is charged with the related offence, and

(b) a court imposes on him a condition of bail under section 3(6D) of the *Bail Act* 1976 (duty to impose condition to undergo relevant assessment etc.).

(2) For the purposes of section 3(6D) of the 1976 Act, a relevant assessment (within the meaning of that Act) is to be treated as having been carried out if—

(a) a person attends an initial assessment and remains for its duration, and

(b) the initial assessor is satisfied that the initial assessment fulfilled the purposes of a relevant assessment.

(3) For the purposes of paragraph 6B(2)(b) of Schedule 1 to the 1976 Act (exceptions to right to bail for drug users in certain areas), a person is to be treated as having undergone a relevant assessment (within the meaning of that Act) if—

(a) the person attends an initial assessment and remains for its duration, and

(b) the initial assessor is satisfied that the initial assessment fulfilled the purposes of a relevant assessment.

(4) An initial assessor may disclose information relating to an initial assessment for the purpose of enabling a court considering an application for bail by the person concerned to determine whether subsection (2) or (3) applies.

(5) Nothing in subsection (1) affects—

(a) the validity of anything done in connection with the requirement before it ceases to have effect, or

(b) any liability which the person may have for an offence under section 12(3) or 14(3) committed before the requirement ceases to have effect.

(6) In subsection (1), "the related offence" is the offence in respect of which the condition specified in subsection (1A) or (2) of section 63B of *PACE* is satisfied in relation to the taking of the sample mentioned in section 9(1)(a) of this Act.

Orders under this Part and guidance

18–88 **18.**—(1) A statutory instrument containing an order under section 9(4) or 10(5) must not be made unless a draft of the instrument has been laid before, and approved by a resolution of, each House of Parliament.

(2) Any such order may—

(a) make different provision for different police areas;

(b) make such provision as the Secretary of State considers appropriate in connection with requiring persons who have not attained the age of 18 to attend and remain for the duration of an initial assessment or a follow-up assessment (as the case may be), including provision amending this Part.

(3) In exercising any functions conferred by this Part, a police officer and a suitably qualified person must have regard to any guidance issued by the Secretary of State for the purposes of this Part.

Interpretation

19.—(1) This section applies for the purposes of this Part. **18–89**

(2) "Class A drug" and "misuse" have the same meanings as in the *Misuse of Drugs Act* 1971.

(3) "Specified", in relation to a Class A drug, has the same meaning as in Part 3 of the *Criminal Justice and Court Services Act* 2000.

(4) "Initial assessment" and "initial assessor" must be construed in accordance with section 9(3).

(5) "Follow-up assessment" and "follow-up assessor" must be construed in accordance with section 10(3).

(6) "Suitably qualified person" means a person who has such qualifications or experience as are from time to time specified by the Secretary of State for the purposes of this Part.

(7) "Police support officer" means a person who is employed by a police authority under section 15(1) of the *Police Act* 1996 and who is under the direction and control of the chief officer of police of the police force maintained by that authority.

(8) "PACE" means the *Police and Criminal Evidence Act* 1984.

tion with consulting persons who have not attained the age of [illegible] [illegible] the adoption of [illegible] [illegible] as the [illegible]

[illegible]

[illegible]

[illegible]

(3) [illegible]

(5) [illegible]

[illegible] the Paper [illegible]

Chapter 19

REVENUE AND CUSTOMS OFFENCES

I. INTRODUCTION

A. Customs and Excise Management Act 1979

(1) Definitions

Customs and Excise Management Act 1979, s.1

Interpretation

1.—(1) In this Act, unless the context otherwise requires— **19–1**

"aerodrome" means any area of land or water designed, equipped, set apart of commonly used for affording facilities for the landing and departure of aircraft;

"approved wharf" has the meaning given by section 20 section 20A below;

"armed forces" means the Royal Navy, the Royal Marines, the regular army and the regular air force, and any reserve or auxiliary force of any of those services which has been called out on permanent service, or embodied;

"assigned matter" means any matter in relation to which the Commissioners, or officers of Revenue and Customs, have a power or duty;

"boarding station" means a boarding station for the time being appointed under section 19 below;

"boundary" means the land boundary of Northern Ireland;

"British ship" means a British ship within the meaning of the *Merchant Shipping Act* 1894, *British Nationality Act* 1948, *Merchant Shipping Act* 1995;

"claimant" , in relation to proceedings for the condemnation of any thing as being forfeited, means a person claiming that the thing is not liable to forfeiture;

"coasting ship" has the meaning given by section 69 below;

"commander", in relation to an aircraft, includes any person having or taking the charge or command of the aircraft;

"the Commissioners" means the Commissioners for Her Majesty's Revenue and Customs;

"Community transit goods"—

(a) in relation to imported goods, means —

(i) goods which have been imported under the internal or external

Community transit procedure for transit through the United Kingdom with a view to exportation where the importation was and the transit and exportation are to be part of one Community transit operation; or

(ii) goods which have, at the port or airport at which they were imported, been placed under the internal or external Community transit procedure for transit through the United Kingdom with a view to exportation where the transit and exportation are to be part of one Community transit operation;

(b) in relation to goods for exportation, means—

(i) goods which have been imported as mentioned in paragraph (a)(i) of this definition and are to be exported as part of the Community transit operation in the course of which they were imported; or

(ii) goods which have, under the internal or external Community transit procedure, transited the United Kingdom from the port or airport at which they were imported and are to be exported as part of the Community transit operation which commenced at that port or airport and for the purposes of paragraph (a)(i) above the Isle of Man shall be treated as if it were part of the United Kingdom;

"container" includes any bundle or package and any baggage, box, cask or other receptacle whatsoever;

"the customs and excise Acts" means the Customs and Excise Acts 1979 and any other enactment for the time being in force relating to customs or excise;

"the Customs and Excise Acts 1979" means —

this Act,
the *Customs and Excise Duties (General Reliefs) Act* 1979,
the *Alcoholic Liquor Duties Act* 1979,
the *Hydrocarbon Oil Duties Act* 1979, and
the *Tobacco Products Duty Act* 1979;

"customs and excise airport" has the meaning given by section 21(7) below;

"customs and excise station" has the meaning given by section 26 below;

"designation order" has the meaning given by section 100A(5);

"drawback goods" means goods in the case of which a claim for drawback has been or is to be made;

"dutiable goods", except in the expression "dutiable or restricted goods", means goods of a class or description subject to any duty of customs or excise, whether or not those goods are in fact chargeable with that duty, and whether or not that duty has been paid thereon;

"dutiable or restricted goods" has the meaning given by section 52 below;

"examination station" has the meaning given by section 22 section 22A below;

"excise duty point" has the meaning given by section 1 of the *Finance (No. 2) Act* 1992;

"excise licence trade" means , subject to subsection (5) below, a trade or business for the carrying on of which an excise licence is required;

"excise warehouse" means a place of security approved by the Commissioners under subsection (1) (whether or not it is also approved under subsection (2)) of section 92 below, and, except in that section, also includes a distiller's warehouse;

"exporter", in relation to goods for exportation or for use as stores, includes the shipper of the goods and any person performing in relation to an aircraft functions corresponding with those of a shipper;

"free zone" has the meaning given by section 100A(2);

"free zone goods" are goods which are within a free zone;

"goods" includes stores and baggage;

"holiday" , in relation to any part of the United Kingdom, means any day that is a bank holiday in that part of the United Kingdom under the *Banking and Financial Dealings Act* 1971, Christmas Day, Good Friday and the day appointed for the purposes of customs and excise for the celebration of Her Majesty's birthday;

"hovercraft" means a hovercraft within the meaning of the *Hovercraft Act* 1968;

"importer" , in relation to any goods at any time between their importation and the time when they are delivered out of charge, includes any owner or other person for the time being possessed of or beneficially interested in the goods and, in relation to goods imported by means of a pipe-line, includes the owner of the pipe-line;

"justice" and "justice of the peace" in Scotland includes a sheriff and in Northern Ireland, in relation to any powers and duties which can under any enactment for the time being in force be exercised and performed only by a resident magistrate, means a resident magistrate;

"land" and "landing", in relation to aircraft, include alighting on water;

"law officer of the Crown" means the Attorney General or for the purpose of criminal proceedings in Scotland, the Lord Advocate or, for the purpose of civil proceedings in Scotland, the appropriate Law Officer within the meaning of section 4A of the *Crown Suits (Scotland) Act* 1857 or in Northern Ireland the Attorney General for Northern Ireland;

"licence year" , in relation to an excise licence issuable annually, means the period of 12 months ending on the date on which that licence expires in any year;

"master", in relation to a ship, includes any person having or taking the charge or command of the ship;

"night" means the period between 11 pm and 5 am;

"occupier" , in relation to any bonded premises, includes any person who has given security to the Crown in respect of those premises;

"officer" means , subject to section 8(2) below, a person commissioned by the Commissioners;

"owner", in relation to an aircraft, includes the operator of the aircraft; "owner" , in relation to a pipe-line, means (except in the case of a pipe-line vested in the Crown which in pursuance of arrangements in that behalf is operated by another) the person in whom the line is vested and, in the said excepted case, means the person operating the line;

"perfect entry" means an entry made in accordance with regulation 5 of the *Customs Controls on Importation of Goods Regulations* 1991 or warehousing regulations as the case may require;

"pipe-line" has the meaning given by section 65 of the *Pipe-lines Act* 1962 (that Act being taken, for the purposes of this definition, to extend to Northern Ireland);

"port" means a port appointed by the Commissioners under section 19 below;

"prescribed area" means such an area in Northern Ireland adjoining the boundary as the Commissioners may by regulations prescribe;

"prescribed sum", in relation to the penalty provided for an offence, has the meaning given by section 171(2) below;

"prohibited or restricted goods" means goods of a class or description of which the importation, exportation or carriage coastwise is for the time being prohibited or restricted under or by virtue of any enactment;

"proper", in relation to the person by, with or to whom, or the place at which, anything is to be done, means the person or place appointed or authorised in that behalf by the Commissioners;

"proprietor", in relation to any goods, includes any owner, importer, exporter, shipping or other person for the time being possessed of or beneficially interested in those goods;

"Queen's warehouse" means any place provided by the Crown or appointed by the Commissioners for the deposit of goods for security thereof and of the duties chargeable thereon;

"registered excise dealer and shipper" means a revenue trader approved and registered by the Commissioners under section 100G below;

"registered excise dealers and shippers regulations" means regulations under section 100G below;

"representative", in relation to any person from whom the Commissioners assess an amount as being excise duty due, means his personal representative, trustee in bankruptcy or interim or permanent trustee, any receiver or liquidator appointed in relation to him or any of his property or any other person acting in a representative capacity in relation to him;

"the revenue trade provisions of the customs and excise Acts" means —

(a) the provisions of the customs and excise Acts relating to the protection, security, collection or management of the revenues derived from the duties of excise on goods produced or manufactured in the United Kingdom;

(b) the provisions of the customs and excise Acts relating to any activity or facility for the carrying on or provision of which an excise licence is required;
(c) the provisions of the *Betting and Gaming Duties Act* 1972 (so far as not included in paragraph (b) above); and
(d) the provisions of Chapter II of Part I of the *Finance Act* 1993;
(e) the provisions of sections 10 to 15 of, and Schedule 1 to, the *Finance Act* 1997;

"revenue trader" means —
(a) any person carrying on a trade or business subject to any of the revenue trade provisions of the customs and excise Acts, and; or which consists of or includes—
(i) the buying, selling, importation, exportation, dealing in or handling of any goods of a class or description which is subject to a duty of excise (whether or not duty is chargeable on the goods);
(ia) the buying, selling, importation, exportation, dealing in or handling of tickets or chances on the taking of which lottery duty is or will be chargeable;
(ib) being (within the meaning of sections 10 to 15 of the *Finance Act* 1997 the provider of any premises for gaming;
(ic) the organisation, management or promotion of *Gaming Act* 1968 Betting, Gaming, Lotteries and Amusements (Northern Ireland) Order 1985gaming within the meaning of the *Betting and Gaming Duties Act* 1981 (see section 33(1)), or
(ii) the financing or facilitation of any such transactions or activities as are mentioned in sub-paragraph (i), (ia), (ib) or (ic) above,

whether or not that trade or business is an excise licence trade, and;
(b) any person who is a wholesaler or an occupier of an excise warehouse (so far as not included in paragraph (a) above), and includes a registered club;

"ship" and "vessel" include any boat or other vessel whatsoever (and, to the extent provided in section 2 below, any hovercraft);

"shipment" includes loading into an aircraft, and "shipped" and cognate expressions shall be construed accordingly;

"stores" means , subject to subsection (4) below, goods for use in a ship or aircraft and includes fuel and spare parts and other articles of equipment, whether or not for immediate fitting;

"tons register" means the tons of a ship's net tonnage as ascertained and registered according to the tonnage regulations of the *Merchant Shipping Act* 1894 *Merchant Shipping Act* 1995 or, in the case of a ship which is not registered under that Act, ascertained in like manner as if it were to be so registered;

"transit goods", except in the expression "Community transit goods", means imported goods entered on importation for transit or transhipment;

"transit or transhipment" , in relation to the entry of goods, means transit through the United Kingdom or transhipment with a view to the re-exportation of the goods in question or transhipment of those goods for use as stores;

"transit shed" has the meaning given by section 25 section 25A below;

"tribunal" means the First-tier Tribunal or, where determined by or under Tribunal Procedure Rules, the Upper Tribunal;

"United Kingdom waters" means any waters (including inland waters) within the seaward limits of the territorial sea of the United Kingdom;

"vehicle" includes a railway vehicle;

"victualling warehouse" means a place of security approved by the Commissioners under subsection (2) (whether or not it is also a place approved under subsection (1) of section 92 below).

"warehouse", except in the expressions "Queen's warehouse" and "distiller's warehouse", means a place of security approved by the Commissioners under subsection (1) or (2) or subsections (1) and (2) of section 92 below and, except in that section, also includes a distiller's warehouse; and "warehoused" and cognate expressions shall, subject to subsection (4) of that section and any regulations made by virtue of section 93(2)(da)(i) or (ee) or (4) below, be construed accordingly;

"warehousing regulations" means regulations under section 93 below.

(2) This Act and the other Acts included in the Customs and Excise Acts 1979 shall be construed as one Act but where a provision of this Act refers to this Act that reference is not to be construed as including a reference to any of the others.

(3) Any expression used in this Act or in any instrument made under this Act to which a meaning is given by any other Act included in the Customs and Excise Acts 1979 has, except where the context otherwise requires, the same meaning in this Act or any such instrument as in that Act; and for ease of reference the Table below indicates the expressions used in this Act to which a meaning is given by any other such Act—

Alcoholic Liquor Duties Act 1979

"beer"
"brewer" and "registered brewer"
"cider"
"compounder"
"distiller"
"distiller's warehouse"
"dutiable alcoholic liquor"
"licensed", in relation to producers of wine or made-wine
"made-wine"
"producer of made-wine"
"producer of wine"
"proof"
"rectifier"
"registered club"
"spirits"
"wholesaler"
"wine"

Hydrocarbon Oil Duties Act 1979

"rebate"
"refinery"

Tobacco Products Duty Act 1979

"tobacco products"

(4) Goods for use in a ship or aircraft as merchandise for sale to persons carried in the ship or aircraft shall be treated for the purposes of the customs and excise Acts as stores if, and only if—

(a) the goods are to be sold by retail either—
  (i) in the course of a relevant journey, or
  (ii) for consumption on board;
 and
(b) the goods are not treated as exported by virtue of regulations under section 12 of the *Customs and Excise Duties (General Reliefs) Act* 1979 (goods for use in naval ships or establishments).

(4A) For the purposes of subsection (4) above a relevant journey is any journey beginning in the United Kingdom and having an immediate destination outside the member States.

(4B) In relation to goods treated as stores by virtue of subsection (4) above, any reference in the customs and excise Acts to the consumption of stores shall be construed as referring to the sale of the goods as mentioned in paragraph (a) of that subsection.

(5) A person who deals in or sells tobacco products in the course of a trade or business carried on by him shall be deemed for the purposes of this Act to be carrying on an excise licence trade (and to be a revenue trader) notwithstanding that no excise licence is required for carrying on that trade or business.

(6) In computing for the purposes of this Act any period expressed therein as a period of clear days no account shall be taken of the day of the event from which the period is computed or of any Sunday or holiday.

(7) The provisions of this Act in so far as they relate to customs duties apply, notwithstanding that any duties are imposed for the benefit of the Communities, as if the revenue from duties so imposed remained part of the revenues of the Crown.

[This section is printed as amended by the *Isle of Man Act* 1979, s.13 and Sched. 1; the *Betting and Gaming Duties Act* 1981, s.34(1) and Sched. 5, para. 5(a); the *Finance Act* 1981, s.11(1) and Sched. 8, Pt I, para. 1(1), (2); the *Finance Act* 1984, s.8 and Sched. 4, Pt II, para. 1; the *Finance (No.2) Act* 1987, s.103(3); the *Territorial Sea Act* 1987, s.3(1), (4), Sched. 1, para. 4(1) and Sched. 2; the *Finance Act* 1991, s.11(1), (2); the *Customs Controls on Importation of Goods Regulations* 1991 (S.I. 1991 No.2724), reg. 6(1) and (2); the *Finance (No.2) Act* 1992, s.3 and Sched. 2; the *Finance Act* 1993, s.30; and the *Merchant Shipping Act* 1995, Sched. 13. Immaterial definitions in subs. (1) have been omitted.]

Customs and Excise Management Act 1979, s.5

Time of importation, exportation, etc.

19–2 **5.**—(1) The provisions of this section shall have effect for the purposes of the customs and excise Acts.

(2) Subject to subsections (3) and (6) below, the time of importation of any goods shall be deemed to be—

(a) where the goods are brought by sea, the time when the ship carrying them comes within the limits of a port;

(b) where the goods are brought by air, the time when the aircraft carrying them lands in the United Kingdom or the time when the goods are unloaded in the United Kingdom, whichever is the earlier;

(c) where the goods are brought by land, the time when the goods are brought across the boundary into Northern Ireland.

(3) In the case of goods brought by sea of which entry is not required under regulation 5 of the *Customs Controls on Importation of Goods Regulations* 1991, the time of importation shall be deemed to be the time when the ship carrying them came within the limits of the port at which the goods are discharged.

(4) Subject to subsections (5) and (7) below, the time of exportation of any goods from the United Kingdom shall be deemed to be—

(a) where the goods are exported by sea or air, the time when the goods are shipped for exportation;

(b) where the goods are exported by land, the time when they are cleared by the proper officer at the last customs and excise station on their way to the boundary.

(5) In the case of goods of a class or description with respect to the exportation of which any prohibition or restriction is for the time being in force under or by virtue of any enactment which are exported by sea or air, the time of exportation shall be deemed to be the time when the exporting ship or aircraft departs from the last port or customs and excise airport at which it is cleared before departing for a destination outside the United Kingdom.

(6) Goods imported by means of a pipe-line shall be treated as imported at the time when they are brought within the limits of a port or brought across the boundary into Northern Ireland.

(7) Goods exported by means of a pipe-line shall be treated as exported at the time when they are charged into that pipe-line for exportation.

(8) A ship shall be deemed to have arrived at or departed from a port at the time when the ship comes within or, as the case may be, leaves the limits of that port.

[This section is printed as amended by the *Customs and Excise (Single Market etc.) Regulations* 1992 (S.I. 1992 No.3095), reg.10(1), Sched. 1, para. 3.]

(2) Proceedings in the magistrates' court

19–3 No proceedings for an offence under this Act shall be instituted except by or with the consent of the Director of Revenue and Customs Prosecutions, or by order of, or with the consent of, the Commissioners for Her Majesty's Revenue and Customs: *Customs and Excise Management Act* 1979, s.145. Where proceedings are begun by way of information and summons, the information should be in the name of an officer. Where an information fails to name the informant, the omission does not invalidate the information: *Rubin v. DPP* [1990] 2 Q.B. 80; 89 Cr.App.R. 44. Proceedings may not be commenced for an indictable offence after twenty years have elapsed since the day the offence was committed and for a summary offence after three years but, subject to that, a summary offence may be commenced within six months from the date upon which sufficient evidence to warrant the proceedings came to the knowledge of the prosecuting authority: s.146A. A certificate to the latter fact is sufficient. The fact that officers of HMRC have sufficient evidence to warrant a prosecution does not impute knowledge to the Director of Revenue and Customs Prosecutions: *Revenue and Customs Prosecutions Office v. NE Plastics Ltd* [2009] 2 Cr.App.R. 21. Proceedings may be commenced in any court having jurisdiction in the place where the person charged with the offence resides or is found, where anything was seized or detained in connection with the charge, or where the offence was committed: s.148.

Where two or more persons are liable for an offence they may be proceeded against **19–4** jointly or severally and shall each be liable for the full amount of any pecuniary penalty although the court may mitigate that penalty: s.150.

Proceedings take place in the normal way save that:

— the court may not change from committal proceedings to a summary trial without the consent of the Commissioners or, where the proceedings were brought in the name of the Attorney-General, his consent;

— the prosecutor may appeal to the Crown Court or request that the magistrates' court states a case for the opinion of the High Court: s.147.

II. OFFENCES IN CONNECTION WITH COMMISSIONERS, OFFICERS, ETC.

A. IMPERSONATING A REVENUE AND CUSTOMS OFFICER

(1) Definition

Commissioners for Revenue and Customs Act 2005, s.30

Impersonation

30.—(1) A person commits an offence if he pretends to be a Commissioner or an officer of **19–5** Revenue and Customs with a view to obtaining—

(a) admission to premises,

(b) information, or

(c) any other benefit.

(2) A person guilty of an offence under this section shall be liable on summary conviction to—

(a) imprisonment for a period not exceeding 51 weeks,

(b) a fine not exceeding level 5 on the standard scale, or

(c) both.

(3) In the application of this section to Scotland or Northern Ireland the reference in subsection (2)(a) to 51 weeks shall be taken as a reference to six months.

(2) Allocation

This offence is triable summarily. **19–6**

(3) Elements of the offence

The prosecution must prove that the defendant pretended to be a Commissioner or **19–7** an officer of Revenue and Customs with a view to obtaining:

— admission to premises;

— information; or

— any other benefit.

(4) Sentence

19–8 The maximum penalty is six months' imprisonment, a £5000 fine or both. The reference in s.30(2) to 51 weeks shall have effect as if it were a reference to six months: *Commissioners for Revenue and Customs Act* 2005, s.55(4).

B. OBSTRUCTION

(1) Definition

Commissioners for Revenue and Customs Act 2005, s.31

Obstruction

19–9 **31.**—(1) A person commits an offence if without reasonable excuse he obstructs—

(a) an officer of Revenue and Customs,

(b) a person acting on behalf of the Commissioners or an officer of Revenue and Customs, or

(c) a person assisting an officer of Revenue and Customs.

(2) A person guilty of an offence under this section shall be liable on summary conviction to—

(a) imprisonment for a period not exceeding 51 weeks,

(b) a fine not exceeding level 3 on the standard scale, or

(c) both.

(3) In the application of this section to Scotland or Northern Ireland the reference in subsection (2)(a) to 51 weeks shall be taken as a reference to six months.

(2) Allocation

19–10 This offence is triable summarily.

(3) Elements of the offence

19–11 The prosecution must prove that the defendant has without reasonable excuse obstructed:

— an officer of Revenue and Customs,

— a person acting on behalf of the Commissioners or an officer of Revenue and Customs, or

— a person assisting an officer of Revenue and Customs.

In *George and Davies* [1981] Crim.L.R.185 the giving of a false name was held to be obstruction.

(4) Sentence

19–12 The maximum penalty is six months' imprisonment or a fine of £1000 or both. The reference in s.31(2) to 51 weeks shall have effect as if it were a reference to six months: *Commissioners for Revenue and Customs Act* 2005, s.55(5).

C. ASSAULT

(1) Definition

Commissioners for Revenue and Customs Act 2005, s.32

Assault

19–13 **32.**—(1) A person commits an offence if he assaults an officer of Revenue and Customs.

(2) A person guilty of an offence under this section shall be liable on summary conviction to—

(a) imprisonment for a period not exceeding 51 weeks,

(b) a fine not exceeding level 5 on the standard scale, or
(c) both.

(3) In the application of this section to Scotland or Northern Ireland the reference in subsection (2)(a) to 51 weeks shall be taken as a reference to six months.

(2) Allocation

This offence is triable summarily. 19–14

(3) Elements of the offence

The prosecution must prove that the defendant intentionally or recklessly assaulted an officer of Revenue and Customs. Unlike the offence of assaulting a police officer, there is no requirement that the officer was acting in the execution of his duty. 19–15

(4) Sentence

The maximum penalty is six months' imprisonment or a fine of £1000 or both. The reference in section 32(2) to 51 weeks shall have effect as if it were a reference to six months: *Commissioners for Revenue and Customs Act* 2005, s.55(6). 19–16

III. OFFENCES OF ILLEGAL IMPORTATION AND EXPORTATION

A. ILLEGAL IMPORTATION

(1) Definition

Customs and Excise Management Act 1979, s.50

Penalty for improper importation of goods.

50.—(1) Subsection (2) below applies to goods of the following descriptions, that is to say— 19–17

(a) goods chargeable with a duty which has not been paid; and
(b) goods the importation, landing or unloading of which is for the time being prohibited or restricted by or under any enactment.

(2) If any person with intent to defraud Her Majesty of any such duty or to evade any such prohibition or restriction as is mentioned in subsection (1) above—

(a) unships or lands in any port or unloads from any aircraft in the United Kingdom or from any vehicle in Northern Ireland any goods to which this subsection applies, or assists or is otherwise concerned in such unshipping, landing or unloading; or
(b) removes from their place of importation or from any approved wharf, examination station, transit shed or customs and excise station any goods to which this subsection applies or assists or is otherwise concerned in such removal,

he shall be guilty of an offence under this subsection and may be detained.

(3) If any person imports or is concerned in importing any goods contrary to any prohibition or restriction for the time being in force under or by virtue of any enactment with respect to those goods, whether or not the goods are unloaded, and does so with intent to evade the prohibition or restriction, he shall be guilty of an offence under this subsection and may be detained.

(4) Subject to subsection or (5A) (5), (5A), (5B) or (5C) below, a person guilty of an offence under subsection (2) or (3) above shall be liable—

(a) on summary conviction, to a penalty of the prescribed sum or of three times the value of the goods, whichever is the greater, or to imprisonment for a term not exceeding 6 months, or to both; or
(b) on conviction on indictment, to a penalty of any amount, or to imprisonment for a term not exceeding 7 years, or to both.

(5) In the case of an offence under subsection (2) or (3) above in connection with a prohibition or restriction on importation having effect by virtue of section 3 of the *Misuse of Drugs Act* 1971, subsection (4) above shall have effect subject to the modifications specified in Schedule 1 to this Act.

(5A) In the case of—

(a) an offence under subsection (2) or (3) above committed in Great Britain in connection with a prohibition or restriction on the importation of any weapon or ammunition that is of a kind mentioned in section 5(1)(a), (ab), (aba), (ac), (ad), (ae), (af) or (c) or (1A)(a) of the *Firearms Act* 1968,

(b) any such offence committed in Northern Ireland in connection with a prohibition or restriction on the importation of any weapon or ammunition that is of a kind mentioned in Article 6(1)(a), (ab), (ac), (ad), (ae) or (c) or (1A)(a) of the *Firearms (Northern Ireland) Order* 1981, or

(c) any such offence committed in connection with the prohibition contained in section 20 of the *Forgery and Counterfeiting Act* 1981,

subsection (4)(b) above shall have effect as if for the words "7 years" there were substituted the words "10 years".

(5B) In the case of an offence under subsection (2) or (3) above in connection with the prohibition contained in regulation 2 of the *Import of Seal Skins Regulations* 1996, subsection (4) above shall have effect as if-

(a) for paragraph (a) there were substituted the following—

"(a) on summary conviction, to a fine not exceeding the statutory maximum or to imprisonment for a term not exceeding three months, or to both"

; and

(b) in paragraph (b) for the words "7 years" there were substituted the words "2 years".

(5C) In the case of an offence under subsection (2) or (3) above in connection with a prohibition or restriction relating to the importation of nuclear material, subsection (4)(b) above shall have effect as if for the words "7 years" there were substituted the words "14 years".

(6) If any person—

(a) imports or causes to be imported any goods concealed in a container holding goods of a different description; or

(b) directly or indirectly imports or causes to be imported or entered any goods found, whether before or after delivery, not to correspond with the entry made thereof,

he shall be liable on summary conviction to a penalty of three times the value of the goods or level 3 on the standard scale, whichever is the greater.

(7) In any case where a person would, apart from this subsection, be guilty of—

(a) an offence under this section in connection with the importation of goods contrary to a prohibition or restriction; and

(b) a corresponding offence under the enactment or other instrument imposing the prohibition or restriction, being an offence for which a fine or other penalty is expressly provided by that enactment or other instrument,

he shall not be guilty of the offence mentioned in paragraph (a) of this subsection.

(2) Allocation

19–18 This offence is triable either way.

(3) Elements of the offence

19–19 The prosecution must prove that (section 50(2)):

— the goods are taxable or prohibited or restricted;

— the defendant has either landed or assisted in the landing of the goods or has removed or assisted in the removal of the goods from an approved area; or

— the defendant either does not intend to pay the duty or intends to evade the prohibition or restriction.

The prosecutor must prove that the defendant (section 50(3)):

— has imported prohibited or restricted goods; or

— intended to evade the prohibition or restriction.

By virtue of s.154, once importation has been proved it is presumed to be unlawful unless the defence can prove otherwise. For time of importation see s.5 above. An intention to evade is necessary: *Frailey v. Charlton* [1920] 1 K.B. 147. In *Smith (Donald)* [1973] Q.B. 924; 57 Cr.App.R. 737, it was held that there can be no goods which are merely "unloaded" or "landed" and not imported; goods on board an aircraft are imported into the country when it lands and are exported when placed on another about to depart. In *Hurford-Jones*, 65 Cr.App.R. 263, it was held that it is not a defence that D had an honest mind and that he did not believe he was breaking the law. The word "evade" has its normal English meaning of "get around" or "avoid" and does not carry the connotation of fraud, as the word "avoid" does in income tax law.

(4) Sentence

The maximum penalty is a fine of £5000 or a penalty of three times the value of the goods, whichever is the greater or imprisonment for a term not exceeding six months, or both. **19–20**

There are enhanced penalties under s.50(5) and Sched. 1 for certain types of goods. In the case of drugs, where the drug concerned is a Class A or B drug, on summary conviction, the penalty is six months' imprisonment, a fine of £5000 or three times the value of the goods, whichever is the greater. If the drug is a Class C drug, on summary conviction, the maximum penalty is three months' imprisonment, a fine not exceeding £500 or three times the value of the goods, whichever is the greater.

B. IMPROPER UNLOADING OF GOODS LOADED ETC. FOR EXPORTATION

(1) Definition

Customs and Excise Management Act 1979, s.67

Offences in relation to exportation of goods.

67.—(1) If any goods which have been loaded or retained on board any ship or aircraft for exportation are not exported to and discharged at a place outside the United Kingdom but are unloaded in the United Kingdom, then, unless— **19–21**

(a) the unloading was authorised by the proper officer; and

(b) except where that officer otherwise permits, any duty chargeable and unpaid on the goods is paid and any drawback or allowance paid in respect thereof is repaid,

the master of the ship or the commander of the aircraft and any person concerned in the unshipping, relanding, landing, unloading or carrying of the goods from the ship or aircraft without such authority, payment or repayment shall each be guilty of an offence under this section.

(2) The Commissioners may impose such conditions as they see fit with respect to any goods loaded or retained as mentioned in subsection (1) above which are permitted to be unloaded in the United Kingdom.

(3) If any person contravenes or fails to comply with, or is concerned in any contravention of or failure to comply with, any condition imposed under subsection (2) above he shall be guilty of an offence under this section.

(4) Where any goods loaded or retained as mentioned in subsection (1) above or brought to a customs and excise station for exportation by land are—

(a) goods from warehouse, other than goods which have been kept, without being warehoused, in a warehouse by virtue of section 92(4) below;

(b) transit goods;

(c) other goods chargeable with a duty which has not been paid;

(d) drawback goods,

then if any container in which the goods are held is without the authority of the proper officer opened, or any mark, letter or device on any such container or on any lot of the goods is without that authority cancelled, obliterated or altered, every person concerned in the opening, cancellation, obliteration or alteration shall be guilty of an offence under this section.

(5) Any goods in respect of which an offence under this section is committed shall be li-

able to forfeiture and any person guilty of an offence under this section shall be liable on summary conviction to a penalty of three times the value of the goods or level 3 on the standard scale, whichever is the greater.

(2) Allocation

19–22 This offence is triable summarily.

(3) Elements of the offence

19–23 The prosecution must prove that:
- — the goods are intended for export;
- — the goods have been loaded on a vessel or aircraft;
- — the goods have been unloaded without authorisation; or
- — the duty has not been paid.

(4) Sentence

19–24 The maximum penalty is forfeiture of goods and a fine of three times the value of the goods or a fine not exceeding level three, *i.e.* £1000, whichever is the greater.

C. ILLEGAL EXPORTATION

(1) Definition

Customs and Excise Management Act 1979, s.68

Offences in relation to exportation of prohibited or restricted goods.

19–25 **68.**—(1) If any goods are—

(a) exported or shipped as stores; or

(b) brought to any place in the United Kingdom for the purpose of being exported or shipped as stores,

and the exportation or shipment is or would be contrary to any prohibition or restriction for the time being in force with respect to those goods under or by virtue of any enactment, the goods shall be liable to forfeiture and the exporter or intending exporter of the goods and any agent of his concerned in the exportation or shipment or intended exportation or shipment shall each be liable on summary conviction to a penalty of three times the value of the goods or level 3 on the standard scale, whichever is the greater.

(2) Any person knowingly concerned in the exportation or shipment as stores, or in the attempted exportation or shipment as stores, of any goods with intent to evade any such prohibition or restriction as is mentioned in subsection (1) above shall be guilty of an offence under this subsection and may be detained.

(3) Subject to subsection (4) or (4A), (4A) or (4B) below, a person guilty of an offence under subsection (2) above shall be liable—

(a) on summary conviction, to a penalty of the prescribed sum or of three times the value of the goods, whichever is the greater, or to imprisonment for a term not exceeding 6 months, or to both; or

(b) on conviction on indictment, to a penalty of any amount, or to imprisonment for a term not exceeding 7 years, or to both.

(4) In the case of an offence under subsection (2) above in connection with a prohibition or restriction on exportation having effect by virtue of section 3 of the *Misuse of Drugs Act* 1971, subsection (3) above shall have effect subject to the modifications specified in Schedule 1 to this Act.

(4A) In the case of an offence under subsection (3) above in connection with the prohibition contained in section 21 of the Forgery and Counterfeiting Act 1981, subsection (3)(b) above shall have effect as if for the words "2 years" there were substituted the words "10 years".]

(5) If by virtue of any such restriction as is mentioned in subsection (1) above any goods may be exported only when consigned to a particular place or person and any goods so

consigned are delivered to some other place or person, the ship, aircraft or vehicle in which they were exported shall be liable to forfeiture unless it is proved to the satisfaction of the Commissioners that both the owner of the ship, aircraft or vehicle and the master of the ship, commander of the aircraft or person in charge of the vehicle—

(a) took all reasonable steps to secure that the goods were delivered to the particular place to which or person to whom they were consigned; and

(b) did not connive at or, except under duress, consent to the delivery of the goods to that other place or person.

(6) In any case where a person would, apart from this subsection, be guilty of—

(a) an offence under subsection (1) or (2) above; and

(b) a corresponding offence under the enactment or instrument imposing the prohibition or restriction in question, being an offence for which a fine or other penalty is expressly provided by that enactment or other instrument,

he shall not be guilty of the offence mentioned in paragraph (a) of this subsection.

(2) Allocation

This offence is triable either way. **19–26**

(3) Elements of the offence

The prosecution must prove: **19–27**

— the goods are prohibited from being exported;

— the goods have either been brought to a place to be exported or have been exported; or

— the defendant knew of the plan to export the goods and intended to evade the prohibition.

There is a statutory defence. In *Garrett v. Arthur Churchill (Glass) Ltd* [1970] 1 Q.B. 92, it was said that the question whether a defendant was knowingly concerned in the exportation of goods with intent to evade the prohibition should be treated as one question. In *Uxbridge Justices, ex p. Sofaer*, 85 Cr.App.R. 367, it was held that destruction of the goods will not necessarily prejudice the defendant or amount to a breach natural justice, where secondary evidence in the form of photographs can be put before the court.

(4) Sentence

The maximum penalty is a fine of £5000, or three times the value of the goods, **19–28** whichever is the greater, or imprisonment for a term not exceeding six months or both. The enhanced penalties provided for drug exportation are the same as those provided under s.67, and are provided by Sched. 1 to the Act and subs. (4) and (4A) of s.68.

D. CONTROL OF PERSONS ENTERING OR LEAVING THE UK

(1) Definition

Customs and Excise Management Act 1979, s.78

Customs and excise control of persons entering or leaving the United Kingdom

19–29 **78.**—(1) Any person entering the United Kingdom shall, at such place and in such manner as the Commissioners may direct, declare any thing contained in his baggage or carried with him which—

(a) he has obtained outside the United Kingdom; or

(b) being dutiable goods or chargeable goods, he has obtained in the United Kingdom without payment of duty or tax,

and in respect of which he is not entitled to exemption from duty and tax by virtue of any order under section 13 of the *Customs and Excise Duties (General Reliefs) Act* 1979 (personal reliefs).

In this subsection "chargeable goods" means goods on the importation of which value added tax is chargeable or goods obtained in the United Kingdom before 1st April 1973 which are chargeable goods within the meaning of the *Purchase Tax Act* 1963; and "tax" means value added tax or purchase tax.

(1A) Subsection (1) above does not apply to a person entering the United Kingdom from the Isle of Man as respects anything obtained by him in the Island unless it is chargeable there with duty or value added tax and he has obtained it without payment of the duty or tax.

(1B) Subsection (1) above does not apply to a person entering the United Kingdom from another member State, except—

(a) where he arrives at a customs and excise airport in an aircraft in which he began his journey in a place outside the member States; or

(b) as respects such of his baggage as—

(i) is carried in the hold of the aircraft in which he arrives at a customs and excise airport, and

(ii) notwithstanding that it was transferred on one or more occasions from aircraft to aircraft at an airport in a member State, began its journey by air from a place outside the member States.

(2) Any person entering or leaving the United Kingdom shall answer such questions as the proper officer may put to him with respect to his baggage and any thing contained therein or carried with him, and shall, if required by the proper officer, produce that baggage and any such thing for examination at such place as the Commissioners may direct.

(2A) Subject to subsection (1A) above, where the journey of a person arriving by air in the United Kingdom is continued or resumed by air to a destination in the United Kingdom which is not the place where he is regarded for the purposes of this section as entering the United Kingdom, subsections (1) and (2) above shall apply in relation to that person on his arrival at that destination as they apply in relation to a person entering the United Kingdom.

(3) Any person failing to declare any thing or to produce any baggage or thing as required by this section shall be liable on summary conviction to a penalty of three times the value of the thing not declared or of the baggage or thing not produced, as the case may be, or level 3 on the standard scale, whichever is the greater.

(4) Any thing chargeable with any duty or tax which is found concealed, or is not declared, and any thing which is being taken into or out of the United Kingdom contrary to any prohibition or restriction for the time being in force with respect thereto under or by virtue of any enactment, shall be liable to forfeiture.

[This section is printed as amended by the *Isle of Man Act* 1979, s.13, Sched. 1; the *CJA* 1982, ss.38, 46; the *Finance (No.2) Act* 1992, s.5; and the *Customs and Excise (Single Market etc.) Regulations* 1992 (S.I. 1992 No.3095), reg.3(10).]

(2) Allocation

19–30 This offence is triable summarily: s.78(3).

(3) Elements of the offence

The prosecution must prove: **19–31**
— the goods are dutiable;
— they were bought outside the UK; or
— they were not declared or produced.

It is an absolute offence: *Customs and Excise Commissioners, ex p. Claus*, 86 Cr.App.R. 189. The offence is committed once there was a failure to declare goods which should have been declared and it is irrelevant that a voluntary declaration takes place at some later stage. The provision applies only to persons entering or leaving the United Kingdom, and there is no requirement to show that there are reasonable grounds to suspect that the person entering or leaving is carrying a prohibited or restricted article or a dutiable article on which duty has not been paid. This distinction is however, qualified by the *Finance Act (No.2)* 1992, s.4 (see *post* § 19–33). In *Lucien* [1995] Crim.L.R. 807, the Court of Appeal dismissed the argument that the cocaine concealed in shoes that were worn by the defendant were neither part of his baggage nor "carried with him". The mere fact that a person comes to an airport to meet or collect someone in whose bags drugs are identified does not constitute reasonable objective grounds to suspect involvement in drug smuggling: *Perpont* [2004] EWCA Crim 2562.

(4) Sentence

The maximum penalty is a fine of three times the value of the goods or a fine not exceeding level three, *i.e.* £1000, whichever is greater. **19–32**

Finance (No.2) Act 1992, s.4

Enforcement powers

4.—(1) Except in a case falling within subsection (1A) or (2) below, the powers to which this section applies shall not be exercisable in relation to any person or thing entering or leaving the United Kingdom so as to prevent, restrict or delay the movement of that person or thing between different member States. **19–33**

(1A) The first case in which a power to which this section applies may be exercised as mentioned in subsection (1) above is where it is necessary to exercise the power in order to ascertain whether the movement in question is or is not in fact between different member States.

(2) The second case in which a power to which this section applies may be exercised as mentioned in subsection (1) above is where it is necessary to exercise the power for purposes connected with—

(a) securing the collection of any EU customs duty or giving effect to any Community legislation relating to any such duty;
(b) the enforcement of any prohibition or restriction for the time being in force by virtue of any Community legislation with respect to the movement of goods into or out of the member States;
(c) the enforcement of any prohibition or restriction for the time being in force by virtue of any enactment with respect to the importation or exportation of goods into or out of the United Kingdom; or
(d) searching for cash that is recoverable property or intended for use in unlawful conduct.

(3) Subject to subsection (4) below, this section applies to any power which is conferred on the Commissioners of Customs and Excise or any officer or constable under any of the following provisions of the *Customs and Excise Management Act* 1979, that is to say—

(a) section 21 (control of movement of aircraft into and out of the United Kingdom);
(b) section 26 (power to regulate movement by land into and out of Northern Ireland);
(c) section 27 (officers' powers of boarding);
(d) section 28 (officers' powers of access);
(e) section 29 (officers' powers to detain ships);
(f) section 34 (power to prevent flight of aircraft);

(g) section 78 (questions as to baggage of person entering or leaving the United Kingdom);

(ga) section 157A (general information powers in relation to persons entering or leaving the United Kingdom);

(h) section 164 (powers of search).

(4) The Treasury may by order made by statutory instrument add any power conferred by any enactment contained in the customs and excise Acts to the powers to which this section applies; and a statutory instrument containing an order under this subsection shall be subject to annulment in pursuance of a resolution of either House of Parliament.

(5) In this section—

"cash" has the meaning given by section 289(6) and (7) of the *Proceeds of Crime Act* 2002;

"EU customs duty" includes any agricultural levy of the Economic Community;

"the customs and excise Acts" and "goods" have the same meanings as in the *Customs and Excise Management Act* 1979;

"recoverable property" has the same meaning as in section 316(1) of the *Proceeds of Crime Act* 2002; and

"unlawful conduct" has the same meaning as in section 241 of that Act;

and for the purposes of this section a power shall be taken to be exercised otherwise than in relation to a person or thing entering or leaving the United Kingdom in any case where the power is exercisable irrespective of whether the person or thing in question is entering or leaving the United Kingdom.

(6) This section shall come into force on 1st January 1993.

19–34 Section 78 does not provide a basis for permitting customs officers to conduct rubdown, strip or intimate searches. This power is only exercisable by virtue of s.164 of the 1979 Act: *Lucien, ante*.

19–35 The *Channel Tunnel (Customs and Excise) Order* 1990 (S.I. 1990 No.2167), Sched. 1, para. 17B as amended by the *Channel Tunnel (Miscellaneous Provisions) Order* 1994 (S.I. 1994 No.1405) provides that for the purposes of s.78 of the 1979 Act:

(a) a person intending to travel to the United Kingdom through the tunnel who has entered a control zone in France or Belgium shall be treated as being a person entering the United Kingdom,

(b) a person who has travelled from the United Kingdom through the tunnel and is in such a control zone shall be treated as still being a person leaving the United Kingdom, and

(c) concealment shall be taken to include concealment in such a control zone.

E. SMUGGLING

(1) Definition

Customs and Excise Management Act 1979, s.85(1)

Penalty for interfering with revenue vessels, etc.

19–36 **85.**—(1) Any person who save for just and sufficient cause interferes in any way with any ship, aircraft, vehicle, buoy, anchor, chain, rope or mark which is being used for the purposes of any functions of the Commissioners under Parts III to VII of this Act shall be liable on summary conviction to a penalty of level 1 on the standard scale.

(2) Allocation

19–37 This offence is triable summarily.

(3) Elements of the offence

19–38 The prosecution must prove that the defendant:

— interfered with a customs vessel/vehicle/aircraft *etc.*; and

— had no just cause.

(4) Sentence

The maximum penalty is a level one fine, *i.e.* £200. **19–39**

F. UNTRUE DECLARATIONS

(1) Definition

Customs and Excise Management Act 1979, s.167

Untrue declarations, etc.

167.—(1) If any person either knowingly or recklessly— **19–40**

(a) makes or signs, or causes to be made or signed, or delivers or causes to be delivered to the Commissioners or an officer, any declaration, notice, certificate or other document whatsoever; or

(b) makes any statement in answer to any question put to him by an officer which he is required by or under any enactment to answer,

being a document or statement produced or made for any purpose of any assigned matter, which is untrue in any material particular, he shall be guilty of an offence under this subsection and may be detained; and any goods in relation to which the document or statement was made shall be liable to forfeiture.

(2) Without prejudice to subsection (4) below, a person who commits an offence under subsection (1) above shall be liable—

(a) on summary conviction, to a penalty of the prescribed sum, or to imprisonment for a term not exceeding 6 months, or to both; or

(b) on conviction on indictment, to penalty of any amount, or to imprisonment for a term not exceeding 2 years, or to both.

(3) If any person—

(a) makes or signs, or causes to be made or signed, or delivers or causes to be delivered to the Commissioners or an officer, any declaration, notice, certificate or other document whatsoever; or

(b) makes any statement in answer to any question put to him by an officer which he is required by or under any enactment to answer.

being a document or statement produced or made for any purpose of any assigned matter, which is untrue in any material particular, then, without prejudice to subsection (4) below, he shall be liable on summary conviction to a penalty of level 4 on the standard scale.

(4) Where by reason of any such document or statement as is mentioned in subsection (1) or (3) above the full amount of any duty payable is not paid or any overpayment is made in respect of any drawback, allowance, rebate or repayment of duty, the amount of the duty unpaid or of the overpayment shall be recoverable as a debt due to the Crown or may be summarily recovered as a civil debt.

(5) An amount of excise duty, or the amount of an overpayment in respect of any drawback, allowance, rebate or repayment of any excise duty, shall not be recoverable as mentioned in subsection (4) above unless the Commissioners have assessed the amount of the duty or of the overpayment as being excise duty due from the person mentioned in subsection (1) or (3) above and notified him or his representative accordingly.

[Subsections (1)–(3) are printed as amended by the *CJA* 1982, ss.38 and 46; and *PACE* 1984, s.114(1). Subsection (5) was inserted by the *Finance Act* 1997, s.50 and Sched. 6, para. 5.]

(2) Allocation

This offence is triable either way. **19–41**

(3) Elements of the offence

The prosecution must prove that the defendant: **19–42**

Part III

— made a certificate or statement which was untrue; or
— knew or was reckless as to whether it was untrue.

(4) Sentence

19–43 The maximum penalty is six months' imprisonment and/or a fine not exceeding £5000. The duty may also be reclaimed.

G. COUNTERFEITING DOCUMENTS

(1) Definition

Customs and Excise Management Act 1979, s.168

Counterfeiting documents, etc.

19–44 **168.**—(1) If any person—

(a) counterfeits or falsifies any document which is required by or under any enactment relating to an assigned matter or which is used in the transaction of any business relating to an assigned matter; or
(b) knowingly accepts, receives or uses any such document so counterfeited or falsified; or
(c) alters any such document after it is officially issued; or
(d) counterfeits any seal, signature, initials or other mark of, or used by, any officer for the verification of such a document or for the security of goods or for any other purpose relating to an assigned matter,

he shall be guilty of an offence under this section and may be detained.

(2) A person guilty of an offence under this section shall be liable—

(a) on summary conviction, to a penalty of the prescribed sum, or to imprisonment for a term not exceeding 6 months, or to both; or
(b) on conviction on indictment, to a penalty of any amount, or to imprisonment for a term not exceeding 2 years, or to both.

[This section is printed as amended by *PACE* 1984, s.114(1).]

(2) Allocation

19–45 This offence is triable either way: s.168(2).

(3) Elements of the offence

19–46 The prosecution must prove that the defendant either:
— forged or falsified a document;
— accepted or used such a document;
— altered an official document; or
— forged a seal etc.

(4) Sentence

19–47 When tried summarily, the maximum penalty is six months' imprisonment, a fine not exceeding the prescribed sum, or both: s.168(2)(b).

H. FRAUDULENT EVASION OF DUTY

(1) Definition

Customs and Excise Management Act 1979, s.170

Penalty for fraudulent evasion of duty, etc.

19–48 **170.**—(1) Without prejudice to any other provision of the Customs and Excise Acts 1979, if any person—

(a) knowingly acquires possession of any of the following goods, that is to say—
(i) goods which have been unlawfully removed from a warehouse or Queen's warehouse;
(ii) goods which are chargeable with a duty which has not been paid;
(iii) goods with respect to the importation or exportation of which any prohibition or restriction is for the time being in force under or by virtue of any enactment; or
(b) is in any way knowingly concerned in carrying, removing, depositing, harbouring, keeping or concealing or in any manner dealing with any such goods,

and does so with intent to defraud Her Majesty of any duty payable on the goods or to evade any such prohibition or restriction with respect to the goods he shall be guilty of an offence under this section and may be detained.

(2) Without prejudice to any other provision of the Customs and Excise Acts 1979, if any person is, in relation to any goods, in any way knowingly concerned in any fraudulent evasion or attempt at evasion—
(a) of any duty chargeable on the goods;
(b) of any prohibition or restriction for the time being in force with respect to the goods under or by virtue of any enactment; or
(c) of any provision of the Customs and Excise Acts 1979 applicable to the goods,

he shall be guilty of an offence under this section and may be detained.

(3) Subject to subsection (4), (4A), (4B) or (4C) below, a person guilty of an offence under this section shall be liable—
(a) on summary conviction, to a penalty of the prescribed sum or of three times the value of the goods, whichever is the greater, or to imprisonment for a term not exceeding 6 months, or to both; or
(b) on conviction on indictment, to a penalty of any amount, or to imprisonment for a term not exceeding 7 years, or to both.

(4) In the case of an offence under this section in connection with prohibition or restriction on importation or exportation having effect by virtue of section 3 of the *Misuse of Drugs Act* 1971, subsection (3) above shall have effect subject to the modifications specified in Schedule 1 to this Act.

(4A) In the case of—
(a) an offence under subsection (2) or (3) above committed in Great Britain in connection with a prohibition or restriction on the importation or exportation of any weapon or ammunition that is of a kind mentioned in section 5(1)(a), (ab), (aba), (ac), (ad), (ae), (af) or (c) or (1A)(a) of the *Firearms Act* 1968,
(b) any such offence committed in Northern Ireland in connection with a prohibition or restriction on the importation or exportation of any weapon or ammunition that is of a kind mentioned in Article 6(1)(a), (ab), (ac), (ad), (ae) or (c) or (1A)(a) of the *Firearms (Northern Ireland) Order* 1981, or
(c) any such offence committed in connection with the prohibitions contained in sections 20 and 21 of the *Forgery and Counterfeiting Act* 1981,

subsection (3)(b) above shall have effect as if for the words "7 years" there were substituted the words "10 years".

(4B) In the case of an offence under subsection (1) or (2) above in connection with the prohibition contained in regulation 2 of the *Import of Seal Skins Regulations* 1996, subsection (3) above shall have effect as if-
(a) for paragraph (a) there were substituted the following-
"(a) on summary conviction, to a fine not exceeding the statutory maximum or to imprisonment for a term not exceeding three months, or to both"

; and
(b) in paragraph (b) for the words "7 years" there were substituted the words "2 years".

(4C) In the case of an offence under subsection (1) or (2) above in connection with a prohibition or restriction relating to the importation, exportation or shipment as stores of nuclear material, subsection (3)(b) above shall have effect as if for the words "7 years" there were substituted the words "14 years".

(5) In any case where a person would, apart from this subsection, be guilty of—
(a) an offence under this section in connection with a prohibition or restriction; and

(b) a corresponding offence under the enactment or other instrument imposing the prohibition or restriction, being an offence for which a fine or other penalty is expressly provided by that enactment or other instrument,

he shall not be guilty of the offence mentioned in paragraph (a) of this subsection.

(6) Where any person is guilty of an offence under this section, the goods in respect of which the offence was committed shall be liable to forfeiture.

[This section is printed as amended by the *Forgery and Counterfeiting Act* 1981, s.23(3) (insertion of subs. (4A); the *PACE Act* 1984, s.144(1); the *Finance Act* 1988, s.12(1)(a) (substitution of "7 years" for "2 years" in subs. 3(b))); the *Finance (No.2) Act* 1992, s.3, Sched. 2, para. 7; and the *Import of Seal Skins Regulations* 1996 (S.I. 1996 No.2686).]

(2) Allocation

19–49 This offence is triable either way.

(3) Elements of the offence

19–50 The prosecution must prove:

— the goods fall within the categories listed in s.170(1)(a);

— possession or knowledge of the removal, keeping or hiding of goods subject to a prohibition or restriction; or

— an intention not to pay the duty or to evade a prohibition or restriction.

The prosecution must prove that there has been an importation and must establish a link between the offence and the prohibited importation: *Watts and Stack*, 70 Cr.App.R. 187. In this case, the Court of Appeal held that it was not enough to prove that the defendants were dealing in cocaine; it must also be proved that there was some prohibited importation in order to prove the "intention" to evade.

Further, the prosecution must prove that the defendant knows that the goods are subject to a prohibition or restriction and that the operation he is concerned with is an operation designed to get around that prohibition or restriction; but it does not have to prove that the defendant knows the precise category of goods involved: *Hussain* [1969] 2 Q.B. 567; 53 Cr.App.R. 448; *Shivpuri* [1987] A.C. 1; 83 Cr.App.R. 178; *Forbes* [2002] 2 A.C. 512; [2002] 1 Cr.App.R. 1. In *Taaffe* [1984] A.C. 539; 78 Cr.App.R. 301 it was held that the accused was to be judged on the facts as he believed them to be. In that case, T mistakenly believed that he was illegally importing currency (which he wrongly believed was subject to a prohibition), whereas he was importing cannabis; it was held that if the jury accepted his version of events, he should be acquitted. By contrast, in *Ellis*, 84 Cr.App.R. 235, it was held that it did not matter what goods E thought he was importing provided he thought those goods were subject to a prohibition against importation, and the goods he thought he was importing as well as the actual goods he was importing were subject to such a prohibition. In *Cohen* [1951] 1 K.B. 505; 34 Cr.App.R. 239, it was held that possession raises a presumption that goods are knowingly in the defendant's possession.

The prosecution must prove specific intent to be knowingly concerned in any fraudulent evasion of a prohibition; recklessness is insufficient: *Panayi (No.2) and Karte* [1989] 1 W.L.R. 187.

Trans-shipment within Heathrow airport customs area from one aircraft coming from one country to another aircraft going to another country falls within the section: *Smith* [1973] Q.B. 924; 57 Cr.App.R. 737. Steps taken abroad leading to fraudulent evasion in this country can lead to a charge in this country: *Wall*, 59 Cr.App.R. 58. A person prepared to look after a parcel sent from abroad for a friend, knowing that the parcel was likely to contain drugs having been promised some for himself, can be charged with fraudulent evasion: *Att.-Gen.'s Reference (No.1 of 1998)*, 163 J.P. 390. If an undercover customs officer undertook the importation, the organiser could still be convicted (in this case of an attempt): *Latif* [1996] 2 Cr.App.R. 92. The offence is a continuing one: *Green* [1976] Q.B. 985; 62 Cr.App.R. 74; *Neal*, 77 Cr.App.R. 283. In the latter case the provision of a barn for the concealment of goods was sufficient evidence of being "knowingly concerned". The offence may be committed at any time after the actual importation and at any place: *Ardalan*, 56 Cr.App.R. 320 It is no defence that the defendant has acted fraudulently only after the goods have been imported innocently: *Ciaparra*, 87 Cr.App.R. 316. In this case, the defendant only became involved after the drug had been imported and baking powder had been substituted for the drug. In *Mitchell* [1992] Crim.L.R. 594, it was held that unsolicited receipt of drugs followed by knowing retention was sufficient to allow a jury to convict. In *Williams*, 55 Cr.App.R. 275, it was held that an agreement to sell cannabis after it has been imported into this country was sufficiently close to the act of actual importation to make W knowingly concerned in it. The burden of proof is on the defendant to show that the duty has been paid: s.154.

(4) Sentence

The maximum sentence is a fine of £5000 or three times the value of the goods **19–51**
concerned, whichever is the greater, and/or imprisonment for a term not exceeding six months.

The Sentencing Guidelines Council definitive guideline issued in October 2009—sentencing for fraud—statutory offences, reflects the Court of Appeal decision in *Czyzewski* [2004] 1 Cr.App.R.(S.) 49. The guideline may be found on the Sentencing Council's website at: *http://sentencingcouncil.judiciary.gov.uk/docs/web_sentencing_for_fraud_statutory_offences.pdf*. An extract from the guidance appears below.

Professional smuggling will be evidenced by a complex operation with many people **19–52**
involved; financial accounting or budgets; obtaining goods from several different sources; integration of freight movements with commercial organisations; sophisticated concealment methods such as forged documents or specially adapted vehicles; varying of methods and routes; links with illicit overseas organisations and when the amount of goods smuggled is in the order of half a million cigarettes (equates approximately to evasion of £75,000 worth of duty): this is not a precise indication but the value of the goods could be a potential indicator of professional smuggling.

Forfeiture and deprivation orders should be considered and disqualification from driving.

REVENUE FRAUD (AGAINST HM REVENUE AND CUSTOMS (HMRC))

Maximum penalty: Fraud (prosecuted under *Fraud Act* 2006), 10 years custody For all other offences, 7 years custody

	Amount obtained or intended to be obtained				
Nature of offence	**£500,000 or more Starting point based on: £750,000***	**£100,000 or more and less than £500,000 Starting point based on: £300,000***	**£20,000 or more and less than £100,000 Starting point based on: £60,000***	**£5,000 or more and less than £20,000 Starting point based on: £12,500***	**Less than £5,000 Starting point based on: £2,500***
Fraudulent from the outset, professionally planned **and either** fraud carried out over a significant period of time **or** multiple frauds	**Starting point:** 5 years custody **Range:** 4–7 years custody	**Starting point:** 4 years custody **Range:** 3–5 years custody	**Starting point:** 2 years custody **Range:** 18 months–3 years custody		
Fraudulent from the outset **and either** fraud carried out over a significant period of time **or** multiple frauds	**Starting point:** 4 years custody **Range:** 3–7 years custody	**Starting point:** 3 years custody **Range:** 2–4 years custody	**Starting point:** 15 months custody **Range:** 18 weeks–30 months custody	**Starting point:** 12 weeks custody **Range:** Community order (HIGH)–12 months custody	**Starting point:** Community order (HIGH) **Range:** Community order (LOW)–6 weeks custody
Not fraudulent from the outset **and either** fraud carried out over a significant period of time **or** multiple frauds	**Starting point:** 3 years custody **Range:** 2–6 years custody	**Starting point:** 2 years custody **Range:** 12 months–3 years custody	**Starting point:** 36 weeks custody **Range:** 12 weeks–18 months custody	**Starting point:** 6 weeks custody **Range:** Community order (MEDIUM) –26 weeks custody	**Starting point:** Community order (MEDIUM) **Range:** Fine–Community order (HIGH)
Single fraudulent transaction, fraudulent from the outset			**Starting point:** 26 weeks custody **Range:** 6 weeks–12 months custody	**Starting point:** Community order (HIGH) **Range:** Fine–18 weeks custody	**Starting point:** Community order (LOW) **Range:** Fine–Community order (MEDIUM)

	Amount obtained or intended to be obtained				
Nature of offence	**£500,000 or more Starting point based on: £750,000***	**£100,000 or more and less than £500,000 Starting point based on: £300,000***	**£20,000 or more and less than £100,000 Starting point based on: £60,000***	**£5,000 or more and less than £20,000 Starting point based on: £12,500***	**Less than £5,000 Starting point based on: £2,500***
Single fraudulent transaction, not fraudulent from the outset			**Starting point:** 12 weeks custody **Range:** Community order (MEDIUM) –36 weeks custody	**Starting point:** Community order (MEDIUM) **Range:** Fine–6 weeks custody	**Starting point:** Fine **Range:** Fine–Community order (LOW)

* Where the actual amount is greater or smaller than the figure on which the starting point is based, that is likely to be one of the factors that will move the sentence within the range (see paragraph 6 on page 28).

Additional aggravating factors	Additional mitigating factors
1. Number involved in the offence and role of the offender 2. Use of another person's identity 3. Making repeated importations, particularly in the face of warnings from the authorities 4. Dealing in goods with an additional health risk 5. Disposing of goods to under-aged purchasers	1. Peripheral involvement 2. Misleading or incomplete advice

I. TAKING STEPS TO EVADE EXCISE DUTY

(1) Definition

Customs and Excise Management Act 1979, s.170B

Offence of taking preparatory steps for evasion of excise duty

170B.—(1) If any person is knowingly concerned in the taking of any steps with a view to the fraudulent evasion, whether by himself or another, of any duty of excise on any goods, he shall be liable— **19–53**

(a) on summary conviction, to a penalty of the prescribed sum or of three times the amount of the duty, whichever is the greater, or to imprisonment for a term not exceeding six months or to both; and

(b) on conviction on indictment, to a penalty of any amount or to imprisonment for a term not exceeding seven years or to both.

(2) Where any person is guilty of an offence under this section, the goods in respect of which the offence was committed shall be liable to forfeiture.

[This section was inserted by the *Finance (No.2) Act* 1992, s.3 and Sched. 2, para. 8.]

(2) Allocation

19–54 This offence is triable either way: s.170B(1).

(3) Elements of the offence

19–55 The prosecution must prove that:

— steps have been taken to evade duty; and

— the defendant knew what he was doing.

Under legislation relating to value added tax, taking steps has been held to include omissions: *McCarthy* [1981] S.T.C. 298, CA.

(4) Sentence

19–56 The maximum sentence is imprisonment for a term not exceeding six months or a £5000 fine or three times the value of the goods, or both.

CHAPTER 20

REGULATORY OFFENCES

Part III

I. AEROPLANES AND AIRPORTS

A. OFFENCES IN RELATION TO CERTAIN DANGEROUS ARTICLES

(1) Definition

Aviation Security Act 1982, s.4

Offences in relation to certain dangerous articles

20–1 **4.**—(1) It shall be an offence for any person without lawful authority or reasonable excuse (the proof of which shall lie on him) to have with him—

(a) in any aircraft registered in the United Kingdom, whether at a time when the aircraft is in the United Kingdom or not, or

(b) in any other aircraft at a time when it is in, or in flight over, the United Kingdom, or

(c) in any part of an aerodrome in the United Kingdom, or

(d) in any air navigation installation in the United Kingdom which does not form part of an aerodrome,

any article to which this section applies.

(2) This section applies to the following articles, that is to say—

(a) any firearm, or any article having the appearance of being a firearm, whether capable of being discharged or not;

(b) any explosive, any article manufactured or adapted (whether in the form of a bomb, grenade or otherwise) so as to have the appearance of being an explosive, whether it is capable of producing a practical effect by explosion or not, or any article marked or labelled so as to indicate that it is or contains an explosive; and

(c) any article (not falling within either of the preceding paragraphs) made or adapted for use for causing injury to or incapacitating a person or for destroying or damaging property, or intended by the person having it with him for such use, whether by him or by any other person.

(3) For the purposes of this section a person who is for the time being in an aircraft, or in part of an aerodrome, shall be treated as having with him in the aircraft, or in that part of the aerodrome, as the case may be, an article to which this section applies if—

(a) where he is in an aircraft, the article, or an article in which it is contained, is in the aircraft and has been caused (whether by him or by any other person) to be brought there as being, or as forming part of, his baggage on a flight in the aircraft or has been caused by him to be brought there as being, or as forming part of, any other property to be carried on such a flight, or

(b) where he is in part of an aerodrome (otherwise than in an aircraft), the article, or an article in which it is contained, is in that or any other part of the aerodrome and has been caused (whether by him or by any other person) to be brought into the aerodrome as being, or as forming part of, his baggage on a flight from that aerodrome or has been caused by him to be brought there as being, or as forming part of, any other property to be carried on such a flight on which he is also to be carried.

notwithstanding that the circumstances may be such that (apart from this subsection) he would not be regarded as having the article with him in the aircraft or in a part of the aerodrome, as the case may be.

(4) A person guilty of an offence under this section shall be liable—

(a) on summary conviction, to a fine not exceeding the statutory maximum or to imprisonment for a term not exceeding three months or to both;

(b) on conviction on indictment, to a fine or to imprisonment for a term not exceeding five years or to both.

(5) Nothing in subsection (3) above shall be construed as limiting the circumstances in which a person would, apart from that subsection, be regarded as having an article with him as mentioned in subsection (1) above.

(2) Allocation

This offence is triable either way: section (4). **20–2**

(3) Sentence

When tried summarily, the maximum penalty for this offence is a fine not exceeding the statutory maximum, imprisonment for a term not exceeding three months or both. **20–3**

Aviation Security Act 1982, s.8

Prosecution of offences and proceedings

8.—(1) Proceedings for an offence under any of the preceding provisions of this Part of this Act (other than sections 4 and 7) shall not be instituted— **20–4**

(a) in England and Wales, except by, or with the consent of, the Attorney General; and

(b) in Northern Ireland, except by, or with the consent of, the Attorney General for Northern Ireland.

(2) As respects Scotland, for the purpose of conferring on the sheriff jurisdiction to entertain proceedings for an offence under or by virtue of section 2, 3 or 6(2)(b) or (c) of this Act, any such offence shall, without prejudice to any jurisdiction exercisable apart from this subsection, be deemed to have been committed in any place in Scotland where the offender may for the time being be.

B. AIRPORT BYELAWS

Airports Act 1986, ss.63, 64

Airport byelaws

63.—(1) Where an airport is either— **20–5**

(a) designated for the purposes of this section by an order made by the Secretary of State, or

(b) managed by the Secretary of State,

the airport operator (whether the Secretary of State or some other person) may make byelaws for regulating the use and operation of the airport and the conduct of all persons while within the airport.

(2) Any such byelaws may, in particular, include byelaws—

(a) for securing the safety of aircraft, vehicles and persons using the airport and preventing danger to the public arising from the use and operation of the airport;

(b) for controlling the operation of aircraft within, or directly above, the airport for the purpose of limiting or mitigating the effect of noise, vibration and atmospheric pollution caused by aircraft using the airport;

(c) for preventing obstruction within the airport;

(d) for regulating vehicular traffic anywhere within the airport, except on roads within the airport to which the road traffic enactments apply, and in particular (with that exception) for imposing speed limits on vehicles within the airport and for restricting or regulating the parking of vehicles or their use for any purpose or in any manner specified in the byelaws;

(e) for prohibiting waiting by hackney carriages except at standings appointed by such person as may be specified in the byelaws;

(f) for prohibiting or restricting access to any part of the airport;

(g) for preserving order within the airport and preventing damage to property within it;

(h) for regulating or restricting advertising within the airport;
(i) for requiring any person, if so requested by a constable or airport official, to leave the airport or any particular part of it, or to state his name and address and the purpose of his being within the airport;
(j) for securing the safe custody and redelivery of any property which, while not in proper custody, is found within the airport or in an aircraft within the airport, and in particular—
  (i) for requiring charges to be paid in respect of any such property before it is redelivered; and
  (ii) for authorising the disposal of any such property if it is not redelivered before the end of such period as may be specified in the byelaws;
(k) for restricting the area which is to be taken as constituting the airport for the purposes of the byelaws.

(3) In paragraph (d) of subsection (2) "the road traffic enactments" means the enactments (whether passed before or after this Act) relating to road traffic, including the lighting and parking of vehicles, and any order or other instrument having effect by virtue of any such enactment.

(4) In paragraph (i) of subsection (2) "airport official" means a person authorised by the airport operator; and any such official shall not exercise any power under a byelaw made by virtue of that paragraph without producing written evidence of his authority if required to do so.

(5) Byelaws made under this section by a person other than the Secretary of State shall not have effect until they are confirmed by the Secretary of State, and the provisions of Schedule 3 shall apply to any such byelaws.

(6) Before any byelaws are made by the Secretary of State under this section, he shall take such steps as appear to him to be appropriate for giving public notice of the proposed byelaws and for affording an opportunity for representations to be made with respect to them; and the Secretary of State shall have regard to any such representations and may then make the byelaws in the form proposed or in that form with such modifications as he thinks fit.

(7) Any byelaws made by the Secretary of State under this section shall be made by statutory instrument.

(8) Section 236(9) of the *Local Government Act* 1972 and section 202(13) of the *Local Government (Scotland) Act* 1973 (notice of byelaws made by one local authority to be given to another) and section 237 of the Act of 1972 and section 203 of the Act of 1973 (penalties) shall not apply to any byelaws made by a local authority under this section.

Byelaws: penalties and power to revoke in certain cases

20–6 **64.**—(1) Any person contravening any byelaws made under section 63 shall be liable on summary conviction to a fine not exceeding such amount as, subject to subsection (2) of this section, may be specified by the byelaws in relation to the contravention.

(2) The maximum fines that byelaws may specify by virtue of subsection (1) are fines of an amount at the fourth level on the standard scale or of a lower amount.

(3) Where any person other than the Secretary of State has made any byelaw in relation to any airport by virtue of section 63(2)(b), the Secretary of State may, after consulting that person, by order—
(a) revoke or vary that byelaw if the Secretary of State considers it appropriate to do so by reason of his having designated the airport for the purposes of section 78 of the 1982 Act (regulation of noise and vibration from aircraft); or
(b) revoke or vary that byelaw to the extent that it appears to the Secretary of State to be inconsistent with the safety of persons or vehicles using the airport, of aircraft or of the general public or to be inconsistent with any international obligation of the United Kingdom.

20–7 The following airports in England and Wales have been designated:

Biggin Hill, Birmingham, Blackpool, Bournemouth (Hurn), Bristol, Cardiff-Wales, Coventry, East Midlands, Exeter, Humberside, Leeds/Bradford, Liverpool, London-Gatwick, London-Heathrow, London-Stanstead, Luton, Manchester, Newcastle, Norwich, Southampton, Southend, Tees-side: *Airport Byelaws (Designation) Order* 1987, (S.I. 1987 No. 380) and Bainbridge, Carlisle, Gloucester/Cheltenham, Redhill and Swansea: *Airport Byelaws (Designation) (No.2) Order* 1987 (S.I. 1987 No. 2246).

II. ANIMALS

A. ANIMAL WELFARE

The *Animal Welfare Act* 2006 consolidates and updates the law relating to the treatment of animals, other than those in the wild. The Act is designed to promote the welfare of animals and duties of those responsible for animals and rights of protection for animals are provided for. **20–8**

Sections 1–3 define the categories of animal;

Sections 4–8 set out the offences of animal cruelty and animal fighting;

Sections 9–17 relate to the promotion of animal welfare supported by a system of inspection, licensing and registration all governed by Codes of Practice;

Sections 18–21 give powers to remove animals in distress;

Sections 30–35 provide for powers of prosecution and penalties and orders on conviction.

The Act is lengthy and detailed and the sections set out below are those most likely to be referred to in the magistrates courts. These provisions came into force on April 6, 2007 under the *Animal Welfare Act (Commencement No.1) Order* (S.I. 2007 No. 499).

(1) Definition

Animal Welfare Act 2006, s.4

Unnecessary suffering

4.—(1) A person commits an offence if— **20–9**

(a) an act of his, or a failure of his to act, causes an animal to suffer,

(b) he knew, or ought reasonably to have known, that the act, or failure to act, would have that effect or be likely to do so,

(c) the animal is a protected animal, and

(d) the suffering is unnecessary.

(2) A person commits an offence if—

(a) he is responsible for an animal,

(b) an act, or failure to act, of another person causes the animal to suffer,

(c) he permitted that to happen or failed to take such steps (whether by way of supervising the other person or otherwise) as were reasonable in all the circumstances to prevent that happening, and

(d) the suffering is unnecessary.

(3) The considerations to which it is relevant to have regard when determining for the purposes of this section whether suffering is unnecessary include—

(a) whether the suffering could reasonably have been avoided or reduced;

(b) whether the conduct which caused the suffering was in compliance with any relevant enactment or any relevant provisions of a licence or code of practice issued under an enactment;

(c) whether the conduct which caused the suffering was for a legitimate purpose, such as—

(i) the purpose of benefiting the animal, or

(ii) the purpose of protecting a person, property or another animal;

(d) whether the suffering was proportionate to the purpose of the conduct concerned;

(e) whether the conduct concerned was in all the circumstances that of a reasonably competent and humane person.

(4) Nothing in this section applies to the destruction of an animal in an appropriate and humane manner.

Animal Welfare Act 2006, s.8

Fighting etc.

8.—(1) A person commits an offence if he— **20–10**

(a) causes an animal fight to take place, or attempts to do so;
(b) knowingly receives money for admission to an animal fight;
(c) knowingly publicises a proposed animal fight;
(d) provides information about an animal fight to another with the intention of enabling or encouraging attendance at the fight;
(e) makes or accepts a bet on the outcome of an animal fight or on the likelihood of anything occurring or not occurring in the course of an animal fight;
(f) takes part in an animal fight;
(g) has in his possession anything designed or adapted for use in connection with an animal fight with the intention of its being so used;
(h) keeps or trains an animal for use for in connection with an animal fight;
(i) keeps any premises for use for an animal fight.

(2) A person commits an offence if, without lawful authority or reasonable excuse, he is present at an animal fight.

[(3) *A person commits an offence if, without lawful authority or reasonable excuse, he—*
(a) *knowingly supplies a video recording of an animal fight,*
(b) *knowingly publishes a video recording of an animal fight,*
(c) *knowingly shows a video recording of an animal fight to another, or*
(d) *possesses a video recording of an animal fight, knowing it to be such a recording, with the intention of supplying it.*]

[(4) *Subsection (3) does not apply if the video recording is of an animal fight that took place—*
(a) *outside Great Britain, or*
(b) *before the commencement date.*]

[(5) *Subsection (3) does not apply—*
(a) *in the case of paragraph (a), to the supply of a video recording for inclusion in a programme service;*
(b) *in the case of paragraph (b) or (c), to the publication or showing of a video recording by means of its inclusion in a programme service;*
(c) *in the case of paragraph (d), by virtue of intention to supply for inclusion in a programme service.*]

[(6) *Provision extending the application of an offence under subsection (3), so far as relating to the provision of information society services, may be made under section 2(2) of the European Communities Act 1972 (c. 68) (powers to implement Community obligations by regulations) notwithstanding the limits imposed by paragraph 1(1)(d) of Schedule 2 to that Act on the penalties with which an offence may be punishable on summary conviction.*]

(7) In this section—

"animal fight" means an occasion on which a protected animal is placed with an animal, or with a human, for the purpose of fighting, wrestling or baiting;

"commencement date" means the date on which subsection (3) comes into force;

"information society services" has the meaning given in Article 2(a) of Directive 2000/31/EC of the European Parliament and of the Council of 8 June 2000 on certain legal aspects of information society services, in particular electronic commerce in the Internal Market (Directive on electronic commerce);

"programme service" has the same meaning as in the *Communications Act* 2003 (c. 21);

"video recording" means a recording, in any form, from which a moving image may by any means be reproduced and includes data stored on a computer disc or by other electronic means which is capable of conversion into a moving image.

(8) In this section—
(a) references to supplying or publishing a video recording are to supplying or publishing a video recording in any manner, including, in relation to a video recording in the form of data stored electronically, by means of transmitting such data;
(b) references to showing a video recording are to showing a moving image reproduced from a video recording by any means.

[The subsections printed in italics are not yet in force.]

Animal Welfare Act 2006, s.9

Duty of person responsible for animal to ensure welfare

9.—(1) A person commits an offence if he does not take such steps as are reasonable in all the circumstances to ensure that the needs of an animal for which he is responsible are met to the extent required by good practice. **20–11**

(2) For the purposes of this Act, an animal's needs shall be taken to include—

(a) its need for a suitable environment,

(b) its need for a suitable diet,

(c) its need to be able to exhibit normal behaviour patterns,

(d) any need it has to be housed with, or apart from, other animals, and

(e) its need to be protected from pain, suffering, injury and disease.

(3) The circumstances to which it is relevant to have regard when applying subsection (1) include, in particular—

(a) any lawful purpose for which the animal is kept, and

(b) any lawful activity undertaken in relation to the animal.

(4) Nothing in this section applies to the destruction of an animal in an appropriate and humane manner.

(2) Allocation

The offences are triable summarily: s.35. **20–12**

The offences may be prosecuted by the local authority as well as the CPS: s.30. The time limit for prosecutions is three years from the date of commission of the offence and six months from the time when evidence sufficient to justify proceedings comes to the prosecutor's knowledge. Section 31.

(3) Elements of the offence

Animal Welfare Act 2006, s.1

Animals to which the Act applies

1.—(1) In this Act, except subsections (4) and (5), "animal" means a vertebrate other than man. **20–13**

(2) Nothing in this Act applies to an animal while it is in its foetal or embryonic form.

(3) The appropriate national authority may by regulations for all or any of the purposes of this Act—

(a) extend the definition of "animal" so as to include invertebrates of any description;

(b) make provision in lieu of subsection (2) as respects any invertebrates included in the definition of "animal";

(c) amend subsection (2) to extend the application of this Act to an animal from such earlier stage of its development as may be specified in the regulations.

(4) The power under subsection (3)(a) or (c) may only be exercised if the appropriate national authority is satisfied, on the basis of scientific evidence, that animals of the kind concerned are capable of experiencing pain or suffering.

(5) In this section, "vertebrate" means any animal of the Sub-phylum Vertebrata of the Phylum Chordata and "invertebrate" means any animal not of that Sub-phylum.

Animal Welfare Act, s.2

"Protected animal"

2. An animal is a "protected animal" for the purposes of this Act if— **20–14**

(a) it is of a kind which is commonly domesticated in the British Islands,

(b) it is under the control of man whether on a permanent or temporary basis, or

(c) it is not living in a wild state.

Animal Welfare Act 2006, s.3

Responsibility for animals

3.—(1) In this Act, references to a person responsible for an animal are to a person responsible for an animal whether on a permanent or temporary basis. **20–15**

(2) In this Act, references to being responsible for an animal include being in charge of it.

(3) For the purposes of this Act, a person who owns an animal shall always be regarded as being a person who is responsible for it.

(4) For the purposes of this Act, a person shall be treated as responsible for any animal for which a person under the age of 16 years of whom he has actual care and control is responsible.

(4) Sentence

Animal Welfare Act 2006, s.32

Imprisonment or fine

20–16 **32.**—(1) A person guilty of an offence under any of sections 4, 5, 6(1) and (2), 7 and 8 shall be liable on summary conviction to—

(a) imprisonment for a term not exceeding 51 weeks, or

(b) a fine not exceeding £20,000,

or to both.

(2) A person guilty of an offence under section 9, 13(6) or 34(9) shall be liable on summary conviction to—

(a) imprisonment for a term not exceeding 51 weeks, or

(b) a fine not exceeding level 5 on the standard scale,

or to both.

(3) A person guilty of an offence under regulations under section 12 or 13 shall be liable on summary conviction to such penalty by way of imprisonment or fine as may be provided by regulations under that section.

(4) A person guilty of any other offence under this Act shall be liable on summary conviction to—

(a) imprisonment for a term not exceeding 51 weeks, or

(b) a fine not exceeding level 4 on the standard scale,

or to both.

(5) In relation to an offence committed before the commencement of section 281(5) of the *Criminal Justice Act* 2003 (c. 44), the reference in each of subsections (1)(a), (2)(a) and (4)(a) to 51 weeks is to be read as a reference to 6 months.

Animal Welfare Act 2006, s.33

Deprivation

20–17 **33.**—(1) If the person convicted of an offence under any of sections 4, 5, 6(1) and (2), 7, 8 and 9 is the owner of an animal in relation to which the offence was committed, the court by or before which he is convicted may, instead of or in addition to dealing with him in any other way, make an order depriving him of ownership of the animal and for its disposal.

(2) Where the owner of an animal is convicted of an offence under section 34(9) because ownership of the animal is in breach of a disqualification under section 34(2), the court by or before which he is convicted may, instead of or in addition to dealing with him in any other way, make an order depriving him of ownership of the animal and for its disposal.

(3) Where the animal in respect of which an order under subsection (1) or (2) is made has any dependent offspring, the order may include provision depriving the person to whom it relates of ownership of the offspring and for its disposal.

(4) Where a court makes an order under subsection (1) or (2), it may—

(a) appoint a person to carry out, or arrange for the carrying out of, the order;

(b) require any person who has possession of an animal to which the order applies to deliver it up to enable the order to be carried out;

(c) give directions with respect to the carrying out of the order;

(d) confer additional powers (including power to enter premises where an animal to which the order applies is being kept) for the purpose of, or in connection with, the carrying out of the order;

(e) order the offender to reimburse the expenses of carrying out the order.

(5) Directions under subsection (4)(c) may—

(a) specify the manner in which an animal is to be disposed of, or
(b) delegate the decision about the manner in which an animal is to be disposed of to a person appointed under subsection (4)(a).

(6) Where a court decides not to make an order under subsection (1) or (2) in relation to an offender, it shall—
(a) give its reasons for the decision in open court, and
(b) if it is a magistrates' court, cause them to be entered in the register of its proceedings.

(7) Subsection (6) does not apply where the court makes an order under section 34(1) in relation to the offender.

(8) In subsection (1), the reference to an animal in relation to which an offence was committed includes, in the case of an offence under section 8, an animal which took part in an animal fight in relation to which the offence was committed.

(9) In this section, references to disposing of an animal include destroying it.

Animal Welfare Act 2006, s.34

Disqualification

34.—(1) If a person is convicted of an offence to which this section applies, the court by or before which he is convicted may, instead of or in addition to dealing with him in any other way, make an order disqualifying him under any one or more of subsections (2) to (4) for such period as it thinks fit. **20–18**

(2) Disqualification under this subsection disqualifies a person—
(a) from owning animals,
(b) from keeping animals,
(c) from participating in the keeping of animals, and
(d) from being party to an arrangement under which he is entitled to control or influence the way in which animals are kept.

(3) Disqualification under this subsection disqualifies a person from dealing in animals.

(4) Disqualification under this subsection disqualifies a person—
(a) from transporting animals, and
(b) from arranging for the transport of animals.

(5) Disqualification under subsection (2), (3) or (4) may be imposed in relation to animals generally, or in relation to animals of one or more kinds.

(6) The court by which an order under subsection (1) is made may specify a period during which the offender may not make an application under section 43(1) for termination of the order.

(7) The court by which an order under subsection (1) is made may—
(a) suspend the operation of the order pending an appeal, or
(b) where it appears to the court that the offender owns or keeps an animal to which the order applies, suspend the operation of the order, and of any order made under section 35 in connection with the disqualification, for such period as it thinks necessary for enabling alternative arrangements to be made in respect of the animal.

(8) Where a court decides not to make an order under subsection (1) in relation to an offender, it shall—
(a) give its reasons for the decision in open court, and
(b) if it is a magistrates' court, cause them to be entered in the register of its proceedings.

(9) A person who breaches a disqualification imposed by an order under subsection (1) commits an offence.

(10) This section applies to an offence under any of sections 4, 5, 6(1) and (2), 7, 8, 9 and 13(6) and subsection (9).

The Magistrates' Courts Sentencing Guidelines 2008 issued by the Sentencing Guidelines Council apply to offences of animal cruelty and specifically to offences under section 4 (unnecessary suffering), s.8 (fighting etc.) and section 9 (breach of duty to ensure welfare). **20–19**

These lists of factors are not exhaustive and general sentencing factors apply.

STARTING POINT AND RANGE OF SENTENCE

(BASED ON A FIRST TIME OFFENDER PLEADING NOT GUILTY)

Examples of nature of activity	Starting Point	Range
One impulsive act causing little or no injury; short term neglect	Band C fine	Band B fine to medium level community order
Several incidents of deliberate ill-treatment/frightening animal(s); medium term neglect	High level community order	Medium level community order to 12 weeks custody
Attempt to kill/torture; animal baiting/conducting or permitting cock-fighting etc; prolonged neglect	18 weeks custody	12 to 26 weeks custody.

AGGRAVATING AND MITIGATING FACTORS

Factors indicating higher culpability	Factors indicating lower culpability
1. Offender in position of special responsibility 2. Adult involves children in offending 3. Animal(s) kept for a livelihood 4. Use of weapon 5. Offender ignored advice/warnings 6. Offence committed for commercial gain **Factors indicating greater degree of harm** 1. Serious injury or death 2. Several animals affected	1. Offender induced by others 2. Ignorance of appropriate care 3. Offender with limited capacity

Ancillary orders such as deprivation and disqualification must also be considered.

B. DANGEROUS DOGS

(1) Legislation

Dogs Act 1871, s.2

Dangerous dogs may be destroyed

2. Any court of summary jurisdiction may take cognizance of a complaint that a dog is dangerous, and not kept under proper control, and if it appears to the court having cognizance of such complaint that such dog is dangerous, the court may make an order in a summary way directing the dog to be kept by the owner under proper control or destroyed **20–20**

A complaint may be made by a police officer: *Smith v. Baker*, 125 J.P. 53.

The court has jurisdiction to hear a complaint under this section even if the conduct **20–21** complained of occurred outside of the commission area. Jurisdiction is founded on the location of the animal at the time when the summons is applied for and the complaint relates to the dangerousness of the animal which should be kept under proper control no matter where it might be: *Shufflebottom v. Chief Constable of Greater Manchester* (2003) 167 J.P. 153.

The term "dangerous" is to be given its ordinary, every day meaning and the question of whether it is kept under "proper control" is a question of fact for the court. The dog does not have to be dangerous only to human beings or livestock. The fact that it is dangerous to other dogs is sufficient: *Briscoe v. Shattock* (1998) 163 J.P. 201. But the fact that a dog killed two pet rabbits on one occasion was held not to make it dangerous because it was in the nature of dogs to hunt and kill other small animals: *Sansom v. Chief Constable of Kent* [1981] Crim.L.R. 617.

The court may order destruction of the animal and further powers are contained in s.1 of the *Dangerous Dogs Act* 1989, *post*.

Costs may be ordered under s.64 of the *Magistrates Courts Act* 1980.

Dangerous Dogs Act 1989, s.1

Additional powers of court on complaint about dangerous dog

1.—(1) Where a magistrates' court makes an order under section 2 of the *Dogs Act* 1871 directing a dog to be destroyed it may also— **20–22**

(a) appoint a person to undertake its destruction and require any person having custody of the dog to deliver it up for that purpose; and

(b) if it thinks fit, make an order disqualifying the owner for having custody of a dog for such period as is specified in the order.

(2) An appeal shall lie to the Crown Court against any order under section 2 of that Act or under subsection (1) above; and, unless the owner of a dog which is ordered to be delivered up and destroyed gives notice to the court that made the order that he does not intend to appeal against it, the dog shall not be destroyed pursuant to the order—

(a) until the end of the period within which notice of appeal to the Crown Court against the order can be given; and

(b) if notice of appeal is given within that period, until the appeal is determined or withdrawn.

(3) Any person who fails to comply with an order under section 2 of the said Act of 1871 to keep a dog under proper control or to deliver a dog up for destruction as required by an order under subsection (1)(a) above is guilty of an offence and liable on summary conviction to a fine not exceeding level 3 on the standard scale and the court may, in addition, make an order disqualifying him for having custody of a dog for such period as is specified in the order.

(4) A person who is disqualified for having custody of a dog by virtue of an order made under subsection (1)(b) or (3) above may, at any time after the end of the period of one year beginning with the date of the order, apply to the court that made it (or any magistrates' court acting for the same petty sessions area as that court) for a direction terminating the disqualification.

(5) On an application under subsection (4) above the court may—

(a) having regard to the applicant's character, his conduct since the disqualification was imposed and any other circumstances of the case, grant or refuse the application; and

(b) order the applicant to pay all or any part of the costs of the application;

and where an application in respect of an order is refused no further application in respect of that order shall be entertained if made before the end of the period of one year beginning with the date of the refusal.

(6) Any person who has custody of a dog in contravention of an order made under subsection (1)(b) or (3) above is guilty of an offence and liable on summary conviction to a fine not exceeding level 5 on the standard scale.

(7) This section shall apply to Scotland subject to the following adaptations—

(a) in subsection (1) for the words "magistrates' court" there shall be substituted the words "court of summary jurisdiction";

(b) in subsection (2)—

(i) for the words "shall lie to the Crown Court" there shall be substituted the words "may be made to the High Court within a period of 7 days commencing with the date of the order";

(ii) for paragraph (a) there shall be substituted—

"(a) until the end of the said period of 7 days;and ";

(c) in subsection (4) the words "(or any magistrates' court acting for the same petty sessions area as that court)" shall be omitted.

(2) Definition

Dangerous Dogs Act 1991, s.1

Dogs bred for fighting

20–23 **1.**—(1) This section applies to—

(a) any dog of the type known as the pit bull terrier;

(b) any dog of the type known as the Japanese tosa; and

(c) any dog of any type designated for the purposes of this section by an order of the Secretary of State, being a type appearing to him to be bred for fighting or to have the characteristics of a type bred for that purpose.

(2) No person shall—

(a) breed, or breed from, a dog to which this section applies;

(b) sell or exchange such a dog or offer, advertise or expose such a dog for sale or exchange;

(c) make or offer to make a gift of such a dog or advertise or expose such a dog as a gift;

(d) allow such a dog of which he is the owner or of which he is for the time being in charge to be in a public place without being muzzled and kept on a lead; or

(e) abandon such a dog of which he is the owner or, being the owner or for the time being in charge of such a dog, allow it to stray.

(3) After such day as the Secretary of State may by order appoint for the purposes of this subsection no person shall have any dog to which this section applies in his possession or custody except—

(a) in pursuance of the power of seizure conferred by the subsequent provisions of this Act; or

(b) in accordance with an order for its destruction made under those provisions;

but the Secretary of State shall by order make a scheme for the payment to the owners of such dogs who arrange for them to be destroyed before that day of sums specified in or determined under the scheme in respect of those dogs and the cost of their destruction.

(4) Subsection (2)(b) and (c) above shall not make unlawful anything done with a view to the dog in question being removed from the United Kingdom before the day appointed under subsection (3) above.

(5) The Secretary of State may by order provide that the prohibition in subsection (3) above shall not apply in such cases and subject to compliance with such conditions as are

specified in the order and any such provision may take the form of a scheme of exemption containing such arrangements (including provision for the payment of charges or fees) as he thinks appropriate.

(6) A scheme under subsection (3) or (5) above may provide for specified functions under the scheme to be discharged by such persons or bodies as the Secretary of State thinks appropriate.

(7) Any person who contravenes this section is guilty of an offence and liable on summary conviction to imprisonment for a term not exceeding six months or a fine not exceeding level 5 on the standard scale or both except that a person who publishes an advertisement in contravention of subsection (2)(b) or (c)—

(a) shall not on being convicted be liable to imprisonment if he shows that he published the advertisement to the order of someone else and did not himself devise it; and

(b) shall not be convicted if, in addition, he shows that he did not know and had no reasonable cause to suspect that it related to a dog to which this section applies.

(8) An order under subsection (1)(c) above adding dogs of any type to those to which this section applies may provide that subsections (3) and (4) above shall apply in relation to those dogs with the substitution for the day appointed under subsection (3) of a later day specified in the order.

(9) The power to make orders under this section shall be exercisable by statutory instrument which, in the case of an order under subsection (1) or (5) or an order containing a scheme under subsection (3), shall be subject to annulment in pursuance of a resolution of either House of Parliament.

(3) Allocation

This offence is triable summarily. **20–24**

(4) Elements of the offence

This section applies specifically to dogs bred for fighting. The appointed day referred **20–25** to in s.1(3) was November 30, 1991 (S.I. 1991 No. 1742). The word "type" has wider and different meaning from the description "breed". It was held to include any dog which had a substantial amount or most of the physical characteristics of the breed of dog in question, *e.g.* a pitbull terrier: *Crown Court at Knightsbridge ex p. Dunne* [1993] 4 All E.R. 491. An offence is committed if the dog is in a car, when the car itself is in a public place: *Bates v. DPP* (1993) 157 J.P. 1004.

This is an absolute offence and it is no defence to a charge of allowing a dog to be off the lead and unmuzzled for the owner to say he was intoxicated at the time: *DPP v. Kellet* (1994) 158 J.P. 1138. Nor is it a defence for the owner to say that the dog was not muzzled or kept on a lead as a necessity to avoid serious harm to the dog itself: *Cichon v. DPP* [1994] Crim.L.R.

(5) Sentence

The sentence is a maximum of six months' imprisonment or a fine not exceeding **20–26** level 5 or both. After commencement of the relevant provisions, the maximum custodial sentence in a magistrates' court will be 12 months' imprisonment: *Criminal Justice Act* 2003, ss.154 and 282.

The court also has power to make destruction and disqualification orders under ss.4 and 4A (see *post*).

(1) Definition

Dangerous Dogs Act 1991, s.3

Keeping dogs under proper control

3.—(1) If a dog is dangerously out of control in a public place— **20–27**

(a) the owner; and

(b) if different, the person for the time being in charge of the dog,

is guilty of an offence, or, if the dog while so out of control injures any person, an aggravated offence, under this subsection.

(2) In proceedings for an offence under subsection (1) above against a person who is the owner of a dog but was not at the material time in charge of it, it shall be a defence for the accused to prove that the dog was at the material time in the charge of a person whom he reasonably believed to be a fit and proper person to be in charge of it.

(3) If the owner or, if different, the person for the time being in charge of a dog allows it to enter a place which is not a public place but where it is not permitted to be and while it is there—

(a) it injures any person; or

(b) there are grounds for reasonable apprehension that it will do so,

he is guilty of an offence, or, if the dog injures any person, an aggravated offence, under this subsection.

(4) A person guilty of an offence under subsection (1) or (3) above other than an aggravated offence is liable on summary conviction to imprisonment for a term not exceeding six months or a fine not exceeding level 5 on the standard scale or both; and a person guilty of an aggravated offence under either of those subsections is liable—

(a) on summary conviction, to imprisonment for a term not exceeding six months or a fine not exceeding the statutory maximum or both;

(b) on conviction on indictment, to imprisonment for a term not exceeding two years or a fine or both.

(5) It is hereby declared for the avoidance of doubt that an order under section 2 of the *Dogs Act* 1871 (order on complaint that dog is dangerous and not kept under proper control)—

(a) may be made whether or not the dog is shown to have injured any person; and

(b) may specify the measures to be taken for keeping the dog under proper control, whether by muzzling, keeping on a lead, excluding it from specified places or otherwise.

(6) If it appears to a court on a complaint under section 2 of the said Act of 1871 that the dog to which the complaint relates is a male and would be less dangerous if neutered the court may under that section make an order requiring it to be neutered.

(7) The reference in section 1(3) of the *Dangerous Dogs Act* 1989 (penalties) to failing to comply with an order under section 2 of the said Act of 1871 to keep a dog under proper control shall include a reference to failing to comply with any other order made under that section; but no order shall be made under that section by virtue of subsection (6) above where the matters complained of arose before the coming into force of that subsection.

(2) Allocation

20–28 This offence is triable summarily only unless it is an aggravated offence in which case it is triable either way. An offence is aggravated under s.3(1) if, while the dog is out of control, it injures any person.

(3) Elements of the offence

20–29 This section applies to any kind of dog. A dog is defined as being dangerously out of control "on any occasion on which there are grounds for reasonable apprehension that it will injure any person, whether or not it actually does so, but references to a dog injuring a person or there being grounds for reasonable apprehension that it will do so do not include references to any case in which the dog is being used for a lawful purpose by a constable or a person in the service of the Crown.": s.10(3) of the Act. This is an objective test.

Where a dog had never shown a propensity to attack and was on a lead on the pavement, it was held that the dog was 'out of control' because it bit and injured an innocent passer-by who exhibited no provocative behaviour. The definition in s.10(3) was held not to be exclusive and the straight forward words of s.3 applied directly to the way the dog behaved and the lack of control by its handler. *Gedminintaite and Collier* (2008) 172 J.P. 413.

A public place is "any street, road or other place, (whether or not enclosed) to which the public have or are permitted to have access whether for payment or otherwise and includes the common parts of a building containing two or more separate dwellings.": s.10(2) of the Act.

In *Bogdal* (2008) 172 J.P. 178 it was held that a driveway shared between a private residence and a private residential home was not a public place for the purposes of this statute. The public did not have a right of access to the driveway as it led only to the two residences concerned so the dog involved was not dangerously out of control in a public place whilst on the driveway.

An offence may be committed in a public place if the dog is dangerously out of control. An offence may also be committed in a place which is not a public place and where the dog is not permitted to be but only if the dog injures any person or there is a reasonable apprehension that it will do so: s.3(3). This offence is aggravated if a person is injured.

In *L v. CPS* [2010] 174 J.P. 209 D.C. the defendant was held to be in charge of a dog even when he had handed physical control to another for a short period whist he tied his shoelace and the dog attacked a person at that time.

(4) Defence

This is an absolute offence. It is no defence for the owner to say that they never re- **20–30**
alised that the dog would behave in a dangerous manner: *Bezzina* 158 J.P. 671.

The offence may be committed by the owner of the dog or any person for the time being in charge of the dog. The defence under s.3(2) requires clear and plain evidence that the owner has placed the dog in the charge of another identifiable person: *Huddart* [1999] Crim.L.R. 568.

(5) Sentence

For a summary offence the sentence is a maximum term of imprisonment of six **20–31**
months or a fine not exceeding level 5 or both.

On conviction on indictment the sentence is a maximum term of imprisonment of two years and a fine or both. The court also has power to make destruction and disqualification orders under ss.4 and 4A, *post*.

When imposing sentence the courts should look at the consequences of the offence. The nature and extent of the obligations of dog owners had to be marked by a custodial sentence when there was a seriously aggravated offence. In a case where a pack of five dogs attacked and seriously injured a boy of seven in a public park, a sentence of three months' imprisonment was held to be appropriate for a defendant of good character who entered a plea of guilty: *Cox*, (2004) 2 Cr.App.R.(S) 54. In *Jamal Richards* [2009] 1 Cr.App.R. (S) 48 the appellant owned two pit-bull dogs which escaped from his yard and attacked and bit a postman who sustained deep lacerations and permanent scarring. The appeal was against a sentence of 9 months custody. The appeal court recognised the need to take into account the serious consequences to the victim but in light of the young age of the defendant and his genuine remorse and pleas of guilty it was held that the sentence should be reduced to 4 months. However in *Joel Lee* [2009] EWCA Crim 2046 the appeal court stated that previous cases were not guideline cases setting a maximum sentence of 4 months as each case depended on its individual facts but where the appellants two dogs attacked and severely injured a 72 year old neighbour the sentence was reduced from 10 to 6 months custody. On commencement of the relevant provisions, the maximum custodial sentence in a magistrates' court will be 12 months' imprisonment: *Criminal Justice Act* 2003, ss.154 and 282.

(6) Other penalties

Dangerous Dogs Act 1991, ss.4, 4A, 4B

Destruction and disqualification orders

4.—(1) Where a person is convicted of an offence under section 1 or 3(1) or (3) above or of **20–32**
an offence under an order made under section 2 above the court—

Part III

(a) may order the destruction of any dog in respect of which the offence was committed and, subject to subsection (1A) below, shall do so in the case of an offence under section 1 or an aggravated offence under section 3(1) or (3) above; and

(b) may order the offender to be disqualified, for such period as the court thinks fit, for having custody of a dog.

(1A) Nothing in subsection (1)(a) above shall require the court to order the destruction of a dog if the court is satisfied—

(a) that the dog would not constitute a danger to public safety; and

(b) where the dog was born before 30th November 1991 and is subject to the prohibition in section 1 (3) above, that there is a good reason why the dog has not been exempted from that prohibition.

(2) Where a court makes an order under subsection (1)(a) above for the destruction of a dog owned by a person other than the offender, the owner may appeal to the Crown Court against the order.

(3) A dog shall not be destroyed pursuant to an order under subsection (1)(a) above—

(a) until the end of the period for giving notice of appeal against the conviction or against the order; and

(b) if notice of appeal is given within that period, until the appeal is determined or withdrawn,

unless the offender and, in a case to which subsection (2) above applies, the owner of the dog give notice to the court that made the order that there is to be no appeal.

(4) Where a court makes an order under subsection (1)(a) above it may—

(a) appoint a person to undertake the destruction of the dog and require any person having custody of it to deliver it up for that purpose; and

(b) order the offender to pay such sum as the court may determine to be the reasonable expenses of destroying the dog and of keeping it pending its destruction.

(5) Any sum ordered to be paid under subsection (4)(b) above shall be treated for the purposes of enforcement as if it were a fine imposed on conviction.

(6) Any person who is disqualified for having custody of a dog by virtue of an order under subsection (1)(b) above may, at any time after the end of the period of one year beginning with the date of the order, apply to the court that made it (or a magistrates' court acting for the same petty sessions area as that court) for a direction terminating the disqualification.

(7) On an application under subsection (6) above the court may—

(a) having regard to the applicant's character, his conduct since the disqualification was imposed and any other circumstances of the case, grant or refuse the application; and

(b) order the applicant to pay all or any part of the costs of the application;

and where an application in respect of an order is refused no further application in respect of that order shall be entertained if made before the end of the period of one year beginning with the date of the refusal.

(8) Any person who—

(a) has custody of a dog in contravention of an order under subsection (1)(b) above; or

(b) fails to comply with a requirement imposed on him under subsection (4)(a) above,

is guilty of an offence and liable on summary conviction to a fine not exceeding level 5 on the standard scale.

(9) In the application of this section to Scotland—

(a) in subsection (2) for the words "Crown Court against the order" there shall be substituted the words "High Court of Justiciary against the order within the period of seven days beginning with the date of the order";

(b) for subsection (3)(a) there shall be substituted—

"(a) until the end of the period of seven days beginning with the date of the order";

(c) for subsection (5) there shall be substituted—

"(5) section 221 of the *Criminal Procedure (Scotland) Act* 1995 shall apply in relation to the recovery of sums ordered to be paid under subsection (4)(b) above as it applies to fines ordered to be recovered by civil diligence in pursuance of Part XI of that Act."

; and

(d) in subsection (6) the words "(or a magistrates' court acting for the same petty sessions area as that court)" shall be omitted.

Contingent destruction orders

4A.—(1) Where— 20–33

(a) a person is convicted of an offence under section 1 above or an aggravated offence under section 3(1) or (3) above;

(b) the court does not order the destruction of the dog under section 4(1)(a) above; and

(c) in the case of an offence under section 1 above, the dog is subject to the prohibition in section 1(3) above.

the court shall order that, unless the dog is exempted from that prohibition within the requisite period, the dog shall be destroyed.

(2) Where an order is made under subsection (1) above in respect of a dog, and the dog is not exempted from the prohibition in section 1(3) above within the requisite period, the court may extend that period.

(3) Subject to subsection (2) above, the requisite period for the purposes of such an order is the period of two months beginning with the date of the order.

(4) Where a person is convicted of an offence under section 3(1) or (3) above, the court may order that, unless the owner of the dog keeps it under proper control, the dog shall be destroyed.

(5) An order under subsection (4) above—

(a) may specify the measures to be taken for keeping the dog under proper control, whether by muzzling, keeping on a lead, excluding it from specified places or otherwise; and

(b) if it appears to the court that the dog is a male and would be less dangerous if neutered, may require it to be neutered.

(6) Subsections (2) to (4) of section 4 above shall apply in relation to an order under subsection (1) or (4) above as they apply in relation to an order under subsection (1)(a) of that section.

Destruction orders otherwise than on a conviction

4B.—(1) Where a dog is seized under section 5(1) or (2) below and it appears to a justice of the peace, or in Scotland a justice of the peace or sheriff— 20–34

(a) that no person has been or is to be prosecuted for an offence under this Act or an order under section 2 above in respect of that dog (whether because the owner cannot be found or for any other reason); or

(b) that the dog cannot be released into the custody or possession of its owner without the owner contravening the prohibition in section 1(3) above,

he may order the destruction of the dog and, subject to subsection (2) below, shall do so if it is one to which section 1 above applies.

(2) Nothing in subsection (1)(b) above shall require the justice or sheriff to order the destruction of a dog if he is satisfied—

(a) that the dog would not constitute a danger to public safety; and

(b) where the dog was born before 30th November 1991 and is subject to the prohibition in section 1(3) above, that there is a good reason why the dog has not been exempted from that prohibition.

(3) Where in a case falling within subsection (1)(b) above the justice or sheriff does not order the destruction of the dog, he shall order that, unless the dog is exempted from the prohibition in section 1(3) above within the requisite period, the dog shall be destroyed.

(4) Subsections (2) to (4) of section 4 above shall apply in relation to an order under subsection (1)(b) or (3) above as they apply in relation to an order under subsection (1)(a) of that section.

(5) Subsections (2) and (3) of section 4A above shall apply in relation to an order under subsection (3) above as they apply in relation to an order under subsection (1) of that section, except that the reference to the court in subsection (2) of that section shall be construed as a reference to the justice or sheriff.

[These sections are printed as amended by the *Dangerous Dogs (Amendment) Act 1997*, s.1(4), s.2 and s.3(1).]

Part III

20–35 Before an order of destruction is made, the rules of natural justice require that the owner, if he has not already been notified, should be advised of the hearing and be given the opportunity to attend court and make representations: *Trafford Magistrates' Court ex p. Riley* (1996) 160 J.P. 418.

The power under s.4B may not be exercised where a prosecution has been discontinued but if there is a further new incident involving the dog then fresh proceedings may be instituted after seizure and this will not be an abuse of the courts powers: *Walton Street Justices ex p. Crothers* (1996) 160 J.P. 427.

In *Holland* [2003] 1 Cr.App.R.(S.) 60, CA, a disqualification order disqualifying the appellant for 10 years from keeping a dog, and an order for the destruction of the dog, was upheld in a case where a bull terrier attacked a child. It was held that whilst the destruction order was mandatory under s.4(1)(a) and s.4(1A) of the 1991 Act unless the judge was satisfied that the dog did not constitute a danger to public safety, the order disqualifying the appellant from having the custody of the dog was discretionary. The disqualification order had been made to protect the victim child from anxiety when she visited her grandparents who lived next to the owner of the bull terrier. The Court stated that in cases of this kind, a balance should be struck between the sensitivities of the victim on the one hand and restriction on the freedom of the custodian on the other. The disqualification order prohibited the appellant from keeping any dog at all. The statute made provision for a disqualified person to apply to a court for a direction terminating the disqualification and it would be open to the appellant to make such an application in due course, so the disqualification order was upheld.

A destruction order is justifiable although a dog may not be proved to be inherently dangerous by nature but only likely to bite because of the way in which it was kept and cared for. The power to order a dog to be destroyed was designed to protect the public and the court had to consider the position as it was in relation to the animal's care so if it had not been shown that the dog did not constitute a danger to public safety the order should be made; *Donnelly* [2007] EWCA Crim 2548.

In *Flack* (2008) 2 Cr.App.R.(S) 70 it was held that on conviction the court should consider a contingent destruction order before deciding that a final order was necessary.

See also *Davies* [2010] EWCA Crim 1923 where a destruction order in respect of a dangerous dog was quashed because the court had failed to consider first whether a contingent order should be made. In *Baballa* [2011] 1 C.App.R.(S.) 329 it was held that the court should make a contingent destruction order if satisfied that the dog would not constitute a danger to public safety if as an exempted dog the animal were kept in accordance with various conditions including muzzling, neutering, being kept on a lead and undergoing training. It would seem also that a condition of a contingent destruction order can include transferring ownership of the dog and requiring the animal to be re-housed away from an irresponsible (and in this case –disqualified) owner; *Devon* [2011] EWCA Crim 1073.

Dangerous Dogs Act 1991, s.5

Seizure, entry of premises and evidence.

20–36 **5.**—(1) A constable or an officer of a local authority authorised by it to exercise the powers conferred by this subsection may seize—

(a) any dog which appears to him to be a dog to which section 1 above applies and which is in a public place—

(i) after the time when possession or custody of it has become unlawful by virtue of that section; or

(ii) before that time, without being muzzled and kept on a lead;

(b) any dog in a public place which appears to him to be a dog to which an order under section 2 above applies and in respect of which an offence against the order has been or is being committed; and

(c) any dog in a public place (whether or not one to which that section or such an order applies) which appears to him to be dangerously out of control.

(2) If a justice of the peace is satisfied by information on oath, or in Scotland a justice of

the peace or sheriff is satisfied by evidence on oath, that there are reasonable grounds for believing—

(a) that an offence under any provision of this Act or of an order under section 2 above is being or has been committed; or

(b) that evidence of the commission of any such offence is to be found,

on any premises he may issue a warrant authorising a constable to enter those premises (using such force as is reasonably necessary) and to search them and seize any dog or other thing found there which is evidence of the commission of such an offence.

(3) A warrant issued under this section in Scotland shall be authority for opening lockfast places and may authorise persons named in the warrant to accompany a constable who is executing it.

(5) If in any proceedings it is alleged by the prosecution that a dog is one to which section 1 or an order under section 2 above applies it shall be presumed that it is such a dog unless the contrary is shown by the accused by such evidence as the court considers sufficient; and the accused shall not be permitted to adduce such evidence unless he has given the prosecution notice of his intention to do so not later than the fourteenth day before that on which the evidence is to be adduced.

[This section is printed as amended by the *Dangerous Dogs (Amendment) Act* 1997, s.3(2).]

Dangerous Dogs Act 1991, s.6

Dogs owned by young persons

6. Where a dog is owned by a person who is less than sixteen years old any reference to its owner in section 1(2)(d) or (e) or 3 above shall include a reference to the head of the household, if any, of which that person is a member or, in Scotland, to the person who has his actual care and control. **20–37**

III. CONSUMER PROTECTION

A. PROHIBITION OF FALSE TRADE DESCRIPTIONS

(1) Definition

Trade Descriptions Act 1968, ss.1–6

Prohibition of false trade descriptions

1.—(1) Any person who, in the course of a trade or business,— **20–38**

(a) applies a false trade description to any goods; or

(b) supplies or offers to supply any goods to which a false trade description is applied;

shall, subject to the provisions of this Act, be guilty of an offence.

(2) Sections 2 to 6 of this Act shall have effect for the purposes of this section and for the interpretation of expressions used in this section, wherever they occur in this Act.

Trade description

2.—(1) A trade description is an indication, direct or indirect, and by whatever means given, of any of the following matters with respect to any goods or parts of goods, that is to say— **20–39**

(a) quantity, size or gauge;

(b) method of manufacture, production, processing or reconditioning;

(c) composition;

(d) fitness for purpose, strength, performance, behaviour or accuracy;

(e) any physical characteristics not included in the preceding paragraphs;

(f) testing by any person and results thereof;

(g) approval by any person or conformity with a type approved by any person;

(h) place or date of manufacture, production, processing or reconditioning;

(i) person by whom manufactured, produced, processed or reconditioned;

(j) other history, including previous ownership or use.

(2) The matters specified in subsection (1) of this section shall be taken—

(a) in relation to any animal, to include sex, breed or cross, fertility and soundness;

(b) in relation to any semen, to include the identity and characteristics of the animal from which it was taken and measure of dilution.

(3) In this sections "quantity" includes length, width, height, area, volume, capacity, weight and number.

(4) Notwithstanding anything in the preceding provisions of this section, the following shall be deemed not to be trade descriptions, that is to say, any description or mark applied in pursuance of—

(b) section 2 of the *Agricultural Produce (Grading and Marking) Act* 1928 (as amended by the *Agricultural Produce (Grading and Marking) Amendment Act* 1931) or any corresponding enactment of the Parliament of Northern Ireland;

(c) the *Plant Varieties and Seeds Act* 1964;

(d) the *Agriculture and Horticulture Act* 1964 or any Community grading rules within the meaning of Part III of that Act;

(e) the *Seeds Act (Northern Ireland) 1965*;

(f) the *Horticulture Act (Northern Ireland)* 1966;

any statement made in respect of, or mark applied to, any material in pursuance of Part IV of the *Agriculture Act* 1970, any name or expression to which a meaning has been assigned under section 70 of that Act when applied to any material in the circumstances specified in that section any mark prescribed by a system of classification compiled under section 5 of the *Agriculture Act* 1967 and any designation, mark or description applied in pursuance of a scheme brought into force under section 6(1) or an order made under section 25(1) of the *Agriculture Act* 1970.

(g) the *Consumer Protection Act* 1987;

(h) the *Plant Varieties Act* 1997.

(5) Notwithstanding anything in the preceding provisions of this section, (a) where provision is made under the *Food Act* 1984, the *Food and Drugs (Scotland) Act* 1956 the *Food Safety Act* 1990 or the *Food and Drugs Act (Northern Ireland)* 1958 or the *Consumer Protection Act* 1987 prohibiting the application of a description except to goods in the case of which the requirements specified in that provision are complied with, that description, when applied to such goods, shall be deemed not to be a trade description.

(b) where by virtue of any provision made under Part V of the *Medicines Act* 1968 (or made under any provisions of the said Part V as applied by an order made under section 104 or section 105 of that Act) anything which, in accordance with this Act, constitutes the application of a trade description to goods is subject to any requirements or restrictions imposed by that provision, any particular description specified in that provision, when applied to goods in circumstances to which those requirements or restrictions are applicable, shall be deemed not to be a trade description

False trade description

20–40 **3.**—(1) A false trade description is a trade description which is false to a material degree.

(2) A trade description which, though not false, is misleading, that is to say, likely to be taken for such an indication of any of the matters specified in section 2 of this Act as would be false to a material degree, shall be deemed to be a false trade description.

(3) Anything which, though not a trade description, is likely to be taken for an indication of any of those matters and, as such an indication, would be false to a material degree, shall be deemed to be a false trade description.

(4) A false indication, or anything likely to be taken as an indication which would be false, that any goods comply with a standard specified or recognised by any person or implied by the approval of any person shall be deemed to be a false trade description, if there is no such person or no standard so specified, recognised or implied.

Applying a trade description to goods

20–41 **4.**—(1) A person applies a trade description to goods if he—

(a) affixes or annexes it to or in any manner marks it on or incorporates it with—

(i) the goods themselves, or

(ii) anything in, on or with which the goods are supplied; or

(b) places the goods in, on or with anything which the trade description has been affixed or annexed to, marked on or incorporated with, or places any such thing with the goods; or

(c) uses the trade description in any manner likely to be taken as referring to the goods.

(2) An oral statement may amount to the use of a trade description.

(3) Where goods are supplied in pursuance of a request in which a trade description is used and the circumstances are such as to make it reasonable to infer that the goods are supplied as goods corresponding to that trade description, the person supplying the goods shall be deemed to have applied that trade description to the goods.

Trade descriptions used in advertisements

5.—(1) The following provisions of this section shall have effect where in an advertisement a trade description is used in relation to any class of goods. **20–42**

(2) The trade description shall be taken as referring to all goods of the class, whether or not in existence at the time the advertisement is published—

(a) for the purpose of determining whether an offence has been committed under paragraph (a) of section 1(1) of this Act; and

(b) where goods of the class are supplied or offered to be supplied by a person publishing or displaying the advertisement, also for the purpose of determining whether an offence has been committed under paragraph (b) of the said section 1(1).

(3) In determining for the purposes of this section whether any goods are of a class to which a trade description used in an advertisement relates regard shall be had not only to the form and content of the advertisement but also to the time, place, manner and frequency of its publication and all other matters making it likely or unlikely that a person to whom the goods are supplied would think of the goods as belonging to the class in relation to which the trade description is used in the advertisement.

Offer to supply

6. A person exposing goods for supply or having goods in his possession for supply shall be deemed to offer to supply them. **20–43**

Part III

(2) Allocation

This offence is triable either way: *Trade Descriptions Act* 1968, s.18. **20–44**

(3) Elements of the offence

"In the course of a trade or business"

Professionals are not excluded from the scope of the Act; the term "trade or business" applies to them as well: *Roberts v. Leonard* (1995) 159 J.P. 711. A person engaging in a hobby of repairing and selling cars in his spare time was held not to be subject to the act as his activities could not be termed a "trade or business" for the purposes of s.1: *Blakemore v. Bellamy* (1982) 147 J.P. 89. **20–45**

There needs to be some degree of regularity in the transactions for them to form part of the normal practice of a business, however this does not necessarily mean that a one-off venture in the nature of trade carried out with a view to profit would not fall under the scope of s.1(1): *Davies v. Sumner* [1984] 3 All E.R. 831.

The Act does not apply to an expert who gives an opinion in respect of the condition of goods: *Wycombe Marsh Garages Ltd v. Fowler* [1972] 3 All E.R. 248.

Trade description

The particular words complained of must be looked at as a whole: *Evans v. British Doughnut Co Ltd* [1944] 1 K.B. 102. Where functional goods are supplied with instructions for their use the goods must be fit for use in accordance with those instructions as understood by the reasonable purchaser: *Janbo Trading Ltd. v. Dudley MBC* (1993) 157 J.P. 1056. **20–46**

This is a strict liability offence and the prosecution do not have to prove dishonesty: *Alec Norman Garages Ltd v. Phillips* (1984) 148 J.P. 741. **20–47**

False trade descriptions are sometimes used in the second-hand car market. The Act provides for the offence of applying a false description, which might be done by an unscrupulous trader and also the offence of supplying goods to which a false trade description has been applied, which might be an offence committed by the less than careful trader. Whether an advertising slogan used to encourage buyers amounts to a false trade description is a matter of fact in each case but there is no requirement to prove that the buyer has actually been deceived. Where a car was described as being in 'excellent condition throughout' it was no defence to say that the car was in as good a condition as could be expected for a car of its age and mileage and in an unrepaired state. It was held that a false trade description had been applied as there were 17 defects in the car: *Chidwick v. Beer* [1974] R.T.R. 415. To say a car is in "showroom condition throughout" cannot be described as mere puff but it was held to be a false trade description as the car had defects requiring repair. The term referred to the interior, exterior and mechanical condition of the car and not just it's appearance: *Hawkins v. Smith* [1978] Crim.L.R. 578.

When the mileage on a car is altered the false reading on the odometer is capable of amounting to a false trade description: *Hammerton Cars Ltd v. London Borough of Redbridge* [1976] 3 All E.R. 758. A trader who alters the reading himself cannot hide behind any disclaimer that may be attached to the vehicle but where the car is supplied or offered for supply a disclaimer may neutralise any trade description attached if it is "bold, precise and compelling": *Norman v. Bennett* [1974] R.T.R. 441, *Southwood* [1987] 3 All E.R. 556.

(4) Sentence

20–48 When tried summarily the maximum penalty for this offence is a fine not exceeding the statutory maximum: *Trade Descriptions Act* 1968, s.18.

Trade Descriptions Act 1968, s.20

Offences by corporations

20–49 **20.**—(1) Where an offence under this Act which has been committed by a body corporate is proved to have been committed with the consent and connivance of, or to be attributable to any neglect on the part of, any director, manager, secretary or other similar officer of the body corporate, or any person who was purporting to act in any such capacity, he as well as the body corporate shall be guilty of that offence and shall be liable to be proceeded against and punished accordingly.

(2) In this section "director", in relation to any body corporate established by or under any enactment for the purpose of carrying on under national ownership any industry or part of an industry or undertaking, being a body corporate whose affairs are managed by the members thereof, means a member of that body corporate.

20–50 There must be evidence of conduct that amounts to neglect. In *Lewin v. Bland* (1984) 148 J.P. 69 the defendant was the managing director of a garage that dealt in cars and he instructed his service manager to complete a service book in respect of a second hand car that had been sold. The book was completed inaccurately by his employee and the director was prosecuted for applying a false trade description. It was held that there was no evidence of neglect and the defendant was entitled to expect that his employee would follow his instructions properly without the need to check his work. The conviction was quashed.

Trade Descriptions Act 1968, s.19

Time limit for prosecutions

20–51 **19.**—(1) No prosecution for an offence under this Act shall be commenced after the expiration of three years from the commission of the offence or one year from its discovery by the prosecutor, whichever is the earlier.

(2) Notwithstanding anything in section 127(1) of the *Magistrates' Courts Act* 1980, a magistrates' court may try an information for an offence under this Act if the information was laid at any time within twelve months from the commission of the offence.

(3) Notwithstanding anything in section 23 of the *Summary Jurisdiction (Scotland) Act* 1954 (limitation of time for proceedings in statutory offences) summary proceedings in Scotland for an offence under this section may be commenced at any time within twelve months from the time when the offence was committed, and subsection (2) of the said section 23 shall apply for the purposes of this subsection as it applies for the purposes of that section.

(4) Subsections (2) and (3) of this section do not apply where—

(a) the offence was committed by the making of an oral statement; or

(b) the offence was one of supplying goods to which a false trade description is applied, and the trade description was applied by an oral statement; or

(c) the offence was one where a false trade description is deemed to have been applied to goods by virtue of section 4(3) of this Act and the goods were supplied in pursuance of an oral request.

An offence is discovered when all the relevant facts necessary to found a charge are disclosed to the prosecution: *Newham London Borough v. Co-operative Retail Services Ltd* (1985) 149 J.P. 421. In *R. (Donnachie) v. Cardiff Magistrates' Court* [2007] 1 W.L.R. 3085 the claimant was prosecuted for altering the odometers of motor vehicles which were sold by auction. It was held that the offence was committed when the odometer was altered and not just at the point when the sale was confirmed by the auction house. It was also held that the prosecutor was the local authority who brought the case and not the individual employee who laid the information. The time limit applied from when any employee of the local authority first discovered the offence and not from when the person laying the information was informed of it. **20–52**

The time limit for these either way offences is three years, (s.19(1)).

(5) Defences

Trade Descriptions Act 1968, ss.24, 25

Defence of mistake, accident, etc.

24.—(1) In any proceedings for an offence under this Act it shall, subject to subsection (2) of this section, be a defence for the person charged to prove— **20–53**

(a) that the commission of the offence was due to a mistake or to reliance on information supplied to him or to the act or default of another person, an accident or some other cause beyond his control; and

(b) that he took all reasonable precautions and exercised all due diligence to avoid the commission of such an offence by himself or any person under his control.

(2) If in any case the defence provided by the last foregoing subsection involves the allegation that the commission of the offence was due to the act or default of another person or to reliance on information supplied by another person, the person charged shall not, without leave of the court, be entitled to rely on that defence unless, within a period ending seven clear days before the hearing, he has served on the prosecutor a notice in writing giving such information identifying or assisting in the identification of that other person as was then in his possession.

(3) In any proceedings for an offence under this Act of supplying or offering to supply goods to which a false trade description is applied it shall be a defence for the person charged to prove that he did not know, and could not with reasonable diligence have ascertained, that the goods did not conform to the description or that the description had been applied to the goods.

Innocent publication of advertisement

25. In proceedings for an offence under this Act committed by the publication of an advertisement it shall be a defence for the person charged to prove that he is a person whose business it is to publish or arrange for the publication of advertisements and that he received the advertisement for publication in the ordinary course of business and did not know and had no reason to suspect that its publication would amount to an offence under this Act. **20–54**

The defence under s.24(1) is available to those charged with applying a false trade description and those charged with supplying or offering to supply goods to which a false trade description has been applied. The defendant must prove on a balance of **20–55** probabilities that he has done all that could be reasonably expected of him to investigate the person whom he says was responsible for the default: *McGuire v. Sittingbourne Co-op Society Ltd* [1976] Crim.L.R. 268. Notice of the details of the third party must be served on the prosecution, s.24(2).

The defence under subs. (3) is only available to those charged with supplying or offering to supply goods with a false trade description. The test of "reasonable diligence" is whether, in view of all the circumstances and the defendant's position as a trader, he used all diligence to ascertain whether the goods conformed to their description. A car salesman should be put on inquiry by an abnormally low odometer reading for a vehicle and although he may not be under a duty to trace the entire history of the car he should have made some inquiries and carefully examined the vehicle: *Simmons v. Ravenhill* (1983) 148 J.P. 109.

B. CRIMINAL LIABILITY FOR MAKING OR DEALING WITH INFRINGING ARTICLES ETC.

(1) Definition

Copyright, Design and Patents Act 1988, s.107

Criminal liability for making or dealing with infringing articles, &c.

20–56 **107.**—(1) A person commits an offence who, without the licence of the copyright owner—

(a) makes for sale or hire, or

(b) imports into the United Kingdom otherwise than for his private and domestic use, or

(c) possesses in the course of a business with a view to committing any act infringing the copyright, or

(d) in the course of a business—

(i) sells or lets for hire, or

(ii) offers or exposes for sale or hire, or

(iii) exhibits in public, or

(iv) distributes, or

(e) distributes otherwise than in the course of a business to such an extent as to affect prejudicially the owner of the copyright,

an article which is, and which he knows or has reason to believe is, an infringing copy of a copyright work.

(2) A person commits an offence who—

(a) makes an article specifically designed or adapted for making copies of a particular copyright work, or

(b) has such an article in his possession,

knowing or having reason to believe that it is to be used to make infringing copies for sale or hire or for use in the course of a business.

(2A) A person who infringes copyright in a work by communicating the work to the public—

(a) in the course of a business, or

(b) otherwise than in the course of a business to such an extent as to affect prejudicially the owner of the copyright,

commits an offence if he knows or has reason to believe that, by doing so, he is infringing copyright in that work.

(3) Where copyright is infringed (otherwise than by reception of a communication to the public)—

(a) by the public performance of a literary, dramatic or musical work, or

(b) by the playing or showing in public of a sound recording or film,

any person who caused the work to be so performed, played or shown is guilty of an offence if he knew or had reason to believe that copyright would be infringed.

(4) A person guilty of an offence under subsection (1)(a), (b), (d)(iv) or (e) is liable—

(a) on summary conviction to imprisonment for a term not exceeding six months or a fine not exceeding the statutory maximum, or both;

(b) on conviction on indictment to a fine or imprisonment for a term not exceeding ten years, or both.

(4A) A person guilty of an offence under subsection (2A) is liable—

(a) on summary conviction to imprisonment for a term not exceeding three months or a fine not exceeding the statutory maximum, or both;

(b) on conviction on indictment to a fine or imprisonment for a term not exceeding two years, or both.

(5) A person guilty of any other offence under this section is liable on summary conviction to imprisonment for a term not exceeding six months or a fine not exceeding level 5 on the standard scale, or both.

(6) Sections 104 to 106 (presumptions as to various matters connected with copyright) do not apply to proceedings for an offence under this section; but without prejudice to their application in proceedings for an order under section 108 below.

[This section is printed as amended by the *Copyright etc. and Trade Marks (Offences and Enforcement) Act* 2002, s.1.]

(2) Allocation

This offence is triable either way: *Copyright, Design and Patents Act* 1988, s.107(4). **20–57**

Copyright, Designs and Patents Act 1988, s.110

Offence by body corporate: liability of officers

110.—(1) Where an offence under section 107 committed by a body corporate is proved to have been committed with the consent or connivance of a director, manager, secretary or other similar officer of the body, or a person purporting to act in any such capacity, he as well as the body corporate is guilty of the offence and liable to be proceeded against and punished accordingly. **20–58**

(2) In relation to a body corporate whose affairs are managed by its members "director" means a member of the body corporate.

Part III

(3) Sentence

When tried summarily, the maximum sentence for this offence is imprisonment for a period not exceeding six months, a fine not exceeding the statutory maximum or both: *Copyright, Design and Patents Act* 1988, s.107(4). As regards offences concerning publication rights, the maximum punishment on summary conviction is imprisonment for a term not exceeding three months, or a fine not exceeding level five on the standard scale or both: *Copyright and Related Rights Regulations* 1996, (S.I. 1996 No. 2967). On commencement of the relevant provisions, the maximum custodial sentence in a magistrates' court will be 12 months' imprisonment: *Criminal Justice Act* 2003, ss.154 and 282. **20–59**

In *Carter* (1992) 13 Cr.App.R.(S.) 576, CA, a suspended sentence of nine months' imprisonment imposed for making and hiring pirate video tapes was upheld by the Court of Appeal, Jowitt J. stating that "counterfeiting of video films is a serious offence. In effect to make and distribute pirate copies of films is to steal from the true owner of the copyright, the property for which he has to expend money in order to possess it. It is an offence really of dishonesty." **20–60**

C. UNAUTHORISED USE OF TRADE MARK

(1) Definition

Trade Marks Act 1994, s.92

Unauthorised use of trade mark, &c. in relation to goods

92.—(1) A person commits an offence who with a view to gain for himself or another, or with intent to cause loss to another, and without the consent of the proprietor— **20–61**

(a) applies to goods or their packaging a sign identical to, or likely to be mistaken for, a registered trade mark, or

(b) sells or lets for hire, offers or exposes for sale or hire or distributes goods which bear, or the packaging of which bears, such a sign, or

(c) has in his possession, custody or control in the course of a business any such goods with a view to the doing of anything, by himself or another, which would be an offence under paragraph (b).

(2) A person commits an offence who with a view to gain for himself or another, or with intent to cause loss to another, and without the consent of the proprietor—

(a) applies a sign identical to, or likely to be mistaken for, a registered trade mark to material intended to be used—

(i) for labelling or packaging goods,

(ii) as a business paper in relation to goods, or

(iii) for advertising goods, or

(b) uses in the course of a business material bearing such a sign for labelling or packaging goods, as a business paper in relation to goods, or for advertising goods, or

(c) has in his possession, custody or control in the course of a business any such material with a view to the doing of anything, by himself or another, which would be an offence under paragraph (b).

(3) A person commits an offence who with a view to gain for himself or another, or with intent to cause loss to another, and without the consent of the proprietor—

(a) makes an article specifically designed or adapted for making copies of a sign identical to, or likely to be mistaken for, a registered trade mark, or

(b) has such an article in his possession, custody or control in the course of a business,

knowing or having reason to believe that it has been, or is to be, used to produce goods, or material for labelling or packaging goods, as a business paper in relation to goods, or for advertising goods.

(4) A person does not commit an offence under this section unless—

(a) the goods are goods in respect of which the trade mark is registered, or

(b) the trade mark has a reputation in the United Kingdom and the use of the sign takes or would take unfair advantage of, or is or would be detrimental to, the distinctive character or the repute of the trade mark.

(5) It is a defence for a person charged with an offence under this section to show that he believed on reasonable grounds that the use of the sign in the manner in which it was used, or was to be used, was not an infringement of the registered trade mark.

(6) A person guilty of an offence under this section is liable—

(a) on summary conviction to imprisonment for a term not exceeding six months or a fine not exceeding the statutory maximum, or both;

(b) on conviction on indictment to a fine or imprisonment for a term not exceeding ten years, or both.

(2) Allocation

20-62 This offence is triable either way: *Trade Marks Act* 1994, s.92(6).

Trade Marks Act 1994, s.101

Offences by partnerships and bodies corporate

20-63 **101.**—(1) Proceedings for an offence under this Act alleged to have been committed by a partnership shall be brought against the partnership in the name of the firm and not in that of the partners; but without prejudice to any liability of the partners under subsection (4) below.

(2) The following provisions apply for the purposes of such proceedings as in relation to a body corporate—

(a) any rules of court relating to the service of documents,

(b) in England and Wales or Northern Ireland, Schedule 3 to the *Magistrates' Courts Act* 1980 or Schedule 4 to the *Magistrates' Courts (Northern Ireland) Order* 1981 (procedure on charge of offence).

(3) A fine imposed on a partnership on its conviction in such proceedings shall be paid out of the partnership assets.

(4) Where a partnership is guilty of an offence under this Act, every partner, other than a partner who is proved to have been ignorant of or to have attempted to prevent the commission of the offence, is also guilty of the offence and liable to be proceeded against and punished accordingly.

(5) Where an offence under this Act committed by a body corporate is proved to have been committed with the consent or connivance of a director, manager, secretary or other similar officer of the body, or a person purporting to act in any such capacity, he as well as the body corporate is guilty of the offence and liable to be proceeded against and punished accordingly.

(3) Elements of the offence

In *Johnstone* [2003] 2 Cr.App.R. 33, CA, the defendant was involved in activities relating to bootleg recordings on CDs of performances of well known bands all of whom had registered their names as trade marks. He claimed that the use of the names of the bands on the CD covers was not an indication of "trade origin" under the terms of s.11 of the Act but simply described the performer whose music was on the CD. It was held by the House of Lords that the inclusion of the artists' names did not amount to an offence against s.92 as the names were not an indication of "trade origin". Whether it was such an indication was a question of fact in each case and the onus of proof was on the prosecution; the test was how the use of the sign would be perceived by the average consumer of the type of goods in question. The defendant was held to be not guilty of the offence. **20–64**

In *Kousar* [2009] EWCA Crim 139 the issue of "possession, control or custody" of counterfeit goods was considered. The defendant was the wife of a man who was convicted of unauthorised use of a trade mark. Goods were found on his market stall and in his van and in the loft of the family home. His wife was charged jointly as a principal offender. On appeal her conviction was quashed. The court said that proof of knowledge or acquiescence of the presence of the goods in the home was not sufficient to prove possession and there was no evidence she had the ability or right to control the goods nor that she was a participant in the husband's business. The outcome may have been different had she been charged with aiding and abetting the offence.

(4) Defences

Section 92(5) of the 1994 Act provides that a person will have a defence to a charge under the section if he can prove he believed on reasonable grounds that the use of the sign in the manner in which it was used, or was to be used, was not an infringement of the registered trade mark. **20–65**

In *Torbay Council v. Singh* [1999] 2 Cr.App.R. 451, DC, the defendant sold children's clothes bearing the identical logo to that of the registered trade mark of the 'Teletubbies'. He was assured by his supplier that the goods were not counterfeit and did not infringe any trade mark. He pleaded not guilty on the basis of the defence afforded by s.92(5) and that he believed on reasonable grounds that his use of the sign in the manner in which it was used was not an infringement of the registered trade mark. As he was ignorant of the existence of the registered trade mark it was argued that there had been no infringement. The court on appeal held that the subsection did not speak of a reasonable belief in the absence of a registration. It spoke of a reasonable belief that the "manner" of use of the sign did not infringe "the registered trade mark" which presupposed an awareness by a defendant of the existence of the registration against which he could match his manner of use of the allegedly offending sign. The trader could not rely on his ignorance as a defence to a charge under s.92. This case was overruled by the *Johnstone* case (above) where the House of Lords said that it made no sense to confine the defence of s.92(5) to cases where the defendant is aware of the existence of the trade mark but to exclude those where he is not. It was held that the defence did apply when the defendant was unaware of the registration.

20–66 However, subs. 92(5) does afford a defence for the trader who honestly and reasonably believes that his goods are genuine. In *Rhodes* [2002] EWCA Crim 1390, it was held that s.92(5) of the *Trade Marks Act* 1994 provides a broad general defence albeit subject to the limitation that a person will be deemed to know about any registered trade mark so that he could not, relying on that subsection, assert a defence that he was ignorant of it. The defendant with an honest and reasonable belief in the authenticity of the goods will be able to rely on the defence in s.92(5).

In *Essex Trading Standards v. Singh* [2009] EWHC 520 (Admin) the defendant was charged with an offence of trade mark infringement. He was helping out a sick friend by working at his market stall selling trainers which bore a Nike trade mark. He said his friend was a drug addict and he had asked him if the shoes were counterfeit and he had been assured they were not. The magistrates found that the statutory defence had been made out and acquitted the defendant. On appeal by the prosecution it was held that the burden under s.92(5) was to show that there were objectively reasonable grounds to believe the goods were genuine and the defendant had to show he had acted not only honestly but also reasonably. On the facts of the case it was held that the defendant had not sought any independent evidence of the genuineness of the goods and in fact could hardly have done less to establish their genuineness and he had not acted reasonably. On that basis the decision of the magistrates was quashed as being one no reasonable bench could have reached.

The fact that the counterfeit material was of such poor quality that no customer would be confused by the trademark used does not amount to a defence. In this case the defendant had in his possession several DVDs and CDs bearing the trade mark of EMI and other companies of similar repute. The defence was that the recordings were so poor that no-one would think they were produced by those companies. The court dismissed this argument and said that the proprietor of a trade mark or logo should be able to control its use as a badge of origin and the standing of that trade mark is damaged if goods of variable quality bearing that mark are on the market. *Boulter* [2008] EWCA Crim 2375.

(5) Sentence

20–67 When tried summarily, the maximum penalty for this offence is imprisonment for a period not exceeding six months, a fine not exceeding the statutory maximum or both: *Trade Marks Act* 1994, s.92(6). After commencement of the relevant provisions, the maximum custodial sentence in a magistrates' court will be 12 months' imprisonment: *Criminal Justice Act* 2003, ss.154 and 282.

The Magistrates' Courts Sentencing Guidelines 2008 include this offence.

STARTING POINT AND SENTENCE RANGE

(BASED ON A FIRST TIME OFFENDER PLEADING NOT GUILTY)

Examples of nature of activity	**Starting Point**	**Range**
Small number of counterfeit items	Band C fine	Band B fine to low level community order
Larger number of counterfeit items but no involvement in wider operation	Medium level community order plus fine	Low level community order to 12 weeks custody plus fine

Examples of nature of activity	Starting Point	Range
High number of counterfeit items or involvement in wider operation e.g. manufacture or distribution	12 weeks custody	6 weeks custody to Crown Court
Central role in large scale operation	Crown Court	Crown Court

AGGRAVATING AND MITIGATING FACTORS

Factors indicating higher culpability	Factor indicating lower culpability
1. High degree of professionalism 2. High level of profit **Factor indicating greater degree of harm** 1. Purchasers at risk of harm e.g. from counterfeit drugs	1. Mistake or ignorance about provenance of goods

D. SELLING FOOD NOT OF THE NATURE, SUBSTANCE OR QUALITY DEMANDED

(1) Definition

Food Safety Act 1990, s.14

Selling food not of the nature or substance or quality demanded

14.—(1) Any person who sells to the purchaser's prejudice any food which is not of the nature or substance or quality demanded by the purchaser shall be guilty of an offence. **20–68**

(2) In subsection (1) above the reference to sale shall be construed as a reference to sale for human consumption; and in proceedings under that subsection it shall not be a defence that the purchaser was not prejudiced because he bought for analysis or examination.

(2) Allocation

This offence is triable either way: *Food Safety Act* 1990, s.35. **20–69**

The person may be a limited company: *ICR Haulage Ltd* [1944] K.B. 551.

Vicarious liability applies so that a servant who sells on behalf of his master may be convicted: *Goodfellow v. Johnson* [1966] 1 Q.B. 83, and a master can be liable for the sale by his servant who has authority to sell: *United Dairies (London) Ltd v. Beckenham Corp* [1963] 1 Q.B. 434.

Food Safety Act 1990, s.36

Offences by bodies corporate

20–70 **36.**—(1) Where an offence under this Act which has been committed by a body corporate is proved to have been committed with the consent or connivance of, or to be attributable to any neglect on the part of—

(a) any director, manager, secretary or other similar officer of the body corporate; or

(b) any person who was purporting to act in any such capacity,

he as well as the body corporate shall be deemed to be guilty of that offence and shall be liable to be proceeded against and punished accordingly.

(2) In subsection (1) above "director", in relation to any body corporate established by or under any enactment for the purpose of carrying on under national ownership any industry or part of an industry or undertaking, being a body corporate whose affairs are managed by its members, means a member of that body corporate.

(3) Elements of the offence

Food Safety Act 1990, s.1

Meaning of "food" and other basic expressions

20–71 **1.**—(1) In this Act "food" includes—

(a) drink;

(b) articles and substances of no nutritional value which are used for human consumption;

(c) chewing gum and other products of a like nature and use; and

(d) articles and substances used as ingredients in the preparation of food or anything falling within this subsection.

(2) In this Act "food" does not include—

(a) live animals or birds, or live fish which are not used for human consumption while they are alive;

(b) fodder or feeding stuffs for animals, birds or fish;

(c) controlled drugs within the meaning of the *Misuse of Drugs Act* 1971; or

(d) subject to such exceptions as may be specified in an order made by the Secretary of State—

(i) medicinal products within the meaning of the *Medicines Act* 1968 in respect of which product licences within the meaning of that Act are for the time being in force; or

(ii) other articles or substances in respect of which such licences are for the time being in force in pursuance of orders under section 104 or 105 of that Act (application of Act to other articles and substances).

(3) In this Act, unless the context otherwise requires—

"business" includes the undertaking of a canteen, club, school, hospital or institution, whether carried on for profit or not, and any undertaking or activity carried on by a public or local authority;

"commercial operation", in relation to any food or contact material, means any of the following, namely—

(a) selling, possessing for sale and offering, exposing or advertising for sale;

(b) consigning, delivering or serving by way of sale;

(c) preparing for sale or presenting, labelling or wrapping for the purpose of sale;

(d) storing or transporting for the purpose of sale;

(e) importing and exporting; and, in relation to any food source, means deriving food from it for the purpose of sale or for purposes connected with sale;

"contact material" means any article or substance which is intended to come into contact with food;

"food business" means any business in the course of which commercial operations with respect to food or food sources are carried out;

"food premises" means any premises used for the purposes of a food business;

"food source" means any growing crop or live animal, bird or fish from which food is intended to be derived (whether by harvesting, slaughtering, milking, collecting eggs or otherwise);

"premises" includes any place, any vehicle, stall or moveable structure and, for such purposes as may be specified in an order made by the Secretary of State, any ship or aircraft of a description so specified.

(4) The reference in subsection (3) above to preparing for sale shall be construed, in relation to any contact material, as a reference to manufacturing or producing for the purpose of sale.

[This section is printed as amended by *Medicines for Human Use (Marketing Authorisations Etc.) Regulations* 1994 (S.I. 1994 No. 3144) and the *Food Standards Act* 1999, Sched. 5, para. 8.]

A sale will not be prejudicial to the purchaser where it is brought to his notice that **20–72** the article offered to him is not of the same nature or quality as the article he has asked for: *Sandys v. Jackson* (1905) 69 J.P. 171. The fact that the goods are sold below the market price is not *prima facie* evidence of their quality deficiency: *Heywood v. Whitehead* (1897) 76 L.T. 781.

In the absence of a prescribed minimum standard for the product in question, where there is sufficient evidence for the justices to decide what is a proper standard for that product and that the product in question was below it, the justices will be entitled to find that the retailers are guilty of selling an article which was not the article demanded: *Tonkin v. Victor Value and Piper Products* [1962] 1 W.L.R. 339, DC.

(4) Defences

Food Safety Act 1990, s.21

Defence of due diligence

21.—(1) In any proceedings for an offence under any of the preceding provisions of this Part **20–73** (in this section referred to as "the relevant provision"), it shall, subject to subsection (5) below, be a defence for the person charged to prove that he took all reasonable precautions and exercised all due diligence to avoid the commission of the offence by himself or by a person under his control.

(2) Without prejudice to the generality of subsection (1) above, a person charged with an offence under section 8, 14 or 15 above who neither—

(a) prepared the food in respect of which the offence is alleged to have been committed; nor

(b) imported it into Great Britain,

shall be taken to have established the defence provided by thatsubsection if he satisfies the requirements of subsection (3) or (4) below.

(3) A person satisfies the requirements of this subsection if he proves—

(a) that the commission of the offence was due to an act or default of another person who was not under his control, or to reliance on information supplied by such a person;

(b) that he carried out all such checks of the food in question as were reasonable in all the circumstances, or that it was reasonable in all the circumstances for him to rely on checks carried out by the person who supplied the food to him; and

(c) that he did not know and had no reason to suspect at the time of the commission of the alleged offence that his act or omission would amount to an offence under the relevant provision.

(4) A person satisfies the requirements of this subsection if he proves—

(a) that the commission of the offence was due to an act or default of another person who was not under his control, or to reliance on information supplied by such a person;

(b) that the sale or intended sale of which the alleged offence consisted was not a sale or intended sale under his name or mark; and

(c) that he did not know, and could not reasonably have been expected to know, at the time of the commission of the alleged offence that his act or omission would amount to an offence under the relevant provision.

(5) If in any case the defence provided by subsection (1) above involves the allegation that the commission of the offence was due to an act or default of another person, or to reliance on information supplied by another person, the person charged shall not, without leave of the court, be entitled to rely on that defence unless—

(a) at least seven clear days before the hearing; and

(b) where he has previously appeared before a court in connection with the alleged offence, within one month of his first such appearance,

he has served on the prosecutor a notice in writing giving such information identifying or assisting in the identification of that other person as was then in his possession.

(6) In subsection (5) above any reference to appearing before a court shall be construed as including a reference to being brought before a court.

20–74 In *Carrick DC v. Taunton Vale Meat Traders' Ltd* (1994) 158 J.P. 347, DC, it was held that an error of judgement by a meat inspector is a valid defence to the charge of supplying meat unfit for human consumption under the *Food Safety Act* 1990. No further precautions were deemed necessary to determine the fitness of the meat for human use. The defendant had had the meat examined by a meat inspector, and was therefore not liable for the inspector's error of judgement.

(5) Sentence

20–75 When tried summarily, the maximum penalty for this offence is six months' imprisonment or a fine not exceeding £20,000 or both: *Food Safety Act* 1990, s.35 (see *post*, § 20–87). After commencement of the relevant provisions, the maximum custodial sentence in a magistrates' court will be 12 months' imprisonment: *Criminal Justice Act* 2003, ss.154 and 282.

E. FALSELY DESCRIBING OR PRESENTING FOOD

(1) Definition

Food Safety Act 1990 s.15

Falsely describing or presenting food

20–76 **15.**—(1) Any person who gives with any food sold by him, or displays with any food offered or exposed by him for sale or in his possession for the purpose of sale, a label, whether or not attached to or printed on the wrapper or container, which—

(a) falsely describes the food; or

(b) is likely to mislead as to the nature or substance or quality of the food,

shall be guilty of an offence.

(2) Any person who publishes, or is a party to the publication of, an advertisement (not being such a label given or displayed by him as mentioned in subsection (1) above) which—

(a) falsely describes any food; or

(b) is likely to mislead as to the nature or substance or quality of any food,

shall be guilty of an offence.

(3) Any person who sells, or offers or exposes for sale, or has in his possession for the purpose of sale, any food the presentation of which is likely to mislead as to the nature or substance or quality of the food shall be guilty of an offence.

(4) In proceedings for an offence under subsection (1) or (2) above, the fact that a label or advertisement in respect of which the offence is alleged to have been committed contained an accurate statement of the composition of the food shall not preclude the court from finding that the offence was committed.

(5) In this section references to sale shall be construed as references to sale for human consumption.

(2) Allocation

20–77 The offences created under this section are triable either way: *Food Safety Act* 1990, s.35. The section creates distinct offences and the summons must be clear as to which of the offences is being alleged: *Ward v. Barking and Dagenham LBC* [2000] E.H.L.R. 263, QBD.

(3) Defences

In addition to the defence available under s.21 of the 1990 Act, see *ante*, § 16–113, the defendant may be able to rely on the defence relating to publication in the course of business established by s.22. **20–78**

Food Safety Act 1990, s.22

Defence of publication in the course of business

22. In proceedings for an offence under any of the preceding provisions of this Part consisting of the advertisement for sale of any food, it shall be a defence for the person charged to prove— **20–79**

(a) that he is a person whose business it is to publish or arrange for the publication of advertisements; and

(b) that he received the advertisement in the ordinary course of business and did not know and had no reason to suspect that its publication would amount to an offence under that provision.

(4) Sentence

When tried summarily, the maximum penalty for this offence is six months' imprisonment or a fine not exceeding the statutory maximum or both: *Food Safety Act* 1990, s.35, see *post*, § 20–87. After commencement of the relevant proceedings, the maximum custodial sentence in a magistrates' court will be 12 months' imprisonment: *Criminal Justice Act* 2003, ss.154 and 282. **20–80**

F. FOOD SAFETY AND CONSUMER PROTECTION

(1) Regulations

Food Safety Act 1990, s.16

Food safety and consumer protection

16.—(1) The Secretary of State may by regulations make— **20–81**

(a) provision for requiring, prohibiting or regulating the presence in food or food sources of any specified substance, or any substance of any specified class, and generally for regulating the composition of food;

(b) provision for securing that food is fit for human consumption and meets such microbiological standards (whether going to the fitness of the food or otherwise) as may be specified by or under the regulations;

(c) provision for requiring, prohibiting or regulating the use of any process or treatment in the preparation of food;

(d) provision for securing the observance of hygienic conditions and practices in connection with the carrying out of commercial operations with respect to food or food sources;

(e) provision for imposing requirements or prohibitions as to, or otherwise regulating, the labelling, marking, presenting or advertising of food, and the descriptions which may be applied to food; and

(f) such other provision with respect to food or food sources, including in particular provision for prohibiting or regulating the carrying out of commercial operations with respect to food or food sources, as appears to them to be necessary or expedient—

(i) for the purpose of securing that food complies with food safety requirements or in the interests of the public health; or

(ii) for the purpose of protecting or promoting the interests of consumers.

(2) The Secretary of State may also by regulations make provision—

(a) for securing the observance of hygienic conditions and practices in connection with the carrying out of commercial operations with respect to contact materials which are intended to come into contact with food intended for human consumption;

(b) for imposing requirements or prohibitions as to, or otherwise regulating, the labelling, marking or advertising of such materials, and the descriptions which may be applied to them; and

(c) otherwise for prohibiting or regulating the carrying out of commercial operations with respect to such materials.

(3) Without prejudice to the generality of subsection (1) above, regulations under that subsection may make any such provision as is mentioned in Schedule 1 to this Act.

(4) In making regulations under subsection (1) above, the Secretary of State shall have regard to the desirability of restricting, so far as practicable, the use of substances of no nutritional value as foods or as ingredients of foods.

(5) In subsection (1) above and Schedule 1 to this Act, unless the context otherwise requires—

(a) references to food shall be construed as references to food intended for sale for human consumption; and

(b) references to food sources shall be construed as references to food sources from which such food is intended to be derived.

(2) Elements of the offence

20–82 A multitude of regulations have been made applying to various specific foodstuffs. The *Food Safety (General Food Hygiene) Regulations* 1995 (S.I. 1995 No. 1763) as amended apply to proprietors of food businesses. The regulations impose a duty on proprietors to ensure that the preparation, processing, manufacturing, packaging storing, transportation, distribution, handling and offering for sale or supply of food are carried out hygienically: reg.4. Schedule 1 to the regulations sets out the rules of hygiene that must be complied with. Offences against s.16 should state separately each specific requirement that it is alleged has been breached.

In *Asda Food Stores Ltd v. Wandsworth Borough Council* [2007] EWHC 433, Admin, it was held that the *Food Safety etc. Regulations* create more than one offence in a single regulation and it was not duplicitous or over-charging to prosecute for two separate offences under reg.4(2) when one offence related to failing to ensure adequate procedures were in place to control pests and the other related to failing to place food so as to minimize the risk of contamination. The regulations refer to different ways in which and different times at which the offences can be committed and the prosecution could charge and specify the offences separately even where they were committed under one regulation only.

(3) Sentence

20–83 When tried summarily, the maximum penalty for failure to comply with regulations made under this section is six months' imprisonment or a fine not exceeding the statutory maximum or both: *Food Safety Act* 1990, s.35, see *post*, § 20–87. After commencement of the relevant provisions, the maximum custodial sentence in a magistrates' court will be 12 months' imprisonment: *Criminal Justice Act* 2003, ss.154 and 282.

Food Safety Act 1990, ss.20, 34

Offences due to fault of another person

20–84 **20.** Where the commission by any person of an offence under any of the preceding provisions of this Part is due to an act or default of some other person, that other person shall be guilty of the offence; and a person may be charged with and convicted of the offence by virtue of this section whether or not proceedings are taken against the first-mentioned person.

Time limit for prosecutions

20–85 **34.** No prosecution for an offence under this Act which is punishable under section 35(2) below shall be begun after the expiry of—

(a) three years from the commission of the offence; or

(b) one year from its discovery by the prosecutor,

whichever is the earlier.

In the case of a continuing offence discovery may occur on any day that the offence continues to be committed: *Thames Metropolitan Stipendiary Magistrate ex p. London Borough of Hackney* (1994) 158 J.P. 305. **20–86**

Food Safety Act 1990, s.35

Punishment of offences

35.—(1) A person guilty of an offence under section 33(1) above shall be liable on summary conviction to a fine not exceeding level 5 on the standard scale or to imprisonment for a term not exceeding three months or to both. **20–87**

(2) A person guilty of any other offence under this Act shall be liable—

(a) on conviction on indictment, to a fine or to imprisonment for a term not exceeding two years or to both;

(b) on summary conviction, to a fine not exceeding the relevant amount or to imprisonment for a term not exceeding six months or to both.

(3) In subsection (2) above "the relevant amount" means—

(a) in the case of an offence under section 7, 8 or 14 above, £ 20,000;

(b) in any other case, the statutory maximum.

(4) If a person who is—

(a) licensed under section 1 of the *Slaughterhouses Act* 1974 to keep a knacker's yard;

(b) registered under section 4 of the *Slaughter of Animals (Scotland) Act* 1980 in respect of any premises for use as a slaughterhouse; or

(c) licensed under section 6 of the *Slaughter of Animals (Scotland) Act* 1980 to use any premises as a knacker's yard,

is convicted of an offence under Part II of this Act, the court may, in addition to any other punishment, cancel his licence or registration.

Part III

Section 33(1) referred to in this section is the offence of obstructing officers acting under their powers in the Act. Section 7 is the offence of rendering food injurious to health and s.8 is the offence of selling food not in compliance with food safety requirements.

IV. HIGHWAYS

A. OFFENCES UNDER THE HIGHWAYS ACT 1980

Highways Act 1980, s.328

Meaning of "highway"

328.—(1) In this Act, except where the context otherwise requires, "highway" means the whole or a part of a highway other than a ferry or waterway. **20–88**

(2) Where a highway passes over a bridge or through a tunnel, that bridge or tunnel is to be taken for the purposes of this Act to be a part of the highway.

(3) In this Act, "highway maintainable at the public expense" and any other expression defined by reference to a highway is to be construed in accordance with the foregoing provisions of this section.

Section 329 includes further lengthy provisions on interpretation.

Highways Act 1980, s.312

Restriction on institution of proceedings

312.—(1) Subject to subsection (3) below, proceedings for an offence under any provision of this Act to which this section applies or under byelaws made under any such provision shall not, without the written consent of the Attorney General, be taken by any person other than the **20–89**

person aggrieved, or a highway authority or council having an interest in the enforcement of the provision or byelaws in question.

(2) This section applies to sections 167 and 177 above and to the provisions of this Act specified in Schedule 22 to this Act.

(3) A constable may take proceedings—

(a) for an offence under paragraph (b) of section 171(6) above; or

(b) for an offence under paragraph (c) of that subsection consisting of failure to perform a duty imposed by section 171(5)(a) above; or

(c) for an offence under section 174 above,

without the consent of the Attorney General.

The offences referred to in this section are as follows: s.171(6) is one of failing without reasonable excuse to comply with directions relating to placing traffic signs in connection with a deposit or excavation; s.171(5) imposes a duty of signposting, fencing and lighting of obstructions and excavations on the highway; s.174 details the precautions to be taken by persons executing works in the street. The police may prosecute these offences.

Highways Act 1980, Sched. 22

SCHEDULE 22

PROVISIONS OF THIS ACT TO WHICH SECTIONS 288, 294, 312, 338, 339 AND 341 OF THIS ACT APPLY

Provisions contained in Part IV

20–90 1. Section 36(6) and (7) and section 38.

Provisions contained in Part V

2. Section 66(2) to (8), sections 73 and 77 and section 96(4) and (5).

Provisions contained in Part IX

3. Sections 133, and 151 to 153, section 154(1), and 154(4) so far as relating to a notice under 154(1), sections 163 and 165, sections 171 to 174, 176, 178 and 179, section 180 other than subsection (2) and subsection (4) so far as relating to subsection (2), and section 185.

Provisions contained in Part X

4. Sections 186 to 188, 190 to 107, 200 and 201.

Provisions contained in Part XI

5. The private street works code, sections 226 and 228, section 230(1) to (6), and sections 231, 233, 236 and 237.

Provisions contained in Part XII

6. Section 239(6) and section 241.

Provisions contained in Part XIV

7. Sections 286, 295, 297, 303, 304, and 305.

Highways Act 1980, s.314

Offences by body corporate

20–91 **314.**—(1) Where an offence under any provision of this Act to which this section applies is committed by a body corporate and it is proved to have been committed with the consent or connivance of, or to be attributable to any neglect on the part of, any director, manager, secretary or other similar officer of the body corporate or any person who was purporting to act in any such capacity, he as well as the body corporate is guilty of that offence and liable to be proceeded against and punished accordingly.

(2) Where the affairs of a body corporate are managed by its members, subsection (1) above applies in relation to the acts and defaults of a member in connection with his functions of management as if he were a director of the body corporate.

(3) This section applies to sections 139, 140, 167, 168, 177 and 181 above.

[This section is printed as amended by the *New Roads and Street Works Act* 1991, Sched. 8.]

The offences referred to in this section are: s.139 relates to the control of builders' skips; s.140 covers the removal of builders' skips; s.167 provides for powers relating to retaining walls near streets; s.168 relates to building operations affecting public safety; and section 177 imposes a restriction on the construction of buildings over highways. **20–92**

Highways Act 1980, s.319

Judges and justices not to be disqualified by liability to rates

319. The judge of any court or a justice of the peace is not disqualified for acting in cases arising under this Act by reason only of his being as one of several ratepayers, or as one of any other class of persons, liable in common with the others to contribute to, or to be benefited by, any rate or fund out of which any expenses of a council are to be defrayed. **20–93**

B. Damage to Highway

(1) Definition

Highways Act 1980, s.131

Penalty for damaging highway etc.

131.—(1) If a person, without lawful authority or excuse— **20–94**

(a) makes a ditch or excavation in a highway which consists of or comprises a carriageway, or

(b) removes any soil or turf from any part of a highway, except for the purpose of improving the highway and with the consent of the highway authority for the highway, or

(c) deposits anything whatsoever on a highway so as to damage the highway, or

(d) lights any fire, or discharges any firearm or firework, within 50 feet from the centre of a highway which consists of or comprises a carriageway, and in consequence thereof the highway is damaged,

he is guilty of an offence.

(2) If a person without lawful authority or excuse pulls down or obliterates a traffic sign placed on or over a highway, or a milestone or direction post (not being a traffic sign) so placed, he is guilty of an offence; but it is a defence in any proceedings under this subsection to show that the traffic sign, milestone or post was not lawfully so placed.

(3) A person guilty of an offence under this section is liable to a fine not exceeding level three on the standard scale.

[This section is printed as amended by the *Criminal Justice Act* 1982, ss.35, 38 and 46.]

(2) Allocation

This offence is triable summarily: *Highways Act* 1980, s.310. **20–95**

(3) Sentence

The maximum penalty for the offences under this section is a fine not exceeding level three on the standard scale. **20–96**

C. Wilful Obstruction

(1) Definition

Highways Act 1980, s.137

Penalty for wilful obstruction

137.—(1) If a person, without lawful authority or excuse, in any way wilfully obstructs the **20–97**

free passage along a highway he is guilty of an offence and liable to a fine not exceeding level 3 on the standard scale.

(2) [...]

[This section is printed as amended by the *Criminal Justice Act* 1982, ss.38 and 46 and partially repealed by the *Police and Criminal Evidence Act* 1984, Sched. 7.]

(2) Allocation

20–98 This offence is triable summarily: *Highways Act* 1980, s.310.

(3) Elements of the offence

20–99 Lawful authority is given by permits and licences granted to market and street traders and those collecting for charitable causes. A lawful excuse may be found if the activities engaged in are lawful in themselves and they may or may not be reasonable.

The test of whether a particular use of a highway by a vehicle, such as a van selling hot-dogs, constitutes an obstruction is whether the use is unreasonable having regard to all the circumstances including its duration, position and purpose and whether it causes an actual, rather than a potential obstruction: *Nagy v. Weston* [1965] 1 All E.R. 78. It is sufficient to constitute the offence that the accused, without lawful authority or excuse, by exercise of his free will does something or omits to do something, which causes an obstruction or the continuance of an obstruction: *Arrowsmith v. Jenkins* [1963] 2 Q.B. 561. In *Waltham Forest LBC v. Mills* [1980] R.T.R. 201, QBD, the defendant conducted a business of serving tea and snacks to the public from a mobile snack bar which he stationed on a part of the highway which had been designated as a layby. People who stopped to buy snacks parked their motorcycles and cars in the layby and, on some occasions when the layby entrance was blocked by motorcycles, on the side of the carriageway itself. It was held that this constituted an unreasonable obstruction of the highway and that selling refreshments on the highway was of itself an unreasonable user. In *Hertfordshire County Council v. Bolden* (1987) 151 J.P. 252, the defendant owned premises adjoining a public highway. He sometimes used part of the highway verge bordering his premises for the display and sale of garden produce. It was held that such activities could form unreasonable obstructions for the purpose of the offence under s.137, that such obstructions could not be said to be *de minimis* and hence outside the scope of s.137 and that the fact that they did not cause inconvenience to anyone did not mean that they were insufficient to constitute offences.

20–100 As regards peaceful picketing under s.134 of the *Industrial Relations Act* 1971 (now the *Trade Union and Labour Relations Act (Consolidation) Act* 1992, s.220), in *Broome v. DPP* [1974] 1 All E.R. 314, it was held that s.134 made lawful the attendance of pickets only for the purposes specified therein and did not require the person whom it was sought to persuade to submit to any constraint or restriction of his right to personal freedom. Hence whilst a driver can be invited to stop and listen to the protest, he cannot be compelled to stop by a blockade on the highway. Where the highway is obstructed by a peaceful protest the question of whether the use of the highway is reasonable or not must be considered: *Hirst v. Chief Constable of West Yorkshire* (1987) 85 Cr.App.R. 143.

The onus is on the prosecution to prove that the defendant was obstructing the highway without lawful authority or excuse. A defendant does not acquire a license to perform an unlawful act through the fact that the police or other prosecuting authority have refrained from prosecuting in respect of the alleged obstruction for a number of years: *Redbridge London Borough v. Jacques* (1971) 1 All E.R. 260.

20–101 In *Westminster City Council v. Haw* (2002) EWHC 2073, it was held that the art.10 right to freedom of expression contained in the ECHR is not a trump card to authorise any protest, but rather is a significant consideration to take into account when considering the reasonableness of the obstruction of the highway. In this case the court held that there was a wilful obstruction as protest placards encroached onto the pavement but the defendant's activities were neither unlawful nor unreasonable.

(4) Sentence

The maximum penalty for this offence is a fine not exceeding level three on the standard scale. 20–102

D. BUILDERS' SKIPS

(1) Definition

Highways Act 1980, s.139

Control of builders' skips

139.—(1) A builders' skip shall not be deposited on a highway without the permission of the highway authority for the highway. 20–103

(2) A permission under this section shall be a permission for a person to whom it is granted to deposit, or cause to be deposited, a skip on the highway specified in the permission, and a highway authority may grant such permission either unconditionally or subject to such conditions as may be specified in the permission including, in particular, conditions relating to—

(a) the siting of the skip;
(b) its dimensions;
(c) the manner in which it is to be coated with paint and other material for the purpose of making it immediately visible to oncoming traffic;
(d) the care and disposal of its contents;
(e) the manner in which it is to be lighted or guarded;
(f) its removal at the end of the period of permission.

(3) If a builder's skip is deposited on a highway without a permission granted under this section, the owner of the skip is, subject to subsection (6) below, guilty of an offence and liable to a fine not exceeding level 3 on the standard scale.

(4) Where a builder's skip has been deposited on a highway in accordance with a permission granted under this section, the owner of the skip shall secure—

(a) that the skip is properly lighted during the hours of darkness and, where regulations made by the Secretary of State under this section require it to be marked in accordance with the regulations (whether with reflecting or fluorescent material or otherwise), that it is so marked;
(b) that the skip is clearly and indelibly marked with the owner's name and with his telephone number or address;
(c) that the skip is removed as soon as practicable after it has been filled;
(d) that each of the conditions subject to which that permission was granted is complied with;

and, if he fails to do so, he is, subject to subsection (6) below, guilty of an offence and liable to a fine not exceeding level 3 on the standard scale.

(5) Where the commission by any person of an offence under this section is due to the act or default of some other person, that other person is guilty of the offence, and a person may be charged with and convicted of the offence by virtue of this subsection whether or not proceedings are taken against the first-mentioned person.

(6) In any proceedings for an offence under this section it is a defence, subject to subsection (7) below, for the person charged to prove that the commission of the offence was due to the act or default of another person and that he took all reasonable precautions and exercised all due diligence to avoid the commission of such an offence by himself or any person under his control.

(7) A person charged with an offence under this section is not, without leave of the court, entitled to rely on the defence provided by subsection (6) above unless, within a period ending 7 clear days before the hearing, he has served on the prosecutor a notice in writing giving such information identifying or assisting in the identification of that other person as was then in his possession.

(8) Where any person is charged with an offence under any other enactment for failing to secure that a builder's skip which has been deposited on a highway in accordance with a permission granted under this section was properly lighted during the hours of darkness, it is a defence for the person charged to prove that the commission of the offence was due

to the act or default of another person and that he took all reasonable precautions and exercised all due diligence to avoid the commission of such an offence by himself or any person under his control.

(9) Where a person is charged with obstructing, or interrupting any user of, a highway by depositing a builder's skip on it, it is a defence for the person charged to prove that the skip was deposited on it in accordance with a permission granted under this section and either—

(a) that each of the requirements of subsection (4) above had been complied with; or

(b) that the commission of any offence under that subsection was due to the act or default of another person and that he took all reasonable precautions and exercised all due diligence to avoid the commission of such an offence by himself or any person under his control.

(10) Nothing in this section is to be taken as authorising the creation of a nuisance or of a danger to users of a highway or as imposing on a highway authority by whom a permission has been granted under this section any liability for any injury, damage or loss resulting from the presence on a highway of the skip to which the permission relates.

(11) In this section section 140 and section 140A below—

"builder's skip" means a container designed to be carried on a road vehicle and to be placed on a highway or other land for the storage of builders' materials, or for the removal and disposal of builders' rubble, waste, household and other rubbish or earth; and

"owner", in relation to a builder's skip which is the subject of a hiring agreement, being an agreement for a hiring of not less than one month, or a hire purchase agreement, means the person in possession of the skip under that agreement.

[This section is printed as amended by the *Criminal Justice Act* 1982, ss.38 and 46, the *Transport Act* 1982, s.65 and the *New Roads and Street Works Act* 1991, Sched. 8.]

(2) Allocation

20–104 This offence is triable summarily: *Highways Act* 1980, s.310.

(3) Elements of the offence

20–105 Depositing means more than just placing, putting down or delivering the skip. The offence applies to incidents of leaving or allowing the skip to remain: *Craddock v. Green* [1983] R.T.R. 479.

Permission granted by the local authority must be in writing and specific to the location: *York City Council v. Poller* [1976] R.T.R. 479 and *Highways Act* 1980, s.320.

For the purposes of subs. 4(a) the relevant regulations are the *Builders' Skips (Markings) Regulations* 1984 (S.I. 1984 No. 1933).

It is a defence under subs. 6 to prove that the commission of the offence was due to the act or default of a person other than the person charged and that due diligence was exercised to avoid the commission of the offence. The other person does not have to be identified: *P.G.M. Building Co Ltd v. Kensington and Chelsea (Royal) LBC* [1982] R.T.R. 107. See also *York City Council v. Poller* [1976] R.T.R. 37. Note the requirements contained in subs. (7) concerning the requirement that a defendant seeking to rely on the defence established by subs. (6) must serve on the prosecutor a notice in writing giving information identifying or assisting in the identification of that other person as was then in his possession within a period ending seven clear days before the hearing.

(4) Sentence

20–106 The maximum penalty for the offences under this section is fine not exceeding level 3 on the standard scale.

E. REMOVAL OF BUILDERS' SKIPS

(1) Definition

Highways Act 1980, s.140

Removal of builders' skips

140.—(1) The following provisions of this section have effect in relation to a builder's skip deposited on a highway notwithstanding that it was deposited on it in accordance with a permission granted under section 139 above. **20–107**

(2) The highway authority for the highway or a constable in uniform may require the owner of the skip to remove or reposition it or cause it to be removed or repositioned.

(3) A person required to remove or reposition, or cause to be removed or repositioned, a skip under a requirement made by virtue of subsection (2) above shall comply with the requirement as soon as practicable, and if he fails to do so he is guilty of an offence and liable to a fine not exceeding level 3 on the standard scale.

(4) The highway authority for the highway or a constable in uniform may themselves remove or reposition the skip or cause it to be removed or repositioned.

(5) Where a skip is removed under subsection (4) above, the highway authority or, as the case may be, the chief officer of police shall, where practicable, notify the owner of its removal, but if the owner cannot be traced, or if after a reasonable period of time after being so notified he has not recovered the skip, the highway authority or chief officer of police may dispose of the skip and its contents.

(6) Any expenses reasonably incurred by a highway authority or chief officer of police in the removal or repositioning of a skip under subsection (4) above or the disposal of a skip under subsection (5) above may be recovered from the owner of the skip in any court of competent jurisdiction or summarily as a civil debt.

(7) Any proceeds of the disposal of a skip under subsection (5) above shall be used in the first place to meet the expenses reasonably incurred in the removal and disposal of the skip and thereafter any surplus shall be given to the person entitled to it if he can be traced and if not may be retained by the highway authority or the chief officer of police, as the case may be; and any surplus so retained by a chief officer of police shall be paid into the police fund.

(8) References in this section to expenses incurred in the removal of a skip include references to expenses incurred in storing the skip until it is recovered by the owner or, as the case may be, disposed of.

(9) The owner of a skip is not guilty of an offence under section 139(4) above of failing to secure that a condition relating to the siting of the skip was complied with if the failure resulted from the repositioning of the skip under subsection (3) or (4) above.

[This section is printed as amended by the *Criminal Justice Act* 1982, ss.38 and 46.]

(2) Allocation

This offence is triable summarily: *Highways Act* 1980, s.310. **20–108**

(3) Elements of the offence

A requirement that a skip be removed must be communicated to a potential offender by a constable in uniform going to that person and telling him of the requirement: *Worthing Justices ex p. Waste Management Ltd* (1988) 152 J.P. 362. **20–109**

(4) Sentence

The maximum penalty for the offence under this section is a fine not exceeding level three on the standard scale. **20–110**

V. IMMIGRATION

A. ILLEGAL ENTRY AND SIMILAR OFFENCES

(1) Definition

Immigration Act 1971, s.24

Illegal entry and similar offences

20–111 **24.**—(1) A person who is not a British citizen shall be guilty of an offence punishable on summary conviction with a fine of not more than level 5 on the standard scale or with imprisonment for not more than six months, or with both, in any of the following cases—

(a) if contrary to this Act he knowingly enters the United Kingdom in breach of a deportation order or without leave;

(b) if, having only a limited leave to enter or remain in the United Kingdom, he knowingly either—

(i) remains beyond the time limited by the leave; or

(ii) fails to observe a condition of the leave;

(c) if, having lawfully entered the United Kingdom without leave by virtue of section 8(1) above, he remains without leave beyond the time allowed by section 8(1);

(d) if, without reasonable excuse, he fails to comply with any requirement imposed on him under Schedule 2 to this Act to report to a medical officer of health or to attend, or submit to a test or examination, as required by such an officer;

(e) if, without reasonable excuse, he fails to observe any restriction imposed on him under Schedule 2 or 3 to this Act as to residence, as to his employment or occupation or as to reporting to the police, to an immigration officer or to the Secretary of State;

(f) if he leaves a train in the United Kingdom after being placed on board under Schedule 2 or 3 to this Act with a view to his removal from the United Kingdom;

(g) if he leaves or seeks to leave the United Kingdom through the tunnel system in contravention of a restriction imposed by or under an Order in Council under section 3(7) of this Act.

(1A) A person commits an offence under subsection (1)(b)(i) above on the day when he first knows that the time limited by his leave has expired and continues to commit it throughout any period during which he is in the United Kingdom thereafter; but a person shall not be prosecuted under that provision more than once in respect of the same limited leave.

(3) The extended time limit for prosecutions which is provided for by section 28 below shall apply to offences under subsection (1)(a) and (c) above.

(4) In proceedings for an offence against subsection (1)(a) above of entering the United Kingdom without leave—

(a) any stamp purporting to have been imprinted on a passport or other travel document by an immigration officer on a particular date for the purpose of giving leave shall be presumed to have been duly so imprinted, unless the contrary is proved;

(b) proof that a person had leave to enter the United Kingdom shall lie on the defence if, but only if, he is shown to have entered within six months before the date when the proceedings were commenced.

(2) Allocation

20–112 This offence is triable summarily: *Immigration Act* 1971, s.24.

(3) Elements of the offence

20–113 Section 8 allows for seamen and aircraft crew who arrive in the UK to enter without leave and remain in the country until their vessel leaves again.

The power to give or refuse leave to enter or remain in the UK is only exercisable in writing: s.4(1). To prosecute under s.24 there must be evidence of a written notice. A defective stamp in a passport which omitted to note that leave was limited did not amount to sufficient notice although verbal information had been given: *Lamptey v. Owen* [1982] Crim.L.R. 42.

These are continuing offences which may be prosecuted at any time whilst the limited leave or conditions on leave apply: *Manickavasagar v. Metropolitan Police Commissioner* [1987] Crim.L.R. 50.

Immigration Act 1971, s.28

Proceedings

28.—(1) Where the offence is one to which, under section 24 or 26 above, an extended time limit for prosecutions is to apply, then— **20–114**

(a) an information relating to the offence may in England and Wales be tried by a magistrates' court if it is laid within six months after the commission of the offence, or if it is laid within three years after the commission of the offence and not more than two months after the date certified by an officer of police above the rank of chief superintendent to be the date on which evidence sufficient to justify proceedings came to the notice of an officer of the police force to which he belongs; and

(b) summary proceedings for the offence may in Scotland be commenced within six months after the commission of the offence, or within three years after the commission of the offence and not more than two months after the date on which evidence sufficient in the opinion of the Lord Advocate to justify proceedings came to his knowledge; and

(c) a complaint charging the commission of the offence may in Northern Ireland be heard and determined by a magistrates' court if it is made within six months after the commission of the offence, or if it is made within three years after the commission of the offence and not more than two months after the date certified by an officer of police not below the rank of assistant chief constable to be the date on which evidence sufficient to justify the proceedings came to the notice of the police in Northern Ireland.

(2) For purposes of subsection (1)(b) above proceedings shall be deemed to be commenced on the date on which a warrant to apprehend or to cite the accused is granted, if such warrant is executed without undue delay; and a certificate of the Lord Advocate as to the date on which such evidence as is mentioned in subsection (1)(b) came to his knowledge shall be conclusive evidence.

(3) For the purposes of the trial of a person for an offence under this Part of this Act, the offence shall be deemed to have been committed either at the place at which it actually was committed or at any place at which he may be.

(4) Any powers exercisable under this Act in the case of any person may be exercised notwithstanding that proceedings for an offence under this Part of this Act have been taken against him.

The certificate of awareness of sufficient evidence may be signed after a not guilty **20–115**
plea is entered but before the trial begins. The court does not start to try the case until evidence is called: *Quazi v. DPP* (1988) 152 J.P. 385.

(4) Sentence

The maximum penalty for this offence is a fine of not more than level 5 on the stan- **20–116**
dard scale, imprisonment for a period of not more than six months or both: *Immigration Act* 1971, s.24(1). After commencement of the relevant provisions, the maximum custodial sentence in a magistrates' court will be 12 months' imprisonment: *Criminal Justice Act* 2003, ss.154 and 282.

A recommendation for deportation can be made by a court on convicting a person where the defendant is over 18 and not a British citizen of an imprisonable offence—see Sentencing, Pt IV.

Part III

B. DECEPTION

(1) Definition

Immigration Act 1971, s.24A

Deception

20–117 **24A.**—(1) A person who is not a British citizen is guilty of an offence if, by means which include deception by him—

(a) he obtains or seeks to obtain leave to enter or remain in the United Kingdom; or

(b) he secures or seeks to secure the avoidance, postponement or revocation of enforcement action against him.

(2) "Enforcement action", in relation to a person, means—

(a) the giving of directions for his removal from the United Kingdom ("directions") under Schedule 2 to this Act or section 10 of the *Immigration and Asylum Act* 1999;

(b) the making of a deportation order against him under section 5 of this Act; or

(c) his removal from the United Kingdom in consequence of directions or a deportation order.

(3) A person guilty of an offence under this section is liable—

(a) on summary conviction, to imprisonment for a term not exceeding six months or to a fine not exceeding the statutory maximum, or to both; or

(b) on conviction on indictment, to imprisonment for a term not exceeding two years or to a fine, or to both.

[This section was inserted by the *Asylum and Immigration Act* 1996, s.28.]

(2) Allocation

20–118 This offence is triable either way: s.24A(3). The extended time limit for prosecutions provided under s.28 applies to this section: s.24A(4).

(3) Sentence

20–119 The maximum penalty for an offence under this section is imprisonment for a term not exceeding six months, a fine not exceeding the statutory maximum or both: s.24(3). After commencement of the relevant provisions, the maximum custodial sentence in a magistrates' court will be 12 months' imprisonment: *Criminal Justice Act* 2003, ss.154 and 282. A recommendation for deportation can be made by a court on convicting a person over 18 who is not a British citizen of an imprisonable offence—see Sentencing, Pt IV.

C. ASSISTING ILLEGAL ENTRY AND HARBOURING

(1) Definition

Immigration Act 1971, s.25

Assisting unlawful immigration to member State

20–120 **25.**—(1) A person commits an offence if he—

(a) does an act which facilitates the commission of a breach of immigration law by an individual who is not a citizen of the European Union,

(b) knows or has reasonable cause for believing that the act facilitates the commission of a breach of immigration law by the individual, and

(c) knows or has reasonable cause for believing that the individual is not a citizen of the European Union.

(2) In subsection (1) "immigration law" means a law which has effect in a member State and which controls, in respect of some or all persons who are not nationals of the State, entitlement to—

(a) enter the State,
(b) transit across the State, or
(c) be in the State.

(3) A document issued by the government of a member State certifying a matter of law in that State—

(a) shall be admissible in proceedings for an offence under this section, and
(b) shall be conclusive as to the matter certified.

(4) Subsection (1) applies to anything done—

(a) in the United Kingdom,
(b) outside the United Kingdom by an individual to whom subsection (5) applies, or
(c) outside the United Kingdom by a body incorporated under the law of a part of the United Kingdom.

(5) This subsection applies to—

(a) a British citizen,
(b) a British overseas territories citizen,
(c) a British National (Overseas),
(d) a British Overseas citizen,
(e) a person who is a British subject under the *British Nationality Act* 1981, and
(f) a British protected person within the meaning of that Act.

(6) A person guilty of an offence under this section shall be liable—

(a) on conviction on indictment, to imprisonment for a term not exceeding 14 years, to a fine or to both, or
(b) on summary conviction, to imprisonment for a term not exceeding six months, to a fine not exceeding the statutory maximum or to both.

[This section is printed as amended by the *Criminal Law Act* 1977, s.28, the *MCA* 1980, s.32(2), the *British Nationality Act* 1981, Sched. 4, the *Criminal Justice Act* 1982, ss.38 and 46, the *Asylum and Immigration Act* 1996, s.5 and the *Immigration and Asylum Act* 1999, s.29 and Scheds 14 and 16 and the *British Overseas Territories Act* 2002, s.2(3).] **20–121**

Part III

(2) Allocation

This offence is triable either way: s.25(1). The extended time limit for prosecutions provided under s.28 applies to this section: s.25(4). **20–122**

(3) Elements of the offence

The offence under s.25(1) can relate to the implementation of arrangements for facilitating entry which, on usual principles, would be completed by the carrying out of such arrangements, irrespective of whether or not entry has taken place. The charge can properly relate to a would-be or intending illegal entrant, as opposed to someone who had already become an illegal entrant by reason of passing through or attempting to pass through immigration control by concealment or deception: *Eyck* [2000] All E.R. 569, CA. In *Eyck* (*ante*) the Court held that it was a matter for the jury to decide whether it had been proved that passengers carried in a car driven by the defendant onto a UK-bound ferry intended to enter or seek to enter illegally and whether the defendant was knowingly concerned in carrying out arrangements for facilitating such illegal entry. If they so decided, a conviction under s.25 would be appropriate. The Court also held that an offence under s.25(1)(b) may relate to an intending asylum claimant. **20–123**

It is a crime to assist illegal immigrants to leave their disembarkation port, even if they have already technically entered the United Kingdom. In *Amat Jit Singh* (1973) 1 All E.R. 122, CA, Lawton L.J. stated that s.25 defines the offences which can be committed by those who help illegal entrants. He continued: **20–124**

> The help may come in two ways: the illegal entrant may be given help to get into the United Kingdom or he may be helped after he has arrived here. Section 25 (1) was intended to deal with the first kind of help; section 25 (2) with the second: but they are not mutually exclusive.

The help to get in may be, and often is, continued without any break long after the illegal entry has been effected. There may be no dividing line between helping to effect entry and helping by way of harbouring…Now those who are minded to enter the United Kingdom illegally have no wish to be discovered as soon as they disembark. Effective arrangements for an illegal entry would be likely to include plans for getting the entrant away as quickly as possible from the point of disembarkation. Those who made or carried out such plans would be facilitating entry into the United Kingdom.'

20–125 Section 25(2) creates two separate offences of harbouring: the first involves knowledge that a person is an "illegal entrant" as defined in s.33 and the second, knowledge that the person was an "overstayer" as defined in s.24. The prosecution must state in the information the illegal status relied upon for alleging that the accused knew or believed that status to exist. If the prosecution intends to establish one or other of the offences it must lay separate informations, otherwise it will lay itself open to arguments of duplicity: *Rahman and Qadir v. DPP* [1993] Crim.L.R. 874.

(4) Sentence

20–126 On summary conviction the maximum sentence is six months' imprisonment and/or the maximum fine. After commencement of the relevant provisions, the maximum custodial sentence in a magistrates' court will be 12 months' imprisonment: *Criminal Justice Act* 2003, ss.154 and 282. In *Sackey* [2004] 2 Cr.App.R. 556 the court held that a period of imprisonment for three years on a guilty plea was the guideline so such cases will generally be committed to the Crown Court for sentence.

D. ILLEGAL ENTRY AND SIMILAR OFFENCES

(1) Definition

Asylum and Immigration (Treatment of Claimants) Act 2004, s.2

Entering United Kingdom without passport, &c.

20–127 **2**—(1) A person commits an offence if at a leave or asylum interview he does not have with him an immigration document which—

(a) is in force, and

(b) satisfactorily establishes his identity and nationality or citizenship.

(2) A person commits an offence if at a leave or asylum interview he does not have with him, in respect of any dependent child with whom he claims to be travelling or living, an immigration document which—

(a) is in force, and

(b) satisfactorily establishes the child's identity and nationality or citizenship.

(3) But a person does not commit an offence under subsection (1) or (2) if—

(a) the interview referred to in that subsection takes place after the person has entered the United Kingdom, and

(b) within the period of three days beginning with the date of the interview the person provides to an immigration officer or to the Secretary of State a document of the kind referred to in that subsection.

(4) It is a defence for a person charged with an offence under subsection (1)—

(a) to prove that he is an EEA national,

(b) to prove that he is a member of the family of an EEA national and that he is exercising a right under the Community Treaties in respect of entry to or residence in the United Kingdom,

(c) to prove that he has a reasonable excuse for not being in possession of a document of the kind specified in subsection (1),

(d) to produce a false immigration document and to prove that he used that document as an immigration document for all purposes in connection with his journey to the United Kingdom, or

(e) to prove that he travelled to the United Kingdom without, at any stage since he set out on the journey, having possession of an immigration document.

(5) It is a defence for a person charged with an offence under subsection (2) in respect of a child—

(a) to prove that the child is an EEA national,

(b) to prove that the child is a member of the family of an EEA national and that the child is exercising a right under the Community Treaties in respect of entry to or residence in the United Kingdom,

(c) to prove that the person has a reasonable excuse for not being in possession of a document of the kind specified in subsection (2),

(d) to produce a false immigration document and to prove that it was used as an immigration document for all purposes in connection with the child's journey to the United Kingdom, or

(e) to prove that he travelled to the United Kingdom with the child without, at any stage since he set out on the journey, having possession of an immigration document in respect of the child.

(6) Where the charge for an offence under subsection (1) or (2) relates to an interview which takes place after the defendant has entered the United Kingdom—

(a) subsections (4)(c) and (5)(c) shall not apply, but

(b) it is a defence for the defendant to prove that he has a reasonable excuse for not providing a document in accordance with subsection (3).

(7) For the purposes of subsections (4) to (6)—

(a) the fact that a document was deliberately destroyed or disposed of is not a reasonable excuse for not being in possession of it or for not providing it in accordance with subsection (3), unless it is shown that the destruction or disposal was—

(i) for a reasonable cause, or

(ii) beyond the control of the person charged with the offence, and

(b) in paragraph (a)(i) "reasonable cause" does not include the purpose of—

(i) delaying the handling or resolution of a claim or application or the taking of a decision,

(ii) increasing the chances of success of a claim or application, or

(iii) complying with instructions or advice given by a person who offers advice about, or facilitates, immigration into the United Kingdom, unless in the circumstances of the case it is unreasonable to expect non-compliance with the instructions or advice.

(8) A person shall be presumed for the purposes of this section not to have a document with him if he fails to produce it to an immigration officer or official of the Secretary of State on request.

(9) A person guilty of an offence under this section shall be liable—

(a) on conviction on indictment, to imprisonment for a term not exceeding two years, to a fine or to both, or

(b) on summary conviction, to imprisonment for a term not exceeding twelve months, to a fine not exceeding the statutory maximum or to both.

(10) If a constable or immigration officer reasonably suspects that a person has committed an offence under this section he may arrest the person without warrant.

(11) An offence under this section shall be treated as—

(a) a relevant offence for the purposes of sections 28B and 28D of the *Immigration Act* 1971 (c. 77) (search, entry and arrest), and

(b) an offence under Part III of that Act (criminal proceedings) for the purposes of sections 28(4), 28E, 28G and 28H (search after arrest, &c.) of that Act.

(12) In this section—

"EEA national" means a national of a State which is a contracting party to the Agreement on the European Economic Area signed at Oporto on 2nd May 1992 (as it has effect from time to time),

"immigration document" means —

(a) a passport, and

(b) a document which relates to a national of a State other than the United Kingdom and which is designed to serve the same purpose as a passport, and

"leave or asylum interview" means an interview with an immigration officer or an official of the Secretary of State at which a person–

(a) seeks leave to enter or remain in the United Kingdom, or
(b) claims that to remove him from or require him to leave the United Kingdom would breach the United Kingdom's obligations under the Refugee Convention or would be unlawful under section 6 of the *Human Rights Act* 1998 (c. 42) as being incompatible with his Convention rights.

(13) For the purposes of this section—
(a) a document which purports to be, or is designed to look like, an immigration document, is a false immigration document, and
(b) an immigration document is a false immigration document if and in so far as it is used—
(i) outside the period for which it is expressed to be valid,
(ii) contrary to provision for its use made by the person issuing it, or
(iii) by or in respect of a person other than the person to or for whom it was issued.

(14) Section 11 of the *Immigration Act* 1971 (c. 77) shall have effect for the purpose of the construction of a reference in this section to entering the United Kingdom.

(15) In so far as this section extends to England and Wales, subsection (9)(b) shall, until the commencement of section 154 of the *Criminal Justice Act* 2003 (c. 44) (increased limit on magistrates' power of imprisonment), have effect as if the reference to twelve months were a reference to six months.

(16) In so far as this section extends to Scotland, subsection (9)(b) shall have effect as if the reference to twelve months were a reference to six months.

(17) In so far as this section extends to Northern Ireland, subsection (9)(b) shall have effect as if the reference to twelve months were a reference to six months.

This section came into force on September 22, 2004.

(2) Allocation

20–128 This offence is triable either way: s.2(9).

(3) Elements of the offence

20–129 This offence was introduced to counter the effect of people arriving in the UK who destroyed or otherwise disposed of forged travel documents prior to going through immigration procedures. A person at a leave or asylum interview commits an offence if he does not have a valid passport or other document serving the same purpose as a passport which establishes identity and nationality or citizenship. The offence may be committed at the port of entry on arrival or at a later interview when 3 days may be allowed to produce the relevant documents. The statute provides defences under subs. 4 which include having a reasonable excuse for not being in possession of such a document. Deliberate destruction or disposal of the document does not amount to a reasonable excuse in itself unless there was reasonable cause to destroy or dispose of the document or the destruction or disposal was beyond the control of the person charged. A reasonable excuse might arise if a person is travelling in a family group and someone else had custody of the passports or where individuals are intimidated or threatened to such an extent by a third party that it is reasonable to expect that instructions to destroy or dispose of the document would be followed. In *Navabi* [2005] EWCA Crim 2865 it was held that a request for asylum is not a reasonable excuse under s.2(4)(c) for not being in possession of the relevant document. There is a reverse burden of proof on the defendant but it is compatible with art. 6 ECHR.

In *Thet v. DPP* [2007] 1 W.L.R. 2022 the complex provisions of s.2 of the *Asylum and Immigration (Treatment of Claimants) Act* 2004 were considered. The appellant was a Burmese national who arrived in the UK and passed through immigration control with a false passport which was later returned to an agent. He subsequently attended asylum screening interviews and was unable to produce any travel documents either false or genuine. He claimed that he was unable to obtain a passport in his country of origin because he had been a political prisoner. The statutory defence under s.2(3) and 2(6)(b) was put forward at trial but rejected on the basis that the provisions applied only to any false immigration documents that may have been used on the journey and not to any non-existent genuine passport. On appeal it was held that the Act could not be restrictively interpreted to apply only to any false documents used on the journey. It was said that the natural reading of the section allowed for the defendant to rely on the defence of reasonable excuse for the failure to produce a genuine passport as well as false documents. The court observed that the statute was ambiguous and poorly drafted and accepted that this interpretation could well undermine the purpose of the legislation but as the outcome did not lead to absurdity that was the only proper way in which the section could be interpreted.

This case could have a profound effect on prosecutions against persons arriving in this country without valid travel documents. If the inability to obtain a passport in their home country provides a defence for failing to produce a proper travel document the courts may find defendants disposing of false travel documents before passing through immigration and raising this defence at the earliest opportunity.

Mohammed and Osman [2008] 1 W.L.R. 1130 gave further detailed consideration to the interpretation of s.2 offences. The defendants were both Somalian nationals who entered the UK on false passports. The defence submitted that the 'immigration document' defined in the Act at s.2(12) must refer to a genuine and valid passport, and as the journey had begun with no such document the defendants were entitled to rely on the defence in s.2(4)(e) that they travelled without having possession of an immigration document. It was argued that their failure to produce a false travel document did not deprive the defendants of that defence. On appeal the convictions were quashed because the judge at trial had failed to direct the jury that they must consider whether the explanations given by both defendants for their failure to produce the documents may have been reasonable under s.2(4)(c). However, the defence argument that the section applied only to genuine documents was not accepted. The court said that the statute must be interpreted to preserve the meaning of s.2(4)(d)—whereby a false immigration document is produced and proved to have been used for the entire journey to the UK—and also to limit the defence in s.2(4)(c) imposed by s.2(7) whereby certain circumstances are held not to amount to a reasonable excuse or cause. Through a rather tortuous argument the court appears to have applied the reasoning used in the case of *Thet* but the judgment serves to demonstrate the difficulty of interpretation the Act presents. This case confirms that the section applies to failure to produce either false or genuine immigration documents and in particular that the defence of s.2(4)(e) applies only to those travelling with no documents at all, whether false or genuine.

Part III

(4) Sentence

On summary conviction the maximum sentence is six months' imprisonment and/or a fine at level 5. After commencement of the relevant provisions, the maximum custodial sentence in a magistrates' court will be 12 months' imprisonment: *Criminal Justice Act* 2003, ss.154 and 282. **20–130**

On conviction on indictment the maximum sentence is two years or a fine or both. Guidelines following forged passport cases indicate the starting point for a guilty plea and no previous convictions would be four months' imprisonment. In *Wang* [2005] 2 Cr.App.R.(S.) 79, a sentence of 10 months' imprisonment for an offence under this section was reduced to two months on appeal. See also *Lu Zhu Ai* (2006) 1 Cr.App.R.(S.). 5 where it was held that a five-month sentence of imprisonment for an offence of failing to have immigration documents was appropriate taking into account mitigation but also considering the deterrent effect of the sentence.

VI. POLICE

A. POWER TO MAKE ORDERS IN RESPECT OF PROPERTY IN POSSESSION OF POLICE

Police (Property) Act 1897, s.1

Power to make orders with respect to property in possession of police

20–131 **1.**—(1) Where any property has come into the possession of the police in connexion with their investigation of a suspected offence, a court of summary jurisdiction may, on application, either by an officer of police or by a claimant of the property, make an order for the delivery of the property to the person appearing to the magistrate or court to be the owner thereof, or, if the owner cannot be ascertained, make such order with respect to the property as to the magistrate or court may seem meet.

(2) An order under this section shall not affect the right of any person to take within six months from the date of the order legal proceedings against any person in possession of property delivered by virtue of the order for the recovery of the property, but on the expiration of those six months the right shall cease.

20–132 The police come into possession of property when investigating offences but if the charge is dropped or the accused acquitted and there is a dispute over ownership, it may be necessary for an order to be applied for to allow the police to release the property. If no relevant order is made at the end of the proceedings, the police or a claimant may apply to the magistrates court' for an order under the *Police (Property) Act* 1897. The court will decide who appears to be the "owner" of the property.

An application is made by way of complaint for a summons and costs may be ordered under s.64 of the *Magistrates' Courts Act* 1980: *Uxbridge Justices ex p. Metropolitan Police Commissioner* [1981] Q.B. 829.

20–133 The court should not make use of this procedure when there are real difficulties in deciding ownership or if questions of legal ownership are in dispute and the word "owner" should be given its ordinary and popular meaning: *Raymond Lyons & Co v. Metropolitan Police Commissioner* [1975] Q.B. 321. The fact that proceedings are pending at the County Court for delivery of the property does not of itself make the issue complex and beyond the magistrates' jurisdiction: *Maidstone Magistrates' Court ex p. Knight* (2000) WL 1027029. The fact that the owner of the property may have come by it illegally is irrelevant. The question at issue is who has good or better possessory title: *Costello v. Chief Constable of Derbyshire* [2001] 3 All E.R. 150 and *Haley v. Chief Constable of Northumbria* (2002) 166 J.P. 719. The morality of the claim is also irrelevant and where a claimant was acquitted of soliciting murder, it was held that the nature of the charge was not a good reason for the magistrates declining to return the £10,000 that was paid to a police officer who posed as a hired assassin: *R. (Carter) v. Ipswich Magistrates' Court* [2002] EWHC 332.

20–134 The police may come into possession of property taken from the accused on arrest and the return of the property may be sought during the proceedings by the defendant under the *Magistrates' Courts Act* 1980.

Magistrates' Courts Act 1980, s.48

Return of property taken from accused.

20–135 **48.** Where a summons or warrant has been issued requiring any person to appear or be brought before a magistrates' court to answer to an information, or where any person has been arrested without a warrant for an offence, and property has been taken from him after the issue of the summons or warrant or, as the case may be, on or after his arrest without a warrant, the police shall report the taking of the property, with particulars of the property, to the magistrates' court which deals with the case; and, if the court, being of opinion that the whole or any part of the property can be returned to the accused consistently with the interests of justice and the safe custody of the accused, so directs, the property, or such part of it as the court directs, shall be returned to the accused or to such other person as he may require.

This provision relates only to a person who has been charged and who wishes to reclaim his property: *Arnell v. Harris* [1945] K.B. 60. It only covers property taken from the person of the defendant so if the property was taken from his premises at the time of arrest, there is no power to order its return under this section, but if the court is of the opinion that the property seized should be returned as a necessary part of the defence case it has the discretion to refuse to proceed. *Southampton Magistrates' Court ex p. Newman* [1988] 3 All E.R. 669. 20–136

B. IMPERSONATION OF A POLICE OFFICER

(1) Definition

Police Act 1996, s.90

Impersonation, etc.

90.—(1) Any person who with intent to deceive impersonates a member of a police force or special constable, or makes any statement or does any act calculated falsely to suggest that he is such a member or constable, shall be guilty of an offence and liable on summary conviction to imprisonment for a term not exceeding six months or to a fine not exceeding level 5 on the standard scale, or to both. 20–137

(2) Any person who, not being a constable, wears any article of police uniform in circumstances where it gives him an appearance so nearly resembling that of a member of a police force as to be calculated to deceive shall be guilty of an offence and liable on summary conviction to a fine not exceeding level 3 on the standard scale.

(3) Any person who, not being a member of a police force or special constable, has in his possession any article of police uniform shall, unless he proves that he obtained possession of that article lawfully and has possession of it for a lawful purpose, be guilty of an offence and liable on summary conviction to a fine not exceeding level 1 on the standard scale.

(4) In this section—

(a) "article of police uniform" means any article of uniform or any distinctive badge or mark or document of identification usually issued to members of police forces or special constables, or anything having the appearance of such an article, badge, mark or document.

(aa) "member of a police force" includes a member of the British Transport Police Force, and

(b) "special constable" means a special constable appointed for a police area.

[This section is printed as amended by the *Anti-Terrorism, Crime and Security Act* 2001, Sched. 7.]

(2) Allocation

The offences in this section are triable summarily: s.90(1), (2), (3). 20–138

(3) Elements of the offence

It is an offence to wear a uniform which is likely to deceive persons into thinking that one is a police officer, even if that deception is not intended. In *Turner v. Shearer* [1973] 1 All E.R. 397, DC, the defendant was wearing secondhand articles of police uniform, and persons were misled into thinking that he was a police officer. The defendant did not intend to mislead anyone. The Divisional Court held that "calculated" meant "likely," not "intended" and the defendant was convicted. 20–139

(4) Sentence

The offence under subs. (1) carries a maximum penalty of six months imprisonment, a fine not exceeding the statutory maximum or both: s.90(1). The offence under subs. (2) carries a maximum penalty of a fine not exceeding level three on the standard scale: 20–140 s.90(2). The offence under subs. (3) carries a maximum penalty of a fine not exceeding level one on the standard scale: s.90(3). After commencement of the relevant provisions, the maximum custodial sentence in a magistrates' court will be 12 months' imprisonment: *Criminal Justice Act* 2003, ss.154 and 282.

VII. PRISONS

A. HARBOURING AN ESCAPED PRISONER

(1) Definition

Criminal Justice Act 1961, s.22

20–141 **22.**—(1) [...]

(2) If any person knowingly harbours a person who has escaped from a prison or other institution to which the said section thirty-nine applies, or who, having been sentenced in any part of the United Kingdom or in any of the Channel Islands or the Isle of Man to imprisonment or detention, is otherwise unlawfully at large, or gives to any such person any assistance with intent to prevent, hinder or interfere with his being taken into custody, he shall be liable—

(a) on summary conviction, to imprisonment for a term not exceeding six months or to a fine not exceeding one hundred pounds, or to both;

(b) on conviction on indictment, to imprisonment for a term not exceeding ten years, or to a fine, or to both.

(3) In the following enactments (which make provision for the application of sections thirty-nine to forty-two of the *Prison Act* 1952) that is to say, subsection (3) of section one hundred and twenty-two of the *Army Act* 1955, subsection (3) of section one hundred and twenty-two of the *Air Force Act* 1955 and subsection (3) of section eighty-two of the *Naval Discipline Act* 1957, references to the said section thirty-nine shall be construed as including references to subsection (2) of this section.

(4) [...]

(2) Allocation

20–142 This offence is triable either way: s.22(2).

(3) Elements of the offence

20–143 In *Darch v. Weight* (1984) 79 Cr.App.R. 40, CA it was held that "harbour" meant to shelter or provide refuge and that could be done irrespective of any interest in the premises concerned. Merely giving assistance to an escaped prisoner without actually sheltering him would not amount to "harbouring" him. The defendant was a lodger in a house into which the landlady admitted three escaped prisoners. Both she and the landlady were charged and convicted, though the landlady's conviction was later quashed by the Crown Court. On the defendant's appeal, the Divisional Court held that as the defendant had done no positive act to provide shelter, she was not guilty of "harbouring" under s.22(2) of the 1961 Act.

The yard of a police station is not a "prison or other institution" within the meaning of the *Prison Act* 1952, s.39: *Nicoll v. Catron* (1985) 81 Cr.App.R. 339, DC.

(4) Sentence

20–144 When tried summarily, the maximum penalty for this offence is imprisonment for a term not exceeding six months, a fine not exceeding the statutory maximum or both: *CJA* 1961, s.22(2)(a). On commencement of the relevant provisions, the maximum custodial sentence in a magistrates' court will be 12 months' imprisonment: *Criminal Justice Act* 2003, ss.154 and 282.

In *Forbes* [2011] 1 Cr.App.R.(S.) 23 a sentence of 16 months imprisonment was reduced on appeal to 8 months. It was held that mitigating circumstances, such as the fact that the offender was of previous good character, had not initially been aware that the prisoner was unlawfully at large and also that she was the carer for a severely disabled relative had not been sufficiently taken into account. Although custody for an offence of this nature was justified the length of sentence was held to be manifestly excessive.

B. ESCAPE FROM CUSTODY

The offence of escaping from custody and being unlawfully at large is a common law offence, triable only on indictment. In *Dhillon* (2006) 1 W.L.R. 1535 the essential ingredients of the offence of escape were considered in detail. For the offence to be made out the defendant must actually be in custody; he must know or be reckless as to his being in custody and the custody must be lawful. In this case the defendant had been arrested as an illegal immigrant but had then been accompanied to hospital. In the apparent absence of any officers he later walked out of the hospital. It was held that he had not committed the offence of escape as there was no continuity of custody and no evidence that the defendant was aware of any constraint placed upon him. In *Iqbal (Shaid)* [2011] 1 Cr.App.R. 24 the appellant had been stopped by police on suspicion of involvement with a drugs conspiracy. He was hand cuffed and told to wait for other officers to arrive to arrest him. He did not, but tried to run away. It was held that as he had not at this stage been arrested but was only restrained or controlled by police prior to arrest the common law offence of escape from custody did not cover his situation. The court drew an analogy with the position of a person who attends voluntarily at a police station but is then free to leave at any time up to and until he is arrested and charged which clearly confirms that without arrest, the police have no broad power to detain a citizen. In *Golding* (2007) 2 Cr.App.R.(S.) 49 the defendant returned to an open prison from his day release but then later that same day he absconded. He was convicted of escaping from lawful custody and was sentenced to 10 months imprisonment. On appeal the sentence was upheld and the court said that escape from custody subverted the process of the courts and prisons and the defendant had only been recaptured at considerable public expense. The *Prisoners (Return to Custody) Act* 1995 which created a summary only offence restricted to a maximum custodial sentence of six months was held not to have affected the common law offence and level of sentence. **20–145**

C. REMAINING AT LARGE

(1) Definition

Prisoners (Return to Custody) Act 1995, s.1

Remaining at large after temporary release

1.—(1) Subject to subsection (2) below, a person who has been temporarily released in pursuance of rules made under section 47(5) of the *Prison Act* 1952 (rules for temporary release) is guilty of an offence if— **20–146**

(a) without reasonable excuse, he remains unlawfully at large at any time after becoming so at large by virtue of the expiry of the period for which he was temporarily released; or

(b) knowing or believing an order recalling him to have been made and while unlawfully at large by virtue of such an order, he fails, without reasonable excuse, to take all necessary steps for complying as soon as reasonably practicable with that order.

(1A) A person who has been temporarily released in pursuance of an intermittent custody order made under section 183 of the *Criminal Justice Act* 2003 is guilty of an offence if, without reasonable excuse, he remains unlawfully at large at any time after becoming so at large by virtue of the expiry of the period for which he was temporarily released.

(2) Subsection (1) above shall not apply in the case of a person temporarily released from a secure training centre.

(3) A person guilty of any offence under this section shall be liable, on summary conviction, to imprisonment for a term not exceeding six months or to a fine not exceeding level 5 on the standard scale, or to both.

(4) An offence under this section shall be taken to be committed at the place where the offender was required to be detained immediately before being temporarily released.

(5) A person shall be deemed for the purposes of this section to be unlawfully at large whenever he is deemed to be so at large for the purposes of section 49 of the *Prison Act 1952 (which confers powers of arrest).*

(6) This section shall not apply where the period of temporary release expired, or the order of recall was made, before the commencement of this section.

[This section is printed as amended by the *Criminal Justice Act* 2003 s. 186(5).]

(2) Allocation

20–147 This offence is triable summarily only; s.1(3).

(3) Elements of the offence

20–148 *Montgomery* (2008) 1 W.L.R. 636 highlighted the importance of preferring the correct charge for escapes. In this case the defendant had failed to return to an open prison after his permitted day release expired. The charge of escaping from lawful custody was held to be wrongly brought as the defendant had been neither confined nor was he under the direct control of a representative of any authority at the time of his escape. The proper charge was one under the *Prisoners (Return to Custody) Act* 1995.

(4) Sentence

20–149 The maximum sentence is a period of imprisonment for six months or a fine at level 5 or both.

VIII. PUBLIC HEALTH

A. PROHIBITION ON UNLICENSED DISPOSAL OF WASTE

(1) Definition

Control of Pollution Act 1974, s.3

Prohibition of unlicensed disposal of waste

20–150 **3.**—(1) Except in prescribed cases, a person shall not—

(a) deposit controlled waste on any land or cause or knowingly permit controlled waste to be deposited on any land; or

(b) use any plant or equipment, or cause or knowingly permit any plant or equipment to be used, for the purpose of disposing of controlled waste or of dealing in a prescribed manner with controlled waste,

unless the land on which the waste is deposited or, as the case may be, which forms the site of the plant or equipment is occupied by the holder of a licence issued in pursuance of section 5 of this Act (in this Part of this Act referred to as a "disposal licence") which authorises the deposit or use in question and the deposit or use is in accordance with the conditions, if any, specified in the licence.

(2) Except in a case falling within the following subsection, a person who contravenes any of the provisions of the preceding subsection shall, subject to subsection (4) of this section, be guilty of an offence and liable on summary conviction to a fine of an amount not exceeding £400 or on conviction on indictment to imprisonment for a term not exceeding two years or a fine or both.

(3) A person who contravenes paragraph (a) of subsection (1) of this section in a case where—

(a) the waste in question is of a kind which is poisonous, noxious or polluting; and
(b) its presence on the land is likely to give rise to an environmental hazard; and
(c) it is deposited on the land in such circumstances or for such a period that whoever deposited it there may reasonably be assumed to have abandoned it there or to have brought it there for the purpose of its being disposed of (whether by himself or others) as waste,

shall, subject to the following subsection, be guilty of an offence and liable on summary conviction to imprisonment for a term not exceeding six months or a fine not exceeding £400 or both or, on conviction on indictment, to imprisonment for a term not exceeding five years or a fine or both.

(4) It shall be a defence for a person charged with an offence under this section to prove—

(a) that he—
 (i) took care to inform himself, from persons who were in a position to provide the information, as to whether the deposit or use to which the charge relates would be in contravention of subsection (1) of this section, and
 (ii) did not know and had no reason to suppose that the information given to him was false or misleading and that the deposit or use might be in contravention of that subsection; or
(b) that he acted under instructions from his employer and neither knew nor had reason to suppose that the deposit or use was in contravention of the said subsection (1); or
(c) in the case of an offence of making, causing or permitting a deposit or use otherwise than in accordance with conditions specified in a disposal licence, that he took all such steps as were reasonably open to him to ensure that the conditions were complied with; or
(d) that the acts specified in the charge were done in an emergency in order to avoid danger to the public and that, as soon as reasonably practicable after they were done, particulars of them were furnished to the disposal authority in whose area the acts were done.

(5) In this section and subsections (5) and (6) of the following section 'land' includes land covered with waters where the land is above the low-water mark of ordinary spring tides and the waters are not inland waters (within the meaning of Chapter I of Part III of the *Water Act* 1989).

[This section will be repealed by the *Environmental Protection Act* 1990, Sched. 16, when it comes into force.]

(2) Allocation

This offence is triable either way: section (3)(c). **20–151**

(3) Elements of the offence

The offence of depositing controlled waste is committed when waste is left on land from which it will later be removed, and does not occur only when the waste reaches its final place of deposit: *Metropolitan Stipendiary Magistrate ex p. London Waste Regulation Authority* [1993] 3 All E.R. 113, QBD. This finding was approved in *Smith (David Brian)* [1999] Env.L.R. 433, CA, the Court emphasising that the purpose of the 1974 Act was to protect the environment from the consequences of dumping waste and it would diminish its efficacy if the meaning of "deposit" under s.3(1) was restricted to "final deposit". **20–152**

Controlled waste is defined in s.30(1) of the 1974 Act as "household, industrial and commercial waste or any such waste." Section 30(5) provides that:

"(a) household waste consists of waste from a private dwelling or residential home or from premises forming part of a university or school or other educational establishment or forming part of a hospital or nursing home (b) industrial waste consists of waste from any factory within the meaning of the *Factories Act* 1961 and any premises occupied by a body corporate established by or under any enactment for the purpose of carrying on under national ownership any industry or part of an industry or any undertaking, excluding waste from any mine or quarry and (c) commercial waste consists of waste from premises used wholly or mainly for the purposes of a trade or business or the purposes of sport, recreation or entertainment excluding—

(i) household and industrial waste and (ii) waste from any mine or quarry and waste from premises used for agriculture within the meaning of the *Agriculture Act* 1947 or, in Scotland, the *Agriculture (Scotland) Act* 1948, and (iii) waste of any other description prescribed for the purposes of this sub-paragraph."

(4) Defences

20–153 Section 3(4) provides a defence to a charge under this section. In *Durham CC v. Peter Connors Industrial Services Ltd* [1993] Env.L.R. 197, QBD, it was held that in order to establish a defence under s.3(4) it had to be shown that the defendant company charged with depositing waste had received information about each specific deposit to which a charge related and then a judgment on whether that deposit might contravene the section could be formed. The defendant company had operated a blanket system of checks whereby drivers were instructed to check, so far as possible, that there were no toxic materials in the waste deposited. There was no reason for the defendant to believe that the information from the drivers was false or misleading but it was not specific enough to provide a defence under s.3(4).

(5) Sentence

20–154 This offence is triable either way with a maximum sentence on summary conviction of a fine not exceeding £400. If the offence is aggravated under subs. (3), the maximum offence on summary conviction is a fine not exceeding £400 or six months' imprisonment. After commencement of the relevant provisions, the maximum custodial sentence in a magistrates' court will be 12 months' imprisonment: *Criminal Justice Act* 2003, ss.154 and 282.

B. PROHIBITION ON UNAUTHORISED OR HARMFUL DEPOSIT TREATMENT OF WASTE

(1) Definition

Environmental Protection Act 1990, s.33

Prohibition on unauthorised or harmful deposit, treatment or disposal etc. of waste

20–155 **33.**—(1) Subject to subsection (2) and (3) below and, in relation to Scotland, to section 54 below, a person shall not—

(a) deposit controlled waste, or knowingly cause or knowingly permit controlled waste to be deposited in or on any land unless a waste management licence authorising the deposit is in force and the deposit is in accordance with the licence;

(b) treat, keep or dispose of controlled waste, or knowingly cause or knowingly permit controlled waste to be treated, kept or disposed of—

(i) in or on any land, or

(ii) by means of any mobile plant,

except under and in accordance with a waste management licence;

(c) treat, keep or dispose of controlled waste in a manner likely to cause pollution of the environment or harm to human health.

(2) Subsection (1) above does not apply in relation to household waste from a domestic property which is treated, kept or disposed of within the curtilage of the dwelling by or with the permission of the occupier of the dwelling.

(3) Subsection (1)(a), (b) or (c) above do not apply in cases prescribed in regulations made by the Secretary of State and the regulations may make different exceptions for different areas.

(4) The Secretary of State, in exercising his power under subsection (3) above, shall have regard in particular to the expediency of excluding from the controls imposed by waste management licences—

(a) any deposits which are small enough or of such a temporary nature that they may be so excluded;

(b) any means of treatment or disposal which are innocuous enough to be so excluded;

(c) cases for which adequate controls are provided by another enactment than this section.

(5) Where controlled waste is carried in and deposited from a motor vehicle, the person who controls or is in a position to control the use of the vehicle shall, for the purposes of subsection (1)(a) above, be treated as knowingly causing the waste to be deposited whether or not he gave any instructions for this to be done.

(6) A person who contravenes subsection (1) above or any condition of a waste management licence commits an offence.

(7) It shall be a defence for a person charged with an offence under this section to prove—

(a) that he took all reasonable precautions and exercised all due diligence to avoid the commission of the offence; or

(b) that he acted under instructions from his employer and neither knew nor had reason to suppose that the acts done by him constituted a contravention of subsection (1) above; or

(c) that the acts alleged to constitute the contravention were done in an emergency in order to avoid danger to human health in a case where—

(i) he took all such steps as were reasonably practicable in the circumstances for minimising pollution of the environment and harm to human health; and

(ii) particulars of the acts were furnished to the waste regulation authority as soon as reasonably practicable after they were done.

(8) Except in a case falling within subsection (9) below, a person who commits an offence under this section shall be liable—

(a) on summary conviction, to imprisonment for a term not exceeding six months or a fine not exceeding £20,000 or both; and

(b) on conviction on indictment, to imprisonment for a term not exceeding two years or a fine or both.

(9) A person who commits an offence under this section in relation to special waste shall be liable—

(a) on summary conviction, to imprisonment for a term not exceeding six months or a fine not exceeding £20,000 or both;

(b) on conviction on indictment, to imprisonment for a term not exceeding five years or a fine or both.

[This section is printed as amended by the *Environment Act* 1995, Sched. 22.]

(2) Allocation

This offence is triable either way: s.33(8). **20–156**

(3) Elements of the offence

The requirement as to knowledge relates to knowledge that the waste is being deposited, rather than knowledge that the deposit breaches the license conditions. In *Shanks & McEwan (Teesside) Ltd v. Environment Agency* [1999] Q.B. 333, QBD, it was held that it was sufficient for the prosecution to prove that the company had on the relevant day knowingly operated and held out the site for the reception and deposit of controlled waste, and that the deposit had not been in accordance with a condition of the licence. **20–157**

The burden of proof that a defendant had deposited or accepted delivery of "special waste" will lie on the prosecution. However, the burden of proving that the deposit of waste was conducted with prior approval will lie on the defendant, the standard of proof being on the balance of probabilities: *Environment Agency v. ME Foley Contractors Ltd* [2002] 1 W.L.R. 1754, QBD.

In *Thames Water Utilities Ltd v. Bromley Magistrates' Court* [2009] 1 All E.R. 744 it was held that water waste escaping from a public sewage system was controlled waste within the meaning of s.33.

(4) Defence

20–158 Subsection (6) provides a defence of due diligence, acting under employer instructions or acting under conditions of emergency.

(5) Sentence

20–159 When tried summarily, the maximum penalty for this offence is imprisonment for a term not exceeding six months, a fine not exceeding £20,000 or both. On commencement of the relevant provisions, the maximum custodial sentence in a magistrates' court will be 12 months' imprisonment: *Criminal Justice Act* 2003, ss.154 and 282.

C. LEAVING LITTER

(1) Definition

Environmental Protection Act 1990, s.87

Offence of leaving litter

20–160 **87.**—(1) If any person throws down, drops or otherwise deposits in, into or from any place to which this section applies, and leaves, any thing whatsoever in such circumstances as to cause, or contribute to, or tend to lead to, the defacement by litter of any place to which this section applies, he shall, subject to subsection (2) below, be guilty of an offence.

(2) No offence is committed under this section where the depositing and leaving of the thing was—

(a) authorised by law, or
(b) done with the consent of the owner, occupier or other person or authority having control of the place in or into which that thing was deposited.

(3) This section applies to any public open place and, in so far as the place is not a public open place, also to the following places—

(a) any relevant highway or relevant road and any trunk road which is a special road;
(b) any place on relevant land of a principal litter authority;
(c) any place on relevant Crown land;
(d) any place on relevant land of any designated statutory undertaker;
(e) any place on relevant land of any designated educational institution;
(f) any place on relevant land within a litter control area of a local authority.

(4) In this section "public open place" means a place in the open air to which the public are entitled or permitted to have access without payment; and any covered place open to the air on at least one side and available for public use shall be treated as a public open place.

(5) A person who is guilty of an offence under this section shall be liable on summary conviction to a fine not exceeding level 4 on the standard scale.

(6) A local authority, with a view to promoting the abatement of litter, may take such steps as the authority think appropriate for making the effect of subsection (5) above known to the public in their area.

(7) In any proceedings in Scotland for an offence under this section it shall be lawful to convict the accused on the evidence of one witness.

(2) Allocation

20–161 This offence is triable summarily only: s.87(5).

(3) Elements of the offence

20–162 A telephone kiosk will not be regarded as a "public open space" or a covered place available for public use as they are not open to air on at least one side, but instead have three fixed sides and one door which was usually closed except for access: *DPP v. Felix* [1998] Crim.L.R. 657. The court added that the phrase "otherwise deposits in" was extremely wide and that "deposits" meant no more than places or puts.

The word "litter" should be given its natural meaning of "miscellaneous rubbish left lying about". This will include commercial waste: *Westminster City Council v. Riding* (1996) Env.L.R. 95, QBD.

(4) Sentence

The maximum penalty for this offence is a fine not exceeding level four on the standard scale: s.87(5). **20–163**

D. Health and Safety Offences

(1) Health and Safety at Work Act 1974

Sections 2–7 of the Act impose general duties on employers to ensure the health and safety and welfare at work of their employees and other persons who may be affected by the employer's undertaking, *e.g.* sub-contractors: s.2. A similar duty is imposed on self-employed persons and their workforce who are not employees: s.3. **20–164**

Persons concerned with premises have a duty relating to health and safety towards persons other than their employees who use premises as a place of work: s.4.

Manufacturers have a duty as regards articles and substances for use at work: s.6.

Employees also have a general duty to take reasonable care for their own health and safety and that of other people affected by their actions: s.7.

(2) Definition

Health and Safety at Work Act 1974 s.33

Offences

33.—(1) It is an offence for a person— **20–165**

(a) to fail to discharge a duty to which he is subject by virtue of sections 2 to 7;

(b) to contravene section 8 or 9;

(c) to contravene any health and safety regulations or any requirement or prohibition imposed under any such regulations (including any requirement or prohibition to which he is subject by virtue of the terms of or any condition or restriction attached to any licence, approval, exemption or other authority issued, given or granted under the regulations);

(d) to contravene any requirement imposed by or under regulations under section 14 or intentionally to obstruct any person in the exercise of his powers under that section;

(e) to contravene any requirement imposed by an inspector under section 20 or 25;

(f) to prevent or attempt to prevent any other person from appearing before an inspector or from answering any question to which an inspector may by virtue of section 20(2) require an answer;

(g) to contravene any requirement or prohibition imposed by an improvement notice or a prohibition notice (including any such notice as modified on appeal);

(h) intentionally to obstruct an inspector in the exercise or performance of his powers or duties or to obstruct a customs officer in the exercise of his powers under section 25A;

(i) to contravene any requirement imposed by a notice under section 27(1);

(j) to use or disclose any information in contravention of section 27(4) or 28;

(k) to make a statement which he knows to be false or recklessly to make a statement which is false where the statement is made—

(i) in purported compliance with a requirement to furnish any information imposed by or under any of the relevant statutory provisions; or

(ii) for the purpose of obtaining the issue of a document under any of the relevant statutory provisions to himself or another person;

(l) intentionally to make a false entry in any register, book, notice or other document required by or under any of the relevant statutory provisions to be kept, served or given or, with intent to deceive, to make use of any such entry which he knows to be false;

(m) with intent to deceive, to use a document issued or authorised to be issued under any of the relevant statutory provisions or required for any purpose thereunder or to make or have in his possession a document so closely resembling any such document as to be calculated to deceive;

(n) falsely to pretend to be an inspector;

(o) to fail to comply with an order made by a court under section 42.

(2) Schedule 3A (which specifies the mode of trial and maximum penalty applicable to offences under this section and the existing statutory provisions) has effect.

(3) Schedule 3A is subject to any provision made by virtue of section 15(6)(c) or (d).

[This section is printed as amended by the *Health and Safety (Offences) Act* 2008 which came into force on January 16, 2009]

The *Health and Safety (Offences) Act* 2008 revises the mode of trial and maximum penalties under the *Health and Safety at Work Act* 1974. The mode of trial for several offences has been varied and maximum penalties increased. The Act does not apply to offences committed before the January 16, 2009 when it came into force.

(3) Allocation

20–166 The allocation of offences is set out in the Table to Sched. 3A (see below).

Health and Safety at Work Act 1974, s.34(1)–(4), 36–38

Extension of time for bringing summary proceedings

20–167 **34.**—(1) Where—

(a) a special report on any matter to which section 14 of this Act applies is made by virtue of subsection (2)(a) of that section; or

(b) a report is made by the person holding an inquiry into any such matter by virtue of subsection (2)(b) of that section; or

(c) a coroner's inquest is held touching the death of any person whose death may have been caused by an accident which happened while he was at work or by a disease which he contracted or probably contracted at work or by any accident, act or omission which occurred in connection with the work of any person whatsoever; or

(d) a public inquiry into any death that may have been so caused is held under the *Fatal Accidents and Sudden Deaths Inquiry (Scotland) Act* 1976,

and it appears from the report or, in a case falling within paragraph (c) or (d) above, from the proceedings at the inquest or inquiry, that any of the relevant statutory provisions was contravened at a time which is material in relation to the subject-matter of the report, inquest or inquiry, summary proceedings against any person liable to be proceeded against in respect of the contravention may be commenced at any time within three months of the making of the report or, in a case falling within paragraph (c) or (d) above, within three months of the conclusion of the inquest or inquiry.

(2) Where an offence under any of the relevant statutory provisions is committed by reason of a failure to do something at or within a time fixed by or under any of those provisions, the offence shall be deemed to continue until that thing is done.

(3) Summary proceedings for an offence to which this subsection applies may be commenced at any time within six months from the date on which there comes to the knowledge of a responsible enforcing authority evidence sufficient in the opinion of that authority to justify a prosecution for that offence; and for the purposes of this subsection—

(a) a certificate of an enforcing authority stating that such evidence came to its knowledge on a specified date shall be conclusive evidence of that fact; and

(b) a document purporting to be such a certificate and to be signed by or on behalf of the enforcing authority in question shall be presumed to be such a certificate unless the contrary is proved.

(4) The preceding subsection applies to any offence under any of the relevant statutory provisions which a person commits by virtue of any provision or requirement to which he is subject as the designer, manufacturer, importer or supplier of any thing; and in that subsection "responsible enforcing authority" means an enforcing authority within whose field of responsibility the offence in question lies, whether by virtue of section 35 or otherwise.

Offences due to fault of other person

36.—(1) Where the commission by any person of an offence under any of the relevant statutory provisions is due to the act or default of some other person, that other person shall be guilty of the offence, and a person may be charged with and convicted of the offence by virtue of this subsection whether or not proceedings are taken against the first-mentioned person. **20–168**

(2) Where there would be or have been the commission of an offence under section 33 by the Crown but for the circumstance that that section does not bind the Crown, and that fact is due to the act or default of a person other than the Crown, that person shall be guilty of the offence which, but for that circumstance, the Crown would be committing or would have committed, and may be charged with and convicted of that offence accordingly.

(3) The preceding provisions of this section are subject to any provision made by virtue of section 15(6).

Offences by bodies corporate

37.—(1) Where an offence under any of the relevant statutory provisions committed by a body corporate is proved to have been committed with the consent or connivance of, or to have been attributable to any neglect on the part of, any director, manager, secretary or other similar officer of the body corporate or a person who was purporting to act in any such capacity, he as well as the body corporate shall be guilty of that offence and shall be liable to be proceeded against and punished accordingly. **20–169**

(2) Where the affairs of a body corporate are managed by its members, the preceding subsection shall apply in relation to the acts and defaults of a member in connection with his functions of management as if he were a director of the body corporate.

Restriction on institution of proceedings in England and Wales

38. Proceedings for an offence under any of the relevant statutory provisions shall not, in England and Wales, be instituted except by an inspector or the Environment Agency or by or with the consent of the Director of Public Prosecutions. **20–170**

(4) Sentence

Health and Safety at Work Act 1974, Sched. 3A

SCHEDULE 3A

OFFENCES: MODE OF TRIAL AND MAXIMUM PENALTY

1. The mode of trial and maximum penalty applicable to each offence listed in the first column of the following table are as set out opposite that offence in the subsequent columns of the table. **20–171**

Offence	*Mode of trial*	*Penalty on summary conviction*	*Penalty on conviction on indictment*
An offence under section 33(1)(a) consisting of a failure to discharge a duty to which a person is subject by virtue of sections 2 to 6.	Summarily or on indictment.	Imprisonment for a term not exceeding 12 months, or a fine not exceeding £20,000, or both.	Imprisonment for a term not exceeding two years, or a fine, or both.
An offence under section 33(1)(a) consisting of a failure to discharge a duty to which a person is subject by virtue of section 7.	Summarily or on indictment.	Imprisonment for a term not exceeding 12 months, or a fine not exceeding the statutory maximum, or both.	Imprisonment for a term not exceeding two years, or a fine, or both.
An offence under section 33(1)(b) consisting of a contravention of section 8.	Summarily or on indictment.	Imprisonment for a term not exceeding 12 months, or a fine not exceeding £20,000, or both.	Imprisonment for a term not exceeding two years, or a fine, or both.
An offence under section 33(1)(b) consisting of a contravention of section 9.	Summarily or on indictment.	A fine not exceeding £20,000.	A fine.
An offence under section 33(1)(c).	Summarily or on indictment.	Imprisonment for a term not exceeding 12 months, or a fine not exceeding £20,000, or both.	Imprisonment for a term not exceeding two years, or a fine, or both.
An offence under section 33(1)(d).	Summarily only.	A fine not exceeding level 5 on the standard scale.	
An offence under section 33(1)(e), (f) or (g).	Summarily or on indictment.	Imprisonment for a term not exceeding 12 months, or a fine not exceeding £20,000, or both.	Imprisonment for a term not exceeding two years, or a fine, or both.
An offence under section 33(1)(h).	Summarily only.	Imprisonment for a term not exceeding 51 weeks (in England and Wales) or 12 months (in Scotland), or a fine not exceeding level 5 on the standard scale, or both.	
An offence under section 33(1)(i).	Summarily or on indictment.	A fine not exceeding the statutory maximum.	A fine.

An offence under section 33(1)(j).	Summarily or on indictment.	Imprisonment for a term not exceeding 12 months, or a fine not exceeding the statutory maximum, or both.	Imprisonment for a term not exceeding two years, or a fine, or both.
An offence under section 33(1)(k), (l) or (m).	Summarily or on indictment.	Imprisonment for a term not exceeding 12 months, or a fine not exceeding £20,000, or both.	Imprisonment for a term not exceeding two years, or a fine, or both.
An offence under section 33(1)(n).	Summarily only.	A fine not exceeding level 5 on the standard scale.	
An offence under section 33(1)(o).	Summarily or on indictment.	Imprisonment for a term not exceeding 12 months, or a fine not exceeding £20,000, or both.	Imprisonment for a term not exceeding two years, or a fine, or both.
An offence under the existing statutory provisions for which no other penalty is specified.	Summarily or on indictment.	Imprisonment for a term not exceeding 12 months, or a fine not exceeding £20,000, or both.	Imprisonment for a term not exceeding two years, or a fine, or both.

2.—(1) This paragraph makes transitional modifications of the table as it applies to England and Wales.

(2) In relation to an offence committed before the commencement of section 154(1) of the *Criminal Justice Act* 2003 (general limit on magistrates' court's powers to imprison), a reference to imprisonment for a term not exceeding 12 months is to be read as a reference to imprisonment for a term not exceeding six months.

(3) In relation to an offence committed before the commencement of section 281(5) of that Act (alteration of penalties for summary offences), a reference to imprisonment for a term not exceeding 51 weeks is to be read as a reference to imprisonment for a term not exceeding six months.

[This Schedule is printed as amended by the *Health and Safety (Offences) Act* 2008 which came into force on January 16, 2009.]

For guidelines on the level of fine to be imposed and the factors to be taken into account when sentencing companies for offences in breach of health and safety legislation: see *Howe and Son (Engineers) Ltd* [1999] 2 All E.R. 249. The court must take into the account the seriousness of the offence and the means of the corporate offender. In *B. & Q.* [2005] EWCA Crim 2297 it was held that the totality of the criminality of the defendant company must be considered including the degree of repetition and management failures. Fines of £550,000 were upheld as not manifestly excessive. The court also said that such fines imposed on large companies should be paid immediately or within days. Also in *P. & O. Ferries (Irish Sea) Ltd* [2005] 2 Cr.App.R.(S.) 21 the court held that fines for breach of Health and Safety requirements had to be significant so as to penalise large companies. A reduced fine of £200,000 was substituted on appeal where the breach had led to a fatality.

Reference is made to these offences in the *Magistrates' Courts Sentencing Guidelines 2008*. No specific guidelines have been drawn up but mitigating and aggravating factors are considered.

IX. PUBLIC TRANSPORT

20–172 Public transport includes trains, underground railways and buses. This section covers the railways but regulations apply to other forms of public transport. For the purposes of this section, the principles explained apply equally to similar offences committed on other modes of transport but they are covered by specific, separate regulations etc.

A. OBSTRUCTION OF THE OFFICERS OF ANY RAILWAY COMPANY, TRESPASSING UPON ANY RAILWAY

(1) Definition

Railway Regulation Act 1840, s.16

For punishment of persons obstructing the officers of any railway company, or trespassing upon any railway

20–173 **16.** If any person shall wilfully obstruct or impede any officer or agent of any railway company in the execution of his duty upon any railway, or upon or in any of the stations or other works or premises connected therewith, or if any person shall wilfully trespass upon any railway, or any of the stations or other works or premises connected therewith, and shall refuse to quit the same upon request to him made by any officer or agent of the said company, every such person so offending, and all others aiding or assisting therein, shall, upon conviction by a magistrates' court, at the discretion of the court, forfeit to her Majesty any sum not exceeding level 1 on the standard scale level 3 on the standard scale and in default of payment thereof shall or may be imprisoned.

[This section is printed as amended by the *Summary Jurisdiction Act* 1848, s.4, the *Statute Law Revision (No.2) Act* 1888, the *Statute Law Revision Act* 1892, the *Mag-*

istrates' Courts Act 1952, Sched. 6, the *British Railways Act* 1965, s.35(1), the *London Transport Act* 1965, s.34(1), the *British Railways Act* 1977, Sched. 1, the *CJA* 1982, s.46 and the *Police and Criminal Evidence Act* 1984, Sched. 6.]

(2) Allocation

This offence is triable summarily. **20–174**

(3) Elements of the offence

The word "railway" extends to all railways constructed under the powers of any Act of Parliament and intended for the conveyance of passengers in or upon carriages drawn or impelled by the power of steam or by any other mechanical power; "company" includes the proprietors for the time being of any such railway: *Railway Regulation Act* 1840, s.21. **20–175**

The ambit of s.16 was considered in *R. (Mair) v. Criminal Injuries Compensation Board* [2002] P.I.Q.R. P4, QBD. The applicant was a railway employee seeking to challenge the refusal of the CICB to award him compensation for post traumatic stress disorder suffered as a result of watching a young boy lose his arm beneath the wheels of a train. The applicant argued that his PTSD was attributable to "an offence of trespass on a railway." The application was dismissed, the court finding that there had been no offence committed at the time of the incident. The section makes it an offence to refuse to leave railway premises when required, but the injured boy had only been required to leave the train and there was no implicit request to leave the track or the platform. Hence a request to leave a train will not found a charge of trespass if the individual chooses to remain on the train platform. Stanley Burnton J. explained the working of section 16 by stating:

> 'It can be seen that there are two parts of that particular statutory provision. The first part is concerned with a person who wilfully obstructs or impedes any officer or agent of a railway company in the execution of his duties. It is not suggested that that provision applied in this case. The second part is concerned with wilful trespass on a railway, and the words are "or if any person shall trespass upon any railway, or any of the stations or any works or premises connected therewith, and shall refuse to quit the same upon request to him made by any officer or agent of the said company".
>
> Pausing there for a moment, the words clearly refer to premises or land or works, works in the sense of an electrical substation. They do not refer to a train as such, and it is not suggested that they do. That is the first point. The second point is that the provision requires a refusal on the part of the offender to quit the same upon a request. If there is no request and a refusal to comply with the request, there is no offence committed under that part of this statute.'

A railway company can exclude anyone not wishing to use the railway, or anyone unwilling to comply with conditions: *Perth General Station Committee v. Ross* (1897) A.C. 479.

(4) Sentence

The offence under s.16 of the 1840 Act carries a maximum penalty of one month's imprisonment or a fine not exceeding level three on the standard scale. **20–176**

B. PENALTY FOR TRESPASSING ON RAILWAYS

(1) Definition

Regulation of Railways Act 1868, s.23

23. If any person shall be or pass upon any railway, except for the purpose of crossing the same at any authorized crossing, after having once received warning by the company which works such railway, or by any of their agents or servants, not to go or pass thereon, every person **20–177**

so offending shall forfeit and pay any sum not exceeding level 1 on the standard scale for every such offence.

[This section is printed as amended by the *Regulation of Railways Act* 1871, s.14, the *Criminal Law Act* 1977, s.31 and the *CJA* 1982, s.46.]

(2) Allocation

20–178 This offence is triable summarily.

(3) Sentence

20–179 This offence is punishable by a fine not exceeding level 1 on the standard scale.

C. PENALTY FOR AVOIDING PAYMENT OF FARE

(1) Definition

Regulation of Railways Act 1889, s.5

20–180 **5.**—(1) Every passenger by a railway shall, on request by an officer or servant of a railway company, either produce, and if so requested deliver up, a ticket showing that his fare is paid, or pay his fare from the place whence he started, or give the officer or servant his name and address; and in case of default shall be liable on summary conviction to a fine not exceeding level 2 on the standard scale

(2) If a passenger having failed either to produce, or if requested to deliver up, a ticket showing that his fare is paid, or to pay his fare, refuses or fails on request by an officer or servant of a railway company, to give his name and address, any officer of the company or any constable may detain him until he can be conveniently brought before some justice or otherwise discharged by due course of law.

(3) If any person—

(a) Travels or attempts to travel on a railway without having previously paid his fare, and with intent to avoid payment thereof; or

(b) Having paid his fare for a certain distance, knowingly and wilfully proceeds by train beyond that distance without previously paying the additional fare for the additional distance, and with intent to avoid payment thereof; or

(c) Having failed to pay his fare, gives in reply to a request by an officer of a railway company a false name or address,

he shall be liable on summary conviction to a fine not exceeding level 3 on the standard scale, or, in the discretion of the court to imprisonment for a term not exceeding three months

(4) The liability of an offender to punishment under this section shall not prejudice the recovery of any fare payable by him.

(5) In this section—

(a) "railway company" includes an operator of a train, and

(b) "operator", in relation to a train, means the person having the management of that train for the time being.

[This section is printed as amended by the *Transport Act* 1962, ss.84(2) and 93(1), the *British Railways Act* 1965, s.35(5), the *British Railways Act* 1971, s.18, the *British Railways Act* 1977, Sched. 1, the *CJA* 1982, ss.35 and 46, the *Police and Criminal Evidence Act* 1984, Sched. 7 and (SI 1994/857).]

(2) Allocation

20–181 This offence is triable summarily: s.5(2)(c).

(3) Elements of the offence

20–182 The "fare" means the fare by the train and the class of carriage in which the passenger travels; a person who had purchased a workman's ticket, marked "not transferable," which had been issued by a railway company to another person, from that person, and had travelled on the railway without having purchased a ticket from the railway company, had travelled on the railway "without having previously paid his fare, and with intent to avoid payment thereof" within the meaning of the statute: *Reynolds v. Beasley* [1919] 1 K.B. 215. A person travelling in a first class carriage with a second class ticket and fraudulently intending to avoid payment of a first class fare may be convicted for "without having previously paid his fare": *Gillingham v. Walker* (1881) 45 J.P. 470.

Proof of intent to avoid payment is the necessary mental element of the offence, this intent does not have to be to defraud: *Browning v. Floyd* (1946). A person is still travelling on a railway for the purpose of *Regulation of Railways Act* 1889, s.5, after he has alighted from his train and before he passes the ticket barrier. If, therefore, he conceives an intention to avoid payment of his fare at that stage he is guilty of an offence against the section: *Bremme v. Dubury* [1964] All E.R. 193, DC.

The intention to avoid payment does not have to be permanent. Where a fare was underpaid and the defendant said he intended to pay the excess if he were later tracked down and requested to do so this did not provide a defence: *Corbyn v. Saunders* [1978] 2 All E.R. 697.

(4) Sentence

These offences are triable summarily only. The maximum penalties are three months imprisonment or a level 3 fine for an offence under s.5(3) and a fine at level 2 for an offence under s.5(1). **20–183**

The Magistrates' Courts Sentencing Guidelines 2008 include these offences.

STARTING POINTS AND SENTENCING RANGE

(BASED ON A FIRST TIME OFFENDER PLEADING NOT GUILTY)

Examples of nature of activity	Starting Point	Range
Failing to produce ticket or pay fare on request	Band A fine	Conditional discharge to Band B fine
Travelling on the railway without having paid the fare or knowingly and wilfully travelling beyond the distance paid for with intent to avoid payment	Band B fine	Band A fine to band C fine

AGGRAVATING AND MITIGATING FACTORS

Factor indicating higher culpability	Factors indicating lower culpability
1. Offensive or intimidating language or behaviour towards railway staff **Factor indicating greater degree of harm** 1. High level of loss caused or intended to be caused.	Nil

X. SCHOOL ATTENDANCE

A. FAILING TO SECURE REGULAR ATTENDANCE AT SCHOOL

(1) Definition

Education Act 1996, s.444

Offence: failure to secure regular attendance at school of registered pupil

20–184 **444.**—(1) If a child of compulsory school age who is a registered pupil at a school fails to attend regularly at the school, his parent is guilty of an offence.

(1A) If in the circumstances mentioned in subsection (1) the parent knows that his child is failing to attend regularly at the school and fails to cause him to do so, he is guilty of an offence.

(1B) It is a defence for a person charged with an offence under subsection (1A) to prove that he had a reasonable justification for his failure to cause the child to attend regularly at the school.

(2) Subsections (2A) to (6) below apply in proceedings for an offence under this section in respect of a child who is not a boarder at the school at which he is a registered pupil.

(2A) The child shall not be taken to have failed to attend regularly at the school by reason of his absence from the school at any time if the parent proves that at that time the child was prevented from attending by reason of sickness or any unavoidable cause.

(3) The child shall not be taken to have failed to attend regularly at the school by reason of his absence from the school—

(a) with leave, or

(b) ...

(c) on any day exclusively set apart for religious observance by the religious body to which his parent belongs.

(3A) Subsections (3B) and (3D) apply where the child's home is in England.

(3B) The child shall not be taken to have failed to attend regularly at the school if the parent proves that—

(a) the local education authority have a duty to make travel arrangements in relation to the child under section 508B(1) for the purpose of facilitating the child's attendance at the school and have failed to discharge that duty, or

(b) the local education authority have a duty to make travel arrangements in relation to the child by virtue of subsection (2)(c) of section 508E (school travel schemes) for the purpose of facilitating the child's attendance at the school and have failed to discharge that duty.

(3C) For the purposes of subsection (3B)—

(a) the reference to "travel arrangements" in paragraph (a) has the same meaning as in section 508B, and

(b) the reference to "travel arrangements" in paragraph (b) has the same meaning as in paragraph 3 of Schedule 35C

(3D) Where the school is an independent school which is not a qualifying school, the child shall not be taken to have failed to attend regularly at the school if the parent proves—

(a) that the school is not within walking distance of the child's home,

(b) that no suitable arrangements have been made by the local education authority for boarding accommodation for him at or near the school, and

(c) that no suitable arrangements have been made by the local education authority for enabling him to become a registered pupil at a qualifying school nearer to his home.

(3E) For the purposes of subsection (3D), "qualifying school" has the same meaning as it has for the purposes of Schedule 35B (meaning of "eligible child" for the purposes of section 508B).

(3F) Subsection (4) applies where the child's home is in Wales.

(4) The child shall not be taken to have failed to attend regularly at the school if the parent proves—

(a) that the school at which the child is a registered pupil is not within walking distance of the child's home, and

(b) that no suitable arrangements have been made by the local education authority...for any of the following—

(i) his transport to and from the school,

(ii) boarding accommodation for him at or near the school, or

(iii) enabling him to become a registered pupil at a school nearer to his home.

(5) In subsections (3D) and (4) "walking distance"—

(a) in relation to a child who is under the age of eight, means 3.218688 kilometres (two miles), and

(b) in relation to a child who has attained the age of eight, means 4.828032 kilometres (three miles),

in each case measured by the nearest available route.

(6) If it is proved that the child has no fixed abode, subsections (3B), (3D) and (4) shall not apply, but it is a defence for the parent to prove—

(a) that he is engaged in a trade or business of such a nature as to require him to travel from place to place,

(b) that the child has attended at a school as a registered pupil as regularly as the nature of that trade or business permits, and

(c) if the child has attained the age of six, that he has made at least 200 attendances during the period of 12 months ending with the date on which the proceedings were instituted.

(7) In proceedings for an offence under this section in respect of a child who is a boarder at the school at which he is a registered pupil, the child shall be taken to have failed to attend regularly at the school if he is absent from it without leave during any part of the school term [unless the parent proves that at that time the child was] prevented from being present by reason of sickness or any unavoidable cause.

(7A) Where—

(a) a child of compulsory school age has been excluded for a fixed period on disciplinary grounds from a school in England which is—

(i) a maintained school,

(ii) a pupil referral unit,

(iii) an Academy,

(iv) a city technology college, or

(v) a city college for the technology of the arts,

(b) he remains for the time being a registered pupil at the school,

(c) the appropriate authority make arrangements for the provision of full-time education for him at the school during the period of exclusion, and

(d) the exclusion does not affect the application of subsections (1) to (7) to the child's attendance at the school on any day to which the arrangements relate.

(7B) In subsection (7A)(c) "the appropriate authority" means—

(a) in relation to a maintained school, the governing body of the school,

(b) in relation to a pupil referral unit, the local education authority, and

(c) in relation to any school mentioned in subsection (7A)(a)(iii) to (v), the proprietor of the school.

(8) A person guilty of an offence under subsection (1) is liable on summary conviction to a fine not exceeding level 3 on the standard scale.

(8A) A person guilty of an offence under subsection (1A) is liable on summary conviction—

(a) to a fine not exceeding level 4 on the standard scale, or

(b) to imprisonment for a term not exceeding three months [51 weeks], or both.

(8B) If, on the trial of an offence under subsection (1A), the court finds the defendant not guilty of that offence but is satisfied that he is guilty of an offence under subsection (1), the court may find him guilty of that offence.

(9) In this section "leave", in relation to a school, means leave granted by any person authorised to do so by the governing body or proprietor of the school.

[This section is printed as amended by the *School Standards and Framework Act* 1998, s.140 and Scheds 30 and 31, the *Criminal Justice and Court Services Act* 2000, s.72, the *Criminal Justice Act* 2003, s.280 and Sched. 26 and the *Education and Inspections Act* 2006, ss.82, 109, 184, 188, 194 and Sched. 18. The *Education and Inspections Act* 2006, s.82 came into force on September 1, 2007 by virtue of the *Education and Inspections Act 2006 (Commencement No.5 and Savings Provisions) Order* 2007 (S.I. 2007 No. 1801).]

(2) Allocation

20–185 These offences are triable summarily only.

(3) Elements of the offence

20–186 Under the Act every local education authority has a duty to secure that education is available at primary, secondary and higher level to meet the needs of the population of their area. The Act places a duty on parents to ensure attendance at school of their children. Subsection (1) creates the offence of failing to attend school regularly and subs. (1A) creates the aggravated offence of knowing that a pupil is failing to attend school and failing without reasonable justification to cause the child to attend school. The latter offence requires an element of knowledge and connivance which attracts a more severe sentence on conviction.

Compulsory school age is defined as lasting between the ages of 5 to 16 years of age: s.8. The presumption that a child is of compulsory school age is rebuttable by the parent; s.445. The definition of parent includes a person with parental responsibility or one who cares for the child: s.576.

20–187 Unavoidable cause in subs. 3(b) does not include the chronic illness of a parent or other family duties: *Jenkins v. Howells* [1949] 2 K.B. 218. The test of "unavoidable cause" is higher than that of "reasonable cause": *Jarman v. Mid Glamorgan Education Authority* (1985) L.S. Gaz.R. 1249.

In *Telford and Wrekin Council v. Ashley* [2001] C.L.Y. 1986, MC, a single parent was convicted of failing to secure her son's attendance at school. Over a four-month period, the boy's attendance had been recorded at 14 per cent. There had been five home visits by the Education Welfare Officer, together with two pupil planning meetings and both parents had received oral and written warnings, including a final written warning, and the boy had been excluded from school twice. The mother asserted a defence of duress based on the physical and verbal abuse she had endured from her son following her attempts to make him attend school. The justices held that whilst the defence of duress was applicable to charges under s.444 of the Act, notwithstanding the special defence of "unavoidable cause" provided for in that section, it could not be established that verbal abuse, accompanied by "pushing and shoving away" of the parent by the child, constituted duress so as to afford a parent a defence to a charge under s.444 of the Act.

In *Bath and North East Somerset District Council v. Warman* [1999] E.L.R. 81, [1999] Ed.C.R. 517, QBD, a mother was prosecuted for failing to secure her daughter's attendance at school. The daughter had left home in mid 1997, whilst she was aged 15, and gone to live with her long-term boyfriend. The mother did not discover where she was living until Christmas 1997. The mother had objected to the daughter leaving home but could not stop her. She did not contact the police or social services because she did not think that they would do anything and she did not in any event think that her daughter would be at risk. The Divisional Court held that the circumstances of the case did not give rise to an unavoidable cause for the child's absence from school, and the justices' decision to acquit the mother was wrong. The case was remitted with a direction to convict, with a recommendation that the appropriate penalty would be a conditional discharge, the court questioning the propriety of prosecuting the mother for a criminal offence. **20–188**

In *R. (P.) v. Liverpool City Magistrates' Court* [2006] E.L.R. 386, s.444(1A) of the *Education Act* 1996 was considered. The defendant was found guilty under the section. Her defence was that her son was a big and self-willed boy and that she had done everything she could to ensure he went to school short of physically dragging him there. The magistrates decided that the offence was almost one of strict liability which placed a reverse burden of proof on the defendant. In addition they said that she should have inquired into alternative forms of education for her son. On appeal it was held that there was no reverse burden of proof but the court could only convict if satisfied beyond reasonable doubt that no reasonable justification existed. This did not impose on the parent a requirement to explore all other alternative avenues for schooling. The availability of other forms of education was held to have no relevance to any failure to attend at the school where a child was registered.

In subs. 4(a) the route is not prevented from being available because of fears for the child's safety walking along that route alone. The pupil may need to be accompanied to guard against perceived dangers but the route remains available: *Essex County Council v. Rogers* [1987] A.C. 66.

Under subs. 4(b)(iii), it is the arrangements that must be suitable and not the choice of school nearer to the pupil's home: *Dyfed County Council ex p. S.* [1995] 1 F.C.R. 113.

The *Education Act* 2005, s.116, inserts s.444ZA into this Act which applies s.444 to alternative educational provision. It came into force on September 1, 2005.

Section 444 has been amended to take account of the change in travel provisions made by the Act. Under s.508 the local education authority now has a duty to make travel arrangements to facilitate a child's attendance at school and it may be a defence to a charge under s.444 if that duty has not been fulfilled.

The section has also been amended so that there is now a statutory defence under s.444(1B) where reasonable justification for the failure to secure attendance can be proved. Section 444(2A) also provides that there is not a failure to attend if it is proved that the child was prevented from attending by reason of sickness or any unavoidable cause. The case law on "unavoidable cause" will continue to apply. This makes it clear that there is a reverse burden of proof on the defendant.

(4) Sentence

The maximum penalty for the offence established by subs. (1) is a fine not exceeding level 3 on the standard scale. The maximum penalty for the offence established by subs. 1A is a fine not exceeding level 4 on the standard scale, imprisonment for a term not exceeding three months or both. After commencement of the relevant provisions, the maximum custodial sentence in a magistrates' court will be 12 months' imprisonment: *Criminal Justice Act* 2003, ss.154 and 282. **20–189**

The Magistrates Courts Sentencing Guidelines issued in May 2008 include the offences of school non-attendance under s.444(1) and 444(1A).

STARTING POINTS AND SENTENCING RANGES

(BASED ON A FIRST TIME OFFENDER PLEADING NOT GUILTY)

Examples of nature of activity	**Starting Point**	**Range**
Short period following previous good attendance (s.444(1))	Band A fine	Conditional Discharge to Band A fine
Erratic attendance for a long time	Band B fine	Band B fine to band C fine
Colluding in and condoning non-attendance or deliberately instigating non-attendance (s.444(1A))	Medium level community order	Low level community order to high level community order

AGGRAVATING AND MITIGATING FACTORS

Factors indicating higher culpability	**Factors indicating lower culpability**
1. Parental collusion (s.444(1) only) 2. Lack of parental effort to ensure attendance 3. Threats to teachers and /or officials 4. Refusal to co-operate with school and /or officials **Factors indicating greater degree of harm** 1. More than one child 2. Harmful effect on other children in the family	1. Parent unaware of child's whereabouts 2. Parent tried to ensure attendance 3. Parent concerned by child's allegations of bullying/ unable to get school to address bullying

Parenting orders may also be made following the commission of an offence under this section: *Crime and Disorder Act* 1998, s.8.

Crime and Disorder Act 1998, s.8

Parenting orders

20–190 **8.**—(1) This section applies where, in any court proceedings—

(a) a child safety order is made in respect of a child;

(b) an anti-social behaviour order or sex offender order is made in respect of a child or young person;

(c) a child or young person is convicted of an offence; or

(d) a person is convicted of an offence under section 443 (failure to comply with school attendance order) or section 444 (failure to secure regular attendance at school of registered pupil) of the *Education Act* 1996.

(2) Subject to subsection (3) and section 9(1) below and to section 19(5) of, and paragraph 13(5) of Schedule 1 to, the *Powers of Criminal Courts (Sentencing) Act* 2000, if in the proceedings the court is satisfied that the relevant condition is fulfilled, it may make a parenting order in respect of a person who is a parent or guardian of the child or young person or, as the case may be, the person convicted of the offence under section 443 or 444 ("the parent").

(3) A court shall not make a parenting order unless it has been notified by the Secretary of State that arrangements for implementing such orders are available in the are in which it appears to the court that the parent resides or will reside and the notice has not been withdrawn.

(4) A parenting order is an order which requires the parent—

(a) to comply, for a period not exceeding twelve months, with such requirements as are specified in the order; and

(b) subject to subsection (5) below, to attend, for a concurrent period not exceeding three months and not more than once in any week, such counselling or guidance sessions as may be specified in directions given by the responsible officer;

and in this subsection "week" means a period of seven days beginning with a Sunday.

(5) A parenting order may, but need not, include such a requirement as is mentioned in subsection (4)(b) above in any case where such an order has been made in respect of the parent on a previous occasion.

(6) The relevant condition is that the parenting order would be desirable in the interests of preventing—

(a) in a case falling within paragraph (a) or (b) of subsection (1) above, any repetition of the kind of behaviour which led to the child safety order, anti-social behaviour order or sex offender order being made;

(b) in a case falling within paragraph (c) of that subsection, the commission of any further offence by the child or young person;

(c) in a case falling within paragraph (d) of that subsection, the commission of any further offence under section 443 or 444 of the *Education Act* 1996.

(7) The requirements that may be specified under subsection (4)(a) above are those which the court considers desirable in the interests of preventing any such repetition or, as the case may be, the commission of any such further offence.

(8) In this section and section 9 below "responsible officer", in relation to a parenting order, means one of the following who is specified in the order, namely—

(a) an officer of a local probation board;

(b) a social worker of a local authority social services department; and

(bb) a person nominated by a person appointed as chief education officer under section 532 of the *Education Act* 1996.

(c) a member of a youth offending team.

See also *Bath and North East Somerset District Council v. Warman* (*ante*), where the court recommended a conditional discharge as an appropriate penalty in the circumstances of the offence, and Rose L.J. stated "one can well understand that it is of the highest importance that the parents of children should be persuaded to comply with the statutory obligation which bears upon them in the terms of the section of the Act to ensure that their children do go to school. But, for my part, I have some doubt as to whether, in the particular circumstances of this case, the prosecution of the mother for a criminal offence was a wholly desirable exercise." **20–191**

XI. SOCIAL SECURITY

A. DISHONEST REPRESENTATIONS FOR OBTAINING BENEFIT

(1) Definition

Social Security Administration Act 1992, s.111A

Dishonest representations for obtaining benefit etc.

20–192 **111A.**—(1) If a person dishonestly—

(a) makes a false statement or representation; or

(b) produces or furnishes, or causes or allows to be produced or furnished, any document or information which is false in a material particular;

with a view to obtaining any benefit or other payment or advantage under the relevant social security legislation (whether for himself or for some other person), he shall be guilty of an offence.

(1A) A person shall be guilty of an offence if—

(a) there has been a change of circumstances affecting any entitlement of his to any benefit or other payment or advantage under any provision of the relevant social security legislation;

(b) the change is not a change that is excluded by regulations from the changes that are required to be notified;

(c) he knows that the change affects an entitlement of his to such a benefit or other payment or advantage; and

(d) he dishonestly fails to give a prompt notification of that change in the prescribed manner to the prescribed person.

(1B) A person shall be guilty of an offence if—

(a) there has been a change of circumstances affecting any entitlement of another person to any benefit or other payment or advantage under any provision of the relevant social security legislation;

(b) the change is not a change that is excluded by regulations from the changes that are required to be notified;

(c) he knows that the change affects an entitlement of that other person to such a benefit or other payment or advantage; and

(d) he dishonestly causes or allows that other person to fail to give a prompt notification of that change in the prescribed manner to the prescribed person.

(1C) This subsection applies where—

(a) there has been a change of circumstances affecting any entitlement of a person ('the claimant') to any benefit or other payment or advantage under any provision of the relevant social security legislation;

(b) the benefit, payment or advantage is one in respect of which there is another person ('the recipient') who for the time being has a right to receive payments to which the claimant has, or (but for the arrangements under which they are payable to the recipient) would have, an entitlement; and

(c) the change is not a change that is excluded by regulations from the changes that are required to be notified.

(1D) In a case where subsection (1C) above applies, the recipient is guilty of an offence if—

(a) he knows that the change affects an entitlement of the claimant to a benefit or other payment or advantage under a provision of the relevant social security legislation;

(b) the entitlement is one in respect of which he has a right to receive payments to which the claimant has, or (but for the arrangements under which they are payable to the recipient) would have, an entitlement; and

(c) he dishonestly fails to give a prompt notification of that change in the prescribed manner to the prescribed person.

(1E) In a case where that subsection applies, a person other than the recipient is guilty of an offence if—

(a) he knows that the change affects an entitlement of the claimant to a benefit or other payment or advantage under a provision of the relevant social security legislation;

(b) the entitlement is one in respect of which the recipient has a right to receive payments to which the claimant has, or (but for the arrangements under which they are payable to the recipient) would have, an entitlement; and

(c) he dishonestly causes or allows the recipient to fail to give a prompt notification of that change in the prescribed manner to the prescribed person.

(1F) In any case where subsection (1C) above applies but the right of the recipient is confined to a right, by reason of his being a person to whom the claimant is required to make payments in respect of a dwelling, to receive payments of housing benefit—

(a) a person shall not be guilty of an offence under subsection (1D) or (1E) above unless the change is one relating to one or both of the following—

(i) the claimant's occupation of that dwelling;

(ii) the claimant's liability to make payments in respect of that dwelling;

but

(b) subsections (1D)(a) and (1E)(a) above shall each have effect as if after "knows" there were inserted "or could reasonably be expected to know".

(1G) For the purposes of subsections (1A) to (1E) above a notification of a change is prompt if, and only if, it is given as soon as reasonably practicable after the change occurs.

(3) A person guilty of an offence under this section shall be liable—

(a) on summary conviction, to imprisonment for a term not exceeding six months, or to a fine not exceeding the statutory maximum, or to both; or

(b) on conviction on indictment, to imprisonment for a term not exceeding seven years, or to a fine, or to both.

(4) In the application of this section to Scotland, in subsections (1) to (1E) for "dishonestly" substitute "knowingly".

(2) Allocation

These offences are triable either way: *Social Security Administration Act* 1992, s.111A(3). **20–193**

Social Security Administration Act 1992, s.116

Legal Proceedings

116.—(1) Any person authorised by the Secretary of State in that behalf may conduct any proceedings under any provision of this Act other than section 114 or under any provision of the *Jobseekers Act* 1995 before a magistrates' court although not a barrister or solicitor. **20–194**

(2) Notwithstanding anything in any Act—

(a) proceedings for an offence under this Act other than an offence relating to housing benefit or council tax benefit, or for an offence under the *Jobseekers Act* 1995, may be begun at any time within the period of 3 months from the date on which evidence, sufficient in the opinion of the Secretary of State to justify a prosecution for the offence, comes to his knowledge or within a period of 12 months from the commission of the offence, whichever period last expires; and

(b) proceedings for an offence under this Act relating to housing benefit or council tax benefit may be begun at any time within the period of 3 months from the date on which evidence, sufficient in the opinion of the appropriate authority to justify a prosecution for the offence, comes to the authority's knowledge or within a period of 12 months from the commission of the offence, whichever period last expires.

(2A) Subsection (2) above shall not be taken to impose any restriction on the time when proceedings may be begun for an offence under section 111A above.

(3) For the purposes of subsection (2) above—

(a) a certificate purporting to be signed by or on behalf of the Secretary of State as to the date on which such evidence as is mentioned in paragraph (a) of that subsection came to his knowledge shall be conclusive evidence of that date; and

(b) a certificate of the appropriate authority as to the date on which such evidence as is mentioned in paragraph (b) of that subsection came to the authority's knowledge shall be conclusive evidence of that date.

(4) In subsection (2) and (3) above "the appropriate authority" means, in relation to an offence which relates to housing benefit and concerns any dwelling—

(b) if it relates to a rent rebate, the authority who are the appropriate housing authority by virtue of that subsection; and

(c) if it relates to rent allowance, the authority who are the appropriate local authority by virtue of that subsection.

(5) In subsection (2) and (3) above "the appropriate authority" means, in relation to an offence relating to council tax benefit, such authority as is prescribed in relation to the offence.

(5A) In relation to proceedings for an offence under section 114 above, the references in subsections (2)(a) and (3)(a) to the Secretary of State shall have effect as references to the Inland Revenue.

(7) In the application of this section to Scotland, the following provisions shall have effect in substitution for subsections (1) to (5A) above—

(a) proceedings for an offence under this Act or the *Jobseekers Act* 1995 may, notwithstanding anything in section 136 of the *Criminal Procedure (Scotland) Act* 1995, be commenced at any time within the period of 3 months from the date on which evidence, sufficient in the opinion of the Lord Advocate to justify proceedings, comes to his knowledge, or within the period of 12 months from the commission of the offence, whichever period last expires;

(aa) this subsection shall not be taken to impose any restriction on the time when proceedings may be commenced for an offence under section 111A above;

(b) for the purposes of this subsection—

(i) a certificate purporting to be signed by or on behalf of the Lord Advocate as to the date on which such evidence as is mentioned above came to his knowledge shall be conclusive evidence of that date; and

(ii) subsection (3) of section 136 of the said *Act of* 1995 (date of commencement of proceedings) shall have effect as it has effect for the purposes of that section.

[This section is printed as amended by the *Local Government Finance Act* 1992, Sched. 9, the *Jobseekers Act* 1995, Sched. 2, the *Social Security Administration (Fraud) Act* 1997, Sched. 1, the *Social Security Contributions (Transfer of Functions etc.) Act* 1999, Sched. 1 and the *Welfare Reform and Pensions Act* 1999, Sched. 11.]

(3) Elements of the offence

20–195 This section does not apply to cases where the benefit or other payment or advantage is or relates to, or the failure to notify relates to tax credit: *Tax Credit Act* 1999, Sched. 2.

The prosecution must prove dishonesty.

The right to free legal advice under *PACE* Code C 3.15 will not apply to interviews conducted at the offices of the Benefits Agency: *R. (Secretary of State for Social Security) v. South Central Division Magistrates, Daily Telegraph*, November 28, 2000.

In *Passmore (Paul Darren)* [2008] 1 Cr.App.R. 12, it was held that the fact that a claimant formed a company was not a change in circumstances that had to be disclosed under s.111A(1A). The change in circumstances has to be one that the claimant knows will affect the entitlement to benefits. Here the formation of the company had only the potential to affect entitlement. As the statute was penal in nature it was interpreted in favour of the claimant and convictions under the section were quashed. In *R. v. T.* [2009] EWCA Crim 1426 the defendant was charged under s.111A (1B) of the *Social Security Administration Act* 1992 with an offence of 'allowing' another to fail to give prompt notification of a change of circumstances affecting benefit payment. His partner had continued to claim benefits when he was maintaining a common household with her and she had not notified that change of circumstances. The interpretation of the word 'allow' in these circumstances fell to be considered. It was held that by standing by and doing nothing the defendant did no positive act of allowing the offence to be committed so his conviction was quashed. In *Smith v. North Somerset Council* (2007) 171 J.P. 509 the calculation of time limits for prosecution were considered. The appellant had been in receipt of a student loan which she failed to disclose as a change in circumstances. She received overpayments for several months and the prosecution was commenced 21 months after the first overpayment. It was argued that the 12 month limit had expired since it started to run from the first failure to disclose. On appeal it was held that this was a continuing offence so the time limit ran from the last occasion on which she had claimed benefits and failed to disclose the change in circumstances.

(4) Sentence

When tried summarily, the maximum penalty for this offence is imprisonment for a term not exceeding six months, a fine not exceeding the statutory maximum or both. After commencement of the relevant provisions, the maximum custodial sentence in a magistrates' court will be 12 months' imprisonment: *Criminal Justice Act* 2003, ss.154 and 282. The Magistrates' Courts Sentencing Guidelines cover these offences. See § 20–201. **20–196**

In *Heath* [2003] H.L.R. 7, the defendant was aged 36. She was a mother of four children and was in receipt of income support, housing benefit and council tax benefit. She then obtained work as a cleaner in a cinema at weekends. Initially that was on a part-time basis and did not affect her entitlement to benefits; however, she later began working full-time without informing, as she should have done, the Benefits Agency. She was subsequently charged with three offences of making false statements to obtain benefits, contrary to s.111A of the *Social Security Administration Act* 1992, to which she pleaded guilty. Her original sentence of 12 months', imprisonment was reduced on appeal. The Court substituted a sentence of five months' imprisonment, given the net loss to the taxpayer, the early plea, the fact that initially her claims were lawful, and that there was no evidence pointing to luxurious living, indeed the reverse and having regard to the fact that she had four children to support.

Offences under s.111(A) of the *Social Security Administration Act* 1992 are now covered by guidelines issued by the Sentencing Guidelines Council. The definitive guideline on offences of fraud incorporates benefit fraud. The guidelines are included at § 15–112, *ante*.

For additional guidance on sentencing see *Stewart* [1987] 2 All E.R. 383, CA, but bearing in mind the warning issued by Mr Justice Mitchell in *Heath* (*ante*) that it has of course to be remembered that £10,000 in 1987 is not worth the same today. In *Stewart*, relevant factors to be taken into account when sentencing for this offence included (1) a guilty plea; (2) the amount involved and the length of time over which the defalcations were persisted in; (3) the circumstances in which the offence began; (4) the use to which the money so obtained was put; (5) previous character; (6) matters special to the offender; and (7) any voluntary payment of the amounts overpaid. **20–197**

In *Graham, Whatley* [2005] 1 Cr.App.R. 115 it was held that where imprisonment was necessary for benefit fraud cases, 9 to 12 months would usually be sufficient in a contested case where the amount overpaid was less than £20,000. The aggravating and mitigating factors identified in Stewart continue to be approved.

In *Areh* [2008] EWCA Crim 1817 a sentence of 15 months imprisonment was quashed and a community order of two years with requirements was substituted for a defendant charged with four offences of making false statements or representations in respect of claims for housing and council tax benefits. An over-payment of over £50,000 was obtained over four years. The defendant was 60 years old and of previous good character. On appeal it was held that a custodial sentence was not wrong in principle but as an act of mercy and based on information not available to the sentencing judge relating to the adverse impact the defendant's incarceration was having on her severely autistic daughter the community sentence would be substituted.

B. FALSE REPRESENTATIONS FOR OBTAINING BENEFIT

(1) Definition

Social Security Administration Act 1992, s.112

False representations for obtaining benefit etc.

20-198 **112.**—(1) If a person for the purpose of obtaining any benefit or other payment under the relevant social security legislation whether for himself or some other person, or for any other purpose connected with that legislation—

(a) makes a statement or representation which he knows to be false; or

(b) produces or furnishes, or knowingly causes or knowingly allows to be produced or furnished, any document or information which he knows to be false in a material particular,

he shall be guilty of an offence.

(1A) A person shall be guilty of an offence if—

(a) there has been a change of circumstances affecting any entitlement of his to any benefit or other payment or advantage under any provision of the relevant social security legislation;

(b) the change is not a change that is excluded by regulations from the changes that are required to be notified;

(c) he knows that the change affects an entitlement of his to such a benefit or other payment or advantage; and

(d) he fails to give a prompt notification of that change in the prescribed manner to the prescribed person.

(1B) A person is guilty of an offence under this section if—

(a) there has been a change of circumstances affecting any entitlement of another person to any benefit or other payment or advantage under any provision of the relevant social security legislation;

(b) the change is not a change that is excluded by regulations from the changes that are required to be notified;

(c) he knows that the change affects an entitlement of that other person to such a benefit or other payment or advantage; and

(d) he causes or allows that other person to fail to give a prompt notification of that change in the prescribed manner to the prescribed person.

(1C) In a case where subsection (1C) of section 111A above applies, the recipient is guilty of an offence if—

(a) he knows that the change affects an entitlement of the claimant to a benefit or other payment or advantage under a provision of the relevant social security legislation;

(b) the entitlement is one in respect of which he has a right to receive payments to which the claimant has, or (but for the arrangements under which they are payable to the recipient) would have, an entitlement; and

(c) he fails to give a prompt notification of that change in the prescribed manner to the prescribed person.

(1D) In a case where that subsection applies, a person other than the recipient is guilty of an offence if—

(a) he knows that the change affects an entitlement of the claimant to a benefit or other payment or advantage under a provision of the relevant social security legislation;

(b) the entitlement is one in respect of which the recipient has a right to receive payments to which the claimant has, or (but for the arrangements under which they are payable to the recipient) would have, an entitlement; and

(c) he causes or allows the recipient to fail to give a prompt notification of that change in the prescribed manner to the prescribed person.

(1E) Subsection (1F) of section 111A above applies in relation to subsections (1C) and (1D) above as it applies in relation to subsections (1D) and (1E) of that section.

(1F) For the purposes of subsections (1A) to (1D) above a notification of a change is prompt if, and only if, it is given as soon as reasonably practicable after the change occurs.

(2) A person guilty of an offence under this section shall be liable on summary conviction to a fine not exceeding level 5 on the standard scale, or to imprisonment for a term not exceeding 3 months, or to both.

[This section is printed as amended by the *Social Security Administration (Fraud) Act* 1997, s.14 and Sched. 1, the *Child Support, Pensions and Social Security Act* 2000, Sched. 6 and the *Social Security Fraud Act* 2001, s.16(3).]

(2) Allocation

This offence is triable summarily. For provisions relating to the institution of legal **20–199** proceedings, see *ante*, s.116 of the 1992 Act.

(3) Elements of the offence

This section does not apply to cases where the benefit or other payment or advantage **20–200** is or relates to, or the failure to notify relates to tax credit: *Tax Credit Act* 1999, Sched. 2.

It is not necessary to prove that the false statement was made with the intention to defraud the Department of Social Security. The offence is made out when it is proved that the defendant made a statement that he knew to be false: *DSS v. Bavi* (1996) C.O.D. 260, QBD.

An applicant for housing benefit will be required to declare whether he was the registered owner of a property other than his main home. In *Fairbank v. Lambeth Magistrates' Court* [2002] EWHC 785, QBD, the defendant's failure to do so constituted a false representation under the *Social Security Administration Act* 1992, s.112 notwithstanding his claim that he held the property on trust for another.

But in *R. (on the application of Pearson) v Greenwich Magistrates' Court* [2008] EWHC 300 (Admin) which concerned an application for Council Tax Benefit, it was held that failure to complete answers in an application form did not amount to a false statement. This case centres more on the complexity of questions asked in the form and indicates that evidence of positive conduct in making a false statement is required.

See also *Coventry City Council v. Vassell* [2011] EWHC 1542 (Admin) where the defendant was charged with offences under s.112(1A) after it was said he had failed to notify the Housing Department of his change in circumstances so that he continued to receive housing benefit and council tax benefit. He had informed the Job Centre of the change and his JSA had stopped. He was acquitted in the magistrates' court and that decision was appealed. On appeal it was held that a person is not guilty of an offence under this section when he was aware only that the change could affect his entitlement as opposed to definitely would affect it. It was held that it was open to the convicting court to find that he believed his entitlement to the other benefits was unaffected and that his notification to the Job Centre was sufficient. It was not a 'knowing' failure to notify with the requisite mens rea. It was also observed that the word 'prompt' should be given its natural meaning and it was a matter of fact for the court to decide whether any notification had been promptly given.

(4) Sentence

The maximum penalty for this offence is a fine not exceeding level five on the stan- **20–201** dard scale, imprisonment for a term not exceeding three months or both. After commencement of the relevant provisions, the maximum custodial sentence in a magistrates' court will be 12 months' imprisonment: *Criminal Justice Act* 2003, ss.154 and 282.

Sentencing guidelines can be found in the cases of *Heath* and *Stewart*, *ante*.

The Magistrates' Courts Sentencing Guidelines 2008 also cover these offences.

STARTING POINTS AND SENTENCING RANGE

(BASED ON A FIRST TIME OFFENDER PLEADING NOT GUILTY)

Examples of nature of activity	**Starting Point**	**Range**
Claim fraudulent from the start, up to £5,000 obtained (S.111A or s.112.)	Medium level community order	Band B fine to high level community order
Claim fraudulent from the start more than £5,000 but less than £20,000 obtained	12 weeks custody	Medium level community order to Crown Court
Claim fraudulent from the start, large scale professional offending	Crown Court	Crown Court

AGGRAVATING AND MITIGATING FACTORS

Factors indicating higher culpability	**Factors indicating lower culpability**
1. Offending carried out over a long period 2. Offender acting in unison with one or more others 3. Planning 4. Offender motivated by greed or desire to live beyond his/her means 5. False identities or other personal details used 6. False or forged documents used 7. Official documents altered or falsified	1. Pressurised by others 2. Claim initially legitimate **Factors indicating a lesser degree of harm** 1. Voluntary repayment of amounts overpaid

XII. STREET TRADING

A. UNLICENSED STREET TRADING

(1) Definition

London Local Authorities Act 1990, s.38

20–202 **38.**—(1) A person who—

(a) is not the holder of a street trading licence or a temporary licence and who engages in street trading in a borough; or

(b) is the holder of a temporary licence and who engages in street trading in a borough on a day or in a place not specified in that temporary licence;

shall be guilty of an offence and shall be liable on summary conviction to a fine not exceeding level 3 on the standard scale.

(2) In any proceedings for an offence under this section or for an offence of aiding, abetting, counselling or procuring the commission of an offence under this section where it is shown that—

(a) any article or thing was displayed (whether or not in or on any receptacle) in any street; or

(b) any receptacle or equipment used in the provision of any service was available in any street in such circumstances that a service was being offered;

the article or thing shall be presumed to have been exposed or offered for sale and the receptacle or equipment shall be presumed to have been available for the provision of a service at such time and in such position as it was displayed or available by the person having care or control or appearing to have care and control thereof unless in either case, it is shown to the satisfaction of the court that the article or thing or receptacle or equipment was brought into that street for some purpose other than for the purpose of selling it or exposing or offering it for sale or using it in the course of the provision of the service in a street.

(3) Where an offence under this section committed by a body corporate is proved to have been committed with the consent or connivance of, or to be attributable to any neglect on the part of, any director, manager, secretary or other similar officer of the body corporate, or any person who was purporting to act in any such capacity, he, as well as the body corporate, shall be guilty of the offence and liable to the same maximum penalty as the body corporate.

(4) If an authorised officer or a constable has reasonable grounds for suspecting that a person has committed an offence under this section he may seize any article or thing being offered or exposed for sale or receptacle being used by that person which may be required to be used in evidence in any proceedings in respect of that offence or may be thesubject of forfeiture under subsection (5) below, provided that no article or thing which is of a perishable nature shall be seized under the provisions of this subsection.

(4A)

(a) The following provisions of this subsection shall have effect where any article or thing (including any receptacle) is seized under subsection (4) above and references in those provisions to proceedings are to proceedings in respect of the alleged offence in relation to which the article or thing is seized.

(b) Subject to paragraph (e) below, at the conclusion of the proceedings the article or thing shall be returned to the person from whom it was seized unless the court orders it to be forfeited under subsection (5) below.

(c) Subject to paragraph (d) below, where a receptacle seized under subsection (4) above is a motor vehicle used for ice cream trading, the borough council or the Commissioner of Police of the Metropolis (as the case may be) shall, within three days of the receipt of an application in writing by the owner or registered keeper of the vehicle, permit him to remove it.

(d) Paragraph (c) above shall not apply where—

(i) the owner or registered keeper of the vehicle has been convicted of an offence under this Part of this Act; or

(ii) the owner or registered keeper of the vehicle is being prosecuted for a previous alleged offence under this Part of this Act; or

(iii) the vehicle has been used in the commission of such an offence or previous alleged offence;

if the offence or previous alleged offence was committed or is alleged to have been committed no more than three years before the seizure and (in the case of an alleged offence) the proceedings are continuing.

(e) If no proceedings are instituted before the expiration of a period of 28 days beginning with the date of seizure, or any proceedings instituted within that period are discontinued, at the expiration of that period or, as the case may be, on the discontinuance of the proceedings, the article or thing shall be returned to the person from whom it was seized unless it has not proved possible, after diligent enquiry, to identify that person and ascertain his address.

(f) Where the article or thing is not returned because it has not proved possible to identify the person from whom it was seized and ascertain his address the borough council (whether the article or thing was seized by a constable or by an authorised officer) may apply to a magistrates' court for an order as to the manner in which it should be dealt with.

(5) Subject to subsection (6) below the court by or before which a person is convicted of an offence under this section or for an offence of aiding, abetting, counselling or procuring the commission of an offence under this section may order anything produced to the court, and shown to the satisfaction of the court to relate to the offence, to be forfeited and dealt with in such manner as the court may order.

(6) The court shall not order anything to be forfeited under subsection (5) above where a person claiming to be the owner of or otherwise interested in it applies to be heard by the court, unless an opportunity has been given to him to show cause why the order should not be made and in considering whether to make such an order a court shall have regard—

(i) to the value of the property; and

(ii) to the likely financial and other effects on the offender of the making of the order (taken together with any other order that the court contemplates making).

(7) An authorised officer shall produce his authority if required to do so by the person having care or control of anything seized in pursuance of the powers in subsection (4) above.

(8)

(a) This subsection shall have effect where—

(i) an article, thing or receptacle is seized under subsection (4) above; and

(ii)

(A) not less than six months have passed since the date of the seizure and no information has been laid against any person for an offence under this section in respect of the acts or circumstances which occasioned the seizure; or

(B) proceedings for such an offence have been brought and either the person charged has been acquitted (whether or not on appeal) and the time for appealing against or challenging the acquittal (where applicable) has expired without an appeal or challenge being brought, or the proceedings (including any appeal) have been withdrawn by, or have failed for want of prosecution by, the person by whom the original proceedings were brought.

(b) When this subsection has effect a person who has or at the time of seizure had a legal interest in the article, thing or receptacle seized may recover compensation from the borough council or (where it is seized by a constable) the Commissioner of Police of the Metropolis by civil action in the County Court in respect of any loss suffered by him as a result of the seizure.

(c) The court may not make an order for compensation under paragraph (b) above unless it is satisfied that seizure was not lawful under subsection (4) above.

[This section is printed as amended by the *London Local Authorities Act* 1994, s.6.]

(2) Allocation

20–203 This offence is triable summarily only: s.38(1).

(3) Elements of the offence

20–204 In *Onasanya v. Newham LBC* [2006] 4 All E.R. 459 the defendant was convicted of street trading. He displayed a "For Sale" sign in his car and left the vehicle parked on the public highway when he went to a doctor's appointment. He also had another vehicle which displayed a "For Sale" sign but he said he had lent that to a friend whilst he was out of the country and had expected the car to be kept in a garage. On appeal the issue was considered as to whether displaying such a sign on a car and leaving it in the highway amounted to street trading without a licence. It was held that s.38(2) provided a statutory defence if the item (in this case a car) was brought into the street for some purpose other than street trading. The fact that there may be more than one purpose for the presence of the car on the street did not prevent the defence from applying. The question to be asked was why the car was on the street and in no other place at the material time. In the first case the car was on the street as the defendant attended his GP and in the second case the vehicle was left parked on the street for the convenience of the borrower who left it close to his home. The defendant was acquitted on both charges.

Unlicensed street trading can range from selling small items from a box or tray to selling food from barbecues or braziers or ice-cream or hot-dogs from vans. Such trading is allowed but only under the control of licences issued by local authorities.

Items used in illegal street trading can be seized in an effort to prevent further offending. Perishables cannot be seized but grills and cooking utensils, vans and carts can be removed and forfeiture proceedings be taken.

In the case of ice-cream vans, the owner or keeper of the vehicle that has been seized has a limited right to have the vehicle returned. If there is a history of offending in relation to the owner or the vehicle then forfeiture proceedings may follow. In such applications the owner of any goods subject to possible forfeiture must be given the opportunity to attend court to show cause why the items should not be forfeited.

The power to order forfeiture contained in subs. (5) only applies to goods produced to the court. Goods can be produced to the court either by being brought physically into the courtroom or by the making of arrangements for the court to view the goods. Alternatively, in appropriate circumstances, a written statement could be made under the *Criminal Justice Act* 1967, s.9: *R. (London Borough of Islington) v. Jordan* (2002) 167 J.P. 1, DC. Where there is a late objection to the non-production of the goods magistrates have power to adjourn the matter to some later date to allow the item to be produced or to arrange to view the goods at some convenient occasion on the same or a future date (*ibid.*).

(4) Sentence

The maximum penalty for this offence is a fine not exceeding level 3 on the standard scale: s.38(1). The court also has a power to forfeit the relevant goods under s.38(5). **20–205**

XIII. TELEVISION LICENCES

The *Communications Act* 2003 covers the provision and regulation of electronic communication networks and broadcasting. It also deals with the "licensing of TV reception" in Pt 4. Television receivers must be authorised for installation or use by a licence. **20–206**

(1) Definition

Communications Act 2003, ss.363–365

Licence required for use of TV receiver

363.—(1) A television receiver must not be installed or used unless the installation and use of the receiver is authorised by a licence under this Part. **20–207**

(2) A person who installs or uses a television receiver in contravention of subsection (1) is guilty of an offence.

(3) A person with a television receiver in his possession or under his control who—

(a) intends to install or use it in contravention of subsection (1), or

(b) knows, or has reasonable grounds for believing, that another person intends to install or use it in contravention of that subsection,

is guilty of an offence.

(4) A person guilty of an offence under this section shall be liable, on summary conviction, to a fine not exceeding level 3 on the standard scale.

(5) Subsection (1) is not contravened by anything done in the course of the business of a dealer in television receivers solely for one or more of the following purposes—

(a) installing a television receiver on delivery;

(b) demonstrating, testing or repairing a television receiver.

(6) The Secretary of State may by regulations exempt from the requirement of a licence under subsection (1) the installation or use of television receivers—

(a) of such descriptions,

(b) by such persons,

(c) in such circumstances, and

(d) for such purposes,

as may be provided for in the regulations.

(7) Regulations under subsection (6) may make any exemption for which such regulations provide subject to compliance with such conditions as may be specified in the regulations.

TV licences

20–208 **364.**—(1) A licence for the purposes of section 363 ("a TV licence")—

(a) may be issued by the BBC subject to such restrictions and conditions as the BBC think fit; and

(b) must be issued subject to such restrictions and conditions as the Secretary of State may require by a direction to the BBC.

(2) The matters to which the restrictions and conditions subject to which a TV licence may be issued may relate include, in particular—

(a) the description of television receivers that may be installed and used under the licence;

(b) the persons authorised by the licence to install and use a television receiver;

(c) the places where the installation and use of the television receiver is authorised by the licence;

(d) the circumstances in which the installation and use of such a receiver is so authorised;

(e) the purposes for which the installation and use of such a receiver is so authorised;

(f) the use of such receiver in a manner that causes, or may cause, interference (within the meaning of the *Wireless Telegraphy Act* 1949) with wireless telegraphy.

(3) The restrictions and conditions subject to which a TV licence may be issued do not include—

(a) a provision conferring a power of entry to any premises; or

(b) a provision prohibited by a direction to the BBC by the Secretary of State.

(4) A TV licence shall continue in force, unless previously revoked by the BBC, for such period as may be specified in the licence.

(5) The BBC may revoke or modify a TV licence, or the restrictions or conditions of such a licence—

(a) by a notice to the holder of the licence; or

(b) by a general notice published in such manner as may be specified in the licence.

(6) It shall be the duty of the BBC to exercise their power under subsection (5) to revoke or modify a TV licence, or any of its restrictions or conditions, if they are directed to do so by the Secretary of State.

(7) A direction by the Secretary of State under this section may be given either generally in relation to all TV licences (or all TV licences of a particular description) or in relation to a particular licence.

(8) A notice under subsection (5)(a) must be given—

(a) in the manner specified in the licence; or

(b) if no manner of service is so specified, in the manner authorised by section 394.

(9) For the purposes of the application, in relation to the giving of such a notice, of—

(a) section 394; and

(b) section 7 of the *Interpretation Act* 1978 (service by post) in its application for the purposes of that section,

a person's proper address is any address where he is authorised by a TV licence to install or use a TV receiver or, if there is no such address, his last known address.

TV licence fees

20–209 **365.**—(1) A person to whom a TV licence is issued shall be liable to pay—

(a) on the issue of the licence (whether initially or by way of renewal), and

(b) in such other circumstances as regulations made by the Secretary of State may provide,

such sum (if any) as may be provided for by any such regulations.

(2) Sums which a person is liable to pay by virtue of regulations under subsection (1) must be paid to the BBC and are to be recoverable by them accordingly.

(3) The BBC are entitled, in such cases as they may determine, to make refunds of sums received by them by virtue of regulations under this section.

(4) Regulations under this section may include provision—

(a) for the means by which an entitlement to a concession must be established; and

(b) for the payment of sums by means of an instalment scheme set out in the regulations.

(5) The reference to a concession in subsection (4) is a reference to any concession under which a person is, on the satisfaction of specified requirements—

(a) exempted from the liability to pay a sum in respect of a TV licence; or

(b) required to pay only a reduced sum in respect of such a licence.

(6) The consent of the Treasury shall be required for the making of any regulations under this section by the Secretary of State.

(7) Subject to subsection (8), sums received by the BBC by virtue of any regulations under this section must be paid into the Consolidated Fund.

(8) The BBC may retain, out of the sums received by them by virtue of regulations under this section, any sums they require for making refunds of sums so received.

(2) Allocation

The offence is triable summarily only. The procedure where the offence is committed by a body corporate is contained in s.404 of the *Communications Act* 2003. **20–210**

Communications Act 2003, s.404

Criminal liability of company directors etc.

404.—(1) Where an offence under any enactment to which this section applies is committed by a body corporate and is proved to have been committed with the consent or connivance of, or to be attributable to any neglect on the part of— **20–211**

(a) a director, manager, secretary or other similar officer of the body corporate, or

(b) a person who was purporting to act in any such capacity,

he (as well as the body corporate) is guilty of that offence and shall be liable to be proceeded against and punished accordingly.

(2) Where an offence under any enactment to which this section applies—

(a) is committed by a Scottish firm, and

(b) is proved to have been committed with the consent or connivance of, or to be attributable to any neglect on the part of a partner of the firm,

he (as well as the firm) is guilty of that offence and shall be liable to be proceeded against and punished accordingly.

(3) In this section "director", in relation to a body corporate whose affairs are managed by its members, means a member of the body corporate.

(4) The enactments to which this section applies are every enactment contained in—

(a) this Act;

(b) the *Wireless Telegraphy Act* 1949;

(c) the *Marine, etc.,Broadcasting (Offences) Act* 1967;

(d) the *Wireless Telegraphy Act* 1967; or

(e) the *Telecommunications Act* 1984.

(5) Section 14(2) of the *Wireless Telegraphy Act* 1949 (which is superseded by this section) shall cease to have effect.

(3) Elements of the offence

This Act replaces the provisions of the *Wireless Telegraphy Act* 1949 in so far as it applied to licences for television sets. Relevant regulations came into force on April 1, **20–212**

2004 in the *Communications (Television Licensing) Regulations* 2004 (S.I. 2004 No. 692). Interpretation of the various terms used in the statute are found in the Act itself.

Communications Act 2003, ss.367–368

Interpretation of provisions about dealer notification

20–213 **367.**—(1) Section 6 of the *Wireless Telegraphy Act* 1967 (interpretation of provisions requiring notification of sale and hire of television sets) shall be amended as follows.

(2) In subsection (1), for the definitions of "television dealer", "television programme" and "television set" there shall be substituted—

"television dealer" means a person of any description specified in regulations made by the Secretary of State setting out the descriptions of persons who are to be television dealers for the purposes of this Part;

"television set" means any apparatus of a description specified in regulations made by the Secretary of State setting out the descriptions of apparatus that are to be television sets for the purposes of this Part.

(3) After that subsection there shall be inserted—

(1A) Regulations under subsection (1) defining a television set may provide for references to such a set to include references to software used in association with apparatus.

Meanings of "television receiver" and "use"

20–214 **368.**—(1) In this Part "television receiver" means any apparatus of a description specified in regulations made by the Secretary of State setting out the descriptions of apparatus that are to be television receivers for the purposes of this Part.

(2) Regulations under this section defining a television receiver may provide for references to such a receiver to include references to software used in association with apparatus.

(3) References in this Part to using a television receiver are references to using it for receiving television programmes.

(4) The power to make regulations under this section defining a television receiver includes power to modify subsection (3).

20–215 The definition of a television receiver is found in reg.9.

Communications (Television Licensing) Regulations 2004, reg.9

Meaning of "television receiver"

20–216 **9.**—(1) In Part 4 of the Act (licensing of TV reception), "television receiver" means any apparatus installed or used for the purpose of receiving (whether by means of wireless telegraphy or otherwise) any television programme service, whether or not it is installed or used for any other purpose.

(2) In this regulation, any reference to receiving a television programme service includes a reference to receiving by any means any programme included in that service, where that programme is received at the same time (or virtually the same time) as it is received by members of the public by virtue of its being broadcast or distributed as part of that service.

20–217 A television licence applies to the specified location recorded on the licence and authorises the person living there or anyone else living at the premises or visiting or working there to install and use either black and white or colour television sets at that address. The location may include not only premises but also a vehicle, vessel or caravan. The regulations set the amount of the fees and also provide for concessions in certain circumstances.

The offences are those of using or installing the receiver, or of intending to use or install it or knowing that someone else intends to use or install it. This dispenses with the need for the prosecution to prove that the television receiver was actually being used without a licence but still requires the intention to be proved.

(4) Defence

20–218 Section 363(5) exempts television dealers from having a licence where the receiver is being installed on delivery or the receiver is being demonstrated, tested or repaired.

(5) Powers to enforce

Communications Act 2003, s.366

Powers to enforce TV licensing

366.—(1) If a justice of the peace, a sheriff in Scotland or a lay magistrate in Northern Ireland is satisfied by information on oath that there are reasonable grounds for believing— **20–219**

(a) that an offence under section 363 has been or is being committed,

(b) that evidence of the commission of the offence is likely to be on premises specified in the information, or in a vehicle so specified, and

(c) that one or more of the conditions set out in subsection (3) is satisfied,

he may grant a warrant under this section.

(2) A warrant under this section is a warrant authorising any one or more persons authorised for the purpose by the BBC or by OFCOM—

(a) to enter the premises or vehicle at any time (either alone or in the company of one or more constables); and

(b) to search the premises or vehicle and examine and test any television receiver found there.

(3) Those conditions are—

(a) that there is no person entitled to grant entry to the premises or vehicle with whom it is practicable to communicate;

(b) that there is no person entitled to grant access to the evidence with whom it is practicable to communicate;

(c) that entry to the premises or vehicle will not be granted unless a warrant is produced;

(d) that the purpose of the search may be frustrated or seriously prejudiced unless the search is carried out by a person who secures entry immediately upon arriving at the premises or vehicle.

(4) A person is not to enter premises or a vehicle in pursuance of a warrant under this section at any time more than one month after the day on which the warrant was granted.

(5) The powers conferred by a warrant under this section on a person authorised by OFCOM are exercisable in relation only to a contravention or suspected contravention of a condition of a TV licence relating to interference with wireless telegraphy.

(6) A person authorised by the BBC, or by OFCOM, to exercise a power conferred by a warrant under this section may (if necessary) use such force as may be reasonable in the exercise of that power.

(7) Where a person has the power by virtue of a warrant under this section to examine or test any television receiver found on any premises, or in any vehicle, it shall be the duty—

(a) of a person who is on the premises or in the vehicle, and

(b) in the case of a vehicle, of a person who has charge of it or is present when it is searched,

to give the person carrying out the examination or test all such assistance as that person may reasonably require for carrying it out.

(8) A person is guilty of an offence if he—

(a) intentionally obstructs a person in the exercise of any power conferred on that person by virtue of a warrant under this section; or

(b) without reasonable excuse, fails to give any assistance that he is under a duty to give by virtue of subsection (7).

(9) A person guilty of an offence under subsection (8) shall be liable, on summary conviction, to a fine not exceeding level 5 on the standard scale.

(10) In this section—

"interference", in relation to wireless telegraphy, has the same meaning as in the *Wireless Telegraphy Act* 1949; and

"vehicle" includes vessel, aircraft or hovercraft.

(11) In the application of this section to Scotland, the reference in subsection (1) to information on oath shall have effect as a reference to evidence on oath.

(12) In the application of this section to Northern Ireland, the reference in subsection (1) to a lay magistrate shall have effect, in relation to times before the coming into force of

sections 9 and 10 of the *Justice (Northern Ireland) Act* 2002, as a reference to a justice of the peace.

Warrants of entry and search of premises may be granted together with a power to test equipment found there. The conditions of the section must be met and it is an offence intentionally to obstruct or fail to assist any person executing the warrant.

(6) Sentence

20–220 The maximum penalty is a fine not exceeding level 3.

The Magistrates' Courts Sentencing Guidelines 2008 cover this offence.

STARTING POINT AND SENTENCING RANGE

(BASED ON A FIRST TIME OFFENDER PLEADING NOT GUILTY)

Examples of nature of activity	**Starting Point**	**Range**
Up to 6 months unlicensed use	Band A fine	Band A fine
Over 6 months unlicensed use	Band B fine	Band A to band B fine

AGGRAVATING AND MITIGATING FACTORS

Factors indicating higher culpability	**Factors indicating lower culpability**
Nil	1. Accidental oversight or belief licence held 2. Confusion over responsibility 3. Licence obtained immediately

XIV. VIDEO RECORDINGS

A. SUPPLYING VIDEO RECORDINGS OF UNCLASSIFIED WORK

(1) Definition

Video Recordings Act 1984, s.9

Supplying video recording of unclassified work

20–221 **9.**—(1) A person who supplies or offers to supply a video recording containing a video work in respect of which no classification certificate has been issued is guilty of an offence unless—

(a) the supply is, or would if it took place be, an exempted supply, or

(b) the video work is an exempted work.

(2) It is a defence to a charge of committing an offence under this section to prove that the accused believed on reasonable grounds—

(a) that the video work concerned or, if the video recording contained more than one work to which the charge relates, each of those works was either an exempted work or a work in respect of which a classification certificate had been issued, or

(b) that the supply was, or would if it took place be, an exempted supply by virtue of section 3(4) or (5) of this Act.

(3) A person guilty of an offence under this section shall be liable—

(a) on conviction on indictment, to imprisonment for a term not exceeding two years or a fine or both,

(b) on summary conviction, to imprisonment for a term not exceeding six months or a fine not exceeding £20,000 or both.

[This section is printed as amended by the *Criminal Justice and Public Order Act* 1994, s.88.]

(2) Allocation

This offence is triable either way: s.9(3). **20–222**

Video Recordings Act 1984, s.15

Time limit for prosecutions

15.—(1) No prosecution for an offence under this Act shall be brought after the expiry of the period of three years beginning with the date of the commission of the offence or one year beginning with the date of its discovery by the prosecutor, whichever is earlier. **20–223**

(2) In Scotland, the reference in subsection (1) above to the date of discovery by the prosecutor shall be construed as a reference to the date on which evidence sufficient in the opinion of the Lord Advocate to warrant proceedings came to his knowledge.

(3) For the purposes of subsection (2) above—

(a) a certificate signed by the Lord Advocate or on his behalf and stating the date on which evidence came to his knowledge shall be conclusive evidence of that fact;

(b) a certificate purporting to be signed as mentioned in paragraph (a) above shall be presumed to be so signed unless the contrary is proved; and

(c) a prosecution shall be deemed to be brought on the date on which a warrant to apprehend or to cite the accused is granted provided that the warrant is executed without undue delay.

Video Recordings Act 1984, s.16

Offences by bodies corporate

16.—(1) Where an offence under this Act committed by a body corporate is proved to have been committed with the consent or connivance of, or to be attributable to any neglect on the part of, any director, manager, secretary or other similar officer of the body corporate, or any person who was purporting to act in any such capacity, he as well as the body corporate shall be guilty of the offence and shall be liable to be proceeded against and punished accordingly. **20–224**

(2) Where the affairs of a body corporate are managed by its members, subsection (1) above shall apply in relation to the acts and defaults of a member in connection with his functions of management as if he were a director of the body corporate.

(3) Defence

Video Recordings Act 1984, s.14A

14A. Without prejudice to any defence specified in the preceding provisions of this Act in relation to a particular offence, it is a defence to a charge of committing any offence under this Act to prove— **20–225**

(a) that the commission of the offence was due to the act or default of a person other than the accused, and

(b) that the accused took all reasonable precautions and exercised all due diligence to avoid the commission of the offence by any person under his control.

In *Bilon v. W.H. Smith Trading Limited* (2001) 165 J.P. 701, QBD, the defendant had supplied a video recording in respect of which no classification certificate had been issued. The recording had been in the form of a CD Rom attached to the cover of a magazine which had been supplied to the defendant by a long standing supplier. The defendant relied on the statutory defence contained in the *Video Recordings Act* 1984, **20–226** s.14A(b), contending that it had taken all reasonable precautions and had exercised all due diligence. The Court held that they were entitled to rely on the defence of due diligence, despite having taken no positive steps to avoid the commission of the offence. Under s.14A(b) of the 1984 Act, the retailer merely had to show that he had acted without negligence. The defendant had traded with the supplier for 20 years, the supplier was a reputable publisher, and had supplied the defendant with discs previously without any cause for concern. In all the circumstances, it had not been negligent for the defendant to rely on the supplier not to supply a disc and magazine without the defendant having first ensured that the disc had obtained the necessary classification certificate.

(4) Sentence

20–227 When tried summarily the maximum penalty for this offence is imprisonment for a term not exceeding six months, a fine not exceeding the £20,000 or both: s.9(3)(b). After commencement of the relevant provisions, the maximum custodial sentence in a magistrates' court will be 12 months' imprisonment: *Criminal Justice Act* 2003, ss.154 and 282.

Video Recordings Act 1984, s.21

Forfeiture

20–228 **21.**—(1) Where a person is convicted of any offence under this Act, the court may order any video recording—

(a) produced to the court, and

(b) shown to the satisfaction of the court to relate to the offence,

to be forfeited.

(2) The court shall not order any video recording to be forfeited under subsection (1) above if a person claiming to be the owner of it or otherwise interested in it applies to be heard by the court, unless an opportunity has been given to him to show cause why the order should not be made.

(3) References in this section to a video recording include a reference to any spool, case or other thing on or in which the recording is kept.

(4) An order made under subsection (1) above in any proceedings in England and Wales or Northern Ireland shall not take effect until the expiration of the ordinary time within which an appeal may be instituted or, where such an appeal is duly instituted, until the appeal is finally decided or abandoned; and for this purpose—

(a) an application for a case to be stated or for leave to appeal shall be treated as the institution of an appeal; and

(b) where a decision on appeal is subject to a further appeal, the appeal is not finally decided until the expiration of the ordinary time within which a further appeal may be instituted or, where a further appeal is duly instituted, until the further appeal is finally decided or abandoned.

(5) [*Scotland*]

B. POSSESSION OF VIDEO RECORDINGS OF UNCLASSIFIED WORK FOR THE PURPOSES OF SUPPLY

(1) Definition

Video Recordings Act 1984, s.10

Possession of video recording of unclassified work for the purposes of supply

20–229 **10.**—(1) Where a video recording contains a video work in respect of which no classification certificate has been issued, a person who has the recording in his possession for the purpose of supplying it is guilty of an offence unless—

(a) he has it in his possession for the purpose only of a supply which, if it took place, would be an exempted supply, or

(b) the video work is an exempted work.

(2) It is a defence to a charge of committing an offence under this section to prove—

(a) that the accused believed on reasonable grounds that the video work concerned or, if the video recording contained more than one work to which the charge relates, each of those works was either an exempted work or a work in respect of which a classification certificate had been issued,

(b) that the accused had the video recording in his possession for the purpose only of a supply which he believed on reasonable grounds would, if it took place, be an exempted supply by virtue of section 3(4) or (5) of this Act, or

(c) that the accused did not intend to supply the video recording until a classification certificate had been issued in respect of the video work concerned.

(3) A person guilty of an offence under this section shall be liable—

(a) on conviction on indictment, to imprisonment for a term not exceeding two years or a fine or both,

(b) on summary conviction, to imprisonment for a term not exceeding six months or a fine not exceeding £20,000 or both.

(2) Allocation

This offence is triable either way: s.10(3). The provisions as to time limits for proceedings and offences by corporations detailed above apply to charges under this section. **20-230**

(3) Defences

The defence established by s.14A of the 1984 Act (*ante*) is applicable to a charge under this section. **20-231**

(4) Sentence

When tried summarily the maximum penalty for this offence is imprisonment for a term not exceeding six months, a fine not exceeding the £20,000 or both: s.9(3)(b). After commencement of the relevant provisions, the maximum custodial sentence in a magistrates' court will be 12 months' imprisonment: *Criminal Justice Act* 2003, ss.154 and 282. The provisions regarding forfeiture detailed above are applicable to a charge under this section. **20-232**

C. Supplying a Video Recording of Classified Work in Breach of Classification

(1) Definition

Video Recordings Act 1984, s.11

Supplying video recording of classified work in breach of classification

11.—(1) Where a classification certificate issued in respect of a video work states that no video recording containing that work is to be supplied to any person who has not attained the age specified in the certificate, a person who supplies or offers to supply a video recording containing that work to a person who has not attained the age so specified is guilty of an offence unless the supply is, or would if it took place be, an exempted supply. **20-233**

(2) It is a defence to a charge of committing an offence under this section to prove—

(a) that the accused neither knew nor had reasonable grounds to believe that the classification certificate contained the statement concerned,

(b) that the accused neither knew nor had reasonable grounds to believe that the person concerned had not attained that age, or

(c) that the accused believed on reasonable grounds that the supply was, or would if it took place be, an exempted supply by virtue of section 3(4) or (5) of this Act.

(3) A person guilty of an offence under this section shall be liable, on summary conviction, to imprisonment for a term not exceeding six months or a fine not exceeding level 5 on the standard scale or both.

[This section is printed as amended by the *Criminal Justice and Public Order Act* 1994, s.88.]

(2) Allocation

20–234 This offence is triable summarily: s.11(3). The provisions as to time limits for proceedings and offences by corporations detailed above apply to charges under this section.

(3) Elements of the offence

20–235 The offence consists of supplying a classified video to a person under the specified age. A Trading Standards Officer instructed his son, who was under 18 to go and buy a video meant for over 18s for the purposes of an investigation. The defence claimed that the boy's evidence should be inadmissible. The court held that in the absence of any evidence that the witness was acting as an "agent provocateur" his evidence was admissible: *Ealing London Borough v. Woolworths Plc* [1995] Crim.L.R. 58.

(4) Defences

20–236 The defence established by s.14A of the 1984 Act, *ante*, is applicable to a charge under this section.

(5) Sentence

20–237 The maximum penalty for this offence is imprisonment for a term not exceeding six months, a fine of level five on the standard scale or both: s.11(3). After commencement of the relevant provisions, the maximum custodial sentence in a magistrates' court will be 12 months' imprisonment: *Criminal Justice Act* 2003, ss.154 and 282. The provisions regarding forfeiture detailed above are applicable to a charge under this section.

CHAPTER 21

CORRUPTION, OFFENCES AGAINST PUBLIC MORALS AND POLICY AND OFFENCES AGAINST PUBLIC JUSTICE

I. BRIBERY

(1) Introduction

Bribery

The *Bribery Act* 2010 is designed to modernise and consolidate the law on bribery and corruption. The offences at common law of bribery and embracery are abolished and the statutes relating to the prevention of corruption, dating from 1889, 1906 and 1916 are all repealed. **21–1**

The new act creates two main new offences of active and passive bribery. One covers conduct by a person who offers a bribe and the other covers conduct by the person who receives a bribe. There is also a new specific offence of bribery of a foreign official and a new offence of commercial organisations failing to prevent bribery.

The statute is relatively complex in terms of the expression of the offences and the definitions. Guidance has been issued to prosecutors and to commercial organisations to assist in the understanding of the act and its implications. The Act came fully into force on the July 1, 2011 by virtue of the *Bribery Act 2010 (Commencement) Order* 2011 (S.I. 2011 No. 1418). There are transitional provisions so that offences committed before the coming into force of the act are still dealt with under the old law.

(2) Bribery of another person

(a) *Definition*

Bribery Act 2010, s.1

Offences of bribing another person

1.—(1) A person ("P") is guilty of an offence if either of the following cases applies. **21–2**

(2) Case 1 is where—

(a) P offers, promises or gives a financial or other advantage to another person, and

(b) P intends the advantage—

(i) to induce a person to perform improperly a relevant function or activity, or

(ii) to reward a person for the improper performance of such a function or activity.

(3) Case 2 is where—

(a) P offers, promises or gives a financial or other advantage to another person, and

(b) P knows or believes that the acceptance of the advantage would itself constitute the improper performance of a relevant function or activity.

(4) In case 1 it does not matter whether the person to whom the advantage is offered, promised or given is the same person as the person who is to perform, or has performed, the function or activity concerned.

(5) In cases 1 and 2 it does not matter whether the advantage is offered, promised or given by P directly or through a third party.

(b) *Allocation*

21–3 An offence under this section is triable either way. See s.11 (*post*).

(c) *Elements*

21–4 The prosecution must prove that a person (P)

— offers, promises or gives

— a financial or other advantage to another person

and intends the advantage to

— induce a person to perform improperly a relevant function or activity

or

— reward a person for the improper performance of a relevant function or activity.

This section relates to the giver of a bribe. The section identifies two separate situations in which the offence may be committed.

Case 1 applies in circumstances where the advantage is intended to induce or reward a person to act improperly as regards a relevant function or activity.

Case 2 applies to circumstances where the advantage is offered, given or promised when it is known or believed that the acceptance of the advantage would itself constitute improper performance of a relevant function or activity.

In case 1 it is irrelevant whether the person offered the bribe is the one to perform the function or activity and in both cases 1 and 2 it is irrelevant whether the bribe is made directly or through a third party.

The terms "relevant function or activity" and "improper performance" are defined in sections 3 and 4. See § 21–16 *et seq.*

(d) *Sentence*

21–5 On summary conviction the sentence is a maximum of 12 months' imprisonment or a fine not exceeding the statutory maximum or both.

Until s.154(1) of the *Criminal Justice Act* 2003 comes into force the reference to 12 months is read as being 6 months. See s.11 (*post*).

(3) Receiving a bribe

(a) *Definition*

Bribery Act 2010, s.2

Offences relating to being bribed

21–6 **2.**—(1) A person ("R") is guilty of an offence if any of the following cases applies.

(2) Case 3 is where R requests, agrees to receive or accepts a financial or other advantage intending that, in consequence, a relevant function or activity should be performed improperly (whether by R or another person).

(3) Case 4 is where—

(a) R requests, agrees to receive or accepts a financial or other advantage, and

(b) the request, agreement or acceptance itself constitutes the improper performance by R of a relevant function or activity.

(4) Case 5 is where R requests, agrees to receive or accepts a financial or other advantage

as a reward for the improper performance (whether by R or another person) of a relevant function or activity.

(5) Case 6 is where, in anticipation of or in consequence of R requesting, agreeing to receive or accepting a financial or other advantage, a relevant function or activity is performed improperly—

(a) by R, or

(b) by another person at R's request or with R's assent or acquiescence.

(6) In cases 3 to 6 it does not matter—

(a) whether R requests, agrees to receive or accepts (or is to request, agree to receive or accept) the advantage directly or through a third party,

(b) whether the advantage is (or is to be) for the benefit of R or another person.

(7) In cases 4 to 6 it does not matter whether R knows or believes that the performance of the function or activity is improper.

(8) In case 6, where a person other than R is performing the function or activity, it also does not matter whether that person knows or believes that the performance of the function or activity is improper.

(b) *Allocation*

This offence is triable either way. See s.11 (*post*). **21–7**

(c) *Elements*

The prosecution must prove that the receiver (R) **21–8**

— requests, agrees to receive or accepts

— a financial or other advantage

and any one of three sets of circumstances as follows applies—

Case 3 applies to situations where there is an intention that a relevant function or activity should be performed improperly by himself or another as a result.

Case 4 applies to a situation where the very act of requesting, agreeing to receive or accepting the advantage amounts to an improper performance of a relevant function or activity by him.

Case 5 applies to a bribe being taken as a reward for an improper performance either by the receiver or another.

In case 6 the prosecution must prove that

— the request, agreement to receive or acceptance of

— a financial or other advantage

is anticipated as regards improper performance by R of a relevant function or activity by R himself or another person at his request or with his agreement.

In all these cases it is irrelevant whether the bribe is received directly or through a third party or whether the advantage is directly for the receiver or someone else.

In case 6 it is irrelevant whether the other person performing the function or activity knows or believes the performance is improper.

The terms "relevant function or activity" and "improper performance" are defined in sections 3 and 4. See § 21–16 *et seq.*

(d) *Sentence*

On summary conviction the sentence is a maximum of 12 months' imprisonment or a fine not exceeding the statutory maximum or both. **21–9**

Until s.154(1) of the *Criminal Justice Act* 2003 comes into force the reference to 12 months is read as being 6 months. See s.11 (*post*).

(4) Bribery of foreign officials

(a) *Definition*

Bribery Act 2010, s.6

Bribery of foreign public officials

21–10 **6.**—(1) A person ("P") who bribes a foreign public official ("F") is guilty of an offence if P's intention is to influence F in F's capacity as a foreign public official.

(2) P must also intend to obtain or retain—

(a) business, or

(b) an advantage in the conduct of business.

(3) P bribes F if, and only if—

(a) directly or through a third party, P offers, promises or gives any financial or other advantage—

(i) to F, or

(ii) to another person at F's request or with F's assent or acquiescence, and

(b) F is neither permitted nor required by the written law applicable to F to be influenced in F's capacity as a foreign public official by the offer, promise or gift.

(4) References in this section to influencing F in F's capacity as a foreign public official mean influencing F in the performance of F's functions as such an official, which includes—

(a) any omission to exercise those functions, and

(b) any use of F's position as such an official, even if not within F's authority.

(5) "Foreign public official" means an individual who—

(a) holds a legislative, administrative or judicial position of any kind, whether appointed or elected, of a country or territory outside the United Kingdom (or any subdivision of such a country or territory),

(b) exercises a public function—

(i) for or on behalf of a country or territory outside the United Kingdom (or any subdivision of such a country or territory), or

(ii) for any public agency or public enterprise of that country or territory (or subdivision), or

(c) is an official or agent of a public international organisation.

(6) "Public international organisation" means an organisation whose members are any of the following—

(a) countries or territories,

(b) governments of countries or territories,

(c) other public international organisations,

(d) a mixture of any of the above.

(7) For the purposes of subsection (3)(b), the written law applicable to F is—

(a) where the performance of the functions of F which P intends to influence would be subject to the law of any part of the United Kingdom, the law of that part of the United Kingdom,

(b) where paragraph (a) does not apply and F is an official or agent of a public international organisation, the applicable written rules of that organisation,

(c) where paragraphs (a) and (b) do not apply, the law of the country or territory in relation to which F is a foreign public official so far as that law is contained in—

(i) any written constitution, or provision made by or under legislation, applicable to the country or territory concerned, or

(ii) any judicial decision which is so applicable and is evidenced in published written sources.

(8) For the purposes of this section, a trade or profession is a business.

(b) *Allocation*

21–11 This offence is triable either way. See s.11 (*post*).

(c) *Elements*

21–12 This section introduces the specific offence of bribery of a foreign public official.

The prosecution must prove P
— bribes
— a foreign public official (F)
— with the intention to influence F in their capacity as an official
and
— with an intention to obtain or retain
— business or an advantage in the conduct of business.

Definitions are given within the section of "bribe" and "influence".

Definitions are given also of "foreign public official" and "public international organisations".

Both the law in the United Kingdom and the law in the country of the official may be considered (provided it is written law) as may the written rules of any public international organisation to which the official is attached.

(d) *Sentence*

On summary conviction the sentence is a maximum of 12 months' imprisonment or a fine not exceeding the statutory maximum or both. **21–13**

Until s.154(1) of the *Criminal Justice Act* 2003 comes into force the reference to 12 months is read as being 6 months. See s.11 (*post*).

(5) Bribery and commercial organisations

(a) *Definition*

Bribery Act 2010, s.7

Failure of commercial organisations to prevent bribery

7.—(1) A relevant commercial organisation ("C") is guilty of an offence under this section if a person ("A") associated with C bribes another person intending— **21–14**

(a) to obtain or retain business for C, or

(b) to obtain or retain an advantage in the conduct of business for C.

(2) But it is a defence for C to prove that C had in place adequate procedures designed to prevent persons associated with C from undertaking such conduct.

(3) For the purposes of this section, A bribes another person if, and only if, A—

(a) is, or would be, guilty of an offence under section 1 or 6 (whether or not A has been prosecuted for such an offence), or

(b) would be guilty of such an offence if section 12(2)(c) and (4) were omitted.

(4) See section 8 for the meaning of a person associated with C and see section 9 for a duty on the Secretary of State to publish guidance.

(5) In this section—

"partnership" means—

(a) a partnership within the *Partnership Act* 1890, or

(b) a limited partnership registered under the *Limited Partnerships Act* 1907, or a firm or entity of a similar character formed under the law of a country or territory outside the United Kingdom,

"relevant commercial organisation" means—

(a) a body which is incorporated under the law of any part of the United Kingdom and which carries on a business (whether there or elsewhere),

(b) any other body corporate (wherever incorporated) which carries on a business, or part of a business, in any part of the United Kingdom,

(c) a partnership which is formed under the law of any part of the United Kingdom and which carries on a business (whether there or elsewhere), or

(d) any other partnership (wherever formed) which carries on a business, or part of a business, in any part of the United Kingdom, and, for the purposes of this section, a trade or profession is a business.

(b) *Allocation*

21–15 This offence is triable on indictment only and carries a fine. See s.11 (*post*).

(6) General definitions

Bribery Act 2010, ss.3, 4, 5

Function or activity to which bribe relates

21–16 **3.**—(1) For the purposes of this Act a function or activity is a relevant function or activity if—

(a) it falls within subsection (2), and

(b) meets one or more of conditions A to C.

(2) The following functions and activities fall within this subsection—

(a) any function of a public nature,

(b) any activity connected with a business,

(c) any activity performed in the course of a person's employment,

(d) any activity performed by or on behalf of a body of persons (whether corporate or unincorporate).

(3) Condition A is that a person performing the function or activity is expected to perform it in good faith.

(4) Condition B is that a person performing the function or activity is expected to perform it impartially.

(5) Condition C is that a person performing the function or activity is in a position of trust by virtue of performing it.

(6) A function or activity is a relevant function or activity even if it—

(a) has no connection with the United Kingdom, and

(b) is performed in a country or territory outside the United Kingdom.

(7) In this section "business" includes trade or profession.

Improper performance to which bribe relates

21–17 **4.**—(1) For the purposes of this Act a relevant function or activity—

(a) is performed improperly if it is performed in breach of a relevant expectation, and

(b) is to be treated as being performed improperly if there is a failure to perform the function or activity and that failure is itself a breach of a relevant expectation.

(2) In subsection (1) "relevant expectation"—

(a) in relation to a function or activity which meets condition A or B, means the expectation mentioned in the condition concerned, and

(b) in relation to a function or activity which meets condition C, means any expectation as to the manner in which, or the reasons for which, the function or activity will be performed that arises from the position of trust mentioned in that condition.

(3) Anything that a person does (or omits to do) arising from or in connection with that person's past performance of a relevant function or activity is to be treated for the purposes of this Act as being done (or omitted) by that person in the performance of that function or activity.

Expectation test

21–18 **5.**—(1) For the purposes of sections 3 and 4, the test of what is expected is a test of what a reasonable person in the United Kingdom would expect in relation to the performance of the type of function or activity concerned.

(2) In deciding what such a person would expect in relation to the performance of a function or activity where the performance is not subject to the law of any part of the United Kingdom, any local custom or practice is to be disregarded unless it is permitted or required by the written law applicable to the country or territory concerned.

(3) In subsection (2) "written law" means law contained in—

(a) any written constitution, or provision made by or under legislation, applicable to the country or territory concerned, or

(b) any judicial decision which is so applicable and is evidenced in published written sources.

[The next paragraph is § 21–20.]

These sections give definitions which relate to all the offences under the act. Section 5 introduces an "expectation test". This imposes an objective test of what a reasonable person in the UK would expect to happen in relation to the performance of the type of relevant function or activity. **21–20**

If the performance is not subject to the law of the UK, then local custom and practice in any other jurisdiction is still to be disregarded unless it forms part of the written law of that jurisdiction where the function or activity is performed. The section contains a definition of "written law".

(7) Consent to prosecution

Bribery Act 2010, s.10

Consent to prosecution

10.—(1) No proceedings for an offence under this Act may be instituted in England and Wales except by or with the consent of— **21–21**

(a) the Director of Public Prosecutions,

(b) the Director of the Serious Fraud Office, or

(c) the Director of Revenue and Customs Prosecutions.

(2) No proceedings for an offence under this Act may be instituted in Northern Ireland except by or with the consent of—

(a) the Director of Public Prosecutions for Northern Ireland, or

(b) the Director of the Serious Fraud Office.

(3) No proceedings for an offence under this Act may be instituted in England and Wales or Northern Ireland by a person—

(a) who is acting—

(i) under the direction or instruction of the Director of Public Prosecutions, the Director of the Serious Fraud Office or the Director of Revenue and Customs Prosecutions, or

(ii) on behalf of such a Director, or

(b) to whom such a function has been assigned by such a Director,

except with the consent of the Director concerned to the institution of the proceedings.

(4) The Director of Public Prosecutions, the Director of the Serious Fraud Office and the Director of Revenue and Customs Prosecutions must exercise personally any function under subsection (1), (2) or (3) of giving consent.

(5) The only exception is if—

(a) the Director concerned is unavailable, and

(b) there is another person who is designated in writing by the Director acting personally as the person who is authorised to exercise any such function when the Director is unavailable.

(6) In that case, the other person may exercise the function but must do so personally.

(7) Subsections (4) to (6) apply instead of any other provisions which would otherwise have enabled any function of the Director of Public Prosecutions, the Director of the Serious Fraud Office or the Director of Revenue and Customs Prosecutions under subsection (1), (2) or (3) of giving consent to be exercised by a person other than the Director concerned.

(8) No proceedings for an offence under this Act may be instituted in Northern Ireland by virtue of section 36 of the *Justice (Northern Ireland) Act* 2002 (delegation of the functions of the Director of Public Prosecutions for Northern Ireland to persons other than the Deputy Director) except with the consent of the Director of Public Prosecutions for Northern Ireland to the institution of the proceedings.

(9) The Director of Public Prosecutions for Northern Ireland must exercise personally any function under subsection (2) or (8) of giving consent unless the function is exercised personally by the Deputy Director of Public Prosecutions for Northern Ireland by virtue of

section 30(4) or (7) of the Act of 2002 (powers of Deputy Director to exercise functions of Director).

(10) Subsection (9) applies instead of section 36 of the Act of 2002 in relation to the functions of the Director of Public Prosecutions for Northern Ireland and the Deputy Director of Public Prosecutions for Northern Ireland under, or (as the case may be) by virtue of, subsections (2) and (8) above of giving consent.

21–22 The consent of the DPP, the Director of the Serious Fraud Office or the Director of Revenue and Customs Prosecutions is required for the prosecution of any offence under this Act.

(8) Penalties

Bribery Act 2010, s.11

Penalties

21–23 **11.**—(1) An individual guilty of an offence under section 1, 2 or 6 is liable—

(a) on summary conviction, to imprisonment for a term not exceeding 12 months, or to a fine not exceeding the statutory maximum, or to both,

(b) on conviction on indictment, to imprisonment for a term not exceeding 10 years, or to a fine, or to both.

(2) Any other person guilty of an offence under section 1, 2 or 6 is liable—

(a) on summary conviction, to a fine not exceeding the statutory maximum,

(b) on conviction on indictment, to a fine.

(3) A person guilty of an offence under section 7 is liable on conviction on indictment to a fine.

(4) The reference in subsection (1)(a) to 12 months is to be read—

(a) in its application to England and Wales in relation to an offence committed before the commencement of section 154(1) of the *Criminal Justice Act* 2003, and

(b) in its application to Northern Ireland,

as a reference to 6 months.

(9) Territoriality

Bribery Act 2010, s.12

Offences under this Act: territorial application

21–24 **12.**—(1) An offence is committed under section 1, 2 or 6 in England and Wales, Scotland or Northern Ireland if any act or omission which forms part of the offence takes place in that part of the United Kingdom.

(2) Subsection (3) applies if—

(a) no act or omission which forms part of an offence under section 1, 2 or 6 takes place in the United Kingdom,

(b) a person's acts or omissions done or made outside the United Kingdom would form part of such an offence if done or made in the United Kingdom, and

(c) that person has a close connection with the United Kingdom.

(3) In such a case—

(a) the acts or omissions form part of the offence referred to in subsection (2)(a), and

(b) proceedings for the offence may be taken at any place in the United Kingdom.

(4) For the purposes of subsection (2)(c) a person has a close connection with the United Kingdom if, and only if, the person was one of the following at the time the acts or omissions concerned were done or made—

(a) a British citizen,

(b) a British overseas territories citizen,

(c) a British National (Overseas),

(d) a British Overseas citizen,

(e) a person who under the *British Nationality Act* 1981 was a British subject,

(f) a British protected person within the meaning of that Act,

(g) an individual ordinarily resident in the United Kingdom,
(h) a body incorporated under the law of any part of the United Kingdom,
(i) a Scottish partnership.

(5) An offence is committed under section 7 irrespective of whether the acts or omissions which form part of the offence take place in the United Kingdom or elsewhere.

(6) Where no act or omission which forms part of an offence under section 7 takes place in the United Kingdom, proceedings for the offence may be taken at any place in the United Kingdom.

(7) Subsection (8) applies if, by virtue of this section, proceedings for an offence are to be taken in Scotland against a person.

(8) Such proceedings may be taken—
(a) in any sheriff court district in which the person is apprehended or in custody, or
(b) in such sheriff court district as the Lord Advocate may determine.

(9) In subsection (8) "sheriff court district" is to be read in accordance with section 307(1) of the *Criminal Procedure (Scotland) Act* 1995.

This section clarifies the extent of the application of the act as regards conduct outside of the jurisdiction of the UK. It applies to offences under sections 1, 2 or 6. **21–25**

The act applies where any part of the offence is committed within the UK. It also applies where the conduct occurs entirely outside of the UK but the acts or omissions concerned would amount to an offence within the UK and the offender has a close connection with the UK as defined in s.12(4).

(10) Statutory Defences

Bribery Act 2010, s.13

Defence for certain bribery offences etc.

13.—(1) It is a defence for a person charged with a relevant bribery offence to prove that the person's conduct was necessary for— **21–26**
(a) the proper exercise of any function of an intelligence service, or
(b) the proper exercise of any function of the armed forces when engaged on active service.

(2) The head of each intelligence service must ensure that the service has in place arrangements designed to ensure that any conduct of a member of the service which would otherwise be a relevant bribery offence is necessary for a purpose falling within subsection (1)(a).

(3) The Defence Council must ensure that the armed forces have in place arrangements designed to ensure that any conduct of—
(a) a member of the armed forces who is engaged on active service, or
(b) a civilian subject to service discipline when working in support of any person falling within paragraph (a),

which would otherwise be a relevant bribery offence is necessary for a purpose falling within subsection (1)(b).

(4) The arrangements which are in place by virtue of subsection (2) or (3) must be arrangements which the Secretary of State considers to be satisfactory.

(5) For the purposes of this section, the circumstances in which a person's conduct is necessary for a purpose falling within subsection (1)(a) or (b) are to be treated as including any circumstances in which the person's conduct—
(a) would otherwise be an offence under section 2, and
(b) involves conduct by another person which, but for subsection (1)(a) or (b), would be an offence under section 1.

(6) In this section—

"active service" means service in—
(a) an action or operation against an enemy,
(b) an operation outside the British Islands for the protection of life or property, or
(c) the military occupation of a foreign country or territory,

"armed forces" means Her Majesty's forces (within the meaning of the *Armed Forces Act* 2006)

Part III

"civilian subject to service discipline" and "enemy" have the same meaning as in the Act of 2006,

"GCHQ" has the meaning given by section 3(3) of the *Intelligence Services Act* 1994,

"head" means—

(a) in relation to the Security Service, the Director General of the Security Service,

(b) in relation to the Secret Intelligence Service, the Chief of the Secret Intelligence Service, and

(c) in relation to GCHQ, the Director of GCHQ,

"intelligence service" means the Security Service, the Secret Intelligence Service or GCHQ,

"relevant bribery offence" means—

(a) an offence under section 1 which would not also be an offence under section 6,

(b) an offence under section 2,

(c) an offence committed by aiding, abetting, counselling or procuring the commission of an offence falling within paragraph (a) or (b),

(d) an offence of attempting or conspiring to commit, or of inciting the commission of, an offence falling within paragraph (a) or (b), or

(e) an offence under Part 2 of the *Serious Crime Act* 2007 (encouraging or assisting crime) in relation to an offence falling within paragraph (a) or (b).

The only statutory defences apply to members of the intelligence services or the armed forces when on active service. The defence covers offences under s.1 (but not if it would also be an offence under s.6—bribery of a foreign public official) and s.2 and aiding and abetting, counselling or procuring the commission of offences or attempting or conspiring to commit or inciting the commission of the offences.

(11) Bodies Corporate

Bribery Act 2010, s.14

Offences under sections 1, 2 and 6 by bodies corporate etc.

21–27 **14.**—(1) This section applies if an offence under section 1, 2 or 6 is committed by a body corporate or a Scottish partnership.

(2) If the offence is proved to have been committed with the consent or connivance of—

(a) a senior officer of the body corporate or Scottish partnership, or

(b) a person purporting to act in such a capacity,

the senior officer or person (as well as the body corporate or partnership) is guilty of the offence and liable to be proceeded against and punished accordingly.

(3) But subsection (2) does not apply, in the case of an offence which is committed under section 1, 2 or 6 by virtue of section 12(2) to (4), to a senior officer or person purporting to act in such a capacity unless the senior officer or person has a close connection with the United Kingdom (within the meaning given by section 12(4)).

(4) In this section—

"director", in relation to a body corporate whose affairs are managed by its members, means a member of the body corporate,

"senior officer" means—

(a) in relation to a body corporate, a director, manager, secretary or other similar officer of the body corporate, and

(b) in relation to a Scottish partnership, a partner in the partnership.

21–28 The offences can be committed by companies. Any senior officer of a company is also guilty of an offence if it is committed with his consent or connivance.

(12) Abuses in respect of honours

(a) *Definition*

Honours (Prevention of Abuses) Act 1925, s.1

Punishment of abuses in connection with the grant of honours

1.—(1) If any person accepts or obtains or agrees to accept or attempts to obtain from any person, for himself or for any other person, or for any purpose, any gift, money or valuable consideration as an inducement or reward for procuring or assisting or endeavouring to procure the grant of a dignity or title of honour to any person, or otherwise in connection with such a grant, he shall be guilty of a misdemeanour. **21–29**

(2) If any person gives, or agrees or proposes to give, or offers to any person any gift, money or valuable consideration as an inducement or reward for procuring or assisting or endeavouring to procure the grant of a dignity or title of honour to any person, or otherwise in connection with such a grant, he shall be guilty of a misdemeanour.

(3) Any person guilty of a misdemeanour under this Act shall be liable on conviction on indictment to imprisonment for a term not exceeding two years or to a fine or to both such imprisonment and such fine, or on summary conviction to imprisonment for a term not exceeding three months or to a fine not exceeding the prescribed amount, or to both such imprisonment and such fine, and where the person convicted (whether on indictment or summarily) received any such gift, money, or consideration as aforesaid which is capable of forfeiture, he shall in addition to any other punishment be liable to forfeit the same to Her Majesty.

(4) [*Repealed by* Administration of Justice (Miscellaneous Provisions) Act *1933, Sched. 3, and* Criminal Justice Act (Northern Ireland) *1945, Sched. 4*.]

[This section is printed as amended by the *CLA* 1977 s.32(1); and the *MCA* 1980, s.32(2) (substitution of reference to "the prescribed sum"). In subs. (3), "12" is substituted for "three", as from a day to be appointed, by the *CJA* 2003, s.282(2) and (3). The increase has no application to offences committed before the substitution takes effect: s.282(4).]

(b) *Allocation*

This offence is triable either way: s.1(3) (*ante*). **21–30**

(c) *Elements of the offence*

The prosecution must prove that: **21–31**

— the defendant accepted or obtained, or agreed to accept or obtain from any person,
— for himself or for any other person, or for any purpose,
— any gift, money or valuable consideration as an inducement or reward,
— for procuring or assisting or endeavouring to procure the grant of a dignity or title of honour to any person or otherwise in connection with such a grant;

OR

— the defendant gave, agreed, or proposed to give, or offered,
— to any person,
— any gift, money or valuable consideration as an inducement or reward,
— for procuring or assisting or endeavouring to procure the grant of a dignity or title of honour to any person or otherwise in connection with such a grant.

(d) Sentence

When tried summarily, the maximum penalty for this offence is three months' imprisonment, a fine not exceeding the statutory maximum or both: s.1(3), *ante*. As from the date of commencement of the *Criminal Justice Act* 2003, s.282(2) and (3), the maximum custodial sentence on summary conviction will be increased to 12 months; but only in respect of offences committed on or after that date: s.282(4). **21–32**

II. OFFENCES AGAINST PUBLIC MORALS AND POLICY

A. BIGAMY

(1) Definition

Offences against the Person Act 1861, s.57

21–33 **57.** Whosoever, being married, shall marry any other person during the life of the former husband or wife, whether the second marriage shall have taken place in England or Ireland or elsewhere, shall be guilty of felony, and being convicted thereof shall be liable to be imprisoned for any term not exceeding seven years...

Provided, that nothing in this section contained shall extend to any second marriage contracted elsewhere than in England and Ireland by any other than a subject of Her Majesty, or to any person marrying a second time whose husband or wife shall have been continually absent from such person for the space of seven years then last past, and shall not have been known by such person to be living within that time, or shall extend to any person who, at the time of such second marriage, shall have been divorced from the bond of the first marriage, or to any person whose former marriage shall have been declared void by the sentence of any court of competent jurisdiction.

(2) Allocation

21–34 This offence is triable either way: *Magistrates' Courts Act* 1980, s.17(1), and Sched. 1.

(3) Elements of the offence

21–35 The prosecution must prove that:
— the defendant was married,
— when he "married" another person,
— during the life of the former husband or wife.

"Being married"

21–36 The time for determining whether a person was "married" within the meaning of section 57 is the time of the alleged bigamous ceremony. Accordingly, although the marriage which is to be the foundation for a prosecution for bigamy must be a monogamous marriage, since a potentially polygamous marriage may in certain circumstances change its character and become monogamous (*e.g.* by a change in domicile to a country where monogamy is part of the law, or by a change in the law of the country where the marriage was celebrated), a charge of bigamy is well founded where such a change has occurred by the time of the alleged bigamous ceremony of marriage: *Sagoo* [1975] Q.B. 885, CA.

The first marriage must be strictly proved by the production of the certificate of the registrar of marriages: *Lindsay*, 66 J.P. 505. The words "or elsewhere" in the statute mean that the marriage can have taken place in any other part of the world. A British subject resident in England is liable to be convicted of bigamy although both marriages were solemnised in Scotland: *Topping* (1856) Dears. 647.

"Second marriage"

21–37 Where a person, already bound by an existing marriage, goes through with another person a form of marriage known to and recognised by the law as capable of producing a valid marriage, for the purpose of a pretended and fictitious marriage, such person is guilty of bigamy, notwithstanding any special circumstances which, independently of the bigamous character of the marriage, may constitute a legal disability in the parties, or make the form of marriage resorted to inapplicable to their case. Hence, in *Allen* (1872) L.R. 1 C.C.R. 367, a defendant who went through a ceremony of marriage with his wife's niece, whilst his wife was still living was properly found guilty of bigamy, despite the fact that the second marriage would be void for reasons of consanguinity. The validity of the second marriage is immaterial: *Robinson*, 26 Cr.App.R. 129, CCA.

(4) Defences

To establish the defence of seven years' absence provided in the statute, the defendant must not have known at any period during the seven years that the spouse was alive: *Cullen* (1840) 9 C & P. 681. **21–38**

The defence of seven years' absence of the lawful husband or wife continues to be available in relation to a third or subsequent marriage: *Taylor* [1950] 2 All E.R. 170, CCA.

An honest belief on reasonable grounds as to the invalidity of a previous marriage, will be a good defence to a charge of bigamy: *King* [1964] 1 Q.B. 285, CCA. An honest and reasonable belief at the time of the second marriage that the first marriage had been dissolved will also be a good defence: *Gould* [1968] 2 Q.B. 65, CA; as will an honest belief on reasonable grounds that the first spouse had died before the second marriage, even though the seven years of continued absence specified in the Act had not expired: *Tolson* (1889) 23 Q.B.D. 168, CCR. **21–39**

(5) Sentence

When tried summarily, the maximum penalty for this offence is six months' imprisonment, a fine not exceeding the prescribed sum or both: *Magistrates' Courts Act* 1980, s.32(1). As from the date of commencement of the *Criminal Justice Act* 2003, s.282(1), the maximum custodial sentence on summary conviction will be increased to 12 months; but only in respect of offences committed on or after that date: s.282(4). **21–40**

A custodial sentence should be passed where the innocent party has been deceived and suffered some injury or distress as a consequence *Smith (James)*, 15 Cr.App.R.(S.) 407, CA (bracket was four to six months) and *Seed* [2007] 2 Cr.App.R.(S.) 69, although if the bigamy is only discovered after two parties have separated, this is said to lessen the distress that otherwise might have been caused and the custodial sentence passed should reflect this: *Ballard* [2007] 2 Cr.App.R.(S.) 94 (six months reduced to three months on appeal).

Marriage to evade immigration control will require the imposition of a deterrent sentence and hence a custodial sentence is inevitable: *Cairns* [1997] 1 Cr.App.R.(S.) 118 (nine months' imprisonment upheld in the case of a man who married for money to enable the woman to evade immigration control).

In *Khan* [2005] 2 Cr.App.R.(S.) 45, one of the appellants, Mrs Khan, was sentenced to consecutive terms of 12 and 15 months' imprisonment for two offences of bigamy, both marriages had been designed to circumvent immigration controls. The Court of Appeal held that deterrent sentences were legitimate where immigration controls were flouted and the sentence was upheld. The other appellant had aided and abetted the second of Mrs Khan's marriages and was sentenced to two years' imprisonment, this was reduced 18 months imprisonment.

B. OBSCENE OR INDECENT PUBLICATIONS OR DISPLAYS, ETC.

(1) Outraging public decency

For the offence of outraging public decency, see *ante*, § 14–54. **21–41**

(2) Obscene publications

(a) *Definition*

Obscene Publications Act 1959, s.2

Prohibition of publication of obscene matter

2.—(1) Subject as hereinafter provided, any person who, whether for gain or not, publishes **21–42**

an obscene article or who has an obscene article for publication for gain (whether gain to himself or gain to another) shall be liable—

(a) on summary conviction to a fine not exceeding the prescribed sum or to imprisonment for a term not exceeding six months;

(b) on conviction on indictment to a fine or to imprisonment for a term not exceeding five years or both.

(3) A prosecution for an offence against this section shall not be commenced more than two years after the commission of the offence.

(3A) Proceedings for an offence under this section shall not be instituted except by or with the consent of the Director of Public Prosecutions in any case where the article in question is a moving picture film of a width of not less than sixteen millimetres and the relevant publication or the only other publication which followed or could reasonably have been expected to follow from the relevant publication took place or (as the case may be) was to take place in the course of an exhibition of a film; and in this subsection "the relevant publication" means—

(a) in the case of any proceedings under this section for publishing an obscene article, the publication in respect of which the defendant would be charged if the proceedings were brought; and

(b) in the case of any proceedings under this section for having an obscene article for publication for gain, the publication which, if the proceedings were brought, the defendant would be alleged to have had in contemplation.

21–43 (4) A person publishing an article shall not be proceeded against for an offence at common law consisting of the publication of any matter contained or embodied in the article where it is of the essence of the offence that the matter is obscene.

(4A) Without prejudice to subsection (4) above, a person shall not be proceeded against for an offence at common law—

(a) in respect of an exhibition of a film or anything said or done in the course of an exhibition of a film, where it is of the essence of the common law offence that the exhibition or, as the case may be, what was said or done was obscene, indecent, offensive, disgusting or injurious to morality; or

(b) in respect of an agreement to give an exhibition of a film or to cause anything to be said or done in the course of such an exhibition where the common law offence consists of conspiring to corrupt public morals or to do any act contrary to public morals or decency.

(5) A person shall not be convicted of an offence against this section if he proves that he had not examined the article in respect of which he is charged and had no reasonable cause to suspect that it was such that his publication of it would make him liable to be convicted of an offence against this section.

(6) In any proceedings against a person under this section the question whether an article is obscene shall be determined without regard to any publication by another person unless it could reasonably have been expected that the publication by the other person would follow from publication by the person charged.

(7) In this section "exhibition of a film" has the same meaning as in the *Cinemas Act* 1985.

[This section is printed as amended by the *Criminal Justice and Immigration Act* 2008, s.71.]

For the application of this section to matter in sound or television programmes or intended to be included therein, see Sched. 15 to the *Broadcasting Act* 1990.

For the definition of "film exhibition", see section 21 of the 1985 Act (as amended by the *Broadcasting Act* 1990, s.203(1), and Sched. 20, para. 40).

Obscene Publications Act 1964, s.1

Obscene articles intended for publication for gain

21–44 **1.**—(1) [*Amends the* Obscene Publications Act *1959*.]

(2) For the purpose of any proceedings for an offence against the said section 2 a person shall be deemed to have an article for publication for gain if with a view to such publication he has the article in his ownership, possession or control.

(3) In proceedings brought against a person under the said section 2 for having an obscene article for publication for gain the following provisions shall apply in place of subsections (5) and (6) of that section, that is to say,—

(a) he shall not be convicted of that offence if he proves that he had not examined the article and had no reasonable cause to suspect that it was such that his having it would make him liable to be convicted of an offence against that section; and

(b) the question whether the article is obscene shall be determined by reference to such publication for gain of the article as in the circumstances it may reasonably be inferred he had in contemplation and to any further publication that could reasonably be expected to follow from it, but not to any other publication.

(4) Where articles are seized under section 3 of the *Obscene Publications Act* 1959 (which provides for the seizure and forfeiture of obscene articles kept for publication for gain), and a person is convicted under section 2 of that Act of having them for publication for gain, the court on his conviction shall order the forfeiture of those articles: **21–45**

Provided that an order made by virtue of this subsection (including an order so made on appeal) shall not take effect until the expiration of the ordinary time within which an appeal in the matter of the proceedings in which the order was made may be instituted or, where such an appeal is duly instituted, until the appeal is finally decided or abandoned; and for this purpose—

(a) an application for a case to be stated or for leave to appeal shall be treated as the institution of an appeal; and

(a) where a decision on appeal is subject to a further appeal, the appeal shall not be deemed to be finally decided until the expiration of the ordinary time within which a further appeal may be instituted or, where a further appeal is duly instituted, until the further appeal is finally decided or abandoned.

(5) References in section 3 of the *Obscene Publications Act* 1959 and this section to publication for gain shall apply to any publication with a view to gain, whether the gain is to accrue by way of consideration for the publication or in any other way.

For section 3 of the 1959 Act, see *post* § 21–61.

Obscene Publications Act 1964, s.2

Negatives, etc. for production of obscene articles

2.—(1) The *Obscene Publications Act* 1959 (as amended by this Act) shall apply in relation to anything which is intended to be used, either alone or as one of a set, for the reproduction or manufacture therefrom of articles containing or embodying matter to be read, looked at or listened to, as if it were an article containing or embodying that matter so far as that matter is to be derived from it or from the set. **21–46**

(2) For the purposes of the *Obscene Publications Act* 1959 (as so amended) an article shall be deemed to be had or kept for publication if it is had or kept for the reproduction or manufacture therefrom of articles for publication; and the question whether an article so had or kept is obscene shall—

(a) for purposes of section 2 of the Act be determined in accordance with section 1(3)(b) above as if any reference there to publication of the article were a reference to publication of articles reproduced or manufactured from it; and

(b) for purposes of section 3 of the Act be determined on the assumption that articles reproduced or manufactured from it would be published in any manner likely having regard to the circumstances in which it was found, but in no other manner.

Section 3 of the 1959 Act relates to powers of search and seizure: see *post*, § 21–61.

(b) *Allocation*

This offence is triable either way: *Obscene Publications Act* 1959, s.2(1) (*ante* § 21–42). **21–47**

(c) *Elements of the offence*

The prosecution must prove that: **21–48**

— the defendant published, or had for publication for gain,

— an obscene article.

"Obscene"

Obscene Publications Act 1959, s.1(1)

Test of obscenity

21–49 **1.**—(1) For the purposes of this Act an article shall be deemed to be obscene if its effect or (where the article comprises two or more distinct items) the effect of any one of its items is, if taken as a whole, such as to tend to deprave and corrupt persons who are likely, having regard to all relevant circumstances, to read, see or hear the matter contained or embodied in it.

21–50 The test of obscenity is whether the effect of the article was such as to tend to deprave and corrupt persons who were likely to read it, so that obscenity depends on the article and not the author; it follows that intention and the defendant's honesty of purpose will be irrelevant: *Shaw v. DPP* [1962] A.C. 220, HL. Obscenity and depravity are not confined to sex, and include material that advocates drug taking: *John Calder (Publications) Ltd v. Powell* [1965] 1 Q.B. 508, DC. It also includes material that tends to induce violence: *DPP v. A. and B.C. Chewing Gum Ltd* [1968] 1 Q.B. 159, DC.

21–51 The sole test of obscenity is that provided by the Act: *Anderson* [1972] 1 Q.B. 304, CA. The test for obscenity in an article consisting of individual items is to be applied to the items individually; if the test shows one item to be obscene it is enough to make the whole article obscene: *ibid*. The quality of indecency is to be determined by looking at the article alleged to be indecent and nothing else. It is an objective test: *O'Carroll* [2003] EWCA Crim 2338.

The meaning of the words "deprave" and "corrupt" were articulated by Byrne J. in the "Lady Chatterley" case:

> "To deprave means to make morally bad, to pervert, to debase or to corrupt morally. To corrupt means to render morally unsound or rotten, to destroy the moral purity or chastity, to pervert or ruin good quality, to debase, to defile" (*Penguin Books Ltd* [1961] Crim. L.R. 176 at 177).

This definition was approved in *Calder and Boyars Ltd* [1969] 1 Q.B. 151, CA. The words "deprave and corrupt" refer primarily to the effect on the minds, including the emotions, of the persons who read or see the article: *DPP v. Whyte* [1972] A.C. 849, HL.

21–52 In *Calder and Boyars Ltd, ante*, the Court of Appeal stated that the jury should have been directed to consider whether the effect of the book was to tend to deprave or corrupt a significant proportion of those persons likely to read it. However, in *DPP v. Whyte, ante*, Lord Pearson observed (at p. 865) that although such a direction had been suitable on the facts of the case, the phrase "significant proportion" cannot be safely transplanted to cases of a different character. The statutory definition of obscenity contains no requirement as to the number of persons or as to the proportion of its readers which the article will tend to corrupt or deprave. That definition—

> ". . . refers to 'persons', which means some persons, though I think in a suitable case, if the number of persons likely to be affected is so small as to be negligible - really negligible - the *de minimis* principle might be applied. But if a seller of pornographic books has a large number of customers who are not likely to be corrupted by such books, he does not thereby acquire a licence to expose for sale or sell such books to a small number of customers who are likely to be corrupted by them" (*ibid.*, at p. 866).

Lords Simon (at p.868), Cross (at p.869) and Salmon (at p.873) accepted the "significant proportion" test, Lord Cross saying that a significant proportion of a class means a part which is not numerically negligible but which may be much less than half (at p.870). Lord Wilberforce did not specifically consider this issue. The justices had found that the class of likely customers for the defendant's pornographic publications was middle-aged men whose morals were already in a state of depravity and corruption, and they had not been satisfied, therefore, that the publications would have a tendency to deprave and corrupt a significant proportion (see *ante*) of likely readers. The House of Lords held that the Act was not merely concerned with the once and for all corruption of the wholly innocent; it equally protected the less innocent from further corruption and the addict from feeding or increasing his addiction.

"Article"

Obscene Publications Act 1959, s.1(2)

1.—(2) In this Act "article" means any description of article containing or embodying matter to be read or looked at or both, any sound record, and any film or other record of a picture or pictures. **21–53**

"Publishes"

Obscene Publications Act 1959, s.1(3)–(6)

1.—(3) For the purposes of this Act a person publishes an article who— **21–54**

(a) distributes, circulates, sells, lets on hire, gives, or lends it, or who offers it for sale or for letting on hire; or

(b) in the case of an article containing or embodying matter to be looked at or a record, shows, plays or projects it, or, where the matter is data stored electronically, transmits that data.

(4) For the purposes of this Act a person also publishes an article to the extent that any matter recorded on it is included by him in a programme included in a programme service.

(5) Where the inclusion of any matter in a programme so included would, if that matter were recorded matter, constitute the publication of an obscene article for the purposes of this Act by virtue of subsection (4) above, this Act shall have effect in relation to the inclusion of that matter in that programme as if it were recorded matter.

(6) In this section "programme" and "programme service" have the same meaning as in the *Broadcasting Act* 1990.

Part III

For the definitions of "programme" and "programme service", see sections 202(1) and 201 of the 1990 Act, respectively.

The forms of publication included in the definition in s.1(3)(a) fall into three distinct groups: in the first group, comprising the words "sells, lets on hire, gives, or lends", publication is to an individual; in the second group, comprising the words "distributes, circulates", publication is on a wider scale involving more than one person; in the third group, a mere offer for sale or letting on hire constitutes publication: *Barker*, 46 Cr.App.R. 227, CCA. **21–55**

In *Barker*, the court went on to say that in a case falling within the first group, assuming that publication is proved, the first issue for the court is whether the effect of the article was such as to tend to deprave and corrupt the individual to whom it was published. The second issue is whether any other person or persons were likely to see the article. In this connection, the issue is not whether republication has or has not taken place, but whether it could reasonably have been expected. If the answer to the second issue is "yes", a third issue will arise, namely, whether the article is such as to tend to deprave and corrupt the person or persons to whom republication could reasonably have been expected. On the first issue, a jury should take into consideration both the article itself and the age or occupation of the person to whom it was published, if there is evidence on this. On the second issue, whether republication could reasonably have been expected, age and occupation are relevant, but they are not the only relevant factors. On the third issue, considerations similar to those involved in the first are applicable. It was further held that the fact that the defendant was wholly unaware of the age or occupation of the person to whom the article had been published is irrelevant. A person who sells potentially obscene matter to an unknown applicant takes the risk **21–56** that the latter is someone whom the article would tend to deprave and corrupt. On the other hand, if the unknown applicant is not of that type, the defendant's ignorance of the applicant's character cannot make the article obscene.

Uploading or downloading of a webpage will constitute publication: *Perrin* [2002] 4 *Archbold News* 2, CA.

(d) *Defence*

Obscene Publications Act 1959, s.4

Defence of public good

21–57 **4.**—(1) Subject to subsection (1A) of this section a person shall not be convicted of an offence against section two of this Act, and an order for forfeiture shall not be made under the foregoing section, if it is proved that publication of the article in question is justified as being for the public good on the ground that it is in the interests of science, literature, art or learning, or of other objects of general concern.

(1A) Subsection (1) of this section shall not apply where the article in question is a moving picture film or soundtrack, but—

(a) a person shall not be convicted of an offence against section 2 of this Act in relation to any such film or soundtrack, and

(b) an order for forfeiture of any such film or soundtrack shall not be made under section 3 of this Act,

if it is proved that publication of the film or soundtrack is justified as being for the public good on the ground that it is in the interests of drama, opera, ballet or any other art, or of literature or learning.

(2) It is hereby declared that the opinion of experts as to the literary, artistic, scientific or other merits of an article may be admitted in any proceedings under this Act either to establish or to negative the said ground.

(3) In this section "moving picture soundtrack" means any sound record designed for playing with a moving picture film, whether incorporated with the film or not.

21–58 Only after is has been established that the article in question is obscene and that it was published by the defendant does the issue of whether the defendant has successfully established a defence fall to be considered: *DPP v. Jordan* [1977] A.C. 699, HL.

The "other objects" and the nature of the "general concern" referred to in subsection (1) fall within the same area as science, literature, art and learning already mentioned, so that expert evidence relating to the alleged beneficial effect of the material on the sexual behaviour and attitudes of some particular persons will not be admissible: *ibid*.

(e) *Sentence*

21–59 When tried summarily, the maximum penalty for this offence is six months' imprisonment, a fine not exceeding the statutory maximum or both: s.2(1) of the 1959 Act (*ante*, § 21–42). As from the date of commencement of the *Criminal Justice Act* 2003, s.282(2) and (3), the maximum custodial sentence on summary conviction will be increased to 12 months; but only in respect of offences committed on or after that date: s.282(4). Once section 181 of the 2003 Act is brought into force, custodial sentences of less than 12 months will consist of a custody plus order (see *post*, Ch.23).

21–60 See *Holloway*, 4 Cr.App.R.(S.) 128, CA; *Pace* [1998] 1 Cr.App.R.(S.) 121, CA; *Ibrahim* [1998] 1 Cr.App.R.(S.) 157, CA; and *Tunnicliffe and Greenwood* [1999] 2 Cr.App.R.(S.) 88, CA (all cases involving "front men" in video shops). In the last of these, it was said that a prison sentence would not always be necessary. For a case involving the shopkeeper himself, see *Singh (Jasjit)* [1999] 2 Cr.App.R.(S.) 160, CA.

In *Snowden* [2010] 1 Cr.App.R.(S.) 233(39), CA. a 53-year-old of good character pleaded guilty at the earliest opportunity to seven counts of publishing an obscene article. 2,840 pornographic DVDs were recovered from the defendant's home, 55 were categorised as obscene for the purposes of the Act; at least 69 obscene DVDs containing "extreme obscenity". They had been sold commercially throughout the preceding six years. After a reduction to the sentence of 20 per cent for the early guilty plea, full credit not being due owing to the strength of the evidence, a total sentence of 30 months' imprisonment was upheld on appeal.

(f) *Search and seizure*

Obscene Publications Act 1959, s.3

Powers of search and seizure

3.—(1) If a justice of the peace is satisfied by information on oath that there is reasonable ground for suspecting that, in any premises, or on any stall or vehicle, being premises or a stall or vehicle specified in the information, obscene articles are, or are from time to time, kept for publication for gain, the justice may issue a warrant under his hand empowering any constable to enter (if need be by force) and search the premises, or to search the stall or vehicle and to seize and remove any articles found therein or thereon which the constable has reason to believe to be obscene articles and to be kept for publication for gain. **21–61**

(2) A warrant under the foregoing subsection shall, if any obscene articles are seized under the warrant, also empower the seizure and removal of any documents found in the premises or, as the case may be, on the stall or vehicle which relate to a trade or business carried on at the premises or from the stall or vehicle.

(3) Subject to subsection (3A) of this section any articles seized under subsection (1) of this section shall be brought before a justice of the peace acting in the local justice area in which the articles were seized, who may thereupon issue a summons to the occupier of the premises or, as the case may be, the user of the stall or vehicle to appear on a day specified in the summons before a magistrates' court acting in that local justice area to show cause why the articles or any of them should not be forfeited; and if the court is satisfied, as respects any of the articles, that at the time when they were seized they were obscene articles kept for publication for gain, the court shall order those articles to be forfeited:

Provided that if the person summoned does not appear, the court shall not make an order unless service of the summons is proved.

Provided also that this subsection does not apply in relation to any article seized under subsection (1) of this section which is returned to the occupier of the premises or, as the case may be, to the user of the stall or vehicle in or on which it was found.

(3A) Without prejudice to the duty of a court to make an order for the forfeiture of an article where section 1(4) of the *Obscene Publications Act* 1964 applies (orders made on conviction), in a case where by virtue of subsection (3A) of section 2 of this Act proceedings under the said section 2 for having an article for publication for gain could not be instituted except by or with the consent of the Director of Public Prosecutions, no order for the forfeiture of the article shall be made under this section unless the warrant under which the article was seized was issued on an information laid by or on behalf of the Director of Public Prosecutions

(4) In addition to the person summoned, any other person being the owner, author or maker of any of the articles brought before the court, or any other person through whose hands they had passed before being seized, shall be entitled to appear before the court on the day specified in the summons to show cause why they should not be forfeited. **21–62**

(5) Where an order is made under this section for the forfeiture of any articles, any person who appeared, or was entitled to appear, to show cause against the making of the order may appeal to the Crown Court, and no such order shall take effect until the expiration of the period within which notice of appeal to the Crown Court may be given against the order, or, if before the expiration thereof notice of appeal is duly given or application is made for the statement of a case for the opinion of the High Court, until the final determination or abandonment of the proceedings on the appeal or case.

(6) If as respects any articles brought before it the court does not order forfeiture, the court may if it thinks fit order the person on whose information the warrant for the seizure of the articles was issued to pay such costs as the court thinks reasonable to any person who has appeared before the court to show cause why those articles should not be forfeited; and costs ordered to be paid under this subsection shall be enforceable as a civil debt.

(7) For the purposes of this section the question whether an article is obscene shall be determined on the assumption that copies of it would be published in any manner likely having regard to the circumstances in which it was found, but in no other manner.

Part III

(8) [*Repeal of* Obscene Publications Act *1857*.]

(3) Sending injurious, indecent or obscene articles, etc., by post

(a) *Definition*

Postal Services Act 2000, s.85

Prohibition on sending certain articles by post

21–63 **85.**—(1) A person commits an offence if he sends by post a postal packet which encloses any creature, article or thing of any kind which is likely to injure other postal packets in course of their transmission by post or any person engaged in the business of a postal operator.

(2) Subsection (1) does not apply to postal packets which enclose anything permitted (whether generally or specifically) by the postal operator concerned.

(3) A person commits an offence if he sends by post a postal packet which encloses—

(a) any indecent or obscene print, painting, photograph, lithograph, engraving, cinematograph film or other record of a picture or pictures, book, card or written communication, or

(b) any other indecent or obscene article (whether or not of a similar kind to those mentioned in paragraph (a)).

(4) A person commits an offence if he sends by post a postal packet which has on the packet, or on the cover of the packet, any words, marks or designs which are of an indecent or obscene character.

(5) A person who commits an offence under this section shall be liable—

(a) on summary conviction, to a fine not exceeding the statutory maximum,

(b) on conviction on indictment, to a fine or to imprisonment for a term not exceeding twelve months or to both.

(b) *Allocation*

21–64 This offence is triable either way: s.85(5) (*ante*).

(c) *Elements of the offence*

21–65 The prosecution must prove that:

— the defendant sent by post,

— a packet which encloses any creature, article or thing of any kind,

— which is likely to injure other postal packets in the course of their transmission by post or any person engaged in the business of a postal operator;

OR

— the defendant sent by post,

— any indecent or obscene print, painting, photograph, lithograph, engraving, cinematograph film or other record of a picture or pictures, book, card or written communication or any other indecent or obscene article;

OR

— the defendant sent by post,

— any postal packet which has on the packet or the cover of the packet,

— any words, marks or designs which are of an indecent or obscene character.

21–66 The meaning of "obscene" in section 11 of the *Post Office Act* 1953, on which this provision is closely modelled, was held to be the ordinary meaning of that word which includes "shocking, lewd and indecent": see *Anderson* [1972] 1 Q.B. 304, CA. The test is objective, and the character of the addressee and the effect on the recipient are immaterial: see *Straker* [1965] Crim.L.R. 229, CCA.

(d) *Sentence*

21–67 When tried summarily, the maximum penalty for this offence is a fine not exceeding the statutory maximum: *Postal Services Act* 2000, s.85(5).

Where the offence involves neither direct corruption nor commercial exploitation of pornography, and offender is of previous good character, a custodial sentence need not be imposed: *Littleford*, 6 Cr.App.R.(S.) 272, CA.

(4) Printing, publishing, selling, etc., works harmful to children

(a) *Definition*

Children and Young Persons (Harmful Publications) Act 1955, s.2

Penalty for printing, publishing, selling, &c., works to which this Act applies

2.—(1) A person who prints, publishes, sells or lets on hire a work to which this Act applies, or has any such work in his possession for the purpose of selling it or letting it on hire, shall be guilty of an offence and liable, on summary conviction, to imprisonment for a term not exceeding *four months* [51 weeks] or to a fine not exceeding level 3 on the standard scale or to both: **21–68**

Provided that, in any proceedings taken under this subsection against a person in respect of selling or letting on hire a work or of having it in his possession for the purpose of selling it or letting it on hire, it shall be a defence for him to prove that he had not examined the contents of the work and had no reasonable cause to suspect that it was one to which this Act applies.

(2) A prosecution for an offence under this section shall not, in England or Wales, be instituted except by, or with the consent, of the Attorney General.

[This section is printed as amended by the *CJA* 1982, ss.38 and 46. "51 weeks" is substituted for "four months" as from a day to be appointed by the *CJA* 2003, s.280(2), and Sched. 26, para. 15; but not in relation to any offence committed before the amendment takes effect: *ibid.* s.280(3).]

As to the works to which the Act applies, see *post*, § 21–71.

(b) *Allocation*

This offence is triable summarily: s.2(1) (*ante*). **21–69**

(c) *Elements of the offence*

The prosecution must prove that: **21–70**

- the defendant printed, published, sold or let out on hire, or had in his possession,
- a work to which the Act applies (as to which, see *post*, § 21–71),
- for the purposes of selling it or letting it on hire.

Children and Young Persons (Harmful Publications) Act 1955, s.1

Works to which this Act applies

1. This Act applies to any book, magazine or other like work which is of a kind likely to fall into the hands of children or young persons and consists wholly or mainly of stories told in pictures (with or without the addition of written matter), being stories portraying— **21–71**

(a) the commission of crimes; or

(b) acts of violence or cruelty; or

(c) incidents of a repulsive or horrible nature;

in such a way that the work as a whole would tend to corrupt a child or young person into whose hands it might fall.

Section 5(2) of the 1955 Act defines "child" and "young person" by reference to the definitions of those expressions in section 107(1) of the *Children and Young Persons Act* 1933, *viz.* a child is a person under the age of 14 years, and a young person is one who has attained the age of 14 years but is under the age of 18 years. **21–72**

(d) *Defence*

See the proviso to section 2(1) (*ante*). **21–73**

Part III

(e) *Sentence*

21–74 The maximum penalty for this offence is four months' imprisonment, or a fine not exceeding level 3, or both: s.2(1) (*ante*). As from the date of commencement of the *Criminal Justice Act* 2003, s.280(2) and Sched. 26, para. 15, the maximum custodial sentence on summary conviction will be increased to 51 weeks; but only in respect of offences committed on or after that date: s.280(3).

(5) Obscene, etc., theatrical performances

(a) *Definition*

Theatres Act 1968, s.2

Prohibition of presentation of obscene performances of plays

21–75 **2.**—(1) For the purposes of this section a performance of a play shall be deemed to be obscene if, taken as a whole, its effect was such as to tend to deprave and corrupt persons who were likely, having regard to all relevant circumstances, to attend it.

(2) Subject to sections 3 and 7 of this Act, if an obscene performance of a play is given, whether in public or private, any person who (whether for gain or not) presented or directed that performance shall be liable—

(a) on summary conviction, to a fine not exceeding the prescribed sum or to imprisonment for a term not exceeding *six* [12] months;

(b) on conviction on indictment, to a fine or to imprisonment for a term not exceeding three years, or both.

(3) A prosecution on indictment for an offence under this section shall not be commenced more than two years after the commission of the offence.

(4) No person shall be proceeded against in respect of a performance of a play or anything said or done in the course of such a performance—

(a) for an offence at common law where it is of the essence of the offence that the performance or, as the case may be, what was said or done was obscene, indecent, offensive, disgusting or injurious to morality; or

(b) [*repealed by* Indecent Displays (Control) Act *1981*]

(c) [*repealed by* Civic Government (Scotland) Act *1982*]

and no person shall be proceeded against for an offence at common law of conspiring to corrupt public morals, or to do any act contrary to public morals or decency, in respect of an agreement to present or give a performance of a play, or to cause anything to be said or done in the course of such a performance.

[This section is printed as amended by the *MCA* 1980, s.32(2). In subs. (2)(a), "12" is substituted for "six", as from a day to be appointed, by the *CJA* 2003, s.282(2) and (3). The increase has no application to offences committed before the substitution takes effect: s.282(4).]

Proceedings for an offence under this section may not be instituted except by or with the consent of the Attorney-General: s.8.

A judicial decision that s.2(4) of the *Theatres Act* 1968 prevented prosecution on the grounds of blasphemous libel was appealed in *R. v. City of Westminster Magistrates' Court* [2007] EWHC 2785 (Admin). The attempted prosecution related to alleged lewd and blasphemous content of the theatrical work "Jerry Springer: the Opera". The decision was upheld: the 1968 Act having been passed to abolish censorship of live theatrical performances. Furthermore, in accordance with European Convention on Human Rights 1950, Art.10, the protection of freedom of speech had to be accorded to the unpopular, tasteless or offensive.

(b) *Allocation*

21–76 This offence is triable either way: s.2(2) (*ante*).

(c) *Evidence, etc.*

Theatres Act 1968, ss.9, 10

Script as evidence of what was performed

9.—(1) Where a performance of a play was based on a script, then, in any proceedings for an offence under section 2... or 6 of this Act alleged to have been committed in respect of that performance— **21–77**

(a) an actual script on which that performance was based shall be admissible as evidence of what was performed and of the manner in which the performance or any part of it was given; and

(b) if such a script is given in evidence on behalf of any party to the proceedings then, except in so far as the contrary is shown, whether by evidence given on behalf of the same or any other party, the performance shall be taken to have been given in accordance with that script.

(2) In this Act "script", in relation to a performance of a play, means the text of the play (whether expressed in words or in musical or other notation) together with any stage or other directions for its performance, whether contained in a single document or not.

[This section is printed as repealed in part by the *Public Order Act* 1986, s.40, and Sched. 3.]

Power to make copies of scripts

10.—(1) If a police officer of or above the rank of superintendent has reasonable grounds for suspecting— **21–78**

(a) that an offence under section 2... or 6 of this Act has been committed by any person in respect of a performance of a play; or

(b) that a performance of a play is to be given and that an offence under the said section 2... or 6 is likely to be committed by any person in respect of that, performance,

he may make an order in writing under this section relating to that person and that performance.

(2) Every order made under this section shall be signed by the police officer by whom it is made, shall name the person to whom it relates, and shall describe the performance to which it relates in a manner sufficient to enable that performance to be identified.

(3) Where an order under this section has been made, any police officer, on production if so required of the order—

(a) may require the person named in the order to produce, if such a thing exists, an actual script on which the performance was or, as the case may be, will be based; and

(b) if such a script is produced to him, may require the person so named to afford him an opportunity of causing a copy thereof to be made.

(4) Any person who without reasonable excuse fails to comply with a requirement under subsection (3) above shall be liable on summary conviction to a fine not exceeding level 3 on the standard scale.

(5) Where, in the case of a performance of a play based on a script, a copy of an actual script on which that performance was based has been made by or on behalf of a police officer by virtue of an order under this section relating to that performance, section 9(1) of this Act shall apply in relation to that copy as it applies in relation to an actual script on which the performance was based.

[This section is printed as amended, and repealed in part, by the *CJA* 1982, ss.38 and 46; and the *Public Order Act* 1986, s.40, and Sched. 3.]

(d) *Liability of corporate officers*

Theatres Act 1968, s.16

Offences by bodies corporate

16. Where any offence under this Act committed by a body corporate is proved to have been committed with the consent or connivance of, or to be attributable to any neglect on the part of, **21–79**

any director, manager, secretary or other similar officer of the body corporate, or any person purporting to act in any such capacity, he as well as the body corporate shall be guilty of that offence and shall be liable to be proceeded against and punished accordingly.

(e) *Elements of the offence*

21–80 The prosecution must prove that:

— the defendant,
— presented or directed a performance of a play,
— the effect of which (taken as a whole) was such as to tend to deprave and corrupt persons who were likely, having regard to all relevant circumstances, to have attended it.

Theatres Act 1968, s.18

Interpretation

21–81 **18.**—(1) In this Act—

"licensing authority" means—...

(c) [*Scotland*];

"play" means—

(a) any dramatic piece, whether involving improvisation or not, which is given wholly or in part by one or more persons actually present and performing and in which the whole or a major proportion of what is done by the person or persons performing, whether by way of speech, singing or action, involves the playing of a role; and

(b) any ballet given wholly or in part by one or more persons actually present and performing, whether or not it falls within paragraph (a) of this definition;

"police officer" means a member, or in Scotland a constable, of a police force;

"premises" includes any place;

"public performance" includes any performance in a public place within the meaning of the *Public Order Act* 1936 and any performance which the public or any section thereof are permitted to attend, whether on payment or otherwise;

"script" has the meaning assigned by section 9(2) of this Act.

(2) For the purposes of this Act—

(a) a person shall not be treated as presenting a performance of a play by reason only of his taking part therein as a performer;

(b) a person taking part as a performer in a performance of a play directed by another person shall be treated as a person who directed the performance if without reasonable excuse he performs otherwise than in accordance with that person's direction; and

(c) a person shall be taken to have directed a performance of a play given under his direction notwithstanding that he was not present during the performance;

and a person shall not be treated as aiding or abetting the commission of an offence under section 2 or 6 of this Act in respect of a performance of a play by reason only of his taking part in that performance as a performer.

[This section is printed as repealed in part by the *Public Order Act* 1986, s.40, and Sched. 3; and the *Licensing Act* 2003, ss.198(1) and 199, Sched. 6, paras 43 and 47, and Sched. 7.]

(f) *Defence and exceptions*

Theatres Act 1968, ss.3, 7

Defence of public good

21–82 **3.**—(1) A person shall not be convicted of an offence under section 2 of this Act if it is proved that the giving of the performance in question was justified as being for the public good on the ground that it was in the interest of drama, opera, ballet or any other art, or of literature or learning.

(2) It is hereby declared that the opinion of experts as to the artistic, literary or other merits of a performance of a play may be admitted in any proceedings for an offence under section 2 of this Act either to establish or negative the said ground.

As to this provision, see *ante*, §§ 21–57, 21–58.

Exceptions for performances given in certain circumstances

7.—(1) Nothing in sections 2 to 4 of this Act shall apply in relation to a performance of a play given on a domestic occasion in a private dwelling. **21–83**

(2) Nothing in sections 2 to 6 of this Act shall apply in relation to a performance of a play given solely or primarily for one or more of the following purposes, that is to say—

(a) rehearsal; or

(b) to enable—

(i) a record or cinematograph film to be made from or by means of the performance; or

(ii) the performance to be broadcast; or

(iii) the performance to be included in a programme service (within the meaning of the *Broadcasting Act* 1990) other than a sound or television broadcasting service;

but in any proceedings for an offence under section 2 or 6 of this Act alleged to have been committed in respect of a performance of a play if it is proved that the performance was attended by persons other than persons directly connected with the giving of the performance or the doing in relation thereto of any of the things mentioned in paragraph (b) above, the performance shall be taken not to have been given solely or primarily for one or more of the said purposes unless the contrary is shown.

(3) In this section—

"broadcast" means broadcast by wireless telegraphy (within the meaning of the *Wireless Telegraphy Act* 1949), whether by way of sound broadcasting or television;

"cinematograph film" means any print, negative, tape or other article on which a performance of a play or any part of such a performance is recorded for the purposes of visual reproduction;

"record" means any record or similar contrivance for reproducing sound, including the sound-track of a cinematograph film.

[This section is printed as amended, and repealed in part, by the *Public Order Act* 1986, s.40, and Sched. 3; the *Cable and Broadcasting Act* 1984, s.57, Sched. 5, para. 21, and Sched. 6; and the *Broadcasting Act* 1990, s.203(1), and Sched. 20, para. 13.]

[As further amended by the *Coroners and Justice Act* 2009, s.178, Sched. 23, Pt 2, which came into force on the January 12, 2010: see the *Coroners and Justice Act* 2009, s.182(2)(e).]

(g) *Sentence*

When tried summarily, the maximum penalty for this offence is imprisonment for a term not exceeding six months or a fine not exceeding the prescribed sum or both: s.2(2)(a) (*ante*, § 21–75). As from the date of commencement of the *Criminal Justice Act* 2003, s.282(2) and (3), the maximum custodial sentence on summary conviction will be increased to 12 months; but only in respect of offences committed on or after that date: s.282(4). **21–84**

(6) Theatrical performances intended, or likely, to provoke breach of the peace

(a) *Definition*

Theatres Act 1968, s.6

Provocation of breach of peace by means of public performance of a play

6.—(1) Subject to section 7 of this Act, if there is given a public performance of a play involv- **21–85**

ing the use of threatening, abusive or insulting words or behaviour, any person who (whether for gain or not) presented or directed that performance shall be guilty of an offence under this section if—

(a) he did so with intent to provoke a breach of the peace; or

(b) the performance, taken as a whole, was likely to occasion a breach of the peace.

(2) A person guilty of an offence under this section shall be liable on summary conviction to a fine not exceeding level 5 on the standard scale or to imprisonment for a term not exceeding *six months* [51 weeks] or to both.

[This section is printed as amended by the *CLA* 1977, ss.15 and 30, and Sched. 1; and the *CJA* 1982, s.46; and as amended, as from a day to be appointed, by the *CJA* 2003, s.281(4) and (5) (substitution of "51 weeks" for "six months"); but this has no application in relation to an offence before the amendment comes into force: s.281(6).]

Proceedings for an offence under this section may not be instituted except by or with the consent of the Attorney-General: s.8.

(b) *Allocation*

21–86 This offence is triable summarily: s.6(2) (*ante*).

(c) *Elements of the offence*

21–87 The prosecution must prove:

— the giving of a public performance of a play,

— involving the use of threatening, abusive or insulting words or behaviour,

— the defendant presented or directed the performance,

— he did so with intent to provoke a breach of the peace, or the performance, taken as a whole, was likely to occasion a breach of the peace.

21–88 As to the meaning of "play" and "public performance", see section 18 (*ante*, § 21–81). As to the script as evidence of what was performed, see section 9 (*ante*, § 21–77).

(d) *Defence*

21–89 As to certain performances being excepted from section 6, see section 7(2) (*ante*, § 21–83).

(e) *Sentence*

21–90 The maximum penalty for this offence is a fine not exceeding level 5 on the standard scale, six months' imprisonment, or both: s.6(2) (*ante*, § 21–85). As from the date of commencement of the *Criminal Justice Act* 2003, s.281(4) and (5), the maximum custodial sentence on summary conviction will be increased to 12 months; but only in respect of offences committed on or after that date: s.281(6).

(7) Indecent displays

(a) *Definition*

Indecent Displays (Control) Act 1981, s.1

Indecent displays

21–91 **1.**—(1) If any indecent matter is publicly displayed the person making the display and any person causing or permitting the display to be made shall be guilty of an offence.

(2) Any matter which is displayed in or so as to be visible from any public place shall, for the purposes of this section, be deemed to be publicly displayed.

(3) In subsection (2) above, "public place", in relation to the display of any matter, means any place to which the public have or are permitted to have access (whether on payment or otherwise) while that matter is displayed except—

(a) a place to which the public are permitted to have access only on payment which is or includes payment for that display; or

(b) a shop or any part of a shop to which the public can only gain access by passing beyond an adequate warning notice; but the exclusions contained in paragraphs (a) and (b) above shall only apply where persons under the age of 18 years are not permitted to enter while the display in question is continuing.

(4) Nothing in this section applies in relation to any matter—

(a) included by any person in a television broadcasting service or other television programme service (within the meaning of the *Broadcasting Act* 1990);

(b) included in the display of an art gallery or museum and visible only from within the gallery or museum; or

(c) displayed by or with the authority of, and visible only from within a building occupied by, the Crown or any local authority; or

(d) included in a performance of a play (within the meaning of paragraph 14(1) of Schedule 1 to the *Licensing Act* 2003) in England and Wales or of a play (within the meaning of the *Theatres Act* 1968) in Scotland; or

(e) included in an exhibition of a film, within the meaning of paragraph 15 of Schedule 1 to the *Licensing Act* 2003, in England and Wales, or a film exhibition, as defined in the *Cinemas Act* 1985 in Scotland—

(i) given in a place which as regards that exhibition is required to be licensed under section 1 of that Act or by virtue only of section 5, 7 or 8 of that Act is not required to be so licensed; or

(ii) which is an exhibition to which section 6 of that Act applies given by an exempted organisation as defined by subsection (6) of that section.

(5) In this section "matter" includes anything capable of being displayed, except that it does not include an actual human body or any part thereof; and in determining for the purpose of this section whether any displayed matter is indecent—

(a) there shall be disregarded any part of that matter which is not exposed to view; and

(b) account may be taken of the effect of juxtaposing one thing with another.

(6) A warning notice shall not be adequate for the purposes of this section unless it complies with the following requirements—

(a) The warning notice must contain the following words, and no others—

"WARNING

Persons passing beyond this notice will find material on display which they may consider indecent. No admittance to persons under 18 years of age."

(b) The word "WARNING" must appear as a heading.

(c) No pictures or other matter shall appear on the notice.

(d) The notice must be so situated that no one could reasonably gain access to the shop or part of the shop in question without being aware of the notice and it must be easily legible by any person gaining such access.

[This section is printed as amended by the *Broadcasting Act* 1990, s.203(1), and Sched. 20, para. 30; the *Cinemas Act* 1985, s.24(1), and Sched. 2, para. 13; and the *Licensing Act* 2003, s.198(1), and Sched. 6, para. 80.]

(b) *Allocation*

This offence is triable either way: *Indecent Displays (Control) Act* 1981, s.4(1). **21–92**

(c) *Liability of corporate officers*

Indecent Displays (Control) Act 1981, s.3

Offences by corporations

3.—(1) Where a body corporate is guilty of an offence under this Act and it is proved that the offence occurred with the consent or connivance of, or was attributable to any neglect on the part of, any director, manager, secretary or other officer of the body, or any person who was purporting to act in any such capacity he, as well as the body corporate, shall be deemed to be guilty of that offence and shall be liable to be proceeded against and punished accordingly. **21–93**

(2) Where the affairs of a body corporate are managed by its members, subsection (1) shall apply in relation to the acts and defaults of a member in connection with his functions of management as if he were a director of the body corporate.

(d) *Sentence*

21–94 When tried summarily, the maximum penalty is a fine not exceeding the statutory maximum: *Indecent Displays (Control) Act* 1981, s.4(1)(a). When tried on indictment, the offence carries two years' imprisonment, or a fine, or both: *ibid.*, s.4(1)(b).

(e) *Search and seizure*

Indecent Displays (Control) Act 1981, s.2

Powers of arrest, seizure and entry

21–95 **2.**—(1) [...]

(2) A constable may seize any article which he has reasonable grounds for believing to be or to contain indecent matter and to have been used in the commission of an offence under this Act.

(3) In England and Wales, a justice of the peace if satisfied on information on oath that there are reasonable grounds for suspecting that an offence under this Act has been or is being committed on any premises and, in Scotland, a sheriff or justice of the peace on being so satisfied on evidence on oath, may issue a warrant authorising any constable to enter the premises specified in the information or, as the case may be, evidence (if need be by force) ... seize any article which the constable has reasonable grounds for believing to be or to contain indecent matter and to have been used in the commission of an offence under this Act.

[Subs. (1) and the words omitted from subs. (3) were repealed by the *PACE Act* 1984, s.119(2), and Sched. 7, Pt 1.]

III. OFFENCES AGAINST PUBLIC JUSTICE

A. CONTEMPT OF COURT

(1) General

21–96 The *Contempt of Court Act* 1981 gave statutory powers to magistrates to deal with contempt in the face of the court. In addition, magistrates have powers of enforcement in respect of fine defaulters under sections 75 to 96 of the *Magistrates' Courts Act* 1980, and to punish defaults in respect of other orders under section 63 of that Act, which provides that any person disobeying an order of a magistrates' court to do anything other than the payment of money may be fined up to a maximum of £50 a day for every day during which he is in default or a sum not exceeding £5,000, or the court may commit him to custody until he has remedied his default or for a period not exceeding two months.

(2) Definition

Contempt of Court Act 1981, s.12

Offences of contempt of magistrates' courts

21–97 **12.**—(1) A magistrates' court has jurisdiction under this section to deal with any person who—

(a) wilfully insults the justice or justices, any witness before or officer of the court or any solicitor or counsel having business in the court, during his or their sitting or attendance in court or in going to or returning from the court; or

(b) wilfully interrupts the proceedings of the court or otherwise misbehaves in court.

(2) In any such case the court may order any officer of the court, or any constable, to

take the offender into custody and detain him until the rising of the court; and the court may, if it thinks fit, commit the offender to custody for a specified period not exceeding one month or impose on him a fine not exceeding £2,500, or both.

(2A) A fine imposed under subsection (2) above shall be deemed, for the purposes of any enactment, to be a sum adjudged to be paid by a conviction.

(4) A magistrates' court may at any time revoke an order of committal made under subsection (2) and, if the offender is in custody, order his discharge.

(5) Section 135 of the *Powers of Criminal Courts (Sentencing) Act* 2000 (limits on fines in respect of young persons) and the following provisions of the *Magistrates' Courts Act* 1980 apply in relation to an order under this section as they apply in relation to a sentence on conviction or finding of guilty of an offence; and those provisions of the *Magistrates' Courts Act* 1980 are sections 75 to 91 (enforcement); section 108 (appeal to Crown Court); section 136 (overnight detention in default of payment); and section 142(1) (power to rectify mistakes).

[This section is printed as amended, and repealed in part, by the *CJA* 1982, s.78, and Sched. 16; the *CJA* 1991, s.17(3), and Sched. 4, Pts I and V; the *CJA* 1993, s.65(3) and (4), and Sched. 3, para. 6(4); and the *PCC(S)A* 2000, s.165(1), and Sched. 9, para. 83.]

Although the wording of s.12(5) seems to suggest that only sentence can be appealed, *Haw v. Westminster Magistrates Court* [2008] 2 All E.R. 326 confirmed that the intended purpose of the section was to provide an appeal in relation to both conviction and sentence.

Magistrates' Courts Act 1980, s.97(4)

Summons to witness and warrant for his arrest

97.—(4) If any person attending or brought before a magistrates' court refuses without just excuse to be sworn or give evidence, or to produce any document or thing, the court may commit him to custody until the expiration of such period not exceeding one month as may be specified in the warrant or until he sooner gives evidence or produces the document or thing or impose on him a fine not exceeding £2,500 or both. **21–98**

[Subs. (4) is printed as amended by the *Contempt of Court Act* 1981, s.14, and Sched. 2, Pt III, para. 7; and the *CJA* 1991, s.17(3)(a) and (e), and Sched. 4, Pts I and V, para. 2.]

Part III

(3) Allocation

These offences are triable summarily only. **21–99**

(4) Elements of the offence

For the offence under section 12 of the *Contempt of Court Act* 1981, the prosecution must prove that: **21–100**

- — the defendant wilfully insulted the justice or justices, or any witness before or officer of the court or any solicitor or counsel having business in the court,
- — during his or their sitting or attendance in court or in going to or returning from the court.

OR

- — that the defendant wilfully interrupted the proceedings of the court or otherwise misbehaved in court.

Regarding the offence under section 97(4) of the 1980 Act, the prosecution must prove that:

- — the defendant was attending or brought before a magistrates' court, and
- — refused without just excuse to be sworn or give evidence, or to produce any document or thing.

As regards contempt in the face of the court under section 12, a person "wilfully" interrupts the proceedings of the court if he commits the acts causing disruption **21–101** deliberately with the intention that they should interrupt the proceedings of the court or if, knowing that there is a risk that his acts will interrupt the proceedings, he nevertheless goes on deliberately to do those acts: *Bodden v. Metropolitan Police Commr* [1990] 2 Q.B. 397, CA. Section 12(a) does not apply to the making of threats: *R. v. Havant JJ., ex p. Palmer*, 149 J.P. 609, DC, though threats may constitute "misbehaviour" under paragraph (b) (witness, after giving his evidence, threatening to "get" the defendant and his solicitor who were waiting outside court whilst the magistrates considered their decision).

21–102 In construing the words "otherwise misbehaves" regard has to be had to the fact that the 1981 Act is a criminal statute and that the other prohibitions in section 12 are qualified by the word "wilfully". There has to be some element of defiance in the alleged contemnor's conduct: *Re Hooker* [1990] C.O.D. 190, DC.

The *Consolidated Criminal Practice Direction*, para. V.54 (contempt in the face of a magistrates' court) (*post*, Appendix F–63) sets out the relevant principles governing the exercise of magistrates' powers under these sections. It includes advice that before using the power to commit, the offender should be warned to desist or face the prospect of being detained. It also says that where the contempt consists of insults or misbehaviour, in the majority of cases an apology and a promise as to future conduct should suffice for a court to order the defendant's release.

In *Phelps* [2010] 2 Cr.App.R.(S.) 1 it was said that a sentencing judge had acted hastily in sentencing a contemnor under summary procedure without giving him an opportunity to apologise and provide mitigation. The contempt in this case was serious as the defendant had spat at and punched the officers in the dock. It was held that the court does need to act promptly to deal with incidents of contempt but in most cases a cooling off period should be allowed which can be given by adjourning the case temporarily with the contemnor being kept in custody and being given the opportunity to calm down and seek legal advice. In this case a sentence of imprisonment for two years for the contempt was reduced to 21 months.

The Practice Direction also gives guidance on how trials for contempt should be dealt with, going before a different bench on the same day if possible.

(5) Sentence

21–103 The maximum penalty for this offence under section 12 is imprisonment for a term not exceeding one month, or a fine not exceeding £2,500, or both. The court may also order that the defendant be detained until the rising of the court. The maximum penalty for the offence under section 97 is committal to custody until the defendant gives evidence, or produces the relevant document, or for a period not exceeding one month, or a fine not exceeding £2,500, or both.

B. PERJURY AND OFFENCES AKIN TO PERJURY

(1) Introduction

21–104 Perjury, contrary to section 1(1) of the *Perjury Act* 1911 is triable only on indictment. All other offences under the 1911 Act are triable either way, either by virtue of express provision in the 1911 Act (see ss.3 and 4) or by virtue of the *Magistrates' Courts Act* 1980, s.17(1), and Sched. 1, para. 14. This includes the offences contrary to section 89 of the *Criminal Justice Act* 1967 (*post*, § 21–105) and section 106 of the 1980 Act (*post*, § 21–106), which are effectively assimilated into the 1911 Act on account of subsection (2) in each section.

(2) False statements for the purposes of criminal proceedings

(a) *Definition*

Criminal Justice Act 1967, s.89

False written statements tendered in evidence

89.—(1) If any person in a written statement tendered in evidence in criminal proceedings by virtue of section 9 of this Act wilfully makes a statement material in those proceedings which he knows to be false or does not believe to be true, he shall be liable on conviction on indictment to imprisonment for a term not exceeding two years or a fine or both. **21–105**

(2) The *Perjury Act* 1911 shall have effect as if this section were contained in that Act.

[This section is printed as amended, and repealed in part, by the *Armed Forces Act* 1976, s.22(5), and Sched. 9, para. 15; and the *MCA* 1980, s.154(3), and Sched. 9; and as amended, as from a day to be appointed, by the *Armed Forces Act* 2006, s.378(2), and Sched. 17 (omission of words from "or in proceedings" to "*Air Force Act* 1955").]

[As further amended by the *Armed Forced Act* 2006 s.378(2)].

Magistrates' Courts Act 1980, s.106

False written statements tendered in evidence

106.—(1) *If any person in a written statement admitted in evidence in criminal proceedings by virtue of section 5B above wilfully makes a statement material in those proceedings which he knows to be false or does not believe to be true, he shall be liable on conviction on indictment to imprisonment for a term not exceeding 2 years or a fine or both.* **21–106**

(2) *The* Perjury Act *1911 shall have effect as if this section were contained in that Act.*

[This section is printed as amended by the *CPIA* 1996, s.47, and Sched. 1, Pt I, paras 1 and 12. It is repealed, as from a day to be appointed, by the *CJA* 2003, ss.41 and 332, Sched. 3, para. 51(1) and (6)(c), and Sched. 37, Pt 4.]

(b) *Allocation*

These offences are triable either way: see *ante*, § 21–104. **21–107**

(c) *Elements of the offences*

The prosecution must prove that: **21–108**

- the defendant, in a written statement tendered in evidence in criminal proceedings or in proceedings before a court-martial, or in a written statement admitted in evidence in criminal proceedings,
- wilfully made a statement,
- material in those proceedings,
- which he knew to be false or did not believe to be true.

Wilfully

The prosecution are required to prove that the statement was made deliberately and not inadvertently or by mistake: *Millward* [1985] Q.B. 519, CA. **21–109**

Materiality

The matter of materiality is an issue to be determined objectively by the judge. The defendant's belief on the materiality of the statement is irrelevant: *Millward*, *ante*. **21–110**

Falsity

The defendant may be convicted where the statement that he believed to be false **21–111** turns out to be true, as the sections only require the making of a statement which is known or believed to be untrue.

Perjury Act 1911, s.13

Corroboration

21–112 **13.** A person shall not be liable to be convicted of any offence against this Act, or of any offence declared by any other Act to be perjury or subornation of perjury, or to be punishable as perjury or subornation of perjury, solely upon the evidence of one witness as to the falsity of any statement alleged to be false.

In *Cooper* [2010] 1 W.L.R. 2390 it was held that the evidence of a single witness as to the falsity of a statement cannot be corroborated by the production of business records compiled by the same witness. Such a record was not independent and did not comply with the requirements of s.13.

(d) *Sentence*

21–113 As these offences are triable either way by virtue of section 17(1) of, and Sched. 1 to, the *MCA* 1980 (see *ante*, § 21–104), the maximum penalties on summary conviction are prescribed by section 32(1) of that Act (six months' imprisonment (amended to 12 months, as from a day to be appointed, by the *CJA* 2003, s.282(1), but not in relation to an offence committed before the amendment takes effect: s.282(4)) or a fine not exceeding the prescribed sum): see *post*, § 23–129.

(3) False statements for the purposes of judicial proceedings abroad

(a) *Definition*

Perjury Act 1911, s.1A

False unsworn statement under Evidence (Proceedings in Other Jurisdictions) Act 1975

21–114 **1A.** If any person, in giving any testimony (either orally or in writing) otherwise than on oath, where required to do so by an order under section 2 of the *Evidence (Proceedings in Other Jurisdictions) Act* 1975, makes a statement—

(a) which he knows to be false in material particular, or

(b) which is false in a material particular and which he does not believe to be true,

he shall be guilty of an offence and shall be liable on conviction on indictment to imprisonment for a term not exceeding two years or a fine or both.

[This section was inserted by the 1975 Act, s.8(1), and Sched. 1.]

(b) *Allocation*

21–115 This offence is triable either way: see *ante*, § 21–104.

(c) *Elements of the offence*

21–116 The prosecution must prove that:

— the defendant, in giving any testimony, otherwise than on oath,

— where required to do so under section 2 of the 1975 Act

— made a statement which

— he knew to be false in a material particular or

— which was false in a material particular and he did not believe it to be true.

As to falsity, and its proof, see *ante*, §§ 21–111, 21–112.

(d) *Sentence*

21–117 See *ante*, § 21–113.

(4) False statements on oath otherwise than in a judicial proceeding

(a) *Definition*

Perjury Act 1911, s.2

False statements on oath made otherwise than in a judicial proceedings

2.— If any person— **21–118**

(1) being required or authorised by law to make any statement on oath for any purpose, and being lawfully sworn (otherwise than in a judicial proceeding) wilfully makes a statement which is material for that purpose and which he knows to be false or does not believe to be true; or

(2) wilfully uses any false affidavit for the purposes of the *Bills of Sale Act* 1878, as amended by any subsequent enactment,

he shall be guilty of a misdemeanour, and, on conviction thereof on indictment, shall be liable to imprisonment for a term not exceeding seven years, or to a fine or to both such imprisonment and fine.

(b) *Allocation*

This offence is triable either way: see *ante*, § 21–104. **21–119**

(c) *Elements of the offence*

The prosecution must prove (para. (1)) that: **21–120**

— the defendant was required or authorised by law to make any statement on oath for any purpose, and
— was lawfully sworn (otherwise than in a judicial proceeding), and
— wilfully made a statement which was material for that purpose, and
— which he knew to be false or did not believe was true.

For the meaning of "wilfully", see *ante* § 21–109.
For the meaning of "falsity" and proof thereof, see *ante* §§ 21–111, 21–112.

(d) *Sentence*

See *ante*, § 21–113. **21–121**

(5) False statements with reference to marriage

(a) *Definition*

Perjury Act 1911, s.3

False statements, &c. with reference to marriage

3.—(1) If any person— **21–122**

(a) for the purpose of procuring a marriage, or a certificate or licence for marriage, knowingly and wilfully makes a false oath, or makes or signs a false declaration, notice or certificate required under any Act of Parliament for the time being in force relating to marriage; or

(b) knowingly and wilfully makes, or knowingly and wilfully causes to be made, for the purposes of being inserted in any register of marriage, a false statement as to any particular required by law to be known and registered relating to any marriage; or

(c) forbids the issue of any certificate or licence for marriage by falsely representing himself to be a person whose consent to the marriage is required by law knowing such representation to be false, or

(d) with respect to a declaration made under section 16(1A) or 27B(2) of the *Marriage Act* 1949—

(i) enters a caveat under subsection (2) of the said section 16, or

Part III

(ii) makes a statement mentioned in subsection (4) of the said section 27B, which he knows to be false in a material particular,

he shall be guilty of a misdemeanour, and, on conviction thereof on indictment, shall be liable to imprisonment for a term not exceeding seven years, or to a fine or to both such imprisonment and fine and on summary conviction thereof shall be liable to a penalty not exceeding the prescribed sum.

(2) No prosecution for knowingly and wilfully making a false declaration for the purpose of procuring any marriage out of the district in which the parties or one of them dwell shall take place after the expiration of eighteen months from the solemnization of the marriage to which the declaration refers.

[This section is printed as amended by the *CJA* 1925, s.28; the *Marriage (Prohibited Degrees of Relationship) Act* 1986, s.4; and the *MCA* 1980, s.32(2).]

(b) *Allocation*

21–123 This offence is triable either way: s.3(1), *ante*.

(c) *Elements of the offence*

21–124 The prosecution must prove that:

— the defendant for the purpose of procuring a marriage, or a certificate or licence for marriage,

— knowingly and wilfully made a false oath, or made or signed a false declaration, notice or certificate, required under an Act of Parliament, or

— knowingly and wilfully made, or knowingly and wilfully caused to be made, for the purposes of being inserted in any register of marriage, a false statement as to any particular required by law to be known and registered relating to any marriage, or

— forbade the issue of any certificate or licence for marriage by falsely representing himself to be a person whose consent to the marriage was required by law knowing such representation to be false, or

— with respect to a declaration made under section 16(1A) or 27B(2) of the *Marriage Act* 1949,

entered a caveat under section 16(2), or

made a statement mentioned in section 27B(4),

— which he knew to be false in a material particular.

(d) *Sentence*

21–125 When tried summarily, the maximum penalty for this offence is a fine not exceeding the prescribed sum (*i.e.* £5,000: see s.32(9) of the *MCA* 1980, § 23–28).

(6) False statements in relation to births and deaths

(a) *Definition*

Perjury Act 1911, s.4

False statements, &c. as to births or deaths

21–126 **4.**—(1) If any person—

(a) wilfully makes any false answer to any question put to him by any registrar of births or deaths relating to the particulars required to be registered concerning any birth or death, or, wilfully gives to any such registrar any false information concerning any birth or death or the cause of any death; or

(b) wilfully makes any false certificate or declaration under or for the purposes of any Act relating to the registration of births or deaths, or, knowing any such certificate or declaration to be false, uses the same as true or gives or sends the same as true to any person; or

(c) wilfully makes, gives or uses any false statement or declaration as to a child born alive as having been still-born, or as to the body of a deceased person or a still-born child in any coffin, or falsely pretends that any child born alive was still-born; or

(d) makes any false statement with intent to have the same inserted in any register of births or deaths:

he shall be guilty of a misdemeanour and shall be liable—

(i) on conviction thereof on indictment to imprisonment for a term not exceeding seven years, or to a fine; and

(ii) on summary conviction thereof, to a penalty not exceeding the prescribed sum.

(1A) For the purposes of subsection (1)(a), information which a person is required to provide to a registrar of births or deaths for the purposes of subsection (1) of section 2B of the *Births and Deaths Registration Act* 1953 (duties of unmarried mother when acting alone) is to be taken to be information concerning a birth.

(2) A prosecution on indictment for an offence against this section shall not be commenced more than three years after the commission of the offence.

[This section is printed as amended by the *MCA* 1980, s.32(2).]

[Sub-section, 1A, is inserted by *Welfare Reform Act* 2009, s.61(3), (4), in force from a day to be appointed].

(b) *Allocation*

This offence is triable either way: s.4(1) (*ante*). **21–127**

(c) *Sentence*

When tried summarily, the maximum penalty for this offence is a fine not exceeding the prescribed sum (as to which, see *ante*, § 21–125). **21–128**

Part III

(7) False statutory declarations and other statements not on oath

(a) *Definition*

Perjury Act 1911, s.5

False statutory declarations and other false statements without oath

5. If any person knowingly and wilfully makes (otherwise than on oath) a statement false in a material particular, and the statement is made— **21–129**

(a) in a statutory declaration; or

(b) in an abstract, account, balance sheet, book, certificate, declaration, entry, estimate, inventory, notice, report, return, or other document which he is authorised or required to make, attest, or verify, by any public general Act of Parliament for the time being in force; or

(c) in any oral declaration or oral answer which he is required to make by, under, or in pursuance of any public general Act of Parliament for the time being in force,

he shall be guilty of a misdemeanour and shall be liable on conviction thereof on indictment to imprisonment, for any term not exceeding two years, or to a fine or to both such imprisonment and fine.

(b) *Allocation*

This offence is triable either way: see *ante*, § 21–104. **21–130**

(c) *Elements of the offence*

The prosecution must prove that: **21–131**

— the defendant knowingly and wilfully made,

— otherwise than on oath,

— a statement false in a material particular, and
— the statement was made
in a statutory declaration, or
in an abstract, account balance sheet, book, certificate, declaration, entry, estimate, inventory, notice, report, return, or other document which he was authorised to make, attest or verify by any public general Act of Parliament for the time being in force, or
in any oral declaration or oral answer which he was required to make by, under or in pursuance of any such Act of Parliament.

(d) *Sentence*

21–132 See *ante*, § 21–113.

(8) False declarations to obtain registration

(a) *Definition*

Perjury Act 1911, s.6

False declarations, &c. to obtain registration, &c. for carrying on a vocation

21–133 **6.** If any person—
(a) procures or attempts to procure himself to be registered on any register or roll kept under or in pursuance of any public general Act of Parliament for the time being in force of persons qualified by law to practise any vocation or calling; or
(b) procures or attempts to procure a certificate of the registration of any person on any such register or roll as aforesaid,

by wilfully making or producing or causing to be made or produced either verbally or in writing, any declaration, certificate, or representation which he knows to be false or fraudulent, he shall be guilty of a misdemeanour and shall be liable on conviction thereof on indictment to imprisonment for any term not exceeding twelve months, or to a fine, or to both such imprisonment and fine.

(b) *Allocation*

21–134 This offence is triable either way: see *ante*, § 21–104.

(c) *Elements of the offence*

21–135 The prosecution must prove that:
— the defendant procured, or attempted to procure himself to be registered on any register or roll kept under or in pursuance of any public general Act of Parliament for the time being in force of persons qualified by law to practice any vocation or calling, or
— procured or attempted to procure a certificate of the registration of any person on any such register or roll as aforesaid,
— by wilfully making or producing or causing to be made or produced either verbally or in writing, any declaration, certificate, or representation,
— which he knew to be false or fraudulent.

(d) *Sentence*

21–136 See *ante*, § 21–113.

C. INTIMIDATION OF WITNESSES, JURORS AND OTHERS

(1) Definition

Criminal Justice and Public Order Act 1994, s.51

21–137 **51.**—(1) A person commits an offence if—

(a) he does an act which intimidates, and is intended to intimidate, another person ("the victim"),

(b) he does the act knowing or believing that the victim is assisting in the investigation of an offence or is a witness or potential witness or a juror or potential juror in proceedings for an offence, and

(c) he does it intending thereby to cause the investigation or the course of justice to be obstructed, perverted or interfered with.

(2) A person commits an offence if—

(a) he does an act which harms, and is intended to harm, another person or, intending to cause another person to fear harm, he threatens to do an act which would harm that other person,

(b) he does or threatens to do the act knowing or believing that the person harmed or threatened to be harmed ("the victim)", or some other person, has assisted in an investigation into an offence or has given evidence or particular evidence in proceedings for an offence, or has acted as a juror or concurred in a particular verdict in proceedings for an offence, and

(c) he does or threatens to do it because of that knowledge or belief.

(3) For the purposes of subsections (1) and (2) it is immaterial that the act is or would be done, or that the threat is made—

(a) otherwise than in the presence of the victim, or

(b) to a person other than the victim.

(4) The harm that may be done or threatened may be financial as well as physical (whether to the person or a person's property) and similarly as respects an intimidatory act which consists of threats.

(5) The intention required by subsection (1)(c) and the motive required by subsection (2)(c) above need not be the only or the predominating intention or motive with which the act is done or, in the case of subsection (2), threatened.

(6) A person guilty of an offence under this section shall be liable—

(a) on conviction on indictment, to imprisonment for a term not exceeding five years or a fine or both;

(b) on summary conviction, to imprisonment for a term not exceeding six months or a fine not exceeding the statutory maximum or both.

(7) If, in proceedings against a person for an offence under subsection (1) above, it is proved that he did an act falling within paragraph (a) with the knowledge or belief required by paragraph (b), he shall be presumed, unless the contrary is proved, to have done the act with the intention required by paragraph (c) of that subsection.

(8) If, in proceedings against a person for an offence under subsection (2) above, it is proved that he did or threatened to do an act falling within paragraph (a) within the relevant period—

(a) he did an act which harmed, and was intended to harm, another person, or

(b) intending to cause another person fear of harm, he threatened to do an act which would harm that other person,

and that he did the act, or (as the case may be) threatened to do the act with the knowledge or belief required by paragraph (b), he shall be presumed, unless the contrary is proved, to have done the act or (as the case may be) threatened to do the act with the motive required by paragraph (c) of that subsection.

(9) In this section—

"investigation into an offence" means such an investigation by the police or other person charged with the duty of investigating offences or charging offenders;

"offence" includes an alleged or suspected offence;

"potential" in relation to a juror, means a person who has been summoned for jury service at the court at which proceedings for the offence are pending; *and*

["public prosecutor", "requisition" and "written charge" have the same meaning as in section 29 of the *Criminal Justice Act* 2003;]

"the relevant period" —

(a) in relation to a witness or juror in any proceedings for an offence, means the period beginning with the institution of the proceedings and ending with the first anniversary of the conclusion of the trial or, if there is an appeal or a reference under section 9 or 11 of the *Criminal Appeal Act* 1995, of the conclusion of the appeal;

(b) in relation to a person who has, or is believed by the accused to have, assisted in an investigation into an offence, but was not also a witness in proceedings for an offence, means the period of one year beginning with any act of his, or any act believed by the accused to be an act of his, assisting in the investigation; and

(c) in relation to a person who both has, or is believed by the accused to have, assisted in the investigation into an offence and was a witness in proceedings for the offence, means the period beginning with any act of his, or any act believed by the accused to be an act of his, assisting in the investigation and ending with the anniversary mentioned in paragraph (a) above.

(10) For the purposes of the definition of the relevant period in subsection (9) above—

(a) proceedings for an offence are instituted at the earliest of the following times—

(i) when a justice of the peace issues a summons or warrant under section 1 of the *Magistrates' Courts Act* 1980 in respect of the offence;

[(ia) when a public prosecutor issues a written charge and requisition in respect of the offence;]

(ii) when a person is charged with the offence after being taken into custody without a warrant;

(iii) when a bill of indictment is preferred by virtue of section 2(2)(b) of the *Administration of Justice (Miscellaneous Provisions) Act* 1933;

(b) proceedings at a trial of an offence are concluded with the occurrence of any of the following, the discontinuance of the prosecution, the discharge of the jury without a finding otherwise than in circumstances where the proceedings are continued without a jury, the acquittal of the accused or the sentencing of or other dealing with the accused for the offence of which he was convicted; and

(c) proceedings on an appeal are concluded on the determination of the appeal or the abandonment of the appeal.

(11) This section is in addition to, and not in derogation of, any offence subsisting at common law.

[This section is printed as amended by the *Criminal Appeal Act* 1995, s.29(1), and Sched. 2, para. 19; the *YJCEA* 1999, s.67(1), and Sched. 4, para. 22; and the *CJA* 2003, s.331, and Sched. 36, paras 62 and 64; and, as from a day or days to be appointed, by the *CJA* 2003 as follows: by s.282(2) and (3) (substitution of "12" for "six" in subs. (6), but not in relation to an offence committed before the date of commencement: s.282(4)); and by s.331, and Sched. 36, para. 11 (omission of italicised word and insertion of words in square brackets in subss. (9) and (10)).]

(2) Allocation

21–138 Offences under this section are triable either way: s.51(6) (*ante*).

(3) Elements of the offence

21–139 For an offence under section 51(1), the prosecution must prove that the defendant:

— did an act which intimidated another person (but see *Patrascu, post*),

— he did the act intending that it should intimidate the other person,

— he did the act knowing or believing that the person intimidated was assisting in the investigation of an offence or was a witness or potential witness or a juror or a potential juror in proceedings for an offence, and

— he did it intending thereby to cause the investigation or the course of justice to be obstructed, perverted or interfered with.

For an offence under section 51(2), the prosecution must prove that the defendant:

— did an act which harmed, and which was intended to harm another person or, intending to cause another person to fear harm, he threatened to do an act which would harm that other person,

— he did or threatened to do the act knowing or believing that the person harmed or threatened, or some other person, had assisted an investigation into an of-

fence or had given evidence in proceedings for an offence, or had acted as a juror or concurred in a particular verdict in proceedings for an offence, and
— he did the act or threatened to do it because of that knowledge or belief.

Intimidation

A person may be guilty of an offence contrary to section 51(1) notwithstanding that the victim is not actually intimidated; a person does an act which intimidates another person within section 51(1)(a) if he puts the victim in fear, which is the ordinary meaning of "intimidate"; but the person also does so if he seeks to deter the victim from some relevant action by threat or violence; a threat unaccompanied by violence may be sufficient, and the threat need not necessarily be a threat of violence; the act must be intended to intimidate and must involve pressure which amounts to improper pressure; but the intimidation does not necessarily have to be successful in the sense that the victim does not actually have to be deterred or put in fear; an act may amount to intimidation and thus intimidate, even though the victim is sufficiently steadfast not to be intimidated: *Patrascu* [2005] 1 Cr.App.R. 35, CA. **21–140**

Investigation

There must be an investigation under way at the time of the alleged act; it is insufficient that the defendant believed this to be the case: *Singh (B.)* [1999] Crim.L.R. 681, CA. **21–141**

Harm

See subsection (4). Financial harm aside, "harm" in section 51 refers to physical harm and does not include physical assaults (such as spitting), which do not cause injury: *Normanton* [1998] Crim.L.R. 220, CA. **21–142**

Intention and motive

See subsections (5), (7) and (8). The reverse burden provision in subsection (7) was held not to breach the presumption of innocence under Article 6(2) of the European Convention on Human Rights: *Att.-Gen.'s Reference (No. 1 of 2004)*; *R. v. Edwards*; *R. v. Denton*; *R. v. Hendley*; *R. v. Crowley* [2004] 1 W.L.R. 2111, CA. **21–143**

Offences of intimidation under s.51 can potentially be dealt with as a contempt of court. In *S* [2008] Crim.L.R. 716 the defendant appealed against a conviction for contempt of court on the basis that matter should instead have been charged under the specific offences created under s.51(1) and s.51(2) of the *Criminal Justice and Public Order Act* 1994. During his trial for causing death by careless driving whilst unfit through drink or drugs the defendant had approached the main prosecution witness after she had given evidence on the first day and left the court building and behaved in an intimidating and frightening manner towards her. It was held, dismissing the appeal, that the procedure followed was almost indistinguishable from the procedure that would have been followed under the *Criminal Justice and Public Order Act* 1994 and by exercising his discretion to deal with the matter as the judge did, it enabled the matter to be dealt with promptly, ensuring no similar incidents would occur during the trial or pending the retrial.

(4) Sentence

When tried summarily, the maximum penalty for either offence is imprisonment for a term not exceeding six months, or a fine not exceeding the statutory maximum, or both (s.51(6)). After commencement of the relevant provisions, the maximum custodial sentence will be 12 months' imprisonment, but not in relation to an offence committed before their commencement (see *ante*, § 21–137). **21–144**

Part III

The fact that Parliament thought it necessary to enact section 51 was ample reason for holding that an offence contrary to it, that involved an assault, contained an extra element of criminality, above and beyond the assault: *Watmore* [1998] 2 Cr.App.R.(S.) 46, CA.

In *R. v. Parry* [2007] 1 Cr.App.R.(S.) 356, 62, the appellant faced acharge of assault for slapping the victim and subsequently said to him regarding the charge "if you carry on with this and don't drop the charges then something bad will happen to you." He was convicted of intimidation and sentenced to six months' imprisonment, which was upheld on appeal. It was not manifestly excessive.

Part IV

Sentencing

Chapter 22

GENERAL PRINCIPLES OF SENTENCING

I. THE PURPOSES OF SENTENCING

22–1 Sentencing can range from a relatively complex task to a relatively straightforward one. At its most difficult, it is a complex balance in which conflicting goals have to be addressed. The main sentencing statutes currently in force are the *Criminal Justice Act* 2003 and the *Powers of Criminal Courts (Sentencing) Act* 2000 (*PCC(S)A* 2000). Much of the *Powers of Criminal Courts (Sentencing) Act* 2000 has been repealed and replaced by provisions in the *Criminal Justice Act* 2003, predominantly for offences committed on or after April 4, 2005 though some of the provisions have been amended, sometimes significantly. The most recent amendments are contained in the *Criminal Justice and Immigration Act* 2008 and the *Coroners and Justice Act* 2009. The most significant provisions yet to come into force replace custodial sentences of less than 12 months with the custody plus order. In addition to the statutory provisions, the Sentencing Guidelines Council has issued guidelines on matters of general principle including the approach to the assessment of the seriousness of the offence, the response to violence occurring in a domestic context and the approach to the giving of a reduction in sentence on account of the entry of a guilty plea (as revised). Much of these guidelines has been incorporated into the revised *Magistrates' Court Sentencing Guidelines* (issued by the Sentencing Guidelines Council in May 2008) and, since the training for judges, magistrates and court staff has included these guidelines, practitioners will need to be familiar with them. Relevant parts are included at the appropriate point in this work. The full text can be found at *www.sentencingcouncil.judiciary.gov.uk*. All SGC guidelines are deemed to have been made by the Sentencing Council created by the *Coroners and Justice Act* 2009 and effective from April 2010.

Section 142 of the 2003 Act requires every court to have regard to five specified purposes—punishment, reduction of crime, reform and rehabilitation, protection of the public and the making of reparation to those affected by the offence. Sentencing of youths (those aged under 18 at the time of conviction) is excluded from this obligation: s.142(2)(a). Although s.9 of the *Criminal Justice and Immigration Act* 2008 inserts a new s.142A into the 2003 Act setting out the purposes of sentencing for youths, that has not been brought into force. For youths, there is a clear obligation to treat the prevention of offending by young people as the principal aim (s.37 of the *Crime and Disorder Act* 1998) supported by the obligation to have regard to the welfare of the youth: *Children and Young Persons Act* 1933, s.44. A salutary warning concerning the degree of care needing to be taken by prosecutors and defence alike can be seen in *R. v. O* [2008] EWCA Crim. 2835. A young girl appeared before the Crown Court charged with an offence of possessing a false identity card. During the course of the proceedings, information became available that there was a real possibility that the defendant was a "victim of a sex trafficking operation". The defendant was initially thought to have been an adult but was likely to have been 16 or 17 years old. The Court and the advocates proceeded on the basis of a custodial sentence being inevitable.

One of the grounds of appeal invoked the Council of Europe Convention on Action against Trafficking in Human Beings (Council of Europe Treaty Series 197/1975) which is intended to protect the human rights of the victims of trafficking. Article 10 requires the States Parties to identify and protect victims of trafficking; there is a particular focus on the protection of trafficked children. Article 10(3) provides that where the age of a victim is uncertain, and there are reasons to believe that he or she is a child (that is a person defined as someone under 18 (Article 4D)) then he or she is to be presumed to be a child.

At the time, the United Kingdom was a signatory to this Convention but had not ratified it; accordingly, Article 18 of the Vienna Convention on the Law of Treaties creates an obligation to refrain from acts which would defeat the object and purpose of the Convention. Indeed, the United Kingdom has taken some measures expressly to support that purpose. In particular, there are two protocols, one on the prosecution of defendants charged with immigration offences who might be trafficked victims and one on prosecution of young offenders charged with offences who might be trafficked victims. The Court of Appeal understood that both were incorporated into the Code for Crown Prosecutors. The Convention was ratified in December 2008 and the United Kingdom is now fully bound by it.

Under the first protocol, where a "credible" trafficked victim is prosecuted for an immigration offence, which includes possession of a false identity document, prosecutors are required to consider whether the public interest is best served in continuing the prosecution. The prosecution should set in hand appropriate enquiries into the question whether the person has in fact been trafficked and review the case. In its judgment, the Court noted that, in the case of young defendants, the Code states:

> "Where there is clear evidence that the youth has a credible defence of duress, the case should be discontinued on evidential grounds. Where the information concerning coercion is less certain, further details should be sought from the police and youth offender teams, so that the public interest in continuing a prosecution can be considered carefully. Prosecutors should also be alert to the fact that an appropriate adult in interview could be the trafficker or a person allied to the trafficker.
>
> Any youth who might be a trafficked victim should be afforded the protection of our child care legislation if there are concerns that they have been working under duress or if their well being has been threatened.
>
> In these circumstances, the youth may well then become a victim or witness for a prosecution

against those who have exploited them. The younger a child is, the more careful investigators and prosecutors have to be in deciding whether it is right to ask them to become involved in a criminal trial"

In a strongly worded judgment, the Court noted that, in this case, there was:

24. " ... material before the defence which should plainly have raised at least the apprehension that this appellant had been trafficked to the United Kingdom for the purposes of prostitution. The defence had information from her suggesting that she was at most 17, as counsel indeed submitted to the court, and perhaps only 16. From the custody record the Crown should have appreciated that she might have been a very young person.

25. No steps were taken by the defence to investigate the history. No consideration was given by the defence as to whether she might have a defence of duress. The possibility that she might have been trafficked was ignored. There is nothing in the transcript to suggest that any thought had been given to the State's possible duty to protect her as a young victim. Nobody considered that if she was 17 or less, she should not have been in the Crown Court at all. Counsel for the defence thought it right to refer to "an inevitable prison sentence". The judge passed what she described as an "inevitable prison sentence" of 8 months. If the appellant was 17 or less, a sentence of imprisonment as such was unlawful. For good measure the judge sentenced her without a report.

26. This appeal against conviction must obviously be allowed. We would put it most simply on the footing that the common law and Article 6 of the European Convention on Human Rights alike require far higher standards of procedural protection than were given here. There was no fair trial. We hope that such a shameful set of circumstances never occurs again. Prosecutors must be aware of the protocols which, although not in the text books are enshrined in their Code. Defence lawyers must respond by making enquiries, if there is before them credible material showing that they have a client who might have been the victim of trafficking, especially a young client. Where there is doubt about the age of a defendant who is a possible victim of trafficking, proper inquiries must be made, indeed statute so required. All this is obvious. It matches with what was said by the report of a joint Committee in the House of Lords and House of Commons on human trafficking published in October 2006 (see in particular paragraphs 134 and 159). We hope that this case serves as a lesson to drive these messages home"

This part of the judgment has been set out in full given the importance of the issue and the obvious need for the provisions of the protocols to be more widely known.

In the light of continuing concerns about practice, the Court of Appeal (Criminal Division) has considered 5 cases where it was asserted that the defendants were (or had been) victims of people trafficking: *LM and others v. R.* [2010] EWCA Crim. 2327; [2011] 1 Cr.App.R. 12. Giving the judgment, the Vice President, Hughes L.J., described the effect of the Convention and set out the three stages that a prosecutor should undertake—

1. is there a reason to believe that the person has been trafficked? if so,
2. if there is clear evidence of a common law defence (*e.g.* duress, necessity), the case will be discontinued on evidential grounds; **but** even where there is no such evidence
3. if the offence may have been committed as a result of a compulsion arising from the trafficking, prosecutors should consider whether the public interest is in proceeding to prosecution.

In relation to the first stage, the State is obliged to take active steps to consider whether trafficking is a realistic possibility; it is not enough to await an assertion from the defendant.

The Court of Appeal was at pains to point out that the Convention does not state that no trafficked victim should be prosecuted for any offence or for any offence arising out of the trafficking nor does it provide a defence to any charge. Rather, it places an obligation on the State to give careful consideration to whether or not public policy calls for prosecution and punishment where the defendant is a trafficked victim and the crime was committed under some compulsion (in a broad sense). Acknowledging that the decision will be highly fact sensitive, the judgment sought to give some general propositions which are set out below:

Part IV

"i) If there is evidence on which a common law defence of duress or necessity is likely to succeed, the case will no doubt not be proceeded with on ordinary evidential grounds independent of the convention, but additionally there are likely to be public policy grounds under the convention leading to the same conclusion.

ii) But cases in which it is not in the public interest to prosecute are not limited to these [see above].

iii) It may be reasonable to prosecute if the defendant's assertion that she was trafficked meets the reasonable grounds test, but has been properly considered and rejected by the Crown for good evidential reason. The fact that a person passes the threshold test as a person of whom there are reasonable grounds to believe she has been trafficked is not conclusive that she has. Conversely, it may well be that, in other cases, that the real possibility of trafficking and a nexus of compulsion (in the broad sense) means that public policy points against prosecution.

iv) There is normally no reason not to prosecute, even if the defendant has previously been a trafficked victim, if the offence appears to have been committed outwith any reasonable nexus of compulsion (in the broad sense) occasioned by the trafficking, and hence is outside Article 26.

v) A more difficult judgment is involved if the victim has been a trafficked victim and retains some nexus with the trafficking, but has committed an offence which arguably calls, in the public interest, for prosecution in court. Some of these may be cases of a cycle of abuse. It is well known that one tool of those in charge of trafficking operations is to turn those who were trafficked and exploited in the past into assistants in the exploitation of others. Such a cycle of abuse is not uncommon in this field, as in other fields, for example that of abuse of children. In such a case, the question which must be actively confronted by the prosecutor is whether or not the offence committed is serious enough, despite any nexus with trafficking, to call for prosecution. That will depend on all the circumstances of the case, and normally no doubt particularly on the gravity of the offence alleged, the degree of continuing compulsion, and the alternatives reasonably available to the defendant."

Whilst there is power to stay prosecutions for abuse, the Court of Appeal emphasised the limitations on that power in this context—"Criminal courts in England and Wales do not decide whether a person ought to be prosecuted or not. They decide whether an offence has been committed. They may, however, also have to decide whether a legal process to which a person is entitled, or to which he has a legitimate expectation, has been neglected to his disadvantage". Concern was again expressed that the provisions of the Convention are not sufficiently known amongst the legal profession.

Criminal Justice Act 2003, s.142

Purposes of sentencing

22–2 **142.**—(1) Any court dealing with an offender in respect of his offence must have regard to the following purposes of sentencing—

(a) the punishment of offenders,

(b) the reduction of crime (including its reduction by deterrence),

(c) the reform and rehabilitation of offenders,

(d) the protection of the public, and

(e) the making of reparation by offenders to persons affected by their offences.

(2) Subsection (1) does not apply—

(a) in relation to an offender who is aged under 18 at the time of conviction,

(b) to an offence the sentence for which is fixed by law,

(c) to an offence the sentence for which falls to be imposed under section 51A(2) of the *Firearms Act* 1968 (minimum sentence for certain firearms offences), under subsection (2) of section 110 or 111 of the *Sentencing Act* (required custodial sentences) under section 29(4) or (6) of the *Violent Crime Reduction Act* 2006 (minimum sentences in certain cases of using someone to mind a weapon) or under any of sections 225(2) or 226(2) of this Act (dangerous offenders), or

(d) in relation to the making under Part 3 of the *Mental Health Act* 1983 of a hospital order (with or without a restriction order), an interim hospital order, a hospital direction or a limitation direction.

(3) In this Chapter "sentence", in relation to an offence, includes any order made by a court when dealing with the offender in respect of his offence; and "sentencing" is to be construed accordingly.

The sentencing framework established by the 2003 Act follows the previous framework in the 2000 Act in having as its central concept the seriousness of the offence. The assessment of seriousness determines whether any of the sentencing thresholds has been crossed, indicating what type of sentence is likely to be most appropriate. It is also the key element in determining the length of a custodial sentence, the onerousness of requirements to be included in a community order and the amount of any fine imposed. **22–3**

Section 148 of the 2003 Act provides that a court must not pass a community sentence on an offender unless it is of the opinion that the offence, or the combination of the offence and one or more offences associated with it, was *serious enough* to warrant such a sentence. Section 152 provides that the court must not pass a custodial sentence unless it is of the opinion that the offence, or the combination of the offence and one or more offences associated with it, was *so serious* that neither a fine alone nor a community sentence can be justified for the offence. Whilst this is the same basic criterion as the *PCC(S)A* 2000, it is articulated a little differently. In its draft guideline on custodial sentences of less than 12 months the Sentencing Guidelines Council suggests that, taking together this revised wording and the change in character of community orders and the potential increase in onerousness of a custody plus order, the custodial threshold is now higher than it was.

By s.143 of the 2003 Act, any assessment of seriousness requires the court to consider both the culpability of the offender and any harm that was caused, intended to be caused or might foreseeably have been caused. When a court is considering sentence, it will be looking to identify the factors that assist it in determining both culpability and harm. Having done that, the court will take into account mitigating factors personal to the offender and then, having determined sentence, apply any reduction on account of a guilty plea. It is well established that a court will take account of injury caused to the victim of a crime. A court is not, however, required to gather extensive detail about the level of that injury. In *R. (Holme) v. Liverpool Magistrates' Court* (2005) 169 J.P. 306, the defendant was convicted of dangerous driving at a magistrates' court after a trial. The Divisional Court concluded both that (even though no specific information was given) the effect of the accident should have been recognised by the court given the nature of the impact between the defendant's vehicle and the victim and that the sentence imposed was about right. The court affirmed the importance of a court being aware of the injuries to a victim in such cases and was concerned that the justices in this case appeared to consider it was not a relevant matter. It was stated: **22–4**

> "... benches of magistrates, when sentencing, should not consider it necessary that they should either hear oral evidence or receive medical reports which go into great detail. But, that said, a balance has to be struck in cases such as this between the injuries of the victim being expanded on to some degree to enable a balanced view to be formed by the court, and extensive detail being canvassed in court in too great detail. It would be helpful for magistrates to say, when they do sentence in a case in which there have been injuries, something to the effect that they have taken them into account. That is what they are entitled to do. Should this course be adopted there would be no reason for misunderstanding to occur as appears in this case to have occurred." (At para. 53, *per* Newman J.)

The guideline from the Sentencing Guidelines Council on seriousness (*Overarching Principles: Seriousness*) identifies 4 levels of criminal culpability. The offender who is most culpable is the one who has the *intention* to cause harm. The more the offence is planned rather than spontaneous, the higher the culpability. When this is combined with the level of harm caused, intended or foreseeable it will show the seriousness of the offence. The next level of culpability is where the offender is *reckless* as to whether harm is caused. In this context, the Council describes recklessness as "where the offender appreciates at least some harm would be caused but proceeds giving no thought to the consequences even though the extent of the risk would be obvious to most people". The third level of culpability is where the offender has knowledge of the specific risks entailed by his actions even though he does not intend to cause the harm that results. Finally, the lower level of culpability arises where the offender is guilty of negligence. The Council recognises that there are cases where liability is strict and there needs to be no proof of culpability in order to secure a conviction; however, even in those circumstances, the extent to which the offender was culpable is likely to be a key factor in determining the approach to sentence. It is the culpability of the offender that is the *initial* factor in determining seriousness.

22–5 The guideline also describes (at paras 1.8–1.14) different types of harm that are likely to be caused and the amount of harm will clearly also be a critical factor in assessing seriousness. Culpability will be greater where an offender deliberately causes more harm than is necessary in order to commit the offence—the burglar who vandalises the property as well as stealing what is there, the robber who uses unnecessary violence over and above what is needed to take the property from the victim. The guidelines also draw attention (para. 1.18) to those circumstances where far greater harm was caused than was intended or was within the control of the offender; in those circumstances, a court will be looking to assess the extent to which that level of harm could have been foreseen.

A court is sometimes asked to approach the assessment of the seriousness of an offence on the basis that offences of this type have become particularly prevalent and so normal sentencing practice should change. Again this is addressed by the Sentencing Guidelines Council in its guideline on seriousness. It states that, whilst seriousness should be assessed on the basis of the harm and culpability of the particular offence rather than as part of a "collective social harm", it is nonetheless legitimate for the overall approach to sentencing levels for particular offences to be directed by their cumulative effect. Where there are exceptional local circumstances which suggest that prevalence should influence sentencing levels, the Council asserts that, as the pivotal issue will be the harm being caused to the community, "It is essential that sentencers both have supporting evidence from an external source (for example the local Criminal Justice Board) to justify claims that a particular crime is prevalent in their area and are satisfied that there is a compelling need to treat the offence more seriously than elsewhere." It is emphasised that sentencing patterns should return to normal once the exceptional circumstances cease to exist. This was reinforced by the Court of Appeal in *Oosthuizen* [2006] 1 Cr.App.R.(S.) 73. In this case, a judge had been dealing with an offence of street robbery and formed the view that this was becoming a prevalent offence in the area and sentenced accordingly. The attention of the judge had not been drawn to the guideline. The Court of Appeal disapproved of the approach of the judge (and an earlier authority of the Court of Appeal) emphasising in strong terms the legal obligation to have regard to a guideline issued by the Sentencing Guidelines Council. The Court stated:

> "15. … If, in any particular town or city, there are statistics available to the Crown Prosecution Service, the Local Criminal Justice Board or otherwise, which demonstrate a prevalence greater than that nationally of a particular type of offence, those statistics can and should be made available to the Court.
>
> 16. In the absence of such statistics or other evidence identifying particular prevalence in a particular area, a judge, however experienced in a particular area, should not make the assumption that prevalence of that offence is more marked in the area with which he is familiar than it is nationally. Such an assumption will be particularly hazardous when, as in the present case, there is either a guideline decision of this Court, or a guideline issued by the Sentencing Guidelines Council, or specific guidance in relation to particular offences, intended to be of national application. *Lobban*, as the Lord Chief Justice pointed out, was not, strictly speaking, a guideline case, but it did afford guidance which was intended to be of general application. It follows that the learned judge was not entitled to impose, for reasons of local deterrence, a sentence higher than would otherwise be appropriate for that particular kind of offence by reference to national guidance."

The Court of Appeal has found it necessary to remind courts of this approach. In *Lanham and Willis* [2008] EWCA Crim. 2450 the defendants had been found in possession of 12 lengths of lead which they admitted to stealing from the roof of a building. At the Crown Court, in imposing sentence, the Judge had indicated that there had been a spate of such thefts in the locality and a deterrent sentence was necessary. On appeal, attention was drawn to the judgment in *Oosthuizen* (above) and to the guidelines stating that it was essential both that sentencers had supporting evidence from an external source to justify any claim that a particular crime was prevalent and that the court was satisfied that there was a "compelling need" to treat the offence more seriously than elsewhere. However experienced the court was, assumptions should not be made in the absence of statistical or other evidence.

An example of the response to crimes believed to be prevalent nationally can be seen in the decision of the Court of Appeal in *Povey* [2008] EWCA Crim. 1261. Considerable public concern was being expressed about the possession and use of knives. In its judgment, the Court of Appeal noted the extent of possession and use and the harm caused. For the time being, it was stated that a court should focus on the sentencing purposes of reduction of crime (including by deterrence) and public protection. Accordingly, the *Magistrates' Court Sentencing Guidelines* should normally be applied towards the top end of the sentencing range. No time limit was set. In fact, those guidelines already provided for custodial sentences in most circumstances for simple possession of a knife since having a particularly dangerous weapon is an aggravating factor which would justify an increase from the starting point for all offensive weapons (a high community order). Generally, a knife could be expected to be found to be "particularly dangerous" in comparison with other weapons likely to be prosecuted under these provisions.

Guideline: Overarching Principles: Seriousness

F. PREVALENCE

1.38 The seriousness of an individual case should be judged on its own dimensions of harm and culpability rather than as part of a collective social harm. It is legitimate for the overall approach to sentencing levels for particular offences to be guided by their cumulative effect. However, it would be wrong to further penalise individual offenders by increasing sentence length for committing an individual offence of that type. **22–6**

1.39 There may be exceptional local circumstances that arise which may lead a court to decide that prevalence should influence sentencing levels. The pivotal issue in such cases will be the harm being caused to the community. It is essential that sentencers both have supporting evidence from an external source (for example the local Criminal Justice Board) to justify claims that a particular crime is prevalent in their area and are satisfied that there is a compelling need to treat the offence more seriously than elsewhere.

The key factor in determining whether sentencing levels should be enhanced in response to prevalence will be the level of harm being caused in the locality. Enhanced sentences should be exceptional and in response to exceptional circumstances. Sentencers must sentence within the sentencing guidelines once the prevalence has been addressed.

Criminal Justice Act 2003, s.143

Determining the seriousness of an offence

143.—(1) In considering the seriousness of any offence, the court must consider the offender's culpability in committing the offence and any harm which the offence caused, was intended to cause or might forseeably have caused. **22–7**

(2) In considering the seriousness of an offence ("the current offence") committed by an offender who has one or more previous convictions, the court must treat each previous conviction as an aggravating factor if (in the case of that conviction) the court considers that it can reasonably be so treated having regard, in particular, to—

(a) the nature of the offence to which the conviction relates and its relevance to the current offence, and

(b) the time that has elapsed since the conviction.

(3) In considering the seriousness of any offence committed while the offender was on bail, the court must treat the fact that it was committed in those circumstances as an aggravating factor.

(4) Any reference in subsection (2) to a previous conviction is to be read as a reference to—

(a) a previous conviction by a court in the United Kingdom, [...][

(aa) a previous conviction by a court in another member State of a relevant offence under the law of that State,][

(b) a previous conviction of a service offence within the meaning of the *Armed Forces Act* 2006 ("conviction" here including anything that under section 376(1) and (2) of that Act is to be treated as a conviction) [, or]][

(c) a finding of guilt in respect of a member State service offence.][

(5) Subsections (2) and (4) do not prevent the court from treating—

(a) a previous conviction by a court outside both the United Kingdom and any other member State, or

(b) a previous conviction by a court in any member State (other than the United Kingdom) of an offence which is not a relevant offence,

as an aggravating factor in any case where the court considers it appropriate to do so.

(6) For the purposes of this section—

(a) an offence is "relevant" if the offence would constitute an offence under the law of any part of the United Kingdom if it were done in that part at the time of the conviction of the defendant for the current offence,

(b) "member State service offence" means an offence which—

(i) was the subject of proceedings under the service law of a member State other than the United Kingdom, and

(ii) would constitute an offence under the law of any part of the United Kingdom, or a service offence (within the meaning of the *Armed Forces Act* 2006), if it were done in any part of the United Kingdom, by a member of Her Majesty's forces, at the time of the conviction of the defendant for the current offence,

(c) "Her Majesty's forces" has the same meaning as in the *Armed Forces Act* 2006, and

(d) "service law", in relation to a member State other than the United Kingdom, means the law governing all or any of the naval, military or air forces of that State.]

22–8 A court must take into account two aspects directly relevant to the offence itself—the culpability of the offender and the harm which was caused, intended or could have been caused. No guidance is given in the Act as to different types of harm or the people by whom the harm has been/could have been suffered. A person damaging property in a minor way as part of a campaign by activists against certain (lawful) activity may be playing a part in a chain of events that causes serious financial harm to the country as a whole by deterring inward investment. To incorporate that level of harm is likely to be seen as stretching the chain too far. However, those sentenced for importing illegal drugs will be sentenced on the basis of the harm those drugs will have the potential to do to people far removed in the chain of events from the importer. Perhaps the link then is generally the extent to which the harm is an inevitable consequence of the conduct.

A more radical requirement is set out in s.143(2). There has long been an issue about the significance of previous convictions given the obligation to ensure that a sentence is not greater than is commensurate with the seriousness of the offence. This provision seeks to circumvent that by causing a previous conviction to aggravate the seriousness of the current offence, presumably because it influences the decision as to culpability.

II. ESTABLISHMENT OF SENTENCING GUIDELINES COUNCIL AND SENTENCING COUNCIL

22–9 Since its establishment in 2004, the Sentencing Guidelines Council issued guidelines for many of the most common offences and issues faced by a magistrates' court when imposing sentence. Part of the aim of the Council was to produce guidelines that are readily accessible and this has been seen in the publication of revised Magistrates' Court Sentencing Guidelines in May 2008. Most of the important information relating to sentencing in a magistrates' court can be found in the guidelines but reference may still need to be made to the full offence guidelines where more detail is required concerning issues relating to a specific offence. From April 2010, a new Sentencing Council has taken responsibility for those guidelines and guidelines issued by the SGC are deemed to have been made by the council.

The first guideline issued by the Council relates to offences of assault sentenced on or after June 13, 2011 and replaces an earlier Sentencing Guidelines Council guideline. Many of the offences included are triable either way or summary only and so the relevant entries in the *Magistrates' Court Sentencing Guidelines* are also replaced.

As well as dealing with individual offences, the guidelines deal with more general issues such as the extent of the reduction in sentence following a guilty plea and the significance of previous convictions. The Council has also published information about sentencing. In April 2005 (and subsequent revisions), the Council published a compendium of guideline judgments of the Court of Appeal designed to give readier access to important sentencing decisions pending the publication of its own guidelines. In July 2008, an addendum was published summarising the statutory provisions and associated case law concerning the application of the "dangerous offender" provisions to both youths and adults. Whilst not of direct application in a magistrates' court, these provisions may occasionally have an impact when a court is determining whether a case should be sentenced in the Crown Court. These provisions have been changed substantially by the *Criminal Justice and Immigration Act* 2008. Information on the Council and any guidelines can be found at *www.sentencingcouncil.judiciary.gov.uk*.

Judicial consideration concerning the effect of a guideline was given in *Oosthuizen* [2006] 1 Cr.App.R.(S.) 73. In an earlier case, a constitution of the Court of Appeal had expressed doubt about a part of the Council guideline on Seriousness. However, this constitution (headed by the Vice President) drew attention to the legal obligation to have regard to any guideline whilst retaining the discretion to reach a different conclusion in relation to the case under consideration.

> "Individual judges and indeed constitutions of this Court may, from time to time, disagree with some aspect of a guideline issued by the Sentencing Guidelines Council. But it is not open to them to disregard what the Council says. On the contrary, by virtue of the statutory duty imposed by [*Criminal Justice Act* 2003] section 172, they must have regard to guidelines so issued. It does not necessarily follow that in every case a guideline will be followed. As was pointed out by Lord Woolf CJ in *Last & Ors* [2005] EWCA Crim. 106, para. 16: 'The fact that every Court must have regard to the relevant guideline does not mean that it has to be followed.'"

Similar sentiments were expressed in *Bowering* [2006] 2 Cr.App.R.(S.) 10 and in *Gisbourne* [2005] EWCA Crim. 2491. Where no definitive guideline exists, a court may be referred to the advice of the Sentencing Advisory Panel. In certain circumstances, and with due recognition of the status of such documents (including the fact that the definitive guideline may be different), this is acceptable. In *R. (W.) v. Brent Youth Court* [2006] EWHC Admin 95; (2006) 170 J.P. 198, the DC stated that "In cases where there is no guidance from the Sentencing Guidelines Council it is permissible and helpful for the court to consider any relevant publication of the Sentencing Advisory Panel". In *R. (DPP) v. Camberwell Youth Court* [2005] 1 Cr.App.R. 6, Kennedy L.J. said "that, although the Sentencing Advisory Panel's advice has no legal force, as it has yet to be acted upon, it is helpful as an indication of a considered response to a sentencing problem. In short, providing that the court recognises that the advice does not carry legal force, it is legitimate and helpful to consider such a publication." However, where there are existing guidelines it is unlikely that a court will be expected to act upon proposals that are made as part of the process of developing a definitive guideline. In *Valentas* [2010] EWCA Crim. 200, a court was urged to take account of proposals made in a Consultation Paper issued by the Sentencing Advisory Panel when sentencing a drug courier; for a limited group of couriers, the Consultation Paper proposed an approach significantly different from that derived from Court of Appeal guideline judgments. Citing the authorities noted above, the Court of Appeal identified a "very clear principle" emerging from them—whilst proposals may be of considerable interest as part of the "background which sentencing judges may wish to bear in mind, they are not guidance and provide no justification for the Court of Appeal to interfere with a decision based on an existing guideline. That would be to prejudge the outcome of a carefully structured process".

In relation to guidelines issued (or deemed to be issued) by the Sentencing Council, the definition of what constituted a departure from a guideline is different from that which applied in relation to guidelines issued by the Sentencing Guidelines Council. A court may depart from a Sentencing Council guideline when it is in the interests of justice to do so. Reasons for a departure need to be given where a sentence is imposed outside the "offence range" for the offence, that is the range from the bottom of the range for the least serious category set out within the guidelines to the top of the range for the most serious category. *Criminal Justice Act* 2003, s.174(2)

Typically, an offence guideline issued by the Sentencing Guidelines Council will apply to a first time offender who has been convicted after pleading not guilty; the Sentencing Council has taken a slightly different approach although, in practice, it is unlikely that any difference will be seen. The Council has provided that its guideline applies to all defendants (whether or not there are any previous convictions) with any relevant previous convictions becoming a factor which is taken into account at the second stage of the assessment of seriousness at which point it might increase seriousness. In order to avoid double counting, it is inevitable that the starting point identified in Stage 1 of the process will, therefore, be based on an offender with no qualifying convictions as in guidelines issued by the Sentencing Guidelines Council. Guidelines typically identify three types of activity (Sentencing Guidelines Council) or three categories based on relative culpability and harm (Sentencing Council) falling within the broad definition of the offence and then provide a starting point and a range. In order to assist in the consistent interpretation of these terms, the Sentencing Guidelines Council and Sentencing Advisory Panel have published definitions:

MEANING OF "RANGE", "STARTING POINT" AND "FIRST TIME OFFENDER" WITHIN SENTENCING GUIDELINES COUCIL GUIDELINES

A Council guideline is generally for a *first time offender* convicted after a trial. It commonly provides a *starting point* based on an assessment of the seriousness of the offence and a *range* within which sentence will normally fall for most cases.

A clear, consistent understanding of each of these terms is essential and the Council and the Sentencing Advisory Panel have agreed the meanings set out in paragraphs 1(a)–(d) below.

They are set out in a format that follows the structured approach to a sentencing decision which identifies first those aspects that affect the assessment of the seriousness of the offence, then those aspects that form part of personal mitigation and, finally, any reduction for a guilty plea.

In practice, the boundaries between these stages will not always be as clear cut but the underlying principles will remain the same.

In accordance with section 174 of the *Criminal Justice Act* 2003, a court is obliged to "*state in open court, in ordinary language and in general terms, its reasons for deciding on the sentence passed*".

In particular, "*where guidelines indicate that a sentence of a particular kind, or within a particular range, would normally be appropriate and the sentence is of a different kind, or is outside that range*" the court must give its reasons for imposing a sentence of a different kind or outside the range.

Assessing the seriousness of the offence

—1.

(a) The guidelines apply to an offence that can be committed in a variety of circumstances with different levels of seriousness. It will apply to a **first time offender** who has been convicted after a trial (that is, any case in which there has not been a guilty plea). Within the guidelines, a **first time offender** is a person who does not have a conviction which, by virtue of section 143(2) of the *Criminal Justice Act* 2003, must be treated as an aggravating factor.

(b) As an aid to consistency of approach, a guideline will describe a number of types of activity which would fall within the broad definition of the offence. These will be set out in a column generally headed "type/nature of activity" or "examples of nature of activity".

(c) The expected approach is for a court to identify the description that most nearly matches the particular facts of the offence for which sentence is being imposed. This will identify a **starting point** from which the sentencer can depart to reflect aggravating or mitigating factors affecting the seriousness of the offence (beyond those contained in the description itself) to reach a **provisional sentence**.

(d) The range is the bracket into which the **provisional sentence** will normally fall after having regard to factors which aggravate or mitigate the seriousness of the offence. The particular circumstances may, however, make it appropriate that the provisional sentence falls outside the range.

2. Where the offender has previous convictions which aggravate the seriousness of the current offence, that may take the **provisional sentence** beyond the **range** given particularly where there are significant other aggravating factors present.

Personal Mitigation

—3. Once the **provisional sentence** has been identified (by reference to the factors affecting the seriousness of the offence), the court will take into account any relevant factors of **personal** mitigation. Again, this may take the provisional sentence outside the range.

Reduction for guilty plea

—4. Where there has been a guilty plea, any reduction attributable to that plea will be applied to the sentence at this stage. This reduction may take the sentence below the **range** provided.

III. FUNCTION OF THE PROSECUTION IN RELATION TO SENTENCE

There is a substantial difference in the range and the volume of the workload between the Crown Court and the magistrates' courts. Not every prosecutor in a magistrates' court is a solicitor or barrister; not only do lay presenters appear on behalf of the Crown Prosecution Service, but also other prosecutors can authorise suitable individuals to prosecute on their behalf. In addition, the volume of cases and the speed of throughput is much greater in a magistrates' court and the existing guidelines are published more systematically. **22–10**

The Code for Crown Prosecutors makes specific provision for the role of the Crown Prosecutor in relation to sentence. It states:

The Prosecutors' Role in Sentencing

11.1 Sentencing is a decision for the court, but prosecutors have a duty to offer assistance to the sentencing court in reaching its decision as to the appropriate sentence by drawing the court's attention to the following factors:

(a) any aggravating or mitigating factors disclosed by the prosecution case;
(b) any Victim Personal Statement;
(c) where appropriate, evidence of the impact of the offending on a community;
(d) any statutory provisions or sentencing guidelines which may assist;
(e) any relevant statutory provisions relating to ancillary orders (such as anti-social behaviour orders).

11.2 Prosecutors may also offer assistance to the court by making submissions, in the light of all the above factors, as to the sentencing range within which the current offence falls.

11.3 In all complex cases or where there is the potential for misunderstanding, the prosecutor must set out in writing the aggravating and mitigating factors that he or she will outline when informing the court of the case in the sentencing hearing. In all other cases, this approach should be considered and undertaken if it will be of benefit to the court or the public to understand the case.

11.4 It is the duty of the prosecutor to apply for compensation and ancillary orders, such as anti-social behaviour orders and confiscation orders, in all appropriate cases. When considering which ancillary orders to apply for, the prosecutor must always have regard to the victim's needs, including the question of their future protection.

11.5 Prosecutors should challenge any assertion made by the defence in mitigation that is inaccurate, misleading or derogatory. If the defence persists in the assertion, and it appears relevant to the sentence, the court should be invited to hear evidence to determine the facts and sentence accordingly.

11.6 Prosecutors must comply with the "Attorney General's Guidelines on the Acceptance of Pleas and the Prosecutor's Role in the Sentencing Exercise" which set out in greater detail the extent of prosecutor's duties and role in the sentencing process.

This part of the Code follows the line of authority set out *post* which is also summarised in the Attorney General's guidance referred to in para. 11.6 of the Code. This guidance can be found at *www.attorneygeneral.gov.uk/publications*. This guidance emphasises the important role of the prosecutor "in protecting the victim's interest in the criminal justice process, not least in the acceptance of pleas and the sentencing exercise": at [A1]. The requirement to draw to the attention of the court any "sentencing guidelines which may assist" is likely to be influenced greatly in practice by differences between a magistrates' court and the Crown Court, not least the presence of the legal adviser to the magistrates and the existence of definitive guidelines especially the *Magistrates' Court Sentencing Guidelines*. The compendium of existing guideline decisions referred to *ante* should also assist busy advocates to find a relevant authority: see *www.sentencingcouncil.judiciary.gov.uk*.

Further legal guidance is provided under the heading *Sentencing General Principles* (revised in March 2010): *http://www.cps.gov.uk/legal/s_to_u/sentencing_-_general_principles/*. This includes information regarding *Newton* hearings, Victim Personal Statements and reduction for a Guilty Plea.

22–11 In *Att.-Gen.'s Reference (No.52 of 2003)* (*Webb*) [2003] EWCA Crim. 3731 it was emphasised that prosecuting counsel had a duty to draw relevant guideline cases to the attention of the court (see now para. 11.1 of the code at 22.10 above) and that it would be wrong for a judge to suggest that counsel should not do his duty. Prosecuting counsel, it was said, should be meticulous in drawing relevant guidelines to the attention of the judge and in having copies available if required. Whilst this is a desirable situation also in the magistrates' court, it is legitimate to expect the legal adviser to the magistrates to fulfil that function in normal circumstances. However, prosecution and defence advocates should always be aware of the existence of relevant guidance and be prepared to draw it to the attention of the court should the court seem to be unaware of it.

22–12 Whilst Prosecution Counsel should be able to present the court with sufficient information about the offence to enable the court to assess its seriousness, it is not part of the function to influence the court with regard to that assessment. However, if a defendant is not legally represented it is proper to inform the judge of any mitigating circumstances about which counsel is instructed.

As noted in para. 11.5 of the code at 22.10 above (and in Part E of the Attorney General's Guidance) counsel should draw the attention of the Court to any assertion of material fact put forward in mitigation which prosecuting counsel believes to be untrue; if the defence persist in this assertion, prosecuting counsel should invite the Court to consider requiring the issue to be determined through a *Newton* hearing (see *post*, § 25–2): para. 10.8(e) of the *Code of Conduct of the Bar, s.3 Written Standards for the Conduct of Professional Work* (8th Edn.). For defence counsel, the same rules apply to mitigation as to any other court proceedings. Defence counsel should notify the prosecution of anything which counsel is instructed to submit in mitigation which casts aspersions on the conduct or character of a victim or witness in the case. The purpose of this is to give prosecuting counsel sufficient opportunity to consider whether or not to challenge these assertions. For defence counsel, the same rules apply to mitigation as to any other court proceedings. Defence counsel should notify the prosecution of anything which counsel is instructed to submit in mitigation which casts aspersions on the conduct or character of a victim or witness in the case. The purpose of this is to give prosecuting counsel sufficient opportunity to consider whether or not to challenge these assertions.

Paragraph 708(g) of the *Code of Conduct of the Bar* provides that a barrister must not make statements or ask questions which are merely scandalous or intended or calculated only to vilify insult or annoy either a witness or some other person. The barrister must also, if possible, avoid naming in open court a third party whose conduct would be impugned thereby (para. 708(h)).

The obligations were re-emphasised with some force by the Court of Appeal (Crim. **22–13**
Div.) in *Cain and others* [2006] EWCA Crim. 3233. Giving the judgment of the court, Lord Phillips C.J. stated:

> "It is not satisfactory for a prosecuting advocate, having secured a conviction, to sit back and leave sentencing to the defence. Nor can an advocate, when appearing for the prosecution for the purpose of sentence on a plea of guilty, limit the assistance that he provides to the court to the outlining of the facts and details of the defendant's previous convictions.
>
> The advocate for the prosecution should always be ready to assist the court by drawing attention to any statutory provisions that govern the court's sentencing powers. It is the duty of the prosecuting advocate to ensure that the judge does not, through inadvertence, impose a sentence that is outside his powers. The advocate for the prosecution should also be in a position to offer to draw the judge's attention to any relevant sentencing guidelines or guideline decisions of this court."

This obligation applies also to the defence advocate. The Court recognised the judge's duty to pass a lawful sentence but noted that advocates may well have had more time to prepare a case than the judge. Lord Phillips stated:

> "It is of course the duty of a judge to impose a lawful sentence, but sentencing has become a complex matter and a judge will often not see the papers very long before the hearing and does not have the time for preparation that advocates should enjoy. In these circumstances a judge relies on the advocates to assist him with sentencing. It is unacceptable for advocates not to ascertain and be prepared to assist the judge with the legal restrictions on the sentence that he can impose on their clients."

Although the judgment states that it applies equally to a magistrates' court, whilst advocates need to be aware of the guidance and law as they apply to a magistrates' court and to be prepared to draw them to the attention of the court, as pointed out *ante* there will also be a legal adviser (justices' clerk or assistant justices' clerk) present who can be expected to fulfil that function in normal circumstances. In addition, the *Criminal Procedure Rules* 2011 (see Appendix G–1) states the overriding objective of the rules that criminal cases be dealt with justly. This includes ensuring that appropriate information is available to the court when sentence is considered: r.1(2)(f).

The *Criminal Proceedings and Investigations Act* 1996, ss.58 to 60 give the court power to restrict the reporting of false or irrelevant assertions made during a speech in mitigation. Where there are substantial grounds for concluding that an assertion is both derogatory and either false or irrelevant to sentence (s.58(4)), the court may make an order which makes it an offence to publish that assertion: ss.59 and 60. An order may be made before the court determines sentences (s.58(7)), in which case it ceases on sentence being passed, or it may be made as soon as reasonably practicable after sentence in which case, unless earlier revoked, it will cease to be effective after 12 months: s.58(8).

Criminal Procedure and Investigations Act 1996, ss.58–60

Orders in respect of certain assertions

58.—(1) This section applies where a person has been convicted of an offence and a speech **22–14**
in mitigation is made by him or on his behalf before—

(a) a court determining what sentence should be passed on him in respect of the offence, or

Part IV

(b) a magistrates' court determining whether he should be committed to the Crown Court for sentence.

(2) This section also applies where a sentence has been passed on a person in respect of an offence and a submission relating to the sentence is made by him or on his behalf before—

(a) a court hearing an appeal against or reviewing the sentence, or

(b) a court determining whether to grant leave to appeal against the sentence.

(3) Where it appears to the court that there is a real possibility that an order under subsection (8) will be made in relation to the assertion, the court may make an order under subsection (7) in relation to the assertion.

(4) Where there are substantial grounds for believing—

(a) that an assertion forming part of the speech or submission is derogatory to a person's character (for instance, because it suggests that his conduct is or has been criminal, immoral or improper), and

(b) that the assertion is false or that the facts asserted are irrelevant to the sentence,

the court may make an order under subsection (8) in relation to the assertion.

(5) An order under subsection (7) or (8) must not be made in relation to an assertion if it appears to the court that the assertion was previously made—

(a) at the trial at which the person was convicted of the offence, or

(b) during any other proceedings relating to the offence.

(6) Section 59 has effect where a court makes an order under subsection (7) or (8).

(7) An order under this subsection—

(a) may be made at any time before the court has made a determination with regard to sentencing;

(b) may be revoked at any time by the court;

(c) subject to paragraph (b), shall cease to have effect when the court makes a determination with regard to sentencing.

(8) An order under this subsection—

(a) may be made after the court has made a determination with regard to sentencing, but only if it is made as soon as is reasonably practicable after the making of the determination;

(b) may be revoked at any time by the court;

(c) subject to paragraph (b), shall cease to have effect at the end of the period of 12 months beginning with the day on which it is made;

(d) may be made whether or not an order has been made under subsection (7) with regard to the case concerned.

(9) For the purposes of subsection (7) and (8) the court makes a determination with regard to sentencing—

(a) when it determines what sentence should be passed (where this section applies by virtue of subsection (1)(a);

(b) when it determines whether the person should be committed to the Crown Court for sentence (where this section applies by virtue of subsection (1)(b));

(c) when it determines what the sentence should be (where this section applies by virtue of subsection (2)(a));

(d) when it determines whether to grant leave to appeal (where this section applies by virtue of subsection (2)(b).

Restriction on reporting of assertions

22–15 **59.**—(1) Where a court makes an order under section 58(7) or (8) in relation to any assertion, at any time when the order has effect the assertion must not—

(a) be published in Great Britain in a written publication available to the public, or

(b) be included in a relevant programme for reception in Great Britain.

(2) In this section—

"relevant programme" means a programme included in a programme service, within the meaning of the *Broadcasting Act* 1990;

"written publication" includes a film, a soundtrack and any other record in permanent form but does not include an indictment or other document prepared for use in particular legal proceedings.

(3) For the purposes of this section an assertion is published or included in a programme if the material published or included—

(a) names the person about whom the assertion is made or, without naming him, contains enough to make it likely that members of the public will identify him as the person about whom it is made, and

(b) reproduces the actual wording of the matter asserted or contains its substance.

Reporting of assertions: offences

60.—(1) If an assertion is published or included in a relevant programme in contravention of section 59, each of the following persons is guilty of an offence— **22–16**

(a) in the case of publication in a newspaper or periodical, any proprietor, any editor and any publisher of the newspaper or periodical;

(b) in the case of publication in any other form, the person publishing the assertion;

(c) in the case of an assertion included in a relevant programme, any body corporate engaged in providing the service in which the programme is included and any person having functions in relation to the programme corresponding to those of an editor of a newspaper.

(2) A person guilty of an offence under this section is liable on summary conviction to a fine of an amount not exceeding level 5 on the standard scale.

(3) Where a person is charged with an offence under this section it is a defence to prove that at the time of the alleged offence—

(a) he was not aware, and neither suspected nor had reason to suspect, that an order under section 58(7) or (8) had effect at that time, or

(b) he was not aware, and neither suspected nor had reason to suspect, that the publication or programme in question was of, or (as the case may be) included, the assertion in question.

(4) Where an offence under this section committed by a body corporate is proved to have been committed with the consent or connivance of, or to be attributable to any neglect on the part of—

(a) a director, manager, secretary or other similar officer of the body corporate, or

(b) a person purporting to act in any such capacity,

he as well as the body, corporate is guilty of the offence and liable to be proceeded against and punished accordingly.

(5) In relation to a body corporate whose affairs are managed by its members "director" in subsection (4) means a member of the body corporate.

(6) Subsection (2) and (3) of section 59 apply for the purposes of this section as they apply for the purposes of that.

IV. LEGAL REPRESENTATION

There is no obligation on a person to be legally represented (although there are certain things that an unrepresented defendant cannot do). However, the court must not impose a custodial sentence on an offender who is not legally represented unless an opportunity to apply for legal representation at public expense has been given and not taken, an application has been refused because of the offender's financial resources or, though taken, has been withdrawn on the ground of the conduct of the defendant: *PCC(S)A* 2000, s.83(1)–(3). **22–17**

For magistrates' courts, this additional requirement applies where a defendant aged 21 or over on conviction who is liable to receive imprisonment has not previously been so sentenced and is not legally represented: s.83(1) and (2). For defendants aged 18–20 on conviction, it applies regardless of whether a custodial sentence has previously been imposed—the only criterion is lack of legal representation: s.83(2).

Powers of Criminal Courts (Sentencing) Act 2000, s.83

Restriction on imposing custodial sentences on persons not legally represented

83.—(1) A magistrates' court on summary conviction, or the Crown Court on committal for sentence or on conviction on indictment, shall not pass a sentence of imprisonment on a person who— **22–18**

(a) is not legally represented in that court, and

Part IV

(b) has not been previously sentenced to that punishment by a court in any part of the United Kingdom,

unless he is a person to whom subsection (3) below applies.

(2) A magistrates' court on summary conviction, or the Crown Court on committal for sentence or on conviction on indictment, shall not—

(a) pass a sentence of detention under section 90 or 91 below,

(b) pass a sentence of custody for life under section 93 or 94 below,

(c) pass a sentence of detention in a young offender institution, or

(d) make a detention and training order,

on or in respect of a person who is not legally represented in that court unless he is a person to whom subsection (3) below applies.

(3) This subsection applies to a person if either—

(a) he was granted a right to representation funded by the Legal Services Commission as part of the Criminal Defence Service but the right was withdrawn because of his conduct or because it appeared that his financial resources were such that he was not eligible to be granted such a right;

(aa) he applied for such representation and the application was refused because it appeared that his financial resources were such that he was not eligible to be granted a right to it; or

(b) having been informed of his right to apply for such representation and having had the opportunity to do so, he refused or failed to apply.

(4) For the purposes of this section a person is to be treated as legally represented in a court if, but only if, he has the assistance of counsel or a solicitor to represent him in the proceedings in that court at some time after he is found guilty and before he is sentenced.

(5) For the purposes of subsection (1)(b) above a previous sentence of imprisonment which has been suspended and which has not taken effect under section 119 below or under section 19 of the *Treatment of Offenders Act (Northern Ireland)* 1968 shall be disregarded.

(6) In this section "sentence of imprisonment" does not include a committal for contempt of court or any kindred offence.

V. FUNCTION OF THE LEGAL ADVISER (COURT CLERK) IN RELATION TO SENTENCE

22–19 The *Consolidated Criminal Practice Direction*, V.55 (clerk retiring with justices, see Appendix F, F–68) makes it clear that the justices' clerk is responsible for the advice tendered to justices in the area either directly or through a legal adviser. Job titles will vary but the term "legal adviser" has generally superseded that of "court clerk". The term "assistant to a Justices' Clerk" seems to be becoming the normal legal term following the implementation of the provisions in the *Courts Act* 2003 creating a unified court administration for the Crown Court and magistrates' courts. Both Direction 55 and the Legal Adviser competences (published by the Justices' Clerks' Society) make it clear that sentencing advice should be given and that it is the responsibility of the legal adviser to do so whether or not that advice is requested. Advice on sentencing will be required:

— where the plea before venue procedure is adopted, and the court is unsure of its sentencing powers;

— when the court is considering the issue of mode of trial and it needs to decide whether the sentencing powers would be sufficient should the defendant be convicted; and

— when passing sentence.

Direction 55.3 provides that it is the responsibility of the legal adviser to provide the justices with any advice they require to properly perform their functions whether or not the justices have requested that advice on, amongst other matters, the range of penalties available, the relevant decisions of the superior courts or other guidelines, other issues relevant to the matter before the court and the appropriate decision making structure to be applied in any given case. Paragraph 7 confirms that any legal advice given to justices other than in open court should clearly be stated to be provisional, and the adviser should subsequently repeat the substance of the advice in open court and give the parties an opportunity to make any representations they wish on that provisional advice. This procedure will ensure that any party can challenge the advice given where necessary.

VI. PRE-SENTENCE REPORTS

A. PROBATION SERVICE NATIONAL STANDARDS

(1) Legislative framework

The statutory provisions are complemented by national standards which set out the responsibilities of the offender manager, the nature and extent of contact required between the offender and the offender manager, sentence planning, enforcement and work with victims of crime. An Appendix sets out the specifications for bail information reports, pre-sentence reports and drug rehabilitation requirement reviews and reports. The National Standards for the Management of Offenders were published in September 2007 and can be found at *www.noms.justice.gov.uk*. **22–20**

Criminal Justice Act 2003, ss.156–158

Pre-sentence reports and other requirements

156.—(1) In forming any such opinion as is mentioned in section 148(1) or (2)(b), section 152(2) or section 153(2), or in section 1(4)(b) or (c) of the *Criminal Justice and Immigration Act* 2008 (youth rehabilitation orders with intensive supervision and surveillance or fostering) a court must take into account all such information as is available to it about the circumstances of the offence or (as the case may be) of the offence and the offence or offences associated with it, including any aggravating or mitigating factors. **22–21**

(2) In forming any such opinion as is mentioned in section 148(2)(a), the court may take into account any information about the offender which is before it.

(3) Subject to subsection (4), a court must obtain and consider a pre-sentence report before—

(a) in the case of a custodial sentence, forming any such opinion as is mentioned in section 152(2), section 153(2), section 225(1)(b), section 226(1)(b), section 227(1)(b) or section 228(1)(b)(i), or

(b) in the case of a community sentence, forming any such opinion as is mentioned in section 148(1) or 2(b), or in section 1(4)(b) or (c) of the *Criminal Justice and Immigration Act* 2008, or any opinion as to the suitability for the offender of the particular requirement or requirements to be imposed by the community order or youth rehabilitation order.

(4) Subsection (3) does not apply if, in the circumstances of the case, the court is of the opinion that it is unnecessary to obtain a pre-sentence report.

(5) In a case where the offender is aged under 18, the court must not form the opinion mentioned in subsection (4) unless—

(a) there exists a previous pre-sentence report obtained in respect of the offender, and

(b) the court has had regard to the information contained in that report, or, if there is more than one such report, the most recent report.

(6) No custodial sentence or community sentence is invalidated by the failure of a court to obtain and consider a pre-sentence report before forming an opinion referred to in subsection (3), but any court on an appeal against such a sentence—

(a) must, subject to subsection (7), obtain a pre-sentence report if none was obtained by the court below, and

(b) must consider any such report obtained by it or by that court.

(7) Subsection (6)(a) does not apply if the court is of the opinion—

(a) that the court below was justified in forming an opinion that it was unnecessary to obtain a pre-sentence report, or

(b) that, although the court below was not justified in forming that opinion, in the circumstances of the case at the time it is before the court, it is unnecessary to obtain a pre-sentence report.

(8) In a case where the offender is aged under 18, the court must not form the opinion mentioned in subsection (7) unless—

(a) there exists a previous pre-sentence report obtained in respect of the offender, and

(b) the court has had regard to the information contained in that report, or, if there is more than one such report, the most recent report.

Additional requirements in case of mentally disordered offender

22–22 **157.**—(1) Subject to subsection (2), in any case where the offender is or appears to be mentally disordered, the court must obtain and consider a medical report before passing a custodial sentence other than one fixed by law.

(2) Subsection (1) does not apply if, in the circumstances of the case, the court is of the opinion that it is unnecessary to obtain a medical report.

(3) Before passing a custodial sentence other than one fixed by law on an offender who is or appears to be mentally disordered, a court must consider—

(a) any information before it which relates to his mental condition (whether given in a medical report, a pre-sentence report or otherwise), and

(b) the likely effect of such a sentence on that condition and on any treatment which may be available for it.

(4) No custodial sentence which is passed in a case to which subsection (1) applies is invalidated by the failure of a court to comply with that subsection, but any court on an appeal against such a sentence—

(a) must obtain a medical report if none was obtained by the court below, and

(b) must consider any such report obtained by it or by that court.

(5) In this section "mentally disordered", in relation to any person, means suffering from a mental disorder within the meaning of the *Mental Health Act* 1983 (c. 20).

(6) In this section "medical report" means a report as to an offender's mental condition made or submitted orally or in writing by a registered medical practitioner who is approved for the purposes of section 12 of the *Mental Health Act* 1983 by the Secretary of State as having special experience in the diagnosis or treatment of mental disorder.

(7) Nothing in this section is to be taken to limit the generality of section 156.

Meaning of "pre-sentence report"

22–23 **158.**—(1) In this Part "pre-sentence report" means a report which—

(a) with a view to assisting the court in determining the most suitable method of dealing with an offender, is made or submitted by an appropriate officer, and

(b) contains information as to such matters, presented in such manner, as may be prescribed by rules made by the Secretary of State.

(1A) Subject to any rules made under subsection (1)(b) and to subsection (1B), the court may accept a pre-sentence report given orally in open court.

(1B) But a pre-sentence report that—

(a) relates to an offender aged under 18, and

(b) is required to be obtained and considered before the court forms an opinion mentioned in section 156(3)(a),

must be in writing.

(2) In subsection (1) "an appropriate officer" means—

(a) where the offender is aged 18 or over, an officer of a local probation board, or an officer of a provider of probation services and

(b) where the offender is aged under 18, an officer of a local probation board, or an officer of a provider of probation services, a social worker of a local authority social services department or a member of a youth offending team.

(2) Assessment before sentence

Pre-sentence reports

22–24 The preparation of such a report will be in accordance with the Probation Circular

12/2007, which is effective from June 1, 2007 and the National Standards published in 2007.

There are three types of reports—standard delivery, fast delivery and oral reports. All are "pre-sentence reports" for the purposes of s.158 (see *ante*, § 22–23). Whilst a court has to be given the information needed to reach a sentencing decision, probation court officers can assist by advising the court of the report type most likely to best meet the need of the court.

The Circular states that an oral report is most suitable in low seriousness cases or where a court needs current information of the offender's progress against a sentence plan that already exists. Both the standard and fast delivery reports provide a fuller assessment. The fast delivery report will be based on OGRS and on an OASys risk of harm screening; the standard delivery report will be based on an OASys assessment. The practise of providing oral reports has been recognised in statute since the amendment to s.158, but written reports are mandatory for young offenders facing custody.

Probation court officers are reminded through the Circular both of the need to "engage proactively" with a court to identify those cases where no probation involvement is required and of the advantages of early identification (ideally pre-hearing) of those cases where a report may be required. Where a report proposes a Community Order or a Suspended Sentence Order, it should detail the proposed arrangements and the sentence plan objectives. Where a programme is part of the proposal, the report should confirm that the offender is eligible and suitable and that the programme is available. Where a drug rehabilitation requirement is proposed, the informed consent of the offender should be confirmed in the report.

The provisions of s.156 continue to require a court to obtain and consider a pre-sentence report in specified circumstances: s.156(3). That obligation may be avoided where the court considers that it is "unnecessary" to obtain such a report: s.156(4). Where the offender is under 18 years, the court may only reach that conclusion if there is a pre-sentence report already in existence which the court has considered: s.156(5). This is a little more restrictive than the previous provisions since it does not exempt a court dealing with an indictable only offence. **22–25**

Where an offender is mentally disordered, there is a presumption that, before imposing a custodial sentence, a magistrates' court will obtain a medical report: s.157. Such a report may again be written or oral and must be by a registered medical practitioner approved by the Secretary of State as having special experience in this area: s.157(6). See *post*, Ch.28.

Section 159 of the 2003 Act governs the disclosure of reports. The court must give a copy of the report to the offender or the offender's legal representative (s.159(2)(a)) and to the prosecutor (s.159(2)(c)) subject to the discretion of the court where that prosecutor is not of a description prescribed by order and the court considers that disclosure would be inappropriate (s.159(4)).

The *Pre-Sentence Report Disclosure (Description of Prosecutors) Order* 1998 (S.I. 1998 No.191) prescribes the following descriptions of prosecutors for the purposes of s.159(4): a Crown Prosecutor, any other person acting on behalf of the Crown Prosecution Service, a person acting on behalf of the Commissioners of Revenue and Customs, the Secretary of State for Social Security, or the Director of the Serious Fraud Office. For these prosecutors, the court does not have a discretion and must give the prosecutor a copy of the report. In relation to an offender who is under 18 years, the court must also give a copy to any parent or guardian present in court (s.159(2)(b)). However, where an offender is under 18 and the court considers that disclosure of anything in the report would be likely to create a risk of significant harm to the offender, then it can withhold a complete copy of the report from the offender and/or the parent or guardian. The expectation must be that it would be possible to provide a partial copy, though it is still necessary to provide a complete copy to the offender's legal representative. Where an offender under 18 years is a person for whom a local authority has parental responsibility and is either in the care of the local authority or provided with accommodation by the authority, a copy of the report is to be given to the authority not to the parent or guardian: s.159(6). **22–26**

22–27 In an ideal world, the report will be delivered to the court and to the parties at least a day ahead of the court hearing which will give all parties the opportunity to consider its contents. This can be done by electronic means but it is a process which must be under the control of the court—the report is to the court; the statutory obligation to ensure copies are given out is also placed on the court.

However, in reality, the report will almost always be delivered to a magistrates' court on the day of the hearing and there will be local arrangements to ensure that copies get to the appropriate parties.

A report is a key element in assisting a court to decide the appropriate sentence; it also enables the commencement of post sentence planning and so needs to be done thoroughly and effectively. At its heart is the assessment of the risk of the offender re-offending and an analysis of ways in which any risk can be reduced.

In a magistrates' court, the court that passes sentence will often consist of different people from those who ordered the pre-sentence report. It is highly desirable that the court ordering the report identifies clearly what it sees as the issues both in terms of the assessment of seriousness of the offences committed and in terms of the offender's personal circumstances. This approach has been endorsed by the Sentencing Guidelines Council in its guidance on the approach to the imposition of sentences under the 2003 Act (see *post*, § 22–38).

22–28 When proceeding to sentence after a PSR has been prepared, the normal sequence will be for the court to hear from the prosecutor setting out the circumstances of the offence and any previous criminal activity of the defendant, for the court to consider the pre-sentence report (though it may have taken an opportunity to read the report in advance of hearing from the prosecution) and then for the court to hear from the defendant or his legal representative.

After hearing from the prosecution and reading the report, the court may wish to consider certain issues in detail—for instance, the report may have suggested a community order with certain requirements which seem to the court to be highly commendable or the court may have taken a completely different view from the report writer on either sentence or the seriousness of certain events. It is quite legitimate to put the defence on notice before the court is addressed, perhaps by way of "The court has read the report and heard from the prosecution. On what we know so far we can see merit in following the proposal in the pre-sentence report—do you wish to persuade us otherwise?" Where there is agreement, that can readily be identified. Where there is disagreement, the defence knows clearly what the issues are for the court and this enables the defence advocate to address those issues directly rather than having to try to guess what the court is thinking.

(3) Pre-sentence reports

22–29 Regarding the facts of the offence given to the probation officer for the preparation of a PSR, the offender may sometimes give an account which differs from that given by the prosecution. Guidance as to the approach of the court was given in *Tolera* [1999] 1 Cr.App.R. 29. Whilst this part of the pre-sentence report would, of course, be read by the court, it was not ordinarily to form part of the factual basis for the passing of sentence. If a defendant wishes to rely on this part of the pre-sentence report for the purposes of sentence, the defence should make this clear, and the prosecution should be forewarned. The issue could then be resolved, if necessary by the calling of evidence.

Criminal Justice Act 2003, s.159

Disclosure of pre-sentence reports

22–30 **159.**—(1) This section applies where the court obtains a pre-sentence report, other than a report given orally in open court.

(2) Subject to subsections (3) and (4), the court must give a copy of the report—

(a) to the offender or his legal representative,

(b) if the offender is aged under 18, to any parent or guardian of his who is present in court, and

(c) to the prosecutor, that is to say, the person having the conduct of the proceedings in respect of the offence.

(3) If the offender is aged under 18 and it appears to the court that the disclosure to the offender or to any parent or guardian of his of any information contained in the report would be likely to create a risk of significant harm to the offender, a complete copy of the report need not be given to the offender or, as the case may be, to that parent or guardian.

(4) If the prosecutor is not of a description prescribed by order made by the Secretary of State, a copy of the report need not be given to the prosecutor if the court considers that it would be inappropriate for him to be given it.

(5) No information obtained by virtue of subsection (2)(c) may be used or disclosed otherwise than for the purpose of—

(a) determining whether representations as to matters contained in the report need to be made to the court, or

(b) making such representations to the court.

(6) In relation to an offender aged under 18 for whom a local authority have parental responsibility and who—

(a) is in their care, or

(b) is provided with accommodation by them in the exercise of any social services functions,

references in this section to his parent or guardian are to be read as references to that authority.

(7) In this section and section 160—

"harm" has the same meaning as in section 31 of the *Children Act* 1989 (c. 41);

"local authority" and "parental responsibility" have the same meanings as in that Act;

"social services functions", in relation to a local authority, has the meaning given by section 1A of the *Local Authority Social Services Act* 1970 (c. 42).

VII. OTHER REPORTS

Other reports may be obtained or are required to be obtained in certain other **22–31** circumstances. Whenever a report is obtained which is not a PSR, the court is obliged to ensure that a copy of the report is given to the offender or to his legal representative. Where the offender is under 18 years, s.160 sets out the power of the court to control or restrict distribution of such a report. These provisions mirror those in relation to pre-sentence reports in s.159 (see *ante*).

Criminal Justice Act 2003, s.160

Other reports of local probation boards, providers of probation services and members of youth offending teams

160.—(1) This section applies where— **22–32**

(a) a report by an officer of a local probation board, an officer of a provider of probation services or a member of a youth offending team is made to any court (other than a youth court) with a view to assisting the court in determining the most suitable method of dealing with any person in respect of an offence, and

(b) the report is not a pre-sentence report.

(2) Subject to subsection (3), the court must give a copy of the report—

(a) to the offender or his legal representative, and

(b) if the offender is aged under 18, to any parent or guardian of his who is present in court.

(3) If the offender is aged under 18 and it appears to the court that the disclosure to the offender or to any parent or guardian of his of any information contained in the report would be likely to create a risk of significant harm to the offender, a complete copy of the report need not be given to the offender, or as the case may be, to that parent or guardian.

(4) In relation to an offender aged under 18 for whom a local authority have parental responsibility and who—

(a) is in their care, or

(b) is provided with accommodation by them in the exercise of any social services functions, references in this section to his parent or guardian are to be read as references to that authority.

VIII. PRE-SENTENCE DRUG TESTING

22–33 Testing may take place whilst a person is in police detention (see *ante*, Ch.18) and there is a further power (not yet in force) to require a person to provide samples to find out whether there are traces of certain illegal drugs present in the body. The offender must be aged 14 years or over and the court must be considering a community sentence or a suspended sentence.

Criminal Justice Act 2003, s.161

Pre-sentence drug testing

22–34 **161.**—(1) Where a person is convicted of an offence and the court is considering passing a community sentence or a suspended sentence, it may make an order under subsection (2) for the purpose of ascertaining whether the offender has any specified Class A drug in his body.

(2) The order requires the offender to provide, in accordance with the order, samples of any description specified in the order.

(3) Where the offender has not attained the age of 17, the order must provide for the samples to be provided in the presence of an appropriate adult.

(4) If it is proved to the satisfaction of the court that the offender has, without reasonable excuse, failed to comply with the order it may impose on him a fine of an amount not exceeding level 4.

(5) In subsection (4) "level 4" means the amount which, in relation to a fine for a summary offence, is level 4 on the standard scale.

(6) The court may not make an order under subsection (2) unless it has been notified by the Secretary of State that the power to make such orders is exercisable by the court and the notice has not been withdrawn.

(8) In this section—

"appropriate adult", in relation to a person under the age of 17, means—

(a) his parent or guardian or, if he is in the care of a local authority or voluntary organisation, a person representing that authority or organisation, or

(c) if no person falling within paragraph (a) or (b) is available, any responsible person aged 18 or over who is not a police officer or a person employed by the police;

"specified Class A drug" has the same meaning as in Part 3 of the *Criminal Justice and Court Services Act* 2000 (c. 43).

See also ss.35, 36 of the *Mental Health Act* 1983 for the power to remand a mentally disordered offender to hospital for a report on his medical condition, see *post*, §§ 28–9—28–14.

IX. ADJOURNMENTS AFTER CONVICTION AND BEFORE SENTENCE

22–35 A court may need to adjourn the proceedings to allow for the preparation of reports. This power is contained in s.10(3) of the *Magistrates' Courts Act* 1980.

Magistrates' Courts Act 1980, s.10

Adjournment of trial

22–36 **10.**—(1) A magistrates' court may at any time, whether before or after beginning to try an information, adjourn the trial, and may do so, notwithstanding anything in this Act, when composed of a single justice.

(2) The court may when adjourning either fix the time and place at which the trial is to be resumed, or, unless it remands the accused, leave the time and place to be determined later by the court; but the trial shall not be resumed at that time and place unless the court is satisfied that the parties have had adequate notice thereof.

(3) A magistrates' court may, for the purpose of enabling inquiries to be made or of

determining the most suitable method of dealing with the case, exercise its power to adjourn after convicting the accused and before sentencing him or otherwise dealing with him; but, if it does so, the adjournment shall not be for more than 4 weeks at a time unless the court remands the accused in custody and, where it so remands him, the adjournment shall not be for more than 3 weeks at a time.

(3A) A youth court shall not be required to adjourn any proceedings for an offence at any stage by reason only of the fact—

(a) that the court commits the accused for trial for another offence; or

(b) that the accused is charged with another offence.

(4) On adjourning the trial of an information the court may remand the accused and, where the accused has attained the age of 18 years, shall do so if the offence is triable either way and—

(a) on the occasion on which the accused first appeared, or was brought, before the court to answer to the information he was in custody or, having been released on bail, surrendered to the custody of the court; or

(b) the accused has been remanded at any time in the course of proceedings on the information;

and, where the court remands the accused, the time fixed for the resumption of the trial shall be that at which he is required to appear or be brought before the court in pursuance of the remand or would be required to be brought before the court but for section 128(3A) below.

Where a magistrates' court adjourns for reports after conviction, what is said at the time can restrict the options of the court that passes sentence. Great care, therefore, needs to be taken to ensure that justice is done. The defendant should invariably be told clearly that he must not assume from the fact that the court has ordered an assessment or investigation, that he is likely to receive any particular form of sentence or that a custodial sentence is ruled out: *Chamberlain* (1995) 16 Cr.App.R.(S.) 473, CA. Guidance from the Sentencing Guidelines Council (*New Sentences: Criminal Justice Act 2003*) regarding the approach to sentence and to the ordering of a pre-sentence report demonstrates that more precision is required from a court in terms of both the purposes of sentencing in the case in question and the court's assessment of seriousness on the basis of the information before it. This may reduce the difficulties previously experienced because courts will be more precise about the issues relevant to sentence. **22–37**

Guideline: New Sentences: Criminal Justice Act 2003

Section 1—Community Sentences & Deferred Sentences

Part 1: Community Sentences

B. IMPOSING A COMMUNITY SENTENCE—THE APPROACH

(i) Requirements

(a) Information for Sentencers

1.1.15 In many cases, a pre-sentence report will be pivotal in helping a sentencer decide whether to impose a custodial sentence or whether to impose a community sentence and, if so, whether particular requirements, or combinations of requirements, are suitable for an individual offender. The court must always ensure (especially where there are multiple requirements) that the restriction on liberty placed on the offender is proportionate to the seriousness of the offence committed. The court must also consider the likely effect of one requirement on another, and that they do not place conflicting demands upon the offender. **22–38**

1.1.16 The Council supports the approach proposed by the Panel at paragraph 78 of its Advice that, having reached the provisional view that a community sentence is the most appropriate disposal, the sentencer should request a pre-sentence report, indicating which of the three sentencing ranges is relevant and the purpose(s) of sentencing that the package of requirements is required to fulfil. Usually the most helpful way for the court to do this would be to produce a written note for the report writer, copied on the court file. If it is known that the same tribunal and defence advocate will be present at the sentencing hearing and a probation officer is present in court when the request for a report is made, it may not be nec-

Part IV

essary to commit details of the request to writing. However, events may change during the period of an adjournment and it is good practice to ensure that there is a clear record of the request for the court. These two factors will guide the Probation Service in determining the nature and combination of requirements that may be appropriate and the onerousness and intensity of those requirements. A similar procedure should apply when ordering a pre-sentence report when a custodial sentence is being considered.

22–39 Where the court fails to warn the offender that all sentencing options remain open to the court, a legitimate expectation may be created in the mind of the offender that a non-custodial sentence may be imposed by the sentencing court. In *Inner London Crown Court, ex p. Mentesh* [2001] 1 Cr.App.R.(S.) 94, the offender submitted that the magistrates' actions in adjourning sentence to permit preparation of a further report in addition to the pre-sentence report had created a legitimate expectation that, if all went well, he would receive a non-custodial sentence and that the expectation should have been honoured by the sentencing court. The questions were:

a) whether, when the magistrates adjourned the case, they created an expectation on the part of the applicant that if all went well he would receive a non-custodial sentence,
b) whether it was legitimate, if there were such an expectation, that it should have been honoured by the sentencing court, and
c) whether anything had intervened to change the position.

22–40 Following *Gillam* (1980) 2 Cr.App.R.(S.) 267 and *Chamberlain* (*ante*), the Court held that this case was squarely within the situations envisaged by previous authorities as giving rise to a legitimate expectation of a non-custodial sentence and the appeal against sentence was allowed. In *Southampton Magistrates' Court, ex p. Sansome* [1999] 1 Cr.App.R.(S.) 112, CA, the offender was tried summarily, despite representations by the prosecutor that the case should be heard by the Crown Court. The matter was then adjourned for a pre-sentence report which recommended a probation order. After considering the pre-sentence report, the Court decided to commit the offender to the Crown Court for sentence. Upholding this order, Schiemann L.J. said that nothing in the case constituted the breaking of a promise by the court, hence the decision to commit to the Crown Court for sentence could not be interfered with. However, in circumstances in which a reasonable expectation of a non-custodial sentence is created in the mind of the offender, and a favourable report is received, then, should the magistrates' court commit the offender to the Crown Court for sentence, the Crown Court should not impose a custodial sentence: *Rennes* (1985) 7 Cr.App.R.(S.) 343, CA. See also *Gutteridge v. DPP* (1987) 9 Cr.App.R.(S.) 279, DC. The need for particular care when one bench is adjourning for sentence without reserving sentence to itself was emphasised again in *Thornton v. DPP* [2010] EWHC 346. The defendant had been charged with an offence under s.4 of the *Public Order Act* 1986. Having heard both the prosecution and the defence following a guilty plea, magistrates adjourned the case for a PSR indicating that a medium level community order was under consideration having concluded that the offence fell within the middle of the three levels of seriousness in the *Magistrates' Court Sentencing Guidelines*. When the case came for sentence, a District Judge considered that the offence was much more serious and, having heard argument, concluded that she was able to impose a custodial sentence, albeit suspended. That decision was upheld by the Divisional Court which agreed that the offence was far more serious and should have been placed in the most serious level in the guidelines. Since the decision to place it in the middle level was one no reasonable bench could have reached, there could be no legitimate entitlement on the part of the defendant. As a subsidiary point, the Divisional Court noted the likely intention of the magistrates' court that the indication of a medium community order was for the benefit of the Probation service rather than for the defendant; if that was the case, it needed to have been made clear to the defendant. In *Hudd* [2010] EWCA Crim. 48, the court drew a distinction between circumstances where the defendant had "a hope" that there would be a non-custodial sentence and those where there was a "legitimate expectation". The defendant had been charged with a serious wounding (s.20) and had spent the equivalent of a 12 month sentence on remand; when adjourning for a PSR, the Crown Court made a number of comments that showed that a non-custodial sentence was certainly not ruled out. The imposition of a suspended sentence order was appealed unsuccessfully though the defence case was weakened by the fact that it had argued for an immediate custodial sentence in the Crown Court (since that would have led to the defendant's immediate release!). A process has been established to enable a defendant to seek an indication of likely sentence: *Goodyear* [2005] 3 All E.R. 117. However, this procedure does not apply in a magistrates' court (though see Pt X, below).

It is an improper exercise of power for a court to adjourn solely to enable an offender to be sentenced as an adult. The date of conviction is taken to be the date of the finding of guilt or plea of guilty, not the date sentence is passed: *Danga* [1992] Q.B. 476, CA. When approaching sentence for an individual who has crossed a significant threshold between the date of the commission of the offence and the date of sentence, the court should start from a sentence appropriate if sentencing had taken place at the date of the commission of the offence: *Overarching Principles: Sentencing Youths*, Part 5; Sentencing Guidelines Council, November 2009. **22–41**

X. INDICATION OF SENTENCE

When brought into force, as part of the changes to the allocation procedure (see *ante*, Ch.7) a defendant may seek an indication of sentence before consenting to an either way offence being heard in a magistrates' court. **22–42**

Magistrates' Courts Act 1980, ss.20 and 20A

Procedure where summary trial appears more suitable

20.—(1) If, where a court has considered as required by section 19(1) above, it appears to the court that the offence is more suitable for summary trial, the following provisions of this section shall apply (unless excluded by section 23 below). **22–43**

(2) 2The court shall explain to the accused in ordinary language—

(a) that it appears to the court more suitable for him to be tried summarily for the offence, and that he can either consent to be so tried or, of he wishes, be tried by a jury; and

(b) that if he is tried summarily and is convicted by the court, he may be committed for sentence to the Crown Court under [section 3 of the *Powers of Criminal Courts (Sentencing) Act* 2000] if the convicting court, [is of such opinion as is mentioned in subsection (2) of that section].

(3) After explaining to the accused as provided by subsection (2) above, the court shall ask him whether he consents to be tried summarily or wishes to be tried by a jury, and—

(a) if he consents to be tried summarily, shall proceed to the summary trial of the information;

(b) if he does not so consent, shall proceed to inquire into the information as examining justices.

When in force, *Criminal Justice Act* 2003, Sched. 3, para. 6 will substitute s.20 as shown below and insert new s.20A.

Procedure where summary trial appears more suitable

20.—(1) If the court decides under section 19 above that the offence appears to it more suitable for summary trial, the following provisions of this section shall apply (unless they are excluded by section 23 below).

(2) The court shall explain to the accused in ordinary language—

(a) that it appears to the court more suitable for him to be tried summarily for the offence;

(b) that he can either consent to be so tried or, if he wishes, be tried on indictment; and

(c) that if he is tried summarily and is convicted by the court, he may be committed for sentence to the Crown Court under section 3 or (if applicable) under section

3A of the *Powers of Criminal Courts (Sentencing) Act* 2000 if the committing court is of such opinion as is mentioned in subsection (2) of the applicable section.

(3) The accused may then request an indication ("an indication of sentence") of whether a custodial sentence or non-custodial sentence would be more likely to be imposed if he were to be tried summarily for the offence and to plead guilty.

(4) If the accused requests an indication of sentence, the court may, but need not, give such an indication.

(5) If the accused requests and the court gives an indication of sentence, the court shall ask the accused whether he wishes, on the basis of the indication, to reconsider the indication of plea which was given, or is taken to have been given, under section 17A or 17B above.

(6) If the accused indicates that he wishes to reconsider the indication under section 17A or 17B above, the court shall ask the accused whether (if the offence were to proceed to trial) he would plead guilty or not guilty.

(7) If the accused indicates that he would plead guilty the court shall proceed as if—

(a) the proceedings constituted from that time the summary trial of the information; and

(b) section 9(1) above were complied with and he pleaded guilty under it.

(8) Subsection (9) below applies where—

(a) the court does not give an indication of sentence (whether because the accused does not request one or because the court does not agree to give one);

(b) the accused either—

(i) does not indicate, in accordance with subsection (5) above, that he wishes; or

(ii) indicates, in accordance with subsection (5) above, that he does not wish, to reconsider the indication of plea under section 17A or 17B above; or

(c) the accused does not indicate, in accordance with subsection (6) above, that he would plead guilty.

(9) The court shall ask the accused whether he consents to be tried summarily or wishes to be tried on indictment and—

(a) if he consents to be tried summarily, shall proceed to the summary trial of the information; and

(b) if he does not so consent, shall proceed in relation to the offence in accordance with section 51(1) of the *Crime and Disorder Act* 1998.

Procedure where summary trial appears more suitable: supplementary

22–44 **20A.**—(1) Where the case is dealt with in accordance with section 20(7) above, no court (whether a magistrates' court or not) may impose a custodial sentence for the offence unless such a sentence was indicated in the indication of sentence referred to in section 20 above.

(2) Subsection (1) above is subject to sections 3A(4), 4(8) and 5(3) of the *Powers of Criminal Courts (Sentencing) Act* 2000.

(3) Except as provided in subsection (1) above—

(a) an indication of sentence shall not be binding on any court (whether a magistrates' court or not); and

(b) no sentence may be challenged or be the subject of appeal in any court on the ground that it is not consistent with an indication of sentence.

(4) Subject to section 20(7) above, the following shall not for any purpose be taken to constitute the taking of a plea—

(a) asking the accused under section 20 above whether (if the offence were to proceed to trial) he would plead guilty or not guilty; or

(b) an indication by the accused under that section of how he would plead.

(5) Where the court gives an indication of sentence under section 20 above, it shall cause each such indication to be entered in the register.

(6) In this section and in section 20 above, references to a custodial sentence are to a custodial sentence within the meaning of section 76 of the *Powers of Criminal Courts (Sentencing) Act* 2000, and references to a non-custodial sentence shall be construed accordingly.

The approach to this provision has been considered by the Sentencing Advisory

Panel in its advice to the Sentencing Guidelines Council and the key elements have been set out by the Council in its draft National Allocation Guidelines: *www.sentencing-guidelines.gov.uk*.

4. Indication of Sentence

A. THE STATUTORY PROCEDURE

4.1 If it is clear whether or not a custodial sentence is likely, it will normally be helpful for a court to give the indication requested unless there is a good reason for not doing so. **22–45**

4.2 The key elements of the approach to giving a sentence indication are:

(i) A court should assess the type of sentence realistically possible in the light of the facts as presented by the prosecution, with the additional element of a guilty plea tendered at this stage in the proceedings, and subject to defence representations as to the accuracy of the factual outline of the case. Wherever possible, the key elements of the basis upon which the indication is given should be recorded in writing.

(ii) A court should proceed with caution where an offender is unrepresented. The offender should be advised of the availability of independent legal advice. The Justices' Clerk (or assistant to the Justices' Clerk) present in court has a duty to assist the unrepresented party, and this will include drawing to the attention of an unrepresented defendant that there is an entitlement to request an indication of sentence.

(iii) A court should not give an indication of sentence where there are alternative charges unless the prosecution has indicated that an agreement as to acceptable pleas has been established following discussions with the defence, and there is an appropriate factual basis upon which an indication could be given.

(iv) The prosecution must ensure that the court is fully informed of the facts of the case and any relevant background.

(v) The court is entitled to expect that the Justices' Clerk (or assistant to the Justices' Clerk) present in court, and the prosecution and defence advocates, will ensure that the court considers any relevant guidelines or other authorities affecting sentence.

(vi) The information presented to the court will not include personal mitigation except in so far as it has influenced the facts of the case presented to the court or it is actively agreed by the prosecution advocate.

(vii) Any indication given must be recorded in writing and entered onto the court register.

B. REDUCTION IN SENTENCE FOR A GUILTY PLEA

4.14 In order to set the maximum type of sentence in cases where the offence is close to the threshold for a custodial sentence, a magistrates' court would have to consider whether the maximum reduction in sentence for a guilty plea would potentially be available where a guilty plea is forthcoming only after a sentence indication has been given. **22–46**

4.15 The Guideline, Reduction in Sentence for a Guilty Plea, at paragraph 4.3 (as amended) states:

4.3 The level of reduction should reflect the stage at which the offender indicated a willingness to admit guilt to the offence for which he is eventually sentenced:

(i) the largest recommended reduction will not normally be given unless the offender indicated willingness to admit guilt at the **first reasonable opportunity**; when this occurs will vary from case to case (*see Annex 1 for illustrative examples*);

(ii) where the admission of guilt comes later than the **first reasonable opportunity,** the reduction for guilty plea will be less than one third.

(iii) where the plea of guilty comes very late, it is still appropriate to give some reduction;

(iv) if after pleading guilty there is a *Newton* hearing and the offender's version of the circumstances of the offence is rejected, this should be taken into account in determining the level of reduction;

(v) if the not guilty plea was entered and maintained for tactical reasons (such as to retain privileges whilst on remand), a late guilty plea should attract very little, if any, discount.

In considering further when the "first reasonable opportunity" occurs, Annex 2 of the Guideline

(Annex 1 in the revised guideline) emphasises the purpose of giving the reduction which is in recognition of "the benefits that come from a guilty plea both for those directly involved in the case in question but also in enabling Courts more quickly to deal with other outstanding cases".

4.16 There may only be a relatively short time gap between the opportunity to give an indication prior to allocation and the opportunity after an indication of sentence. However, the court will have had to consider allocation and determine summary trial and will then have to consider its response to the request for an indication of sentence. In those circumstances, it would appear that delay had taken place that could have been avoided and this will influence the extent of the reduction.

Where a guilty plea is indicated after the court has given an indication of the likely sentence, the appropriate reduction in sentence for the guilty plea should be a maximum of one quarter.

22–47 The power is much more restricted than that available in the Crown Court as set out in *Goodyear* [2006] 1 Cr.App.R.(S.) 6. However, the Council has accepted the advice of the Sentencing Advisory Panel that the principles of *Goodyear* can be applied within the context of the more limited, statutory, procedure provided for a magistrates' court. Whilst there is a discretion to refuse to give an indication of sentence, when it is clear whether or not a custodial sentence is likely a court is expected to give the indication except where it has a serious concern that it would be unable to do justice either to the defendant or to others. The court is entitled to ensure that it has been given enough information to decide whether or not a custodial sentence ought to be available for consideration by the court that imposes sentence and will normally be more cautious about giving an indication to one of a number of co-defendants than to a sole defendant. If there is no firm factual basis, it would be inappropriate for an indication to be given, even though it is probably not as necessary (or practicable) to reduce that basis to writing as it is in the Crown Court. Other circumstances where a refusal may be appropriate include situations where a defendant is considered already to be under inappropriate pressure to plead guilty (perhaps from a co-defendant) or where there is concern about whether the defendant appreciates that a plea of guilty should only be entered where the defendant is guilty of the offence charged or where there is concern that the court could not judge properly the differing levels of culpability or responsibility amongst co-defendants. It is unlikely that a court will give reasons for its decision following the reasoning set out in *Goodyear*.

XI. POWERS OF YOUTH COURT TO REMIT TO ADULT COURT, AND SENTENCING POWERS OF ADULT COURT DEALING WITH YOUTH

22–48 An adult court has limited sentencing powers in respect of young offenders convicted in an adult court: see *post*, Ch.27. Where a youth appearing in a youth court becomes 18 years old before sentence is passed, the youth court has the additional option of remitting the case to the adult court for sentence and that court will have its usual range of sentencing options. However, see *Overarching Principles: Sentencing Youths*, Part 5; Sentencing Guidelines Council, November 2009 emphasising that the starting point for sentence should be that which would have been passed if the defendant had been sentenced on the date on which the offence was committed.

Powers of Criminal Courts (Sentencing) 2000, s.9

Power of youth court to remit offender who attains age of 18 to magistrates' court other than youth court for sentence

22–49 **9.**—(1) Where a person who appears or is brought before a youth court charged with an offence subsequently attains the age of 18, the youth court may, at any time after conviction and before sentence, remit him for sentence to a magistrates' court (other than a youth court).

(2) Where an offender is remitted under subsection (1) above, the youth court shall adjourn proceedings in relation to the offence, and—

(a) section 128 of the *Magistrates' Courts Act* 1980 (remand in custody or on bail) and all other enactments, whenever passed, relating to remand or the granting of bail in criminal proceedings shall have effect, in relation to the youth court's power or duty to remand the offender on that adjournment, as if any reference to the court to or before which the person remanded is to be brought or appear after remand were a reference to the court to which he is being remitted; and

(b) subject to subsection (3) below, the court to which the offender is remitted ("the other court") may deal with the case in any way in which it would have power to deal with it if all proceedings relating to the offence which took place before the youth court had taken place before the other court.

(3) Where an offender is remitted under subsection (1) above, section 8(6) above (duty of adult magistrates' court to remit young offenders to youth court for sentence) shall not apply to the court to which he is remitted.

(4) Where an offender is remitted under subsection (1) above he shall have no right of appeal against the order of remission (but without prejudice to any right of appeal against an order made in respect of the offence by the court to which he is remitted).

(5) In this section—

(a) "enactment" includes an enactment contained in any order, regulation or other instrument having effect by virtue of an Act; and

(b) "bail in criminal proceedings" has the same meaning as in the *Bail Act* 1976.

XII. POWERS TO REMIT A YOUTH WHO APPEARS IN THE ADULT COURT TO THE YOUTH COURT FOR SENTENCE

The presumption is that a youth convicted in the adult court will be remitted to a youth court (usually the one for the area in which the youth resides) for sentence. The only circumstance in which a youth can be sentenced in an adult magistrates' court is where the sentence to be passed comes within s.8(7) or (8), that is, a referral order, a fine (note lower maximum penalties for youths), an absolute or conditional discharge or an order binding over parents to take proper control of the youth. If one of these sentences is being used, ancillary orders (such as endorsement or disqualification from driving) can also be made. **22–50**

Powers of Criminal Courts (Sentencing) Act 2000, s.8

Power and duty to remit young offenders to youth courts for sentence

8.—(1) Subsection (2) below applies where a child or young person (that is to say, any person aged under 18) is convicted by or before any court of an offence other than homicide. **22–51**

(2) The court may and, if it is not a youth court, shall unless satisfied that it would be undesirable to do so, remit the case—

(a) if the offender was committed for trial or sent to the Crown Court for trial under section 51 or 51A of the *Crime and Disorder Act* 1998, to a youth court acting for the place where he was sent to the Crown Court for trial;

(b) in any other case, to a youth court acting either for the same place as the remitting court or for the place where the offender habitually resides;

but in relation to a magistrates' court other than a youth court this subsection has effect subject to subsection (6) below.

(3) Where a case is remitted under subsection (2) above, the offender shall be brought before a youth court accordingly, and that court may deal with him in any way in which it might have dealt with him if he had been tried and convicted by that court.

(4) A court by which an order remitting a case to a youth court is made under subsection (2) above—

(a) may, subject to section 25 of the *Criminal Justice and Public Order Act* 1994 (restrictions on granting bail), give such directions as appear to be necessary with respect to the custody of the offender or for his release on bail until he can be brought before the youth court; and

(b) shall cause to be transmitted to the designated officer for the youth court a certificate setting out the nature of the offence and stating—

(i) that the offender has been convicted of the offence; and

(ii) that the case has been remitted for the purpose of being dealt with under the preceding provisions of this section.

(5) Where a case is remitted under subsection (2) above, the offender shall have no right of appeal against the order of remission, but shall have the same right of appeal against any order of the court to which the case is remitted as if he had been convicted by that court.

(6) Without prejudice to the power to remit any case to a youth court which is conferred on a magistrates' court other than a youth court by subsection (1) and (2) above, where such a magistrates' court convicts a child or young person of an offence it must exercise that power unless the case falls within subsection (7) or (8) below.

(7) The case falls within this subsection if the court would, were it not so to remit the case, be required by section 16(2) below to refer the offender to a youth offender panel (in which event the court may, but need not, so remit the case).

(8) The case falls within this subsection if it does not fall within subsection (7) above but the court is of the opinion that the case is one which can properly be dealt with by means of—

(a) an order discharging the offender absolutely or conditionally, or

(b) an order for the payment of a fine, or

(c) an order (under section 150 below) requiring the offender's parent or guardian to enter into a recognizance to take proper care of him and exercise proper control over him,

with or without any other order that the court has power to make when absolutely or conditionally discharging an offender.

(9) In subsection (8) above "care" and "control" shall be construed in accordance with section 150(11) below.

(10) A document purporting to be a copy of an order made by a court under this section shall, if it purports to be certified as a true copy by the designated officer for the court, be evidence of the order.

XIII. APPROACH TO SENTENCE

A. STRUCTURE OF DECISION

22–52 The standard approach to sentencing on which magistrates have been trained for many years commences with an assessment of the seriousness of the offence (which sets the ceiling above which the sentence imposed should never rise) and then considers circumstances relevant to the offender which may mitigate the level of penalty that the offence would otherwise deserve. The *Magistrates' Court Sentencing Guidelines* explain the structure of the guidelines by reference to that approach.

Magistrates' Court Sentencing Guidelines

SENTENCING STRUCTURE

1. OFFENCE SERIOUSNESS (CULPABILITY AND HARM)

A. IDENTIFY THE APPROPRIATE STARTING POINT

- Consider which of the examples of offence activity corresponds most closely to the circumstances of the case to identify the appropriate **starting point**.
- Starting points are based on a **first time offender pleading not guilty**.
- The range of sentences, including a fine, community order or custodial sentence are defined in the guidelines.
  (i) fine—pages 148–155;
  (ii) community order—pages 160–162;
  (iii) custodial sentence—pages 163–164.
- The terms 'starting point', 'range' and 'first time offender' are explained in the guidelines.

B. CONSIDER THE EFFECT OF AGGRAVATING AND MITIGATING FACTORS

- Move up or down from the starting point to reflect aggravating or mitigating factors that affect the seriousness of the offence to reach a provisional sentence.
- Common aggravating and mitigating factors are set out, relevant factors are also identified in the individual offence guidelines. **These lists are not exhaustive.**

- Do not double-count any aggravating or mitigating factors in the description of the activity used to reach the starting point.
- The **range** is the bracket into which the provisional sentence will normally fall but the court is not precluded from going outside the range where the facts justify it.
- Previous convictions which aggravate the seriousness of the current offence may take the provisional sentence beyond the range, especially if there are significant other aggravating factors present.

2. FORM A PRELIMINARY VIEW OF THE APPROPRIATE SENTENCE, THEN CONSIDER OFFENDER MITIGATION

- Matters of offender mitigation may include remorse and admissions to police in interview.

3. CONSIDER A REDUCTION FOR A GUILTY PLEA

- Apply the sliding scale reduction for a guilty plea to punitive elements of the sentence.
- Application of the reduction may take the sentence below the range in some cases.

4. CONSIDER ANCILLARY ORDERS, INCLUDING COMPENSATION

- Guidance on available ancillary orders is given.
- Consider compensation in every case where the offending has resulted in personal injury, loss or damage—give reasons if order not made … .

5. DECIDE SENTENCE
GIVE REASONS

- Review the total sentence to ensure that it is proportionate to the offending behaviour and properly balanced.
- Give reasons for the sentence passed, including any ancillary orders.
- State if the sentence has been reduced to reflect a guilty plea; indicate what the sentence would otherwise have been.
- Explain if the sentence is of a different kind or outside the range indicated in the guidelines.

In its first guideline, the Sentencing Council has set out a structure which, whilst bearing many similarities to that in the *Magistrates' Court Sentencing Guidelines*, also has some differences reflecting the more general terms in which the offence categories are defined. The Council provides for nine steps starting with a determination of the offence category derived from an assessment of relative harm and culpability. The second step then provides for starting points and ranges and for movement from the provided starting point in the light of "additional factual elements providing the context of the offence and factors relating to the offender". Further steps provide for the reduction for a guilty plea, an assessment of whether the dangerous provisions ought to be considered, consideration of the totality principle where sentence is for multiple offences, ancillary orders, the giving of reasons and allowance for time on remand. Whichever structure is to be followed, the court will first assess the seriousness of the offence itself, ensuring that it takes into account all factors which make this particular offence more or less serious. This will include statutory aggravating factors such as the fact that the offence was committed whilst the offender was on bail. The existence of "recent and relevant" previous convictions makes the offence more serious. In any case, they are likely to indicate that the offender was more culpable since they demonstrate that he was clearly aware that what was being done was wrong. There is a different approach where an offence is aggravated by reason of one or more of the elements of race, religion, disability or sexual orientation: see § 22–67, *post*. Where those factors apply, the court will first determine what the sentence would have been without such a factor and then increase it to take account of that factor.

Having formed a view of the seriousness of the offence, personal mitigation is considered and the sentence may be reduced accordingly. The absence of previous convictions is likely to be relevant only in so far as it supports a contention of positive good character since the law now requires that the presence of "recent and relevant" previous convictions will make an offence more serious. Sentence is then determined taking account of other relevant factors such as any reduction for entering a timely guilty plea.

B. FACTUAL BASIS FOR SENTENCE

22–53 A defendant wishing to ask the court to pass sentence on a basis other than that disclosed in the prosecution case has to make that quite clear. Where a plea of guilty is tendered on the basis of facts which the Crown could not accept, and the discrepancy between the two accounts is such that the choice between them will potentially have a significant effect on the level of sentence, then the court has to consider resolving the issue by hearing evidence—a *Newton* hearing (see *Newton* (1983) 77 Cr.App.R. 13). When faced with differing versions of the facts of the offence, the choices available to the court are:

(a) to hear evidence and come to a conclusion or

(b) to hear no evidence, though, in the event of a substantial conflict between the versions of events, the version of the defendant must "so far as possible be accepted."

If the court does hear evidence, the normal rules of procedure apply, the court should apply the criminal standard of proof and must announce that it has done so when passing sentence: *Kerrigan* (1993) 14 Cr.App.R.(S.) 179, CA.

22–54 The procedure to be adopted following a guilty plea in such circumstances was further examined by Lord Bingham C.J. in *Tolera* [1999] 1 Cr.App.R. 29:

> "a) where a defendant pleads guilty and gives an account of the offence which the *prosecution* does not challenge, but which the *court* feels unable to accept, the court should make it clear before sentence that it did not accept the defence account. Failing any other resolution, evidence can be called and the prosecution can explore matters which the court wishes to explore.
>
> b) regarding the facts of the offence given to the probation officer for the preparation of a pre-sentence report, an offender may sometimes give an account which differs from that which emerged in the prosecution case. Whilst this part of the pre-sentence report would, of course, be read by the court, it was not ordinarily to form part of the factual basis for the passing of sentence. If the defendant wished to rely on this part of the pre-sentence report for the purposes of sentence, the defence should make this clear, and the prosecution should be forewarned. The issue could then be resolved, if necessary, by the calling of evidence."

22–55 In *Tolera*, the Court held that there was an onus on the prosecution to rebut an allegation that the defendant had been subject to a degree of compulsion, falling short of duress, to act as a drug courier. *Tolera* was followed in *Artwell* [2001] EWCA Crim. 1387, CA where the offender appealed against his sentence of six years' imprisonment imposed for being concerned in the supply of heroin. He contended that there had been a large discrepancy between his basis of plea and the prosecution's case that he was the main organiser. The judge had not held a *Newton* hearing on this matter and had not clarified why he did not accept the defence account of the facts. The Court of Appeal held that the judge should have clarified why he did not accept the defence account and, failing a resolution, should have a held a *Newton* hearing. The offender's sentence was reduced from six years' imprisonment to three. If there is a meaningful discrepancy between the way in which the Crown put the case and the way in which the defence asked the court to sentence, there should either be a *Newton* hearing or the court has to be faithful to the basis of the plea.

Following the holding of a *Newton* hearing, the accused may still be entitled to receive some credit for his guilty plea in the form of a reduction of sentence. In its guideline in relation to the reduction in sentence following a guilty plea (revised July 2007), the Sentencing Guidelines Council considered the approach where such a hearing had been necessary. The Council states that the purpose of the reduction is to generate the benefits that come from an early guilty plea, in particular, the saving for victims and witnesses of the anxiety and apprehension surrounding the possible need to give evidence and the saving in time and resources. The maximum reduction would only be given where there was a guilty plea at the first reasonable opportunity. Even where there has been such a plea, if it subsequently becomes necessary to adduce evidence because of a dispute of essential facts and the offender's version of events is not wholly accepted, then at least some of the benefits will be lost: *Guideline: 4.3(iv)*.

A *Newton* hearing will not be necessary: **22–56**

(i) where the difference in the two versions of the facts of the case is immaterial to the sentence. In *Hall* (1984) 6 Cr.App.R.(S.) 321, the Court of Appeal held that the additional facts which the defendant disputed would not have affected the sentence, and in such a case the judge should proceed only on the defendant's version of events.

(ii) where the defence version can be described as "manifestly false" or "wholly implausible": *Walton* (1987) 9 Cr.App.R.(S.) 107, *Att.-Gen.'s Ref Nos 3 and 4 of 1996 (Alan Anthony Healy and Robert William Taylor)* [1997] 1 Cr.App.R.(S.) 29, CA.

(iii) where the matters put forward do not challenge the prosecutor's version of events, but rather challenge extraneous matters, such as the background of the offence. These matters are likely to be outside the knowledge of the prosecution: *Broderick* (1994) 15 Cr.App.R.(S.) 476, CA.

A helpful summary of the limitations on the *Newton* hearing procedure is set out in *Underwood* [2004] EWCA Crim. 2256. In particular, it emphasises that care needs to be taken where guilty pleas are accepted on lesser charges to those originally preferred, especially in case involving multiple defendants. A *Newton* hearing will be unnecessary where the impact of any dispute on the sentencing decision will be minimal.

The Court of Appeal has expressed concern that this guidance is either overlooked or ignored: *Temple* [2008] EWCA Crim. 2511. In particular, the Court emphasised the obligation on the defence to alert the prosecutor where a plea was entered on a different factual basis from that in the prosecution case, the need for a written and signed agreement where the basis of plea was agreed, the entitlement of the court to take a different view from that agreed upon and the circumstances in which a hearing was not necessary where there remained a dispute. In this case, the Court concluded that the facts as asserted by the defence, if true, would have made the offence worse than in the prosecution case and the court was quite justified in declining to convene a hearing.

Where a *Newton* hearing has taken place in a magistrates' court and the defendant has then been committed for sentence, the Crown Court may allow the findings of fact to be re-opened but is unlikely to do so unless there has been some significant development or matter which has occurred since the magistrates' court reached its conclusion: *Gillan v. DPP* [2007] EWHC Admin 380. Accordingly, it is important that the Crown Court is properly informed of the facts found by the magistrates' court: *Warley J.J. ex p. DPP* [1999] 1 W.L.R. 216.

C. GENERAL AGGRAVATING FACTORS

As described earlier (see *ante*, § 22–4), provisions in the *Criminal Justice Act* 2003 **22–57** concern the determination of the seriousness of an offence. As stated there, the issues of culpability and harm are paramount. There are, however, other factors which, if present, will make the offence more serious. In particular, s.143(2) of the *Criminal Justice Act* 2003 provides for the presence of recent and relevant convictions to be a factor aggravating the seriousness of the offence and s.143(3) of the *Criminal Justice Act* 2003 provides that the fact that an offence was committed while the offender was on bail must be treated as an aggravating factor. Further general guidance has been given by the Sentencing Guidelines Council where violence occurs in a domestic context: see guideline *Overarching Principles: Domestic Violence*, December 2006, *www.sentencingcouncil.judiciary.gov.uk* and § 22–59, *post*.

In its guideline on the assessment of seriousness published in December 2004, the **22–58** Sentencing Guidelines Council collated the most important aggravating factors of general application. Following the two-prong approach to the assessment of seriousness (culpability and harm), those factors are separated into those that suggest higher culpability and those that suggest a more than usually serious degree of harm. Inevitably, some of those factors will be an essential element of some offences and, therefore, care needs to be taken to avoid "double counting": see § 22–64, *post*.

22–59 The Sentencing Guidelines Council guideline *Overarching Principles: Domestic Violence* applies to all offences sentenced on or after December 18, 2006. As is pointed out in the Foreword to the guideline, there is no specific offence of domestic violence and the guideline needs to encompass a wide range of circumstances and conduct. There is a clear statement not only that offences committed in a domestic context are no less serious than offences committed in any other context but also that, because an offence is committed in a domestic context, it is likely to have aggravating factors present that make it more serious.

In a magistrates' court there will be a wide range of offences dealt with, some in specialist courts, some in the ordinary mix of business. Often fine judgements will need to be made about the nature of the sanction necessary to reduce the risk of future violence and to protect the victim.

The guideline sets out 4 issues of principle:

Guideline: Overarching Principles: Domestic Violence

E. FACTORS TO TAKE INTO CONSIDERATION

The following points of principle should be considered by a court when imposing sentence for any offence of violence committed in domestic context.

1. Offences committed in a domestic context should be regarded as being no less serious than offences committed in a non-domestic context.

2. Many offences of violence in a domestic context are dealt with in a magistrates' court as an offence of common assault or assault occasioning actual bodily harm because the injuries sustained are relatively minor. Offences involving serious violence will warrant a custodial sentence in the majority of cases.

3. Some offences will be specified offences for the purposes of the dangerous offender provisions. In such circumstances, consideration will need to be given to whether there is a significant risk of serious harm to members of the public, which include, of course, family members. If so, the court will be required to impose a life sentence, imprisonment for public protection or an extended sentence.

4. Where the custody threshold is only just crossed, so that if a custodial sentence is imposed it will be a short sentence, the court will wish to consider whether the better option is a suspended sentence order or a community order, including in either case a requirement to attend an accredited domestic violence programme. Such an option will only be appropriate where the court is satisfied that the offender genuinely intends to reform his or her behaviour and that there is a real prospect of rehabilitation being successful. Such a situation is unlikely to arise where there has been a pattern of abuse.

22–60 The guideline also sets out aggravating and mitigating factors most likely to occur and these are set out *post*. They recognise that the violence is likely to take place in the context of a relationship and that it may include an abuse of both trust and of power. Some victims will be particularly vulnerable and a court must be alert to this possibility. The guideline draws attention to the impact of domestic violence on children both through witnessing the violence and through being aware of it occurring even when it is not witnessed.

Whilst the guideline draws attention to the general sentencing principle that the good character of the defendant can be relevant to sentence, it points out the ability of an offender to have "two personae" which can make it possible for domestic violence to continue for long periods.

Guideline: Overarching Principles: Domestic Violence

C. AGGRAVATING AND MITIGATING FACTORS

3.1 Since domestic violence takes place within the context of a current or past relationship, the history of the relationship will often be relevant in assessing the gravity of the offence. Therefore, a court is entitled to take into account anything occurring within the relationship as a whole, which may reveal relevant aggravating or mitigating factors.

3.2 The following aggravating and mitigating factors (which are not intended to be exhaustive) are of particular relevance to offences committed in a domestic context, and should be read alongside the general factors set out in the Council guideline *Overarching Principles: Seriousness*.

Aggravating Factors

(i) Abuse of trust and abuse of power

3.3 The guideline *Overarching Principles: Seriousness* identifies abuse of a position of trust and abuse of power as factors that indicate higher culpability. Within the nature of relationship required to meet the definition of domestic violence set out above, trust implies a mutual expectation of conduct that shows consideration, honesty, care and responsibility. In some such relationships, one of the parties will have the power to exert considerable control over the other.

3.4 In the context of domestic violence:

- an *abuse of trust*, whether through direct violence or emotional abuse, represents a violation of this understanding;
- an *abuse of power* in a relationship involves restricting another individual's autonomy which is sometimes a specific characteristic of domestic violence. This involves the exercise of control over an individual by means which may be psychological, physical, sexual, financial or emotional.

3.5 Where an abuse of trust or abuse of power is present, it will aggravate the seriousness of an offence. These factors are likely to exist in many offences of violence within a domestic context.

3.6 However, the breadth of the definition of domestic violence (set out in 1.1 above) encompasses offences committed by a former spouse or partner. Accordingly, there will be circumstances where the abuse of trust or abuse of power may be a very minor feature of an offence or may be deemed no longer to exist—for example, where the offender and victim have been separated for a long period of time.

(ii) Victim is particularly vulberable

3.7 For cultural, religious, language, financial or any other reasons, some victims of domestic violence may be more vulnerable than others, not least because these issues may make it almost impossible for the victim to leave a violent relationship.

3.8 Where a perpetrator has exploited a victim's vulnerability (for instance, when the circumstances have been used by the perpetrator to prevent the victim from seeking and obtaining help), an offence will warrant a higher penalty.

3.9 Age, disability or the fact that the victim was pregnant or had recently given birth at the time of the offence may make a victim particularly vulnerable.

3.10 Any steps taken to prevent the victim reporting an incident or obtaining assistance will usually aggravate the offence.

(iii) Impact on Children

3.11 Exposure of children to an offence (either directly or indirectly) is an aggravating factor.

3.12 Children are likely to be adversely affected by directly witnessing violence or other abuse and by being aware of it taking place while they are elsewhere in the home.

(iv) Using contact arrangements with a child to instigate an offence

3.13 An offence will be aggravated where an offender exploits contact arrangements with a child in order to commit an offence.

(v) A proven history of violence or threats by the offender in a domestic setting

3.14 It is important that an assessment of the seriousness of an offence recognises the cumulative effect of a series of violent incidents or threats over a prolonged period, where such conduct has been proved or accepted.

3.15 Where an offender has previously been convicted of an offence involving domestic violence either against the same or a different partner, this is likely to be a statutory aggravating factor.

(vi) A history of disobedience to court orders

3.16 A breach of an order that has been imposed for the purpose of protecting a victim can cause significant harm or anxiety. Where an offender's history of disobedience has had this effect, it will be an aggravating factor.

Part IV

3.17 Commission of the offence in breach of a non-molestation order imposed in civil proceedings, in breach of a sentence (such as a conditional discharge) imposed for similar offending, or while subject to an ancillary order, such as a restraining order, will aggravate the seriousness of the offence.

3.18 The appropriate response to breach of a civil order is dealt with in a separate guideline *Breach of a Protective Order*.

(vii) Victim forced to leave home

3.19 An offence will be aggravated if, as a consequence, the victim is forced to leave home.

Mitigating Factors

(i) Positive good character

3.20 As a general principle of sentencing, a court will take account of an offender's positive good character. However, it is recognised that one of the factors that can allow domestic violence to continue unnoticed for lengthy periods is the ability of the perpetrator to have two personae. In respect of an offence of violence in a domestic context, an offender's good character in relation to conduct outside the home should generally be of no relevance where there is a proven pattern of behaviour.

3.21 Positive good character is of greater relevance in the rare case where the court is satisfied that the offence was an isolated incident.

(ii) Provocation

3.22 It may be asserted that the offence, at least in part, has been provoked by the conduct of the victim. Such assertions need to be treated with great care, both in determining whether they have a factual basis and in considering whether in the circumstances the alleged conduct amounts to provocation sufficient to mitigate the seriousness of the offence.

3.23 For provocation to be a mitigating factor, it will usually involve actual or anticipated violence including psychological bullying. Provocation is likely to have more of an effect as mitigation if it has taken place over a significant period of time.

22–61 The guideline also addresses the issue of how a court should approach situations where a victim expresses a wish for a particular type of sentence, generally one more lenient than might otherwise be thought appropriate. The guideline states very clearly that victims should not be put in a situation where they can be seen to have responsibility for the choice of sentence. Nonetheless, it also recognises that there will be situations where a victim genuinely and reasonably wishes a relationship to continue. A court should proceed with considerable caution in such circumstances.

Guideline: Overarching Principles: Domestic Violence

D. OTHER FACTORS INFLUENCING SENTENCE

Wishes of the victim and effect of the sentence

4.1 As a matter of general principle, a sentence imposed for an offence of violence should be determined by the seriousness of the offence, not by the expressed wishes of the victim.

4.2 There are a number of reasons why it may be particularly important that this principle is observed in a case of domestic violence:

- it is undesirable that a victim should feel a responsibility for the sentence imposed;
- there is a risk that a plea for mercy made by a victim will be induced by threats made by, or by a fear of, the offender;
- the risk of such threats will be increased if it is generally believed that the severity of the sentence may be affected by the wishes of the victim.

4.3 Nonetheless, there may be circumstances in which the court can properly mitigate a sentence to give effect to the expressed wish of the victim that the relationship be permitted to continue. The court must, however, be confident that such a wish is genuine, and that giving effect to it will not expose the victim to a real risk of further violence. Critical conditions are likely to be the seriousness of the offence and the history of the relationship. It is vitally important that the court has up-to-date information in a pre-sentence report and victim personal statement.

4.4 Either the offender or the victim (or both) may ask the court to take into consideration the interests of any children and to impose a less severe sentence. The court will wish to have regard not only to the effect on the children if the relationship is disrupted but also to the likely effect on the children of any further incidents of domestic violence.

D. The Assessment of Culpability and Harm

Guideline: Overarching Principles: Seriousness

D. Assessment of Culpability and Harm

(i) Aggravating Factors

1.20 Sentencing guidelines for a particular offence will normally include a list of aggravating features which, if present in an individual instance of the offence, would indicate either a higher than usual level of culpability on the part of the offender, or a greater than usual degree of harm caused by the offence (or sometimes both). **22–62**

1.21 The lists below bring together the most important aggravating features with potential application to more than one offence or class of offences. They include some factors (such as the vulnerability of victims or abuse of trust) which are integral features of certain offences; in such cases, the presence of the aggravating factor is already reflected in the penalty for the offence and ***cannot be used as justification for increasing the sentence further***. The lists are not intended to be comprehensive and the aggravating factors are not listed in any particular order of priority. On occasions, two or more of the factors listed will describe the same feature of the offence and care needs to be taken to avoid "doublecounting". Those factors starred with an asterisk are statutory aggravating factors where the statutory provisions are in force.

1.22 Factors indicating higher culpability:

- Offence committed whilst on bail for other offences*
- Failure to respond to previous sentences*
- Offence was racially or religiously aggravated*
- Offence motivated by, or demonstrating, hostility to the victim based on his or her sexual orientation (or presumed sexual orientation)*
- Offence motivated by, or demonstrating, hostility based on the victim's disability (or presumed disability)*
- Previous conviction(s), particularly where a pattern of repeat offending is disclosed*
- Planning of an offence
- An intention to commit more serious harm than actually resulted from the offence
- Offenders operating in groups or gangs
- "Professional" offending
- Commission of the offence for financial gain (where this is not inherent in the offence itself)
- High level of profit from the offence
- An attempt to conceal or dispose of evidence
- Failure to respond to warnings or concerns expressed by others about the offender's behaviour
- Offence committed whilst on licence
- Offence motivated by hostility towards a minority group, or a member or members of it
- Deliberate targeting of vulnerable victim(s)
- Commission of an offence while under the influence of alcohol or drugs
- Use of a weapon to frighten or injure victim
- Deliberate and gratuitous violence or damage to property, over and above what is needed to carry out the offence
- Abuse of power
- Abuse of a position of trust

1.23 Factors indicating a more than usually serious degree of harm:

- Multiple victims
- An especially serious physical or psychological effect on the victim, even if unintended
- A sustained assault or repeated assaults on the same victim
- Victim is particularly vulnerable
- Location of the offence (for example, in an isolated place)

- Offence is committed against those working in the public sector or providing a service to the public
- Presence of others *e.g.* relatives, especially children or partner of the victim
- Additional degradation of the victim (*e.g.* taking photographs of a victim as part of a sexual offence)
- In property offences, high value (including sentimental value) of property to the victim, or substantial consequential loss (*e.g.* where the theft of equipment causes serious disruption to a victim's life or business)

Previous convictions

22–63 The significance of previous convictions in assessing sentence has been the subject of debate for many years. At one extreme, the argument is that, once a person has been punished and that punishment completed, then the significance of the offence should be at an end. At the other, is the argument now contained in the *Criminal Justice Act* 2003 that each previous conviction should aggravate the seriousness of the current offence. The existence of a previous conviction for the same offence prevents any argument that the defendant was unaware of the significance of what was being done.

In practice, courts have tended to treat the absence of previous convictions as mitigating factor rather than the existence as an aggravating factor but the statutory provisions now ensure that those convictions (where recent and relevant) influence the assessment of the seriousness of the offence. There will be some circumstances where statute prescribes a minimum sentence where there have been previous convictions—for magistrates' courts, this tends to be for road traffic offences where, for instance, disqualification generally follows the acquisition of 12 penalty points and higher periods of disqualification become the minimum where previous disqualifications have been imposed.

In recent years there has been a considerable increase in the number of disposals that can be imposed as an alternative to prosecution. A fixed penalty is available for an increasing number of offences and there are now also penalty notices for disorder. Cautions are frequently used and now there are also conditional cautions. There is also a cannabis warning which is a verbal warning accompanied by confiscation of cannabis which, depending on the circumstances, can be issued on the street or in a police station. There are also a number of agencies which have the power to impose administrative penalties. A short guide to the circumstances in which these disposals can be used—*Out-of-court disposals for adults*—can be found at *www.cjsonline.gov.uk*.

The *Magistrates' Court Sentencing Guidelines* published by the Sentencing Guidelines Council sets out (pp.188–9) how a court should respond when considering sentence for a person who has been subject to one of these disposals. The guidance covers situations where such a disposal has been offered but declined, where it has been accepted but not fully complied with and where it would have been offered save for an occurrence beyond the control of the offender and prosecution has been pursued instead.

A "recent and relevant" previous conviction, by statute, aggravates the seriousness of an offence. However, many of these disposals are not "convictions" for these purposes though many may appear on an offender's record or be brought to the attention of the court through one means or another. In such circumstances, the existence of those previous orders cannot make the current offence more serious but may influence the choice of sentence from amongst those available to the court. Some of these sanctions do not require there to be an admission of guilt and this must be taken into account whenever a court is considering what weight (if any) to place on them (see, for example, *Hamer* [2010] EWCA Crim. 2053; [2011] 1 W.L.R. 528 in connection with a penalty notice for disorder). The extent of the sentences available will be determined by the court's assessment of the seriousness of the current offence, *i.e.* a custodial offence is only available (whether immediate or suspended) if the custody threshold has been crossed.

Offence committed whilst on bail

22–64 If the offence is committed whilst the offender was on bail for some other matter, the court has to treat that fact as a factor that aggravates the seriousness of the present offence: *Criminal Justice Act* 2003, s.143(3).

Religious or racial aggravation; aggravation related to disability or sexual orientation

The existence of an element of racial or religious aggravation may cause a particular offence to be committed in an aggravated fashion with a higher maximum penalty (for example, certain assaults or criminal damage). Even where that is not the case, the existence of racial or religious aggravation (as defined in s.28 of the *Crime and Disorder Act* 1998) will make the offence more serious. This approach is continued in s.145 of the *Criminal Justice Act* 2003 and extended by s.146, to aggravation related to disability or sexual orientation. **22–65**

A new, but similar, provision was introduced by the 2003 Act in relation to disability or sexual orientation. Disability is defined as "any physical or mental impairment". Where hostility on such a basis is found to exist, a court must treat it as an aggravating factor.

These factors can arise in two circumstances:

(i) Where the offence was motivated by hostility based on membership of a racial or religious group, on sexual orientation or on disability. The hostility need not be the whole motivation for the offence, it may be just a part of the motivation. The victim does not need to be a member of the racial or religious group or a person of the sexual orientation or possessing the disability in question as long as the offence is at least partially motivated by hostility to persons who do. Thus an offence would be aggravated where it was committed against a person who is not disabled but is motivated by hostility against someone that that person is supporting who is disabled.

(ii) Where the offender demonstrated hostility to the victim based on the membership of a racial or religious group, sexual orientation or disability of the victim. This includes presumed, as well as actual, orientation or disability. This hostility may be demonstrated at the time the offence is committed or immediately after or before it is committed.

The court must state in open court that the offence has been committed in the circumstances covered by this provision.

The House of Lords has given consideration to the meaning of "racial group" in the context of the aggravated form of certain offences. The term used was "bloody foreigners" and the defence sought to argue that this was too wide to be a "racial group" within the meaning of the legislation. The House of Lords did not accept the argument. The statute intended a broad non-technical approach and the essence was denial of equal respect and dignity to all people which was damaging not only to the victims but also to the community as a whole: *Rogers* [2007] UKHL 8.

It is clear that only part of the motivation for the offences needs to be racial *etc.* In *Johnson v. DPP* [2008] EWHC 509, the Divisional Court agreed that it was open to a court to find a racially aggravated offence proved on the basis of threatening, abusive or insulting words or behaviour based partly on the victim's presumed membership of a racial group and partly on the victim's occupation.

The approach of the court was set out in *R. (DPP) v. Dykes* [2008] EWHC 2775; (2009) 173 J.P. 88. In determining whether the offence was racially aggravated within the terms of s.28 of the *Crime and Disorder Act* 1998 (see below), the court must focus on whether the remark in question had been made, whether it demonstrated racial hostility and, then, that remark having been made during the commission of an offence, whether either subs. 1(a) or 1(b) was engaged.

The approach to sentencing has been set out by the Court of Appeal in *Kelly and Donnelly* [2001] 2 Cr.App.R.(S.) 73 and is now summarised and incorporated into the *Magistrates' Court Sentencing Guidelines* at p.178. Having re-stated the requirement that an offender must first be put on notice that a court is minded to consider that an offence has been aggravated on the grounds of race, religion, disability or sexual orientation, the guideline sets out the approach to be followed. The guideline states that a high level of aggravation is likely to be indicated where, as far as the offender's intention was concerned, the element of aggravation based on race, religion, disability or sexual orientation was planned or the offence was part of a pattern of offending by the offender or the offender was a member of, or was associated with, a group promoting hostility based on race, religion, disability or sexual orientation or the incident was deliberately set up to be offensive or humiliating to the victim or to the group of which the victim is a member.

As far as the aggravation concerned the impact on the victim or others, relevant factors indicating greater seriousness would include that the offence was committed in the victim's home, the victim was providing a service to the public, the timing or location of the offence was calculated to maximise the harm or distress it caused, the expressions of hostility were repeated or prolonged, the offence caused fear and distress throughout a local community or more widely or the offence caused particular distress to the victim and/or the victim's family.

The guideline provides that, at the lower end of the scale, the aggravation may be regarded as less serious if it was limited in scope or duration, the offence was not motivated by hostility on the basis of race, religion, disability or sexual orientation, and the element of hostility or abuse was minor or incidental.

22–66 Since there are a limited number of racially or religiously aggravated offences, a situation may arise where a defendant has been charged with both the standard offence and the racially or religiously aggravated offence. If found guilty of the standard offence but acquitted of the aggravated offence, can the court in its approach to sentencing still take into account racial or religious aggravation as an aggravating factor? In *G. and T. v. DPP* (2004) 168 J.P. 313, a youth had been charged (with others) with racially aggravated common assault and racially aggravated affray. Prior to trial, the racially aggravated elements were withdrawn from both offences before it was realised that there was no such offence as racially aggravated affray! The defendant was convicted and the District Judge took account of racial aggravation as a statutory aggravating factor in relation to the affray conviction. Allowing the defendant's appeal, the Divisional Court recognised the unusual circumstances in this case. In other cases there may be a different result. Whilst it is for the court to determine on the material before it the seriousness of the offence, "... nevertheless, the court is circumscribed by the ambit of the offence which is charged and the ambit of the offence for which the defendant is convicted." In the circumstances of this case, the defendant had been led to suppose that it was not necessary to deal with issues of racial aggravation because of the decisions in relation to the charges and so it was not open to the court to introduce those issues when considering sentence.

It now appears clear that, where the prosecution has withdrawn a charge of which this form of statutory aggravation is an essential element, the court cannot then impose a sentence for the standard offence which takes account of such aggravation.

Criminal Justice Act 2003, s.145

Increase in sentences for racial or religious aggravation

22–67 **145.**—(1) This section applies where a court is considering the seriousness of an offence other than one under sections 29 to 32 of the *Crime and Disorder Act* 1998 (racially or religiously aggravated assaults, criminal damage, public order offences and harassment etc).

(2) If the offence was racially or religiously aggravated, the court—

(a) must treat that fact as an aggravating factor, and

(b) must state in open court that the offence was so aggravated.

(3) Section 28 of the *Crime and Disorder Act* 1998 (meaning of "racially or religiously aggravated") applies for the purposes of this section as it applies for the purposes of sections 29 to 32 of that Act.

Crime and Disorder Act 1998, s.28

Meaning of "racially or religiously aggravated"

28.—(1) An offence is racially aggravated for the purposes of sections 29 to 32 below if— **22–68**

(a) at the time of committing the offence, or immediately before or after doing so, the offender demonstrates towards the victim of the offence hostility based on the victim's membership (or presumed membership) of a racial or religious group; or

(b) the offence is motivated (wholly or partly) by hostility towards members of a racial or religious group based on their membership of that group.

(2) In subsection (1)(a) above—

"membership", in relation to a racial or religious group, includes association with members of that group;

"presumed" means presumed by the offender.

(3) It is immaterial for the purposes of paragraph (a) or (b) of subsection (1) above whether or not the offender's hostility is also based, to any extent, on any other factor not mentioned in that paragraph.

(4) In this section "racial group" means a group of persons defined by reference to race, colour, nationality (including citizenship) or ethnic or national origins.

(5) In this section "religious group" means a group of persons defined by reference to religious belief or lack of religious belief.

Criminal Justice Act 2003, s.146

Increase in sentences for aggravation related to disability or sexual orientation

146.—(1) This section applies where the court is considering the seriousness of an offence committed in any of the circumstances mentioned in subsection (2). **22–69**

(2) Those circumstances are—

(a) that, at the time of committing the offence, or immediately before or after doing so, the offender demonstrated towards the victim of the offence hostility based on—

(i) the sexual orientation (or presumed sexual orientation) of the victim, or

(ii) a disability (or presumed disability) of the victim, or

(b) that the offence is motivated (wholly or partly)—

(i) by hostility towards persons who are of a particular sexual orientation, or

(ii) by hostility towards persons who have a disability or a particular disability.

(3) The court—

(a) must treat the fact that the offence was committed in any of those circumstances as an aggravating factor, and

(b) must state in open court that the offence was committed in such circumstances.

(4) It is immaterial for the purposes of paragraph (a) or (b) of subsection (2) whether or not the offender's hostility is also based, to any extent, on any other factor not mentioned in that paragraph.

(5) In this section "disability" means any physical or mental impairment.

Antecedents

Courts rely heavily on information regarding previous convictions provided through the prosecution. Drawn from national records, there are times when the information is not as current as it ought to be and courts need to be on their guard in case there are apparent disparities between information sources. The prosecution will tender a list of previous convictions at the conclusion of its presentation once a defendant has been found guilty. Alternatively, for road traffic offenders, this information may come from the defendant's driving licence or from a copy of the driving record. **22–70**

In addition to offences of which an offender has been convicted by a court, conditional cautions are citable. However, since a conditional caution is not a previous conviction, it will not be capable of being a statutory aggravating factor so as to make the current offence more serious. Whilst Penalty Notices for Disorder and Fixed Penalties are not citable, they may nonetheless come to the attention of the court, particularly where they have resulted in the endorsement of a driving licence. The *Magistrates' Court Sentencing Guidelines* suggests that, in each case, the existence of such sanctions should not be treated as making the current offence more serious but might influence sentence selection within the range of options available.

For the standards for the provision of information of antecedents, see the *Consolidated Criminal Practice Direction*, para. III.27 (see Appendix F).

22–71 An antecedents statement should not refer to the fact that the offender has been acquitted on a previous occasion. Where an offender disputes a statement of fact contained in an antecedents statement, it must be proved by admissible evidence or omitted from the evidence placed before the court: *Sargeant* (1974) 60 Cr.App.R. 74, CA. Particular care must be taken where the defendant denies that the record of a particular conviction relates to him.

Rehabilitation of offenders

22–72 One aspect of the approach to the rehabilitation of offenders is that many sentences will become "spent" after a specified period. This means that the conviction does not have to be declared except in certain prescribed circumstances. The time scales for youths are less than for adults. One exception relates to criminal proceedings before a magistrates' court. A court is entitled to take into account convictions that are spent under the *Rehabilitation of Offenders Act* 1974. However, a court does not have an unfettered discretion, it must be demonstrated that justice cannot be done without the admission of such evidence for spent convictions to be admitted: *Hastings Magistrates' Court, ex p. McSpirit* (1998) 162 J.P. 44. In practice, the normal approach will be to ignore spent convictions.

Rehabilitation of Offenders Act 1974, s.5

Rehabilitation periods for particular sentences

22–73 **5.**—(1) The sentences excluded from rehabilitation under this Act are—

(a) a sentence of imprisonment for life;

(b) a sentence of imprisonment, youth custody or corrective training for a term exceeding thirty months;

(c) a sentence of preventive detention;

(d) a sentence of detention during Her Majesty's pleasure or for life under section 90 or 91 of the *Powers of Criminal Courts (Sentencing) Act* 2000 or under section 209 or 218 of the *Armed Forces Act* 2006, or under section 205(2) or (3) of the *Criminal Procedure (Scotland) Act* 1975, or a sentence of detention for a term exceeding thirty months passed under section 91 of the said Act of 2000 (young offenders convicted of grave crimes) or under section 206 of the said Act of 1975 (detention of children convicted on indictment) and

(e) a sentence of custody for life; and

(f) a sentence of imprisonment for public protection under section 225 of the *Criminal Justice Act* 2003, a sentence of detention for public protection under section 226 of that Act or an extended sentence under section 227 or 228 of that Act (including any sentence within this paragraph passed as a result of any sections 219 to 222 of the *Armed Forces Act* 2006);

and any other sentence is a sentence subject to rehabilitation under this Act.

(1A) In subsections (1)(d)—

(a) references to section 209 of the *Armed Forces Act* 2006 include reference to section 71A(4) of the *Army Act* 1955 or *Air Force Act* 1955 or section 43A(a) of the *Naval Discipline Act* 1957;

(b) the reference to section 218 of the *Armed Forces Act* 2006 includes reference to section 71A(3) of *Army Act* 1955 or *Air Force Act* 1955 or section 43A(3) of the *Naval Discipline Act* 1957.

(2) For the purposes of this Act—

(a) the rehabilitation period applicable to a sentence specified in the first column of

Table A below is the period specified in the second column of that Table in relation to that sentence, or, where the sentence was imposed on a person who was under eighteen years of age at the date of his conviction, half that period; and

(b) the rehabilitation period applicable to a sentence specified in the first column of Table B below is the period specified in the second column of that Table in relation to that sentence;

reckoned in either case from the date of the conviction in respect of which the sentence was imposed.

TABLE A: REHABILITATION PERIODS SUBJECT TO REDUCTION BY HALF FOR PERSONS UNDER 18

Sentence	*Rehabilitation period*
A sentence of imprisonment or youth custody or corrective training for a term exceeding six months but not exceeding thirty months.	Ten years
A sentence of cashiering, discharge with ignominy or dismissal with disgrace from Her Majesty's service.	Ten years
A sentence of imprisonment or youth custody for a term not exceeding six months.	Seven years
A sentence of dismissal from Her Majesty's service.	Seven years
Any sentence of service detention within the meaning of the Armed Forces Act 2006, or any sentence of detention corresponding to such a sentence, in respect of conviction in service disciplinary proceedings.	Five years
A fine or any other sentence subject to rehabilitation under this Act, not being a sentence to which Table B below or any of subsection (3) to (8) below applies.	Five years

22–74

TABLE B: REHABILITATION PERIODS FOR CERTAIN SENTENCES CONFINED TO YOUNG OFFENDERS

Sentence	*Rehabilitation period*
A sentence of Borstal training.	Seven years
A custodial order under section 71AA of the *Army Act* 1955 or the *Air Force Act* 1955, or under section 43AA of the *Naval Discipline Act* 1957, where the maximum period of detention specified in the order is more than six months.	Seven years
A custodial order under Schedule 5A to the *Army Act* 1955 or the *Air Force Act* 1955, or under Schedule 4A to the *Naval Discipline Act* 1957, where the maximum period of detention specified in the order is more than six months.	Seven years

22–75

Part IV

22–75

Sentence	*Rehabilitation period*
A sentence of detention for a term exceeding six months but not exceeding thirty months passed under section 91 of the *Powers of Criminal Courts (Sentencing) Act* 2000 or under s.209 of the *Armed Forces Act* 2006 or under 206 of the *Criminal Procedure (Scotland) Act* 1975.	Five years
A sentence of detention for a term not exceeding six months passed under any provisions mentioned in the fourth entry in this Table.	Three years
An order for detention in a detention centre made under section 4 of the *Criminal Justice Act* 1982, section 4 of the *Criminal Justice Act* 1961.	Three years
A custodial order under any of the Schedules to the said Acts of 1955 and 1957 mentioned above, where the maximum period of detention specified in the order is six months or less.	Three years
A custodial order under section 71AA of the said Acts of 1955, or section 43AA of the said act of 1957, where the maximum period of detention specified in the order is six months or less.	Three years

(2A) Table B applies in relation to a sentence under section 71A(4) of the *Army Act* 1955 or *Air Force Act* 1955 or section 43A(4) of the *Naval Discipline Act* 1957 as it applies in relation to one under section 209 of the *Armed Forces Act* 2006.

22–76 (3) The rehabilitation period applicable—

(a) to an order discharging a person absolutely for an offence; and
(b) to the discharge by a children's hearing under section 69(1)(b) and (12) of the *Children (Scotland) Act* 1995 of the referral of a child's case;

shall be six months from the date of conviction.

(4) Where in respect of a conviction a person was conditionally discharged, bound over to keep the peace or be of good behaviour, the rehabilitation period applicable to the sentence shall be one year from the date of conviction or a period beginning with that date and ending when the order for conditional discharge or (as the case may be) the recognizance or bond of caution to keep the peace or be of good behaviour ceases or ceased to have effect, whichever is the longer.

(4A) Where in respect of a conviction a probation order or a community order under section 177 of the *Criminal Justice Act* 2003 or a service community order or overseas community order under the *Armed Forces Act* 2006 was made, the rehabilitation period applicable to the sentence shall be—

(a) in the case of a person aged eighteen years or over at the date of his conviction, five years from the date of conviction;
(b) in the case of a person aged under the age of eighteen years at the date of his conviction, two and a half years from the date of conviction or a period beginning with the date of conviction and ending when the order in question ceases or ceased to have effect, whichever is the longer.

(4B) Where in respect of a conviction a referral order (within the meaning of the *Powers of Criminal Courts (Sentencing) Act* 2000) is made in respect of the person convicted, the rehabilitation period applicable to the sentence shall be—

(a) if a youth offender contract takes effect under section 23 of that Act between him and a youth offender panel, the period beginning with the date of conviction and ending on the date when (in accordance with section 24 of that Act) the contract ceases to have effect;
(b) if no such contract so takes effect, the period beginning with the date of conviction and having the same length as the period for which such a contract would (ignoring any order under paragraph 11 or 12 of Schedule 1 to that Act) have had effect had one so taken effect.

(4C) Where in respect of a conviction an order is made in respect of the person convicted under paragraph 11 or 12 of Schedule 1 to the *Powers of Criminal Courts (Sentencing) Act* 2000 (extension of period for which youth offender contract has effect), the rehabilitation period applicable to the sentence shall be—

(a) if a youth offender contract takes effect under section 23 of that Act between the offender and a youth offender panel, the period beginning with the date of conviction and ending on the date when (in accordance with section 24 of that Act) the contract ceases to have effect;

(b) if no such contract so takes effect, the period beginning with the date of conviction and having the same length as the period for which, in accordance with the order, such a contract would have had effect had one so taken effect.

(5) Where in respect of a conviction any of the following sentences was imposed, that is to say—

(a) an order under section 57 of the *Children and Young Persons Act* 1933 or section 61 of the *Children and Young Persons (Scotland) Act* 1937 committing the person convicted to the care of a fit person;

(b) a supervision order under any provision of either of those Acts or of the *Children and Young Persons Act* 1963.

(c) an order under section 413 of the *Criminal Procedure (Scotland) Act* 1975 committing a child for the purpose of his undergoing residential training:

(d) an approved school order under section 61 of the said Act of 1937;

(da) a youth rehabilitation order under Part 1 of the *Criminal Justice and Immigration Act* 2008;

(e) a supervision order under section 63(1) of the *Powers of Criminal Courts (Sentencing) Act* 2000; or

(f) a supervision requirement under any provision of the *Children (Scotland) Act* 1995;

(g) a community supervision order under Schedule 5A to the *Army Act* 1955 or the *Air Force Act* 1955, or under Schedule 4A to the *Naval Discipline Act* 1957;

the rehabilitation period applicable to the sentence shall be one year from the date of conviction or a period beginning with that date and ending when the order or requirement ceases or ceased to have effect, whichever is the longer.

(6) Where in respect of a conviction any of the following orders was made, that is to say—

(a) an order under section 54 of the said Act of 1933 committing the person convicted to custody in a remand home;

(b) an approved school order under section 57 of the said Act of 1933;

(c) an attendance centre order under section 60 of the *Powers of Criminal Courts (Sentencing) Act* 2000; or

(d) a secure training order under section 1 of the *Criminal Justice and Public Order Act* 1994;

the rehabilitation period applicable to the sentence shall be a period beginning with the date of conviction and ending one year after the date on which the order ceases or ceased to have effect.

(6A) Where in respect of a conviction a detention and training order was made under section 100 of the *Powers of Criminal Courts (Sentencing) Act* 2000, or an order under section 211 of the *Armed Forces Act* 2006 was made, the rehabilitation period applicable to the sentence shall be—

(a) in the case of a person aged fifteen years or over at the date of his conviction, five years if the order was, and three and a half years if the order was not, for a term exceeding six months;

(b) in the case of a person aged under fifteen years at the date of his conviction, a period beginning with that date and ending one year after the date on which the order ceases to have effect.

(7) Where in respect of a conviction a hospital order under Part III of the *Mental Health Act* 1983 or under Pt VI of the *Criminal Procedure (Scotland) Act* 1995 was made, the rehabilitation period applicable to the sentence shall be the period of five years from the date of conviction or a period beginning with that date and ending two years after the date on which the hospital order ceases or ceased to have effect, whichever is the longer.

(8) Where in respect of a conviction an order was made imposing on the person convicted any disqualification, disability, prohibition or other penalty, the rehabilitation period applicable to the sentence shall be a period beginning with the date of conviction and

ending on the date on which the disqualification, disability, prohibition or penalty (as the case may be) ceases or ceased to have effect.

(9) For the purposes of this section—

(a) "sentence of imprisonment" includes a sentence of detention under section 207 or 415 of the *Criminal Procedure (Scotland) Act* 1975 and a sentence of penal servitude, and "term of imprisonment" shall be construed accordingly;

(b) consecutive terms of imprisonment or of detention under section 91 of the *Powers of Criminal Courts (Sentencing) Act* 2000 or section 209 of the *Armed Forces Act* 2006 or section 206 of the said Act of 1975, and terms which are wholly or partly concurrent (being terms of imprisonment or detention imposed in respect of offences of which a person was convicted in the same proceedings) shall be treated as a single term;

(c) no account shall be taken of any subsequent variation, made by a court in dealing with a person in respect of a suspended sentence of imprisonment, of the term originally imposed; and

(d) a sentence imposed by a court outside Great Britain shall be treated as a sentence of that one of the descriptions mentioned in this section which most nearly corresponds to the sentence imposed.

(10) References in this section to the period during which a probation order, or a supervision order under the *Powers of Criminal Courts (Sentencing) Act* 2000, or a supervision requirement under the *Children (Scotland) Act* 1995, is or was in force include references to any period during which any order or requirement to which this subsection applies, being an order or requirement made or imposed directly or indirectly in substitution for the first-mentioned order or requirement, is or was in force.

This subsection applies—

(a) to any such order or requirement as is mentioned above in this subsection;

(b) to any order having effect under section 25(2) of the *Children and Young Persons Act* 1969 as if it were a training school order in Northern Ireland; and

(c) to any supervision order made under section 72(2) of the said Act of 1968 and having effect as a supervision order under the *Children and Young Persons Act (Northern Ireland)* 1950.

(11) The Secretary of State may by order—

(a) substitute different periods or terms for any of the periods or terms mentioned in subsection (1) to (8) above; and

(b) substitute a different age for the age mentioned in subsection (2)(a) above.

Rehabilitation of Offenders Act 1974, s.6

The rehabilitation period applicable to a conviction

22–77 **6.**—(1) Where only one sentence is imposed in respect of a conviction (not being a sentence excluded from rehabilitation under this Act) the rehabilitation period applicable to the conviction is, subject to the following provisions of this section, the period applicable to the sentence in accordance with section 5 above.

(2) Where more than one sentence is imposed in respect of a conviction (whether or not in the same proceedings) and none of the sentences imposed is excluded from rehabilitation under this Act, then, subject to the following provisions of this section, if the periods applicable to those sentences in accordance with section 5 above differ, the rehabilitation period applicable to the conviction shall be the longer or the longest (as the case may be) of those periods.

(3) Without prejudice to subsection (2) above, where in respect of a conviction a person was conditionally discharged or a probation order was made and after the end of the rehabilitation period applicable to the conviction in accordance with subsection (1) or (2) above he is dealt with, in consequence of a breach of conditional discharge or a breach of the order, for the offence for which the order for conditional discharge or a breach of the order was made, then, if the rehabilitation period applicable to the conviction in accordance with subsection (2) above (taking into account any sentence imposed when he is so dealt with) ends later than the rehabilitation period previously applicable to the conviction, he shall be treated for the purposes of this Act as not having become a rehabilitated person in respect of that conviction, and the conviction shall for those purposes be treated as not having become spent, in relation to any period falling before the end of the new rehabilitation period.

(4) Subject to subsection (5) below, where during the rehabilitation period applicable to a conviction—

(a) the person convicted is convicted of a further offence; and

(b) no sentence excluded from rehabilitation under this Act is imposed on him in respect of the later conviction;

if the rehabilitation period applicable in accordance with this section to either of the convictions would end earlier than the period so applicable in relation to the other, the rehabilitation period which would (apart from this subsection) end the earlier shall be extended so as to end at the same time as the other rehabilitation period.

(5) Where the rehabilitation period applicable to a conviction is the rehabilitation period applicable in accordance with section 5(8) above to an order imposing on a person any disqualification, disability, prohibition or other penalty, the rehabilitation period applicable to another conviction shall not by virtue of subsection (4) above be extended by reference to that period; but if any other sentence is imposed in respect of the first-mentioned conviction for which a rehabilitation period is prescribed by any other provision of section 5 above, the rehabilitation period applicable to another conviction shall, where appropriate, be extended under subsection (4) above by reference to the rehabilitation period applicable in accordance with that section to that sentence or, where more than one such sentence is imposed, by reference to the longer or longest of the periods so applicable to those sentences, as if the period in question were the rehabilitation period applicable to the first-mentioned conviction.

(6) For the purposes of subsection (4)(a) above there shall be disregarded—

(a) any conviction in England and Wales of a summary offence or of a scheduled offence (within the meaning of section 22 of the *Magistrates' Courts Act* 1980) tried summarily in pursuance of subsection (2) of that section (summary trial where value involved is small);

(b) any conviction in Scotland of an offence which is not excluded from the jurisdiction of inferior courts of summary jurisdiction by virtue of section 4 of the *Summary Jurisdiction (Scotland) Act* 1954 (certain crimes not to be tried in inferior courts of summary jurisdiction);

(bb) any conviction in service disciplinary proceedings for an offence listed in Schedule 1 to this Act; and

(c) any conviction by or before a court outside Great Britain of an offence in respect of conduct which, if it had taken place in any part of Great Britain, would not have constituted an offence under the law in force in that part of Great Britain.

E. MITIGATION

(1) General

A court has a wide discretion concerning what it chooses to take into account as mitigation. Factors may mitigate the seriousness of an offence or may relate to the offence itself or to the offender and thus be relevant to the selection of sentence within the limits fixed by the seriousness if the offence. In relation to the sentences for individual offences, they are set out in earlier chapters that relate to those offences. **22–78**

There may be times when a court has some difficulty in accepting what is put forward either as a description of the circumstances of the offence or as the circumstances of the offender. If a significant issue is put forward by the defence which the prosecution or the court is not prepared to accept as accurate, this will normally need to be resolved by the hearing of evidence—a *Newton* hearing (see *ante*, § 22–53, for a general discussion of the approach where there is a dispute about the factual basis on which sentence is to be passed).

However, situations are not always so straightforward to identify and defence advocates will often be instructed to put forward versions of events or the conduct of the defendant that it would not be appropriate to spend large amounts of court time disputing.

The offender or his/her legal representative should be able to address the court in mitigation, notwithstanding that the offender has been convicted by a jury after having denied the charge led against him: *Jones*, unreported, August 6, 1979, CA. The same principle applies where a defendant is convicted after a trial in a magistrates' court. The judge is also under a duty of fairness to alert defence counsel to the possibility that he may impose a sentence which the defence counsel is not anticipating. This is to allow defence counsel to make submissions on this issue: *Scott* (1989) 11 Cr.App.R.(S.) 249.

(2) General mitigating circumstances

22–79 Factors that generally assist a court in determining the level of culpability or harm are set out in the guideline on seriousness issued by the Sentencing Guidelines Council in December 2004 at paragraphs 1.20–1.29. The statutory provisions are contained in s.166 of the *Criminal Justice Act* 2003. The most significant change from the previous provisions is in s.166(2) where it is made clear that, even where the initial assessment of seriousness takes a case over the custody threshold (and therefore so serious that a community sentence could not be justified), nonetheless personal mitigation may allow a court to impose a community sentence. Whilst this was the approach of many courts under the previous framework, it is helpful to have this clarification.

Criminal Justice Act 2003, s.166

Savings for powers to mitigate sentences and deal appropriately with mentally disordered offenders

22–80 **166.**—(1) Nothing in—

(a) section 148 (imposing community sentences),

(b) section 152, 153 or 157 (imposing custodial sentences),

(c) section 156 (pre-sentence reports and other requirements),

(d) section 164 (fixing of fines),

(e) paragraph 3 of Schedule 1 to the *Criminal Justice and Immigration Act* 2008 (youth rehabilitation order with intensive supervision and surveillance), or

(f) paragraph 4 of Schedule 1 to that Act (youth rehabilitation order with fostering),

prevents a court from mitigating an offender's sentence by taking into account any such matters as, in the opinion of the court, are relevant in mitigation of sentence.

(2) Section 152(2) does not prevent a court, after taking into account such matters, from passing a community sentence even though it is of the opinion that the offence, or the combination of the offence and one or more offences associated with it, was so serious that a community sentence could not normally be justified for the offence.

(3) Nothing in the sections mentioned in subsection (1)(a) to (f) prevents a court—

(a) from mitigating any penalty included in an offender's sentence by taking into account any other penalty included in that sentence, and

(b) in the case of an offender who is convicted of one or more other offences, from mitigating his sentence by applying any rule of law as to the totality of sentences.

(4) Subsections (2) and (3) are without prejudice to the generality of subsection (1).

(5) Nothing in the sections mentioned in subsection (1)(a) to (f) is to be taken—

(a) as requiring a court to pass a custodial sentence, or any particular custodial sentence, on a mentally disordered offender, or

(b) as restricting any power (whether under the *Mental Health Act* 1983 or otherwise) which enables a court to deal with such an offender in the manner it considers to be most appropriate in all the circumstances.

(6) In subsection (5) "mentally disordered", in relation to a person, means suffering from a mental disorder within the meaning of the *Mental Health Act* 1983.

Guideline: Overarching Principles: Seriousness

D. ASSESSMENT OF CULPABILITY AND HARM

(ii) Mitigating factors

22–81 **1.24** Some factors may indicate that an offender's culpability is **unusually** low, or that the harm caused by an offence is less than usually serious.

1.25 Factors indicating significantly lower culpability:

- A greater degree of provocation than normally expected
- Mental illness or disability
- Youth or age, where it affects the responsibility of the individual defendant
- The fact that the offender played only a minor role in the offence

(iii) Personal mitigation

1.26 Section 166(1) Criminal Justice Act 2003 makes provision for a sentencer to take account of any matters that "in the opinion of the court, are relevant in mitigation of sentence".

1.27 When the court has formed an initial assessment of the seriousness of the offence, then it should consider any offender mitigation. The issue of remorse should be taken into account at this point along with other mitigating features such as admissions to the police in interview.

(iv) Reduction for a guilty plea

1.28 Sentencers will normally reduce the severity of a sentence to reflect an early guilty plea. This subject is covered by a separate guideline and provides a sliding scale reduction with a normal maximum one-third reduction being given to offenders who enter a guilty plea at the first reasonable opportunity.

1.29 Credit may also be given for ready co-operation with the authorities. This will depend on the particular circumstances of the individual case.

(3) Mitigation for assistance

An offender who materially assists the police, perhaps by disclosing information of **22–82** value to an investigation of offences committed by others, or relating to the involvement of others in the offence for which he is charged, may expect some degree of discount from the court: *Sinfield* (1981) 3 Cr.App.R.(S.) 258, CA. The size of the discount depends on the individual facts of the case: *Rose and Sapiano* (1980) 2 Cr.App.R.(S.) 239, CA. There is no "tariff" for people who give evidence against co-defendants, each case must be approached on its own particular facts, weighing up the criminality of the admitted offences against the offender's assistance to and co-operation with the police, and taking into account the public interest in encouraging others to come forward. Whilst most cases of this type will be dealt with in the Crown Court, there will be occasions when they will appear for sentence in a magistrates' court, perhaps with the additional complication that a lesser (summary only) charge has been preferred as a part of the response to the assistance given. Additional powers have now been provided to enable the prosecuting and enforcement authorities to encourage the giving of assistance. These include immunity from prosecution, undertakings regarding the giving of evidence and the provision of reductions in sentence: *Serious Organised Crime and Police Act* 2005, s.71. The powers relating to reduction in sentence may only be exercised by the Crown Court.

The formal scheme under ss.71–75 of the *Serious Organised Crime and Police Act* 2005 is complemented by the perpetuation of the previous, non-statutory, scheme for situations which do not fit within the statutory scheme and the Court of Appeal considered the impact of the statutory scheme in *H, D, Chaudhury* [2009] EWCA Crim. 2485; [2010] 2 Cr.App.R.(S.) 18. The Lord Chief Justice, Lord Judge, summarised the key elements of the statutory scheme and confirmed that it did not abolish the previous scheme but that any discount under the non-statutory scheme was likely to be less than under the statutory scheme both because the information was likely to be of less value and also because the means by which it was given was less readily susceptible to a safeguarding review. The non-statutory scheme envisaged that the information would be provided before sentence was imposed but an exception might arise where an offender sought to provide assistance and take advantage of the scheme before sentence was imposed but, through oversight or misadventure, the court was ignorant of it.

In *Ruddock* [2010] EWCA Crim. 1093 the defendant (who had pleaded guilty to a number of serious offences including robbery) gave information leading to the conviction of 17 other offenders and the detection of others in addition (this was given under the non-statutory ("text") system). In this case, a reduction of 25 per cent was considered appropriate.

The discount should be calculated by deciding what would have been the appropriate sentence had the offence not been admitted by the defendant and been contested at trial. The judge should then make an appropriate reduction which adequately reflects the nature and importance of the information and assistance actually given: *Sehitoglu and Ozakan* [1998] 1 Cr.App.R.(S.) 89, CA.

22–83 In *King* (1985) 7 Cr.App.R.(S.) 227 it was held that the correct approach is for the court first to assess the gravity and number of the offences committed by the defendant, which should result in what might be called a starting figure. The amount by which that figure should be reduced would depend on a number of variable features including the quality and quantity of the material disclosed by the informer, its accuracy and his willingness to confront other criminals or give evidence against them and the degree to which the offender had put himself and his family at risk of reprisal. The amount of that mitigation would vary from about one half to two thirds, according to the circumstances. The sentence must be tailored to punish the defendant, but at the same time reward him for the help he has given and to demonstrate to offenders that it is worth their while to disclose the criminal activities of others for the benefit of the law-abiding public in general: *Sivan* (1988) 10 Cr.App.R.(S.) 282, CA.

22–84 Further guidance on how to assess the accuracy of the information offered, given the defendant's desire to preserve anonymity, was stated in *Sivan, ante*. Lord Lane C.J. stated that, in important cases, it might be desirable for the court to have a letter from a senior officer in the investigating agency, unconnected with the case, who has examined all the facts and is able to certify that the facts are as reported by the officers conducting the investigation. There should be a statement in writing from the officer in charge of the investigation setting out those facts which will be certified by the senior unconnected officer. It would also be advisable in the more important cases to have the officer in charge of the investigation available to give evidence if necessary, whether in court or in the judge's chambers as the situation may demand. The shorthand writer should also be present taking a note of what transpires in the judge's private room.

Credit should only be given if the information is offered early enough for it to be potentially useful: *Debbag and Izzet* (1991) 12 Cr.App.R.(S.) 733, CA. This aversion to encouraging a system of negotiation is particularly so where the information offered proves to be of no practical assistance to the authorities. See also *A. and B.* [1999] 1 Cr.App.R.(S.) 52, CA and *X.* (1994) 15 Cr.App.R.(S.) 750, CA.

In *X. (No.2)* [1999] 2 Cr.App.R.(S.) 294, CA, guidance was given on the appropriate approach when the defendant disagrees with the police account of the assistance he has given to the investigation of the case. Hughes J. stated:

22–85 "We consider that the proper principles to be followed in a case of this kind are as follows:

1. It is convenient to remember that a document of this kind, although supplied by a police officer, is supplied at the request of the defendant.

2. Except to the extent that the defendant's contention that he has given assistance is supported by the police, it will not generally be likely that the sentencing judge will be able to make any adjustment in sentence. A defendant's unsupported assertion to that effect is not normally likely to be a reliable basis for mitigation.

3. It follows from that, that courts must rely very heavily upon the greatest possible care being taken, in compiling such a document for the information of the judge. The judge will have to rely upon it, without investigation, if police inquiries are not to be damaged or compromised and other suspects, guilty or innocent, are not to be affected.

We have to express our regret that the document in the present case had not been prepared with sufficient care. Those who prepare such documents, and senior officers who verify them, must realise the importance of ensuring that they are complete and accurate.

4. Except in very unusual circumstances, it will not be necessary, nor will it be desirable for a document of this kind to contain the kind of details which would attract a public interest immunity application. We should observe that, as it seems to us, the document in the present case did not do so.

5. If very exceptionally such a document does contain information attracting a public interest immunity consideration, then the usual rules about the conduct of such an application will apply. In particular, the *Crown Court (Criminal Procedure and Investigations Act 1996)*

(Disclosure) Rules 1997, will apply. It will of course be a case in which the defence can and should be told of the public interest immunity application.

6. Absent any consideration of public interest immunity, which we take to be the general position, a document of this kind should be shown to counsel for the defence, who will no doubt discuss its contents with the defendant. That is not, we emphasise, because it will be necessary to debate its contents, but it is so that there should be no room for any unfounded suspicion that the judge has been told something potentially adverse to the defendant without his knowing about it. On general principles, a defendant is entitled to see documents put before the trial judge on which he is to be sentenced. Expeditions to the judge's chambers should not be necessary in these cases. There should never normally be any question of evidence being given, nor of an issue being tried upon the question of the extent of the information provided. To that extent, we entirely agree with the learned judge.

7. If the defendant wishes to disagree with the contents of such a document, it is not appropriate for there to be cross-examination of the policeman, whether in court or in chambers. The policeman is not a Crown witness, he has simply supplied material for the judge, at the request of the defendant. It would no doubt be possible, in an appropriate case, for a defendant to ask for an adjournment to allow any opportunity for further consideration to be given to the preparation of the document. Otherwise, if the defendant does not accept what the document says, his remedy is not to rely upon it.

Quite apart from the position of the police officer as an officer reporting at the request of the defendant, cross-examination on the usefulness of the information would almost inevitably be contrary to the public interest. It would be likely to damage inquiries still in train, trials yet to come, suspects guilty or innocent and quite possibly the defendant in the instant case. In a limited number of cases, such a request for cross-examination might even have been set up deliberately for such purpose, although we do not, for a moment, say that would have been the position here.

8. No doubt, the learned judge should ordinarily disregard such a document, if asked by the defendant to do so. In such case, he will no doubt not then be minded to entertain any submission that the defendant has given valuable assistance to the police.

9. If the judge does take the document into consideration he will, no doubt, say no more than is in accordance with the present practice, namely that he has taken into consideration all the information about the defendant, with which he has been provided."

(4) Mitigation where the offender avoids apprehension for a substantial period of time

Where the offender avoids apprehension for a substantial period of time, the sentencer may make such allowance in mitigation as he feels proper: *Bird* (1987) 9 Cr.App.R.(S.) 77, CA. **22-86**

However, this principle does not extend to cases involving sexual abuse within a family, which are very likely to remain undetected for substantial periods: *Tiso* (1990) 12 Cr.App.R.(S.) 122, CA.

(5) Mitigation where the offender committed the offence as a young person but convicted of them as an adult

In cases where an offender has committed offences as a youth but is not convicted of them for many years, the proper approach for the sentencing judge is to identify the sentence which would have been passed if the defendant had been sentenced within a reasonable period after committing the offences and to take that sentence as a starting point in determining the proper sentence to be imposed. **22-87**

In particular, where an offence is committed by an offender under eighteen, but the conviction occurs after attaining the age of eighteen the starting point for consideration of the appropriate sentence is the sentence that the offender would have been likely to receive if he had been sentenced at the date of the commission of the offence: *Overarching Principles—Sentencing Youths*, Part 5: Sentencing Guidelines Council, November 2009. In accordance with general sentencing principles, a sentence may also be discounted to reflect the youth of the offender: *Overarching Principles: Seriousness* at 1.25: *www.sentencingcouncil.judiciary.gov.uk*.

In *Bowker* [2007] EWCA Crim. 1608, the defendant was convicted of a serious offence of violent disorder committed two days before his 18th birthday. He was a key participant in the event and sentenced on the same basis as the two other defendants (both of whom were well over 18 at the time of the offence). The sentence was 28 months detention, above the maximum that could have been imposed if he had been sentenced as a 17-year-old. The court rejected an argument that the European Convention on Human Rights required the sentence not to exceed the maximum that could have been imposed on a 17-year-old. The purpose of art. 7(1) was to prevent retrospective increases in maximum penalties and a defendant must be taken to be aware of how the law applies depending on age. Attention was drawn to the change in approach to sentencing once a person attains the age of 18. The aims set out in s.142 of the *Criminal Justice Act* 2003 apply to those aged 18 or over at the time of conviction and therefore shift the focus away from those that apply to youths. This had not been a case where there had been delays in reporting or in investigation and, given the role of the defendant and the fact that he was just short of his 18th birthday, the court considered it relevant to examine whether it was just that he be treated significantly differently from those who were over 18 at the time of the offence. The court agreed that there should have been a difference and that a sentence of 24 months would properly reflect the part that the defendant played, his age and the plea. This would have been the maximum sentence if sentenced as a 17-year-old.

(6) Mitigation due to personal characteristics of the offender

22–88 A sentencer may give credit for meritorious conduct that is unrelated to the offence for which he is to be sentenced: *Alexander* [1997] 2 Cr.App.R.(S.) 74; but great care needs to be paid to whether that is appropriate. Whilst such credit may be acceptable in relation to non violent offences, it may be less so where the offender has inflicted injury on another person. So, for instance, a person with a good record of public service who is convicted of assaults taking place in a domestic context may not merit any reduction in sentence whereas such a person convicted of theft may do; see Sentencing Guidelines Council guideline *Overarching Principles—Domestic Violence* para. 3.20 and § 22–62, *ante*.

The hardship inflicted on the offender's family may be a mitigating factor in exceptional cases: *Summers* (1979) 1 Cr.App.R.(S.) 13. In *Whitehead* [1996] 1 Cr.App.R.(S.) 111, CA the case was described as "finely balanced as to whether a custodial sentence was required or not." The matter tipping the balance in favour of a non-custodial sentence was the position of the three children, aged nine, seven and five. As a result of both parents being sent to prison, they were deprived of the care of both father and mother. The factor relating to the children was decisive in coming to the conclusion that the imprisonment was inappropriate and a 50-hour community service order was imposed.

Ill-health should not affect the length of the sentence imposed, but in exceptional cases the court could reduce the sentence imposed as an act of mercy: *Moore* (1994) 15 Cr.App.R.(S.) 97. Asperger's syndrome, an abnormality of development related to autism, characterised by subtle abnormalities of social interaction, preoccupation with special interests and abnormalities of personality may persuade the court to take an exceptional course: *Gibson* [2001] EWCA 656. A short life expectancy may also persuade the court to reduce the sentence it would otherwise impose: *Lewis* [2001] EWCA Crim. 935.

(7) Mitigation relating to the circumstances of the offence

22–89 The fact that the offence was committed under the influence of alcohol is not normally a mitigating factor: *Bradley* (1980) 2 Cr.App.R.(S.) 12 nor is the fact that the offence was committed to provide money to support an addiction: *Lawrence* (1988) 10 Cr.App.R.(S.) 463, CA.

See also Sentencing Guidelines Council definitive guidelines: *Overarching Principles: Seriousness*, para. 1.22; *Theft and Burglary in a building other than a dwelling*, para. 16, *www.sentencingcouncil.judiciary.gov.uk*.

The use of an agent provocateur to facilitate commission of the offence will not be a mitigating factor unless the officer concerned has acted improperly: *Underhill* (1979) 1 Cr.App.R.(S.) 270, CA; *Springer* [1999] 1 Cr.App.R.(S.) 217, CA. Entrapment as a result of the conduct of journalists rather than police officers will also result in mitigation of sentence: *Tonnessen* [1998] 2 Cr.App.R.(S.) 328, CA.

(8) Mitigation relating to mentally disordered offenders

Section 166(5) of the *CJA* 2003 makes it clear that the court is not fettered in regard **22–90** to making appropriate orders regarding mentally disordered offenders by the criteria for other sentences. An offender is mentally disordered if suffering from a mental disorder within the meaning of the *Mental Health Act* 1983: s.1. See *post*, Ch.28.

(9) The totality principle

A defendant will often face more than one offence, sometimes arising out of the same **22–91** circumstances, sometimes arising out of different circumstances. Each offence must receive a sentence (even if it is "no separate penalty"). As well as looking at the appropriate sentence for each offence, the court must also consider the appropriate sentence for the totality of the offending before it. When the court has calculated the sentence appropriate for each offence, it should then consider the aggregate sentence and decide whether the total sentence is just and appropriate: *Hewitt* [1980] Crim. L.R. 116; *Jones* [1996] 1 Cr.App.R.(S.) 153.

The effect of this is confirmed in section 166(3)(b) of the *CJA* 2003. In the explanatory material, the *Magistrates' Court Sentencing Guidelines* provides (at p.147): "the overall sentence must be just and appropriate having regard to the totality of the offending; the court should not simply aggregate the sentences considered suitable for the individual offences. The court's assessment of the totality of the offending may result in an overall sentence above the range indicated for the individual offences, including a sentence of a different type": *www.sentencingcouncil.judiciary.gov.uk*. A particular difficulty can arise where an offence has a maximum penalty that has become too low in comparison with other equivalent offences; in such circumstances, particular care needs to be taken to comply with the proper approach to the use of consecutive sentences, that is, that the offences should be distinct or separate events. This issue was considered again by a strong constitution of the Court of Appeal (Criminal Division) in *Ralphs* [2010] 2 Cr.App.R.(S.) 30 in which the judgment was given by the Lord Chief Justice. The defendant pleaded guilty to 9 counts arising from the possession of guns and ammunition; it was accepted that he was a 'minder' and he was sentenced to a total of 6 years imprisonment. The Attorney General sought to persuade the court that this was unduly lenient and that sentences totalling well into double figures should have been imposed – the maximum sentence for any of the offences was 10 years. Recognising this as an attempt to circumvent the statutory maximum sentence on the grounds that it was too low, the Court rejected that part of the application (although increasing the sentence to 8 years overall); it was for Parliament to address the situation not for the Courts to set aside well established principles of which Parliament must be deemed to have been aware when providing the statutory maximum. A generally recognised example of a situation where difficulties may be encountered is the maximum sentence for dangerous driving. A useful reminder of the circumstances in which maximum sentences should be considered for such offences can be found in *Butt* [2006] EWCA Crim. 47. The driving consisted of driving on the wrong side of the road whilst trying to evade the police; the driver was the worse for both drink and drugs. Upholding a sentence of 18 months' imprisonment (after a guilty plea), the Court of Appeal drew attention to existing guidance on the circumstances in which it is appropriate to use the maximum as a starting point. Similarly, it may be appropriate to consider consecutive sentences where the driver both drove dangerously and drove with excess alcohol or was disqualified. Although the general practice is to impose concurrent sentences where the offences arose from a single incident, nonetheless there is a well recognised practice that, in circumstances such as these, consecutive sentences may be imposed. In *Hardy* [2006] 2 Cr.App.R.(S.) 4, the defendant was convicted of dangerous driving, driving whilst disqualified and failing to provide a specimen. Consecutive sentences totalling two years were imposed in the Crown Court. Upholding those sentences and the approach, the Court of Appeal stated that, whilst consecutive sentences would not generally be appropriate where the matters arose out of the same incident "it would be bizarre that this man would in fact have a licence to drive with excess alcohol and while disqualified without any added penalty." An approach that may have less offended general sentencing principle would have been to have treated the alcohol and disqualification as aggravating factors and increased the sentence accordingly; however, the low maximum penalty does not allow that to happen so readily and this is perhaps another example of the problems that arise when maximum sentences are allowed to remain at a level that is too low.

22-92 This principle applies to community penalties and financial orders as well as to custodial sentences. In magistrates' courts, the issue is more likely to arise in relation to financial penalties than to custodial or community sentences with the additional obligation to set the penalty in the light of the resources available to the defendant.

Generally, financial penalties are in addition to other financial penalties imposed whereas community penalties will each start from the day of imposition. Custodial penalties are either concurrent with each other or consecutive to others as specified by the court at the time of sentence.

F. TAKING OFFENCES INTO CONSIDERATION AND SPECIMEN CHARGES

22-93 When passing sentence for the principal offence, the court may take into consideration other offences admitted by the defendant but which have not been charged, and in respect of which there will not be a conviction. The practice of taking offences into consideration has no statutory foundation, and has been described as "a convention under which if a court is informed that there are outstanding charges against a prisoner who is before it for a particular offence the court can, if the prisoner admits the offences and asks that they should be taken into account, take them into account." Lord Goddard C.J. in *Batchelor* (1952) 36 Cr.App.R. 64.

However, an offence should not be taken into consideration if the public interest requires that it should be the subject of a separate trial: *McClean*, 6 Cr.App.R.(S.) 26, CA. A court should also not take into consideration an offence which it is not empowered to try, hence a magistrates' court could not take into consideration a charge triable only on indictment: *Simons* (1953) 37 Cr.App.R. 120, CA.

Generally, offences that an offender asks to have taken into consideration are no more serious than the conviction offence. However, in *Lavery* [2008] EWCA Crim. 2499, the offender was sentenced for an offence of robbery and asked for four other offences of robbery to be taken into consideration. The court formed the view that one of more of those offences should have been the subject of separate prosecution and were significantly more serious than the conviction offence. The prosecution, however, declined (despite the relevant provisions in the Crown Prosecution Service Code of Practice) and the court felt obliged to proceed by taking the offences into consideration. On appeal, it was argued that the sentence was too high and that the offence taken into consideration should not have justified such a sentence. The Court of Appeal dismissed that proposition; "There is no reason in principle why an offence to be taken into consideration, and which is of a more serious nature than the index offence or offences, should not result in a higher sentence than would otherwise have been the case as the sentence will reflect the defendant's overall criminality" *per* Lord Judge, C.J.

Some puzzlement as to the principles behind this practice were expressed by the Court of Appeal (Criminal Division) in *Sinfield* [2005] EWCA Crim. 3638. In *Miles* [2006] EWCA Crim. 256, the court considered the issue further. It was emphasised that the sentence is intended to reflect the overall criminality of the offender. Asking for offences to be taken into consideration may bring credit to an offender by virtue of assistance given in clearing up crimes that would not otherwise have been cleared up and by demonstrating a genuine determination to wipe the slate clean. In this case, the offender was committing burglary as a consequence of long term addiction to drugs, had drawn the additional offences to the notice of the police and had already successfully completed a detoxification programme whilst in prison awaiting sentence. On the other hand, such offences may demonstrate a pattern of criminal activity involving careful planning or may reveal offences committed on bail or a return to crime shortly after sentence for earlier crimes. In those circumstances, they may substantially increase the sentence imposed. The approach has been reviewed in an advice published by the Sentencing Advisory Panel in March 2010: *www.sentencingcouncil.judiciary.gov.uk* and the extent to which a sentence will change as a result of offences taken into consideration was again considered in *Shilton* [2010] EWCA Crim. 990. The defendant had pleaded guilty to 15 offences of theft and asked for a further 19 to be taken into consideration. These were all thefts from stores in the area, generally of food, alcohol and toiletries, and the total value was just under £3000. On some occasions, the value of goods taken was relatively high—in one theft £325 of alcohol was stolen. The offences were committed to fund a drug habit. At the Crown Court, a sentence of 30 months imprisonment was imposed; the Judge stated that this was one month for each offence but, having taken the 19 offences into consideration, a total of 30 months—in essence doubling what would otherwise have been the sentence. Allowing the appeal against sentence, the Court of Appeal noted that there was a balance to be struck between the aggravation arising from the larger number of offences and the effect of the frankness of the defendant in admitting them. Recognising that that balance will not always be neutral, doubling sentence gave undue weight to the additional offences; the custodial sentence was reduced to 22 months.

An offence should not be taken into consideration where the court is required to disqualify the offender from driving or to endorse his driving licence in the event of conviction, as such measures cannot be taken where the offence is taken into consideration. **22–94**

In *DPP v. Anderson* (1978) 142 J.P. 391, it was held that if justice is to be done the practice of taking cases into consideration should not be followed except with the express and unequivocal assent of the offender. Hence he should be informed explicitly of each offence which the judge proposes to be taken into consideration and should explicitly admit that he committed them and should state his desire that they should be taken into consideration in determining the sentence passed upon him.

A similar practice has grown up in relation to specimen charges. The prosecution may select a small number of occasions where an offence has been committed knowing that similar offences have taken place on other occasions. Providing the defendant clearly accepts responsibility for all offences, the court can sentence on the basis of the whole course of conduct.

Part IV

G. Credit for Guilty Plea

Criminal Justice Act 2003, s.144

Reduction in sentences for guilty pleas

144.—(1) In determining what sentence to pass on an offender who has pleaded guilty to an offence in proceedings before that or another court, a court must take into account— **22–95**

(a) the stage in the proceedings for the offence at which the offender indicated his intention to plead guilty, and

(b) the circumstances in which this indication was given.

(2) In the case of an offence the sentence for which falls to be imposed under subsection (2) of section 110 or 111 of the Sentencing Act, nothing in that subsection prevents the court, after taking into account any matter referred to in subsection (1) of this section, from imposing any sentence which is not less than 80 per cent of that specified in that subsection.

The Sentencing Guidelines Council has published a definitive guideline which all courts must follow. **22–96**

Guideline: Reduction in Sentence for a Guilty Plea

B. Statement of Purpose

22–97 **2.1** When imposing a custodial sentence, statute requires that a court must impose the shortest term that is commensurate with the seriousness of the offence(s). Similarly, when imposing a community order, the restrictions on liberty must be commensurate with the seriousness of the offence(s). Once that decision is made, a court is required to give consideration to the reduction for any guilty plea. As a result, the final sentence after the reduction for a guilty plea will be less than the seriousness of the offence requires.

2.2 A reduction in sentence is appropriate because a guilty plea avoids the need for a trial (thus enabling other cases to be disposed of more expeditiously), shortens the gap between charge and sentence, saves considerable cost, and, in the case of an early plea, saves victims and witnesses from the concern about having to give evidence. The reduction principle derives from the need for the effective administration of justice and not as an aspect of mitigation.

2.3 Where a sentencer is in doubt as to whether a custodial sentence is appropriate, the reduction attributable to a guilty plea will be relevant consideration. Where this is amongst the factors leading to the imposition of a non-custodial sentence, there will be no need to apply a further reduction on account of the guilty plea. A similar approach is appropriate where the reduction for a guilty plea is amongst the factors leading to the imposition of a financial penalty or discharge instead of a community order.

2.4 When deciding the most appropriate length of sentence, the sentencer should address separately the issue of remorse, together with any other mitigating features, before calculating the reduction for the guilty plea. Similarly, assistance to the prosecuting or enforcement authorities is a separate issue which may attract a reduction in sentence under other procedures though care will need to be taken to ensure that there is no "double counting".

2.5 The implications of other offences that an offender has asked to be taken into consideration should be reflected in the sentence before the reduction for guilty plea has been applied.

2.6 A reduction in sentence should only be applied to the **punitive elements** of a penalty. The guilty plea reduction has no impact on sentencing decisions in relation to ancillary orders, including orders of disqualification from driving.

C. Application of the Reduction Principle

Recommended Approach

3.1 The court decides sentence for the offence(s) taking into account aggravating and mitigating factors and any other offences that have been formally admitted (TICs)

↓

The court selects the amount of the reduction by reference to the sliding scale

↓

The court applies the reduction

↓

When pronouncing sentence the court should usually state what the sentence would have been if there had been no reduction as a result of the guilty plea.

D. Determining the Level of Reduction

4.1 The level of reduction should be a proportion of the total sentence imposed, with the proportion calculated by reference to the circumstances in which the guilty plea was indicated, in particular the stage in the proceedings. The greatest reduction will be given where the plea was indicated at the "first reasonable opportunity".

4.2 Save where section 144(2) of the 2003 Act applies, the level of the reduction will be gauged on a sliding scale ranging from a recommended one third (where the guilty plea was entered at the first reasonable opportunity in relation to the offence for which sentence is being imposed), reducing to a recommended one quarter (where a trial date has been set) and to a recommended one tenth (for a guilty plea entered at the 'door of the court' or after the trial has begun). *See diagram below*.

4.3 The level of reduction should reflect the stage at which the offender indicated a *willingness to admit guilt* to the offence for which he is eventually sentenced:

(i) the largest recommended reduction will not normally be given unless the offender indicated willingness to admit guilt at the **first reasonable opportunity**; when this occurs will vary from case to case (*see Annex 1 for illustrative examples*);

(ii) where the admission of guilt comes later than the first reasonable opportunity, the reduction for guilty plea will normally be less than one third;

(iii) where the plea of guilty comes very late, it is still appropriate to give some reduction;

(iv) if after pleading guilty there is a Newton hearing and the offender's version of the circumstances of the offence is rejected, this should be taken into account in determining the level of reduction;

(v) if the not guilty plea was entered and maintained for tactical reasons (such as to retain privileges whilst on remand), a late guilty plea should attract very little, if any, discount.

In each category, there is a presumption that the recommended reduction will be given unless there are good reasons for a lower amount.

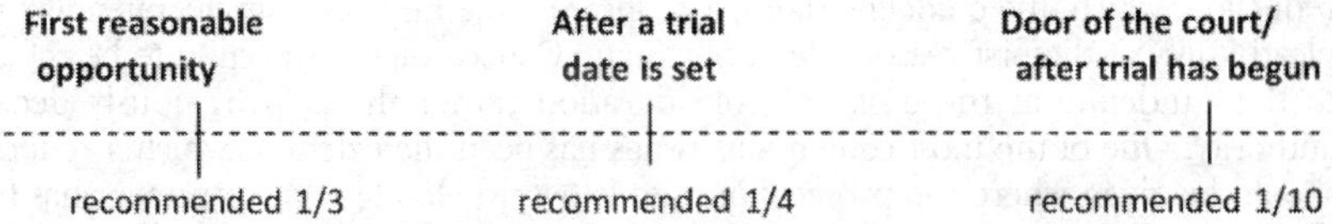

E. WITHHOLDING A REDUCTION

On the basis of dangerousness

5.1 Where a sentence for a "dangerous offender" is imposed under the provisions in the *Criminal Justice Act* 2003, whether the sentence requires the calculation of a minimum term or is an extended sentence, the approach will be the same as for any other determinate sentence (see also paragraph 7 below).

Where the prosecution case is overwhelming

5.2 The purpose of giving credit is to encourage those who are guilty to plead at the earliest opportunity. Any defendant is entitled to put the prosecution to proof and so every defendant who is guilty should be encouraged to indicate that guilt at the first reasonable opportunity.

5.3 Where the prosecution case is overwhelming, it may not be appropriate to give the full reduction that would otherwise be given. Whilst there is a presumption in favour of the full reduction being given where a plea has been indicated at the first reasonable opportunity, the fact that the prosecution case is overwhelming without relying on admissions from the defendant may be a reason justifying departure from the guideline.

5.4 Where a court is satisfied that a lower reduction should be given for this reason, a recommended reduction of 20% is likely to be appropriate where the guilty plea was indicated at the first reasonable opportunity.

5.5 A Court departing from a guideline must state the reasons for doing so.

Where the maximum penalty for the offence is thought to be too low

5.6 The sentencer is bound to sentence for the offence with which the offender has been charged, and to which he has pleaded guilty. The sentencer cannot remedy perceived defects (for example an inadequate charge or maximum penalty) by refusal of the appropriate discount.

Where jurisdictional issues arise

(i) Where two or more summary only offences are to be sentenced

5.7 When the total sentence for both or all of the offences is 6 months imprisonment, a court may determine to impose consecutive sentences which, even allowing for a reduction for a guilty plea where appropriate on each offence, would still result in the imposition of the maximum sentence available. In such circumstances, in order to achieve the purpose for which the reduction principle has been established, some modest allowance should normally be given against the total sentence for the entry of a guilty plea.

(ii) Where a maximum sentence might still be imposed

5.8 Despite a guilty plea being entered which would normally attract a reduction in sentence, a magistrates' court may impose a sentence of imprisonment of 6 months for a single either-way offence where, but for the plea, that offence would have been committed to the Crown Court for sentence.

5.9 Similarly, a detention and training order of 24 months may be imposed on an offender aged under 18 if the offence is one which would but for the plea have attracted a sentence of long-term detention in excess of 24 months under the *Powers of Criminal Courts (Sentencing) Act* 2000, section 91.

22–98 This guideline seeks to define clearly the purpose of the reduction, the means of calculating the amount of that reduction and the significance of other factors, such as the offender being caught in circumstances where the prosecution case was "overwhelming", on which differing views have developed. The primary purpose of the guideline is to ensure consistency of approach and, by making the existence of the reduction better known and understood, to better achieve Parliament's aim in providing for such a reduction, which, the guideline states, is to increase the number of guilty offenders who plead guilty at the first reasonable opportunity. Courts will be expecting to be referred to this guideline as the basis for consideration rather than to previously decided authority. One of the most contentious issues has been the extent to which a reduction should be given where the prosecution case is overwhelming. One argument has been that, since the purpose of the reduction principle is purely pragmatic and since many defendants will continue to plead not guilty even in the face of a strong prosecution case, no distinction should be made based on the strength of that case. The contrary position has been that it is unjust to give a full reduction where the defendant is faced with a very strong case, particularly where the strength of the case is independent of any admission from the defendant. In the 2004 guideline, the Sentencing Guidelines Council accepted the first argument. However, in the light of a small number of exceptional cases and continuing concern about this aspect of the guideline, the revised guideline has opened the way for greater discretion: see paras 5.2–5.5. Although there is a presumption in favour of the full reduction where a plea has been entered at the first reasonable opportunity, departure from the guideline may be justified where the prosecution case is overwhelming without reliance on admissions from the defendant. In such circumstances, the recommended reduction of one third reduces to 20 per cent. No guidance is given on the circumstances in which the prosecution case can be said to be "overwhelming" and this is likely to be an area where different views are taken. The obligation to give reasons will be important in such circumstances.

In *Shepherd* [2010] EWCA Crim. 46; [2010] 2 Cr.App.R.(S.) 54, (a case of causing death by careless driving: see § 17–45, *ante*), the Crown Court (with some justification, it appears) considered that the charge should have been causing death by dangerous driving and imposed a sentence of 4 years following a guilty plea. The Court of Appeal considered it wrong in the circumstances to start from the maximum sentence but accepted that this was a case where the prosecution case was overwhelming and where it would not be appropriate to allow the full reduction. Although not stated, there appears to have been a sense that this defendant was fortunate to have avoided conviction for a more serious offence and this is likely to have had an influence on the approach adopted.

A further important (and related) aspect for a magistrates' court is the approach where a court is sentencing an offender for two or more offences where the maximum sentence overall is six months imprisonment. This could be where there are several summary only offences (*e.g.* two or more offences of driving whilst disqualified) or one either way offence and one or more summary only offences (*e.g.* theft and assault on a police officer and/or an offence under s.4 of the *Public Order Act* 1986). In such circumstances, it would be permissible to impose consecutive sentences resulting in the maximum of six months whilst allowing for the reduction in each individual case. However, the guideline provides (para.5.7) that there should still be some "modest allowance" against the total sentence in order to give some encouragement towards a guilty plea.

The guideline states that the reduction should apply to the punitive elements of a sentence not to the rehabilitative elements. However, it also makes it clear that the principle applies to the sentence itself and not to the ancillary orders. In those circumstances, for example, neither the length of the disqualification nor the number of penalty points will be affected by any reduction based solely on the reduction for a guilty plea in accordance with the guideline.

Having stated that the reduction is purely pragmatic (para.2.2), the guideline emphasises that issues of personal mitigation and remorse should be dealt with separately and before calculating the reduction on account of the guilty plea.

The scale of the reduction should never exceed one third and this will apply to the punitive (rather than rehabilitative) elements of the sentence—for example, within a community sentence, it would reduce the period of a curfew or unpaid work requirement but not a drug rehabilitation requirement. That maximum of one third will only be available where the guilty plea is entered at the "first reasonable opportunity". The Guideline recognises the difficulty of defining this term in a way that can be consistently applied and elaborates on it in Annex 1 to the guideline.

Guideline: Reduction in Sentence for a Guilty Plea

ANNEX 1

First Reasonable Opportunity

1. The critical time for determining the reduction for a guilty plea is the first reasonable opportunity for the defendant to have indicated a willingness to plead guilty. This opportunity will vary with a wide range of factors and the Court will need to make a judgement on the particular facts of the case before it. **22–99**

2. The key principle is that the purpose of giving a reduction is to recognise the benefits that come from a guilty plea not only for those directly involved in the case in question but also in enabling Courts more quickly to deal with other outstanding cases.

3. This Annex seeks to help Courts to adopt a consistent approach by giving examples of circumstances where a determination will have to be made:

a) the first reasonable opportunity may be the first time that a defendant appears before the court and has the opportunity to plead guilty;

b) but the court may consider that it would be reasonable to have expected an indication of willingness even earlier, perhaps whilst under interview;

Note: *For a) and b) to apply, the Court will need to be satisfied that the defendant (and any legal adviser) would have had sufficient information about the allegations*

c) where an offence triable either way is committed to the Crown Court for trial and the defendant pleads guilty at the first hearing in that Court, the reduction will be less than if there had been an indication of a guilty plea given to the magistrates' court (recommended reduction of one third) but more than if the plea had been entered after a trial date had been set (recommended reduction of one quarter), and is likely to be in the region of 30%;

d) where an offence is triable only on indictment, it may well be that the first reasonable opportunity would have been during the police station stage; where that is not the case, the first reasonable opportunity is likely to be at the first hearing in the Crown Court;

(e) where a defendant is convicted after pleading guilty to an alternative (lesser) charge to that to which he/she had originally pleaded not guilty, the extent of any reduction will be determined by the stage at which the defendant first formally indicated to the court willingness to plead guilty to the lesser charge, and the reason why that lesser charge was proceeded with in preference to the original charge.

If a guilty plea is entered later than the first reasonable opportunity, the degree of reduction will reduce. This follows the principle behind the reduction that it is designed to spare both the anxiety of victims and witnesses caused by prolonged court proceedings in which they may have to give evidence and the potential waste of police, prosecution and court time. Accordingly, if a guilty plea is entered after the trial date is set but before trial is due to commence, the reduction is not to exceed one quarter. If the plea is entered at the "door of the court" or even after the trial has begun, a reduction should still be given but this should not exceed 10 per cent. **22–100**

The Guideline makes clear that, even with the reduction applied to the full, there will be circumstances where a defendant who pleads guilty will still receive the maximum sentence available in a magistrates' court. This would be the case where, for example, in the absence of a guilty plea, the case would have been committed to the Crown Court for sentence: paras 5.8–5.9. The guilty plea may also justify a change in the type of sentence, perhaps from a custodial sentence to a non-custodial sentence or from a community sentence to a fine: para.2.3.

The Guideline also emphasises the benefit of a court stating what the sentence would have been if there had been no reduction as a result of the guilty plea: para.3.1.

22–101 Section 144 does not confer a statutory discount, the issue remains one in the discretion of the court. Where a court takes a guilty plea into account, it is important that it states that it has done so, for the benefit of the defendant and a later appeal court: *Fearon* [1996] 2 Cr.App.R.(S.) 25, CA; *Aroride* [1999] 2 Cr.App.R.(S.) 406, CA.

H. EXPLANATIONS OF SENTENCE

22–102 Giving reasons for a decision is now widely accepted as important both for the benefit of those directly involved in a case and for the wider understanding of the court process. In addition, giving of reasons helps to fulfil obligations under the European Convention on Human Rights to ensure a fair trial. Reasons should enable an interested observer to understand the significant factors in a decision. The more the decision differs from what might be considered a normal sentence in the circumstances, the more extensive the reasons should be. A court will also need to be aware of the anxiety being experienced by the defendant and that what is said is tempered to the occasion.

The requirements were previously contained in a range of provisions (primarily in the *PCC(S)A* 2000) but are now brought together in s.174 of the *Criminal Justice Act* 2003.

In relation to offences committed on or after April 6, 2010, s.174 has been amended (by Sched. 22 to the *Coroners and Justice Act* 2009) and that version is set out immediately below. However, for offences committed before that date, s.174 continues to apply in its unamended form and so that is reproduced also.

Criminal Justice Act 2003, s.174 (as amended by Coroners and Justice Act 2009)

Duty to give reasons for, and explain effect of, sentence

174.—(1) Subject to subsections (3) and (4), any court passing sentence on an offender—

(a) must state in open court, in ordinary language and in general terms, its reasons for deciding on the sentence passed, and

(b) must explain to the offender in ordinary language—

(i) the effect of the sentence,

(ii) where the offender is required to comply with any order of the court forming part of the sentence, the effects of non-compliance with the order,

(iii) any power of the court, on the application of the offender or any other person, to vary or review any order of the court forming part of the sentence, and

(iv) where the sentence consists of or includes a fine, the effects of failure to pay the fine.

(2) In complying with subsection (1)(a), the court must—

(a) identify any definitive sentencing guidelines relevant to the offender's case and explain how the court discharged any duty imposed on it by section 125 of the *Coroners and Justice Act* 2009,

(aa) where the court did not follow any such guidelines because it was of the opinion that it would be contrary to the interests of justice to do so, state why it was of that opinion,

(b) where the sentence is a custodial sentence and the duty in subsection (2) of section 152 is not excluded by subsection (1)(a) or (b) or (3) of that section or any other statutory provision, state that it is of the opinion referred to in section 152(2) and why it is of that opinion,

(c) where the sentence is a community sentence, other than one consisting of or including a youth rehabilitation order with intensive supervision and surveillance or fostering, and the case does not fall within section 151(2), state that it is of the opinion that section 148(1) applies and why it is of that opinion,

(ca) where the sentence consists of or includes a youth rehabilitation order with intensive supervision and surveillance and the case does not fall within paragraph 5(2) of Schedule 1 to the *Criminal Justice and Immigration Act* 2008, state that it is of the opinion that section 1(4)(a) to (c) of that Act and section 148(1) of this Act apply and why it is of that opinion,

(cb) where the sentence consists of or includes a youth rehabilitation order with fostering, state that it is of the opinion that section 1(4)(a) to (c) of the *Criminal Justice and Immigration Act* 2008 and section 148(1) of this Act apply and why it is of that opinion,

(d) where as a result of taking into account any matter referred to in section 144(1), the court imposes a punishment on the offender which is less severe than the punishment it would otherwise have imposed, state that fact, and

(e) in any case, mention any aggravating or mitigating factors which the court has regarded as being relevant to the case.

(3) Subsection (1)(a) does not apply—

(a) to an offence the sentence for which is fixed by law (provision relating to sentencing for such an offence being made by section 270), or

(b) to an offence the sentence for which falls to be impose under section 51A(2) of the *Firearms Act* 1968 (c. 27), under subsection (2) of section 110 or 111 of the *Sentencing* Act or under section 29(4) or (6) of the *Violent Crime Reduction Act* 2006 (required custodial sentences).

(4) The Lord Chancellor may by order—

(a) prescribe cases in which subsection (1)(a) or (b) does not apply, and

(b) prescribe cases in which the statement referred to in subsection (1)(a) or the explanation referred to in subsection (1)(b) may be made in the absence of the offender, or may be provided in written form.

(4A) Subsection (4B) applies where—

(a) a court passes a custodial sentence in respect of an offence on an offender who is aged under 18, and

(b) the circumstances are such that the court must, in complying with subsection (1)(a), make the statement referred to in subsection (2)(b).

(4B) That statement must include—

(a) a statement by the court that it is of the opinion that a sentence consisting of or including a youth rehabilitation order with intensive supervision and surveillance or fostering cannot be justified for the offence, and

(b) a statement by the court why it is of that opinion.

(5) Where a magistrates' court passes a custodial sentence, it must cause any reason stated by virtue of subsection (2)(b) to be specified in the warrant of commitment and entered on the register.

(6) In this section—

"definitive sentencing guidelines" mean sentencing guidelines issued by the Sentencing Council for England and Wales under section 120 of the *Coroners and Justice Act* 2009 as definitive guidelines, as revised by any subsequent guidelines so issued,

"the register" has the meaning given by section 163 of the *Sentencing* Act.

Criminal Justice Act 2003, s.174

Duty to give reasons for, and explain effect of, sentence

174.—(1) Subject to subsections (3) and (4), any court passing sentence on an offender— **22–103**

(a) must state in open court, in ordinary language and in general terms, its reasons for deciding on the sentence passed, and

(b) must explain to the offender in ordinary language—

(i) the effect of the sentence,

(ii) where the offender is required to comply with any order of the court forming part of the sentence, the effects of non-compliance with the order,

(iii) any power of the court, on the application of the offender or any other person, to vary or review any order of the court forming part of the sentence, and

(iv) where the sentence consists of or includes a fine, the effects of failure to pay the fine.

(2) In complying with subsection (1)(a), the court must—

(a) where guidelines indicate that a sentence of a particular kind, or within a particular range, would normally be appropriate for the offence and the sentence is of a different kind, or is outside that range, state the court's reasons for deciding on a sentence of a different kind or outside that range,

(b) where the sentence is a custodial sentence and the duty in subsection (2) of section 152 is not excluded by subsection (1)(a) or (b) or (3) of that section or any statutory provision, state that it is of the opinion referred to in section 152(2) and why it is of that opinion,

(c) where the sentence is a community sentence, other than one consisting of or including a youth rehabilitation order with intensive supervision and surveillance or fostering, and the case does not fall within section 151(2), state that it is of the opinion that section 148(1) applies and why it is of that opinion,

(ca) where the sentence consists of or includes a youth rehabilitation order with intensive supervision and surveillance and the case does not fall within paragraph 5(2) of Schedule 1 to the *Criminal Justice and Immigration Act* 2008, state that it is of the opinion that section 1(4)(a) to (c) of that Act and section 148(1) of this Act apply and why it is of that opinion,

(cb) where the sentence consists of or includes a youth rehabilitation order with fostering, state that it is of the opinion that section 1(4)(a) to (c) of the *Criminal Justice and Immigration Act* 2008 and section 148(1) of this Act apply and why it is of that opinion,

(d) where as a result of taking into account any matter referred to in section 144(1), the court imposes a punishment on the offender which is less severe than the punishment it would otherwise have imposed, state that fact, and

(e) in any case, mention any aggravating or mitigating factors which the court has regarded as being of particular importance.

(3) Subsection (1)(a) does not apply—

(a) to an offence the sentence for which is fixed by law (provision relating to sentencing for such an offence being made by section 270), or

(b) to an offence the sentence for which falls to be imposed under section 51A(2) of the *Firearms Act* 1968 (c 27) or under subsection (2) of section 110 or 111 of the Sentencing Act or under section 29(4) or (6) of the *Violent Crime Reduction Act* 2006 (required custodial sentences).

(4) The Secretary of State may by order—

(a) prescribe cases in which subsection (1)(a) or (b) does not apply, and

(b) prescribe cases in which the statement referred to in subsection (1)(a) or the explanation referred to in subsection (1)(b) may be made in the absence of the offender, or may be provided in written form.

(4A) Subsection (4B) applies where—

(a) a court passes a custodial sentence in respect of an offence on an offender who is aged 18 or under, and

(b) the circumstances are such that the court must, in complying with subsection (1)(a), make the statement referred to in subsection (2)(b).

(4B) That statement must include—

(a) a statement by the court that it is of the opinion that a sentence consisting of or including a youth rehabilitation order with intensive supervision and surveillance or fostering cannot be justified for the offence, and

(b) a statement by the court why it is of that opinion.

(5) Where a magistrates' court passes a custodial sentence, it must cause any reason stated by virtue of subsection (2)(b) to be specified in the warrant of commitment and entered on the register.

(6) In this section—

"guidelines" has the same meaning as in section 172;

"the register" has the meaning given by section 163 of the Sentencing Act.

There is a general obligation to state in ordinary language the reasons for deciding on the sentence to be passed and to explain to the offender the effect of the sentence, including what might happen if he fails to comply with the order of the court: s.174(1). Where a relevant guideline has been issued by the Sentencing Guidelines Council and the sentence is outside the range suggested in that guideline, the reasons must also show why that decision has been made: s.174(2)(a). **22–104**

More specific obligations require a court:

— when passing a custodial sentence to state why the offence is so serious than nothing other than custody is justified;

— when passing a community sentence, to state why the offence was serious enough to warrant such a sentence (unless it was based on some other rationale such as that contained in s.151(2) of the *Criminal Justice Act* 2003 when in force);

— when reducing a sentence on account of the defendant's guilty plea, to state that that has been done;

— always to draw attention to any aggravating or mitigating factors that were of particular importance in determining sentence.

When the court has taken other offences into consideration when passing sentence, it should expressly state that it has done so.

Victims are likely to want to know the reasons for the decision, the public are entitled to know what is going on in the criminal justice system and to have confidence in it and ill-informed criticism in the media may be reduced if reasons have been given in public and recorded. **22–105**

A clear example was seen in *Major* [2010] EWCA Crim. 3016. Although the defendant had been acquitted, the Crown Court used its power to impose a restraining order under s.5A of the *Protection from Harassment Act* 1997 (see § 23–254, *post*). Recognising that this power had been given to courts because there were cases where there was clear evidence that a victim needed protection from harassment but there was insufficient evidence to convict on the charge before the court, it was essential that the court identified the factual basis for imposing such an order.

However, the primary purpose of explanations is to ensure that there is a clear understanding of what the court has chosen to do, and why, which is for the benefit of those directly involved in the case as well as for the wider public. The extent to which this is needed will vary from case to case both with the complexity of the case itself and the extent to which the court is making a decision different from what might reasonably have been expected. Much of the detailed explanation of the consequences of the sentence (which is primarily for the benefit of the offender) is likely to be lost in the apprehension of the moment and it is hoped that clarification will come as to better ways in which such information can be conveyed which both reduces the burden on the court and increases the understanding of the offender of what is expected as a result of the sentence imposed. **22–106**

The principle of giving clear explanations is carried through to the point of requesting a pre-sentence report by the definitive guideline issued by the Sentencing Guidelines Council in December 2004 (*New Sentences: Criminal Justice Act 2003*). Wherever a court requests a pre-sentence report (note the wide definition under the 2003 Act which includes reports now commonly known by other name) it will be expected to give clear guidance on the objectives of sentencing it is seeking to achieve and on those factors that make the offence more or less serious: see *ante*, § 22–37.

If a case has to be adjourned, and a differently constituted court sits on the next occasion, the later court must know the reasons for the decision of the earlier court.

CHAPTER 23

SPECIFIC SENTENCES

I. SPECIFIC ASPECTS OF SENTENCING

A. DEFERMENT OF SENTENCE

(1) Legislation

Powers of Criminal Courts (Sentencing) Act 2000, ss.1–1D

DEFERMENT OF SENTENCE

1.—(1) The Crown Court or a magistrates' court may defer passing sentence on an offender **23–1**
for the purpose of enabling the court, or any other court to which it falls to deal with him, to have regard in dealing with him to—

(a) his conduct after conviction (including, where appropriate, the making by him of reparation for his offence); or

(b) any change in his circumstances;

but this is subject to subsections (3) and (4) below.

(2) Without prejudice to the generality of subsection (1) above, the matters to which the court to which it falls to deal with the offender may have regard by virtue of paragraph (a) of that subsection include the extent to which the offender has complied with any requirements imposed under subsection (3)(b) below.

(3) The power conferred by subsection (1) above shall be exercisable only if—

(a) the offender consents;

(b) the offender undertakes to comply with any requirements as to his conduct during the period of the deferment that the court considers it appropriate to impose; and

(c) the court is satisfied, having regard to the nature of the offence and the character and circumstances of the offender, that it would be in the interests of justice to exercise the power.

(4) Any deferment under this section shall be until such date as may be specified by the court, not being more than six months after the date on which the deferment is announced by the court; and, subject to section 1D(3) below, where the passing of sentence has been deferred under this section it shall not be further so deferred.

(5) Where a court has under this section deferred passing sentence on an offender, it shall forthwith give a copy of the order deferring the passing of sentence and setting out any requirements imposed under subsection (3)(b) above—

(a) to the offender,

(b) where an officer of a local probation board has been appointed to act as a supervisor in relation to him, to that board,

(ba) where an officer of a provider of probation services has been appointed to act as a supervisor in relation to him, to that provider, and

(c) where a person has been appointed under section 1A(2)(b) below to act as a supervisor in relation to him, to that person.

(6) Notwithstanding any enactment, a court which under this section defers passing sentence on an offender shall not on the same occasion remand him.

(7) Where—

(a) a court which under this section has deferred passing sentence on an offender proposes to deal with him on the date originally specified by the court, or

(b) the offender does not appear on the day so specified,

the court may issue a summons requiring him to appear before the court at a time and place specified in the summons, or may issue a warrant to arrest him and bring him before the court at a time and place specified in the warrant.

(8) Nothing in this section or sections 1A to 1D below shall affect—

(a) the power of the Crown Court to bind over an offender to come up for judgment when called upon; or

(b) the power of any court to defer passing sentence for any purpose for which it may lawfully do so apart from this section.

Further provision about undertakings

23–2 **1A.**—(1) Without prejudice to the generality of paragraph (b) of section 1(3) above, the requirements that may be imposed by virtue of that paragraph include requirements as to the residence of the offender during the whole or any part of the period of deferment.

(2) Where an offender has undertaken to comply with any requirements imposed under section 1(3)(b) above the court may appoint—

(a) an officer of a local probation board or an officer of a provider of probation services, or

(b) any other person whom the court thinks appropriate,

to act as a supervisor in relation to him.

(3) A person shall not be appointed under subsection (2)(b) above without his consent.

(4) It shall be the duty of a supervisor appointed under subsection (2) above—

(a) to monitor the offender's compliance with the requirements; and

(b) to provide the court to which it falls to deal with the offender in respect of the offence in question with such information as the court may require relating to the offender's compliance with the requirements.

Breach of undertakings

1B.—(1) A court which under section 1 above has deferred passing sentence on an offender may deal with him before the end of the period of deferment if— **23–3**

(a) he appears or is brought before the court under subsection (3) below; and

(b) the court is satisfied that he has failed to comply with one or more requirements imposed under section 1(3)(b) above in connection with the deferment.

(2) Subsection (3) below applies where—

(a) a court has under section 1 above deferred passing sentence on an offender;

(b) the offender undertook to comply with one or more requirements imposed under section 1(3)(b) above in connection with the deferment; and

(c) a person appointed under section 1A(2) above to act as a supervisor in relation to the offender has reported to the court that the offender has failed to comply with one or more of those requirements.

(3) Where this subsection applies, the court may issue—

(a) a summons requiring the offender to appear before the court at a time and place specified in the summons; or

(b) a warrant to arrest him and bring him before the court at a time and place specified in the warrant.

Conviction of offence during period of deferment

1C.—(1) A court which under section 1 above has deferred passing sentence on an offender may deal with him before the end of the period of deferment if during that period he is convicted in Great Britain of any offence. **23–4**

(2) Subsection (3) below applies where a court has under section 1 above deferred passing sentence on an offender in respect of one or more offences and during the period of deferment the offender is convicted in England and Wales of any offence ("the later offence").

(3) Where this subsection applies, then (without prejudice to subsection (1) above and whether or not the offender is sentenced for the later offence during the period of deferment), the court which passes sentence on him for the later offence may also, if this has not already been done, deal with him for the offence or offences for which passing of sentence has been deferred, except that—

(a) the power conferred by this subsection shall not be exercised by a magistrates' court if the court which deferred passing sentence was the Crown Court; and

(b) the Crown Court, in exercising that power in a case in which the court which deferred passing sentence was a magistrates' court, shall not pass any sentence which could not have been passed by a magistrates' court in exercising that power.

(4) Where a court which under section 1 above has deferred passing sentence on an offender proposes to deal with him by virtue of subsection (1) above before the end of the period of deferment, the court may issue—

(a) a summons requiring him to appear before the court at a time and place specified in the summons; or

(b) a warrant to arrest him and bring him before the court at a time and place specified in the warrant.

Deferment of sentence: supplementary

1D.—(1) In deferring the passing of sentence under section 1 above a magistrates' court shall be regarded as exercising the power of adjourning the trial conferred by section 10(1) of the Magistrates' Courts Act 1980, and accordingly sections 11(1) and 13(1) to (3A) and (5) of that Act (non-appearance of the accused) apply (without prejudice to section 1(7) above) if the offender does not appear on the date specified under section 1(4) above. **23–5**

(2) Where the passing of sentence on an offender has been deferred by a court ("the original court") under section 1 above, the power of that court under that section to deal with the offender at the end of the period of deferment and any power of that court under section 1B(1) or 1C(1) above, or of any court under section 1C(3) above, to deal with the offender—

(a) is power to deal with him, in respect of the offence for which passing of sentence has been deferred, in any way in which the original court could have dealt with him if it had not deferred passing sentence; and

(b) without prejudice to the generality of paragraph (a) above, in the case of a magistrates' court, includes the power conferred by section 3 below to commit him to the Crown Court for sentence.

(3) Where—

(a) the passing of sentence on an offender in respect of one or more offences has been deferred under section 1 above, and

(b) a magistrates' court deals with him in respect of the offence or any of the offences by committing him to the Crown Court under section 3 below,

the power of the Crown Court to deal with him includes the same power to defer passing sentence on him as if he had just been convicted of the offence or offences on indictment before the court.

(4) Subsection (5) below applies where—

(a) the passing of sentence on an offender in respect of one or more offences has been deferred under section 1 above;

(b) it falls to a magistrates' court to determine a relevant matter; and

(c) a justice of the peace is satisfied—

(i) that a person appointed under section 1A(2)(b) above to act as a supervisor in relation to the offender is likely to be able to give evidence that may assist the court in determining that matter; and

(ii) that that person will not voluntarily attend as a witness.

(5) The justice may issue a summons directed to that person requiring him to attend before the court at the time and place appointed in the summons to give evidence.

(6) For the purposes of subsection (4) above a court determines a relevant matter if it—

(a) deals with the offender in respect of the offence, or any of the offences, for which the passing of sentence has been deferred; or

(b) determines, for the purposes of section 1B(1)(b) above, whether the offender has failed to comply with any requirements imposed under section 1(3)(b) above."

(2) Purpose and effect

23–6 These provisions provide the potential to give new life to a sentence that was considered all but finished with by filling some of the gaps that had created problems. Most notably, there is now formal provision for the court to require undertakings from the offender to be complied with during the period of deferment (s.1(3) and s.1A), a power to appoint a person to oversee the completion of those undertakings (s.1A(2)) and the option of bringing the offender back to court for sentence earlier than the end of the period of deferment if those undertakings are not being complied with (s.1B). In addition, the Sentencing Guidelines Council has included within its definitive guidelines, published in December 2004 (New Sentences: *Criminal Justice Act* 2003), guidance on circumstances when it might be appropriate to defer sentence. The Guideline draws attention to the wide range of sentencing options available under the new framework and concludes that a deferred sentence is likely to be used only in limited circumstances. The Guideline sets out the purpose and possible benefits.

Guideline: New Sentences: Criminal Justice Act 2003

Section 1—Community Sentences & Deferred Sentences

Part 2: Deferred Sentences

B. USE OF DEFERRED SENTENCES

23–7 **1.2.6** ...A deferred sentence enables the court to review the conduct of the defendant before passing sentence, having first prescribed certain requirements. It also provides several opportunities for an offender to have some influence as to the sentence passed–

a) it tests the commitment of the offender not to re-offend;

b) it gives the offender an opportunity to do something where progress can be shown within a short period;

c) it provides the offender with an opportunity to behave or refrain from behaving in a particular way that will be relevant to sentence.

(3) General

There are now 3 conditions that need to be satisfied before sentence can be deferred: **23–8**

(i) the court must be satisfied that deferral is in the interests of justice (subsection 1(3)(c)). In reaching that conclusion the court must have regard both to the offence and to the character and circumstances of the offender.

(ii) the offender must consent (subsection 1(3)(a)).

(iii) the offender must undertake to comply with requirements imposed by the court (subsection 1(3)(b)).

The extent of the requirements are at the discretion of the court and may include a residence requirement: s.1A(1). Given that the purpose of deferment is to enable the offender to influence sentence, it is imperative that the offender and the court are absolutely clear about what is expected. Again this is underlined by the Sentencing Guidelines Council:

Guideline: New Sentences: Criminal Justice Act 2003

Section 1—Community Sentences & Deferred Sentences

Part 2: Deferred Sentences

B. USE OF DEFERRED SENTENCES

1.2.8 A court may impose any conditions during the period of deferment that it considers appropriate. These could be specific requirements as set out in the provisions for community sentences, or requirements that are drawn more widely. These should be specific, measurable conditions so that the offender knows exactly what is required and the court can assess compliance; the restriction on liberty should be limited to ensure that the offender has a reasonable expectation of being able to comply whilst maintaining his or her social responsibilities. **23–9**

1.2.9 Given the need for clarity in the mind of the offender and the possibility of sentence by another court, the court should give a clear indication (and make a written record) of the type of sentence it would be minded to impose if it had not decided to defer and ensure that the offender understands the consequences of failure to comply with the court's wishes during the deferral period.

When deferring sentence, the sentencer must make clear the consequence of not complying with any requirements and should indicate the type of sentence it would be minded to impose. Sentencers should impose specific, measurable conditions that do not involve a serious restriction on liberty.

Part IV

The court may appoint a supervisor to oversee the completion of the requirements it has imposed. This may be an officer of a local probation board or any other appropriate person willing to undertake the role: s.1A(2, 3). The supervisor's role is to monitor compliance with the requirements and to inform the court, as requested, about that compliance: s.1A(4). If the requirements are not complied with, the supervisor will be expected to draw that to the attention of the court (s.1B(2)) which may issue a summons or a warrant to bring the offender before the court: s.1B(3). An offender brought before the court following such a summons or a warrant who has not complied with one or more of the requirements may be sentenced by the court even though the period of deferment has not ended: s.1B(1). **23–10**

As before, there are strong suggestions that, in most circumstances, a court would expect to impose sentence at the earliest opportunity and that the decision to defer is likely to be relatively infrequent.

Guideline: New Sentences: Criminal Justice Act 2003

Section 1—Community Sentences & Deferred Sentences

Part 2: Deferred Sentences

B. USE OF DEFERRED SENTENCES

23–11 **1.2.7** Given the new power to require undertakings and the ability to enforce those undertakings before the end of the period of deferral, the decision to defer sentence should be predominantly for a small group of cases at either the custody threshold or the community sentence threshold where the sentencer feels that there would be particular value in giving the offender the opportunities listed because, if the offender complies with the requirements, a different sentence will be justified at the end of the deferment period. This could be a community sentence instead of a custodial sentence or a fine or discharge instead of a community sentence. It may, rarely, enable a custodial sentence to be suspended rather than imposed immediately.

The use of deferred sentences should be predominantly for a small group of cases close to a significant threshold where, should the defendant be prepared to adapt his behaviour in a way clearly specified by the sentencer, the court may be prepared to impose a lesser sentence.

(4) Convictions during period of deferment

23–12 If the defendant is convicted anywhere in Great Britain (*i.e.* England, Wales and Scotland) of another offence committed during the period of deferral, the *court that has deferred sentence* may deal with the defendant before the end of the period of deferment: s.1C(1). In order to bring the defendant before the court, a summons or a warrant may be issued: s.1C(4).

If a defendant subject to a deferred sentence is convicted in England and Wales of an offence, then *the court dealing with the later offence* may be able to deal with the offence on which sentence was deferred even though it was not the court which deferred sentence: s.1C(2), (3). However, a magistrates' court may not sentence for an offence that is subject to a deferred sentence imposed by the Crown Court: s.1C(3)(a). A Crown Court sentencing for an offence on which a magistrates' court has deferred sentence is limited to the maximum sentence that a magistrates' court could have passed: s.1C(3)(b). This limit applies even though one of the options available to a magistrates' court at the end of the period of deferment is to commit the defendant to the Crown Court for sentence: s.1D(2)(b).

(5) Sentence after deferment

23–13 The approach to sentence at the end of the period of deferment was also considered in *George*, 79 Cr.App.R.26.

(i) be clear about the purpose of the deferment and any requirement imposed by the deferring court
(ii) decide whether the defendant has substantially conformed or attempted to conform with the expectations of the deferring court.
(iii) if he has, then the defendant may legitimately expect that an immediate custodial sentence will not be imposed: *Smith* (1979) 1 Cr.App.R.(S.) 339.
(iv) if he has not, then the court should state clearly how the defendant has failed to do what the court required.

B. ABSOLUTE AND CONDITIONAL DISCHARGE

(1) Legislation

Powers of Criminal Courts (Sentencing) Act 2000, s.12

Absolute and conditional discharge

23–14 **12.**—(1) Where a court by or before which a person is convicted of an offence (not being an offence the sentence for which is fixed by law or falls to be imposed under section 110(2) or 111(2) below, section 51A(2) of the *Firearms Act* 1968, sections 225(2) or 226(2) of the *Criminal Justice Act* 2003 or section 29(4) or (6) of the *Violent Crime Reduction Act* 2006) is of the opinion, having regard to the circumstances including the nature of the offence and the character of the offender, that it is inexpedient to inflict punishment, the court may make an order either—

(a) discharging him absolutely; or

(b) if the court thinks fit, discharging him subject to the condition that he commits no offence during such period, not exceeding three years from the date of the order, as may be specified in the order.

(2) Subsection (1)(b) above has effect subject to section 66(4) of the *Crime and Disorder Act* 1998 (effect of reprimands and warnings).

(3) An order discharging a person subject to such a condition as is mentioned in subsection (1)(b) above is in this Act referred to as an "order for conditional discharge"; and the period specified in any such order is in this Act referred to as "the period of conditional discharge".

(4) [*repealed*]

(5) If (by virtue of section 13 below) a person conditionally discharged under this section is sentenced for the offence in respect of which the order for conditional discharge was made, that order shall cease to have effect.

(6) On making an order for conditional discharge, the court may, if it thinks it expedient for the purpose of the offender's reformation, allow any person who consents to do so to give security for the good behaviour of the offender.

(7) Nothing in this section shall be construed as preventing a court, on discharging an offender absolutely or conditionally in respect of any offence, from making an order for costs against the offender or imposing any disqualification on him or from making in respect of the offence an order under section 130, 143 or 148 below (compensation orders, deprivation orders and restitution orders).

(2) Purpose and effect

An offender suffers no penalty for the offence providing (in the case of a conditional discharge) that he commits no further offence during the period specified. If he does, the court that deals with him for the later offence may also sentence him for the offence subject to the discharge. **23–15**

(3) General

When making an order of conditional discharge, the court must explain to the offender, in ordinary language, that, if he commits another offence during the period of the conditional discharge, he will be liable to be sentenced for the original offence: *Criminal Justice Act* 2003, s.174(1). This task does not have to be undertaken by the court; an undertaking from the defendant's counsel that they will explain the effect of the order will suffice: *Wehner* [1977] 3 All E.R. 553. **23–16**

A discharge may not be combined with a fine for the same offence: *Sanck* (1990) 12 Cr.App.R.(S.) 155. A conditional discharge may be combined with an ancillary order such as a compensation order, a restitution order, an order to pay the costs of the prosecution, or a order depriving the offender of his rights in property under s.143 of the 2000 Act, or a recommendation for deportation order. A court which makes an order of discharge may exercise any power arising out of the *Road Traffic Offenders Act* 1988, ss.34, 35, 36 or 44 and must comply with any mandatory requirement of those sections: s.46 of the 1988 Act.

Magistrates' courts should not make an order of discharge in respect of an offence committed during the currency of a suspended sentence of imprisonment imposed by the Crown Court, the offender should be committed to the Crown Court so that both elements can be dealt with together: *Moore* [1995] Q.B. 353.

Powers of Criminal Courts (Sentencing) Act 2000, ss.13–15

Commission of further offence by person conditionally discharged

13.—(1) If it appears to the Crown Court, where that court has jurisdiction in accordance with subsection (2) below, or to a justice of the peace having jurisdiction in accordance with that subsection, that a person in whose case an order for conditional discharge has been made— **23–17**

(a) has been convicted by a court in Great Britain of an offence committed during the period of conditional discharge, and

(b) has been dealt with in respect of that offence,

that court or justice may, subject to subsection (3) below, issue a summons requiring that person to appear at the place and time specified in it or a warrant for his arrest.

(2) Jurisdiction for the purposes of subsection (1) above may be exercised—

(a) if the order for conditional discharge was made by the Crown Court, by that court;

(b) if the order was made by a magistrates' court, by a justice of the peace.

(3) A justice of the peace shall not issue a summons under this section except on information and shall not issue a warrant under this section except on information in writing and on oath.

(4) A summons or warrant issued under this section shall direct the person to whom it relates to appear or to be brought before the court by which the order for conditional discharge was made.

(5) If a person in whose case an order for conditional discharge has been made by the Crown Court is convicted by a magistrates' court of an offence committed during the period of conditional discharge, the magistrates' court—

(a) may commit him to custody or release him on bail until he can be brought or appear before the Crown Court; and

(b) if it does so, shall send to the Crown Court a copy of the minute or memorandum of the conviction entered in the register, signed by the designated officer by whom the register is kept.

(6) Where it is proved to the satisfaction of the court by which an order for conditional discharge was made that the person in whose case the order was made has been convicted of an offence committed during the period of conditional discharge, the court may deal with him, for the offence for which the order was made, in any way in which it could deal with him if he had just been convicted by or before that court of that offence.

(7) If a person in whose case an order for conditional discharge has been made by a magistrates' court—

(a) is convicted before the Crown Court of an offence committed during the period of conditional discharge, or

(b) is dealt with by the Crown Court for any such offence in respect of which he was committed for sentence to the Crown Court,

the Crown Court may deal with him, for the offence for which the order was made, in any way in which the magistrates' court could deal with him if it had just convicted him of that offence.

(8) If a person in whose case an order for conditional discharge has been made by a magistrates' court is convicted by another magistrates' court of any offence committed during the period of conditional discharge, that other court may, with the consent of the court which made the order, deal with him, for the offence for which the order was made, in any way in which the court could deal with him if it had just convicted him of that offence.

(9) Where an order for conditional discharge has been made by a magistrates' court in the case of an offender under 18 years of age in respect of an offence triable only on indictment in the case of an adult, any powers exercisable under subsection (6), (7) or (8) above by that or any other court in respect of the offender after he attains the age of 18 shall be powers to do either or both of the following—

(a) to impose a fine not exceeding £5,000 for the offence in respect of which the order was made;

(b) to deal with the offender for that offence in any way in which a magistrates' court could deal with him if it had just convicted him of an offence punishable with imprisonment for a term not exceeding six months.

(10) The reference in subsection (6) above to a person's having been convicted of an offence committed during the period of conditional discharge is a reference to his having been so convicted by a court in Great Britain.

Effect of discharge

23–18 **14.**—(1) Subject to subsection (2) below, a conviction of an offence for which an order is made under section 12 above discharging the offender absolutely or conditionally shall be deemed not to be a conviction for any purpose other than the purposes of the proceedings in which the order is made and of any subsequent proceedings which may be taken against the offender under section 13 above.

(2) Where the offender was aged 18 or over at the time of his conviction of the offence in question and is subsequently sentenced (under section 13 above) for that offence, subsection (1) above shall cease to apply to the conviction.

(3) Without prejudice to subsections (1) and (2) above, the conviction of an offender who is discharged absolutely or conditionally under section 12 above shall in any event be disregarded for the purposes of any enactment or instrument which—

(a) imposes any disqualification or disability upon convicted persons; or

(b) authorises or requires the imposition of any such disqualification or disability.

(4) Subsections (1) to (3) above shall not affect—

(a) any right of an offender discharged absolutely or conditionally under section 12 above to rely on his conviction in bar of any subsequent proceedings for the same offence;

(b) the restoration of any property in consequence of the conviction of any such offender; or

(c) the operation, in relation to any such offender, of any enactment or instrument in force on 1st July 1974 which is expressed to extend to persons dealt with under section 1(1) of the *Probation of Offenders Act* 1907 as well as to convicted persons.

(5) In subsections (3) and (4) above—

"enactment" includes an enactment contained in a local Act; and

"instrument" means an instrument having effect by virtue of an Act.

(6) Subsection (1) above has effect subject to section 50(1A) of the *Criminal Appeal Act* 1968 and section 108(1A) of the *Magistrates' Courts Act* 1980 (rights of appeal); and this subsection shall not be taken to prejudice any other enactment that excludes the effect of subsection (1) or (3) above for particular purposes.

(7) Without prejudice to paragraph 1(3) of Schedule 11 to this Act (references to provisions of this Act to be construed as including references to corresponding old enactments), in this section—

(a) any reference to an order made under section 12 above discharging an offender absolutely or conditionally includes a reference to an order which was made under any provision of Part I of the *Powers of Criminal Courts Act* 1973 (whether or not reproduced in this Act) discharging the offender absolutely or conditionally;

(b) any reference to an offender who is discharged absolutely or conditionally under section 12 includes a reference to an offender who was discharged absolutely or conditionally under any such provision.

Discharge: Supplementary

15.—(1) The Secretary of State may by order direct that subsection (1) of section 12 above shall be amended by substituting, for the maximum period specified in that subsection as originally enacted or as previously amended under this subsection, such period as may be specified in the order. **23–19**

(2) Where an order for conditional discharge has been made on appeal, for the purposes of section 13 above it shall be deemed—

(a) if it was made on an appeal brought from a magistrates' court, to have been made by that magistrates' court;

(b) if it was made on an appeal brought from the Crown Court or from the criminal division of the Court of Appeal, to have been made by the Crown Court.

(3) In proceedings before the Crown Court under section 13 above, any question whether any person in whose case an order for conditional discharge has been made has been convicted of an offence committed during the period of conditional discharge shall be determined by the court and not by the verdict of a jury.

C. FINANCIAL PENALTIES

(1) Purpose and effect

A financial penalty is the sanction most often imposed in magistrates' courts. There are three main types—the fine itself, a compensation order (which can be a sentence in itself or an ancillary order) and an order to pay the costs of the prosecution. In addition, **23–20** where a court imposes a fine, it must (in most circumstances) impose a surcharge of £15, commonly called a "victims' surcharge". A fine is primarily a punishment for the current offence and a deterrent to future offending and so is designed to make sufficient impact on the spending power of the defendant to cause a degree of hardship commensurate with the seriousness of the offence.

A compensation order is primarily concerned with reparation, making financial compensation for the harm or loss caused by the offence. Where there is not enough money to pay a fine and compensation, then it is the compensation that must take priority. Where both a fine and compensation are ordered, money paid by the defendant is allocated first to paying off the compensation and then to any fines.

An order for costs reimburses, or contributes to, the costs incurred by the prosecution in bringing the case to court. Such an order takes priority over a fine but not over compensation.

The "victims' surcharge" should be imposed in each case where a court imposes a fine for an offence committed on or after April 1, 2007. It should be announced as a separate ingredient in the sentence. Where there are insufficient means to pay both the fine and the surcharge, it is the fine that must be reduced: *Criminal Justice Act* 2003, s.164(4A). Where there are insufficient means to pay both the surcharge and any compensation order, it is the surcharge that must be reduced (and may be avoided altogether): *Criminal Justice Act* 2003, s.161A(3). A surcharge will take priority over any order for costs. The surcharge will be enforceable as a fine.

(2) Assessment of amount

23–21 Fines are in the lowest tier of sanctions and there is no threshold criteria that need to be passed before a financial penalty can be imposed. However, any amount imposed must be balanced by the resources available to the defendant. In most circumstances, a fine must be capable of being paid within one year, compensation within no more than three years. Even where an offence is serious enough to justify a community sentence, a court may still impose a financial penalty instead where appropriate. This principle is re-affirmed by the Sentencing Guidelines Council in its definitive guideline, published in December 2004, which confirms that the crossing of a sentencing threshold empowers a court to impose a particular sentence but does not require it to do so.

Guideline: Overarching Principles: Seriousness

E. THE SENTENCING THRESHOLDS

The Threshold for Community Sentences

23–22 **1.36** Sentencers should consider all of the disposals available (within or below the threshold passed) at the time of sentence before reaching the provisional decision to make a community sentence, so that, even where the threshold for a community sentence has been passed, a financial penalty or discharge may still be an appropriate penalty.

The approach to the assessment of a fine is dealt with extensively within the *Magistrates' Court Sentencing Guidelines* issued by the Sentencing Guidelines Council in May 2008 and effective in relation to all cases sentenced on or after August 4, 2008. Having determined that a fine is the appropriate sentence, a court is required to take account of both the seriousness of the offence and the financial circumstances of the offender: *Criminal Justice Act* 2003, s.164. Those financial circumstances may have the effect of increasing or decreasing the level of the fine. There is a separate structure for the decision making process in the guidelines which is set out in the guidelines at p.153. A court will identify both the fine band and the place of the offence within that band by reference to the seriousness of the offence before taking into account the offender's financial circumstances. Any reduction for a guilty plea will follow as will consideration of any ancillary orders including compensation.

The guidelines provide for 3 levels of fine (bands A, B and C) which are used as starting points for offences; there are two further levels (bands D and E) which indicate an appropriate level where the offence is sufficiently serious to have crossed the community or custody threshold but the court nevertheless feels it appropriate to impose a fine.

The bands are translated into a monetary amount by means of a proportion of relevant weekly income—band A is 50%, band B is 100% and band C is 150%. Relevant weekly income has three possible meanings:

i) where the offender is in receipt of earned income of more than £100 per week after deduction of tax and national insurance, the relevant weekly income is that amount;

ii) where the offender has earned income of £100 or less or where the primary source of income is state benefit, there is a deemed relevant weekly income of £100;

iii) where there is no information on which a court can base its assessment, there is a deemed relevant weekly income of £350.

In most circumstances, this will be all the information that a court will need. Further guidance is provided for those circumstances where the court has no reliable information about the financial circumstances of the offender, where the offence has a "commercial" element (that is, where the offender is seeking to gain a significant commercial benefit) and where the offender incurs expenditure which is "out of the ordinary" and which "substantially reduces the ability to pay" so that a fine based on the standard approach would produce "undue hardship".

Occasionally a court will be faced with a situation where it has the power to impose a fine much larger than normal. In such circumstances, where the defendant is a publicly funded body, a court may take account of how the fine is to be paid. Whilst public bodies are not immune from criminal prosecution because they have no shareholders, "if a very substantial financial penalty will inhibit the proper performance by a statutory body of the public function that it has been set up to perform that is not something to be disregarded. In the present case there is nothing to suggest that the cost of any fine can simply be recouped from customers by raising charges": *Milford Haven Port Authority* [2000] 2 Cr.App.R.(S) 423 cited with approval in *Southampton University Hospital NHS Trust* [2006] EWCA Crim 2971. Since there were no substantial aggravating factors, the court was prepared to take this factor into account and to reduce the fine from £100,000 to £40,000.

Situations may arise where a company has been prosecuted for an offence but, prior to sentence, has incurred substantial expenditure in seeking to make good the damage caused by the offence. The approach to the calculation of fine and compensation was considered in *Thames Water Utilities Ltd.* [2010] EWCA Crim 202. The defendant had allowed poisonous substances to escape from its plant and substantial damage was caused to a river used extensively for leisure purposes. Prior to conviction, the defendant had spent (or pledged) £500,000 in compensation and for future improvement. It was asserted that the Crown Court had taken insufficient account of this when imposing the financial penalties and the Court of Appeal set out a number of principles. As in any other situation, the first stage in assessing the amount of a fine would be the assessment of the seriousness of the offence and the second would be the consideration of the means of the offender. The court should then calculate a notional fine incorporating both the punishment and deterrent elements, the latter being the amount over and above the punishment element that "brings the necessary message home to the offender's managers and shareholders (and thereby to others)": at [54]. Consideration will then be given to the payment of compensation and the extent to which it should be in addition to (or deducted from) the notional fine.

The departure from the normal process comes at this point as a court will then consider the extent to which the offender has "brought the message home to itself" and whether that should result in a reduction in the amount of the notional fine. The cost of corrective action should not be taken into account (since that should be the minimum response in most circumstances) whereas the making of substantial voluntary reparation is likely to be a significant mitigating feature sufficient to reduce the amount of the fine, possibly removing all the deterrent element. In exceptional cases, a reduction in the punishment element may also be justified.

Following this stage, the court will revert to the normal process of taking account of offender mitigation and any reduction for a guilty plea. Although not referred to in the judgment, this approach appears to follow the principle underlying the approach of the Sentencing Guidelines Council to voluntary restitution as seen, for example, in its definitive guideline on *Sentencing for fraud—Statutory Offences* at para. 44, *www.sentencingcouncil.judiciary.gov.uk*.

23–23 A court is obliged to inquire into the financial circumstances of the offender before fixing the amount of a fine: *Criminal Justice Act* 2003, s.164. The onus is on the offender to disclose evidence of his financial situation; if he does not, the court is entitled to draw whatever inferences it sees fit, and may conclude that the offender is being evasive about his financial circumstances and has the means to pay: *Higgins* (1988) 10 Cr.App.R.(S.) 144. Failure to comply with an order to disclose financial circumstances (s.162(1)) is itself an offence: s.162(3).

There is nothing wrong in principle with the fine being paid in instalments. Where a compensation order is being paid, the instalment period may quite properly be longer than one year, provided that it is not an undue burden and too severe a punishment for the offender, having regard to the nature of the offence and the offender. There is authority that a two year period will seldom be too long and in exceptional circumstances, a three year period might prove unassailable: *Olliver and Olliver* (1989) 11 Cr.App.R.(S.) 10, CA. However, a court will always need to ensure that there is a realistic prospect of the order being paid and will be conscious of the impact on the victim also where payments received from a court extend over a lengthy period. Schedule 5, Pt 3 to the *Courts Act* 2003 requires a court (when allowing time for payment on imposition) to make an attachment of earnings order or a deduction from benefit order in respect of an "existing defaulter" (as defined) unless that is impracticable and, for others, to make such an order with the consent of the person on whom the financial penalty has been imposed.

23–24 Where an offender has spent time in custody on remand before a fine is imposed, credit should be given for that time when the amount of the fine is determined: *Warden* [1996] 2 Cr.App.R.(S.) 269, CA.

A fine cannot be imposed at the same time as a discharge (*PCC(S)A* 2000, s.12(1)) unless the offender is being sentenced for two or more offences: *Sanck* (1990) 12 Cr.App.R.(S.) 155. It will only rarely be appropriate to combine a fine with a custodial sentence in a magistrates' court. One of the effects of a custodial sentence is to reduce the employability of the offender and it is unlikely to aid the objective of reducing crime by having an offender released from custody with a continuing obligation to pay fines to the court. This may be different where a defendant has substantial savings or where the order seeks to reclaim the proceeds of the crime.

The *Magistrates' Court Sentencing Guidelines* provides:

Imposition of fines with custodial sentences

39. A fine and a custodial sentence may be imposed for the same offence although there will be few circumstances in which this is appropriate, particularly where the custodial sentence is to be served immediately. One example might be where an offender has profited financially from an offence but there is no obvious victim to whom compensation can be awarded. Combining these sentences is most likely to be appropriate only where the custodial sentence is short and/or the offender clearly has, or will have, the means to pay.

40. Care must be taken to ensure that the overall sentence is proportionate to the seriousness of the offence and that better off offenders are not able to 'buy themselves out of custody'.

Criminal Justice Act 2003, ss.161A, 162, 164

Surcharges

Court's duty to order payment of surcharge

161A.—(1) A court when dealing with a person for one or more offences must also (subject to subsections (2) and (3)) order him to pay a surcharge. **23–25**

(2) Subsection (1) does not apply in such cases as may be prescribed by an order made by the Secretary of State.

(3) Where a court dealing with an offender considers—

(a) that it would be appropriate to make a compensation order, but

(b) that he has insufficient means to pay both the surcharge and appropriate compensation,

the court must reduce the surcharge accordingly (if necessary to nil).

(4) For the purposes of this section a court does not "deal with" a person if it—

(a) discharges him absolutely, or

(b) makes an order under the *Mental Health Act* 1983 in respect of him.

By virtue of the *Criminal Justice Act 2003 (Surcharge) (No.2) Order* 2007 (S.I. 2007 No.1079), the amount of the surcharge is £15. The requirement does not apply to cases where the court is not imposing a fine—see also *ante*, § 23–20 and s.164(4A), *post*.

Powers to order statement as to offender's financial circumstances

162.—(1) Where an individual has been convicted of an offence, the court may, before sentencing him, make a financial circumstances order with respect to him. **23–26**

(2) Where a magistrates' court has been notified in accordance with section 12(4) of the *Magistrates' Courts Act* 1980 that an individual desires to plead guilty without appearing before the court, the court may make a financial circumstances order with respect to him.

(3) In this section "a financial circumstances order" means, in relation to any individual, an order requiring him to give to the court, within such period as may be specified in the order, such a statement of his financial circumstances as the court may require.

(4) An individual who without reasonable excuse fails to comply with a financial circumstances order is liable on summary conviction to a fine not exceeding level 3 on the standard scale.

(5) If an individual, in furnishing any statement in pursuance of a financial circumstances order—

(a) makes a statement which he knows to be false in a material particular,

(b) recklessly furnishes a statement which is false in a material particular, or

(c) knowingly fails to disclose any material fact,

he is liable on summary conviction to a fine not exceeding level 4 on the standard scale.

(6) Proceedings in respect of an offence under subsection (5) may, notwithstanding anything in section 127(1) of the *Magistrates' Courts Act* 1980 (limitation of time), be commenced at any time within two years from the date of the commission of the offence or within six months from its first discovery by the prosecutor, whichever period expires the earlier.

Fixing of fines

164.—(1) Before fixing the amount of any fine to be imposed on an offender who is an individual, a court must inquire into his financial circumstances. **23–27**

(2) The amount of any fine fixed by a court must be such as, in the opinion of the court, reflects the seriousness of the offence.

(3) In fixing the amount of any fine to be imposed on an offender (whether an individual or other person), a court must take into account the circumstances of the case including, among other things, the financial circumstances of the offender so far as they are known, or appear, to the court.

(4) Subsection (3) applies whether taking into account the financial circumstances of the offender has the effect of increasing or reducing the amount of the fine.

(4A) In applying subsection (3), a court must not reduce the amount of a fine on account of any surcharge it orders the offender to pay under section 161A, except to the extent that he has insufficient means to pay both.

(5) Where—

(a) an offender has been convicted in his absence in pursuance of section 11 or 12 of the *Magistrates' Courts Act* 1980 (non-appearance of accused), or

(b) an offender—

(i) has failed to furnish a statement of his financial circumstances in response to a request which is an official request for the purposes of section 20A of the *Criminal Justice Act* 1991 (offence of making false statement as to financial circumstances),

(ii) has failed to comply with an order under section 162(1), or

(iii) has otherwise failed to co-operate with the court in its inquiry into his financial circumstances,

and the court considers that it has insufficient information to make a proper determination of the financial circumstances of the offender, it may make such determination as it thinks fit.

Criminal Justice Act 1982, s.37

The standard scale of fines for summary offences

23–28 **37.**—(1) There shall be a standard scale of fines for summary offences, which shall be known as "the standard scale".

(2) The standard scale is shown below—

Level on the scale	Amount of fine
1	£200
2	£500
3	£1,000
4	£2,500
5	£5,000.

(3) Where any enactment (whether contained in an Act passed before or after this Act) provides—

(a) that a person convicted of a summary offence shall be liable on conviction to a fine or a maximum fine by reference to a specified level on the standard scale; or

(b) confers power by subordinate instrument to make a person liable on conviction of a summary offence (whether or not created by the instrument) to a fine or maximum fine by reference to a specified level on the standard scale,

it is to be construed as referring to the standard scale for which this section provides as that standard scale has effect from time to time by virtue either of this section or of an order under section 143 of the *Magistrates' Courts Act* 1980.

Magistrates' Courts Act 1980, s.32

Penalties on summary conviction for offences triable either way

23–29 **32.**—(1) On summary conviction of any of the offences triable either way listed in Schedule 1 to this Act a person shall be liable to imprisonment for a term not exceeding 6 months (increased to 12 months on the bringing into force of *Criminal Justice Act* 2003, s.282) or to a fine not exceeding the prescribed sum or both, except that—

(a) a magistrates' court shall not have power to impose imprisonment for an offence so listed if the Crown Court would not have that power in the case of an adult convicted of it on indictment.

(2) For any offence triable either way which is not listed in Schedule 1 to this Act, being an offence under a relevant enactment, the maximum fine which may be imposed on summary conviction shall by virtue of this subsection be the prescribed sum unless the offence is one for which by virtue of an enactment other than this subsection a larger fine may be imposed on summary conviction.

(3) Where, by virtue of any relevant enactment, a person summarily convicted of an offence triable either way would, apart from this section, be liable to a maximum fine of one amount in the case of a first conviction and of a different amount in the case of a second or

subsequent conviction, subsection (2) above shall apply irrespective of whether the conviction is a first, second or subsequent one.

(4) Subsection (2) above shall not affect so much of any enactment as (in whatever words) makes a person liable on summary conviction to a fine not exceeding a specified amount for each day on which a continuing offence is continued after conviction or the occurrence of any other specified event.

(5) Subsection (2) above shall not apply on summary conviction of any of the following offences—

(a) offences under section 5(2) of the *Misuse of Drugs Act* 1971 (having possession of a controlled drug) where the controlled drug in relation to which the offence was committed was a Class B or Class C drug;

(b) offences under the following provisions of that Act, where the controlled drug in relation to which the offence was committed was a Class C drug, namely—

(i) section 4(2) (production, or being concerned in the production, of a controlled drug);

(ii) section 4(3) (supplying or offering a controlled drug or being concerned in the doing of either activity by another);

(iii) section 5(3) (having possession of a controlled drug with intent to supply it to another);

(iv) section 8 (being the occupier, or concerned in the management, of premises and permitting or suffering certain activities to take place there);

(v) section 12(6) (contravention of direction prohibiting practitioner etc. from possessing, supplying etc. controlled drugs); or

(vi) section 13(3) (contravention of direction prohibiting practitioner etc. from prescribing, supplying etc. controlled drugs).

(6) Where, as regards any offence triable either way, there is under any enactment (however framed or worded) a power by subordinate instrument to restrict the amount of the fine which on summary conviction can be imposed in respect of that offence—

(a) subsection (2) above shall not affect that power or override any restriction imposed in the exercise of that power; and

(b) the amount to which that fine may be restricted in the exercise of that power shall be any amount less than the maximum fine which could be imposed on summary conviction in respect of the offence apart from any restriction so imposed.

(8) In subsection (5) above "controlled drug", "Class B drug" and "Class C drug" have the same meaning as in the *Misuse of Drugs Act* 1971.

(9) In this section—

"fine" includes a pecuniary penalty but does not include a pecuniary forfeiture or pecuniary compensation;

"the prescribed sum" means £5,000 or such sum as is for the time being substituted in this definition by an order in force under section 143(1) below;

"relevant enactment" means an enactment contained in the *Criminal Law Act* 1977 or in any Act passed before, or in the same Session as, that Act.

Powers of Criminal Courts (Sentencing) Act 2000, s.135

Limit on fines imposed by magistrates' courts in respect of young offenders

135.—(1) Where a person aged under 18 is found guilty by a magistrates' court of an offence for which, apart from this section, the court would have power to impose a fine of an amount exceeding £1,000, the amount of any fine imposed by the court shall not exceed £1,000. **23–30**

(2) In relation to a person aged under 14, subsection (1) above shall have effect as if for "£1,000", in both places where it occurs, there were substituted "£250".

Magistrates' Courts Act 1980, ss. 82(1), (6), 88, 89

Restriction on power to impose imprisonment for default

82.—(1) A magistrates' court shall not on the occasion of convicting an offender of an offence issue a warrant of commitment for a default in paying any sum adjudged to be paid by the conviction unless— **23–31**

Part IV

(a) in the case of an offence punishable with imprisonment, he appears to the court to have sufficient means to pay the sum forthwith;

(b) it appears to the court that he is unlikely to remain long enough at a place of abode in the United Kingdom to enable payment of the sum to be enforced by other methods; or

(c) on the occasion of that conviction the court sentences him to immediate imprisonment, youth custody or detention in a detention centre for that or another offence or he is already serving a sentence of custody for life, or a term of imprisonment, youth custody, detention under section 9 of the *Criminal Justice Act* 1982 or detention in a detention centre.

(6) Where a magistrates' court issues a warrant of commitment on the ground that one of the conditions mentioned in subsection (1) ... above is satisfied, it shall state that fact, specifying the ground, in the warrant.

Supervision pending payment

23–32 **88.**—(1) Where any person is adjudged to pay a sum by a summary conviction and the convicting court does not commit him to prison forthwith in default of payment, the court may, either on the occasion of the conviction or on a subsequent occasion, order him to be placed under the supervision of such person as the court may from time to time appoint.

(2) An order placing a person under supervision in respect of any sum shall remain in force so long as he remains liable to pay the sum or any part of it unless the order ceases to have effect or is discharged under subsection (3) below.

(3) An order under this section shall cease to have effect on the making of a transfer of fine order under section 89 below with respect to the sum adjudged to be paid and may be discharged by the court that made it, without prejudice in either case to the making of a new order.

(4) Where a person under 21 years old has been adjudged to pay a sum by a summary conviction and the convicting court does not commit him to detention under section 108 of the *Powers of Criminal Courts (Sentencing) Act* 2000 forthwith in default of payment, the court shall not commit him to such detention in default of payment of the sum, or for want of sufficient distress to satisfy the sum, unless he has been placed under supervision in respect of the sum or the court is satisfied that it is undesirable or impracticable to place him under supervision.

(5) Where a court, being satisfied as aforesaid, commits a person under 21 years old to such detention without an order under this section having been made, the court shall state the grounds on which it is so satisfied in the warrant of commitment.

(6) Where an order placing a person under supervision with respect to a sum is in force, a magistrates' court shall not commit him to prison in default of payment of the sum, or for want of sufficient distress to satisfy the sum, unless the court has before committing him taken such steps as may be reasonably practicable to obtain from the person appointed for his supervision an oral or written report on the offender's conduct and means and has considered any report so obtained, in addition, in a case where an inquiry is required by section 82 above, to that inquiry.

Transfer of fine order

23–33 **89.**—(1) Where a magistrates' court in a local justice area has, or is treated by any enactment as having, adjudged a person by a conviction to pay a sum and it appears to the court, or where that sun is the subject of a collection order, it appears to the court or the fines officer as the case may be, that the person residing in England and Wales, the court or the fines officer, as the case may be, may make a transfer of fine order, that is to say, an order making payment enforceable in another local justice area and that area shall be specified in the order.

(2) As from the date on which a transfer of fine order is made with respect to any sum, all functions under this Part of this Act or under Schedule 5 to the Courts Act 2003 relating to that sum which, if no order had been made, would have been exercisable by any court or person mentioned in column 1 of the Table below shall be exercisable by the court or person mentioned in the corresponding entry in column 2, and not otherwise.

Column 1	*Column 2*
(A) The court which made the order.	
(B) A court acting in the same local justice area as was the fines officer who made the order.	In either case, a court acting in the local justice area specified in the order.
The designated officer for the court mentioned in the row above.	The designated officer for the court mentioned in the row above.
(A) The fines officer who made the order.	
(B) A fines officer acting in the same local justice area as was the court which made the order.	In either case, a fines officer acting in the local justice area specified in the order.

(2A) The functions of the court under this part of this Act to which subsection (2) above, relates shall be deemed to include the court's power to apply the Secretary of State under any regulations made by him under section 24(1)(a) of the *Criminal Justice Act* 1991 (power to deduct fines etc. from income support).

(3) A court or a fines officer, as the case may be, by which or whom functions in relation to any sum are for the time being exercisable by virtue of a transfer of fine order may make a further transfer of fine order with respect to that sum.

(4) In this section and sections 90 and 91 below, references to this Part of this Act do not include references to section 81(1) above.

D. POWER TO ORDER PERIODICAL PAYMENTS

Magistrates' Courts Act 1980, s.75

Power to dispense with immediate payment

75.—(1) A magistrates' court by whose conviction or order a sum is adjudged to be paid may, instead of requiring immediate payment, allow time for payment, or order payment by instalments. **23–34**

(2) Where a magistrates' court has allowed time for payment, the court may, on application by or on behalf of the person liable to make the payment, allow further time or order payment by instalments.

(2A.–2C.) [*Omitted.*]

(3) Where a court has ordered payment by instalments and default is made in the payment of any one instalment, proceedings may be taken as if the default had been made in the payment of all the instalments then unpaid.

E. POWER TO ORDER APPEARANCE BEFORE THE COURT IF ANY PART OF THE SUM REMAINS UNPAID

Magistrates' Courts Act 1980, s.86

Power of magistrates' court to fix day for appearance of offender at means inquiry etc.

86.—(1) A magistrates' court which has exercised in relation to a sum adjudged to be paid by a conviction either of the powers conferred by section 75(1) above shall have power, either then or later, to fix a day on which, if the relevant condition is satisfied, the offender must appear in person before the court for either or both of the following purposes, namely— **23–35**

(a) to enable an inquiry into his means to be made under section 82 above;

(b) to enable a hearing required by subsection (5) of the said section 82 to be held.

(1A) Where the power which the court has exercised is the power to allow time for payment of a sum ("the adjudged sum"), the relevant condition is satisfied if any part of that sum remains unpaid on the day fixed by the court.

(1B) Where the power which the court has exercised is the power to order payment by instalments, the relevant condition is satisfied if an instalment which has fallen due remains unpaid on the day fixed by the court.

(2) Except as provided in subsection (3) below, the power to fix a day under this section shall be exercisable only in the presence of the offender.

(3) Where a day has been fixed under this section, the court may fix a later day in subsection for the day previously fixed, and may do so—

(a) when composed of a single justice; and

(b) whether the offender is present or not.

(4) Subject to subsection (5) below, if on the day fixed under this section—

(a) the relevant condition is satisfied; and

(b) the offender fails to appear in person before the court,

the court may issue a warrant to arrest him and bring him before the court; and subsection (3) of section 83 above shall apply in relation to a warrant issued under this section.

(5) Where under subsection (3) above a later day has in the absence of the offender been fixed in substitution for a day previously fixed under this section, the court shall not issue a warrant under this section unless it is proved to the satisfaction of the court, on oath or in such other manner as may be prescribed, that notice in writing of the substituted day was served on the offender not less than what appears to the court to be a reasonable time before that day.

II. COMMUNITY ORDERS

A. COMMUNITY SENTENCES

(1) General

23–36 In relation to adults, a community sentence is a sentence which consists of a community order. A community order consists of one or more "requirements" as provided for by the Act.

23–37 A community order can consist of any number of the requirements set out in ss.177 and 199–214 of the *Criminal Justice Act* 2003. An order may be supported by electronic monitoring: s.177(3) and (4) and s.215. Once the threshold is passed (s.148(1)), whilst a court is able to choose from any (or all!) of these requirements, it must ensure that the restriction on liberty is commensurate with the seriousness of the offence, that the requirements are suitable for the offender and that interlocking requirements are compatible with each other: ss.148(2) and 177(6). As far as practicable, the requirements should not interfere with the religious beliefs, employment or education of the offender: s.217. There are some requirements which can only be made where the court has been informed that a suitable programme etc. is available for the offender; and some where a court must await confirmation that there are suitable facilities in the area before such requirements can be imposed: s.218. Whenever a community order is made, the offender must keep in touch with the "responsible officer" (see *post*) in the way prescribed by that officer and must notify any change of address: s.220(1). Although not a "requirement", this obligation is enforceable as if it were a requirement (see *post*, § 23–47: s.220(2). It should be noted that it is also possible to make a "supervision requirement" as a requirement of the order (see *post*, § 23–90): s.213. When imposing a community order, a court must stipulate a date by which all the requirements in the order must be complied with. This date must not be more than three years after the date of the order: *Criminal Justice Act* 2003, s.177(5). Some requirements also have their own time restrictions (for example, a curfew requirement or an unpaid work requirement) and the options available following breach are sometimes affected by the date set under s.177(5) (since that date cannot be extended). The interaction between the various dates and the principles that should govern the setting of the overall date has been the subject of differing views. In November 2008, the Magistrates' Association, the District Bench and the Justices' Clerks' Society issued an advice designed to assist in achieving a consistent interpretation. That advice recommends that the section 177(5) date should be for a period sufficient for all requirements to be completed but should not extend artificially beyond that time simply in case of a future breach. In addition, an order should be deemed to be no longer in force once all the requirements have been completed (even if still within the time set under s.177(5)) thereby avoiding the possibility of re-sentence for the original offence should the subject of the order commit a further offence. There is no entirely satisfactory solution to the problems caused by the current legislation but this approach seems likely to be just in most circumstances. By virtue of s.178 of the *Criminal Justice Act* 2003, there is an order making power enabling the Secretary of State to enable a court that makes a Community Order to provide for that order to be reviewed periodically. Such an order has been made to allow periodic reviews at the Liverpool Community Justice Centre and at the Salford Magistrates' Court both of which are piloting different approaches to community justice arising from consideration of the Red Hook project in the USA. This pilot has now been extended to cover 10 other pilot courts.

(2) Guidelines

In addition to the statutory provisions, a definitive guideline issued by the Sentencing **23–38**
Guidelines Council in December 2004 (*Overarching Principles: Seriousness*) sets out the approach to matching the seriousness of the offence and the characteristics of the offender to the order made. In a further guideline (*New Sentences: Criminal Justice Act* 2003), paras 1.1.9—1.1.14 emphasise the need for a rigorous approach to determining both the need for an order and the content of that order. It is noted that there is evidence that, where an offender has a low risk of re-offending, an inappropriate order can actually increase the chances of re-offending rather than reduce them. It is also noted that the consequences of breach of a community sentence may well be a custodial sentence and great care needs to be taken in ensuring that every requirement (and combination of requirements) properly matches the statutory obligation both to balance the restriction on liberty with the seriousness of the offence and to make the requirement(s) the most suitable for the offender: *Criminal Justice Act* 2003, s.148. The court must always have clearly in its mind the objectives of sentencing that it is seeking to achieve.

Guideline: New Sentences: Criminal Justice Act 2003

Section 1—Community Sentences & Deferred Sentences

Part 1: Community Sentences

B. IMPOSING A COMMUNITY SENTENCE—THE APPROACH

1.1.9 On pages 8 and 9 of the Seriousness guideline the two thresholds for the imposition of **23–39**
a community sentence are considered. Sentencers must consider all of the disposals available (within or below the threshold passed) at the time of sentence, and reject them before reaching the provisional decision to make a community sentence, so that even where the threshold for a community sentence has been passed a financial penalty or discharge may still be an appropriate penalty. Where an offender has a low risk of reoffending, particular care needs to be taken in the light of evidence that indicates that there are circumstances where inappropriate intervention can increase the risk of re-offending rather than decrease it. In addition, recent improvements in enforcement of financial penalties make them a more viable sentence in a wider range of cases.

1.1.10 Where an offender is being sentenced for a non-imprisonable offence or offences, great care will be needed in assessing whether a community sentence is appropriate since failure to comply could result in a custodial sentence.

1.1.11 Having decided (in consultation with the Probation Service where appropriate) that a community sentence is justified, the court must decide which requirements should be included in the community order. The requirements or orders imposed will have the effect of restricting the offender's liberty, whilst providing punishment in the community, rehabilitation for the offender, and/or ensuring that the offender engages in reparative activities.

The key issues arising are:
(i) **which requirements to impose;**
(ii) **how to make allowance for time spent on remand; and**
(iii) **how to deal with breaches.**

Part IV

(i) Requirements

1.1.12 When deciding which requirements to include, the court must be satisfied on three matters–

(i) that the **restriction on liberty is commensurate with the seriousness** of the offence(s);

(ii) that the **requirements are the most suitable** for the offender; and

(iii) that, where there are two or more requirements included, they are **compatible with each other**.

1.1.13 Sentencers should have the possibility of breach firmly in mind when passing sentence for the original offence. If a court is to reflect the seriousness of an offence, there is little value in setting requirements as part of a community sentence that are not demanding enough for an offender. On the other hand, there is equally little value in imposing requirements that would "set an offender up to fail" and almost inevitably lead to sanctions for a breach.

In community sentences, the guiding principles are proportionality and suitability. Once a court has decided that the offence has crossed the community sentence threshold and that a community sentence is justified, the initial factor in defining which requirements to include in a community sentence should be the seriousness of the offence committed.

1.1.14 This means that "seriousness" is an important factor in deciding whether the Court chooses the low, medium or high range (see below) but, having taken that decision, selection of the content of the order within the range will be determined by a much wider range of factors.

- **Sentencing ranges must remain flexible enough to take account of the suitability of the offender, his or her ability to comply with particular requirements and their availability in the local area.**
- **The justification for imposing a community sentence in response to persistent petty offending is the persistence of the offending behaviour rather than the seriousness of the offences being committed. The requirements imposed should ensure that the restriction on liberty is proportionate to the seriousness of the offending, to reflect the fact that the offences, of themselves, are not sufficiently serious to merit a community sentence.**

Once made, an order will name the local justice area in which the offender will reside (s.216) and a copy of that order must be given to those persons set out in s.219.

Criminal Justice Act 2003, ss.147–8, 150A 177, 216, 217, 219, 220

General restrictions on community sentences

Meaning of "community sentence" etc.

23–40 **147.**—(1) In this Part "community sentence" means a sentence which consists of or includes—

(a) a community order (as defined by section 177),

(c) a youth rehabilitation order.

Restrictions on imposing community sentences

23–41 **148.**—(1) A court must not pass a community sentence on an offender unless it is of the opinion that the offence, or the combination of the offence and one or more offences associated with it, was serious enough to warrant such a sentence.

(2) Where a court passes a community sentence—

(a) the particular requirement or requirements forming part of the community order, or as the case may be, youth rehabilitation order, comprised in the sentence must be such as, in the opinion of the court, is, or taken together are, the most suitable for the offender, and

(b) the restrictions on liberty imposed by the order must be such as in the opinion of the court are commensurate with the seriousness of the offence, or the combination of the offence and one or more offences associated with it.

(2A) Subsection (2) is subject to paragraph 3(4) of Schedule 1 to the *Criminal Justice and Immigration Act* 2008 (youth rehabilitation order with intensive supervision and surveillance.

(4) Subsections (1) and (2)(b) have effect subject to section 151(2).

(5) The fact that by virtue of any provision of this section—

(a) a community sentence may be passed in relation to an offence; or

(b) particular restrictions on liberty may be imposed by a community order or youth rehabilitation order,

does not require a court to pass such a sentence or to impose those restrictions.

Community order available only for offences punishable with imprisonment or for persistent offenders previously fined

150A.—(1) The power to make a community order is only exercisable in respect of an offence if— **23–42**

(a) the offence is punishable with imprisonment; or

(b) in any other case, section 151(2) confers power to make such an order.

(2) For the purposes of this section and section 151 an offence triable either way that was tried summarily is to be regarded as punishable with imprisonment only if it is so punishable by the sentencing court (and for this purpose section 148(1) is to be disregarded)

CHAPTER 2

COMMUNITY ORDERS: OFFENDERS AGED 16 OR OVER

Community orders

177.—(1) Where a person aged 18 or over is convicted of an offence, the court by or before which he is convicted may make an order (in this Part referred to as a "community order") imposing on him any one or more of the following requirements— **23–43**

(a) an unpaid work requirement (as defined by section 199),

(b) an activity requirement (as defined by section 201),

(c) a programme requirement (as defined by section 202),

(d) a prohibited activity requirement (as defined by section 203),

(e) a curfew requirement (as defined by section 204),

(f) an exclusion requirement (as defined by section 205),

(g) a residence requirement (as defined by section 206),

(h) a mental health treatment requirement (as defined by section 207),

(i) a drug rehabilitation requirement (as defined by section 209),

(j) an alcohol treatment requirement (as defined by section 212),

(k) a supervision requirement (as defined by section 213), and

(l) in a case where the offender is aged under 25, an attendance centre requirement (as defined by section 214).

(2) Subsection (1) has effect subject to sections 150 and 218 and to the following provisions of Chapter 4 relating to particular requirements—

(a) section 199(3) (unpaid work requirement),

(b) section 201(3) and (4) (activity requirement),

(c) section 202(4) and (5) (programme requirement),

(d) section 203(2) (prohibited activity requirement),

(e) section 207(3) (mental health treatment requirement),

(f) section 209(2) (drug rehabilitation requirement), and

(g) section 212(2) and (3) (alcohol treatment requirement).

(3) Where the court makes a community order imposing a curfew requirement or an exclusion requirement, the court must also impose an electronic monitoring requirement (as defined by section 215) unless—

(a) it is prevented from doing so by section 215(2) or 218(4), or

(b) in the particular circumstances of the case, it considers it inappropriate to do so.

(4) Where the court makes a community order imposing an unpaid work requirement, an activity requirement, a programme requirement, a prohibited activity requirement, a

Part IV

residence requirement, a mental health treatment requirement, a drug rehabilitation requirement, an alcohol treatment requirement, a supervision requirement or an attendance centre requirement, the court may also impose an electronic monitoring requirement unless prevented from doing so by section 215(2) or 218(4).

(5) A community order must specify a date, not more than three years after the date of the order, by which all the requirements in it must have been complied with; and a community order which imposes two or more different requirements falling within subsection (1) may also specify an earlier date or dates in relation to compliance with any one or more of them.

(6) Before making a community order imposing two or more different requirements falling within subsection (1), the court must consider whether, in the circumstances of the case, the requirements are compatible with each other.

Provisions applying to relevant orders generally

Local justice area to be specified in relevant order

23–44 **216.**—(1) A community order or suspended sentence order must specify the local justice area in which the offender resides or will reside.

(2) A custody plus order or an intermittent custody order must specify the local justice area in which the offender will reside—

(a) in the case of a custody plus order, during the licence period as defined by section 181(3)(b), or

(b) in the case of an intermittent custody order, during the licence periods as defined by section 183(3).

Requirement to avoid conflict with religious beliefs, etc

23–45 **217.**—(1) The court must ensure, as far as practicable, that any requirement imposed by a relevant order is such as to avoid—

(a) any conflict with the offender's religious beliefs or with the requirements of any other relevant order to which he may be subject; and

(b) any interference with the times, if any, at which he normally works or attends any educational establishment.

(2) The responsible officer in relation to an offender to whom a relevant order relates must ensure, as far as practicable, that any instruction given or requirement imposed by him in pursuance of the order is such as to avoid the conflict or interference mentioned in subsection (1).

(3) The Secretary of State may by order provide that subsection (1) or (2) is to have effect with such additional restrictions as may be specified in the order.

Provision of copies of relevant orders

23–46 **219.**—(1) The court by which any relevant order is made must forthwith provide copies of the order—

(a) to the offender,

(b) if the offender is aged 18 or over, to an officer of a local probation board assigned to the court, or an officer of a provider of probation services acting at the court

(c) if the offender is aged 16 or 17, to an officer of a local probation board assigned to the court, an officer of a provider of probation services acting at the court or to a member of a youth offending team assigned to the court, and

(d) where the order specifies a local justice area in which the court making the order does not act, to the local probation board acting for that area, or, as the case may be, a provider of probation services acting in that area.

(2) Where a relevant order imposes any requirement specified in the first column of Schedule 14, the court by which the order is made must also forthwith provide the person specified in relation to that requirement in the second column of that Schedule with a copy of so much of the order as relates to that requirement.

(3) Where a relevant order specifies a local justice area in which the court making the order does not act, the court making the order must provide to the magistrates' court acting in that area—

(a) a copy of the order, and

(b) such documents and information relating to the case as it considers likely to be of assistance to a court acting in that area in the exercise of its functions in relation to the order.

Duty of offender to keep in touch with responsible officer

220.—(1) An offender in respect of whom a community order or a suspended sentence order is in force— **23–47**

(a) must keep in touch with the responsible officer in accordance with such instructions as he may from time to time be given by that officer, and

(b) must notify him of any change of address.

(2) The obligation imposed by subsection (1) is enforceable as if it were a requirement imposed by the order.

Under s.150A, a community order can only be imposed for imprisonable offences and imprisonment must be available to the sentencing court.

In considering whether the threshold has been crossed, the court may take into account both the offence itself and any other offence "associated with it". **23–48**

The fact that the threshold has been crossed does not require the court to pass a community sentence (s.148(5)). That decision simply sets an upper limit on the most severe type of sentence that can be imposed. Prior to deciding on the sentence to be imposed, the court will: **23–49**

— first decide whether the threshold has been crossed (s.148(1)) and
— then decide which order is most suitable for the offender (s.148(2)(a)) whilst
— ensuring that the restrictions on liberty that result from the imposition of the order(s) are commensurate with the seriousness of the offence(s) (s.148(2)(b)).

It is in making a community sentence that the conflict is often most apparent between the needs of the offender in order to reduce the likelihood of re-offending and the need to maintain the balance between the seriousness of the offence and the severity of the sanction. This can be seen in the shift away from financial penalties towards a community sentence. It may also be a factor in the increased use of custody since a person who has offended again after (or during) such a sentence is more likely to receive a custodial sentence. **23–50**

Prior to making a community sentence, a court will consider what information it has and what else is needed. Information about the offence will assist the court particularly in relation to the threshold of seriousness and the extent to which any order(s) need to restrict the liberty of the defendant. Information about the offender will particularly assist in relation to deciding the most suitable order for the offender. **23–51**

Given the open ended nature of the sentence, there is clear scope for widely differing applications. The resolution of this has been the Guideline issued by the Sentencing Guidelines Council on December 16, 2004 after extensive consultation: *New Sentences: Criminal Justice Act 2003*. As well as providing the basis of training for the judiciary, justices' clerks and legal advisers, the approach adopted by the Council has been imported into the guidance issued to probation officers. The Guideline emphasises the primacy of the assessment of "seriousness" of the offence as the starting point for sentence. Setting the scene by emphasising the importance of clarity of thought in the process of deciding what requirements to include in an order to ensure both that the order properly reflects that seriousness and also realistically attempts to achieve the goals that the court considers important, the Guideline establishes three levels of seriousness. These provide a framework within which a court can consistently deal with the need to reflect the seriousness of the offence whilst allowing the flexibility to meet the other statutory obligations of suitability and compatibility. The key parts of the guideline are summarised in the *Magistrates' Court Sentencing Guidelines* at p.160. **23–52**

Guideline: New Sentences: Criminal Justice Act 2003

Section 1—Community Sentences & Deferred Sentences

Part 1: Community Sentences

B. IMPOSING A COMMUNITY SENTENCE—THE APPROACH

(i) Requirements

(b) Ranges of Sentence Within the Community Sentence Band

23–53 **1.1.18** To enable the court to benefit from the flexibility that community sentences provide and also to meet its statutory obligations, any structure governing the use of community requirements must allow the courts to choose the most appropriate sentence for each individual offender.

1.1.19 Sentencers have a statutory obligation to pass sentences that are commensurate with the seriousness of an offence. However, within the range of sentence justified by the seriousness of the offence(s), courts will quite properly consider those factors that heighten the risk of the offender committing further offences or causing further harm with a view to lessening that risk. The extent to which requirements are imposed must be capable of being varied to ensure that the restriction on liberty is commensurate with the seriousness of the offence.

1.1.20 The Council recognises that it would be helpful for sentencers to have a framework to help them decide on the most appropriate use of the new community sentence. While there is no single guiding principle, the seriousness of the offence that has been committed is an important factor. Three sentencing ranges (low, medium and high) within the community sentence band can be identified. It is not possible to position particular types of offence at firm points within the three ranges because the seriousness level of an offence is largely dependent upon the culpability of the offender and this is uniquely variable. The difficulty is particularly acute in relation to the medium range where it is clear that requirements will need to be tailored across a relatively wide range of offending behaviour.

1.1.21 In general terms, the lowest range of community sentence would be for those offenders whose offence was relatively minor within the community sentence band and would include persistent petty offenders whose offences only merit a community sentence by virtue of failing to respond to the previous imposition of fines. Such offenders would merit a "light touch" approach, for example, normally a single requirement such as a short period of unpaid work, or a curfew, or a prohibited activity requirement or an exclusion requirement (where the circumstances of the case mean that this would be an appropriate disposal without electronic monitoring).

1.1.22 The top range would be for those offenders who have only just fallen short of a custodial sentence and for those who have passed the threshold but for whom a community sentence is deemed appropriate.

1.1.23 In all three ranges there must be sufficient flexibility to allow the sentence to be varied to take account of the suitability of particular requirements for the individual offender and whether a particular requirement or package of requirements might be more effective at reducing any identified risk of re-offending. It will fall to the sentencer to ensure that the sentence strikes the right balance between proportionality and suitability.

There should be three sentencing ranges (low, medium and high) within the community sentence band based upon seriousness.

It is not intended that an offender necessarily progress from one range to the next on each sentencing occasion. The decision as to the appropriate range each time is based upon the seriousness of the new offence(s).

The decision on the nature and severity of the requirements to be included in a community sentence should be guided by:

(i) **the assessment of offence seriousness (LOW, MEDIUM OR HIGH);**
(ii) **the purpose(s) of sentencing the court wishes to achieve;**
(iii) **the risk of re-offending;**
(iv) **the ability of the offender to comply, and**
(v) **the availability of requirements in the local area.**

The resulting restriction on liberty must be a proportionate response to the offence that was committed.

1.1.24 Below we set out a non-exhaustive description of examples of requirements that might be appropriate in the three sentencing ranges. These examples focus on punishment in the community, although it is recognised that not all packages will necessarily need to include a punitive requirement. There will clearly be other requirements of a rehabilitative nature, such as a treatment requirement or an accredited programme, which may be appropriate depending on the specific needs of the offender and assessment of suitability. Given the intensity of such interventions, it is expected that these would normally only be appropriate at medium and high levels of seriousness, and where assessed as having a medium or high risk of re-offending. In addition, when passing sentence in any one of the three ranges, the court should consider whether a rehabilitative intervention such as a programme requirement, or a restorative justice intervention might be suitable as an additional or alternative part of the sentence.

Low

1.1.25 For offences only just crossing the community sentence threshold (such as persistent petty offending, some public order offences, some thefts from shops, or interference with a motor vehicle, where the seriousness of the offence or the nature of the offender's record means that a discharge or fine is inappropriate).

1.1.26 Suitable requirements might include:

- 40 to 80 hours of unpaid work or
- a curfew requirement within the lowest range (*e.g.* up to 12 hours per day for a few weeks) or
- an exclusion requirement (where the circumstances of the case mean that this would be an appropriate disposal without electronic monitoring) lasting a few months or
- a prohibited activity requirement or
- an attendance centre requirement (where available).

1.1.27 Since the restriction on liberty must be commensurate with the seriousness of the offence, particular care needs to be taken with this band to ensure that this obligation is complied with. In most cases, only one requirement will be appropriate and the length may be curtailed if additional requirements are necessary.

Medium

1.1.28 For offences that obviously fall within the community sentence band such as handling stolen goods worth less than £1000 acquired for resale or somewhat more valuable goods acquired for the handler's own use, some cases of burglary in commercial premises, some cases of taking a motor vehicle without consent, or some cases of obtaining property by deception.

1.1.29 Suitable requirements might include:

- a greater number (*e.g.* 80 to 150) of hours of unpaid work or
- an activity requirement in the middle range (20 to 30 days) or
- a curfew requirement within the middle range (*e.g.* up to 12 hours for 2–3 months) or
- an exclusion requirement lasting in the region of 6 months or
- a prohibited activity requirement.

1.1.30 Since the restriction on liberty must be commensurate with the seriousness of the offence, particular care needs to be taken with this band to ensure that this obligation is complied with.

High

1.1.31 For offences that only just fall below the custody threshold or where the custody threshold is crossed but a community sentence is more appropriate in all the circumstances, for example some cases displaying the features of a standard domestic burglary committed by a first-time offender.

1.1.32 More intensive sentences which combine two or more requirements may be appropriate at this level. Suitable requirements might include an unpaid work order of between 150 and 300 hours; an activity requirement up to the maximum 60 days; an exclusion order lasting in the region of 12 months; a curfew requirement of up to 12 hours a day for 4–6 months.

(3) Implementation of the order

Responsible officer

In terms of the implementation of the order, the key person is designated as the **23–54**
"responsible officer": *Criminal Justice Act* 2003, s.197. This person will vary with the

nature of the requirement imposed. The duty imposed on that officer is also set out: *Criminal Justice Act* 2003, s.198.

Criminal Justice Act 2003, ss.197–198

Meaning of "the responsible officer"

23–55 **197.**—(1) For the purposes of this Part, "the responsible officer", in relation to an offender to whom a relevant order relates, means—

(a) in a case where the order—

(i) imposes a curfew requirement or an exclusion requirement but no other requirement mentioned in section 177(1) or, as the case requires, section 182(1) or 190(1), and

(ii) imposes an electronic monitoring requirement,

the person who under section 215(3) is responsible for the electronic monitoring required by the order;

(b) in a case where the only requirement imposed by the order is an attendance centre requirement, the officer in charge of the attendance centre in question;

(c) in any other case, the qualifying officer who, as respects the offender, is for the time being responsible for discharging the functions conferred by this Part on the responsible officer.

(2) The following are qualifying officers for the purposes of subsection (1)(c)—

(a) in a case where the offender is aged under 18 st the time when the relevant order is made—

(i) an officer of a local probation broad appointed for or assigned to the local justice area for the time being specified in the order or, (as the case may be) an officer of a provider of probation services acting in the local justice area for the time being specified in the order;

(ii) a member of the youth offending team established by a local authority for the time being specified in the order,

(b) in any other case, an officer of a local probation board appointed for or assigned to the local justice area for the time being specified in the order, or (as the case may be) an officer of a provider of probation services acting in the local justice area for the time being specified in the order.

(3) The Secretary of State may by order—

(a) amend subsections (1) and (2), and

(b) make any other amendments of this Part that appear to him to be necessary or expedient in consequence of any amendment made by virtue of paragraph (a).

(4) An order under subsection (3) may, in particular, provide for the court to determine which of two or more descriptions of "responsible officer" is to apply in relation to any relevant order.

Duties of responsible officer

23–56 **198.**—(1) Where a relevant order has effect, it is the duty of the responsible officer—

(a) to make any arrangements that are necessary in connection with the requirements imposed by the order,

(b) to promote the offender's compliance with those requirements, and

(c) where appropriate, to take steps to enforce those requirements.

(2) In this section "responsible officer" does not include a person falling within section 197(1)(a).

23–57 A more restricted duty falls on those responsible for curfew or exclusion requirements or for electronic monitoring than on those responsible for other requirements. In essence, this is because those obligations will be contracted out whilst the other requirements are most likely to remain under the responsibility of the National Offender Management Service.

B. ELECTRONIC MONITORING REQUIREMENT

23–58 The availability of electronic monitoring has become a well used option that has enabled a court to ensure that its order is being obeyed and, consequentially, to be more sparing in the use of custodial sentences. In relation to some of the requirements being imposed, the imposition of electronic monitoring is obligatory. In other circumstances, the court may have the power to make such an order. In its Guideline, *New Sentences: Criminal Justice Act 2003*, the Sentencing Guidelines Council (at para. 1.1.33) emphasises the "primary purpose of promoting and monitoring compliance with other requirements" imposed by the court and that this most arises in situations where "the punishment of the offender and/or the need to safeguard the public and prevent re-offending are the most important concerns".

Criminal Justice Act 2003, ss.177, 215

Community orders

177.—(3) Where the court makes a community order imposing a curfew requirement or an exclusion requirement, the court must also impose an electronic monitoring requirement (as defined by section 215) unless— **23–59**

(a) it is prevented from doing so by section 215(2) or 218(4), or

(b) in the particular circumstances of the case, it considers it inappropriate to do so.

(4) Where the court makes a community order imposing an unpaid work requirement, an activity requirement, a programme requirement, a prohibited activity requirement, a residence requirement, a mental health treatment requirement, a drug rehabilitation requirement, an alcohol treatment requirement, a supervision requirement or an attendance centre requirement, the court may also impose an electronic monitoring requirement unless prevented from doing so by section 215(2) or 218(4).

Electronic monitoring requirement

215.—(1) In this Part "electronic monitoring requirement", in relation to a relevant order, means a requirement for securing the electronic monitoring of the offender's compliance with other requirements imposed by the order during a period specified in the order, or determined by the responsible officer in accordance with the relevant order. **23–60**

(2) Where—

(a) it is proposed to include in a relevant order a requirement for securing electronic monitoring in accordance with this section, but

(b) there is a person (other than the offender) without whose co-operation it will not be practicable to secure the monitoring,

the requirement may not be included in the order without that person's consent.

(3) A relevant order which includes an electronic monitoring requirement must include provision for making a person responsible for the monitoring; and a person who is made so responsible must be of a description specified in an order made by the Secretary of State.

(4) Where an electronic monitoring requirement is required to take effect during a period determined by the responsible officer in accordance with the relevant order, the responsible officer must, before the beginning of that period, notify—

(a) the offender,

(b) the person responsible for the monitoring, and

(c) any person falling within subsection (2)(b),

of the time when the period is to begin.

C. COMMUNITY ORDERS — REQUIREMENTS

The heart of the new community order is the requirements. Each has its own limits and options. Some requirements can only be included where specifically recommended by a probation officer. Subject to that and to the qualifying criteria, most requirements are available for all adult offenders. The exception is the Attendance Centre requirement which has an upper age limit. **23–61**

D. UNPAID WORK REQUIREMENT

(1) General

The work will generally be for the benefit of the community though this may be to **23–62** the community as a whole or to an individual or smaller group within the community. Although primarily designed as having a large element of punishment and of reparation to the community, it is quite common for the involvement of the offender to lead on to continuing beneficial contact with the community group initially involved.

The court will need to be satisfied that the offender is suitable to perform work. In reaching that conclusion, the court may hear from an "appropriate officer", that is an officer of a local probation board.

(2) Content

23–63 The court will specify the number of hours to be completed. In total, there has to be not less than 40 hours nor more than 300 hours: s.199(2). Those hours will normally be completed within a maximum of 12 months (s.200(2)) though this period may be extended by the court (Sched. 8, para. 20—see further in Enforcement at §§ 24–123 and 24–151, *post*).

If the court is making several orders on the same occasion, it is possible to make the hours in each order consecutive to each other: s.199(5). The maximum may not exceed 300 hours. In practice, making concurrent orders is usually simpler both for the defendant and the public to understand and also for the management of the orders. This is permissible because of the power of the court in assessing both the seriousness of the offence and the extent of restriction on liberty to consider both the offence and other offences associated with it: s.148(1).

Criminal Justice Act 2003, ss.199–200

Unpaid work requirement

23–64 **199.**—(1) In this Part "unpaid work requirement", in relation to a relevant order, means a requirement that the offender must perform unpaid work in accordance with section 200.

(2) The number of hours which a person may be required to work under an unpaid work requirement must be specified in the relevant order and must be in the aggregate—

(a) not less than 40, and

(b) not more than 300.

(3) A court may not impose an unpaid work requirement in respect of an offender unless after hearing (if the courts thinks necessary) an officer of a local probation board or an officer of a provider of probation services, the court is satisfied that the offender is a suitable person to perform work under such a requirement.

(5) Where the court makes relevant orders in respect of two or more offences of which the offender has been convicted on the same occasion and includes unpaid work requirements in each of them, the court may direct that the hours of work specified in any of those requirements is to be concurrent with or additional to those specified in any other of those orders, but so that the total number of hours which are not concurrent does not exceed the maximum specified in subsection (2)(b).

Obligations of person subject to unpaid work requirement

23–65 **200.**—(1) An offender in respect of whom an unpaid work requirement of a relevant order is in force must perform for the number of hours specified in the order such work at such times as he may be instructed by the responsible officer.

(2) Subject to paragraph 20 of Schedule 8 and paragraph 18 of Schedule 12 (power to extend order), the work required to be performed under an unpaid work requirement of a community order or a suspended sentence order must be performed during a period of twelve months.

(3) Unless revoked, a community order imposing an unpaid work requirement remains in force until the offender has worked under it for the number of hours specified in it.

(4) Where an unpaid work requirement is imposed by a suspended sentence order, the supervision period as defined by section 189(1)(a) continues until the offender has worked under the order for the number of hours specified in the order, but does not continue beyond the end of the operational period as defined by section 189(1)(b)(ii).

E. Activity Requirement, Programme Requirement, Prohibited Activity Requirement

(1) General

The Activity Requirement is in s.201, the programme Requirement in s.202 and the Prohibited Activity Requirement in s.203. In the case of an Activity or Prohibited Activity Requirement, a court must consult a probation officer before making the order. In the case of a Programme Requirement, a court may only include it within a community order if the programme is an "accredited programme" (s.202(2)), is recommended to the court by a probation officer as being suitable for the offender (s.202(4)(a)) and is available at a place to be specified by the court (s.202(4)(b)). **23–66**

Criminal Justice Act 2003, ss.201–203

Activity requirement

201.—(1) In this Part "activity requirement", in relation to a relevant order, means a requirement that the offender must do either or both of the following— **23–67**

(a) present himself to a person or persons specified in the relevant order at a place or places so specified on such number of days as may be so specified;

(b) participate in activities specified in the order on such number of days as may be so specified.

(2) The specified activities may consist of or include activities whose purpose is that of reparation, such as activities involving contact between offenders and persons affected by their offences.

(3) A court may not include an activity requirement in a relevant order unless—

(a) it has consulted an officer of a local probation board or an officer of a provider of probation services; and

(b) it is satisfied that it is feasible to secure compliance with the requirement.

(4) A court may not include an activity requirement in a relevant order if compliance with that requirement would involve the co-operation of a person other than the offender and the offender's responsible officer, unless that other person consents to its inclusion.

(5) The aggregate of the number of days specified under subsection (1)(a) and (b) must not exceed 60.

(6) A requirement such as is mentioned in subsection (1)(a) operates to require the offender—

(a) in accordance with instructions given by his responsible officer, to present himself at a place or places on the number of days specified in the order, and

(b) while at any place, to comply with instructions given by, or under the authority of, the person in charge of that place.

(7) A place specified under subsection (1)(a) must be—

(a) a community rehabilitation centre, or

(b) a place that has been approved as providing facilities suitable for persons subject to activity requirements—

(i) where the premises are situated in the area of a local probation board, by that board, or

(ii) in any other case, by a provider of probation services authorised to do so by arrangements under section 3 of the Offender Management Act 2007.

(8) Where the place specified under subsection (1)(a) is a community rehabilitation centre, the reference in subsection (6)(a) to the offender presenting himself at the specified place includes a reference to him presenting himself elsewhere than at the centre for the purpose of participating in activities in accordance with instructions given by, or under the authority of, the person in charge of the centre.

(9) A requirement to participate in activities operates to require the offender—

(a) in accordance with instructions given by his responsible officer, to participate in activities on the number of days specified in the order, and

(b) while participating, to comply with instructions given by, or under the authority of, the person in charge of the activities.

(10) In this section "community rehabilitation centre" means premises—

(a) at which non-residential facilities are provided for use in connection with the rehabilitation of offenders, and
(b) which are for the time being approved by the Secretary of State as providing facilities suitable for persons subject to relevant orders.

Programme requirement

23–68 **202.**—(1) In this Part "programme requirement", in relation to a relevant order, means a requirement that the offender must participate in an accredited programme specified in the order at a place so specified on such number of days as may be so specified.

(2) In this Part "accredited programme" means a programme that is for the time being accredited by the Secretary of State for the purposes of this section.

(3) In this section—
(a) "programme" means a systematic set of activities.

(4) A court may not include a programme requirement in a relevant order unless—
(a) the accredited programme which the court proposes to specify in the order has been recommended to the court as being suitable for the offender by an officer of a local probation board or an officer of a provider of probation services; and
(b) the court is satisfied that the programme is (or, where the relevant order is a custody plus order or an intermittent custody order, will be) available at the place proposed to be specified.

(5) A court may not include a programme requirement in a relevant order if compliance with that requirement would involve the co-operation of a person other than the offender and the offender's responsible officer, unless that other person consents to its inclusion.

(6) A requirement to attend an accredited programme operates to require the offender—
(a) in accordance with instructions given by the responsible officer, to participate in the accredited programme at the place specified in the order on the number of days specified in the order, and
(b) while at that place, to comply with instructions given by, or under the authority of, the person in charge of the programme.

(7) A place specified in an order must be a place that has been approved as providing facilities suitable for persons subject to programme requirements—
(a) where the premises are situated in the area of a local probation board, by that board, or
(b) in any other case, by a provider of probation services authorised to do so by section 3 of the Offender Management Act 2007.

Prohibited activity requirement

23–69 **203.**—(1) In this Part "prohibited activity requirement", in relation to a relevant order, means a requirement that the offender must refrain from participating in activities specified in the order—
(a) on a day or days so specified, or
(b) during a period so specified.

(2) A court may not include a prohibited activity requirement in a relevant order unless it has consulted an officer of a local probation board or an officer of a provider of probation services.

(3) The requirements that may by virtue of this section be included in a relevant order include a requirement that the offender does not possess, use or carry a firearm within the meaning of the *Firearms Act* 1968.

F. CURFEW REQUIREMENT

(1) General

23–70 The Curfew Requirement is designed to keep a person in a certain place at specified times. Although it may have an element that helps reduce the likelihood of the offender committing further offences, its primary purpose is to impose punishment by restricting the liberty of the offender.

Prior to imposing the requirement, the court must consider information about the place(s) where the offender will have to be and the attitude of those people who are likely to be affected by the fact that the offender is required to be there: s.204(6).

(2) Content

The obligation on the offender is to remain at a specified place for the periods specified in the order. Those periods must add up to no less than two hours and no more than 12 hours in any one day: s.204(2). The order must not continue for more than six months: s.204(3). **23–71**

The hours and the place may vary from time to time: s.204(2). Compliance with the order will often be monitored electronically; in these circumstances, the consent of anyone other than the offender who is involved in the monitoring will need to be obtained: s.215(2) (see *ante*, § 23–60) although blanket contracts will have been made for this purpose.

Criminal Justice Act 2003, s.204

Curfew requirement

204.—(1) In this Part "curfew requirement", in relation to a relevant order, means a requirement that the offender must remain, for periods specified in the relevant order, at a place so specified. **23–72**

(2) A relevant order imposing a curfew requirement may specify different places or different periods for different days, but may not specify periods which amount to less than two hours or more than twelve hours in any day.

(3) A community order or suspended sentence order which imposes a curfew requirement may not specify periods which fall outside the period of six months beginning with the day on which it is made.

(4) A custody plus order which imposes a curfew requirement may not specify a period which falls outside the period of six months beginning with the first day of the licence period as defined by section 181(3)(b).

(5) An intermittent custody order which imposes a curfew requirement must not specify a period if to do so would cause the aggregate number of days on which the offender is subject to the requirement for any part of the day to exceed 182.

(6) Before making a relevant order imposing a curfew requirement, the court must obtain and consider information about the place proposed to be specified in the order (including information as to the attitude of persons likely to be affected by the enforced presence there of the offender).

G. EXCLUSION REQUIREMENT

(1) General

The Exclusion Requirement prohibits the offender from entering a place specified for the period prescribed. That period may not exceed two years when the requirement is included within a community order: s.205(2). As with a curfew requirement, different places can be specified for different periods or days. **23–73**

Criminal Justice Act 2003, s.205

Exclusion requirement

205.—(1) In this Part "exclusion requirement", in relation to a relevant order, means a provision prohibiting the offender from entering a place specified in the order for a period so specified. **23–74**

(2) Where the relevant order is a community order, the period specified must not be more than two years.

(3) An exclusion requirement—

(a) may provide for the prohibition to operate only during the periods specified in the order, and

(b) may specify different places for different periods or days.

(4) In this section "place" includes an area.

H. RESIDENCE REQUIREMENT

(1) General

23–75 As well as providing where the offender must reside (s.206(1)), the court may authorise residence elsewhere with the prior approval of the "responsible officer" (s.206(2)). This introduces welcome flexibility for circumstances where the accommodation in the order ceases to be available or suitable. The place of residence specified by the court may only be a hostel or other institution where that is on the recommendation of a probation officer (s.206(4)).

Criminal Justice Act 2003, s.206

Residence requirement

23–76 **206.**—(1) In this Part, "residence requirement", in relation to a community order or a suspended sentence order, means a requirement that, during a period specified in the relevant order, the offender must reside at a place specified in the order.

(2) If the order so provides, a residence requirement does not prohibit the offender from residing, with the prior approval of the responsible officer, at a place other than that specified in the order.

(3) Before making a community order or suspended sentence order containing a residence requirement, the court must consider the home surroundings of the offender.

(4) A court may not specify a hostel or other institution as the place where an offender must reside, except on the recommendation of an officer of a local probation board or an officer of a provider of probation services.

I. MENTAL HEALTH TREATMENT REQUIREMENT

(1) General

23–77 This requirement enables a court to make provision for treatment for an offender's mental condition. This treatment may be as a resident or non-resident patient or in some other way but the court may only describe the treatment in those general terms: s.207(2). The criteria that must be satisfied before an order is made are set out in s.207(3). The offender must be willing to comply with the requirement; the offender's mental condition must both require and be susceptible to treatment (but not be such as to require the making of a hospital or guardianship order) and the court must be satisfied that arrangements can be made for that treatment. Where the offender is under treatment as a resident patient as a result of this requirement, the remit of the "responsible officer" is limited to that necessary for the purpose of any revocation or amendment of the order (s.207(4)).

Criminal Justice Act 2003, s.207–208

Mental health treatment requirement

23–78 **207.**—(1) In this Part, "mental health treatment requirement", in relation to a community order or suspended sentence order, means a requirement that the offender must submit, during a period or periods specified in the order, to treatment by or under the direction of a registered medical practitioner or a registered psychologist (or both, for different periods) with a view to the improvement of the offender's mental condition.

(2) The treatment required must be such one of the following kinds of treatment as may be specified in the relevant order—

(a) treatment as a resident patient in an independent hospital or care home within the meaning of the *Care Standards Act* 2000 or a hospital within the meaning of the *Mental Health Act* 1983, but not in hospital premises where high security psychiatric services within the meaning of that Act are provided;

(b) treatment as a non-resident patient at such institution or place as may be specified in the order;

(c) treatment by or under the direction of such registered medical practitioner or registered psychologist (or both) as may be so specified;

but the nature of the treatment is not to be specified in the order except as mentioned in paragraph (a), (b) or (c).

(3) A court may not by virtue of this section include a mental health treatment requirement in a relevant order unless—

(a) the court is satisfied, on the evidence of a registered medical practitioner approved for the purposes of section 12 of the *Mental Health Act* 1983, that the mental condition of the offender—

(i) is such as requires and may be susceptible to treatment, but

(ii) is not such as to warrant the making of a hospital order or guardianship order within the meaning of that Act;

(b) the court is also satisfied that arrangements have been or can be made for the treatment intended to be specified in the order (including arrangements for the reception of the offender where he is to be required to submit to treatment as a resident patient); and

(c) the offender has expressed his willingness to comply with such a requirement.

(4) While the offender is under treatment as a resident patient in pursuance of a mental health requirement of a relevant order, his responsible officer shall carry out the supervision of the offender to such extent only as may be necessary for the purpose of the revocation or amendment of the order.

(5) Subsections (2) and (3) of section 54 of the *Mental Health Act* 1983 have effect with respect to proof for the purposes of subsection (3)(a) of an offender's mental condition as they have effect with respect to proof of an offender's mental condition for the purposes of section 37(2)(a) of that Act.

(6) In this section and section 208, "registered psychologist" means a person registered in the part of the register maintained under the *Health Professions Order 2001* which relates to practitioner psychologists.

Mental health treatment at place other than that specified in order

208.—(1) Where the medical practitioner or registered psychologist by whom or under whose direction an offender is being treated for his mental condition in pursuance of a mental health treatment requirement is of the opinion that part of the treatment can be better or more conveniently given in or at an institution or place which— **23–79**

(a) is not specified in the relevant order, and

(b) is one in or at which the treatment of the offender will be given by or under the direction of a registered medical practitioner or registered psychologist,

he may, with the consent of the offender, make arrangements for him to be treated accordingly.

(2) Such arrangements as are mentioned in subsection (1) may provide for the offender to receive part of his treatment as a resident patient in an institution or place notwithstanding that the institution or place is not one which could have been specified for that purpose in the relevant order.

(3) Where any such arrangements as are mentioned in subsection (1) are made for the treatment of an offender—

(a) at the medical practitioner or registered psychologist by whom the arrangements are made shall give notice in writing to the offender's responsible officer, specifying the institution or place in or at which the treatment is to be carried out; and

(b) the treatment provided for by the arrangements shall be deemed to be treatment to which he is required to submit in pursuance of the relevant order.

J. DRUG REHABILITATION REQUIREMENT

(1) General

The aim of a drug rehabilitation requirement is to provide a chance for an offender to break (or reduce) his drug addiction and thereby cease offending: s.209(1)(a). An order will consist of treatment by a suitably qualified person (s.209(1)(a)), and the provision of samples as and when required to ascertain the presence of drugs in the body **23–80** (s.209(1)(b)). The treatment may be residential or non-residential as specified in the order (s.209(4)). There is power to establish reviews of progress by the court: s.210.

These must be established if the treatment and testing period exceeds 12 months: s.210(1). The treatment and testing period must be made for not less than six months: s.209(3). A court must first be satisfied both that the offender is either dependent on drugs or has a tendency to misuse them and that this dependency or propensity both requires treatment and is susceptible to treatment.

It must then be satisfied that arrangements can be made for the treatment it is intended to require. This type of requirement can only be included where an officer of a local probation board recommends it as suitable for the offender: s.209(2). The requirement may only be included if the offender expresses willingness to comply: s.209(2)(d).

(2) When to include this requirement

23–81 This is often an even more complex balancing exercise than usual since those most needing treatment will often have committed offences that are both serious and prolific. A spate of judicial consideration led to the Court of Appeal (Criminal Division) reviewing the authorities and identifying some of the most relevant factors: *Att.-Gen.'s Reference (No.64 of 2003) (Boujettif, Harrison)* [2004] 2 Cr.App.R.(S.) 22. Although these were decided in the context of the making of a Drug Treatment and Testing Order (DTTO) under the previous legislation, the principles are likely to continue to be applicable. The Court concluded that, although a DTTO may well be suitable where a substantial number of offences have been committed, such an order is not likely to be appropriate for an offender who has committed a substantial number of serious offences which either involve minor violence or have had a particularly damaging effect on the victim(s)—"excessive weight must not be given to the prospect of rehabilitation at the expense of proper regard for the criminality of the offender": Rose V.P. at para. 14. It was also noted that a DTTO is more likely to be effective early in a criminal career but that there will be exceptional cases justifying such orders at other times. There must be clear evidence that the offender is determined to be free from drugs. Further consideration was given to the decision whether to make such an order in the context of offences serious enough to be sentenced in the Crown Court in *Woods* [2005] EWCA Crim 2065; [2006] 1 Cr.App.R. (S.) 83. The Court of Appeal summarised propositions arising from a range of cases much of which will apply equally in a magistrates' court and these are set out *post* as an extract from the judgment. Proposition 6 is likely to be the most significant.

1) A drug treatment and testing order is designed for, amongst others, repeat offenders whose offending is driven by drug dependence. Such offenders will often be those who would otherwise have to be sent to prison and it may well be not for a short period. Such an order is not a soft option. It imposes significant obligations on the offender and the court retains quite intensive supervision of his progress and the power to substitute imprisonment if he fails.
2) That the defendant has been a prolific offender does not necessarily mean that a drug treatment and testing order will not be the right order. On the other hand, there will plainly be cases in which the nature of the offence or the scale of offending is such that only a custodial sentence is justified.
3) A drug treatment and testing order is an expensive order. It is in the interests neither of the public nor the offender for such an order to be made where there are not reasonable prospects of it succeeding. That would only divert scarce resources from other more deserving cases and, in addition, increase the risk that the defendant will offend again, thus depriving the public of protection against him and making it likely that, if he is caught, he will spend in the end even longer in prison. Conversely, no one should expect 100 per cent success rate and some lapse is often a feature of an order which turns out substantially successful.
4) It follows that the judge has difficult balancing decisions to be made at two stages—
   (a) does the case warrant adjournment for a report on the possible availability of such an order,

(b) if there is such a report and it is favourable, is a drug treatment and testing order the right disposal?

5) We think that we should underline that a judge is not under an obligation to adjourn for a report in every case in which it is represented to him that the cause of offending is drug dependence and that the defendant would welcome a drug treatment and testing order. To adjourn for a report if there is no prospect of such an order being made would be wasteful and additionally would unjustifiably raise false expectations in the defendant.

6) Experienced trial judges sitting in criminal cases now have considerable knowledge of drug treatment and testing orders because they supervise their working. At the stage of considering whether or not to seek a report, they know to look (inter alia) for possible signs that such an order might be effective. Generally they will have the assistance of the standard pre-sentence report. They are likely to look for indications that the defendant is likely to engage with the order, and that he has sufficient stability in his home life to have reasonable prospects of its succeeding. They are also right at that stage to consider the nature of his offending. The gravity of the offences or the personal characteristics of the defendant, such as repeated breaches of community orders, might demonstrate that a drug treatment and testing order will plainly be inappropriate. They should not, however, reject the possibility of a DTTO simply on the ground that the defendant is a repeat thief or burglar for whom otherwise a custodial sentence would be inevitable. That is precisely the kind of offender who may—we emphasise may—be suitable. The Vice President, Rose L.J., put it this way in *Robinson*—

'It is well known that a high proportion of criminal offences against people and property are committed in order to provide funds to feed the drug habit of the perpetrator. If there were fewer drug addicts, it is likely that there would be fewer criminal offences. Accordingly, in our judgment, judges should be alert to pass sentences which have a realistic prospect of reducing drug addiction whenever it is possible sensibly to do so.'

7) If a report is obtained, then the judge has a second, often a very difficult, decision to make. The decision is, it should be remembered, his and not that of the probation officer. It is the judge who has to weigh in the balance the public interest as well as the interests of the defendant. It is the judge who has to assess the criminality of the defendant as well as the desirability and prospects of rehabilitation. In *Attorney-General's Reference No 28 of 2001*, which was a case of street robberies, this court held that a drug treatment and testing order was in that case an unduly lenient sentence. Judge L.J. put it in a single sentence—

'It gave excessive weight to the issue of rehabilitation and wholly insufficient weight to the actual criminality of the offender.'

8) If at either stage the judge has properly addressed the issue before him and exercised his judgment, we think it will be in comparatively rare cases that it would be right for this court to say that he has arrived at a decision which has erred in principle."

A further example of how to approach the balance was given by the Court of Appeal (Criminal Division) in *Att.-Gen.'s Reference (No.101 of 2009) (Matheson)* [2010] 2 Cr.App.R.(S.) 81. The defendant had developed a chronic drug habit; he supplied a small number of other users with cocaine and cannabis. The defence sought to argue that this fell within the approach set out in *Afonso* [2004] EWCA Crim 2342 (see § 18–18 *ante*) but this was firmly rejected as that was not providing for offenders who (whether or not addicts themselves), for largely commercial motives, stocked and repeatedly supplied small quantities of Class A drugs—there was little difference between those who used the profit to buy drugs for his own use and those who used it for some other purpose. However, the Court emphasised that drug rehabilitation requirements were "capable of being constructive, of capitalising on motivation to change and thus capable of being very much in the public interest". In giving the judgment, Hughes VP stated that there were two principal conditions in which such an order can properly be made—the offence must be of a kind where the imposition of a non-custodial sentence will not undermine public confidence in the criminal justice system and there must be "a proper basis justifying a real reason to believe the defendant wants to rid himself of drugs".

(3) Review of the court

In *Robinson* [2002] 2 Cr.App.R.(S.) 95, guidance was issued as to the treatment of of- **23–82** fenders who commit further offences whilst the subject of a drug treatment and testing order.

Although this guidance was issued in the context of the making of a Drug Treatment and Testing Order (DTTO) under the previous legislation, the principles are likely to continue to be applicable. However, the more restricted options following the breach of an order (see *post*, § 24–83) may affect some of the choices available to the court. The fact that an order is being made in relation to someone with a drug dependency suggests that a court needs to take care to ensure that the purpose of its order is achieved wherever possible. In its guideline, *New Sentences: Criminal Justice Act* 2003, the Sentencing Guidelines Council emphasised that the primary response to the breach of an order was the importance of a court seeking to ensure that an offender complied with an order that it had made. The review provisions enable a court to take a more active role in ensuring that compliance and this is likely to benefit all involved. The offender will benefit by being required to account for his/her conduct to the court that made the order, the "responsible officer" will benefit from having the authority of the court to reinforce the requirements imposed and the court will benefit from seeing directly the outcome of an order that it has made. By s.210, the court that includes a drug rehabilitation requirement within a Community Order may provide for review hearings. The treatment and testing period must be for at least six months; if it is for more than 12 months, the review process must be undertaken, if it is for 12 months or less, the court has a discretion. The reviews must be no more frequently held than monthly, initially (at least) at a court hearing which the offender attends and which receives a report in writing from the responsible officer on the offender's progress and on the results of the samples taken to test whether there have been drugs in the offender's body: s.210(1).

At such a hearing, the court may amend the drug rehabilitation requirement with the offender's agreement but may not reduce the treatment and testing period below the minimum of six months: s.211(1), (2). If the offender does not agree to the amendment, the court may revoke the community order and re-sentence the offender: s.211(3).

If the court considers the offender"s progress to be satisfactory, it can provide for future reviews to be without a hearing: s.211(6). That can be revoked should the progress cease to be satisfactory: s.211(7).

Criminal Justice Act 2003, s.209–211

Drug rehabilitation requirement

23–83 **209.**—(1) In this Part "drug rehabilitation requirement", in relation to a community order or suspended sentence order, means a requirement that during a period specified in the order ("the treatment and testing period") the offender—

(a) must submit to treatment by or under the direction of a specified person having the necessary qualifications or experience with a view to the reduction or elimination of the offender's dependency on or propensity to misuse drugs, and

(b) for the purpose of ascertaining whether he has any drug in his body during that period, must provide samples of such description as may be so determined, at such times or in such circumstances as may (subject to the provisions of the order) be determined by the responsible officer or by the person specified as the person by or under whose direction the treatment is to be provided.

(2) A court may not impose a drug rehabilitation requirement unless—

(a) it is satisfied—

(i) that the offender is dependent on, or has a propensity to misuse, drugs, and

(ii) that his dependency or propensity is such as requires and may be susceptible to treatment,

(b) it is also satisfied that arrangements have been or can be made for the treatment intended to be specified in the order (including arrangements for the reception of the offender where he is to be required to submit to treatment as a resident),

(c) the requirement has been recommended to the court as being suitable for the offender by an officer of a local probation board or an officer of a provider of probation services, and

(d) the offender expresses his willingness to comply with the requirement.

(3) The treatment and testing period must be at least six months.

(4) The required treatment for any particular period must be—

(a) treatment as a resident in such institution or place as may be specified in the order, or

(b) treatment as a non-resident in or at such institution or place, and at such intervals, as may be so specified;

but the nature of the treatment is not to be specified in the order except as mentioned in paragraph (a) or (b) above.

(5) The function of making a determination as to the provision of samples under provision included in the community order or suspended sentence order by virtue of subsection (1)(b) is to be exercised in accordance with guidance given from time to time by the Secretary of State.

(6) A community order or suspended sentence order imposing a drug rehabilitation requirement must provide that the results of tests carried out on any samples provided by the offender in pursuance of the requirement to a person other than the responsible officer are to be communicated to the responsible officer.

(7) In this section "drug" means a controlled drug as defined by section 2 of the *Misuse of Drugs Act* 1971.

Drug rehabilitation requirement: provision for review by court

210.—(1) A community order or suspended sentence order imposing a drug rehabilitation requirement may (and must if the treatment and testing period is more than 12 months)— **23–84**

(a) provide for the requirement to be reviewed periodically at intervals of not less than one month,

(b) provide for each review of the requirement to be made, subject to section 211(6), at a hearing held for the purpose by the court responsible for the order (a "review hearing"),

(c) require the offender to attend each review hearing,

(d) provide for the responsible officer to make to the court responsible for the order, before each review, a report in writing on the offender's progress under the requirement, and

(e) provide for each such report to include the test results communicated to the responsible officer under section 209(6) or otherwise and the views of the treatment provider as to the treatment and testing of the offender.

(2) In this section references to the court responsible for a community order or suspended sentence order imposing a drug rehabilitation requirement are references—

(a) where a court is specified in the order in accordance with subsection (3), to that court;

(b) in any other case, to the court by which the order is made.

(3) Where the area specified in a community order or suspended sentence order which is made by a magistrates' court and imposes a drug rehabilitation requirement is not the area for which the court acts, the court may, if it thinks fit, include in the order provision specifying for the purposes of subsection (2) a magistrates' court which acts for the area specified in the order.

(4) Where a community order or suspended sentence order imposing a drug rehabilitation requirement has been made on an appeal brought from the Crown Court or from the criminal division of the Court of Appeal, for the purposes of subsection (2)(b) it shall be taken to have been made by the Crown Court.

Periodic review of drug rehabilitation requirement

211.—(1) At a review hearing (within the meaning given by subsection (1) of section 210) the court may, after considering the responsible officer's report referred to in that subsection, amend the community order or suspended sentence order, so far as it relates to the drug rehabilitation requirement. **23–85**

(2) The court—

(a) may not amend the drug rehabilitation requirement unless the offender expresses his willingness to comply with the requirement as amended,

(b) may not amend any provision of the order so as to reduce the period for which the drug rehabilitation requirement has effect below the minimum specified in section 209(3), and

(c) except with the consent of the offender, may not amend any requirement or provision of the order while an appeal against the order is pending.

(3) If the offender fails to express his willingness to comply with the drug rehabilitation requirement as proposed to be amended by the court, the court may—

(a) revoke the community order, or the suspended sentence order and the suspended sentence to which it relates, and

(b) deal with him, for the offence in respect of which the order was made, in any way in which he could have been dealt with for that offence by the court which made the order if the order had not been made.

(4) In dealing with the offender under subsection (3)(b), the court—

(a) shall take into account the extent to which the offender has complied with the requirements of the order, and

(b) may impose a custodial sentence (where the order was made in respect of an offence punishable with such a sentence) notwithstanding anything in section 152(2).

(6) If at a review hearing (as defined by section 210(1)(b)) the court, after considering the responsible officer's report, is of the opinion that the offender's progress under the requirement is satisfactory, the court may so amend the order as to provide for each subsequent review to be made by the court without a hearing.

(7) If at a review without a hearing the court, after considering the responsible officer's report, is of the opinion that the offender's progress under the requirement is no longer satisfactory, the court may require the offender to attend a hearing of the court at a specified time and place.

(8) At that hearing the court, after considering that report, may—

(a) exercise the powers conferred by this section as if the hearing were a review hearing, and

(b) so amend the order as to provide for each subsequent review to be made at a review hearing.

(9) In this section any reference to the court, in relation to a review without a hearing, is to be read—

(a) in the case of the Crown Court, as a reference to a judge of the court;

(b) in the case of a magistrates' court, as a reference to a justice of the peace. [...].

[This section was repealed by the *Courts Act 2003 (Consequential Provisions) Order* 2005 (S.I. 2005 No.886).]

K. ALCOHOL TREATMENT REQUIREMENT

(1) General

23–86 This requirement obliges an offender to submit to treatment by a suitably qualified person for the period set by the court: s.212(1). The minimum period is six months: s.212(4). A court may only impose the requirement if satisfied that the offender is dependent on alcohol, that the dependency both requires and is susceptible to treatment and that arrangements can be made for the treatment to be required.

Criminal Justice Act 2003, s.212

Alcohol treatment requirement

23–87 **212.**—(1) In this Part "alcohol treatment requirement", in relation to a community order or suspended sentence order, means a requirement that the offender must submit during a period specified in the order to treatment by or under the direction of a specified person having the necessary qualifications or experience with a view to the reduction or elimination of the offender's dependency on alcohol.

(2) A court may not impose an alcohol treatment requirement in respect of an offender unless it is satisfied—

(a) that he is dependent on alcohol,

(b) that his dependency is such as requires and may be susceptible to treatment, and

(c) that arrangements have been or can be made for the treatment intended to be specified in the order (including arrangements for the reception of the offender where he is to be required to submit to treatment as a resident).

(3) A court may not impose an alcohol treatment requirement unless the offender expresses his willingness to comply with its requirements.

(4) The period for which the alcohol treatment requirement has effect must be not less than six months.

(5) The treatment required by an alcohol treatment requirement for any particular period must be—

(a) treatment as a resident in such institution or place as may be specified in the order,

(b) treatment as a non-resident in or at such institution or place, and at such intervals, as may be so specified, or

(c) treatment by or under the direction of such person having the necessary qualification or experience as may be so specified;

but the nature of the treatment shall not be specified in the order except as mentioned in paragraph (a), (b) or (c) above.

L. SUPERVISION REQUIREMENT

(1) General

The Supervision Requirement is an optional requirement which places an obligation on the offender to attend appointments with the "responsible officer", or another person designated by the responsible officer. This requirement will last for the duration of the Community Order. The purpose of this requirement is to promote the offender's rehabilitation (s.213(2)). In the absence of this requirement, the responsible officer will have the obligations set out by s.198 (see *ante*) to make the arrangements necessary to ensure compliance with the requirements of the order, but will not have the authority or the obligation to make appointments for the purpose of promoting the offender's rehabilitation. This recognises that there will be situations where a Community Order is primarily about punishment or where there is no further beneficial work that needs to be done outside that taking place within the context of another requirement and enables the task of the responsible officer to accurately reflect what is required. **23–88**

Criminal Justice Act 2003, s.213

Supervision requirement

213.—(1) In this Part "supervision requirement", in relation to a relevant order, means a requirement that, during the relevant period, the offender must attend appointments with the responsible officer or another person determined by the responsible officer, at such time and place as may be determined by the officer. **23–89**

(2) The purpose for which a supervision requirement may be imposed is that of promoting the offender's rehabilitation.

(3) In subsection (1) "the relevant period" means—

(a) in relation to a community order, the period for which the community order remains in force,

(b) in relation to a custody plus order, the licence period as defined by section 181(3)(b),

(c) in relation to an intermittent custody order, the licence periods as defined by section 183(3), and

(d) in relation to a suspended sentence order, the supervision period as defined by section 189(1)(a).

M. ATTENDANCE CENTRE REQUIREMENT

(1) General

An Attendance Centre Requirement enables the equivalent of an Attendance Centre **23–90**

Part IV

Order to be included within a Community Order. It may also be made as a sentence in its own right in the youth court since, by virtue of the provisions of Sched. 32, para. 102 to the *Criminal Justice Act* 2003, s.60 of the *PCC(S)A* 2000 continues in force in relation to those aged 16 or under. Where an appropriate centre is available, a requirement may be made on an offender aged under 25.

(2) Purpose and effect

23–91 This order is available for youths and adults. In relation to youths, see Ch.34 later in this work. For adults, there are a small number of centres available. An order will require the offender to attend at the centre as required until the hours fixed by the court are completed. Attendance is designed both to be a punishment (by intruding into the offender's time, and by requiring them to be at a certain place for a certain period and to obey the requirements of the centre) and to offer an opportunity for a positive challenge to continuing criminality. A centre is generally run by the police or by the Youth Offending Team.

(3) Content

23–92 The court has the power to require a minimum of 12 hours attendance and a maximum of 36 hours for this age range (18 years and above). The court will specify the centre to be attended and will fix the date and time of the offender's first attendance. Attendance on any one day must not exceed three hours; in practice, it tends to be two hours on each attendance.

The court must be satisfied that the specified centre is reasonably accessible to the offender given his age, the means of transport available and any other relevant circumstance. As far as practicable, the court should also seek to ensure that attendance at the centre will not conflict with the defendant's religious beliefs, the requirements of any other community penalties to which the defendant may be subject or interfere with normal work or education.

Criminal Justice Act 2003, s.214

Requirements available only in case of offenders aged under 25

Attendance centre requirement

23–93 **214.**—(1) In this Part "attendance centre requirement", in relation to a relevant order, means a requirement that the offender must attend at an attendance centre specified in the relevant order for such number of hours as may be so specified.

(2) The aggregate number of hours for which the offender may be required to attend at an attendance centre must not be less than 12 or more than 36.

(3) The court may not impose an attendance centre requirement unless the court is satisfied that the attendance centre to be specified in it is reasonably accessible to the offender concerned, having regard to the means of access available to him and any other circumstances.

(4) The first time at which the offender is required to attend at the attendance centre is a time notified to the offender by the responsible officer.

(5) The subsequent hours are to be fixed by the officer in charge of the centre, having regard to the offender's circumstances.

(6) An offender may not be required under this section to attend at an attendance centre on more than one occasion on any day, or for more than three hours on any occasion.

(7) A requirement to attend at an attendance centre for any period on any occasion operates as a requirement, during that period, to engage in occupation, or receive instruction, under the supervision of and in accordance with instructions given by, or under the authority of, the officer in charge of the centre, whether at the centre or elsewhere.

N. OFFENDER RESIDENT IN SCOTLAND OR NORTHERN IRELAND

23–94 Given the different provisions that apply in some circumstances in Scotland and

Northern Ireland, specific provision is made where a court wishes to make a Community Order in respect of an offender who resides in Scotland or Northern Ireland or in order to ensure that an order is enforceable.

Criminal Justice Act 2003, Sched. 9

Section 180 SCHEDULE 9

TRANSFER OF COMMUNITY ORDERS TO SCOTLAND OR NORTHERN IRELAND

PART 1

SCOTLAND

1.—(1) Where the court considering the making of a community order is satisfied that the offender resides in Scotland, or will reside there when the order comes into force, the court may not make a community order in respect of the offender unless it appears to the court— **23–95**

(a) in the case of an order imposing a requirement mentioned in sub-paragraph (2), that arrangements exist for persons to comply with such a requirement in the locality in Scotland in which the offender resides, or will be residing when the order comes into force, and that provision can be made for him to comply with the requirement under those arrangements, and

(b) in any case, that suitable arrangements for his supervision can be made by the council constituted under section 2 of the *Local Government etc. (Scotland) Act* 1994 in whose area he resides, or will be residing when the order comes into force.

(2) The requirements referred to in sub-paragraph (1)(a) are—

(a) an unpaid work requirement,

(b) an activity requirement,

(c) a programme requirement,

(d) a mental health treatment requirement,

(e) a drug rehabilitation requirement,

(f) an alcohol treatment requirement, and

(g) an electronic monitoring requirement.

(3) Where—

(a) the appropriate court for the purposes of paragraph 16 of Schedule 8 (amendment by reason of change of residence) is satisfied that an offender in respect of whom a community order is in force proposes to reside or is residing in Scotland, and

(b) it appears to the court that the conditions in sub-paragraph (1)(a) and (b) are satisfied,

the power of the court to amend the order under Part 4 of Schedule 8 includes power to amend it by requiring it to be complied with in Scotland and the offender to be supervised in accordance with the arrangements referred to in sub-paragraph (1)(b).

(4) For the purposes of sub-paragraph (3), any reference in sub-paragraph (1)(a) and (b) to the time when the order comes into force is to be treated as a reference to the time when the amendment comes into force.

(5) The court may not by virtue of sub-paragraph (1) or (3) require an attendance centre requirement to be complied with in Scotland.

(6) A community order made or amended in accordance with this paragraph must—

(a) specify the locality in Scotland in which the offender resides or will be residing when the order or amendment comes into force;

(b) specify as the corresponding order for the purposes of this Schedule an order that may be made by a court in Scotland;

(c) specify as the appropriate court for the purposes of subsection (4) of section 228 of the *Criminal Procedure (Scotland) Act* 1995 a court of summary jurisdiction (which, in the case of an offender convicted on indictment, must be the sheriff court) having jurisdiction in the locality specified under paragraph (a);

and section 216 (*local justice area* to be specified) does not apply in relation to an order so made or amended.

Part IV

23–96 2.—(1) Where a court is considering the making or amendment of a community order by virtue of paragraph 1, Chapter 4 of Part 12 of this Act has effect subject to the following modifications.

(2) Any reference to the responsible officer has effect as a reference to the officer of a council constituted under section 2 of the *Local Government etc. (Scotland) Act* 1994 responsible for the offender's supervision or, as the case may be, discharging in relation to him the functions in respect of community service orders assigned by sections 239 to 245 of the *Criminal Procedure (Scotland) Act* 1995.

(3) The following provisions are omitted—

(a) subsection (7) of section 201 (activity requirement),

(b) subsection (7) of section 202 (programme requirement),

(c) subsection (4) of section 206 (residence requirement), and

(d) subsection (4) of section 218 (availability of arrangements in local area).

(4) In section 207 (mental health treatment requirement), for subsection (2)(a) there is substituted—

"(a) treatment as a resident patient in a hospital within the meaning of the *Mental Health (Care and Treatment) (Scotland) Act* 2003, not being a State hospital within the meaning of that Act;".

(5) In section 215 (electronic monitoring requirement), in subsection (3), the words from "and" onwards are omitted.

PART 2

NORTHERN IRELAND

23–97 3.—(1) Where the court considering the making of a community order is satisfied that the offender resides in Northern Ireland, or will reside there when the order comes into force, the court may not make a community order in respect of the offender unless it appears to the court—

(a) in the case of an order imposing a requirement mentioned in sub-paragraph (2), that arrangements exist for persons to comply with such a requirement in the petty sessions district in Northern Ireland in which the offender resides, or will be residing when the order comes into force, and that provision can be made for him to comply with the requirement under those arrangements, and

(b) in any case, that suitable arrangements for his supervision can be made by the Probation Board for Northern Ireland.

(2) The requirements referred to in sub-paragraph (1) are—

(a) an unpaid work requirement,

(b) an activity requirement,

(c) a programme requirement,

(d) a mental health treatment requirement,

(e) a drug rehabilitation requirement,

(f) an alcohol treatment requirement,

(g) an attendance centre requirement, and

(h) an electronic monitoring requirement.

(3) Where—

(a) the appropriate court for the purposes of paragraph 16 of Schedule 8 (amendment by reason of change of residence) is satisfied that the offender to whom a community order relates proposes to reside or is residing in Northern Ireland, and

(b) it appears to the court that the conditions in sub-paragraphs (1)(a) and (b) are satisfied,

the power of the court to amend the order under Part 4 of Schedule 8 includes power to amend it by requiring it to be complied with in Northern Ireland and the offender to be supervised in accordance with the arrangements referred to in sub-paragraph (1)(b).

(4) For the purposes of sub-paragraph (3), any reference in sub-paragraph (1)(a) and (b) to the time when the order comes into force is to be treated as a reference to the time when the amendment comes into force.

(5) A community order made or amended in accordance with this paragraph must

specify the petty sessions district in Northern Ireland in which the offender resides or will be residing when the order or amendment comes into force; and section 216 (local justice area to be specified) does not apply in relation to an order so made or amended.

(6) A community order made or amended in accordance with this paragraph must also specify as the corresponding order for the purposes of this Schedule an order that may be made by a court in Northern Ireland.

4.—(1) Where a court is considering the making or amendment of a community order by virtue of paragraph 3, Chapter 4 of Part 12 of this Act has effect subject to the following modifications. **23–98**

(2) Any reference to the responsible officer has effect as a reference to the probation officer responsible for the offender's supervision or, as the case may be, discharging in relation to the offender the functions conferred by Part 2 of the *Criminal Justice (Northern Ireland) Order* 1996 (S.I. 1996/No.3160 (N.I. 24)).

(3) The following provisions are omitted—

(a) subsection (7) of section 201 (activity requirement),

(b) subsection (7) of section 202 (programme requirement),

(c) subsection (4) of section 206 (residence requirement), and

(d) subsection (4) of section 218 (availability of arrangements in local area).

(4) In section 207 (mental health treatment requirement), for subsection (2)(a) there is substituted—

"(a) treatment (whether as an in-patient or an out-patient) at such hospital as may be specified in the order, being a hospital within the meaning of the *Health and Personal Social Services (Northern Ireland) Order* 1972, approved by the Department of Health, Social Services and Public Safety for the purposes of paragraph 4(3) of Schedule 1 to the *Criminal Justice (Northern Ireland) Order* 1996 (S.I. 1996/No.3160 (N.I. 24));".

(5) In section 214 (attendance centre requirement), any reference to an attendance centre has effect as a reference to a day centre, as defined by paragraph 3(6) of Schedule 1 to the *Criminal Justice (Northern Ireland) Order* 1996 (S.I. 1996/No.3160 (N.I. 24)).

(6) In section 215 (electronic monitoring requirement), in subsection (3), the words from "and" onwards are omitted.

PART 3

GENERAL PROVISIONS

5. In this Part of this Schedule— **23–99**

"corresponding order" means the order specified under paragraph 1(6)(b) or 3(6);

"home court" means —

(a) if the offender resides in Scotland, or will be residing there at the relevant time, the sheriff court having jurisdiction in the locality in which he resides or proposes to reside, and

(b) if he resides in Northern Ireland, or will be residing there at the relevant time, the court of summary jurisdiction acting for the petty sessions district in which he resides or proposes to reside;

"the local authority officer concerned", in relation to an offender, means the officer of a council constituted under section 2 of the *Local Government etc. (Scotland) Act* 1994 responsible for his supervision or, as the case may be, discharging in relation to him the functions in respect of community service orders assigned by sections 239 to 245 of the *Criminal Procedure (Scotland) Act* 1995;

"the probation officer concerned", in relation to an offender, means the probation officer responsible for his supervision or, as the case may be, discharging in relation to him the functions conferred by Part 2 of the *Criminal Justice (Northern Ireland) Order* 1996;

"the relevant time" means the time when the order or the amendment to it comes into force.

6. Where a community order is made or amended in accordance with paragraph 1 or 3, the court which makes or amends the order must provide the home court with a copy **23–100**

Part IV

of the order as made or amended, together with such other documents and information relating to the case as it considers likely to be of assistance to that court; and paragraphs (b) to (d) of subsection (1) of section 219 (provision of copies of relevant orders) do not apply.

23–101 7. In section 220 (duty of offender to keep in touch with responsible officer) the reference to the responsible officer is to be read in accordance with paragraph 2(2) or 4(2).

23–102 8. Where a community order is made or amended in accordance with paragraph 1 or 3, then, subject to the following provisions of this Part of this Schedule—

(a) the order is to be treated as if it were a corresponding order made in the part of the United Kingdom in which the offender resides, or will be residing at the relevant time, and

(b) the legislation relating to such orders which has effect in that part of the United Kingdom applies accordingly.

23–103 9. Before making or amending a community order in those circumstances the court must explain to the offender in ordinary language—

(a) the requirements of the legislation relating to corresponding orders which has effect in the part of the United Kingdom in which he resides or will be residing at the relevant time,

(b) the powers of the home court under that legislation, as modified by this Part of this Schedule, and

(c) its own powers under this Part of this Schedule.

23–104 10. The home court may exercise in relation to the community order any power which it could exercise in relation to the corresponding order made by a court in the part of the United Kingdom in which the home court exercises jurisdiction, by virtue of the legislation relating to such orders which has effect in that part, except the following—

(a) any power to discharge or revoke the order (other than a power to revoke the order where the offender has been convicted of a further offence and the court has imposed a custodial sentence),

(b) any power to deal with the offender for the offence in respect of which the order was made,

(c) in the case of a community order imposing an unpaid work requirement, any power to vary the order by substituting for the number of hours of work specified in it any greater number than the court which made the order could have specified, and

(d) in the case of a community order imposing a curfew requirement, any power to vary the order by substituting for the period specified in it any longer period than the court which made the order could have specified.

23–105 11. If at any time while legislation relating to corresponding orders which has effect in Scotland or Northern Ireland applies by virtue of paragraph 7 to a community order made in England and Wales—

(a) it appears to the home court—

(i) if that court is in Scotland, on information from the local authority officer concerned, or

(ii) if that court is in Northern Ireland, upon a complaint being made to a justice of the peace acting for the petty sessions district for the time being specified in the order,

that the offender has failed to comply with any of the requirements of the order, or

(b) it appears to the home court—

(i) if that court is in Scotland, on the application of the offender or of the local authority officer concerned, or

(ii) if it is in Northern Ireland, on the application of the offender or of the probation officer concerned,

that it would be in the interests of justice for a power conferred by paragraph 13 or 14 of Schedule 8 to be exercised,

the home court may require the offender to appear before the court which made the order or the court which last amended the order in England and Wales.

23–106 12. Where an offender is required by virtue of paragraph 11 to appear before a court in England and Wales that court—

(a) may issue a warrant for his arrest, and

(b) may exercise any power which it could exercise in respect of the community order if the offender resided in England and Wales,

and any enactment relating to the exercise of such powers has effect accordingly, and with any reference to the responsible officer being read as a reference to the local authority officer or probation officer concerned.

13. Paragraph 12(b) does not enable the court to amend the community order unless— **23–107**

(a) where the offender resides in Scotland, it appears to the court that the conditions in paragraph 1(1)(a) and (b) are satisfied in relation to any requirement to be imposed, or

(b) where the offender resides in Northern Ireland, it appears to the court that the conditions in paragraph 3(1)(a) and (b) are satisfied in relation to any requirement to be imposed.

14. The preceding paragraphs of this Schedule have effect in relation to the amendment of a community order by virtue of paragraph 12(b) as they have effect in relation to the amendment of such an order by virtue of paragraph 1(3) or 3(3). **23–108**

15. Where an offender is required by virtue of paragraph (a) of paragraph 11 to appear before a court in England and Wales— **23–109**

(a) the home court must send to that court a certificate certifying that the offender has failed to comply with such of the requirements of the order as may be specified in the certificate, together with such other particulars of the case as may be desirable, and

(b) a certificate purporting to be signed by the clerk of the home court is admissible as evidence of the failure before the court which made the order.

III. CUSTODIAL SENTENCES

A. COMMITTAL FOR SENTENCE

If a magistrates' court has convicted a person aged 18 or over of an offence triable either way, it may form the view that the defendant requires a sentence that only the Crown Court has the power to impose. In those circumstances, the magistrates' court may have the power to commit the defendant to the Crown Court for sentence. The decision will be accompanied by a decision on whether the defendant should be remanded in custody or on bail. There have been suggestions that, since the committal is for a sentence beyond the powers of the magistrates' court, that committal should be in custody in most circumstances. However, that approach confuses two distinct decisions—that on the appropriate sentence and that on what is necessary to ensure the defendant attends court, etc. The better approach is to start from the basis of the status of the defendant before committal. Generally speaking, a defendant on bail up to committal would remain on bail pending sentence in the Crown Court whereas a defendant in custody would remain in custody: *Rafferty* [1999] 1 Cr.App.R. 235. **23–110**

The court considers that the offence (or the combination of the offence and one or more offences associated with it) was so serious that the Crown Court should have the power to deal with the offender as if the offender had been convicted at the Crown Court, it may commit the offender for sentence: s.3(2). These powers apply equally to a corporation: s.3(5). **23–111**

A defendant committed to the Crown Court for sentence in relation to an either way offence will generally be susceptible to the whole range of sentencing powers available to the Court but other cases may in certain circumstances also be committed and then the Crown Court will be restricted to the powers available to a magistrates' court. Where a defendant is committed for sentence for an either way offence, the court may also commit for sentence any other offence that is imprisonable or endorsable of which the court has convicted the defendant: s.6. **23–112**

An additional power to commit for sentence is provided in respect of offenders who may require a sentence of imprisonment for public protection or an extended sentence. This power is available where an offender aged 18 or over is convicted of a "specified offence". This is defined in section 224 as a "specified violent offence or a specified sexual offence"—these are set out in Sched. 15 to the Act and contain a wide variety of offences that commonly come before a magistrates' court. It is not limited to those circumstances where a defendant has indicated a guilty plea during the initial (allocation) procedure nor is it constrained by the giving of an indication of a non-custodial sentence following a request under s.19 of the *Magistrates' Courts Act* 1980 for an indication of sentence.

Detailed consideration has been given to the assessment of the criterion for use of one of these sentences for public protection. Such a sentence was mandatory where the court imposing sentence considered that "there was a significant risk to members of the public of serious harm occasioned by the commission by the offender of further specified offences" but the *Criminal Justice and Immigration Act* 2008 has introduced considerably greater discretion in the imposition of such sentences.

In most circumstances an offender likely to be sentenced as a dangerous offender will have committed an offence that would in any case need to be sentenced in the Crown Court. Generally, imprisonment for public protection or an extended sentence may only be imposed where a court would otherwise have imposed a sentence of at least four years. The exception to this is where an offender has a previous conviction for one of the very serious offences listed in Sched. 15A to the 2003 Act (as inserted by s.13(2) and Sched. 5 to the *Criminal Justice and Immigration Act* 2008), In those circumstances there is no lower limit on a minimum term within a sentence of imprisonment of public protection and the shortest custodial term within an extended sentence will be 12 months.

Principles set out under the unamended legislation continue to be relevant and the key principles were described in the leading case of *Lang* [2006] 2 Cr.App.R. (S.) 3.

> "In our judgment, the following factors should be borne in mind when a sentencer is assessing significant risk—
>
> (i) The risk identified must be significant. This is a higher threshold than mere possibility of occurrence and in our view can be taken to mean (as in the Oxford Dictionary) 'noteworthy, of considerable amount or importance'.
>
> (ii) In assessing the risk of further offences being committed, the sentencer should take into account the nature and circumstances of the current offence; the offender's history of offending including not just the kind of offence but its circumstances and the sentence passed, details of which the prosecution must have available, and, whether the offending demonstrates any pattern; social and economic factors in relation to the offender including accommodation, employability, education, associates, relationships and drug or alcohol abuse; and the offender's thinking, attitude towards offending and supervision and emotional state. Information in relation to these matters will most readily, though not exclusively, come from antecedents and pre-sentence probation and medical reports. The Guide for sentences for public protection issued in June 2005 for the National Probation Service affords valuable guidance for probation officers. The guidance in relation to assessment of dangerousness in paragraph 5 is compatible with the terms of this judgment. The sentencer will be guided, but not bound by, the assessment of risk in such reports. A sentencer who contemplates differing from the assessment in such a report should give both counsel the opportunity of addressing the point.
>
> (iii) If the foreseen specified offence is serious, there will clearly be some cases, though not by any means all, in which there may be a significant risk of serious harm. For example, robbery is a serious offence. But it can be committed in a wide variety of ways many of which do not give rise to a significant risk of serious harm. Sentencers must therefore guard against assuming there is a significant risk of serious harm merely because the foreseen specified offence is serious.
>
> (iv) If the foreseen specified offence is not serious, there will be comparatively few cases in which a risk of serious harm will properly be regarded as significant. The huge variety of offences in Schedule 15, includes many which, in themselves, are not suggestive of serious harm. Repetitive violent or sexual offending at a relatively low level without serious harm does not of itself give rise to a significant risk of serious harm in the future. There may, in such cases, be some risk of future victims being more adversely affected than past victims but this, of itself, does not give rise to significant risk of serious harm.

(v) In relation to the rebuttable assumption to which section 229(3) gives rise, the court is accorded a discretion if, in the light of information about the current offence, the offender and his previous offences, it would be unreasonable to conclude that there is a significant risk. The exercise of such a discretion is, historically, at the very heart of judicial sentencing and the language of the statute indicates that judges are expected, albeit starting from the assumption, to exercise their ability to reach a reasonable conclusion in the light of the information before them. It is to be noted that the assumption will be rebutted, if at all, as an exercise of judgment: the statute includes no reference to the burden or standard of proof. As we have indicated *ante*, it will usually be unreasonable to conclude that the assumption applies unless information about the offences, pattern of behaviour and offender show a significant risk of serious harm from further offences.

(vi) It cannot have been Parliament's intention, in a statute dealing with the liberty of the subject, to require the imposition of indeterminate sentences for the commission of relatively minor offences. On the contrary, Parliament's repeatedly expressed intention is to protect the public from serious harm (compare the reasoning of the Court in relation to automatic life sentences in *Offen* [2001] 2 Cr.App.R. (S.) 10, paras 96 to 99."

A magistrates' court will be dealing with specified offences that are not serious offences and it seems that the risk criterion is set at quite a high level for such offences. Where there is a risk of further offences, unless those further offences would be "serious offences" within the terms of the Act, the Court of Appeal stated that it was likely to be rare for there to be a "significant risk of serious harm". The effect of the legislative changes in the *Criminal Justice and Immigration Act* 2008 were considered in *C.* [2008] EWCA Crim 2790. The court noted that (apart from life imprisonment) imprisonment for public protection was the most draconian sentence available to a court. Emphasising that the primary question is the nature and extent of the risk posed by the offender and the most appropriate method of addressing it to provide public protection, the court indicated that imprisonment for public protection should not be imposed where the "overall sentencing package provides appropriate protection".

Powers of Criminal Court (Sentencing) Act 2000, ss.3, 3C, 4–6

Committal for sentence on summary trial of offence triable either way

3.—(1) Subject to subsection (4) below, this section applies where on the summary trial of an offence triable either way a person aged 18 or over is convicted of the offence. **23–113**

(2) If the court is of the opinion—

(a) that the offence or the combination of the offence and one or more offences associated with it was so serious that the Crown Court should, in the court's opinion, have the power to deal with the offender in any way it could deal with him if he had been convicted on indictment,

the court may commit the offender in custody or on bail to the Crown Court for sentence in accordance with section 5(1) below.

(3) Where the court commits a person under subsection (2) above, section 6 below (which enables a magistrates' court, where it commits a person under this section in respect of an offence, also to commit him to the Crown Court to be dealt with in respect of certain other offences) shall apply accordingly.

(4) This section does not apply in relation to an offence as regards which this section is excluded by section 17D or 33 of the *Magistrates' Courts Act* 1980 (certain offences where value involved is small).

(5) The preceding provisions of this section shall apply in relation to a corporation as if—

(a) the corporation were an individual aged 18 or over; and

(b) in subsection (2) above, the words "in custody or on bail" were omitted

Committal for sentence of dangerous young offenders

3C.—(1) This section applies where on the summary trial of a specified offence a person aged under 18 is convicted of the offence. **23–114**

(2) If, in relation to the offence, it appears to the court that the criteria for the imposition of a sentence under section 226(3) or 228(2) of the *Criminal Justice Act* 2003 would be met, the court must commit the offender in custody or on bail to the Crown Court for sentence in accordance with section 5A(1) below.

(3) Where the court commits a person under subsection (2) above, section 6 below (which enables a magistrates' court, where it commits a person under this section in respect of an offence, also to commit him to the Crown Court to be dealt with in respect of certain other offences) shall apply accordingly.

(4) Nothing in this section shall prevent the court from committing a specified offence to the Crown Court for sentence under section 3B above if the provisions of that section are satisfied.

(5) In this section, references to a specified offence are to a specified offence within the meaning of section 224 of the *Criminal Justice Act* 2003.

Committal for sentence on indication of guilty plea to offence triable either way

23–115 **4.**—(1) This section applies where—

(a) a person aged 18 or over appears or is brought before a magistrates' court ("the court") on an information charging him with an offence triable either way ("the offence");

(b) he or his representative indicates that he would plead guilty if the offence were to proceed to trial; and

(c) proceeding as if section 9(1) of that Act were complied with and he pleaded guilty under it, the court convicts him of the offence.

(2) If the court has committed the offender to the Crown Court for trial for one or more related offences, that is to say, one or more offences which, in its opinion, are related to the offence, it may commit him in custody or on bail to the Crown Court to be dealt with in respect of the offence in accordance with section 5(1) below.

(3) If the power conferred by subsection (2) above is not exercisable but the court is still to inquire, as examining justices, into one or more related offences—

(a) it shall adjourn the proceedings relating to the offence until after it has made those determinations; and

(b) if it commits the offender to the Crown Court for trial for one or more related offences, it may then exercise that power.

(4) Where the court—

(a) under subsection (2) above commits the offender to the Crown Court to be dealt with in respect of the offence, and

(b) does not state that, in its opinion, it also has power so to commit him under section 3(2) above,

section 5(1) below shall not apply unless he is convicted before the Crown Court of one or more of the related offences.

(5) Where section 5(1) below does not apply, the Crown Court may deal with the offender in respect of the offence in any way in which the magistrates' court could deal with him if it had just convicted him of the offence.

(6) Where the court commits a person under subsection (2) above, section 6 below (which enables a magistrates' court, where it commits a person under this section in respect of an offence, also to commit him to the Crown Court to be dealt with in respect of certain other offences) shall apply accordingly.

(7) For the purposes of this section one offence is related to another if, were they both to be prosecuted on indictment, the charges for them could be joined in the same indictment.

Power of Crown Court on committal for sentence under ss.3 and 4

23–116 **5.**—(1) Where an offender is committed by a magistrates' court for sentence under section 3 or 4 above, the Crown Court shall inquire into the circumstances of the case and may deal with the offender in any way in which it could deal with him if he had just been convicted of the offence on indictment before the court.

(2) In relation to committals under section 4 above, subsection (1) above has effect subject to section 4(4) and (5) above.

Committal for sentence in certain cases where offender committed in respect of another offence

23–117 **6.**—(1) This section applies where a magistrates' court ("the committing court") commits a person in custody or on bail to the Crown Court under any enactment mentioned in subsection (4) below to be sentenced or otherwise dealt with in respect of an offence ("the relevant offence").

(2) Where this section applies and the relevant offence is an indictable offence, the committing court may also commit the offender, in custody or on bail as the case may require, to the Crown Court to be dealt with in respect of any other offence whatsoever in respect of which the committing court has power to deal with him (being an offence of which he has been convicted by that or any other court).

(3) Where this section applies and the relevant offence is a summary offence, the committing court may commit the offender, in custody or on bail as the case may require, to the Crown Court to be dealt with in respect of—

(a) any other offence of which the committing court has convicted him, being either—

(i) an offence punishable with imprisonment; or

(ii) an offence in respect of which the committing court has a power or duty to order him to be disqualified under section 34, 35 or 36 of the *Road Traffic Offenders Act* 1988 (disqualification for certain motoring offences); or

(b) any suspended sentence in respect of which the committing court has under para. 11(1) of Sched. 12 to the *Criminal Justice Act* 2003 power to deal with him.

(4) The enactments referred to in subsection (1) above are—

(a) the *Vagrancy Act* 1824 (incorrigible rogues);

(b) sections 3 to 4A above (committal for sentence for offences triable either way);

(c) section 13(5) below (conditionally discharged person convicted of further offence);

(d) [...]

(e) para. 11(2) of Sched. 12 to the *Criminal Justice Act* 2003 (committal to Crown Court where offender convicted during operational period of suspended sentence).

Where a court adjourns a case after conviction, care needs to be taken to avoid restricting the power of the next court to commit for sentence by raising a legitimate expectation in the mind of the defendant that he will not be committed. In *Feltham Justices, ex p. Rees* [2001] 2 Cr.App.R.(S.) 1, DC Rose L.J. outlined the circumstances leading to a finding of a legitimate expectation which may fetter the power of the Court to commit for sentence. In that case, the critical factors leading to a finding that there was a legitimate expectation were that: **23–118**

— the justices had been addressed as to the adequacy of their sentencing powers on behalf of the applicant,

— the justices had specifically invited the applicant's solicitor to mitigate before them,

— the solicitor had proceeded to mitigate before them,

— the justices had then adjourned, apparently to consider the impact of that sentence, and that adjournment lasted some ten minutes.

— when the justices returned to court, they said that "they" were unable to sentence him on that date as "they" would require more information in the form of a pre-sentence report.

The justices had stated that they were "leaving all options open" but, in the light of the events listed *ante*, something more specific was needed if anything other than sentencing in the magistrates' court was envisaged. If justices have in mind that one of the options which is open to them is to commit for sentence, they should specifically say so. Even more care now needs to be taken since courts will be following the guideline of the Sentencing Guidelines Council to state clearly the purposes of sentencing and its assessment of seriousness when adjourning for such a report. It is likely that courts will become more ready to commit for sentence prior to receiving such a report in future. **23–119**

See also Bingham L.J. in *Nottingham Magistrates' Court, ex p. Davidson* [2000] 1 Cr.App.R.(S.) 167, CA and Potts J. in *Horseferry Road Magistrates' Court, ex p. Rugless* [2000] 1 Cr.App.R.(S.) 484, CA.

When the Court adjourns sentence after specifically indicating to the defendant that he will not be committed for sentence, unless there is a change in the relevant circumstances, the offender may not be committed for sentence: *Norwich Magistrates' Court, ex p. Elliot* [2000] 1 Cr.App.R.(S.) 152, CA, where Otton L.J. referred to the "seminal **23–120** judgment" of Kennedy L.J. in *Warley Justices, ex p. DPP* [1999] 1 Cr.App.R.(S.) 156, QBD, where he summarised the position as regards triable either way offences, following a guilty plea by the defendant:

> "If, after allowance has been made for the plea of guilty, it appears to the court that it will or may be possible for the court to sentence properly by deploying its statutory power—if necessary to the full—then, as it seems to me, the court should proceed to hear the case in the normal way, and, so long as a committal for sentence remains a possibility, care should be taken to ensure that nothing is said or done which might indicate to an accused that that option has been ruled out.
>
> If a court, initially minded to commit at an early stage of the proceedings, is persuaded not to adopt that course at that stage it can keep the option open by saying that is what it is going to do, and then for example, arranging for the preparation of a pre-sentence report. But if it says that it is satisfied that the case is not one in which it will be necessary for it to commit to the Crown Court for sentence, and then adjourns for the pre-sentence report, when the matter comes back before a differently constituted bench that second bench is likely to consider that so far as committal for sentence is concerned its hands are tied."

23–121 The decision to commit for sentence must be based on the assessment of the adequacy of the magistrates' sentencing powers to deal with the offence, not whether the offence would have been triable on indictment had the "plea before venue" procedure not been adopted. In making this assessment, the appropriate allowance should be made for the guilty plea. Where this discount results in sentence being able to be imposed in the magistrates' court, it would be helpful if this could be stated: *Warley Magistrates' Court, ex p. DPP, ante*. The definitive guideline issued by the Sentencing Guidelines Council on reductions for a guilty plea covers the situation where a guilty plea has been entered and that fact alone enables a court to decide not to commit the case for sentence. In such circumstances, it is legitimate for the magistrates' court to impose the maximum sentence available to it since the effect of the guilty plea has been to allow that court to pass sentence rather than to commit for sentence. The fact that that has been done should be stated clearly by the court (Guideline: *Reduction in Sentence for a Guilty Plea*, para. 5.8).

A magistrates' court may also commit for sentence if it considers that, although a financial penalty is appropriate, the limits on the level of financial penalties it can impose is too low to deal with the offence: *North Essex Justices, ex p. Lloyd* [2001] 2 Cr.App.R.(S.) 86.

23–122 Where the Court is dealing with an offender who has breached a community order made by a magistrates' court by revoking the order, the Court may not commit him to the Crown Court for sentence for the offence in relation to which the order was made: *Jordan* [1998] 2 Cr.App.R.(S.) 83, DC. The magistrates may still deal with an offender who has been unlawfully committed: *Norfolk JJ, ex p. DPP* [1950] 2 K.B. 558, DC. Where a magistrates' court has revoked an order made by the Crown Court, such an offender may be committed to the Crown Court for sentence and remanded in custody or on bail: Sched. 8(9)(b).

B. SENTENCES OF IMPRISONMENT

(1) Purpose and effect

23–123 Committing a person to a custodial sentence is the most severe punishment available and is hedged around by a number of conditions that need to be fulfilled:

- — the offence (or combination of the offence and one or more other associated with it) must be so serious that no other sentence is justified (with a few exceptions),
- — the defendant must be legally represented (or have not taken the opportunity to be),
- — in most circumstances, a pre-sentence report will be required and
- — the length of the sentence must be no more than is commensurate with the seriousness of the offence.

In its Guideline, *Overarching Principles: Seriousness*, published in December 2004, the Sentencing Guidelines Council considered the threshold that has to be passed. The Council emphasises that the purpose of the threshold test is "to reserve prison as a punishment for the most serious offences" (para. 1.32). There is also a firm reminder that the passing of the threshold is only one of the early steps in determining sentence. The test is based on the seriousness of the offence alone. Other factors then come into play which may justify a non-custodial sentence (para. 1.32). The Guideline sets out (at para. 1.33) a series of questions to be asked by the court when considering a custodial sentence.

Criminal Justice Act 2003, ss.152–153

General restrictions on imposing discretionary custodial sentences

152.—(1) This section applies where a person is convicted of an offence punishable with a custodial sentence other than one— **23–124**

(a) fixed by law, or

(b) falling to be imposed under section 51A(2) of the *Firearms Act* 1968, under section 110(2) or 111(2) of the Sentencing Act, under section 29(4) or (6) of the *Violent Crime Reduction Act* 2006 or under any of sections 225(a) to 226(2) of this Act.

(2) The court must not pass a custodial sentence unless it is of the opinion that the offence, or the combination of the offence and one or more offences associated with it, was so serious that neither a fine alone nor a community sentence can be justified for the offence.

(3) Nothing in subsection (2) prevents the court from passing a custodial sentence on the offender if—

(a) he fails to express his willingness to comply with a requirement which is proposed by the court to be included in a community order and which requires an expression of such willingness, or

(b) he fails to comply with an order under section 161(2) (pre-sentence drug testing).

Length of discretionary custodial sentences: general provision

153.—(1) This section applies where a court passes a custodial sentence other than one fixed by law or falling to be imposed under section 225 or 226. **23–125**

(2) Subject to section 51A(2) of the *Firearms Act* 1968, sections 110(2) and 111(2) of the Sentencing Act, section 29(4) or (6) of the *Violent Crime Reduction Act* 2006 and sections 227(2) and 228(2) of this Act, the custodial sentence must be for the shortest term (not exceeding the permitted maximum) that in the opinion of the court is commensurate with the seriousness of the offence, or the combination of the offence and one or more offences associated with it.

Magistrates' Courts Act 1980, s.132

Minimum term

132. A magistrates' court shall not impose imprisonment for less than five days. **23–126**

Criminal Justice Act 2003, ss.157–158

Additional requirements in case of mentally disordered offender

157.—(1) Subject to subsection (2), in any case where the offender is or appears to be mentally disordered, the court must obtain and consider a medical report before passing a custodial sentence other than one fixed by law. **23–127**

(2) Subsection (1) does not apply if, in the circumstances of the case, the court is of the opinion that it is unnecessary to obtain a medical report.

(3) Before passing a custodial sentence other than one fixed by law on an offender who is or appears to be mentally disordered, a court must consider—

(a) any information before it which relates to his mental condition (whether given in a medical report, a pre-sentence report or otherwise), and

(b) the likely effect of such a sentence on that condition and on any treatment which may be available for it.

(4) No custodial sentence which is passed in a case to which subsection (1) applies is invalidated by the failure of a court to comply with that subsection, but any court on an appeal against such a sentence—

(a) must obtain a medical report if none was obtained by the court below, and

(b) must consider any such report obtained by it or by that court.

(5) In this section "mentally disordered", in relation to any person, means suffering from a mental disorder within the meaning of the *Mental Health Act* 1983.

(6) In this section "medical report" means a report as to an offender's mental condition made or submitted orally or in writing by a registered medical practitioner who is approved for the purposes of section 12 of the *Mental Health Act* 1983 by the Secretary of State as having special experience in the diagnosis or treatment of mental disorder.

(7) Nothing in this section is to be taken to limit the generality of section 156.

Meaning of "pre-sentence report"

23–128 **158.**—(1) In this Part "pre-sentence report" means a report which—

(a) with a view to assisting the court in determining the most suitable method of dealing with an offender, is made or submitted by an appropriate officer, and

(b) contains information as to such matters, presented in such manner, as may be prescribed by rules made by the Secretary of State.

(1A) Subject to any rules made under subsection (1)(b) and to subsection (1B), the court may accept a pre-sentence report given orally in open court.

(1B) But a pre-sentence report that—

(a) relates to an offender aged under 18, and

(b) is required to be obtained and considered before the court forms an opinion mentioned in section 156(3)(a),

must be in writing.

(2) In subsection (1) "an appropriate officer" means—

(a) where the offender is aged 18 or over, an officer of a local probation board or an officer of a provider of probation services, and

(b) where the offender is aged under 18, an officer of a local probation board or an officer of a provider of probation services, a social worker of a local authority or a member of a youth offending team.

(2) Guideline

Guideline: Overarching Principles: Seriousness

E. The Sentencing Thresholds

23–129 **1.30** Assessing the seriousness of an offence is only the first step in the process of determining the appropriate sentence in an individual case. Matching the offence to a type and level of sentence is a separate and complex exercise assisted by the application of the respective threshold tests for custodial and community sentences.

The Custody Threshold

1.32 In applying the threshold test, sentencers should note:

- the clear intention of the threshold test is to reserve prison as a punishment for the most serious offences;
- it is impossible to determine definitively which features of a particular offence make it serious enough to merit a custodial sentence;
- passing the custody threshold does not mean that a custodial sentence should be deemed inevitable, and custody can still be avoided in the light of personal mitigation or where there is a suitable intervention in the community which provides sufficient restriction (by way of punishment) while addressing the rehabilitation of the offender to prevent future crime. For example, a prolific offender who currently could expect a short custodial sentence (which, in advance of custody plus, would have no provision for supervision on release) might more appropriately receive a suitable community sentence.

1.33 The approach to the imposition of a custodial sentence under the new framework should be as follows:

(a) has the custody threshold been passed?

(b) if so, is it unavoidable that a custodial sentence be imposed?

(c) if so, can that sentence be suspended? (sentencers should be clear that they would have imposed a custodial sentence if the power to suspend had not been available)

(d) if not, can the sentence be served intermittently?
(e) if not, impose a sentence which takes immediate effect for the term commensurate with the seriousness of the offence.

Custody is primarily for those convicted of violent offences, serious sexual offences and, perhaps, for persistent petty offenders. Considerable judicial and Parliamentary scrutiny has been given to the circumstances in which a custodial sentence is justified. The starting point is the seriousness of the offence. In considering that, the Court must treat as an aggravating factor each recent and relevant previous conviction of the offender (*Criminal Justice Act* 2003, s.143(2)) and must treat it as an aggravating factor if the offence was committed while the offender was on bail (s.143(3)), or where there was hostility based on sexual orientation or disability (s.146), or was racially or religiously aggravated (s.145). **23–130**

An offence which is deliberate and premeditated or which involves an excessive response to provocation; an offence which inflicts personal injury or mental trauma, particularly if permanent, will usually be more serious than one which inflicts financial loss only: *Howells* [1999] 1 Cr.App.R. 98, CA.

Where offending has been fuelled by addiction to drink or drugs, the Court may be inclined to look more favourably on an offender who has already demonstrated (by taking practical steps to that end) a genuine, self-motivated determination to address his addiction: see *ante*, § 23–87 in relation to drug rehabilitation requirements.

Youth and immaturity, while affording no defence, will often justify a less rigorous penalty than would be appropriate for an adult.

Some leniency will often be given to an offender of previous good character, the more so if there is evidence of positive good character (such as solid employment record or faithful discharge of family duties) as opposed to a mere absence of previous convictions. It will sometimes be appropriate to take account of family responsibilities, or physical or mental disability. However, care will be need to be taken to ensure that it is appropriate to do so. Where the primary purpose of the sentence is to show society's disapproval of the conduct (such as offences of violence in a domestic context), previous good character may be less significant. Similarly where offences are serious but likely to be committed by first offenders (for example, serious fraud on an employer). **23–131**

Particular care should be taken when considering whether to impose a custodial sentence on a woman or on anyone on whom other people are dependent for their physical care.

While the Court will never impose a custodial sentence unless satisfied that it is necessary to do so, there will be even greater reluctance to impose a custodial sentence on an offender who has never before served such a sentence: *Seed, Stark* [2007] EWCA Crim 254.

Where the Court is of the opinion that an offence, or the combination of an offence and one or more offences associated with it, is so serious that neither a fine alone or a community sentence can be justified and that such a sentence should be passed, the sentence imposed should be no longer than is necessary to meet the penal purpose which the Court has in mind: *Ollerenshaw* [1999] 1 Cr.App.R.(S.) 65, CA. In any case, it must be no longer than is commensurate with the seriousness of the offence: s.153(2). **23–132**

The need for caution in the selection of a custodial sentence was emphasised in *Kefford* [2002] EWCA Crim 519 where Lord Woolf C.J. stated that those who are responsible for imposing sentences have to take into account the impact on the prison system of the number of prisoners the prison estate is being required to accommodate at the present time. Whilst, the Court did not intend to deter courts from sending to prison for the appropriate period those who commit offences involving violence or intimidation or other grave crimes, there were other categories of offence where a community punishment or a fine can sometimes be a more appropriate form of sentence than imprisonment. Lord Woolf gave the example of economic crimes, such as obtaining undue credit by fraud, which may not, especially in the case of an offender of hitherto good character, require a custodial sentence.

23–133 See generally on the assessment of the seriousness of an offence in "General Principles of Sentencing" at § 22–3, *ante*.

The maximum sentence of imprisonment provided should be reserved for the worst forms of that offence: *Byrne* (1975) 62 Cr.App.R. 159, CA. When the sentencer is considering whether an offence is one of the worst examples of its kind, he should have regard to cases that have been encountered in practice, rather than unlikely or imaginary examples: *Ambler* [1976] Crim.L.R. 266. The maximum penalty for an offence should not normally be imposed where there is substantial mitigation: *Cade* (1984) 6 Cr.App.R.(S.) 28, CA. Most imprisonable offences are triable either way and so a magistrates' court will often have the option of committing for sentence for the more serious offences. However, for those summary offences that are imprisonable, a court will give credit for any guilty plea and also bear in mind that the longest sentence available should be reserved for the worst type of offending.

(3) Concurrent and consecutive sentences

Magistrates' Courts Act 1980, s.133

Consecutive terms of imprisonment

23–134 **133.**—(1) Subject to section 265 of the *Criminal Justice Act* 2003 a magistrates' court imposing imprisonment or youth custody on any person may order that the term of imprisonment or youth custody shall commence on the expiration of any other term of imprisonment or youth custody imposed by that or any other court; but where a magistrates' court imposes two or more terms of imprisonment or youth custody to run consecutively the aggregate of such terms shall not, subject to the provisions of this section, exceed 6 months.

(2) If two or more of the terms imposed by the court are imposed in respect of an offence triable either way which was tried summarily otherwise than in pursuance of section 22(2) above, the aggregate of the terms so imposed and any other terms imposed by the court may exceed 6 months but shall not, subject to the following provisions of this section, exceed 12 months.

(2A) In relation to the imposition of terms of detention in a young offender institution subsection (2) above shall have effect as if the reference to an offence triable either way were a reference to such an offence or an offence triable only on indictment.

(3) The limitations imposed by subsection 1 above shall not operate to reduce the aggregate of the terms that the court may impose in respect of any offences below the term which the court has power to impose in respect of any one of those offences.

(4) Where a person has been sentenced by a magistrates' court to imprisonment and a fine for the same offence, a period of imprisonment imposed for non-payment of the fine, or for want of sufficient distress to satisfy the fine, shall not be subject to the limitations imposed by the preceding subsections.

(5) For the purposes of this section a term of imprisonment shall be deemed to be imposed in respect of an offence if it is imposed as a sentence or in default of payment of a sum adjudged to be paid by the conviction or for want of sufficient distress to satisfy such a sum.

Criminal Justice Act 2003, ss.263, 264

Concurrent terms

23–135 **263.**—(1) This section applies where—

(a) a person ("the offender") has been sentenced to two or more terms of imprisonment which are wholly or partly concurrent, and

(b) the sentences were passed on the same occasion or, where they were passed on different occasions, the person has not been released under this Chapter at any time during the period beginning with the first and ending with the last of those occasions.

(2) Where this section applies—

(a) nothing in this Chapter requires the Secretary of State to release the offender in respect of any of the terms unless and until he is required to release him in respect of each of the others,

(b) section 244 does not authorise the Secretary of State to release him on licence under that section in respect of any of the terms unless and until that section authorises the Secretary of State to do so in respect of each of the others, on and after his release under this Chapter the offender is to be on licence for so long, and subject to such conditions, as is required by this Chapter in respect of any of the sentences.

(3) Where the sentences include one or more sentences of twelve months or more and one or more sentences of less than twelve months, the terms of the licence may be determined by the Secretary of State in accordance with section 250(4)(b), without regard to the requirements of any custody plus order or intermittent custody order.

(4) In this section "term of imprisonment" includes a determinate sentence of detention under section 91 of the Sentencing Act or under section 228 of this Act or a sentence of detention in a young offender institution under section 96 of the Sentencing Act or section 227 of this Act.

Consecutive terms

264.—(1) This section applies where— **23–136**

(a) a person ("the offender") has been sentenced to two or more terms of imprisonment which are to be served consecutively on each other, and

(b) the sentences were passed on the same occasion or, where they were passed on different occasions, the person has not been released under this Chapter at any time during the period beginning with the first and ending with the last of those occasions, and

(c) none of those terms is a term to which an intermittent custody order relates.

(2) Nothing in this Chapter requires the Secretary of State to release the offender on licence until he has served a period equal in length to the aggregate of the length of the custodial periods in relation to each of the terms of imprisonment.

(3) Where any of the terms of imprisonment is a term of twelve months or more, the offender is, on and after his release under this Chapter, to be on licence—

(a) until he would, but for his release, have served a term equal in length to the aggregate length of the terms of imprisonment, and

(b) subject to such conditions as are required by this Chapter in respect of each of those terms of imprisonment.

(4) Where each of the terms of imprisonment is a term of less than twelve months, the offender is, on and after his release under this Chapter, to be on licence until the relevant time, and subject to such conditions as are required by this Chapter in respect of any of the terms of imprisonment, and none of the terms is to be regarded for any purpose as continuing after the relevant time.

(5) In subsection (4) "the relevant time" means the time when the offender would, but for his release, have served a term equal in length to the aggregate of—

(a) all the custodial periods in relation to the terms of imprisonment, and

(b) the longest of the licence periods in relation to those terms.

(6) In this section—

(a) "custodial period"—

(i) in relation to an extended sentence imposed under section 227 or 228, means one half of the appropriate custodial term determined under that section,

(ii) in relation to a term of twelve months or more, means one-half of the term, and

(iii) in relation to a term of less than twelve months complying with section 181, means the custodial period as defined by subsection (3)(a) of that section;

(b) "licence period", in relation to a term of less than twelve months complying with section 181, has the meaning given by subsection (3)(b) of that section.

(7) This section applies to a determinate sentence of detention under section 91 of the Sentencing Act or under section 228 of this Act or a sentence of detention in a young offender institution under section 96 of the Sentencing Act or section 227 of this Act as it applies to a term of imprisonment of 12 months or more.

An offender who is convicted of more than one offence must be given separate sen- **23–137** tences on each. These sentences may run concurrently or consecutively, or there may be a mixture of concurrent and consecutive sentences. If the court fails to make clear whether the sentences are concurrent or consecutive, it is presumed that the sentences are concurrent.

Where a prison sentence is passed on an offender already serving a prison sentence, the court must make it clear whether this sentence is to be served consecutively or concurrently with the existing sentence.

The restriction on maximum sentences only applies to terms of imprisonment imposed on the same occasion, and the court may order that the sentence of imprisonment is to commence on the expiration of a term imposed by another court even though the offender will serve longer than the statutory maximum: *Prime* (1983) 5 Cr.App.R.(S.) 127, CA. However, this is subject to the totality principle: *Watts* [2000] 1 Cr.App.R.(S.) 460, CA.

23–138 Consecutive sentences should not generally be imposed for offences which arise out of the same transaction: *Jones* (1980) 2 Cr.App.R.(S.) 152, CA; *Noble* [2003] 1 Cr.App.R.(S.) 65, CA. The importance of this as a general principle was emphasised by the Court of Appeal (Criminal Division) in *Ralphs* [2010] 2 Cr.App.R.(S.) 30 in which the Court was urged (but declined) to impose consecutive sentences in order to circumvent what the prosecution perceived to be too low maximum sentence. However, the fact that this is not an absolute principle was emphasised in *Noble*, where it was said that the principle may admit of exceptions in exceptional circumstances. Consecutive sentences may be inappropriate where the offences concerned form a series of similar offences against the same victim, and are committed over a short period of time: *Paddon*, March 3, 1971, CA (Crim. Div.); however, care must be taken to avoid undue lenience—it is not necessarily less serious, for example, to assault the same person three times over a week period than it is to assault three different people. An application of this principle can be seen in *Bain* [2005] 2 Cr.App.R.(S) 53. The defendant was aged 19. In the course of driving dangerously, serious injuries were caused to a passenger in the vehicle that he was driving. He was charged with dangerous driving and with causing grievous bodily harm (s.20). Dangerous driving attracts a maximum of two years' imprisonment, GBH a maximum of five years. The Court of Appeal held that there was nothing wrong in principle in charging such offences even though they arose from the same course of conduct. However, since the offences did arise out of the same course of conduct, concurrent sentences should have been imposed that reflected the totality of the offending conduct. Where the offences import different or additional aspects, it may be appropriate to consider consecutive sentences. So, for example, where the driver both drove dangerously and drove with excess alcohol or disqualified, although the general practice is to impose concurrent sentences where the offences arose from a single incident, nonetheless there is a well recognised practice that, in such circumstances consecutive sentences may be imposed. In *Hardy* [2006] 2 Cr.App.R.(S.) 4, the defendant was convicted of dangerous driving, driving whilst disqualified and failing to provide a specimen. Consecutive sentences totalling two years were imposed in the Crown Court. Upholding those sentences and the approach, the Court of Appeal stated that, whilst consecutive sentences would not generally be appropriate where the matters arose out of the same incident "it would be bizarre that this man would in fact have a licence to drive with excess alcohol and while disqualified without any added penalty." An approach that may have less offended general sentencing principle would have been to have treated the alcohol and disqualification as aggravating factors and increased the sentence accordingly; however, the low maximum penalty does not allow that to happen so readily and this is perhaps another example of the problems that arise when maximum sentences are allowed to remain at a level that is too low.

Consecutive sentences may be appropriate where the offender uses violence to escape: *Bunch*, November 6, 1971, or where violence is used to resist arrest: *Wellington* (1988) 10 Cr.App.R.(S.) 384.

(4) Time served prior to imposition of sentence

Criminal Justice Act 2003, ss.240–242

Crediting of periods of remand in custody: terms of imprisonment and detention

240.—(1) This section applies where— 23–139

(a) a court sentences an offender to imprisonment for a term in respect of an offence committed after the commencement of this section, and

(b) the offender has been remanded in custody (within the meaning given by section 242) in connection with the offence or a related offence, that is to say, any other offence the charge for which was founded on the same facts or evidence.

(2) It is immaterial for that purpose whether the offender—

(a) has also been remanded in custody in connection with other offences; or

(b) has also been detained in connection with other matters.

(3) Subject to subsection (4), the court must direct that the number of days for which the offender was remanded in custody in connection with the offence or a related offence is to count as time served by him as part of the sentence.

(4) Subsection (3) does not apply if and to the extent that—

(a) rules made by the Secretary of State so provide in the case of—

(i) a remand in custody which is wholly or partly concurrent with a sentence of imprisonment, or

(ii) sentences of imprisonment for consecutive terms or for terms which are wholly or partly concurrent, or

(b) it is in the opinion of the court just in all the circumstances not to give a direction under that subsection.

(5) Where the court gives a direction under subsection (3), it shall state in open court—

(a) the number of days for which the offender was remanded in custody, and

(b) the number of days in relation to which the direction is given.

(6) Where the court does not give a direction under subsection (3), or gives such a direction in relation to a number of days less than that for which the offender was remanded in custody, it shall state in open court—

(a) that its decision is in accordance with rules made under paragraph (a) of subsection (4), or

(b) that it is of the opinion mentioned in paragraph (b) of that subsection and what the circumstances are.

(7) For the purposes of this section a suspended sentence—

(a) is to be treated as a sentence of imprisonment when it takes effect under paragraph 8(2)(a) or (b) of Schedule 12, and

(b) is to be treated as being imposed by the order under which it takes effect.

(8) For the purposes of the reference in subsection (3) to the term of imprisonment to which a person has been sentenced (that is to say, the reference to his "sentence"), consecutive terms and terms which are wholly or partly concurrent are to be treated as a single term if—

(a) the sentences were passed on the same occasion, or

(b) where they were passed on different occasions, the person has not been released under this Chapter at any time during the period beginning with the first and ending with the last of those occasions.

(9) Where an offence is found to have been committed over a period of two or more days, or at some time during a period of two or more days, it shall be taken for the purposes of subsection (1) to have been committed on the last of those days.

(10) This section applies to a determinate sentence of detention under section 91 of the Sentencing Act or section 228 of this Act or a sentence of detention in a young offender institution under section 96 of the Sentencing Act or section 227 of this Act as it applies to an equivalent sentence of imprisonment.

[This section is printed as inserted by the *Criminal Justice Act 2003 (Sentencing) (Transitory Provisions) Order* 2005 (S.I. 2005 No.643).]

Crediting periods of remand on bail: terms of imprisonment and detention

240A.—(1) This section applies where— 23–140

Part IV

(a) a court sentences an offender to imprisonment for a term in respect of an offence committed on or after 4th April 2005,

(b) the offender was remanded on bail by a court in course of or in connection with proceedings for the offence, or any related offence, after the coming into force of section 21 of the *Criminal Justice and Immigration Act* 2008, and

(c) the offender's bail was subject to a qualifying curfew condition and an electronic monitoring condition ("the relevant conditions").

(2) Subject to subsection (4), the court must direct that the credit period is to count as time served by the offender as part of the sentence.

(3) The "credit period" is the number of days represented by half of the sum of—

(a) the day on which the offender's bail was first subject to conditions that, had they applied throughout the day in question, would have been relevant conditions, and

(b) the number of other days on which the offender's bail was subject to those conditions (excluding the last day on which it was so subject),

rounded up to the nearest whole number.

(4) Subsection (2) does not apply if and to the extent that—

(a) rules made by the Secretary of State so provide, or

(b) it is in the opinion of the court just in all the circumstances not to give a direction under that subsection.

(5) Where as a result of paragraph (a) or (b) of subsection (4) the court does not give a direction under subsection (2), it may give a direction in accordance with either of those paragraphs to the effect that a period of days which is less than the credit period is to count as time served by the offender as part of the sentence.

(6) Rules made under subsection (4)(a) may, in particular, make provision in relation to

(a) sentences of imprisonment for consecutive terms;

(b) sentences of imprisonment for terms which are wholly or partly concurrent;

(c) periods during which a person granted bail subject to the relevant conditions is also subject to electronic monitoring required by an order made by a court or the Secretary of State.

(7) In considering whether it is of the opinion mentioned in subsection (4)(b) the court must, in particular, take into account whether or not the offender has, at any time whilst on bail subject to the relevant conditions, broken either or both of them.

(8) Where the court gives a direction under subsection (2) or (5) it shall state in open court—

(a) the number of days on which the offender was subject to the relevant conditions, and

(b) the number of days in relation to which the direction is given.

(9) Subsection (10) applies where the court—

(a) does not give a direction under subsection (2) but gives a direction under subsection (5), or

(b) decides not to give a direction under this section.

(10) The court shall state in open court—

(a) that its decision is in accordance with rules made under paragraph (a) of subsection (4), or

(b) that it is of the opinion mentioned in paragraph (b) of that subsection and what the circumstances are.

(11) Subsections (7) to (10) of section 240 apply for the purposes of this section as they apply for the purposes of that section but as if—

(a) in subsection (7)—

(i) the reference to a suspended sentence is to be read as including a reference to a sentence to which an order under section 118(1) of the *Sentencing Act* relates;

(ii) in paragraph (a) after "Schedule 12" there were inserted "or section 119(1)(a) or (b) of the *Sentencing Act*"; and

(b) in subsection (8) the reference to subsection (3) of section 240 is to be read as a reference to subsection (2) of this section and, in paragraph (b), after "Chapter" there were inserted "or Part 2 of the *Criminal Justice Act* 1991".

(12) In this section—

"electronic monitoring condition" means any electronic monitoring requirements imposed under section 3(6ZAA) of the Bail Act 1976 for the purpose of securing the electronic monitoring of a person's compliance with a qualifying curfew condition;

"qualifying curfew condition" means a condition of bail which requires the person granted bail to remain at one or more specified places for a total of not less than 9 hours in any given day; and

"related offence" means an offence, other than the offence for which the sentence is imposed ("offence A"), with which the offender was charged and the charge for which was founded on the same facts or evidence as offence A.

Effect of direction under section 240 or 240A on release on licence

241.—(1) In determining for the purposes of this Chapter or Chapter 3 (prison sentences of less than twelve months) whether a person to whom a direction under section 240 or 240A relates— **23–141**

(a) has served, or would (but for his release) have served, a particular proportion of his sentence, or

(b) has served a particular period,

the number of days specified in the direction are to be treated as having been served by him as part of that sentence or period.

(1A) In subsection (1) the reference to a direction under section 240 includes a direction under section 246 of the *Armed Forces Act* 2006.

(2) In determining for the purposes of section 183 (intermittent custody) whether any part of a sentence to which an intermittent custody order relates is a licence period, the number of custodial days, as defined by subsection (3) of that section, is to be taken to be reduced by the number of days specified in a direction under section 240 or 240A.

Interpretation of sections 240, 240A and 241

242.—(1) For the purposes of sections 240, 240A and 241, the definition of "sentence of imprisonment" in section 305 applies as if for the words from the beginning of the definition to the end of paragraph (a) there were substituted— **23–142**

" 'sentence of imprisonment' does not include a committal—

(a) in default of payment of any sum of money, other than one adjudged to be paid on a conviction,";

and references in those sections to sentencing an offender to imprisonment, and to an offender's sentence, are to be read accordingly.

(2) References in sections 240 and 241 to an offender's being remanded in custody are references to his being—

(a) remanded in or committed to custody by order of a court,

(b) remanded or committed to local authority accommodation under section 23 of the *Children and Young Persons Act* 1969 and kept in secure accommodation or detained in a secure training centre pursuant to arrangements under subsection (7A) of that section, or

(c) remanded, admitted or removed to hospital under section 35, 36, 38 or 48 of the *Mental Health Act* 1983.

(3) In subsection (2), "secure accommodation" has the same meaning as in section 23 of the *Children and Young Persons Act* 1969.

Remand in Custody (Effect of Concurrent and Consecutive Sentences of Imprisonment) Rules 2005 (S.I. 2005 No.2054)

1.—(1) These Rules may be cited as the *Remand in Custody (Effect of Concurrent and Consecutive Sentences of Imprisonment) Rules* 2005 and shall come into force on the day after the day on which they are made. **23–143**

(2) In these Rules "the 2003 Act" means the *Criminal Justice Act* 2003.

2. Section 240(3) of the 2003 Act does not apply in relation to a day for which an offender was remanded in custody— **23–144**

(a) if on that day he was serving a sentence of imprisonment (and it was not a day on which he was on licence under Chapter 6 of Part 12 of the 2003 Act or Part 2 of the *Criminal Justice Act* 1991); or

(b) where the term of imprisonment referred to in subsection (1) of that section is ordered to be served consecutively on another term of imprisonment, if the length of that other term falls to be reduced by the same day by virtue of section 67 of the *Criminal Justice Act* 1967.

23–145 Where an offender has spent time in custody before being made subject to a community order, and is later sentenced to custody for the same offence, the sentence should be reduced to allow for the time spent in custody on remand before the order was made, since that will not be automatically credited to the time to be served under the sentence.

Where an offender is sentenced to a custodial sentence and has been remanded on bail under s.3AB of the *Bail Act* 1976 (inserted by Sched. 11, para. 4 to the *Criminal Justice and Immigration Act* 2008) where a condition of that bail was a curfew subject to electronic monitoring, there will be a presumption that credit will be given against the length of the sentence. For each day on which the offender was subject to a curfew to remain in one place for no less than 9 hours, one half day will be allowed against sentence. The day on which the condition was imposed will be included, the last day on which it was applicable will be excluded (no doubt this will often be the day of sentence or of a later remand in custody). Any part days will be rounded up in favour of the offender. Bail may only qualify under this provision where it has been granted under the new section 3AB that is, where bail would not have been granted if it had not been possible to impose electronic monitoring.

Where an offender who is sentenced to imprisonment has previously been in custody on remand for that or a related offence, the court must direct that that time is to be counted as time served as part of the sentence: *Criminal Justice Act* 2003, s.240. It is of no consequence if the offender has also been remanded in custody for other offences. A court may decline to credit all the days to sentence in certain circumstances, one of which is where the court considers that it would be just to so decline: s.240(4). In such a circumstance, the court must declare in open court the number of days on remand, the number for which credit is being given and the circumstances that have led it to conclude that it is just to reduce the number of days that count: s.240(5), (6). The circumstances that count as a remand in custody are set out in s.242(2). They are court ordered remands and so do not include time when an offender was in police custody prior to charge or between charge and first appearance.

Two exceptions are provided by *Criminal Justice Act* 2003, s.240(4). One is where, in the opinion of the court, it is just not to give such a direction. The other exception provides for rules to be made by the Secretary of State. The *Remand in Custody (Effect of Concurrent and Consecutive Sentences of Imprisonment) Rules* 2005 (S.I. 2005 No.2054) have been made. They aim to prevent a court from making a direction that would have the effect of causing the remand days to be counted twice and provide for two circumstances. The first circumstance is where an offender has been remanded in custody for two or more offences for which sentence is imposed on different days. The second instance is where sentence is imposed on one occasion for an offence committed prior to April 4, 2005 and for an offence committed on or after that date. In respect of the earlier offence, the time on remand would be deducted from the sentence automatically and so it would be inappropriate for a court to make a further direction. An accompanying circular (HOC 37/2005) points out that the day on which sentence is imposed will be regarded as a sentence day and will not be regarded as a remand day. Accordingly, it does not need to be included in any direction under these provisions. Proper exercise of this duty requires accurate and timely information being provided to the court, an obligation emphasised by the Court of Appeal in *Oosthuizen* [2006] 1 Cr.App.R.(S.) 73. The importance of stating the effect of a custodial sentence, and whether or not days on remand should count towards the sentence, was emphasised in *Barber* [2006] EWCA Crim 162. The court should state the position clearly and unambiguously and both the prosecution and defence legal representatives should be alert to bring the requirements of the provisions to the attention of the court if it appeared that they were being overlooked. The court should put defence legal representatives on notice if it was considering that some or all of the days should not count. It was not proper to withhold credit for days spent in custody prior to a change of plea to guilty, *Vaughan* [2008] EWCA Crim 1613. The strength of the presumption in favour of allowing credit for the whole of the qualifying period was emphasised in *McGrail* [2009] EWCA Crim 1400. Following conviction for robbery in which the defendant had pleaded guilty at a late stage, the Judge declined to give credit for the 154 days spent in custody on remand. Although the reasoning was not clear for that decision, it was apparent that the Judge had little sympathy for the defendant and that the late plea may have been amongst the reasons. Allowing the appeal on this point, the Court of Appeal noted that the 2003 Act obliges a court to direct that the time should count towards the sentence unless that would be unjust; in this case, there appeared to be no reason to justify a determination that it would be unjust. In *Gordon* [2007] EWCA Crim 165, the Court of Appeal reviewed various issues arising from these provisions particularly where a court was dealing with offences committed before and after the date on which these provisions were commenced. Where the credit arises from time on remand or bail, the court must announce both the number of days on which the offender was subject to qualifying conditions and the number of days credit given. Credit need not be given where a court considers that it would be just in all the circumstances not to do so or where the offender falls within situations set out in rules designed to cover situations where there are consecutive sentences or where the offender is subject to electronic monitoring under otherprovisions: s.240A(4). Reasons need to be given in such circumstances and, as with credit for time on remand in custody, it is likely to be rare for a court to refuse credit in the interests of justice. The *Remand on Bail (Disapplication of Credit Period) Rules* 2008 have been made and are effective from November 3, 2008: S.I. 2008 No.2793. They seek to prevent double counting of a qualifying period where consecutive sentences are being imposed or where the offender is subject to a curfew and electronic monitoring for other purposes as well as the bail condition, including early or temporary release from a custodial sentence and a requirement within a community order or a suspended sentence order.

Offences committed before April 4, 2005 continue to be governed by the previous provisions contained in s.67 of the *Criminal Justice Act* 1967. A reminder was given about the need to give reasons where a court decided not to direct that time spent on remand should count towards sentence or to direct that a lesser time should count: *Criminal Justice Act* 2003, s.240(6). It was also confirmed that it was possible to adjourn the sentencing hearing in part where further calculation was needed, the court having indicated the appropriate period to be taken into account. In February 2007, the Senior Presiding Judge notified courts of a revised procedure to ensure that the correct information on periods that count should be conveyed accurately to the court imposing sentence. As well as reproducing the agreed procedures and forms, the Senior Presiding Judge emphasised the duty on advocates to agree the number of days for which a prisoner had been remanded in custody and which, therefore, were available to be credited against sentence. If there was a dispute, that should be resolved by the advocates before the hearing but, if that was not possible, the court would have the ambit of the dispute clearly defined. The continuing difficulties in obtaining accurate information about qualifying periods on remand prompted the Court of Appeal to emphasise again the importance of using appropriate wording to minimise the risk of unnecessary appeals or re-listing of cases. The Court noted that this was even more important now that the credit can extend to certain periods on bail. In *Nnaji* [2009] EWCA Crim 468 the Court suggested wording along the following lines: "The defendant will receive full credit for the full period of time spent in custody on remand and half the time spent under curfew if the curfew qualified under the provisions of s.240. On the information before me the total period is XX days but if this period is mistaken, this Court will order an amendment of the record for the correct period to be recorded."

Continuing problems regarding the calculation of the days spent on a qualifying remand led the Senior Presiding Judge, Goldring L.J., to write to Presiding and Resident Judges in September 2010 drawing attention to the formula to be used when ss.240 and 240A are engaged. This is the formula set out above derived from the decision in *Nnaji* [2009] 2 Cr.App.R.(S.) 107 as adopted in *Irving and Squires* [2010] 2 Cr.App.R.(S.) 75. Continuing failures to follow this approach were severely criticised by the Court of Appeal in *Boutell, Ricketts* (2010) 174 J.P. 546 and defence advocates in particular were reminded of their duty to enquire into these matters at the sentencing hearing.

Summary of approach

23–146 Noting the very considerable complexities arising from the effect of the statutory provisions, the Court of Appeal has set out four things which the courts and practitioners "must do": *Squires* [2010] EWCA Crim 189.

(i) a court must use the formula set out in *Nnaji* (see above);
(ii) when imposing a curfew and tagging condition on bail, every court must use the form provided by the Court Service—"Record of Electronic Monitoring of Curfew Bail"—which should follow the defendant from court to court;
(iii) defence and prosecution advocates should both ascertain (from the court record or their own systems) whether the defendant has been subject to curfew and tagging and, if so, for what periods;
(iv) the Court of Appeal will be reluctant to grant long extensions of time in which to appeal when the sole complaint is an error in calculation—this should be picked up at an early stage.

Where the period on remand is such that a custodial sentence that is the "shortest commensurate with the seriousness of the offence" would result in the immediate release of the offender, the court should not impose a sentence that would make the punishment more severe. In *Hemmings* [2008] 1 Cr.App.R.(S.) 106 it was stated "A sentence of a community order, and all the more so one coupled with requirements which have a real impact on the offender's liberty, is a form of punishment. It does not seem to us to be right that the appellant should receive a substantial further punishment in circumstances where he has already received what was in practice the maximum punishment by way of imprisonment which the law could have imposed". In *Barrett* [2010] EWCA Crim 365 the offender was convicted of two offences for which the maximum custodial sentence in total was 6 months; he had spent 4 months in custody on remand so, even if the maximum sentence was imposed, would have been entitled to immediate release. The offences arose out of a domestic dispute and it was clear that the court wished to do what it could to protect the victim; a suspended sentence order was imposed so that the offender had the threat of imprisonment hanging over him as an incentive to comply with requirements. The Court of Appeal allowed the offender's appeal since the effect of the sentence was to impose a punishment more severe than the maximum for the offence; that was wrong in principle. A conditional discharge was imposed for a period short enough for it to expire on or before the date on which the appeal was determined so ensuring the offender was not subject to any further penalty. If that principle had been followed by the sentencing court, it is submitted that the proper course would have been to impose a custodial sentence (assuming the offence(s) were sufficiently serious) since that would ensure that the record properly reflected the seriousness of the offender's conduct.

C. SUSPENDED SENTENCES ORDERS

(1) Purpose and effect

23–147 This is an order that a period of imprisonment imposed by the court will not need to be served by the defendant unless he commits another imprisonable offence during the "operational period".

23–148 Profound changes have been made to these provisions by the *Criminal Justice Act* 2003 not least the ability to link the imposition of a custodial sentence (albeit suspended) with requirements to be undertaken. As well as the statutory provisions, a definitive guideline was issued by the Sentencing Guidelines Council in December 2004 (*New Sentences: Criminal Justice Act* 2003) which sets out the approach to the various decisions that have to be made as part of the imposition of this sentence. In particular, the Council emphasises the importance of a court ensuring that it would have imposed a custodial sentence if there had been no power to suspend. The provisions in the Act were drafted to apply when "custody plus" was in force; for offences committed prior to commencement, transitional provisions enable the power to be used within the previous sentencing powers. These provisions enable a Crown Court which imposes a prison sentence of up to 12 months to suspend it for between six months and two years. Inexplicably, as a result of the transitional provisions, a magistrates' court intending to suspend sentence is restricted to a sentence totalling six months even when sentencing for two or more either way offences. The approach, the issues, the extent of requirements and the approach to breach of an order are clearly set out in the guidelines. An additional power is that to establish reviews by the court of compliance with the requirements contained within the order (ss.191, 192).

An issue has been raised as to whether a court must impose a requirement when making a suspended sentence order or whether it is sufficient simply to suspend the sentence of imprisonment. *Criminal Justice Act* 2003, s.189 requires a court first to determine that it must impose a sentence of imprisonment. Having made that decision, the section empowers a court to impose one or more requirements and to suspend the sentence of imprisonment. It would appear that the power to suspend does not arise unless a requirement is imposed: *Lees-Wolfenden* [2006] EWCA Crim 3068.

Criminal Justice Act 2003, ss.189–190

Suspended sentences of imprisonment

189.—(1) A court which passes a sentence of imprisonment or, in the case of a person aged at least 18 but under 21, detention in a young offender institution for a term of at least 14 days but not more than twelve months, or in the case of a magistrates' court, at least 14 days but not more than six months may— **23–149**

(a) order the offender to comply during a period specified for the purposes of this paragraph in the order (in this Chapter referred to as "the supervision period") with one or more requirements falling within section 190(1) and specified in the order, and

(b) order that the sentence of imprisonment or detention in a young offender institution is not to take effect unless either—

(i) during the supervision period the offender fails to comply with a requirement imposed under paragraph (a), or

(ii) during a period specified in the order for the purposes of this sub-paragraph (in this Chapter referred to as "the operational period") the offender commits in the United Kingdom another offence (whether or not punishable with imprisonment),

and (in either case) a court having power to do so subsequently orders under paragraph 8 of Schedule 12 that the original sentence is to take effect.

(2) Where two or more sentences imposed on the same occasion are to be served consecutively, the power conferred by subsection (1) is not exercisable in relation to any of them unless the aggregate of the terms of the sentences does not exceed twelve months, or in the case of a magistrates' court, six months.

(3) The supervision period and the operational period must each be a period of not less than six months and not more than two years beginning with the date of the order.

(4) The supervision period must not end later than the operational period.

(5) A court which passes a suspended sentence on any person for an offence may not impose a community sentence in his case in respect of that offence or any other offence of which he is convicted by or before the court or for which he is dealt with by the court.

(6) Subject to any provision to the contrary contained in the *Criminal Justice Act* 1967, the Sentencing Act or any other enactment passed or instrument made under any enactment after 31st December 1967, a suspended sentence which has not taken effect under paragraph 8 of Schedule 12 is to be treated as a sentence of imprisonment or in the case of a person aged at

Part IV

least 18 but under 21, a sentence of detention in a young offender institution for the purposes of all enactments and instruments made under enactments.

(7) In this Part—

(a) "suspended sentence order" means an order under subsection (1),

(b) "suspended sentence" means a sentence to which a suspended sentence order relates, and

(c) "community requirement", in relation to a suspended sentence order, means a requirement imposed under subsection (1)(a).

Imposition of requirements by suspended sentence order

23–150 **190.**—(1) The requirements falling within this subsection are—

(a) an unpaid work requirement (as defined by section 199),

(b) an activity requirement (as defined by section 201),

(c) a programme requirement (as defined by section 202),

(d) a prohibited activity requirement (as defined by section 203),

(e) a curfew requirement (as defined by section 204),

(f) an exclusion requirement (as defined by section 205),

(g) a residence requirement (as defined by section 206),

(h) a mental health treatment requirement (as defined by section 207),

(i) a drug rehabilitation requirement (as defined by section 209),

(j) an alcohol treatment requirement (as defined by section 212),

(k) a supervision requirement (as defined by section 213), and

(l) in a case where the offender is aged under 25, an attendance centre requirement (as defined by section 214).

(2) Section 189(1)(a) has effect subject to section 218 and to the following provisions of Chapter 4 relating to particular requirements—

(a) section 199(3) (unpaid work requirement),

(b) section 201(3) and (4) (activity requirement),

(c) section 202(4) and (5) (programme requirement),

(d) section 203(2) (prohibited activity requirement),

(e) section 207(3) (mental health treatment requirement),

(f) section 209(2) (drug rehabilitation requirement), and

(g) section 212(2) and (3) (alcohol treatment requirement).

(3) Where the court makes a suspended sentence order imposing a curfew requirement or an exclusion requirement, it must also impose an electronic monitoring requirement (as defined by section 215) unless—

(a) the court is prevented from doing so by section 215(2) or 218(4), or

(b) in the particular circumstances of the case, it considers it inappropriate to do so.

(4) Where the court makes a suspended sentence order imposing an unpaid work requirement, an activity requirement, a programme requirement, a prohibited activity requirement, a residence requirement, a mental health treatment requirement, a drug rehabilitation requirement, an alcohol treatment requirement, a supervision requirement or an attendance centre requirement, the court may also impose an electronic monitoring requirement unless the court is prevented from doing so by section 215(2) or 218(4).

(5) Before making a suspended sentence order imposing two or more different requirements falling within subsection (1), the court must consider whether, in the circumstances of the case, the requirements are compatible with each other.

(2) Guideline

Guideline: New Sentences: Criminal Justice Act 2003

Section 2—Custodial Sentences

Part 2: Suspended Sentences

B. IMPOSING A SUSPENDED SENTENCE

23–151 **2.2.6** A suspended sentence is a sentence of imprisonment. It is subject to the same criteria as a sentence of imprisonment which is to commence immediately. In particular, this requires a court to be satisfied that the custody threshold has been passed and that the length of the term is the shortest term commensurate with the seriousness of the offence.

2.2.7 A court which passes a prison sentence of less than 12 months may suspend it for between 6 months and 2 years (the operational period). During that period, the court can impose one or more requirements for the offender to undertake in the community. The requirements are identical to those available for the new community sentence.

2.2.8 The period during which the offender undertakes community requirements is "the supervision period" when the offender will be under the supervision of a "responsible officer"; this period may be shorter than the operational period. The court may periodically review the progress of the offender in complying with the requirements and the reviews will be informed by a report from the responsible officer.

The power to suspend a sentence is expected to come into force earlier than the provisions implementing "custody plus" and transitional provisions are expected to enable any sentence of imprisonment of under 12 months to be suspended. This guideline therefore is written in the language of the expected transitional provisions.

2.2.9 If the offender fails to comply with a requirement during the supervision period, or commits a further offence during the operational period, the suspended sentence can be activated in full or in part or the terms of the supervision made more onerous. There is a presumption that the suspended sentence will be activated either in full or in part. **23–152**

(i) The decision to suspend

2.2.10 There are many similarities between the suspended sentence and the community sentence. In both cases, requirements can be imposed during the supervision period and the court can respond to breach by sending the offender to custody. The crucial difference is that the suspended sentence is a prison sentence and is appropriate only for an offence that passes the custody threshold and for which imprisonment is the only option. A community sentence may also be imposed for an offence that passes the custody threshold where the court considers that to be appropriate. **23–153**

2.2.11 The full decision making process for imposition of custodial sentences under the new framework (including the custody threshold test) is set out in paragraphs 1.31–1.33 of the Seriousness guideline. For the purposes of suspended sentences the relevant steps are:

(a) **has the custody threshold been passed?**

(b) **if so, is it unavoidable that a custodial sentence be imposed?**

(c) **if so, can that sentence be suspended? (sentencers should be clear that they would have imposed a custodial sentence if the power to suspend had not been available)**

(d) if not, can the sentence be served intermittently?

(e) if not, impose a sentence which takes immediate effect for the term commensurate with the seriousness of the offence.

(ii) Length of sentence

2.2.12 Before making the decision to suspend sentence, the court must already have decided that a prison sentence is justified and should also have decided the length of sentence that would be the shortest term commensurate with the seriousness of the offence if it were to be imposed immediately. The decision to suspend the sentence should not lead to a longer term being imposed than if the sentence were to take effect immediately. **23–154**

A prison sentence that is suspended should be for the same term that would have applied if the offender were being sentenced to immediate custody.

2.2.13 When assessing the length of the operational period of a suspended sentence, the court should have in mind the relatively short length of the sentence being suspended and the advantages to be gained by retaining the opportunity to extend the operational period at a later stage (see below).

23–155 **The operational period of a suspended sentence should reflect the length of the sentence being suspended. As an approximate guide, an operational period of up to 12 months might normally be appropriate for a suspended sentence of up to 6 months and an operational period of up to 18 months might normally be appropriate for a suspended sentence of up to 12 months.**

(iii) Requirements

23–156 **2.2.14** The court will set the requirements to be complied with during the supervision period. Whilst the offence for which a suspended sentence is imposed is generally likely to be more serious than one for which a community sentence is imposed, the imposition of the custodial sentence is a clear punishment and deterrent. In order to ensure that the overall terms of the sentence are commensurate with the seriousness of the offence, it is likely that the requirements to be undertaken during the supervision period would be less onerous than if a community sentence had been imposed. These requirements will need to ensure that they properly address those factors that are most likely to reduce the risk of re-offending.

Because of the very clear deterrent threat involved in a suspended sentence, requirements imposed as part of that sentence should generally be less onerous than those imposed as part of a community sentence. A court wishing to impose onerous or intensive requirements on an offender should reconsider its decision to suspend sentence and consider whether a community sentence might be more appropriate.

(3) Review of suspended sentence order

23–157 It will be possible for a court to provide for a Suspended Sentence Order to be reviewed periodically by the court. It will be for the court to determine the frequency and nature of the review (s.191(1)). At such a hearing, the court may amend the community requirements. There is also power to dispense with the attendance of the offender where progress is satisfactory (s.192(4)). This can apply just to the next hearing or to all future hearings. If the latter, that can be rescinded if the progress ceases to be satisfactory (s.192(5)).

If, at a review hearing, the court forms the view that the offender has failed to comply with the requirements without reasonable excuse, the hearing must be adjourned for the purpose of a hearing under Sched. 12 to enforce the order.

Criminal Justice Act 2003, ss.191–192

Power to provide for review of suspended sentence order

23–158 **191.**—(1) A suspended sentence order may—

(a) provide for the order to be reviewed periodically at specified intervals,

(b) provide for each review to be made, subject to section 192(4), at a hearing held for the purpose by the court responsible for the order (a "review hearing"),

(c) require the offender to attend each review hearing, and

(d) provide for the responsible officer to make to the court responsible for the order, before each review, a report on the offender's progress in complying with the community requirements of the order.

(2) Subsection (1) does not apply in the case of an order imposing a drug rehabilitation requirement (provision for such a requirement to be subject to review being made by section 210).

(3) In this section references to the court responsible for a suspended sentence order are references—

(a) where a court is specified in the order in accordance with subsection (4), to that court;

(b) in any other case, to the court by which the order is made.

(4) Where the area specified in a suspended sentence order made by a magistrates' court is not the area for which the court acts, the court may, if it thinks fit, include in the

order provision specifying for the purpose of subsection (3) a magistrates' court which acts for the area specified in the order.

(5) Where a suspended sentence order has been made on an appeal brought from the Crown Court or from the criminal division of the Court of Appeal, it is to be taken for the purposes of subsection (3)(b) to have been made by the Crown Court.

Periodic reviews of suspended sentence order

192.—(1) At a review hearing (within the meaning of subsection (1) of section 191) the court may, after considering the responsible officer's report referred to in that subsection, amend the community requirements of the suspended sentence order, or any provision of the order which relates to those requirements. **23–159**

(2) The court—

(a) may not amend the community requirements of the order so as to impose a requirement of a different kind unless the offender expresses his willingness to comply with that requirement,

(b) may not amend a mental health treatment requirement, a drug rehabilitation requirement or an alcohol treatment requirement unless the offender expresses his willingness to comply with the requirement as amended,

(c) may amend the supervision period only if the period as amended complies with section 189(3) and (4),

(d) may not amend the operational period of the suspended sentence, and

(e) except with the consent of the offender, may not amend the order while an appeal against the order is pending.

(3) For the purposes of subsection (2)(a)—

(a) a community requirement falling within any paragraph of section 190(1) is of the same kind as any other community requirement falling within that paragraph, and

(b) an electronic monitoring requirement is a community requirement of the same kind as any requirement falling within section 190(1) to which it relates.

(4) If before a review hearing is held at any review the court, after considering the responsible officer's report, is of the opinion that the offender's progress in complying with the community requirements of the order is satisfactory, it may order that no review hearing is to be held at that review; and if before a review hearing is held at any review, or at a review hearing, the court, after considering that report, is of that opinion, it may amend the suspended sentence order so as to provide for each subsequent review to be held without a hearing.

(5) If at a review held without a hearing the court, after considering the responsible officer's report, is of the opinion that the offender's progress under the order is no longer satisfactory, the court may require the offender to attend a hearing of the court at a specified time and place.

(6) If at a review hearing the court is of the opinion that the offender has without reasonable excuse failed to comply with any of the community requirements of the order, the court may adjourn the hearing for the purpose of dealing with the case under paragraph 8 of Schedule 12.

(7) At a review hearing the court may amend the suspended sentence order so as to vary the intervals specified under section 191(1).

(8) In this section any reference to the court, in relation to a review without a hearing, is to be read—

(a) in the case of the Crown Court, as a reference to a judge of the court, and

(b) in the case of a magistrates' court, as a reference to a justice of the peace.

(4) Offender who resides in Scotland or Northern Ireland

Given the different provisions that apply in some circumstances in Scotland and Northern Ireland, specific provision is made where a court wishes to make a Suspended Sentence Order which contains requirements in respect of an offender who resides in either Scotland or Northern Ireland. **23–160**

Part IV

Criminal Justice Act 2003, ss.195, 194

Interpretation of Chapter

Interpretation of Chapter 3

23–161 **195.** In this Chapter—

"custodial period", in relation to a term of imprisonment imposed in accordance with section 181, has the meaning given by subsection (3)(a) of that section;

"licence period" —

(a) in relation to a term of imprisonment imposed in accordance with section 181, has the meaning given by subsection (3)(b) of that section, and

(b) in relation to a term of imprisonment to which an intermittent custody order relates, has the meaning given by section 183(3);

"the number of custodial days", in relation to a term of imprisonment to which an intermittent custody order relates, has the meaning given by section 183(3);

"operational period" and "supervision period", in relation to a suspended sentence, are to be read in accordance with section 189(1);

"sentence of imprisonment" does not include a committal for contempt of court or any kindred offence.

Transfer of suspended sentence orders to Scotland or Northern Ireland

23–162 **194.** Schedule 13 (transfer of suspended sentence orders to Scotland or Northern Ireland) shall have effect.

Criminal Justice Act 2003, Sched. 13

Section 194 SCHEDULE 13

TRANSFER OF SUSPENDED SENTENCE ORDERS TO SCOTLAND OR NORTHERN IRELAND

PART 1

SCOTLAND

23–163 1.—(1) Where the court considering the making of a suspended sentence order is satisfied that the offender resides in Scotland, or will reside there when the order comes into force, the court may not make a suspended sentence order in respect of the offender unless it appears to the court—

(a) in the case of an order imposing a requirement mentioned in subparagraph (2), that arrangements exist for persons to comply with such a requirement in the locality in Scotland in which the offender resides, or will be residing when the order comes into force, and that provision can be made for him to comply with the requirement under those arrangements, and

(b) in any case, that suitable arrangements for his supervision can be made by the local authority in whose area he resides, or will be residing when the order comes into force.

(2) The requirements referred to in sub-paragraph (1)(a) are—

(a) an unpaid work requirement,

(b) an activity requirement,

(c) a programme requirement,

(d) a mental health treatment requirement,

(e) a drug rehabilitation requirement,

(f) an alcohol treatment requirement, and

(g) an electronic monitoring requirement.

(3) Where—

(a) the appropriate court for the purposes of paragraph 14 of Schedule 12 (amendment by reason of change of residence) is satisfied that an offender in respect of whom a suspended sentence order is in force proposes to reside or is residing in Scotland, and

(b) it appears to the court that the conditions in sub-paragraph (1)(a) and (b) are satisfied,

the power of the court to amend the order under Part 3 of Schedule 12 includes power to amend it by requiring it to be complied with in Scotland and the offender to be supervised in accordance with the arrangements referred to in sub-paragraph (1)(b).

(4) For the purposes of sub-paragraph (3), any reference in sub-paragraph (1)(a) and (b) to the time when the order comes into force is to be treated as a reference to the time when the amendment comes into force.

(5) The court may not by virtue of sub-paragraph (1) or (3) require an attendance centre requirement to be complied with in Scotland.

(6) The court may not provide for an order made in accordance with this paragraph to be subject to review under section 191 or 210; and where an order which is subject to review under either of those sections is amended in accordance with this paragraph, the order shall cease to be so subject.

2. A suspended sentence order made or amended in accordance with paragraph 1 must— **23–164**

(a) specify the local authority area in which the offender resides or will be residing when the order or amendment comes into force, and

(b) require the local authority for that area to appoint or assign an officer who will be responsible for discharging in relation to him the functions conferred on responsible officers by Part 12 of this Act;

and section 216 ([local justice area] to be specified) does not apply in relation to an order so made or amended.

3.—(1) Where a court makes or amends a suspended sentence order in accordance with paragraph 1, the court must provide the relevant documents to— **23–165**

(a) the local authority for the area specified in the order, and

(b) the sheriff court having jurisdiction in the locality in which the offender resides or proposes to reside;

and paragraphs (b) to (d) of subsection (1) of section 219 (provision of copies of relevant orders) do not apply in relation to an order so made or amended.

(2) In this paragraph, "the relevant documents" means—

(a) a copy of the order as made or amended, and

(b) such other documents and information relating to the case as the court making or amending the order considers likely to be of assistance.

4.—(1) In relation to the making or amendment of a suspended sentence order in accordance with paragraph 1, and (except for the purposes of paragraph 20) in relation to an order so made or amended, Chapter 4 of Part 12 of this Act has effect subject to the following modifications. **23–166**

(2) Any reference to the responsible officer has effect as a reference to the officer appointed or assigned under paragraph 2(b).

(3) The following provisions are omitted—

(a) subsection (7) of section 201 (activity requirement),

(b) subsection (7) of section 202 (programme requirement),

(c) subsection (4) of section 206 (residence requirement),

(d) subsection (4) of section 218 (availability of arrangements in local area).

(4) In section 207 (mental health treatment requirement), for subsection (2)(a) there is substituted—

"(a) treatment as a resident patient in a hospital within the meaning of the *Mental Health (Care and Treatment) (Scotland) Act* 2003, not being a state hospital within the meaning of that Act;".

(5) In section 215 (electronic monitoring requirement), in subsection (3), the words from "and" onwards are omitted.

5. In this Part of this Schedule "local authority" means a council constituted under section 2 of the *Local Government etc. (Scotland) Act* 1994; and any reference to the area of such an authority is a reference to the local government area within the meaning of that Act. **23–167**

PART 2

NORTHERN IRELAND

23–168 6.—(1) Where the court considering the making of a suspended sentence order is satisfied that the offender resides in Northern Ireland, or will reside there when the order comes into force, the court may not make a suspended sentence order in respect of the offender unless it appears to the court—

(a) in the case of an order imposing a requirement mentioned in subparagraph (2), that arrangements exist for persons to comply with such a requirement in the petty sessions district in Northern Ireland in which the offender resides, or will be residing when the order comes into force, and that provision can be made for him to comply with the requirement under those arrangements, and

(b) in any case, that suitable arrangements for his supervision can be made by the Probation Board for Northern Ireland.

(2) The requirements referred to in sub-paragraph (1)(a) are—

(a) an unpaid work requirement,
(b) an activity requirement,
(c) a programme requirement,
(d) a mental health treatment requirement,
(e) a drug rehabilitation requirement,
(f) an alcohol treatment requirement,
(g) an attendance centre requirement, and
(h) an electronic monitoring requirement.

(3) Where—

(a) the appropriate court for the purposes of paragraph 14 of Schedule 12 (amendment by reason of change of residence) is satisfied that an offender in respect of whom a suspended sentence order is in force proposes to reside or is residing in Northern Ireland, and

(b) it appears to the court that the conditions in sub-paragraphs (1)(a) and (b) are satisfied,

the power of the court to amend the order under Part 3 of Schedule 12 includes power to amend it by requiring it to be complied with in Northern Ireland and the offender to be supervised in accordance with the arrangements referred to in sub-paragraph (1)(b).

(4) For the purposes of sub-paragraph (3), any reference in sub-paragraph (1)(a) and (b) to the time when the order comes into force is to be treated as a reference to the time when the amendment comes into force.

(5) The court may not provide for an order made in accordance with this paragraph to be subject to review under section 191 or 210; and where an order which is subject to review under either of those sections is amended in accordance with this paragraph, the order shall cease to be so subject.

23–169 7. A suspended sentence order made or amended in accordance with paragraph 6 must—

(a) specify the petty sessions district in Northern Ireland in which the offender resides or will be residing when the order or amendment comes into force, and

(b) require the Probation Board for Northern Ireland to appoint or assign a probation officer who will be responsible for discharging in relation to him the functions conferred on responsible officers by Part 12 of this Act;

and section 216 ([local justice area] to be specified) does not apply in relation to an order so made or amended.

23–170 8.—(1) Where a court makes or amends a suspended sentence order in accordance with paragraph 6, the court must provide the relevant documents to—

(a) the Probation Board for Northern Ireland, and

(b) the court of summary jurisdiction acting for the petty sessions district in which the offender resides or proposes to reside;

and paragraphs (b) to (d) of subsection (1) of section 219 (provision of copies of relevant orders) do not apply in relation to an order so made or amended.

(2) In this paragraph, "the relevant documents" means—

(a) a copy of the order as made or amended, and

(b) such other documents and information relating to the case as the court making or amending the order considers likely to be of assistance.

9.—(1) In relation to the making or amendment of a suspended sentence order in accordance with paragraph 6, and (except for the purposes of paragraph 20) in relation to an order so made or amended, Chapter 4 of Part 12 of this Act has effect subject to the following modifications. **23–171**

(2) Any reference to the responsible officer has effect as a reference to the probation officer appointed or assigned under paragraph 7(b).

(3) The following provisions are omitted—

(a) subsection (7) of section 201 (activity requirement),

(b) subsection (7) of section 202 (programme requirement),

(c) subsection (4) of section 206 (residence requirement),

(d) subsection (4) of section 218 (availability of arrangements in local area).

(4) In section 207 (mental health treatment requirement), for subsection (2)(a) there is substituted—

"(a) treatment (whether as an in-patient or an out-patient) at such hospital as may be specified in the order, being a hospital within the meaning of the Health and Personal Social Services (Northern Ireland) Order 1972, approved by the Department of Health, Social Services and Public Safety for the purposes of paragraph 4(3) of Schedule 1 to the Criminal Justice (Northern Ireland) Order 1996 (S.I. 1996/ 3160 (N.I. 24));".

(5) In section 214 (attendance centre requirement), any reference to an attendance centre has effect as a reference to a day centre, as defined by paragraph 3(6) of Schedule 1 to the Criminal Justice (Northern Ireland) Order 1996 (S.I. 1996/3160 (N.I. 24).

(6) In section 215 (electronic monitoring requirement), in subsection (3), the words from "and" onwards are omitted.

PART 3

GENERAL PROVISIONS: BREACH OR AMENDMENT

10. This Part of this Schedule applies at any time while a suspended sentence order made or amended in accordance with paragraph 1 or 6 is in force in respect of an offender. **23–172**

11. In this Part of this Schedule— **23–173**

"home court" means —

(a) if the offender resides in Scotland, or will be residing there at the relevant time, the sheriff court having jurisdiction in the locality in which the offender resides or proposes to reside, and

(b) if he resides in Northern Ireland, or will be residing there at the relevant time, the court of summary jurisdiction acting for the petty sessions district in which he resides or proposes to reside;

"local authority" and "local authority area" are to be read in accordance with paragraph 5;

"original court" means the court in England and Wales which made or last amended the order;

"the relevant officer" means —

(a) where the order specifies a local authority area in Scotland, the local authority officer appointed or assigned under paragraph 2(b), and

(b) where the court specifies a petty sessions district in Northern Ireland, the probation officer appointed or assigned under paragraph 7(b);

"the relevant time" means the time when the order or the amendment to it comes into force.

12.—(1) Where this Part of this Schedule applies, Schedule 12 has effect subject to the following modifications. **23–174**

(2) Any reference to the responsible officer has effect as a reference to the relevant officer.

(3) Any reference to a magistrates' court acting in the local justice area concerned has

effect as a reference to a magistrates' court acting in the same local justice area as the original court; and any reference to a justice of the peace acting in the local justice area concerned has effect as a reference to a justice of the peace acting in the same local justice area as that court.

(4) Any reference to the appropriate court has effect as a reference to the original court.

(5) In paragraphs 4 and 5, any reference to causing an information to be laid before a justice of the peace has effect—

(a) if the home court is in Scotland, as a reference to providing information to the home court with a view to it issuing a citation, and

(b) if the home court is in Northern Ireland, as a reference to making a complaint to a justice of the peace in Northern Ireland.

(5A) In paragraph 6(3)(b), the words "before a magistrates' court acting in the local justice area in which the offender resides or, if it is not known where he resides," are omitted.

(6) In paragraph 14—

(a) if the home court is in Scotland—

(i) any reference to the [local justice area] concerned has effect as a reference to the local authority area specified in the order, and

(ii) any other reference to a [local justice area] has effect as a reference to a local authority area, and

(b) if the home court is in Northern Ireland—

(i) any reference to the [local justice area] concerned has effect as a reference to the petty sessions district specified in the order, and

(ii) any other reference to a [local justice area] has effect as a reference to a petty sessions district.

(7) Paragraph 22 is omitted.

(8) No court in England and Wales may—

(a) exercise any power in relation to any failure by the offender to comply with any community requirement of the order unless the offender has been required in accordance with paragraph 14(1)(b) or (2)(a) of this Schedule to appear before that court;

(b) exercise any power under Part 3 of Schedule 12 unless the offender has been required in accordance with paragraph 15(2) or 16 of this Schedule to appear before that court.

[This paragraph is printed as substituted by the *Courts Act 2003 (Consequential Provisions) Order* 2005 (S.I. 2005 No.886).]

23–175 13.—(1) Sub-paragraph (2) applies where it appears to the home court—

(a) if that court is in Scotland, on information from the relevant officer, or

(b) if that court is in Northern Ireland, upon a complaint being made by the relevant officer,

that the offender has failed without reasonable excuse to comply with any of the community requirements of the suspended sentence order.

(2) The home court may—

(a) if it is in Scotland—

(i) issue a citation requiring the offender to appear before it at the time specified in the citation, or

(ii) issue a warrant for the offender's arrest;

(b) if it is in Northern Ireland–

(i) issue a summons requiring the offender to appear before it at the time specified in the summons, or

(ii) issue a warrant for the offender's arrest.

23–176 14.—(1) The court before which an offender appears or is brought by virtue of paragraph 13 must—

(a) determine whether the offender has failed without reasonable excuse to comply with any of the community requirements of the suspended sentence order, or

(b) require the offender to appear before the original court.

(2) If the home court determines that the offender has failed without reasonable excuse to comply with any of the community requirements of the order—

(a) the home court must require the offender to appear before the original court, and

(b) when the offender appears before the original court, paragraph 8 of Schedule 12 applies as if it had already been proved to the satisfaction of the original court that the offender failed without reasonable excuse to comply with such of the community requirements of the order as may have been determined.

(3) An offender who is required by any of the following community requirements of a suspended sentence order—

(a) a mental health treatment requirement,

(b) a drug rehabilitation requirement, or

(c) an alcohol treatment requirement,

to submit to treatment for his mental condition, or his dependency on or propensity to misuse drugs or alcohol, is not to be treated for the purposes of sub-paragraph (2) as having failed to comply with that requirement on the ground only that he had refused to undergo any surgical, electrical or other treatment if, in the opinion of the court, his refusal was reasonable having regard to all the circumstances.

(4) The evidence of one witness shall, for the purposes of sub-paragraph (2), be sufficient.

(5) Where the home court is in Scotland and the order contains an electronic monitoring requirement, section 245H of the *Criminal Procedure (Scotland) Act* 1995 (documentary evidence) applies to proceedings under this paragraph as it applies to proceedings under section 245F of that Act (breach of restriction of liberty order).

(6) Where an offender is required by virtue of sub-paragraph (2) to appear before the original court—

(a) the home court must send to the original court a certificate certifying that the offender has failed without reasonable excuse to comply with the requirements of the order in the respect specified, and

(b) such a certificate signed by the clerk of the home court is admissible before the original court as conclusive evidence of the matters specified in it.

15.—(1) The home court may exercise any power under Part 3 of Schedule 12 (amendment of suspended sentence order) as if it were the original court, except that the home court may not exercise the power conferred by paragraph 15(4) of that Schedule. **23–177**

(2) Where paragraph 15(4) of Schedule 12 applies the home court must require the offender to appear before the original court.

(3) Subject to sub-paragraph (4), where the home court proposes to exercise the power conferred by paragraph 15(1) of Schedule 12, otherwise than on the application of the offender, the court—

(a) if it is in Scotland—

(i) must issue a citation requiring the offender to appear before it, and

(ii) if he does not appear in answer to the citation, may issue a warrant for the offender's arrest;

(b) if it is in Northern Ireland—

(i) must issue a summons requiring the offender to appear before it, and

(ii) if he does not appear in answer to the summons, may issue a warrant for the offender's arrest;

and paragraph 20 of Schedule 12 does not apply to the home court.

(4) Sub-paragraph (3) does not apply to an order cancelling any community requirement of a suspended sentence order.

(5) Where the home court is considering amending a suspended sentence order, any reference in Chapter 4 of Part 12 of this Act to a local probation board has effect as a reference to a local authority in Scotland or, as the case may be, the Probation Board for Northern Ireland.

16. Where by virtue of paragraph 15 any application is made to the home court under Part 3 of Schedule 12, the home court may (instead of dealing with the application) require the offender to appear before the original court. **23–178**

17. No court may amend or further amend a suspended sentence order unless it ap- **23–179**

pears to the court that the conditions in paragraph 1(1)(a) and (b) or, as the case may be, paragraph 6(1)(a) and (b) are satisfied in relation to any requirement to be imposed; but this paragraph does not apply to any amendment by virtue of paragraph 20(2).

23–180 18. The preceding paragraphs of this Schedule have effect in relation to any amendment of a suspended order by any court as they have effect in relation to the amendment of such an order by virtue of paragraph 1(3) or 6(3).

23–181 19. On the making of an order amending a suspended sentence order—

(a) the court must provide copies of the amending order to the offender and the relevant officer, and

(b) in the case of an amending order which substitutes a new local authority area or petty sessions district, paragraphs 2 and 3 or, as the case may be, 7 and 8 have effect in relation to the order as they have effect in relation to an order made or amended in accordance with paragraph 1 or 6.

23–182 20.—(1) This paragraph applies where the home court is satisfied that the offender is residing or proposes to reside in England and Wales.

(2) Subject to sub-paragraphs (3) and (4), the home court may, and on the application of the relevant officer must, amend the suspended sentence order by requiring it to be complied with in England and Wales.

(3) The court may not amend under this paragraph a suspended sentence order which contains requirements which, in the opinion of the court, cannot be complied within the local justice area in which the offender is residing or proposes to reside unless, in accordance with paragraph 15 of Schedule 12 it either—

(a) cancels those requirements, or

(b) substitutes for those requirements other requirements which can be complied with if the offender resides in that area.

(4) The court may not amend under this paragraph any suspended sentence order imposing a programme requirement unless it appears to the court that the accredited programme specified in the requirement is available in the local justice area in England and Wales in which the offender is residing or proposes to reside.

(5) The suspended sentence order as amended must specify the petty sessions area in which the offender resides or proposes to reside.

(6) On the making under this paragraph of an order amending a suspended sentence order, the home court must—

(a) provide copies of the amending order to the offender, the relevant officer and the local probation board acting in the new local justice area, or (as the case may be) a provider of probation services operating in the new local justice area and

(b) provide the magistrates' court acting in that area with a copy of the amending order and such other documents and information relating to the case as the home court considers likely to be of assistance to a court acting in that area in the exercise of its functions in relation to the order.

(7) Where an order has been amended under this paragraph, the preceding paragraphs of this Schedule shall cease to apply to the order as amended.

PART 4

SUPPLEMENTARY

23–183 21. Subsections (1) and (3) of section 245C of the *Criminal Procedure (Scotland) Act* 1995 (provision of remote monitoring) have effect as if they included a reference to the electronic monitoring of the community requirements of a suspended sentence order made or amended in accordance with paragraph 1 of this Schedule.

23–184 22.—(1) Section 4 of the *Summary Jurisdiction (Process) Act* 1881 (which provides, among other things, for service in England and Wales of Scottish citations or warrants) applies to any citation or warrant issued under paragraph 13(2)(a) or 15(3)(a) as it applies to a citation or warrant granted under section 134 of the *Criminal Procedure (Scotland) Act* 1995.

(2) A summons issued by a court in Northern Ireland under paragraph 13(2)(b) or 15(3)(b) may, in such circumstances as may be prescribed by rules of court, be served in England and Wales or Scotland.

(5) Breach of suspended sentence order

A Suspended Sentence Order may be breached either by the commission of a further offence or by failure to comply with the requirements without reasonable excuse. Note that the further offence does not need to be punishable by imprisonment (Sched. 12, para. 8(1)(b) to the *Criminal Justice Act* 2003). There is a presumption in favour of implementing the suspended sentence either in full or with a reduced custodial term: see further at 24–133, *post*. Where a court considers that such implementation would be unjust (Sched. 12, para. 8(3)) in all the circumstances (including the extent of compliance so far and the facts of the later offence (Sched. 12, para. 8(4)), then the court may only amend the order in one of three ways—imposing more onerous requirements, extending the supervision period or extending the operational period. There is no power to alter the custodial term at this stage, nor to "take no action". Where the breach is of one of the requirements, the Sentencing Guidelines Council's Guideline emphasises that the primary purpose of enforcement is to ensure that the order of the court is complied with. A court has required the offender to undertake certain requirements and the court can legitimately expect the offender to fulfil the obligation imposed by the court. However, it would have been made clear to the offender when sentence was passed that a custodial sentence would follow non-compliance, and, in many circumstances, there is likely to be little alternative. This again emphasises the need for particular care in choosing between a Community Order and a Suspended Sentence Order. **23–185**

D. Release from Custody

(1) Purpose and effect

A defendant will be released before the end of the period ordered by the court. There are rules that govern the earliest date of release which can be a complex blend of periods spent in custody on remand, the length of the sentence ordered by the court, and the availability of home detention curfew. In terms of sentencing in a magistrates' court, the critical distinction is that a person sentenced to under 12 months is currently released unconditionally on completing one half of the sentence whereas a person sentenced to 12 months will be released on licence on serving one half of the sentence: *Criminal Justice Act* 2003, s.244. There is also a discretionary power to release earlier on licence: s.246. **23–186**

A person released early in these ways may be recalled.

The *Powers of Criminal Courts (Sentencing) Act* 2000 made provision for a person serving a sentence of less than 12 months to be returned to prison when a further offence was committed after his early release. This is still scheduled to be repealed but it has been preserved pending the full introduction of the new sentence regime of the *Criminal Justice Act* 2003.

The complexities that may arise from the different regimes that apply to sentences depending on whether or not the offence was committed on or after April 4, 2005 were extensively considered by the Court of Appeal in *Costello* [2010] EWCA Crim 371. In a seminal judgment, Hughes L.J. recited the various combinations of events and options available. Since the issues are rarely likely to arise in a magistrates' court, they are not detailed in this work.

Powers of the Criminal Courts (Sentencing) Act 2000 s.116

Power to order return to prison etc. where offence committed during original sentence

116.—(1) This section applies to a person if—

(a) he has been serving a determinate sentence of imprisonment which he began serving on or after 1st October 1992;

(b) he is released under Part II of the *Criminal Justice Act* 1991 (early release of prisoners)

(c) before the date on which he would (but for his release) have served his sentence in full, he commits an offence punishable with imprisonment ("the new offence"); and

(d) whether before or after that date, he is convicted of the new offence.

(2) Subject to subsection (3) below, the court by or before which a person to whom this section applies is convicted of the new offence may, whether or not it passes any other sentence on him, order him to be returned to prison for the whole or any part of the period which—

(a) begins with the date of the order; and

(b) is equal in length to the period between the date on which the new offence was committed and the date mentioned in subsection (1)(c) above.

(3) A magistrates' court—

(a) shall not have power to order a person to whom this section applies to be returned to prison for a period of more than six months; but

(b) subject to section 25 of the *Criminal Justice and Public Order Act* 1994 (restrictions on granting bail), may commit him in custody or on bail to the Crown Court to be dealt with under subsection (4) below.

(4) Where a person is committed to the Crown Court under subsection (3) above, the Crown Court may order him to be returned to prison for the whole or any part of the period which—

(a) begins with the date of the order; and

(b) is equal in length to the period between the date on which the new offence was committed and the date mentioned in subsection (1)(c) above.

(5) Subsection (3)(b) above shall not be taken to confer on the magistrates' court a power to commit the person to the Crown Court for sentence for the new offence, but this is without prejudice to any such power conferred on the magistrates' court by any other provision of this Act.

(6) The period for which a person to whom this section applies is ordered under subsection (2) or (4) above to be returned to prison—

(a) shall be taken to be a sentence of imprisonment for the purposes of Part II of the *Criminal Justice Act* 1991 and this section;

(b) shall, as the court may direct, either be served before and be followed by, or be served concurrently with, the sentence imposed for the new offence; and

(c) in either case, shall be disregarded in determining the appropriate length of that sentence.

(7) As a consequence of subsection (6)(a) above, the court shall not be prevented by section 84 above from making any direction authorised by subsection (6)(b) above.

(8) Where the new offence is found to have been committed over a period of two or more days, or at some time during a period of two or more days, it shall be taken for the purposes of this section to have been committed on the last of those days.

(9) For the purposes of sections 9 and 10 of the *Criminal Appeal Act* 1968 (rights of appeal), any order made in respect of a person by the Crown Court under subsection (2) or (4) above shall be treated as a sentence passed on him for the offence for which the sentence referred to in subsection (1) above was passed.

(10) This section and section 117 below apply to persons serving—

(a) determinate sentences of detention under section 91 above, or

(b) sentences of detention in a young offender institution,

as they apply to persons serving equivalent sentences of imprisonment; and references in this section and section 117 to imprisonment or prison shall be construed accordingly.

(11) In this section "sentence of imprisonment" does not include a committal for contempt of court or any kindred offence.

[This section is printed as preserved by the *Criminal Justice Act 2003 (Commencement No.8 and Transitional Savings Provisions) Order* 2005; S.I. No.950 of 2005.]

Criminal Justice Act 2003, ss.244–246, 248–253

Duty to release prisoners

23–187 **244.**—(1) As soon as a fixed-term prisoner, other than a prisoner to whom section 247 applies, has served the requisite custodial period, it is the duty of the Secretary of State to release him on licence under this section.

(2) Subsection (1) is subject to section 245.

(3) In this section "the requisite custodial period" means—

(a) in relation to a person serving a sentence of imprisonment for a term of twelve months or more or any determinate sentence of detention under section 91 or 96 of the Sentencing Act, one-half of his sentence,

(b) in relation to a person serving a sentence of imprisonment for a term of less than twelve months (other than one to which an intermittent custody order relates), the custodial period within the meaning of section 181,

(c) in relation to a person serving a sentence of imprisonment to which an intermittent custody order relates, any part of the term which for the purposes of section 183(3) section 183 (as read with section 263(2) or 264A(2) in the case of concurrent or consecutive sentences) is not a licence period], and

(d) in relation to a person serving two or more concurrent or consecutive sentences none of which falls within paragraph (c), the period determined under sections 263(2) and 264(2).

Restrictions on operation of section 244(1) in relation to intermittent custody prisoners

245.—(1) Where an intermittent custody prisoner returns to custody after being unlawfully at large within the meaning of section 49 of the Prison Act 1952 at any time during the currency of his sentence, section 244(1) does not apply until— **23–188**

(a) the relevant time (as defined in subsection (2)), or

(b) if earlier, the date on which he has served in prison the number of custodial days required by the intermittent custody order.

(2) In subsection (1)(a) "the relevant time" means—

(a) in a case where, within the period of 72 hours beginning with the return to custody of the intermittent custody prisoner, the Secretary of State or the responsible officer has applied to the court for the amendment of the intermittent custody order under paragraph 6(1)(b) of Schedule 10, the date on which the application is withdrawn or determined, and

(b) in any other case, the end of that 72-hour period.

(3) Section 244(1) does not apply in relation to an intermittent custody prisoner at any time after he has been recalled under section 254, unless after his recall the Board has directed his further release on licence.

Power to release prisoners on licence before required to do so

246.—(1) Subject to subsections (2) to (4), the Secretary of State may— **23–189**

(a) release on licence under this section a fixed-term prisoner, other than an intermittent custody prisoner, at any time during the period of 135 days ending with the day on which the prisoner will have served the requisite custodial period, and

(b) release on licence under this section an intermittent custody prisoner when 135 or less of the required custodial days remain to be served.

(2) Subsection (1)(a) does not apply in relation to a prisoner unless—

(a) the length of the requisite custodial period is at least 6 weeks, and

(b) he has served—

(i) at least 4 weeks of that period, and

(ii) at least one-half of that period.

(3) Subsection (1)(b) does not apply in relation to a prisoner unless—

(a) the number of required custodial days is at least 42, and

(b) the prisoner has served—

(i) at least 28 of those days, and

(ii) at least one-half of the total number of those days.

(4) Subsection (1) does not apply where—

(a) the sentence is imposed under section 227 or 228,

(b) the sentence is for an offence under section 1 of the *Prisoners (Return to Custody) Act* 1995,

(c) the prisoner is subject to a hospital order, hospital direction or transfer direction under section 37, 45A or 47 of the *Mental Health Act* 1983,

(d) the sentence was imposed by virtue of paragraph 9(1)(b) or (c) or 10(1)(b) or (c) of Schedule 8 in a case where the prisoner has failed to comply with a curfew requirement of a community order,

(e) the prisoner is subject to the notification requirements of Part 2 of the *Sexual Offences Act* 2003,

(f) the prisoner is liable to removal from the United Kingdom,

(g) the prisoner has been released on licence under this section during the currency of the sentence, and has been recalled to prison under section 255(1)(a),

(h) the prisoner has been released on licence under section 248 during the currency of the sentence, and has been recalled to prison under section 254, or

(i) in the case of a prisoner to whom a direction under section 240 or 240A relates, the interval between the date on which the sentence was passed and the date on which the prisoner will have served the requisite custodial period is less than 14 days or, where the sentence is one of intermittent custody, the number of the required custodial days remaining to be served is less than 14.

(4A) In subsection (4)—

(a) the reference in paragraph (d) to a community order includes a service community order or overseas community order under the *Armed Forces Act* 2006; and

(b) the reference in paragraph (i) to a direction under section 240 includes a direction under section 246 of that Act.

(5) The Secretary of State may by order—

(a) amend the number of days for the time being specified in subsection (1)(a) or (b), (3) or (4)(i),

(b) amend the number of weeks for the time being specified in subsection (2)(a) or (b)(i), and

(c) amend the fraction for the time being specified in subsection (2)(b)(ii) or (3)(b)(ii).

(6) In this section—

"the required custodial days", in relation to an intermittent custody prisoner, means —

(a) the number of custodial days specified under section 183, or

(b) in the case of two or more sentences of intermittent custody which are consecutive, the aggregate of the numbers so specified, or

(c) in the case of two or more sentences of intermittent custody which are wholly or partly concurrent, the aggregate of the numbers so specified less the number of days that are to be served concurrently;

"the requisite custodial period" in relation to a person serving any sentence other than a sentence of intermittent custody, has the meaning given by paragraph (a), (b) or (d) of section 244(3);

"sentence of intermittent custody" means a sentence to which an intermittent custody order relates.

Power to release prisoners on compassionate grounds

23–190 **248.**—(1) The Secretary of State may at any time release a fixed-term prisoner on licence if he is satisfied that exceptional circumstances exist which justify the prisoner's release on compassionate grounds.

(2) Before releasing under this section a prisoner to whom section 247 applies, the Secretary of State must consult the Board, unless the circumstances are such as to render such consultation impracticable.

Duration of licence

23–191 **249.**—(1) Subject to subsections (2) and (3), where a fixed-term prisoner is released on licence, the licence shall, subject to any revocation under section 254 or 255, remain in force for the remainder of his sentence.

(2) Where an intermittent custody prisoner is released on licence under section 244, the licence shall, subject to any revocation under section 254, remain in force—

(a) until the time when he is required to return to prison at the beginning of the next custodial period of the sentence, or

(b) where it is granted at the end of the last custodial period, for the remainder of his sentence.

(3) Subsection (1) has effect subject to sections 263(2) (concurrent terms) and 264(3) and

(4) (consecutive terms) and subsection (2) has effect subject to section 264A(3) (consecutive terms: intermittent custody).

(4) In subsection (2) "custodial period", in relation to a sentence to which an intermittent custody order relates, means any period which is not a licence period as defined by 183(3).

Licence conditions

250.—(1) In this section— **23–192**

(a) "the standard conditions" means such conditions as may be prescribed for the purposes of this section as standard conditions, and

(b) "prescribed" means prescribed by the Secretary of State by order.

(2) Subject to subsection (6) and section 251, any licence under this Chapter in respect of a prisoner serving one or more sentences of imprisonment of less than twelve months and no sentence of twelve months or more—

(a) must include—

(i) the conditions required by the relevant court order, and

(ii) so far as not inconsistent with them, the standard conditions, and

(b) may also include—

(i) any condition which is authorised by section 62 of the *Criminal Justice and Court Services Act* 2000 (electronic monitoring) or section 64 of that Act (drug testing requirements) and which is compatible with the conditions required by the relevant court order, and

(ii) such other conditions of a kind prescribed for the purposes of this paragraph as the Secretary of State may for the time being consider to be necessary for the protection of the public and specify in the licence.

(2A) If the sentence (or, if more than one, each sentence) that the prisoner is serving is one in relation to which no custody plus or intermittent custody order is in force, subsection (2) has effect as if there were omitted—

(a) paragraph (a)(i);

(b) the words "so far as not inconsistent with them," in paragraph (a)(ii); and

(c) the words from "and which" in paragraph (b)(i).

(3) For the purposes of subsection (2)(a)(i), any reference in the relevant court order to the licence period specified in the order is, in relation to a prohibited activity requirement, exclusion requirement, residence requirement or supervision requirement, to be taken to include a reference to any other period during which the prisoner is released on licence under section 246 or 248.

(4) Any licence under this Chapter in respect of a prisoner serving a sentence of imprisonment or detention in a young offender institution for a term of twelve months or more (including such a sentence imposed under section 227) or any sentence of detention under section 91 of the Sentencing Act or section 228 of this Act—

(a) must include the standard conditions, and

(b) may include—

(i) any condition authorised by section 62 or 64 of the *Criminal Justice and Court Services Act* 2000 or section 28 of the Offender Management Act 2007, and

(ii) such other conditions of a kind prescribed by the Secretary of State for the purposes of this paragraph as the Secretary of State may for the time being specify in the licence.

(5) A licence under section 246 must also include a curfew condition complying with section 253.

(6) Where—

(a) a licence under section 246 is granted to a prisoner serving one or more sentences of imprisonment of less than 12 months and no sentence of 12 months or more, and

(b) the relevant court order requires the licence to be granted subject to a condition requiring his compliance with a curfew requirement (as defined by section 204),

that condition is not to be included in the licence at any time while a curfew condition required by section 253 is in force.

(7) The preceding provisions of this section have effect subject to section 263(3) (concur-

Part IV

rent terms), section 264(3) and (4), (consecutive terms) and section 264A(3) (consecutive terms: intermittent custody).

(8) In exercising his powers to prescribe standard conditions or the other conditions referred to in subsection (4)(b)(ii), the Secretary of State must have regard to the following purposes of the supervision of offenders while on licence under this Chapter—

(a) the protection of the public,
(b) the prevention of re-offending, and
(c) securing the successful re-integration of the prisoner into the community.

Licence conditions on re-release of prisoner serving sentence of less than 12 months

23–193 **251.**—(1) In relation to any licence under this Chapter which is granted to a prisoner serving one or more sentences of imprisonment of less than twelve months and no sentence of twelve months or more on his release in pursuance of a decision of the Board under section 254 or 256, subsections (2) and (3) apply instead of section 250(2).

(2) The licence—

(a) must include the standard conditions, and
(b) may include—
    (i) any condition authorised by section 62 or 64 of the *Criminal Justice and Court Services Act* 2000, and
    (ii) such other conditions of a kind prescribed by the Secretary of State for the purposes of section 250(4)(b)(ii) as the Secretary of State may for the time being specify in the licence.

(3) In exercising his powers under subsection (2)(b)(ii), the Secretary of State must have regard to the terms of the relevant court order (if any).

(4) In this section "the standard conditions" has the same meaning as in section 250.

Duty to comply with licence conditions

23–194 **252.**—(1) A person subject to a licence under this Chapter must comply with such conditions as may for the time being be specified in the licence.

(2) But where—

(a) the licence relates to a sentence of imprisonment passed by a service court,
(b) no custody plus order was made in relation to the sentence, or such an order was made but subsequently revoked, and
(c) the person is residing outside the British Islands,

the conditions specified in the licence apply to him only so far as it is practicable for him to comply with them where he is residing.

Curfew condition to be included in licence under section 246

23–195 **253.**—(1) For the purposes of this Chapter, a curfew condition is a condition which—

(a) requires the released person to remain, for periods for the time being specified in the condition, at a place for the time being so specified (which may be premises approved by the Secretary of State under section 13 of the *Offender Management Act 2007*), and
(b) includes requirements for securing the electronic monitoring of his whereabouts during the periods for the time being so specified.

(2) The curfew condition may specify different places or different periods for different days, but may not specify periods which amount to less than 9 hours in any one day (excluding for this purpose the first and last days of the period for which the condition is in force).

(3) The curfew condition is to remain in force until the date when the released person would (but for his release) fall to be released on licence under section 244.

(4) Subsection (3) does not apply in relation to a released person to whom an intermittent custody order relates; and in relation to such a person the curfew condition is to remain in force until the number of days during which it has been in force is equal to the number of the required custodial days, as defined in section 246(6), that remained to be served at the time when he was released under section 246.

(5) The curfew condition must include provision for making a person responsible for monitoring the released person's whereabouts during the periods for the time being specified in the condition; and a person who is made so responsible shall be of a description specified in an order made by the Secretary of State.

(6) Nothing in this section is to be taken to require the Secretary of State to ensure that arrangements are made for the electronic monitoring of released persons' whereabouts in any particular part of England and Wales.

E. COMPENSATION ORDERS

(1) Purpose and effect

A compensation order enables a court to require an offender to provide financial compensation for loss or harm caused by the offence. It is designed for use in simple, straightforward circumstances. It can either be a sentence in its own right or an ancillary order. If no order is made in circumstances where the court has the power to make such an order, then the court must give its reasons for not making the compensation order. This emphasises the importance of this part of the sentencing task which directly recognises the impact of the crime on any victim. **23–196**

The existence of civil liability is not a precondition to the making of a compensation order: *Chappel* (1985) 80 Cr.App.R. 31, CA. Causation must be established before a compensation order is made, though the court does not need to apply the strict test of causation applied in the field of tort: *Derby* (1990) 12 Cr.App.R.(S.) 502, CA.

Powers of Criminal Courts (Sentencing) Act 2000, ss.130, 131

Compensation orders against convicted persons

130.—(1) A court by or before which a person is convicted of an offence, instead of or in addition to dealing with him in any other way, may, on application or otherwise, make an order (in this Act referred to as a "compensation order") requiring him— **23–197**

(a) to pay compensation for any personal injury, loss or damage resulting from that offence or any other offence which is taken into consideration by the court in determining sentence; or

(b) to make payments for funeral expenses or bereavement in respect of a death resulting from any such offence, other than a death due to an accident arising out of the presence of a motor vehicle on a road;

but this is subject to the following provisions of this section and to section 131 below.

(2) Where the person is convicted of an offence the sentence for which is fixed by law or falls to be imposed under section 110(2) or 111(2) above, section 51A(2) of the *Firearms Act* 1968 or section 225(2) or 226(2) of the *Criminal Justice Act* 2003 or section 29(4) or (6) of the *Violent Crime Reduction Act* 2006, subsection (1) above shall have effect as if the words "instead of or" were omitted.

(3) A court shall give reasons, on passing sentence, if it does not make a compensation order in a case where this section empowers it to do so.

(4) Compensation under subsection (1) above shall be of such amount as the court considers appropriate, having regard to any evidence and to any representations that are made by or on behalf of the accused or the prosecutor.

(5) In the case of an offence under the *Theft Act* 1968, where the property in question is recovered, any damage to the property occurring while it was out of the owner's possession shall be treated for the purposes of subsection (1) above as having resulted from the offence, however and by whomever the damage was caused.

(6) A compensation order may only be made in respect of injury, loss or damage (other than loss suffered by a person's dependants in consequence of his death) which was due to an accident arising out of the presence of a motor vehicle on a road, if—

(a) it is in respect of damage which is treated by subsection (5) above as resulting from an offence under the *Theft Act* 1968; or

(b) it is in respect of injury, loss or damage as respects which—

(i) the offender is uninsured in relation to the use of the vehicle; and

(ii) compensation is not payable under any arrangements to which the Secretary of State is a party.

(7) Where a compensation order is made in respect of injury, loss or damage due to an accident arising out of the presence of a motor vehicle on a road, the amount to be paid may include an amount representing the whole or part of any loss of or reduction in preferential rates of insurance attributable to the accident.

(8) A vehicle the use of which is exempted from insurance by section 144 of the *Road Traffic Act* 1988 is not uninsured for the purposes of subsection (6) above.

(9) A compensation order in respect of funeral expenses may be made for the benefit of any one who incurred the expenses.

(10) A compensation order in respect of bereavement may be made only for the benefit of a person for whose benefit a claim for damages for bereavement could be made under section 1A of the *Fatal Accidents Act* 1976; and the amount of compensation in respect of bereavement shall not exceed the amount for the time being specified in section 1A(3) of that Act [presently £11,800].

(11) In determining whether to make a compensation order against any person, and in determining the amount to be paid by any person under such an order, the court shall have regard to his means so far as they appear or are known to the court.

(12) Where the court considers—

(a) that it would be appropriate both to impose a fine and to make a compensation order, but

(b) that the offender has insufficient means to pay both an appropriate fine and appropriate compensation,

the court shall give preference to compensation (though it may impose a fine as well).

Limit on amount payable under compensation order of magistrates' court.

23–198 **131.**—(1) The compensation to be paid under a compensation order made by a magistrates' court in respect of any offence of which the court has convicted the offender shall not exceed £5,000.

(2) The compensation or total compensation to be paid under a compensation order or compensation orders made by a magistrates' court in respect of any offence or offence taken into consideration in determining sentence shall not exceed the difference (if any) between—

(a) the amount or total amount which under subsection (1) above is the maximum for the offence or offences of which the offender has been convicted; and

(b) the amount or total amounts (if any) which are in fact ordered to be paid in respect of that offence or those offences

23–199 Where there are limited financial resources, compensation takes priority over a fine and the "victims' surcharge" (see *ante*, § 23–20). Similarly, where both compensation and confiscation are available sentences, compensation is the first priority. If it is possible to impose both penalties, that course may be followed. If not the court can reduce the amount of the confiscation order by virtue of s.71(1C) of the *Criminal Justice Act* 1988, or make no confiscation order, or make both confiscation and compensation orders and add a direction under s.72(7) of the 1988 Act: *Mitchell and Mitchell* [2001] 2 Cr.App.R.(S.) 29, CA.

A compensation order may not be made in respect of admitted offences which have not been charged or formally taken into consideration: *Hose* (1995) 16 Cr.App.R.(S.) 682, CA.

The thorny question of whether to make a compensation order when imposing a custodial sentence fell to be considered again in *Cooper* [2004] EWCA Crim 950. The defendant had had a serious argument with his wife and completely lost self control. He got into his motor vehicle (for which he was not insured) and drove it around a housing estate. During that drive he damaged five other vehicles (three deliberately) as well as some gates and fences. He was self-employed as a tree surgeon. Whilst upholding the sentence of 18 months' imprisonment (for dangerous driving) and the three year disqualification from driving, the Court of Appeal set aside the compensation order. Confirming that "the court must have regard to the means of the offender when making such orders, so far as those means are known to the court, and that the compensation should not be of such an amount that the offender has no prospect of paying it from his available resources within a reasonable time", the court stated that the defendant would "need to re-establish himself in his chosen trade as a tree surgeon. He will have no little difficulty doing that without the ability to drive and his disqualification will have some years to run at that stage."

The amount of the order will be such as the court considers appropriate having regard to any evidence and to any representations that are made by or on behalf of the accused or the prosecutor up to the maximum of £5000 for each offence of which the defendant is convicted. Where the defendant challenges the basis on which any compensation order is made and real issues are raised as to whether the claimants have suffered any, and if so what loss, evidence must be received to establish the defendant's liability to pay compensation: *Horsham Justices, ex p. Richards* [1985] 2 All E.R. 1114, DC.

The *Magistrates' Court Sentencing Guidelines* gives more detailed guidance both on the approach to making an order and to the level of compensation that should be considered as a starting point. These levels are consistent with those used by the Criminal Injuries Compensation Authority (which makes no award where the loss is less than £1,000) and include physical injury, mental injury and physical and sexual abuse. The guidelines emphasise the importance of ascertaining the wishes of the victim of the crime as part of the process of considering a compensation order stressing that compensation is intended to benefit the victim not to inflict further harm: Guidelines, p.165, para. 6. Whilst it is likely to be possible to agree any financial loss, there will be cases in which that is not possible. The Guidelines suggest a slightly more flexible approach than has been adopted in the past by stating that the amount of the order should represent the "agreed or likely loss": Guidelines, p.165, para. 7. **23–200**

This trend has been continued in *Pola* [2009] EWCA Crim 655 in which serious injury was caused following breaches of obligations under health and safety legislation. It was argued that compensation orders should be confined to simple and straightforward cases where the amount of compensation can be readily and easily ascertained. The Court of Appeal rejected that approach and upheld the decision to award £90,000 noting that this was within the means of the offender (and that fines had been adjusted to ensure that it could be paid) and that the injured person would not benefit under any insurance policy, would not qualify under the criminal injuries compensation scheme, would be unlikely to succeed in civil action because of the appellant's means and was not entitled to state benefits either in this country or in his home country (Slovakia). The suggested bracket for damages was between £58,000 and £96,000 with some features suggesting a higher award could be justified. Attention was drawn to other cases in which a court had determined compensation in the face of complex issues and disputed evidence and to the growing expertise of courts developing from confiscation proceedings. Here, there was a clear causal link between the conviction and the injury, there was sufficient evidence to show that the gravity of the injury would justify an award far in excess of what the court was contemplating and there was no more convenient or practicable alternative route available to the injured person. The order was within the means of the defendant and was just and proper in the context of his culpability.

Magistrates' Court Sentencing Guidelines

COMPENSATION

1. The court must consider making a compensation order in any case where personal injury, loss or damage has resulted from the offence. It can either be a sentence in its own right or an ancillary order. The court must give reasons if it decides not to order compensation. **23–201**

2. Up to £5,000 compensation may be imposed in respect of each offence of which the offender has been convicted. Compensation may also be ordered in respect of offences taken into consideration. The total amount of compensation must not exceed the maximum available for the offence(s) of which the offender has been convicted so that, for example, where an offender has been convicted of two offences, the maximum amount of compensation able to be awarded is £10,000 regardless of the number of offences taken into consideration.

3. Where the personal injury, loss or damage arises from a road accident, a compensation order may be made only if there is a conviction for an offence under the Theft Act 1968, or the offender is uninsured and the Motor Insurers' Bureau will not cover the loss. Compensation paid by the Motor Insurers' Bureau is subject to an excess of £300.

4. Subject to consideration of the victim's views (see paragraph 6 below), the court must order compensation wherever possible and should not have regard to the availability of other sources such as civil litigation or the Criminal Injuries Compensation Scheme. Any amount paid by an offender under a compensation order will generally be deducted from a subsequent civil award or payment under the Scheme to avoid double compensation.

5. Compensation may be ordered for such amount as the court considers appropriate having regard to any evidence and any representations made by the offender or prosecutor. The court must also take into account the offender's means (see also paragraphs 11–13 below).

6. Compensation should benefit, not inflict further harm on, the victim. Any financial recompense from the offender may cause distress. A victim may or may not want compensation from the offender and assumptions should not be made either way. The victim's views are properly obtained through sensitive discussion by the police or witness care unit, when it can be explained that the offender's ability to pay will ultimately determine whether, and how much, compensation is ordered and whether the compensation will be paid in one lump sum or by instalments. If the victim does not want compensation, this should be made known to the court and respected.

7. In cases where it is difficult to ascertain the full amount of the loss suffered by the victim, consideration should be given to making a compensation order for an amount representing the agreed or likely loss. Where relevant information is not immediately available, it may be appropriate to grant an adjournment for it to be obtained.

8. The court should consider two types of loss:

- financial loss sustained as a result of the offence such as the cost of repairing damage or, in case of injury, any loss of earnings or medical expenses;
- pain and suffering caused by the injury (including terror, shock or distress) and any loss of facility. This should be assessed in light of all factors that appear to the court to be relevant, including any medical evidence, the victim's age and personal circumstances.

9. The tables below suggest starting points for compensating physical and mental injuries commonly encountered in a magistrates' court. They have been developed to be consistent with the approach in the Criminal Injuries Compensation Authority tariff (revised 2001), available at: *www.cica.gov.uk*.

PHYSICAL INJURY

Type of injury	**Description**	**Starting point**
Graze	Depending on size	Up to £75
Bruise	Depending on size	Up to £100
Cut: no permanent scar	Depending on size and whether stitched	£100-500
Black eye		£125
Eye	Blurred or double vision lasting up to 6 weeks	Up to £1,000
	Blurred or double vision lasting for 6 to 13 weeks	£1,000
	Blurred or double vision lasting for more than 13 weeks (recovery expected)	£1,750
Brain	Concussion lasting one week	£1,500
Nose	Undisplaced fracture of nasal bone	£1,000
	Displaced fracture requiring manipulation	£2,000
	Deviated nasal septum requiring septoplasty	£2,000
Loss of non-front tooth	Depending on cosmetic effect	£1,250
Loss of front tooth		£1,750
Facial scar	Minor disfigurement (permanent)	£1,500

Type of injury	Description	Starting point
Arm	Fractured humerus, radius, ulna (substantial recovery)	£3,300
Shoulder	Dislocated (substantial recovery)	£1,750
Wrist	Dislocated/fractured—including scaphoid fracture (substantial recovery) Fractured—colles type (substantial recovery)	£3,300 £4,400
Sprained wrist, ankle	Disabling for up to 6 weeks Disabling for 6 to 13 weeks Disabling for more than 13 weeks	Up to £1,000 £1,000 £2,500
Finger	Fractured finger other than index finger (substantial recovery) Fractured index finger (substantial recovery) Fractured thumb (substantial recovery)	£1,000 £1,750 £2,000
Leg	Fractured fibula (substantial recovery) Fractured femur, tibia (substantial recovery)	£2,500 £3,800
Abdomen	Injury requiring laparotomy	£3,800

MENTAL INJURY

Description	Starting point
Temporary mental anxiety (including terror, shock, distress), not medically verified	Up to £1,000
Disabling mental anxiety, lasting more than 6 weeks, medically verified*	£1,000
Disability mental illness, lasting up to 28 weeks, confirmed by psychiatric diagnosis*	£2,500

* In this context, 'disabling' means a person's functioning is significantly impaired in some important aspect of his or her life, such as impaired work or school performance or significant adverse effects on social relationships.

10. The following table, which is also based on the Criminal Injuries Compensation Authority tariff, sets out suggested starting points for compensating physical and sexual abuse. It will be rare for cases involving this type of harm to be dealt with in a magistrates' court and it will be important to **consult your legal adviser for guidance in these situations.**

PHYSICAL AND SEXUAL ABUSE

Type of abuse	Description	Starting point
Physical abuse of adult	Intermittent physical assaults resulting in accumulation of healed wounds, burns or scalds, but with no appreciable disfigurement	£2,000

Part IV

Type of abuse	Description	Starting point
Physical abuse of child	Isolated or intermittent assault(s) resulting in weals, hair pulled from scalp etc	£1,000
	Intermittent physical assaults resulting in accumulation of healed wounds, burns or scalds, but with no appreciable disfigurement	£2,000
Sexual abuse of adult	Non-penetrative indecent physical acts over clothing	£1,000
	Non-penetrative indecent act(s) under clothing	£2,000
Sexual abuse of child (under 18)	Non-penetrative indecent physical act(s) over clothing	£1,000
	Non-penetrative frequent assaults over clothing or non-penetrative indecent act under clothing	£2,000
	Repetitive indecent acts under clothing	£3,300

11. Once the court has formed a preliminary view of the appropriate level of compensation, it must have regard to the means of the offender so far as they are known. Where the offender has little money, the order may have to be scaled down or additional time allowed to pay; the court may allow compensation to be paid over a period of up to three years in appropriate cases.

12. The fact that a custodial sentence is imposed does not, in itself, make it inappropriate to order compensation; however, it may be relevant to whether the offender has the means to satisfy the order.

13. Where the court considers that it would be appropriate to impose a fine and a compensation order but the offender has insufficient means to pay both, priority should be given to compensation. Compensation also takes priority over the victim surcharge where the offender's means are an issue.

23–202 A compensation order must not be made on the basis of pure speculation as to the offender's future prospects: *Ellis* (1994) 158 J.P. 386, though when considering the defendant's means the court may have regard to possible future income: *Ford* [1977] Crim.L.R. 114.

23–203 Once the court has made a preliminary calculation of the appropriate compensation, it will then consider the means of the offender before making an order. Ideally, orders should be capable of being paid within one year but periods of up to two or even three years have been accepted where there is a real likelihood of the order being paid.

IV. ANCILLARY ORDERS

A. DEPRIVATION AND CONFISCATION ORDERS

(1) Purpose and effect

23–204 These are part of a package of powers to enable the court to remove property from an offender where that property was used to assist the commission of the crime or is part of the proceeds of the crime. It is a potentially complex area of the law and this section briefly summarises the key points that a busy practitioner will need.

Where property was lawfully seized from a defendant or in his possession or under his control at the time he was apprehended, on conviction (or on the offence being taken into consideration), the court can order that he be deprived of any rights over that property if satisfied that the property had been used (or intended to be used) to assist the commission of any offence, not just the offence for which the defendant was apprehended or subsequently convicted.

Where the offence is punishable by imprisonment under the Road Traffic Acts and consists of driving (or attempting to drive or being in charge of) a motor vehicle or failing to provide a specimen for analysis or of failing to stop after and/or report an accident, then the vehicle being used is deemed to have been used for the purpose of committing the offence: s.143(6) and (7).

In deciding whether or not to make an order, the court must consider the value of the property and the likely effect on the offender of making the order—the higher the value, the more careful the court will need to be in deciding whether the order is appropriate.

Powers of Criminal Courts (Sentencing) Act 2000, ss.143–145

Powers to deprive offender of property used etc. for purposes of crime

143.—(1) Where a person is convicted of an offence and the court by or before which he is **23–205**
convicted is satisfied that any property which has been lawfully seized from him, or which was in his possession or under his control at the time when he was apprehended for the offence or when a summons in respect of it was issued—

(a) has been used for the purpose of committing, or facilitating the commission of, any offence, or

(b) was intended by him to be used for that purpose,

the court may (subject to subsection (5) below) make an order under this section in respect of that property.

(2) Where a person is convicted of an offence and the offence, or an offence which the court has taken into consideration in determining his sentence, consists of unlawful possession of property which—

(a) has been lawfully seized from him, or

(b) was in his possession or under his control at the time when he was apprehended for the offence of which he has been convicted or when a summons in respect of that offence was issued,

the court may (subject to subsection (5) below) make an order under this section in respect of that property.

(3) An order under this section shall operate to deprive the offender of his rights, if any, in the property to which it relates, and the property shall (if not already in their possession) be taken into the possession of the police.

(4) Any power conferred on a court by subsection (1) or (2) above may be exercised—

(a) whether or not the court also deals with the offender in any other way in respect of the offence of which he has been convicted; and

(b) without regard to any restrictions on forfeiture in any enactment contained in an Act passed before 29th July 1988.

(5) In considering whether to make an order under this section in respect of any property, a court shall have regard—

(a) to the value of the property; and

(b) to the likely financial and other effects on the offender of the making of the order (taken together with any other order that the court contemplates making).

(6) Where a person commits an offence to which this subsection applies by—

(a) driving, attempting to drive, or being in charge of a vehicle, or

(b) failing to comply with a requirement made under section 7 or 7A of the *Road Traffic Act* 1988 (failure to provide specimen for analysis or laboratory test or to give permission for such a test in the course of an investigation into whether the offender had committed an offence while driving, attempting to drive or being in charge of a vehicle, or

(c) failing, as the driver of a vehicle, to comply with subsection (2) or (3) of section 170 of the *Road Traffic Act* 1988 (duty to stop and give information or report accident),

the vehicle shall be regarded for the purposes of subsection (1) above (and section 144(1)(b) below) as used for the purpose of committing the offence (and for the purpose of committing any offence of aiding, abetting, counselling or procuring the commission of the offence).

(7) Subsection (6) above applies to—

(a) an offence under the *Road Traffic Act* 1988 which is punishable with imprisonment;

(b) an offence of manslaughter; and

Part IV

(c) an offence under section 35 of the *Offences Against the Person Act* 1861 (wanton and furious driving).

(8) Facilitating the commission of an offence shall be taken for the purposes of subsection (1) above to include the taking of any steps after it has been committed for the purpose of disposing of any property to which it relates or of avoiding apprehension or detection.

Property which is in possession of police by virtue of section 143

23–206 **144.**—(1) The *Police (Property) Act* 1897 shall apply, with the following modifications, to property which is in the possession of the police by virtue of section 143 above—

(a) no application shall be made under section 1(1) of that Act by any claimant of the property after the end of six months from the date on which the order in respect of the property was made under section 143 above; and

(b) no such application shall succeed unless the claimant satisfies the court either—

(i) that he had not consented to the offender having possession of the property; or

(ii) where an order is made under subsection (1) of section 143 above, that he did not know, and had no reason to suspect, that the property was likely to be used for the purpose mentioned in that subsection.

(2) In relation to property which is in the possession of the police by virtue of section 143 above, the power to make regulations under section 2 of the *Police (Property) Act* 1897 (disposal of property in cases where the owner of the property has not been ascertained and no order of a competent court has been made with respect to it) shall, subject to subsection (3) below, include power to make regulations for disposal (including disposal by vesting in the relevant authority) in cases where no application by a claimant of the property has been made within the period specified in subsection (1)(a) above or no such application has succeeded.

(3) The regulations may not provide for the vesting in the relevant authority of property in relation to which an order has been made under section 145 below (court order as to application of proceeds of forfeited property).

(4) Nothing in subsection (2A)(a) or (3) of section 2 of the *Police (Property) Act* 1897 limits the power to make regulations under that section by virtue of subsection (2) above.

(5) In this section "relevant authority" has the meaning given by section 2(2B) of the *Police (Property) Act* 1897.

Application of proceeds of forfeited property.

23–207 **145.**—(1) Where a court makes an order under section 143 above in a case where—

(a) the offender has been convicted of an offence which has resulted in a person suffering personal injury, loss or damage, or

(b) any such offence is taken into consideration by the court in determining sentence, the court may also make an order that any proceeds which arise from the disposal of the property and which do not exceed a sum specified by the court shall be paid to that person.

(2) The court may make an order under this section only if it is satisfied that but for the inadequacy of the offender's means it would have made a compensation order under which the offender would have been required to pay compensation of an amount not less than the specified amount.

(3) An order under this section has no effect—

(a) before the end of the period specified in section 144(1)(a) above; or

(b) if a successful application under section 1(1) of the *Police (Property) Act* 1897 has been made.

The power does not extend to real property: *Khan (Sultan Ashraf)* [1984] 1 W.L.R. 1405, CA.

23–208 As noted *ante*, the power under s.143(1) is widely drawn and is not restricted to property used in the offences currently before the court and an order may be made in respect of property intended to be used by the offender to commit any offence. In *O'Farrell* [1988] Crim.L.R. 387, the court ordered the forfeiture of a large sum of money found on a person convicted of supplying illegal drugs. The defendant sought to argue that the order could not be made as there was no evidence that the money was the proceeds of the current offence and that it was intended for use to fund future offences but the Court of Appeal agreed that the order had been rightly made.

An order should not be made unless the court has information before it relating to the value of the property concerned and the effect on the offender of making the order: *Ball* [2003] 2 Cr.App.R.(S.) 18, CA. A deprivation order made against one offender, where several offenders are responsible for a single offence may give rise to an objectionable disparity: *Burgess* [2001] 2 Cr.App.R.(S.) 5, CA.

A deprivation order may be made in addition to other sentences imposed in respect of the same offence. The order should be seen as part of the overall penalty, and the other sentences imposed should be adjusted accordingly: *Joyce* [1991] R.T.R. 241, CA. In *Highbury Corner Stipendiary Magistrate, ex p. Di Matteo* [1992] 1 All E.R. 102, DC, Watkins L.J. said that a court considering whether to make an order under s.143 should have regard to the totality principle and to the two matters specifically set out in subs. (5)—the value of the property concerned and the likely financial and other effects on the offender of making the order—taken together with any other order that the court was considering making. **23–209**

In *Priestly* [1996] 2 Cr.App.R.(S.) 144, CA, a sentence of four years' imprisonment for applying false trademarks to perfumes and clothing so as to resemble goods manufactured by famous manufacturers was reduced to three years, to take account of an order made under the *Powers of Criminal Courts Act* 1973, s.43 (now *PCC(S)A* 2000, s.143). The Court held that the sentencer had failed to take into account the effect of the order as part of the total sentence, as was required by *Joyce* (1989) 11 Cr.App.R.(S.) 253, CA, and the sentence of four years imprisonment should be reduced to one of three.

A deprivation order will only be suitable in cases where it will not be difficult to implement. In *Troth* [1980] Crim.L.R. 249, a case concerning partnership property, it was held that difficulties would arise in the implementation of a deprivation order where the property was subject to encumbrances, and it might be appropriate to impose "an increased financial penalty…in lieu of making a forfeiture order." **23–210**

The power to order forfeiture of particular objects is also provided by various statutes. See the *Misuse of Drugs Act* 1971, s.27; *Firearms Act* 1968, s.52; *Salmon and Freshwater Fisheries Act* 1975, Sched. 4, para. 5 (fish and fishing tackle); *Licensing Act* 1964, ss.161, 162 (intoxicating liquor); *Obscene Publications Act* 1959, s.3 (obscene articles); *Prevention of Crime Act* 1953, s.1 (offensive weapons) and *Wireless Telegraphy Act* 1949, s.14 (wireless telegraphy apparatus).

B. Confiscation Orders under the Criminal Justice Act 1988

The provisions of the *Criminal Justice Act* 1988, (ss.71 to 102) are repealed with effect from March 24, 2003 by the *Proceeds of Crime Act* 2002. The repeal does not apply to offences committed before that date and so the provisions of the *Criminal Justice Act* 1988 will continue to apply. However, orders under the 2002 Act can only be made in the Crown Court. **23–211**

Confiscation orders may be made by a magistrates' court in respect of a limited number of summary offences, which are listed in Sched. 4 to the 1988 Act.

C. Recommendation for Deportation

(1) Purpose and effect

When fully in force, the provisions in the *UK Borders Act* 2007 will mean that it will rarely be necessary for a court to make a recommendation for deportation. Deportation will automatically be considered for any qualifying offender sentenced to any custodial sentence for a wide range of offences (including almost all offences for which a custodial sentence is commonly imposed) and, for other offences, to a sentence of 12 months imprisonment or more. The list of qualifying offences is contained in the *Nationality, Immigration and Asylum Act 2002 (Specification of Particularly Serious Crimes) Order* 2004, S.I. 2004 No.1910. These provisions have been brought into force in part **23–212** by the *UK Borders Act (Commencement No.3 and Transitional Provisions) Order* 2008, S.I. 2008 No.1818. From August 1, 2008, s.32 of the 2007 Act provides for an offender who is a "foreign criminal", that is a person who is not a British citizen and is convicted in the UK of an offence, who is sentenced to 12 months imprisonment or more to be subject to the automatic making of a deportation order. Exceptions apply as set out in s.33 of the Act but are not set out in this work as they apply to the Secretary of State not to a court. At the time of going to print, it was not known when the provisions will be brought into force to apply this process to custodial sentences of any length. Until those provisions are brought into force fully, the existing approach continues and, subject to various limitations, a court which sentences a person aged 17 or over who is not a British citizen may, where the offence is one that is punishable with imprisonment, recommend to the Home Secretary that the defendant be deported from the United Kingdom. This order is additional to any sentence passed and must be preceded by formal notice of the possibility of the order being made. That notice must be given at least seven days before the making of the order is considered: s.6(2).

The approach has been considered by the Court of Appeal (Criminal Division) in *Kluxen* [2011] 1 W.L.R. 218. Confirming that a recommendation is no longer needed in the circumstances described above, the Court also confirmed (in para. 10) that it is not necessary for a court to explain that it is not making the recommendation. The Court also stated (at para. 28) that, where the 2007 Act does not apply, it will rarely be appropriate to recommend deportation; where in such a case, exceptionally, a court does consider whether to make a recommendation, it should apply the test set out in *Nazari* (see para. 23–220 *post*) in tandem with the *Bouchereau* test (see para. 23–218 *post*) whether or not the offender is an EU citizen. The court should not take into account the offender's convention rights, the political situation in the country of destination or the impact on innocent people not before the court; these are all matters for the Secretary of State to consider. Similarly, it is inappropriate for a court to reduce an otherwise correct sentence simply because a consequence is that the sentence triggers the automatic deportation provisions: *Mintchev* [2011] EWCA Crim 499.

There is a further restriction on the court that limits the exercise of the power in relation to citizens of the European Community exercising their right to free movement under the Treaty of Rome. Such citizens may only be recommended for deportation if the court considers that the continued presence of the defendant in the UK represents a "genuine and sufficiently serious threat to the requirements of public policy affecting one of the fundamental interests of society". In such a case, reasons must be given for that view: *Nazari* [1980] 1 W.L.R. 1366.

There are also exceptions provided in ss.7 and 8 protecting long standing residents and also seamen, aircrews and other special cases such as members of diplomatic missions.

23–213 The Home Secretary will consider any recommendation but is not bound to order deportation.

Immigration Act 1971, ss.3(6), (8), 6, 7

General provisions for regulation and control

23–214 **3.**—(6) Without prejudice to the operation of subsection (5) above, a person who is not a British citizen shall also be liable to deportation from the United Kingdom if, after he has attained the age of seventeen, he is convicted of an offence for which he is punishable with imprisonment and on his conviction is recommended for deportation by a court empowered by this Act to do so.

(8) When any question arises under this Act whether or not a person is a British citizen, or is entitled to any exemption under this Act, it shall lie on the person asserting it to prove that he is.

Recommendations by court for deportation

23–215 **6.**—(1) Where under section 3(6) above a person convicted of an offence is liable to deportation on the recommendation of a court, he may be recommended for deportation by any court having power to sentence him for the offence unless the court commits him to be sentenced or further dealt with for that offence by another court…

(2) A court shall not recommend a person for deportation unless he has been given not less than seven days notice in writing stating that a person is not liable to deportation if he is a British citizen, describing the persons who are British citizens and stating (so far as material) the effect of section 3(8) above and section 7 below; but the powers of adjournment conferred by section 10(3) of the *Magistrates' Courts Act* 1980, section 179 or 380 of the *Criminal Procedure (Scotland) Act* 1975 or any corresponding enactment for the time being in force in Northern Ireland shall include power to adjourn, after convicting an offender, for the purpose of enabling a notice to be given to him under this subsection or, if a notice was so given to him less than seven days previously, for the purpose of enabling the necessary seven days to elapse.

(3) For purposes of section 3(6) above—

(a) a person shall be deemed to have attained the age of seventeen at the time of his conviction if, on consideration of any available evidence, he appears to have done so to the court making or considering a recommendation for deportation; and

(b) the question whether an offence is one for which a person is punishable with imprisonment shall be determined without regard to any enactment restricting the imprisonment of young offenders or persons who have not previously been sentenced to imprisonment;

and for purposes of deportation a person who on being charged with an offence is found to have committed it shall, notwithstanding any enactment to the contrary and notwithstanding that the court does not proceed to conviction, be regarded as a person convicted of the offence, and references to conviction shall be construed accordingly.

(4) Notwithstanding any rule of practice restricting the matters which ought to be taken into account in dealing with an offender who is sentenced to imprisonment, a recommendation for deportation may be made in respect of an offender who is sentenced to imprisonment for life.

(5) Where a court recommends or purports to recommend a person for deportation, the validity of the recommendation shall not be called in question except on an appeal against the recommendation or against the conviction on which it is made; but—

(a) the recommendation shall be treated as a sentence for the purpose of any enactment providing an appeal against sentence

(6) A deportation order shall not be made on the recommendation of a court so long as an appeal or further appeal is pending against the recommendation or against the conviction on which it was made; and for this purpose an appeal or further appeal shall be treated as pending (where one is competent but has not been brought) until the expiration of the time for bringing that appeal or, in Scotland, until the expiration of twenty-eight days from the date of the recommendation.

(7) [*Scotland*]

Exemption from deportation for certain existing residents

7.—(1) Notwithstanding anything in section 3(5) or (6) above but subject to the provisions of this section, a Commonwealth citizen or citizen of the Republic of Ireland who was such a citizen at the coming into force of this Act and was then ordinarily resident in the United Kingdom— **23–216**

(b) shall not be liable to deportation under section 3(5)(a) or (b) or 10 of the *Immigration and Asylum Act* 1999 if at the time of the Secretary of State's decision he had for the last five years been ordinarily resident in the United Kingdom and Islands;

(c) shall not on conviction of an offence be recommended for deportation under section 3(6) if at the time of the conviction he had for the last five years been ordinarily resident in the United Kingdom and Islands.

(2) A person who has at any time become ordinarily resident in the United Kingdom or in any of the Islands shall not be treated for the purposes of this section as having ceased to be so by reason only of his having remained there in breach of the immigration laws.

(3) The "last five years" before the material time under subsection (1)(b) or (c) above is to be taken as a period amounting in total to five years exclusive of any time during which the person claiming exemption under this section was undergoing imprisonment or detention by virtue of a sentence passed for an offence on a conviction in the United Kingdom and Islands, and the period for which he was imprisoned or detained by virtue of the sentence amounted to six months or more.

(4) For purposes of subsection (3) above—

(a) "sentence" includes any order made on conviction of an offence; and
(b) two or more sentences for consecutive (or partly consecutive) terms shall be treated as a single sentence; and
(c) a person shall be deemed to be detained by virtue of a sentence—
(i) at any time when he is liable to imprisonment or detention by virtue of the sentence, but is unlawfully at large; and
(ii) (unless the sentence is passed after the material time) during any period of custody by which under any relevant enactment the term to be served under the sentence is reduced.

In paragraph (c)(ii) above "relative enactment" means section 240 of the *Criminal Justice Act* 2003 and any similar enactment which is for the time being or has (before or after the passing of this Act) been in force in any part of the United Kingdom and Islands.

(5) Nothing in this section shall be taken to exclude the operation of section 3(8) above in relation to an exemption under this section.

Immigration Act 1971, s.8(2), (3), (3A)

Exceptions for seamen, aircrews and other special cases

23–217 **8.**—(2) The Secretary of State may by order exempt any person or class of persons, either unconditionally or subject to such conditions as may be imposed by or under the order, from all or any of the provisions of this Act relating to those who are not British citizens.

An order under this subsection, if made with respect to a class of persons, shall be made by statutory instrument, which shall be subject to annulment in pursuance of a resolution of either House of Parliament.

(3) Subject to subsection (3A) below, the provisions of this Act relating to those who are not British citizens shall not apply to any person so long as he is a member of a mission (within the meaning of the *Diplomatic Privileges Act* 1964), a person who is a member of the family and forms part of the household of such a member, or a person otherwise entitled to the like immunity from jurisdiction as is conferred by that Act on a diplomatic agent.

(3A) For the purposes of subsection (3), a member of a mission other than a diplomatic agent (as defined by the 1964 Act) is not to count as a member of a mission unless—
(a) he was resident outside the United Kingdom, and was not in the United Kingdom, when he was offered a post as such a member; and
(b) he has not ceased to be such a member after having taken up the post.

23–218 A British citizen may not be deported. A "British citizen" is, broadly, a person who has a right of abode in the UK. Persons who have the right of abode in the United Kingdom are entirely free from United Kingdom immigration control. They do not need to obtain the permission of an immigration officer to enter the UK, and may live and work here without restriction. Under s.2 of the *Immigration Act* 1971 (which was amended by s.39 of the *British Nationality Act* 1981), all British citizens and certain Commonwealth citizens have the right of abode in the United Kingdom. This is in contrast to persons given leave to enter or remain in the United Kingdom for a specific purpose, who are expected to leave the country when their limited right to enter or remain expires or when their reasons for being here no longer apply. A recommendation for deportation cannot be made in the case of a Commonwealth citizen or a citizen of the Irish Republic who was resident in the UK when the 1971 Act came into force (*i.e.* January 1, 1973) and has been ordinarily resident in the UK for at least the five years immediately prior to the date of conviction.

EU nationals in the UK exercising their right of free movement under the Treaty of Rome may be deported only if the requirements of EU law are satisfied. The court must consider that the continued presence of the offender in the UK represents "a genuine and sufficiently serious threat to the requirements of public policy affecting one of the fundamental interests of society": *Bouchereau* [1978] Q.B. 732, ECJ. This decision is primarily about likely future conduct rather than criminal history (though the one is often deduced from the other): *Kraus* (1982) 4 Cr.App.R.(S.) 113. Reasons must be given to the Home Secretary and to the offender.

Deportation can only take place if another country or territory agrees to accept the deportee. Where a person subject to deportation proceedings lodges a claim for asylum (at any stage in the process) there must be a stay in the removal.

Immigration Rules, para. 364 provides:

> ". . . in considering whether deportation is the right course on the merits, the public interest will be balanced against any compassionate circumstances of the case . . ."

In *R. v. Secretary of State for the HD, ex p. Santillo* [1981] Q.B. 778, CA, the Court held that the existence of previous criminal convictions is not of itself a basis for making a recommendation. However, if the court considers that the previous record, including the offence with which the court is directly concerned, renders it likely that the person before them will offend again, the court may take account of the previous convictions since the possibility of re-offending is a very important factor in deciding whether to recommend deportation and taking account of it is permitted by the Council Directive. The Court also held that the sentencer should give reasons if a recommendation is to be made and that the reasons should include "some indication of the extent to which the current and previous criminal convictions of the accused have been taken into account and, in so far as this has been done, the light which in the view of the court, such conviction or convictions throw on the likely nature of the accused's personal conduct in the future." **23–219**

Where a sentencer is considering making a deportation order (see para. 23–212, *ante*) he should alert the offender or his counsel, so that mitigation can be advanced in relation to the making of an order: *Omojudi* (1992) 13 Cr.App.R.(S.) 346, CA. There is a formal obligation (s.6(2)) to ensure that the person concerned has received written notice setting out that a British citizen is not liable to deportation with information on who is a British citizen. This notice must be given at least seven days before making a recommendation **23–220**

When a court makes a recommendation for deportation, it should give its reasons for doing so in adequate detail: *Rodney* [1996] 2 Cr.App.R.(S.) 230, CA. General guidance as to the making of deportation orders was given in *Nazari* [1980] 1 W.L.R. 1366, CA, where Lawton L.J. said:

> "We now indicate some guidelines which Courts should keep in mind when considering whether to make an order recommending deportation. But we stress that these are guidelines, not rigid rules. There may well be considerations which take a particular case out of the guidelines; that is a matter which will depend on the evidence.
>
> First, the Court must consider ... whether the accused's continued presence in the United Kingdom is to its detriment. This country has no use for criminals of other nationalities, particularly if they have committed serious crimes or have long criminal records ... The more serious the crime and the longer the record the more obvious it is that there should be an order recommending deportation. On the other hand, a minor offence would not merit an order recommending deportation. In the Greater London area, for example, shoplifting is an offence which is frequently committed by visitors to this country. Normally an arrest for shoplifting followed by conviction, even if there were more than one offence being dealt with, would not merit a recommendation for deportation. But a series of shoplifting offences on different occasions may justify a recommendation for deportation. Even a first offence of shoplifting might merit a recommendation if the offender were a member of a gang carrying out a planned raid on a departmental store.
>
> Secondly, the Courts are not concerned with the political systems which operate in other countries ... The Court has no knowledge of those matters over and above that which is common knowledge; and that may he wrong. In our judgment it would be undesirable for this Court or any other Court to express views about regimes which exist outside the United Kingdom...It is for the Home Secretary to decide in each case whether an offender's return to his country of origin would have consequences which would make his compulsory return unduly harsh.
>
> The next ... is the effect that an order recommending deportation will have upon others who are not before the Court and who are innocent persons. This Court and all other Courts would have no wish to break up families or impose hardship on innocent people.
>
> We wish to state clearly and firmly that all a Court does when it makes a recommendation for

Part IV

deportation is to indicate to the Secretary of State that in the opinion of the Court it is to the detriment of this country that the accused should remain here ... No doubt he will take into account the personal circumstances of each person whose case he is considering, and that will include the political situation in the country to which he will have to go if an order of deportation is made. These are matters solely for the Secretary of State."

23–221 In deciding whether to make an order recommending deportation, the key issue for the sentencer is whether the continued presence of the defendant in the U.K. would be to the detriment of the community: *Craviot*o (1990) 12 Cr.App.R.(S.) 71, CA. Where the offender has dependants who are resident in the U.K., the detriment caused to them by his removal must be balanced against the potential detriment that will arise from his continued presence in the country: *Craviot*o (*ante*). Article 8 of the European Convention on Human Rights states:

1. Everyone has the right to respect for his private and family life, his home and his correspondence.

2. There shall be no interference by a public authority with the exercise of this right except such as is in accordance with the law and is necessary in a democratic society in the interests of national security, public safety or the economic well-being of the country, for the prevention of disorder or crime, for the protection of health or morals, or for the protection of the rights and freedoms of others.

However, it appears that a court is not required to consider in detail the defendant's rights under art. 8 of the European Convention on Human Rights: *Carmona* [2006] EWCA Crim. 508.

In *Aziz* [2004] EWCA Crim 1700, it was emphasised that the making of a recommendation is not part of the punishment for the offence and does not justify reducing the sentence imposed. The defendant (or his legal representative) must be given the opportunity to address the court specifically on whether or not the recommendation should be made. In *R. (N., Kenya) v. Secretary of State for the Home Department* [2004] EWCA Civ 1094, the responsibility for determining the balance between the public interest and the compassionate circumstances of the case was examined as between the Home Secretary and an adjudicator considering an appeal against the decision of the Home Secretary to deport the offender. It is unclear to what extent the court must take account of the impact of deportation on the family of the offender. Given that it is at this stage simply a recommendation, one school of thought suggests that this is not a relevant issue for the court which is concerned only whether the continued presence of the offender would be to the detriment of the United Kingdom. Another school of thought suggests that the European Convention on Human Rights requires courts to take that into account through a combination of the application of art. 6 and art. 8. At present, the balance seems to be towards the former view that this is an issue for the Home Secretary rather than the court. An indication of a shift in view can be seen in *Harris* [2004] EWCA Crim 1738, where the Court of Appeal quashed a recommendation made in respect of an offender sentenced to three years nine months imprisonment for supplying drugs on the grounds that he had been in the country for 8 years and had built up "very strong roots". However, in *Dennis* [2004] EWCA Crim 2146, the Court of Appeal upheld a recommendation in respect of an offender convicted of supplying drugs holding that "... whilst [the defendant] has not apparently offended hitherto, the charges of drug dealing are extremely serious. They are more than potentially detrimental to the interests of this country."

Where a person enters the UK illegally, a recommendation for deportation may be appropriate, but the sentencer is not obliged to make a recommendation for deportation in every case involving an infringement of the Act: *Akan* (1972) 56 Cr.App.R. 716, CA. In *Ahemed* [2006] 1 Cr.App.R.(S.) 78, the defendant had pleaded guilty to obtaining leave to enter the U.K. by submitting documents purporting to show that his marriage to a co-accused was subsisting. In fact, it was a bogus marriage designed to facilitate the obtaining of indefinite leave to enter or remain in the UK. The defendant asserted that he was of previous good character, that he had obtained an extension of leave to remain of only a few days and that the Secretary of State had ample powers to remove him under an administrative power. The Court agreed with the prosecution that entering into a wholly bogus marriage and then using it as a means to deceive the Home Office in order to further prospects of remaining indefinitely was sufficient to justify a finding that his continued presence was to the detriment of the UK. The defendant's behaviour went well beyond the commission of a "mere" immigration offence. In *Benabbas* [2006] 1 Cr.App.R.(S.) 94, the defendant, an Algerian national, had pleaded guilty to using a forged instrument which was a stolen French passport. He admitted that he had bought the passport in France. The Court reviewed the authorities (confirming the leading authority of *Nazari* [1980] 1 W.L.R. 1366) and considered in particular the contrasting approaches where a defendant's presence in the country was lawful and regular and that where it was (as in this case) illegal or irregular. It stated that, where a defendant's presence in this country was lawful and regular, the *Nazari* approach involved a relatively straightforward exercise of balancing the aggravation of the defendant's wrongdoing, present, past and potential, against the mitigation which he could pray in aid, which included the interests of his family. That balance might on occasions be a difficult one to find. However, the test and the elements in it were plain and personal to the defendant. The detriment had to be judged by reference to the public interest and the requirements of public policy. The court was in no position to embark on any assessment of what would happen to the defendant on return to his country of origin. Whether a recommendation was made or not, those matters were ultimately for the Secretary of State. Where a defendant's presence in the UK was illegal or irregular, the position could be more complicated. Where the illegality or irregularity was the entirely irrelevant to the offence for which the defendant was sentenced, the general principle was that such incidental illegality or irregularity in the status of the defendant was irrelevant because the defendant was to be sentenced for the offence of which he had been convicted and not for his incidental status under statute. Even so the defendant's status, if indeed it was clear, was not entirely irrelevant. It was part of the defendant's personal conduct which, as a matter of public interest, could be taken into account as part of the balancing exercise. The sentencing judge was correct in Benabbas to say that the use of stolen and forged passports undermined the good order of society. Such a view was consistent with authority (see *Bouchereau* [1978] Q.B. 732). It was right to distinguish between the case of a person who entered the UK by fraudulent means and a case of a person who was in the country unlawfully and was convicted of an offence unconnected with his status and the circumstances in which he entered the country. Whilst in this case the defendant was not charged with use of his forged passport to gain entry, it was overwhelmingly likely that he did so use it, or at least that he presented himself at the EU citizen entry channel thereby representing that he was a holder of a passport issued by a Member State. Although the defendant had not been in trouble since arriving in the UK and he had since been in employment, his failure to disclose his true address was a serious matter. As a result of the suppression of his Algerian passport and of his true address, nothing at all was known about him beyond his employment. The judge was therefore right to say that the defendant's use of a forged passport undermined the good order of society and that his presence in the U.K. would be a detriment to this country under the *Nazari* principles.

The sentencer should not consider circumstances of a personal nature which make it **23–222**
difficult for the offender to return to his country of origin when considering whether to make a recommendation for deportation: *Bali* [2001] 2 Cr.App.R.(S.) 104, CA.

D. COSTS

The court has the power to compensate a party for costs incurred in relation to the **23–223**
prosecution: see *post*, Ch.30.

E. BINDING OVER

(1) Purpose and effect

A requirement to be bound over is an order designed to prevent future misconduct. **23–224**

It is an ancient power deriving statutory authority from one of the oldest statutes still in force as well as being provided for in more recent legislation. As with many crime prevention powers, it is designed to be flexible and easy to use. No formal procedure is required under the 1361 Act (though anyone who a court is proposing to be bound over must have proper opportunity to resist such an order if they wish); the 1980 Act requires a formal commencement though this can be done orally.

The order requires the person against whom it is made to enter into a recognisance to guarantee future conduct. In essence, this is a promise to pay a specified sum of money if the terms of the order are breached. It is a useful power made on over 20,000 occasions each year in magistrates' courts. Its use has come before the European Court of Human Rights, primarily because it can be used even where a person is acquitted of any offence and because of the lack of clarity in defining the conduct that will cause a court to consider whether the recognisance should be forfeited: *Steel v. United Kingdom* [1998] E.H.R.R. 603. A recommendation by the Law Commission that the power be abolished (Binding Over, Law Com. No.222 (Cm. 2439)) was not widely supported and the Home Office has consulted on ways in which the power can be used in ways that comply with obligations on fairness, certainty and proportionality (*Binding Over; A Power for the 21st Century*: HO 2002). This has led to an amendment to the Consolidated Criminal Practice Direction: see III.31 in Appendix F below.

23–225 If a court orders a person to enter into a recognisance and they decline to do so, then, if the order is being made under the 1361 Act, the court has no sanction and cannot require the recognisance to be entered into. If the order is being made under the 1980 Act, then the court has the power to commit to custody for up to six months in default of entering into the recognisance; however, it is likely that the exercise of this power would be held to be out of proportion to the nature of the order being made. Clearly, if a person misbehaves in a way that contravenes the criminal law they can in any case be prosecuted for that offence; a bind over is designed for lower levels of misconduct and may gradually be superseded by the Anti-Social Behaviour Order (see *post*, §§ 23–241 *et seq.*).

Justices of the Peace Act 1361

23–226 …First, that in every county of England shall be assigned for the keeping of the peace, one lord, and with him three or four of the most worthy in the county, with some learned in the law, and they shall have power to restrain the offenders, rioters, and all other barators and to pursue, arrest, take, and chastise them according their trespass or offence; and to cause them to be imprisoned and duly punished according to the law and customs of the realm, and according to that which to them shall seem best to do by their discretions and good advisement; … and to take of all them that they may find by indictment, or by suspicion, and put them in prison; and to take of all them that be [not] of good fame, where they shall be found, sufficient surety and mainprise of their good behaviour towards the King and his people, and the other duly to punish; to the intent that the people be not by such rioters or rebels troubled nor endamaged, nor the peace blemished, nor merchants nor other passing by the highways of the realm disturbed, nor [put in the peril which may happen] of such offenders: …

Magistrates' Courts Act 1980, s.115

Binding over to keep the peace or be of good behaviour

23–227 **115.**—(1) The power of a magistrates' court on the complaint of any person to adjudge any other person to enter into a recognizance, with or without sureties, to keep the peace or to be of good behaviour towards the complainant shall be exercised by order on complaint.

(2) Where a complaint is made under this section, the power of the court to remand the defendant under subsection (5) of section 55 above shall not be subject to the restrictions imposed by subsection (6) of that section.

(3) If any person ordered by a magistrates' court under subsection (1) above to enter into a recognizance, with or without sureties, to keep the peace or to be of good behaviour fails to comply with the order, the court may commit him to custody for a period not exceeding 6 months or until he sooner complies with the order.

The use of the power to bind over to keep the peace does not depend on conviction: **23–228**
it may be used against any person where a future breach of the peace is apprehended including a witness who has given evidence: *Sheldon v. Broomfield JJ.* [1964] 2 Q.B. 573, DC. The *Consolidated Criminal Practice Direction* provides that a court must be satisfied that a breach of the peace which involves violence or an imminent threat of violence has occurred or that there is a real risk of violence in the future: III.31.2. See Appendix F. Previous authorities stated that it is not possible to include specific conditions in an order binding over a person to keep the peace: *Randall* (1986) 8 Cr.App.R.(S.) 433, CA. However, considerable concerns have been expressed about the uncertainty contained in being bound over to keep the peace and/or be of good behaviour. If a person is to be sanctioned for conduct, then it needs to be clear what conduct will lead to the sanction being invoked. The *Consolidated Criminal Practice Direction* provides that a court should not bind over anyone "to be of good behaviour" nor should it bind anyone over, in general terms, "to keep the peace"—the order must identify the specific conduct or activity from which the individual must refrain: III.31.3. Those details should be specified in a written order and served on all relevant parties: III.31.4.

An example of where the proper approach was not followed occurred in the context of making a binding over order following acquittal: *Emohare v. Thames Magistrates' Court* [2009] EWHC Admin 689. The defendant had been stopped whilst driving home from hospital (following medical treatment to his shoulder and arm) and questioned about a bag snatch in the area. He was aggressive and, when a police officer took hold of his arm, he reacted by swinging his head which caught the officer's head—he was charged with assault. The court was not sure that the assault was more than an involuntary reaction to the pain caused when the police officer took hold of his arm and acquitted the defendant. Nonetheless, the court considered the defendant's conduct to be reprehensible and, having invited representations, bound him over for two years to keep the peace. This order was overturned on appeal. The Court had not considered the relevant provisions of the Consolidated Criminal Practice Direction which emphasised the importance of the court being satisfied either that a breach of the peace involving violence (or an imminent threat of violence) had occurred or that there was a real risk of violence in the future; on the facts found, neither condition could have been satisfied. Even if the bind over had been justified, the court had not made the order in the specific terms required by the para. III.31 (see above).

When making an order, the court should set out its reasons together with the amount of the recognisance and the length of the order which should not generally exceed 12 months: III.31.4. See Appendix F.

Before making an order, a court must give affected parties the opportunity to make representations and particular care has to be taken when the potential subject of the order has been a witness in the proceedings: III.31.5. Evidence should be heard where there is no sufficient admission and a court should always hear enough (by representation or evidence) to enable it to satisfy itself both that an order is appropriate and what the terms of it should be: III.31.6. A court needs to be satisfied beyond reasonable doubt before making an order and the burden is on the prosecutor or complainant: III.31.8.

A person who refuses to be bound over to keep the peace may be committed to **23–229**
prison by the magistrates' court: *Magistrates' Courts Act* 1980, s.115(3). A person under 21 and over 18 who refuses to be bound over by a magistrates' court may be detained under the *PCC(S)A* 2000, s.108. An offender under the age of 18 who refuses to be bound over by the magistrates' court may be ordered to attend at an attendance centre: *PCC(S)A* 2000, s.60(1)(b).

In *Steel v. United Kingdom* (1999) 38 E.H.R.R. 603, the European Court of Human Rights determined that the committal to prison of two protesters who refused to be bound over to keep the peace fell within the scope of art. 5(1)(b) for non-compliance with the order of a court, and that whilst binding orders are in rather vague and general terms, they were specific enough for the purposes of art. 5(1)(b). However, use of this sanction to secure compliance with this type of order is likely to be seen as disproportionate and, in practice, the order is made with the consent, or at least acquiescence, of the subject of the order. The *Consolidated Criminal Practice Direction* now provides steps to be taken before this power is used. The court must consider whether there is a realistic alternative (such as continuing with a prosecution) and must give an opportunity for the potential subject to take legal advice for which public funding should generally be granted. If that opportunity is declined, the court should give a final opportunity and ensure that the consequences are clearly understood: III.31.12-14.

23–230 Where a person who has been bound over has been proved to have broken the terms of the recognisance, the court has power to order the person to pay the amount of the recognisance, but there is no power to order a sentence of imprisonment or otherwise for the breach itself.

Where the fact of breach is contested, the court should hear representations and evidence before determining whether a breach has occurred: III.31.7. Again, the court must be satisfied beyond reasonable doubt and the burden of proof is on the prosecution: III.31.9.

F. ANTI-SOCIAL BEHAVIOUR ORDERS

(1) Purpose and effect

23–231 This is an order with a potentially very wide scope that may be made to control a wide range of behaviour that is deemed to be anti-social. An order can be made as a result of a specific application (*Crime and Disorder Act* 1998, s.1) or by a court that has convicted a defendant of an offence (*ibid.* s.1C) in which case no application is needed though the prosecutor can apply: s.1C(3). Evidence can be led by either the prosecution or the defence and is not restricted to that which would be admissible in relation to the offence itself: s.1C(3A) and (3B) as inserted by the *Anti-Social Behaviour Act* 2003. The order will be additional to the sentence passed for the offence: s.1C(4) Proceedings under section 1C may be adjourned. This power may be exercisable even though sentence has been passed for the offence itself and it is only the making of an ASBO that remains to be determined. The court may issue a warrant of arrest for failure to attend subsequent hearings.

The order will prohibit the offender from doing anything described in the order: s.1C(2). The order will last for the period specified in the order which must be at least two years: s.1(7) as applied by s.1C(9).

For some, making the order is sufficient but, for others, making an order without providing additional support is unlikely to be successful in achieving the aims of the order. One example of this is s.1G and 1H of the *Crime and Disorder Act* 1998, inserted by the *Drugs Act* 2005, s.20. This provides for an "intervention order" in addition to an ASBO where a court is satisfied that misuse of controlled drugs is affecting the behaviour of the person to be subject to the ASBO and that, if an intervention order is made, "appropriate activities" (as defined in s.1G(10)) will be available. Such an order may not exceed 6 months. Failure to comply with an intervention order is a summary offence punishable with a fine not exceeding level 4 (currently £2,500).

The legislative provisions have been much amended; we have set out below those provisions that appear most relevant to criminal proceedings in a consolidated form. In addition, there is now provision enabling the grant of an injunction in relation to gang-related violence: *Policing and Crime Act* 2009 (as amended by the *Crime and Security Act* 2010) in force from January 31, 2011. Since these are civil proceedings and are not dealt with in a magistrates' court, they are not covered in this work.

23–232 A person who does not comply with the order commits an offence punishable by up to six months' imprisonment or the statutory maximum fine on summary conviction or to imprisonment for up to five years or an unlimited fine on conviction on indictment. The maximum period of imprisonment on summary conviction will increase to 12 months on the implementation of the *Criminal Justice Act* 2003, s.282.

Crime and Disorder Act 1998, ss.1, 1A, 1AA, 1AB, 1C, 1CA, 1D, 1E, 1G, 1H, 1I, 1J, 1K

Anti-social behaviour orders

1.—(1) An application for an order under this section may be made by a relevant authority if it appears to the authority that the following conditions are fulfilled with respect to any person aged 10 or over, namely— **23–233**

(a) that the person has acted, since the commencement date, in an anti-social manner, that is to say, in a manner that caused or was likely to cause harassment, alarm or distress to one or more persons not of the same household as himself; and

(b) that such an order is necessary to protect relevant persons from further anti-social acts by him.

(1A) In this section and sections 1AA, 1B, 1C, 1CA, 1E, 1F and 1K "relevant authority" means—

(a) the council for a local government area;

(aa) in relation to England, a county council;

(b) the chief officer of police of any police force maintained for a police area;

(c) the chief constable of the British Transport Police Force;

(d) any person registered under section 1 of the *Housing Act* 1996 (c.52) as a social landlord who provides or manages any houses or hostel in a local government area; or

(e) a housing action trust established by order in pursuance of section 62 of the *Housing Act* 1988.

(1B) In this section "relevant persons" means—

(a) in relation to a relevant authority falling within paragraph (a) of subsection (1A), persons within the local government area of that council;

(aa) in relation to a relevant authority falling within paragraph (aa) of subsection (1A), persons within the county of the county council;

(b) in relation to a relevant authority falling within paragraph (b) of that subsection, persons within the police area;

(c) in relation to a relevant authority falling within paragraph (c) of that subsection—

(i) persons who are within or likely to be within a place specified in section 31(1)(a) to (f) of the *Railways and Transport Safety Act* 2003 in a local government area; or

(ii) persons who are within or likely to be within such a place;

(d) in relation to a relevant authority falling within paragraph (d) or (e) of that subsection—

(i) persons who are residing in or who are otherwise on or likely to be on premises provided or managed by that authority; or

(ii) persons who are in the vicinity of or likely to be in the vicinity of such premises.

(3) Such an application shall be made by complaint to the magistrates' court.

(4) If, on such an application, it is proved that the conditions mentioned in subsection (1) above are fulfilled, the magistrates' court may make an order under this section (an "anti-social behaviour order") which prohibits the defendant from doing anything described in the order.

(5) For the purpose of determining whether the condition mentioned in subsection (1)(a) above is fulfilled, the court shall disregard any act of the defendant which he shows was reasonable in the circumstances.

(5A) Nothing in this section affects the operation of section 127 of the *Magistrates' Courts Act* 1980 (limitation of time in respect of informations laid or complaints made in magistrates' court).

(6) The prohibitions that may be imposed by an anti-social behaviour order are those necessary for the purpose of protecting persons (whether relevant persons or persons elsewhere in England and Wales) from further anti-social acts by the defendant.

(7) An anti-social behaviour order shall have effect for a period (not less than two years) specified in the order or until further order.

(8) Subject to subsection (9) below, the applicant or the defendant may apply by complaint to the court which made an anti-social behaviour order for it to be varied or discharged by a further order.

(9) Except with the consent of both parties, no anti-social behaviour order shall be discharged before the end of the period of two years beginning with the date of service of the order.

(10) If without reasonable excuse a person does anything which he is prohibited from doing by an anti-social behaviour order, he is guilty of an offence and liable—

(a) on summary conviction, to imprisonment for a term not exceeding six months or to a fine not exceeding the statutory maximum, or to both; or

(b) on conviction on indictment, to imprisonment for a term not exceeding five years or to a fine, or to both.

(10A) The following may bring proceedings for an offence under subsection (10)—

(a) a council which is a relevant authority;

(b) the council for the local government area in which a person in respect of whom an anti-social behaviour order has been made resides or appears to reside.

(10B) If proceedings for an offence under subsection (10) are brought in a youth court section 47(2) of the *Children and Young Persons Act* 1933 has effect as if the persons entitled to be present at a sitting for the purposes of those proceedings include one person authorised to be present by a relevant authority.

(10C) In proceedings for an offence under subsection (10), a copy of the original anti-social behaviour order, certified as such by the proper officer of the court which made it, is admissible as evidence of its having been made and of its contents to the same extent that oral evidence of those things is admissible in those proceedings.

(10D) In relation to proceedings brought against a child or a young person for an offence under subsection (10)—

(a) section 49 of the *Children and Young Persons Act* 1933 (restrictions on reports of proceedings in which children and young persons are concerned) does not apply in respect of the child or young person against whom the proceedings are brought;

(b) section 45 of the *Youth Justice and Criminal Evidence Act* 1999 (power to restrict reporting of criminal proceedings involving persons under 18) does so apply.

(10E) If, in relation to any such proceedings, the court does exercise its power to give a direction under section 45 of the *Youth Justice and Criminal Evidence Act* 1999, it shall give its reasons for doing so.

(11) Where a person is convicted of an offence under subsection (10) above, it shall not be open to the court by or before which he is so convicted to make an order under subsection (1)(b) (conditional discharge) of section 12 of the *Powers of Criminal Courts (Sentencing) Act* 2000 in respect of the offence.

(12) In this section—

"child" and "young person" shall have the same meaning as in the *Children and Young Persons Act* 1933;

"the commencement date" means the date of the commencement of this section;

"local government area" means—

(a) in relation to England, a district or London borough, the City of London, the Isle of Wight and the Isles of Scilly;

(b) in relation to Wales, a county or county borough.

Power of Secretary of State to add to relevant authorities

23–234 **1A.**—(1) The Secretary of State may by order provide that the chief officer of a body of constables maintained otherwise than by a police authority is, in such cases and circumstances as may be prescribed by the order, to be a relevant authority for the purposes of section 1 above.

(2) The Secretary of State may by order—

(a) provide that a person or body of any other description specified in the order is, in such cases and circumstances as may be prescribed by the order, to be a relevant authority for the purposes of such of sections 1 above and 1B, 1CA, and E below as are specified in the order; and

(b) prescribe the description of persons who are to be "relevant persons" in relation to that person or body.

Individual support orders

23–235 **1AA.**—(1) This section applies where a court makes an anti-social behaviour order in respect of a defendant who is a child or young person when that order is made.

(1A) This section also applies where—

(a) an anti-social behaviour order has previously been made in respect of such a defendant;
(b) an application is made by complaint to the court which made that order, by the relevant authority which applied for it, for an order under this section; and
(c) at the time of the hearing of the application—
(i) the defendant is still a child or young person, and
(ii) the anti-social behaviour order is still in force.

(1B) The court must consider whether the individual support conditions are fulfilled and, if satisfied that they are, must make an individual support order.

(2) An individual support order is an order which—
(a) requires the defendant to comply, for a period not exceeding six months, with such requirements as are specified in the order; and
(b) requires the defendant to comply with any directions given by the responsible officer with a view to the implementation of the requirements under paragraph (a) above.

(3) The individual support conditions are—
(a) that an individual support order would be desirable in the interests of preventing any repetition of the kind of behaviour which led to the making of—
(i) the anti-social behaviour order, or
(ii) an order varying that order (in a case where the variation is made as a result of further anti-social behaviour by the defendant);
(b) that the defendant is not already subject to an individual support order; and
(c) that the court has been notified by the Secretary of State that arrangements for implementing individual support orders are available in the area in which it appears to it that the defendant resides or will reside and the notice has not been withdrawn.

(4) If the court is not satisfied that the individual support conditions are fulfilled, it shall state in open court that it is not so satisfied and why it is not.

(5) The requirements that may be specified under subsection (2)(a) above are those that the court considers desirable in the interests of preventing any repetition of the kind of behaviour mentioned in subsection (3)(a) above.

(6) Requirements included in an individual support order, or directions given under such an order by a responsible officer, may require the defendant to do all or any of the following things—
(a) to participate in activities specified in the requirements or directions at a time or times so specified;
(b) to present himself to a person or persons so specified at a place or places and at a time or times so specified;
(c) to comply with any arrangements for his education so specified.

(7) But requirements included in, or directions given under, such an order may not require the defendant to attend (whether at the same place or at different places) on more than two days in any week; and "week" here means a period of seven days beginning with a Sunday.

(8) Requirements included in, and directions given under, an individual support order shall, as far as practicable, be such as to avoid—
(a) any conflict with the defendant's religious beliefs; and
(b) any interference with the times, if any, at which he normally works or attends school or any other educational establishment.

(9) Before making an individual support order, the court shall obtain from a social worker of a local authority or a member of a youth offending team any information which it considers necessary in order—
(a) to determine whether the individual support conditions are fulfilled, or
(b) to determine what requirements should be imposed by an individual support order if made,
and shall consider that information.

(10) In this section and section 1AB below "responsible officer", in relation to an individual support order, means one of the following who is specified in the order, namely—
(a) a social worker of a local authority;
(b) a person nominated by a person appointed as chief education officer under section 532 of the *Education Act* 1996;

Part IV

(c) a member of a youth offending team.

Individual support orders: explanation, breach, amendment etc.

23–236 **1AB.**—(1) Before making an individual support order, the court shall explain to the defendant in ordinary language—

(a) the effect of the order and of the requirements proposed to be included in it;

(b) the consequences which may follow (under subsection (3) below) if he fails to comply with any of those requirements; and

(c) that the court has power (under subsection (6) below) to review the order on the application either of the defendant or of the responsible officer.

(2) The power of the Secretary of State under section 174(4) of the *Criminal Justice Act* 2003 includes power by order to—

(a) prescribe cases in which subsection (1) above does not apply; and

(b) prescribe cases in which the explanation referred to in that subsection may be made in the absence of the defendant, or may be provided in written form.

(3) If the person in respect of whom an individual support order is made fails without reasonable excuse to comply with any requirement included in the order, he is guilty of an offence and liable on summary conviction to a fine not exceeding—

(a) if he is aged 14 or over at the date of his conviction, £1,000;

(b) if he is aged under 14 then, £250.

(4) No referral order under section 16(2) or (3) of the *Powers of Criminal Courts (Sentencing) Act* 2000 (referral of young offenders to youth offender panels) may be made in respect of an offence under subsection (3) above.

(5) If the anti-social behaviour order as a result of which an individual support order was made ceases to have effect, the individual support order (if it has not previously ceased to have effect) ceases to have effect when the anti-social behaviour order does.

(5A) The period specified as the term of an individual support order made on an application under section 1AA(1A) above must not be longer than the remaining part of the term of the anti-social behaviour order as a result of which it is made.

(6) On an application made by complaint by—

(a) the person subject to an individual support order, or

(b) the responsible officer,

the court which made the individual support order may vary or discharge it by a further order.

(7) If the anti-social behaviour order as a result of which an individual support order was made is varied, the court varying the anti-social behaviour order may by a further order vary or discharge the individual support order.

Orders on conviction in criminal proceedings

23–237 **1C.**—(1) This section applies where a person (the "offender") is convicted of a relevant offence.

(2) If the court considers—

(a) that the offender has acted, at any time since the commencement date, in an anti-social manner, that is to say in a manner that caused or was likely to cause harassment, alarm or distress to one or more persons not of the same household as himself, and

(b) that an order under this section is necessary to protect persons in any place in England and Wales from further anti-social acts by him,

it may make an order which prohibits the offender from doing anything described in the order.

(3) The court may make an order under this section—

(a) if the prosecutor asks it to do so, or

(b) if the court thinks it is appropriate to do so.

(3A) For the purpose of deciding whether to make an order under this section the court may consider evidence led by the prosecution and the defence.

(3B) It is immaterial whether evidence led in pursuance of subsection (3A) would have been admissible in the proceedings in which the offender was convicted.

(4) An order under this section shall not be made except—

(a) in addition to a sentence imposed in respect of the relevant offence; or

(b) in addition to an order discharging him conditionally

(4A) The court may adjourn any proceedings in relation to an order under this section even after sentencing the offender.

(4B) If the offender does not appear for any adjourned proceedings, the court may further adjourn the proceedings or may issue a warrant for his arrest.

(4C) But the court may not issue a warrant for the offender's arrest unless it is satisfied that he has had adequate notice of the time and place of the adjourned proceedings.

(5) An order under this section takes effect on the day on which it is made, but the court may provide in any such order that such requirements of the order as it may specify shall, during any period when the offender is detained in legal custody, be suspended until his release from that custody.

(9) Subsections (7), (10), (10C), (10D), (10E) and (11) of section 1 apply for the purposes of the making and effect of orders made by virtue of this section as they apply for the purposes of the making and effect of anti-social behaviour orders.

(9ZA) An order under this section made in respect of a person under the age of 17, or an order varying such an order, may specify a relevant authority (other than the chief officer of police mentioned in section 1K(2)(a)) as being responsible for carrying out a review under section 1J of the operation of the order.

(9A) The council for the local government area in which a person in respect of whom an anti-social behaviour order has been made resides or appears to reside may bring proceedings under section 1(10) (as applied by subsection (9) above) for breach of an order under subsection (2) above.

(9AA) Sections 1AA and 1AB apply in relation to orders under this section, with any necessary modifications, as they apply in relation to anti-social behaviour orders.

(9AB) In their application by virtue of subsection (9AA), sections 1AA(1A)(b) and 1AB(6) have effect as if the words "by complaint" were omitted.

(9AC) In its application by virtue of subsection (9AA), section 1AA(1A)(b) has effect as if the reference to the relevant authority which applied for the anti-social behaviour order were a reference to the chief officer of police, or other relevant authority, responsible under section 1K(2)(a) or (b) for carrying out a review of the order under this section.

(9B) Subsection (9C) applies in relation to proceedings in which an order under subsection (2) is made against a child or young person who is convicted of an offence.

(9C) In so far as the proceedings relate to the making of the order—

(a) section 49 of the *Children and Young Persons Act* 1933 (restrictions on reports of proceedings in which children and young persons are concerned) does not apply in respect of the child or young person against whom the order is made;

(b) section 39 of that Act (power to prohibit publication of certain matter) does so apply.

(10) In this section—

"child" and "young person" have the same meaning as in the *Children and Young Persons Act* 1933;

"the commencement date" has the same meaning as in section 1 above;

"the court" in relation to an offender means—

(a) the court by or before which he is convicted of the relevant offence; or

(b) if he is committed to the Crown Court to be dealt with for that offence, the Crown Court; and

"relevant offence" means an offence committed after the coming into force of section 64 of the *Police Reform Act* 2002.

Variation and discharge of orders under section 1C

1CA.—(1) An offender subject to an order under section 1C may apply to the court which made it for it to be varied or discharged. **23–238**

(2) If he does so, he must also send written notice of his application to the Director of Public Prosecutions.

(3) The Director of Public Prosecutions may apply to the court which made an order under section 1C for it to be varied or discharged.

(4) A relevant authority may also apply to the court which made an order under section 1C for it to be varied or discharged if it appears to it that—

(a) in the case of variation, the protection of relevant persons from anti-social acts by the person subject to the order would be more appropriately effected by a variation of the order;

(b) in the case of discharge, that it is no longer necessary to protect relevant persons from anti-social acts by him by means of such an order.

(5) If the Director of Public Prosecutions or a relevant authority applies for the variation or discharge of an order under section 1C, he or it must also send written notice of the application to the person subject to the order.

(6) In the case of an order under section 1C made by a magistrates' court, the references in subsections (1), (3) and (4) to the court by which the order was made include a reference to any magistrates' court acting in the same local justice area as that court.

(7) No order under section 1C shall be discharged on an application under this section before the end of the period of two years beginning with the day on which the order takes effect, unless—

(a) in the case of an application under subsection (1), the Director of Public Prosecutions consents, or

(b) in the case of an application under subsection (3) or (4), the offender consents.

Interim Orders

23–239 **1D.**—(1) This section applies where—

(a) an application is made for an anti-social behaviour order;

(b) an application is made for an order under section 1B;

(c) a request is made by the prosecution for an order under section 1C; or

(d) the court is minded to make an order under section 1C of its own motion.

(2) If, before determining the application or request, or before deciding whether to make an order under section 1C of its own motion, the court considers that it is just to make an order under this section pending the determination of that application or request or before making that decision, it may make such an order.

(3) An order under this section is an order which prohibits the defendant from doing anything described in the order.

(4) An order under this section—

(a) shall be for a fixed period;

(b) may be varied, renewed or discharged;

(c) shall, if it has not previously ceased to have effect, cease to have effect on the determination of the application or request mentioned in subsection (1), or on the court's making a decision as to whether or not to make an order under section 1C of its own motion.

(5) In relation to cases to which this section applies by virtue of paragraph (a) or (b) of subsection (1), subsections (6), (8) and (10) to (12) of section 1 apply for the purposes of the making and effect of orders under this section as they apply for the purposes of the making and effect of anti-social behaviour orders.

(6) In relation to cases to which this section applies by virtue of paragraph (c) or (d) of subsection (1)—

(a) subsections (6) and (10) to (12) of section 1 apply for the purposes of the making and effect of orders under this section as they apply for the purposes of the making and effect of anti-social behaviour orders; and

(b) section 1CA applies for the purposes of the variation or discharge of an order under this section as it applies for the purposes of the variation or discharge of an order under section 1C.

Consultation requirements

23–240 **1E.**—(1) This section applies to—

(a) applications for an anti-social behaviour order; and

(b) applications for an order under section 1B.

(2) Before making an application to which this section applies, the council for a local government area shall consult the chief officer of police of the police force maintained for the police area within which that local government area lies.

(3) Before making an application to which this section applies, a chief officer of police shall consult the council for the local government area in which the person in relation to whom the application is to be made resides or appears to reside.

(4) Before making an application to which this section applies, a relevant authority other than a council for a local government area or a chief officer of police shall consult—

(a) the council for the local government area in which the person in relation to whom the application is to be made resides or appears to reside; and

(b) the chief officer of police of the police force maintained for the police area within which that local government area lies.

(5) Subsection (4)(a) does not apply if the relevant authority is a county council for a county in which there are no districts.

Intervention orders

1G.—(1) This section applies if, in relation to a person who has attained the age of 18, a relevant authority— **23–241**

(a) makes an application for an anti-social behaviour order or an order under section 1B above (the behaviour order),

(b) has obtained from an appropriately qualified person a report relating to the effect on the person's behaviour of the misuse of controlled drugs or of such other factors as the Secretary of State by order prescribes, and

(c) has engaged in consultation with such persons as the Secretary of State by order prescribes for the purpose of ascertaining that, if the report recommends that an order under this section is made, appropriate activities will be available.

(2) The relevant authority may make an application to the court which is considering the application for the behaviour order for an order under this section (an intervention order).

(3) If the court—

(a) makes the behaviour order, and

(b) is satisfied that the relevant conditions are met,

it may also make an intervention order.

(4) The relevant conditions are—

(a) that an intervention order is desirable in the interests of preventing a repetition of the behaviour which led to the behaviour order being made (trigger behaviour);

(b) that appropriate activities relating to the trigger behaviour or its cause are available for the defendant;

(c) that the defendant is not (at the time the intervention order is made) subject to another intervention order or to any other treatment relating to the trigger behaviour or its cause (whether on a voluntary basis or by virtue of a requirement imposed in pursuance of any enactment);

(d) that the court has been notified by the Secretary of State that arrangements for implementing intervention orders are available in the area in which it appears that the defendant resides or will reside and the notice has not been withdrawn.

(5) An intervention order is an order which—

(a) requires the defendant to comply, for a period not exceeding six months, with such requirements as are specified in the order, and

(b) requires the defendant to comply with any directions given by a person authorised to do so under the order with a view to the implementation of the requirements under paragraph (a) above.

(6) An intervention order or directions given under the order may require the defendant—

(a) to participate in the activities specified in the requirement or directions at a time or times so specified;

(b) to present himself to a person or persons so specified at a time or times so specified.

(7) Requirements included in, or directions given under, an intervention order must, as far as practicable, be such as to avoid—

(a) any conflict with the defendant's religious beliefs, and

(b) any interference with the times (if any) at which he normally works or attends an educational establishment.

(8) If the defendant fails to comply with a requirement included in or a direction given under an intervention order, the person responsible for the provision or supervision of appropriate activities under the order must inform the relevant authority of that fact.

(9) The person responsible for the provision or supervision of appropriate activities is a person of such description as is prescribed by order made by the Secretary of State.

(10) In this section—

"appropriate activities" means such activities, or activities of such a description, as are prescribed by order made by the Secretary of State for the purposes of this section;

"appropriately qualified person" means a person who has such qualifications or experience as the Secretary of State by order prescribes;

"controlled drug" has the same meaning as in the *Misuse of Drugs Act* 1971;

"relevant authority" means a relevant authority for the purposes of section 1 above.

(11) An order under this section made by the Secretary of State may make different provision for different purposes.

(12) This section and section 1H below apply to a person in respect of whom a behaviour order has been made subject to the following modifications—

(a) in subsection (1) above paragraph (a) must be ignored;

(b) in subsection (2) above, for "is considering the application for" substitute "made";

(c) in subsection (3) above paragraph (a), the word "and" following it and the word "also" must be ignored.

Intervention orders: explanation, breach, amendment etc.

23–242 **1H.**—(1) Before making an intervention order the court must explain to the defendant in ordinary language—

(a) the effect of the order and of the requirements proposed to be included in it,

(b) the consequences which may follow (under subsection (3) below) if he fails to comply with any of those requirements, and

(c) that the court has power (under subsection (5) below) to review the order on the application either of the defendant or of the relevant authority.

(2) The power of the Secretary of State under section 174(4) of the *Criminal Justice Act* 2003 includes power by order to—

(a) prescribe cases in which subsection (1) does not apply, and

(b) prescribe cases in which the explanation referred to in that subsection may be made in the absence of the defendant, or may be provided in written form.

(3) If a person in respect of whom an intervention order is made fails without reasonable excuse to comply with any requirement included in the order he is guilty of an offence and liable on summary conviction to a fine not exceeding level 4 on the standard scale.

(4) If the behaviour order as a result of which an intervention order is made ceases to have effect, the intervention order (if it has not previously ceased to have effect) ceases to have effect when the behaviour order does.

(5) On an application made by—

(a) a person subject to an intervention order, or

(b) the relevant authority,

the court which made the intervention order may vary or discharge it by a further order.

(6) An application under subsection (5) made to a magistrates' court must be made by complaint.

(7) If the behaviour order as a result of which an intervention order was made is varied, the court varying the behaviour order may by a further order vary or discharge the intervention order.

(8) Expressions used in this section and in section 1G have the same meaning in this section as in that section.

Special measures for witnesses

23–243 **1I.**—(1) This section applies to the following proceedings—

(a) any proceedings in a magistrates' court on an application for an anti-social behaviour order,

(b) any proceedings in a magistrates' court or the Crown Court so far as relating to the issue whether to make an order under section 1C, and

(c) any proceedings in a magistrates' court so far as relating to the issue whether to make an order under section 1D.

(2) Chapter 1 of Part 2 of the *Youth Justice and Criminal Evidence Act* 1999 (special measures directions in the case of vulnerable and intimidated witnesses) shall apply in relation to any such proceedings as it applies in relation to criminal proceedings, but with—

(a) the omission of the provisions of that Act mentioned in subsection (3) (which make provision appropriate only in the context of criminal proceedings), and
(b) any other necessary modifications.

(3) The provisions are—
(a) section 17(4),
(b) section 21(1)(b) and (5) to (7),
(c) section 22(1)(b) and (2)(b) and (c),
(d) section 27(10), and
(e) section 32.

(4) Any rules of court made under or for the purposes of Chapter 1 of Part 2 of that Act shall apply in relation to proceedings to which this section applies—
(a) to such extent as may be provided by rules of court, and
(b) subject to such modifications as may be so provided.

(5) Section 47 of that Act (restrictions on reporting special measures directions etc.) applies, with any necessary modifications, in relation to—
(a) a direction under section 19 of the Act as applied by this section, or
(b) a direction discharging or varying such a direction,
and sections 49 and 51 of that Act (offences) apply accordingly.

Review of orders under sections 1, 1B and 1C

1J.—(1) This section applies where— 23–244
(a) an anti-social behaviour order,
(b) an order under section 1B, or
(c) an order under section 1C,
has been made in respect of a person under the age of 17.

(2) If—
(a) the person subject to the order will be under the age of 18 at the end of a period specified in subsection (3) (a "review period"), and
(b) the term of the order runs until the end of that period or beyond,
then before the end of that period a review of the operation of the order shall be carried out.

(3) The review periods are—
(a) the period of 12 months beginning with—
(i) the day on which the order was made, or
(ii) if during that period there is a supplemental order (or more than one), the date of the supplemental order (or the last of them);
(b) a period of 12 months beginning with—
(i) the day after the end of the previous review period, or
(ii) if during that period there is a supplemental order (or more than one), the date of the supplemental order (or the last of them).

(4) In subsection (3) "supplemental order" means—
(a) a further order varying the order in question;
(b) an individual support order made in relation to the order in question on an application under section 1AA(1A).

(5) Subsection (2) does not apply in relation to any review period if the order is discharged before the end of that period.

(6) A review under this section shall include consideration of—
(a) the extent to which the person subject to the order has complied with it;
(b) the adequacy of any support available to the person to help him comply with it;
(c) any matters relevant to the question whether an application should be made for the order to be varied or discharged.

(7) Those carrying out or participating in a review under this section shall have regard to any guidance issued by the Secretary of State when considering—
(a) how the review should be carried out;
(b) what particular matters should be dealt with by the review;
(c) what action (if any) it would be appropriate to take in consequence of the findings of the review.

Responsibility for, and participation in, reviews under section 1J

1K.—(1) A review under section 1J of an anti-social behaviour order or an order under section 1B shall be carried out by the relevant authority that applied for the order. 23–245

(2) A review under section 1J of an order under section 1C shall be carried out—

(a) (except where paragraph (b) applies) by the appropriate chief officer of police;

(b) where a relevant authority is specified under section 1C(9ZA), by that authority.

(3) A local authority, in carrying out a review under section 1J, shall act in co-operation with the appropriate chief officer of police; and it shall be the duty of that chief officer to co-operate in the carrying out of the review.

(4) The chief officer of police of a police force, in carrying out a review under section 1J, shall act in co-operation with the appropriate local authority; and it shall be the duty of that local authority to co-operate in the carrying out of the review.

(5) A relevant authority other than a local authority or chief officer of police, in carrying out a review under section 1J, shall act in co-operation with—

(a) the appropriate local authority, and

(b) the appropriate chief officer of police;

and it shall be the duty of that local authority and that chief officer to co-operate in the carrying out of the review.

(6) A chief officer of police or other relevant authority carrying out a review under section 1J may invite the participation in the review of a person or body not required by subsection (3), (4) or (5) to co-operate in the carrying out of the review.

(7) In this section—

"the appropriate chief officer of police" means the chief officer of police of the police force maintained for the police area in which the person subject to the order resides or appears to reside;

"the appropriate local authority" means the council for the local government area (within the meaning given in section 1(12)) in which the person subject to the order resides or appears to reside."

(2) Fulfilment of criteria

23–246 The criteria that must be fulfilled before a court makes an order in respect of a person convicted of an offence are that:

— the offender has acted in an anti-social manner at any time since the commencement of this provision (December 2, 2002) and

— that an order is necessary to protect other people in England and Wales from further anti-social acts from him.

In *Birmingham City Council v. Dixon* [2009] EWHC Admin 761 the applicant sought to use evidence of conduct after the dates stated in the application to substantiate the evidence on which the application was based. This conduct had taken place whilst the person in respect of whom the application was made had been subject to an interim order. The District Judge ruled that the evidence was inadmissible since it was not relevant to either of the criteria on which the decision to make an order had to be based. The Divisional Court disagreed with that conclusion holding that (whilst not removing the obligation to prove the allegations specified in the complaint) such evidence might be relevant either in showing a propensity to behave in an anti-social manner or in substantiating the need for an order.

23–247 An "anti-social manner" is a manner that causes (or is likely to cause) harassment, alarm or distress to one or more people who are not of the same household as the offender: s.1CA.

Once made, an order can be varied or discharged but no application for discharge may be made until two years have elapsed: s.1C(6) and (8). If an order is made in relation to a person who is to remain in custody, then the provisions of the order may be suspended until release: s.1C(5). Although it may not be appropriate to make an order where a defendant is sentenced to a long period in custody, that is unlikely to be an issue in a magistrates' court: see *post*, *P*. Changes to the *Prosecution of Offences Act* 1985 give to the DPP the power to take over proceedings for variation or discharge of an ASBO made under s.1C.

23–248 For consideration of the standard of proof to be applied when the court is considering making an ASBO: *R. (McCann) v. Manchester Crown Court* [2003] 1 A.C. 787,

HL. More detailed consideration was given to the making of orders under this provision in *C. v. Sunderland Youth Court* [2004] 1 Cr.App.R.(S.) 76 and in *P.* [2004] 2 Cr.App.R.(S.) 63. In the *Sunderland* case, the Divisional Court was reviewing an order made in a youth court. It emphasised that courts must act fairly and take account of all relevant considerations. Whilst that will vary with each case, the basis for both the order itself and its scope must be absolutely clear and the terms of the order must be clearly and accurately explained to the defendant by the court. The written order must correctly reflect the order made by the court.

In *P.*, the Court of Appeal considered a range of issues arising from sentencing in the Crown Court including the making of an order under s.1C. Endorsing the comments in the *Sunderland* case, six key principles emerged:

- the test for making the order is the necessity to protect the public from further anti-social acts by the offender
- the terms of the order must be precise
- the terms of the order must be capable of being understood by the offender
- the findings of fact giving rise to the making of the order must be recorded
- the order must be explained to the offender
- the exact terms of the order must both be pronounced in open court and accurately reproduced in the written order.

The Court considered whether it could be said that an order was "necessary" where a person had been sentenced to a substantial period in custody which would be followed by a period on licence in the community. Whilst provisions in the order (such as geographical constraints) may effectively supplement licence conditions, generally it would not be possible for a court to be satisfied that such an order was necessary when it would only become operative after a substantial period in custody—here the Crown Court had been dealing with a youth and the sentence was four years detention (reduced to three on appeal). This approach was emphasised again by the Court of Appeal in *Thomas* (2008) 172 J.P. 545. An adult offender was sentenced to 8 years and 6 months for street robbery, drug and other offences. He was also made subject to an anti-social behaviour order for 10 years suspended until after release. His appeal against the anti-social behaviour order was successful. Given that he would be on licence for over 4 years on release, there could be no necessity for an order. However, it is ultimately an issue for the court as to whether such an order is necessary. In *Barclay* [2011] EWCA Crim 32, the Court of Appeal reviewed sentences imposed on those who had been openly dealing in Class A drugs in an area where such dealing was rife and causing considerable public disquiet; the dealing was accompanied by widespread intimidation directed towards both individuals and organisations. Upholding both lengthy custodial sentences and ASBOs of between three and five years from release, the Court drew attention to the wider anti-social behaviour taking place in the area to which such an order could be an effective deterrent. **23–249**

Necessity for an order was also considered in *Belaid* [2008] EWCA Crim 2153. The defendant was a long term heroin and crack addict who funded his habit by stealing bags and contents in public places (such as railway stations, bars and cafes) where they had been put down temporarily. He was sentenced to 30 months imprisonment and made subject to an anti-social behaviour order for 3 years from release prohibiting him from entering 16 named main line railway stations in London. His appeal against the anti-social behaviour order was allowed; since the defendant would be on licence for at least 15 months after release, conditions on that licence were much more likely to be effective and so it could not be said that the order was necessary. This is less likely to be the case in a magistrates' court but may be the case in a youth court where the maximum custodial sentence can be 24 months.

As emphasised in *P.*, the nature of an ASBO is such that clarity about the terms of the order is of high importance and the written order must correctly reflect the order made by the court. An ingenious attempt was made to circumvent the terms of an order when the written order was at variance with the terms announced by the court in *R.* **23–250**

(Walkling) v. DPP (2004) 168 J.P. 65. An order was made in a magistrates' court for two years. The defendant was present when the order was made. The written order recorded that the appellant was subject to the terms of the order until a specified date which was one day less than the two years. The defendant breached the order and sought to evade responsibility by arguing that the order was a nullity. That was given short shrift—the order was that pronounced by the court and the difference in the written order did not have any effect on the nature of the breach. The Court was also very concerned that parts of the order were both too vague and general and could not readily be understood by a person of the age and educational attainment of the offender.

One of the more important recent judgments is that in *Boness; Bebbington* (2005) 169 J.P. 621. This reviews a wide range of authorities and situations and seeks to provide substantial clarification.

i) Whilst an order may be made indefinitely (it must be for at least two years), that is not advisable. Not every part of an order need be required to last for at least two years and so the original provisions can be removed or amended during the first two years without avoiding the order provided that there must be at least one prohibition that does last for at least two years: *Lonerghan v. Lewes Crown Court* (2005) 169 J.P. 324.

ii) Two statutory criteria are provided—that the offender has acted in an anti-social manner in the past and that an order is necessary to protect persons from further anti-social acts by the offender. Once a court has decided that an order is necessary, it must consider what prohibitions to include. Each order (and each prohibition within an order) must be targeted at the individual and at the type of anti-social behaviour that it is aimed to prevent. The court should consider carefully the need for an order or for a particular prohibition against the background of the case—it is not appropriate to utilise a standard order: *Boness* (2005) 169 J.P. 621.

iii) The order must be proportionate to the legitimate aim pursued and commensurate with the risk to be guarded against: *ibid.*

iv) The order must be clear so that the offender will know precisely what it is he is prohibited from doing: ibid. An example of a condition too widely drawn can be seen in *R. (W.) v. DPP* [2005] EWCA Civ 1333 where the Court considered one of the conditions of an order that restrained W (a youth) from "Committing any criminal offence". There is a long running issue as to the extent that it is appropriate or lawful for an ASBO to prohibit what is already a criminal offence (see *below*). This case confirmed that orders must be sufficiently certain for the subject to know what is prohibited—it was not possible for a person (certainly a youth) to know what was and what was not a criminal offence.

v) Furthermore, it was accepted that, where an order is plainly invalid (as the order was in this case), it was open to a magistrates' court to consider submissions to that effect without the need for proceedings before the High Court to declare the order (or at least the critical part of it) to be invalid. Note that this aspect has been doubted by later authorities.

vi) The order must also be clear in a way that enables any breach to be identified and enforced.

vii) There is no requirement that the acts prohibited by an ASBO should, in themselves, give rise to harassment, alarm or distress (*McGrath* [2005] EWCA Crim. 353) though the order must be designed to prevent further such acts from taking place. If such parts of the order are breached but there is no harassment, alarm or distress caused, that may influence the approach to sentence (see *post*).

viii) The purpose of an ASBO is not to punish the offender; it is to prevent further anti-social acts. A court should not allow itself to be persuaded to reduce the sentence that it would otherwise impose because it is making an ASBO: *Lonerghan*.

ix) A number of orders have sought to prohibit conduct that would also be a criminal offence in its own right. This is now generally disapproved of: *Boness* (at. paras. 31–39) subject to a small number of exceptions. An ASBO is designed to enable intervention before a criminal act is committed and it should be targeting the preparatory or preliminary acts rather than the crimes themselves. Thus, in relation to orders made to increase the maximum sentence available (for example, driving whilst disqualified which carries a maximum of 6 months imprisonment), such an order should not be made unless the court is satisfied that the normal range of penalties would be insufficient deterrence. Where the offence itself is punishable with imprisonment, the court doubted whether the availability of a longer period would be significant and such a requirement would, therefore, fail the test of necessity. It may be different where the maximum penalty is a non-custodial sentence. The part of the judgment in *P.* (see *ante*) that suggested that there is unlikely to be any harm in reminding offenders that certain matters constitute criminal conduct by including prohibitions in the ASBO was doubted. The test should not be whether the offender needs reminding but whether the prohibitions are necessary. The later case of *Lamb* (see *post*) considered how to approach sentencing for a breach where the acts of the offender not only breached the terms of the order but were themselves a criminal offence with a lower maximum penalty for that for beaching the ASBO.

A further summary of the process and criteria to be considered has been set out by the Court of Appeal (Criminal Division). In *Wadmore, Foreman* [2006] EWCA Crim. 686 the Court considered a range of decisions including that of the House of Lords in *McCann* [2003] 1 A.C. 787, and of the Court of Appeal in *Boness, Bebbington* [2005] EWCA Crim 2395. It identified ten principles (statutory references are to the *Crime and Disorder Act* 1998 as amended):

(1) Proceedings under s.1C are civil in nature, so that hearsay evidence is admissible, but a court must be satisfied to a criminal standard that the defendant has acted in the anti-social manner alleged.

(2) The test of "*necessity*" set out in s.1C(2)(b) requires the exercise of judgement or evaluation; it does not require proof beyond reasonable doubt that the order is "necessary".

(3) It was particularly important that the findings of fact giving rise to the making of the order are recorded by the Court.

(4) The terms of the order made must be precise and capable of being understood by the offender.

(5) The conditions in the order must be enforceable in the sense that the conditions should allow a breach to be readily identified and capable of being proved. Therefore the conditions should not impose generic prohibitions, but should identify and prohibit the particular type of anti-social behaviour that gives rise to the necessity of an ASBO.

(6) There is power under s.1C(5) to suspend the starting point of an ASBO until an offender has been released from a custodial sentence. However, where a custodial sentence in excess of a few months is passed and the offender is liable to be released on licence and is thus subject to recall, the circumstances will be limited in which there would be a demonstrable necessity to make a suspended ASBO, to take effect on release. There might be cases where geographical restraints could supplement licence conditions.

(7) Because the test for making an ASBO and prohibiting an offender from doing something is one of necessity, each separate order prohibiting a person from doing a specified thing must be necessary to protect persons from anti-social behaviour by the offender. Therefore, each order must be specifically fashioned to deal with the offender concerned. The court has to ask: "is this order necessary to protect persons in any place in England and Wales from further anti-social acts by him".

(8) Not all conditions set out in an ASBO have to run for the full term of the ASBO itself. The test must always be is what is necessary to deal with the particular anti-social behaviour of the offender and what is proportionate in the circumstances.

(9) The order is there to protect others from anti-social behaviour by the offender. Therefore the court should not impose an order which prohibits an offender from committing specified criminal offences if the sentence which could be passed following conviction for the offence should be a sufficient deterrent.

(10) It is unlawful to make an ASBO as if it were a further sentence or punishment. An ASBO must therefore not be used merely to increase the sentence of imprisonment that the offender is to receive.

Another example demonstrating the need for care in determining whether an order is necessary can be found in *Barnard* [2006] EWCA Crim 2041. The defendant had been sentenced to 15 months imprisonment for theft from a motor vehicle. He had 11 previous convictions many for dishonesty offences. There was ample evidence that he habitually committed crimes against vehicles parked on the streets of West London and caused considerable distress. The court also made an ASBO covering the whole of Greater London and prohibiting the carrying of a stone or rock or similar object for breaking glass. In revoking the order, the court stated that:

> "On the question of whether an ASBO was necessary in the present case, ... the Crown agreed that the purpose of an ASBO is preventative and that the test is one of necessity. [Counsel] submitted that, in this case, there was a real need for an ASBO because it could enable the police to act before the offender actually committed his crimes. However, we found ourselves unable to accept that submission. We can envisage this offender loitering in the streets near some parked cars. If he is known to the police he will be watched, as he was in the instant case, with, in this case, the assistance of CCTV, and if he attacks a car he will be arrested. [Counsel's] submission was that the police would be able to stop and search him for stones and rocks and other items for breaking glass before he could use them. However, in our view an order to that effect is likely to be of very limited use. The description of this offence demonstrated that it was the work of a few seconds. We do not think that the power given by this ASBO would provide any useful addition to the police's existing powers to arrest and initiate a prosecution. Accordingly, we are persuaded that this is not a case in which an ASBO should have been imposed. One is not necessary for the protection of the public from further anti-social acts. We stress that we are most sympathetic to the task of the police in trying to monitor and prevent this type of prevalent crime. But we do think that ordinary policing methods are the way in which it must be done and not by the imposition of an ASBO which does no more than to seek to prohibit the commission of a crime. We would add that if we had been minded to uphold the ASBO in this case we would have cut it down in both time and place, heeding the advice in *Boness* that such orders must be proportionate in the circumstances."

23–251 The first point from *Boness* (above) indicated that an indefinite order would not usually be advisable. Unusually, the Court of Appeal has upheld an anti-social behaviour order that was without limitation of time: *Bowker* [2007] EWCA Crim 1608. The 18-year-old defendant had been convicted of a serious offence of violent disorder arising from an incident outside a night club in Wigan. He received a custodial sentence and the court made an anti-social behaviour order. The prohibition in the order was not to enter Wigan Town centre on any day between 10pm and 7am. The evidence suggested a significant risk that the defendant would become involved in violence if at liberty to attend a night club in Wigan. Since he did not live in Wigan and was only excluded during hours when the primary purpose could only have been to go to a night club, the court accepted that it was an appropriate condition. Whilst the length was a cause for concern, the court noted the power to apply for the order to be modified in due course and determined that it would not be right to interfere with an order considered necessary in the context of violence with which the judge would have been familiar.

A further example of such an order can be found in *Avery* [2009] EWCA Crim 2670; [2010] 2 Cr.App.R.(S.) 33, a case arising out of concerted attacks against those connected with Huntingdon Life Sciences in which the defendants were convicted of conspiracy to commit blackmail. The Court of Appeal (Criminal Division) agreed with the Crown Court that some of the defendants were "lifelong veteran fanatical animal rights activists" who were unlikely to change their activities on release from prison. Should there be such a change, there was a right to apply for variation of the order. Responding to arguments that such an order infringed rights under arts 10 and 11 of the European Convention on Human Rights, the Court of Appeal (Criminal Division) considered that the restriction was proportionate to the aim to be achieved noting the comments of Bingham MR in *Burrows v. Asadani* [1995] 1 W.L.R. 1372 that "Respect for the freedom of the aggressor should never lead a court to deny necessary protection to the victim".

Many cases have emphasised the importance of the terms of an anti-social behaviour order being clear, precise, targeted to the individual and the type of behaviour it is aimed to prevent and both proportionate to the aim of the order and commensurate with the risk to be guarded against. In *N. v. DPP* [2007] EWHC 883 Admin; (2007) 171 J.P. 393, the subject of the order was 15 years old. One of the prohibitions was against "congregating in groups of 3 or more in a public place other than when with adults over the age of 21 years". The Divisional Court accepted that N's behaviour was likely to be worse when in the company of others but that this condition would prohibit him from attending sporting or other outdoor events. The prohibition agreed by the parties and endorsed by the court was "prohibited from congregating in a public place in a group of 2 or more persons in a manner causing or likely to cause any person to fear for their own safety".

In *R. (on the application of B) v. Greenwich Magistrates' Court* (2009) 173 J.P. 52, an order was made containing a prohibition on "wearing any article of clothing with an attached hood in any public place in the London Borough of Greenwich, whether the hood is up or down". On appeal, the defendant argued that that prohibition was unreasonable and that it infringed the right to freedom of expression guaranteed by art. 10 of the European Convention on Human Rights. The defendant was a member of a gang which, it was agreed, intimidated members of the public through language and gestures; the hooded tops were worn to help conceal identity. The District Judge (Magistrates' Court) was satisfied that this prohibition would "reduce the swagger, menace and fear of anti-social behaviour". The Divisional Court upheld the prohibition; on the facts found, it satisfied the requirements.

In *M. v. DPP* [2007] EWHC 1032 Admin; (2007) 171 J.P. 457, the Divisional Court considered a prohibition "not to knowingly associate with a person or persons whilst such persons are engaged in attempting or conspiring to commit any criminal offence in England and Wales". Unsurprisingly, the court removed the prohibition. Even assuming it prohibited the defendant from associating with those he knew to be committing a criminal offence (which is not quite what it says), it still required the exercise of a value judgement that might require the defendant to make an instant decision about what was being done and, in particular, whether that had reached the stage of being a conspiracy.

A further issue was considered by the Divisional Court in *R. (on the application of Cooke) v. DPP* (2009) 173 J.P. 596. The defendant had numerous previous convictions for public order offences; having been convicted of causing harassment, alarm and distress he was made subject to an anti-social behaviour order. During the hearing, the court had been informed that the defendant had been diagnosed as suffering from a "borderline personality disorder and post-traumatic stress disorder". It was argued that an order was not necessary because the defendant's mental state was such that he would be unable to understand and comply with the terms of the order. However, the court found that the defendant was able to understand what the order meant and what behaviour would breach it. Confirming that it would be wrong to make an order on a person who, by reason of mental health, would not be able to understand or comply with the order, the Divisional Court nonetheless confirmed that the fact that a person would be likely to breach an order because of a personality disorder was not, in itself, a good reason for not making the order.

Procedural Rules are in the *Criminal Procedure Rules 2011* (S.I. 2011 No. 1709), Pt 50 (Civil behaviour orders after verdict or finding) applies where the defendant has been charged on or after April 7, 2008 and in any other case where the court so orders; given the benefits of the rules and the general discretion of the court in r. 50.9 (see below), it can be anticipated that these rules will be adopted in most cases.

Amongst the provisions in Pt 50, some apply specifically to "behaviour orders"; these include full and interim anti-social behaviour orders made under s.1C and s.1D, football banning orders, restraining orders made on conviction or acquittal and sexual offences prevention orders.

Rule 50.2 sets out rules of general application. Other than for an interim order, a behaviour order must not be made unless the subject of it has had the opportunity to consider the proposed order and the reasons for it and to make representations at a hearing; that opportunity does not need to have been taken up. The safeguard for an interim order is that, if the subject of the order is not present when it is made, that order has no effect unless a document recording the order is handed to the subject not more than 7 days after it was made.

Rule 50.3 sets out the procedure to be followed where, if the defendant was convicted of an offence, the prosecution would wish the court to make an anti-social behaviour order. The prosecutor is under an obligation to serve a notice (in the prescribed form) setting out the intention to apply for an order; in that notice, the relevant facts are to be summarised, the evidence to be relied upon is to be identified (including a copy of any written statement to be relied on that has not already been served) as is the order sought. As soon as practicable (and without awaiting verdict in the criminal case), this notice must be served on the court, the defendant and anyone else on whom the order "would be likely to have a significant adverse effect". The defendant is then under an obligation to serve written notice of evidence on the court and the prosecutor, again as soon as practicable and without awaiting verdict.

Where a court indicates that it may wish to make an anti-social behaviour order on its own initiative, r. 50.4 requires each party to serve notice of any particular evidence which it wishes the court to take into account. That notice must be served on the court and on every other party.

Where any evidence is hearsay, the party wishing to introduce it must notify the court and any person directly affected: r. 50.6. A procedure is provided where a party intends to seek the permission of the court to cross examine a person who made a statement that is sought to be relied upon as hearsay: r. 50.7. Application must be in writing not more than 7 days after service of the notice indicating an intention to rely on hearsay evidence; that application must be served on the court, on the party intending to introduce the hearsay evidence and every one on whom notice has been served regarding that introduction.

Whilst a court may determine the application without a hearing, it may not dismiss it without giving the applicant an opportunity to make representations at a hearing; nor may a court allow it unless everyone on whom notice is served has had at least 7 days in which to make representations, including on whether or not there should be a hearing.

Rule 50.8 sets out a process for where a party wishes to challenge the "credibility or consistency" of a person who made the statement intended to be introduced as hearsay. Written warning must be served. If the party then chooses to introduce the evidence as oral evidence, further notice must be served to that effect.

Applications to vary or revoke an anti-social behaviour order are now governed by r. 50.5 which is subject to the statutory provisions. Application must be in writing together with notice of any particular evidence that a party wishes the court to take into account. Such an application can be determined with or without a hearing; however, an application may not be dismissed without allowing the applicant an opportunity to make representations at a hearing; nor may it be allowed by the court unless everyone on whom notice is served has had at least 14 days in which to make representations: r. 50.5(5). Where application is to a magistrates' court, it must be by complaint and the court must issue a summons for the hearing: r. 50.5(6).

In relation to any of these provisions, a court has discretion to shorten or extend the time limits or to allow notices or applications to be in a different form from that prescribed or, indeed, to be given orally rather than in writing: r. 50.9.

In *R. (on the application of Langley) v. Preston Crown Court* (2009) 172 J.P. 605, the Divisional Court had to consider complex provisions relating to the right to appeal against a variation of an anti-social behaviour order. In this case, the anti-social behaviour order had been made for 3.5 years in "stand alone" proceedings initiated by a local authority. Before it expired, it was varied by a magistrates' court (on the application of the local authority) by extending it for a further 2 years. Having reviewed the relevant statutory provisions and case law, the Divisional Court concluded that:

- in the county court, there is a right of appeal against an order or its variation to the High Court or Court of Appeal (as appropriate) but only with permission which would only be given if there was a real prospect of success or other good reason—a rehearing would be exceptional;
- in the Crown Court, where an order is made on conviction, there is a right of appeal against an order (and probably a variation) to the Court of Appeal with leave; any appeal would normally be allowed only if the decision was wrong in principle or in some way manifestly excessive;
- in a magistrates' court, whether made on conviction or in stand alone proceedings, there is an appeal to the Crown Court against an order but not against variation; however, in respect of a variation, case stated or judicial review is available.

This position appeared to the court to be consistent since, in all cases, an appellate court will be able to consider key issues concerning whether the decision on variation was reasonable, rational and proportional.

(3) Breach proceedings

The issue of how to deal with the breach of an order has been much litigated. The Sentencing Guidelines Council has now published a definitive guideline which applies to sentences imposed on or after January 5, 2009. The guideline emphasises that **23–252**

Nature of failure & harm	Starting Point	Range
Serious harassment, alarm or distress has been caused or where such harm was intended	**26 weeks custody**	**Custody threshold — 2 years custody**
Lesser degree of harassment, alarm or distress, where such harm was intended, or where it would have been likely if the offender had not been apprehended	**6 weeks custody**	**Community Order (Medium) — 26 weeks custody**
No harassment, alarm or distress, was actually caused by the breach and none was intended by the offender	**Community Order (LOW)**	**Fine Band B — Community Order (MEDIUM)**

Part IV

Aggravating factors	Mitigating Factors
1. Offender has a history of disobedience to court orders 2. Breach was committed immediately or shortly after the order was made 3. Breach was committed subsequent to earlier breach proceedings arising from the same order 4. Targeting of a person the order was made to protect or a witness in the original proceedings	1. Breach occurred after a long period of compliance 2. The prohibition(s) breached was not fully understood, especially where the interim order was made without notice

23–253 An order can be breached only if its terms are not complied with "without reasonable excuse". The question of where the burden of proof lies arose for decision in *Charles* [2009] EWCA Crim 1570. The Court affirmed the approach set out in the *Guide for the Judiciary on Anti-Social Behaviour Orders* (2007) which (at para. 6.5) states that the prosecution must prove a breach of the order to the criminal standard and that, if the defendant raises the evidential issue of reasonable excuse, that it is for the prosecution to prove lack of reasonable excuse. In *Nicholson* [2006] EWCA Crim 1518 the Court of Appeal (Criminal Division) considered the extent to which ignorance, forgetfulness or misunderstanding of the terms of the order could be capable of being a reasonable excuse. The defendant had been made subject to an anti-social behaviour order which included a prohibition on being within 500 metres of a named building. She subsequently was part of a demonstration within that area. She asserted that she had a reasonable excuse because she had never heard the building in question referred to by the name given in the order and mistakenly believed she was entitled to attend the demonstration. The judge considered the offence to be one of strict liability and that the defence should be narrowly construed. Accordingly, ignorance, forgetfulness or misunderstanding of the terms of the order could not be a reasonable excuse. The Court reviewed the authorities and concluded that, in this case, the issue should have been left to the jury to consider. The Court recognised the danger that such a defence might be used to frustrate the effective application and enforcement of the law but considered that the issue would be highly fact sensitive and should, therefore, be suitable for determination by a jury.

Some earlier cases may be helpful in indicating where a sentence beyond the top range of the guideline might be justified.

In *Braxton* [2004] EWCA Crim 1374, the judgment quotes, with support, a statement in the Court of Appeal judgment in an earlier appeal by the defendant:

> "... a sentence close to the maximum should really be reserved for cases in which the anti-social behaviour order had itself been the subject of persistent and prolonged breaches, or where the breaches ... had consisted of conduct more serious than abusive, offensive and insulting language or conduct, in other words, in which the behaviour was truly intimidating."

In *Anthony* [2005] EWCA Crim 2055, the defendant had made a habit of abusing GP surgery and hospital staff, usually when she was the worse for drink. She had breached an ASBO on eight occasions including assaulting a doctor, spitting at a police officer and kicking a female security officer. Offences occurred the day following the making of the ASBO. The Court agreed that the four-year sentence was appropriate, less the maximum discount resulting from early guilty pleas.

Similarly, in *Thomas* [2004] EWCA Crim. 1173, a persistent shoplifter was held to have merited an 18-month sentence for flagrantly and consistently breaching an ASBO. This defendant had acquired 237 convictions for 451 offences, 263 of which were for shoplifting or theft.

G. RESTRAINING ORDERS

In accordance with s.5A of the *Protection from Harassment Act* 1997, a court before which a person is acquitted of any offence may make a restraining order prohibiting that person from doing anything prescribed in that order; the court must consider that it is necessary to make such an order so as to protect a person from harassment by the person acquitted. Similarly, in accordance with s.5 of the 1997 Act, a court sentencing an offender for any offence may make a restraining order for the protection of the victim of the offence or any other person from conduct which amounts to harassment or which will cause a fear of violence; such an order will be additional to sentence or other order. In respect of either power, the court may limit the order to a specified period or may make it effective until further order. As with an ASBO, failure to comply is an offence punishable with a maximum sentence of five years imprisonment. **23–254**

Restraining orders on conviction.

5.—(1) A court sentencing or otherwise dealing with a person ("the defendant") convicted of an offence may (as well as sentencing him or dealing with him in any other way) make an order under this section. **23–255**

(2) The order may, for the purpose of protecting the victim or victims of the offence, or any other person mentioned in the order, from conduct which—

(a) amounts to harassment, or

(b) will cause a fear of violence,

prohibit the defendant from doing anything described in the order.

(3) The order may have effect for a specified period or until further order.

(3A) In proceedings under this section both the prosecution and the defence may lead, as further evidence, any evidence that would be admissible in proceedings for an injunction under section 3.

(4) The prosecutor, the defendant or any other person mentioned in the order may apply to the court which made the order for it to be varied or discharged by a further order.

(4A) Any person mentioned in the order is entitled to be heard on the hearing of an application under subsection (4).

(5) If without reasonable excuse the defendant does anything which he is prohibited from doing by an order under this section, he is guilty of an offence.

(6) A person guilty of an offence under this section is liable—

(a) on conviction on indictment, to imprisonment for a term not exceeding five years, or a fine, or both, or

(b) on summary conviction, to imprisonment for a term not exceeding six months, or a fine not exceeding the statutory maximum, or both.

(7) A court dealing with a person for an offence under this section may vary or discharge the order in question by a further order.

Restraining orders on acquittal

5A—(1) A court before which a person ("the defendant") is acquitted of an offence may, if it considers it necessary to do so to protect a person from harassment by the defendant, make an order prohibiting the defendant from doing anything described in the order.

(2) Subsections (3) to (7) of section 5 apply to an order under this section as they apply to an order under that one.

(3) Where the Court of Appeal allow an appeal against conviction they may remit the case to the Crown Court to consider whether to proceed under this section.

(4) Where–

(a) the Crown Court allows an appeal against conviction, or

(b) a case is remitted to the Crown Court under subsection (3),

the reference in subsection (1) to a court before which a person is acquitted of an offence is to be read as referring to that court.

(5) A person made subject to an order under this section has the same right of appeal against the order as if–

(a) he had been convicted of the offence in question before the court which made the order, and

(b) the order had been made under section 5.

Interpretation of this group of sections.

7.—(1) This section applies for the interpretation of sections 1 to 5A.

(2) References to harassing a person include alarming the person or causing the person distress.

(3) A "course of conduct" must involve—

(a) in the case of conduct in relation to a single person (see section 1(1)), conduct on at least two occasions in relation to that person, or

(b) in the case of conduct in relation to two or more persons (see section 1(1A)), conduct on at least one occasion in relation to each of those persons.

(3A) A person's conduct on any occasion shall be taken, if aided, abetted, counselled or procured by another–

(a) to be conduct on that occasion of the other (as well as conduct of the person whose conduct it is); and

(b) to be conduct in relation to which the other's knowledge and purpose, and what he ought to have known, are the same as they were in relation to what was contemplated or reasonably foreseeable at the time of the aiding, abetting, counselling or procuring.

(4) "Conduct" includes speech.

(5) References to a person, in the context of the harassment of a person, are references to a person who is an individual.

23–256 A restraining order is a civil behavioural order for the purposes of the *Criminal Procedure Rules* 2011 (S.I. 2011 No. 1709) (as amended) (see Appendix G *post*) and Part 50 contains provisions governing the process to be followed when the making, variation or revocation of an order is to be considered. Judicial consideration has been given to the approach to be adopted when making an order following acquittal. In *Major* [2010] EWCA Crim 3016, the Court of Appeal (Criminal Division) (presided over by the Lord Chief Justice, Lord Judge) was urged to accept that such an order should be made only rarely or on uncontested facts. The Court did not accept that argument. Recognising that Parliament had created the power in order to deal with situations where there was clear evidence that a victim needed protection though insufficient to convict, the court noted that the power related to a future risk and, whilst evidence given in the trial may be sufficient, further evidence may also be adduced following the procedures set out in the *Criminal Procedure Rules* 2011 (S.I. 2011 No. 1709) (as amended). That evidence does not need to establish that harassment has taken place; it is sufficient if it establishes which, in the opinion of the court, if repeated might amount to harassment and an order is necessary to prevent it. It is important that the factual basis for the order is set out clearly by the court.

Breach of A Restraining Order

23–257 Whether the order is made on conviction or following acquittal, the person subject to the order commits an offence if, without reasonable excuse, that person does anything which he is prohibited from doing by the order: s.5(5). The offence is triable either way with a maximum penalty of 5 years imprisonment or an unlimited fine on indictment or six months imprisonment or a fine up to the statutory maximum if dealt with summarily. In addition, the court dealing with the breach may vary or discharge the order: s.5(7).

The approach to sentence for such a breach is set out in the guideline *Breach of a Protective Order* published by the Sentencing Guidelines Council in December 2006: *www.sentencingcouncil.judiciary.gov.uk*. The guideline emphasises the importance of getting the order right in the first place – the terms of the order should be "necessary and proportionate": para. 3.1—and also the need to have as the primary aim the importance of ensuring that the order is complied with since its purpose is the protection of an individual from harm: para. 3.3–4. The sentencing starting points (unusually, those points are ranges and there are no separate ranges) reflect the impact of the breach on the person that the order was designed to protect. Once there is some violence or some significant physical or psychological harm, a custodial sentence will be the starting point even where there has only been a single contact. Aggravating factors draw attention to the need to protect those who are particularly vulnerable, including children.

BREACH OF A PROTECTIVE ORDER

A. Statutory Provisions

1.1 For the purposes of this guideline, two protective orders are considered:

(i) Restraining Order

1.2 It is an offence contrary to the *Protection from Harassment Act* 1997 to behave in a way which a person knows (or ought to know) causes someone else harassment (section 2) or fear of violence (section 4). When imposing sentence on an offender, a court may also impose a restraining order to prevent future conduct causing harassment or fear of violence.

1.3 An offence under these provisions may have occurred in a domestic context or may have occurred in other contexts. The *Domestic Violence, Crime and Victims Act* 2004 provides for such orders also to be made on conviction for any offence or following acquittal.

1.4 It is an offence contrary to section 5(5) of the Act to fail to comply with the restraining order without reasonable excuse. That offence is punishable with a maximum of five years imprisonment.

(ii) Non-Molestation Order

1.5 Section 42 of the *Family Law Act* 1996 provides that, during family proceedings, a court may make a non-molestation order containing either or both of the following provisions:

(a) *provision prohibiting a person ("the respondent") from molesting another person who is associated with the respondent;*

(b) *provision prohibiting the respondent from molesting a relevant child.*

1.6 Section 1 of the *Domestic Violence, Crime and Victims Act* 2004 inserts a new section 42A into the 1996 Act. Section 42A (1) will provide that it is an offence to fail to comply with the order without reasonable excuse. That offence is punishable with a maximum of five years imprisonment.

1.7 In addition, breach of a non-molestation order may be dealt with as a contempt of court.

B. Sentencing for Breach

2.1 The facts that constitute a breach of a protective order may or may not also constitute a substantive offence. Where they do constitute a substantive offence, it is desirable that the substantive offence and the breach of the order should be charged as separate counts. Where necessary, consecutive sentences should be considered to reflect the seriousness of the counts and achieve the appropriate totality.

2.2 Sometimes, however, only the substantive offence or only the breach of the order will be charged. The basic principle is that the sentence should reflect all relevant aspects of the offence so that, provided the facts are not in issue, the result should be the same, regardless of whether one count or two has been charged. For example:

(i) **if the substantive offence only has been charged, the fact that it constitutes breach of a protective order should be treated as an aggravating factor;**

(ii) **if breach of the protective order only has been charged, the sentence should reflect the nature of the breach, namely, the conduct that amounts to the substantive offence, aggravated by the fact that it is also breach of an order.**

2.3 If breach of a protective order has been charged where no substantive offence was involved, the sentence should reflect the circumstances of the breach, including whether it was an isolated breach, or part of a course of conduct in breach of

Part IV

the order; whether it was planned or unpre-meditated; and any consequences of the breach, including psychiatric injury or distress to the person protected by the order.

C. Factors Influencing Sentencing

3.1 **In order to ensure that a protective order achieves the purpose it is intended for—protecting the victim from harm—it is important that the terms of the order are necessary and proportionate.**

3.2 The circumstances leading to the making of one of the protective orders will vary widely. Whilst a restraining order will be made in criminal proceedings, it will almost certainly result from offences of markedly different levels of seriousness or even acquittal. A nonmolestation order will have been made in civil proceedings and, again, may follow a wide variety of conduct by the subject of the order.

3.3 **In all cases the order will have been made to protect an individual from harm and action in response to breach should have as its primary aim the importance of ensuring that the order is complied with and that it achieves the protection that it was intended to achieve.**

3.4 **When sentencing for a breach of an order, the main aim should be to achieve future compliance with that order where that is realistic.**

The nature and context of the originating conduct or offence

3.5 The nature of the original conduct or offence is relevant in so far as it allows a judgement to be made on the level of harm caused to the victim by the breach and the extent to which that harm was intended by the offender.

3.6 If the original offence was serious, conduct which breaches the order might have a severe effect on the victim where in other contexts such conduct might appear minor. Even indirect contact, such as telephone calls, can cause significant harm or anxiety for a victim.

3.7 However, sentence following a breach is for the breach alone and must avoid punishing the offender again for the offence or conduct as a result of which the order was made.

The nature and context of the conduct that caused the breach

3.8 **The protective orders are designed to protect a victim. When dealing with a breach, a court will need to consider the extent to which the conduct amounting to breach put the victim at risk of harm.**

3.9 There may be exceptional cases where the nature of the breach is particularly serious but has not been dealt with by a separate offence being charged. In these cases, the risk posed by the offender and the nature of the breach will be particularly significant in determining the response. Where the order is breached by the use of physical violence, the starting point should normally be a custodial sentence.

3.10 Non-violent behaviour and/or indirect contact can also cause (or be intended to cause) a high degree of harm and anxiety. In such circumstances, it is likely that the custody threshold will have been crossed.

3.11 Where an order was made in civil proceedings, its purpose may have been to cause the subject of the order to modify behaviour rather than to imply that the conduct was especially serious. If so, it is likely to be disproportionate to impose a custodial sentence for a breach of the order if the breach did not involve threats or violence.

3.12 In some cases where a breach might result in a short custodial sentence but the court is satisfied that the offender genuinely intends to reform his or her behaviour and there is a real prospect of rehabilitation, the court may consider it appropriate to impose a sentence that will allow this. This may mean imposing a suspended sentence order or a community order (where appropriate with a requirement to attend an accredited domestic violence programme).

3.13 **Breach of a protective order will generally be more serious than breach of a conditional discharge.** Not only is a breach of a protective order an offence in its own right but it also undermines a specific prohibition imposed by the court. Breach of a conditional discharge amounts to an offender failing to take a chance that has been provided by the court.

D. Aggravating and Mitigating Factors

4.1 Many of the aggravating factors which apply to an offence of violence in a domestic context will apply also to an offence arising from breach of a protective order.

Aggravating Factors

(i) *Victim is particularly vulnerable*

4.2 For cultural, religious, language, financial or any other reasons, some victims may be more vulnerable than others. This vulnerability means that the terms of a protective order are particularly important and a violation of those terms will warrant a higher penalty than usual.

4.3 Age, disability or the fact that the victim was pregnant or had recently given birth at the time of the offence may make a victim particularly vulnerable.

4.4 Any steps taken to prevent the victim reporting an incident or obtaining assistance will usually aggravate the offence.

(ii) *Impact on children*

4.5 If a protective order is imposed in order to protect children, either solely or in addition to another victim, then a breach of that order will generally be more serious.

(iii) *A proven history of violence or threats by the offender*

4.6 Of necessity, a breach of a protective order will not be the first time an offender has caused fear or harassment towards a victim. However, the offence will be more serious if the breach is part of a series of prolonged violence or harassment towards the victim or the offender has a history of disobedience to court orders.

4.7 Where an offender has previously been convicted of an offence involving domestic violence, either against the same or a different person, or has been convicted for a breach of an order, this is likely to be a statutory aggravating factor.

(iv) *Using contact arrangements with a child to instigate an offence*

4.8 An offence will be aggravated where an offender exploits contact arrangements with a child in order to commit an offence.

(v) *Victim is forced to leave home*

4.9 A breach will be aggravated if, as a consequence, the victim is forced to leave home.

(vi) *Additional aggravating factors*

4.10 In addition to the factors listed above, the following will aggravate a breach of an order:

- the offence is a further breach, following earlier breach proceedings;
- the breach was committed immediately or shortly after the order was made.

Mitigating Factors

(i) *Breach was committed after a long period of compliance*

4.11 If the court is satisfied that the offender has complied with a protective order for a substantial period before a breach is committed, the court should take this into account when imposing sentence for the breach. The history of the relationship and the specific nature of the contact will be relevant in determining its significance as a mitigating factor.

(ii) *Victim initiated contact*

4.12 If the conditions of an order are breached following contact from the victim, this should be considered as mitigation. It is important to consider the history of the relationship and the specific nature of the contact in determining its significance as a mitigating factor.

4.13 Nonetheless it is important for the court to make clear that it is the responsibility of the offender and not the victim to ensure that the order is complied with.

E. Factors to take into Consideration

Aims of sentencing

(a) When sentencing for a breach of a protective order (which would have been imposed to protect a victim from further harm), the main aim should be to achieve future compliance with that order.

(b) A court will need to assess the level of risk posed by the offender. If the offender requires treatment or assistance for mental health or other issues, willingness to undergo treatment or accept help may influence sentence.

1. Key Factors

(a) The nature of the conduct that caused the breach of the order, in particular, whether the contact was direct or indirect, although it is important to recognise that indirect contact is capable of causing significant harm or anxiety.

(b) **There may be exceptional cases where the nature of the breach is particularly serious but has not been dealt with by a separate offence being charged. In these cases the risk posed by the offender and the nature of the breach will be particularly significant in determining the response.**

(c) The nature of the original conduct or offence is relevant to sentencing for the breach in so far as it allows a judgement to be made on the level of harm caused to the victim by the breach, and the extent to which that harm was intended by the offender.

(d) The sentence following a breach is for the breach alone and must avoid punishing the offender again for the offence or conduct as a result of which the order was made.

(e) Where violence is used to breach a restraining order or a molestation order, custody is the starting point for sentence.

(f) Non-violent conduct in breach may cross the custody threshold where a high degree of harm or anxiety has been caused to the victim.

(g) Where an order was made in civil proceedings, its purpose may have been to cause the subject of the order to modify behaviour rather than to imply that the conduct was especially serious. If so, it is likely to be disproportionate to impose a custodial sentence for a breach of the order if the breach did not involve threats or violence.

(h) In some cases where a breach might result in a short custodial sentence but the court is satisfied that the offender genuinely intends to reform his or her behaviour and there is a real prospect of rehabilitation, the court may consider it appropriate to impose a sentence that will allow this. This may mean imposing a suspended sentence order or a community order (where appropriate with a requirement to attend an accredited domestic violence programme).

(i) While, in principle, consecutive sentences may be imposed for each breach of which the offender is convicted, the overall sentence should reflect the totality principle.

2. General

(a) Breach of a protective order should be considered more serious than a breach of a conditional discharge.

(b) The principle of reduction in sentence for a guilty plea should be applied as set out in the Council guideline *Reduction in Sentence for a Guilty Plea*.

3. Non-custodial sentences

(a) It is likely that all breaches of protective orders will pass the threshold for a community sentence. The reference in the starting points to medium and low range community orders refers to the Council guideline *New Sentences: Criminal Justice Act 2003* paragraphs 1.1.18–1.1.32.

(b) In accordance with general principle, the fact that the seriousness of an offence crosses a particular threshold does not preclude the court from imposing another type of sentence of a lower level where appropriate.

BREACH OF A PROTECTIVE ORDER

Breach of a Restraining Order
Section 5(5) Protection from Harassment Act 1997

Breach of a Non-Molestation Order
*Section 42A Family Law Act 1996**

Maximum Penalty: 5 years imprisonment

Where the conduct is particularly serious, it would normally be charged as a separate offence. These starting points are based on the premise that the activity has either been prosecuted separately as an offence or is not of a character sufficient to justify prosecution of it as an offence in its own right.

Nature of activity	Starting points
	Custodial Sentence
Breach (whether one or more) involving significant physical violence and significant physical or psychological harm to the victim	More than 12 months The length of the custodial sentence imposed will depend on the nature and seriousness of the breach(es).
More than one breach involving some violence and/or significant physical or psychological harm to the victim	26-39 weeks custody [Medium/High Custody Plus order]**
Single breach involving some violence and/or significant physical or psychological harm to the victim	13-26 weeks custody [Low/Medium Custody Plus order]**
	Non-Custodial Sentence
More than one breach involving no/minimal contact or some direct contact	MEDIUM range community order
Single breach involving no/minimal direct contact	LOW range community order

Additional aggravating factors	Additional mitigating factors
1. Victim is particularly vulnerable. 2. Impact on children. 3. A proven history of violence or threats by the offender. 4. Using contact arrangements with a child to instigate an offence. 5. Victim is forced to leave home. 6. Offence is a further breach, following earlier breach proceedings. 7. Offender has a history of disobedience to court orders. 8. Breach was committed immediately or shortly after the order was made.	1. Breach occurred after a long period of compliance. 2. Victim initiated contact.

consequences of the breach)

Non-Custodial sentence

Additional contributing factors

Additional mitigating factors

CHAPTER 24

EXCLUSION, ALTERATION AND ENFORCEMENT

I. ANCILLARY ORDERS

A. BANNING ORDERS UNDER FOOTBALL SPECTATORS ACT 1989

(1) Purpose and effect

Disorder at and around professional football matches had become a major source of public disorder. As part of the response to that, courts were given powers under the 1989 Act to restrict the activities of those considered likely to cause trouble. This was refined and developed by the *Football (Disorder) Act* 2000, in particular Sched. 1 which makes a series of amendments to Pt II of, and the Schedule to, the 1989 Act. The *Violent Crime Reduction Act* 2006 also amends the statute. **24–1**

An order may be made either on conviction of a "relevant offence" or after a specific complaint seeking simply an order under these provisions. Where a person is convicted of a relevant offence (see s.14(8)—an offence to which Sched. 1 to the 1989 Act applies) and the court is satisfied that there are reasonable grounds for believing that making a banning order will help to prevent violence or disorder (defined in s.14C), then that order can be made in addition to the sentence for the offence: s.14A(4). The prosecution can appeal against the failure to make a banning order.Where it is a magistrates' court that does not make the order, that appeal is to the Crown Court: s.14A(5A). If the court adjourns proceedings, it may remand the offender: s.14A(4BA). If that remand is on bail, conditions may include a requirement not to leave England and Wales before the court appearance and, if a match or tournament outside the UK is involved, a requirement for the surrender of the offender's passport.

Part IV

The procedure governing the making of a football banning order on conviction is set out in Pt 50 to the *Criminal Procedure Rules* 2011 (S.I. 2011 No. 1709): see Appendix G, *post*. These provisions are described in detail in § 23–273, *ante*. Provisions applying to a football banning order are r.50.2—rules of general application; r.50.4–8—provisions regarding evidence; r.50.5—applications to vary or revoke orders and r.50.9—general discretion of court regarding time limits and forms.

24–2 The main effects of the order are to require the subject of the order to report to a police station within five days, prohibit the subject from entering premises to attend regulated football matches (s.14(4)), make arrangements for the surrender of the subject's passport when certain matches outside the UK are imminent (s.14E(3)) and make whatever additional requirements are necessary. Minimum and maximum periods for the order are specified: s.14F. There are also obligations to notify the enforcing authority of circumstances including changes of name or address and the making of an appeal or an application for termination of the order: s.14E(2A), (2B). Notification must be within seven days of the occurrence of the event starting with the day on which that event occurred: s.14E(2C).

Football Spectators Act 1989, s.1

Scope and interpretation of this Part

24–3 **1.**—(1) This Part of this Act applies in relation to association football matches played in England and Wales which are designated football matches and the following provisions have effect for its interpretation.

(2) "Designated football match" means any such match of a description for the time being designated for the purposes of this Part by order made by the Secretary of State or a particular such match so designated.

(4) An order under subsection (2) above—

(a) may designate descriptions of football matches wherever played or when played at descriptions of ground or in any area specified in the order.

(8) Each of the following periods is "relevant to" a designated football match, that is to say—

(a) the period beginning—

(i) two hours before the start of the match, or

(ii) two hours before the time at which it is advertised to start, or

(iii) with the time at which spectators are first admitted to the premises,

whichever is the earliest, and ending one hour after the end of the match;

(b) where a match advertised to start at a particular time on a particular day is postponed to a later day, or does not take place, the period in the advertised day beginning two hours before and ending one hour after that time.

(9) A person is a "responsible person" in relation to any designated football match at any premises if he is a person concerned in the management of the premises or in the organisation of the match.

(10) The power to make an order under subsection (2) above is exercisable by statutory instrument which shall be subject to annulment in pursuance of a resolution of either House of Parliament.

(11) The imposition under this Part of this Act of restrictions on the persons who may attend as spectators at any designated football match does not affect any other right of any person to exclude persons from admission to the premises at which the match is played.

Football Spectators Act 1989, s.14

Main definitions

24–4 **14.**—(1) This section applies for the purposes of this Part.

(2) "Regulated football match" means an association football match (whether in England and Wales or elsewhere) which is a prescribed match or a match of a prescribed description.

(3) "External tournament" means a football competition which includes regulated football matches outside England and Wales.

(4) "Banning order" means an order made by the court under this Part which—

(a) in relation to regulated football matches in England and Wales, prohibits the person who is subject to the order from entering any premises for the purpose of attending such matches, and

(b) in relation to regulated football matches outside England and Wales, requires that person to report at a police station in accordance with this Part.

(5) "Control period", in relation to a regulated football match outside England and Wales, means the period—

(a) beginning five days before the day of the match, and

(b) ending when the match is finished or cancelled.

(6) "Control period", in relation to an external tournament, means any period described in an order made by the Secretary of State—

(a) beginning five days before the day of the first football match outside England and Wales which is included in the tournament, and

(b) ending when the last football match outside England and Wales which is included in the tournament is finished or cancelled,

but, for the purposes of paragraph (a), any football match included in the qualifying or pre-qualifying stages of the tournament is to be left out of account

(7) References to football matches are to football matches played or intended to be played.

(8) "Relevant offence" means an offence to which Schedule 1 to this Act applies.

See the *Football Spectators (Prescription) Order* 2004 (S.I. 2004 No. 2409) (as amended by S.I. 2006 No. 71) for football matches in England and Wales and outside England and Wales that are regulated football matches for the purposes of Pt II of the 1989 Act. **24–5**

Football Spectators Act 1989, ss.14A–14C, 14E–14H, 14J

Banning orders made on conviction of an offence

14A.—(1) This section applies where a person (the "offender") is convicted of a relevant offence. **24–6**

(2) If the court is satisfied that there are reasonable grounds to believe that making a banning order would help to prevent violence or disorder at or in connection with any regulated football matches, it must make such an order in respect of the offender.

(3) If the court is not so satisfied, it must in open court state that fact and give its reasons.

(3A) For the purpose of deciding whether to make an order under this section the court may consider evidence led by the prosecution and the defence.

(3B) It is immaterial whether evidence led in pursuance of subsection (3A) would have been admissible in the proceedings in which the offender was convicted.

(4) A banning order may only be made under this section—

(a) in addition to a sentence imposed in respect of the relevant offence, or

(b) in addition to an order discharging him conditionally.

(4A) The court may adjourn any proceedings in relation to an order under this section even after sentencing the offender.

(4B) If the offender does not appear for any adjourned proceedings, the court may further adjourn the proceedings or may issue a warrant for his arrest.

(4BA) If the court adjourns or further adjourns any proceedings under subsection (4A) or (4B), the court may remand the offender.

(4BB) A person who, by virtue of subsection (4BA), is remanded on bail may be required by the conditions of his bail—

(a) not to leave England and Wales before his appearance before the court, and

(b) if the control period relates to a regulated football match outside the United Kingdom or to an external tournament which includes such matches, to surrender his passport to a police constable, if he has not already done so.

(4C) The court may not issue a warrant under subsection (4B) above for the offender's arrest unless it is satisfied that he has had adequate notice of the time and place of the adjourned proceedings.

(5) A banning order may be made as mentioned in subsection (4)(b) above in spite of

Part IV

anything in sections 12 and 14 of the *Powers of the Criminal Courts (Sentencing) Act* 2000 (which relate to orders discharging a person absolutely or conditionally and their effect).

(5A) The prosecution has a right of appeal against a failure by the court to make a banning order under this section—

(a) where the failure is by a magistrates' court, to the Crown Court; and

(b) where it is by the Crown Court, to the Court of Appeal.

(5B) An appeal under subsection (5A)(b) may be brought only if the Court of Appeal gives permission or the judge who decided not to make an order grants a certificate that his decision is fit for appeal.

(5C) An order made on appeal under this section (other than one directing that an application be re-heard by the court from which the appeal was brought) is to be treated for the purposes of this Part as if it were an order of the court from which the appeal was brought.

(6) In this section, "the court" in relation to an offender means—

(a) the court by or before which he is convicted of the relevant offence, or

(b) if he is committed to the Crown Court to be dealt with for that offence, the Crown Court.

Banning orders made on a complaint

24–7 **14B.**—(1) An application for a banning order in respect of any person may be made by—

(a) the relevant chief officer, or

(b) the Director of Public Prosecutions,

if it appears to him that the condition in subsection (2) is met.

(1A) In subsection (1) "the relevant chief officer" means—

(a) the chief officer of police of any police force maintained for a police area; or

(b) the chief constable of the British Transport Police Force.

(2) That condition is that the respondent has at any time caused or contributed to any violence or disorder in the United Kingdom or elsewhere.

(3) The application is to be made by complaint to a magistrates' court.

(4) If—

(a) it is proved on the application that the condition in subsection (2) above is met, and

(b) the court is satisfied that there are reasonable grounds to believe that making a banning order would help to prevent violence or disorder at or in connection with any regulated football matches,

the court must make a banning order in respect of the respondent.

(5) If the magistrates' court adjourns proceedings on an application under this section, the court may remand the person in respect of whom the application is made.

(6) A person who, by virtue of subsection (5) above, is remanded on bail under section 128 of the *Magistrates' Courts Act* 1980 may be required by the conditions of his bail—

(a) not to leave England and Wales before his appearance before the court, and

(b) if the control period relates to a regulated football match outside the United Kingdom or to an external tournament which includes such matches, to surrender his passport to a police constable, if he has not already done so.

Banning orders: supplementary

24–8 **14C.**—(1) In this Part, "violence" means violence against persons or property and includes threatening violence and doing anything which endangers the life of any person.

(2) In this Part, "disorder" includes—

(a) stirring up hatred against a group of persons defined by reference to colour, race, nationality (including citizenship) or ethnic or national origins, or against an individual as a member of such a group,

(b) using threatening, abusive or insulting words or behaviour or disorderly behaviour,

(c) displaying any writing or other thing which is threatening, abusive or insulting.

(3) In this Part, "violence" and "disorder" are not limited to violence or disorder in connection with football.

(4) The magistrates' court may take into account the following matters (among others),

so far as they consider it appropriate to do so, in determining whether to make an order under section 14B above—

(a) any decision of a court or tribunal outside the United Kingdom,

(b) deportation or exclusion from a country outside the United Kingdom,

(c) removal or exclusion from premises used for playing football matches, whether in the United Kingdom or elsewhere,

(d) conduct recorded on video or by any other means.

(5) In determining whether to make such an order—

(a) the magistrates' court may not take into account anything done by the respondent before the beginning of the period of ten years ending with the application under section 14B(1) above, except circumstances ancillary to a conviction,

(b) before taking into account any conviction for a relevant offence, where a court made a statement under section 14A(3) above (or section 15(2A) below or section 30(3) of the *Public Order Act* 1986), the magistrates' court must consider the reasons given in the statement,

and in this subsection "circumstances ancillary to a conviction" has the same meaning as it has for the purposes of section 4 of the *Rehabilitation of Offenders Act* 1974 (effect of rehabilitation).

(6) Subsection (5) does not prejudice anything in the *Rehabilitation of Offenders Act* 1974.

Banning orders: general

14E.—(1) On making a banning order, a court must in ordinary language explain its effect to the person subject to the order. **24–9**

(2) A banning order must require the person subject to the order to report initially at a police station in England and Wales specified in the order within the period of five days beginning with the day on which the order is made.

(2A) A banning order must require the person subject to the order to give notification of the events mentioned in subsection (2B) to the enforcing authority.

(2B) The events are—

(a) a change of any of his names;

(b) the first use by him after the making of the order of a name for himself that was not disclosed by him at the time of the making of the order;

(c) a change of his home address;

(d) his acquisition of a temporary address;

(e) a change of his temporary address or his ceasing to have one;

(f) his becoming aware of the loss of his travel authorisation;

(g) receipt by him of a new travel authorisation;

(h) an appeal made by him in relation to the order;

(i) an application made by him under section 14H(2) for termination of the order;

(j) an appeal made by him under section 23(3) against the making of a declaration of relevance in respect of an offence of which he has been convicted.

(2C) A notification required by a banning order by virtue of subsection (2A) must be given before the end of the period of seven days beginning with the day on which the event in question occurs and—

(a) in the case of a change of a name or address or the acquisition of a temporary address, must specify the new name or address;

(b) in the case of a first use of a previously undisclosed name, must specify that name; and

(c) in the case of a receipt of a new travel authorisation, must give details of that travel authorisation.

(3) A banning order must impose a requirement as to the surrender in accordance with this Part, in connection with regulated football matches outside the United Kingdom, of the travel authorisation of the person subject to the order.

(5) In the case of a person detained in legal custody—

(a) the requirement under this section to report at a police station, and

(b) any requirement imposed under section 19 below,

is suspended until his release from custody.

(6) If—

(a) he is released from custody more than five days before the expiry of the period for which the order has effect, and

(b) he was precluded by his being in custody from reporting initially,

the order is to have effect as if it required him to report initially at the police station specified in the order within the period of five days beginning with the date of his release.

(8) In the section—

"declaration of relevance" has the same meaning as in section 23;

"home address", in relation to any person, means the address of his sole or main residence;

"loss", includes theft or destruction;

"new", includes replacement;

"temporary address", in relation to any person, means the address (other than his home address) of a place at which he intends to reside, or has resided, for a period of at least four weeks.

Period of banning orders

24–10 **14F.**—(1) Subject to the following provisions of this Part, a banning order has effect for a period beginning with the day on which the order is made.

(2) The period must not be longer than the maximum or shorter than the minimum.

(3) Where the order is made under section 14A above in addition to a sentence of imprisonment taking immediate effect, the maximum is ten years and the minimum is six years; and in this subsection "imprisonment" includes any form of detention.

(4) In any other case where the order is made under section 14A above, the maximum is five years and the minimum is three years.

(5) Where the order is made under section 14B above, the maximum is five years and the minimum is three years.

Additional requirements of orders

24–11 **14G.**—(1) A banning order may, if the court making the order thinks fit, impose additional requirements on the person subject to the order in relation to any regulated football matches.

(2) The court by which a banning order was made may, on an application made by—

(a) the person subject to the order, or

(b) the person who applied for the order or who was the prosecutor in relation to the order,

vary the order so as to impose, replace or omit any such requirements.

(3) In the case of a banning order made by a magistrates' court, the reference in subsection (2) above to the court by which it was made includes a reference to any magistrates' court acting in the same local justice area as that court.

Termination of orders

24–12 **14H.**—(1) If a banning order has had effect for at least two-thirds of the period determined under section 14F above, the person subject to the order may apply to the court by which it was made to terminate it.

(2) On the application, the court may by order terminate the banning order as from a specified date or refuse the application.

(3) In exercising its powers under subsection (2) above, the court must have regard to the person's character, his conduct since the banning order was made, the nature of the offence or conduct which led to it and any other circumstances which appear to it to be relevant.

(4) Where an application under subsection (1) above in respect of a banning order is refused, no further application in respect of the order may be made within the period of six months beginning with the day of the refusal.

(5) The court may order the applicant to pay all or any part of the costs of an application under this section.

(6) In the case of a banning order made by a magistrates' court, the reference in subsection (1) above to the court by which it was made includes a reference to any magistrates' court acting in the same local justice area as that court.

Offences

24–13 **14J.**—(1) A person subject to a banning order who fails to comply with—

(a) any requirement imposed by the order, or

(b) any requirement imposed under section 19(2B) or (2C) below,

is guilty of an offence.

(2) A person guilty of an offence under this section is liable on summary conviction to imprisonment for a term not exceeding six months, or a fine not exceeding level 5 on the standard scale, or both.

Football Spectators Act 1989, s.18

Information

18.—(1) Where a court makes a banning order, the designated officer for the court (in the case of a magistrates' court) or the appropriate officer (in the case of the Crown Court)— **24–14**

(a) shall give a copy of it to the person to whom it relates;
(b) shall (as soon as reasonably practicable) send a copy of it to the enforcing authority and to any prescribed person;
(c) shall (as soon as reasonably practicable) send a copy of it to the police station (addressed to the officer responsible for the police station) at which the person subject to the order is to report initially; and
(d) in a case where the person subject to the order is detained in legal custody, shall (as soon as reasonably practicable) send a copy of it to the person in whose custody he is detained.

(2) Where a court terminates a banning order under section 14H above, the designated officer for the court (in the case of a magistrates' court) or the appropriate officer (in the case of the Crown Court)—

(a) shall give a copy of the terminating order to the person to whom the banning order relates;
(b) shall (as soon as reasonably practicable) send a copy of it to the enforcing authority; and
(c) in a case where the person subject to the banning order is detained in legal custody, shall (as soon as reasonably practicable) send a copy of the terminating order to the person in whose custody he is detained.

(3) Where a person subject to a banning order is released from custody and, in the case of a person who has not reported initially to a police station, is released more than five days before the expiry of the banning order, the person in whose custody he is shall (as soon as reasonably practicable) give notice of his release to the enforcing authority.

Article 5 of S.I. 2000 No. 2126 prescribes the Football Banning Orders Authority as the enforcing authority for the purposes of Pt II of the 1989 Act, and the Chief Executive of the Football Association for the purposes of s.18(1) and (2) of that Act. **24–15**

For banning orders arising out of offences outside England and Wales, see s.22 of the 1989 Act and a series of orders made thereunder.

Football Spectators Act 1989, s.22A

Other interpretation, etc.

22A.—(1) In this Part— **24–16**

"British citizen" has the same meaning as in the *British Nationality Act* 1981,
"country" includes territory,
"enforcing authority" means a prescribed organisation established by the Secretary of State under section 57 of the *Police Act* 1996 (central police organisations),
"passport" means a United Kingdom passport within the meaning of the *Immigration Act* 1971,
"prescribed" means prescribed by an order made by the Secretary of State.
"travel authorisation", in relation to a person, means one or both of the following—,

(a) any UK passport (within the meaning of the *Immigration Act* 1971) that has been issued to him;
(b) any ID card issued to him under the *Identity Cards Act* 2006 which records that he is a British citizen.

(2) The Secretary of State may, if he considers it necessary or expedient to do so in order to secure the effective enforcement of this Part, by order provide for section 14(5) and (6) above to have effect in relation to any, or any description of, regulated football match or external tournament as if, for any reference to the number of days (not exceeding ten) specified in the order.

Part IV

(3) Any power of the Secretary of State to make an order under this Part is exercisable by statutory instrument.

(4) An instrument containing an order made by the Secretary of State under this Part shall be subject to annulment in pursuance of a resolution of either House of Parliament.

Football Spectators Act 1989, s.23

Further provision about, and appeals against, declarations of relevance

24–17 **23.**—(1) Subject to subsection (2) below, a court may not make a declaration of relevance as respects any offence unless it is satisfied that the prosecutor gave notice to the defendant, at least five days before the first day of the trial, that it was proposed to show that the offence related to football matches, to a particular football match or to particular football matches (as the case may be).

(2) A court may, in any particular case, make a declaration of relevance notwithstanding that notice to the defendant as required by subsection (1) above has not been given if he consents to waive the giving of full notice or the court is satisfied that the interests of justice do not require more notice to be given.

(3) A person convicted of an offence as respects which the court makes a declaration of relevance may appeal against the making of the declaration of relevance as if the declaration were included in any sentence passed on him for the offence, and accordingly—

(a) in section 10(3) of the *Criminal Appeal Act* 1968 (appeals against sentence by Crown Court), in paragraph (c), after the sub-paragraph (iv) inserted by section 15(7) above there shall be inserted

"or

(v) a declaration of relevance under the *Football Spectators Act* 1989;";

(b) in section 50(1) of that Act (meaning of "sentence"), at the end there shall be inserted the words "and a declaration of relevance under the *Football Spectators Act* 1989"; and

(c) in section 108(3) of the *Magistrates' Courts Act* 1980 (right of appeal to the Crown Court), at the end there shall be inserted the words "and also includes a declaration of relevance under the *Football Spectators Act* 1989".

(4) A banning order made upon a person's conviction of a relevant offence shall be quashed if the making of a declaration of relevance as respects that offence is reversed on appeal.

(5) In this section "declaration of relevance" means a declaration by a court for the purposes of Schedule 1 to this Act that an offence related to football matches, or that it related to one or more particular football matches.

Football Spectators Act 1989, Sched. 1

SCHEDULE 1

OFFENCES

24–18 1. This Schedule applies to the following offences:

(a) any offence under section 14J(1) or 21C(2) of this Act,

(b) any offence under section 2 or 2A of the *Sporting Events (Control of Alcohol etc.) Act* 1985 (alcohol, containers and fireworks) committed by the accused at any football match to which this Schedule applies or while entering or trying to enter the ground,

(c) any offence under section 4A or 5 of the *Public Order Act* 1986 (harassment, alarm or distress) or any provision of Part 3 or 3A of that Act (hatred by reference to race etc.) committed during a period relevant to a football match to which this Schedule applies at any premises while the accused was at, or was entering or leaving or trying to enter or leave, the premises,

(d) any offence involving the use or threat of violence by the accused towards another person committed during a period relevant to a football match to which this Schedule applies at any premises while the accused was at, or was entering or leaving or trying to enter or leave, the premises,

(e) any offence involving the use or threat of violence towards property committed during a period relevant to a football match to which this Schedule applies at any premises while the accused was at, or was entering or leaving or trying to enter or leave, the premises,

(f) any offence involving the use, carrying or possession of an offensive weapon or a firearm committed during a period relevant to a football match to which this Schedule applies at any premises while the accused was at, or was entering or leaving or trying to enter or leave, the premises,

(g) any offence under section 12 of the *Licensing Act* 1872 (persons found drunk in public places, etc.) of being found drunk in a highway or other public place committed while the accused was on a journey to or from a football match to which this Schedule applies being an offence as respects which the court makes a declaration that the offence related to football matches,

(h) any offence under section 91(1) of the *Criminal Justice Act* 1967 (disorderly behaviour while drunk in a public place) committed in a highway or other public place while the accused was on a journey to or from a football match to which this Schedule applies being an offence as respects which the court makes a declaration that the offence related to football matches,

(j) any offence under section 1 of the *Sporting Events (Control of Alcohol etc.) Act* 1985 (alcohol on coaches or trains to or from sporting events) committed while the accused was on a journey to or from a football match to which this Schedule applies being an offence as respects which the court makes a declaration that the offence related to football matches,

(k) any offence under section 4A or 5 of the *Public Order Act* 1986 (harassment, alarm or distress) or any provision of Part 3 or 3A of that Act (hatred by reference to race etc.) committed while the accused was on a journey to or from a football match to which this Schedule applies being an offence as respects which the court makes a declaration that the offence related to football matches,

(l) any offence under section 4 or 5 of the *Road Traffic Act* 1988 (driving etc. when under the influence of drink or drugs or with an alcohol concentration above the prescribed limit) committed while the accused was on a journey to or from a football match to which this Schedule applies being an offence as respects which the court makes a declaration that the offence related to football matches,

(m) any offence involving the use or threat of violence by the accused towards another person committed while one or each of them was on a journey to or from a football match to which this Schedule applies being an offence as respects which the court makes a declaration that the offence related to football matches,

(n) any offence involving the use or threat of violence towards property committed while the accused was on a journey to or from a football match to which this Schedule applies being an offence as respects which the court makes a declaration that the offence related to football matches,

(o) any offence involving the use, carrying or possession of an offensive weapon or a firearm committed while the accused was on a journey to or from a football match to which this Schedule applies being an offence as respects which the court makes a declaration that the offence related to football matches,

(p) any offence under the *Football (Offences) Act* 1991,

(q) any offence under section 4A or 5 of the *Public Order Act* 1986 (harassment, alarm or distress) or any provision of Part 3 or 3A of that Act (hatred by reference to race etc.) —

(i) which does not fall within paragraph (c) or (k) above,

(ii) which was committed during a period relevant to a football match to which this Schedule applies, and

(iii) as respects which the court makes a declaration that the offence related to that match or to that match and any other football match which took place during that period,

(r) any offence involving the use or threat of violence by the accused towards another person—

(i) which does not fall within paragraph (d) or (m) above,

(ii) which was committed during a period relevant to a football match to which this Schedule applies, and

(iii) as respects which the court makes a declaration that the offence related to that match or to that match and any other football match which took place during that period,

(s) any offence involving the use or threat of violence towards property—
  (i) which does not fall within paragraph (e) or (n) above,
  (ii) which was committed during a period relevant to a football match to which this Schedule applies, and
  (iii) as respects which the court makes a declaration that the offence related to that match or to that match and any other football match which took place during that period,

(t) any offence involving the use, carrying or possession of an offensive weapon or a firearm—
  (i) which does not fall within paragraph (f) or (o) above,
  (ii) which was committed during a period relevant to a football match to which this Schedule applies, and
  (iii) as respects which the court makes a declaration that the offence related to that match or to that match and any other football match which took place during that period,

(u) any offence under section 166 of the *Criminal Justice and Public Order Act* 1994 (sale of tickets by unauthorised persons) which relates to tickets for a football match.

24–19 2. Any reference to an offence in paragraph 1 above includes—
  (a) a reference to any attempt, conspiracy or incitement to commit that offence, and
  (b) a reference to aiding and abetting, counselling or procuring the commission of that offence.

24–20 3. For the purposes of paragraphs 1(g) to (o) above—
  (a) a person may be regarded as having been on a journey to or from a football match to which this Schedule applies whether or not he attended or intended to attend the match, and
  (b) a person's journey includes breaks (including overnight breaks).

4.—(1) In this Schedule, "football match" means a match which is a regulated football match for the purposes of Part II of this Act.

(2) For the purposes of this Schedule each of the following periods is 'relevant to' a football match to which this Schedule applies—
  (a) in the case of a match which takes place on the day on which it is advertised to take place, the period—
    (i) beginning 24 hours before whichever is the earlier of the start of the match and the time at which it was advertised to start; and
    (ii) ending 24 hours after it ends;
  (b) in the case of a match which does not take place on the day on which it was advertised to take place, the period—
    (i) beginning 24 hours before the time at which it was advertised to start on that day; and
    (ii) ending 24 hours after that time.

24–21 An order may be made following many of the incidents set out in Sched. 1 only where the court makes a declaration that the offence "related to football matches": see, for example, Sched. 1 para. 1(m). This is essentially a question of fact but one that has come before the appeal courts from time to time. In *Parkes* (2011) 175 J.P. 33, the Court of Appeal concluded that the issue is the "spark" for the violence. In this case, supporters of one team (whose match had been cancelled) knew that supporters of another team (not involved in the cancelled match but whose team had been involved in a match that had taken place) would be in a particular public house; there was hostility between the two groups. The court had no difficulty in finding that the offences that ensued were related to the match that took place and were clearly related to football. In those circumstances, banning orders could lawfully be made.

24–22 In *Gough v. Chief Constable of the Derbyshire Constabulary* [2002] 3 W.L.R. 289, CA, it was held that in order to justify the restriction on freedom of movement imposed by the banning order, an order should only be made where there are strong grounds for concluding that the individual who is the subject of the order has a propensity for taking part in football hooliganism. The principle of proportionality requires that the restraints on the individual's freedom of movement should be imposed following individual consideration of the case, should not be based simply on the individual's criminal record, should be rationally connected to the objective of preventing English football hooliganism abroad and should be the minimum necessary to achieve that legitimate objective.

When considering the conditions in s.14B, the appropriate standard of proof must also be applied, this standard being practically indistinguishable from the criminal standard of proof, given the consequences that will follow if the conditions for the banning order are made out. This follows the approach adopted regarding an application for an anti-social behaviour order and recommended in relation to an application for a Bind Over, see *ante*, §§ 23–231 and 23–224.

B. Disqualification from Driving when Vehicle Used for Purposes of Crime

Powers of Criminal Courts (Sentencing) Act 2000, ss.146, 147

Driving disqualification for any offence

146.—(1) The court by or before which a person is convicted of an offence committed after 31st December 1997 may, instead of or in addition to dealing with him in any other way, order him to be disqualified, for such period as it thinks fit, for holding or obtaining a driving licence. **24–23**

(2) Where the person is convicted of an offence the sentence for which is fixed by law or falls to be imposed under section 110(2) or 111(2) above, section 51A(2) of the *Firearms Act* 1968, section 225(2) and 226(2) of the *Criminal Justice Act* 2003 or section 29(4) or (6) of the *Violent Crime Reduction Act* 2006; subsection (1) above shall have effect as if the words "instead of or" were omitted.

(3) A court shall not make an order under subsection (1) above unless the court has been notified by the Secretary of State that the power to make such orders is exercisable by the court and the notice has not been withdrawn.

(4) A court which makes an order under this section disqualifying a person for holding or obtaining a driving licence shall require him to produce—

(a) any such licence held by him together with its counterpart;

(aa) in the case where he holds a Northern Ireland licence (within the meaning of Part 3 of the *Road Traffic Act* 1988), his Northern Ireland licence and its counterpart (if any); or

(b) in the case where he holds a Community licence (within the meaning of Part III of the *Road Traffic Act* 1988), his Community licence and its counterpart (if any).

(5) In this section—

"driving licence" means a licence to drive a motor vehicle granted under Part III of the *Road Traffic Act* 1988;

"counterpart" —

(a) in relation to a driving licence, has the meaning given in relation to such a licence by section 108(1) of that Act;

(aa) in relation to a Northern Ireland licence, has the meaning given by section 109A of that Act; and

(b) in relation to a Community licence, has the meaning given by section 99B of that Act.

Driving disqualification where vehicle used for purposes of crime

147.—(1) This section applies where a person— **24–24**

(a) is convicted before the Crown Court of an offence punishable on indictment with imprisonment for a term of two years or more; or

(b) having been convicted by a magistrates' court of such an offence, is committed under section 3 above to the Crown Court for sentence.

(2) This section also applies where a person is convicted by or before any court of common assault or of any other offence involving an assault (including an offence of aiding, abetting, counselling or procuring, or inciting to the commission of, an offence).

(3) If, in a case to which this section applies by virtue of subsection (1) above, the Crown Court is satisfied that a motor vehicle was used (by the person convicted or by anyone else) for the purpose of committing, or facilitating the commission of, the offence in question, the court may order the person convicted to be disqualified, for such period as the court thinks fit, for holding or obtaining a driving licence.

(4) If, in a case to which this section applies by virtue of subsection (2) above, the court is satisfied that the assault was committed by driving a motor vehicle, the court may order the person convicted to be disqualified, for such period as the court thinks fit, for holding or obtaining a driving licence.

(5) A court which makes an order under this section disqualifying a person for holding or obtaining a driving licence shall require him to produce—

(a) any such licence held by him together with its counterpart; or

(b) in the case where he holds a Community licence (within the meaning of Part III of the *Road Traffic Act* 1988), his Community licence and its counterpart (if any).

(6) Facilitating the commission of an offence shall be taken for the purposes of this section to include the taking of any steps after it has been committed for the purpose of disposing of any property to which it relates or of avoiding apprehension or detection.

(7) In this section "driving licence" and "counterpart" have the meanings given by section 146(5) above.

[Sections 147A and 147B are inserted by Sched. 16, para. 5 to the *Coroners and Justice Act* 2009 when in force.]

Extension of disqualification where custodial sentence also imposed

147A.—(1) This section applies where a person is convicted of an offence for which the court—

(a) imposes a custodial sentence, and

(b) orders the person to be disqualified under section 146 or 147 for holding or obtaining a driving licence.

(2) The order under section 146 or 147 must provide for the person to be disqualified for the appropriate extension period, in addition to the discretionary disqualification period.

(3) The discretionary disqualification period is the period for which, in the absence of this section, the court would have disqualified the person under section 146 or 147.

(4) The appropriate extension period is—

(a) where an order under section 82A(2) of this Act (determination of tariffs) is made in relation to the custodial sentence, a period equal to the part of the sentence specified in that order;

(b) in the case of a detention and training order under section 100 of this Act (offenders under 18: detention and training orders), a period equal to half the term of that order;

(c) where an order under section 181 of the *Criminal Justice Act* 2003 (prison sentences of less than 12 months) is made in relation to the custodial sentence, a period equal to the custodial period specified pursuant to section 181(3)(a) of that Act less any relevant discount;

(d) where an order under section 183 of that Act (intermittent custody orders) is made in relation to the custodial sentence, a period equal to the number of custodial days specified pursuant to section 183(1)(a) of that Act less any relevant discount;

(e) where section 227 of that Act (extended sentence for certain violent or sexual offences: persons 18 or over) applies in relation to the custodial sentence, a period equal to half the term imposed pursuant to section 227(2C)(a) of that Act calculated after that term has been reduced by any relevant discount;

(f) where section 228 of that Act (extended sentence for certain violent or sexual offences: persons under 18) applies in relation to the custodial sentence, a period equal to half the term imposed pursuant to section 228(2B)(a) of that Act calculated after that term has been reduced by any relevant discount;

(g) where an order under section 269(2) of that Act (determination of minimum term in relation to mandatory life sentence: early release) is made in relation to the custodial sentence, a period equal to the part of the sentence specified in that order;

(h) in any other case, a period equal to half the custodial sentence imposed calculated after that sentence has been reduced by any relevant discount.

(5) If a period determined under subsection (4) includes a fraction of a day, that period is to be rounded up to the nearest number of whole days.

(6) The "relevant discount" is the total number of days to count as time served by virtue of a direction under—

(a) section 240 of the *Criminal Justice Act* 2003 (crediting periods of remand in custody), or

(b) section 240A of that Act (crediting periods of remand on bail).

(7) This section does not apply where—

(a) the custodial sentence was a suspended sentence,

(b) the court has made an order under section 269(4) of the *Criminal Justice Act* 2003 (determination of minimum term in relation to mandatory life sentence: no early release) in relation to the custodial sentence, or

(c) the court has made an order under section 82A(4) of this Act (determination of minimum term in relation to discretionary life sentence: no early release) in relation to the custodial sentence.

(8) Subsection (9) applies where an amending order provides that the proportion of a prisoner's sentence referred to in section 244(3)(a) or 247(2) of the *Criminal Justice Act* 2003 (release of prisoners in certain circumstances) is to be read as a reference to another proportion ("the new proportion").

(9) The Secretary of State may by order—

(a) if the amending order makes provision in respect of section 244(3)(a) of that Act, provide that the proportion specified in subsection (4)(h) of this section is to be read, in the case of a custodial sentence to which the amending order applies, as a reference to the new proportion;

(b) if the amending order makes provision in respect of section 247(2) of that Act, provide that the proportion specified in subsection (4)(e) and (f) of this section is to be read, in the case of a custodial sentence to which the amending order applies, as a reference to the new proportion.

(10) In this section—

"amending order", means an order under section 267 of the *Criminal Justice Act* 2003 (alteration by order of relevant proportion of sentence);

"driving licence" means a licence to drive a motor vehicle granted under Part 3 of the *Road Traffic Act* 1988;

"suspended sentence" has the meaning given by section 189 of the *Criminal Justice Act* 2003.

Part IV

Effect of custodial sentence in other cases

147B.—(1) This section applies where a person is convicted of an offence for which a court proposes to order the person to be disqualified under section 146 or 147 for holding or obtaining a driving licence and—

(a) the court proposes to impose on the person a custodial sentence (other than a suspended sentence) for another offence, or

(b) at the time of sentencing for the offence, a custodial sentence imposed on the person on an earlier occasion has not expired.

(2) In determining the period for which the person is to be disqualified under section 146 or 147, the court must have regard to the consideration in subsection (3) if and to the extent that it is appropriate to do so.

(3) The consideration is the diminished effect of disqualification as a distinct punishment if the person who is disqualified is also detained in pursuance of a custodial sentence.

(4) If the court proposes to order the person to be disqualified under section 146 or 147 and to impose a custodial sentence for the same offence, the court may not in relation to that disqualification take that custodial sentence into account for the purposes of subsection (2).

(5) In this section "suspended sentence" has the same meaning as in section 147A.

Section 146 is significantly wider than the power under s.147 in that it is available to **24–25**
both the Crown Court and magistrates' courts, it is not limited to any particular offence, and it is not necessary that the offence should be connected in any way with the use of a

motor vehicle. The s.147 power is, therefore, only likely to be used for offences committed before the powers under s.146 became available.

When in force, s.147A will require a court imposing both a custodial sentence and disqualification from driving under these provisions to extend the period of disqualification so that the period of disqualification, in effect, starts at the point at which the offender is likely to be released from the custodial sentence. Section 147B applies where a court is imposing the custodial sentence and the disqualification for different offences; in those circumstances the court must consider the diminished effect of the disqualification and may, but is not obliged to, increase the period of disqualification: s.147B(2).

Home Office guidance that accompanied the implementation of s.146 suggests that the power should be used where the offence is in some way linked to the use of a vehicle although that is not necessary under the terms of the section. Any order needs to be proportionate to the offence and it may be that any disqualification for an offence where no vehicle or driving is involved would fall on that ground. In *Cliff* [2005] R.T.R. 11, the defendant committed an offence of affray. In the sequence of events leading up to the offence, it was clear that he had driven a motor vehicle whilst under the influence of drink and/or drugs but there was no offence charged relating to that driving. The court imposed a sentence of 15 months' imprisonment and two years' disqualification under s.146. On appeal, it was argued that it was wrong in principle to impose the disqualification because there was no link between the offence and the driving. The Court of Appeal disagreed although it reduced the period of disqualification to nine months. It is not necessary for the offence to be connected to the use of a motor car and the section provides an additional punishment available to the court. However, the Court also said that such an order cannot be imposed arbitrarily and there must be "sufficient reason" for it. No guidance was given as to what might constitute a sufficient reason but the Court drew attention to the driving that had occurred and to the fact that it was under the heavy influence of drink, drugs or both. However, in *Sofekun* [2008] EWCA Crim 2035, the Court of Appeal reviewed the approach and stated that the judgment in *Cliff* should not be taken "to have created any restrictions on the exercise of the power which cannot otherwise be found in the statutory provision itself": *per* Judge P. Since the statutory provision has no restriction, the order may be made whenever the court consider it to be appropriate.

In another case, an offender had been disqualified under s.147, a more restricted power.He had been convicted of engaging in sexual activity in the presence of a child by masturbating whilst driving his car close to young girls: *Bowling* [2008] EWCA Crim 1148. In the commentary on the case at [2008] Crim.L.R. 727, it is observed that the court could alternatively have imposed an anti-social behaviour order in such circumstances which would have brought the court two advantages. First, the order could have been more closely tailored to the needs arising from the case; whereas a disqualification covers driving in every situation, a prohibition could have limited the restriction to driving in the circumstances likely to cause harassment, alarm or distress whilst leaving the offender able to drive in other situations where use of a vehicle would be necessary, such as for travel to and from employment. Secondly, the sanction available on breach is more extensive than for driving whilst disqualified which, in the circumstances of this particular case, may have been advantageous.

An offender who receives a custodial sentence should not be disqualified from driving for such a term that he will be prevented from securing employment upon his release from prison: *Wright* (1979) 1 Cr.App.R.(S.) 82, CA. However, there is no absolute principle that an offender's period of disqualification should come to an end before he is released from prison: *Arif* (1985) 7 Cr.App.R.(S.) 92, CA. In its definitive guideline covering four offences of causing death by driving, the Sentencing Guidelines Council has stated that a court should take into account any period in custody when determining the length of disqualification. For each of the offences in that guideline, Parliament has provided for a minimum period of disqualification implying that the punitive element of such an order is significant as well as the public safety element. In such circumstances, a court imposing a custodial sentence may well consider imposing disqualification for a period that ensures that the minimum term is served following release.

C. Disqualification of Company Directors

(1) Purpose and effect

Where a person is convicted of certain offences concerned with the management of a company, the court may disqualify that person for a maximum of five years from being a company director, from acting as a receiver of the property of a company or of being directly or indirectly involved in the promotion, formation or management of a company or of acting as an insolvency practitioner. **24–26**

The power arises on conviction for the offences described in s.5(1) of the 1986 Act. If it is an either way offence, the disqualification can follow any conviction of a qualifying offence. If it is a summary only offence, disqualification can follow only where there have been at least three default orders or convictions in the five years preceding the date of conviction: s.5(2) and (3).

Company Directors Disqualification Act 1986, ss.1, 5

Disqualification orders: general.

1.—(1) In the circumstances specified below in this Act a court may, and under sections 6 and 9A shall, make against a person a disqualification order, that is to say an order that for a period specified in the order— **24–27**

(a) he shall not be a director of a company, act as receiver of a company's property or in any way, whether directly or indirectly, be concerned or take part in the promotion, formation or management of a company unless (in each case) he has the leave of the court, and

(b) he shall not act as an insolvency practitioner.

(2) In each section of this Act which gives to a court power or, as the case may be, imposes on it the duty to make a disqualification order there is specified the maximum (and, in section 6, the minimum) period of disqualification which may or (as the case may be) must be imposed by means of the order and, unless the court otherwise orders, the period of disqualification so imposed shall begin at the end of the period of 21 days beginning with the date of the order.

(3) Where a disqualification order is made against a person who is already subject to such an order or to a disqualification undertaking, the periods specified in those orders or, as the case may be, in the order and the undertaking shall run concurrently.

(4) A disqualification order may be made on grounds which are or include matters other than criminal convictions, notwithstanding that the person in respect of whom it is to be made may be criminally liable in respect of those matters.

Disqualification on summary conviction

5.—(1) An offence counting for the purposes of this section is one of which a person is convicted (either on indictment or summarily) in consequence of a contravention of, or failure to comply with, any provision of the companies legislation requiring a return, account or other document to be filed with, delivered or sent, or notice of any matter to be given, to the registrar of companies (whether the contravention or failure is on the person's own part or on the part of any company). **24–28**

(2) Where a person is convicted of a summary offence counting for those purposes, the court by which he is convicted (or, in England and Wales, any other magistrates' court acting in the same local justice area) may make a disqualification order against him if the circumstances specified in the next subsection are present.

(3) Those circumstances are that, during the 5 years ending with the date of the conviction, the person has had made against him, or has been convicted of, in total not less than 3 default orders and offences counting for the purposes of this section; and those offences may include that of which he is convicted as mentioned in subsection (2) and any other offence of which he is convicted on the same occasion.

(4) For the purposes of this section—

(a) the definition of "summary offence" in Schedule 1 to the *Interpretation Act* 1978 applies for Scotland as for England and Wales, and

(b) "default order" means the same as in section 3(3)(b).

(4A) In this section "the companies legislation" means the *Companies Acts* and Parts 1 to 7 of the *Insolvency Act* 1986 (company insolvency and winding up).

(5) The maximum period of disqualification under this section is 5 years.

24–29 The "management" of a company has been held to apply to cases of obtaining by deception and similar activities committed during the course of trading by the company: *Corbin* (1984) 6 Cr.App.R.(S.) 17, DC; *Austen* (1985) 7 Cr.App.R.(S.) 214, CA and *Georgiou*, 87 Cr.App.R. 207, CA.

A disqualification order should not be combined with a compensation order, if the effect of the order would be to deprive the offender of his means to earn money with which to pay compensation: *Holmes* (1992) 13 Cr.App.R.(S.) 29, CA.

D. DRINKING BANNING ORDERS

(1) Purpose and effect

24–30 This power included in the *Violent Crime Reduction Act* 2006 enables a court to impose any prohibition on the subject of the order that is "necessary" for the purpose of "protecting other persons from criminal or disorderly conduct by the subject while he is under the influence of alcohol". This includes protecting property from unlawful loss or damage (s.14(2)) and so may be usable in relation to those who persistently steal from shops whilst under the influence of alcohol. The order must include any necessary prohibitions on the subject entering premises licensed for the sale of alcohol by retail and those holding a club premises certificate for a similar purpose: s.1(3). An order must have effect for at least two months but for no more than two years: s.2(1). Individual provisions may have effect for different periods but never for less than two months nor more than two years: s.2(2). An order may be permitted to cease earlier than the designated time if the subject completes an "approved course" specified in the order: ss.2(3), 12 and 13.

Where an order is being made on conviction, the court must first be satisfied both that the proposed subject has, after the commencement of s.3 of the Act, "engaged in criminal or disorderly conduct while under the influence of alcohol" and that an order is necessary to protect others from such conduct by the subject while under the influence of alcohol.

The court may consider evidence led by the prosecution or the defence; that evidence need not have been admissible in criminal proceedings: s.7(1) and (2). An order may be made as an ancillary order not as a sentence in its own right: s.7(3); however, the consideration of the banning order may be adjourned even after sentence has been imposed for the offence itself: s.7(4). An interim order may be made: s.9(2).

An order may be varied or discharged; however, an order may not be discharged on application unless either half of the length of the order has been completed or the DPP has consented to earlier discharge: s.8(6). If an order is breached without reasonable excuse, the maximum penalty is a fine of level 4 (currently £2,500): s.11.

Violent Crime Reduction Act 2006, ss.1, 2, 3, 6, 7, 8, 9, 10, 11, 14

Drinking banning orders

24–31 **1.**—(1) A drinking banning order is an order that prohibits the individual against whom it is made ("the subject") from doing the things described in the order.

(2) Such an order may impose any prohibition on the subject which is necessary for the purpose of protecting other persons from criminal or disorderly conduct by the subject while he is under the influence of alcohol.

(3) The prohibitions imposed by such an order must include such prohibition as the court making it considers necessary, for that purpose, on the subject's entering—

(a) premises in respect of which there is a premises licence authorising the use of the premises for the sale of alcohol by retail; and

(b) premises in respect of which there is a club premises certificate authorising the use of the premises for the supply of alcohol to members or guests.

(4) A drinking banning order may not impose a prohibition on the subject that prevents him—

(a) from having access to a place where he resides;

(b) from attending at any place which he is required to attend for the purposes of any employment of his or of any contract of services to which he is a party;

(c) from attending at any place which he is expected to attend during the period for which the order has effect for the purposes of education or training or for the purpose of receiving medical treatment; or

(d) from attending at any place which he is required to attend by any obligation imposed on him by or under an enactment or by the order of a court or tribunal.

(5) Expressions used in subsection (3) and in the *Licensing Act* 2003 or in a Part of that Act have the same meanings in that subsection as in that Act or Part.

Duration of drinking banning orders

2.—(1) A drinking banning order has effect for a period specified in the order ("the specified period"), which must be not less than two months and not more than two years. **24–32**

(2) A drinking banning order may provide that different prohibitions contained in the order have effect for different periods; but, in each case, the period ("the prohibition period") must be not less than two months and not more than two years.

(3) A drinking banning order may include provision for—

(a) the order, or

(b) a prohibition contained in it,

to cease to have effect before the end of the specified period or the prohibition period if the subject satisfactorily completes the approved course specified in the order.

(4) Provision under subsection (3) must fix the time at which the order or the prohibition will cease to have effect if the subject satisfactorily completes the specified approved course as whichever is the later of—

(a) the time specified in the order in accordance with subsection (5); and

(b) the time when he does satisfactorily complete that course.

(5) The time specified for the purposes of subsection (4)(a) must be a time after the expiry of at least half the specified period or (as the case may be) the prohibition period.

(6) Provision under subsection (3) may be included in a drinking banning order only if—

(a) the court making the order is satisfied that a place on the specified approved course will be available for the subject; and

(b) the subject has agreed to the inclusion of the provision in question in the order.

(7) Before making provision under subsection (3), the court must inform the subject in ordinary language (whether in writing or otherwise) about—

(a) the effect of including the provision in the order;

(b) what, in general terms, attendance on the course will involve if he undertakes it;

(c) any fees he will be required to pay for the course if he undertakes it; and

(d) when he will have to pay any such fees.

(8) Where a court makes a drinking banning order which does not include provision under subsection (3), it must give its reasons for not including such provision in open court.

(9) The Secretary of State may by regulations amend subsection (5) so as to modify the earliest time (after the completion of the specified approved course) when by virtue of that subsection—

(a) a drinking banning order, or

(b) a prohibition contained in such an order,

may cease to have effect.

Orders on an application to magistrates' court

3.—(1) An application to a magistrates' court for the making of a drinking banning order against an individual may be made by a relevant authority if— **24–33**

(a) it appears to the authority that the conditions in subsection (2) are satisfied with respect to the individual; and

(b) the individual is aged 16 or over.

(2) The conditions are—

(a) that the individual has, after the commencement of this section, engaged in criminal or disorderly conduct while under the influence of alcohol; and

(b) that such an order is necessary to protect other persons from further conduct by him of that kind while he is under the influence of alcohol.

(3) An application under this section to a magistrates' court has to be made by complaint.

(4) Before making an application under this section, a relevant authority must consult the appropriate persons.

(5) If, on an application under this section with respect to an individual, it is proved that the conditions in subsection (2) are satisfied in his case, the magistrates' court may make a drinking banning order against him.

(6) Nothing in this section affects the operation of section 127 of the Magistrates' Courts Act 1980 (c. 43) (limitation of time in respect of informations laid or complaints made in magistrates' court).

Orders on conviction in criminal proceedings

24–34 **6.**—(1) This section applies where—

(a) an individual aged 16 or over is convicted of an offence (the "offender"); and

(b) at the time he committed the offence, he was under the influence of alcohol.

(2) The court must consider whether the conditions in section 3(2) are satisfied in relation to the offender.

(3) If the court decides that the conditions are satisfied in relation to the offender, it may make a drinking banning order against him.

(4) If the court—

(a) decides that the conditions are satisfied in relation to the offender, but

(b) does not make a drinking banning order,

it must give its reasons for not doing so in open court.

(5) If the court decides that the conditions are not satisfied in relation to the offender, it must state that fact in open court and give its reasons.

Supplementary provision about orders on conviction

24–35 **7.**—(1) For the purpose of deciding whether to make a drinking banning order under section 6 the court may consider evidence led by the prosecution and evidence led by the defence.

(2) It is immaterial whether the evidence would have been admissible in the proceedings in which the offender was convicted.

(3) A drinking banning order under section 6 must not be made except—

(a) in addition to a sentence imposed in respect of the offence; or

(b) in addition to an order discharging the offender conditionally.

(4) The court may adjourn any proceedings in relation to a drinking banning order under section 6 even after sentencing the offender.

(5) If the offender does not appear for any adjourned proceedings, the court may further adjourn the proceedings or may issue a warrant for his arrest.

(6) But the court may not issue a warrant for the offender's arrest unless it is satisfied that he has had adequate notice of the time and place of the adjourned proceedings.

(7) A drinking banning order under section 6 takes effect on—

(a) the day on which it is made; or

(b) if on that day the offender is detained in legal custody, the day on which he is released from that custody.

(8) Subsection (9) applies in relation to proceedings in which a drinking banning order is made under section 6 against a young person.

(9) In so far as the proceedings relate to the making of the order—

(a) section 49 of the *Children and Young Persons Act* 1933 (restrictions on reports of proceedings in which children and young persons are concerned) does not apply in respect of the young person against whom the order is made; and

(b) section 39 of that Act (power to prohibit publication of certain matters) does so apply.

(10) In section 3(2)(fa) of the *Prosecution of Offences Act* 1985 (functions of the Director), after the first occurrence of "conviction of certain offences)" insert ", section 6 of the Violent Crime Reduction Act 2006 (orders on conviction in criminal proceedings)".

(11) In this section and section 6 "the court" in relation to an offender means—

(a) the court by or before which he is convicted of the offence; or
(b) if he is committed to the Crown Court to be dealt with for the offence, the Crown Court.

Variation or discharge of orders under s.6

8.—(1) The following persons may apply to the court which made a drinking banning order under section 6 for the order to be varied or discharged by a further order— **24–36**

(a) the subject;
(b) the Director of Public Prosecutions; or
(c) a relevant authority.

(2) If the subject makes an application under subsection (1), he must also send notice of his application to the Director of Public Prosecutions.

(3) If the Director of Public Prosecutions or a relevant authority makes an application under subsection (1), he or it must also send notice of the application to the subject.

(4) In the case of an order under section 6 made by a magistrates' court, the reference in subsection (1) to the court which made the order includes a reference to a relevant local court.

(5) An order under section 6 may not be varied so as to extend the specified period to more than two years.

(6) No order under section 6 is to be discharged on an application under subsection (1)(a) unless—

(a) it is discharged from a time after the end of the period that is half the duration of the specified period; or
(b) the Director of Public Prosecutions has consented to its earlier discharge.

(7) In section 3 of the *Prosecution of Offences Act* 1985 (c. 23) (functions of the Director of Public Prosecutions), in subsection (2) after paragraph (fc) insert—

"(fd) where it appears to him appropriate to do so, to have the conduct of applications under section 8(1)(b) of the *Violent Crime Reduction Act* 2006 for the variation or discharge of orders made under section 6 of that Act;

(fe) where it appears to him appropriate to do so, to appear on any application under section 8(1)(a) of that Act by a person subject to an order under section 6 of that Act for the variation or discharge of the order."

Interim orders

9.—(1) This section applies in each of the following cases— **24–37**

(a) where an application is made for a drinking banning order;
(b) where the court is required under section 6 to consider whether the conditions for making a drinking banning order are satisfied.

(2) Before—

(a) determining the application, or
(b) considering whether the conditions are satisfied,

the court may make an order under this section ("an interim order") if it considers that it is just to do so.

(3) Where this section applies by virtue of subsection (1)(a), an application for an interim order against an individual—

(a) may be made without notice being given to that individual; and
(b) may be heard in the absence of that individual.

(4) The following permission is required for the making or hearing of an application in accordance with subsection (3)—

(a) in the case of proceedings in the county court, the permission of the court; and
(b) in the case of an application to a magistrates' court, the permission of the proper officer.

(5) Permission may only be given under subsection (4) if the court or proper officer is satisfied—

(a) that it is necessary for the application to be made without notice being given to the individual in question; and
(b) that it is not necessary for the application to be heard in the presence of the individual.

(6) An interim order—

(a) may contain any provision that may be contained in a drinking banning order; but

(b) has effect, unless renewed, only for such fixed period of not more than four weeks as may be specified in the order.

(7) An interim order—

(a) may be renewed (on one or more occasions) for a period of not more than four weeks from the end of the period when it would otherwise cease to have effect;

(b) must cease to have effect (if it has not previously done so) on the determination of the application mentioned in subsection (1)(a) or on the court's making its decision whether to make a drinking banning order under section 6.

(8) Section 5 applies in relation to an interim order made in a case falling within subsection (1)(a) as it applies in relation to a drinking banning order made under section 3 or 4, but with the omission of section 5(5) and (6).

(9) Section 8 applies in relation to an interim order made in a case falling within subsection (1)(b) as it applies in relation to a drinking banning order made under section 6, but with the omission of section 8(5) and (6).

Appeals

24–38 **10.**—(1) An appeal lies to the Crown Court against the making by a magistrates' court of a drinking banning order under section 3 or 6.

(2) On such an appeal the Crown Court—

(a) may make such orders as may be necessary to give effect to its determination of the appeal;

(b) may also make such incidental or consequential orders as appear to it to be just.

(3) An order of the Crown Court made on an appeal under this section (other than one directing that an application be re-heard by a magistrates' court) shall be treated for the purposes of sections 5 and 8 as an order of the magistrates' court from which the appeal was brought.

Breach of drinking banning orders

24–39 **11.**—(1) If the subject of a drinking banning order or of an interim order does, without reasonable excuse, anything that he is prohibited from doing by the order, he is guilty of an offence.

(2) A person guilty of an offence under subsection (1) shall be liable, on summary conviction, to a fine not exceeding level 4 on the standard scale.

(3) If a person is convicted of an offence under subsection (1), it is not open to the court by or before which he is convicted to make an order under subsection (1)(b) (conditional discharge) of section 12 of the *Powers of Criminal Courts (Sentencing) Act* 2000 (c. 6).

(4) A local authority may bring proceedings for an offence under subsection (1).

(5) The Secretary of State may by order provide that a person of a description specified in the order may bring proceedings for an offence under subsection (1) in such cases and such circumstances as may be prescribed by the order.

(6) In proceedings for an offence under subsection (1), a copy of the original drinking banning order or interim order, certified as such by the proper officer of the court which made it, is admissible as evidence—

(a) of its having been made, and

(b) of its contents,

to the same extent that oral evidence of those things is admissible in those proceedings.

(7) If proceedings for an offence under subsection (1) are brought in a youth court, section 47(2) of the *Children and Young Persons Act* 1933 (c. 12) has effect as if the persons entitled to be present for the purposes of those proceedings included one person authorised to be present by a relevant authority.

(8) In relation to proceedings brought against a young person for an offence under subsection (1)—

(a) section 49 of the *Children and Young Persons Act* 1933 (restrictions on reports of proceedings in which children and young persons are concerned) does not apply in respect of the young person against whom the proceedings are brought; and

(b) section 45 of the *Youth Justice and Criminal Evidence Act* 1999 (c. 23) (power to restrict reporting on criminal proceedings involving persons under 18) does so apply.

(9) If, in relation to any such proceedings, the court does exercise its power to give a

direction under section 45 of the *Youth Justice and Criminal Evidence Act* 1999, it must give its reasons for doing so.

(10) Subject to paragraph 2(2) of Schedule 2 to the *Youth Justice and Criminal Evidence Act* 1999, until section 45 of that Act comes into force, the references to it in this section are to be read as references to section 39 of the *Children and Young Persons Act* 1933 (power to prohibit publication of certain matters).

Interpretation of Chapter 1

14.—(1) In this Chapter— **24–40**

"appropriate persons", in relation to an application for a drinking banning order or an application referred to in section 4(6)(b) or (c), means such of the following as is not a party to the application—

(a) the chief officer of police of the police force for the police area where the conduct to which the application relates occurred;

(b) the chief officer of police of the police force for the police area in which the individual to whose conduct the application relates normally resides;

(c) every local authority in whose area the place where that individual normally resides is situated; and

(d) the Chief Constable of the British Transport Police Force;

"approved course" means a course approved by the Secretary of State for the purposes of section 2;

"drinking banning order" means an order under section 3, 4 or 6;

"interim order" means an order under section 9;

"local authority" means —

(a) a county council in England;

(b) a district council in England;

(c) a London borough council;

(d) the Common Council of the City of London;

(e) the Council of the Isles of Scilly;

(f) a county council or a county borough council in Wales;

"proper officer" —

(a) in relation to a magistrates' court, means the justices' clerk; and

(b) in relation to any other court, means the clerk of the court;

"relevant authority" means —

(a) the chief officer of police of a police force for a police area;

(b) the Chief Constable of the British Transport Police Force;

(c) a local authority;

"relevant local court", in relation to a drinking banning order, means a magistrates' court acting for the local justice area in which the subject normally resides;

"specified period", in relation to a drinking banning order, means the period specified in the order for the purposes of section 2(1) as the period for which the order is to have effect;

"subject", in relation to an order, means the individual against whom it is made;

"young person" has the same meaning as in the *Children and Young Persons Act* 1933 (see section 107(1) of that Act).

(2) References in this Chapter to protecting persons from criminal or disorderly conduct include references to protecting their property from unlawful loss or damage.

(3) The Secretary of State may by order provide that a person of a description specified in the order is to be regarded as a relevant authority for such purposes of the provisions of this Chapter as are specified in the order.

(4) A power of the Secretary of State to make an order or regulations under this Chapter shall be exercisable by statutory instrument.

(5) Every such power includes power—

(a) to make different provision for different cases;

(b) to make provision subject to such exemptions and exceptions as the Secretary of State thinks fit; and

(c) to make such incidental, supplemental, consequential and transitional provision as he thinks fit.

(6) No regulations shall be made under section 2 unless a draft of the regulations has been laid before Parliament and approved by a resolution of each House.

(7) A statutory instrument containing—

(a) regulations under section 12 or 13, or

(b) an order under section 11 or this section,

shall be subject to annulment in pursuance of a resolution of either House of Parliament.

(8) The power under subsection (5) to make incidental, supplemental and consequential provision includes power to modify so much of this section as defines "appropriate persons".

E. POWER TO RECTIFY SENTENCE

24–41 If a party considers a sentence to be wrong, generally it may only seek to rectify that by utilising the appeal procedure, an option more readily open to the defence than to the prosecution. However, there will be circumstances where it is subsequently recognised that a mistake has been made and a power has been provided to magistrates' courts which avoids the necessity for an appeal to be made.

This power exists wherever a court considers it necessary in the interests of justice. A hearing convened to consider such a change should only take place when notice has been given to all relevant parties and the court should take steps to enable everyone with an interest to be heard before a decision is made. The change could be to replace a sentence or part of a sentence which is wrong in law (*e.g.* one year mandatory disqualification imposed where the law requires a minimum of three years) or to change a sentence because of new information becoming available that makes the original sentence less just. Although this is a widely drawn power, it is one that needs to be used with care where it is proposed to make a major change to a sentence for reasons other than a mistake or omission. In *R. (Holme) v. Liverpool Magistrates' Court* (2005) 169 J.P. 306, the defendant was convicted of dangerous driving at a magistrates' court after a trial. A sentence of 50 hours community service was imposed together with disqualification for 12 months and until a test had been passed. Subsequently, information came to light which gave considerably more information about the effect of the offence on the victim than had been formally presented to the court when considering sentence. Approximately five months after sentence, the CPS sought (successfully) to persuade the court to re-open the case with a view to re-considering sentence. The DC allowed the defendant's appeal against that decision. The DC concluded both that (even though no specific information was given) the effect of the accident should have been recognised by the court given the nature of the impact between the defendant's vehicle and the victim and that the sentence imposed was about right. In that context, although the requirement to exercise the power within 28 days had been removed by Parliament, it is a power which, in such circumstances, needed to be exercised speedily. A similar power in the Crown Court for correcting sentence (or for commencing an appeal against an unduly lenient sentence) had to be exercised within 28 days [now 56 days]. The DC emphasised that, not least because of the importance of finality, it would only be in very rare circumstances that it would be appropriate to resort to s.142 to consider an increase in sentence, particularly if that increase brought about the possibility of a custodial sentence as opposed to another form of disposal.

The restrictive interpretation of the wide terms of the statute has been continued in *Zykin v. Crown Prosecution Service* [2009] EWHC 1469; (2009) 173 J.P. 361. The applicant was subject to a confiscation order made in the Crown Court. In enforcement proceedings in a magistrates' court, the court ordered the applicant to serve a further 364 days imprisonment consecutive to the custodial sentence imposed for the substantive offence. Approximately two months later, the applicant asked the magistrates' court to re-open the determination in accordance with the power under s.142 but the court declined on the grounds that it was being asked to sit as an appeal court from its own decision. Dismissing the applicant's appeal from that decision, the Divisional Court confirmed that the section did not confer a wide and general power but was generally (and correctly) to be regarded as a "slip rule"; here there was no suggestion that the court had erred in any way and so the refusal was correct. Similarly, the power should not be used to deal with an application which should properly be made under other provisions: *Trigger v. Northampton Magistrates' Court* (2011) 175 J.P. 101.

Magistrates' Courts Act 1980, s.142

Power of magistrates' court to re-open cases to rectify mistakes etc.

142.—(1) A magistrates' court may vary or rescind a sentence or other order imposed or made by it when dealing with an offender if it appears to the court to be in the interests of justice to do so, and it is hereby declared that this power extends to replacing a sentence or order which for any reason appears to be invalid by another which the court has power to impose or make. **24–42**

(1A) The power conferred on a magistrates' court by subsection (1) above shall not be exercisable in relation to any sentence or order imposed or made by it when dealing with an offender if—

(a) the Crown Court has determined an appeal against—

(i) that sentence or order;

(ii) the conviction in respect of which that sentence or order was imposed or made; or

(iii) any other sentence or order imposed or made by the magistrates' court when dealing with the offender in respect of that conviction (including a sentence or order replaced by that sentence or order); or

(b) the High Court has determined a case stated for the opinion of that court on any question arising in any proceeding leading to or resulting from the imposition or making of the sentence or order.

(2) Where a person is convicted by a magistrates' court and it subsequently appears to the court that it would be in the interests of justice that the case should be heard again by different justices, the court may so direct.

(2A) The power conferred on a magistrates' court by subsection (2) above shall not be exercisable in relation to a conviction if—

(a) the Crown Court has determined an appeal against—

(i) the conviction; or

(ii) any sentence or order imposed or made by the magistrates' court when dealing with the offender in respect of the conviction; or

(b) the High Court has determined a case stated for the opinion of that court on any question arising in any proceeding leading to or resulting from the conviction.

(3) Where a court gives a direction under subsection (2) above—

(a) the conviction and any sentence or other order imposed or made in consequence thereof shall be of no effect; and

(b) section 10(4) above shall apply as if the trial of the person in question had been adjourned.

(5) Where a sentence or order is varied under subsection (1) above, the sentence or other order, as so varied, shall take effect from the beginning of the day on which it was originally imposed or made, unless the court otherwise directs.

II. POWER TO ENFORCE FINANCIAL PENALTIES

A. INTRODUCTION

The court has a variety of options when dealing with an offender who has failed to pay a sum adjudged to be payable upon conviction. **24–43**

B. POWER TO REMIT THE FINE

A court has the power to remit a fine that has been ordered. The power under s.85 of the 1980 Act requires a change in the circumstances of the defaulter: s.85(1). For these purposes, the definition of a fine is tighter than elsewhere or in common use and care needs to be taken to ensure that the penalty is truly a "fine" for these purposes: s.85(4). The most commonly found exception is an "excise penalty", which is the equivalent of a fine for some offences mainly those arising from use of a vehicle without a vehicle excise licence. **24–44**

The power under s.129 covers situations where the court has fixed the amount of a fine in the absence of information about means from the offender and, that information having subsequently been provided, the court considers that a lower fine (or no fine) would have been imposed if that had been known. In those circumstances, the court can remit some or all of the fine imposed.

Magistrates' Courts Act 1980, s.85

Power to remit fine

24–45 **85.**—(1) Where a fine has been imposed on conviction of an offender by a magistrates' court, the court may at any time remit the whole or any part of the fine, but only if it thinks it just to do so having regard to a change of circumstances which has occurred—

(a) where the court is considering whether to issue a warrant of commitment after the issue of such a warrant in respect of the fine has been postponed under subsection (2) of section 77 above, since the relevant time as defined in subsection (4) of that section; and

(b) in any other case, since the date of the conviction.

(2) Where the court remits the whole or part of the fine after a term of imprisonment has been fixed, it shall also reduce the term by an amount which bears the same proportion to the whole term as the amount remitted bears to the whole or, as the case may be, shall remit the whole term.

(2A) Where the court remits the whole or part of the fine after an order has been made under section 35(2)(a) or (b) of the *Crime (Sentences) Act* 1997, it shall also reduce the total number of hours or days to which the order relates by a number which bears the same proportion as the amount remitted bears to the whole sum or, as the case may be, shall revoke the order.

(2B) Where the court remits the whole or part of the fine after a work order has been made under Schedule 6 to the *Courts Act* 2003 (discharge of fines by unpaid work), it shall also reduce the number of hours specified in the order by a number which bears the same proportion as the amount remitted bears to the whole sum or, as the case may be, shall revoke the order.

(3) In calculating any reduction required by subsection (2), (2A) or (2B) above any fraction of a day or hour shall be left out of account.

(4) Notwithstanding the definition of "fine" in section 150(1) below, references in this section to a fine do not include any other sum adjudged to be paid on conviction, whether as a pecuniary penalty, forfeiture, compensation or otherwise.

24–46 The magistrates may not remit the whole or any part of a fine imposed by the Crown Court, without the consent of the Crown Court: *PCC(S)A* 2000, s.140(5). Neither costs nor compensation can be remitted but, with the consent of the beneficiary of the order, can be written out of the court records. When in force, Sched. 32, para. 28 to the *Criminal Justice Act* 2003 amends s.85(2A) of the 1980 Act by replacing the reference to the *Crime (Sentences) Act* 1997 with one to s.300(2) of the *Criminal Justice Act* 2003.

Criminal Justice Act 2003, s.165

Remission of fines

24–47 **165.**—(1) This section applies where a court has, in fixing the amount of a fine, determined the offender's financial circumstances under section 164(5).

(2) If, on subsequently inquiring into the offender's financial circumstances, the court is satisfied that had it had the results of that inquiry when sentencing the offender it would—

(a) have fixed a smaller amount, or

(b) not have fined him,

it may remit the whole or part of the fine.

(3) Where under this section the court remits the whole or part of a fine after a term of imprisonment has been fixed under section 139 of the *Sentencing Act* (powers of Crown Court in relation to fines) or section 82(5) of the *Magistrates' Courts Act* 1980 (magistrates' powers in relation to default) it must reduce the term by the corresponding proportion.

(4) In calculating any reduction required by subsection (3), any fraction of a day is to be ignored.

C. IMPRISONMENT IN DEFAULT OF PAYMENT

The power to commit to prison in default of payment of a fine is hedged around by many safeguards—it is the final step to be used only where every other option has been shown to be inappropriate or unsuccessful. This section is not an exhaustive study of this complex area but is designed to assist the busy practitioner in identifying the key points in the enforcement process. It is subject to rapid change as provisions to improve enforcement in the *Courts Act* 2003 and the *Criminal Justice Act* 2003 are introduced, sometimes after being piloted in a limited number of areas. **24-48**

The conditions in which the court may order imprisonment in default of payment are set out in s.82 of the 1980 Act. A court may impose imprisonment as an alternative to payment on the day of conviction only if the offender has the means to pay immediately or is unlikely to remain at a place of abode in the United Kingdom for long enough for the fine to be enforced by other means. The minimum period for committal to prison is five days at the point of imposition (though this can be reduced by part payment) and the maximum is on a sliding scale depending on the amount owed. However, shorter periods can be imposed that are not *imprisonment* but have the same effect—see ss.135 and 136, *post* § 24-80 and 24-82.

If commitment was not ordered at the point of sentence, it can only subsequently be ordered if the defaulter is already in custody serving a sentence or following a means inquiry: s.82(3). If the offence was punishable by imprisonment and the offender appears to the court to have the resources to pay straightaway, then the court can commit the person to prison in default of payment. Otherwise, commitment can only follow a decision that the default is due to the offender's wilful refusal or culpable neglect *and* that the court has considered or tried every other means of securing payment and each is inappropriate or unsuccessful: s.82(4). Generally the alternatives include allowing payment by instalments, issuing a distress warrant to seize the goods of the defaulter, making a money payment supervision order to assist the offender to manage their financial affairs in a way that allows the fine to be paid and either an attachment of earnings order or deduction from a qualifying state benefit. Additional initiatives are being taken to provide viable alternatives which increase the likelihood of a fine being paid.

When a means inquiry is conducted, the offender should be examined in detail on income, capital or savings, expenditure, circumstances of original failure to pay sums as they come due, failure to pay in accordance with any terms subsequently set by the court, likelihood of paying in the future: *R. v. Newport Pagnell Justices ex p. Smith* (1988) 152 J.P. 475. **24-49**

Wilful refusal or culpable neglect pursuant to s.82(3) must be demonstrated to the criminal standard of proof: *R. v. South Tyneside Justices ex. p. Martin, Independent*, September 20, 1995. The terms "wilful refusal" and "culpable neglect" denote deliberate defiance or reckless disregard of a court order: *R. v. Luton Magistrates' Court ex p. Sullivan* [1992] 2 F.L.R. 196. The defaulter should be given proper opportunity to put his case, and all relevant factors must have been taken into account before the court concludes that the default is due to "wilful failure" or "culpable neglect": *R. v. York Magistrates' Court ex p. Grimes* (1997) 161 J.P. 550. In *Louis v. Ealing Magistrates' Court* [2009] EWHC Admin 521, Mr Louis had been fined £1,600 by the Crown Court for eight trade mark offences. The payment rate fixed by the Crown Court was subsequently varied downwards by a magistrates' court. Although not paying at the rate specified, Mr Louis made small, regular payments so that by the time of the hearing he had paid £600. However, finding that he had consistently failed to make regular payments and that he should have made greater efforts to obtain work, the court found "wilful refusal" and activated the period of committal in default (making no allowance for the part payment, it would appear). The Divisional Court recited the text in this paragraph and was satisfied that the court had properly considered the various options available to it. However, it allowed the appeal on the ground that the court had not properly explained the basis on which it had rejected the evidence from Mr Louis particularly as it seemed to the Divisional Court that he had made significant efforts; if there was evidence to the contrary, the court should have highlighted it and not simply asserted that he should have made more effort. The court has an absolute duty to consider all other means of dealing with the defaulter: *R.. v. Exeter City Magistrates' Court ex p. Sugar* (1993) 157 J.P. 766. These other methods are listed in s.82(4A) of the 1980 Act, see *post*.

The implications of art. 8 of the European Convention on Human Rights must be considered when making a decision as to whether to order imprisonment in default of payment; it appears committal will not be an appropriate response where the case involves a single mother with a large number of children with a very limited income, doing her level best to balance one monetary obligation against another. Whilst there might be a case in which the pursuit of the aim to make a mother comply with her legal obligations overrode the rights of her children to have the benefit of her care at home, committal must be a remedy of final resort if all else has failed: *R. (Stokes) v. Gwent Magistrates' Court* (2001) 165 J.P. 766, *per* Brooke L.J. If the defaulter is employed, the fact that his earnings fluctuate from week to week does not preclude the making of an attachment of earnings order: *R. v. Stockport Justices ex p. Conlon* [1997] 2 All E.R. 204.

24–50 Where the offender is already serving a sentence of custody for life, or a term of imprisonment or detention under s.108 of the *PCC(S)A* 2000 or detention in a young offenders' institution, the magistrates' court may order imprisonment, or detention in the case of offenders aged 18–20, under s.82(3) of the *MCA* 1980. This is often a convenient way of ensuring that a person released from custody is able to start again without debts to the court.

However, some care will need to be taken before proceeding too readily to wiping out debts to the court. In *Clacton Justices ex p. Commissioners of Customs and Excise* (1988) 152 J.P. 129, DC it was held that in exercising their discretion whether to issue a warrant of commitment or a warrant of distress to enforce payment of a fine, it was essential for the justices to consider the defaulter's means and to ascertain whether the prosecution held any assets belonging to him. The defendant cannot be allowed to choose between payment of his fine and imprisonment. In the instant case, the Customs and Excise Commissioners held, unknown to the magistrates, a substantial sum of money belonging to the defaulter. Bingham L.J. stated that had the magistrates known this, it was difficult to suppose that they would have concluded otherwise than that a warrant of distress would, if necessary, lie.

In *R. v. Grimsby and Cleethorpes Justices ex p. Walters* [1997] 1 W.L.R. 89, it was held that where an offender had just been sentenced to imprisonment for substantive offences, he was then "already serving a term of imprisonment" within the terms of the *Magistrates' Courts Act* 1980, s.82(3)(a), and it was open to justices to sentence him in the same judgment to a consecutive term for failure to pay fines and a compensation order. Any sentence will take effect immediately after it is pronounced.

Magistrates' Courts Act 1980, s.82(2)–(6)

24–51 **82.**—(2) A magistrates' court shall not in advance of the issue of a warrant of commitment fix a term of imprisonment which is to be served by an offender in the event of a default in paying a sum adjudged to be paid by a conviction, except where it has power to issue a warrant of commitment forthwith, but postpones issuing the warrant under section 77(2) above.

(3) Where on the occasion of the offender's conviction a magistrates' court does not issue a warrant of commitment for a default in paying any such sum as aforesaid or fix a term of imprisonment under the said section 77(2) which is to be served by him in the event of any such default, it shall not thereafter issue a warrant of commitment for any such default or for want of sufficient distress to satisfy such a sum unless—

(a) he is already serving a sentence of custody for life, or a term of imprisonment, youth custody, detention under section 9 of the *Criminal Justice Act* 1982 or detention in a detention centre; or

(b) the court has since the conviction inquired into his means in his presence on at least one occasion.

(4) Where a magistrates' court is required by subsection (3) above to inquire into a

person's means, the court may not on the occasion of the inquiry or at any time thereafter issue a warrant of commitment for a default in paying any such sum unless—

(a) in the case of an offence punishable with imprisonment, the offender appears to the court to have sufficient means to pay the sum forthwith; or

(b) the court—

(i) is satisfied that the default is due to the offender's wilful refusal or culpable neglect; and

(ii) has considered or tried all other methods of enforcing payment of the sum and it appears to the court that they are inappropriate or unsuccessful.

(4A) The methods of enforcing payment mentioned in subsection (4)(b)(ii) above are—

(a) a warrant of distress under section 76 above;

(b) an application to the High Court or county court for enforcement under section 87 below;

(c) an order under section 88 below;

(d) an attachment of earnings order; and

(e) if the offender is under the age of 25, an order under section 17 of the *Criminal Justice Act* 1982 (attendance centre orders).

(4B) The cases in which the offender's default may be regarded for the purposes of subsection (4)(b)(i) as being attributable to his wilful refusal or culpable neglect include any case in which–

(a) he has refused, otherwise than on reasonable grounds, to consent to a work order proposed to be made under Schedule 6 to the *Courts Act* 2003 (discharge of fines by unpaid work), or

(b) he has without reasonable excuse failed to comply with such an order.

(5) After the occasion of an offender's conviction by a magistrates' court, the court shall not, unless—

(a) the court has previously fixed a term of imprisonment under section 77(2) above which is to be served by the offender in the event of a default in paying a sum adjudged to be paid by the conviction; or

(b) the offender is serving a sentence of custody for life, or a term of imprisonment, youth custody, detention under section 9 of the *Criminal Justice Act* 1982 or detention in a detention centre,

issue a warrant of commitment for a default in paying the sum or fix such a term except at a hearing at which the offender is present.

(5A) A magistrates' court may not issue a warrant of commitment under subsection (5) above at a hearing at which the offender is not present unless the justices' chief executive for the court has first served on the offender a notice in writing stating that the court intends to hold a hearing to consider whether to issue such a warrant and giving the reason why the court so intends.

(5B) Where after the occasion of an offender's conviction by a magistrates' court the court holds a hearing for the purpose of considering whether to issue a warrant of commitment for default in paying a sum adjudged to be paid by the conviction, it shall consider such information about the offender's means as is available to it unless it has previously—

(a) inquired into the offender's means; and

(b) postponed the issue of the warrant of commitment under section 77(2) above.

(5C) A notice under subsection (5A) above—

(a) shall state the time and place appointed for the hearing; and

(b) shall inform the offender that, if he considers that there are grounds why the warrant should not be issued, he may make representations to the court in person or in writing,

but the court may exercise its powers in relation to the issue of a warrant whether or not he makes representations.

(5D) Except as mentioned in subsection (5E) below, the time stated in a notice under subsection (5A) above shall not be earlier than 21 days after the issue of the notice.

(5E) Where a magistrates' court exercises in relation to an offender the power conferred by section 77(2) above and at the same hearing issues a notice under subsection (5A) above in relation to him, the time stated in the notice may be a time on any day following the end of the period for which the issue of the warrant of commitment has been postponed.

(5F) A notice under subsection (5A) above to be served on any person shall be deemed to be served on that person if it is sent by registered post or the recorded delivery service addressed to him at his last known address, notwithstanding that the notice is returned as undelivered or is for any other reason not received by that person.

(6) Where a magistrates' court issues a warrant of commitment on the ground that one of the conditions mentioned in subsection (1) or (4) above is satisfied, it shall state that fact, specifying the ground, in the warrant.

D. POWER TO MAKE A MONEY PAYMENTS SUPERVISION ORDER

Magistrates' Courts Act 1980, s.88

Supervision pending payment

24–52 **88.**—(1) Where any person is adjudged to pay a sum by a summary conviction and the convicting court does not commit him to prison forthwith in default of payment, the court may, either on the occasion of the conviction or on a subsequent occasion, order him to be placed under the supervision of such person as the court may from time to time appoint.

(2) An order placing a person under supervision in respect of any sum shall remain in force so long as he remains liable to pay the sum or any part of it unless the order ceases to have effect or is discharged under subsection (3) below.

(3) An order under this section shall cease to have effect on the making of a transfer of fine order under section 89 below with respect to the sum adjudged to be paid and may be discharged by the court that made it, without prejudice in either case to the making of a new order.

(4) Where a person under 21 years old has been adjudged to pay a sum by a summary conviction and the convicting court does not commit him to detention under section 108 of the *Powers of Criminal Courts (Sentencing) Act* 2000 forthwith in default of payment, the court shall not commit him to such detention in default of payment of the sum, or for want of sufficient distress to satisfy the sum, unless he has been placed under supervision in respect of the sum or the court is satisfied that it is undesirable or impracticable to place him under supervision.

(5) Where a court, being satisfied as aforesaid, commits a person under 21 years old to such detention without an order under this section having been made, the court shall state the grounds on which it is so satisfied in the warrant of commitment.

(6) Where an order placing a person under supervision with respect to a sum is in force, a magistrates' court shall not commit him to prison in default of payment of the sum, or for want of sufficient distress to satisfy the sum, unless the court has before committing him taken such steps as may be reasonably practicable to obtain from the person appointed for his supervision an oral or written report on the offender's conduct and means and has considered any report so obtained, in addition, in a case where an inquiry is required by section 82 above, to that inquiry.

E. POWER TO ORDER A DISTRESS WARRANT

Magistrates' Courts Act 1980, ss.76–78

Enforcement of sums adjudged to be paid

24–53 **76.**—(1) Subject to the following provisions of this Part of this Act, and to section 132 below, where default is made in paying a sum adjudged to be paid by a conviction or order of a magistrates' court, the court may issue a warrant of distress for the purposes of levying the sum or issue a warrant committing the defaulter to prison.

(2) A warrant of commitment may be issued as aforesaid either—

(a) where it appears on the return to a warrant of distress that the money and goods of the defaulter are insufficient to satisfy the sum with the costs and charges of levying the sum; or

(b) instead of a warrant of distress.

(3) The period for which a person may be committed to prison under such a warrant as aforesaid shall not, subject to the provisions of any enactment passed after 31st December 1879, exceed the period applicable to the case under Schedule 4 to this Act.

(4) Where proceedings are brought for the enforcement of a magistrates' court maintenance order under this section, the court may vary the order by exercising one of its powers under paragraphs (a) to (d) of section 59(3) above.

(5) Subsections (4), (5) and (7) of section 59 above shall apply for the purposes of subsection (4) above as they apply for the purposes of that section.

(6) Subsections (4) and (5) above shall not have effect in relation to a maintenance order which is not a qualifying maintenance order (within the meaning of section 59 above).

Postponement of issue of warrant

77.—(1) Where a magistrates' court has power to issue a warrant of distress under this Part of this Act, it may, if it thinks it expedient to do so, postpone the issue of the warrant until such time and on such conditions, if any, as the court thinks just. **24–54**

(2) Where a magistrates' court has power to issue a warrant of commitment under this Part of this Act, it may, if it thinks it expedient to do so, fix a term of imprisonment or detention under section 108 of the *Powers of Criminal Courts (Sentencing) Act* 2000 (detention of persons aged 18 to 20 for default) and postpone the issue of the warrant until such time and on such conditions, if any, as the court thinks just.

(3) A magistrates' court shall have power at any time to do either or both of the following—

(a) to direct that the issue of the warrant of commitment shall be postponed until a time different from that to which it was previously postponed;

(b) to vary any of the conditions on which its issue is postponed,

but only if it thinks it just to do so having regard to a change of circumstances since the relevant time.

(4) In this section "the relevant time" means—

(a) where neither of the powers conferred by subsection (3) above has been exercised previously, the date when the issue of the warrant was postponed under subsection (2) above; and

(b) in any other case, the date of the exercise or latest exercise of either or both of the powers.

(5) Without prejudice to the generality of subsection (3) above, if on an application by a person in respect of whom issue of a warrant has been postponed it appears to a justice of the peace acting for the petty sessions area in which the warrant has been or would have been issued that since the relevant time there has been a change of circumstances which would make it just for the court to exercise one or other or both of the powers conferred by that subsection, he shall refer the application to the court.

(6) Where such an application is referred to the court—

(a) the clerk of the court shall fix a time and place for the application to be heard; and

(b) the designated officer for the court shall give the applicant notice of that time and place.

(7) Where such a notice has been given but the applicant does not appear at the time and place specified in the notice, the court may proceed with the consideration of the application in his absence.

(8) If a warrant of commitment in respect of the sum adjudged to be paid has been issued before the hearing of the application, the court shall have power to order that the warrant shall cease to have effect and, if the applicant has been arrested in pursuance of it, to order that he shall be released, but it shall only make an order under this subsection if it is satisfied that the change of circumstances on which the applicant relies was not put before the court when it was determining whether to issue the warrant.

Defect in distress warrant and irregularity in its execution

78.—(1) A warrant of distress issued for the purpose of levying a sum adjudged to be paid by the conviction or order of a magistrates' court shall not, if it states that the sum has been so adjudged to be paid, be held void by reason of any defect in the warrant. **24–55**

(2) A person acting under a warrant of distress shall not be deemed to be a trespasser from the beginning by reason only of any irregularity in the execution of the warrant.

(3) Nothing in this section shall prejudice the claim of any person for special damages in respect of any loss caused by a defect in the warrant or irregularity in its execution.

(4) If any person removes any goods marked in accordance with rules of court as articles impounded in the execution of a warrant of distress, or defaces or removes any such mark, he shall be liable on summary conviction to a fine not exceeding level 1 on the standard scale.

(5) If any person charged with the execution of a warrant of distress wilfully retains from the proceeds of a sale of the goods on which distress is levied, or otherwise exacts, any greater costs and charges than those properly payable, or makes any improper charge, he shall be liable on summary conviction to a fine not exceeding level 1 on the standard scale.

F. POWER TO MAKE AN ATTENDANCE CENTRE ORDER

24–56 The court may order an attendance centre order where a centre is available to the court and the offender is under 25 years of age.

Powers of Criminal Courts (Sentencing) Act 2000, s.60

Attendance centre orders.

60.—(1) Where—

(a) a court would have power, but for section 89 below (restrictions on imprisonment of young offenders and defaulters), to commit a person aged under 21 to prison in default of payment of any sum of money or for failing to do or abstain from doing anything required to be done or left undone, or

(b) a court has power to commit a person aged at least 21 but under 25 to prison in default of payment of any sum of money,

the court may, if it has been notified by the Secretary of State that an attendance centre is available for the reception of persons of his description, order him to attend at such a centre, to be specified in the order, for such number of hours as may be so specified.

(2) An order under subsection (1) above is in this Act referred to as an "attendance centre order".

(3) The aggregate number of hours for which an attendance centre order may require a person to attend at an attendance centre shall not be less than 12 except where—

(a) he is aged under 14; and

(b) the court is of the opinion that 12 hours would be excessive, having regard to his age or any other circumstances.

(4) The aggregate number of hours shall not exceed 12 except where the court is of the opinion, having regard to all the circumstances, that 12 hours would be inadequate, and in that case—

(a) shall not exceed 24 where the person is aged under 16; and

(b) shall not exceed 36 where the person is aged 16 or over but under 21 or (where subsection (1)(c) above applies) under 25.

(5) A court may make an attendance centre order in respect of a person before a previous attendance centre order made in respect of him has ceased to have effect, and may determine the number of hours to be specified in the order without regard—

(a) to the number specified in the previous order; or

(b) to the fact that order is still in effect.

(6) An attendance centre order shall not be made unless the court is satisfied that the attendance centre to be specified in it is reasonably accessible to the person concerned, having regard to his age, the means of access available to him and any other circumstances.

(7) The times at which a person is required to attend at an attendance centre shall, as for as practicable, be such as to avoid—

(a) any conflict with his religious beliefs or with the requirements of any other youth community order to which he may be subject; and

(b) any interference with the times, if any, at which he normally works or attends school or any other educational establishment.

(8) The first time at which the person is required to attend at an attendance centre shall be a time at which the centre is available for his attendance in accordance with the notification of the Secretary of State, and shall be specified in the order.

(9) The subsequent times shall be fixed by the officer in charge of the centre, having regard to the person's circumstances.

(10) A person shall not be required under this section to attend at an attendance centre on more than one occasion on any day, or for more than three hours on any occasion.

(11) Where a court makes an attendance centre order, the designated officer for the court shall—

(a) deliver or send a copy of the order to the officer in charge of the attendance centre specified in it; and

(b) deliver a copy of the order to the person in respect of whom it is made or send a copy by registered post or the recorded delivery service addressed to his last or usual place of abode.

(12) Where a person ("the defaulter") has been ordered to attend at an attendance centre in default of the payment of any sum of money—

(a) on payment of the whole sum to any person authorised to receive it, the attendance centre order shall cease to have effect;

(b) on payment of a part of the sum to any such person, the total number of hours for which the defaulter is required to attend at the centre shall be reduced proportionately, that is to say by such number of complete hours as bears to the total number the proportion most nearly approximating to, without exceeding, the proportion which the part bears to the whole sum.

G. Collection Orders

At § 24–48, *ante*, reference was made to the many changes being introduced to improve the enforcement of financial penalties. Some of these provisions are contained in the *Courts Act* 2003, some in the *Criminal Justice Act* 2003. **24–57**

The majority of the new provisions are contained in s.97 of, and Sched. 5 to, the *Courts Act* 2003 which provides for "collection orders". Whenever compensation is imposed (Sched. 5, para. 7A) or the court concludes that the offender is an existing defaulter (para. 8), unless it would be impracticable or inappropriate to do so, the court must make an attachment of earnings order (AEO) or application for benefit deductions (ABD). In other cases, the court may make an AEO or ABD with the offender's consent (para. 9). In every case in which a fine or compensation order is imposed, the court must make a collection order unless this would be impracticable or inappropriate (para. 12). The collection order must state the amount of the sum due, whether the court considers the offender to be an existing defaulter, whether an AEO or ABD has been made and information about the effect of the order, if the court has not made an AEO or ABD, the payment terms and, if an AEO or ABD has been made, the reserve terms (that is, the payment terms that will apply if the AEO or ABD fails). Commonly, a reserve term provides for payment in full within 14 days. If an offender defaults on a collection order and is not already subject to an AEO or ABD, a fines officer must make an AEO or ABD. Where this would be impracticable or inappropriate, or where the offender is already subject to an AEO or ABD, a fines officer must either issue a "further steps" notice advising that the officer intends to take any of the enforcement action listed *post* or refer the case to a magistrates' court. In relation to the enforcement of financial penalties, information of assistance to the court or its officers may be held by the Government for other purposes. Access to this information has been increased by the implementation from November 3, 2008 of s.41 of the *Criminal Justice and Immigration Act* 2008 inserting new paras 9A–9C into Sched. 5 to the *Criminal Justice Act* 2003. These provisions enable a designated officer of a magistrates' court to request disclosure of specified information to assist a court in determining whether to make an Application for Benefit Deduction. The information able to be sought is the full name of the person liable to pay the penalty, any address(es), date of birth, National Insurance number and benefit status.

A fines officer is able to take enforcement action to the extent of the making of an AEO or ABD, the issuing of a distress warrant, the registering of the sum in the register of judgments and orders, the taking of enforcement proceedings in the High Court or county court or the making of a clamping order. A magistrates' court may order the sale of the vehicle if the sum remains unpaid one month after the vehicle was clamped. The care that must be taken in following the procedures set down by law was emphasised in *R. (on the application of Guest) v. Woking Magistrates' Court* [2008] EWHC 2649. A distress warrant had been issued following the issue of a "further steps order". However, that order had been issued at a time when an application for deduction of

Part IV

benefits was still pending and so the payer could not be said to be "in default under the collection order", the prerequisite on which the court was relying.

Where a fines officer refers the case to a magistrates' court, the court may vary the payment terms or reserve terms or take any of the enforcement steps available to a fines officer. Additionally, where the court is satisfied that the default is due to wilful refusal or culpable neglect, it may increase the fine by up to 50 per cent (para. 42A) or discharge the collection order and exercise any of the court's standard fine enforcement powers.

The case may also be referred to a magistrates' court if an offender appeals against a "further steps" notice issued by a fines officer. Standard fine enforcement powers are normally available where a collection order is not made or a case is referred to a magistrates' court by a fines officer or an offender appeals against a "further steps" notice issued by a fines officer. Section 97 of, and Sched. 6 to, the Act provide the details of how fines may be discharged by unpaid work. The power is not dissimilar to the power under s.300 of the *Criminal Justice Act* 2003 to impose an unpaid work requirement or a curfew order instead of issuing a warrant of commitment to prison in default of payment. By the *Discharge of Fines by Unpaid Work (Prescribed Hourly Sum) Order* 2004 (S.I. 2004 No. 2196), an hour's work discharges £6 worth of financial penalty. This is exempted from the provisions setting the national minimum wage: *National Minimum Wage Act* 1998, s.45A as inserted by Sched. 8, para. 382 to the *Courts Act* 2003. Such an order may be made only where, in view of the payer's financial circumstances, no other available means of enforcing the sum is likely to be practicable or appropriate. If so and the payer is both suitable for unpaid work and consents to the order, then the order may be made: *Courts Act* 2003, Sched. 6, para. 2. An offender who unreasonably refuses to consent to such an order may be found guilty of wilful refusal or culpable neglect and therefore susceptible to committal in default (see *ante*, § 24–48). The amount of hours is calculated by dividing the amount due by the "prescribed hourly sum" and rounding up to the next whole number: Sched. 6, para. 3(3).

Courts Act 2003, Sched. 6

Section 97(2) SCHEDULE 6

DISCHARGE OF FINES BY UNPAID WORK

Introductory

24–58 1.—(1) This schedule applies if a person aged 18 or over ("P") is liable to pay a sum which is or is treated for the purposes of Part 3 of the 1980 Act as a sum adjudged to be paid by conviction of a magistrates' court.

(2) In this Schedule–

"the prescribed hourly sum" means such sum as may be prescribed by regulations;

"regulations" means regulations made under this schedule by the lord chancellor;

"the relevant court" means –

(a) the court imposing the liability to pay the relevant sum, or

(b) if that liability has previously been imposed, the magistrates' court responsible for enforcing payment of the relevant sum;

"the relevant sum" means the sum for which P is liable as mentioned in sub-paragraph (1), but excluding any pecuniary compensation, any pecuniary forfeiture or any sum due in respect of prosecution costs.

Cases where work order may be made

24–59 2.—(1) The relevant court may, on the application of a fines officer or of its own motion, make an order under this Schedule (a "work order") where—

(a) it appears to the court that in view of P's financial circumstances all the following methods of enforcing payment of the relevant sum are likely to be impracticable or inappropriate—

(i) a warrant of distress under section 76 of the 1980 Act,

(ii) an application to the high court or county court for enforcement under section 87 of the 1980 Act,

(iii) an order under section 88 of the 1980 Act,

(iv) an attachment of earnings order,

(v) an application for deductions to be made by virtue of section 24 of the *Criminal Justice Act* 1991 (recovery of fines etc. By deductions from income support etc.), and

(vi) a collection order under Schedule 5,

(b) it appears to the court that P is a suitable person to perform unpaid work under this Schedule, and

(c) P consents to the making of the order.

(2) A court which is considering the making of a work order may issue a summons requiring P to appear before the court.

(3) A magistrates' court which is considering the making of a work order may order Pto give to the court, within a specified period, such a statement of his means as the court may require.

(4) Subsections (2) to (4) of section 84 of the 1980 Act (offences in respect of statement of means) apply to an order made under sub-paragraph (3) as they apply to an order made under subsection (1) of that section.

Provisions of order

3.—(1) A work order is an order requiring P to perform unpaid work for a specified number of hours, in accordance with instructions to be given by the fines officer, in order to discharge by virtue of this Schedule his liability for the relevant sum. **24–60**

(2) The order must also—

(a) state the amount of the relevant sum,

(b) specify a fines office to which the order is allocated, and

(c) specify a person ("the supervisor") who is to act as supervisor in relation to P.

(3) The specified number of hours is to be determined by dividing the relevant sum by the prescribed hourly sum and, where the result is not a whole number, adjusting the result upwards to the next whole number.

(4) A work order must specify a date ("the specified date") not later than which the required hours of unpaid work must be performed.

(5) In the following provisions of this Schedule "the fines officer", in relation to P, means any fines officer working at the fines office specified in the work order.

Effect of order on enforcement of payment

4.—(1) Where a work order has been made in respect of the relevant sum, payment of that sum may not be enforced against P unless the order is revoked. **24–61**

(2) On making a work order, the court must revoke any order relating to the enforcement of the payment of the relevant sum.

Appointment of, and duties of, supervisor

5.—(1) A person may not be appointed as the supervisor without his consent. **24–62**

(2) It is the duty of the supervisor—

(a) to monitor P's compliance with the requirements of the work order, and

(b) to provide the court with such information as the court may require relating to P's compliance with those requirements.

Obligations of person subject to work order, and effect of compliance

6.—(1) Where a work order is in force, P must perform for the number of hours specified in the order such work, at such places and at such times as he may be instructed by the fines officer. **24–63**

(2) The fines officer must ensure, as far as practicable, that any instructions given to P in pursuance of the work order are such as to avoid—

(a) any conflict with P's religious beliefs, and

(b) any interference with the times, if any, at which he normally works or attends school or any other educational establishment.

(3) If not later than the specified date P performs work in accordance with the instructions of the fines officer for the specified number of hours, his liability to pay the relevant sum is discharged.

Effect of payment

7.—(1) Where a work order has been made in respect of any sum— **24–64**

(a) on payment of the whole of the sum to any person authorised to receive it, the work order ceases to have effect, and

(b) on payment of part of the sum to any such person, the number of hours specified in the order is to be taken to be reduced by a proportion corresponding to that which the part paid bears to the whole of the relevant sum.

(2) In calculating any reduction required by sub-paragraph (1)(b), any fraction of an hour is to be disregarded.

Revocation or variation of order

24–65 8.—(1) If, on the application of the fines officer, it appears to the relevant court that P is failing or has failed to comply with a work order without reasonable excuse, the court must revoke the order.

(2) If, on the application of the fines officer, it appears to the relevant court—

(a) that P has failed to comply with a work order but has a reasonable excuse for the failure, or

(b) that, because of a change in circumstances since the order was made, P is unlikely to be able to comply with a work order,

the court may revoke the order or postpone the specified date.

(3) The relevant court may of its own motion revoke a work order if it appears to the court that, because of a change in circumstances since the order was made, P is unlikely to be able to comply with the order.

(4) A work order may be revoked under any of sub-paragraphs (1) to (3), or varied under sub-paragraph (2), before the specified date (as well as on or after that date).

(5) Regulations may provide for the fines officer to have the power to issue a summons for the purpose of ensuring that P attends the court to which an application has been made under sub-paragraph (1) or (2).

Allowing for work done

24–66 9.—(1) If it appears to the court revoking a work order under paragraph 8(1), (2) or (3) that P has performed at least one hour of unpaid work in accordance with the instructions of the fines officer, the court must by order specify the number of hours of work that have been performed; and for this purpose any fraction of an hour is to be disregarded.

(2) Where the court has specified a number of hours under this paragraph, P's liability to pay the relevant sum is discharged to the extent of the prescribed hourly sum in respect of each hour.

Effect of revocation

24–67 10.—(1) Where a work order is revoked under paragraph 8(1), (2) or (3), immediate payment of the relevant sum (subject to any reduction under paragraph 9(2)) may be enforced against P.

(2) Sub-paragraph (1) does not limit the court's power, on or after the revocation of the work order, to allow time for payment or to direct payment by instalments.

Order not directly enforceable

24–68 11. The obligations of P under a work order are not enforceable against him except by virtue of paragraph 10(1).

Evidence of supervisor

24–69 12.—(1) This paragraph applies where—

(a) it falls to a court to determine whether P has performed unpaid work in accordance with a work order, and

(b) the court is satisfied—

(i) that the supervisor is likely to be able to give evidence that may assist the court in determining that matter, and

(ii) that the supervisor will not voluntarily attend as a witness.

(2) The court may issue a summons directed to that person requiring him to attend before the court at the time and place appointed in the summons to give evidence.

Provision of information

24–70 13. Regulations may—

(a) require a work order to contain prescribed information,

(b) require the court making a work order to give a copy of the order to such persons as may be prescribed, and

(c) require the court revoking or varying a work order to give notice of the revocation or variation to such persons as may be prescribed.

When in force, the *Criminal Justice Act* 2003 provisions enable a court to make a "default order" which will require completion of an unpaid work requirement or a curfew requirement as an alternative to commitment to prison. This power is not limited by the same criteria as the power under the *Courts Act* 2003, can be accompanied by electronic monitoring and will be enforced in the same way as a Community Order. Schedule 31 to the *Criminal Justice Act* 2003 provides for matching the amount in default to the extent of the requirement and provides for the lower minimum of 20 hours under the unpaid work requirement compared with a minimum of 40 hours where the requirement is made following conviction. If the order is not complied with and the court decides to revoke the requirement and to re-sentence, the powers of re-sentence are the powers of enforcing the default rather than the powers of sentence for the offence for which the financial penalty was imposed: Sched. 31, para. 4(3). **24–71**

Criminal Justice Act 2003, s.300 and Sched. 31

Power to impose unpaid work requirement or curfew requirement or attendance centre requirement on fine defaulter

300.—(1) Subsection (2) applies in any case where, in respect of a person aged 16 or over, a magistrates' court— **24–72**

(a) has power under Part 3 of the *Magistrates*' Courts Act 1980 to issue a warrant of commitment for default in paying a sum adjudged to be paid by a conviction (other than a sum ordered to be paid under section 6 of the *Proceeds of Crime Act* 2002), or

(b) would, but for section 89 of the *Sentencing Act* (restrictions on custodial sentences for persons under 18), have power to issue such a warrant for such default.

(2) The magistrates' court may, instead of issuing a warrant of commitment or, as the case may be, proceeding under section 81 of the *Magistrates*' Courts Act 1980 (enforcement of fines imposed on young offender), order the person in default to comply with—

(a) an unpaid work requirement (as defined by section 199), or

(b) a curfew requirement (as defined by section 204).

(c) in a case where the person is aged under 25, an attendance centre requirement (as defined by section 214)

(3) In this part "default order" means an order under subsection (2).

(4) Subsections (3) and (4) of section 177 (which relate to electronic monitoring) have effect in relation to a default order as they have effect in relation to a community order.

(5) Where a magistrates' court has power to make a default order, it may, if it thinks it expedient to do so, postpone the making of the order until such time and on such conditions (if any) as it thinks just.

(6) Schedule 8 (breach, revocation or amendment of community order), Schedule 9 (transfer of community orders to Scotland or Northern Ireland) and Chapter 4 (further provisions about orders under Chapters 2 and 3) have effect in relation to default orders as they have effect in relation to community orders, but subject to the modifications contained in Schedule 31.

(7) Where a default order has been made for default in paying any sum—

(a) on payment of the whole sum to any person authorised to receive it, the order shall cease to have effect, and

(b) on payment of a part of the sum to any such person, the total number of hours or days to which the order relates is to be taken to be reduced by a proportion corresponding to that which the part paid bears to the whole sum.

(8) In calculating any reduction required by subsection (7)(b), any fraction of a day or hour is to be disregarded.

SCHEDULE 31

DEFAULT ORDERS: MODIFICATION OF PROVISIONS RELATING TO COMMUNITY ORDERS

General

24–73 **3A.** In its application to a default order, section 214(2) (attendance centre requirement) is modified by the substitution for "not be less than 12 or more than 36" of "be—

(a) not less than 12, and

(b) in the case of an amount in default which is specified in the first column of the following Table, not more than the number of hours set out opposite that amount in the second column.

Amount	*Number of hours*
An amount not exceeding £200	18 hours
An amount exceeding £200 but not exceeding £500	21 hours
An amount exceeding £500 but not exceeding £1,000	24 hours
An amount exceeding £1,000 but not exceeding £2,500	30 hours
An amount exceeding £2,500	36 hours

Enforcement, revocation and amendment of default order

24–74 4.—(1) In its application to a default order, Schedule 8 (breach, revocation or amendment of community orders) is modified as follows.

(2) Any reference to the offence in respect of which the community order was made is to be taken to be a reference to the default in respect of which the default order was made.

(3) Any power of the court to revoke the community order and deal with the offender for the offence is to be taken to be a power to revoke the default order and deal with him in any way in which the court which made the default order could deal with him for his default in paying the sum in question.

(4) In paragraph 4 the reference to the Crown Court is to be taken as a reference to a magistrates' court.

(5) The following provisions are omitted

(a) paragraph 9(1)(c) and (8),

(b) paragraph 12,

(c) paragraph 13(5),

(d) paragraph 15,

(e) paragraph 17(5),

(f) paragraph 21(4), and

(g) paragraph 23(2)(b).

Power to alter amount of money or number of hours or days

24–75 5. The secretary of state may by order amend paragraph 2, 3 or 3A by substituting for any reference to an amount of money or a number of hours or days there specified a reference to such other amount or number as may be specified in the order.

24–76 When in force, s.301 of the *Criminal Justice Act* 2003 will enable a court to utilise driving disqualification for up to 12 months instead of issuing a warrant of commitment.

Criminal Justice Act 2003, s.301

Fine defaulters: driving disqualification

24–77 **301.**—(1) Subsection (2) applies in any case where a magistrates' court—

(a) has power under Part 3 of the *Magistrates*' Courts Act 1980 to issue a warrant of commitment for default in paying a sum adjudged to be paid by a conviction (other than a sum ordered to be paid under section 6 of the *Proceeds of Crime Act* 2002), or

(b) would, but for section 89 of the *Sentencing Act* (restrictions on custodial sentences for persons under 18), have power to issue such a warrant for such default.

(2) The magistrates' court may, instead of issuing a warrant of commitment or, as the

case may be, proceeding under section 81 of the *Magistrates*' Courts Act 1980 (enforcement of fines imposed on young offenders), order the person in default to be disqualified, for such period not exceeding twelve months as it thinks fit, for holding or obtaining a driving licence.

(3) Where an order has been made under subsection (2) for default in paying any sum—

(a) on payment of the whole sum to any person authorised to receive it, the order shall cease to have effect, and

(b) on payment of part of the sum to any such person, the total number of weeks or months to which the order relates is to be taken to be reduced by a proportion corresponding to that which the part paid bears to the whole sum.

(4) In calculating any reduction required by subsection (3)(b) any fraction of a week or month is to be disregarded.

(5) The Secretary of State may by order amend subsection (2) by substituting, for the period there specified, such other period as may be specified in the order.

(6) A court which makes an order under this section disqualifying a person for holding or obtaining a driving licence shall require him to produce—

(a) any such licence held by him together with its counterpart; or

(b) in the case where he holds a Community licence (within the meaning of Part 3 of the *Road Traffic Act* 1988), his Community licence and its counterpart (if any).

(7) In this section—

"driving licence" means a licence to drive a motor vehicle granted under Part 3 of the *Road Traffic Act* 1988;

"counterpart" —

(a) in relation to a driving licence, has the meaning given in relation to such a licence by section 108(1) of that act; and

(b) in relation to a Community licence, has the meaning given by Section 99B of that Act.

By Sched. 8, para. 220 to the *Courts Act* 2003, a new subs. 4B will be added to enable a court to find wilful refusal or culpable neglect where an offender has unreasonably refused to consent to a work order or has failed to comply with such an order without reasonable excuse. **24–78**

H. POWER TO ORDER DETENTION

A widely used power (both as a sentence in its own right and as an order in respect of unpaid fines) is the power to order detention within the precincts of the court (or at any police station) for a specified period not later than 8 p.m. on the day on which the order is made. This is not a period of imprisonment and so does not have to meet the criteria for a custodial sentence or for imprisonment in default of a fine. However, it is a sentence for an offence and, where used in response to default on payment of a fine, it removes liability to pay the fine. It can be used either after time has been allowed for payment of the fine or where immediate payment is required. **24–79**

Magistrates' Courts Act 1980, s.135

Detention of offender for one day in court-house or police station

135.—(1) A magistrates' court that has power to commit to prison a person convicted of an offence, or would have that power but for section 82 or 88 above, may order him to be detained within the precincts of the court-house or at any police station until such hour, not later than 8 o'clock in the evening of the day on which the order is made, as the court may direct, and, if it does so, shall not, where it has power to commit him to prison, exercise that power. **24–80**

(2) A court shall not make such an order under this section as will deprive the offender of a reasonable opportunity of returning to his abode on the day of the order.

(3) This section shall have effect in relation to a person aged 18 or over but less than 21 as if references in it to prison were references to detention under section 108 of the *Powers of Criminal Courts (Sentencing) Act* 2000 (detention of persons aged 18 to 20 for default).

I. POWER TO ORDER DETENTION OVERNIGHT

This power enables a defendant aged 18 or over to discharge responsibility for pay- **24–81**

Part IV

ment of a fine by serving a night in custody. As it is not imprisonment (since it is "detention"), the court does not have to be satisfied of all that it must if ordering imprisonment in default. The effect of the warrant (which can be issued in the absence of the defaulter) is to require the defaulter to be arrested and detained in a police station until the 8 a.m. that follows arrest. However, the police may release the defaulter between 4 a.m. and 8 a.m. in the circumstances set out in s.136(3).

Magistrates' Courts Act 1980, s.136

Committal to custody overnight at police station for non-payment of sum adjudged by conviction

24–82 **136.**—(1) A magistrates' court that has power to commit to prison a person in default of payment of a sum adjudged to be paid by a summary conviction, or would have that power but for section 82 or 88 above, may issue a warrant for his detention in a police station, and, if it does so, shall not, where it has power to commit him to prison, exercise that power.

(2) A warrant under this section—

(a) shall authorise the person executing it,

to arrest the defaulter and take him to a police station, and

(b) shall require the officer in charge of the station to detain him there until 8 o'clock in the morning of the day following that on which he is arrested, or, if he is arrested between midnight and 8 o'clock in the morning, until 8 o'clock in the morning of the day on which he is arrested.

(3) Notwithstanding subsection (2)(b) above, the officer may release the defaulter at any time within 4 hours before 8 o'clock in the morning if the officer thinks it expedient to do so in order to enable him to go to his work or for any other reason appearing to the officer to be sufficient.

(4) This section shall have effect in relation to a person aged 18 or over but less than 21 as if references in it to prison were references to detention under section 108 of the *Powers of Criminal Courts (Sentencing) Act* 2000 (detention of persons aged 18 to 20 for default).

III. ENFORCEMENT OF COMMUNITY ORDERS

A. LEGISLATIVE FRAMEWORK

(1) General

24–83 In addition to the statutory provisions, a definitive guidelines issued by the Sentencing Guidelines Council sets out the approach to dealing with those who fail to comply with the order of the court.

24–84 Decisions on enforcement of a community sentence are often complex and finely balanced. On the one hand, there is the need to reinforce the authority of the court which made the order and of the supervisor in the knowledge that the prospect of a more severe sentence can be a major incentive assisting the offender to comply with the order. On the other hand, there is a desire to see the order properly completed and the realisation of the benefits that it brings particularly where the life style of the offender makes it more difficult to adjust to the self discipline required to complete an order.

(2) Breach provisions

24–85 There is only a narrow range of options available once a breach is proved. A court may either re-sentence or make the original order more onerous. There is no power to impose a financial penalty for the breach and allow the order to continue nor to impose no sanction for the breach.

24–86 Responsibility for determining whether to take action on a breach starts with the "responsible officer" (see *ante*, § 23–47 and s.197). The trigger is a failure, without reasonable excuse, to comply with any of the requirements of the community order. The responsible officer must either give the offender a warning or initiate court proceedings (Sched. 8, paras 5 and 6). A warning may not be given if the offender has already been given a warning within the preceding 12 months in relation to failing to comply with the requirements of the order (Sched. 8, para. 5). This can be any requirements of the order and is not limited to the same requirements as those subject to the later action. In relation to orders where the responsible officer is an officer of a local probation board, the process of enforcement set out in statute is complemented by requirements in National Standards.

Where there is a second breach and proceedings initiated, the breach that resulted in the warning can also be included in the information bringing the matter before the court following the second breach. In *West Yorkshire Probation Board v. Tinker, Robinson* [2009] EWHC Admin 2468, the Divisional Court affirmed that a warning did not expunge the breach in respect of which it had been given and could legitimately be included in an information following a second breach. The warning did not act as a punishment and did not deal with the breach.

If court proceedings are started, this will be by the laying of an information before a Justice of the Peace if the order was made by a magistrates' court or before the Crown Court if that is where the order was made. However, a Crown Court may (in the Community Order) direct that any failure to comply in respect of an order made in the Crown Court is to be dealt with by a magistrates' court and, in those circumstances, the information will be laid before a Justice of the Peace: Sched. 8, para. 5(4). Where there are a number of failures that are to be brought before the court, the question can arise as to whether there should be separate informations for each failure or whether a single information covering all failures is lawful. In its News Sheet 09/2004 of June 8, 2004, the Justices' Clerks' Society concludes that a single information is generally sufficient. In the same way as an allegation of theft from a shop may encompass a range of items stolen from different places in the shop, so the failure to comply with the order may be evidenced in different ways. The essence is the failure to comply with the order rather than the individual events that demonstrate that. Where some instances are disputed, it will be open to the court to amend the information or to make appropriate findings. Issues may arise concerning whether the person before the court is the person subject to the Community Order. This is an issue similar to that where the prosecution has to prove that the defendant to a charge of driving whilst disqualified is a disqualified driver. In *West Yorkshire Probation Board v. Boulter* (2005) 169 J.P. 601, a person subject to a community rehabilitation order was brought before a magistrates' court on a warrant for breaching the order. The proceedings were adjourned. The defendant did not attend subsequent hearings but was legally represented. Justices accepted defence submissions that the prosecution had failed to prove that the person summoned to appear was the person made subject to the order and that the coincidence of names, date of birth and address was insufficient to prove identity beyond reasonable doubt. The DC upheld the prosecution appeal: **24–87**

> "When magistrates have evidence that the person before them has the same name, date of birth and address as the person previously convicted, it was open to them to draw an inference that he is the same person. Whether that inference is to be drawn in any particular case depends on all the facts of that case."

Where all three of those personal details coincided, it was to be expected that justices would draw such an inference unless there was some other factor which cast doubt on the inference.

See *ante*, § 17–118 and, in particular, the case of *Pattison v. DPP* [2005] EWHC 2938, Admin; (2006) J.P. 51, which has reviewed all the leading authorities (including *Boulter*) and set out some general principles of approach.

It will not be a "reasonable excuse" where an offender does not undertake unpaid work because an appeal has been lodged against the making of the order: *West Midlands' Probation Board v. Sutton Coldfield Magistrates' Court* (2008) 172 J.P. 169. An order is effective immediately it is made until revoked or varied or there is a successful appeal. There is no power to suspend an order pending an appeal.

If the court is satisfied that the offender has failed to comply and that that failure is without reasonable excuse, Sched. 8, para. 9 provides the court with two options. *The first option* is to amend the terms of the Community Order, but this may only be by imposing more onerous requirements. They must be requirements that the court could include if it was making the Community Order at that point: Sched. 8, para. 9(1)(a). This entails the obligation to ensure both the suitability for the offender and the continued matching of the restriction on liberty to the seriousness of the offence. It is not limited to increasing the onerousness of requirements already part of the order (*e.g.* increasing the hours of unpaid work) but could enable the inclusion of a new requirement (*e.g.* a curfew order). Where unpaid work is inserted as a new requirement, the minimum number of hours is reduced to 20 hours: Sched. 8, Pt 2. The court can extend the duration of any requirements (*e.g.* more unpaid work, longer curfew) but may not extend the overall length of the order: Sched. 8, para. 9(3). Additional restrictions apply in relation to those requirements including treatment—the mental health requirement, the alcohol treatment requirement and the drug rehabilitation requirement. The right to reasonably refuse certain treatment within such an order is preserved: Sched. 8, para. 11(1). Similarly, amendments to such requirements must have the agreement of the offender: Sched. 8, para. 11(2).

How much more onerous will be for the court to decide in the light of the breach and all the circumstances. No minimum level is prescribed. The general approach to dealing with breaches has been considered by the Sentencing Guidelines Council in its guidance on *New Sentences: Criminal Justice Act* 2003 (see *post*).

24–88 *The second option* is to re-sentence for the offence(s) in relation to which the Community Order was made: Sched. 8, para. 9(1)(b). Where that offence was not punishable by imprisonment, nonetheless the court may impose a custodial sentence (where the offender is aged 18 or over) if there has been wilful and persistent failure to comply with the requirements of the order: Sched. 8, para. 9(1)(c). A custodial sentence may be imposed on re-sentencing for an imprisonable offence even though the custody threshold was not passed for that offence, again provided the failure to comply with the requirements of the order is wilful and persistent: Sched. 8, para. 9(4). From time to time, a magistrates' court will be required to deal with a failure to comply by an offender aged 18 or over who was under 18 when the order was imposed. Issues have arisen concerning how to re-sentence when the offence leading to the order would have been triable only on indictment if the offender had been an adult rather than a youth. By Sched. 8, para. 12, in such cases the court may re-sentence by imposing a fine of up to £5,000 and/or imposing imprisonment for up to the maximum available in the magistrates' court for an adult offender (in the *Criminal Justice Act* 2003 this is expressed as 51 weeks but is restricted to six months in the transitional provisions pending the introduction of custody plus). It appears that there is no power to commit an offender to the Crown Court for sentence for the original offence where the community order was made by a magistrates' court. In *Andrews* [2006] EWCA Crim 2228, the Court considered and upheld the lines of authority culminating in *River Jordan* [1998] 2 Cr.App.R.(S.) 83 under the previous statutory provisions. Although in *Andrews* the Court speculated that the provisions in the 2003 Act were differently worded, it appeared to be referring to the later provisions that concerned revocation of the order rather than the provisions of paras 9 and 10 of the Schedule . Where a magistrates' court is entitled to sentence an offender following breach of a Crown Court imposed community order, it may commit such an offender to the Crown Court for sentence: Sched. 8, para. 9(6).

If the offender is re-sentenced, the court must revoke the Community Order if it has not already expired: Sched. 8, para. 9(5).

24–89 Whichever route the court chooses to follow, it must take into account the extent to which the requirements of the Community Order have been complied with. Thus the offender who fails to comply with a requirement in a relatively minor way towards the end of the order (perhaps having to be brought to court because there was an earlier warning) will be dealt with less severely than an offender who has made no serious attempt to comply. In *Noble* [2008] EWCA Crim 1473, the defendant had been subject to a community punishment order of 200 hours imposed (and enforced) under the previous legislative provisions. Having breached the order, he was made subject to a further community punishment order of 240 hours. On appeal, the court noted that the defendant had completed 80 of the original hours, had a good and valid reason for all but two of the alleged absences, and had been required to spend 12 days in custody before being finally dealt with for the breach. He having completed a further 70–80 hours of the new order, the Court reduced that order to 80 hours directing that the completed hours counted towards it.

A number of cases have considered the obligation to take into account time spent on a qualifying remand prior to the imposition of a community order when imposing a custodial sentence following breach or revocation of the order. In particular, a community order should not be imposed following a period on remand in excess of the maximum custodial sentence available for the offences but, where it has and the court is re-sentencing following breach or revocation, the Court of Appeal (Criminal Division) has frequently substituted a conditional discharge terminating on the date of the appeal for any custodial sentence imposed. In *Bell* [2010] EWCA Crim 1075 the defendant breached a community order made in relation to an offence with a maximum penalty of six months imprisonment when he had spent five months in custody on remand. The Court of Appeal (Criminal Division) allowed the appeal against the imposition of a custodial sentence following that breach, substituting a conditional discharge expected to expire on the day of the judgment.

Where an offender has spent time on a qualifying remand before being sentenced to a community order and is then made subject to a custodial sentence, the court imposing the custodial sentence must take account of the time on remand. However, one of the factors that led a court to impose a community order rather than a custodial sentence (or influenced it in determining the requirements to be included within it in accordance with the provisions of s.149 of the *Criminal Justice Act* 2003) may have been the period on remand. Whilst the Sentencing Guidelines Council guideline *New Sentences: Criminal Justice Act 2003* provides (at para. 1.1.39) that, where the custodial sentence was to be 12 months or more, that should still be imposed (even though the offender might be released immediately) because of the power to make the offender subject to licence conditions, the same does not apply where the sentence would be less than 12 months. It is to be expected, therefore, that an offender may be made subject to a community order because (at least in part) of time spent on remand and the issue will arise as to whether credit should again be allowed against a subsequent custodial sentence following breach of the order or revocation consequent upon the commission of further offences. In *Whitehouse* [2010] EWCA Crim 1927 the defendant, having spent six months in custody on remand, was made subject to a community order following conviction for burglary and other offences. During that order, he committed further offences which led to the order being revoked and sentences totalling 12 months imprisonment being imposed for both the new and the old offences but no allowance made for the 6 months on remand (not least, it seems, because the Judge was not made aware of it). Reviewing that decision, the Court of Appeal confirmed that the sentencing court was not required to ignore the realities of what had happened and determined that it would be unjust in these circumstances to give credit for the time on remand (there appeared to be general agreement that the defendant could not have complained if sentences totalling two years had been imposed). Although not expressly overruling *Stickley* [2007] EWCA Crim 3184, the Court did indicate that it sided with those who considered that it should be reviewed.

Dealing effectively with breaches of an order is an important task for a court. On the **24–90**
one hand, a court has identified requirements designed both to reflect the seriousness of the offence and the suitability of the offender and it is important that the court ensures that everything possible is done to enable the purposes of its order to be achieved. On the other hand, offenders cannot be seen to ignore the order of a court without a suitable sanction. In its guideline on *New Sentences: Criminal Justice Act* 2003 the Sentencing Guidelines Council sets out the approach to be adopted; this is summarised

in the *Magistrates' Court Sentencing Guidelines* at p.43. Emphasising that the *primary* objective is to ensure the completion of the requirements, courts are urged to be vigilant to ensure that there is a realistic prospect of the purposes of the order being achieved.

(3) New sentences under the Criminal Justice Act 2003

Guideline: New Sentences: Criminal Justice Act 2003

Section 1—Community Sentences & Deferred Sentences

Part 1: Community Sentences

B. IMPOSING A COMMUNITY SENTENCE—THE APPROACH

(iii) Breaches

24–91 **1.1.44** When increasing the onerousness of requirements, the court must consider the impact on the offender's ability to comply and the possibility of precipitating a custodial sentence for further breach. For that reason, and particularly where the breach occurs towards the end of the sentence, the court should take account of compliance to date [and may consider that extending the supervision or operational periods will be more sensible;] in other cases it might choose to add punitive or rehabilitative requirements instead. In making these changes the court must be mindful of the legislative restrictions on the overall length of community sentences and on the supervision and operational periods allowed for each type of requirement.

1.1.45 The court dealing with breach of a community sentence should have as its primary objective ensuring that the requirements of the sentence are finished, and this is important if the court is to have regard to the statutory purposes of sentencing. A court that imposes a custodial sentence for breach without giving adequate consideration to alternatives is in danger of imposing a sentence that is not commensurate with the seriousness of the original offence and is solely a punishment for breach. This risks undermining the purposes it has identified as being important. Nonetheless, courts will need to be vigilant to ensure that there is a realistic prospect of the purposes of the order being achieved.

Having decided that a community sentence is commensurate with the seriousness of the offence, the primary objective when sentencing for breach of requirements is to ensure that those requirements are completed.

1.1.46 A court sentencing for breach must take account of the extent to which the offender has complied with the requirements of the community order, the reasons for breach and the point at which the breach has occurred. Where a breach takes place towards the end of the operational period and the court is satisfied that the offender's appearance before the court is likely to be sufficient in itself to ensure future compliance, then given that it is not open to the court to make no order, an approach that the court might wish to adopt could be to re-sentence in a way that enables the original order to be completed properly—for example, a differently constructed community sentence that aims to secure compliance with the purposes of the original sentence.

It should be noted that the Sentencing Guidelines Council guideline at 1.1.44 suggests that it is possible to extend the "supervision and operational periods" when acting in response to breach of a community sentence. The Council has noted that it is not possible to extend the supervision period (which must always be for the length of the order) and there is no operational period. It appears that these words have been inadvertently carried forward from the part of the guideline relating to a Suspended Sentence Order.

24–92 **1.1.47** If the court decides to increase the onerousness of an order, it must give careful consideration, with advice from the Probation Service, to the offender's ability to comply. A custodial sentence should be the last resort, where all reasonable efforts to ensure that an offender completes a community sentence have failed.

- **The Act allows for a custodial sentence to be imposed in response to breach of a community sentence. Custody should be the last resort, reserved for those cases of deliberate and repeated breach where all reasonable efforts to ensure that the offender complies have failed.**
- **Before increasing the onerousness of requirements, sentencers should take account of the offender's ability to comply and should avoid precipitating further breach by overloading the offender with too many or conflicting requirements.**
- **There may be cases where the court will need to consider re-sentencing to a differently constructed community sentence in order to secure compliance with the purposes of the original sentence, perhaps where there has already been partial compliance or where events since the sentence was imposed have shown that a different course of action is likely to be effective.**

B. REVOCATION ON APPLICATION

There is power to revoke a Community Order. In a magistrates' court, this may be exercised in relation to an order made by a magistrates' court or to one made by the Crown Court which includes a direction that any failure to comply is to be dealt with by a magistrates' court: Sched. 8, para. 13(1). Either the offender or the responsible officer may apply for revocation. The power arises only where the court considers that it is in the interests of justice either to revoke the order or for the offender to be re-sentenced. This must be based on circumstances arising since the making of the order (which include the good progress of the offender under the order): Sched. 8, para. 13(1) and (3). If it is not the offender's application, then the court must summons the offender to appear. Should the offender fail to attend in response to the summons, the court may issue a warrant. There appears to be no power to issue a warrant until there has been a failure to appear in response to a summons. This is in contrast to the power when dealing with a breach of the order. **24–93**

The court may either revoke the order or revoke it and re-sentence. If the court re-sentences, it must take account of the extent of compliance with the order: Sched. 8, para. 13(4). There is a right of appeal to the Crown Court against sentence passed in these circumstances: Sched. 8, para. 13(5). No application to revoke an order under Sched. 8, para. 13 can be made whilst appeal against the Community Order is pending: Sched. 8, para. 24. **24–94**

C. REVOCATION FOLLOWING SUBSEQUENT CONVICTION

A further power to revoke or to revoke and re-sentence arises where an offender subject to a Community Order is convicted of an offence. This power can be exercised by a magistrates' court when the Community Order was made by a magistrates' court. Again, the criterion is that the court considers that the exercise of these powers is in the interests of justice based on circumstances since the Community Order was made. This ensures that a court does not need to allow two potentially inconsistent sentences to run alongside each other whilst also avoiding the need for a specific application to revoke the order following, for example, a custodial sentence: Sched. 8, para. 21. If the offender is convicted in a magistrates' court but is subject to a Community Order made by the Crown Court, the court may commit the offender on bail or in custody to be dealt with: Sched. 8, para. 22. The Crown Court may only deal with an offender under these provisions where committed (see *ante*) or where convicted at the Crown Court: Sched. 9, para. 23. Where conviction takes place in the magistrates' court and there is no committal, the Crown Court will only have the power to revoke if an application is made under Sched. 8, para. 14 or breach proceedings are initiated. **24–95**

D. AMENDMENT

Different provisions are made for five different circumstances for amendment —change of residence, general requirements, treatment requirements, drug rehabilita- **24–96** tion requirement and unpaid work requirement: Sched. 9, Pt 4. If the application is not made by the offender, the court must issue a summons for the offender's attendance. If the offender does not attend, a warrant may be issued: Sched. 8, para. 25(1). This process is not necessary in relation to the limited changes specified in para. 25(2).

Criminal Justice Act 2003, s.179, Sched. 8

Breach, revocation or amendment of community order

24–97 **179.** Schedule 8 (which relates to failures to comply with the requirements of community orders and to the revocation or amendment of such orders) shall have effect.

Section 179 SCHEDULE 8

BREACH, REVOCATION OR AMENDMENT OF COMMUNITY ORDER

PART 1

PRELIMINARY

Interpretation

24–98 1. In this Schedule—

"the offender", in relation to a community order, means the person in respect of whom the order is made;

"the local justice area concerned", in relation to a community order, means the local justice area for the time being specified in the order;

"the responsible officer" has the meaning given by section 197.

24–99 2. In this Schedule—

(a) references to a drug rehabilitation requirement of a community order being subject to review are references to that requirement being subject to review in accordance with section 210(1)(b);

(b) references to the court responsible for a community order imposing a drug rehabilitation requirement which is subject to review are to be construed in accordance with section 210(2).

24–100 3. For the purposes of this Schedule—

(a) a requirement falling within any paragraph of section 177(1) is of the same kind as any other requirement falling within that paragraph, and

(b) an electronic monitoring requirement is a requirement of the same kind as any requirement falling within section 177(1) to which it relates.

Orders made on appeal

24–101 4. Where a community order has been made on appeal, it is to be taken for the purposes of this Schedule to have been made by the Crown Court.

PART 2

BREACH OF REQUIREMENT OF ORDER

Duty to give warning

24–102 5.—(1) If the responsible officer is of the opinion that the offender has failed without reasonable excuse to comply with any of the requirements of a community order, the officer must give him a warning under this paragraph unless—

(a) the offender has within the previous twelve months been given a warning under this paragraph in relation to a failure to comply with any of the requirements of the order, or

(b) the officer causes an information to be laid before a justice of the peace in respect of the failure.

(2) A warning under this paragraph must—

(a) describe the circumstances of the failure,

(b) state that the failure is unacceptable, and

(c) inform the offender that, if within the next twelve months he again fails to comply with any requirement of the order, he will be liable to be brought before a court.

(3) The responsible officer must, as soon as practicable after the warning has been given, record that fact.

(4) In relation to any community order which was made by the Crown Court and does not include a direction that any failure to comply with the requirements of the order is to be dealt with by a magistrates' court, the reference in sub-paragraph (1)(b) to a justice of the peace is to be read as a reference to the Crown Court.

Breach of order after warning

6.—(1) If— **24–103**

(a) the responsible officer has given a warning under paragraph 5 to the offender in respect of a community order, and

(b) at any time within the twelve months beginning with the date on which the warning was given, the responsible officer is of the opinion that the offender has since that date failed without reasonable excuse to comply with any of the requirements of the order,

the officer must cause an information to be laid before a justice of the peace in respect of the failure in question.

(2) In relation to any community order which was made by the Crown Court and does not include a direction that any failure to comply with the requirements of the order is to be dealt with by a magistrates' court, the reference in sub-paragraph (1) to a justice of the peace is to be read as a reference to the Crown Court.

Issue of summons or warrant by justice of the peace

7.—(1) This paragraph applies to— **24–104**

(a) a community order made by a magistrates' court, or

(b) any community order which was made by the Crown Court and includes a direction that any failure to comply with the requirements of the order is to be dealt with by a magistrates' court.

(2) If at any time while a community order to which this paragraph applies is in force it appears on information to a justice of the peace concerned that the offender has failed to comply with any of the requirements of the order, the justice may—

(a) issue a summons requiring the offender to appear at the place and time specified in it, or

(b) if the information is in writing and on oath, issue a warrant for his arrest.

(3) Any summons or warrant issued under this paragraph must direct the offender to appear or be brought—

(a) in the case of a community order imposing a drug rehabilitation requirement which is subject to review, before the magistrates' court responsible for the order, or

(b) in any other case, before a magistrates' court acting in the local justice area in which the offender resides or, if it is not known where he resides, before a magistrates' court acting for the local justice area concerned.

(4) Where a summons issued under sub-paragraph (2)(a) requires the offender to appear before a magistrates' court and the offender does not appear in answer to the summons, the magistrates' court may issue a warrant for the arrest of the offender.

Issue of summons or warrant by Crown Court

8.—(1) This paragraph applies to a community order made by the Crown Court which **24–105** does not include a direction that any failure to comply with the requirements of the order is to be dealt with by a magistrates' court.

(2) If at any time while a community order to which this paragraph applies is in force it appears on information to the Crown Court that the offender has failed to comply with any of the requirements of the order, the Crown Court may—

(a) issue a summons requiring the offender to appear at the place and time specified in it, or

(b) if the information is in writing and on oath, issue a warrant for his arrest.

(3) Any summons or warrant issued under this paragraph must direct the offender to appear or be brought before the Crown Court.

(4) Where a summons issued under sub-paragraph (2)(a) requires the offender to appear before the Crown Court and the offender does not appear in answer to the summons, the Crown Court may issue a warrant for the arrest of the offender.

Powers of magistrates' court

24–106 9.—(1) If it is proved to the satisfaction of a magistrates' court before which an offender appears or is brought under paragraph 7 that he has failed without reasonable excuse to comply with any of the requirements of the community order, the court must deal with him in respect of the failure in any one of the following ways—

(a) by amending the terms of the community order so as to impose more onerous requirements which the court could include if it were then making the order;

(b) where the community order was made by a magistrates' court, by dealing with him, for the offence in respect of which the order was made, in any way in which the court could deal with him if he had just been convicted by it of the offence;

(c) where—

(i) the community order was made by a magistrates' court,

(ii) the offence in respect of which the order was made was not an offence punishable by imprisonment,

(iii) the offender is aged 18 or over, and

(iv) the offender has wilfully and persistently failed to comply with the requirements of the order,

by dealing with him, in respect of that offence, by imposing a sentence of imprisonment or, in the case of a person aged at least 18 but under 21, detention in a young offender institution, for a term not exceeding 6 months.

(2) In dealing with an offender under sub-paragraph (1), a magistrates' court must take into account the extent to which the offender has complied with the requirements of the community order.

(3) In dealing with an offender under sub-paragraph (1)(a), the court may extend the duration of particular requirements (subject to any limit imposed by Chapter 4 of Part 12 of this Act) but may not extend the period specified under section 177(5).

(3A) Where—

(a) the court is dealing with the offender under sub-paragraph (1)(a), and

(b) the community order does not contain an unpaid work requirement, section 199(2)(a) applies in relation to the inclusion of such a requirement as if for "40" there were substituted "20".

(4) In dealing with an offender under sub-paragraph (1)(b), the court may, in the case of an offender who has wilfully and persistently failed to comply with the requirements of the community order, impose a custodial sentence (where the order was made in respect of an offence punishable with such a sentence) notwithstanding anything in section 152(2).

(5) Where a magistrates' court deals with an offender under sub-paragraph (1)(b) or (c), it must revoke the community order if it is still in force.

(5A) Where a magistrates' court dealing with an offender under sub-paragraph (1)(a) would not otherwise have the power to amend the community order under paragraph 16 (amendment by reason of change of residence), that paragraph has effect as if the references to the appropriate court were references to the court dealing with the offender.

(6) Where a community order was made by the Crown Court and a magistrates' court would (apart from this sub-paragraph) be required to deal with the offender under sub-paragraph (1)(a), (b) or (c), it may instead commit him to custody or release him on bail until he can be brought or appear before the Crown Court.

(7) A magistrates' court which deals with an offender's case under subparagraph (6) must send to the Crown Court—

(a) a certificate signed by a justice of the peace certifying that the offender has failed to comply with the requirements of the community order in the respect specified in the certificate, and

(b) such other particulars of the case as may be desirable;

and a certificate purporting to be so signed is admissible as evidence of the failure before the Crown Court.

(8) A person sentenced under sub-paragraph (1)(b) or (c) for an offence may appeal to the Crown Court against the sentence.

Powers of Crown Court

24–107 10.—(1) Where under paragraph 8 or by virtue of paragraph 9(6) an offender appears or is brought before the Crown Court and it is proved to the satisfaction of that court that he has failed without reasonable excuse to comply with any of the requirements of the community order, the Crown Court must deal with him in respect of the failure in any one of the following ways—

(a) by amending the terms of the community order so as to impose more onerous requirements which the Crown Court could impose if it were then making the order;

(b) by dealing with him, for the offence in respect of which the order was made, in any way in which he could have been dealt with for that offence by the court which made the order if the order had not been made;

(c) where—

(i) the offence in respect of which the order was made was not an offence punishable by imprisonment,

(ii) the offender is aged 18 or over,

(iii) the offender has wilfully and persistently failed to comply with the requirements of the order,

by dealing with him, in respect of that offence, by imposing a sentence of imprisonment or, in the case of a person aged at least 18 but under 21, detention in a young offender institution, for a term not exceeding 6 months.

(2) In dealing with an offender under sub-paragraph (1), the Crown Court must take into account the extent to which the offender has complied with the requirements of the community order.

(3) In dealing with an offender under sub-paragraph (1)(a), the court may extend the duration of particular requirements (subject to any limit imposed by Chapter 4 of Part 12 of this Act) but may not extend the period specified under section 177(5).

(3A) Where—

(a) the court is dealing with the offender under sub-paragraph (1)(a), and

(b) the community order does not contain an unpaid work requirement, section 199(2)(a) applies in relation to the inclusion of such a requirement as if for "40" there were substituted "20".

(4) In dealing with an offender under sub-paragraph (1)(b), the Crown Court may, in the case of an offender who has wilfully and persistently failed to comply with the requirements of the community order, impose a custodial sentence (where the order was made in respect of an offence punishable with such a sentence) notwithstanding anything in section 152(2).

(5) Where the Crown Court deals with an offender under sub-paragraph (1)(b) or (c), it must revoke the community order if it is still in force.

(6) In proceedings before the Crown Court under this paragraph any question whether the offender has failed to comply with the requirements of the community order is to be determined by the court and not by the verdict of a jury.

Restriction of powers in paragraphs 9 and 10 where treatment required

11.—(1) An offender who is required by any of the following requirements of a community order— **24–108**

(a) a mental health treatment requirement,

(b) a drug rehabilitation requirement, or

(c) an alcohol treatment requirement,

to submit to treatment for his mental condition, or his dependency on or propensity to misuse drugs or alcohol, is not to be treated for the purposes of paragraph 9 or 10 as having failed to comply with that requirement on the ground only that he had refused to undergo any surgical, electrical or other treatment if, in the opinion of the court, his refusal was reasonable having regard to all the circumstances.

(2) A court may not under paragraph 9(1)(a) or 10(1)(a) amend a mental health treatment requirement, a drug rehabilitation requirement or an alcohol treatment requirement unless the offender expresses his willingness to comply with the requirement as amended.

PART 3

REVOCATION OF ORDER

Revocation of order with or without re-sentencing: powers of magistrates' court

13.—(1) This paragraph applies where a community order, other than an order made **24–109** by the Crown Court and falling within paragraph 14(1)(a), is in force and on the application of the offender or the responsible officer it appears to the appropriate magistrates' court that, having regard to circumstances which have arisen since the order was made, it would be in the interests of justice—

(a) for the order to be revoked, or

(b) for the offender to be dealt with in some other way for the offence in respect of which the order was made.

(2) The appropriate magistrates' court may—

(a) revoke the order, or

(b) both—

(i) revoke the order, and

(ii) deal with the offender, for the offence in respect of which the order was made, in any way in which it could deal with him if he had just been convicted by the court of the offence.

(3) The circumstances in which a community order may be revoked under subparagraph (2) include the offender's making good progress or his responding satisfactorily to supervision or treatment (as the case requires).

(4) In dealing with an offender under sub-paragraph (2)(b), a magistrates' court must take into account the extent to which the offender has complied with the requirements of the community order.

(5) A person sentenced under sub-paragraph (2)(b) for an offence may appeal to the Crown Court against the sentence.

(6) Where a magistrates' court proposes to exercise its powers under this paragraph otherwise than on the application of the offender, it must summon him to appear before the court and, if he does not appear in answer to the summons, may issue a warrant for his arrest.

(7) In this paragraph "the appropriate magistrates' court" means—

(a) in the case of an order imposing a drug rehabilitation requirement which is subject to review, the magistrates' court responsible for the order, and

(b) in the case of any other community order, a magistrates' court acting in the local justice area concerned.

Revocation of order with or without re-sentencing: powers of Crown Court

24–110 14.—(1) This paragraph applies where—

(a) there is in force a community order made by the Crown Court which does not include a direction that any failure to comply with the requirements of the order is to be dealt with by a magistrates' court, and

(b) the offender or the responsible officer applies to the Crown Court for the order to be revoked or for the offender to be dealt with in some other way for the offence in respect of which the order was made.

(2) If it appears to the Crown Court to be in the interests of justice to do so, having regard to circumstances which have arisen since the order was made, the Crown Court may—

(a) revoke the order, or

(b) both—

(i) revoke the order, and

(ii) deal with the offender, for the offence in respect of which the order was made, in any way in which he could have been dealt with for that offence by the court which made the order if the order had not been made.

(3) The circumstances in which a community order may be revoked under subparagraph (2) include the offender's making good progress or his responding satisfactorily to supervision or treatment (as the case requires).

(4) In dealing with an offender under sub-paragraph (2)(b), the Crown Court must take into account the extent to which the offender has complied with the requirements of the order.

(5) Where the Crown Court proposes to exercise its powers under this paragraph otherwise than on the application of the offender, it must summon him to appear before the court and, if he does not appear in answer to the summons, may issue a warrant for his arrest.

PART 4

AMENDMENT OF ORDER

Amendment by reason of change of residence

16.—(1) This paragraph applies where, at any time while a community order is in force in respect of an offender, the appropriate court is satisfied that the offender proposes to change, or has changed, his residence from the local justice area concerned to another local justice area. **24–111**

(2) Subject to sub-paragraphs (3) and (4), the appropriate court may, and on the application of the responsible officer must, amend the community order by substituting the other local justice area for the area specified in the order.

(3) The court may not under this paragraph amend a community order which contains requirements which, in the opinion of the court, cannot be complied with unless the offender continues to reside in the local justice area concerned unless, in accordance with paragraph 17, it either—

(a) cancels those requirements, or

(b) substitutes for those requirements other requirements which can be complied with if the offender ceases to reside in that area.

(4) The court may not amend under this paragraph a community order imposing a programme requirement unless it appears to the court that the accredited programme specified in the requirement is available in the other local justice area.

(5) In this paragraph "the appropriate court" means—

(a) in relation to any community order imposing a drug rehabilitation requirement which is subject to review, the court responsible for the order,

(b) in relation to any community order which was made by the Crown Court and does not include any direction that any failure to comply with the requirements of the order is to be dealt with by a magistrates' court, the Crown Court, and

(c) in relation to any other community order, a magistrates' court acting in the local justice area concerned.

Amendment of requirements of community order

17.—(1) The appropriate court may, on the application of the offender or the responsible officer, by order amend a community order— **24–112**

(a) by cancelling any of the requirements of the order, or

(b) by replacing any of those requirements with a requirement of the same kind, which the court could include if it were then making the order.

(2) The court may not under this paragraph amend a mental health treatment requirement, a drug rehabilitation requirement or an alcohol treatment requirement unless the offender expresses his willingness to comply with the requirement as amended.

(3) If the offender fails to express his willingness to comply with a mental health treatment requirement, drug rehabilitation requirement or alcohol treatment requirement as proposed to be amended by the court under this paragraph, the court may—

(a) revoke the community order, and

(b) deal with him, for the offence in respect of which the order was made, in any way in which he could have been dealt with for that offence by the court which made the order if the order had not been made.

(4) In dealing with the offender under sub-paragraph (3)(b), the court—

(a) must take into account the extent to which the offender has complied with the requirements of the order, and

(b) may impose a custodial sentence (where the order was made in respect of an offence punishable with such a sentence) notwithstanding anything in section 152(2).

(5) Paragraph 12 applies for the purposes of this paragraph as it applies for the purposes of paragraph 9, but as if for the words "paragraph 9(1)(b)" there were substituted "paragraph 17(3)(b)".

(6) In this paragraph "the appropriate court" has the same meaning as in paragraph 16.

Amendment of treatment requirements of community order on report of practitioner

18.—(1) Where the medical practitioner or other person by whom or under whose **24–113** direction an offender is, in pursuance of any requirement to which this subparagraph applies, being treated for his mental condition or his dependency on or propensity to misuse drugs or alcohol—

(a) is of the opinion mentioned in sub-paragraph (3), or

(b) is for any reason unwilling to continue to treat or direct the treatment of the offender,

he must make a report in writing to that effect to the responsible officer and that officer must apply under paragraph 17 to the appropriate court for the variation or cancellation of the requirement.

(2) The requirements to which sub-paragraph (1) applies are—

(a) a mental health treatment requirement,

(b) a drug rehabilitation requirement, and

(c) an alcohol treatment requirement.

(3) The opinion referred to in sub-paragraph (1) is—

(a) that the treatment of the offender should be continued beyond the period specified in that behalf in the order,

(b) that the offender needs different treatment,

(c) that the offender is not susceptible to treatment, or

(d) that the offender does not require further treatment.

(4) In this paragraph "the appropriate court" has the same meaning as in paragraph 16.

Amendment in relation to review of drug rehabilitation requirement

24–114 19. Where the responsible officer is of the opinion that a community order imposing a drug rehabilitation requirement which is subject to review should be so amended as to provide for each subsequent periodic review (required by section 211) to be made without a hearing instead of at a review hearing, or vice versa, he must apply under paragraph 17 to the court responsible for the order for the variation of the order.

Extension of unpaid work requirement

24–115 20.—(1) Where—

(a) a community order imposing an unpaid work requirement is in force in respect of any offender, and

(b) on the application of the offender or the responsible officer, it appears to the appropriate court that it would be in the interests of justice to do so having regard to circumstances which have arisen since the order was made,

the court may, in relation to the order, extend the period of twelve months specified in section 200(2).

(2) In this paragraph "the appropriate court" has the same meaning as in paragraph 16.

PART 5

POWERS OF COURT IN RELATION TO ORDER FOLLOWING SUBSEQUENT CONVICTION

Powers of magistrates' court following subsequent conviction

24–116 21.—(1) This paragraph applies where—

(a) an offender in respect of whom a community order made by a magistrates' court is in force is convicted of an offence by a magistrates' court, and

(b) it appears to the court that it would be in the interests of justice to exercise its powers under this paragraph, having regard to circumstances which have arisen since the community order was made.

(2) The magistrates' court may—

(a) revoke the order, or

(b) both—

(i) revoke the order, and

(ii) deal with the offender, for the offence in respect of which the order was made, in any way in which he could have been dealt with for that offence by the court which made the order if the order had not been made.

(3) In dealing with an offender under sub-paragraph (2)(b), a magistrates' court must take into account the extent to which the offender has complied with the requirements of the community order.

(4) A person sentenced under sub-paragraph (2)(b) for an offence may appeal to the Crown Court against the sentence.

22.—(1) Where an offender in respect of whom a community order made by the Crown Court is in force is convicted of an offence by a magistrates' court, the magistrates' court may commit the offender in custody or release him on bail until he can be brought before the Crown Court. **24–117**

(2) Where the magistrates' court deals with an offender's case under subparagraph (1), it must send to the Crown Court such particulars of the case as may be desirable.

Powers of Crown Court following subsequent conviction

23.—(1) This paragraph applies where— **24–118**

(a) an offender in respect of whom a community order is in force—
   (i) is convicted of an offence by the Crown Court, or
   (ii) is brought or appears before the Crown Court by virtue of paragraph 22 or having been committed by the magistrates' court to the Crown Court for sentence, and

(b) it appears to the Crown Court that it would be in the interests of justice to exercise its powers under this paragraph, having regard to circumstances which have arisen since the community order was made.

(2) The Crown Court may—

(a) revoke the order, or
(b) both—
   (i) revoke the order, and
   (ii) deal with the offender, for the offence in respect of which the order was made, in any way in which he could have been dealt with for that offence by the court which made the order if the order had not been made.

(3) In dealing with an offender under sub-paragraph (2)(b), the Crown Court must take into account the extent to which the offender has complied with the requirements of the community order.

PART 6

SUPPLEMENTARY

24.—(1) No order may be made under paragraph 16, and no application may be made under paragraph 13, 17 or 20, while an appeal against the community order is pending. **24–119**

(2) Sub-paragraph (1) does not apply to an application under paragraph 17 which—

(a) relates to a mental health treatment requirement, a drug rehabilitation requirement or an alcohol treatment requirement, and
(b) is made by the responsible officer with the consent of the offender.

25.—(1) Subject to sub-paragraph (2), where a court proposes to exercise its powers under Part 4 or 5 of this Schedule, otherwise than on the application of the offender, the court— **24–120**

(a) must summon him to appear before the court, and
(b) if he does not appear in answer to the summons, may issue a warrant for his arrest.

(2) This paragraph does not apply to an order cancelling a requirement of a community order or reducing the period of any requirement, or substituting a new local justice area or a new place for the one specified in the order.

25A.—(1) This paragraph applies to any hearing relating to an offender held by a magistrates' court in any proceedings under this Schedule.

(2) The court may adjourn the hearing, and, where it does so, may—

(a) direct that the offender be released forthwith, or
(b) remand the offender.

(3) Where the court remands the offender under sub-paragraph (2)—

(a) it must fix the time and place at which the hearing is to be resumed, and

(b) that time and place must be the time and place at which the offender is required to appear or be brought before the court by virtue of the remand.

(4) Where the court adjourns the hearing under sub-paragraph (2) but does not remand the offender—

(a) it may fix the time and place at which the hearing is to be resumed, but

(b) if it does not do so, it must not resume the hearing unless it is satisfied that the offender and the responsible officer have had adequate notice of the time and place for the resumed hearing.

(5) The powers of a magistrates' court under this paragraph may be exercised by a single justice of the peace, notwithstanding anything in the *Magistrates' Courts Act* 1980.

(6) This paragraph—

(a) applies to any hearing in any proceedings under this Schedule in place of section 10 of the *Magistrates' Courts Act* 1980 (adjournment of trial) where that section would otherwise apply, but

(b) is not to be taken to affect the application of that section to hearings of any other description.

24–121 26. Paragraphs 9(1)(a), 10(1)(a) and 17(1)(b) have effect subject to the provisions mentioned in subs. (2) of s.177, and to subss. (3) and (6) of that section.

24–122 27.—(1) On the making under this Schedule of an order revoking or amending a community order, the proper officer of the court must—

(a) provide copies of the revoking or amending order to the offender and the responsible officer,

(b) in the case of an amending order which substitutes a new petty sessions area, provide a copy of the amending order to—

(i) the local probation board acting for that areaor (as the case may be) a provider of probation services operating in that area

(ii) the magistrates' court acting in that area,

(c) in the case of an amending order which imposes or amends a requirement specified in the first column of Schedule 14, provide a copy of so much of the amending order as relates to that requirement to the person specified in relation to that requirement in the second column of that Schedule.

(d) where the court acts in a local justice area other than the one specified in the order prior to the revocation or amendment, provide a copy of the revoking or amending order to a magistrates' court acting in the area so specified.

(2) Where under sub-paragraph (1)(b) the proper officer of the court provides a copy of an amending order to a magistrates' court acting in a different area, the officer must also provide to that court such documents and information relating to the case as it considers likely to be of assistance to a court acting in that area in the exercise of its functions in relation to the order.

(3) In this paragraph "proper officer" means—

(a) in relation to a magistrates' court, the designated officer for the court; and

(b) in relation to the Crown Court, the appropriate officer.

IV. ENFORCEMENT OF SUSPENDED SENTENCE ORDER

(1) General

24–123 A suspended sentence order may be breached by a failure to comply with the requirements of the order without reasonable excuse or by the commission of a further offence (not necessarily an imprisonable offence) during the operational period. Where it is alleged that there has been a breach as a result of failure to comply with the requirements of the order, the procedure follows closely that for breach of a Community Order. The responsible officer must either warn or institute proceedings and no more than one warning can be given in a 12 month period. Where there is a second breach and proceedings initiated, the breach that resulted in the warning can also be included in the information bringing the matter before the court following the second breach. In *West Yorkshire Probation Board v. Tinker, Robinson* [2009] EWHC Admin 2468, the Divisional Court affirmed that a warning did not expunge the breach in respect of which it had been given and could legitimately be included in an information following a second breach. The warning did not act as a punishment and did not deal with the breach. A Crown Court may, when making a suspended sentence order, direct that any failure to comply with the requirements should be dealt with in a magistrates' court. In the absence of such a direction, proceedings commence at the level of court at which the order had been made: Sched. 12, paras 4–6.

Where the offender is convicted of a further offence committed during the operational period, the suspended sentence may be dealt with in the Crown Court regardless of which level of court made the order and in a magistrates' court if the order was imposed in a magistrates' court: Sched. 12, para. 11. If a magistrates' court convicts the offender of an offence committed during the operational period of a Crown Court imposed suspended sentence order, that court may commit the offender to the Crown Court on bail or in custody: Sched. 12, para. 11(2)(a). If it does not do so, it must notify the Crown Court that the offender has been convicted (Sched. 12, para. 11(2)(b)) and the Crown Court can initiate proceedings to deal with the issue: Sched. 12, para. 12. Similarly, if a magistrates' court which imposed a suspended sentence order discovers that the offender has been convicted of a further offence but the suspended sentence has not been dealt with, that court may issue process in order for it to deal with the suspended sentence: Sched. 12, para. 12. **24–124**

The importance of the timely initiation of proceedings for breach was emphasised in *West Yorkshire Probation Board v. Cruickshanks* (2010) 174 J.P. 305. The defendant had been made subject to a suspended sentence order for 12 months during which he was required to complete 150 hours unpaid work. Breach proceedings were initiated alleging that he had failed to work on three occasions. Because of injuries sustained in a road traffic accident, the defendant was unable to complete work within the 12 months specified and had a reasonable excuse for not doing so. Whilst he completed some work after that time, he failed to attend on other dates and the Board sought to enforce the order. The Divisional Court noted that there is a difference between community orders and suspended sentence orders in that a community order will, by statute, continue until the hours have been worked whereas a suspended sentence order cannot continue beyond the operational period. Whilst there are limited powers to extend the time for compliance with an unpaid work requirement within a suspended sentence order (12 months), that was not available in this case because the operational period itself was only 12 months. Accordingly, as the operational period had expired, the Board could not proceed. **24–125**

If the failure to comply with a requirement is proved or if the offender is convicted of another offence committed during the operational period, the options open to the court are set out in Sched. 12, para. 8. As with the suspended sentence itself, the statutory wording reflects the introduction of custody plus and so there are transitional provisions pending implementation of that sentence. The choices for the court are to implement the suspended sentence in full, to implement it with a reduced term or to amend the order. Any amendment must impose more onerous requirements and/or extend the supervision period and/or extend the operational period. If the extensions are considered, they cannot take the orders beyond the maximum periods that could have been imposed when the order was made: Sched. 12, para. 8(2)(c). There is a presumption that the court will implement the suspended sentence either in full or with the reduced term unless the court considers that it would be unjust: Sched. 12, para. 8(3). In *Nobbs v. DPP* [2009] R.T.R. 9, the defendant had pleaded guilty to driving with excess alcohol (127mg per 100ml in blood) and using a vehicle without insurance. He was in breach of a 2 year suspended sentence imposed 13 months earlier for offences of assault occasioning actual bodily harm and criminal damage. He had complied with the terms of the supervision order. The suspended sentence was activated in full and a further one month sentence imposed for the later offence. The defendant appealed citing

Part IV

the Sentencing Guidelines Council guidelines and seeking to argue that, although the new offence was imprisonable, it was not one for which imprisonment would otherwise be imposed and, therefore, the suspended sentence should not have been activated. That argument was rejected by both the Crown Court and the Court of Appeal. Recognising that imprisonment would not have been imposed for the later offence when considered in isolation, nonetheless the defendant had a history both of alcohol related offending and of failure to comply with community sentences; in addition, there was a considerable period of the operational period yet to be completed when the offence was committed.

24–126 When activating a suspended sentence order, by Sched. 12, para. 8(4) a court must take account of the extent to which a defendant has complied with the requirements imposed under the order. In *Kavanagh* [2011] 1 Cr.App.R.(S.) 63 the defendant had completed all of the requirements under the order including over 200 hours of unpaid work. The defendant was convicted of offences committed during the operational period and the Crown Court activated the suspended sentence in full (32 weeks). On appeal, the Court of Appeal (Criminal Division) reduced the period to eight weeks because of the extent of the compliance. Further issues arise on sentencing following breach from the effect of the statutory obligations concerning the allowance for time on remand (either in custody or, in some circumstances, on bail) where the qualifying remand was before the suspended sentence order was imposed. Where a defendant has spent time on a qualifying remand that matches (or exceeds) the time that would be served if the court imposed the maximum custodial sentence available for the offence, a suspended sentence should order not be made. In *Barrett* [2010] 2 Cr.App.R.(S.) 86 the defendant was convicted of a number of offences for which the maximum sentence in total was six months imprisonment. He was sentenced to 12 weeks imprisonment suspended for 12 months although he had already spent four months on remand in custody, in effect a period in excess of that which would have been spent in custody if the maximum available sentence had been imposed. Applying the principles noted in relation to *Hemmings* [2007] EWCA Crim 2413 (see *ante*, § 23–146), the Court imposed a conditional discharge designed to ensure that the defendant was no longer at risk of re-sentence for the original offence. In *Shariff* [2010] 2 Cr.App.R.(S.) 39 a court imposed a 36 weeks custodial sentence suspended for two years. The defendant had spent 104 days on remand in custody (the equivalent of a 30 week custodial sentence). When the defendant failed to comply with the requirements attached to the order, the Crown Court activated the sentence in full declining to give any credit for the time on remand pointing out that otherwise the defendant would have known that there was very little sanction in the suspended sentence order because he had already served much of the term of that sentence. The Court of Appeal (Criminal Division) considered there was no valid reason for directing that the time on remand should not count towards the sentence. In *Carruthers v. Hampshire Probation Service* [2010] EWHC 1961; (2010) 174 J.P. 553 the defendant had been convicted of eight offences of theft, one of assault and three motoring offences; in the magistrates' court he was sentenced to a total of six months imprisonment suspended for 12 months and the District Judge stated specifically that, if the terms of the order were breached, the 26 days spent on remand should not count towards the sentence. This decision was taken because the District Judge considered that a 12 month sentence would have been appropriate but statute did not permit a sentence of that length to be suspended in a magistrates' court. Whilst sympathising, the Divisional Court considered that the time for making determinations about whether credit should be given is when the suspended sentence order is being activated not when it is being imposed. It is unfortunate that immediate custodial sentences totalling 12 months could have been imposed by the magistrates' court but a sentence which is to be suspended cannot currently exceed six months because of the "transitional" arrangements introduced when the provisions relating to a suspended sentence order were brought into force but not those relating to "custody plus".

Reasons must be given for not implementing the suspended sentence.

24–127 In its guideline, *New Sentences: Criminal Justice Act* 2003, the Sentencing Guidelines Council issued guidance on the approach to breaches.

(2) New sentences under the Criminal Justice Act 2003

Guideline: New Sentences: Criminal Justice Act 2003

Section 2—Custodial Sentences

Part 2: Suspended Sentences

C. BREACHES

2.2.15 The essence of a suspended sentence is to make it abundantly clear to an offender that failure to comply with the requirements of the order or commission of another offence will almost certainly result in a custodial sentence. Where an offender has breached any of the requirements without reasonable excuse for the first time, the responsible officer must either give a warning or initiate breach proceedings. Where there is a further breach within a twelve-month period, breach proceedings must be initiated. **24–128**

2.2.16 Where proceedings are brought the court has several options, including extending the operational period. However, the presumption (which also applies where breach is by virtue of the commission of a further offence) is that the suspended prison sentence will be activated (either with its original custodial term or a lesser term) unless the court takes the view that this would, in all the circumstances, be unjust. In reaching that decision, the court may take into account both the extent to which the offender has complied with the requirements and the facts of the new offence.

2.2.17 Where a court considers that the sentence needs to be activated, it may activate it in full or with a reduced term. Again, the extent to which the requirements have been complied with will be very relevant to this decision.

2.2.18 If a court amends the order rather than activating the suspended prison sentence, it must either make the requirements more onerous, or extend the supervision or operational periods (provided that these remain within the limits defined by the Act). In such cases, the court must state its reasons for not activating the prison sentence, which could include the extent to which the offender has complied with requirements or the facts of the subsequent offence.

2.2.19 If an offender near the end of an operational period (having complied with the requirements imposed) commits another offence, it may be more appropriate to amend the order rather than activate it.

2.2.20 If a new offence committed is of a less serious nature than the offence for which the suspended sentence was passed, it may justify activating the sentence with a reduced term or amending the terms of the order.

2.2.21 It is expected that any activated suspended sentence will be consecutive to the sentence imposed for the new offence.

2.2.22 If the new offence is non-imprisonable, the sentencer should consider whether it is appropriate to activate the suspended sentence at all.

Where the court decides to amend a suspended sentence order rather than activate the custodial sentence, it should give serious consideration to extending the supervision or operational periods (within statutory limits) rather than making the requirements more onerous.

(3) Legislation

Criminal Justice Act 2003, Sched. 12

Section 193 SCHEDULE 12

BREACH OR AMENDMENT OF SUSPENDED SENTENCE ORDER, AND EFFECT OF FURTHER CONVICTION

PART 1

PRELIMINARY

Interpretation

1. In this Schedule— **24–129**

"the offender", in relation to a suspended sentence order, means the person in respect of whom the order is made;

"the local justice area concerned", in relation to a suspended sentence order, means the local justice area for the time being specified in the order;

"the responsible officer" has the meaning given by section 197.

24–130 2. In this Schedule—

(a) any reference to a suspended sentence order being subject to review is a reference to such an order being subject to review in accordance with section 191(1)(b) or to a drug rehabilitation requirement of such an order being subject to review in accordance with section 210(1)(b);

(b) any reference to the court responsible for a suspended sentence order which is subject to review is to be construed in accordance with section 191(3) or, as the case may be, 210(2).

Orders made on appeal

24–131 3. Where a suspended sentence order is made on appeal it is to be taken for the purposes of this Schedule to have been made by the Crown Court.

PART 2

BREACH OF COMMUNITY REQUIREMENT OR CONVICTION OF FURTHER OFFENCE

Duty to give warning in relation to community requirement

24–132 4.—(1) If the responsible officer is of the opinion that the offender has failed without reasonable excuse to comply with any of the community requirements of a suspended sentence order, the officer must give him a warning under this paragraph unless—

(a) the offender has within the previous twelve months been given a warning under this paragraph in relation to a failure to comply with any of the community requirements of the order, or

(b) the officer causes an information to be laid before a justice of the peace in respect of the failure.

(2) A warning under this paragraph must—

(a) describe the circumstances of the failure,

(b) state that the failure is unacceptable, and

(c) inform the offender that if within the next twelve months he again fails to comply with any requirement of the order, he will be liable to be brought before a court.

(3) The responsible officer must, as soon as practicable after the warning has been given, record that fact.

(4) In relation to any suspended sentence order which is made by the Crown Court and does not include a direction that any failure to comply with the community requirements of the order is to be dealt with by a magistrates' court, the reference in sub-paragraph (1)(b) to a justice of the peace is to be read as a reference to the Crown Court.

Breach of order after warning

24–133 5.—(1) If—

(a) the responsible officer has given a warning under paragraph 4 to the offender in respect of a suspended sentence order, and

(b) at any time within the twelve months beginning with the date on which the warning was given, the responsible officer is of the opinion that the offender has since that date failed without reasonable excuse to comply with any of the community requirements of the order,

the officer must cause an information to be laid before a justice of the peace in respect of the failure in question.

(2) In relation to any suspended sentence order which is made by the Crown Court and does not include a direction that any failure to comply with the community requirements of the order is to be dealt with by a magistrates' court, the reference in sub-paragraph (1) to a justice of the peace is to be read as a reference to the Crown Court.

Issue of summons or warrant by justice of the peace

24–134 6.—(1) This paragraph applies to—

(a) a suspended sentence order made by a magistrates' court, or

(b) any suspended sentence order which was made by the Crown Court and includes a direction that any failure to comply with the community requirements of the order is to be dealt with by a magistrates' court.

(2) If at any time while a suspended sentence order to which this paragraph applies is in force it appears on information to a justice of the peace that the offender has failed to comply with any of the community requirements of the order, the justice may—

(a) issue a summons requiring the offender to appear at the place and time specified in it, or

(b) if the information is in writing and on oath, issue a warrant for his arrest.

(3) Any summons or warrant issued under this paragraph must direct the offender to appear or be brought—

(a) in the case of a suspended sentence order which is subject to review, before the court responsible for the order,

(b) in any other case, before a magistrates' court acting in the local justice area in which the offender resides or, if it is not known where he resides, before a magistrates' court acting in the local justice area concerned.

(4) Where a summons issued under sub-paragraph (2)(a) requires the offender to appear before a magistrates' court and the offender does not appear in answer to the summons, the magistrates' court may issue a warrant for the arrest of the offender.

Issue of summons or warrant by Crown Court

7.—(1) This paragraph applies to a suspended sentence order made by the Crown Court which does not include a direction that any failure to comply with the community requirements of the order is to be dealt with by a magistrates' court. **24–135**

(2) If at any time while a suspended sentence order to which this paragraph applies is in force it appears on information to the Crown Court that the offender has failed to comply with any of the community requirements of the order, the Crown Court may—

(a) issue a summons requiring the offender to appear at the place and time specified in it, or

(b) if the information is in writing and on oath, issue a warrant for his arrest.

(3) Any summons or warrant issued under this paragraph must direct the offender to appear or be brought before the Crown Court.

(4) Where a summons issued under sub-paragraph (1)(a) requires the offender to appear before the Crown Court and the offender does not appear in answer to the summons, the Crown Court may issue a warrant for the arrest of the offender.

Powers of court on breach of community requirement or conviction of further offence

8.—(1) This paragraph applies where— **24–136**

(a) it is proved to the satisfaction of a court before which an offender appears or is brought under paragraph 6 or 7 or by virtue of section 192(6) that he has failed without reasonable excuse to comply with any of the community requirements of the suspended sentence order, or

(b) an offender is convicted of an offence committed during the operational period of a suspended sentence (other than one which has already taken effect) and either—

(i) he is so convicted by or before a court having power under paragraph 11 to deal with him in respect of the suspended sentence, or

(ii) he subsequently appears or is brought before such a court.

(2) The court must consider his case and deal with him in one of the following ways—

(a) the court may order that the suspended sentence is to take effect with its original term unaltered,

(b) the court may order that the sentence is to take effect subject to the substitution for the original term of a lesser term.

(c) the court may amend the order by doing any one or more of the following—

(i) imposing more onerous community requirements which the court could include if it were then making the order,

(ii) subject to subsections (3) and (4) of section 189, extending the supervision period, or

(iii) subject to subsection (3) of that section, extending the operational period.

(3) The court must make an order under sub-paragraph (2)(a) or (b) unless it is of the

Part IV

opinion that it would be unjust to do so in view of all the circumstances, including the matters mentioned in sub-paragraph (4); and where it is of that opinion the court must state its reasons.

(4) The matters referred to in sub-paragraph (3) are—

(a) the extent to which the offender has complied with the community requirements of the suspended sentence order, and

(b) in a case falling within sub-paragraph (1)(b), the facts of the subsequent offence.

(4A) Where a magistrates' court dealing with an offender under sub-paragraph (2)(c) would not otherwise have the power to amend the suspended sentence order under paragraph 14 (amendment by reason of change of residence), that paragraph has effect as if the references to the appropriate court were references to the court dealing with the offender.

(5) Where a court deals with an offender under sub-paragraph (2) in respect of a suspended sentence, the appropriate officer of the court must notify the appropriate officer of the court which passed the sentence of the method adopted.

(6) Where a suspended sentence order was made by the Crown Court and a magistrates' court would (apart from this sub-paragraph) be required to deal with the offender under sub-paragraph (2)(a), (b) or (c) it may instead commit him to custody or release him on bail until he can be brought or appear before the Crown Court.

(7) A magistrates' court which deals with an offender's case under subparagraph (6) must send to the Crown Court—

(a) a certificate signed by a justice of the peace certifying that the offender has failed to comply with the community requirements of the suspended sentence order in the respect specified in the certificate, and

(b) such other particulars of the case as may be desirable;

and a certificate purporting to be so signed is admissible as evidence of the failure before the Crown Court.

(8) In proceedings before the Crown Court under this paragraph any question whether the offender has failed to comply with the community requirements of the suspended sentence order and any question whether the offender has been convicted of an offence committed during the operational period of the suspended sentence is to be determined by the court and not by the verdict of a jury.

Further provisions as to order that suspended sentence is to take effect

24–137 9.—(1) When making an order under paragraph 8(2)(a) or (b) that a sentence is to take effect (with or without any variation of the original term, the court—

(b) may order that the sentence is to take effect immediately or that the term of that sentence is to commence on the expiry of another term of imprisonment passed on the offender by that or another court.

(2) The power to make an order under sub-paragraph (1)(b) has effect subject to section 265 (restriction on consecutive sentences for released prisoners).

(3) For the purpose of any enactment conferring rights of appeal in criminal cases, any order made by the court under paragraph 8(2)(a) or (b) is to be treated as a sentence passed on the offender by that court for the offence for which the suspended sentence was passed.

Restriction of powers in paragraph 8 where treatment required

24–138 10.—(1) An offender who is required by any of the following community requirements of a suspended sentence order—

(a) a mental health treatment requirement,

(b) a drug rehabilitation requirement, or

(c) an alcohol treatment requirement,

to submit to treatment for his mental condition, or his dependency on or propensity to misuse drugs or alcohol, is not to be treated for the purposes of paragraph 8(1)(a) as having failed to comply with that requirement on the ground only that he had refused to undergo any surgical, electrical or other treatment if, in the opinion of the court, his refusal was reasonable having regard to all the circumstances.

(2) A court may not under paragraph 8(2)(c)(i) amend a mental health treatment requirement, a drug rehabilitation requirement or an alcohol treatment requirement unless the offender expresses his willingness to comply with the requirement as amended.

Court by which suspended sentence may be dealt with under paragraph 8(1)(b)

11.—(1) An offender may be dealt with under paragraph 8(1)(b) in respect of a suspended sentence by the Crown Court or, where the sentence was passed by a magistrates' court, by any magistrates' court before which he appears or is brought. **24–139**

(2) Where an offender is convicted by a magistrates' court of any offence and the court is satisfied that the offence was committed during the operational period of a suspended sentence passed by the Crown Court—

(a) the court may, if it thinks fit, commit him in custody or on bail to the Crown Court, and

(b) if it does not, must give written notice of the conviction to the appropriate officer of the Crown Court.

Procedure where court convicting of further offence does not deal with suspended sentence

12.—(1) If it appears to the Crown Court, where that court has jurisdiction in accordance with sub-paragraph (2), or to a justice of the peace having jurisdiction in accordance with that sub-paragraph— **24–140**

(a) that an offender has been convicted in the United Kingdom of an offence committed during the operational period of a suspended sentence, and

(b) that he has not been dealt with in respect of the suspended sentence,

that court or justice may, subject to the following provisions of this paragraph, issue a summons requiring the offender to appear at the place and time specified in it, or a warrant for his arrest.

(2) Jurisdiction for the purposes of sub-paragraph (1) may be exercised—

(a) if the suspended sentence was passed by the Crown Court, by that court;

(b) if it was passed by a magistrates' court, by a justice acting in the local justice area for which the court acted.

(3) Where—

(a) an offender is convicted in Scotland or Northern Ireland of an offence, and

(b) the court is informed that the offence was committed during the operational period of a suspended sentence passed in England or Wales,

the court must give written notice of the conviction to the appropriate officer of the court by which the suspended sentence was passed.

(4) Unless he is acting in consequence of a notice under sub-paragraph (3), a justice of the peace may not issue a summons under this paragraph except on information and may not issue a warrant under this paragraph except on information in writing and on oath.

(5) A summons or warrant issued under this paragraph must direct the offender to appear or be brought before the court by which the suspended sentence was passed.

PART 3

AMENDMENT OF SUSPENDED SENTENCE ORDER

Cancellation of community requirements of suspended sentence order

13.—(1) Where at any time while a suspended sentence order is in force, it appears to the appropriate court on the application of the offender or the responsible officer that, having regard to the circumstances which have arisen since the order was made, it would be in the interests of justice to do so, the court may cancel the community requirements of the suspended sentence order. **24–141**

(2) The circumstances in which the appropriate court may exercise its power under sub-paragraph (1) include the offender's making good progress or his responding satisfactorily to supervision.

(3) In this paragraph "the appropriate court" means—

(a) in the case of a suspended sentence order which is subject to review, the court responsible for the order,

(b) in the case of a suspended sentence order which was made by the Crown Court and does not include any direction that any failure to comply with the community requirements of the order is to be dealt with by a magistrates' court, the Crown Court, and

(c) in any other case, a magistrates' court acting in the local justice area concerned.

Amendment by reason of change of residence

24–142 14.—(1) This paragraph applies where, at any time while a suspended sentence order is in force, the appropriate court is satisfied that the offender proposes to change, or has changed, his residence from the petty sessions area concerned to another local justice area.

(2) Subject to sub-paragraphs (3) and (4), the appropriate court may, and on the application of the responsible officer must, amend the suspended sentence order by substituting the other local justice area for the area specified in the order.

(3) The court may not amend under this paragraph a suspended sentence order which contains requirements which, in the opinion of the court, cannot be complied with unless the offender resides in the local justice area concerned unless, in accordance with paragraph 15 it either—

(a) cancels those requirements, or

(b) substitutes for those requirements other requirements which can be complied with if the offender does not reside in that area.

(4) The court may not amend under this paragraph any suspended sentence order imposing a programme requirement unless it appears to the court that the accredited programme specified in the requirement is available in the other local justice area.

(5) In this paragraph "the appropriate court" has the same meaning as in paragraph 13.

Amendment of community requirements of suspended sentence order

24–143 15.—(1) At any time during the supervision period, the appropriate court may, on the application of the offender or the responsible officer, by order amend any community requirement of a suspended sentence order—

(a) by cancelling the requirement, or

(b) by replacing it with a requirement of the same kind, which the court could include if it were then making the order.

(2) For the purposes of sub-paragraph (1)—

(a) a requirement falling within any paragraph of section 190(1) is of the same kind as any other requirement falling within that paragraph, and

(b) an electronic monitoring requirement is a requirement of the same kind as any requirement falling within section 190(1) to which it relates.

(3) The court may not under this paragraph amend a mental health treatment requirement, a drug rehabilitation requirement or an alcohol treatment requirement unless the offender expresses his willingness to comply with the requirement as amended.

(4) If the offender fails to express his willingness to comply with a mental health treatment requirement, drug rehabilitation requirement or alcohol treatment requirement as proposed to be amended by the court under this paragraph, the court may—

(a) revoke the suspended sentence order and the suspended sentence to which it relates, and

(b) deal with him, for the offence in respect of which the suspended sentence was imposed, in any way in which it could deal with him if he had just been convicted by or before the court of the offence.

(5) In dealing with the offender under sub-paragraph (4)(b), the court must take into account the extent to which the offender has complied with the requirements of the order.

(6) In this paragraph "the appropriate court" has the same meaning as in paragraph 13.

Amendment of treatment requirements on report of practitioner

24–144 16.—(1) Where the medical practitioner or other person by whom or under whose direction an offender is, in pursuance of any requirement to which this subparagraph applies, being treated for his mental condition or his dependency on or propensity to misuse drugs or alcohol—

(a) is of the opinion mentioned in sub-paragraph (3), or

(b) is for any reason unwilling to continue to treat or direct the treatment of the offender,

he must make a report in writing to that effect to the responsible officer and that officer must apply under paragraph 15 to the appropriate court for the variation or cancellation of the requirement.

(2) The requirements to which sub-paragraph (1) applies are—
- (a) a mental health treatment requirement,
- (b) a drug rehabilitation requirement, and
- (c) an alcohol treatment requirement.

(3) The opinion referred to in sub-paragraph (1) is—
- (a) that the treatment of the offender should be continued beyond the period specified in that behalf in the order,
- (b) that the offender needs different treatment,
- (c) that the offender is not susceptible to treatment, or
- (d) that the offender does not require further treatment.

(4) In this paragraph "the appropriate court" has the same meaning as in paragraph 13.

Amendment in relation to review of drug rehabilitation requirement

17. Where the responsible officer is of the opinion that a suspended sentence order imposing a drug rehabilitation requirement which is subject to review should be so amended as to provide for each periodic review (required by section 211) to be made without a hearing instead of at a review hearing, or vice versa, he must apply under paragraph 15 to the court responsible for the order for the variation of the order. **24–145**

Extension of unpaid work requirement

18.—(1) Where— **24–146**
- (a) a suspended sentence order imposing an unpaid work requirement is in force in respect of the offender, and
- (b) on the application of the offender or the responsible officer, it appears to the appropriate court that it would be in the interests of justice to do so having regard to circumstances which have arisen since the order was made,

the court may, in relation to the order, extend the period of twelve months specified in section 200(2).

(2) In this paragraph "the appropriate court" has the same meaning as in paragraph 13.

Supplementary

19.—(1) No application may be made under paragraph 13, 15 or 18, and no order may be made under paragraph 14, while an appeal against the suspended sentence is pending. **24–147**

(2) Sub-paragraph (1) does not apply to an application under paragraph 15 which—
- (a) relates to a mental health treatment requirement, a drug rehabilitation requirement or an alcohol treatment requirement, and
- (b) is made by the responsible officer with the consent of the offender.

20.—(1) Subject to sub-paragraph (2), where a court proposes to exercise its powers under paragraph 15, otherwise than on the application of the offender, the court— **24–148**
- (a) must summon him to appear before the court, and
- (b) if he does not appear in answer to the summons, may issue a warrant for his arrest.

(2) This paragraph does not apply to an order cancelling any community requirement of a suspended sentence order.

21. Paragraphs 8(2)(c) and 15(1)(b) have effect subject to the provisions mentioned in subsection (2) of section 190, and to subsections (3) and (5) of that section. **24–149**

22.—(1) On the making under this Schedule of an order amending a suspended sentence order, the proper officer of the court must— **24–150**
- (a) provide copies of the amending order to the offender and the responsible officer,
- (b) in the case of an amending order which substitutes a new local justice area, provide a copy of the amending order to—
  - (i) the local probation board acting for that area, and
  - (ii) the magistrates' court acting in that area, and

(c) in the case of an amending order which imposes or amends a requirement specified in the first column of Schedule 14, provide a copy of so much of the amending order as relates to that requirement to the person specified in relation to that requirement in the second column of that Schedule, and

(d) where the court acts in a local justice area other than the one specified in the order prior to the revocation or amendment, provide a copy of the revoking or amending order to a magistrates' court acting in the local justice area so specified.

(2) Where under sub-paragraph (1)(b) the proper officer of the court provides a copy of an amending order to a magistrates' court acting in a different area, the officer must also provide to that court such documents and information relating to the case as it considers likely to be of assistance to a court acting in that area in the exercise of its functions in relation to the order.

(3) In this paragraph "proper officer" means—

(a) in relation to a magistrates' court, the designated officer for the court; and

(b) in relation to the Crown Court, the appropriate officer.

V. BREACH OF REQUIREMENTS OF ATTENDANCE CENTRE ORDER

Powers of Criminal Courts (Sentencing) Act 2000, Sched. 5

SCHEDULE 5

BREACH, REVOCATION AND AMENDMENT OF ATTENDANCE CENTRE ORDERS

Breach of order or attendance centre rules

24–151 1.—(1) Where an attendance centre order is in force and it appears on information to a justice that the offender—

(a) has failed to attend in accordance with the order, or

(b) while attending has committed a breach of rules made under section 222(1)(d) or (e) of the *Criminal Justice Act* 2003 which cannot be adequately dealt with under those rules,

the justice may issue a summons requiring the offender to appear at the place and time specified in the summons or, if the information is in writing and on oath, may issue a warrant for the offender's arrest.

(2) Any summons or warrant issued under this paragraph shall direct the offender to appear or be brought—

(a) before a magistrates' court acting for the [local justice area] in which the offender resides; or

(b) if it is known where the offender resides, before a magistrates' court acting for the [local justice area] in which is situated the attendance centre which the offender is required to attend by the order or by virtue of an order under paragraph 5(1)(b) below.

24–152 2.—(1) If it is proved to the satisfaction of the magistrates' court before which an offender appears or is brought under paragraph 1 above that he has failed without reasonable excuse to attend as mentioned in sub-paragraph (1)(a) of that paragraph or has committed such a breach of rules as is mentioned in sub-paragraph (1)(b) of that paragraph, that court may deal with him in any one of the following ways—

(a) it may impose on him a fine not exceeding £1,000;

(b) where the attendance centre order was made by a magistrates' court, it may deal with him, for the offence in respect of which the order was made, in any way in which he could have been dealt with for that offence by the court which made the order if the order had not been made; or

(c) where the order was made by the Crown Court, it may commit him to custody or release him on bail until he can be brought or appear before the Crown Court.

(2) Any exercise by the court of its power under sub-paragraph (1)(a) above shall be without prejudice to the continuation of the order.

(3) A fine imposed under sub-paragraph (1)(a) above shall be deemed, for the purposes of any enactment, to be a sum adjudged to be paid by a conviction.

(4) Where a magistrates' court deals with an offender under sub-paragraph (1)(b) above, it shall revoke the attendance centre order if it is still in force.

(5) In dealing with an offender under sub-paragraph (1)(b) above, a magistrates' court—

(a) shall take into account the extent to which the offender has complied with the requirements of the attendance centre order; and

(b) in the case of an offender who has wilfully and persistently failed to comply with those requirements, may impose a custodial sentence notwithstanding anything in section 152(2) of the *Criminal Justice Act* 2003.

(5A) Where a magistrates' court dealing with an offender under sub-paragraph (1)(a) above would not otherwise have the power to amend the order under paragraph 5(1)(b) below (substitution of different attendance centre), that paragraph has effect as if references to an appropriate magistrates' court were references to the court dealing with the offender.

(6) A person sentenced under sub-paragraph (1)(b) above for an offence may appeal to the Crown Court against the sentence.

(7) A magistrates' court which deals with an offender's case under sub-paragraph (1)(c) above shall send to the Crown Court—

(a) a certificate signed by a justice of the peace giving particulars of the offender's failure to attend or, as the case may be, the breach of the rules which he has committed; and

(b) such other particulars of the case as may be desirable;

and a certificate purporting to be so signed shall be admissible as evidence of the failure or the breach before the Crown Court.

3. [Crown Court]

Revocation of order with or without re-sentencing

4.—(1) Where an attendance centre order is in force in respect of an offender, an appropriate court may, on an application made by the offender or by the officer in charge of the relevant attendance centre, revoke the order. **24–153**

(2) In sub-paragraph (1) above "an appropriate court" means—

(a) where the court which made the order was the Crown Court and there is included in the order a direction that the power to revoke the order is reserved to that court, the Crown Court;

(b) in any other case, either of the following—

(i) a magistrates' court acting in the local justice area in which the relevant attendance centre is situated;

(ii) the court which made the order.

(3) Any power conferred by this paragraph—

(a) on a magistrates' court to revoke an attendance centre order made by such a court, or

(b) on the Crown Court to revoke an attendance centre order made by the Crown Court,

includes power to deal with the offender, for the offence in respect of which the order was made, in any way in which he could have been dealt with for that offence by the court which made the order if the order had not been made.

(4) A person sentenced by a magistrates' court under sub-paragraph (3) above for an offence may appeal to the Crown Court against the sentence.

(5) The proper officer of a court which makes an order under this paragraph revoking an attendance centre order shall—

(a) deliver a copy of the revoking order to the offender or send a copy by registered post or the recorded delivery service addressed to the offender's last or usual place of abode; and

(b) deliver or send a copy to the officer in charge of the relevant attendance centre.

(6) In this paragraph "the relevant attendance centre", in relation to an attendance centre order, means the attendance centre specified in the order or substituted for the attendance centre so specified by an order made by virtue of paragraph 5(1)(b) below.

(7) In this paragraph "proper officer" means—

(a) in relation to a magistrates' court, the designated officer for the court; and

(b) in relation to the Crown Court, the appropriate officer.

Amendment of order

24–154 5.—(1) Where an attendance centre order is in force in respect of an offender, an appropriate magistrates' court may, on an application made by the offender or by the officer in charge of the relevant attendance centre, by order—

(a) vary the day or hour specified in the order for the offender's first attendance at the relevant attendance centre; or

(b) substitute for the relevant attendance centre an attendance centre which the court is satisfied is reasonably accessible to the offender, having regard to his age, the means of access available to him and any other circumstances.

(2) In sub-paragraph (1) above "an appropriate magistrates' court" means—

(a) a magistrates' court acting in the local justice area in which the relevant attendance centre is situated; or

(b) (except where the attendance centre order was made by the Crown Court) the magistrates' court which made the order.

(3) The designated officer for a court which makes an order under this paragraph shall—

(a) deliver a copy to the offender or send a copy by registered post or the recorded delivery service addressed to the offender's last or usual place of abode; and

(b) deliver or send a copy—

(i) if the order is made by virtue of sub-paragraph (1)(a) above, to the officer in charge of the relevant attendance centre; and

(ii) if it is made by virtue of sub-paragraph (1)(b) above, to the officer in charge of the attendance centre which the order as amended will require the offender to attend.

(4) In this paragraph "the relevant attendance centre" has the meaning given by paragraph 4(6) above.

Part V

Youth Courts

Chapter 25

JURISDICTIONAL ISSUES

I. INTRODUCTION

The youth court is part of the magistrates' court system. It is a court of summary jurisdiction that hears charges against children and young defendants aged between 10 and 17 years inclusive. It is conclusively presumed that no child under the age of 10 years can be guilty of any offence. Children over this age are subject to the criminal law in the same way as defendants in the adult magistrates' court. Courtroom procedure closely mirrors that of the adult court. However, the procedure is modified to reflect the age group that the youth court deals with. The geography of the courtroom is made less formal. The use of ordinary straightforward language is encouraged. Emphasis is put on the necessity of the court communicating and engaging directly with the defendants and their families. In the youth court it is usual to speak and refer to defendants by their first names. **25–1**

The Sentencing Guidelines Council issued the guideline "Overarching Principles—Sentencing Youths" in November 2009. This covers in detail the general approach to sentencing and the sentences available for youths. See § 27–13 *et seq.* for the full text.

II. THE YOUTH JUSTICE SYSTEM AND THE YOUTH COURT

(1) Aims and considerations

Crime and Disorder Act 1998, s.37

Aim of the youth justice system

37.—(1) It shall be the principal aim of the youth justice system to prevent offending by children and young persons. **25–2**

(2) In addition to any other duty to which they are subject, it shall be the duty of all persons and bodies carrying out functions in relation to the youth justice system to have regard to that aim.

Children and Young Persons Act 1933, s.44

General considerations.

44.—(1) Every court in dealing with a child or young person who is brought before it, either **25–3**

as an offender or otherwise, shall have regard to the welfare of the child or young person, and shall in a proper case take steps for removing him from undesirable surroundings, and for securing that proper provision is made for his education and training.

25–4 It is the duty of each local authority to establish for their area one or more Youth Offending Teams (*Crime and Disorder Act* 1998, s.39).

Youth Offending Teams (YOT) play a vital part in the work of the youth court. There are now 155 YOTs covering all of England and Wales. The duty of the YOT is to co-ordinate the provision of youth justice services for all those in the authority's area. It is customary for a representative from the YOT to attend each sitting of the youth court and the YOT plays a most important part in assisting in the work of the court. More particularly the YOT will assist in dealing with the following matters—

(a) investigating and confirming the personal circumstances and antecedents of defendants;
(b) the provision of bail support (with or without an ISSP programme);
(c) the preparation of appropriate written reports required by the court as part of the sentencing process;
(d) the administration of many of the non-custodial penalties imposed by the youth court;
(e) the prosecution of defendants who have breached community penalties.

Defence advocates will obtain much important information by conferring with the YOT prior to the hearing of their clients case.

Intellectual Capacity of the defendant

25–5 A child or young person facing criminal proceedings must be of sufficient intellectual capacity to be able to effectively participate in his trial.

In *R. (P.) v.West London Youth Court* [2006] 1 W.L.R. 1219 the Divisional Court considered the application of a 15-year-old who sought judicial review of a decision by the youth court not to stay proceedings against him on the basis of abuse of process.

It was contended on his behalf that his intellectual capacity was such that he could not effectively participate in the court proceedings and therefore could not have a fair trial. In dismissing the application for judicial review the court emphasised the specialist nature of the youth court jurisdiction and went on to set out a number of steps that could, and should, be taken by that Court to ensure that a defendant with learning difficulties would be able to effectively participate in his trial. The minimum requirements for a fair trial were:

(1) The defendant has to understand what he is said to have done wrong;
(2) The court has to be satisfied that the defendant when he had done wrong by act or omission had the means of knowing that was wrong;
(3) The defendant had to understand what, if any, defences were available to him;
(4) He had to have a reasonable opportunity to make relevant representations if he wished; and
(5) He had to have the opportunity to consider what representation he wished to make once he had understood the issues involved.

He had therefore to be able to give proper instructions and participate by way of providing answers to questions and suggesting questions to his lawyers in the circumstances of the trial as they arose.

In *CPS v. P* [2007] EWCA 946 (Admin) the CPS successfully appealed against the decision of a Youth Court to stay proceedings in respect of a 13-year-old on the grounds that he did not have a sufficient level of maturity or intellectual capacity to understand and participate effectively in the proceedings against him based on the contents of psychological and psychiatric reports produced to the Court. There being no statutory procedure laid down for dealing with overlapping capacity issues, the Court of Appeal suggested the following approach:

(1) Particularly in the case of a young child with marked learning or disability

problems, appropriate consideration should be given by the relevant authorities as to whether or not civil proceedings under the *Children Act* 1989 are more appropriate than criminal prosecution.

(2) If criminal proceedings are begun, the Youth Court has inherent jurisdiction to stay proceedings as an abuse of process under the same principles that apply to the adult Magistrates Court. However, it will only be in exceptional cases that this power should be exercised on the basis of the "capacity" of a young defendant before any evidence is heard.

(3) Medical evidence may be of great importance in considering these issues but it must almost always be set in the context of other evidence relating to the child, including the court's own observations. It is the court's opinion of the child's level of understanding which must determine whether or not a criminal trial proceeds.

(4) The medical evidence should be considered as part of the evidence in the case, not the sole evidence on a free standing application for abuse of process. The court might conclude that with assistance from his legal advisor and suitable adjustment to the procedure of the court, the trial can properly proceed.

(5) The court has a duty to keep under continuing review the question of whether or not the trial should continue.

(6) If the criminal trial is halted, the Youth Court must then go on to consider whether or not to switch to a fact finding hearing. The court can then proceed to consider seeking further medical evidence with a view to making an order under the *Mental Health Act* 1983.

In *R. v. T* [2008] 3 W.L.R. 923 the Court of Appeal in considering the decision in *CPS v. P* (see above) held that there is no separate defence of *doli incapax* remaining after s.34 of the *Crime and Disorder Act* 1998 abolished the presumption.

(2) Preliminary issues

Children and Young Persons Act 1933, s.34A

Attendance at court of parent or guardian

34A.—(1) Where a child or young person is charged with an offence or is for any other reason brought before a court, the court— **25–6**

(a) may in any case; and

(b) shall in the case of a child or a young person who is under the age of sixteen years,

require a person who is a parent or guardian of his to attend at the court during all the stages of the proceedings, unless and to the extent that the court is satisfied that it would be unreasonable to require such attendance, having regard to the circumstances of the case.

(2) In relation to a child or young person for whom a Local Authority have parental responsibility and who—

(a) is in their care; or

(b) is provided with accommodation by them in the exercise of any functions (in particular those under the *Children Act* 1989) which are social services functions within the meaning of the *Local Authority Social Services Act* 1970,

the reference in subsection (1) above to a person who is a parent or guardian of his shall be construed as a reference to that Authority, where he is allowed to live with such a person, as including such a reference.

In this subsection "local authority" and "parental responsibility" have the same meanings as in the *Children Act* 1989.

It is essential that parents or guardians of young defendants attend the youth court with them. Section 34A above makes such attendance mandatory where the youth is under 16 years of age unless the court is satisfied that it would be unreasonable to require such attendance in all the circumstances of the case. If a defendant appears without a parent, the court must enquire as to why they are unaccompanied, and **25–7** consider taking steps to ensure attendance. The court may write to the parent or guardian requesting attendance. Alternatively a summons may be issued and, if this does not remedy the situation, a warrant obtained.

Having secured parental attendance the court will be anxious to allow parents to address the court and to contribute to the hearing generally. It is important that the court engages with both the defendant and his family.

(3) Press and publicity

25–8 Persons who may be present at the sitting of a youth court are—

(a) members and officers of the court;

(b) parties to the case together with their solicitors and counsel, and other persons directly concerned in that case;

(c) accredited representatives of news agencies;

(d) the court may especially authorise other persons to be present who have good cause to be there.

Accredited press representatives are therefore allowed to observe and report on court proceedings in the youth court and their presence in the courtroom cannot be objected to by the parties. However, the press is restricted in the details it may report. More particularly no report of any proceedings in a youth court should reveal the name, address or school, or include any particulars likely to lead to the identification of any child or young person concerned in those proceedings. This restriction includes details of young witnesses who are concerned in the court proceedings and the publication of pictures.

Children and Young Persons Act 1933, s.49

Restrictions on reports of proceedings in which children or young persons are concerned.

25–9 **49.**—(1) The following prohibitions apply (subject to subsection (5) below) in relation to any proceedings to which this section applies, that is to say—

(a) no report shall be published which reveals the name, address or school of any child or young person concerned in the proceedings or includes any particulars likely to lead to the identification of any child or young person concerned in the proceedings; and

(b) no picture shall be published or included in a programme service as being or including a picture of any child or young person concerned in the proceedings.

(2) The proceedings to which this section applies are—

(a) proceedings in a youth court;

(b) proceedings on appeal from a youth court (including proceedings by way of case stated);

(c) proceedings under section 15 or 16 of the *Children and Young Persons Act* 1969 (proceedings for varying or revoking supervision orders); and

(d) proceedings on appeal from a magistrates' court arising out of proceedings under section 15 or 16 of that Act (including proceedings by way of case stated).

(3) The reports to which this section applies are reports in a newspaper and reports included in a programme service; and similarly as respects pictures.

(4) For the purposes of this section a child or young person is "concerned" in any proceedings whether as being the person against or in respect of whom the proceedings are taken or as being a witness in the proceedings.

(4A) If a court is satisfied that it is in the public interest to do so, it may, in relation to a child or young person who has been convicted of an offence, by order dispense to any specified extent with the requirements of this section in relation to any proceedings before it to which this section applies by virtue of subsection (2)(a) or (b) above, being proceedings relating to—

(a) the prosecution or conviction of the offender for the offence;

(b) the manner in which he, or his parent or guardian, should be dealt with in respect of the offence;

(c) the enforcement, amendment, variation, revocation or discharge of any order made in respect of the offence;

(d) where an attendance centre order is made in respect of the offence, the enforcement of any rules made under section 16(3) of the *Criminal Justice Act* 1982; or

(e) where a detention and training order is made, the enforcement of any requirements imposed under section 76(6)(b) of the *Crime and Disorder Act* 1998.

(4B) A court shall not exercise its power under subsection (4A) above without—

(a) affording the parties to the proceedings an opportunity to make representations; and

(b) taking into account any representations which are duly made.

(5) Subject to subsection (7) below, a court may, in relation to proceedings before it to which this section applies, by order dispense to any specified extent with the requirements of this section in relation to a child or young person who is concerned in the proceedings if it is satisfied—

(a) that it is appropriate to do so for the purpose of avoiding injustice to the child or young person; or

(b) that, as respects a child or young person to whom this paragraph applies who is unlawfully at large, it is necessary to dispense with those requirements for the purpose of apprehending him and bringing him before a court or returning him to the place in which he was in custody.

(6) Paragraph (b) of subsection (5) above applies to any child or young person who is charged with or has been convicted of—

(a) a violent offence,

(b) a sexual offence, or

(c) an offence punishable in the case of a person aged 21 or over with imprisonment for fourteen years or more.

(7) The court shall not exercise its power under subsection (5)(b) above—

(a) except in pursuance of an application by or on behalf of the Director of Public Prosecutions; and

(b) unless notice of the application has been given by the Director of Public Prosecutions to any legal representative of the child or young person.

(8) The court's power under subsection (5) above may be exercised by a single justice.

(9) If a report or picture is published or included in a programme service in contravention of subsection (1) above, the following persons, that is to say—

(a) in the case of publication of a written report or a picture as part of a newspaper, any proprietor, editor or publisher of the newspaper;

(b) in the case of the inclusion of a report or picture in a programme service, any body corporate which provides the service and any person having functions in relation to the programme corresponding to those of an editor of a newspaper,

shall be liable on summary conviction to a fine not exceeding level 5 on the standard scale.

(10) In any proceedings under section 15 or 16 of the *Children and Young Persons Act* 1969 (proceedings for varying or revoking supervision orders) before a magistrates' court other than a youth court or on appeal from such a court it shall be the duty of the magistrates' court or the appellate court to announce in the course of the proceedings that this section applies to the proceedings; and if the court fails to do so this section shall not apply to the proceedings.

(11) In this section—

"legal representative" means an authorised advocate or authorised litigator, as defined by section 119(1) of the *Courts and Legal Services Act* 1990;

"programme" and "programme service" have the same meaning as in the *Broadcasting Act* 1990;

"sexual offence" has the same meaning as in section 31(1) of the *Criminal Justice Act* 1991;

"specified" means specified in an order under this section;

"violent offence" has the same meaning as in section 31(1) of the *Criminal Justice Act* 1991;

and a person who, having been granted bail, is liable to arrest (whether with or without a warrant) shall be treated as unlawfully at large.

The youth court may order the lifting of press restrictions to any extent that it specifies in certain specific circumstances: **25–10**

(1) that it is appropriate to do so for the purpose of avoiding injustice to the child or young person subject to the application;

(2) in respect of a child or young person who has been convicted of an offence and

the court is satisfied that it is in the public interest that details of their identity are given in the press;

(3) where a defendant has been charged with or convicted of a violent or sexual offence or an offence punishable with imprisonment for 14 years or more if he/she is unlawfully at large and the court is satisfied on the application of the DPP that it is necessary to identify him in the press for the purpose of apprehending him to bring him before a court or to return him to the place in which he was held in custody.

The youth court's power to dispense with reporting restrictions under s.49 should be exercised with the greatest care and caution. International law and practice emphasises the necessity of protecting the privacy of children and young persons involved in legal proceedings. In the case of *McKerry v. Teesdale and Wear Valley J.J.* [2000] Crim.L.R. 594, the Divisional Court stated that the need for the full and fair reporting of the administration of justice must be balanced against the welfare of the youth involved. It would be wholly wrong to invoke the power by way of additional punishment and it would only be "very rarely" that the statutory criteria for "naming and shaming" would be met.

(4) Legal representation

25–11 A majority of youths who appear before the youth court will be legally represented either under the duty solicitor scheme or as a result of instructing their own lawyers. Representation orders are applied for in the youth court in the same way as in the adult magistrates' court. The applications are considered under the Widgery criteria and decided on the basis of the interests of justice. In considering such an application the age of the applicant must be taken into account. In *Scunthorpe Justices, ex p. S., The Times*, March 5, 1998, DC it was held that a refusal to grant legal aid to a 16-year-old defendant who wished to challenge a police constable as to whether he had acted in the execution of his duty was said to be irrational, as the expertise required to cross examine police witnesses and find, select and proof defence witnesses is beyond that of a defendant aged 16 years.

(5) Reprimands and final warnings (section 65 of the Crime and Disorder Act 1998)

25–12 These have replaced police cautions for young people. They are not court orders and cannot be ordered by the court. However, they are frequently cited when the court is told about a defendants antecedent history, in dealing with issues relating to bail and sentencing.

A reprimand will be given for first time offenders and for less serious offences. However, if the offence is sufficiently serious a final warning may be given instead of a reprimand. A final warning is given to offenders who have been reprimanded previously. Once a final warning is given the offender cannot receive a further reprimand or final warning except where the new offence has been committed more than two years since the previous warning and is not sufficiently serious to be charged.

When a final warning is given, the YOT will be notified and the young person should be assessed with a view to work being done with him to prevent offending.

Before the police can give a reprimand or final warning the offender must admit the offence.

25–13 Reprimands and final warnings may be relevant in making a bail decision for a youth. They will also be relevant in assessing his/her antecedent history for the purpose of sentencing. It should be noted that a young person who re-offends and is convicted within two years of receiving a final warning cannot be given a conditional discharge (*Crime and Disorder Act* 1998, s.66) unless there are exceptional circumstances relating to the offence itself or the offender. See *post*, § 27–17.

After a defendant has been charged the youth court is sometimes asked to adjourn proceedings against him/her to allow a reprimand or final warning to be administered. This situation was considered by the Divisional Court in *F. v. CPS* (2004) 168 J.P. 93. In that case the court was asked to judicially review the decision of the CPS not to discontinue a prosecution after a decision had been made by the police not to administer a final warning. The Divisional Court emphasised that final warnings are meant to be administered quickly and that it was clearly envisaged that they should be given before charge. It would only be in exceptional circumstances that the police should administer a final warning or reprimand when the defendant had already been charged and had appeared before a court.

In *R. (H.) v. Guildford Youth Court* [2008] EWHC 506 (Admin) the Divisional Court quashed the decision of a Youth Court not to stay proceedings. The defendant had admitted a serious assault in his interview with the police after his lawyer had been told by police that he would receive a final warning and not be prosecuted. He subsequently was prosecuted. It was held that a promise from a police officer in charge of the case was something that there was a clear public interest in upholding. The proceedings were be stayed as an abuse of process.

III. AGE AND JURISDICTION

(1) Presumption and determination of age

The youth court's jurisdiction is founded upon the age of the defendant. Therefore the court is under a duty to establish that the defendant is aged between 10 and 17 years. Additionally, the powers of the youth court in respect of bail, remand, and sentencing vary widely between the different age groups within the court jurisdiction. **25–14**

In the vast majority of cases coming before the youth court establishing the age of a defendant does not cause any problem, however if an issue as to age does arise it is dealt with by the following statutory procedure.

Children and Young Persons Act 1933, s.99(1)

Presumption and determination of age

99.—(1) Where a person, whether charged with an offence or not, is brought before any court otherwise than for the purpose of giving evidence, and it appears to the court that he is a child or young person, the court shall make due inquiry as to the age of that person, and for that purpose shall take such evidence as may be forthcoming at the hearing of the case, but an order or judgment of the court shall not be invalidated by any subsequent proof that the age of that person has not been correctly stated to the court, and the age presumed or declared by the court to be the age of the person so brought before it shall, for the purposes of this Act, be deemed to be the true age of that person, and, where it appears to the court that the person so brought before it has attained the age of eighteen years, that person shall for the purposes of this Act be deemed not to be a child or young person. **25–15**

If the youth court is not satisfied that it has been given accurate information regarding a defendant's age, this section places a duty on the court to determine the age of the defendant. For the purposes of determining age the court can hear oral evidence and consider both domestic or foreign documentation. The court can also take into account the physical appearance of the defendant in the courtroom. The YOT, with its wide experience of dealing with young people, may also have a valuable part to play in such hearings. At the end of the hearing the court will deem the defendant to be of a certain age or within a certain age group. If new relevant evidence emerges at future hearings of the case, the court may re-open the question of age and alter its original decision. However, this must be based on new factors that have come to light. **25–16**

In *B. v. The Mayor and Burgesses of the London Borough of Merton* (2003) EWHC 1689 (Admin) the Court reviewed the procedure used by the defendant Borough in determining the age of an asylum seeker from the Ivory Coast. The Court emphasised the difficulties of determining age simply by physical observation and set out the following guidelines:

(a) Assessment of age is difficult but not complex. It does not require a trial and an informal enquiry is satisfactory if it meets reasonable standards of fairness.

(b) Assessment by physical appearance will only be sufficient in the most obvious cases. In other cases full enquiry must be made as to the personal circumstances of the individual concerned taking into account ethnic and cultural issues.

(c) The conclusions reached by such enquiry should be explained to the individual concerned and he should be given the opportunity to answer the points made.

(d) While the procedure used at such an enquiry should be informal it may be helpful for a note to be taken and shown to the individual concerned. An interpreter should also be present if needed.

In *N. v. Staines Magistrates' Court* (2009) EWHC 3081 (Admin) the Court considered the fairness of the deeming of the age of the defendant by the Youth Court. It was held that providing the procedure used in such deeming was "*Merton* compliant" the decision reached would seldom be interfered with on appeal. It seems therefore that the principles laid down in the *Merton* case apply to deeming age in the Youth Court. A rapid deeming of a defendant based solely on the Court's visual assessment of him/her will only be appropriate in the most obvious cases. In all other cases an adjournment will be required in order for a full *Merton* assessment to take place.

(2) Crossing the age barrier

25–17 The situation sometimes arises that a defendant who has been charged with an offence when under the age of 18 years, attains that age before proceedings against him in the youth court have been concluded. This has important implications for the defendant. It is submitted that the most common situations are as follows:

(1) If a young person is charged with an offence whilst he is 17 years of age but turns 18 years of age before his first appearance before the court, then the youth court does not have jurisdiction to deal with him: *Uxbridge Youth Court, ex p. H.* (1998) 162 J.P. 327.

(2) If the young person has appeared before the youth court when under 18 years of age but attains 18 during the proceedings then the following rules apply:

If, before summary trial in the youth court or, after conviction in the youth court but before sentence, the youth court may remit the person to the adult magistrates' court for the same area as the youth court.

Powers of Criminal Courts (Sentencing) Act 2000, s.9(1), (2)

25–18 **9.**—(1) Where a person who appears or is brought before a youth court charged with an offence subsequently attains the age of 18, the youth court may, at any time after conviction and before sentence, remit him for sentence to a magistrates' court (other than a youth court).

(2) Where an offender is remitted under subsection (1) above, the youth court shall adjourn proceedings in relation to the offence, and—

(a) section 128 of the *Magistrates' Courts Act* 1980 (remand in custody or on bail) and all other enactments, whenever passed, relating to remand or the granting of bail in criminal proceedings shall have effect, in relation to the youth court's power or duty to remand the offender on that adjournment, as if any reference to the court to or before which the person remanded is to be brought or appear after remand were a reference to the court to which he is being remitted; and

(b) subject to subsection (3), the court to which the offender is remitted ("the other court") may deal with the case in any way in which it would have power to deal with it if all proceedings relating to the offence which took place before the youth court had taken place before the other court.

25–19 Section 9 of the *PCC(S)A* 2000 gives the youth court discretion whether or not to remit to the magistrates' court. If the youth court decides to retain the case the enabling provision to do so is below.

Although s.9 does not, in terms, exclude indictable only offences from the power to remit to the adult court, it plainly makes no sense to remit a person to an adult court if that court has no power to sentence him. In the case of *R. (Denny) v. Acton Youth Court* [2004] 1 W.L.R. 3051, the youth court convicted an 18-year-old defendant of attempted robbery. The offence had been committed when the defendant was 17 years of age. The youth court sought to remit him to the adult court for sentence. It was held that a youth court should never remit under s.9 in relation to an offence which would be triable only on indictment in the case of an adult.

Children and Young Persons Act 1963, s.29

29.—(1) Where proceedings in respect of a young person are begun for an offence and he attains the age of eighteen before the conclusion of the proceedings, the court may deal with the case and make any order which it could have made if he had not attained that age. **25–20**

If, during the course of proceedings against a defendant who the court believes to be under 18 years of age, it emerges that the defendant is in fact 18 or over the youth court has discretion to continue to deal with the defendant under the provision below. **25–21**

Children and Young Persons Act 1933, s.48(1)

48.—(1) A youth court sitting for the purpose of hearing a charge against a person who is believed to be a child or young person may, if it thinks fit to do so, proceed with the hearing and determination of the charge, notwithstanding that it is discovered that the person in question is not a child or young person. **25–22**

If a defendant under 18 appears before the youth court charged with an offence which is "either way" in the case of an adult (not being a grave crime) and he attains the age of 18 years before his plea is taken, he may apply to the youth court to be remitted to the adult court. Once a defendant has attained 18 years of age he has the right to elect trial by jury in respect of either way charges. However, it seems that if a defendant has entered his plea prior to his 18th birthday it is then "too late" for him to elect Crown Court trial although his trial in the youth court will not commence until after his 18th birthday. It is submitted that this is the interpretation to be given to the judgment in *Islington North Juvenile Court, ex p. Daley* [1982] 2 All E.R. 974. During his leading judgment Lord Diplock stated: **25–23**

> "it seems to me that reason and justice combine to indicate that the only appropriate date at which to determine whether an accused person has attained an age which entitles him to elect trial by jury for offences which under section 18 or section 22 are triable either way is the date of his appearance before the court on the occasion when the court makes its decision as to mode of trial".

If the defendant is charged with a "grave crime" under s.24 of the *Magistrates' Courts Act* 1980 and the youth court decides to retain jurisdiction before the defendant attains 18 years, the matter must remain for summary trial in the youth court. The defendant does not, on attaining 18 years acquire a right of trial before a jury: *Nottingham Justices, ex p. Taylor* [1991] 4 All E.R. 860. If the defendant attains 18 years before the mode of trial decision, then the youth court has no power to proceed, and the case should be remitted to the adult court in accordance with s.9 of the *PCC(S)A* 2000 (see § 25–18, *ante*).

No matter whether the original charges are summary, either way or indictable, the youth court has no jurisdiction to deal with any further fresh charges after the defendant has turned 18 years. This is irrespective of whether the fresh charges arise from the same circumstances: *Chelsea Justices, ex p. DPP* [1963] 3 All E.R. 657.

Part V

(3) Sentencing across the age barrier

In *Ghafoor* [2002] Crim.L.R. 739, the Court of Appeal considered the approach to be adopted where a court sentences a defendant who crosses a relevant age threshold between the date of the commission of an offence and the date of conviction. The judgments of the court made it clear that the starting point for sentencing a defendant in such circumstances is the sentence that the defendant would have been likely to receive **25–24** if he had been sentenced on the date of the commission of the offence. The "starting point" principle is a powerful factor in deciding sentence although other factors might have to be considered. However, a court would have to have good reason for departing from the starting point sentence and passing a sentence higher than would have been passed at the date of the commission of the offence.

In *L.M.* [2003] 2 Cr.App.R.(S.) 26, a 14-year-old defendant who was not a "persistent offender" was convicted when 15 years old of an offence of inflicting grievous bodily harm. He was sentenced to a detention and training order. He could not have received a custodial sentence when 14 but was eligible for such a sentence once he became 15. It was held that it was wrong for a detention and training order to be imposed as applying *Ghafoor* (*ante*) the starting point for sentence should be the sentence which he would have been likely to receive if he had been sentenced at the date of the commission of the offence when only 14 years old. In *R.* (2006) 150 S.J.L.B. 1607 the Court dealt with an appeal by a 15-year-old female who received an 18 month DTO for the offence of wounding with intent. On the date of the offence she was 14 years old and was not a persistent young offender (see *post*, § 27–99). In applying the case of *Ghafoor* the Court stated that the emphasis for young offenders should be rehabilitation not retribution and deterrence. The starting point for sentencing the appellant was how she would have been sentenced on the date of the offence, when she could not have received a DTO. The order was quashed and substituted by a supervision order.

In *Kevin Robson* [2007] 1 Cr.App.R.(S.) 54 the Court of Appeal held that the age of an offender for the purposes of determining which statutory sentencing regime applied to him under the provisions of the *Criminal Justice Act* 2003 was the offender's age at the date of conviction and not of sentence.

If an order of conditional discharge was made in respect of a young person, the youth court may deal with a breach of that order even though the person is over 18 years of age: *Children and Young Persons Act* 1933, s.48(2).

If the order of conditional discharge was made by the youth court for an offence which is indictable only in the case of an adult, and the accused has attained 18 years when breached, the re-sentencing courts powers are set out in the *PCC(S)A* 2000, s.13(9):

(a) to impose a fine not exceeding £5,000 for the offence in respect of which the order was made;
(b) to deal with the offender for that offence in any way in which a magistrates' court could deal with him if it had just convicted him of an offence punishable with imprisonment for a term not exceeding six months.

If, during the duration of a supervision order, breach proceedings are brought, and the offender has attained 18 years, then the proceedings are brought in the adult court. If the breach proceedings are commenced in the youth court whilst the offender is under 18 years, then they remain in the youth court to be concluded there: *PCC(S)A* 2000, Sched. 7, para. 1.

IV. *JURISDICTION, GRAVE CRIMES AND DANGEROUSNESS*

Magistrates' Courts Act 1980, s.24(1)

25–25 **24.**—(1) Where a person under the age of 18 years appears or is brought before a magistrates' court on an information charging him with an indictable offence other than one falling within subsection (1B) below, he shall be tried summarily unless—

(a) the offence is such as is mentioned in subsection (1) or (2) of section 91 of the *Powers of Criminal Courts (Sentencing) Act* 2000 (under which a young person convicted on indictment of certain grave crimes may be sentenced to be detained for long periods) and the court considers that if he is found guilty of the offence it ought to be possible to sentence him in pursuance of subsection (3) of that section; or
(b) he is charged jointly with a person who has attained the age of 18 and the court considers it necessary in the interests of justice to commit them both for trial;

and accordingly in a case falling within paragraph (a) or (b) of this subsection the court shall commit the accused for trial if either it is of the opinion that there is sufficient evidence to put him on trial or it has power under section 6(2) above so to commit him without consider of the evidence.

It should be noted that possession of prohibited weapons and ammunition, contrary to s.5 of the *Firearms Act* 1968, as amended by s.287 of the *Criminal Justice Act* 2003, now requires a minimum 5-year sentence to be imposed if the offence was: **25–26**

(a) committed after January 22, 2004; and

(b) at the time of the offence, the defendant was aged 16 years or over.

Section 39 of the *Anti-Social Behaviour Act* 2003 extended the list of prohibited weapons contained in s.5, by adding any air rifle, air gun or air pistol which uses or is designed or adapted for use with a self-contained gas cartridge system. A young person fitting these criteria must be committed to the Crown Court for trial and in the event of conviction, for a sentence of detention to be passed under s.91 of the *PCC(S)A* 2000.

The plea before venue procedure that takes place in the adult court does not apply to young people who do not have a right to elect Crown Court trial. The youth court has jurisdiction to try either way and indictable offences other than offences of homicide. However, if the offence alleged is one of the grave crimes (see s.91 of the *PCC(S)A* 2000), s.24(1), *ante*, jurisdiction must be considered by the youth court. **25–27**

In such cases the youth court must consider whether it should retain jurisdiction and try the case, or whether it should decline jurisdiction and, if there is a case to answer, commit the defendant to the Crown Court. In such cases the court must consider the seriousness of the allegation and decide whether its own powers of punishment are sufficient or whether the allegation is of such a serious nature that, if found guilty, it ought to be possible to sentence the defendant to detention under s.91 of the *PCC(S)A* 2000.

The decision the youth court makes as to whether to accept jurisdiction is a most important one which may have a profound effect on the outcome of the case for the defendant. If the youth court accepts jurisdiction, and the defendant pleads guilty or is convicted, the youth court has no power to commit him/her to the Crown Court for sentence unless the "dangerousness" provisions apply (see § 25–40, *post*). In such cases the defendant must, therefore, be sentenced in accordance with the powers of the youth court. **25–28**

The youth court's powers to impose a custodial sentence are limited in the following ways:

(a) In the case of defendants aged 10 or 11 years of age, the youth court has no power at all to impose a custodial sentence.

(b) In the case of defendants aged from 12 to 14 years, the court has power to impose a detention and training order for a maximum of two years but only if it is of the opinion that the defendant is a persistent offender. If not, the youth court has no power to impose a custodial sentence (persistent offender—see detention and training order, § 27–79, *post*).

(c) Defendants aged 15, 16 and 17 years can be sentenced to a detention and training order up to a maximum of two years: *PCC(S)A* 2000, s.103.

If, however, the youth court decline jurisdiction and commit the defendant to the Crown Court for trial, he/she may then be sentenced by the Crown Court under s.91, below.

In *R. (on the application of D.) v Sheffield Youth Court* [2008] EWHC 601 (Admin), a 17-year-old who appeared with others at the adult magistrates court was allowed to enter a plea of guilty to offences of supplying Class A drugs. The question of jurisdiction and the grave crime procedure was not considered. It was held that this did not render subsequent steps invalid, and, in addition, the Youth Court did not have the power to re-open the s.24 procedure.

V. PUNISHMENT OF CERTAIN GRAVE CRIMES—PCC(S)A 2000, SECTION 91

(1) Sentencing

25–29 Where a young offender is convicted on indictment of certain grave crimes, he may be sentenced to long-term detention. This sentence is available:

(a) where a person of at least 10 but not more than 17 years is convicted on indictment of any offence punishable in the case of an adult with imprisonment of 14 years or more not being an offence the sentence for which is fixed by law; or an offence under section 14 (indecent assault on a woman) or section 15 (indecent assault on a man) of the *Sexual Offences Act* 1956. Or an offence under the-*Sexual Offences Act* 2003 which is capable of being committed for trial at the Crown Court under the Grave Crime provisions.

(b) where a young person is convicted of an offence under section 1 of the *Road Traffic Act* 1988 (causing death by dangerous driving); or an offence under section 3A of the *Road Traffic Act* 1988 (causing death by careless driving while under the influence of drink or drugs).

Section 91 of the *PCC(S)A* 2000 is available to the Crown Court if a young person is convicted on indictment of a grave crime. Detention under s.91 can be imposed upon defendants aged 10 to 17 years.

(2) The application of section 24

25–30 The application of s.24 by the youth court has been the subject of much litigation, and scrutiny by the higher courts. There is a considerable body of case law and there is also guidance in SGC overarching principles at para. 12.8. See *post*, § 27–13 *et seq.* It is submitted that the following are the principles for the court to apply:

(1) The test that the youth court must apply is whether the court considers that if convicted it ought to be possible to sentence the defendant in pursuance of s.91 of the *PCC(S)A* 2000. There must be a real possibility of such a sentence, not a vague or theoretical one. If the court is of a view that such a sentence is a real possibility, the court has no further discretion and must decline jurisdiction: *R. (D. & N.) v. Sheffield Youth Court* (2003) 167 J.P. 159, QBD.

(2) The youth court will hear the facts of the prosecution case. The defendant's criminal record will be considered: *R. (Tullet) v. Medway Magistrates' Court* (2003) 167 J.P. 541 and 896. The court must also consider defence submissions both on the undisputed facts of the prosecution case and any other factors relating to the defendant, his character, and his personal circumstances. Contentious mitigation should be ignored.

(3) In *R. (W.) v. Southampton Youth Court*; *R. (K.) v. Wirral Borough Magistrates' Court* [2003] 1 Cr.App.R.(S.) 87, the Lord Chief Justice emphasised the importance of trials for young offenders taking into account the needs of defendants of that age group: "While the need to impose the appropriate sentence is important, so is the need to ensure that wherever possible the trial should take place in the appropriate setting. That is more satisfactorily achieved in a Youth Court than in a Crown Court." The youth court should start therefore with a strong presumption against sending young offenders to the Crown Court unless satisfied that it is clearly required, notwithstanding the fact that the forum will not be as appropriate as the youth court. The younger the defendant is, so the stronger the presumption that he/she should be tried in the youth court. In *CPS v. Newcastle upon Tyne Youth Court* (2010) EWHC 2773 (Admin) the Court considered the question of jurisdiction where a 17-year-old was charged with rape. The judgement of Mr Justice Langstaff deals with the application of s.24 in detail particularly in relation to the application of Sentencing Guidelines.

(4) In *R. (W. F. and B.) v. DPP*, DC, January 13, 2006, the decision of a Youth Court to decline jurisdiction in respect of a 12-year-old defendant charged with raping a 13-year-old was upheld. However, the Court stated that it was possible that there were circumstances in which it would be appropriate for a Youth Court to accept jurisdiction in cases of rape. The definition of rape contained in the *Sexual Offences Act* 2003 now covers a much wider range of sexual activity than had previously been the case. Therefore, in deciding jurisdiction the Youth Court must consider each case on its own facts. The Youth Court will now be a suitable venue for the trial of many such cases. See also *CPS v. Newcastle upon Tyne Youth Court* (2010) EWHC 2773 (Admin).

The procedure to be adopted for Sexual Offences in the Youth Court is now set out in a Protocol issued by the Senior Presiding Judge dated 31.3.10. This is dealt with in detail at § 25–37, *post*.

(5) In deciding whether it ought to be possible to sentence a defendant to detention under s.91 the youth court must consider the sentencing powers of the Crown Court and the guidance given on the exercise of those powers. If there is no real possibility of such a sentence, committal is inappropriate. In assessing a likely sentence, the youth court should take into account the age of the defendant. Youths aged 15 to 17 years will receive a substantially shorter sentence of custody than adults convicted of a similar crime. Those aged between 10 and 12 years are unlikely to receive any custodial sentence unless the crime is extremely grave. The same applies to the 12 to 15 age group unless they are persistent young offenders. Only in exceptional circumstances will it be appropriate to pass a sentence of less than two years detention under s.91 on a defendant who would be eligible for a detention and training order were he not too young for such an order to be made. This issue was considered in *Manchester City Youth Court* [2002] 1 Cr.App.R.(S.) 573 and in *W. v. Thetford Youth Justices v. DPP* [2003] 1 Cr.App.R.(S.) 67. In his judgment Gage J. said:

"in respect of offenders under 15 a custodial sentence will ordinarily only be available in the form of a detention and training order. If the court is prohibited from making such an order in general an order under section 91 will not be appropriate. I remain of the opinion that where an offence or offences are likely to attract a sentence of less than two years custody the appropriate sentence will be a detention and training order. In the case of an offender under 15, who is not a persistent offender, or a child under 12, the most likely sentence will be non-custodial sentence. It follows that in most cases the appropriate place of trial will be the youth court. I remain of the view that the mere fact that a youth court, unable to make a short detention and training order, considers that the option to pass a short custodial sentence should be available, does not mean that it should decline jurisdiction. It seems to me that Parliament intended that generally a non-custodial sentence should be passed. Perhaps it would be better to say that cases involving offenders under 15 for whom a detention and training order is not available will only rarely attract a period of detention under section 91; the more rarely if the offender is under 12".

See also *Balham Youth Court, ex p. R. (Admin)*, unreported, September 13, 2002.

In *C. v. Balham Youth Court* (2003) 167 J.P. 525, QBD the youth court declined jurisdiction in dealing with a 14-year-old charged with robbery. On appeal the court held that where an offender is not able to be made the subject of a custodial sentence in the youth court because of his age, he should only be committed to the Crown Court for trial if a sentence of two years of more could be expected or if there were exceptional circumstances. The court stated that there was a general principle that first time offenders aged 13 or 14 should not be detained in custody and it was only rarely that a youth under 15 should be give a custodial sentence of under two years. **25–31**

In the case of *A.* (2005) CA (Crim. Div.) June 14, 2005 it was emphasised that youths aged 15–17 years will receive a substantially shorter sentence of custody than adults convicted of a similar crime.

25–32 This approach has been firmly emphasised in two further cases. In *R. (M.W.) v. West London Youth Court* [2004] EWHC 1144, two 14-year-old defendants were charged with robbery of a mobile telephone. Both were of good character and appealed against the decision of the youth court to decline jurisdiction. Allowing their appeal, it was held that neither defendant faced the real possibility of a sentence of, or approaching, two years in length and that therefore, the youth court should have retained jurisdiction. Subsequently, in the case of *R. (H.A. and O.) v. Southampton Youth Court* [2005] 2 Cr.App.R.(S.) 30, the three 13-year-old defendants were charged with indecent assault on a male of the same age. The circumstances of the assault were such that the youth court declined jurisdiction. On appeal it was held that jurisdiction should have been retained. In the course of his judgment, Leveson J. sought to summarise the law in a way that could be put before the youth court whenever this issue arose as follows:

(a) The general policy of the legislator is that those who are under 18 years of age and in particular children of under 15 years of age should, wherever possible, be tried in the youth court. A trial in the Crown Court with the inevitably greater formality and greatly increased number of people involved (including a jury and the public) should be reserved for the most serious of cases.

(b) It is a further policy of the legislature that, generally speaking, first time offenders aged 12–14 and all offenders under 12 should not be detained in custody and decisions as to jurisdiction should have regard to the fact that the exceptional power to detain for grave offences should not be used to water down the general principle. Those under 15 will rarely attract a period of detention and, even more rarely, those who are under 12.

(c) In each case the Court should ask itself whether there is a real prospect, having regard to his/her age, that this defendant whose case they are considering might require a sentence of, or in excess of, two years or, alternatively, whether although the sentence might be less than two years, there is some unusual feature of the case which justifies declining jurisdiction, bearing in mind that the absence of the power to impose a detention and training order because the defendant is under 15 is not an unusual feature. See SGC overarching principles 12.11 (see § 27–14, *post*) and also *CPS v. Newcastle upon Tyne Youth Court* (2010) EWHC 2883 (Admin). It would now seem that the Youth Court must contemplate a sentence at the Crown Court of something no less than $2^1/_2$ years or more as being a real possibility.

In deciding the issue of jurisdiction in relation to defendants of different age groups it is submitted that the following principles should be applied. The reader is also referred to see "Overarching Principles" at § 27–13, *post*.

(3) Defendants aged 10 or 11 years of age

25–33 Such defendants should only be committed to the Crown Court when charged with exceptionally serious offences of such gravity that in spite of his/her age a custodial sentence exceeding two years is a realistic possibility. Committal to the Crown Court in other circumstances will be rare. In *T.*, CA (Crim. Div.), November 9, 2004, a 10-year-old pleaded guilty to robbery, false imprisonment, and inflicting grievous bodily harm. He was sentenced to three years' detention under s.91. On appeal it was emphasised that it was very rare for a Court to make such an order in respect of such a young defendant. However, in this particular case it was essential both in the public interest and in the long term interest of the appellant himself. An unusual feature of the case is that the pre-sentence report also recommended a s.91 order in view of the circumstances of the offence and the defendant's chaotic and traumatic childhood.

(4) Defendants aged 12, 13 and 14 years

(a) *Non-persistent offenders*

The youth court has no power to make detention and training orders in respect of this age group unless it finds that the defendant is a persistent offender. For definition of "persistent offender" see *post*, § 27–79. **25–34**

If this is not the case there is a very strong presumption that trial should take place in the youth court. If, however, the youth court finds that in all the circumstances of the case the sentencing court ought to have available to it power to impose a custodial sentence greater than two years then, in spite of the defendants age, it should commit to the Crown Court.

(b) *Persistent young offenders*

If the defendant is a persistent offender the youth court has power to impose a detention and training order of up to two years. If, in spite of the defendant's young age, the youth court finds that there is a real possibility that a sentence in excess of two years will be imposed, and that therefore the sentencing court ought to have such powers available to it, the youth court should commit for trial. **25–35**

(5) Defendants aged 15, 16 and 17 years

The youth court has power to make a detention and training order up to a maximum of two years for this age group whether or not they are persistent offenders. In dealing with jurisdiction the youth court must ask itself whether the circumstances of the alleged crime are so serious that the sentencing court ought to have available to it powers of custody exceeding two years and that such a sentence is more than a vague or theoretical possibility. **25–36**

Once a youth court has made a decision retaining jurisdiction, albeit in ignorance of a legal provision, the only power to review such decision is limited to the circumstances specified in s.25 of the *Magistrates' Courts Act* 1980: *Grimsby and Cleethorpes Magistrates' Court* [2004] EWHC 2240.

The preferred way to challenge the decision of a youth court to accept jurisdiction is by way of Judicial Review and not an application for a voluntary bill of indictment: *R. (DPP) the Camberwell Youth Court, The Times*, August 12, 2004, QB.

VI. SEXUAL OFFENCES IN THE YOUTH COURT

A Protocol has been issued by the Senior Presiding Judge dated 31.3.10 setting out a procedure to be applied in the Youth Court in all cases involving allegations of sexual offences which are capable of being committed for trial at the Crown Court under the Grave Crimes provisions. **25–37**

In summary the procedure is:

(a) such cases should be listed before an authorised District Judge (Magistrates Court) to decide whether jurisdiction should be retained or the case committed to the Crown Court for trial.

(b) If jurisdiction is retained and the allegation involved actual, or attempted, penetrative activity, the case must be tried by an authorised DJ(MC).

(c) If the allegation is not of that nature the authorised DJ(MC) must consider whether it is so serious and/or complex that it must be tried by an authorised DJ(MC), or whether the case is suitable to be heard on any DJ(MC) or any Youth Court Bench.

(d) If it is not practicable for an authorised DJ(MC) to decide jurisdiction any DJ(MC) or any Youth Court Bench may consider that issue. If jurisdiction is retained the case papers, including a detailed case summary and a note of any representations made by the parties must be sent to an authorised DJ(MC) to

Part V

consider. That DJ(MC) must decide whether the case should be tried by an authorised DJ(MC) or whether it is suitable to be heard by any DJ(MC) or any Youth Court Bench. If the case involves actual, or alleged, penetrative activity, the trial must be heard by an authorised DJ(MC).

(e) In all cases involving actual or alleged penetrative activity or in cases that must be tried by a DJ(MC), all further procedural hearings should, as far as practicable, be heard by an authorised DJ(MC).

A number of District Judge (Magistrates' Courts) have been specifically authorised to hear cases involving serious sexual offence which fall short of requiring committal to the Crown Court.

VII. DANGEROUS DEFENDANTS IN THE YOUTH COURT

A. DANGEROUS OFFENDERS AND GRAVE CRIMES

25–38 The *Criminal Justice Act* 2003 creates new powers of sentencing designed to protect the public from dangerous offenders. The new sentences are not available to the youth court, whose powers of custodial sentence remain unchanged. However, the Act gives the youth court powers to send youths to the Crown Court for trial or to commit them for sentence to the Crown Court if they are charged or convicted of a "specified offence". Schedule 15 to the *Criminal Justice Act* 2003 sets out some 153 offences which are so specified. If a youth appears before the youth court and is charged or convicted of a specified offence "dangerousness" must be considered. Some of the "specified" offences are also offences that are mentioned under *PCC(S)A* 2000, s.91 (see *ante*, § 25–25). These offences are therefore both specified offences and grave crimes under section 91. In such circumstances the youth court must consider both procedures.

B. PRE-TRIAL PROCEDURE

Criminal Justice Act 2003, Sched. 3, para. 18

25–39 18. For section 51 [of the *Crime and Disorder Act* 1998] (no committal proceedings for indictable-only offences) there is substituted—

Sending cases to the Crown Court: children and young persons

51A.—(1) This section is subject to sections 24A and 24B of the *Magistrates' Courts Act* 1980 (which provide for certain offences involving children or young persons to be tried summarily).

(2) Where a child or young person appears or is brought before a magistrates' court ("the court") charged with an offence and any of the conditions mentioned in subsection (3) below is satisfied, the court shall send him forthwith to the Crown Court for trial for the offence.

(3) Those conditions are—

(d) that the offence is a specified offence (within the meaning of section 224 of the *Criminal Justice Act* 2003) and it appears to the court that if he is found guilty of the offence the criteria for the imposition of a sentence under section 226(3) or 228(2) of that Act would be met.

[Note, section 51A(3)(d) is the only part of this section that presently applies.]

25–40 This section requires a child or young person to be sent from the youth court to the Crown Court for trial if he is charged with a specified offence and it appears to the youth court that if he were convicted of it the criteria for the imposition of an indeterminate sentence under s.226 of the 2003 Act or an extended sentence under s.228 of the 2003 Act would be met. The assessment of dangerousness is made under the provisions of s.229 of the *Criminal Justice Act* 2003, see *post*.

In the case of *R. (DPP) v. South East Surrey Youth Court* [2006] 1 W.L.R. 2543 the DPP applied for judicial review of a decision of the youth court declining to send a youth for trial at the Crown Court under the dangerousness procedure for an offence of assault occasioning actual bodily harm (a specified offence). The Court had committed the defendant for trial to the Crown Court in respect of a completely separate charge of robbery under the s.91 *PCC(S)A* procedure. On appeal the Court emphasised it was not open to the youth court to ignore the provisions of s.51A of the 2003 Act. However, in considering the applicability of s.51A the youth court should bear in mind the following factors:

(1) The policy is that those who are under 18 should wherever possible be tried in a youth court which is designed for their specific needs.

(2) The youth court should bear in mind the guidance given in the case of *Lang*— (see *post*) to non-serious specified offences.

(3) In relation to defendants under 18 years of age there is a need to be particularly rigorous before concluding that there is a significant risk of serious harm by the commission of further specified offences. Such a conclusion is unlikely to be appropriate in the absence of a pre-sentence report following assessment by a youth offender team.

(4) In most cases where a non-serious specified offence was charged, an assessment of dangerousness would not be appropriate until after conviction when, if the dangerous criteria were met, the defendant could then be committed to the Crown Court for sentence.

In *B. v. Barking Youth Court* [2006] EWHC 2121 (Admin), the 16-year-old defendant sought to judicially review the decision of the youth court to send him for trial to the Crown Court under the provisions of s.51A (see *ante*). The defendant was charged with robbery (a specified offence) in which passengers on the London Underground at night were threatened, and their property taken. On appeal the Court repeated the judgment in the *South East Surrey Youth Court* case (*ante*). It was clearly desirable that criminal process against young defendants be dealt with expeditiously and those advising such offenders should use their best endeavours to obtain reports on the dangerousness issue at an early stage. In this case no such reports had been obtained but the defence had not asked for an adjournment to do so. In all the circumstances the magistrates were entitled to conclude that the dangerousness criteria had been met. The appeal was dismissed.

C. POST-CONVICTION PROCEDURE

Powers of the Criminal Courts (Sentencing) Act 2000, s.3C

Committal for sentence of dangerous young offenders

3C.—(1) This section applies where on the summary trial of a specified offence a person aged under 18 is convicted of the offence. **25–41**

(2) If, in relation to the offence, it appears to the court that the criteria for the imposition of a sentence under section 226(3) or 228(2) of the *Criminal Justice Act* 2003 would be met, the court must commit the offender in custody or on bail to the Crown Court for sentence in accordance with section 5A(1) below.

(3) Where the court commits a person under subsection (2) above, section 6 below (which enables a magistrates' court, where it commits a person under this section in respect of an offence, also to commit him to the Crown Court to be dealt with in respect of certain other offences) shall apply accordingly.

(4) Nothing in this section shall prevent the court from committing a specified offence to the Crown Court for sentence under section 3B above if the provisions of that section are satisfied.

(5) In this section, references to a specified offence are to a specified offence within the meaning of section 224 of the *Criminal Justice Act* 2003.

This section above allows the youth court to commit to the Crown Court for sentence defendants who have been convicted of a specified offence if the dangerousness provisions apply. The cases of *R. (DPP) v. South East Surrey Youth Court* (see *ante*, § 25–40) and *Lang* (see *post*, § 25–45) both give helpful guidance on the approach to be taken in dealing with young defendants. **25–42**

The assessment of dangerousness

25–43 Before deciding whether to send a youth to the Crown Court for trial or commit him for sentence after conviction under the above provisions the youth court must assess "dangerousness" if the charge or conviction is for a specified offence.

Criminal Justice Act 2003, s.229(1), (2)

The assessment of dangerousness

25–44 **229.**—(1) This section applies where—

(a) a person has been convicted of a specified offence, and

(b) it falls to a court to assess under any of sections 225 to 228 whether there is a significant risk to members of the public of serious harm occasioned by the commission by him of further such offences.

(2) If at the time when that offence was committed the offender had not been convicted in any part of the United Kingdom of any relevant offence or was aged under 18, the court in making the assessment referred to in subsection (1)(b)—

(a) must take into account all such information as is available to it about the nature and circumstances of the offence,

(b) may take into account any information which is before it about any pattern of behaviour of which the offence forms part, and

(c) may take into account any information about the offender which is before it.

25–45 This section sets out matters to be taken into account by the youth court in assessing dangerousness. In *Lang* [2006] 1 W.L.R. 2509 the Court of Appeal dealt with a number of cases relating to dangerousness and gave guidance as to the principles applicable to the new sentences for both adults and youths. In relation to those under 18 the court emphasised the importance of bearing in mind the capacity of young people to change and develop for the better. In respect of youths this approach was further developed in the case of *R. (DPP) v. South East Surrey Youth Court* (see *ante*, § 25–40). It seems that both youth and adult courts at all levels have found the "dangerousness" provisions complex and somewhat confusing. It is to be hoped that this will be ended by the full implementation of the provisions of the *CJA* 2003. The reader is referred to *D. (Hollie Louise)* [2006] 1 Cr.App.R.(S.) 104, which sets out the Court of Appealapproach to the sentencing of a 13-year-old girl convicted of a number of specified offences. The reader is also referred to the case of *Shaffi (Zulfiqar)* [2006] 2 Cr.App.R.(S.) 92. This case involves an adult appellant. However, the judgment of the court emphasises the need for a significant evidential basis before establishing that a victim had suffered serious psychological harm within the meaning of the Act.

See Specific Sentences, *ante*, §§ 23–110–23–123.

The reader is referred to the SGC Overarching Principles at § 27–13, *post*.

25–46 Since a young offender should normally be dealt with in a youth court, where a young person charged with a specified offence would not otherwise be committed or sent to the Crown Court for trial, generally it is preferable for the decision whether to commit under these provisions to be made after conviction.

Chapter 26

BAIL IN THE YOUTH COURT

I. INTRODUCTION

The youth court has power to remand a young person on bail, into local authority accommodation (with or without a security requirement) or into custody. The powers vary greatly, dependant upon the age and gender of the defendant as shown on the flow charts (see *post*, §§ 26–29—26–31). **26–1**

The initial decision to be made by the youth court is whether bail, conditional or unconditional, should be granted.

The *Bail Act* 1976 applies to all youths, the only difference being that the accused may be refused bail for his "own welfare" rather than his "own protection", as is the case with adult offenders: *Bail Act* 1976, Sched. 1. The presumption in favour of granting unconditional bail contained in s.4 of the *Bail Act* 1976 applies equally to youths. It is only if bail is refused that the complex provisions of s.23 of the *CYPA* 1969 have to be invoked.

In deciding whether to grant bail, with or without conditions, the court must take into account its statutory duties to prevent offending and also consider the welfare of the defendant. The Youth Offending Team (YOT) plays a vital role in any application for bail. More especially, the YOT will provide the court with up to date information relating to: **26–2**

(a) the defendant's antecedents;
(b) his record in complying with previous bail conditions and any community penalties including referral orders;
(c) his home situation, health and welfare;
(d) confirmation of his attendance at school, college or work.

In addition, the YOT will investigate the viability of appropriate bail conditions which may meet the concerns of the court especially by way of a Bail Support Programme or an Intensive Supervision and Surveillance Programme (ISSP), see *post*, § 26–7.

If a remand into custody is contemplated by the court, the YOT will, in the case of 15 and 16–year–old males, carry out the "vulnerability" assessment as required by s.23(5A) of the *CYPA* 1969, (see *post*, § 26–19).

A remand into local authority accommodation is a refusal of bail and custody time limits apply in the same way as to a remand into custody.

Under s.115 of the *Coroners and Justice Act* 2009 the magistrates' court was prohibited from considering the issue of bail in respect of a defendant charged with murder (see § 5–2a, *ante*). The section is silent on the position of children and young persons facing such a charge but in *R. (A.) Lewisham Youth Court v. DPP* [2011] EWHC 1193 Admin it was held that a Youth Court cannot grant bail to a child or young person charged with murder as that is a decision for the Crown Court but in determining the form of custody for such a defendant the Youth Court should still apply the criteria of s.23 of the *Children and Young Persons Act* 1969 as they would in any other case (see *post*, § 26–10 *et seq*).

Part V

II. THE BAIL APPLICATION

26–3 When the defendant is charged with offences that are not imprisonable, bail may only be refused in the circumstances specified in Sched. 1, Pt II of the 1976 Act. These circumstances are:

(1) The defendant has previously refused to surrender to bail, and in view of that failure, the court believes that the defendant would fail to surrender if released on bail on this occasion: Sched. 1, Pt II, para. 2.
(2) The court is satisfied that the defendant should be kept in custody for his own welfare: Sched. 1, Pt II, para. 3.
(3) The defendant is in custody in pursuance of a sentence of a court or of any authority acting under any of the Service Acts: Sched. 1, Pt II, para. 4.
(4) The defendant has been arrested under the 1976 Act for failing to surrender to the custody of the court or for being in breach of conditions of bail or likely to be in breach of such conditions: Sched. 1, Pt II, para. 5.

26–4 When the defendant is charged with offences that are punishable with imprisonment in the case of an adult offender, bail may be refused only in the circumstances specified in Sched. 1, Pt 1 of the 1976 Act. These circumstances are:

(1) The court is satisfied that there are substantial grounds for believing that the defendant would fail to surrender to custody, commit an offence whilst on bail, or interfere with witnesses or otherwise obstruct the course of justice whether in relation to himself or another person: Sched. 1, Pt I, para. 2.
(2) The defendant is charged with or convicted of an indictable offence (whether or not triable either way) committed whilst on bail in criminal proceedings: Sched. 1, Pt I, para. 2A.
(3) The defendant is in custody in pursuance of a sentence of a court or of any authority acting under any of the *Service Acts*: Sched. 1, Pt 1, para. 3.
(4) The court is satisfied that it has not been practicable to obtain sufficient information for the purpose of taking the decisions required regarding bail due to lack of time since the proceedings started: Sched. 1, Pt I, para 5
(5) The defendant had been released on bail in or in connection with proceedings for an offence, and had been arrested under s.7 of the 1976 Act for failing to surrender to the custody of the court or being in breach of conditions of bail or likely to be in breach of such conditions: Sched. 1, Pt I, para. 6.
(6) Where the court is adjourned for enquiries or for a report to be prepared and it a ppears to the court impracticable to complete the inquiries or make the report unless the defendant is kept in custody: Sched. 1, Pt I, para. 7.

(1) Conditions on bail

26–5 Conditions may be imposed following a grant of bail in the circumstances described in para. 8 of Sched. 1, Pt I to the 1976 Act. These circumstances are when the court believes the conditions imposed are necessary to prevent a failure to surrender to custody, the commission of an offence whilst on bail or the interference with witnesses or any other obstruction of justice. Conditions may also be imposed if they are necessary for the purpose of enabling further inquiries to be made or a report to be made to assist the court in dealing with the offence.

Where the defendant is aged 17 years, electronic tagging may be used to monitor his compliance with the relevant conditions: *Bail Act* 1976, s.3.

Where the defendant is aged between 12 and 16 years electronic tagging may be used in accordance with the conditions laid down in s.3AA of the 1976 Act.

Bail Act 1976, s.3AA(1)–(5), (11)

Conditions for the imposition of electronic monitoring requirements: children and young persons

26–6 **3AA.**—(1) A court may not impose electronic monitoring requirements on a child or young person unless each of the following conditions is met.

(2) The first condition is that the child or young person has attained the age of twelve years.

(3) The second condition is that—

(a) the child or young person is charged with or has been convicted of a violent or sexual offence, or an offence punishable in the case of an adult with imprisonment for a term of fourteen years or more; or

(b) he is charged with or has been convicted of one or more imprisonable offences which, together with any other imprisonable offences of which he has been convicted in any proceedings—

(i) amount, or

(ii) would, if he were convicted of the offences with which he is charged, amount, to a recent history of repeatedly committing imprisonable offences while remanded on bail or to local authority accommodation.

(4) The third condition is that the court is satisfied that the necessary provision for dealing with the person concerned can be made under arrangements for the electronic monitoring of persons released on bail that are currently available in each local justice area which is a relevant area.

(5) The fourth condition is that a youth offending team has informed the court that in its opinion the imposition of electronic monitoring requirements will be suitable in the case of the child or young person.

(6)–(10) [Omitted]

(11) In this section "local authority accommodation" has the same meaning as in the *Children and Young Persons Act* 1969 (c. 54).

(12) [Omitted]

[This section is printed as amended by the *Criminal Justice and Immigration Act* 2008, Sched. 11 and the *Criminal Justice and Immigration Act* 2008 (Commencement No.3 and Transitional Provisions) Order 2008 (S.I. 2008 No.2712) which came into force on November 3, 2008.]

(2) Intensive Supervision and Surveillance Programme (ISSP)

This programme is intended for the most prolific and serious young offenders. **26–7**
Complete guidance is set out in relation to Supervision Orders (see sentencing—*post*, §§ 27–42 *et seq.*). The principal aim, when used as part of a bail package or as part of the conditions relating to a remand into local authority accommodation, is to prevent the commission of further offences. This is achieved by addressing the needs of young offenders by placing a particular emphasis on education and training. The programme is available for 10- to 17-year-olds but eligibility requires that the defendant fulfils the necessary criteria (see *post*, §§ 27–61—27–65).

Electronic tagging is available but not voice verification. The YOT will carry out an assessment as to suitability and make proposals on the content of the ISSP. Advocates and courts should be aware that the ISSP programme is a limited resource. It is a non-statutory scheme funded by the Youth Justice Board and even if a defendant is deemed a suitable candidate there may not be an ISSP programme available within the defendant's local authority.

Part V

III. REFUSAL OF BAIL

(1) Remands available following a refusal of bail

Options available to the court are entirely dependant on the age and gender of the **26–8**
defendant.

(a) *Defendants aged 10 or 11 years*

(i) Remand to a local authority under section 23 of the Children Act 1989

Following a refusal of bail, the defendant must be remanded to local authority ac- **26–9** commodation, with or without conditions, under s.23 of the *Children and Young Persons Act* 1969.

Children and Young Persons Act 1969, s.23

Remands and committals to local authority accommodation

26–10 **23.**—(1) Where—

(a) a court remands a child or young person charged with or convicted of one or more offences or commits him for trial or sentence; and

(b) he is not released on bail,

the remand or committal shall be to local authority accommodation; and in the following provisions of this section, any reference (however expressed) to a remand shall be construed as including a reference to a committal.

(2) A court remanding a person to local authority accommodation shall designate the local authority who are to receive him; and that authority shall be—

(a) in the case of a person who is being looked after by a local authority, that authority; and

(b) in any other case, the local authority in whose area it appears to the court that he resides or the offence or one of the offences was committed.

(3) Where a person is remanded to local authority accommodation, it shall be lawful for any person acting on behalf of the designated authority to detain him.

(4)–(6) [security requirements, see below]

(7) Subject to section 23AA below, a court remanding a person to local authority accommodation without imposing a security requirement may, after consultation with the designated authority, require that person to comply with

(a) any such conditions as could be imposed under section 3(6) of the *Bail Act* 1976 if he were then being granted bail; and

(b) any conditions imposed for the purpose of securing the electronic monitoring of his compliance with any other condition imposed under this subsection.

(7A) [security requirements, see below]

(7B) [security requirements, see below]

(8) Where a court imposes on a person any such conditions as are mentioned in subsection (7) above, it shall be its duty to explain to him in open court and in ordinary language why it is imposing those conditions; and a magistrates' court shall cause a reason stated by it under this subsection to be specified in the warrant of commitment and to be entered in the register.

(9) A court remanding a person to local authority accommodation without imposing a security requirement may, after consultation with the designated authority, impose on that authority requirements—

(a) for securing compliance with any conditions imposed on that person under subsection (7) above; or

(b) stipulating that he shall not be placed with a named person.

(10) Where a person is remanded to local authority accommodation, a relevant court—

(a) may, on the application of the designated authority, impose on that person any such conditions as could be imposed under subsection (7) above if the court were then remanding him to such accommodation; and

(b) where it does so, may impose on that authority any requirements for securing compliance with the conditions so imposed.

(11) Where a person is remanded to local authority accommodation, a relevant court may, on the application of the designated authority or that person, vary or revoke any conditions or requirements imposed under subsections (7), (9) or (10) above.

(12) In this section—

"children's home" has the same meaning as in the *Care Standards Act* 2000;

"court" and "magistrates' court" include a justice;

"imprisonable offence" means an offence punishable in the case of an adult with imprisonment;

"prescribed description" means a description prescribed by reference to age or sex or both by an order of the Secretary of State;

"relevant court", in relation to a person remanded to local authority accommodation, means the court by which he was so remanded, or any magistrates' court having jurisdiction in the place where he is for the time being;

"secure accommodation" means accommodation which is provided in a children's home in respect of which a person is registered under Part II of the *Care Standards Act* 2000 for the purpose of restricting liberty, and is approved for that purpose by the Secretary of State or the National Assembly for Wales;

"sexual offence" and "violent offence" have the same meanings as in the *PCC(S)A* 2000;

"young person" means a person who has attained the age of fourteen years and is under the age of seventeen years.

but, for the purposes of the definition of "secure accommodation", "local authority accommodation" includes any accommodation falling within section 61(2) of the *Criminal Justice Act* 1991.

(13) In this section—

(a) any reference to a person who is being looked after by a local authority shall be construed in accordance with section 22 of the *Children Act* 1989;

(b) any reference to consultation shall be construed as a reference to such consultation (if any) as is reasonably practicable in all the circumstances of the case; and

(c) any reference, in relation to a person charged with or convicted of a violent or sexual offence, to protecting the public from serious harm from him shall be construed as a reference to protecting members of the public from death or serious personal injury, whether physical or psychological, occasioned by further such offences committed by him.

(14) This section has effect subject to—

(b) section 128(7) of that Act (remands to the custody of a constable for periods of not more than three days),

but section 128(7) shall have effect in relation to a child or young person as if for the reference to three clear days there were substituted a reference to twenty-four hours.

Electronic monitoring may not be used to monitor compliance with the local authority remand conditions. **26–11**

(ii) Remand in secure accommodation under s.25 of the Children Act 1989

Power exists under the *Children Act* 1989 to make a Secure Accommodation order. **26–12**
This power exists under the civil jurisdiction of the court. If the court indicate to the YOT that the availability of secure accommodation should be investigated and invite the YOT to make enquiries, the YOT *may* subsequently make an application for such an order on behalf of the local authority in which the defendant is ordinarily resident. It is entirely an issue for the local authority as to whether this application is made or not.

Children Act 1989, s.25

Use of accommodation for restricting liberty

25.—(1) Subject to the following provisions of this section, a child who is being looked after **26–13**
by a local authority may not be placed, and, if placed, may not be kept, in accommodation provided for the purpose of restricting liberty ("secure accommodation") unless it appears—

(a) that—

(i) he has a history of absconding and is likely to abscond from any other description of accommodation; and

(ii) if he absconds, he is likely to suffer significant harm; or

(b) that if he is kept in any other description of accommodation he is likely to injure himself or other persons.

(2) [powers of Secretary of State]

(3) It shall be the duty of a court hearing an application under this section to determine whether any relevant criteria for keeping a child in secure accommodation are satisfied in his case.

(4) If a court determines that any such criteria are satisfied, it shall make an order authorising the child to be kept in secure accommodation and specifying the maximum period for which he may be so kept.

(5) On any adjournment of the hearing of an application under this section, a court may make an interim order permitting the child to be kept during the period of the adjournment in secure accommodation.

(6) No court shall exercise the powers conferred by this section in respect of a child who is not legally represented in that court unless, having been informed of his right to apply for representation funded by the Legal Services Commission as part of the Community Legal Service or Criminal Defence Service and having had the opportunity to do so, he refused or failed to apply.

(7) [powers of Secretary of State]

(8) The giving of an authorisation under this section shall not prejudice any power of any court in England and Wales or Scotland to give directions relating to the child to whom the authorisation relates.

(9) This section is subject to section 20(8).

26–14 Regulation 4 of the *Children (Secure Accommodation) Regulations* 1991 provides that a child under 13 may only be placed in secure accommodation with the approval of the Secretary of State for Health. Regulation 5(2)(a) provides that 16- and 17-year-olds accommodated under s.20(5) of the *Children Act* 1989 (which allows the local authority to provide accommodation for any person aged 16 to 20 years if they consider that doing so would safeguard or promote his own welfare) may not be placed in secure accommodation. Children detained under any provision of the *Mental Health Act* 1983 may not be the subject of an order under section 25.

Proceedings for a secure accommodation order are not criminal proceedings within the meaning of Art. 6 of the ECHR: *Re C. (A Child) (Secure Accommodation order: Representation)* (2001) 2 F.L.R 169. However, a child facing such an application is entitled to the minimum rights to a fair trial set out in Art. 6(3) of the European Convention. The requirement that the defendant is legally represented may, in exceptional cases, be satisfied where the defendant's solicitor is only served with the application on the day of the hearing. However, the preferred course of action in such circumstances would be the making of an interim order under s.25(5) of the *Children Act* 1989, which would authorise further detention in secure accommodation, and allow the defence adequate time to prepare its case: *Re C. (ante), per* Thorpe and Brooke L.JJ.

26–15 A court may make a secure accommodation order under s.25 of the *Children Act* 1989 where the criteria for detention in secure accommodation in s.23 of the *Children and Young Persons Act* are not satisfied: *Re G. (A Child) (Secure Accommodation order)* (2001) 1 F.L.R. 884. However, where a child has been remanded to local authority accommodation under s.23 of the *Children and Young Persons Act* 1969, the court may only make an order for secure accommodation where the criteria in reg.6(2) of the *Children (Secure Accommodation) Regulations* 1991 are satisfied: *Re W. and D. (Secure Accommodation)* [1995] 2 F.L.R. 807.

(b) *Defendants aged 12, 13 or 14 years, and girls aged 15 or 16*

(i) Remand in secure accommodation following refusal of bail

26–16 The court has the same powers to remand to local authority accommodation following refusal of bail as it does in the context of defendants aged 10 or 11 years. The additional powers are:

— The court may, after consultation with the YOT, impose a security requirement requiring the local authority to place and keep the youth in secure accommodation. A security requirement is defined in s.23(4) of the 1969 Act as a requirement that the youth be placed in secure accommodation, which is described in s.23(12) of the 1969 Act as accommodation which is provided in a children's home in respect of which a person is registered under Pt II of the *Care Standards Act* 2000 for the purpose of restricting liberty. The conditions relating to the imposition of a security requirement are contained in s.23 of the 1969 Act.

— The provisions of the *CYPA* 1969, s.23AA can be made as a requirement of a remand into local authority accomodation.

(ii) Electronic monitoring on remand to local authority accommodation

Children and Young Persons Act 1969, s.23AA(1)–(6)

Electronic monitoring of conditions of remand

23AA.—(1) A court shall not impose a condition on a person under section 23(7)(b) above (an "electronic monitoring condition") unless each of the following requirements is fulfilled. **26–17**

(2) The first requirement is that the person has attained the age of twelve years.

(3) The second requirement is that—

(a) the person is charged with or has been convicted of a violent or sexual offence, or an offence punishable in the case of an adult with imprisonment for a term of fourteen years or more; or

(b) he is charged with or has been convicted of one or more imprisonable offence which, together with any other imprisonable offences of which he has been convicted in any proceedings—

(i) amount, or

(ii) would, if he were convicted of the offences with which he is charged, amount,

to a recent history of repeatedly committing imprisonable offences while remanded on bail or to local authority accommodation.

(4) The third requirement is that the court—

(a) has been notified by the Secretary of State that electronic monitoring arrangements are available in each petty sessions area which is a relevant area; and

(b) is satisfied that the necessary provision can be made under those arrangements.

(5) The fourth requirement is that a youth offending team has informed the court that in its opinion the imposition of such a condition will be suitable in the person's case.

(6) Where a court imposes an electronic monitoring condition, the condition shall include provision for making a person responsible for the monitoring; and a person who is made so responsible shall be of a description specified in an order made by the Secretary of State.

Thus, the court must consider the following questions when considering the use of electronic monitoring: **26–18**

(1) Is the youth aged 12–16?

(2) Is the offence a violent or sexual offence? OR

(3) Does it carry a punishment of 14 years or more in the case of an adult offender? OR

(4) Is the defendant charged with or convicted of one or more imprisonable offences which together with any other imprisonable offences which relate to the defendant amounts to or would amount to a recent history of repeatedly committing imprisonable offences whilst remanded on bail or remanded to local authority accommodation?

(iii) Security requirement

Children and Young Persons Act 1969, s.23(4)–(5A), (6), (7A)–(8)

23.—(4) Subject to subsections (5) and (5A) below, a court remanding a person to local authority accommodation may, after consultation with the designated authority, require that authority to comply with a security requirement, that is to say, a requirement that the person in question be placed and kept in secure accommodation. **26–19**

(5) A court shall not impose a security requirement except in respect of a child who has attained the age of twelve, or a young person, who (in either case) is of a prescribed description, and then only if—

(a) he is charged with or has been convicted of a violent or sexual offence, or an of-

Part V

fence punishable in the case of an adult with imprisonment for a term of fourteen years or more; or

(b) he is charged with or has been convicted of one or more imprisonable offences which, together with any other imprisonable offences of which he has been convicted in any proceedings—

(i) amount, or

(ii) would, if he were convicted of the offences with which he is charged, amount,

to a recent history of repeatedly committing imprisonable offences while remanded on bail or to local authority accommodation,

and (in either case) the condition set out in subsection (5AA) below is satisfied.

(5AA) The condition mentioned in subsection (5) above is that the court is of the opinion, after considering all the options for the remand of the person, that only remanding him to local authority accommodation with a security requirement would be adequate—

(a) to protect the public from serious harm from him; or

(b) to prevent the commission by him of imprisonable offences.

(5A) A court shall not impose a security requirement in respect of a child or young person who is not legally represented in the court unless—

(a) he was granted a right to representation funded by the Legal Services Commission as part of the Criminal Defence Service but the right was withdrawn because of his conduct or because it appeared that his financial resources were such that he was not eligible to be granted such a right;

(aa) he applied for such representation and the application was refused because it appeared that his financial resources were such that he was not eligible to be granted a right to it; or

(b) having been informed of his right to apply for such representation and had the opportunity to do so, he refused or failed to apply.

(6) Where a court imposes a security requirement in respect of a person, it shall be its duty—

(a) to state in open court that it is of such opinion as is mentioned in subsection (5AA) above; and

(b) to explain to him in open court and in ordinary language why it is of that opinion;

and a magistrates' court shall cause a reason stated by it under paragraph (b) above to be specified in the warrant of commitment and to be entered in the register.

(7A) Where a person is remanded to local authority accommodation and a security requirement is imposed in respect of him—

(a) the designated local authority may, with the consent of the Secretary of State, arrange for the person to be detained, for the whole or any part of the period of the remand or committal, in a secure training centre; and

(b) his detention there pursuant to the arrangements shall be lawful.

(7B) Arrangements under subsection (7A) above may include provision for payments to be made by the authority to the Secretary of State.

(8) Where a court imposes on a person any such conditions as are mentioned in subsection (7) above, it shall be its duty to explain to him in open court and in ordinary language why it is imposing those conditions; and a Magistrates' Court shall cause a reason stated by it under this subsection to be specified in the warrant of commitment and to be entered in the register.

26–20 In *H. (Steven) (Remand: Violent Offences)* [1999] C.L.Y. 1027, the offender was refused bail pending committal for sentence for the offence of taking a vehicle without consent, aggravated by damage caused to another vehicle. The prosecution submitted that the offender should be remanded to a remand centre on account of his having committed a violent offence. The court held that for an offence to be violent it was not necessary that physical harm should have been caused to a person. A collision with a car with people in it, in the circumstances of the offence, could lead to injury to a person. Hence this was a violent offence and remand to a remand centre was appropriate.

Thus the relevant questions for the court when considering the imposition of a security requirement are:

(1) Is the youth aged 12–14, or a girl aged 15–16?
(2) Is the offence a violent or sexual offence? OR
(3) An offence punishable in the case of an adult with a term of imprisonment for 14 years or more? OR
(4) Is the defendant charged with or convicted of one or more imprisonable offences which together with any other imprisonable offences which relate to the defendant amounts to or would amount to a recent history of repeatedly committing imprisonable offences while remanded on bail ore remanded to local authority accommodation? AND
(5) Is the court of the opinion that only remanding the defendant to local authority accommodation with a security requirement would be adequate to protect the public from serious harm from him or to prevent the commission by him of imprisonable offences? AND
(6) Is the defendant legally represented?

The court may only impose a security requirement following consultation with the designated local authority, the length of consultation being that which is reasonably practicable in all the circumstances of the case: s.23(13)(b) of the 1969 Act. The court imposing the security requirement must also state in open court and explain to the youth in ordinary language why it is of the opinion that a security requirement is necessary. **26–21**

(c) *Male defendants who are aged 15 or 16 years*

The options available to a court dealing with a male youth aged 15 or 16 are the same as those available for dealing with defendants aged 12 to 14 and 15 and 16-year-old females. However, s.23 of the *Children and Young Persons Act* 1969 is modified in relation to male youths of 15 or 16 years. The effect of these modifications is that the defendant will be remanded to local authority accommodation unless the court considers him to be an offender to whom s.23(5), as modified, applies. **26–22**

The modification of s.23 was effected by s.98(2)–(6) of the *Crime and Disorder Act* 1998, as amended by s.130 of the *Criminal Justice and Police Act* 2001. The modified statute reads:

Children and Young Persons Act 1969, s.23

Remands and committals to local authority accommodation

23.—(1) Where— **26–23**

(a) a court remands a child or young person charged with or convicted of one or more offences or commits him for trial or sentence; and
(b) he is not released on bail,

the remand or committal shall be to local authority accommodation; and in the following provisions of this section, any reference (however expressed) to a remand shall be construed as including a reference to a committal.

(2) A court remanding a person to local authority accommodation shall designate the local authority who are to receive him; and that authority shall be—

(a) in the case of a person who is being looked after by a local authority, that authority; and
(b) in any other case, the local authority in whose area it appears to the court that he resides or the offence or one of the offences was committed.

(3) Where a person is remanded to local authority accommodation, it shall be lawful for any person acting on behalf of the designated authority to detain him.

(4) Where a court, after consultation with a probation officer, a social worker of a local authority social services department or a member of a youth offending team, declares a person to be one to whom subsection (5) below applies—

(a) it shall remand him to local authority accommodation and require him to be placed and kept in secure accommodation, if—
(i) it also, after such consultation, declares him to be a person to whom subsection (5A) below applies; and

Part V

(ii) it has been notified that secure accommodation is available for him;

(b) it shall remand him to a remand centre, if paragraph (a) above does not apply and it has been notified that such a centre is available for the reception from the court of persons to whom subsection (5) below applies; and

(c) it shall remand him to a prison, if neither paragraph (a) nor paragraph (b) above applies.

(4A) A court shall not declare a person who is not legally represented in the court to be a person to whom subsection (5) below applies unless—

(a) he applied for legal aid and the application was refused on the ground that it did not appear his means were such that he required assistance; or

(b) having been informed of his right to apply for legal aid and had the opportunity to do so, he refused or failed to apply.

(5) This subsection applies to a person who—

(a) is charged with or has been convicted of a violent or sexual offence, or an offence punishable in the case of an adult with imprisonment for a term of fourteen years or more; or

(b) has a recent history of absconding while remanded to local authority accommodation, and is charged with or has been convicted of an imprisonable offence alleged or found to have been committed while he was so remanded,

if (in either case) the court is of the opinion that only remanding him to a remand centre or prison, or to local authority accommodation with a requirement that he be placed and kept in secure accommodation, would be adequate to protect the public from serious harm from him.

(5AA) The condition mentioned in subsection (5) above is that the court is of the opinion, after considering all the options for the remand of the person, that only remanding him to local authority accommodation with a security requirement would be adequate—

(a) to protect the public from serious harm from him; or

(b) to prevent the commission by him of imprisonable offences.

(5A) This subsection applies to a person if the court is of opinion that, by reason of his physical or emotional immaturity or a propensity of his to harm himself, it would be undesirable for him to be remanded to a remand centre or a prison.

(6) Where a court declares a person to be one to whom subsection (5) above applies, it shall be its duty—

(a) to state in open court that it is of such opinion as is mentioned in subsection (5AA) above; and

(b) to explain to him in open court and in ordinary language why it is of that opinion;

and a Magistrates' Court shall cause a reason stated by it under paragraph (b) above to be specified in the warrant of commitment and to be entered in the register.

(7) Subject to section 23AA below, a court remanding a person to local authority accommodation without imposing a security requirement (that is to say a requirement imposed under subsection (4)(a) above that the person be placed and kept in secure accommodation) may, after consultation with the designated authority, require that person to comply with

(a) any such conditions as could be imposed under section 3(6) of the *Bail Act* 1976 if he were then being granted bail; and

(b) any conditions imposed for the purpose of securing the electronic monitoring of his compliance with any other condition imposed under this subsection.

(7A) Where a person is remanded to local authority accommodation and a security requirement is imposed in respect of him—

(a) the designated local authority may, with the consent of the Secretary of State, arrange for the person to be detained, for the whole or any part of the period of the remand or committal, in a secure training centre; and

(b) his detention there pursuant to the arrangements shall be lawful.

(7B) Arrangements under subsection (7A) above may include provision for payments to be made by the authority to the Secretary of State.

(8) Where a court imposes on a person any such conditions as are mentioned in subsection (7) above, it shall be its duty to explain to him in open court and in ordinary language why it is imposing those conditions; and a magistrates' court shall cause a reason stated by it under this subsection to be specified in the warrant of commitment and to be entered in the register.

(9) A court remanding a person to local authority accommodation without imposing a security requirement may after consultation with the designated authority impose on that authority requirements—

(a) for securing compliance with any conditions imposed on that person under subsection (7) above; or

(b) stipulating that he shall not be placed with a named person.

(9A) Where a person is remanded to local authority accommodation without the imposition of a security requirement, a relevant court may, on the application of the designated authority, declare him to be a person to whom subsection (5) above applies; and on its doing so, subsection (4) above shall apply.

[Subsections (10)–(14) unchanged by the modifications.]

Hence the relevant questions for the court when considering whether to remand the defendant in local authority accommodation or custody are: **26–24**

(1) Is the youth a male aged 15–16?

(2) Is the offence violent or sexual? OR

(3) Is the offence punishable in the case of an adult with imprisonment for a term of 14 years or more? OR

(4) Has the defendant been charged with or convicted of one or more imprisonable offences which together with any other imprisonable offences of which he has been convicted in any proceedings amount to or would if he were convicted of the offences with which he has been charged amount to a recent history of repeatedly committing imprisonable offences while remanded on bail or remanded to local authority accommodation? AND

(5) Is the court of the opinion that only remanding the defendant to the local authority accommodation with a security requirement would be adequate to protect the public from serious harm from him or prevent the commission by him of imprisonable offences?

In *Croydon Youth Court, ex p. Grinham (A Minor)*, *The Times*, May 3, 1995, the Court of Appeal held that under s.23(5) a court has to be satisfied that a young person whom it was considering remanding was liable to cause harm that could sensibly be described as serious, on account of the nature of the offence or offences that might be committed, and not merely the risk of repetition. It is not the case that following commission of an offence punishable in the case of an adult with imprisonment for a term of fourteen years or more, the court can conclude that only remanding the offender to a remand centre would be adequate to protect the public from serious harm from him. Leggatt L.J. cited the example of the offence of burglary of a dwelling, stating that such an offence is: **26–25**

> "not necessarily calculated to cause serious harm if, *e.g.* the burglar is careful only to enter unoccupied houses in daylight and steal television sets. A series of such offences, if apprehended, could not be aggregated so as to render serious such harm as might be caused by them".

The issue of vulnerability was examined in *R. (S.R.) v. Nottingham Magistrates' Court* (2002) 166 J.P.N. 209. An offender described as emotionally immature, with a limited range of coping strategies such as to render him at greater risk of self-harm should he be placed in a punitive and stressful environment such as a Young Offenders Institution, was found to be vulnerable for the purposes of s.5A of the 1969 Act by the Divisional Court. The court also held that a young person who had been told by justices that they regarded him as vulnerable for remand purposes, had a legitimate expectation that such a conclusion would subsist up until the time of sentencing unless he was told that his status might change or another compelling reason existed to alter his status. **26–26**

In *R. (M.) v. Inner London Crown Court* [2006] 1 W.L.R. 3406, Admin, the Court considered an appeal by way of judicial review against the decision of the Crown Court to remand in custody a 16-year-old male charged with attempted robbery. The judgment of the Court sets out a structured approach in dealing with the "labyrinthine" provisions of s.23.

(d) *Defendants aged 17 years*

26–27 A defendant of either gender aged 17 will be treated in the same way as an adult, hence refusal of bail will lead to remand in custody. See *ante*, Ch.5 on Bail.

IV. APPEAL AGAINST REFUSAL OF BAIL: YOUTHS

26–28 Youths have the same rights as adults to appeal against bail decisions. See *ante*, § 5–39.

26–29 **FLOWCHART FOR BAIL DECISION MAKING**

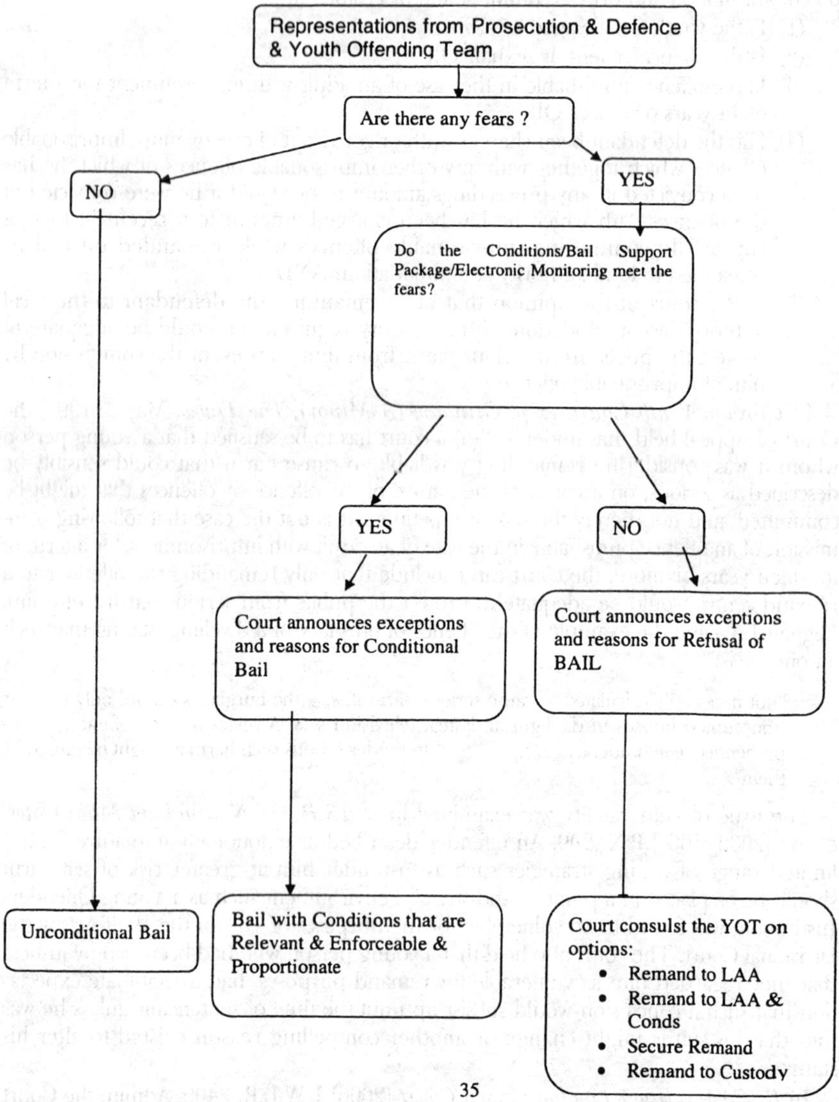

DECISION MAKING PROCESS FOR SECURE REMAND OF 15-16 YR OLDS BOYS UNDER SEC 23(5) CYPA 1969 (AS AMENDED) BY CJPOA 2001 26–30

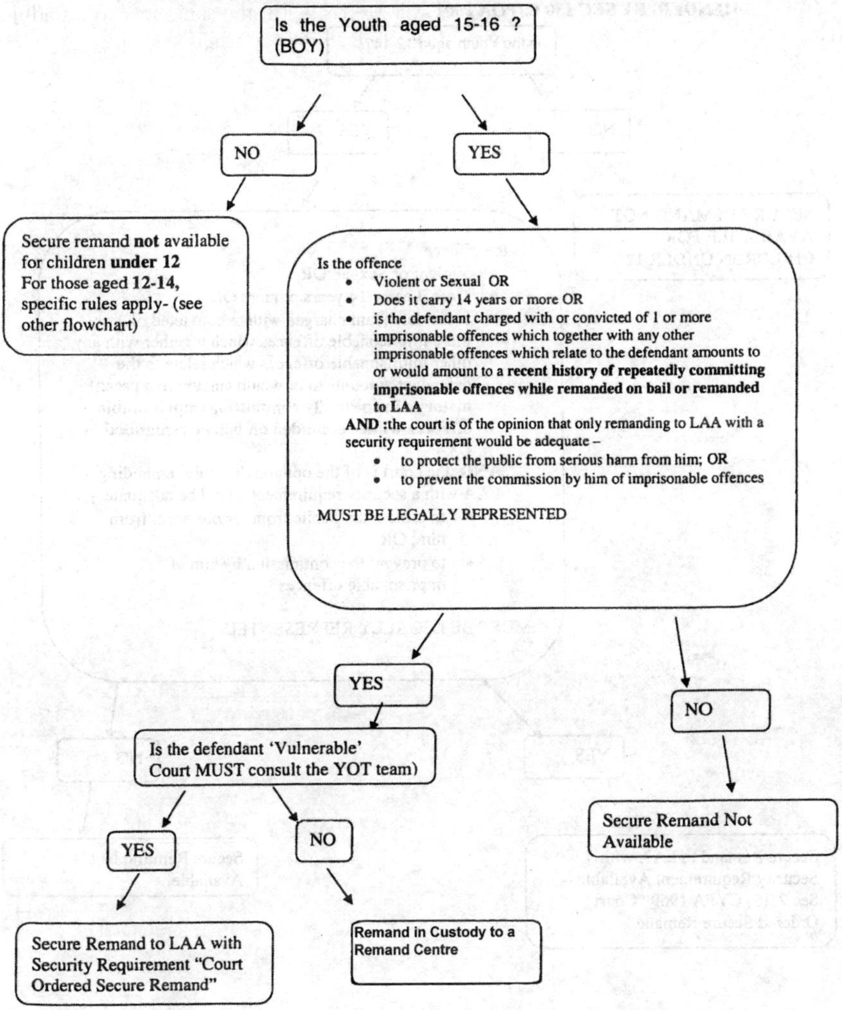

Is the Youth aged 15-16 ? (BOY)
NO
YES
Secure remand not available for children under 12
For those aged 12-14, specific rules apply- (see other flowchart)
Is the offence
Violent or Sexual OR
Does it carry 14 years or more OR
is the defendant charged with or convicted of 1 or more imprisonable offences which together with any other imprisonable offences which relate to the defendant amounts to or would amount to a recent history of repeatedly committing imprisonable offences while remanded on bail or remanded to LAA
AND :the court is of the opinion that only remanding to LAA with a security requirement would be adequate –
to protect the public from serious harm from him; OR
to prevent the commission by him of imprisonable offences
MUST BE LEGALLY REPRESENTED
YES
NO
Is the defendant 'Vulnerable'
Court MUST consult the YOT team)
Secure Remand Not Available
YES
NO
Secure Remand to LAA with Security Requirement "Court Ordered Secure Remand"
Remand in Custody to a Remand Centre

Part V

26–31 DECISION MAKING PROCESS FOR SECURE REMAND OF 12-14 YR OLDS BOYS AND 12-16 YEAR OLD GIRLS UNDER SEC 23(5) CYPA 1969 (AS *AMENDED) BY SEC 130 CJPOA 2001*

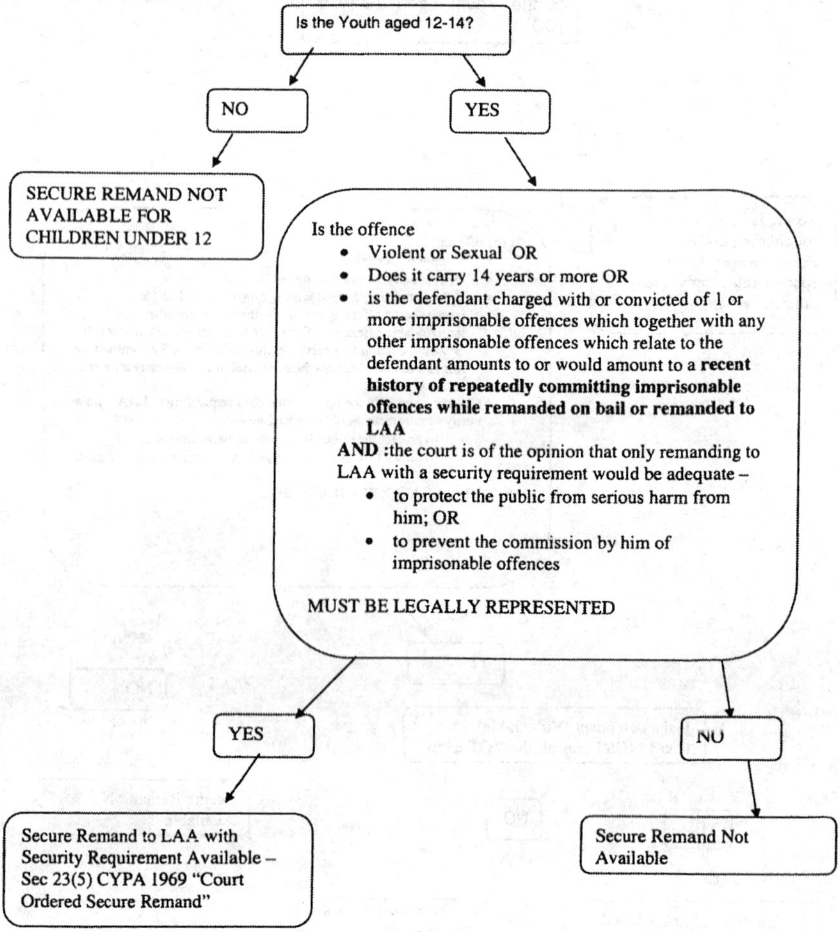

Chapter 27

SENTENCING IN THE YOUTH COURT

I. INTRODUCTION

27–1 The youth court is given wide and flexible powers of sentence. Sentencing young offenders is a difficult duty, which involves balancing the seriousness of the offence and offending history, against the welfare and needs of young offenders, many of whom have led highly disrupted lives. The availability of the various orders set out in this chapter partly depend on the age of the offender. In addition some of the orders can be combined with each other to produce a sentencing "package" specifically designed to meet the needs of individual offenders (see the sentence availability and combination charts, *post*).

The principal aim of the youth justice system is to prevent offending: *Crime and Disorder Act* 1998, s.37 (see *ante*, § 25–2). This is, therefore, the youth courts' principal aim in the sentencing process. The court must also have regard to the welfare principle: *Children and Young Persons Act* 1933, s.44 (see *ante*, § 25–3).

27–2 The aim of "preventing offending" may be given a wide interpretation. In *Inner London Crown Court, ex p. N. and S.* [2001] 1 Cr.App.R.(S.) 99 the Divisional Court stated (although the point had not been argued before them) that "in the light of s.37 of the Act (*CDA* 1998—see *ante*) in appropriate cases, the need to impose a deterrent sentence in relation to an offender under the age of 18 may take priority over s.44 of the *Children and Young Person Act* 1933, which requires the court to promote the welfare of the individual offender".

The welfare of young offenders remains a vitally important issue for the youth court to consider. However, the principal aim of the youth justice system is to "prevent offending". The welfare principal is therefore of relevance and importance to the sentencing court in so far as it is consistent with achieving the prevention of offending by the offender.

The *Criminal Justice and Immigration Act* 2008 sets out a new framework for sentencing young people aged under 18. The Court may make a Youth Rehabilitation Order (YRO) selecting any one or more of 15 requirements which in general terms reflect the disposals previously available. The purposes of sentencing are also redefined to emphasise the statutory objective of preventing offending while having regard to the welfare of the offender, protection of the public, reparation by the offender, together with punishment, reform and rehabilitation.

The Act makes substantial changes in youth court sentencing in the following respects:

(a) The Act sets out statutory purposes of sentencing defendants under 18 years.

(b) Substantial alterations are made to the Referral Orders (see *post*, § 27–21) and these provisions are now in force for offences committed after April 27, 2009.

(c) The Act introduces major changes to community penalties for youths.

Purposes of sentencing

Criminal Justice Act 2003, s.142A

Purposes etc. of sentencing: offenders under 18

142A.—(1) This section applies where a Court is dealing with an offender aged under 18 in respect of the offence.

(2) The Court must have regard to—

(a) the principle aim of the Youth Justice system (which is to prevent offending (or re-offending) by persons aged under 18; see Section 37(1) of the *Crime and Disorder Act* 1998,

(b) In accordance with S44 of the *Children and Young Persons Act* 1933, the welfare of the offender, and

(c) the purposes of sentencing mentioned in sub-section 3 (so far as it is not required to do so by paragraph (a)).

(3) Those purposes of sentencing are—

(a) the punishment of offenders

(b) the reform and rehabilitation of offenders

(c) the protection of the public, and

(d) the making of reparation by offenders to persons affected by their offences.

(4) This section does not apply—

(a) to an offence the sentence for which is fixed by law

(b) to an offence the sentence for which falls to be imposed under:—

(i) Section 51A(2) of the *Firearms Act* 1968

(ii) Section 29(6) of the *Violent Crime Reduction Act* 2006 or

(iii) Section 226(2) of this Act.

(c) In relation to the making under Part 3 of the *Mental Health Act* 1983 of a hospital order (with or without a restriction order,) an interim hospital order, a hospital direction or limitation direction."

(2) In section 142 of the *Criminal Justice Act* 2003 (purposes of sentencing in relation to offenders aged 18 or over at the time of conviction)—

(a) In the heading, at the end insert "offenders aged 18 or over", and

(b) in subsection (2)(a) omit "at the time of conviction".

(3) In section 44 of the *Children and Young Persons Act* 1933 (c.12) (general considerations) after sub section (1) insert—

(1A) Subsection (1) is to be read with paragraphs (a) and (c) of section 142A (2) of the *Criminal Justice Act* 2003 (which require a court dealing with an offender aged under 18 also to have regard to the principal aim of the youth justice system and the specified purposes of sentencing.)

(1B) Accordingly, in determining in the case of an offender whether it should take steps as mentioned in subsection (1), the court shall also have regard to the matters mentioned in those paragraphs.

(4) In section 42(1) of the *Crime and Disorder Act* 1998 after the definition of "local authority" insert—"offending includes re-offending".

The SGC Definitive Guideline "Overarching Principles—Sentencing Youths" sets out a general approach to the Sentencing of Youths and gives guidance to the appropriate use of individual sentences available to the Youth Court

The Guidelines as they apply to the Youth Court are extremely important and are reproduced in full at § 27–102, *post*.

II. SENTENCING POWERS

Like the adult magistrates' court, the youth court sentencing powers fall into the following categories: **27–3**

1. First Tier Penalties
   — absolute and conditional discharge
   — compensation order
   — fine
   — referral order
   — reparation order
2. Community Penalties
   — The Youth Rehabilitation Order
3. Custodial Sentence
   — The detention and training order
4. Ancillary Orders
   — compensation
   — costs
   — anti-social behaviour order
   — parenting order
   — parental bindover

Statutory restrictions on imposing community and custodial sentences apply to youths in the same way as they apply to adult offenders. **27–4**

(1) Statutory restrictions

Criminal Justice Act 2003, s.148(1)–(3)

Restrictions on imposing community sentences

148.—(1) A court must not pass a community sentence on an offender unless it is of the opinion that the offence, or the combination of the offence and one or more offences associated with it, was serious enough to warrant such a sentence. **27–5**

(2) Where a court passes a community sentence which consists of or includes a community order—

(a) the particular requirement or requirements forming part of the community order must be such as, in the opinion of the court, is, or taken together are, the most suitable for the offender, and

(b) the restrictions on liberty imposed by the order must be such as in the opinion of the court are commensurate with the seriousness of the offence, or the combination of the offence and one or more offences associated with it.

(3) Where a court passes a community sentence which consists of or includes one or more youth community orders—

(a) the particular order or orders forming part of the sentence must be such as, in the opinion of the court, is, or taken together are, the most suitable for the offender, and

(b) the restrictions on liberty imposed by the order or orders must be such as in the opinion of the court are commensurate with the seriousness of the offence, or the combination of the offence and one or more offences associated with it.

[This act replaces the *Powers of Criminal Courts (Sentencing) Act* 2000, s.35(1)–(3).]

Criminal Justice Act 2003, s.152

General restrictions on imposing discretionary custodial sentences.

152.—(1) This section applies where a person is convicted of an offence punishable with a custodial sentence other than one— **27–6**

(a) fixed by law; or

(b) falling to be imposed under section 51A(2) of the *Firearms Act* 1968 (c. 27), under

Part V

section 110(2) or 111(2) of the *Sentencing Act*, under section 29(4) or (6) of the *Violent Crime Reduction Act* 2006 or under any of sections 225 to 228 of this Act.

(2) The court must not pass a custodial sentence unless it is of the opinion that the offence, or the combination of the offence and one or more offences associated with it, was so serious that neither a fine alone nor a community sentence can be justified for the offence.

(3) Nothing in subsection (2) prevents the court from passing a custodial sentence on the offender if—

(a) he fails to express his willingness to comply with a requirement which is proposed by the court to be included in a community order and which requires an expression of such willingness, or

(b) he fails to comply with an order under section 161(2) (pre-sentence drug testing).

[This act replaces the *Powers of Criminal Courts (Sentencing) Act* 2000, s.79(1)–(3)(b).]

Powers of Criminal Courts (Sentencing) Act 2000, s.151(1)–(2)

Effect of previous convictions and of offending while on bail.

27–7 **151.**—(1) In considering the seriousness of any offence, the court may take into account any previous convictions of the offender or any failure of his to respond to previous sentences.

(2) In considering the seriousness of any offence committed while the offender was on bail, the court shall treat the fact that it was committed in those circumstances as an aggravating factor.

27–8 In coming to its decision as to an appropriate sentence therefore, the youth court must take, as its starting point the seriousness of the offence and/or offences associated with it, including any aggravating or mitigating factors. In assessing the seriousness of the offence the court must take into account the offender's criminal record.

Powers of Criminal Courts (Sentencing) Act 2000, s.152(1)–(2)

Reduction in sentences for guilty pleas

27–9 **152.**—(1) In determining what sentence to pass on an offender who has pleaded guilty to an offence in proceedings before that or another court, a court shall take into account—

(a) the stage in the proceedings for the offence at which the offender indicated his intention to plead guilty; and

(b) the circumstances in which this indication was given.

(2) If, as a result of taking into account any matter referred to in subsection (1) above the court imposes a punishment on the offender which is less severe than the punishment it would otherwise have imposed, it shall state in open court that it has done so.

27–10 If the offender has pleaded guilty he is entitled to be given credit for his plea and that may be reflected in the sentence he receives.

In *Christopher Pitt* [2002] 1 Cr.App.R.(S.) 46 the Court of Appeal dealt with an appeal against an 18-months' detention and training order made against a 17-year-old defendant. The grounds of the appeal were that insufficient credit had been given to the appellant for his plea of guilty and also time he had spent in custody on remand. The Court of Appeal reduced the appellant's sentence to 12 months, that being the next "step down" from the 18-month sentence originally imposed.

(2) Procedure

27–11 The court will hear mitigation put forward by the defence. In the youth court, such mitigation will inevitably refer to the contents of a pre-sentence report.

Written reports on defendants in the youth court are usually prepared by the YOT on the order of the court. Such reports play a vitally important role in the sentencing process. The court will indicate the type of penalty it has in mind on ordering the report. A report dealing with the offender's suitability for community penalties may be requested. Alternatively the court may indicate a specified penalty that it has in mind. If the court is considering a community penalty it must be satisfied that the offence or offences are serious enough to justify that type of penalty.

If the court considers that the offence or offences are so serious that a custodial sentence may be justified a full pre-sentence report will be ordered which must deal with the offender's suitability for such a order.

The contents of pre-sentence reports are governed by national standards. Such **27–12**
reports should include an analysis of the offence, an assessment of the offender, an assessment of his/her risk of re-offending and risk to the community, and a conclusion which may include a recommendation for the court's consideration. The court will expect the young offender, his parents, and his legal representative to be aware of the contents of any report that the YOT has prepared before the sentencing hearing begins.

This section will now go on to describe each of the various sentences the youth court has power to impose. In considering the approach to each sentencing power reference should be made to the SGC Overarching Principles.

III. SENTENCING GUIDELINES COUNCIL — OVERARCHING PRINCIPLES IN THE YOUTH COURT

GENERAL APPROACH

1. STATUTORY PROVISIONS

1.1 Offence seriousness is the starting point for sentencing. In considering the seriousness **27–13**
of any offence, the court must consider the offender's culpability in committing the offence and any harm which the offence caused, was intended to cause or might foreseeably have caused. In imposing sentence, the restrictions on liberty must be commensurate with the seriousness of the offence.

1.2 When sentencing an offender aged under 18, a court must have regard to:

(a) the principal aim of the youth justice system (to prevent offending by children and young persons); and

(b) the welfare of the offender.

1.3 In addition to the statutory provisions, a court sentencing a young offender must be aware of obligations under a range of international conventions which emphasise the importance of avoiding "criminalisation" of young people whilst ensuring that they are held responsible for their actions and, where possible, take part in repairing the damage that they have caused. This includes recognition of the damage caused to the victims and understanding by the young person that the deed was not acceptable. Within a system that provides for both the acknowledgement of guilt and sanctions which rehabilitate, the intention is to establish responsibility and, at the same time, to promote re-integration rather than to impose retribution.

2. SENTENCING PRINCIPLES

2.1 **The approach to sentence will be individualistic.**

2.2 The youth of the offender is widely recognised as requiring a different approach from that which would be adopted in relation to an adult. Even within the category of "youth", the response to an offence is likely to be very different depending on whether the offender is at the lower end of the age bracket, in the middle or towards the top end; in many instances, the maturity of the offender will be at least as important as the chronological age.

2.3 However, the sentence must remain proportionate to the seriousness of the present offence (except in the rare circumstances where the criteria for a sentence under the dangerous offender provisions are met) and should not impose greater restrictions on liberty than the seriousness of the offence justifies simply to deal with the risk of re-offending. Particular care will need to be taken where a young person has committed a relatively less serious offence but there is a high risk of re-offending.

2.4 Whilst a court is required to aggravate the seriousness of an offence where there are previous convictions (if the court considers that to be reasonable taking account both of the offence and the time that had elapsed since the previous conviction) **a sentence that follows re-offending does not need to be more severe than the previous sentence solely because there had been a previous conviction.**

(i) Approach to determining sentence

2.5 When determining sentence, the court will:

(1) **Assess the culpability of the offender and the harm caused (or intended or foreseeable) taking into account aggravating and mitigating factors relating to the offence.**

The assessment of offence seriousness will fix the most severe penalty that can be imposed and will determine whether an offence has crossed the necessary threshold to enable the court to impose a community or custodial sentence.

Even where the custody threshold has been crossed, a court is not required to impose a custodial sentence; similarly with the community sentence threshold.

Harm may be to individual victims or to the community or society at large. Of the four levels of culpability for sentencing purposes, intention is the highest followed by recklessness, knowledge and negligence. Even within those levels there will be gradations of seriousness.

Statutory aggravating factors (including previous convictions) will be relevant in assessing the seriousness of an offence.

(2) **Consider any mitigating factors that apply to the offender and any reduction for a guilty plea.**

When considering the maturity of the offender and its relevance to the sentence, it will only be in the most exceptional case that this will require more information than is available to the court through the representations of the advocates and any pre-sentence report.

(3) **Having taken account of all these factors, a court must then determine sentence including any relevant ancillary orders.**

The overall impact of the sentence and the ancillary orders must be considered to ensure that the restrictions on liberty are no more than is commensurate with the seriousness of the offence.

(ii) The principal aim of the youth justice system

2.6 By section 37 of the *Crime and Disorder Act* 1998, the principal aim of the youth justice system is to prevent offending by children and young people. For the offender, it incorporates the need to demonstrate that such conduct is not acceptable in a way that makes an impact on the offender whilst also identifying and seeking to address any other factors that make offending more likely. For any victim of the offence and society as a whole, it incorporates the need to demonstrate that the law is being effectively enforced and to sustain confidence in the rule of law.

(iii) The welfare of the offender

2.7 By section 44 of the *Children and Young Persons Act* 1933, "Every court in dealing with a child or young person who is brought before it, either as an offender or otherwise, shall have regard to the *welfare* of the child or young person, and shall in a proper case take steps for removing him from undesirable surroundings, and for securing that proper provision is made for his education and training".

2.8 In other requirements or obligations, different terminology—best interests, *well-being* or *welfare*—may be used. Generally, although there are shades of difference between the meanings, it is unlikely that different decisions will arise solely from those differences.

2.9 Accordingly, since "welfare" is the term used in the legislation applicable to England and Wales, that is the term used in this guideline. Welfare includes the obligation to secure proper provision for education and training, where appropriate to remove from undesirable surroundings and the need to choose the best option for the young person taking account of the circumstances of the offence.

In having regard to the "welfare" of the young person, a court should ensure that it is alert to:

- **the high incidence of mental health problems amongst young people in the criminal justice system;**
- **the high incidence of those with learning difficulties or learning disabilities amongst young people in the criminal justice system;**
- **the effect that speech and language difficulties might have on the ability of the young person (or any adult with them) to communicate with the court, to understand the sanction imposed or to fulfil the obligations resulting from that sanction;**
- **the extent to which young people anticipate that they will be discriminated against by those in authority and the effect that it has on the way that they conduct themselves during court proceedings;**
- **the vulnerability of young people to self harm, particularly within a custodial environment;**
- **the extent to which changes taking place during adolescence can lead to experimentation;**
- **the effect on young people of experiences of loss or of abuse.**

2.10 In the light of the high incidence of these impairments amongst young people in custody or subject to a community sentence, and taking account of the fact that the principal aim of the youth justice system is preventing offending, a court should always seek to ensure that it has access to information about how best to identify and respond to those impairments and, where necessary, that a proper assessment has taken place in order to enable the most appropriate sentence to be imposed.

(iv) The purpose of sentencing

2.11 As set out in paragraph 1 above, a court sentencing a person under the age of 18 is obliged to have regard to the principal aim of the youth justice system (to prevent offending by children and young persons) and to the welfare of the offender. As the principal aim of the youth justice system is the prevention of offending by children and young people, the emphasis should be on approaches that seem most likely to be effective with young people.

3. EFFECT ON SENTENCEOF THE OFFENDER BEING A YOUNG PERSON

3.1 In addition to the distinctive range of penalties available for youths, there is an expectation that, generally, a young person will be dealt with less severely than an adult offender, although this distinction diminishes as the offender approaches age 18 (subject to an assessment of maturity and criminal sophistication). In part, this is because young people are unlikely to have the same experience and capacity as an adult to realise the effect of their actions on other people or to appreciate the pain and distress caused and because a young person is likely to be less able to resist temptation, especially where peer pressure is exerted.

3.2 Additionally, in most cases a young person is likely to benefit from being given greater opportunity to learn from mistakes without undue penalisation or stigma, especially as a court sanction might have a significant effect on the prospects and opportunities of the young person, and, therefore, on the likelihood of effective integration into society.

3.3 When sentencing a young offender whose offence involves sexual activity but there is no evidence of a coercive or abusive relationship or of anything other than consensual activity, a court will need to be aware that a desire to explore gender identity or sexual orientation may result in offending behaviour. Depending on the seriousness of the offending behaviour, offender mitigation may arise where that behaviour stems from sexual immaturity or confusion.

3.4 Individual sanctions are likely to have a greater impact on a youth than on an adult, especially lengths of time spent in a custodial establishment, not least because of the exposure to influences likely to entrench criminal conduct (to which a young person may be more susceptible than an adult) and the greater risk of self harm than exists in relation to an adult.

3.5 It is also important to consider whether the young offender lacks the maturity fully to appreciate the consequences of his conduct and the extent to which the offender has been acting on an impulsive basis and the offender's conduct has been affected by inexperience, emotional volatility or negative influences.

3.6 Factors regularly present in the background of those juveniles who commit offences include: low family income, poor housing, poor employment records, low educational attainment, early experience of offending by other family members or of violence or abuse (often accompanied by harsh and erratic discipline within the home) and the misuse of drugs. There is also evidence that those young people who are "looked after" have been more at risk of being drawn into the criminal justice system than other young people acting in similar ways.

3.7 It is clear that these factors do not cause delinquency (since many who have experienced them do not commit crime); nonetheless, there is a strong association and any response to criminal activity amongst young people will need to recognise the presence of such factors if it is to be effective.

The following factors have led to a different approach to the sentencing of young people who offend (compared with the approach for adult offenders) and will affect the sentence imposed in an individual case:

- **offending by a young person is frequently a phase which passes fairly rapidly and therefore the reaction to it needs to be kept well balanced in order to avoid alienating the young person from society;**
- **a criminal conviction at this stage of a person's life may have a disproportionate impact on the ability of the young person to gain meaningful employment and play a worthwhile role in society;**
- **the impact of punishment is felt more heavily by young people in the sense that any sentence will seem to be far longer in comparison with their relative age compared with adult offenders;**
- **young people may be more receptive to changing the way they conduct themselves and be able to respond more quickly to interventions;**
- **young people should be given greater opportunity to learn from their mistakes;**
- **young people will be no less vulnerable than adults to the contaminating influences that can be expected within a custodial context and probably more so.**

4. THE RELEVANT CONSIDERATIONS

4.1 This guideline sets out a process that will enable the various obligations and requirements to be applied consistently. It is, however, only a framework and is intended to apply to the generality of cases.

In determining the sentence, the key elements are:

- **the age of the offender (chronological and emotional),**
- **the seriousness of the offence,**
- **the likelihood of further offences being committed, and**
- **the extent of harm likely to result from those further offences.**

The approach to sentence will be individualistic.

Proper regard should be had to the mental health and capability of the young person, and to any learning disability, learning difficulty, speech and language difficulty or other disorder, any of which is likely to affect the likelihood of those purposes being achieved.

4.2 The younger an offender (taking account of maturity and not just chronological age) the more likely it is that considering the welfare of the young person will be of greater significance. Since many young people "grow out of" crime, the obligation to have regard to the welfare of a young person who has offended might in some circumstances be best manifested by protecting that person from the adverse effects of intervention in his or her life rather than by providing for some positive action.

4.3 The requirement to have regard to the welfare of a young person is subject to the obligation to impose only those restrictions on liberty that are commensurate with the seriousness of the offence; accordingly, a court should not impose greater restrictions because of other factors in the young person's life.

4.4 In relation to custodial sentences, the reconviction rate is high and there are concerns about the effect on vulnerable young people of being in closed conditions. Risks commonly found are those of self harm and suicide and, in relation to female offenders, the additional impact on the offender herself and on the child if the offender is the primary carer of a child or is pregnant. Since a court is obliged to have regard to the welfare of the young person, it must have regard to these issues when considering sentence.

4.5 Particular care should be taken where an offender has mental health problems, learning disabilities, learning difficulties or other disabilities. Research shows that there is a high incidence of these issues in young people in the youth justice system and, in particular, in custody.

4.6 These issues are not always able to be identified at an early stage in the proceedings leading to sentence. As a result, a court needs to be alert to the possibility that the conduct of the young person (and that of any adult accompanying them in court) might be affected by issues relating to mental health, learning or communication, or some other form of disability that has not previously been identified.

4.7 In such circumstances, care needs to be taken in ensuring that the young person is able to take a proper part in the court proceedings, is able to understand what the court requires as a result of the sentence imposed and that that sentence properly takes account of difficulties in compliance that may arise from those issues.

4.8 Some young people may attend court believing that they will be discriminated against or otherwise unfairly treated; this might be for any of a wide range of reasons including ethnicity and sexuality. However unjustified that belief is, a court will need to be alert to the fact that the young person's behaviour in court might be affected by it.

4.9 The obligations to treat the prevention of offending by children and young persons as the principal aim of sentencing and to have regard to their welfare both require a court to consider the impairments and life experiences noted above, not only in determining the sentence to be imposed, but also in determining the length or content of that sentence.

The proper approach for the Crown Court, a magistrates' court or a youth court when sentencing a young offender is for the court, within a sentence that is no more restrictive on liberty than is proportionate to the seriousness of the offence(s), to seek to impose a sentence that takes proper account of the matters to which the court must have regard (see paragraph 1 above) by:

- **confronting the young offender with the consequences of the offending and helping the young offender to develop a sense of personal responsibility—these consequences may be experienced by the offender himself or herself, by the family of the offender, by the victim(s) of the offence and/or by the community;**
- **tackling the particular factors (personal, family, social, educational or health) that put the young person at risk of offending;**
- **strengthening those factors that reduce the risk that the young person will continue to offend;**
- **encouraging reparation to victims;**
- **defining, agreeing and reinforcing the responsibilities of parents.**

5. Crossing a significant age threshold between commission of an offence and sentence

5.1 There will be occasions when an increase in the age of an offender will result in the maximum sentence on the date of *conviction* being greater than that available on the date on which the offence was *committed*.

5.2 In such circumstances, the approach should be:

- where an offender crosses a relevant age threshold between the date on which the offence was committed and the date of conviction or sentence, a court should take as its starting point the sentence likely to have been imposed on the date on which the offence was committed;
- where an offender attains the age of 18 after committing the offence but before conviction, section 142 of the *Criminal Justice Act* 2003 applies (whilst section 37 of the 1998 Act and section 44 of the 1933 Act (see 2.6–2.10 above) apply to those aged under 18) and the sentencing disposal has to take account of the matters set out in that section;
- it will be rare for a court to have to consider passing a sentence more severe than the maximum it would have had jurisdiction to pass at the time the offence was committed even where an offender has subsequently attained the age of 18;
- however, a sentence at or close to that maximum may be appropriate, especially where a serious offence was committed by an offender close to the age threshold.

6. Persistent offenders

6.1 Certain sentences are available only where the offender is a "persistent offender"—in particular, a youth rehabilitation order with intensive supervision and surveillance or with fostering in relation to an offender aged between 10 and 14 and a detention and training order in relation to an offender aged between 12 and 14. This criterion does not have to be met before the Crown Court imposes long term detention (see paragraph 12 below) or detention for life.

6.2 Similarly, additional powers may be available to a court where a youth rehabilitation order has been breached "wilfully and persistently".

6.3 "Persistent offender" is not defined in legislation but has been considered by the Court of Appeal on a number of occasions. However, following the implementation of the 2008 Act, the sentencing framework is different from that when the definition was judicially developed, particularly the greater emphasis on the requirement to use a custodial sentence as "a measure of last resort".

6.4 A dictionary definition of "persistent offender" is "persisting or having a tendency to persist"; "persist" is defined as "to continue firmly or obstinately in a course of action in spite of difficulty or opposition".

6.5 In determining whether an offender is a persistent offender for these purposes, a court should consider the simple test of whether the young person is one who persists in offending:

i) in most circumstances, the normal expectation is that the offender will have had some contact with authority in which the offending conduct was challenged before being classed as "persistent"; a finding of persistence in offending may be derived from information about previous convictions but may also arise from orders which require an admission or finding of guilt—these include reprimands, final warnings, restorative justice disposals and conditional cautions; since they do not require such an admission, penalty notices for disorder are unlikely to be sufficiently reliable;

ii) a young offender is certainly likely to be found to be persistent (and, in relation to a custodial sentence, the test of being a measure of last resort is most likely to be satisfied) where the offender has been convicted of, or made subject to a pre-court disposal that involves an admission or finding of guilt in relation to, imprisonable offences on at least 3 occasions in the past 12 months.

6.6 Even where a young person is found to be a persistent offender, a court is not obliged to impose the custodial sentence or youth rehabilitation order with intensive supervision and surveillance or fostering that becomes available as a result of that finding. The other tests continue to apply and it is clear that Parliament expects custodial sentences to be imposed only rarely on those aged 14 or less.

7. ENFORCING THE RESPONSIBILITIES OF PARENTS AND GUARDIANS

7.1 A significant difference arising from the procedures for dealing with young people who commit criminal offences is the importance attached to the presence of a parent, carer or appropriate adult at key stages, especially when sentence is imposed. In addition, specific provisions exist to enable a court to reinforce the responsibilities of a parent or guardian.

7.2 The statutory framework clearly envisages the attendance of an adult with a degree of responsibility for the young person; this obligation reflects the principal aim of reducing offending, recognising that that is unlikely to be achieved by the young person alone. A court must be aware of a risk that a young person will seek to avoid this requirement either by urging the court to proceed in the absence of an adult or in arranging for a person to come to court who purports to have (but in reality does not have) the necessary degree of responsibility.

7.3 Insistence on attendance may produce a delay in the case before the court; however, it is important that this obligation is maintained and that it is widely recognised that a court will require such attendance, especially when imposing sentence. If a court proceeds in the absence of a responsible adult, it should ensure that the outcome of the hearing is properly communicated.

7.4 Where a person under the age of 18 is convicted of an offence, the court is under a duty to **bind over a parent or guardian** if satisfied that such a course of action would be desirable in the interest of preventing the commission of further offences. Such an order may not be made where the court imposes a referral order. Similarly, the court has the power to make a **parenting order** where it would be desirable in the interest of preventing the commission of any further offence. Where the offender is aged 16 or less and the court considers that a parenting order would be desirable, there is a presumption in favour of the order being made and reasons must be given if it is not made. In most circumstances where an order is necessary, it is more likely that a parenting order will be appropriate.

7.5 When considering whether to impose a parenting order, the court should give careful consideration to the strength of the familial relationships and to any diversity issues that might impact on the achievement of the purposes of the order. Such factors and issues arising may be documented in a pre-sentence report.

7.6 Particular issues may arise in relation to an offender who is, or who runs the risk of, experiencing familial abuse or rejection on the grounds of sexual orientation. In considering such factors, which may be documented in a pre-sentence report the court must take care not to disclose facts about an offender's sexual orientation without his or her consent. Similar issues might arise in a family where racial tensions exist.

SENTENCES

8. REFERRAL ORDERS

8.1 Where an offender is being sentenced in a youth court or a magistrates' court, a referral order is a mandatory sentence in many circumstances in which a young person is to be sentenced for the first time and is discretionary in a wider range of situations. In particular, it is possible to make an order on a second conviction where a referral order was not made following the first conviction. **27–14**

8.2 When an order is made, the court determines the length of the order (between 3 months and 12 months) but the action taken during that order is decided by a Youth Offender Panel consisting of members of the community supported by a member of a Youth Offending Team. Any victim of the offence may be invited to attend the meeting of the Panel at which the terms are agreed.

8.3 When determining the length of an order, although the needs of the offender are a factor, the primary consideration in most circumstances is the relative seriousness of the offence. Given the mandatory nature of the order in many circumstances, it is less likely that the needs of the offender will be considered in a pre-sentence report. This consideration is more likely to take place once the order has been made and in preparation for the Panel meeting since, within the period of the order, the Youth Offender Panel will agree what needs to be undertaken by the young person both in the light of the nature of the offence and of the young person's needs.

8.4 **A court should be prepared to use the whole range of periods allowed; in general, orders of 10–12 months should be made only for the more serious offences.**

8.5 Typically, the length of an order should be between 3–5 months for offences where the court assesses seriousness to be relatively low, between 5–7 months for an offence of medium level seriousness and between 7–9 months for an offence where the court considers seriousness to be relatively high. In determining which level applies, a court may find assistance in section 2 of the Youth Court Bench Book issued by the Judicial Studies Board which provides indications of the level of seriousness of an average offence of the types described.

9. FINANCIAL ORDERS

9.1 A court may impose a fine for any offence. In accordance with statutory requirements, where financial orders are being considered, priority must be given to compensation orders and, where an order for costs is to be made alongside a fine, the amount of the costs must not exceed the amount of the fine.

9.2 In practice, many young people who offend have few financial resources. Where a young person is in receipt of the *Education Maintenance Allowance* or a similar provision which is related to the means of the offender or those with whom the offender lives, a court will need to consider the extent to which making a deduction from the allowance would prejudice the access of the young person to education or training.

9.3 **As a general rule, it will rarely be appropriate to take the allowance into account as a resource from which a financial penalty may be paid, especially where the recipient is a young person who is living independently or as part of a household primarily dependent on state benefit.**

10. YOUTH REHABILITATION ORDERS

10.1 The *Criminal Justice and Immigration Act* 2008 provides for a single community sentence (the youth rehabilitation order) within which a court may include one or more requirements variously designed to provide for punishment, for protection of the public, for reducing reoffending and for reparation.

10.2 A youth rehabilitation order with intensive supervision and surveillance or with fostering is also provided but may be imposed only where a custodial sentence otherwise would have been appropriate (see 10.23 below).

(i) Threshold and availability

10.3 In order for a court to be able to impose a youth rehabilitation order, it must be satisfied that the offence is "serious enough". Even where an offence crosses this threshold, a court is not obliged to make a youth rehabilitation order.

10.4 In determining the content and length of an order, the guiding principles are proportionality and suitability since statute provides that the restrictions on liberty within such an order must be commensurate with the seriousness of the offence and that, taken together, the requirements within the order are the most suitable for the offender.

10.5 In contrast to the provisions relating to adult offenders, a court may impose a youth rehabilitation order (other than one with intensive supervision and surveillance or fostering) for an offence that is not imprisonable.

10.6 A youth rehabilitation order is not an available sentence where the "compulsory referral conditions" are found to exist; accordingly, the order will not be available in a youth court or other magistrates' court for a first time offender who has pleaded guilty to an imprisonable offence.

(ii) Effect of a guilty plea

10.7 Where a court is considering sentence for an offence for which a custodial sentence is justified, a guilty plea may be one of the factors that persuades a court that it can properly impose a youth rehabilitation order instead and no further adjustment to the sentence needs to be made to fulfil the obligation to give credit for that plea.

10.8 Where the provisional sentence is already a youth rehabilitation order, the necessary reduction for a guilty plea should apply to those requirements within the order that are primarily punitive rather than to those which are primarily rehabilitative.

(iii) Approach to determining nature and extent of requirements

10.9 In determining the nature and extent of requirements to be included within an order and the length of that order, the key factors are the assessment of the seriousness of the offence, the objective(s) the court wishes to achieve, the risk of re-offending, the ability of the offender to comply, and the availability of requirements in the local area.

10.10 Since a court must determine that the offence (or combination of offences) is "serious enough" to justify such an order, a court will be able to determine the nature and extent of the requirements within the order primarily by reference to the likelihood of the young person re-offending and to the risk of the young person causing serious harm. This is in accordance with the principal aim of the youth justice system and the welfare principle.

10.11 Before making an order a court will consider a pre-sentence report. In preparing that report, (following national standards and practice guidance) the Youth Offending Team (YOT) will be seeking to identify an appropriate balance between the seriousness of the offence, the risk of harm in the future from any further offences the young person might commit and the needs of the young person.

10.12 In most cases, the assessment by the YOT will be undertaken by use of Asset supported by professional judgement. An initial assessment will calculate the risk of re-offending; where necessary, an additional assessment will assess the risk of serious harm likely to be involved in further offending.

10.13 Those assessments will be reviewed by the YOT in the context of all other available information and the report will identify a level of intervention for the court to consider. There are three intervention levels:

- **Standard level**—for those who show a low likelihood of reoffending **and** a low risk of serious harm; in those circumstances, the order primarily will seek to repair the harm caused by the offence—typically, this will involve interventions to meet the requirements of the order and the engagement of parents in those interventions and/or in supporting the young person;
- **Enhanced level**—for those who show a medium likelihood of reoffending **or** a medium risk of serious harm; in those circumstances, the order will, in addition, seek to enable help or change as appropriate —typically, this will involve greater activity in motivating the young person and in addressing the reasons for non-compliance with the law and may involve external interventions;
- **Intensive level**—for those with a high likelihood of reoffending or a high or very high risk of serious harm; in those circumstances, the order will, in addition, seek to ensure control of the young person as necessary to minimise the risk of further offending or of serious harm—typically this will involve additional controls, restrictions and monitoring.

10.14 For the broad generality of offences where a youth rehabilitation order is to be imposed, this approach will enable the writer of a pre-sentence report to make proposals that match the obligations on the court to balance the various statutory obligations that apply.

10.15 Where a young person is assessed as presenting a **high risk of re-offending or of causing serious harm** despite having committed a relatively less serious offence, the emphasis is likely to be on requirements that are primarily rehabilitative or for the protection of the public. Care will need to be taken to ensure both that the requirements are "those most suitable for the offender" and that the restrictions on liberty are commensurate with the seriousness of the offence.

10.16 Where a young person is assessed as presenting a **low risk despite having committed a relatively high seriousness offence**, the emphasis is likely to be on requirements that are primarily punitive, again ensuring that restrictions on liberty are commensurate with the seriousness of the offence. In relation to young offenders, the primary purpose of punitive sanctions is to achieve acknowledgement by the young person of responsibility for his or her actions and, where possible, to take a proper part in repairing the damage caused.

(iv) Length of order

10.17 When imposing a youth rehabilitation order, the court must fix a period within which the requirements of the order are to be completed; this must not be more than 3 years from the date on which the order comes into effect. Where the order contains two or more requirements, the order may specify an earlier date for any of those requirements.

10.18 The period specified as the overall period for the order will normally commence on the day the order is made but, where the young person is already subject to a detention and training order, the court may specify that the youth rehabilitation order will take effect either on the day that supervision begins in relation to the detention and training order or on the expiry of the term of that order.

10.19 It is not possible to make a youth rehabilitation order when the young person is already subject to another youth rehabilitation order or to a reparation order unless the court revokes those orders.

10.20 The overall length of an order has three main consequences:

- where a supervision requirement is included, the obligation to attend appointments as directed by the responsible officer continues for the whole period;
- where a young person is in breach of a youth rehabilitation order, one of the sanctions available to a court is to amend the order by including within it any requirement that it would have had power to include when the order was made; however, that new requirement must be capable of being complied with before the expiry of the overall period;
- a young person is liable to re-sentence for the offence(s) for which the order was made if convicted of another offence whilst the order is in force.

10.21 In determining the length of an order, a court should allow sufficient time for the order as a whole to be complied with, recognising that the young person is at risk of further sanction throughout the whole of the period, but allowing sufficient flexibility should a sanction need to be imposed for breach of the order. Where appropriate, an application for early discharge may be made.

(v) Determining the requirements and the length of an order – summary

10.22 As set out in paragraph 2.1 above, the approach to the sentencing of a youth will be individualistic. Where a court is satisfied that an offence has crossed the community sentence threshold and that such a sentence is necessary or has crossed the custody threshold but is an offence for which a youth rehabilitation order is nonetheless considered to be appropriate, taking account of the assessment in the pre-sentence report, the consideration process that the court should follow is:

I) **what requirements are most suitable for the offender?**
II) **what overall period is necessary to ensure that all requirements may be satisfactorily completed?**
III) **are the restrictions on liberty that result from those requirements commensurate with the seriousness of the offence?**

(vi) Orders with intensive supervision and surveillance or with fostering

10.23 Such orders may be made where:

- the court is dealing with a young person for an offence punishable with imprisonment;
- that offence (or combination of offences) crosses the custody threshold; and
- custody would be an appropriate sentence.

If the offender was under 15 at the time of conviction, such an order may be imposed only where the offender is a "persistent offender".

10.24 When imposing such an order, the court must give its reasons for concluding that the offence(s) cross(es) the community sentence threshold and that the requirements set out above have been met.

(a) With intensive supervision and surveillance

10.25 A youth rehabilitation order with intensive supervision and surveillance is an order that contains an "extended activity requirement", that is, an activity requirement with a maximum of 180 days. As a result, there are further obligations to include a supervision requirement and a curfew requirement.

10.26 Where appropriate, a youth rehabilitation order with intensive supervision and surveillance may also include additional requirements, although the order as a whole must comply with the obligation that the requirements must be those most suitable for the offender and that any restrictions on liberty must be commensurate with the seriousness of the offence.

10.27 When imposing such an order, a court must ensure that the requirements are not so onerous as to make the likelihood of breach almost inevitable.

(b) With fostering

10.28 Where a fostering requirement is included within a youth rehabilitation order, it will require the offender to reside with a local authority foster parent for a specified period; that period must not exceed 12 months. The court must be satisfied that a significant factor in the offence was the circumstances in which the young person was living and that the imposition of a fostering requirement would assist in the rehabilitation of the young person. It is likely that other rights will be engaged (such as those under Article 8 of the European Convention on Human Rights) and any interference with such rights must be proportionate.

10.29 Before including this requirement, the court must consult both the young person's parent or guardian (unless impracticable) and the local authority; it cannot be included unless the offender was legally represented in court when the court was considering whether or not to impose the requirement or, having had the opportunity to be represented, the offender has not applied for representation or that right was withdrawn because of the offender's conduct. This requirement may be included only where the court has been notified that arrangements are available in the area of the relevant local authority.

10.30 A fostering requirement cannot be included with intensive supervision and surveillance and it cannot be included in a youth rehabilitation order unless the higher criteria described above have been met. Where appropriate, a youth rehabilitation order with fostering may also include other requirements (and must include supervision) although the order as a whole must comply with the obligation that the requirements must be those most suitable for the offender and that any restrictions on liberty must be commensurate with the seriousness of the offence.

10.31 It is unlikely that the statutory criteria will be met in many cases; where they are met and the court is considering making an order, care should be taken to ensure that there is a well developed plan for the care and support of the young person throughout the period of the order and following conclusion of the order. A court will need to be provided with sufficient information, including proposals for education and training during the order and plans for the offender on completion of the order.

(vii) Breaches

10.32 Where a young person fails to comply with a youth rehabilitation order, the "responsible officer" must consider whether there was a reasonable excuse. If the officer considers that there was no reasonable excuse and this is the first failure to comply with the order without reasonable excuse, the officer must issue a "warning".

10.33 The warning will describe the circumstances of the failure to comply, a statement that the failure is not acceptable and a warning that a further failure to comply may lead to the order being referred back to the court. In most circumstances, two warnings will be permitted within a 12 month period before the matter is referred back to court.

10.34 There is a presumption in favour of referring the matter back to court after a third failure to comply and a discretionary power to do so after the second failure to comply.

10.35 Breach of an order brought before a court may arise from a failure to keep an appointment or otherwise co-operate with the responsible officer or may arise from a failure to comply with one or more of the other requirements of the order.

10.36 Even where a breach has been proved, a court is not obliged to make any order but may allow the youth rehabilitation order to continue as imposed. In contrast with the powers in relation to an adult offender, there is no obligation on the court to make an order more onerous. Where a court determines that a sanction is necessary, it has the power to:

- impose a fine (in which case the order continues in its original form);
- amend the terms of the order; or
- revoke the order and re-sentence the offender.

10.37 If amending the terms of the order, the court may impose any requirement that it could have imposed when making the order and this may be in addition to, or in substitution for, any requirements contained in the order. If the youth rehabilitation order did not contain an unpaid work requirement and the court includes such a requirement using this power, the minimum period of unpaid work is 20 hours; this will give greater flexibility when responding to less serious breaches or where there are significant other requirements to be complied with.

10.38 A court may not amend the terms of a youth rehabilitation order that did not include an extended activity requirement or a fostering requirement by inserting them at this stage; should these requirements be considered appropriate following breach, the offender must be re-sentenced and the original youth rehabilitation order revoked.

10.39 Before imposing a custodial sentence as a result of re-sentencing following breach, a court should be satisfied that the YOT and other local authority services have taken all steps necessary to ensure that the young person has been given appropriate opportunity and support necessary for compliance.

10.40 Where the failure arises primarily from non-compliance with reporting or other similar obligations and a sanction is necessary, the most appropriate response is likely to be the inclusion of (or increase in) a primarily punitive requirement such as the curfew requirement, unpaid work, the exclusion requirement and the prohibited activity requirement or in the imposition of a fine. However, continuing failure to comply with the order is likely to lead to revocation of the order and re-sentencing for the original offence.

10.41 Where the offender has "wilfully and persistently" failed to comply with the order, and the court proposes to sentence again for the offence(s) in respect of which the order was made, additional powers are available. These additional powers include:

- the making of a youth rehabilitation order with intensive supervision and surveillance even though the offence is not imprisonable or a custodial sentence would not have been imposed if the order had not been available

- even though the offence is not imprisonable, the imposition of a detention and training order for 4 months for breach of a youth rehabilitation order with intensive supervision and surveillance imposed following wilful and persistent breach of an order made for a non-imprisonable offence.

10.42 In considering whether the failure to comply is "persistent", account should be taken of the principles set out in paragraph 6 above.

The primary objective when sentencing for breach of a youth rehabilitation order is to ensure that the young person completes the requirements imposed by the court.

Where the failure arises primarily from non-compliance with reporting or other similar obligations, where a sanction is necessary, the most appropriate is likely to be the inclusion of (or increase in) a primarily punitive requirement.

A court must ensure that it has sufficient information to enable it to understand why the order has been breached and that all steps have been taken by the YOT and other local authority services to give the young person appropriate opportunity and support. This will be particularly important if the court is considering imposing a custodial sentence as a result of the breach.

Where a court is determining whether the young person has "wilfully and persistently" breached an order, it should apply the same approach as when determining whether an offender is a "persistent offender". In particular, almost certainly a young person will have "persistently" breached a youth rehabilitation order where there have been three breaches (each resulting in an appearance before a court) demonstrating a lack of willingness to comply with the order.

11. CUSTODIAL SENTENCES

11.1 There is a statutory presumption that a person aged under 18 will be dealt with summarily, usually in a youth court; in such circumstances, the maximum custodial sentence will be a detention and training order of no more than 24 months. Such an order may be made only for the periods prescribed —4, 6, 8, 10, 12, 18 or 24 months.

11.2 The custodial sentences available in the Crown Court are:

- detention and training order of up to 24 months;
- long term detention —in relation to a young person convicted 53 in the Crown Court, under section 91 of the *Powers of Criminal Courts (Sentencing) Act* 2000;
- extended sentence of detention or detention for public protection – where a young person is sent for trial or committed for sentence to the Crown Court to be dealt with under the dangerous offender provisions; in each case, the minimum period to be spent in custody under the sentence must be two years;
- detention at Her Majesty's pleasure—for offences of murder.

11.3 A detention and training order may not be imposed on an offender aged 10 or 11 years at the time of conviction; an order may be imposed in relation to an offender aged between 12 and 14 at the time of conviction only if the offender is a "persistent offender" (see paragraph 6 above). However, the persistent offender criterion does not have to be met before the Crown Court imposes long term detention or detention for life in relation to offenders who are under 15 years of age.

11.4 A pre-sentence report must be considered before a custodial sentence is imposed.

(i) Threshold and approach

11.5 Under both domestic law and international convention, a custodial sentence must be imposed only as a "measure of last resort"; statute provides that such a sentence may be imposed only where an offence is "so serious that neither a community sentence nor a fine alone can be justified"

11.6 For a first time offender who has pleaded guilty to an imprisonable offence, in most circumstances a referral order will be the most appropriate sentence.

11.7 Since the minimum length of a custodial sentence in the youth court is 4 months (significantly in excess of the minimum available in relation to an adult offender) and since the term of a custodial sentence must be the shortest commensurate with the seriousness of the offence, it is inevitable that the custody threshold is higher in the case of a young person than in the case of an adult—any case that warrants a detention and training order of less than four months must result in a non-custodial sentence.

11.8 In relation to a person under the age of 18, in determining whether an offence has crossed the custody threshold a court will need to consider whether the offence has resulted (or could reasonably have resulted) in serious harm. In determining whether a custodial sentence is unavoidable, generally, a court will need to take account both of the seriousness of the offence (particularly the extent to which it caused (or was likely to cause) serious harm) and of the risk of serious harm in the future. A custodial sentence is most likely to be unavoidable where it is necessary to protect the public from serious harm.

11.9 In addition, a court must take account of:

i) the requirement to have regard to the principal aim of the youth justice system;

ii) the requirement to have regard to the welfare of the offender and the evidence that the risks associated with young offenders in a custodial setting are high.

11.10 Even where the threshold is crossed, a court is not required to impose a custodial sentence.

11.11 Before deciding to impose a custodial sentence on a young offender, the court must ensure that all the statutory tests are satisfied—namely:

i) that the offender cannot properly be dealt with by a fine alone or by a youth rehabilitation order,

ii) that a youth rehabilitation order with intensive supervision and surveillance or with fostering cannot be justified, and

iii) that custody is the last resort

and in doing so should take account of the circumstances, age and maturity of the young offender.

11.12 When a custodial sentence is imposed, a court must state its reasons for being satisfied that the offence(s) is (are) so serious that no other sanction is appropriate and, in particular, why a youth rehabilitation order with intensive supervision and surveillance or with fostering cannot be justified. This justification will need to be based on the principles set out in the statutory framework.

Where the offence(s) has crossed the custody threshold, the statutory tests are likely to be satisfied only where a custodial sentence will be more effective in preventing offending by children and young persons. The obligation to have regard to the welfare of the offender will require a court to take account of a wide range of issues including those relating to mental health, capability and maturity.

(ii) Length of sentence

11.13 A court imposing a custodial sentence is required to set the shortest term commensurate with the seriousness of the offence(s). Offence specific guidelines do not generally provide starting points or ranges for offenders aged under 18 because of the wide range of issues that are likely to arise and the marked differences in the sentencing framework depending on the age of the offender. Where they are provided, they are for offenders aged 17 with a provision that, for younger offenders, a court should consider whether a lower starting point is justified in recognition of the offender's age and maturity.

11.14 Any approach needs to take account of the general sentencing rules that apply where there is more than one offence or more than one defendant. Where the offence has been committed by offender(s) aged 18 or over and by offender(s) aged under 18, the court will need to consider the role of each offender and the number of offenders involved.

11.15 Where the primary offender is under the age of 18, a court is likely to determine sentence for that offender first giving proper weight to the offender's age and maturity; that will provide a framework within which sentence for the offender(s) over 18 can be determined. Where the primary offender is over 18, a court is likely to determine sentence for that offender first; that will provide a framework within which sentence for the offender(s) under 18 can be determined giving proper weight to age and maturity.

11.16 Where an offence crosses the custodial threshold **and** the court determines that a custodial sentence is unavoidable:

- **where the offender is aged 15, 16 or 17, the court will need to consider • the maturity of the offender as well as chronological age. Where there is no offence specific guideline, it may be appropriate, depending on maturity, to consider a**

Part V

starting point from half to three quarters of that which would have been identified for an adult offender.

It will be particularly important to consider maturity when the court has to sentence more than one offender. When the offenders are of different ages, including when one or more is over 18, the court will also need to have proper regard to parity between their sentences.

The closer an offender was to age 18 when the offence was committed and the greater the maturity of the offender or the sophistication of the offence, the closer the starting point is likely to be to that appropriate for an adult. Some offenders will be extremely mature, more so than some offenders who are over 18, whilst others will be significantly less mature.

For younger offenders, greater flexibility will be required to reflect the potentially wide range of culpability.

Where an offence shows considerable planning or sophistication, a court may need to adjust the approach upwards.

Where the offender is particularly immature, the court may need to adjust the approach downwards.

- **where the offender is aged 14 or less**, sentence should normally be imposed in a youth court (except in cases of homicide or where the young person comes within the "dangerous offender" criteria); the length of a custodial sentence will normally be shorter than for an offender aged 15–17 convicted of the same offence.
- **an offender aged 14 years or less** should be sentenced to long term detention only where that is necessary for the protection of the public either because of the risk of serious harm from future offending or because of the persistence of offending behaviour; exceptionally, such a sentence may be appropriate where an offender aged 14 years or less has committed a very serious offence but is not a persistent offender and there is no risk of serious harm from future offending.

11.17 In determining the term of a detention and training order, the court must take account of any period for which the offender has been remanded in custody or on bail subject to a qualifying curfew condition and electronic monitoring. As the available terms are specified, the proper approach in taking a remand period into account is to reduce, if possible, the sentence otherwise appropriate to reflect that period. Where a short custodial sentence was being considered, the court might conclude that a non-custodial sentence was appropriate.

11.18 On the implementation of the relevant parts of schedule 3 to the *Criminal Justice Act* 2003, a "plea before venue" procedure will be introduced for offenders under the age of 18 and will include a general power to commit for sentence where a court accepts jurisdiction following indication of a guilty plea. As with adult offenders, where a young person could have been dealt with in the Crown Court but the youth court has retained jurisdiction, where appropriate the maximum period of 24 months may be imposed following a guilty plea at the first reasonable opportunity where that plea was a factor in retaining a case for sentence in the youth court.

12. TRIAL AND SENTENCING OF CASES IN THE CROWN COURT

12.1 There is a clear principle (established both in statute and in domestic and European case law) that cases involving young offenders should be tried and sentenced in the youth court wherever possible. This section summarises the relevant statutory provisions and case law.

12.2 It has long been recognised that the Crown Court should be reserved for the most serious cases, noting the greater formality of the proceedings and the increased number of people likely to be present. These factors present additional obstacles in ensuring that proceedings in the Crown Court involving young offenders are conducted in accordance with international obligations.

12.3 Accordingly, it is rare for a young offender to be tried or sentenced in the Crown Court and for a sentence beyond the powers of the youth court to be imposed, except where that sentence is substantially beyond those powers.

12.4 A youth will appear in the Crown Court for trial and sentence only:

i) when charged with "homicide";
ii) when subject to a minimum statutory sentence;
iii) when charged with a "grave crime" and a youth court has determined that, if convicted, a sentence beyond its powers should be available; or
iv) when charged together with an adult offender who has been sent to the Crown Court and it has been determined that the cases should be kept together.

12.5 Where a sentence under the "dangerous offender" provisions is likely to be needed the youth may be committed for trial or for sentence.

(i) Homicide

12.6 An exception to the presumption that a person aged under 18 should be tried summarily arises where the young person is charged with an offence of "homicide". For a case falling within this description, there is no discretion and it must be sent to the Crown Court for trial. The meaning of "homicide" is not defined in statute.

(ii) Statutory minimum sentences

12.7 A further exception to the presumption in favour of summary trial arises where a young person is charged with an offence which has a statutory minimum custodial sentence and the criteria for that sentence would be likely to be satisfied if the young person were convicted. A sentence of long term detention may be imposed following committal where these mandatory sentence provisions apply; before there can be a departure from the minimum sentence prescribed, a court must find that there are "exceptional circumstances".

(iii) "Grave crimes"

12.8 A further exception to the statutory presumption in favour of summary trial arises where a young person is charged with a "grave crime" and a youth court has determined that, if convicted, a sentence beyond its powers should be available. In such circumstances, a young person may be sentenced by the Crown Court to long term detention under section 91 of the *Powers of Criminal Courts (Sentencing) Act* 2000. At present, such a sentence may be imposed only by the Crown Court and only where the offender was **convicted** in the Crown Court, and that court considers that neither a community order nor a detention and training order is suitable.

12.9 An offence comes within section 91 where:

- it is punishable with 14 years imprisonment or more for an adult (but is not a sentence fixed by law), or
- is an offence contrary to sections 3, 13, 25 or 26 of the *Sexual Offences Act* 2003, or
- is one of a number of specified offences in relation to firearms, ammunition and weapons which are subject to a minimum term but in respect of which a court has found exceptional circumstances justifying a lesser sentence.

12.10 This general power should be used rarely since:

i) it is the general policy of Parliament that those under 18 should be tried in the youth court wherever possible;

ii) trial in the Crown Court under this provision should be reserved for the most serious cases, recognising the greater formality of the proceedings and the greatly increased number of people involved;

iii) offenders aged under 15 will rarely attract a period of detention under this provision and those under 12 even more rarely.

12.11 Accordingly,

i) **a young person aged 10 or 11 (or aged 12–14 but not a persistent offender) should be committed to the Crown Court under this provision only where charged with an offence of such gravity that, despite the normal prohibition on a custodial sentence for a person of that age, a sentence exceeding two years is a realistic possibility;**

ii) **a young person aged 12–17 (for which a detention and training order could be imposed) should be committed to the Crown Court under this provision only where charged with an offence of such gravity that a sentence substantially beyond the 2 year maximum for a detention and training order is a realistic possibility.**

(iv) Dangerous offenders

12.12 There are rigorous statutory tests which must be satisfied before a court may conclude that a youth is a "dangerous offender" and requires sentence under the dangerous offender provisions in the *Criminal Justice Act* 2003 (as amended). Such a sentence may be imposed only where an equivalent determinate sentence of at least 4 years would have been imposed. Criteria relating to future offending and the risk of serious harm must be assessed in the light of the maturity of the offender, the possibility of change in a much shorter time than would apply for an adult and the wider circumstances of the young person.

12.13 At present, the provisions by which a potentially "dangerous" young offender reaches the Crown Court are overlapping to some extent as a result of the only partial implementation of the provisions of the Criminal Justice Act 2003, which introduce a new section 51A to the *Crime and Disorder Act* 1998. This new section requires a young offender to be sent for trial where it appears that the criteria for imposition of a sentence under the dangerous offender provisions will be met on conviction. However, the power to commit for sentence following conviction in a youth court or magistrates' court is preserved.

12.14 The nature of the offence is likely to be very significant in determining both whether the offender meets the risk and harm criteria and, even if so, whether a sentence under the provisions is necessary (given that there is now wide discretion).

Since a young offender should normally be dealt with in a youth court, where a young person charged with a specified offence would not otherwise be committed or sent to the Crown Court for trial, generally it is preferable for the decision whether to commit under these provisions to be made after conviction.

(v) Jointly charged with an adult

12.15 A further exception to the presumption in favour of summary trial arises where a young person is charged jointly with a person aged 18 or over; if the court considers it necessary to commit them both for trial it will have the power to commit the young person to the Crown Court for trial.

12.16 Any presumption in favour of sending a youth to the Crown Court to be tried jointly with an adult must be balanced with the general presumption that young offenders should be dealt with in a youth court.

12.17 When deciding whether to separate the youth and adult defendants, a court must consider:

- he young age of the offender, particularly where the age gap between the adult and youth is substantial,
- the immaturity and intellect of the youth,
- the relative culpability of the youth compared with the adult and whether or not the role played by the youth was minor, and
- any lack of previous convictions on the part of the youth compared with the adult offender.

12.18 A very significant factor will be whether the trial of the adult and youth could be severed without inconvenience to witnesses or injustice to the case as a whole, including whether there are benefits in the same tribunal sentencing all offenders. In most circumstances, a single trial of all issues is likely to be most in the interests of justice.

(vi) Remittal from the Crown Court

12.19 Where a young person is convicted before the Crown Court of an offence other than homicide, there is an obligation to remit the young person to a youth court for sentence unless that is "undesirable". In considering whether remittal is "undesirable", a court should balance the need for expertise in the sentencing of young offenders with the benefits of sentence being imposed by the court which had determined guilt.

12.20 Particular attention should be given to the presumption where a young person appears before the Crown Court only because he or she is jointly charged with an adult offender. A referral order is not available in the Crown Court for a first time offender and such orders may now be made following a second conviction in certain circumstances.

IV. ABSOLUTE AND CONDITIONAL DISCHARGES

(1) Purpose and effect

Powers of Criminal Courts (Sentencing) Act 2000, s.12

Absolute and conditional discharge

12.—(1) Where a court by or before which a person is convicted of an offence (not being an offence the sentence for which is fixed by law or falls to be imposed under section 110(2) or 111(2) below, section 51A(2) of the *Firearms Act* 1968, section 225, 226, 227 or 228 of the *Criminal Justice Act* 2003 or section 29(4) or (6) of the *Violent Crime Reduction Act* 2006) is of the opinion, having regard to the circumstances including the nature of the offence and the character of the offender, that it is inexpedient to inflict punishment, the court may make an order either— **27–15**

(a) discharging him absolutely; or

(b) if the court thinks fit, discharging him subject to the condition that he commits no offence during such period, not exceeding 3 years from the date of the order as may be specified in the order.

(2) Subsection (1)(b) above has effect subject to section 66(4) of the *Crime and Disorder Act* 1998 (effect of reprimands and warnings).

(3)–(7) [*omitted*]

(2) Reprimands and warnings

Crime and Disorder Act 1998, ss.65, 66

Reprimands and warnings

65.—(1) Subsections (2) to (5) below apply where— **27–16**

(a) a constable has evidence that a child or young person (the offender) has committed an offence;

(b) the constable considers that the evidence is such that, if the offender were prosecuted for the offence, there would be a realistic prospect of his being convicted;

(c) the offender admits to the constable that he committed the offence;

(d) the offender has not previously been convicted of an offence; and

(e) the constable is satisfied that it would not be in the public interest for the offender to be prosecuted.

(2) Subject to subsection (4) below, the constable may reprimand the offender if the offender has not previously been reprimanded or warned.

(3) The constable may warn the offender if—

(a) the offender has not previously been warned; or

(b) where the offender has previously been warned, the offence was committed more than 2 years after the date of the previous warning and the constable considers the offence to be not so serious as to require a charge to be brought;

but no person may be warned under paragraph (b) above more than once.

(4) Where the offender has not been previously reprimanded, the constable shall warn rather than reprimand the offender if he considers the offence to be so serious as to require a warning.

(5) The constable shall—

(a) give any reprimand or warning at a police station and, where the offender is under the age of 17, in the presence of an appropriate adult; and

(b) explain to the offender and, where he is under that age, the appropriate adult in ordinary language—

(i) in the case of a reprimand, the effect of subsection (5)(a) of section 66 below; and

(ii) in the case of a warning, the effect of subsections (1), (2), (4) and (5)(b) and (c) of that section, and any guidance issued under subsection (3) of that Section.

(6)–(9) [*omitted*]

Effect of reprimands and warnings

27–17 **66.**—(1)–(3) [*omitted*]

(4) Where a person who has been warned under section 65 above is convicted of an offence committed within 2 years of the warning, the court by or before which he is so convicted—

(a) shall not make an order under subsection (1)(b) (conditional discharge) of section 12 of the *Powers of Criminal Courts (Sentencing) Act* 2000 in respect of the offence unless it is of the opinion that there are exceptional circumstances relating to the offence or the offender which justify its doing so; and

(b) where it does so, shall state in open court that it is of that opinion and why it is.

(5)–(6) [*omitted*]

27–18 The youth court may order the absolute discharge of an offender if, after assessing the seriousness of the case and taking into account personal mitigation, it is of the opinion that punishment is inappropriate.

If the youth court is of the view that immediate punishment is inappropriate providing the offender does not re-offend, it may discharge the offender on condition that he he/she does not re-offend for a period of a maximum of three years.

(3) Breach

27–19 If the offender does re-offend within the period of that conditional discharge he will be in breach of that order and will be liable to be sentenced for the original offence as well as being sentenced for the new offence that he has committed.

The use of orders of conditional discharge is restricted for young offenders. If the offender commits an offence within two years of receiving a warning under s.65, above, the youth court shall not make an order of conditional discharge unless it is of the opinion that there are exceptional circumstances which either relate to the offence or the offender which justify such an order. There is no definition in statute or case law as to what circumstances might be regarded as "exceptional" under this section.

(4) Conditional discharge orders

27–20 Conditional discharge orders used to be frequently imposed by the youth court, especially upon those falling to be sentenced by the court for the first time. However, this category of offender now usually falls to be dealt with by way of a referral order.

It should be noted that an order of absolute discharge may be made in respect of an offender who would otherwise be made the subject of a referral order under *PCC(S)A* 2000, s.16.

V. REFERRAL ORDERS

(1) Purpose and effect

Powers of Criminal Courts (Sentencing) Act 2000, s.16

Duty and power to refer certain young offenders to youth offender panels

27–21 **16.**—(1) This section applies where a youth court or other magistrates' court is dealing with a person aged under 18 for an offence and—

(a) neither the offence nor any connected offence is one for which the sentence is fixed by law;

(b) the court is not in respect of the offence or any connected offence, proposing to impose a custodial sentence on the offender or make a hospital order in his case; and

(c) the court is not proposing to discharge him absolutely in respect of the offence.

(2) If—

(a) the compulsory referral conditions are satisfied in accordance with section 17 below; and

(b) referral is available to the court,

the court shall sentence the offender for the offence by ordering him to be referred to a youth offender panel.

(3) If—

(a) the discretionary referral conditions are satisfied in accordance with section 17 below; and

(b) referral is available to the court,

the court may sentence the offender for the offence by ordering him to be referred to a youth offender panel.

(4) For the purposes of this part an offence is connected with another if the offender falls to be dealt with for it at the same time as he is dealt with for the other offence (whether or not he is convicted of the offences at the same time or by or before the same court).

(5)–(7) *[omitted]*

Referral orders are a mandatory sentence for young offenders appearing before a youth or magistrates' court for the first time. On making such an order, the defendant is referred to a youth offender panel. **27–22**

The referral order must—

(a) specify the youth offending team responsible for implementing the order;

(b) require the offender to attend each meeting of a youth offender panel to be established by the team for the offender; and

(c) specify the period for which any youth offender contract taking effect between the offender and the panel is to have effect being a period of not less than 3 months nor more than 12 months.

The panel consists of a YOT officer and two community volunteers who are not members of a YOT. It is the defendant's responsibility to attend the panel. One of the main purposes of a referral order is for the panel to engage in a dialogue with the young offender and his parents or guardian. The panel is not a court and formalities are kept to a minimum. To this end, on making a referral order the youth court shall make an order requiring at least one parent or guardian to attend meetings with the YOT unless the court considers that it would be unreasonable to make such an order.

At the meetings members of the panel will speak to the defendant and his family. The aims of the panel are to stop further offending, help the offender right the wrong he did to his victim, and help the offender with any problems he might have. To this end they will discuss with him why he committed the crime in question. They will speak to him about other relevant aspects of his life. The victim may well be present at one or more of the meetings. The panel will then agree with the defendant a youth offender contract, which is a programme of behaviour aimed at preventing re-offending. It is for the sentencing court to specify the length of the contract which can be from 3 to 12 months duration. It is for the panel (and not the court) to agree the terms of the youth offender contract.

"A court should be prepared to use the whole range of periods allowed (3–12 months). In general, orders of 10–12 months should be made only for the more serious offences"—SGC Overarching Principles p.8.4.

If the referral conditions set out in s.17(1), *post*, are satisfied the court must make a referral order if the offence is an imprisonable one. **27–23**

Powers of Criminal Courts (Sentencing) Act 2000, s.17(1)

The referral conditions

17.—(1) For the purposes of section 16(2) above and subsection (2) below the compulsory referral conditions are satisfied in relation to an offence if the offence is an offence punishable with imprisonment and the offender— **27–24**

(a) pleaded guilty to the offence and to any connected offence; and

(b) has never been convicted by or before a court in the United Kingdom of any offence other than the offence and any connected offence.

(2) For the purposes of section 16(3) above, the discretionary referral conditions are satisfied in relation to an offence if—

(a) the compulsory referral conditions are not satisfied in relation to the offence;
(b) the offender pleaded guilty—
(i) to the offence; or
(ii) if the offender is being dealt with by the court for the offence and any connected offence, to at least one of those offences; and
(c) subsection (2A), (2B) or (2C) below is satisfied in relation to the offender.

(2A) This subsection is satisfied in relation to the offender if the offender has never been convicted by or before a court in the United Kingdom ("a UK court") of any offence other than the offence and any connected offence.

(2B) This subsection is satisfied in relation to the offender if the offender has been dealt with by a UK court for any offence other than the offence and any connected offence on only one previous occasion, but was not referred to a youth offender panel under section 16 above on that occasion.

(2C) This subsection is satisfied in relation to the offender if—
(a) the offender has been dealt with by a UK court for any offence other than the offence and any connected offence on one or more previous occasions, but has been referred to a youth offender panel under section 16 above on only one previous occasion;
(b) an appropriate officer recommends to the court as suitable for the offender a referral to a youth offender panel under that section in respect of the offence; and
(c) the court considers that there are exceptional circumstances which justify ordering the offender to be so referred.

(2D) In subsection (2C)(b) above "appropriate officer" means—
(a) a member of a youth offending team;
(b) an officer of a local probation board; or
(c) an officer of a provider of probation services.

(3) The Secretary of State may by regulations make such amendments of this section as he considers appropriate for altering in any way the descriptions of offenders in the case of which the compulsory referral conditions or the discretionary referral conditions fall to be satisfied for the purposes of section 16(2) or (3) above (as the case may be).

(4) Any description of offender having effect for those purposes by virtue of such regulations may be framed by reference to such matters as the Secretary of State considers appropriate, including (in particular) one or more of the following—
(a) the offender's age;
(b) how the offender has pleaded;
(c) the offence (or offences) of which the offender has been convicted;
(d) the offender's previous convictions (if any);
(e) how (if at all) the offender has been previously punished or otherwise dealt with by any court; and
(f) any characteristics or behaviour of, or circumstances relating to, any person who has at any time been charged in the same proceedings as the offender (whether or not in respect of the same offence).

27–25 A referral order cannot be made unless the offender pleads guilty to the offence with which he is charged. The order is clearly designed to encourage young people to admit their guilt by restricting the courts powers of sentence and allowing the conviction to become "spent" at an earlier stage.

Rehabilitation of Offenders Act 1974, s.5(4B)

27–26 **5.**—(4B) Where in respect of a conviction a referral order (within the meaning of the *Powers of Criminal Courts (Sentencing) Act* 2000 is made in respect of the person convicted, the rehabilitation period applicable to the sentence shall be—
(a) if a youth offender contract takes effect under section 23 of that Act between him and a youth offender panel, the period beginning with the date of conviction and ending on the date when (in accordance with section 24 of that Act) the contract ceases to have effect;
(b) if no such contract so takes effect, the period beginning with the date of conviction and having the same length as the period for which such a contract would

(ignoring any order under paragraph 11 or 12 of Schedule 1 to that Act) have had any effect had one so taken effect.

Referral orders are therefore available to the Court in the following circumstances: **27–27**

(a) The defendant pleads guilty to an imprisonable offence under s.17(1) above in which case the compulsory Referral Order conditions apply.

(b) The defendant pleads guilty to a non-imprisonable offence under s.17(2) above in which case the discretionary Referral Order conditions apply.

The provisions for discretionary Referral Orders will be satisfied if:

(a) The compulsory conditions are not satisfied.

(b) The offender has pleaded guilty to the offence

or

(c) The offender is being dealt with by the court for the offence and any connected offence

and

(d) Subsection (2A), (2B), (2C) is satisfied in relation to the offender.

The previous prohibition concerning those who had been conditionally discharged is abolished. If a defendant has only been before a court once before and was conditionally discharged there is a strong argument that he would fall within the compulsory provisions. The significance of the provision is an expansion of the power to make a discretionary Referral Order.

The effect of subs. (2B) would seem to be that where an offender has pleaded guilty to a first offence, but has not received a Referral Order, the court will now have discretion to make such an order.

The effect of subs. (2C) would appear to be that the court has a discretion to make a Referral Order in respect of a persistent young offender. The section states that the court must consider whether there are "exceptional circumstances" to justify this order. There will no doubt be substantial litigation to define what can constitute "exceptional circumstances" in the context of this section.

Where the first time offender is charged with a mix of imprisonable and non-imprisonable offences and in other respects qualifies for a referral order and the court make a referral order in respect of the imprisonable offences, it must also make a referral order in respect of the non-imprisonable offences.

On making a referral order the court must nominate the appropriate YOT responsible for the defendant. If the defendant is under 16 years of age the court must include a requirement that at least one of his parents attend the meetings with the youth offender panel.

On making a referral order the court can also make orders for compensation, forfeiture and deprivation and costs. The court may make a parenting order when making a referral order: *CJA* 2003, Sched. 34.

If the court is minded to make a parenting order with a referral order, it must first obtain and consider a report from the YOT, a local authority social worker, or a probation officer dealing with the need for such an order and what requirements might be included.

(3) Breach of referral order

Breaches and Extensions of Referral Orders

Powers of Criminal Courts (Sentencing) Act 2000, s.27B

Extension of period for which young offender contract has effect

27B.—(1) This section applies where at any time— **27–28**

(a) a youth offender contract has taken effect under section 23 above for a period which is less than twelve months;

(b) that period has not ended; and

(c) having regard to circumstances which have arisen since the contract took effect, it appears to the youth offender panel to be in the interests of justice for the length of that period to be extended.

(2) The panel may refer the offender back to the appropriate court requesting it to extend the length of that period.

(3) The requested period of extension must not exceed three months.

Powers of Criminal Courts (Sentencing) Act 2000, Sched. 1, Pt 1ZA

Referral back to appropriate court: extension of period for which contract has effect

9ZB.—(1) This Part of this Schedule applies where a youth offender panel refers an offender back to the appropriate court under section 27B of this Act with a view to the court extending the period for which the offender's youth offender contract has effect.

(2) For the purposes of this Part of this Schedule and that section the appropriate court is—

(a) in the case of an offender aged under 18 at the time when (in pursuance of the referral back) the offender first appears before the court, a youth court acting in the local justice area in which it appears to the youth offender panel that the offender resides or will reside; and

(b) otherwise, a magistrates' court (other than a youth court) acting in that area.

Mode of referral back to court

9ZC. The panel shall make the referral by sending a report to the appropriate court explaining why the offender is being referred back to it.

Power of court

9ZD.—(1) If it appears to the appropriate court that it would be in the interests of justice to do so having regard to circumstances which have arisen since the contract took effect, the court may make an order extending the length of the period for which the contract has effect.

(2) An order under sub-paragraph (1) above—

(a) must not extend that period by more than three months; and

(b) must not so extend that period as to cause it to exceed twelve months.

(3) In deciding whether to make an order under sub-paragraph (1) above, the court shall have regard to the extent of the offender's compliance with the terms of the contract.

(4) The court may not make an order under sub-paragraph (1) above unless—

(a) the offender is present before it; and

(b) the contract has effect at the time of the order.

Supplementary

9ZE. The following paragraphs of Part 1 of this Schedule apply for the purposes of this Part of this Schedule as they apply for the purposes of that Part—

(a) paragraph 3 (bringing the offender before the court);

(b) paragraph 4 (detention and remand of arrested offender); and

(c) paragraph 9ZA (power to adjourn hearing and remand offender).

(4) Further convictions during referral

Powers of Criminal Courts (Sentencing) Act 2000, Sched. 1, Pt II, paras 10–12

Extension of referral for further offences

27–29 10.—(1) Paragraphs 11 and 12 below apply where, at a time when an offender aged under 18 is subject to referral, a youth court or other magistrates' court is dealing with him for an offence in relation to which paragraphs (a) to (c) of section 16(1) of this Act are applicable.

(2) But paragraphs 11 and 12 do not apply unless the offenders compliance period is less than 12 months.

Extension where further offences committed pre-referral

27–30 11. If—

(a) the occasion on which the offender was referred back to the panel is the only other occasion on which it has fallen to a court in the United Kingdom to deal with the offender for any offence or offences, and

(b) the offender committed the offence mentioned in paragraph 10 above, and any connected offence, before he was referred to the panel,

the relevant court many sentence the offender for the offence by making an order extending his compliance period.

Extension where further offence committed after referral

12.—(1) If— 27–31

(a) paragraph 11(a) above applies, but

(b) the offender committed the offence mentioned in paragraph 10 above or any connected offence, after he was referred to the panel,

the relevant court may sentence the offender for the offence by making an order extending his compliance period but only if the requirements of sub-paragraph (2) below are complied with.

(2) Those requirements are that the court must—

(a) be satisfied, on the basis of a report made to it by the relevant body that there are exceptional circumstances which indicate that, even though the offender has re-offended since being referred to the panel, extending his compliance period is likely to help prevent further re-offending by him; and

(b) state in open court that it is so satisfied and why it is.

(3) In sub paragraph (2) above "the relevant body" means the panel to which the offender has been referred, or if no contact has yet taken effect between the offender and the panel under section 23 of this Act, the specified team.

Paragraphs 10, 11 and 12 above deal with the situation where the offender has been further convicted during the course of his referral order. These paragraphs allow the original referral order to be extended in respect of the new offence. However, it should be noted that orders made under paras 11 or 12 above must not extend the offender's referral order so as to cause it to exceed 12 months.

There are two scenarios. Under para. 11 above, the new offence is committed before the referral order was made. In such a case, the court has discretion to sentence the offender for the offence by making an order extending the compliance period, as long as it does not exceed 12 months in total. Under para. 12 above a new offence has been committed after the referral order was made. Under these circumstances the court may also extend the existing referral order up to the 12-month limit. However, before doing so the court must be satisfied with those matters set out in para. 12(2)(a) and (b), *ante*. 27–32

In either scenario, the youth court has discretion as to whether to extend the existing referral order. This will depend on the aggravating and mitigating factors that apply to the new offence. Additionally the court will wish to have a verbal or written report from the YOT indicating the offender's progress on the existing referral order. If the court considers that extending the referral order is inappropriate the offender will be sentenced in some other way for the new offence. This will have implications for the original referral order.

Powers of Criminal Courts (Sentencing) Act 2000, Sched. 1, Pt II, para. 14

Further convictions which lead to revocation of referral

14.—(1) This paragraph applies where, at a time when an offender is subject to referral, a court in England and Wales deals with him for an offence (whether committed before or after he was referred to the Panel) by making an order other than— 27–33

(a) an order under paragraph 11 or 12 above; or

(b) an order discharging him absolutely.

(2) In such a case the order of the court shall have the effect of revoking—

(a) the referral order (or orders); and

(b) any related order (or orders) under paragraph 11 or 12 above.

(3) Where any order is revoked by virtue of sub-paragraph (2) above, the court may, if it appears to the court that it would be in the interests of justice to do so, deal with the of-

fender for the offence in respect of which the revoked order was made in any way which (assuming section 16 of this Act had not applied) he could have been dealt with for that offence by the court which made the order.

(4) When dealing with the offender under sub-paragraph (3) above, the court shall, where a contract has taken effect between the offender and the panel under section 23 of this Act, have regard to the extent of his compliance with the terms of the contract.

Powers of Criminal Courts (Sentencing) Act 2000, s.27A

Revocation of referral order where offender making good progress etc.

27A.—(1) This section applies where, having regard to circumstances which have arisen since a youth offender contract took effect under section 23 above, it appears to the youth offender panel to be in the interests of justice for the referral order (or each of the referral orders) to be revoked.

(2) The panel may refer the offender back to the appropriate court requesting it—

(a) to exercise only the power conferred by sub-paragraph (2) of paragraph 5 of Schedule 1 to this Act to revoke the order (or each of the orders); or

(b) to exercise both—

(i) the power conferred by that sub-paragraph to revoke the order (or each of the orders); and

(ii) the power conferred by sub-paragraph (4) of that paragraph to deal with the offender for the offence in respect of which the revoked order was made.

(3) The circumstances in which the panel may make a referral under subsection (2) above include the offender's making good progress under the contract.

(4) Where—

(a) the panel makes a referral under subsection (2) above in relation to any offender and any youth offender contract, and

(b) the appropriate court decides not to exercise the power conferred by paragraph 5(2) of Schedule 1 to this Act in consequence of that referral,

the panel may not make a further referral under that subsection in relation to that offender and contract during the relevant period except with the consent of the appropriate court.

(5) In subsection (4) above "the relevant period" means the period of 3 months beginning with the date on which the appropriate court made the decision mentioned in paragraph (b) of that subsection.

(3) In paragraph 1(1) of Schedule 1 (youth offender panels: further court proceedings), for "or 27(4)" substitute ", 27(4) or 27A(2)".

Breaches are dealt with in an amended Pt 3 of the *PCC(S)A* 2000 and the *CJIA* 2008 inserts new requirements concerning the extension of Referral Orders and the revocation of Referral Orders where an offender is making good progress.

VI. FINES AND OTHER FINANCIAL PENALTIES

A. FINES

27–34 The amount of a fine imposed by the youth court on a young offender must reflect the seriousness of the offence and the defendant's financial circumstances.

The maximum fine which may be imposed on a youth is dependent upon his age: *PCC(S)A* 2000, s.135, Pt III. The amounts are as follows:

(a) 10–13 years of age inclusive—the maximum fine is £250.

(b) 14–17 years of age inclusive—the maximum fine is £1,000.

Where the fine is imposed on a youth under the age of 16 years, the court is under a duty to order that the fine, compensation or costs awarded, be paid by the parent or guardian of the youth instead of by the youth himself, unless the court is satisfied that:

(a) the parent or guardian cannot be found;

(b) it would be unreasonable to make an order for payment having regard to the circumstances of the case.

Where the youth has attained the age of 16, the court duty to make an order against the parent or guardian is discretionary: *PCC(S)A* 2000, s.137, Pt III.

Before making an order against a parent or guardian the youth court must give such person the opportunity of being heard. If the parent or guardian has not attended, the court must require their attendance. If they fail to attend an order for payment may be made against them in their absence. When a fine or compensation is ordered to be paid by a parent or guardian, their means or financial circumstances must be taken into consideration. If, having imposed a financial penalty, the parent or guardian fails to pay, then enforcement powers will apply in the adult court.

Upon imposing a fine against a young offender the youth court may grant time to pay, fix periodical payments, or make a money payment supervision order. If there is default in payment, the court also has power:

(a) to make an attendance centre order (Attendance Centre—see *post*, § 27–47); or
(b) to order the parent or guardian (who must be given an opportunity to attend) to pay the fine, if the court is satisfied that the offender has had the means to pay the sum or any instalment of it on which he has defaulted and has refused or neglected to pay.

Where the offender is under the age of 18 years the youth court does not have power to fix a term of detention in default of payment of a fine.

B. COMPENSATION

Powers of Criminal Courts (Sentencing) Act 2000, s.137

Power to order parent or guardian to pay fine, costs, compensation or surcharge.

137.—(1) Where— **27–35**

(a) a child or young person (that is to say, any person aged under 18) is convicted of any offence for the commission of which a fine or costs may be imposed or a compensation order may be made, and
(b) the court is of the opinion that the case would best be met by the imposition of a fine or costs or the making of such an order, whether with or without any other punishment, the court shall order that the fine, compensation or costs awarded be paid by the parent or guardian of the child or young person instead of by the child or young person himself, unless the court is satisfied—
    (i) that the parent or guardian cannot be found; or
    (ii) that it would be unreasonable to make an order for payment, having regard to the circumstances of the case.

(1A) Where but for this subsection a court would order a child or young person to pay a surcharge under section 161A of the *Criminal Justice Act* 2003, the court shall order that the surcharge be paid by the parent or guardian of the child or young person instead of by the child or young person himself, unless the court is satisfied—

(a) that the parent or guardian cannot be found; or
(b) that it would be unreasonable to make an order for payment, having regard to the circumstances of the case.

(2) Where but for this subsection a court would impose a fine on a child or young person under—

(a) paragraph 4(1)(a) or 5(1)(a) of Schedule 3 to this Act (breach of curfew, probation, community service, combination or drug treatment and testing order),
(b) paragraph 2(1)(a) of Schedule 5 to this Act (breach of attendance centre order or attendance centre rules),
(c) paragraph 2(2)(a) of Schedule 7 to this Act (breach of supervision order),
(d) paragraph 2(2)(a) of Schedule 8 to this Act (breach of action plan order or reparation order),
(e) section 104(3)(b) above (breach of requirements of supervision under a detention and training order), or
(f) section 4(3)(b) of the *Criminal Justice and Public Order Act* 1994 (breach of requirements of supervision under a secure training order),

the court shall order that the fine be paid by the parent or guardian of the child or young person instead of by the child or young person himself, unless the court is satisfied—

Part V

(i) that the parent or guardian cannot be found; or

(ii) that it would be unreasonable to make an order for payment, having regard to the circumstances of the case.

(3) In the case of a young person aged 16 or over, [subsections (1) to (2)] above shall have effect as if, instead of imposing a duty, they conferred a power to make such an order as is mentioned in those subsections.

(4) Subject to subsection (5) below, no order shall be made under this section without giving the parent or guardian an opportunity of being heard.

(5) An order under this section may be made against a parent or guardian who, having been required to attend, has failed to do so.

(6) A parent or guardian may appeal to the Crown Court against an order under this section made by a magistrates' court.

(7) A parent or guardian may appeal to the Court of Appeal against an order under this section made by the Crown Court, as if he had been convicted on indictment and the order were a sentence passed on his conviction.

(8) In relation to a child or young person for whom a local authority have parental responsibility and who—

(a) is in their care, or

(b) is provided with accommodation by them in the exercise of any functions (in particular those under the *Children Act* 1989) which are social services functions within the meaning of the *Local Authority Social Services Act* 1970,

references in this section to his parent or guardian shall be construed as references to that authority.

(9) In subsection (8) above "local authority" and "parental responsibility" have the same meanings as in the *Children Act* 1989.

27–36 A compensation order may be made against a young offender as a penalty in itself or in addition to other penalties that the court has imposed.

Compensation is governed by s.137 of the *PCC(S)A* 2000. If the youth court decides that the victim of the offence has suffered a loss that deserved to be compensated and that the case would be appropriately dealt with by the imposition of a fine, costs or a compensation order with or without other punishment the court may make a compensation order. If the offender is under 16 the order for payment must be made against the parent or guardian. If over 16, such order may be made against the parent or guardian. The principles for payment and enforcement of a compensation order are similar to those as for a fine.

If a local authority has parental responsibility for a youth who is fined his parent or guardian shall be construed to be a reference to that Authority. Therefore an order for payment of a fine, costs or compensation may be made against such a local authority, unless the court is satisfied that it would be unreasonable to make an order for payment, having regard to the circumstances of the case.

C. COSTS

27–37 Costs incurred by the prosecution can be awarded against the defendant and his parents/guardian may be ordered to pay in the same way as for a financial penalty. There is no maximum figure for costs. However, if a fine is imposed as well as costs, the amount of costs ordered by the court cannot exceed the amount of any fine imposed: s.18(5) of the *Prosecution of Offences Act* 1985, see *post*, § 30–22.

VII. REPARATION ORDER

(1) Purpose and effect

Powers of Criminal Courts (Sentencing) Act 2000, s.73

Reparation orders

27–38 **73.**—(1) Where a child or young person (that is to say any person aged under 18) is convicted of an offence other than one for which the sentence is fixed by law, the court by or before which he is convicted may make an order requiring him to make reparation specified in the order—

(a) to a person or person so specified; or

(b) to the community at large;

and any person so specified must be a person identified by the court as a victim of the offence or a person otherwise affected by it.

(2)–(4) [*omitted*]

(5) Before making a reparation order, a court shall obtain and consider a written report by an officer of a local probation board, a social worker of a local authority or a member of a youth offending team indicating—

(a) the type of work that is suitable for the offender

and

(b) the attitude of the victim or victims to the requirements proposed to be included in the order.

(6)–(8) [*omitted*]

Powers of Criminal Courts (Sentencing) Act 2000, s.74(1A)

74.—(1A) The Youth Court has power to make a Reparation order that must not require the offender to work for more than 24 hours in aggregate or to require the offender to make reparation to any person without the consent of that person (*PCC(S)A* 2000 section 74(1)). **27–39**

The requirements that the court specifies in a reparation order must be commensurate with the seriousness of the offence or offences that the court is dealing with: *PCC(S)A* 2000, s.74(2).

The work to be done under the order will normally be undertaken under the supervision of the youth offending team, and must be completed within three months.

The requirements specified in a reparation order shall, as far as practicable, be such as to avoid conflict with the offenders religious beliefs or with the requirements of any community order to which he may be subject and should not cause any interference with the times at which he attends work, school or any other educational establishment: *PCC(S)A* 2000, s.74(3).

The legislation clearly envisages and stresses the importance of victim participation in the reparation process. If the victim is unwilling to co-operate or cannot be found the YOT will normally recommend a form of reparation to the community generally. **27–40**

A reparation order is based on the concept of "restorative justice". Apart from reparation orders, a reparative element is often included as part of an action plan, supervision order, or community rehabilitation order, see *post*, §§ 27–42—27–48.

(2) Breach

Breach, revocation and amendment of reparation orders are dealt with under Sched. 8 of the *PCC(S)A (Sentencing) Act* 2000. **27–41**

VIII. YOUTH REHABILITATION ORDERS

(1) Requirements on Youth Rehabilitation Orders

Criminal Justice and Immigration Act 2008, s.1

Youth Rehabilitation Orders

1.—(1) Where a person aged under 18 is convicted of an offence, the court by or before which the person is convicted may in accordance with Schedule 1 make an order (in this Part referred to as a "youth rehabilitation order") imposing on the person any one or more of the following requirements— **27–42**

(a) an activity requirement (see paragraphs 6 to 8 of Schedule 1),

(b) a supervision requirement (see paragraph 9 of that Schedule),

(c) in a case where the offender is aged 16 or 17 at the time of the conviction, an unpaid work requirement (see paragraph 10 of that Schedule),

(d) a programme requirement (see paragraph 11 of that Schedule),
(e) an attendance centre requirement (see paragraph 12 of that Schedule),
(f) a prohibited activity requirement (see paragraph 13 of that Schedule),
(g) a curfew requirement (see paragraph 14 of that Schedule),
(h) an exclusion requirement (see paragraph 15 of that Schedule),
(i) a residence requirement (see paragraph 16 of that Schedule),
(j) a local authority residence requirement (see paragraph 17 of that Schedule),
(k) treatment a mental health requirement (see paragraph 20 of that Schedule),
(l) a drug treatment requirement (see paragraph 22 of that Schedule),
(m) a drug testing requirement (see paragraph 23 of that Schedule),
(n) an intoxicating substance treatment requirement (see paragraph 24 of that Schedule), and
(o) an education requirement (see paragraph 25 of that Schedule).

(2) A youth rehabilitation order—
(a) may also impose an electronic monitoring requirement (see paragraph 26 of Schedule 1), and
(b) must do so if paragraph 2 of that Schedule so requires.

(3) A youth rehabilitation order may be—
(a) a youth rehabilitation order with intensive supervision and surveillance (see paragraph 3 of Schedule 1), or
(b) a youth rehabilitation order with fostering (see paragraph 4 of that Schedule).

(4) But a court may only make an order mentioned in subsection (3)(a) or (b) if—
(a) the court is dealing with the offender for an offence which is punishable with imprisonment,
(b) the court is of the opinion that the offence, or the combination of the offence and one or more offences associated with it, was so serious that, but for paragraph 3 or 4 of Schedule 1, a custodial sentence would be appropriate (or, if the offender was aged under 12 at the time of conviction, would be appropriate if the offender had been aged 12), and
(c) if the offender was aged under 15 at the time of conviction, the court is of the opinion that the offender is a persistent offender.

(5) Schedule 1 makes further provision about youth rehabilitation orders.

(6) This section is subject to—
(a) sections 148 and 150 of the *Criminal Justice Act* 2003 (c. 44) (restrictions on community sentences etc.), and
(b) the provisions of Parts 1 and 3 of Schedule 1.

Youth Rehabilitation Orders are now in force. There is one order and the sentencer can choose from a menu of requirements to tailor make an order. Some of the requirements may be incompatible and some may have specific pre-conditions. The requirements that may be attached to a generic order are listed. The Act makes provision for two specific youth rehabilitation orders namely a youth rehabilitation order with intensive supervision and surveillance or a youth rehabilitation order with fostering under s.1(3) of the *Criminal Justice and Immigration Act* 2008. There are pre-conditions which need to be satisfied for each order and care needs to be taken when making these orders to check that the mandatory requirements are added and that the pre-conditions are met. The requirements which may be added to a generic order are dealt with below.

The "SGC Overarching Principle" gives the following guidance on determining the length of a YRO and its requirements:

> "The approach to the sentencing of a youth will be individualistic. Where a court is satisfied that an offence has crossed the community sentence Threshold and that such a sentence is necessary or has crossed the custody threshold but is an offence for which a YRO is nonetheless considered to be appropriate, taking account of the assessment in the PSR, the consideration process that the Court should follow is:
>
> 1. What requirements are most suitable for offender?
> 2. What overall period is necessary to ensure that all requirements may be satisfactorily completed?

3. Are the restrictions on liberty that result from those requirements commensurate with the seriousness of the offence?"

Activity Requirement

Criminal Justice and Immigration Act 2008, Sched. 1, paras 6–8

Activity requirement

6.—(1) In this Part of this Act "activity requirement", in relation to a youth rehabilitation order, means a requirement that the offender must do any or all of the following— **27–43**

(a) participate, on such number of days as may be specified in the order, in activities at a place, or places, so specified;

(b) participate in an activity, or activities, specified in the order on such number of days as may be so specified;

(c) participate in one or more residential exercises for a continuous period or periods comprising such number or numbers of days as may be specified in the order;

(d) in accordance with paragraph 7, engage in activities in accordance with instructions of the responsible officer on such number of days as may be specified in the order.

(2) Subject to paragraph 3(2), the number of days specified in the order under sub-paragraph (1) must not, in aggregate, be more than 90.

(3) A requirement such as is mentioned in sub-paragraph (1)(a) or (b) operates to require the offender, in accordance with instructions given by the responsible officer, on the number of days specified in the order in relation to the requirement—

(a) in the case of a requirement such as is mentioned in sub-paragraph (1)(a), to present himself or herself at a place specified in the order to a person of a description so specified, or

(b) in the case of a requirement such as is mentioned in sub-paragraph (1)(b), to participate in an activity specified in the order,

and, on each such day, to comply with instructions given by, or under the authority of, the person in charge of the place or the activity (as the case may be).

(4) Where the order requires the offender to participate in a residential exercise, it must specify, in relation to the exercise—

(a) a place, or

(b) an activity.

(5) A requirement to participate in a residential exercise operates to require the offender, in accordance with instructions given by the responsible officer—

(a) if a place is specified under sub-paragraph (4)(a)—

(i) to present himself or herself at the beginning of the period specified in the order in relation to the exercise, at the place so specified to a person of a description specified in the instructions,

and

(ii) to reside there for that period,

(b) if an activity is specified under sub-paragraph (4)(b), to participate, for the period specified in the order in relation to the exercise, in the activity so specified,

and, during that period, to comply with instructions given by, or under the authority of, the person in charge of the place or the activity (as the case may be).

Activity requirement: instructions of responsible officer under paragraph 6(1)(d)

7.—(1) Subject to sub-paragraph (3), instructions under paragraph 6(1)(d) relating to any day must require the offender to do either of the following—

(a) present himself or herself to a person or persons of a description specified in the instructions at a place so specified;

(b) participate in an activity specified in the instructions.

(2) Any such instructions operate to require the offender, on that day or while participating in that activity, to comply with instructions given by, or under the authority of, the person in charge of the place or, as the case may be, the activity.

(3) If the order so provides, instructions under paragraph 6(1)(d) may require the offender to participate in a residential exercise for a period comprising not more than 7 days, and, for that purpose—

(a) to present himself or herself at the beginning of that period to a person of a description specified in the instructions at a place so specified and to reside there for that period, or

(b) to participate for that period in an activity specified in the instructions.

(4) Instructions such as are mentioned in sub-paragraph (3)—

(a) may not be given except with the consent of a parent or guardian of the offender,

and

(b) operate to require the offender, during the period specified under that sub-paragraph, to comply with instructions given by, or under the authority of, the person in charge of the place or activity specified under sub-paragraph (3)(a) or (b) (as the case may be).

Activity requirement: further provisions

8.—(1) Instructions given by, or under the authority of, a person in charge of any place under any of the following provisions—

(a) paragraph 6(3),

(b) paragraph 6(5),

(c) paragraph 7(2), or

(d) paragraph 7(4)(b),

may require the offender to engage in activities otherwise than at that place.

(2) An activity specified—

(a) in an order under paragraph 6(1)(b), or

(b) in instructions given under paragraph 6(1)(d),

may consist of or include an activity whose purpose is that of reparation, such as an activity involving contact between an offender and persons affected by the offences in respect of which the order was made.

(3) A court may not include an activity requirement in a youth rehabilitation order unless—

(a) it has consulted a member of a youth offending team, an officer of a local probation board or an officer of a provider of probation services,

(b) it is satisfied that it is feasible to secure compliance with the requirement,

and

(c) it is satisfied that provision for the offender to participate in the activities proposed to be specified in the order can be made under the arrangements for persons to participate in such activities which exist in the local justice area in which the offender resides or is to reside.

(4) A court may not include an activity requirement in a youth rehabilitation order if compliance with that requirement would involve the co-operation of a person other than the offender and the responsible officer, unless that other person consents to its inclusion.

There is no age restriction on an activity requirement, if the YRO is a generic Order as opposed to a YRO with ISS or a YRO with Fostering, and the offence need not be an imprisonable offence. In addition the generic requirement should not exceed 90 days in aggregate (*Criminal Justice and Immigration Act* 2008 Sched. 1, para. 6(2)) but this is not the case if the YRO is to be a YRO with ISS.

The activity may comprise of an element of reparation (Sched. 1, para. 8(2)) only if the activity requirement has been made pursuant to Sched. 1, para. 6(1)(d) or (b). It is arguable that if an activity requirement is made pursuant to Sched. 1, para. 6(1)(a) or (c) then it cannot contain an element of reparation. The sentencer will need to look at the activity that is proposed and decide which paragraph it falls under before determining if an element of reparation can be specified as an activity. Care will need to be taken when making an activity requirement.

Supervision Requirement

Criminal Justice and Immigration Act 2008, Sched. 1, para. 9

Supervision requirement

27–44 9. In this Part of this Act "supervision requirement", in relation to a youth rehabilitation order, means a requirement that, during the period for which the order remains in force, the offender must attend appointments with the responsible officer or another person determined by the responsible officer, at such times and places as may be determined by the responsible officer.

Where a supervision requirement is added, there is no age limit and the offences need not be imprisonable offences.

Unpaid Work Requirement

Criminal Justice and Immigration Act 2008, Sched. 1, para. 10

Unpaid work requirement

10.—(1) In this Part of this Act "unpaid work requirement", in relation to a youth rehabilitation order, means a requirement that the offender must perform unpaid work in accordance with this paragraph. **27–45**

(2) The number of hours which a person may be required to work under an unpaid work requirement must be specified in the youth rehabilitation order and must be, in aggregate—

(a) not less than 40, and
(b) not more than 240.

(3) A court may not impose an unpaid work requirement in respect of an offender unless—

(a) after hearing (if the court thinks necessary) an appropriate officer, the court is satisfied that the offender is a suitable person to perform work under such a requirement,

and

(b) the court is satisfied that provision for the offender to work under such a requirement can be made under the arrangements for persons to perform work under such a requirement which exist in the local justice area in which the offender resides or is to reside.

(4) In sub-paragraph (3)(a) "an appropriate officer" means a member of a youth offending team, an officer of a local probation board or an officer of a provider of probation services.

(5) An offender in respect of whom an unpaid work requirement of a youth rehabilitation order is in force must perform for the number of hours specified in the order such work at such times as the responsible officer may specify in instructions.

(6) Subject to paragraph 17 of Schedule 2, the work required to be performed under an unpaid work requirement of a youth rehabilitation order must be performed during the period of 12 months beginning with the day on which the order takes effect.

(7) Unless revoked, a youth rehabilitation order imposing an unpaid work requirement remains in force until the offender has worked under it for the number of hours specified in it.

There is an age restriction. The offender must be aged 16 or 17 ***at the time of conviction*** (s.1(1)(c) of the *Criminal Justice and Immigration Act* 2008). The hours are "not less than 40 and no more than 240". It must not be added unless the requirements of Sched. 1, paras 3 and 4 have been complied with. The order remains in force until the offender has worked under it for the number of hours specified in it. Breaches are covered under Sched. 2, para. 17 to the *Criminal Justice and Immigration Act* 2008 and according to the provisions of that Schedule, the work must be completed within 12 months and it remains in force until it has been worked or the order has been revoked. The requirement can be imposed for a non-imprisonable offence.

Part V

Programme Requirement

Criminal Justice and Immigration Act 2008, Sched. 1, para. 11

Programme requirement

11.—(1) In this Part of this Act "programme requirement", in relation to a youth reha- **27–46** bilitation order, means a requirement that the offender must participate in a systematic set of activities ("a programme") specified in the order at a place or places so specified on such number of days as may be so specified.

(2) A programme requirement may require the offender to reside at any place specified in the order under sub-paragraph (1) for any period so specified if it is necessary for the offender to reside there for that period in order to participate in the programme.

(3) A court may not include a programme requirement in a youth rehabilitation order unless—

(a) the programme which the court proposes to specify in the order has been recommended to the court by—

(i) a member of a youth offending team,

(ii) an officer of a local probation board,

or

(iii) an officer of a provider of probation services,

as being suitable for the offender, and

(b) the court is satisfied that the programme is available at the place or places proposed to be specified.

(4) A court may not include a programme requirement in a youth rehabilitation order if compliance with that requirement would involve the co-operation of a person other than the offender and the offender's responsible officer, unless that other person consents to its inclusion.

(5) A requirement to participate in a programme operates to require the offender—

(a) in accordance with instructions given by the responsible officer to participate in the programme at the place or places specified in the order on the number of days so specified,

and

(b) while at any of those places, to comply with instructions given by, or under the authority of, the person in charge of the programme.

There is no age restriction. The requirement may be attached to a YRO for a non-imprisonable offence. The offender must participate in a systematic set of activities and the nature of the activity in a programme requirement must be recommended to the court by one of the named persons in para. 11(3) and the the programme must be available at the place or places specified. If this involves the co-operation of a third party other than the offender or the responsible officer then that third party must consent. This is worth noting from a practical application but may in fact only relate to situations where the programme may have a reparation element.

Attendance Centre Requirement

Criminal Justice and Immigration Act 2008, Sched. 1, para. 12

Attendance centre requirement

27–47 12.—(1) In this Part of this Act "attendance centre requirement", in relation to a youth rehabilitation order, means a requirement that the offender must attend at an attendance centre specified in the order for such number of hours as may be so specified.

(2) The aggregate number of hours for which the offender may be required to attend at an attendance centre—

(a) if the offender is aged 16 or over at the time of conviction, must be—

(i) not less than 12, and

(ii) not more than 36;

(b) if the offender is aged 14 or over but under 16 at the time of conviction, must be—

(i) not less than 12, and

(ii) not more than 24;

(c) if the offender is aged under 14 at the time of conviction, must not be more than 12.

(3) A court may not include an attendance centre requirement in a youth rehabilitation order unless it—

(a) has been notified by the Secretary of State that—

(i) an attendance centre is available for persons of the offender's description, and

(ii) provision can be made at the centre for the offender,

and

(b) is satisfied that the attendance centre proposed to be specified is reasonably accessible to the offender, having regard to the means of access available to the offender and any other circumstances.

(4) The first time at which the offender is required to attend at the attendance centre is a time notified to the offender by the responsible officer.

(5) The subsequent hours are to be fixed by the officer in charge of the centre—

(a) in accordance with arrangements made by the responsible officer,

and

(b) having regard to the offender's circumstances.

(6) An offender may not be required under this paragraph to attend at an attendance centre—

(a) on more than one occasion on any day, or

(b) for more than three hours on any occasion.

(7) A requirement to attend at an attendance centre for any period on any occasion operates as a requirement—

(a) to attend at the centre at the beginning of the period,

and

(b) during that period, to engage in occupation, or receive instruction, under the supervision of and in accordance with instructions given by, or under the authority of, the officer in charge of the centre, whether at the centre or elsewhere.

This requirement is fairly self explanatory but it is age limited and it can be attached to a YRO for a non imprisonable offence.

Prohibited Activity Requirement

Criminal Justice and Immigration Act 2008, Sched. 1, para. 13

Prohibited activity requirement

13.—(1) In this Part of this Act "prohibited activity requirement", in relation to a youth rehabilitation order, means a requirement that the offender must refrain from participating in activities specified in the order— **27–48**

(a) on a day or days so specified,

or

(b) during a period so specified.

(2) A court may not include a prohibited activity requirement in a youth rehabilitation order unless it has consulted—

(a) a member of a youth offending team,

(b) an officer of a local probation board,

or

(c) an officer of a provider of probation services.

(3) The requirements that may by virtue of this paragraph be included in a youth rehabilitation order include a requirement that the offender does not possess, use or carry a firearm within the meaning of the *Firearms Act* 1968 (c. 27).

This is not age limited and can be attached to a YRO where the offence is non-imprisonable. The Court must consult the YOT, Probation or an officer who provides Probation services before it attaches a prohibited activity to a YRO.

Curfew Requirement

Criminal Justice and Immigration Act 2008, Sched. 1, para. 14

Curfew requirement

14.—(1) In this Part of this Act "curfew requirement", in relation to a youth rehabilita- **27–49** tion order, means a requirement that the offender must remain, for periods specified in the order, at a place so specified.

(2) A youth rehabilitation order imposing a curfew requirement may specify different places or different periods for different days, but may not specify periods which amount to less than 2 hours or more than 12 hours in any day.

(3) A youth rehabilitation order imposing a curfew requirement may not specify periods which fall outside the period of 6 months beginning with the day on which the requirement first takes effect.

(4) Before making a youth rehabilitation order imposing a curfew requirement, the court must obtain and consider information about the place proposed to be specified in the order (including information as to the attitude of persons likely to be affected by the enforced presence there of the offender).

This is not age limited and it may be attached to a YRO for a non-imprisonable offence. Under Sched. 1, para. 2(2) to the *Criminal Justice and Immigration Act* 2008, the court must attach an electronic monitoring requirement in addition to a curfew requirement unless it is inappropriate or the court is prevented from doing so under the terms of Sched. 1, para. 26(3) or (6) to the *Criminal Justice and Immigration Act* 2008. The Court must not add the electronic monitoring requirement unless it is mandatory to do so, or it is necessary to ensure compliance with other requirements. This would mean that it cannot be added as a sole requirement.

Exclusion Requirement

Criminal Justice and Immigration Act 2008, Sched. 1, para. 15

Exclusion requirement

27–50 15.—(1) In this Part of this Act "exclusion requirement", in relation to a youth rehabilitation order, means a provision prohibiting the offender from entering a place specified in the order for a period so specified.

(2) The period specified must not be more than 3 months.

(3) An exclusion requirement—

(a) may provide for the prohibition to operate only during the periods specified in the order,

or

(b) may specify different places for different periods or days.

(4) In this paragraph "place" includes an area.

The requirement is not age limited and the offence need not be imprisonable, but the court must attach a requirement of electronic monitoring whenever it attaches an exclusion requirement having regard to the provisions of Sched. 1, para. 2(2) and para. 26(3) and (6).

Residence Requirement

Criminal Justice and Immigration Act 2008, Sched. 1, para. 16

Residence requirement

27–51 16.—(1) In this Part of this Act, "residence requirement", in relation to a youth rehabilitation order, means a requirement that, during the period specified in the order, the offender must reside—

(a) with an individual specified in the order, or

(b) at a place specified in the order.

(2) A court may not by virtue of sub-paragraph (1)(a) include in a youth rehabilitation order a requirement that the offender reside with an individual unless that individual has consented to the requirement.

(3) In this paragraph, a residence requirement falling within sub-paragraph (1)(b) is referred to as "a place of residence requirement".

(4) A court may not include a place of residence requirement in a youth rehabilitation order unless the offender was aged 16 or over at the time of conviction.

(5) If the order so provides, a place of residence requirement does not prohibit the offender from residing, with the prior approval of the responsible officer, at a place other than that specified in the order.

(6) Before making a youth rehabilitation order containing a place of residence requirement, the court must consider the home surroundings of the offender.

(7) A court may not specify a hostel or other institution as the place where an offender must reside for the purposes of a place of residence requirement except on the recommendation of—

(a) a member of a youth offending team,

(b) an officer of a local probation board,

(c) an officer of a provider of probation services, or

(d) a social worker of a local authority.

The court must consult before imposing a residence requirement, the offender must be aged 16 or over ***at the time of conviction***. It can specify that the offender lives with a named individual or at a named place. If the requirement is attached on the basis of a place rather than an individual, then the requirement is referred to as a "place of residence requirement". There appears to be no power for the court to specify that the offender should ***not*** reside with a named individual under a residence requirement.

Local Authority Residence Requirement

Criminal Justice and Immigration Act 2008, Sched. 1, para. 17

Local authority residence requirement

17.—(1) In this Part of this Act, "local authority residence requirement", in relation to a youth rehabilitation order, means a requirement that, during the period specified in the order, the offender must reside in accommodation provided by or on behalf of a local authority specified in the order for the purposes of the requirement. **27–52**

(2) A youth rehabilitation order which imposes a local authority residence requirement may also stipulate that the offender is not to reside with a person specified in the order.

(3) A court may not include a local authority residence requirement in a youth rehabilitation order made in respect of an offence unless it is satisfied—

(a) that the behaviour which constituted the offence was due to a significant extent to the circumstances in which the offender was living,

and

(b) that the imposition of that requirement will assist in the offender's rehabilitation.

(4) A court may not include a local authority residence requirement in a youth rehabilitation order unless it has consulted—

(a) a parent or guardian of the offender (unless it is impracticable to consult such a person),

and

(b) the local authority which is to receive the offender.

(5) A youth rehabilitation order which imposes a local authority residence requirement must specify, as the local authority which is to receive the offender, the local authority in whose area the offender resides or is to reside.

(6) Any period specified in a youth rehabilitation order as a period for which the offender must reside in accommodation provided by or on behalf of a local authority must—

(a) not be longer than 6 months, and

(b) not include any period after the offender has reached the age of 18

There is a time restriction, the requirement should not be longer than 6 months. The court should not include any period after the offender has reached the age of 18. There is no other restriction as to age. The offence need not be imprisonable. The court must observe the pre-conditions in para. 17(3) and the offender may be excluded from residing with a named individual and that individual must be named in the order.

In addition, para. 19 (see *post*) must be observed and the court may not impose the requirement unless the offender was legally represented at the relevant time in court, or either of the conditions below is satisfied, namely,

(a) that the offender was granted a right to representation funded by the Legal Services Commission as part of the Criminal Defence Service for the purposes of the proceedings but the right was withdrawn because of the offender's conduct,

and

(b) that the offender has been informed of the right to apply for such representation for the purposes of the proceedings and has had the opportunity to do so, but nevertheless refused or failed to apply.

Mental Health Treatment Requirement

Criminal Justice and Immigration Act 2008, Sched. 1, para. 20

Mental health treatment requirement

27–53 20.—(1) In this Part of this Act "mental health treatment requirement", in relation to a youth rehabilitation order, means a requirement that the offender must submit, during a period or periods specified in the order, to treatment by or under the direction of a registered medical practitioner or a chartered psychologist (or both, for different periods) with a view to the improvement of the offender's mental condition.

(2) The treatment required during a period specified under sub-paragraph (1) must be such one of the following kinds of treatment as may be specified in the youth rehabilitation order—

(a) treatment as a resident patient in an independent hospital or care home within the meaning of the Care Standards Act 2000 (c. 14) or a hospital within the meaning of the Mental Health Act 1983 (c. 20), but not in hospital premises where high security psychiatric services within the meaning of that Act are provided;

(b) treatment as a non-resident patient at such institution or place as may be specified in the order;

(c) treatment by or under the direction of such registered medical practitioner or chartered psychologist (or both) as may be so specified;

but the order must not otherwise specify the nature of the treatment.

(3) A court may not include a mental health treatment requirement in a youth rehabilitation order unless—

(a) the court is satisfied, on the evidence of a registered medical practitioner approved for the purposes of section 12 of the *Mental Health Act* 1983 (c. 20), that the mental condition of the offender—

(i) is such as requires and may be susceptible to treatment, but

(ii) is not such as to warrant the making of a hospital order or guardianship order within the meaning of that Act,

(b) the court is also satisfied that arrangements have been or can be made for the treatment intended to be specified in the order (including, where the offender is to be required to submit to treatment as a resident patient, arrangements for the reception of the offender),

and

(c) the offender has expressed willingness to comply with the requirement.

(4) While the offender is under treatment as a resident patient in pursuance of a mental health treatment requirement of a youth rehabilitation order, the responsible officer is to carry out the supervision of the offender to such extent only as may be necessary for the purpose of the revocation or amendment of the order.

(5) Subsections (2) and (3) of section 54 of the *Mental Health Act* 1983 have effect with respect to proof of an offender's mental condition for the purposes of sub-paragraph (3)(a) as they have effect with respect to proof of an offender's mental condition for the purposes of section 37(2)(a) of that Act.

(6) In this paragraph and paragraph 21, "chartered psychologist" means a person for the time being listed in the British Psychological Society's Register of Chartered Psychologists.

Criminal Justice and Immigration Act 2008, Sched. 1, para. 21

Mental health treatment at place other than that specified in order

21.—(1) Where the registered medical practitioner or chartered psychologist by whom or under whose direction an offender is being treated in pursuance of a mental health treatment requirement is of the opinion that part of the treatment can be better or more conveniently given in or at an institution or place which— **27–54**

(a) is not specified in the youth rehabilitation order, and

(b) is one in or at which the treatment of the offender will be given by or under the direction of a registered medical practitioner or chartered psychologist,

the medical practitioner or psychologist may make arrangements for the offender to be treated accordingly.

(2) Such arrangements as are mentioned in sub-paragraph (1) may only be made if the offender has expressed willingness for the treatment to be given as mentioned in that sub-paragraph.

(3) Such arrangements as are mentioned in sub-paragraph (1) may provide for part of the treatment to be provided to the offender as a resident patient in an institution or place notwithstanding that the institution or place is not one which could have been specified for that purpose in the youth rehabilitation order.

(4) Where any such arrangements as are mentioned in sub-paragraph (1) are made for the treatment of an offender—

(a) the registered medical practitioner or chartered psychologist by whom the arrangements are made must give notice in writing to the offender's responsible officer, specifying the institution or place in or at which the treatment is to be carried out, and

(b) the treatment provided for by the arrangements is deemed to be treatment to which the offender is required to submit in pursuance of the youth rehabilitation order.

There is no age limitation and there appears to be no requirement that the offence should be an imprisonable offence. Under a Mental Health Treatment Requirement, the court should take care to observe that it cannot give specific direction as to the nature of the treatment. The court must be satisfied that arrangements have been made or can be made for the treatment intended to be specified in the order including arrangements with the institution where the offender is expected to be a resident patient. Where the registered medical practitioner or chartered psychologist by whom or under whose direction an offender is being treated in pursuance of a mental health treatment requirement is of the opinion that part of the treatment can be better or more conveniently given in or at an institution or place which is not specified in the youth rehabilitation order, and is one in or at which the treatment of the offender will be given by or under the direction of a registered medical practitioner or chartered psychologist, the medical practitioner or psychologist may make arrangements for the offender to be treated accordingly.

It is therefore possible for the mental health treatment to take place at a place that has not been specified in the order providing that the offender has expressed willingness for the treatment to take place elsewhere. The mechanics or arranging this are covered in para. 21 and it appears that the court need not make a formal amendment.

Drug Treatment Requirement

Criminal Justice and Immigration Act 2008, Sched. 1, para. 22

Drug treatment requirement

22.—(1) In this Part of this Act, "drug treatment requirement", in relation to a youth rehabilitation order, means a requirement that the offender must submit, during a period or periods specified in the order, to treatment, by or under the direction of a person so specified having the necessary qualifications or experience ("the treatment provider"), with a view to the reduction or elimination of the offender's dependency on, or propensity to misuse, drugs. **27–55**

(2) A court may not include a drug treatment requirement in a youth rehabilitation order unless it is satisfied—

(a) that the offender is dependent on, or has a propensity to misuse, drugs,

and

(b) that the offender's dependency or propensity is such as requires and may be susceptible to treatment.

(3) The treatment required during a period specified under sub-paragraph (1) must be such one of the following kinds of treatment as may be specified in the youth rehabilitation order—

(a) treatment as a resident in such institution or place as may be specified in the order,

or

(b) treatment as a non-resident at such institution or place, and at such intervals, as may be so specified,

but the order must not otherwise specify the nature of the treatment.

(4) A court may not include a drug treatment requirement in a youth rehabilitation order unless—

(a) the court has been notified by the Secretary of State that arrangements for implementing drug treatment requirements are in force in the local justice area in which the offender resides or is to reside

(b) the court is satisfied that arrangements have been or can be made for the treatment intended to be specified in the order (including, where the offender is to be required to submit to treatment as a resident, arrangements for the reception of the offender),

(c) the requirement has been recommended to the court as suitable for the offender by a member of a youth offending team, an officer of a local probation board or an officer of a provider of probation services,

and

(d) the offender has expressed willingness to comply with the requirement.

(5) In this paragraph "drug" means a controlled drug as defined by section 2 of the *Misuse of Drugs Act* 1971 (c. 38).

Drug Testing Requirement

Criminal Justice and Immigration Act 2008, Sched. 1, para. 23

Drug testing requirement

27–56 23.—(1) In this Part of this Act, "drug testing requirement", in relation to a youth rehabilitation order, means a requirement that, for the purpose of ascertaining whether there is any drug in the offender's body during any treatment period, the offender must, during that period, provide samples in accordance with instructions given by the responsible officer or the treatment provider.

(2) In sub-paragraph (1)—

(a) "drug" has the same meaning as in paragraph 22,

(b) "treatment period" means a period specified in the youth rehabilitation order as a period during which the offender must submit to treatment as mentioned in sub-paragraph (1) of that paragraph, and

(c) "the treatment provider" has the meaning given by that sub-paragraph.

(3) A court may not include a drug testing requirement in a youth rehabilitation order unless—

(a) the court has been notified by the Secretary of State that arrangements for implementing drug testing requirements are in force in the local justice area in which the offender resides or is to reside,

(b) the order also imposes a drug treatment requirement,

and

(c) the offender has expressed willingness to comply with the requirement.

(4) A youth rehabilitation order which imposes a drug testing requirement

(a) must specify for each month the minimum number of occasions on which samples are to be provided, and

(b) may specify—

(i) times at which and circumstances in which the responsible officer or treatment provider may require samples to be provided,

and

(ii) descriptions of the samples which may be so required.

(5) A youth rehabilitation order which imposes a drug testing requirement must provide for the results of tests carried out otherwise than by the responsible officer on samples provided by the offender in pursuance of the requirement to be communicated to the responsible officer.

A court may not include a drug treatment requirement in a youth rehabilitation order unless it is satisfied—

(a) that the offender is dependent on, or has a propensity to misuse, drugs, and

(b) that the offender's dependency or propensity is such as requires and may be susceptible to treatment.

If the court makes a requirement of Drug Treatment, it must also attach a requirement of Drug Testing (para. 23(3)(b)). It is not age limited and the offence need not be imprisonable. The offender must express willingness to comply with both requirements and the offender must be assessed as suitable. The order must specify for each month, the minimum number of occasions on which samples are to be provided and may specify the times and circumstances in which the responsible officer or treatment provider may require samples to be provided and descriptions of the samples which may be so required. The court should take care to observe that it cannot give specific direction as to the nature of the treatment. The court must be satisfied that arrangements have been made or can be made for the treatment intended to be specified in the order including arrangements with the institution where the offender is expected to be a resident patient

Intoxicating substance treatment Requirement

Criminal Justice and Immigration Act 2008, Sched. 1, para. 24

Intoxicating substance treatment requirement

24.—(1) In this Part of this Act, "intoxicating substance treatment requirement", in relation to a youth rehabilitation order, means a requirement that the offender must submit, during a period or periods specified in the order, to treatment, by or under the direction of a person so specified having the necessary qualifications or experience, with a view to the reduction or elimination of the offender's dependency on or propensity to misuse intoxicating substances. **27–57**

(2) A court may not include an intoxicating substance treatment requirement in a youth rehabilitation order unless it is satisfied—

(a) that the offender is dependent on, or has a propensity to misuse, intoxicating substances,

and

(b) that the offender's dependency or propensity is such as requires and may be susceptible to treatment.

(3) The treatment required during a period specified under sub-paragraph (1) must be such one of the following kinds of treatment as may be specified in the youth rehabilitation order—

(a) treatment as a resident in such institution or place as may be specified in the order,

or

(b) treatment as a non-resident at such institution or place, and at such intervals, as may be so specified,

but the order must not otherwise specify the nature of the treatment.

(4) A court may not include an intoxicating substance treatment requirement in a youth rehabilitation order unless—

(a) the court is satisfied that arrangements have been or can be made for the treatment intended to be specified in the order (including, where the offender is to be required to submit to treatment as a resident, arrangements for the reception of the offender),

(b) the requirement has been recommended to the court as suitable for the offender by a member of a youth offending team, an officer of a local probation board or an officer of a provider of probation services,

and

(c) the offender has expressed willingness to comply with the requirement.

(5) In this paragraph "intoxicating substance" means—

(a) alcohol,

or

(b) any other substance or product (other than a drug) which is, or the fumes of which are, capable of being inhaled or otherwise used for the purpose of causing intoxication.

(6) In sub-paragraph (5)(b) "drug" means a controlled drug as defined by section 2 of the *Misuse of Drugs Act* 1971 (c. 38).

A court may not include an intoxicating substance treatment requirement in a youth rehabilitation order unless it is satisfied of the pre-conditions under para. 24(2).

There is no power to attach a testing requirement. The requirement is not age limited and the offence need not be imprisonable. The offender must express willingness to comply with the requirement and the offender must be assessed as suitable. The court cannot give specific direction as to the nature of the treatment. The court must be satisfied that arrangements have been made or can be made for the treatment intended to be specified in the order including arrangements with the institution where the offender is expected to be a resident patient.

Education Requirement

Criminal Justice and Immigration Act 2008, Sched. 1, para. 25

Education requirement

27–58 25.—(1) In this Part of this Act "education requirement", in relation to a youth rehabilitation order, means a requirement that the offender must comply, during a period or periods specified in the order, with approved education arrangements

(2) For this purpose, "approved education arrangements" means arrangements for the offender's education—

(a) made for the time being by the offender's parent or guardian,

and

(b) approved by the local education authority specified in the order.

(3) The local education authority so specified must be the local education authority for the area in which the offender resides or is to reside.

(4) A court may not include an education requirement in a youth rehabilitation order unless—

(a) it has consulted the local education authority proposed to be specified in the order with regard to the proposal to include the requirement,

and

(b) it is satisfied—

(i) that, in the view of that local education authority, arrangements exist for the offender to receive efficient full-time education suitable to the offender's age, ability, aptitude and special educational needs (if any),

and

(ii) that, having regard to the circumstances of the case, the inclusion of the education requirement is necessary for securing the good conduct of the offender or for preventing the commission of further offences.

(5) Any period specified in a youth rehabilitation order as a period during which an offender must comply with approved education arrangements must not include any period after the offender has ceased to be of compulsory school age.

(6) In this paragraph, "local education authority" and "parent" have the same meanings as in the *Education Act* 1996 (c. 56).

There is no age limit, save that of compulsory school age and the offence need not be imprisonable. The court must consult the local education authority for the area in which the offender resides or is to reside.

The court must be satisfied that the pre-conditions in para. 25(4)(b) are met.

Electronic Monitoring Requirement

Criminal Justice and Immigration Act 2008, Sched. 1, para. 26

Electronic monitoring requirement

26.—(1) In this Part of this Act "electronic monitoring requirement", in relation to a youth rehabilitation order, means a requirement for securing the electronic monitoring of the offender's compliance with other requirements imposed by the order during a period specified in the order or determined by the responsible officer in accordance with the order. **27–59**

(2) Where an electronic monitoring requirement is required to take effect during a period determined by the responsible officer in accordance with the youth rehabilitation order, the responsible officer must, before the beginning of that period, notify—

(a) the offender,

(b) the person responsible for the monitoring,

and

(c) any person falling within sub-paragraph (3)(b),

of the time when the period is to begin.

(3) Where—

(a) it is proposed to include an electronic monitoring requirement in a youth rehabilitation order, but

(b) there is a person (other than the offender) without whose co-operation it will not be practicable to secure that the monitoring takes place,

the requirement may not be included in the order without that person's consent.

(4) A youth rehabilitation order which imposes an electronic monitoring requirement must include provision for making a person responsible for the monitoring.

(5) The person who is made responsible for the monitoring must be of a description specified in an order made by the Secretary of State.

(6) A court may not include an electronic monitoring requirement in a youth rehabilitation order unless the court—

(a) has been notified by the Secretary of State that arrangements for electronic monitoring of offenders are available—

(i) in the local justice area proposed to be specified in the order,

and

(ii) for each requirement mentioned in the first column of the Table in sub-paragraph (7) which the court proposes to include in the order, in the area in which the relevant place is situated,

and

(b) is satisfied that the necessary provision can be made under the arrangements currently available.

(7) For the purposes of sub-paragraph (6), "relevant place", in relation to a requirement mentioned in the first column of the following Table which the court proposes to include in the order, means the place mentioned in relation to it in the second column of the Table.

Proposed requirement of youth rehabilitation order	*Relevant place*
Curfew requirement.	The place which the court proposes to specify in the order for the purposes of that requirement.
Exclusion requirement.	The place (within the meaning of paragraph 15) which the court proposes to specify in the order.
Attendance centre requirement.	The attendance centre which the court proposes to specify in the order.

Criminal Justice and Immigration Act 2008, Sched. 1, para. 2

Electronic monitoring requirement

27–60 2.—(1) Sub-paragraph (2) applies to a youth rehabilitation order which—

(a) imposes a curfew requirement (whether by virtue of paragraph 3(4)(b) or otherwise), or

(b) imposes an exclusion requirement.

(2) The order must also impose an electronic monitoring requirement unless—

(a) in the particular circumstances of the case, the court considers it inappropriate for the order to do so, or

(b) the court is prevented by paragraph 26(3) or (6) from including such a requirement in the order.

(3) Subsection (2)(a) of section 1 has effect subject to paragraph 26(3) and (6).

As stated above, there are situations where the court must attach an electronic monitoring requirement and in other situations the court may attach the requirement. Schedule 1, para. 2 states that the court must impose an electronic monitoring requirement when it imposes a curfew requirement or an exclusion requirement. In addition it states that the court must also impose an electronic monitoring requirement unless the exceptions listed apply.

YRO with fostering and YRO with ISS

27–61 There are two further types of youth rehabilitation orders. These are specific orders. Great care needs to be taken when making these orders as there are quite a number of preconditions. In addition there are mandatory requirements. The court may be prohibited from adding certain requirements and may mix and match the other requirements.

These two orders are youth rehabilitation orders with fostering and youth rehabilitation orders with Intensive Supervision and Surveillance, (ISS). Section 1(3) of the *Criminal Justice and Immigration Act* 2008.

Youth Rehabilitation Order with fostering

27–62 The court may not make a YRO with fostering unless the provisions of s.1(4)(a) and (b) of the *Criminal Justice and Immigration Act* 2008 have been complied with.

The offences must be imprisonable and so serious that a custodial sentence would be appropriate. There is no definition of "persistent", the existing case law in relation to Detention and Training Orders may assist. The offender must be represented or have been given the opportunity of representation and have refused it.

Criminal Justice and Immigration Act 2008, Sched. 1, para. 4

Youth rehabilitation order with fostering

4.—(1) This paragraph applies where paragraphs (a) to (c) of section 1(4) are satisfied.

(2) If the court is satisfied—

(a) that the behaviour which constituted the offence was due to a significant extent to the circumstances in which the offender was living, and

(b) that the imposition of a fostering requirement (see paragraph 18) would assist in the offender's rehabilitation,

it may make a youth rehabilitation order in accordance with section 1 which imposes a fostering requirement.

(3) But a court may not impose a fostering requirement unless—

(a) it has consulted the offender's parents or guardians (unless it is impracticable to do so),

and

(b) it has consulted the local authority which is to place the offender with a local authority foster parent.

(4) A youth rehabilitation order which imposes a fostering requirement must also impose a supervision requirement.

(5) This paragraph has effect subject to paragraphs 18(7) and 19 (pre-conditions to imposing fostering requirement).

(6) A youth rehabilitation order which imposes a fostering requirement is referred to in this Part of this Act as "a youth rehabilitation order with fostering" (whatever other requirements mentioned in section 1(1) or (2) it imposes).

Fostering Requirement

Criminal Justice and Immigration Act 2008, Sched. 1, para. 18

Fostering requirement

18.—(1) In this Part of this Act "fostering requirement", in relation to a youth rehabilitation order, means a requirement that, for a period specified in the order, the offender must reside with a local authority foster parent. **27–63**

(2) A period specified in a youth rehabilitation order as a period for which the offender must reside with a local authority foster parent must—

(a) end no later than the end of the period of 12 months beginning with the date on which the requirement first has effect (but subject to paragraphs 6(9), 8(9) and 16(2) of Schedule 2),

and

(b) not include any period after the offender has reached the age of 18.

(3) A youth rehabilitation order which imposes a fostering requirement must specify the local authority which is to place the offender with a local authority foster parent under section 23(2)(a) of the *Children Act* 1989 (c. 41).

(4) The authority so specified must be the local authority in whose area the offender resides or is to reside.

(5) If at any time during the period specified under sub-paragraph (1), the responsible officer notifies the offender—

(a) that no suitable local authority foster parent is available,

and

(b) that the responsible officer has applied or proposes to apply under Part 3 or 4 of Schedule 2 for the revocation or amendment of the order,

the fostering requirement is, until the determination of the application, to be taken to require the offender to reside in accommodation provided by or on behalf of a local authority.

(6) In this paragraph, "local authority foster parent" has the same meaning as it has in the Children Act 1989.

Pre-conditions to imposing fostering requirement

Criminal Justice and Immigration Act 2008, Sched. 1, para. 19

19.—(1) A court may not include a local authority residence requirement or a fostering requirement in a youth rehabilitation order in respect of an offender unless— **27–64**

(a) the offender was legally represented at the relevant time in court,

and

(b) either of the conditions in sub-paragraph (2) is satisfied.

(2) Those conditions are—

(a) that the offender was granted a right to representation funded by the Legal Services Commission as part of the Criminal Defence Service for the purposes of the proceedings but the right was withdrawn because of the offender's conduct,

and

(b) that the offender has been informed of the right to apply for such representation for the purposes of the proceedings and has had the opportunity to do so, but nevertheless refused or failed to apply.

(3) In this paragraph—

"the proceedings" means—

(a) the whole proceedings,

or

(b) the part of the proceedings relating to the imposition of the local authority residence requirement or the fostering requirement;

"the relevant time" means the time when the court is considering whether to impose that requirement.

The court must have regard to paras 18 and 19, must consult with the local authority and must attach a supervision requirement as well. When imposed, the YRO is referred to as a "YRO with fostering". This specific type of order must contain a fostering requirement and it is the only order that may have a fostering requirement. The YRO with fostering may have other requirements which come from s.1(1) and 1(2) of the *Criminal Justice and Immigration Act* 2008. These must be distinguished from the menu of requirements listed in Sched. 1, para. 4 .

There is a time limit for the requirement, it must end no later than the end of the period of 12 months beginning with the date on which the requirement first has effect.

It must not include any period after the offender has reached 18.

The court may not include a fostering requirement in a youth rehabilitation order unless the court has been notified by the Secretary of State that arrangements for implementing such a requirement are available in the area of the local authority which is to place the offender with a local authority foster parent.

There is no effect upon the power of a local authority to place with a local authority foster parent an offender in respect of whom a local authority residence requirement is imposed.

Youth Rehabilitation Order with Intensive Supervision And Surveillance (ISS)

27–65 The YRO with Intensive Supervision and Surveillance is basically a YRO with an extended activity requirement, supervision requirement, curfew requirement and an electronic monitoring requirement. These requirements are mandatory and the activity requirement must be no less than 90 and no more than 180 days. Other requirements under s.1(1) of the *Criminal Justice and Immigration Act* 2008 may be added but the court cannot add a fostering requirement with an ISS order. The court may only make a YRO with Intensive Supervision and Surveillance when the provisions of s.1(4)(a) and (b) of the *Criminal Justice and Immigration Act* 2008 have been complied with. The offences must be imprisonable and so serious that a custodial sentence would be appropriate. There is no definition of 'persistent', the existing case law in relation to Detention and Training Orders may assist.

Youth Rehabilitation Order with Intensive Supervision and Surveillance

Criminal Justice and Immigration Act 2008, Sched. 1, paras 3, 5

Youth rehabilitation order with intensive supervision and surveillance

27–66 3.—(1) This paragraph applies where paragraphs (a) to (c) of section 1(4) are satisfied.

(2) The court, if it makes a youth rehabilitation order which imposes an activity requirement, may specify in relation to that requirement a number of days which is more than 90 but not more than 180.

(3) Such an activity requirement is referred to in this Part of this Act as "an extended activity requirement".

(4) A youth rehabilitation order which imposes an extended activity requirement must also impose—

(a) a supervision requirement,

and

(b) a curfew requirement (and, accordingly, if so required by paragraph 2, an electronic monitoring requirement).

(5) A youth rehabilitation order which imposes an extended activity requirement (and other requirements in accordance with sub-paragraph (4)) is referred to in this Part of this Act as "a youth rehabilitation order with intensive supervision and surveillance" (whether or not it also imposes any other requirement mentioned in section 1(1)).

Intensive supervision and surveillance and fostering: further provisions

5.—(1) A youth rehabilitation order with intensive supervision and surveillance may not impose a fostering requirement.

(2) Nothing in—

(a) section 1(4)(b), or

(b) section 148(1) or (2)(b) of the *Criminal Justice Act* 2003 (c. 44) (restrictions on imposing community sentences),

prevents a court from making a youth rehabilitation order with intensive supervision and surveillance in respect of an offender if the offender fails to comply with an order under section 161(2) of the *Criminal Justice Act* 2003 (pre-sentence drug testing).

Provisions Applying Where Court Proposes to Make Youth Rehabilitation Order

Criminal Justice and Immigration Act 2008, Sched. 1, para. 28

Family circumstances

28. Before making a youth rehabilitation order, the court must obtain and consider information about the offender's family circumstances and the likely effect of such an order on those circumstances. **27–67**

Criminal Justice and Immigration Act 2008, Sched. 1, para. 29

Compatibility of requirements, requirement to avoid conflict with religious beliefs, etc.

29.—(1) Before making—

(a) a youth rehabilitation order imposing two or more requirements,

and

(b) two or more youth rehabilitation orders in respect of associated offences,

the court must consider whether, in the circumstances of the case, the requirements to be imposed by the order or orders are compatible with each other.

(2) Sub-paragraph (1) is subject to paragraphs 2, 3(4) and 4(4).

(3) The court must ensure, as far as practicable, that any requirement imposed by a youth rehabilitation order is such as to avoid—

(a) any conflict with the offender's religious beliefs,

(b) any interference with the times, if any, at which the offender normally works or attends school or any other educational establishment,

and

(c) any conflict with the requirements of any other youth rehabilitation order to which the offender may be subject.

(4) The Secretary of State may by order provide that sub-paragraph (3) is to have effect with such additional restrictions as may be specified in the order.

Criminal Justice and Immigration Act 2008, Sched. 1, para. 30

Date of taking effect and other existing orders

30.—(1) Subject to sub-paragraph (2), a youth rehabilitation order takes effect on the day after the day on which the order is made.

(2) If a detention and training order is in force in respect of an offender, a court making a youth rehabilitation order in respect of the offender may order that it is to take effect instead—

(a) when the period of supervision begins in relation to the detention and training order in accordance with section 103(1)(a) of the *Powers of Criminal Courts (Sentencing) Act* 2000 (c. 6),

or

(b) on the expiry of the term of the detention and training order.

(3) In sub-paragraph (2)—

(a) the references to a detention and training order include an order made under section 211 of the *Armed Forces Act* 2006 (c. 52) (detention and training orders made by service courts);

and

(b) the reference to section 103(1)(a) of the *Powers of Criminal Courts (Sentencing) Act* 2000 includes that provision as applied by section 213(1) of the *Armed Forces Act* 2006.

(4) A court must not make a youth rehabilitation order in respect of an offender at a time when—

(a) another youth rehabilitation order,

or

(b) a reparation order made under section 73(1) of the *Powers of Criminal Courts (Sentencing) Act* 2000 (c. 6),

is in force in respect of the offender, unless when it makes the order it revokes the earlier order.

(5) Where the earlier order is revoked under sub-paragraph (4), paragraph 24 of Schedule 2 (provision of copies of orders) applies to the revocation as it applies to the revocation of a youth rehabilitation order.

Criminal Justice and Immigration Act 2008, Sched. 1, para. 31

Concurrent and consecutive orders

31.—(1) This paragraph applies where the court is dealing with an offender who has been convicted of two or more associated offences.

(2) If, in respect of one of the offences, the court makes an order of any of the following kinds—

(a) a youth rehabilitation order with intensive supervision and surveillance,

(b) a youth rehabilitation order with fostering, or

(c) any other youth rehabilitation order,

it may not make an order of any other of those kinds in respect of the other offence, or any of the other offences.

(3) If the court makes two or more youth rehabilitation orders with intensive supervision and surveillance, or with fostering, both or all of the orders must take effect at the same time (in accordance with paragraph 30(1) or (2)).

(4) Where the court includes requirements of the same kind in two or more youth rehabilitation orders, it must direct, in relation to each requirement of that kind, whether—

(a) it is to be concurrent with the other requirement or requirements of that kind, or any of them,

or

(b) it and the other requirement or requirements of that kind, or any of them, are to be consecutive.

(5) But the court may not direct that two or more fostering requirements are to be consecutive.

(6) Where the court directs that two or more requirements of the same kind are to be consecutive—

(a) the number of hours, days or months specified in relation to one of them is additional to the number of hours, days, or months specified in relation to the other or others,

but

(b) the aggregate number of hours, days or months specified in relation to both or all of them must not exceed the maximum number which may be specified in relation to any one of them.

(7) For the purposes of sub-paragraphs (4) and (6), requirements are of the same kind if they fall within the same paragraph of Part 2 of this Schedule.

Provisions Applying Where Court Makes Youth Rehabilitation Order etc.

Criminal Justice and Immigration Act 2008, Sched. 1, paras 32, 33, 34, 35 and 36

Date for compliance with requirements to be specified in order

32.—(1) A youth rehabilitation order must specify a date, not more than 3 years after the date on which the order takes effect, by which all the requirements in it must have been complied with **27–68**

(2) A youth rehabilitation order which imposes two or more different requirements falling within Part 2 of this Schedule may also specify an earlier date or dates in relation to compliance with any one or more of them.

(3) In the case of a youth rehabilitation order with intensive supervision and surveillance, the date specified for the purposes of sub-paragraph (1) must not be earlier than 6 months after the date on which the order takes effect.

Local justice area to be specified in order

33. A youth rehabilitation order must specify the local justice area in which the offender resides or will reside.

Provision of copies of orders

34.—(1) The court by which any youth rehabilitation order is made must forthwith provide copies of the order—

(a) to the offender,

(b) if the offender is aged under 14, to the offender's parent or guardian,

and

(c) to a member of a youth offending team assigned to the court, to an officer of a local probation board assigned to the court or to an officer of a provider of probation services.

(2) Sub-paragraph (3) applies where a youth rehabilitation order—

(a) is made by the Crown Court, or

(b) is made by a magistrates' court which does not act in the local justice area specified in the order.

(3) The court making the order must—

(a) provide to the magistrates' court acting in the local justice area specified in the order—

(i) a copy of the order,

and

(ii) such documents and information relating to the case as it considers likely to be of assistance to a court acting in that area in the exercise of its functions in relation to the order,

and

(b) provide a copy of the order to the local probation board acting for that area or (as the case may be) a provider of probation services operating in that area.

(4) Where a youth rehabilitation order imposes any requirement specified in the first column of the following Table, the court by which the order is made must also forthwith provide the person specified in relation to that requirement in the second column of that Table with a copy of so much of the order as relates to that requirement.

Requirement	*Person to whom copy of requirement is to be given*
An activity requirement specifying a place under paragraph 6(1)(a).	The person in charge of that place.
An activity requirement specifying an activity under paragraph 6(1)(b).	The person in charge of that activity.
An activity requirement specifying a residential exercise under paragraph 6(1)(c).	The person in charge of the place or activity specified under paragraph 6(4) in relation to that residential exercise.
An attendance centre requirement.	The officer in charge of the attendance centre specified under paragraph 12(1).
An exclusion requirement imposed for the purpose (or partly for the purpose) of protecting a person from being approached by the offender.	The person intended to be protected.
A residence requirement requiring residence with an individual.	The individual specified under paragraph 16(1)(a).
A place of residence requirement (within the meaning of paragraph 16) relating to residence in an institution	The person in charge of the institution.
A local authority residence requirement.	The local authority specified under paragraph 17(1).
A mental health treatment requirement.	The person in charge of the institution or place specified under sub-paragraph (2)(a) or (b) of paragraph 20, or the person specified under sub-paragraph (2)(c) of that paragraph.
A drug treatment requirement.	The treatment provider specified under paragraph 22(1).
A drug testing requirement.	The treatment provider specified under paragraph 22(1).
An intoxicating substance treatment requirement	The person specified under paragraph 24(1).
An education requirement.	The local education authority specified under paragraph 25(2).
An electronic monitoring requirement.	Any person who by virtue of paragraph 26(4) will be responsible for the electronic monitoring. Any person without whose consent the requirement could not have been included in the order.

Power to provide for court review of orders

35.—(1) The Secretary of State may by order—

(a) enable or require a court making a youth rehabilitation order to provide for the order to be reviewed periodically by that or another court,

(b) enable a court to amend a youth rehabilitation order so as to include or remove a provision for review by a court,

and

(c) make provision as to the timing and conduct of reviews and as to the powers of the court on a review.

(2) An order under this paragraph may, in particular, make provision in relation to youth rehabilitation orders corresponding to any provision made by sections 191 and 192 of the *Criminal Justice Act* 2003 (c. 44) (reviews of suspended sentence orders) in relation to suspended sentence orders.

(3) An order under this paragraph may repeal or amend any provision of—

(a) this Part of this Act, or
(b) Chapter 1 of Part 12 of the *Criminal Justice Act* 2003 (general provisions about sentencing).

Order made by Crown Court: direction in relation to further proceedings

36.—(1) Where the Crown Court makes a youth rehabilitation order, it may include in the order a direction that further proceedings relating to the order be in a youth court or other magistrates' court (subject to paragraph 7 of Schedule 2).

(2) In sub-paragraph (1), "further proceedings", in relation to a youth rehabilitation order, means proceedings—
(a) for any failure to comply with the order within the meaning given by paragraph 1(2)(b) of Schedule 2, or
(b) on any application for amendment or revocation of the order under Part 3 or 4 of that Schedule.

Breach of Youth Rehabilitation Orders

Criminal Justice and Immigration Act 2008, Sched. 2, paras 5, 6, 7 and 18

Issue of summons or warrant by justice of the peace

5.—(1) If at any time while a youth rehabilitation order is in force it appears on information to a justice of the peace that an offender has failed to comply with a youth rehabilitation order, the justice may— **27–69**
(a) issue a summons requiring the offender to appear at the place and time specified in it, or
(b) if the information is in writing and on oath, issue a warrant for the offender's arrest.

(2) Any summons or warrant issued under this paragraph must direct the offender to appear or be brought—
(a) if the youth rehabilitation order was made by the Crown Court and does not include a direction under paragraph 36 of Schedule 1, before the Crown Court, and
(b) in any other case, before the appropriate court.

(3) In sub-paragraph (2), "appropriate court" means—
(a) if the offender is aged under 18, a youth court acting in the relevant local justice area, and
(b) if the offender is aged 18 or over, a magistrates' court (other than a youth court) acting in that local justice area

(4) In sub-paragraph (3), "relevant local justice area" means—
(a) the local justice area in which the offender resides, or
(b) if it is not known where the offender resides, the local justice area specified in the youth rehabilitation order.

(5) Sub-paragraphs (6) and (7) apply where the offender does not appear in answer to a summons issued under this paragraph.

(6) If the summons required the offender to appear before the Crown Court, the Crown Court may—
(a) unless the summons was issued under this sub-paragraph, issue a further summons requiring the offender to appear at the place and time specified in it, or
(b) in any case, issue a warrant for the arrest of the offender.

(7) If the summons required the offender to appear before a magistrates' court, the magistrates' court may issue a warrant for the arrest of the offender.

Powers of magistrates' court

6.—(1) This paragraph applies where—
(a) an offender appears or is brought before a youth court or other magistrates' court under paragraph 5, and
(b) it is proved to the satisfaction of the court that the offender has failed without reasonable excuse to comply with the youth rehabilitation order.

Part V

(2) The court may deal with the offender in respect of that failure in any one of the following ways—

(a) by ordering the offender to pay a fine of an amount not exceeding—

(i) £250, if the offender is aged under 14, or

(ii) £1,000, in any other case;

(b) by amending the terms of the youth rehabilitation order so as to impose any requirement which could have been included in the order when it was made—

(i) in addition to, or

(ii) in substitution for, any requirement or requirements already imposed by the order;

(c) by dealing with the offender, for the offence in respect of which the order was made, in any way in which the court could have dealt with the offender for that offence (had the offender been before that court to be dealt with for it).

(3) Sub-paragraph (2)(b) is subject to sub-paragraphs (6) to (9).

(4) In dealing with the offender under sub-paragraph (2), the court must take into account the extent to which the offender has complied with the youth rehabilitation order.

(5) A fine imposed under sub-paragraph (2)(a) is to be treated, for the purposes of any enactment, as being a sum adjudged to be paid by a conviction.

(6) Any requirement imposed under sub-paragraph (2)(b) must be capable of being complied with before the date specified under paragraph 32(1) of Schedule 1.

(7) Where—

(a) the court is dealing with the offender under sub-paragraph (2)(b), and

(b) the youth rehabilitation order does not contain an unpaid work requirement,

paragraph 10(2) of Schedule 1 applies in relation to the inclusion of such a requirement as if for "40" there were substituted "20".

(8) The court may not under sub-paragraph (2)(b) impose—

(a) an extended activity requirement, or

(b) a fostering requirement,

if the order does not already impose such a requirement.

(9) Where—

(a) the order imposes a fostering requirement (the "original requirement"), and

(b) under sub-paragraph (2)(b) the court proposes to substitute a new fostering requirement ("the substitute requirement") for the original requirement,

paragraph 18(2) of Schedule 1 applies in relation to the substitute requirement as if the reference to the period of 12 months beginning with the date on which the original requirement first had effect were a reference to the period of 18 months beginning with that date.

(10) Where—

(a) the court deals with the offender under sub-paragraph (2)(b), and

(b) it would not otherwise have the power to amend the youth rehabilitation order under paragraph 13 (amendment by reason of change of residence),

that paragraph has effect as if references in it to the appropriate court were references to the court which is dealing with the offender.

(11) Where the court deals with the offender under sub-paragraph (2)(c), it must revoke the youth rehabilitation order if it is still in force.

(12) Sub-paragraphs (13) to (15) apply where—

(a) the court is dealing with the offender under sub-paragraph (2)(c), and

(b) the offender has wilfully and persistently failed to comply with a youth rehabilitation order.

(13) The court may impose a youth rehabilitation order with intensive supervision and surveillance notwithstanding anything in section 1(4)(a) or (b).

(14) If—

(a) the order is a youth rehabilitation order with intensive supervision and surveillance, and

(b) the offence mentioned in sub-paragraph (2)(c) was punishable with imprisonment,

the court may impose a custodial sentence notwithstanding anything in section 152(2) of the *Criminal Justice Act* 2003 (c. 44) (general restrictions on imposing discretionary custodial sentences).

(15) If—

(a) the order is a youth rehabilitation order with intensive supervision and surveillance which was imposed by virtue of sub-paragraph (13) or paragraph 8(12), and

(b) the offence mentioned in sub-paragraph (2)(c) was not punishable with imprisonment,

for the purposes of dealing with the offender under sub-paragraph (2)(c), the court is to be taken to have had power to deal with the offender for that offence by making a detention and training order for a term not exceeding 4 months.

(16) An offender may appeal to the Crown Court against a sentence imposed under sub-paragraph (2)(c).

Power of magistrates' court to refer offender to Crown Court

7.—(1) Sub-paragraph (2) applies if—

(a) the youth rehabilitation order was made by the Crown Court and contains a direction under paragraph 36 of Schedule 1, and

(b) a youth court or other magistrates' court would (apart from that sub-paragraph) be required, or has the power, to deal with the offender in one of the ways mentioned in paragraph 6(2).

(2) The court may instead—

(a) commit the offender in custody, or

(b) release the offender on bail,

until the offender can be brought or appear before the Crown Court.

(3) Where a court deals with the offender's case under sub-paragraph (2) it must send to the Crown Court—

(a) a certificate signed by a justice of the peace certifying that the offender has failed to comply with the youth rehabilitation order in the respect specified in the certificate, and

(b) such other particulars of the case as may be desirable;

and a certificate purporting to be so signed is admissible as evidence of the failure before the Crown Court.

Powers of magistrates' court following subsequent conviction

18.—(1) This paragraph applies where—

(a) a youth rehabilitation order is in force in respect of an offender, and

(b) the offender is convicted of an offence (the "further offence") by a youth court or other magistrates' court ("the convicting court").

(2) Sub-paragraphs (3) and (4) apply where—

(a) the youth rehabilitation order—

(i) was made by a youth court or other magistrates' court, or

(ii) was made by the Crown Court and contains a direction under paragraph 36 of Schedule 1, and

(b) the convicting court is dealing with the offender for the further offence.

(3) The convicting court may revoke the order.

(4) Where the convicting court revokes the order under sub-paragraph (3), it may deal with the offender, for the offence in respect of which the order was made, in any way in which it could have dealt with the offender for that offence (had the offender been before that court to be dealt with for the offence).

(5) The convicting court may not exercise its powers under sub-paragraph (3) or (4) unless it considers that it would be in the interests of justice to do so, having regard to circumstances which have arisen since the youth rehabilitation order was made.

(6) In dealing with an offender under sub-paragraph (4), the sentencing court must take into account the extent to which the offender has complied with the order.

(7) A person sentenced under sub-paragraph (4) for an offence may appeal to the Crown Court against the sentence.

(8) Sub-paragraph (9) applies where—

(a) the youth rehabilitation order was made by the Crown Court and contains a direction under paragraph 36 of Schedule 1, and

(b) the convicting court would, but for that sub-paragraph, deal with the offender for the further offence.

(9) The convicting court may, instead of proceeding under sub-paragraph (3)—

(a) commit the offender in custody, or

(b) release the offender on bail,

until the offender can be brought before the Crown Court.

(10) Sub-paragraph (11) applies if the youth rehabilitation order was made by the Crown court and does not contain a direction under paragraph 36 of Schedule 1.

(11) The convicting court may—

(a) commit the offender in custody, or

(b) release the offender on bail,

until the offender can be brought or appear before the Crown Court.

(12) Where the convicting court deals with an offender's case under sub-paragraph (9) or (11), it must send to the Crown Court such particulars of the case as may be desirable.

Any breach of a youth rehabilitation order by failing to comply with the requirements is dealt with under this schedule. The powers on breach range from imposing a fine to amending the requirements by addition or substitution or revocation and re-sentence. If the breach is brought to court when the offender has reached the age of 18 then it must be dealt with at the magistrates' court (para. 5(3)) although any sentence on revocation must be one which would have been imposed at the Youth Court (para. 6(2)(c)). Where an offender is convicted of an offence during the currency of a Youth Rehabilitation Order this does not constitute a breach but under para. 30 (see § 27–67, *ante*) the court is prohibited from making another order when one is already in force unless the earlier order is revoked when the subsequent sentence is imposed. The practice is that the earlier order will be revoked but if a new youth rehabilitation order is made it will incorporate the earlier offences previously covered by the original order by way of re-sentence.

Where the original order was made by the Crown Court, the Youth Court may only deal with breach if the Crown Court has made a direction permitting it to do so under para. 36 (see § 27–68, *ante*) It will be necessary for a copy of the Crown Court order to be obtained for confirmation that such a direction has been made. Similarly if the defendant is convicted of another offence during the currency of an order made by the Crown Court, in the absence of such a direction the Youth Court will have no power to revoke the order and re-sentence but may commit the offender in custody or on bail to the Crown Court (see Sched. 2, para. 18).

IX. DETENTION AND TRAINING ORDER

(1) Purpose and effect

Powers of Criminal Courts (Sentencing) Act 2000, s.79(2)

27–70 **79.**—(2) The court shall not pass a custodial sentence on the offender unless it is of the opinion—

(a) that the offence or the combination of the offence and one or more offences associated with it, was so serious that only such a sentence can be justified for the offence; or

(b) where the offence is a violent or sexual offence, that only such a sentence would be adequate to protect the public from serious harm from him.

Powers of Criminal Courts (Sentencing) Act 2000, ss.100–103

Offenders under 18: detention and training orders

27–71 **100.**—(1) Subject to sections 90 and 91 above, sections 226 and 228 of the Criminal Justice Act 2003, and subsection (2) below, where—

(a) a child or young person (that is to say any person aged under 18) is convicted of an offence which is punishable with imprisonment in the case of a person aged 21 or over, and

(b) the court is of the opinion that subsection (2) of section 152 of the Criminal Justice Act 2003 applies or the case falls within subsection (3) of that section, the sentence that the court is to pass is a detention and training order.

(2) A court shall not make a detention and training order—

(a) in the case of an offender under the age of 15 at the time of conviction unless it is of the opinion that he is a persistent offender;

(b) In the case of an offender under the age of 12 at that time unless—

(i) it is of the opinion that only a custodial sentence would be adequate to protect the public from further offending by him; and

(ii) the offence was committed on or after such date as the Secretary of State may by order appoint.

(3) A detention and training order is an order that the offender in respect of whom it is made shall be subject, for the term specified in the order, to a period of detention and training followed by a period of supervision.

Term of order, consecutive terms and taking account of remands

101.—(1) Subject to subsection (2) below, the term of a detention and training order made in respect of an offence (whether by a magistrates' court or otherwise) shall be 4, 6, 8, 10, 12, 18 or 24 months. **27–72**

(2) The term of a detention and training order may not exceed the maximum term of imprisonment that the Crown Court could (in the case of an offender aged 21 or over) impose for the offence.

(3) Subject to subsections (4) and (6) below, a court making a detention and training order may order that its term shall commence on the expiry of the term of any other detention and training order made by that or any other court.

(4) A court shall not make in respect of an offender a detention and training order the effect of which would be that he would be subject to detention and training orders for a term which exceeds 24 months.

(5) Where the term of the detention and training order to which an offender would otherwise be subject exceeds 24 months, the excess shall be treated as remitted.

(6) A court making a detention and training order shall not order that its term shall commence on the expiry of the term of a detention and training order under which the period of supervision has already begun under section 103(1).

(7) Where a detention and training order ("the new order") is made in respect of an offender who is subject to a detention and training order under which the period of supervision has begun ("the old order"), the old order shall be disregarded in determining—

(a) for the purpose of subsection (4) above whether the effect of the new order would be that the offender would be subject to detentionand training orders for a term which exceeds 24 months; and

(b) for the purposes of subsection (5) above whether the term of detention and training orders to which the offender would (apart from that subsection) be subject exceeds 24 months.

(8) In determining the term of the detention and training order for an offence, the court shall take into account any period for which the offender has been remanded in custody in connection with the offence, or any other offence, the charge for which was founded on the same facts or evidence.

(9) Where a court proposes to make a detention and training order in respect of an offender for two or more offences—

(a) subsection (8) above shall not apply; but

(b) in determining the total term of the detention and training orders it proposes to make in respect of the offender, the court shall take into account of the total period (if any) for which he has been remanded in custody in connection with any of those offences, or any other offence the charge for which was founded on the same facts or evidence.

(10) Once a period of remand has, under subsection (8) or (9) above been taken account of in relation to a detention and training order made in respect of an offender for any offence or offences, it shall not subsequently be taken into account (under either of those subsections) in relation to such an order made in respect of the offender for any other offence or offences.

(11) Any reference in subsection (8) or (9) above to an offender's being remanded in custody is a reference to his being—

(a) held in police detention;

(b) remanded in or committed to custody by order of the court;

(c) remanded or committed to local authority accommodation under section 23 of the *Children and Young Person Act* 1969 and placed and kept in secure accommodation or detained in a secure training centre pursuant to arrangements under subsection (7A) of that section; or

(d) remanded, admitted or removed to hospital under sections 35, 36, 38 or 48 of the *Mental Health Act* 1983.

(12) A person is in police detention for the purposes of subsection (11) above—

(a) at any time when he is in police detention for the purposes of the *Police and Criminal Evidence Act* 1984; and

(b) at any time when he is detained under section 41 of the *Terrorism Act* 2000;

and in that subsection "secure accommodation" has the same meaning as in section 23 of the *Children and Young Person Act* 1969.

(12A) Section 243 of the *Criminal Justice Act* 2003 (persons extradited to the United Kingdom) applies in relation to a person sentenced to a detention and training order as it applies in relation to a fixed-term prisoner, with the reference in subsection (2) of that section to section 240 being read as a reference to subsection (8) above.

(13) For the purpose of any reference in sections 102–105 below to the term of a detention and training order, consecutive terms of such orders and terms of such order which are wholly or partly concurrent shall be treated as a single term if—

(a) the orders were made on the same occasion; or

(b) where they were made on different occasions, the offender has not been released (by virtue of subsection (2), (3), (4) or (5) of section 102 below) at any time during the period beginning with the first and ending with the last of those occasions.

The period of detention and training

27–73 **102.**—(1) An offender shall serve the period of detention and training under a detention and training order in such secure accommodation as may be determined by the Secretary of State or by such other person as may be authorised by him for that purpose.

(2) Subject to subsections (3)–(5) below, the period of detention and training under a detention and training order shall be one half of the term of the order.

(3) The Secretary of State may at any time release the offender if he is satisfied that if exceptional circumstances exist which justify the offenders release on compassionate grounds.

(4) The Secretary of State may release the offender—

(a) In the case of an order for a term of 8 months or more, but less than 18 months, one month before the half way point of the term of the order; and

(b) in the case of an order for a term of 18 months or more, one month or two months before that point.

(5) If a youth court so orders on an application made by the Secretary of State for the purpose, the Secretary of State shall release the offender—

(a) in the case of an order for a term of 8 months or more, but less than 18 months, one month after the half way point of the term of the order; and

(b) in the case of an order for a term of 18 months or more, one month or two months after that point.

(6) An offender detained in pursuance of a detention and training order shall be deemed to be in legal custody.

The period of supervision

27–74 **103.**—(1) The period of supervision of an offender who is subject to a detention and training order—

(a) shall begin with the offender's release whether at the half way point of the term of the order or otherwise; and

(b) subject to subsection (2) below shall end when the term of the order ends.

(2) The Secretary of State may by order provide that the period of supervision shall end at such point during the term of a detention and training order as may be specified in the order under this subsection.

(3) During the period of supervision the offender shall be under the supervision of—

(a) an officer of a local probation board;

(b) a social worker of a local authority; or

(c) a member of a youth offending team;

and the category of person to supervise the offender shall be determined from time to time by the Secretary of State.

(4) Where the supervision is to be provided by a probation officer, the probation officer shall be an officer appointed for or assigned to the petty sessions area within which the offender resides for the time being.

(5) Where the supervision is provided by—

(a) a social worker of a local authority, or

(b) a member of a youth offending team,

the social worker or member shall be a social worker of, or a member of a youth offending team established by, the local authority within whose area the offender resides for the time being.

(6)–(7) [*omitted*]

(2) Overarching Principles

Section 11 of the SGC Guidelines sets out most important Principles that must be applied by the Youth Court on considering the imposition of a custodial sentence. (See *ante*, § 27–14). **27–75**

(3) Procedure

The detention and training order is the only custodial sentence for young offenders appearing in the youth court. The court's power to impose a custodial sentence is restricted. **27–76**

A detention and training order may be imposed for fixed periods of 4, 6, 8, 10, 12, 18 or 24 months.

If the court having considered the facts of the case and the defendants antecedent history considers that a detention and training order may be appropriate it must first order the preparation of a full written pre-sentence report, unless there exists a previous report: *PCC(S)A* 2000, s.81. The report must specifically address custody as a sentencing option.

The offence itself must be one which is punishable with a minimum of four months' imprisonment in the adult court and is also so serious that only a custodial sentence of four months or over can be justified. Following the making of a detention and training order the offender is held in a custodial institution for one half of the duration of the order. He is then released into the community under the supervision of the YOT. Such supervision may included electronic tagging and an intensive supervision and surveillance programme. However, this is a matter purely for the YOT and does not involve an order of the court. **27–77**

In determining the appropriate term of a detention and training order the court must take into account any period for which the offender has been remanded in custody. This includes time held in police detention, remanded to local authority accommodation and secure accommodation or remanded or admitted to hospital under the *Mental Health Act* 1983, ss.35, 36, 38 or 48. Although the court must take such periods of custody into account it is not required to discount the sentence on a one to one basis nor is the court required to fine tune the appropriate sentence by taking into account a few days spent in custody: *B.* [2000] Crim.L.R. 870, CA. In *Inner London Crown Court, ex p. N.S.* [2000] Crim.L.R. 871, CA, two offenders had each been sentenced to a detention and training order (DTO) of four months. Each appealed on the basis that the three days that they had both spent in custody on remand had not been taken into account in deciding the term of the DTO. The court held that it was neither appropriate or desirable that any precise reflection should be given, in the making of a DTO, of two or three days spent in custody. If a more substantial time of weeks or months had been spent on remand the proper approach would have been to reduce sentence to reflect that period. In *Andrew James Eagles* [2007] 1 Cr.App.R.(S.) 99 in considering an appeal against a DTO on the grounds that the time spent on remand by the defendant had not been taken properly into account, the Court of Appealapplied a mathematical approach in allowing the appeal.

27–78 In determining the length of a detention and training order the court must also take into account a plea of guilty in accordance with *PCC(S)A* 2000, s.152. In *Marley* [2002] 2 Cr.App.R.(S.) 21 a detention and training order of 24 months was reduced to 18 months on the ground that the appellant had pleaded guilty and it was inappropriate to impose the maximum sentence available. The provisions relating to detention and training orders were restricted as to their length. If the maximum sentence of 24 months was not to be imposed, the next permissible length below that level was 18 months.

In *Pye v. Leeds Youth Court* [2006] EWHC 2527, DC, October 3, 2006, a youth received a sentence of a four-month DTO for criminal damage to the value of £50. On appeal it was held that such a sentence was unlawful. The maximum sentence an adult could have received in such circumstances was three months' imprisonment. The *Powers of Criminal Courts (Sentencing) Act* 2000, s.101(2) applied. Youth was a mitigating factor not an aggravating one. The youth court had no power to impose a custodial sentence under these circumstances.

(4) Definition of "persistency"

27–79 Youths aged between 12 and 14 years cannot be given a detention and training order unless they are persistent offenders. In deciding whether a defendant is "persistent" it is appropriate to apply the currently understood meaning of that word. The court should assess whether the defendant's criminal behaviour demonstrates a sufficient degree of persistence. Previous findings of guilt and findings of guilt made after the commission of the offence in question will all count in assessing the defendant's criminal behaviour as will cautions, reprimands and final warnings: *Charlton* (2000) 164 J.P. 685. It is not necessary that a defendant should have committed a string of offences or that he has failed to comply with previous orders of the court: *B.* [2001] Crim.L.R. 50. However, in *J.D.* (2001) 165 J.P. 1, a 14-year-old charged with affray was held not to be a persistent offender although he had a previous finding of guilt for handling stolen goods and a caution for a similar offence. The offence of affray was a different type of offence than those he had committed before. In *Smith* [2000] Crim.L.R. 613, a 14-year-old who had pleaded guilty to robbery, offensive weapon and false imprisonment, all committed over a two-day period, was held to be a persistent offender although he had no previous convictions. In *G.* (2004), CA (Crim. Div.) a 14-year-old appellant appealed against an 18-month DTO on the grounds that he was not a "persistent offender". He had pleaded guilty to charges of possessing firearms, possessing ammunition, and possessing cannabis with intent to supply. He had received a conditional discharge for theft in 2002 and a six-month supervision order for aggravated vehicle taking in 2003. It was held that the instant offences were very serious, normally justifying an immediate custodial sentence. However, they had taken place at the very end of a supervision order and it was held that his criminal behaviour was not persistent. The sentence was quashed and a two-year supervision order substituted.

(5) Consecutive periods of detention

27–80 The youth court may impose consecutive detention and training orders for summary offences up to an aggregate of 24 months: *C. v. DPP* [2002] 1 Cr.App.R.(S.) 45. However, in *Norris* (2000) 164 J.P. 689 it was held that in passing a consecutive DTO upon an offender who was already serving such a sentence the aggregate of the two orders did not have to correspond with one of the periods set out in s.101 of the *PCC(S)A* 2000.

Where an offender is already serving a period of detention under s.91 of the *PCC(S)A* 2000 there is no power to impose a consecutive detention and training order for a further offence as the two sentencing regimes are incompatible.

(6) Offenders attaining 18 years during the course of proceedings

27–81 Where an offender attains 18 years of age during the course of proceedings the starting point for sentence is that which he would have been likely to receive had he been sentenced on the date of the commission of the offence: *Ghafoor* [2002] Crim.L.R. 739: see *ante*, § 25–24. In *Aldis v. DPP* [2002] 2 Cr.App.R.(S.) 88 it was held that an 18-year-old offender was correctly sentenced to a detention and training order as he had committed the offence when he was 17 years old. He appealed on the basis that, as an 18-year-old at the time of sentence, he should have received a term of custody in a young offenders' institute.

(7) Imposition and duration of detention and training orders

There are a number of decisions giving guidance as to when a sentencing court should impose a detention and training order and the appropriate length of such an order. The reader will note that several of the following cases involve convictions for the offence of robbery. This is currently a prevalent offence in the youth court jurisdiction. The reader is referred to the Sentencing Guidelines Council Sentencing Guidelines relating to the offence of robbery and more especially that part that deals with particular factors to be taken into account when dealing with young offenders. See *www.sentencing-guidelines.gov.uk*. **27–82**

Att.-Gen's References (Nos 4 and 7 of 2002) (Lobban and Sawyers) (Q) [2002] 2 Cr.App.R.(S.) 77, CA

In this case the Court of Appeal held that street robberies of mobile phones would be punished severely. Custodial sentences would be the only option available irrespective of the age of the offender or his previous good character, unless there are exceptional circumstances. The sentencing bracket would be 18 months to three years where no weapon is used.

L. [2003] All E.R. (D) 37 (APR)

In this case the 15-year-old defendants had both pleaded guilty to burglary and each were sentenced to a 12-month DTO. On appeal it was held that the circumstances of the burglary put it at the lower end of the scale. A custodial sentence could have been avoided as both defendants were young and had entered timely pleas. Each defendant had served the equivalent of a four-month sentence and the sentence of 12-months was reduced to four months accordingly.

F.A. [2003] 2 Cr.App.R.(S.)

In this case two applicants of good character had admitted a number of robberies of fellow pupils at their school. Each was sentenced to a DTO of eight months. On appeal the court held that pupils at school who indulge in a campaign of intimidation and violence could expect to be dealt with severely. The sentences were upheld.

Hahn [2003] Cr.App.R.(S.) 106, CA

In this case it was held that as the appellant was 17 years old at the date of conviction the power of the sentencing court was limited to a detention and training order. The power to order detention under s.91 of the *PCC(S)A* 2000 may be exercised only in cases where the offender was convicted of a "grave crime". Before imposing such a sentence the court must be of the opinion that none of the other methods in which the case might be dealt with was suitable. In this particular case it was held that a detention and training order was a suitable sentence and the appeal was allowed accordingly.

A. (2005) CA (Criminal Division) June 14, 2005

See *ante*, § 25–30. The defendant, who was 14 years old at the time of the offence and 15 years on sentence was the ringleader of a gang of six youths who robbed a young victim of his property including his mobile phone. No weapon was used. The defendant had several previous convictions for crimes of violence and dishonesty. It was held that although no weapon had been used, the robbery had involved an attack by six people. A starting point of four years custody was appropriate. However, the defendant's age had to be recognised and taken into account. Responsibility at 15 years of age was not that of an older man and a sentence of three years for a 15-year-old was longer than a three year sentence for someone of a greater age. The sentence of three years detention was quashed and a two year detention and training order substituted.

T. (Att.-Gen's Reference Numbers 102 and 103 of 2006), CA

The sixteen-year-old defendant together with an adult was convicted of robbery. The offence involved threats made to a young victim with a knife, forcing him to take the defendants to his home, which they ransacked, and subsequently using gratuitous violence on the victim. The prosecution appealed against a sentence of a DTO for eighteen months. It was held that the aggravating features of the case meant that an adult would have received a prison sentence between five and six years. However, the Court had to bear in mind the appellant's age. Accordingly the sentence imposed was held to be too lenient and a sentence of four years' detention substituted under *PCC(S)A* 2000, s.91 (see *ante*, § 25–29).

P. (Att.-Gen.'s Reference Numbers 102 and 103 of 2006), CA

The defendant was seventeen years old and had pleaded guilty to two counts of assault leading to serious injury. Three days before sentence he had received a supervision order in the youth court in respect of another matter. The Court deferred sentence for six months in respect of the assault charges on the basis that the judge said she felt obliged to see whether the supervision order would be effective. On appeal it was held that the deferral was unduly lenient and was only applicable if a non-custodial sentence for the offences in question was a real possibility. This was not the case in view of the gravity of the offences. The judge should not have felt obliged to respect the supervision order. An extended sentence of two-and-a-half years' custody was substituted.

R. (2006) 150 S.J.L.B. 1607

See *ante*, § 25–24. The female defendant was 14 years old at the time of the offence and pleaded guilty to wounding with intent. She had been persistently bullied at school by the victim and had taken two knives with her in order to keep herself safe. The victim found out about the knives and challenged the defendant, punching her in the face several times. The defendant then produced one of the knives and stabbed the victim in the ribs causing a superficial wound. The defendant pleaded guilty to the offence and received an 18-month DTO. The custodial sentence was quashed in view of the defendant's age at the time of the offence (see *ante*, § 25–24). The Court stated that were it not for her age there would have been no alternative but to impose a custodial sentence. However, 18 months would have been excessive and would have been reduced to six months on appeal.

(8) Breaches of supervision requirements in a detention and training order

Powers of Criminal Courts (Sentencing) Act 2000, s.103(1), (3)

27–83 **103.**—(1) The period of supervision of an offender who is subject to a detention and training order—

(a) shall be given with the offender's release whether at the half way point of the term of the order or otherwise; and

(b) subject to subsection (2) below, shall end when the term of the order ends.

(3) During the period of supervision the offender shall be under the supervision of—

(a) an officer of a local probation board;

(b) a social worker of a local authority; or

(c) a member of a youth offending team;

and the category of person to supervise the offender shall be determined from time to time by the Secretary of State.

In *H. v. Doncaster Youth Court* [2009] EWHC 3463 (Admin) the appellant youth appealed against a decision of the Youth Court ordering his return to detention following a breach of a Detention and Training Order. He had been released under supervision and had breached the terms of such supervision for the second time. He was returned to detention under the above section. It was held that the words "remainder of the term of the detention and training order" meant the period between the occasion on which it was proved to the satisfaction of the Youth Court that an offender had failed to comply with the requirements of this section and the expiry of the order.

Powers of Criminal Courts (Sentencing) Act 2000, s.104(1), (3)

Breach of supervision requirements

104.—(1) Where a detention and training order is in force in respect of an offender and it appears on information to a justice of the peace that the offender has failed to comply with requirements under section 103(6)(b) above, the justice— **27–84**

(a) may issue a summons requiring the offender to appear at the place and time specified in the summons; or

(b) if the information is in writing and on oath, may issue a warrant for the offender's arrest.

(3) If it is proved to the satisfaction of the youth court before which an offender appears or is brought under this section that he has failed to comply with requirements under section 103(6)(b) above, that court may—

(a) order the offender to be detained, in such secure accommodation as the Secretary of State may determine, for such period, not exceeding the shorter of three months or the remainder of the term of the detention and training order, as the court may specify; or

(b) impose on the offender a fine not exceeding level 3 on the standard scale.

(9) Committing an offence during the currency of a detention and training order

Powers of Criminal Courts (Sentencing) Act 2000, s.105(2), (3)

Offences during currency of order

105.—(2) Subject to section 8(6) above (duty of adult magistrates' court to remit young offenders to youth court for sentence), the court by or before which a person to whom this section applies is convicted of the new offence may, whether or not it passes any other sentence on him, order him to be detained in such secure accommodation as the Secretary of State may determine for the whole or any part of the period which— **27–85**

(a) begins with the date of the court's order; and

(b) is equal in length to the period between the date on which the new offence was committed and the date mentioned in subsection (1) above.

(3) The period for which a person to whom this section applies is ordered under subsection (2) above to be detained in secure accommodation—

(a) shall, as the court may direct, either be served before and be followed by, or be served concurrently with, any sentence imposed for the new offence; and

(b) in either case, shall be disregarded in determining the appropriate length of that sentence.

The power to deal with a person for an offence committed during the currency of a detention and training order arises if that person after his release and before the date on which the term of the order ends, commits an offence punishable with imprisonment in the case of a person aged 21 or over, and before or after that date, he is convicted of that offence ("the new offence"). **27–86**

Part V

X. PARENTING ORDER

(1) Purpose and effect

Crime and Disorder Act 1998, ss.8–10

Parenting orders

27–87 **8.**—(1) This section applies where, in any court proceedings—

(a) a child safety order is made in respect of a child or the court determines on an application under section 12(6) below that a child has failed to comply with any requirement included in such an order;

(aa) a parental compensation order is made in relation to a child's behaviour;

(b) an anti-social behaviour order or sex offender order is made in respect of a child or young person;

(c) a child or young person is convicted of an offence; or

(d) a person is convicted of an offence under section 443 (failure to comply with school attendance order) or section 444 (failure to secure regular attendance at school of registered pupil) of the *Education Act* 1996.

(2) Subject to subsection (3) and section 9(1) below, if in the proceedings the court is satisfied that the relevant condition is fulfilled, it may make a parenting order in respect of a person who is a parent or guardian of the child or young person or, as the case may be, the person convicted of the offence under section 443 or 444 ("the parent").

(3) A court shall not make a parenting order unless it has been notified by the Secretary of State that arrangements for implementing such orders are available in the are in which it appears to the court that the parent resides or will reside and the notice has not been withdrawn.

(4) A parenting order is an order which requires the parent—

(a) to comply, for a period not exceeding twelve months, with such requirements as are specified in the order; and

(b) subject to subsection (5) below, to attend, for a concurrent period not exceeding three months, such counselling or guidance programme as may be specified in directions given by the responsible officer.

(5) A parenting order may, but need not, include such a requirement as is mentioned in subsection (4)(b) above in any case where a parenting order under this section or any other enactment has been made in respect of the parent on a previous occasion.

(6) The relevant condition is that the parenting order would be desirable in the interests of preventing—

(a) in a case falling within paragraph (a), (aa) or (b) of subsection (1) above, any repetition of the kind of behaviour which led to the child safety order, parental compensation order, anti-social behaviour order or sex offender order being made;

(b) in a case falling within paragraph (c) of that subsection, the commission of any further offence by the child or young person;

(c) in a case falling within paragraph (d) of that subsection, the commission of any further offence under section 443 or 444 of the *Education Act* 1996.

(7) The requirements that may be specified under subsection (4)(a) above are those which the court considers desirable in the interests of preventing any such repetition or, as the case may be, the commission of any such further offence.

(7A) A counselling or guidance programme which a parent is required to attend by virtue of subsection (4)(b) above may be or include a residential course but only if the court is satisfied—

(a) that the attendance of the parent at a residential course is likely to be more effective than his attendance at a non-residential course in preventing any such repetition or, as the case may be, the commission of any such further offence, and

(b) that any interference with family life which is likely to result from the attendance of the parent at a residential course is proportionate in all the circumstances.

(8) In this section and section 9 below "responsible officer", in relation to a parenting order, means one of the following who is specified in the order, namely—

(a) an officer of a local probation board;

(b) a social worker of a local authority; and

(bb) a person nominated by a person appointed as chief education officer under section 532 of the *Education Act* 1996.

(c) a member of a youth offending team

Parenting orders: supplemental.

9.—(1) Where a person under the age of 16 is convicted of an offence, the court by or before which he is so convicted— **27–88**

(a) if it is satisfied that the relevant condition is fulfilled, shall make a parenting order; and

(b) if it is not so satisfied, shall state in open court that it is not and why it is not.

(1A) The requirements of subsection (1) do not apply where the court makes a referral order in respect of the offence.

(1B) If an anti-social behaviour order is made in respect of a person under the age of 16 the court which makes the order—

(a) must make a parenting order if it is satisfied that the relevant condition is fulfilled;

(b) if it is not so satisfied, must state in open court that it is not and why it is not.

(2) Before making a parenting order—

(a) in a case falling within paragraph (a) of subsection (1) of section 8 above;

(b) in a case falling within paragraph (b) or (c) of that subsection, where the person concerned is under the age of 16; or

(c) in a case falling within paragraph (d) of that subsection, where the person to whom the offence related is under that age,

a court shall obtain and consider information about the person's family circumstances and the likely effect of the order on those circumstances.

(2A) In a case where a court proposes to make both a referral order in respect of a child or young person convicted of an offence and a parenting order, before making the parenting order the court shall obtain and consider a report by an appropriate officer—

(a) indicating the requirements proposed by that officer to be included in the parenting order;

(b) indicating the reasons why he considers those requirements would be desirable in the interests of preventing the commission of any further offence by the child or young person; and

(c) if the child or young person is aged under 16, containing the information required by subsection (2) above.

(2B) In subsection (2A) above "an appropriate officer" means—

(a) an officer of a local probation board;

(b) a social worker of a local authority; or

(c) a member of a youth offending team.

(3) Before making a parenting order, a court shall explain to the parent in ordinary language—

(a) the effect of the order and of the requirements proposed to be included in it;

(b) the consequences which may follow (under subsection (7) below) if he fails to comply with any of those requirements; and

(c) that the court has power (under subsection (5) below) to review the order on the application either of the parent or of the responsible officer.

(4) Requirements specified in, and directions given under, a parenting order shall, as far as practicable, be such as to avoid—

(a) any conflict with the parent's religious beliefs; and

(b) any interference with the times, if any, at which he normally works or attends an educational establishment.

(5) If while a parenting order is in force it appears to the court which made it, on the application of the responsible officer or the parent, that it is appropriate to make an order under this subsection, the court may make an order discharging the parenting order or varying it—

(a) by cancelling any provision included in it; or

(b) by inserting in it (either in addition to or in substitution for any of its provisions) any provision that could have been included in the order if the court had then had power to make it and were exercising the power.

(6) Where an application under subsection (5) above for the discharge of a parenting order is dismissed, no further application for its discharge shall be made under that subsection by any person except with the consent of the court which made the order.

(7) If while a parenting order is in force the parent without reasonable excuse fails to comply with any requirement included in the order, or specified in directions given by the responsible officer, he shall be liable on summary conviction to a fine not exceeding level 3 on the standard scale.

(7A) In this section "referral order" means an order under section 16(2) or (3) of the *Powers of Criminal Courts (Sentencing) Act* 2000 (referral of offender to youth offender panel).

Appeals against parenting orders.

27–89 **10.**—(1) An appeal shall lie—

(a) to the High court against the making of a parenting order by virtue of paragraph (a) of subsection (1) of section 8 above; and

(b) to the Crown Court against the making of a parenting order by virtue of paragraph (b) of that subsection.

(2) On an appeal under subsection (1) above the High court or the Crown Court—

(a) may make such orders as may be necessary to give effect to its determination of the appeals; and

(b) may also make such incidental or consequential orders as appear to it to be just.

(3) Any order of the High court or the Crown Court made on an appeal under subsection (1) above (other than one directing that an application be re-heard by a magistrates' court) shall, for the purposes of subsections (5) to (7) of section 9 above, be treated as if it were an order of the court from which the appeal was brought and not an order of the High Court or the Crown Court.

(4) A person in respect of whom a parenting order is made by virtue of section 8(1)(c) above shall have the same right of appeal against the making of the order as if—

(a) the offence that led to the making of the order were an offence committed by him; and

(b) the order were a sentence passed on him for the offence.

(5) A person in respect of whom a parenting order is made by virtue of section 8(1)(d) above shall have the same right of appeal against the making of the order as if the order were a sentence passed on him for the offence that led to the making of the order.

(6) The Lord Chancellor may by order make provision as to the circumstances in which appeals under subsection (1)(a) above may be made against decisions taken by courts on questions arising in connection with the transfer, or proposed transfer, of proceedings by virtue of any order under paragraph 2 of Schedule 11 (jurisdiction) to the *Children Act* 1989 ("the 1989 Act").

(7) Except to the extent provided for in any order made under subsection (6) above, no appeal may be made against any decision of a kind mentioned in that subsection.

(8) The Lord Chief Justice may nominate a judicial office holder (as defined in section 109(4) of the *Constitutional Reform Act* 2005) to exercise his functions under this section.

(2) Procedure

27–90 In summary, a parenting order may be imposed where:

(a) a child safety order is made in respect of a child;

(b) an anti-social behaviour order or a sex offender order is made in respect of a child or young person;

(c) a child or young person is convicted of an offence;

(d) a person is convicted of an offence under s.443 (failure to comply with school attendance order) or s.444 (failure to secure regular attendance at school of registered pupil) of the *Education Act* 1996;

(e) a youth court may make a parenting order when making a referral order.

27–91 The parenting order consists of two elements; compliance with such requirements as are specified in the order and attendance at counselling or guidance sessions. These measures are designed to encourage parents to accept responsibility for their children's offending and to provide appropriate support and discipline to prevent further offending. The order may not be made unless the court has received notification from the Secretary of State that arrangements for implementing such orders are available in the area in which it appears to the court that the parent resides or will reside and the notice has not been withdrawn: *Crime and Disorder Act* 1998, s.8(3). The order may be imposed for a maximum of twelve months, and the requirement to attend counselling or guidance session may last for a maximum period of three months with attendance a maximum of one session a week: *Crime and Disorder Act* 1998, s.8(4).

The order is mandatory where the offender is under 16 and the court considers that the relevant condition (prevention of re-offending) is satisfied; where the court does not consider the relevant condition to be satisfied, it must state in open court why it has arrived at that conclusion: *Crime and Disorder Act* 1998, s.9(1). The order is discretionary in the case of offenders aged 16 or 17. The court does not have to obtain a pre-sentence report, but the court should obtain and consider information about the person's family circumstances and the likely effect of the order on those circumstances: *Crime and Disorder Act* 1998, s.9(2). Before making the order, the court must explain to the parent in ordinary language: **27–92**

(1) The effect of the order and of the requirements proposed to be included in it.
(2) The consequences which may follow if he fails to comply with any of those requirements.
(3) That the court has power to review the order on the application either of the parent or of the responsible officer: *Crime and Disorder Act* 1998, s.9(4).

The requirements specified in the order must also be such as to avoid any conflict with the parents religious beliefs, and any interference with the times at which he normally works or attends an educational establishment: *Crime and Disorder Act* 1998, s.9(5). **27–93**

There is no longer a prohibition against a court making a parenting order at the same time as making a referral order. However, the obligation to make such an order, or to give reasons for not doing so, does not apply when a referral order is made: *Criminal Justice Act* 2003, s.324 and Sched. 34.

The court may vary or discharge the parenting order following an application made to the court by the responsible officer or the parent: s.9(5). If an application for variation or discharge is made and dismissed, a further such application may not proceed without the consent of the court which refused the original application: s.9(6). A person in respect of whom a parenting order is made by virtue of paras (c) or (d) of s.8 of the 1998 Act will have the same right of appeal against the making of the order as if the order were a sentence passed on him for the offence: *Crime and Disorder Act* 1998, s.10(4).

(3) Breach

Breach of a parenting order will result in the parent being liable upon summary conviction to a fine not exceeding level three on the standard scale: s.9(7). **27–94**

XI. ANTI-SOCIAL BEHAVIOUR ORDERS

(1) Purpose and effect

An application for an ASBO against a child or young person as a free standing civil order is heard in the adult magistrates' court. The youth court has no jurisdiction to hear an application for such an order. However, the youth court has jurisdiction to make an ASBO on conviction for a criminal offence. **27–95**

Crime and Disorder Act 1998, s.1C

Orders on conviction in criminal proceedings

1C.—(1) This section applies where a person (the "offender") is convicted of a relevant offence. **27–96**

Part V

(2) If the court considers—

(a) that the offender has acted, at any time since the commencement date, in an anti-social manner, that is to say in a manner that caused or was likely to cause harassment, alarm or distress to one or more persons not of the same household as himself, and

(b) that an order under this section is necessary to protect persons in any place in England and Wales from further anti-social acts by him,

it may make an order which prohibits the offender from doing anything described in the order.

(3) The court may make an order under this section—

(a) if the prosecutor asks it to do so, or

(b) if the court thinks it is appropriate to do so.

(3A) For the purpose of deciding whether to make an order under this section the court may consider evidence led by the prosecution and the defence.

(3B) It is immaterial whether evidence led in pursuance of subsection (3A) would have been admissible in the proceedings in which the offender was convicted.

(4) An order under this section shall not be made except—

(a) in addition to a sentence imposed in respect of the relevant offence; or

(b) in addition to an order discharging him conditionally.

(4A) The court may adjourn any proceedings in relation to an order under this section even after sentencing the offender.

(4B) If the offender does not appear for any adjourned proceedings, the court may further adjourn the proceedings or may issue a warrant for his arrest.

(4C) But the court may not issue a warrant for the offender's arrest unless it is satisfied that he has had adequate notice of the time and place of the adjourned proceedings.

(5) An order under this section takes effect on the day on which it is made, but the court may provide in any such order that such requirements of the order as it may specify shall, during any period when the offender is detained in legal custody, be suspended until his release from that custody.

(9) Subsections (7), (10), (10C), (10D), (10E) and (11) of section 1 apply for the purposes of the making and effect of orders made by virtue of this section as they apply for the purposes of the making and effect of anti-social behaviour orders.

(9A) The council for the local government area in which a person in respect of whom an anti-social behaviour order has been made resides or appears to reside may bring proceedings under section 1(10) (as applied by subsection (9) above) for breach of an order under subsection (2) above.

(9B) Subsection (9C) applies in relation to proceedings in which an order under subsection (2) is made against a child or young person who is convicted of an offence.

(9C) In so far as the proceedings relate to the making of the order—

(a) section 49 of the *Children and Young Persons Act* 1933 (c. 12) (restrictions on reports of proceedings in which children and young persons are concerned) does not apply in respect of the child or young person against whom the order is made;

(b) section 39 of that Act (power to prohibit publication of certain matter) does so apply.

(10) In this section—

"child" and "young person" have the same meaning as in the *Children and Young Persons Act* 1933;

"the commencement date" has the same meaning as in section 1 above;

"the court" in relation to an offender means—

(a) the court by or before which he is convicted of the relevant offence; or

(b) if he is committed to the Crown Court to be dealt with for that offence, the Crown Court; and

"relevant offence" means an offence committed after the coming into force of section 64 of the *Police Reform Act* 2002.

(2) Procedure

27–97 The youth court may make an ASBO where an offender is convicted of an offence on or after December 2, 2002. The Court must consider that the offender has acted at any time since April 1, 1999 in a manner that was likely to cause harassment, alarm or distress to one or more persons not of the same household as himself. Having reached this conclusion the Court must then go on to consider whether an ASBO is necessary to protect persons in any place in England and Wales from further anti-social acts by the defendant. It must be proved to the criminal standard of proof that anti-social behaviour has been committed by the defendant, but the civil rules of evidence apply. The question of whether an order is necessary is a matter of judgment and evaluation by the Court.

The need for an order and the wording of appropriate prohibitions has been looked at extensively by the Court of Appeal in a number of decisions. The principles set out in those decisions apply equally to youths as they do to adults. In dealing with youths, however, the welfare provisions in s.44(1) of the *CYPA* 1933 must be taken into account (see *ante*, § 25–3). In *R. (A.) v. Leeds Magistrates' Court* [2004] EWHC 554, Admin, the Court held that welfare was a primary consideration but not the paramount consideration which was the interests of the public.

27–98 The youth court may make an ASBO under s.1C upon the application of any agency concerned in the case that would be entitled to apply for such an order. In addition the youth court may make an order of its own volition.

In *Sheffield Magistrates' Court* [2004] EWHC 1830 the appellant youth appealed against an ASBO made against him. The applicant for the ASBO was the same local authority to whom he was in care pursuant to an order made under s.31 of the *Children Act* 1989. The Court was asked to consider whether the potential for conflict was such that a local authority could ever apply for an ASBO in respect of a child in its care. It was held that a local authority was not prevented from applying for an ASBO in such circumstances provided that measures were taken to prevent a breach of the rights of that child in connection with such an application.

27–99 Section 1C does not prescribe any particular procedure when consideration is given as to whether an ASBO should be made on conviction. However, the youth court must act fairly and have regard to all relevant considerations. In *C. v. (1) Sunderland Youth Court (2) Northumbria Police and (3) CPS* [2004] 1 Cr.App.R.(S.) 76, DC a youth applied for judicial review of the youth court's decision to impose an ASBO under s.1(C) of the *CDA* 1998. The application was allowed, the court emphasising the importance of fairness, careful consideration of evidence, and clarity as to the reasons for its decision. It was also said to be vital that the terms of an ASBO were clearly and accurately explained to the offender by the court.

In the case of *P.*, *The Times*, February 19, 2004, CA a youth was sentenced to detention for four years. In addition an ASBO for two years was made, suspended until his release from custody. On appeal the ASBO was quashed because it was not possible for the court to determine that an ASBO was necessary to protect the public at a future date in view of the length of the sentence coupled with a 12-month period on licence. The court also confirmed the principles set out in *C. v. Sunderland Youth Court*—above.

In *Shane Tony* [2004] EWCA Crim. 287, the Court of Appeal identified the following principles in relation to the making of an ASBO on conviction:

- (a) The test for making an order is one of necessity to protect the public from further anti social acts by the offender.
- (b) The terms of the order must be precise and capable of being understood by the offender.
- (c) The findings of fact giving rise to the making of the order must be recorded.
- (d) The order must be explained to the offender.
- (e) The exact terms of the order must be pronounced in open court and the written order must accurately reflect the order pronounced.

In *R. (on the application of B) (Claimant) v. Greenwich Magistrates' Court* [2009] H.L.R. 24 the claimant appealed against the decision of the Magistrates' Court to make him the subject of an ASBO a condition of which prevented him from wearing a hooded top in a particular London Borough. It was submitted that the order was unreasonable and restricted his freedom to wear whatever style of garment he might wish. It was held that the top had been worn to cause fear and that the prohibition in the order was properly directed towards that fear and was therefore necessary and proportionate.

(3) Breach of ASBO

27–100 The ASBO is a civil proceedings order with criminal penalties if breached. If without reasonable excuse a person does anything which he is prohibited from doing by an ASBO, he shall be guilty of an offence which when tried summarily carries a penalty of imprisonment for a term not exceeding six months, a fine not exceeding the statutory maximum or both. Where a person is convicted of breach of ASBO the Court may not make an order of Conditional Discharge: s.1 of the *Crime and Disorder Act* 1998 (see *ante*, §§ 23–231 *et seq.*).

Breach proceedings against youths, whether in respect of a civil ASBO or an ASBO made on conviction are prosecuted in the youth court. The offence is not a "grave crime" or "scheduled" offence and there is therefore no power to send the matter to the Crown Court. On conviction in the youth court the referral order, community penalty and detention and training order apply in the same way as they do for other offences involving youths. The maximum sentence for breach of an ASBO in appropriate circumstances is a two-year DTO.

(4) Publicity in ASBO cases in the youth court

27–101 The restrictions on press and publicity in the youth court are set out under §§ 25–8–25–10, *ante*. However, in respect of ASBOs against youths different rules apply:

(i) As regard orders made on conviction in the youth court the restrictions on reporting set out in s.49 remain (see § 25–9, *ante*). However, s.1C(9C) of the 1998 Act provides that s.49 does not apply in relation to youths against whom an ASBO is made on conviction in so far as the proceedings relate to the making of the order. This means that, unless the Court exercises its discretion under s.39 of the 1933 Act, details of the child or young person may be published. However, details of the criminal offence which led to the order being made remain subject to automatic reporting restrictions.

(ii) Proceedings for breach of an ASBO in the youth court are not subject to s.49 and may be reported. However, it seems that the youth court may make an order prohibiting such reporting under the provisions of s.39 of the 1933 Act.

XII. OVERARCHING PRINCIPLES—SENTENCING YOUTHS

GENERAL APPROACH

1. STATUTORY PROVISIONS

27–102 1.1 Offence seriousness is the starting point for sentencing. In considering the seriousness of any offence, the court must consider the offender's culpability in committing the offence and any harm which the offence caused, was intended to cause or might foreseeably have caused. In imposing sentence, the restrictions on liberty must be commensurate with the seriousness of the offence.

1.2 When sentencing an offender aged under 18, a court must have regard to:

(a) the principal aim of the youth justice system (to prevent offending by children and young persons); and

(b) the welfare of the offender.

1.3 In addition to the statutory provisions, a court sentencing a young offender must be aware of obligations under a range of international conventions which emphasise the importance of avoiding "criminalisation" of young people whilst ensuring that they are held responsible for their actions and, where possible, take part in repairing the damage that they have caused. This includes recognition of the damage caused to the victims and understanding by the young person that the deed was not acceptable. Within a system that provides for both the acknowledgement of guilt and sanctions which rehabilitate, the intention is to establish responsibility and, at the same time, to promote re-integration rather than to impose retribution.

2. SENTENCING PRINCIPLES

2.1 **The approach to sentence will be individualistic.**

2.2 The youth of the offender is widely recognised as requiring a different approach from that which would be adopted in relation to an adult. Even within the category of "youth", the response to an offence is likely to be very different depending on whether the offender is at the lower end of the age bracket, in the middle or towards the top end; in many instances, the maturity of the offender will be at least as important as the chronological age.

2.3 However, the sentence must remain proportionate to the seriousness of the present offence (except in the rare circumstances where the criteria for a sentence under the dangerous offender provisions are met) and should not impose greater restrictions on liberty than the seriousness of the offence justifies simply to deal with the risk of re-offending. Particular care will need to be taken where a young person has committed a relatively less serious offence but there is a high risk of re-offending.

2.4 Whilst a court is required to aggravate the seriousness of an offence where there are previous convictions (if the court considers that to be reasonable taking account both of the offence and the time that had elapsed since the previous conviction) **a sentence that follows re-offending does not need to be more severe than the previous sentence solely because there had been a previous conviction.**

(i) Approach to determining sentence

2.5 When determining sentence, the court will:

(1) **Assess the culpability of the offender and the harm caused (or intended or foreseeable) taking into account aggravating and mitigating factors relating to the offence.**

The assessment of offence seriousness will fix the most severe penalty that can be imposed and will determine whether an offence has crossed the necessary threshold to enable the court to impose a community or custodial sentence.

Even where the custody threshold has been crossed, a court is not required to impose a custodial sentence; similarly with the community sentence threshold.

Harm may be to individual victims or to the community or society at large. Of the four levels of culpability for sentencing purposes, intention is the highest followed by recklessness, knowledge and negligence. Even within those levels there will be gradations of seriousness.

Statutory aggravating factors (including previous convictions) will be relevant in assessing the seriousness of an offence.

(2) **Consider any mitigating factors that apply to the offender and any reduction for a guilty plea.**

When considering the maturity of the offender and its relevance to the sentence, it will only be in the most exceptional case that this will require more information than is available to the court through the representations of the advocates and any pre-sentence report.

(3) **Having taken account of all these factors, a court must then determine sentence including any relevant ancillary orders.**

The overall impact of the sentence and the ancillary orders must be considered to ensure that the restrictions on liberty are no more than is commensurate with the seriousness of the offence.

(ii) The principal aim of the youth justice system

2.6 By section 37 of the *Crime and Disorder Act* 1998, the principal aim of the youth justice system is to prevent offending by children and young people. For the offender, it incorporates the need to demonstrate that such conduct is not acceptable in a way that makes an impact on the offender whilst also identifying and seeking to address any other factors that make offending more likely. For any victim of the offence and society as a whole, it incorporates the need to demonstrate that the law is being effectively enforced and to sustain confidence in the rule of law.

(iii) The welfare of the offender

2.7 By section 44 of the *Children and Young Persons Act* 1933, "Every court in dealing with a child or young person who is brought before it, either as an offender or otherwise, shall have regard to the *welfare* of the child or young person, and shall in a proper case take steps for removing him from undesirable surroundings, and for securing that proper provision is made for his education and training".

2.8 In other requirements or obligations, different terminology—best interests, *well-being* or *welfare*—may be used. Generally, although there are shades of difference between the meanings, it is unlikely that different decisions will arise solely from those differences.

2.9 Accordingly, since "welfare" is the term used in the legislation applicable to England and Wales, that is the term used in this guideline. Welfare includes the obligation to secure proper provision for education and training, where appropriate to remove from undesirable surroundings and the need to choose the best option for the young person taking account of the circumstances of the offence.

In having regard to the "welfare" of the young person, a court should ensure that it is alert to:

- **the high incidence of mental health problems amongst young people in the criminal justice system;**
- **the high incidence of those with learning difficulties or learning disabilities amongst young people in the criminal justice system;**
- **the effect that speech and language difficulties might have on the ability of the young person (or any adult with them) to communicate with the court, to understand the sanction imposed or to fulfil the obligations resulting from that sanction;**
- **the extent to which young people anticipate that they will be discriminated against by those in authority and the effect that it has on the way that they conduct themselves during court proceedings;**
- **the vulnerability of young people to self harm, particularly within a custodial environment;**
- **the extent to which changes taking place during adolescence can lead to experimentation;**
- **the effect on young people of experiences of loss or of abuse.**

2.10 In the light of the high incidence of these impairments amongst young people in custody or subject to a community sentence, and taking account of the fact that the principal aim of the youth justice system is preventing offending, a court should always seek to ensure that it has access to information about how best to identify and respond to those impairments and, where necessary, that a proper assessment has taken place in order to enable the most appropriate sentence to be imposed.

(iv) The purpose of sentencing

2.11 As set out in paragraph 1 above, a court sentencing a person under the age of 18 is obliged to have regard to the principal aim of the youth justice system (to prevent offending by children and young persons) and to the welfare of the offender. As the principal aim of the youth justice system is the prevention of offending by children and young people, the emphasis should be on approaches that seem most likely to be effective with young people.

3. EFFECT ON SENTENCEOF THE OFFENDER BEING A YOUNG PERSON

3.1 In addition to the distinctive range of penalties available for youths, there is an expectation that, generally, a young person will be dealt with less severely than an adult offender, although this distinction diminishes as the offender approaches age 18 (subject to an assessment of maturity and criminal sophistication). In part, this is because young people are unlikely to have the same experience and capacity as an adult to realise the effect of their actions on other people or to appreciate the pain and distress caused and because a young person is likely to be less able to resist temptation, especially where peer pressure is exerted.

3.2 Additionally, in most cases a young person is likely to benefit from being given greater opportunity to learn from mistakes without undue penalisation or stigma, especially as a court sanction might have a significant effect on the prospects and opportunities of the young person, and, therefore, on the likelihood of effective integration into society.

3.3 When sentencing a young offender whose offence involves sexual activity but there is no evidence of a coercive or abusive relationship or of anything other than consensual activity, a court will need to be aware that a desire to explore gender identity or sexual orientation may result in offending behaviour. Depending on the seriousness of the offending behaviour, offender mitigation may arise where that behaviour stems from sexual immaturity or confusion.

3.4 Individual sanctions are likely to have a greater impact on a youth than on an adult, especially lengths of time spent in a custodial establishment, not least because of the exposure to influences likely to entrench criminal conduct (to which a young person may be more susceptible than an adult) and the greater risk of self harm than exists in relation to an adult.

3.5 It is also important to consider whether the young offender lacks the maturity fully to appreciate the consequences of his conduct and the extent to which the offender has been acting on an impulsive basis and the offender's conduct has been affected by inexperience, emotional volatility or negative influences.

3.6 Factors regularly present in the background of those juveniles who commit offences include: low family income, poor housing, poor employment records, low educational attainment, early experience of offending by other family members or of violence or abuse (often accompanied by harsh and erratic discipline within the home) and the misuse of drugs. There is also evidence that those young people who are "looked after" have been more at risk of being drawn into the criminal justice system than other young people acting in similar ways.

3.7 It is clear that these factors do not cause delinquency (since many who have experienced them do not commit crime); nonetheless, there is a strong association and any response to criminal activity amongst young people will need to recognise the presence of such factors if it is to be effective.

The following factors have led to a different approach to the sentencing of young people who offend (compared with the approach for adult offenders) and will affect the sentence imposed in an individual case:

- **offending by a young person is frequently a phase which passes fairly rapidly and therefore the reaction to it needs to be kept well balanced in order to avoid alienating the young person from society;**
- **a criminal conviction at this stage of a person's life may have a disproportionate impact on the ability of the young person to gain meaningful employment and play a worthwhile role in society;**
- **the impact of punishment is felt more heavily by young people in the sense that any sentence will seem to be far longer in comparison with their relative age compared with adult offenders;**
- **young people may be more receptive to changing the way they conduct themselves and be able to respond more quickly to interventions;**
- **young people should be given greater opportunity to learn from their mistakes;**
- **young people will be no less vulnerable than adults to the contaminating influences that can be expected within a custodial context and probably more so.**

Part V

4. THE RELEVANT CONSIDERATIONS

4.1 This guideline sets out a process that will enable the various obligations and requirements to be applied consistently. It is, however, only a framework and is intended to apply to the generality of cases.

In determining the sentence, the key elements are:

- **the age of the offender (chronological and emotional),**
- **the seriousness of the offence,**

- **the likelihood of further offences being committed, and**
- **the extent of harm likely to result from those further offences.**

The approach to sentence will be individualistic.

Proper regard should be had to the mental health and capability of the young person, and to any learning disability, learning difficulty, speech and language difficulty or other disorder, any of which is likely to affect the likelihood of those purposes being achieved.

4.2 The younger an offender (taking account of maturity and not just chronological age) the more likely it is that considering the welfare of the young person will be of greater significance. Since many young people "grow out of" crime, the obligation to have regard to the welfare of a young person who has offended might in some circumstances be best manifested by protecting that person from the adverse effects of intervention in his or her life rather than by providing for some positive action.

4.3 The requirement to have regard to the welfare of a young person is subject to the obligation to impose only those restrictions on liberty that are commensurate with the seriousness of the offence; accordingly, a court should not impose greater restrictions because of other factors in the young person's life.

4.4 In relation to custodial sentences, the reconviction rate is high and there are concerns about the effect on vulnerable young people of being in closed conditions. Risks commonly found are those of self harm and suicide and, in relation to female offenders, the additional impact on the offender herself and on the child if the offender is the primary carer of a child or is pregnant. Since a court is obliged to have regard to the welfare of the young person, it must have regard to these issues when considering sentence.

4.5 Particular care should be taken where an offender has mental health problems, learning disabilities, learning difficulties or other disabilities. Research shows that there is a high incidence of these issues in young people in the youth justice system and, in particular, in custody.

4.6 These issues are not always able to be identified at an early stage in the proceedings leading to sentence. As a result, a court needs to be alert to the possibility that the conduct of the young person (and that of any adult accompanying them in court) might be affected by issues relating to mental health, learning or communication, or some other form of disability that has not previously been identified.

4.7 In such circumstances, care needs to be taken in ensuring that the young person is able to take a proper part in the court proceedings, is able to understand what the court requires as a result of the sentence imposed and that that sentence properly takes account of difficulties in compliance that may arise from those issues.

4.8 Some young people may attend court believing that they will be discriminated against or otherwise unfairly treated; this might be for any of a wide range of reasons including ethnicity and sexuality. However unjustified that belief is, a court will need to be alert to the fact that the young person's behaviour in court might be affected by it.

4.9 The obligations to treat the prevention of offending by children and young persons as the principal aim of sentencing and to have regard to their welfare both require a court to consider the impairments and life experiences noted above, not only in determining the sentence to be imposed, but also in determining the length or content of that sentence.

The proper approach for the Crown Court, a magistrates' court or a youth court when sentencing a young offender is for the court, within a sentence that is no more restrictive on liberty than is proportionate to the seriousness of the offence(s), to seek to impose a sentence that takes proper account of the matters to which the court must have regard (see paragraph 1 above) by:

- **confronting the young offender with the consequences of the offending and helping the young offender to develop a sense of personal responsibility—these consequences may be experienced by the offender himself or herself, by the family of the offender, by the victim(s) of the offence and/or by the community;**
- **tackling the particular factors (personal, family, social, educational or health) that put the young person at risk of offending;**
- **strengthening those factors that reduce the risk that the young person will continue to offend;**
- **encouraging reparation to victims;**
- **defining, agreeing and reinforcing the responsibilities of parents.**

5. CROSSING A SIGNIFICANT AGE THRESHOLD BETWEEN COMMISSION OF AN OFFENCE AND SENTENCE

5.1 There will be occasions when an increase in the age of an offender will result in the maximum sentence on the date of *conviction* being greater than that available on the date on which the offence was *committed*.

5.2 In such circumstances, the approach should be:

- where an offender crosses a relevant age threshold between the date on which the offence was committed and the date of conviction or sentence, a court should take as its starting point the sentence likely to have been imposed on the date on which the offence was committed;
- where an offender attains the age of 18 after committing the offence but before conviction, section 142 of the*Criminal Justice Act* 2003 applies (whilst section 37 of the 1998 Act and section 44 of the 1933 Act (see 2.6–2.10 above) apply to those aged under 18) and the sentencing disposal has to take account of the matters set out in that section;
- it will be rare for a court to have to consider passing a sentence more severe than the maximum it would have had jurisdiction to pass at the time the offence was committed even where an offender has subsequently attained the age of 18;
- however, a sentence at or close to that maximum may be appropriate, especially where a serious offence was committed by an offender close to the age threshold.

6. PERSISTENT OFFENDERS

6.1 Certain sentences are available only where the offender is a "persistent offender"—in particular, a youth rehabilitation order with intensive supervision and surveillance or with fostering in relation to an offender aged between 10 and 14 and a detention and training order in relation to an offender aged between 12 and 14. This criterion does not have to be met before the Crown Court imposes long term detention (see paragraph 12 below) or detention for life.

6.2 Similarly, additional powers may be available to a court where a youth rehabilitation order has been breached "wilfully and persistently".

6.3 "Persistent offender" is not defined in legislation but has been considered by the Court of Appeal on a number of occasions. However, following the implementation of the 2008 Act, the sentencing framework is different from that when the definition was judicially developed, particularly the greater emphasis on the requirement to use a custodial sentence as "a measure of last resort".

6.4 A dictionary definition of "persistent offender" is "persisting or having a tendency to persist"; "persist" is defined as "to continue firmly or obstinately in a course of action in spite of difficulty or opposition".

6.5 In determining whether an offender is a persistent offender for these purposes, a court should consider the simple test of whether the young person is one who persists in offending:

i) in most circumstances, the normal expectation is that the offender will have had some contact with authority in which the offending conduct was challenged before being classed as "persistent"; a finding of persistence in offending may be derived from information about previous convictions but may also arise from orders which require an admission or finding of guilt—these include reprimands, final warnings, restorative justice disposals and conditional cautions; since they do not require such an admission, penalty notices for disorder are unlikely to be sufficiently reliable;

ii) a young offender is certainly likely to be found to be persistent (and, in relation to a custodial sentence, the test of being a measure of last resort is most likely to be satisfied) where the offender has been convicted of, or made subject to a pre-court disposal that involves an admission or finding of guilt in relation to, imprisonable offences on at least 3 occasions in the past 12 months.

6.6 Even where a young person is found to be a persistent offender, a court is not obliged to impose the custodial sentence or youth rehabilitation order with intensive supervision and surveillance or fostering that becomes available as a result of that finding. The other tests continue to apply and it is clear that Parliament expects custodial sentences to be imposed only rarely on those aged 14 or less.

7. ENFORCING THE RESPONSIBILITIES OF PARENTS AND GUARDIANS

7.1 A significant difference arising from the procedures for dealing with young people

Part V

who commit criminal offences is the importance attached to the presence of a parent, carer or appropriate adult at key stages, especially when sentence is imposed. In addition, specific provisions exist to enable a court to reinforce the responsibilities of a parent or guardian.

7.2 The statutory framework clearly envisages the attendance of an adult with a degree of responsibility for the young person; this obligation reflects the principal aim of reducing offending, recognising that that is unlikely to be achieved by the young person alone. A court must be aware of a risk that a young person will seek to avoid this requirement either by urging the court to proceed in the absence of an adult or in arranging for a person to come to court who purports to have (but in reality does not have) the necessary degree of responsibility.

7.3 Insistence on attendance may produce a delay in the case before the court; however, it is important that this obligation is maintained and that it is widely recognised that a court will require such attendance, especially when imposing sentence. If a court proceeds in the absence of a responsible adult, it should ensure that the outcome of the hearing is properly communicated.

7.4 Where a person under the age of 18 is convicted of an offence, the court is under a duty to **bind over a parent or guardian** if satisfied that such a course of action would be desirable in the interest of preventing the commission of further offences. Such an order may not be made where the court imposes a referral order. Similarly, the court has the power to make a **parenting order** where it would be desirable in the interest of preventing the commission of any further offence. Where the offender is aged 16 or less and the court considers that a parenting order would be desirable, there is a presumption in favour of the order being made and reasons must be given if it is not made. In most circumstances where an order is necessary, it is more likely that a parenting order will be appropriate.

7.5 When considering whether to impose a parenting order, the court should give careful consideration to the strength of the familial relationships and to any diversity issues that might impact on the achievement of the purposes of the order. Such factors and issues arising may be documented in a pre-sentence report.

7.6 Particular issues may arise in relation to an offender who is, or who runs the risk of, experiencing familial abuse or rejection on the grounds of sexual orientation. In considering such factors, which may be documented in a pre-sentence report the court must take care not to disclose facts about an offender's sexual orientation without his or her consent. Similar issues might arise in a family where racial tensions exist.

SENTENCES

8. REFERRAL ORDERS

8.1 Where an offender is being sentenced in a youth court or a magistrates' court, a referral order is a mandatory sentence in many circumstances in which a young person is to be sentenced for the first time and is discretionary in a wider range of situations. In particular, it is possible to make an order on a second conviction where a referral order was not made following the first conviction.

8.2 When an order is made, the court determines the length of the order (between 3 months and 12 months) but the action taken during that order is decided by a Youth Offender Panel consisting of members of the community supported by a member of a Youth Offending Team. Any victim of the offence may be invited to attend the meeting of the Panel at which the terms are agreed.

8.3 When determining the length of an order, although the needs of the offender are a factor, the primary consideration in most circumstances is the relative seriousness of the offence. Given the mandatory nature of the order in many circumstances, it is less likely that the needs of the offender will be considered in a pre-sentence report. This consideration is more likely to take place once the order has been made and in preparation for the Panel meeting since, within the period of the order, the Youth Offender Panel will agree what needs to be undertaken by the young person both in the light of the nature of the offence and of the young person's needs.

8.4 **A court should be prepared to use the whole range of periods allowed; in general, orders of 10–12 months should be made only for the more serious offences.**

8.5 Typically, the length of an order should be between 3–5 months for offences where the court assesses seriousness to be relatively low, between 5–7 months for an offence of medium level seriousness and between 7–9 months for an offence where the court considers seriousness to be relatively high. In determining which level applies, a court may find assistance in section 2 of the Youth Court Bench Book issued by the Judicial Studies Board which provides indications of the level of seriousness of an average offence of the types described.

9. FINANCIAL ORDERS

9.1 A court may impose a fine for any offence. In accordance with statutory requirements, where financial orders are being considered, priority must be given to compensation orders and, where an order for costs is to be made alongside a fine, the amount of the costs must not exceed the amount of the fine.

9.2 In practice, many young people who offend have few financial resources. Where a young person is in receipt of the *Education Maintenance Allowance* or a similar provision which is related to the means of the offender or those with whom the offender lives, a court will need to consider the extent to which making a deduction from the allowance would prejudice the access of the young person to education or training.

9.3 **As a general rule, it will rarely be appropriate to take the allowance into account as a resource from which a financial penalty may be paid, especially where the recipient is a young person who is living independently or as part of a household primarily dependent on state benefit.**

10. YOUTH REHABILITATION ORDERS

10.1 The *Criminal Justice and Immigration Act* 2008 provides for a single community sentence (the youth rehabilitation order) within which a court may include one or more requirements variously designed to provide for punishment, for protection of the public, for reducing reoffending and for reparation.

10.2 A youth rehabilitation order with intensive supervision and surveillance or with fostering is also provided but may be imposed only where a custodial sentence otherwise would have been appropriate (see 10.23 below).

(i) Threshold and availability

10.3 In order for a court to be able to impose a youth rehabilitation order, it must be satisfied that the offence is "serious enough". Even where an offence crosses this threshold, a court is not obliged to make a youth rehabilitation order.

10.4 In determining the content and length of an order, the guiding principles are proportionality and suitability since statute provides that the restrictions on liberty within such an order must be commensurate with the seriousness of the offence and that, taken together, the requirements within the order are the most suitable for the offender.

10.5 In contrast to the provisions relating to adult offenders, a court may impose a youth rehabilitation order (other than one with intensive supervision and surveillance or fostering) for an offence that is not imprisonable.

10.6 A youth rehabilitation order is not an available sentence where the "compulsory referral conditions" are found to exist; accordingly, the order will not be available in a youth court or other magistrates' court for a first time offender who has pleaded guilty to an imprisonable offence.

(ii) Effect of a guilty plea

10.7 Where a court is considering sentence for an offence for which a custodial sentence is justified, a guilty plea may be one of the factors that persuades a court that it can properly impose a youth rehabilitation order instead and no further adjustment to the sentence needs to be made to fulfil the obligation to give credit for that plea.

10.8 Where the provisional sentence is already a youth rehabilitation order, the necessary reduction for a guilty plea should apply to those requirements within the order that are primarily punitive rather than to those which are primarily rehabilitative.

(iii) Approach to determining nature and extent of requirements

10.9 In determining the nature and extent of requirements to be included within an order and the length of that order, the key factors are the assessment of the seriousness of the offence, the objective(s) the court wishes to achieve, the risk of re-offending, the ability of the offender to comply, and the availability of requirements in the local area.

10.10 Since a court must determine that the offence (or combination of offences) is "serious enough" to justify such an order, a court will be able to determine the nature and extent of the requirements within the order primarily by reference to the likelihood of the young person re-offending and to the risk of the young person causing serious harm. This is in accordance with the principal aim of the youth justice system and the welfare principle.

10.11 Before making an order a court will consider a pre-sentence report. In preparing that report, (following national standards and practice guidance) the Youth Offending Team (YOT) will be seeking to identify an appropriate balance between the seriousness of the offence, the risk of harm in the future from any further offences the young person might commit and the needs of the young person.

10.12 In most cases, the assessment by the YOT will be undertaken by use of Asset supported by professional judgement. An initial assessment will calculate the risk of re-offending; where necessary, an additional assessment will assess the risk of serious harm likely to be involved in further offending.

10.13 Those assessments will be reviewed by the YOT in the context of all other available information and the report will identify a level of intervention for the court to consider. There are three intervention levels:

- **Standard level**—for those who show a low likelihood of reoffending **and** a low risk of serious harm; in those circumstances, the order primarily will seek to repair the harm caused by the offence—typically, this will involve interventions to meet the requirements of the order and the engagement of parents in those interventions and/or in supporting the young person;
- **Enhanced level**—for those who show a medium likelihood of reoffending **or** a medium risk of serious harm; in those circumstances, the order will, in addition, seek to enable help or change as appropriate —typically, this will involve greater activity in motivating the young person and in addressing the reasons for non-compliance with the law and may involve external interventions;
- **Intensive level**—for those with a high likelihood of reoffending or a high or very high risk of serious harm; in those circumstances, the order will, in addition, seek to ensure control of the young person as necessary to minimise the risk of further offending or of serious harm—typically this will involve additional controls, restrictions and monitoring.

10.14 For the broad generality of offences where a youth rehabilitation order is to be imposed, this approach will enable the writer of a pre-sentence report to make proposals that match the obligations on the court to balance the various statutory obligations that apply.

10.15 Where a young person is assessed as presenting a **high risk of re-offending or of causing serious harm** despite having committed a relatively less serious offence, the emphasis is likely to be on requirements that are primarily rehabilitative or for the protection of the public. Care will need to be taken to ensure both that the requirements are "those most suitable for the offender" and that the restrictions on liberty are commensurate with the seriousness of the offence.

10.16 Where a young person is assessed as presenting a **low risk despite having committed a relatively high seriousness offence**, the emphasis is likely to be on requirements that are primarily punitive, again ensuring that restrictions on liberty are commensurate with the seriousness of the offence. In relation to young offenders, the primary purpose of punitive sanctions is to achieve acknowledgement by the young person of responsibility for his or her actions and, where possible, to take a proper part in repairing the damage caused.

(iv) Length of order

10.17 When imposing a youth rehabilitation order, the court must fix a period within which the requirements of the order are to be completed; this must not be more than 3 years from the date on which the order comes into effect. Where the order contains two or more requirements, the order may specify an earlier date for any of those requirements.

10.18 The period specified as the overall period for the order will normally commence on the day the order is made but, where the young person is already subject to a detention and training order, the court may specify that the youth rehabilitation order will take effect either on the day that supervision begins in relation to the detention and training order or on the expiry of the term of that order.

10.19 It is not possible to make a youth rehabilitation order when the young person is already subject to another youth rehabilitation order or to a reparation order unless the court revokes those orders.

10.20 The overall length of an order has three main consequences:

- where a supervision requirement is included, the obligation to attend appointments as directed by the responsible officer continues for the whole period;
- where a young person is in breach of a youth rehabilitation order, one of the sanctions available to a court is to amend the order by including within it any requirement that it would have had power to include when the order was made; however, that new requirement must be capable of being complied with before the expiry of the overall period;
- a young person is liable to re-sentence for the offence(s) for which the order was made if convicted of another offence whilst the order is in force.

10.21 In determining the length of an order, a court should allow sufficient time for the order as a whole to be complied with, recognising that the young person is at risk of further sanction throughout the whole of the period, but allowing sufficient flexibility should a sanction need to be imposed for breach of the order. Where appropriate, an application for early discharge may be made.

(v) Determining the requirements and the length of an order – summary

10.22 As set out in paragraph 2.1 above, the approach to the sentencing of a youth will be individualistic. Where a court is satisfied that an offence has crossed the community sentence threshold and that such a sentence is necessary or has crossed the custody threshold but is an offence for which a youth rehabilitation order is nonetheless considered to be appropriate, taking account of the assessment in the pre-sentence report, the consideration process that the court should follow is:

I) **what requirements are most suitable for the offender?**

II) **what overall period is necessary to ensure that all requirements may be satisfactorily completed?**

III) **are the restrictions on liberty that result from those requirements commensurate with the seriousness of the offence?**

(vi) Orders with intensive supervision and surveillance or with fostering

10.23 Such orders may be made where:

- the court is dealing with a young person for an offence punishable with imprisonment;
- that offence (or combination of offences) crosses the custody threshold; and
- custody would be an appropriate sentence.

If the offender was under 15 at the time of conviction, such an order may be imposed only where the offender is a "persistent offender".

10.24 When imposing such an order, the court must give its reasons for concluding that the offence(s) cross(es) the community sentence threshold and that the requirements set out above have been met.

(a) With intensive supervision and surveillance

10.25 A youth rehabilitation order with intensive supervision and surveillance is an order that contains an "extended activity requirement", that is, an activity requirement with a maximum of 180 days. As a result, there are further obligations to include a supervision requirement and a curfew requirement.

10.26 Where appropriate, a youth rehabilitation order with intensive supervision and surveillance may also include additional requirements, although the order as a whole must comply with the obligation that the requirements must be those most suitable for the offender and that any restrictions on liberty must be commensurate with the seriousness of the offence.

10.27 When imposing such an order, a court must ensure that the requirements are not so onerous as to make the likelihood of breach almost inevitable.

(b) With fostering

10.28 Where a fostering requirement is included within a youth rehabilitation order, it will require the offender to reside with a local authority foster parent for a specified period; that period must not exceed 12 months. The court must be satisfied that a significant factor in the offence was the circumstances in which the young person was living and that the imposition of a fostering requirement would assist in the rehabilitation of the young person. It is likely that other rights will be engaged (such as those under Article 8 of the European Convention on Human Rights) and any interference with such rights must be proportionate.

10.29 Before including this requirement, the court must consult both the young person's parent or guardian (unless impracticable) and the local authority; it cannot be included unless the offender was legally represented in court when the court was considering whether or not to impose the requirement or, having had the opportunity to be represented, the offender has not applied for representation or that right was withdrawn because of the offender's conduct. This requirement may be included only where the court has been notified that arrangements are available in the area of the relevant local authority.

10.30 A fostering requirement cannot be included with intensive supervision and surveillance and it cannot be included in a youth rehabilitation order unless the higher criteria described above have been met. Where appropriate, a youth rehabilitation order with fostering may also include other requirements (and must include supervision) although the order as a whole must comply with the obligation that the requirements must be those most suitable for the offender and that any restrictions on liberty must be commensurate with the seriousness of the offence.

10.31 It is unlikely that the statutory criteria will be met in many cases; where they are met and the court is considering making an order, care should be taken to ensure that there is a well developed plan for the care and support of the young person throughout the period of the order and following conclusion of the order. A court will need to be provided with sufficient information, including proposals for education and training during the order and plans for the offender on completion of the order.

(vii) Breaches

10.32 Where a young person fails to comply with a youth rehabilitation order, the "responsible officer" must consider whether there was a reasonable excuse. If the officer considers that there was no reasonable excuse and this is the first failure to comply with the order without reasonable excuse, the officer must issue a "warning".

10.33 The warning will describe the circumstances of the failure to comply, a statement that the failure is not acceptable and a warning that a further failure to comply may lead to the order being referred back to the court. In most circumstances, two warnings will be permitted within a 12 month period before the matter is referred back to court.

10.34 There is a presumption in favour of referring the matter back to court after a third failure to comply and a discretionary power to do so after the second failure to comply.

10.35 Breach of an order brought before a court may arise from a failure to keep an appointment or otherwise co-operate with the responsible officer or may arise from a failure to comply with one or more of the other requirements of the order.

10.36 Even where a breach has been proved, a court is not obliged to make any order but may allow the youth rehabilitation order to continue as imposed. In contrast with the powers in relation to an adult offender, there is no obligation on the court to make an order more onerous. Where a court determines that a sanction is necessary, it has the power to:

- impose a fine (in which case the order continues in its original form);
- amend the terms of the order; or
- revoke the order and re-sentence the offender.

10.37 If amending the terms of the order, the court may impose any requirement that it could have imposed when making the order and this may be in addition to, or in substitution for, any requirements contained in the order. If the youth rehabilitation order did not contain an unpaid work requirement and the court includes such a requirement using this power, the minimum period of unpaid work is 20 hours; this will give greater flexibility when responding to less serious breaches or where there are significant other requirements to be complied with.

10.38 A court may not amend the terms of a youth rehabilitation order that did not include an extended activity requirement or a fostering requirement by inserting them at this stage; should these requirements be considered appropriate following breach, the offender must be re-sentenced and the original youth rehabilitation order revoked.

10.39 Before imposing a custodial sentence as a result of re-sentencing following breach, a court should be satisfied that the YOT and other local authority services have taken all steps necessary to ensure that the young person has been given appropriate opportunity and support necessary for compliance.

10.40 Where the failure arises primarily from non-compliance with reporting or other similar obligations and a sanction is necessary, the most appropriate response is likely to be the inclusion of (or increase in) a primarily punitive requirement such as the curfew requirement, unpaid work, the exclusion requirement and the prohibited activity requirement or in the imposition of a fine. However, continuing failure to comply with the order is likely to lead to revocation of the order and re-sentencing for the original offence.

10.41 Where the offender has "wilfully and persistently" failed to comply with the order, and the court proposes to sentence again for the offence(s) in respect of which the order was made, additional powers are available. These additional powers include:

- the making of a youth rehabilitation order with intensive supervision and surveillance even though the offence is not imprisonable or a custodial sentence would not have been imposed if the order had not been available
- even though the offence is not imprisonable, the imposition of a detention and training order for 4 months for breach of a youth rehabilitation order with intensive supervision and surveillance imposed following wilful and persistent breach of an order made for a non-imprisonable offence.

10.42 In considering whether the failure to comply is "persistent", account should be taken of the principles set out in paragraph 6 above.

The primary objective when sentencing for breach of a youth rehabilitation order is to ensure that the young person completes the requirements imposed by the court.

Where the failure arises primarily from non-compliance with reporting or other similar obligations, where a sanction is necessary, the most appropriate is likely to be the inclusion of (or increase in) a primarily punitive requirement.

A court must ensure that it has sufficient information to enable it to understand why the order has been breached and that all steps have been taken by the YOT and other local authority services to give the young person appropriate opportunity and support. This will be particularly important if the court is considering imposing a custodial sentence as a result of the breach.

Where a court is determining whether the young person has "wilfully and persistently" breached an order, it should apply the same approach as when determining whether an offender is a "persistent offender". In particular, almost certainly a young person will have "persistently" breached a youth rehabilitation order where there have been three breaches (each resulting in an appearance before a court) demonstrating a lack of willingness to comply with the order.

11. CUSTODIAL SENTENCES

11.1 There is a statutory presumption that a person aged under 18 will be dealt with summarily, usually in a youth court; in such circumstances, the maximum custodial sentence will be a detention and training order of no more than 24 months. Such an order may be made only for the periods prescribed —4, 6, 8, 10, 12, 18 or 24 months.

11.2 The custodial sentences available in the Crown Court are:

- detention and training order of up to 24 months;
- long term detention —in relation to a young person convicted 53 in the Crown Court, under section 91 of the *Powers of Criminal Courts (Sentencing) Act* 2000;
- extended sentence of detention or detention for public protection – where a young person is sent for trial or committed for sentence to the Crown Court to be dealt with under the dangerous offender provisions; in each case, the minimum period to be spent in custody under the sentence must be two years;

Part V

- detention at Her Majesty's pleasure—for offences of murder.

11.3 A detention and training order may not be imposed on an offender aged 10 or 11 years at the time of conviction; an order may be imposed in relation to an offender aged between 12 and 14 at the time of conviction only if the offender is a "persistent offender" (see paragraph 6 above). However, the persistent offender criterion does not have to be met before the Crown Court imposes long term detention or detention for life in relation to offenders who are under 15 years of age.

11.4 A pre-sentence report must be considered before a custodial sentence is imposed.

(i) Threshold and approach

11.5 Under both domestic law and international convention, a custodial sentence must be imposed only as a "measure of last resort"; statute provides that such a sentence may be imposed only where an offence is "so serious that neither a community sentence nor a fine alone can be justified"

11.6 For a first time offender who has pleaded guilty to an imprisonable offence, in most circumstances a referral order will be the most appropriate sentence.

11.7 Since the minimum length of a custodial sentence in the youth court is 4 months (significantly in excess of the minimum available in relation to an adult offender) and since the term of a custodial sentence must be the shortest commensurate with the seriousness of the offence, it is inevitable that the custody threshold is higher in the case of a young person than in the case of an adult—any case that warrants a detention and training order of less than four months must result in a non-custodial sentence.

11.8 In relation to a person under the age of 18, in determining whether an offence has crossed the custody threshold a court will need to consider whether the offence has resulted (or could reasonably have resulted) in serious harm. In determining whether a custodial sentence is unavoidable, generally, a court will need to take account both of the seriousness of the offence (particularly the extent to which it caused (or was likely to cause) serious harm) and of the risk of serious harm in the future. A custodial sentence is most likely to be unavoidable where it is necessary to protect the public from serious harm.

11.9 In addition, a court must take account of:

i) the requirement to have regard to the principal aim of the youth justice system;
ii) the requirement to have regard to the welfare of the offender and the evidence that the risks associated with young offenders in a custodial setting are high.

11.10 Even where the threshold is crossed, a court is not required to impose a custodial sentence.

11.11 Before deciding to impose a custodial sentence on a young offender, the court must ensure that all the statutory tests are satisfied—namely:

i) that the offender cannot properly be dealt with by a fine alone or by a youth rehabilitation order,
ii) that a youth rehabilitation order with intensive supervision and surveillance or with fostering cannot be justified, and
iii) that custody is the last resort

and in doing so should take account of the circumstances, age and maturity of the young offender.

11.12 When a custodial sentence is imposed, a court must state its reasons for being satisfied that the offence(s) is (are) so serious that no other sanction is appropriate and, in particular, why a youth rehabilitation order with intensive supervision and surveillance or with fostering cannot be justified. This justification will need to be based on the principles set out in the statutory framework.

Where the offence(s) has crossed the custody threshold, the statutory tests are likely to be satisfied only where a custodial sentence will be more effective in preventing offending by children and young persons. The obligation to have regard to the welfare of the offender will require a court to take account of a wide range of issues including those relating to mental health, capability and maturity.

(ii) Length of sentence

11.13 A court imposing a custodial sentence is required to set the shortest term commensurate with the seriousness of the offence(s). Offence specific guidelines do not generally provide starting points or ranges for offenders aged under 18 because of the wide range of issues that are likely to arise and the marked differences in the sentencing framework depending on the age of the offender. Where they are provided, they are for offenders aged 17 with a provision that, for younger offenders, a court should consider whether a lower starting point is justified in recognition of the offender's age and maturity.

11.14 Any approach needs to take account of the general sentencing rules that apply where there is more than one offence or more than one defendant. Where the offence has been committed by offender(s) aged 18 or over and by offender(s) aged under 18, the court will need to consider the role of each offender and the number of offenders involved.

11.15 Where the primary offender is under the age of 18, a court is likely to determine sentence for that offender first giving proper weight to the offender's age and maturity; that will provide a framework within which sentence for the offender(s) over 18 can be determined. Where the primary offender is over 18, a court is likely to determine sentence for that offender first; that will provide a framework within which sentence for the offender(s) under 18 can be determined giving proper weight to age and maturity.

11.16 Where an offence crosses the custodial threshold **and** the court determines that a custodial sentence is unavoidable:

- **where the offender is aged 15, 16 or 17, the court will need to consider • the maturity of the offender as well as chronological age. Where there is no offence specific guideline, it may be appropriate, depending on maturity, to consider a starting point from half to three quarters of that which would have been identified for an adult offender.**

  It will be particularly important to consider maturity when the court has to sentence more than one offender. When the offenders are of different ages, including when one or more is over 18, the court will also need to have proper regard to parity between their sentences.

  The closer an offender was to age 18 when the offence was committed and the greater the maturity of the offender or the sophistication of the offence, the closer the starting point is likely to be to that appropriate for an adult. Some offenders will be extremely mature, more so than some offenders who are over 18, whilst others will be significantly less mature.

  For younger offenders, greater flexibility will be required to reflect the potentially wide range of culpability.

  Where an offence shows considerable planning or sophistication, a court may need to adjust the approach upwards.

  Where the offender is particularly immature, the court may need to adjust the approach downwards.
- **where the offender is aged 14 or less**, sentence should normally be imposed in a youth court (except in cases of homicide or where the young person comes within the "dangerous offender" criteria); the length of a custodial sentence will normally be shorter than for an offender aged 15–17 convicted of the same offence.
- **an offender aged 14 years or less** should be sentenced to long term detention only where that is necessary for the protection of the public either because of the risk of serious harm from future offending or because of the persistence of offending behaviour; exceptionally, such a sentence may be appropriate where an offender aged 14 years or less has committed a very serious offence but is not a persistent offender and there is no risk of serious harm from future offending.

11.17 In determining the term of a detention and training order, the court must take account of any period for which the offender has been remanded in custody or on bail subject to a qualifying curfew condition and electronic monitoring. As the available terms are specified, the proper approach in taking a remand period into account is to reduce, if possible, the sentence otherwise appropriate to reflect that period. Where a short custodial sentence was being considered, the court might conclude that a non-custodial sentence was appropriate.

11.18 On the implementation of the relevant parts of schedule 3 to the *Criminal Justice Act* 2003, a "plea before venue" procedure will be introduced for offenders under the age of 18 and will include a general power to commit for sentence where a court accepts jurisdiction following indication of a guilty plea. As with adult offenders, where a young person could have been dealt with in the Crown Court but the youth court has retained jurisdiction, where appropriate the maximum period of 24 months may be imposed following a guilty plea at the first reasonable opportunity where that plea was a factor in retaining a case for sentence in the youth court.

12. TRIAL AND SENTENCING OF CASES IN THE CROWN COURT

12.1 There is a clear principle (established both in statute and in domestic and European case law) that cases involving young offenders should be tried and sentenced in the youth court wherever possible. This section summarises the relevant statutory provisions and case law.

12.2 It has long been recognised that the Crown Court should be reserved for the most serious cases, noting the greater formality of the proceedings and the increased number of people likely to be present. These factors present additional obstacles in ensuring that proceedings in the Crown Court involving young offenders are conducted in accordance with international obligations.

12.3 Accordingly, it is rare for a young offender to be tried or sentenced in the Crown Court and for a sentence beyond the powers of the youth court to be imposed, except where that sentence is substantially beyond those powers.

12.4 A youth will appear in the Crown Court for trial and sentence only:

i) when charged with "homicide";
ii) when subject to a minimum statutory sentence;
iii) when charged with a "grave crime" and a youth court has determined that, if convicted, a sentence beyond its powers should be available; or
iv) when charged together with an adult offender who has been sent to the Crown Court and it has been determined that the cases should be kept together.

12.5 Where a sentence under the "dangerous offender" provisions is likely to be needed the youth may be committed for trial or for sentence.

(i) Homicide

12.6 An exception to the presumption that a person aged under 18 should be tried summarily arises where the young person is charged with an offence of "homicide". For a case falling within this description, there is no discretion and it must be sent to the Crown Court for trial. The meaning of "homicide" is not defined in statute.

(ii) Statutory minimum sentences

12.7 A further exception to the presumption in favour of summary trial arises where a young person is charged with an offence which has a statutory minimum custodial sentence and the criteria for that sentence would be likely to be satisfied if the young person were convicted. A sentence of long term detention may be imposed following committal where these mandatory sentence provisions apply; before there can be a departure from the minimum sentence prescribed, a court must find that there are "exceptional circumstances".

(iii) "Grave crimes"

12.8 A further exception to the statutory presumption in favour of summary trial arises where a young person is charged with a "grave crime" and a youth court has determined that, if convicted, a sentence beyond its powers should be available. In such circumstances, a young person may be sentenced by the Crown Court to long term detention under section 91 of the *Powers of Criminal Courts (Sentencing) Act* 2000. At present, such a sentence may be imposed only by the Crown Court and only where the offender was **convicted** in the Crown Court, and that court considers that neither a community order nor a detention and training order is suitable.

12.9 An offence comes within section 91 where:

- it is punishable with 14 years imprisonment or more for an adult (but is not a sentence fixed by law), or
- is an offence contrary to sections 3, 13, 25 or 26 of the *Sexual Offences Act* 2003, or
- is one of a number of specified offences in relation to firearms, ammunition and weapons which are subject to a minimum term but in respect of which a court has found exceptional circumstances justifying a lesser sentence.

12.10 This general power should be used rarely since:

i) it is the general policy of Parliament that those under 18 should be tried in the youth court wherever possible;

ii) trial in the Crown Court under this provision should be reserved for the most serious cases, recognising the greater formality of the proceedings and the greatly increased number of people involved;

iii) offenders aged under 15 will rarely attract a period of detention under this provision and those under 12 even more rarely.

12.11 Accordingly,

i) **a young person aged 10 or 11 (or aged 12–14 but not a persistent offender) should be committed to the Crown Court under this provision only where charged with an offence of such gravity that, despite the normal prohibition on a custodial sentence for a person of that age, a sentence exceeding two years is a realistic possibility;**

ii) **a young person aged 12–17 (for which a detention and training order could be imposed) should be committed to the Crown Court under this provision only where charged with an offence of such gravity that a sentence substantially beyond the 2 year maximum for a detention and training order is a realistic possibility.**

(iv) Dangerous offenders

12.12 There are rigorous statutory tests which must be satisfied before a court may conclude that a youth is a "dangerous offender" and requires sentence under the dangerous offender provisions in the *Criminal Justice Act* 2003 (as amended). Such a sentence may be imposed only where an equivalent determinate sentence of at least 4 years would have been imposed. Criteria relating to future offending and the risk of serious harm must be assessed in the light of the maturity of the offender, the possibility of change in a much shorter time than would apply for an adult and the wider circumstances of the young person.

12.13 At present, the provisions by which a potentially "dangerous" young offender reaches the Crown Court are overlapping to some extent as a result of the only partial implementation of the provisions of the Criminal Justice Act 2003, which introduce a new section 51A to the *Crime and Disorder Act* 1998. This new section requires a young offender to be sent for trial where it appears that the criteria for imposition of a sentence under the dangerous offender provisions will be met on conviction. However, the power to commit for sentence following conviction in a youth court or magistrates' court is preserved.

12.14 The nature of the offence is likely to be very significant in determining both whether the offender meets the risk and harm criteria and, even if so, whether a sentence under the provisions is necessary (given that there is now wide discretion).

Since a young offender should normally be dealt with in a youth court, where a young person charged with a specified offence would not otherwise be committed or sent to the Crown Court for trial, generally it is preferable for the decision whether to commit under these provisions to be made after conviction.

(v) Jointly charged with an adult

12.15 A further exception to the presumption in favour of summary trial arises where a young person is charged jointly with a person aged 18 or over; if the court considers it necessary to commit them both for trial it will have the power to commit the young person to the Crown Court for trial.

12.16 Any presumption in favour of sending a youth to the Crown Court to be tried jointly with an adult must be balanced with the general presumption that young offenders should be dealt with in a youth court.

12.17 When deciding whether to separate the youth and adult defendants, a court must consider:

- he young age of the offender, particularly where the age gap between the adult and youth is substantial,
- the immaturity and intellect of the youth,
- the relative culpability of the youth compared with the adult and whether or not the role played by the youth was minor, and
- any lack of previous convictions on the part of the youth compared with the adult offender.

12.18 A very significant factor will be whether the trial of the adult and youth could be severed without inconvenience to witnesses or injustice to the case as a whole, including whether there are benefits in the same tribunal sentencing all offenders. In most circumstances, a single trial of all issues is likely to be most in the interests of justice.

(vi) Remittal from the Crown Court

12.19 Where a young person is convicted before the Crown Court of an offence other than homicide, there is an obligation to remit the young person to a youth court for sentence unless that is "undesirable". In considering whether remittal is "undesirable", a court should balance the need for expertise in the sentencing of young offenders with the benefits of sentence being imposed by the court which had determined guilt.

12.20 Particular attention should be given to the presumption where a young person appears before the Crown Court only because he or she is jointly charged with an adult offender. A referral order is not available in the Crown Court for a first time offender and such orders may now be made following a second conviction in certain circumstances.

Part VI

Mentally Disordered Offenders

Chapter 28

MENTALLY DISORDERED OFFENDERS

I. MENTAL HEALTH ACT 2007

The *Mental Health Act* 2007 received the Royal Assent on July 19, 2007. Part 1 of the 2007 Act amends the *Mental Health Act* 1983. Chapter 1 amends key provisions of the 1983 Act; s.1 removes the categories of "severe mental impairment", "mental impairment" and "psychopathic disorder" from the current definition of mental disorder, and amends s.1 of the *Mental Health Act* 1983 so that "mental disorder" means 'any disorder or disability of the mind'. Section 2 of the 2007 Act provides that a person with learning disability shall not be considered by reason of that disability to be (a) suffering from mental disorder or (b) requiring treatment in hospital for mental disorder unless that disability is associated with abnormally aggressive or seriously irresponsible conduct on his part. Section 3 provides that dependence on alcohol or drugs is not considered to be a disorder or disability of the mind. This replaces the current exclusions for promiscuity or other immoral conduct, sexual deviancy or dependence on alcohol and drugs. Section 4 of the 2007 Act introduces a requirement that treatment be "appropriate" and "available" which will apply to the making of Hospital Orders under s.37 of the 1983 Act, remanding an individual to hospital for treatment under s.36 of the 1983 Act, Interim Hospital Orders under s.38 of the 1983 Act and transfers to hospital under ss.47 and 48 of the 1983 Act. **28–1**

Sections 1–5 of the *Mental Health Act* 2007 came into force on November 3, 2008 (*Mental Health Act 2007 (Commencement No. 6 and After-care under Supervision: Savings, Modifications and Transitional Provisions) Order* 2008 (S.I. 2008 No. 1210)); *Mental Health Act 2007 (Commencement No. 7 and Transitional Provisions) Order* 2008 (S.I. 2008 No. 1900)). Section 11 and s.14 of the *Mental Health Act* 2007 came into force on the same date (*Mental Health Act 2007 (Commencement No. 7 and Transitional Provisions) Order* 2008 (S.I. 2008 No. 1900)).

Chapter 2 of the 2007 Act amends the definitions of certain professional roles in the 1983 Act. Of relevance to the magistrates' court are provisions that amend the relevant professionals who may exercise roles under Pt 3 of the *Mental Health Act* 1983. Section 10 of the 2007 Act amends ss.35, 36 and 37 of the *Mental Health Act* 1983 so that **28–2** "approved clinician" replaces "registered medical practitioner". Section 14 defines "approved clinician" as "a person approved by the Secretary of State (in relation to England) or by the Welsh Ministers (in relation to Wales) to act as an approved clinician for the purposes of this Act".

28–3 Chapter 3 of the 2007 Act concerns amendments to current safeguards for patients, which fall outside the scope of this work. Chapter 4 concerns the introduction of Supervised Community Treatment Orders. Section 32 inserts new ss.17A–17G into the *Mental Health Act* 1983, permitting a responsible clinician to discharge an individual from hospital subject to recall to hospital should the individual not comply with community treatment, or should they require medical treatment in hospital for their mental disorder and there is a risk of harm to the health or safety of the patient or to other persons if the patient were not recalled to hospital for that purpose. Offenders who have been discharged from hospital following the imposition of a Hospital Order under s.37 of the 1983 Act can be made subject to such orders.

28–4 The *Mental Health Act* 2007 inserts ss.17A, 17B, 17C, 17D, 17E, 17F and 17G into the *Mental Health Act* 1983 which introduce community treatment orders. Sections 17A–17E and 17G came into force on November 3, 2008 (*Mental Health Act 2007 (Commencement No. 7 and Transitional Provisions) Order* 2008 (S.I. 2008 No. 1900)), and s.17F came into force on April 1, 2008 (*Mental Health Act 2007 (Commencement No. 4) Order* 2008 (S.I. 2008 No. 745)); *Mental Health Act 2007 (Commencement No. 6 and After-care under Supervision: Savings, Modifications and Transitional Provisions) Order* 2008 (S.I. 2008 No. 1210)).

These orders allow patients with a mental disorder to be discharged from hospital subject to the possibility of recall to hospital if necessary. The orders are an attempt to address the situation where some patients leave hospital and discontinue treatment, leading to a deterioration in their health such as to require hospital detention. The orders can only be imposed by a responsible clinician ("the approved clinician with overall responsibility for the patient's case": *Mental Health Act* 2007, s.9) and are available to patients treated under a hospital order imposed by the court under s.37 of the *Mental Health Act* 1983.

Mental Health Act 1983, ss.17A–17G

Community treatment orders

28–5 **17A.**—(1) The responsible clinician may by order in writing discharge a detained patient from hospital subject to his being liable to recall in accordance with section 17E below.

(2) A detained patient is a patient who is liable to be detained in a hospital in pursuance of an application for admission for treatment.

(3) An order under subsection (1) above is referred to in this Act as a "community treatment order".

(4) The responsible clinician may not make a community treatment order unless—

(a) in his opinion, the relevant criteria are met; and

(b) an approved mental health professional states in writing—

(i) that he agrees with that opinion; and

(ii) that it is appropriate to make the order—

(5) The relevant criteria are—

(a) the patient is suffering from mental disorder of a nature or degree which makes it appropriate for him to receive medical treatment;

(b) it is necessary for his health or safety or for the protection of other persons that he should receive such treatment;

(c) subject to his being liable to be recalled as mentioned in paragraph (d) below, such treatment can be provided without his continuing to be detained in a hospital;

(d) it is necessary that the responsible clinician should be able to exercise the power under section 17E(1) below to recall the patient to hospital; and

(e) appropriate medical treatment is available for him.

(6) In determining whether the criterion in subsection (5)(d) above is met, the

responsible clinician shall, in particular, consider, having regard to the patient's history of mental disorder and any other relevant factors, what risk there would be of a deterioration of the patient's condition if he were not detained in a hospital (as a result, for example, of his refusing or neglecting to receive the medical treatment he requires for his mental disorder).

(7) In this Act—

"community patient" means a patient in respect of whom a community treatment order is in force;

"the community treatment order", in relation to such a patient, means the community treatment order in force in respect of him; and

"the responsible hospital", in relation to such a patient, means the hospital in which he was liable to be detained immediately before the community treatment order was made, subject to section 19A below.

Conditions

17B.—(1) A community treatment order shall specify conditions to which the patient is to be subject while the order remains in force. **28–6**

(2) But, subject to subsection (3) below, the order may specify conditions only if the responsible clinician, with the agreement of the approved mental health professional mentioned in section 17A(4)(b) above, thinks them necessary or appropriate for one or more of the following purposes—

(a) ensuring that the patient receives medical treatment;
(b) preventing risk of harm to the patient's health or safety;
(c) protecting other persons.

(3) The order shall specify—

(a) a condition that the patient make himself available for examination under section 20A below; and
(b) a condition that, if it is proposed to give a certificate under Part 4A of this Act in his case, he make himself available for examination so as to enable the certificate to be given.

(4) The responsible clinician may from time to time by order in writing vary the conditions specified in a community treatment order.

(5) He may also suspend any conditions specified in a community treatment order.

(6) If a community patient fails to comply with a condition specified in the community treatment order by virtue of subsection (2) above, that fact may be taken into account for the purposes of exercising the power of recall under section 17E(1) below.

(7) But nothing in this section restricts the exercise of that power to cases where there is such a failure.

Duration of community treatment order

17C. A community treatment order shall remain in force until– **28–7**

(a) the period mentioned in section 20A(1) below (as extended under any provision of this Act) expires, but this is subject to sections 21 and 22 below;
(b) the patient is discharged in pursuance of an order under section 23 below or a direction under section 72 below;
(c) the application for admission for treatment in respect of the patient otherwise ceases to have effect; or
(d) the order is revoked under section 17F below, whichever occurs first.

Effect of community treatment order

17D.—(1) The application for admission for treatment in respect of a patient shall not cease to have effect by virtue of his becoming a community patient. **28–8**

(2) But while he remains a community patient—

(a) the authority of the managers to detain him under section 6(2) above in pursuance of that application shall be suspended; and
(b) reference (however expressed) in this or any other Act, or in any subordinate legislation (within the meaning of the *Interpretation Act* 1978), to patients liable to be detained, or detained, under this Act shall not include him.

(3) And section 20 below shall not apply to him while he remains a community patient.

(4) Accordingly, authority for his detention shall not expire during any period in which that authority is suspended by virtue of subsection (2)(a) above.

Power to recall to hospital

28–9 **17E.**—(1) The responsible clinician may recall a community patient to hospital if in his opinion—

(a) the patient requires medical treatment in hospital for his mental disorder; and

(b) there would be a risk of harm to the health or safety of the patient or to other persons if the patient were not recalled to hospital for that purpose.

(2) The responsible clinician may also recall a community patient to hospital if the patient fails to comply with a condition specified under section 17B(3) above.

(3) The hospital to which a patient is recalled need not be the responsible hospital.

(4) Nothing in this section prevents a patient from being recalled to a hospital even though he is already in the hospital at the time when the power of recall is exercised; references to recalling him shall be construed accordingly.

(5) The power of recall under subsections (1) and (2) above shall be exercisable by notice in writing to the patient.

(6) A notice under this section recalling a patient to hospital shall be sufficient authority for the managers of that hospital to detain the patient there in accordance with the provisions of this Act.

Powers in respect of recalled patients

28–10 **17F.**—(1) This section applies to a community patient who is detained in a hospital by virtue of a notice recalling him there under section 17E above.

(2) The patient may be transferred to another hospital in such circumstances and subject to such conditions as may be prescribed in regulations made by the Secretary of State (if the hospital in which the patient is detained is in England) or the Welsh Ministers (if that hospital is in Wales).

(3) If he is so transferred to another hospital, he shall be treated for the purposes of this section (and section 17E above) as if the notice under that section were a notice recalling him to that other hospital and as if he had been detained there from the time when his detention in hospital by virtue of the notice first began.

(4) The responsible clinician may by order in writing revoke the community treatment order if—

(a) in his opinion, the conditions mentioned in section 3(2) above are satisfied in respect of the patient; and

(b) an approved mental health professional states in writing—

(i) that he agrees with that opinion; and

(ii) that it is appropriate to revoke the order.

(5) The responsible clinician may at any time release the patient under this section, but not after the community treatment order has been revoked.

(6) If the patient has not been released, nor the community treatment order revoked, by the end of the period of 72 hours, he shall then be released.

(7) But a patient who is released under this section remains subject to the community treatment order.

(8) In this section—

(a) "the period of 72 hours" means the period of 72 hours beginning with the time when the patient's detention in hospital by virtue of the notice under section 17E above begins; and

(b) references to being released shall be construed as references to being released from that detention (and accordingly from being recalled to hospital).

Effect of revoking community treatment order

28–11 **17G.**—(1) This section applies if a community treatment order is revoked under section 17F above in respect of a patient.

(2) Section 6(2) above shall have effect as if the patient had never been discharged from hospital by virtue of the community treatment order.

(3) The provisions of this or any other Act relating to patients liable to be detained (or detained) in pursuance of an application for admission for treatment shall apply to the

patient as they did before the community treatment order was made, unless otherwise provided.

(4) If, when the order is revoked, the patient is being detained in a hospital other than the responsible hospital, the provisions of this Part of this Act shall have effect as if—

(a) the application for admission for treatment in respect of him were an application for admission to that other hospital; and

(b) he had been admitted to that other hospital at the time when he was originally admitted in pursuance of the application.

(5) But, in any case, section 20 below shall have effect as if the patient had been admitted to hospital in pursuance of the application for admission for treatment on the day on which the order is revoked.

Chapters 5, 6, 7 and 8 of Pt 1 of the *Mental Health Act* 2007 fall outside the scope of this work. Part 2 of the *Mental Health Act* 2007 amends the *Domestic Crime and Victims Act* 2004 to increase the rights of victims where the offender concerned has been sent to hospital, and also amends the *Mental Capacity Act* 2005. The amendments affected by Pt 2 also fall outside the scope of this work. **28–12**

II. DEFINITION OF MENTAL DISORDER

Mental Health Act 1983, s.1

Application of Act: "mental disorder"

1.—(1) The provisions of this Act shall have effect with respect to the reception, care and treatment of mentally disordered patients, the management of their property and other related matters. **28–13**

(2) In this Act—

'mental disorder" means any disorder or disability of the mind; and

"mentally disordered" shall be construed accordingly; and other expressions shall have the meanings assigned to them in section 145 below.

(2A) But a person with learning disability shall not be considered by reason of that disability to be—

(a) suffering from mental disorder for the purposes of the provisions mentioned in subsection (2B) below; or

(b) requiring treatment in hospital for mental disorder for the purposes of sections 17E and 50 to 53 below, unless that disability is associated with abnormally aggressive or seriously irresponsible conduct on his part.

(2B) The provisions are—

(a) sections 3, 7, 17A, 20 and 20A below;

(b) sections 35 to 38, 45A, 47, 48 and 51 below; and

(c) section 72(1)(b) and (c) and (4) below.

(3) Dependence on alcohol or drugs is not considered to be a disorder or disability of the mind for the purposes of subsection (2) above.

(4) In subsection (2A) above, "learning disability" means a state of arrested or incomplete development of the mind which includes significant impairment of intelligence and social functioning.

[This section is printed as amended by the *Mental Health Act* 2007, ss.1–3; the *Mental Health Act 2007 (Commencement No. 6 and After-care under Supervision: Savings, Modifications and Transitional Provisions) Order* 2008 (S.I 2008 No. 1210): *Mental Health Act 2007 (Commencement No. 7 and Transitional Provisions) Order* 2008 (S.I. 2008 No. 1900) which came into force on November 3, 2008.]

III. DIVERSION FROM THE CRIMINAL JUSTICE SYSTEM

Two government policy documents encourage the diversion of mentally disordered offenders from the criminal justice system in appropriate cases. First, Home Office Circular 66/90 (*Provision for Mentally Disordered Offenders*) provides that government policy is to divert mentally disordered persons from the criminal justice system in **28–14** cases where the public interest does not require their prosecution. Chief Officers of Police are therefore asked to ensure that, taking into account the public interest, consideration is always given to alternatives to prosecution, including taking no further action where appropriate and that effective arrangements are established with local health and social services authorities to ensure their speedy involvement when mentally disordered persons are taken into police custody. Where a prosecution is considered necessary, non-penal disposals should be used wherever appropriate and the police, courts and probation services should work with their local health and social services to make effective use of the provisions of the *Mental Health Act* 1983 and the services which exist to help the mentally disordered offender.

Secondly, further advice is contained in Home Office Circular 12/95 *Mentally Disordered Offenders—Inter-Agency Working*.

28–15 In deciding whether a prosecution should be commenced or continued prosecutors should have regard to The Code for Crown Prosecutors (2004). The Code (at para. 5.10) provides some common public interest factors against prosecution, which include: if the prosecution is likely to have a bad effect on the victim's physical or mental health (always bearing in mind the seriousness of the offence) and whether the defendant is, or was at the time of the offence, suffering from significant mental or physical ill heath. The Code identifies the need for prosecutors to "balance the desirability of diverting a defendant who is suffering from significant mental or physical ill health with the need to safeguard the general public". The Code is reproduced in full in Appendix E.

IV. BAIL

(1) Bail from the police station

28–16 After charge at the police station, the general right to bail for persons accused of offences in the magistrates' courts applies to the mentally disordered offender. The offender must be granted bail unless one of the conditions specified in s.38(1) of the *Police and Criminal Evidence Act* 1984 applies. Bail may be refused in specified circumstances, some of which may apply in the case of an accused who is suspected of suffering from mental disorder: see *ante*, Ch.5.

(2) Bail at the magistrates' court

28–17 The *Bail Act* 1976 applies to mentally disordered offenders as to any other offender. Note the exceptions to right to bail where there are grounds for believing that the defendant may abscond, commit an offence or interfere with witnesses. The court may exercise its power to remand in custody for the defendant's own protection (*Bail Act* 1976, Sched. 1, Pt 1, para. 3).

Post conviction the court may exercise its power to impose a requirement that the offender makes himself available for the purpose of enabling enquiries or a report to be made to assist the court in dealing with him for the offence: *Bail Act* 1976, s.3(6)(d).

If a defendant is remanded in custody, the Home Secretary may direct that the defendant be transferred from prison to a hospital for the purpose of the preparation of medical reports on the accused's psychiatric condition: *Mental Health Act* 1983, s.48(2)(b). A transfer under s.48 may be ordered before or after conviction. It is an administrative alternative to a remand to hospital ordered by a court under s.35 or s.38, see *post*, §§ 28–18 and 28–36.

Mental Health Act 1983, s.35

Remand to hospital for report on accused's mental condition

28–18 **35.**—(1) Subject to the provisions of this section, the Crown Court or a magistrates' court may remand an accused person to a hospital specified by the court for a report on his mental condition.

(2) For the purposes of this section an accused person is—

(a) in relation to the Crown Court, any person who is awaiting trial before the court for an offence punishable with imprisonment or who has been arraigned before the court for such an offence and has not yet been sentenced or otherwise dealt with for the offence on which he has been arraigned;

(b) in relation to a magistrates' court, any person who has been convicted by the court of an offence punishable on summary conviction with imprisonment and any person charged with such an offence if the court is satisfied that he did the act or made the omission charged or he has consented to the exercise by the court of the powers conferred by this section.

(3) Subject to subsection (4) below, the powers conferred by this section may be exercised if—

(a) the court is satisfied, on the written or oral evidence of a registered medical practitioner, that there is reason to suspect that the accused person is suffering from mental disorder; and

(b) the court is of the opinion that it would be impracticable for a report on his mental condition to be made if he were remanded on bail;

but those powers shall not be exercised by the Crown Court in respect of a person who has been convicted before the court if the sentence for the offence of which he has been convicted is fixed by law.

(4) The court shall not remand an accused person to a hospital under this section unless satisfied, on the written or oral evidence of the approved clinician who would be responsible for making the report or of some other person representing the managers of the hospital, that arrangements have been made for his admission to that hospital and for his admission to it within the period of seven days beginning with the date of the remand; and if the court is so satisfied it may, pending his admission, give directions for his conveyance to and detention in a place of safety.

(5) Where a court has remanded an accused person under this section it may further remand him if it appears to the court, on the written or oral evidence of the approved clinician responsible for making the report, that a further remand is necessary for completing the assessment of the accused person's mental condition.

(6) The power of further remanding an accused person under this section may be exercised by the court without his being brought before the court if he is represented by an authorised person who is given an opportunity of being heard.

(7) An accused person shall not be remanded or further remanded under this section for more than 28 days at a time or for more than 12 weeks in all; and the court may at any time terminate the remand if it appears to the court that it is appropriate to do so.

(8) An accused person remanded to hospital under this section shall be entitled to obtain at his own expense an independent report on his mental condition from a registered medical practitioner or approved clinician chosen by him and to apply to the court on the basis of it for his remand to be terminated under subsection (7) above.

(9) Where an accused person is remanded under this section—

(a) a constable or any other person directed to do so by the court shall convey the accused person to the hospital specified by the court within the period mentioned in subsection (4) above; and

(b) the managers of the hospital shall admit him within that period and thereafter detain him in accordance with the provisions of this section.

(10) If an accused person absconds from a hospital to which he has been remanded under this section, or while being conveyed to or from that hospital, he may be arrested without warrant by any constable and shall, after being arrested, be brought as soon as practicable before the court that remanded him; and the court may thereupon terminate the remand and deal with him in any way in which it could have dealt with him if he had not been remanded under this section.

[This section is printed as amended by the *Legal Services Act* 2007, Sched. 21, para. 54.]

Whilst the proceedings remain in the magistrates' court, this power to remand to hospital for assessment only arises if the defendant has been convicted of an offence which is punishable with imprisonment on summary conviction or if the defendant is **28–19** charged with such an offence and the court have made a finding (without convicting) that the defendant did the act or made the omission charged, in accordance with s.37(3), see below.

V. HOSPITAL ORDERS WITHOUT CONVICTION

(1) Mental Health Act 1983, s.37(3)

28–20 Section 37(3) of the *Mental Health Act* 1983 provides that where a person is tried summarily for an act or omission which would, upon conviction, warrant a hospital order, the court may impose such an order once it is satisfied that the accused did the act or made the omission charged. The order is also available where the offender is charged with an offence triable either way and he elects trial by indictment: *Ramsgate Justices, ex p. Kazmarek* (1984) 80 Cr.App.R. 366. The order is also available where the offender was unable to consent to summary trial: *Lincolnshire (Kesteven) Justices, ex p. O'Connor* [1983] 1 W.L.R. 335, DC.

The court must still have the reports of two registered medical practitioners testifying to the mental state of the accused, and a hospital bed must be available before this power becomes exercisable.

Because s.37(3) gives the court the power to make a hospital order without convicting the accused, it has been held that it is not necessary that a trial be held: *Lincolnshire (Kesteven) Justices, ex p. O'Connor*, above. To satisfy the court that the defendant did the act or made the omission charged, the prosecution need only prove the ingredients which comprise the *actus reus* of the offence:*Antoine* [2000] 2 All E.R. 208, HL.

Whilst a finding under s.37(3) is not a conviction, a defendant against whom such an order is made has a right of appeal as if it were a conviction: *Mental Health Act* 1983, s.45.

In *Surat Singh v. Stratford Magistrates' Court* (2008) 1 Cr.App.R. 2, the Court was invited to consider whether the court can proceed to make a Hospital Order under s.37(3) where there is a possibility that the accused may be able to establish the defence of insanity and thus be entitled to an acquittal. The Court held that the defence of insanity could be relied upon in the magistrates' court and if established by the accused in a case to which it was relevant, it prevented conviction. Although there was no entitlement to a trial of the issue of insanity, the interests of justice had to be considered individually in each case. If it was clear that it was a possibility the magistrates' court should invite submissions upon the course to be adopted. In particular, careful consideration had to be given to any reason advanced as to why the issue of insanity should be tried. Such an application should be resolved having regard to the interests of justice. Even if an order under s.37(3) was likely, an accused was entitled to a full consideration of whether there should be a trial of the issue of insanity; neither s.37(3) of the 1983 Act nor s.11 of the *Powers of Criminal Courts (Sentencing) Act* 2000 bore on the question of whether insanity was a defence to a charge brought in the magistrates' court. The sections merely established a coherent scheme for dealing with most defendants in the magistrates' court who were suffering from mental illness when they appeared. The natural reading of s.37(3) was that it provided the magistrates' court with the power, in an appropriate case, to abstain from convicting or acquitting, and instead to make a hospital or guardianship order provided the conditions of the subsection were met.

(2) Fitness to plead

28–21 The question of fitness to plead is not relevant to proceedings in the magistrates' court. The issue of fitness to plead arises only under the *Criminal Procedure (Insanity) Act* 1964 and the *Criminal Procedure (Insanity and Unfitness to Plead) Act* 1991, which apply only to proceedings in the Crown Court. The magistrates may commit an accused charged with an offence triable either way to the Crown Court, where the issue may be raised, though this power is not available if the accused is charged with an offence triable only summarily: *R. v. Metropolitan Stipendiary Magistrate Tower Bridge, ex p. Antifowosi* (1985) 144 J.P. 752.

The fact that a court of higher authority has previously held that a person was unfit to plead does not make it an abuse of process to try that person for subsequent criminal acts: *CPS v. P* [2007] EWHC 946, QBD.

(3) Insanity

Although the *Trial of Lunatics Act* 1883, s.2(1) provides that the special verdict of **28–22** not guilty by reason of insanity may only be returned by a jury, the defence is not limited to trials on indictment. The legal definition of insanity is that the accused was, at the time of commission of the act in question, labouring under a defect of reason, from disease of the mind as not to know the nature and the quality of the act he was doing, or if he did know it, he did not know it was wrong: *M'Naghten's case* (1843) 10 Cl. & Fin. 200.

A disorder which impairs the accused's mental faculties of reason, memory and understanding so as to render him unaware of what he was doing, or unaware of the fact that what he was doing was wrong will be a "disease of the mind" causing a "defect of reason" within the M'Naghten Rules, whether the aetiology of the impairment was organic or functional and whether it was permanent or transient and intermittent: *Sullivan* (1984) A.C 156.

Insanity is a defence to any criminal charge as it operates as to render absent the **28–23** *mens rea* element of the crime. Insanity may therefore be raised against a charge tried summarily, though the court may not return the special verdict of "not guilty by reason of insanity": *Trial of Lunatics Act* 1883, *ante*. In *DPP v. Harper* [1997] 1 W.L.R. 1406, the respondent had been acquitted of driving a motor vehicle with an excess of alcohol in his blood, contrary to s.5(1)(a) of the *Road Traffic Act* 1988, on grounds of insanity. The prosecution appealed to the Divisional Court of the Queen's Bench Division, who granted the appeal holding that no defence of insanity is available in cases where the offence is one of strict liability. McCowan L.J. stated:

> "[I]nsanity can be a defence in the magistrates' court, but only if the offence charged is one in which *mens rea* is an element. Every man is assumed to be sane at the time of an alleged offence and, accordingly, the burden is on the accused to establish insanity at the time of the commission of the offence on the balance of probabilities. The defence is based on the absence of *mens rea*, but none is required for the offence of driving with an excess of alcohol. Hence, the defence of insanity has no relevance to such a charge, as it is an offence of strict liability." [at p.1409]

In *Johnson* [2007] EWCA Crim. 1978, CA, the appellant appealed against his convic- **28–24** tion for wounding with intent to cause grievous bodily harm. Two psychiatrists agreed that the appellant was suffering from paranoid schizophrenia at the time of the offence. They also agreed that at the time, the appellant knew his actions were against the law; however, one psychiatrist asserted the appellant did not consider what he had done to be morally wrong. The trial judge had concluded that there was no basis for considering the defence of insanity as the appellant knew that what he was doing was against the law. The appellant submitted that on a proper reading of the M'Naghten Rules, he was entitled to a verdict of not guilty by reason of insanity on the grounds that, although he knew that what he was doing was against the law, on the basis of his mental condition at the time he felt there was a moral justification for doing so. The Court of Appeal dismissed his appeal, holding that although the issue was one of great importance, the court could only assess verdicts of not guilty by reason of insanity in light of the M'Naghten Rules. The issue was the meaning of "wrong" in the context of the appellant's behaviour and it had been unequivocally held in *R. v. Windle* [1952] 2 Q.B. 826, CCA, that the meaning of "wrong" was that it was contrary to law and did not have a vague meaning that might vary according to the opinion of different persons whether a particular act might or might not be justified.

In addition to the inability to return the special verdict, the 1983 Act makes no provision for committal to the Crown Court by the magistrates for imposition of a restriction order under section 41 upon a person who has been acquitted of an offence by reason of insanity. The magistrates only have such a power to commit to the Crown Court for that purpose in the case of a person convicted of an imprisonable offence, whether indictable or summary only. This situation has been described as a "legislative lacuna": *R. v. Horseferry Road Magistrates' Court, ex p. K.* [1996] 2 Cr.App.R. 574, DC.

VI. SENTENCING POWERS

A. PRE-SENTENCE REPORTS

28–25 Section 11 of the *Powers of Criminal Courts (Sentencing) Act* 2000 gives the court power to order a medical report on the offender's physical or mental condition when it considers such a report necessary for disposal of the case. The power arises when the offence is triable summarily, and punishable with imprisonment and the court is satisfied that the offender did the act or made the omission charged.

Powers of Criminal Courts (Sentencing) Act 2000, s.11

Remand by magistrates' court for medical examination

28–26 **11.**—(1) If, on the trial by a magistrates' court of an offence punishable on summary conviction with imprisonment, the court—

(a) is satisfied that the accused did the act or made the omission charged, but

(b) is of the opinion that an inquiry ought to be made into his physical or mental condition before the method of dealing with him is determined,

the court shall adjourn the case to enable a medical examination and report to be made, and shall remand him.

(2) An adjournment under subsection (1) above shall not be for more than three weeks at a time where the court remands the accused in custody, nor for more than four weeks at a time where it remands him on bail.

(3) Where on an adjournment under subsection (1) above the accused is remanded on bail, the court shall impose conditions under paragraph (d) of section 3(6) of the Bail Act 1976 and the requirements imposed as conditions under that paragraph shall be or shall include requirements that the accused—

(a) undergo medical examination by a registered medical practitioner or, where the inquiry is into his mental condition and the court so directs, two such practitioners; and

(b) for that purpose attend such an institution or place, or on such practitioner, as the court directs and, where the inquiry is into his mental condition, comply with any other directions which may be given to him for that purpose by any person specified by the court or by a person of any class so specified.

28–27 When exercising this power, the court must send a statement to the doctor where the offender is to be examined listing reasons for the request and any information before the court about the offender's mental and physical condition: *Criminal Procedure Rules*, r.49.1.

In addition, the *Criminal Justice Act* 2003, s.157(1) requires the Court, where the offender appears to be mentally disordered, to obtain and consider a medical report when passing a custodial sentence other than one fixed by law. However, this requirement does not apply if, in the circumstances of the case, the court is of the opinion that it is unnecessary to obtain a medical report.

In *Blouet v. Bath & Wansdyke Magistrates Court* [2009] EWHC 759, the claimant applied for permission to seek judicial review of a decision of the magistrates' court declining to order a fact-finding exercise under s.11 of the *Powers of Criminal Courts (Sentencing) Act* 2000. The claimant, who suffered from Asperger's syndrome and had a history of mental health problems, had been charged with an offence. While one psychiatric report concluded he was not fit to plead, a second concluded that he was fit to plead and that he did not have a mental disorder requiring attention under the *Mental Health Act* 1983. Instead of adjourning the matter for a fact-finding hearing to determine whether or not the claimant had done the act with which he was charged, the court adjourned the matter for trial. The claimant submitted that the first psychiatric report was sufficient to trigger a fact-finding hearing.

The Court refused the application, stating that where the question of a fact-finding hearing arose, the judge should have before him up-to-date medical evidence. If there was a possibility of an order being made under s.37(3) of the 1983 Act, he was to try the issue in accordance with s.11(1) of the 2000 Act. If there then arose an obligation to adjourn for further reports; that was what had to happen. A trial and a finding within s.11(1) were not the same thing.

Lord Justice Goldring outlined the procedure the court is to follow:

> "The approach which the district judge should follow is this. First, there should be up-to-date - and I emphasise the words "up-to-date" - medical evidence before him. If there is a possibility of a Section 37 (3) order being made, he will then try the issue in accordance with Section 11 (1) of the Act. If thereafter there arises the obligation to adjourn for further reports then that is what must happen. It may of course be that - given the up-to-date reports which he will then have - only a very short adjournment will be needed or, if everyone agrees that in the circumstances it is not, the matter can proceed under Section 37 (3) if that be appropriate" (para. 9).

In *R. (on the application of Varma) v. Redbridge Magistrates' Court* [2009] EWHC 836 (Admin), DC, the claimant applied for judicial review of a decision of the defendant magistrates' court to convict him of an offence of driving whilst disqualified. The appellant had initially pleaded guilty to the offence but was deemed unfit to plead in respect of separate proceedings in the Crown Court on the basis of medical reports. A successful application was made to withdraw his guilty plea, a not guilty plea was entered and a trial of the issues listed. A further medical report was ordered and directions given, with a mental health disposal anticipated. However, following an application by the Crown based on a further medical report which found that the appellant was fit to plead, the matter proceeded to trial, despite the appellant's request for an adjournment for further consideration of the medical evidence. The appellant did not give evidence and was convicted. A report prepared after conviction concluded that the appellant was unfit to be tried. The magistrates' court and the Crown declined to sign a consent order quashing the conviction.

Granting the application, the Court held that as the Crown had given no effective notice of its proposed course for the case, which was contrary to the directions given by the district judge, the magistrates' court was quite wrong not to grant the adjournment sought by the appellant to allow the medical evidence to be called. The court was also wrong to proceed on the basis of the further report, as it was not agreed, was not in evidence and was contradicted by four other medical reports. The court should not have embarked on a summary trial as if there was no problem with the appellant's understanding and the court should not have acceded to the Crown's submission that any unfairness in the trial could be corrected on appeal. The trial was not fair and the conviction had to be quashed. The case was remitted to the magistrates' court to be reconsidered by a different bench to determine whether the appellant committed the acts alleged and to make appropriate orders under s.37(3) of the *Mental Health Act* 1983.

Criminal Justice Act 2003, s.157

Additional requirements in case of mentally disordered offender

157.—(1) Subject to subsection (2), in any case where the offender is or appears to be mentally disordered, the court must obtain and consider a medical report before passing a custodial sentence other than one fixed by law. **28–28**

(2) Subsection (1) does not apply if, in the circumstances of the case, the court is of the opinion that it is unnecessary to obtain a medical report.

(3) Before passing a custodial sentence other than one fixed by law on an offender who is or appears to be mentally disordered, a court must consider–

(a) any information before it which relates to his mental condition (whether given in a medical report, a pre-sentence report or otherwise), and

(b) the likely effect of such a sentence on that condition and on any treatment which may be available for it.

(4) No custodial sentence which is passed in a case to which subsection (1) applies is invalidated by the failure of a court to comply with that subsection, but any court on an appeal against such a sentence—

(a) must obtain a medical report if none was obtained by the court below, and

(b) must consider any such report obtained by it or by that court.

(5) In this section "mentally disordered", in relation to any person, means suffering from a mental disorder within the meaning of the *Mental Health Act* 1983.

(6) In this section "medical report" means a report as to an offender's mental condition made or submitted orally or in writing by a registered medical practitioner who is approved for the purposes of section 12 of the *Mental Health Act* 1983 by the Secretary of State as having special experience in the diagnosis or treatment of mental disorder.

(7) Nothing in this section is to be taken to limit the generality of section 156.

28–29 See the *Criminal Procedure Rules*, r.49.1.

Where the court receives conflicting medical evidence in psychiatric reports, the court is entitled to prefer the evidence of one expert, and must resolve the issue in the light of the evidence and all the circumstances of the case: *Reid* [2005] EWCA Crim. 392, CA.

B. HOSPITAL/GUARDIANSHIP ORDER

Mental Health Act 1983, s.37

Powers of courts to order hospital admission or guardianship.

28–30 **37.**—(1) Where a person is convicted before the Crown Court of an offence punishable with imprisonment other than an offence the sentence for which is fixed by law, or is convicted by a magistrates' court of an offence punishable on summary conviction with imprisonment, and the conditions mentioned in subsection (2) below are satisfied, the court may by order authorise his admission to and detention in such hospital as may be specified in the order or, as the case may be, place him under the guardianship of a local social services authority or of such other person approved by a local social services authority as may be so specified.

(1A) In the case of an offence the sentence for which would otherwise fall to be imposed—

(a) under section 51A(2) of the *Firearms Act* 1968,

(b) under section 110(2) or 111(2) of the *Powers of Criminal Courts (Sentencing) Act* 2000,

(c) under section 225(2) or 226(2) of the *Criminal Justice Act* 2003 or

(d) under section 29(4) or (6) of the *Violent Crime Reduction Act* 2006 (minimum sentences in certain cases of using someone to mind a weapon).

nothing in those provisions shall prevent a court from making an order under subsection (1) above for the admission of the offender to a hospital.

(1B) References in subsection (1A) above to a sentence falling to be imposed under any of the provisions mentioned in that subsection are to be read in accordance with section 305(4) of the *Criminal Justice Act* 2003.

(2) The conditions referred to in subsection (1) above are that—

(a) the court is satisfied, on the written or oral evidence of two registered medical practitioners, that the offender is suffering from mental disorder and that either—

(i) the mental disorder from which the offender is suffering is of a nature or degree which makes it appropriate for him to be detained in a hospital for medical treatment and appropriate medical treatment is available for him; or

(ii) in the case of an offender who has attained the age of 16 years, the mental disorder is of a nature or degree which warrants his reception into guardianship under this Act; and

(b) the court is of the opinion, having regard to all the circumstances including the nature of the offence and the character and antecedents of the offender, and to the other available methods of dealing with him, that the most suitable method of disposing of the case is by means of an order under this section.

(3) Where a person is charged before a magistrates' court with any act or omission as an offence and the court would have power, on convicting him of that offence, to make an order under subsection (1) above in his case, then, if the court is satisfied that the accused did the act or made the omission charged, the court may, if it thinks fit, make such an order without convicting him.

(4) An order for the admission of an offender to a hospital (in this Act referred to as "a hospital order") shall not be made under this section unless the court is satisfied on the written or oral evidence of the approved clinician who would have overall responsibility for his case or of some other person representing the managers of the hospital that arrangements have been made for his admission to that hospital, and for his admission to it within the period of 28 days beginning with the date of the making of such an order; and the court may, pending his admission within that period, given such directions as it thinks fit for his conveyance to and detention in a place of safety.

(5) If within the said period of 28 days it appears to the Secretary of State that by reason of an emergency or other special circumstances it is not practicable for the patient to be received into the hospital specified in the order, he may give directions for the admission of the patient to such other hospital as appears to be appropriate instead of the hospital so specified; and where such directions are given—

(a) the Secretary of State shall cause the person having the custody of the patient to be informed, and

(b) the hospital order shall have effect as if the hospital specified in the directions were substituted for the hospital specified in the order.

(6) An order placing an offender under the guardianship of a local social services authority or of any other person (in this Act referred to as "a guardianship order") shall not be made under this section unless the court is satisfied that that authority or person is willing to receive the offender into guardianship.

(7) *Repealed*.

(8) Where an order is made under this section, the court shall not—

(a) pass sentence of imprisonment or impose a fine or make a community order (within the meaning of Part 12 of the *Criminal Justice Act* 2003 or a youth rehabilitation order (within the meaning of Part 1 of the *Criminal Justice and Immigration Act* 2008) in respect of the offence,

(b) if the order under this section is a hospital order, make a referral order (within the meaning of the *Powers of Criminal Courts (Sentencing) Act* 2000 in respect of the offence, or

(c) make in respect of the offender an order under section 150 of that Act (binding over of parent or guardian), but the court may make any other order which it has power to make apart from this section; and for the purposes of this subsection "sentence of imprisonment" includes any sentence or order for detention.

[This section is printed as amended by the *Criminal Justice and Immigration Act* 2008, Sched. 28, para. 1.]

The court must be satisfied on the evidence of two registered medical practitioners that the offender is suffering from a mental disorder, as defined in s.1 of the 1983 Act, of a nature or degree which makes it appropriate for him to be detained and treated in hospital for medical treatment and the court is of the opinion that this would be the most suitable method of disposal of the case. The court may make a hospital order without the offender's consent. **28–31**

The hospital order has the "sole purpose" of ensuring "that the offender receives the medical care and attention which he needs in the hope and expectation of course that the result will be to avoid the commission of further criminal acts": *Birch* (1989) 11 Cr.App.R.(S.) 202 The Court of Appeal also outlined the appropriate approach of a court when sentencing a mentally disordered offender: **28–32**

> "First he should decide whether a period of compulsory detention is apposite. If the answer is that it is not, or may not be, the possibility of a probation order with a condition of out-patient treatment should be considered...

> Secondly the judge will ask himself whether the conditions contained in section 37(2)(a) for the making of a hospital order are satisfied. Here the judge acts on the evidence of the doctors. If he is left in doubt, he may wish to avail himself of the valuable provisions of sections 38 and 39.
>
> If the judge concludes that the conditions empowering him to make an order are satisfied, he will consider whether to make such an order, or whether "the most suitable method of disposing of the case (section 37(2)(b)) is to impose a sentence of imprisonment".

28–33 Where the psychiatric evidence given to a court is incomplete at the time of sentence in that it fails to give a full picture of the defendant's mental state at the time of the offence, fresh evidence as to the mental state of the defendant may be submitted, and it may be appropriate to replace a sentence of imprisonment with a hospital order under s.37 of the *Mental Health Act* 1983: *Roden* [2006] EWCA Crim. 1121, CA. In this case, the appellant appealed against concurrent sentences of six years' imprisonment imposed after he pleaded guilty to two counts of arson with intent to endanger life. A psychiatrist had given evidence that the appellant had no diagnosable mental disorder and was not mentally ill at the time of the offence. After sentencing, the appellant began to exhibit psychotic symptoms, and was transferred to a mental hospital. His Responsible Medical Officer concluded he was suffering from paranoid schizophrenia and had done so since before starting the fire.

The Court of Appeal held that the Responsible Medical Officer's evidence satisfied the requirements of the *Criminal Appeal Act* 1968, s.23(2), it was expedient in the interests of justice to receive it, and that the psychiatric evidence before the judge had been incomplete as it failed to give a full picture of the appellant's mental state at the time of the offence. The Court stated that the fresh evidence satisfied the criteria for making a hospital order under s.37(2) and had that evidence been before the judge, it would have been appropriate to make such an order. It was, therefore, appropriate to replace the appellant's sentence with a hospital order, together with a restriction order under s.41 of the *Mental Health Act* 1983.

28–34 The decision whether to make a hospital order lies within the court's discretion; there is no presumption that where an offender meets the conditions for a hospital order, a hospital order will be made. The offender's needs, specifically those relating to his psychiatric condition, are an important matter for the judge but they are not overriding: *Khelifi* [2006] 2 Cr.App.R.(S.) 100, CA. In this case, the appellant had been involved to a major extent in a serious and sophisticated fraud. There was evidence that he had been genuinely suffering from paranoid schizophrenia since 1994 and that he was at risk of self-harm if not treated. However, the Court of Appeal held that a sentence of imprisonment was not wrong in principle, though the appellant's circumstances and his basis of plea justified a reduction in the sentence from five years to three-and-a-half years' imprisonment.

This decision has been received with caution. For example, writing in *Criminal Law Week*, James Richardson states:

> "it should be remembered that prison is no place for the mentally ill, and that expectations about particular offenders being transferred promptly to hospital under s.37 are not always realised, and that delays may lead to a serious deterioration in the prisoner's mental health". (CLW/06/40/31)

Section 37(4) must be strictly applied with the details of the admitting hospital and date of expiry of the 28 days clearly noted on the order *R. (D.B.) v. Notts Healthcare NHS Trust* (2009) 2 All E.R. 792, CA.

28–35 See also *Criminal Procedure Rules*, r.49.2.

C. INTERIM HOSPITAL ORDERS

Mental Health Act 1983, s.38

Interim hospital orders

28–36 **38.**—(1) Where a person is convicted before the Crown Court of an offence punishable with imprisonment (other than an offence the sentence for which is fixed by law) or is convicted by a magistrates' court of an offence punishable on summary conviction with imprisonment and the court before or by which he is convicted is satisfied, on the written or oral evidence of two registered medical practitioners—

(a) that the offender is suffering from mental disorder ; and

(b) that there is reason to suppose that the mental disorder from which the offender is suffering is such that it may be appropriate for a hospital order to be made in his case,

the court may, before making a hospital order or dealing with him in some other way, make an order (in this Act referred to as "an interim hospital order") authorising his admission to such hospital as may be specified in the order and his detention there in accordance with this section.

(2) In the case of an offender who is subject to an interim hospital order the court may make a hospital order without his being brought before the court if he is represented by an authorised person who is given an opportunity of being heard.

(3) At least one of the registered medical practitioners whose evidence is taken into account under subsection (1) above shall be employed at the hospital which is to be specified in the order.

(4) An interim hospital order shall not be made for the admission of an offender to a hospital unless the court is satisfied, on the written or oral evidence of the approved clinician who would have overall responsibility for his case or of some other person representing the managers of the hospital, that arrangements have been made for his admission to that hospital and for his admission to it within the period of 28 days beginning with the date of the order; and if the court is so satisfied the court may, pending his admission, given directions for his conveyance to and detention in a place of safety.

(5) An interim hospital order—

(a) shall be in force for such period, not exceeding 12 weeks, as the court may specify when making the order; but

(b) may be renewed for further periods of not more than 28 days at a time if it appears to the court, on the written or oral evidence of the responsible clinician, that the continuation of the order is warranted; but no such order shall continue in force for more than twelve months in all and the court shall terminate the order if it makes a hospital order in respect of the offender or decides after considering the written or oral evidence of the responsible clinician to deal with the offender in some other way.

(6) The power of renewing an interim hospital order may be exercised without the offender being brought before the court if he is represented by counsel or a solicitor and his counsel or solicitor is given an opportunity of being heard.

(7) If an offender absconds from a hospital in which he is detained in pursuance of an interim hospital order, or while being conveyed to or from such a hospital, he may be arrested without warrant by a constable and shall, after being arrested, be brought as soon as practicable before the court that made the order; and the court may thereupon terminate the order and deal with him in any way in which it could have dealt with him if no such order had been made.

[This section is printed as amended by the *Legal Services Act* 2007, Sched. 21, para. 56.]

Where a court is unable to make an interim hospital order under s.37(3) due to the absence of any illness of such a nature or degree to warrant compulsory detention in hospital, the court is still able to make an guardianship order under s.37(3) of the *Mental Health Act* 1983. A court cannot therefore order that a defendant suffering from a disorder that does not warrant hospital treatment must enter a formal plea, and be subject to normal criminal procedure; the guardianship order remains an option and must be considered: *R. (Bartram) v. Southend Magistrates' Court* [2004] EWHC 2691, QBD. **28–37**

D. COMMUNITY ORDERS WITH A CONDITION OF MEDICAL TREATMENT

Criminal Justice Act 2003, s.207

Mental health treatment requirement

207.—(1) In this Part, "mental health treatment requirement", in relation to a community or- **28–38**

der or suspended sentence order, means a requirement that the offender must submit, during a period or periods specified in the order, to treatment by or under the direction of a registered medical practitioner or a registered psychologist (or both, for different periods) with a view to the improvement of the offender's mental condition.

(2) The treatment required must be such one of the following kinds of treatment as may be specified in the relevant order—

(a) treatment as a resident patient in [a] care home within the meaning of the *Care Standards Act* 2000 (c. 14 [, an independent hospital] or a hospital within the meaning of the *Mental Health Act* 1983 (c. 20), but not in hospital premises where high security psychiatric services within the meaning of that Act are provided;

(b) treatment as a non-resident patient at such institution or place as may be specified in the order;

(c) treatment by or under the direction of such registered medical practitioner or registered psychologist (or both) as may be so specified;

but the nature of the treatment is not to be specified in the order except as mentioned in paragraph (a), (b) or (c).

(3) A court may not by virtue of this section include a mental health treatment requirement in a relevant order unless—

(a) the court is satisfied, on the evidence of a registered medical practitioner approved for the purposes of section 12 of the *Mental Health Act* 1983, that the mental condition of the offender—

(i) is such as requires and may be susceptible to treatment, but

(ii) is not such as to warrant the making of a hospital order or guardianship order within the meaning of that Act;

(b) the court is also satisfied that arrangements have been or can be made for the treatment intended to be specified in the order (including arrangements for the reception of the offender where he is to be required to submit to treatment as a resident patient); and

(c) the offender has expressed his willingness to comply with such a requirement.

(4) While the offender is under treatment as a resident patient in pursuance of a mental health requirement of a relevant order, his responsible officer shall carry out the supervision of the offender to such extent only as may be necessary for the purpose of the revocation or amendment of the order.

[(4A) In subsection (2) "independent hospital"—

(a) in relation to England, means a hospital as defined by section 275 of the *National Health Service Act* 2006 that is not a health service hospital as defined by that section; and

(b) in relation to Wales, has the same meaning as in the *Care Standards Act* 2000.

(5) Subsections (2) and (3) of section 54 of the *Mental Health Act* 1983 (c. 20) have effect with respect to proof for the purposes of subsection (3)(a) of an offender's mental condition as they have effect with respect to proof of an offender's mental condition for the purposes of section 37(2)(a) of that Act.

(6) In this section and section 208, "registered psychologist" means a person registered in the part of the register maintained under the Health Professions Order 2001 which relates to practitioner psychologists.

[This section is printed as amended by the *Health Care and Associated Professions (Miscellaneous Amendments and Practitioner Psychologists) Order* 2009 (S.I. 2009 No. 1182) Sched. 5(1), para.7(a)(i) and (b).]

28–39 Before making such an order, the court must be satisfied that arrangements have been or can be made for the treatment intended to be specified in the order (including arrangements for the reception of the offender where he is to be required to submit to treatment as a resident patient) and the offender has consented to the treatment: *Criminal Justice Act* 2003, s.207(3).

E. IMPRISONMENT

28–40 When considering passing a sentence of imprisonment, other than one fixed by law, on an offender who is or appears to be suffering from some form of mental disorder, the court must obtain and consider a medical report: *Criminal Justice Act* 2003, s.157 (see *ante*, § 28–28).

The power to impose an extended sentence (either under the *Powers of Criminal Courts (Sentencing) Act* 2000 in respect of offences committed before April 4, 2005 or under the *Criminal Justice Act* 2003 for offences committed after April 4, 2005) should be considered, and may influence the magistrates in their decision whether or not to commit to the Crown Court for sentence. **28–41**

Where the court obtains a medical report to assist in determining whether an extended sentence would be appropriate, it is essential that for the guidance of the sentencing judge it addresses the risk of serious harm posed by the offender: *S.* [2006] 2 Cr.App.R.(S.) 35, CA. **28–42**

F. Hospital Order with Restriction Order

The magistrates' court has no power to attach to a hospital order an order restricting discharge from hospital: *Mental Health Act* 1883, s.41. If a restriction order may be necessary the magistrates court should exercise its power in cases triable either way to decline jurisdiction or commit to the Crown Court for sentence (on which, see *ante*, § 23–112. **28–43**

If the offender is aged over 14, and he has been convicted of a summary offence punishable with imprisonment, if the court considers that all the conditions for the making of a hospital order are satisfied and a restriction order (*Mental Health Act* 1983, s.41) is necessary for the effective punishment of the offender it should commit to the Crown Court for sentence: *Mental Health Act* 1983, s.43.

Where an offender is committed under s.43(1) and the magistrates' court by which he is committed is satisfied on written or oral evidence that arrangements have been made for admission of the offender to hospital, the court may order the offender to be detained in hospital until the case is disposed of by the Crown Court: *Mental Health Act* 1983, s.44.

Part VII

Legal Aid and Costs

Chapter 29

LEGAL REPRESENTATION

I. CRIMINAL DEFENCE REPRESENTATION ORDERS

A. General

The *Access to Justice Act* 1999 established a new framework for the public funding of legal representation in the criminal courts. It created the Legal Services Commission to replace the Legal Aid Board, and the Criminal Defence Service, which secures access to legal advice, assistance and representation in criminal matters. The Community Legal Service, also created by the Act, deals with the public funding of civil matters. The Act has been supplemented by regulations. The *Criminal Defence Service Act* 2006 came into force on October 2, 2006 and amended the *Access to Justice Act* 1999 so that the Legal Services Commission now has responsibility for administering the legal aid system. The Commission has power to delegate some function to court officers. The interests of justice test applies and a means test has now been reintroduced. The new system is set out in the Regulations all of which came into force on October 2, 2006. The *Criminal Defence Service (General) (No.2) (Amendment) Regulations* 2006 (S.I. 2006 No. 2490) amend the 2001 regulations of the same name to recognise the transfer of responsibility for granting legal aid from the court to the Legal Services Commission. **29–1**

The *Criminal Defence Service (Representation Orders and Consequential Amendments) Regulations* 2006 (S.I. 2006 No. 2493) empower the Legal Services Commission to grant legal aid instead of the court.

The *Criminal Defence Service (Representation Orders: Appeals etc.) Regulations* 2006 (S.I. 2006 No. 2494) as amended provided a right of appeal against a refusal on the interests of justice grounds to the Legal Services Commission and then the court.

The *Criminal Defence Service (Financial Eligibility) Regulations* 2006 (S.I. 2006 No. 2492) set out the criteria to be applied in the means test and imposes a duty to report any changes of circumstances which might affect eligibility for legal aid. These regulations have been amended by the *Criminal Defence Service (Financial Eligibility) (Amendment) Regulations* 2007 (S.I. 2007 No. 777), which came into force on April 2, 2007 and increased the financial eligibility limits and the cost of living allowances for all applications made on or after that date.

The *Criminal Defence Service (General) (No.2) (Amendment No.2) Regulations* 2007 (S.I. 2007 No. 2936) amend the regulations in a variety of ways.

Any reference to "solicitor" is changed to " litigator" and there are new definitions for the terms "representative" and " advocate". A "litigator" is the person named on the representation order as representing an assisted person, being a solicitor, firm of solicitors or other appropriately qualified person. A "representative" is defined as a litigator or advocate. An advocate is a barrister, a solicitor with higher courts advocacy qualifications or a solicitor who is exercising automatic rights of audience in the Crown Court. Where cases are sent to the Crown Court under s.51 of the *Crime and Disorder Act* 1998 the proceedings at the magistrates' court are now treated as being preliminary proceedings and so are covered by the Crown Court order as and when it is granted. Where a representation order has been made to cover magistrates' court proceedings only but there is an appeal to the Crown Court against the decision of that court then application can be made for a representation order to cover the appeal. That application may be made orally or in writing to the magistrates' court or the Crown Court. Application for representation in the case of an appeal by way of case stated to the High Court may also be made to the magistrates' court either orally or in writing. Representation by a Q.C. or more than one advocate can now be granted in exceptional extradition cases. The regulations are also amended to make reference to the *Extradition Act* 2003.

A magistrates' court representation order which extends to cover Crown Court proceedings may cover representation by a "junior advocate" which means any advocate who is not a Q.C.

The *Criminal Defence Service (Financial Eligibility) (Amendment No.2) Regulations* 2007 (S.I. 2007 No. 2937) also amend the original regulations so that all applicants under the age of 18, irrespective of whether they are in education or not, are automatically financially eligible for legal representation.

The authority which reviews decisions on financial eligibility is given the new power to quash decisions thereby allowing a re-application to be made. It also makes reference to payments made through the Independent Living Fund which are disregarded in the calculation of gross income.

The *Criminal Defence Service (General) (No.2) (Amendment) Regulations* 2008 (S.I. 2008 No. 725) provide for proceedings relating to serious crime prevention orders made under the *Serious Crime Act* 2007 to be regarded as criminal proceedings for the purpose of Legal Aid. Increases are also made in respect of the financial eligibility limits relating to the lowest and highest levels of income relevant to eligibility for legal aid, the costs of living allowances and the figures used to calculate the level of disposable income. They apply to applications made on or after April 7, 2008. The *Criminal Defence Service (Financial Eligibility) (Amendment) Regulations* 2008 (S.I. 2008 No. 723) also increase the financial eligibility limits and cost of living allowance. They apply to applications made on or before April 7, 2008.

The *Criminal Defence Service (Financial Eligibility) (Amendment) Regulations* 2009 (S.I. 2009 No. 2878) extend the cases in which a person may be financially eligible to receive publicly funded representation to proceedings where a defendant is committed from the magistrate' court to the Crown Court for sentence. This is a staged amendment which comes into force at different dates in 2010 throughout the country in accordance with the Schedule attached to the statutory instrument.

The *Criminal Justice and Immigration Act* 2008, s.56 provides for a provisional grant of legal aid to be made. The section came into force on the July 14, 2008 following the *Criminal Justice and Immigration Act 2008 (Commencement No.2 and Transitional and Saving Provisions) Order* 2008 (S.I. 2008 No. 1586). It amends Sched. 3 to the *Access to Justice Act* 1999 (*post*) which deals with the right to representation. Regulations have yet to be made identifying the circumstances in which such a provisional grant could be made and the conditions that might apply but it would be intended to cover any applicant involved in an investigation that might result in criminal proceedings and would only be granted for the purposes of criminal proceedings that may result from the investigation.

Financial eligibility

29–2 Applicants are automatically eligible for legal aid if:

- they are under 18; or
- they are under 18 and in full time education; or
- they are in receipt of a passporting benefit, *i.e.* income support, income based jobseekers allowance or guarantee credit under the *State Pension Credit Act* 2002;
- they earn less than a gross annual income of £12,475 once allowances are taken into account for partners and dependants.

Applicants are ineligible if their gross annual income, taking into account allowances for partners and dependants exceeds £22, 325. The allowances to be made are listed in the Schedule to the *Criminal Defence Service (Financial Eligibility) Regulations* 2006 as amended. Applicants whose income falls between the two amounts are subject to a means assessment to calculate the disposable income and where that falls below £3, 398 then they are eligible for legal aid.

There is no discretion in respect of the means test and assessment. An arithmetical formula is applied and applicants either pass or fail the test. The income of a co-habiting partner is also taken into account but if that partner is in receipt of a passporting benefit then the applicant is automatically eligible. The income of a partner will be disregarded if the applicant is separated from the partner even though they may still share accommodation. The partner's income will also be disregarded where they are a complainant or witness in the case against the applicant. This also applies to same sex partnerships.

A general application form must be completed and a means form unless the applicant is automatically eligible.

Some cases must be referred to the Commission. This includes cases where the applicant or their partner is self-employed, a company director, a partner in a firm or where they have assets subject to a freezing order or an injunction.

The court staff have a discretion to refer any applications where there is:

- an aura of wealth, (*i.e.* no income but an expensive address);
- fraudulent claims on the application form;
- high profile applicant;
- no income declared;
- outgoings exceeding income.

Under Sched. 3 to the *Access to Justice Act* 1999 which deals with the right to representation (post) the relevant authority can request information from the Secretary of State and the Commissioner for Her Majesty's Revenue and Customs to facilitate the making of a decision on the applicant's eligibility. See § 29–22, *post*.

Supporting evidence

The applicant must supply supporting documentary evidence of income with the application: **29–3**

- Benefits—National Insurance number;
- Employment—Wage slips;
- Accommodation costs—Bank statements where the rent or mortgage payment exceeds £500 per month;
- Child care costs—Bank statement where costs exceed £500 per month;
- Self-employed—Business accounts or tax statements.

If the applicant is in custody and has no access to supporting evidence of income then he may make a statement of truth of income. Where the interests of justice test is passed but the means are still being assessed an early cover payment may be made to legal representatives provided the application is lodged with the court within two days of the defendant being charged or within five days in respect of an applicant in custody. A fixed fee may be payable where legal aid is refused provided the defendant is seen within 10 days of charge.

In *Southwark Law Centre v. Legal Services Commission* [2007] 4 All E.R. 754 it was held that under reg.24 of the *Community Legal Service (Financial) Regulations* 2000 any rent payable is deductible in calculating disposable income. The fact that the rent has not been paid does not mean that the LSC can disregard it.

Appeals

29–4 Any appeal against a refusal on grounds of financial ineligibility must be made to the LSC. If the applicant fails the means test an application for hardship review can be made if there is an inability to pay. If further more detailed or accurate information of financial circumstances becomes available the application can be submitted again to the court. An appeal against a refusal on the interests of justice is still made to the court. See *post*, § 29–51.

The application forms and the means calculator are all available on-line at *www.legalservices.gov.uk/docs/forms*.

29–5 Legal aid is available to defendants to ensure that legal representation is provided. Legal assistance is not automatic in criminal cases in the magistrates' court. The circumstances and impact of the charge will be taken into account in assessing whether it is in the interests of justice that representation should be paid for from public funds. Schedule 3, para. 5 to the *Access to Justice Act* 1999 lists the factors that are relevant. Once the interests of justice test is met the grant of legal aid is subject to means.

In the magistrates' court the application will be considered by a "proper officer of the court" who will usually be a trained member of staff to whom the power to grant legal representation orders has been delegated by the Legal Services Commission. The application must identify fully the reasons why it is in the interests of justice for an order to be granted in accordance with the provisions of Sched. 3 to the Act, otherwise the application may be refused. Information and evidence of means must also be provided. The form must also be signed and dated.

B. The Human Rights Act 1998

29–6 Under Art. 6(3)(c) of the European Convention on Human Rights everyone charged with a criminal offence has the right "to defend himself in person or through legal assistance of his own choosing or, if he does not have sufficient means to pay for legal assistance, to be given it free when the interests of justice require it."

In the magistrates' court, applications for legal representation will be granted if the interests of justice require it. The interests of justice tests are included in the *Access to Justice Act* 1999 and European case law also gives an indication of the factors to be taken into account when assessing the interests of justice. The complexity of the case is relevant; *Benham v. UK* [1996] 22 E.H.R.R. 293 as is the ability of the defendant to comprehend and present his case: *Hoang v. France* [1993] 16 E.H.R.R. 53. The likelihood of a custodial sentence is an important factor: *Benham v. UK, ante*.

29–7 The legal representation granted must be "practical and effective" and it is not sufficient for a lawyer to be merely nominated by the state. The system for legal aid must ensure that advice and assistance is given: *Artico v. Italy* [1981] 3 E.H.R.R. 1.

The choice of lawyer is not absolute. Where legal aid is concerned, the wishes of the defendant will be given consideration but the state can override those wishes where necessary. Also the right to conduct a complex case unrepresented may be restricted: *Croissant v. Germany* [1993] 16 E.H.R.R. 135. Article 6 requires the hearing to be "fair" and if the conduct or incompetence of a legal representative assigned under a scheme affects the fairness of the trial, a court may be obliged to intervene: *Nangle* [2001] Crim.L.R. 506.

A defence application for an adjournment of criminal proceedings should normally be granted where the defendant has not had the opportunity to apply for legal representation. In such circumstances the right to legal representation (or to a proper opportunity to apply for it) will normally outweigh other considerations, such as the convenience of the other parties and the use of court resources: *Berry Trade Ltd v. Moussavi* [2002] 1 W.L.R. 1910.

C. THE LEGAL SERVICES COMMISSION

(1) Constitution of the Commission

Access to Justice Act 1999, ss.1–2

Legal Services Commission

1.—(1) There shall be a body known as the Legal Services Commission (in this Part referred to as "the Commission"). **29–8**

(2) The Commission shall have the functions relating to—

(a) the Community Legal Service, and

(b) the Criminal Defence Service,

which are conferred or imposed on it by the provisions of this Act or any other enactment.

(3) The Commission shall consist of—

(a) not fewer than seven members, and

(b) not more than twelve members;

but the Lord Chancellor may by order substitute for either or both of the numbers for the time being specified in paragraphs (a) and (b) such other number or numbers as he thinks appropriate.

(4) The members of the Commission shall be appointed by the Lord Chancellor; and the Lord Chancellor shall appoint one of the members to chair the Commission.

(5) In appointing persons to be members of the Commission the Lord Chancellor shall have regard to the desirability of securing that the Commission includes members who (between them) have experience in or knowledge of—

(a) the provision of services which the Commission can fund as part of the Community Legal Service or Criminal Defence Service,

(b) the work of the courts,

(c) consumer affairs,

(d) social conditions, and

(e) management.

(6) Schedule 1 (which makes further provision about the Commission) has effect.

Power to replace Commission with two bodies

2.—(1) The Lord Chancellor may by order establish in place of the Commission two bodies— **29–9**

(a) one to have functions relating to the Community Legal Service, and

(b) the other to have functions relating to the Criminal Defence Service.

(2) The order may make any consequential, incidental, supplementary or transitional provisions, and any savings, which appear to the Lord Chancellor to be appropriate.

(3) The order shall include amendments of—

(a) any provisions of, or amended by, this Part which refer to the Commission, and

(b) any other enactments which so refer,

to replace references to the Commission with references to either or both of the bodies established by the order.

(2) Powers of the Commission

Access to Justice Act 1999, s.3

Powers of Commission

3.—(1) Subject to the provisions of this Part, the Commission may do anything which it considers— **29–10**

(a) is necessary or appropriate for, or for facilitating, the discharge of its functions, or

(b) is incidental or conducive to the discharge of its functions.

(2) In particular, the Commission shall have power—

(a) to enter into any contract,

(b) to make grants (with or without conditions),
(c) to make loans,
(d) to invest money,
(e) to promote or assist in the promotion of publicity relating to its functions,
(f) to undertake any inquiry or investigation which it may consider appropriate in relation to the discharge of any of its functions, and
(g) to give the Lord Chancellor any advice which it may consider appropriate in relation to matters concerning any of its functions.

(3) Subsections (1) and (2) do not confer on the Commission power to borrow money.

(4) The Commission may make such arrangements as it considers appropriate for the discharge of its functions, including the delegation of any of its functions.

(5) The Lord Chancellor may by order require the Commission—
(a) to delegate any function specified in the order or to delegate any function so specified to a person (or person of a description) so specified,
(b) not to delegate any function so specified or not to delegate any function so specified to a person (or person of a description) so specified, or
(c) to make arrangements such as are specified in the order in relation to the delegation of any function so specified.

29–11 The Commission has made arrangements under s.3(4) of the *Access to Justice Act* 1999. The Review Panel Arrangements, which are effective from April 1, 2000, provide for the creation of a Review Panel, the appointment from that Panel of Funding Review Committees and Cost Committees and the regulation of the proceedings of those committees. The Commission has also made the Criminal Defence Service Duty Solicitor Arrangements 2001, which govern the provision of advice and assistance by duty solicitors at police stations and magistrates' courts.

D. CRIMINAL DEFENCE SERVICE

(1) The role of the Criminal Defence Service

Access to Justice Act 1999, s.12

Criminal Defence Service

29–12 **12.**—(1) The Commission shall establish, maintain and develop a service known as the Criminal Defence Service for the purpose of securing that individuals involved in criminal investigations or criminal proceedings have access to such advice, assistance and representation as the interests of justice require.

(2) In this Part "criminal proceedings" means—
(a) proceedings before any court for dealing with an individual accused of an offence,
(b) proceedings before any court for dealing with an individual convicted of an offence (including proceedings in respect of a sentence or order),
(c) proceedings for dealing with an individual under section 9 of, or paragraph 6 of Schedule 1 to, the *Extradition Act* 1989,
(d) proceedings for binding an individual over to keep the peace or to be of good behaviour under section 115 of the *Magistrates' Courts Act* 1980 and for dealing with an individual who fails to comply with an order under that section,
(e) proceedings on an appeal brought by an individual under section 44A of the *Criminal Appeal Act* 1968,
(f) proceedings for contempt committed, or alleged to have been committed, by an individual in the face of a court, and
(g) such other proceedings concerning an individual, before any such court or other body, as may be prescribed.

(3) The Commission shall fund services as part of the Criminal Defence Service in accordance with sections 13 to 15.

(4) The Commission may accredit, or authorise others to accredit, persons or bodies providing services which may be funded by the Commission as part of the Criminal Defence Service; and any system of accreditation shall include provision for the monitoring

of the services provided by accredited persons and bodies and for the withdrawal of accreditation from any providing services of unsatisfactory quality.

(5) The Commission may charge—

(a) for accreditation,

(b) for monitoring the services provided by accredited persons and bodies, and

(c) for authorising accreditation by others;

and persons or bodies authorised to accredit may charge for accreditation, and for such monitoring, in accordance with the terms of their authorisation.

(6) The Lord Chancellor may by order require the Commission to discharge the functions in subsections (4) and (5) in accordance with the order.

Additional criminal proceedings have been prescribed by the *Criminal Defence Service (General) (No.2) Regulations* 2001. The Rules included here relate specifically to the magistrates' court. The *Criminal Defence Service (General) (No.2) (Amendment) Regulations* 2005 (S.I. 2005 No. 2784) extend the list of related proceedings, which although not strictly criminal are eligible for legal aid. It includes certain intervention orders under the *Crime and Disorder Act* 1998 as amended by the *Drugs Act* 2005; certain parenting orders under the *Anti-Social Behaviour Act* 2003; certain orders under the *Sexual Offences Act* 2003 and restraining orders following acquittal of offences under the *Protection from Harassment Act* 1997. The order came into force on October 31, 2005 except in respect of offences that are not yet themselves in force. **29–13**

Part VII

Criminal Defence Service (General) (No.2) Regulations 2001, reg.3(1)–(2)

Criminal proceedings

3.—(1) For the purposes of this regulation, "the 1998 Act" means the *Crime and Disorder Act* 1998. **29–14**

(2) The following proceedings are criminal proceedings for the purposes of section 12(2)(g) of the Act—

(a) civil proceedings in a magistrates' court arising from failure to pay a sum due or to obey an order of that court where such failure carries the risk of imprisonment;

(b) proceedings under sections 1, 1D and 4 of the 1998 Act relating to anti-social behaviour orders;1

(ba) proceedings under sections 1G and 1H of the 1998 Act relating to intervention orders, in which an application for an anti-social behaviour order has been made;

(c) proceedings under section 8(1)(b) of the 1998 Act relating to parenting orders made where an anti-social behaviour order or a sex offender order is made in respect of a child;

(d) proceedings under section 8(1)(c) of the 1998 Act relating to parenting orders made on the conviction of a child;

(e) proceedings under section 9(5) of the 1998 Act to discharge or vary a parenting order made as mentioned in sub-paragraph (c) or (d);

(f) proceedings under section 10 of the 1998 Act to appeal against a parenting order made as mentioned in sub-paragraph (c) or (d);

(g) proceedings under sections 14B, 14D, 14G, 14H, 21B and 21D of the *Football Spectators Act* 1989 (banning orders and references to a court);

(h) proceedings under section 137 of the *Financial Services and Markets Act* 2000 to appeal against a decision of the Financial Services and Markets Tribunal;

(i) proceedings under sections 2, 5 and 6 of the *Anti-Social Behaviour Act* 2003 relating to closure orders;

(j) proceedings under sections 20, 22, 26 and 28 of the *Anti-Social Behaviour Act* 2003 relating to parenting orders in cases of exclusion from school and parenting orders in respect of criminal conduct and anti-social behaviour;

(k) proceedings under sections 97, 100 and 101 of the *Sexual Offences Act* 2003 relating to notification orders and interim notification orders;

(l) proceedings under sections 104, 108, 109 and 110 of the *Sexual Offences Act* 2003 relating to sexual offences prevention orders and interim sexual offences prevention orders;

(m) proceedings under sections 114, 118 and 119 of the *Sexual Offences Act* 2003 relating to foreign travel orders;

(n) proceedings under sections 123, 125, 126 and 127 of the*Sexual Offences Act* 2003 relating to risk of sexual harm orders and interim risk of sexual harm orders;

(o) proceedings under Part 1A of Schedule 1 to the *Powers of Criminal Courts (Sentencing) Act* 2000 relating to parenting orders for failure to comply with orders under section 20 of that Act;

(q) proceedings before the Crown Court or the Court of Appeal relating to serious crime prevention orders and arising by virtue of section 19, 20, 21 or 24 of the *Serious Crime Act* 2007;

(r) proceedings under sections 100, 101, 103, 104 and 106 of the *Criminal Justice and Immigration Act* 2008 relating to violent offender orders and interim violent offender orders;

(s) proceedings under sections 3, 5, 9 and 10 of the *Violent Crime Reduction Act* 2006 relating to drinking banning orders and interim orders.

(3) Proceedings—

(a) in the Crown Court, following committal for sentence by a magistrates' court;

(b) to quash an acquittal under the *Criminal Procedure and Investigations Act* 1996; and

(c) for confiscation and forfeiture in connection with criminal proceedings under RSC Order 115 in Schedule 1 to the *Civil Procedure Rules* 1998 are to be regarded as incidental to the criminal proceedings from which they arise.

(4) Applications for judicial review or habeas corpus relating to any criminal investigations or proceedings are not to be regarded as incidental to such criminal investigations or proceedings.

(5) Proceedings in a magistrates' court in which the court sends an assisted person for trial in the Crown Court under section 51 of the *Crime and Disorder Act* 1998 are to be regarded as preliminary to the proceedings in the Crown Court.

[This regulation is printed as amended by the *Criminal Defence Service (General) (No.2) (Amendment) Regulations* 2002, *Criminal Defence Service (General) (No.2) (Amendment) Regulations* 2004, the *Criminal Defence Service (General) (No.2) (Amendment) Regulations* 2005, *Criminal Defence Service (General) (No.2) (Amendment No.2) Regulations* 2007, *Criminal Defence Service (General) (No.2) (Amendment) Regulations* 2008, *Criminal Defence Service (General) (No.2) (Amendment No.2) Regulations* 2009, *Criminal Defence Service (General) (No.2) (Amendment No.3) Regulations* 2009, the *Football (Disorder) Act* 2000 and the *Criminal Justice Act* 2003.]

29–15 Case law under previous legislation clarified the meaning of "criminal proceedings". In *Recorder of Liverpool, ex. p. McCann*, *The Times*, May 4, 1994, DC the court held that an application for the removal of a driving disqualification under the *Road Traffic Offenders Act* 1988, s.42 qualified as "criminal proceedings" because they were proceedings "in respect of a sentence". In *Redbridge Magistrates' Court, ex. p. Guppy* (1995) 159 J.P. 622, it was held that proceedings for the enforcement of a compensation order were criminal proceedings in respect of sentence and so were eligible for legal aid. Applications under s.42(2) of the *Drug Trafficking Act* 1994 for the continued detention of cash seized under s.2(1), or for the forfeiture of that cash did not fall within the definition as the applicant was neither charged with nor convicted of an offence: *Crawley Justices, ex. p. Ohakwe*, *The Times*, May 26, 1994.

Under the regulations the "hybrid offences" of anti-social behaviour orders and parenting orders introduced by the *Crime and Disorder Act* 1998 qualify for legal representation. Football banning orders drink banning orders and violent offender orders are also covered. A surety may be eligible for legal representation under the provision that defines some civil proceedings as criminal for the purposes of legal representation if there is a risk of imprisonment in default of payment of a sum of money: reg.3(2)(a), *ante*.

(2) Funding of legal services in criminal proceedings

Access to Justice Act 1999, s.13

Advice and assistance

13.—(1) The Commission shall fund such advice and assistance as it considers appropriate— **29–16**

(a) for individuals who are arrested and held in custody at a police station or other premises, and

(b) in prescribed circumstances, for individuals who—

(i) are not within paragraph (a) but are involved in investigations which may lead to criminal proceedings,

(ii) are before a court or other body in such proceedings, or

(iii) have been the subject of such proceedings;

and the assistance which the Commission may consider appropriate includes assistance in the form of advocacy.

(2) The Commission may comply with the duty imposed by subsection (1) by—

(a) entering into contracts with persons or bodies for the provision of advice or assistance by them,

(b) making payments to persons or bodies in respect of the provision of advice or assistance by them,

(c) making grants or loans to persons or bodies to enable them to provide, or facilitate the provision of, advice or assistance,

(d) establishing and maintaining bodies to provide, or facilitate the provision of, advice or assistance,

(e) making grants to individuals to enable them to obtain advice or assistance,

(f) employing persons to provide advice or assistance, or

(g) doing anything else which it considers appropriate for funding advice and assistance.

(3) The Lord Chancellor may by order require the Commission to discharge the function in subsection (2) in accordance with the order.

(4) The Commission may fund advice and assistance by different means—

(a) in different areas in England and Wales, and

(b) in relation to different descriptions of cases.

[This section is reprinted as amended by the *Criminal Defence Service (Advice and Assistance) Act* 2001, s.1(1), which provides that the amendment be retrospective in its effect.]

The Legal Services Commission is empowered to secure the services referred to in s.12 through contracts with lawyers in private practice or by providing salaried defenders employed directly by the commission. This means that a suspect's choice of legal representation is limited to contracted or salaried defenders although the intention is to provide a choice in all but exceptional cases. This does not offend against the ECHR. The right to have a lawyer of one's own choosing under Art. 6(3)(c) is not absolute, particularly where the representation is being publicly funded: *Croissant v. Germany* (see *ante*, § 29–7). As a general rule the defendant's choice of lawyer should be respected and there must be relevant and sufficient justification to appoint a lawyer against his wishes: *Goddi v. Italy* [1984] 6 E.H.R.R. 457. It might be argued that the scheme for control of legal firms supplying defence services by the Legal Services Commission ensures a high standard of service and so is justified. Private solicitors may only undertake publicly funded criminal defence work if they have a contract to provide such services with the Criminal Defence Service: *Criminal Defence Service (General) (No.2) Regulations* 2001 (S.I. 2001 No. 1437), r.11. In 2001 the Legal Services Commission began a four-year trial of its own defender service comprised of six offices staffed by people employed directly by the Commission. **29–17**

Criminal Defence Service (General) (No.2) Regulations 2001, regs 4–5

Advice and assistance—scope

4. The Commission shall fund such advice and assistance, including advocacy assistance, as it considers appropriate in relation to any individual who: **29–18**

Part VII

(a) is the subject of an investigation which may lead to criminal proceedings;
(b) is the subject of criminal proceedings;
(c) requires advice and assistance regarding his appeal or potential appeal against the outcome of any criminal proceedings or an application to vary a sentence;
(d) requires advice and assistance regarding his sentence;
(e) requires advice and assistance regarding his application or potential application to the Criminal Cases Review Commission;
(f) requires advice and assistance regarding his treatment or discipline in prison (other than in respect of actual or contemplated proceedings regarding personal injury, death or damage to property);
(g) is the subject of proceedings before the Parole Board;
(h) requires advice and assistance regarding representations to the Home Office in relation to a mandatory life sentence or other parole review;
(i) is a witness in criminal proceedings and requires advice regarding self-incrimination;[…]
(j) is a volunteer or
(k) is detained under Schedule 7 to the *Terrorism Act* 2000.

[This regulation is reprinted as amended by the *Criminal Defence Service (General) (Amendment) (No.2) Regulations* 2002, reg.6.]

29–19 A volunteer is any person who voluntarily attends at a police station or elsewhere to assist with an investigation without having been arrested. Pursuant to its obligations under this section the Legal Services Commission has established the Police Station Duty Solicitor Scheme and the Magistrates' Courts Duty Solicitor Scheme so that those who require advice and assistance at a police station or court have access to a duty solicitor who is accredited by the Commission. A Duty Solicitor will be available at most courts on a daily basis to provide advice for unrepresented defendants. In busy courts there may well be a "bail" duty solicitor and a "custody" duty solicitor.

Advice and assistance—financial eligibility

29–20 **5.**—(1) The following advice and assistance may be granted without reference to the financial resources of the individual:

(a) all advice and assistance provided to an individual who is arrested and held in custody at a police station or other premises;
(b) all advocacy assistance before a magistrates' court or the Crown Court;
(c) all advice and assistance provided by a court duty solicitor in accordance with his contract with the Commission;
(d) all advice and assistance provided to a volunteer during his period of voluntary attendance;
(e) all advice and assistance provided to an individual being interviewed in connection with a serious service offence; and
(f) all advice and assistance provided in respect of an individual who is the subject of an identification procedure carried out by means of video recordings in connection with that procedure, notwithstanding the individual's non-attendance at a police station at the time the procedure is carried out.

(2) For the purposes of paragraph (1), a serious service offence is an offence under the *Army Act* 1955, the *Air Force Act* 1955 or the *Naval Discipline Act* 1957 which cannot be dealt with summarily.

[This regulation is reprinted as amended by the *Arms Forces Discipline Act* 2000 and the *Criminal Defence Service (General) (No.2) (Amendment) Regulations* 2003, reg.4(2).]

E. REPRESENTATION

(1) General

Access to Justice Act 1999, s.14

Representation

29–21 **14.**—(1) Schedule 3 (which makes provision about the grant of a right to representation in criminal proceedings and about the provisional grant of a right to representation in prescribed circumstances) has effect; and the Commission shall fund representation to which an individual has been granted or provisionally granted a right in accordance with that Schedule.

(2) Subject to the following provisions, the Commission may comply with the duty imposed by subsection (1) by—

(a) entering into contracts with persons or bodies for the provision of representation by them,

(b) making payments to persons or bodies in respect of the provision of representation by them,

(c) making grants or loans to persons or bodies to enable them to provide, or facilitate the provision of, representation,

(d) establishing and maintaining bodies to provide, or facilitate the provision of, representation,

(e) making grants to individuals to enable them to obtain representation,

(f) employing persons to provide representation, or

(g) doing anything else which it considers appropriate for funding representation.

(3) The Lord Chancellor—

(a) shall by order make provision about the payments which may be made by the Commission in respect of any representation provided by non-contracted private practitioners, and

(b) may by order make any other provision requiring the Commission to discharge the function in subsection (2) in accordance with the order.

(4) For the purposes of subsection (3)(a) representation is provided by a non-contracted private practitioner if it is provided, otherwise than pursuant to a contract entered into by the Commission, by a person or body which is neither—

(a) a person or body in receipt of grants or loans made by the Commission as part of the Criminal Defence Service, nor

(b) the Commission itself or a body established or maintained by the Commission.

(5) The provision which the Lord Chancellor is required to make by order under subsection (3)(a) includes provision for reviews of, or appeals against, determinations required for the purposes of the order.

(6) The Commission may fund representation by different means—

(a) in different areas in England and Wales, and

(b) in relation to different descriptions of cases.

(2) The right to representation

Access to Justice Act 1999, Sched. 3, para. 1(1)–(3)

1.—(1) A right to representation for the purposes of any kind of criminal proceedings before a court may be granted to an individual such as is mentioned in relation to that kind of proceedings in section 12(2). **29–22**

(2) A right to representation for the purposes of criminal proceedings may also be granted to an individual to enable him to resist an appeal to the Crown Court otherwise than in an official capacity.

(3) In this Schedule "court" includes any body before which criminal proceedings take place.

Individuals to whom right may be provisionally granted

1A.—(1) Regulations may provide that, in prescribed circumstances, and subject to any prescribed conditions, a right to representation may be provisionally granted to an individual where—

(a) the individual is involved in an investigation which may result in criminal proceedings, and

(b) the right is so granted for the purposes of criminal proceedings that may result from the investigation.

(2) Regulations under sub-paragraph (1) may, in particular, make provision about—

(a) the stage in an investigation at which a right to representation may be provisionally granted;

(b) the circumstances in which a right which has been so granted—
(i) is to become, or be treated as if it were, a right to representation under paragraph 1, or
(ii) is to be, or may be, withdrawn.

Information requests

6.—(1) The relevant authority may make an information request to—
(a) the Secretary of State, or
(b) the Commissioners,
for the purpose of facilitating the making of a decision by the authority about the application of paragraph 3B(1) or (2), or regulations under paragraph 3B(3), in relation to an individual.

(2) An information request made to the Secretary of State is a request for the disclosure of some or all of the following information—
(a) the individual's full name;
(b) the individual's address;
(c) the individual's date of birth;
(d) the individual's national insurance number;
(e) the individual's benefit status;
(f) information of any description specified in regulations.

(3) An information request made to the Commissioners is a request for the disclosure of some or all of the following information—
(a) whether or not the individual is employed;
(b) the name and address of the employer (if the individual is employed);
(c) the individual's national insurance number;
(d) information of any description specified in regulations made with the agreement of the Commissioners.

(4) The information that may be specified under subsection (3)(d) includes, in particular, information relating to the individual's income (as defined in the regulations) for a period so specified.

(5) On receiving an information request, the Secretary of State or (as the case may be) the Commissioners may disclose the information requested to the relevant authority.

Restrictions on disclosure

7.—(1) A person to whom information is disclosed under paragraph 6(5), or this sub-paragraph, may disclose the information to any person to whom its disclosure is necessary or expedient in connection with facilitating the making of a decision by the relevant authority about the application of paragraph 3B(1) or (2), or regulations under paragraph 3B(3), in relation to an individual.

(2) A person to whom such information is disclosed commits an offence if the person—
(a) discloses or uses the information, and
(b) the disclosure is not authorised by sub-paragraph (1) or (as the case may be) the use is not for the purpose of facilitating the making of such a decision as is mentioned in that sub-paragraph.

(3) But it is not an offence under sub-paragraph (2)—
(a) to disclose any information in accordance with any enactment or order of a court or for the purposes of any proceedings before a court; or
(b) to disclose any information which has previously been lawfully disclosed to the public.

(4) It is a defence for a person charged with an offence under sub-paragraph (2) to prove that the person reasonably believed that the disclosure or use was lawful.

(5) A person guilty of an offence under sub-paragraph (2) is liable—
(a) on conviction on indictment, to imprisonment for a term not exceeding 2 years or a fine or both;
(b) on summary conviction, to imprisonment for a term not exceeding 12 months or a fine not exceeding the statutory maximum or both.

(6) In sub-paragraph (5)(b) the reference to 12 months is to be read as a reference to 6 months in relation to an offence committed before the commencement of section 154(1) of the *Criminal Justice Act* 2003.

(7) Nothing in section 20 applies in relation to the disclosure of information to which

sub-paragraph (1) applies.

Paragraphs 6 and 7: supplementary

8.—(1) This paragraph applies for the purposes of paragraphs 6 and 7.

(2) "Benefit status", in relation to an individual, means whether or not the individual is in direct or indirect receipt of any prescribed benefit or benefits and, if so (in the case of each benefit)—

(a) which benefit the individual is so receiving, and

(b) (in prescribed cases) the amount the individual is so receiving by way of the benefit.

(3) "The Commissioners" means the Commissioners for Her Majesty's Revenue and Customs.

(4) "Information" means information held in any form.

(5) Nothing in paragraph 6 or 7 authorises the making of a disclosure which contravenes the *Data Protection Act* 1998."

[This Sched. is printed as amended by the *Criminal Justice and Immigration Act* 2008 s.56 which came into force on July 14, 2008; the *Criminal Justice and Immigration Act* 2008 (Commencement No.2 and Transitional and Saving Provisions) Order 2008 (S.I. 2008 No. 1586)]

The Criminal Defence Service must fund representation to an individual who has been granted a right of representation. Legal aid is not available to corporations. **29–23**

(3) Application for representation order

Criminal Defence Service (General) (No.2) Regulations 2001, reg.6

Representation order

6.—(1) The date of any representation order is the date on which the application for the grant of such an order is received in accordance with these Regulations. **29–24**

(2) Any application for the grant of a representation order in respect of proceedings in the Crown Court or the Court of Appeal which are mentioned in section 12(2)(a) to (f) of the Act and in regulation 3(2)(h), shall be made in accordance with regulations 9 and 10.

(3) Any application for the grant of a representation order in respect of the proceedings mentioned in regulation 3(2) (criminal proceedings for the purposes of section 12(2)(g) of the Act)[, except those mentioned in regulation 3(2)(h)]:

(a) shall be made to the Commission; and

(b) may be granted only by the Commission or a person acting on behalf of the Commission where such function has been delegated in accordance with section 3(4) of the Act.

(4) Where an application under paragraph (3) is refused, the Commission shall provide to the applicant:

(a) written reasons for the refusal; and

(b) details of the appeal process.

(5) Where the person who requires representation is aged less than 18, the application for the grant of a representation order may be made by his parent or guardian on his behalf.

(6) The appropriate officer of each court shall keep a record of every application to that court for a representation order, and of its outcome.

(7) The appropriate officer shall send to the Lord Chancellor such information from the record mentioned in paragraph (6) as the Lord Chancellor may request.

The LSC has delegated the function to grant legal aid to court staff: see *ante*, § 29–1. **29–25**

Criminal Defence Service (General) (No.2) Regulations 2001, reg.7

General power to grant representation

7. The court, a judge of the court, or the registrar of criminal appeals may grant a represen- **29–26**

Part VII

tation order at any stage of criminal proceedings (other than criminal proceedings in a magistrates' court) in the circumstances set out in these Regulations whether or not an application has been made for such an order.

[This regulation is reprinted as amended by the *Criminal Defence Service (General) (No.2) (Amendment) Regulations* 2002, reg.9.]

29–27 The LSC has not delegated its power to grant representation to the district judge or justices in court. All applications must be submitted in writing to court staff so the interests of justice and financial eligibility may be assessed.

Criminal Defence Service (General) (No.2) Regulations 2001, reg.18

29–28 **18.** Where an individual is committed or sent for trial by a lower court to a higher court, or appeals or applies for leave to appeal from a lower court to a higher court, the appropriate officer of the lower court shall send to the appropriate officer of the higher court the following documents:

(a) a copy of any representation order previously made in respect of the same proceedings; and

(b) a copy of any application for a representation order which has been refused.

29–29 A copy of the criminal defence representation order (CDRO) or a notice of refusal will be sent to the Crown Court with the committal documents.

Access to Justice Act 1999, Sched. 3, para. 5

29–30 **5.**—(1) Any question as to whether power to grant or provisionally grant, a right to representation should be exercised shall be determined according to the interests of justice.

(2) In deciding what the interests of justice consist of in relation to any individual, the following factors must be taken into account—

(a) whether the individual would, if any matter arising in the proceedings is decided against him, be likely to lose his liberty or livelihood or suffer serious damage to his reputation,

(b) whether the determination of any matter arising in the proceedings may involve consideration of a substantial question of law,

(c) whether the individual may be unable to understand the proceedings or to state his own case,

(d) whether the proceedings may involve the tracing, interviewing or expert cross-examination of witnesses on behalf of the individual, and

(e) whether it is in the interests of another person that the individual be represented.

(2A) For the purposes of sub-paragraph (2), "proceedings" includes, in the context of a provisional grant of a right to representation, proceedings that may result from the investigation in which the individual is involved.

(3) The Lord Chancellor may by order amend sub-paragraph (2) by adding new factors or varying any factor.

(4) Regulations may prescribe circumstances in which the grant, or provisional grant, of a right to representation shall be taken to be in the interests of justice.

[This paragraph is printed as amended by the *Criminal Justice and Immigration Act* 2008, s.56.]

Regulations governing the provisional grant of a right to representation have yet to be issued.

29–31 A criminal defence representation order will be granted if it is in the interests of justice according to these criteria. The test in Sched. 3, para. 5 to the *Access to Justice Act* 1999 is similar to that which governed the discretion to grant legal aid in the now-repealed *Legal Aid Act* 1988, s.22(2). Cases concerning that section are of assistance in interpreting the test in the *Access to Justice Act* 1999.

When assessing whether a conviction might lead to deprivation of liberty, loss of livelihood or damage to reputation, the authority asked to grant a representation order should consider the nature of the facts alleged by the prosecution in the particular case rather than the maximum penalty that might theoretically be imposed Although the offence may carry a maximum of five years' imprisonment, the court must make a subjective assessment of the likelihood of loss of liberty having regard to the circumstances of the case: *Highgate Justices, ex. p. Lewis* [1977] Crim.L.R. 611.

In *Liverpool City Magistrates' Court, ex. p. McGhee* (1994) 158 J.P. 275, the court considered that the imposition of a community punishment order could not be regarded as depriving the accused of his liberty but it could still be a relevant factor when deciding whether to grant a right of representation.

In *Chester Magistrates' Court, ex. p. Ball* (1999) 163 J.P. 757, DC, the refusal to **29–32** grant legal aid was quashed where justices had considered only the likelihood of loss of liberty in the event of conviction and had failed to have regard to whether a conviction was likely to lead to serious damage to the reputation of the defendant. In *Brigg Justices, ex. p. Lynch* (1984) 148 J.P. 214, legal aid was justified because of the serious consequences of a conviction to the reputation and livelihood of a solider who had been charged with indecent exposure.

A defendant who intended to raise a special reason in order to avoid a disqualification from driving on conviction of driving with excess alcohol in his blood was eligible for legal aid in the interests of justice. The suggestion was that his drink had been laced and so the advice and assistance could extend to the instruction of an expert witness. The case was likely to be complex and the obtaining of an expert witness and possible cross-examination of another expert witness meant that the criteria were met: *Gravesend Magistrates' Court, ex. p. Baker* (1997) 161 J.P. 765, DC.

In *Scunthorpe Justices, ex. p. S., The Times*, March 5, 1998, DC the refusal to grant legal aid to a 16-year-old charged with obstruction of a police officer in the execution of his duty was quashed as irrational where there was an issue as to whether the officer was acting in the execution of his duty. The expertise required for the purpose of cross examining the officer and for tracing and taking evidence from defence witnesses and the need to trace and interview them was beyond that of a 16-year-old and a conviction would have damaged a young man of good character on the threshold of his life. If the court is of the view that there is insufficient information about alleged defence witnesses, it should adjourn the matter rather than refuse the application. The inability to understand or follow proceedings may relate to the complexity of the case or individual factors affecting the applicant, such as his age, mental or physical health or language difficulties. In *R. (Matara) v. Brent Magistrates' Court*, 169 J.P. 576, DC it was held that a Criminal Defence Representation Order should have been granted to an applicant who needed an interpreter where his defence to a drink drive charge was that he had not understood what was said to him on arrest. The assistance of an interpreter did not address the question of whether without benefit of legal representation he would be able to state his case and have a fair trial. These issues may also be relevant as to whether it would be in the interests of another person such as the victim or witnesses for the defendant to be represented so that cross-examination in person by the defendant may be avoided where appropriate. It is generally not sufficient to simply tick or mark "yes" on the form. Full details in the application form indicating which of the criteria apply and the reasons why, should ensure that applications are dealt with expeditiously.

Where an application for a representation order is made at the conclusion of proceed- **29–33** ings in a magistrates' court, the interests of justice test should be applied on the basis of the facts as they appeared at the time when the solicitor was first consulted and not on the basis of hindsight. Where the defendant was charged with an imprisonable offence in relation to which there was a real and practical (not simply a theoretical) risk of imprisonment, an application made at the end of the proceedings should have been granted. It was not open to the appropriate officer to refuse the application on the ground that there was, in the end, no risk of imprisonment because the prosecution had substituted a charge of a non-imprisonable offence to which the defendant had pleaded guilty: *Horseferry Road Magistrates, ex. p. Punatar & Co*; [2002] EWHC 1196, Admin.

(4) Selection of the representative

Access to Justice Act 1999, s.15

Selection of representative

29–34 **15.**—(1) An individual who has been granted or provisionally granted a right to representation in accordance with Schedule 3 may select any representative or representatives willing to act for him; and, where he does so, the Commission is to comply with the duty imposed by section 14(1) by funding representation by the selected representative or representatives.

(2) Regulations may provide that in prescribed circumstances—

(a) the right conferred by subsection (1) is not to apply in cases of prescribed descriptions,

(b) an individual who has been provided with advice or assistance funded by the Commission under section 13 by a person whom he chose to provide it for him is to be taken to have selected that person as his representative pursuant to that right,

(c) that right is not to include a right to select a representative of a prescribed description,

(d) that right is to select only a representative of a prescribed description,

(e) that right is to select not more than a prescribed number of representatives to act at any one time, and

(f) that right is not to include a right to select a representative in place of a representative previously selected.

(3) Regulations under subsection (2)(b) may prescribe circumstances in which an individual is to be taken to have chosen a person to provide advice or assistance for him.

(4) Regulations under subsection (2) may not provide that only a person employed by the Commission, or by a body established and maintained by the Commission, may be selected.

(5) Regulations may provide that in prescribed circumstances the Commission is not required to fund, or to continue to fund, representation for an individual by a particular representative (but such provision shall not prejudice any right of the individual to select another representative).

(6) The circumstances which may be prescribed by regulations under subsection (2) or (5) include that a determination has been made by a prescribed body or person.

29–35 The prescribed description is contained in r.11 and includes an employee in the Criminal Defence Service or a lawyer who is franchised from the Legal Services Commission.

Criminal Defence Service (General) (No.2) Regulations 2001, reg.16A

29–36 **16A.** Where an individual who is granted a right to representation is one of two or more co-defendants whose cases are to be heard together, that individual must select the same representative as a co-defendant unless there is, or is likely to be, a conflict of interest.

Co-defendants should be represented by one solicitor unless there is a conflict of interest. That conflict must be clearly identified in the application where separate representation is sought.

(5) Employment by Legal Services Commission

Criminal Defence Service (General) (No.2) Regulations 2001, regs 11–12

29–37 **11.**—(1) The right conferred by section 15(1) of the Act, as regards representation in respect of any proceedings to which this regulation applies, shall be exercisable only in relation to those representatives who are:

(a) employed by the Commission to provide such representation; or

(b) authorised to provide such representation under a crime franchise contract with the Commission which commences on or after 2nd April 2001 and specifies the rate of remuneration for such representation.

(2) This regulation applies to:

(a) any criminal proceedings in a magistrates' court;
(b) any proceedings in the Crown Court mentioned in regulation 3(2);
(c) any appeal by way of case stated from a magistrates' court; and
(d) any proceedings which are preliminary or incidental to proceedings mentioned in sub-paragraphs (a) to (c).

(3) This regulation does not apply to proceedings referred to in section 12(2)(f) of the Act (proceedings for contempt in the face of a court).

(6) Representation by an advocate

12.—(1) A representation order for the purposes of proceedings before a magistrates' court may only include representation by an advocate in the case of: **29–38**

(a) any indictable offence, including an offence which is triable either way; or
(b) proceedings under section 9 of, or paragraph 6 of Schedule 1 to, the *Extradition Act* 1989

where the court is of the opinion that, because of circumstances which make the proceedings unusually grave or difficult, representation by both a solicitor and an advocate would be desirable.

(2) A representation order for the purposes of proceedings before a magistrates' court may not include representation by an advocate other than as provided in paragraph (1).

Before the court can properly exercise its discretion to assign counsel in a case other than a charge of murder, the applicant must show not only that the case is of unusual gravity or difficulty but also that circumstances lead to the conclusion that such representation is desirable in the particular proceedings—whether summary trial or committal proceedings. The proper approach is to recognise that in a large number of cases which might in themselves be grave or difficult it is nevertheless possible at an early stage for any competent solicitor to realise that no useful purpose would be likely to be served in the interests of his client in opposing, for example a simple committal for trial under s.6(2) of the *Magistrates' Courts Act* 1980. The mere multiplicity of simple, straightforward charges could not make it desirable for counsel to be instructed. The facts in relation to a single charge might be so complex that it is desirable that counsel should at least advise whether there were good grounds for opposing a committal under s.6(2). Assignment of counsel may be justified if a submission of no case to answer is to be made in a case of some gravity and weight: *Guildford Justices, ex. p. Scott* [1975] Crim.L.R. 286. **29–39**

The principle of equality of arms under the ECHR, art. 6 does not require that a defendant should be represented by leading counsel merely because the prosecution were so represented. What is required is that the defendant be properly represented by an advocate who could ensure that the defendant's case was properly and adequately put before the court: *Lea (Att.-Gen's Reference (No.82a of 2000))*; *Shatwell* [2002] 2 Cr.App.R. 24, CA. Rule 14, para. 14 of the regulations makes provision for representation by Queen's Counsel to be ordered in the magistrates court but only at the time when a murder charge is sent to the Crown Court or a case prosecuted by the SFO is transferred. **29–40**

(7) Representation by advocate only

Criminal Defence Service (General) (No.2) Regulations 2001, reg.15

15. The court may grant a representation order for representation by an advocate alone: **29–41**

(a) in any proceedings referred to in section 12(2)(f) of the Act;
(b) in respect of an appeal to the Court of Appeal or the Courts-Martial Appeal Court; or
(c) in cases of urgency where it appears to the court that there is no time to instruct a solicitor:
 (i) in respect of an appeal to the Crown Court; or
 (ii) in proceedings in which a person is committed to or appears before the Crown Court for trial or sentence, or appears or is brought before that court to be dealt with.

29–42 A CDRO may be granted to a solicitor and it is open to them to brief counsel if they see fit but this rule restricts the circumstances in which an order can specify representation by a barrister.

Criminal Defence Service (General) (No.2) Regulations 2001, reg.22

29–43 **22.** Where a representation order has been made, the assisted person's solicitor or advocate whether acting under a representation order or otherwise shall not receive or be a party to the making of any payment for work done in connection with the proceedings in respect of which the representation order was made except such payments as may be made:

(a) by the Lord Chancellor or the Commission; or

(b) in respect of any expenses or fees incurred in:

(i) preparing, obtaining or considering any report, opinion or further evidence, whether provided by an expert witness or otherwise; or

(ii) obtaining any transcripts or recordings

where an application for an authority to incur such fees or expenses has been refused by the Costs Committee.

(8) High cost cases

Criminal Defence Service (General) (No.2) Regulations 2001, reg.23

29–44 **23.**—(1) This regulation applies to very high cost cases where funded services are provided.

(2) Any solicitor who has conduct of a case which is a very high cost case shall notify the Commission in writing accordingly as soon as is practicable.

(3) Where a solicitor fails to comply with the provisions of this regulation without good reason, and as a result there is a loss to public funds, the court or Costs Committee, as appropriate, may refuse payment of his costs up to the extent of such loss.

(4) No payment under paragraph (3) shall be refused unless the solicitor has been given a reasonable opportunity to show why it should not be refused.

29–45 Very high cost cases by definition will rarely be dealt with in the magistrates' court but the original application for legal representation will be made there. The applicant or his solicitor should note the high cost of the case on the application at the earliest opportunity. The Court has a duty to check that the LSC have been notified and will advise that failure to notify may mean costs will not be recovered: *Practice Direction (Costs: Criminal Proceedings)* May, 2004.

(9) Expenditure, expert witnesses

29–46 Case law under the previous legislation clarified the situation relating to expert evidence that could be commissioned at public expense. In *Silcott, Braithwaite and Raghip*, *The Times*, December 9, 1991, the Court of Appeal said that lawyers are under a duty not to involve the legal aid fund in unnecessary expenditure. It was not appropriate to continue to obtain reports until one favourable to the defence case was found. The fund would allow for one or at the most two expert's reports to be commissioned. "Expert shopping" was to be discouraged but in this case there were exceptional circumstances where the need for a further expert opinion could be demonstrated. Counsel should advise on evidence in support of an extension of the representation order to obtain expert's reports and the courts must rely on the proper professional standards being observed by all the lawyers concerned.

The court has no power to authorise the incurring of costs under a representation order for an expert witness, although it may express an opinion as to the desirability of the order being so extended: *Donnelly* [1998] Crim.L.R. 131, CA.

(10) Change of representative

Criminal Defence Service (General) (No.2) Regulations 2001, reg.16

29–47 **16.**—(1) Where a representation order has been granted an application may be made to the court before which the proceedings are heard to select a representative in place of a representative previously selected, and any such application shall state the grounds on which it is made.

(2) The court may:

(a) grant the application where:

(i) the representative considers himself to be under a duty to withdraw from the case in accordance with his professional rules of conduct and, in such a case, the representative shall provide details of the nature of such duty;

(ii) there is a breakdown in the relationship between the assisted person and the representative such that effective representation can no longer be provided and, in such a case, the representative shall provide details of the nature of such breakdown;

(iii) through circumstances beyond his control, the representative is no longer able to represent the assisted person; or

(iv) some other substantial compelling reason exists; or

(b) refuse the application.

When legal advice and assistance is being publicly funded under a CDRO the court has a duty to scrutinise the justification for changing solicitors which may result in a duplication of work and costs. A request for a change of representation should be in writing clearly explaining the reasons for the application. The court will require confirmation that the original solicitor is aware of and consents to the transfer. If there is no consent then representations should be heard. **29–48**

In a case where a defendant went through three different legal representatives in a trial and finally ended up representing himself it was held that although sufficient time must be given for the preparation of the defence case this does not entitle the defendant to manipulate or abuse the court process so as to cause delay and effectively derail the trial. The appeal against conviction was not allowed. The first team of representatives withdrew because they were "professionally embarrassed" and the other two withdrew because they said the court would not allow sufficient time for preparation. The case involved several co-defendants who would have been affected by any delay and the defendant appeared to keep changing his instructions throughout the trial; *Ulcay and Toygun* (2008) 1 W.L.R. 1209.

(11) Withdrawal of representation order

Criminal Defence Service (General) (No.2) Regulations 2001, reg.17

17.—(1) Where any charge or proceedings against the assisted person are varied, the court before which the proceedings are heard or, in respect of any proceedings mentioned in regulation 3(2)(a) to (g), the Commission, must— **29–49**

(a) consider whether the interests of justice continue to require that he be represented in respect of the varied charge or proceedings; and

(b) withdraw the representation order if the interests of justice do not so require.

(1A) The court before which the proceedings are heard or, in respect of any proceedings mentioned in regulation 3(2)(a) to (g), the Commission, must consider whether to withdraw the representation order in any of the following circumstances—

(a) where the assisted person declines to accept the order in the terms which are offered;

(b) otherwise at the request of the assisted person; or

(c) where the representative named in the representation order declines to continue to represent the assisted person.

(2) Where representation is withdrawn, the appropriate officer or the Commission, as appropriate, shall provide written notification to the assisted person and to the solicitor (or, where there was no solicitor assigned, to the advocate), who shall inform any assigned advocate (or, where notification is given to the advocate, any other assigned advocate).

(3) On any subsequent application by the assisted person for a representation order in respect of the same proceedings,

(a) he must declare the withdrawal of the previous representation order and the reason for it; and

(b) where the representation order was withdrawn in the circumstances set out in paragraph (1) or paragraph (1A)(a) or (b) and a representation order is subsequently granted, the court or the Commission, as appropriate, must select the same representative, unless it considers that there are good reasons why it should select a different representative.

29–50 A CDRO may be withdrawn because of a breakdown in the relationship between the defendant and the solicitor. A fresh application for representation may then be made; but the same representative may be appointed.

(12) Appeal against refusal to grant representation

Criminal Defence Service (Representation Order: Appeals etc) Regulations 2006, reg.4

Renewed applications and appeals: magistrates' courts

29–51 **4.**—(1) In this regulation "court" means the magistrates' court in which the proceedings in respect of which the individual is seeking a representation order are being or are to be heard and includes a single justice and a District Judge (Magistrates' Courts).

(2) Where the representation authority refuses to grant a representation order to an individual on the grounds that the interests of justice do not require such an order to be granted, the individual may renew the application for a representation order to that authority.

(3) The representation authority must grant the representation order or refuse the application.

(4) Where the representation authority refuses the application, the individual may appeal to the court against the refusal.

(5) The court must either—

(a) decide that it would be in the interests of justice for a representation order to be granted; or

(b) dismiss the appeal.

(6) Where the court makes a decision under paragraph (5)(a), the individual may apply to the representation authority for a representation order; and—

(a) if the individual states in writing, verified by a statement of truth, that the individual's financial resources have not changed since the date of the original application so as to make the individual financially ineligible for a representation order, the authority must grant such an order; or

(b) if the resources may have so changed, the representation authority must determine whether the individual is financially eligible to be granted a representation order in accordance with the *Criminal Defence Service (Financial Eligibility) Regulations* 2006 and, if the individual is so eligible, must grant such an order."

[This regulation is printed as substituted by the *Criminal Defence Service (Representation Orders: Appeals etc.) (Amendment) Regulations* 2010 (S.I. 2010 No. 1186) which came into force on April 6, 2010.]

Where an individual who is involved in criminal proceedings has been refused publicly funded representation on the grounds that the interests of justice do not require the grant of a representation order, a renewed application may be made to the authority responsible for granting representation orders in magistrates' court, *i.e.* the Legal Services Commission. If the application is still refused, an appeal may be made to the court.

Chapter 30

COSTS

Part VII

I. INTRODUCTION

The *Prosecution of Offences Act* 1985, Pt II governs the award of costs in criminal proceedings. It has been supplemented by the *Costs in Criminal Cases (General) Regulations* 1986 made under ss.19 and 20. The magistrates' court has power to make a defendant's costs order and a prosecution costs order for payment of costs from central or public funds. An order can also be made for the convicted defendant to pay the costs of the prosecution. The court may make a wasted costs order against either the prosecution or defence to cover any costs incurred by a party as a result of an unnecessary or improper act or omission by the other party to the proceedings. The court may also make an order for wasted costs against legal representatives. The *Courts Act* 2003 also adds a power for the court to award costs against third parties. The magistrates' court has no inherent jurisdiction to award the payment of costs in criminal cases. Any party making an application for costs must identify the statutory authority for the court to do so. **30–1**

The *Criminal Procedure Rules* 2011 (S.I. 2011 No. 1709) came into force on April 5, 2010 and include rules to cover all applications for costs orders in the criminal courts. Part 76 has been inserted replacing the rules in Pt 78. There are five sections which cover general information, costs out of central funds, costs paid by one party to another, other costs orders and the assessment of costs. See Appendix G.

General

The *Prosecution of Offences Act* 1985 covers criminal proceedings only. It does not extend to applications such as those under the *Police Property Act* 1897 for the release of property being held by the police: *Daventry Justices, ex p. Chief Constable of Northamptonshire Police* (2001) A.C.D. 92. An application for access orders by Customs and Excise under the *Value Added Tax Act* 1994 was held not to be criminal proceedings as no person had been charged and a wasted costs order could not be made in the course of the application: *Customs and Excise Commissioners v. City of London Magistrates' Court* [2000] 4 All E.R. 763. There is power under s.64 of the *Magistrates' Courts Act* 1980 for the court to make an award of costs in civil cases where a complaint is made, which may be relevant in some applications. **30–2**

Human Rights Act 1998

No absolute right to costs or expenses can be read into the European Convention on **30–3**

Human Rights: *Lutz v. Germany* [1988] 10 E.H.R.R. 182. As a general principle, case law indicates that on acquittal costs should normally be awarded: *Sekanina v. Austria* [1993] 17 E.H.R.R. 221. If costs are refused to a defendant where the case has been dismissed or discontinued this could amount to a breach of Art.6 as a violation of the presumption of innocence where the reasons for the refusal amount in substance to a determination of guilt: *Minelli v. Switzerland* [1983] 5 E.H.R.R. 554. Where, however, a court refers to the state of suspicion against the defendant in support of its exercise of its discretion to refuse costs, there is no violation of the presumption of innocence: *Leutscher v. Netherlands* [1997] 24 E.H.R.R. 181. The possibility of the presumption of innocence being violated would appear to be more likely in relation to acquittals as compared to cases where the case is discontinued through a technicality: *Sekanina v. Austria, ante.*

II. COSTS, ORDERS AND ENFORCEMENT

A. GUIDES TO THE AWARD OF COSTS IN CRIMINAL PROCEEDINGS

30–4 On July 30, 2010 the Lord Chief Justice handed down a *Practice Direction (Costs in Criminal Proceedings)* to take effect immediately. This revokes the 2004 *Practice Direction (Costs: Criminal Proceedings)* and also the *Amendment to the Practice Direction on Costs in Criminal Proceedings (Value Added Tax on Disbursements)* issued in 2007.

The new Practice Direction applies to Magistrates' Courts and now makes reference to the relevant Parts of the *Criminal Procedure Rules* 2011 in relation to costs. The text is reported at [2011] 1 Cr.App.R. 13.

Part 76 of the *Criminal Procedure Rules* 2011 covers costs—see Appendix G G–316.

B. DEFENDANT'S COSTS ORDERS

Prosecution of Offences Act 1985, s.16

Defence costs

30–5 **16.**—(1) Where—

(a) an information laid before a justice of the peace for any area, charging any person with an offence, is not proceeded with;

(b) a magistrates' court inquiring into an indictable offence as examining justices determines not to commit the accused for trial;

(c) a magistrates' court dealing summarily with an offence dismisses the information;

that court or, in a case falling within paragraph (a) above, a magistrates' court for that area, may make an order in favour of the accused for a payment to be made out of central funds in respect of his costs (a "defendant's costs order").

(2)–(5) deal with the powers of other courts to order costs.

(6) A defendant's costs order shall, subject to the following provisions of this section, be for the payment out of central funds, to the person in whose favour the order is made, of such amount as the court considers reasonably sufficient to compensate him for any expenses properly incurred by him in the proceedings.

(7) Where a court makes a defendant's costs order but is of the opinion that there are circumstances which make it inappropriate that the person in whose favour the order is made should recover the full amount mentioned in subsection (6) above, the court shall—

(a) assess what amount would, in its opinion, be just and reasonable; and

(b) specify that amount in the order.

(9) Subject to subsection (7) above, the amount to be paid out of central funds in pursuance of a defendant's costs order shall—

(a) be specified in the order, in any case where the court considers it appropriate for the amount to be so specified and the person in whose favour the order is made agrees the amount; and

(b) in any other case, be determined in accordance with regulations made by the Lord Chancellor for the purposes of this section.

(10) Subsection (6) above shall have effect, in relation to any case falling within subsection (1)(a) or (2)(a) above, as if for the words "in the proceedings" there were substituted the words "in or about the defence".

(11) Where a person ordered to be retried is acquitted at his retrial, the costs which may be ordered to be paid out of central funds under this section shall include—

(a) any costs which, at the original trial, could have been ordered to be so paid under this section if he had been acquitted; and

(b) if no order was made under this section in respect of his expenses on appeal, any sums for the payment of which such an order could have been made.

(12) [Refers to Crown Court powers.]

[This section is reprinted as amended by the *Criminal Justice and Public Order Act* 1994, Sched. 9, para. 25(a).]

At the end of a case in the magistrates' court where the defendant is found not guilty **30–6** of a charge tried summarily or is discharged on committal or the case is not proceeded with by the prosecution, he may apply for his costs to be paid out of central funds under this section. The application may be made in court immediately. The court may then, if the amount claimed is specified or can be readily assessed, make a defendant's costs order for the required amount to be paid out of central funds. The determined total figure must be expressed in the order: *Judd* [1971] 1 All E.R. 127. In *Galandauer v. Snaresbrook Crown Court* [2006] EWHC 1633 the appellant was partially successful in an appeal against sentence dealt with at the Crown Court but the judge only allowed him a reduced amount of costs. He appealed against that reduction which led to him being awarded about a quarter of what he had originally claimed. On appeal it was held that if the court intended that only a proportion of costs claimed should be paid then the reasons why the full amount was not considered justified must be clearly identified. There must be a rational basis for deciding that the amount ordered was just and reasonable. As this had not happened in this case the appeal challenging the reduction was upheld. If the amount is yet to be properly quantified or cannot be agreed then the court may order that the amount be "taxed" or assessed by an appropriate officer of the court under the regulations. Where a DCO is to be taxed, the claim must be submitted within three months: regs (6) and (12) of the *Costs in Criminal Cases (General Regulations)* 1986. There is no right of appeal to the Crown Court against the decision of the appropriate officer on costs: (s.108 of the *Magistrates' Courts Act* 1980) and any assessment of a claim can only be challenged by way of judicial review.

If an application for a costs order is not made immediately in court it may be made at a later date: *Bolton Justices, ex p. Wildish* (1983) 147 J.P. 309, DC; *Liverpool Magistrates' Court, ex p. Abiaka* [1999] (96) 14 L.S.G. 32, DC. The court must be satisfied that one of the circumstances listed in s.16, *ante*, apply. A case is not proceeded with when a notice of discontinuance is served by the prosecution and the court retains the jurisdiction to award costs to the defendant to cover the expense of preparation for the trial: *Denning v. DPP* [1991] 2 Q.B. 532. The reason why the case is not proceeded with is irrelevant. Where a case was unable to proceed because the information was found to have been laid out of time it was held that the court still had power to make an award of costs in favour of a defendant: *Patel v. Blakely* [1988] R.T.R. 65, DC.

A defendant's costs order may be made in favour of a parent or guardian of a child **30–7** or young person. The reference to "the accused" in s.16 covers a parent or guardian including a local authority looking after a child or young person: *Preston Crown Court, ex p. Lancashire CC*; *Burnley Crown Court, ex p. Same* [1999] 1 W.L.R. 142, DC.

The exception to the entitlement of a defendant's costs order, especially on acquittal is very narrow despite the court's discretion to make such an order: *South West Surrey Magistrates' Court, ex p. James* [2001] Crim.L.R. 690, DC. This is in accordance with European case law. The *Practice Direction (Costs: Criminal Proceedings)* [2011] 1 Cr.App.R. 13 covers defence costs orders. In Pt 2 it says that an order for defence costs should normally be made on acquittal unless there are positive reasons for not doing so. An example is given where a defendant's own conduct brings suspicion on him and misleads the prosecution into thinking that the case against him was stronger than it is. The directions also confirm that the court retains a discretion whether to order defence costs or not. It has been held that when an information is dismissed after a trial the fact that a prosecution was properly brought and was not malicious is irrelevant and does not constitute a good reason for a refusal to make a defendant's costs order: *Birmingham Juvenile Court, ex p. H.* (1992) 156 J.P. 445. In cases of discontinuance the conduct of the defendant must be carefully considered as it may provide a reason for refusal. The fact that the defendant has brought the prosecution on himself was held to amount to a reason for not making an order: *Spens, Independent,* March 18, 1992. But the suggestion that the defendant brought the prosecution on himself must be based on strong independent evidence in order to provide a positive reason to refuse costs: *Mooney v. Cardiff Magistrates' Court* (1999) 164 J.P. 220. Where the prosecution decided to offer a caution a decision to refuse costs to the acquitted defendant was quashed. No reasons had been given for the refusal and the court appeared to have based it on the fact that the defendant had brought suspicion on himself but failed to consider also whether he had misled the prosecution. It was held that the expression in Practice Direction was to be read conjunctively so both aspects had to be satisfied; *Dowler v. Merseyrail* 173 J.P. 332. Where a costs order was refused to a defendant whose case was dismissed in the absence of a prosecution witness, it was held that this could interfere with the presumption of innocence under Art. 6 as it indicated a determination of guilt: *R. (Barrington) v. Preston Crown Court* [2001] EWHC 599 (Admin). See also *Hussain v. UK* (2006) 43 E.H.R.R. 22 (ECHR) where it was held that a refusal of a costs order for the defendant where the judge commented that he had been acquitted only because of the failure of a key witness to give evidence was held to be incompatible with the presumption of innocence under Art. 6.

The *Practice Direction 2010* at 2.1.1 states that when declining to make a Defendant's Costs Order the court should explain in open court that the reason for not making an order does not involve any suggestion that the defendant is guilty of any criminal conduct but the order is refused because of a positive reason that must be identified. Where the defence used an "ambush" defence in a drink drive case and secured an acquittal following an appeal by way of case stated the application for a Defendant's Costs Order following the successful appeal was refused as the application was considered to be entirely without merit. The court observed that the *Criminal Procedure Rules* must be complied with and the failure of the defence to raise issues and make them clear to the prosecution and court at an early stage was held to amount to a good reason for refusing costs. *Cox v. DPP* [2010] WL 5590245.

In *Emohare v. Thames Magistrates' Court* (2009) 173 J.P. 303 a defendants costs order was refused following an acquittal for an offence of assaulting a police officer in the execution of his duty. The court said that the defendant's behaviour had been reprehensible and he had brought the prosecution on himself. It was also observed by the court that the defendant had been fortunate not to have faced a charge under the *Public Order Act* 1986. The reasoning of the court was held on appeal to be suggestive of the fact that the court regarded him as guilty despite the acquittal and this was not a proper basis for refusing the costs order. The Practice Direction had to be followed closely and the presumption of innocence should not be seen to be infringed by a refusal of costs. In *R. (On the application of Spiteri) v. Basildon Crown Court* [2009] 173 J.P. 327 the defendant was acquitted in a drink and drive case as a result of what was described as an "unmeritorious technicality". Costs were refused because it was said that he had brought the prosecution on himself. On appeal it was held to be wrong in principle and contrary to the presumption of innocence to approach the issue of costs on the basis that the defendant was in truth guilty of the offence. It was also said that the bringing of the prosecution on oneself alone was not a sufficient positive reason to refuse costs as the Practice Direction went on to say that there must also have been some misleading of the prosecution into thinking that the case against the defendant was stronger than it was.

30–8 The amount ordered to be taxed is for expenses "properly incurred" by the defendant. The court or the appropriate officer will consider whether the defendant has incurred costs and to what amount.

Under the *Prosecution of Offences Act* 1985, s.21(4A), the costs of a defendant who has the benefit of a criminal defence representation order shall not, for the purposes of a defendant's costs order, be taken to include any expenses incurred on his behalf by the Legal Services Commission or the Lord Chancellor. The costs are paid out of public funds in any event so he incurs no costs. A costs order may be appropriate in limited circumstances, for example, if the defendant was not legally aided until a late stage in the proceedings and paid for early representation personally.

A defendant who had legal aid had originally engaged an American lawyer to act for him when he was being investigated by the Serious Fraud Office. On his acquittal he claimed for the fees paid to the US lawyer which were disallowed. On appeal it was held that he could be entitled to the costs if he could show they were reasonably incurred and of a reasonable amount. The court would have to have regard to all the circumstances including the question of duplication of work; *Brewer v. Secretary of State for Justice* [2009] 3 All E.R. 861.

But see *Hayes* [2008] Costs L.R. which seems to indicate that a defendant's costs order will not be made to cover any private payment made before legal aid was granted.

Costs are incurred by a defendant when he is liable to his solicitors for the costs of his defence even if a third party, such as his employer or an insurance company has undertaken or is liable to pay any of the costs. Only if there is an express or implied agreement in binding form that in no circumstances would the solicitor seek to recover costs from the defendant could it be said that the defendant had incurred no costs: *Miller and Glennie* (1984) 78 Cr.App.R. 71, QBD.

Defence solicitors may be instructed privately with a contract to pay legal expenses **30–9**
but no money actually changing hands until the case is concluded. Difficulties might then arise as to whether costs were actually "incurred by the defendant". In the case of *R. (McCormick) v. Liverpool City Magistrates* [2001] 2 All E.R. 705, the precise meaning of "incurred" was considered in detail. One defendant had entered into a contract with his solicitor that he would not be expected to make any payment not within the ambit of public funds. Another defendant had instructed a solicitor privately but had not made any payment to him during the progression of the case. Both were refused DCOs as the court took the view that in these circumstances no legal costs had been incurred. It was held on appeal against the refusals that in the first case a liability had been incurred because the defendant may have been ordered to pay costs outside the ambit of public funds. In the second case the Act and Regulations were held only to require that costs be incurred and not actually paid by the defendant. In both cases it was held that the financial ability of the defendants to pay any costs incurred was not relevant and in the circumstances the refusals of the DCOs were quashed.

In *Jain, The Times*, December 10, 1987, CA, a defendant's costs order was made in favour of a named person other than the defendant, who had financed the proceedings. However, the judgment does not specify how the court dealt with the question of whether the Act allows costs awards in favour of persons other than the defendant.

A solicitor who represents himself in person in criminal proceedings incurs costs in **30–10**
conducting his own case. He may claim for the fees chargeable by him had he been representing a defendant and not himself: *Stafford, Stone and Eccleshall Magistrates' Court, ex p. Robinson* [1988] 1 W.L.R. 369. A barrister who was represented by counsel in criminal proceedings was entitled to claim costs for his representation and also for the work he had done himself in preparing his own defence. The Code of Conduct prevented him from representing himself in a professional capacity: *Khan v. Lord Chancellor* [2003] 1 W.L.R. 2385.

A person in respect of whom a defendant's costs order is made may also be paid subsistence allowance and travelling expenses in relation to his attendances at court under reg.23 of the *Costs on Criminal Cases (General) Regulations* 1986. The rates are fixed by the Lord Chancellor. No claim can be made for loss of earnings or loss of time.

There is no provision in criminal proceedings under the *Prosecution of Offences Act* 1985 or the Regulations to award interest on costs: *Westminster City Council v. Wingrove* [1991] 1 Q.B. 652.

Costs in Criminal Cases (General) Regulations 1986, regs 4–8, 12

PART III

COSTS OUT OF CENTRAL FUNDS

Application and definitions

30–11 **4.** This Part of these Regulations applies to costs payable out of central funds in pursuance of an order made under or by virtue of Part II of the Act and in this Part of these Regulations—

"applicant" means the person in whose favour a costs order has been made;

"appropriate authority" has the meaning assigned to it by regulation 5;

"costs judge" means a costs judge of the Supreme Court;

"costs order" means an order made under or by virtue of Part II of the Act for the payment of costs out of central funds;

"disbursements" do not include any payment made out of central funds to a witness, interpreter or medical practitioner in accordance with Part V of these Regulations;

"expenses" means out of pocket expenses, travelling expenses and subsistence allowance;

"presiding judge" means the judge who presided at the hearing in respect of which the costs are payable; and

The appropriate authority

30–12 **5.**—(1) Costs shall be determined by the appropriate authority in accordance with these Regulations.

(2) Subject to paragraph (3), the appropriate authority shall be—

(a) the registrar of criminal appeals in the case of proceedings in the Court of Appeal,

(b) the master of the Crown Office in the case of proceedings in a Divisional Court of the Queen's Bench Division,

(c) an officer appointed by the Lord Chancellor in the case of proceedings in the Crown Court or, subject to sub-paragraph (d), a magistrates' court,

(d) the justices' clerk in the case of proceedings in a magistrates' court, where the costs consist solely of expenses claimed by the applicant.

(3) The appropriate authority may appoint or authorise the appointment of determining officers to act on its behalf under these Regulations in accordance with directions given by it or on its behalf.

Claims for costs

30–13 **6.**—(1) Subject to regulation 12, no claim for costs shall be entertained unless it is submitted within three months of the date on which the costs order was made.

(2) Subject to paragraph (3), a claim for costs shall be submitted to the appropriate authority, in such form and manner as it may direct and shall be accompanied by receipts or other evidence of the applicant's payment of the costs claimed, and any receipts or other documents in support of any disbursements claimed.

(3) A claim shall—

(a) summarise the items of work done by a solicitor;

(b) state, where appropriate, the dates on which items of work were done, the time taken and the sums claimed,

(c) specify any disbursements claimed, including counsel's fees, the circumstances in which they were incurred and the amounts claimed in respect of them, and

(d) contain either full particulars, including the date and outcome, of any claim for payment in respect of services funded for the applicant as part of the Criminal Defence Service, or a certificate by the solicitor that he has not made, and will not make, any such claim.

(4) Where there are any special circumstances which should be drawn to the attention of the appropriate authority, the applicant shall specify them.

(5) The applicant shall supply such further particulars, information and documents as the appropriate authority may require.

Determination of rates and scales of costs payable out of central funds

7.—(1) The appropriate authority shall consider the claim, any further particulars, information or documents submitted by the applicant under regulation 6 and shall allow costs in respect of— **30–14**

(a) such work as appears to it to have been actually and reasonably done; and

(b) such disbursements as appear to it to have been actually and reasonably incurred.

(2) Any doubts which the appropriate authority may have as to whether the costs were reasonably incurred or were reasonable in amount shall be resolved against the applicant.

(3) The costs awarded shall not exceed the costs actually incurred.

(4) The Lord Chancellor shall, with the consent of the Treasury and for the purposes of this regulation, determine the rates and scales of costs in respect of work and disbursements payable out of central funds.

[This regulation is printed as amended by the *Costs in Criminal Cases (General) (Amendment) Regulations* 2009 (S.I. 2009 No. 2720) which came into force with effect from October 30, 2009.]

Payment of costs

8.—(1) When the appropriate authority has determined the costs payable to an applicant in accordance with these Regulations, the appropriate authority shall notify the applicant of the costs payable and authorise payment accordingly. **30–15**

(2) Where the costs payable under paragraph (1) are varied as a result of a redetermination under regulation 9, an appeal to a costs judge under regulation 10, or an appeal to the High Court under regulation 11, then—

(a) where the costs are increased, the appropriate authority shall authorise payment of the increase;

(b) where the costs are decreased, the applicant shall repay the amount of such decrease; and

(c) where the payment of the costs of an appeal is ordered under regulation 10(14) or 11(8), the appropriate authority shall authorise such payment to the applicant.

Time limits

12.—(1) Subject to paragraph (2), the time limit within which there must be made or instituted— **30–16**

(a) a claim for costs by an applicant under regulation 6, an application for a redetermination under regulation 9, or a request for an appropriate authority to give reasons for its decision on a redetermination under regulation 9;

(b) an appeal to a costs judge under regulation 10 or an application for a certificate under regulation 11; or

(c) an appeal to the High Court under regulation 11;

may, for good reason, be extended by the appropriate authority, the Senior Costs Judge or the High Court, as the case may be.

(2) Where an applicant without good reason has failed (or, if an extension were not granted, would fail) to comply with a time limit, the appropriate authority, the Senior Costs Judge or the High Court, as the case may be, may, in exceptional circumstances, extend the time limit and shall consider whether it is reasonable in the circumstances to reduce the costs; provided that the costs shall not be reduced unless the representative has been allowed a reasonable opportunity to show cause orally or in writing why the costs should not be reduced.

(3) An applicant may appeal to the Senior Costs Judge against a decision made under this regulation by an appropriate authority in respect of proceedings other than proceedings before a magistrates' court and such an appeal shall be instituted within 21 days of the decision being given by giving notice in writing to the Senior Costs Judge specifying the grounds of appeal.

[These regulations are printed as amended by the *Costs in Criminal Cases (Gen-*

eral) (Amendments) Regulations 2005 (S.I. 2005 No. 2622) and the *Costs in Criminal Cases (General) (Amendment) Regulations Order* 2008 (S.I. 2008 No. 2448) which came into force on October 13, 2008].]

30–17 These regulations outline the procedure to be used when costs awarded under a defendant's costs order are assessed. The *Costs in Criminal Cases (General) (Amendment) Regulations Order 2008* (S.I. 2008 No. 2448) moved the responsibility for the taxation of costs under a defendant's costs order from the justices' clerk to a National Taxing Team. The NTT is based at the Crown Court. There is no appeal against the decision of the NTT except on an internal basis or by judicial review. The court will issue a defendant's costs order certificate which must be submitted to the NTT with any claim for costs. The magistrates' court retains responsibility for the payment of expenses to witnesses of fact; for expert witnesses and interpreters but will not deal with legal costs. If defence costs can be agreed between parties the court may make an award of a specified sum at hearing but this is unlikely to occur where costs may exceed £1,000. The amended regulations also provide for the payment of expenses for intermediaries appointed under s.29 of the *Youth Justice and Criminal Evidence Act* 1999. A claim for costs must be submitted within three months of the order for costs being made by the court but the appropriate officer has a discretion to extend that time limit (regulation 12). The *Costs in Criminal Cases (General) (Amendment) Regulations* 2009 (S.I. 2009 No. 2720) came into force on October 30, 2009. Regulation 7 was amended to provide that the Lord Chancellor in agreement with the Treasury shall set the rates and scales at which payment for legal costs and disbursements are paid from central funds rather than the scales being determined by a taxing officer. A new funding scheme implemented by the Lord Chancellor under these Regulations which purported to set the scales and restrict the rates at which costs from central funds could be claimed has now been held unlawful. The recovery of costs limited to legal aid rates was challenged and was held to be in contravention of the *Prosecution of Offences Act* 1985, s.16(6) which requires a successful defendant to be 'reasonably sufficiently' compensated for their costs: *R. (On the application of the Law Society) v. Lord Chancellor* [2011] 1 All E.R. 32.

30–18 Claims may be disallowed if the grade and cost of the solicitor or counsel instructed is considered to be too expensive. The test is not whether a more junior lawyer could have dealt with the case just as competently but whether it was reasonable in all the circumstances to instruct a more senior barrister: *Dudley Magistrates' Court, ex p. Power City Stores Ltd* (1990) 154 J.P. 654. For a defendant charged with common assault and battery the instruction of a solicitor of more than four years' standing was reasonable as was the agreement to incur costs using a flat hourly rate: *North Sefton Justices, ex p. Hale, The Times*, January 29, 2002, DC.

It may be reasonable to instruct solicitors who are not local and so may be more expensive, but the reasons for doing so must be advanced: *Wraith v. Sheffield Forgemasters* (1998) 1 All E.R. 82. Higher rates may be allowed for specialist lawyers if it is reasonable to incur such costs and the rate charged is justifiable in view of higher overheads *etc.*: *Jones v. Secretary of State for Wales* [1997] 2 All E.R. 507.

30–19 An application to extend the time limit within which a claim should be submitted may be made either before or after the limit of three months expires. The appropriate officer will then decide if there is good reason to extend the limit. An extension of time may also be granted if there are "exceptional circumstances" which led to the delay despite the fact that there was no good reason for it: *Clerk to the North Kent Justices, ex p. McGoldrick & Co* (1996) 160 J.P. 30. *R. (on the application of Leask) v. South Western Magistrates' Court* (2007) 171 J.P. 489, considered the circumstances in which an extension of the time limit to apply for taxation of costs can be given. The applicant claimed that his lawyer had sought advice of court staff and was told that no time limit applied to such applications. On review the court refused to accept that explanation and said that no good reason existed to extend the time limit as the lawyer should have verified for himself the procedure for claiming costs and any limitation of time. It was held that this decision was flawed as the court had not had regard to whether any exceptional reason applied to justify an extension of the time limit. It was held that the regulation provided a two step approach and both elements must be considered. Under the amended reg.12 the taxing officer may penalise the applicant for late applications by reducing the amount awarded but the applicant must be allowed to make representations about the proposed reduction of costs.

C. PROSECUTION COSTS

Prosecution of Offences Act 1985, s.17

Prosecution costs

17.—(1) Subject to subsection (2) below, the court may— **30–20**

(a) in any proceedings in respect of an indictable offence; and

(b) in any proceedings before a Divisional Court of the Queen's Bench Division or the House of Lords in respect of a summary offence;

order the payment out of central funds of such amount as the court considers reasonably sufficient to compensate the prosecutor for any expenses properly incurred by him in the proceedings.

(2) No order under this section may be made in favour of—

(a) a public authority; or

(b) a person acting—

(i) on behalf of a public authority; or

(ii) in his capacity as an official appointed by such an authority.

(3) Where a court makes an order under this section but is of the opinion that there are circumstances which make it inappropriate that the prosecution should recover the full amount mentioned in subsection (1) above, the court shall—

(a) assess what amount would, in its opinion, be just and reasonable; and

(b) specify that amount in the order.

(4) Subject to subsection (3) above, the amount to be paid out of central funds in pursuance of an order under this section shall—

(a) be specified in the order, in any case where the court considers it appropriate for the amount to be so specified and the prosecutor agrees the amount; and

(b) in any other case, be determined in accordance with regulations made by the Lord Chancellor for the purposes of this section.

(5) Where the conduct of proceedings to which subsection (1) above applies is taken over by the Crown Prosecution Service, that subsection shall have effect as if it referred to the prosecutor who had the conduct of the proceedings before the intervention of the Service and to expenses incurred by him up to the time of intervention.

(6) In this section "public authority" means—

(a) a police force within the meaning of section 3 of this Act;

(b) the Crown Prosecution Service or any other government department;

(c) a local authority or other authority or body constituted for purposes of—

(i) the public service or of local government; or

(ii) carrying on under national ownership any industry or undertaking or part of an industry or undertaking; or

(d) any other authority or body whose members are appointed by Her Majesty or by any Minister of the Crown or government department or whose revenues consist wholly or mainly of money provided by Parliament.

The Crown Prosecution Service and the police are already publicly funded so there is **30–21** no power to order their costs from central funds. This section refers to private prosecutions for either way offences and does not cover summary only cases. Costs may be awarded irrespective of the outcome of the case but the court has a discretion whether to order costs and to what amount. Expenses for a private prosecutor may include legal expenses, secretarial costs and travel expenses but a claim cannot be made for compensation for lost time: *Stockport Magistrates, ex p. Cooper* (1984) 148 J.P. 261.

D. Award of Costs against Accused

Prosecution of Offences Act 1985, s.18

Award of costs against accused

30–22 **18.**—(1) Where—

(a) any person is convicted of an offence before a magistrates' court;

(b) the Crown Court dismisses an appeal against such a conviction or against the sentence imposed on that conviction; or

(c) any person is convicted of an offence before the Crown Court;

the court may make such order as to the costs to be paid by the accused to the prosecutor as it considers just and reasonable.

(2) Relates to the Court of Appeal…

(3) The amount to be paid by the accused in pursuance of an order under this section shall be specified in the order.

(4) Where any person is convicted of an offence before a magistrates' court and—

(a) under the conviction the court orders payment of any sum as a fine, penalty, forfeiture or compensation; and

(b) the sum so ordered to be paid does not exceed £5;

the court shall not order the accused to pay any costs under this section unless in the particular circumstances of the case it considers it right to do so.

(5) Where any person under the age of eighteen is convicted of an offence before a magistrates' court, the amount of any costs ordered to be paid by the accused under this section shall not exceed the amount of any fine imposed on him.

(6) Relates to the Court of Appeal…

[This section is reprinted as amended by the *Criminal Justice and Public Order Act* 1994, Sched. 9, para. 26.]

Costs in Criminal Cases (General) Regulations 1986, reg.14

Application of sections 16, 17 and 18 of the Act

30–23 **14.**—(1) Sections 17 and 18 of the Act shall apply to proceedings in the Crown Court in respect of a person committed by a magistrates' court to that Court—

(a) with a view to his being sentenced for an indictable offence in accordance with section 42 of the *Powers of Criminal Courts Act* 1973; or

(b) with a view to his being sentenced by the Crown Court under section 6(6) or 9(3) of the *Bail Act* 1976 or

(c) with a view to the making of a hospital order with an order restricting his discharge under Part III of the *Mental Health Act* 1983,

as they apply where a person is convicted in proceedings before the Crown Court.

(2) Section 18 of the Act shall apply to proceedings in the Crown Court—

(a) in respect of a person committed by a magistrates' court as an incorrigible rogue under section 5 of the *Vagrancy Act* 1824 as if he were committed for trial before the Crown Court and as if the committing court were examining justices; and

(b) in respect of an appeal under section 14 of the *Vagrancy Act* 1824 as if the hearing of the appeal were a trial on indictment and as if the magistrates' court from which the appeal was brought were examining justices.

(3) Section 18 of the Act shall apply to proceedings in a magistrates' court or the Crown Court for dealing with an offender—

(a) under any of the following provisions of the *Powers of Criminal Courts (Sentencing) Act* 2000—

(i) section 13 (commission of further offence by person conditionally discharged);

(ii) section 119(1) or 123 (power of court on conviction of further offence to deal with suspended sentence and breach of requirement of suspended sentence supervision order);

(iii) paragraph 5 of Schedule 1 (power of court on referral back from panel);

(iv) Part II of Schedule 3 (breach of requirement of certain community orders);

(v) paragraphs 1 to 3 of Schedule 5 (breach etc of attendance centre order);
(vi) paragraphs 2 to 4 of Schedule 7 (breach of requirement of supervision order);
(vii) paragraphs 2 to 4 of Schedule 8 (breach of requirement of action plan order or reparation order); and
(b) under either of the following provisions of the *Criminal Justice Act* 2003—
(i) Part 2 of Schedule 8 (breach of requirement of community order);
(ii) Part 2 of Schedule 12 (breach of community requirement of suspended sentence order or conviction of further offence)
as if the offender had been tried in those proceedings for the offence for which the order was made or the sentence passed.

(4) Section 16 of the Act shall apply to proceedings in a magistrates' court or the Crown Court in which it is alleged that an offender required to enter into a recognisance to keep the peace or be of good behaviour has failed to comply with a condition of that recognisance, as if that failure were an indictable offence.

[This regulation is printed as amended by the *Costs in Criminal Cases (General) (Amendment) Regulations* Order 2008 (S.I. 2008 No. 2448) which came into force on October 13, 2008.]

The amended reg.14 clarifies the proceedings in respect of which a prosecutor has the right to apply for costs and in particular includes cases where breach of court orders are being dealt with. **30–24**

The Crown Prosecution Service may make application to the court for costs of prosecuting the case to be paid by the convicted defendant. The court has a discretion whether to make the order and must specify the amount in accordance with s.18(3). This must be done in court as there is no provision for prosecution costs to be taxed. Where a fine is less than £5, the presumption is that no costs will be ordered and for a person under the age of 18, any costs awarded must not be greater than the amount of any fine imposed: ss.18(4) and (5).

The prosecution will state the amount of costs sought and may be required to submit full details if the amount claimed is high. The court will always retain a discretion in fixing the amount ordered to be paid.

Costs payable under such an order were held to be limited to such items as would be payable to the prosecution out of central funds were such an order possible. So counsels' fees, the DPP's costs and witness expenses could be claimed but the jury expenses and cost of security on a trial could not be included: *Maher* [1983] Q.B. 784.

In *Dickinson* [2010] EWCA Crim. 2143 the Judge at the Crown Court ordered costs based on a national scale drawn up by the Crown Prosecution Service. The defendant was fined £200 and ordered to pay £1,200 costs. The appeal was on the basis that a scale should not be applied and that the costs order was grossly disproportionate. On appeal it was held that such a scale can be relied upon as it provides a fair and reasonable guide and avoids the need for the CPS to provide itemised bills in every case. As the order was neither wrong in principle nor manifestly excessive it would not be interfered with. This recognises the practice of the CPS in Magistrates' Courts to apply for standard costs in most cases.

The importance of identifying the power to order costs was stressed in *Nuthoo* [2010] EWCA Crim. 2383 where a prosecution was brought by a local authority. It was confirmed that such a prosecutor was entitled to an order for costs under the *Prosecution of Offences Act* 1985 s.18 and that order is enforceable as if it had been adjudged to be paid on conviction. Section 18 is not restricted in its application to only the Crown Prosecution Service and it was confirmed that the same principles apply when assessing costs for any prosecutor as they do to an application for costs by the Crown Prosecution Service.

Issues have arisen over whether the costs of the investigation can be included. It was held that the order for prosecution costs did not extend to cover the costs of the investigation, particularly when, as in the case, a different body carried out the investigation: *Seymour* (1987) 9 Cr.App.R.(S.) 395. In *Neville (Westminster City Council) v.* **30–25**

Gardner Merchant Ltd (1983) 82 L.G.R. 577 it was held that that the court did have the discretion to include the cost of time spent by a salaried Environmental Health Officer in conducting the investigation and inspecting premises under the *Food Safety (General Food Hygiene) Regulations* 1995 (S.I. 1995 No. 1763). This was especially so if the investigation arose from a specific complaint rather than coming to light through a routine inspection.

In *Associated Octel Ltd* [1997] 1 Cr.App.R. 435, CA, the court said that the costs incurred by the prosecuting authority (the Health and Safety Executive), in investigating a case for prosecution could be recovered under a prosecution costs order. In such a case it was advisable for the prosecution to serve notice on the defence of the full details of the claim so that the defence could consider the claim and make representations.

In *Balshaw v. CPS* [2009] 1 W.L.R. 2301, the CPS claimed for the costs of an accountancy report from KPMG commissioned by the police after charge. It was held to be "just and reasonable" to make an order to cover those costs as they were relevant to the investigation and the trial and the CPS were to pass them on to the police to compensate for fees paid.

In cases where a defendant would have paid a fixed penalty if the option had been offered to him but the case ended up in court, it was held to be incumbent upon the court to either not award any costs or to give cogent reasons as to why costs would be awarded: *R. (Ritson) v. County Durham Magistrates' Court* (2002) 166 J.P. 218.

30–26 The prosecution will request a specific amount but the court has a discretion as to exactly how much it will order to be paid by the defence. In exercising this discretion there are several factors to take into account. The means of the defendant are relevant and it was suggested that an amount that could be paid off within 12 months would be reasonable: *Nottingham Justices, ex p. Fohmann* (1987) 84 Cr.App.R. 316, DC.

The court is obliged when fixing the amount to be paid to investigate the defendant's financial situation with adequate thoroughness and it was held not to be reasonable to make an order for costs that was five times the amount of the fines when the defendant had debts exceeding his savings: *Newham Justices, ex p. Samuels* [1991] C.O.D. 412, DC. Even if the financial situation is investigated with thoroughness the award made may be subject to quashing on appeal if it is considered that no reasonable court could have made such an order on the information obtained: *Croydon Justices, ex p. Summers* [1993] C.O.D. 202, DC. The court, however, declined to determine whether there ought to be some proportionality between fines and costs awards. In *BPS Advertising Ltd v. Barnet LBC* (2007) 171 J.P. 223, QBD it was said that costs awarded should not be grossly disproportionate to the fine imposed. In this case the defendants were fined the maximum for an offence under the *Town and Country Planning Act* 1990 with costs of almost seven times the amount of the fine. On appeal the costs were cut by two-thirds as they were considered to be over-inflated.

30–27 Where the defendant faces multiple charges it is not appropriate to multiply the costs by the number of summonses which related to offences all resulting from one incident. The defendant was summonsed for 37 offences under the *Food Safety (General Food Hygiene) Regulations* 1995 (S.I. 1995 No. 1763) and separate costs orders were made in respect of each summons after written pleas of guilty were accepted. The costs ordered were held to be excessive: *Tottenham Justices, ex p. Joshi* (1982) 75 Cr.App.R. 72, DC. In a case of multiple offences it is acceptable to order a global figure of costs more truly reflecting the work done.

In *Splain* [2010] EWCA Crim. 49 the defendant was originally charged with 17 offences but was convicted of only three. He was ordered to pay costs of £22,045 which was the total amount of costs incurred by the prosecution. It was held this was disproportionate and unfair and the figure was reduced on appeal to £10,000 which was held to be a fair overall assessment of the proportion of costs payable. The court warned that it was not necessary to take a purely mathematical approach but a reduction was appropriate in view of the acquittal on many of the charges.

30–28 An award of costs should not be made with a view to punishing the defendant for the way in which he chose to conduct his case but if his actions necessarily incur higher costs as for example by electing jury trial then this will inevitably be reflected in the amount ordered: *Hayden* (1964) 60 Cr.App.R. 304, CA. In *Northallerton Magistrates' Court, ex p. Dove* [2000] 1 Cr.App.R.(S.) 136, DC, the court held on appeal that where the costs ordered were almost five times the amount of the fine imposed that this was "grossly disproportionate". The court took the opportunity to issue guidelines for the assessment of prosecution costs to be paid by the defendant as follows:

1. The defendant's means and liability for any other financial order should be ascertained so that any order did not exceed a reasonable sum he was able to pay.
2. The sum should never be more than the costs incurred.
3. It was compensation for the prosecutor and not further punishment for the defendant.
4. The costs order should be proportionate to the fine and if the total amount is excessive, the costs should be reduced.
5. The onus was on the defendant to provide details of means and if he failed to do so, the court could deduce his financial circumstances from all available evidence.
6. The defendant must be given the opportunity to produce evidence of his means and should be put on notice of any unusual costs order intended.

In *Dickinson* [2010] EWCA Crim. 2143 the court said that there was no principle that a financial penalty including costs should be payable within a year. The issue was that the amount should not be beyond the means of the defendant so that it was an undue burden or too severe a punishment.

A fine and costs against a company may be payable over a longer period of time than **30–29** would be regarded as reasonable for an individual defendant. In determining the appropriate amount for directors, the court should consider, on the one hand, the need to avoid the risk of double punishment which may arise where the directors of a small company were also its shareholders, and on the other, that it is important to mark the personal responsibility of the directors: *Rollco Screw and Rivet Co Ltd* [1999] 2 Cr.App.R. 436, CA.

The court has discretion to make a prosecution costs order whether the defendant pleads guilty or not guilty. On a guilty plea the costs should be greatly reduced because the expense of preparation and conduct of a trial is avoided. The stage at which the guilty plea is tendered will be relevant in assessing the amount of costs to be ordered. The court has a discretion to award costs on a written plea of guilty dealt with under s.12 of the *Magistrates' Courts Act* 1980. The application for costs should be notified to the defendant in the paperwork sent to him but it does not form part of the statement of facts so would not technically need to be read out by the legal adviser in court. It was held to be sufficient for the claim for costs to be drawn to the court's attention by the legal adviser: *Coventry Magistrates' Court, ex p. DPP* [1990] 3 All E.R. 277.

Where there are several defendants and only some of them have the ability to pay, it **30–30** is wrong to divide the total cost of the prosecution between those defendants. If it is not possible to say what part of the total costs is attributable to any defendant, the court should divide the total costs between the total number of defendants, and order those who do have sufficient means to pay their share only: *Ronson and Parnes* (1992) 13 Cr.App.R.(S.) 153, CA; *Harrison* [1993] 14 Cr.App.R.(S.) 419, CA.

In a case where corporate defendants were held to bear a greater responsibility for criminal conduct than the individual co-defendants it was held appropriate for the company to be ordered to pay a greater amount of costs: *Fresha Bakeries* [2003] 1 Cr.App.R.(S.) 44.

E. WASTED COSTS AWARDS

Prosecution of Offences Act 1985, s.19(1), (3)–(4)

Provision for orders as to costs in other circumstances

30–31 **19.**—(1) The Lord Chancellor may by regulations make provision empowering magistrates' courts, the Crown Court and the Court of Appeal, in any case where the court is satisfied that one party to criminal proceedings has incurred costs as a result of an unnecessary or improper act or omission by, or on behalf of, another party to the proceedings, to make an order as to the payment of those costs.

(2)–(5) [*contain the content of Regulations made under subsection (1) above*]

(3) The Lord Chancellor may by regulations make provision for the payment out of central fund, in such circumstances and in relation to such criminal proceedings as may be specified, of such sums as appear to the court to be reasonably necessary—

(a) to compensate any witness in the proceedings, and any other person who in the opinion of the court necessarily attends for the purposes of the proceedings otherwise than to give evidence, for the expense, trouble or loss of time properly incurred in or incidental to his attendance,

(b) to cover the proper expenses of an interpreter who is required because of the accused's lack of English;

(c) to compensate a duly qualified medical practitioner who—

(i) makes a report otherwise than in writing for the purposes of section 11 of the *Powers of Criminal Courts(Sentencing) Act* 2000 (remand for medical examination); or

(ii) makes a written report to a court in pursuance of a request to which section 32(2) of the *Criminal Justice Act* 1967 (report by medical practitioner on medical condition of offender) applies;

for the expenses properly incurred in or incidental to his reporting to the court.

(d) to cover the proper fee or costs of a person appointed by the Crown Court under section 4A of the *Criminal Procedure (Insanity) Act* 1964 to put the case for the defence.

(e) To cover the proper fee or costs of a legal representative appointed under section 38(4) of the *Youth Justice and Criminal Evidence Act* 1999 (defence representation for purposes of cross-examination) and any expenses properly incurred in providing such a person with evidence or other material in connection with his appointment.

(3A) In subsection (3)(a) above "attendance" means attendance at the court or elsewhere.

(4) [Court of Appeal.]

[This section is reprinted as amended by the *Access to Justice Act* 1999, Sched. 4, para. 28.]

30–32 This section provides for an order to be made for wasted costs between parties and also for payments from public funds to witnesses. Pursuant to the power in s.19, the Lord Chancellor has made the *Costs in Criminal Cases (General) Regulations* 1986 which in Pt V sets out the witnesses who are entitled to be paid allowances and the *Costs in Criminal Cases (General) Regulations* 1986— Rates of Allowances which fixes the amounts to be paid. The rates are amended periodically.

In *R. (on the application of Crowch) v. DPP* [2008] EWHC 948(Admin) it was confirmed that a defendant who represented himself was not entitled under the 1986 *Regulations* when applying for a wasted costs order to claim for costs or expenses incurred by way of time spent travelling to court or preparing his case. The applicant through no fault of his own, had had to attend court twice in abortive hearings and had lost a considerable amount of money on the journeys and by taking time off from his work in relation to the case but it was held that the law did not allow for any reimbursement of such losses.

Costs in Criminal Cases (General) Regulations 1986, reg.3, Part II Costs Unnecessarily or Improperly Incurred

Unnecessary or improper acts and omissions

30–33 **3.**—(1) Subject to the provisions of this regulation, where at any time during criminal proceedings—

(a) a magistrates' court,
(b) the Crown Court, or
(c) the Court of Appeal

is satisfied that costs have been incurred in respect of the proceedings by one of the parties as a result of an unnecessary or improper act or omission by, or on behalf of, another party to the proceedings, the court may, after hearing the parties, order that all or part of the costs so incurred by that party shall be paid to him by the other party.

(2) When making an order under paragraph (1), the court may take into account any other order as to costs which has been made in respect of the proceedings.

(3) An order made under paragraph (1) shall specify the amount of costs to be paid in pursuance of the order.

(4) Where an order under paragraph (1) has been made, the court may take that order into account when making any other order as to costs in respect of the proceedings.

(5) No order under paragraph (1) shall be made by a magistrates' court which requires a person under the age of seventeen who has been convicted of an offence to pay an amount by way of costs which exceeds the amount of any fine imposed on him.

[This Regulation is printed as amended by the *Costs in Criminal Cases (General) (Amendment) Regulations Order* 2008 (S.I. 2008 No. 2448) which came into force on October 13, 2008.]

An order under s.19, in common with other orders under the Act, may only be made in respect of criminal proceedings. The power to award a wasted costs order acts not only as a compensation to any party who incurs extra costs but also as an encouragement to all parties involved in a criminal case to act with diligence and expedition. An application can be made at any time during the proceedings or at the conclusion of the case. The order is made between the parties. **30–34**

The court must be satisfied that the costs were incurred as a result of "an unnecessary or improper act or omission." The word "improper" used in conjunction with "unnecessary" was held to encompass an act or omission resulting in costs which would not have been incurred in the proper conduct of the party's case: *DPP v. Denning* [1991] 2 Q.B. 532. *Per curiam* the court observed that "improper" did not connote "grave impropriety".

A causal connection must be shown to exist between the unnecessary or improper act or omission and the incurring of the costs or expenses claimed under the order. Where the prosecution was ordered to pay wasted costs which covered the costs of a Crown Court case when no evidence was offered following committal, the court said that inquiries must be made into whether the prosecution's negligence was the cause of the defence costs: *Crown Court at Wood Green, ex p. DPP* [1993] 1 W.L.R. 723. In *A.* (2005) 149 S.J. 1350 a wasted costs order was made against the prosecution when they failed to disclose, within a reasonable time, information vital to the defence that affected the safety of the convictions. **30–35**

Where the defendant has the benefit of a criminal defence representation order then for the purposes of s.19 of the *Prosecution of Offences Act* 1985 his costs shall be taken to include the cost of representation publicly funded for him: *Prosecution of Offences Act* 1985, s.21(4A)(b). A wasted costs order may not be appropriate against the prosecution in the case of a legally aided defendant as it simply means the transfer of public funds. Only in extraordinary cases or where the conduct of the police and the Crown Prosecution Service is open to criticism may it be appropriate to make an order. Otherwise the costs of the defence should be borne by the legal aid fund: *Oxford City Justices, ex p. Chief Constable Thames Valley Police*, *The Times*, April 24, 1987. Under the amended reg.3 the court now has a discretion rather than a duty to take into account any other order made in the proceedings as to costs.

This section only allows for orders to be made between the parties. Orders cannot be made against solicitors or counsel personally under s.19: *Crown Court at Isleworth, ex p. Montague & Co* [1990] C.O.D. 86, DC. As to costs awarded against representatives personally, see *post*, § 30–36. **30–36**

In *DPP v. Bury Magistrates' Court* [2007] EWHC 3256 (Admin) it was stressed that the proper section under the Act must be identified. In this case the application purported to be under s.19A against the Crown Prosecutor. On appeal the application was treated as being brought under s.19 since the prosecution was actually a party to the proceedings. Consideration was also given to the effect that the applicant's failure to comply with their own obligations under the *Criminal Procedure Rules* might have on the quantum of wasted costs.

F. ORDERS FOR COSTS AGAINST LEGAL REPRESENTATIVES

Prosecution of Offences Act 1985, s.19A

Costs against legal representatives

30–37 **19A.**—(1) In any criminal proceedings—

(a) the Court of Appeal;

(b) the Crown Court;

(c) a magistrates' court,

may disallow, or (as the case may be) order the legal or other representative concerned to meet, the whole of any wasted costs or such part of them as may be determined in accordance with regulations.

(2) Regulations shall provide that a legal or other representative against whom action is taken by a magistrates' court under subsection (1) may appeal to the Crown Court and that a legal or other representative against whom action is taken by the Crown Court under subsection (1) may appeal to the Court of Appeal.

(3) In this section—

"legal or other representative" in relation to any proceedings, means a person who is exercising a right of audience, or right to conduct litigation, on behalf of any party to the proceedings;

"regulations" means regulations made by the Lord Chancellor; and

"wasted costs" means any costs incurred by a party—

(a) as a result of any improper, unreasonable or negligent act or omission on the part of any representative or any employee of a representative; or

(b) which, in the light of any such act or omission occurring after they were incurred, the court considers it is unreasonable to expect that party to pay.

Costs in Criminal Cases (General) Regulations 1986, regs 3A–3D

PART IIA

WASTED COSTS ORDERS

Application and definitions

30–38 **3A.** This Part of these Regulations applies to action taken by a court under section 19A of the Act and in this Part of these regulations—

"wasted costs order" means any action taken by a court under section 19A of the Act; and

"interested party" means the party benefiting from the wasted costs order and, where he was legally aided, or an order for the payment of costs out of central funds was made in his favour, shall include the authority responsible for determining costs payable in respect of work done under the legal aid order or out of central funds as the case may be.

General

30–39 **3B.**—(1) A wasted costs order may provide for the whole or any part of the wasted costs to be disallowed or ordered to be paid and the court shall specify the amount of such costs.

(2) *Repealed.*

(3) When making a wasted costs order the court may take into account any other order as to costs in respect of the proceedings and order into account when making any other such order.

(4) *Repealed.*

[This regulation is printed as amended by the *Costs in Criminal Cases (General) (Amendment) Regulations* 2009 (S.I. 2009 No. 2720) which came into force with effect from October 30, 2009.]

Appeals

3C.—(1) A legal or other representative against whom the wasted costs order is made may appeal— **30–40**

(a) in the case of an order made by a magistrates' court, to the Crown Court, and

(b) in the case of an order made at first instance by the Crown Court, to the Court of Appeal.

(2–5) *Repealed.*

(6) The appeal court may affirm, vary or revoke the order as it thinks fit

[This regulation is printed as amended by the *Costs in Criminal Cases (General) (Amendment) Regulations* 2009 (S.I. 2009 No. 2720) which came into force with effect from October 30, 2009.]

Recovery of sums due under a wasted costs order

3D. Where the person required to make a payment in respect of sums due under a wasted costs order fails to do so, the payment may be recovered summarily as a sum adjudged to be paid as a civil debt by order of a magistrates' court by the party benefiting from the order, save that where he was legally aided or an order for the payment of costs out of central funds was made in his favour, the power to recover shall be exercisable by the Lord Chancellor. **30–41**

Extra costs may arise when a lawyer is at fault in the conduct of a case before the court. The court has power to order legal representatives to pay personally or be disallowed his own costs when wasted costs are incurred as a result of his actions or omissions. Wasted costs are defined in s.19A. The *Costs in Criminal Cases (General) (Amendment) Regulations* 2009 (S.I. 2009 No. 2720) came into force on October 30, 2009. Procedural elements are removed from some of the existing regulations as these aspects are now covered by the new Pt 76 of the *Criminal Procedure Rules* 2011. The regulations which apply to wasted costs orders have been amended accordingly and reference must be made to the *CPR* to ascertain the procedure applying to such applications. See Appendix G. **30–42**

This is a harsh measure and case law provides some guidance on how the Act and regulations should be applied. In *Re A Barrister (Wasted Costs Order) (No. 1 of 1991)* [1993] Q.B. 293, the Court of Appeal gave the following guidance for the making of wasted costs orders against legal representatives.

1. There is a clear need for any court or judge intending to exercise the wasted costs jurisdiction to formulate carefully and concisely the complaint and the grounds upon which such an order may be sought. The measures are draconian and the grounds must be clear and particular.
2. Where necessary a transcript of the relevant part of the proceedings under discussion should be available. And in accordance with the Rules, a transcript of a wasted costs hearing must be made.
3. A defendant involved in a case where such proceedings are contemplated should be present, if after discussion, with counsel, it is thought that his interests may be affected and he should certainly be present and represented if the matter might affect the course of his trial. Regulation 3B(2) of the *Costs in Criminal Cases (General) (Amendment) Regulations* 1991 furthermore requires that before a wasted costs order is made "the court shall allow the legal or other representative and any party to the proceedings to make representations." There may be cases where it may be appropriate for counsel for the Crown to be present.
4. A three-stage test or approach is recommended when a wasted costs order is contemplated. (i) Has there been an improper, unreasonable or negligent act or

omission? (ii) As a result, have any costs been incurred by a party? (iii) If these questions are answered in the affirmative, should the court exercise its discretion to disallow or order the representative to meet the whole or any party of the relevant costs, and if so what specific sum is involved?

5. It is inappropriate to propose any deal or settlement that the representative might forgo fees. The judge should formally state his complaint, in chambers, and invite the representative to make his or her own comments. After any other party has been heard the judge should give a formal ruling. Discursive conversations may be unfair and should certainly not take place.
6. The judge must specify the sum to be disallowed or ordered. Alternatively the relevant available procedure should be substituted, should it be impossible to fix the sum.

30–43 In this case the wasted costs order was made against counsel whose unexplained and unrefuted remark led the judge to discharge the jury. Because the proper procedure was not followed the order was held invalid. The procedure in the magistrates' court will be slightly different as no full transcripts are taken so the hearing will be recorded only by way of the notes made by the legal adviser. The suggestion of dealing with the matter in chambers is not applicable to the magistrates' court although the court may be cleared in sensitive cases. The general principles enunciated should otherwise be followed. This guidance was approved in *Re Mintz (Wasted Costs Order), The Times*, July 16, 1999, CA, where an order was made against counsel who failed to reach prompt agreement about the removal of certain passages from interview transcripts. The judge did not indicate his complaint in chambers; counsel was not invited to make representations and the amount of costs was not specified. These irregularities led to the order being quashed. Failure to allow representations is in breach of reg.3B and failure to specify the amount ordered is a fatal flaw. See also *Re Wiseman Lee (Solicitors) (Wasted Costs Order) (No. 5 of 2000), The Times*, April 5, 2001 and *Harry Jagdev & Co (Wasted Costs Order) (No. 2 of 1999), The Times*, August 12, 1999.

30–44 Because of the procedural irregularities in these cases, the courts did not go into the question of whether the conduct complained of justified the making of such an order. Guidance on this issue is found in *Ridehalgh v. Horsefield* [1994] Ch. 205, CA. The court considered a number of applications and reviewed the level of conduct that could be said to give rise to wasted costs. It was stated that "improper, unreasonable and negligent" were words that bore their established meaning.

1. Improper included conduct that amounted to any significant breach of a substantial duty imposed by a relevant code of professional conduct and included conduct so regarded by the consensus of professional opinion.
2. Unreasonable described conduct which did not permit of a reasonable explanation.
3. Negligent was to be understood in a non-technical way to denote a failure to act with the competence reasonably to be expected of ordinary members of the profession.

30–45 It was further said that the conduct so characterised had to be established to be directly causative of any wasted costs. From the cases under consideration it was held that such an order was not appropriate for a solicitor pursuing a hopeless case. It was not improper, unreasonable or negligent to act for a defendant whose case was doomed to failure. Also late acceptance of a brief by counsel which led to delay in the case was held to be neither improper nor unnecessary as the "cab rank" principle applied and counsel was obliged to accept the case. The failure of a solicitor to pick up an urgent fax which led to a witness unnecessarily attending court through counsel and incurring costs was held not to amount to a "serious error" or "serious misconduct" so as to justify the making of a wasted costs order against the legal representatives; *Angela Taylor Solicitors* [2008] EWCA Crim. 3085. In *Boodhoo* [2007] 1 Cr.App.R. 32 a wasted costs order was made against a solicitor who had withdrawn from representing a defendant who failed to attend for trial. The trial court wished to proceed in the defendant's absence but considered itself unable to do so as counsel said that the instructing solicitors would withdraw. The wasted costs order was made against the solicitor on the basis that his actions had led to the trial not proceeding. On appeal it was held that the behaviour of the solicitor was neither improper nor negligent. Nor did the appeal court consider that the decision to withdraw from the case was unreasonable. On the facts of the case it was held that the appellant was entitled to conclude that he could not properly represent the defendant at trial. The defendant had indicated he would not attend at his trial yet his defence rested on alibi evidence. In those circumstances it was held not to be unreasonable for the solicitor to conclude that he should withdraw.

This case demonstrates the importance of ensuring that the provisions of s.19(3) are not only applied but that a full explanation is given as to the finding of an improper, negligent or unreasonable act or ommission. The court said that the role of the independent, professional advocate in the administration of justice had to be borne in mind and it should not be undermined by illegitimate pressures. It appears that a wasted costs order should not be made simply as a mark of the court's displeasure when a certain course of action is taken but must be clearly justified because of impropriety, negligence or unreasonableness.

In *Re P. (A Barrister) (Wasted Costs Order)* [2002] 1 Cr.App.R. 207, CA it was held that a judge could decline to deal with an application for a wasted costs order arising from a case he has dealt with but the fact that the judge had expressed views in relation to the conduct of the barrister against whom the order was sought did not of itself amount to bias or the appearance of bias. The appeal court took the view that it was in the interest of both the public and the profession to retain the summary nature of the procedure which was quick, economical and effective so it was acceptable for the trial judge to deal with wasted costs and not adjourn the matter to another court. It was also held that the standard of proof was the normal civil standard unless the allegation was one of serious misconduct or crime. In this case the misconduct complained of was an inference by the defence that the defendant was of good character when in fact he had spent convictions. The jury was discharged as a result of hearing about the convictions and the wasted costs order was upheld.

G. AWARD OF COSTS AGAINST THIRD PARTIES

Prosecution of Offences Act 1985 s.19B

Provision for award of costs against third parties

19B.—(1) The Lord Chancellor may by regulations make provision empowering magistrates' courts, the Crown Court and the Court of Appeal to make a third party costs order if the condition in subsection (3) is satisfied. **30–46**

(2) A "third party costs order" is an order as to the payment of costs incurred by a party to criminal proceedings by a person who is not a party to those proceedings ("the third party").

(3) The condition is that—

(a) there has been serious misconduct (whether or not constituting a contempt of court) by the third party, and

(b) the court considers it appropriate, having regard to that misconduct, to make a third party costs order against him.

(4) Regulations made under this section may, in particular—

(a) specify types of misconduct in respect of which a third party costs order may not be made;

(b) allow the making of a third party costs order at any time;

(c) make provision for any other order as to costs which has been made in respect of the proceedings to be varied on, or taken account of in, the making of a third party costs order;

(d) make provision for account to be taken of any third party costs order in the making of any other order as to costs in respect of the proceedings.

(5) Regulations made under this section in relation to magistrates' courts must provide

that the third party may appeal to the Crown Court against a third party costs order made by a magistrates' court.

(6) Regulations made under this section in relation to the Crown Court must provide that the third party may appeal to the Court of Appeal against a third party costs order made by the Crown Court.

[This section was inserted by the *Courts Act* 2003, s.93.]

30–47 This section allows the Lord Chancellor to make regulations giving powers to the courts, including magistrates' courts, to make an order for costs against a person who is not a party to the proceedings, known as a "third party costs order".

An order can only be made if the serious misconduct condition is met and the court considers such an order to be appropriate. The *Costs in Criminal Cases (General) (Amendment) Regulations* 2004 (S.I. 2004 No.2408) came into force on October 18, 2004 and make provision for third party costs orders to be made in respect of any misconduct occurring after that date. The Regulations set out the procedure to be followed so that an order may be made at any time after the proceedings or also during the proceedings if the court decides there are good reasons for the order to be made then. There is a right of appeal to the Crown Court and the order is enforceable as a civil debt in the magistrates' court.

H. ENFORCEMENT

Magistrates' Courts Act 1980, s.76

Enforcement of sums adjudged to be paid

30–48 **76.**—(1) Subject to the following provi sions of this Part of this Act, and to section 132 below, where default is made in paying a sum adjudged to be paid by a conviction or order of a magistrates' court, the court may issue a warrant of distress for the purposes of levying the sum or issue a warrant committing the defaulter to prison.

(2) A warrant of commitment may be issued as aforesaid either—

(a) where it appears on the return to a warrant of distress that the money and goods of the defaulter are insufficient to satisfy the sum with the costs and charges of levying the sum; or

(b) instead of a warrant of distress.

(3) The period for which a person may be committed to prison under such a warrant as aforesaid shall not, subject to the provisions of any enactment passed after 31st December 1879, exceed the period applicable to the case under Schedule 4 to this Act.

(4)–(6) [apply to civil maintenance orders.]

[This section is reprinted as amended by the *Criminal Justice Act* 1982, s.78 and Sched. 16.]

30–49 Costs may be enforced in the same way as fines, see *ante*, Ch.24. A sum adjudged to be paid by a conviction or order includes costs, damages or compensation: s.150(3) of the *Magistrates' Courts Act* 1980. Any period of imprisonment ordered in default of payment cannot be less than five days: *Magistrates' Courts Act* 1980, s.132. Maximum periods of imprisonment in default are fixed according to the amount ordered to be paid. There is no power to remit costs, but nominal default orders may be made.

APPENDIX A

PACE CODES
(CODES OF PRACTICE ISSUED UNDER THE POLICE AND CRIMINAL EVIDENCE ACT 1984)

I. INTRODUCTION

Section 66 of the *Police and Criminal Evidence Act* 1984 requires the Secretary of State to issue codes of practice in connection with the exercise of various statutory powers and other procedures. **A–1**

At present there are eight codes issued under that section:

— Code A (stop and search): see *post*, Appendix A–2 *et seq.*

— Code B (search and seizure): see *post*, Appendix A–18 *et seq.*

— Code C (detention, treatment and questioning of persons): see *post*, Appendix A–38 *et seq.*

— Code D (identification): see *post*, Appendix A–112 *et seq.*

— Code E (tape recording of interviews): see *post*, Appendix A–162 *et seq.*

— Code F (visual recording of interviews): see *post*, Appendix A–180 *et seq.*

— Code G (arrest): see *post*, Appendix A–203 *et seq.*

— Code H (detention etc. under the *Terrorism Act* 2000) (not reproduced in this work).

With effect from January 1, 2006, the *Police and Criminal Evidence Act 1984 (Codes of Practice) Order* 2005 (S.I. 2005 No. 3503) revised Codes A to F and added a new Code G. **A–1a**

With effect from effect from July 25, 2006, the *Police and Criminal Evidence Act 1984 (Code of Practice C and Code of Practice H) Order* 2006 (S.I. 2006 No. 1938) revised Code C and added a new Code H.

With effect from August 31, 2006, the *Police and Criminal Evidence Act 1984 (Codes of Practice) (Revisions to Code A) Order* 2006 (S.I. 2006 No. 2165) made further revisions Code A.

With effect from February 1, 2008, the *Police and Criminal Evidence Act 1984 (Codes of Practice) Order* 2008 (S.I. 2008 No. 167) made further revisions to Codes A to E.

With effect from October 27, 2008, the *Police and Criminal Evidence Act 1984 (Codes of Practice) (Revisions to Code A) Order* 2008 (S.I. 2008 No. 2638) made further revisions to Code A

With effect from January 1, 2009, the *Police and Criminal Evidence Act 1984 (Codes of Practice) (Revisions to Code A) (No. 2) Order* 2008 (S.I. 2008 No. 3146) made further revisions to Code A.

With effect from May 1, 2010, the *Police and Criminal Evidence Act 1984 (Codes of Practice) (Revisions to Codes E and F) Order* 2010 (S.I. 2010 No. 1108) made further revisions to Codes E and F.

With effect from March 7, 2011, the *Police and Criminal Evidence Act 1984 (Codes of Practice) (Revisions of Codes A, B and D) Order* 2011 (S.I. 2011 No. 412) made further revisions to Codes A, B and D.

The Codes printed in this Appendix incorporate these amendments.

II. CODE A (STOP AND SEARCH)

A. Code of Practice for the Exercise by:

Police Officers of Statutory Powers of Stop and Search
Police Officers and Police Staff of Requirements to Record Public Encounters

Commencement—Transitional arrangements

A–2 This code applies to any search by a police officer or any public encounter taking place after midnight, twenty-one days after the day on which the *Police and Criminal Evidence Act 1984 (Codes of Practice) (Revision of Codes A, B and D) Order 2010* [*sic*] is made.

General

This code of practice must be readily available at all police stations for consultation by police officers, police staff, detained persons and members of the public.

The notes for guidance included are not provisions of this code, but are guidance to police officers and others about its application and interpretation. Provisions in the annexes to the code are provisions of this code.

This code governs the exercise by police officers of statutory powers to search a person or a vehicle without first making an arrest. The main stop and search powers to which this code applies are set out in Annex A, but that list should not be regarded as definitive. [See *Note 1*.] In addition, it covers requirements on police officers and police staff to record encounters not governed by statutory powers.

This code does not apply to:

(a) the powers of stop and search under;

(i) *Aviation Security Act* 1982, section 27(2);

(ii) *Police and Criminal Evidence Act* 1984, section 6(1) (which relates specifically to powers of constables employed by statutory undertakers on the premises of the statutory undertakers);

(b) searches carried out for the purposes of examination under Schedule 7 to the *Terrorism Act* 2000 and to which the Code of Practice issued under paragraph 6 of Schedule 14 to the *Terrorism Act* 2000 applies.

A:1 Principles governing stop and search

A–3 **A:**1.1 Powers to stop and search must be used fairly, responsibly, with respect for people being searched and without unlawful discrimination. The *Equality Act* 2010 makes it unlawful for police officers to discriminate against, harass or victimise any person on the grounds of the "protected characteristics" of age, disability, gender reassignment, race, religion or belief, sex and sexual orientation, marriage and civil partnership, pregnancy and maternity when using their powers. When police forces are carrying out their functions they also have a duty to have regard to the need to eliminate unlawful discrimination, harassment and victimisation and to take steps to foster good relations.

A:1.2 The intrusion on the liberty of the person stopped or searched must be brief and detention for the purposes of a search must take place at or near the location of the stop.

A:1.3 If these fundamental principles are not observed the use of powers to stop and search may be drawn into question. Failure to use the powers in the proper manner reduces their effectiveness. Stop and search can play an important role in the detection and prevention of crime, and using the powers fairly makes them more effective.

A:1.4 The primary purpose of stop and search powers is to enable officers to allay or confirm suspicions about individuals without exercising their power of arrest. Officers may be required to justify the use or authorisation of such powers, in relation both to individual searches and the overall pattern of their activity in this regard, to their supervisory officers or in court. Any misuse of the powers is likely to be harmful to policing and lead to mistrust of the police. Officers must also be able to explain their actions to the member of the public searched. The misuse of these powers can lead to disciplinary action.

A:1.5 An officer must not search a person, even with his or her consent, where no power to search is applicable. Even where a person is prepared to submit to a search voluntarily, the person must not be searched unless the necessary legal power exists, and the search must be in accordance with the relevant power and the provisions of this code. The only exception, where an officer does not require a specific power, applies to searches of persons entering sports grounds or other premises carried out with their consent given as a condition of entry.

A:2 Explanation of powers to stop and search

A:2.1 This code applies to powers of stop and search as follows: A–4

(a) powers which require reasonable grounds for suspicion, before they may be exercised; that articles unlawfully obtained or possessed are being carried, or under section 43 of the *Terrorism Act* 2000 that a person is a terrorist;

(b) authorised under section 60 of the *Criminal Justice and Public Order Act* 1994, based upon a reasonable belief that incidents involving serious violence may take place or that people are carrying dangerous instruments or offensive weapons within any locality in the police area or that it is expediant to use the powers to find such insruments or weapons that have been used in incidents of serious violence;

(c) authorised under section 44(1) and (2) of the *Terrorism Act* 2000 based upon a consideration that the exercise of the power is necessary for the prevention of acts of terrorism (see paragraph 2.18A), and;

(d) powers to search a person who has not been arrested in the exercise of a power to search premises (see Code B, paragraph 2.4).

Searches requiring reasonable grounds for suspicion

A:2.2 Reasonable grounds for suspicion depend on the circumstances in each case. There must be an objective basis for that suspicion based on facts, information, and/or intelligence which are relevant to the likelihood of finding an article of a certain kind or, in the case of searches under section 43 of the *Terrorism Act* 2000, to the likelihood that the person is a terrorist. Reasonable suspicion can never be supported on the basis of personal factors. It must rely on intelligence or information about, or some specific behaviour by the person concerned. For example, unless the police have a description of a suspect, a person's physical appearance (including any of the "protected characteristics" set out in the *Equality Act* 2010 (see paragraph 1.1)), or the fact that the person is known to have a previous conviction, cannot be used alone or in combination with each other, or in combination with any other factor, as the reason for searching that person. Reasonable suspicion cannot be based on generalisations or stereotypical images of certain groups or categories of people as more likely to be involved in criminal activity. A person's religion cannot be considered as reasonable grounds for suspicion and should never be considered as a reason to stop or stop and search an individual. A–5

Appendices

A:2.3 Reasonable suspicion can sometimes exist without specific information or intelligence and on the basis of the behaviour of a person. For example, if an officer encounters someone on the street at night who is obviously trying to hide something, the officer may (depending on the other surrounding circumstances) base such suspicion on the fact that this kind of behaviour is often linked to stolen or prohibited articles being carried. Similarly, for the purposes of section 43 of the *Terrorism Act* 2000, suspicion that a person is a terrorist may arise from the person's behaviour at or near a location which has been identified as a potential target for terrorists.

A:2.4 However, reasonable suspicion should normally be linked to accurate and current intelligence or information, such as information describing an article being carried, a suspected offender, or a person who has been seen carrying a type of article known to have been stolen recently from premises in the area. Searches based on accurate and current intelligence or information are more likely to be effective. Targeting searches in a particular area at specified crime problems increases their effectiveness and minimises inconvenience to law-abiding members of the public. It also helps in justifying the use of searches both to those who are searched and to the public. This does not however prevent stop and search powers being exercised in other locations where such powers may be exercised and reasonable suspicion exists.

A:2.5 Searches are more likely to be effective, legitimate, and secure public confidence when reasonable suspicion is based on a range of factors. The overall use of these powers is more likely to be effective when up to date and accurate intelligence or information is communicated to officers and they are well-informed about local crime patterns.

A:2.6 Where there is reliable information or intelligence that members of a group or gang habitually carry knives unlawfully or weapons or controlled drugs, and wear a distinctive item of clothing or other means of identification to indicate their membership of the group or gang, that distinctive item of clothing or other means of identification may provide reasonable grounds to stop and search a person. [See *Note 9*.]

A:2.7 A police officer may have reasonable grounds to suspect that a person is in innocent possession of a stolen or prohibited article or other item for which he or she is empowered to search. In that case the officer may stop and search the person even though there would be no power of arrest.

A:2.8 Under section 43(1) of the *Terrorism Act* 2000 a constable may stop and search a person whom the officer reasonably suspects to be a terrorist to discover whether the person is in possession of anything which may constitute evidence that the person is a terrorist. These searches may only be carried out by an officer of the same sex as the person searched (see Annex F). An authorisation under section 44(1) of the *Terrorism Act* 2000 allows vehicles to be stopped and searched by a constable in uniform who reasonably suspects that articles which could be used in connection with terrorism will be found in the vehicle or in anything in or on that vehicle. See paragraph 2.18A below.

A:2.9 An officer who has reasonable grounds for suspicion may detain the person concerned in order to carry out a search. Before carrying out a search the officer may ask questions about the person's behaviour or presence in circumstances which gave rise to the suspicion. As a result of questioning the detained person, the reasonable grounds for suspicion necessary to detain that person may be confirmed or, because of a satisfactory explanation, be eliminated. [See *Notes 2* and *3*.] Questioning may also reveal reasonable grounds to suspect the possession of a different kind of unlawful article from that originally suspected. Reasonable grounds for suspicion however cannot be provided retrospectively by such questioning during a person's detention or by refusal to answer any questions put.

A:2.10 If, as a result of questioning before a search, or other circumstances which come to the attention of the officer, there cease to be reasonable grounds for suspecting that an article is being carried of a kind for which there is a power to stop and search, no search may take place. [See *Note 3*.] In the absence of any other lawful power to detain, the person is free to leave at will and must be so informed.

A:2.11 There is no power to stop or detain a person in order to find grounds for a search. Police officers have many encounters with members of the public which do not involve detaining people against their will. If reasonable grounds for suspicion emerge during such an encounter, the officer may search the person, even though no grounds existed when the encounter began. If an officer is detaining someone for the purpose of a search, he or she should inform the person as soon as detention begins.

Searches authorised under section 60 of the Criminal Justice and Public Order Act 1994

A:2.12 Authority for a constable in uniform to stop and search under section 60 of the *Criminal Justice and Public Order Act* 1994 may be given if the authorising officer reasonably believes:

(a) that incidents involving serious violence may take place in any locality in the officer's police area, and it is expedient to use these powers to prevent their occurrence;

(b) that persons are carrying dangerous instruments or offensive weapons without good reason in any locality in the officer's police area or

(c) that an incident involving serious violence has taken place in the officer's police area, a dangerous incident or offensive weapon used in the incident is being carried by a person in any locality in that police area, and it is expedient to use these powers to find that instrument or weapon.

A:2.13 An authorisation under section 60 may only be given by an officer of the rank of inspector or above, in writing, or orally if paragraph 2.12(c) applies and it is not practicable to give the authorisation in writing. The authorisation (whether written or oral) must specify the grounds on which it was given, the locality in which the powers may be exercised and the period of time for which they are in force. The period authorised shall be no longer than appears reasonably necessary to prevent, or seek to prevent incidents of serious violence, or to deal with the problem of carrying dangerous instruments or offensive weapons. It may not exceed 24 hours. An oral authorisation given where paragraph 2.12(c) applies must be recorded in writing as soon as practicable. [See *Notes 10–13*.]

A:2.14 If an inspector gives an authorisation, he or she must, as soon as practicable, inform an officer of or above the rank of superintendent. This officer may direct that the authorisation shall be extended for a further 24 hours, if violence or the carrying of dangerous instruments or offensive weapons has occurred, or is suspected to have occurred, and the continued use of the powers is considered necessary to prevent or deal with further such activity. That direction must also be given in writing at the time or as soon as practicable afterwards. [See *Note 12*.]

A:2.14A The selection of persons and vehicles under section 60 to be stopped and, if appropriate, searched should reflect an objective assessment of the nature of the incident or weapon in question and the individuals and vehicles thought likely to be associated with that incident or those weapons (see *Notes 10 and 11*). The powers must not be used to stop and search persons and vehicles for reasons unconnected with the purpose of the authorisation. When selecting persons and vehicles to be stopped in response to a specific threat or incident, officers must take care not to discriminate unlawfully against anyone on the grounds of any of the protected characteristics set out in the *Equality Act* 2010 (see paragraph 1.1).

A:2.14B The driver of a vehicle which is stopped under section 60 and any person who is searched under section 60 are entitled to a written statement to that effect if they apply within twelve months from the day the vehicle was stopped or the person was searched. This statement is a record which states that the vehicle was stopped or (as the case may be) that the person was searched under section 60 and it may form part of the search record or be supplied as a separate record.

Powers to require removal of face coverings

A:2.15 Section 60AA of the *Criminal Justice and Public Order Act* 1994 also provides a power to demand the removal of disguises. The officer exercising the power must reasonably believe that someone is wearing an item wholly or mainly for the purpose of concealing identity. There is also a power to seize such items where the officer believes that a person intends to wear them for this purpose. There is no power to stop and search for disguises. An officer may seize any such item which is discovered when exercising a power of search for something else, or which is being carried, and which the officer reasonably believes is intended to be used for concealing anyone's identity. This power can only be used if an authorisation given under section 60, or under section 60AA, is in force. [See *Note 4*] **A–6**

A:2.16 Authority under section 60AA for a constable in uniform to require the removal of disguises and to seize them may be given if the authorising officer reasonably believes that activities may take place in any locality in the officer's police area that are likely to involve the commission of offences and it is expedient to use these powers to prevent or control these activities.

A:2.17 An authorisation under section 60AA may only be given by an officer of the rank of inspector or above, in writing, specifying the grounds on which it was given, the locality in which the powers may be exercised and the period of time for which they are in force. The period authorised shall be no longer than appears reasonably necessary to prevent, or seek to prevent the commission of offences. It may not exceed 24 hours. [See *Notes 10–13*.]

A:2.18 An inspector who gives an authorisation must, as soon as practicable, inform an officer of or above the rank of superintendent. This officer may direct that the authorisation shall be extended for a further 24 hours, if crimes have been committed, or are suspected to have been committed, and the continued use of the powers is considered necessary to prevent or deal with further such activity. This direction must also be given in writing at the time or as soon as practicable afterwards. [See *Note 12*.]

Searches authorised under section 44 of the Terrorism Act 2000

A:2.18A The European Court of Human Rights has ruled that the stop and search powers under sections 44 to 47 of the *Terrorism Act* 2000 are not compatible with the right to a private life under Article 8 of the European Convention on Human Rights. Neither the European Court ruling nor the provisions of this code can amend these statutory provisions. However, in an oral statement made by the Home Secretary in the House of Commons on 8 July 2010, interim guidelines were announced pending a review (with a view to legislative amendment) of these provisions to ensure that police do not exercise any powers under section 44 in a way which would be incompatible with Convention rights. Under these guidelines: **A–7**

(i) Authorisations under section 44(1) should be given, and may be confirmed by the Secretary of State, only:

- in relation to searches of vehicles and anything in or on vehicles, but not searches of drivers or passengers or anything being carried by a driver or passenger; and
- if such searches are considered necessary for the prevention of acts of terrorism.

Note: section 44(3) provides that an authorising officer may give an authorisa-

Appendices

tion when they consider it is "expedient" for the prevention of acts of terrorism, but the test now to be applied is that of necessity—taking account of all of the circumstances.

(ii) A search of a vehicle or of anything in or on a vehicle under section 44(1) should only be carried out if it is reasonably suspected that articles which could be used in connection with terrorism will be found in the vehicle or in anything in or on that vehicle.

Note: this now applies despite the provision in section 45(1)(b) which allows the power to be exercised whether or not the constable has grounds for suspecting the presence of such articles.

(iii) Authorisations to search pedestrians, drivers of vehicles and passengers in vehicles and anything carried by a driver or passenger, are not to be given under section 44(1) or (2) and if given, will not be confirmed. For these searches police must rely on the power under section 43 which requires the person who may be searched to be reasonably suspected of being a terrorist, but does not authorise the removal of headgear or footwear in public.

The provisions of paragraphs 2.1, 2.8, 2.19 to 2.26, 3.5, Annex A, paragraphs 15 and 16, and Annex C, paragraph 1, are amended by this code to reflect these guidelines.

A:2.19 An officer of the rank of assistant chief constable (or equivalent) or above, may give authority under section 44 of the *Terrorism Act* 2000 for a constable in uniform to exercise the power to stop and search any vehicle and anything in or on any vehicle, in the whole or any part or parts of the authorising officer's police area. An authorisation may only be given if the officer considers it is necessary for the prevention of acts of terrorism.

A:2.20 If an authorisation is given orally at first, it must be confirmed in writing by the officer who gave it as soon as reasonably practicable.

A:2.21 When giving an authorisation, the officer must specify the geographical area in which the power may be used, and the time and date that the authorisation ends (up to a maximum of 28 days from the time the authorisation was given). [See *Notes 12* and *13*.]

A:2.22 The officer giving an authorisation under section 44(1) must cause the Secretary of State to be informed, as soon as reasonably practicable, that such an authorisation has been given. An authorisation which is not confirmed by the Secretary of State within 48 hours of its having been given, shall have effect up until the end of that 48 hour period or the end of the period specified in the authorisation (whichever is the earlier). [See *Note 14*.]

A:2.23 Following notification of the authorisation, the Secretary of State may:

(i) cancel the authorisation with immediate effect or with effect from such other time as he or she may direct;

(ii) confirm it but for a shorter period than that specified in the authorisation; or

(iii) confirm the authorisation as given.

A:2.24 When an authorisation under section 44 is given, a constable in uniform may exercise the power:

(a) only for the purpose of stopping and searching a vehicle and anything in or on a vehicle for articles of a kind which could be used in connection with terrorism (see paragraph 2.25); and

(b) only if there are reasonable grounds for suspecting the presence of such articles. See paragraphs 2.2 to 2.11, "Searches requiring reasonable grounds for suspicion"

A:2.24A When a community support officer on duty and in uniform has been conferred powers under section 44(1) of the *Terrorism Act* 2000 by a chief officer of their force, the exercise of this power must comply with the requirements of this code of practice, including the recording requirements.

A:2.25 Paragraphs 2.2 to 2.11 above ("Searches requiring reasonable grounds for suspicion") are to be applied to the stopping and searching of vehicles when an authorisation under section 44(1) is given.

A:2.26 The powers under sections 43 and 44(1) of the *Terrorism Act* 2000 allow a constable to search only for articles which could be used for terrorist purposes. However, this would not prevent a search being carried out under other powers if, in the course of exercising these powers, the officer formed reasonable grounds for suspicion.

Powers to search in the exercise of a power to search premises

A–8 **A:**2.27 The following powers to search premises also authorise the search of a person, not under arrest, who is found on the premises during the course of the search:

(a) section 139B of the *Criminal Justice Act* 1988 under which a constable may enter school premises and search the premises and any person on those premises for any bladed or pointed article or offensive weapon;

(b) under a warrant issued under section 23(3) of the *Misuse of Drugs Act* 1971 to search premises for drugs or documents but only if the warrant specifically authorises the search of persons found on the premises; and

(c) under a search warrant or order issued under paragraph 1, 3 or 11 of Schedule 5 to the *Terrorism Act* 2000 to search premises and any person found there for material likely to be of substantial value to a terrorist investigation.

A:2.28 Before the power under section 139B of the *Criminal Justice Act* 1988 may be exercised, the constable must have reasonable grounds to believe that an offence under section 139A of the *Criminal Justice Act* 1988 (having a bladed or pointed article or offensive weapon on school premises) has been or is being committed. A warrant to search premises and persons found therein may be issued under section 23(3) of the *Misuse of Drugs Act* 1971 if there are reasonable grounds to suspect that controlled drugs or certain documents are in the possession of a person on the premises.

A:2.29 The powers in paragraph 2.27 do not require prior specific grounds to suspect that the person to be searched is in possession of an item for which there is an existing power to search. However, it is still necessary to ensure that the selection and treatment of those searched under these powers is based upon objective factors connected with the search of the premises, and not upon personal prejudice.

A:3 Conduct of searches

A:3.1 All stops and searches must be carried out with courtesy, consideration and respect for the person concerned. This has a significant impact on public confidence in the police. Every reasonable effort must be made to minimise the embarrassment that a person being searched may experience. [See *Note 4*.] **A–9**

Appendices

A:3.2 The co-operation of the person to be searched must be sought in every case, even if the person initially objects to the search. A forcible search may be made only if it has been established that the person is unwilling to co-operate or resists. Reasonable force may be used as a last resort if necessary to conduct a search or to detain a person or vehicle for the purposes of a search.

A:3.3 The length of time for which a person or vehicle may be detained must be reasonable and kept to a minimum. Where the exercise of the power requires reasonable suspicion, the thoroughness and extent of a search must depend on what is suspected of being carried, and by whom. If the suspicion relates to a particular article which is seen to be slipped into a person's pocket, then, in the absence of other grounds for suspicion or an opportunity for the article to be moved elsewhere, the search must be confined to that pocket. In the case of a small article which can readily be concealed, such as a drug, and which might be concealed anywhere on the person, a more extensive search may be necessary. In the case of searches mentioned in paragraph 2.1(b), (c), and (d), which do not require reasonable grounds for suspicion, officers may make any reasonable search to look for items for which they are empowered to search. [See *Note 5*.]

A:3.4 The search must be carried out at or near the place where the person or vehicle was first detained. [See *Note 6*.]

A:3.5 There is no power to require a person to remove any clothing in public other than an outer coat, jacket or gloves, except under section 60AA of the *Criminal Justice and Public Order Act* 1994 (which empowers a constable to require a person to remove any item worn to conceal identity). [See *Notes 4* and *6*.] A search in public of a person's clothing which has not been removed must be restricted to superficial examination of outer garments. This does not, however, prevent an officer from placing his or her hand inside the pockets of the outer clothing, or feeling round the inside of collars, socks and shoes if this is reasonably necessary in the circumstances to look for the object of the search or to remove and examine any item reasonably suspected to be the object of the search. For the same reasons, subject to the restrictions on the removal of headgear, a person's hair may also be searched in public (see paragraphs 3.1 and 3.3).

A:3.6 Where on reasonable grounds it is considered necessary to conduct a more thorough search (*e.g.* by requiring a person to take off a T-shirt), this must be done out of public view, for example, in a police van unless paragraph 3.7 applies, or police station if there is one nearby. [See *Note 6*.] Any search involving the removal of more than an outer coat, jacket, gloves, headgear or footwear, or any other item concealing identity, may only be made by an officer of the same sex as the person searched and may not be made in the presence of anyone of the opposite sex unless the person being searched specifically requests it. [See *Notes 4, 7* and *8*.]

A:3.7 Searches involving exposure of intimate parts of the body must not be conducted as a routine extension of a less thorough search, simply because nothing is found in the course of the initial search. Searches involving exposure of intimate parts of the body may be carried out only at a nearby police station or other nearby location which is out of public view (but not a police vehicle). These searches must be conducted in accordance with paragraph 11 of Annex A to Code C except that an intimate search mentioned in paragraph 11(f) of Annex A to Code C may not be authorised or carried out under any stop and search powers. The other provisions of Code C do not apply to the conduct and recording of searches of persons detained at police stations in the exercise of stop and search powers. [See *Note 7*.]

Steps to be taken prior to a search

A–10 **A:**3.8 Before any search of a detained person or attended vehicle takes place the officer must take reasonable steps, if not in uniform (see paragraph 3.9), to show their warrant card to the person to be searched or in charge of the vehicle to be searched and whether or not in uniform, to give that person the following information:

(a) that they are being detained for the purposes of a search;

(b) the officer's name (except in the case of enquiries linked to the investigation of terrorism, or otherwise where the officer reasonably believes that giving his or her name might put him or her in danger, in which case a warrant or other identification number shall be given) and the name of the police station to which the officer is attached;

(c) the legal search power which is being exercised; and

(d) a clear explanation of:

(i) the object of the search in terms of the article or articles for which there is a power to search; and

(ii) in the case of:

- the power under section 60 of the *Criminal Justice and Public Order Act* 1994 (see paragraph 2.1(b)), the nature of the power, the authorisation and the fact that it has been given;
- the power under section 44 of the *Terrorism Act* 2000, the nature of the power, the authorisation and the fact that it has been given and the grounds for suspicion; (see paragraph 2.1(c) and 2.18A);
- all other powers requiring reasonable suspicion (see paragraph 2.1(a)), the grounds for that suspicion;

(e) that they are entitled to a copy of the record of the search if one is made (see section 4 below) if they ask within 3 months from the date of the search and:

(i) if they are not arrested and taken to a police station as a result of the search and it is practicable to make the record on the spot, that immediately after the search is completed they will be given, if they request, either:

- a copy of the record, or
- a receipt which explains how they can obtain a copy of the full record or access to an electronic copy of the record, or

(ii) if they are arrested and taken to a police station as a result of the search, that the record will be made at the station as part of their custody record and they will be given, if they request, a copy of their custody record which includes a record of the search as soon as practicable whilst they are at the station. [See *Note 16*.]

A:3.9 Stops and searches under the powers mentioned in paragraphs 2.1(b), and (c) may be undertaken only by a constable in uniform.

A:3.10 The person should also be given information about police powers to stop and search and the individual's rights in these circumstances.

A:3.11 If the person to be searched, or in charge of a vehicle to be searched, does not appear to understand what is being said, or there is any doubt about the person's ability to understand English, the officer must take reasonable steps to bring information regarding the person's rights and any relevant provisions of this code to his or her attention. If the person is deaf or cannot understand English and is accompanied by someone, then the officer must try to establish whether that person can interpret or otherwise help the officer to give the required information.

A:4 Recording requirements

(a) Searches which do not result in an arrest

A:4.1 When an officer carries out a search in the exercise of any power to which this code applies and the search does not result in the person searched or person in charge of the vehicle searched being arrested and taken to a police station, a record must be made of it, electronically or on paper, unless there are exceptional circumstances which make this wholly impracticable (*e.g.* in situations involving public disorder or when the recording officer's presence is urgently required elsewhere). If a record is to be made, the officer carrying out the search must make the record on the spot unless this is not practicable, in which case the officer must make the record as soon as practicable after the search is completed. [See *Note 16.*] **A–11**

A:4.2 If the record is made at the time, the person who has been searched or who is in charge of the vehicle that has been searched must be asked if they want a copy and if they do, they must be given immediately, either:

- a copy of the record, or
- a receipt which explains how they can obtain a copy of the full record or access to an electronic copy of the record.

A:4.2A An officer is not required to provide a copy of the full record or a receipt at the time if they are called to an incident of higher priority. [See *Note 21.*]

(b) Searches which result in an arrest

A:4.2B If a search in the exercise of any power to which this code applies results in a person being arrested and taken to a police station, the officer carrying out the search is responsible for ensuring that a record of the search is made as part of their custody record. The custody officer must then ensure that the person is asked if they want a copy of the record and if they do, that they are given a copy as soon as practicable. [See *Note 16.*]

(c) Record of search

A:4.3 The record of a search must always include the following information:

(a) a note of the self-defined ethnicity, and if different, the ethnicity as perceived by the officer making the search, of the person searched or of the person in charge of the vehicle searched (as the case may be) [see *Note 18*];

(b) the date, time and place the person or vehicle was searched [see *Note 6*];

(c) the object of the search in terms of the article or articles for which there is a power to search;

(d) in the case of:

- the power under section 60 of the *Criminal Justice and Public Order Act* 1994 (see paragraph 2.1(b)), the nature of the power, the authorisation and the fact that it has been given [see *Note 17*];
- the power under section 44 of the *Terrorism Act* 2000, the nature of the power, the authorisation and the fact that it has been given and the grounds for suspicion [see paragraphs 2.1(c) and 2.18A and *Note 17*];
- all other powers requiring reasonable suspicion (see paragraph 2.1(a)), the grounds for that suspicion;

(e) subject to paragraph 3.8(b), the identity of the officer carrying out the search. [See *Note 15.*]

A:4.3A For the purposes of completing the search record, there is no requirement to record the name, address and date of birth of the person searched or the person in charge of a vehicle which is searched and the person is under no obligation to provide this information.

A:4.4 Nothing in paragraph 4.3 requires the names of police officers to be shown on the search record or any other record required to be made under this code in the case of enquiries linked to the investigation of terrorism or otherwise where an officer reasonably believes that recording names might endanger the officers. In such cases the record must show the officers' warrant or other identification number and duty station.

A:4.5 A record is required for each person and each vehicle searched. However, if a person is in a vehicle and both are searched, and the object and grounds of the search are the same, only one record need be completed. If more than one person in a vehicle is searched, separate records for each search of a person must be made. If only a vehicle is searched, the self-defined ethnic background of the person in charge of the vehicle must be recorded, unless the vehicle is unattended.

A:4.6 The record of the grounds for making a search must, briefly but informatively, explain the reason for suspecting the person concerned, by reference to the person's behaviour and/or other circumstances.

A:4.7 Where officers detain an individual with a view to performing a search, but the need to search is eliminated as a result of questioning the person detained, a search should not be carried out and a record is not required. [See paragraph 2.10, *Notes 3* and *22A*.]

A:4.8 After searching an unattended vehicle, or anything in or on it, an officer must leave a notice in it (or on it, if things on it have been searched without opening it) recording the fact that it has been searched.

A:4.9 The notice must include the name of the police station to which the officer concerned is attached and state where a copy of the record of the search may be obtained and how (if applicable) an electronic copy may be accessed and where any application for compensation should be directed.

A:4.10 The vehicle must if practicable be left secure.

Recording of encounters not governed by statutory powers

A:4.11 *Not used.*

A:4.12 There is no national requirement for an officer who requests a person in a public place to account for themselves, *i.e.* their actions, behaviour, presence in an area or possession of anything, to make any record of the encounter or to give the person a receipt. [See *Notes 22A* and *22B*.]

A:5 Monitoring and supervising the use of stop and search powers

A–12 **A:**5.1 Supervising officers must monitor the use of stop and search powers and should consider in particular whether there is any evidence that they are being exercised on the basis of stereotyped images or inappropriate generalisations. Supervising officers should satisfy themselves that the practice of officers under their supervision in stopping, searching and recording is fully in accordance with this code. Supervisors must also examine whether the records reveal any trends or patterns which give cause for concern, and if so take appropriate action to address this.

A:5.2 Senior officers with area or force-wide responsibilities must also monitor the broader use of stop and search powers and, where necessary, take action at the relevant level.

A:5.3 Supervision and monitoring must be supported by the compilation of comprehensive statistical records of stops and searches at force, area and local level. Any apparently disproportionate use of the powers by particular officers or groups of officers or in relation to specific sections of the community should be identified and investigated.

A:5.4 In order to promote public confidence in the use of the powers, forces in consultation with police authorities must make arrangements for the records to be scrutinised by representatives of the community, and to explain the use of the powers at a local level. [See *Note 19*.]

Notes for Guidance

Officers exercising stop and search powers

A–13 **A:**1 *This code does not affect the ability of an officer to speak to or question a person in the ordinary course of the officer's duties without detaining the person or exercising any element of compulsion. It is not the purpose of the code to prohibit such encounters between the police and the community with the co-operation of the person concerned and neither does it affect the principle that all citizens have a duty to help police officers to prevent crime and discover offenders. This is a civic rather than a legal duty; but when a police officer is trying to discover whether, or by whom, an offence has been committed he or she may question any person from whom useful information might be obtained, subject to the restrictions imposed by Code C. A person's unwillingness to reply does not alter this entitlement, but in the absence of a power to arrest, or to detain in order to search, the person is free to leave at will and cannot be compelled to remain with the officer.*

A:2 *In some circumstances preparatory questioning may be unnecessary, but in general a brief conversation or exchange will be desirable not only as a means of avoiding unsuccessful searches, but to explain the grounds for the stop/search, to gain cooperation and reduce any tension there might be surrounding the stop/search.*

A:3 *Where a person is lawfully detained for the purpose of a search, but no search in the event takes place, the detention will not thereby have been rendered unlawful.*

A:4 *Many people customarily cover their heads or faces for religious reasons—for example, Muslim women, Sikh men, Sikh or Hindu women, or Rastafarian men or women. A police officer cannot order the removal of a head or face covering except where there is reason to believe that the item is being worn by the individual wholly or mainly for the purpose of disguising identity, not simply because it disguises identity. Where there may be religious sensitivities about ordering the removal of such an item, the officer should permit the item to be removed out of public view. Where practicable, the item should be removed in the presence of an officer of the same sex as the person and out of sight of anyone of the opposite sex [see Annex F].*

A:5 *A search of a person in public should be completed as soon as possible.*

A:6 *A person may be detained under a stop and search power at a place other than where the person was first detained, only if that place, be it a police station or elsewhere, is nearby. Such a place should be located within a reasonable travelling distance using whatever mode of travel (on foot or by car) is appropriate. This applies to all searches under stop and search powers, whether or not they involve the removal of clothing or exposure of intimate parts of the body (see paragraphs 3.6 and 3.7) or take place in or out of public view. It means, for example, that a search under the stop and search power in section 23 of the* Misuse of Drugs Act *1971 which involves the compulsory removal of more than a person's outer coat, jacket or gloves cannot be carried out unless a place which is both nearby the place they were first detained and out of public view, is available. If a search involves exposure of intimate parts of the body and a police station is not nearby, particular care must be taken to ensure that the location is suitable in that it enables the search to be conducted in accordance with the requirements of paragraph 11 of Annex A to Code C.*

A:7 *A search in the street itself should be regarded as being in public for the purposes of paragraphs 3.6 and 3.7 above, even though it may be empty at the time a search begins. Although there is no power to require a person to do so, there is nothing to prevent an officer from asking a person voluntarily to remove more than an outer coat, jacket or gloves in public.*

A:8 Not used

A:9 *Other means of identification might include jewellery, insignias, tattoos or other features which are known to identify members of the particular gang or group.*

Authorising officers

A:10 *The powers under section 60 are separate from and additional to the normal stop and search powers which require reasonable grounds to suspect an individual of carrying an offensive weapon (or other article). Their overall purpose is to prevent serious violence and the widespread carrying of weapons which might lead to persons being seriously injured by disarming potential offenders or finding weapons that have been used in circumstances where other powers would not be sufficient. They should not therefore be used to replace or circumvent the normal powers for dealing with routine crime problems. A particular example might be an authorisation to prevent serious violence or the carrying of offensive weapons at a sports event by rival team supporters when the expected general appearance and age range of those likely to be responsible, alone, would not be sufficiently distinctive to support reasonable suspicion (see paragraph 2.6). The purpose of the powers under section 60AA is to prevent those involved in intimidatory or violent protests using face coverings to disguise identity.* **A–14**

A:11 *Authorisations under section 60 require a reasonable belief on the part of the authorising officer. This must have an objective basis, for example: intelligence or relevant information such as a history of antagonism and violence between particular groups; previous incidents of violence at, or connected with, particular events or locations; a significant increase in knife-point robberies in a limited area; reports that individuals are regularly carrying weapons in a particular locality; information following an incident in which weapons were used about where the weapons might be found or in the case of section 60AA previous incidents of crimes being committed while wearing face coverings to conceal identity.*

A:12 *It is for the authorising officer to determine the period of time during which the powers mentioned in paragraph 2.1(b) and (c) may be exercised. The officer should set the minimum period he or she considers necessary to deal with the risk of violence, the carrying of knives or offensive weapons, or terrorism or to find dangerous instruments or weapons that have been used. A direction to extend the period authorised under the powers mentioned in paragraph 2.1(b) may be given only once. Thereafter further use of the powers requires a new authorisation. There is no provision to extend an authorisation of the powers mentioned in paragraph 2.1(c); further use of the powers requires a new authorisation.*

A:13 *It is for the authorising officer to determine the geographical area in which the use of the powers is to be authorised. In doing so the officer may wish to take into account factors such as the nature and venue of the anticipated incident or the incident which has taken place, the number of people who may be in the immediate area of that incident, their access to surrounding areas and the anticipated or actual level of violence. The officer should not set a geographical area which is wider than that he or she believes necessary for the purpose of preventing anticipated violence, the carrying of knives or offensive weapons, acts of terrorism, finding a dangerous instrument or weapon that has been used or, in the case of section 60AA, the prevention of commission of offences. It is particularly important to ensure that constables exercising such powers are fully aware of where they may be used. If the area specified is smaller than the whole force area, the officer giving the authorisation should specify either the streets which form the boundary of the area or a divisional boundary within the force area. If the power is to be used in response to a threat or incident that straddles police force areas, an officer from each of the forces concerned will need to give an authorisation.*

A:14 *An officer who has authorised the use of powers under section 44(1) of the* Terrorism Act *2000 must take immediate steps to send a copy of the authorisation to the National Joint Unit, Metropolitan Police Special Branch, who will forward it to the Secretary of State. The Secretary of State should be informed of the reasons for the authorisation. The National Joint Unit will inform the force concerned, within 48 hours of the authorisation being made, whether the Secretary of State has confirmed or cancelled or altered the authorisation. See paragraph 2.18A.*

Recording

A–15 **A:**15 *Where a stop and search is conducted by more than one officer the identity of all the officers engaged in the search must be recorded on the record. Nothing prevents an officer who is present but not directly involved in searching from completing the record during the course of the encounter.*

A:16 *When the search results in the person searched or in charge of a vehicle which is searched being arrested, the requirement to make the record of the search as part of the person's custody record does not apply if the person is granted "street bail" after arrest (see section 30A of* PACE*) to attend a police station and is not taken in custody to the police station. An arrested person's entitlement to a copy of the search record which is made as part of their custody record does not affect their entitlement to a copy of their custody record or any other provisions of* PACE *Code C section 2 (custody records).*

A:17 *It is important for monitoring purposes to specify whether the authority for exercising a stop and search power was given under section 60 of the* Criminal Justice and Public Order Act *1994, or under section 44(1) of the* Terrorism Act *2000.*

A:18 *Officers should record the self-defined ethnicity of every person stopped according to the categories used in the 2001 census question listed in Annex B. The person should be asked to select one of the five main categories representing broad ethnic groups and then a more specific cultural background from within this group. The ethnic classification should be coded for recording purposes using the coding system in Annex B. An additional "Not stated" box is available but should not be offered to respondents explicitly. Officers should be aware and explain to members of the public, especially where concerns are raised, that this information is required to obtain a true picture of stop and search activity and to help improve ethnic monitoring, tackle discriminatory practice, and promote effective use of the powers. If the person gives what appears to the officer to be an "incorrect" answer* (e.g. *a person who appears to be white states that they are black), the officer should record the response that has been given and then record their own perception of the person's ethnic background by using the PNC classification system. If the "Not stated" category is used the reason for this must be recorded on the form.*

A:19 *Arrangements for public scrutiny of records should take account of the right to confidentiality of those stopped and searched. Anonymised forms and/or statistics generated from records should be the focus of the examinations by members of the public.*

A:20 Not used

A:21 *In situations where it is not practicable to provide a written copy of the record or immediate access to an electronic copy of the record or a receipt of the search at the time (see paragraph 4.2A above), the officer should consider giving the person details of the station which they may attend for a copy of the record. A receipt may take the form of a simple business card which includes sufficient information to locate the record should the person ask for copy, for example, the date and place of the search, a reference number or the name of the officer who carried out the search (unless paragraph 4.4 applies).*

A:22 Not used

A:22A *Where there are concerns which make it necessary to monitor any local disproportionality, forces have discretion to direct officers to record the self-defined ethnicity of persons they request to account for themselves in a public place or who they detain with a view to searching but do not search. Guidance should be provided locally and efforts made to minimise the bureaucracy involved. Records should be closely monitored and supervised in line with paragraphs 5.1 to 5.4 and forces can suspend or re-instate recording of these encounters as appropriate.*

A:22B *A person who is asked to account for themselves should, if they request, be given information about how they can report their dissatisfaction about how they have been treated.*

Definition of offensive weapon

A:23 *"Offensive weapon" is defined as any article made or adapted for use for causing injury to the person, or intended by the person having it with him for such use or by someone else. There are three categories of offensive weapons: those made for causing injury to the person; those adapted for such a purpose; and those not so made or adapted, but carried with the intention of causing injury to the person. A firearm, as defined by section 57 of the* Firearms Act *1968, would fall within the definition of offensive weapon if any of the criteria above apply.*

Appendices

A–16

ANNEX A

Summary of main stop and search powers

This table relates to stop and search powers only. Individual statutes below may contain other police powers of entry, search and seizure.

POWER	Object of search	Extent of Search	Where Exercisable
Unlawful articles general			
1. *Public Stores Act* 1875, s.6	HM Stores stolen or unlawfully obtained	Persons, vehicles and vessels	Anywhere where the constabulary powers are exercisable
2. *Firearms Act* 1968, s.47	Firearms	Persons and vehicles	A public place, or anywhere in the case of reasonable suspicion of offences of carrying firearms with criminal intent or trespassing with firearms
3. *Misuse of Drugs Act* 1971, s.23	Controlled drugs	Persons and vehicles	Anywhere
4. *Customs and Excise Management Act* 1979, s.163	Goods: (a) on which duty has not been paid; (b) being unlawfully removed, imported or exported; (c) otherwise liable to forfeiture to HM Revenue and Customs	Vehicles and vessels only	Anywhere
5. *Aviation Security Act* 1982, s.27(1)	Stolen or unlawfully obtained goods	Airport employees and vehicles carrying airport employees or aircraft or any vehicle in a cargo area whether or not carrying an employee	Any designated airport

6. *Police and Criminal Evidence Act* 1984, s.1	Stolen goods; articles for use in certain *Theft Act* offences; offensive weapons, including bladed or sharply-pointed articles (except folding pocket knives with a bladed cutting edge not exceeding 3 inches); prohibited possession of a category 4 (display grade) firework, any person under 18 in possession of an adult firework in a public place.	Persons and vehicles	Where there is public access
	Criminal damage: articles made, adapted or intended for use in destroying or damaging property	Persons and vehicles	Where there is public access
7. *Sporting Events (Control of Alcohol etc.) Act* 1985, s.7	Intoxicating liquor	Persons, coaches and trains	Designated sports grounds or coaches and trains travelling to or from a designated sporting event.
8. *Crossbows Act* 1987, s.4	Crossbows or parts of crossbows (except crossbows with a draw weight of less than 1.4 kilograms)	Persons and vehicles	Anywhere except dwellings
9. *Criminal Justice Act* 1988 s.139B	Offensive weapons, bladed or sharply pointed article	Persons	School premises
Evidence of game and wildlife offences			
10. *Poaching Prevention Act* 1862, s.2	Game or poaching equipment	Persons and vehicles	A public place
11. *Deer Act* 1991, s.12	Evidence of offences under the Act	Persons and vehicles	Anywhere except dwellings
12. *Conservation of Seals Act* 1970, s.4	Seals or hunting equipment	Vehicles only	Anywhere
13. *Protection of Badgers Act* 1992, s.11	Evidence of offences under the Act	Persons and vehicles	Anywhere
14. *Wildlife and Countryside Act* 1981, s.19	Evidence of wildlife offences	Persons and vehicles	Anywhere except dwellings
Other			
15. *Terrorism Act* 2000, s.43(1)	Anything which may constitute evidence that the person is a terrorist	Persons	Anywhere

16. *Terrorism Act* 2000, s.44(1)	Articles of a kind which could be used in connection with terrorism	Vehicles and anything in or on vehicles (see paragraph 2.18A)	Anywhere within the area or locality authorised under subsection (1)
17. [*Not used.*]			
18. Paragraphs 7 and 8 of Schedule 7 to the *Terrorism Act* 2000	Anything relevant to determining if a person being examined falls within section 40(1)(b)	Persons, vehicles, vessels etc. (*Note: these searches are subject to the code of practice and issued under paragraph 6 of Schedule 14 to the* Terrorism Act *2000*)	Ports and airports
19. Section 60 *Criminal Justice and Public Order Act* 1994	Offensive weapons or dangerous instruments to prevent incidents of serious violence or to deal with the carrying of such items or find such items which have been used in incidents of serious violence	Persons and vehicles	Anywhere within a locality authorised under subsection (1)

ANNEX B

Self-Defined ethnic classification categories

A–17

White	**W**
A. *White—British*	W1
B. *White—Irish*	*W2*
C. *Any other White background*	*W9*
Mixed	**M**
D. *White and Black Caribbean*	*M1*
E. *White and Black African*	*M2*
F. *White and Asian*	*M3*
G. *Any other Mixed Background*	*M9*
Asian/ Asian—British	**A**
H. *Asian—Indian*	*A1*
I. *Asian—Pakistani*	*A2*
J. *Asian—Bangladeshi*	*A3*
K. *Any other Asian background*	*A9*
Black / Black—British	***B***
L. *Black—Caribbean*	*B1*
M. *Black African*	*B2*
N. *Any other Black background*	*B9*
Other	**O**
O. *Chinese*	*O1*
P. *Any other*	*O9*
Not stated	NS

ANNEX C

Summary of powers of community support officers to search and seize

The following is a summary of the search and seizure powers that may be exercised by a community support officer (CSO) who has been designated with the relevant powers in accordance with Part 4 of the *Police Reform Act* 2002. A–17a

When exercising any of these powers, a CSO must have regard to any relevant provisions of this code, including section 3 governing the conduct of searches and the steps to be taken prior to a search.

1. Power to stop and search not requiring consent				
Designation	**Power conferred**	**Object of Search**	**Extent of Search**	**Where Exercisable**
Police Reform Act 2002, Schedule 4, paragraph 15	*Terrorism Act* 2000, s.44(1)(a) and (d) and 45(2) (see paragraph 2.18A)	Items intended to be used in connection with terrorism	(a) Vehicles or anything carried in or on the vehicle	Anywhere within area of locality authorised and in the company and under the supervision of a constable.
2. Powers to search requiring the consent of the person and seizure A CSO may detain a person using reasonable force where necessary as set out in Part 1 of Schedule 4 to the *Police Reform Act* 2002. If the person has been lawfully detained, the CSO may search the person provided that person gives consent to such a search in relation to the following:				
Designation	**Powers conferred**	**Object of Search**	**Extent of Search**	**Where Exercisable**
Police Reform Act 2002, Schedule 4, paragraph 7A	(a) *Criminal Justice and Police Act* 2001, s.12(2)	(a) Alcohol or a container for alcohol	(a) Persons	(a) Designated public place
	(b) *Confiscation of Alcohol (Young Persons) Act* 1997, s.1	(b) Alcohol	(b) Persons under 18 years old	(b) Public place
	(c) *Children and Young Persons Act* 1933, s.7(3)	(c) Tobacco or cigarette papers	(c) Persons under 16 years old found smoking	(c) Public place
3. Powers to search not requiring the consent of the person and seizure A CSO may detain a person using reasonable force where necessary as set out in Part 1 of Schedule 4 to the *Police Reform Act* 2002. If the person has been lawfully detained, the CSO may search the person without the need for that person's consent in relation to the following:				
Designation	**Power conferred**	**Object of Search**	**Extent of Search**	**Where Exercisable**
Police Reform Act 2002, Schedule 4, paragraph 2A	*Police and Criminal Evidence Act* 1984, s.32	(a) Objects that might be used to cause physical injury to the person or the CSO.	Persons made subject to a requirement to wait.	Any place where the requirement to wait has been made.
		(b) Items that might be used to assist escape.		
4. Powers to seize without consent This power applies when drugs are found in the course of any search mentioned above.				
Designation	**Power conferred**	**Object of Seizure**		**Where Exercisable**
Police Reform Act 2002, Schedule 4, paragraph 7B	*Police Reform Act* 2002, Schedule 4, paragraph 7B	Controlled drugs in a person's possession.		Any place where the person is in possession of the drug.

Annex D—Deleted

Annex E—Deleted

ANNEX F

Establishing gender of persons for the purpose of searching

A:1. Certain provisions of this and other codes explicitly state that searches and other procedures may only be carried out by, or in the presence of, persons of the same sex as the person subject to the search or other procedure. (See paragraphs 2.8 and 3.6 and Note 4 of this code, Code C, paragraph 4.1 and Annex A, paragraphs 5, 6, 11 and 12 (searches, strip and intimate searches of detainees under sections 54 and 55 of *PACE*), Code D, paragraph 5.5 and Note 5F (searches, examinations and photographing of detainees under section 54A of *PACE*) and 6.9 (taking samples) and Code H, paragraph 4.1 and Annex A, paragraphs 6, 7 and 12 (searches, strip and intimate searches under sections 54 and 55 of *PACE* and 43(2) of the *Terrorism Act* of persons arrested under section 41 of the *Terrorism Act* 2000.) **A–17b**

A:2. All searches should be carried out with courtesy, consideration and respect for the person concerned. Police officers should show particular sensitivity when dealing with transsexual or transvestite persons (see *Notes F1* and *F2*). The following approach is designed to minimise embarrassment and secure the co-operation of the person subject to the search.

(a)

Consideration

A:3. At law, the gender of an individual is their gender as registered at birth unless they possess a gender recognition certificate as issued under section 9 of the *Gender Recognition Act* 2004, in which case the person's gender is the acquired gender. **A–17c**

(a) If there is no doubt as to the sex of a person, or there is no reason to suspect that the person is not the sex that they appear to be, they should be dealt with as that sex.

(b) A person who possesses a gender recognition certificate must be treated as their acquired gender.

(c) If the police are not satisfied that the person possesses a gender recognition certificate and there is doubt as to a person's gender, the person should be asked what gender they consider themselves to be. If the person expresses a preference to be dealt with as a particular gender, they should be asked to sign the search record, the officer's notebook or, if applicable, their custody record, to indicate and confirm their preference. If appropriate, the person should be treated as being that gender.

(d) If a person is unwilling to make such an election, efforts should be made to determine the predominant lifestyle of the person. For example, if they appear to live predominantly as a woman, they should be treated as such.

(e) If there is still doubt, the person should be dealt with according to the sex that they were born.

A:5. [*sic*] Once a decision has been made about which gender an individual is to be treated as, where possible before an officer searches that person, the officer should be advised of the doubt as to the person's gender. This is important so as to maintain the dignity of the officer(s) concerned.

(b)

Documentation

A:6. Where the gender of the detainee is established under paragraphs 2(b) to (e) above the decision should be recorded either on the search record, in the officer's notebook or, if applicable, in the person's custody record. **A–17d**

A:7. Where the person elects which gender they consider themselves to be under paragraph 2(c) but is not treated as their elected gender, the reason must be recorded in the search record, in the officer's notebook or, if applicable, in the person's custody record.

Note for guidance

A–17e **A:**F1 *Transsexual means a person who is proposing to undergo, is undergoing or has undergone a process (or part of a process) for the purpose of gender reassignment which is a protected characteristic under the* Equality Act *2010 (see paragraph 1.1) by changing physiological or other attributes of their sex. It would apply to a woman making the transition to being a man and a man making the transition to being a woman as well as to a person who has only just started out on the process of gender reassignment and to a person who has completed the process. Both would share the characteristic of gender reassignment with each having the characteristics of one sex, but with certain characteristics of the other sex.*

A:F2 *Transvestite means a person of one gender who dresses in the clothes of a person of the opposite gender.*

A:F3 *Similar principles will apply to police officers and police staff whose duties involve carrying out, or being present at, any of the searches and other procedures mentioned in paragraph 1. Chief officers are responsible for providing corresponding operational guidance and instructions for the deployment of any transsexual officers and staff under their direction and control.*

III. CODE B (SEARCH AND SEIZURE)

A–18 The text that follows is of the version of the code that came into force on March 7, 2011: see *ante*, Appendix A–1.

For authorities in relation to Code B, see, in particular, §§ 15–104 and 15–151 in the main work.

B. Code of Practice for Searches of Premises by Police Officers and the Seizure of Property Found by Police Officers on Persons or Premises

Commencement—transitional arrangements

A–19 This code applies to applications for warrants made after midnight, twenty-one days after the day on which the *Police and Criminal Evidence Act 1984 (Codes of Practice) (Revision of Codes A, B and D) Order* 2010 [*sic*] is made, and to searches and seizures taking place after that time.

B:1 Introduction

A–20 **B:**1.1 This code of practice deals with police powers to:

- search premises
- seize and retain property found on premises and persons.

B:1.1A These powers may be used to find:

- property and material relating to a crime
- wanted persons
- children who abscond from local authority accommodation where they have been remanded or committed by a court.

B:1.2 A justice of the peace may issue a search warrant granting powers of entry, search and seizure, *e.g.* warrants to search for stolen property, drugs, firearms and evidence of serious offences. Police also have powers without a search warrant. The main ones provided by the *Police and Criminal Evidence Act* 1984 (*PACE*) include powers to search premises:

- to make an arrest
- after an arrest.

B:1.3 The right to privacy and respect for personal property are key principles of the *Human Rights Act* 1998. Powers of entry, search and seizure should be fully and clearly justified before use because they may significantly interfere with the occupier's privacy. Officers should consider if the necessary objectives can be met by less intrusive means.

B:1.3A Powers to search and seize must be used fairly, responsibly, with respect for people who occupy premises being searched or are in charge of property being seized and without unlawful discrimination. The *Equality Act* 2010 makes it unlawful for police officers to discriminate against, harass or victimise any person on the grounds of the "protected characteristics" of age, disability, gender reassignment, race, religion or belief, sex and sexual orientation, marriage and civil partnership, pregnancy and maternity when using their powers. When police forces are carrying out their functions they also have a duty to have regard to the need to eliminate unlawful discrimination, harassment and victimisation and to take steps to foster good relations.

B:1.4 In all cases, police should therefore:

- exercise their powers courteously and with respect for persons and property
- only use reasonable force when this is considered necessary and proportionate to the circumstances.

B:1.5 If the provisions of *PACE* and this code are not observed, evidence obtained from a search may be open to question.

B:2 General

B:2.1 This code must be readily available at all police stations for consultation by: **A–21**

- police officers
- police staff
- detained persons
- members of the public.

B:2.2 The *Notes for Guidance* included are not provisions of this code.

B:2.3 This code applies to searches of premises:

(a) by police for the purposes of an investigation into an alleged offence, with the occupier's consent, other than:
- routine scene of crime searches;
- calls to a fire or burglary made by or on behalf of an occupier or searches following the activation of fire or burglar alarms or discovery of insecure premises;
- searches when paragraph 5.4 applies;
- bomb threat calls;

(b) under powers conferred on police officers by *PACE*, sections 17, 18 and 32;

(c) undertaken in pursuance of search warrants issued to and executed by constables in accordance with *PACE*, sections 15 and 16; [see *Note* 2A];

(d) subject to paragraph 2.6, under any other power given to police to enter premises with or without a search warrant for any purpose connected with the investigation into an alleged or suspected offence. [See *Note 2B*].

For the purposes of this code, "premises" as defined in *PACE*, section 23, includes any place, vehicle, vessel, aircraft, hovercraft, tent or movable structure and any offshore installation as defined in the *Mineral Workings (Offshore Installations) Act* 1971, section 1. See *Note 2D*.

B:2.4 A person who has not been arrested but is searched during a search of premises should be searched in accordance with Code A. See *Note 2C*.

B:2.5 This code does not apply to the exercise of a statutory power to enter premises or to inspect goods, equipment or procedures if the exercise of that power is not dependent on the existence of grounds for suspecting that an offence may have been committed and the person exercising the power has no reasonable grounds for such suspicion.

B:2.6 This code does not affect any directions or requirements of a search warrant, order or other power to search and seize lawfully exercised in England or Wales that any item or evidence seized under that warrant, order or power be handed over to a police force, court, tribunal, or other authority outside England or Wales. For example, warrants and orders issued in Scotland or Northern Ireland, see *Note 2B(f)* and search warrants and powers provided for in sections 14 to 17 of the *Crime (International Co-operation) Act* 2003.

B:2.7 When this code requires the prior authority or agreement of an officer of at least inspector or superintendent rank, that authority may be given by a sergeant or chief inspector authorised to perform the functions of the higher rank under *PACE*, section 107.

B:2.8 Written records required under this code not made in the search record shall, unless otherwise specified, be made:

- in the recording officer's pocket book ("pocket book" includes any official report book issued to police officers) or
- on forms provided for the purpose.

B:2.9 Nothing in this code requires the identity of officers, or anyone accompanying them during a search of premises, to be recorded or disclosed:

(a) in the case of enquiries linked to the investigation of terrorism; or

(b) if officers reasonably believe recording or disclosing their names might put them in danger.

In these cases officers should use warrant or other identification numbers and the name of their police station. Police staff should use any identification number provided to them by the police force. See *Note 2E*.

B:2.10 The "officer in charge of the search" means the officer assigned specific duties and responsibilities under this code. Whenever there is a search of premises to which this code applies one officer must act as the officer in charge of the search. See *Note 2F*.

B:2.11 In this code:

(a) "designated person" means a person other than a police officer, designated under the *Police Reform Act* 2002, Part 4 who has specified powers and duties of police officers conferred or imposed on them; [see *Note 2G*];

(b) any reference to a police officer includes a designated person acting in the exercise or performance of the powers and duties conferred or imposed on them by their designation;

(c) a person authorised to accompany police officers or designated persons in the execution of a warrant has the same powers as a constable in the execution of the warrant and the search and seizure of anything related to the warrant. These powers must be exercised in the company and under the supervision of a police officer. See *Note 3C*.

B:2.12 If a power conferred on a designated person:

(a) allows reasonable force to be used when exercised by a police officer, a designated person exercising that power has the same entitlement to use force;

(b) includes power to use force to enter any premises, that power is not exercisable by that designated person except:

(i) in the company and under the supervision of a police officer; or

(ii) for the purpose of:

- saving life or limb; or
- preventing serious damage to property.

B:2.13 Designated persons must have regard to any relevant provisions of the codes of practice.

Notes for guidance

A–22 **B:**2A PACE *sections 15 and 16 apply to all search warrants issued to and executed by constables under any enactment,* e.g. *search warrants issued by a*:

(a) *justice of the peace under the*:

Theft Act *1968, section 26—stolen property*;

Misuse of Drugs Act *1971, section 23—controlled drugs*;

PACE, *section 8—evidence of an indictable offence*;

Terrorism Act *2000, Schedule 5, paragraph 1*;

Prevention of Terrorism Act 2005, section 7C—*monitoring compliance with control order (see paragraph 10.1)*;

(b) *circuit judge under*:

PACE, *Schedule 1*;

Terrorism Act *2000, Schedule 5, paragraph 11*.

B:2B *Examples of the other powers in paragraph 2.3(d) include*:

(a) Road Traffic Act *1988, section 6E(1) giving police power to enter premises under section 6E(1) to*:

- *require a person to provide a specimen of breath; or*
- *arrest a person following*:

– *a positive breath test*;

– *failure to provide a specimen of breath*;

(b) Transport and Works Act *1992, section 30(4) giving police powers to enter premises mirroring the powers in (a) in relation to specified persons working on transport systems to which the Act applies;*

(c) Criminal Justice Act *1988, section 139B giving police power to enter and search school premises for offensive weapons, bladed or pointed articles;*

(d) Terrorism Act *2000, Schedule 5, paragraphs 3 and 15 empowering a superintendent in urgent cases to give written authority for police to enter and search premises for the purposes of a terrorist investigation;*

(e) Explosives Act *1875, section 73(b) empowering a superintendent to give written authority for police to enter premises, examine and search them for explosives;*

(f) *search warrants and production orders or the equivalent issued in Scotland or Northern Ireland endorsed under the* Summary Jurisdiction (Process) Act *1881 or the* Petty Sessions (Ireland) Act *1851 respectively for execution in England and Wales;*

(g) *sections 7A and 7B* of the Prevention of Terrorism Act 2005, *searches connected with the enforcement of control orders (see paragraph 10.1).*

B:2C *The* Criminal Justice Act *1988, section 139B provides that a constable who has reasonable grounds to believe an offence under the* Criminal Justice Act *1988, section 139A has or is being committed may enter school premises and search the premises and any persons on the premises for any bladed or pointed article or offensive weapon. Persons may be searched under a warrant issued under the* Misuse of Drugs Act *1971, section 23(3) to search premises for drugs or documents only if the warrant specifically authorises the search of persons on the premises. Powers to search premises under certain terrorism provisions also authorise the search of persons on the premises, for example, under paragraphs 1, 2, 11 and 15 of Schedule 5 to the* Terrorism Act *2000 and section 52 of the* Anti-terrorism, Crime and Security Act *2001.*

B:2D *The* Immigration Act *1971, Part III and Schedule 2 gives immigration officers powers to enter and search premises, seize and retain property, with and without a search warrant. These are similar to the powers available to police under search warrants issued by a justice of the peace and without a warrant under* PACE, *sections 17, 18, 19 and 32 except they only apply to specified offences under the* Immigration Act *1971 and immigration control powers. For certain types of investigations and enquiries these powers avoid the need for the Immigration Service to rely on police officers becoming directly involved. When exercising these powers, immigration officers are required by the* Immigration and Asylum Act *1999, section 145 to have regard to this code's corresponding provisions. When immigration officers are dealing with persons or property at police stations, police officers should give appropriate assistance to help them discharge their specific duties and responsibilities.*

B:2E *The purpose of paragraph 2.9(b) is to protect those involved in serious organised crime investigations or arrests of particularly violent suspects when there is reliable information that those arrested or their associates may threaten or cause harm to the officers or anyone accompanying them during a search of premises. In cases of doubt, an officer of inspector rank or above should be consulted.*

B:2F *For the purposes of paragraph 2.10, the officer in charge of the search should normally be the most senior officer present. Some exceptions are:*

(a) *a supervising officer who attends or assists at the scene of a premises search may appoint an officer of lower rank as officer in charge of the search if that officer is*

- *more conversant with the facts;*
- *a more appropriate officer to be in charge of the search;*

(b) *when all officers in a premises search are the same rank. The supervising officer if available must make sure one of them is appointed officer in charge of the search, otherwise the officers themselves must nominate one of their number as the officer in charge;*

(c) *a senior officer assisting in a specialist role. This officer need not be regarded as having a general supervisory role over the conduct of the search or be appointed or expected to act as the officer in charge of the search.*

Except in (c), nothing in this note diminishes the role and responsibilities of a supervisory officer who is present at the search or knows of a search taking place.

B:2G *An officer of the rank of inspector or above may direct a designated investigating officer not to wear a uniform for the purposes of a specific operation.*

B:3 Search warrants and production orders

(a) Before making an application

A–23 **B:**3.1 When information appears to justify an application, the officer must take reasonable steps to check the information is accurate, recent and not provided maliciously or irresponsibly. An application may not be made on the basis of information from an anonymous source if corroboration has not been sought. See *Note 3A*.

B:3.2 The officer shall ascertain as specifically as possible the nature of the articles concerned and their location.

B:3.3 The officer shall make reasonable enquiries to:

(i) establish if:

- anything is known about the likely occupier of the premises and the nature of the premises themselves;
- the premises have been searched previously and how recently;

(ii) obtain any other relevant information.

B:3.4 An application:

(a) to a justice of the peace for a search warrant or to a circuit judge for a search warrant or production order under *PACE*, Schedule 1 must be supported by a signed written authority from an officer of inspector rank or above; [Note: if the case is an urgent application to a justice of the peace and an inspector or above is not readily available, the next most senior officer on duty can give the written authority];

(b) to a circuit judge under the *Terrorism Act* 2000, Schedule 5 for

- a production order;
- search warrant; or
- an order requiring an explanation of material seized or produced under such a warrant or production order

must be supported by a signed written authority from an officer of superintendent rank or above.

B:3.5 Except in a case of urgency, if there is reason to believe a search might have an adverse effect on relations between the police and the community, the officer in charge shall consult the local police/community liaison officer:

- before the search; or
- in urgent cases, as soon as practicable after the search.

(b) Making an application

B:3.6 A search warrant application must be supported in writing, specifying:

(a) the enactment under which the application is made, see *Note 2A*;

(b)

(i) whether the warrant is to authorise entry and search of:

- one set of premises; or
- if the application is under *PACE* section 8, or Schedule 1, paragraph 12, more than one set of specified premises or all premises occupied or controlled by a specified person, and

(ii) the premises to be searched;

(c) the object of the search, see *Note 3B*;

(d) the grounds for the application, including, when the purpose of the proposed search is to find evidence of an alleged offence, an indication of how the evidence relates to the investigation;

(da) where the application is under *PACE* section 8, or Schedule 1, paragraph 12 for a single warrant to enter and search:

(i) more than one set of specified premises, the officer must specify each set of premises which it is desired to enter and search;

(ii) all premises occupied or controlled by a specified person, the officer must specify:

- as many sets of premises which it is desired to enter and search as it is reasonably practicable to specify;

- the person who is in occupation or control of those premises and any others which it is desired to search;
- why it is necessary to search more premises than those which can be specified;
- why it is not reasonably practicable to specify all the premises which it is desired to enter and search;

(db) whether an application under *PACE* section 8 is for a warrant authorising entry and search on more than one occasion, and if so, the officer must state the grounds for this and whether the desired number of entries authorised is unlimited or a specified maximum;

(e) there are no reasonable grounds to believe the material to be sought, when making application to a:

(i) justice of the peace or a circuit judge consists of or includes items subject to legal privilege;

(ii) justice of the peace, consists of or includes excluded material or special procedure material;

[Note: this does not affect the additional powers of seizure in the *Criminal Justice and Police Act* 2001, Part 2 covered in paragraph 7.7, see *Note 3B*];

(f) if applicable, a request for the warrant to authorise a person or persons to accompany the officer who executes the warrant, see *Note 3C*.

B:3.7 A search warrant application under *PACE*, Schedule 1, paragraph 12(a), shall if appropriate indicate why it is believed service of notice of an application for a production order may seriously prejudice the investigation. Applications for search warrants under the *Terrorism Act* 2000, Schedule 5, paragraph 11 must indicate why a production order would not be appropriate.

B:3.8 If a search warrant application is refused, a further application may not be made for those premises unless supported by additional grounds.

Notes for guidance

B:3A *The identity of an informant need not be disclosed when making an application, but the officer should be prepared to answer any questions the magistrate or judge may have about:* **A–24**

- *the accuracy of previous information from that source*
- *any other related matters.*

B:3B *The information supporting a search warrant application should be as specific as possible, particularly in relation to the articles or persons being sought and where in the premises it is suspected they may be found. The meaning of "items subject to legal privilege", "excluded material" and "special procedure material" are defined by* PACE, *sections 10, 11 and 14 respectively.*

B:3C *Under* PACE, *section 16(2), a search warrant may authorise persons other than police officers to accompany the constable who executes the warrant. This includes,* e.g. *any suitably qualified or skilled person or an expert in a particular field whose presence is needed to help accurately identify the material sought or to advise where certain evidence is most likely to be found and how it should be dealt with. It does not give them any right to force entry, but it gives them the right to be on the premises during the search and to search for or seize property without the occupier's permission.*

B:4 Entry without warrant—particular powers

(a) Making an arrest etc

B:4.1 The conditions under which an officer may enter and search premises without a warrant are set out in *PACE*, section 17. It should be noted that this section does not create or confer any powers of arrest. See other powers in *Note 2B(a)*. **A–25**

(b) Search of premises where arrest takes place or the arrested person was immediately before arrest

B:4.2 When a person has been arrested for an indictable offence, a police officer has power under *PACE*, section 32 to search the premises where the person was arrested or where the person was immediately before being arrested.

(c) Search of premises occupied or controlled by the arrested person

B:4.3 The specific powers to search premises which are occupied or controlled by a person arrested for an indictable offence are set out in *PACE*, section 18. They may not be exercised, except if section 18 (5) applies, unless an officer of inspector rank or above has given written authority. That authority should only be given when the authorising officer is satisfied that the premises are occupied or controlled by the arrested person and that the necessary grounds exist. If possible the authorising officer should record the authority on the Notice of Powers and Rights and, subject to paragraph 2.9, sign the notice. The record of the grounds for the search and the nature of the evidence sought as required by section 18(7) of the Act should be made in:

- the custody record if there is one, otherwise
- the officer's pocket book, or
- the search record.

B:5 Search with consent

A–26 **B:**5.1 Subject to paragraph 5.4, if it is proposed to search premises with the consent of a person entitled to grant entry the consent must, if practicable, be given in writing on the Notice of Powers and Rights before the search. The officer must make any necessary enquiries to be satisfied the person is in a position to give such consent. See *Notes 5A* and *5B*.

B:5.2 Before seeking consent the officer in charge of the search shall state the purpose of the proposed search and its extent. This information must be as specific as possible, particularly regarding the articles or persons being sought and the parts of the premises to be searched. The person concerned must be clearly informed they are not obliged to consent, that any consent given can be withdrawn at any time, including before the search starts or while it is under way and anything seized may be produced in evidence. If at the time the person is not suspected of an offence, the officer shall say this when stating the purpose of the search.

B:5.3 An officer cannot enter and search or continue to search premises under paragraph 5.1 if consent is given under duress or withdrawn before the search is completed.

B:5.4 It is unnecessary to seek consent under paragraphs 5.1 and 5.2 if this would cause disproportionate inconvenience to the person concerned. See *Note 5C*.

Notes for guidance

A–27 **B:**5A *In a lodging house, hostel or similar accommodation, every reasonable effort should be made to obtain the consent of the tenant, lodger or occupier. A search should not be made solely on the basis of the landlord's consent.*

B:5B *If the intention is to search premises under the authority of a warrant or a power of entry and search without warrant, and the occupier of the premises co-operates in accordance with paragraph 6.4, there is no need to obtain written consent.*

B:5C *Paragraph 5.4 is intended to apply when it is reasonable to assume innocent occupiers would agree to, and expect, police to take the proposed action, e.g. if:*

- *a suspect has fled the scene of a crime or to evade arrest and it is necessary quickly to check surrounding gardens and readily accessible places to see if the suspect is hiding*
- *police have arrested someone in the night after a pursuit and it is necessary to make a brief check of gardens along the pursuit route to see if stolen or incriminating articles have been discarded.*

B:6 Searching premises—general considerations

(a) Time of searches

A–28 **B:**6.1 Searches made under warrant must be made within three calendar months of the date of the warrant's issue.

B:6.2 Searches must be made at a reasonable hour unless this might frustrate the purpose of the search.

B:6.3 When the extent or complexity of a search mean it is likely to take a long time, the officer in charge of the search may consider using the seize and sift powers referred to in section 7.

B:6.3A A warrant under *PACE*, section 8 may authorise entry to and search of premises on more than one occasion if, on the application, the justice of the peace is satisfied that it is necessary to authorise multiple entries in order to achieve the purpose for which the warrant is issued. No premises may be entered or searched on any subsequent occasions without the prior written authority of an officer of the rank of inspector who is not involved in the investigation. All other warrants authorise entry on one occasion only.

B:6.3B Where a warrant under *PACE*, section 8, or Schedule 1, paragraph 12 authorises entry to and search of all premises occupied or controlled by a specified person, no premises which are not specified in the warrant may be entered and searched without the prior written authority of an officer of the rank of inspector who is not involved in the investigation.

(b) Entry other than with consent

B:6.4 The officer in charge of the search shall first try to communicate with the occupier, or any other person entitled to grant access to the premises, explain the authority under which entry is sought and ask the occupier to allow entry, unless:

(i) the search premises are unoccupied;
(ii) the occupier and any other person entitled to grant access are absent;
(iii) there are reasonable grounds for believing that alerting the occupier or any other person entitled to grant access would frustrate the object of the search or endanger officers or other people.

B:6.5 Unless sub-paragraph 6.4(iii) applies, if the premises are occupied the officer, subject to paragraph 2.9, shall, before the search begins:

(i) identify him or herself, show their warrant card (if not in uniform) and state the purpose of and grounds for the search;
(ii) identify and introduce any person accompanying the officer on the search (such persons should carry identification for production on request) and briefly describe that person's role in the process.

B:6.6 Reasonable and proportionate force may be used if necessary to enter premises if the officer in charge of the search is satisfied the premises are those specified in any warrant, or in exercise of the powers described in paragraph 4.1 to 4.3, and if:

(i) the occupier or any other person entitled to grant access has refused entry;
(ii) it is impossible to communicate with the occupier or any other person entitled to grant access; or
(iii) any of the provisions of paragraph 6.4 apply.

(c) Notice of powers and rights

B:6.7 If an officer conducts a search to which this code applies the officer shall, unless it is impracticable to do so, provide the occupier with a copy of a notice in a standard format: **A–29**

(i) specifying if the search is made under warrant, with consent, or in the exercise of the powers described in paragraphs 4.1 to 4.3; [Note: the notice format shall provide for authority or consent to be indicated, see paragraphs 4.3 and 5.1];
(ii) summarising the extent of the powers of search and seizure conferred by *PACE* and other relevant legislation as appropriate;
(iii) explaining the rights of the occupier, and the owner of the property seized;
(iv) explaining compensation may be payable in appropriate cases for damages [*sic*] caused entering and searching premises, and giving the address to send a compensation application, see *Note 6A*;
(v) stating this code is available at any police station.

B:6.8 If the occupier is:

- present, copies of the notice and warrant shall, if practicable, be given to them before the search begins, unless the officer in charge of the search reasonably believes this would frustrate the object of the search or endanger officers or other people;
- not present, copies of the notice and warrant shall be left in a prominent place on the premises or appropriate part of the premises and endorsed, subject to paragraph 2.9 with the name of the officer in charge of the search, the date and time of the search.

The warrant shall be endorsed to show this has been done.

(d) Conduct of searches

B:6.9 Premises may be searched only to the extent necessary to achieve the purpose of the search, having regard to the size and nature of whatever is sought.

B:6.9A A search may not continue under:

- a warrant's authority once all the things specified in that warrant have been found;
- any other power once the object of that search has been achieved.

B:6.9B No search may continue once the officer in charge of the search is satisfied whatever is being sought is not on the premises. See *Note 6B*. This does not prevent a further search of the same premises if additional grounds come to light supporting a further application for a search warrant or exercise or further exercise of another power. For example, when, as a result of new information, it is believed articles previously not found or additional articles are on the premises.

B:6.10 Searches must be conducted with due consideration for the property and privacy of the occupier and with no more disturbance than necessary. Reasonable force may be used only when necessary and proportionate because the co-operation of the occupier cannot be obtained or is insufficient for the purpose. See *Note 6C*.

B:6.11 A friend, neighbour or other person must be allowed to witness the search if the occupier wishes unless the officer in charge of the search has reasonable grounds for believing the presence of the person asked for would seriously hinder the investigation or endanger officers or other people. A search need not be unreasonably delayed for this purpose. A record of the action taken should be made on the premises search record including the grounds for refusing the occupier's request.

B:6.12 A person is not required to be cautioned prior to being asked questions that are solely necessary for the purpose of furthering the proper and effective conduct of a search, see Code C, paragraph 10.1(c). For example, questions to discover the occupier of specified premises, to find a key to open a locked drawer or cupboard or to otherwise seek co-operation during the search or to determine if a particular item is liable to be seized.

B:6.12A If questioning goes beyond what is necessary for the purpose of the exemption in Code C, the exchange is likely to constitute an interview as defined by Code C, paragraph 11.1A and would require the associated safeguards included in Code C, section 10.

(e) Leaving premises

A–30 B:6.13 If premises have been entered by force, before leaving the officer in charge of the search must make sure they are secure by:

- arranging for the occupier or their agent to be present;
- any other appropriate means.

(f) Searches under PACE Schedule 1 or the Terrorism Act 2000, Schedule 5

B:6.14 An officer shall be appointed as the officer in charge of the search, see paragraph 2.10, in respect of any search made under a warrant issued under *PACE Act* 1984, Schedule 1 or the *Terrorism Act* 2000, Schedule 5. They are responsible for making sure the search is conducted with discretion and in a manner that causes the least possible disruption to any business or other activities carried out on the premises.

B:6.15 Once the officer in charge of the search is satisfied material may not be taken from the premises without their knowledge, they shall ask for the documents or other records concerned. The officer in charge of the search may also ask to see the index to files held on the premises, and the officers conducting the search may inspect any files which, according to the index, appear to contain the material sought. A more extensive search of the premises may be made only if:

- the person responsible for them refuses to:
  - produce the material sought, or
  - allow access to the index;
- it appears the index is:
  - inaccurate, or
  - incomplete;
- for any other reason the officer in charge of the search has reasonable grounds for believing such a search is necessary in order to find the material sought.

Notes for guidance

A–31 B:6A *Whether compensation is appropriate depends on the circumstances in each case. Compensation for damage caused when effecting entry is unlikely to be appropriate if the search was lawful, and the force used can be shown to be reasonable, proportionate and necessary to effect entry. If the wrong premises are searched by mistake everything possible should be done at the earliest opportunity to allay any sense of grievance and there should normally be a strong presumption in favour of paying compensation.*

B:6B *It is important that, when possible, all those involved in a search are fully briefed about any powers to be exercised and the extent and limits within which it should be conducted.*

B:6C *In all cases the number of officers and other persons involved in executing the warrant should be determined by what is reasonable and necessary according to the particular circumstances.*

B:7 Seizure and retention of property

(a) Seizure

B:7.1 Subject to paragraph 7.2, an officer who is searching any person or premises under any statutory power or with the consent of the occupier may seize anything: **A–32**

(a) covered by a warrant;

(b) the officer has reasonable grounds for believing is evidence of an offence or has been obtained in consequence of the commission of an offence but only if seizure is necessary to prevent the items being concealed, lost, disposed of, altered, damaged, destroyed or tampered with;

(c) covered by the powers in the *Criminal Justice and Police Act* 2001, Part 2 allowing an officer to seize property from persons or premises and retain it for sifting or examination elsewhere.

See *Note 7B*.

B:7.2 No item may be seized which an officer has reasonable grounds for believing to be subject to legal privilege, as defined in *PACE*, section 10, other than under the *Criminal Justice and Police Act* 2001, Part 2.

B:7.3 Officers must be aware of the provisions in the *Criminal Justice and Police Act* 2001, section 59, allowing for applications to a judicial authority for the return of property seized and the subsequent duty to secure in section 60, see paragraph 7.12(iii).

B:7.4 An officer may decide it is not appropriate to seize property because of an explanation from the person holding it but may nevertheless have reasonable grounds for believing it was obtained in consequence of an offence by some person. In these circumstances, the officer should identify the property to the holder, inform the holder of their suspicions and explain the holder may be liable to civil or criminal proceedings if they dispose of, alter or destroy the property.

B:7.5 An officer may arrange to photograph, image or copy, any document or other article they have the power to seize in accordance with paragraph 7.1. This is subject to specific restrictions on the examination, imaging or copying of certain property seized under the *Criminal Justice and Police Act* 2001, Part 2. An officer must have regard to their statutory obligation to retain an original document or other article only when a photograph or copy is not sufficient.

B:7.6 If an officer considers information stored in any electronic form and accessible from the premises could be used in evidence, they may require the information to be produced in a form:

- which can be taken away and in which it is visible and legible; or
- from which it can readily be produced in a visible and legible form.

(b) Criminal Justice and Police Act 2001: specific procedures for seize and sift powers

B:7.7 The *Criminal Justice and Police Act* 2001, Part 2 gives officers limited powers to seize property from premises or persons so they can sift or examine it elsewhere. Officers must be careful they only exercise these powers when it is essential and they do not remove any more material than necessary. The removal of large volumes of material, much of which may not ultimately be retainable, may have serious implications for the owners, particularly when they are involved in business or activities such as journalism or the provision of medical services. Officers must carefully consider if removing copies or images of relevant material or data would be a satisfactory alternative to removing originals. When originals are taken, officers must be prepared to facilitate the provision of copies or images for the owners when reasonably practicable. See *Note 7C*. **A–33**

B:7.8 Property seized under the *Criminal Justice and Police Act* 2001, sections 50 or 51 must be kept securely and separately from any material seized under other powers. An examination under section 53 to determine which elements may be retained must be carried out at the earliest practicable time, having due regard to the desirability of allowing the person from whom the property was seized, or a person with an interest in the property, an opportunity of being present or represented at the examination.

B:7.8A All reasonable steps should be taken to accommodate an interested person's request to be present, provided the request is reasonable and subject to the need to prevent harm to, interference with, or unreasonable delay to the investigatory process. If an examination proceeds in the absence of an interested person who asked to attend or their representative, the officer who exercised the relevant seizure power must give that person a written notice of why the examination was carried out in those circumstances. If it is necessary for security reasons or to maintain confidentiality officers may exclude interested persons from decryption or other processes which facilitate the examination but do not form part of it. See *Note 7D*.

B:7.9 It is the responsibility of the officer in charge of the investigation to make sure property is returned in accordance with sections 53 to 55. Material which there is no power to retain must be:

- separated from the rest of the seized property;
- returned as soon as reasonably practicable after examination of all the seized property.

B:7.9A Delay is only warranted if very clear and compelling reasons exist, *e.g.* the:

- unavailability of the person to whom the material is to be returned;
- need to agree a convenient time to return a large volume of material.

B:7.9B Legally privileged, excluded or special procedure material which cannot be retained must be returned:

- as soon as reasonably practicable;
- without waiting for the whole examination.

B:7.9C As set out in section 58, material must be returned to the person from whom it was seized, except when it is clear some other person has a better right to it. See *Note 7E*.

B:7.10 When an officer involved in the investigation has reasonable grounds to believe a person with a relevant interest in property seized under section 50 or 51 intends to make an application under section 59 for the return of any legally privileged, special procedure or excluded material, the officer in charge of the investigation should be informed as soon as practicable and the material seized should be kept secure in accordance with section 61. See *Note 7C*.

B:7.11 The officer in charge of the investigation is responsible for making sure property is properly secured. Securing involves making sure the property is not examined, copied, imaged or put to any other use except at the request, or with the consent, of the applicant or in accordance with the directions of the appropriate judicial authority. Any request, consent or directions must be recorded in writing and signed by both the initiator and the officer in charge of the investigation. See *Notes 7F* and *7G*.

B:7.12 When an officer exercises a power of seizure conferred by sections 50 or 51 they shall provide the occupier of the premises or the person from whom the property is being seized with a written notice:

(i) specifying what has been seized under the powers conferred by that section;

(ii) specifying the grounds for those powers;

(iii) setting out the effect of sections 59 to 61 covering the grounds for a person with a relevant interest in seized property to apply to a judicial authority for its return and the duty of officers to secure property in certain circumstances when an application is made;

(iv) specifying the name and address of the person to whom:

- notice of an application to the appropriate judicial authority in respect of any of the seized property must be given;
- an application may be made to allow attendance at the initial examination of the property.

B:7.13 If the occupier is not present but there is someone in charge of the premises, the notice shall be given to them. If no suitable person is available, so the notice will easily be found it should either be:

- left in a prominent place on the premises;
- attached to the exterior of the premises.

(c) Retention

B:7.14 Subject to paragraph 7.15, anything seized in accordance with the above provisions may be retained only for as long as is necessary. It may be retained, among other purposes: **A-34**

(i) for use as evidence at a trial for an offence;

(ii) to facilitate the use in any investigation or proceedings of anything to which it is inextricably linked, see *Note 7H*;

(iii) for forensic examination or other investigation in connection with an offence;

(iv) in order to establish its lawful owner when there are reasonable grounds for believing it has been stolen or obtained by the commission of an offence.

B:7.15 Property shall not be retained under paragraph 7.14(i), (ii) or (iii) if a copy or image would be sufficient.

(d) Rights of owners etc

B:7.16 If property is retained, the person who had custody or control of it immediately before seizure must, on request, be provided with a list or description of the property within a reasonable time.

B:7.17 That person or their representative must be allowed supervised access to the property to examine it or have it photographed or copied, or must be provided with a photograph or copy, in either case within a reasonable time of any request and at their own expense, unless the officer in charge of an investigation has reasonable grounds for believing this would:

(i) prejudice the investigation of any offence or criminal proceedings; or

(ii) lead to the commission of an offence by providing access to unlawful material such as pornography.

A record of the grounds shall be made when access is denied.

Notes for guidance

B:7A *Any person claiming property seized by the police may apply to a magistrates' court under the* Police (Property) Act *1897 for its possession and should, if appropriate, be advised of this procedure.* **A-35**

B:7B *The powers of seizure conferred by* PACE, *sections 18(2) and 19(3) extend to the seizure of the whole premises when it is physically possible to seize and retain the premises in their totality and practical considerations make seizure desirable. For example, police may remove premises such as tents, vehicles or caravans to a police station for the purpose of preserving evidence.*

B:7C *Officers should consider reaching agreement with owners and/or other interested parties on the procedures for examining a specific set of property, rather than awaiting the judicial authority's determination. Agreement can sometimes give a quicker and more satisfactory route for all concerned and minimise costs and legal complexities.*

B:7D *What constitutes a relevant interest in specific material may depend on the nature of that material and the circumstances in which it is seized. Anyone with a reasonable claim to ownership of the material and anyone entrusted with its safe keeping by the owner should be considered.*

B:7E *Requirements to secure and return property apply equally to all copies, images or other material created because of seizure of the original property.*

B:7F *The mechanics of securing property vary according to the circumstances; "bagging up",* i.e. *placing material in sealed bags or containers and strict subsequent control of access is the appropriate procedure in many cases.*

B:7G *When material is seized under the powers of seizure conferred by* PACE, *the duty to retain it under the code of practice issued under the* Criminal Procedure and Investigations Act *1996 is subject to the provisions on retention of seized material in* PACE, *section 22.*

B:7H *Paragraph 7.14(ii) applies if inextricably linked material is seized under the* Criminal Justice and Police Act *2001, sections 50 or 51. Inextricably linked material is material it is not reasonably practicable to separate from other linked material without prejudicing the use of that other material in any investigation or proceedings. For example, it may not be possible to separate items of data held on computer disk without damaging their evidential integrity. Inextricably linked material must not be examined, imaged, copied or used for any purpose other than for proving the source and/or integrity of the linked material.*

B:8 Action after searches

B:8.1 If premises are searched in circumstances where this code applies, unless the exceptions **A-36**

in paragraph 2.3(a) apply, on arrival at a police station the officer in charge of the search shall make or have made a record of the search, to include:

(i) the address of the searched premises;

(ii) the date, time and duration of the search;

(iii) the authority used for the search:

- if the search was made in exercise of a statutory power to search premises without warrant, the power which was used for the search:
- if the search was made under a warrant or with written consent;
  - a copy of the warrant and the written authority to apply for it, see paragraph 3.4; or
  - the written consent;

  shall be appended to the record or the record shall show the location of the copy warrant or consent;

(iv) subject to paragraph 2.9, the names of:

- the officer(s) in charge of the search;
- all other officers and any authorised persons who conducted the search;

(v) the names of any people on the premises if they are known;

(vi) any grounds for refusing the occupier's request to have someone present during the search, see paragraph 6.11;

(vii) a list of any articles seized or the location of a list and, if not covered by a warrant, the grounds for their seizure;

(viii) whether force was used, and the reason;

(ix) details of any damage caused during the search, and the circumstances;

(x) if applicable, the reason it was not practicable;

(a) to give the occupier a copy of the notice of powers and rights, see paragraph 6.7;

(b) before the search to give the occupier a copy of the notice, see paragraph 6.8;

(xi) when the occupier was not present, the place where copies of the notice of powers and rights and search warrant were left on the premises, see paragraph 6.8.

B:8.2 On each occasion when premises are searched under warrant, the warrant authorising the search on that occasion shall be endorsed to show:

(i) if any articles specified in the warrant were found and the address where found;

(ii) if any other articles were seized;

(iii) the date and time it was executed and if present, the name of the occupier or if the occupier is not present the name of the person in charge of the premises;

(iv) subject to paragraph 2.9, the names of the officers who executed it and any authorised persons who accompanied them;

(v) if a copy, together with a copy of the notice of powers and rights was:

- handed to the occupier;
- or endorsed as required by paragraph 6.8; and left on the premises and where.

B:8.3 Any warrant shall be returned within three calendar months of its issue or sooner on completion of the search(es) authorised by that warrant, if it was issued by a:

- justice of the peace, to the designated officer for the local justice area in which the justice was acting when issuing the warrant; or
- judge, to the appropriate officer of the court concerned.

B:9 Search registers

A–37 **B:**9.1 A search register will be maintained at each sub-divisional or equivalent police station. All search records required under paragraph 8.1 shall be made, copied, or referred to in the register. See *Note 9A*.

Note for guidance

B:9A *Paragraph 9.1 also applies to search records made by immigration officers. In these* *cases, a search register must also be maintained at an immigration office. See also Note 2D.*

B:10 Searches under sections 7A, 7B and 7C of the Prevention of Terrorism Act 2005 in connection with control orders

B:10.1 This code applies to the powers under sections 7A, 7B and 7C of the *Prevention of Terrorism Act* 2005 to enter and search premises subject to the modifications in the following paragraphs. **A–37a**

B:10.2 In paragraph 2.3(d), the reference to the investigation into an alleged or suspected offence include [*sic*] the enforcement of obligations imposed by or under a control order made under the *Prevention of Terrorism Act* 2005.

B:10.3 References to the purpose and object of the search, the nature of articles sought and what may be seized and retained include (as appropriate):

- in relation section [*sic*] 7A (absconding), determining whether the controlled person has absconded and if it appears so, any material or information that may assist in the pursuit and arrest of the controlled person;
- in relation to section 7B (failure to grant access to premises), determining whether any control order obligations have been contravened and if it appears so, any material or information that may assist in determining whether the controlled person is complying with the obligations imposed by the control order or in investigating any apparent contravention of those obligations;
- in relation to section 7C (monitoring compliance), determining whether the controlled person is complying with their control order obligations, and any material that may assist in that determination;
- evidence in relation to an offence under section 9 of the *Prevention of Terrorism Act* 2005 (offences relating to control orders).

IV. CODE C (DETENTION, TREATMENT AND QUESTIONING OF PERSONS)

The text that follows is of the version of the code that came into force on February 1, 2008: see *ante*, Appendix A–1. **A–38**

For authorities in relation to Code C, see, in particular, §§ 15–210 *et seq.* (right of access to solicitor), § 15–251 (general), § 15–352 (confessions), § 15–425 (sufficient evidence for prosecution to succeed), §§ 15–452 *et seq.* (discretionary exclusion of evidence) in the main work.

C. Code of Practice for the Detention, Treatment and Questioning of Persons by Police Officers

Commencement—Transitional arrangements

This code applies to people in police detention after midnight on January 31, 2008, notwithstanding that their period of detention may have commenced before that time. **A–39**

C:1 General

C:1.1 All persons in custody must be dealt with expeditiously, and released as soon as the need for detention no longer applies. **A–40**

C:1.1A A custody officer must perform the functions in this code as soon as practicable. A custody officer will not be in breach of this code if delay is justifiable and reasonable steps are taken to prevent unnecessary delay. The custody record shall show when a delay has occurred and the reason. See *Note 1H*.

C:1.2 This code of practice must be readily available at all police stations for consultation by:

- police officers;

- police staff;
- detained persons;
- members of the public.

C:1.3 The provisions of this code:

- include the *Annexes*;
- do not include the *Notes for Guidance*.

C:1.4 If an officer has any suspicion, or is told in good faith, that a person of any age may be mentally disordered or otherwise mentally vulnerable, in the absence of clear evidence to dispel that suspicion, the person shall be treated as such for the purposes of this code. See *Note 1G*.

C:1.5 If anyone appears to be under 17, they shall be treated as a juvenile for the purposes of this code in the absence of clear evidence that they are older.

C:1.6 If a person appears to be blind, seriously visually impaired, deaf, unable to read or speak or has difficulty orally because of a speech impediment, they shall be treated as such for the purposes of this code in the absence of clear evidence to the contrary.

A–41 **C:**1.7 "The appropriate adult" means, in the case of a:

(a) juvenile:

(i) the parent, guardian or, if the juvenile is in local authority or voluntary organisation care, or is otherwise being looked after under the *Children Act* 1989, a person representing that authority or organisation;

(ii) a social worker of a local authority;

(iii) failing these, some other responsible adult aged 18 or over who is not a police officer or employed by the police;

(b) person who is mentally disordered or mentally vulnerable: see *Note 1D*;

(iv) a relative, guardian or other person responsible for their care or custody;

(v) someone experienced in dealing with mentally disordered or mentally vulnerable people but who is not a police officer or employed by the police;

(vi) failing these, some other responsible adult aged 18 or over who is not a police officer or employed by the police.

C:1.8 If this code requires a person be given certain information, they do not have to be given it if at the time they are incapable of understanding what is said, are violent or may become violent or in urgent need of medical attention, but they must be given it as soon as practicable.

C:1.9 References to a custody officer include any:—

- police officer; or
- designated staff custody officer acting in the exercise or performance of the powers and duties conferred or imposed on them by their designation,

performing the functions of a custody officer. See *Note 1J*.

C:1.9A When this code requires the prior authority or agreement of an officer of at least inspector or superintendent rank, that authority may be given by a sergeant or chief inspector authorised to perform the functions of the higher rank under the *Police and Criminal Evidence Act* 1984 (*PACE*), section 107.

C:1.10 Subject to paragraph 1.12, this Code applies to people in custody at police stations in England and Wales, whether or not they have been arrested, and to those removed to a police station as a place of safety under the *Mental Health Act* 1983, sections 135 and 136. Section 15 applies solely to people in police detention, *e.g.* those brought to a police station under arrest or arrested at a police station for an offence after going there voluntarily.

C:1.11 People detained under the *Terrorism Act* 2000, Schedule 8 and section 41 and other provisions of that Act are not subject to any part of this code. Such persons are subject to the code of practice for detention, treatment and questioning of persons by police officers detained [*sic*] under that Act.

C:1.12 This code's provisions do not apply to people in custody:

(i) arrested on warrants issued in Scotland by officers under the *Criminal Justice and Public Order Act* 1994, section 136(2), or arrested or detained without warrant by officers from a police force in Scotland under section 137(2); in these cases, police powers and duties and the person's rights and entitlements whilst at a police station in England or Wales are the same as those in Scotland;

(ii) arrested under the *Immigration and Asylum Act* 1999, section 142(3) in order to have their fingerprints taken;

(iii) whose detention is authorised by an immigration officer under the *Immigration Act* 1971;

(iv) who are convicted or remanded prisoners held in police cells on behalf of the Prison Service under the *Imprisonment (Temporary Provisions) Act* 1980;

(v) [*not used*];

(vi) detained for searches under stop and search powers except as required by Code A.

The provisions on conditions of detention and treatment in sections 8 and 9 must be considered as the minimum standards of treatment for such detainees.

C:1.13 In this Code:

(a) "designated person" means a person other than a police officer, designated under the *Police Reform Act* 2002, Part 4 who has specified powers and duties of police officers conferred or imposed on them;

(b) reference to a police officer includes a designated person acting in the exercise or performance of the powers and duties conferred or imposed on them by their designation.

C:1.14 Designated persons are entitled to use reasonable force as follows:— **A–42**

(a) when exercising a power conferred on them which allows a police officer exercising that power to use reasonable force, a designated person has the same entitlement to use force; and

(b) at other times when carrying out duties conferred or imposed on them that also entitle them to use reasonable force, for example:

- when at a police station carrying out the duty to keep detainees for whom they are responsible under control and to assist any other police officer or designated person to keep any detainee under control and to prevent their escape;
- when securing, or assisting any other police officer or designated person in securing, the detention of a person at a police station;
- when escorting, or assisting any other police officer or designated person in escorting, a detainee within a police station;
- for the purpose of saving life or limb; or
- preventing serious damage to property.

C:1.15 Nothing in this code prevents the custody officer, or other officer given custody of the detainee, from allowing police staff who are not designated persons to carry out individual procedures or tasks at the police station if the law allows. However, the officer remains responsible for making sure the procedures and tasks are carried out correctly in accordance with the codes of practice. Any such person must be:

(a) a person employed by a police authority maintaining a police force and under the control and direction of the chief officer of that force;

(b) employed by a person with whom a police authority has a contract for the provision of services relating to persons arrested or otherwise in custody.

C:1.16 Designated persons and other police staff must have regard to any relevant provisions of the codes of practice.

C:1.17 References to pocket books include any official report book issued to police officers or other police staff.

Notes for guidance

C:1A *Although certain sections of this code apply specifically to people in custody at police stations, those there voluntarily to assist with an investigation should be treated with no less consideration,* e.g. *offered refreshments at appropriate times, and enjoy an absolute right to obtain legal advice or communicate with anyone outside the police station.* **A–43**

C:1B *A person, including a parent or guardian, should not be an appropriate adult if they:*

- *are*
  - *suspected of involvement in the offence;*
  - *the victim;*
  - *a witness;*

– *involved in the investigation;*

- *received admissions prior to attending to act as the appropriate adult.*

Note: If a juvenile's parent is estranged from the juvenile, they should not be asked to act as the appropriate adult if the juvenile expressly and specifically objects to their presence.

C:1C *If a juvenile admits an offence to, or in the presence of, a social worker or member of a youth offending team other than during the time that person is acting as the juvenile's appropriate adult, another appropriate adult should be appointed in the interest of fairness.*

C:1D *In the case of people who are mentally disordered or otherwise mentally vulnerable, it may be more satisfactory if the appropriate adult is someone experienced or trained in their care rather than a relative lacking such qualifications. But if the detainee prefers a relative to a better qualified stranger or objects to a particular person their wishes should, if practicable, be respected.*

C:1E *A detainee should always be given an opportunity, when an appropriate adult is called to the police station, to consult privately with a solicitor in the appropriate adult's absence if they want. An appropriate adult is not subject to legal privilege.*

C:1F *A solicitor or independent custody visitor (formerly a lay visitor) present at the police station in that capacity may not be the appropriate adult.*

C:1G *"Mentally vulnerable" applies to any detainee who, because of their mental state or capacity, may not understand the significance of what is said, of questions or of their replies. "Mental disorder" is defined in the* Mental Health Act *1983, section 1(2) as "mental illness, arrested or incomplete development of mind, psychopathic disorder and any other disorder or disability of mind". When the custody officer has any doubt about the mental state or capacity of a detainee, that detainee should be treated as mentally vulnerable and an appropriate adult called.*

C:1H *Paragraph 1.1A is intended to cover delays which may occur in processing detainees* e.g. *if:*

- *a large number of suspects are brought into the station simultaneously to be placed in custody;*
- *interview rooms are all being used;*
- *there are difficulties contacting an appropriate adult, solicitor or interpreter.*

C:1I *The custody officer must remind the appropriate adult and detainee about the right to legal advice and record any reasons for waiving it in accordance with section 6.*

C:1J *The designation of police staff custody officers applies only in police areas where an order commencing the provisions of the* Police Reform Act *2002, section 38 and Schedule 4A, for designating police staff custody officers is in effect.*

C:1K *This code does not affect the principle that all citizens have a duty to help police officers to prevent crime and discover offenders. This is a civic rather than a legal duty; but when a police officer is trying to discover whether, or by whom, an offence has been committed he is entitled to question any person from whom he thinks useful information can be obtained, subject to the restrictions imposed by this code. A person's declaration that he is unwilling to reply does not alter this entitlement.*

C:2 Custody records

A–44 **C:**2.1A When a person is brought to a police station:

- under arrest;
- is arrested [*sic*] at the police station having attended there voluntarily; or
- attends [*sic*] a police station to answer bail,

they should be brought before the custody officer as soon as practicable after their arrival at the station or, if appropriate, following arrest after attending the police station voluntarily. This applies to designated and non-designated police stations. A person is deemed to be "at a police station" for these purposes if they are within the boundary of any building or enclosed yard which forms part of that police station.

C:2.1 A separate custody record must be opened as soon as practicable for each person brought to a police station under arrest or arrested at the station having gone there voluntarily or attending a police station in answer to street bail. All information recorded under this code must be recorded as soon as practicable in the custody record unless otherwise specified. Any audio or video recording made in the custody area is not part of the custody record.

C:2.2 If any action requires the authority of an officer of a specified rank, subject to paragraph 2.6A, their name and rank must be noted in the custody record.

C:2.3 The custody officer is responsible for the custody record's accuracy and completeness and for making sure the record or copy of the record accompanies a detainee if they are transferred to another police station. The record shall show the:

- time and reason for transfer;
- time a person is released from detention.

C:2.4 A solicitor or appropriate adult must be permitted to consult a detainee's custody record as soon as practicable after their arrival at the station and at any other time whilst the person is detained. Arrangements for this access must be agreed with the custody officer and may not unreasonably interfere with the custody officer's duties.

C:2.4A When a detainee leaves police detention or is taken before a court they, their legal representative or appropriate adult shall be given, on request, a copy of the custody record as soon as practicable. This entitlement lasts for 12 months after release.

C:2.5 The detainee, appropriate adult or legal representative shall be permitted to inspect the original custody record after the detainee has left police detention provided they give reasonable notice of their request. Any such inspection shall be noted in the custody record.

C:2.6 Subject to paragraph 2.6A, all entries in custody records must be timed and signed by the maker. Records entered on computer shall be timed and contain the operator's identification.

C:2.6A Nothing in this code requires the identity of officers or other police staff to be recorded or disclosed:

(a) [*not used*]

(b) if the officer or police staff reasonably believe recording or disclosing their name might put them in danger.

In these cases, they shall use their warrant or other identification numbers and the name of their police station. See *Note 2A*.

C:2.7 The fact and time of any detainee's refusal to sign a custody record, when asked in accordance with this code, must be recorded.

Note for guidance

C:2A *The purpose of paragraph 2.6A(b) is to protect those involved in serious organised crime investigations or arrests of particularly violent suspects when there is reliable information that those arrested or their associates may threaten or cause harm to those involved. In cases of doubt, an officer of inspector rank or above should be consulted.* **A–45**

C:3 Initial action

(a) Detained persons—normal procedure

C:3.1 When a person is brought to a police station under arrest or arrested at the station having gone there voluntarily, the custody officer must make sure the person is told clearly about the following continuing rights which may be exercised at any stage during the period in custody: **A–46**

(i) the right to have someone informed of their arrest as in section 5;

(ii) the right to consult privately with a solicitor and that free independent legal advice is available;

(iii) the right to consult these codes of practice. See *Note 3D*.

C:3.2 The detainee must also be given:

- a written notice setting out:
  - the above three rights;
  - the arrangements for obtaining legal advice;
  - the right to a copy of the custody record as in paragraph 2.4A;
  - the caution in the terms prescribed in section 10;
- an additional written notice briefly setting out their entitlements while in custody, see *Notes 3A* and *3B*.

Note: the detainee shall be asked to sign the custody record to acknowledge receipt of these notices. Any refusal must be recorded on the custody record.

C:3.3 A citizen of an independent Commonwealth country or a national of a foreign country, including the Republic of Ireland, must be informed as soon as practicable about their rights of communication with their High Commission, embassy or consulate; see *section 7*;

C:3.4 The custody officer shall:

- record the offence(s) that the detainee has been arrested for and the reason(s) for the arrest on the custody record; see paragraph 10.3 and Code G paragraphs 2.2 and 4.3;
- note on the custody record any comment the detainee makes in relation to the arresting officer's account but shall not invite comment. If the arresting officer is not physically present when the detainee is brought to a police station, the arresting officer's account must be made available to the custody officer remotely or by a third party on the arresting officer's behalf. If the custody officer authorises a person's detention the detainee must be informed of the grounds as soon as practicable and before they are questioned about any offence;
- note any comment the detainee makes in respect of the decision to detain them but shall not invite comment;
- not put specific questions to the detainee regarding their involvement in any offence, nor in respect of any comments they may make in response to the arresting officer's account or the decision to place them in detention. Such an exchange is likely to constitute an interview as in paragraph 11.1A and require the associated safeguards in section 11.

See paragraph 11.13 in respect of unsolicited comments.

C:3.5 The custody officer shall:

(a) ask the detainee, whether at this time, they:

(i) would like legal advice, see paragraph 6.5;

(ii) want someone informed of their detention, see section 5;

(b) ask the detainee to sign the custody record to confirm their decisions in respect of (a);

(c) determine whether the detainee:

(i) is, or might be, in need of medical treatment or attention, see section 9;

(ii) requires:

- an appropriate adult;
- help to check documentation;
- an interpreter;

(d) record the decision in respect of (c).

C:3.6 When determining these needs the custody officer is responsible for initiating an assessment to consider whether the detainee is likely to present specific risks to custody staff or themselves. Such assessments should always include a check on the Police National Computer, to be carried out as soon as practicable, to identify any risks highlighted in relation to the detainee. Although such assessments are primarily the custody officer's responsibility, it may be necessary for them to consult and involve others, *e.g.* the arresting officer or an appropriate health care professional, see paragraph 9.13. Reasons for delaying the initiation or completion of the assessment must be recorded.

C:3.7 Chief officers should ensure that arrangements for proper and effective risk assessments required by paragraph 3.6 are implemented in respect of all detainees at police stations in their area.

C:3.8 Risk assessments must follow a structured process which clearly defines the categories of risk to be considered and the results must be incorporated in the detainee's custody record. The custody officer is responsible for making sure those responsible for the detainee's custody are appropriately briefed about the risks. If no specific risks are identified by the assessment, that should be noted in the custody record. See *Note 3E* and paragraph 9.14.

C:3.9 The custody officer is responsible for implementing the response to any specific risk assessment, *e.g.*:

- reducing opportunities for self harm;
- calling a health care professional;
- increasing levels of monitoring or observation.

C:3.10 Risk assessment is an ongoing process and assessments must always be subject to review if circumstances change.

C:3.11 If video cameras are installed in the custody area, notices shall be prominently displayed showing cameras are in use. Any request to have video cameras switched off shall be refused.

(b) Detained persons—special groups

C:3.12 If the detainee appears deaf or there is doubt about their hearing or speaking ability or ability to understand English, and the custody officer cannot establish effective communication, the custody officer must, as soon as practicable, call an interpreter for assistance in the action under paragraphs 3.1–3.5. See section 13. **A–47**

C:3.13 If the detainee is a juvenile, the custody officer must, if it is practicable, ascertain the identity of a person responsible for their welfare. That person:

- may be:
  - the parent or guardian;
  - if the juvenile is in local authority or voluntary organisation care, or is otherwise being looked after under the *Children Act* 1989, a person appointed by that authority or organisation to have responsibility for the juvenile's welfare;
  - any other person who has, for the time being, assumed responsibility for the juvenile's welfare;
- must be informed as soon as practicable that the juvenile has been arrested, why they have been arrested and where they are detained. This right is in addition to the juvenile's right in section 5 not to be held incommunicado. See *Note 3C*.

C:3.14 If a juvenile is known to be subject to a court order under which a person or organisation is given any degree of statutory responsibility to supervise or otherwise monitor them, reasonable steps must also be taken to notify that person or organisation (the "responsible officer"). The responsible officer will normally be a member of a youth offending team, except for a curfew order which involves electronic monitoring when the contractor providing the monitoring will normally be the responsible officer.

C:3.15 If the detainee is a juvenile, mentally disordered or otherwise mentally vulnerable, the custody officer must, as soon as practicable:

- inform the appropriate adult, who in the case of a juvenile may or may not be a person responsible for their welfare, as in paragraph 3.13, of:
  - the grounds for their detention;
  - their whereabouts;
- ask the adult to come to the police station to see the detainee.

C:3.16 It is imperative that a mentally disordered or otherwise mentally vulnerable person, detained under the *Mental Health Act* 1983, section 136, be assessed as soon as possible. If that assessment is to take place at the police station, an approved social worker and a registered medical practitioner shall be called to the station as soon as possible in order to interview and examine the detainee. Once the detainee has been interviewed, examined and suitable arrangements made for their treatment or care, they can no longer be detained under section 136. A detainee must be immediately discharged from detention under section 136 if a registered medical practitioner, having examined them, concludes they are not mentally disordered within the meaning of the Act.

C:3.17 If the appropriate adult is:

- already at the police station, the provisions of paragraphs 3.1 to 3.5 must be complied with in the appropriate adult's presence;
- not at the station when these provisions are complied with, they must be complied with again in the presence of the appropriate adult when they arrive.

C:3.18 The detainee shall be advised that:

- the duties of the appropriate adult include giving advice and assistance;
- they can consult privately with the appropriate adult at any time.

C:3.19 If the detainee, or appropriate adult on the detainee's behalf, asks for a solicitor to be called to give legal advice, the provisions of section 6 apply.

C:3.20 If the detainee is blind, seriously visually impaired or unable to read, the custody officer shall make sure their solicitor, relative, appropriate adult or some other person likely to take an interest in them and not involved in the investigation is available to help check any documentation. When this code requires written consent or signing the person assisting may be asked to sign instead, if the detainee prefers. This paragraph does not require an appropriate adult to be called solely to assist in checking and signing documentation for a person who is not a juvenile, or mentally disordered or otherwise mentally vulnerable (see paragraph 3.15).

(c) Persons attending a police station voluntarily

A–48 **C:**3.21 Anybody attending a police station voluntarily to assist with an investigation may leave at will unless arrested. See *Note 1K*. If it is decided they shall not be allowed to leave, they must be informed at once that they are under arrest and brought before the custody officer, who is responsible for making sure they are notified of their rights in the same way as other detainees. If they are not arrested but are cautioned as in section 10, the person who gives the caution must, at the same time, inform them they are not under arrest, they are not obliged to remain at the station but if they remain at the station they may obtain free and independent legal advice if they want. They shall be told the right to legal advice includes the right to speak with a solicitor on the telephone and be asked if they want to do so.

C:3.22 If a person attending the police station voluntarily asks about their entitlement to legal advice, they shall be given a copy of the notice explaining the arrangements for obtaining legal advice. See paragraph 3.2.

(d) Documentation

C:3.23 The grounds for a person's detention shall be recorded, in the person's presence if practicable.

C:3.24 Action taken under paragraphs 3.12 to 3.20 shall be recorded.

(e) Persons answering street bail

C:3.25 When a person is answering street bail, the custody officer should link any documentation held in relation to arrest with the custody record. Any further action shall be recorded on the custody record in accordance with paragraphs 3.23 and 3.24 above.

Notes for guidance

A–49 **C:**3A *The notice of entitlements should:*

- *list the entitlements in this code, including:*
  - *visits and contact with outside parties, including special provisions for Commonwealth citizens and foreign nationals;*
  - *reasonable standards of physical comfort;*
  - *adequate food and drink;*
  - *access to toilets and washing facilities, clothing, medical attention, and exercise when practicable;*
- *mention the:*
  - *provisions relating to the conduct of interviews;*
  - *circumstances in which an appropriate adult should be available to assist the detainee and their statutory rights to make representation whenever the period of their detention is reviewed.*

C:3B *In addition to notices in English, translations should be available in Welsh, the main minority ethnic languages and the principal European languages, whenever they are likely to be helpful. Audio versions of the notice should also be made available.*

C:3C *If the juvenile is in local authority or voluntary organisation care but living with their parents or other adults responsible for their welfare, although there is no legal obligation to inform them, they should normally be contacted, as well as the authority or organisation unless suspected of involvement in the offence concerned. Even if the juvenile is not living with their parents, consideration should be given to informing them.*

C:3D *The right to consult the codes of practice does not entitle the person concerned to delay unreasonably any necessary investigative or administrative action whilst they do so. Examples of action which need not be delayed unreasonably include:*

- *procedures requiring the provision of breath, blood or urine specimens under the* Road Traffic Act *1988 or the* Transport and Works Act *1992;*
- *searching detainees at the police station;*
- *taking fingerprints, footwear impressions or non-intimate samples without consent for evidential purposes.*

C:3E *Home Office Circular 32/2000 provides more detailed guidance on risk assessments* *and identifies key risk areas which should always be considered.*

C:4 Detainee's property

(a) Action

C:4.1 The custody officer is responsible for: A–50

(a) ascertaining what property a detainee:

(i) has with them when they come to the police station, whether on:

- arrest or re-detention on answering to bail;
- commitment to prison custody on the order or sentence of a court;
- lodgement at the police station with a view to their production in court from prison custody;
- transfer from detention at another station or hospital;
- detention under the *Mental Health Act* 1983, section 135 or 136;
- remand into police custody on the authority of a court;

(ii) might have acquired for an unlawful or harmful purpose while in custody;

(b) the safekeeping of any property taken from a detainee which remains at the police station.

The custody officer may search the detainee or authorise their being searched to the extent they consider necessary, provided a search of intimate parts of the body or involving the removal of more than outer clothing is only made as in Annex A. A search may only be carried out by an officer of the same sex as the detainee. See *Note 4A*.

C:4.2 Detainees may retain clothing and personal effects at their own risk unless the custody officer considers they may use them to cause harm to themselves or others, interfere with evidence, damage property, effect an escape or they are needed as evidence. In this event the custody officer may withhold such articles as they consider necessary and must tell the detainee why.

C:4.3 Personal effects are those items a detainee may lawfully need, use or refer to while in detention but do not include cash and other items of value.

(b) Documentation

C:4.4 It is a matter for the custody officer to determine whether a record should be made of the property a detained person has with him or had taken from him on arrest. Any record made is not required to be kept as part of the custody record but the custody record should be noted as to where such a record exists. Whenever a record is made the detainee shall be allowed to check and sign the record of property as correct. Any refusal to sign shall be recorded.

C:4.5 If a detainee is not allowed to keep any article of clothing or personal effects, the reason must be recorded.

Notes for guidance

C:4A PACE, *section 54(1) and paragraph 4.1 require a detainee to be searched when it is clear the custody officer will have continuing duties in relation to that detainee or when that detainee's behaviour or offence makes an inventory appropriate. They do not require every detainee to be searched,* e.g. *if it is clear a person will only be detained for a short period and is not to be placed in a cell, the custody officer may decide not to search them. In such a case the custody record will be endorsed "not searched", paragraph 4.4 will not apply, and the detainee will be invited to sign the entry. If the detainee refuses, the custody officer will be obliged to ascertain what property they have in accordance with paragraph 4.1.* A–51

C:4B *Paragraph 4.4 does not require the custody officer to record on the custody record property in the detainee's possession on arrest if, by virtue of its nature, quantity or size, it is not practicable to remove it to the police station.*

C:4C *Paragraph 4.4 does not require items of clothing worn by the person be recorded unless withheld by the custody officer as in paragraph 4.2.*

C:5 Right not to be held incommunicado

(a) Action

C:5.1 Any person arrested and held in custody at a police station or other premises may, on A–52 request, have one person known to them or likely to take an interest in their welfare informed at public expense of their whereabouts as soon as practicable. If the person cannot be contacted the detainee may choose up to two alternatives. If they cannot be contacted, the person in charge of detention or the investigation has discretion to allow further attempts until the information has been conveyed. See *Notes 5C* and *5D*.

C:5.2 The exercise of the above right in respect of each person nominated may be delayed only in accordance with Annex B.

C:5.3 The above right may be exercised each time a detainee is taken to another police station.

C:5.4 The detainee may receive visits at the custody officer's discretion. See *Note 5B*.

C:5.5 If a friend, relative or person with an interest in the detainee's welfare enquires about their whereabouts, this information shall be given if the suspect agrees and Annex B does not apply. See *Note 5D*.

C:5.6 The detainee shall be given writing materials, on request, and allowed to telephone one person for a reasonable time, see *Notes 5A* and *5E*. Either or both these privileges may be denied or delayed if an officer of inspector rank or above considers sending a letter or making a telephone call may result in any of the consequences in:

(a) Annex B, paragraphs 1 and 2 and the person is detained in connection with an indictable offence; or

(b) [*not used*].

Nothing in this paragraph permits the restriction or denial of the rights in paragraphs 5.1 and 6.1.

C:5.7 Before any letter or message is sent, or telephone call made, the detainee shall be informed that what they say in any letter, call or message (other than in a communication to a solicitor) may be read or listened to and may be given in evidence. A telephone call may be terminated if it is being abused. The costs can be at public expense at the custody officer's discretion.

C:5.7A Any delay or denial of the rights in this section should be proportionate and should last no longer than necessary.

(b) Documentation

C:5.8 A record must be kept of any:

(a) request made under this section and the action taken;

(b) letters, messages or telephone calls made or received or visit received;

(c) refusal by the detainee to have information about them given to an outside enquirer. The detainee must be asked to countersign the record accordingly and any refusal recorded.

Notes for guidance

A–53 **C**:5A *A person may request an interpreter to interpret a telephone call or translate a letter.*

C:5B *At the custody officer's discretion, visits should be allowed when possible, subject to having sufficient personnel to supervise a visit and any possible hindrance to the investigation.*

C:5C *If the detainee does not know anyone to contact for advice or support or cannot contact a friend or relative, the custody officer should bear in mind any local voluntary bodies or other organisations who might be able to help. Paragraph 6.1 applies if legal advice is required.*

C:5D *In some circumstances it may not be appropriate to use the telephone to disclose information under paragraphs 5.1 and 5.5.*

C:5E *The telephone call at paragraph 5.6 is in addition to any communication under paragraphs 5.1 and 6.1.*

C:6 Right to legal advice

(a) Action

A–54 **C**:6.1 Unless Annex B applies, all detainees must be informed that they may at any time consult and communicate privately with a solicitor, whether in person, in writing or by telephone, and that free independent legal advice is available. See paragraph 3.1, *Note 6B* and *Note 6J*.

C:6.2 *Not Used*

C:6.3 A poster advertising the right to legal advice must be prominently displayed in the charging area of every police station. See *Note 6H*.

C:6.4 No police officer should, at any time, do or say anything with the intention of dissuading a detainee from obtaining legal advice.

C:6.5 The exercise of the right of access to legal advice may be delayed only as in Annex B. Whenever legal advice is requested, and unless Annex B applies, the custody officer must act without delay to secure the provision of such advice. If, on being informed or reminded of this right, the detainee declines to speak to a solicitor in person, the officer should point out that the right includes the right to speak with a solicitor on the telephone. If the detainee continues to waive this right the officer should ask them why and any reasons should be recorded on the custody record or the interview record as appropriate. Reminders of the right to legal advice must be given as in paragraphs 3.5, 11.2, 15.4, 16.4, 2B of Annex A, 3 of Annex K and 16.5 and Code D, paragraphs 3.17(ii) and 6.3. Once it is clear a detainee does not want to speak to a solicitor in person or by telephone they should cease to be asked their reasons. See *Note 6K*.

C:6.5A In the case of a juvenile, an appropriate adult should consider whether legal advice from a solicitor is required. If the juvenile indicates that they do not want legal advice, the appropriate adult has the right to ask for a solicitor to attend if this would be in the best interests of the person. However, the detained person cannot be forced to see the solicitor if he is adamant that he does not wish to do so.

C:6.6 A detainee who wants legal advice may not be interviewed or continue to be interviewed until they have received such advice unless:

(a) Annex B applies, when the restriction on drawing adverse inferences from silence in Annex C will apply because the detainee is not allowed an opportunity to consult a solicitor; or

(b) an officer of superintendent rank or above has reasonable grounds for believing that:

(i) the consequent delay might:

- lead to interference with, or harm to, evidence connected with an offence;
- lead to interference with, or physical harm to, other people;
- lead to serious loss of, or damage to, property;
- lead to alerting other people suspected of having committed an offence but not yet arrested for it;
- hinder the recovery of property obtained in consequence of the commission of an offence;

(ii) when a solicitor, including a duty solicitor, has been contacted and has agreed to attend, awaiting their arrival would cause unreasonable delay to the process of investigation;

[Note: in these cases the restriction on drawing adverse inferences from silence in Annex C will apply because the detainee is not allowed an opportunity to consult a solicitor];

(c) the solicitor the detainee has nominated or selected from a list:

(i) cannot be contacted;

(ii) has previously indicated they do not wish to be contacted; or

(iii) having been contacted, has declined to attend; and

the detainee has been advised of the Duty Solicitor Scheme but has declined to ask for the duty solicitor; in these circumstances the interview may be started or continued without further delay provided an officer of inspector rank or above has agreed to the interview proceeding; [Note: the restriction on drawing adverse inferences from silence in *Annex C* will not apply because the detainee is allowed an opportunity to consult the duty solicitor];

(d) the detainee changes their mind, about wanting legal advice. In these circumstances the interview may be started or continued without delay provided that:

(i) the detainee agrees to do so, in writing or on the interview record made in accordance wtih Code E or F; and

(ii) an officer of inspector rank or above has inquired about the detainee's reasons for their change of mind and gives authority for the interview to proceed.

Confirmation of the detainee's agreement, their change of mind, the reasons for it if given and, subject to paragraph 2.6A, the name of the authorising officer shall be recorded in the written interview record or the interview record made in accordance with Code E or F. See *Note 6I*. [Note: In these circumstances the restriction on drawing adverse inferences from silence in Annex C will not apply because the detainee is allowed an opportunity to consult a solicitor if they wish.]

A–55 **C:**6.7 If paragraph 6.6(b)(i) applies, once sufficient information has been obtained to avert the risk, questioning must cease until the detainee has received legal advice unless paragraph 6.6(a), (b)(ii), (c) or (d) applies.

C:6.8 A detainee who has been permitted to consult a solicitor shall be entitled on request to have the solicitor present when they are interviewed unless one of the exceptions in paragraph 6.6 applies.

C:6.9 The solicitor may only be required to leave the interview if their conduct is such that the interviewer is unable properly to put questions to the suspect. See *Notes 6D* and *6E*.

C:6.10 If the interviewer considers a solicitor is acting in such a way, they will stop the interview and consult an officer not below superintendent rank, if one is readily available, and otherwise an officer not below inspector rank not connected with the investigation. After speaking to the solicitor, the officer consulted will decide if the interview should continue in the presence of that solicitor. If they decide it should not, the suspect will be given the opportunity to consult another solicitor before the interview continues and that solicitor given an opportunity to be present at the interview. See *Note 6E*.

C:6.11 The removal of a solicitor from an interview is a serious step and, if it occurs, the officer of superintendent rank or above who took the decision will consider if the incident should be reported to the Law Society. If the decision to remove the solicitor has been taken by an officer below superintendent rank, the facts must be reported to an officer of superintendent rank or above who will similarly consider whether a report to the Law Society would be appropriate. When the solicitor concerned is a duty solicitor, the report should be both to the Law Society and to the Legal Services Commission.

C:6.12 "Solicitor" in this code means:

- a solicitor who holds a current practising certificate;
- an accredited or probationary representative included on the register of representatives maintained by the Legal Services Commission.

C:6.12A An accredited or probationary representative sent to provide advice by, and on behalf of, a solicitor shall be admitted to the police station for this purpose unless an officer of inspector rank or above considers such a visit will hinder the investigation and directs otherwise. Hindering the investigation does not include giving proper legal advice to a detainee as in *Note 6D*. Once admitted to the police station, paragraphs 6.6 to 6.10 apply.

C:6.13 In exercising their discretion under paragraph 6.12A, the officer should take into account in particular:

- whether:
  - the identity and status of an accredited or probationary representative have been satisfactorily established;
  - they are of suitable character to provide legal advice, *e.g.* a person with a criminal record is unlikely to be suitable unless the conviction was for a minor offence and not recent;
- any other matters in any written letter of authorisation provided by the solicitor on whose behalf the person is attending the police station. See *Note 6F*.

C:6.14 If the inspector refuses access to an accredited or probationary representative or a decision is taken that such a person should not be permitted to remain at an interview, the inspector must notify the solicitor on whose behalf the representative was acting and give them an opportunity to make alternative arrangements. The detainee must be informed and the custody record noted.

C:6.15 If a solicitor arrives at the station to see a particular person, that person must, unless Annex B applies, be so informed whether or not they are being interviewed and asked if they would like to see the solicitor. This applies even if the detainee has declined legal advice or, having requested it, subsequently agreed to be interviewed without receiving advice. The solicitor's attendance and the detainee's decision must be noted in the custody record.

(b) Documentation

C:6.16 Any request for legal advice and the action taken shall be recorded.

C:6.17 A record shall be made in the interview record if a detainee asks for legal advice and an interview is begun either in the absence of a solicitor or their representative, or they have been required to leave an interview.

Notes for guidance

C:6A *In considering if paragraph 6.6(b) applies, the officer should, if practicable, ask the solicitor for an estimate of how long it will take to come to the station and relate this to the time detention is permitted, the time of day* (i.e. *whether the rest period under paragraph 12.2 is imminent) and the requirements of other investigations. If the solicitor is on their way or is to set off immediately, it will not normally be appropriate to begin an interview before they arrive. If it appears necessary to begin an interview before the solicitor's arrival, they should be given an indication of how long the police would be able to wait before 6.6(b) applies so there is an opportunity to make arrangements for someone else to provide legal advice.* **A–56**

C:6B [See note C:6B2, *post.*]

C:6B1 [See note C:6B2, *post.*]

C:6B2 ***With effect from 21 April 2008,*** *the contents of Notes for Guidance 6B and 6B1 above will be superseded by this paragraph in all police forces areas in England and Wales by the following. A detainee who asks for legal advice to be paid for by himself should be given an opportunity to consult a specific solicitor or another solicitor from that solicitor's firm. If this solicitor is unavailable by these means, they may choose up to two alternatives. If these attempts are unsuccessful, the custody officer has discretion to allow further attempts until a solicitor has been contacted and agrees to provide legal advice. Otherwise, publicly funded legal advice shall in the first instance be accessed by telephoning a call centre authorised by the Legal Services Commission (LSC) to deal with calls from the police station. The Defence Solicitor Call Centre will determine whether legal advice should be limited to telephone advice or whether a solicitor should attend. Legal advice will be by telephone if a detainee is:*

- *detained for a non-imprisonable offence,*
- *arrested on a bench warrant for failing to appear and being held for production before the court (except where the solicitor has clear documentary evidence available that would result in the client being released from custody),*
- *arrested on suspicion of driving with excess alcohol (failure to provide a specimen, driving whilst unfit/drunk in charge of a motor vehicle), or*
- *detained in relation to breach of police or court bail conditions.*

An attendance by a solicitor for an offence suitable for telephone advice will depend on whether limited exceptions apply, such as:

- *whether the police are going to carry out an interview or an identification parade,*
- *whether the detainee is eligible for assistance from an appropriate adult,*
- *whether the detainee is unable to communicate over the telephone,*
- *whether the detainee alleges serious maltreatment by the police.*

Apart from carrying out these duties, an officer must not advise the suspect about any particular firm of solicitors.

C:6C *Not Used*

C:6D *A detainee has a right to free legal advice and to be represented by a solicitor. Legal advice by telephone advice may be provided in respect of those offences listed in Note for Guidance 6B1 and 6B2 above. The Defence Solicitor Call Centre will determine whether attendance is required by a solicitor. The solicitor's only role in the police station is to protect and advance the legal rights of their client. On occasions this may require the solicitor to give advice which has the effect of the client avoiding giving evidence which strengthens a prosecution case. The solicitor may intervene in order to seek clarification, challenge an improper question to their client or the manner in which it is put, advise their client not to reply to particular questions, or if they wish to give their client further legal advice. Paragraph 6.9 only applies if the solicitor's approach or conduct prevents or unreasonably obstructs proper questions being put to the suspect or the suspect's response being recorded. Examples of unacceptable conduct include answering questions on a suspect's behalf or providing written replies for the suspect to quote.*

C:6E *An officer who takes the decision to exclude a solicitor must be in a position to satisfy the court the decision was properly made. In order to do this they may need to witness what is happening.*

C:6F *If an officer of at least inspector rank considers a particular solicitor or firm of solicitors is persistently sending probationary representatives who are unsuited to provide legal* *advice, they should inform an officer of at least superintendent rank, who may wish to take the matter up with the Law Society.*

A–57 **C:**6G *Subject to the constraints of Annex B, a solicitor may advise more than one client in an investigation if they wish. Any question of a conflict of interest is for the solicitor under their professional code of conduct. If, however, waiting for a solicitor to give advice to one client may lead to unreasonable delay to the interview with another, the provisions of paragraph 6.6(b) may apply.*

C:6H *In addition to a poster in English, a poster or posters containing translations into Welsh, the main minority ethnic languages and the principal European languages should be displayed wherever they are likely to be helpful and it is practicable to do so.*

C:6I *Paragraph 6.6(d) requires the authorisation of an officer of inspector rank or above to the continuation of an interview when a detainee who wanted legal advice changes their mind. It is permissible for such authorisation to be given over the telephone, if the authorising officer is able to satisfy themselves about the reason for the detainee's change of mind and is satisfied it is proper to continue the interview in those circumstances.*

C:6J *Whenever a detainee exercises their right to legal advice by consulting or communicating with a solicitor, they must be allowed to do so in private. This right to consult or communicate in private is fundamental. If the requirement for privacy is compromised because what is said or written by the detainee or solicitor for the purpose of giving and receiving legal advice is overheard, listened to, or read by others without the informed consent of the detainee, the right will effectively have been denied. When a detainee chooses to speak to a solicitor on the telephone, they should be allowed to do so in private unless this is impractical because of the design and layout of the custody area or the location of telephones. However, the normal expectation should be that facilities will be available, unless they are being used, at all police stations to enable detainees to speak in private to a solicitor either face to face or over the telephone.*

C:6K *A detainee is not obliged to give reasons for declining legal advice and should not be pressed to do so.*

C:7 Citizens of independent Commonwealth countries or foreign nationals

(a) Action

A–58 **C:**7.1 Any citizen of an independent Commonwealth country or a national of a foreign country, including the Republic of Ireland, may communicate at any time with the appropriate High Commission, embassy or consulate. The detainee must be informed as soon as practicable of:

- this right;
- their right, upon request, to have their High Commission, embassy or consulate told of their whereabouts and the grounds for their detention. Such a request should be acted upon as soon as practicable.

C:7.2 If a detainee is a citizen of a country with which a bilateral consular convention or agreement is in force requiring notification of arrest, the appropriate High Commission, embassy or consulate shall be informed as soon as practicable, subject to paragraph 7.4. The countries to which this applies as at 1 April 2003 are listed in Annex F.

C:7.3 Consular officers may visit one of their nationals in police detention to talk to them and, if required, to arrange for legal advice. Such visits shall take place out of the hearing of a police officer.

C:7.4 Notwithstanding the provisions of consular conventions, if the detainee is a political refugee whether for reasons of race, nationality, political opinion or religion, or is seeking political asylum, consular officers shall not be informed of the arrest of one of their nationals or given access or information about them except at the detainee's express request.

(b) Documentation

A–59 **C:**7.5 A record shall be made when a detainee is informed of their rights under this section and of any communications with a High Commission, embassy or consulate.

Note for guidance

A–60 **C:**7A *The exercise of the rights in this section may not be interfered with even though Annex*

B applies.

C:8 Conditions of detention

(a) Action

C:8.1 So far as it is practicable, not more than one detainee should be detained in each cell. **A–61**

C:8.2 Cells in use must be adequately heated, cleaned and ventilated. They must be adequately lit, subject to such dimming as is compatible with safety and security to allow people detained overnight to sleep. No additional restraints shall be used within a locked cell unless absolutely necessary and then only restraint equipment, approved for use in that force by the chief officer, which is reasonable and necessary in the circumstances having regard to the detainee's demeanour and with a view to ensuring their safety and the safety of others. If a detainee is deaf, mentally disordered or otherwise mentally vulnerable, particular care must be taken when deciding whether to use any form of approved restraints.

C:8.3 Blankets, mattresses, pillows and other bedding supplied shall be of a reasonable standard and in a clean and sanitary condition. See *Note 8A*.

C:8.4 Access to toilet and washing facilities must be provided.

C:8.5 If it is necessary to remove a detainee's clothes for the purposes of investigation, for hygiene, health reasons or cleaning, replacement clothing of a reasonable standard of comfort and cleanliness shall be provided. A detainee may not be interviewed unless adequate clothing has been offered.

C:8.6 At least two light meals and one main meal should be offered in any 24 hour period. See *Note 8B*. Drinks should be provided at meal times and upon reasonable request between meals. Whenever necessary, advice shall be sought from the appropriate health care professional, see *Note 9A*, on medical and dietary matters. As far as practicable, meals provided shall offer a varied diet and meet any specific dietary needs or religious beliefs the detainee may have. The detainee may, at the custody officer's discretion, have meals supplied by their family or friends at their expense. See *Note 8A*.

C:8.7 Brief outdoor exercise shall be offered daily if practicable.

C:8.8 A juvenile shall not be placed in a police cell unless no other secure accommodation is available and the custody officer considers it is not practicable to supervise them if they are not placed in a cell or that a cell provides more comfortable accommodation than other secure accommodation in the station. A juvenile may not be placed in a cell with a detained adult.

(b) Documentation

C:8.9 A record must be kept of replacement clothing and meals offered. **A–62**

C:8.10 If a juvenile is placed in a cell, the reason must be recorded.

C:8.11 The use of any restraints on a detainee whilst in a cell, the reasons for it and, if appropriate, the arrangements for enhanced supervision of the detainee whilst so restrained, shall be recorded. See paragraph 3.9.

Notes for guidance

C:8A *The provisions in paragraph 8.3 and 8.6 respectively are of particular importance in the case of a person likely to be detained for an extended period. In deciding whether to allow meals to be supplied by family or friends, the custody officer is entitled to take account of the risk of items being concealed in any food or package and the officer's duties and responsibilities under food handling legislation.* **A–63**

C:8B *Meals should, so far as practicable, be offered at recognised meal times, or at other times that take account of when the detainee last had a meal.*

C:9 Care and treatment of detained persons

(a) General

C:9.1 Nothing in this section prevents the police from calling the police surgeon or, if appropriate, some other health care professional, to examine a detainee for the purposes of obtaining evidence relating to any offence in which the detainee is suspected of being involved. See *Note 9A*. **A–64**

C:9.2 If a complaint is made by, or on behalf of, a detainee about their treatment since their arrest, or it comes to notice that a detainee may have been treated improperly, a report must be made as soon as practicable to an officer of inspector rank or above not connected with the investigation. If the matter concerns a possible assault or the possibility of the unnecessary or unreasonable use of force, an appropriate health care professional must also be called as soon as practicable.

C:9.3 Detainees should be visited at least every hour. If no reasonably foreseeable risk was identified in a risk assessment, see paragraphs 3.6–3.10, there is no need to wake a sleeping detainee. Those suspected of being intoxicated through drink or drugs or having swallowed drugs, see *Note 9CA*, or whose level of consciousness causes concern must, subject to any clinical directions given by the appropriate health care professional, see paragraph 9.13:

- be visited and roused at least every half hour;
- have their condition assessed as in Annex H;
- and clinical treatment arranged if appropriate.

See *Notes 9B, 9C* and *9H*.

C:9.4 When arrangements are made to secure clinical attention for a detainee, the custody officer must make sure all relevant information which might assist in the treatment of the detainee's condition is made available to the responsible health care professional. This applies whether or not the health care professional asks for such information. Any officer or police staff with relevant information must inform the custody officer as soon as practicable.

(b) Clinical treatment and attention

A–65 **C:**9.5 The custody officer must make sure a detainee receives appropriate clinical attention as soon as reasonably practicable if the person:

(a) appears to be suffering from physical illness; or

(b) is injured; or

(c) appears to be suffering from a mental disorder; or

(d) appears to need clinical attention.

C:9.5A This applies even if the detainee makes no request for clinical attention and whether or not they have already received clinical attention elsewhere. If the need for attention appears urgent, *e.g.* when indicated as in Annex H, the nearest available health care professional or an ambulance must be called immediately.

C:9.5B The custody officer must also consider the need for clinical attention as set out in Note for Guidance 9C in relation to those suffering the effects of alcohol or drugs.

C:9.6 Paragraph 9.5 is not meant to prevent or delay the transfer to a hospital if necessary of a person detained under the *Mental Health Act* 1983, section 136. See *Note 9D*. When an assessment under that Act takes place at a police station, see paragraph 3.16, the custody officer must consider whether an appropriate health care professional should be called to conduct an initial clinical check on the detainee. This applies particularly when there is likely to be any significant delay in the arrival of a suitably qualified medical practitioner.

C:9.7 If it appears to the custody officer, or they are told, that a person brought to a station under arrest may be suffering from an infectious disease or condition, the custody officer must take reasonable steps to safeguard the health of the detainee and others at the station. In deciding what action to take, advice must be sought from an appropriate health care professional. See *Note 9E*. The custody officer has discretion to isolate the person and their property until clinical directions have been obtained.

A–66 **C:**9.8 If a detainee requests a clinical examination, an appropriate health care professional must be called as soon as practicable to assess the detainee's clinical needs. If a safe and appropriate care plan cannot be provided, the police surgeon's advice must be sought. The detainee may also be examined by a medical practitioner of their choice at their expense.

C:9.9 If a detainee is required to take or apply any medication in compliance with clinical directions prescribed before their detention, the custody officer must consult the appropriate health care professional before the use of the medication. Subject to the restrictions in paragraph 9.10, the custody officer is responsible for the safekeeping of any medication and for making sure the detainee is given the opportunity to take or apply prescribed or approved medication. Any such consultation and its outcome shall be noted in the custody record.

C:9.10 No police officer may administer or supervise the self-administration of medically prescribed controlled drugs of the types and forms listed in the *Misuse of Drugs Regulations* 2001, Schedule 2 or 3. A detainee may only self-administer such drugs under the personal supervision of the registered medical practitioner authorising their use. Drugs listed in Schedule 4 or 5 may be distributed by the custody officer for self-administration if they have consulted the registered medical practitioner authorising their use, this may be done by telephone, and both parties are satisfied self-administration will not expose the detainee, police officers or anyone else to the risk of harm or injury.

C:9.11 When appropriate health care professionals administer drugs or other medications, or supervise their self-administration, it must be within current medicines legislation and the scope of practice as determined by their relevant professional body.

C:9.12 If a detainee has in their possession, or claims to need, medication relating to a heart condition, diabetes, epilepsy or a condition of comparable potential seriousness then, even though paragraph 9.5 may not apply, the advice of the appropriate health care professional must be obtained.

C:9.13 Whenever the appropriate health care professional is called in accordance with this section to examine or treat a detainee, the custody officer shall ask for their opinion about:

- any risks or problems which police need to take into account when making decisions about the detainee's continued detention;
- when to carry out an interview if applicable; and
- the need for safeguards.

C:9.14 When clinical directions are given by the appropriate health care professional, whether orally or in writing, and the custody officer has any doubts or is in any way uncertain about any aspect of the directions, the custody officer shall ask for clarification. It is particularly important that directions concerning the frequency of visits are clear, precise and capable of being implemented. See *Note 9F*.

(c) Documentation

C:9.15 A record must be made in the custody record of: **A–67**

(a) the arrangements made for an examination by an appropriate health care professional under paragraph 9.2 and of any complaint reported under that paragraph together with any relevant remarks by the custody officer;

(b) any arrangements made in accordance with paragraph 9.5;

(c) any request for a clinical examination under paragraph 9.8 and any arrangements made in response;

(d) the injury, ailment, condition or other reason which made it necessary to make the arrangements in (a) to (c), see *Note 9G*;

(e) any clinical directions and advice, including any further clarifications, given to police by a health care professional concerning the care and treatment of the detainee in connection with any of the arrangements made in (a) to (c), see *Note 9F*;

(f) if applicable, the responses received when attempting to rouse a person using the procedure in Annex H, see *Note 9H*.

C:9.16 If a health care professional does not record their clinical findings in the custody record, the record must show where they are recorded. See *Note 9G*. However, information which is necessary to custody staff to ensure the effective ongoing care and well being of the detainee must be recorded openly in the custody record, see paragraph 3.8 and Annex G, paragraph 7.

C:9.17 Subject to the requirements of section 4, the custody record shall include:

- a record of all medication a detainee has in their possession on arrival at the police station;
- a note of any such medication they claim to need but do not have with them.

Notes for guidance

C:9A *A "health care professional" means a clinically qualified person working within the scope of practice as determined by their relevant professional body. Whether a health care professional is "appropriate" depends on the circumstances of the duties they carry out at the time.* **A–68**

C:9B *Whenever possible juveniles and mentally vulnerable detainees should be visited more frequently.*

C:9C *A detainee who appears drunk or behaves abnormally may be suffering from illness, the effects of drugs or may have sustained injury, particularly a head injury which is not apparent. A detainee needing or dependent on certain drugs, including alcohol, may experience harmful effects within a short time of being deprived of their supply. In these circumstances, when there is any doubt, police should always act urgently to call an appropriate health care professional or an ambulance. Paragraph 9.5 does not apply to minor ailments or injuries which do not need attention. However, all such ailments or injuries must be recorded in the custody record and any doubt must be resolved in favour of calling the appropriate health care professional.*

C:9CA *Paragraph 9.3 would apply to a person in police custody by order of a magistrates' court under the* Criminal Justice Act *1988, section 152 (as amended by the* Drugs Act *2005, section 8) to facilitate the recovery of evidence after being charged with drug possession or drug trafficking and suspected of having swallowed drugs. In the case of the healthcare needs of a person who has swallowed the drugs, the custody officer subject to any clinical directions, should consider the necessity for rousing every half hour. This does not negate the need for regular visiting of the suspect in the cell.*

C:9D *Whenever practicable, arrangements should be made for persons detained for assessment under the* Mental Health Act *1983, section 136 to be taken to a hospital. There is no power under that Act to transfer a person detained under section 136 from one place of safety to another place of safety for assessment.*

C:9E *It is important to respect a person's right to privacy and information about their health must be kept confidential and only disclosed with their consent or in accordance with clinical advice when it is necessary to protect the detainee's health or that of others who come into contact with them.*

C:9F *The custody officer should always seek to clarify directions that the detainee requires constant observation or supervision and should ask the appropriate health care professional to explain precisely what action needs to be taken to implement such directions.*

C:9G *Paragraphs 9.15 and 9.16 do not require any information about the cause of any injury, ailment or condition to be recorded on the custody record if it appears capable of providing evidence of an offence.*

C:9H *The purpose of recording a person's responses when attempting to rouse them using the procedure in Annex H is to enable any change in the individual's consciousness level to be noted and clinical treatment arranged if appropriate.*

C:10 Cautions

(a) When a caution must be given

A–69 C:10.1 A person whom there are grounds to suspect of an offence, see *Note 10A*, must be cautioned before any questions about an offence, or further questions if the answers provide the grounds for suspicion, are put to them if either the suspect's answers or silence (*i.e.* failure or refusal to answer or answer satisfactorily) may be given in evidence to a court in a prosecution. A person need not be cautioned if questions are for other necessary purposes, *e.g.*:

- (a) solely to establish their identity or ownership of any vehicle;
- (b) to obtain information in accordance with any relevant statutory requirement, see paragraph 10.9;
- (c) in furtherance of the proper and effective conduct of a search, *e.g.* to determine the need to search in the exercise of powers of stop and search or to seek co-operation while carrying out a search;
- (d) to seek verification of a written record as in paragraph 11.13.

C:10.2 Whenever a person not under arrest is initially cautioned, or reminded they are under caution, that person must at the same time be told they are not under arrest and are free to leave if they want to. See *Note 10C*.

C:10.3 A person who is arrested, or further arrested, must be informed at the time, or as soon as practicable thereafter, that they are under arrest and the grounds for their arrest, see paragraph 3.4, *Note 10B* and Code G, paragraphs 2.2 and 4.3.

C:10.4 As per Code G, section 3, a person who is arrested, or further arrested, must also be cautioned unless:

- (a) it is impracticable to do so by reason of their condition or behaviour at the time;

(b) they have already been cautioned immediately prior to arrest as in paragraph 10.1.

(b) Terms of the cautions

C:10.5 The caution which must be given on:

(a) arrest;

(b) all other occasions before a person is charged or informed they may be prosecuted, see section 16,

should, unless the restriction on drawing adverse inferences from silence applies, see Annex C, be in the following terms:

"You do not have to say anything. But it may harm your defence if you do not mention when questioned something which you later rely on in court. Anything you do say may be given in evidence."

Where the use of the Welsh Language is appropriate, a constable may provide the caution directly in Welsh in the following terms:

"Does dim rhaid i chi ddweud dim byd. Ond gall niweidio eich amddiffyniad os na fyddwch chi'n sôn, wrth gael eich holi, am rywbeth y byddwch chi'n dibynnu arno nes ymlaen yn y Llys. Gall unrhyw beth yr ydych yn ei ddweud gael ei roi fel tystiolaeth."

See *Note 10G*.

C:10.6 Annex C, paragraph 2 sets out the alternative terms of the caution to be used when the restriction on drawing adverse inferences from silence applies. **A–70**

C:10.7 Minor deviations from the words of any caution given in accordance with this code do not constitute a breach of this code, provided the sense of the relevant caution is preserved. See *Note 10D*.

C:10.8 After any break in questioning under caution, the person being questioned must be made aware they remain under caution. If there is any doubt the relevant caution should be given again in full when the interview resumes. See *Note 10E*.

C:10.9 When, despite being cautioned, a person fails to co-operate or to answer particular questions which may affect their immediate treatment, the person should be informed of any relevant consequences and that those consequences are not affected by the caution. Examples are when a person's refusal to provide:

- their name and address when charged may make them liable to detention;
- particulars and information in accordance with a statutory requirement, *e.g.* under the *Road Traffic Act* 1988, may amount to an offence or may make the person liable to a further arrest.

(c) Special warnings under the Criminal Justice and Public Order Act 1994, sections 36 and 37

C:10.10 When a suspect interviewed at a police station or authorised place of detention after arrest fails or refuses to answer certain questions, or to answer satisfactorily, after due warning, see *Note 10F*, a court or jury may draw such inferences as appear proper under the *Criminal Justice and Public Order Act* 1994, sections 36 and 37. Such inferences may only be drawn when: **A–71**

(a) the restriction on drawing adverse inferences from silence, see Annex C, does not apply; and

(b) the suspect is arrested by a constable and fails or refuses to account for any objects, marks or substances, or marks on such objects found:

- on their person;
- in or on their clothing or footwear;
- otherwise in their possession; or
- in the place they were arrested;

(c) the arrested suspect was found by a constable at a place at or about the time the offence for which that officer has arrested them is alleged to have been committed, and the suspect fails or refuses to account for their presence there.

When the restriction on drawing adverse inferences from silence applies, the suspect may still be asked to account for any of the matters in (b) or (c) but the special warning described in paragraph 10.11 will not apply and must not be given.

C:10.11 For an inference to be drawn when a suspect fails or refuses to answer a question about one of these matters or to answer it satisfactorily, the suspect must first be told in ordinary language:

(a) what offence is being investigated;

(b) what fact they are being asked to account for;

(c) this fact may be due to them taking part in the commission of the offence;

(d) a court may draw a proper inference if they fail or refuse to account for this fact;

(e) a record is being made of the interview and it may be given in evidence if they are brought to trial.

(d) Juveniles and persons who are mentally disordered or otherwise mentally vulnerable

C:10.12 If a juvenile or a person who is mentally disordered or otherwise mentally vulnerable is cautioned in the absence of the appropriate adult, the caution must be repeated in the adult's presence.

(e) Documentation

C:10.13 A record shall be made when a caution is given under this section, either in the interviewer's pocket book or in the interview record.

Notes for guidance

A–72 **C:**10A *There must be some reasonable, objective grounds for the suspicion, based on known facts or information which are relevant to the likelihood the offence has been committed and the person to be questioned committed it.*

C:10B *An arrested person must be given sufficient information to enable them to understand they have been deprived of their liberty and the reason they have been arrested,* e.g. *when a person is arrested on suspicion of committing an offence they must be informed of the suspected offence's nature, when and where it was committed. The suspect must also be informed of the reason or reasons why the arrest is considered necessary. Vague or technical language should be avoided.*

C:10C *The restriction on drawing inferences from silence, see Annex C, paragraph 1, does not apply to a person who has not been detained and who therefore cannot be prevented from seeking legal advice if they want, see paragraph 3.21.*

C:10D *If it appears a person does not understand the caution, the person giving it should explain it in their own words.*

C:10E *It may be necessary to show to the court that nothing occurred during an interview break or between interviews which influenced the suspect's recorded evidence. After a break in an interview or at the beginning of a subsequent interview, the interviewing officer should summarise the reason for the break and confirm this with the suspect.*

C:10F *The* Criminal Justice and Public Order Act *1994, sections 36 and 37 apply only to suspects who have been arrested by a constable or Customs and Excise officer and are given the relevant warning by the police or customs officer who made the arrest or who is investigating the offence. They do not apply to any interviews with suspects who have not been arrested.*

C:10G *Nothing in this code requires a caution to be given or repeated when informing a person not under arrest they may be prosecuted for an offence. However, a court will not be able to draw any inferences under the* Criminal Justice and Public Order Act *1994, section 34, if the person was not cautioned.*

C:11 Interviews—general

(a) Action

A–73 **C:**11.1A An interview is the questioning of a person regarding their involvement or suspected involvement in a criminal offence or offences which, under paragraph 10.1, must be carried out under caution. Whenever a person is interviewed they must be informed of the nature of the offence, or further offence. Procedures under the *Road Traffic Act* 1988, section 7 or the *Transport and Works Act* 1992, section 31 do not constitute interviewing for the purpose of this code.

C:11.1 Following a decision to arrest a suspect, they must not be interviewed about the relevant offence except at a police station or other authorised place of detention, unless the consequent delay would be likely to:

(a) lead to:
- interference with, or harm to, evidence connected with an offence;
- interference with, or physical harm to, other people; or
- serious loss of, or damage to, property;

(b) lead to alerting other people suspected of committing an offence but not yet arrested for it; or

(c) hinder the recovery of property obtained in consequence of the commission of an offence.

Interviewing in any of these circumstances shall cease once the relevant risk has been averted or the necessary questions have been put in order to attempt to avert that risk.

C:11.2 Immediately prior to the commencement or re-commencement of any interview at a police station or other authorised place of detention, the interviewer should remind the suspect of their entitlement to free legal advice and that the interview can be delayed for legal advice to be obtained, unless one of the exceptions in paragraph 6.6 applies. It is the interviewer's responsibility to make sure all reminders are recorded in the interview record.

C:11.3 [*Not Used.*]

C:11.4 At the beginning of an interview the interviewer, after cautioning the suspect, see section 10, shall put to them any significant statement or silence which occurred in the presence and hearing of a police officer or other police staff before the start of the interview and which have not been put to the suspect in the course of a previous interview. See *Note 11A*. The interviewer shall ask the suspect whether they confirm or deny that earlier statement or silence and if they want to add anything.

C:11.4A A significant statement is one which appears capable of being used in evidence against the suspect, in particular a direct admission of guilt. A significant silence is a failure or refusal to answer a question or answer satisfactorily when under caution, which might, allowing for the restriction on drawing adverse inferences from silence, see Annex C, give rise to an inference under the *Criminal Justice and Public Order Act* 1994, Part III.

C:11.5 No interviewer may try to obtain answers or elicit a statement by the use of oppression. Except as in paragraph 10.9, no interviewer shall indicate, except to answer a direct question, what action will be taken by the police if the person being questioned answers questions, makes a statement or refuses to do either. If the person asks directly what action will be taken if they answer questions, make a statement or refuse to do either, the interviewer may inform them what action the police propose to take provided that action is itself proper and warranted.

C:11.6 The interview or further interview of a person about an offence with which that person has not been charged or for which they have not been informed they may be prosecuted, must cease when:

(a) the officer in charge of the investigation is satisfied all the questions they consider relevant to obtaining accurate and reliable information about the offence have been put to the suspect, this includes allowing the suspect an opportunity to give an innocent explanation and asking questions to test if the explanation is accurate and reliable, *e.g.* to clear up ambiguities or clarify what the suspect said;

(b) the officer in charge of the investigation has taken account of any other available evidence; and

(c) the officer in charge of the investigation, or in the case of a detained suspect, the custody officer, see paragraph 16.1, reasonably believes there is sufficient evidence to provide a realistic prospect of conviction for that offence. See *Note 11B*.

This paragraph does not prevent officers in revenue cases or acting under the confiscation provisions of the *Criminal Justice Act* 1988 or the *Drug Trafficking Act* 1994 from inviting suspects to complete a formal question and answer record after the interview is concluded.

(b) Interview records

C:11.7 A–74

(a) An accurate record must be made of each interview, whether or not the interview takes place at a police station.

(b) The record must state the place of interview, the time it begins and ends, any interview breaks and, subject to paragraph 2.6A, the names of all those present; and must be made on the forms provided for this purpose or in the interviewer's pocket book or in accordance with the Codes of Practice E or F.

(c) Any written record must be made and completed during the interview, unless this would not be practicable or would interfere with the conduct of the interview, and must constitute either a verbatim record of what has been said or, failing this, an account of the interview which adequately and accurately summarises it.

C:11.8 If a written record is not made during the interview it must be made as soon as practicable after its completion.

C:11.9 Written interview records must be timed and signed by the maker.

C:11.10 If a written record is not completed during the interview the reason must be recorded in the interview record.

C:11.11 Unless it is impracticable, the person interviewed shall be given the opportunity to read the interview record and to sign it as correct or to indicate how they consider it inaccurate. If the person interviewed cannot read or refuses to read the record or sign it, the senior interviewer present shall read it to them and ask whether they would like to sign it as correct or make their mark or to indicate how they consider it inaccurate. The interviewer shall certify on the interview record itself what has occurred. See *Note 11E*.

C:11.12 If the appropriate adult or the person's solicitor is present during the interview, they should also be given an opportunity to read and sign the interview record or any written statement taken down during the interview.

C:11.13 A written record shall be made of any comments made by a suspect, including unsolicited comments, which are outside the context of an interview but which might be relevant to the offence. Any such record must be timed and signed by the maker. When practicable the suspect shall be given the opportunity to read that record and to sign it as correct or to indicate how they consider it inaccurate. See *Note 11E*.

C:11.14 Any refusal by a person to sign an interview record when asked in accordance with this code must itself be recorded.

(c) Juveniles and mentally disordered or otherwise mentally vulnerable people

A–75 **C:**11.15 A juvenile or person who is mentally disordered or otherwise mentally vulnerable must not be interviewed regarding their involvement or suspected involvement in a criminal offence or offences, or asked to provide or sign a written statement under caution or record of interview, in the absence of the appropriate adult unless paragraphs 11.1, 11.18 to 11.20 apply. See *Note 11C*.

C:11.16 Juveniles may only be interviewed at their place of education in exceptional circumstances and only when the principal or their nominee agrees. Every effort should be made to notify the parent(s) or other person responsible for the juvenile's welfare and the appropriate adult, if this is a different person, that the police want to interview the juvenile and reasonable time should be allowed to enable the appropriate adult to be present at the interview. If awaiting the appropriate adult would cause unreasonable delay, and unless the juvenile is suspected of an offence against the educational establishment, the principal or their nominee can act as the appropriate adult for the purposes of the interview.

C:11.17 If an appropriate adult is present at an interview, they shall be informed:

- they are not expected to act simply as an observer; and
- the purpose of their presence is to:
  - advise the person being interviewed;
  - observe whether the interview is being conducted properly and fairly;
  - facilitate communication with the person being interviewed.

(d) Vulnerable suspects–urgent interviews at police stations

C:11.18. The following persons may not be interviewed unless an officer of superintendent rank or above considers delay will lead to the consequences in paragraph 11.1(a) to (c), and is satisfied the interview would not significantly harm the person's physical or mental state (see Annex G):

(a) a juvenile or person who is mentally disordered or otherwise mentally vulnerable if at the time of the interview the appropriate adult is not present;

(b) anyone other than in (a) who at the time of the interview appears unable to:

- appreciate the significance of questions and their answers; or
- understand what is happening because of the effects of drink, drugs or any illness, ailment or condition;

(c) a person who has difficulty understanding English or has a hearing disability, if at the time of the interview an interpreter is not present.

C:11.19 These interviews may not continue once sufficient information has been obtained to avert the consequences in paragraph 11.1(a) to (c).

C:11.20. A record shall be made of the grounds for any decision to interview a person under paragraph 11.18.

Notes for guidance

C:11A *Paragraph 11.4 does not prevent the interviewer from putting significant statements and silences to a suspect again at a later stage or a further interview.* **A–76**

C:11B *The* Criminal Procedure and Investigations Act *1996 code of practice, paragraph 3.4 states "In conducting an investigation, the investigator should pursue all reasonable lines of enquiry, whether these point towards or away from the suspect. What is reasonable will depend on the particular circumstances." Interviewers should keep this in mind when deciding what questions to ask in an interview.*

C:11C *Although juveniles or people who are mentally disordered or otherwise mentally vulnerable are often capable of providing reliable evidence, they may, without knowing or wishing to do so, be particularly prone in certain circumstances to provide information that may be unreliable, misleading or self-incriminating. Special care should always be taken when questioning such a person, and the appropriate adult should be involved if there is any doubt about a person's age, mental state or capacity. Because of the risk of unreliable evidence it is also important to obtain corroboration of any facts admitted whenever possible.*

C:11D *Juveniles should not be arrested at their place of education unless this is unavoidable. When a juvenile is arrested at their place of education, the principal or their nominee must be informed.*

C:11E *Significant statements described in paragraph 11.4 will always be relevant to the offence and must be recorded. When a suspect agrees to read records of interviews and other comments and sign them as correct, they should be asked to endorse the record with,* e.g. *"I agree that this is a correct record of what was said" and add their signature. If the suspect does not agree with the record, the interviewer should record the details of any disagreement and ask the suspect to read these details and sign them to the effect that they accurately reflect their disagreement. Any refusal to sign should be recorded.*

C:12 Interviews in police stations

(a) Action

C:12.1 If a police officer wants to interview or conduct enquiries which require the presence of a detainee, the custody officer is responsible for deciding whether to deliver the detainee into the officer's custody. **A–77**

C:12.2 Except as below, in any period of 24 hours a detainee must be allowed a continuous period of at least 8 hours for rest, free from questioning, travel or any interruption in connection with the investigation concerned. This period should normally be at night or other appropriate time which takes account of when the detainee last slept or rested. If a detainee is arrested at a police station after going there voluntarily, the period of 24 hours runs from the time of their arrest and not the time of arrival at the police station. The period may not be interrupted or delayed, except:

(a) when there are reasonable grounds for believing not delaying or interrupting the period would:

(i) involve a risk of harm to people or serious loss of, or damage to, property;

(ii) delay unnecessarily the person's release from custody;

(iii) otherwise prejudice the outcome of the investigation;

(b) at the request of the detainee, their appropriate adult or legal representative;

(c) when a delay or interruption is necessary in order to:

(i) comply with the legal obligations and duties arising under section 15;

(ii) to take action required under section 9 or in accordance with medical advice.

If the period is interrupted in accordance with (a), a fresh period must be allowed. Interruptions under (b) and (c), do not require a fresh period to be allowed.

C:12.3 Before a detainee is interviewed the custody officer, in consultation with the officer in charge of the investigation and appropriate health care professionals as necessary, shall assess whether the detainee is fit enough to be interviewed. This means determining and considering the risks to the detainee's physical and mental state if the interview took place and determining what safeguards are needed to allow the interview to take place. See *Annex G*. The custody officer shall not allow a detainee to be interviewed if the custody officer considers it would cause significant harm to the detainee's physical or mental state. Vulnerable suspects listed at paragraph 11.18 shall be treated as always being at some risk during an interview and these persons may not be interviewed except in accordance with paragraphs 11.18 to 11.20.

C:12.4 As far as practicable interviews shall take place in interview rooms which are adequately heated, lit and ventilated.

C:12.5 A suspect whose detention without charge has been authorised under *PACE*, because the detention is necessary for an interview to obtain evidence of the offence for which they have been arrested, may choose not to answer questions but police do not require the suspect's consent or agreement to interview them for this purpose. If a suspect takes steps to prevent themselves being questioned or further questioned, *e.g.* by refusing to leave their cell to go to a suitable interview room or by trying to leave the interview room, they shall be advised their consent or agreement to interview is not required. The suspect shall be cautioned as in section 10, and informed if they fail or refuse to co-operate, the interview may take place in the cell and that their failure or refusal to co-operate may be given in evidence. The suspect shall then be invited to co-operate and go into the interview room.

C:12.6 People being questioned or making statements shall not be required to stand.

A–78 **C:**12.7 Before the interview commences each interviewer shall, subject to paragraph 2.6A, identify themselves and any other persons present to the interviewee.

C:12.8 Breaks from interviewing should be made at recognised meal times or at other times that take account of when an interviewee last had a meal. Short refreshment breaks shall be provided at approximately two hour intervals, subject to the interviewer's discretion to delay a break if there are reasonable grounds for believing it would:

(i) involve a:
- risk of harm to people;
- serious loss of, or damage to, property;

(ii) unnecessarily delay the detainee's release;

(iii) otherwise prejudice the outcome of the investigation.

See *Note 12B*.

C:12.9 If during the interview a complaint is made by or on behalf of the interviewee concerning the provisions of this code, the interviewer should:

(i) record it in the interview record;

(ii) inform the custody officer, who is then responsible for dealing with it as in section 9.

(b) Documentation

A–79 **C:**12.10 A record must be made of the:
- time a detainee is not in the custody of the custody officer, and why;
- reason for any refusal to deliver the detainee out of that custody.

C:12.11 A record shall be made of:

(a) the reasons it was not practicable to use an interview room; and

(b) any action taken as in paragraph 12.5.

The record shall be made on the custody record or in the interview record for action taken whilst an interview record is being kept, with a brief reference to this effect in the custody record.

C:12.12 Any decision to delay a break in an interview must be recorded, with reasons, in the interview record.

C:12.13 All written statements made at police stations under caution shall be written on forms provided for the purpose.

C:12.14 All written statements made under caution shall be taken in accordance with Annex D. Before a person makes a written statement under caution at a police station they shall be reminded about the right to legal advice. See *Note 12A*.

Notes for guidance

A–80 **C:**12A *It is not normally necessary to ask for a written statement if the interview was re-*

corded in writing and the record signed in accordance with paragraph 11.11 or audibly or visually recorded in accordance with Code E or F. Statements under caution should normally be taken in these circumstances only at the person's express wish. A person may however be asked if they want to make such a statement.

C:12B *Meal breaks should normally last at least 45 minutes and shorter breaks after two hours should last at least 15 minutes. If the interviewer delays a break in accordance with paragraph 12.8 and prolongs the interview, a longer break should be provided. If there is a short interview, and another short interview is contemplated, the length of the break may be reduced if there are reasonable grounds to believe this is necessary to avoid any of the consequences in paragraph 12.8(i) to (iii).*

C:13 Interpreters

(a) General

C:13.1 Chief officers are responsible for making sure appropriate arrangements are in place for provision of suitably qualified interpreters for people who: **A–81**

- are deaf;
- do not understand English.

Whenever possible, interpreters should be drawn from the National Register of Public Service Interpreters (NRPSI) or the Council for the Advancement of Communication with Deaf People (CACDP) Directory of British Sign Language/English Interpreters.

(b) Foreign languages

C:13.2 Unless paragraphs 11.1, 11.18 to 11.20 apply, a person must not be interviewed in the absence of a person capable of interpreting if:

(a) they have difficulty understanding English;

(b) the interviewer cannot speak the person's own language;

(c) the person wants an interpreter present.

C:13.3 The interviewer shall make sure the interpreter makes a note of the interview at the time in the person's language for use in the event of the interpreter being called to give evidence, and certifies its accuracy. The interviewer should allow sufficient time for the interpreter to note each question and answer after each is put, given and interpreted. The person should be allowed to read the record or have it read to them and sign it as correct or indicate the respects in which they consider it inaccurate. If the interview is audibly recorded or visually recorded, the arrangements in Code E or F apply.

C:13.4 In the case of a person making a statement to a police officer or other police staff other than in English:

(a) the interpreter shall record the statement in the language it is made;

(b) the person shall be invited to sign it;

(c) an official English translation shall be made in due course.

(c) Deaf people and people with speech difficulties

C:13.5 If a person appears to be deaf or there is doubt about their hearing or speaking ability, they must not be interviewed in the absence of an interpreter unless they agree in writing to being interviewed without one or paragraphs 11.1, 11.18 to 11.20 apply. **A–82**

C:13.6 An interpreter should also be called if a juvenile is interviewed and the parent or guardian present as the appropriate adult appears to be deaf or there is doubt about their hearing or speaking ability, unless they agree in writing to the interview proceeding without one or paragraphs 11.1, 11.18 to 11.20 apply.

C:13.7 The interviewer shall make sure the interpreter is allowed to read the interview record and certify its accuracy in the event of the interpreter being called to give evidence. If the interview is audibly recorded or visually recorded, the arrangements in Code E or F apply.

(d) Additional rules for detained persons

C:13.8 All reasonable attempts should be made to make the detainee understand that interpreters will be provided at public expense.

C:13.9 If paragraph 6.1 applies and the detainee cannot communicate with the solicitor because of language, hearing or speech difficulties, an interpreter must be called. The interpreter may not be a police officer or any other police staff when interpretation is needed for the purposes of obtaining legal advice. In all other cases a police officer or other police staff may only interpret if the detainee and the appropriate adult, if applicable, give their agreement in writing or if the interview is audibly recorded or visually recorded as in Code E or F.

C:13.10 When the custody officer cannot establish effective communication with a person charged with an offence who appears deaf or there is doubt about their ability to hear, speak or to understand English, arrangements must be made as soon as practicable for an interpreter to explain the offence and any other information given by the custody officer.

(e) Documentation

C:13.11 Action taken to call an interpreter under this section and any agreement to be interviewed in the absence of an interpreter must be recorded.

C:14 Questioning—special restrictions

A–83 **C:**14.1 If a person is arrested by one police force on behalf of another and the lawful period of detention in respect of that offence has not yet commenced in accordance with *PACE*, section 41 no questions may be put to them about the offence while they are in transit between the forces except to clarify any voluntary statement they make.

C:14.2 If a person is in police detention at a hospital they may not be questioned without the agreement of a responsible doctor. See *Note 14A*.

Note for guidance

A–84 **C:**14A *If questioning takes place at a hospital under paragraph 14.2, or on the way to or from a hospital, the period of questioning concerned counts towards the total period of detention permitted.*

C:15 Reviews and extensions of detention

(a) Persons detained under PACE

A–85 **C:**15.1 The review officer is responsible under *PACE*, section 40 for periodically determining if a person's detention, before or after charge, continues to be necessary. This requirement continues throughout the detention period and except as in paragraph 15.10, the review officer must be present at the police station holding the detainee. See *Notes 15A* and *15B*.

C:15.2 Under *PACE*, section 42, an officer of superintendent rank or above who is responsible for the station holding the detainee may give authority any time after the second review to extend the maximum period the person may be detained without charge by up to 12 hours. Further detention without charge may be authorised only by a magistrates' court in accordance with *PACE*, sections 43 and 44. See *Notes 15C, 15D* and *15E*.

C:15.2A Section 42(1) of *PACE* as amended extends the maximum period of detention for indictable offences from 24 hours to 36 hours. Detaining a juvenile or mentally vulnerable person for longer than 24 hours will be dependent on the circumstances of the case and with regard to the person's:

(a) special vulnerability;

(b) the legal obligation to provide an opportunity for representations to be made prior to a decision about extending detention;

(c) the need to consult and consider the views of any appropriate adult; and

(d) any alternatives to police custody.

C:15.3 Before deciding whether to authorise continued detention the officer responsible under paragraphs 15.1 or 15.2 shall give an opportunity to make representations about the detention to:

(a) the detainee, unless in the case of a review as in paragraph 15.1, the detainee is asleep;

(b) the detainee's solicitor if available at the time; and

(c) the appropriate adult if available at the time.

C:15.3A Other people having an interest in the detainee's welfare may also make representations at the authorising officer's discretion.

C:15.3B Subject to paragraph 15.10, the representations may be made orally in person or by telephone or in writing. The authorising officer may, however, refuse to hear oral representations from the detainee if the officer considers them unfit to make representations because of their condition or behaviour. See *Note 15C*.

C:15.3C The decision on whether the review takes place in person or by telephone or by video conferencing (see *Note 15G*) is a matter for the review officer. In determining the form the review may take, the review officer must always take full account of the needs of the person in custody. The benefits of carrying out a review in person should always be considered, based on the individual circumstances of each case with specific additional consideration if the person is:

(a) a juvenile (and the age of the juvenile); or

(b) mentally vulnerable; or

(c) has [*sic*] been subject to medical attention for other than routine minor ailments; or

(d) there are presentational or community issues around the person's detention.

C:15.4 Before conducting a review or determining whether to extend the maximum period of detention without charge, the officer responsible must make sure the detainee is reminded of their entitlement to free legal advice, see paragraph 6.5, unless in the case of a review the person is asleep. **A–86**

C:15.5 If, after considering any representations, the officer decides to keep the detainee in detention or extend the maximum period they may be detained without charge, any comment made by the detainee shall be recorded. If applicable, the officer responsible under paragraph 15.1 or 15.2 shall be informed of the comment as soon as practicable. See also paragraphs 11.4 and 11.13.

C:15.6 No officer shall put specific questions to the detainee:

- regarding their involvement in any offence; or
- in respect of any comments they may make;
  - when given the opportunity to make representations; or
  - in response to a decision to keep them in detention or extend the maximum period of detention.

Such an exchange could constitute an interview as in paragraph 11.1A and would be subject to the associated safeguards in section 11 and, in respect of a person who has been charged, paragraph 16.5. See also paragraph 11.13.

C:15.7 A detainee who is asleep at a review, see paragraph 15.1, and whose continued detention is authorised must be informed about the decision and reason as soon as practicable after waking.

C:15.8 [*Not used.*]

(b) Telephone review of detention

C:15.9 *PACE*, section 40A provides that the officer responsible under section 40 for reviewing the detention of a person who has not been charged, need not attend the police station holding the detainee and may carry out the review by telephone. **A–87**

C:15.9A *PACE*, section 45A(2) provides that the officer responsible under section 40 for reviewing the detention of a person who has not been charged, need not attend the police station holding the detainee and may carry out the review by video conferencing facilities. (See *Note 15G*.)

C:15.9B A telephone review is not permitted where facilities for review by video conferencing exist and it is practicable to use them.

C:15.9C The review officer can decide at any stage that a telephone review or review by video conferencing should be terminated and that the review will be conducted in person. The reasons for doing so should be noted in the custody record. See *Note 15F*.

C:15.10 When a telephone review is carried out, an officer at the station holding the detainee shall be required by the review officer to fulfil that officer's obligations under *PACE* section 40 or this code by:

(a) making any record connected with the review in the detainee's custody record;

(b) if applicable, making a record in (a) in the presence of the detainee; and

(c) giving the detainee information about the review.

C:15.11 When a telephone review is carried out, the requirement in paragraph 15.3 will be satisfied:

(a) if facilities exist for the immediate transmission of written representations to the review officer, *e.g.* fax or email message, by giving the detainee an opportunity to make representations:
   (i) orally by telephone; or
   (ii) in writing using those facilities; and
(b) in all other cases, by giving the detainee an opportunity to make their representations orally by telephone.

(d) Documentation

C:15.12 It is the officer's responsibility to make sure all reminders given under paragraph 15.4 are noted in the custody record.

C:15.13 The grounds for, and extent of, any delay in conducting a review shall be recorded.

C:15.14 When a telephone review is carried out, a record shall be made of:
(a) the reason the review officer did not attend the station holding the detainee;
(b) the place the review officer was;
(c) the method representations, oral or written, were made to the review officer, see paragraph 15.11.

C:15.15 Any written representations shall be retained.

C:15.16 A record shall be made as soon as practicable about the outcome of each review or determination whether to extend the maximum detention period without charge or an application for a warrant of further detention or its extension. If paragraph 15.7 applies, a record shall also be made of when the person was informed and by whom. If an authorisation is given under *PACE*, section 42, the record shall state the number of hours and minutes by which the detention period is extended or further extended. If a warrant for further detention, or extension, is granted under section 43 or 44, the record shall state the detention period authorised by the warrant and the date and time it was granted.

Notes for guidance

A–88 **C:**15A *Review officer for the purposes of:*
- PACE, *sections 40 and 40A means, in the case of a person arrested but not charged, an officer of at least inspector rank not directly involved in the investigation and, if a person has been arrested and charged, the custody officer.*

C:15B *The detention of persons in police custody not subject to the statutory review requirement in paragraph 15.1 should still be reviewed periodically as a matter of good practice. Such reviews can be carried out by an officer of the rank of sergeant or above. The purpose of such reviews is to check the particular power under which a detainee is held continues to apply, any associated conditions are complied with and to make sure appropriate action is taken to deal with any changes. This includes the detainee's prompt release when the power no longer applies, or their transfer if the power requires the detainee be taken elsewhere as soon as the necessary arrangements are made. Examples include persons:*
(a) *arrested on warrant because they failed to answer bail to appear at court;*
(b) *arrested under the* Bail Act *1976, section 7(3) for breaching a condition of bail granted after charge;*
(c) *in police custody for specific purposes and periods under the* Crime (Sentences) Act *1997, Schedule 1;*
(d) *convicted, or remand prisoners, held in police stations on behalf of the Prison Service under the* Imprisonment (Temporary Provisions) Act *1980, section 6;*
(e) *being detained to prevent them causing a breach of the peace;*
(f) *detained at police stations on behalf of the Immigration Service.*
(g) *detained by order of a magistrates' court under the* Criminal Justice Act *1988, section 152 (as amended by the* Drugs Act *2005, section 8) to facilitate the recovery of evidence after being charged with drug possession or drug trafficking and suspected of having swallowed drugs.*

The detention of persons remanded into police detention by order of a court under the Magistrates' Courts Act *1980, section 128 is subject to a statutory requirement to review that detention. This is to make sure the detainee is taken back to court no later than the end of the period authorised by the court or when the need for their detention by police ceases, whichever is the sooner.*

C:15C *In the case of a review of detention, but not an extension, the detainee need not be woken for the review. However, if the detainee is likely to be asleep, e.g. during a period of rest allowed as in paragraph 12.2, at the latest time a review or authorisation to extend detention may take place, the officer should, if the legal obligations and time constraints permit, bring forward the procedure to allow the detainee to make representations. A detainee not asleep during the review must be present when the grounds for their continued detention are recorded and must at the same time be informed of those grounds unless the review officer considers the person is incapable of understanding what is said, violent or likely to become violent or in urgent need of medical attention.*

C:15D *An application to a magistrates' court under* PACE, *sections 43 or 44 for a warrant of further detention or its extension should be made between 10am and 9pm, and if possible during normal court hours. It will not usually be practicable to arrange for a court to sit specially outside the hours of 10am to 9pm. If it appears a special sitting may be needed outside normal court hours but between 10am and 9pm, the clerk to the justices should be given notice and informed of this possibility, while the court is sitting if possible.*

C:15E *In paragraph 15.2, the officer responsible for the station holding the detainee includes a superintendent or above who, in accordance with their force operational policy or police regulations, is given that responsibility on a temporary basis whilst the appointed long-term holder is off duty or otherwise unavailable.*

C:15F *The provisions of* PACE, *section 40A allowing telephone reviews do not apply to reviews of detention after charge by the custody officer. When video conferencing is not required, they allow the use of a telephone to carry out a review of detention before charge. The procedure under* PACE, *section 42 must be done in person.*

C:15G *The use of video conferencing facilities for decisions about detention under section 45A of* PACE *is subject to the introduction of regulations by the Secretary of State.*

C:16 Charging detained persons

(a) Action

C:16.1 When the officer in charge of the investigation reasonably believes there is sufficient evidence to provide a realistic prospect of the detainee's conviction for the offence (see paragraph 11.6) they shall without delay, and subject to the following qualification, inform the custody officer who will be responsible for considering whether the detainee should be charged. See *Notes 11B* and *16A*. When a person is detained in respect of more than one offence it is permissible to delay informing the custody officer until the above conditions are satisfied in respect of all the offences, but see paragraph 11.6. If the detainee is a juvenile, mentally disordered or otherwise mentally vulnerable, any resulting action shall be taken in the presence of the appropriate adult if they are present at the time. See *Notes 16B* and *16C*. **A–89**

C:16.1A Where guidance issued by the Director of Public Prosecutions under section 37A is in force the custody officer must comply with that guidance in deciding how to act in dealing with the detainee. See *Notes 16AA* and *16AB*.

C:16.1B Where in compliance with the DPP's Guidance the custody officer decides that the case should be immediately referred to the CPS to make the charging decision, consultation should take place with a Crown Prosecutor as soon as is reasonably practicable. Where the Crown Prosecutor is unable to make the charging decision on the information available at that time, the detainee may be released without charge and on bail (with conditions if necessary) under section 37(7)(a). In such circumstances, the detainee should be informed that they are being released to enable the Director of Public Prosecutions to make a decision under section 37B.

C:16.2 When a detainee is charged with or informed they may be prosecuted for an offence, see *Note 16B*, they shall, unless the restriction on drawing adverse inferences from silence applies, see Annex C, be cautioned as follows:

> *"You do not have to say anything. But it may harm your defence if you do not mention now something which you later rely on in court. Anything you do say may be given in evidence.".*

Where the use of the Welsh Language is appropriate, a constable may provide the caution directly in Welsh in the following terms:

> *"Does dim rhaid i chi ddweud dim byd. Ond gall niweidio eich amddiffyniad os na fyddwch chi'n sôn, yn awr, am rywbeth y byddwch chi'n dibynnu arno nes ymlaen yn y llys. Gall un-*

rhyw beth yr ydych yn ei ddweud gael ei roi fel tystiolaeth."

Annex C, paragraph 2 sets out the alternative terms of the caution to be used when the restriction on drawing adverse inferences from silence applies.

C:16.3 When a detainee is charged they shall be given a written notice showing particulars of the offence and, subject to paragraph 2.6A, the officer's name and the case reference number. As far as possible the particulars of the charge shall be stated in simple terms, but they shall also show the precise offence in law with which the detainee is charged. The notice shall begin:

"You are charged with the offence(s) shown below." Followed by the caution.

If the detainee is a juvenile, mentally disordered or otherwise mentally vulnerable, the notice should be given to the appropriate adult.

C:16.4 If, after a detainee has been charged with or informed they may be prosecuted for an offence, an officer wants to tell them about any written statement or interview with another person relating to such an offence, the detainee shall either be handed a true copy of the written statement or the content of the interview record brought to their attention [*sic*]. Nothing shall be done to invite any reply or comment except to:

(a) caution the detainee, *"You do not have to say anything, but anything you do say may be given in evidence."*; where the use of the Welsh Language is appropriate, caution the detainee in the following terms: *"Does dim rhaid i chi ddweud dim byd, ond gall unrhyw beth yr ydych yn ei ddweud gael ei roi fel tystiolaeth."*; and

(b) remind the detainee about their right to legal advice.

C:16.4A If the detainee:

- cannot read, the document may be read to them;
- is a juvenile, mentally disordered or otherwise mentally vulnerable, the appropriate adult shall also be given a copy, or the interview record shall be brought to their attention.

A–90 **C:**16.5 A detainee may not be interviewed about an offence after they have been charged with, or informed they may be prosecuted for it, unless the interview is necessary:

- to prevent or minimise harm or loss to some other person, or the public;
- to clear up an ambiguity in a previous answer or statement;
- in the interests of justice for the detainee to have put to them, and have an opportunity to comment on, information concerning the offence which has come to light since they were charged or informed they might be prosecuted.

Before any such interview, the interviewer shall:

(a) caution the detainee, *"You do not have to say anything, but anything you do say may be given in evidence."*; where the use of the Welsh Language is appropriate, the interviewer shall caution the detainee, *"Does dim rhaid i chi ddweud dim byd, ond gall unrhyw beth yr ydych yn ei ddweud gael ei roi fel tystiolaeth."*;

(b) remind the detainee about their right to legal advice.

See *Note 16B*.

C:16.6 The provisions of paragraphs 16.2 to 16.5 must be complied with in the appropriate adult's presence if they are already at the police station. If they are not at the police station then these provisions must be complied with again in their presence when they arrive unless the detainee has been released. See *Note 16C*.

C:16.7 When a juvenile is charged with an offence and the custody officer authorises their continued detention after charge, the custody officer must try to make arrangements for the juvenile to be taken into the care of a local authority to be detained pending appearance in court unless the custody officer certifies it is impracticable to do so or, in the case of a juvenile of at least 12 years old [*sic*], no secure accommodation is available and there is a risk to the public of serious harm from that juvenile, in accordance with *PACE*, section 38(6). See *Note 16D*.

(b) Documentation

C:16.8 A record shall be made of anything a detainee says when charged.

C:16.9 Any questions put in an interview after charge and answers given relating to the offence shall be recorded in full during the interview on forms for that purpose and the record signed by the detainee or, if they refuse, by the interviewer and any third parties present. If the questions are audibly recorded or visually recorded the arrangements in Code E or F apply.

C:16.10 If it is not practicable to make arrangements for a juvenile's transfer into local authority care as in paragraph 16.7, the custody officer must record the reasons and complete a certificate to be produced before the court with the juvenile. See *Note 16D*.

Notes for guidance

C:16A *The custody officer must take into account alternatives to prosecution under the* Crime and Disorder Act *1998, reprimands and warning applicable to persons under 18, and in national guidance on the cautioning of offenders, for persons aged 18 and over.* **A–91**

C:16AA *When a person is arrested under the provisions of the* Criminal Justice Act *2003 which allow a person to be re-tried after being acquitted of a serious offence which is a qualifying offence specified in Schedule 5 to that Act and not precluded from further prosecution by virtue of section 75(3) of that Act the detention provisions of* PACE *are modified and make an officer of the rank of superintendant or above who has not been directly involved in the investigation responsible for determining whether the evidence is sufficient to charge.*

C:16AB *Where guidance issued by the Director of Public Prosecutions under section 37B is in force, a custody officer who determines in accordance with that guidance that there is sufficient evidence to charge the detainee, may detain that person for no longer than is reasonably necessary to decide how that person is to be dealt with under* PACE *section 37(7)(a) to (d), including, where appropriate, consultation with the duty prosecutor. The period is subject to the maximum period of detention before charge determined by* PACE, *sections 41* to *44. Where in accordance with the guidance the case is referred to the CPS for decision, the custody officer should ensure that an officer involved in the investigation sends to the CPS such information as is specified in the guidance.*

C:16B *The giving of a warning or the service of the Notice of Intended Prosecution required by the* Road Traffic Offenders Act *1988, section 1 does not amount to informing a detainee they may be prosecuted for an offence and so does not preclude further questioning in relation to that offence.*

C:16C *There is no power under* PACE *to detain a person and delay action under paragraphs 16.2 to 16.5 solely to await the arrival of the appropriate adult. After charge, bail cannot be refused, or release on bail delayed, simply because an appropriate adult is not available, unless the absence of that adult provides the custody officer with the necessary grounds to authorise detention after charge under* PACE, *section 38.*

C:16D *Except as in paragraph 16.7, neither a juvenile's behaviour nor the nature of the offence provides grounds for the custody officer to decide it is impracticable to arrange the juvenile's transfer to local authority care. Similarly, the lack of secure local authority accommodation does not make it impracticable to transfer the juvenile. The availability of secure accommodation is only a factor in relation to a juvenile aged 12 or over when the local authority accommodation would not be adequate to protect the public from serious harm from them. The obligation to transfer a juvenile to local authority accommodation applies as much to a juvenile charged during the daytime as to a juvenile to be held overnight, subject to a requirement to bring the juvenile before a court under* PACE, *section 46.*

C:17 Testing persons for the presence of specified Class A drugs

(a) *Action*

C:17.1 This section of Code C applies only in selected police stations in police areas where the provisions for drug testing under section 63B of *PACE* (as amended by section 5 of the *Criminal Justice Act* 2003 and section 7 of the *Drugs Act* 2005) are in force and in respect of which the Secretary of State has given a notification to the relevant chief officer of police that arrangements for the taking of samples have been made. Such a notificiation will cover either a police area as a whole or particular stations within a police area. The notification indicates whether the testing applies to those arrested or charged or under the age of 18 as the case may be and testing can only take place in respect of the persons so indicated in the notification. Testing cannot be carried out unless the relevant notification has been given and has not been withdrawn. See *Note 17F*. **A–91a**

C:17.2 A sample of urine or a non-intimate sample may be taken from a person in police detention for the purpose of ascertaining whether he has any specified Class A drug in his body only where they have been brought before the custody officer and;

(a) either the arrest condition, see paragraph 17.3, or the charge condition, see paragraph 17.4, is met;

(b) the age condition, see paragraph 17.5, is met;

(c) the notification condition is met in relation to the arrest condition, the charge condition, or the age condition, as the case may be; (testing on charge and/or arrest must be specifically provided for in the notification for the power to apply; in addition, the fact that testing of under 18s is authorised must be expressly provided for in the notification before the power to test such persons applies); see paragraph 17.1; and

(d) a police officer has requested the person concerned to give the sample (the request condition).

C:17.3 The arrest condition is met where the detainee:

(a) has been arrested for a trigger offence, see *Note 17E*, but not charged with that offence; or

(b) has been arrested for any other offence but not charged with that offence and a police officer of inspector rank or above, who has reasonable grounds for suspecting that their misuse of any specified Class A drug caused or contributed to the offence, has authorised the sample to be taken.

C:17.4 The charge condition is met where the detainee:

(a) has been charged with a trigger offence, or

(b) has been charged with any other offence and a police officer of inspector rank or above, who has reasonable grounds for suspecting that the detainee's misuse of any specified Class A drug caused or contributed to the offence, has authorised the sample to be taken.

C:17.5 The age condition is met where:

(a) in the case of a detainee who has been arrested but not charged as in paragraph 17.3, they are aged 18 or over;

(b) in the case of a detainee who has been charged as in paragraph 17.4, they are aged 14 or over.

C:17.6 Before requesting a sample from the person concerned, an officer must:

(a) inform them that the purpose of taking the sample is for drug testing under *PACE*; this is to ascertain whether they have a specified Class A drug present in their body;

(b) warn them that if, when so requested, they fail without good cause to provide a sample they may be liable to prosecution;

(c) where the taking of the sample has been authorised by an inspector or above in accordance with paragraph 17.3(b) or 17.4(b) above, inform them that the authorisation has been given and the grounds for giving it;

(d) remind them of the following rights, which may be exercised at any stage during the period in custody:

(i) the right to have someone informed of their arrest [see section 5];

(ii) the right to consult privately with a solicitor and that free independent legal advice is available [see section 6]; and

(iii) the right to consult these codes of practice [see section 3].

C:17.7 In the case of a person who has not attained the age of 17—

(a) the making of the request for a sample under paragraph 17.2(d) above;

(b) the giving of the warning and the information under paragraph 17.6 above; and

(c) the taking of the sample,

may not take place except in the presence of an appropriate adult. (See *Note 17G*.)

C:17.8 Authorisation by an officer of the rank of inspector or above within paragraph 17.3(b) or 17.4(b) may be given orally or in writing but, if it is given orally, it must be confirmed in writing as soon as practicable.

C:17.9 If a sample is taken from a detainee who has been arrested for an offence but not charged with that offence as in paragraph 17.3, no further sample may be taken during the same continuous period of detention. If during that same period the charge condition is also met in respect of that detainee, the sample which has been taken shall be treated as being taken by virtue of the charge condition, see paragraph 17.4, being met.

C:17.10 A detainee from whom a sample may be taken may be detained for up to six hours from the time of the charge if the custody officer reasonably believes the detention is necessary to enable a sample to be taken. Where the arrest condition is met, a detainee whom the custody officer has decided to release on bail without charge may continue to be detained, but not beyond 24 hours from the relevant time (as defined in section 41(2) of *PACE*), to enable a sample to be taken.

C:17.11 A detainee in respect of whom the arrest condition is met, but not the charge condition, see paragraphs 17.3 and 17.4, and whose release would be required before a sample can be taken had they not continued to be detained as a result of being arrested for a further offence which does not satisfy the arrest condition, may have a sample taken at any time within 24 hours after the arrest for the offence that satisfies the arrest condition.

(b) *Documentation*

C:17.12 The following must be recorded in the custody record:

(a) if a sample is taken following authorisation by an officer of the rank of inspector or above, the authorisation and the grounds for suspicion;

(b) the giving of a warning of the consequences of failure to provide a sample;

(c) the time at which the sample was given; and

(d) the time of charge or, where the arrest condition is being relied upon, the time of arrest and, where applicable, the fact that a sample taken after arrest but before charge is to be treated as being taken by virtue of the charge condition, where that is met in the same period of continuous detention. See paragraph 17.9.

(c) *General*

C:17.13 A sample may only be taken by a prescribed person. See *Note 17C*.

C:17.14 Force may not be used to take any sample for the purpose of drug testing.

C:17.15 The terms "Class A drug" and "misuse" have the same meanings as in the *Misuse of Drugs Act* 1971. "Specified" (in relation to a Class A drug) and "trigger offence" have the same meanings as in Part III of the *Criminal Justice and Court Services Act* 2000.

C:17.16 Any sample taken:

(a) may not be used for any purpose other than to ascertain whether the person concerned has a specified Class A drug present in his body; and

(b) can be disposed of as clinical waste unless it is to be sent for further analysis in cases where the test result is disputed at the point when the result is known, or where medication has been taken, or for quality assurance purposes.

(d) *Assessment of misuse of drugs*

C:17.17 Under the provisions of Part 3 of the *Drugs Act* 2005, where a detainee has tested positive for a specified Class A drug under section 63B of *PACE* a police officer may, at any time before the person's release from the police station, impose a requirement on the detainee for them to attend an initial assessment of their drug misuse by a suitably qualified person and to remain for its duration. Where such a requirement is imposed, the officer must, at the same time, impose a second requirement on the detainee to attend and remain for a follow-up assessment. The officer must inform the detainee that the second requirement will cease to have effect if, at the initial assessment they are informed that a follow-up assessment is not necessary. These requirements may only be imposed on a person if:

(a) they have reached the age of 18;

(b) notification has been given by the Secretary of State to the relevant chief officer of police that arrangements for conducting initial and follow-up assessments have been made for those from whom samples for testing have been taken at the police station where the detainee is in custody.

C:17.18 When imposing a requirement to attend an initial assessment and a follow-up assessment the police officer must:

(a) inform the person of the time and place at which the initial assessment is to take place;

(b) explain that this information will be confirmed in writing; and

(c) warn the person that they may be liable to prosecution if they fail without good cause to attend the initial assessment and remain for its duration and if they fail to attend the follow-up assessment and remain for its duration (if so required).

C:17.19 Where a police officer has imposed a requirement to attend an initial assessment and a follow-up assessment in accordance with paragraph 17.17, he must, before the person is released from detention, give the person notice in writing which:

(a) confirms their requirement to attend and remain for the duration of the assessments; and

(b) confirms the information and repeats the warning referred to in paragraph 17.18.

C:17.20 The following must be recorded in the custody record:

(a) that the requirement to attend an initial assessment and a follow-up assessment has been imposed; and

(b) the information, explanation, warning and notice given in accordance with paragraphs 17.17 and 17.19.

C:17.21 Where a notice is given in accordance with paragraph 17.19, a police officer can give the person a further notice in writing which informs the person of any change to the time or place at which the initial assessment is to take place and which repeats the warning referred to in paragraph 17.18(c).

C:17.22 Part 3 of the *Drugs Act* 2005 also requires police officers to have regard to any guidance issued by the Secretary of State in respect of the assessment provisions.

Notes for Guidance

C:17A *When warning a person who is asked to provide a urine or non-intimate sample in accordance with paragraph 17.6(b), the following form of words may be used:*

"You do not have to provide a sample, but I must warn you that if you fail or refuse without good cause to do so, you will commit an offence for which you may be imprisoned, or fined, or both.".

Where the Welsh language is appropriate, the following form of words may be used:

"Does dim rhaid i chi roi sampl, ond mae'n rhaid i mi eich rhybuddio y byddwch chi'n cyflawni trosedd os byddwch chi'n methu neu yn gwrthod gwneud hynny heb reswm da, ac y gellir, oherwydd hynny, eich carcharu, eich dirwyo, neu'r ddau."

C:17B *A sample has to be sufficient and suitable. A sufficient sample is sufficient in quantity and quality to enable drug testing analysis to take place. A suitable sample is one which, by its nature, is suitable for a particular form of drug analysis.*

C:17C *A prescribed person in paragraph 17.13 is one who is prescribed in regulations made by the Secretary of State under section 63B(6) of the* Police and Criminal Evidence Act *1984. [The regulations are currently contained in regulation S.I. 2001 No. 2645, the* Police and Criminal Evidence Act 1984 (Drug Testing Persons in Police Detention) (Prescribed Persons) Regulations *2001.]*

C:17D *Samples, and the information derived from them, may not be subsequently used in the investigation of any offence or in evidence against the persons from whom they were taken.*

C:17E *Trigger offences are:*

1. Offences under the following provisions of the Theft Act *1968*:

section 1	*(theft)*
section 8	*(robbery)*
section 9	*(burglary)*
section 10	*(aggravated burglary)*
section 12	*(taking a motor vehicle or other conveyance without authority)*
section 12A	*(aggravated vehicle-taking)*
section 22	*(handling stolen goods)*
section 25	*(going equipped for stealing, etc.)*

2. Offences under the following provisions of the Misuse of Drugs Act *1971, if committed in respect of a specified Class A drug:—*

section 4	*(restriction on production and supply of controlled drugs)*
section 5(2)	*(possession of a controlled drug)*
section 5(3)	*(possession of a controlled drug with intent to supply)*

3. Offences under the following provisions of the Fraud Act 2006:

section 1	*(fraud)*

section 6 *(possession etc. of articles for use in frauds)*
section 7 *(making or supplying articles for use in frauds)*

3A. *An offence under section 1(1) of the* Criminal Attempts Act *1981 if committed in respect of an offence under—*

(a) any of the following provisions of the Theft Act *1968*

section 1 *(theft)*
section 8 *(robbery)*
section 9 *(burglary)*
section 22 *(handling stolen goods)*

(b) section 1 of the Fraud Act *2006*

4. *Offences under the following provisions of the* Vagrancy Act *1824*:

section 3 *(begging)*
section 4 *(persistent begging)*

C:17F *The power to take samples is subject to notification by the Secretary of State that appropriate arrangements for the taking of samples have been made for the police area as a whole or for the particular police station concerned for whichever of the following is specified in the notification*:

(a) *persons in respect of whom the arrest condition is met;*
(b) *persons in respect of whom the charge condition is met;*
(c) *persons who have not attained the age of 18.*

Note: Notification is treated as having been given for the purposes of the charge condition in relation to a police area, if testing (on charge) under section 63B(2) of PACE was in force immediately before section 7 of the Drugs Act *2005 was brought into force; and for the purposes of the age condition, in relation to a police area or police station, if immediately before that day, notification that arrangements had been made for the taking of samples from persons under the age of 18 (those aged 14–17) had been given and had not been withdrawn.*

C:17G *Appropriate adult in paragraph 17.7 means the person's—*

(a) *parent or guardian or, if they are in the care of a local authority or voluntary organisation, a person representing that authority or organisation; or*
(b) *a social worker of a local authority; or*
(c) *if no person falling within (a) or (b) above is available, any responsible person aged 18 or over who is not a police officer or a person employed by the police.*

ANNEX A

Intimate and strip searches

A *Intimate search*

C:1. An intimate search consists of the physical examination of a person's body orifices other than the mouth. The intrusive nature of such searches means the actual and potential risks associated with intimate searches must never be underestimated. **A–92**

(a)

Action

C:2. Body orifices other than the mouth may be searched only: **A–93**

(a) if authorised by an officer of inspector rank or above who has reasonable grounds for believing that the person may have concealed on themselves:
 (i) anything which they could and might use to cause physical injury to themselves or others at the station; or
 (ii) a Class A drug which they intended to supply to another or to export;

and the officer has reasonable grounds for believing that an intimate search is the only means of removing those items; and

(b) if the search is under paragraph 2(a)(ii) (a drug offence search), the detainee's appropriate consent has been given in writing.

C:2A. Before the search begins, a police officer, designated detention officer or staff custody officer, must tell the detainee:—

(a) that the authority to carry out the search has been given;

(b) the grounds for giving the authorisation and for believing that the article cannot be removed without an intimate search.

C:2B Before a detainee is asked to give appropriate consent to a search under paragraph 2(a)(ii) (a drug offence search) they must be warned that if they refuse without good cause their refusal may harm their case if it comes to trial, see *Note A6*. This warning may be given by a police officer or member of police staff. A detainee who is not legally represented must be reminded of their entitlement to have free legal advice, see Code C, paragraph 6.5, and the reminder noted in the custody record.

C:3. An intimate search may only be carried out by a registered medical practitioner or registered nurse, unless an officer of at least inspector rank considers this is not practicable and the search is to take place under paragraph 2(a)(i), in which case a police officer may carry out the search. See *Notes A1* to *A5*.

C:3A. Any proposal for a search under paragraph 2(a)(i) to be carried out by someone other than a registered medical practitioner or registered nurse must only be considered as a last resort and when the authorising officer is satisfied the risks associated with allowing the item to remain with the detainee outweigh the risks associated with removing it. See *Notes A1* to *A5*.

C:4. An intimate search under:

- paragraph 2(a)(i) may take place only at a hospital, surgery, other medical premises or police station;
- paragraph 2(a)(ii) may take place only at a hospital, surgery or other medical premises and must be carried out by a registered medical practitioner or a registered nurse.

C:5. An intimate search at a police station of a juvenile or mentally disordered or otherwise mentally vulnerable person may take place only in the presence of an appropriate adult of the same sex, unless the detainee specifically requests a particular adult of the opposite sex who is readily available. In the case of a juvenile the search may take place in the absence of the appropriate adult only if the juvenile signifies in the presence of the appropriate adult they do not want the adult present during the search and the adult agrees. A record shall be made of the juvenile's decision and signed by the appropriate adult.

C:6. When an intimate search under paragraph 2(a)(i) is carried out by a police officer, the officer must be of the same sex as the detainee. A minimum of two people, other than the detainee, must be present during the search. Subject to paragraph 5, no person of the opposite sex who is not a medical practitioner or nurse shall be present, nor shall anyone whose presence is unnecessary. The search shall be conducted with proper regard to the sensitivity and vulnerability of the detainee.

(b)

Documentation

A–94 **C:**7. In the case of an intimate search the following shall be recorded as soon as practicable, in the detainee's custody record:

(a) for searches under paragraphs 2(a)(i) and (ii);

- the authorisation to carry out the search;
- the grounds for giving the authorisation;
- the grounds for believing the article could not be removed without an intimate search;
- which parts of the detainee's body were searched;
- who carried out the search;
- who was present;
- the result;

(b) for searches under paragraph 2(a)(ii):

- the giving of the warning required by paragraph 2B;

- the fact that the appropriate consent was given or (as the case may be) refused, and if refused, the reason given for the refusal (if any).

C:8. If an intimate search is carried out by a police officer, the reason why it was impracticable for a registered medical practitioner or registered nurse to conduct it must be recorded.

B *Strip search*

C:9. A strip search is a search involving the removal of more than outer clothing. In this code, outer clothing includes shoes and socks. **A–95**

(a)

Action

C:10. A strip search may take place only if it is considered necessary to remove an article which a detainee would not be allowed to keep, and the officer reasonably considers the detainee might have concealed such an article. Strip searches shall not be routinely carried out if there is no reason to consider that articles are concealed. **A–96**

The conduct of strip searches

C:11. When strip searches are conducted:

(a) a police officer carrying out a strip search must be the same sex as the detainee;

(b) the search shall take place in an area where the detainee cannot be seen by anyone who does not need to be present, nor by a member of the opposite sex except an appropriate adult who has been specifically requested by the detainee;

(c) except in cases of urgency, where there is risk of serious harm to the detainee or to others, whenever a strip search involves exposure of intimate body parts, there must be at least two people present other than the detainee, and if the search is of a juvenile or mentally disordered or otherwise mentally vulnerable person, one of the people must be the appropriate adult. Except in urgent cases as above, a search of a juvenile may take place in the absence of the appropriate adult only if the juvenile signifies in the presence of the appropriate adult that they do not want the adult to be present during the search and the adult agrees. A record shall be made of the juvenile's decision and signed by the appropriate adult. The presence of more than two people, other than an appropriate adult, shall be permitted only in the most exceptional circumstances;

(d) the search shall be conducted with proper regard to the sensitivity and vulnerability of the detainee in these circumstances and every reasonable effort shall be made to secure the detainee's co-operation and minimise embarrassment. Detainees who are searched shall not normally be required to remove all their clothes at the same time, *e.g.* a person should be allowed to remove clothing above the waist and redress before removing further clothing;

(e) if necessary to assist the search, the detainee may be required to hold their arms in the air or to stand with their legs apart and bend forward so a visual examination may be made of the genital and anal areas provided no physical contact is made with any body orifice;

(f) if articles are found, the detainee shall be asked to hand them over. If articles are found within any body orifice other than the mouth, and the detainee refuses to hand them over, their removal would constitute an intimate search, which must be carried out as in Part A;

(g) a strip search shall be conducted as quickly as possible, and the detainee allowed to dress as soon as the procedure is complete.

(b)

Documentation

C:12. A record shall be made on the custody record of a strip search including the reason it was considered necessary, those present and any result. **A–97**

Notes for guidance

C:A1 *Before authorising any intimate search, the authorising officer must make every rea-* **A–98**

sonable effort to persuade the detainee to hand the article over without a search. If the detainee agrees, a registered medical practitioner or registered nurse should whenever possible be asked to assess the risks involved and, if necessary, attend to assist the detainee.

C:A2 *If the detainee does not agree to hand the article over without a search, the authorising officer must carefully review all the relevant factors before authorising an intimate search. In particular, the officer must consider whether the grounds for believing an article may be concealed are reasonable.*

C:A3 *If authority is given for a search under paragraph 2(a)(i), a registered medical practitioner or registered nurse shall be consulted whenever possible. The presumption should be that the search will be conducted by the registered medical practitioner or registered nurse and the authorising officer must make every reasonable effort to persuade the detainee to allow the medical practitioner or nurse to conduct the search.*

C:A4 *A constable should only be authorised to carry out a search as a last resort and when all other approaches have failed. In these circumstances, the authorising officer must be satisfied the detainee might use the article for one or more of the purposes in paragraph 2(a)(i) and the physical injury likely to be caused is sufficiently severe to justify authorising a constable to carry out the search.*

C:A5 *If an officer has any doubts whether to authorise an intimate search by a constable, the officer should seek advice from an officer of superintendent rank or above.*

C:A6 *In warning a detainee who is asked to consent to an intimate drug offence search, as in paragraph 2B, the following form of words may be used:*

> *"You do not have to allow yourself to be searched, but I must warn you that if you refuse without good cause, your refusal may harm your case if it comes to trial.".*

Where the use of the Welsh Language is appropriate, the following form of words may be used:

> *"Nid oes rhaid i chi roi caniatâd i gael eich archwilio, ond mae'n rhaid i mi eich rhybuddio os gwrthodwch heb reswm da, y gallai eich penderfyniad i wrthod wneud niwed i'ch achos pe bai'n dod gerbron llys."*

ANNEX B

Delay in notifying arrest or allowing access to legal advice

A *Persons detained under PACE*

A–99 **C:**1. The exercise of the rights in section 5 or section 6, or both, may be delayed if the person is in police detention, as in *PACE*, section 118(2), in connection with an indictable offence, has not yet been charged with an offence and an officer of superintendent rank or above, or inspector rank or above only for the rights in section 5, has reasonable grounds for believing their exercise will:

(i) lead to:
- interference with, or harm to, evidence connected with an indictable offence; or
- interference with, or physical harm to, other people; or

(ii) lead to alerting other people suspected of having committed an indictable offence but not yet arrested for it; or

(iii) hinder the recovery of property obtained in consequence of the commission of such an offence.

C:2. These rights may also be delayed if the officer has reasonable grounds to believe that:

(i) the person detained for an indictable offence has benefited from their criminal conduct (decided in accordance with Part 2 of the *Proceeds of Crime Act* 2002); and

(ii) the recovery of the value of the property constituting that benefit will be hindered by the exercise of either right.

C:3. Authority to delay a detainee's right to consult privately with a solicitor may be given only if the authorising officer has reasonable grounds to believe the solicitor the detainee wants to consult will, inadvertently or otherwise, pass on a message from the detainee or act in some other way which will have any of the consequences specified under paragraphs 1 or 2. In these circumstances the detainee must be allowed to choose another solicitor. See *Note B3*.

C:4. If the detainee wishes to see a solicitor, access to that solicitor may not be delayed on the grounds they might advise the detainee not to answer questions or the solicitor was initially asked to attend the police station by someone else. In the latter case the detainee must be told the solicitor has come to the police station at another person's request, and must be asked to sign the custody record to signify whether they want to see the solicitor.

C:5. The fact the grounds for delaying notification of arrest may be satisfied does not automatically mean the grounds for delaying access to legal advice will also be satisfied.

C:6. These rights may be delayed only for as long as grounds exist and in no case beyond 36 hours after the relevant time as in *PACE*, section 41. If the grounds cease to apply within this time, the detainee must, as soon as practicable, be asked if they want to exercise either right, the custody record must be noted accordingly, and action taken in accordance with the relevant section of the code.

C:7. A detained person must be permitted to consult a solicitor for a reasonable time before any court hearing.

B *[Not used.]*

C *Documentation*

C:13. The grounds for action under this annex shall be recorded and the detainee informed of them as soon as practicable. **A–100**

C:14. Any reply given by a detainee under paragraphs 6 or 11 must be recorded and the detainee asked to endorse the record in relation to whether they want to receive legal advice at this point.

D *Cautions and special warnings*

C:15. When a suspect detained at a police station is interviewed during any period for which access to legal advice has been delayed under this annex, the court or jury may not draw adverse inferences from their silence.

Notes for guidance

C:B1 *Even if Annex B applies in the case of a juvenile, or a person who is mentally disordered or otherwise mentally vulnerable, action to inform the appropriate adult and the person responsible for a juvenile's welfare if that is a different person, must nevertheless be taken as in paragraph 3.13 and 3.15.* **A–101**

C:B2 *In the case of Commonwealth citizens and foreign nationals, see Note 7A.*

C:B3 *A decision to delay access to a specific solicitor is likely to be a rare occurrence and only when it can be shown the suspect is capable of misleading that particular solicitor and there is more than a substantial risk that the suspect will succeed in causing information to be conveyed which will lead to one or more of the specified consequences.*

ANNEX C

Restriction on drawing adverse inferences from silence and terms of the caution when the restriction applies

(a)

The restriction on drawing adverse inferences from silence

C:1. The *Criminal Justice and Public Order Act* 1994, sections 34, 36 and 37 as amended by the *Youth Justice and Criminal Evidence Act* 1999, section 58 describe the conditions under **A–102**

which adverse inferences may be drawn from a person's failure or refusal to say anything about their involvement in the offence when interviewed, after being charged or informed they may be prosecuted. These provisions are subject to an overriding restriction on the ability of a court or jury to draw adverse inferences from a person's silence. This restriction applies:

(a) to any detainee at a police station, see *Note 10C*, who, before being interviewed, see section 11, or being charged or informed they may be prosecuted, see section 16, has:
  (i) asked for legal advice, see section 6, paragraph 6.1;
  (ii) not been allowed an opportunity to consult a solicitor, including the duty solicitor, as in this code; and
  (iii) not changed their mind about wanting legal advice, see section 6, paragraph 6.6(d);
  – [note the condition in (ii) will
    – apply when a detainee who has asked for legal advice is interviewed before speaking to a solicitor as in section 6, paragraph 6.6(a) or (b);
    – not apply if the detained person declines to ask for the duty solicitor, see section 6, paragraphs 6.6(c) and (d)];

(b) to any person charged with, or informed they may be prosecuted for, an offence who:
  (i) has had brought to their notice a written statement made by another person or the content of an interview with another person which relates to that offence, see section 16, paragraph 16.4;
  (ii) is interviewed about that offence, see section 16, paragraph 16.5; or
  (iii) makes a written statement about that offence, see Annex D paragraphs 4 and 9.

(b)

Terms of the caution when the restriction applies

C:2. When a requirement to caution arises at a time when the restriction on drawing adverse inferences from silence applies, the caution shall be:

"You do not have to say anything, but anything you do say may be given in evidence.".

Where the use of the Welsh Language is appropriate, the caution may be used directly in Welsh in the following terms:

"Does dim rhaid i chi ddweud dim byd, ond gall unrhyw beth yr ydych chi'n ei ddweud gael ei roi fel tystiolaeth."

C:3. Whenever the restriction either begins to apply or ceases to apply after a caution has already been given, the person shall be re-cautioned in the appropriate terms. The changed position on drawing inferences and that the previous caution no longer applies shall also be explained to the detainee in ordinary language. See *Note C2*.

Notes for guidance

C:C1 *The restriction on drawing inferences from silence does not apply to a person who has not been detained and who therefore cannot be prevented from seeking legal advice if they want to, see paragraphs 10.2 and 3.15.*

C:C2 *The following is suggested as a framework to help explain changes in the position on drawing adverse inferences if the restriction on drawing adverse inferences from silence:*

(a) begins to apply:

"The caution you were previously given no longer applies. This is because after that caution:
(i) you asked to speak to a solicitor but have not yet been allowed an opportunity to speak to a solicitor;" see paragraph 1(a); or
"(ii) you have been charged with/informed you may be prosecuted." See paragraph 1(b).
"This means that from now on, adverse inferences cannot be drawn at court and your defence will not be harmed just because you choose to say nothing. Please listen carefully to the caution I am about to give you because it will apply from now on. You will see that it does not say anything about your defence being harmed.";

(b) ceases to apply before or at the time the person is charged or informed they may be prosecuted, see paragraph 1(a);

"The caution you were previously given no longer applies. This is because after that caution

you have been allowed an opportunity to speak to a solicitor. Please listen carefully to the caution I am about to give you because it will apply from now on. It explains how your defence at court may be affected if you choose to say nothing.".

ANNEX D

Written statements under caution

(a)

Written by a person under caution

C:1. A person shall always be invited to write down what they want to say. A–103

C:2. A person who has not been charged with, or informed they may be prosecuted for, any offence to which the statement they want to write relates, shall:

(a) unless the statement is made at a time when the restriction on drawing adverse inferences from silence applies, see Annex C, be asked to write out and sign the following before writing what they want to say:

"I make this statement of my own free will. I understand that I do not have to say anything but that it may harm my defence if I do not mention when questioned something which I later rely on in court. This statement may be given in evidence.";

(b) if the statement is made at a time when the restriction on drawing adverse inferences from silence applies, be asked to write out and sign the following before writing what they want to say;

"I make this statement of my own free will. I understand that I do not have to say anything. This statement may be given in evidence.".

C:3. When a person, on the occasion of being charged with or informed they may be prosecuted for any offence, asks to make a statement which relates to any such offence and wants to write it they shall:

(a) unless the restriction on drawing adverse inferences from silence, see Annex C, applied when they were so charged or informed they may be prosecuted, be asked to write out and sign the following before writing what they want to say:

"I make this statement of my own free will. I understand that I do not have to say anything but that it may harm my defence if I do not mention when questioned something which I later rely on in court. This statement may be given in evidence.";

(b) if the restriction on drawing adverse inferences from silence applied when they were so charged or informed they may be prosecuted, be asked to write out and sign the following before writing what they want to say:

"I make this statement of my own free will. I understand that I do not have to say anything. This statement may be given in evidence.".

C:4. When a person, who has already been charged with or informed they may be prosecuted for any offence, asks to make a statement which relates to any such offence and wants to write it they shall be asked to write out and sign the following before writing what they want to say:

"I make this statement of my own free will. I understand that I do not have to say anything. This statement may be given in evidence.".

C:5. Any person writing their own statement shall be allowed to do so without any prompting except a police officer or police staff may indicate to them which matters are material or question any ambiguity in the statement.

(b)

Written by a police officer or other police staff

C:6. If a person says they would like someone to write the statement for them, a police officer, or other police staff shall write the statement. A–104

C:7. If the person has not been charged with, or informed they may be prosecuted for, any offence to which the statement they want to make relates they shall, before starting, be asked to sign, or make their mark, to the following:

(a) unless the statement is made at a time when the restriction on drawing adverse inferences from silence applies, see Annex C:

"I,..................., wish to make a statement. I want someone to write down what I say. I understand that I do not have to say anything but that it may harm my defence if I do not mention when questioned something which I later rely on in court. This statement may be given in evidence.";

(b) if the statement is made at a time when the restriction on drawing adverse inferences from silence applies:

"I,..................., wish to make a statement. I want someone to write down what I say. I understand that I do not have to say anything. This statement may be given in evidence.".

C:8. If, on the occasion of being charged with or informed they may be prosecuted for any offence, the person asks to make a statement which relates to any such offence they shall before starting be asked to sign, or make their mark to, the following:

(a) unless the restriction on drawing adverse inferences from silence applied, see Annex C, when they were so charged or informed they may be prosecuted:

"I,..................., wish to make a statement. I want someone to write down what I say. I understand that I do not have to say anything but that it may harm my defence if I do not mention when questioned something which I later rely on in court. This statement may be given in evidence.";

(b) if the restriction on drawing adverse inferences from silence applied when they were so charged or informed they may be prosecuted:

"I,..................., wish to make a statement. I want someone to write down what I say. I understand that I do not have to say anything. This statement may be given in evidence.".

C:9. If, having already been charged with or informed they may be prosecuted for any offence, a person asks to make a statement which relates to any such offence they shall before starting, be asked to sign, or make their mark to:

"I,..................., wish to make a statement. I want someone to write down what I say. I understand that I do not have to say anything. This statement may be given in evidence.".

C:10. The person writing the statement must take down the exact words spoken by the person making it and must not edit or paraphrase it. Any questions that are necessary, *e.g.* to make it more intelligible, and the answers given must be recorded at the same time on the statement form.

C:11. When the writing of a statement is finished the person making it shall be asked to read it and to make any corrections, alterations or additions they want. When they have finished reading they shall be asked to write and sign or make their mark on the following certificate at the end of the statement:

"I have read the above statement, and I have been able to correct, alter or add anything I wish. This statement is true. I have made it of my own free will.".

C:12. If the person making the statement cannot read, or refuses to read it, or to write the above mentioned certificate at the end of it or to sign it, the person taking the statement shall read it to them and ask them if they would like to correct, alter or add anything and to put their signature or make their mark at the end. The person taking the statement shall certify on the statement itself what has occurred.

ANNEX E

Summary of provisions relating to mentally disordered and otherwise mentally vulnerable people

A–105 **C:**1. If an officer has any suspicion, or is told in good faith, that a person of any age may be mentally disordered or otherwise mentally vulnerable, or mentally incapable of understanding the significance of questions or their replies that person shall be treated as mentally disordered or otherwise mentally vulnerable for the purposes of this code. See paragraph 1.4.

C:2. In the case of a person who is mentally disordered or otherwise mentally vulnerable, "the appropriate adult" means:

(a) a relative, guardian or other person responsible for their care or custody;

(b) someone experienced in dealing with mentally disordered or mentally vulnerable people but who is not a police officer or employed by the police;

(c) failing these, some other responsible adult aged 18 or over who is not a police officer or employed by the police.

See paragraph 1.7(b) and Note 1D.

C:3. If the custody officer authorises the detention of a person who is mentally vulnerable or appears to be suffering from a mental disorder, the custody officer must as soon as practicable inform the appropriate adult of the grounds for detention and the person's whereabouts, and ask the adult to come to the police station to see them. If the appropriate adult:

- is already at the station when information is given as in paragraphs 3.1 to 3.5 the information must be given in their presence;
- is not at the station when the provisions of paragraph 3.1 to 3.5 are complied with these provisions must be complied with again in their presence once they arrive.

See paragraphs 3.15 to 3.17.

C:4. If the appropriate adult, having been informed of the right to legal advice, considers legal advice should be taken, the provisions of section 6 apply as if the mentally disordered or otherwise mentally vulnerable person had requested access to legal advice. See paragraph 3.19 and *Note E1*.

C:5. The custody officer must make sure a person receives appropriate clinical attention as soon as reasonably practicable if the person appears to be suffering from a mental disorder or in urgent cases immediately call the nearest health care professional or an ambulance. It is not intended these provisions delay the transfer of a detainee to a place of safety under the *Mental Health Act* 1983, section 136 if that is applicable. If an assessment under that Act is to take place at a police station, the custody officer must consider whether an appropriate health care professional should be called to conduct an initial clinical check on the detainee. See paragraph 9.5 and 9.6.

C:6. It is imperative a mentally disordered or otherwise mentally vulnerable person detained under the *Mental Health Act* 1983, section 136 be assessed as soon as possible. If that assessment is to take place at the police station, an approved social worker and registered medical practitioner shall be called to the station as soon as possible in order to interview and examine the detainee. Once the detainee has been interviewed, examined and suitable arrangements been made for their treatment or care, they can no longer be detained under section 136. A detainee should be immediately discharged from detention if a registered medical practitioner having examined them, concludes they are not mentally disordered within the meaning of the Act. See paragraph 3.16.

C:7. If a mentally disordered or otherwise mentally vulnerable person is cautioned in the absence of the appropriate adult, the caution must be repeated in the appropriate adult's presence. See paragraph 10.12.

C:8. A mentally disordered or otherwise mentally vulnerable person must not be interviewed or asked to provide or sign a written statement in the absence of the appropriate adult unless the provisions of paragraphs 11.1 or 11.18 to 11.20 apply. Questioning in these circumstances may not continue in the absence of the appropriate adult once sufficient information to avert the risk has been obtained. A record shall be made of the grounds for any decision to begin an interview in these circumstances. See paragraphs 11.1, 11.15 and 11.18 to 11.20.

C:9. If the appropriate adult is present at an interview, they shall be informed they are not expected to act simply as an observer and the purposes of their presence are to:

- advise the interviewee;
- observe whether or not the interview is being conducted properly and fairly;
- facilitate communication with the interviewee.

See paragraph 11.17.

C:10. If the detention of a mentally disordered or otherwise mentally vulnerable person is reviewed by a review officer or a superintendent, the appropriate adult must, if available at the time, be given an opportunity to make representations to the officer about the need for continuing detention. See paragraph 15.3. **A–106**

C:11. If the custody officer charges a mentally disordered or otherwise mentally vulnerable person with an offence or takes such other action as is appropriate when there is sufficient evidence for a prosecution this must be done in the presence of the appropriate adult. The written notice embodying any charge must be given to the appropriate adult. See paragraphs 16.1 to 16.4A.

C:12. An intimate or strip search of a mentally disordered or otherwise mentally vulnerable person may take place only in the presence of the appropriate adult of the same sex, unless the detainee specifically requests the presence of a particular adult of the opposite sex. A strip search may take place in the absence of an appropriate adult only in cases of urgency when there is a risk of serious harm to the detainee or others. See Annex A, paragraphs 5 and 11(c).

C:13. Particular care must be taken when deciding whether to use any form of approved restraints on a mentally disordered or otherwise mentally vulnerable person in a locked cell. See paragraph 8.2.

Notes for guidance

A–107 **C:**E1 *The purpose of the provision at paragraph 3.19 is to protect the rights of a mentally disordered or otherwise mentally vulnerable detained person who does not understand the significance of what is said to them. If the detained person wants to exercise the right to legal advice, the appropriate action should be taken and not delayed until the appropriate adult arrives. A mentally disordered or otherwise mentally vulnerable detained person should always be given an opportunity, when an appropriate adult is called to the police station, to consult privately with a solicitor in the absence of the appropriate adult if they want.*

C:E2 *Although people who are mentally disordered or otherwise mentally vulnerable are often capable of providing reliable evidence, they may, without knowing or wanting to do so, be particularly prone in certain circumstances to provide information that may be unreliable, misleading or self-incriminating. Special care should always be taken when questioning such a person, and the appropriate adult should be involved if there is any doubt about a person's mental state or capacity. Because of the risk of unreliable evidence, it is important to obtain corroboration of any facts admitted whenever possible.*

C:E3 *Because of the risks referred to in Note E2, which the presence of the appropriate adult is intended to minimise, officers of superintendent rank or above should exercise their discretion to authorise the commencement of an interview in the appropriate adult's absence only in exceptional cases, if it is necessary to avert an immediate risk of serious harm. See paragraphs 11.1, 11.18 to 11.20.*

ANNEX F

Countries with which bilateral consular conventions or agreements requiring notification of the arrest and detention of their nationals are in force as at 1 April 2003

A–108

Armenia	Italy
Austria	Japan
Azerbaijan	Kazakhstan
Belarus	Macedonia
Belgium	Mexico
Bosnia-Herzegovina	Moldova
Bulgaria	Mongolia
China*	Norway
Croatia	Poland
Cuba	Romania
Czech Republic	Russia
Denmark	Slovak Republic
Egypt	Slovenia
France	Spain
Georgia	Sweden
German Federal Republic	Tajikistan
Greece	Turkmenistan
Hungary	Ukraine

USA Yugoslavia
Uzbekistan

* Police are required to inform Chinese officials of arrest/detention in the Manchester consular district only. This comprises Derbyshire, Durham, Greater Manchester, Lancashire, Merseyside, North South and West Yorkshire, and Tyne and Wear.

ANNEX G

Fitness to be interviewed

C:1. This annex contains general guidance to help police officers and health care professionals assess whether a detainee might be at risk in an interview. **A–109**

C:2. A detainee may be at risk in an interview if it is considered that:

(a) conducting the interview could significantly harm the detainee's physical or mental state;

(b) anything the detainee says in the interview about their involvement or suspected involvement in the offence about which they are being interviewed **might** be considered unreliable in subsequent court proceedings because of their physical or mental state.

C:3. In assessing whether the detainee should be interviewed, the following must be considered:

(a) how the detainee's physical or mental state might affect their ability to understand the nature and purpose of the interview, to comprehend what is being asked and to appreciate the significance of any answers given and make rational decisions about whether they want to say anything;

(b) the extent to which the detainee's replies may be affected by their physical or mental condition rather than representing a rational and accurate explanation of their involvement in the offence;

(c) how the nature of the interview, which could include particularly probing questions, might affect the detainee.

C:4. It is essential health care professionals who are consulted consider the functional ability of the detainee rather than simply relying on a medical diagnosis, *e.g.* it is possible for a person with severe mental illness to be fit for interview. **A–110**

C:5. Health care professionals should advise on the need for an appropriate adult to be present, whether reassessment of the person's fitness for interview may be necessary if the interview lasts beyond a specified time, and whether a further specialist opinion may be required.

C:6. When health care professionals identify risks they should be asked to quantify the risks. They should inform the custody officer:

- whether the person's condition:
  - is likely to improve;
  - will require or be amenable to treatment; and
- indicate how long it may take for such improvement to take effect.

C:7. The role of the health care professional is to consider the risks and advise the custody officer of the outcome of that consideration. The health care professional's determination and any advice or recommendations should be made in writing and form part of the custody record.

C:8. Once the health care professional has provided that information, it is a matter for the custody officer to decide whether or not to allow the interview to go ahead and if the interview is to proceed, to determine what safeguards are needed. Nothing prevents safeguards being provided in addition to those required under the code. An example might be to have an appropriate health care professional present during the interview, in addition to an appropriate adult, in order constantly to monitor the person's condition and how it is being affected by the interview.

ANNEX H

Detained person: observation list

C:1. If any detainee fails to meet any of the following criteria, an appropriate health care professional or an ambulance must be called. **A–111**

C:2. When assessing the level of rousability, consider:

Rousability—can they be woken?

- go into the cell
- call their name
- shake gently

Response to questions—can they give appropriate answers to questions such as:

- What's your name?
- Where do you live?
- Where do you think you are?

Response to commands—can they respond appropriately to commands such as:

- Open your eyes!
- Lift one arm, now the other arm!

C:3. Remember to take into account the possibility or presence of other illnesses, injury, or mental condition, a person who is drowsy and smells of alcohol may also have the following:

- Diabetes
- Epilepsy
- Head injury
- Drug intoxication or overdose
- Stroke

ANNEX I

[Not used]

ANNEX J

[Not used]

ANNEX K

X-rays and ultrasound scans

(a)

Action

A–111a **C**:1. *PACE*, section 55A allows a person who has been arrested and is in police detention to have an x-ray taken of them or an ultrasound scan to be carried out on them (or both) if:

(a) authorised by an officer of inspector rank or above who has reasonably grounds for believing that the detainee:

(i) may have swallowed a Class A drug; and

(ii) was in possession of that Class A drug with the intention of supplying it to another or to export; and

(b) the detainee's appropriate consent has been given in writing.

C:2. Before an x-ray is taken or an ultrasound scan carried out, a police officer, designated detention officer or staff custody officer must tell the detainee:—

(a) that the authority has been given; and

(b) the grounds for giving the authorisation.

C:3. Before a detainee is asked to give appropriate consent to an x-ray or an ultrasound scan, they must be warned that if they refuse without good cause their refusal may harm their case if it comes to trial, see *Notes K1* and *K2*. This warning may be given by a police officer or member of police staff. A detainee who is not legally represented must be reminded of their entitlement to have free legal advice, see Code C, paragraph 6.5, and the reminder noted in the custody record.

C:4. An x-ray may be taken, or an ultrasound scan may be carried out, only by a registered medical practitioner or registered nurse, and only at a hospital, surgery or other medical premises.

(b)

Documentation

C:5. The following shall be recorded as soon as practicable in the detainee's custody record:
(a) the authorisation to take the x-ray or carry out the ultrasound scan (or both);
(b) the grounds for giving the authorisation;
(c) the giving of the warning required by paragraph 3; and
(d) the fact that the appropriate consent was given or (as the case may be) refused, and if refused, the reason given for the refusal (if any); and
(e) if an x-ray is taken or an ultrasound scan carried out:
- where it was taken or carried out;
- who took it or carried it out;
- who was present;
- the result.

Paragraphs 1.4–1.7 of this code apply and an appropriate adult should be present when consent is sought to any procedure under this annex.

Notes for guidance

C:K1 *If authority is given for an x-ray to be taken or an ultrasound scan to be carried out (or both), consideration should be given to asking a registered medical practitioner or registered nurse to explain to the detainee what is involved and to allay any concerns the detainee might have about the effect which taking an x-ray or carrying out an ultrasound scan might have on them. If appropriate consent is not given, evidence of the explanation may, if the case comes to trial, be relevant to determining whether the detainee had a good cause for refusing.* **A–111b**

C:K2 *In warning a detainee who is asked to consent to an x-ray being taken or an ultrasound scan being carried out (or both), as in paragraph 3, the following form of words may be used:*

"You do not have to allow an x-ray of you to be taken or an ultrasound scan to be carried out on you, but I must warn you that if you refuse without good cause, your refusal may harm your case if it comes to trial.".

Where the use of the Welsh Language is appropriate, the following form of words may be provided in Welsh:

"Does dim rhaid i chi ganiatáu cymryd sgan uwchsain neu belydr-x (neu'r ddau) arnoch, ond mae'n rhaid i mi eich rhybuddio os byddwch chi'n gwrthod gwneud hynny heb reswm da, fe allai hynny niweidio eich achos pe bai'n dod gerbron llys."

V. CODE D (IDENTIFICATION)

The text that follows is of the version of the code that came into force on March 7, 2011 see *ante*, Appendix A–1. **A–112**

In connection with Code D, see also §§ 14–29 *et seq.* (application of code), §§ 14–33 *et seq.* (identification parades), § 14–39 (group identification, confrontation and video identification), §§ 14–40 *et seq.* (effect of breaches), §§ 14–43 *et seq.* (photographs), §§ 14–46 *et seq.* (video recordings), and § 15–234 (photographs) in the main work.

D. Code of Practice for the Identification of Persons by Police Officers

Commencement—Transitional arrangements **A–113**

This code has effect in relation to any identification procedure carried out after midnight, twenty-one days after the day on which the *Police and Criminal Evidence Act 1984 (Codes of Practice) (Revision of Codes A, B and D) Order 2010* [*sic*] is made.

D:1 Introduction

D:1.1 This code of practice concerns the principal methods used by police to identify people in **A–114**

connection with the investigation of offences and the keeping of accurate and reliable criminal records. The powers and procedures in this code must be used fairly, responsibly, with respect for the people to whom they apply and without unlawful discrimination. The *Equality Act* 2010 makes it unlawful for police officers to discriminate against, harass or victimise any person on the grounds of the "protected characteristics" of age, disability, gender reassignment, race, religion or belief, sex and sexual orientation, marriage and civil partnership, pregnancy and maternity when using their powers. When police forces are carrying out their functions they also have a duty to have regard to the need to eliminate unlawful discrimination, harassment and victimisation and to take steps to foster good relations.

D:1.2 In this code, identification by an eye-witness arises when a witness who has seen the offender committing the crime and is given an opportunity to identify a person suspected of involvement in the offence in a video identification, identification parade or similar procedure. These eye-witness identification procedures (see Part A of section 3 below) are designed to:

- test the witness's ability to identify the suspect as the person they saw on a previous occasion;
- provide safeguards against mistaken identification.

While this code concentrates on visual identification procedures, it does not preclude the police making use of aural identification procedures such as a "voice identification parade", where they judge that appropriate.

D:1.2A In this code, separate provisions in Part B of section 3 below apply when any person, including a police officer, is asked if they recognise anyone they see in an image as being someone they know and to test their claim that they recognise that person as someone who is known to them. Except where stated, these separate provisions are not subject to the eye-witnesses identification procedures described in paragraph 1.2.

D:1.3 Identification by fingerprints applies when a person's fingerprints are taken to:

- compare with fingerprints found at the scene of a crime;
- check and prove convictions;
- help to ascertain a person's identity.

D:1.3A Identification using footwear impressions applies when a person's footwear impressions are taken to compare with impressions found at the scene of a crime.

D:1.4 Identification by body samples and impressions includes taking samples such as blood or hair to generate a DNA profile for comparison with material obtained from the scene of a crime, or a victim.

D:1.5 Taking photographs of arrested people applies to recording and checking identity and locating and tracing persons who:

- are wanted for offences;
- fail to answer their bail.

D:1.6 Another method of identification involves searching and examining detained suspects to find, *e.g.*, marks such as tattoos or scars which may help establish their identity or whether they have been involved in committing an offence.

D:1.7 The provisions of the *Police and Criminal Evidence Act* 1984 (*PACE*) and this code are designed to make sure fingerprints, samples, impressions and photographs are taken, used and retained, and identification procedures carried out, only when justified and necessary for preventing, detecting or investigating crime. If these provisions are not observed, the application of the relevant procedures in particular cases may be open to question.

D:2 General

A–115 **D:**2.1 This code must be readily available at all police stations for consultation by:

- police officers and police staff;
- detained persons;
- members of the public.

D:2.2 The provisions of this code:

- include the Annexes;
- do not include the *Notes for guidance*.

D:2.3 Code C, paragraph 1.4, regarding a person who may be mentally disordered or otherwise mentally vulnerable and the *Notes for guidance* applicable to those provisions apply to this code.

D:2.4 Code C, paragraph 1.5, regarding a person who appears to be under the age of 17 applies to this code.

D:2.5 Code C, paragraph 1.6, regarding a person who appears to be blind, seriously visually impaired, deaf, unable to read or speak or has difficulty communicating orally because of a speech impediment applies to this code.

D:2.6 In this code: **A–116**

- "appropriate adult" means the same as in Code C, paragraph 1.7;
- "solicitor" means the same as in Code C, paragraph 6.12;

and the *Notes for guidance* applicable to those provisions apply to this code;

- where a search or other procedure under this code may only be carried out or observed by a person of the same sex as the person to whom the search or procedure applies, the gender of the detainee and other persons present should be established and recorded in line with Annex F of Code A.

D:2.7 References to custody officers include those performing the functions of custody officer, see paragraph 1.9 of Code C.

D:2.8 When a record of any action requiring the authority of an officer of a specified rank is made under this code, subject to paragraph 2.18, the officer's name and rank must be recorded.

D:2.9 When this code requires the prior authority or agreement of an officer of at least inspector or superintendent rank, that authority may be given by a sergeant or chief inspector who has been authorised to perform the functions of the higher rank under *PACE*, section 107.

D:2.10 Subject to paragraph 2.18, all records must be timed and signed by the maker.

D:2.11 Records must be made in the custody record, unless otherwise specified. References to "pocket book" include any official report book issued to police officers or police staff. **A–117**

D:2.12 If any procedure in this code requires a person's consent, the consent of a:

- mentally disordered or otherwise mentally vulnerable person is only valid if given in the presence of the appropriate adult;
- juvenile is only valid if their parent's or guardian's consent is also obtained unless the juvenile is under 14, when their parent's or guardian's consent is sufficient in its own right. If the only obstacle to an identification procedure in section 3 is that a juvenile's parent or guardian refuses consent or reasonable efforts to obtain it have failed, the identification officer may apply the provisions of paragraph 3.21. See *Note 2A*.

D:2.13 If a person is blind, seriously visually impaired or unable to read, the custody officer or identification officer shall make sure their solicitor, relative, appropriate adult or some other person likely to take an interest in them and not involved in the investigation is available to help check any documentation. When this code requires written consent or signing, the person assisting may be asked to sign instead, if the detainee prefers. This paragraph does not require an appropriate adult to be called solely to assist in checking and signing documentation for a person who is not a juvenile, or mentally disordered or otherwise mentally vulnerable (see *Note 2B* and Code C paragraph 3.15).

D:2.14 If any procedure in this code requires information to be given to or sought from a suspect, it must be given or sought in the appropriate adult's presence if the suspect is mentally disordered, otherwise mentally vulnerable or a juvenile. If the appropriate adult is not present when the information is first given or sought, the procedure must be repeated in the presence of the appropriate adult when they arrive. If the suspect appears deaf or there is doubt about their hearing or speaking ability or ability to understand English, and effective communication cannot be established, the information must be given or sought through an interpreter.

D:2.15 Any procedure in this code involving the participation of a suspect who is mentally disordered, otherwise mentally vulnerable or a juvenile must take place in the presence of the appropriate adult. See Code C, paragraph 1.4.

D:2.15A Any procedure in this code involving the participation of a witness who is or appears to be mentally disordered, otherwise mentally vulnerable or a juvenile should take place in the presence of a pre trial support person unless the witness states that they do not want a support person to be present. A support person must not be allowed to prompt any identification of a suspect by a witness. See *Note 2AB*.

D:2.16 References to:

- "taking a photograph", include the use of any process to produce a single, still or moving, visual image;

- "photographing a person", should be construed accordingly;
- "photographs", "films", "negatives" and "copies" include relevant visual images recorded, stored, or reproduced through any medium;
- "destruction" includes the deletion of computer data relating to such images or making access to that data impossible.

D:2.17 Except as described, nothing in this code affects the powers and procedures:

(i) for requiring and taking samples of breath, blood and urine in relation to driving offences, etc, when under the influence of drink, drugs or excess alcohol under the:

- *Road Traffic Act* 1988, sections 4 to 11;
- *Road Traffic Offenders Act* 1988, sections 15 and 16;
- *Transport and Works Act* 1992, sections 26 to 38;

(ii) under the *Immigration Act* 1971, Schedule 2, paragraph 18, for taking photographs and fingerprints from persons detained under that Act, Schedule 2, paragraph 16 (administrative controls as to control on entry etc.); for taking fingerprints in accordance with the *Immigration and Asylum Act* 1999, sections 141 and 142(3), or other methods for collecting information about a person's external physical characteristics provided for by regulations made under that Act, section 144;

(iii) under the *Terrorism Act* 2000, Schedule 8, for taking photographs, fingerprints, skin impressions, body samples or impressions from people:

- arrested under that Act, section 41,
- detained for the purposes of examination under that Act, Schedule 7, and to whom the code of practice issued under that Act, Schedule 14, paragraph 6, applies ("the terrorism provisions"); see *Note 2C*;

(iv) for taking photographs, fingerprints, skin impressions, body samples or impressions from people who have been:

- arrested on warrants issued in Scotland, by officers exercising powers under the *Criminal Justice and Public Order Act* 1994, section 136(2);
- arrested or detained without warrant by officers from a police force in Scotland exercising their powers of arrest or detention under the *Criminal Justice and Public Order Act* 1994, section 137(2) (cross border powers of arrest etc.).

Note: in these cases, police powers and duties and the person's rights and entitlements whilst at a police station in England and Wales are the same as if the person had been arrested in Scotland by a Scottish police officer.

2.18 Nothing in this code requires the identity of officers or police staff to be recorded or disclosed:

(a) in the case of enquiries linked to the investigation of terrorism;

(b) if the officers or police staff reasonably believe recording or disclosing their names might put them in danger.

In these cases, they shall use warrant or other identification numbers and the name of their police station. *See Note 2D.*

A–118 **D:**2.19 In this code:

(a) "designated person" means a person other than a police officer, designated under the *Police Reform Act* 2002, Part 4, who has specified powers and duties of police officers conferred or imposed on them;

(b) any reference to a police officer includes a designated person acting in the exercise or performance of the powers and duties conferred or imposed on them by their designation.

D:2.20 If a power conferred on a designated person:

(a) allows reasonable force to be used when exercised by a police officer, a designated person exercising that power has the same entitlement to use force;

(b) includes power to use force to enter any premises, that power is not exercisable by that designated person except:

(i) in the company, and under the supervision, of a police officer; or

(ii) for the purpose of:

- saving life or limb; or

- preventing serious damage to property.

D:2.21 Nothing in this code prevents the custody officer, or other officer given custody of the detainee, from allowing police staff who are not designated persons to carry out individual procedures or tasks at the police station if the law allows. However, the officer remains responsible for making sure the procedures and tasks are carried out correctly in accordance with the codes of practice. Any such person must be:

(a) a person employed by a police authority maintaining a police force and under the control and direction of the chief officer of that force;

(b) employed by a person with whom a police authority has a contract for the provision of services relating to persons arrested or otherwise in custody.

D:2.22 Designated persons and other police staff must have regard to any relevant provisions of the codes of practice.

Notes for guidance

D:2A *For the purposes of paragraph 2.12, the consent required from a parent or guardian may, for a juvenile in the care of a local authority or voluntary organisation, be given by that authority or organisation. In the case of a juvenile, nothing in paragraph 2.12 requires the parent, guardian or representative of a local authority or voluntary organisation to be present to give their consent, unless they are acting as the appropriate adult under paragraphs 2.14 or 2.15. However, it is important that a parent or guardian not present is fully informed before being asked to consent. They must be given the same information about the procedure and the juvenile's suspected involvement in the offence as the juvenile and appropriate adult. The parent or guardian must also be allowed to speak to the juvenile and the appropriate adult if they wish. Provided the consent is fully informed and is not withdrawn, it may be obtained at any time before the procedure takes place.* **A–119**

D:2AB *The* Youth Justice and Criminal Evidence Act *1999 guidance "Achieving Best Evidence in Criminal Proceedings" indicates that a pre-trial support person should accompany a vulnerable witness during any identification procedure unless the witness states that they do not want a support person to be present. It states that this support person should not be (or not be likely to be) a witness in the investigation.*

D:2B *People who are seriously visually impaired or unable to read may be unwilling to sign police documents. The alternative,* i.e. *their representative signing on their behalf, seeks to protect the interests of both police and suspects.*

D:2C *Photographs, fingerprints, samples and impressions may be taken from a person detained under the terrorism provisions to help determine whether they are, or have been, involved in terrorism, as well as when there are reasonable grounds for suspecting their involvement in a particular offence.*

D:2D *The purpose of paragraph 2.18(b) is to protect those involved in serious organised crime investigations or arrests of particularly violent suspects when there is reliable information that those arrested or their associates may threaten or cause harm to the officers. In cases of doubt, an officer of inspector rank or above should be consulted.*

D:3 Identification and recognition of suspects

(A) Identification of a suspect by an eye-witness

D:3.0 This part applies when an eye-witness has seen the offender committing the crime or in any other circumstances which tend to prove or disprove the involvement of the person they saw in the crime, for example, close to the scene of the crime, immediately before or immediately after it was committed. It sets out the procedures to be used to test the ability of that eye-witness to identify a person suspected of involvement in the offence as the person they saw on the previous occasion. Except where stated, this part does not apply to the procedures described in Part B and *Note 3AA*. **A–120**

D:3.1 A record shall be made of the suspect's description as first given by a potential witness. This record must:

(a) be made and kept in a form which enables details of that description to be accurately produced from it, in a visible and legible form, which can be given to the suspect or the suspect's solicitor in accordance with this code; and

(b) unless otherwise specified, be made before the witness takes part in any identification procedures under paragraphs 3.5 to 3.10, 3.21 or 3.23.

A copy of the record shall where practicable, be given to the suspect or their solicitor before any procedures under paragraphs 3.5 to 3.10, 3.21 or 3.23 are carried out. See *Note 3E*.

(a) Cases when the suspect's identity is not known

D:3.2 In cases when the suspect's identity is not known, a witness may be taken to a particular neighbourhood or place to see whether they can identify the person they saw on a previous occasion. Although the number, age, sex, race, general description and style of clothing of other people present at the location and the way in which any identification is made cannot be controlled, the principles applicable to the formal procedures under paragraphs 3.5 to 3.10 shall be followed as far as practicable. For example:

(a) where it is practicable to do so, a record should be made of the witness's description of the suspect, as in paragraph 3.1(a), before asking the witness to make an identification;

(b) care must be taken not to direct the witness's attention to any individual unless, taking into account all the circumstances, this cannot be avoided; however, this does not prevent a witness being asked to look carefully at the people around at the time or to look towards a group or in a particular direction, if this appears necessary to make sure that the witness does not overlook a possible suspect simply because the witness is looking in the opposite direction and also to enable the witness to make comparisons between any suspect and others who are in the area; see *Note 3F*;

(c) where there is more than one witness, every effort should be made to keep them separate and witnesses should be taken to see whether they can identify a person independently;

(d) once there is sufficient information to justify the arrest of a particular individual for suspected involvement in the offence, *e.g.*, after a witness makes a positive identification, the provisions set out from paragraph 3.4 onwards shall apply for any other witnesses in relation to that individual;

(e) the officer or police staff accompanying the witness must record, in their pocket book, the action taken as soon as, and in as much detail, as possible. The record should include: the date, time and place of the relevant occasion the witness claims to have previously seen the suspect; where any identification was made; how it was made and the conditions at the time (*e.g.* the distance the witness was from the suspect, the weather and light); if the witness's attention was drawn to the suspect; the reason for this; and anything said by the witness or the suspect about the identification or the conduct of the procedure.

D:3.3 A witness must not be shown photographs, computerised or artist's composite likenesses or similar likenesses or pictures (including "E-fit" images) if the identity of the suspect is known to the police and the suspect is available to take part in a video identification, an identification parade or a group identification. If the suspect's identity is not known, the showing of such images to a witness to obtain identification evidence must be done in accordance with Annex E.

(b) Cases when the suspect is known and available

A–121 **D:**3.4 If the suspect's identity is known to the police and they are available, the identification procedures set out in paragraphs 3.5 to 3.10 may be used. References in this section to a suspect being "known" mean there is sufficient information known to the police to justify the arrest of a particular person for suspected involvement in the offence. A suspect being "available" means they are immediately available or will be within a reasonably short time and willing to take an effective part in at least one of the following which it is practicable to arrange:

- video identification;
- identification parade; or
- group identification.

Video identification

D:3.5 A "video identification" is when the witness is shown moving images of a known suspect, together with similar images of others who resemble the suspect. Moving images must be used unless:

- the suspect is known but not available (see paragraph 3.21 of this code); or
- in accordance with paragraph 2A of Annex A of this code, the identification officer does not consider that replication of a physical feature can be achieved or that it is not possible to conceal the location of the feature on the image of the suspect.

The identification officer may then decide to make use of video identification but using **still** images.

D:3.6 Video identifications must be carried out in accordance with Annex A.

Identification parade

D:3.7 An "identification parade" is when the witness sees the suspect in a line of others who resemble the suspect.

D:3.8 Identification parades must be carried out in accordance with Annex B.

Group identification

D:3.9 A "group identification" is when the witness sees the suspect in an informal group of people.

D:3.10 Group identifications must be carried out in accordance with Annex C.

Arranging identification procedures

D:3.11 Except for the provisions in paragraph 3.19, the arrangements for, and conduct of, the identification procedures in paragraphs 3.5 to 3.10 and circumstances in which an identification procedure must be held shall be the responsibility of an officer not below inspector rank who is not involved with the investigation, "the identification officer". Unless otherwise specified, the identification officer may allow another officer or police staff, see paragraph 2.21, to make arrangements for, and conduct, any of these identification procedures. In delegating these procedures, the identification officer must be able to supervise effectively and either intervene or be contacted for advice. No officer or any other person involved with the investigation of the case against the suspect, beyond the extent required by these procedures, may take any part in these procedures or act as the identification officer. This does not prevent the identification officer from consulting the officer in charge of the investigation to determine which procedure to use. When an identification procedure is required, in the interest of fairness to suspects and witnesses, it must be held as soon as practicable.

Circumstances in which an eye-witness identification procedure must be held

D:3.12 Whenever: A–122

(i) an eye witness has identified a suspect or purported to have identified them prior to any identification procedure set out in paragraphs 3.5 to 3.10 having been held; or

(ii) there is a witness available who expresses an ability to identify the suspect, or where there is a reasonable chance of the witness being able to do so, and they have not been given an opportunity to identify the suspect in any of the procedures set out in paragraphs 3.5 to 3.10,

and the suspect disputes being the person the witness claims to have seen, an identification procedure shall be held unless it is not practicable or it would serve no useful purpose in proving or disproving whether the suspect was involved in committing the offence, for example:

- where the suspect admits being at the scene of the crime and gives an account of what took place and the eye-witness does not see anything which contradicts that;
- when it is not disputed that the suspect is already known to the witness who claims to have recognised them when seeing them commit the crime.

D:3.13 An eye-witness identification procedure may also be held if the officer in charge of the investigation considers it would be useful.

Selecting an identification procedure

D:3.14 If, because of paragraph 3.12, an identification procedure is to be held, the suspect shall initially be offered a video identification unless:

(a) a video identification is not practicable; or

(b) an identification parade is both practicable and more suitable than a video identification; or

(c) paragraph 3.16 applies.

The identification officer and the officer in charge of the investigation shall consult each other to determine which option is to be offered. An identification parade may not be practicable because of factors relating to the witnesses, such as their number, state of health, availability and travelling requirements. A video identification would normally be more suitable if it could be arranged and completed sooner than an identification parade. Before an option is offered the suspect must also be reminded of their entitlement to have free legal advice, see Code C, paragraph 6.5.

D:3.15 A suspect who refuses the identification procedure first offered shall be asked to state their reason for refusing and may get advice from their solicitor and/or if present, their appropriate adult. The suspect, solicitor and/or appropriate adult shall be allowed to make representations about why another procedure should be used. A record should be made of the reasons for refusal and any representations made. After considering any reasons given, and representations made, the identification officer shall, if appropriate, arrange for the suspect to be offered an alternative which the officer considers suitable and practicable. If the officer decides it is not suitable and practicable to offer an alternative identification procedure, the reasons for that decision shall be recorded.

D:3.16 A group identification may initially be offered if the officer in charge of the investigation considers it is more suitable than a video identification or an identification parade and the identification officer considers it practicable to arrange.

Notice to suspect

A–123 **D:**3.17 Unless paragraph 3.20 applies, before a video identification, an identification parade or group identification is arranged, the following shall be explained to the suspect:

(i) the purposes of the video identification, identification parade or group identification;

(ii) their entitlement to free legal advice; see Code C, paragraph 6.5;

(iii) the procedures for holding it, including their right to have a solicitor or friend present;

(iv) that they do not have to consent to or co-operate in a video identification, identification parade or group identification;

(v) that if they do not consent to, and co-operate in, a video identification, identification parade or group identification, their refusal may be given in evidence in any subsequent trial and police may proceed covertly without their consent or make other arrangements to test whether a witness can identify them, see paragraph 3.21;

(vi) whether, for the purposes of the video identification procedure, images of them have previously been obtained, see paragraph 3.20, and if so, that they may co-operate in providing further, suitable images to be used instead;

(vii) if appropriate, the special arrangements for juveniles;

(viii) if appropriate, the special arrangements for mentally disordered or otherwise mentally vulnerable people;

(ix) that if they significantly alter their appearance between being offered an identification procedure and any attempt to hold an identification procedure, this may be given in evidence if the case comes to trial, and the identification officer may then consider other forms of identification, see paragraph 3.21 and *Note 3C*;

(x) that a moving image or photograph may be taken of them when they attend for any identification procedure;

(xi) whether, before their identity became known, the witness was shown photographs, a computerised or artist's composite likeness or similar likeness or image by the police, see *Note 3B;*

(xii) that if they change their appearance before an identification parade, it may not be practicable to arrange one on the day or subsequently and, because of the appearance change, the identification officer may consider alternative methods of identification, see *Note 3C;*

(xiii) that they or their solicitor will be provided with details of the description of the suspect as first given by any witnesses who are to attend the video identification, identification parade, group identification or confrontation, see paragraph 3.1.

D:3.18 This information must also be recorded in a written notice handed to the suspect. The suspect must be given a reasonable opportunity to read the notice, after which, they should be asked to sign a second copy to indicate if they are willing to co-operate with the making of a video or take part in the identification parade or group identification. The signed copy shall be retained by the identification officer.

D:3.19 The duties of the identification officer under paragraphs 3.17 and 3.18 may be performed by the custody officer or other officer not involved in the investigation if:

(a) it is proposed to release the suspect in order that an identification procedure can be arranged and carried out and an inspector is not available to act as the identification officer, see paragraph 3.11, before the suspect leaves the station; or

(b) it is proposed to keep the suspect in police detention whilst the procedure is arranged and carried out and waiting for an inspector to act as the identification officer, see paragraph 3.11, would cause unreasonable delay to the investigation.

The officer concerned shall inform the identification officer of the action taken and give them the signed copy of the notice. See *Note 3C*

D:3.20 If the identification officer and officer in charge of the investigation suspect, on reasonable grounds that if the suspect was given the information and notice as in paragraphs 3.17 and 3.18, they would then take steps to avoid being seen by a witness in any identification procedure, the identification officer may arrange for images of the suspect suitable for use in a video identification procedure to be obtained before giving the information and notice. If suspect's [*sic*] images are obtained in these circumstances, the suspect may, for the purposes of a video identification procedure, co-operate in providing new images which if suitable, would be used instead, see paragraph 3.17(vi).

(c) Cases when the suspect is known but not available

D:3.21 When a known suspect is not available or has ceased to be available, see paragraph 3.4, the identification officer may make arrangements for a video identification (see Annex A). If necessary, the identification officer may follow the video identification procedures but using still images. Any suitable moving or still images may be used and these may be obtained covertly if necessary. Alternatively, the identification officer may make arrangements for a group identification. See *Note 3D*. These provisions may also be applied to juveniles where the consent of their parent or guardian is either refused or reasonable efforts to obtain that consent have failed (see paragraph 2.12). **A–124**

D:3.22 Any covert activity should be strictly limited to that necessary to test the ability of the witness to identify the suspect.

D:3.23 The identification officer may arrange for the suspect to be confronted by the witness if none of the options referred to in paragraphs 3.5 to 3.10 or 3.21 are practicable. A "confrontation" is when the suspect is directly confronted by the witness. A confrontation does not require the suspect's consent. Confrontations must be carried out in accordance with Annex D.

D:3.24 Requirements for information to be given to, or sought from, a suspect or for the suspect to be given an opportunity to view images before they are shown to a witness, do not apply if the suspect's lack of co-operation prevents the necessary action.

(d) Documentation

D:3.25 A record shall be made of the video identification, identification parade, group identification or confrontation on forms provided for the purpose. **A–125**

D:3.26 If the identification officer considers it is not practicable to hold a video identification or identification parade requested by the suspect, the reasons shall be recorded and explained to the suspect.

D:3.27 A record shall be made of a person's failure or refusal to co-operate in a video identification, identification parade or group identification and, if applicable, of the grounds for obtaining images in accordance with paragraph 3.20.

(e) Showing films and photographs of incidents and information released to the media

D:3.28 Nothing in this code inhibits showing films, photographs or other images to the public through the national or local media, or to police officers for the purposes of recognition and tracing suspects. However, when such material is shown to obtain evidence of recognition, the procedures in Part B will apply. See *Note 3AA*. **A–126**

D:3.29 When a broadcast or publication is made, see paragraph 3.28, a copy of the relevant material released to the media for the purposes of recognising or tracing the suspect, shall be kept. The suspect or their solicitor shall be allowed to view such material before any eye-witness identification procedures under paragraphs 3.5 to 3.10, 3.21 or 3.23 of Part A are carried out, provided it is practicable and would not unreasonably delay the investigation. Each eye-witness involved in the procedure shall be asked, after they have taken part, whether they have seen any film, photograph or image relating to the offence or any description of the suspect which has been broadcast or published in any national or local media or on any social networking site and if they have, they should be asked to give details of the circumstances, such as the date and place as relevant. Their replies shall be recorded. This paragraph does not affect any separate requirement under the *Criminal Procedure and Investigations Act* 1996 to retain material in connection with criminal investigations.

(f) Destruction and retention of photographs taken or used in eye-witness identification procedures

D:3.30 *PACE*, section 64A, see paragraph 5.12, provides powers to take photographs of suspects and allows these photographs to be used or disclosed only for purposes related to the prevention or detection of crime, the investigation of offences or the conduct of prosecutions by, or on behalf of, police or other law enforcement and prosecuting authorities inside and outside the United Kingdom or the enforcement of a sentence. After being so used or disclosed, they may be retained but can only be used or disclosed for the same purposes.

D:3.31 Subject to paragraph 3.33, the photographs (and all negatives and copies), of suspects not taken in accordance with the provisions in paragraph 5.12 which are taken for the purposes of, or in connection with, the identification procedures in paragraphs 3.5 to 3.10, 3.21 or 3.23 must be destroyed unless the suspect:

(a) is charged with, or informed they may be prosecuted for, a recordable offence;

(b) is prosecuted for a recordable offence;

(c) is cautioned for a recordable offence or given a warning or reprimand in accordance with the *Crime and Disorder Act* 1998 for a recordable offence; or

(d) gives informed consent, in writing, for the photograph or images to be retained for purposes described in paragraph 3.30.

D:3.32 When paragraph 3.31 requires the destruction of any photograph, the person must be given an opportunity to witness the destruction or to have a certificate confirming the destruction if they request one within five days of being informed that the destruction is required.

D:3.33 Nothing in paragraph 3.31 affects any separate requirement under the *Criminal Procedure and Investigations Act* 1996 to retain material in connection with criminal investigations.

(B) Evidence of recognition by showing films, photographs and other images

A–126a **D:**3.34 This part of this section applies when, for the purposes of obtaining evidence of recognition, any person, including a police officer:

(a) views the image of an individual in a film, photograph or any other visual medium; and

(b) is asked whether they recognise that individual as someone who is known to them.

See *Notes 3AA* and *3G*.

D:3.35 The films, photographs and other images shall be shown on an individual basis to avoid any possibility of collusion and to provide safeguards against mistaken recognition (see *Note 3G*), the showing shall as far as possible follow the principles for video identification if the suspect is known, see Annex A, or identification by photographs if the suspect is not known, see Annex E.

D:3.36 A record of the circumstances and conditions under which the person is given an opportunity to recognise the individual must be made and the record must include:

(a) whether the person knew or was given information concerning the name or identity of any suspect;

(b) what the person has been told *before* the viewing about the offence, the person(s) depicted in the images or the offender and by whom;

(c) how and by whom the witness was asked to view the image or look at the individual;

(d) whether the viewing was alone or with others and if with others, the reason for it;

(e) the arrangements under which the person viewed the film or saw the individual and by whom those arrangements were made;

(f) whether the viewing of any images was arranged as part of a mass circulation to police and the public or for selected persons;

(g) the date time and place images were viewed or further viewed or the individual was seen;

(h) the times between which the images were viewed or the individual was seen;

(i) how the viewing of images or sighting of the individual was controlled and by whom;

(j) whether the person was familiar with the location shown in any images or the place where they saw the individual and if so, why;

(k) whether or not on this occasion, the person claims to recognise any image shown, or any individual seen, as being someone known to them, and if they do:

(i) the reason;

(ii) the words of recognition;

(iii) any expressions of doubt;

(iv) what features of the image or the individual triggered the recognition.

D:3.37 The record under paragraph 3.36 may be made by:

- the person who views the image or sees the individual and makes the recognition;
- the officer or police staff in charge of showing the images to the person or in charge of the conditions under which the person sees the individual.

Notes for guidance

D:3AA *The eye-witness identification procedures in Part A should not be used to test whether a witness can recognise a person as someone they know and would be able to give evidence of recognition along the lines that "On (describe date, time location) I saw an image of an individual who I recognised as AB." In these cases, the procedures in Part B shall apply.* **A–127**

D:3A *Except for the provisions of Annex E, paragraph 1, a police officer who is a witness for the purposes of this part of the code is subject to the same principles and procedures as a civilian witness.*

D:3B *When a witness attending an identification procedure has previously been shown photographs, or been shown or provided with computerised or artist's composite likenesses, or similar likenesses or pictures, it is the officer in charge of the investigation's responsibility to make the identification officer aware of this.*

D:3C *The purpose of paragraph 3.19 is to avoid or reduce delay in arranging identification procedures by enabling the required information and warnings, see sub-paragraphs 3.17(ix) and 3.17(xii), to be given at the earliest opportunity.*

D:3D *Paragraph 3.21 would apply when a known suspect deliberately makes themselves "unavailable" in order to delay or frustrate arrangements for obtaining identification evidence. It also applies when a suspect refuses or fails to take part in a video identification, an identification parade or a group identification, or refuses or fails to take part in the only practicable options from that list. It enables any suitable images of the suspect, moving or still, which are available or can be obtained, to be used in an identification procedure. Examples include images from custody and other CCTV systems and from visually recorded interview records, see Code F, Note for Guidance 2D.*

D:3E *When it is proposed to show photographs to a witness in accordance with Annex E, it is the responsibility of the officer in charge of the investigation to confirm to the officer responsible for supervising and directing the showing, that the first description of the suspect given by that witness has been recorded. If this description has not been recorded, the procedure under Annex E must be postponed. See Annex E, paragraph 2.*

D:3F *The admissibility and value of identification evidence obtained when carrying out the procedure under paragraph 3.2 may be compromised if:*

(a) before a person is identified, the witness's attention is specifically drawn to that person; or

(b) the suspect's identity becomes known before the procedure.

D:3G *The admissibility and value of evidence of recognition obtained when carrying out the procedures in Part B may be compromised if before the person is recognised, the witness who has claimed to know them is given or is made, or becomes aware of, information about the person which was not previously known to them personally but which they have purported to rely on to support their claim that the person is in fact known to them.*

D:4 Identification by fingerprints and footwear impressions

(A) Taking fingerprints in connection with a criminal investigation

(a) General **A–128**

D:4.1 References to "fingerprints" means any record, produced by any method, of the skin pattern and other physical characteristics or features of a person's:

(i) fingers; or

(ii) palms.

(b) Action

D:4.2 A person's fingerprints may be taken in connection with the investigation of an offence only with their consent or if paragraph 4.3 applies. If the person is at a police station consent must be in writing.

D:4.3 *PACE*, section 61, provides powers to take fingerprints without consent from any person over the age of ten years:

(a) under section 61(3), from a person detained at a police station in consequence of being arrested for a recordable offence, see *Note 4A*, if they have not had their fingerprints taken in the course of the investigation of the offence unless those previously taken fingerprints are not a complete set or some or all of those fingerprints are not of sufficient quality to allow satisfactory analysis, comparison or matching;

(b) under section 61(4), from a person detained at a police station who has been charged with a recordable offence, see *Note 4A*, or informed they will be reported for such an offence if they have not had their fingerprints taken in the course of the investigation of the offence unless those previously taken fingerprints are not a complete set or some or all of those fingerprints are not of sufficient quality to allow satisfactory analysis, comparison or matching;

(c) under section 61(4A), from a person who has been bailed to appear at a court or police station if the person:

(i) has answered to bail for a person whose fingerprints were taken previously and there are reasonable grounds for believing they are not the same person; or

(ii) who has answered to bail claims to be a different person from a person whose fingerprints were previously taken;

and in either case, the court or an officer of inspector rank or above, authorises the fingerprints to be taken at the court or police station (an inspector's authority may be given in writing or orally and confirmed in writing, as soon as practicable);

(ca) under section 61(5A) from a person who has been arrested for a recordable offence and released if the person:

(i) is on bail and has not had their fingerprints taken in the course of the investigation of the offence, or;

(ii) has had their fingerprints taken in the course of the investigation of the offence, but they do not constitute a complete set or some, or all, of the fingerprints are not of sufficient quality to allow satisfactory analysis, comparison or matching;

(cb) under section 61(5B) from a person not detained at a police station who has been charged with a recordable offence or informed they will be reported for such an offence if they have not had their fingerprints taken in the course of the investigation or their fingerprints have been taken in the course of the investigation of the offence, but they do not constitute a complete set or some, or all, of the fingerprints are not of sufficient quality to allow satisfactory analysis, comparison or matching;

(d) under section 61(6), from a person who has been:

(i) convicted of a recordable offence;

(ii) given a caution in respect of a recordable offence which, at the time of the caution, the person admitted; or

(iii) warned or reprimanded under the *Crime and Disorder Act* 1998, section 65, for a recordable offence, if, since their conviction, caution, warning or reprimand their fingerprints have not been taken or their fingerprints which have been taken since then do not constitute a complete set or some, or all, of the fingerprints are not of sufficient quality to allow satisfactory analysis, comparison or matching, and in either case, an officer of inspector rank or above, is satisfied that taking the fingerprints is necessary to assist in the prevention or detection of crime and authorises the taking;

(e) under section 61(6A) from a person a constable reasonably suspects is committing or attempting to commit, or has committed or attempted to commit, any offence if either:

- the person's name is unknown and cannot be readily ascertained by the constable; or
- the constable has reasonable grounds for doubting whether a name given by the person is their real name; note: fingerprints taken under this power are not regarded as having been taken in the course of the investigation of an offence; [see *Note 4C*];

(f) under section 61(6D) from a person who has been convicted outside England and Wales of an offence which if committed in England and Wales would be a qualifying offence as defined by *PACE*, section 65A (see *Note 4AB*) if:

(i) the person's fingerprints have not been taken previously under this power or their fingerprints have been so taken on a previous occasion but they do not constitute a complete set or some, or all, of the fingerprints are not of sufficient quality to allow satisfactory analysis, comparison or matching; and

(ii) a police officer of inspector rank or above is satisfied that taking fingerprints is necessary to assist in the prevention or detection of crime and authorises them to be taken.

D:4.4 *PACE*, section 63A(4) and Schedule 2A provide powers to:

(a) make a requirement (in accordance with Annex G) for a person to attend a police station to have their fingerprints taken in the exercise of certain powers in paragraph 4.3 above when that power applies at the time the fingerprints would be taken in accordance with the requirement; those powers are:

(i) section 61(5A)—persons arrested for a recordable offence and released, see paragraph 4.3(ca): the requirement may not be made more than six months from the day the investigating officer was informed that the fingerprints previously taken were incomplete or below standard;

(ii) section 61(5B)—persons charged etc. with a recordable offence, see paragraph 4.3(cb): the requirement may not be made more than six months from:

- the day the person was charged or reported if fingerprints have not been taken since then; or
- the day the investigating officer was informed that the fingerprints previously taken were incomplete or below standard;

(iii) section 61(6)—person convicted, cautioned, warned or reprimanded for a recordable offence in England and Wales, see paragraph 4.3(d): where the offence for which the person was convicted etc is also a qualifying offence (see *Note 4AB*), there is no time limit for the exercise of this power; where the conviction etc. is for a recordable offence which is not a qualifying offence, the requirement may not be made more than two years from:

- the day the person was convicted, cautioned, warned or reprimanded, or the day Schedule 2A comes into force (if later), if fingerprints have not been taken since then; or
- the day an officer from the force investigating the offence was informed that the fingerprints previously taken were incomplete or below standard or the day Schedule 2A comes into force (if later);

(v) [sic] section 61(6D)—a person who has been convicted of a qualifying offence (see *Note 4AB*) outside England and Wales, see paragraph 4.3(g): there is no time limit for making the requirement;

note: a person who has had their fingerprints taken under any of the powers in section 61 mentioned in paragraph 4.3 on two occasions in relation to any offence may not be required under Schedule 2A to attend a police station for their fingerprints to be taken again under section 61 in relation to that offence, unless authorised by an officer of inspector rank or above; the fact of the authorisation and the reasons for giving it must be recorded as soon as practicable;

(b) arrest, without warrant, a person who fails to comply with the requirement.

D:4.5 A person's fingerprints may be taken, as above, electronically.

D:4.6 Reasonable force may be used, if necessary, to take a person's fingerprints without their consent under the powers as in paragraphs 4.3 and 4.4.

D:4.7 Before any fingerprints are taken:

(a) without consent under any power mentioned in paragraphs 4.3 and 4.4 above, the person must be informed of:

(i) the reason their fingerprints are to be taken;

(ii) the power under which they are to be taken; and

(iii) the fact that the relevant authority has been given if any power mentioned in paragraph 4.3(c), (d) or (f) applies;

(b) with or without consent at a police station or elsewhere, the person must be informed:

(i) that their fingerprints may be subject of a speculative search against other fingerprints, see *Note 4B*; and

(ii) that their fingerprints may be retained in accordance with Annex F, Part (a) unless they were taken under the power mentioned in paragraph 4.3(e) when they must be destroyed after they have being [*sic*] checked (see *Note 4C*).

(c) Documentation

D:4.8A A record must be made as soon as practicable after the fingerprints are taken, of:

- the matters in paragraph 4.7(a)(i) to (iii) and the fact that the person has been informed of those matters; and
- the fact that the person has been informed of the matters in paragraph 4.7(b)(i) and (ii).

The record must be made in the person's custody record if they are detained at a police station when the fingerprints are taken.

D:4.8 If force is used, a record shall be made of the circumstances and those present.

D:4.9 *Not used*

(B) Taking fingerprints in connection with immigration enquiries

Action

A–129 **D**:4.10 A person's fingerprints may be taken and retained for the purposes of immigration law enforcement and control in accordance with powers and procedures other than under *PACE* and for which the UK Border Agency (not the police) are responsible. Details of these powers and procedures which are under the *Immigration Act* 1971, Schedule 2 and *Immigration and Asylum Act* 1999, section 141, including modifications to the *PACE* Codes of Practice are contained in Chapter 24 of the operational instructions and guidance manual which is published by the UK Border Agency (see *Note 4D*).

D:4.11 *Not used*

D:4.12 *Not used*

D:4.13 *Not used*

D:4.14 *Not used*

D:4.15 *Not used*

(C) Taking footwear impressions in connection with a criminal investigation

(a) Action

D:4.16 Impressions of a person's footwear may be taken in connection with the investigation of an offence only with their consent or if paragraph 4.17 applies. If the person is at a police station consent must be in writing.

D:4.17 *PACE*, section 61A, provides power for a police officer to take footwear impressions without consent from any person over the age of ten years who is detained at a police station:

(a) in consequence of being arrested for a recordable offence, see *Note 4A*; or if the detainee has been charged with a recordable offence, or informed they will be reported for such an offence; and

(b) the detainee has not had an impression of their footwear taken in the course of the investigation of the offence unless the previously taken impression is not complete or is not of sufficient quality to allow satisfactory analysis, comparison or matching (whether in the case in question or generally).

D:4.18 Reasonable force may be used, if necessary, to take a footwear impression from a detainee without consent under the power in paragraph 4.17.

D:4.19 Before any footwear impression is taken with, or without, consent as above, the person must be informed:

(a) of the reason the impression is to be taken;

(b) that the impression may be retained and may be subject of a speculative search against other impressions, see *Note 4B*, unless destruction of the impression is required in accordance with Annex F, Part (a); and

(c) that if their footwear impressions are required to be destroyed, they may witness their destruction as provided for in Annex F, Part (a).

(b) Documentation

D:4.20 A record must be made as soon as possible, of the reason for taking a person's footwear impressions without consent. If force is used, a record shall be made of the circumstances and those present.

D:4.21 A record shall be made when a person has been informed under the terms of paragraph 4.19(b), of the possibility that their footwear impressions may be subject of a speculative search.

Notes for guidance

D:4A *References to "recordable offences" in this code relate to those offences for which convictions, cautions, reprimands and warnings may be recorded in national police records: see* PACE, *section 27(4). The recordable offences current at the time when this code was prepared, are any offences which carry a sentence of imprisonment on conviction (irrespective of the period, or the age of the offender or actual sentence passed) as well as the non-imprisonable offences under the* Vagrancy Act *1824, sections 3 and 4 (begging and persistent begging), the* Street Offences Act *1959, section 1 (loitering or soliciting for purposes of prostitution), the* Road Traffic Act *1988, section 25 (tampering with motor vehicles), the* Criminal Justice and Public Order Act *1994, section 167 (touting for car hire services) and others listed in the* National Police Records (Recordable Offences) Regulations *2000 as amended.*

D:4AB *A qualifying offence is one of the offences specified in* PACE, *section 65A. These indictable offences which concern the use or threat of violence or unlawful force against persons, sexual offences and offences against children include, for example, murder, manslaughter, false imprisonment, kidnapping and other offences such as:*

- *sections 4, 16, 18, 20 to 24 or 47 of the* Offences Against the Person Act *1861;*
- *sections 16 to 18 of the* Firearms Act *1968;*
- *sections 9 or 10 of the* Theft Act *1968 or under section 12A of that Act involving an accident which caused a person's death;*
- *section 1 of the* Criminal Damage Act *1971 required to be charged as arson;*
- *section 1 of the* Protection of Children Act *1978 and;*
- *sections 1 to 19, 25, 26, 30 to 41, 47 to 50, 52, 53, 57 to 59, 61 to 67, 69 and 70 of the* Sexual Offences Act *2003.*

D:4B *Fingerprints, footwear impressions or a DNA sample (and the information derived from it) taken from a person arrested on suspicion of being involved in a recordable offence, or charged with such an offence, or informed they will be reported for such an offence, may be subject of a speculative search. This means the fingerprints, footwear impressions or DNA sample may be checked against other fingerprints, footwear impressions and DNA records held by, or on behalf of, the police and other law enforcement authorities in, or outside, the UK, or held in connection with, or as a result of, an investigation of an offence inside or outside the UK. Fingerprints, footwear impressions and samples taken from a person suspected of committing a recordable offence but not arrested, charged or informed they will be reported for it, may be subject to a speculative search only if the person consents in writing. The following is an example of a basic form of words:*

> *"I consent to my fingerprints, footwear impressions and DNA sample and information derived from it being retained and used only for purposes related to the prevention and detection of a crime, the investigation of an offence or the conduct of a prosecution either nationally or internationally.*
>
> *I understand that my fingerprints, footwear impressions or DNA sample may be checked against other fingerprint, footwear impressions and DNA records held by or on behalf of relevant law enforcement authorities, either nationally or internationally.*
>
> *I understand that once I have given my consent for my fingerprints, footwear impressions or DNA sample to be retained and used I cannot withdraw this consent."*

See Annex F regarding the retention and use of fingerprints and footwear impressions taken with consent for elimination purposes.

D:4C *The power under section 61(6A) of* PACE *described in paragraph 4.3(e) allows fingerprints of a suspect who has not been arrested to be taken in connection with any offence (whether recordable or not) using a mobile device and then checked on the street against the database containing the national fingerprint collection. Fingerprints taken under this power cannot be retained after they have been checked. The results may make an arrest for the suspected offence based on the name condition unnecessary (see code G, paragraph 2.9(a)) and enable the offence to be disposed of without arrest, for example, by summons/charging by post, penalty notice or words of advice. If arrest for a non-recordable offence is necessary for any* *other reasons, this power may also be exercised at the station. Before the power is exercised, the officer should:*

- *inform the person of the nature of the suspected offence and why they are suspected of committing it;*
- *give them a reasonable opportunity to establish their real name before deciding that their name is unknown and cannot be readily ascertained or that there are reasonable grounds to doubt that a name they have given is their real name;*
- *as applicable, inform the person of the reason why their name is not known and cannot be readily ascertained or of the grounds for doubting that a name they have given is their real name, including, for example, the reason why a particular document the person has produced to verify their real name, is not sufficient.*

D:4D *Powers to take fingerprints without consent for immigration purposes are given to police and immigration officers under the:*

(a) Immigration Act *1971, Schedule 2, paragraph 18(2), when it is reasonably necessary for the purposes of identifying a person detained under the* Immigration Act *1971, Schedule 2, paragraph 16 (detention of person liable to examination or removal), and*

(b) Immigration and Asylum Act *1999, section 141(7) when a person:*

- *fails without reasonable excuse to produce, on arrival, a valid passport with a photograph or some other document satisfactorily establishing their identity and nationality;*
- *is refused entry to the UK but is temporarily admitted if an immigration officer reasonably suspects the person might break a residence or reporting condition;*
- *is subject to directions for removal from the UK;*
- *has been arrested under the* Immigration Act *1971, Schedule 2, paragraph 17;*
- *has made a claim for asylum;*
- *is a dependant of any of the above.*

The Immigration and Asylum Act *1999, section 142(3), also gives police and immigration officers power to arrest without warrant a person who fails to comply with a requirement imposed by the Secretary of State to attend a specified place for fingerprinting.*

D:5 Examinations to establish identity and the taking of photographs

(A) Detainees at police stations

(a) *Searching or examination of detainees at police stations*

A–130 **D:**5.1 *PACE*, section 54A(1), allows a detainee at a police station to be searched or examined or both, to establish:

(a) whether they have any marks, features or injuries that would tend to identify them as a person involved in the commission of an offence and to photograph any identifying marks, see paragraph 5.5; or

(b) their identity, see *Note 5A*.

A person detained at a police station to be searched under a stop and search power, see Code A, is not a detainee for the purposes of these powers.

D:5.2 A search and/or examination to find marks under section 54A(1)(a) may be carried out without the detainee's consent, see paragraph 2.12, only if authorised by an officer of at least inspector rank when consent has been withheld or it is not practicable to obtain consent, see *Note 5D*.

D:5.3 A search or examination to establish a suspect's identity under section 54A(1)(b) may be carried out without the detainee's consent, see paragraph 2.12, only if authorised by an officer of at least inspector rank when the detainee has refused to identify themselves or the authorising officer has reasonable grounds for suspecting the person is not who they claim to be.

D:5.4 Any marks that assist in establishing the detainee's identity, or their identification as a person involved in the commission of an offence, are identifying marks. Such marks may be photographed with the detainee's consent, see paragraph 2.12; or without their consent if it is withheld or it is not practicable to obtain it, see *Note 5D*.

D:5.5 A detainee may only be searched, examined and photographed under section 54A, by a police officer of the same sex.

D:5.6 Any photographs of identifying marks, taken under section 54A, may be used or disclosed only for purposes related to the prevention or detection of crime, the investigation of offences or the conduct of prosecutions by, or on behalf of, police or other law enforcement and prosecuting authorities inside, and outside, the UK. After being so used or disclosed, the photograph may be retained but must not be used or disclosed except for these purposes, see *Note 5B*.

D:5.7 The powers, as in paragraph 5.1, do not affect any separate requirement under the *Criminal Procedure and Investigations Act* 1996 to retain material in connection with criminal investigations.

D:5.8 Authority for the search and/or examination for the purposes of paragraphs 5.2 and 5.3 may be given orally or in writing. If given orally, the authorising officer must confirm it in writing as soon as practicable. A separate authority is required for each purpose which applies.

D:5.9 If it is established a person is unwilling to co-operate sufficiently to enable a search and/or examination to take place or a suitable photograph to be taken, an officer may use reasonable force to:

(a) search and/or examine a detainee without their consent; and

(b) photograph any identifying marks without their consent.

D:5.10 The thoroughness and extent of any search or examination carried out in accordance with the powers in section 54A must be no more than the officer considers necessary to achieve the required purpose. Any search or examination which involves the removal of more than the person's outer clothing shall be conducted in accordance with Code C, Annex A, paragraph 11.

D:5.11 An intimate search may not be carried out under the powers in section 54A.

(b) *Photographing detainees at police stations and other persons elsewhere than at a police station*

D:5.12 Under *PACE*, section 64A, an officer may photograph: **A–131**

(a) any person whilst they are detained at a police station; and

(b) any person who is elsewhere than at a police station and who has been:

(i) arrested by a constable for an offence;

(ii) taken into custody by a constable after being arrested for an offence by a person other than a constable;

(iii) made subject to a requirement to wait with a community support officer under paragraph 2(3) or (3B) of Schedule 4 to the *Police Reform Act* 2002;

(iiia) given a direction by a constable under section 27 of the *Violent Crime Reduction Act* 2006.

(iv) given a penalty notice by a constable in uniform under Chapter 1 of Part 1 of the *Criminal Justice and Police Act* 2001, a penalty notice by a constable under section 444A of the *Education Act* 1996, or a fixed penalty notice by a constable in uniform under section 54 of the *Road Traffic Offenders Act* 1988;

(v) given a notice in relation to a relevant fixed penalty offence (within the meaning of paragraph 1 of Schedule 4 to the *Police Reform Act* 2002) by a community support officer by virtue of a designation applying that paragraph to him;

(vi) given a notice in relation to a relevant fixed penalty offence (within the meaning of paragraph 1 of Schedule 5 to the *Police Reform Act* 2002) by an accredited person by virtue of accreditation specifying that that paragraph applies to him; or

(vii) given a direction to leave and not return to a specified location for up to 48 hours by a police constable (under section 27 of the *Violent Crime Reduction Act* 2006).

D:5.12A Photographs taken under *PACE*, section 64A:

(a) may be taken with the person's consent, or without their consent if consent is withheld or it is not practicable to obtain their consent, see *Note 5E*; and

(b) may be used or disclosed only for purposes related to the prevention or detection of crime, the investigation of offences or the conduct of prosecutions by, or on behalf of, police or other law enforcement and prosecuting authorities inside and outside the United Kingdom or the enforcement of any sentence or order made by a court when dealing with an offence. After being so used or disclosed, they may be retained but can only be used or disclosed for the same purposes. See *Note 5B*.

D:5.13 The officer proposing to take a detainee's photograph may, for this purpose, require the person to remove any item or substance worn on, or over, all, or any part of, their head or face. If they do not comply with such a requirement, the officer may remove the item or substance.

D:5.14 If it is established the detainee is unwilling to co-operate sufficiently to enable a suitable photograph to be taken and it is not reasonably practicable to take the photograph covertly, an officer may use reasonable force, see *Note 5F*,

(a) to take their photograph without their consent; and

(b) for the purpose of taking the photograph, remove any item or substance worn on, or over, all, or any part of, the person's head or face which they have failed to remove when asked.

D:5.15 For the purposes of this code, a photograph may be obtained without the person's consent by making a copy of an image of them taken at any time on a camera system installed anywhere in the police station.

(c) *Information to be given*

A–132 **D**:5.16 When a person is searched, examined or photographed under the provisions as in paragraph 5.1 and 5.12, or their photograph obtained as in paragraph 5.15, they must be informed of the:

(a) purpose of the search, examination or photograph;

(b) grounds on which the relevant authority, if applicable, has been given; and

(c) purposes for which the photograph may be used, disclosed or retained.

This information must be given before the search or examination commences or the photograph is taken, except if the photograph is:

(i) to be taken covertly;

(ii) obtained as in paragraph 5.15, in which case the person must be informed as soon as practicable after the photograph is taken or obtained.

(d) *Documentation*

D:5.17 A record must be made when a detainee is searched, examined, or a photograph of the person, or any identifying marks found on them, are [*sic*] taken. The record must include the:

(a) identity, subject to paragraph 2.18, of the officer carrying out the search, examination or taking the photograph;

(b) purpose of the search, examination or photograph and the outcome;

(c) detainee's consent to the search, examination or photograph, or the reason the person was searched, examined or photographed without consent;

(d) giving of any authority as in paragraphs 5.2 and 5.3, the grounds for giving it and the authorising officer.

D:5.18 If force is used when searching, examining or taking a photograph in accordance with this section, a record shall be made of the circumstances and those present.

(B) Persons at police stations not detained

A–133 **D**:5.19 When there are reasonable grounds for suspecting the involvement of a person in a criminal offence, but that person is at a police station **voluntarily** and not detained, the provisions of paragraphs 5.1 to 5.18 should apply, subject to the modifications in the following paragraphs.

D:5.20 References to the "person being detained" and to the powers mentioned in paragraph 5.1 which apply only to detainees at police stations shall be omitted.

D:5.21 Force may not be used to:

(a) search and/or examine the person to:

(i) discover whether they have any marks that would tend to identify them as a person involved in the commission of an offence; or

(ii) establish their identity, see *Note 5A*;

(b) take photographs of any identifying marks, see paragraph 5.4; or

(c) take a photograph of the person.

D:5.22 Subject to paragraph 5.24, the photographs of persons or of their identifying marks which are not taken in accordance with the provisions mentioned in paragraphs 5.1 or 5.12, must be destroyed (together with any negatives and copies) unless the person:

(a) is charged with, or informed they may be prosecuted for, a recordable offence;

(b) is prosecuted for a recordable offence;

(c) is cautioned for a recordable offence or given a warning or reprimand in accordance with the *Crime and Disorder Act* 1998 for a recordable offence; or

(d) gives informed consent, in writing, for the photograph or image to be retained as in paragraph 5.6.

D:5.23 When paragraph 5.22 requires the destruction of any photograph, the person must be given an opportunity to witness the destruction or to have a certificate confirming the destruction provided they so request the certificate within five days of being informed the destruction is required.

D:5.24 Nothing in paragraph 5.22 affects any separate requirement under the *Criminal Procedure and Investigations Act* 1996 to retain material in connection with criminal investigations.

Notes for guidance

D:5A *The conditions under which fingerprints may be taken to assist in establishing a person's identity, are described in section 4.* **A–134**

D:5B *Examples of purposes related to the prevention or detection of crime, the investigation of offences or the conduct of prosecutions include:*

(a) *checking the photograph against other photographs held in records or in connection with, or as a result of, an investigation of an offence to establish whether the person is liable to arrest for other offences;*

(b) *when the person is arrested at the same time as other people, or at a time when it is likely that other people will be arrested, using the photograph to help establish who was arrested, at what time and where;*

(c) *when the real identity of the person is not known and cannot be readily ascertained or there are reasonable grounds for doubting a name and other personal details given by the person are their real name and personal details; in these circumstances, using or disclosing the photograph to help to establish or verify their real identity or determine whether they are liable to arrest for some other offence,* e.g. *by checking it against other photographs held in records or in connection with, or as a result of, an investigation of an offence;*

(d) *when it appears any identification procedure in section 3 may need to be arranged for which the person's photograph would assist;*

(e) *when the person's release without charge may be required, and if the release is:*

(i) *on bail to appear at a police station, using the photograph to help verify the person's identity when they answer their bail and if the person does not answer their bail, to assist in arresting them; or*

(ii) *without bail, using the photograph to help verify their identity or assist in locating them for the purposes of serving them with a summons to appear at court in criminal proceedings;*

(f) *when the person has answered to bail at a police station and there are reasonable grounds for doubting they are the person who was previously granted bail, using the photograph to help establish or verify their identity;*

(g) *when the person arrested on a warrant claims to be a different person from the person named on the warrant and a photograph would help to confirm or disprove their claim;*

(h) *when the person has been charged with, reported for, or convicted of, a recordable offence and their photograph is not already on record as a result of (a) to (f) or their photograph is on record but their appearance has changed since it was taken and the person has not yet been released or brought before a court.*

D:5C *There is no power to arrest a person convicted of a recordable offence solely to take their photograph. The power to take photographs in this section applies only where the person is in custody as a result of the exercise of another power,* e.g. *arrest for fingerprinting under* PACE, *section 27.*

D:5D *Examples of when it would not be practicable to obtain a detainee's consent, see paragraph 2.12, to a search, examination or the taking of a photograph of an identifying mark include:*

(a) *when the person is drunk or otherwise unfit to give consent;*

(b) *when there are reasonable grounds to suspect that if the person became aware a search or examination was to take place or an identifying mark was to be photographed, they would take steps to prevent this happening,* e.g. *by violently resisting, covering or concealing the mark etc and it would not otherwise be possible to carry out the search or examination or to photograph any identifying mark;*

(c) *in the case of a juvenile, if the parent or guardian cannot be contacted in sufficient time to allow the search or examination to be carried out or the photograph to be taken.*

D:5E *Examples of when it would not be practicable to obtain the person's consent, see paragraph 2.12, to a photograph being taken include:*

(a) *when the person is drunk or otherwise unfit to give consent;*

(b) *when there are reasonable grounds to suspect that if the person became aware a photograph, suitable to be used or disclosed for the use and disclosure described in paragraph 5.6, was to be taken, they would take steps to prevent it being taken,* e.g. *by violently resisting, covering or distorting their face etc, and it would not otherwise be possible to take a suitable photograph;*

(c) *when, in order to obtain a suitable photograph, it is necessary to take it covertly; and*

(d) *in the case of a juvenile, if the parent or guardian cannot be contacted in sufficient time to allow the photograph to be taken.*

D:5F *The use of reasonable force to take the photograph of a suspect elsewhere than at a police station must be carefully considered. In order to obtain a suspect's consent and co-operation to remove an item of religious headwear to take their photograph, a constable should consider whether in the circumstances of the situation the removal of the headwear and the taking of the photograph should be by an officer of the same sex as the person. It would be appropriate for these actions to be conducted out of public view.*

D:6 Identification by body samples and impressions

(A) General

A–135 **D:**6.1 References to:

(a) an "intimate sample" mean a dental impression or sample of blood, semen or any other tissue fluid, urine, or pubic hair, or a swab taken from any part of a person's genitals or from a person's body orifice other than the mouth;

(b) a "non-intimate sample" means:

(i) a sample of hair, other than pubic hair, which includes hair plucked with the root, see *Note 6A*;

(ii) a sample taken from a nail or from under a nail;

(iii) a swab taken from any part of a person's body other than a part from which a swab taken would be an intimate sample;

(iv) saliva;

(v) a skin impression which means any record, other than a fingerprint, which is a record, in any form and produced by any method, of the skin pattern and other physical characteristics or features of the whole, or any part of, a person's foot or of any other part of their body.

(B) Action

(a) *Intimate samples*

A–136 **D:**6.2 *PACE*, section 62, provides that intimate samples may be taken under:

(a) section 62(1), from a person in police detention only:

(i) if a police officer of inspector rank or above has reasonable grounds to believe such an impression or sample will tend to confirm or disprove the suspect's involvement in a recordable offence, see *Note 4A*, and gives authorisation for a sample to be taken; and

(ii) with the suspect's written consent;

(b) section 62(1A), from a person not in police detention but from whom two or more nonintimate samples have been taken in the course of an investigation of an offence and the samples, though suitable, have proved insufficient if:

(i) a police officer of inspector rank or above authorises it to be taken; and

(ii) the person concerned gives their written consent; see *Notes 6B* and *6C*;

(c) section 62(2A), from a person convicted outside England and Wales of an offence which if committed in England and Wales would be qualifying offence [*sic*] as defined by *PACE*, section 65A (see *Note 4AB*) from whom two or more non-intimate samples taken under section 63(3E) (see paragraph 6.6(h)) have proved insufficient if:

(i) a police officer of inspector rank or above is satisfied that taking the sample is necessary to assist in the prevention or detection of crime and authorises it to be taken; and

(ii) the person concerned gives their written consent.

D:6.2A *PACE*, section 63A(4) and Schedule 2A provide powers [*sic*] to:

(a) [*sic*] make a requirement (in accordance with Annex G) for a person to attend a police station to have an intimate sample taken in the exercise of one of the following powers in paragraph 6.2 when that power applies at the time the sample is to be taken in accordance with the requirement or after the person's arrest if they fail to comply with the requirement:

(i) section 62(1A)—persons from whom two or more non-intimate samples have been taken and proved to be insufficient, see paragraph 6.2(b); there is no time limit for making the requirement;

(ii) section 62(2A)—persons convicted outside England and Wales from whom two or more non-intimate samples taken under section 63(3E) (see paragraph 6.6(h)) have proved insufficient, see paragraph 6.2(c); there is no time limit for making the requirement.

D:6.3 Before a suspect is asked to provide an intimate sample, they must be:

(a) informed:

(i) of the reason, including the nature of the suspected offence (except if taken under paragraph 6.2(c) from a person convicted outside England and Wales;

(ii) that authorisation has been given and the provisions under which given;

(iii) that a sample taken at a police station may be subject of a speculative search;

(b) warned that if they refuse without good cause their refusal may harm their case if it comes to trial, see *Note 6D*. If the suspect is in police detention and not legally represented, they must also be reminded of their entitlement to have free legal advice, see Code C, paragraph 6.5, and the reminder noted in the custody record. If paragraph 6.2(b) applies and the person is attending a station voluntarily, their entitlement to free legal advice as in Code C, paragraph 3.21 shall be explained to them.

D:6.4 Dental impressions may only be taken by a registered dentist. Other intimate samples, except for samples of urine, may only be taken by a registered medical practitioner or registered nurse or registered paramedic.

(b) *Non-intimate samples*

D:6.5 A non-intimate sample may be taken from a detainee only with their written consent or if paragraph 6.6 applies. **A–137**

D:6.6 A non-intimate sample may be taken from a person without the appropriate consent in the following circumstances:

(a) under section 63(2A) from a person who is in police detention as a consequence of being arrested for a recordable offence and who has not had a non-intimate sample of the same type and from the same part of the body taken in the course of the investigation of the offence by the police or they have had such a sample taken but it proved insufficient;

(b) under section 63(3) from a person who is being held in custody by the police on the authority of a court if an officer of at least the rank of inspector authorises it to be taken; an authorisation may be given:

(i) if the authorising officer has reasonable grounds for suspecting the person of involvement in a recordable offence and for believing that the sample will tend to confirm or disprove that involvement, and

(ii) in writing or orally and confirmed in writing, as soon as practicable;

but an authorisation may not be given to take from the same part of the body a further non-intimate sample consisting of a skin impression unless the previously taken impression proved insufficient;

(c) under section 63(3ZA) from a person who has been arrested for a recordable offence and released if the person:

(i) is on bail and has not had a sample of the same type and from the same part of the body taken in the course of the investigation of the offence, or

(ii) has had such a sample taken in the course of the investigation of the offence, but it proved unsuitable or insufficient;

(d) under section 63(3A), from a person (whether or not in police detention or held in custody by the police on the authority of a court) who has been charged with a recordable offence or informed they will be reported for such an offence if the person:

(i) has not had a non-intimate sample taken from them in the course of the investigation of the offence;

(ii) has had a sample so taken, but it proved unsuitable or insufficient, see *Note 6B*; or

(iii) has had a sample taken in the course of the investigation of the offence and the sample has been destroyed and in proceedings relating to that offence there is a dispute as to whether a DNA profile relevant to the proceedings was derived from the destroyed sample;

(e) under section 63(3B), from a person who has been:

(i) convicted of a recordable offence;

(ii) given a caution in respect of a recordable offence which, at the time of the caution, the person admitted; or

(iii) warned or reprimanded under the *Crime and Disorder Act* 1998, section 65, for a recordable offence,

if, since their conviction, caution, warning or reprimand a non-intimate sample has not been taken from them or a sample which has been taken since then has proved to be unsuitable or insufficient and in either case, an officer of inspector rank or above, is satisfied that taking the fingerprints [*sic*] is necessary to assist in the prevention or detection of crime and authorises the taking;

(f) under section 63(3C) from a person to whom section 2 of the *Criminal Evidence (Amendment) Act* 1997 applies (persons detained following acquittal on grounds of insanity or finding of unfitness to plead);

(g) under section 63(3E) from a person who has been convicted outside England and Wales of an offence which if committed in England and Wales would be a qualifying offence as defined by *PACE*, section 65A (see *Note 4AB*) if:

(i) a non-intimate sample has not been taken previously under this power or unless a sample was so taken but was unsuitable or insufficient; and

(ii) a police officer of inspector rank or above is satisfied that taking a sample is necessary to assist in the prevention or detection of crime and authorises it to be taken.

D:6.6A *PACE*, section 63A(4) and Schedule 2A provide powers to:

(a) make a requirement (in accordance with Annex G) for a person to attend a police station to have a non-intimate sample taken in the exercise of one of the following powers in paragraph 6.6 when that power applies at the time the sample would be taken in accordance with the requirement:

(i) section 63(3ZA)—persons arrested for a recordable offence and released, see paragraph 6.6(c); the requirement may not be made more than six months from the day the investigating officer was informed that the sample previously taken was unsuitable or insufficient;

(ii) section 63(3A)—persons charged etc. with a recordable offence, see paragraph 6.6(d); the requirement may not be made more than six months from:

- the day the person was charged or reported if a sample has not been taken since then; or

- the day the investigating officer was informed that the sample previously taken was unsuitable or insufficient;

(iii) section 63(3B)—person convicted, cautioned, warned or reprimanded for a recordable offence in England and Wales, see paragraph 6.6(e); where the offence for which the person was convicted etc is also a qualifying offence (see *Note 4AB*), there is no time limit for the exercise of this power; where the conviction etc was for a recordable offence that is not a qualifying offence, the requirement may not be made more than two years from:

- the day the person was convicted, cautioned, warned or reprimanded, or the day Schedule 2A comes into force (if later), if a samples [*sic*] has not been taken since then; or
- the day an officer from the force investigating the offence was informed that the sample previously taken was unsuitable or insufficient or the day Schedule 2A comes into force (if later);

(iv) section 63(3E)—a person who has been convicted of qualifying offence (see *Note 4AB*) outside England and Wales, see paragraph 6.6(h); there is no time limit for making the requirement;

note: a person who has had a non-intimate sample taken under any of the powers in section 63 mentioned in paragraph 6.6 on two occasions in relation to any offence may not be required under Schedule 2A to attend a police station for a sample to be taken again under section 63 in relation to that offence, unless authorised by an officer of inspector rank or above; the fact of the authorisation and the reasons for giving it must be recorded as soon as practicable;

(b) arrest, without warrant, a person who fails to comply with the requirement.

D:6.7 Reasonable force may be used, if necessary, to take a non-intimate sample from a person without their consent under the powers mentioned in paragraph 6.6.

D:6.8 Before any non-intimate sample is taken:

(a) without consent under any power mentioned in paragraphs 6.6 and 6.6A, the person must be informed of:

(i) the reason for taking the sample;

(ii) the power under which the sample is to be taken;

(iii) the fact that the relevant authority has been given if any power mentioned in paragraph 6.6(b), (e) or (h) applies;

(b) with or without consent at a police station or elsewhere, the person must be informed:

(i) that their sample or information derived from it may be subject of a speculative search against other samples and information derived from them, see *Note 6E* and

(ii) that their sample and the information derived from it may be retained in accordance with Annex F, Part (a).

(c) *Removal of clothing*

D:6.9 When clothing needs to be removed in circumstances likely to cause embarrassment to the person, no person of the opposite sex who is not a registered medical practitioner or registered health care professional shall be present (unless in the case of a juvenile, mentally disordered or mentally vulnerable person, that person specifically requests the presence of an appropriate adult of the opposite sex who is readily available), nor shall anyone whose presence is unnecessary. However, in the case of a juvenile, this is subject to the overriding proviso that such a removal of clothing may take place in the absence of the appropriate adult only if the juvenile signifies in their presence, that they prefer the adult's absence and they agree.

(c) *Documentation*

D:6.10 A record must be made as soon as practicable after the sample is taken of:

- the matters in paragraph 6.8(a)(i) to (iii) and the fact that the person has been informed of those matters; and
- the fact that the person has been informed of the matters in paragraph 6.8(b)(i) and (ii).

D:6.10A If force is used, a record shall be made of the circumstances and those present.

D:6.11 A record must be made of a warning given as required by paragraph 6.3.

Notes for guidance

A–138 **D:**6A *When hair samples are taken for the purpose of DNA analysis (rather than for other purposes such as making a visual match), the suspect should be permitted a reasonable choice as to what part of the body the hairs are taken from. When hairs are plucked, they should be plucked individually, unless the suspect prefers otherwise and no more should be plucked than the person taking them reasonably considers necessary for a sufficient sample.*

(a) *An insufficient sample is one which is not sufficient either in quantity or quality to provide information for a particular form of analysis, such as DNA analysis. A sample may also be insufficient if enough information cannot be obtained from it by analysis because of loss, destruction, damage or contamination of the sample or as a result of an earlier, unsuccessful attempt at analysis.*

(b) *An unsuitable sample is one which, by its nature, is not suitable for a particular form of analysis.*

D:6C *Nothing in paragraph 6.2 prevents intimate samples being taken for elimination purposes with the consent of the person concerned but the provisions of paragraph 2.12 relating to the role of the appropriate adult, should be applied. Paragraph 6.2(b) does not, however, apply where the non-intimate samples were previously taken under the* Terrorism Act *2000, Schedule 8, paragraph 10.*

D:6D *In warning a person who is asked to provide an intimate sample as in paragraph 6.3, the following form of words may be used:*

"You do not have to provide this sample/allow this swab or impression to be taken, but I must warn you that if you refuse without good cause, your refusal may harm your case if it comes to trial."

D:6E *Fingerprints or a DNA sample and the information derived from it taken from a person arrested on suspicion of being involved in a recordable offence, or charged with such an offence, or informed they will be reported for such an offence, may be subject of a speculative search. This means they may be checked against other fingerprints and DNA records held by, or on behalf of, the police and other law enforcement authorities in or outside the UK or held in connection with, or as a result of, an investigation of an offence inside or outside the UK. Fingerprints and samples taken from any other person,* e.g. *a person suspected of committing a recordable offence but who has not been arrested, charged or informed they will be reported for it, may be subject to a speculative search only if the person consents in writing to their fingerprints being subject of such a search. The following is an example of a basic form of words:*

"I consent to my fingerprints/DNA sample and information derived from it being retained and used only for purposes related to the prevention and detection of a crime, the investigation of an offence or the conduct of a prosecution either nationally or internationally.

I understand that this sample may be checked against other fingerprint/DNA records held by or on behalf of relevant law enforcement authorities, either nationally or internationally.

I understand that once I have given my consent for the sample to be retained and used I cannot withdraw this consent."

See Annex F regarding the retention and use of fingerprints and samples taken with consent for elimination purposes.

D:6F *Samples of urine and non-intimate samples taken in accordance with sections 63B and 63C of* PACE *may not be used for identification purposes in accordance with this code. See Code C note for guidance 17D.*

ANNEX A

Video identification

(a) *General*

A–139 **D:**1 The arrangements for obtaining and ensuring the availability of a suitable set of images to be used in a video identification must be the responsibility of an identification officer, who has no direct involvement with the case.

D:2 The set of images must include the suspect and at least eight other people who, so far as possible, resemble the suspect in age, general appearance and position in life. Only one suspect shall appear in any set unless there are two suspects of roughly similar appearance, in which case they may be shown together with at least twelve other people.

D:2A If the suspect has an unusual physical feature, *e.g.* a facial scar, tattoo or distinctive hairstyle or hair colour which does not appear on the images of the other people that are available to be used, steps may be taken to:

(a) conceal the location of the feature on the images of the suspect and the other people; or

(b) replicate that feature on the images of the other people.

For these purposes, the feature may be concealed or replicated electronically or by any other method which it is practicable to use to ensure that the images of the suspect and other people resemble each other. The identification officer has discretion to choose whether to conceal or replicate the feature and the method to be used. If an unusual physical feature has been described by the witness, the identification officer should, if practicable, have that feature replicated. If it has not been described, concealment may be more appropriate.

D:2B If the identification officer decides that a feature should be concealed or replicated, the reason for the decision and whether the feature was concealed or replicated in the images shown to any witness shall be recorded.

D:2C If the witness requests to view an image where an unusual physical feature has been concealed or replicated without the feature being concealed or replicated, the witness may be allowed to do so.

D:3 The images used to conduct a video identification shall, as far as possible, show the suspect and other people in the same positions or carrying out the same sequence of movements. They shall also show the suspect and other people under identical conditions unless the identification officer reasonably believes:

(a) because of the suspect's failure or refusal to co-operate or other reasons, it is not practicable for the conditions to be identical; and

(b) any difference in the conditions would not direct a witness's attention to any individual image.

D:4 The reasons identical conditions are not practicable shall be recorded on forms provided for the purpose.

D:5 Provision must be made for each person shown to be identified by number.

D:6 If police officers are shown, any numerals or other identifying badges must be concealed. If a prison inmate is shown, either as a suspect or not, then either all, or none of, the people shown should be in prison clothing.

D:7 The suspect or their solicitor, friend, or appropriate adult must be given a reasonable opportunity to see the complete set of images before it is shown to any witness. If the suspect has a reasonable objection to the set of images or any of the participants, the suspect shall be asked to state the reasons for the objection. Steps shall, if practicable, be taken to remove the grounds for objection. If this is not practicable, the suspect and/or their representative shall be told why their objections cannot be met and the objection, the reason given for it and why it cannot be met shall be recorded on forms provided for the purpose. **A–140**

D:8 Before the images are shown in accordance with paragraph 7, the suspect or their solicitor shall be provided with details of the first description of the suspect by any witnesses who are to attend the video identification. When a broadcast or publication is made, as in paragraph 3.28, the suspect or their solicitor must also be allowed to view any material released to the media by the police for the purpose of recognising or tracing the suspect, provided it is practicable and would not unreasonably delay the investigation.

D:9 The suspect's solicitor, if practicable, shall be given reasonable notification of the time and place the video identification is to be conducted so a representative may attend on behalf of the suspect. The suspect may not be present when the images are shown to the witness(es). In the absence of the suspect's solicitor, the viewing itself shall be recorded on video. No unauthorised people may be present.

(b) *Conducting the video identification*

D:10 The identification officer is responsible for making the appropriate arrangements to make **A–141**

sure, before they see the set of images, witnesses are not able to communicate with each other about the case, see any of the images which are to be shown, see, or be reminded of, any photograph or description of the suspect or be given any other indication as to the suspect's identity, or overhear a witness who has already seen the material. There must be no discussion with the witness about the composition of the set of images and they must not be told whether a previous witness has made any identification.

D:11 Only one witness may see the set of images at a time. Immediately before the images are shown, the witness shall be told that the person they saw on a specified earlier occasion may, or may not, appear in the images they are shown and that if they cannot make a positive identification, they should say so. The witness shall be advised that at any point, they may ask to see a particular part of the set of images or to have a particular image frozen for them to study. Furthermore, it should be pointed out to the witness that there is no limit on how many times they can view the whole set of images or any part of them. However, they should be asked not to make any decision as to whether the person they saw is on the set of images until they have seen the whole set at least twice.

D:12 Once the witness has seen the whole set of images at least twice and has indicated that they do not want to view the images, or any part of them, again, the witness shall be asked to say whether the individual they saw in person on a specified earlier occasion has been shown and, if so, to identify them by number of the image. The witness will then be shown that image to confirm the identification, see paragraph 17.

D:13 Care must be taken not to direct the witness's attention to any one individual image or give any indication of the suspect's identity. Where a witness has previously made an identification by photographs, or a computerised or artist's composite or similar likeness, the witness must not be reminded of such a photograph or composite likeness once a suspect is available for identification by other means in accordance with this code. Nor must the witness be reminded of any description of the suspect.

D:14 After the procedure, each witness shall be asked whether they have seen any broadcast or published films or photographs, or any descriptions of suspects relating to the offence and their reply shall be recorded.

(c) *Image security and destruction*

D:15 Arrangements shall be made for all relevant material containing sets of images used for specific identification procedures to be kept securely and their movements accounted for. In particular, no-one involved in the investigation shall be permitted to view the material prior to it being shown to any witness.

D:16 As appropriate, paragraph 3.30 or 3.31 applies to the destruction or retention of relevant sets of images.

(d) *Documentation*

D:17 A record must be made of all those participating in, or seeing, the set of images whose names are known to the police.

D:18 A record of the conduct of the video identification must be made on forms provided for the purpose. This shall include anything said by the witness about any identifications or the conduct of the procedure and any reasons it was not practicable to comply with any of the provisions of this code governing the conduct of video identifications.

ANNEX B

Identification parades

(a) *General*

A–142 **D:**1 A suspect must be given a reasonable opportunity to have a solicitor or friend present, and the suspect shall be asked to indicate on a second copy of the notice whether or not they wish to do so.

D:2 An identification parade may take place either in a normal room or one equipped with a screen permitting witnesses to see members of the identification parade without being seen. The procedures for the composition and conduct of the identification parade are the same in both cases, subject to paragraph 8 (except that an identification parade involving a screen may take place only when the suspect's solicitor, friend or appropriate adult is present or the identification parade is recorded on video).

D:3 Before the identification parade takes place, the suspect or their solicitor shall be provided with details of the first description of the suspect by any witnesses who are attending the identification parade. When a broadcast or publication is made as in paragraph 3.28, the suspect or their solicitor should also be allowed to view any material released to the media by the police for the purpose of recognising or tracing the suspect, provided it is practicable to do so and would not unreasonably delay the investigation.

(b) *Identification parades involving prison inmates*

D:4 If a prison inmate is required for identification, and there are no security problems about the person leaving the establishment, they may be asked to participate in an identification parade or video identification.

D:5 An identification parade may be held in a Prison Department establishment but shall be conducted, as far as practicable under normal identification parade rules. Members of the public shall make up the identification parade unless there are serious security, or control, objections to their admission to the establishment. In such cases, or if a group or video identification is arranged within the establishment, other inmates may participate. If an inmate is the suspect, they are not required to wear prison clothing for the identification parade unless the other people taking part are other inmates in similar clothing, or are members of the public who are prepared to wear prison clothing for the occasion.

(c) *Conduct of the identification parade*

D:6 Immediately before the identification parade, the suspect must be reminded of the procedures governing its conduct and cautioned in the terms of Code C, paragraphs 10.5 or 10.6, as appropriate. **A–143**

D:7 All unauthorised people must be excluded from the place where the identification parade is held.

D:8 Once the identification parade has been formed, everything afterwards, in respect of it, shall take place in the presence and hearing of the suspect and any interpreter, solicitor, friend or appropriate adult who is present (unless the identification parade involves a screen, in which case everything said to, or by, any witness at the place where the identification parade is held, must be said in the hearing and presence of the suspect's solicitor, friend or appropriate adult or be recorded on video).

D:9 The identification parade shall consist of at least eight people (in addition to the suspect) who, so far as possible, resemble the suspect in age, height, general appearance and position in life. Only one suspect shall be included in an identification parade unless there are two suspects of roughly similar appearance, in which case they may be paraded together with at least twelve other people. In no circumstances shall more than two suspects be included in one identification parade and where there are separate identification parades, they shall be made up of different people.

D:10 If the suspect has an unusual physical feature, *e.g.*, a facial scar, tattoo or distinctive hairstyle or hair colour which cannot be replicated on other members of the identification parade, steps may be taken to conceal the location of that feature on the suspect and the other members of the identification parade if the suspect and their solicitor, or appropriate adult, agree. For example, by use of a plaster or a hat, so that all members of the identification parade resemble each other in general appearance.

D:11 When all members of a similar group are possible suspects, separate identification parades shall be held for each unless there are two suspects of similar appearance when they may appear on the same identification parade with at least twelve other members of the group who are not suspects. When police officers in uniform form an identification parade any numerals or other identifying badges shall be concealed.

D:12 When the suspect is brought to the place where the identification parade is to be held, they shall be asked if they have any objection to the arrangements for the identification parade or to any of the other participants in it and to state the reasons for the objection. The suspect may obtain advice from their solicitor or friend, if present, before the identification parade proceeds. If the suspect has a reasonable objection to the arrangements or any of the participants, steps shall, if practicable, be taken to remove the grounds for objection. When it is not practicable to do so, the suspect shall be told why their objections cannot be met and the objection, the reason given for it and why it cannot be met, shall be recorded on forms provided for the purpose.

D:13 The suspect may select their own position in the line, but may not otherwise interfere with the order of the people forming the line. When there is more than one witness, the suspect must be told, after each witness has left the room, that they can, if they wish, change position in the line. Each position in the line must be clearly numbered, whether by means of a number laid on the floor in front of each identification parade member or by other means.

A–144 **D:**14 Appropriate arrangements must be made to make sure, before witnesses attend the identification parade, they are not able to:

(i) communicate with each other about the case or overhear a witness who has already seen the identification parade;

(ii) see any member of the identification parade;

(iii) see, or be reminded of, any photograph or description of the suspect or be given any other indication as to the suspect's identity; or

(iv) see the suspect before or after the identification parade.

D:15 The person conducting a witness to an identification parade must not discuss with them the composition of the identification parade and, in particular, must not disclose whether a previous witness has made any identification.

D:16 Witnesses shall be brought in one at a time. Immediately before the witness inspects the identification parade, they shall be told the person they saw on a specified earlier occasion may, or may not, be present and if they cannot make a positive identification, they should say so. The witness must also be told they should not make any decision about whether the person they saw is on the identification parade until they have looked at each member at least twice.

D:17 When the officer or police staff (see paragraph 3.11) conducting the identification procedure is satisfied the witness has properly looked at each member of the identification parade, they shall ask the witness whether the person they saw on a specified earlier occasion is on the identification parade and, if so, to indicate the number of the person concerned, see paragraph 28.

D:18 If the witness wishes to hear any identification parade member speak, adopt any specified posture or move, they shall first be asked whether they can identify any person(s) on the identification parade on the basis of appearance only. When the request is to hear members of the identification parade speak, the witness shall be reminded that the participants in the identification parade have been chosen on the basis of physical appearance only. Members of the identification parade may then be asked to comply with the witness's request to hear them speak, see them move or adopt any specified posture.

A–145 **D:**19 If the witness requests that the person they have indicated remove anything used for the purposes of paragraph 10 to conceal the location of an unusual physical feature, that person may be asked to remove it.

D:20 If the witness makes an identification after the identification parade has ended, the suspect and, if present, their solicitor, interpreter or friend shall be informed. When this occurs, consideration should be given to allowing the witness a second opportunity to identify the suspect.

D:21 After the procedure, each witness shall be asked whether they have seen any broadcast or published films or photographs or any descriptions of suspects relating to the offence and their reply shall be recorded.

D:22 When the last witness has left, the suspect shall be asked whether they wish to make any comments on the conduct of the identification parade.

(d) *Documentation*

D:23 A video recording must normally be taken of the identification parade. If that is impracticable, a colour photograph must be taken. A copy of the video recording or photograph shall be supplied, on request, to the suspect or their solicitor within a reasonable time.

D:24 As appropriate, paragraph 3.30 or 3.31, should apply to any photograph or video taken as in paragraph 23.

D:25 If any person is asked to leave an identification parade because they are interfering with its conduct, the circumstances shall be recorded.

D:26 A record must be made of all those present at an identification parade whose names are known to the police.

D:27 If prison inmates make up an identification parade, the circumstances must be recorded.

D:28 A record of the conduct of any identification parade must be made on forms provided for the purpose. This shall include anything said by the witness or the suspect about any identifications or the conduct of the procedure, and any reasons it was not practicable to comply with any of this code's provisions.

ANNEX C

Group identification

(a) *General*

D:1 The purpose of this annex is to make sure, as far as possible, group identifications follow the principles and procedures for identification parades so the conditions are fair to the suspect in the way they test the witness's ability to make an identification. **A–146**

D:2 Group identifications may take place either with the suspect's consent and co-operation or covertly without their consent.

D:3 The location of the group identification is a matter for the identification officer, although the officer may take into account any representations made by the suspect, appropriate adult, their solicitor or friend.

D:4 The place where the group identification is held should be one where other people are either passing by or waiting around informally, in groups such that the suspect is able to join them and be capable of being seen by the witness at the same time as others in the group. For example people leaving an escalator, pedestrians walking through a shopping centre, passengers on railway and bus stations, waiting in queues or groups or where people are standing or sitting in groups in other public places.

D:5 If the group identification is to be held covertly, the choice of locations will be limited by the places where the suspect can be found and the number of other people present at that time. In these cases, suitable locations might be along regular routes travelled by the suspect, including buses or trains or public places frequented by the suspect.

D:6 Although the number, age, sex, race and general description and style of clothing of other people present at the location cannot be controlled by the identification officer, in selecting the location the officer must consider the general appearance and numbers of people likely to be present. In particular, the officer must reasonably expect that over the period the witness observes the group, they will be able to see, from time to time, a number of others whose appearance is broadly similar to that of the suspect. **A–147**

D:7 A group identification need not be held if the identification officer believes, because of the unusual appearance of the suspect, none of the locations it would be practicable to use, satisfy the requirements of paragraph 6 necessary to make the identification fair.

D:8 Immediately after a group identification procedure has taken place (with or without the suspect's consent), a colour photograph or video should be taken of the general scene, if practicable, to give a general impression of the scene and the number of people present. Alternatively, if it is practicable, the group identification may be video recorded.

D:9 If it is not practicable to take the photograph or video in accordance with paragraph 8, a photograph or film of the scene should be taken later at a time determined by the identification officer if the officer considers it practicable to do so.

D:10 An identification carried out in accordance with this code remains a group identification even though, at the time of being seen by the witness, the suspect was on their own rather than in a group.

D:11 Before the group identification takes place, the suspect or their solicitor shall be provided with details of the first description of the suspect by any witnesses who are to attend the identification. When a broadcast or publication is made, as in paragraph 3.28, the suspect or their solicitor should also be allowed to view any material released by the police to the media for the purposes of recognising or tracing the suspect, provided that it is practicable and would not unreasonably delay the investigation.

D:12 After the procedure, each witness shall be asked whether they have seen any broadcast or published films or photographs or any descriptions of suspects relating to the offence and their reply recorded.

(b) *Identification with the consent of the suspect*

A–148 **D:**13 A suspect must be given a reasonable opportunity to have a solicitor or friend present. They shall be asked to indicate on a second copy of the notice whether or not they wish to do so.

D:14 The witness, the person carrying out the procedure and the suspect's solicitor, appropriate adult, friend or any interpreter for the witness, may be concealed from the sight of the individuals in the group they are observing, if the person carrying out the procedure considers this assists the conduct of the identification.

D:15 The person conducting a witness to a group identification must not discuss with them the forthcoming group identification and, in particular, must not disclose whether a previous witness has made any identification.

D:16 Anything said to, or by, the witness during the procedure about the identification should be said in the presence and hearing of those present at the procedure.

D:17 Appropriate arrangements must be made to make sure, before witnesses attend the group identification, they are not able to:

(i) communicate with each other about the case or overhear a witness who has already been given an opportunity to see the suspect in the group;

(ii) see the suspect; or

(iii) see, or be reminded of, any photographs or description of the suspect or be given any other indication of the suspect's identity.

D:18 Witnesses shall be brought one at a time to the place where they are to observe the group. Immediately before the witness is asked to look at the group, the person conducting the procedure shall tell them that the person they saw may, or may not, be in the group and that if they cannot make a positive identification, they should say so. The witness shall be asked to observe the group in which the suspect is to appear. The way in which the witness should do this will depend on whether the group is moving or stationary.

Moving group

A–149 **D:**19 When the group in which the suspect is to appear is moving, *e.g.* leaving an escalator, the provisions of paragraphs 20 to 24 should be followed.

D:20 If two or more suspects consent to a group identification, each should be the subject of separate identification procedures. These may be conducted consecutively on the same occasion.

D:21 The person conducting the procedure shall tell the witness to observe the group and ask them to point out any person they think they saw on the specified earlier occasion.

D:22 Once the witness has been informed as in paragraph 21 the suspect should be allowed to take whatever position in the group they wish.

D:23 When the witness points out a person as in paragraph 21 they shall, if practicable, be asked to take a closer look at the person to confirm the identification. If this is not practicable, or they cannot confirm the identification, they shall be asked how sure they are that the person they have indicated is the relevant person.

D:24 The witness should continue to observe the group for the period which the person conducting the procedure reasonably believes is necessary in the circumstances for them to be able to make comparisons between the suspect and other individuals of broadly similar appearance to the suspect as in paragraph 6.

Stationary groups

A–150 **D:**25 When the group in which the suspect is to appear is stationary, *e.g.* people waiting in a queue, the provisions of paragraphs 26 to 29 should be followed.

D:26 If two or more suspects consent to a group identification, each should be subject to separate identification procedures unless they are of broadly similar appearance when they may appear in the same group. When separate group identifications are held, the groups must be made up of different people.

D:27 The suspect may take whatever position in the group they wish. If there is more than one witness, the suspect must be told, out of the sight and hearing of any witness, that they can, if they wish, change their position in the group.

D:28 The witness shall be asked to pass along, or amongst, the group and to look at each person in the group at least twice, taking as much care and time as possible according to the circumstances, before making an identification. Once the witness has done this, they shall be asked whether the person they saw on the specified earlier occasion is in the group and to indicate any such person by whatever means the person conducting the procedure considers appropriate in the circumstances. If this is not practicable, the witness shall be asked to point out any person they think they saw on the earlier occasion.

D:29 When the witness makes an indication as in paragraph 28, arrangements shall be made, if practicable, for the witness to take a closer look at the person to confirm the identification. If this is not practicable, or the witness is unable to confirm the identification, they shall be asked how sure they are that the person they have indicated is the relevant person.

All cases

D:30 If the suspect unreasonably delays joining the group, or having joined the group, deliberately conceals themselves [*sic*] from the sight of the witness, this may be treated as a refusal to co-operate in a group identification. **A–151**

D:31 If the witness identifies a person other than the suspect, that person should be informed what has happened and asked if they are prepared to give their name and address. There is no obligation upon any member of the public to give these details. There shall be no duty to record any details of any other member of the public present in the group or at the place where the procedure is conducted.

D:32 When the group identification has been completed, the suspect shall be asked whether they wish to make any comments on the conduct of the procedure.

D:33 If the suspect has not been previously informed, they shall be told of any identifications made by the witnesses.

(c) *Identification without the suspect's consent*

D:34 Group identifications held covertly without the suspect's consent should, as far as practicable, follow the rules for conduct of group identification by consent. **A–152**

D:35 A suspect has no right to have a solicitor, appropriate adult or friend present as the identification will take place without the knowledge of the suspect.

D:36 Any number of suspects may be identified at the same time.

(d) *Identifications in police stations*

D:37 Group identifications should only take place in police stations for reasons of safety, security or because it is not practicable to hold them elsewhere.

D:38 The group identification may take place either in a room equipped with a screen permitting witnesses to see members of the group without being seen, or anywhere else in the police station that the identification officer considers appropriate.

D:39 Any of the additional safeguards applicable to identification parades should be followed if the identification officer considers it is practicable to do so in the circumstances.

(e) *Identifications involving prison inmates*

D:40 A group identification involving a prison inmate may only be arranged in the prison or at a police station. **A–153**

D:41 When a group identification takes place involving a prison inmate, whether in a prison or in a police station, the arrangements should follow those in paragraphs 37 to 39. If a group identification takes place within a prison, other inmates may participate. If an inmate is the suspect, they do not have to wear prison clothing for the group identification unless the other participants are wearing the same clothing.

(f) *Documentation*

D:42 When a photograph or video is taken as in paragraph 8 or 9, a copy of the photograph or video shall be supplied on request to the suspect or their solicitor within a reasonable time.

D:43 Paragraph 3.30 or 3.31, as appropriate, shall apply when the photograph or film taken in accordance with paragraph 8 or 9 includes the suspect.

D:44 A record of the conduct of any group identification must be made on forms provided for the purpose. This shall include anything said by the witness or suspect about any identifications or the conduct of the procedure and any reasons why it was not practicable to comply with any of the provisions of this code governing the conduct of group identifications.

ANNEX D

Confrontation by a witness

A–154 **D:**1 Before the confrontation takes place, the witness must be told that the person they saw may, or may not, be the person they are to confront and that if they are not that person, then the witness should say so.

D:2 Before the confrontation takes place the suspect or their solicitor shall be provided with details of the first description of the suspect given by any witness who is to attend. When a broadcast or publication is made, as in paragraph 3.28, the suspect or their solicitor should also be allowed to view any material released to the media for the purposes of recognising or tracing the suspect, provided it is practicable to do so and would not unreasonably delay the investigation.

D:3 Force may not be used to make the suspect's face visible to the witness.

D:4 Confrontation must take place in the presence of the suspect's solicitor, interpreter or friend unless this would cause unreasonable delay.

D:5 The suspect shall be confronted independently by each witness, who shall be asked "Is this the person?". If the witness identifies the person but is unable to confirm the identification, they shall be asked how sure they are that the person is the one they saw on the earlier occasion.

D:6 The confrontation should normally take place in the police station, either in a normal room or one equipped with a screen permitting a witness to see the suspect without being seen. In both cases, the procedures are the same except that a room equipped with a screen may be used only when the suspect's solicitor, friend or appropriate adult is present or the confrontation is recorded on video.

D:7 After the procedure, each witness shall be asked whether they have seen any broadcast or published films or photographs or any descriptions of suspects relating to the offence and their reply shall be recorded.

ANNEX E

Showing photographs

(a) *Action*

A–155 **D:**1 An officer of sergeant rank or above shall be responsible for supervising and directing the showing of photographs. The actual showing may be done by another officer or police staff, see paragraph 3.11.

D:2 The supervising officer must confirm the first description of the suspect given by the witness has been recorded before they are shown the photographs. If the supervising officer is unable to confirm the description has been recorded they shall postpone showing the photographs.

D:3 Only one witness shall be shown photographs at any one time. Each witness shall be given as much privacy as practicable and shall not be allowed to communicate with any other witness in the case.

D:4 The witness shall be shown not less than twelve photographs at a time, which shall, as far as possible, all be of a similar type.

D:5 When the witness is shown the photographs, they shall be told the photograph of the person they saw may, or may not, be amongst them and if they cannot make a positive identification, they should say so. The witness shall also be told they should not make a decision until they have viewed at least twelve photographs. The witness shall not be prompted or guided in any way but shall be left to make any selection without help.

D:6 If a witness makes a positive identification from photographs, unless the person identified is otherwise eliminated from enquiries or is not available, other witnesses shall not be shown photographs. But both they, and the witness who has made the identification, shall be asked to attend a video identification, an identification parade or group identification unless there is no dispute about the suspect's identification.

D:7 If the witness makes a selection but is unable to confirm the identification, the person showing the photographs shall ask them how sure they are that the photograph they have indicated is the person they saw on the specified earlier occasion. **A–156**

D:8 When the use of a computerised or artist's composite or similar likeness has led to there being a known suspect who can be asked to participate in a video identification, appear on an identification parade or participate in a group identification, that likeness shall not be shown to other potential witnesses.

D:9 When a witness attending a video identification, an identification parade or group identification has previously been shown photographs or computerised or artist's composite or similar likeness (and it is the responsibility of the officer in charge of the investigation to make the identification officer aware that this is the case), the suspect and their solicitor must be informed of this fact before the identification procedure takes place.

D:10 None of the photographs shown shall be destroyed, whether or not an identification is made, since they may be required for production in court. The photographs shall be numbered and a separate photograph taken of the frame or part of the album from which the witness made an identification as an aid to reconstituting it.

(b) *Documentation*

D:11. Whether or not an identification is made, a record shall be kept of the showing of photographs on forms provided for the purpose. This shall include anything said by the witness about any identification or the conduct of the procedure, any reasons it was not practicable to comply with any of the provisions of this code governing the showing of photographs and the name and rank of the supervising officer. **A–157**

D:12 The supervising officer shall inspect and sign the record as soon as practicable.

ANNEX F

Fingerprints, footwear impressions and samples—destruction and speculative searches

(a)

Fingerprints, footwear impressions and samples taken in connection with a criminal investigation from a person suspected of committing the offence under investigation

D:1 The retention and destruction of fingerprints, footwear impressions and samples taken in connection with a criminal investigation from a person suspected of committing the offence under investigation is subject to *PACE*, section 64. **A–158**

(b)

Fingerprints, footwear impressions and samples taken in connection with a criminal investigation from a person not suspected of committing the offence under investigation

D:2 When fingerprints, footwear impressions or DNA samples are taken from a person in connection with an investigation and the person is not suspected of having committed the offence, see *Note F1*, they must be destroyed as soon as they have fulfilled the purpose for which they were taken unless:

(a) they were taken for the purposes of an investigation of an offence for which a person has been convicted; and

(b) fingerprints, footwear impressions or samples were also taken from the convicted person for the purposes of that investigation.

However, subject to paragraph 2, the fingerprints, footwear impressions and samples, and the information derived from samples, may not be used in the investigation of any offence or in evidence against the person who is, or would be, entitled to the destruction of the fingerprints, footwear impressions and samples, see *Note F2*.

D:3 The requirement to destroy fingerprints, footwear impressions and DNA samples, and information derived from samples, and restrictions on their retention and use in paragraph 1 do not apply if the person gives their written consent for their fingerprints, footwear impressions or sample to be retained and used after they have fulfilled the purpose for which they were taken, see *Note F1*.

D:4 When a person's fingerprints, footwear impressions or sample are to be destroyed:

(a) any copies of the fingerprints and footwear impressions must also be destroyed;

(b) the person may witness the destruction of their fingerprints, footwear impressions or copies if they ask to do so within five days of being informed destruction is required;

(c) access to relevant computer fingerprint data shall be made impossible as soon as it is practicable to do so and the person shall be given a certificate to this effect within three months of asking; and

(d) neither the fingerprints, footwear impressions, the sample, or any information derived from the sample, may be used in the investigation of any offence or in evidence against the person who is, or would be, entitled to its destruction.

D:5 Fingerprints, footwear impressions or samples, and the information derived from samples, taken in connection with the investigation of an offence which are not required to be destroyed, may be retained after they have fulfilled the purposes for which they were taken but may be used only for purposes related to the prevention or detection of crime, the investigation of an offence or the conduct of a prosecution in, as well as outside, the UK and may also be subject to a speculative search. This includes checking them against other fingerprints, footwear impressions and DNA records held by, or on behalf of, the police and other law enforcement authorities in, as well as outside, the UK.

(b) [sic] *Fingerprints taken in connection with Immigration Service enquiries*

A–159 **D:**6 See paragraph 4.10.

Notes for guidance

A–160 **D:**F1 *Fingerprints, footwear impressions and samples given voluntarily for the purposes of elimination play an important part in many police investigations. It is, therefore, important to make sure innocent volunteers are not deterred from participating and their consent to their fingerprints, footwear impressions and DNA being used for the purposes of a specific investigation is fully informed and voluntary. If the police or volunteer seek to have the fingerprints, footwear impressions or samples retained for use after the specific investigation ends, it is important the volunteer's consent to this is also fully informed and voluntary.*

Examples of consent for:

- *DNA/fingerprints/footwear impressions—to be used only for the purposes of a specific investigation;*
- *DNA/fingerprints/footwear impressions—to be used in the specific investigation* ***and*** *retained by the police for future use.*

To minimise the risk of confusion, each consent should be physically separate and the volunteer should be asked to sign **each consent**.

(a) DNA:

(i) DNA sample taken for the purposes of elimination or as part of an intelligence-led screening and to be used only for the purposes of that investigation and destroyed afterwards:

"I consent to my DNA/mouth swab being taken for forensic analysis. I understand that the sample will be destroyed at the end of the case and that my profile will only be compared to the crime stain profile from this enquiry. I have been advised that the person taking the

sample may be required to give evidence and/or provide a written statement to the police in relation to the taking of it.".

(ii) DNA sample to be retained on the National DNA database and used in the future:

"I consent to my DNA sample and information derived from it being retained and used only for purposes related to the prevention and detection of a crime, the investigation of an offence or the conduct of a prosecution either nationally or internationally.

I understand that this sample may be checked against other DNA records held by, or on behalf of, relevant law enforcement authorities, either nationally or internationally.

I understand that once I have given my consent for the sample to be retained and used I cannot withdraw this consent.".

(b) Fingerprints:

(i) Fingerprints taken for the purposes of elimination or as part of an intelligence-led screening and to be used only for the purposes of that investigation and destroyed afterwards:

"I consent to my fingerprints being taken for elimination purposes. I understand that the fingerprints will be destroyed at the end of the case and that my fingerprints will only be compared to the fingerprints from this enquiry. I have been advised that the person taking the fingerprints may be required to give evidence and/or provide a written statement to the police in relation to the taking of it.".

(ii) Fingerprints to be retained for future use:

"I consent to my fingerprints being retained and used only for purposes related to the prevention and detection of a crime, the investigation of an offence or the conduct of a prosecution either nationally or internationally.

I understand that my fingerprints may be checked against other records held by, or on behalf of, relevant law enforcement authorities, either nationally or internationally.

I understand that once I have given my consent for my fingerprints to be retained and used I cannot withdraw this consent.".

(c) Footwear impressions:

(i) Footwear impressions taken for the purposes of elimination or as part of an intelligence-led screening and to be used only for the purposes of that investigation and destroyed afterwards:

"I consent to my footwear impressions being taken for elimination purposes. I understand that the footwear impressions will be destroyed at the end of the case and that my footwear impressions will only be compared to the footwear impressions from this enquiry. I have been advised that the person taking the footwear impressions may be required to give evidence and/or provide a writtens statement to the police in relation to the taking of it.".

(ii) Footwear impressions to be retained for future use:

"I consent to my footwear impressions being retained and used only for purposes related to the prevention and detection of a crime, the investigation of an offence or the conduct of a prosecution, either nationally or internationally.

I understand that my footwear impressions may be checked against other records held by, or on behalf of, relevant law enforcement authorities, either nationally or internationally.

I understand that once I have given my consent for my footwear impressions to be retained and used I cannot withdraw this consent.".

D:F2 *The provisions for the retention of fingerprints, footwear impressions and samples in paragraph 1 allow for all fingerprints, footwear impressions and samples in a case to be available for any subsequent miscarriage of justice investigation.* **A–161**

ANNEX G

Requirement for a person to attend a police station for fingerprints and samples

D:1 A requirement under Schedule 2A for a person to attend a police station to have fingerprints or samples taken: **A–161a**

(a) must give the person a period of at least seven days within which to attend the police station; and

(b) may direct them to attend at a specified time of day or between specified times of day.

D:2 When specifying the period and times of attendance, the officer making the requirements must consider whether the fingerprints or samples could reasonably be taken at a time when the person is required to attend the police station for any other reason. See *Note G1*.

D:3 An officer of the rank of inspector or above may authorise a period shorter than 7 days if there is an urgent need for person's fingerprints or sample for the purposes of the investigation of an offence. The fact of the authorisation and the reasons for giving it must be recorded as soon as practicable.

D:4 The constable making a requirement and the person to whom it applies may agree to vary it so as to specify any period within which, or date or time at which, the person is to attend. However, variation shall not have effect for the purposes of enforcement, unless it is confirmed by the constable in writing.

Notes for guidance

A–161b **D:**G1 *The specified period within which the person is to attend need not fall within the period allowed (if applicable) for making the requirement.*

D:G2 *To justify the arrest without warrant of a person who fails to comply with a requirement, (see paragraph 4.4(b) above), the officer making the requirement, or confirming a variation, should be prepared to explain how, when and where the requirement was made or the variation was confirmed and what steps were taken to ensure the person understood what to do and the consequences of not complying with the requirement.*

VI. CODE E (TAPE RECORDING OF INTERVIEWS)

A–162 The text that follows is of the version of the code that came into force on May 1, 2010: see *ante*, Appendix A–1.

For further details of the application of the code, and as to commencement of the governing legislation, see § 15–224, *ante*.

E. Code of Practice on Audio Recording Interviews with Suspects

Commencement—Transitional arrangements

A–162a This code applies to interviews carried out after midnight on 1 May 2010, notwithstanding that the interview may have commenced before that time.

E:1 General

A–163 **E:**1.1 This code of practice must be readily available for consultation by:

- police officers;
- police staff;
- detained persons;
- members of the public.

E:1.2 The *Notes for Guidance* included are not provisions of this code.

E:1.3 Nothing in this code shall detract from the requirements of Code C, the code of practice for the detention, treatment and questioning of persons by police officers.

E:1.4 This code does not apply to those people listed in Code C, paragraph 1.12.

E:1.5 The term:

- "appropriate adult" has the same meaning as in Code C, paragraph 1.7;
- "solicitor" has the same meaning as in Code C, paragraph 6.12.

E:1.5A Recording of interviews shall be carried out openly to instil confidence in its reliability as an impartial and accurate record of the interview.

A–164 **E:**1.6 In this code:

(aa) "recording media" means any removable, physical audio recording medium (such as magnetic tape, optical disc or solid state memory) which can be played and copied;

(a) "designated person" means a person other than a police officer, designated under the

Police Reform Act 2002, Part 4 who has specified powers and duties of police officers conferred or imposed on them;

(b) any reference to a police officer includes a designated person acting in the exercise or performance of the powers and duties conferred or imposed on them by their designation;

(c) "secure digital network" is a computer network system which enables an original interview recording to be stored as a digital multi media file or a series of such files, on a secure file server which is accredited by the National Accreditor for Police Information Systems in the National Police Improvement Agency (NPIA) in accordance with the UK Government Protective Marking Scheme (see section 7 of this code).

E:1.7 Sections 2 to 6 of this code set out the procedures and requirements which apply to all interviews together with the provisions which apply only to interviews recorded using removable media. Section 7 sets out the provisions which apply to interviews recorded using a secure digital network and specifies the provisions in sections 2 to 6 which do not apply to secure digital network recording.

E:1.8 Nothing in this code prevents the custody officer, or other officer given custody of the detainee, from allowing police staff who are not designated persons to carry out individual procedures or tasks at the police station if the law allows. However, the officer remains responsible for making sure the procedures and tasks are carried out correctly in accordance with this code. Any such police staff must be: **A–165**

(a) a person employed by a police authority maintaining a police force and under the control and direction of the chief officer of that force; or

(b) employed by a person with whom a police authority has a contract for the provision of services relating to persons arrested or otherwise in custody.

E:1.9 Designated persons and other police staff must have regard to any relevant provisions of the codes of practice.

E:1.10 References to pocket book [*sic*] include any official report book issued to police officers or police staff.

E:1.11 References to a custody officer include those performing the functions of a custody officer as in paragraph 1.9 of Code C.

E:2 Recording and sealing master recordings

E:2.1 [*Not used*] **A–166**

E:2.2 One recording, the master recording, will be sealed in the suspect's presence. A second recording will be used as a working copy. The master recording is either of the two recordings used in a twin deck/drive machine or the only recording in a single deck/drive machine. The working copy is either the second/third recording used in a twin/triple deck/drive machine or a copy of the master recording made by a single deck/drive machine. See *Notes 2A* and *2B*. [*This paragraph does not apply to interviews recorded using a secure digital network, see paragraphs 7.4 to 7.6.*]

E:2.3 Nothing in this code requires the identity of officers or police staff conducting interviews to be recorded or disclosed:

(a) in the case of enquiries linked to the investigation of terrorism (see paragraph 3.2); or

(b) if the interviewer reasonably believes recording or disclosing their name might put them in danger.

In these cases interviewers should use warrant or other identification numbers and the name of their police station. See *Note 2C*.

Notes for guidance

E:2A *The purpose of sealing the master recording in the suspect's presence is to show the recording's integrity is preserved. If a single deck/drive machine is used the working copy of the master recording must be made in the suspect's presence and without the master recording leaving their sight. The working copy shall be used for making further copies if needed.* **A–167**

E:2B *[Not used.]*

E:2C *The purpose of paragraph 2.3(b) is to protect those involved in serious organised crime investigations or arrests of particularly violent suspects when there is reliable information* *that those arrested or their associates may threaten or cause harm to those involved. In cases of doubt, an officer of inspector rank or above should be consulted.*

E:3 Interviews to be audio recorded

A–168 **E:**3.1 Subject to paragraphs 3.3 and 3.4, audio recording shall be used at police stations for any interview:

(a) with a person cautioned under Code C, section 10 in respect of any indictable offence, including an offence triable either way, see *Note 3A*;

(b) which takes place as a result of an interviewer exceptionally putting further questions to a suspect about an offence described in paragraph 3.1(a) after they have been charged with, or told they may be prosecuted for, that offence, see Code C, paragraph 16.5;

(c) when an interviewer wants to tell a person, after they have been charged with, or informed they may be prosecuted for, an offence described in paragraph 3.1(a), about any written statement or interview with another person, see Code C, paragraph 16.4.

E:3.2 The *Terrorism Act* 2000 makes separate provision for a code of practice for the audio recording of interviews of those arrested under section 41 of, or detained under Schedule 7 to, the Act. The provisions of this code do not apply to such interviews. See *Note 3C*.

E:3.3 The custody officer may authorise the interviewer not to audio record the interview when it is:

(a) not reasonably practicable because of equipment failure or the unavailability of a suitable interview room or recording equipment and the authorising officer considers, on reasonable grounds, that the interview should not be delayed; or

(b) clear from the outset there will not be a prosecution.

Note: in these cases the interview should be recorded in writing in accordance with Code C, section 11. In all cases the custody officer shall record the specific reasons for not audio recording. See *Note 3B*.

E:3.4 If a person refuses to go into or remain in a suitable interview room, see Code C, paragraph 12.5, and the custody officer considers, on reasonable grounds, that the interview should not be delayed the interview may, at the custody officer's discretion, be conducted in a cell using portable recording equipment or, if none is available, recorded in writing as in Code C, section 11. The reasons for this shall be recorded.

E:3.5 The whole of each interview shall be audio recorded, including the taking and reading back of any statement.

E:3.6 A sign or indicator which is visible to the suspect must show when the recording equipment is recording.

Notes for guidance

A–169 **E:**3A *Nothing in this code is intended to preclude audio recording at police discretion of interviews at police stations with people cautioned in respect of offences not covered by paragraph 3.1, or responses made by persons after they have been charged with, or told they may be prosecuted for, an offence, provided this code is complied with.*

E:3B *A decision not to audio record an interview for any reason may be the subject of comment in court. The authorising officer should be prepared to justify that decision.*

E:3C *If, during the course of an interview under this code, it becomes apparent that the interview should be conducted under one of the terrorism codes for recording of interviews the interview should only continue in accordance with the relevant code.*

E:4 The interview

(a) General

A–170 **E:**4.1 The provisions of Code C:

- sections 10 and 11, and the applicable *Notes for Guidance* apply to the conduct of interviews to which this code applies;
- paragraphs 11.7 to 11.14 apply only when a written record is needed.

E:4.2 Code C, paragraphs 10.10, 10.11 and Annex C describe the restriction on drawing adverse inferences from a suspect's failure or refusal to say anything about their involvement in the offence when interviewed or after being charged or informed they may be prosecuted, and how it affects the terms of the caution and determines if and by whom a special warning under sections 36 and 37 of the *Criminal Justice and Public Order Act* 1994 can be given.

(b) Commencement of interviews

E:4.3 When the suspect is brought into the interview room the interviewer shall, without delay but in the suspect's sight, load the recorder with new recording media and set it to record. The recording media must be unwrapped or opened in the suspect's presence. [*This paragraph does not apply to interviews recorded using a secure digital network, see paragraphs 7.4 and 7.5*].

E:4.4 The interviewer should tell the suspect about the recording process and point out the sign or indicator which shows that the recording equipment is activated and recording. See paragraph 3.6. The interviewer shall:

(a) say the interview is being audibly recorded;
(b) subject to paragraph 2.3, give their name and rank and that of any other interviewer present;
(c) ask the suspect and any other party present, *e.g.* a solicitor, to identify themselves;
(d) state the date, time of commencement and place of the interview;
(e) state the suspect will be given a notice about what will happen to the copies of the recording. [*This sub-paragraph does not apply to interviews recorded using a secure digital network, see paragraphs 7.4 and 7.6 to 7.7.*]

See *Note 4A*.

E:4.5 The interviewer shall:

- caution the suspect, see Code C, section 10;
- remind the suspect of their entitlement to free legal advice, see Code C, paragraph 11.2.

E:4.6 The interviewer shall put to the suspect any significant statement or silence, see Code C, paragraph 11.4.

(c) Interviews with deaf persons

E:4.7 If the suspect is deaf or is suspected of having impaired hearing, the interviewer shall make a written note of the interview in accordance with Code C, at the same time as audio recording it in accordance with this code. See *Notes 4B* and *4C*. **A–171**

(d) Objections and complaints by the suspect

E:4.8 If the suspect objects to the interview being audibly recorded at the outset, during the interview or during a break, the interviewer shall explain that the interview is being audibly recorded and that this code requires the suspect's objections to be recorded on the audio recording. When any objections have been audibly recorded or the suspect has refused to have their objections recorded, the interviewer shall say they are turning off the recorder, give their reasons and turn it off. The interviewer shall then make a written record of the interview as in Code C, section 11. If, however, the interviewer reasonably considers they may proceed to question the suspect with the audio recording still on, the interviewer may do so. This procedure also applies in cases where the suspect has previously objected to the interview being visually recorded, see Code F 4.8, and the investigating officer has decided to audibly record the interview. See *Note 4D*.

E:4.9 If in the course of an interview a complaint is made by or on behalf of the person being questioned concerning the provisions of this code or Code C, the interviewer shall act as in Code C, paragraph 12.9. See *Notes 4E* and *4F*.

E:4.10 If the suspect indicates they want to tell the interviewer about matters not directly connected with the offence and they are unwilling for these matters to be audio recorded, the suspect should be given the opportunity to tell the interviewer at the end of the formal interview.

(e) Changing recording media

E:4.11 When the recorder shows the recording media only has a short time left, the interviewer shall tell the suspect the recording media are coming to an end and round off that part of the interview. If the interviewer leaves the room for a second set of recording media, the suspect shall not be left unattended. The interviewer will remove the recording media from the recorder and insert the new recording media which shall be unwrapped or opened in the suspect's presence.

The recorder should be set to record on the new media. To avoid confusion between the recording media, the interviewer shall mark the media with an identification number immediately after they are removed from the recorder. [*This paragraph does not apply to interviews recorded using a secure digital network as this does not use removable media, see paragraphs 1.6(c), 7.4 and 7.14 to 7.15.*]

(f) Taking a break during interview

A–172 **E:**4.12 When a break is taken, the fact that a break is to be taken, the reason for it and the time shall be recorded on the audio recording.

E:4.12A When the break is taken and the interview room vacated by the suspect, the recording media shall be removed from the recorder and the procedures for the conclusion of an interview followed, see paragraph 4.18.

E:4.13 When a break is a short one and both the suspect and an interviewer remain in the interview room, the recording may be stopped. There is no need to remove the recording media and when the interview recommences the recording should continue on the same recording media. The time the interview recommences shall be recorded on the audio recording.

E:4.14 After any break in the interview the interviewer must, before resuming the interview, remind the person being questioned that they remain under caution or, if there is any doubt, give the caution in full again. See *Note 4G*.

[*Paragraphs 4.12 to 4.14 do not apply to interviews recorded using a secure digital network, see paragraphs 7.4 and 7.8 to 7.10.*]

(g) Failure of recording equipment

E:4.15 If there is an equipment failure which can be rectified quickly, *e.g.* by inserting new recording media, the interviewer shall follow the appropriate procedures as in paragraph 4.11. When the recording is resumed the interviewer shall explain what happened and record the time the interview recommences. If, however, it will not be possible to continue recording on that recorder and no replacement recorder is readily available, the interview may continue without being audibly recorded. If this happens, the interviewer shall seek the custody officer's authority as in paragraph 3.3. See *Note 4H*. [*This paragraph does not apply to interviews recorded using a secure digital network, see paragraphs 7.4 and 7.11.*]

(h) Removing recording media from the recorder

E:4.16 When recording media is removed from the recorder during the interview, they shall be retained and the procedures in paragraph 4.18 followed. [*This paragraph does not apply to interviews recorded using a secure digital network as this does not use removable media, see 1.6(c), 7.4 and 7.14 to 7.15.*]

(i) Conclusion of interview

E:4.17 At the conclusion of the interview, the suspect shall be offered the opportunity to clarify anything he or she has said and asked if there is anything they want to add.

E:4.18 At the conclusion of the interview, including the taking and reading back of any written statement, the time shall be recorded and the recording shall be stopped. The interviewer shall seal the master recording with a master recording label and treat it as an exhibit in accordance with force standing orders. The interviewer shall sign the label and ask the suspect and any third party present during the interview to sign it. If the suspect or third party refuse to sign the label an officer of at least inspector rank, or if not available the custody officer, shall be called into the interview room and asked, subject to paragraph 2.3, to sign it.

E:4.19 The suspect shall be handed a notice which explains:

- how the audio recording will be used;
- the arrangements for access to it;
- that if the person is charged or informed they will be prosecuted, a copy of the audio recording will be supplied as soon as practicable or as otherwise agreed between the suspect and the police or on the order of the court.

[*Paragraphs 4.17 to 4.19 do not apply to interviews recorded using a secure digital network, see paragraphs 7.4 and 7.12 to 7.13.*]

Notes for guidance

A–173 **E:**4A *For the purpose of voice identification the interviewer should ask the suspect and any other people present to identify themselves.*

E:4B *This provision is to give a person who is deaf or has impaired hearing equivalent rights of access to the full interview record as far as this is possible using audio recording.*

E:4C *The provisions of Code C, section 13 on interpreters for deaf persons or for interviews with suspects who have difficulty understanding English continue to apply.*

E:4D *The interviewer should remember that a decision to continue recording against the wishes of the suspect may be the subject of comment in court.*

E:4E *If the custody officer is called to deal with the complaint, the recorder should, if possible, be left on until the custody officer has entered the room and spoken to the person being interviewed. Continuation or termination of the interview should be at the interviewer's discretion pending action by an inspector under Code C, paragraph 9.2.*

E:4F *If the complaint is about a matter not connected with this code or Code C, the decision to continue is at the interviewer's discretion. When the interviewer decides to continue the interview, they shall tell the suspect the complaint will be brought to the custody officer's attention at the conclusion of the interview. When the interview is concluded the interviewer must, as soon as practicable, inform the custody officer about the existence and nature of the complaint made.* **A–174**

E:4G *The interviewer should remember that it may be necessary to show to the court that nothing occurred during a break or between interviews which influenced the suspect's recorded evidence. After a break or at the beginning of a subsequent interview, the interviewer should consider summarising on the record the reason for the break and confirming this with the suspect.*

E:4H *Where the interview is being recorded and the media or the recording equipment fails the officer conducting the interview should stop the interview immediately. Where part of the interview is unaffected by the error and is still accessible on the media, that media shall be copied and sealed in the suspect's presence and the interview recommenced using new equipment/media as required. Where the content of the interview has been lost in its entirety the media should be sealed in the suspect's presence and the interview begun again. If the recording equipment cannot be fixed or no replacement is immediately available the interview should be recorded in accordance with Code C, section 11.*

E:5 After the interview

E:5.1 The interviewer shall make a note in their pocket book that the interview has taken place, was audibly recorded, its time, duration and date and the master recording's identification number. **A–175**

E:5.2 If no proceedings follow in respect of the person whose interview was recorded, the recording media must be kept securely as in paragraph 6.1 and *Note 6A*.

[*This section (paragraphs 5.1, 5.2 and Note 5A) does not apply to interviews recorded using a secure digital network, see paragraphs 7.4 and 7.14 to 7.15.*]

Note for guidance

E:5A *Any written record of an audibly recorded interview should be made in accordance with national guidelines approved by the Secretary of State, and with regard to the advice contained in the Manual of Guidance for the preparation, processing and submission of prosecution files.* **A–176**

E:6 Media security

E:6.1 The officer in charge of each police station at which interviews with suspects are recorded shall make arrangements for master recordings to be kept securely and their movements accounted for on the same basis as material which may be used for evidential purposes, in accordance with force standing orders. See *Note 6A*. **A–177**

E:6.2 A police officer has no authority to break the seal on a master recording required for criminal trial or appeal proceedings. If it is necessary to gain access to the master recording, the police officer shall arrange for its seal to be broken in the presence of a representative of the Crown Prosecution Service. The defendant or their legal adviser should be informed and given a reasonable opportunity to be present. If the defendant or their legal representative is present they shall be invited to reseal and sign the master recording. If either refuses or neither is present this should be done by the representative of the Crown Prosecution Service. See *Notes 6B* and *6C*.

E:6.3 If no criminal proceedings result or the criminal trial and, if applicable, appeal proceedings to which the interview relates have been concluded, the chief officer of police is responsible for establishing arrangements for breaking the seal on the master recording, if necessary.

E:6.4 When the master recording seal is broken, a record must be made of the procedure followed, including the date, time, place and persons present.

[*This section (paragraphs 6.1 to 6.4 and Notes 6A to 6C) does not apply to interviews recorded using a secure digital network, see paragraphs 7.4 and 7.14 to 7.15.*]

Notes for guidance

A–178 **E:**6A *This section is concerned with the security of the master recording sealed at the conclusion of the interview. Care must be taken of working copies of recordings because their loss or destruction may lead to the need to access master recordings.*

E:6B *If the recording has been delivered to the Crown Court for their keeping after committal for trial the crown prosecutor will apply to the chief clerk of the Crown Court centre for the release of the recording for unsealing by the crown prosecutor.*

A–179 **E:**6C *Reference to the Crown Prosecution Service or to the crown prosecutor in this part of the code should be taken to include any other body or person with a statutory responsibility for prosecution for whom the police conduct any audibly recorded interviews.*

E:7 Recording of interviews by secure digital network

A–179a **E:**7.1 A secure digital network does not use removable media and this section specifies the provisions which will apply when a secure digital network is used.

E:7.2 [*Not used*]

E:7.3 The following requirements are solely applicable to the use of a secure digital network for the recording of interviews.

Application of sections 1 to 6 of Code E

A–179b **E:**7.4 Sections 1 to 6 of Code E above apply except for the following paragraphs:

- paragraph 2.2 under "Recording and sealing of master recordings"
- paragraph 4.3 under "(b) Commencement of interviews"
- paragraph 4.4 (e) under "(b) Commencement of interviews"
- paragraphs 4.11 – 4.19 under "(e) Changing recording media", "(f) Taking a break during interview", "(g) Failure of recording equipment", "(h) Removing recording media from the recorder" and (i) "Conclusion of the interview"
- paragraphs 6.1 – 6.4 and Notes 6A to 6C under "Media security".

Commencement of interview

A–179c **E:**7.5 When the suspect is brought into the interview room, the interviewer shall without delay and in the sight of the suspect, switch on the recording equipment and enter the information necessary to log on to the secure network and start recording.

E:7.6 The interviewer must then provide inform the suspect that the interview is being recorded using a secure digital network and that recording has commenced.

E:7.7 In addition to the requirements of paragraph 4.4(a) – (d) above, the interviewer must inform the person that:

- they will be given access to the recording of the interview in the event that they are charged or informed that they will be prosecuted but if they are not charged or informed that they will be prosecuted they will only be given access as agreed with the police or on the order of a court; and
- they will be given a written notice at the end of the interview setting out their rights to access the recording and what will happen to the recording.

Taking a break during interview

A–179d **E:**7.8 When a break is taken, the fact that a break is to be taken, the reason for it and the time shall be recorded on the audio recording. The recording shall be stopped and the procedures in paragraphs 7.12 and 7.13 for the conclusion of an interview followed.

E:7.9 When the interview recommences the procedures in paragraphs 7.5 to 7.7 for commencing an interview shall be followed to create a new file to record the continuation of the interview. The time the interview recommences shall be recorded on the audio recording.

E:7.10 After any break in the interview the interviewer must, before resuming the interview, remind the person being questioned that they remain under caution or, if there is any doubt, give the caution in full again. See *Note 4G*.

Failure of recording equipment

E:7.11 If there is an equipment failure which can be rectified quickly, *e.g.* by commencing a new secure digital network recording, the interviewer shall follow the appropriate procedures as in paragraphs 7.8 to 7.10. When the recording is resumed the interviewer shall explain what happened and record the time the interview recommences. If, however, it is not possible to continue recording on the secure digital network the interview should be recorded on removable media as in paragraph 4.3 unless the necessary equipment is not available. If this happens the interview may continue without being audibly recorded and the interviewer shall seek the custody officer's authority as in paragraph 3.3. See *Note 4H*. **A–179e**

Conclusion of interview

E:7.12 At the conclusion of the interview, the suspect shall be offered the opportunity to clarify anything he or she has said and asked if there is anything they want to add. **A–179f**

E:7.13 At the conclusion of the interview, including the taking and reading back of any written statement:

(a) the time shall be orally recorded;

(b) the suspect shall be handed a notice which explains:

- how the audio recording will be used,
- the arrangements for access to it,
- that if they are charged or informed that they will be prosecuted, they will be given access to the recording of the interview either electronically or by being given a copy on removable recording media, but if they are not charged or informed that they will prosecuted, they will only be given access as agreed with the police or on the order of a court; see *Note 7A*;

(c) the suspect must be asked to confirm that he or she has received a copy of the notice at paragraph 7.13(b) above; if the suspect fails to accept or to acknowledge receipt of the notice, the interviewer will state for the recording that a copy of the notice has been provided to the suspect and that he or she has refused to take a copy of the notice or has refused to acknowledge receipt;

(d) the time shall be recorded and the interviewer shall notify the suspect that the recording is being saved to the secure network. The interviewer must save the recording in the presence of the suspect. The suspect should then be informed that the interview is terminated.

After the interview

E:7.14 The interviewer shall make a note in their pocket book that the interview has taken place, was audibly recorded, its time, duration and date and the original recording's identification number.

E:7.15 If no proceedings follow in respect of the person whose interview was recorded, the recordings must be kept securely as in paragraphs 7.16 and 7.17.

See Note 5A

Security of secure digital network interview records

E:7.16 Interview record files are stored in read only format on non-removable storage devices, for example, hard disk drives, to ensure their integrity. The recordings are first saved locally to a secure non-removable device before being transferred to the remote network device. If for any reason the network connection fails, the recording remains on the local device and will be transferred when the network connections are restored.

E:7.17 Access to interview recordings, including copying to removable media, must be strictly controlled and monitored to ensure that access is restricted to those who have been given specific permission to access for specified purposes when this is necessary. For example, police officers and CPS lawyers involved in the preparation of any prosecution case, persons interviewed if they have been charged or informed they may be prosecuted and their legal representatives.

Note for guidance

A–179g **E:**7A *The notice at paragraph 7.13 above should provide a brief explanation of the secure digital network and how access is strictly limited to the recording. The notice should also explain the access rights of the suspect, his or her legal representative, the police and the prosecutor to the recording of the interview. Space should be provided on the form to insert the date and the file reference number for the interview.*

VII. CODE F (VISUAL RECORDING OF INTERVIEWS)

A–180 The text that follows is of the version of the code that came into force on May 1, 2010: see *ante*, Appendix A–1.

The *Police and Criminal Evidence Act 1984 (Visual Recording of Interviews) (Certain Police Areas) Order* 2002 (S.I. 2002 No. 1069) (made under s.60A(1)(b) and (2)) required the visual recording of interviews held by police officers at Basingstoke, Portsmouth, Southampton, Chatham, Gravesend, Tonbridge, Bromley, Colindale, Edmonton, Redditch, Telford and Worcester police stations and commencing after midnight on May 7, 2002.

The *Police and Criminal Evidence Act 1984 (Visual Recording of Interviews) (Certain Police Areas) (No. 2) Order* 2002 (S.I. 2002 No. 2527) (made under s.60A(1)(b) and (2)) required the visual recording of interviews held by police officers at Harlow, Colchester, and Southend police stations and commencing after midnight on October 29, 2002.

The *Police and Criminal Evidence Act 1984 (Visual Recording of Interviews) (Certain Police Areas) Order* 2003 (S.I. 2003 No. 2463) revoked S.I. 2002 No. 1069 and S.I. 2002 No. 2527 (*ante*) as from November 1, 2003, so that visual recording of interviews in the police areas specified in those orders was no longer mandatory.

As at March 9, 2011, there was no requirement on any police force to make visual recordings of interviews, but police officers who choose to make such recordings will still be required to have regard to the provisions of this code.

F. Code of Practice on Visual Recordings With Sound Of Interviews With Suspects

Commencement—Transitional arrangements

A–180a The contents of this code should be considered if an interviewing officer decides to make a visual recording with sound of an interview with a suspect after midnight on 1 May 2010. There is no statutory requirement under *PACE* to visually record interviews.

F:1. General

A–181 **F:**1.1 This code of practice must be readily available for consultation by police officers and other police staff, detained persons and members of the public.

F:1.2 The notes for guidance included are not provisions of this code. They form guidance to police officers and others about its application and interpretation.

F:1.3 Nothing in this code shall be taken as detracting in any way from the requirements of the Code of Practice for the Detention, Treatment and Questioning of Persons by Police Officers (Code C). [See *Note 1A*.]

F:1.4 The interviews to which this code applies are set out in paragraphs 3.1–3.3.

F:1.5 In this code, the term "appropriate adult", "solicitor" and "interview" have the same meaning as those set out in Code C. The corresponding provisions and Notes for Guidance in Code C applicable to those terms shall also apply where appropriate.

F:1.5A The visual recording of interviews shall be carried out openly to instil confidence in its reliability as an impartial and accurate record of the interview.

F:1.6 Any reference in this code to visual recording shall be taken to mean visual recording with sound and in this code:

(aa) "recording media" means any removable, physical audio recording medium (such as magnetic tape, optical disc or solid state memory) which can be played and copied;

(a) "designated person" means a person other than a police officer, designated under the Police Reform Act 2002, Part 4 who has specified powers and duties of police officers conferred or imposed on them;

(b) any reference to a police officer includes a designated person acting in the exercise or performance of the powers and duties conferred or imposed on them by their designation;

(c) "secure digital network" is a computer network system which enables an original interview recording to be stored as a digital multi media file or a series of such files, on a secure file server which is accredited by the National Accreditor for Police Information Systems in the National Police Improvement Agency (NPIA) in accordance with the UK Government Protective Marking Scheme (see section 7 of this code).

F:1.7 References to "pocket book" in this code include any official report book issued to police officers.

Note for guidance

F:1A *As in paragraph 1.9 of Code C, references to custody officers include those carrying out the functions of a custody officer.*

F:2. Recording and sealing of master recordings

F:2.1 [*Not used*] **A–182**

F:2.2 The camera(s) shall be placed in the interview room so as to ensure coverage of as much of the room as is practicably possible whilst the interviews are taking place. [See *Note 2A*.]

F:2.3 The certified recording medium will be of a high quality, new and previously unused. When the certified recording medium is placed in the recorder and switched on to record, the correct date and time, in hours, minutes and seconds will be superimposed automatically, second by second, during the whole recording. [See *Note 2B*.] See section 7 regarding the use of a secure digital network to record the interview.

F:2.4 One copy of the certified recording medium, referred to in this code as the master copy, will be sealed before it leaves the presence of the suspect. A second copy will be used as a working copy. [See *Note 2C* and *2D*.]

F:2.5 Nothing in this code requires the identity of an officer to be recorded or disclosed if:

(a) the interview or record relates to a person detained under the *Terrorism Act* 2000 (see paragraph 3.2); or

(b) otherwise where the officer reasonably believes that recording or disclosing their name might put them in danger.

In these cases, the officer will have their back to the camera and shall use their warrant or other identification number and the name of the police station to which they are attached. Such instances and the reasons for them shall be recorded in the custody record. [See *Note 2E*.]

Notes for guidance

F:2A *Interviewing officers will wish to arrange that, as far as possible, visual recording arrangements are unobtrusive. It must be clear to the suspect, however, that there is no opportunity to interfere with the recording equipment or the recording media.* **A–183**

F:2B *In this context, the certified recording media should be capable of having an image of the date and time superimposed upon them as they record the interview.*

F:2C *The purpose of sealing the master copy before it leaves the presence of the suspect is to establish their confidence that the integrity of the copy is preserved.*

F:2D *The recording of the interview may be used for identification procedures in accordance with paragraph 3.21 or Annex E of Code D.*

F:2E *The purpose of the* [sic] *paragraph 2.5(b) is to protect police officers and others involved in the investigation of serious organised crime or the arrest of particularly violent suspects when there is reliable information that those arrested or their associates may threaten or cause harm to the officers, their families or their personal property.*

F:3. Interviews to be visually recorded

A–184 **F:**3.1 Subject to paragraph 3.2 below, if an interviewing officer decides to make a visual recording, these are the areas where it might be appropriate:

(a) with a suspect in respect of an indictable offence (including an offence triable either way) [see *Notes 3A* and *3B*];

(b) which takes place as a result of an interviewer exceptionally putting further questions to a suspect about an offence described in sub-paragraph (a) above after they have been charged with, or informed they may be prosecuted for, that offence [see *Note 3C*];

(c) in which an interviewer wishes to bring to the notice of a person, after that person has been charged with, or informed they may be prosecuted for an offence described in sub-paragraph (a) above, any written statement made by another person, or the content of an interview with another person [see *Note 3D*];

(d) with, or in the presence of, a deaf or deaf/blind or speech impaired person who uses sign language to communicate;

(e) with, or in the presence of anyone who requires an "appropriate adult"; or

(f) in any case where the suspect or their representative requests that the interview be recorded visually.

A–185 **F:**3.2 The *Terrorism Act* 2000 makes separate provision for a code of practice for the video recording of interviews in a police station of those detained under Schedule 7 or section 41 of the Act. The provisions of this code do not therefore apply to such interviews [see *Note 3E*].

F:3.3 The custody officer may authorise the interviewing officer not to record the interview visually:

(a) where it is not reasonably practicable to do so because of failure of the equipment, or the non-availability of a suitable interview room, or recorder and the authorising officer considers on reasonable grounds that the interview should not be delayed until the failure has been rectified or a suitable room or recorder becomes available; in such cases the custody officer may authorise the interviewing officer to audio record the interview in accordance with the guidance set out in Code E;

(b) where it is clear from the outset that no prosecution will ensue; or

(c) where it is not practicable to do so because at the time the person resists being taken to a suitable interview room or other location which would enable the interview to be recorded, or otherwise fails or refuses to go into such a room or location, and the authorising officer considers on reasonable grounds that the interview should not be delayed until these conditions cease to apply.

In all cases the custody officer shall make a note in the custody records [*sic*] of the reasons for not taking a visual record. [See *Note 3F*.]

F:3.4 When a person who is voluntarily attending the police station is required to be cautioned in accordance with Code C prior to being interviewed, the subsequent interview shall be recorded, unless the custody officer gives authority in accordance with the provisions of paragraph 3.3 above for the interview not to be so recorded.

F:3.5 The whole of each interview shall be recorded visually, including the taking and reading back of any statement.

F:3.6 A sign or indicator which is visible to the suspect must show when the visual recording equipment is recording.

Notes for guidance

A–186 **F:**3A *Nothing in the code is intended to preclude visual recording at police discretion of interviews at police stations with people cautioned in respect of offences not covered by paragraph 3.1, or responses made by interviewees after they have been charged with or informed they may be prosecuted for, an offence, provided that this code is complied with.*

F:3B *Attention is drawn to the provisions set out in Code C about the matters to be considered when deciding whether a detained person is fit to be interviewed.*

F:3C *Code C sets out the circumstances in which a suspect may be questioned about an offence after being charged with it.*

F:3D *Code C sets out the procedures to be followed when a person's attention is drawn after charge, to a statement made by another person. One method of bringing the content of an interview with another person to the notice of a suspect may be to play him a recording of that interview.*

F:3E *If, during the course of an interview under this code, it becomes apparent that the interview should be conducted under one of the terrorism codes for video recording of interviews the interview should only continue in accordance with the relevant code.*

F:3F *A decision not to record an interview visually for any reason may be the subject of comment in court. The authorising officer should therefore be prepared to justify their decision in each case.*

F:4. The interview

(a) General

F:4.1 The provisions of Code C in relation to cautions and interviews and the Notes for Guidance applicable to those provisions shall apply to the conduct of interviews to which this code applies. **A–187**

F:4.2 Particular attention is drawn to those parts of Code C that describe the restrictions on drawing adverse inferences from a suspect's failure or refusal to say anything about their involvement in the offence when interviewed, or after being charged or informed they may be prosecuted and how those restrictions affect the terms of the caution and determine 'whether a special warning under sections 36 and 37 of the *Criminal Justice and Public Order Act* 1994 can be given.

(b) Commencement of interviews

F:4.3 When the suspect is brought into the interview room the interviewer shall without delay, but in sight of the suspect, load the recording equipment and set it to record. The recording media must be unwrapped or otherwise opened in the presence of the suspect. [See *Note 4A*]. **A–188**

F:4.4 The interviewer shall then tell the suspect formally about the visual recording and point out the sign or indicator which shows that the recording equipment is activated and recording. See paragraph 3.6. The interviewer shall:

(a) explain the interview is being visually recorded;
(b) subject to paragraph 2.5, give his or her name and rank, and that of any other interviewer present;
(c) ask the suspect and any other party present (*e.g.* his solicitor) to identify themselves;
(d) state the date, time of commencement and place of the interview; and
(e) state that the suspect will be given a notice about what will happen to the recording.

F:4.5 The interviewer shall then caution the suspect, which should follow that set out in Code C, and remind the suspect of their entitlement to free and independent legal advice and that they can speak to a solicitor on the telephone.

F:4.6 The interviewer shall then put to the suspect any significant statement or silence (*i.e.* failure or refusal to answer a question or to answer it satisfactorily) which occurred before the start of the interview, and shall ask the suspect whether they wish to confirm or deny that earlier statement or silence or whether they wish to add anything. The definition of a "significant" statement or silence is the same as that set out in Code C.

(c) Interviews with the deaf

F:4.7 If the suspect is deaf or there is doubt about their hearing ability, the provisions of Code C on interpreters for the deaf or for interviews with suspects who have difficulty in understanding English continue to apply. **A–189**

(d) Objections and complaints by the suspect

F:4.8 If the suspect raises objections to the interview being visually recorded either at the outset or during the interview or during a break in the interview, the interviewer shall explain the fact **A–190**

that the interview is being visually recorded and that the provisions of this code require that the suspect's objections shall be recorded on the visual recording. When any objections have been visually recorded or the suspect has refused to have their objections recorded, the interviewer shall say that they are turning off the recording equipment, give their reasons and turn it off. If a separate audio recording is being maintained, the officer shall ask the person to record the reasons for refusing to agree to visual recording of the interview. Paragraph 4.8 of Code E will apply if the person objects to audio recording of the interview. The officer shall then make a written record of the interview. If the interviewer reasonably considers they may proceed to question the suspect with the visual recording still on, the interviewer may do so. See *Note 4G*.

F:4.9 If in the course of an interview a complaint is made by the person being questioned, or on their behalf, concerning the provisions of this code or of Code C, then the interviewer shall act in accordance with Code C, record it in the interview record and inform the custody officer. [See *4B* and *4C*.]

F:4.10 If the suspect indicates that they wish to tell the interviewer about matters not directly connected with the offence of which they are suspected and that they are unwilling for these matters to be recorded, the suspect shall be given the opportunity to tell the interviewer about these matters after the conclusion of the formal interview.

(e) Changing the recording media

A–191 **F:**4.11 In instances where the recording medium is not of sufficient length to record all of the interview with the suspect, further certified recording medium will be used. When the recording equipment indicates that the recording medium has only a short time left to run, the interviewer shall advise the suspect and round off that part of the interview. If the interviewer wishes to continue the interview but does not already have further certified recording media with him, they shall obtain a set. The suspect should not be left unattended in the interview room. The interviewer will remove the recording media from the recording equipment and insert the new ones which have been unwrapped or otherwise opened in the suspect's presence. The recording equipment shall then be set to record. Care must be taken, particularly when a number of sets of recording media have been used, to ensure that there is no confusion between them. This could be achieved by marking the sets of recording media with consecutive identification numbers.

(f) Taking a break during the interview

A–192 **F:**4.12 When a break is to be taken during the course of an interview and the interview room is to be vacated by the suspect, the fact that a break is to be taken, the reason for it and the time shall be recorded. The recording equipment must be turned off and the recording media removed. The procedures for the conclusion of an interview set out in paragraph 4.19, below, should be followed.

F:4.13 When a break is to be a short one, and both the suspect and a police officer are to remain in the interview room, the fact that a break is to be taken, the reasons for it and the time shall be recorded on the recording media. The recording equipment may be turned off, but there is no need to remove the recording media. When the interview is recommenced the recording shall continue on the same recording media and the time at which the interview recommences shall be recorded.

F:4.14 When there is a break in questioning under caution, the interviewing officer must ensure that the person being questioned is aware that they remain under caution. If there is any doubt the caution must be given again in full when the interview resumes. [See *Notes 4D* and *4E*.]

(g) Failure of recording equipment

A–193 **F:**4.15 If there is a failure of equipment which can be rectified quickly, the appropriate procedures set out in paragraph 4.12 shall be followed. When the recording is resumed the interviewer shall explain what has happened and record the time the interview recommences. If, however, it is not possible to continue recording on that particular recorder and no alternative equipment is readily available, the interview may continue without being recorded visually. In such circumstances, the procedures set out in paragraph 3.3 of this code for seeking the authority of the custody officer will be followed. [See *Note 4F*.]

(h) Removing used recording media from recording equipment

A–194 **F:**4.16 Where used recording media are removed from the recording equipment during the course of an interview, they shall be retained and the procedures set out in paragraph 4.18 below followed.

(i) Conclusion of interview

F:4.17 Before the conclusion of the interview, the suspect shall be offered the opportunity to clarify anything he or she has said and asked if there is anything that they wish to add. **A–195**

F:4.18 At the conclusion of the interview, including the taking and reading back of any written statement, the time shall be recorded and the recording equipment switched off. The master recording shall be removed from the recording equipment, sealed with a master recording label and treated as an exhibit in accordance with the force standing orders. The interviewer shall sign the label and also ask the suspect and any third party present during the interview to sign it. If the suspect or third party refuses to sign the label, an officer of at least the rank of inspector, or if one is not available, the custody officer, shall be called into the interview room and asked, subject to paragraph 2.5, to sign it.

F:4.19 The suspect shall be handed a notice which explains the use which will be made of the recording and the arrangements for access to it. The notice will also advise the suspect that a copy of the tape shall be supplied as soon as practicable if the person is charged or informed that he will be prosecuted.

Notes for guidance

F:4A *The interviewer should attempt to estimate the likely length of the interview and ensure that an appropriate quantity of certified recording media and labels with which to seal the master copies are available in the interview room.* **A–196**

F:4B *Where the custody officer is called immediately to deal with the complaint, wherever possible the recording equipment should be left to run until the custody officer has entered the interview room and spoken to the person being interviewed. Continuation or termination of the interview should be at the discretion of the interviewing officer pending action by an inspector as set out in Code C.*

F:4C *Where the complaint is about a matter not connected with this code of practice or Code C, the decision to continue with the interview is at the discretion of the interviewing officer. Where the interviewing officer decides to continue with the interview, the person being interviewed shall be told that the complaint will be brought to the attention of the custody officer at the conclusion of the interview. When the interview is concluded, the interviewing officer must, as soon as practicable, inform the custody officer of the existence and nature of the complaint made.*

F:4D *In considering whether to caution again after a break, the officer should bear in mind that he may have to satisfy a court that the person understood that he was still under caution when the interview resumed.*

F:4E *The officer should bear in mind that it may be necessary to satisfy the court that nothing occurred during a break in an interview or between interviews which influenced the suspect's recorded evidence. On the re-commencement of an interview, the officer should consider summarising on the record the reason for the break and confirming this with the suspect.*

F:4F *If any part of the recording media breaks or is otherwise damaged during the interview, it should be sealed as a master copy in the presence of the suspect and the interview resumed where it left off. The undamaged part should be copied and the original sealed as a master tape in the suspect's presence, if necessary after the interview. If equipment for copying is not readily available, both parts should be sealed in the suspect's presence and the interview begun again.*

F:4G *The interviewer should be aware that a decision to continue recording against the wishes of the suspect may be the subject of comment in court.*

F:5. After the interview

F:5.1 The interviewer shall make a note in his or her pocket book of the fact that the interview has taken place and has been recorded, its time, duration and date and the identification number of the master copy of the recording media. **A–197**

F:5.2 Where no proceedings follow in respect of the person whose interview was recorded, the recording media must nevertheless be kept securely in accordance with paragraph 6.1 and Note 6A.

Note for guidance

F:5A *Any written record of a recorded interview shall be made in accordance with national* *guidelines approved by the Secretary of State, and with regard to the advice contained in the Manual of Guidance for the preparation, processing and submission of files.*

F:6. Master copy security

(a) General

A–198 **F:**6.1 The officer in charge of the police station at which interviews with suspects are recorded shall make arrangements for the master copies to be kept securely and their movements accounted for on the same basis as other material which may be used for evidential purposes, in accordance with force standing orders. [See *Note 6A*.]

(b) Breaking master copy seal for criminal proceedings

A–199 **F:**6.2 A police officer has no authority to break the seal on a master copy which is required for criminal trial or appeal proceedings. If it is necessary to gain access to the master copy, the police officer shall arrange for its seal to be broken in the presence of a representative of the Crown Prosecution Service. The defendant or their legal adviser shall be informed and given a reasonable opportunity to be present. If the defendant or their legal representative is present they shall be invited to reseal and sign the master copy. If either refuses or neither is present, this shall be done by the representative of the Crown Prosecution Service. [See *Notes 6B* and *6C*.]

(c) Breaking master copy seal: other cases

A–200 **F:**6.3 The chief officer of police is responsible for establishing arrangements for breaking the seal of the master copy where no criminal proceedings result, or the criminal proceedings, to which the interview relates, have been concluded and it becomes necessary to break the seal. These arrangements should be those which the chief officer considers are reasonably necessary to demonstrate to the person interviewed and any other party who may wish to use or refer to the interview record that the master copy has not been tampered with and that the interview record remains accurate. [See *Note 6D*.]

F:6.4 Subject to paragraph 6.6, a representative of each party must be given a reasonable opportunity to be present when the seal is broken, the master copy copied and re-sealed.

F:6.5 If one or more of the parties is not present when the master copy seal is broken because they cannot be contacted or refuse to attend or paragraph 6.6 applies, arrangements should be made for an independent person such as a custody visitor, to be present. Alternatively, or as an additional safeguard, arrangement should be made for a film or photographs to be taken of the procedure.

F:6.6 Paragraph 6.5 does not require a person to be given an opportunity to be present when:

(a) it is necessary to break the master copy seal for the proper and effective further investigation of the original offence or the investigation of some other offence; and

(b) the officer in charge of the investigation has reasonable grounds to suspect that allowing an opportunity might prejudice any such an investigation or criminal proceedings which may be brought as a result or endanger any person. [See *Note 6E*.]

(e) Documentation

A–201 **F:**6.7 When the master copy seal is broken, copied and re-sealed, a record must be made of the procedure followed, including the date time and place and persons present.

Notes for guidance

A–202 **F:**6A *This section is concerned with the security of the master copy which will have been sealed at the conclusion of the interview. Care should, however, be taken of working copies since their loss or destruction may lead unnecessarily to the need to have access to master copies.*

F:6B *If the master copy has been delivered to the Crown Court for their keeping after committal for trial the crown prosecutor will apply to the chief clerk of the Crown Court centre for its release for unsealing by the crown prosecutor.*

F:6C *Reference to the Crown Prosecution Service or to the crown prosecutor in this part of the code shall be taken to include any other body or person with a statutory responsibility for prosecution for whom the police conduct any recorded interviews.*

F:6D *The most common reasons for needing access to master copies that are not required for* *criminal proceedings arise from civil actions and complaints against police and civil actions between individuals arising out of allegations of crime investigated by police.*

F:6E *Paragraph 6.6 could apply, for example, when one or more of the outcomes or likely outcomes of the investigation might be: (i) the prosecution of one or more of the original suspects; (ii) the prosecution of someone previously not suspected, including someone who was originally a witness; and (iii) any original suspect being treated as a prosecution witness and when premature disclosure of any police action, particularly through contact with any parties involved, could lead to a real risk of compromising the investigation and endangering witnesses.*

F:7. Visual recording of interviews by secure digital network

F:7.1 This section applies if an officer wishes to make a visual recording with sound of an interview mentioned in section 3 of this code using a secure digital network which does not use removable media (see paragraph 1.6(c) above). **A–202a**

F:7.3 [*sic*] The provisions of sections 1 to 6 of this code which relate or apply only to removable media will not apply to a secure digital network recording.

F:7.4 The statutory requirement and provisions for the audio recording of interviews using a secure digital network set out in section 7 of Code E should be applied to the visual recording with sound of interviews mentioned in section 3 of this code as if references to audio recordings of interviews include visual recordings with sound.

VIII. CODE G (ARREST)

The first version of Code G came into force on January 1, 2006, to coincide with the commencement of the substantial changes to the provisions of the *PACE Act* 1984 relating to the powers of arrest of police constables. As from that date, all offences became arrestable offences, but the lawfulness of an arrest by a constable for an offence became dependent on the constable having "reasonable grounds for believing that for any of the reasons mentioned in subsection (5) [of section 24] it is necessary to arrest the person in question". For the substituted section 24, see § 15–163 in the main work. **A–203**

As to the content of this code, paragraph 2.1 significantly over-simplifies the requirements of a lawful arrest, and there is an error in paragraph 2.3. This states that a constable may arrest without warrant "in relation to any offence, except for the single exception [*sic*] listed in Note for Guidance 1". That note recites the powers of arrest for offences under the *CLA* 1967, ss.4(1) and 5(1) (assisting offenders/ concealment of evidence) require that the offences to which they relate must carry a maximum term of at least five years' imprisonment. This, however, is to confuse the ingredients of the offence and the power of arrest.

G. Code of Practice for the Statutory Power of Arrest by Police Officers

Commencement **A–203a**

This code applies to any arrest made by a police officer after midnight on 31 December 2005.

G:1 Introduction

G:1.1 This code of practice deals with statutory power of police to arrest persons suspected of involvement in a criminal offence. **A–204**

G:1.2 The right to liberty is a key principle of the *Human Rights Act* 1998. The exercise of the power of arrest represents an obvious and significant interference with that right.

G:1.3 The use of the power must be fully justified and officers exercising the power should consider if the necessary objectives can be met by other, less intrusive means. Arrest must never be used simply because it can be used. Absence of justification for exercising the powers of arrest may lead to challenges should the case proceed to court. When the power of arrest is exercised it is essential that it is exercised in a non-discriminatory and proportionate manner.

G:1.4 Section 24 of the *Police and Criminal Evidence Act* 1984 (as substituted by section 110 of the *Serious Organised Crime and Police Act* 2005) provides the statutory power of arrest. If the provisions of the Act and this code are not observed, both the arrest and the conduct of any subsequent investigation may be open to question.

G:1.5 This code of practice must be readily available at all police stations for consultation by police officers and police staff, detained persons and members of the public.

G:1.6 The notes for guidance are not provisions of this code.

G:2 Elements of arrest under section 24 PACE

A–205 **G:**2.1 A lawful arrest requires two elements:

A person's involvement or suspected involvement or attempted involvement in the commission of a criminal offence;

AND

reasonable grounds for believing that the person's arrest is necessary.

G:2.2 Arresting officers are required to inform the person arrested that they have been arrested, even if this fact is obvious, and of the relevant circumstances of the arrest in relation to both elements and to inform the custody officer of these on arrival at the police station. See Code C, paragraph 3.4.

Involvement in the commision of an offence

A–206 **G:**2.3 A constable may arrest without warrant in relation to any offence, except for the single exception listed in *Note for Guidance* 1. A constable may arrest anyone:

- who is about to commit an offence or is in the act of committing an offence;
- whom the officer has reasonable grounds for suspecting is about to commit an offence or to be committing an offence;
- whom the officer has reasonable grounds to suspect of being guilty of an offence which he or she has reasonable grounds for suspecting has been committed;
- anyone [*sic*] who is guilty of an offence which has been committed or anyone whom the officer has reasonable grounds for suspecting to be guilty of that offence.

Necessity criteria

A–207 **G:**2.4 The power of arrest is only exercisable if the constable has reasonable grounds for believing that it is necessary to arrest the person. The criteria for what may constitute necessity are set out in paragraph 2.9. It remains an operational decision at the discretion of the arresting officer as to:

- what action he or she may take at the point of contact with the individual;
- the necessity criterion or criteria (if any) which applies to the individual; and
- whether to arrest, report for summons, grant street bail, issue a fixed penalty notice or take any other action that is open to the officer.

G:2.5 In applying the criteria, the arresting officer has to be satisfied that at least one of the reasons supporting the need for arrest is satisfied.

G:2.6 Extending the power of arrest to all offences provides a constable with the ability to use that power to deal with any situation. However, applying the necessity criteria requires the constable to examine and justify the reason or reasons why a person needs to be taken to a police station for the custody officer to decide whether the person should be placed in police detention.

G:2.7 The criteria below are set out in section 24 of *PACE* as substituted by section 110 of the *Serious Organised Crime and Police Act* 2005. The criteria are exhaustive. However, the circumstances that may satisfy those criteria remain a matter for the operational discretion of individual officers. Some examples are given below of what those circumstances may be.

G:2.8 In considering the individual circumstances, the constable must take into account the situation of the victim, the nature of the offence, the circumstances of the suspect and the needs of the investigative process.

A–208 **G:**2.9 The criteria are that the arrest is necessary:

(a) to enable the name of the person in question to be ascertained (in the case where the constable does not know, and cannot readily ascertain, the person's name, or has reasonable grounds for doubting whether a name given by the person as his name is his real name);

(b) correspondingly as regards the person's address;

an address is a satisfactory address for service of summons if the person will be at it for a sufficiently long period for it to be possible to serve him or her with a summons; or, that some other person at that address specified by the person will accept service of the summons on their behalf;

(c) to prevent the person in question—

(i) causing physical injury to himself or any other person;

(ii) suffering physical injury;

(iii) causing loss or damage to property;

(iv) committing an offence against public decency (only applies where members of the public going about their normal business cannot reasonably be expected to avoid the person in question); or

(v) causing an unlawful obstruction of the highway;

(d) to protect a child or other vulnerable person from the person in question;

(e) to allow the prompt and effective investigation of the offence or of the conduct of the person in question;

this may include cases such as:

(i) where there are reasonable grounds to believe that the person:

- has made false statements;
- has made statements which cannot be readily verified;
- has presented false evidence;
- may steal or destroy evidence;
- may make contact with co-suspects or conspirators;
- may intimidate or threaten or make contact with witnesses;
- where it is necessary to obtain evidence by questioning [*sic*]; or

(ii) when considering arrest in connection with an indictable offence, there is a need to:

- enter and search any premises occupied or controlled by a person;
- search the person;
- prevent contact with others;
- take fingerprints, footwear impressions, samples or photographs of the suspect;

(iii) ensuring compliance with statutory drug testing requirements;

(f) to prevent any prosecution for the offence from being hindered by the disappearance of the person in question;

this may arise if there are reasonable grounds for believing that:

- if the person is not arrested he or she will fail to attend court;
- street bail after arrest would be insufficient to deter the suspect from trying to evade prosecution.

G:3 Information to be given on arrest

(a) Cautions—when a caution must be given (taken from Code C section 10)

G:3.1 A person whom there are grounds to suspect of an offence (see *Note 2*) must be cautioned before any questions about an offence, or further questions if the answers provide the grounds for suspicion, are put to them if either the suspect's answers or silence (*i.e.* failure or refusal to answer or answer satisfactorily) may be given in evidence to a court in a prosecution. A person need not be cautioned if questions are for other necessary purposes *e.g.*: **A–209**

(a) solely to establish their identify or ownership of any vehicle;

(b) to obtain information in accordance with any relevant statutory requirement;

(c) in furtherance of the proper and effective conduct of a search, *e.g.* to determine the need to search in the exercise of powers to stop and search or to seek co-operation while carrying out a search;

(d) to seek verification of a written record as in Code C, paragraph 11.13;

(e) when examining a person in accordance with the *Terrorism Act* 2000, Schedule 7 and the Code of Practice for Examining Officers issued under that Act, Schedule 14, paragraph 6.

G:3.2 Whenever a person not under arrest is initally cautioned, or reminded they are under caution, that person must at the same time be told they are not under arrest and are free to leave if they want to.

G:3.3 A person who is arrested, or further arrested, must be informed at the time, or as soon as practicable thereafter, that they are under arrest and the grounds for their arrest, see *Note 3*.

G:3.4 A person who is arrested, or further arrested, must also be cautioned unless:

(a) it is impracticable to do so by reason of their condition or behaviour at the time;

(b) they have already been cautioned immediately prior to arrest as in paragraph 3.1.

(c) [sic] Terms of the caution (taken from Code C section 10)

A–210 **G:**3.5 The caution, which must be given on arrest, should be in the following terms:

"You do not have to say anything. But it may harm your defence if you do not mention when questioned something which you later rely on in court. Anything you do say may be given in evidence.".

See *Note 5*.

G:3.6 Minor deviations from the words of any caution given in accordance with this code do not constitute a breach of this code, provided the sense of the relevant caution is preserved. See *Note 6*.

G:3.7 When, despite being cautioned, a person fails to co-operate or to answer particular questions which may affect their immediate treatment, the person should be informed of any relevant consequences and that those consequences are not affected by the caution. Examples are when a person's refusal to provide:

- their name and address when charged may make them liable to detention;
- particulars and information in accordance with a statutory requirement, *e.g.* under the *Road Traffic Act* 1988, may amount to an offence or may make the person liable to a further arrest.

G:4 Records of arrest

(a) General

A–211 **G:**4.1 The arresting officer is required to record in his pocket book or by other methods used for recording information:

- the nature and cirumstances of the offence leading to the arrest;
- the reason or reasons why arrest was necessary;
- the giving of the caution;
- anything said by the person at the time of the arrest.

G:4.2 Such a record should be made at the time of the arrest unless impracticable to do. If not made at that time, the record should then be completed as soon as possible thereafter.

G:4.3 On arrival at the police station, the custody officer shall open the custody record (see paragraph 1.1A and section 2 of Code C). The information given by the arresting officer on the circumstances and reason or reasons for arrest shall be recorded as part of the custody record. Alternatively, a copy of the record made by the officer in accordance with paragraph 4.1 above shall be attached as part of the custody record. See paragraph 2.2 and Code C, paragraphs 3.4 and 10.3.

G:4.4 The custody record will serve as a record of the arrest. Copies of the custody record will be provided in accordance with paragraphs 2.4 and 2.4A of Code C and access for inspection of the original record in accordance with paragraph 2.5 of Code C.

(b) Interviews and arrests

G:4.5 Records of interviews, significant statements or silences will be treated in the same way as set out in sections 10 and 11 of Code C and in Code E (audio recording of interviews).

Notes for guidance

A–212 **G:**1 *The powers of arrest for offences under section 4(1) and 5(1) of the* Criminal Law Act

1967 require that the offences to which they relate must carry a sentence fixed by law or one which a first time offender aged 18 or over could be sentenced to 5 years or more imprisonment.

G:2 *There must be some reasonable, objective grounds for the suspicion, based on known facts or information which are relevant to the likelihood the offence has been committed and the person to be questioned committed it.*

G:3 *An arrested person must be given sufficient information to enable them to understand they have been deprived of their liberty and the reason they have been arrested, e.g. when a person is arrested on suspicion of committing an offence they must be informed of the suspected offence's nature, when and where it was committed. The suspect must also be informed of the reason or reasons why arrest is considered necessary. Vague or technical language should be avoided.*

G:4 *Nothing in this code requires a caution to be given or repeated when informing a person not under arrest they may be prosecuted for an offence. However, a court will not be able to draw any inferences under the* Criminal Justice and Public Order Act *1994, section 34, if the person was not cautioned.*

G:5 *If it appears a person does not understand the caution, the people giving it should explain it in their own words.*

G:6 *The powers available to an officer as the result of an arrest – for example, entry and search of premises, holding a person incommunicado, setting up road blocks – are only available in respect of indictable offences and are subject to the specific requirements on authorisation as set out in the 1984 Act and relevant PACE code of practice.*

Appendix B

CODE OF PRACTICE ON DISCLOSURE

Under Part II of the Criminal Procedure and Investigations Act 1996

Introduction

Pursuant to sections 23 and 25 of the 1996 Act, the Secretary of State prepared and published codes of practice governing the action the police must take in recording and retaining material obtained in the course of a criminal investigation and regulating its supply to the prosecutor for a decision on disclosure.

The first code came into force on the day appointed for the purpose of Part I of the 1996 Act, namely April 1, 1997 (S.I. 1997 No. 1033). It was revised with effect from April 4, 2005: *Criminal Procedure and Investigations Act 1996 (Code of Practice) Order* 2005 (S.I. 2005 No. 985).

Code of practice under Part II

Preamble

This code of practice is issued under Part II of the *Criminal Procedure and Investigations Act* 1996 ('the Act'). It sets out the manner in which police officers are to record, retain and reveal to the prosecutor material obtained in a criminal investigation and which may be relevant to the investigation, and related matters. **B–1**

Introduction

1.1 This code of practice applies in respect of criminal investigations conducted by police officers which begin on or after the day on which this code comes into effect. Persons other than police officers who are charged with the duty of conducting an investigation as defined in the Act are to have regard to the relevant provisions of the code, and should take these into account in applying their own operating procedures. **B–2**

1.2 This code does not apply to persons who are not charged with the duty of conducting an investigation as defined in the Act.

1.3 Nothing in this code applies to material intercepted in obedience to a warrant issued under section 2 of the *Interception of Communications Act* 1985 or section 5 of the *Regulation of Investigatory Powers Act* 2000, or to any copy of that material as defined in section 10 of the 1985 Act or section 15 of the 2000 Act.

1.4 This code extends only to England and Wales.

Definitions

2.1 In this code: **B–3**

- a *criminal investigation* is an investigation conducted by police officers with a view to it being ascertained whether a person should be charged with an offence, or whether a person charged with an offence is guilty of it. This will include:
  - investigations into crimes that have been committed;
  - investigations whose purpose is to ascertain whether a crime has been committed, with a view to the possible institution of criminal proceedings; and
  - investigations which begin in the belief that a crime may be committed, for example

when the police keep premises or individuals under observation for a period of time, with a view to the possible institution of criminal proceedings;

- charging a person with an offence includes prosecution by way of summons;
- an *investigator* is any police officer involved in the conduct of a criminal investigation. All investigators have a responsibility for carrying out the duties imposed on them under this code, including in particular recording information, and retaining records of information and other material;
- the *officer in charge of an investigation* is any police officer involved in the conduct of a criminal investigation. All investigators have a responsibility for carrying out the duties imposed on them under this code, including in particular recording information, and retaining records of information and other material;
- the *disclosure officer* is the person responsible for examining material retained by the police during the investigation; revealing material to the prosecutor during the investigation and any criminal proceedings resulting from it, and certifying that he has done this; and disclosing material to the accused at the request of the prosecutor;
- the *prosecutor* is the authority responsible for the conduct, on behalf of the Crown, of criminal proceedings resulting from a specific criminal investigation;
- *material* is material of any kind, including information and objects, which is obtained in the course of a criminal investigation and which may be relevant to the investigation. This includes not only material coming into the possession of the investigator (such as documents seized in the course of searching premises) but also material generated by him (such as interview records);
- material may be *relevant to the investigation* if it appears to an investigator, or to the officer in charge of an investigation, or to the disclosure officer, that it has some bearing on any offence under investigation or any person being investigated, or on the surrounding circumstances of the case, unless it is incapable of having any impact on the case;
- *sensitive material* is material, the disclosure of which, the disclosure officer believes, would give rise to a real risk of serious prejudice to an important public interest;
- references to *prosecution disclosure* are to the duty of the prosecutor under sections 3 and 7A of the Act to disclose material which is in his possession or which he has inspected in pursuance of this code, and which might reasonably be considered capable of undermining the case against the accused, or of assisting the case for the accused;
- references to the disclosure of material to a person accused of an offence include references to the disclosure of material to his legal representative;
- references to police officers and to the chief officer of police include those employed in a police force as defined in section 3(3) of the *Prosecution of Offences Act* 1985.

As to the meaning of "criminal investigation", see *DPP v. Metten*, unreported, January 22, 1999, DC (§ 12–72 in the main work).

General responsibilities

B–4 3.1 The functions of the investigator, the officer in charge of an investigation and the disclosure officer are separate. Whether they are undertaken by one, two or more persons will depend on the complexity of the case and the administrative arrangements within each police force. Where they are undertaken by more than one person, close consultation between them is essential to the effective performance of the duties imposed by this code.

3.2 In any criminal investigation, one or more deputy disclosure officers may be appointed to assist the disclosure officer, and a deputy disclosure officer may perform any function of a disclosure officer as defined in paragraph 2.1.

3.3 The chief officer of police for each police force is responsible for putting in place arrangements to ensure that in every investigation the identity of the officer in charge of an investigation and the disclosure officer is recorded. The chief officer of police for each police force shall ensure that disclosure officers and deputy disclosure officers have sufficient skills and authority, commensurate with the complexity of the investigation, to discharge their functions effectively. An individual must not be appointed as disclosure officer, or continue in that role, if that is likely to result in a conflict of interest, for instance, if the disclosure officer is the victim of the alleged crime which is the subject of the investigation. The advice of a more senior officer must always be sought if there is doubt as to whether a conflict of interest precludes an individual acting as disclosure officer. If thereafter the doubt remains, the advice of a prosecutor should be sought.

3.4 The officer in charge of an investigation may delegate tasks to another investigator, to civilians employed by the police force, or to other persons participating in the investigation under arrangements for joint investigations, but he remains responsible for ensuring that these have been carried out and for accounting for any general policies followed in the investigation. In particular, it is an essential part of his duties to ensure that all material which may be relevant to an investigation is retained, and either made available to the disclosure officer or (in exceptional circumstances) revealed directly to the prosecutor.

3.5 In conducting an investigation, the investigator should pursue all reasonable lines of inquiry, whether these point towards or away from the suspect. What is reasonable in each case will depend on the particular circumstances. For example, where material is held on computer, it is a matter for the investigator to decide which material on the computer it is reasonable to inquire into, and in what manner.

3.6 If the officer in charge of an investigation believes that other persons may be in possession of material that may be relevant to the investigation, and if this has not been obtained under paragraph 3.5 above, he should ask the disclosure officer to inform them of the existence of the investigation and to invite them to retain the material in case they receive a request for its disclosure. The disclosure officer should inform the prosecutor that they may have such material. However, the officer in charge of an investigation is not required to make speculative enquiries of other persons; there must be some reason to believe that they may have relevant material. That reason may come from information provided to the police by the accused or from other inquiries made or from some other source.

3.7 If, during a criminal investigation, the officer in charge of an investigation or disclosure officer for any reason no longer has responsibility for the functions falling to him, either his supervisor or the police officer in charge of criminal investigations for the police force concerned must assign someone else to assume that responsibility. That person's identity must be recorded, as with those initially responsible for these functions in each investigation.

Appendices

Recording of information

4.1 If material which may be relevant to the investigation consists of information which is not recorded in any form, the officer in charge of an investigation must ensure that it is recorded in a durable or retrievable form (whether in writing, on video or audio tape, or on computer disk). **B–5**

4.2 Where it is not practicable to retain the initial record of information because it forms part of a larger record which is to be destroyed, its contents should be transferred as a true record to a durable and more easily-stored form before that happens.

4.3 Negative information is often relevant to an investigation. If it may be relevant it must be recorded. An example might be a number of people present in a particular place at a particular time who state that they saw nothing unusual.

4.4 Where information which may be relevant is obtained, it must be recorded at the time it is obtained or as soon as practicable after that time. This includes, for example, information obtained in house-to-house enquiries, although the requirement to record information promptly does not require an investigator to take a statement from a potential witness where it would not otherwise be taken.

Retention of material

(a) Duty to retain material

5.1 The investigator must retain material obtained in a criminal investigation which may be relevant to the investigation. Material may be photographed, video-recorded, captured digitally or otherwise retained in the form of a copy rather than the original at any time, if the original is perishable; the original was supplied to the investigator rather than generated by him and is to be returned to its owner; or the retention of a copy rather than the original is reasonable in all the circumstances. **B–6**

5.2 Where material has been seized in the exercise of the powers of seizure conferred by the *Police and Criminal Evidence Act* 1984, the duty to retain it under this code is subject to the provisions on the retention of seized material in section 22 of that Act.

5.3 If the officer in charge of an investigation becomes aware as a result of developments in the case that material previously examined but not retained (because it was not thought to be relevant) may now be relevant to the investigation, he should, wherever practicable, take steps to obtain it or ensure that it is retained for further inspection or for production in court if required.

5.4 The duty to retain material includes in particular the duty to retain material falling into the following categories, where it may be relevant to the investigation:

— crime reports (including crime report forms, relevant parts of incident report books or police officer's notebooks);

— custody records;

— records which are derived from tapes of telephone messages (for example, 999 calls) containing descriptions of an alleged offence or offender;

— final versions of witness statements (and draft versions where their content differs from the final version), including any exhibits mentioned (unless these have been returned to their owner on the understanding that they will be produced in court if required);

— interview records (written records, or audio or video tapes, of interviews with actual or potential witnesses or suspects);

— communications between the police and experts such as forensic scientists, reports of work carried out by experts, and schedules of scientific material prepared by the expert for the investigator, for the purposes of criminal proceedings;

— records of the first description of a suspect by each potential witness who purports to identify or describe the suspect, whether or not the description differs from that of subsequent descriptions by that or other witnesses;

— any material casting doubt on the reliability of a witness.

5.5 The duty to retain material, where it may be relevant to the investigation, also includes in particular the duty to retain material which may satisfy the test for prosecution disclosure in the Act, such as:

— information provided by an accused person which indicates an explanation for the offence with which he has been charged;

— any material casting doubt on the reliability of a confession;

— any material casting doubt on the reliability of a prosecution witness.

5.6 The duty to retain material falling into these categories does not extend to items which are purely ancillary to such material and possess no independent significance (for example, duplicate copies of records or reports).

(b) Length of time for which material is to be retained

5.7 All material which may be relevant to the investigation must be retained until a decision is taken whether to institute proceedings against a person for an offence.

5.8 If a criminal investigation results in proceedings being instituted, all material which may be relevant must be retained at least until the accused is acquitted or convicted or the prosecutor decides not to proceed with the case.

5.9 Where the accused is convicted, all material which may be relevant must be retained at least until:

— the convicted person is released from custody, or discharged from hospital, in cases where the court imposes a custodial sentence or a hospital order;

— six months from the date of conviction, in all other cases.

If the court imposes a custodial sentence or hospital order and the convicted person is released from custody or discharged from hospital earlier than six months from the date of conviction, all material which may be relevant must be retained at least until six months from the date of conviction.

5.10 If an appeal against conviction is in progress when the release or discharge occurs, or at the end of the period of six months specified in paragraph 5.9, all material which may be relevant must be retained until the appeal is determined. Similarly, if the Criminal Cases Review Commission is considering an application at that point in time, all material which may be relevant must be retained at least until the Commission decides not to refer the case to the Court.

Preparation of material for prosecutor

(a) Introduction

6.1 The officer in charge of the investigation, the disclosure officer or an investigator may seek advice from the prosecutor about whether any particular item of material may be relevant to the investigation. **B–7**

6.2 Material which may be relevant to an investigation, which has been retained in accordance with this code, and which the disclosure officer believes will not form part of the prosecution case, must be listed on a schedule.

6.3 Material which the disclosure officer does not believe is sensitive must be listed on a schedule of non-sensitive material. The schedule must include a statement that the disclosure officer does not believe the material is sensitive.

6.4 Any material which is believed to be sensitive must be either listed on a schedule of sensitive material or, in exceptional circumstances, revealed to the prosecutor separately. If there is no sensitive material, the disclosure officer must record this fact on a schedule of sensitive material.

6.5 Paragraphs 6.6 to 6.11 below apply to both sensitive and non-sensitive material. Paragraphs 6.12 to 6.14 apply to sensitive material only.

(b) Circumstances in which a schedule is to be prepared

6.6 The disclosure officer must ensure that a schedule is prepared in the following circumstances:

— the accused is charged with an offence which is triable only on indictment;

— the accused is charged with an offence which is triable either way, and it is considered either that the case is likely to be tried on indictment or that the accused is likely to plead not guilty at a summary trial;

— the accused is charged with a summary offence, and it is considered that he is likely to plead not guilty.

6.7 In respect of either way and summary offences, a schedule may not be needed if a person has admitted the offence, or if a police officer witnessed the offence and that person has not denied it.

6.8 If it is believed that the accused is likely to plead guilty at a summary trial, it is not necessary to prepare a schedule in advance. If, contrary to this belief, the accused pleads not guilty at a summary trial, or the offence is to be tried on indictment, the disclosure officer must ensure that a schedule is prepared as soon as is reasonably practicable after that happens.

(c) Way in which material is to be listed on schedule

6.9 The disclosure officer should ensure that each item of material is listed separately on the schedule, and is numbered consecutively. The description of each item should make clear the nature of the item and should contain sufficient detail to enable the prosecutor to decide whether he needs to inspect the material before deciding whether or not it should be disclosed.

6.10 In some enquiries it may not be practicable to list each item of material separately. For example, there may be many items of a similar or repetitive nature. These may be listed in a block and described by quantity and generic title.

6.11 Even if some material is listed in a block, the disclosure officer must ensure that any items among that material which might satisfy the test for prosecution disclosure are listed and described individually.

(d) Treatment of sensitive material

6.12 Subject to paragraph 6.13 below, the disclosure officer must list on a sensitive schedule any material, the disclosure of which he believes would give rise to a real risk of serious prejudice to an important public interest, and the reason for that belief. The schedule must include a statement that the disclosure officer believes the material is sensitive. Depending on the circumstances, examples of such material may include the following among others:

— material relating to national security;
— material received from the intelligence and security agencies;
— material relating to intelligence from foreign sources which reveals sensitive intelligence gathering methods;
— material given in confidence;
— material relating to the identity or activities of informants, or undercover police officers, or witnesses, or other persons supplying information to the police who may be in danger if their identities are revealed;
— material revealing the location of any premises or other place used for police surveillance, or the identity of any person allowing a police officer to use them for surveillance;
— material revealing, either directly or indirectly, techniques and methods relied upon by a police officer in the course of a criminal investigation, for example covert surveillance techniques, or other methods of detecting crime;
— material whose disclosure might facilitate the commission of other offences or hinder the prevention and detection of crime;
— material upon the strength of which search warrants were obtained;
— material containing details of persons taking part in identification parades;
— material supplied to an investigator during a criminal investigation which has been generated by an official of a body concerned with the regulation or supervision of bodies corporate or of persons engaged in financial activities, or which has been generated by a person retained by such a body;
— material supplied to an investigator during a criminal investigation which relates to a child or young person and which has been generated by a local authority social services department, an Area Child Protection Committee or other party contacted by an investigator during the investigation;
— material relating to the private life of a witness.

6.13 In exceptional circumstances, where an investigator considers that material is so sensitive that its revelation to the prosecutor by means of an entry on the sensitive schedule is inappropriate, the existence of the material must be revealed to the prosecutor separately. This will apply only where compromising the material would be likely to lead directly to the loss of life, or directly threaten national security.

6.14 In such circumstances, the responsibility for informing the prosecutor lies with the investigator who knows the detail of the sensitive material. The investigator should act as soon as is reasonably practicable after the file containing the prosecution case is sent to the prosecutor. The investigator must also ensure that the prosecutor is able to inspect the material so that he can assess whether it is disclosable and, if so, whether it needs to be brought before a court for a ruling on disclosure.

Revelation of material to prosecutor

B–8 7.1 The disclosure officer must give the schedules to the prosecutor. Wherever practicable this should be at the same time as he gives him the file containing the material for the prosecution case (or as soon as is reasonably practicable after the decision on mode of trial or the plea, in cases to which paragraph 6.8 applies).

7.2 The disclosure officer should draw the attention of the prosecutor to any material an investigator has retained (including material to which paragraph 6.13 applies) which may satisfy the test for prosecution disclosure in the Act, and should explain why he has come to that view.

7.3 At the same time as complying with the duties in paragraphs 7.1 and 7.2, the disclosure officer must give the prosecutor a copy of any material which falls into the following categories (unless such material has already been given to the prosecutor as part of the file containing the material for the prosecution case):
— information provided by an accused person which indicates an explanation for the offence with which he has been charged;
— any material casting doubt on the reliability of a confession;
— any material casting doubt on the reliability of a prosecution witness;

— any other material which the investigator believes may satisfy the test for prosecution disclosure in the Act.

— any other material which the investigator believes may fall within the test for primary prosecution disclosure in the Act.

7.4 If the prosecutor asks to inspect material which has not already been copied to him, the disclosure officer must allow him to inspect it. If the prosecutor asks for a copy of material which has not already been copied to him, the disclosure officer must give him a copy. However, this does not apply where the disclosure officer believes, having consulted the officer in charge of the investigation, that the material is too sensitive to be copied and can only be inspected.

7.5 If material consists of information which is recorded other than in writing, whether it should be given to the prosecutor in its original form as a whole, or by way of relevant extracts recorded in the same form, or in the form of a transcript, is a matter for agreement between the disclosure officer and the prosecutor.

Subsequent action by disclosure officer

8.1 At the time a schedule of non-sensitive material is prepared, the disclosure officer may not know exactly what material will form the case against the accused, and the prosecutor may not have given advice about the likely relevance of particular items of material. Once these matters have been determined, the disclosure officer must give the prosecutor, where necessary, an amended schedule listing any additional material: **B–9**

— which may be relevant to the investigation,

— which does not form part of the case against the accused,

— which is not already listed on the schedule, and

— which he believes is not sensitive,

unless he is informed in writing by the prosecutor that the prosecutor intends to disclose the material to the defence.

8.2 Section 7A of the Act imposes a continuing duty on the prosecutor, for the duration of criminal proceedings against the accused, to disclose material which satisfies the test for disclosure (subject to public interest considerations). To enable him to do this, any new material coming to light should be treated in the same way as the earlier material.

8.3 In particular, after a defence statement has been given, the disclosure officer must look again at the material which has been retained and must draw the attention of the prosecutor to any material which might reasonably be considered capable of undermining the case for the prosecution against the accused or of assisting the case for the accused; and he must reveal it to him in accordance with paragraphs 7.4 and 7.5 above.

Certification by disclosure officer

9.1 The disclosure officer must certify to the prosecutor that to the best of his knowledge and belief, all relevant material which has been retained and made available to him has been revealed to the prosecutor in accordance with this code. He must sign and date the certificate. It will be necessary to certify not only at the time when the schedule and accompanying material is submitted to the prosecutor, and when relevant material which has been retained is reconsidered after the accused has given a defence statement, but also whenever a schedule is otherwise given or material is otherwise revealed to the prosecutor. **B–10**

Disclosure of material to accused

10.1 If material has not already been copied to the prosecutor, and he requests its disclosure to the accused on the ground that: **B–11**

— it satisfies the test for prosecution disclosure, or

— it satisfies the test for prosecution disclosure, or

the disclosure officer must disclose it to the accused.

10.2 If material has been copied to the prosecutor, and it is to be disclosed, whether it is disclosed by the prosecutor or the disclosure officer is a matter of agreement between the two of them.

10.3 The disclosure officer must disclose material to the accused either by giving him a copy or by allowing him to inspect it. If the accused person asks for a copy of any material which he has been allowed to inspect, the disclosure officer must give it to him, unless in the opinion of the disclosure officer that is either not practicable (for example because the material consists of an object which cannot be copied, or because the volume of material is so great), or not desirable (for example because the material is a statement by a child witness in relation to a sexual offence).

10.4 If material which the accused has been allowed to inspect consists of information which is recorded other than in writing, whether it should be given to the accused in its original form or in the form of a transcript is matter for the discretion of the disclosure officer. If the material is transcribed, the disclosure officer must ensure that the transcript is certified to the accused as a true record of the material which has been transcribed.

10.5 If a court concludes that an item of sensitive material satisfies the prosecution disclosure test and that the interests of the defence outweigh the public interest in withholding disclosure, it will be necessary to disclose the material if the case is to proceed. This does not mean that sensitive documents must always be disclosed in their original form: for example, the court may agree that sensitive details still requiring protection should be blocked out, or that documents may be summarised, or that the prosecutor may make an admission about the substance of the material under section 10 of the *Criminal Justice Act* 1967.

APPENDIX C

ATTORNEY-GENERAL'S GUIDELINES ON DISCLOSURE

I. INTRODUCTION

As superintendent of the public prosecuting authorities, the Attorney General has provided guidelines on various aspects of the law touching on prosecutions. The guidelines are not binding and do not have the effect of law but are nevertheless expected to be followed by prosecutors. The guidelines reproduced in this appendix are as follows: **C–1**

- Guidelines on disclosure (as last revised in April 2005): see *post*, Appendix C–2.
- Guidelines on the prosecutor's role in applications for witness anonymity orders under the *Criminal Evidence (Witness Anonymity) Act* 2008 (issued on July 21, 2008): see *post*, Appendix C–23.
- Guidelines on the acceptance of pleas and the prosecutor's role in the sentencing exercise (as last revised on June 8, 2007): see *post*, Appendix C–27.

II. ATTORNEY-GENERAL'S GUIDELINES ON DISCLOSURE

[*These guidelines were published with a foreword and commentary which are not reproduced here.*] **C–1a**

Disclosure of Unused Material in Criminal Proceedings

Introduction

1. Every accused person has a right to a fair trial, a right long embodied in our law and guaranteed under Article 6 of the European Convention on Human Rights (ECHR). A fair trial is the proper object and expectation of all participants in the trial process. Fair disclosure to an accused is an inseparable part of a fair trial. **C–2**

2. What must be clear is that a fair trial consists of an examination not just of all the evidence the parties wish to rely on but also all other relevant subject matter. A fair trial should not require consideration of irrelevant material and should not involve spurious applications or arguments which serve to divert the trial process from examining the real issues before the court.

3. The scheme set out in the *Criminal Procedure and Investigations Act* 1996 (as amended by the *Criminal Justice Act* 2003) (the Act) is designed to ensure that there is fair disclosure of material which may be relevant to an investigation and which does not form part of the prosecution case. Disclosure under the Act should assist the accused in the timely preparation and presentation of their case and assist the court to focus on all the relevant issues in the trial. Disclosure which does not meet these objectives risks preventing a fair trial taking place.

4. This means that the disclosure regime set out in the Act must be scrupulously followed. These Guidelines build upon the existing law to help to ensure that the legislation is operated more effectively, consistently and fairly.

5. Disclosure must not be an open ended trawl of unused material. A critical element to fair and proper disclosure is that the defence play their role to ensure that the prosecution are directed to material which might reasonably be considered capable of undermining the prosecution case or assisting the case for the accused. This process is key to ensuring prosecutors make informed determinations about disclosure of unused material. **C–3**

6. Fairness does recognise that there are other interests that need to be protected, including those of victims and witnesses who might otherwise be exposed to harm. The scheme of the Act protects those interests. It should also ensure that material is not disclosed which overburdens the participants in the trial process, diverts attention from the relevant issues, leads to unjustifiable delay, and is wasteful of resources.

7. Whilst it is acknowledged that these Guidelines have been drafted with a focus on Crown Court proceedings the spirit of the Guidelines must be followed where they apply to proceedings in the magistrates' court.

General Principles

C–4 8. Disclosure refers to providing the defence with copies of, or access to, any material which might reasonably be considered capable of undermining the case for the prosecution against the accused, or of assisting the case for the accused, and which has not previously been disclosed.

9. Prosecutors will only be expected to anticipate what material might weaken their case or strengthen the defence in the light of information available at the time of the disclosure decision, and this may include information revealed during questioning.

10. Generally, material which can reasonably be considered capable of undermining the prosecution case against the accused or assisting the defence case will include anything that tends to show a fact inconsistent with the elements of the case that must be proved by the prosecution. Material can fulfil the disclosure test:

(a) by the use to be made of it in cross-examination; or
(b) by its capacity to support submissions that could lead to:
  (i) the exclusion of evidence; or
  (ii) a stay of proceedings; or
  (iii) a court or tribunal finding that any public authority had acted incompatibly with the accused 's rights under the ECHR, or
(c) by its capacity to suggest an explanation or partial explanation of the accused's actions.

C–5 11. In deciding whether material may fall to be disclosed under *paragraph 10*, especially *(b)(ii)*, prosecutors must consider whether disclosure is required in order for a proper application to be made. The purpose of this paragraph is not to allow enquiries to support speculative arguments or for the manufacture of defences.

12. Examples of material that might reasonably be considered capable of undermining the prosecution case or of assisting the case for the accused are:

(i) Any material casting doubt upon the accuracy of any prosecution evidence.
(ii) Any material which may point to another person, whether charged or not (including a co-accused) having involvement in the commission of the offence.
(iii) Any material which may cast doubt upon the reliability of a confession.
(iv) Any material that might go to the credibility of a prosecution witness.
(v) Any material that might support a defence that is either raised by the defence or apparent from the prosecution papers.
(vi) Any material which may have a bearing on the admissibility of any prosecution evidence.

13. It should also be borne in mind that while items of material viewed in isolation may not be reasonably considered to be capable of undermining the prosecution case or assisting the accused, several items together can have that effect.

14. Material relating to the accused's mental or physical health, intellectual capacity, or to any ill treatment which the accused may have suffered when in the investigator's custody is likely to fall within the test for disclosure set out in *paragraph 8* above.

Defence Statements

C–6 15. A defence statement must comply with the requirements of section 6A of the Act. A comprehensive defence statement assists the participants in the trial to ensure that it is fair. The trial process is not well served if the defence make general and unspecified allegations and then seek far-reaching disclosure in the hope that material may turn up to make them good. The more detail a defence statement contains the more likely it is that the prosecutor will make an informed decision about whether any remaining undisclosed material might reasonably be considered capable of undermining the prosecution case or of assisting the case for the accused, or whether to advise the investigator to undertake further enquiries. It also helps in the management of the trial by narrowing down and focussing on the issues in dispute. It may result in the prosecution discontinuing the case. Defence practitioners should be aware of these considerations when advising their clients.

16. Whenever a defence solicitor provides a defence statement on behalf of the accused it will be deemed to be given with the authority of the solicitor's client.

Continuing Duty of Prosecutor to Disclose

17. Section 7A of the Act imposes a continuing duty upon the prosecutor to keep under review at all times the question of whether there is any unused material which might reasonably be considered capable of undermining the prosecution case against the accused or assisting the case for the accused and which has not previously been disclosed. This duty arises after the prosecutor has complied with the duty of initial disclosure or purported to comply with it and before the accused is acquitted or convicted or the prosecutor decides not to proceed with the case. If such material is identified, then the prosecutor must disclose it to the accused as soon as is reasonably practicable. **C–7**

18. As part of their continuing duty of disclosure, prosecutors should be open, alert and promptly responsive to requests for disclosure of material supported by a comprehensive defence statement. Conversely, if no defence statement has been served or if the prosecutor considers that the defence statement is lacking specificity or otherwise does not meet the requirements of section 6A of the Act, a letter should be sent to the defence indicating this. If the position is not resolved satisfactorily, the prosecutor should consider raising the issue at a hearing for directions to enable the court to give a warning or appropriate directions.

19. When defence practitioners are dissatisfied with disclosure decisions by the prosecution and consider that they are entitled to further disclosure, applications to the court should be made pursuant to section 8 of the Act and in accordance with the procedures set out in the Criminal Procedure Rules. Applications for further disclosure should not be made as ad hoc applications but dealt with under the proper procedures.

Applications for Non-disclosure in the Public Interest

20. Before making an application to the court to withhold material which would otherwise fall to be disclosed, on the basis that to disclose would give rise to a real risk of serious prejudice to an important public interest, prosecutors should aim to disclose as much of the material as they properly can (for example, by giving the defence redacted or edited copies or summaries). Neutral material or material damaging to the defendant need not be disclosed and must not be brought to the attention of the court. It is only in truly borderline cases that the prosecution should seek a judicial ruling on the disclosability of material in its possession. **C–8**

21. Prior to or at the hearing, the court must be provided with full and accurate information. Prior to the hearing the prosecutor and the prosecution advocate must examine all material, which is the subject matter of the application and make any necessary enquiries of the investigator. The prosecutor (or representative) and/or investigator should attend such applications.

22. The principles set out at paragraph 36 of *R v H & C* should be rigorously applied firstly by the prosecutor and then by the court considering the material. It is essential that these principles are scrupulously attended to to ensure that the procedure for examination of material in the absence of the accused is compliant with Article 6 of ECHR.

Responsibilities

Investigators and Disclosure Officers

23. Investigators and disclosure officers must be fair and objective and must work together with prosecutors to ensure that disclosure obligations are met. A failure to take action leading to inadequate disclosure may result in a wrongful conviction. It may alternatively lead to a successful abuse of process argument, an acquittal against the weight of the evidence or the appellate courts may find that a conviction is unsafe and quash it. **C–9**

24. Officers appointed as disclosure officers must have the requisite experience, skills, competence and resources to undertake their vital role. In discharging their obligations under the Act, code, common law and any operational instructions, investigators should always err on the side of recording and retaining material where they have any doubt as to whether it may be relevant.

25. An individual must not be appointed as disclosure officer, or continue in that role, if that is likely to result in a conflict of interest, for instance, if the disclosure officer is the victim of the alleged crime which is the subject of investigation. The advice of a more

Appendices

senior investigator must always be sought if there is doubt as to whether a conflict of interest precludes an individual acting as the disclosure officer. If thereafter a doubt remains, the advice of a prosecutor should be sought.

C–10 26. There may be a number of disclosure officers, especially in large and complex cases. However, there must be a lead disclosure officer who is the focus for enquiries and whose responsibility it is to ensure that the investigator's disclosure obligations are complied with. Disclosure officers, or their deputies, must inspect, view or listen to all relevant material that has been retained by the investigator, and the disclosure officer must provide a personal declaration to the effect that this task has been undertaken.

27. Generally this will mean that such material must be examined in detail by the disclosure officer or the deputy, but exceptionally the extent and manner of inspecting, viewing or listening will depend on the nature of material and its form. For example, it might be reasonable to examine digital material by using software search tools, or to establish the contents of large volumes of material by dip sampling. If such material is not examined in detail, it must nonetheless be described on the disclosure schedules accurately and as clearly as possible. The extent and manner of its examination must also be described together with justification for such action.

28. Investigators must retain material that may be relevant to the investigation. However, it may become apparent to the investigator that some material obtained in the course of an investigation because it was considered potentially relevant, is in fact incapable of impact. It need not then be retained or dealt with in accordance with these Guidelines, although the investigator should err on the side of caution in coming to this conclusion and seek the advice of the prosecutor as appropriate.

C–11 29. In meeting the obligations in *paragraph 6.9* and *8.1* of the Code, it is crucial that descriptions by disclosure officers in non-sensitive schedules are detailed, clear and accurate. The descriptions may require a summary of the contents of the retained material to assist the prosecutor to make an informed decision on disclosure. Sensitive schedules must contain sufficient information to enable the prosecutor to make an informed decision as to whether or not the material itself should be viewed, to the extent possible without compromising the confidentiality of the information.

30. Disclosure officers must specifically draw material to the attention of the prosecutor for consideration where they have any doubt as to whether it might reasonably be considered capable of undermining the prosecution case or of assisting the case for the accused.

31. Disclosure officers must seek the advice and assistance of prosecutors when in doubt as to their responsibility as early as possible. They must deal expeditiously with requests by the prosecutor for further information on material, which may lead to disclosure.

Prosecutors

C–12 32. Prosecutors must do all that they can to facilitate proper disclosure, as part of their general and personal professional responsibility to act fairly and impartially, in the interests of justice and in accordance with the law. Prosecutors must also be alert to the need to provide advice to, and where necessary probe actions taken by, disclosure officers to ensure that disclosure obligations are met.

33. Prosecutors must review schedules prepared by disclosure officers thoroughly and must be alert to the possibility that relevant material may exist which has not been revealed to them or material included which should not have been. If no schedules have been provided, or there are apparent omissions from the schedules, or documents or other items are inadequately described or are unclear, the prosecutor must at once take action to obtain properly completed schedules. Likewise schedules should be returned for amendment if irrelevant items are included. If prosecutors remain dissatisfied with the quality or content of the schedules they must raise the matter with a senior investigator, and if necessary, persist, with a view to resolving the matter satisfactorily.

34. Where prosecutors have reason to believe that the disclosure officer has not discharged the obligation in *paragraph 26* to inspect, view or listen to relevant material, they must at once raise the matter with the disclosure officer and, if it is believed that the officer has not inspected, viewed or listened to the material, request that it be done.

C–13 35. When prosecutors or disclosure officers believe that material might reasonably be considered capable of undermining the prosecution case or assisting the case for the accused, prosecutors must always inspect, view or listen to the material and satisfy themselves that the prosecution can properly be continued having regard to the disclosability of the material reviewed. Their judgement as to what other material to inspect, view or listen to will depend on the circumstances of each case.

36. Prosecutors should copy the defence statement to the disclosure officer and investigator as soon as reasonably practicable and prosecutors should advise the investigator if, in their view, reasonable and relevant lines of further enquiry should be pursued.

37. Prosecutors cannot comment upon, or invite inferences to be drawn from, failures in defence disclosure otherwise than in accordance with section 11 of the Act. Prosecutors may cross-examine the accused on differences between the defence case put at trial and that set out in his or her defence statement. In doing so, it may be appropriate to apply to the judge under section 6E of the Act for copies of the statement to be given to a jury, edited if necessary to remove inadmissible material. Prosecutors should examine the defence statement to see whether it points to other lines of enquiry. If the defence statement does point to other reasonable lines of inquiry further investigation is required and evidence obtained as a result of these enquiries may be used as part of the prosecution case or to rebut the defence.

38. Once initial disclosure is completed and a defence statement has been served requests for disclosure should ordinarily only be answered if the request is in accordance with and relevant to the defence statement. If it is not, then a further or amended defence statement should be sought and obtained before considering the request for further disclosure. **C–14**

39. Prosecutors must ensure that they record in writing all actions and decisions they make in discharging their disclosure responsibilities, and this information is to be made available to the prosecution advocate if requested or if relevant to an issue.

40. If the material does not fulfil the disclosure test there is no requirement to disclose it. For this purpose, the parties' respective cases should not be restrictively analysed but must be carefully analysed to ascertain the specific facts the prosecution seek to establish and the specific grounds on which the charges are resisted. Neutral material or material damaging to the defendant need not be disclosed and must not be brought to the attention of the court. Only in truly borderline cases should the prosecution seek a judicial ruling on the disclosability of material in its hands.

41. If prosecutors are satisfied that a fair trial cannot take place where material which satisfies the disclosure test cannot be disclosed, and that this cannot or will not be remedied including by, for example, making formal admissions, amending the charges or presenting the case in a different way so as to ensure fairness or in other ways, they must not continue with the case.

Prosecution Advocates

42. Prosecution advocates should ensure that all material that ought to be disclosed under the Act is disclosed to the defence. However, prosecution advocates cannot be expected to disclose material if they are not aware of its existence. As far as is possible, prosecution advocates must place themselves in a fully informed position to enable them to make decisions on disclosure. **C–15**

43. Upon receipt of instructions, prosecution advocates should consider as a priority all the information provided regarding disclosure of material. Prosecution advocates should consider, in every case, whether they can be satisfied that they are in possession of all relevant documentation and that they have been instructed fully regarding disclosure matters. Decisions already made regarding disclosure should be reviewed. If as a result, the advocate considers that further information or action is required, written advice should be promptly provided setting out the aspects that need clarification or action. Prosecution advocates must advise on disclosure in accordance with the Act. If necessary and where appropriate a conference should be held to determine what is required.

44. The prosecution advocate must keep decisions regarding disclosure under review until the conclusion of the trial. The prosecution advocate must in every case specifically consider whether he or she can satisfactorily discharge the duty of continuing review on the basis of the material supplied already, or whether it is necessary to inspect further material or to reconsider material already inspected. Prosecution advocates must not abrogate their responsibility under the Act by disclosing material which could not be considered capable of undermining the prosecution case or of assisting the case for the accused.

45. Prior to the commencement of a trial, the prosecuting advocate should always make

decisions on disclosure in consultation with those instructing him or her and the disclosure officer. After a trial has started, it is recognised that in practice consultation on disclosure issues may not be practicable; it continues to be desirable, however, whenever this can be achieved without affecting unduly the conduct of the trial.

46. There is no basis in law or practice for disclosure on a "counsel to counsel" basis.

Involvement of Other Agencies

Material held by Government departments or other Crown bodies

C–16 47. Where it appears to an investigator, disclosure officer or prosecutor that a Government department or other Crown body has material that may be relevant to an issue in the case, reasonable steps should be taken to identify and consider such material. Although what is reasonable will vary from case to case, the prosecution should inform the department or other body of the nature of its case and of relevant issues in the case in respect of which the department or body might possess material, and ask whether it has any such material.

48. It should be remembered that investigators, disclosure officers and prosecutors cannot be regarded to be in constructive possession of material held by Government departments or Crown bodies simply by virtue of their status as Government departments or Crown bodies.

49. Departments in England and Wales should have identified personnel as established Enquiry Points to deal with issues concerning the disclosure of information in criminal proceedings.

50. Where, after reasonable steps have been taken to secure access to such material, access is denied the investigator, disclosure officer or prosecutor should consider what if any further steps might be taken to obtain the material or inform the defence.

Material held by Other Agencies

C–17 51. There may be cases where the investigator, disclosure officer or prosecutor believes that a third party (for example, a local authority, a social services department, a hospital, a doctor, a school, a provider of forensic services) has material or information which might be relevant to the prosecution case. In such cases, if the material or information might reasonably be considered capable of undermining the prosecution case or of assisting the case for the accused prosecutors should take what steps they regard as appropriate in the particular case to obtain it.

52. If the investigator, disclosure officer or prosecutor seeks access to the material or information but the third party declines or refuses to allow access to it, the matter should not be left. If despite any reasons offered by the third party it is still believed that it is reasonable to seek production of the material or information, and the requirements of section 2 of the *Criminal Procedure (Attendance of Witnesses) Act* 1965 or as appropriate section 97 of the *Magistrates' Courts Act* 1980 are satisfied, then the prosecutor or investigator should apply for a witness summons causing a representative of the third party to produce the material to the Court.

53. Relevant information which comes to the knowledge of investigators or prosecutors as a result of liaison with third parties should be recorded by the investigator or prosecutor in a durable or retrievable form (for example potentially relevant information revealed in discussions at a child protection conference attended by police officers).

54. Where information comes into the possession of the prosecution in the circumstances set out in *paragraphs 51–53* above, consultation with the other agency should take place before disclosure is made: there may be public interest reasons which justify withholding disclosure and which would require the issue of disclosure of the information to be placed before the court.

Other Disclosure

Disclosure Prior to Initial Disclosure

C–18 55. Investigators must always be alive to the potential need to reveal and prosecutors to the potential need to disclose material, in the interests of justice and fairness in the particular circumstances of any case, after the commencement of proceedings but before their duty arises under the Act. For instance, disclosure ought to be made of significant information that might affect a bail decision or that might enable the defence to contest the committal proceedings.

56. Where the need for such disclosure is not apparent to the prosecutor, any disclosure will depend on what the accused chooses to reveal about the defence. Clearly, such disclosure will not exceed that which is obtainable after the statutory duties of disclosure arise.

Summary Trial

57. The prosecutor should, in addition to complying with the obligations under the Act, provide to the defence all evidence upon which the Crown proposes to rely in a summary trial. Such provision should allow the accused and their legal advisers sufficient time properly to consider the evidence before it is called. **C–19**

Material Relevant to Sentence

58. In all cases the prosecutor must consider disclosing in the interests of justice any material, which is relevant to sentence (e.g. information which might mitigate the seriousness of the offence or assist the accused to lay blame in part upon a co-accused or another person). **C–20**

Post-conviction

59. The interests of justice will also mean that where material comes to light after the conclusion of the proceedings, which might cast doubt upon the safety of the conviction, there is a duty to consider disclosure. Any such material should be brought immediately to the attention of line management. **C–21**

60. Disclosure of any material that is made outside the ambit of Act will attract confidentiality by virtue of *Taylor v SFO* [1998].

Applicability of these Guidelines

61. Although the relevant obligations in relation to unused material and disclosure imposed on the prosecutor and the accused are determined by the date on which the investigation began, these Guidelines should be adopted with immediate effect in relation to all cases submitted to the prosecuting authorities in receipt of these Guidelines save where they specifically refer to the statutory or Code provisions of the *Criminal Justice Act* 2003 that do not yet apply to the particular case. **C–22**

III. ATTORNEY-GENERAL' GUIDELINES ON THE PROSECUTOR'S ROLE IN APPLICATIONS FOR WITNESS ANONYMITY ORDERS UNDER THE CRIMINAL EVIDENCE (WITNESS ANONYMITY) ACT 2008

A.

Foreword

A:1 Every defendant has a right to a fair trial. An important aspect of a fair trial is the right of the defendant to be confronted by, and to challenge, those who accuse him or her. **C–23**

A:2 Making an application for a witness anonymity order is therefore a serious step, to be taken by the prosecutor only where there are genuine grounds to believe that the court would not otherwise hear evidence that should be available to it in the interests of justice; that other measures falling short of anonymity would not be sufficient; and that the defendant will have a fair trial if the order is made.

A:3 Anonymous witness testimony is not necessarily incompatible with Article 6, even when it is the sole or decisive evidence against the accused. But whether the measures used to allow a witness to give evidence anonymously in any particular case would make the trial unfair has to be evaluated with care on the facts of each case.

A:4 When assessing whether and in what terms to make an application for a witness anonymity order, prosecutors have overriding duties to be fair, independent and objective. These guidelines set out the overarching principles by which a prosecutor should consider, and if appropriate apply for, a witness anonymity order in accordance with the considerations set out in the *Criminal Evidence (Witness Anonymity) Act* 2008.

B.

THE PROSECUTOR'S DUTIES

C–24 **B:**1 The effect of a witness anonymity order is to prevent the defendant from knowing the identity of a witness. Without this information the defendant's ability to investigate and challenge the accuracy or credibility of the witness's evidence may be limited.

B:2 When considering whether to make a witness anonymity order the court will consider to what extent the defendant needs to know the identity of the witness in order to challenge the witness's evidence effectively. This question will often be central to the question of whether, having regard to all the circumstances, the witness anonymity order sought would be consistent with a fair trial.

B:3 The prosecutor's role is:

— To act with scrupulous fairness.

— To examine with care, and probe where appropriate, the material provided in support of the application and the evidential basis for it. Prosecutors should in particular objectively assess any statement made by the witness or witnesses in question and the grounds on which it is based.

— To be satisfied before making the application that, viewed objectively, it can properly be said that the order is necessary and in the interests of justice and that the defendant can receive a fair trial.

— To put before the court all material that is relevant to the application. Courts will rely to a significant extent upon the prosecutor and the investigator to provide relevant material. Material will be relevant if the prosecutor relies upon it to support the application, or if it may tend to undermine or qualify the justification for making the order at all, or for making it in the form sought by the prosecutor. Material is particularly relevant if credibility is or may be in issue, for example if there is a known link between the witness and the defendant or a co-accused.

— To disclose as much relevant material to the defence as possible without identifying the witness, including material that may tend to cast doubt on the credibility, reliability or accuracy of the witness's evidence.

B:4 The role of the prosecutor as an independent and impartial minister of justice is of paramount importance. Applications should only be authorised by prosecutors at an appropriately senior level within the prosecuting authority.

B:5 The interests of justice include the interests of the victim or victims, the interests of the witness or witnesses, the interests of the defendant and any co-defendants and the wider public interest.

B:6 Prosecutors should take all necessary and reasonable steps consistent with a fair trial and the interests of justice to ensure the safety of a witness or the avoidance of real harm to the public interest or the protection of property.

C.

APPLICATIONS BY DEFENDANTS

C–25 **C:**1 The Act permits a defendant (as well as a prosecutor) to apply for a Witness Anonymity Order. Prosecutors should respond to such applications independently and objectively. Prosecutors should examine critically, but fairly, the basis for any application and any material put forward in support of any application.

C:2 The prosecutor should provide the court with all material within the prosecutor's possession or control that is relevant to the defendant's application.

D.

APPOINTMENT AND ROLE OF SPECIAL COUNSEL IN APPLICATIONS FOR WITNESS ANONYMITY

D:1 The Act makes no statutory provision for the appointment of Special Counsel. **C–26**

D:2 A criminal court may invite the Attorney General to appoint Special Counsel. However, in line with authority, such an appointment:

— Should be regarded as '... exceptional, never automatic, a course of last and never first resort.' *R. v. H and C.* [2004] 2 A.C. 134, HL. The need for Special Counsel has to be shown.

— The court will take account of the seriousness of the issue that the court has to determine in the particular case. Whether credibility is at issue is likely to be an important consideration. The court will also need to consider the extent to which Special Counsel could further the defendant's case.

— The court itself can be expected to perform a role of testing and probing the case which is presented on the application. When coupled with the prosecutor's duty to put all relevant material before the court, this may often be sufficient to enable a fair and informed decision to be reached without the need to appoint Special Counsel.

D:3 Where appointed, the role of Special Counsel is to make representations on behalf of the accused in any closed proceedings.

D:4 The Attorney General will consider each invitation to appoint Special Counsel on its merits, having regard to the all the relevant circumstances of the case. In particular, in this context, to the basis of the application, whether it is opposed, the basis upon which it is opposed and the particular considerations that the court wishes Special Counsel to address.

D:5 A prosecutor making an application for a witness anonymity order should always be prepared to assist the court to consider whether the circumstances are such that exceptionally the appointment of Special Counsel may be called for. When appropriate a prosecutor should draw to the attention of the court any aspect of an application for a witness anonymity order or any aspect of the case that may, viewed objectively, call for the appointment of Special Counsel.

D:6 When a court decides to invite the Attorney General to appoint Special Counsel the prosecutor should (regardless of any steps taken by the court or any defendant) ensure that the Attorney General's Office is promptly notified; and assist in ensuring that the Attorney General receives all the information needed to take a decision.

D:7 Where Special Counsel is appointed, he or she will initially be provided by the prosecutor with any open material made available to the accused regarding the application (and any other open material requested by Special Counsel). Special Counsel may then seek instructions from the defendant and his legal representatives. Only then will Special Counsel be provided by the prosecutor with the closed or un-redacted material provided to the court.

Attorney-General's Guidelines on the Acceptance of Pleas and the Prosecutor's Role in the Sentencing Exercise

A. Foreword

A:1. Prosecutors have an important role in protecting the victim's interests in the criminal justice process, not least in the acceptance of pleas and the sentencing exercise. The basis of plea, particularly in a case that is not contested, is the vehicle through which the victim's voice is heard. Factual inaccuracies in pleas in mitigation cause distress and offence to victims, the families of victims and witnesses. This can take many forms but may be most acutely felt when the victim is dead and the family hears inaccurate assertions about the victim's character or lifestyle. Prosecution advocates are reminded that they are required to adhere to the standards set out in the Victim's Charter, which places the needs of the victim at the heart of the criminal justice process, and that they will be subject to a similar obligation in respect of the Code of Practice for Victims of Crime when it comes into force. **C–27**

Appendices

A:2. The principle of fairness is central to the administration of justice. The implementation of *Human Rights Act* 1998 [*sic*] in October 2000 incorporated into domestic law the principle of fairness to the accused articulated in the European Convention on Human Rights. Accuracy and reasonableness of plea plays an important part in ensuring fairness both to the accused and to the victim.

A:3. The Attorney General's Guidelines on the Acceptance of Pleas issued on December 7, 2000 highlighted the importance of transparency in the conduct of justice. The basis of plea agreed by the parties in a criminal trial is central to the sentencing process. An illogical or unsupported basis of plea can lead to the passing of an unduly lenient sentence and has a consequential effect where consideration arises as to whether to refer the sentence to the Court of Appeal under section 36 of the *Criminal Justice Act* 1988.

A:4. These Guidelines, which expand upon and now replace the Guidelines issued on the 7 December 2000 [*sic*], give guidance on how prosecutors should meet these objectives of protection of victims' interests and of securing fairness and transparency in the process. They take into account the guidance issued by the Court of Appeal (Criminal) Division [*sic*] in *R. v. Beswick* [1996] 1 Cr.App.R. 343, *R. v. Tolera* [1999] 1 Cr.App.R. 25 and *R. v. Underwood* [2005] 1 Cr.App.R 13. They complement the Bar Council Guidance on Written Standards for the Conduct of Professional Work issued with the 7th edition of the Code of Conduct for the Bar of England and Wales and the Law Society's Professional Conduct Rules. When considering the acceptance of a guilty plea prosecution advocates are also reminded of the need to apply "The Farquharson Guidelines on The Role and Responsibilities of the Prosecution Advocate".

A:5. The Guidelines should be followed by all prosecutors and those persons designated under section 7 of the *Prosecution of Offences Act* 1985 (designated caseworkers) and apply to prosecutions conducted in England and Wales.

B. General Principles

C–28 **B**:1. Justice in this jurisdiction, save in the most exceptional circumstances, is conducted in public. This includes the acceptance of pleas by the prosecution and sentencing.

B:2. The Code for Crown Prosecutors governs the prosecutor's decision-making prior to the commencement of the trial hearing and sets out the circumstances in which pleas to a reduced number of charges, or less serious charges, can be accepted.

B:3. When a case is listed for trial and the prosecution form the view that the appropriate course is to accept a plea before the proceedings commence or continue, or to offer no evidence on the indictment or any part of it, the prosecution should whenever practicable speak to the victim or the victim's family, so that the position can be explained. The views of the victim or the family may assist in informing the prosecutor's decision as to whether it is the [*sic*] public interest, as defined by the Code for Crown Prosecutors, to accept or reject the plea. The victim or victim's family should then be kept informed and decisions explained once they are made at court.

B:4. The appropriate disposal of a criminal case after conviction is as much a part of the criminal justice process as the trial of guilt or innocence. The prosecution advocate represents the public interest, and should be ready to assist the court to reach its decision as to the appropriate sentence. This will include drawing the court's attention to:

- any victim personal statement or other information available to the prosecution advocate as to the impact of the offence on the victim;
- where appropriate, to any evidence of the impact of the offending on a community;
- any statutory provisions relevant to the offender and the offences under consideration;
- any relevant sentencing guidelines and guideline cases; and
- the aggravating and mitigating factors of the offence under consideration;

The prosecution advocate may also offer assistance to the court by making submissions, in the light of all these factors, as to the appropriate sentencing range.

In all cases, it is the prosecution advocate's duty to apply for appropriate ancillary orders, such as anti-social behaviour orders and confiscation orders. When considering which ancillary orders to apply for, prosecution advocates must always have regard to the victim's needs, including the question of his or her future protection.

C. The Basis of Plea

C–29 **C**:1. The basis of a guilty plea must not be agreed on a misleading or untrue set of facts and must take proper account of the victim's interests. An illogical or insupportable basis of plea will inevitably result in the imposition of an inappropriate sentence and is capable of damaging public confidence in the criminal justice system.

C:2. When the defendant indicates an acceptable plea, the defence advocate should reduce the basis of the plea to writing. This should be done in all cases save for those in which the issue is simple or where the defendant has indicated that the guilty plea has been or will be tendered on the basis of the prosecution case.

C:3. The written basis of plea must be considered with great care, taking account of the position of any other relevant defendant where appropriate. The prosecution should not lend itself to any agreement whereby a case is presented to the sentencing judge on a misleading or untrue set of facts or on a basis that is detrimental to the victim's interests. There will be cases where a defendant seeks to mitigate on the basis of assertions of fact which are outside the scope of the prosecution's knowledge. A typical example concerns the defendant's state of mind. If a defendant wishes to be sentenced on this basis, the prosecution advocate should invite the judge not to accept the defendant's version unless he or she gives evidence on oath to be tested in cross-examination.

C:4. The prosecution advocate should show the prosecuting authority any written record relating to the plea and agree with them the basis on which the case will be opened to the court.

C:5. It is the responsibility of the prosecution advocate thereafter to ensure that the defence advocate is aware of the basis on which the plea is accepted by the prosecution and the way in which the prosecution case will be opened to the court.

C:6. In all cases before the Crown Court, and in cases before the magistrates' court where the issues are complex or there is scope for misunderstanding, the prosecution must commit to writing the aggravating and mitigating factors that will form the opening of the prosecution case as well as any statutory limitations on sentencing. The prosecution will address, where relevant, the factors outlined at B4 including the matters set out in the next sub-paragraph.

The matters to be dealt with are:

- the aggravating and mitigating factors of the offence (not personal mitigation);
- any statutory provisions relevant to the offender and the offence under consideration so that the judge is made aware of any statutory limitations on sentencing;
- any relevant sentencing guidelines and guideline cases;
- identifying any victim personal statement or other information available to the prosecution advocate as to the impact of the offence on the victim;
- where appropriate, any evidence of the impact of the offending on a community;
- an indication, where applicable, of an intention to apply for any ancillary orders, such as anti-social behaviour orders and confiscation orders, and so far as possible, indicating the nature of the order to be sought.

C:7. When the prosecution advocate has agreed the written basis of plea submitted by the defence advocate, he or she should endorse the document accordingly. If the prosecution advocate takes issue with all or part of the written basis of plea, he or she should set out in writing what is accepted and what is rejected or not accepted. Where there is a dispute about a particular fact which the defence advocate believes to be effectively immaterial to the sentencing decision, the difference should be recorded so that the judge can make up his or her own mind. The signed original document should be made available to the trial judge and thereafter lodged with the court papers, as it will form part of the record of the hearing.

C:8. Where a defendant declines to admit an offence that he or she previously indicated should be taken into consideration, the prosecution advocate should indicate to the defence advocate and the court that, subject to further review, the offence may now form the basis of a new prosecution.

C:9. Where the basis of plea cannot be agreed and the discrepancy between the two accounts is such as to have a potentially significant effect on the level of sentence, it is the duty of the defence advocate so to inform the court before the sentencing process begins. There remains an overriding duty on the prosecution advocate to ensure that the sentencing judge is made aware of the discrepancy and of the consideration which must be given to the holding of a *Newton* hearing to resolve the issue. The court should be told where a derogatory reference to a victim, witness or third party is not accepted, even though there may be no effect on sentence.

C:10. Whenever an agreement as to the basis of plea is made between the prosecution and defence, any such agreement will be subject to the approval of the trial judge, who may of his or her own motion disregard the agreement and direct that a *Newton* hearing should be held to determine the proper basis on which sentence should be passed.

D. Sentence Indications

D:1. Only in the Crown Court may sentence indications be sought. Advocates there are **C–30**

reminded that indications as to sentence should not be sought from the trial judge unless issues between the prosecution and defence have been addressed and resolved. Therefore, in difficult or complicated cases, no less than seven days notice in writing of an intention to seek an indication should normally be given to the prosecution and the court. When deciding whether the circumstances of a case require such notice to be given, defence advocates are reminded that prosecutors should not agree a basis of plea unless and until the necessary consultation has taken place first with the victim and/or the victim's family and second, in the case of an independent prosecution advocate, with the prosecuting authority.

D:2. If there is no final agreement about the plea to the indictment, or the basis of plea, and the defence nevertheless proceeds to seek an indication of sentence, which the judge appears minded to give, the prosecution advocate should remind him or her of the guidance given in *R. v. Goodyear (Karl)* [2005] EWCA 888 [*sic*] that normally speaking an indication of sentence should not be given until the basis of the plea has been agreed or the judge has concluded that he or she can properly deal with the case without the need for a trial of the issue.

D:3. If an indication is sought, the prosecution advocate should normally enquire whether the judge is in possession of or has access to all the evidence relied on by the prosecution, including any victim personal statement, as well as any information about relevant previous convictions recorded against the defendant.

D:4. Before the judge gives the indication, the prosecution advocate should draw the judge's attention to any minimum or mandatory statutory sentencing requirements. Where the prosecution advocate would be expected to offer the judge assistance with relevant guideline cases or the views of the Sentencing Guidelines Council, he or she should invite the judge to allow them to do so. Where it applies, the prosecution advocate should remind the judge that the position [*sic*] of the Attorney General to refer any sentencing decision as unduly lenient is unaffected. In any event, the prosecution advocate should not say anything which may create the impression that the sentence indication has the support or approval of the Crown.

E. Pleas in Mitigation

C–31 **E:**1. The prosecution advocate must challenge any assertion by the defence in mitigation which is derogatory to a person's character (for instance, because it suggests that his or her conduct is or has been criminal, immoral or improper) and which is either false or irrelevant to proper sentencing considerations. If the defence advocate persists in that assertion, the prosecution advocate should invite the court to consider holding a *Newton* hearing to determine the issue.

E:2. The defence advocate must not submit in mitigation anything that is derogatory to a person's character without giving advance notice in writing so as to afford the prosecution advocate the opportunity to consider their position under paragraph E:1. When the prosecution advocate is so notified they must take all reasonable steps to establish whether the assertions are true. Reasonable steps will include seeking the views of the victim. This will involve seeking the views of the victim's family if the victim is deceased, and the victim's parents or legal guardian where the victim is a child. Reasonable steps may also include seeking the views of the police or other law enforcement authority, as appropriate. An assertion which is derogatory to a person's character will rarely amount to mitigation unless it has a causal connection to the circumstances of the offence or is otherwise relevant to proper sentencing considerations.

E:3. Where notice has not been given in accordance with paragraph E:2, the prosecution advocate must not acquiesce in permitting mitigation which is derogatory to a person's character. In such circumstances, the prosecution advocate should draw the attention of the court to the failure to give advance notice and seek time, and if necessary, an adjournment to investigate the assertion in the same way as if proper notice had been given. Where, in the opinion of the prosecution advocate, there are substantial grounds for believing that such an assertion is false or irrelevant to sentence, he or she should inform the court of their opinion and invite the court to consider making an order under section 58(8) of the *Criminal Procedure and Investigations Act* 1996, preventing publication of the assertion.

E:4. Where the prosecution advocate considers that the assertion is, if true, relevant to sentence, or the court has so indicated, he or she should seek time, and if necessary an adjournment, to establish whether the assertion is true. If the matter cannot be resolved to the satisfaction of the parties, the prosecution advocate should invite the court to consider holding a *Newton* hearing to determine the issue.

Appendix D

PROTOCOL FOR THE PROVISION OF ADVANCE INFORMATION, PROSECUTION EVIDENCE AND DISCLOSURE OF UNUSED MATERIAL IN THE MAGISTRATES' COURTS

Introduction

With effect from May 15, 2006, in four (unspecified) pilot sites, a judicial protocol has effect for the purposes of establishing firm principles for the management of advance information, evidence and disclosure in the magistrates' court for police, prosecution and defence practitioners, legal advisors and the judiciary. The protocol is said to be "regarded as best practice to ensure the administration of justice is not delayed by inappropriate or inadequate provision or applications for advance information, evidence or disclosure." **D–1**

Although the protocol is intended to apply in the pilot sites, it is expected that courts and practitioners in all areas will use and refer to the document for guidance.

It should be noted that Part 1 of the protocol relates to the provision of advance information under Part 21 of the *Criminal Procedure Rules* 2005 prior to replacement of that part with the new "initial details" regime applicable to both summary only and either way cases.

Protocol for the Provision of Advance Information, Prosecution Evidence and Disclosure of Unused Material in the Magistrates' Courts

Introduction

i. This protocol is a guide to all those involved in the control and management of criminal proceedings in magistrates' courts. The provision of advance information, prosecution evidence, and disclosure of unused material are important procedural steps in criminal trials, but widely misunderstood, particularly as to exactly what material the defence are entitled and the procedures to be followed. All too frequently applications by the parties and decisions by the court in this area have been based either on misconceptions as to the true nature of the law or a general laxity of approach (however well-intentioned). This failure properly to apply the binding provisions as regards disclosure has proved extremely and unnecessarily costly and has obstructed justice. **D–2**

ii. This protocol identifies the different types of material that may be available in magistrates' courts, sets out the simple procedures that should be followed and aims to clarify the stages at which relevant duties arise.

iii. This protocol must be read in the context of general case management, which is to be regarded as an essential duty of the court. The new *Criminal Procedure Rules* 2005 impose duties and burdens on all the participants in a criminal trial, including the judge, and the preparation and conduct of criminal trials is dependent on and subject to these rules: *R. v. K. and others* [2006] EWCA Crim. 724.

iv. The duty of courts to manage proceedings, and the requirement on the parties to conduct them, in order to achieve the overriding objective in Part 1 of the Rules, means there has to be a complete culture change. Nothing less is required to stem unnecessary delays and prevent potential obstructions to achieving justice. The summary trial process must not be delayed or unnecessarily complicated by inappropriate handling of prosecution material or misconceived applications in relation to such material.

v. It is essential that judges, magistrates and the parties are clear as to the law and procedure relating to provision of advance information, prosecution evidence and disclosure of unused material, act within the framework of the legislation and recognise and accept the

Appendices

role of the court in overseeing this process. This protocol is in part the reciprocal in magistrates' courts proceedings of Disclosure: A Protocol for the Control and Management of Unused Material in the Crown Court. The Court of Appeal made clear in *R v K* [2006] EWCA Crim 724 that 'the protocol should be applied by trial judges, and those who act for the prosecution and the defence should ensure that they have familiarised themselves with it'. This protocol should be regarded similarly.

vi. Magistrates will need to rely heavily on their legal advisers for guidance on the matters covered by this protocol. Legal advisers should ensure that they are familiar with the statutory provisions and applicable case law, and should draw the attention of the parties and the magistrates to this protocol. Any case which raises difficult issues of disclosure should be referred to a District Judge (Magistrates' Courts) for directions, where such a judge is available.

PART 1 ADVANCED INFORMATION

D–3 [*The contents of this part of the protocol are not reproduced in this work in view of the replacement of the "advance information" rules with the new "initial details" rules in Part 21 of the* Criminal Procedure Rules.]

PART 2 PROSECUTION EVIDENCE

D–4 **2.1.** The provision of prosecution evidence in summary trials is a duty on the prosecution that arises **only after** a not-guilty plea has been entered. It is not regulated by any statutory provisions, but is covered by the Attorney General's Guidelines on Disclosure (April 2005). Paragraph 57 requires the prosecution to provide the defendant with all the evidence upon which they intend to rely at trial (in so far as it has not already been provided as advance information, where that duty arises) to allow the defendant and his legal adviser sufficient time properly to consider the evidence before it is called. Standard directions[1] currently set a time limit of 28 days from plea for prosecution to provide such evidence.

2.2. Prosecutors should act to ensure directions are complied with, to avoid delays. However, late provision of such evidence should not automatically result in a trial being adjourned. The court must take into account the nature of the evidence being provided late and form a view as to how long is required to properly consider it. In the majority of cases, a competent advocate will be able to deal with the material then and there by the court allowing time before the trial commences, or even during the course of the trial.

PART 3 UNUSED PROSECUTION MATERIAL AND DEFENCE STATEMENT

Disclosure of unused prosecution material

D–5 **3.1.** This is a duty on the prosecution that arises **only after** a not-guilty plea has been entered[2]. Disclosure of unused material is governed by the *Criminal Procedure and Investigations Act* 1996[3]. The test for whether material should be disclosed will depend upon the date when the criminal investigation commenced (see Annex A). Standard directions allow 28 days following plea for initial disclosure to be provided.

3.2. The majority of cases are likely to be subject to the new disclosure regime which applies where the criminal investigation commenced on or after April 4, 2005. The law is set out in the *CPIA* as amended by Part V of the *Criminal Justice Act* 2003. The April 2005 edition of the Code of Practice under section 23(1) of the *CPIA* applies (see S.I. 2005 No. 985). The amended test for disclosure of unused material requires the prosecutor to disclose *any prosecution material which might reasonably be considered capable of undermining the case for the prosecution against the accused or of assisting the case for the accused*. This one test applies throughout.

3.3. Justice requires that the prosecution complies fully with its legal duties of disclosure. The overarching principle relating to disclosure is that prosecution material must be disclosed at the appropriate stage in the proceedings, but **only if** it satisfies the appropriate statutory test for disclosure. It is the duty of the court to oversee and manage the process to see that the overriding objective in Part 1 of the *Criminal Procedure Rules* is achieved.

3.4. While the disclosure of unused material is undoubtedly essential to achieving justice, it is also essential that summary trials are not delayed or over-complicated by inappropriate disclosure of prosecution material or misconceived applications in relation to such material[4].

The defence statement

3.5. Provision of a defence statement is voluntary where matters are tried summarily in the magistrate's court (s.6 of the *CPIA*). However in the absence of a defence statement, the defendant **cannot** make an application for specific disclosure under section 8 of the *CPIA*, and the court **cannot** make any orders for disclosure of unused prosecution material. Service of the defence statement is therefore a critical stage in the disclosure process, and timely service is crucial for the proper consideration of disclosure issues well in advance of the trial date. Defence advocates **must** give consideration at an early stage as to whether to serve such a statement.

3.6. In the past, defence statements have contained little more than an assertion that the defendant is not guilty. Reiteration of the defendant's plea is not the purpose of a defence statement: *R. v. Bryant* [2005] EWCA Crim 2079 (*per* Judge LJ at [12]). Defence statements must comply with the requirements set out in the *CPIA*.

3.7. Enhanced requirements now apply to defence statements under section 6A of the *CPIA*[5], as amended by the *Criminal Justice Act* 2003. The defence statement must spell out, in detail, the nature of the defence, and particular defences relied upon; it must identify the matters of fact upon which the defendant takes issue with the prosecution, and the reason why, in relation to each disputed matter of fact. It must further identify any point of law (including points as to the admissibility of evidence, or abuse of process) which the defendant proposes to take, and identify authorities relied on in relation to each point of law (see s.6A(1) of the *CPIA*). Where an alibi defence is relied upon, the particulars given must comply with section 6A(2)(a) and (b) of the *CPIA*. **Courts will expect to see defence statements that contain a clear and detailed exposition of the issues of fact and law in the case.**

3.8. Courts should examine the defence statement with care to ensure that it complies with the formalities required by the *CPIA*. As was stated at [35] in *R. v. H. and C.* [2004] 2 A.C. 134, HL:

"The trial process is not well served if the defence are permitted to make general and unspecified allegations and then seek far-reaching disclosure in the hope that material may turn up to make them good. Neutral material or material damaging to the defendant need not be disclosed and should not be brought to the attention of the court."

3.9. Standard directions require that a defence statement, if there is to be one, must be served within 14 days of the date upon which the prosecution has complied with, or purported to comply with the duty to provide initial disclosure.[6] Courts will expect to see the standard timeframe met. However, there may be some rare occasions where it is simply not possible to serve a properly drafted defence statement within the 14 day period; well-founded defence applications for an extension of time under regulation 3(1) of the *Criminal Procedure and Investigations Act 1996 (Defence Disclosure Time Limits) Regulations* 1997 may therefore be granted. Such applications **must** be made in writing in accordance with rule 25.7 of the *Criminal Procedure Rules*, and **must** be made **before** the time limit expires (reg. 3(2)[7]).

3.10. Late service of a defence statement does not, of itself, permit the prosecution to ignore it, nor does it preclude the court from considering a proper application under section 8 of the *CPIA* (*DPP v Wood*; *DPP v McGillicuddy* [2005] EWHC 2986). However, where late service of a defence statement results in potential delay in the proceedings, any application to adjourn for further disclosure or to make an application under section 8 of the *CPIA*, must be scrutinised carefully and if granted, the court should give consideration to the issue of wasted costs, or even drawing matters to the attention of the Legal Services Commission.

3.11. Courts must, of course, be alert to ensure that defendants do not suffer because of the failings of their lawyer, but there must be a clear indication to the professions that if justice is to be done, proper consideration must be given to disclosure issues at an early stage and not left.

3.12. It is vital to a fair trial that the prosecution is mindful of its continuing duty of disclosure, and must particularly review disclosure in the light of the issues identified in any defence statement. While the defence may indicate what items of unused material they are interested in and why, such requests must relate to prosecution material (*i.e.* not third party material) and matters properly raised in the defence statement (*DPP v. Wood*; *DPP v. McGillicuddy* [2005] EWHC 2986).

3.13. The court should not allow the prosecution to abdicate its statutory responsibility for reviewing the unused material by the expedient of allowing the defence to inspect (or providing copies of) everything on the unused material schedule, irrespective of whether it satisfies the relevant test for disclosure. Additionally, indications should not be given by individual prosecutors that disclosure will be provided of material that does not satisfy the relevant test. Such indications often result in fruitless adjournments for the promised material to be provided and applications to the court for directions in relation to such material, causing unreasonable expectations and delay, and unjustifiable public cost.

3.14. The prosecution must disclose material *only* if it meets the appropriate test for disclosure. Where the appropriate test is satisfied, it is for the prosecutor to decide the form in which disclosure is made. Disclosure need not be in the same form as that in which the information was recorded.

3.15. If the defence have a reasonable basis to claim disclosure has been inadequate, they must make a formal application under section 8 of the *CPIA*. The procedure for making such an application is set out in rule 25.6 of the *Criminal Procedure Rules*. This requires **written notice** in the form prescribed by rule 25.6(2). The prosecutor is entitled to 14 days within which to agree to provide the specific disclosure requested or to request a hearing in order to make representations in relation to the defence application (rule 25.6(5)). Courts should insist that the procedural rules are complied with and not agree to 'list' section 8 applications or consider *ad hoc* applications for disclosure at case management hearings without formal application being made as prescribed by the rules. **Courts must not hear such applications or purport to make directions for disclosure under section 8 in the absence of a defence statement**.

The court's duty to enforce the statutory scheme

3.16. For cases being dealt with summarily, following the entry of a not guilty plea, the standard directions in relation to disclosure will apply, unless specifically disapplied or varied. It may be appropriate to consider reducing the standard time allowed *e.g.* where the defendant is refused bail and an early trial date is fixed; where the defendant is a persistent young offender. However extensions of time should not be given lightly or as a matter of course.

3.17. If extensions of time are sought, then an appropriately detailed explanation in support must be given. It is not sufficient merely for the prosecutor to say that the papers have not yet been received, or were delivered late by the police (or other investigator): the court will need to know why there are no papers, or why they have been delivered late. Likewise, where the defendant has been dilatory in serving a voluntary defence statement, it is not enough simply to say insufficient instructions have been taken to meet the 14-day time limit: the court will need to know why this has occurred, and what arrangements have been made to rectify the situation.

3.18. Delays and failures by prosecution and defence in meeting their obligations to progress matters to trial are damaging to the timely, fair and efficient hearing of the case, and courts should identify and deal with all such failures firmly and fairly. The parties must not rely upon the court or others to remind them to act; they must take responsibility for meeting their obligations and to that end must monitor compliance with directions and take any necessary action at an early stage.

3.19. There is an expectation and duty (rule 3.3 of the *Criminal Procedure Rules*) on the parties to have matters listed at the earliest opportunity for further consideration where directions have not been complied with, or the case is not trial ready. In appropriate cases, to save unnecessary costs, such applications may be made in writing[8]. Applications to adjourn for disclosure made very late or on the day of trial without any good reason for failure to apply earlier in the proceedings should be dealt with robustly.

PART 4 THIRD PARTY DISCLOSURE

D–6 **4.1.** The disclosure of unused material that remains in the hands of a third party is an area of the law that causes difficulty. The *CPIA* and code of practice are not directed to creating duties for third parties to follow: see *DPP v Wood*; *DPP v McGillicuddy* (*supra*). There is no specific procedure governing the disclosure of material held by third parties in criminal proceedings. The provisions of section 97 of the *Magistrates' Courts Act* 1980 can be used in order to obtain material in the hands of a third party. However the test to be applied is not the same test as under the *CPIA*. The material in question must be 'material' evidence, *i.e.* immediately admissible in evidence in the proceedings (see *R. v. Reading JJ, ex p. Berkshire County Council* [1996] 1 Cr.App.R. 239, *R. v. Derby Magistrates' Court, ex p. B.* [1996] AC 487; [1996] 1 Cr.App.R. 385, *R v Alibhai and others* [2004] EWCA Crim. 681).

4.2. Material held by government departments or other Crown agencies will not be prosecution material for the purposes of section 3(2) or section 8(4) of the *CPIA*, if it has not been inspected, recorded and retained during the course of the relevant criminal investigation. However, the Attorney-General's Guidelines impose a duty on the investigators and prosecutors to consider whether such departments or bodies have material which may satisfy the test for disclosure under the Act. Where this is the case, they must seek appropriate disclosure from such bodies, who should themselves have an identified point for such enquiries (see paras 47 to 51 of the Guidelines).

4.3. Where material is held by a third party such as a local authority, a social services department, hospital or business, investigators and prosecutors may seek to make arrangements to inspect the material with a view to applying the appropriate test for disclosure to it and determining whether any or all of the material should be retained, recorded and, in due course, disclosed to the defendant. In considering the latter, the investigators and the prosecution will establish whether the holder of the material wishes to raise public interest immunity (PII) issues[9], as a result of which the material may have to be placed before the court.

4.4. Where a third party declines to allow inspection of the material, or requires the prosecution to obtain an order before handing over copies of the material, the prosecutor will need to consider whether it is appropriate to obtain a witness summons under section 97 of the *Magistrates' Court Act* 1980, if the statutory requirements are satisfied, and where the prosecutor considers that the material may satisfy the appropriate test for disclosure. *R. v. Alibhai* (*supra*) makes it clear that the prosecutor has a "margin of consideration" in this regard.

4.5. Where issues are raised in relation to allegedly relevant third party material, the court must ascertain whether inquiries with the third party are likely to be appropriate, and, if so, identify who is going to make the request, what material is to be sought, from whom is the material to be sought and within what time scale the matter must be resolved.

4.6. The court should also consider what action would be appropriate in the light of the third party failing or refusing to comply with a request, including inviting the defence to make the request on its own behalf. Where the prosecutor does not consider it appropriate to seek such a summons, the defence should consider doing so, provided always that the appropriate statutory test will be met. The defence must not sit back and expect the prosecution to make all the running. The court should specifically enquire whether any such application is to be made by the defence and set out a clear timetable. The objectionable practice of late applications being made in the few days before trial must end.

4.7. 'Fishing' expeditions in relation to third party material—whether by prosecution or the defence—must be discouraged, and in appropriate cases, the court should consider making an order for wasted costs where an application is clearly unmeritorious and ill-conceived. When considering applications concerning technical material relating to approved devices used in the detection of road traffic offences (*e.g.* breathalyser machines, speed check devices, *etc.*) the observations made in *R. v. Skegness Magistrates' Court, ex p. Cardy* [1985] R.T.R. 49 remain relevant[10]. See also *DPP v. Wood*; *DPP v. McGillicuddy* (*supra*).

4.8. Applications for a witness summons must identify what documents are sought and why they are said to be material evidence. This is particularly relevant where attempts are made to access the medical reports of those who allege that they are victims of crime. Victims do not waive the confidentiality of their medical records, or their right to privacy under Article 8 of the European Convention on Human Rights, by the mere fact of making a complaint against the defendant. Courts should be alert to balance the rights of victims against the real and proven needs of the defence. The court, as a public authority, must ensure that any interference with the Article 8 rights of those entitled to privacy is in accordance with the law and necessary in pursuit of a legitimate public interest. General and unspecified requests to trawl through such records should be refused. If material is held by any person in relation to family proceedings then careful consideration should be given to whether such material is permitted to be disclosed for the purpose sought without application to the family court.

PART 5 CCTV, POLICE CRIME REPORTS, RECORDS OF EMERGENCY CALLS, PREVIOUS CONVICTIONS OF WITNESSES AND DISCIPLINARY RECORDS OF POLICE OFFICERS

5.1. Disclosure of this type of routine prosecution material frequently causes problems in summary proceedings and courts are too often asked to grant adjournments to allow for its inspection, or inappropriate directions sought for its disclosure. In the case of CCTV, it is important that prosecutors should be in a position to properly inform defence advocates and the court as to whether such material is available, and whether it will form part of the prosecution case. However, there is nothing special about CCTV, and it must be treated like any other form of material, in line with the guidance given in this protocol. Note: The pilots will examine best practice in relation to the time for the provision of CCTV evidence and the ability to play it in court. **D–7**

5.2. Careful consideration must be given to the stage reached in the proceedings. There

Appendices

is no duty on the prosecution to provide the defence with material prior to plea unless the defendant is charged with an either-way offence and thereby entitled to request advance information; the duty is limited to that set out in Part 1. The court should only adjourn to allow inspection of a document referred to in advance information, where it is clear that it exists, is in the hands of the prosecutor and the prosecutor proposes to adduce it as evidence in the proceedings. Even where the duty to provide advance information arises, the court may still properly refuse an adjournment for service or inspection of such material if satisfied that the case for the accused would not be substantially prejudiced by the accused not having sight of it before the first hearing to determine venue and enter a plea.

5.3. Following a not-guilty plea, CCTV material secured by the police forms part of the prosecution material and should be dealt with like any other material(assuming it is relevant material): it will either be prosecution evidence[11] (to be disclosed under the Attorney General's Guidelines in advance of trial), or unused material[12].

5.4. If it is unused material, it should only be disclosed if it meets the appropriate test for disclosure under the *CPIA*[13]. Disclosure may be by way of provision of copies or by allowing the defendant to inspect the material.

5.5. If the prosecutor forms the view that the CCTV does not meet the test for disclosure, in order to obtain disclosure, the defence *must* make a written application under section 8 of the *CPIA* (and must, therefore, have served a defence statement) before the court can give consideration to whether it should order disclosure of the CCTV. It is improper for courts to make general directions requiring the prosecutor to disclosure such material within a specified time without a proper application and scrutiny of the matter in compliance with the *CPIA*.

5.6. Where such material is not in the possession of the police, but may be the property of a third party, the guidance in Part 4 above in relation to third party material will apply.

5.7. Crime reports and records of emergency calls are routinely provided by some prosecutors as part of a bundle of disclosure documents irrespective of whether the material (or all of the material) in question satisfies the appropriate test for disclosure. This practice does not comply with the overarching principle in paragraph 3.3 of this protocol, and must cease. Such material must be dealt with in the same way as any other prosecution material. There are few cases where it is likely to form part of the prosecution case. It will generally be unused material and so it should therefore be dealt with properly under the statutory framework of the *CPIA*.

5.8. Previous convictions of witnesses and disciplinary proceedings relating to officers involved in any investigation may be part of the prosecution material and are likely to be unused material. Again, such material must be dealt with in the same way as any other unused prosecution material in compliance with the *CPIA*. Whilst the defence advocates and the prosecutor should co-operate to resolve all issues of disclosure, the practice of defence advocates sending letters as a matter of routine to the prosecutor requesting such material must cease. If the material falls to be disclosed under the *CPIA*, then the prosecutor must deal with it under the *CPIA* and in the time allowed by the standard directions. If it is not considered disclosable, then a proper written application must be made by the defence under section 8 of the *CPIA*.

5.9. Courts must take control over issues relating to this type of material, and should be scrupulous about not allowing it to delay the progress of proceedings. In particular, courts should guard against granting unnecessary adjournments or making inappropriate directions and orders at an early stage in proceedings.

CONCLUSION

The public rightly expects that the delays and failures that have been present in some cases in the past where there has been scant adherence to sound disclosure principles will be eradicated by observation of this Protocol. The new regime under the *Criminal Justice Act* 2003 and the *Criminal Procedure Rules* 2005 gives courts the power to change the culture in which such cases are tried. It is now the duty of judges and magistrates to actively manage disclosure issues in every case. The court must seize the initiative and drive the case along towards an efficient, effective and timely resolution, having regard to the overriding objective of Part 1 of the *Criminal Procedure Rules*. In this way the interests of justice will be better served and public confidence in the criminal justice system will be increased.

ANNEX A: THE APPROPRIATE TEST FOR DISCLOSURE OF UNUSED PROSECUTION MATERIAL

Investigations commenced on or after April 1, 1997, but before April, 4 2005

D–8 **i.** For criminal investigations commenced on or after April 1, 1997, but before April 4,

2005, the *CPIA* in its original form will apply, with separate tests for disclosure of unused prosecution material at the primary and secondary disclosure stages. The 1997 edition of the Code of Practice issued under section 23(1) of the *CPIA* (S.I. 1997 No. 1033) applies.

ii. At the **primary stage**, material falls to be disclosed *if, in the opinion of the prosecutor, it might undermine the case for the prosecution against the accused*. At the **secondary stage**, (*i.e.* following service of a defence statement) material falls to be disclosed *if it might reasonably be expected to assist the accused's defence as disclosed by the defence statement.*

CJA 2003 amendment to CPIA—investigations commenced on or after April 4, 2005

iii. The majority of cases are likely to be subject to the new disclosure regime where the criminal investigation has commenced on or after April 4, 2005. The law is set out in the *CPIA* as amended by Part V of the *Criminal Justice Act* 2003. There is now a single amended test for disclosure which applies to both initial and secondary disclosure. The April 2005 edition of the Code of Practice under section 23(1) of the *CPIA* applies (see S.I. 2005 No. 985).

iv. The amended test for disclosure *is prosecution material which might reasonably be considered capable of undermining the case for the prosecution against the accused or of assisting the case for the accused.*

ANNEX B: THE DUTY TO GATHER AND RECORD UNUSED MATERIAL

i. For the statutory scheme to work properly, investigators and disclosure officers responsible for the gathering, inspection, retention and recording of relevant unused prosecution material must perform their tasks thoroughly, scrupulously and fairly. In this, they must adhere to the appropriate provisions of the *CPIA* Code of Practice. **D–9**

ii. It is crucial that the police appoint competent disclosure officers, who have sufficient knowledge of the issues in the case, avoiding any conflict of interest. For example, an officer who is an alleged victim of an assault should not be appointed disclosure officer in any investigation in relation to that matter. Officers need to be sufficiently trained to make a proper assessment of the unused prosecution material in the light of the relevance test under paragraph 2.1 of the Code, with a view to preparing full and accurate schedules of the retained material.

iii. In any criminal investigation, the disclosure officer must retain material that may be relevant to an investigation. This material must be listed on schedules (separate schedules are required for sensitive and non-sensitive material) in accordance with the Code of Practice. Each item listed on the schedule should contain sufficient detail to enable the prosecutor to decide whether or not the material falls to be disclosed. The schedules must be sent to the prosecutor. Wherever possible this should be at the same time as the file containing the material for the prosecution case but the duty to disclose does not end at this point and must continue while relevant material is received even after conviction.

iv. Scheduling of the relevant material must be completed properly and expeditiously, so as to enable the prosecution to comply promptly with the duty to provide disclosure. On occasions, material which is clearly to be used as prosecution evidence will erroneously appear on the unused material schedule, while other relevant material may be omitted. Disclosure officers must have proper regard to what information they include on the schedule, and if necessary seek guidance. Prosecutors must properly scrutinise schedules, and where it is obvious that material has not been included which should be listed, ensure that the schedules are returned to the disclosure officer to be amended. For example, in a straightforward case, a prosecutor might expect to see the following listed on the non-sensitive unused material schedule[14]:

- custody record;
- records of emergency calls and/or crime reports;
- unused CCTV footage if seized by police in the course of the particular investigation;
- record of examination of the defendant by the police doctor;
- the notice given to the defendant in relation to provision of copies of audio tapes of the interview under caution at the police station;
- previous convictions of witnesses;
- incident report books of officers not intended to give evidence at trial.

The non-sensitive unused material schedule will be provided to the defendant in line with the Code of Practice so that the defendant is aware of what material is in the hands of the prosecutor, but not intended to be used as prosecution evidence. Therefore, proper listing of material on the unused material schedule and appropriate scrutiny of it by the prosecutor is vital to the proper implementation of the statutory scheme.

v. In magistrates' courts, the duty to provide disclosure will be triggered on sending to the Crown Court under s.51 or 51A *Crime and Disorder Act* 1998, on committal for trial, or on entering a not guilty plea. There is an expectation that indictable-only cases will be sent to the Crown Court on first appearance. Where cases are triable summarily, pleas should be entered upon first appearance following charge. Investigators, disclosure officers and prosecutors must promptly and properly discharge their responsibilities under the Act and statutory Code, in order to ensure that justice is not delayed, denied or frustrated and directions complied with.

vi. CPS lawyers advising the police pre-charge at police stations should consider conducting a preliminary review of the unused material generated by the investigation, where this is practicable, so as to give early advice on disclosure issues. Otherwise, prosecutors should conduct a preliminary review of disclosure at the same time as the initial review of the evidence. It is critical that the important distinction between the evidence in the case, on the one hand, and any unused material, on the other, is not blurred. Items such as exhibits should be treated as such and the obligation to serve them is not affected by the statutory disclosure regime.

vii. Where the single test for disclosure applies under the amended *CPIA*, the prosecutor is under a duty to consider, at an early stage of proceedings, whether there is any unused prosecution material which is reasonably capable of assisting the case for the defendant. What a defendant has said following arrest or charge, or in interview or given in a prepared statement can be a useful guide to making an objective assessment of the material which would satisfy this test.

---

[1] Reference to 'standard directions' in this protocol means the default directions set out in the case progression forms for use in magistrates' courts in accordance with the Consolidated Criminal Practice Direction.

[2] Duties also arise in relation to cases being sent or committed for trial to the Crown Court, for which see Disclosure: A Protocol for the Control and Management of Unused Material in the Crown Court.

[3] There may be occasions when the prosecutor, pursuant to surviving common law rules of disclosure, ought to disclose an item or items of unused material in advance of disclosure under the *CPIA*., e.g. to assist a defendant in making a bail application. However, once the *CPIA* is triggered, the common law no longer applies. See *R. v. DPP, ex p. Lee* [1999] 2 Cr.App.R. 304, DC. The circumstances in which common law disclosure should be given will be rare and the surviving common law rules must not be cited in an attempt to obtain disclosure before the statutory duty arises, or wider disclosure than would be available under the *CPIA*.

[4] Section 17 of the *CPIA* prohibits parties from using or disclosing unused material for any purpose unconnected with the proceedings. This is to ensure privacy and confidentiality of those who may have provided the material. Applications can be made to the court for permission to use or disclose protected material. Material, once displayed or communicated to the public in open court, is no longer so protected.

[5] Where the pre-April 4, 2005, *CPIA* disclosure regime applies, the defendant must, in the defence statement, set out the nature of the defence in general terms, indicate the matters upon which the defendant takes issue with the prosecution and set out (in relation to each such matter) why issue is taken (see s.5(6) of the Act, pre-amendment). Any alibi defence relied upon should comply with the formalities in section 5(7) of the Act, pre-amendment.

[6] See also regulation 2 of the *Criminal Procedure and Investigations Act 1996 (Defence Disclosure Time Limits) Regulations* 1997.

[7] Applications must specify why it is not possible to provide a defence statement before the expiration of the time period and specify the number of days by which the accused wishes that period to be extended.

[8] See *R. v. K. and others* (*supra*) when dealing with matters preliminary to trial, if the judge thought it right to do so, case management powers permitted him to deal with issues of disclosure exclusively by reference to written submissions and also to limit them to a length specified by him. A judge was not bound to hear oral submissions and was entitled to put a time limit on them. Case management submissions are case specific and no particular method of approach is prescribed. The necessary public element of any hearing is sufficiently achieved if the defendants are supplied with copies of written submissions if they wish to see them, and similarly the media present for any hearing.

[9] Public interest immunity applications are rarely heard in relation to proceedings in the magistrates' court. In the event of such an application, the guidance set out in the Crown Court Protocol should be followed. Section 16 of the *CPIA* gives such a party a right to make representations to the court.

[10] *Per* Goff J (later Lord Goff) "It is important to bear in mind … that a witness summons must not be issued under s.97 of the Act of 1980 as a disguised attempt to obtain discovery. Nor can a witness summons be issued under s.97 summoning a person to produce documents at the hearing, when the docu-

ments are not likely to be material evidence, but it is merely desired to have them in court for the purposes of cross-examination."

[11] See Part 2 above.

[12] See Part 3 above.

[13] See Annex A.

[14] This is not intended to be an exhaustive list, but merely illustrative of the type of material that might appear on the schedule.

Appendices

APPENDIX E

CODE FOR CROWN PROSECUTORS

The sixth edition of the Code for Crown Prosecutors was issued by the Director of Public Prosecutors in February 2010 under s.10 of the *Prosecution of Offences Act* 1985. It replaces all previous editions of the code. **E–1**

Code for Crown Prosecutors (February 2010 edition)

Introduction

1.1 The Crown Prosecution Service (CPS) is the principal public prosecution service for England and Wales. In January 2010, it merged with the Revenue and Customs Prosecutions Office (RCPO). The service is headed by the Director of Public Prosecutions (DPP) who is also the Director of Revenue and Customs Prosecutions. The DPP exercises his functions independently, subject to the superintendence of the Attorney General who is accountable to Parliament for the work of the prosecution service. **E–2**

1.2 The DPP is responsible for issuing the Code for Crown Prosecutors (the Code) under section 10 of the *Prosecution of Offences Act* 1985. The Code gives guidance to prosecutors on the general principles to be applied when making decisions about prosecutions. This is the sixth edition of the Code and replaces all earlier versions.

1.3 In this Code, the term "prosecutors" is used to describe members of the prosecution service who are designated as Crown Prosecutors; prosecutors who are members of the RCPO; Associate Prosecutors who are designated under section 7A of the *Prosecution of Offences Act* 1985 and who exercise their powers in accordance with the instructions issued by the DPP; and other members of the RCPO who are designated by the DPP in his capacity as the Director of the Revenue and Customs Prosecutions under section 39 of the *Commissioners for Revenue and Customs Act* 2005.

1.4 In this Code, the expression "police or other investigators" is used to describe members of all those investigative agencies, including the Serious Organised Crime Agency and the UK Border Agency, who prepare and present cases to the prosecution service.

1.5 Although the prosecution service works closely with the police and other investigators, it is independent of them. The independence of prosecutors is of fundamental constitutional importance.

1.6 The prosecution service co-operates with the investigating and prosecuting agencies of other jurisdictions to facilitate enquiries and prosecutions both in England and Wales and abroad.

1.7 In accordance with section 36(2) of the *Commissioners for Revenue and Customs Act* 2005, prosecutors from the RCPO who are acting in that capacity must have regard to the Code for Crown Prosecutors issued by the DPP.

1.8 In this Code, the term "suspect" is used to describe a person who is not yet the subject of formal criminal proceedings; the term "defendant" is used to describe a person who has been charged or summonsed; and the term "offender" is used to describe a person who has admitted his or her guilt to a police officer or other investigator or prosecutor, or who has been found guilty in a court of law.

1.9 The Code is one of two key published and publicly available documents that explain the purpose and work of the prosecution service. The second is the Core Quality Standards booklet. Only the Code is issued by law.

1.10 Together, they let the public know what prosecutors do; how they take their decisions; and the level of service that the prosecution service is committed to providing in every key aspect of its work.

1.11 The Code and the Core Quality Standards booklet are available from the contact points listed on the back cover of this booklet.

General Principles

E–3 2.1 The decision to prosecute or to offer an individual an out-of court disposal is a serious step. Fair and effective prosecution is essential to the maintenance of law and order. It is the duty of prosecutors to make sure that the right person is prosecuted for the right offence and to bring offenders to justice wherever possible. Casework decisions taken fairly, impartially and with integrity help to deliver justice for victims, witnesses, defendants and the public.

2.2 It is the duty of prosecutors to review, to advise on and to prosecute cases or to offer an appropriate out-of-court disposal to the offender. Prosecutors must ensure that the law is properly applied; that all relevant evidence is put before the court; and that obligations of disclosure are complied with, in accordance with the principles set out in this Code.

2.3 Although each case must be considered on its own facts and on its own merits, there are general principles that apply to the way in which prosecutors must approach every case.

2.4 Prosecutors must be fair, independent and objective. They must not let any personal views about the ethnic or national origin, gender, disability, age, religion or belief, political views, sexual orientation, or gender identity of the suspect, victim or any witness influence their decisions. Neither must prosecutors be affected by improper or undue pressure from any source. Prosecutors must always act in the interests of justice and not solely for the purpose of obtaining a conviction.

2.5 The prosecution service is a public authority for the purposes of current, relevant equality legislation. Prosecutors are bound by the duties set out in this legislation.

2.6 The prosecution service is also a public authority for the purposes of the *Human Rights Act* 1998. Prosecutors must apply the principles of the European Convention on Human Rights, in accordance with the *Human Rights Act* 1998, at each stage of a case. Prosecutors must also comply with any guidelines issued by the Attorney General and with the policies of the prosecution service issued on behalf of the DPP. They must also comply with the *Criminal Procedure Rules* currently in force.

The Decision Whether to Prosecute

E–4 3.1 In more serious or complex cases, prosecutors decide whether a person should be charged with a criminal offence, and, if so, what that offence should be. They make their decisions in accordance with this Code and the DPP's Guidance on Charging. The police apply the same principles in deciding whether to charge or summons a person in those cases for which they are responsible.

3.2 The police and other investigators are responsible for conducting enquiries into an allegation that a crime may have been committed. Every case that prosecutors receive from the police or other investigators is reviewed. Prosecutors must ensure that they have all the information they need to make an informed decision about how best to deal with the case. This will often involve prosecutors providing guidance and advice to the police and other investigators about lines of inquiry, evidential requirements, and assistance in any pre-charge procedures throughout the investigative and prosecuting process. However, prosecutors cannot direct the police or other investigators.

3.3 Prosecutors should identify and, where possible, seek to rectify evidential weaknesses, but, subject to the Threshold Test (see section 5), they should swiftly stop cases which do not meet theevidential stage of the Full Code Test (see section 4) and which cannot be strengthened by further investigation, or where the public interest clearly does not require a prosecution (see section 4). Although the prosecutor primarily considers the evidence and information supplied by the police and other investigators, the suspect or those acting on his or her behalf may also submit evidence or information to the prosecutor via the police or other investigators, prior to charge, to help to inform the prosecutor'sdecision.

3.4 Prosecutors must only start or continue a prosecution when the case has passed both stages of the Full Code Test (see section 4). The exception is when the Threshold Test (see section 5) may be applied where it is proposed to apply to the court to keep the suspect in custody after charge, and the evidence required to apply the Full Code Test is not yet available.

3.5 Prosecutors must make sure that they do not allow a prosecution to start or continue where to do so would be seen by the courts as oppressive or unfair so as to amount to an abuse of the process of the court.

3.6 Review is a continuing process and prosecutors must take account of any change in circumstances that occurs as the case develops. Wherever possible, they should talk to the investigator first if they are thinking about changing the charges or stopping the case. Prosecutors and investigators work closely together, but the final responsibility for the decision whether or not a case should go ahead rests with the prosecution service.

3.7 Parliament has decided that a limited number of very serious or sensitive offences should only be taken to court with the agreement of the DPP. These are called "consent" cases. In such cases, the DPP or prosecutors acting on his behalf apply the Code in deciding whether to give consent to a prosecution.

[The next paragraph is § E-6.]

The Full Code Test

4.1 The Full Code Test has two stages: (i) the evidential stage; followed by (ii) the public interest stage. **E–6**

4.2 In the vast majority of cases, prosecutors should only decide whether to prosecute after the investigation has been completed and after all the available evidence has been reviewed. However, there will be cases where it is clear, prior to the collection and consideration of all the likely evidence, that the public interest does not require a prosecution. In these rare instances, prosecutors may decide that the case should not proceed further.

4.3 Prosecutors should only take such a decision when they are satisfied that the broad extent of the criminality has been determined and that they are able to make a fully informed assessment of the public interest. If prosecutors do not have sufficient information to take such a decision, the investigation should proceed and a decision taken later in accordance with the Full Code Test set out in this section.

4.4 Prosecutors must follow any guidance issued by the DPP to ensure that decisions in these cases are appropriate and correct.

The Evidential Stage

4.5 Prosecutors must be satisfied that there is sufficient evidence to provide a realistic prospect of conviction against each suspect on each charge. They must consider what the defence case may be, and how it is likely to affect the prospects of conviction. A case which does not pass the evidential stage must not proceed, no matter how serious or sensitive it may be.

4.6 A realistic prospect of conviction is an objective test based solely upon the prosecutor's assessment of the evidence and any information that he or she has about the defence that might be put forward by the suspect. It means that an objective, impartial and reasonable jury or bench of magistrates or judge hearing a case alone, properly directed and acting in accordance with the law, is more likely than not to convict the defendant of the charge alleged. This is a different test from the one that the criminal courts themselves must apply. A court may only convict if it is sure that the defendant is guilty.

4.7 When deciding whether there is sufficient evidence to prosecute, prosecutors must consider whether the evidence can be used and whether it is reliable. There will be many cases in which the evidence does not give any cause for concern. But there will also be cases in which the evidence may not be as strong as it first appears. In particular, prosecutors will need to consider the following issues.

Can the evidence be used in court?

a) Is it likely that the evidence will be excluded by the court? There are legal rules that might mean that evidence which seems relevant cannot be given at a trial. For example, is it likely that the evidence will be excluded because of the way in which it was obtained?

b) Is the evidence hearsay? If so, is the court likely to allow it to be presented under any of the exceptions which permit such evidence to be given in court?

c) Does the evidence relate to the bad character of the suspect? If so, is the court likely to allow it to be presented?

Is the evidence reliable?

d) What explanation has the suspect given? Is a court likely to find it credible in the light of the evidence as a whole? Does the evidence support an innocent explanation?

e) Is there evidence which might support or detract from the reliability of a confession? Is its reliability affected by factors such as the suspect's level of understanding?

f) Is the identification of the suspect likely to be questioned? Is the evidence of his or her identity strong enough? Have the appropriate identification procedures been carried out? If not, why not? Will any failure to hold the appropriate identification procedures lead to the evidence of identification being excluded?

g) Are there concerns over the accuracy, reliability or credibility of the evidence of any witness?

h) Is there further evidence which the police or other investigators should reasonably be asked to find which may support or undermine the account of the witness?

i) Does any witness have any motive that may affect his or her attitude to the case?

j) Does any witness have a relevant previous conviction or out-of-court disposal which may affect his or her credibility?

k) Is there any further evidence that could be obtained that would support the integrity of evidence already obtained?

4.8 Where it is considered that it would be helpful in assessing the reliability of a witness' evidence or in better understanding complex evidence, an appropriately trained and authorised prosecutor should conduct a pre-trial interview with the witness in accordance with the relevant Code of Practice.

4.9 Prosecutors should not ignore evidence because they are not sure that it can be used or is reliable. But they should look closely at it when deciding if there is a realistic prospect of conviction.

The Public Interest Stage

E–7 4.10 In 1951, Sir Hartley Shawcross, who was then Attorney General, made the classic statement on public interest: "[i]t has never been the rule in this country – I hope it never will be – that suspected criminal offences must automatically be the subject of prosecution". He added that there should be a prosecution: "wherever it appears that the offence or the circumstances of its commission is or are of such a character that a prosecution in respect thereof is required in the public interest" (House of Commons Debates, Volume 483, 29 January 1951). This approach has been endorsed by Attorneys General ever since.

4.11 Accordingly, where there is sufficient evidence to justify a prosecution or to offer an out-of-court disposal, prosecutors must go on to consider whether a prosecution is required in the public interest.

4.12 A prosecution will usually take place unless the prosecutor is sure that there are public interest factors tending against prosecution which outweigh those tending in favour, or unless the prosecutor is satisfied that the public interest may be properly served, in the first instance, by offering the offender the opportunity to have the matter dealt with by an out-of-court disposal (see section 7). The more serious the offence or the offender's record of criminal behaviour, the more likely it is that a prosecution will be required in the public interest.

4.13 Assessing the public interest is not simply a matter of adding up the number of factors on each side and seeing which side has the greater number. Each case must be considered on its own facts and on its own merits. Prosecutors must decide the importance of each public interest factor in the circumstances of each case and go on to make an overall assessment. It is quite possible that one factor alone may outweigh a number of other factors which tend in the opposite direction. Although there may be public interest factors tending against prosecution in a particular case, prosecutors should consider whether nonetheless a prosecution should go ahead and for those factors to be put to the court for consideration when sentence is passed.

4.14 The absence of a factor does not necessarily mean that it should be taken as a factor tending in the opposite direction. For example, just because the offence was not "carried out by a group" does not transform the "factor tending in favour of a prosecution" into a "factor tending against prosecution".

4.15 Some common public interest factors which should be considered when deciding on the most appropriate course of action to take are listed below. The following lists of public interest factors are not exhaustive and each case must be considered on its own facts and on its own merits.

Some common public interest factors tending in favour of prosecution

4.16 A prosecution is more likely to be required if:

a) a conviction is likely to result in a significant sentence;
b) a conviction is likely to result in an order of the court in excess of that which a prosecutor is able to secure through a conditional caution;
c) the offence involved the use of a weapon or the threat of violence;
d) the offence was committed against a person serving the public (for example, a member of the emergency services; a police or prison officer; a health or social welfare professional; or a provider of public transport);
e) the offence was premeditated;
f) the offence was carried out by a group;
g) the offence was committed in the presence of, or in close proximity to, a child;
h) the offence was motivated by any form of discrimination against the victim's ethnic or national origin, gender, disability, age, religion or belief, political views, sexual orientation or gender identity; or the suspect demonstrated hostility towards the victim based on any of those characteristics;
i) the offence was committed in order to facilitate more serious offending;
j) the victim of the offence was in a vulnerable situation and the suspect took advantage of this;
k) there was an element of corruption of the victim in the way the offence was committed;
l) there was a marked difference in the ages of the suspect and the victim and the suspect took advantage of this;
m) there was a marked difference in the levels of understanding of the suspect and the victim and the suspect took advantage of this;
n) the suspect was in a position of authority or trust and he or she took advantage of this;
o) the suspect was a ringleader or an organiser of the offence;
p) the suspect's previous convictions or the previous out-of - court disposals which he or she has received are relevant to the present offence;
q) the suspect is alleged to have committed the offence in breach of an order of the court;
r) a prosecution would have a significant positive impact on maintaining community confidence;
s) there are grounds for believing that the offence is likely to be continued or repeated.

Some common public interest factors tending against prosecution

4.17 Some common public interest factors tending against prosecution

A prosecution is less likely to be required if:

a) the court is likely to impose a nominal penalty;
b) the seriousness and the consequences of the offending can be appropriately dealt with by an out-of-court disposal which the suspect accepts and with which he or she complies (see section 7);
c) the suspect has been subject to any appropriate regulatory proceedings, or any punitive or relevant civil penalty which remains in place or which has been satisfactorily discharged, which adequately addresses the seriousness of the offending and any breach of trust involved;
d) the offence was committed as a result of a genuine mistake or misunderstanding;
e) the loss or harm can be described as minor and was the result of a single incident, particularly if it was caused by a misjudgement ;
f) there has been a long delay between the offence taking place and the date of the trial, unless:
    - the offence is serious;
    - the delay has been caused wholly or in part by the suspect;
    - the offence has only recently come to light;
    - the complexity of the offence has meant that there has been a long investigation; or
    - new investigative techniques have been used to re-examine previously unsolved crimes and, as a result, a suspect has been identified.
g) a prosecution is likely to have an adverse effect on the victim's physical or mental health, always bearing in mind the seriousness of the offence and the views of the victim about the effect of a prosecution on his or her physical or mental health;
h) the suspect played a minor role in the commission of the offence;
i) the suspect has put right the loss or harm that was caused (but a suspect must not

Appendices

avoid prosecution or an out-of-court disposal solely because he or she pays compensation or repays the sum of money he or she unlawfully obtained);

j) the suspect is, or was at the time of the offence, suffering from significant mental or physical ill health, unless the offence is serious or there is a real possibility that it may be repeated. Prosecutors apply Home Office guidelines about how to deal with mentally disordered offenders and must balance a suspect's mental or physical ill health with the need to safeguard the public or those providing care services to such persons;

k) a prosecution may require details to be made public that could harm sources of information, international relations or national security.

The views of victims or their families

4.18 In deciding whether a prosecution is required in the public interest, prosecutors should take into account any views expressed by the victim regarding the impact that the offence has had. In appropriate cases, for example, a case of homicide or where the victim is a child or an adult who lacks capacity as defined by the Mental Capacity Act 2005, prosecutors should take into account any views expressed by the victim's family.

4.19 However, the prosecution service does not act for victims or their families in the same way as solicitors act for their clients, and prosecutors must form an overall view of the public interest.

4.20 Where prosecutors have a responsibility to explain their decision to the victim, for example, when they stop a case or substantially alter the charge in a case, they must comply with the Code of Practice for Victims of Crime and all relevant CPS Guidance. Prosecutors must follow any agreed procedures, including abiding by any time period within which such decisions should be notified to the victim.

The Threshold Test

E–8 5.1 Prosecutors will apply the Full Code Test wherever possible. However, there will be cases where the suspect presents a substantial bail risk if released and not all the evidence is available at the time when he or she must be released from custody unless charged.

5.2 In such cases, prosecutors may apply the Threshold Test in order to make a charging decision.

When the Threshold Test may be applied

5.3 The Threshold Test may only be applied where the prosecutor is satisfied that all the following four conditions are met:

a) there is insufficient evidence currently available to apply the evidential stage of the Full Code Test; and

b) there are reasonable grounds for believing that further evidence will become available within a reasonable period;and

c) the seriousness or the circumstances of the case justifies themaking of an immediate charging decision; and

d) there are continuing substantial grounds to object to bail inaccordance with the *Bail Act* 1976 and in all thecircumstances of the case an application to withhold bail may properly be made.

5.4 Where any of the above conditions is not met, the ThresholdTest cannot be applied and the suspect cannot be charged. Suchcases must be referred back to the custody officer who willdetermine whether the person may continue to be detained orreleased on bail, with or without conditions.

5.5 There are two parts to the evidential consideration of the Threshold Test.

The first part of the Threshold Test – is there reasonable suspicion?

5.6 First, the prosecutor must be satisfied that there is at least a reasonable suspicion that the person to be charged has committed the offence.

5.7 In determining whether reasonable suspicion exists, the prosecutor must consider the evidence which is currently available. This may take the form of witness statements, material or other information, provided the prosecutor is satisfied that:

a) it is relevant; and
b) it is capable of being put into an admissible format for presentation in court; and
c) it would be used in the case.

5.8 If this part of the Threshold Test is satisfied, the prosecutor should proceed to the second part of the Threshold Test.

The second part of the Threshold Test – will there be a realistic prospect of conviction?

5.9 Secondly, the prosecutor must be satisfied that there are reasonable grounds for believing that the continuing investigation will provide further evidence, within a reasonable period of time, so that all the evidence taken together is capable of establishing a realistic prospect of conviction in accordance with the Full Code Test.

5.10 The further evidence must be identifiable and not merely speculative.

5.11 In reaching a decision under this second part of the Threshold Test, the prosecutor must consider:

a) the nature, extent and admissibility of any likely further evidence and the impact it will have on the case;
b) the charges that all the evidence will support;
c) the reasons why the evidence is not already available;
d) the time required to obtain the further evidence and whether any consequential delay is reasonable in all the circumstances.

5.12 If both parts of the Threshold Test are satisfied, prosecutors must apply the public interest stage of the Full Code Test based onthe information available at that time.

Reviewing the Threshold Test

5.13 A decision to charge under the Threshold Test must be kept under review. The evidence must be regularly assessed to ensure that the charge is still appropriate and that continued objection to the granting of bail is justified. The Full Code Test must be applied as soon as is reasonably practicable and in any event before the expiry of any applicable custody time limit or extended custody time limit.

Selection of Charges

6.1 Prosecutors should select charges which: **E–9**

a) reflect the seriousness and extent of the offending supported by the evidence;
b) give the court adequate powers to sentence and impose appropriate post-conviction orders; and
c) enable the case to be presented in a clear and simple way.

6.2 This means that prosecutors may not always choose or continue with the most serious charge where there is a choice.

6.3 Prosecutors should never go ahead with more charges than are necessary just to encourage a defendant to plead guilty to a few. In the same way, they should never go ahead with a more serious charge just to encourage a defendant to plead guilty to a less serious one.

6.4 Prosecutors should not change the charge simply because of the decision made by the court or the defendant about where the case will be heard.

6.5 Prosecutors must take account of any relevant change in circumstances as the case progresses after charge.

Out-of-Court Disposals

7.1 The prosecution service is responsible for deciding whether to offer an offender a **E–10**
conditional caution in certain cases. In such cases, the Full Code Test must be met. Prosecutors will offer a conditional caution where it is a proportionate response to the seriousness and the consequences of the offending and where the conditions offered meet the aims of rehabilitation, reparation or punishment within the terms of the *Criminal Justice Act* 2003.

7.2 A conditional caution is not a criminal conviction but it forms part of the offender's criminal record and may be cited in court in any subsequent proceedings. It may also be taken into consideration by prosecutors if the offender re-offends. Prosecutors may offer a conditional caution where, having taken into account the views of the victim, they consider that it is in the interests of the suspect, victim or community to do so.

7.3 Prosecutors must follow the relevant Code of Practice and the DPP's Guidance on Conditional Cautioning when deciding whether to offer an offender a conditional caution.

7.4 The offer of a conditional caution which is accepted and complied with takes the place of a prosecution. If the offer of a conditional caution is refused or the suspect does not make the required admission of guilt to the person who seeks to administer the conditional caution, a prosecution must follow for the original offence. If the terms of the conditional caution are not complied with, the prosecutor will reconsider the public interest and decide whether to charge the offender. Usually, a prosecution should be brought for the original offence.

7.5 Only prosecutors can decide whether to authorise the offer of a simple caution to an offender for an offence that may only be heard in the Crown Court. The occasions when this will be an appropriate disposal will be exceptional.

7.6 In all other cases, prosecutors may direct that a simple caution be offered in accordance with CPS and Home Office Guidance, or suggest, for example, the issue of a Penalty Notice for Disorder. The issue of a Penalty Notice for Disorder is, however, a decision for the police.

7.7 Prosecutors must be satisfied that the Full Code Test is met and that there is a clear admission of guilt by the offender in any case in which they authorise or direct a simple caution to be offered by the police.

7.8 The acceptance of a simple caution or other out-of-court disposal which is complied with takes the place of a prosecution. If the offer of a simple caution is refused, a prosecution must follow for the original offence. If any other out-of-court disposal is not accepted, prosecutors will apply the Full Code Test, upon receipt of the case from the police or other investigators, and decide whether to prosecute the offender.

Youths

E–10a 8.1 For the purposes of the criminal law, a youth is a person under 18 years of age.

8.2 Prosecutors must bear in mind in all cases involving youths that the United Kingdom is a signatory to the United Nations 1989 Convention on the Rights of the Child and the United Nations 1985 Standard Minimum Rules for the Administration of Juvenile Justice. In addition, prosecutors must have regard to the principal aim of the youth justice system which is to prevent offending by children and young people. Prosecutors must consider the interests of the youth when deciding whether it is in the public interest to prosecute.

8.3 Prosecutors should not avoid a decision to prosecute simply because of the suspect's age. The seriousness of the offence or the youth's past behaviour is very important.

8.4 Cases involving youths are usually only referred to the prosecution service for prosecution if the youth has already received a reprimand and final warning, unless the offence is so serious that neither is appropriate or the child or young person does not admit committing the offence.

8.5 Reprimands, final warnings and conditional cautions (see section 7) are intended to prevent re-offending and the fact that a further offence has occurred may indicate that those previous disposals have not been effective. The public interest will usually require a prosecution in such cases.

Mode of Trial

E–11 9.1 Prosecutors must have regard to the current Magistrates' Court Sentencing Guidelines and the relevant Practice Direction when making submissions to the court about where the defendant should be tried.

E–12 9.2 Speed must never be the only reason for asking for a case to stay in the magistrates' courts. But prosecutors should consider the effect of any likely delay if a case is committed or sent to the Crown Court, and the possible effect on any victim or witness if the case is delayed.

Venue for trial in cases involving youths

E–12a 9.3 Generally, prosecutors must bear in mind that youths should be tried in the youth court, wherever possible. It is the court which is best designed to meet their specific needs. A trial of a youth in the Crown Court should be reserved for the most serious cases or where the interests of justice require a youth to be jointly tried with an adult.

Accepting Guilty Pleas

10.1 Defendants may want to plead guilty to some, but not all, of the charges. Alternatively, they may want to plead guilty to a different, possibly less serious, charge because they are admitting only part of the crime. **E–13**

10.2 Prosecutors should only accept the defendant's plea if they think the court is able to pass a sentence that matches the seriousness of the offending, particularly where there are aggravating features. Prosecutors must never accept a guilty plea just because it is convenient.

10.3 In considering whether the pleas offered are acceptable, prosecutors should ensure that the interests and, where possible, the views of the victim, or in appropriate cases the views of the victim's family, are taken into account when deciding whether it is in the public interest to accept the plea. However, the decision rests with the prosecutor.

10.4 It must be made clear to the court on what basis any plea is advanced and accepted. In cases where a defendant pleads guilty to the charges but on the basis of facts that are different from the prosecution case, and where this may significantly affect sentence, the court should be invited to hear evidence to determine what happened, and then sentence on that basis.

10.5 Where a defendant has previously indicated that he or she will ask the court to take an offence into consideration when sentencing, but then declines to admit that offence at court, prosecutors will consider whether a prosecution is required for that offence. Prosecutors should explain to the defence advocate and the court that the prosecution of that offence may be subject to further review.

10.6 Particular care must be taken when considering pleas which would enable the defendant to avoid the imposition of a mandatory minimum sentence. When pleas are offered, prosecutors also must bear in mind the fact that ancillary orders can be made with some offences but not with others.

10.7 Prosecutors must comply with the "Attorney General's Guidelines on the Acceptance of Pleas and the Prosecutor's Role in the Sentencing Exercise" which set out in greater detail the extent of prosecutors' duties and role in the acceptance of guilty pleas.

Appendices

The Prosecutor's Role in Sentencing

11.1 Sentencing is a decision for the court, but prosecutors have a duty to offer assistance to the sentencing court in reaching its decision as to the appropriate sentence by drawing the court's attention to the following factors: **E–14**

a) any aggravating or mitigating factors disclosed by the prosecution case;
b) any Victim Personal Statement;
c) where appropriate, evidence of the impact of the offending on a community;
d) any statutory provisions, sentencing guidelines, or guideline cases which may assist; and
e) any relevant statutory provisions relating to ancillary orders (such as anti-social behaviour orders).

11.2 Prosecutors may also offer assistance to the court by making submissions, in the light of all the above factors, as to the sentencing range within which the current offence falls.

11.3 In all complex cases or where there is the potential for misunderstanding, the prosecutor must set out in writing the aggravating and mitigating factors that he or she will outline when informing the court of the case in the sentencing hearing. In all other cases, this approach should be considered and undertaken if it will be of benefit to the court or the public to understand the case.

11.4 It is the duty of the prosecutor to apply for compensation and ancillary orders, such as anti-social behaviour orders and confiscation orders, in all appropriate cases. When considering which ancillary orders to apply for, the prosecutor must always have regard to the victim's needs, including the question of their future protection.

11.5 Prosecutors should challenge any assertion made by the defence in mitigation that is inaccurate, misleading or derogatory. If the defence persist in the assertion, and it appears relevant to the sentence, the court should be invited to hear evidence to determine the facts and sentence accordingly.

11.6 Prosecutors must comply with the "Attorney General's Guidelines on the Acceptance of Pleas and the Prosecutor's Role in the Sentencing Exercise" which set out in greater detail the extent of prosecutors' duties and role in the sentencing process.

Reconsidering a Prosecution Decision

E–14a 12.1 People should be able to rely on decisions taken by the prosecution service. Normally, if the prosecution service tells a suspect or defendant that there will not be a prosecution, or that the prosecution has been stopped, the case will not start again. But occasionally there are special reasons why the prosecution service will overturn a decision not to prosecute or to deal with the case by way of an out-of-court disposal or when it will restart the prosecution, particularly if the case is serious.

12.2 These reasons include:

a) rare cases where a new look at the original decision shows that it was wrong and, in order to maintain confidence in the criminal justice system, a prosecution should be brought despite the earlier decision;
b) cases which are stopped so that more evidence which is likely to become available in the fairly near future can be collected and prepared. In these cases, the prosecutor will tell the defendant that the prosecution may well start again;
c) cases which are stopped because of a lack of evidence but where more significant evidence is discovered later; and
d) cases involving a death in which a review following the findings of an inquest concludes that a prosecution should be brought, notwithstanding any earlier decision not to prosecute.

12.3 There may also be exceptional cases in which, following an acquittal of a serious offence, a prosecutor may, with the written consent of the DPP, apply to the Court of Appeal for an order quashing the acquittal and requiring the defendant to be retried.

E–15 This is a public document.

Further copies of this document and information about alternative languages and formats are available from:

CPS Communication Division

Rose Court

Southwark Bridge

London SE1 9HF

Email: publicity.branchcps.gsi.gov.uk

For information about the Crown Prosecution Service, and to view or download an electronic copy of this document, please visit our website: www.cps.gov.uk

CPS Policy Directorate

Appendix F

CONSOLIDATED CRIMINAL PRACTICE DIRECTION

In July 2002 Lord Woolf C.J. issued a consolidation (with some amendments) of existing practice directions, practice statements and practice notes as they affect proceedings in the Court of Appeal (Criminal Division), the Crown Court and the magistrates' courts: see Consolidated Criminal Practice Direction [2002] 2 Cr.App.R. 35. The consolidation has since been subject to various amendments (as to which, see *post*). **F–1**

The consolidation does not include the practice directions which relate to costs (for which, see Practice Direction (Costs in Criminal Proceedings) [2011] 1 Cr.App.R. 13 and it does not include the Attorney-General's guidelines. It is expressly "not a comprehensive statement of the practice and procedure of the criminal courts" and throughout the document words connoting the masculine include the feminine. It is divided into the following parts:

Part I	Directions of general application;
Part II	Further directions applying in the Court of Appeal (Criminal Division) (not reproduced in this appendix);
Part III	Further directions applying in the Crown Court and magistrates' courts;
Part IV	Further Directions applying in the Crown Court (not reproduced in this appendix);
Part V	Further directions applying in the magistrates' courts;
Annex A	List of practice directions, practice notes and practice statements included in the consolidation (in chronological order) (not reproduced in this appendix);
Annex B	List of practice directions, practice notes and practice statements not included in the consolidation, but no longer applicable in criminal proceedings (in chronological order) (not reproduced in this appendix)
Annex C	Explanations for the imposition of custodial sentences: forms of words (not reproduced in this appendix)
Annex D	*Criminal Procedure Rules*: list of forms and their related rule numbers (not reproduced in this appendix)
Annex E	The case management forms (Part 3of the *Criminal Procedure Rules*) (not reproduced in this appendix).

History of amendment

Since the consolidation, the practice direction has been amended by the following instruments: **F–1a**

- — Amendment No. 1 to the Consolidated Criminal Practice Direction (Support for Witnesses Giving Evidence by Live Television Link) (unreported).
- — Amendment No. 2 to the Consolidated Criminal Practice Direction (Appeals Against Sentence – the Provision of Notice to the Prosecution) (unreported).
- — Amendment No. 3 to the Consolidated Criminal Practice Direction (Bail: Failure to Surrender and Trials in Absence) [2004] 1 Cr.App.R. 28.
- — Amendment No. 4 to the Consolidated Criminal Practice Direction (Guidance to Jurors) [2004] 2 Cr.App.R. 1.
- — Amendment No. 5 to the Consolidated Criminal Practice Direction (Listing of Appeals against Conviction and Sentence in the Court of Appeal Criminal Division) [2004] 2 Cr.App.R. 2.

— Consolidated Criminal Practice Direction (Amendment No. 6) (Mandatory Life Sentences) [2004] 2 Cr.App.R. 24 (now removed).
— Amendment No. 7 to the Consolidated Criminal Practice Direction (Explanations for the Imposition of Custodial Sentences) [2004] 2 Cr.App.R. 25.
— Amendment No. 8 to the Consolidated Criminal Practice Direction (Mandatory Life Sentences) [2005] 1 Cr.App.R. 8.
— Amendment No. 9 to the Consolidated Criminal Practice Direction (Jury Service) [2005] 2 Cr.App.R. 16.
— Amendment No. 10 to the Consolidated Criminal Practice Direction (Forms for Use in Criminal Proceedings) [2005] 2 Cr.App.R. 17.
— Amendment No. 11 to the Consolidated Criminal Practice Direction (Case Management) [2005] 2 Cr.App.R. 18.
— Amendment No. 12 to the Consolidated Criminal Practice Direction (Classification and Allocation of Crown Court Business) [2005] 2 Cr.App.R. 33.
— Amendment No. 13 to the Consolidated Criminal Practice Direction (Forms for Use in Criminal Proceedings) [2006] 2 Cr.App.R. 22.
— Amendment No. 14 to the Consolidated Criminal Practice Direction (Forms for Use in Criminal Proceedings) [2007] 1 Cr. App. R. 22.
— Amendment No. 15 to the Consolidated Criminal Practice Direction (Treatment of Vulnerable Defendants; Settling the Indictment; Management of Cases to be Heard in the Crown Court; Forms for Use in Criminal Proceedings) [2007] 2 Cr.App.R. 20.
— Amendment No. 16 to the Consolidated Criminal Practice Direction (Forms for use in appeals to the Court of Appeal (Criminal Division)) [2008] 1 Cr.App.R. 15.
— Amendment No. 17 to the Consolidated Criminal Practice Direction (Arraignment in two stage trials) [2008] 1 Cr.App.R. 32.
— Practice Direction (Court Dress) (No. 4) [2008] 1 Cr.App.R. 31.
— Amendment No. 19 to the Consolidated Criminal Practice Direction (Part 50 forms of notice of intention to apply for certain behaviour orders if the defendant is convicted, and proposed application) [2008] 2 Cr.App.R. 16.
— Amendment No. 20 to the Consolidated Criminal Practice Direction (Court Dress) [2009] 1 Cr.App.R. 4.
— Amendment No. 21 to the Consolidated Criminal Practice Direction (Criminal Proceedings: Witness Anonymity Orders; Forms) [2009] 1 Cr.App.R. 5.
— Amendment No. 22 to the Consolidated Criminal Practice Direction (Criminal Proceedings: Victim Personal Statements; Pleas of Guilty in the Crown Court; Forms) [2009] 1 W.L.R. 1396.
— Amendment No. 23 to the Consolidated Criminal Practice Direction (Criminal Proceedings: Forms) [2009] 1 W.L.R. 2239.
— Consolidated Criminal Practice Direction (Amendment No. 24) (Criminal Proceedings: Witness Anonymity Orders (2); Forms) [2010] 2 Cr.App.R. 6
— Consolidated Criminal Practice Direction (Amendment No. 25) (Criminal Proceedings: Listing, Case Management) [2011] 1 Cr.App.R. 7.

This appendix sets out relevant extracts from the practice direction with all above amendments incorporated.

CONTENTS

F–2 **Part I: Directions Of General Application**

PART I: DIRECTIONS OF GENERAL APPLICATION

Part I: Directions of General Application

I.1. Court Dress

F–3 **I.1.1** In magistrates' courts, advocates appear without robes or wigs. In all other courts, Queen's Counsel wear a short wig and a silk (or stuff) gown over a court coat with bands, junior counsel wear a short wig and stuff gown with bands. Solicitors and other advocates authorised under the *Courts and Legal Services Act* 1990 wear a black stuff gown with bands; they may wear short wigs in circumstances where they would be worn by Queen's Counsel or junior counsel.

I.1.2 High Court Judges hearing criminal cases shall wear the winter criminal robe year-round. Scarlet summer robes are no longer issued or worn.

I.2. Unofficial Tape Recording of Proceedings

F–4 **I.2.1** Section 9 of the *Contempt of Court Act* 1981 contains provisions governing the unofficial use of tape recorders in court. Section 9(1) provides that it is a contempt of court (a) to use in court, or bring into court for use, any tape recorder or other instrument for recording sound, except with the leave of the Court; (b) to publish a recording of legal proceedings made by means of any such instrument, or any recording derived directly or indirectly from it, by playing it in the hearing of the public or any section of the public, or to dispose of it or any recording so derived, with a view to such publication; (c) to use any such recording in contravention of any conditions of leave granted under paragraph (a). These provisions do not apply to the making or use of sound recordings for purposes of official transcripts of the proceedings, upon which the Act imposes no restriction whatever.

I.2.2 The discretion given to the Court to grant, withhold or withdraw leave to use tape recorders or to impose conditions as to the use of the recording is unlimited, but the following factors may be relevant to its exercise: (a) the existence of any reasonable need on the part of the applicant for leave, whether a litigant or a person connected with the press or broadcasting, for the recording to be made; (b) the risk that the recording could be used for the purpose of briefing witnesses out of court; (c) any possibility that the use of the recorder would disturb the proceedings or distract or worry any witnesses or other participants.

I.2.3 Consideration should always be given whether conditions as to the use of a recording made pursuant to leave should be imposed. The identity and role of the applicant for leave and the nature of the subject matter of the proceedings may be relevant to this.

I.2.4 The particular restriction imposed by section 9(1)(b) applies in every case, but may not be present to the mind of every applicant to whom leave is given. It may therefore be desirable on occasion for this provision to be drawn to the attention of those to whom leave is given.

I.2.5 The transcript of a permitted recording is intended for the use of the person given leave to make it and is not intended to be used as, or to compete with, the official transcript mentioned in section 9(4).

I.3. Restrictions on Reporting Proceedings

F–5 **I.3.1** Under section 4(2) of the *Contempt of Court Act* 1981 a court may, where it appears necessary for avoiding a substantial risk of prejudice to the administration of justice in the proceedings before it or in any others pending or imminent, order that publication of any report of the proceedings or part thereof be postponed for such time as the court thinks necessary for that purpose. Section 11 of the Act provides that a court may prohibit the publication of any name or other matter in connection with the proceedings before it which it has allowed to be withheld from the public.

I.3.2 When considering whether to make such an order there is nothing which precludes the court from hearing a representative of the press. Indeed it is likely that the court will wish to do so.

I.3.3 It is necessary to keep a permanent record of such orders for later reference. For this purpose all orders made under section 4(2) must be formulated in precise terms having regard to the decision in *R v Horsham Justices ex parte Farquharson* [1982] Q.B. 762; 76 Cr.App.R. 87, and orders under both sections must be committed to writing either by the judge personally or by the clerk of the court under the judge's directions. An order must state (a) its precise scope, (b) the time at which it shall cease to have effect, if appropriate, and (c) the specific purpose of making the order. Courts will normally give notice to the press in some form that an order has been made under either section of theAct and the court staff should be prepared to answer any enquiry about a specific case, but it is, and will remain, the responsibility of those reporting cases, and their editors, to ensure that no breach of any orders occurs and the onus rests on them to make enquiry in any case of doubt.

I.4. Availability of Judgments given in the Court of Appeal and the High Court

I.4.1 Reference should be made to paragraph 9 of *Practice Direction (Court of Appeal-(Civil Division))* [1999]1 W.L.R. 1027; [1999] 2 All E.R. 490. **F–6**

I.5. Wards of Court

I.5.1 Where a child has been interviewed by the police in connection with contemplated criminal proceedings and the child subsequently becomes a ward of court, no leave of the wardship court is required for the child to be called as a witness in those proceedings. Where, however, the police desire to interview a child who is already a ward of court, application must, other than in the exceptional cases referred to in paragraph I.5.3, be made to the wardship court, on summons and on notice to all parties, for leave for the police to do so. Where, however, a party may become the subject of a criminal investigation and it is considered necessary for the ward to be interviewed without that party knowing that the police are making inquiries, the application for leave may be made *ex parte* to a judge without notice to that party. Notice, should, where practicable, be given to the reporting officer. **F–7**

I.5.2 Where leave is given the order should, unless some special reason requires the contrary, give leave for any number of interviews which may be required by the prosecution or the police. If it is desired to conduct any interview beyond what has been permitted by the order, a further application should be made.

I.5.3 The exceptional cases are those where the police need to deal with complaints or alleged offences concerning wards and it is appropriate, if not essential, for action to be taken straight away without the prior leave of the wardship court. Typical examples may be: (a) serious offences against the ward, such as rape, where medical examination and the collection of scientific evidence ought to be carried out promptly; (b) where the ward is suspected by the police of having committed a criminal act and the police wish to interview him about it; (c) where the police wish to interview the ward as a potential witness. The list is not exhaustive; there will inevitably be other instances where immediate action is appropriate. In such cases the police should notify the parent or foster parent with whom the ward is living or other "appropriate adult" within the Code of Practice for the Detention, Treatment and Questioning of Persons by Police Officers, so that that adult has the opportunity of being present when the police interview the child. Additionally, if practicable, the reporting officer (if one has been appointed) should be notified and invited to attend the police interview or to nominate a third party to attend on his behalf. A record of the interview or a copy of any statement made by the ward should be supplied to the reporting officer. Where the ward has been interviewed without the reporting officer's knowledge, he should be informed at the earliest opportunity. So too, if it be the case that the police wish to conduct further interviews. The wardship court should be appraised of the situation at the earliest possible opportunity thereafter by the reporting officer, the parent, foster parent (through the local authority) or other responsible adult.

I.5.4 No evidence or documents in the wardship proceedings or information about the proceedings should be disclosed in the criminal proceedings without leave of the wardship court.

I.6. Spent Convictions

I.6.1 The effect of section 4(1) of the *Rehabilitation of Offenders Act* 1974 is that a person who has become a rehabilitated person for the purpose of the Act in respect of a conviction (known as a "spent" conviction) shall be treated for all purposes in law as a person who has not committed or been charged with or prosecuted for or convicted of or sentenced for the offence or offences which were the subject of that conviction. **F–8**

I.6.2 Section 4(1) of the 1974 Act does not apply, however, to evidence given in criminal proceedings: section 7(2)(a). Convictions are often disclosed in such criminal proceedings. When the Bill was before the House of Commons on 28 June 1974 the hope was expressed that the Lord Chief Justice would issue a Practice Direction for the guidance of the Crown Court with a view to reducing disclosure of spent convictions to a minimum and securing uniformity of approach. The direction is set out in the following paragraphs. The same approach should be adopted in all courts of criminal jurisdiction.

I.6.3 During the trial of a criminal charge, reference to previous convictions (and therefore to spent convictions) can arise in a number of ways. The most common is when the character of the accused or a witness is sought to be attacked by reference to his criminal record, but there are, of course, cases where previous convictions are relevant and admissible as, for instance, to prove system.

Appendices

I.6.4 It is not possible to give general directions which will govern all these different situations, but it is recommended that both court and advocates should give effect to the general intention of Parliament by never referring to a spent conviction when such reference can reasonably be avoided.

I.6.5 After a verdict of guilty the court must be provided with a statement of the defendant's record for the purposes of sentence. The record supplied should contain all previous convictions, but those which are spent should, so far as practicable, be marked as such.

I.6.6 No one should refer in open court to a spent conviction without the authority of the judge, which authority should not be given unless the interests of justice so require.

I.6.7 When passing sentence the judge should make no reference to a spent conviction unless it is necessary to do so for the purpose of explaining the sentence to be passed.

I.7. Explanations for the Imposition of Custodial Sentences

F–9 **I.7.1** The practical effect of custodial sentences imposed by the courts is almost entirely governed by statutory provisions. Those statutory provisions, changed by Parliament from time to time, are not widely understood by the general public. It is desirable that when sentence is passed the practical effect of the sentence should be understood by the defendant, any victim and any member of the public who is present in court or reads a full report of the proceedings.

I.7.2 Whenever a custodial sentence is imposed on an offender the court should explain the practical effect of the sentence in addition to complying with existing statutory requirements. This will be no more than an explanation; the sentence will be that pronounced by the court.

I.7.3 Sentencers should give the explanation in terms of their own choosing, taking care to ensure that the explanation is clear and accurate. No form of words is prescribed. Annexed to this Practice Direction are short statements which may, adapted as necessary, be of value as models (see Annex C). These statements are based on the statutory provisions in force on 1 January 1998 and will, of course, require modification if those provisions are materially amended.

I.7.4 Sentencers will continue to give such explanation as they judge necessary of ancillary orders relating to matters such as disqualification, compensation, confiscation, costs and so on.

I.7.5 The power of the Secretary of State to release a prisoner early under supervision is not part of the sentence. The judge is therefore not required in his sentencing remarks to provide an explanation of this power. However, in explaining the effect of custodial sentences the judge should not say anything which conflicts with the existence of this power.

I.8. Words to be Used when Passing Sentence

F–10 **I.8.1** Where a court passes on a defendant more than one term of imprisonment the court should state in the presence of the defendant whether the terms are to be concurrent or consecutive. Should this not be done the court clerk should ask the court, before the defendant leaves court, to do so.

I.8.2 If a prisoner is, at the time of sentence, already serving two or more consecutive terms of imprisonment and the court intends to increase the total period of imprisonment, it should use the expression "consecutive to the total period of imprisonment to which you are already subject" rather than "at the expiration of the term of imprisonment you are now serving", lest the prisoner be not then serving the last of the terms to which he is already subject.

I.9. Substitution of Suspended Sentences for Immediate Custodial Sentences

F–11 **I.9.1** Where an appellate court substitutes a suspended sentence of imprisonment for one having immediate effect, the court should have in mind any period the appellant has spent in custody. If the court is of the opinion that it would be fair to do so, an approximate adjustment to the term of the suspended sentence should be made. Whether or not the court makes such adjustment, it should state that it had that period in mind. The court should further indicate that the operational period of suspension runs from the date the court passes the suspended sentence.

I.10. References to the European Court of Justice

I.10.1 These are the subject of Practice Direction: References to the European Court of Justice by the Court of Appeal and the High Court under Article 177 of the EC Treaty [1999] 1 WLR 260; [1999] 1 Cr.App.R. 452, to which reference should be made. **F–12**

I.11. Devolution Issues

I.11.1 These are the subject of Practice Direction: (Supreme Court) (Devolution Issues) [1999] 1WLR 1592; [1999] 3 All ER 466; [1999] 2 Cr App R 486, to which reference should be made. **F–13**

I.12. Preparation of Judgments: Neutral Citation

I.12.1 Since 11 January 2001 every judgment of the Court of Appeal, and of the Administrative Court, and since 14 January 2002 every judgment of the High Court, has been prepared and issued as approved with single spacing, paragraph numbering (in the margins) and no page numbers. In courts with more than one judge the paragraph numbering continues sequentially through each judgment and does not start again at the beginning of each judgment. Indented paragraphs are not numbered. A unique reference number is given to each judgment. For judgments of the Court of Appeal this number is given by the official shorthand writers. For judgments of the High Court it is provided by the Mechanical Recording Department at the Royal Courts of Justice. Such a number will also be furnished, on request to the Mechanical Recording Department, Royal Courts of Justice, Strand, London WC2A 2LL (Tel: 020 7947 7771), to High Court judgments delivered outside London. **F–14**

I.12.2 Each Court of Appeal judgment starts with the year, followed by EW (for England and Wales), then CA (for Court of Appeal), followed by Civ or Crim and finally the sequential number. For example *Smith v Jones* [2001] EWCA Civ 10.

I.12.3 In the High Court, represented by HC, the number comes before the divisional abbreviation and, unlike Court of Appeal judgments, the latter is bracketed: (Ch), (Pat), (QB), (Admin), (Comm), (Admlty), (TCC) or (Fam) as appropriate. For example, [2002] EWHC 123 (Fam) or [2002] EWHC 124 (QB) or [2002] EWHC 125 (Ch).

I.12.4 This "neutral citation", as it is called, is the official number attributed to the judgment and must always be used at least once when the judgment is cited in a later judgment. Once the judgment is reported this neutral citation appears in front of the familiar citation from the law reports series. Thus: *Smith v Jones* [2001] EWCA 10; [2001] Q.B. 124; [2001] 2 All E.R. 364, *etc*.

I.12.5 Paragraph numbers are referred to in square brackets. When citing a paragraph from a High Court judgment it is unnecessary to include the descriptive word in brackets: (Admin), (QB) or whatever. When citing a paragraph from a Court of Appeal judgment, however, Civ or Crim is included. If it is desired to cite more than one paragraph of a judgment each numbered paragraph should be enclosed with a square bracket. Thus paragraph 59 in *Green v White* [2002] EWHC 124 (QB) would be cited: *Green v White* [2002] EWHC 124 at [59]; paragraphs 30–35 in *Smith v Jones* would be *Smith v Jones* [2001] EWCA Civ 10 at [30]–[35]; similarly, where a number of paragraphs are cited: *Smith v Jones* [2001] EWCA Civ 10 at [30], [35] and [40–43].

I.12.6 If a judgment is cited more than once in a later judgment it is helpful if only one abbreviation is used, *e.g. Smith v Jones* or Smith's case, but preferably not both (in the same judgment.)

I.13 Bail: Failure to Surrender to Suurender and Trials in Absence

I.13.1 The following directions take effect immediately. **F–15**

I.13.2 The failure of the defendants to comply with the terms of their bail by not surrendering can undermine the administration of justice. It can disrupt proceedings. The resulting delays impact on victims, witnesses and other court users and also waste costs. A defendant's failure to surrender affects not only the case with which he is concerned, but also the courts' ability to administer justice more generally by damaging the confidence of victims, witnesses and the public in the effectiveness of the court system and the judiciary. It is, therefore most important that defendants who are granted bail appreciate the significance of the obligation to surrender to custody in accordance with the terms of their bail and that courts take appropriate action if they fail to do so.

I.13.3 There are at least three courses of action for the courts to consider taking:—

(a) imposing penalties for the failure to surrender;

(b) revoking bail or imposing more stringent bail conditions; and

(c) conducting trials in the absence of the defendant.

Penalties for Failure to Surrender

F–16 **I.13.4** A defendant who commits a section 6(1) or section 6(2) *Bail Act* 1976 offence commits an offence that stands apart from the proceedings in respect of which bail was granted. The seriousness of the offence can be reflected by an appropriate penalty being imposed for the *Bail Act* offence.

I.13.5 The common practice at present of courts automatically deferring disposal of a section 6(1) or section 6(2) *Bail Act* 1976 offence (failure to surrender) until the conclusion of the proceedings in respect of which bail was granted should no longer be followed. Instead, courts should now deal with defendants as soon as is practicable. In deciding what is practicable, the Court must take into account when the proceedings in respect of which bail was granted are expected to conclude, the seriousness of the offence for which the defendant is already being prosecuted, the type of penalty that might be imposed for the breach of bail and the original offence as well as any other relevant circumstances. If there is no good reason for postponing dealing with the breach until after the trial, the breach should be dealt with as soon as practicable. If the disposal of the breach of bail is deferred, then it is still necessary to consider imposing a separate penalty at the trial and the sentence for the breach of the bail should usually be custodial and consecutive to any other custodial sentence (as to which see I.13.13). In addition, bail should usually be revoked in the meantime (see I.13.14 to 16). In the case of offences which cannot, or are unlikely to, result in a custodial sentence, trial in the absence of the defendant may be a pragmatic sensible response to the situation (see I.13.17 to I.13.19). This is not a penalty for the *Bail Act* offence and a penalty may also be imposed for the *Bail Act* offence.

Initiating Proceedings—Bail granted by a police officer

I.13.6 When a person has been granted bail by a police officer to attend court and subsequently fails to surrender to custody, the decision whether to initiate proceedings for a section 6(1) or section 6(2) offence will be for the police/prosecutor.

I.13.7 The offence in this form is a summary offence and should be initiated as soon as practicable after the offence arises in view of the six month time limit running from the failure to surrender. It should be dealt with on the first appearance after arrest, unless an adjournment is necessary, as it will be relevant in considering whether to grant bail again.

Initiating Proceedings—Bail granted by a court

I.13.8 When a person has been granted bail by a court and subsequently fails to surrender to custody, on arrest that person should normally be brought as soon as appropriate before the court at which the proceedings in respect of which bail was granted are to be heard. (The six months time limit does not apply where bail was granted by the court). Should the defendant commit another offence outside the jurisdiction of the bail court, the *Bail Act* offence should, where practicable, be dealt with by the new court at the same time as the new offence. If impracticable, the defendant may, if this is appropriate, be released formally on bail by the new court so that the warrant may be executed for his attendance before the first court in respect of the substantive and *Bail Act* offences.

I.13.9 Given that bail was granted by a court, it is more appropriate that the court itself should initiate the proceedings by its own motion. The court will be invited to take proceedings by the prosecutor, if the prosecutor considers proceedings are appropriate.

Conduct of Proceedings

I.13.10 Proceedings under section 6 *Bail Act* 1976 may be conducted either as a summary offence or as a criminal contempt of court. Where the court is invited to take proceedings by the prosecutor, the prosecutor will conduct the proceedings and, if the matter is contested, call the evidence. Where the court initiates proceedings without such an invitation the same role can be played by the prosecutor at the request of the court, where this is practicable.

I.13.11 The burden of proof is on the defendant to prove that he had reasonable cause for his failure to surrender to custody (section 6(3) of the *Bail Act* 1976).

Proceedings to be progressed to disposal as soon as is practicable

I.13.12 If the court decides to proceed, the section 6 *Bail Act* offence should be concluded as soon as practicable.

Sentencing for a Bail Act offence

I.13.13 In principle, a custodial sentence for the offence of failing to surrender should be ordered to be served consecutively to any other sentence imposed at the same time for another offence unless there are circumstances that make this inappropriate (see White & McKinnon).

Relationship between the Bail Act Offence and Further Remands on Bail or in Custody.

I.13.14 When a defendant has been convicted of a *Bail Act* offence, the court should review the remand status of the defendant, including the conditions of that bail, in respect of the main proceedings for which bail had been granted. **F-17**

I.13.15 Failure by the defendant to surrender or a conviction for failing to surrender to bail in connection with the main proceedings will be significant factors weighing against the re-granting of bail or, in the case of offences which do not normally give rise to a custodial sentence, in favour of trial in the absence of the offender.

I.13.16 Whether or not an immediate custodial sentence has been imposed for the *Bail Act* offence, the court may, having reviewed the defendant's remand status, also remand the defendant in custody in the main proceedings.

Trials in Absence

I.13.17 A defendant has a right, in general, to be present and to be represented at his trial. However, a defendant may choose not to exercise those rights by voluntarily absenting himself and failing to instruct his lawyers adequately so that they can represent him and, in the case of proceedings before the magistrates' court, there is an express statutory power to hear trials in the defendant's absence (s.11 of the *Magistrates' Courts Act* 1980). In such circumstances, the court has discretion whether the trial should take place in his/her absence. **F-18**

I.13.18 The court must exercise its discretion to proceed in the absence of the defendant with the utmost care and caution. The overriding concern must be to ensure that such a trial is as fair as circumstances permit and leads to a just outcome.

I.13.19 Due regard should be had to the judgment of Lord Bingham in *R v. Jones* [2003] A.C. 1, [2002] 2 All E.R. 113 in which Lord Bingham identified circumstances to be taken into account before proceeding, which include: the conduct of the defendant, the disadvantage to the defendant, public interest, the effect of any delay and whether the attendance of the defendant could be secured at a later hearing. Other relevant considerations are the seriousness of the offence and likely outcome if the defendant is found guilty. If the defendant is only likely to be fined for a summary offence this can be relevant since the costs that a defendant might otherwise be ordered to pay as a result of an adjournment could be disproportionate. In the case of summary proceedings the fact that there can be an appeal that is a complete rehearing is also relevant, as is the power to re-open the case under s142 of the *Magistrates' Court Act* 1980.

PART III: FURTHER DIRECTIONS APPLYING IN THE CROWN COURT AND MAGISTRATES' COURTS

PART III: FURTHER DIRECTIONS APPLYING IN THE CROWN COURT AND MAGISTRATES' COURTS

I.14 Forms

I.14.1 This Practice Direction supplements Part 5 (forms) of the *Criminal Procedure Rules*. **F-19**

I.14.2 The forms set out in Annex D, or forms to that effect, are to be used in the criminal courts on or after 4th April, 2005, when the *Criminal Procedure Rules* come into force. Almost all are identical to those in use before that date, and accordingly a form in use before that date which corresponds with one set out in Annex D may still be used in connection with the rule to which it applies.

I.14.3 The table at the beginning of Annex D lists the forms set out in that Annex and—

— shows the rule in connection with which each form applies

— describes each form

- in the case of a form in use before the *Criminal Procedure Rules* came into force, shows the legislation by which the form was prescribed and by what number (if any) it was known.

I.15 Witness Anonymity Orders

F-20 **I.15.1** Pending the making by the Criminal Procedure Rule Committee of specific rules for the purpose, this direction sets out the procedure to be followed on an application for a witness anonymity order. The court's power to make such an order is conferred by the *Criminal Evidence (Witness Anonymity) Act* 2008 (in this direction, 'the Act'). The court's power to give case management directions is conferred by Part 3 of the *Criminal Procedure Rules*. Section 3 of the Act provides specific relevant powers and obligations.

Case management

I.15.2 Where such an application is proposed, with the parties' active assistance the court should set a realistic timetable, in accordance with the duties imposed by rules 3.2 and 3.3. Where possible, the trial judge should determine the application, and any hearing should be attended by the parties' trial advocates.

Service of evidence and disclosure of prosecution material pending an application

I.15.3 Where the prosecutor proposes an application for a witness anonymity order it is not necessary for that application to have been determined before the proposed evidence is served. In most cases an early indication of what that evidence will be if an order is made will be consistent with a party's duties under rules 1.2 and 3.3. The prosecutor should serve with the other prosecution evidence a witness statement setting out the proposed evidence, redacted in such a way as to prevent disclosure of the witness' identity, as permitted by section 3(4) of the Act. Likewise the prosecutor should serve with other prosecution material disclosed under the *Criminal Procedure and Investigations Act* 1996 any such material appertaining to the witness, similarly redacted.

The application

F-21 **I.15.4** An application for a witness anonymity order should be made as early as possible and within the period for which rule 29.3 provides. The application must comply with the requirements of that rule and with those of rule 29.19. In accordance with rules 1.2 and 3.3, the applicant must provide the court with all available information relevant to the considerations to which the Act requires a court to have regard.

I.15.5 The application (to be served on all parties and on the court) must comply with rule 29.19(1).

I.15.6 Other, confidential, information that supports the application, including the identity of the witness, must be presented separately to the court in accordance with rule 29.19(2).

I.15.7 Such information will be received by the court in accordance with rule 29.19(3).

Response to the application

F-22 **I.15.8** A party upon whom an application for a witness anonymity order is served must serve a response on the other parties and on the court within 14 days: rule 29.22. That period may be extended or shortened in the court's discretion: rule 29.5.

I.15.9 To avoid the risk of injustice a respondent must actively assist the court. If not already done, a respondent defendant should serve a defence statement under section 5 or 6 of the *Criminal Procedure and Investigations Act* 1996, so that the court is fully informed of what is in issue. The prosecutor's continuing duty to disclose material under section 7A of the *Criminal Procedure and Investigations Act* 1996 may be engaged by a defendant's application for a witness anonymity order. Therefore a prosecutor's response should include confirmation that that duty has been considered. Nothing disclosed under the 1996 Act by a respondent prosecutor to a respondent defendant should contain anything that might reveal the witness' identity. A respondent prosecutor must provide an applicant defendant and the court with all available information relevant to the considerations to which the Act requires a court to have regard, whether or not that information falls to be disclosed under the 1996 Act: r.29.22(6).

Determination of the application

F-23 **I.15.10** All parties must have an opportunity to make oral representations to the court on an application for a witness anonymity order: section 87(6) of the Act. However, a hearing may not be needed if none is sought: r.29.18(1)(a). Where, for example, the witness is an investigator who is recognisable by the defendant but known only by an assumed name, and there is no likelihood that the witness' credibility will be in issue, then the court may indicate a provisional decision and invite representations within a defined period, usually 14 days, including representations about whether there should be a hearing. In such a case, where the parties do not object the court may make an order without a hearing. Or where the court provisionally considers an application to be misconceived, an applicant may choose to withdraw it without requiring a hearing. Where the court directs a hearing of the application then it should allow adequate time for service of the representations in response.

I.15.11 The hearing of an application for a witness anonymity order usually should be in private: r.29.18(1)(a). The court has power to hear a party in the absence of a defendant and that defendant's representatives: section 87(7) of the Act and r.29.18(1)(b). In the Crown Court, a recording of the proceedings will be made, in accordance with r.65.8(2). The Crown Court officer must treat such a recording in the same way as the recording of an application for a public interest ruling. It must be kept in secure conditions, and the arrangements made by the Crown Court officer for any transcription must impose restrictions that correspond with those under r.65.9(2)(a).

I.15.12 At a hearing the court will proceed in accordance with r.29.19(3).

I.15.13 Where confidential supporting information is presented to the court before the last stage of the hearing, the court may prefer not to read that information until that last stage.

I.15.14 The court may adjourn the hearing at any stage, and should do so if its duty under r.3.2 so requires.

I.15.15 On a prosecutor's application, the court is likely to be assisted by the attendance of a senior investigator or other person of comparable authority who is familiar with the case.

I.15.16 During the last stage of the hearing it is essential that the court test thoroughly the information supplied in confidence in order to satisfy itself that the conditions prescribed by the Act are met. At that stage, if the court concludes that this is the only way in which it can satisfy itself as to a relevant condition or consideration, exceptionally it may invite the applicant to present the proposed witness to be questioned by the court. Any such questioning should be carried out at such a time, and the witness brought to the court in such a way, as to prevent disclosure of his or her identity.

I.15.7 The court may ask the Attorney General to appoint special counsel to assist. However, it must be kept in mind that, 'Such an appointment will always be exceptional, never automatic; a course of last and never first resort. It should not be ordered unless and until the trial judge is satisfied that no other course will adequately meet the overriding requirement of fairness to the defendant': *R. v. H* [2004] 2 A.C. 134, at [22]. Whether to accede to such a request is a matter for the Attorney General, and adequate time should be allowed for the consideration of such a request.

I.15.18 Following a hearing the court should announce its decision on an application for a witness anonymity order in the parties' presence and in public: r.29.4(2). The court should give such reasons as it is possible to give without revealing the witness' identity. In the Crown Court, the court will be conscious that reasons given in public may be reported and reach the jury. Consequently, the court should ensure that nothing in its decision or its reasons could undermine any warning it may give jurors under section 90(2) of the Act. A record of the reasons must be kept. In the Crown Court, the announcement of those reasons will be recorded.

Order

I.15.19 Where the court makes a witness anonymity order it is essential that the measures to be taken are clearly specified in a written record of that order approved by the court and issued on its behalf. An order made in a magistrates' court must be recorded in the court register, in accordance with rule 5.4. **F–23a**

I.15.20 Self-evidently, the written record of the order must not disclose the identity of the witness to whom it applies. However, it is essential that there be maintained some means of establishing a clear correlation between witness and order, and especially where in the same proceedings witness anonymity orders are made in respect of more than one witness, specifying different measures in respect of each. Careful preservation of the application for the order, including any confidential information presented to the court, ordinarily will suffice for this purpose.

Discharge or variation of the order

F–23b **I.15.21** Section 91 of the Act allows the court to discharge or vary a witness anonymity order: on application, if there has been a material change of circumstances since the order was made or since any previous variation of it; or on its own initiative. Rule 29.21 allows the parties to apply for the variation of a pre-trial direction where circumstances have changed.

I.15.22 The court should keep under review the question of whether the conditions for making an order are met. In addition, consistently with the parties' duties under rr.1.2 and 3.3, it is incumbent on each, and in particular on the applicant for the order, to keep the need for it under review.

I.15.23 Where the court considers the discharge or variation of an order, the procedure that it adopts should be appropriate to the circumstances. As a general rule, that procedure should approximate to the procedure for determining an application for an order. The court may need to hear further representations by the applicant for the order in the absence of a respondent defendant and that defendant's representatives.

Retention of confidential material

F–23c **I.15.24** If retained by the court, confidential material must be stored in secure conditions by the court officer. Alternatively, subject to such directions as the court may give, such material may be committed to the safe keeping of the applicant or any other appropriate person in exercise of the powers conferred by r.29.6. If the material is released to any such person, the court should ensure that it will be available to the court at trial.

III.21 Classification of Crown Court Business and Allocation to Crown Court Centres

Classification

F–23d **III.21.1 For the purposes of trial in the Crown Court offences are classified as follows:** Class 1:

(a) Misprision of treason and treason felony;
(b) Murder;
(c) Genocide;
(d) Torture, hostage-taking and offences under the *War Crimes Act* 1991;
(e) An offence under the *Official Secrets Acts*;
(f) Manslaughter;
(g) Infanticide;
(h) Child destruction;
(i) Abortion (section 58 of the *Offences against the Person Act* 1861);
(j) Sedition;
(k) An offence under section 1 of the *Geneva Conventions Act* 1957;
(l) Mutiny;
(m) Piracy;
(n) Soliciting, incitement, attempt or conspiracy to commit any of the above offences.

Class 2:

(a) Rape;
(b) Sexual intercourse with a girl under 13;
(c) Incest with girl under 13;
(d) Assault by penetration;
(e) Causing a person to engage in sexual activity, where penetration is involved;
(f) Rape of a child under 13;
(g) Assault of a child under 13 by penetration;
(h) Causing or inciting a child under 13 to engage in sexual activity, where penetration is involved;
(i) Sexual activity with a person with a mental disorder, where penetration is involved;
(j) Inducement to procure sexual activity with a mentally disordered person where penetration is involved;

(k) Paying for sexual services of a child where child is under 13 and penetration is involved;
(l) Committing an offence with intent to commit a sexual offence, where the offence is kidnapping or false imprisonment;
(m) Soliciting, incitement, attempt or conspiracy to commit any of the above offences.

Class 3:
All other offences not listed in classes 1 or 2.

Cases committed, transferred or sent for trial

III.21.2 The magistrates' court, upon either committing a person for trial under section 6 of the *Magistrates' Courts Act* 1980, or sending a person under section 51 of the *Crime and Disorder Act* 1998, shall: **F–23e**

(a) if the offence or any of the offences is included in Class 1, specify the most convenient location of the Crown Court where a High Court Judge, or, where a Circuit Judge duly authorised by the Lord Chief Justice to try class 1 cases, regularly sits.
(b) if the offence or any of the offences is included in Class 2, specify the most convenient location of the Crown Court where a Judge duly authorised to try Class 2 regularly sits. These courts on each Circuit will be identified by the Presiding Judges, with the concurrence of the Lord Chief Justice.
(c) where an offence is in Class 3 the magistrates' court shall specify the most convenient location of the Crown Court.

Where a case is transferred under section 4 of the *Criminal Justice Act* 1987 or section 53 of the *Criminal Justice Act* 1991, the authority shall, in specifying the proposed place of trial in the notice of transfer, comply with the provisions of this paragraph.

III.21.3 In selecting the most convenient location of the Crown Court the justices shall have regard to the considerations referred to in section 7 of the *Magistrates' Courts Act* 1980 and section 51(10) of the *Crime and Disorder Act* 1998 and the location or locations of the Crown Court designated by a Presiding Judge as the location to which cases should normally be committed from their court.

III.21.4 Where on one occasion a person is committed in respect of a number of offences all the committals shall be to the same location of the Crown Court and that location shall be the one where a High Court Judge regularly sits if such a location is appropriate for any of the offences.

Committals following breach

III.21.5 Where, in the Crown Court, a community order or an order for conditional discharge has been made, or a suspended sentence has been passed, and the offender is subsequently found or alleged to be in breach before a magistrates' court which decides to commit the offender to the Crown Court, he shall be committed in accordance with paragraphs III.21.6, III.21.7 or III.21.8. **F–23f**

III.21.6 He shall be committed to the location of the Crown Court where the order was made or the suspended sentence was passed, unless it is inconvenient, impracticable or inappropriate to do so in all the circumstances.

III.21.7 If, for whatever reason, he is not so committed and the order was made or sentence passed by a High Court Judge, he shall be committed to the most convenient location of the Crown Court where a High Court Judge regularly sits.

III.21.8 In all other cases he shall be committed to the most convenient location of the Crown Court.

III.21.9 In selecting the most convenient location of the Crown Court, the justices shall have regard to the locations of the Crown Court designated by a Presiding Judge as the locations to which cases should normally be committed from their court.

Notice of transfer in cases of serious or complex fraud

III.21.10 Where a notice of transfer is served under section 4 of the *Criminal Justice Act* 1987 the proposed place of trial to be specified in the notice shall be one of the Crown Court centres designated by the Senior Presiding Judge. **F–23g**

Notice of transfer in child witness cases

Appendices

F–23h **III.21.11** Where a notice of transfer is served under section 53 of the *Criminal Justice Act* 1991 (child witness cases) the proposed place of trial to be specified in accordance with paragraph 1(1) of Schedule 6 to the Act shall be a Crown Court centre which is equipped with live television link facilities.

III.22 Applications for Evidence to be given in Welsh

F–24 **III.22.1** If a defendant in a court in England asks to give or call evidence in the Welsh language the case should not be transferred to Wales. In ordinary circumstances interpreters can be provided on request.

III.23 Use of the Welsh Language in Courts in Wales

F–25 **III.23.1** The purpose of this direction is to reflect the principle of the *Welsh Language Act* 1993 that in the administration of justice in Wales the English and Welsh languages should be treated on a basis of equality.

General

F–26 **III.23.2** It is the responsibility of the legal representatives in every case in which the Welsh language may be used by any witness or party or in any document which may be placed before the court to inform the court of that fact so that appropriate arrangements can be made for the listing of the case.

III.23.3 If the possible use of the Welsh language is known at the time of committal, transfer or appeal to the Crown Court, the court should be informed immediately after committal or transfer or when the notice of appeal is lodged. Otherwise the court should be informed as soon as possible use of the Welsh language becomes known.

III.23.4 If costs are incurred as a result of failure to comply with these directions, a wasted costs order may be made against the defaulting party and/or his legal representatives.

III.23.5 The law does not permit the selection of jurors in a manner which enables the court to discover whether a juror does or does not speak Welsh or to secure a jury whose members are bilingual to try a case in which the Welsh language may be used.

Plea and directions hearings

F–27 **III.23.6** An advocate in a case in which the Welsh language may be used must raise that matter at the plea and directions hearing and endorse details of it on the judge's questionnaire so that appropriate directions may be given for the progress of the case.

Listing

F–28 **III.23.7** The listing officer, in consultation with the resident judge, should ensure that a case in which the Welsh language may be used is listed (a) wherever practicable before a Welsh speaking judge, and (b) in a court in Wales with simultaneous translation facilities.

Interpreters

F–29 **III.23.8** Whenever an interpreter is needed to translate evidence from English into Welsh or from Welsh into English, the court manager in whose court the case is to be heard shall ensure that the attendance is secured of an interpreter whose name is included in the list of approved court interpreters.

Jurors

F–30 **III.23.9** The jury bailiff when addressing the jurors at the start of their period of jury service shall inform them that each juror may take an oath or affirm in Welsh or English as he wishes.

III.23.10 After the jury has been selected to try a case, and before it is sworn, the court officer swearing in the jury shall inform the jurors in open court that each juror may take an oath or affirm in Welsh or English as he wishes.

Witnesses

F–31 **III.23.11** When each witness is called the court officer administering the oath or affirmation shall inform the witness that he may be sworn or affirm Welsh or English as he wishes.

Opening/closing of courts

III.23.12 Unless it is not reasonably practicable to do so, the opening and closing of the court should be performed in Welsh and English. **F-32**

Role of liaison judge

III.23.13 If any question or problem arises concerning the implementation of paragraphs III.23.1–III.23.12, contact should in the first place be made with the liaison judge for Welsh language matters on circuit. **F-33**

III.24 Evidence by Written Statement

III.24.1 Where the prosecution proposes to tender written statements in evidence either under sections 5A and 5B of the *Magistrates' Courts Act* 1980 or section 9 of the *Criminal Justice Act* 1967 it will frequently be not only proper, but also necessary for the orderly presentation of the evidence, for certain statements to be edited. This will occur either because a witness has made more than one statement whose contents should conveniently be reduced into a single, comprehensive statement or where a statement contains inadmissible, prejudicial or irrelevant material. Editing of statements should in all circumstances be done by a Crown Prosecutor (or by a legal representative, if any, of the prosecutor if the case is not being conducted by the Crown Prosecution Service) and not by a police officer. **F-34**

Composite statements

III.24.2 A composite statement giving the combined effect of two or more earlier statements or settled by a person referred to in paragraph III.24.1 must be prepared in compliance with the requirements of sections 5A and 5B of the 1980 Act or section 9 of the 1967 Act as appropriate and must then be signed by the witness. **F-35**

Editing single statements

III.24.3 There are two acceptable methods of editing single statements. **F-36**

a. By marking *copies* of the statement in a way which indicates the passages on which the prosecution will not rely. This merely indicates that the prosecution will not seek to adduce the evidence so marked. The *original signed statement* to be tendered to the court is not marked in any way. The marking on the copy statement is done by lightly striking out the passages to be edited so that what appears beneath can still be read, or by bracketing, or by a combination of both. It is not permissible to produce a photocopy with the deleted material obliterated, since this would be contrary to the requirement that the defence and the court should be served with copies of the signed original statement. Whenever the striking out/bracketing method is used, it will assist if the following words appear at the foot of the frontispiece or index to any bundle of copy statements to be tendered:

'The prosecution does not propose to adduce evidence of those passages of the attached copy statements which have been struck out 30 and/or bracketed (nor will it seek to do so at the trial unless a notice of further evidence is served).'

b. By obtaining a fresh statement, signed by the witness, which omits the offending material, applying the procedure in paragraph III.24.2.

III.24.4 In most cases where a single statement is to be edited, the striking out/bracketing method will be the more appropriate, but the taking of a fresh statement is preferable in the following circumstances:

a. When a police (or other investigating) officer's statement contains details of interviews with more suspects than are eventually charged, a fresh statement should be prepared and signed omitting all details of interview with those not charged except, insofar as it is relevant, for the bald fact that a certain named person was interviewed at a particular time, date and place.

b. When a suspect is interviewed about more offences than are eventually made the subject of committal charges, a fresh statement should be prepared and signed omitting all questions and answers about the uncharged offences unless either they might appropriately be taken into consideration or evidence about those offences is admissible on the charges preferred, such as evidence of system. It may, however, be desirable to replace the omitted questions and answers with a phrase such as:

Appendices

"After referring to some other matters, I then said ... ", so as to make it clear that part of the interview has been omitted.

c. A fresh statement should normally be prepared and signed if the only part of the original on which the prosecution is relying is only a small proportion of the whole, although it remains desirable to use the alternative method if there is reason to believe that the defence might itself wish to rely, in mitigation or for any other purpose, on at least some of those parts which the prosecution does not propose to adduce.

d. When the passages contain material which the prosecution is entitled to withhold from disclosure to the defence.

III.24.5 Prosecutors should also be aware that, where statements are to be tendered under section 9 of the 1967 Act in the course of *summary* proceedings, there will be a need to prepare fresh statements excluding inadmissible or prejudicial material rather than using the striking out or bracketing method.

III.24.6 None of the above principles applies, in respect of committal proceedings, to documents which are exhibited (including statements under caution and signed contemporaneous notes). Nor do they apply to oral statements of a defendant which are recorded in the witness statements of interviewing police officers, except in the circumstances referred to in paragraph III.24.4(b). All this material should remain in its original state in the committal bundles, any editing being left to prosecuting counsel at the Crown Court (after discussion with defence counsel and, if appropriate, the trial judge).

III.24.7 Whenever a fresh statement is taken from a witness, a copy of the earlier, unedited statement(s) of that witness will be given to the defence in accordance with the Attorney General's guidelines on the disclosure of unused material (*Practice Note* [1982] 1 All E.R. 734) unless there are grounds under paragraph 6 of the guidelines for withholding such disclosure.

III.25 Bail During Trial

F–37 **III.25.1** Paragraphs III.25.2 to III.25.5 are to be read subject to the *Bail Act* 1976, especially section 4.

III.25.2 Once a trial has begun the further grant of bail, whether during the short adjournment or overnight, is in the discretion of the trial judge. It may be a proper exercise of this discretion to refuse bail during the short adjournment if the accused cannot otherwise be segregated from witnesses and jurors.

III.25.3 An accused who was on bail while on remand should not be refused overnight bail during the trial unless in the opinion of the judge there are positive reasons to justify this refusal. Such reasons are likely to be:

(a) that a point has been reached where there is a real danger that the accused will abscond, either because the case is going badly for him, or for any other reason;

(b) that there is a real danger that he may interfere with witnesses or jurors.

III.25.4 There is no universal rule of practice that bail shall not be renewed when the summing-up has begun. Each case must be decided in the light of its own circumstances and having regard to the judge's assessment from time to time of the risks involved.

III.25.5 Once the jury has returned a verdict a further renewal of bail should be decided in the light of the gravity of the offence and the likely sentence to be passed in all the circumstances of the case.

III.26 Facts to be Stated on Pleas of Guilty

F–38 **III.26.1** To enable the press and the public to know the circumstances of an offence of which an accused has been convicted and for which he is to be sentenced, in relation to each offence to which an accused has pleaded guilty the prosecution shall state those facts in open court before sentence is imposed.

III.27 Antecedents

Standard for the provision of information of antecedents in the Crown Court and magistrates' courts

F–39 **III.27.1** In the Crown Court the police will provide brief details of the circumstances of the last three similar convictions and/or of convictions likely to be of interest to the court, the latter being judged on a case by case basis. This information should be provided separately and attached to the antecedents as set out below.

III.27.2 Where the current alleged offence could constitute a breach of an existing community order, *e.g.* community rehabilitation order, and it is known that that order is still in force then, to enable the court to consider the possibility of revoking that order, details of the circumstances of the offence leading to the community order should be included in the antecedents as set out below.

Preparation of antecedents and standard formats to be used

III.27.3 In magistrates' courts and the Crown Court: **F–40**

Personal details and summary of convictions and cautions—Police National Computer ["PNC"] Court/Defence/Probation Summary Sheet;
Previous convictions—PNC Court/Defence/Probation printout, supplemented by Form MG16 if the police force holds convictions not shown on PNC;
Recorded cautions—PNC Court/Defence/Probation printout, supplemented by Form MG17 if the police force holds cautions not shown on PNC.
And, in addition, in the Crown Court:
Circumstances of the last three similar convictions;
Circumstances of offence leading to a community order still in force;
Form MG(c). The detail should be brief and include the date of the offence.

Provision of antecedents to the court and parties

Crown Court

III.27.4 The Crown Court antecedents will be prepared by the police immediately following committal proceedings, including committals for sentence, transfers under section 4 of the *Criminal Justice Act* 1987 or section 53 of the *Criminal Justice Act* 1991 or upon receipt of a notice of appeal, excluding non-imprisonable motoring offences. **F–41**

III.27.5 Seven copies of the antecedents will be prepared in respect of each defendant. Two copies are to be provided to the Crown Prosecution Service ["CPS"] direct, the remaining five to be sent to the Crown Court. The court will send one copy to the defence and one to the Probation Service. The remaining copies are for the court's use. Where following conviction a custodial order is made one copy is to be attached to the order sent to the prison.

III.27.6 The antecedents must be provided, as above, within 21 days of committal or transfer in each case. Any points arising from them are to be raised with the police by the defence solicitor as soon as possible and, where there is time, at least seven days before the hearing date so that the matter can be resolved prior to that hearing.

III.27.7 Seven days before the hearing date the police will check the record of convictions. Details of any additional convictions will be provided using the standard format above. These will be provided as above and attached to the documents already supplied. Details of any additional outstanding cases will also be provided at this stage.

Magistrates' courts

III.27.8 The magistrates' court antecedents will be prepared by the police and submitted to the CPS with the case file.

III.27.9 Five copies of the antecedents will be prepared in respect of each defendant and provided to the CPS who will be responsible for distributing them to others at the sentencing hearing. Normally two copies will be provided to the court, one to the defence and one to the Probation Service when appropriate. Where following conviction a custodial order is made, one of the court's copies is to be attached to the order sent to the prison.

III.27.10 In instances where antecedents have been provided to the court some time before the hearing the police will, if requested to do so by the CPS, check the record of convictions. Details of any additional convictions will be provided using the standard format above. These will be provided as above and attached to the documents already supplied. Details of any additional outstanding cases will also be provided at this stage.

III.27.11 The above arrangements whereby the police provide the antecedents to the CPS for passing on to others will apply unless there is a local agreement between the CPS and the court that alters that arrangement.

III.28 Victim Personal Statements

F–42 **III.28.1** This section draws attention to the Victim Personal Statement scheme, which started on 1 October 2001, to give victims a more formal opportunity to say how a crime has affected them. It may help to identify whether they have a particular need for information, support and protection. It will also enable the court to take the statement into account when determining sentence. In some circumstances, it may be appropriate for relatives of a victim to make a Victim Personal Statement, for example where the victim has died as a result of the relevant criminal conduct.

III.28.2 When a police officer takes a statement from a victim the victim will be told about the scheme and given the chance to make a Victim Personal Statement. The decision about whether or not to make a victim personal statement is entirely for the victim. A Victim Personal Statement may be made or updated at any time prior to the disposal of the case. It will not normally be appropriate for a Victim Personal Statement to be made after the disposal of the case; there may be rare occasions between sentence and appeal when an update to the Victim Personal Statement may be necessary, for example, when the victim was injured and the final prognosis was not available at the date of sentence. If the court is presented with a victim personal statement the following approach should be adopted:

(a) The victim personal statement and any evidence in support should be considered and taken into account by the court prior to passing sentence.

(b) Evidence of the effects of an offence on the victim contained in the victim personal statement or other statement, must be in proper form, that is a witness statement made under section 9 of the *Criminal Justice Act* 1967 or an expert's report, and served upon the defendant's solicitor or the defendant, if he is not represented, prior to sentence. Except where inferences can properly be drawn from the nature of or circumstances surrounding the offence, a sentencer must not make assumptions unsupported by evidence about the effects of an offence on the victim.

(c) The court must pass what it judges to be the appropriate sentence having regard to the circumstances of the offence and of the offender, taking into account, so far as the court considers it appropriate, the impact on the victim. The opinions of the victim or the victim's close relatives as to what the sentence should be are therefore not relevant, unlike the consequence of the offence on them. Victims should be advised of this. If, despite the advice, opinions as to sentence are included in the statement, the court should pay no attention to them.

(d) The court should consider whether it is desirable in its sentencing remarks to refer to the evidence provided on behalf of the victim.

III.29 Support for Witnesses giving Evidence by Live Television Link

F–43 **III.29.1** This section of the Practice Direction is made pursuant to Rule 7 of the *Crown Court (Special Measures Directions and Directions Prohibiting Cross-examination) Rules* 2002 and Rule 7 of the *Magistrates' Courts (Special Measures Directions) Rules* 2002 and supersedes previous guidance given by the Senior Presiding Judges, Lord Justice Tasker Watkins in 1991 and Lord Justice Auld in 1998.

III.29.2 An increased degree of flexibility is now appropriate as to who can act as supporter of a witness giving evidence by live television link. Where a special measures direction is made enabling a vulnerable, intimidated or child witness to give evidence by means of a live television link, the trial judge will make a direction as to the identity of the witness supporter. Where practical, the direction will be made before the trial commences. In giving the direction, the trial judge will balance all relevant interests—see paragraph 1.11 of the guidance "*Achieving Best Evidence*". The witness supporter should be completely independent of the witness and his or her family and have no previous knowledge of or personal involvement in the case. The supporter should also be suitably trained so as to understand the obligations of, and comply with, the National Standards relating to witness supporters. Providing these criteria are met, the witness supporter need not be an usher or court official. Thus, for example, the functions of the witness supporter may be performed by a representative of the Witness Service.

III.29.3 Where the witness supporter is someone other than the court usher, the usher should continue to be available both to assist the witness and the witness supporter, and to ensure that the judge's requirements are properly complied with in the CCTV room.

III.30.1 Treatment of Vulnerable Defendants

F–44 **III.30.1** This direction applies to proceedings in the Crown Court and in magistrates' courts on the trial, sentencing or (in the Crown Court) appeal of (a) children and young persons under 18 or (b) adults who suffer from a mental disorder within the meaning of the *Mental Health Act* 1983 or who have any other significant impairment of intelligence and social function. In this direction such defendants are referred to collectively as "vulnerable defendants". The purpose of this direction is to extend to proceedings in relation to such persons in the adult courts procedures analogous to those in use in youth courts.

III.30.2 The steps which should be taken to comply with paragraphs III.30.3 to III.30.17 should be judged, in any given case, taking account of the age, maturity and development (intellectual, social and emotional) of the defendant concerned and all other circumstances of the case.

The overriding principle

III.30.3 A defendant may be young and immature or may have a mental disorder within the meaning of the *Mental Health Act* 1983 or some other significant impairment of intelligence and social function such as to inhibit his understanding of and participation in the proceedings. The purpose of criminal proceedings is to determine guilt, if that is in issue, and decide on the appropriate sentence if the defendant pleads guilty or is convicted. All possible steps should be taken to assist a vulnerable defendant to understand and participate in those proceedings. The ordinary trial process should, so far as necessary, be adapted to meet those ends. Regard should be had to the welfare of a young defendant as required by section 44 of the *Children and Young Persons Act* 1933, and generally to Parts 1 and 3 of the *Criminal Procedure Rules* (the overriding objective and the court's powers of case management).

Before the trial, sentencing or appeal

III.30.4 If a vulnerable defendant, especially one who is young, is to be tried jointly with one who is not, the court should consider at the plea and case management hearing, or at a case management hearing in a magistrates' court, whether the vulnerable defendant should be tried on his own and should so order unless of the opinion that a joint trial would be in accordance with Part 1 of the *Criminal Procedure Rules* (the overriding objective) and in the interests of justice. If a vulnerable defendant is tried jointly with one who is not, the court should consider whether any of the modifications set out in this direction should apply in the circumstances of the joint trial and so far as practicable make orders to give effect to any such modifications.

III.30.5 At the plea and case management hearing, or at a case management hearing in a magistrates' court, the court should consider and so far as practicable give directions on the matters covered in paragraphs III.30.9 to III.30.17.

III.30.6 It may be appropriate to arrange that a vulnerable defendant should visit, out of court hours and before the trial, sentencing or appeal hearing, the courtroom in which that hearing is to take place so that he can familiarise himself with it.

III.30.7 If any case against a vulnerable defendant has attracted or may attract widespread public or media interest, the assistance of the police should be enlisted to try and ensure that the defendant is not, when attending the court, exposed to intimidation, vilification or abuse. Section 41 of the *Criminal Justice Act* 1925 prohibits the taking of photographs of defendants and witnesses (among others) in the court building or in its precincts, or when entering or leaving those precincts. A direction informing media representatives that the prohibition will be enforced may be appropriate.

III.30.8 The court should be ready at this stage, if it has not already done so, where relevant to make a reporting restriction under section 39 of the *Children and Young Persons Act* 1933 or, on an appeal to the Crown Court from a youth court, to remind media representatives of the application of section 49 of that Act. Any such order, once made, should be reduced to writing and copies should on request be made available to anyone affected or potentially affected by it.

The trial, sentencing or appeal hearing

III.30.9 Subject to the need for appropriate security arrangements the proceedings should, if practicable, be held in a courtroom in which all the participants are on the same or almost the same level.

III.30.10 A vulnerable defendant, especially if he is young, should normally, if he wishes, be free to sit with members of his family or others in a like relationship, and with some other suitable supporting adult such as a social worker, and in a place which permits easy, informal communication with his legal representatives. The court should ensure that a suitable supporting adult is available throughout the course of the proceedings.

III.30.11 At the beginning of the proceedings the court should ensure that what is to take place has been explained to a vulnerable defendant in terms he can understand, and at trial in the Crown Court it should ensure in particular that the role of the jury has been explained. It should remind those representing the vulnerable defendant and the supporting adult of their responsibility to explain each step as it takes place, and at trial to explain the possible consequences of a guilty verdict. Throughout the trial the court should continue to ensure, by any appropriate means, that the defendant understands what is happening and what has been said by those on the bench, the advocates and witnesses.

III.30.12 A trial should be conducted according to a timetable which takes full account of a vulnerable defendant's ability to concentrate. Frequent and regular breaks will often be appropriate. The court should ensure, so far as practicable, that the trial is conducted in simple, clear language that the defendant can understand and that cross-examination is conducted by questions that are short and clear.

III.30.13 A vulnerable defendant who wishes to give evidence by live link in accordance with section 33A of the *Youth Justice and Criminal Evidence Act* 1999 may apply for a direction to that effect. Before making such a direction the court must be satisfied that it is in the interests of justice to do so, and that the use of a live link would enable the defendant to participate more effectively as a witness in the proceedings. The direction will need to deal with the practical arrangements to be made, including the room from which the defendant will give evidence, the identity of the person or persons who will accompany him, and how it will be arranged for him to be seen and heard by the court.

III.30.14 In the Crown Court robes and wigs should not be worn unless the court for good reason orders that they should. It may be appropriate for the court to be robed for sentencing in a grave case even though it has sat without robes for trial. It is generally desirable that those responsible for the security of a vulnerable defendant who is in custody, especially if he is young, should not be in uniform, and that there should be no recognisable police presence in the courtroom save for good reason.

III.30.15 The court should be prepared to restrict attendance by members of the public in the court room to a small number, perhaps limited to those with an immediate and direct interest in the outcome. The court should rule on any challenged claim to attend.

III.30.16 Facilities for reporting the proceedings (subject to any restrictions under section 39 or 49 of the *Children and Young Persons Act* 1933) must be provided. But the court may restrict the number of reporters attending in the courtroom to such number as is judged practicable and desirable. In ruling on any challenged claim to attend in the court room for the purpose of reporting the court should be mindful of the public's general right to be informed about the administration of justice.

III.30.17 Where it has been decided to limit access to the courtroom, whether by reporters or generally, arrangements should be made for the proceedings to be relayed, audibly and if possible visually, to another room in the same court complex to which the media and the public have access if it appears that there will be a need for such additional facilities. Those making use of such a facility should be reminded that it is to be treated as an extension of the court room and that they are required to conduct themselves accordingly.

III.30.18 Where the court is called upon to exercise its discretion in relation to any procedural matter falling within the scope of this practice direction but not the subject of specific reference, such discretion should be exercised having regard to the principles in paragraph III.30.3.

III.31.1 Binding Over Orders and Conditional Discharges

F–45 **III.31.1** This direction takes into account the judgments of the European Court of Human Rights in *Steel v United Kingdom* 28 E.H.R.R. 603, [1998] Crim.L.R. 893 and in *Hashman and Harrup v United Kingdom* 30 E.H.R.R. 241, [2000] Crim.L.R. 185. Its purpose is to give practical guidance, in the light of those two judgments, on the practice of imposing binding over orders. The direction applies to orders made under the court's common law powers, under the *Justices of the Peace Act* 1361, under section 1(7) of the *Justices of the Peace Act* 1968 and under section 115 of the *Magistrates' Courts Act* 1980. This direction also gives guidance concerning the court's power to bind over parents or guardians under section 150 of the *Powers of Criminal Courts (Sentencing) Act* 2000 and the Crown Court's power to bind over to come up for judgment. The court's power to impose a conditional discharge under section 12 of the *Powers of Criminal Courts (Sentencing) Act* 2000 is also covered by this direction.

Binding over to keep the peace

III.31.2 Before imposing a binding over order, the court must be satisfied that a breach of the peace involving violence or an imminent threat of violence has occurred or that there is a real risk of violence in the future. Such violence may be perpetrated by the individual who will be subject to the order or by a third party as a natural consequence of the individual's conduct.

III.31.3 In light of the judgment in *Hashman and Harrup*, courts should no longer bind an individual over "to be of good behaviour". Rather than binding an individual over to "keep the peace" in general terms, the court should identify the specific conduct or activity from which the individual must refrain.

Written order

III.31.4 When making an order binding an individual over to refrain from specified types of conduct or activities, the details of that conduct or those activities should be specified by the court in a written order served on all relevant parties. The court should state its reasons for the making of the order, its length and the amount of the recognisance. The length of the order should be proportionate to the harm sought to be avoided and should not generally exceed 12 months.

Evidence

III.31.5 Sections 51 to 57 of the *Magistrates' Courts Act* 1980 set out the jurisdiction of the magistrates' court to hear an application made on complaint and the procedure which is to be followed. This includes a requirement under section 53 to hear evidence and the parties before making any order. This practice should be applied to all cases in the magistrates' court and the Crown Court where the court is considering imposing a binding over order. The court should give the individual who would be subject to the order and the prosecutor the opportunity to make representations, both as to the making of the order and as to its terms. The court should also hear any admissible evidence the parties wish to call and which has not already been heard in the proceedings. Particularly careful consideration may be required where the individual who would be subject to the order is a witness in the proceedings.

III.31.6 Where there is an admission which is sufficient to found the making of a binding over order and/or the individual consents to the making of the order, the court should nevertheless hear sufficient representations and, if appropriate, evidence, to satisfy itself that an order is appropriate in all the circumstances and to be clear about the terms of the order.

III.31.7 Where there is an allegation of breach of a binding over order and this is contested, the court should hear representations and evidence, including oral evidence, from the parties before making a finding.

Burden of proof

III.31.8 The court should be satisfied beyond reasonable doubt of the matters complained of before a binding over order may be imposed. Where the procedure has been commenced on complaint, the burden of proof rests on the complainant. In all other circumstances, the burden of proof rests upon the prosecution.

III.31.9 Where there is an allegation of breach of a binding over order, the court should be satisfied beyond reasonable doubt that a breach has occurred before making any order for forfeiture of a recognisance. The burden of proof shall rest on the prosecution.

Recognisance

III.31.10 The court must be satisfied on the merits of the case that an order for binding over is appropriate and should announce that decision before considering the amount of the recognisance. The individual who is made subject to the binding over order should be told he has a right of appeal from the decision.

III.31.11 When fixing the amount of the recognisance, courts should have regard to the individual's financial resources and should hear representations from the individual or his legal representatives regarding finances.

Refusal to enter into a recognisance

III.31.12 If there is any possibility that an individual will refuse to enter a recognisance, the court should consider whether there are any appropriate alternatives to a binding over order (for example, continuing with a prosecution). Where there are no appropriate alternatives and the individual continues to refuse to enter into the recognisance, the magistrates' court may use its power under section 115(3) of the *Magistrates' Courts Act* 1980, and the Crown Court may use its common law power, to commit the individual to custody.

III.31.13 Before the court exercises a power to commit the individual to custody, the individual should be given the opportunity to see a duty solicitor or another legal representative and be represented in proceedings if the individual so wishes. Public funding should generally be granted to cover representation.

III.31.14 In the event that the individual does not take the opportunity to seek legal advice, the court shall give the individual a final opportunity to comply with the request and shall explain the consequences of a failure to do so.

Antecedents

III.31.15 Courts are reminded of the provisions of section 7(5) of the *Rehabilitation of Offenders Act* 1974 which excludes from a person's antecedents any order of the court "with respect to any person otherwise than on a conviction".

Binding over to come up for judgment

III.31.16 If the Crown Court is considering binding over an individual to come up for judgment, the court should specify any conditions with which the individual is to comply in the meantime and not specify that the individual is to be of good behaviour.

Binding over of parent or guardian

III.31.17 Where a court is considering binding over a parent or guardian under section 150 of the *Powers of Criminal Courts (Sentencing) Act* 2000 to enter into a recognisance to take proper care of and exercise proper control over a child or young person, the court should specify the actions which the parent or guardian is to take.

Security for good behaviour

III.31.18 Where a court is imposing a conditional discharge under section 12 of the *Powers of Criminal Courts (Sentencing) Act* 2000, it has the power, under section 12(6) to make an order that a person who consents to do so give security for the good behaviour of the offender. When making such an order, the court should specify the type of conduct from which the offender is to refrain.

PART V: FURTHER DIRECTIONS APPLYING IN THE MAGISTRATES' COURTS

PART V: FURTHER DIRECTIONS APPLYING IN THE MAGISTRATES' COURTS

V.51 Mode of Trial

F–46 **V.51.1** The purpose of these guidelines is to help magistrates decide whether or not to commit defendants charged with "either way" offences for trial in the Crown Court. Their object is to provide guidance not direction. They are not intended to impinge on a magistrate's duty to consider each case individually and on its own particular facts. These guidelines apply to all defendants aged 18 and above.

General mode of trial considerations

F–47 **V.51.2** Section 19 of the *Magistrates' Courts Act* 1980 requires magistrates to have regard to the following matters in deciding whether an offence is more suitable for summary trial or trial on indictment:

(a) the nature of the case;

(b) whether the circumstances make the offence one of a serious character;

(c) whether the punishment which a magistrates' court would have power to inflict for it would be adequate;

(d) any other circumstances which appear to the court to make it more suitable for the offence to be tried in one way rather than the other;

(e) any representations made by the prosecution or the defence.

V.51.3 Certain general observations can be made:

(a) the court should never make its decision on the grounds of convenience or expedition;

(b) the court should assume for the purpose of deciding mode of trial that the prosecution version of the facts is correct;

(c) the fact that the offences are alleged to be specimens is a relevant consideration (although, it has to be borne in mind that difficulties can arise in sentencing in relation to specimen counts see *R v Clark* [1996] 2 Cr App R (S) 351 and *R v Canavan and others* [1998] 1 Cr App R (S) 243); the fact that the defendant will be asking for other offences to be taken into consideration, if convicted, is not;

(d) where cases involve complex questions of fact or difficult questions of law, including difficult issues of disclosure of sensitive material, the court should consider committal for trial;

(e) where two or more defendants are jointly charged with an offence each has an individual right to elect his mode of trial;

(f) in general, except where otherwise stated, either way offences should be tried summarily unless the court considers that the particular case has one or more of the features set out in paragraphs V.51.4 to V.51.18 and that its sentencing powers are insufficient;

(g) the court should also consider its power to commit an offender for sentence under sections 3 and 4 of the *Powers of Criminal Courts (Sentencing) Act* 2000, if information emerges during the course of the hearing which leads it to conclude that the offence is so serious, or the offender such a risk to the public, that its powers to sentence him are inadequate. This means that committal for sentence is no longer determined by reference to the character and antecedents of the offender.

Features relevant to individual offences

V.51.4 Where reference is made in these guidelines to property or damage of "high value" it means a figure equal to at least twice the amount of the limit (currently £5,000) imposed by statute on a magistrates' court when making a compensation order. **F–48**

Burglary: Dwelling-house

V.51.5 Cases should be tried summarily unless the court considers that one or more of the following features is present in the case *and* that its sentencing powers are insufficient. Magistrates should take account of their powers under sections 3 and 4 of the *Powers of Criminal Courts (Sentencing) Act* 2000 to commit for sentence, see paragraph V.51.3(g). **F–49**

(a) Entry in the daytime when the occupier (or another) is present;

(b) Entry at night of a house which is normally occupied, whether or not the occupier (or another) is present;

(c) The offence is alleged to be one of a series of similar offences;

(d) When soiling, ransacking, damage or vandalism occurs;

(e) The offence has professional hallmarks;

(f) The unrecovered property is of high value: see paragraph V.51.4 for definition of high value;

(g) The offence is racially motivated.

Note: Attention is drawn to paragraph 28(c) of Schedule 1 to the *Magistrates' Courts Act* 1980 by which offences of burglary in a dwelling cannot be tried summarily if any person in the dwelling was subjected to violence or the threat of violence.

Burglary: Non-dwelling

V.51.6 Cases should be tried summarily unless the court considers that one or more of the following features is present in the case *and* that its sentencing powers are insufficient. Magistrates should take account of their powers under sections 3 and 4 of the *Powers of Criminal Courts (Sentencing) Act* 2000 to commit for sentence, see paragraph V.51.3(g). **F–50**

(a) Entry of a pharmacy or doctor's surgery;

(b) Fear is caused or violence is done to anyone lawfully on the premises (e.g. nightwatchman, security guard);

(c) The offence has professional hallmarks;

(d) Vandalism on a substantial scale;

(e) The unrecovered property is of high value: see paragraph V.51.4 for definition of high value;

(f) The offence is racially motivated.

Theft and fraud

F–51 **V.51.7** Cases should be tried summarily unless the court considers that one or more of the following features is present in the case *and* that its sentencing powers are insufficient. Magistrates should take account of their powers under sections 3 and 4 of the *Powers of Criminal Courts (Sentencing) Act* 2000 to commit for sentence, see paragraph V.51.3(g).

(a) Breach of trust by a person in a position of substantial authority, or in whom a high degree of trust is placed;

(b) Theft or fraud which has been committed or disguised in a sophisticated manner;

(c) Theft or fraud committed by an organised gang;

(d) The victim is particularly vulnerable to theft or fraud, e.g. the elderly or infirm;

(e) The unrecovered property is of high value: see paragraph V.51.4 for definition of high value.

Handling

F–52 **V.51.8** Cases should be tried summarily unless the court considers that one or more of the following features is present in the case *and* that its sentencing powers are insufficient. Magistrates should take account of their powers under sections 3 and 4 of the *Powers of Criminal Courts (Sentencing) Act* 2000 to commit for sentence, see paragraph V.51.3(g).

(a) Dishonest handling of stolen property by a receiver who has commissioned the theft;

(b) The offence has professional hallmarks;

(c) The property is of high value: see paragraph V.51.4 for definition of high value.

Social security frauds

F–53 **V.51.9** Cases should be tried summarily unless the court considers that one or more of the following features is present in the case *and* that its sentencing powers are insufficient. Magistrates should take account of their powers under sections 3 and 4 of the *Powers of Criminal Courts (Sentencing) Act* 2000 to commit for sentence, see paragraph V.51.3(g).

(a) Organised fraud on a large scale;

(b) The frauds are substantial and carried out over a long period of time.

Violence (sections 20 and 47 of the Offences against the Person Act 1861)

F–54 **V.51.10** Cases should be tried summarily unless the court considers that one or more of the following features is present in the case *and* that its sentencing powers are insufficient. Magistrates should take account of their powers under sections 3 and 4 of the *Powers of Criminal Courts (Sentencing) Act* 2000 to commit for sentence, see paragraph V.51.3(g).

(a) The use of a weapon of a kind likely to cause serious injury;

(b) A weapon is used and serious injury is caused;

(c) More than minor injury is caused by kicking or head-butting;

(d) Serious violence is caused to those whose work has to be done in contact with the public or are likely to face violence in the course of their work;

(e) Violence to vulnerable people, *e.g.* the elderly and infirm;

(f) The offence has clear racial motivation.

Note: the same considerations apply to cases of domestic violence.

Public Order Act Offences

F–55 **V.51.11** Cases should be tried summarily unless the court considers that one or more of the following features is present in the case *and* that its sentencing powers are insufficient. Magistrates should take account of their powers under sections 3 and 4 of the *Powers of Criminal Courts (Sentencing) Act* 2000 to commit for sentence, see paragraph V.51.3(g).

(a) Cases of *violent disorder* should generally be committed for trial;

(b) *Affray*;

(i) Organised violence or use of weapons;

(ii) Significant injury or substantial damage;

(iii) The offence has clear racial motivation;

(iv) An attack on police officers, ambulance staff, fire-fighters and the like.

Violence to and neglect of children

V.51.12 Cases should be tried summarily unless the court considers that one or more of the following features is present in the case *and* that its sentencing powers are insufficient. Magistrates should take account of their powers under sections 3 and 4 of the *Powers of Criminal Courts (Sentencing) Act* 2000 to commit for sentence, see paragraph V.51.3(g): **F–56**

(a) Substantial injury;

(b) Repeated violence or serious neglect, even if the physical harm is slight;

(c) Sadistic violence, *e.g.* deliberate burning or scalding.

Indecent assault

V.51.13 Cases should be tried summarily unless the court considers that one or more of the following features is present in the case *and* that its sentencing powers are insufficient. Magistrates should take account of their powers under sections 3 and 4 of the *Powers of Criminal Courts (Sentencing) Act* 2000 to commit for sentence, see paragraph V.51.3(g). **F–57**

(a) Substantial disparity in age between victim and defendant, and a more serious assault;

(b) Violence or threats of violence;

(c) Relationship of trust or responsibility between defendant and victim;

(d) Several more serious similar offences;

(e) The victim is particularly vulnerable;

(f) Serious nature of the assault.

Unlawful sexual intercourse

V.51.14 Cases should be tried summarily unless the court considers that one or more of the following features is present in the case *and* that its sentencing powers are insufficient. Magistrates should take account of their powers under sections 3 and 4 of the *Powers of Criminal Courts (Sentencing) Act* 2000 to commit for sentence, see paragraph V.51.3(g). **F–58**

(a) Wide disparity of age;

(b) Breach of position of trust;

(c) The victim is particularly vulnerable.

Note: Unlawful sexual intercourse with a girl *under 13* is triable only on indictment.

Drugs

V.51.15 Class A: **F–59**

(a) Supply; possession with intent to supply:

These cases should be committed for trial.

(b) Possession:

Should be committed for trial unless the amount is consistent only with personal use.

V.51.16 Class B:

(a) Supply; possession with intent to supply:

Should be committed for trial unless there is only small scale supply for no payment.

(b) Possession:

Should be committed for trial when the quantity is substantial and not consistent only with personal use.

Dangerous driving and aggravated vehicle taking

V.51.17 Cases should be tried summarily unless the court considers that one or more of the following features is present in the case *and* that its sentencing powers are insufficient. Magistrates should take account of their powers under sections 3 and 4 of the *Powers of Criminal Courts (Sentencing) Act* 2000 to commit for sentence, see paragraph V.51.3(g). **F–60**

(a) Alcohol or drugs contributing to the dangerous driving;

(b) Grossly excessive speed;

(c) Racing;

(d) Prolonged course of dangerous driving;

(e) Other related offences;

(f) Significant injury or damage sustained.

Criminal damage

F–61 **V.51.18** Cases should be tried summarily unless the court considers that one or more of the following features is present in the case *and* that its sentencing powers are insufficient. Magistrates should take account of their powers under sections 3 and 4 of the *Powers of Criminal Courts (Sentencing) Act* 2000 to commit for sentence, see paragraph V.51.3(g).

(a) Deliberate fire-raising;

(b) Committed by a group;

(c) Damage of a high value;

(d) The offence has clear racial motivation.

Note: Offences set out in Schedule 2 to the *Magistrates' Courts Act* 1980 (which includes offences of criminal damage which do not amount to arson) *must* be tried summarily if the value of the property damaged or destroyed is £5,000 or less.

V.52 Committal for Sentence and Appeals to Crown Court

F–62 **V.52.2** Any case notes should be sent to the Crown Court when there is an appeal, thereby making them available to the judge if the judge requires them in order to decide before the hearing questions of listing or representation or the like. They will also be available to the court during the hearing if it becomes necessary or desirable for the court to see what happened in the lower court. On a committal for sentence or an appeal, any reasons given by the magistrates for their decision should be included with the notes.

V.53 Bail before Committal for Trial

F–63 **V.53.1** Rules 19 and 20 of the *Crown Court Rules* 1982 SI 1982/1109 apply to these applications.

V.53.2 Before the Crown Court can deal with an application it must be satisfied that the magistrates' court has issued a certificate under section 5(6A) of the *Bail Act* 1976 that it heard full argument on the application for bail before it refused the application. A copy of the certificate will be issued to the applicant and not sent directly to the Crown Court. It will therefore be necessary for the applicant's solicitors to attach a copy of the certificate to the bail application form. If the certificate is not enclosed with the application form it will be difficult to avoid some delay in listing.

Venue

F–64 **V.53.3** Applications should be made to the court to which the defendant will be or would have been committed for trial. In the event of an application in a purely summary case, it should be made to the Crown Court centre which normally receives class 4 work. The hearing will be listed as a chambers matter unless a judge has directed otherwise.

V.54 Contempt in the Face of the Magistrates' Court

General

F–65 **V.54.1** Section 12 of the *Contempt of Court Act* 1981 gives magistrates' courts the power to detain until the court rises, someone, whether a defendant or another person present in court, who wilfully insults anyone specified in section 12 or who interrupts proceedings. In any such case, the court may order any officer of the court, or any constable, to take the offender into custody and detain him until the rising of the court; and the court may, if it thinks fit, commit the offender to custody for a specified period not exceeding one month or impose a fine not exceeding level 4 on the standard scale or both. This power can be used to stop disruption of their proceedings. Detention is until the person can be conveniently dealt with without disruption of the proceedings. Prior to the court using the power the offender should be warned to desist or face the prospect of being detained.

V.54.2 Magistrates' courts also have the power to commit to custody any person attending or brought before a magistrates' court who refuses without just cause to be sworn or to give evidence under section 97(4) of the *Magistrates' Courts Act* 1980, until the expiration of such period not exceeding one month as may be specified in the warrant or until he sooner gives evidence or produces the document or thing, or impose on him a fine not exceeding £2,500, or both.

V.54.3 In the exercise of any of these powers, as soon as is practical, and in any event prior to an offender being proceeded against, an offender should be told of the conduct which it is alleged to constitute his offending in clear terms. When making an order under section 12 the justices should state their findings of fact as to the contempt.

V.54.4 Exceptional situations require exceptional treatment. While this direction deals with the generality of situations, there will be a minority of situations where the application of the direction will not be consistent with achieving justice in the special circumstances of the particular case. Where this is the situation, the compliance with the direction should be modified so far as is necessary so as to accord with the interests of justice.

V.54.5 The power to bind persons over to be of good behaviour in respect of their conduct in court should cease to be exercised.

Contempt consisting of wilfully insulting anyone specified in section 12 or interrupting proceedings

V.54.6 In the case of someone who wilfully insults anyone specified in section 12 or interrupts proceedings, if an offender expresses a willingness to apologise for his misconduct, he should be brought back before the court at the earliest convenient moment in order to make the apology and to give undertakings to the court to refrain from further misbehaviour. **F–66**

V.54.7 In the majority of cases, an apology and a promise as to future conduct should be sufficient for justices to order an offender's release. However, there are likely to be certain cases where the nature and seriousness of the misconduct requires the justices to consider using their powers under section 12(2) of the *Contempt of Court* 1981 Act either to fine or to order the offender's committal to custody.

Where an offender is detained for contempt of court

V.54.8 Anyone detained under either of these provisions in paragraphs V.54.1 or V.54.2 should be seen by the duty solicitor or another legal representative and be represented in proceedings if they so wish. Public funding should generally be granted to cover representation. The offender must be afforded adequate time and facilities in order to prepare his case. The matter should be resolved the same day if at all possible. **F–67**

V.54.9 The offender should be brought back before the court before the justices conclude their daily business. The justices should ensure that he understands the nature of the proceedings, including his opportunity to apologise or give evidence and the alternative of them exercising their powers.

V.54.10 Having heard from the offender's solicitor, the justices should decide whether to take further action.

Sentencing of an offender who admits being in contempt

V.54.11 If an offence of contempt is admitted the justices should consider whether they are able to proceed on the day or whether to adjourn to allow further reflection. The matter should be dealt with on the same day if at all possible. If the justices are of the view to adjourn they should generally grant the offender bail unless one or more of the exceptions to the right to bail in the *Bail Act* 1976 are made out. **F–68**

V.54.12 When they come to sentence the offender where the offence has been admitted, the justices should first ask the offender if he has any objection to them dealing with the matter. If there is any objection to the justices dealing with the matter a differently constituted panel should hear the proceedings. If the offender's conduct was directed to the justices, it will not be appropriate for the same bench to deal with the matter.

V.54.13 The justices should consider whether an order for the offender's discharge is appropriate, taking into account any time spent on remand, whether the offence was admitted and the seriousness of the contempt. Any period of committal should be for the shortest time commensurate with the interests of preserving good order in the administration of justice.

Trial of the issue where the contempt is not admitted

V.54.14 Where the contempt is not admitted the justices' powers are limited to making arrangements for a trial to take place. They should not at this stage make findings against the offender. **F–69**

V.54.15 In the case of a contested contempt the trial should take place at the earliest opportunity and should be before a bench of justices other than those before whom the alleged contempt took place. If a trial of the issue can take place on the day such arrangements should be made taking into account the offender's rights under Article 6 of the European Convention for the Protection of Human Rights and Fundamental Freedoms (Rome, 4 November 1950; TS 71 (1953); Cmd 8969). If the trial cannot take place that day the justices should again bail the offender unless there are grounds under the *Bail Act* 1976 to remand him in custody.

V.54.16 The offender is entitled to call and examine witnesses where evidence is relevant. If the offender is found by the court to have committed contempt the court should again consider first whether an order for his discharge from custody is sufficient to bring proceedings to an end. The justices should also allow the offender a further opportunity to apologise for his contempt or to make representations. If the justices are of the view that they must exercise their powers to commit to custody under section 12(2) of the 1981 Act, they must take into account any time spent on remand and the nature and seriousness of the contempt. Any period of committal should be for the shortest period of time commensurate with the interests of preserving good order in the administration of justice.

V.55 Clerk Retiring with Justices

F–70 **V.55.1** A justices' clerk is responsible for:

(a) the legal advice tendered to the justices within the area;

(b) the performance of any of the functions set out below by any member of his staff acting as legal adviser;

(c) ensuring that competent advice is available to justices when the justices' clerk is not personally present in court; and

(d) the effective delivery of case management and the reduction of unnecessary delay.

V.55.2 Where a person other than the justices' clerk (a "legal adviser"), who is authorised to do so, performs any of the functions referred to in this direction he will have the same responsibilities as the justices' clerk. The legal adviser may consult the justices' clerk or other person authorised by the justices' clerk for that purpose before tendering advice to the bench. If the justices' clerk or that person gives any advice directly to the bench, he should give the parties or their advocates an opportunity of repeating any relevant submissions prior to the advice being given.

V.55.3 It shall be the responsibility of the legal adviser to provide the justices with any advice they require properly to perform their functions, whether or not the justices have requested that advice, on:

(a) questions of law (including European Court of Human Rights jurisprudence and those matters set out in section 2(1) of the *Human Rights Act* 1998);

(b) questions of mixed law and fact;

(c) matters of practice and procedure;

(d) the range of penalties available;

(e) any relevant decisions of the superior courts or other guidelines;

(f) other issues relevant to the matter before the court; and

(g) the appropriate decision-making structure to be applied in any given case.

In addition to advising the justices it shall be the legal adviser's responsibility to assist the court, where appropriate, as to the formulation of reasons and the recording of those reasons.

V.55.4 A justices' clerk or legal adviser must not play any part in making findings of fact, but may assist the bench by reminding them of the evidence, using any notes of the proceedings for this purpose.

V.55.5 A justices' clerk or legal adviser may ask questions of witnesses and the parties in order to clarify the evidence and any issues in the case. A legal adviser has a duty to ensure that every case is conducted fairly.

V.55.6 When advising the justices the justices' clerk or legal adviser, whether or not previously in court, should:

(a) ensure that he is aware of the relevant facts; and

(b) provide the parties with the information necessary to enable the parties to make any representations they wish as to the advice before it is given.

V.55.7 At any time justices are entitled to receive advice to assist them in discharging their responsibilities. If they are in any doubt as to the evidence which has been given, they should seek the aid of their legal adviser, referring to his notes as appropriate. This should ordinarily be done in open court. Where the justices request their adviser to join them in the retiring room, this request should be made in the presence of the parties in court. Any legal advice given to the justices other than in open court should be clearly stated to be provisional and the adviser should subsequently repeat the substance of the advice in open court and give the parties an opportunity to make any representations they wish on that provisional advice. The legal adviser should then state in open court whether the provisional advice is confirmed or if it is varied the nature of the variation.

V.55.8 The performance of a legal adviser may be appraised by a person authorised by the magistrates' courts committee to do so. For that purpose the appraiser may be present in the justices' retiring room. The content of the appraisal is confidential, but the fact that an appraisal has taken place, and the presence of the appraiser in the retiring room, should be briefly explained in open court.

V.55.9 The legal adviser is under a duty to assist unrepresented parties to present their case, but must do so without appearing to become an advocate for the party concerned.

V.55.10 The role of legal advisers in fine default proceedings or any other proceedings for the enforcement of financial orders, obligations or penalties is to assist the court. They must not act in an adversarial or partisan manner. With the agreement of the justices a legal adviser may ask questions of the defaulter to elicit information which the justices will require to make an adjudication, for example to facilitate his explanation for the default. A legal adviser may also advise the justices in the normal way as to the options open to them in dealing with the case. It would be inappropriate for the legal adviser to set out to establish wilful refusal or neglect or any other type of culpable behaviour, to offer an opinion on the facts, or to urge a particular course of action upon the justices. The duty of impartiality is the paramount consideration for the legal adviser at all times, and this takes precedence over any role he may have as a collecting officer. The appointment of other staff to "prosecute" the case for the collecting officer is not essential to ensure compliance with the law, including the *Human Rights Act* 1998. Whether to make such appointments is a matter for the justices' chief executive.

V.56 Case Management in Magistrates' Courts

V.56.1 This section of the practice direction supplements the rules in Part 3 of the *Criminal Procedure Rules* as they apply to the management of cases in magistrates' courts. Where time limits or other directions in the Consolidated Criminal Practice Direction appear inconsistent with this section, the directions in this section take precedence. To avoid unnecessary and wasted hearings the parties should be allowed adequate time to prepare the case, having regard to the time limits for applications and notices set by the Criminal Procedure Rules and by other legislation. When those time limits have expired the parties will be expected to be fully prepared. **F–71**

Cases to be tried summarily by the magistrates' court

V.56.2 The case progression form to be used is set out in annex E with guidance notes. The form, read with the notes, constitutes a case progression timetable for the effective preparation of a case.

Cases sent, committed or transferred to the Crown Court for trial

V.56.3 The case progression forms set out in annex E with guidance notes are to be used in connection with cases that are sent to the Crown Court for trial under section 51 of the *Crime and Disorder Act* 1998 and cases that are committed to the Crown Court for trial under section 6 of the *Magistrates' Courts Act* 1980. In a case transferred to the Crown Court for trial under section 4(1) of the *Criminal Justice Act* 1987 or under section 53(1) of the *Criminal Justice Act* 1991 the directions contained in the case progression form used for committal for trial apply as if the case had been committed on the date of the notice of transfer.

V.56.4 A preliminary hearing ('PH') is not required in every case sent for trial under section 51 of the *Crime and Disorder Act* 1998: see rule 12.2 (which altered the Crown Court rule from which it derived). A PH should be ordered only where such a hearing is considered necessary. The PH should be held about 14 days after sending.

V.56.5 Whether or not a magistrates' court orders a PH, a plea and case management hearing ('PCMH') should be ordered in every case sent or committed to the Crown Court for trial. The PCMH should be held within about 7 weeks after committal for trial, within about 14 weeks after sending for trial where a defendant is in custody and within about 17 weeks after sending for trial where a defendant is on bail.

Use of the forms: directions that apply by default

V.56.6 The case progression forms to be used in magistrates' courts contain directions some of which are determined by *Criminal Procedure Rules* or by other legislation and some of which are discretionary, as explained in the guidance notes. All those directions apply in every case unless the court otherwise orders.

APPENDIX G

CRIMINAL PROCEDURE RULES

The *Criminal Procedure Rules* 2011 (S.I. 2011 No. 1709) consolidated and amended the *Criminal Procedure Rules* 2010 (as amended by S.I. 2010 No. 1921 and S.I. 2010 No. 3026) and the previous consolidation of the *Criminal Procedure Rules* 2005 (as amended by S.I. 2006 No. 353, S.I. 2006 No. 2636, S.I. 2007 No. 699, S.I. 2007 No. 2317, S.I. 2007 No. 3662, S.I. 2008 No. 2076, S.I. 2008 No. 3269, S.I. 2009 No. 2087). The new rules have effect from October 3, 2011; but, unless the court otherwise directs, the new rules do not affect any right or duty existing under the 2010 rules.

Criminal Procedure Rules 2011 (S.I. 2011 No. 1709)

ARRANGEMENT OF RULES

Appendices

Evidence

Part 27: Witness statements (*post*, G–158).
Part 28: Witness summonses, warrants and orders (*post*, G–160).
Part 29: Measures to assist a witness or defendant to give evidence (*post*, G–168).
Part 30: [*Empty*]
Part 31: Restriction on cross-examination by a defendant acting in person (*post*, G–178).
Part 32: International co-operation (*post*, G–182).
Part 33: Expert evidence (*post*, G–191).
Part 34: Hearsay evidence (*post*, G–199).
Part 35: Evidence of bad character (*post*, G–207).
Part 36: Evidence of a complainant's previous sexual behaviour (*post*, G–216).

Trial

Part 37: Trial and sentence in a magistrates' court (*post*, G–223).
Part 38: [*Empty*]
Part 39: Trial on indictment (these rules are not reproduced in this work).
Part 40: Tainted acquittals (*post*, G–238).
Part 41: Retrial following acquittal for serious offence (not reproduced in this work).

Sentencing

Part 42: Sentencing procedures in special cases (*post*, G–263).
Part 43: [*Empty*]
Part 44: Breach, revocation and amendment of community and other orders (*post*, G–266).
Part 45: [*Empty*]
Part 46: [*Empty*]
Part 47: [*Empty*]
Part 48: [*Empty*]
Part 49: [*Empty*]
Part 50: Civil behaviour orders after verdict or finding (*post*, G–275).
Part 51: [*Empty*]
Part 52: Enforcement of fines and other orders for payment (*post*, G–280).
Part 53: [*Empty*]
Part 54: [*Empty*]
Part 55: Road traffic penalties (*post*, G–296).

Confiscation and related proceedings

Part 56: Confiscation proceedings under the *Criminal Justice Act* 1988 and the *Drug Trafficking Ac* 1994 (not reproduced in this work).
Part 57: *Proceeds of Crime Act* 2002: rules applicable to all proceedings (not reproduced in this work
Part 58: *Proceeds of Crime Act* 2002: rules applicable only to confiscation proceedings (not reproduce in this work).
Part 59: *Proceeds of Crime Act* 2002: rules applicable only to restraint proceedings (not reproduced i this work).
Part 60: *Proceeds of Crime Act* 2002: rules applicable only to receivership proceedings (not reproduce in this work).
Part 61: *Proceeds of Crime Act* 2002: rules applicable to restraint and receivership proceedings (not reproduced in this work).

Contempt of court

Part 62: Contempt of court (*post*, G–299a).

Appeal

Part 63: Appeal to the Crown Court (*post*, G–300)
Part 64: Appeal to the High Court by way of case stated (*post*, G–309)
Part 65: Appeal to the Court of Appeal: general rules (not reproduced in this work).

PART 1 THE OVERRIDING OBJECTIVE

Contents of this Part

The overriding objective

1.1.—(1) The overriding objective of this new code is that criminal cases be dealt with justly. **G–1**

(2) Dealing with a criminal case justly includes—

(a) acquitting the innocent and convicting the guilty;

(b) dealing with the prosecution and the defence fairly;

(c) recognising the rights of a defendant, particularly those under Article 6 of the European Convention on Human Rights;

(d) respecting the interests of witnesses, victims and jurors and keeping them informed of the progress of the case;

(e) dealing with the case efficiently and expeditiously;

(f) ensuring that appropriate information is available to the court when bail and sentence are considered; and

(g) dealing with the case in ways that take into account—

(i) the gravity of the offence alleged,

(ii) the complexity of what is in issue,

(iii) the severity of the consequences for the defendant and others affected, and

(iv) the needs of other cases.

The duty of the participants in a criminal case

1.2.—(1) Each participant, in the conduct of each case, must— **G–1a**

Appendices

(a) prepare and conduct the case in accordance with the overriding objective;
(b) comply with these Rules, practice directions and directions made by the court; and
(c) at once inform the court and all parties of any significant failure (whether or not that participant is responsible for that failure) to take any procedural step required by these Rules, any practice direction or any direction of the court. A failure is significant if it might hinder the court in furthering the overriding objective.

(2) Anyone involved in any way with a criminal case is a participant in its conduct for the purposes of this rule.

The application by the court of the overriding objective

G–1b **1.3.** The court must further the overriding objective in particular when—
(a) exercising any power given to it by legislation (including these Rules);
(b) applying any practice direction; or
(c) interpreting any rule or practice direction.

PART 2 UNDERSTANDING AND APPLYING THE RULES

Contents of this Part

When the Rules apply

G–2 **2.1.**—(1) In general, the Criminal Procedure Rules apply—
(a) in all criminal cases in magistrates' courts and in the Crown Court; and
(b) in all cases in the criminal division of the Court of Appeal.

(2) If a rule applies only in one or two of those courts, the rule makes that clear.

(3) The Rules apply on and after 3rd October, 2011, but unless the court otherwise directs they do not affect a right or duty existing under The *Criminal Procedure Rules* 2010.

Definitions

G–2a **2.2**—(1) In these Rules, unless the context makes it clear that something different is meant:

'business day' means any day except Saturday, Sunday, Christmas Day, Boxing Day, Good Friday, Easter Monday or a bank holiday;

'court' means a tribunal with jurisdiction over criminal cases. It includes a judge, recorder, District Judge (Magistrates' Court), lay justice and, when exercising their judicial powers, the Registrar of Criminal Appeals, a justices' clerk or assistant clerk;

'court officer means the appropriate member of the staff of a court;

'justices' legal adviser' means a justices' clerk or an assistant to a justices' clerk;

'live link' means an arrangement by which a person can see and hear, and be seen and heard by, the court when that person is not in court;

"Practice Direction" means the Lord Chief Justice's Consolidated Criminal Practice Direction, as amended, and "Criminal Costs Practice Direction" means the Lord Chief Justice's Practice Direction (Costs in Criminal Proceedings), as amended; and

'public interest ruling' means a ruling about whether it is in the public interest to disclose prosecution material under sections 3(6), 7A(8) or 8(5) of the *Criminal Procedure and Investigations Act* 1996.

'Registrar' means the Registrar of Criminal Appeals or a court officer acting with the Registrar's authority.

(2) Definitions of some other expressions are in the rules in which they apply.

References to Acts of Parliament and to Statutory Instruments

2.3. In these Rules, where a rule refers to an Act of Parliament or to subordinate legislation by title and year, subsequent references to that Act or to that legislation in the rule are shortened: so, for example, after a reference to the *Criminal Procedure and Investigations Act* 1996 that Act is called 'the 1996 Act'; and after a reference to the *Criminal Procedure and Investigations Act 1996 (Defence Disclosure Time Limits) Regulations* 1997 those Regulations are called 'the 1997 Regulations'. **G–2b**

The glossary

2.4. The glossary at the end of the Rules is a guide to the meaning of certain legal expressions used in them. **G–2c**

Representatives

2.5.—(1) Under these Rules, unless the context makes it clear that something different is meant, anything that a party may or must do may be done— **G–2d**

(a) by a legal representative on that party's behalf;

(b) by a person with the corporation's written authority, where that party is a corporation;

(c) with the help of a parent, guardian or other suitable supporting adult where that party is a defendant—

(i) who is under 18, or

(ii) whose understanding of what the case involves is limited.

(2) Anyone with a prosecutor's authority to do so may, on that prosecutor's behalf—

(a) serve on the magistrates' court officer, or present to a magistrates' court, an information under section 1 of the *Magistrates' Courts Act* 1980; or

(b) issue a written charge and requisition under section 29 of the *Criminal Justice Act* 2003.

PART 3 CASE MANAGEMENT

Contents of this Part

The scope of this Part

3.1. This Part applies to the management of each case in a magistrates' court and in the Crown Court (including an appeal to the Crown Court) until the conclusion of that case. **G–3**

The duty of the court

3.2.—(1) The court must further the overriding objective by actively managing the case. **G–4**

Appendices

(2) Active case management includes—
(a) the early identification of the real issues;
(b) the early identification of the needs of witnesses;
(c) achieving certainty as to what must be done, by whom, and when, in particular by the early setting of a timetable for the progress of the case;
(d) monitoring the progress of the case and compliance with directions;
(e) ensuring that evidence, whether disputed or not, is presented in the shortest and clearest way;
(f) discouraging delay, dealing with as many aspects of the case as possible on the same occasion, and avoiding unnecessary hearings;
(g) encouraging the participants to co-operate in the progression of the case; and
(h) making use of technology.

(3) The court must actively manage the case by giving any direction appropriate to the needs of that case as early as possible

The duty of the parties

G–5 **3.3.** Each party must—
(a) actively assist the court in fulfilling its duty under rule 3.2, without or if necessary with a direction; and
(b) apply for a direction if needed to further the overriding objective.

Case progression officers and their duties

G–6 **3.4.**—(1) At the beginning of the case each party must, unless the court otherwise directs—
(a) nominate an individual responsible for progressing that case; and
(b) tell other parties and the court who he is and how to contact him.

(2) In fulfilling its duty under rule 3.2, the court must where appropriate—
(a) nominate a court officer responsible for progressing the case; and
(b) make sure the parties know who he is and how to contact him.

(3) In this Part a person nominated under this rule is called a case progression officer.

(4) A case progression officer must—
(a) monitor compliance with directions;
(b) make sure that the court is kept informed of events that may affect the progress of that case;
(c) make sure that he can be contacted promptly about the case during ordinary business hours;
(d) act promptly and reasonably in response to communications about the case; and
(e) if he will be unavailable, appoint a substitute to fulfil his duties and inform the other case progression officers.

The court's case management powers

G–7 **3.5.**—(1) In fulfilling its duty under rule 3.2 the court may give any direction and take any step actively to manage a case unless that direction or step would be inconsistent with legislation, including these Rules.

(2) In particular, the court may—
(a) nominate a judge, magistrate or justices' legal adviser to manage the case;
(b) give a direction on its own initiative or on application by a party;
(c) ask or allow a party to propose a direction;
(d) for the purpose of giving directions, receive applications and representations by letter, by telephone or by any other means of electronic communication, and conduct a hearing by such means;
(e) give a direction—
(i) at a hearing, in public or private, or
(ii) without a hearing;
(f) fix, postpone, bring forward, extend or cancel a hearing;
(g) shorten or extend (even after it has expired) a time limit fixed by a direction;
(h) require that issues in the case should be determined separately, and decide in what order they will be determined; and (i) specify the consequences of failing to comply with a direction.

(3) A magistrates' court may give a direction that will apply in the Crown Court if the case is to continue there.

(4) The Crown Court may give a direction that will apply in a magistrates' court if the case is to continue there.

(5) Any power to give a direction under this Part includes a power to vary or revoke that direction.

(6) If a party fails to comply with a rule or a direction, the court may—

(a) fix, postpone, bring forward, extend, cancel or adjourn a hearing;

(b) exercise its powers to make a costs order; and

(c) impose such other sanction as may be appropriate.

Application to vary a direction

3.6.—(1) A party may apply to vary a direction if— **G–8**

(a) the court gave it without a hearing;

(b) the court gave it at a hearing in his absence; or

(c) circumstances have changed.

(2) A party who applies to vary a direction must—

(a) apply as soon as practicable after he becomes aware of the grounds for doing so; and

(b) give as much notice to the other parties as the nature and urgency of his application permits.

Agreement to vary a time limit fixed by a direction

3.7.—(1) The parties may agree to vary a time limit fixed by a direction, but only if— **G–9**

(a) the variation will not—

(i) affect the date of any hearing that has been fixed, or

(ii) significantly affect the progress of the case in any other way;

(b) the court has not prohibited variation by agreement; and

(c) the court's case progression officer is promptly informed.

(2) The court's case progression officer must refer the agreement to the court if he doubts the condition in paragraph (1)(a) is satisfied.

Case preparation and progression

3.8.—(1) At every hearing, if a case cannot be concluded there and then the court must give directions so that it can be concluded at the next hearing or as soon as possible after that. **G–10**

(2) At every hearing the court must, where relevant—

(a) if the defendant is absent, decide whether to proceed nonetheless;

(b) take the defendant's plea (unless already done) or if no plea can be taken then find out whether the defendant is likely to plead guilty or not guilty;

(c) set, follow or revise a timetable for the progress of the case, which may include a timetable for any hearing including the trial or (in the Crown Court) the appeal;

(d) in giving directions, ensure continuity in relation to the court and to the parties' representatives where that is appropriate and practicable; and

(e) where a direction has not been complied with, find out why, identify who was responsible, and take appropriate action.

(3) In order to prepare for a trial in the Crown Court, the court must conduct a plea and case management hearing unless the circumstances make that unnecessary.

(4) In order to prepare for the trial, the court must take every reasonable step to encourage and to facilitate the attendance of witnesses when they are needed.

Readiness for trial or appeal

3.9.—(1) This rule applies to a party's preparation for trial or appeal, and in this rule and rule 3.10 trial includes any hearing at which evidence will be introduced. **G–11**

(2) In fulfilling his duty under rule 3.3, each party must—

(a) comply with directions given by the court;

(b) take every reasonable step to make sure his witnesses will attend when they are needed;

(c) make appropriate arrangements to present any written or other material; and

Appendices

(d) promptly inform the court and the other parties of anything that may—
(i) affect the date or duration of the trial or appeal, or
(ii) significantly affect the progress of the case in any other way.
(3) The court may require a party to give a certificate of readiness.

Conduct of a trial or an appeal

G–12 **3.10.** In order to manage a trial or an appeal, the court—
(a) must establish, with the active assistance of the parties, what are the disputed issues;
(b) must consider setting a timetable that—
(i) takes account of those issues and of any timetable proposed by a party, and
(ii) may limit the duration of any stage of the hearing;
(c) may require a party to identify—
(i) which witnesses that party wants to give evidence in person,
(ii) the order in which that party wants those witnesses to give their evidence,
(iii) whether that party requires an order compelling the attendance of a witness,
(iv) what arrangements are desirable to facilitate the giving of evidence by a witness,
(v) what arrangements are desirable to facilitate the participation of any other person, including the defendant,
(vi) what written evidence that party intends to introduce,
(vii) what other material, if any, that person intends to make available to the court in the presentation of the case, and
(viii) whether that party intends to raise any point of law that could affect the conduct of the trial or appeal; and
(d) may limit—
(i) the examination, cross-examination or re-examination of a witness, and
(ii) the duration of any stage of the hearing.

Case management forms and records

G–13 **3.11.**—(1) The case management forms set out in the Practice Direction must be used, and where there is no form then no specific formality is required.
(2) The court must make available to the parties a record of directions given.
(3) Where a person is entitled or required to attend a hearing, the court officer must give as reasonably practicable to—
(a) that person; and
(b) that person's custodian (if any).

PART 4 SERVICE OF DOCUMENTS

Contents of this Part

When this Part applies

4.1. The rules in this Part apply to the service of every document in a case to which these Rules apply, subject to any special rules in other legislation (including other Parts of these Rules) or in the Practice Direction. **G–14**

4.2.—(1) A document may be served by any of the methods described in rules 4.3 to 4.6 (subject to rule 4.7), or in rule 4.8. **G–15**

(2) Where a document may be served by electronic means, the general rule is that the person serving it will use that method.

Service by handing over a document

4.3.—(1) A document may be served on— **G–16**

(a) an individual by handing it to him or her;

(b) a corporation by handing it to a person holding a senior position in that corporation;

(c) an individual or corporation who is legally represented in the case by handing it to that representative;

(d) the prosecution by handing it to the prosecutor or to the prosecution representative;

(e) the court officer by handing it to a court officer with authority to accept it at the relevant court office; and

(f) the Registrar of Criminal Appeals by handing it to a court officer with authority to accept it at the Criminal Appeal Office.

(2) If an individual is under 18, a copy of a document served under paragraph (1)(a) must be handed to his or her parent, or another appropriate adult, unless no such person is readily available.

Service by leaving or posting a document

4.4—(1) A document may be served by leaving it at the appropriate address for service under this rule or by sending it to that address by first class post or by the equivalent of first class post. **G–17**

(2) The address for service under this rule on—

(a) an individual is an address where it is reasonably believed that he or she will receive it;

(b) a corporation is its principal office, and if there is no readily identifiable principal office then any place where it carries on its activities or business;

(c) an individual or corporation who is legally represented in the case is that representative's office;

(d) the prosecution is the prosecutor's office;

(e) the court officer is the relevant court office; and

(f) the Registrar of Criminal Appeals is the Criminal Appeal Office, Royal Courts of Justice, Strand, London, WC2A 2LL.

Service through a document exchange

4.5. A document may be served by document exchange (DX) where— **G–18**

(a) the person to be served—

(i) has given a DX box number, and

(ii) has not refused to accept service by DX; or

(b) the person to be served is legally represented in the case and the representative has given a DX box number.

Service by electronic means

4.6.—(1) A document may be served by electronic means where— **G–19**

(a) the person to be served—

(i) has given an electronic address, and

(ii) has not refused to accept service by that method; or

(b) the person to be served is legally represented in the case and the representative has given an electronic address.

(2) Where a document is served under this rule the person serving it need not provide a paper copy as well.

Documents that must be served by specified methods

G–20 **4.7.**—(1) The documents listed in paragraph (2) may be served—

(a) on an individual, only under rule 4.3(1)(a) (handing over) or rule 4.4(1) and (2)(a) (leaving or posting); and

(b) on a corporation, only under rule 4.3(1)(b) (handing over) or rule 4.4(1) and (2)(b) (leaving or posting).

(2) Those documents are—

(a) a summons, requisition or witness summons;

(b) notice of an order under section 25 of the *Road Traffic Offenders Act* 1988;

(c) a notice of registration under section 71(6) of that Act;

(d) notice of a hearing to review the postponement of the issue of a warrant of detention or imprisonment under section 77(6) of the *Magistrates' Courts Act* 1980;

(e) notice under section 86 of that Act of a revised date to attend a means inquiry;

(f) any notice or document served under Part 19 (bail in magistrates' courts and the Crown Court);

(g) notice under rule 37.15(a) of when and where an adjourned hearing will resume;

(h) notice under rule 42.5(3) of an application to vary or discharge a compensation order;

(i) notice under rule 42.10(2)(c) of the location of the sentencing or enforcing court;

(j) a collection order, or notice requiring payment, served under rule 52.2(a).

(k) any notice or document served under Part 19.

(3) An application or written statement, and notice, under rule 62.9 alleging contempt of court may be served—

(a) on an individual, only under rule 4.3(1)(a) (by handing it to him or her);

(b) on a corporation, only under rule 4.3(1)(b) (by handing it to a person holding a senior position in that corporation).

Service by person in custody

G–21 **4.8.**—(1) A person in custody may serve a document by handing it to the custodian addressed to the person to be served.

(2) The custodian must—

(a) endorse it with the time and date of receipt;

(b) record its receipt; and

(c) forward it promptly to the addressee.

Service by another method

G–22 **4.9.**—(1) The court may allow service of a document by a method—

(a) other than those described in rules 4.3 to 4.6 and in rule 4.8;

(b) other than one specified by rule 4.7, where that rule applies.

Date of service

G–23 **4.10.**—(1) A document served under rule 4.3 or rule 4.8 is served on the day it is handed over.

(2) Unless something different is shown, a document served on a person by any other method is served—

(a) in the case of a document left at an address, on the next business day after the day on which it was left;

(b) in the case of a document sent by first class post or by the equivalent of first class post, on the second business day after the day on which it was posted or despatched;

(c) in the case of a document served by document exchange, on the second business day after the day on which it was left at the addressee's DX or at a correspondent DX;

(d) in the case of a document transmitted by electronic means, on the next business day after it was transmitted; and

(e) in any case, on the day on which the addressee responds to it if that is earlier.

(3) Unless something different is shown, a document produced by a court computer system is to be taken as having been sent by first class post or by the equivalent of first class post, to the addressee on the business day after the day on which it was produced.

(4) Where a document is served on or by the court officer, 'business day' does not include a day on which the court office is closed.

Proof of service

4.11. The person who serves a document may prove that by signing a certificate explaining how and when it was served. **G–24**

Court's power to give directions about service

4.12.—(1) The court may specify the time as well as the date by which a document must be— **G–25**

(a) served under rule 4.3 or rule 4.8; or

(b) transmitted by electronic means if it is served under rule 4.6.

(2) The court may treat a document as served if the addressee responds to it even if it was not served in accordance with the rules in this Part.

PART 5 FORMS AND COURT RECORDS

Contents of this Part

SECTION 1: FORMS

Forms

5.1. The forms set out in the Practice Direction and in the Criminal Costs Practice Direction shall be used as appropriate in connection with the rules to which they apply. **G–26**

Forms in Welsh

5.2.—(1) Any Welsh language form set out in the Practice Direction, or in the Criminal Costs Practice Direction, is for use in connection with proceedings in courts in Wales. **G–27**

Appendices

(2) Both a Welsh form and an English form may be contained in the same document.

(3) Where only a Welsh form, or only the corresponding English form, is served—

(a) the following words in Welsh and English must be added:

"Darperir y ddogfen hon yn Gymraeg / Saesneg os bydd arnoch ei heisiau. Dylech wneud cais yn ddi-oed i (swyddog y llys) (rhodder yma'r cyfeiriad)

This document will be provided in Welsh / English if you require it. You should apply immediately to (the court officer) (address)"; and

(b) the court officer, or the person who served the form, must, on request, supply the corresponding form in the other language to the person served.

Signature of forms

G–28 **5.3.**—(1) This rule applies where a form provides for its signature.

(2) Unless other legislation otherwise requires, signature may be by any written or electronic authentication of the form by, or with the authority of, the signatory.

SECTION 2: COURT RECORDS

Duty to make records

G–29 **5.4.**—(1) For each case, as appropriate, the court officer must record, by such means as the Lord Chancellor directs—

(a) each charge or indictment against the defendant;
(b) the defendant's plea to each charge or count;
(c) each acquittal, conviction, sentence, determination, direction or order;
(d) each decision about bail;
(e) the power exercised where the court commits or adjourns the case to another court—
  (i) for sentence, or
  (ii) for the defendant to be dealt with for breach of a community order, a deferred sentence, a conditional discharge, or a suspended sentence of imprisonment, imposed by that other court;
(f) the court's reasons for a decision, where legislation requires those reasons to be recorded;
(g) any appeal;
(h) each party's presence or absence at each hearing;
(i) any consent that legislation requires before the court can proceed with the case, or proceed to a decision;
(j) in a magistrates' court—
  (i) any indication of sentence given in connection with the allocation of a case for trial, and
  (ii) the registration of a fixed penalty notice for enforcement as a fine, and any related endorsement on a driving licence;
(k) in the Crown Court, any request for assistance or other communication about the case received from a juror; and
(l) the identity of—
  (i) the prosecutor,
  (ii) the defendant,
  (iii) any other applicant to whom these Rules apply,
  (iv) the parties' legal representatives, if any, and
  (v) the judge, magistrate or magistrates, justices' legal adviser or other person who made each recorded decision.

(2) Such records must include—

(a) each party's and representative's address, including any electronic address and telephone number available;
(b) the defendant's date of birth, if available; and
(c) the date of each event and decision recorded.

Recording and transcription of proceedings in the Crown Court

G–30 **5.5.**—(1) Where someone may appeal to the Court of Appeal, the court officer must—

(a) arrange for the recording of the proceedings in the Crown Court, unless the court otherwise directs; and

(b) arrange for the transcription of such a recording if—

(i) the Registrar wants such a transcript, or

(ii) anyone else wants such a transcript (but that is subject to the restrictions in paragraph (2)).

(2) Unless the court otherwise directs, a person who transcribes a recording of proceedings under such arrangements—

(a) must not supply anyone other than the Registrar with a transcript of a recording of—

(i) a hearing in private, or

(ii) information to which reporting restrictions apply;

(b) subject to that, must supply any person with any transcript for which that person asks—

(i) in accordance with the transcription arrangements made by the court officer, and

(ii) on payment by that person of any fee prescribed.

(3) A party who wants to hear a recording of proceedings must—

(a) apply—

(i) in writing to the Registrar, if an appeal notice has been served where Part 65 applies (Appeal to the Court of Appeal: general rules), or

(ii) orally or in writing to the Crown Court officer; (b) explain the reasons for the request; and

(c) pay any fee prescribed.

(4) If the Crown Court or the Registrar so directs, the Crown Court officer must allow that party to hear a recording of—

(a) a hearing in public;

(b) a hearing in private, if the applicant was present at that hearing.

Custody of case materials

5.6. Unless the court otherwise directs, in respect of each case the court officer may— **G–31**

(a) keep any evidence, application, representation or other material served by the parties; or

(b) arrange for the whole or any part to be kept by some other appropriate person, subject to—

(i) any condition imposed by the court, and

(ii) the rules in Part 63 (Appeal to the Crown Court) and Part 65 (Appeal to the Court of Appeal: general rules) about keeping exhibits pending any appeal.

Supply to a party of information or documents from records or case materials

5.7.—(1) This rule applies where a party wants information, or a copy of a document, from records or case materials kept by the court officer (for example, in case of loss, or to establish what is retained). **G–32**

(2) Such a party must—

(a) apply to the court officer;

(b) specify the information or document required; and

(c) pay any fee prescribed.

(3) The application—

(a) may be made orally, giving no reasons, if paragraph (4) requires the court officer to supply the information or document requested;

(b) must be in writing, unless the court otherwise permits, and must explain for what purpose the information is required, in any other case.

(4) The court officer must supply to the applicant party—

(a) a copy of any document served by, or on, that party (but not of any document not so served);

(b) by word of mouth, or in writing, as requested—

(i) information that was received from that party in the first place,

(ii) information about any direction or order directed to that party, or made on an application by that party, or at a hearing in public,

(iii) information about the outcome of the case.

(5) If the court so permits, the court officer may supply to the applicant party, by word of mouth or in writing, as requested, information that paragraph (4) does not require the court officer to supply.

Supply to the public, including reporters, of information about a case

G–32za **5.8.**—(1) This rule applies where a member of the public, including a reporter, wants information about a case from the court officer.

(2) Such a person must—

(a) apply to the court officer;

(b) specify the information requested; and

(c) pay any fee prescribed.

(3) The application—

(a) may be made orally, giving no reasons, if paragraph (4) requires the court officer to supply the information requested;

(b) must be in writing, unless the court otherwise permits, and must explain for what purpose the information is required, in any other case.

(4) The court officer must supply to the applicant—

(a) any information listed in paragraph (6), if—

(i) the information is available to the court officer,

(ii) the supply of the information is not prohibited by a reporting restriction, and

(iii) the trial has not yet concluded, or the verdict was not more than 6 months ago; and

(b) details of any reporting or access restriction ordered by the court.

(5) The court officer will supply that information—

(a) by word of mouth; or

(b) by such other arrangements as the Lord Chancellor directs.

(6) The information that paragraph (4) requires the court officer to supply is—

(a) the date of any hearing in public, unless any party has yet to be notified of that date;

(b) each alleged offence and any plea entered;

(c) the court's decision at any hearing in public, including any decision about—

(i) bail, or

(ii) the committal, sending or transfer of the case to another court;

(d) whether the case is under appeal;

(e) the outcome of any trial and any appeal; and

(f) the identity of—

(i) the prosecutor,

(ii) the defendant,

(iii) the parties' representatives, including their addresses, and

(iv) the judge, magistrate or magistrates, or justices' legal adviser by whom a decision at a hearing in public was made.

(7) If the court so directs, the court officer will—

(a) supply to the applicant, by word of mouth, other information about the case; or

(b) allow the applicant to inspect or copy a document, or part of a document, containing information about the case.

(8) The court may determine an application to which paragraph (7) applies—

(a) at a hearing, in public or in private; or

(b) without a hearing.

Supply of written certificate or extract from records

G–32zb **5.9.**—(1) This rule applies where legislation—

(a) allows a certificate of conviction or acquittal, or an extract from records kept by the court officer, to be introduced in evidence in criminal proceedings; or

(b) requires such a certificate or extract to be supplied by the court officer to a specified person for a specified purpose.

(2) A person who wants such a certificate or extract must—
(a) apply in writing to the court officer;
(b) specify the certificate or extract required;
(c) explain under what legislation and for what purpose it is required;
(d) and pay any fee prescribed.

(3) If the application satisfies the requirements of that legislation, the court officer must supply the certificate or extract requested—
(a) to a party;
(b) unless the court otherwise directs, to any other applicant.

PART 6 INVESTIGATION ORDERS

Contents of this Part

SECTION 1: UNDERSTANDING AND APPLYING THIS PART

When this Part applies

6.1.—(1) Sections 2 and 3 of this Part apply where, for the purposes of a terrorist investigation— **G–32a**

(a) a Circuit judge can make, vary or discharge—
(i) an order for the production of, or for giving access to, material, or for a statement of its location, under paragraphs 5 and 10 of Schedule 5 to the *Terrorism Act* 2000,
(ii) an explanation order, under paragraphs 10 and 13 of Schedule 5 to the 2000 Act,
(iii) a customer information order, under paragraphs 1 and 4 of Schedule 6 to the 2000 Act;

(b) a Circuit judge can make, and the Crown Court can vary or discharge, an account monitoring order, under paragraphs 2 and 4 of Schedule 6A to the 2000 Act.

(2) Sections 2 and 4 of this Part apply where, for the purposes of a confiscation investigation or a money laundering investigation, a Crown Court judge can make, and the Crown Court can vary or discharge—

(a) a production order, under sections 345 and 351 of the *Proceeds of Crime Act* 2002;

(b) an order to grant entry, under sections 347 and 351 of the 2002 Act;

(c) a disclosure order, under sections 357 and 362 of the 2002 Act;

(d) a customer information order, under sections 363 and 369 of the 2002 Act;

(e) an account monitoring order, under sections 370 and 375 of the 2002 Act(75).

(3) Rule 6.5 and Section 5 of this Part apply where—

(a) a justice of the peace can make or discharge an investigation anonymity order, under sections 76 and 80 of the *Coroners and Justice Act* 2009;

(b) a Crown Court judge can determine an appeal against—

(i) (i) a refusal of such an order, under section 79 of the 2009 Act,

(ii) a decision on an application to discharge such an order, under section 80(6) of the 2009 Act.

Meaning of 'court', 'applicant' and 'respondent'

G–32b **6.2.** In this Part—

(a) a reference to the 'court' includes a reference to any justice of the peace or judge who can exercise a power to which this Part applies;

(b) 'applicant' means any person who can apply for an order to which this Part applies; and

(c) 'respondent' means a person against whom such an order is sought or made.

SECTION 2: GENERAL RULES

Exercise of court's powers

G–32c **6.3.**—(1) The court must determine an application for an order—

(a) at a hearing (which will be in private unless the court otherwise directs); and

(b) in the applicant's presence.

(2) The court must not determine such an application in the absence of the respondent or any other person affected, unless—

(a) the absentee has had at least 2 business days in which to make representations; or

(b) the court is satisfied that—

(i) the applicant cannot identify or contact the absentee,

(ii) it would prejudice the investigation if the absentee were present, or

(iii) it would prejudice the investigation to adjourn or postpone the application so as to allow the absentee to attend.

(3) The court may determine an application to vary or discharge an order—

(a) at a hearing (which will be in private unless the court otherwise directs), or without a hearing; and

(b) in the absence of—

(i) the applicant,

(ii) the respondent,

(iii) any other person affected by the order.

Court's power to vary requirements under this Part

G–32d **6.4.**—(1) The court may—

(a) shorten or extend (even after it has expired) a time limit under this Part;

(b) dispense with a requirement for service under this Part (even after service was required); and

(c) consider an application made orally instead of in writing.

(2) A person who wants an extension of time must—

(a) apply when serving the application for which it is needed; and

(b) explain the delay.

Custody of documents

6.5. Unless the court otherwise directs, the court officer may— **G–32e**

(a) keep a written application; or

(b) arrange for the whole or any part to be kept by some other appropriate person, subject to any conditions that the court may impose.

SECTION 5: ORDERS UNDER THE CORONERS AND JUSTICE ACT 2009

Exercise of court's powers

6.23.—(1) The court may determine an application for an investigation anonymity order, and any appeal against the refusal of such an order— **G–32f**

(a) at a hearing (which will be in private unless the court otherwise directs); or

(b) without a hearing.

(2) The court must determine an application to discharge an investigation anonymity order, and any appeal against the decision on such an application—

(a) at a hearing (which will be in private unless the court otherwise directs); and

(b) in the presence of the person specified in the order, unless—

(i) that person applied for the discharge of the order,

(ii) that person has had an opportunity to make representations, or

(iii) the court is satisfied that it is not reasonably practicable to communicate with that person.

(3) The court may consider an application or an appeal made orally instead of in writing.

Application for an investigation anonymity order

6.24.—(1) This rule applies where an applicant wants a magistrates' court to make an investigation anonymity order. **G–32g**

(2) The applicant must—

(a) apply in writing;

(b) serve the application on the court officer;

(c) identify the person to be specified in the order, unless—

(i) the applicant wants the court to determine the application at a hearing, or

(ii) the court otherwise directs;

(d) explain how the proposed order meets the conditions prescribed by section 78 of the *Coroners and Justice Act* 2009;

(e) say if the applicant intends to appeal should the court refuse the order;

(f) attach any material on which the applicant relies; and

(g) propose the terms of the order.

(3) At any hearing of the application, the applicant must—

(a) identify to the court the person to be specified in the order, unless—

(i) the applicant has done so already, or

(ii) the court otherwise directs; and

(b) unless the applicant has done so already, inform the court if the applicant intends to appeal should the court refuse the order.

Application to discharge an investigation anonymity order

6.25.—(1) This rule applies where one of the following wants a magistrates' court to discharge an investigation anonymity order— **G–32h**

(a) an applicant; or

(b) the person specified in the order.

(2) That applicant or the specified person must—

(a) apply in writing as soon as practicable after becoming aware of the grounds for doing so;

(b) serve the application on—
(i) the court officer, and as applicable
(ii) the applicant for the order, and
(iii) the specified person;
(c) explain—
(i) what material circumstances have changed since the order was made, or since any previous application was made to discharge it, and
(ii) why it is appropriate for the order to be discharged; and
(d) attach—.
(i) a copy of the order, and
(ii) any material on which the applicant relies.

(3) A party must inform the court if that party intends to appeal should the court discharge the order

Appeal

G–32i **6.26.**—(1) This rule applies where one of the following ('the appellant') wants to appeal to the Crown Court—
(a) the applicant for an investigation anonymity order, where a magistrates' court has refused to make the order;
(b) a party to an application to discharge such an order, where a magistrates' court has decided that application.

(2) The appellant must—
(a) serve on the Crown Court officer a copy of the application to the magistrates' court; and
(b) where the appeal concerns a discharge decision, notify each other party, not more that 21 days after the decision against which the appellant wants to appeal.

(3) The Crown Court must hear the appeal without justices of the peace.

PART 7 STARTING A PROSECUTION IN A MAGISTRATES' COURT

Contents of this Part

When this Part applies

G–33 **7.1.**—(1) This Part applies in a magistrates' court where—
(a) a prosecutor wants the court to issue a summons or warrant under section 1 of the *Magistrates' Courts Act* 1980;
(b) a public prosecutor—
(i) wants the court to issue a warrant under section 1 of the *Magistrates' Courts Act* 1980, or
(ii) issues a written charge and requisition under section 29 of the *Criminal Justice Act* 2003; or
(c) a person who is in custody is charged with an offence.

(2) In this Part, 'public prosecutor' means one of those public prosecutors listed in section 29 of the *Criminal Justice Act* 2003.

Information and written charge

G–34 **7.2.**—(1) A prosecutor who wants the court to issue a summons must—

(a) serve an information in writing on the court officer; or

(b) unless other legislation prohibits this, present an information orally to the court, with a written record of the allegation that it contains.

(2) A prosecutor who wants the court to issue a warrant must—

(a) serve on the court officer—

(i) an information in writing, or

(ii) a copy of a written charge that has been issued; or

(b) present to the court either of those documents.

(3) A public prosecutor who issues a written charge must notify the court officer immediately.

(4) A single document may contain—

(a) more than one information; or

(b) more than one written charge.

(5) Where an offence can be tried only in a magistrates' court, then unless other legislation otherwise provides—

(a) a prosecutor must serve an information on the court officer or present it to the court; or

(b) a public prosecutor must issue a written charge, not more than 6 months after the offence alleged.

(6) Where an offence can be tried in the Crown Court then—

(a) a prosecutor must serve an information on the court officer or present it to the court; or

(b) a public prosecutor must issue a written charge, within any time limit that applies to that offence.

Allegation of offence in information or charge

7.3.—(1) An allegation of an offence in an information or charge must contain— **G–35**

(a) a statement of the offence that—

(i) describes the offence in ordinary language, and

(ii) identifies any legislation that creates it; and

(b) such particulars of the conduct constituting the commission of the offence as to make clear what the prosecutor alleges against the defendant.

(2) More than one incident of the commission of the offence may be included in the allegation if those incidents taken together amount to a course of conduct having regard to the time, place or purpose of commission.

Summons, warrant and requisition

7.4.—(1) The court may issue or withdraw a summons or warrant— **G–36**

(a) without giving the parties an opportunity to make representations; and

(b) without a hearing, or at a hearing in public or in private.

(2) A summons, warrant or requisition may be issued in respect of more than one offence.

(3) A summons or requisition must—

(a) contain notice of when and where the defendant is required to attend the court;

(b) specify each offence in respect of which it is issued;

(c) in the case of a summons, identify—

(i) the court that issued it, unless that is otherwise recorded by the court officer, and

(ii) the court office for the court that issued it; and

(d) in the case of a requisition, identify the person under whose authority it is issued.

(4) A summons may be contained in the same document as an information.

(5) A requisition may be contained in the same document as a written charge.

(6) Where the court issues a summons—

(a) the prosecutor must—

(i) serve it on the defendant, and

(ii) notify the court officer; or

(b) the court officer must—

(i) serve it on the defendant, and

(ii) notify the prosecutor.

(7) Where a public prosecutor issues a requisition that prosecutor must—

(a) serve on the defendant—

(i) the requisition, and

(ii) the written charge; and

(b) serve a copy of each on the court officer.

(8) Unless it would be inconsistent with other legislation, a replacement summons or requisition may be issued without a fresh information or written charge where the one replaced—

(a) was served by leaving or posting it under rule 4.7 (documents that must be served only by handing them over, leaving or posting them); but

(b) is shown not to have been received by the addressee.

(9) A summons or requisition issued to a defendant under 18 may require that defendant's parent or guardian to attend the court with the defendant, or a separate summons or requisition may be issued for that purpose.

[This rule is printed as amended by the *Criminal Procedure (Amendment) Rules* 2010 (S.I. 2010 No. 1921), r.6.]

[The next paragraph is § G–42.]

PART 8 DISCONTINUING A PROSECUTION

Contents of this Part

When this Part applies

G–42 **8.1.**—(1) This Part applies where—

(a) the Director of Public Prosecutions, or the Director of Revenue and Customs Prosecutions, can discontinue a case in a magistrates' court, under section 23 of the *Prosecution of Offences Act* 1985;

(b) the Director of Public Prosecutions, or another public prosecutor, can discontinue a case sent for trial in the Crown Court, under section 23A of the *Prosecution of Offences Act* 1985.

(2) In this Part, "prosecutor" means one of those authorities.

Discontinuing a case

G–43 **8.2.**—(1) A prosecutor exercising a power to which this Part applies must serve notice on—

(a) the court officer;

(b) the defendant; and

(c) any custodian of the defendant.

(2) Such a notice must—

(a) identify—

(i) the defendant and each offence to which the notice relates,

(ii) the person serving the notice, and

(iii) the power that that person is exercising;

(b) explain—

(i) in the copy of the notice served on the court officer, the reasons for discontinuing the case,

(ii) that the notice brings the case to an end,

(iii) if the defendant is in custody for any offence to which the notice relates, that the defendant must be released from that custody, and

(iv) if the notice is under section 23 of the 1985 Act, that the defendant has a right to require the case to continue.

(3) Where the defendant is on bail, the court officer must notify—

(a) any surety; and

(b) any person responsible for monitoring or securing the defendant's compliance with a condition of bail.

Duty of Director of Public Prosecutions

8.3.—(1) This rule applies where a prosecutor serves a notice to discontinue under section 23 of the 1985 Act. **G–44**

(2) A defendant who wants the case to continue must serve notice—

(a) on the court officer; and

(b) not more than 35 days after service of the notice to discontinue.

(3) If the defendant serves such a notice, the court officer must—

(a) notify the prosecutor; and

(b) refer the case to the court.

[The next paragraph is § G–47.]

PART 10 COMMITTAL FOR TRIAL

Contents of this Part

Restrictions on reports of committal proceedings

10.1.—(1) Except in a case where evidence is, with the consent of the accused, to be tendered in his absence under section 4(4)(b) of the *Magistrates' Courts Act* 1980 (absence caused by ill health), a magistrates' court acting as examining justices shall before admitting any evidence explain to the accused the restrictions on reports of committal proceedings imposed by section 8 of that Act and inform him of his right to apply to the court for an order removing those restrictions. **G–47**

(2) Where a magistrates' court has made an order under section 8(2) of the 1980 Act removing restrictions on the reports of committal proceedings, such order shall be entered in the register.

(3) Where the court adjourns any such proceedings to another day, the court shall, at the beginning of any adjourned hearing, state that the order has been made.

Committal for trial without consideration of the evidence

10.2.—(1) This rule applies to committal proceedings where the accused has a solicitor acting for him in the case and where the court has been informed that all the evidence falls within section 5A(2) of the *Magistrates' Courts Act* 1980. **G–48**

(2) A magistrates' court inquiring into an offence in committal proceedings to which this rule applies shall cause the charge to be written down, if this has not already been done, and read to the accused and shall then ascertain whether he wishes to submit that there is insufficient evidence to put him on trial by jury for the offence with which he is charged.

(3) If the court is satisfied that the accused or, as the case may be, each of the accused does not wish to make such a submission as is referred to in paragraph (2) it shall, after receiving any written evidence falling within section 5A(3) of the 1980 Act, determine whether or not to commit the accused for trial without consideration of the evidence, and where it determines not to so commit the accused it shall proceed in accordance with rule 10.3.

Consideration of evidence at committal proceedings

G–49 **10.3.**—(1) This rule does not apply to committal proceedings where under section 6(2) of the *Magistrates' Courts Act* 1980 a magistrates' court commits a person for trial without consideration of the evidence.

(2) A magistrates' court inquiring into an offence as examining justices, having ascertained—

(a) that the accused has no legal representative acting for him in the case; or

(b) that the accused's legal representative has requested the court to consider a submission that there is insufficient evidence to put the accused on trial by jury for the offence with which he is charged, as the case may be, shall permit the prosecutor to make an opening address to the court, if he so wishes, before any evidence is tendered.

(3) After such opening address, if any, the court shall cause evidence to be tendered in accordance with sections 5B(4), 5C(4), 5D(5) and 5E(3) of the 1980 Act, that is to say by being read out aloud, except where the court otherwise directs or to the extent that it directs that an oral account be given of any of the evidence.

(4) The court may view any exhibits produced before the court and may take possession of them.

(5) After the evidence has been tendered the court shall hear any submission which the accused may wish to make as to whether there is sufficient evidence to put him on trial by jury for any indictable offence.

(6) The court shall permit the prosecutor to make a submission—

(a) in reply to any submission made by the accused in pursuance of paragraph (5); or

(b) where the accused has not made any such submission but the court is nevertheless minded not to commit him for trial.

(7) After hearing any submission made in pursuance of paragraph (5) or (6) the court shall, unless it decides not to commit the accused for trial, cause the charge to be written down, if this has not already been done, and, if the accused is not represented by counsel or a solicitor, shall read the charge to him and explain it in ordinary language.

Objection to committal statements being read at trial

G–50 **10.4.**—(1) This rule applies where—

(a) a written statement is admitted as evidence in committal proceedings;

(b) under Schedule 2 to the *Criminal Procedure and Investigations Act* 1996, the statement may be introduced in evidence at trial; and

(c) a party wants to object to that.

(2) Such a party must serve notice of objection—

(a) on each other party and on the Crown Court officer;

(b) not more than 14 days after the defendant is committed for trial.

(3) A prosecutor who introduces a written statement in committal proceedings must serve with it on the defendant a notice—

(a) of the right to object, and of the time limit; and

(b) that if the defendant does not object, the prosecutor may decide not to call the witness to give evidence in person at trial, but to rely on the written statement instead.

(4) The magistrates' court that commits the defendant for trial must remind the defendant of that right to object.

(5) The Crown Court may extend the time limit under this rule, even after it has

expired.

Material to be sent to court of trial

10.5.—(1) As soon as practicable after the committal of any person for trial, and in any case within 4 days from the date of his committal (not counting Saturdays, Sundays, Good Friday, Christmas Day or Bank Holidays), the magistrates' court officer shall, subject to the provisions of section 7 of the *Prosecution of Offences Act* 1985 (which relates to the sending of documents and things to the Director of Public Prosecutions), send to the Crown Court officer— **G–51**

(a) the information, if it is in writing;

(b)

(i) the evidence tendered in accordance with section 5A of the *Magistrates' Courts Act* 1980 and, where any of that evidence consists of a copy of a deposition or documentary exhibit which is in the possession of the court, any such deposition or documentary exhibit, and

(ii) a certificate to the effect that that evidence was so tendered;

(c) any notification by the prosecutor under section 5D(2) of the 1980 Act;

(d) a copy of the record made in pursuance of section 5 of the *Bail Act* 1976 relating to the grant or withholding of bail in respect of the accused on the occasion of the committal;

(e) any recognizance entered into by any person as surety for the accused together with a statement of any enlargement thereof under section 129(4) of the 1980 Act;

(f) a list of the exhibits produced in evidence before the justices or treated as so produced;

(g) such of the exhibits referred to in paragraph (1)(f) as have been retained by the justices;

(h) the names and addresses of any interpreters engaged for the defendant for the purposes of the committal proceedings, together with any telephone numbers at which they can be readily contacted, and details of the languages or dialects in connection with which they have been so engaged;

(i) if the committal was under section 6(2) of the 1980 Act (committal for trial without consideration of the evidence), a statement to that effect;

(j) if the magistrates' court has made an order under section 8(2) of the 1980 Act (removal of restrictions on reports of committal proceedings), a statement to that effect;

(k) the certificate of the examining justices as to the costs of the prosecution under the Costs in Criminal Cases (General) Regulations 1986;

(l) if any person under the age of 18 is concerned in the committal proceedings, a statement whether the magistrates' court has given a direction under section 39 of the *Children and Young Persons Act* 1933 (prohibition of publication of certain matter in newspapers);

(m) a copy of any representation order previously made in the case;

(n) a copy of any application for a representation order previously made in the case which has been refused; and

(o) any documents relating to an appeal by the prosecution against the granting of bail.

(2) The period of 4 days specified in paragraph (1) may be extended in relation to any committal for so long as the Crown Court officer directs, having regard to the length of any document mentioned in that paragraph or any other relevant circumstances.

PART 11 TRANSFER FOR TRIAL OF SERIOUS FRAUD CASES OR CASES INVOLVING CHILDREN

Contents of this Part

Appendices

Interpretation of this Part

G–52 **11.1.**—(1) In this Part, 'notice of transfer' means a notice referred to in section 4(1) of the *Criminal Justice Act* 1987 or section 53(1) of the *Criminal Justice Act* 1991.

(2) Where this Part requires a document to be given or sent, or a notice to be communicated in writing, it may, with the consent of the addressee, be sent by electronic communication.

(3) Electronic communication means a communication transmitted (whether from one person to another, from one device to another or from a person to a device or vice versa)—

(a) by means of an electronic communications network (within the meaning of the *Communications Act* 2003); or

(b) by other means but while in an electronic form.

Transfer on bail

G–53 **11.2.**—(1) Where a person in respect of whom notice of transfer has been given—

(a) is granted bail under section 5(3) or (7A) of the *Criminal Justice Act* 1987 by the magistrates' court to which notice of transfer was given; or

(b) is granted bail under paragraph 2(1) or (7) of Schedule 6 to the *Criminal Justice Act* 1991 by the magistrates' court to which notice of transfer was given, the magistrates' court officer shall give notice thereof in writing to the governor of the prison or remand centre to which the said person would have been committed by that court if he had been committed in custody for trial.

(2) Where notice of transfer is given under section 4(1) of the 1987 Act in respect of a corporation the magistrates' court officer shall give notice thereof to the governor of the prison to which would be committed a male over 21 committed by that court in custody for trial.

Notice where person removed to hospital

G–54 **11.3.** Where a transfer direction has been given by the Secretary of State under section 47 or 48 of the *Mental Health Act* 1983 in respect of a person remanded in custody by a magistrates' court and, before the direction ceases to have effect, notice of transfer is given in respect of that person, the magistrates' court officer shall give notice thereof in writing—

(a) to the governor of the prison to which that person would have been committed by that court if he had been committed in custody for trial; and

(b) to the managers of the hospital where he is detained.

Variation of arrangements for bail

G–55 **11.4.**—(1) A person who intends to make an application to a magistrates' court under section 3(8) of the *Bail Act* 1976 as that subsection has effect under section 3(8A) of that Act shall give notice thereof in writing to the magistrates' court officer, and to the designated authority or the defendant, as the case may be, and to any sureties concerned.

(2) Where, on an application referred to in paragraph (1), a magistrates' court varies or imposes any conditions of bail, the magistrates' court officer shall send to the Crown Court officer a copy of the record made in pursuance of section 5 of the 1976 Act relating to such variation or imposition of conditions.

Documents to be sent to the Crown Court

G–56 **11.5.** As soon as practicable after a magistrates' court to which notice of transfer has been given has discharged the functions reserved to it under section 4(1) of the *Criminal Justice Act* 1987 or section 53(3) of the*Criminal Justice Act* 1991, the magistrates' court officer shall send to the Crown Court officer—

(a) a list of the names, addresses and occupations of the witnesses;
(b) a copy of the record made in pursuance of section 5 of the *Bail Act* 1976 relating to the grant of withholding of bail in respect of the accused;
(c) any recognizance entered into by any person as surety for the accused together with a statement of any enlargement thereof;
(d) a copy of any representation order previously made in the case; and
(e) a copy of any application for a representation order previously made in the case which has been refused.

PART 12 SENDING FOR TRIAL

Contents of this Part

Documents to be sent to the Crown Court

12.1.—(1) As soon as practicable after any person is sent for trial (pursuant to section 51 of the *Crime and Disorder Act* 1998), and in any event within 4 days from the date on which he is sent (not counting Saturdays, Sundays, Good Friday, Christmas Day or Bank Holidays), the magistrates' court officer shall, subject to section 7 of the *Prosecution of Offences Act* 1985 (which relates to the sending of documents and things to the Director of Public Prosecutions), send to the Crown Court officer— **G–57**

(a) the information, if it is in writing;
(b) the notice required by section 51(7) of the 1998 Act;
(c) a copy of the record made in pursuance of section 5 of the *Bail Act* 1976 relating to the granting or withholding of bail in respect of the accused on the occasion of the sending;
(d) any recognizance entered into by any person as surety for the accused together with any enlargement thereof under section 129(4) of the *Magistrates' Courts Act* 1980;
(e) the names and addresses of any interpreters engaged for the defendant for the purposes of the appearance in the magistrates' court, together with any telephone numbers at which they can be readily contacted, and details of the languages or dialects in connection with which they have been so engaged;
(f) if any person under the age of 18 is concerned in the proceedings, a statement whether the magistrates' court has given a direction under section 39 of the *Children and Young Persons Act* 1933 (prohibition of publication of certain matter in newspapers);
(g) a copy of any representation order previously made in the case;
(h) a copy of any application for a representation order previously made in the case which has been refused; and
(i) any documents relating to an appeal by the prosecution against the granting of bail.

(2) The period of 4 days specified in paragraph (1) may be extended in relation to any sending for trial for so long as the Crown Court officer directs, having regard to any relevant circumstances.

Time for first appearance of accused sent for trial

12.2. A Crown Court officer to whom notice has been given under section 51(7) of the *Crime and Disorder Act* 1998, shall list the first Crown Court appearance of the person to whom the notice relates in accordance with any directions given by the magistrates' court. **G–58**

[The next paragraph is § G–73.]

Appendices

PART 16 RESTRICTIONS ON REPORTING AND PUBLIC ACCESS

Contents of this Part

SECTION 1: GENERAL RULES

G–73 **16.1.**—(1) This Part applies where the court can—

(a) impose a restriction on—

(i) reporting what takes place at a public hearing, or

(ii) public access to what otherwise would be a public hearing;

(b) vary or remove a reporting or access restriction that is imposed by legislation;

(c) withhold information from the public during a public hearing;

(d) order a trial in private;

(e) allow there to take place during a hearing—

(i) sound recording, or

(ii) communication by electronic means.

(2) This Part does not apply to arrangements required by legislation, or directed by the court, in connection with—

(a) sound recording during a hearing, or the transcription of such a recording; or

(b) measures to assist a witness or defendant to give evidence.

Exercise of court's powers to which this Part applies

G–74 **16.2.**—(1) When exercising a power to which this Part applies, as well as furthering the overriding objective, in accordance with rule 1.3, the court must have regard to the importance of—

(a) dealing with criminal cases in public; and

(b) allowing a public hearing to be reported to the public.

(2) The court may determine an application under this Part—

(a) at a hearing, in public or in private; or

(b) without a hearing.

(3) But the court must not exercise a power to which this Part applies unless each party and any other person directly affected—

(a) is present; or

(b) has had an opportunity—

(i) to attend, or
(ii) to make representations.

Court's power to vary requirements under this Part

16.3.—(1) The court may— G–75

(a) shorten or extend (even after it has expired) a time limit under this Part;
(b) require an application to be made in writing instead of orally;
(c) consider an application or representations made orally instead of in writing;
(d) dispense with a requirement to—
(i) give notice, or
(ii) serve a written application.

(2) Someone who wants an extension of time must—

(a) apply when making the application or representations for which it is needed; and
(b) explain the delay.

SECTION 2: REPORTING AND ACCESS RESTRICTIONS

Reporting and access restrictions

16.4.—(1) This rule applies where the court can— G–76

(a) impose a restriction on—
(i) reporting what takes place at a public hearing, or
(ii) public access to what otherwise would be a public hearing;
(b) withhold information from the public during a public hearing.

(2) The court may do so—

(a) on application by a party; or
(b) on its own initiative.

(3) A party who wants the court to do so must—

(a) apply as soon as reasonably practicable;
(b) notify—
(i) each other party, and
(ii) such other person (if any) as the court directs;
(c) specify the proposed terms of the order, and for how long it should last;
(d) explain—
(i) what power the court has to make the order, and
(ii) why an order in the terms proposed is necessary;
(e) where the application is for a reporting direction in respect of a witness under section 46 of the *Youth Justice and Criminal Evidence Act* 1999, explain—
(i) how the witness is eligible for assistance, and
(ii) why a reporting direction would be likely to improve the quality of the witness' evidence, or the level of co-operation the witness gives the applicant in connection with the preparation of the applicant's case.

Varying or removing restrictions

16.5.—(1) This rule applies where the court can vary or remove a reporting or access restriction. G–77

(2) The court may do so—

(a) on application by a party or person directly affected; or
(b) on its own initiative.

(3) A party or person who wants the court to do so must—

(a) apply as soon as reasonably practicable;
(b) notify—
(i) each other party, and
(ii) such other person (if any) as the court directs;
(c) specify the restriction;
(d) explain, as appropriate, why it should be varied or removed.

Trial in private

G–78 **16.6.**—(1) This rule applies where the court can order a trial in private.

(2) A party who wants the court to do so must—

(a) apply in writing not less than 5 business days before the trial is due to begin; and

(b) serve the application on—

(i) the court officer, and

(ii) each other party.

(3) The applicant must explain—

(a) the reasons for the application;

(b) how much of the trial the applicant proposes should be in private; and

(c) why no measures other than trial in private will suffice, such as—

(i) reporting restrictions,

(ii) an admission of facts,

(iii) the introduction of hearsay evidence,

(iv) a direction for a special measure under section 19 of the *Youth Justice and Criminal Evidence Act* 1999,

(v) a witness anonymity order under section 86 of the *Coroners and Justice Act* 2009, or

(vi) arrangements for the protection of a witness.

(4) Where the application includes information that the applicant thinks ought not be revealed to another party, the applicant must—

(a) omit that information from the part of the application that is served on that other party;

(b) mark the other part to show that, unless the court otherwise directs, it is only for the court; and

(c) in that other part, explain why the applicant has withheld that information from that other party.

(5) The court officer must at once—

(a) display notice of the application somewhere prominent in the vicinity of the courtroom; and

(b) give notice of the application to reporters by such other arrangements as the Lord Chancellor directs.

(6) The application must be determined at a hearing which—

(a) will be in private, unless the court otherwise directs;

(b) if the court so directs, may be, wholly or in part, in the absence of a party from whom information has been withheld; and

(c) in the Crown Court, must be after the defendant is arraigned but before the jury is sworn.

(7) At the hearing of the application—

(a) the general rule is that the court will receive, in the following sequence—

(i) representations first by the applicant and then by each other party, in all the parties' presence, and then

(ii) further representations by the applicant, in the absence of a party from whom information has been withheld; but

(b) the court may direct other arrangements for the hearing.

(8) The court must not hear a trial in private until—

(a) the business day after the day on which it orders such a trial, or

(b) the disposal of any appeal against, or review of, any such order, if later.

Representations in response

G–79 **16.7.**—(1) This rule applies where a party, or person directly affected, wants to make representations about an application.

(2) Such a party or person must—

(a) serve the representations on—

(i) the court officer,

(ii) the applicant,

(iii) each other party, and

(iv) such other person (if any) as the court directs;

(b) do so as soon as reasonably practicable after notice of the application; and
(c) ask for a hearing, if that party or person wants one, and explain why it is needed.
(3) Representations must—
(a) explain the reasons for any objection;
(b) specify any alternative terms proposed.

Order about restriction or trial in private

16.8.—(1) This rule applies where the court— **G–80**
(a) orders, varies or removes a reporting or access restriction; or
(b) orders a trial in private.
(2) The court officer must—
(a) record the court's reasons for the decision; and
(b) as soon as reasonably practicable, arrange for notice of the decision to be—
(i) displayed somewhere prominent in the vicinity of the courtroom, and
(ii) communicated to reporters by such other arrangements as the Lord Chancellor directs.

SECTION 3: SOUND RECORDING AND ELECTRONIC COMMUNICATION

Sound recording and electronic communication

16.9.—(1) This rule applies where the court can give permission to— **G–81**
(a) bring into a hearing for use, or use during a hearing, a device for—
(i) recording sound, or
(ii) communicating by electronic means; or
(b) publish a sound recording made during a hearing.
(2) The court may give such permission—
(a) on application; or
(b) on its own initiative.
(3) A person who wants the court to give such permission must—
(a) apply as soon as reasonably practicable;
(b) notify—
(i) each party, and
(ii) such other person (if any) as the court directs; and
(c) explain why the court should permit the use or publication proposed.
(4) As a condition of the applicant using such a device, the court may direct arrangements to minimise the risk of its use—
(a) contravening a reporting restriction;
(b) disrupting the hearing; or
(c) compromising the fairness of the hearing, for example by affecting—
(i) the evidence to be given by a witness, or
(ii) the verdict of a jury.
(5) Such a direction may require that the device is used only—
(a) in a specified part of the courtroom;
(b) for a specified purpose;
(c) for a purpose connected with the applicant's activity as a member of a specified group, for example representatives of news-gathering or reporting organisations;
(d) at a specified time, or in a specified way.

Forfeiture of unauthorised sound recording

16.10.—(1) This rule applies where someone without the court's permission— **G–82**
(a) uses a device for recording sound during a hearing; or
(b) publishes a sound recording made during a hearing.
(2) The court may exercise its power to forfeit the device or recording—
(a) on application by a party, or on its own initiative;

(b) provisionally, despite rule 16.2(3), to allow time for representations.

(3) A party who wants the court to forfeit a device or recording must—

(a) apply as soon as reasonably practicable;

(b) notify—

(i) as appropriate, the person who used the device, or who published the recording, and

(ii) each other party; and

(c) explain why the court should exercise that power.

[The next paragraph is § G-84.]

PART 17 EXTRADITION

Contents of this Part

Refusal to make an order of committal

G–84 **17.1.**—(1) Where a magistrates' court refuses to make an order of committal in relation to a person in respect of the offence or, as the case may be, any of the offences to which the authority to proceed relates and the state, country or colony seeking the surrender of that person immediately informs the court that it intends to make an application to the court to state a case for the opinion of the High Court, if the magistrates' court makes an order in accordance with section 10(2) of the *Extradition Act* 1989 releasing that person on bail, the court officer shall forthwith send a copy of that order to the Administrative Court Office.

(2) Where a magistrates' court refuses to make an order of committal in relation to a person in respect of the offence or, as the case may be, any of the offences to which the authority to proceed relates and the state, country or colony seeking his surrender wishes to apply to the court to state a case for the opinion of the High Court under section 10(1) of the 1989 Act, such application must be made to the magistrates' court within the period of 21 days following the day on which the court refuses to make the order of committal unless the court grants a longer period within which the application is to be made.

(3) Such an application shall be made in writing and shall identify the question or questions of law on which the opinion of the High Court is sought.

(4) Within 21 days after receipt of an application to state a case under section 10(1) of

the 1989 Act, the magistrates' court officer shall send a draft case to the solicitor for the state, country or colony and to the person whose surrender is sought or his solicitor and shall allow each party 21 days within which to make representations thereon; within 21 days after the latest day on which such representations may be made the court of committal shall, after considering any such representations and making such adjustments, if any, to the draft case as it thinks fit, state and sign the case which the court officer shall forthwith send to the solicitor for the state, country or colony.

Notice of waiver

17.2.—(1) A notice given under section 14 of, or paragraph 9 of Schedule 1 to, the *Extradition Act* 1989 (notice of waiver under the simplified procedure) shall be in the form set out in the Practice Direction or a form to the like effect. **G–85**

(2) Such a notice shall be signed in the presence of the Senior District Judge (Chief Magistrate) or another District Judge (Magistrates' Courts) designated by him for the purposes of the Act, a justice of the peace or a justices' clerk.

(3) Any such notice given by a person in custody shall be delivered to the Governor of the prison in whose custody he is.

(4) If a person on bail gives such notice he shall deliver it to, or send it by post in a registered letter or by recorded delivery service addressed to, the Secretary of State for the Home Department, c/o the Extradition Section, Home Office, 5th Floor, Fry Building, 2 Marsham Street, London, SW1P 4DF.

Notice of consent

17.3.—(1) A person arrested in pursuance of a warrant under section 8 of or paragraph 5 of Schedule 1 to the *Extradition Act* 1989 may at any time consent to his return; and where such consent is given in accordance with the following provisions of this rule, the Senior District Judge (Chief Magistrate) or another District Judge (Magistrates' Courts) designated by him for the purposes of the Act may order the committal for return of that person in accordance with section 14(2) of that Act or, as the case may be, paragraph 9(2) of Schedule 1 to the Act. **G–86**

(2) A notice of consent for the purposes of this rule shall be given in the form set out in the Practice Direction and shall be signed in the presence of the Senior District Judge (Chief Magistrate) or another District Judge (Magistrates' Courts) designated by him for the purposes of the 1989 Act.

Notice of consent (parties to 1995 Convention)

17.4.—(1) This rule applies as between the United Kingdom and states other than the Republic of Ireland that are parties to the Convention drawn up on the basis of Article 31 of the Treaty on European Union on Simplified Extradition Procedures between the Member States of the European Union, in relation to which section 14A of the *Extradition Act* 1989 applies by virtue of section 34A and Schedule 1A of that Act. **G–87**

(2) Notice of consent for the purposes of section 14A(3) of the 1989 Act shall be given in the form set out in the Practice Direction and shall be signed in the presence of the Senior District Judge (Chief Magistrate) or another District Judge (Magistrates' Courts) designated by him for the purposes of that Act.

(3) The Senior District Judge (Chief Magistrate) or another District Judge (Magistrates' Courts) designated by him for the purposes of the Act may order the committal for return of a person if he gives consent under section 14A of the 1989 Act in accordance with paragraph (2) above before he is committed under section 9 of that Act.

Consent to early removal to Republic of Ireland

17.5.—(1) A notice given under section 3(1)(a) of the *Backing of Warrants (Republic of Ireland) Act* 1965 (consent to surrender earlier than is otherwise permitted) shall be signed in the presence of a justice of the peace or a justices' clerk. **G–88**

(2) Any such notice given by a person in custody shall be delivered to the Governor of the prison in whose custody he is.

(3) If a person on bail gives such notice, he shall deliver it to, or send it by post in a registered letter or by recorded delivery service addressed to, the police officer in charge of the police station specified in his recognizance.

(4) Any such notice shall be attached to the warrant ordering the surrender of that person.

Appendices

Bail pending removal to Republic of Ireland

G–89 **17.6.**—(1) The person taking the recognizance of a person remanded on bail under section 2(1) or 4(3) of the *Backing of Warrants (Republic of Ireland) Act* 1965 shall furnish a copy of the recognizance to the police officer in charge of the police station specified in the recognizance.

(2) The court officer for a magistrates' court which ordered a person to be surrendered and remanded him on bail shall deliver to, or send by post in a registered letter or by recorded delivery service addressed to, the police officer in charge of the police station specified in the recognizance the warrant ordering the person to be surrendered.

(3) The court officer for a magistrates' court which refused to order a person to be delivered under section 2 of the 1965 Act but made an order in accordance with section 2A(2) of that Act releasing that person on bail, upon the chief officer of police immediately informing the court that he intended to make an application to the court to state a case for the opinion of the High Court, shall forthwith send a copy of that order to the Administrative Court Office.

Delivery of warrant issued in Republic of Ireland

G–90 **17.7.**—(1) The court officer for a magistrates' court which ordered a person to be surrendered under section 2(1) of the *Backing of Warrants (Republic of Ireland) Act* 1965 shall deliver to, or send by post in a registered letter or by recorded delivery service addressed to—

(a) if he is remanded in custody under section 5(1)(a) of the 1965 Act, the prison Governor to whose custody he is committed;

(b) if he is remanded on bail under section 5(1)(b) of the 1965 Act, the police officer in charge of the police station specified in the recognizance; or

(c) if he is committed to the custody of a constable pending the taking from him of a recognizance under section 5(1) of the 1965 Act, the police officer in charge of the police station specified in the warrant of commitment, the warrant of arrest issued by a judicial authority in the Republic of Ireland and endorsed in accordance with section 1 of the 1965 Act.

(2) The Governor or police officer to whom the said warrant of arrest is delivered or sent shall arrange for it to be given to the member of the police force of the Republic into whose custody the person is delivered when the person is so delivered.

Verification of warrant etc. issued in Republic of Ireland

G–91 **17.8.**—(1) A document purporting to be a warrant issued by a judicial authority in the Republic of Ireland shall, for the purposes of section 7(a) of the *Backing of Warrants (Republic of Ireland) Act* 1965, be verified by a certificate purporting to be signed by a judicial authority, a clerk of a court or a member of the police force of the Republic and certifying that the document is a warrant and is issued by a judge or justice of a court or a peace commissioner.

(2) A document purporting to be a copy of a summons issued by a judicial authority in the Republic shall, for the purposes of section 7(a) of the 1965 Act, be verified by a certificate purporting to be signed by a judicial authority, a clerk of a court or a member of the police force of the Republic and certifying that the document is a true copy of such a summons.

(3) A deposition purporting to have been made in the Republic, or affidavit or written statement purporting to have been sworn therein, shall, for the purposes of section 7(c) of the 1965 Act, be verified by a certificate purporting to be signed by the person before whom it was sworn and certifying that it was so sworn.

Application to state a case where court declines to order removal to Republic of Ireland

G–92 **17.9.**—(1) Where a magistrates' court refuses to make an order in relation to a person under section 2 of the *Backing of Warrants (Republic of Ireland) Act* 1965, any application to the court under section 2A(1) of that Act to state a case for the opinion of the High Court on any question of law arising in the proceedings must be made to the court by the chief officer of police within the period of 21 days following the day on which the order was refused, unless the court grants a longer period within which the application is to be made.

(2) Such an application shall be made in writing and shall identify the question or questions of law on which the opinion of the High Court is sought.

Draft case where court declines to order removal to Republic of Ireland

G–93 **17.10.** Within 21 days after receipt of an application to state a case under section 2A(1) of the *Backing of Warrants (Republic of Ireland) Act* 1965, the magistrates' court officer shall send a draft case to the applicant or his solicitor and to the person to whom the warrant relates or his solicitor and shall allow each party 21 days within which to make representations thereon; within 21 days after the latest day on which such representations may be made the court shall, after considering such representations and making such adjustments, if any, to the draft case as it thinks fit, state and sign the case which the court officer shall forthwith send to the applicant or his solicitor.

Forms for proceedings for removal to Republic of Ireland

17.11. Where a requirement is imposed by the *Backing of Warrants (Republic of Ireland) Act* 1965 for the use of a form, and an appropriate form is contained in the Practice Direction, that form shall be used. **G–94**

PART 18 WARRANTS FOR ARREST, DETENTION OR IMPRISONMENT

Contents of this Part

When this Part applies

18.1.—(1) This Part applies where the court can issue a warrant for arrest, detention or imprisonment. **G–95**

(2) In this Part, "defendant" means anyone against whom such a warrant is issued.

Terms of a warrant for arrest

18.2. A warrant for arrest must require the person(s) to whom it is directed to arrest the defendant and— **G–96**

(a) bring the defendant to a court—
  (i) specified in the warrant, or
  (ii) required or allowed by law; or
(b) release the defendant on bail (with conditions or without) to attend court at a date, time and place—
  (i) specified in the warrant, or
  (ii) to be notified by the court.

Terms of a warrant for detention or imprisonment

18.3.—(1) A warrant for detention or imprisonment must— **G–97**

(a) require the person(s) to whom it is directed to—
  (i) arrest the defendant,
  (ii) take the defendant to any place specified in the warrant, and
  (iii) deliver the defendant to the custodian of that place; and
(b) require that custodian to keep the defendant in custody, as ordered by the court, until in accordance with the law—
  (i) the defendant is delivered to the appropriate court or place, or
  (ii) the defendant is released.

(2) Where a magistrates' court remands a defendant to police detention under section 128(7) or section 136 of the *Magistrates' Courts Act* 1980, or to customs detention under section 152 of the Criminal Justice Act 1988, the warrant it issues must—

(a) be directed, as appropriate, to—
(i) a constable, or
(ii) an officer of Her Majesty's Revenue and Customs; and
(b) require that constable or officer to keep the defendant in custody—
(i) for a period (not exceeding the maximum permissible) specified in the warrant, or
(ii) until in accordance with the law the defendant is delivered to the appropriate court or place.

Information to be included in a warrant

G–98 **18.4.**—(1) A warrant must identify—
(a) the person(s) to whom it is directed;
(b) the defendant against whom it was issued;
(c) the reason for its issue;
(d) the court that issued it, unless that is otherwise recorded by the court officer; and
(e) the court office for the court that issued it.

(2) A warrant for detention or imprisonment must contain a record of any decision by the court under—
(a) section 23 of the *Children and Young Persons Act* 1969 (remand to local authority accommodation);
(b) section 80 of the *Magistrates' Courts Act* 1980 (application of money found on defaulter to satisfy sum adjudged); or
(c) section 82(1) or (4) of the 1980 Act (conditions for issue of a warrant).

(3) A warrant that contains an error is not invalid, as long as—
(a) it was issued in respect of a lawful decision by the court; and
(b) it contains enough information to identify that decision.

Execution of a warrant

G–99 **18.5.**—(1) A warrant may be executed—
(a) by any person to whom it is directed; or
(b) if the warrant was issued by a magistrates' court, by anyone authorised to do so by section 125 (warrants), 125A (civilian enforcement officers) or 125B (execution by approved enforcement agency) of the *Magistrates' Courts Act* 1980.

(2) The person who executes a warrant must—
(a) explain, in terms the defendant can understand, what the warrant requires, and why;
(b) show the defendant the warrant, if that person has it; and
(c) if the defendant asks—
(i) arrange for the defendant to see the warrant, if that person does not have it, and
(ii) show the defendant any written statement of that person's authority required by section 125A or 125B of the 1980 Act.

(3) The person who executes a warrant of arrest that requires the defendant to be released on bail must—
(a) make a record of—
(i) the defendant's name,
(ii) the reason for the arrest,
(iii) the defendant's release on bail, and
(iv) when and where the warrant requires the defendant to attend court; and
(b) serve the record on—
(i) the defendant, and
(ii) the court officer.

(4) The person who executes a warrant of detention or imprisonment must—
(a) take the defendant—
(i) to any place specified in the warrant, or
(ii) if that is not immediately practicable, to any other place at which the defendant may be lawfully detained (and the warrant then has effect as if it specified that place);

(b) obtain a receipt from the custodian; and
(c) notify the court officer that the defendant has been taken to that place.

Warrants that cease to have effect on payment

18.6.—(1) This rule applies to a warrant issued by a magistrates' court under any of the following provisions of the *Magistrates' Courts Act* 1980— **G–100**

(a) section 76 (enforcement of sums adjudged to be paid);
(b) section 83 (process for securing attendance of offender);
(c) section 86 (power of magistrates' court to fix day for appearance of offender at means inquiry, etc.);
(d) section 136 (committal to custody overnight at police station for non-payment of sum adjudged by conviction).

(2) The warrant no longer has effect if—

(a) the sum in respect of which the warrant was issued is paid to the person executing it;
(b) that sum is offered to, but refused by, that person; or
(c) that person is shown a receipt for that sum given by—
(i) the court officer, or
(ii) the authority to which that sum is due.

Warrant issued when the court office is closed

18.7.—(1) This rule applies where the court issues a warrant when the court office is closed. **G–101**

(2) The applicant for the warrant must, not more than 72 hours later, serve on the court officer—

(a) a copy of the warrant; and
(b) any written material that was submitted to the court.

[The next paragraph is § G–111.]

Appendices

PART 19 BAIL IN MAGISTRATES' COURTS AND THE CROWN COURT

Contents of this Part

Application to a magistrates' court to vary conditions of bail

G–111 **19.1.**—(1) An application under section 43B(1) of the *Magistrates' Courts Act* 1980, or section 47(1E) of the *Police and Criminal Evidence Act* 1984, to vary conditions of police bail, shall—

(a) be made in writing;

(b) contain a statement of the grounds upon which it is made;

(c) where the applicant has been bailed following charge, specify the offence with which he was charged and, in any other case, specify the offence under investigation;

(d) specify, or be accompanied by a copy of the note of, the reasons given by the custody officer for imposing or varying the conditions of bail;

(e) specify the name and address of any surety provided by the applicant before his release on bail to secure his surrender to custody; and

(f) specify the address at which the applicant would reside, if the court imposed a condition of residence.

(2) Any such application shall be sent to the court officer for—

(a) the magistrates' court appointed by the custody officer as the court before which the applicant has a duty to appear; or

(b) if no such court has been appointed, a magistrates' court acting for the local justice area in which the police station at which the applicant was granted bail or at which the conditions of his bail were varied, as the case may be, is situated,

(3) The court officer to whom an application is sent under paragraph (2) above shall serve not less than 24 hours' notice in writing of the date, time and place fixed for the hearing of the application on—

(a) the applicant;

(b) the prosecutor or, if the applicant has not been charged, the chief officer of police or other investigator, together with a copy of the application; and

(c) any surety in connection with bail in criminal proceedings granted to, or the conditions of which were varied by a custody officer in relation to, the applicant.

(4) The time fixed for the hearing shall be not later than 72 hours after receipt of the application. In reckoning for the purposes of this paragraph any period of 72 hours, no account shall be taken of Christmas Day, Boxing Day, Good Friday, any bank holiday, or any Saturday or Sunday.

(5) A party who wants a magistrates' court to vary or impose conditions of bail under section 3(8) of the *Bail Act* 1976, must—

(a) serve notice, not less than 24 hours before the hearing at which that party intends to apply, on—

(i) the court officer, and

(ii) the other party; and

(b) in that notice—

(i) specify the variation or conditions proposed, and

(ii) explain the reasons.

(6) If the magistrates' court hearing an application under section 43B(1) of the 1980 Act or section 47(1E) of the 1984 Act discharges or enlarges any recognizance entered into by any surety or increases or reduces the amount in which that person is bound, the court officer shall forthwith give notice thereof to the applicant and to any such surety.

(7) The court—

(a) vary or waive a time limit under paragraph (3) or (5) of this rule; and

(b) allow a notice to be—

(i) in a different form to one set out in the Practice Direction, or

(ii) given orally.

Appendices

Application to a magistrates' court to reconsider grant of police bail

19.2.—(1) The appropriate court for the purposes of section 5B of the *Bail Act* 1976 in relation to the decision of a constable to grant bail shall be— **G–112**

(a) the magistrates' court appointed by the custody officer as the court before which the person to whom bail was granted has a duty to appear; or

(b) if no such court has been appointed, a magistrates' court acting for the local justice area in which the police station at which bail was granted is situated.

(2) An application under section 5B(1) of the 1976 Act shall—

(a) be made in writing;

(b) contain a statement of the grounds on which it is made;

(c) specify the offence which the proceedings in which bail was granted were connected with, or for;

(d) specify the decision to be reconsidered (including any conditions of bail which have been imposed and why they have been imposed);

(e) specify the name and address of any surety provided by the person to whom the application relates to secure his surrender to custody; and

(f) contain notice of the powers available to the court under section 5B of the 1976 Act.

(3) The court officer to whom an application is sent under paragraph (2) above shall serve notice in writing of the date, time and place fixed for the hearing of the application on—

(a) the prosecutor who made the application;

(b) the person to whom bail was granted, together with a copy of the application; and

(c) any surety specified in the application.

(4) The time fixed for the hearing shall be not later than 72 hours after receipt of the application. In reckoning for the purpose of this paragraph any period of 72 hours, no account shall be taken of Christmas Day, Good Friday, any bank holiday or any Sunday.

(5) At the hearing of an application under section 5B of the 1976 Act the court shall consider any representations made by the person affected (whether in writing or orally) before taking any decision under that section with respect to him; and, where the person affected does not appear before the court, the court shall not take such a decision unless it is proved to the satisfaction of the court, on oath or in the manner set out by rule 4.11, that the notice required to be given under paragraph (3) of this rule was served on him before the hearing.

(6) Where the court proceeds in the absence of the person affected in accordance with paragraph (6)—

(a) if the decision of the court is to vary the conditions of bail or impose conditions in respect of bail which has been granted unconditionally, the court officer shall notify the person affected;

(b) if the decision of the court is to withhold bail, the order of the court under section 5B(5)(b) of the 1976 Act (surrender to custody) shall be signed by the justice issuing it or state his name and be authenticated by the signature of the clerk of the court.

Notice of change of time for appearance before magistrates' court

G–113 **19.3.** Where—

(a) a person has been granted bail under the *Police and Criminal Evidence Act* 1984 subject to a duty to appear before a magistrates' court and the court before which he is to appear appoints a later time at which he is to appear; or

(b) a magistrates' court further remands a person on bail under section 129 of the *Magistrates' Courts Act* 1980 in his absence, it shall give him and his sureties, if any, notice thereof.

Directions by a magistrates' court as to security, etc

G–114 **19.4.** Where a magistrates' court, under section 3(5) or (6) of the*Bail Act* 1976, imposes any requirement to be complied with before a person's release on bail, the court may give directions as to the manner in which and the person or persons before whom the requirement may be complied with.

Requirements to be complied with before release on bail granted by a magistrates' court

G–115 **19.5.**—(1) Where a magistrates' court has fixed the amount in which a person (including any surety) is to be bound by a recognizance, the recognizance may be entered into—

(a) in the case of a surety where the accused is in a prison or other place of detention, before the governor or keeper of the prison or place as well as before the persons mentioned in section 8(4)(a) of the *Bail Act* 1976;

(b) in any other case, before a justice of the peace, a justices' clerk, a magistrates' court officer, a police officer who either is of the rank of inspector or above or is in charge of a police station or, if the person to be bound is in a prison or other place of detention, before the governor or keeper of the prison or place; or

(c) where a person other than a police officer is authorised under section 125A or 125B of the *Magistrates' Courts Act* 1980 to execute a warrant of arrest providing for a recognizance to be entered into by the person arrested (but not by any other person), before the person executing the warrant.

(2) The court officer for a magistrates' court which has fixed the amount in which a person (including any surety) is to be bound by a recognizance or, under section 3(5), (6) or (6A) of the 1976 Act imposed any requirement to be complied with before a person's release on bail or any condition of bail shall issue a certificate showing the amount and conditions, if any, of the recognizance, or as the case may be, containing a statement of the requirement or condition of bail; and a person authorised to take the recognizance or do anything in relation to the compliance with such requirement or condition of bail shall not be required to take or do it without production of such a certificate as aforesaid.

(3) If any person proposed as a surety for a person committed to custody by a magistrates' court produces to the governor or keeper of the prison or other place of detention in which the person so committed is detained a certificate to the effect that he is acceptable as a surety, signed by any of the justices composing the court or the clerk of the court and signed in the margin by the person proposed as surety, the governor or keeper shall take the recognizance of the person so proposed.

(4) Where the recognizance of any person committed to custody by a magistrates' court

or of any surety of such a person is taken by any person other than the court which committed the first-mentioned person to custody, the person taking the recognizance shall send it to the court officer for that court: Provided that, in the case of a surety, if the person committed has been committed to the Crown Court for trial or under any of the enactments mentioned in rule 43.1(1), the person taking the recognizance shall send it to the Crown Court officer.

Notice to governor of prison, etc, where release from custody is ordered by a magistrates' court

19.6. Where a magistrates' court has, with a view to the release on bail of a person in custody, fixed the amount in which he or any surety of such a person shall be bound or, under section 3(5), (6) or (6A) of the *Bail Act* 1976, imposed any requirement to be complied with before his release or any condition of bail— **G–116**

(a) the magistrates' court officer shall give notice thereof to the governor or keeper of the prison or place where that person is detained by sending him such a certificate as is mentioned in rule 19.5(2); and

(b) any person authorised to take the recognizance of a surety or do anything in relation to the compliance with such requirement shall, on taking or doing it, send notice thereof by post to the said governor or keeper and, in the case of a recognizance of a surety, shall give a copy of the notice to the surety.

Release when notice received by governor of prison that recognizances have been taken or requirements complied with

19.7. Where a magistrates' court has, with a view to the release on bail of a person in custody, fixed the amount in which he or any surety of such a person shall be bound or, under section 3(5) or (6) of the *Bail Act* 1976, imposed any requirement to be complied with before his release and given notice thereof in accordance with this Part to the governor or keeper of the prison or place where that person is detained, the governor or keeper shall, when satisfied that the recognizances of all sureties required have been taken and that all such requirements have been complied with, and unless he is in custody for some other cause, release him. **G–117**

Notice from a magistrates' court of enlargement of recognizances

19.8.—(1) If a magistrates' court before which any person is bound by a recognizance to appear enlarges the recognizance to a later time under section 129 of the *Magistrates' Courts Act* 1980 in his absence, it shall give him and his sureties, if any, notice thereof. **G–118**

(2) If a magistrates' court, under section 129(4) of the 1980 Act, enlarges the recognizance of a surety for a person committed for trial on bail, it shall give the surety notice thereof.

Further remand by a youth court

19.9. Where a child or young person has been remanded, and the period of remand is extended in his absence in accordance with section 48 of the *Children and Young Persons Act* 1933, notice shall be given to him and his sureties (if any) of the date at which he will be required to appear before the court. **G–119**

Notes of argument in magistrates' court bail hearings

19.10. Where a magistrates' court hears full argument as to bail, the clerk of the court shall take a note of that argument. **G–120**

Bail records to be entered in register of a magistrates' court

19.11. Any record required by section 5 of the *Bail Act* 1976 to be made by a magistrates' court (together with any note of reasons required by section 5(4) to be included and the particulars set out in any certificate granted under section 5(6A)) shall be made by way of an entry in the register. **G–121**

Notification of bail decision by a magistrate after arrest while on bail

19.12. Where a person who has been released on bail and is under a duty to surrender into the custody of a court is brought under section 7(4)(a) of the *Bail Act* 1976 before a justice of the peace, the justice shall cause a copy of the record made in pursuance of section 5 of that Act relating to his decision under section 7(5) of that Act in respect of that person to be sent to the court officer for that court: Provided that this rule shall not apply where the court is a magis- **G–122**

Appendices

trates' court acting for the same local justice area as that for which the justice acts.

Transfer of remand hearings

G–123 **19.13.**—(1) Where a magistrates' court, under section 130(1) of the *Magistrates' Courts Act* 1980, orders that an accused who has been remanded in custody be brought up for any subsequent remands before an alternate magistrates' court, the court officer for the first-mentioned court shall, as soon as practicable after the making of the order and in any case within 2 days thereafter (not counting Sundays, Good Friday, Christmas Day or bank holidays), send to the court officer for the alternate court—

(a) a statement indicating the offence or offences charged;

(b) a copy of the record made by the first-mentioned court in pursuance of section 5 of the *Bail Act* 1976 relating to the withholding of bail in respect of the accused when he was last remanded in custody;

(c) a copy of any representation order previously made in the same case;

(d) a copy of any application for a representation order;

(e) if the first-mentioned court has made an order under section 8(2) of the 1980 Act (removal of restrictions on reports of committal proceedings), a statement to that effect.

(f) a statement indicating whether or not the accused has a solicitor acting for him in the case and has consented to the hearing and determination in his absence of any application for his remand on an adjournment of the case under sections 5, 10(1) and 18(4) of the 1980 Act together with a statement indicating whether or not that consent has been withdrawn;

(g) a statement indicating the occasions, if any, on which the accused has been remanded under section 128(3A) of the 1980 Act without being brought before the first-mentioned court; and

(h) if the first-mentioned court remands the accused under section 128A(198) of the 1980 Act on the occasion upon which it makes the order under section 130(1) of that Act, a statement indicating the date set under section 128A(2) of that Act.

(2) Where the first-mentioned court is satisfied as mentioned in section 128(3A) of the 1980 Act, paragraph (1) shall have effect as if for the words 'an accused who has been remanded in custody be brought up for any subsequent remands before' there were substituted the words 'applications for any subsequent remands of the accused be made to'.

(3) The court officer for an alternate magistrates' court before which an accused who has been remanded in custody is brought up for any subsequent remands in pursuance of an order made as aforesaid shall, as soon as practicable after the order ceases to be in force and in any case within 2 days thereafter (not counting Sundays, Good Friday, Christmas Day or bank holidays), send to the court officer for the magistrates' court which made the order—

(a) a copy of the record made by the alternate court in pursuance of section 5 of the 1976 Act relating to the grant or withholding of bail in respect of the accused when he was last remanded in custody or on bail;

(b) a copy of any representation order made by the alternate court;

(c) a copy of any application for a representation order made to the alternate court;

(d) if the alternate court has made an order under section 8(2) of the 1980 Act removal of restrictions on reports of committal proceedings), a statement to that effect;

(e) a statement indicating whether or not the accused has a solicitor acting for him in the case and has consented to the hearing and determination in his absence of any application for his remand on an adjournment of the case under sections 5, 10(1) and 18(4) of the 1980 Act together with a statement indicating whether or not that consent has been withdrawn; and

(f) a statement indicating the occasions, if any, on which the accused has been remanded by the alternate court under section 128(3A) of the 1980 Act without being brought before that court.

(4) Where the alternate court is satisfied as mentioned in section 128(3A) of the 1980 Act paragraph (2) above shall have effect as if for the words 'an accused who has been remanded in custody is brought up for any subsequent remands' there shall be substituted the words 'applications for the further remand of the accused are to be made'

Notice of further remand in certain cases

G–124 **19.14.** Where a transfer direction has been given by the Secretary of State under section 47 of the *Mental Health Act* 1983 in respect of a person remanded in custody by a magistrates' court and the direction has not ceased to have effect, the court officer shall give notice in writing to the managers of the hospital where he is detained of any further remand under section 128 of the Magistrates' Courts Act 1980.

Cessation of transfer direction

19.15 Where a magistrates' court directs, under section 52(5) of the *Mental Health Act* 1983, that a transfer direction given by the Secretary of State under section 48 of that Act in respect of a person remanded in custody by a magistrates' court shall cease to have effect, the court officer shall give notice in writing of the court's direction to the managers of the hospital specified in the Secretary of State's direction and, where the period of remand has not expired or the person has been committed to the Crown Court for trial or to be otherwise dealt with, to the Governor of the prison to which persons of the sex of that person are committed by the court if remanded in custody or committed in custody for trial. **G–125**

Lodging an appeal against a grant of bail by a magistrates' court

19.16.—(1) Where the prosecution wishes to exercise the right of appeal, under section 1 of the *Bail (Amendment) Act* 1993, to a judge of the Crown Court against a decision to grant bail, the oral notice of appeal must be given to the justices' clerk and to the person concerned, at the conclusion of the proceedings in which such bail was granted and before the release of the person concerned. **G–126**

(2) When oral notice of appeal is given, the justices' clerk shall announce in open court the time at which such notice was given.

(3) A record of the prosecution's decision to appeal and the time the oral notice of appeal was given shall be made in the register and shall contain the particulars set out.

(4) Where an oral notice of appeal has been given the court shall remand the person concerned in custody by a warrant of commitment.

(5) On receipt of the written notice of appeal required by section 1(5) of the 1993 Act, the court shall remand the person concerned in custody by a warrant of commitment, until the appeal is determined or otherwise disposed of.

(6) A record of the receipt of the written notice of appeal shall be made in the same manner as that of the oral notice of appeal under paragraph (3).

(7) If, having given oral notice of appeal, the prosecution fails to serve a written notice of appeal within the two hour period referred to in section 1(5) of the 1993 Act the justices' clerk shall, as soon as practicable, by way of written notice (served by a court officer) to the persons in whose custody the person concerned is, direct the release of the person concerned on bail as granted by the magistrates' court and subject to any conditions which it imposed.

(8) If the prosecution serves notice of abandonment of appeal on a court officer, the justices' clerk shall, forthwith, by way of written notice (served by the court officer) to the governor of the prison where the person concerned is being held, or the person responsible for any other establishment where such a person is being held, direct his release on bail as granted by the magistrates' court and subject to any conditions which it imposed.

(9) A court officer shall record the prosecution's failure to serve a written notice of appeal, or its service of a notice of abandonment.

(10) Where a written notice of appeal has been served on a magistrates' court officer, he shall provide as soon as practicable to a Crown Court officer a copy of that written notice, together with—

(a) the notes of argument made by the court officer for the court under rule 19.10; and

(b) a note of the date, or dates, when the person concerned is next due to appear in the magistrates' court, whether he is released on bail or remanded in custody by the Crown Court.

(11) References in this rule to 'the person concerned' are references to such a person within the meaning of section 1 of the 1993 Act.

Crown Court procedure on appeal against grant of bail by a magistrates' court

19.17.—(1) This rule shall apply where the prosecution appeals under section 1 of the *Bail (Amendment) Act* 1993 against a decision of a magistrates' court granting bail and in this rule, 'the person concerned' has the same meaning as in that Act. **G–126a**

(2) The written notice of appeal required by section 1(5) of the 1993 Act shall be in the form set out in the Practice Direction and shall be served on—

(a) the magistrates' court officer; and

(b) the person concerned.

(3) The Crown Court officer shall enter the appeal and give notice of the time and place of the hearing to—

(a) the prosecution;

(b) the person concerned or his legal representative; and

(c) the magistrates' court officer.

(4) The person concerned shall be entitled to be present at the hearing of the appeal.

(5) Where a person concerned has not been able to instruct a solicitor to represent him at the appeal, he may give notice to the Crown Court requesting that the Official Solicitor shall represent him at the appeal, and the court may, if it thinks fit, assign the Official Solicitor to act for the person concerned accordingly.

(6) At any time after the service of written notice of appeal under paragraph (2), the prosecution may abandon the appeal by giving notice in writing in the form set out in the Practice Direction.

(7) The notice of abandonment required by the preceding paragraph shall be served on—

(a) the person concerned or his legal representative;

(b) the magistrates' court officer; and

(c) the Crown Court officer.

(8) Any record required by section 5 of the*Bail Act* 1976 (together with any note of reasons required by subsection (4) of that section to be included) shall be made by way of an entry in the file relating to the case in question and the record shall include the following particulars, namely—

(a) the effect of the decision;

(b) a statement of any condition imposed in respect of bail, indicating whether it is to be complied with before or after release on bail; and

(c) where bail is withheld, a statement of the relevant exception to the right to bail (as provided in Schedule 1 to the 1976 Act) on which the decision is based.

(9) The Crown Court officer shall, as soon as practicable after the hearing of the appeal, give notice of the decision and of the matters required by the preceding paragraph to be recorded to—

(a) the person concerned or his legal representative;

(b) the prosecution;

(c) the police;

(d) the magistrates' court officer; and

(e) the governor of the prison or person responsible for the establishment where the person concerned is being held.

(10) Where the judge hearing the appeal grants bail to the person concerned, the provisions of rule 19.18(9) (informing the Court of any earlier application for bail) and rule 19.22 (conditions attached to bail granted by the Crown Court) shall apply as if that person had applied to the Crown Court for bail.

(11) The notices required by paragraphs (3), (5), (7) and (9) of this rule may be served under rule 4.6 (service by fax, e-mail or other electronic means) and the notice required by paragraph (3) may be given by telephone.

(12) The Crown Court may hear an appeal to which this rule applies in public or in private.

Application or appeal to the Crown Court relating to bail

G–126b **19.18.**—(1) This rule applies where—

(a) an application to the Crown Court relating to bail is made otherwise than during the hearing of proceedings in the Crown Court;

(b) a defendant appeals under section 16 of the *Criminal Justice Act* 2003.

(2) Subject to paragraph (7) below, notice in writing of intention to make such an application to the Crown Court shall, at least 24 hours before it is made, be given to the prosecutor and if the prosecution is being carried on by the Crown Prosecution Service, to the appropriate Crown Prosecutor or, if the application is to be made by the prosecutor or a constable under section 3(8) of the *Bail Act* 1976, to the person to whom bail was granted.

(3) On receiving notice under paragraph (2), the prosecutor or appropriate Crown Public Prosecutor or, as the case may be, the person to whom bail was granted shall—

(a) notify the Crown Court officer and the applicant that he wishes to be represented at the hearing of the application;

(b) notify the Crown Court officer and the applicant that he does not oppose the application; or

(c) give to the Crown Court officer, for the consideration of the Crown Court, a written statement of his reasons for opposing the application, at the same time sending a copy of the statement to the applicant.

(4) A notice under paragraph (2) shall be in the form set out in the Practice Direction or a form to the like effect, and the applicant shall give a copy of the notice to the Crown Court officer.

(5) Except in the case of an application made by the prosecutor or a constable under section 3(8) of the 1976 Act, the applicant shall not be entitled to be present on the hearing of his application unless the Crown Court gives him leave to be present.

(6) Where a person who is in custody or has been released on bail desires to make an application relating to bail and has not been able to instruct a solicitor to apply on his behalf under the preceding paragraphs of this rule, he may give notice in writing to the Crown Court of his desire to make an application relating to bail, requesting that the Official Solicitor shall act for him in the application, and the Court may, if it thinks fit, assign the Official Solicitor to act for the applicant accordingly.

(7) Where the Official Solicitor has been so assigned the Crown Court may, if it thinks fit, dispense with the requirements of paragraph (2) and deal with the application in a summary manner.

(8) Any record required by section 5 of the 1976 Act (together with any note of reasons required by section 5(4) to be included) shall be made by way of an entry in the file relating to the case in question and the record shall include the following particulars, namely—

(a) the effect of the decision;

(b) a statement of any condition imposed in respect of bail, indicating whether it is to be complied with before or after release on bail;

(c) where conditions of bail are varied, a statement of the conditions as varied; and

(d) where bail is withheld, a statement of the relevant exception to the right to bail (as provided in Schedule 1 to the 1976 Act) on which the decision is based.

(9) Every person who makes an application to the Crown Court relating to bail shall inform the Court of any earlier application to the High Court or the Crown Court relating to bail in the course of the same proceedings.

(10) The Crown Court may hear an application appeal to which this rule applies in public or in private.

Notice to governor of prison of committal on bail

19.19.—(1) Where the accused is committed or sent for trial on bail, a magistrates' court officer shall give notice thereof in writing to the governor of the prison to which persons of the sex of the person committed or sent are committed or sent by that court if committed or sent in custody for trial and also, if the person committed or sent is under 21, to the governor of the remand centre to which he would have been committed or sent if the court had refused him bail. **G–127**

(2) Where a corporation is committed or sent for trial, a magistrates' court officer shall give notice thereof to the governor of the prison to which would be committed or sent a man committed or sent by that court in custody for trial.

Notices on committal of person subject to transfer direction

19.20. Where a transfer direction has been given by the Secretary of State under section 48 of the *Mental Health Act* 1983 in respect of a person remanded in custody by a magistrates' court and, before the direction ceases to have effect, that person is committed or sent for trial, a magistrates' court officer shall give notice— **G–128**

(a) to the governor of the prison to which persons of the sex of that person are committed or sent by that court if committed or sent in custody for trial; and

(b) to the managers of the hospital where he is detained.

Variation of arrangements for bail on committal to the Crown Court

19.21. Where a magistrates' court has committed or sent a person on bail to the Crown **G–129**

Appendices

Court for trial or under any of the enactments mentioned in rule 43.1(1) and subsequently varies any conditions of the bail or imposes any conditions in respect of the bail, the magistrates' court officer shall send to the Crown Court officer a copy of the record made in pursuance of section 5 of the *Bail Act* 1976 relating to such variation or imposition of conditions.

Conditions attached to bail granted by the Crown Court

G–130 **19.22.**—(1) Where the Crown Court grants bail, the recognizance of any surety required as a condition of bail may be entered into before an officer of the Crown Court or, where the person who has been granted bail is in a prison or other place of detention, before the governor or keeper of the prison or place as well as before the persons specified in section 8(4) of the *Bail Act* 1976.

(2) Where the Crown Court under section 3(5) or (6) of the 1976 Act imposes a requirement to be complied with before a person's release on bail, the Court may give directions as to the manner in which and the person or persons before whom the requirement may be complied with.

(3) A person who, in pursuance of an order made by the Crown Court for the grant of bail, proposes to enter into a recognizance or give security must, unless the Crown Court otherwise directs, give notice to the prosecutor at least 24 hours before he enters into the recognizance or gives security as aforesaid.

(4) Where, in pursuance of an order of the Crown Court, a recognizance is entered into or any requirement imposed under section 3(5) or (6) of the 1976 Act is complied with (being a requirement to be complied with before a person's release on bail) before any person, it shall be his duty to cause the recognizance or, as the case may be, a statement of the requirement to be transmitted forthwith to the court officer; and a copy of the recognizance or statement shall at the same time be sent to the governor or keeper of the prison or other place of detention in which the person named in the order is detained, unless the recognizance was entered into or the requirement was complied with before such governor or keeper.

(5) (5) Where, in pursuance of section 3(5) of the 1976 Act, security has been given in respect of a person granted bail with a duty to surrender to the custody of the Crown Court and either—

(a) that person surrenders to the custody ot the Court; or

(b) that person having failed to surrender to the custody of the Court, the Court decides not to order the forfeiture of the security, the court officer shall as soon as practicable give notice of the surrender to custody or, as the case may be, of the decision not to forfeit the security to the person before whom the security was given.

Estreat of recognizances in respect of person bailed to appear before the Crown Court

G–131 **19.23.**—(1) Where a recognizance has been entered into in respect of a person granted bail to appear before the Crown Court and it appears to the Court that a default has been made in performing the conditions of the recognizance, other than by failing to appear before the Court in accordance with any such condition, the Court may order the recognizance to be estreated.

(2) Where the Crown Court is to consider making an order under paragraph (1) for a recognizance to be estreated, the court officer shall give notice to that effect to the person by whom the recognizance was entered into indicating the time and place at which the matter will be considered; and no such order shall be made before the expiry of 7 days after the notice required by this paragraph has been given.

Forfeiture of recognizances in respect of person bailed to appear before the Crown Court

G–132 **19.24.**—(1) Where a recognizance is conditioned for the appearance of an accused before the Crown Court and the accused fails to appear in accordance with the condition, the Court shall declare the recognizance to be forfeited.

(2) Where the Crown Court declares a recognizance to be forfeited under paragraph (1), the court officer shall issue a summons to the person by whom the recognizance was entered into requiring him to appear before the Court at a time and place specified in the summons to show cause why the Court should not order the recognizance to be estreated.

(3) At the time specified in the summons the Court may proceed in the absence of the person by whom the recognizance was entered into if it is satisfied that he has been served with the summons.

Grant of bail subject to a condition of residence

19.25.—(1) The defendant must notify the prosecutor of the address at which the defendant would reside if released on bail with a condition of residence— **G–132a**

(a) as soon as practicable after the institution of proceedings, unless already done; and

(b) as soon as practicable after any change of that address.

(2) The prosecutor must help the court to assess the suitability of an address proposed as a condition of residence.

Grant of bail subject to electronic monitoring requirements

19.26.—(1) This rule applies where the court imposes electronic monitoring requirements (where available) as a condition of bail. **G–132b**

(2) The court officer must—

(a) inform the person responsible for the monitoring ('the monitor') of—

(i) the defendant's name, and telephone number (if available),

(ii) the offence or offences with which the defendant is charged,

(iii) details of the place at which the defendant's presence must be monitored,

(iv) the period or periods during which the defendant's presence at that place must be monitored, and

(v) if fixed, the date on which the defendant must surrender to custody;

(b) inform the defendant and, where the defendant is under 16, an appropriate adult, of the monitor's name, and the means by which the monitor may be contacted; and

(c) notify the monitor of any subsequent—

(i) variation or termination of the electronic monitoring requirements, or

(ii) fixing or variation of the date on which the defendant must surrender to custody.

Grant of bail subject to accommodation or support requirements

19.27.—(1) This rule applies where the court imposes as a condition of bail a requirement (where available) that the defendant must— **G–132c**

(a) reside in accommodation provided for that purpose by, or on behalf of, a public authority;

(b) receive bail support provided by, or on behalf of, a public authority.

(2) The court officer must—

(a) inform the person responsible for the provision of any such accommodation or support ('the service provider') of—

(i) the defendant's name, and telephone number (if available),

(ii) the offence or offences with which the defendant is charged,

(iii) details of the requirement,

(iv) any other bail condition, and

(v) if fixed, the date on which the defendant must surrender to custody;

(b) inform the defendant and, where the defendant is under 16, an appropriate adult, of—

(i) the service provider's name, and the means by which the service provider may be contacted, and

(ii) the address of any accommodation in which the defendant must reside; and

(c) notify the service provider of any subsequent—

(i) variation or termination of the requirement

(ii) variation or termination of any other bail condition, and

(iii) fixing or variation of the date on which the defendant must surrender to custody.

Appendices

PART 20 CUSTODY TIME LIMITS

Contents of this Part

Appeal to the Crown Court against decision in respect of a custody time limit

G–133 **20.1.**—(1) This rule applies—

(a) to any appeal brought by an accused, under section 22(7) of the *Prosecution of Offences Act* 1985, against a decision of a magistrates' court to extend, or further extend, a custody time limit imposed by regulations made under section 22(1) of the 1985 Act; and

(b) to any appeal brought by the prosecution, under section 22(8) of the 1985 Act, against a decision of a magistrates' court to refuse to extend, or further extend, such a time limit.

(2) An appeal to which this rule applies shall be commenced by the appellant's giving notice in writing of appeal—

(a) to the court officer for the magistrates' court which took the decision;

(b) if the appeal is brought by the accused, to the prosecutor and, if the prosecution is to be carried on by the Crown Prosecution Service, to the appropriate Crown Prosecutor;

(c) if the appeal is brought by the prosecution, to the accused; and

(d) to the Crown Court officer.

(3) The notice of an appeal to which this rule applies shall state the date on which the custody time limit applicable to the case is due to expire and, if the appeal is brought by the accused under section 22(7) of the 1985 Act, the date on which the custody time limit would have expired had the court decided not to extend or further extend that time limit

(4) On receiving notice of an appeal to which this rule applies, the Crown Court officer shall enter the appeal and give notice of the time and place of the hearing to—

(a) the appellant;

(b) the other party to the appeal; and

(c) the court officer for the magistrates' court which took the decision.

(5) Without prejudice to the power of the Crown Court to give leave for an appeal to be abandoned, an appellant may abandon an appeal to which this rule applies by giving notice in writing to any person to whom notice of the appeal was required to be given by paragraph (2) of this rule not later than the third day preceding the day fixed for the hearing of the appeal:

Provided that, for the purpose of determining whether notice was properly given in accordance with this paragraph, there shall be disregarded any Saturday and Sunday and any day which is specified to be a bank holiday in England and Wales under section 1(1) of the *Banking and Financial Dealings Act* 1971.

Hearing of application or appeal to the Crown Court

G–133a **20.2.** The court may hear in public or in private—

(a) an application under section 22(3) of the 1985 Act to extend a custody time limit;

(b) an appeal to which rule 20.1 applies.

PART 21 INITIAL DETAILS OF THE PROSECUTION CASE

Contents of this Part

When this Part applies

21.1.—(1) This Part applies in a magistrates' court, where the offence is one that can be tried in a magistrates' court. **G–134**

(2) The court may direct that, for a specified period, this Part will not apply—

(a) to any case in that court; or

(b) to any specified category of case.

Providing initial details of the prosecution case

21.2. The prosecutor must provide initial details of the prosecution case by— **G–135**

(a) serving those details on the court officer; and

(b) making those details available to the defendant, at, or before, the beginning of the day of the first hearing.

Content of initial details

21.3. Initial details of the prosecution case must include— **G–136**

(a) a summary of the evidence on which that case will be based; or

(b) any statement, document or extract setting out facts or other matters on which that case will be based; or

(c) any combination of such a summary, statement, document or extract; and

(d) the defendant's previous convictions.

[The next paragraph is § G–140.]

PART 22 DISCLOSURE

Contents of this Part

When this Part applies

22.1. This Part applies— **G–140**

(a) in a magistrates' court and in the Crown Court;

(b) where Parts I and II of the *Criminal Procedure and Investigations Act* 1996 apply.

Prosecution disclosure

22.2.—(1) This rule applies in the Crown Court where, under section 3 of the *Criminal Procedure and Investigations Act* 1996, the prosecutor— **G–140a**

(a) discloses prosecution material to the defendant; or

(b) serves on the defendant a written statement that there is no such material to disclose.

(2) The prosecutor must at the same time so inform the court officer.

Prosecutor's application for public interest ruling

G–140b **22.3.**—(1) This rule applies where—

(a) without a court order, the prosecutor would have to disclose material; and

(b) the prosecutor wants the court to decide whether it would be in the public interest to disclose it.

(2) The prosecutor must—

(a) apply in writing for such a decision; and

(b) serve the application on—

(i) the court officer,

(ii) any person who the prosecutor thinks would be directly affected by disclosure of the material, and

(iii) the defendant, but only to the extent that serving it on the defendant would not disclose what the prosecutor thinks ought not be disclosed.

(3) The application must—

(a) describe the material, and explain why the prosecutor thinks that—

(i) it is material that the prosecutor would have to disclose,

(ii) it would not be in the public interest to disclose that material, and

(iii) no measure such as the prosecutor's admission of any fact, or disclosure by summary, extract or edited copy, adequately would protect both the public interest and the defendant's right to a fair trial;

(b) omit from any part of the application that is served on the defendant anything that would disclose what the prosecutor thinks ought not be disclosed (in which case, paragraph (4) of this rule applies); and

(c) explain why, if no part of the application is served on the defendant.

(4) Where the prosecutor serves only part of the application on the defendant, the prosecutor must—

(a) mark the other part, to show that it is only for the court; and

(b) in that other part, explain why the prosecutor has withheld it from the defendant.

(5) Unless already done, the court may direct the prosecutor to serve an application on—

(a) the defendant;

(b) any other person who the court considers would be directly affected by the disclosure of the material.

(6) The court must determine the application at a hearing which—

(a) will be in private, unless the court otherwise directs; and

(b) if the court so directs, may take place, wholly or in part, in the defendant's absence.

(7) At a hearing at which the defendant is present—

(a) the general rule is that the court will receive, in the following sequence—

(i) representations first by the prosecutor and any other person served with the application, and then by the defendant, in the presence of them all, and then

(ii) further representations by the prosecutor and any such other person in the defendant's absence; but

(b) the court may direct other arrangements for the hearing.

(8) The court may only determine the application if satisfied that it has been able to take adequate account of—

(a) such rights of confidentiality as apply to the material; and

(b) the defendant's right to a fair trial.

(9) Unless the court otherwise directs, the court officer—

(a) must not give notice to anyone other than the prosecutor—

(i) of the hearing of an application under this rule, unless the prosecutor served the application on that person, or

(ii) of the court's decision on the application;

(b) may—

(i) keep a written application or representations, or

(ii) arrange for the whole or any part to be kept by some other appropriate person, subject to any conditions that the court may impose.

Defence disclosure

22.4.—(1) This rule applies where— **G–140c**

(a) under section 5(8) or 6 of the *Criminal Procedure and Investigations Act* 1996, the defendant gives a defence statement;

(b) under section 6C of the 1996 Act, the defendant gives a defence witness notice.

(2) The defendant must serve such a statement or notice on—

(a) the court officer; and

(b) the prosecutor.

[This rule is printed as substituted by the *Criminal Procedure (Amendment No. 2) Rules* 2010 (S.I. 2010 No. 3026)].

Defendant's application for prosecution disclosure

22.5.—(1) This rule applies where the defendant— **G–140d**

(a) has served a defence statement given under the *Criminal Procedure and Investigations Act* 1996; and

(b) wants the court to require the prosecutor to disclose material.

(2) The defendant must serve an application on—

(a) the court officer; and

(b) the prosecutor.

(3) The application must—

(a) describe the material that the defendant wants the prosecutor to disclose;

(b) explain why the defendant thinks there is reasonable cause to believe that—

(i) the prosecutor has that material, and

(ii) it is material that the*Criminal Procedure and Investigations Act* 1996 requires the prosecutor to disclose; and

(c) ask for a hearing, if the defendant wants one, and explain why it is needed.

(4) The court may determine an application under this rule—

(a) at a hearing, in public or in private; or

(b) without a hearing.

(5) The court must not require the prosecutor to disclose material unless the prosecutor—

(a) is present; or

(b) has had at least 14 days in which to make representations.

Review of public interest ruling

22.6.—(1) This rule applies where the court has ordered that it is not in the public interest to disclose material that the prosecutor otherwise would have to disclose, and **G–140e**

(a) the defendant wants the court to review that decision; or

(b) the Crown Court reviews that decision on its own initiative.

(2) Where the defendant wants the court to review that decision, the defendant must—

(a) serve an application on—

(i) the court officer, and

(ii) the prosecutor; and

(b) in the application—

(i) describe the material that the defendant wants the prosecutor to disclose, and

(ii) explain why the defendant thinks it is no longer in the public interest for the prosecutor not to disclose it.

(3) The prosecutor must serve any such application on any person who the prosecutor thinks would be directly affected if that material were disclosed.

(4) The prosecutor, and any such person, must serve any representations on—

(a) the court officer; and

(b) the defendant, unless to do so would in effect reveal something that either thinks ought not be disclosed.

Appendices

(5) The court may direct—

(a) the prosecutor to serve any such application on any person who the court considers would be directly affected if that material were disclosed;

(b) the prosecutor and any such person to serve any representations on the defendant.

(6) The court must review a decision to which this rule applies at a hearing which—

(a) will be in private, unless the court otherwise directs; and

(b) if the court so directs, may take place, wholly or in part, in the defendant's absence.

(7) At a hearing at which the defendant is present—

(a) the general rule is that the court will receive, in the following sequence—

(i) representations first by the defendant, and then by the prosecutor and any other person served with the application, in the presence of them all, and then

(ii) further representations by the prosecutor and any such other person in the defendant's absence; but

(b) the court may direct other arrangements for the hearing.

(8) The court may only conclude a review if satisfied that it has been able to take adequate account of—

(a) such rights of confidentiality as apply to the material; and

(b) the defendant's right to a fair trial.

Defendant's application to use disclosed material

G–140f **22.7.**—(1) This rule applies where a defendant wants the court's permission to use disclosed prosecution material—

(a) otherwise than in connection with the case in which it was disclosed; or

(b) beyond the extent to which it was displayed or communicated publicly at a hearing.

(2) The defendant must serve an application on—

(a) the court officer; and

(b) the prosecutor.

(3) The application must—

(a) specify what the defendant wants to use or disclose; and

(b) explain why.

(4) The court may determine an application under this rule—

(a) at a hearing, in public or in private; or

(b) without a hearing.

(5) The court must not permit the use of such material unless—

(a) the prosecutor has had at least 28 days in which to make representations; and

(b) the court is satisfied that it has been able to take adequate account of any rights of confidentiality that may apply to the material.

Unauthorised use of disclosed material

G–140g **22.8.**—(1) This rule applies where a person is accused of using disclosed prosecution material in contravention of section 17 of the *Criminal Procedure and Investigations Act* 1996.

(2) A party who wants the court to exercise its power to punish that person for contempt of court must comply with the rules in Part 62 (Contempt of court).

(3) The court must not exercise its power to forfeit material used in contempt of court unless—

(a) the prosecutor; and

(b) any other person directly affected by the disclosure of the material, is present, or has had at least 14 days in which to make representations.

Court's power to vary requirements under this Part

G–140h **22.9.** The court may—

(a) shorten or extend (even after it has expired) a time limit under this Part;

(b) allow a defence statement to be in a different written form to one set out in the Practice Direction, as long as it contains what the*Criminal Procedure and Investigations Act* 1996 requires;

(c) allow an application under this Part to be in a different form to one set out in the Practice Direction, or to be presented orally; and
(d) specify the period within which—
(i) any application under this Part must be made, or
(ii) any material must be disclosed, on an application to which rule 22.5 applies (defendant's application for prosecution disclosure).

[The next paragraph is § G–158.]

PART 27 WITNESS STATEMENTS

Contents of this Part

When this Part applies

27.1. This Part applies where a party wants to introduce a written statement in evidence under section 9 of the *Criminal Justice Act* 1967. **G–158**

Content of written statement

27.2. The statement must contain— **G–159**
(a) at the beginning—
(i) the witness' name, and
(ii) the witness' age, if under 18;
(b) a declaration by the witness that—
(i) it is true to the best of the witness' knowledge and belief, and
(ii) the witness knows that if it is introduced in evidence, then it would be an offence wilfully to have stated in it anything that the witness knew to be false or did not believe to be true;
(c) if the witness cannot read the statement, a signed declaration by someone else that that person read it to the witness; and
(d) the witness' signature.

Reference to exhibit

27.3. Where the statement refers to a document or object as an exhibit— **G–159a**
(a) the statement must contain such a description of that exhibit as to identify it clearly; and
(b) the exhibit must be labelled or marked correspondingly, and the label or mark signed by the maker of the statement.

Written statement in evidence

27.4.—(1) A party who wants to introduce in evidence a written statement must— **G–159b**
(a) before the hearing at which that party wants to do so, serve a copy of the statement on—
(i) the court officer, and
(ii) each other party; and
(b) at or before that hearing, serve the statement itself on the court officer.

(2) If that party relies on only part of the statement, that party must mark the copy in such a way as to make that clear.

(3) A prosecutor must serve on a defendant, with the copy of the statement, a notice—
(a) of the right within 7 days of service to object to the introduction of the statement in evidence instead of the witness giving evidence in person; and

(b) that if the defendant does not object in time, the court—
(i) can nonetheless require the witness to give evidence in person, but
(ii) may decide not to do so.

(4) The court may exercise its power to require the witness to give evidence in person—
(a) on application by any party; or
(b) on its own initiative.

(5) A party entitled to receive a copy of a statement may waive that entitlement by so informing—
(a) the party who would have served it; and
(b) the court.

PART 28 WITNESS SUMMONSES, WARRANTS AND ORDERS

Contents of this Part

When this Part applies

G–160 **28.1.**—(1) This Part applies in magistrates' courts and in the Crown Court where—
(a) a party wants the court to issue a witness summons, warrant or order under—
(i) section 97 of the *Magistrates' Courts Act* 1980,
(ii) section 2 of the *Criminal Procedure (Attendance of Witnesses) Act* 1965, or
(iii) section 7 of the *Bankers' Books Evidence Act* 1879;
(b) the court considers the issue of such a summons, warrant or order on its own initiative as if a party had applied; or
(c) one of those listed in rule 28.7 wants the court to withdraw such a summons, warrant or order.

(2) A reference to a 'witness' in this Part is a reference to a person to whom such a summons, warrant or order is directed.

Issue etc. of summons, warrant or order with or without a hearing

G–161 **28.2.**—(1) The court may issue or withdraw a witness summons, warrant or order with or without a hearing.

(2) A hearing under this Part must be in private unless the court otherwise directs.

Application for summons, warrant or order: general rules

G–162 **28.3.**—(1) A party who wants the court to issue a witness summons, warrant or order must apply as soon as practicable after becoming aware of the grounds for doing so.

(2) The party applying must—
(a) identify the proposed witness;
(b) explain—
(i) what evidence the proposed witness can give or produce,

(ii) why it is likely to be material evidence, and
(iii) why it would be in the interests of justice to issue a summons, order or warrant as appropriate.

(3) The application may be made orally unless—
(a) rule 28.5 applies; or
(b) the court otherwise directs.

Written application: form and service

28.4.—(1) An application in writing under rule 28.3 must be in the form set out in the Practice Direction, containing the same declaration of truth as a witness statement. **G–163**

(2) The party applying must serve the application—
(a) in every case, on the court officer and as directed by the court; and
(b) as required by rule 28.5, if that rule applies.

Application for summons to produce a document, etc.: special rules

28.5.—(1) This rule applies to an application under rule 28.3 for a witness summons requiring the proposed witness— **G–164**
(a) to produce in evidence a document or thing; or
(b) to give evidence about information apparently held in confidence, that relates to another person.

(2) The application must be in writing in the form required by rule 28.4.

(3) The party applying must serve the application—
(a) on the proposed witness, unless the court otherwise directs; and
(b) on one or more of the following, if the court so directs—
(i) a person to whom the proposed evidence relates,
(ii) another party.

(4) The court must not issue a witness summons where this rule applies unless—
(a) everyone served with the application has had at least 14 days in which to make representations, including representations about whether there should be a hearing of the application before the summons is issued; and
(b) the court is satisfied that it has been able to take adequate account of the duties and rights, including rights of confidentiality, of the proposed witness and of any person to whom the proposed evidence relates.

(5) This rule does not apply to an application for an order to produce in evidence a copy of an entry in a banker's book.

Application for summons to produce a document, etc.: court's assessment of relevance and confidentiality

28.6.—(1) This rule applies where a person served with an application for a witness summons requiring the proposed witness to produce in evidence a document or thing objects to its production on the ground that— **G–165**
(a) it is not likely to be material evidence; or
(b) even if it is likely to be material evidence, the duties or rights, including rights of confidentiality, of the proposed witness or of any person to whom the document or thing relates, outweigh the reasons for issuing a summons.

(2) The court may require the proposed witness to make the document or thing available for the objection to be assessed.

(3) The court may invite—
(a) the proposed witness or any representative of the proposed witness; or
(b) a person to whom the document or thing relates or any representative of such a person, to help the court assess the objection.

Application to withdraw a summons, warrant or order

28.7.—(1) The court may withdraw a witness summons, warrant or order if one of the following applies for it to be withdrawn— **G–166**
(a) the party who applied for it, on the ground that it no longer is needed;
(b) the witness, on the grounds that—
(i) he was not aware of any application for it, and
(ii) he cannot give or produce evidence likely to be material evidence, or

Appendices

(iii) even if he can, his duties or rights, including rights of confidentiality, or those of any person to whom the evidence relates, outweigh the reasons for the issue of the summons, warrant or order; or

(c) any person to whom the proposed evidence relates, on the grounds that—

(i) he was not aware of any application for it, and

(ii) that evidence is not likely to be material evidence, or

(iii) even if it is, his duties or rights, including rights of confidentiality, or those of the witness, outweigh the reasons for the issue of the summons, warrant or order.

(2) A person applying under the rule must—

(a) apply in writing as soon as practicable after becoming aware of the grounds for doing so, explaining why he wants the summons, warrant or order to be withdrawn; and

(b) serve the application on the court officer and as appropriate on—

(i) the witness,

(ii) the party who applied for the summons, warrant or order, and

(iii) any other person who he knows was served with the application for the summons, warrant or order.

(3) Rule 28.6 applies to an application under this rule that concerns a document or thing to be produced in evidence.

Court's power to vary requirements under this Part

G–167 **28.8.**—(1) The court may—

(a) shorten or extend (even after it has expired) a time limit under this Part; and

(b) where a rule or direction requires an application under this Part to be in writing, allow that application to be made orally instead.

(2) Someone who wants the court to allow an application to be made orally bunder paragraph (1)(b) of this rule must—

(a) give as much notice as the urgency of his application permits to those on whom he would otherwise have served an application in writing; and

(b) in doing so explain the reasons for the application and for wanting the court to consider it orally.

PART 29 MEASURES TO ASSIST A WITNESS OR DEFENDANT TO GIVE EVIDENCE

Contents of this Part

SECTION 1: UNDERSTANDING AND APPLYING THIS PART

When this Part applies

29.1.—(1) This Part applies— **G–168**

(a) where the court can give a direction (a "special measures direction"), under section 19 of the *Youth Justice and Criminal Evidence Act* 1999, on an application or on its own initiative, for any of the following measures—

(i) preventing a witness from seeing the defendant (section 23 of the 1999 Act),

(ii) allowing a witness to give evidence by live link (section 24 of the 1999 Act),

(iii) hearing a witness' evidence in private (section 25 of the 1999 Act),

(iv) dispensing with the wearing of wigs and gowns (section 26 of the 1999 Act),

(v) admitting video recorded evidence (sections 27 and 28 of the 1999 Act),

(vi) questioning a witness through an intermediary (section 29 of the 1999 Act),

(vii) using a device to help a witness communicate (section 30 of the 1999 Act);

(b) where the court can vary or discharge such a direction, under section 20 of the 1999 Act;

(c) where the court can give, vary or discharge a direction (a 'defendant's evidence direction') for a defendant to give evidence—

(i) by live link, under section 33A of the 1999 Act, or

(ii) through an intermediary, under sections 33BA and 33BB of the 1999 Act;

(d) where the court can—

(i) make a witness anonymity order, under section 86 of the *Coroners and Justice Act* 2009, or

(ii) vary or discharge such an order, under section 91, 92 or 93 of the 2009 Act;

(e) where the court can give or discharge a direction (a "live link direction"), on an application or on its own initiative, for a witness to give evidence by live link under—

(i) section 32 of the *Criminal Justice Act* 1988, or

(ii) sections 51 and 52 of the *Criminal Justice Act* 2003;

(f) where the court can exercise any other power it has to give, vary or discharge a direction for a measure to help a witness give evidence.

Meaning of 'witness'

G–169 **29.2.** In this Part, 'witness' means anyone (other than a defendant) for whose benefit an application, direction or order is made.

SECTION 2: GENERAL RULES

Making an application for a direction or order

G–170 **29.3.** A party who wants the court to exercise its power to give or make a direction or order must—

(a) apply in writing as soon as reasonably practicable, and in any event not more than—

(i) 28 days after the defendant pleads not guilty, in a magistrates' court, or

(ii) 14 days after the defendant pleads not guilty, in the Crown Court; and

(b) serve the application on—

(i) the court officer, and

(ii) each other party.

Decisions and reasons

G–171 **29.4.**—(1) A party who wants to introduce the evidence of a witness who is the subject of an application, direction or order must—

(a) inform the witness of the court's decision as soon as reasonably practicable; and

(b) explain to the witness the arrangements that as a result will be made for him or her to give evidence.

(2) The court must announce, at a hearing in public before the witness gives evidence, the reasons for a decision—

(a) to give, make, vary or discharge a direction or order; or

(b) to refuse to do so.

Court's power to vary requirements under this Part

G–172 **29.5.**—(1) The court may—

(a) shorten or extend (even after it has expired) a time limit under this Part; and

(b) allow an application or representations to be made in a different form to one set out in the Practice Direction, or to be made orally.

(2) A person who wants an extension of time must—

(a) apply when serving the application or representations for which it is needed; and

(b) explain the delay.

Custody of documents

G–173 **29.6.** Unless the court otherwise directs, the court officer may—

(a) keep a written application or representations; or
(b) arrange for the whole or any part to be kept by some other appropriate person, subject to any conditions that the court may impose.

Declaration by intermediary

29.7.—(1) This rule applies where— G–174
(a) a video recorded interview with a witness is conducted through an intermediary;
(b) the court directs the examination of a witness or defendant through an intermediary.

(2) An intermediary must make a declaration—
(a) before such an interview begins;
(b) before the examination begins (even if such an interview with the witness was conducted through the same intermediary).

(3) The declaration must be in these terms—

"I solemnly, sincerely and truly declare [or I swear by Almighty God] that I will well and faithfully communicate questions and answers and make true explanation of all matters and things as shall be required of me according to the best of my skill and understanding."

SECTION 3: SPECIAL MEASURES DIRECTIONS

Exercise of court's powers

29.8. The court may decide whether to give, vary or discharge a special measures direction— G–175
(a) at a hearing, in public or in private, or without a hearing;
(b) in a party's absence, if that party—
(i) applied for the direction, variation or discharge, or
(ii) has had at least 14 days in which to make representations.

Special measures direction for a young witness

29.9.—(1) This rule applies where, under section 21 or section 22 of the *Youth Justice and Criminal Evidence Act* 1999, the primary rule requires the court to give a direction for a special measure to assist a child witness or a qualifying witness— G–176
(a) on an application, if one is made; or
(b) on the court's own initiative, in any other case.

(2) A party who wants to introduce the evidence of such a witness must as soon as reasonably practicable—
(a) notify the court that the witness is eligible for assistance;
(b) provide the court with any information that the court may need to assess the witness' views, if the witness does not want the primary rule to apply; and
(c) serve any video recorded evidence on—
(i) the court officer, and
(ii) each other party.

Content of application for a special measures direction

29.10. An applicant for a special measures direction must— G–176a
(a) explain how the witness is eligible for assistance;
(b) explain why special measures would be likely to improve the quality of the witness' evidence;
(c) propose the measure or measures that in the applicant's opinion would be likely to maximise so far as practicable the quality of that evidence;
(d) report any views that the witness has expressed about—
(i) his or her eligibility for assistance,
(ii) the likelihood that special measures would improve the quality of his or her evidence, and
(iii) the measure or measures proposed by the applicant;
(e) in a case in which a child witness or a qualifying witness does not want the primary rule to apply, provide any information that the court may need to assess the witness' views;

Appendices

(f) in a case in which the applicant proposes that the witness should give evidence by live link—
   (i) identify someone to accompany the witness while the witness gives evidence,
   (ii) name that person, if possible, and
   (iii) explain why that person would be an appropriate companion for the witness, including the witness' own views;
(g) in a case in which the applicant proposes the admission of video recorded evidence, identify—
   (i) the date and duration of the recording,
   (ii) which part the applicant wants the court to admit as evidence, if the applicant does not want the court to admit all of it;
(h) attach any other material on which the applicant relies; and
(i) if the applicant wants a hearing, ask for one, and explain why it is needed.

Application to vary or discharge a special measures direction

G–176b **29.11.**—(1) A party who wants the court to vary or discharge a special measures direction must—
(a) apply in writing, as soon as reasonably practicable after becoming aware of the grounds for doing so; and
(b) serve the application on—
   (i) the court officer, and
   (ii) each other party.
(2) The applicant must—
(a) explain what material circumstances have changed since the direction was given (or last varied, if applicable);
(b) explain why the direction should be varied or discharged; and
(c) ask for a hearing, if the applicant wants one, and explain why it is needed.

Application containing information withheld from another party

G–176c **29.12.**—(1) This rule applies where—
(a) an applicant serves an application for a special measures direction, or for its variation or discharge; and
(b) the application includes information that the applicant thinks ought not be revealed to another party.
(2) The applicant must—
(a) omit that information from the part of the application that is served on that other party;
(b) mark the other part to show that, unless the court otherwise directs, it is only for the court; and
(c) in that other part, explain why the applicant has withheld that information from that other party.
(3) Any hearing of an application to which this rule applies—
(a) must be in private, unless the court otherwise directs; and
(b) if the court so directs, may be, wholly or in part, in the absence of a party from whom information has been withheld.
(4) At any hearing of an application to which this rule applies—
(a) the general rule is that the court will receive, in the following sequence—
   (i) representations first by the applicant and then by each other party, in all the parties' presence, and then
   (ii) further representations by the applicant, in the absence of a party from whom information has been withheld; but
(b) the court may direct other arrangements for the hearing.

Representations in response

G–176d **29.13.**—(1) This rule applies where a party wants to make representations about—
(a) an application for a special measures direction;
(b) an application for the variation or discharge of such a direction; or

(c) a direction, variation or discharge that the court proposes on its own initiative.

(2) Such a party must—

(a) serve the representations on—

(i) the court officer, and

(ii) each other party;

(b) do so not more than 14 days after, as applicable—

(i) service of the application, or

(ii) notice of the direction, variation or discharge that the court proposes; and

(c) ask for a hearing, if that party wants one, and explain why it is needed.

(3) Where representations include information that the person making them thinks ought not be revealed to another party, that person must—

(a) omit that information from the representations served on that other party;

(b) mark the information to show that, unless the court otherwise directs, it is only for the court; and

(c) with that information include an explanation of why it has been withheld from that other party.

(4) Representations against a special measures direction must explain—

(a) why the witness is not eligible for assistance; or

(b) if the witness is eligible for assistance, why—

(i) no special measure would be likely to improve the quality of the witness' evidence,

(ii) the proposed measure or measures would not be likely to maximise, so far as practicable, the quality of the witness' evidence, or

(iii) the proposed measure or measures might tend to inhibit the effective testing of that evidence;

(c) In a case in which the admission of video recorded evidence is proposed, why it would not be in the interests of justice for the recording, or part of it, to be admitted as evidence.

(5) Representations against the variation or discharge of a special measures direction must explain why it should not be varied or discharged.

SECTION 4: DEFENDANT'S EVIDENCE DIRECTIONS

Exercise of court's powers

29.14. The court may decide whether to give, vary or discharge a defendant's evidence direction— **G–176e**

(a) at a hearing, in public or in private, or without a hearing;

(b) in a party's absence, if that party—

(i) applied for the direction, variation or discharge, or

(ii) has had at least 14 days in which to make representations.

Content of application for a defendant's evidence direction

29.15. An applicant for a defendant's evidence direction must— **G–176f**

(a) explain how the proposed direction meets the conditions prescribed by the *Youth Justice and Criminal Evidence Act* 1999;

(b) in a case in which the applicant proposes that the defendant give evidence by live link—

(i) identify a person to accompany the defendant while the defendant gives evidence, and

(ii) explain why that person is appropriate;

(c) ask for a hearing, if the applicant wants one, and explain why it is needed.

Application to vary or discharge a defendant's evidence direction

29.16.—(1) A party who wants the court to vary or discharge a defendant's evidence direction must— **G–176g**

(a) apply in writing, as soon as reasonably practicable after becoming aware of the grounds for doing so; and

(b) serve the application on—
(i) the court officer, and
(ii) each other party.

(2) The applicant must—
(a) on an application to discharge a live link direction, explain why it is in the interests of justice to do so;
(b) on an application to discharge a direction for an intermediary, explain why it is no longer necessary in order to ensure that the defendant receives a fair trial;
(c) on an application to vary a direction for an intermediary, explain why it is necessary for the direction to be varied in order to ensure that the defendant receives a fair trial; and
(d) ask for a hearing, if the applicant wants one, and explain why it is needed.

Representations in response

G–176h **29.17.**—(1) This rule applies where a party wants to make representations about—
(a) an application for a defendant's evidence direction;
(b) an application for the variation or discharge of such a direction; or
(c) a direction, variation or discharge that the court proposes on its own initiative.

(2) Such a party must—
(a) serve the representations on—
(i) the court officer, and
(ii) each other party;
(b) do so not more than 14 days after, as applicable—
(i) service of the application, or
(ii) notice of the direction, variation or discharge that the court proposes; and
(c) ask for a hearing, if that party wants one, and explain why it is needed.

(3) Representations against a direction, variation or discharge must explain why the conditions prescribed by the *Youth Justice and Criminal Evidence Act* 1999 are not met.

SECTION 5: WITNESS ANONYMITY ORDERS

Exercise of court's powers

G–176i **29.18.**—(1) The court may decide whether to make, vary or discharge a witness anonymity order—
(a) at a hearing (which will be in private, unless the court otherwise directs), or without a hearing (unless any party asks for one);
(b) in the absence of a defendant.

(2) The court must not exercise its power to make, vary or discharge a witness anonymity order, or to refuse to do so—
(a) before or during the trial, unless each party has had an opportunity to make representations;
(b) on an appeal by the defendant to which applies Part 63 (appeal to the Crown Court) or Part 68 (appeal to the Court of Appeal about conviction or sentence), unless in each party's case—
(i) that party has had an opportunity to make representations, or
(ii) the appeal court is satisfied that it is not reasonably practicable to communicate with that party;
(c) after the trial and any such appeal are over, unless in the case of each party and the witness—
(i) each has had an opportunity to make representations, or
(ii) the court is satisfied that it is not reasonably practicable to communicate with that party or witness.

Content and conduct of application for a witness anonymity order

G–176j **29.19.**—(1) An applicant for a witness anonymity order must—
(a) include in the application nothing that might reveal the witness' identity;
(b) describe the measures proposed by the applicant;

(c) explain how the proposed order meets the conditions prescribed by section 88 of the *Coroners and Justice Act* 2009;
(d) explain why no measures other than those proposed will suffice, such as—
(i) an admission of the facts that would be proved by the witness,
(ii) an order restricting public access to the trial,
(iii) reporting restrictions, in particular under section 46 of the *Youth Justice and Criminal Evidence Act* 1999 or under section 39 of the *Children and Young Persons Act* 1933,
(iv) a direction for a special measure under section 19 of the *Youth Justice and Criminal Evidence Act* 1999,
(v) introduction of the witness' written statement as hearsay evidence, under section 116 of the *Criminal Justice Act* 2003, or
(vi) arrangements for the protection of the witness;
(e) attach to the application—
(i) a witness statement setting out the proposed evidence, edited in such a way as not to reveal the witness' identity,
(ii) where the prosecutor is the applicant, any further prosecution evidence to be served, and any further prosecution material to be disclosed under the *Criminal Procedure and Investigations Act* 1996, similarly edited, and
(iii) any defence statement that has been served, or as much information as may be available to the applicant that gives particulars of the defence; and
(f) ask for a hearing, if the applicant wants one.

(2) At any hearing of the application, the applicant must—
(a) identify the witness to the court, unless at the prosecutor's request the court otherwise directs; and
(b) present to the court, unless it otherwise directs—
(i) the unedited witness statement from which the edited version has been prepared,
(ii) where the prosecutor is the applicant, the unedited version of any further prosecution evidence or material from which an edited version has been prepared, and
(iii) such further material as the applicant relies on to establish that the proposed order meets the conditions prescribed by section 88 of the 2009 Act.

(3) At any such hearing—
(a) the general rule is that the court will receive, in the following sequence—
(i) representations first by the applicant and then by each other party, in all the parties' presence, and then
(ii) information withheld from a defendant, and further representations by the applicant, in the absence of any (or any other) defendant; but
(b) the court may direct other arrangements for the hearing.

(4) Before the witness gives evidence, the applicant must identify the witness to the court—
(a) if not already done;
(b) without revealing the witness' identity to any other party or person; and
(c) unless at the prosecutor's request the court otherwise directs.

Duty of court officer to notify the Director of Public Prosecutions

29.20. The court officer must notify the Director of Public Prosecutions of an application, unless the prosecutor is, or acts on behalf of, a public authority. **G–176k**

Application to vary or discharge a witness anonymity order

29.21.—(1) A party who wants the court to vary or discharge a witness anonymity order, or a witness who wants the court to do so when the case is over, must— **G–176l**
(a) apply in writing, as soon as reasonably practicable after becoming aware of the grounds for doing so; and
(b) serve the application on—
(i) the court officer, and
(ii) each other party.

Appendices

(2) The applicant must—

(a) explain what material circumstances have changed since the order was made (or last varied, if applicable);

(b) explain why the order should be varied or discharged, taking account of the conditions for making an order; and

(c) ask for a hearing, if the applicant wants one.

(3) Where an application includes information that the applicant thinks might reveal the witness' identity, the applicant must—

(a) omit that information from the application that is served on a defendant;

(b) mark the information to show that it is only for the court and the prosecutor (if the prosecutor is not the applicant); and

(c) with that information include an explanation of why it has been withheld.

(4) Where a party applies to vary or discharge a witness anonymity order after the trial and any appeal are over, the party who introduced the witness' evidence must serve the application on the witness.

Representations in response

G–176m **29.22.**—(1) This rule applies where a party or, where the case is over, a witness, wants to make representations about—

(a) an application for a witness anonymity order;

(b) an application for the variation or discharge of such an order; or

(c) a variation or discharge that the court proposes on its own initiative.

(2) Such a party or witness must—

(a) serve the representations on—

(i) the court officer, and

(ii) each other party;

(b) do so not more than 14 days after, as applicable—

(i) service of the application, or

(ii) notice of the variation or discharge that the court proposes; and

(c) ask for a hearing, if that party or witness wants one.

(3) Where representations include information that the person making them thinks might reveal the witness' identity, that person must—

(a) omit that information from the representations served on a defendant;

(b) mark the information to show that it is only for the court (and for the prosecutor, if relevant); and

(c) with that information include an explanation of why it has been withheld.

(4) Representations against a witness anonymity order must explain why the conditions for making the order are not met.

(5) Representations against the variation or discharge of such an order must explain why it would not be appropriate to vary or discharge it, taking account of the conditions for making an order.

(6) A prosecutor's representations in response to an application by a defendant must include all information available to the prosecutor that is relevant to the conditions and considerations specified by sections 88 and 89 of the *Coroners and Justice Act* 2009.

SECTION 6: LIVE LINK DIRECTIONS

Exercise of court's powers

G–176n **29.23.** The court may decide whether to give or discharge a live link direction—

(a) at a hearing, in public or in private, or without a hearing;

(b) in a party's absence, if that party—

(i) applied for the direction or discharge, or

(ii) has had at least 14 days in which to make representations.

Content of application for a live link direction

G–176o **29.24.** An applicant for a live link direction must—

(a) unless the court otherwise directs, identify the place from which the witness will give evidence;

(b) if that place is in the United Kingdom, explain why it would be in the interests of the efficient or effective administration of justice for the witness to give evidence by live link;
(c) if the applicant wants the witness to be accompanied by another person while giving evidence—
(i) name that person, if possible, and
(ii) explain why it is appropriate for the witness to be accompanied;
(d) ask for a hearing, if the applicant wants one, and explain why it is needed.

Application to discharge a live link direction

29.25.—(1) A party who wants the court to discharge a live link direction must— **G–176p**
(a) apply in writing, as soon as reasonably practicable after becoming aware of the grounds for doing so; and
(b) serve the application on— (
(i) the court officer, and
(ii) each other party.
(2) The applicant must—
(a) explain what material circumstances have changed since the direction was given;
(b) explain why it is in the interests of justice to discharge the direction; and
(c) ask for a hearing, if the applicant wants one, and explain why it is needed.

Representations in response

29.26.—(1) This rule applies where a party wants to make representations about— **G–176q**
(a) an application for a live link direction;
(b) an application for the discharge of such a direction; or
(c) a direction or discharge that the court proposes on its own initiative.
(2) Such a party must—
(a) serve the representations on—
(i) the court officer, and
(ii) each other party;
(b) do so not more than 14 days after, as applicable—
(i) service of the application, or
(ii) notice of the direction or discharge that the court proposes; and
(c) ask for a hearing, if that party wants one, and explain why it is needed.
(3) Representations against a direction or discharge must explain, as applicable, why the conditions prescribed by the *Criminal Justice Act* 1988 or the *Criminal Justice Act* 2003 are not met.

[The next paragraph is § G–178.]

PART 31 RESTRICTION ON CROSS-EXAMINATION BY A DEFENDANT ACTING IN PERSON

Contents of this Part

Restrictions on cross-examination of witness

31.1.—(1) This rule and rules 31.2 and 31.3 apply where an accused is prevented from cross-examining a witness in person by virtue of section 34, 35 or 36 of the *Youth Justice and Criminal Evidence Act* 1999. **G–178**

Appendices

(2) The court shall explain to the accused as early in the proceedings as is reasonably practicable that he—

(a) is prevented from cross-examining a witness in person; and

(b) should arrange for a legal representative to act for him for the purpose of cross-examining the witness.

(3) The accused shall notify the court officer within 7 days of the court giving its explanation, or within such other period as the court may in any particular case allow, of the action, if any, he has taken.

(4) Where he has arranged for a legal representative to act for him, the notification shall include details of the name and address of the representative.

(5) The notification shall be in writing.

(6) The court officer shall notify all other parties to the proceedings of the name and address of the person, if any, appointed to act for the accused.

(7) Where the court gives its explanation under paragraph (2) to the accused either within 7 days of the day set for the commencement of any hearing at which a witness in respect of whom a prohibition under section 34, 35 or 36 of the 1999 Act applies may be cross-examined or after such a hearing has commenced, the period of 7 days shall be reduced in accordance with any directions issued by the court.

(8) Where at the end of the period of 7 days or such other period as the court has allowed, the court has received no notification from the accused it may grant the accused an extension of time, whether on its own motion or on the application of the accused.

(9) Before granting an extension of time, the court may hold a hearing at which all parties to the proceedings may attend and be heard.

(10) Any extension of time shall be of such period as the court considers appropriate in the circumstances of the case.

(11) The decision of the court as to whether to grant the accused an extension of time shall be notified to all parties to the proceedings by the court officer.

Appointment of legal representative by the court

G–179 **31.2.**—(1) Where the court decides, in accordance with section 38(4) of the *Youth Justice and Criminal Evidence Act* 1999, to appoint a qualified legal representative, the court officer shall notify all parties to the proceedings of the name and address of the representative.

(2) An appointment made by the court under section 38(4) of the 1999 Act shall, except to such extent as the court may in any particular case determine, terminate at the conclusion of the cross-examination of the witness or witnesses in respect of whom a prohibition under section 34, 35 or 36 of the 1999 Act applies.

Appointment arranged by the accused

G–180 **31.3.**—(1) The accused may arrange for the qualified legal representative, appointed by the court under section 38(4) of the *Youth Justice and Criminal Evidence Act* 1999, to be appointed to act for him for the purpose of cross-examining any witness in respect of whom a prohibition under section 34, 35 or 36 of the 1999 Act applies.

(2) Where such an appointment is made—

(a) both the accused and the qualified legal representative appointed shall notify the court of the appointment; and

(b) the qualified legal representative shall, from the time of his appointment, act for the accused as though the arrangement had been made under section 38(2)(a) of the 1999 Act and shall cease to be the representative of the court under section 38(4).

(3) Where the court receives notification of the appointment either from the qualified legal representative or from the accused but not from both, the court shall investigate whether the appointment has been made, and if it concludes that the appointment has not been made, paragraph (2)(b) shall not apply.

(4) An accused may, notwithstanding an appointment by the court under section 38(4) of the 1999 Act, arrange for a legal representative to act for him for the purpose of cross-examining any witness in respect of whom a prohibition under section 34, 35 or 36 of the 1999 Act applies.

(5) Where the accused arranges for, or informs the court of his intention to arrange for, a legal representative to act for him, he shall notify the court, within such period as the court may allow, of the name and address of any person appointed to act for him.

(6) Where the court is notified within the time allowed that such an appointment has been made, any qualified legal representative appointed by the court in accordance with section 38(4) of the 1999 Act shall be discharged.

(7) The court officer shall, as soon as reasonably practicable after the court receives notification of an appointment under this rule or, where paragraph (3) applies, after the court is satisfied that the appointment has been made, notify all the parties to the proceedings—

(a) that the appointment has been made;

(b) where paragraph (4) applies, of the name and address of the person appointed; and

(c) that the person appointed by the court under section 38(4) of the 1999 Act has been discharged or has ceased to act for the court.

Prohibition on cross-examination of witness

31.4.—(1) An application by the prosecutor for the court to give a direction under section 36 of the *Youth Justice and Criminal Evidence Act* 1999 in relation to any witness must be sent to the court officer and at the same time a copy thereof must be sent by the applicant to every other party to the proceedings. **G–181**

(2) In his application the prosecutor must state why, in his opinion—

(a) the evidence given by the witness is likely to be diminished if cross-examination is undertaken by the accused in person;

(b) the evidence would be improved if a direction were given under section 36(2) of the 1999 Act; and

(c) it would not be contrary to the interests of justice to give such a direction.

(3) On receipt of the application the court officer must refer it—

(a) if the trial has started, to the court of trial; or

(b) if the trial has not started when the application is received—

(i) to the judge or court designated to conduct the trial, or

(ii) if no judge or court has been designated for that purpose, to such judge or court designated for the purposes of hearing that application.

(4) Where a copy of the application is received by a party to the proceedings more than 14 days before the date set for the trial to begin, that party may make observations in writing on the application to the court officer, but any such observations must be made within 14 days of the receipt of the application and be copied to the other parties to the proceedings.

(5) A party to whom an application is sent in accordance with paragraph (1) who wishes to oppose the application must give his reasons for doing so to the court officer and the other parties to the proceedings.

(6) Those reasons must be notified—

(a) within 14 days of the date the application was served on him, if that date is more than 14 days before the date set for the trial to begin;

(b) if the trial has begun, in accordance with any directions issued by the court; or

(c) if neither paragraph (6)(a) nor (b) applies, before the date set for the trial to begin.

(7) Where the application made in accordance with paragraph (1) is made before the date set for the trial to begin and—

(a) is not contested by any party to the proceedings, the court may determine the application without a hearing;

(b) is contested by a party to the proceedings, the court must direct a hearing of the application.

(8) Where the application is made after the trial has begun—

(a) the application may be made orally; and

(b) the court may give such directions as it considers appropriate to deal with the application.

(9) Where a hearing of the application is to take place, the court officer shall notify each party to the proceedings of the time and place of the hearing.

(10) A party notified in accordance with paragraph (9) may be present at the hearing and be heard.

(11) The court officer must, as soon as possible after the determination of an application

made in accordance with paragraph (1), give notice of the decision and the reasons for it to all the parties to the proceedings. (12) A person making an oral application under paragraph (8)(a) must—

(a) give reasons why the application was not made before the trial commenced; and
(b) provide the court with the information set out in paragraph (2).

PART 32 INTERNATIONAL CO-OPERATION

Contents of this Part

Notice required to accompany process served outside the United Kingdom and translations

G–182 **32.1.**—(1) The notice which by virtue of section 3(4)(b) of the*Crime (International Co-operation) Act* 2003 (general requirements for service of process) must accompany any process served outside the United Kingdom must give the information specified in paragraphs (2) and (4) below.

(2) The notice must—

(a) state that the person required by the process to appear as a party or attend as a witness can obtain information about his rights in connection therewith from the relevant authority; and
(b) give the particulars specified in paragraph (4) about that authority.

(3) The relevant authority where the process is served—

(a) at the request of the prosecuting authority, is that authority; or
(b) at the request of the defendant or the prosecutor in the case of a private prosecution, is the court by which the process is served.

(4) The particulars referred to in paragraph (2) are—

(a) the name and address of the relevant authority, together with its telephone and fax numbers and e-mail address; and
(b) the name of a person at the relevant authority who can provide the information referred to in paragraph (2)(a), together with his telephone and fax numbers and e-mail address.

(5) The justices' clerk or Crown Court officer must send, together with any process served outside the United Kingdom—

(a) any translation which is provided under section 3(3)(b) of the 2003 Act; and
(b) any translation of the information required to be given by this rule which is provided to him.

(6) In this rule, 'process' has the same meaning as in section 51(3) of the 2003 Act.

Proof of service outside the United Kingdom

32.2.—(1) A statement in a certificate given by or on behalf of the Secretary of State— **G–183**

(a) that process has been served on any person under section 4(1) of the *Crime (International Co-operation) Act* 2003 (service of process otherwise than by post);

(b) of the manner in which service was effected; and

(c) of the date on which process was served; shall be admissible as evidence of any facts so stated.

(2) In this rule, 'process' has the same meaning as in section 51(3) of the 2003 Act.

Supply of copy of notice of request for assistance abroad

32.3. Where a request for assistance under section 7 of the *Crime (International Co-operation) Act* 2003 is made by a justice of the peace or a judge exercising the jurisdiction of the Crown Court and is sent in accordance with section 8(1) of the 2003 Act, the justices' clerk or the Crown Court officer shall send a copy of the letter of request to the Secretary of State as soon as practicable after the request has been made. **G–184**

Persons entitled to appear and take part in proceedings before a nominated court, and exclusion of the public

32.4. A court nominated under section 15(1) of the *Crime (International Co-operation) Act* 2003 (nominating a court to receive evidence) may— **G–185**

(a) determine who may appear or take part in the proceedings under Schedule 1 to the 2003 Act before the court and whether a party to the proceedings is entitled to be legally represented; and

(b) direct that the public be excluded from those proceedings if it thinks it necessary to do so in the interests of justice.

Record of proceedings to receive evidence before a nominated court

32.5.—(1) Where a court is nominated under section 15(1) of the *Crime (International Co-operation) Act* 2003 the justices' clerk or Crown Court officer shall enter in an overseas record— **G–186**

(a) details of the request in respect of which the notice under section 15(1) of the 2003 Act was given;

(b) the date on which, and place at which, the proceedings under Schedule 1 to the 2003 Act in respect of that request took place;

(c) the name of any witness who gave evidence at the proceedings in question;

(d) the name of any person who took part in the proceedings as a legal representative or an interpreter;

(e) whether a witness was required to give evidence on oath or (by virtue of section 5 of the Oaths Act 1978) after making a solemn affirmation; and

(f) whether the opportunity to cross-examine any witness was refused.

(2) When the court gives the evidence received by it under paragraph 6(1) of Schedule 1 to the 2003 Act to the court or authority that made the request or to the territorial authority for forwarding to the court or authority that made the request, the justices' clerk or Crown Court officer shall send to the court, authority or territorial authority (as the case may be) a copy of an extract of so much of the overseas record as relates to the proceedings in respect of that request.

Interpreter for the purposes of proceedings involving a television or telephone link

32.6.—(1) This rule applies where a court is nominated under section 30(3) (hearing witnesses in the UK through television links) or section 31(4) (hearing witnesses in the UK by telephone) of the *Crime (International Co-operation) Act* 2003. **G–187**

(2) Where it appears to the justices' clerk or the Crown Court officer that the witness to be heard in the proceedings under Part 1 or 2 of Schedule 2 to the 2003 Act ('the relevant proceedings') is likely to give evidence in a language other than English, he shall make arrangements for an interpreter to be present at the proceedings to translate what is said into English.

(3) Where it appears to the justices' clerk or the Crown Court officer that the witness to be heard in the relevant proceedings is likely to give evidence in a language other than

Appendices

that in which the proceedings of the court referred to in section 30(1) or, as the case may be, 31(1) of the 2003 Act ('the external court') will be conducted, he shall make arrangements for an interpreter to be present at the relevant proceedings to translate what is said into the language in which the proceedings of the external court will be conducted.

(4) Where the evidence in the relevant proceedings is either given in a language other than English or is not translated into English by an interpreter, the court shall adjourn the proceedings until such time as an interpreter can be present to provide a translation into English.

(5) Where a court in Wales understands Welsh—

(a) paragraph (2) does not apply where it appears to the justices' clerk or Crown Court officer that the witness in question is likely to give evidence in Welsh;

(b) paragraph (4) does not apply where the evidence is given in Welsh; and

(c) any translation which is provided pursuant to paragraph (2) or (4) may be into Welsh instead of English.

Record of television link hearing before a nominated court

G–188 **32.7.**—(1) This rule applies where a court is nominated under section 30(3) of the *Crime (International Co-operation) Act* 2003.

(2) The justices' clerk or Crown Court officer shall enter in an overseas record—

(a) details of the request in respect of which the notice under section 30(3) of the 2003 Act was given;

(b) the date on which, and place at which, the proceedings under Part 1 of Schedule 2 to that Act in respect of that request took place;

(c) the technical conditions, such as the type of equipment used, under which the proceedings took place;

(d) the name of the witness who gave evidence;

(e) the name of any person who took part in the proceedings as a legal representative or an interpreter; and

(f) the language in which the evidence was given.

(3) As soon as practicable after the proceedings under Part 1 of Schedule 2 to the 2003 Act took place, the justices' clerk or Crown Court officer shall send to the external authority that made the request a copy of an extract of so much of the overseas record as relates to the proceedings in respect of that request.

Record of telephone link hearing before a nominated court

G–189 **32.8.**—(1) This rule applies where a court is nominated under section 31(4) of the *Crime (International Co-operation) Act* 2003.

(2) The justices' clerk or Crown Court officer shall enter in an overseas record—

(a) details of the request in respect of which the notice under section 31(4) of the 2003 Act was given;

(b) the date, time and place at which the proceedings under Part 2 of Schedule 2 to the 2003 Act took place;

(c) the name of the witness who gave evidence;

(d) the name of any interpreter who acted at the proceedings; and

(e) the language in which the evidence was given.

Overseas record

G–190 **32.9.**—(1) The overseas records of a magistrates' court shall be part of the register (within the meaning of section 150(1) of the*Magistrates' Courts Act* 1980).

(2) The overseas records of any court shall not be open to inspection by any person except—

(a) as authorised by the Secretary of State; or

(b) with the leave of the court.

Overseas freezing orders

G–190a **32.10.**—(1) This rule applies where a court is nominated under section 21(1) of the *Crime (International Co-operation) Act* 2003 to give effect to an overseas freezing order.

(2) Where the Secretary of State serves a copy of such an order on the court officer—

(a) the general rule is that the court will consider the order no later than the next business day;

(b) exceptionally, the court may consider the order later than that, but not more than 5 business days after service.

(3) The court must not consider the order unless—

(a) it is satisfied that the chief officer of police for the area in which the evidence is situated has had notice of the order; and

(b) that chief officer of police has had an opportunity to make representations, at a hearing if that officer wants.

(4) The court may consider the order—

(a) without a hearing; or

(b) at a hearing, in public or in private.

PART 33 EXPERT EVIDENCE

Contents of this Part

Reference to expert

33.1. A reference to an 'expert' in this Part is a reference to a person who is required to give or prepare expert evidence for the purpose of criminal proceedings, including evidence required to determine fitness to plead or for the purpose of sentencing. **G–191**

Expert's duty to the court

33.2.—(1) An expert must help the court to achieve the overriding objective by giving objective, unbiased opinion on matters within his expertise. **G–192**

(2) This duty overrides any obligation to the person from whom he receives instructions or by whom he is paid.

(3) This duty includes an obligation to inform all parties and the court if the expert's opinion changes from that contained in a report served as evidence or given in a statement.

Content of expert's report

33.3.—(1) An expert's report must— **G–193**

(a) give details of the expert's qualifications, relevant experience and accreditation;

(b) give details of any literature or other information which the expert has relied on in making the report;

(c) contain a statement setting out the substance of all facts given to the expert which are material to the opinions expressed in the report, or upon which those opinions are based;

(d) make clear which of the facts stated in the report are within the expert's own knowledge;

(e) say who carried out any examination, measurement, test or experiment which the expert has used for the report and—

(i) give the qualifications, relevant experience and accreditation of that person,

(ii) say whether or not the examination, measurement, test or experiment was carried out under the expert's supervision, and

(iii) summarise the findings on which the expert relies;

(f) where there is a range of opinion on the matters dealt with in the report—

(i) summarise the range of opinion, and

(ii) give reasons for his own opinion;

(g) if the expert is not able to give his opinion without qualification, state the qualification;

(h) contain a summary of the conclusions reached;

(i) contain a statement that the expert understands his duty to the court, and has complied and will continue to comply with that duty; and

(j) contain the same declaration of truth as a witness statement.

(2) Only sub-paragraphs (i) and (j) of rule 33.3(1) apply to a summary by an expert of his conclusions served in advance of that expert's report.

Service of expert evidence

G–194 **33.4.**—(1) A party who wants to introduce expert evidence must—

(a) serve it on—

(i) the court officer, and

(ii) each other party;

(b) serve it—

(i) as soon as practicable, and in any event

(ii) with any application in support of which that party relies on that evidence; and

(c) if another party so requires, give that party a copy of, or a reasonable opportunity to inspect—

(i) a record of any examination, measurement, test or experiment on which the expert's findings and opinion are based, or that were carried out in the course of reaching those findings and opinion, and

(ii) anything on which any such examination, measurement, test or experiment was carried out.

(2) A party may not introduce expert evidence if that party has not complied with this rule, unless—

(a) every other party agrees; or

(b) the court gives permission.

Expert to be informed of service of report

G–195 **33.5.** A party who serves on another party or on the court a report by an expert must, at once, inform that expert of that fact.

Pre-hearing discussion of expert evidence

G–196 **33.6.**—(1) This rule applies where more than one party wants to introduce expert evidence.

(2) The court may direct the experts to—

(a) discuss the expert issues in the proceedings; and

(b) prepare a statement for the court of the matters on which they agree and disagree, giving their reasons.

(3) Except for that statement, the content of that discussion must not be referred to without the court's permission.

(4) A party may not introduce expert evidence without the court's permission if the expert has not complied with a direction under this rule.

Court's power to direct that evidence is to be given by a single joint expert

G–197 **33.7.**—(1) Where more than one defendant wants to introduce expert evidence on an issue at trial, the court may direct that the evidence on that issue is to be given by one expert only.

(2) Where the co-defendants cannot agree who should be the expert, the court may—

(a) select the expert from a list prepared or identified by them; or

(b) direct that the expert be selected in another way.

Instructions to a single joint expert

G–198 **33.8.**—(1) Where the court gives a direction under rule 33.7 for a single joint expert to be used, each of the co-defendants may give instructions to the expert.

(2) When a co-defendant gives instructions to the expert he must, at the same time, send a copy of the instructions to the other co-defendant(s).

(3) The court may give directions about—

(a) the payment of the expert's fees and expenses; and

(b) any examination, measurement, test or experiment which the expert wishes to carry out.

(4) The court may, before an expert is instructed, limit the amount that can be paid by way of fees and expenses to the expert.

(5) Unless the court otherwise directs, the instructing co-defendants are jointly and severally liable for the payment of the expert's fees and expenses.

Court's power to vary requirements under this Part

33.9.—(1) The court may— **G–198a**

(a) extend (even after it has expired) a time limit under this Part;

(b) allow the introduction of expert evidence which omits a detail required by this Part.

(2) A party who wants an extension of time must—

(a) apply when serving the expert evidence for which it is required; and

(b) explain the delay.

PART 34 HEARSAY EVIDENCE

Contents of this Part

When this Part applies

34.1. This Part applies— **G–199**

(a) in a magistrates' court and in the Crown Court;

(b) where a party wants to introduce hearsay evidence, within the meaning of section 114 of the *Criminal Justice Act* 2003.

Notice to introduce hearsay evidence

34.2.—(1) This rule applies where a party wants to introduce hearsay evidence for admission under any of the following sections of the *Criminal Justice Act* 2003— **G–200**

(a) section 114(1)(d) (evidence admissible in the interests of justice);

(b) section 116 (evidence where a witness is unavailable);

(c) section 121 (multiple hearsay).

(2) That party must—

(a) serve notice on—

(i) the court officer, and

(ii) each other party;

(b) in the notice—

(i) identify the evidence that is hearsay,

(ii) set out any facts on which that party relies to make the evidence admissible,

(iii) explain how that party will prove those facts if another party disputes them, and

(iv) explain why the evidence is admissible; and

(c) attach to the notice any statement or other document containing the evidence that has not already been served.

(3) A prosecutor who wants to introduce such evidence must serve the notice not more than—

(a) 28 days after the defendant pleads not guilty, in a magistrates' court; or

(b) 14 days after the defendant pleads not guilty, in the Crown Court.

(4) A defendant who wants to introduce such evidence must serve the notice as soon as reasonably practicable.

(5) A party entitled to receive a notice under this rule may waive that entitlement by so informing—

(a) the party who would have served it; and

(b) the court.

Opposing the introduction of hearsay evidence

G–201 **34.3.**—(1) This rule applies where a party objects to the introduction of hearsay evidence.

(2) That party must—

(a) apply to the court to determine the objection;

(b) serve the application on—

(i) the court officer, and

(ii) each other party;

(c) serve the application as soon as reasonably practicable, and in any event not more than 14 days after—

(i) service of notice to introduce the evidence under rule 34.2,

(ii) service of the evidence to which that party objects, if no notice is required by that rule, or

(iii) the defendant pleads not guilty whichever of those events happens last; and

(d) in the application, explain—

(i) which, if any, facts set out in a notice under rule 34.2 that party disputes,

(ii) why the evidence is not admissible,

(iii) any other objection to the application.

(3) The court—

(a) may determine an application—

(i) at a hearing, in public or in private, or

(ii) without a hearing;

(b) must not determine the application unless the party who served the notice—

(i) is present, or

(ii) has had a reasonable opportunity to respond;

(c) may adjourn the application; and

(d) may discharge or vary a determination where it can do so under—

(i) section 8B of the *Magistrates' Courts Act* 1980 (ruling at pre-trial hearing in a magistrates' court), or (ii) section 9 of the *Criminal Justice Act* 1987, or section 31 or 40 of the *Criminal Procedure and Investigations Act* 1996 (ruling at preparatory or other pre-trial hearing in the Crown Court).

Unopposed hearsay evidence

G–202 **34.4.**—(1) This rule applies where—

(a) a party has served notice to introduce hearsay evidence under rule 34.2; and

(b) no other party has applied to the court to determine an objection to the introduction of the evidence.

(2) The court will treat the evidence as if it were admissible by agreement.

Court's power to vary requirements under this Part

G–203 **34.5.**—(1) The court may—

(a) shorten or extend (even after it has expired) a time limit under this Part;

(b) allow an application or notice to be in a different form to one set out in the Practice Direction, or to be made or given orally;

(c) dispense with the requirement for notice to introduce hearsay evidence.

(2) A party who wants an extension of time must—

(a) apply when serving the application or notice for which it is needed; and

(b) explain the delay.

[The next paragraph is § G–207.]

PART 35 EVIDENCE OF BAD CHARACTER

Contents of this Part

When this Part applies

35.1. This Part applies— **G–207**

(a) in a magistrates' court and in the Crown Court;

(b) where a party wants to introduce evidence of bad character, within the meaning of section 98 of the *Criminal Justice Act* 2003.

Content of application or notice

35.2.—(1) A party who wants to introduce evidence of bad character must— **G–208**

(a) make an application under rule 35.3, where it is evidence of a non-defendant's bad character;

(b) give notice under rule 35.4, where it is evidence of a defendant's bad character.

(2) An application or notice must—

(a) set out the facts of the misconduct on which that party relies,

(b) explain how that party will prove those facts (whether by certificate of conviction, other official record, or other evidence), if another party disputes them, and

(c) explain why the evidence is admissible.

Application to introduce evidence of a non-defendant's bad character

35.3.—(1) This rule applies where a party wants to introduce evidence of the bad character of a person other than the defendant. **G–209**

(2) That party must serve an application to do so on—

(a) the court officer; and

(b) each other party.

(3) The applicant must serve the application—

(a) as soon as reasonably practicable; and in any event

(b) not more than 14 days after the prosecutor discloses material on which the application is based (if the prosecutor is not the applicant).

(4) A party who objects to the introduction of the evidence must—

(a) serve notice on—

(i) the court officer, and

(ii) each other party not more than 14 days after service of the application; and

(b) in the notice explain, as applicable—

(i) which, if any, facts of the misconduct set out in the application that party disputes,

(ii) what, if any, facts of the misconduct that party admits instead,

(iii) why the evidence is not admissible, and

(iv) any other objection to the application.

(5) The court—

(a) may determine an application—

(i) at a hearing, in public or in private, or

(ii) without a hearing;

(b) must not determine the application unless each party other than the applicant—

(i) is present, or

(ii) has had at least 14 days in which to serve a notice of objection;

(c) may adjourn the application; and

(d) may discharge or vary a determination where it can do so under—

(i) section 8B of the *Magistrates' Courts Act* 1980 (ruling at pre-trial hearing in a magistrates' court), or

(ii) section 9 of the *Criminal Justice Act* 1987, or section 31 or 40 of the *Criminal Procedure and Investigations Act* 1996 (ruling at preparatory or other pre-trial hearing in the Crown Court).

Notice to introduce evidence of a defendant's bad character

G–210 **35.4.**—(1) This rule applies where a party wants to introduce evidence of a defendant's bad character.

(2) That party must serve notice on—

(a) the court officer; and

(b) each other party.

(3) A prosecutor who wants to introduce such evidence must serve the notice not more than—

(a) 28 days after the defendant pleads not guilty, in a magistrates' court; or

(b) 14 days after the defendant pleads not guilty, in the Crown Court.

(4) A co-defendant who wants to introduce such evidence must serve the notice—

(a) as soon as reasonably practicable; and in any event

(b) not more than 14 days after the prosecutor discloses material on which the notice is based.

(5) A party who objects to the introduction of the evidence must—

(a) apply to the court to determine the objection;

(b) serve the application on—

(i) the court officer, and

(ii) each other party not more than 14 days after service of the notice; and

(c) in the application explain, as applicable—

(i) which, if any, facts of the misconduct set out in the notice that party disputes,

(ii) what, if any, facts of the misconduct that party admits instead,

(iii) why the evidence is not admissible,

(iv) why it would be unfair to admit the evidence, and

(v) any other objection to the notice.

(6) The court—

(a) may determine an application—

(i) at a hearing, in public or in private, or

(ii) without a hearing;

(b) must not determine the application unless the party who served the notice—

(i) is present, or

(ii) has had a reasonable opportunity to respond;

(c) may adjourn the application; and

(d) may discharge or vary a determination where it can do so under—

(i) section 8B of the Magistrates' Courts Act 1980 (ruling at pre-trial hearing in a magistrates' court), or

(ii) section 9 of the *Criminal Justice Act* 1987, or section 31 or 40 of the *Criminal Procedure and Investigations Act* 1996 (ruling at preparatory or other pre-trial hearing in the Crown Court).

(7) A party entitled to receive a notice may waive that entitlement by so informing—

(a) the party who would have served it; and
(b) the court.

Reasons for decisions

35.5. The court must announce at a hearing in public (but in the absence of the jury, if there is one) the reasons for a decision— **G–211**

(a) to admit evidence as evidence of bad character, or to refuse to do so; or
(b) to direct an acquittal or a retrial under section 107 of the *Criminal Justice Act* 2003.

Court's power to vary requirements under this Part

35.6.—(1) The court may— **G–212**

(a) shorten or extend (even after it has expired) a time limit under this Part;
(b) allow an application or notice to be in a different form to one set out in the Practice Direction, or to be made or given orally;
(c) dispense with a requirement for notice to introduce evidence of a defendant's bad character.

(2) A party who wants an extension of time must—

(a) apply when serving the application or notice for which it is needed; and
(b) explain the delay.

[The next paragraph is § G–216.]

PART 36 EVIDENCE OF A COMPLAINANT'S PREVIOUS SEXUAL BEHAVIOUR

Contents of this Part

When this Part applies

36.1. This Part applies in magistrates' courts and in the Crown Court where a defendant wants to— **G–216**

(a) introduce evidence; or
(b) cross-examine a witness about a complainant's sexual behaviour despite the prohibition in section 41 of the *Youth Justice and Criminal Evidence Act* 1999.

Application for permission to introduce evidence or cross-examine

36.2. The defendant must apply for permission to do so— **G–217**

(a) in writing; and
(b) not more than 28 days after the prosecutor has complied or purported to comply with section 3 of the *Criminal Procedure and Investigations Act* 1996 (disclosure by prosecutor).

Content of application

36.3. The application must— **G–218**

(a) identify the issue to which the defendant says the complainant's sexual behaviour is relevant;

(b) give particulars of—
(i) any evidence that the defendant wants to introduce, and
(ii) any questions that the defendant wants to ask;
(c) identify the exception to the prohibition in section 41 of the *Youth Justice and Criminal Evidence Act* 1999 on which the defendant relies; and
(d) give the name and date of birth of any witness whose evidence about the complainant's sexual behaviour the defendant wants to introduce.

Service of application

G–219 **36.4.** The defendant must serve the application on the court officer and all other parties.

Reply to application

G–220 **36.5.** A party who wants to make representations about an application under rule 36.2 must—
(a) do so in writing not more than 14 days after receiving it; and
(b) serve those representations on the court officer and all other parties.

Application for special measures

G–221 **36.6.** If the court allows an application under rule 36.2 then—
(a) a party may apply not more than 14 days later for a special measures direction or for the variation of an existing special measures direction; and
(b) the court may shorten the time for opposing that application.

Court's power to vary requirements under this Part

G–222 **36.7.** The court may shorten or extend (even after it has expired) a time limit under this Part.

PART 37 TRIAL AND SENTENCE IN A MAGISTRATES' COURT

Contents of this Part

When this Part applies

G–223 **37.1.**—(1) This Part applies in a magistrates' court where—
(a) the court tries a case; or
(b) the defendant pleads guilty.
(2) Where the defendant is under 18, in this Part—
(a) a reference to convicting the defendant includes a reference to finding the defendant guilty of an offence; and

(b) a reference to sentence includes a reference to an order made on a finding of guilt.

General rules

37.2.—(1) Where this Part applies— **G–224**

(a) the general rule is that the hearing must be in public; but

(b) the court may exercise any power it has to—

(i) impose reporting restrictions,

(ii) withhold information from the public, or

(iii) order a hearing in private; and

(c) unless the court otherwise directs, only the following may attend a hearing in a youth court—

(i) the parties and their legal representatives,

(ii) a defendant's parents, guardian or other supporting adult,

(iii) a witness,

(iv) anyone else directly concerned in the case, and

(v) a representative of a news-gathering or reporting organisation.

(2) Unless already done, the justices' legal adviser or the court must—

(a) read the allegation of the offence to the defendant;

(b) explain, in terms the defendant can understand (with help, if necessary)—

(i) the allegation, and

(ii) what the procedure at the hearing will be;

(c) ask whether the defendant has been advised about the potential effect on sentence of a guilty plea;

(d) ask whether the defendant pleads guilty or not guilty; and

(e) take the defendant's plea.

(3) The court may adjourn the hearing—

(a) at any stage, to the same or to another magistrates' court; or

(b) to a youth court, where the court is not itself a youth court and the defendant is under 18.

Procedure on plea of not guilty

37.3.—(1) This rule applies— **G–225**

(a) if the defendant has—

(i) entered a plea of not guilty, or

(ii) not entered a plea; or

(b) if, in either case, it appears to the court that there may be grounds for making a hospital order without convicting the defendant.

(2) If a not guilty plea was taken on a previous occasion, the justices' legal adviser or the court must ask the defendant to confirm that plea.

(3) In the following sequence—

(a) the prosecutor may summarise the prosecution case, identifying the relevant law and facts;

(b) the prosecutor must introduce the evidence on which the prosecution case relies;

(c) at the conclusion of the prosecution case, on the defendant's application or on its own initiative, the court—

(i) may acquit on the ground that the prosecution evidence is insufficient for any reasonable court properly to convict, but

(ii) must not do so unless the prosecutor has had an opportunity to make representations;

(d) the justices' legal adviser or the court must explain, in terms the defendant can understand (with help, if necessary)—

(i) the right to give evidence, and

(ii) the potential effect of not doing so at all, or of refusing to answer a question while doing so;

(e) the defendant may introduce evidence;

(f) a party may introduce further evidence if it is then admissible (for example, because it is in rebuttal of evidence already introduced);

(g) the prosecutor may make final representations in support of the prosecution case, where—
(i) the defendant is represented by a legal representative, or
(ii) whether represented or not, the defendant has introduced evidence other than his or her own; and
(h) the defendant may make final representations in support of the defence case.

(4) Where a party wants to introduce evidence or make representations after that party's opportunity to do so under paragraph (3), the court—
(a) may refuse to receive any such evidence or representations; and
(b) must not receive any such evidence or representations after it has announced its verdict.

(5) If the court—
(a) convicts the defendant; or
(b) makes a hospital order instead of doing so, it must give sufficient reasons to explain its decision.

(6) If the court acquits the defendant, it may—
(a) give an explanation of its decision; and
(b) exercise any power it has to make—
(i) a civil behaviour order,
(ii) a costs order.

Evidence of a witness in person

G–226 **37.4.**—(1) This rule applies where a party wants to introduce evidence by calling a witness to give that evidence in person.

(2) Unless the court otherwise directs—
(a) a witness waiting to give evidence must not wait inside the courtroom, unless that witness is—
(i) a party, or
(ii) an expert witness;
(b) a witness who gives evidence in the courtroom must do so from the place provided for that purpose; and
(c) a witness' address must not be announced unless it is relevant to an issue in the case.

(3) Unless other legislation otherwise provides, before giving evidence a witness must take an oath or affirm.

(4) In the following sequence—
(a) the party who calls a witness must ask questions in examination-in-chief;
(b) every other party may ask questions in cross-examination;
(c) the party who called the witness may ask questions in re-examination;
(d) at any time while giving evidence, a witness may refer to a record of that witness' recollection of events, if other legislation so permits;
(e) the party who calls a witness, in examination-in-chief may ask that witness to adopt all or part of such a record as part of that witness' evidence, but only if—
(i) the parties agree, and
(ii) the court so permits;
(f) if the witness adopts any part of such a record—
(i) that part must be read aloud, or
(ii) with the court's permission, its contents may be summarised aloud.

(5) The justices' legal adviser or the court may—
(a) ask a witness questions; and in particular
(b) where the defendant is not represented, ask any question necessary in the defendant's interests.

Evidence by written statement

G–227 **37.5.**—(1) This rule applies where a party introduces in evidence the written statement of a witness.

(2) The party introducing the statement must read or summarise aloud those parts that are relevant to the issues in the case.

Evidence by admission

37.6.—(1) This rule applies where— G–228

(a) a party introduces in evidence a fact admitted by another party; or

(b) parties jointly admit a fact.

(2) Unless the court otherwise directs, a written record must be made of the admission.

Procedure on plea of guilty

37.7.—(1) This rule applies if— G–229

(a) the defendant pleads guilty; and

(b) the court is satisfied that the plea represents a clear acknowledgement of guilt.

(2) The court may convict the defendant without receiving evidence.

Written guilty plea: special rules

37.8.—(1) This rule applies where— G–229a

(a) the offence alleged—

(i) can be tried only in a magistrates' court, and

(ii) is not one specified under section 12(1)(a) of the Magistrates' Courts Act 1980;

(b) the defendant is at least 16 years old;

(c) the prosecutor has served on the defendant—

(i) the summons or requisition,

(ii) the material on which the prosecutor relies to set out the facts of the offence and to provide information relevant to sentence,

(iii) a notice that the procedure set out in this rule applies, and

(iv) a notice for the defendant's use if the defendant wants to plead guilty without attending court; and

(d) the prosecutor has served on the court officer—

(i) copies of those documents, and

(ii) a certificate of service of those documents on the defendant.

(2) A defendant who wants to plead guilty without attending court must, before the hearing date specified in the summons or requisition—

(a) serve a notice of guilty plea on the court officer; and

(b) include with that notice any representations that the defendant wants the court to consider on that date.

(3) A defendant who wants to withdraw such a notice must notify the court officer in writing before the hearing date.

(4) The court may accept such a guilty plea on the hearing date, and if it does so must take account only of—

(a) the material served by the prosecutor on the defendant under this rule; and

(b) any representations by the defendant.

(5) With the defendant's agreement, the court may deal with the case in the same way as under paragraph (4) where the defendant—

(a) is present; and

(b) has served a notice of guilty plea under paragraph (2); or

(c) pleads guilty there and then.

Application to withdraw a guilty plea

37.9.—(1) This rule applies where the defendant wants to withdraw a guilty plea. G–229b

(2) The defendant must apply to do so—

(a) as soon as practicable after becoming aware of the reasons for doing so; and

(b) before sentence.

(3) Unless the court otherwise directs, the application must be in writing and the defendant must serve it on—

(a) the court officer; and

(b) the prosecutor.

(4) The application must—

(a) explain why it would be unjust not to allow the defendant to withdraw the guilty plea;

Appendices

(b) identify—
(i) any witness that the defendant wants to call, and
(ii) any other proposed evidence; and
(c) say whether the defendant waives legal professional privilege, giving any relevant name and date.

Procedure if the court convicts

G–229c **37.10.**—(1) This rule applies if the court convicts the defendant.

(2) The court—
(a) may exercise its power to require—
(i) a statement of the defendant's financial circumstances,
(ii) a pre-sentence report; and
(b) may (and in some circumstances must) remit the defendant to a youth court for sentence where—
(i) the defendant is under 18, and
(ii) the convicting court is not itself a youth court.

(3) The prosecutor must—
(a) summarise the prosecution case, if the sentencing court has not heard evidence;
(b) identify any offence to be taken into consideration in sentencing;
(c) provide information relevant to sentence; and
(d) where it is likely to assist the court, identify any other matter relevant to sentence, including—
(i) aggravating and mitigating factors,
(ii) the legislation applicable, and
(iii) any sentencing guidelines or guideline cases.

(4) The defendant must provide information relevant to sentence, including details of financial circumstances.

(5) Where the defendant pleads guilty but wants to be sentenced on a different basis to that disclosed by the prosecution case—
(a) the defendant must set out that basis in writing, identifying what is in dispute;
(b) the court may invite the parties to make representations about whether the dispute is material to sentence; and
(c) if the court decides that it is a material dispute, the court will—
(i) invite such further representations or evidence as it may require, and
(ii) decide the dispute.

(6) Where the court has power to order the endorsement of the defendant's driving licence, or power to order the disqualification of the defendant from holding or obtaining one—
(a) if other legislation so permits, a defendant who wants the court not to exercise that power must introduce the evidence or information on which the defendant relies;
(b) the prosecutor may introduce evidence; and
(c) the parties may make representations about that evidence or information.

(7) Before the court passes sentence—
(a) the court must—
(i) give the defendant an opportunity to make representations and introduce evidence relevant to sentence, and
(ii) where the defendant is under 18, give the defendant's parents, guardian or other supporting adult, if present, such an opportunity as well; and
(b) the justices' legal adviser or the court must elicit any further information relevant to sentence that the court may require.

(8) If the court requires more information, it may exercise its power to adjourn the hearing for not more than—
(a) 3 weeks at a time, if the defendant will be in custody; or
(b) 4 weeks at a time.

(9) When the court has taken into account all the evidence, information and any report available, the general rule is that the court will—
(a) pass sentence there and then;

(b) explain the sentence, the reasons for it, and its effect, in terms the defendant can understand (with help, if necessary); and

(c) consider exercising any power it has to make a costs or other order.

(10) Despite the general rule—

(a) the court must adjourn the hearing if—

(i) the case started with a summons or requisition, and the defendant is absent, and

(ii) the court considers passing a custodial sentence, or

(iii) the court considers imposing a disqualification (unless it has already adjourned the hearing to give the defendant an opportunity to attend);

(b) the court may exercise any power it has to—

(i) commit the defendant to the Crown Court for sentence (and in some cases it must do so), or

(ii) defer sentence for up to 6 months.

Procedure where a party is absent

37.11.—(1) This rule— **G–229d**

(a) applies where a party is absent; but

(b) does not apply where the defendant has served a notice of guilty plea under rule 37.8 (written guilty plea: special rules).

(2) Where the prosecutor is absent, the court may—

(a) if it has received evidence, deal with the case as if the prosecutor were present; and

(b) in any other case—

(i) enquire into the reasons for the prosecutor's absence, and

(ii) if satisfied there is no good reason, exercise its power to dismiss the allegation.

(3) Where the defendant is absent—

(a) the general rule is that the court will proceed as if the defendant—

(i) were present, and

(ii) had pleaded not guilty (unless a plea already has been taken) and the court must give reasons if it does not do so; but

(b) the general rule does not apply if the defendant is under 18;

(c) the general rule is subject to the court being satisfied that—

(i) any summons or requisition was served on the defendant a reasonable time before the hearing, or

(ii) in a case in which the hearing has been adjourned, the defendant had reasonable notice of where and when it would resume;

(d) the general rule is subject also to rule 37.10(10)(a) (restrictions on passing sentence in the defendant's absence); and

(e) the hearing must be treated as if it had not taken place at all if—

(i) the case started with a summons or requisition,

(ii) the defendant makes a statutory declaration of not having found out about the case until after the hearing began, and

(iii) the defendant serves that declaration on the court officer not more than 21 days after the date of finding out about the case, unless the court extends that time limit.

(4) Where the defendant is absent, the court—

(a) must exercise its power to issue a warrant for the defendant's arrest, if it passes a custodial sentence; and

(b) may exercise its power to do so in any other case, if it does not apply the general rule in paragraph (3)(a) of this rule about proceeding in the defendant's absence.

Provision of documents for the court

37.12.—(1) This rule applies where a party— **G–229e**

(a) introduces in evidence any document; or

(b) relies on any other document in the presentation of that party's case

(2) Unless the court otherwise directs, that party must supply sufficient copies of such a document for—

(a) each other party;
(b) the court; and
(c) the justices' legal adviser.

Place of trial

G–229f **37.13.**—(1) Unless the court otherwise directs, the hearing must take place in a courtroom provided by the Lord Chancellor.

(2) Where the hearing takes place in Wales—
(a) any party or witness may use the Welsh language; and
(b) if practicable, at least one member of the court must be Welsh-speaking.

Duty of justices' legal adviser

G–229g **37.14.**—(1) A justices' legal adviser must attend, unless the court—
(a) includes a District Judge (Magistrates' Courts); and
(b) otherwise directs.

(2) A justices' legal adviser must—
(a) give the court legal advice; and
(b) if necessary, attend the members of the court outside the courtroom to give such advice; but
(c) inform the parties of any such advice given outside the courtroom.

(3) A justices' legal adviser must—
(a) assist an unrepresented defendant;
(b) assist the court by—
(i) making a note of the substance of any oral evidence or representations, to help the court recall that information,
(ii) if the court rules inadmissible part of a written statement introduced in evidence, marking that statement in such a way as to make that clear,
(iii) ensuring that an adequate record is kept of the court's decisions and the reasons for them, and
(iv) making any announcement, other than of the verdict or sentence.

(4) Where the defendant has served a notice of guilty plea to which rule 37.8 (written guilty plea: special rules) applies, a justices' legal adviser must read aloud to the court—
(a) the material on which the prosecutor relies to set out the facts of the offence and to provide information relevant to sentence (or summarise any written statement included in that material, if the court so directs); and
(b) any written representations by the defendant.

Duty of court officer

G–229h **37.15.** The court officer must—
(a) serve on each party notice of where and when an adjourned hearing will resume, unless—
(i) the party was present when that was arranged, or
(ii) the defendant has served a notice of guilty plea to which rule 37.8 applies, and the adjournment is for not more than 4 weeks;
(b) if the reason for the adjournment was to postpone sentence, include that reason in any such notice to the defendant;
(c) unless the court otherwise directs, make available to the parties any written report to which rule 37.10 applies;
(d) where the court has ordered a defendant to provide information under section 25 of the*Road Traffic Offenders Act* 1988, serve on the defendant notice of that order unless the defendant was present when it was made;
(e) serve on the prosecutor—
(i) any notice of guilty plea to which rule 37.8 applies, and
(ii) any declaration served under rule 37.11(3)(e) that the defendant did not know about the case;
(f) record in the magistrates' court register the court's reasons for not proceeding in the defendant's absence where rule 37.11(3)(a) applies; and
(g) give the court such other assistance as it requires.

[The next paragraph is § G–238.]

PART 40 TAINTED ACQUITTALS

Contents of this Part

Time of certification

40.1. Where a person is convicted of an offence as referred to in section 54(1)(b) of the *Criminal Procedure and Investigations Act* 1996 and it appears to the court before which the conviction has taken place that the provisions of section 54(2) are satisfied, the court shall make the certification referred to in section 54(2) at any time following conviction but no later than— **G–238**

(a) immediately after the court sentences or otherwise deals with that person in respect of the offence; or

(b) where the court, being a magistrates' court, commits that person to the Crown Court, or remits him to another magistrates' court, to be dealt with in respect of the offence, immediately after he is so committed or remitted, as the case may be; or

(c) (c) where that person is a child or young person and the court, being the Crown Court, remits him to a youth court to be dealt with in respect of the offence, immediately after he is so remitted.

Form of certification in the Crown Court

40.2. A certification referred to in section 54(2) of the *Criminal Procedure and Investigations Act* 1996 by the Crown Court shall be drawn up in the form set out in the Practice Direction. **G–239**

Service of a copy of the certification

40.3. Where a magistrates' court or the Crown Court makes a certification as referred to in section 54(2) of the *Criminal Procedure and Investigations Act* 1996, the court officer shall, as soon as practicable after the drawing up of the form, serve a copy on the acquitted person referred to in the certification, on the prosecutor in the proceedings which led to the acquittal, and, where the acquittal has taken place before a court other than, or at a different place to, the court where the certification has been made, on— **G–240**

(a) the clerk of the magistrates' court before which the acquittal has taken place; or

(b) the Crown Court officer at the place where the acquittal has taken place.

Entry in register or records in relation to the conviction which occasioned certification

40.4. A clerk of a magistrates' court or an officer of a Crown Court which has made a certification under section 54(2) of the *Criminal Procedure and Investigations Act* 1996 shall enter in the register or records, in relation to the conviction which occasioned the certification, a note of the fact that certification has been made, the date of certification, the name of the acquitted person referred to in the certification, a description of the offence of which the acquitted person has been acquitted, the date of the acquittal, and the name of the court before which the acquittal has taken place. **G–241**

Entry in the register or records in relation to the acquittal

40.5. The court officer of the court before which an acquittal has taken place shall, as soon as **G–242**

Appendices

practicable after receipt of a copy of a form recording a certification under section 54(2) of the *Criminal Procedure and Investigations Act* 1996 relating to the acquittal, enter in the register or records a note that the certification has been made, the date of the certification, the name of the court which has made the certification, the name of the person whose conviction occasioned the making of the certification, and a description of the offence of which that person has been convicted. Where the certification has been made by the same court as the court before which the acquittal has occurred, sitting at the same place, the entry shall be made as soon as practicable after the making of the certification. In the case of an acquittal before a magistrates' court, the entry in the register shall be signed by the clerk of the court.

Display of copy certification form

G–243 **40.6.**—(1) Where a court makes a certification as referred to in section 54(2) of the *Criminal Procedure and Investigations Act* 1996, the court officer shall, as soon as practicable after the drawing up of the form, display a copy of that form at a prominent place within court premises to which place the public has access.

(2) Where an acquittal has taken place before a court other than, or at a different place to, the court which has made the certification under section 54(2) of the 1996 Act in relation to the acquittal, the court officer at the court where the acquittal has taken place shall, as soon as practicable after receipt of a copy of the form recording the certification, display a copy of it at a prominent place within court premises to which place the public has access.

(3) The copy of the form referred to in paragraph (1), or the copy referred to in paragraph (2), shall continue to be displayed as referred to, respectively, in those paragraphs at least until the expiry of 28 days from, in the case of paragraph (1), the day on which the certification was made, or, in the case of paragraph (2), the day on which the copy form was received at the court.

Entry in the register or records in relation to decision of High Court

G–244 **40.7.**—(1) The court officer at the court where an acquittal has taken place shall, on receipt from the Administrative Court Office of notice of an order made under section 54(3) of the *Criminal Procedure and Investigations Act* 1996 quashing the acquittal, or of a decision not to make such an order, enter in the register or records, in relation to the acquittal, a note of the fact that the acquittal has been quashed by the said order, or that a decision has been made not to make such an order, as the case may be.

(2) The court officer of the court which has made a certification under section 54(2) of the 1996 Act shall, on receipt from the Administrative Court Office of notice of an order made under section 54(3) of that Act quashing the acquittal referred to in the certification, or of a decision not to make such an order, enter in the register or records, in relation to the conviction which occasioned the certification, a note that the acquittal has been quashed by the said order, or that a decision has been made not to make such an order, as the case may be.

(3) The entries in the register of a magistrates' court referred to, respectively, in paragraphs (1) and (2) above shall be signed by the magistrates' court officer.

Display of copy of notice received from High Court

G–245 **40.8.**—(1) Where the court officer of a court which has made a certification under section 54(2) of the *Criminal Procedure and Investigations Act* 1996 or before which an acquittal has occurred to which such a certification refers, receives from the Administrative Court Office notice of an order quashing the acquittal concerned, or notice of a decision not to make s uch an order, he shall, as soon as practicable after receiving the notice, display a copy of it at a prominent place within court premises to which place the public has access.

(2) The copy notice referred to in paragraph (1) shall continue to be displayed as referred to in that paragraph at least until the expiry of 28 days from the day on which the notice was received at the court.

[The next paragraph is § G–263.]

PART 42 SENTENCING PROCEDURES IN SPECIAL CASES

Contents of this Part

Reasons for deciding not to follow a guideline or make an order

42.1.—(1) This rule applies where the court decides— **G–263**

(a) not to follow a relevant sentencing guideline;

(b) not to make, where it could—

(i) a reparation order (unless it passes a custodial or community sentence),

(ii) a compensation order, or

(iii) a travel restriction order;

(c) not to order, where it could—

(i) that a suspended sentence of imprisonment is to take effect,

(ii) the endorsement of the defendant's driving record, or

(iii) the defendant's disqualification from driving, for the usual minimum period or at all.

(2) The court must explain why it has not done so, when it explains the sentence that it has passed.

Requirements of community sentence, etc.

42.2.—(1) This rule applies where the court— **G–263a**

(a) imposes a requirement in connection with—

(i) a community sentence,

(ii) a youth rehabilitation order, or

(iii) a suspended sentence of imprisonment; or

(b) orders the defendant to attend meetings with a supervisor.

(2) The court officer must—

(a) notify the defendant and, where the defendant is under 14, an appropriate adult, of—

(i) the requirement or requirements imposed, and

(ii) the name of the responsible officer or supervisor, and the means by which that person may be contacted; and

(b) notify the responsible officer or supervisor, and, where the defendant is under 14, the appropriate qualifying officer (if that is not the responsible officer), of—

(i) the defendant's name, address and telephone number (if available),

(ii) the offence or offences of which the defendant was convicted, and

(iii) the requirement or requirements imposed.

Appendices

(3) If the court imposes an electronic monitoring requirement, the monitor of which is not the responsible officer, the court officer must—

(a) notify the defendant and, where the defendant is under 16, an appropriate adult, of the monitor's name, and the means by which the monitor may be contacted; and

(b) notify the monitor of—

(i) the defendant's name, address and telephone number (if available),

(ii) the offence or offences of which the defendant was convicted,

(iii) the place or places at which the defendant's presence must be monitored,

(iv) the period or periods during which the defendant's presence there must be monitored, and

(v) the responsible officer's name, and the means by which that officer may be contacted.

Notification requirements

G–263b **42.3.**—(1) This rule applies where, on a conviction, sentence or order, legislation requires the defendant—

(a) to notify information to the police; or

(b) to be included in a barred list.

(2) The court must tell the defendant that such requirements apply, and under what legislation.

Variation of sentence

G–263c **42.4.**—(1) This rule—

(a) applies where a magistrates' court or the Crown Court can vary or rescind a sentence or order; and

(b) authorises the Crown Court, in addition to its other powers, to do so within the period of 56 days beginning with another defendant's acquittal or sentencing where—

(i) defendants are tried separately in the Crown Court on the same or related facts alleged in one or more indictments, and

(ii) one is sentenced before another is acquitted or sentenced.

(2) The court may exercise its power—

(a) on application by a party; or

(b) on its own initiative.

(3) A party who wants the court to exercise that power must—

(a) apply in writing as soon as reasonably practicable after—

(i) the sentence or order that that party wants the court to vary or rescind, or

(ii) where paragraph (1)(b) applies, the other defendant's acquittal or sentencing;

(b) serve the application on—

(i) the court officer, and

(ii) each other party; and

(c) in the application—

(i) explain why the sentence should be varied or rescinded,

(ii) specify the variation that the applicant proposes, and

(iii) if the application is late, explain why.

(4) The court must not exercise its power in the defendant's absence unless—

(a) the court makes a variation proposed by the defendant; or

(b) the defendant has had an opportunity to make representations at a hearing (whether or not the defendant in fact attends).

(5) The court may—

(a) extend (even after it has expired) the time limit under paragraph (3), unless the court's power to vary or rescind the sentence cannot be exercised; and

(b) allow an application to be made orally.

Application to vary or discharge a compensation order

42.5.—(1) This rule applies where a magistrates' court can vary or discharge a compensation order on application by the defendant.

(2) A defendant who wants the court to exercise that power must—
(a) apply in writing as soon as practicable after becoming aware of the grounds for doing so;
(b) serve the application on the magistrates' court officer;
(c) where the compensation order was made in the Crown Court, serve a copy of the application on the Crown Court officer; and
(d) in the application, specify the compensation order that the defendant wants the court to vary or discharge and explain (as applicable)—
(i) what civil court finding shows that the injury, loss or damage was less than it had appeared to be when the order was made,
(ii) in what circumstances the person for whose benefit the order was made has recovered the property for the loss of which it was made,
(iii) why a confiscation order makes the defendant now unable to pay compensation in full, or
(iv) in what circumstances the defendant's means have been reduced substantially and unexpectedly, and why they seem unlikely to increase for a considerable period.

(3) The court officer must serve a copy of the application on the person for whose benefit the compensation order was made.

(4) The court must not vary or discharge the compensation order unless—
(a) the defendant, and the person for whose benefit it was made, each has had an opportunity to make representations at a hearing (whether or not either in fact attends); and
(b) where the order was made in the Crown Court, the Crown Court has notified its consent.

Application to remove, revoke or suspend a disqualification or restriction

42.6.—(1) This rule applies where, on application by the defendant, the court can remove, revoke or suspend a disqualification or restriction included in a sentence (except a disqualification from driving). **G–263e**

(2) A defendant who wants the court to exercise such a power must—
(a) apply in writing, no earlier than the date on which the court can exercise the power;
(b) serve the application on the court officer; and
(c) in the application—
(i) specify the disqualification or restriction, and
(ii) explain why the defendant wants the court to remove, revoke or suspend it.

(3) The court officer must serve a copy of the application on the chief officer of police for the local justice area.

Application for a restitution order by the victim of a theft

42.7.—(1) This rule applies where, on application by the victim of a theft, the court can order a defendant to give that person goods obtained with the proceeds of goods stolen in that theft. **G–263f**

(2) A person who wants the court to exercise that power if the defendant is convicted must—
(a) apply in writing as soon as practicable (without waiting for the verdict);
(b) serve the application on the court officer; and
(c) in the application—
(i) identify the goods, and
(ii) explain why the applicant is entitled to them.

(3) The court officer must serve a copy of the application on each party.

(4) The court must not determine the application unless the applicant and each party has had an opportunity to make representations at a hearing (whether or not each in fact attends).

(5) The court may—
(a) extend (even after it has expired) the time limit under paragraph (2); and
(b) allow an application to be made orally.

Appendices

Requests for medical reports, etc.

G–263g **42.8.**—(1) This rule applies where the court—

(a) requests a medical examination of the defendant and a report; or

(b) requires information about the arrangements that could be made for the defendant where the court is considering—

(i) a hospital order, or

(ii) a guardianship order.

(2) Unless the court otherwise directs, the court officer must, as soon as practicable, serve on each person from whom a report or information is sought a note that—

(a) specifies the power exercised by the court;

(b) explains why the court seeks a report or information from that person; and

(c) sets out or summarises any relevant information available to the court.

Information to be supplied on admission to hospital or guardianship

G–263h **42.9.**—(1) This rule applies where the court—

(a) orders the defendant's detention and treatment in hospital; or

(b) makes a guardianship order.

(2) Unless the court otherwise directs, the court officer must, as soon as practicable, serve on (as applicable) the hospital or the guardian—

(a) a record of the court's order;

(b) such information as the court has received that appears likely to assist in treating or otherwise dealing with the defendant, including information about—

(i) the defendant's mental condition,

(ii) the defendant's other circumstances, and

(iii) the circumstances of the offence.

Information to be supplied on committal for sentence, etc.

G–263i **42.10.**—(1) This rule applies where a magistrates' court or the Crown Court convicts the defendant and—

(a) commits or adjourns the case to another court—

(i) for sentence, or

(ii) for the defendant to be dealt with for breach of a deferred sentence, a conditional discharge, or a suspended sentence of imprisonment, imposed by that other court;

(b) deals with a deferred sentence, a conditional discharge, or a suspended sentence of imprisonment, imposed by another court; or

(c) makes an order that another court is, or may be, required to enforce.

(2) Unless the convicting court otherwise directs, the court officer must, as soon as practicable—

(a) where paragraph (1)(a) applies, arrange the transmission from the convicting to the other court of relevant copy court records and other relevant documents, including any—

(i) certificate of conviction,

(ii) magistrates' court register entry,

(iii) record relating to bail,

(iv) note of evidence,

(v) statement or other document introduced in evidence,

(vi) medical or other report,

(vii) representation order or application for such order, and

(viii) interim driving disqualification;

(b) where paragraph (1)(b) or (c) applies, arrange—

(i) the transmission from the convicting to the other court of notice of the convicting court's order, and

(ii) the recording of that order at the other court;

(c) in every case, notify the defendant and, where the defendant is under 14, an appropriate adult, of the location of the other court.

[The next paragraph is § G-266.]

PART 44 BREACH, REVOCATION AND AMENDMENT OF COMMUNITY AND OTHER ORDERS

Contents of this Part

When this Part applies

44.1. This Part applies where— **G–266**

(a) the person responsible for a defendant's compliance with an order to which applies—

(i) Schedule 3, 5, 7 or 8 to the *Powers of Criminal Courts (Sentencing) Act* 2000,

(ii) Schedule 8 or 12 to the *Criminal Justice Act* 2003,

(iii) Schedule 2 to the *Criminal Justice and Immigration Act* 2008, or

(iv) the Schedule to the *Street Offences Act* 1959

wants the court to deal with that defendant for failure to comply;

(b) one of the following wants the court to exercise any power it has to revoke or amend such an order—

(i) the responsible officer or supervisor,

(ii) the defendant, or

(iii) where the legislation allows, a person affected by the order; or

(c) the court considers exercising on its own initiative any power it has to revoke or amend such an order.

Application by responsible officer or supervisor

44.2.—(1) This rule applies where— **G–267**

(a) the responsible officer or supervisor wants the court to—

(i) deal with a defendant for failure to comply with an order to which this Part applies, or

(ii) revoke or amend such an order; or

(b) the court considers exercising on its own initiative any power it has to—

(i) revoke or amend such an order, and

(ii) summon the defendant to attend for that purpose.

(2) Rules 7.2 to 7.4, which deal, among other things, with starting a prosecution in a magistrates' court by information and summons, apply—

(a) as if—

(i) a reference in those rules to an allegation of an offence included a reference to an allegation of failure to comply with an order to which this Part applies, and

(ii) a reference to the prosecutor included a reference to the responsible officer or supervisor; and

(b) with the necessary consequential modifications.

Application by defendant or person affected

44.3.—(1) This rule applies where— **G–267a**

(a) the defendant wants the court to exercise any power it has to revoke or amend an order to which this Part applies; or

(b) where the legislation allows, a person affected by such an order wants the court to exercise any such power.

(2) That defendant, or person affected, must—

(a) apply in writing, explaining why the order should be revoked or amended; and
(b) serve the application on—
(i) the court officer,
(ii) the responsible officer or supervisor, and
(iii) as appropriate, the defendant or the person affected.

Procedure on application by responsible officer or supervisor

G–267b **44.4.**—(1) Except for rule 37.8, the rules in Part 37, which deal with the procedure at a trial in a magistrates' court, apply—
(a) as if—
(i) a reference in those rules to an allegation of an offence included a reference to an allegation of failure to comply with an order to which this Part applies,
(ii) a reference to the court's verdict included a reference to the court's decision to revoke or amend such an order, or to exercise any other power it has to deal with the defendant, and
(iii) a reference to the court's sentence included a reference to the exercise of any such power; and
(b) with the necessary consequential modifications.

(2) The court officer must serve on each party any order revoking or amending an order to which this Part applies.

[The next paragraph is § G-275.]

PART 50 CIVIL BEHAVIOUR ORDERS AFTER VERDICT OR FINDING

Contents of this Part

When this Part applies

G–275 **50.1.**—(1) This Part applies in magistrates' courts and in the Crown Court where the court could decide to make, vary or revoke a civil order—
(a) under a power that the court can exercise after reaching a verdict or making a finding, and
(b) that requires someone to do, or not do, something.

(2) A reference to a 'behaviour order' in this Part is a reference to any such order.

(3) A reference to 'hearsay evidence' in this Part is a reference to evidence consisting of hearsay within the meaning of section 1(2) of the *Civil Evidence Act* 1995.

Behaviour orders: general rules

G–276 **50.2.**—(1) The court must not make a behaviour order unless the person to whom it is directed has had an opportunity—
(a) to consider what order is proposed and why; and

(b) to make representations at a hearing (whether or not that person in fact attends).

(2) That restriction does not apply to making an interim behaviour order, but such an order has no effect unless the person to whom it is directed—

(a) is present when it is made; or

(b) is handed a document recording the order not more than 7 days after it is made.

(3) Where the court decides not to make, where it could—

(a) a football banning order;

(b) a parenting order, after a person under 16 is convicted of disobeying an anti-social behaviour order; or

(c) a drinking banning order,

the court must announce, at a hearing in public, the reasons for its decision.

Application for behaviour order: special rules

50.3.—(1) This rule applies where a prosecutor wants the court to make— **G–277**

(a) an anti-social behaviour order; or

(b) a serious crime prevention order, if the defendant is convicted.

(2) The prosecutor must serve a notice of intention to apply for such an order on—

(a) the court officer;

(b) the defendant against whom the prosecutor wants the court to make the order; and

(c) any person on whom the order would be likely to have a significant adverse effect, as soon as practicable (without waiting for the verdict).

(3) The notice must be in the form set out in the Practice Direction and must—

(a) summarise the relevant facts;

(b) identify the evidence on which the prosecutor relies in support;

(c) attach any written statement that the prosecutor has not already served; and

(d) specify the order that the prosecutor wants the court to make.

(4) The defendant must then—

(a) serve written notice of any evidence on which the defendant relies on—

(i) the court officer, and

(ii) the prosecutor, as soon as practicable (without waiting for the verdict); and

(b) in the notice, identify that evidence and attach any written statement that has not already been served.

(5) This rule does not apply to an application for an interim anti-social behaviour order.

Evidence to assist the court: special rules

50.4.—(1) This rule applies where the court indicates that it may make on its own initiative— **G–278**

(a) a football banning order;

(b) a restraining order;

(c) an anti-social behaviour order; or

(d) a drinking banning order.

(2) A party who wants the court to take account of any particular evidence before making that decision mustµ

(a) serve notice in writing on—

(i) the court officer, and

(ii) every other party, as soon as practicable (without waiting for the verdict); and

(b) in that notice identify that evidence and attach any written statement that has not already been served.

Application to vary or revoke behaviour order

50.5.—(1) The court may vary or revoke a behaviour order if— **G–278a**

(a) the legislation under which it is made allows the court to do so; and

(b) one of the following applies—

(i) the prosecutor,

(ii) the person to whom the order is directed,

(iii) any other person mentioned in the order,

(iv) the relevant authority or responsible officer,

(v) the relevant Chief Officer of Police, or
(vi) the Director of Public Prosecutions.

(2) A person applying under this rule must—
(a) apply in writing as soon as practicable after becoming aware of the grounds for doing so, explaining—
(i) what material circumstances have changed since the order was made, and
(ii) why the order should be varied or revoked as a result; and
(b) serve the application on—
(i) the court officer,
(ii) as appropriate, the prosecutor or defendant, and
(iii) any other person listed in paragraph (1)(b), if the court so directs.

(3) A party who wants the court to take account of any particular evidence before making its decision must, as soon as practicable—
(a) serve notice in writing on—
(i) the court officer,
(ii) as appropriate, the prosecutor or defendant, and
(iii) any other person listed in paragraph (1)(b) on whom the court directed the application to be served; and
(b) in that notice identify the evidence and attach any written statement that has not already been served.

(4) The court may decide an application under this rule with or without a hearing.

(5) But the court must not—
(a) dismiss an application under this rule unless the applicant has had an opportunity to make representations at a hearing (whether or not the applicant in fact attends); or
(b) allow an application under this rule unless everyone required to be served, by this rule or by the court, has had at least 14 days in which to make representations, including representations about whether there should be a hearing.

(6) The court officer must—
(a) serve the application on any person, if the court so directs; and
(b) give notice of any hearing to—
(i) the applicant, and
(ii) any person required to be served, by this rule or by the court.

Notice of hearsay evidence

G–278b **50.6.**—(1) A party who wants to introduce hearsay evidence must—
(a) serve a notice in writing on—
(i) the court officer, and
(ii) every other party directly affected; and
(b) in that notice—
(i) explain that it is a notice of hearsay evidence,
(ii) identify that evidence,
(iii) identify the person who made the statement which is hearsay, or explain why if that person is not identified, and
(iv) explain why that person will not be called to give oral evidence.

(2) A party may serve one notice under this rule in respect of more than one notice and more than one witness.

Cross-examination of maker of hearsay statement

G–278c **50.7.**—(1) This rule applies where a party wants the court's permission to cross-examine a person who made a statement which another party wants to introduce as hearsay.

(2) The party who wants to cross-examine that person must—
(a) apply in writing, with reasons, not more than 7 days after service of the notice of hearsay evidence; and
(b) serve the application on—
(i) the court officer,
(ii) the party who served the hearsay evidence notice, and
(iii) every party on whom the hearsay evidence notice was served.

(3) The court may decide an application under this rule with or without a hearing.

(4) But the court must not—

(a) dismiss an application under this rule unless the applicant has had an opportunity to make representations at a hearing (whether or not the applicant in fact attends); or

(b) allow an application under this rule unless everyone served with the application has had at least 7 days in which to make representations, including representations about whether there should be a hearing.

Credibility and consistency of maker of hearsay statement

50.8.—(1) This rule applies where a party wants to challenge the credibility or consistency of a person who made a statement which another party wants to introduce as hearsay. **G–278d**

(2) The party who wants to challenge the credibility or consistency of that person must—

(a) serve a written notice of intention to do so on—

(i) the court officer, and

(ii) the party who served the notice of hearsay evidence not more than 7 days after service of that hearsay evidence notice; and

(b) in the notice, identify any statement or other material on which that party relies.

(3) The party who served the hearsay notice—

(a) may call that person to give oral evidence instead; and

(b) if so, must serve a notice of intention to do so on—

(i) the court officer, and

(ii) every party on whom he served the hearsay notice not more than 7 days after service of the notice under paragraph (2).

Court's power to vary requirements under this Part

50.9. The court may— **G–278e**

(a) shorten a time limit or extend it (even after it has expired);

(b) allow a notice or application to be given in a different form, or presented orally.

[The next paragraph is § G–280.]

Appendices

PART 52 ENFORCEMENT OF FINES AND OTHER ORDERS FOR PAYMENT

Contents of this Part

When this Part applies

52.1.—(1) This Part applies where a magistrates' court can enforce payment of— **G–280**

(a) a fine, or a sum that legislation requires the court to treat as a fine; or
(b) any other sum that a court has ordered to be paid—
(i) on a conviction, or
(ii) on the forfeiture of a surety.

(2) Rules 52.7 to 52.9 apply where the court, or a fines officer, issues a warrant that requires someone to—
(a) take control of goods or money belonging to the defendant;
(b) remove and sell any such goods; and
(c) pay any such money, and any proceeds of such a sale, to the court officer towards payment of a sum to which this Part applies.

(3) In this Part—
(a) "defendant" means anyone liable to pay a sum to which this Part applies;
(b) "payment terms" means by when, and by what (if any) instalments, such a sum must be paid.

Exercise of court's powers

G–281 **52.2.** The court must not exercise its enforcement powers unless—
(a) the court officer has served on the defendant any collection order or other notice of—
(i) the obligation to pay,
(ii) the payment terms, and
(iii) how and where the defendant must pay; and
(b) the defendant has failed to comply with the payment terms.

Duty to give receipt

G–282 **52.3.**—(1) This rule applies where the defendant makes a payment to—
(a) the court officer specified in an order or notice served under rule 52.2;
(b) another court officer;
(c) any—
(i) custodian of the defendant,
(ii) supervisor appointed to encourage the defendant to pay, or
(iii) responsible officer appointed under a community sentence or a suspended sentence of imprisonment; or
(d) a person executing a warrant to which rule 18.6 (warrants for arrest, detention or imprisonment that cease to have effect on payment) or this Part applies.

(2) The person receiving the payment must—
(a) give the defendant a receipt; and
(b) as soon as practicable transmit the payment to the court officer specified in an order or notice served under rule 52.2, if the recipient is not that court officer.

Appeal against decision of fines officer

G–283 **52.4.**—(1) This rule applies where—
(a) a collection order is in force;
(b) a fines officer makes a decision under one of these paragraphs of Schedule 5 to the *Courts Act* 2003—
(i) paragraph 22 (Application to fines officer for variation of order or attachment of earnings order, etc.),
(ii) paragraph 31 (Application to fines officer for variation of reserve terms), or
(iii) paragraph 37 (Functions of fines officer in relation to defaulters: referral or further steps notice); and
(c) the defendant wants to appeal against that decision.

(2) Unless the court otherwise directs, the defendant must—
(a) appeal in writing not more than 10 business days after the decision;
(b) serve the appeal on the court officer; and
(c) in the appeal—
(i) explain why a different decision should be made, and
(ii) specify the decision that the defendant proposes.

(3) Where the court determines an appeal—

(a) the general rule is that it will do so at a hearing; but
(b) it may do so without a hearing.

Application to reduce a fine or vary payment terms

52.5.—(1) This rule applies where— **G–284**

(a) no collection order is in force; and
(b) the defendant wants the court to—
 (i) reduce the amount of a fine, or
 (ii) vary payment terms.

(2) Unless the court otherwise directs, the defendant must—

(a) apply in writing;
(b) serve the application on the court officer; and
(c) in the application, explain—
 (i) what relevant circumstances have not yet been considered by the court, and
 (ii) why the fine should be reduced, or the payment terms varied.

Claim to avoid fine after penalty notice

52.6.—(1) This rule applies where— **G–285**

(a) a chief officer of police serves on the magistrates' court officer a certificate registering, for enforcement as a fine, a sum payable by a defendant after failure to comply with a penalty notice; and
(b) the court or a fines officer enforces the fine.

(2) A defendant who claims not to be the person to whom the penalty notice was issued must, unless the court otherwise directs—

(a) make that claim in writing; and
(b) serve it on the court officer.

(3) The court officer must—

(a) notify the chief officer of police by whom the certificate was registered; and
(b) refer the case to the court.

(4) Where such a claim is made—

(a) the general rule is that the court will adjourn the enforcement for 28 days and fix a hearing; but
(b) the court may make a different order.

(5) At any such hearing, the chief officer of police must introduce any evidence to contradict the defendant's claim.

Information to be included in a warrant to take goods, etc.

52.7.—(1) A warrant must identify— **G–286**

(a) the person(s) to whom it is directed;
(b) the defendant against whom it was issued;
(c) the sum for which it was issued and the reason that sum is owed;
(d) the court or fines officer who issued it, unless that is otherwise recorded by the court officer; and
(e) the court office for the court or fines officer who issued it.

(2) A person to whom a warrant is directed must record on it the date and time at which it is received.

(3) A warrant that contains an error is not invalid, as long as—

(a) it was issued in respect of a lawful decision by the court or fines officer; and
(b) it contains enough information to identify that decision.

Execution of a warrant to take goods, etc.

52.8.—(1) A warrant may be executed by— **G–287**

(a) any person to whom it is directed; or
(b) anyone authorised to do so by section 125 (warrants), 125A (civilian enforcement officers) or 125B (execution by approved enforcement agency) of the *Magistrates' Courts Act* 1980.

(2) The person who executes a warrant must—

(a) explain, in terms the defendant can understand—
(i) the order or decision that the warrant was issued to enforce,
(ii) the sum for which the warrant was issued, and
(iii) any extra sum payable in connection with the execution of the warrant;
(b) show the defendant the warrant, if that person has it;
(c) if the defendant asks—
(i) arrange for the defendant to see the warrant, if that person does not have it, and
(ii) show the defendant any written statement of that person's authority required by section 125A or 125B of the 1980 Act; and
(d) clearly mark any goods that are taken under the warrant, unless that person removes those goods at once.

(3) These goods must not be taken under the warrant—
(a) clothes or bedding used by the defendant or by anyone living with the defendant;
(b) tools, books, vehicles or other equipment that the defendant needs to use in the defendant's employment, business or vocation, unless the defendant is a corporation.

(4) Unless the court otherwise directs, or the defendant otherwise agrees, if the person who executes the warrant takes household goods they must not be removed until the day of sale.

(5) The warrant no longer has effect if—
(a) there is paid to the person executing it the sum for which it was issued and any extra sum payable in connection with its execution;
(b) those sums are offered to, but refused by, that person; or
(c) that person—
(i) is shown a receipt given under rule 52.3 for the sum for which the warrant was issued, and
(ii) is paid any extra sum payable in connection with its execution.

Sale of goods taken under a warrant

G–288 **52.9.**—(1) Unless the court otherwise directs or the defendant otherwise agrees, goods taken under a warrant must be sold—
(a) at public auction; and
(b) as soon as reasonably practicable after the expiry of 5 business days from the date of execution of the warrant.

(2) After a sale, the person who executed the warrant must, as soon as reasonably practicable—
(a) collect the proceeds of sale;
(b) deduct any sum payable in connection with the execution of the warrant;
(c) pay the court officer specified in an order or notice served under rule 52.2 the sum for which the warrant was issued;
(d) pay any balance remaining to the defendant; and
(e) deliver an account of those deductions and payments to the court officer.

Financial penalties imposed in other European Union member States

G–289 **52.10.**—(1) This rule applies where the Lord Chancellor gives the court officer a request to enforce a financial penalty imposed in another European Union member State.

(2) The court officer must serve on the defendant—
(a) notice of the request for enforcement, and of its effect;
(b) a copy of—
(i) the certificate requesting enforcement, and
(ii) the decision requiring payment to which that certificate relates; and
(c) notice that the procedure set out in this rule applies.

(3) A defendant who wants the court to refuse enforcement must—
(a) serve notice of objection on the court officer;
(b) unless the court otherwise directs, serve that notice not more than 14 days after service of notice of the request; and

(c) in the notice of objection—
  (i) identify each ground for refusal on which the defendant relies,
  (ii) summarise any relevant facts not already included in the certificate and decision served with the notice of the request, and
  (iii) identify any other document that the defendant thinks the court will need to determine the request (and serve any such document with the notice).

(4) The court—
(a) may determine a request for enforcement—
  (i) at a hearing, which will be in public unless the court otherwise directs, or
  (ii) without a hearing; but
(b) must not allow enforcement unless the defendant has had at least 14 days in which to serve notice of objection.

(5) Paragraphs (2) and (3) do not apply if, on receipt of the request, the court decides that a ground for refusal applies.

(6) The court officer must serve on the Lord Chancellor notice of the court's decision.

[The next paragraph is § G-296.]

PART 55 ROAD TRAFFIC PENALTIES

Contents of this Part

Application to remove a disqualification from driving

55.1.—(1) This rule applies where, on application by the defendant, the court can remove a disqualification from driving. **G–296**

(2) A defendant who wants the court to exercise that power must—
(a) apply in writing, no earlier than the date on which the court can exercise the power;
(b) serve the application on the court officer; and
(c) in the application—
  (i) specify the disqualification that the defendant wants the court to remove, and
  (ii) explain why.

(3) The court officer must serve a copy of the application on the chief officer of police for the local justice area.

Information to be supplied on order for endorsement of driving record, etc.

55.2.—(1) This rule applies where the court— **G–297**
(a) convicts the defendant of an offence involving obligatory endorsement, and orders there to be endorsed on the defendant's driving record and on any counterpart licence—
  (i) particulars of the conviction,
  (ii) particulars of any disqualification from driving that the court imposes, and
  (iii) the penalty points to be attributed to the offence;

(b) disqualifies the defendant from driving for any other offence; or
(c) suspends or removes a disqualification from driving.

(2) The court officer must, as soon as practicable, serve on the Secretary of State notice that includes details of—

(a) where paragraph (1)(a) applies—
(i) the local justice area in which the court is acting,
(ii) the dates of conviction and sentence,
(iii) the offence, and the date on which it was committed,
(iv) the sentence, and
(v) the date of birth, and sex, of the defendant, where those details are available;

(b) where paragraph (1)(b) applies—
(i) the date and period of the disqualification,
(ii) the power exercised by the court;

(c) where paragraph (1)(c) applies—
(i) the date and period of the disqualification,
(ii) the date and terms of the order for its suspension or removal,
(iii) the power exercised by the court, and
(iv) where the court suspends the disqualification pending appeal, the court to which the defendant has appealed.

Statutory declaration to avoid fine after fixed penalty notice

G–298 **55.3.**—(1) This rule applies where—

(a) a chief officer of police, or the Secretary of State, serves on the magistrates' court officer a certificate registering, for enforcement as a fine, a sum payable by a defendant after failure to comply with a fixed penalty notice;
(b) the court officer notifies the defendant of the registration; and
(c) the defendant makes a statutory declaration with the effect that—
(i) the fixed penalty notice, or any associated notice sent to the defendant as owner of the vehicle concerned, and
(ii) the registration and any enforcement proceedings
become void.

(2) The defendant must serve that statutory declaration not more than 21 days after service of notice of the registration, unless the court extends that time limit.

(3) The court officer must—

(a) serve a copy of the statutory declaration on the person by whom the certificate was registered,
(b) cancel any endorsement on the defendant's driving record and on any counterpart licence, and
(c) notify the Secretary of State of any such cancellation.

Application for declaration about a course or programme certificate decision

G–299 **55.4.**—(1) This rule applies where the court can declare unjustified—

(a) a course provider's failure or refusal to give a certificate of the defendant's satisfactory completion of an approved course; or
(b) a programme provider's giving of a certificate of the defendant's failure fully to participate in an approved programme.

(2) A defendant who wants the court to exercise that power must—

(a) apply in writing, not more than 28 days after—
(i) the date by which the defendant was required to complete the course, or
(ii) the giving of the certificate of failure fully to participate in the programme;
(b) serve the application on the court officer; and
(c) in the application, specify the course or programme and explain (as applicable)—
(i) that the course provider has failed to give a certificate,
(ii) where the course provider has refused to give a certificate, why the defendant disagrees with the reasons for that decision, or
(iii) where the programme provider has given a certificate, why the defendant disagrees with the reasons for that decision.

(3) The court officer must serve a copy of the application on the course or programme provider.

(4) The court must not determine the application unless the defendant, and the course or programme provider, each has had an opportunity to make representations at a hearing (whether or not either in fact attends).

Appeal against recognition of foreign driving disqualification

55.5.—(1) This rule applies where— **G–299a**

(a) a minister gives a disqualification notice under section 57 of the *Crime (International Co-operation) Act* 2003; and

(b) the person to whom it is given wants to appeal under section 59 of the Act to a magistrates' court.

(2) That person ("the appellant") must serve an appeal notice on—

(a) the court officer, at a magistrates' court in the local justice area in which the appellant lives; and

(b) the minister, at the address given in the disqualification notice.

(3) The appellant must serve the appeal notice within the period for which section 59 of the 2003 Act provides.

(4) The appeal notice must—

(a) attach a copy of the disqualification notice;

(b) explain which of the conditions in section 56 of the 2003 Act is not met, and why section 57 of the Act therefore does not apply; and

(c) include any application to suspend the disqualification, under section 60 of the Act.

(5) The minister may serve a respondent's notice, and must do so if—

(a) the minister wants to make representations to the court; or

(b) the court so directs.

(6) The minister must—

(a) unless the court otherwise directs, serve any such respondent's notice not more than 14 days after—

(i) the appellant serves the appeal notice, or

(ii) a direction to do so;

(b) in any such respondent's notice—

(i) identify the grounds of opposition on which the minister relies,

(ii) summarise any relevant facts not already included in the disqualification and appeal notices, and

(iii) identify any other document that the minister thinks the court will need to decide the appeal (and serve any such document with the notice).

(7) Where the court determines an appeal—

(a) the general rule is that it will do so at a hearing (which will be in public, unless the court otherwise directs); but

(b) it may do so without a hearing.

(8) The court officer must serve on the minister—

(a) notice of the outcome of the appeal; and

(b) notice of any suspension of the disqualification; and

(c) the appellant's driving licence, if surrendered to the court officer.

Appendices

PART 62 CONTEMPT OF COURT

Contents of this Part

Section 1: general rules

SECTION 1: GENERAL RULES

When this Part applies

G–299b **62.1.**—(1) This Part applies where the court can deal with a person for conduct—

(a) in contempt of court; or

(b) in contravention of the legislation to which rules rules 62.5 and 62.9 refer.

(2) In this Part, "respondent" means any such person.

Exercise of court's power to deal with contempt of court

G–299c **62.2.**—(1) The court must determine at a hearing—

(a) an enquiry under rule 62.8;

(b) an allegation under rule 62.9.

(2) The court must not proceed in the respondent's absence unless—

(a) the respondent's behaviour makes it impracticable to proceed otherwise; or

(b) the respondent has had at least 14 days' notice of the hearing, or was present when it was arranged.

(3) If the court hears part of an enquiry or allegation in private, it must announce at a hearing in public—

(a) the respondent's name;

(b) in general terms, the nature of any conduct that the respondent admits, or the court finds proved; and

(c) any punishment imposed.

Notice of suspension of imprisonment by Court of Appeal or Crown Court

62.3.—(1) This rule applies where— **G–299d**

(a) the Court of Appeal or the Crown Court suspends an order of imprisonment for contempt of court; and

(b) the respondent is absent when the court does so.

(2) The respondent must be served with notice of the terms of the court's order—

(a) by any applicant under rule 62.9; or

(b) by the court officer, in any other case.

Application to discharge an order for imprisonment

62.4.—(1) This rule applies where the court can discharge an order for a respondent's imprisonment for contempt of court. **G–299e**

(2) A respondent who wants the court to discharge such an order must—

(a) apply in writing, unless the court otherwise directs, and serve any written application on—

(i) the court officer, and

(ii) any applicant under rule 62.9 on whose application the respondent was imprisoned;

(b) in the application—

(i) explain why it is appropriate for the order for imprisonment to be discharged, and

(ii) give details of any appeal, and its outcome; and

(c) ask for a hearing, if the respondent wants one.

SECTION 2: CONTEMPT OF COURT BY OBSTRUCTION, DISRUPTION, ETC.

Initial procedure on obstruction, disruption, etc.

62.5.—(1) This rule applies where the court observes, or someone reports to the court— **G–299f**

(a) in the Court of Appeal or the Crown Court, obstructive, disruptive, insulting or intimidating conduct, in the courtroom or in its vicinity, or otherwise immediately affecting the proceedings;

(b) in the Crown Court, a contravention of—

(i) section 3 of the *Criminal Procedure (Attendance of Witnesses) Act* 1965 (disobeying a witness summons);

(ii) section 20 of the *Juries Act* 1974 (disobeying a jury summons);

(iii) section 8 of the *Contempt of Court Act* 1981 (obtaining details of a jury's deliberations, *etc.*);

(c) in a magistrates' court, a contravention of—

(i) section 97(4) of the *Magistrates' Courts Act* 1980 (refusing to give evidence), or

(ii) section 12 of the *Contempt of Court Act* 1981 (insulting or interrupting the court, *etc.*);

(d) a contravention of section 9 of the *Contempt of Court Act* 1981 (without the court's permission, recording the proceedings, *etc.*);

(e) any other conduct with which the court can deal as, or as if it were, a criminal contempt of court, except failure to surrender to bail under section 6 of the *Bail Act* 1976.

(2) Unless the respondent's behaviour makes it impracticable to do so, the court must—

(a) explain, in terms the respondent can understand (with help, if necessary)—

(i) the conduct that is in question,

(ii) that the court can impose imprisonment, or a fine, or both, for such conduct,

(iii) (where relevant) that the court has power to order the respondent's immediate temporary detention, if in the court's opinion that is required,

(iv) that the respondent may explain the conduct,

(v) that the respondent may apologise, if he or she so wishes, and that this may persuade the court to take no further action, and

(vi) that the respondent may take legal advice; and

(b) allow the respondent a reasonable opportunity to reflect, take advice, explain and, if he or she so wishes, apologise.

(3) The court may then—

(a) take no further action in respect of that conduct;

(b) enquire into the conduct there and then; or

(c) postpone that enquiry (if a magistrates' court, only until later the same day).

Review after temporary detention

G–299g **62.6.**—(1) This rule applies in a case in which the court has ordered the respondent's immediate temporary detention for conduct to which rule 62.5 applies.

(2) The court must review the case—

(a) if a magistrates' court, later the same day;

(b) in the Court of Appeal or the Crown Court, no later than the next business day.

(3) On the review, the court must—

(a) unless the respondent is absent, repeat the explanations required by rule 62.5(2)(a); and

(b) allow the respondent a reasonable opportunity to reflect, take advice, explain and, if he or she so wishes, apologise.

(4) The court may then—

(a) take no further action in respect of the conduct;

(b) if a magistrates' court, enquire into the conduct there and then; or

(c) if the Court of Appeal or the Crown Court—

(i) enquire into the conduct there and then, or

(ii) postpone the enquiry, and order the respondent's release from such detention in the meantime.

Postponement of enquiry

G–299h **62.7.**—(1) This rule applies where the Court of Appeal or the Crown Court postpones the enquiry.

(2) The court must arrange for the preparation of a written statement containing such particulars of the conduct in question as to make clear what the respondent appears to have done.

(3) The court officer must serve on the respondent—

(a) that written statement;

(b) notice of where and when the postponed enquiry will take place; and

(c) a notice that—

(i) reminds the respondent that the court can impose imprisonment, or a fine or both, for contempt of court, and

(ii) warns the respondent that the court may pursue the postponed enquiry in the respondent's absence, if the respondent does not attend.

Procedure on enquiry

G–299i **62.8.**—(1) At an enquiry, the court must—

(a) ensure that the respondent understands (with help, if necessary) what is alleged, if the enquiry has been postponed from a previous occasion;

(b) explain what the procedure at the enquiry will be; and

(c) ask whether the respondent admits the conduct in question.

(2) If the respondent admits the conduct, the court need not receive evidence.

(3) If the respondent does not admit the conduct, the court will receive—

(a) any statement served under rule 62.7;

(b) any other evidence of the conduct;

(c) any evidence introduced by the respondent; and

(d) any representations by the respondent about the conduct.

(4) If the respondent admits the conduct, or the court finds it proved, the court must—

(a) before imposing any punishment for contempt of court, give the respondent an opportunity to make representations relevant to punishment;

(b) explain, in terms the respondent can understand (with help, if necessary)—

(i) the reasons for its decision, including its findings of fact, and
(ii) the punishment it imposes, and its effect; and
(c) if a magistrates' court, arrange for the preparation of a written record of those findings.

(5) The court that conducts an enquiry—
(a) need not include the same member or members as the court that observed the conduct; but
(b) may do so, unless that would be unfair to the respondent.

SECTION 3: CONTEMPT OF COURT BY FAILURE TO COMPLY WITH COURT ORDER, ETC.

Initial procedure on failure to comply with court order, etc.

62.9.—(1) This rule applies where— **G–299j**
(a) a party, or other person directly affected, alleges—
(i) in the Crown Court, a failure to comply with an order to which rule 6.13 or 6.22 (certain investigation orders), or rule 59.6 (a restraint order), applies,
(ii) in the Court of Appeal or the Crown Court, any other conduct with which that court can deal as a civil contempt of court, or
(iii) in the Crown Court or a magistrates' court, unauthorised use of disclosed prosecution material under section 17 of the *Criminal Procedure and Investigations Act* 1996;
(b) the court deals on its own initiative with conduct to which paragraph (1)(a) applies.

(2) Such a party or person must—
(a) apply in writing and serve the application on the court officer; and
(b) serve on the respondent—
(i) the application, and
(ii) notice of where and when the court will consider the allegation (not less than 14 days after service).

(3) The application must—
(a) identify the respondent;
(b) explain that it is an application for the respondent to be dealt with for contempt of court;
(c) contain such particulars of the conduct in question as to make clear what is alleged against the respondent; an
(d) include a notice warning the respondent that the court—
(i) can impose imprisonment, or a fine, or both, for contempt of court, and
(ii) may deal with the application in the respondent's absence, if the respondent does not attend the hearing.

(4) A court which acts on its own initiative under paragraph (1)(b) must—
(a) arrange for the preparation of a written statement containing the same information as an application; and
(b) arrange for the service on the respondent of—
(i) that written statement, and
(ii) notice of where and when the court will consider the allegation (not less than 14 days after service).

Procedure on hearing

62.10.—(1) At the hearing of an allegation under rule 62.9, the court must— **G–299k**
(a) ensure that the respondent understands (with help, if necessary) what is alleged;
(b) explain what the procedure at the hearing will be; and
(c) ask whether the respondent admits the conduct in question.

(2) If the respondent admits the conduct, the court need not receive evidence.

(3) If the respondent does not admit the conduct, the court will receive—

Appendices

(a) the application or written statement served under rule 62.9;
(b) any other evidence of the conduct;
(c) any evidence introduced by the respondent; and
(d) any representations by the respondent about the conduct.

(4) If the respondent admits the conduct, or the court finds it proved, the court must—
(a) before imposing any punishment for contempt of court, give the respondent an opportunity to make representations relevant to punishment;
(b) explain, in terms the respondent can understand (with help, if necessary)—
(i) the reasons for its decision, including its findings of fact, and
(ii) the punishment it imposes, and its effect; and
(c) in a magistrates' court, arrange for the preparation of a written record of those findings.

Introduction of written witness statement or other hearsay

G–299l **62.11.**—(1) Where rule 62.9 applies, an applicant or respondent who wants to introduce in evidence the written statement of a witness, or other hearsay, must—
(a) serve a copy of the statement, or notice of other hearsay, on—
(i) the court officer, and
(ii) the other party; and
(b) serve the copy or notice—
(i) when serving the application under rule 62.9, in the case of an applicant, or
(ii) not more than 7 days after service of that application or of the court's written statement, in the case of the respondent.

(2) Such service is notice of that party's intention to introduce in evidence that written witness statement, or other hearsay, unless that party otherwise indicates when serving it.

(3) A party entitled to receive such notice may waive that entitlement.

Content of written witness statement

G–299m **62.12.**—(1) This rule applies to a written witness statement served under rule 62.11.

(2) Such a written witness statement must contain a declaration by the person making it that it is true to the best of that person's knowledge and belief.

Content of notice of other hearsay

G–299n **62.13.**—(1) This rule applies to a notice of hearsay, other than a written witness statement, served under rule 62.11.

(2) Such a notice must—
(a) set out the evidence, or attach the document that contains it; and
(b) identify the person who made the statement that is hearsay.

Cross-examination of maker of written witness statement or other hearsay

G–299o **62.14.**—(1) This rule applies where a party wants the court's permission to cross-examine a person who made a statement which another party wants to introduce as hearsay.

(2) The party who wants to cross-examine that person must—
(a) apply in writing, with reasons; and
(b) serve the application on—
(i) the court officer, and
(ii) the party who served the hearsay.

(3) A respondent who wants to cross-examine such a person must apply to do so not more than 7 days after service of the hearsay by the applicant.

(4) An applicant who wants to cross-examine such a person must apply to do so not more than 3 days after service of the hearsay by the respondent.

(5) The court—
(a) may decide an application under this rule without a hearing; but
(b) must not dismiss such an application unless the person making it has had an opportunity to make representations at a hearing.

Credibility and consistency of maker of written witness statement or other hearsay

G–299p **62.15.**—(1) This rule applies where a party wants to challenge the credibility or consistency of a person who made a statement which another party wants to introduce as hearsay.

(2) The party who wants to challenge the credibility or consistency of that person must—

(a) serve a written notice of intention to do so on—

(i) the court officer, and

(ii) the party who served the hearsay; and

(b) in it, identify any statement or other material on which that party relies.

(3) A respondent who wants to challenge such a person's credibility or consistency must serve such a notice not more than 7 days after service of the hearsay by the applicant.

(4) An applicant who wants to challenge such a person's credibility or consistency must serve such a notice not more than 3 days after service of the hearsay by the respondent.

(5) The party who served the hearsay—

(a) may call that person to give oral evidence instead; and

(b) if so, must serve a notice of intention to do so on—

(i) the court officer, and

(ii) the other party

as soon as practicable after service of the notice under paragraph (2).

Magistrates' courts' powers to adjourn, etc.

62.16.—(1) This rule applies where a magistrates' court deals with unauthorised disclosure of prosecution material under sections 17 and 18 of the *Criminal Procedure and Investigations Act* 1996. **G–299o**

(2) The sections of the *Magistrates' Courts Act* 1980 listed in paragraph (3) apply as if in those sections—

(a) "complaint" and "summons" each referred to an application or written statement under rule 62.9;

(b) "complainant" meant an applicant; and

(c) "defendant" meant the respondent.

(3) Those sections are—

(a) section 51(e) (issue of summons on complaint);

(b) section 54(f) (adjournment);

(c) section 55(g) (non-appearance of defendant);

(d) section 97(1)(h) (summons to witness);

(e) section 121(1)(a) (constitution and place of sitting of court);

(f) section 123(b) (defect in process).

(4) Section 127 of the 1980 Act (limitation of time) does not apply.

Court's power to vary requirements under Section 3

62.17.—(1) The court may shorten or extend (even after it has expired) a time limit under rule 62.11, 62.14 or 62.15. **G–299r**

(2) A person who wants an extension of time must—

(a) apply when serving the statement, notice or application for which it is needed; and

(b) explain the delay.

PART 63 APPEAL TO THE CROWN COURT

Content of this Part

Appendices

Hearings and decisions	r.63.7 (*post*, G–306)
Abandoning an appeal	r.63.8 (*post*, G–307)
Court's power to vary requirements under this Part	r.63.9 (*post*, G–308)
Constitution of the Crown Court	r.63.10 (*post*, G–308a)

When this Part applies

G–300 **63.1.**—(1) This Part applies where—

(a) a defendant wants to appeal under—

(i) section 108 of the *Magistrates' Courts Act* 1980,

(ii) section 45 of the *Mental Health Act* 1983,

(iii) paragraph 10 of Schedule 3 to the *Powers of Criminal Courts (Sentencing) Act* 2000, or paragraphs 9(8) or 13(5) of Schedule 8 to the *Criminal Justice Act* 2003,

(iv) section 10 of the *Violent Crime Reduction Act* 2006,

(v) section 42 of the *Counter Terrorism Act* 2008;

(b) the Criminal Cases Review Commission refers a defendant's case to the Crown Court under section 11 of the *Criminal Appeal Act* 1995;

(c) a prosecutor wants to appeal under—

(i) section 14A(5A) of the *Football Spectators Act* 1989, or

(ii) section 147(3) of the *Customs and Excise Management Act* 1979; or

(d) a person wants to appeal under—

(i) section 1 of the Magistrates' Courts (Appeals from Binding Over Orders) Act 1956,

(ii) section 12(5) of the *Contempt of Court Act* 1981,

(iii) regulation 3C or 3H of the *Costs in Criminal Cases (General) Regulations* 1986, or

(iv) section 22 of the *Football Spectators Act* 1989.

(2) A reference to an 'appellant' in this Part is a reference to such a party or person.

Service of appeal notice

G–301 **63.2.**—(1) An appellant must serve an appeal notice on—

(a) the magistrates' court officer; and

(b) every other party.

(2) The appellant must serve the appeal notice—

(a) as soon after the decision appealed against as the appellant wants; but

(b) not more than 21 days after—

(i) sentence or the date sentence is deferred, whichever is earlier, if the appeal is against conviction or against a finding of guilt,

(ii) sentence, if the appeal is against sentence, or

(iii) the order or failure to make an order about which the appellant wants to appeal, in any other case.

(3) The appellant must—

(a) serve with the appeal notice any application for an extension of the time limit under this rule; and

(b) in that application, explain why the appeal notice is late.

Form of appeal notice

G–302 **63.3.** The appeal notice must be in writing and must—

(a) specify—

(i) the conviction or finding of guilt,

(ii) the sentence, or

(iii) the order, or the failure to make an order about which the appellant wants to appeal;

(b) summarise the issues;

(c) in an appeal against conviction—

(i) identify the prosecution witnesses whom the appellant will want to question if they are called to give oral evidence, and
(ii) say how long the trial lasted in the magistrates' court and how long the appeal is likely to last in the Crown Court;
(d) in an appeal against a finding that the appellant insulted someone or interrupted proceedings in the magistrates' court, attach—
(i) the magistrates' court's written findings of fact, and
(ii) the appellant's response to those findings;
(e) say whether the appellant has asked the magistrates' court to reconsider the case; and
(f) include a list of those on whom the appellant has served the appeal notice.

Duty of magistrates' court officer

63.4. The magistrates' court officer must— **G–303**
(a) as soon as practicable serve on the Crown Court officer—
(i) the appeal notice and any accompanying application served by the appellant,
(ii) details of the parties including their addresses,
(iii) a copy of each magistrates' court register entry relating to the decision under appeal and to any application for bail pending appeal, and
(iv) any report received for the purposes of sentencing;
(b) keep any document or object exhibited in the proceedings in the magistrates' court, or arrange for it to be kept by some other appropriate person, until—
(i) 6 weeks after the conclusion of those proceedings, or
(ii) the conclusion of any proceedings in the Crown Court that begin within that 6 weeks; and
(c) provide the Crown Court with any document, object or information for which the Crown Court officer asks, within such period as the Crown Court officer may require.

Appendices

Duty of person keeping exhibit

63.5. A person who, under arrangements made by the magistrates' court officer, keeps a document or object exhibited in the proceedings in the magistrates' court must— **G–304**
(a) keep that exhibit until—
(i) 6 weeks after the conclusion of those proceedings, or
(ii) the conclusion of any proceedings in the Crown Court that begin within that 6 weeks, unless the magistrates' court or the Crown Court otherwise directs; and
(b) provide the Crown Court with any such document or object for which the Crown Court officer asks, within such period as the Crown Court officer may require.

Reference by the Criminal Cases Review Commission

63.6.—(1) The Crown Court officer must, as soon as practicable, serve a reference by the Criminal Cases Review Commission on — **G–305**
(a) the appellant;
(b) every other party; and
(c) the magistrates' court officer.
(2) The appellant may serve an appeal notice on—
(a) the Crown Court officer; and
(b) every other party, not more than 21 days later.
(3) The Crown Court must treat the reference as the appeal notice if the appellant does not serve an appeal notice.

Hearings and decisions

63.7.—(1) The Crown Court as a general rule must hear in public an appeal or reference to which this Part applies, but— **G–306**
(a) may order any hearing to be in private; and
(b) where a hearing is about a public interest ruling, must hold that hearing in private.

(2) The Crown Court officer must give as much notice as reasonably practicable of every hearing to—
(a) the parties;
(b) any party's custodian; and
(c) any other person whom the Crown Court requires to be notified.
(3) The Crown Court officer must serve every decision on—
(a) the parties;
(b) any other person whom the Crown Court requires to be served; and
(c) the magistrates' court officer and any party's custodian, where the decision determines an appeal.
(4) But where a hearing or decision is about a public interest ruling, the Crown Court officer must not—
(a) give notice of that hearing to; or
(b) serve that decision on, anyone other than the prosecutor who applied for that ruling, unless the court otherwise directs.

Abandoning an appeal

G–307 **63.8.**—(1) The appellant—
(a) may abandon an appeal without the Crown Court's permission, by serving a notice of abandonment on—
(i) the magistrates' court officer,
(ii) the Crown Court officer, and
(iii) every other party before the hearing of the appeal begins; but
(b) after the hearing of the appeal begins, may only abandon the appeal with the Crown Court's permission.
(2) A notice of abandonment must be signed by or on behalf of the appellant.
(3) Where an appellant who is on bail pending appeal abandons an appeal—
(a) the appellant must surrender to custody as directed by the magistrates' court officer; and
(b) any conditions of bail apply until then.

Court's power to vary requirements under this Part

G–308 **63.9.** The Crown Court may—
(a) shorten or extend (even after it has expired) a time limit under this Part;
(b) allow an appellant to vary an appeal notice that that appellant has served;
(c) direct that an appeal notice be served on any person;
(d) allow an appeal notice or a notice of abandonment to be in a different form to one set out in the Practice Direction, or to be presented orally.

Constitution of the Crown Court

G–308a **63.10.** On the hearing of an appeal—
(a) the general rule is that the Crown Court must comprise—
(i) a judge of the High Court, a Circuit judge or a Recorder, and
(ii) no less than two and no more than four justices of the peace, none of whom took part in the decision under appeal; and
(b) if the appeal is from a youth court—
(i) each justice of the peace must be qualified to sit as a member of a youth court, and
(ii) the Crown Court must include a man and a woman; but
(c) the Crown Court may include only one justice of the peace and need not include both a man and a woman if—
(i) the presiding judge decides that otherwise the start of the appeal hearing will be delayed unreasonably, or
(ii) one or more of the justices of the peace who started hearing the appeal is absent.

PART 64 APPEAL TO THE HIGH COURT BY WAY OF CASE STATED

Contents of this Part

Application to a magistrates' court to state a case

64.1.—(1) An application under section 111(1) of the *Magistrates' Courts Act* 1980 shall be made in writing and signed by or on behalf of the applicant and shall identify the question or questions of law or jurisdiction on which the opinion of the High Court is sought. **G–309**

(2) Where one of the questions on which the opinion of the High Court is sought is whether there was evidence on which the magistrates' court could come to its decision, the particular finding of fact made by the magistrates' court which it is claimed cannot be supported by the evidence before the magistrates' court shall be specified in such application.

(3) Any such application shall be sent to a court officer for the magistrates' court whose decision is questioned.

Consideration of a draft case by a magistrates' court

64.2.—(1) Within 21 days after receipt of an application made in accordance with rule 64.1, a court officer for the magistrates' court whose decision is questioned shall, unless the justices refuse to state a case under section 111(5) of the *Magistrates' Courts Act* 1980, send a draft case in which are stated the matters required under rule 64.6 (content of case stated) to the applicant or his legal representative and shall send a copy thereof to the respondent or his legal representative. **G–310**

(2) Within 21 days after receipt of the draft case under paragraph (1), each party may make representations thereon. Any such representations shall be in writing and signed by or on behalf of the party making them and shall be sent to the magistrates' court officer.

(3) Where the justices refuse to state a case under section 111(5) of the 1980 Act and they are required by a mandatory order of the High Court under section 111(6) to do so, this rule shall apply as if in paragraph (1)—

(a) for the words 'receipt of an application made in accordance with rule 64.1' there were substituted the words 'the date on which a mandatory order under section 111(6) of the 1980 Act is made'; and

(b) the words 'unless the justices refuse to state a case under section 111(5) of the 1980 Act' were omitted.

Preparation and submission of final case to a magistrates' court

64.3.—(1) Within 21 days after the latest day on which representations may be made under rule 64.2, the justices whose decision is questioned shall make such adjustments, if any, to the draft case prepared for the purposes of that rule as they think fit, after considering any such representations, and shall state and sign the case. **G–311**

(2) A case may be stated on behalf of the justices whose decision is questioned by any 2 or more of them and may, if the justices so direct, be signed on their behalf by the justices' clerk.

(3) Forthwith after the case has been stated and signed a court officer for the court shall send it to the applicant or his legal representative, together with any statement required by rule 64.4.

Extension of time limits by a magistrates' court

64.4.—(1) If a magistrates' court officer is unable to send to the applicant a draft case under rule 64.2(1) within the time required by that paragraph, he shall do so as soon as practicable **G–312**

Appendices

thereafter and the provisions of that rule shall apply accordingly; but in that event a court officer shall attach to the draft case, and to the final case when it is sent to the applicant or his legal representative under rule 64.3(3), a statement of the delay and the reasons for it.

(2) If a magistrates' court officer receives an application in writing from or on behalf of the applicant or the respondent for an extension of the time within which representations on the draft case may be made under rule 64.2(2), together with reasons in writing for it, the justices' clerk may, by notice in writing sent to the applicant, or respondent as the case may be, by the magistrates' court officer, extend the time and the provisions of that paragraph and of rule 64.3 shall apply accordingly; but in that event the court officer shall attach to the final case, when it is sent to the applicant or his legal representative under rule 64.3(3), a statement of the extension and the reasons for it.

(3) If the justices are unable to state a case within the time required by rule 64.3(1), they shall do so as soon as practicable thereafter and the provisions of that rule shall apply accordingly; but in that event a court officer shall attach to the final case, when it is sent to the applicant or his legal representative under rule 64.3(3), a statement of the delay and the reasons for it.

Content of case stated by a magistrates' court

G–313 **64.5.**—(1) A case stated by the magistrates' court shall state the facts found by the court and the question or questions of law or jurisdiction on which the opinion of the High Court is sought.

(2) Where one of the questions on which the opinion of the High Court is sought is whether there was evidence on which the magistrates' court could come to its decision, the particular finding of fact which it is claimed cannot be supported by the evidence before the magistrates' court shall be specified in the case.

(3) Unless one of the questions on which the opinion of the High Court is sought is whether there was evidence on which the magistrates' court could come to its decision, the case shall not contain a statement of evidence.

Application to the Crown Court to state a case

G–314 **64.6.**—(1) An application under section 28 of the *Senior Courts Act* 1981 to the Crown Court to state a case for the opinion of the High Court shall be made in writing to a court officer within 21 days after the date of the decision in respect of which the application is made.

(2) The application shall state the ground on which the decision of the Crown Court is questioned.

(3) After making the application, the applicant shall forthwith send a copy of it to the parties to the proceedings in the Crown Court.

(4) On receipt of the application, the Crown Court officer shall forthwith send it to the judge who presided at the proceedings in which the decision was made.

(5) On receipt of the application, the judge shall inform the Crown Court officer as to whether or not he has decided to state a case and that officer shall give notice in writing to the applicant of the judge's decision.

(6) If the judge considers that the application is frivolous, he may refuse to state a case and shall in that case, if the applicant so requires, cause a certificate stating the reasons for the refusal to be given to him.

(7) If the judge decides to state a case, the procedure to be followed shall, unless the judge in a particular case otherwise directs, be the procedure set out in paragraphs (8) to (12) of this rule.

(8) The applicant shall, within 21 days of receiving the notice referred to in paragraph (5), draft a case and send a copy of it to the Crown Court officer and to the parties to the proceedings in the Crown Court.

(9) Each party to the proceedings in the Crown Court shall, within 21 days of receiving a copy of the draft case under paragraph (8), either—

(a) give notice in writing to the applicant and the Crown Court officer that he does not intend to take part in the proceedings before the High Court;

(b) indicate in writing on the copy of the draft case that he agrees with it and send the copy to a court officer; or

(c) draft an alternative case and send it, together with the copy of the applicant's case, to the Crown Court officer.

(10) The judge shall consider the applicant's draft case and any alternative draft case sent to the Crown Court officer under paragraph (9)(c).

(11) If the Crown Court so orders, the applicant shall, before the case is stated and delivered to him, enter before the Crown Court officer into a recognizance, with or without sureties and in such sum as the Crown Court considers proper, having regard to the means of the applicant, conditioned to prosecute the appeal without delay.

(12) The judge shall state and sign a case within 14 days after either—

(a) the receipt of all the documents required to be sent to a court officer under paragraph (9); or

(b) the expiration of the period of 21 days referred to in that paragraph, whichever is the sooner.

(13) A case stated by the Crown Court shall state the facts found by the Crown Court, the submissions of the parties (including any authorities relied on by the parties during the course of those submissions), the decision of the Crown Court in respect of which the application is made and the question on which the opinion of the High Court is sought.

(14) Any time limit referred to in this rule may be extended either before or after it expires by the Crown Court.

(15) If the judge decides not to state a case but the stating of a case is subsequently required by a mandatory order of the High Court, paragraphs (7) to (14) shall apply to the stating of the case save that—

(a) in paragraph (7) the words 'If the judge decides to state a case' shall be omitted; and

(b) in paragraph (8) for the words 'receiving the notice referred to in paragraph (5)' there shall be substituted the words 'the day on which the mandatory order was made'.

(16) The judge may determine an application to which this rule applies—

(a) at a hearing, in public or in private; or

(b) without a hearing.

[The next paragraph is § G–315a.]

PART 75 REQUEST TO THE EUROPEAN COURT FOR A PRELIMINARY RULING

Contents of this Part

When this Part applies

75.1. This Part applies where the court can request the Court of Justice of the European Union ('the European Court') to give a preliminary ruling, under Article 267 of the Treaty on the Functioning of the European Union. **G–315a**

Preparation of request

75.2.—(1) The court may— **G–315b**

(a) make an order for the submission of a request—

(i) on application by a party, or

(ii) on its own initiative;

(b) give directions for the preparation of the terms of such a request.

(2) The court must—

(a) include in such a request—

(i) the identity of the court making the request,

(ii) the parties' identities,

(iii) a statement of whether a party is in custody,
(iv) a succinct statement of the question on which the court seeks the ruling of the European Court,
(v) a succinct statement of any opinion on the answer that the court may have expressed in any judgment that it has delivered,
(vi) a summary of the nature and history of the proceedings, including the salient facts and an indication of whether those facts are proved, admitted or assumed,
(vii) the relevant rules of national law,
(viii) a summary of the relevant contentions of the parties,
(ix) an indication of the provisions of European Union law that the European Court is asked to interpret, and
(x) an explanation of why a ruling of the European Court is requested;

(b) express the request in terms that can be translated readily into other languages; and
(c) set out the request in a schedule to the order.

Submission of request

G–315c **75.3.**—(1) The court officer must serve the order for the submission of the request on the Senior Master of the Queen's Bench Division of the High Court.

(2) The Senior Master will—
(a) submit the request to the European Court; but
(b) unless the court otherwise directs, postpone the submission of the request until—
(i) the time for any appeal against the order has expired, and
(ii) any appeal against the order has been determined.

Postponement of case pending request

G–315d **75.4.** Where the court orders the submission of a request—
(a) the general rule is that it will adjourn or postpone any further hearing; but
(b) it may otherwise direct.

PART 76 COSTS

Contents of this Part

Appeal to a High Court judge	r.76.13 (*post*, G–328)
Application for an extension of time under Section 5	r.76.14 (*post*, G–329)

SECTION 1: GENERAL

When this Part applies

76.1.—(1) This Part applies where the court can make an order about costs under— **G–316**

(a) Part II of the *Prosecution of Offences Act* 1985 and Part II, IIA or IIB of the *Costs in Criminal Cases (General) Regulations* 1986;

(b) section 109 of the *Magistrates' Courts Act* 1980;

(c) section 52 of the *Senior Courts Act* 1981 and rule 76.6;

(d) section 8 of the *Bankers Books Evidence Act* 1879;

(e) section 2C(8) of the *Criminal Procedure (Attendance of Witnesses) Act* 1965;

(f) section 36(5) of the *Criminal Justice Act* 1972;

(g) section 159(5) and Schedule 3, paragraph 11, of the *Criminal Justice Act* 1988;

(h) section 14H(5) of the *Football Spectators Act* 1989;

(i) section 4(7) of the *Dangerous Dogs Act* 1991; or

(j) Part 3 of the *Serious Crime Act 2007 (Appeals under Section 24) Order* 2008.

(2) In this Part, 'costs' means—

(a) the fees payable to a legal representative;

(b) the disbursements paid by a legal representative; and

(c) any other expenses incurred in connection with the case.

Costs orders: general rules

76.2.—(1) The court must not make an order about costs unless each party and any other person directly affected— **G–317**

(a) is present; or

(b) has had an opportunity—

(i) to attend, or

(ii) to make representations.

(2) The court may make an order about costs—

(a) at a hearing in public or in private; or

(b) without a hearing.

(3) In deciding what order, if any, to make about costs, the court must have regard to all the circumstances, including—

(a) the conduct of all the parties; and

(b) any costs order already made.

(4) If the court makes an order about costs, it must—

(a) specify who must, or must not, pay what, to whom; and

(b) identify the legislation under which the order is made, where there is a choice of powers.

(5) The court must give reasons if it—

(a) refuses an application for a costs order; or

(b) rejects representations opposing a costs order.

(6) If the court makes an order for the payment of costs—

(a) the general rule is that it will be for an amount that is sufficient reasonably to compensate the recipient for costs—

(i) actually, reasonably and properly incurred, and

(ii) reasonable in amount; but

(b) the court may order the payment of—

(i) a proportion of that amount,

(ii) a stated amount less than that amount,

(iii) costs from or until a certain date only,

Appendices

(iv) costs relating only to particular steps taken, or
(v) costs relating only to a distinct part of the case.

(7) On an assessment of the amount of costs, relevant factors include—
(a) the conduct of all the parties;
(b) the particular complexity of the matter or the difficulty or novelty of the questions raised;
(c) the skill, effort, specialised knowledge and responsibility involved;
(d) the time spent on the case;
(e) the place where and the circumstances in which work or any part of it was done; and
(f) any direction or observations by the court that made the costs order.

(8) If the court orders a party to pay costs to be assessed under rule 76.11, it may order that party to pay an amount on account.

(9) An order for the payment of costs takes effect when the amount is assessed, unless the court exercises any power it has to order otherwise.

Court's power to vary requirements under Sections 2, 3 and 4

G–318 **76.2.**—(1) The court may—
(a) extend a time limit for serving an application or representations under section 2, 3 or 4 of this Part, even after it has expired; and
(b) consider an application or representations—
(i) made in a different form to one set out in the Practice Direction, or
(ii) made orally instead of in writing.

(2) A person who wants an extension of time must—
(a) apply when serving the application or representations for which it is needed; and
(b) explain the delay.

SECTION 2: COSTS OUT OF CENTRAL FUNDS

Costs out of central funds

G–319 **76.3.**—(1) This rule applies where the court can order the payment of costs out of central funds.

(2) In this rule, costs—
(a) include—
(i) on an appeal, costs incurred in the court that made the decision under appeal, and
(ii) at a retrial, costs incurred at the initial trial and on any appeal; but
(b) do not include costs funded by the Legal Services Commission.

(3) The court may make an order—
(a) on application by the person who incurred the costs; or
(b) on its own initiative.

(4) Where a person wants the court to make an order that person must—
(a) apply as soon as practicable; and
(b) outline the type of costs and the amount claimed, if that person wants the court to direct an assessment; or
(c) specify the amount claimed, if that person wants the court to assess the amount itself.

(5) The general rule is that the court will make an order, but—
(a) the court may decline to make a defendant's costs order if, for example—
(i) the defendant is convicted of at least one offence, or
(ii) the defendant's conduct led the prosecutor reasonably to think the prosecution case stronger than it was; and
(b) the court may decline to make a prosecutor's costs order if, for example, the prosecution was started or continued unreasonably.

(6) If the court makes an order—
(a) it may direct an assessment under, as applicable—
(i) regulations 4 to 12 of the *Costs in Criminal Cases (General) Regulations* 1986, or

(ii) articles 21 to 28 of the *Serious Crime Act 2007 (Appeals under Section 24) Order* 2008;

(b) it may assess the amount itself, if the recipient agrees;

(c) it must assess the amount itself, in a case in which it decides not to allow an amount that is reasonably sufficient to compensate the recipient for expenses properly incurred in the proceedings.

SECTION 3: PAYMENT OF COSTS BY ONE PARTY TO ANOTHER

Costs on conviction and sentence

76.5.—(1) This rule applies where the court can order a defendant to pay the prosecutor's costs if the defendant is— **G–320**

(a) convicted or found guilty;

(b) dealt with in the Crown Court after committal for sentence there; or

(c) dealt with for breach of a sentence.

(2) The court may make an order—

(a) on application by the prosecutor; or

(b) on its own initiative.

(3) Where the prosecutor wants the court to make an order—

(a) the prosecutor must—

(i) apply as soon as practicable, and

(ii) specify the amount claimed; and

(b) the general rule is that the court will make an order if it is satisfied that the defendant can pay; but

(c) the court may decline to do so.

(4) A defendant who wants to oppose an order must make representations as soon as practicable.

(5) If the court makes an order, it must assess the amount itself.

Costs on appeal

76.6.—(1) This rule— **G–321**

(a) applies where a magistrates' court, the Crown Court or the Court of Appeal can order a party to pay another person's costs on an appeal, or an application for permission to appeal;

(b) authorises the Crown Court, in addition to its other powers, to order a party to pay another party's costs on an appeal to that court, except on an appeal under—

(i) section 108 of the *Magistrates' Courts Act* 1980, or

(ii) section 45 of the *Mental Health Act* 1983.

(2) In this rule, costs include—

(a) costs incurred in the court that made the decision under appeal; and

(b) costs funded by the Legal Services Commission.

(3) The court may make an order—

(a) on application by the person who incurred the costs; or

(b) on its own initiative.

(4) A person who wants the court to make an order must—

(a) apply as soon as practicable;

(b) notify each other party;

(c) specify—

(i) the amount claimed, and

(ii) against whom; and

(d) where an appellant abandons an appeal to the Crown Court by serving a notice of abandonment—

(i) apply in writing not more than 14 days later, and

(ii) serve the application on the appellant and on the Crown Court officer.

(5) A party who wants to oppose an order must—

Appendices

(a) make representations as soon as practicable; and

(b) where the application was under paragraph (4)(d), serve written representations on the applicant, and on the Crown Court officer, not more than 7 days after it was served.

(6) Where the application was under paragraph (4)(d), the Crown Court officer may—

(a) submit it to the Crown Court; or

(b) serve it on the magistrates' court officer, for submission to the magistrates' court.

(7) If the court makes an order, it may direct an assessment under rule 76.11, or assess the amount itself where—

(a) the appellant abandons an appeal to the Crown Court;

(b) the Crown Court decides an appeal, except an appeal under—

(i) section 108 of the *Magistrates' Courts Act* 1980, or

(ii) section 45 of the *Mental Health Act* 1983; or

(c) the Court of Appeal decides an appeal to which Part 69 applies (appeal to the Court of Appeal regarding reporting or public access restriction).

(8) If the court makes an order in any other case, it must assess the amount itself.

Costs on an application

G–322 **76.7.**—(1) This rule applies where the court can order a party to pay another person's costs in a case in which—

(a) the court decides an application for the production in evidence of a copy of a bank record;

(b) a magistrates' court or the Crown Court decides an application to terminate—

(i) a football banning order, or

(ii) a disqualification for having custody of a dog; or

(c) the Crown Court allows an application to withdraw a witness summons.

(2) The court may make an order—

(a) on application by the person who incurred the costs; or

(b) on its own initiative.

(3) A person who wants the court to make an order must—

(a) apply as soon as practicable;

(b) notify each other party; and

(c) specify—

(i) the amount claimed, and

(ii) against whom.

(4) A party who wants to oppose an order must make representations as soon as practicable.

(5) If the court makes an order, it may direct an assessment under rule 76.11, or assess the amount itself.

Costs resulting from unnecessary or improper act, etc.

G–323 **76.8.**—(1) This rule applies where the court can order a party to pay another party's costs incurred as a result of an unnecessary or improper act or omission by or on behalf of the first party.

(2) In this rule, costs include costs funded by the Legal Services Commission.

(3) The court may make an order—

(a) on application by the party who incurred such costs; or

(b) on its own initiative.

(4) A party who wants the court to make an order must—

(a) apply in writing as soon as practicable after becoming aware of the grounds for doing so;

(b) serve the application on—

(i) the court officer (or, in the Court of Appeal, the Registrar), and

(ii) each other party;

(c) in that application specify—

(i) the party by whom costs should be paid,

(ii) the relevant act or omission,

(iii) the reasons why that act or omission meets the criteria for making an order,

(iv) the amount claimed, and
(v) those on whom the application has been served.

(5) Where the court considers making an order on its own initiative, it must—
(a) identify the party against whom it proposes making the order; and
(b) specify—
(i) the relevant act or omission,
(ii) the reasons why that act or omission meets the criteria for making an order, and
(iii) with the assistance of the party who incurred the costs, the amount involved.

(6) A party who wants to oppose an order must—
(a) make representations as soon as practicable; and
(b) in reply to an application, serve written representations on the applicant and on the court officer (or Registrar) not more than 7 days after it was served.

(7) If the court makes an order, it must assess the amount itself.

SECTION 4: OTHER COSTS ORDERS

Costs against a legal representative

76.9.—(1) This rule applies where— G–324
(a) a party has incurred costs—
(i) as a result of an improper, unreasonable or negligent act or omission by a legal or other representative or representative's employee, or
(ii) which it has become unreasonable for that party to have to pay because of such an act or omission occurring after those costs were incurred; and
(b) the court can—
(i) order the representative responsible to pay such costs, or
(ii) prohibit the payment of costs to that representative.

(2) In this rule, costs include costs funded by the Legal Services Commission.

(3) The court may make an order—
(a) on application by the party who incurred such costs; or
(b) on its own initiative.

(4) A party who wants the court to make an order must—
(a) apply in writing as soon as practicable after becoming aware of the grounds for doing so;
(b) serve the application on—
(i) the court officer (or, in the Court of Appeal, the Registrar),
(ii) the representative responsible,
(iii) each other party, and
(iv) any other person directly affected;
(c) in that application specify—
(i) the representative responsible,
(ii) the relevant act or omission,
(iii) the reasons why that act or omission meets the criteria for making an order,
(iv) the amount claimed, and
(v) those on whom the application has been served.

(5) Where the court considers making an order on its own initiative, it must—
(a) identify the representative against whom it proposes making that order; and
(b) specify—
(i) the relevant act or omission,
(ii) the reasons why that act or omission meets the criteria for making an order, and
(iii) with the assistance of the party who incurred the costs, the amount involved.

(6) A representative who wants to oppose an order must—

Appendices

(a) make representations as soon as practicable; and
(b) in reply to an application, serve written representations on the applicant and on the court officer (or Registrar) not more than 7 days after it was served.

(7) If the court makes an order—
(a) the general rule is that it will do so without waiting until the end of the case, but it may postpone making the order; and
(b) it must assess the amount itself.

(8) Instead of making an order, the court may make adverse observations about the representative's conduct for use in an assessment where—
(a) a party's costs are—
(i) funded by the Legal Services Commission, or
(ii) to be paid out of central funds; or
(b) there is to be an assessment under rule 76.11.

Costs against a third party

G–325 **76.10.**—(1) This rule applies where—
(a) there has been serious misconduct by a person who is not a party; and
(b) the court can order that person to pay a party's costs.

(2) In this rule, costs include costs funded by the Legal Services Commission.

(3) The court may make an order—
(a) on application by the party who incurred the costs; or
(b) on its own initiative.

(4) A party who wants the court to make an order must—
(a) apply in writing as soon as practicable after becoming aware of the grounds for doing so;
(b) serve the application on—
(i) the court officer (or, in the Court of Appeal, the Registrar),
(ii) the person responsible,
(iii) each other party, and
(iv) any other person directly affected;
(c) in that application specify—
(i) the person responsible,
(ii) the relevant misconduct,
(iii) the reasons why the criteria for making an order are met,
(iv) the amount claimed, and
(v) those on whom the application has been served.

(5) Where the court considers making an order on its own initiative, it must—
(a) identify the person against whom it proposes making that order; and
(b) specify—
(i) the relevant misconduct,
(ii) the reasons why the criteria for making an order are met, and
(iii) with the assistance of the party who incurred the costs, the amount involved.

(6) A person who wants to oppose an order must—
(a) make representations as soon as practicable; and
(b) in reply to an application, serve written representations on the applicant and on the court officer (or Registrar) not more than 7 days after it was served.

(7) If the court makes an order—
(a) the general rule is that it will do so at the end of the case, but it may do so earlier; and
(b) it must assess the amount itself.

SECTION 5: ASSESSMENT OF COSTS

Assessment and re-assessment

G–326 **76.11.**—(1) This rule applies where the court directs an assessment under—

(a) rule 61.20 (*Proceeds of Crime Act* 2002 – rules applicable to restraint and receivership proceedings, assessment of costs);
(b) rule 76.6 (costs on appeal); or
(c) rule 76.7 (costs on an application).

(2) The assessment must be carried out by the relevant assessing authority, namely—
(a) the court officer, where the direction was given by a magistrates' court or by the Crown Court; or
(b) the Registrar of Criminal Appeals, where the direction was given by the Court of Appeal.

(3) The party in whose favour the court made the costs order ('the applicant') must—
(a) apply for an assessment—
(i) in writing, in any form required by the assessing authority, and
(ii) not more than 3 months after the costs order; and
(b) serve the application on—
(i) the assessing authority, and
(ii) the party against whom the court made the costs order ('the respondent').

(4) The applicant must—
(a) summarise the work done;
(b) specify—
(i) each item of work done, giving the date, time taken and amount claimed,
(ii) any disbursements or expenses, including the fees of any advocate, and
(iii) any circumstances of which the applicant wants the assessing authority to take particular account; and
(c) supply—
(i) receipts or other evidence of the amount claimed, and
(ii) any other information or document for which the assessing authority asks, within such period as that authority may require.

(5) A respondent who wants to make representations about the amount claimed must—
(a) do so in writing; and
(b) serve the representations on the assessing authority, and on the applicant, not more than 21 days after service of the application.

(6) The assessing authority must—
(a) if it seems likely to help with the assessment, obtain any other information or document;
(b) resolve in favour of the respondent any doubt about what should be allowed; and
(c) serve the assessment on the parties.

(7) Where either party wants the amount allowed re-assessed—
(a) that party must—
(i) apply to the assessing authority, in writing and in any form required by that authority,
(ii) serve the application on the assessing authority, and on the other party, not more than 21 days after service of the assessment,
(iii) explain the objections to the assessment,
(iv) supply any additional supporting information or document, and
(v) ask for a hearing, if that party wants one; and
(b) a party who wants to make representations about an application for re-assessment must—
(i) do so in writing,
(ii) serve the representations on the assessing authority, and on the other party, not more than 21 days after service of the application, and
(iii) ask for a hearing, if that party wants one;
(c) the assessing authority—
(i) must arrange a hearing, in public or in private, if either party asks for one,
(ii) subject to that, may re-assess the amount allowed with or without a hearing,
(iii) must re-assess the amount allowed on the initial assessment, taking into account the reasons for disagreement with that amount and any other representations,

(iv) may maintain, increase or decrease the amount allowed on the assessment,
(v) must serve the re-assessment on the parties, and
(vi) must serve written reasons on the parties, if not more than 21 days later either party asks for such reasons.

(8) A time limit under this rule may be extended even after it has expired—
(a) by the assessing authority, or
(b) by the Senior Costs Judge, if the assessing authority declines to do so.

Appeal to a costs judge

G–327 **76.12.**—(1) This rule applies where—
(a) the assessing authority has re-assessed the amount allowed under rule 76.11; and
(b) either party wants to appeal against that amount.

(2) That party must—
(a) serve an appeal notice on—
(i) the Senior Costs Judge,
(ii) the other party, and
(iii) the assessing authority not more than 21 days after service of the written reasons for the re-assessment;
(b) explain the objections to the re-assessment;
(c) serve on the Senior Costs Judge with the appeal notice—
(i) the applications for assessment and re-assessment,
(ii) any other information or document considered by the assessing authority,
(iii) the assessing authority's written reasons for the re-assessment, and
(iv) any other information or document for which a costs judge asks, within such period as the judge may require; and
(d) ask for a hearing, if that party wants one.

(3) A party who wants to make representations about an appeal must—
(a) serve representations in writing on—
(i) the Senior Costs Judge, and
(ii) the applicant not more than 21 days after service of the appeal notice; and
(b) ask for a hearing, if that party wants one.

(4) Unless a costs judge otherwise directs, the parties may rely only on—
(a) the objections to the amount allowed on the initial assessment; and
(b) any other representations and material considered by the assessing authority.

(5) A costs judge—
(a) must arrange a hearing, in public or in private, if either party asks for one;
(b) subject to that, may determine an appeal with or without a hearing;
(c) may—
(i) consult the assessing authority,
(ii) consult the court which made the costs order, and
(iii) obtain any other information or document;
(d) must reconsider the amount allowed by the assessing authority, taking into account the objections to the re-assessment and any other representations;
(e) may maintain, increase or decrease the amount allowed on the re-assessment;
(f) may provide for the costs incurred by either party to the appeal; and
(g) must serve reasons for the decision on—
(i) the parties, and
(ii) the assessing authority.

(6) A costs judge may extend a time limit under this rule, even after it has expired.

Appeal to a High Court judge

G–328 **76.13.**—(1) This rule applies where—
(a) a costs judge has determined an appeal under rule 76.12; and
(b) either party wants to appeal against the amount allowed.

(2) A party who wants to appeal—
(a) may do so only if a costs judge certifies that a point of principle of general importance was involved in the decision on the review; and

(b) must apply in writing for such a certificate and serve the application on—
(i) the costs judge,
(ii) the other party not more than 21 days after service of the decision on the review.

(3) That party must—
(a) appeal to a judge of the High Court attached to the Queen's Bench Division as if it were an appeal from the decision of a master under Part 52 of the Civil Procedure Rules 1998; and
(b) serve the appeal not more than 21 days after service of the costs judge's certificate under paragraph (2).

(4) A High Court judge—
(a) may extend a time limit under this rule even after it has expired;
(b) has the same powers and duties as a costs judge under rule 76.12; and
(c) may hear the appeal with one or more assessors.

Application for an extension of time under Section 5

76.14. . A party who wants an extension of time under rule 76.11, 76.12 or 76.13 must— **G–329**
(a) apply in writing;
(b) explain the delay; and
(c) attach the application, representations or appeal for which the extension of time is needed.

(i) the case judge,

(5) That party must—

(6) The Court judge—

Application for an extension of time under this Chapter

Appendix H

NATIONAL ALLOCATION GUIDELINES 2006

Draft Guidelines

Foreword

The Sentencing Guidelines Council was created in 2004 in order to frame guidelines to assist courts as they deal with criminal cases across the whole of England and Wales. **H–1**

The Council receives advice from the Sentencing Advisory Panel which consults widely before tendering that advice. The Council then produces a draft guideline on which it seeks the views of a limited group as provided by the *Criminal Justice Act* 2003. The Panel's advice to the Council in relation to allocation guidelines is being published simultaneously.

This draft guideline covers the legislative and other factors that should influence the decision whether an either-way offence is retained for trial in a magistrates' court or sent to the Crown Court to be dealt with (the allocation decision). It is within the remit of the Sentencing Guidelines Council to produce guidelines to support that decision and it is important that new guidelines be ready for use when legislative provisions changing the allocation procedure are brought into force.

The new allocation procedure has the added dimension of a sentence indication being given by a magistrates' court once it has decided that a case could be retained. This option is only available after the main part of the allocation decision has been made, but it is a key feature of the new procedures and guidance to courts is critical if consistency of approach is to be achieved. In *R. v. Goodyear*, the Court of Appeal (Criminal Division) considered sentence indications in reference to proceedings in the Crown Court and established a procedure for that Court. Although the procedure and approach of the Crown Court are very different from that in a magistrates' court, most of the principles identified in *Goodyear* can be applied to the statutory sentence indication procedure that follows an allocation decision.

The Panel's advice (and discussion paper that formed the basis of consultation seminars) contains further background details. All documents can be found at *www.sentencing-guidelines.gov.uk* or can be obtained from the Council's Secretariat at 85 Buckingham Gate, London SW1E 6PD.

When the consultation period is concluded (the closing date for responses is April 10, 2006), the Council will consider any responses received and then issue definitive guidelines to which every court must have regard in accordance with section 172 of the 2003 Act.

NATIONAL ALLOCATION GUIDELINES 2006

1. STATEMENT OF PURPOSE

1.1 In accordance with section 19 of the *Magistrates' Courts Act* 1980, where a defendant has not indicated an intention to plead guilty, a magistrates' court must decide whether an offence triable either-way should be sent to the Crown Court for trial. **H–2**

1.2 **The objectives of the allocation procedure are:**

- to ensure (subject to exceptions) that the court that determines guilt also imposes sentence
- where the determination is that trial on indictment is appropriate, the case reaches the Crown Court as soon as possible.

1.3 **The purpose of these guidelines is to provide guidance to those making that decision, applying the legislative criteria in the context of the sentencing framework as provided by the Criminal Justice Act 2003.**

1.4 These guidelines apply:

— to offenders aged 18 and over **and**

— in those cases where a youth is charged together with an adult and the plea before venue procedure applies.

2. STATUTORY CONSIDERATIONS

H–3 2.1 When deciding whether an offence is more suitable for summary trial or trial on indictment, section 19 of the *Magistrates' Courts Act* 1980 (as amended) requires that:

— before making a decision the court will be informed of the accused's previous convictions (if any) and shall consider any representations from the prosecution and defence as to whether summary trial or trial on indictment would be more suitable.

— in making a decision under this section, the court shall consider whether the sentence which a magistrates' court would have power to impose for the offence would be adequate

— the court shall have regard to any allocation guidelines (or revised allocation guidelines) issued as definitive guidelines under section 170 of the *Criminal Justice Act* 2003.

3. PROCEDURE AND PRINCIPLES

H–4 3.1 The court should invite representations from the prosecution and the defence as to the most appropriate venue for trial of the case. The existence of previous convictions recorded against an offender should be brought to the attention of the court at this time.

— **The primary test is the adequacy of the sentencing powers of the court.**

— **A court will start with a general presumption towards trial in a magistrates' court.**

— **The features set out in the following guidelines will need to be considered in order to determine whether the sentencing powers of a magistrates' court are sufficient to deal with the case justly.**

— **In deciding whether the powers of a magistrates' court would be adequate, a court is required to have regard to the approach to the assessment of seriousness set out in the Council Guideline Overarching Principles: Seriousness**

Principles for consideration

3.2 The principles set out below are relevant considerations in relation to the decision of the court as to whether an offence or offences would merit a custodial sentence of 12 months or more. The increased sentencing powers of a magistrates' court mean that more cases can now be dealt with at this level. Accordingly, it is expected that a magistrates' court will retain cases of greater seriousness than has historically been the case.

3.3 ***Adequacy of sentencing powers to be based on an assumption that the prosecution version of the facts is correct***

The issue for the court is the extent of its sentencing powers for the offence(s) charged following conviction based on the prosecution case at its highest.

3.3.1 Given that the allocation decision is only required where a guilty plea indication is not given, the court should allocate either-way cases according to the seriousness of the alleged offence, looking at the case at its worst from the point of view of the defendant. The reduction for a guilty plea principle should not influence the court in making an allocation decision.

3.3.2 The assessment of seriousness will be based upon representations from the prosecution and defence on the nature and circumstances of the offence. These will include factors that aggravate (legislative, general or offence specific aggravating factors) or mitigate the seriousness of the offence, but will not extend to matters of personal mitigation.

3.3.3 The court will have regard to definitive guidelines issued by the Sentencing

Guidelines Council relating both to principles of sentencing and to specific offences, and to relevant judgments of the Court of Appeal (Criminal Division).

3.3.4 In order to properly assess the seriousness of the offending conduct, courts should make efforts to consider together as many outstanding cases as possible where an allocation decision is yet to be made, unless this would result in significant delay or injustice to the prosecution or defence. Where appropriate, consideration may need to be given to transferring a case to another magistrates' court for this purpose, after consultation with that other court.

3.3.5 In assessing the seriousness of the current offence(s), the court must consider the existence and relevance of any previous convictions, taking into consideration the nature of the offence(s) to which the conviction(s) relate(s), the relevance of them to the current offence, and the time that has elapsed since the conviction(s).

3.3.6 Where a defendant has already been convicted of other matters but not yet sentenced, those convictions will be relevant to the assessment of seriousness of the offence(s) currently before the court.

3.3.7 The existence of a suspended sentence order will be relevant to the allocation decision as it will be a recorded conviction. The question of whether the defendant is liable to have the order implemented will be considered following conviction and so is not relevant to the allocation decision.

3.3.8 Where an offence is a specified offence, the issue of whether the offender should be made subject to a sentence for public protection under sections 224-236 of the *Criminal Justice Act* 2003 will be considered following conviction.

3.4 ***Charges and range of conduct to be considered***

3.4.1 The prosecuting authority should ensure that the charge(s) in a particular case present the court with sufficient information to know the extent of the criminality of the defendant. Where, for example, a defendant is alleged to have acted criminally over a long period, the charges need to be constructed with care as a court is not entitled to make assumptions about the extent of criminality where offences are neither admitted nor proved.

3.4.2 The possibility that, after conviction, an offender may ask for other matters to be taken into consideration will not be relevant to the seriousness of the offence before the court when considering allocation. A court could refuse to take additional offences into account when sentencing if they would render the powers of the court inadequate to deal with the case in an appropriate way.

3.5 ***The need for a separate tribunal to determine fact***

3.5.1 The procedures in a magistrates' court are generally likely to be adequate for all cases where sentencing is within the powers of that court. Accordingly, it will rarely be appropriate for a magistrates' court to decline summary trial for an offence within its sentencing range for reasons unconnected with the adequacy of sentence.

3.5.2 However, there may be a few rare and exceptional cases (for example where unusually complex disclosure issues regarding public interest immunity or sensitivity are to be decided) where it will be especially important to have the separation between Judge and jury that is possible in the Crown Court.

3.6 ***Presumption in favour of summary trial***

3.6.1 As many cases as possible should be dealt with in a magistrates' court. However, since there is no general power to commit for sentence after a determination for summary trial, where any uncertainty remains in relation to the adequacy of the sentencing powers available it should be resolved in favour of the case being dealt with in the Crown Court.

As many cases as possible should be dealt with in a magistrates' court. However, since there is no general power to commit for sentence after a determination for summary trial, where any uncertainty remains in relation to the adequacy of the sentencing powers available it should be resolved in favour of the case being dealt with in the Crown Court.

3.6.2 The court is entitled to expect the Justices' Clerk (or assistant to the Justices' Clerk) present in court, and the prosecution and defence advocates, to bring relevant guidelines and authorities to the attention of the court.

3.7 ***Linked cases***

3.7.1 As a general rule, it is preferable for all issues to be dealt with in a single trial.

3.7.2 Where several defendants are contesting charges that are linked, the presumption is that a single trial will be in the interests of justice for the purpose of considering allocation.

3.7.3 Where one or more of the defendants is a youth, any presumption in favour of sending the youth to the Crown Court to be tried jointly with an adult who is being sent must be balanced with the general presumption that young offenders should be dealt with in a youth court. In determining which is the appropriate court, examples of factors that should be considered when deciding whether to separate the youth and adult defendants include:

— the young age of the offender, particularly where the age gap between the adult and youth offender is substantial
— the immaturity and intellect of the youth
— the relative culpability of the youth compared with the adult and whether or not the role played by the youth was minor
— lack of previous convictions on the part of the youth compared with the adult offender
— whether the trial of the adult and youth can be severed without inconvenience to witnesses or injustice to the case as a whole

3.8 ***Any representations by the prosecution or defence***

3.8.1 The assessment of offence seriousness for the purposes of the allocation decision is based on the prosecution case at its highest (see 3.1 above). Defence representations should normally be directed to identifying inaccuracies in the factual outline of the case, assessing the adequacy of the court's sentencing powers and determining the relevance of an offender's previous convictions.

4. INDICATION OF SENTENCE

A. The Statutory Procedure

H–5 The relevant statutory provisions are reproduced at Annex 1.

4.1 If it is clear whether or not a custodial sentence is likely, it will normally be helpful for a court to give the indication requested unless there is a good reason for not doing so.

4.2 The key elements of the approach to giving a sentence indication are:

(i) **A court should assess the type of sentence realistically possible in the light of the facts as presented by the prosecution, with the additional element of a guilty plea tendered at this stage in the proceedings, and subject to defence representations as to the accuracy of the factual outline of the case. Wherever possible, the key elements of the basis upon which the indication is given should be recorded in writing.**

(ii) **A court should proceed with caution where an offender is unrepresented. The offender should be advised of the availability of independent legal advice. The Justices' Clerk (or assistant to the Justices' Clerk) present in court has a duty to assist the unrepresented party, and this will include drawing to the attention of an unrepresented defendant that there is an entitlement to request an indication of sentence.**

(iii) **A court should not give an indication of sentence where there are alternative charges unless the prosecution has indicated that an agreement as to acceptable pleas has been established following discussions with the defence, and there is an appropriate factual basis upon which an indication could be given.**

(iv) **The prosecution must ensure that the court is fully informed of the facts of the case and any relevant background.**

(v) **The court is entitled to expect that the Justices' Clerk (or assistant to the Justices' Clerk) present in court, and the prosecution and defence advocates, will ensure that the court considers any relevant guidelines or other authorities affecting sentence.**

(vi) **The information presented to the court will not include personal mitigation except in so far as it has influenced the facts of the case presented to the court or it is actively agreed by the prosecution advocate.**

(vii) **Any indication given must be recorded in writing and entered onto the court register.**

B. Reduction in Sentence for a Guilty Plea

4.14 In order to set the maximum type of sentence in cases where the offence is close to the threshold for a custodial sentence, a magistrates' court would have to consider whether the maximum reduction in sentence for a guilty plea would potentially be available where a guilty plea is forthcoming only after a sentence indication has been given.

4.15 The Guideline, Reduction in Sentence for a Guilty Plea, at paragraph 4.3 states:

(i) "The maximum reduction will be given only where the offender indicated willingness to admit guilt at the **first reasonable opportunity.** When this occurs will vary from case to case.

(ii) Where the admission of guilt comes later than the first reasonable opportunity, the reduction for guilty plea will be less than one third."

In considering further when the "first reasonable opportunity" occurs, Annex 2 of the Guideline emphasises the purpose of giving the reduction which is in recognition of "the benefits that come from a guilty plea both for those directly involved in the case in question but also in enabling Courts more quickly to deal with other outstanding cases".

4.16 There may only be a relatively short time gap between the opportunity to give an indication prior to allocation and the opportunity after an indication of sentence. However, the court will have had to consider allocation and determine summary trial and will then have to consider its response to the request for an indication of sentence. In those circumstances, it would appear that delay had taken place that could have been avoided and this will influence the extent of the reduction.

Where a guilty plea is indicated after the court has given an indication of the likely sentence, the appropriate reduction in sentence for the guilty plea should be a maximum of one quarter.

Annex 1

Sections 20 and 20A Magistrates' Courts Act 1980

Procedure where summary trial appears more suitable

20.—(1) If the court decides under section 19 above that the offence appears to it more suitable for summary trial, the following provisions of this section shall apply (unless they are excluded by section 23 below). **H-6**

(2) The court shall explain to the accused in ordinary language—

(a) that it appears to the court more suitable for him to be tried summarily for the offence;

(b) that he can either consent to be so tried or, if he wishes, be tried on indictment; and

(c) in the case of a specified offence (within the meaning of section 224 of the *Criminal Justice Act* 2003), that if he is tried summarily and is convicted by the court, he may be committed for sentence to the Crown Court under section 3A of the *Powers of Criminal Courts (Sentencing) Act* 2000 if the committing court is of such opinion as is mentioned in subsection (2) of that section.

(3) The accused may then request an indication ("an indication of sentence") of whether a custodial sentence or non-custodial sentence would be more likely to be imposed if he were to be tried summarily for the offence and to plead guilty.

(4) If the accused requests an indication of sentence, the court may, but need not, give such an indication.

(5) If the accused requests and the court gives an indication of sentence, the court shall ask the accused whether he wishes, on the basis of the indication, to reconsider the indication of plea which was given, or is taken to have been given, under section 17A or 17B above.

(6) If the accused indicates that he wishes to reconsider the indication under section 17A or 17B above, the court shall ask the accused whether (if the offence were to proceed to trial) he would plead guilty or not guilty.

(7) If the accused indicates that he would plead guilty the court shall proceed as if—

(a) the proceedings constituted from that time the summary trial of the information; and

(b) section 9(1) above were complied with and he pleaded guilty under it.

(8) Subsection (9) below applies where—

(a) the court does not give an indication of sentence (whether because the accused does not request one or because the court does not agree to give one);

(b) the accused either—

(i) does not indicate, in accordance with subsection (5) above, that he wishes; or

(ii) indicates, in accordance with subsection (5) above, that he does not wish, to reconsider the indication of plea under section 17A or 17B above; or

(c) the accused does not indicate, in accordance with subsection (6) above, that he would plead guilty.

(9) The court shall ask the accused whether he consents to be tried summarily or wishes to be tried on indictment and—

(a) if he consents to be tried summarily, shall proceed to the summary trial of the information; and

(b) if he does not so consent, shall proceed in relation to the offence in accordance with section 51(1) of the *Crime and Disorder Act* 1998.

[As substituted by the *Criminal Justice Act* 2003, Schedule 3, para. 6.]

Procedure where summary trial appears more suitable: supplementary

H–7 **20A.**—(1) Where the case is dealt with in accordance with section 20(7) above, no court (whether a magistrates' court or not) may impose a custodial sentence for the offence unless such a sentence was indicated in the indication of sentence referred to in section 20 above.

(2) Subsection (1) above is subject to sections 3A(4), 4(8) and 5(3) of the *Powers of Criminal Courts (Sentencing) Act* 2000.

(3) Except as provided in subsection (1) above—

(a) an indication of sentence shall not be binding on any court (whether a magistrates' court or not); and

(b) no sentence may be challenged or be the subject of appeal in any court on the ground that it is not consistent with an indication of sentence.

(4) Subject to section 20(7) above, the following shall not for any purpose be taken to constitute the taking of a plea—

(a) asking the accused under section 20 above whether (if the offence were to proceed to trial) he would plead guilty or not guilty; or

(b) an indication by the accused under that section of how he would plead.

(5) Where the court gives an indication of sentence under section 20 above, it shall cause each such indication to be entered in the register.

(6) In this section and in section 20 above, references to a custodial sentence are to a custodial sentence within the meaning of section 76of the *Powers of Criminal Courts (Sentencing) Act* 2000, and references to a non-custodial sentence shall be construed accordingly.

APPENDIX I

ADULT CRIMINAL CASE MANAGEMENT FRAMEWORK (3RD EDITION)

The Criminal Case Management Framework is a step by step guide for participants in the criminal justice process, setting out best practice in case management so that cases are prepared and conducted appropriately, in accordance with the *Criminal Procedure Rules* and brought to a conclusion efficiently and with the minimum of delay. I–1

Part 1 of the framework, which was published on July 26, 2007, deals with the entire process for adult cases in the magistrates' courts, from pre-charge activity through to conclusion of the case. Part 2 of the framework, which was published on January 18, 2008, covers the process for adult cases in the Crown Court from pre-court through to the conclusion; and also deals with appeals from the magistrates' court. The framework does not cover cases involving offenders under the age of 18 years. A separate youth framework is to be issued in due course.

Relevant extracts from the adult framework are set out as follows.

PART 1

THE MAGISTRATES' COURT

CHAPTER 3

FIRST HEARING

Objectives

(a) To achieve an effective first hearing in compliance with the *Criminal Procedure Rules*. In particular, to ensure that at the first hearing: I–2

- (i) The plea can be taken;
- (ii) The appropriate venue is determined;
- (iii) The real issue(s) are identified;
- (iv) The case (including sentence) can be concluded there and then or, if it really cannot be concluded, directions can be given so that it can be concluded at the next hearing or as soon as possible after that.

(b) To enable directions to be given so that appropriate cases may be committed, sent, or transferred to the Crown Court as soon as possible, and so that such cases may be concluded there without undue delay.

Actions

Representation

3.1.—(a) If he has not already done so and wishes to do so, the defendant should seek representation as soon as possible or see the duty solicitor on the day. I–3

(b) The court administration should determine all applications for legal representation within 48 hours of receipt.

If the defendant does not attend

3.2.—(a) Where the defendant does not attend court, the prosecution advocate will generally apply for a warrant not backed for bail and invite critical scrutiny of any material placed before the court on behalf of the defendant—in particular as to whether it appears to be reliable and

Appendices

relates specifically to the defendant's ability to attend court. A decision by the court not to issue a warrant will not prevent the later determination of whether the defendant has committed an offence contrary to s.6 of the *Bail Act* 1976.

(b) The overriding objective and the case management obligations prescribed by the *Criminal Procedure Rules* apply whether the defendant is present or not. The parties' advocates should prepare for the hearing accordingly and, at the hearing, actively assist the court even if the defendant is absent.

Indictable Only Cases (Crime and Disorder Act 1998, s.51)

3.3.—(a) The defence must expect to be required to give an indication of the likely plea and prepare accordingly.

(b) If a guilty plea is indicated, the parties may apply for directions in relation to the service of papers and indictment, the preparation of a pre-sentence report, and any other matters so that sentence may be passed at the first hearing in the Crown Court. If the case requires management in the Crown Court (for example, to determine any issue arising out of a basis of plea or to decide whether a pre-sentence report is unnecessary) a party may apply for that matter to be decided, by hearing or otherwise, in accordance with local listing practice.

(c) Unless a preliminary hearing would automatically be held in accordance with the practice set by the Resident Judge, the parties should consider whether a preliminary hearing would further the overriding objective (having regard to any guidance notes accompanying the prescribed case progression form). If it would, application should be made for a direction that a preliminary hearing be held on a date fixed in accordance with local listing practice.

(d) The parties should complete the prescribed case management forms and actively consider, having particular regard to the real issue(s), whether the standard directions should be varied or supplemented and, if they should, make application accordingly.

Either way cases

3.4.—(a) **Plea and plea before venue**

(i) The Justices' Issues Group (judicial membership) will decide on local listing practice.

(ii) The defence must expect that the court will, where relevant, take the defendant's plea or if no plea can be taken find out whether he is likely to plead guilty or not guilty and prepare accordingly.

(iii) Where there is a not guilty plea, or no indication is given, it is for the court to determine the venue. (For guidance where a not guilty plea is indicated, the court accepts jurisdiction and the defendant consents to summary trial, see 3.5 (c)).

(iv) Where a guilty plea is indicated, the court will consider the appropriate venue for sentence. (For guidance where jurisdiction is retained, see 3.5 (b)).

(b) **Mode of Trial**

Where the court declines jurisdiction or where the defendant elects Crown Court trial, unless the prosecution is able to proceed there and then, the prosecution shall apply for an adjournment for the service of papers and a committal hearing or transfer.

(c) **Committal or transfer to Crown Court for trial where appropriate**

(See part 6 for detail on the committal and transfer processes).

Summary cases

3.5.—(a) The defendant must expect his plea to be taken and the case must be prepared accordingly.

(b) Where a guilty plea is entered:

(i) The parties should be prepared for the court to pass sentence.

(ii) If the defendant pleads guilty on a basis which is materially different to the prosecution case, the difference(s) should be clearly identified in a written basis of plea and served on the court and the prosecutor. The parties' advocates should be prepared to make submissions to the court in relation to the necessity of a *Newton* hearing.

(iii) The parties should ask that any TICs be put. The police should be told which TICs are accepted. If a previously admitted offence is not accepted, the CPS file should be clearly marked and consideration given to prosecution.

(iv) Whether to submit that a PSR should be prepared should be considered with care. A PSR prepared for an earlier case involving the same defendant may provide enough information.

(v) If a PSR is ordered, the necessary information and assessment(s) should be provided to the court by the Probation Service on the same day if possible. An oral report may be appropriate.

(vi) If the court decides to commit the case to the Crown Court for sentence, the defence should consider with care whether to apply there and then for a PSR so that, if one is ordered, it is ready for the sentencing hearing. This is subject to local practice set by the Resident Judge.

(vii) The court administration should ensure that the memorandum of conviction sent to the Crown Court is accurate.

(viii) If sentence cannot be passed there and then, the parties should be able to provide the court with the appropriate information concerning any application for bail.

(c) Where a plea of not guilty is entered or a *Newton* hearing has been ordered:

(i) The parties should expect and prepare for the court to hold a case management hearing there and then.

(ii) The parties should complete the prescribed case progression forms and consider whether the standard directions should be varied or supplemented and, if they should, make application accordingly.

(iii) The real issue(s) should be explicitly identified.

(iv) Only those witnesses who are relevant to a real, disputed issue should be required to attend the trial. Each party should expect to be required to justify the attendance of each and every witness by explicit reference to a real, disputed issue.

(v) The parties should provide the dates to avoid (and reasons, where available) in relation to the witnesses who are to attend the trial.

(vi) The parties should be able to provide a timetable for those steps which are necessary for the case to be ready for trial so that the court may make directions accordingly.

(vii) The parties should be able to provide a timetable for the trial itself by reference to estimates of the length of: the evidence of each witness (in chief and in cross-examination); presenting agreed evidence; and submissions in relation to points of law.

(viii) The trial will be fixed in accordance with local listing practice.

(ix) If a case management hearing cannot be held at first hearing, sub-paragraphs (ii-)–(vii) above apply to the subsequent case management hearing.

(x) The parties should be able to provide to the court with appropriate information when bail is considered.

The defendant's preparation of his case and attendance at subsequent hearings

3.6.—(a) It is the defendant's responsibility to prepare his case and attend hearings. Any other practices to which this framework refers do not absolve him from those responsibilities.

(b) The defendant or his advocate should be prepared to indicate to the court that the defendant is aware of the importance of preparing his case, keeping appointments with his solicitor, and attending court (knowing the consequences of not doing so).

(c) The court administration should provide the defendant with a written notice of the date of next hearing before the defendant leaves the court.

(d) Where agreed locally, the court administration may offer an additional reminder service, e.g. by text message/telephone, where appropriate.

(e) Agencies should consider the inter-agency agreement 'Managing bail to ensure defendant attendance at court template'.

Responsibilities

Prosecution team

3.7. The Prosecution Advocate should— **I–4**

(a) Prepare and conduct the case to accomplish the actions set out above. Agents should have sufficient instructions and authority to do so.

(b) In the event of a guilty plea, ensure that the Probation Service is given a PSR pack there and then or as directed by local arrangements.

(c) Ensure that the nominated case progression officer and any other member of the prosecution team who is responsible for the conduct of the case know(s) what directions have been made.

Prosecution case progression officer

3.8. To comply with rule 3.4(1) of the *Criminal Procedure Rules*, the prosecution must nominate an individual responsible for progressing the case and tell the other parties who he is and how to contact him.

Police

3.9. The police/court enforcement officer should execute warrants promptly.

Witness care unit

3.10. The Witness Care Unit should—

(a) Notify victims and prosecution witnesses of the outcome of the hearing and of the trial date set.

(b) Share information about victims and prosecution witnesses (e.g. reluctance of witness to attend court or changes in availability) with the prosecution team.

Defence advocate

3.11. The defence should—

(a) Prepare and conduct the case to accomplish the actions set out above.

(b) Ensure that the nominated case progression officer and any other member of the defence team who is responsible for the conduct of the case know(s) what directions have been made.

Magistrates' courts administration

3.12. The court administration should—

(a) deal promptly with applications for representation,

(b) deal promptly with the preparation and issue of warrants within local and/ or national targets,

(c) deal promptly with the sending of cases to the Crown Court,

(d) deal promptly with the preparation of court orders e.g. community orders,

(e) send case progression forms, accurate memorandums of conviction, and any relevant case notes (committals for sentence) to the Crown Court where necessary.

Court case progression officer (CPO)

3.13. Following the first hearing, for matters proceeding to trial/trial of issue, the court case progression officer should—

(a) record details of the prosecution and defence case progression officers,

(b) notify the parties of the name and contact details of the case progression officers,

(c) record the directions made and record the next date of hearing.

National Offender Management Service—Probation Service

3.14. The Probation Service should—

(a) In the event of a guilty plea, obtain a pre-sentence report pack from the prosecution and any appropriate information from the defence/defendant and report to the court on the same day if possible. An oral report may be appropriate.

(b) If a report (oral or written) really cannot be presented to the court on the same day, obtain a pre-sentence report pack from the prosecution and make an appointment with the defendant there and then (or make arrangements to see him in custody) so that the report is ready before the date fixed for sentence.

CHAPTER 4

PREPARATION FOR HEARINGS (TRIALS, NEWTON HEARINGS AND SENTENCE)

Objectives

I–5 (a) To ensure that everything is done so that the case can be concluded at the next hearing or as soon possible after that.

(b) To prepare the case according to the Criminal Procedure Rules and directions by the court.

(c) To tell the court and other parties of anything which might adversely affect the progress of the case and achievement of the overriding objective and to apply promptly for any necessary directions.

(d) To certify readiness, if required by the court.

Actions

Compliance with directions

4.1.—(a) The parties must comply with directions. **I–6**

(b) The parties' and the court's case progression officers must each: monitor compliance with all the directions (whether standard or not); make sure that the court is kept informed of events which may affect the progress of the case (including their own compliance or non-compliance with directions); make sure that they can be contacted promptly about the case during ordinary business hours; act promptly and reasonably in response to communications about the case; and, if unavailable, appoint a substitute.

(c) The parties should only ask for a hearing if a problem cannot otherwise be resolved. Unnecessary hearings must be avoided. Even if a matter cannot be resolved by agreement, a direction may be sought and/or made without a hearing.

Pre-sentence readiness check

4.2.—(a) Each party should review the statutory provisions relevant to the court's sentencing powers and any relevant Sentencing Guidelines Council guidance and guideline cases and consider, where appropriate, drawing them to the attention of the court.

(b) Prosecutors should undertake a review of the statutory provisions relating to any ancillary orders (such as anti-social behaviour orders, confiscation orders, compensation orders) that might be relevant and consider, where appropriate, making applications to the court for such orders and providing drafts of such orders.

(c) If there are technical preconditions to the passing of a particular sentence and/or ancillary order, which will be submitted by a party to be an appropriate sentence and/or ancillary order, that party must ensure that the material to satisfy those preconditions will be available to the court on the day of sentence.

Pre-trial readiness check

4.3.—(a) All the court's directions (standard and case specific) have been complied with.

(b) Every reasonable step (including, where appropriate, seeking the issue of a witness summons) has been taken to make sure that his witnesses will attend when they are needed.

(c) Appropriate arrangements have been made for the presentation of written or other material.

(d) Promptly inform the court and the other parties of anything that may affect the date or duration of the trial or appeal or significantly affect the progress of the case in any other way.

(e) Give a certificate of readiness if required by the court.

Responsibilities

Police

4.4.—(a) Ensure that the prosecution file is completed and submitted to the prosecutor in accordance with the Manual of Guidance. **I–7**

(b) Ensure any actions or requests for information from within the prosecution team are acknowledged, responses are promptly given and any problems identified to the CPS immediately.

(c) Respond promptly to correspondence from prosecution.

Prosecution team

4.5. The prosecution team should ensure that the case is fully prepared and ready for trial, having regard to each topic identified in the prescribed case progression forms, guidance notes and directions. What follows is not intended to be an exhaustive list. The prosecution should, in particular, ensure that—

(a) All directions are complied with.

(b) The case is prepared so as to present the evidence, having regard to the real issues, in the shortest and clearest way.

(c) There is timely disclosure (bearing in mind that only unused material which meets the criteria for disclosure should be disclosed and that the same criteria apply to CCTV recordings as to any other unused material).

(d) Timely pre-trial applications are made (and, where necessary, determined) in relation to: special measures, bad character and hearsay.

(e) There is compliance with Part 33 of the Criminal Procedure Rules in relation to expert evidence.

(f) There is timely service, and any necessary pre-trial editing, of transcripts of interviews (whether with witnesses or defendants).

(g) Witnesses and exhibits will be present at court when needed.

(h) The possibility of a witness failing to attend is anticipated and a timely application made for the issue of a summons.

(i) Arrangements have been made, if appropriate, for staggering the attendance of witnesses.

(j) Interpreters/signers have been arranged.

(k) There is timely service of skeleton arguments and copies/lists of authorities.

(l) If any sound/vision recordings are to be played, the quality is acceptable, a check is made to ensure there is compatible equipment at court and the recordings are provided to the court administration in time to be checked on that equipment.

(m) To consider, before the hearing and as a matter of urgency, the acceptability of a change of plea and/or basis of plea proposed by the defence.

(n) To notify the court immediately of anything which could significantly affect the progress of the case (including intended discontinuance).

(o) To apply for a direction as soon as it becomes apparent that a problem cannot be resolved without one and, in any event, in time to ensure that the hearing is effective.

(p) A certificate of readiness is served if required by the court.

(q) Any matters relevant to sentence can be put before the court, there and then, if the defendant is convicted or enters a late plea of guilty.

(r) The prosecution file complies with the Manual of Guidance and the prosecution advocate is fully briefed so that he has the material and authority to deal with everything which may arise at the hearing.

(s) Should the defence serve s.9 statements upon the prosecution, seeking agreement to avoid the attendance of a witness, ensure careful consideration is given as to whether the witness should be required to attend so that only those witnesses who are needed in relation to the real issue(s) attend court. The defence and court should immediately be informed of any change.

Witness Care Unit

4.6. The Witness Care Unit should—

(a) Notify witnesses of hearing date immediately, tell the CPS of the notification and maintain contact with witnesses.

(b) Use the needs assessment to identify needs and inform the court.

(c) Use the Contact Directory to provide tailored interventions to secure attendance at court.

(d) At once inform the CPS if a witness appears to be unwilling to attend court so that timely application may be made for a witness summons.

(e) Provide the Witness Service with information on witnesses attending court, any special measures and details of any changes in circumstances.

(f) Keep victims/ witnesses informed of special measures and the progress of the case.

(g) Share relevant information about victims and witnesses (e.g reluctance of witness to attend court, changes in availability, difficulties caused by disability or childcare commitments) with the prosecution team.

Defence case progression function

4.7. The defence should ensure that the case is fully prepared and ready for trial, having regard to each topic identified in the prescribed case progression forms, guidance notes, and directions. What follows is not intended to be an exhaustive list. The defence should, in particular, ensure that—

(a) All directions are complied with.

(b) To prepare the case so as to present the evidence, having regard to the real issue(s), in the shortest and clearest way.

(c) There is timely application for further disclosure (bearing in mind the precondition of the service of a defence statement and that only unused material which meets the criteria for disclosure should be disclosed and that the same criteria apply to CCTV recordings as to any other unused material).

(d) Timely pre-trial applications are made (and, where necessary, determined) in relation to: special measures, bad character and hearsay.

(e) There is compliance with Part 33 of the Criminal Procedure Rules and a timely application for public funding in relation to expert evidence.

(f) There is timely service, and any necessary pre-trial editing, of transcripts of interviews (whether with witnesses or defendants).

(g) Witnesses and exhibits will be present at court when needed.

(h) The possibility of a defence witness failing to attend is anticipated and a timely application made for the issue of a summons.

(i) Arrangements have been made, if appropriate, for staggering the attendance of defence witnesses.

(j) Interpreters/signers have been arranged.

(k) There is timely service of skeleton arguments and copies/lists of authorities.

(l) If any sound/vision recordings are to be played, the quality is acceptable, a check is made to ensure there is compatible equipment at court and the recordings are provided to the court administration in time to be checked on that equipment.

(m) The court is informed of any special arrangements which should be made for the defendant, having regard to his needs.

(n) The acceptability of a proposed change of plea and/or basis of plea is discussed with the prosecution, before the hearing and as a matter of urgency.

(o) The witness requirements are proactively reconsidered so that only those witnesses who are needed in relation to the real issue(s) attend court. The prosecution and court should immediately be informed of any change.

(p) The court is notified immediately of anything which could significantly affect the progress of the case (including an intention to plead guilty on an acceptable basis).

(q) Application is made for a direction as soon as it becomes apparent that a problem cannot be resolved without one and, in any event, in time to ensure that the hearing is effective.

(r) The defendant is notified of the time, date and place of the hearing.

(s) The court and CPS are notified if the defendant is in custody to another court (providing sufficient details for a Home Office Production Order to be obtained).

(t) A certificate of readiness is served if required by the court.

(u) Any matters relevant to sentence can be put before the court, there and then, if the defendant is convicted or enters a late plea of guilty.

(v) The defence advocate is fully briefed so that he has the material to deal with everything which may arise at the hearing.

Court case progression officer (CPO)

4.8. The Court Case Progression Officer should—

(a) Monitor directions made by the court and, in the event of non-compliance, refer to the court, if appropriate.

(b) Ensure that any communication received from the parties is dealt with promptly.

(c) Check readiness and take appropriate action. Any application to vacate a trial to be referred to a district judge (magistrates' courts), bench chairman, justices' clerk or deputy justices' clerk in accordance with local arrangements.

(d) Refer the matter to the court for a decision on whether the matter should be listed for further directions.

(e) Remind the defendant of the hearing time, date and venue, where agreed locally.

(f) If any sound/ vision recordings are to be played, check there is compatible equipment at court. The parties should be responsible for checking the quality of their recordings and providing them to the court administration in a timely manner so they can be checked by the court administration on that equipment before the hearing.

Appendices

(g) Ensure that interpreters/signers for defence witnesses are warned to attend if appropriate.

(h) If certificates of readiness are required by the court, provide blank forms to the parties.

Witness Service

4.9. The Witness Service should—

(a) Provide pre-court visits for witnesses when referred and where resources allow.

(b) Share relevant information about victims and witnesses (e.g. reluctance of witness to attend court, changes in availability, difficulties caused by disability or childcare commitments) with the prosecution/defence team.

CHAPTER 5

TRIAL, NEWTON HEARING AND SENTENCE

Objectives

I–8 (a) To achieve the overriding objective of dealing with the case justly.

(b) To ensure that the hearing is effective and proceeds without delay on the day when it is listed.

(c) To ensure that the case is dealt with efficiently, expeditiously and proportionately with the live evidence being confined to the real, disputed issue(s).

Actions

Case management on the day of the hearing

I–9 **5.1.**—(a) The parties should, before the hearing begins, actively assist the court to manage the case. The parties should not wait to be required to do so. This means that, having reconsidered the case and any developments since earlier directions were given, the parties should be able to:

Explicitly identify the real issue(s); and provide the court with:

(i) A list of the witnesses who will be called 'live' to give evidence, in the order in which they will be called.

(ii) A list of any other material which will be made available to the court in the presentation of the case.

(iii) Agreement in relation to the way in which undisputed evidence is to be adduced (e.g. by admission or, if by reading a witness statement, reading only those parts which are relevant).

(iv) Notice of any point of law which could affect the conduct of the hearing.

(v) Details of any special arrangements for the giving of evidence by a witness or the participation of any person, including the defendant.

(vi) A timetable for the hearing (broken down by each witness–examination in chief and cross-examination–and each submission.)

(b) During the hearing, the parties should confine their submissions and questions to the real issue(s) and should be prepared to object if another party starts to explore matters which are irrelevant.

(c) If a witness is required to attend and either is not called or is asked no relevant questions by the party who required his attendance, that party may be required by the court to provide a full explanation.

(d) If the defendant fails to attend, the court will decide whether to proceed in his absence.

(e) If a witness fails to attend court, the party intending to call that witness should determine with the other parties whether the evidence can be agreed or whether he can proceed regardless. If not, the party calling the witness must decide whether to apply to the court for an adjournment and/or a witness summons. He should expect to be required to provide detailed reasons for the witness's non-attendance, whether difficulties were foreseen and the prospects of a witness attending, should the case be adjourned.

(f) If a hearing is ineffective, the parties must be prepared to provide to the court a full explanation and identify the person responsible.

Sentence and committal for sentence

5.2.—(a) Where the defendant wishes other offences to be taken into consideration, the offences should be set out in writing, signed and put before the court. The police should be notified about what TICs have been accepted. If a defendant rejects previously admitted TICs, the CPS file should be clearly marked and consideration given to prosecuting the now denied offences.

(b) The parties must expect the court to proceed to sentence as soon as possible. If a pre-sentence report is required, the Probation Service should consider preparation of a fast delivery report where appropriate. Where a PSR has been prepared for a previous case involving the defendant, sufficient information may be available for sentencing purposes. Where a PSR is required a PSR pack should be given to the Probation Service officer at court on the same day to enable preparation of reports where practicable.

(c) Where the court's sentencing powers are insufficient, the court will consider committing the defendant for sentence.

(i) Cases requiring pre-sentence report(s) or other reports should be identified and the reports prepared in readiness for the hearing in the Crown Court.

(ii) The court administration should ensure an accurate memorandum of conviction is submitted to the Crown Court.

Responsibilities

Prosecution advocate

5.3. In addition to preparing and conducting the case in compliance with the *Criminal Procedure Rules* and the guidance in the 'actions' above, the prosecution advocate should— **I–10**

(a) Consider making an application to proceed in absence if the defendant does not attend.

(b) Check that prosecution witnesses are present when required and meet them to answer any questions they may have about court procedures and to give an indication, where possible, of how long they will have to wait before giving evidence.

(c) Where a witness has not attended, consider making an application for the issue of a summons. The advocate must be in a position to inform the court of the history of contact with the witness.

(d) Endorse the prosecution file with details of the outcome, any directions made and record the next date of hearing or sentence.

(e) Ensure that any requests or actions are brought to the attention of the prosecution team for action.

(f) Where a pre-sentence report is requested, in the event of conviction, ensure the PSR pack is given to the Probation Service officer at court on the same day to enable preparation of reports where practicable.

(g) If the hearing is cracked or ineffective, complete the Cracked and Ineffective Trial Monitoring Form recording the reason for this and place the form before the court for consideration before leaving the court.

(h) Keep the witnesses informed of the progress of the case and apply to the court for their release as soon as practicable if the trial is 'cracked' or ineffective. If the trial 'cracks', the witnesses should remain at the court if there might be a *Newton* hearing. If the trial is ineffective, the witnesses should be asked to remain at court while a new date is fixed.

Police/enforcement officers

5.4. The Police/enforcement officers should—

Use every effort to serve witness summonses and execute warrants promptly.

Witness Care Unit

5.5. The Witness Care Unit should—

(a) Ensure that the tailored interventions are available to secure victims and witnesses attendance at court and provide the support required.

(b) Ensure victims and witnesses are notified of any future hearing date and are informed of the outcome of the hearing.

(c) Thank victims and witnesses for their participation.

Defence advocate

5.6. In addition to preparing and conducting the case in compliance with the *Criminal Procedure Rules* and the guidance in the 'actions' above the defence advocate should—

(a) If the defendant fails to attend, consider whether his professional duty is to remain and to represent the defendant during the course of any trial in absence.

(b) Check that defence witnesses are present when required and meet them.

(c) Where a witness has not attended, consider making an application for the issue of a summons. The advocate must be in a position to inform the court of the history of contact with the witness.

(d) Be ready to present plea in mitigation if the defendant is convicted or enters a late plea of guilty.

(e) Endorse the defence file with details of the outcome, any directions made and record the next date of hearing or sentence.

(f) Ensure that any requests or actions are brought to the attention of the defence team for action.

(g) If the hearing is cracked or ineffective, complete the form recording the reason for this and place the form before the court for consideration before leaving the court.

(h) Be prepared to make a quantified and supported application for a defendant's costs order in a specific sum if the defendant is acquitted.

Magistrates' courts administration

5.7. Court Managers should—

Ensure that audio/video/DVD playback facilities are available for all courts centres where trials take place.

5.8. The court administration should—

(a) Deal promptly with the preparation and issue of warrants within local and/or national targets.

(b) If the hearing is cracked/ineffective, ensure that the 'Cracked and Ineffective Trial Monitoring Form' is completed by the advocates, recording the reasons for the crack/ineffectiveness. The form should be placed before the court for approval before the advocates leave the court.

Witness Service

5.9. The Witness Service should—

(a) Provide support to witnesses during the day and if necessary accompany witnesses to the court room where resources allow.

(b) Where appropriate, share information about victims and witnesses (e.g. reluctance of witness to attend court, changes in availability, difficulties caused by disability or childcare commitments) with the prosecution/defence team.

(c) Bring to the attention of the relevant advocate victim and witness needs not identified elsewhere.

(d) Ensure witness safety and security is considered by the court and that the 'Witness security at court' guidance is followed.

National Offender Management Service–productions from prison custody

5.10. PECS (or the Prison Service, in the case of Category A prisoners) should—

(a) Ensure that all persons in custody are produced at the court when required and taken to each court room promptly.

(b) Notify the court administration immediately of any problems anticipated or arising in respect of the production of persons in custody.

National Offender Management Service–Probation Service

5.11. The Probation Service should—

(a) Obtain a PSR pack from the prosecution and any appropriate information from the defence/defendant and report to the court on the same day if possible. An oral report may be appropriate.

(b) If a report (oral or written) really cannot be presented to the court on the same day, make an appointment with the defendant there and then (or make arrangements to see him in custody) so that the report is ready before the date fixed for sentence.

CHAPTER 6

SENDING, COMMITTAL, OR TRANSFER TO THE CROWN COURT FOR TRIAL

To enable appropriate cases to be committed, sent or transferred to the Crown Court as soon as possible and to give directions so that they may be concluded there without undue delay. **I–11**

Actions

Sending cases triable only on indictment

6.1.—(a) The defence must expect to be required to give an indication of the likely plea and prepare accordingly. **I–12**

(b) If a guilty plea is indicated, the parties may apply for directions in relation to the service of papers and indictment, the preparation of a PSR and any other matters so that sentence may be passed at the first hearing in the Crown Court. If such a case requires management in the Crown Court (for example, to determine any issue arising out of a basis of plea or to decide whether a PSR is unnecessary) a party may apply for that matter to be decided, by hearing or otherwise, in accordance with local listing practice.

(c) Unless a preliminary hearing would automatically be held in accordance with the practice set by the Resident Judge, the parties should consider whether a preliminary hearing would further the overriding objective (having regard to the guidance notes accompanying the prescribed case management form). If it would, application should be made for a direction that a preliminary hearing be held on a date fixed in accordance with local listing practice.

(d) The parties should complete the prescribed case management forms and actively consider, by particular reference to the real issue(s), whether the standard directions should be varied or supplemented and, if they should, make application accordingly.

Committal to Crown Court for trial

6.2.—(a) Where the court declines jurisdiction or the defendant elects Crown Court trial, unless the transfer provisions apply, the prosecution will be required to prepare the case for committal. If the committal cannot take place there and then, the prosecution will apply for an adjournment for the preparation of committal papers. In applying for an adjournment the prosecution should ensure that the application is for the shortest possible period.

(b) After considering any representations by the parties, the court will decide whether to adjourn for committal and if so for how long. The procedure will then be as follows:

(i) There will normally be locally agreed timescales within which the police should provide the prosecution with the committal papers.

(ii) In Full Code cases the key evidence should have been obtained before charge. In Threshold Test cases, the CPS will need to review the case upon receipt of the further evidence from the police. Tighter timescales will apply where the defendant is in custody.

(iii) Obtaining the evidence (the police) and reviewing the evidence (the CPS) may need to be expedited.

(iv) In all cases, the papers should be with the prosecution in good time to enable the prosecution to prepare the case for committal and to serve the papers on the defence sufficiently in advance of the hearing.

(v) The defence must decide whether to concede there is a prima facie case and agree to committal without consideration of the evidence or to require the evidence to be considered by the court. If there is to be a contested committal hearing it is the responsibility of the defence to advise the court in advance so that either a new date can be fixed for the committal or in certain circumstances it may be possible for this to take place on the original hearing date.

(vi) Timescales are subject to the length of any adjournment granted by the court.

(c) If the court commits the case to the Crown Court for trial:

(i) The parties should complete the prescribed case management forms and actively consider, by particular reference to the real issue(s), whether the standard directions should be varied or supplemented and, if they should, make application accordingly.

(ii) The defence must expect to be required to give an indication of the likely plea and prepare accordingly.

Transfer of case

6.3.—(a) The prosecution should serve a notice of transfer and draft indictment upon the court. The case is automatically transferred to the Crown Court and, subject to certain exceptions, the jurisdiction of the magistrates' courts ceases.

(b) The parties should complete the prescribed case management forms (which are the same as for committals for trial) and actively consider, with particular reference to the real issue(s), whether the standard directions should be varied or supplemented and, if they should, make application accordingly.

Responsibilities

Prosecution

I–13 **6.4.** The Prosecution advocate should—

(a) Actively consider the needs of the case, having regard to the real issue(s), consider the standard directions and apply for such variation or additional directions as are needed to further the overriding objective.

(b) Ensure that all directions (including those relating to listing) are communicated to the prosecution case progression officer.

(c) Actively consider whether any further investigation or other action is necessary (which may include responding to requests by the defence) and cause them to be pursued to a set timescale.

(d) Ensure that the defence has been served with the material to which they are entitled.

Witness Care Unit

6.5. The Witness Care Unit should—

Ensure victims and witnesses have been notified of the outcome of the hearing and the next hearing date.

Defence

6.6. The defence advocate should—

(a) Actively consider the needs of the case, having regard to the real issue(s), consider the standard directions and apply for such variation or additional directions as are needed to further the overriding objective.

(b) Ensure that all directions (including those relating to listing) are communicated to the defence case progression officer.

(c) Actively consider whether any further investigation or other action is necessary and, if so, cause it to be pursued to a set timescale.

Magistrates' courts administration

6.7. The Court administration should—

(a) Deal promptly with the preparation of warrants within local and/or national targets.

(b) Deal promptly with the sending of cases to the Crown Court.

(c) Ensure that the notice of transfer is sent to the Crown Court.

(d) Send case progression forms to the Crown Court where necessary.

Case progression officers

6.8. The case progression officers nominated13 by each of the parties and by the court must monitor all the directions (which means that they must find out what they are) and make sure that the court is kept informed of events that may affect the progress of the case.

National Offender Management Service–Productions from Prison Custody

6.9. PECS (or the Prison Service, in the case of Category A prisoners) should—

(a) Ensure that all persons in custody are produced at the court when required and taken to each court room promptly.

(b) Notify the court administration immediately of any problems anticipated or arising in respect of the production of persons in custody.

PART 2

THE CROWN COURT

CHAPTER 6

APPEALS FROM THE MAGISTRATES' COURTS

Objectives

(a) To achieve the overriding objective of dealing with the case justly. **I–14**

(b) To ensure that the hearing is effective and proceeds without delay on the day when it is listed.

(c) To ensure that the case is dealt with efficiently, expeditiously and proportionately with the live evidence being confined to the real issue(s).

Actions

Compliance with directions

6.1.—(a) The parties must comply with directions. If directions are not complied with, the parties must expect the court to investigate the reason, identify who was responsible and take appropriate action. **I–15**

(b) The parties' and the court's CPOs must each monitor compliance with all the directions (whether standard or not), ensure that the court is kept informed of events which may affect the progress of the case (including their own compliance or non-compliance with directions), ensure that they can be contacted promptly about the case during ordinary business hours, act promptly and reasonably in response to communications about the case and, if unavailable, appoint a substitute.

(c) The parties must ask for a hearing only if a problem cannot otherwise be resolved. Unnecessary hearings must be avoided. Even if a matter cannot be resolved by agreement, a direction may be sought and/or made without a hearing by communication between the parties and the court, including by email. "Mentions" should be listed only if there is a compelling reason.

Readiness check (appeals against sentence)

6.2.—(a) Each party must review the statutory provisions relevant to the court's sentencing powers and any relevant Sentencing Guidelines Council guidance and guideline cases and bring them, where appropriate, to the attention of the court.

(b) The respondent must undertake a review of the statutory provisions relating to any ancillary orders (such as anti-social behaviour orders, confiscation orders, compensation orders) that might be relevant.

(c) If there are technical preconditions to the passing of a particular sentence and/or ancillary order, which will be submitted by a party to be an appropriate sentence and/or ancillary order, that party must ensure that the material to satisfy those preconditions will be available to the court on the day of the appeal against sentence.

(d) The police/respondent must make all the victims aware of the Witness Service and explain that they will refer their details to the Witness Service unless they ask the police not to do so.

Readiness check (appeals against conviction)

6.3. Each party must:

(a) Ensure that all the court's directions (standard and case specific) have been complied with.

(b) Ensure that every reasonable step (including, where appropriate, seeking the issue of a witness summons) has been taken to make sure that the witnesses will attend when they are needed.

(c) Check that appropriate arrangements have been made for the presentation of written or other material.

Appendices

(d) Promptly inform the court and the other parties of anything that may affect the date or duration of the appeal or significantly affect the progress of the case in any other way.

(e) Give a certificate of readiness if required by the court.

(f) The police/respondent must make all the victims aware of the Witness Service and explain that they will refer their details to the Witness Service unless they ask the police not to do so.

Responsibilities

Police

I–16 **6.4.** The Police must—

(a) Ensure any actions or requests for information from the respondent are acknowledged, responses are promptly given and any problems identified to the respondent team immediately.

(b) Respond promptly to correspondence from the respondent.

Respondent Team

6.5. The Respondent team must ensure that the case is fully prepared and ready for appeal, having regard to each topic identified in the prescribed case progression forms, guidance notes and directions. What follows is not intended to be an exhaustive list. The respondent must, in particular, ensure that—

(a) All directions are complied with. If directions are not complied with, the respondent must expect the court to investigate the reason, identify who was responsible and take appropriate action.

(b) Correspondence from the appellant is answered in a timely manner, using email where possible.

(c) The case is prepared so as to present the evidence, having regard to the real issues, in the shortest and clearest way (including by way of admissions).

(d) Timely pre-appeal applications are made (and, where necessary, determined), for instance in relation to special measures, bad character and hearsay evidence.

(e) There is compliance with Part 33 of the Criminal Procedure Rules in relation to expert evidence.

(f) Witnesses and exhibits are at court when needed.

(g) The possibility that a witness may fail to attend is considered and a timely application is made for the issue of a summons.

(h) Arrangements have been made, if appropriate, for staggering the attendance of witnesses.

(i) Interpreters/signers have been arranged. In Wales, where the court has been notified that the appellant or witness will use Welsh, the court is responsible for ensuring that interpreters' simultaneous translation equipment has been arranged.

(j) There is timely service of skeleton arguments and copies/ lists of authorities.

(k) If any sound/vision recordings are to be played, a check is made that the quality is acceptable, there is compatible equipment at court and the recordings are provided to the court administration in time to be checked on that equipment.

(l) The court is notified immediately of anything which could significantly affect the progress of the case.

(m) An application is made for a direction as soon as it becomes apparent that a problem cannot be resolved and, in any event, in time to ensure that the hearing is effective.

(n) A certificate of readiness is served if required by the court.

(o) The respondent's file complies with the Manual of Guidance and the respondent advocate is fully briefed so that he has the material and authority to deal with everything which may arise at the hearing.

(p) Should the appellant serve s.9 statements upon the respondent, careful consideration is given as to whether the witness is required to attend so that only those witnesses who are needed in relation to the real issues attend court. The appellant and court must immediately be informed of any change.

Witness Care Unit or equivalent unit for other respondent

6.6. The Witness Care/ equivalent unit should—

(a) Notify the witnesses of the hearing date immediately, inform the respondent of the notification and maintain contact with the witnesses.

(b) Conduct a needs assessment and inform the court and the respondent of any issues that may impact on the attendance at court by a witness or his evidence so as to inform any application for special measures or other issues e.g. disability access.

(c) Ensure support needs are met, using the contact directory to provide tailored interventions, where appropriate, in order to secure the attendance of witnesses at court.

(d) Immediately inform the respondent if a witness appears to be unwilling to attend court so that a timely application can be made for a witness summons.

(e) Provide the Witness Service with information on the witnesses attending court, any special measures, details of any changes in circumstances and any referrals for pre-trial familiarisation visits.

(f) Keep the victims and the witnesses informed of special measures and of the progress of the case.

(g) Share relevant information about the victims and witnesses (e.g. the reluctance of a witness to attend court, changes in availability, the need to make any reasonable adjustments to accommodate needs under the *Disability Discrimination Act* 1995, childcare commitments and the possible need for special measures) with the respondent team.

Appellant case progression function

6.7. The appellant should ensure that the case is fully prepared and ready for appeal, having regard to each topic identified in the prescribed case progression forms, guidance notes and directions. What follows is not intended to be an exhaustive list. The appellant should, in particular, ensure that—

(a) All directions are complied with. If directions are not complied with, they must expect the court to investigate the reason, identify who was responsible and take appropriate action.

(b) Matters raised by the respondent in correspondence are responded to in a timely fashion, using email where possible.

(c) The case is prepared so as to present the evidence, having regard to the real issues, in the shortest and clearest way (including by way of admissions).

(d) Timely pre-trial applications are made (and, where necessary, determined) in relation to: special measures, bad character and hearsay.

(e) There is compliance with Part 33 of the Criminal Procedure Rules and a timely application for public funding in relation to expert evidence.

(f) Witnesses and exhibits are at court when needed.

(g) The possibility that a witness may fail to attend is considered and a timely application is made for the issue of a summons.

(h) Arrangements have been made, if appropriate, for staggering the attendance of witnesses.

(i) Interpreters/signers have been arranged. In Wales, where the court has been notified that the appellant or witness will use Welsh, the court is responsible for ensuring that interpreters' simultaneous translation equipment has been arranged.

(j) There is timely service of skeleton arguments and copies/lists of authorities.

(k) If any sound/vision recordings are to be played, a check is made that the quality is acceptable, there is compatible equipment at court and the recordings are provided to the court administration in time to be checked on that equipment.

(l) The court is informed of any special arrangements which should be made for the appellant, having regard to his needs.

(m) If the appellant is to abandon the appeal, the respondent and the court should be advised in good time so as to avoid the unnecessary attendance of the witnesses.

(n) The witness requirements are proactively reconsidered so that only those witnesses who are needed in relation to the real issues attend court. The respondent and court should immediately be informed of any change.

(o) An application is made for a direction as soon as it becomes apparent that a problem cannot be resolved and, in any event, in time to ensure that the hearing is effective.

(p) The appellant is notified of the time, date, and place of the hearing.

(q) The court and respondent team are notified if the appellant is in custody by order of another court (providing sufficient details for a Home Office Production Order to be obtained).

(r) A certificate of readiness is served if required by the court.

(s) The appellant advocate is fully briefed so that he has the material to deal with everything which may arise at the hearing.

(t) Should the respondent serve s.9 statements upon the appellant, careful consideration is given as to whether the witness is required to attend so that only those witnesses who are needed in relation to the real issues attend court. The respondent and court should immediately be informed of any change.

Crown Court administration

6.8. The Crown Court administration should—

(a) Where court staff have been notified that there are vulnerable or intimidated victims and where adjournments and postponements of scheduled hearings are agreed without a court hearing, ensure that decisions reach the WCU no longer than one working day after the day on which the decision is made and, in cases involving other victims, decisions reach the WCU no later than three working days after the day on which the decision is made.

(b) Where the court has been notified that a vulnerable or intimidated victim is involved, ensure that the WCU is informed of decisions in all cases within one working day of the decision being made and within three days for cases involving other victims.

(c) In accordance with the Witness Charter, and in conjunction with court listing officers ensure, as far as possible, that cases involving a vulnerable or child witness are given priority when listing.

Court case progression officer (CPO)

6.9. The Court Case Progression Officer should—

(a) Monitor directions made by the court and, in the event of non-compliance, refer to the court, if appropriate.

(b) Ensure that any communication received from the parties is dealt with promptly.

(c) Check readiness and take appropriate action. Any application to vacate an appeal is to be referred to the Resident or other nominated judge in accordance with local arrangements.

(d) Refer the matter to the court for a decision on whether the matter should be listed for further directions if a problem cannot otherwise be resolved.

(e) Remind the appellant of the hearing time, date and venue, where agreed locally.

(f) If any sound/vision recordings are to be played, check there is compatible equipment at court. The parties should be responsible for checking the quality of their recordings and providing them to the court administration in a timely manner so they can be checked by the court administration on that equipment before the hearing.

(g) Ensure that interpreters/ signers for appellant witnesses are warned to attend if appropriate. In Wales, where the court has been notified that the appellant or witness will use Welsh, the court is responsible for ensuring that interpreters' simultaneous translation equipment has been arranged.

(h) If certificates of readiness are required by the court, provide blank forms to the parties.

National Offender Management Service–Probation Service

6.10. The Probation Service must—

(a) Obtain a PSR pack from the respondent and any appropriate information from the appellant and report to the court in accordance with local practice, as agreed between the court and the Probation Service. The Probation Service should be in a position to provide an oral report or a FDR report, if appropriate.

(b) If a report (oral or written) cannot be presented to the court on the same day, make an appointment with the appellant if possible there and then, or make arrangements to see him at a later stage, whether he is on bail or in custody, so that the report is ready before the date fixed for sentence.

Witness Service

6.11. The Witness Service must—

(a) Provide pre-court visits for witnesses when referred and where resources allow.

(b) Share relevant information about the victims and the witnesses (e.g. the reluctance of a witness to attend court, changes in availability, the need to make any reasonable adjustments to accommodate needs under the *Disability Discrimination Act* 1995, childcare commitments and possible need for special measures) with the respondent/ appellant team.

National Offender Management Service–Prison Service and prisoner escort services commissioned by PECS

6.12. With persons held in prison custody—

(a) The Prison Service must ensure that the identities of all the persons in custody are notified to the appropriate escort contractor for production at court by the agreed process.

(b) The escort contractor must ensure that all the prisoners notified to them for production at court are delivered to the courthouse and brought before the court by the agreed times.

(c) The escort contractor must notify the court administration immediately of any problems anticipated or arising in respect of the production of persons in custody.

(d) Where the defendant is appearing by way of a prison video link, the Prison Service must ensure that he is available at the appropriate time.

(e) The escort contractor must ensure that there are arrangements in place for the remand forms, prepared by the prisons and attached to the Prison Escort Record forms, to be delivered to the court clerk's office before the hearing.

INDEX

LEGAL TAXONOMY

FROM SWEET & MAXWELL

This index has been prepared using Sweet and Maxwell's Legal Taxonomy. Main index entries conform to keyworks provided by the Legal Taxonomy except where references to specific documents or non-standard terms (denoted by quotation marks) have been included. These keywords provide a means of identifying similar concepts in other Sweet & Maxwell publications and online services to which keywords from the Legal Taxonomy have been applied. Readers may find some minor differences between terms used in the text and those which appear in the index. Suggestions to *taxonomy@sweetandmaxwell.co.uk*

(All references are to paragraph number)

2012

January

M		2	9	16	23	30
T		3	10	17	24	31
W		4	11	18	25	
T		5	12	19	26	
F		6	13	20	27	
S		7	14	21	28	
S	1	8	15	22	29	

February

M		6	13	20	27
T		7	14	21	28
W	1	8	15	22	29
T	2	9	16	23	
F	3	10	17	24	
S	4	11	18	25	
S	5	12	19	26	

March

M		5	12	19	26
T		6	13	20	27
W		7	14	21	28
T	1	8	15	22	29
F	2	9	16	23	30
S	3	10	17	24	31
S	4	11	18	25	

April

M		2	9	16	23	30
T		3	10	17	24	
W		4	11	18	25	
T		5	12	19	26	
F		6	13	20	27	
S		7	14	21	28	
S	1	8	15	22	29	

May

M		7	14	21	28
T	1	8	15	22	29
W	2	9	16	23	30
T	3	10	17	24	31
F	4	11	18	25	
S	5	12	19	26	
S	6	13	20	27	

June

M		4	11	18	25
T		5	12	19	26
W		6	13	20	27
T		7	14	21	28
F	1	8	15	22	29
S	2	9	16	23	30
S	3	10	17	24	

July

M		2	9	16	23	30
T		3	10	17	24	31
W		4	11	18	25	
T		5	12	19	26	
F		6	13	20	27	
S		7	14	21	28	
S	1	8	15	22	29	

August

M		6	13	20	27
T		7	14	21	28
W	1	8	15	22	29
T	2	9	16	23	30
F	3	10	17	24	31
S	4	11	18	25	
S	5	12	19	26	

September

M		3	10	17	24
T		4	11	18	25
W		5	12	19	26
T		6	13	20	27
F		7	14	21	28
S	1	8	15	22	29
S	2	9	16	23	30

October

M	1	8	15	22	29
T	2	9	16	23	30
W	3	10	17	24	31
T	4	11	18	25	
F	5	12	19	26	
S	6	13	20	27	
S	7	14	21	28	

November

M		5	12	19	26
T		6	13	20	27
W		7	14	21	28
T	1	8	15	22	29
F	2	9	16	23	30
S	3	10	17	24	
S	4	11	18	25	

December

M		3	10	17	24	31
T		4	11	18	25	
W		5	12	19	26	
T		6	13	20	27	
F		7	14	21	28	
S	1	8	15	22	29	
S	2	9	16	23	30	